Honoring America

★ **For Americans, the flag has always had a special meaning. It is a symbol of our nation's freedom and democracy.** ★

Flag Etiquette

Over the years, Americans have developed rules and customs concerning the use and display of the flag. One of the most important things every American should remember is to treat the flag with respect.

- The flag should be raised and lowered by hand and displayed only from sunrise to sunset. On special occasions, the flag may be displayed at night, but it should be illuminated.

- The flag may be displayed on all days, weather permitting, particularly on national and state holidays and on historic and special occasions.

- No flag may be flown above the American flag or to the right of it at the same height.

- The flag should never touch the ground or floor beneath it.

- The flag may be flown at half-staff by order of the president, usually to mourn the death of a public official.

- The flag may be flown upside down only to signal distress.

- The flag should never be carried flat or horizontally, but always carried aloft and free.

- When the flag becomes old and tattered, it should be destroyed by burning. According to an approved custom, the Union (stars on blue field) is first cut from the flag; then the two pieces, which no longer form a flag, are burned.

★ ★ ★ ★ ★ ★ ★ ★

The American's Creed

I believe in the United States of America as a Government of the people, by the people, for the people, whose just powers are derived from the consent of the governed; a democracy in a republic; a sovereign Nation of many sovereign States; a perfect union, one and inseparable; established upon those principles of freedom, equality, justice, and humanity for which American patriots sacrificed their lives and fortunes.

I therefore believe it is my duty to my Country to love it; to support its Constitution; to obey its laws; to respect its flag, and to defend it against all enemies.

The Pledge of Allegiance

I pledge allegiance to the Flag of the United States of America and to the Republic for which it stands, one Nation under God, indivisible, with liberty and justice for all.

The Star-Spangled Banner

O! say, can you see, by the dawn's early light,
What so proudly we hail'd at the twilight's last gleaming?
Whose broad stripes and bright stars, thro' the perilous fight,
O'er the ramparts we watched were so gallantly streaming?
And the rockets' red glare, the bombs bursting in air,
Gave proof thro' the night, that our flag was still there.
O! say, does that Star-Spangled Banner yet wave
O'er the land of the free and the home of the brave?

On the shore, dimly seen thro' the mist of the deep,
Where the foe's haughty host in dread silence reposes,
What is that which the breeze, o'er the towering steep,
As it fitfully blows, half conceals, half discloses?
Now it catches the gleam of the morning's first beam,
In full glory reflected now shines on the stream.
'Tis the Star-Spangled Banner. O long may it wave
O'er the land of the free and the home of the brave.

And where is that band who so vauntingly swore,
That the havoc of war and the battle's confusion
A home and a country should leave us no more?
Their blood has wash'd out their foul footstep's pollution.
No refuge could save the hireling and slave
From the terror of flight or the gloom of the grave,
And the Star-Spangled Banner in triumph doth wave
O'er the land of the free and the home of the brave.

O thus be it e'er when free men shall stand
Between their lov'd home and war's desolation,
Blest with vict'ry and peace, may the Heav'n-rescued land
Praise the pow'r that hath made and preserv'd us a nation.
Then conquer we must, when our cause it is just,
And this be our motto, "In God is our Trust."
And the Star-Spangled Banner in triumph shall wave
O'er the land of the free and the home of the brave.

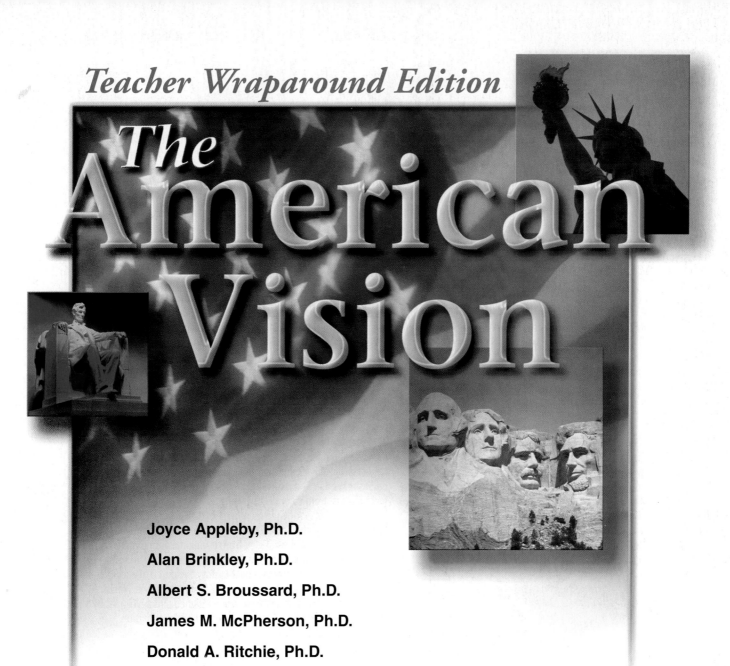

Teacher Wraparound Edition

The American Vision

Joyce Appleby, Ph.D.

Alan Brinkley, Ph.D.

Albert S. Broussard, Ph.D.

James M. McPherson, Ph.D.

Donald A. Ritchie, Ph.D.

NATIONAL
GEOGRAPHIC

**Glencoe
McGraw-Hill**

New York, New York   Columbus, Ohio   Chicago, Illinois   Peoria, Illinois   Woodland Hills, California

Authors

Joyce Appleby, Ph.D., is Professor of History at UCLA. Dr. Appleby's published works include *Inheriting the Revolution: The First Generation of Americans; Capitalism and a New Social Order: The Jeffersonian Vision of the 1790s;* and *Ideology and Economic Thought in Seventeenth-Century England,* which won the Berkshire Prize. She served as president of both the Organization of American Historians and the American Historical Association, and chaired the Council of the Institute of Early American History and Culture at Williamsburg. Dr. Appleby has been elected to the American Philosophical Society and the American Academy of Arts and Sciences, and is a Corresponding Fellow of the British Academy.

Alan Brinkley, Ph.D., is Allan Nevins Professor of American History at Columbia University. His published works include *Voices of Protest: Huey Long, Father Coughlin, and the Great Depression,* which won the 1983 National Book Award; *The End of Reform: New Deal Liberalism in Recession and War; The Unfinished Nation: A Concise History of the American People;* and *Liberalism and its Discontents.* He received the Levenson Memorial Teaching Prize at Harvard University.

Albert S. Broussard, Ph.D., is Professor of History and Graduate Coordinator at Texas A&M University. Before joining the Texas A&M faculty, Dr. Broussard was Assistant Professor of History and Director of the African American Studies Program at Southern Methodist University. Among his publications are the books *Black San Francisco: The Struggle for Racial Equality in the West, 1900–1954* and *African American Odyssey: The Stewarts, 1853–1963.* Dr. Broussard has also served as president of the Oral History Association.

James M. McPherson, Ph.D., is George Henry Davis Professor of American History at Princeton University. Dr. McPherson is the author of 11 books about the Civil War era. These include *Battle Cry of Freedom: The Civil War Era,* for which he won the Pulitzer Prize in 1989, and *For Cause and Comrades: Why Men Fought in the Civil War,* for which he won the 1998 Lincoln Prize. He is a member of many professional historical associations, including the Civil War Preservation Trust.

Donald A. Ritchie, Ph.D., is Associate Historian of the United States Senate Historical Office. Dr. Ritchie received his doctorate in American history from the University of Maryland after service in the U.S. Marine Corps. He has taught American history at various levels, from high school to university. He edits the Historical Series of the Senate Foreign Relations Committee and is the author of several books, including *Doing Oral History, The Oxford Guide to the United States Government,* and *Press Gallery: Congress and the Washington Correspondents,* which received the Organization of American Historians Richard W. Leopold Prize. Dr. Ritchie has served as president of the Oral History Association and as a council member of the American Historical Association.

The National Geographic Society, founded in 1888 for the increase and diffusion of geographic knowledge, is the world's largest nonprofit scientific and educational organization. Since its earliest days, the Society has used sophisticated communication technologies, from color photography to holography, to convey knowledge to its worldwide membership. The School Publishing Division supports the Society's mission by developing innovative educational programs—ranging from traditional print materials to multimedia programs including CD-ROMs, videodiscs, and software. "National Geographic Geography & History," featured in each unit of this textbook, and "National Geographic Moment in Time," featured in chapters 8–29 of this textbook, were designed and developed by the National Geographic Society's School Publishing Division.

About the Cover See page 1135 for a complete explanation of the cover images.

Glencoe/McGraw-Hill

A Division of The McGraw-Hill Companies

Send all inquiries to: Glencoe/McGraw-Hill, 8787 Orion Place, Columbus, OH 43240-4027

ISBN 0-02-664118-6 (Student Edition), ISBN 0-07-824926-0 (Teacher Wraparound Edition)

Printed in the United States of America.

2 3 4 5 6 027/043 06 05 04 03 02

Academic Consultants

Richard G. Boehm
Professor of Geography
Southwest Texas State University
San Marcos, Texas

Assad Nimer Busool
Professor and Chairman of the Department
of Arabic Studies
American Islamic College
Chicago, Illinois

Gloria Contreras
Professor, Department of Teacher Education
and Administration
University of North Texas
Denton, Texas

Frank de Varona
Region Superintendent
Dade County Public Schools
Miami, Florida

Larry Elowitz
Carl Vinson Professor of Political Science
Georgia College and State University
Milledgeville, Georgia

Susan Hartman
Professor of American Women's History
The Ohio State University
Columbus, Ohio

Cole C. Kingseed
Professor of Military History
United States Military Academy
at West Point
West Point, New York

David E. Maas
Professor of History
Wheaton College
Wheaton, Illinois

William E. Nelson, Jr.
Research Professor of Black Studies and
Professor of Political Science
The Ohio State University
Columbus, Ohio

Bernard Reich
Professor of Political Science and
International Affairs
George Washington University
Washington, D.C.

Calbert A. Seciwa
Director, American Indian Institute
Arizona State University
Tempe, Arizona

Athan Theoharis
Professor of History
Marquette University
Milwaukee, Wisconsin

Mark Van Ells
Professor of History
Queensborough Community College
New York, New York

Teacher Reviewers

Ann T. Ackerman
Teacher
Nashua High School
Nashua, New Hampshire

Kelly Robert Berg
Teacher
Killeen Shoemaker High School
Killeen Independent School District
Killeen, Texas

Edward Brickner
Social Studies Teacher
Woodbury High School
Prescott, Wisconsin

P. Nathan Collins
Social Studies Teacher
Buffalo Gap High School
Swoope, Virginia

Carmen Crosse
Teacher and Department Head
Socorro High School
Socorro Independent School District
El Paso, Texas

Bruce L. Eddy
Teacher, History and Social Science
Department
Evanston Township High School
Evanston, Illinois

Bette Gilmore
Campus Instructional Specialist
Killeen Independent School District
Killeen, Texas

George W. Henry, Jr.
History Teacher
Rowland Hall St. Mark's School
Salt Lake City, Utah

Marjorie B. Hollowell
Social Studies Teacher
John A. Holmes High School
Edenton, North Carolina

Pat Jordan
Social Studies Curriculum Consultant
Lubbock ISDR Education Service Center
Region 17
Lubbock, Texas

Merle Knight
Emeritus Social Studies Teacher and
Coordinator of Social Studies
Department
Lewis S. Mills High School
Torrington, Connecticut

Margaret Kress
Social Studies Director
Round Rock Independent School District
Round Rock, Texas

Tom Laichas
History Teacher
Crossroads School
Santa Monica, California

Elizabeth Pederson
Teacher
Grand Prairie High School
Grand Prairie Independent School District
Grand Prairie, Texas

Holly C. Sharpe
Secondary Social Studies Coordinator
Plano Independent School District
Plano, Texas

Denny Shillings
Social Studies Teacher
Homewood Flossmoor High School
Flossmoor, Illinois

Steve Swett
History Teacher
Hingham High School
Hingham, Massachusetts

Jame Wolfe
History Teacher and Department Chair
Suitland High School
Forrestville, Maryland

Contents

Contents

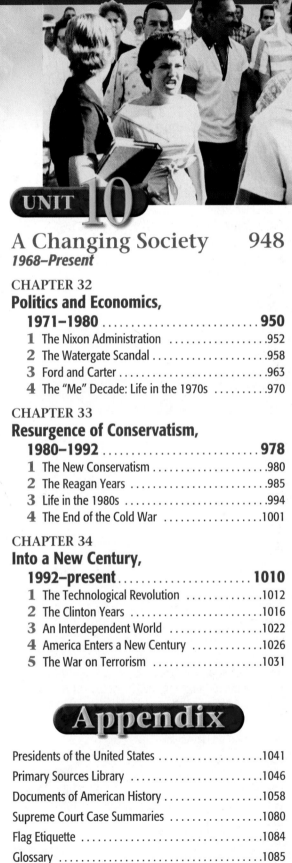

Features

Linking Past & Present

Different Viewpoints

NATIONAL GEOGRAPHIC Geography & History

NATIONAL GEOGRAPHIC MOMENT in HISTORY

World History Connection

World Geography Connection

Features

SKILLBUILDER

Primary Source Quotes

A variety of quotations and excerpts throughout the text express the thoughts, feelings, and life experiences of people, past and present.

Primary Source Quotes

Primary Source Quotes

NATIONAL GEOGRAPHIC Maps

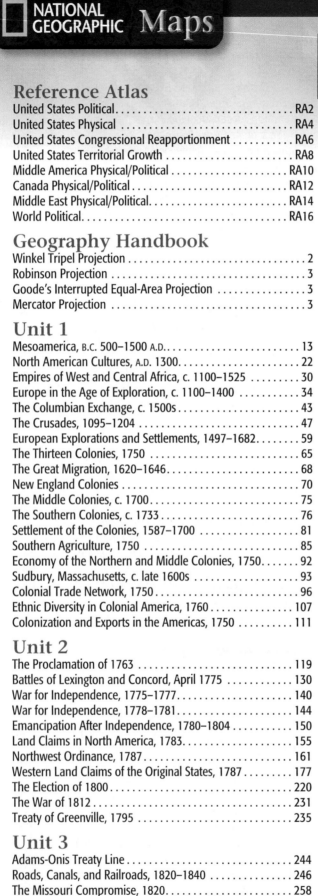

NATIONAL GEOGRAPHIC
Route of the Freedom Riders, 1961

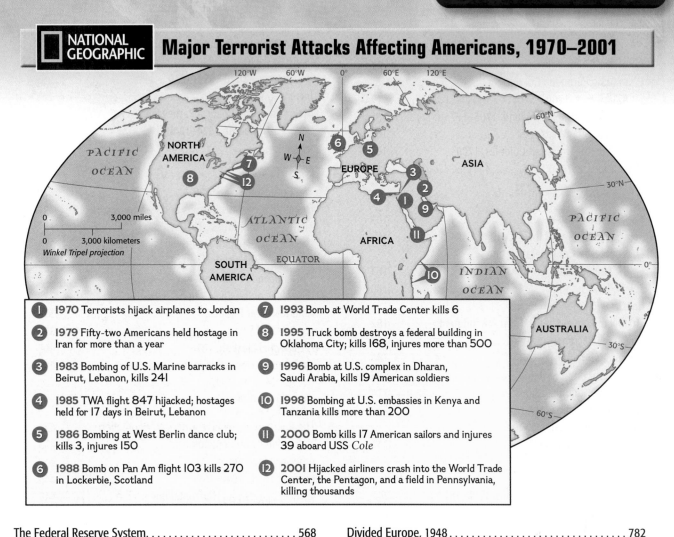

NATIONAL GEOGRAPHIC Major Terrorist Attacks Affecting Americans, 1970–2001

① 1970 Terrorists hijack airplanes to Jordan

② 1979 Fifty-two Americans held hostage in Iran for more than a year

③ 1983 Bombing of U.S. Marine barracks in Beirut, Lebanon, kills 241

④ 1985 TWA flight 847 hijacked; hostages held for 17 days in Beirut, Lebanon

⑤ 1986 Bombing at West Berlin dance club; kills 3, injures 150

⑥ 1988 Bomb on Pan Am flight 103 kills 270 in Lockerbie, Scotland

⑦ 1993 Bomb at World Trade Center kills 6

⑧ 1995 Truck bomb destroys a federal building in Oklahoma City; kills 168, injures more than 500

⑨ 1996 Bomb at U.S. complex in Dharan, Saudi Arabia, kills 19 American soldiers

⑩ 1998 Bombing at U.S. embassies in Kenya and Tanzania kills more than 200

⑪ 2000 Bomb kills 17 American sailors and injures 39 aboard USS *Cole*

⑫ 2001 Hijacked airliners crash into the World Trade Center, the Pentagon, and a field in Pennsylvania, killing thousands

Charts & Graphs

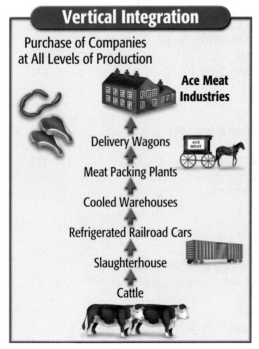

Vertical Integration

Purchase of Companies
at All Levels of Production

Ace Meat Industries

Delivery Wagons

Meat Packing Plants

Cooled Warehouses

Refrigerated Railroad Cars

Slaughterhouse

Cattle

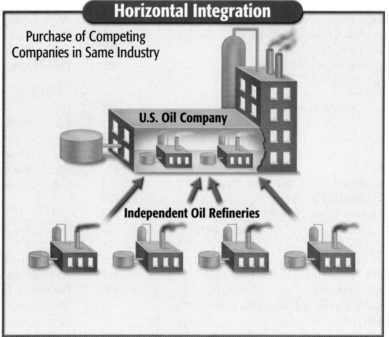

Horizontal Integration

Purchase of Competing
Companies in Same Industry

U.S. Oil Company

Independent Oil Refineries

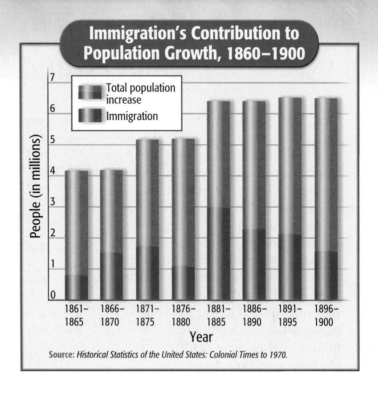

Immigration's Contribution to Population Growth, 1860–1900

Source: *Historical Statistics of the United States: Colonial Times to 1970.*

Reading Strategies

How Can I Help My Students Read and Understand the Textbook?

Social studies teachers do not have to be reading teachers to help students read and understand their textbooks. Often poor readers lack interest in the topic, have trouble concentrating, cannot understand a word or sentence, or are confused as to how the information fits together. These problems can frustrate the student and the teacher, but there are strategies that can be used to improve comprehension and retention of information. Using these reading strategies not only helps poor readers, but also strengthens the reading skills of strong readers.

Activating Prior Knowledge

Activating prior knowledge provides opportunities for students to discover and articulate what they already know about key concepts and ideas. It stimulates student interest and prepares students to incorporate new information into a larger picture. In addition, it helps the teacher to determine a starting place for instruction.

✔ Write the topic on the board and have students brainstorm what they know about it. Record their responses on the board.

✔ Ask general or specific questions about the topic and see how students respond to them.

✔ Present an anticipation guide. An anticipation guide provides a series of statements about an idea or topic. Students read each statement and tell whether they agree or disagree, based on their prior understandings and experiences.

✔ Use a K-W-L-H or K-W-L chart to activate prior knowledge and set reading purposes. Students identify what they already **know** (or think they know) and what they **want** to find out about the topic. After reading, students complete the chart.

K	W	L	H
What I **Know**	What I **Want** to Find Out	What I **Learned**	**How** I Can Learn More

Setting Reading Goals

Reading is a purposeful activity. We read to find answers to specific questions, to satisfy curiosity, and to be entertained.

✔ Have students preview the reading selection. Tell students to read the title, headings, and subheadings. Draw students' attention to diagrams, tables, and other visuals and their captions. Discuss how these will help comprehension.

✔ Prompt students to predict what they might learn in the selection, based on their preview. Invite them to list additional questions they hope to answer through the reading.

Have them identify possible problems, such as unfamiliar words or ideas, to watch for as they read.

✔ Discuss the need to "shift gears" in reading speed and attention when reading. Support students as they plan how best to read a selection—slowly to watch for new vocabulary and ideas or quickly to review previously learned ideas. They can also discuss new information with a buddy as they read.

Developing Vocabulary

Vocabulary knowledge and reading comprehension are closely related.

✔ Before students read, alert students to vocabulary that is crucial for understanding key topics and concepts.

✔ Relate new vocabulary to known words and ideas. After introducing a word and its definition, have students name synonyms or related words they know.

✔ If a student encounters an unfamiliar word while reading, have him or her try to pronounce it aloud. Sometimes saying the word will trigger one's memory of its meaning.

✔ As students read, help them use prefixes (word parts added to the beginning of base words), suffixes (word parts added to the end of base words), and roots (word elements from which other words are formed) as clues to decipher the meaning of words.

✔ Encourage students to use the context of surrounding words and sentences to determine a word's meaning.

✔ If context clues and structural analysis fail to help a student understand an important word as

Tom & DeeAnn McCarthy/CORBIS STOCK MARKET

Common Prefixes	Meanings	Examples
un-, dis-, non-, im- and il-	"not" or "the opposite of"	unwrapped, dishonest, nonprofit, immortal, illogical
re-	"again" or "back"	reform
post-	"after"	postwar
uni-	"one"	uniform

Common Suffixes	Meanings	Examples
-ship, -hood	"state of" or "condition of"	friendship, neighborhood
-ment	"act of" or "state of"	management
-ish	"like"	childish
-ous	"full of" or "like"	joyous

they read, have students find the definition in a glossary or dictionary. If the word is not critical for understanding, have students note the word and read on. Later, have students reread the word in context. If the meaning is still unclear, have students consult the dictionary.

Taking Notes

Taking notes challenges readers to determine what is most important and to organize information in a way that makes sense. Note-taking can also help students stay focused as they read. Reviewing notes can build students' retention of important information.

✔ Have students take notes after they have read long paragraphs in the section rather than the entire chapter. This helps them focus on important ideas and details and prevents them from losing track of the flow of information.

✔ Remind students that as they take notes on the section, they should not take a long time to do it. Students should read, think, write, and move on.

✔ Have students take notes using note cards. Notes should be recorded in the students' own words and labeled with the page number where the entire text appears.

✔ To use notes to review a passage, have students read through the notes, highlighting the most important information. As they review, encourage students to annotate their notes, making connections between related ideas and clarifying difficult concepts.

Summarizing

Summarizing demands that students identify the most important ideas and details to create a streamlined version of the text.

✔ After reading the section, have students recall as much of the information as possible. If the main idea and its supporting details are presented in a certain order, make sure students can recall that organization.

✔ As they summarize, students should try to answer as many of the following questions as possible: *who, what, where, when, why,* and *how.*

✔ If the section does not have a main idea that is clearly stated, have students create one that is concise but comprehensive. Have students state the main idea in a topic sentence at the beginning of their summaries.

✔ Sometimes summaries seem disconnected when details are left out. Students should use connector words such as *and* or *because,* along with introductory or closing statements, to make ideas more connected.✦

Reading Comprehension: Be Aware, Reread, and Connect (BARC)

Advice from Dr. Elizabeth Pryor, Ph.D.
Research Center for Educational Technology
Kent State University, Kent, Ohio

Many students think silent reading means just looking at words and saying them in their heads. They do not make the connection that reading is supposed to make sense! Have you ever read a paragraph or a page and then said to yourself, "What was that?" As a good reader, you were aware of your lack of understanding. Poor readers, on the other hand, just keep on reading the words, unaware that they do not understand them.

What strategies do good readers use when this happens? Most reread the text they did not understand. Before rereading I study key words I might have missed. When I reread, sometimes I "whisper read" so I can hear the text as well as read it. As I reread, I try to connect what I am reading with something I already know. If I reread and still don't understand, I read it a third (or fourth) time. Each rereading increases comprehension.

In summary, **Be aware** of understanding as you read, **reread,** and **connect** the reading to what you already know. **BARC!**

Test-Taking Strategies
How Can I Help My Students Succeed on Tests?

It's not enough for students to learn social studies facts and concepts—they must be able to show what they know in a variety of test-taking situations.

How Can I Help My Students Do Well On Objective Tests?

Objective tests may include multiple choice, true/false, and matching questions. Applying the following strategies can help students do their best on objective tests.

Multiple Choice Questions

✔ Students should read the directions carefully to learn what answer the test requires—the best answer or the right answer. This is especially important when answer choices include "all of the above" or "none of the above."

✔ Advise students to watch for negative words in the questions, such as *not, except, unless,* and *never.* If the question contains a negative, the correct answer choice is the one that does not fit.

✔ Students should try to mentally answer the question before reading the answer choices.

✔ Students should read all the answer choices and cross out those that are obviously wrong. Then they should choose an answer from those that remain.

True/False Questions

✔ It is important that students read the entire question before answering. For an answer to be true, the entire statement must be true. If one part of a statement is false, the answer should be marked *False.*

✔ Remind students to watch for words like *all, never, every,* and *always.* Statements containing these words are often false.

Matching Questions

✔ Students should read through both lists before they mark any answers.

✔ Unless an answer can be used more than once, students should cross out each choice as they use it.

✔ Using what they know about grammar can help students find the right answer. When matching a word with its definition, the definition is often the same part of speech (noun or verb, for example) as the word.

How Can I Help My Students Do Well On Essay Tests?

Essay tests require students to write a thorough and well-organized answer to a question or questions. Help students use the following strategies on essay tests.

Analyze:	To **analyze** means to systematically and critically examine all parts of an issue or event.
Classify or Categorize:	To **classify** or **categorize** means to put people, things, or ideas into groups, based on a common set of characteristics.
Compare and Contrast:	To **compare** is to show how things are similar, or alike. To **contrast** is to show how things are different.
Describe:	To **describe** means to present a sketch or impression. Rich details, especially details that appeal to the senses, flesh out a description.
Discuss:	To **discuss** means to systematically write about all sides of an issue or event.
Evaluate:	To **evaluate** means to make a judgment and support it with evidence.
Explain:	To **explain** means to clarify or make plain.
Illustrate:	To **illustrate** means to provide examples or to show with a picture or other graphic.
Infer:	To **infer** means to read between the lines or to use knowledge and experience to draw conclusions, make a generalization, or form a prediction.
Justify:	To **justify** means to prove or to support a position with specific facts and reasons.
Predict:	To **predict** means to tell what will happen in the future, based on an understanding of prior events and behaviors.
State:	To **state** means to briefly and concisely present information.
Summarize:	To **summarize** means to give a brief overview of the main points of an issue or event.
Trace:	To **trace** means to present the steps or stages in a process or event in sequential or chronological order.

Read the Question

The key to writing successful essays lies in reading and interpreting questions correctly. Teach students to identify and underline key words in the questions, and to use these words to guide them in understanding what the question asks. Help students understand the meaning of some of the most common key words, listed in the chart on page T40.

Plan and Write the Essay

After students understand the question, they should follow the steps below to develop and write their essays.

1. Map out an answer. Make lists, webs, or an outline to plan the response.

2. Decide on an order in which to present the main points.

3. Write an opening statement that directly responds to the essay question.

4. Write the essay. Expand on the opening statement. Support key points with specific facts, details, and reasons.

5. Write a closing statement that brings the main points together.

6. Proofread to check for spelling, grammar, and punctuation.

How Can I Help My Students Prepare for Standardized Tests?

Students can follow the steps below to prepare for a test.

✔ **Read About the Test** Students can familiarize themselves with the format of the test, the types of questions that will be asked, and the amount of time they will have to complete the test.

✔ **Review the Content** Consistent study throughout the school year will help students build social studies knowledge and understanding. If there are specific objectives or standards that are tested on the exam, help students review these facts or skills to be sure they are proficient.

✔ **Practice** Provide practice, ideally with released tests, to build students' familiarity with the content, format, and timing of the actual exam. Students should practice all the types of questions they will encounter on the test—multiple choice, short answer, and extended response.

✔ **Analyze Practice Results** Help students improve test-taking performance by analyzing their test-taking strengths and weaknesses. Spend time discussing students' completed practice tests, explaining why particular answers are right or wrong. Help students identify what kinds of questions they had the most difficulty with. Look for patterns in errors and then tailor your instruction to the appropriate skills or social studies content.✦

Jose L. Pelaez/CORBIS STOCK MARKET

Help Students Learn by Reviewing Graded Tests

Advice from Tara Musslewhite
Humble Independent School District
Humble, Texas

Frequently reviewing graded tests is a great way for students to assess their test-taking skills. It also gives teachers the opportunity to teach test-taking strategies and review content. As the class re-reads each test question, guide students to think logically about their answer choices. Show students how to:

1. Read each question carefully to determine its meaning.
2. Look for key words in the question to support their answers.
3. Recognize synonyms in the answer choices that may match phrases in the question.
4. Narrow down answer choices by eliminating ones that don't make sense.
5. Anticipate the answer before looking at the answer choices.
6. Circle questions of which they are unsure and go back to them later. Sometimes a clue will be found in another question on the test.

Alternative Assessment Strategies

How Can I Go Beyond Tests to Assess Students' Understanding of Social Studies Facts and Concepts?

In response to the growing demand for accountability in the classroom, educators must use multiple assessment measures to accurately gauge student performance. In addition to quizzes, tests, essay exams, and standardized tests, assessment today uses a variety of performance-based measures and portfolio opportunities.

What Are Some Typical Performance-Based Assessments?

There are many kinds of performance-based assessments. They all share one common characteristic: they challenge students to create written or oral reports that demonstrate what they know. One good way to present a performance assessment is in the form of an open-ended question.

Writing

Performance-based writing assessments challenge students to apply their knowledge of social studies concepts and information in various ways. Writing activities are most often completed by one student, rather than by a group.

✔ **Journals** Students write from the perspective of a historical character or a citizen of a particular historical era.

✔ **Letters** Students write a letter from one historical figure to another or from a historical figure to a family member or other audience.

✔ **Position Paper or Editorial** Students explain a controversial issue and present their own opinion and recommendations, supported with strong evidence and convincing reasons.

✔ **Newspaper** Students write a variety of stories from the perspective of a reporter living in a particular time period.

✔ **Biographies and Autobiographies** Students write about historical figures either from the third person point of view (biography) or from the first person (autobiography).

✔ **Creative Stories** Students integrate historical events into a piece of fiction, reflecting the customs, language, and geography of the period.

✔ **Poems and Songs** Students follow the conventions of a particular type of song or poem as they tell about a historical event or person.

✔ **Research Reports** Students synthesize information from a variety of sources into a well-developed report.

Oral Presentations

Oral presentations allow students to demonstrate their social studies literacy before an audience. Oral presentations are often group efforts, although this need not be the case.

✔ **Simulations** Students hold simulations, or reenactments, of actual events, such as trials, acts of civil disobedience, battles, speeches, and so forth.

✔ **Debates** Students debate two or more sides to a historical policy or issue. Students can debate from a contemporary perspective or through role-playing, from the viewpoint of a historical character.

✔ **Interview** Students conduct a mock interview of a historical character or bystander.

✔ **Oral Reports** Students present the results of research efforts in an oral report.

✔ **Skits and Plays** Students use historical events as the basis for a play or skit. Details should accurately reflect the customs, language, and the setting of the period.

Visual Presentations

Visual presentations allow students to demonstrate their social studies understandings in a variety of visual formats. Visual presentations can be either group or individual projects.

✔ **Model** Students make a model to demonstrate or represent a process, place, event, battle, artifact, or custom.

✔ **Museum Exhibit** Students create a rich display of materials around a topic. Typical displays might include models, illustrations, photographs, videos, writings, and audiotaped presentations.

✔ **Graph or Chart** Students analyze and represent historical data in a line graph, bar graph, table, or other chart format.

✔ **Drawing** Students represent or interpret a historical event or period through illustration, including political cartoons.

✔ **Posters and Murals** Posters and murals may include maps, time lines, diagrams, illustrations, photographs, and text that reflect students' understandings of historical information.

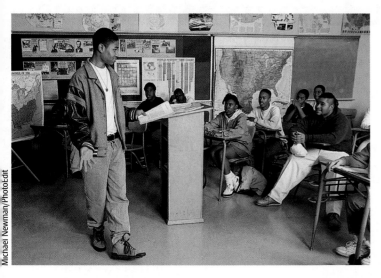

Michael Newman/PhotoEdit

✔ **Quilt** Students sew or draw a design for a patchwork quilt that shows a variety of perspectives, events, or issues related to a key topic.

✔ **Videotapes** Students film a video to show historical fiction or to preserve a simulation of a historical event.

✔ **Multimedia Presentation or Slide Show** Students create a computer-generated multimedia presentation containing historical information and analysis.

How Are Performance Assessments Scored?

There are a variety of means used to evaluate performance tasks. Some or all of the following methods may be used.

✔ **Scoring Rubrics** A scoring rubric is a set of guidelines for assessing the quality of a process and/or product. It sets out criteria used to distinguish acceptable responses from unacceptable ones, generally along a scale from excellent to poor.

✔ **Models of Excellent Work** Teacher-selected models of excellent work give a concrete illustration of what is expected and help students set goals for their own projects.

✔ **Student Self-Assessment** Common methods of self-assessment include ranking work in relation to the model, using a scoring rubric, and writing their own goals and then evaluating how well they have met these goals. Regardless of the method or methods students use, they should be encouraged to evaluate their behaviors, processes, and the finished product.

✔ **Peer or Audience Assessment** Many of the performance tasks target an audience other than the classroom teacher. If possible, the audience of peers should give the student feedback. Have the class create rubrics for specific projects together.

✔ **Observation** As students carry out their performance tasks, you may want to formally observe students at work. Start by developing a checklist, identifying the specific behaviors and knowledge you expect students to demonstrate. Then observe students as they carry out performance tasks and check off these items on your checklist as you observe them.

✔ **Interviews** As a form of ongoing assessment, you may want to conduct interviews with students, asking them to analyze, explain, and assess their participation in performance tasks. When projects take place over an extended period of time, you can hold periodic interviews as well as exit interviews. In this way you can gauge the status of the project and guide students' efforts along the way.✦

Targeting Multiple Intelligences

Advice from John Cartaina
Consultant, New Jersey Council of Social Studies

Authentic performance assessment provides students with different learning styles opportunities to demonstrate their successful learning. The table below lists types of learning styles.

Learning Style	Characteristics of Students
Linguistic	Read regularly, write clearly, and easily understand the written word
Logical-Mathematical	Use numbers, logic, and critical thinking skills
Visual-Spatial	Think in terms of pictures and images
Auditory-Musical	Remember spoken words and produce rhythms and melodies
Kinesthetic	Learn from touch, movement, and manipulating objects
Interpersonal	Understand and work well with other people
Intrapersonal	Have a realistic understanding of their strengths and weaknesses
Naturalist	Can distinguish among, classify, and use features of the environment

You may want to assign activities to students that accommodate their strongest learning styles, but frequently ask them to use their weakest learning styles.

Cooperative Group Strategies

How Can I Use Cooperative Learning to Teach Social Studies?

Today's social and economic climate requires flexibility. Workers must be able to function independently, work well with groups, and engage in fair-minded competition. For this reason, most educators recommend a healthy balance of instructional strategies to foster cooperative, competitive, and individualistic styles of problem solving and learning. Cooperative learning requires students to work together—each with a specific task—to pursue a common goal. Because part of each student's evaluation is determined by the overall quality of the group's work, students help one another accomplish the group goal.

How Do I Form Cooperative Groups?

✔ **Composition** Most experts recommend that cooperative groups be heterogeneous, reflecting a range of student abilities, backgrounds, and learning styles. Thus teachers will want to think in advance about how to balance group membership, rather than assigning students at random.

✔ **Group Size** The size of cooperative groups can change, depending upon the task. Some cooperative tasks are best accomplished in pairs. For most projects, groups of three to five students are ideal.

✔ **Abilities** Consider the tasks and projects the groups will undertake as you make group assignments. You may want to make sure each group has a strong manager, a strong writer, a strong artist, and a good listener.

✔ **Balance** Some teachers use a "family-of-five" approach to grouping. A strong leader heads each group. Two pairs of students with opposing styles or strengths complete the "family." Paired students might exhibit traits such as outgoing and shy, creative and conventional, spontaneous and methodical. Each group continues to work together throughout the semester or year. The goal is for students to develop greater flexibility in their problem-solving abilities and greater respect for the contributions of others.

✔ **Roles** In most instances, you will want to assign a specific role for each student to play in a group, such as designer, moderator, recorder, researcher, presenter, graphic artist, or actor. Roles should be interdependent, requiring students to rely upon one another in order to successfully carry out their individual responsibilities. As students gain experience in working in cooperative groups, turn over more of the responsibility for establishing individual roles and responsibilities to the group.

How Do I Help Groups Run Smoothly?

✔ **Seating Arrangements** Explain how and where groups should sit. Pairs can sit with desks or chairs face-to-face. Larger groups do well with desks or chairs gathered in a circle or with students seated around a table.

✔ **Warm-Ups** Provide an introductory activity for new groups. Even when students know one another, they can benefit by making formal introductions and sharing their thoughts on a sentence starter, such as "If I could go anywhere in the world, I would go to . . ." or "If I could have lived at any period in history, I would choose. . ."

✔ **Rules** Set clear expectations and rules for groups. Typical rules include addressing group members by name, making eye contact, listening politely, expressing disagreement with respect, welcoming others' questions, valuing others' contributions, providing positive feedback, and helping others when asked.

How Do I Use Cooperative Groups in My Classroom?

✔ **Share and Tell** Have students form groups of four. Assign each group member a number between one and four. Ask a factual recall question. Have group members discuss the question and come up with an answer. Call out a number between one and four. The student with that number who is first to raise his or her hand answers the question. The group earns a point for a correct answer.

✔ **Circle Partners** Have the class separate into two equal groups and form two circles, with one circle inside the other. Each student faces a partner in the

PhotoDisc

John Henley/CORBIS STOCK MARKET

opposing circle. Ask a question and have partners discuss the answer. If partners do not know the answer they can ask another pair for help. Then, call on students in the inside circle, the outside circle, or all students to say the answer aloud together.

✔ **In the Know** Provide students with a set of end-of-chapter questions or other questions covering content you want students to master. Tell students to circulate around the room to find someone who can answer a question on the worksheet. After listening to the answer, the student paraphrases it, writes the answer on the worksheet, and asks the "expert" to read and sign off on the answer if it is correct. Students move on to find a student to answer the next question. The process continues until students have completed their worksheets.

✔ **Open-Ended Projects** The best long-term projects for cooperative groups are those that are open-ended and multidimensional. That is, the task or question should have many possible answers and should lend itself to many different presentation possibilities.

Multiple intelligences Appropriate projects should challenge students and allow students of various abilities and backgrounds to contribute significantly to solving the problem and executing the project. One way to assess the validity of a potential project is to see whether it requires the use of many different strengths or "intelligences."

Assigning roles Because of the complexity of long-term projects, it is essential that students have clearly assigned roles and responsibilities. Once cooperative groups are established and successful in your classroom, be sure to vary the assignments given to each student from project to project.

Deadlines Define interim and final deadlines to encourage students to pace their efforts appropriately.

How Do I Assess Group and Individual Efforts?

✔ **Expectations** As with any assignment, set clear guidelines and high expectations for projects. Show models of excellent past projects, if possible, and define what criteria projects must meet to earn the highest grade.

✔ **Group and Individual Grades** Before students begin, define what percentage of the grade will be based on group work and how much will be based on individual effort. Many teachers give two equally weighted grades: a group grade—the same for each team member—and an individual grade.

✔ **Self-Assessment** Provide a checklist or rating scale for each group member. Have students evaluate their own contribution to the group, as well as the contributions of other group members. In addition to assessing the quality of the finished product, students should evaluate the processes they used within the group, such as showing respect for others' ideas. Provide space on the evaluation sheet for students to explain why they rated themselves and group members as they did.◆

Troubleshooting

Advice from Carey Boswell, M.Ed.
Humble Independent School District
Humble, Texas

Modern research overwhelmingly suggests that student learning is enhanced when cooperative groups are used in the classroom. Like many other teachers, I was uncertain of how much learning was taking place when I set up cooperative groups. I struggled with noise and control issues and off-task behavior by some students. I found a solution, though.

A cooperative group activity occurs whenever a student works with another student. Cooperative groups do not have to be large groups. Smaller groups ensure that all students are engaged and contribute to the group effort. Smaller groups also guarantee that members perform multiple tasks so that real learning occurs. I often combine two or more small groups into a larger group for short comparative tasks. After making this small adjustment, I am able to assign cooperative group tasks to students at least once a week and student performance, comprehension, and learning has increased in my classroom.

Web Strategies

How Can I Use the Internet to Teach Social Studies?

Never before have teachers and students had so much information at their fingertips. Besides traditional sources such as books, newspapers, and magazine articles, teachers and students now have access to the Internet and round-the-clock news coverage on television. Yet never before has it been so confusing to determine whether content is reliable. In today's world, social studies teachers must not only use the Internet as a source of up-to-the-minute information for students; they must also teach students how to find and evaluate sources on their own.

What's Available On the Internet?

✔ **Teacher-Focused Web Sites** These Web sites provide teaching tips, detailed lesson plans, and links to other sites of interest to teachers and students.

✔ **Historical Documents** Thousands of primary source documents have now been cataloged and placed on the Web. Some sites provide text-only versions. Others provide photographs of actual documents and artifacts as well as insightful commentary and analysis.

✔ **Geographical Information** The Web holds a variety of geographical resources, from historical, physical, and political maps to interactive mapping programs and information about people and places around the world.

✔ **Statistics** Government Web sites are rich depositories for statistics of all kinds, including census data and information about climate, educa-

tion, the economy, and political processes and patterns.

✔ **Reference Sources** Students can access full-text versions of encyclopedias, dictionaries, atlases, and other reference books, as well as databases containing millions of journal and newspaper articles.

✔ **News** Traditional media sources, including television, radio, newspapers, and newsmagazines, sponsor Internet sites that provide almost instantaneous news updates, as well as in-depth coverage and analysis. Extensive archives facilitate research on past news stories.

✔ **Topical Information** Among the most numerous Web sites are those organized around a particular topic or issue, such as the Civil War or the stock market. These Internet pages may contain essays, analyses, and other commentaries, as well as primary source documents, maps, photographs, video and audio clips, bibliographies, and links to related online resources.

✔ **Organizations** Many organizations such as museums post Web pages

that provide online exhibits, archives, and other information.

Glencoe Online

Glencoe provides an integrated Web curriculum for your textbook. The **Chapter Overview** Web link provides previews and reviews to help students better understand each chapter's organization and content. **Student Web Activities** challenge students to apply what they've learned. **Self-Check Quizzes** at the end of each chapter let you and your students assess their knowledge. You can also find additional links relevant to your state.

Finding Things on the Internet

The greatest asset of the Internet—its vast array of materials—also presents its greatest difficulty—the challenge of finding the specific information needed. Many excellent social studies-specific sites provide links to relevant content. Using Internet search engines can also help you find what you need.

✔ A search engine is an Internet search tool. You type in a keyword, name, or phrase, and the search engine lists the URLs for matching Web sites. However, a search engine may find things that are not at all related or may miss sites that would be useful. The key is to define your search.

✔ Not all search engines are the same. Each seeks out information a little differently. Search engines use different criteria to determine what

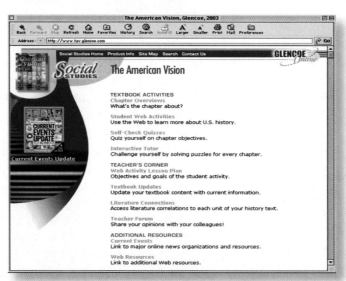

constitutes a "match" for your search topic. The Internet holds numerous articles that compare search engines and offer guidelines for choosing those that best meet your needs.

✔ An advanced search allows you to refine the search by using a phrase or a combination of words. The way to conduct an advanced search varies from search engine to engine. Check the search engine's "Help" feature for information. Encourage students to review this information regularly for each of the search engines they use.

How Do I Teach Students to Evaluate Web Sites?

Anyone can put up a Web site. Web content is easy to change, too, so Webmasters constantly update their Web sites by adding, modifying, and removing content. These characteristics make evaluating Web sites both more challenging and more important than traditional print resources. Teach students to critically evaluate Web resources, using the questions and criteria below.

1 Purpose: What is the purpose of the Web site or Web page? Is it an informational Web page, a news site, a business site, an advocacy site, or a personal Web page? Many sites serve more than one purpose. For instance, a news site may provide current events accompanied by banner ads that market the products advertisers think readers might want.

2 URL: What is the URL, or Web address? Where does the site originate? That can sometimes tell you about the group or business behind the Web page. For example, URLs ending with .edu and .gov indicate that the site is connected to an educational institution or a government agency, respectively. Those ending with a .com suffix usually means that a commercial or business interest hosts the Web site, but may also indicate a personal Web page. A nonprofit organization's Web address may end with .org.

3 Authority: Who wrote the material or created the Web site? What qualifications does this person or group have? Who has ultimate responsibility for the site? If the site is sponsored by an organization, are the organization's goals clearly stated?

4 Accuracy: How reliable is the information? Are sources listed so that they can be verified? Is the Web page free from surface errors in spelling and grammar? How does it compare with other sources you've found on the Web and in print?

5 Objectivity: If the site presents itself as an informational site, is the material free from bias? If there is advertising, is it easy to tell the difference between the ads and other features? If the site mixes factual information with opinion, can you spot the difference between the two? If the site advocates an opinion or viewpoint, is the opinion clearly stated and logically defended?

6 Currency: When was the information first placed on the Web? Is the site updated on a regular basis? When was the last revision? If the information is time-sensitive, are the updates frequent enough?

7 Coverage: What topics are covered on the Web site? What is the depth of coverage? Are all sides of an issue presented? How does the coverage compare with other Web and print sources? ✦

See the *Glencoe Social Studies Guide to Using the Internet* for additional information and teaching strategies.

Avoiding Online Pitfalls

Advice from Jim Matiya
Carl Sandburg High School
Orland Park, Illinois

Integrating technology into your social studies curriculum can have its pitfalls. Because something often goes wrong when you least expect it, here is some advice about technology, computers, and students.

1. Make sure the hyperlinks work—check them yourself.
2. Design assignments that go from easy to complex. Students have varying degrees of success with computers so start with simple, concrete assignments and move to complex, abstract assignments.
3. Vary the selection of sites for students. You can use a search engine and a museum site for one assignment and then use a historical document page and a statistical site for another assignment. Varying the sites makes assignments more interesting.
4. Make sure you have given students enough information to find what you want. Do not give them a question that can lead to thousands of different answers on different sites.
5. Design Web assignments so that students with less Internet experience can achieve some degree of success. Have computer-literate students become mentors for their classmates.
6. Have alternative assignments in case the Internet is temporarily down, the computers are locked inside a closet, or lightning has wiped out a bank of computers.

Primary Source Strategies

How Do I Use Primary Sources in My Classroom?

A primary source is direct evidence of an event, idea, period, or development. It is an oral or written account obtained from actual participants in an event. Examples of primary sources include the following:

✔ official documents (records, statistics)
✔ political declarations, laws, and rules for governance
✔ speeches and interviews
✔ diaries, memoirs, and oral histories
✔ autobiographies
✔ songs and audio recordings
✔ advertisements and posters
✔ letters

Physical objects, such as tools and dishes, can be primary sources; so can visual evidence in the form of fine art, photographs, maps, films, and videotapes.

Why Use Primary Sources in Your Classroom?

Using primary sources to teach transforms the study of social studies from a passive process to an active one. Students become investigators—finding clues, formulating hypotheses and drawing inferences, making judgments, and reaching conclusions. Bringing primary sources into the classroom stimulates students to think critically about events, issues, and concepts rather than simply memorizing dates, names, and generalizations reached by others.

Choosing Primary Sources

✔ Provide exposure to a variety of source types, including historic photographs, folk or popular music, financial records or household accounts, as well as letters, journals, and historic documents.
✔ When choosing print sources, consider the interests and reading levels of your students. Many texts contain challenging vocabulary and unfamiliar sentence structure. You may need to create a reader's guide that defines key vocabulary and paraphrases the main points of the reading.
✔ Some documents may be too long. Decide whether using an excerpt will provide enough information for students to draw conclusions.
✔ Depending upon the topic and your instructional objectives, you may need to provide several different primary sources to expose students to a variety of perspectives.
✔ Decide how students will access the primary sources: through the Internet, the library, a museum, or other print resources. Consider the possibility of an Internet virtual field trip for students.

Moving from URL to URL, students can visit museum sites and other Web pages to view artifacts, interpret economic or census data, and read journals, letters, and official documents.

How Do I Introduce Students to Primary Sources?

Carefully explain the nature of primary sources when you introduce them to students. Although primary sources contain valuable clues, be sure to alert students that primary sources contain biases and prejudices, and must be approached with caution. Every primary source reflects the creator's point of view to some degree.

Using Primary Sources in the Classroom

Primary sources provide a rich source of inspiration for a variety of instructional strategies. They can be used to spark interest in a new topic, foster deeper exploration into a historical era, or assess students' understanding of social studies concepts and facts.

✔ **Pre-Reading Activities** Present a primary source for students to study at the beginning of a new chapter or topic. Have students analyze the source, using the questions and guidelines presented on the next page. Then have students make predictions about what they might learn in the upcoming lessons.

Interpreting a Primary Source

Before students interpret a primary source, they need to know its context. Then they can use questions and guidelines, such as those below, to help them analyze and interpret the primary source.

Print Sources

- Who created the source, and what was the purpose for doing so?
- Did the writer personally experience or witness the event(s)?
- At what point did the writer record the information—as it happened or afterward? How long after?
- Who was the intended audience?
- Was the writer trying to record facts, express an opinion, or persuade others to take action?
- What is the author's main message?
- What values does the document convey?
- What bias does it reflect?
- What information about the topic can you gather from this document?
- Compare this document with what you know about the topic. Does it confirm those ideas or introduce a new perspective?
- How might other accounts about this topic support or modify the message this source delivers?

Visual Sources

- Who created the source, and what was the purpose for doing so?
- What does the image show?
- What mood does the image convey?
- Who or what dominates the image or catches your eye?
- How does the view impact the message?
- What details can you learn from the image?
- What is excluded from view?
- What bias does the visual reflect?
- What information about the topic can you gather from this visual?
- How might other visuals about this topic support or modify the message this one delivers?

Audio Sources

- Who created the source? What was the purpose for creating this source?
- What is the main idea of the audio?
- What mood does the recorder's voice convey?
- What bias does the audio text reflect?
- What information about the topic can you gather from this audio source?
- Compare the information in this source with what you already know about the topic. Does it confirm those ideas or introduce a new perspective?
- How might other sources about this topic support or modify the message that this one delivers?

✔ **Exploring Information** Provide a variety of primary sources related to a topic or time period. Have students compare and contrast the items, analyzing the information, making inferences, and drawing conclusions about the period.

✔ **Evaluation Activities** Have students evaluate a primary source and tell how it supports or refutes what they learned in the textbook. Students can also read a primary source document that provides one perspective on a topic, and then write their own account with another perspective.✦

How to Use the Declaration of Independence in Your Classroom

Advice from Susan Hirsch
East Wake High School
Wendell, North Carolina

Divide students into groups of three or four. Tell students that it is 1777, and one member of their group has been arrested for joining the revolutionary struggle against Great Britain. This person will be sent to London to be tried on charges of treason. Hanging is the punishment for those found guilty of treason. Each group must prepare a defense using only one source—the Declaration of Independence. One person from each group will speak to the class, acting as either the defendant or the defendant's attorney. After all the presentations, the class will vote to determine which person did the best job of defending himself or herself or the client.

Using Maps, Graphs, and Charts

How Can I Use Visuals to Improve Students' Reading Comprehension?

Maps, graphs, and charts are visual tools. By using images rather than words, these tools present complex information in an easy-to-understand format. Teach students the following generalized viewing strategies, and encourage them to apply them as they study each chapter.

✔ **Asking Questions** Students should start by looking over the graphic and asking themselves questions, such as, "What is my purpose for looking at this image?" Then students can identify questions they hope to answer, such as "What is being compared?" or "What are the most important features?"

✔ **Finding Answers** Next, students should use the graphic's structural features, such as the title, labels, colors, and symbols, to help them find the answers to their questions. If the source of the graphic is available, students should also determine its reliability.

✔ **Drawing Conclusions** After studying the visual, students should summarize its main points and draw conclusions.

✔ **Connecting** Before moving on, students should relate what they learned from the visual with what they gained from reading the text selection. Students can examine how the visual supports or extends the meaning of the text.

Maps

Maps show the relative size and location of specific geographic areas.

There are as many different kinds of maps as there are uses for them. Two of the most common general purpose maps are political maps and physical maps. Political maps show human-made boundaries, such as state and country borders. Physical maps show physical features, such as mountains and lakes. Special purpose maps might show battle sites, cultural features, population change over time or land use patterns.

Parts of Maps

All maps contain parts that assist in interpreting the information. Help students learn to identify the following map parts.

✔ **Title** The map title identifies the area shown on the visual. The title can also identify a map's special focus.

✔ **Map Key** The map key, or legend, explains the symbols presented on the map, thus unlocking the map's information.

✔ **Compass Rose** A compass rose is a direction marker. It is a symbol that points out where the cardinal directions—north, south, east, and west—are positioned.

✔ **Scale** A measuring line, often called a scale bar, indicates the relationship between the distances on the map and the actual distances on Earth. Distance on a map can be determined by measuring the distance between points, then multiplying that measure by the number of miles or kilometers specified in the map scale ratio.

NATIONAL GEOGRAPHIC

Cities of Southwest Asia

Black Sea · Hattushah · Caspian Sea · ASIA MINOR · Nineveh · Cyprus · Euphrates River · Tigris River · Sidon · Byblos · Mediterranean Sea · Tyre · Babylon · Memphis · Nile River · Red Sea · ARABIAN PENINSULA · Persian Gulf

30°E · 40°E · 40°N · 30°N

N · W · E · S

0 — 500 miles
0 — 500 kilometers
Lambert Azimuthal Equal-Area projection

✔ **Latitude and Longitude** Mapmakers use lines of latitude and longitude to pinpoint exact locations on maps and globes. The imaginary horizontal lines that circle the globe from east to west are lines of latitude, also called parallels. The imaginary vertical lines are lines of longitude, also called meridians. Both parallels and meridians are measured in degrees.

Graphs

Graphs are a way of showing numbers or statistics in a clear, easy-to-read way. Because graphs summarize and present information visually, many students have an easier time understanding the data and drawing conclusions. The most common types of graphs are bar graphs, line graphs, circle graphs, and pictographs.

Population: Selected Countries

Morocco

Algeria

Egypt

Libya

Tunisia

= 5,000,000

Source: National Geographic Atlas of the World, 7th edition

✔ **Bar Graphs** A bar graph shows how two or more subjects or statistics compare. It provides information along two sides or axes. The horizontal axis is the line across the bottom of the graph. The vertical axis is the line along the side. The bars may be either vertical or horizontal. In most cases the labels on one axis show quantity, while the labels on the opposite axis show the categories of data being compared.

✔ **Line Graphs** A line graph shows change over time. Like a bar graph, it organizes information along the horizontal and vertical axes. The horizontal axis usually shows passing time, such as months, years, or decades. The vertical axis usually shows quantity or amount. Sometimes more than one set of data is shown in a line graph. A double-line graph, for instance, plots data for two related quantities, which may be represented in different colors or patterns.

✔ **Circle Graphs** A circle graph, also called a pie graph, shows how each part or percentage relates to the whole. A circle graph enables a viewer to make comparisons between parts and to analyze the relationship of each part to the whole.

✔ **Pictograph** A pictograph uses rows of small symbols or pictures, each representing a particular amount. Like a bar graph, a pictograph is useful for making comparisons.

Charts

While all charts present information or data in a visual way, the type of chart is often dictated by the nature of the information and by the chart-maker's purposes.

✔ **Tables** Tables show information, including numerical data, in columns and rows. This organized arrangement facilitates comparisons between categories of information. Labels are usually located at the top of each column and on the left-hand side of the table.

✔ **Diagrams** Diagrams are specialized drawings. They can show steps in a process; point out parts of an object, organization, or idea; or explain how something works. Arrows or lines may join parts of a figure and can show relationships between parts or the flow of steps. ✦

Classroom Activity: Create a Graph

Advice from Faith Vautour
Camden Hills Regional High School
Rockport, Maine

Graphs can be difficult to interpret and understand. Help students by having them create their own graph. To help students begin thinking about graphs, separate students into small groups. Then explain that each group should take a quick survey of classmates and make a graph to show their survey results. Suggest that students make either a bar graph, line graph, circle graph, or pictograph to show their data. To prompt students' thinking, ask the following questions.

- *Do you play on a sports team? Which sport(s)?*
- *What do you plan to do after high school?*
- *About how much time do you spend watching TV each day? About how much time did you spend on TV when you were 10 years old? When you were five years old?*

After students are done graphing their data, invite each group to share its work. Discuss the types of graphs students made and their reasons for choosing them. Each group should then take the graph that another group has prepared and transfer the information into another type of graph.

Addressing the Needs of Special Students

How Can I Help ALL my Students Learn Social Studies?

Today's classroom contains students from a variety of backgrounds and with a variety of learning styles, strengths, and challenges. With careful planning, you can address the needs of all students in the social studies classroom. The following tips for instruction can support your efforts to help all students reach their maximum potential.

✔ Survey students to discover their individual differences. Use interest inventories of their unique talents so you can encourage contributions in the classroom.

✔ Be a model for respecting others. Adolescents crave social acceptance. The student with learning differences is especially sensitive to correction and criticism, particularly when it comes from a teacher. Your behavior will set the tone for how students treat one another.

✔ Expand opportunities for success. Provide a variety of instructional activities that reinforce skills and concepts.

✔ Establish measurable objectives and decide how you can best help students meet them.

✔ Celebrate successes and praise "work in progress."

✔ Keep it simple. Point out problem areas if doing so can help a student effect change. Avoid overwhelming students with too many goals at one time.

✔ Assign cooperative group projects that challenge all students to contribute to solving a problem or creating a product.

How Do I Reach Students with Learning Disabilities?

✔ Provide support and structure. Clearly specify rules, assignments, and responsibilities.

✔ Practice skills frequently. Use games and drills to help maintain student interest.

✔ Incorporate many modalities into the learning process. Provide opportunities to say, hear, write, read, and act out important concepts and information.

✔ Link new skills and concepts to those already mastered.

✔ Allow students to record answers on audiotape.

✔ Allow extra time to complete tests and assignments.

✔ Let students demonstrate proficiency with alternative presentations, including oral reports, role plays, art projects, and musical presentations.

✔ Provide outlines, notes, or tape recordings of lecture material.

✔ Pair students with peer helpers, and provide class time for pair interaction.

How Do I Reach Students with Behavioral Disorders?

✔ Provide a structured environment with clear-cut schedules, rules, seat assignments, and safety procedures.

✔ Reinforce appropriate behavior and model it for students.

✔ Cue distracted students back to the task through verbal signals and teacher proximity.

✔ Set very small goals that can be achieved in the short term. Work for long-term improvement in the big areas.

How Do I Reach Students with Physical Challenges?

✔ Openly discuss with the student any uncertainties you have about when to offer aid.

✔ Ask parents or therapists and students what special devices or procedures are needed, and whether any special safety precautions need to be taken.

✔ Welcome students with physical challenges into all activities, including field trips, special events, and projects.

Michael Newman/PhotoEdit

Jose L. Pelaez/CORBIS STOCK MARKET

✔ Provide information to help able-bodied students and adults understand other students' physical challenges.

How Do I Reach Students with Visual Impairments?

✔ Facilitate independence. Modify assignments as needed.
✔ Teach classmates how and when to serve as guides.
✔ Limit unnecessary noise in the classroom if it distracts the student with visual impairments.
✔ Provide tactile models whenever possible.
✔ Foster a spirit of inclusion. Describe people and events as they occur in the classroom. Remind classmates that the student with visual impairments cannot interpret gestures and other forms of nonverbal communication.
✔ Provide taped lectures and reading assignments.
✔ Team the student with a sighted peer for written work.

How Do I Reach Students with Hearing Impairments?

✔ Seat students where they can see your lip movements easily and where they can avoid visual distractions.

✔ Avoid standing with your back to the window or light source.
✔ Use an overhead projector to maintain eye contact while writing.
✔ Seat students where they can see speakers.
✔ Write all assignments on the board, or hand out written instructions.
✔ If the student has a manual interpreter, allow both student and interpreter to select the most favorable seating arrangements.
✔ Teach students to look directly at each other when they speak.

How Do I Reach English Language Learners?

✔ Remember, students' ability to speak English does not reflect their academic abilities.

✔ Try to incorporate the students' cultural experience into your instruction. The help of a bilingual aide may be effective.
✔ Avoid cultural stereotypes.
✔ Pre-teach important vocabulary and concepts.
✔ Encourage students to preview text before they begin reading, noting headings, graphic organizers, photographs, and maps.

How Do I Reach Gifted Students?

✔ Make arrangements for students to take selected subjects early and to work on independent projects.
✔ Ask "what if" questions to develop high-level thinking skills. Establish an environment safe for risk taking.
✔ Emphasize concepts, theories, ideas, relationships, and generalizations.
✔ Promote interest in the past by inviting students to make connections to the present.
✔ Let students express themselves in alternate ways, such as creative writing, acting, debate, simulations, drawing, or music.
✔ Provide students with a catalog of helpful resources, listing such things as agencies that provide free and inexpensive materials, appropriate community services and programs, and community experts.
✔ Assign extension projects that allow students to solve real-life problems related to their communities.✦

Customize Your Classroom!

Advice from Marilyn Gerken
Pickerington Local Schools
Pickerington, Ohio

Provide individualized activities and assignments for a variety of student ability levels. Develop learning packets for chapters and units of study with varying formats, levels, and types of assignments. Assign points and contract students based on their selection of activities to be completed. The activities in the Student Edition can be used for many of the learning activities and assignments.

NCSS Ten Thematic Strands

In *Curriculum Standards for Social Studies: Expectations of Excellence*, the National Council for the Social Studies (NCSS) identified 10 themes that serve as organizing strands for the social studies curriculum at every school level. These themes are interrelated and draw from all of the social science disciplines. Each theme provides student performance expectations in the areas of knowledge, processes, and attitudes. The 10 NCSS themes were the basis for the themes used in *The American Vision*.

Theme and Performance Expectations	Student Pages
I. *Culture* The study of culture helps students understand similarities and differences within groups of people. By studying a culture's beliefs, values, and traditions, students begin to gain a perspective that helps them relate to different groups. In high school, students can understand and use complex cultural concepts such as adaptation, assimilation, and acculturation to explain how culture and cultural systems function. *The American Vision* Related Theme: Culture and Traditions	
A. Analyze and explain the ways groups, societies, and cultures address human needs and concerns.	20–24, 66–71, 91–97, 147–152, 476–480, 620–623, 661–665, 820–825, 970–974
B. Predict how data and experiences may be interpreted by people from diverse cultural perspectives and frames of reference.	52–53, 164–169, 618–619
C. Apply an understanding of culture as an integrated whole that explains the functions and interactions of language, literature, the arts, traditions, beliefs and values, and behavior patterns.	20–24, 66–71, 147–152, 164–169, 210–214, 620–623, 661–665, 773, 820–825, 970–974, 994–999, 1007
D. Compare and analyze societal patterns for preserving and transmitting culture while adapting to environmental or social change.	66–71, 91–97, 210–214, 431, 474–475, 1007
E. Demonstrate the value of cultural diversity, as well as cohesion, within and across groups.	20–24, 750, 970–974, 994–999
F. Interpret patterns of behavior reflecting values and attitudes that contribute or pose obstacles to cross-cultural understanding.	474–475, 618–619, 719–724, 752, 773
G. Construct reasoned judgments about specific cultural responses to persistent human issues.	132–133, 866–886
H. Explain and apply ideas, theories, and modes of inquiry drawn from anthropology and sociology in the examination of persistent issues and social problems.	12–17, 476–480, 481–486
II. *Time, Continuity, and Change* Understanding time, continuity, and change involves being knowledgeable about what things were like in the past and how things change and develop over time. Knowing how to read and reconstruct the past helps students gain a historical perspective. In high school, students examine the past's relationship with the present while extrapolating into the future. They also integrate individual stories about people, events, and situations to form a more complete conception, in which continuity and change persist in time and across cultures. Students will use their knowledge of history to make informed choices and decisions in the present. *The American Vision* Related Theme: Continuity and Change	
A. Demonstrate that historical knowledge and the concept of time are socially influenced constructions that lead historians to be selective in the questions they seek to answer and the evidence they use.	492–497, 599–603
B. Apply key concepts such as time, chronology, causality, change, conflict, and complexity to explain, analyze, and show connections among patterns of historical change and continuity.	240–244, 251–256, 278–282, 306–311, 492–497, 536–541, 562–565, 576–583, 599–603, 610–616, 713–718, 749–754, 828–832
C. Identify and describe significant historical periods and patterns of change within and across cultures, such as the development of ancient cultures and civilizations, the rise of nation-states, and social, economic, and political revolutions.	12–17, 32–37, 42–43, 240–244, 251–256, 278–282, 306–311, 536–541, 562–565, 576–583, 610–616, 713–718, 749–754, 814–819, 920–925
D. Systematically employ processes of critical historical inquiry to reconstruct and reinterpret the past, such as using a variety of sources and checking their credibility, validating and weighing evidence for claims, and searching for causality.	132–133, 306–311, 401, 466, 492–497, 534–535, 536–541, 588, 618–619, 669, 770–771, 788, 898–899, 902–903, 986

Theme and Performance Expectations	Student Pages
E. Investigate, interpret, and analyze multiple historical and contemporary viewpoints within and across cultures related to important events, recurring dilemmas, and persistent issues, while employing empathy, skepticism, and critical judgement.	251–256, 278–282, 452–453, 534–535, 599–603, 610–616, 618–619, 814–819, 828–832, 902–903
F. Apply ideas, theories, and modes of historical inquiry to analyze historical and contemporary developments, and to inform and evaluate actions concerning public policy issues.	251–256, 562–565, 576–583, 610–616, 749–754

III. People, Places, and Environments

The study of people, places, and environments will help students as they create their spatial views and geographic perspectives of the world. Students begin to make informed and critical decisions about the relationship between humans and their environment. In high school, geographic concepts become central to students' comprehension of global connections as they expand their knowledge of diverse cultures, both historical and contemporary.

The American Vision Related Theme: Geography and History

A. Refine mental maps of locales, regions, and the world that demonstrate understanding of relative locations, direction, size, and shape.	12–17, 357–363, 369–373, 420–423, 755–761
B. Create, interpret, use, and synthesize information from various representations of the earth, such as maps, globes, and photographs.	RA2–RA18, 12–17, 18–19, 58–64, 320–324, 357–363, 369–373, 420–423, 464–468, 465, 543, 594, 605, 613, 751, 1002, 1034
C. Use appropriate resources, data sources, and geographic tools such as aerial photographs, satellite images, geographic information systems (GIS), map projections, and cartography to generate, manipulate, and interpret information such as atlases, databases, grid systems, charts, graphs, and maps.	65, 226–227, 312–313, 369–373, 464–468, 992–993
D. Calculate distance, scale, area, and density, and distinguish spatial distribution patterns.	12–17, 320–324, 369–373, 374–375, 474–475, 751, 992–993
E. Describe, differentiate, and explain the relationships among various regional and global patterns of geographic phenomena such as landforms, soils, climate, vegetation, natural resources, and population.	42–43, 84–90, 357–363, 369–373
F. Use knowledge of physical system changes such as seasons, climate and weather, and the water cycle to explain geographic phenomena.	12–17, 755–761
G. Describe and compare how people create places that reflect culture, human needs, government policy, and current values and ideals as they design and build specialized buildings, neighborhoods, shopping centers, urban centers, industrial parks, and the like.	20–24, 58–64, 84–90, 320–324
H. Examine, interpret, and analyze physical and cultural patterns and their interactions, such as land use, settlement patterns, cultural transmission of customs and ideas, and ecosystem changes.	12–17, 42–43, 58–64, 84–90, 308–309, 320–324, 464–468, 755–761
I. Describe and assess ways that historical events have been influenced by, and have influenced, physical and human geographic factors in local, regional, national, and global settings.	18–19, 42–43, 226–227, 320–324, 464–468, 474–475, 560–561, 666–667, 758–759, 762–763, 944–945, 992–993
J. Analyze and evaluate social and economic effects of environmental changes and crises resulting from phenomena such as floods, storms, and drought.	18–19, 42–43, 421–423, 548–549
K. Propose, compare, and evaluate alternative policies for the use of land and other resources in communities, regions, nations, and the world.	558–561, 942, 1020–1021, 1024–1025

Theme and Performance Expectations	Student Pages

IV. Individual Development and Identity

People and culture influence a person's identity. Examining the different forms of human behavior improves one's understanding of social relationships and the development of personal identity. The study of human behavior helps students become aware of how social processes influence a person's identity. In high school, students use methods from the behavioral sciences to examine individuals, societies, and cultures.

The American Vision Related Theme: Individual Action

A.	Articulate personal connections to time, place, and social/cultural system.	284–288, 355, 454–459, 481–486, 508–512, 592–597, 725–730
B.	Identify, describe, and express appreciation for the influence of various historical and contemporary cultures on an individual's daily life.	339, 376–380, 481–486, 550, 750, 752
C.	Describe the ways family, religion, gender, ethnicity, nationality, socioeconomic status, and other group and cultural influences contribute to the development of a sense of self.	98–102, 228–232, 339, 355, 376–380, 431, 454–459, 481–486, 508–512, 550, 725–730, 750, 752, 920–925, 980–984
D.	Apply concepts, methods, and theories about the study of human growth and development, such as physical endowment, learning, motivation, behavior, perception, and personality.	228–232, 481–486, 592–597, 678–681
E.	Examine the interaction of ethnic, national, or cultural influences in specific situations or events.	98–102, 376–380, 425–430, 431, 466, 508–512, 555–559, 589, 592–597, 601–603, 750, 752, 790–795, 920–925, 980–984, 1001–1006
F.	Analyze the role of perceptions, attitudes, values, and beliefs in the development of personal identity.	284–288, 376–380, 431, 508–512, 555–559, 571, 678–681, 725–730, 752, 920–925, 970–974
G.	Compare and evaluate the impact of stereotyping, conformity, acts of altruism, and other behaviors on individuals and groups.	98–102, 284–288, 425–430, 442–446, 752
H.	Work independently and cooperatively within groups and institutions to accomplish goals.	228–232, 678–681
I.	Examine factors that contribute to and damage one's mental health and analyze issues related to mental health and behavioral disorders in contemporary society.	278–282, 552–553

V. Individuals, Groups, and Institutions

Institutions, such as schools, governments, and churches, influence people and often reflect a society's values. Because of the vital role that institutions play in people's lives, it is important that students know how institutions develop, what controls and influences them, and how humans react to them. High school students must understand the traditions and theories that support social and political traditions.

The American Vision Related Theme: Groups and Institutions

A.	Apply concepts such as role, status, and social class in describing the connections and interactions of individuals, groups, and institutions in society.	266–272, 268–269, 398–402, 454–459, 695–700
B.	Analyze group and institutional influences on people, events, and elements of culture in both historical and contemporary settings.	257–260, 266–272, 273–277, 300–304, 332–338, 350–356, 364–368, 386–389, 398–402, 454–459, 626–630, 668–672, 682–688, 695–700, 736–741, 939–943
C.	Describe the various forms institutions take, and explain how they develop and change over time.	257–260, 266–272, 280–281, 300–304, 332–338, 350–356, 386–389, 398–402, 626–630, 668–672, 682–688
D.	Identify and analyze examples of tensions between expressions of individuality and efforts used to promote social conformity by groups and institutions.	273–277, 364–368, 386–389, 736–741, 920–925
E.	Describe and examine belief systems basic to specific traditions and laws in contemporary and historical movements.	257–260, 300–304, 332–338, 364–368, 626–630, 695–700, 736–741, 939–943, 980–984
F.	Evaluate the role of institutions in furthering both continuity and change.	257–260, 266–272, 300–304, 350–356, 364–368, 386–389, 626–630, 668–672, 682–688, 939–943
G.	Analyze the extent to which groups and institutions meet individual needs and promote the common good in contemporary and historical settings.	273–277, 398–402, 668–672, 682–688, 939–943
H.	Explain and apply ideas and modes of inquiry drawn from behavioral science and social theory in the examination of persistent issues and social problems.	476–480, 481–486

Theme and Performance Expectations	Student Pages

VI. Power, Authority, and Governance

Studying structures of power, authority, and governance and their functions in the United States and around the world is important for developing a notion of civic responsibility. Students will identify the purpose and characteristics of various types of government and how people try to resolve conflicts. Students will also examine the relationship between individual rights and responsibilities. High school students study the various systems that have been developed over time to allocate and employ power and authority in the governing process.

The American Vision Related Theme: Government and Democracy

A.	Examine persistent issues involving the rights, roles, and status of the individual in relation to the general welfare.	126–133, 392–393, 546–553, 566–570, 588, 689–694, 752, 764–772, 854–860, 866–872, 920–925
B.	Explain the purpose of government and analyze how its powers are acquired, used, and justified.	134–137, 158–162, 160–161, 172–175, 221–225, 392–393, 469–473, 527–533, 546–553, 548–549, 584–589, 636–639, 669, 689–694, 854–860, 892–895, 910–914, 958–962, 1026–1029
C.	Analyze and explain ideas and mechanisms to meet needs and wants of citizens, regulate territory, manage conflict, establish order and security, and balance competing conceptions of a just society.	20–24, 126–133, 158–162, 172–175, 221–225, 469–473, 548–549, 584–589, 689–694, 854–860, 866–872, 892–895, 910–914, 958–962, 980–984, 1026–1029
D.	Compare and analyze the ways nations and organizations respond to conflicts between forces of unity and forces of diversity.	124–125, 172–175, 174, 392–393, 584–589, 752, 866–872, 920–925, 980–984
E.	Compare different political systems (their ideologies, structure, institutions, processes, and political cultures) with that of the United States, and identify representative political leaders from selected historical and contemporary settings.	172–175, 221–225, 636–639, 958–962, 1026–1029
F.	Analyze and evaluate conditions, actions, and motivations that contribute to conflict and cooperation within and among nations.	42–43, 126–133, 158–162, 172–175, 527–533, 566–570, 764–772, 866–872, 892–895, 910–915, 920–925, 958–962
G.	Evaluate the role of technology in communications, transportation, information-processing, weapons development, or other areas as it contributes to or helps resolve conflicts.	527–533, 1012–1015, 1026–1029
H.	Explain and apply ideas, theories, and modes of inquiry drawn from political science to the examination of persistent ideas and social problems.	126–133, 469–473, 689–694, 854–860, 866–872, 920–925
I.	Evaluate the extent to which governments achieve their stated ideals and policies at home and abroad.	158–162, 172–175, 221–225, 527–533, 546–553, 566–570, 584–589, 689–694, 752, 854–860, 866–872, 892–895
J.	Prepare a public policy paper and present and defend it before an appropriate forum in school or community.	947, 977

VII. Production, Distribution, and Consumption

Societies try to meet people's needs and wants by trying to answer the basic economic questions: What is to be produced? How should goods be produced? How should goods and services be distributed? How should land, labor, capital, and management be allocated? By studying how needs and wants are met, students learn how trade and government economic policies develop. In high school, students develop economic perspectives and a deeper understanding of key economic concepts and processes.

The American Vision Related Theme: Economic Factors

A.	Explain how the scarcity of productive resources (human, capital, technological, and natural) requires the development of economic systems to make decisions about how goods and services are to be produced and distributed.	20–24, 403–407, 436–440, 447–451, 647–650, 656–660, 808–813, 963–969, 985–991, 1016–1021
B.	Analyze the role that supply and demand, prices, incentives, and profits play in determining what is produced and distributed in a competitive market system.	414–419, 436–440, 447–451, 500–507, 656–660, 808–813, 963–969, 985–991
C.	Consider the costs and benefits to society of allocating goods and services through private and public sectors.	452–453, 985–991, 1016–1021
D.	Describe the relationships among the various economic institutions that comprise economic systems such as households, business firms, banks, government agencies, labor unions, and corporations.	403–407, 447–451, 647–650, 656–660, 808–813, 985–991, 1012–1015

Theme and Performance Expectations	Student Pages
E. Analyze the role of specialization and exchange in economic processes.	403–407, 447–451
F. Compare how values and beliefs influence economic decisions in different societies.	20–24, 403–407, 414–419, 647–650, 808–813, 980–984, 1001–1006, 1012–1015, 1016–1021
G. Compare basic economic systems according to how rules and procedures deal with demand, supply, prices, the role of government, banks, labor and labor unions, savings and investments, and capital.	452–453, 500–507, 985–991
H. Apply economic concepts and reasoning when evaluating historical and contemporary social developments and issues.	452–453
I. Distinguish between the domestic and global economic systems, and explain how the two interact.	414–419, 500–507
J. Apply knowledge of production, distribution, and consumption in the analysis of a public issue such as the allocation of health care or the consumption of energy, and devise an economic plan for accomplishing a socially desirable outcome related to that issue.	857–859, 942, 1016–1021, 1022–1025
K. Distinguish between economics as a field of inquiry and the economy.	647–648, 695–700, 987–988

VIII. Science, Technology, and Society

The study of science, technology, and society is ever changing. It raises questions about who will benefit from it and how fundamental values and beliefs can be preserved in a technology-driven society. In high school, students will confront issues that balance the benefits of science and technology against the accompanying social consequences.

The American Vision Related Theme: Science and Technology

A. Identify and describe both current and historical examples of the interaction and interdependence of science, technology, and society in a variety of cultural settings.	32–37, 245–250, 252, 294–297, 415, 470, 640–646, 684–685, 846–851, 873–880, 896–901, 994–999, 1012–1015
B. Make judgments about how science and technology have transformed the physical world and human society and our understanding of time, space, place, and human-environment interactions.	32–37, 42–43, 245–250, 294–297, 365, 415, 470, 538–539, 640–646, 666–667, 797–802, 817, 846–851, 873–880, 994–999, 1012–1015
C. Analyze how science and technology influence the core values, beliefs, and attitudes of society, and how core values, beliefs, and attitudes of society shape scientific and technological change.	32–37, 245–250, 640–646, 790–796, 797–802, 846–851, 873–880, 896–901
D. Evaluate various policies that have been proposed as ways of dealing with social changes resulting from new technologies, such as genetically engineered plants and animals.	538–539, 1012–1015
E. Recognize and interpret varied perspectives about human societies and the physical world using scientific knowledge, ethical standards, and technologies from diverse world cultures.	35–37
F. Formulate strategies and develop policies for influencing public discussions associated with technology-society issues, such as the greenhouse effect.	939–943, 1024–1025

IX. Global Connections

As countries grow more interdependent, understanding global connections among world societies becomes important. Students will analyze emerging global issues in many different fields. They will also investigate relationships among the different cultures of the world. High school students will address critical issues such as peace, human rights, trade, and global ecology.

The American Vision Related Theme: Global Connections

A. Explain how language, art, music, belief systems, and other cultural elements can facilitate global understanding or cause misunderstanding.	50–57, 72–77, 104–109, 797–802, 1031–1037
B. Explain conditions and motivations that contribute to conflict, cooperation, and interdependence among groups, societies, and nations.	26–31, 38–44, 42–43, 50–57, 72–77, 138–145, 520–525, 708–712, 778–782, 783–789, 797–802, 952–957, 984–991, 1001–1006, 1012–1015, 1022–1025

25	26	27	28	29	30	31	32	33	34
	Section 3	Section 3		Section 1		Sections 2, 3	Section 4	Section 3	
		Sections 2, 4		Section 2		Section 1			Sections 2, 3
Section 4					Section 1				
Sections 1, 2		Section 1		Section 1	Section 2			Section 4	Section 5
Section 5			Sections 1, 3		Section 4	Section 4	Section 2		
Section 5	Section 4		Section 3	Section 1	Sections 1, 4	Section 1	Sections 1, 2, 3	Section 1	Section 4
		Sections 1, 2				Section 4	Section 3	Sections 1, 4	Sections 1, 2
	Section 4	Section 3	Section 2	Section 2	Section 2			Section 3	
Sections 1, 2, 3, 4, 5	Sections 1, 2		Section 2				Section 1	Section 2	Sections 3, 5
Section 1	Section 3	Section 4	Section 1	Sections 1, 2, 3	Section 3	Sections 2, 3			
Social Studies Skill	*Critical Thinking Skill*	*Social Studies Skill*	*Critical Thinking Skill*	*Study and Writing Skill*	*Social Studies Skill*	*Critical Thinking Skill*	*Critical Thinking Skill*	*Critical Thinking Skill*	*Social Studies Skill*
Reading a Thematic Map	Making Decisions	Writing a Journal	Problem Solving	Preparing a Bibliography	Conducting an Interview	Analyzing Primary Sources	Analyzing Secondary Sources	Analyzing News Media	Reading a Cartogram

Reading for Information

Think of your textbook as a tool that helps you learn more about the world around you. It is an example of nonfiction writing—it describes real-life events, people, ideas, and places. Here is a menu of reading strategies that will help you become a better textbook reader. As you come to passages in your textbook that you don't understand, refer to these reading strategies for help.

✓ Before You Read

Set a purpose
- Why are you reading the textbook?
- How does the subject relate to your life?
- How might you be able to use what you learn in your own life?

Preview
- Read the chapter title to find what the topic will be.
- Read the subtitles to see what you will learn about the topic.
- Skim the photos, charts, graphs, or maps. How do they support the topic?
- Look for vocabulary words that are boldfaced. What are their definitions?

Draw From Your Own Background
- What have you read or heard concerning new information on the topic?
- How is the new information different from what you already know?
- How will the information that you already know help you understand the new information?

Question

■ What is the main idea?

■ How do the photos, charts, graphs, and maps support the main idea?

Connect

■ Think about people, places, and events in your own life. Are there any similarities with those in your textbook?

■ Can you relate the textbook information to other areas of your life?

Predict

■ Predict events or outcomes by using clues and information that you already know.

■ Change your predictions as you read and gather new information.

Visualize

■ Pay careful attention to details and descriptions.

■ Create graphic organizers to show relationships that you find in the information.

Look For Clues As You Read

Comparison and Contrast Sentences

■ Look for clue words and phrases that signal comparison, such as *similarly, just as, both, in common, also,* and *too.*

■ Look for clue words and phrases that signal contrast, such as *on the other hand, in contrast to, however, different, instead of, rather than, but,* and *unlike.*

Cause-and-Effect Sentences

■ Look for clue words and phrases such as *because, as a result, therefore, that is why, since, so, for this reason,* and *consequently.*

Chronological Sentences

■ Look for clue words and phrases such as *after, before, first, next, last, during, finally, earlier, later, since,* and *then.*

✔ After You Read

Summarize

■ Describe the main idea and how the details support it.

■ Use your own words to explain what you have read.

Assess

■ What was the main idea?

■ Did the text clearly support the main idea?

■ Did you learn anything new from the material?

■ Can you use this new information in other school subjects or at home?

■ What other sources could you use to find more information about the topic?

How Do I Study History?

As you read *The American Vision,* you will be given help in sorting out all the information you encounter. This textbook organizes the events of your nation's past and present around 10 themes. A theme is a concept, or main idea that happens again and again throughout history. By recognizing these themes, you will better understand events of the past and how they affect you today.

Themes in *The American Vision*

Culture and Traditions
Being aware of cultural differences helps us understand ourselves and others. People from around the world for generations have sung of the "land of the Pilgrims' pride, land where our fathers died," even though their ancestors arrived on these shores long after these events occurred.

Continuity and Change
Recognizing our historic roots helps us understand why things are the way they are today. This theme includes political, social, religious, and economic changes that have influenced the way Americans think and act.

Geography and History
Understanding geography helps us understand how humans interact with their environment. The United States succeeded in part because of its rich natural resources and its vast open spaces. In many regions, the people changed the natural landscape to fulfill their wants and needs.

Individual Action

Responsible individuals have often stepped forward to help lead the nation. Americans' strong values helped create such individuals. These values spring in part from earlier times when the home was the center of many activities, including work, education, and spending time with one's family.

Groups and Institutions

Identifying how political and social groups and institutions operate helps us work together. From the beginning, Americans formed groups and institutions to act in support of their economic, political, social, and religious beliefs.

Government and Democracy

Understanding the workings of government helps us become better citizens. Abraham Lincoln explained the meaning of democracy as "government of the people, by the people, for the people." Democracy, at its best, is "among" the people.

Science and Technology

Americans have always been quick to adopt innovations. The nation was settled and built by people who gave up old ways in favor of new. Americans' lives are deeply influenced by technology, the use of science, and machines. Perhaps no machine has so shaped modern life as the automobile. Understanding the role of science and technology helps us see their impact on our society and the roles they will play in the future.

Economic Factors

The free enterprise economy of the United States is consistent with the nation's history of rights and freedoms. Freedom of choice in economic decisions supports other freedoms. Understanding the concept of free enterprise is basic to studying American history.

Global Connections

Being aware of global interdependence helps us make decisions and deal with the difficult issues we will encounter.

Civic Rights and Responsibilities

For a democratic system to survive, its citizens must take an active role in government. The foundation of democracy is the right of every person to take part in government and to voice one's views on issues. An appreciation for the struggle to preserve these freedoms is vital to the understanding of democracy.

Using the Themes

You will find Section Themes at the beginning of every section of your text. You are asked questions that help you put it all together to better understand how ideas and themes are connected across time—and to see why history is important to you today.

REFERENCE ATLAS

NATIONAL GEOGRAPHIC

ATLAS KEY

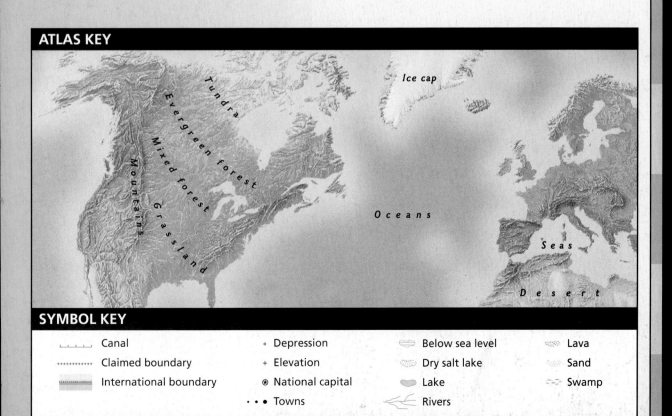

SYMBOL KEY

⌐⌐⌐⌐ Canal	∘ Depression	⊜ Below sea level	≈ Lava
·········· Claimed boundary	+ Elevation	Dry salt lake	Sand
International boundary	⊛ National capital	Lake	⊸ Swamp
	• • Towns	Rivers	

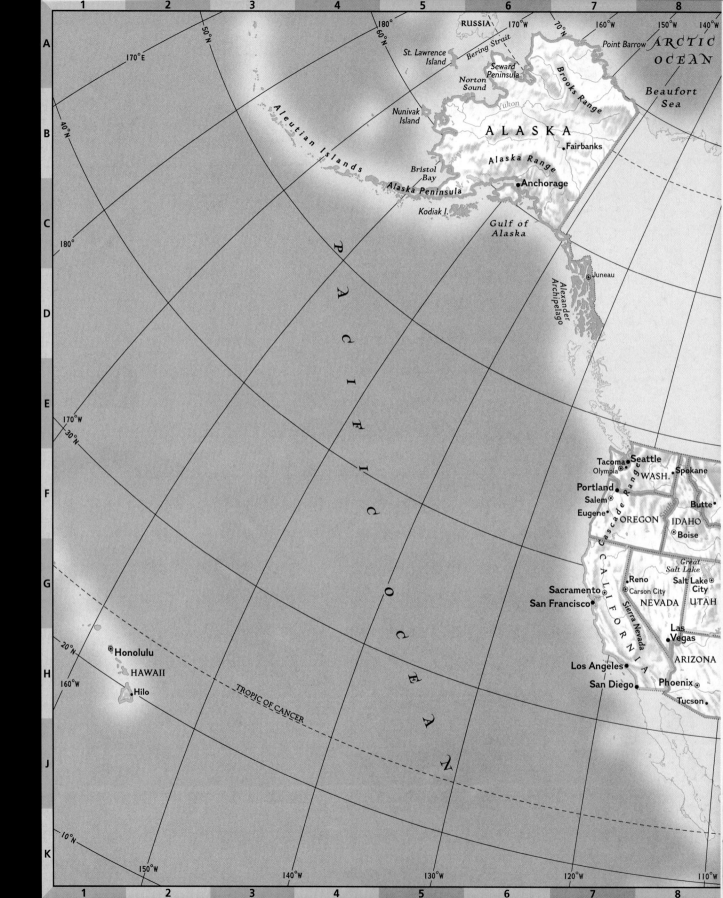

A · B · C · D · E · F · G · H · J · K (row labels on left)

1 · 2 · 3 · 4 · 5 · 6 · 7 · 8 (column labels top and bottom)

170°E · 50°N · 180° · 60°N · 170°W · 70°N · 160°W · 150°W · 140°W

RUSSIA

St. Lawrence Island

Bering Strait

Point Barrow

ARCTIC OCEAN

Seward Peninsula

Norton Sound

Brooks Range

Beaufort Sea

Nunivak Island

ALASKA

Yukon

40°N

Aleutian Islands

Bristol Bay

Alaska Range

Fairbanks

Alaska Peninsula

Anchorage

180°

Kodiak I.

Gulf of Alaska

P A C I F I C

Alexander Archipelago

Juneau

170°W

30°N

O C E A N

Tacoma · Seattle

Olympia · WASH. · Spokane

Portland

Salem · Butte

Eugene · OREGON · IDAHO

Cascade Range

Snake

Boise

Great Salt Lake

20°N

Honolulu

HAWAII

Reno · Salt Lake City

160°W

Hilo

Sacramento · Carson City · NEVADA · UTAH

San Francisco

Sierra Nevada

TROPIC OF CANCER

Las Vegas

ARIZONA

CALIFORNIA

Los Angeles

San Diego · Phoenix

Tucson

10°N

150°W · 140°W · 130°W · 120°W · 110°W

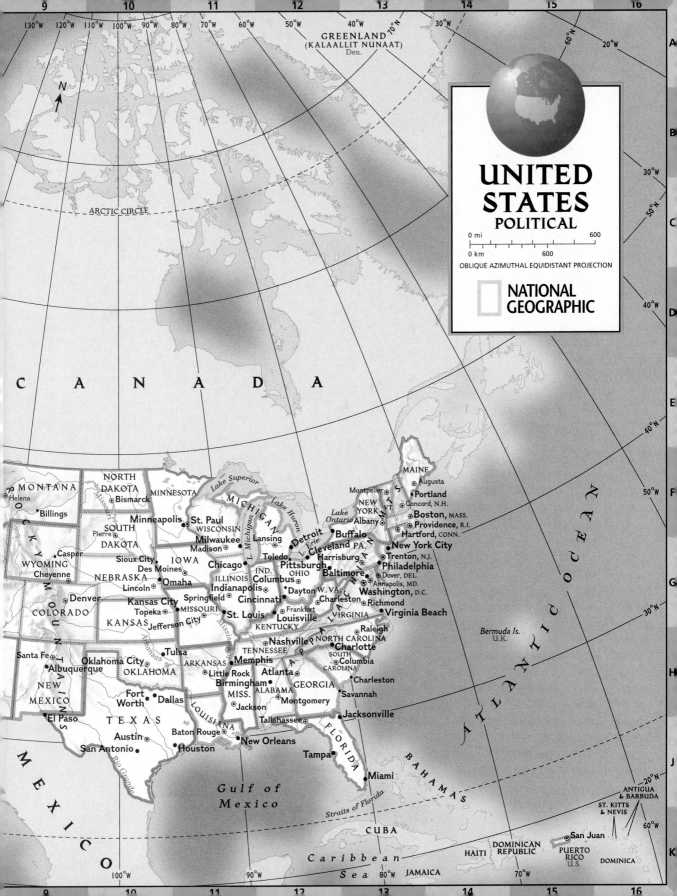

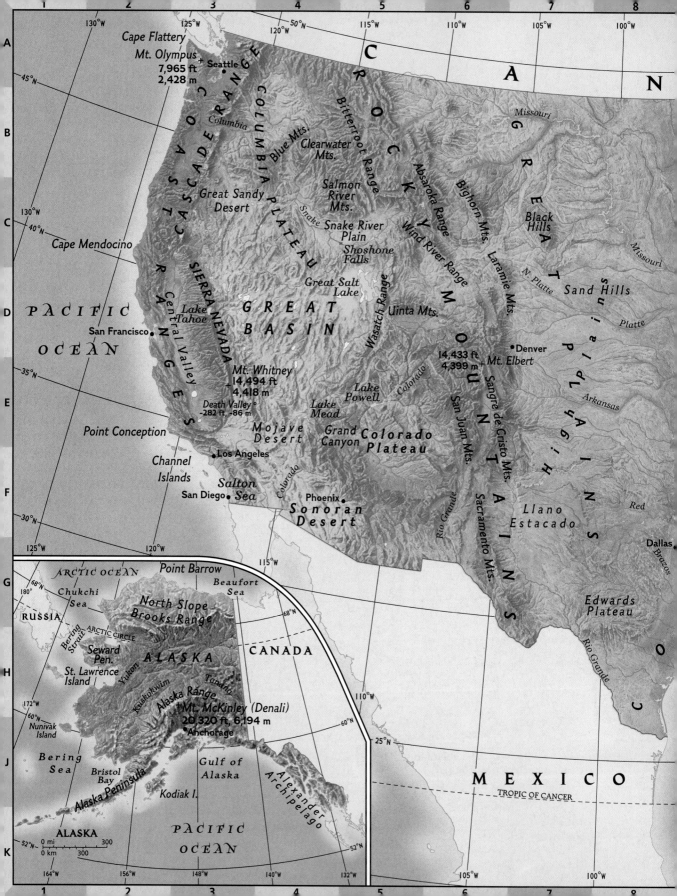

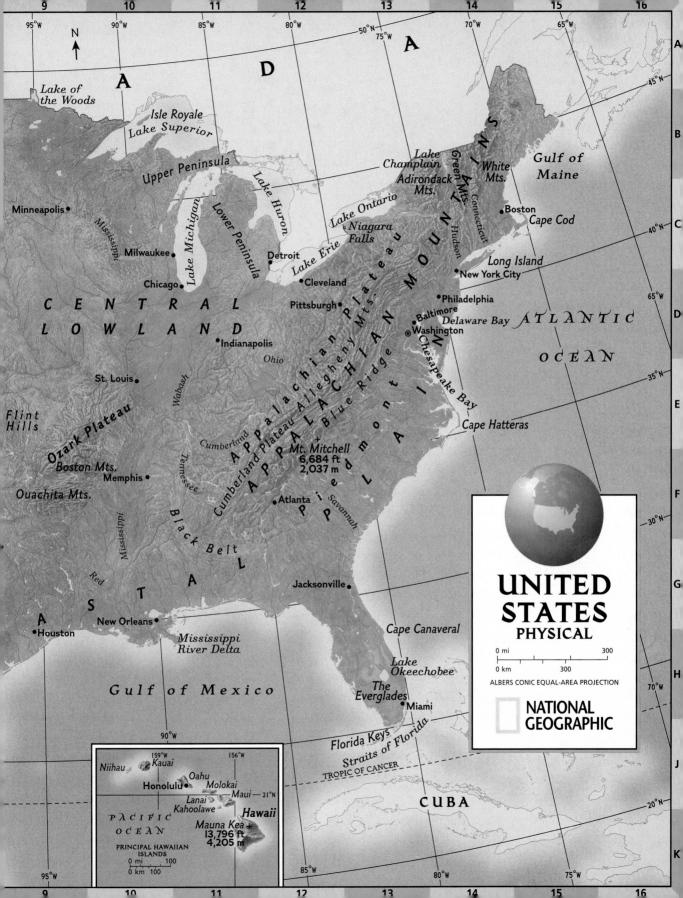

UNITED STATES PHYSICAL

ALBERS CONIC EQUAL-AREA PROJECTION

NATIONAL GEOGRAPHIC

Lake of the Woods

Isle Royale
Lake Superior

Upper Peninsula

Minneapolis

Milwaukee

Lake Michigan

Lower Peninsula

Lake Huron

Detroit

Chicago

Lake Erie

Cleveland

Lake Ontario

Niagara Falls

Lake Champlain

Adirondack Mts.

Green Mts.

White Mts.

Gulf of Maine

Boston

Cape Cod

Connecticut

Hudson

Long Island

New York City

Philadelphia

Baltimore

Washington

Delaware Bay

Chesapeake Bay

ATLANTIC OCEAN

C E N T R A L
L O W L A N D

Indianapolis

Ohio

Wabash

St. Louis

Flint Hills

Ozark Plateau

Boston Mts.

Memphis

Tennessee

Ouachita Mts.

Mississippi

Pittsburgh

Appalachian Plateau

Allegheny Mts.

Cumberland Plateau

APPALACHIAN MOUNTAINS

Blue Ridge

Cumberland

Mt. Mitchell
6,684 ft
2,037 m

Piedmont

Cape Hatteras

Atlanta

Savannah

Black Belt

Red

Mississippi

C O A S T A L   P L A I N

Houston

New Orleans

Mississippi River Delta

Gulf of Mexico

Jacksonville

Cape Canaveral

Lake Okeechobee

The Everglades

Miami

Florida Keys

Straits of Florida

TROPIC OF CANCER

CUBA

C A N A D A

Niihau
Kauai

Honolulu

Oahu
Molokai

Lanai

Kahoolawe

Maui — 21°N

Hawaii

Mauna Kea
13,796 ft
4,205 m

PACIFIC OCEAN

PRINCIPAL HAWAIIAN ISLANDS

0 mi   100
0 km   100

159°W

156°W

90°W

85°W

80°W

75°W

70°W

20°N

N

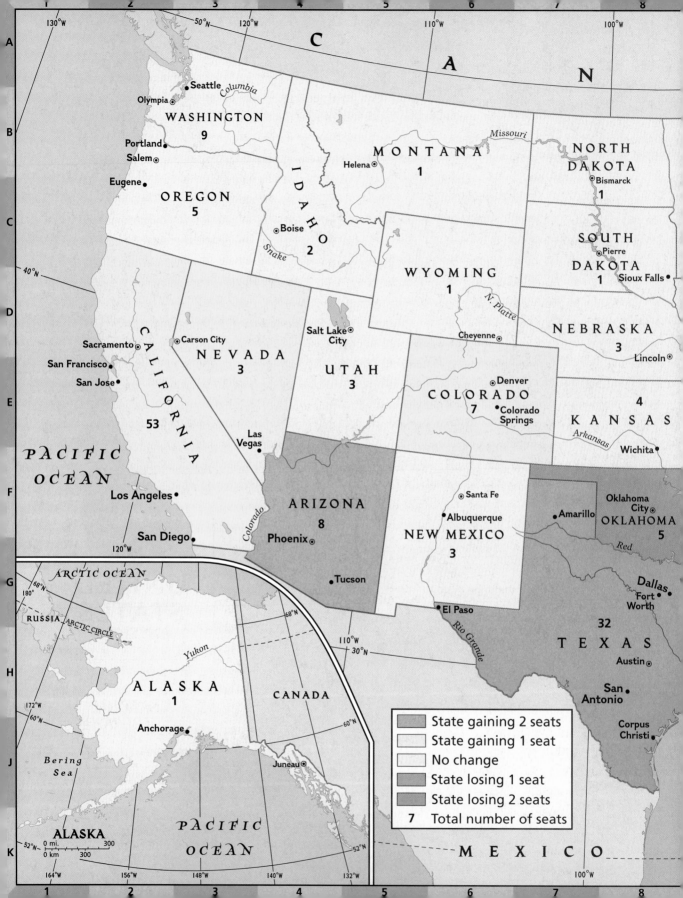

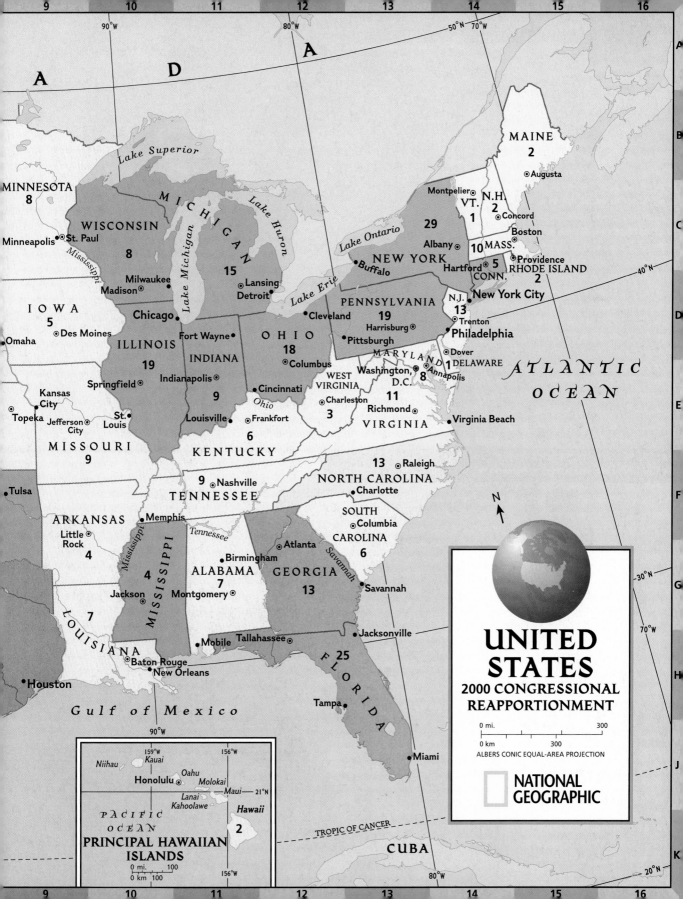

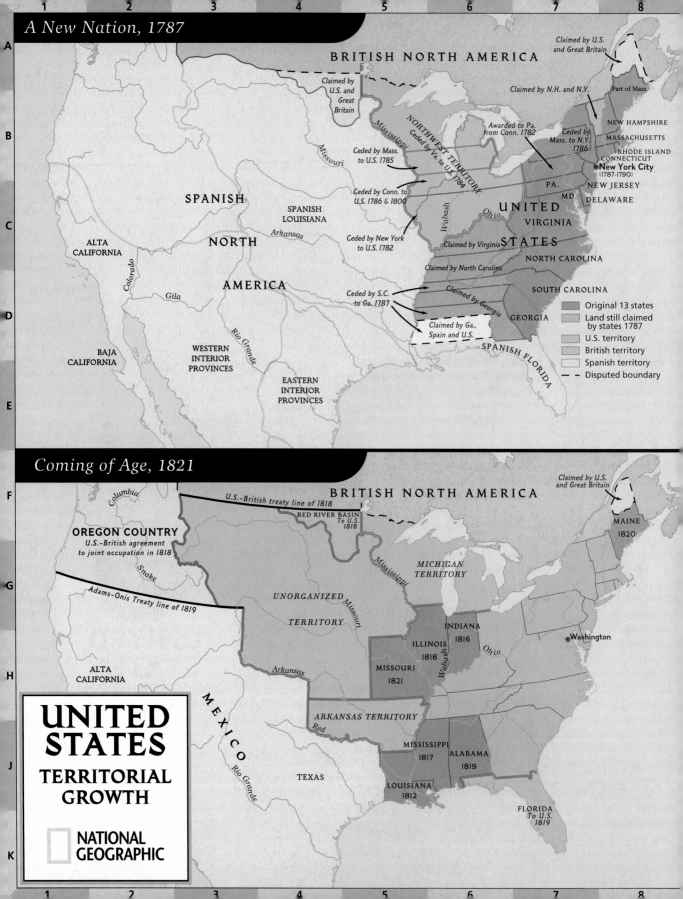

A New Nation, 1787

BRITISH NORTH AMERICA

Claimed by U.S. and Great Britain

Claimed by U.S. and Great Britain

Claimed by N.H. and N.Y.

Part of Mass.

Claimed by U.S. and Great Britain

Mississippi

Missouri

NORTHWEST TERRITORY
Ceded by Va. to U.S. 1784

Awarded to Pa. from Conn. 1782

Ceded by Mass. to N.Y. 1786

NEW HAMPSHIRE

MASSACHUSETTS

RHODE ISLAND
CONNECTICUT

Ceded by Mass. to U.S. 1785

SPANISH

NORTH

AMERICA

SPANISH LOUISIANA

Arkansas

Ceded by Conn. to U.S. 1786 & 1800

Ceded by New York to U.S. 1782

Wabash

Ohio

PA.

MD.

New York City
(1787-1790)

NEW JERSEY

DELAWARE

UNITED
STATES

VIRGINIA

Claimed by Virginia

ALTA
CALIFORNIA

Colorado

Gila

Claimed by North Carolina

NORTH CAROLINA

SOUTH CAROLINA

BAJA
CALIFORNIA

WESTERN
INTERIOR
PROVINCES

Rio Grande

Ceded by S.C. to Ga. 1787

Claimed by Georgia

GEORGIA

EASTERN
INTERIOR
PROVINCES

Claimed by Ga., Spain and U.S.

SPANISH FLORIDA

Original 13 states

Land still claimed by states 1787

U.S. territory

British territory

Spanish territory

– – – Disputed boundary

Coming of Age, 1821

Columbia

BRITISH NORTH AMERICA

U.S.-British treaty line of 1818

RED RIVER BASIN
To U.S.
1818

Claimed by U.S. and Great Britain

MAINE
1820

OREGON COUNTRY
U.S.-British agreement to joint occupation in 1818

Snake

Adams-Onis Treaty line of 1819

UNORGANIZED

TERRITORY

Mississippi

Missouri

MICHIGAN
TERRITORY

INDIANA
1816

Washington

ALTA
CALIFORNIA

Arkansas

ILLINOIS
1818

Wabash

Ohio

MISSOURI
1821

MEXICO

ARKANSAS TERRITORY

Red

Rio Grande

TEXAS

MISSISSIPPI
1817

ALABAMA
1819

LOUISIANA
1812

FLORIDA
To U.S.
1819

UNITED
STATES

TERRITORIAL
GROWTH

**NATIONAL
GEOGRAPHIC**

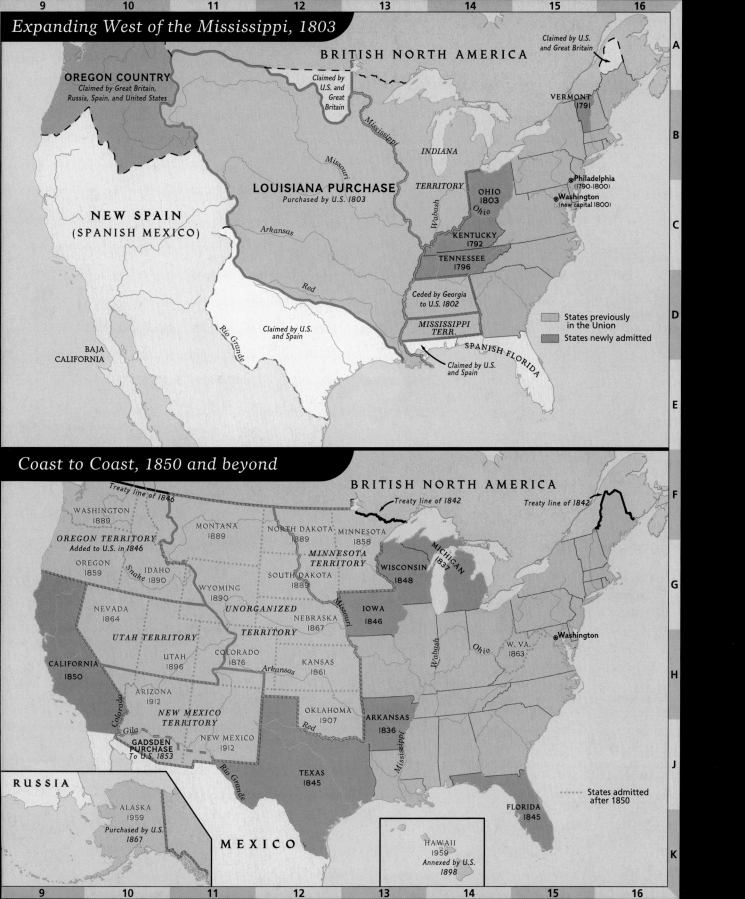

Expanding West of the Mississippi, 1803

BRITISH NORTH AMERICA

Claimed by U.S. and Great Britain

OREGON COUNTRY
Claimed by Great Britain, Russia, Spain, and United States

Claimed by U.S. and Great Britain

VERMONT 1791

INDIANA

Mississippi

Missouri

LOUISIANA PURCHASE
Purchased by U.S. 1803

TERRITORY

Wabash

OHIO 1803

Ohio

Philadelphia (1790-1800)
Washington (new capital 1800)

NEW SPAIN (SPANISH MEXICO)

Arkansas

KENTUCKY 1792

TENNESSEE 1796

Red

Ceded by Georgia to U.S. 1802

Rio Grande

Claimed by U.S. and Spain

MISSISSIPPI TERR.

States previously in the Union

States newly admitted

BAJA CALIFORNIA

SPANISH FLORIDA

Claimed by U.S. and Spain

Coast to Coast, 1850 and beyond

Treaty line of 1846

BRITISH NORTH AMERICA

Treaty line of 1842

Treaty line of 1842

WASHINGTON 1889

MONTANA 1889

NORTH DAKOTA 1889

MINNESOTA 1858

OREGON TERRITORY
Added to U.S. in 1846

MINNESOTA TERRITORY

MICHIGAN 1837

OREGON 1859

Snake

IDAHO 1890

SOUTH DAKOTA 1889

WISCONSIN 1848

WYOMING 1890

UNORGANIZED

Missouri

NEVADA 1864

IOWA 1846

Washington

Wabash

Ohio

W. VA. 1863

UTAH TERRITORY

TERRITORY

NEBRASKA 1867

UTAH 1896

COLORADO 1876

KANSAS 1861

CALIFORNIA 1850

Colorado

Arkansas

ARIZONA 1912

Gila

GADSDEN PURCHASE
To U.S. 1853

NEW MEXICO TERRITORY

OKLAHOMA 1907

Red

ARKANSAS 1836

Mississippi

NEW MEXICO 1912

RUSSIA

Rio Grande

TEXAS 1845

States admitted after 1850

ALASKA 1959
Purchased by U.S. 1867

MEXICO

FLORIDA 1845

HAWAII 1959
Annexed by U.S. 1898

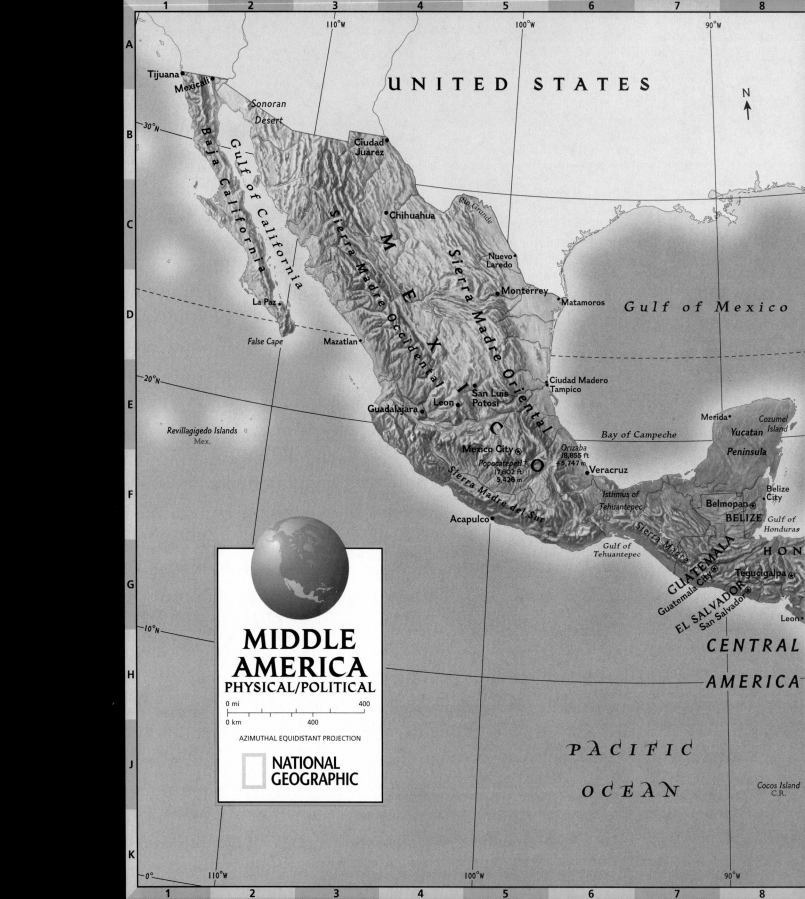

UNITED STATES

Tijuana
Mexicali

Sonoran Desert

30°N

Ciudad Juárez

Chihuahua

Rio Grande

Nuevo Laredo

Monterrey

Matamoros

Gulf of Mexico

La Paz

20°N

False Cape

Mazatlan

Ciudad Madero
Tampico

San Luis Potosí

Leon

Guadalajara

Bay of Campeche

Merida

Cozumel Island

Yucatan

Peninsula

Mexico City
Popocatepetl †
17,802 ft
5,426 m

Orizaba
18,855 ft
5,747 m

Veracruz

Isthmus of Tehuantepec

Belize City

Belmopan

BELIZE *Gulf of Honduras*

Acapulco

Gulf of Tehuantepec

Sierra Madre

HON

GUATEMALA

Guatemala City

Tegucigalpa

EL SALVADOR
San Salvador

Leon

CENTRAL

10°N

AMERICA

MIDDLE
AMERICA
PHYSICAL/POLITICAL

0 mi   400

0 km   400

AZIMUTHAL EQUIDISTANT PROJECTION

NATIONAL
GEOGRAPHIC

PACIFIC

OCEAN

Cocos Island
C.R.

0°

110°W

100°W

90°W

Gulf of California

Baja California

Sierra Madre Occidental

Sierra Madre Oriental

M E X I C O

Sierra Madre del Sur

Revillagigedo Islands
Mex.

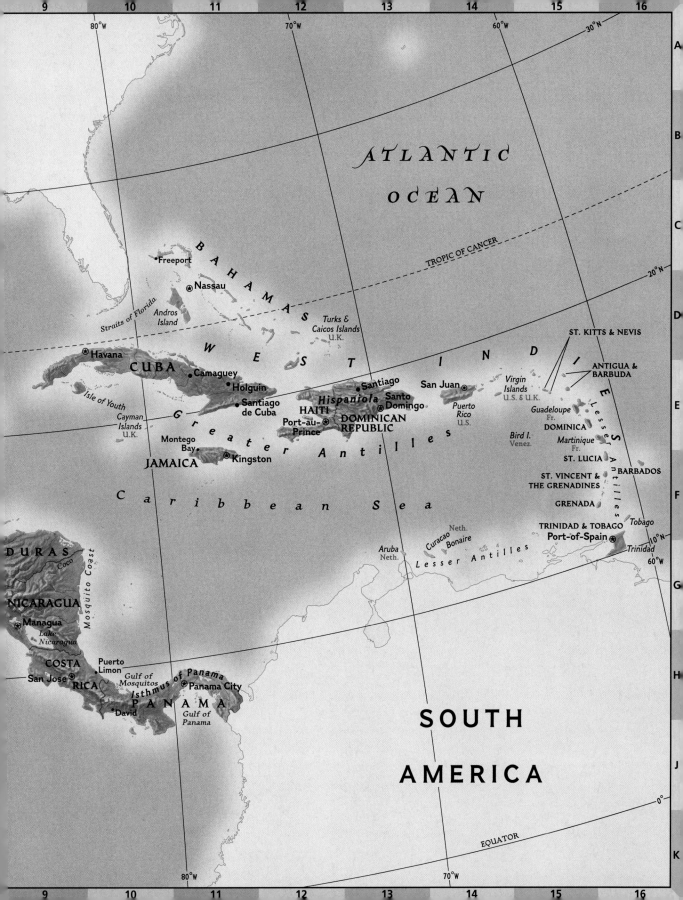

ATLANTIC

OCEAN

TROPIC OF CANCER

•Freeport
BAHAMAS

⊛ Nassau

Straits of Florida
Andros
Island

Turks &
Caicos Islands
U.K.

W E S T   I N D I

ST. KITTS & NEVIS

⊛ Havana
CUBA
•Camaguey
•Holguin

Santiago•
San Juan ⊛

Virgin
Islands
U.S. & U.K.

ANTIGUA &
BARBUDA

Isle of Youth

Cayman
Islands
U.K.

G

•Santiago
de Cuba

Hispaniola
HAITI
Port-au-
Prince ⊛

Santo
Domingo
DOMINICAN
REPUBLIC

Puerto
Rico
U.S.

Guadeloupe
Fr.

DOMINICA

Lesser

Montego
Bay•
JAMAICA
⊛ Kingston

Greater   Antilles

Bird I.
Venez.

Martinique
Fr.

ST. LUCIA

Antilles

BARBADOS

C a r i b b e a n   S e a

ST. VINCENT &
THE GRENADINES

GRENADA

Neth.
Curacao
Bonaire

TRINIDAD & TOBAGO
Port-of-Spain ⊛

Tobago

Trinidad

D U R A S

Coco

Aruba
Neth.

Lesser   Antilles

NICARAGUA

⊛ Managua
Lake
Nicaragua

COSTA
•Puerto
Limon

Gulf of
Mosquitos

Isthmus of Panama

Mosquito Coast

San Jose ⊛
RICA

Panama City ⊛
P A N A M A

SOUTH

•David
Gulf of
Panama

AMERICA

EQUATOR

RUSSIA

ARCTIC OCEAN

Queen

80°N

North Magnetic Pole +

Elizabeth

Prince Patrick I.

Islands

Melville Island

Bathurst Island

Beaufort Sea

Banks Island

Somerset Island

Prince of Wales I.

ALASKA
u.s.

ARCTIC CIRCLE

· Inuvik

Victoria Island

Boothia Peninsula

YUKON

TERRITORY

Mt. Logan
19,551 ft
▲ 5,959 m

Mackenzie Mts.

Mackenzie

Great Bear Lake

N   U   N

Yukon Plateau

® Whitehorse

NORTHWEST

TERRITORIES

Virginia Falls

⊙ Yellowknife

Great Slave Lake

ROCKY

Slave

C   A   N   A   D   I

Coast Mountains

Peace

Lake Athabasca

Queen Charlotte Islands

BRITISH

COLUMBIA

Fraser Plateau

· Prince George

Fraser

M   O   U   N   T   A   I   N   S

Columbia Mts.

ALBERTA

Athabasca

G   R   E   A   T

Churchill ·

Churchill

Nelson

MANITOBA

⊙ Edmonton

SASKATCHEWAN

P A C I F I C

Vancouver Island

· Vancouver

Victoria ⊙

Calgary ·

P   L   A   I   N   S

· Saskatoon

Saskatchewan

Lake Winnipegosis

Lake Winnipeg

O C E A N

⊙ Regina

Winnipeg ⊙

Lake of the Woods

U N I T E D   S T A T E S

60°N

170°W

70°N

170°W

160°W

150°W

130°W

120°W

170°W

160°W

150°W

50°N

140°W

40°N

130°W

120°W

110°W

100°W

CANADA
PHYSICAL/POLITICAL

0 mi   400
0 km   400

AZIMUTHAL EQUIDISTANT PROJECTION

NATIONAL GEOGRAPHIC

Ellesmere Island
Devon Island

GREENLAND
(KALAALLIT NUNAAT)
Den.

ICELAND

Baffin Bay

Melville Peninsula
Foxe Basin
Baffin Island
N U N A V U T
Southampton Island

Davis Strait

Iqaluit

Hudson Strait

Labrador Sea

Ungava Bay

Hudson Bay

Belcher Islands

James Bay

Cartwright

Schefferville
Smallwood Reservoir
Happy Valley-Goose Bay
"Churchill Falls

N E W F O U N D L A N D   L A B R A D O R

Island of Newfoundland

QUEBEC

St. John's
Avalon Peninsula

Manicouagan Reservoir
Sept-Iles

Anticosti I.

St.-Pierre & Miquelon
Fr.

S H I E L D

ONTARIO

Lake Nipigon

Gulf of St. Lawrence

Gaspe Pen.

PRINCE EDWARD ISLAND

Cape Breton I.

ATLANTIC

Chicoutimi

Thunder Bay

Lake Superior

Rouyn-Noranda

Quebec City

NEW BRUNSWICK

Fredericton

Charlottetown

NOVA SCOTIA

OCEAN

Sudbury

Montreal

Ottawa

Saint John

Halifax

Bay of Fundy

St. Lawrence

Lake Huron

Lake Michigan

Toronto
Niagara Falls
London
L. Ontario
L. Erie

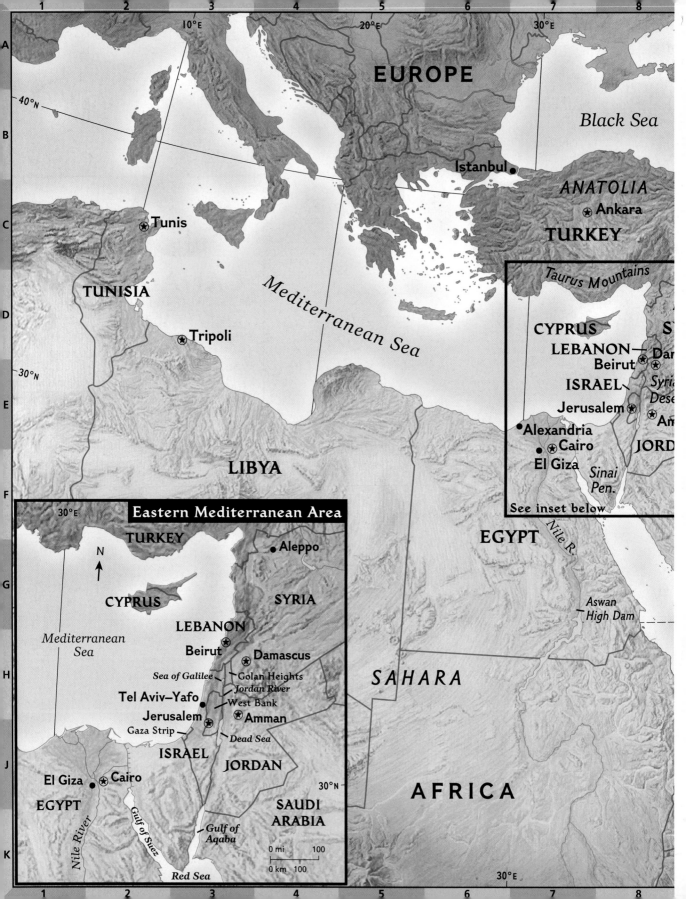

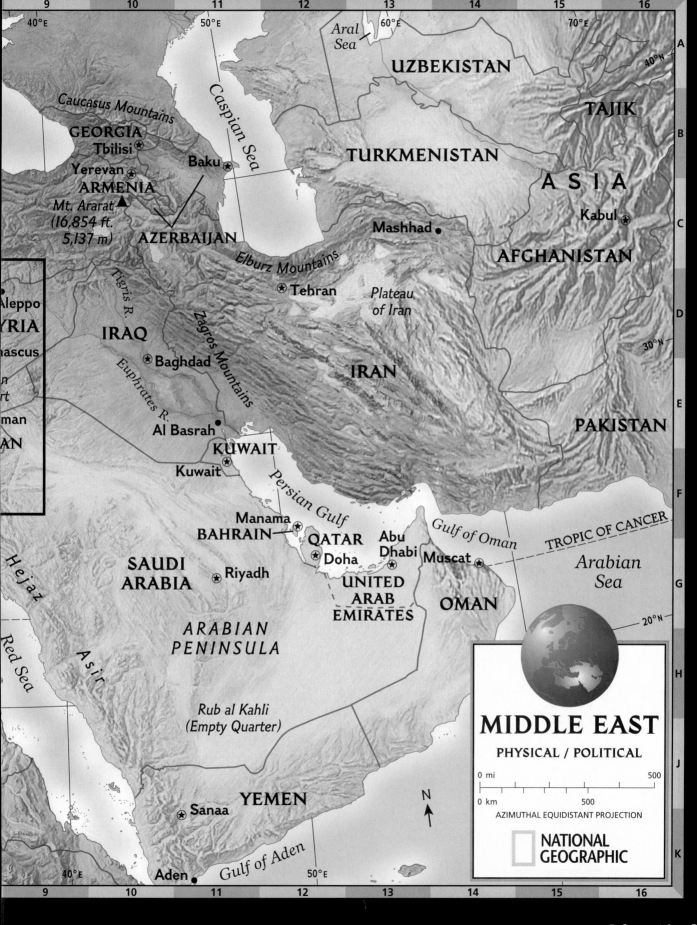

Aral Sea

UZBEKISTAN

TAJIK

Caucasus Mountains

GEORGIA
Tbilisi ✪

Baku ✪

Caspian Sea

TURKMENISTAN

ASIA

Yerevan ✪
ARMENIA

Mashhad •

Kabul ✪

Mt. Ararat ▲
(16,854 ft.
5,137 m)

AZERBAIJAN

Elburz Mountains

AFGHANISTAN

Aleppo •

YRIA

Tigris R.

Tehran ✪

Plateau
of Iran

nascus

IRAQ

Zagros Mountains

30°N

n
rt

Baghdad ✪

IRAN

man

Euphrates R.

AN

Al Basrah •

PAKISTAN

KUWAIT

Kuwait •

Persian Gulf

Manama ✪

Gulf of Oman

TROPIC OF CANCER

BAHRAIN

QATAR

Abu
Dhabi

Arabian
Sea

SAUDI
ARABIA

Riyadh ✪

Doha ✪

UNITED
ARAB
EMIRATES

Muscat ✪

OMAN

Hejaz

20°N

ARABIAN
PENINSULA

MIDDLE EAST

Red Sea

Asir

PHYSICAL / POLITICAL

Rub al Kahli
(Empty Quarter)

0 mi   500

0 km   500

N
↑

AZIMUTHAL EQUIDISTANT PROJECTION

YEMEN

Sanaa ✪

NATIONAL
GEOGRAPHIC

Aden •

Gulf of Aden

40°E

9   10   11   12   13   14   15   16

40°E   50°E   60°E   70°E

40°N

A

B

C

D

E

F

G

H

J

K

9   10   11   12   13   14   15   16

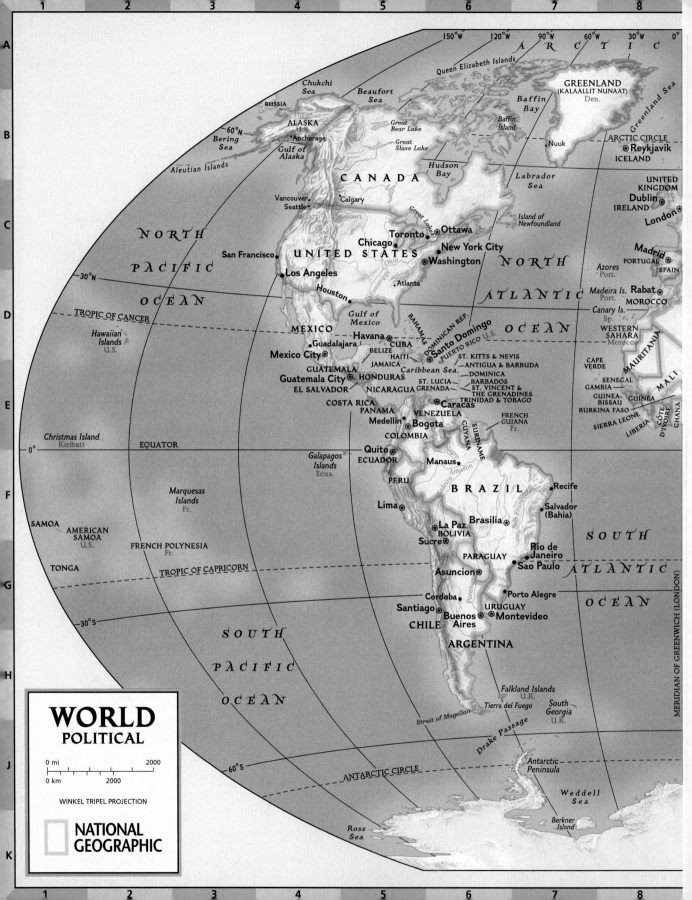

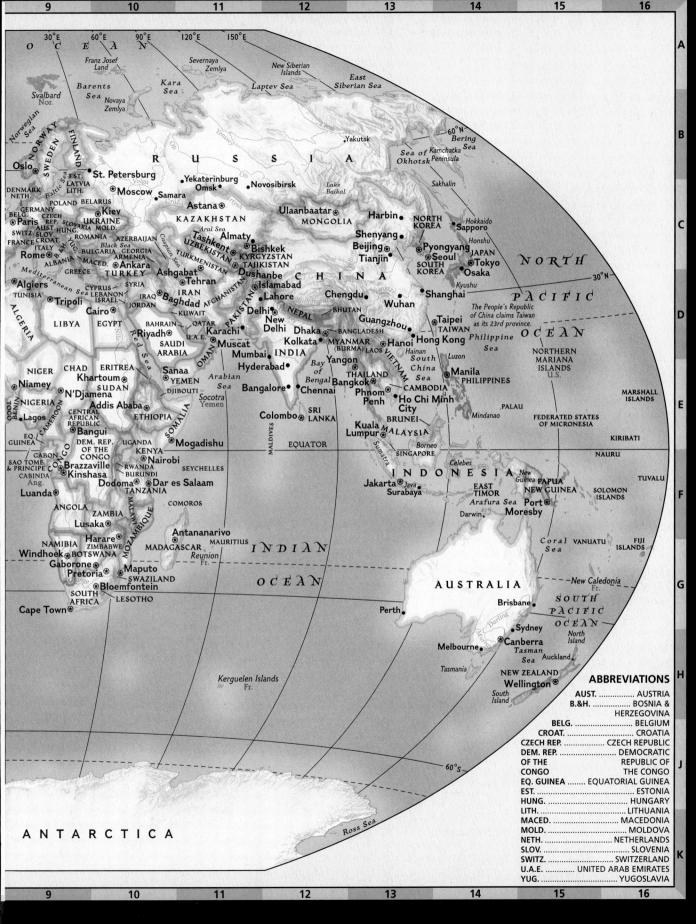

United States States Facts

U.S. Territories

Washington, D.C.
Population: 572,059
Land area: 61 sq. mi.

U.S. Territories

Puerto Rico
Population: 3,808,610
Land area: 3,425 sq. mi.

Guam
Population: 155,000 (est.)
Land area: 209 sq. mi.

U.S. Virgin Islands
Population: 121,000 (est.)
Land area: 134 sq. mi.

American Samoa
Population: 65,000 (est.)
Land area: 77 sq. mi.

The states are listed in the order they were admitted to the Union.

Population figures are based on U.S. Bureau of the Census for 2000. House of Representatives figures are from the Clerk of the House of Representatives. States are not drawn to scale.

1 Delaware
Year Admitted: 1787
Population: 783,600
Land area: 1,955 sq. mi.
Representatives: 1
★ Dover

2 Pennsylvania
Year Admitted: 1787
Population: 12,281,054
Land area: 44,820 sq. mi.
Representatives: 19
Harrisburg ★

3 New Jersey
Year Admitted: 1787
Population: 8,414,350
Land area: 7,419 sq. mi.
Representatives: 13
Trenton ★

9 New Hampshire
Year Admitted: 1788
Population: 1,235,786
Land area: 8,969 sq. mi.
Representatives: 2
Concord ★

10 Virginia
Year Admitted: 1788
Population: 7,078,515
Land area: 39,598 sq. mi.
Representatives: 11
Richmond ★

11 New York
Year Admitted: 1788
Population: 18,976,457
Land area: 47,224 sq. mi.
Representatives: 29
★ Albany

17 Ohio
Year Admitted: 1803
Population: 11,353,140
Land area: 40,953 sq. mi.
Representatives: 18
★ Columbus

18 Louisiana
Year Admitted: 1812
Population: 4,468,976
Land area: 43,566 sq. mi.
Representatives: 7
★ Baton Rouge

19 Indiana
Year Admitted: 1816
Population: 6,080,485
Land area: 35,870 sq. mi.
Representatives: 9
Indianapolis ★

25 Arkansas
Year Admitted: 1836
Population: 2,673,400
Land area: 52,075 sq. mi.
Representatives: 4
Little Rock ★

26 Michigan
Year Admitted: 1837
Population: 9,938,444
Land area: 56,809 sq. mi.
Representatives: 15
Lansing ★

27 Florida
Year Admitted: 1845
Population: 15,982,378
Land area: 53,997 sq. mi.
Representatives: 25
★ Tallahassee

33 Oregon
Year Admitted: 1859
Population: 3,421,399
Land area: 96,003 sq. mi.
Representatives: 5
★ Salem

34 Kansas
Year Admitted: 1861
Population: 2,688,418
Land area: 81,823 sq. mi.
Representatives: 4
Topeka ★

35 West Virginia
Year Admitted: 1863
Population: 1,808,344
Land area: 24,087 sq. mi.
Representatives: 3
★ Charleston

36 Nevada
Year Admitted: 1864
Population: 1,998,257
Land area: 109,806 sq. mi.
Representatives: 3
★ Carson City

42 Washington
Year Admitted: 1889
Population: 5,894,121
Land area: 66,582 sq. mi.
Representatives: 9
★ Olympia

43 Idaho
Year Admitted: 1890
Population: 1,293,953
Land area: 82,751 sq. mi.
Representatives: 2
★ Boise

44 Wyoming
Year Admitted: 1890
Population: 493,782
Land area: 97,105 sq. mi.
Representatives: 1
Cheyenne ★

45 Utah
Year Admitted: 1896
Population: 2,233,169
Land area: 82,168 sq. mi.
Representatives: 3
★ Salt Lake City

4 Georgia
Year Admitted: 1788
Population: 8,186,453
Land area: 57,919 sq. mi.
Representatives: 13
★ Atlanta

5 Connecticut
Year Admitted: 1788
Population: 3,405,565
Land area: 4,845 sq. mi.
Representatives: 5
★ Hartford

6 Massachusetts
Year Admitted: 1788
Population: 6,349,097
Land area: 7,838 sq. mi.
Representatives: 10
Boston ★

7 Maryland
Year Admitted: 1788
Population: 5,296,486
Land area: 9,775 sq. mi.
Representatives: 8
Annapolis ★

8 South Carolina
Year Admitted: 1788
Population: 4,012,012
Land area: 30,111 sq. mi.
Representatives: 6
Columbia ★

12 North Carolina
Year Admitted: 1789
Population: 8,049,313
Land area: 48,718 sq. mi.
Representatives: 13
Raleigh ★

13 Rhode Island
Year Admitted: 1790
Population: 1,048,319
Land area: 1,045 sq. mi.
Representatives: 2
★ Providence

14 Vermont
Year Admitted: 1791
Population: 608,827
Land area: 9,249 sq. mi.
Representatives: 1
★ Montpelier

15 Kentucky
Year Admitted: 1792
Population: 4,041,769
Land area: 39,732 sq. mi.
Representatives: 6
Frankfort ★

16 Tennessee
Year Admitted: 1796
Population: 5,689,283
Land area: 41,220 sq. mi.
Representatives: 9
★ Nashville

20 Mississippi
Year Admitted: 1817
Population: 2,844,658
Land area: 46,914 sq. mi.
Representatives: 4
★ Jackson

21 Illinois
Year Admitted: 1818
Population: 12,419,293
Land area: 55,593 sq. mi.
Representatives: 19
★ Springfield

22 Alabama
Year Admitted: 1819
Population: 4,447,100
Land area: 50,750 sq. mi.
Representatives: 7
Montgomery ★

23 Maine
Year Admitted: 1820
Population: 1,274,923
Land area: 30,865 sq. mi.
Representatives: 2
★ Augusta

24 Missouri
Year Admitted: 1821
Population: 5,595,211
Land area: 68,898 sq. mi.
Representatives: 9
Jefferson City ★

28 Texas
Year Admitted: 1845
Population: 20,851,820
Land area: 261,914 sq. mi.
Representatives: 32
Austin ★

29 Iowa
Year Admitted: 1846
Population: 2,926,324
Land area: 55,875 sq. mi.
Representatives: 5
Des Moines ★

30 Wisconsin
Year Admitted: 1848
Population: 5,363,675
Land area: 54,314 sq. mi.
Representatives: 8
Madison ★

31 California
Year Admitted: 1850
Population: 33,871,648
Land area: 155,973 sq. mi.
Representatives: 53
★ Sacramento

32 Minnesota
Year Admitted: 1858
Population: 4,919,479
Land area: 79,617 sq. mi.
Representatives: 8
Saint Paul ★

37 Nebraska
Year Admitted: 1867
Population: 1,711,263
Land area: 76,878 sq. mi.
Representatives: 3
Lincoln ★

38 Colorado
Year Admitted: 1876
Population: 4,301,261
Land area: 103,730 sq. mi.
Representatives: 7
Denver ★

39 North Dakota
Year Admitted: 1889
Population: 642,200
Land area: 68,994 sq. mi.
Representatives: 1
Bismarck ★

40 South Dakota
Year Admitted: 1889
Population: 754,844
Land area: 75,898 sq. mi.
Representatives: 1
Pierre ★

41 Montana
Year Admitted: 1889
Population: 902,195
Land area: 145,556 sq. mi.
Representatives: 1
★ Helena

46 Oklahoma
Year Admitted: 1907
Population: 3,450,654
Land area: 68,679 sq. mi.
Representatives: 5
Oklahoma City ★

47 New Mexico
Year Admitted: 1912
Population: 1,819,046
Land area: 121,365 sq. mi.
Representatives: 3
★ Santa Fe

48 Arizona
Year Admitted: 1912
Population: 5,130,632
Land area: 113,642 sq. mi.
Representatives: 8
Phoenix ★

49 Alaska
Year Admitted: 1959
Population: 626,932
Land area: 570,374 sq. mi.
Representatives: 1
Juneau ★

50 Hawaii
Year Admitted: 1959
Population: 1,211,537
Land area: 6,432 sq. mi.
Representatives: 2
Honolulu ★

NATIONAL GEOGRAPHIC

1 FOCUS

FYI

The early Inuit labeled distances on their maps with the time it took to travel rather than with miles. A map would show the distance between what is now Nome and Point Barrow (both in Alaska) as 10 days rather than 525 miles (845 km).

Geography Handbook

The story of the United States begins with geography—the study of the earth in all of its variety. Geography describes the earth's land, water, and plant and animal life. It is the study of places and the complex relationships between people and their environments.

The United States is a land of startling physical differences. Within the borders of the United States is a rich variety of landscapes—dense forests, hot deserts, rolling grasslands, and snow-capped mountains. It is also a nation of diverse groups of people. With a total land area of 3,539,230 square miles (9,166,606 sq. km)—the United States is the world's fourth largest country in size. Only Russia, Canada, and China are larger. Because of its size and diversity, the United States has offered people from Europe, Africa, Asia, and other parts of the Americas many opportunities. Today more than 286 million people make the United States their home.

▲ Makapuu Point, Hawaii

◀ Mount Hood, Oregon

EXTENDING THE CONTENT

Careers in Geography Geographers work for the federal government in the Defense Mapping Agency, United States Geologic Survey, Central Intelligence Agency, Army Corps of Engineers, National Science Foundation, Smithsonian Institution, and Office of the Geographer in the Department of State. State environmental and transportation agencies hire geographers as analysts, planners, and cartographers. Some states even have an Office of the State Geographer. In the private sector, geographers work as professors, researchers, and cartographers.

Globes

Photographs from space show the earth in its true form—a great ball spinning around the sun. The most accurate way to depict the earth is as a globe, or a round form. A globe gives a true picture of the earth's relative size and the shape of its landmasses and bodies of water. Globes are proportionally correct, thus showing the true distances and directions between places.

Maps

A map is a flat drawing of the earth's surface. People use maps to locate places, plot routes, and judge distances. Maps can also display useful information about the nation's peoples, such as political boundaries, population densities, or even voting results by city and state.

What advantages does a map have over a globe? Unlike a globe, a map allows you to see all areas of the world at the same time. Maps also show much more detail and can be folded and more easily carried.

Types of Maps

This text uses many different kinds of maps to help you see the connection between geography and the history of the United States.

General-Purpose Maps Maps that show a wide range of general information about a particular area are called **general-purpose maps.** Two of the most common general-purpose maps are physical maps and political maps. **Physical maps** show the location and the shape, or **topography,** of the earth's physical features. **Political maps** show the boundaries between different countries.

Special-Purpose Maps Special-purpose maps, also called **thematic maps,** show information on specific topics, such as climate, land use, or vegetation. Human activities, such as exploration routes, territorial expansion, or battle sites, also appear on special-purpose maps. Colors and map key symbols are very important on these maps.

LANDSAT Maps LANDSAT maps are made from photographs taken by camera-carrying LANDSAT satellites in space. The cameras record millions of energy waves invisible to the human eye. Computers then change this information into pictures of the earth's surface. With LANDSAT images, scientists can study whole mountain ranges, oceans, and geographic regions. Changes to the earth's invironment can also be tracked using the satellite information.

◀ Special-purpose map

▲ LANDSAT map

Geography Handbook 1

2 TEACH

Using Geographic Terms
Survey students' knowledge of geographic terms. Create three columns on the board with the following headings: *Landforms, Bodies of Water,* and *Climates.* List one term that fits each column, such as *canyon, bay,* and *tropical.* Ask students to volunteer as many other terms for each column as they can. Have students turn to pages 6–7 and read the **Geographic Dictionary.** Then have them close their books and continue suggesting terms for each column on the board. **L1**

you don't say...

National Boundaries National boundaries run to the center of the earth and to the top of the atmosphere. Because of this, an airplane pilot needs a country's permission to fly into its air space.

COOPERATIVE LEARNING ACTIVITY

Identifying Place Organize students into groups of four. Have them draw a large outline map of their state on poster board. Then have them research the state's plants, animals, and major economic products, and list these items on the back of the poster. Distribute magazines (gardening, wildlife, and local) and tell students to find and cut out pictures of the items listed on the backs of their posters. Finally, direct students to glue the photos in the appropriate locations on the outline map, creating a montage of distinctive characteristics of the state.

Use the rubric for a cooperative group management plan on pages 81–82 in the *Performance Assessment Activities and Rubrics.*

Geography Handbook

Demonstrating Ideas Write the words *Distance* and *Direction* on the board. **Ask: How do maps show distance and direction?** *(scales and compass roses)* Then, give students practice in determining distance by showing them how to mark a map scale on the edge of a piece of paper. Have students practice measuring the distance between cities on the map on this page. Give students practice in determining direction by having volunteers identify the direction from one city or country to another. **L2**

CURRICULUM CONNECTION

History Until the 1700s, sailors seldom knew exactly where they were because they only had lines of latitude to guide them. John Harrison, an English instrument maker, invented a clock that could keep accurate time at sea. A navigator could determine longitude by figuring the difference between Greenwich Mean Time and the time at the ship's location.

Using Maps

Map Projections Maps, however, do have their limitations. As you can imagine, drawing a round object on a flat surface is very difficult. **Cartographers,** or mapmakers, have drawn many projections, or kinds of maps. Each map projection is a different way of showing the round earth on a flat map. Different map projections include the Winkel Tripel, Robinson, Goode's Interrupted Equal-Area, and Mercator projections. It is impossible to accurately represent the round earth on a flat surface without distorting some part of the earth. Thus, map projections typically distort distance, direction, shape, or area.

Winkel Tripel Projection

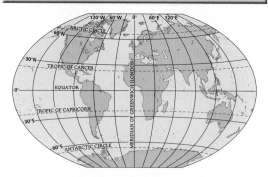

▲ Most general reference maps use the Winkel Tripel projection. Adopted by the National Geographic Society in 1998, this projection provides a better balance between the size and shape of land areas as they are shown on the map.

Reading a Map

Maps include several important tools to help you interpret the information contained on a particular map. Learning to use these map tools will help you read the symbolic language of maps more easily.

Compass Rose A compass rose is a marker that indicates directions. The four cardinal directions—north, south, east, and west—are usually indicated with arrows or points of a star. Sometimes a compass rose may indicate only one direction, because the other directions can be determined in relation to the one given. The compass rose on this map indicates all four cardinal directions.

Key Cartographers use a variety of symbols to represent map information. Because these symbols are graphic and commonly used, most maps can be read and understood by people around the world. To be sure that the symbols are clear, however, every map contains a key—a list that explains what the symbols represent. This key shows symbols used for a battle map in this text. It indicates troop movements, supply lines, and U.S. bases.

Major U.S. and South Vietnamese troop movements

Major North Vietnamese supply lines

U.S. bases

MEETING SPECIAL NEEDS

Visual/Spatial To help students remember the several different categories and examples of maps discussed in this section, guide them in creating a graphic organizer entitled "Types of Maps." Branching from this main head should be three boxes labeled "Political," "Physical," and "Special-Purpose." Have students complete the organizer by taking notes on each of the different types of maps. **L1**

☞ Refer to *Inclusion for the Middle School Social Studies Classroom Strategies and Activities* in the TCR.

Robinson Projection

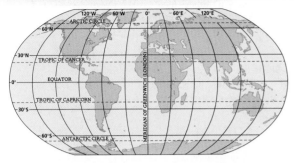

▲ The Robinson projection has minor distortions. The sizes and shapes near the eastern and western edges of the map are accurate, and the outlines of the continents appear much as they do on the globe. The shapes of the polar areas, however, are somewhat flat.

Goode's Interrupted Equal-Area Projection

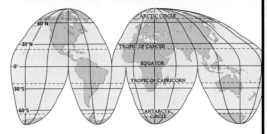

▲ An interrupted projection looks something like a globe that has been cut apart and laid flat. Goode's Interrupted Equal-Area projection shows the true size and shape of the earth's landmasses, but distances are distorted.

Relative Location Relative location is the location of one place in relation to another, while absolute location indicates the exact position of a place on the earth's surface. On this map, the relative location of where the Vietnam War took place is given in relation to the rest of Asia.

Cities and Capitals Cities are symbolized by a solid circle. Sometimes the relative sizes of cities are shown with circles of different sizes. Capitals are represented by a star within a circle.

Boundary Lines On political maps of large areas, boundary lines highlight the borders between different countries, states, or counties.

Scale Bar Every map is a representation of a part of the earth. The scale bar shows the relationship between map measurements and actual distance. Scale can be measured with a ruler to calculate actual distances in standard or metric measurements. On this map, 5/8 inch represents 150 miles (241 km).

Mercator Projection

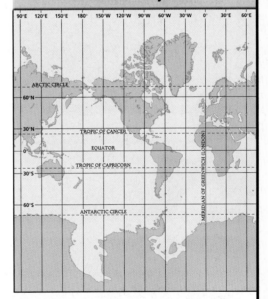

▲ The Mercator projection increasingly distorts size and distance as it moves away from the Equator. However, Mercator projections accurately show true directions and the shapes of the landmasses.

Using a Map Key On slips of paper, write the page number of a map from the textbook and a question that requires the use of the map key. Ask volunteers to select slips and answer the questions. **L1**

Using Special-Purpose Maps Ask volunteers to bring to class special-purpose maps. As an example, explain that the subject of these maps may include hiking trails, ocean currents, energy use, and bus routes. Allow time for volunteers to show and explain their maps. Display selected maps on the wall. **L1** ELL

Classifying Maps Have students work in groups to scan the textbook and classify the maps according to type: physical, political, or special-purpose. Give each group the task of listing page numbers for maps of one type. **L1** ELL

Geography Handbook **3**

COOPERATIVE LEARNING ACTIVITY

Using Absolute Location Organize the class into teams. Have each team record the absolute location (in degrees of latitude and longitude) of 20 named places on the globe (cities, natural features, and so on). Then have teams challenge each other in a round-robin Absolute Location Tournament. In each round, one team will state the latitude and longitude of five places, then time how long it takes the other team to locate the places on a globe. The teams will then switch roles. The team with the better time wins the round.

Use the rubric for a cooperative group management plan on pages 81–82 in the ***Performance Assessment Activities and Rubrics.***

The Elements of Geography

Understanding the Six Essential Elements Have students complete the following activities to learn more about the Six Essential Elements of Geography.

Element 1: The World in Spatial Terms Have students create a map that shows the route they travel from their home to school. Students should identify major roads and human-made landmarks on their maps. Display the maps on the class bulletin board. **L2**

Element 2: Places and Regions Explain that physical characteristics play a part in shaping human characteristics in a given place. For example, Native Americans in Alaska and Native Americans in Florida had widely differing clothing, economic pursuits, architecture, and lifestyles because of the physical characteristics of their regions. Ask students to describe a favorite city, state, or country. Ask them how the physical characteristics in the place might influence characteristics or customs of the inhabitants. **L1**

Element 3: Physical Systems Ask students to think of ways that physical systems affect their lives and cultures. Have students explain how events such as hurricanes influence a region's population and economy. **L2**

To understand how our world is connected, some geographers have broken down the study of geography into five themes. The **Five Themes of Geography** are (1) location, (2) place, (3) human/environment interaction, (4) movement, and (5) regions.

Six Essential Elements

Recently, as suggested in the **Geography Skills for Life**, geographers have broken down the study of geography into **Six Essential Elements**. Being aware of these elements will help you sort out what you are learning about geography.

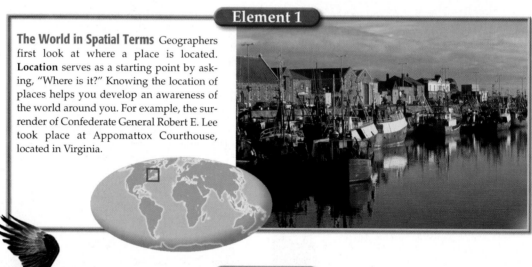

Element 1

The World in Spatial Terms Geographers first look at where a place is located. **Location** serves as a starting point by asking, "Where is it?" Knowing the location of places helps you develop an awareness of the world around you. For example, the surrender of Confederate General Robert E. Lee took place at Appomattox Courthouse, located in Virginia.

Element 2

Place and Regions **Place** has a special meaning in geography. It means more than where an area is located. It also describes what features a place includes. These features may be physical characteristics, such as landforms, climate, and plant or animal life. They may also be human characteristics, including language and way of life. For example, the English settlement of Jamestown was located in a swampy area with mosquitoes and high humidity. This made the way of life difficult for the new settlers.

To help them organize their study, geographers often group places into regions. **Regions** are united by one or more common characteristics. The original thirteen colonies, for instance, were divided into three regions—New England Colonies, Middle Colonies, and Southern Colonies.

4 Geography Handbook

Element 3

Physical Systems When studying places and regions, geographers analyze the ways in which **physical systems**—such as hurricanes, volcanoes, and glaciers—shape the earth's surface. They also look at communities of plants and animals that depend upon one another and their surroundings for survival. Glaciers are an example of a physical system. Near the end of the Ice Age, glaciers melted, raising ocean levels and covering a land bridge that once connected Asia and North America.

Element 4

Human Systems Geographers also examine an area's **human systems,** or how people have shaped our world. They look at how boundary lines are determined and analyze why people settle in certain places and not in others. A key theme in geography is the continual **movement** of people, ideas, and goods. An example of such movement occurred in the 1820s, when Stephen F. Austin organized a group of Americans to settle in the Mexican territory of Texas.

Element 5

Environment and Society "How does the relationship between people and their natural surroundings influence the way people live?" This is one of the questions that the geographic element of **environment and society** answers. This element also shows how people use the environment and how their actions affect it. One example was when some people in the South established large plantations to take advantage of the warm climate and fertile soil.

Element 6

The Uses of Geography Knowledge of geography helps people understand the relationships between people, places, and environment over time. Understanding geography and knowing how to use the tools and technology available to study it prepares you for life in our modern society. Early European explorers, for example, relied on their knowledge of geography to discover lands never seen before by Europeans.

Geography Handbook **5**

Element 4: Human Systems
Call on volunteers to name places from which their families or ancestors moved. Students may describe a move within the United States or a migration from another country. Discuss the reasons that people move to different places. **L1** ELL

Element 5: Environment and Society Give examples of ways that humans use and modify the environment in places they live. For example, people convert fields and forests into towns and irrigate arid land to support farming. Call on students to give examples of the ways people have modified the environment where they live in both positive and negative ways. **L2**

Element 6: The Uses of Geography Have students give examples of ways businesses use geography. Have students explain how various geographic conditions influence where businesses such as gas stations and shopping malls are built. **L2**

EXTENDING THE CONTENT

Regions Geographers organize regions into three parts: formal regions, functional regions, and perceptual regions. A common human property (for example, language, religion, nationality, and political identity) or common physical property (for example, climate, landforms, and vegetation cover) characterize formal regions. Functional regions are organized around a node or focal point with surrounding areas linked to that node through transportation or communication systems or economic associations. Perceptual regions reflect human feelings or attitudes and are defined by subjective images of the area (for example, New England and the Corn Belt).

Constructing a Model Have students use clay to make a model landscape with the features mentioned on pages 6–7. Suggest that students paint the model after the clay dries to make it look more realistic. **L1**

you don't say...

Foreign Geography Terms The terms geographers use to describe the earth come from many different languages. To illustrate this, have students locate the term *mesa* on page 7. Point out that geographers use this word, which means "table" in Spanish, to describe flat-topped, steep-sided hills. Other foreign terms American geographers use include *tsunami,* a Japanese word meaning "overflowing wave," and *fjord,* a Norwegian word meaning "long, narrow bay."

Geographic Dictionary

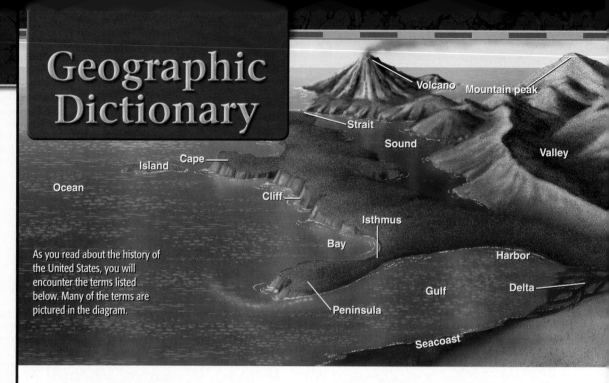

As you read about the history of the United States, you will encounter the terms listed below. Many of the terms are pictured in the diagram.

absolute location exact location of a place on the earth described by global coordinates

basin area of land drained by a given river and its branches; area of land surrounded by lands of higher elevations

bay part of a large body of water that extends into a shoreline, generally smaller than a gulf

canyon deep and narrow valley with steep walls

cape point of land that extends into a river, lake, or ocean

channel wide strait or waterway between two landmasses that lie close to each other; deep part of a river or other waterway

cliff steep, high wall of rock, earth, or ice

continent one of the seven large landmasses on the earth

cultural feature characteristic that humans have created in a place, such as language, religion, housing, and settlement pattern

delta flat, low-lying land built up from soil carried downstream by a river and deposited at its mouth

divide stretch of high land that separates river systems

downstream direction in which a river or stream flows from its source to its mouth

elevation height of land above sea level

Equator imaginary line that runs around the earth halfway between the North and South Poles; used as the starting point to measure degrees of north and south latitude

glacier large, thick body of slowly moving ice

gulf part of a large body of water that extends into a shoreline, generally larger and more deeply indented than a bay

harbor a sheltered place along a shoreline where ships can anchor safely

highland elevated land area such as a hill, mountain, or plateau

hill elevated land with sloping sides and rounded summit; generally smaller than a mountain

island land area, smaller than a continent, completely surrounded by water

isthmus narrow stretch of land connecting two larger land areas

lake a large inland body of water

latitude distance north or south of the Equator, measured in degrees

longitude distance east or west of the Prime Meridian, measured in degrees

lowland land, usually level, at a low elevation

map drawing of the earth shown on a flat surface

meridian one of many lines on the global grid running from the North Pole to the South Pole; used to measure degrees of longitude

COOPERATIVE LEARNING ACTIVITY

Analyzing Maps Organize the class into two teams. Provide one team with a United States map and the other team with a map of your state. Assign each team the following task: Locate every major body of water in your assigned area. Record your findings, including: (1) the name of each major body of water; (2) its relative and/or absolute location; and (3) the type of feature it is— lake, river, bay, and so on. When teams have completed their tasks, have them create a map quiz based on their work. The teams should then trade maps and challenge one another with their quizzes.

Use the rubric for a cooperative group management plan on pages 81–82 in the **Performance Assessment Activities and Rubrics.**

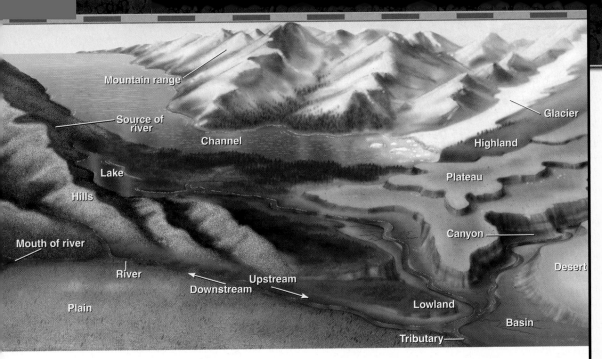

Mountain range
Source of river
Channel
Glacier
Highland
Lake
Plateau
Hills
Mouth of river
Canyon
Desert
River
Upstream
Downstream
Plain
Lowland
Basin
Tributary——

Provide students with an outline map of the United States and colored pencils. Have students use a different color to label each of the following: Appalachian Mountains, Great Lakes, Mississippi River, Atlantic Ocean, Pacific Ocean, Rocky Mountains, Great Plains, and Gulf of Mexico. Have students think about how these features might affect European settlement patterns in North America.

4 CLOSE

Have students describe how a region's physical geography influences its economic development.

mesa broad, flat-topped landform with steep sides; smaller than a plateau

mountain land with steep sides that rises sharply (1,000 feet or more) from surrounding land; generally larger and more rugged than a hill

mountain peak pointed top of a mountain

mountain range a series of connected mountains

mouth (of a river) place where a stream or river flows into a larger body of water

ocean one of the four major bodies of salt water that surround the continents

ocean current stream of either cold or warm water that moves in a definite direction through an ocean

parallel one of many lines on the global grid that circle the earth north or south of the Equator; used to measure degrees of latitude

peninsula body of land jutting into a lake or ocean, surrounded on three sides by water

physical feature characteristic of a place occurring naturally, such as a landform, body of water, climate pattern, or resource

plain area of level land, usually at a low elevation and often covered with grasses

plateau large area of flat or rolling land at a high elevation, about 300–3,000 feet high

Prime Meridian line of the global grid running from the North Pole to the South Pole at Greenwich, England; starting point for measuring degrees of east and west longitude

relief changes in elevation over a given area of land

river large natural stream of water that runs through the land

sea large body of water completely or partly surrounded by land

seacoast land lying next to a sea or ocean

sea level position on land level with surface of nearby ocean or sea

sound body of water between a coastline and one or more islands off the coast

source (of a river) place where a river or stream begins, often in highlands

strait narrow stretch of water joining two larger bodies of water

tributary small river or stream that flows into a larger river or stream; a branch of the river

upstream direction opposite the flow of a river; toward the source of a river or stream

valley area of low land between hills or mountains

volcano mountain created as ash or liquid rock erupts from inside the earth

Geography Handbook **7**

CRITICAL THINKING ACTIVITY

Analyzing Have students use atlases and other resources to plan a cross-country trip through the United States. Have them choose a starting point and destination, then plot the route between the two points. Have them calculate the approximate distance of the journey and how long the journey might take, then list points of interest along the way. Allow time for students to share their itineraries. **L2**

Unit 1 Resources

SUGGESTED PACING CHART

Unit 1 (1 Day)	Chapter 1 (6 Days)	Chapter 2 (5 Days)	Chapter 3 (5 Days)	Unit 1 (2 Days)
Day 1 Introduction	**Day 1** Chapter 1 Intro, Section 1	**Day 1** Chapter 2 Intro, Section 1	**Day 1** Chapter 3 Intro, Section 1	**Day 1** Wrap-Up/Project
	Day 2 Section 2	**Day 2** Section 2	**Day 2** Section 2	**Day 2** Unit 1 Assessment
	Day 3 Section 3	**Day 3** Section 3	**Day 3** Section 3	
	Day 4 Section 4	**Day 4** Section 4	**Day 4** Section 4	
	Day 5 Section 5	**Day 5** Chapter 2 Assessment	**Day 5** Chapter 3 Assessment	
	Day 6 Chapter 1 Assessment			

Use the following tools to easily assess student learning in a variety of ways:

- Performance Assessment Activities and Rubrics
- Chapter and Unit Tests
- Section Quizzes
- Standardized Test Skills Practice Workbook

- tav.glencoe.com
- Interactive Tutor Self-Assessment CD-ROM
- MindJogger Videoquiz
- ExamView® Pro Testmaker CD-ROM
- SAT I/II Test Practice

TEACHING TRANSPARENCIES

Unit 1 Map Overlay Transparencies

Cause-and-Effect Transparency 1

*inter*NET RESOURCES

- tav.glencoe.com

The American Vision
Visit the *American Vision* Web site for history overviews, activities, assessments, and updated charts and graphs.

- www.socialstudies.glencoe.com

Glencoe Social Studies
Visit the Glencoe Web site for social studies activities, updates, and links to other sites.

- www.teachingtoday.glencoe.com

Glencoe Teaching Today
Visit the new Glencoe Web site for teacher development information, teaching tips, Web resources, and educational news.

- www.time.com

TIME Online
Visit the TIME Web site for up-to-date news and special reports.

Unit 1 Resources

ASSESSMENT

Unit 1 Pretests

Unit 1 Posttests

APPLICATION AND ENRICHMENT

American Biography 1

History Simulation and Problem Solving 1

GEOGRAPHY

Geography and History Activity 1

INTERDISCIPLINARY ACTIVITIES

American Literature Reading 1

Economics and History Activity 1

Team-Teaching Interdisciplinary Strategies and Activities 1

BIBLIOGRAPHY

Readings for the Student

Mason, Antony. *Ancient Civilizations of the Americas.* Dorling Kindersley, 2001.

Readings for the Teacher

Brandon, William. *The Last Americans: The Indian in American Culture.* McGraw-Hill, 1974.

Multimedia Resources

Videocassette. *Asia, 1600–1800.* Landmark Films. (26 minutes)

Videocassette. *Mexico Before Cortez.* Social Studies School Service. (14 minutes)

Additional Glencoe Resources for This Unit:

- Glencoe Skillbuilder Interactive Workbook CD-ROM, Level 2
- Social Studies Guide to Using the Internet
- Writer's Guidebook for High School
- Living Constitution
- American Art Prints Strategies and Activities

0:00 Out of Time?

If time does not permit teaching each chapter in this unit, you may want to use the **Reading Essentials and Study Guide** summaries.

Unit Overview

Unit 1 discusses the variety of cultural influences that shaped America from prehistory through the colonial era. **Chapter 1** discusses the converging cultures from prehistory to 1520. **Chapter 2** focuses on the colonization of America by Europeans from 1519 to 1732. **Chapter 3** explores colonial ways of life from 1607 to 1763.

Unit Objectives

After studying this unit, students will be able to:

1. Describe the early civilizations of Mesoamerica.
2. Explain the religious and economic reasons why England became interested in America.
3. Describe colonial culture in the English colonies.

Why It Matters Activity

Have students describe the benefits and challenges of the interactions among Europeans, Africans, and Native Americans in North America.

UNIT

1 Three Worlds Meet

Beginnings to 1763

Why It Matters

The interactions among Native Americans, Europeans, and Africans shaped the history of the Americas. Native Americans struggled to live alongside Europeans and their ever-growing settlements and colonies. Africans tried to adapt to the new continent to which they were brought involuntarily. Studying these early cultural interactions will help you understand the centuries of history that followed. The following resources offer more information about this period in American history.

Primary Sources Library

See pages 1048–1049 for primary source readings to accompany Unit 1.

Use the **American History Primary Source Document Library CD-ROM** to find additional primary sources about the meeting of Native Americans, Europeans, and Africans.

Pre-Cherokee necklace, c. 1300

Cherokee Settlement by Felix Marie Ferdinand Storelli

8

TEAM TEACHING ACTIVITY

Geography Tell students that the world in the 1400s looked very different from the way it looks today. In the 1400s the eastern part of North America was covered by thick forests. Marshland stretched along much of Europe's Mediterranean coast and covered vast areas of northern Germany and Russia. Have interested students research the environment of each continent in the 1400s. Based on their research have them create a world vegetation map. Have them discuss their findings with the class.

> *"Long before they had heard the word Spaniard, they [Native Americans] had properly organized states, wisely ordered by excellent laws, religion, and custom."*
>
> —Bartolomé de Las Casas, 1550

GLENCOE
TECHNOLOGY

CD-ROM
American History Primary Source Document Library CD-ROM
Use the **American History Primary Source Document Library CD-ROM** to access primary source documents related to this period in history.

More About the Art

Have students describe the various structures used by the Cherokee. Have students speculate on the use for each of these types of structures.

SERVICE-LEARNING PROJECT

Organize students into small groups. Have each group research some aspect of your local community's history. Based on their research, have each group contribute to one large display featuring the history of your community. Have students select an appropriate title for the display. If possible, arrange for the display to be enjoyed by the community by placing it in a public building such as a library or town hall.

Refer to **Building Bridges: Connecting Classroom and Community through Service-Learning in Social Studies** from the National Council for the Social Studies for information about service-learning.

Timesaving Tools

TeacherWorks™ **All-In-One Planner and Resource Center**

- **Interactive Teacher Edition** Access your Teacher Wraparound Edition and your classroom resources with a few easy clicks.
- **Interactive Lesson Planner** Planning has never been easier! Organize your week, month, semester, or year with all the lesson helps you need to make teaching creative, timely, and relevant.

Use Glencoe's **Presentation Plus!** multimedia teacher tool to easily present dynamic lessons that visually excite your students. Using Microsoft PowerPoint® you can customize the presentations to create your own personalized lessons.

TEACHING TRANSPARENCIES

Graphic Organizer 1

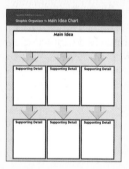

Why It Matters Chapter Transparency 1

APPLICATION AND ENRICHMENT

Linking Past and Present Activity 1

Enrichment Activity 1

Primary Source Reading 1

REVIEW AND REINFORCEMENT

Reteaching Activity 1

Vocabulary Activity 1

Time Line Activity 1

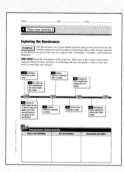

Critical Thinking Skills Activity 1

Meeting NCSS Standards

The following standards are highlighted in Chapter 1:

Section 1	III	People, Places, and Environments: A, B, D, F, H
Section 2	I	Culture: A, C, E
Section 3	IX	Global Connections: B, C, D, E
Section 4	VIII	Science, Technology, and Society: A, B, C
Section 5	IX	Global Connections: B, C, E, F

Local Standards

Chapter 1 Resources

ASSESSMENT AND EVALUATION

Chapter 1 Test Form A

Chapter 1 Test Form B

Standardized Test Skills Practice Workbook Activity 1

Performance Assessment Activities and Rubrics 1

ExamView® Pro Testmaker CD-ROM

MULTIMEDIA

- Vocabulary PuzzleMaker CD-ROM
- Interactive Tutor Self-Assessment CD-ROM
- ExamView® Pro Testmaker CD-ROM
- Audio Program
- American History Primary Source Documents Library CD-ROM
- MindJogger Videoquiz
- Presentation Plus! CD-ROM
- TeacherWorks™ CD-ROM
- Interactive Student Edition CD-ROM
- Glencoe Skillbuilder Interactive Workbook CD-ROM, Level 2
- The *American Vision* Video Program
- American Music: Hits Through History
- American Music: Cultural Traditions

THE HISTORY CHANNEL®

The following videotape programs are available from Glencoe as supplements to Chapter 1:

- **The Secret Mounds of Prehistoric America** (ISBN 1-56-501681-5)
- **The Aztec Empire** (ISBN 0-76-700542-2)
- **Leif Ericsson: Voyages of a Viking** (ISBN 1-56-501673-4)

To order, call Glencoe at 1-800-334-7344. To find classroom resources to accompany many of these videos, check the following home pages:
A&E Television: www.aande.com
The History Channel: www.historychannel.com

SPANISH RESOURCES

The following Spanish language materials are available in the Spanish Resources Binder:

- Spanish Guided Reading Activities
- Spanish Reteaching Activities
- Spanish Quizzes and Tests
- Spanish Vocabulary Activities
- Spanish Summaries
- The Declaration of Independence and United States Constitution Spanish Translation

HISTORY Online

Use our Web site for additional resources. All essential content is covered in the Student Edition.

You and your students can visit tav.glencoe.com, the Web site companion to the *American Vision.* This innovative integration of electronic and print media offers your students a wealth of opportunities. The student text directs students to the Web site for the following options:

- **Chapter Overviews**
- **Self-Check Quizzes**
- **Student Web Activities**
- **Textbook Updates**

Answers to the student Web activities are provided for you in the **Web Activity Lesson Plans.** Additional Web resources and Interactive Tutor Puzzles are also available.

SECTION RESOURCES

Daily Objectives	Reproducible Resources	Multimedia Resources
SECTION 1 **The Migration to America** 1. Explain why scientists believe that the earliest Americans migrated from Asia. 2. Describe the early civilizations of Mesoamerica and the early cultures of North America.	📁 Reproducible Lesson Plan 1–1 📁 Daily Lecture and Discussion Notes 1–1 📁 Guided Reading Activity 1–1* 📁 Section Quiz 1–1* 📁 Reading Essentials and Study Guide 1–1 📁 Performance Assessment Activities and Rubrics	🔖 Daily Focus Skills Transparency 1–1 💿 Interactive Tutor Self-Assessment CD-ROM 💿 ExamView® Pro Testmaker CD-ROM 💿 Presentation Plus! CD-ROM 💿 TeacherWorks™ CD-ROM 🎧 Audio Program 🎵 American Music: Cultural Traditions
SECTION 2 **Native American Cultures** 1. Describe the cultures of Native American groups of the West, the Far North, and the Eastern Woodlands. 2. Describe the agricultural techniques of the Woodlands Native Americans.	📁 Reproducible Lesson Plan 1–2 📁 Daily Lecture and Discussion Notes 1–2 📁 Guided Reading Activity 1–2* 📁 Section Quiz 1–2* 📁 Reading Essentials and Study Guide 1–2 📁 Performance Assessment Activities and Rubrics	🔖 Daily Focus Skills Transparency 1–2 💿 Interactive Tutor Self-Assessment CD-ROM 💿 ExamView® Pro Testmaker CD-ROM 💿 Presentation Plus! CD-ROM 💿 TeacherWorks™ CD-ROM 🎧 Audio Program
SECTION 3 **African Cultures** 1. Describe the culture of early West African kingdoms. 2. Describe the lifestyles of early Central and Southern African peoples.	📁 Reproducible Lesson Plan 1–3 📁 Daily Lecture and Discussion Notes 1–3 📁 Guided Reading Activity 1–3* 📁 Section Quiz 1–3* 📁 Reading Essentials and Study Guide 1–3 📁 Performance Assessment Activities and Rubrics	🔖 Daily Focus Skills Transparency 1–3 💿 Interactive Tutor Self-Assessment CD-ROM 💿 ExamView® Pro Testmaker CD-ROM 💿 Presentation Plus! CD-ROM 💿 TeacherWorks™ CD-ROM 🎧 Audio Program
SECTION 4 **European Cultures** 1. Discuss the impact of the Crusades on Europe's contact with the Middle East. 2. Analyze the impact of the Renaissance on European exploration.	📁 Reproducible Lesson Plan 1–4 📁 Daily Lecture and Discussion Notes 1–4 📁 Guided Reading Activity 1–4* 📁 Section Quiz 1–4* 📁 Reading Essentials and Study Guide 1–4 📁 Performance Assessment Activities and Rubrics	🔖 Daily Focus Skills Transparency 1–4 💿 Interactive Tutor Self-Assessment CD-ROM 💿 ExamView® Pro Testmaker CD-ROM 💿 Presentation Plus! CD-ROM 💿 TeacherWorks™ CD-ROM 🎧 Audio Program
SECTION 5 **Europe Encounters America** 1. Describe Viking and Spanish explorations of North America. 2. Summarize Columbus's journeys and their impact on Native Americans and Europeans.	📁 Reproducible Lesson Plan 1–5 📁 Daily Lecture and Discussion Notes 1–5 📁 Guided Reading Activity 1–5* 📁 Section Quiz 1–5* 📁 Reading Essentials and Study Guide 1–5 📁 Performance Assessment Activities and Rubrics 📁 Interpreting Political Cartoons	🔖 Daily Focus Skills Transparency 1–5 💿 Interactive Tutor Self-Assessment CD-ROM 💿 ExamView® Pro Testmaker CD-ROM 💿 Presentation Plus! CD-ROM 💿 Skillbuilder Interactive Workbook, Level 2 💿 TeacherWorks™ CD-ROM 💿 Vocabulary PuzzleMaker CD-ROM 🎧 Audio Program

`0:00` **OUT OF TIME?**
Assign the Chapter 1 **Reading Essentials and Study Guide.** 📁

*Also Available in Spanish

📁 Blackline Master   🔖 Transparency   💿 CD-ROM   💿 DVD

📕 Poster   🎵 Music Program   🎧 Audio Program   📼 Videocassette

NATIONAL GEOGRAPHIC Teacher's Corner

INDEX TO NATIONAL GEOGRAPHIC MAGAZINE

The following articles relate to this chapter.

- "1491: America Before Columbus," October 1991
- "The Anasazi," April 1996
- "Cherokee," May 1995
- "Dawn of Humans: The First Americans," December 2000
- "Living Iroquois Confederacy," September 1987
- "Pueblo Ancestors Return Home," November 2000

NATIONAL GEOGRAPHIC SOCIETY PRODUCTS AVAILABLE FROM GLENCOE

To order the following products for use with this chapter, contact your local Glencoe sales representative, or call Glencoe at 1-800-334-7344:

- *MapPack: Continents, North America*
- *PicturePack: Geography of North America* (Transparencies)
- *PicturePack: Native Americans Part 1 and Part 2* (Transparencies)
- *PictureShow: Native Americans 1: Eastern Woodlands, Plains* (CD-ROM)
- *PictureShow: Native Americans 2: Southwest, Northwest, Arctic* (CD-ROM)

ADDITIONAL NATIONAL GEOGRAPHIC SOCIETY PRODUCTS

To order the following, call National Geographic at 1-800-368-2728:

- *American Indians: A Brief History* (Video)
- *National Geographic Atlas of the World, Seventh Edition*

NGS ONLINE

Access National Geographic's Web site for current events, atlas updates, activities, links, interactive features, and archives.

www.nationalgeographic.com

From the Classroom of...

Karen O'Connor
San Diego Unified School District
San Diego, CA

The Influence of the East on the West

The Crusades increased contact between Western Europe and the Muslim and Byzantine civilizations. Traders followed the European armies eastward and brought back spices and silk. They also brought back the concept of paying with money instead of trading goods.

Gather students into small groups and ask them to research other areas where the contact between the East and West during this time period influenced European culture. Assign each group one of the following areas: architecture, art, literature, science, or language.

Give them one week to prepare an oral presentation. Their written reports are due one week later.

ADDITIONAL RESOURCES FROM GLENCOE

- American Music: Cultural Traditions
- American Art & Architecture
- Outline Map Resource Book
- U.S. Desk Map
- Building Geography Skills for Life
- Inclusion for the High School Social Studies Classroom Strategies and Activities
- Teaching Strategies for the American History Classroom (Including Block Scheduling Pacing Guides)

KEY TO ABILITY LEVELS

Teaching strategies have been coded.

- **L1** BASIC activities for all students
- **L2** AVERAGE activities for average to above-average students
- **L3** CHALLENGING activities for above-average students
- **ELL** ENGLISH LANGUAGE LEARNER activities

Block Schedule

Activities that are suited to use within the block scheduling framework are identified by:

W*hy It Matters Activity*

Have students explain how they think the events of the late 1400s continue to have an impact on the lives of Americans. Students should evaluate their answers after they have completed the chapter.

GLENCOE
TECHNOLOGY

The *American Vision* Video Program

To learn more about America before 1520, have students view the Chapter 1 video, "America Before the Americans," from the ***American Vision* Video Program.**

 Available in DVD and VHS

MindJogger Videoquiz

Use the **MindJogger Videoquiz** to preview Chapter 1 content.

Available in VHS

1 Converging Cultures

Prehistory to 1520

Why It Matters

Before 1492, the cultures that arose in the Americas had almost no contact with the rest of the world. Then, in the late 1300s, momentous events began taking place that would bring the cultures of Europe and Africa into direct contact with the Americas. This contact had profound effects on the future of the world's civilizations.

The Impact Today

The convergence of the world's cultures in the 1400s launched an era of change that still affects our lives today.

- *Many of our foods, customs, and traditions were originally introduced in the Americas as a result of this cultural contact.*
- *Contact among the cultures of the three continents profoundly changed the society of each.*
- *American society today includes elements of Native American, European, and African cultures.*

The *American Vision* *Video* The Chapter 1 video, "America Before the Americans," examines the early Americas.

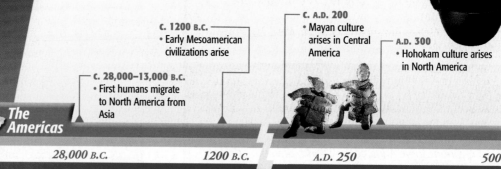

The Americas

c. 28,000–13,000 B.C.
- First humans migrate to North America from Asia

c. 1200 B.C.
- Early Mesoamerican civilizations arise

c. A.D. 200
- Mayan culture arises in Central America

A.D. 300
- Hohokam culture arises in North America

28,000 B.C.   *1200 B.C.*   *A.D. 250*   *500*

World

c. 3000 B.C.
- Sumerians create cuneiform writing

1750 B.C.
- Death of Hammurabi in the Middle East

A.D. 400
- Ghana civilization develops in West Africa

10

TWO-MINUTE LESSON LAUNCHER

Many Americans think American history begins in 1492 when Christopher Columbus landed in America. Ask students why it is important to learn about pre-Columbian historical events. Encourage students to offer examples of events prior to 1492 that helped shape American history.

The Landing of Columbus in San Salvador by Albert Bierstadt, 1893

HISTORY
Online

Introduce students to chapter content and key terms by having them access the **Chapter 1 Overview** at tav.glencoe.com.

More About the Art

Ask: What techniques does the painter use to convey his opinion of the landing party? *(Answers may vary. Students will note that the native peoples are bowing to the landing party. They should also note that the focus of the light is on the landing party, while the land itself is shrouded in darkness. Both convey a sense of superiority and dominance of the landing party.)*

c. 1130
• Drought strikes Native American cliff dwellings at Chaco Canyon

c. 1300
• Cahokia civilization collapses

1492
• Christopher Columbus lands in America

1500s
• Navajo arrive in Southwest of North America

	1100	1200	1300	1400	1500

610
• Muhammed begins teaching ideas of Islam

1240
• Mali empire expands in West Africa

1420s
• Portugal begins exploring African coast

1450
• Songhai empire expands in West Africa

HISTORY
Online

Chapter Overview
Visit the *American Vision* Web site at tav.glencoe.com and click on *Chapter Overviews—Chapter 1* to preview chapter information.

TIME LINE
ACTIVITY

Have students use a globe or world map to identify the approximate location where the events shown on the time line occurred. Encourage students to use library and Internet resources to determine the present-day names of locations. For example, Sumer, home of the Sumerians, was located in the area that is now southern Iraq.

11

GRAPHIC ORGANIZER ACTIVITY

Organizing Information Have students outline Chapter 1, using the format shown below.

I. The Migration to America
  A. The Asian Migration to America
  B. Early Civilizations of Mesoamerica
    1. The Olmec and the Maya
    2. The Toltec and the Aztec
  C. North American Cultures
    1. The Hohokam
    2. The Anasazi

  3. The Adena and Hopewell Cultures
  4. The Mississippian Culture

Students should complete the outline by including all of the section titles and heads in the rest of the chapter.

1 FOCUS

Section Overview
This section describes how the first inhabitants migrated to America and how they lived and developed their cultures.

BELLRINGER
Skillbuilder Activity

Project transparency and have students answer the question.

Available as a blackline master.

Daily Focus Skills Transparency 1–1

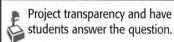

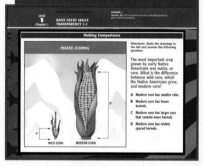

Guide to Reading

Answers to Graphic: Mesoamerica: *Olmec, Mayan, Toltec, Aztec cultures;* North American Southwest: *Hohokam and Anasazi cultures;* North American Midwest: *Adena, Hopewell, and Mississippian cultures*

Preteaching Vocabulary
Have students write a paragraph using at least three of the Key Terms and Names.

SECTION 1 | The Migration to America

Guide to Reading

Main Idea
Native Americans are descended from Asians who probably began migrating to North America approximately 15,000 to 30,000 years ago.

Key Terms and Names
radiocarbon dating, Ice Age, glacier, Beringia, nomad, agricultural revolution, maize, civilization, obsidian, Chaco Canyon, kiva, pueblo, Cahokia

Reading Strategy
Categorizing As you read about the first people to live in North America, complete a graphic organizer similar to the one below by filling in the names of Native American groups who settled in various regions.

Region	Native American Groups
Mesoamerica	
North American Southwest	
North American Midwest	

Reading Objectives
- **Explain** why scientists believe that the earliest Americans migrated from Asia.
- **Describe** the early civilizations of Mesoamerica and the early cultures of North America.

Section Theme
Geography and History Scientists theorize that Asian hunters migrated to North America across a land bridge exposed during the last Ice Age.

Preview of Events

♦30,000 B.C.	♦15,000 B.C.	♦0	♦A.D. 1500

- **c. 28,000–13,000 B.C.** First humans migrate to North America
- **c. 8000–7000 B.C.** Agriculture begins
- **c. 1200 B.C.** Early Mesoamerican civilizations arise
- **c. A.D. 200** Maya culture arises
- **c. A.D. 1300** Cahokia collapses

★ An American Story ★

Folsom point, lying between animal bones

In 1925 an African American cowboy named George McJunkin was riding along a gully near the town of Folsom, New Mexico, when he noticed something gleaming in the dirt. He began digging and found a bone and a flint arrowhead. J.D. Figgins of the Colorado Museum of Natural History knew the bone belonged to a type of bison that had been extinct for 10,000 years. The arrowhead's proximity to the bones implied that human beings had been in America at least 10,000 years, which no one had believed at that time.

The following year, Figgins found another arrowhead embedded in similar bones. In 1927 he led a group of scientists to the find. Anthropologist Frank H.H. Roberts, Jr., wrote, "There was no question but that here was the evidence. . . . The point was still embedded . . . between two of the ribs of the animal skeleton." Further digs turned up more arrowheads, now called Folsom points. Roberts later noted: "The Folsom find was accepted as a reliable indication that man was present in the Southwest at an earlier period than was previously supposed."

—adapted from *The First American: A Story of North American Archaeology*

The Asian Migration to America

No one can say for certain when the first people arrived in America. The Folsom discoveries proved that people were here at least 10,000 years ago, but more recent research suggests that humans arrived much earlier. Presently, scientific speculation points to a

12 CHAPTER 1 Converging Cultures

SECTION RESOURCES

Reproducible Masters
- Reproducible Lesson Plan 1–1
- Daily Lecture and Discussion Notes 1–1
- Guided Reading Activity 1–1
- Section Quiz 1–1
- Reading Essentials and Study Guide 1–1

Transparencies
- Daily Focus Skills Transparency 1–1

- American Art & Architecture

Multimedia
- Interactive Tutor Self-Assessment CD-ROM
- ExamView® Pro Testmaker CD-ROM
- Presentation Plus! CD-ROM
- TeacherWorks™ CD-ROM
- Audio Program
- American Music: Cultural Traditions

period between 15,000 and 30,000 years ago—much earlier than what scientists believed at the time of George McJunkin's discovery.

How long ago the first Americans appeared remains a hotly debated question. Scientists can state much more confidently, however, who these earliest people were, how they arrived in America, and what their lives were like.

To learn the origins of ancient peoples, scientists study their skulls, bones, and teeth. In recent years they have been able to examine DNA—which stands for **d**eoxyribo**n**ucleic **a**cid—a molecule described as the basic building material of all life on Earth. DNA recovered from the bones of people who died many thousands of years ago enables scientists to trace their ethnic, and thus their geographic, origins. From DNA and other evidence, researchers have concluded that the earliest Americans probably came from Asia.

To determine how old objects are, scientists rely on radiocarbon dating. With this method, they measure the radioactivity left in a special type of carbon called carbon 14, which can be taken from fragments of wood and bone. Radiocarbon dating works because all living things absorb carbon. Knowing the rate at which carbon 14 loses its radioactivity, experts can calculate the age of the objects the carbon came from.

Studies of the earth's history offer other important clues. About 100,000 years ago, the earth began to cool gradually, entering what scientists call a period of glaciation. This era is often called the Ice Age. Much of the earth's water froze into huge ice sheets, or glaciers. As ocean levels dropped, they eventually exposed an area of dry land that connected Asia with the part of North America that is now Alaska. The land was named **Beringia,** after Vitus Bering, a later explorer of the region. Scientists think that about 15,000 years ago, people from Asia began trekking eastward across this new land bridge to America in search of food. Others may also have come by boat even earlier, hugging the shoreline of Beringia.

These early arrivals were probably nomads, people who continually moved from place to place. In this case, the people were hunters who stalked herds of animals across Beringia. They hunted such massive prey as the wooly mammoth, as well as antelope, caribou, bison, musk ox, and wild sheep. Wild plants, birds, and fish probably made up an important part of their diet, too. These early peoples did not come all at once. Their migrations probably continued until rising seawater once again submerged the land bridge about 10,000 years ago, creating a waterway that today is called the Bering Strait.

Scientists believe that as the Ice Age ended, the nomads' favorite prey, the wooly mammoth, began to die out, either from too much hunting or because of the changing environment. Faced with a dwindling food supply, early Americans began to make use of other types of food, including fish, shellfish, nuts, and small game.

 Reading Check **Explaining** How do scientists determine the origins of ancient peoples?

Early Civilizations of Mesoamerica

As time passed, early Americans learned how to plant and raise crops. This agricultural revolution occurred between 9,000 and 10,000 years ago in Mesoamerica—*meso* coming from the Greek word for middle. This region includes what is today central and southern Mexico and Central America.

The first crops grown in America included pumpkins, peppers, squashes, gourds, and beans. The most

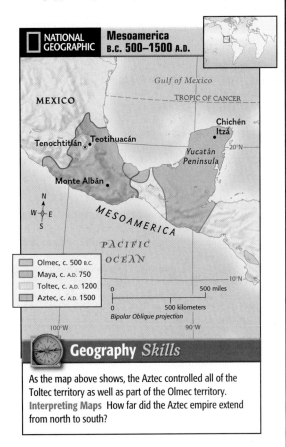

NATIONAL GEOGRAPHIC **Mesoamerica** B.C. 500–1500 A.D.

Gulf of Mexico

MEXICO

TROPIC OF CANCER

Chichén Itzá

Tenochtitlán · Teotihuacán

Yucatán Peninsula

20°N

Monte Albán

MESOAMERICA

PACIFIC OCEAN

Olmec, c. 500 B.C.
Maya, c. A.D. 750
Toltec, c. A.D. 1200
Aztec, c. A.D. 1500

500 miles
500 kilometers
Bipolar Oblique projection

10°N

100°W   90°W

Geography *Skills*

As the map above shows, the Aztec controlled all of the Toltec territory as well as part of the Olmec territory. **Interpreting Maps** How far did the Aztec empire extend from north to south?

CHAPTER 1 Converging Cultures **13**

2 TEACH

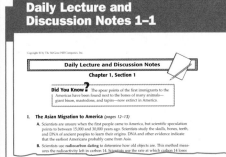

Daily Lecture and Discussion Notes 1–1

Copyright © by The McGraw-Hill Companies, Inc.

Daily Lecture and Discussion Notes
Chapter 1, Section 1

Did You Know? The spear points of the first immigrants to the Americas have been found next to the bones of many animals—giant bison, mastodons, and tapirs—now extinct in America.

I. The Asian Migration to America *(pages 12–13)*

A. Scientists are unsure when the first people came to America, but scientific speculation points to between 15,000 and 30,000 years ago. Scientists study the skulls, bones, teeth, and DNA of ancient peoples to learn their origins. DNA and other evidence indicate that the earliest Americans probably came from Asia.

B. Scientists use **radiocarbon dating** to determine how old objects are. This method measures the radioactivity left in carbon 14. Scientists use the rate at which carbon 14 loses

✓**Reading Check**

Answer: Scientists study the skulls, bones, teeth, and DNA of ancient peoples to trace their ethnic and geographic origins. They often use radiocarbon dating to determine the age of objects. Scientists also study the history of the earth to understand how peoples moved from one area to another.

Drawing a Picture Have students take on the role of an artist 9,000 years ago. Have them draw a picture of life in a typical village in Mesoamerica. Have students consider what record they would want to leave of their existence as they create the drawing. **L1**

Geography *Skills*

Answers: about 500 miles (about 800 kilometers)

Geography Skills Practice
Ask: What was the capital of the Aztec empire? *(Tenochtitlán)*

COOPERATIVE LEARNING ACTIVITY

Creating a Display Have students work in small groups to create a tabletop display featuring pictures, drawings, or models that symbolize important aspects of one of the cultures described in this section. Encourage students to include items that represent the food, art, science, and religion of the culture. The display should include a title and brief description of the culture. Each item displayed should be identified by name and include a brief description.

Use the rubric for a cooperative group management plan on pages 81–82 in the *Performance Assessment Activities and Rubrics.*

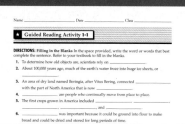
Discussing a Topic Ask students to discuss how members of the early civilizations of Mesoamerica might have spent their time on a typical day. Discuss what people might have eaten, and what different roles people might have had in these early societies. **L1**

A recurring element in the art of the Olmec is the jaguar. The animal appears in carvings and on pottery. Another common image found in Olmec art is a creature that appears to be half jaguar and half human.

History *and the* Humanities

🎵 American Music: Cultural Traditions: "Rain Dance"
🏛 American Art & Architecture: Serpent Mound, Cliff Palace

American Civilizations

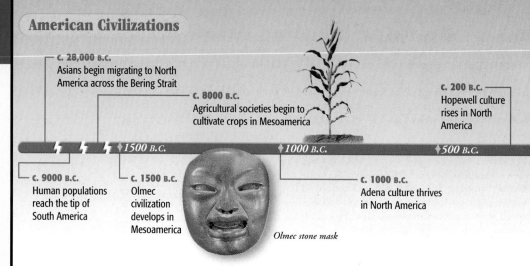

c. 28,000 B.C.
Asians begin migrating to North America across the Bering Strait

c. 8000 B.C.
Agricultural societies begin to cultivate crops in Mesoamerica

c. 200 B.C.
Hopewell culture rises in North America

1500 B.C.   1000 B.C.   500 B.C.

c. 9000 B.C.
Human populations reach the tip of South America

c. 1500 B.C.
Olmec civilization develops in Mesoamerica

c. 1000 B.C.
Adena culture thrives in North America

Olmec stone mask

important crop of all was a large-seeded grass called maize, which is known today as corn. Maize was important because it could be ground into flour to make bread and could be dried and stored for long periods of time.

The shift to agriculture allowed people to abandon their nomadic way of life and stay in one place to tend their crops and store the harvest. With the discovery of agriculture came the first permanent villages. The cultivation of crops also led to many new technologies, including tools for cutting, digging, and grinding. The need to store crops probably led to the development of pottery, and the development of permanent villages led to new construction technologies.

As more people began to live in one place, more complex forms of government developed, as did social classes. People learned specialized skills and traded their products for food and other goods. As these village societies became more complex, America's first civilizations emerged. A civilization is a highly organized society marked by trade, government, the arts, science, and, often, written language.

The Olmec and the Maya Anthropologists think the first people to build a civilization in America were the Olmec. Olmec culture emerged between 1500 and 1200 B.C., near where Veracruz, Mexico, is located today. The Olmec developed a sophisticated society with large villages, temple complexes, and pyramids. They also sculpted imposing monuments, including 8-foot-high heads weighing up to 20 tons, from a hard rock known as basalt. Olmec culture lasted until about 300 B.C.

Olmec ideas spread throughout Mesoamerica, influencing other peoples. One of these peoples constructed the first large city in America, called Teotihuacán (TAY·oh·TEE·wah·KAHN), about 30 miles northeast of where Mexico City is located today. The city was built near a volcano, where there were large deposits of obsidian, or volcanic glass. Obsidian was very valuable. Its sharp, strong edges were perfect for tools and weapons. Teotihuacán built up an elaborate trade network and greatly influenced the development of Mesoamerica. The city lasted from about 300 B.C. to about A.D. 650.

Around A.D. 200, as Teotihuacán's influence spread, the Mayan culture emerged in the Yucatán peninsula and expanded into what is now Central America and southern Mexico. The Maya had a talent for engineering and mathematics. They developed complex and accurate calendars linked to the positions of the stars. They also built great temple pyramids. These pyramids formed the centerpieces of Mayan cities, such as Tikal and Chichén Itzá. Marvels of engineering, some pyramids were 200 feet (61 m) high. Topping each pyramid was a temple where elaborately dressed priests performed ceremonies dedicated to the many Mayan gods.

Although trade and a common culture linked the Mayan people, they were not unified. Each city-state controlled its own territory. Because of the fragmented nature of Mayan society, the different cities frequently went to war.

The Toltec and the Aztec Despite their frequent wars, the Mayan people continued to thrive until the A.D. 900s, when their cities in the Yucatán were abandoned for unknown reasons. Some anthropologists believe Mayan farmers may have exhausted the region's soil. This in turn would have led to famine, riots, and the collapse of the cities. Others believe that invaders from the north devastated the region.

MEETING SPECIAL NEEDS

Interpersonal Have students select one portion of Section 1 to teach to another student. Ask students to read the passage and then teach it to a partner. Have the student doing the teaching ask questions about what has been taught. Direct the student/teacher to review any concepts that the student/learner did not understand. **L1** **ELL**

📁 Refer to *Inclusion for the High School Social Studies Classroom Strategies and Activities* in the TCR.

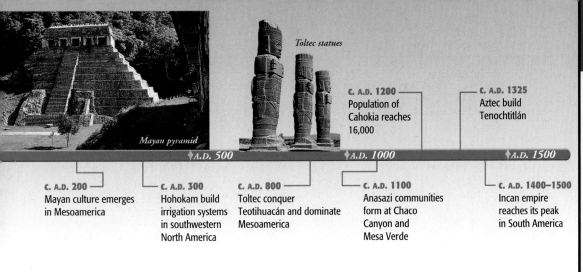

Toltec statues

Mayan pyramid

C. A.D. 1200
Population of
Cahokia reaches
16,000

C. A.D. 1325
Aztec build
Tenochtitlán

♦A.D. 500   ♦A.D. 1000   ♦A.D. 1500

C. A.D. 200
Mayan culture emerges
in Mesoamerica

C. A.D. 300
Hohokam build
irrigation systems
in southwestern
North America

C. A.D. 800
Toltec conquer
Teotihuacán and dominate
Mesoamerica

C. A.D. 1100
Anasazi communities
form at Chaco
Canyon and
Mesa Verde

C. A.D. 1400–1500
Incan empire
reaches its peak
in South America

Mayan cities in the highlands of what is today Guatemala flourished for several more centuries, although by the 1500s, they too were in decline.

In the meantime, people known as the Toltec began building a city called Tula. The Toltec were master architects. They built large pyramids and huge palaces with pillared halls. They were among the first Native Americans to use gold and copper for art and jewelry.

About A.D. 1200, Tula fell to invaders from the north, known as the Chichimec. One group of Chichimec, called the Mexica, established the city of Tenochtitlán (tay·NAWCH·teet·LAHN) in 1325 on the site of what is today Mexico City. The Mexica took the name **Aztec** for themselves, from the name of their original homeland, Aztlán. Aztlán is thought to have been located somewhere in the American Southwest.

The Aztec created a mighty empire by conquering neighboring cities. Using their military power, the Aztec controlled trade in the region and demanded tribute, or payment, from the cities they conquered. They also brought some of the people they conquered to Tenochtitlán to serve as human sacrifices in their religious ceremonies. When the Europeans arrived in the 1500s, an estimated five million people were living under Aztec rule.

✓ **Reading Check** **Examining** How did the shift to agriculture allow early peoples to advance beyond mere survival?

North American Cultures

North of Mesoamerica, other peoples developed their own cultures and civilizations. Many anthropologists think that the agricultural technology of Mesoamerica spread north into the American Southwest and up the Mississippi River. There it transformed many of the scattered hunter-gatherers of North America into farmers.

The Hohokam Beginning in A.D. 300 in what is now south-central Arizona, a group called the Hohokam created a civilization that featured a very elaborate system of irrigation canals. The Hohokam used the Gila and Salt Rivers as their water supply. Their canals carried water hundreds of miles to their farms.

The Hohokam grew large crops of corn, cotton, beans, and squash. They also made decorative red-on-buff pottery and turquoise pendants, and they created the world's first etchings by using cactus juice to etch shells. Hohokam culture flourished for more than 1,000 years. In the 1300s, they began to abandon their irrigation systems, most likely due to floods. Increased competition for farmland probably led to wars and emigration. By 1500 the Hohokam had vanished from history.

The Anasazi Between A.D. 700 and 900, the people living in villages in the Four Corners area, where Utah, Colorado, Arizona, and New Mexico now meet, came together to create a civilization. We know these people only by the name the Navajo gave them—*Anasazi*, or "ancient ones."

In the harsh desert environment of the American Southwest, the Anasazi accumulated water for their crops by building networks of basins and ditches to channel rain into stone-lined depressions with high earthen banks.

Between A.D. 850 and 1100, the Anasazi living in **Chaco Canyon** in what is now northwest New Mexico began constructing large, multi-story buildings of adobe and cut stone with connecting passageways

CHAPTER 1   Converging Cultures   **15**

CHAPTER 1
Section 1, 12–17

Creating a Chart Have students work in pairs to create a bar chart showing the beginning and ending dates for each North American culture mentioned in this section. The finished chart will illustrate the life span of each culture along with its relationship to each of the other cultures. The chart should include a title, labels, and a legend. **L2**

📁 Use the rubric for creating a map, display, or chart on pages 77–78 in the *Performance Assessment Activities and Rubrics.*

FYI

Mayan and Aztec calendars both had 365 days. It is believed that the Mayan calendar was the basis for all calendars in civilized Mesoamerica.

✓ **Reading Check**

Answer: The shift to agriculture allowed people to stay in one place to tend their crops and store their harvest. Because people stayed in one place, permanent villages were established. Village life led to the construction of homes and the development of storage containers. This allowed specialization of skills and more complex forms of government.

 VIDEOCASSETTE
Historic America Electronic Field Trips

View **Tape 1, Chapter 3:** "Cahokia Mounds."

INTERDISCIPLINARY CONNECTIONS ACTIVITY

Visual Arts Have students conduct research about pre-Columbian art using library, museum, and Internet resources. Ask students to focus their research on one of the cultures addressed in this section. Using their findings, have students prepare a short oral presentation. Encourage students to bring books with photographs and illustrations to pass around during their presentations. **L2**

3 ASSESS

Assign Section 1 Assessment as homework or as an in-class activity.

🔘 Have students use the **Interactive Tutor Self-Assessment CD-ROM.**

Picturing History

Answer: A severe drought from around 1130 to 1180 probably caused the Anasazi to abandon their pueblos. Epidemics and attacks from other tribes also may have contributed.

Ask: What building materials did the Anasazi use to construct their buildings? *(adobe and cut stone)*

---

and circular ceremonial rooms called **kivas.** Early Spanish explorers called these structures **pueblos,** the Spanish word for villages. The Anasazi built these pueblos at junctions where streams of rainwater, draining from the canyon, ran together. One particular pueblo in Chaco Canyon, called Pueblo Bonito, covered more than three acres. Its 600 rooms probably housed at least 1,000 people. Later, at Mesa Verde in what is today southwestern Colorado, the Anasazi built equally impressive cliff dwellings.

Beginning around A.D. 1130, Chaco Canyon experienced a devastating drought that lasted at least 50 years. This probably caused the Anasazi to abandon their pueblos. The Mesa Verde pueblos lasted for another 200 years, but when another drought struck in the 1270s, they too were abandoned. Some anthropologists think that epidemics or attacks by hunter-gatherers may have caused the Anasazi civilization to collapse.

The Adena and Hopewell Cultures About the same time that the Olmec people began to build a civilization in Mesoamerica, the people living in North America's eastern woodlands were developing their own unique cultures. The people of the eastern woodlands developed woodworking tools, including stone axes and gouges. They built dugout canoes and made nets to snare birds. They also made clay pots by stacking up coils of clay.

Beginning about 1000 B.C., the people of the region began burying their dead under massive dome-shaped mounds of earth. The most important early mound-building culture was the Adena culture, which lasted from 1000 B.C. to about A.D. 200. The Adena culture originated in the Ohio River valley and spread east into what is now New York and New England.

As the people of the Ohio valley began to plant crops and build permanent settlements between 200 and 100 B.C., another new civilization known as the Hopewell culture rose to prominence. It featured huge, geometric earthworks to serve as ceremonial centers, observatories, and burial places. The Hopewell culture mysteriously began to decline after A.D. 400.

The Mississippian Culture Between A.D. 700 and 900, as agricultural technology and improved strains of maize and beans spread north from Mexico and up the Mississippi River, another new culture—the **Mississippian**—emerged. It began in the Mississippi River valley, where the rich soil of the flood plains

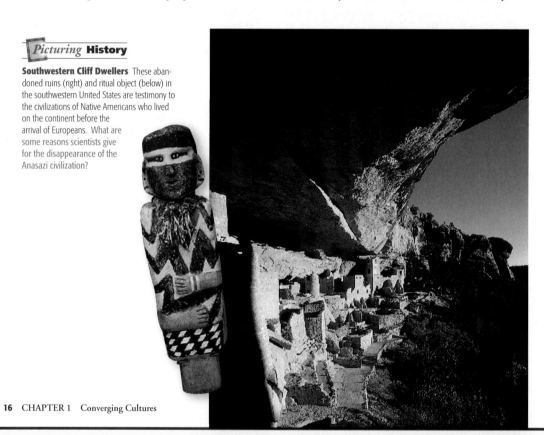

Picturing History

Southwestern Cliff Dwellers These abandoned ruins (right) and ritual object (below) in the southwestern United States are testimony to the civilizations of Native Americans who lived on the continent before the arrival of Europeans. What are some reasons scientists give for the disappearance of the Anasazi civilization?

16 CHAPTER 1 Converging Cultures

CRITICAL THINKING ACTIVITY

Analyzing Ask students to discuss how they think the agricultural revolution in Mesoamerica led to a more highly organized civilization. Focus the discussion on trade, government, the arts, science, and language. Encourage students to make reasonable assumptions based on the information presented in the text. **L2**

was perfectly suited to the intensive cultivation of maize and beans.

The Mississippians were great builders. Eight miles from what is now St. Louis, near Collinsville, Illinois, lie the remains of one of their largest cities, which anthropologists named **Cahokia.** At its peak between about A.D. 1050 and 1250, Cahokia covered 5 square miles (13 sq km), contained over 100 flat-topped pyramids and mounds, and was home to an estimated 16,000 people. Most of the people lived in pole-and-thatch houses that spread out over 2,000 acres (810 ha). The largest pyramid, named Monks Mound, was 100 feet (30.5 m) high, had four levels, and covered 16 acres (6.5 ha). The base of Monks Mound was larger than that of any pyramid in Egypt or Mexico. A log wall with watchtowers and gates surrounded the central plaza and larger pyramids.

From the Mississippi valley, Mississippian culture spread widely, following the Missouri, Ohio, Red, and Arkansas Rivers. Expanding east across the American South, Mississippian culture led to the rise of at least three other large cities with flat-topped mounds—at present-day Spiro, Oklahoma; Moundville, Alabama; and Etowah, Georgia.

Cahokia itself collapsed around A.D. 1300. An attack by other Native Americans may have caused its destruction, or the population may simply have become too large to feed, resulting in famine and emigration. Another possibility is that an epidemic

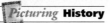 **History**

Adena and Hopewell Culture The Great Serpent Mound in southern Ohio (above) is an example of the earthern mounds built by the Adena culture. The copper falcon (right) is a Hopewell design. These artifacts help scientists learn more about the culture of ancient civilizations. For what did Native Americans use their earthern mounds?

may have devastated the population. Although Cahokia came to an end, many aspects of Mississippian culture survived in the Southeast until the Europeans arrived in America.

✓ **Reading Check** **Explaining** By what route did agricultural technology spread from Mesoamerica into North America?

Reteach
Have students trace a map of North America and mark key locations with the names and dates of the cultures mentioned in this section.

Enrich
Have students research one of the cultures mentioned in this section. Have them use library and Internet resources in order to write a two-page report about the culture. Ask students to include information about some of the unanswered questions about the culture.

4 CLOSE

Ask students to explain the Asian migration to America. Encourage students to offer suggestions about why people from Asia came to America and why they ended up in Mesoamerica.

✓ **Reading Check**

Answer: Many anthropologists think Mesoamerican agricultural technology spread north into the American southwest and up the Mississippi to North America.

SECTION 1 ASSESSMENT

Checking for Understanding
1. **Define:** radiocarbon dating, Ice Age, glacier, nomad, agricultural revolution, maize, civilization, obsidian, kiva, pueblo.
2. **Identify:** Beringia, Aztec, Chaco Canyon, Cahokia.
3. **Explain** how the agricultural revolution led to the establishment of permanent settlements.

Reviewing Themes
4. **Geography and History** How did Asians migrate to America?

Critical Thinking
5. **Evaluating** Choose an early culture group in Mesoamerica or North America. What kind of civilization did this group develop?
6. **Categorizing** Use a graphic organizer like the one below to list the advances of early culture groups in North America.

Culture Groups	Advances

Analyzing Visuals
7. **Picturing History** Study the photographs on this page and on page 16. How did the Native Americans in each region adapt to their environments?

Writing About History
8. **Expository Writing** Using library or Internet resources, find more information on one of the culture groups discussed in this section. Use the information to write an in-depth report about the culture group.

SECTION 1 ASSESSMENT ANSWERS

1. Terms are in blue.
2. Beringia (p. 13), Aztec (p. 15), Chaco Canyon (p. 15), Cahokia (p. 17)
3. Permanent settlements developed as people stayed in one place to tend to their crops.
4. Asians came to America by crossing Beringia on foot or hugging the

Beringian coast in boats.
5. Students should choose one of the cultures discussed in the section.
6. Students' organizers should include advances from each culture group mentioned in the section.
7. The Anasazi built their homes into the canyon walls of the Southwest. The Adena and Hopewell built cer-

emonial earthen mounds in the forested lands of the Midwest.
8. Students' reports will vary. Reports should focus on one culture group and provide information not found in the text.

Geography&History

1 FOCUS

Create three columns on the board and label them: Migration Theory, Potential Problems With Theory, and Evidence Supporting Theory. Have students use the maps, the reading, and any other reference material you supply to fill in the table. Tell students that they may make assumptions about the potential problems that the travelers may have faced.

2 TEACH

Writing Diary Entries Have students choose one of the routes and write diary entries as though they were traveling with the first group of people to use the route. The entries should include one for the first day of the travel, one describing a difficulty they encountered, and one describing their arrival in North or South America. **L1**

Practicing Map Skills Have students look at the maps to answer the following questions. **Ask:** What sites support the coastal route theory? *(Anangula, Ugashik, Ground Hog Bay, Hidden Falls, 49-PET-408, Namu, Borax Lake, and Mostin)* What is the northernmost site where human remains have been found? *(Old Crow)* How old are these human remains? *(more than 13,500 years old)* Where do scientists think people who crossed the Pacific may have landed? *(Quebrada Tacahuay in South America)* **L2**

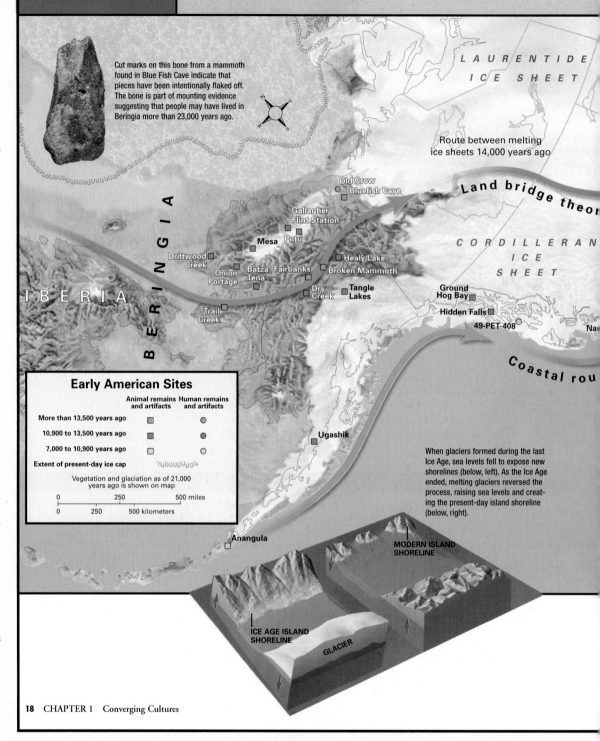

Cut marks on this bone from a mammoth found in Blue Fish Cave indicate that pieces have been intentionally flaked off. The bone is part of mounting evidence suggesting that people may have lived in Beringia more than 23,000 years ago.

Route between melting ice sheets 14,000 years ago

LAURENTIDE ICE SHEET

Land bridge theory

CORDILLERAN ICE SHEET

Old Crow
Bluefish Cave
Gallagher Flint Station
Mesa Putu
Driftwood Creek
Healy Lake
Onion Portage
Batza Tena Fairbanks Broken Mammoth
Dry Creek Tangle Lakes
Trail Creek
Ground Hog Bay
Hidden Falls
49-PET-408

Coastal route

Early American Sites

	Animal remains and artifacts	Human remains and artifacts
More than 13,500 years ago	▪	●
10,900 to 13,500 years ago	▪	●
7,000 to 10,900 years ago	▫	○
Extent of present-day ice cap		

Vegetation and glaciation as of 21,000 years ago is shown on map

0   250   500 miles
0   250   500 kilometers

Ugashik

When glaciers formed during the last Ice Age, sea levels fell to expose new shorelines (below, left). As the Ice Age ended, melting glaciers reversed the process, raising sea levels and creating the present-day island shoreline (below, right).

Anangula

MODERN ISLAND SHORELINE

ICE AGE ISLAND SHORELINE

GLACIER

18 CHAPTER 1 Converging Cultures

EXTENDING THE CONTENT

International Park An international Beringian park was first proposed by scientist Walter Orr Roberts in the 1960s. No action was taken on the proposal for many years. In 1989, however, American and Soviet planning teams presented the concept of an international park during a tour of Native villages in Northwest Alaska and the Chukotka Peninsula in Russia. At a summit conference on June 1, 1990, President Bush and Soviet President Gorbachev agreed to create an international park spanning the Bering Strait. The agreement called for cooperation in studying ecology, archaeology, and cultural heritage on both sides of the Strait. For more information on the proposed park visit http://www.nps.gov/akso/beringia/index.htm.

Land Bridge to America

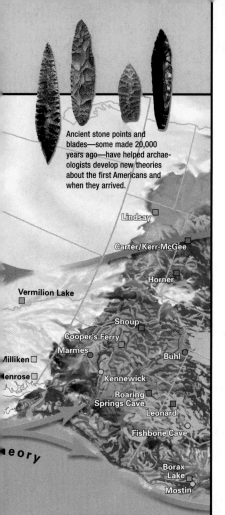

Ancient stone points and blades—some made 20,000 years ago—have helped archaeologists develop new theories about the first Americans and when they arrived.

During the last Ice Age, the Bering Strait that now separates Alaska and Siberia was dry land. Across this so-called land bridge, bands of fur-clad hunter-gatherers from Asia trekked to the northwestern corner of America (purple arrows at left). As they followed herds of woolly mammoths and other big game animals, they slowly spread east through a corridor between two glaciers and then pushed south into the interior of the continent.

These intrepid travelers have been held up as the original Americans. They flourished on the Great Plains and the Southwest of the present-day United States. In less than a thousand years, their descendants had settled most of the hemisphere, from the Arctic Circle to the tip of South America.

The intercontinental land bridge that made this amazing journey possible was up to 1,000 miles (1,609 km) wide. Known as Beringia, it emerged when vast ice sheets absorbed the water, dropping the sea level about 300 feet (91 km) to reveal the floor of the Bering Sea. Many scientists

agree that the Beringia migration began between 14,000 and 15,000 years ago. Recently, however archaeologists have found artifacts that suggest people were in America even before the land corridor had opened. The new evidence has led to theories suggesting other possible routes to the Americas.

One theory proposes that people crossed from northeast Asia in skin-covered boats, skirting the shore and landing occasionally to hunt for food and water (red arrows at left). Continuing south along the coast, they would have reached South America quicker than by any land route (see inset map below). The Pacific crossing theory suggests that migrants from Southeast Asia went south to Australia and across the Pacific Ocean, hopping from island to island until they reached South America. Yet a third theory, the Atlantic crossing theory, suggests that America's earliest inhabitants were from southwestern Europe (modern-day southern France and Spain). Hugging the edge of the glaciers of the North Atlantic, they may have sailed from Iceland and Greenland down to North America. A skull found in Brazil has also prompted some people to consider the possibility of an early migration from Africa.

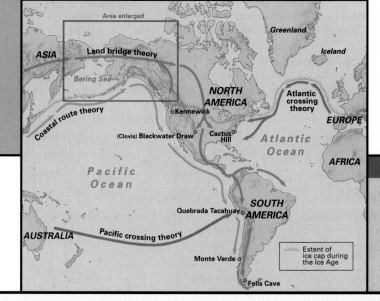

The peopling of the Americas was probably a more complex process than migration across the Bering land bridge alone. Settlers may have arrived in many waves of migration and by a number of routes. As shown in the map at left, they may have traveled from Europe or Australia as well as from Asia.

LEARNING FROM GEOGRAPHY

1. What geographical event made the sea level drop to reveal the land bridge between Asia and America?

2. What other ways may settlers have made their way to the Americas?

CHAPTER 1   Converging Cultures   **19**

NATIONAL GEOGRAPHIC
Geography & History

Geography and History Activity 1

Name _____ Date _____ Class _____

◼ GEOGRAPHY AND HISTORY ACTIVITY 1

Beringia Today: A Unique Region

CLOSE NEIGHBORS

Today the term *Beringia* describes a vast geographic region from the Kolyma River in far eastern Russia to the Mackenzie River in the Northwest Territories of Canada. This region remained relatively ice free during past glaciations when large parts of the earth were covered by glaciers.

The Bering Strait is a somewhat shallow body of water in the central part of Beringia. It separates the Seward Peninsula in Alaska from the Chukotskiy Peninsula in Siberia by a distance of only 55 miles. Situated

we commonly refer to the geological period called the Pleistocene epoch as the Ice Age. This period began 1.6 million years ago. During the final years of the Ice Age, so much of the earth's water was locked up in glaciers that sea levels were significantly lower than they are today. As a result, the land bridge between the continents of Asia and North America appeared.

The continental shelf along the Bering Strait also contributed to the appearance of the land bridge. A continental shelf is an

NGS ONLINE

Access National Geographic's Web site for current events, atlas updates, activities, links, interactive features, and archives at www.nationalgeographic.com.

Beringia The term *Beringia* comes from the name of Vitus Bering, a Danish explorer for the Russian czar in the 1700s. The Bering-Chirikov expedition explored the waters of the North Pacific between Asia and North America. The Bering Strait, which lies between Alaska and Northeast Russia, and Bering Island, located in the Commander Islands, are named after him.

3 ASSESS

Have students answer the Learning from Geography questions.

4 CLOSE

Ask students to state which theory they believe is most credible. Then ask what evidence they believe best supports their chosen theory.

ANSWERS TO LEARNING FROM GEOGRAPHY

1. the last Ice Age
2. Other possibilities include people from northeast Asia traveling by boat along the coastline to North and South America, people from Southeast Asia crossing the Pacific Ocean hopping from island to island, people from southwestern Europe crossing the North Atlantic passing by Iceland and Greenland, or people migrating from Africa.

1 FOCUS

Section Overview

This section explains how geography played a significant role in the development of Native American cultures.

BELLRINGER
Skillbuilder Activity

📖 Project transparency and have students answer the question.

📁 Available as a blackline master.

Daily Focus Skills Transparency 1–2

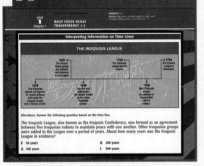

Answers to Graphic: the West: the Southwest–Zuni, Hopi, other Pueblo peoples, Apache, Navajo; the Pacific Coast–Tlingit, Haida, Kwakiutls, Nootkas, Chinook, Salish, Nez Perce, Yakima, Ute, Shoshone, and Pomo; the Great Plains–Pawnee, Kansas, Iowa, and Sioux; **the Far North:** Inuit, Aleut; **the Eastern Woodlands:** Northeast (Algonquian-speaking)–Wampanoag, Narragansett, Pequot, Powhatan Confederacy, Delaware, and Shawnee; Northeast (Iroquoian-speaking)–Huron, Neutral, Erie, Wenro, Seneca, Cayuga, Onondaga, Oneida, and Mohawk; Southeast–Cherokee, Tuscarora, Choctaw, Chickasaw, Natchez, and Creek

Preteaching Vocabulary
Have students look up the proper pronunciation of the Key Terms and Names.

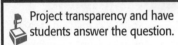

SECTION 2 Native American Cultures

Guide to Reading

Main Idea
The Native Americans of what is today the United States had diverse social structures and religions.

Key Terms and Names
kachina, Algonquian, Iroquoian, slash-and-burn agriculture, longhouse, wigwam, kinship group, Dekanawidah, Hiawatha

Reading Strategy
Categorizing As you read about Native Americans, complete a chart like the one below by filling in the names of the Native American groups who lived in each region.

Region	Groups
West	
Far North	
Eastern Woodlands	

Reading Objectives
• **Describe** the cultures of Native American groups of the West, the Far North, and the Eastern Woodlands.
• **Describe** the agricultural techniques of the Woodlands Native Americans.

Section Theme
Culture and Traditions The cultural differences between Native American groups can be explained by studying the geography where each group lived.

Preview of Events

◆1300	◆1400	◆1500	◆1600

c. 1300
Fighting erupts among the Iroquois

c. 1492
Europeans arrive in the Americas

c. 1500
People of the western Great Plains become nomadic

1500s
Navajo arrive in the Southwest

c. 1570
Iroquois League created

★ An American Story ★

Natchez earthen pyramid

Did the Natchez people of the southeastern United States descend from the Toltec of Mesoamerica? A Natchez man told this story to a European explorer in the mid-1700s:

❝Before we came into this land we lived yonder under the sun (pointing with his finger nearly south-west, by which I understood that he meant Mexico). . . . There our Suns [Mexican rulers were called Suns] had their abode and our nation maintained itself for a long time. . . . Our nation extended itself along the great water [Gulf of Mexico] where this large river [the Mississippi] loses itself; but as our enemies were become very numerous . . . our Suns sent some of their subjects who lived near this river, to examine whether we could return into the country through which it flowed. The country on the east side of the river being found extremely pleasant, the Great Sun, upon the return of those who had examined it, ordered all his subjects who lived in the plains, and who still defended themselves against the ancients of the country, to remove into this land, here to build a temple. . . .❞

—quoted in *America in 1492*

The West

Although Mesoamerican civilization may have shaped Natchez society, the culture of most Native Americans developed in response to their environments. By the time the first Europeans arrived, Native Americans were fragmented into many small groups

---

SECTION RESOURCES

📁 **Reproducible Masters**
• Reproducible Lesson Plan 1–2
• Daily Lecture and Discussion Notes 1–2
• Guided Reading Activity 1–2
• Section Quiz 1–2
• Reading Essentials and Study Guide 1–2

📖 **Transparencies**
• Daily Focus Skills Transparency 1–2

• American Art & Architecture

Multimedia
🔘 Interactive Tutor Self-Assessment CD-ROM
🔘 ExamView® Pro Testmaker CD-ROM
🔘 Presentation Plus! CD-ROM
🔘 TeacherWorks™ CD-ROM
🔘 Audio Program
🔘 American Music: Hits Through History

that had adapted to the different regions of North America. Fragmentation in the American West was especially severe because of the great variations in the region's climate and geography.

The Southwest The descendants of the Anasazi and Hohokam lived in small groups in the arid Southwest. These groups included the Zuni, Hopi, and other Pueblo peoples. The people of the Southwest depended on corn to survive. Farmers cultivated several species of corn whose seeds could withstand the dry soil. With a long taproot, the corn grew deep, reaching moisture far below the surface. The farmers also grew squash and beans.

Among these groups, when a man married, he joined the household of his bride's mother. Within the family, men's and women's work was separate. Men farmed and herded sheep. They also performed most ceremonies, made moccasins, and wove clothing and blankets. It was women's work to take care of the house. In addition, women crafted pottery and baskets and hauled water. The women also helped the men in two occupations—farming and constructing houses.

When boys turned six, they joined the kachina cult. A kachina was a good spirit. The Pueblo people believed kachinas visited their town each year with messages from the gods. Members of the kachina cult would wear masks symbolizing the spirits, and they would dance to bring the spirits to the town.

Sometime around the 1500s, two other peoples—the Apache and the Navajo—came to the region from the far northwest of North America. Although many of the Apache remained primarily nomadic hunters, the Navajo learned farming from the Pueblo people and lived in widely dispersed settlements, where they grew corn, beans, and squash.

The Pacific Coast Many different groups, including the Tlingit, Haida, Kwakiutls, Nootkas, Chinook, and Salish peoples, lived in the lands bordering the Pacific Ocean from what is now southeastern Alaska to Washington state. Although they did not practice agriculture, these groups dwelt in permanent settlements. They looked to the dense coastal forests for lumber, which they used not only to build homes and to fashion canoes, but also to create elaborate works of art, ceremonial masks, and totem poles. They were able to stay in one place because the region's coastal waters and many rivers teemed with fish, particularly salmon. Farther inland, between the Cascade Range and the Rocky Mountains, the Nez Perce, Yakima, and other groups fished, hunted deer, and gathered roots and berries.

South of the Nez Perce's territory, between the Sierra Nevada and Rocky Mountains, the climate was much drier. There, groups such as the Ute and Shoshone lived a nomadic life. Because the land was too arid for farming, they roamed widely in search of food that was often scarce.

West of the Ute lands in what is today central California, several groups enjoyed abundant wildlife and a mild climate. The Pomo, for example, gathered acorns, caught fish in nets and traps, and snared small game and birds. Pomo hunters, working together, would drive deer toward a spot where the village's best archer waited, hidden and disguised in a deer-head mask. Sometimes, the hunters stampeded game into a corral, where the animals could be easily killed. When game was scarce, however, the Pomo relied upon the acorn, which they had learned to convert from a hard, bitter nut into an edible flour.

The Great Plains When Europeans arrived in America, the people of the Great Plains were nomads. Before this, up until about 1500, people living on the Great Plains practiced agriculture. Influenced by the Hopewell and Mississippian cultures, these peoples lived near the Missouri and other rivers, where they could plant corn and find wood to build their homes.

Around 1500 the peoples of the western plains abandoned their villages and became nomads, possibly because of war or drought. Those in the east—including the Pawnee, Kansas, and Iowa peoples—continued to farm as well as hunt. Peoples of the western plains, such as the Sioux, followed migrating buffalo herds on foot and lived in cone-shaped tents called tepees.

Life for the Sioux and others on the Great Plains changed dramatically after they began taming horses. The Spanish had brought horses to North America in the 1500s. Over the next few centuries, as horses either escaped or were stolen, the animals spread northward, eventually reaching the Great Plains. There the Sioux encountered and mastered them, and in the process became some of the world's greatest mounted hunters and warriors.

Sioux men achieved fame in the community through bravery in both hunting and war. Sioux warriors would take the scalps of enemies they had killed, but they could gain even greater glory through

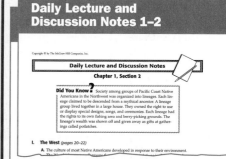

Pacific coast totem pole

2 TEACH

Daily Lecture and Discussion Notes 1–2

Copyright © by The McGraw-Hill Companies, Inc.

Daily Lecture and Discussion Notes

Chapter 1, Section 2

Did You Know? Society among groups of Pacific Coast Native Americans in the Northwest was organized into lineages. Each lineage claimed to be descended from a mythical ancestor. A lineage group lived together in a large house. They owned the right to use or display special designs, songs, and ceremonies. Each lineage had the rights to its own fishing area and berry-picking grounds. The lineage's wealth was showed off and given away as gifts at gatherings called potlatches.

I. **The West** (pages 20–22)
A. The culture of most Native Americans developed in response to their environment.

Creating a Map Have students trace a simple outline map of Canada and the continental United States including Alaska. Ask students to mark the map where each of the Native American cultures mentioned in this section developed. **L1** ELL

📂 Use the rubric for creating a map, display, or chart on pages 77–78 in the *Performance Assessment Activities and Rubrics*.

FYI

Totem poles are large cedar logs that were carved, painted, and mounted vertically by Native American peoples who lived along the northern Pacific coast. Totem poles were used for specific purposes. For example, some totem poles were designed to support the roof of a house while others were created as memorials.

COOPERATIVE LEARNING ACTIVITY

Teaching Your Classmates Group students into home teams of six and assign each member of the team a number from 1 to 6. Divide the section into six parts and number the parts. Have everyone with the number 1 meet to study and discuss part 1 of the section. Do the same for each of the other parts. Reunite the home teams and have each member of the team share his or her knowledge about this section.

Use the rubric for a cooperative group management plan on pages 81–82 in the *Performance Assessment Activities and Rubrics.*

✓ Reading Check

Answer: In dry areas the Native Americans found crops that would grow in the dry soil or they moved from place to place looking for food. In coastal areas, the Native Americans became experts at fishing. In mild climates where wildlife was plentiful, they hunted and trapped animals.

Guided Reading Activity 1–2

★ **Guided Reading Activity 1-2**

DIRECTIONS: Recalling Facts Read the section and answer the questions below. Refer to your textbook to write the answers.

1. The culture of most Native Americans developed in response to what? _____
2. Upon what did the peoples living in the Southwest depend to survive? _____
3. What was the name of a Pueblo good spirit? _____
4. Which peoples lived in the lands bordering the Pacific from southeastern Alaska to Washington State? _____
5. For what did the peoples of the Pacific Coast use lumber? _____
6. Who brought horses to North America? _____

History *and the* Humanities

🎵 American Music: Hits Through History: "Iroquois Round Dance"
🖼 American Art & Architecture: Quilled Buckskin Robe

✓ Reading Check

Answer: the harpoon, the kayak, the dogsled, boots with ivory spikes, goggles, and lamps

Geography *Skills*

Answers:
1. fishing
2. The land was too dry to farm so they hunted migrating buffalo herds.

Geography Skills Practice
Ask: What group lived the farthest north? *(Inuit)*

---

the dangerous but nonviolent act of "counting *coup*," from the French word meaning "blow" or "touch." A warrior would charge into a group of the enemy and simply touch one of them with a stick—as a means of humiliating the enemy—then gallop away.

✓ Reading Check **Contrasting** How did Native Americans respond to the different climates of the American West?

The Far North

Two different Native American groups made the Far North their home. The most northern and widespread were the Inuit, whose territory stretched across the Arctic from present-day Alaska to Greenland. The Aleut settled Alaska's Aleutian Islands.

The Inuit and Aleut depended heavily upon hunting for their livelihood. They hunted seals, walruses, whales, polar bears, caribou, musk oxen, and smaller game. Over time, they invented a wide variety of devices to cope with the harsh environment, including the harpoon, the kayak, the dogsled, boots with ivory spikes for walking on ice, and special goggles to prevent snow blindness. They also were the only Native Americans to develop lamps. They used whale oil and blubber for fuel. Occupying a harsh and unforgiving land, they lived in groups—from a single family to a few hundred people—spaced widely apart.

✓ Reading Check **Identifying** What technologies did the Native Americans of the Far North develop?

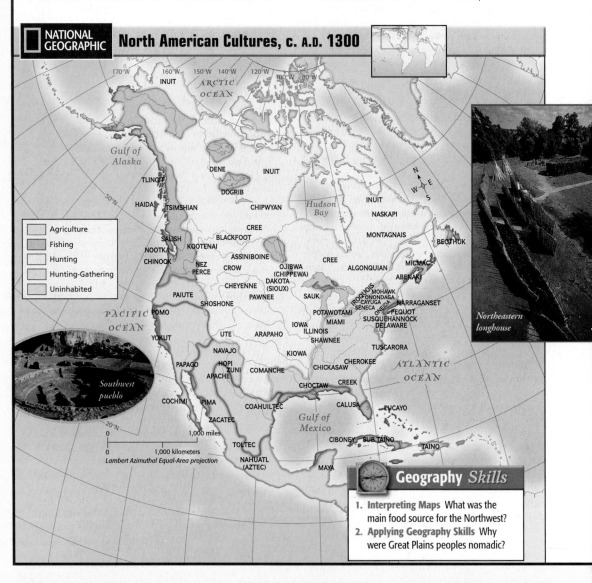

NATIONAL GEOGRAPHIC **North American Cultures, c. A.D. 1300**

Southwest pueblo

Northeastern longhouse

Legend:
- Agriculture
- Fishing
- Hunting
- Hunting-Gathering
- Uninhabited

1,000 miles
1,000 kilometers
Lambert Azimuthal Equal-Area projection

Geography *Skills*

1. **Interpreting Maps** What was the main food source for the Northwest?
2. **Applying Geography Skills** Why were Great Plains peoples nomadic?

MEETING SPECIAL NEEDS

Auditory/Musical Have students work in pairs using dictionary resources to look up the correct pronunciation of the names of each Native American culture discussed in the section. Have students practice saying the names aloud as they write them down. **L1** 🔲

📂 Refer to *Inclusion for the High School Social Studies Classroom Strategies and Activities* in the TCR.

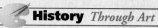
Eastern Woodlands Native Americans hunted the abundant deer in the East by disguising themselves in cleaned deerskins and sneaking very close to their target. French artist Jacques Le Moyne created this illustration in 1591 depicting the practice. What other food sources did Eastern Woodlands peoples have?

🎨 **History** *Through Art*

Answer: corn, beans, squash, fishing in coastal areas
Ask: Native Americans of the Eastern Woodlands incorporated natural elements in decorating their clothing. What are some examples? (*plant dyes; clay or shell beads; animal bone, teeth, or claws; feathers; porcupine quills*)

The Eastern Woodlands

East of the Mississippi River and south of the Great Lakes lay almost a million square miles of woodlands. This landscape supported an amazing range of plant and animal life. Almost all of the Native Americans in the Eastern Woodlands provided for themselves by combining hunting and fishing with farming. Deer were plentiful in the region, and deer meat regularly supplemented the corn, beans, and squash the people planted. Deer hide was also used for clothing.

The Peoples of the Northeast Most of the peoples of the Northeast were divided into two major language groups—those who spoke **Algonquian** (al·GAHN·kwee·UHN) languages and those who spoke **Iroquoian** (IHR·uh·KWOY·uhn) languages. The Algonquian-speaking peoples included most of the groups living in what later became known as New England. Among these peoples were the Wampanoag in Massachusetts, the Narragansett in Rhode Island, and the Pequot in Connecticut. Farther south in what is today Virginia lived the Algonquian-speaking peoples of the Powhatan Confederacy. These groups of Native Americans in New England and Virginia were among the first to encounter English settlers.

Other Algonquian-speaking peoples included the Delaware who lived near the Delaware River and the Shawnee who lived in the Ohio River valley. Many words from the Algonquian language are still used today, including *succotash, hominy, moccasin,* and *papoose.*

Stretching west from the Hudson River across what is today New York and southern Ontario and north to Georgian Bay were the Iroquoian-speaking peoples. They included the Huron, Neutral, Erie, Wenro, Seneca, Cayuga, Onondaga, Oneida, and Mohawk.

Many peoples in the Northeast, including the Algonquians of New England and the Iroquoians of New York, practiced slash-and-burn agriculture. By cutting down parts of forests and then burning the cleared land, they were left with nitrogen-rich ashes, which they then worked into the soil, making it more fertile.

The early peoples of the Northeast used several types of houses. Many villages, enclosed by wooden stockades, had large rectangular longhouses with barrel-shaped roofs covered in bark. Others built wigwams. These dwellings were either conical or dome-shaped and were made using bent poles covered with hides or bark.

All of the Iroquoian peoples, as well as the Algonquian of New England, made beads of white and purple shells that they arranged on strings and wove into belts called wampum. The designs on the wampum recorded important events, treaties, and agreements.

GOVERNMENT

The Iroquois League All of the Iroquoian peoples had similar cultures. They lived in longhouses in large towns, which they protected by building stockades. The people lived in large kinship groups, or extended families, headed by the elder women of each clan. Iroquois women occupied positions of power and importance in their communities. They were responsible for the planting and harvesting of crops. Up to 10 related families lived together in each longhouse.

HISTORY *Online*

Student Web Activity Visit the *American Vision* Web site at tav.glencoe.com and click on **Student Web Activities— Chapter 1** for an activity on America's prehistory.

Conducting Research Have students identify streets, towns, parks, lakes, and other things in their community that have names derived from the names of Native American peoples. Have students make a list of their findings. **L2**

HISTORY *Online*

Objectives and answers to the student activity can be found in the **Web Activity Lesson Plan** at tav.glencoe.com.

3 ASSESS

Assign Section 2 Assessment as homework or as an in-class activity.

🌐 Have students use the **Interactive Tutor Self-Assessment CD-ROM.**

INTERDISCIPLINARY CONNECTIONS ACTIVITY

Science Invite an anthropologist from a museum or local university to visit your class to discuss how he or she researches the cultures and lifestyles of ancient civilizations that no longer exist. Ask the speaker to explain the techniques used in field research and what qualifications and education are needed to enter this field of study. Encourage students to ask questions at the end of the presentation. **L2**

Reading Essentials and Study Guide 1–2

Name _____ Date _____ Class _____

Study Guide
Chapter 1, Section 2
For use with textbook pages 20–24
NATIVE AMERICAN CULTURES

KEY TERMS AND NAMES

kachina a good spirit of the Pueblo people *(page 21)*
Algonquian language of Native Americans who lived in areas that later became known as New England, Delaware, the Ohio River valley, and Virginia *(page 23)*
Iroquoian language of Native Americans who lived in areas that later became known as New York, southern Ontario and north to Georgian Bay *(page 23)*
slash-and-burn agriculture the practice of cutting down forests and then burning the cleared land to use for farming *(page 23)*
longhouses rectangular houses with barrel-shaped roofs covered in bark *(page 23)*
wigwams cone- or dome-shaped houses made with bent poles covered with hides or bark

Section Quiz 1–2

Name _____ Date _____ Class _____

★ **Chapter 1** | Score

Section Quiz 1-2

DIRECTIONS: Matching Match each item in Column A with the items in Column B.
Write the correct letters in the blanks. *(10 points each)*

Column A
___ 1. rectangular house with a barrel-shaped roof covered in bark
___ 2. the most northern Native American group
___ 3. a good spirit
___ 4. a chief of the Mohawk
___ 5. extended families

Column B
A. Hiawatha
B. kinship groups
C. longhouse
D. kachina
E. Inuit

DIRECTIONS: Multiple Choice In the blank at the left, write the letter of the choice that best completes the statement or answers the question. *(10 points each)*

Fact	Fiction	Folklore

Archaeologists have found kernels of popcorn in Utah and Peru that they estimate to be over 1,000 years old. Almost all of the world's popcorn is grown in the United States. According to the Popcorn Board, a non-profit organization sponsored by U.S. Popcorn Processors, the average American eats about 15 gallons of popcorn each year.

Reteach
List the three geographic areas mentioned in this section on separate panels of the board. Have students create an outline using the names of the regions and cultures.

Enrich
Have students pose questions about the Native American cultures addressed in this section and research the answers.

✓ **Reading Check**

Answer: Some Woodland Native Americans practiced slash-and-burn agriculture to clear the land and make it more fertile.

4 CLOSE

Ask students to explain the role of geography in the development of the various Native American cultures.

Fact	Fiction	Folklore

Pass the Popcorn Native Americans perfected the popular American snack of popcorn at least 5,000 years ago. In order to pop, a corn kernel must contain at least 14 percent water. When heated, this water turns into steam, which expands and forces the kernel to explode into its familiar shape. Native Americans developed corn with a high water content suitable for popping, as well as sweet corn to eat off the cob and feed corn for animals. According to legend, popcorn made up part of the menu at the first Thanksgiving feast in 1621.

Despite their similar cultures, war often erupted among the Iroquoian groups. In the late 1500s, five of the nations in western New York—the Seneca, Cayuga, Onondaga, Oneida, and Mohawk—formed an alliance to maintain peace. This alliance was later called the **Iroquois League** or Iroquois Confederacy. Europeans called these five nations the Iroquois, even though other nations spoke Iroquoian as well.

According to Iroquois tradition, **Dekanawidah** (DEK·uh·nuh·WEE·duh), a shaman or tribal elder, and **Hiawatha,** a chief of the Mohawk, founded the League. They were worried that war was tearing the five nations apart at a time when the more powerful Huron people threatened them all. The five nations agreed to the Great Binding Law, a constitution that defined how the confederacy worked.

Although the 50 chiefs who made up the ruling council of the Iroquois League were all men, the women who headed the kinship groups selected them. Council members were appointed for life, but the women could also get rid of an appointee if they disagreed with his actions. In this way, Iroquois women enjoyed considerable political influence.

The Peoples of the Southeast Almost all of the people in the Southeast lived in towns. Women did most of the farming, while the men hunted deer, bear, wildfowl, and even alligator. The Mississippian culture influenced many of the people in the Southeast. The town buildings were arranged around a central plaza. Stockades usually surrounded the towns, although moats and earthen walls were also used. The houses were built out of poles and covered with grass, mud, or thatch.

The Cherokee were the largest group in the Southeast. They lived in what is today western North Carolina and eastern Tennessee. About 20,000 Cherokee lived in some 60 towns when the Europeans arrived. The Cherokee and a nearby group of people called the Tuscarora were Iroquoian speakers. Other people in the Southeast included the Choctaw, Chickasaw, Natchez, and Creek. The Creek were a large group living in what is today Georgia and Alabama. They lived in about 50 villages that were divided into War Towns, where the war leaders lived and men trained for war, and Peace Towns, where the political leaders lived.

By the 1500s, Native Americans had created a wide array of cultures and languages. They had also developed economies and lifestyles well suited to the geography and climate in their particular corners of North America.

✓ **Reading Check** **Analyzing** How did some Woodlands Native Americans increase their crop yield?

SECTION 2 ASSESSMENT

Checking for Understanding
1. **Define:** kachina, slash-and-burn agriculture, longhouse, wigwam, kinship group.
2. **Identify:** Algonquian, Iroquoian, Dekanawidah, Hiawatha.
3. **Explain** why five Native American groups formed the Iroquois League.

Reviewing Themes
4. **Culture and Traditions** How did geography and climate affect the customs and traditions of Native American groups?

Critical Thinking
5. **Analyzing** Why were some Native American groups more nomadic than others?
6. **Categorizing** Use a graphic organizer like the one below to list North American regions and the ways Native Americans living in these regions obtained food.

Region	Ways of Getting Food

Analyzing Visuals
7. **Analyzing Maps** Examine the map of North American cultures on page 22. Which method of acquiring food was used over the largest geographical area of North America?

Writing About History
8. **Descriptive Writing** Take on the role of a Sioux teenager living in North America around 1500. Write a journal entry describing a typical day in your life. Be sure to discuss where you live and how your family obtains food.

24 CHAPTER 1 Converging Cultures

SECTION 2 ASSESSMENT ANSWERS

1. Terms are in blue.
2. Algonquin *(p. 23)*, Iroquoian *(p. 23)*, Dekanawidah *(p. 24)*, Hiawatha *(p. 24)*
3. The Iroquois League was formed in order to keep the peace.
4. Answers will vary. Students should note how customs and traditions were affected by climate using examples from the text.
5. Native American peoples who engaged in farming were less likely to be nomadic than those who primarily hunted for food.
6. Southwest—farmed and herded sheep; Pacific Coast—fished, hunted, gathered roots and berries; Eastern Great Plains—farmed and hunted; Western Great Plains—hunted; Far North: hunted; Northeast—farmed; Southeast—farmed and hunted
7. hunting
8. Students' reports will vary. Journal entries should include details about daily activities, food, and clothing.

American LITERATURE

Among the Native American groups with the richest oral literary traditions are the Iroquois. The Iroquois lived in what is today New York state. For a long time, they were a mighty and warlike people given to fighting amongst themselves. During the 1500s a shaman, or tribal elder, named Dekanawidah urged the Iroquois to stop fighting and unite to protect themselves from their common enemies. Dekanawidah's ideas led to the formation of the Iroquois Confederation of the Five Nations, commonly known as the Iroquois League.

Read to Discover
How did the Iroquois Confederation organize the Confederate Council?

Reader's Dictionary
foundation: basis

unanimous: in complete agreement

render: make; provide

from *The Constitution of the Five Nations*

I am Dekanawidah and with the Five Nations' Confederate Lords I plant the Tree of Great Peace. . . .

The Mohawk Lords are the foundation of the Great Peace and it shall, therefore, be against the Great Binding Law [the constitution] to pass measures in the Confederate Council after the Mohawk Lords have protested against them.

All the business of the Five Nations Confederate Council shall be conducted by the two combined bodies of Confederate Lords. . . . In all cases the procedure must be as follows: when the Mohawk and Seneca Lords have unanimously agreed upon a question, they shall report their decision to the Cayuga and Oneida Lords who shall deliberate upon the question and report a unanimous decision to the Mohawk Lords. The Mohawk Lords will then report the standing of the case to the Firekeepers [the Onondaga], who shall render a decision as they see fit in case of a disagreement by the two bodies. . . .

There shall be one War Chief for each Nation and their duties shall be to carry messages for their Lords and to take up the arms of war in case of emergency. They shall not participate in . . . the Confederate Council.

Whenever a very important matter or a great emergency is presented

before the Confederate Council [that] affects the entire body of the Five Nations . . . the Lords of the Confederacy must submit the matter to the decision of their people and the decision of the people shall affect the decision of the Confederate Council.

Analyzing Literature
1. **Recall and Interpret** Which of the Five Nations settles a dispute within the Confederate Council?
2. **Evaluate and Connect** Which Nation seems to have the most individual power?

Interdisciplinary Activity
Government Imagine that you and several classmates are leaders of five small nations that are going to join together as one. In small groups, develop a new constitution under which all members of the new nation will live.

Block Schedule

Team Teaching This selection from *The Constitution of the Five Nations* can be presented in a team teaching context, in conjunction with English or Language Arts.

Read to Discover
Answer: They organized into two bodies of Lords.

Reinforcing Vocabulary
Have students take turns using one of the terms in a sentence that they speak aloud.

Historical Connection
The portion of *The Constitution of the Five Nations* that appears in the text is only a small part of the complete document which contains more than 12,000 words.

Portfolio Writing Activity
Ask students to find and read the entire document *The Constitution of the Five Nations* and write a summary of the key elements. The document is available at most libraries and on the Internet.

HISTORY Online

Refer to tav.glencoe.com for additional Glencoe Literature titles, lesson plans, and study guides related to this unit.

Answers to Analyzing Literature

1. The Onondaga settle disputes within the Confederate Council.
2. The Mohawk nation appears to have the most individual power since binding laws cannot be passed if Mohawk Lords object to them.

Interdisciplinary Activity
Students' constitutions will vary. To help make the activity more realistic, encourage students to develop descriptions of their nations. Constitutions should deal with maintaining peace, resolving differences, and defense.

1 FOCUS

Section Overview

This section describes the diverse cultures that developed in different parts of Africa. The interaction of people from West Africa and Europe resulted in changes to both the West African and European cultures.

Guide to Reading

Answers to Graphic: West Africa: the Soninke people of Ghana, the Malinke people of Mali, the Sorko of Songhai, the Yoruba people of Ife, and the Edo people of Benin; Central Africa: the kingdom of Kongo

Preteaching Vocabulary
Have students classify the Key Terms and Names as persons, places, or things.

Guide to Reading

Main Idea
Peoples in West, Central, and Southern Africa developed diverse governments and lifestyles.

Key Terms and Names
Sahara, savannah, Islam, Muslim, Soninke, mosque, Malinke, Sorko, Yoruba, matrilineal

Reading Strategy
Organizing As you read about the civilizations and peoples of West, Central, and Southern Africa, complete a graphic organizer similar to the one below by filling in the names of several groups from each region.

West Africa	Central and Southern Africa

Reading Objectives
- *Describe* the culture of early West African kingdoms.
- *Describe* the lifestyles of early Central and Southern African peoples.

Section Theme
Global Connections The interaction of West African and European civilizations created changes in both cultures.

Preview of Events

◆A.D. 400	◆750	◆1100	◆1450

A.D. 400 — West Africa's first empire, Ghana, arises

A.D. 610 — Muhammad begins teaching ideas of Islam

1009 — First Songhai state established

1240 — Mali expands its power

1450 — Songhai empire expands in West Africa

Mansa Musa

★ An African Story ★

In 1324 Mansa Musa, ruler of the Mali empire, made a pilgrimage to the Arabian city of Makkah (Mecca), a place holy to his religion, Islam.

Musa had encouraged scholarship and trade in his realm, establishing his empire's leading city, Timbuktu, as a great center of learning. A man named Mahmoud Kati, a native of the city, wrote a book praising Timbuktu for "the solidity of its institutions, its political liberties, the purity of its morals, the security of persons, its consideration and compassion towards foreigners, its courtesy toward students and men of learning and the financial assistance which it provided for the latter. . . ."

Musa was not the first African king to visit Makkah, but no one there or along his route had ever seen anything as dazzling as his traveling party. With him came 60,000 men, 12,000 of them personal servants he had enslaved. All were lavishly dressed. His vast caravan included 80 camels carrying 300 pounds of gold each.

Along the route, Musa's generous spending brought prosperity to the towns he passed and made his name famous. More importantly, the unmistakable wealth of his empire opened the eyes of North Africans, Arabs, and Europeans to the greatness of the Mali civilization.

—adapted from Wonders of the African World

West Africa

Between the 400s and 1500s, three great empires—Ghana, Mali, and Songhai—rose and fell in West Africa. These realms grew and prospered in large measure by trading in two precious commodities—gold and salt.

⬛ SECTION RESOURCES

📁 Reproducible Masters
- Reproducible Lesson Plan 1–3
- Daily Lecture and Discussion Notes 1–3
- Guided Reading Activity 1–3
- Section Quiz 1–3
- Reading Essentials and Study Guide 1–3

Transparencies
- Daily Focus Skills Transparency 1–3

Multimedia
- 💿 Interactive Tutor Self-Assessment CD-ROM
- 💿 ExamView® Pro Testmaker CD-ROM
- 💿 Presentation Plus! CD-ROM
- 💿 TeacherWorks™ CD-ROM
- 🎧 Audio Program
- 🎵 American Music: Cultural Traditions

GEOGRAPHY

The Lay of the Land Africa's geography helped determine where these empires arose. West Africa is an immense bulge of territory bordered on the north by the Mediterranean Sea and on the west and south by the Atlantic Ocean. Its northern and southern perimeters are well watered and fertile, but between them lies the vast expanse of the **Sahara,** whose name comes from an ancient Arabic word meaning *desert*. At the edges of the Sahara, regions of scrub forest and a kind of rolling grassland called savannah make for a more hospitable landscape.

From the western tip of the continent, where the Atlantic coast curves eastward to form West Africa's southern edge, a tropical rain forest grows. Civilizations both large and small arose in the rain forest and in the savannah along the Niger River, which cuts through West Africa and long served as its major path for east-west migration and trade.

Other important trade routes in West Africa crossed the vast Sahara. Early merchants bravely trekked through the desert using oxen, donkeys, and horses to carry their wares. Although pack oxen could travel a few days without water, long distance trade was rare and risky. For centuries most trade across the Sahara remained local. People living on the edge of the Sahara would exchange food for salt mined in the desert.

When Arab merchants introduced camels to the region between the third and fifth centuries A.D., they revolutionized trans-Saharan trade. Camels could carry more weight than oxen or horses, and they could walk for a much longer period each day. Most importantly, camels could go for over a week without water and could easily withstand the desert's scorching days and cold nights.

Although crossing the Sahara was still risky, camels enabled merchants to open up long-distance trade routes across the desert. Gold, ivory, ostrich feathers, and furs from south of the Sahara soon became more available to North Africa and Europe. As the demand for West African products increased, large trading settlements developed at the northern and southern boundaries of the Sahara.

Islam and West African Civilizations Ideas as well as goods traveled along these African trade routes. Among the most significant of these were the religious ideas of **Islam.**

In the early A.D. 600s, Islam began winning converts outside of its native Arabia. By 711 Islam, whose followers are called **Muslims,** had spread all the way across northern Africa to the Atlantic Ocean. Through both armed conquest and the sense of religious solidarity that Islam promoted, this new creed won wide acceptance.

By the 900s, the nomadic peoples who controlled the trade caravans in the Sahara had become Muslim as well. They in turn carried Islam across the Sahara into the heart of West Africa, where many people living in the region's cities and market towns would eventually embrace it.

The Lure of Gold West Africa prospered primarily because of the gold trade. The Muslim conquest of North Africa greatly increased the demand for gold in the 800s and 900s because the new Muslim states of the region used gold coins.

Later, in the 1200s, trade between Europe and North Africa experienced an economic revival as the rulers of Europe shifted from silver and copper coins to gold coins. By the 1300s, as much as two-thirds of the gold in Europe and North Africa had come from trade with West Africa.

✔ **Reading Check** **Explaining** Why were camels better than horses or oxen for traveling in the desert?

The Empires of West Africa

The African peoples who lived on the southern edge of the Sahara were perfectly positioned to benefit from the growing trade in gold. Being in the middle of the trade, they had access both to the gold from the south and the salt and other goods coming from the north. Their ability to control this trade increased their wealth and power and enabled them to build large empires.

Ghana The earliest empire to emerge was Ghana in the A.D. 400s. Located between the gold mines of Bambuk (just east of present-day Senegal) and the salt mines of Taghaza in the Sahara, the **Soninke,** as the people of Ghana were called, controlled the region's trade and built West Africa's first empire. A visitor from Spain, Abu Hamid al-Andalusi, wrote of Ghana:

Gourd drum from Africa's west coast

2 TEACH

Daily Lecture and Discussion Notes 1–3

Copyright © by The McGraw-Hill Companies, Inc.

Daily Lecture and Discussion Notes
Chapter 1, Section 3

Did You Know ❓ A trade exchange known as "the silent trade" was used by merchants in Ghana. Since many of the traders had no common language, they would place their goods on the ground and then leave. Then the people of Ghana would leave gold beside the goods and then leave. The owners of the goods would return, and if they were satisfied with the amount of gold that was left, they would take it. If not, they would go away again and the people of Ghana would return and add more gold. This process continued until the trade ended.

I. **West Africa** (pages 26–27)

✔ **Reading Check**

Answer: Camels could carry more weight, walk farther each day, and go longer without water than horses or oxen.

Creating a Video Cover Obtain a copy of David Wisniewski's *Sundiata: Lion King of Mali* or Khephra Burns's *Mansa Musa* and read it to the class. Have students design a box cover for a videotape based on the book. Students should draw a dramatic scene of their choice for the front cover, then write a summary of the story for the back that would persuade a viewer to rent the video. **L2**

you don't say...

Salt Salt has been used throughout the ages to season and preserve food. It has also been used in religious ceremonies and as a medium of exchange. The word *salary* is derived from the Latin word *salarium* that referred to the ration of salt issued to soldiers.

COOPERATIVE LEARNING ACTIVITY

Creating Study Cards Organize students into teams of three. Have each team create a set of study cards for each member. The cards should highlight the important topics and concepts presented in this section. Allow teams to determine what each member will contribute to the process. 📖

Use the rubric for a cooperative group management plan on pages 81–82 in the *Performance Assessment Activities and Rubrics.*

Guided Reading Activity 1–3

Name _____ Date _____ Class _____

★ **Guided Reading Activity 1-3**

DIRECTIONS: Outlining Read the section and complete the outline below. Refer to your text-book to fill in the blanks.
I. West Africa

A. The realms of _____ and _____
grew by trading in two precious commodities— _____ and _____

B. West Africa is an immense bulge of territory bordered on the north by the _____ and on the west and south by the _____

C. Ideas as well as goods traveled along the African trade routes. Among the most significant of these were the religious ideas of _____

D. In the 1200s, the rulers of Europe shifted from _____ and _____ coins to _____ coins.

II. The Empires of _____

Writing a Report Have students research the development of one of the African cultures mentioned in this section and write a one-page report about the culture prior to contact with Europeans. **L2**

📁 Use the rubric for a book review, research report, or position paper on pages 89–90 in the *Performance Assessment Activities and Rubrics.*

FYI

📖 History *and the* Humanities

🎵 American Music: Cultural Traditions: "Yarum Praise Songs"

❝In the sands of that country is gold, treasure inexpressible. . . . Merchants trade with salt for it, taking the salt on camels from the salt mines. They . . . travel in the desert as it were upon the sea, having guides to pilot them by the stars or rocks. . . . They take provisions for six months, and when they reach Ghana they weigh their salt and sell it against a certain unit of weight of gold. . . .❞

—quoted in *African Kingdoms*

After the Muslim conquest of North Africa and the Sahara in the 600s and 700s, Ghana's merchants grew wealthy from the gold and salt trade. Muslim traders from the north found a warm welcome in Ghana's capital of Kumbi-Saleh, where the ruler even permitted them to build their own mosques—Muslim places of worship. Ghana's ruler taxed the trade and became very wealthy as well. Most of Ghana's people, however, were farmers and herders who did not profit from the trade.

Despite this success, Ghana's empire had collapsed by the early 1200s. Although Ghana had become a Muslim kingdom in the 1100s, it was hurt by frequent wars with the Muslims of the Sahara. Equally contributing to Ghana's collapse was a change in the environment. Ghana's land was exhausted, and its farmers could no longer feed its people.

At the same time that these factors were combining to weaken Ghana, new gold mines opened in Bure (located in what is today northeast Guinea). Trade routes to these mines bypassed Ghana to the east, depriving Ghana's rulers of the wealth they needed to keep their empire together.

Mali East of Ghana, the **Malinke** people controlled the upper Niger Valley. This enabled them to direct the gold trade from Bure. With their new wealth and

Wooden stool from Ghana

power, the Malinke conquered the Soninke of Ghana and built the empire of Mali.

By the mid-1300s, the empire of Mali had spread east down the Niger River past Timbuktu and west down the Senegal and Gambia Rivers to the Atlantic Ocean. The ruler of Mali was called the *mansa*. The government of Mali was similar to that of Ghana. In both empires, a bureaucracy of scribes and treasurers lived in the capital city with the emperor.

In outlying towns, traditional rulers stayed in power and managed local affairs. To stay in power, local leaders had to collect tribute from the farmers and send a portion to the capital. To enforce the system, the *mansa* kept a large army ready and made army leaders important officials in his government. Although the rulers and traders of Mali adopted Islam, many of the people—especially the farmers—clung to their traditional belief in "spirits of the land," whom they thought ensured the growth of their crops.

The empire of Mali reached its peak in the 1300s under the leadership of **Mansa Musa** and his brother Mansa Sulayman. By that time, new gold mines had opened in the Akan region (located in what is today Ghana), shifting the trade routes farther east and leading to the rise of Timbuktu as a great center of trade and Muslim scholarship.

Akan memorial head

Songhai The **Sorko** people who lived along the middle Niger, east of Mali, built the Songhai empire. The Sorko fashioned canoes and fished for a living. They also used their canoes to control the river and trade with peoples to the north and south, gaining both wealth and power. By the 800s they had created the kingdom of Songhai. Although Songhai had contact with Mali, most of its territory never came under Mali's control.

When Mali began to decline, the ruler of Songhai, **Sonni Ali,** used a powerful army of cavalry backed by a fleet of war canoes to seize Timbuktu in 1468. Until his death in 1492, Ali led his cavalry and war canoes in a series of wars of conquest. After taking Timbuktu, Ali pushed northward into the Sahara to

28 CHAPTER 1 Converging Cultures

MEETING SPECIAL NEEDS

Kinesthetic Tell students that sugarcane became an important crop to Europeans. Explain that harvesting sugarcane requires many laborers and that Europeans enslaved African peoples to perform much of the labor. Have students create a model showing the process of growing and harvesting sugarcane. Encourage students to clearly label the model so that a person observing the model can gain a clear understanding of the process. **L1**

📁 Refer to *Inclusion for the High School Social Studies Classroom Strategies and Activities* in the TCR.

the Taghazi salt mines, and then he expanded southward down the Niger about 200 miles (322 km) to capture the town of Jenne. According to legend, Sonni Ali's army never lost a battle.

Sonni Ali's son and successor proved to be an ineffectual ruler, and within a year a Songhai general named **Askiya Muhammad** seized the throne. Askiya Muhammad, a devout Muslim, revived Timbuktu as a great center of learning, encouraged more trade across the Sahara, and centralized power in the Songhai capital, Gao. Visiting Gao in 1513, a young Moroccan named Leo Africanus wrote:

❝Its inhabitants are rich merchants who travel constantly about the region with their wares. A great many Blacks come to the city bringing quantities of gold with which to purchase goods imported from the Berber country [North Africa] and from Europe, but they never find enough goods on which to spend all their gold and always take half or two-thirds of it home.❞

—quoted in *African Kingdoms*

Songhai remained a powerful and wealthy empire until 1591, when Moroccan troops, armed with guns and cannon, defeated Songhai's armies. After the battle shattered its army, the Songhai empire began to decline.

✔**Reading Check** *Describing* Why did the empire of Ghana begin to decline?

The Forest Kingdoms of Guinea

Ghana, Mali, and Songhai arose on the wide vistas of West Africa's savannah, an open landscape that made it easier to control large territories. The situation differed in the dense, almost impenetrable forests of West Africa's southern coast, an area called Guinea. There, smaller states and kingdoms, such as Ife and Benin, developed.

Both the **Yoruba** people of Ife and the **Edo** people of Benin were a mixture of hunters, farmers, and traders living in small village communities. The rich farmlands and tropical climate enabled the people of the forest kingdoms to produce surplus food that was then used to support rulers, government officials, artisans, and artists. Surplus food was also traded for copper and salt from the Sahara. Ife artists produced some of the most impressive art in West Africa. They carved wood and ivory, made terra-cotta sculptures, and cast metal.

To the south and east of Ife, the Edo people developed the city-state of Benin in the eleventh or twelfth century. By 1400, Benin was a large, walled city measuring several miles across. The ruler of Benin was called the *oba*. In the mid-1400s, **Oba Ewuare** assembled a

Picturing **History**

West African Empire This turreted mosque in Djenné, Mali, dates back to the 1300s. It still provides a vital worship center in the Sahara, much as it did during the days of the West African empires. *Why did so many empires arise in West Africa?*

✔**Reading Check**

Answer: the land was exhausted and the farmers could no longer feed the people

Writing a Biography Have students write a short biography of one of the leaders mentioned in this section. **L2**

📁 Use the rubric for a book review, research report, or position paper on pages 89–90 in the *Performance Assessment Activities and Rubrics.*

Creating a Display Organize students into groups to explore the rich heritage of African textiles. Assign each group a different type of fabric. Examples include kente, mud cloth, strip weaving, adinkra, and adire. Using library and Internet resources, they should research their fabric and create a display that includes information on how the cloth is produced, how it is used, as well as color renditions of patterns used in that type of cloth. **L2**

📁 Use the rubric for creating a map, display, or chart on pages 77–78 in the *Performance Assessment Activities and Rubrics.*

Picturing **History**

Background: Every year on the last day of Ramadan, the faithful gather to apply a fresh coat of adobe to this mosque.

Answer: They were centrally located, well situated to control the trade in gold from the south and salt and other goods coming from the north.

Ask: When did the Muslims take control of North Africa? *(in the 600s and 700s)*

INTERDISCIPLINARY CONNECTIONS ACTIVITY

Performing Arts Have students research the influence of African music and dance on American music. Encourage students to learn about traditional African musical instruments and rhythms. Also encourage students to experience traditional African music and dance through live and recorded performances. **L2**

Geography *Skills*

Answers:

1. Songhai

2. access to water

Geography Skills Practice

Ask: What was the leading city in the Mali kingdom? *(Niani)*

✓ Reading Check

Answer: Unlike the open landscape of the West African savannah, the dense forests of Guinea made it difficult for armies to control large expanses of territory.

✓ Reading Check

Answer: Food surpluses resulted from fertile soil and abundant rainfall.

3 ASSESS

Assign Section 3 Assessment as homework or as an in-class activity.

🌐 Have students use the **Interactive Tutor Self-Assessment CD-ROM.**

Reading Essentials and Study Guide 1–3

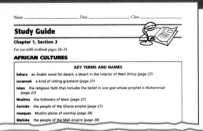

Name _____ Date _____ Class _____

Study Guide

Chapter 1, Section 3

For use with textbook pages 26–31

AFRICAN CULTURES

KEY TERMS AND NAMES

Sahara an Arabic word for desert; a desert in the interior of West Africa *(page 27)*

savannah a kind of rolling grassland *(page 27)*

Islam the religious faith that includes the belief in one god whose prophet is Muhammad *(page 27)*

Muslims the followers of Islam *(page 27)*

Soninke the people of the Ghana empire *(page 27)*

mosques Muslim places of worship *(page 28)*

Malinke the people of the Mali empire *(page 28)*

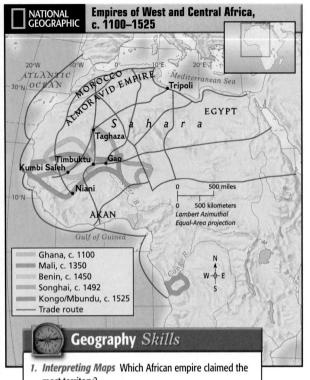

NATIONAL GEOGRAPHIC

Empires of West and Central Africa, c. 1100–1525

- Ghana, c. 1100
- Mali, c. 1350
- Benin, c. 1450
- Songhai, c. 1492
- Kongo/Mbundu, c. 1525
- Trade route

Geography *Skills*

1. *Interpreting Maps* Which African empire claimed the most territory?
2. *Applying Geography Skills* What natural feature determined the location of these empires?

---

powerful army and built Benin into an empire that stretched from the Niger delta west to where the city of Lagos, Nigeria, is located today.

After establishing his empire, Ewuare appointed district chiefs to replace the local rulers he had conquered. Benin's leaders also began trading enslaved people they had captured in war to the Portuguese in exchange for Portuguese goods. They then sold the Portuguese ivory, pepper, gum, and cotton. Later, when Benin collapsed into civil war in the 1700s, many Benin citizens were themselves enslaved and traded to the Portuguese.

✓ Reading Check *Examining* Why were the states and kingdoms smaller in Guinea than in West Africa's savannah area?

Central and Southern Africa

To the southeast of Benin lay the impenetrable reaches of the rain forests. There, the dense vegetation made the movement of people and goods

---

difficult. Many Central African villages, located on rivers, gained a living from fishing but also grew wheat and raised livestock. The villagers had complex family structures and maintained close links to their communities. Other Central Africans lived nomadic lives and subsisted by hunting and gathering.

Like the Iroquois in America, many Central African societies were matrilineal. People traced their lineage, or descent, through their mothers rather than through their fathers. Upon marriage a man became a member of his bride's family.

Though women took responsibility for child rearing and cooking, they also played a major role in trade. In many places the women farmed while the men hunted, fished, and raised livestock. Tribal chiefs were almost always male, but a chief's son could not expect to succeed his father. Instead, the son of the chief's eldest sister inherited the post. Thus, Central and Southern African women of the time enjoyed far more influence and authority than women in many other parts of the world.

The Central African kingdom of Kongo originated around 1400 in a group of prosperous villages along the Zaire River, which flows southwestward through the region to the Atlantic. Fertile soil and abundant rainfall allowed the farmers who lived in these villages to produce food surpluses. By the early 1500s, the Kongo king ruled over a large region from the Atlantic to the Kwango River. South of Kongo, another large kingdom arose among the Mbundu-speaking people in the region that is now Angola.

✓ Reading Check *Analyzing* Why were the peoples of the Kongo able to produce food surpluses?

Slavery

As in other parts of the world, slavery existed in African society. Most of the people enslaved in African societies had been captured in war. A few were convicted criminals who had been enslaved as punishment. Before the Arabs and Europeans began purchasing enslaved Africans, most African societies would either ransom captives back to their people or absorb them into their own society. With hard work and good luck, enslaved Africans had a chance to improve their difficult position. In rare instances, they could purchase their freedom by selling produce they had grown or marry into their captor's society and improve their social status.

CRITICAL THINKING ACTIVITY

Synthesizing Using a blank outline map of Africa that includes the present-day country borders, have students create a historical map showing the land areas controlled by the Ghana, Mali, Songhai, Ife, Benin, and Kongo kingdoms. Tell students to assign a different color to each kingdom and use the color to shade the area of land controlled by each. Have students label the kingdoms and their approximate dates of existence. Remind students that some areas will overlap. **L2**

African slavery began to change with the arrival of Islam. Muslims in the Middle East were permitted to enslave non-Muslims. Arab traders began to trade horses, cotton, and other goods in exchange for enslaved Africans captured in war.

The Gold Trade The gold trade also changed slavery in West Africa. In the early 1400s, the Akan people began mining gold and trading it to the Mali empire. To increase their production, they acquired enslaved Africans from Mali traders for use in clearing the land and mining the gold.

In the 1420s, the Portuguese began exploring the west coast of Africa and trading with West African merchants. They traded European goods for African gold, ivory, pepper, and palm oil. When Portuguese merchants arrived on the coast south of the Akan region, they began to supply the Akan people with enslaved Africans in exchange for gold. They also purchased enslaved Africans to work on Portuguese sugar plantations.

Sugar and Slavery Europeans learned about the cultivation and processing of sugarcane from the Muslims during the 1100s. The introduction of sugar changed the diet of Europeans, who had formerly used honey and fruit juices to sweeten their foods. Demand for sugar began to rise steadily. Eventually about 20 percent of all calories consumed in Europe came from sugar.

Europeans set up sugar plantations on the Mediterranean islands of Cyprus and Sicily. These locations, unlike most of Europe, provided the specific climate and type of soil sugarcane needs to grow well.

Sugarcane cultivation requires heavy manual labor. The cane is tough and thick and has to be chopped down using heavy knives. A huge amount of sugarcane has to be cut to produce a pound of sugar. Consequently, plantation owners needed a large labor force. To get people to do the work, they either had to pay very high wages or find a way to force people to do the work without paying them. As a result, the introduction of sugarcane farming encouraged Europeans to use enslaved workers and to enter into the slave trade.

The first enslaved workers used by the Europeans on sugar farms were captured Muslims and Slavic peoples. Rising demand for sugar in the 1400s led Spain and Portugal to establish sugarcane plantations on the Canary and Madeira Islands off the west coast of Africa. They then brought in enslaved Africans to work the fields. The limited amount of land available to Europeans to plant sugarcane kept their participation in the slave trade limited during the 1400s. This would change dramatically after Europeans introduced sugarcane to America.

As the European demand for slave labor rose following the colonization of America, slavery in Africa completely changed. Traders took enslaved Africans from their homes and sent them across the Atlantic. For the most part, enslaved Africans shipped to America had little chance of winning their freedom. Torn from their own cultures, they had to learn a completely new way of life amid often horrifying conditions.

✓**Reading Check** *Analyzing* Why did Europeans want slaves?

SECTION 3 ASSESSMENT

Checking for Understanding
1. ***Define:*** savannah, mosque, matrilineal.
2. ***Identify:*** Sahara, Islam, Muslim, Soninke, Malinke, Sorko, Yoruba.
3. ***Explain*** why Songhai became a great empire.

Reviewing Themes
4. ***Global Connections*** How did the concept of slavery change as trade between Africa and Europe flourished in the 1500s?

Critical Thinking
5. ***Comparing*** How were Central and Southern African societies different from each other?
6. ***Categorizing*** Use a graphic organizer similar to the one below to list ways of making a living in African cultures.

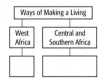

| Ways of Making a Living | |
| West Africa | Central and Southern Africa |

Analyzing Visuals
7. ***Examining Artifacts*** Study the West African artifacts on pages 27 and 28. The skillful handiwork of these items indicates a society able to devote time to artistic pursuits in addition to necessary tasks. What two commodities were essential to the prosperity of West Africa?

Writing About History
8. ***Descriptive Writing*** Imagine you are a Portuguese explorer in West Africa. Write a journal entry describing a West African civilization.

SECTION 3 ASSESSMENT ANSWERS

1. Terms are in blue.
2. Sahara *(p. 27)*, Islam *(p. 27)*, Muslim *(p. 27)*, Soninke *(p. 27)*, Malinke *(p. 28)*, Sorko *(p. 28)*, Yoruba *(p. 29)*
3. Songhai had a powerful army and centralized government.
4. Slavery changed in the 1500s because enslaved Africans were taken from their own culture to America where they had little chance of earning their freedom.
5. Some were agriculturally based with complex family structures. Others were nomadic.
6. West Africa: Ghana–trading, mining; Mali–trading; Songhai–fishing, trading; Guinea–hunting, farming, trading; Central and Southern Africa: fishing, farming, hunting, gathering, raising livestock
7. gold and salt
8. Students' journal entries will vary. Entries should contain detailed observations.

Section Quiz 1–3

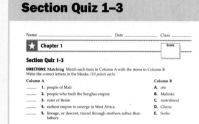

Reteach
Have students explain the importance of trade on the development of African cultures.

Enrich
Have students use library and Internet resources to learn more about slavery in Africa prior to the 1400s. Have them present their findings in the form of a multimedia presentation.

4 CLOSE

Have students list the ways that trading between West Africa and Europe changed cultures in both regions. Have them also identify the ways in which this trade affected American history.

✓**Reading Check**

Answer: Europeans wanted slaves to work on sugarcane plantations.

SECTION 4 European Cultures

1 FOCUS

Section Overview

This section describes European society and the political, social, and scientific events in Europe between 1100 and 1400 that enabled Europeans to explore the world.

BELLRINGER
Skillbuilder Activity

Project transparency and have students answer the question.

Available as a blackline master.

Daily Focus Skills Transparency 1–4

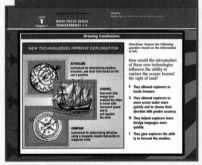

Guide to Reading

Answers to Graphic: Key events include: the Crusades, the invention of a better plow and the horse collar, the collapse of the Mongol empire, the decline of feudalism and emergence of strong states, the Renaissance, technological advances in navigational instruments, and advances in shipbuilding and sailing techniques.

Preteaching Vocabulary

Have students create a simple symbol, icon, or sketch for each of the Key Terms and Names. Ask students to label each drawing.

Guide to Reading

Main Idea
The fall of Rome fragmented Europe. Between 1100 and 1400, several developments helped reunify parts of Europe and encouraged new explorations.

Key Terms and Names
Crusades, Roman Empire, feudalism, manorialism, serf, Renaissance, astrolabe, lateen sail, caravel, Henry the Navigator, Bartolomeu Dias, Vasco da Gama

Reading Strategy
Organizing As you read about European life in the Middle Ages, complete a graphic organizer similar to the one below by filling in the key events that brought Europe out of its long isolation.

End of European Isolation

Reading Objectives
• **Discuss** the impact of the Crusades on Europe's contact with the Middle East.
• **Analyze** the impact of the Renaissance on European exploration.

Section Theme
Science and Technology The Renaissance helped start a scientific revolution that enabled Europeans to explore the world.

Preview of Events

| ◆1095 | ◆1230 | ◆1365 | ◆1500 |

1095
Pope Urban II launches the Crusades

1200s
Mongol empire established

1300s
Renaissance begins in Italy

1420s
Portugal begins exploring the African coast

1497
Vasco da Gama reaches India

★ A European Story ★

Pope Urban II with other Church leaders

In 1095 Pope Urban II, the head of the Roman Catholic Church, was a worried man. The Holy Land, the birthplace of Christianity, was in the hands of Muslims, who, Urban feared, would no longer allow Christians access to holy religious sites. To meet this threat, Urban organized a great meeting of Christians in Clermont, France. On November 18, before a huge outdoor crowd of bishops, knights, and common people, Urban made an impassioned speech, calling on Europeans to seize control of Christianity's holiest sites by armed conquest. A cleric known as Robert the Monk recorded the Pope's speech in these words:

❝Jerusalem is the navel of the world. . . . This is the land which the Redeemer of mankind illuminated by his coming, adorned by his life, consecrated by his passion, redeemed by his death, and sealed by his burial. This royal city, situated in the middle of the world, is now held captive by his enemies. . . . It looks for help from you, especially, because God has bestowed glory in arms upon you more than on any other nation. Undertake this journey, therefore, for the remission of your sins, with the assurance of 'glory which cannot fade' in the kingdom of heaven.❞

—quoted in *The Discoverers*

European Society

Pope Urban II's call to arms launched nearly two centuries of armed struggle to regain the Holy Land. These expeditions were called the **Crusades,** from the Latin word *crux*, meaning "cross." The Crusades helped pry western Europe out of centuries of

SECTION RESOURCES

Reproducible Masters
• Reproducible Lesson Plan 1–4
• Daily Lecture and Discussion Notes 1–4
• Guided Reading Activity 1–4
• Section Quiz 1–4
• Reading Essentials and Study Guide 1–4
• Performance Assessment Activities and Rubrics

Transparencies
• Daily Focus Skills Transparency 1–4

Multimedia
◉ Interactive Tutor Self-Assessment CD-ROM
◉ ExamView® Pro Testmaker CD-ROM
◉ Presentation Plus! CD-ROM
◉ TeacherWorks™ CD-ROM
◉ Audio Program

isolation and triggered a series of events that revolutionized European society and encouraged a new desire for exploration.

For centuries, the **Roman Empire** had dominated much of Europe, imposing a stable social and political order. By A.D. 500, however, the Roman political and economic system had collapsed, isolating western Europe from the rest of the world. Trade declined. Cities, bridges, and roads fell into disrepair. Law and order vanished, and money was no longer used. For most people, life did not extend beyond the tiny villages where they were born, lived, and died. This period, lasting roughly from 500 to 1400, is known as the **Middle Ages.**

Feudalism With the weakening of central government, a new political system known as feudalism developed in western Europe. Under this system, a king would give estates to nobles in exchange for their loyalty and military support. Eventually, the nobles owning the estates became strong enough to assume many of the powers usually held by government. They raised their own armies, dispensed justice, and even minted coins. In return, the nobles swore an oath of loyalty and promised to provide knights, or mounted warriors, for the royal army.

By 1100 feudalism had spread throughout much of Europe. Because the system lacked a strong central government, warfare occurred frequently in feudal society. As a result, most nobles built castles, or fortified manor houses, for defense.

The Manorial System The wealth of a feudal lord came from the labor of the peasants who lived on his land. Since the fall of the Roman Empire, many peasants had worked for large landowners, in part because they could not obtain their own land and in part for protection.

A lord's manor, or estate, varied in size from several hundred to several hundred thousand acres. Each manor included the lord's house, pastures for livestock, fields for crops, forest, and a peasant village. While feudalism describes the political relationships between nobles, manorialism describes the economic ties between nobles and peasants.

In return for protection, peasants provided various services for the lord. Chief among these were farming the lord's land and making various payments of goods. Warfare and bandits made trade difficult, so the manor had to produce nearly everything its residents needed.

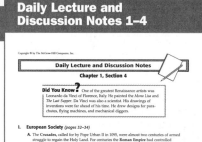

History *Through Art*

The Middle Ages This Bayeaux tapestry and a prayer book show art styles in Europe in the Middle Ages. What aspect of life in the Middle Ages does the tapestry depict?

Peasants rarely left the manor. Most were serfs, people who were bound to the manor and could not leave it without permission. Serfs were not considered enslaved, however, since they could not be sold from the land where they lived and worked. Serfs typically lived in tiny, one-room houses with dirt floors, a hole in the roof for a chimney, and one or two crude pieces of furniture. Coarse bread, a few vegetables, and grain for porridge made up their usual diet. They spent most of their waking hours working. Here, an English monk describes a serf's account of his day:

> ❝I work very hard. I go out at dawn, driving the oxen to the field, and I yoke them to the plough; however hard the winter I dare not stay home for fear of my master; but, having yoked the oxen and made the ploughshare and coulter fast to the plough, every day I have to plough a whole acre or more.❞
>
> —quoted in *Colloquy*

An Improving Economy The economy of western Europe, devastated since the fall of Rome, began to improve around 1000. The invention of a better plow allowed farmers to produce more food, as did the invention of the horse collar, which allowed farmers to use horses instead of oxen. Horses could pull a plow faster than an ox, enabling farmers to plant more crops each year.

CHAPTER 1   Converging Cultures   **33**

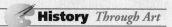
History *Through Art*

Answer: This scene depicts a medieval feast. The tapestry as a whole depicts the events surrounding William the Conqueror's invasion of England in 1066.
Ask: What barriers do you think manorialism created? *(Possible answers include: a barrier between classes in society and barriers to trade.)*

2 TEACH

Daily Lecture and Discussion Notes 1–4

Copyright © by The McGraw-Hill Companies, Inc.

Daily Lecture and Discussion Notes

Chapter 1, Section 4

Did You Know? One of the greatest Renaissance artists was Leonardo da Vinci of Florence, Italy. He painted the *Mona Lisa* and *The Last Supper*. Da Vinci was also a scientist. His drawings of inventions were far ahead of his time. He drew designs for parachutes, flying machines, and mechanical diggers.

I.   **European Society** *(pages 32–34)*

A. The **Crusades**, called for by Pope Urban II in 1095, were almost two centuries of armed struggle to regain the Holy Land. For centuries the **Roman Empire** had controlled much of Europe with stable social and political order. By A.D. 500, however, the empire collapsed. Western Europe became isolated, trade declined, and law and order ended.

Writing a Job Description Have students write a job description for a noble. Encourage students to list any qualifications needed, as well as a description of the work to be done. Have students use employment ads from newspapers and the Internet for examples of job descriptions. **L1**

📁 Use the rubric for a magazine/newspaper/Web site article or help-wanted ad on pages 85–86 in the *Performance Assessment Activities and Rubrics.*

COOPERATIVE LEARNING ACTIVITY

Building a Model Have students work in small groups to build a model of a typical lord's manor and peasant village from the 1100s. Encourage students to supplement the information provided in the text with library and Internet resources. Arrange for students' models to be displayed for classmates. 📦

Use the rubric for a cooperative group management plan on pages 81–82 in the *Performance Assessment Activities and Rubrics.*

Reading Check

Answer: The social order in Europe during the Middle Ages revolved around strong noblemen. Under the political system known as feudalism, a king would give estates to nobles in exchange for loyalty and military support. This political system led to a manorial economic system whereby peasants provided services to nobles in exchange for protection and basic needs such as food and shelter.

Guided Reading Activity 1–4

Creating a Display Have students choose a technological advancement mentioned in this section and create a display showing how the technology worked and how it was used. **L2**

Use the rubric for creating a map, display, or chart on pages 77–78 in the *Performance Assessment Activities and Rubrics.*

Geography *Skills*

Answers:
1. Constantinople
2. the Mongol empire

Geography Skills Practice
Ask: What were Spain's major commercial centers? *(León, Toledo, Valencia, Córdoba, Cádiz)*

The ability of many villages to produce a surplus of food helped to revive trade in Europe and encouraged the growth of towns. Some European rulers succeeded in building strong central governments. Warfare and raids by bandits decreased, and roads were soon filled with traders carrying goods to market. The number of towns in western Europe grew tremendously between 1000 and 1200.

The Church The Roman Catholic Church struggled mightily against the social and political fragmentation of Europe that followed the fall of Rome. In the face of civil chaos and personal insecurity, it promoted stability and order. It had its own laws and courts that dealt with cases related to the clergy, doctrine, marriage, and morals.

Disobedience to Church laws resulted in severe penalties for common persons and rulers alike—including excommunication for those who committed grave offenses. Excommunication barred people from participating in Church rites. They also lost political and legal rights.

Reading Check **Describing** What was the social order in Europe during the Middle Ages?

Expanding Horizons

Pope Urban II's call for Christians to free their religion's holy places from the Muslims launched a period of profound change in Europe. The Crusades

NATIONAL GEOGRAPHIC **Europe in the Age of Exploration, c. 1100–1400**

- Major commercial centers
- ← Major trade routes

0 500 miles
0 500 kilometers
Azimuthal Equidistant projection

Geography *Skills*

1. **Interpreting Maps** Which city was Europe's overland gateway to India?
2. **Applying Geography Skills** Which Eastern empire was crucial for organizing the movement of goods between Europe and China?

MEETING SPECIAL NEEDS

Logical/Mathematical Have students find maps showing common overland and sea trade routes from Europe to China. Then have students use the map scales to calculate the approximate distances of common routes. Ask students to prepare a chart comparing these distances. As an extension, you could ask students to research the approximate time required to make a complete trip and add that detail to the charts. **L2**

Refer to **Inclusion for the High School Social Studies Classroom Strategies and Activities** in the TCR.

helped change western European society by bringing western Europeans into contact with the Muslim and Byzantine civilizations of eastern Europe and the Middle East. The western European presence in this region heightened demand at home for Eastern luxury goods: spices, sugar, melons, tapestries, silk, and other items. Trade increased in the eastern Mediterranean area and especially benefited Italian cities such as Venice, Pisa, and Genoa.

By 1200 Italian and Arab merchants controlled much of the trade in the eastern Mediterranean. Chinese and Indian traders sold silk, spices, and other goods to Arab merchants, who then moved the goods overland to the Mediterranean coast, where they reaped huge profits selling the goods to Italian merchants.

As trade increased, merchants found that many Arab traders would only accept money in payment. European merchants therefore needed a common medium of exchange, and this led to the rise of an economy based on money. The increasing demand for gold from Africa to make gold coins during the 1200s was a direct result of Europe's expanding trade with Asia.

The rise of the Mongol empire in the 1200s helped to increase the flow of goods from China and other parts of Asia. Mongol horsemen swept out of central Asia in the early part of the century and built one of largest empires in world history. The Mongol conquest integrated much of Asia's economy. It broke down trade barriers, opened borders, and secured the roads against bandits, encouraging even more trade between Asia and Europe.

By the 1300s Europe was importing vast quantities of spices, silks, and other goods from Asia. To the frustration of European merchants, however, the Mongol empire collapsed in the 1300s, and Asia again separated into dozens of independent kingdoms and empires. The flow of goods from Asia declined, and the price of spices, already very high, rose even more. Increasingly European merchants and rulers began to look for a route to Asia that bypassed the Muslim kingdoms. If they could not reach China by land, they thought, perhaps they could reach it by sea.

✓ **Reading Check** **Summarizing** Describe the effects of the Crusades on Europe.

New States, New Technology

The wealth that could be earned by trading directly with Asia had given Europeans a compelling motive to begin exploring the world. Before the 1300s, however, western European rulers and merchants did not have the ability to look for a direct sea route to Asia.

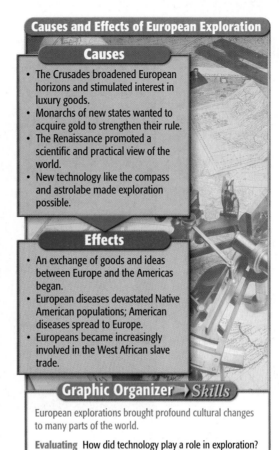

Causes and Effects of European Exploration

Causes

- The Crusades broadened European horizons and stimulated interest in luxury goods.
- Monarchs of new states wanted to acquire gold to strengthen their rule.
- The Renaissance promoted a scientific and practical view of the world.
- New technology like the compass and astrolabe made exploration possible.

Effects

- An exchange of goods and ideas between Europe and the Americas began.
- European diseases devastated Native American populations; American diseases spread to Europe.
- Europeans became increasingly involved in the West African slave trade.

Graphic Organizer *Skills*

European explorations brought profound cultural changes to many parts of the world.

Evaluating How did technology play a role in exploration?

Feudalism had created a society so fragmented and torn by war that no western European kingdom had the wealth to finance exploration and overseas trade. Western Europeans also lacked the technology to even attempt to reach China by sea. Beginning in the 1300s, however, a number of major changes took place in Europe that enabled the Europeans to begin sending ships into the Atlantic Ocean in search of a water route to China.

GOVERNMENT

Strong States Emerge Western Europeans began exploring the world in the 1400s and 1500s for several reasons. First of all, feudalism was in decline. Both the Crusades and trade with Asia had helped to weaken this system. The rise of towns and merchants had provided kings and queens with a new source of wealth they could tax. They could now use their armed forces to open up and protect trade routes and to enforce uniform trade laws and a common currency

CHAPTER 1 Converging Cultures **35**

3 ASSESS

Assign Section 4 Assessment as homework or as an in-class activity.

🖱 Have students use the **Interactive Tutor Self-Assessment CD-ROM.**

Reading Essentials and Study Guide 1–4

Name _____ Date _____ Class _____

Study Guide

Chapter 1, Section 4

For use with textbook pages 32–37

EUROPEAN CULTURES

KEY TERMS AND NAMES

Crusades military expeditions by European Christians in the 1100s and 1200s to regain the Holy Land from the Muslims *(page 32)*

Roman Empire the empire that dominated much of Europe for centuries and collapsed by A.D. 500 *(page 33)*

feudalism the political system that developed in western Europe during the Middle Ages in which the king gave estates to nobles in exchange for their military support *(page 33)*

manorialism the economic system in western Europe during the Middle Ages in which peasants provided services for the lord of the manor in return for his protection *(page 33)*

serf a peasant who worked the land of a manor and who was not allowed to leave it without

Section Quiz 1–4

Name _____ Date _____ Class _____

★ **Chapter 1**   Score ____

Section Quiz 1-4

DIRECTIONS: Matching Match each item in Column A with the items in Column B. Write the correct letters in the blanks. *(10 points each)*

Column A

____ 1. a system in which a king gives estates to nobles in exchange for their loyalty

____ 2. Portuguese prince who set up an astronomical and geographical study center

____ 3. the rebirth of interest in the culture of ancient Greece and Rome

____ 4. a device that uses the sun to determine direction, latitude, and local time

____ 5. armed struggle to regain the Holy Land launched by Pope Urban II

Column B

A. Henry the Navigator

B. Crusades

C. astrolabe

D. feudalism

E. Renaissance

TECHNOLOGY & History

Caravel

The caravel was typical of Spanish and Portuguese ship design during the early years of European world exploration. Ranging in length from 75 to 90 feet (23 to 27 m), caravels were suited for sailing along shallow coastlines. They were not, however, well suited for very long voyages, as they could not carry enough crew and supplies. Caravels were usually rigged with three or four masts, employing both square and triangular sails. *How did the caravel's lateen sails help sailors?*

1 The triangular **lateen sail** caught wind that blew perpendicular to the ship, providing more manueverability.

2 **Ballast stones** were placed in the hull of the ship to provide better balance.

3 A **bilge pump**, operated from the main deck, removed water from storage areas.

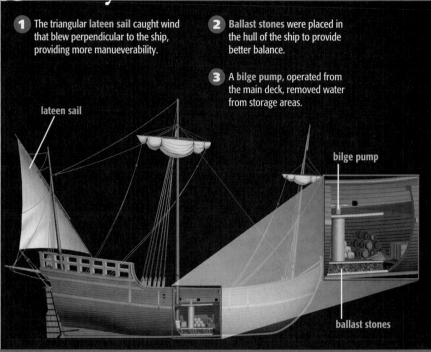

lateen sail

bilge pump

ballast stones

---

within their kingdoms. Merchants, who stood to benefit as well from increased trade, loaned money to monarchs to further finance their operations.

The revenue from trade meant that European rulers did not have to rely as much upon the nobility for support. Increasingly, western European monarchs asserted their power over the nobles. They began to unify their kingdoms and create strong central governments. By the mid-1400s, four strong states—Portugal, Spain, England, and France—had emerged in western Europe. Starting with Portugal in the early 1400s, all four began financing voyages of exploration in the hope of expanding their trade and national power.

The Renaissance Spurs Discoveries The political and economic changes that encouraged western Europeans to begin exploring the world would not have mattered had they not had the technology necessary to launch their expeditions. Fortunately, at about the same time that new unified kingdoms were emerging in western Europe, an intellectual revolution known as the Renaissance began as well. This period began around A.D. 1350 and lasted until around 1600.

Renaissance is a French word that means "rebirth." In this case, it referred to a rebirth of interest in the culture of ancient Greece and Rome. European scholars rediscovered the works of Greek and Roman philosophers, geographers, and mathematicians. They also began to read works by Arab scholars. The Renaissance started with a renewed interest in the past, but it quickly became much more. The Renaissance not only produced spectacular works of art, it also marked a renewed commitment to learning and helped to trigger a scientific revolution.

New Technology If western Europeans were going to find a water route to Asia, they needed navigational instruments that would enable sailors to travel out of sight of land and still find their way home. They also required ships capable of long-distance travel across the ocean. By the early 1400s, Europeans had acquired these technologies.

By studying Arab texts, western Europeans learned about the astrolabe, a device invented by the ancient Greeks and refined by Arab navigators. An astrolabe uses the position of the sun to determine direction, latitude, and local time. Europeans also acquired the

36 CHAPTER 1   Converging Cultures

CRITICAL THINKING ACTIVITY

Interpreting Organize students into small groups. Assign each group one of the following: a bishop, a knight, a noble, or an artisan who works with metal. Have the groups research the Crusades and, from the point of view of their assigned person, write a journal entry expressing their thoughts about the call to "seize control of Christianity's holiest sites." Have each group share its journal entry with the entire class. As a class, discuss the different reactions to the pope's impassioned plea. **L2**

compass from Arab traders. Invented in China, this device reliably showed the direction of magnetic north.

Navigational instruments were important to exploring the world, but not as essential as ships and sails capable of long-distance travel. Late in the 1400s, European shipwrights began to outfit ships with triangle-shaped **lateen sails** perfected by Arab traders. These sails made it possible for ships to sail against the wind. Shipwrights also stopped using a single mast with one large sail. Multiple masts with several smaller sails hoisted one above the other made ships travel much faster. In addition, moving the rudder from the side to the stern made ships easier to steer.

In the 1400s a Portuguese ship called the caravel incorporated all these improvements. A caravel was a small vessel capable of carrying about 130 tons (118 t) of cargo. Because a caravel needed little water to sail, it allowed explorers to venture up shallow inlets and to beach the ships to make repairs. Caravels and ships with similar technology finally enabled Europe to explore the world.

✓ **Reading Check** **Examining** What political and technological developments made it possible for Europeans to begin exploring the world?

Portuguese Exploration

Sailing their caravels, Portuguese explorers became the first Europeans to find a sea route to Asia. In 1419 Prince Henry of Portugal, known as **Henry the Navigator,** set up a center for astronomical and geographical studies at Sagres on Portugal's southwestern tip. He invited mapmakers, astronomers, and shipbuilders from throughout the Mediterranean world to come there to study and plan voyages of exploration.

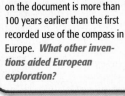

World History Connection

The Compass

While the Europeans made numerous advances in navigation, it was the Chinese who invented one of the more important seafaring tools: the compass. Evidence of this fact includes a Chinese document from 1086 that talks of sea captains relying on a "south-pointing needle" to help them find their way in foggy weather. The date on the document is more than 100 years earlier than the first recorded use of the compass in Europe. *What other inventions aided European exploration?*

Early compasses

Beginning in 1420, Portuguese captains began mapping Africa's west coast. Portuguese explorers discovered the Azores, the Madeira Islands, and Cape Verde. In 1488 a Portuguese ship commanded by **Bartolomeu Dias** reached the southern tip of Africa, later named the Cape of Good Hope. Nine years later, four ships commanded by **Vasco da Gama** sailed from Portugal, rounded Africa, and then headed across to India and landed on India's southwest coast. A water route to eastern Asia had been found.

✓ **Reading Check** **Describing** How did Henry the Navigator help encourage exploration?

SECTION 4 ASSESSMENT

Checking for Understanding

1. **Define:** feudalism, manorialism, serf, Renaissance, astrolabe, caravel.
2. **Identify:** Crusades, Roman Empire, lateen sail, Henry the Navigator, Bartolomeu Dias, Vasco da Gama.
3. **Describe** how feudalism brought about social and political order during the Middle Ages.

Reviewing Themes

4. **Science and Technology** How did scientific advancements affect geographical knowledge?

Critical Thinking

5. **Synthesizing** How did the Renaissance lead to European exploration?
6. **Organizing** Use a graphic organizer similar to the one below to list the effects of the Crusades.

Crusades

7. **Analyzing** If you had been a merchant in Europe during the 1400s, would you have supported attempts to find new routes to Asia? Why or why not?

Analyzing Visuals

8. **Examining Maps** Study the map of European exploration on page 34. How do you think the Crusades assisted the development of the trade routes throughout the European and Asian continents?

Writing About History

9. **Descriptive Writing** Imagine you are a serf living in Europe in the year 1100. Write a letter to a relative describing your daily life.

CHAPTER 1 Converging Cultures **37**

World History Connection

Background: Lodestone is a naturally occurring magnetic ore that when floating on a stick in water naturally points toward north-south orientation. If you know which way is north, you can determine the other directions.
Answer: the astrolabe, lateen sails, multiple masts, the caravel

✓ **Reading Check**

Answer: political: the emergence of strong states; technological: new navigational tools and innovations in shipbuilding

Reteach
Have students explain the significance of the events shown on the time line at the beginning of this section.

Enrich
Have students conduct research on one of the people, places, things, events, or concepts presented in this section. Have them develop a two-minute oral presentation for their classmates.

4 CLOSE

Have students write a paragraph analyzing the impact of the Renaissance on European exploration.

✓ **Reading Check**

Answer: Henry the Navigator set up a center for astronomical and geographic studies and he invited mapmakers, astronomers, and shipbuilders to come there to study and plan voyages of exploration.

1 FOCUS

Section Overview

This section examines how European exploration led to intense interaction and exchange between Europe and the Americas.

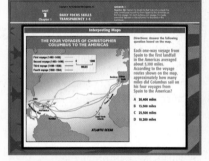
Guide to Reading

Answers to Graphic: Vikings: no permanent settlements or ongoing relationship; Columbus: began exploration of the Americas; Vespucci: continued exploration of the Americas which are named for him; Balboa: first European to reach the Pacific coast of America; Magellan: named the Pacific Ocean and led the crew that was first to circumnavigate the globe

Preteaching Vocabulary
Have students identify the Key Terms and Names that refer to specific individuals and write a one-sentence description of each person.

Guide to Reading

Main Idea
Columbus sought a sea route to Asia. Instead, he landed in the Americas.

Key Terms and Names
Vikings, Christopher Columbus, Claudius Ptolemy, Watling Island, Santo Domingo, Pope Alexander VI, line of demarcation, Amerigo Vespucci, Florida, circumnavigate, Columbian Exchange

Reading Strategy
Organizing As you read about European exploration of the Americas, complete a chart like the one below by filling in the outcome of each exploration listed in the chart.

Exploration	Outcome
Vikings	
Columbus	
Vespucci	
Balboa	
Magellan	

Reading Objectives
• **Describe** Viking and Spanish explorations of North America.
• **Summarize** Columbus's journeys and their impact on Native Americans and Europeans.

Section Theme
Global Connections Material exchanges between Europe and the Americas yielded both positive and negative results.

Preview of Events

♦1000	♦1475	♦1500	♦1525

C. A.D. 1001
Vikings reach North America

1475
Ptolemy's *Geography* revolutionizes mapmaking

1492
Christopher Columbus lands in America

1494
Treaty of Tordesillas

1522
Magellan's expedition circumnavigates the earth

★ An American Story ★

Replicas of Spanish caravels at sea

In 1492 Christopher Columbus led 90 sailors on a voyage into the unknown. On September 9 Columbus noted in his log: "This day we completely lost sight of land, and many men sighed and wept for fear they would not see it again for a long time." As the voyage dragged on, the sailors grew nervous and began plotting mutiny. Columbus wrote:

❝All day long and all night long those who are awake and able to get together never cease to talk to each other in circles, complaining that they will never be able to return home. . . . I am told . . . that if I persist in going onward, the best course of action will be to throw me into the sea some night.❞

Then, on the morning of October 12, the *Pinta's* lookout, Rodrigo de Triana, let out a joyous cry—"Tierra! Tierra!" ("Land! Land!"). At dawn a relieved and triumphant Columbus went ashore. He believed he had arrived in the Indies—islands located southeast of China.

—adapted from *The Log of Christopher Columbus*

The Vikings Arrive in America

Although his historic journey set the stage for permanent European settlement in the Americas, Christopher Columbus was not the first European to arrive there. Strong archaeological evidence credits that accomplishment to the Norse, or **Vikings,** a people who came from Scandinavia.

SECTION RESOURCES

📁 **Reproducible Masters**
• Reproducible Lesson Plan 1–5
• Daily Lecture and Discussion Notes 1–5
• Guided Reading Activity 1–5
• Section Quiz 1–5
• Reading Essentials and Study Guide 1–5
• Interpreting Political Cartoons

📖 **Transparencies**
• Daily Focus Skills Transparency 1–5

Multimedia
⊗ Interactive Tutor Self-Assessment CD-ROM
⊗ ExamView® Pro Testmaker CD-ROM
⊗ Presentation Plus! CD-ROM
⊗ TeacherWorks™ CD-ROM
🎧 Audio Program

Beginning in the late A.D. 700s, Viking ships, called **longboats,** began to venture outward from their homeland. Most headed south, some to trade with the wealthier peoples to the south and others to raid their settlements. Still others braved the violent North Atlantic Ocean and headed west.

In 1001, **Leif Ericsson** and 35 Vikings explored the coast of Labrador and stayed the winter in Newfoundland. Although the Vikings later tried to set up colonies in the region, their attempts failed, in large part because the Native Americans opposed them. Unlike later European colonists, the Vikings did not have better weapons than those of the Native Americans, who outnumbered them. It would take a new series of European expeditions, embarking in the 1400s and 1500s from points much farther south, to establish a permanent European presence in the Americas.

✓ **Reading Check** **Examining** How do we know that Columbus was not the first European in the Americas?

Spain Sends Columbus West

For more than 400 years after the Vikings abandoned their settlements in North America, there is no convincing evidence that Europeans traveled to the Americas. In the mid-1400s, the Renaissance renewed European interest in the world's geography. With many European states eager to find a sea route to Asia, a few persons, including an Italian navigator named **Christopher Columbus,** became interested in sailing west across the Atlantic.

A New Geography By the 1400s most educated Europeans knew that the world was round. On the most accurate European maps of the time, however, only the Mediterranean, Europe, the Middle East, and Africa's northern coast showed any detail. Then a book appeared that revolutionized European exploration.

Twelve centuries earlier, a Greek-educated Egyptian geographer and astronomer named **Claudius Ptolemy** had drawn maps of a round world, complete with 360 lines of longitude, one degree apart, projected onto a flat surface. Ptolemy's *Geography* was rediscovered in 1406 and printed in 1475. It became very influential, and its basic system of lines of latitude and longitude is still used today.

European mariners also consulted the work of a twelfth century Arab geographer named **al-Idrisi,** who had traveled widely in the Middle East. In 1154 al-Idrisi published a geographical survey of as much

of the world as was then known to Europeans and Muslims. By studying the maps of Ptolemy and al-Idrisi, Western mariners finally obtained a reliable idea of the geography of the eastern African coast and the Indian Ocean.

Columbus's Plan Despite its usefulness, Ptolemy's *Geography* had seriously underestimated the distance that each degree of longitude represented, making the earth seem much smaller than it actually was. Basing his own calculations on Ptolemy's, Christopher Columbus predicted with wild optimism that "the end of Spain and the beginning of India are not far apart . . . and it is known that this sea is navigable in a few days' time with favoring wind."

Columbus sought Portuguese financial backing to make a voyage across the Atlantic to Asia. In 1484 he applied to the king of Portugal, who referred him to a committee of experts in navigation. Basing their decision on sources other than Ptolemy's maps, the scholars reasoned correctly that Columbus had greatly underestimated the distance to Asia. Furthermore, when news arrived in 1488 that Bartolomeu Dias had successfully rounded the southern tip of Africa, the Portuguese lost all interest in supporting Columbus.

✎ **History** *Through Art*

Archaeological Evidence This carving of a European figure (left) and Viking calendar (above) prove that the Vikings arrived in North America before Columbus. Why were Vikings unable to colonize successfully?

2 TEACH

Daily Lecture and Discussion Notes 1–5

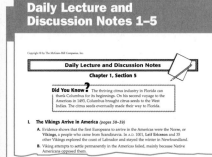

Copyright © by The McGraw-Hill Companies, Inc.

Daily Lecture and Discussion Notes

Chapter 1, Section 5

Did You Know ? The thriving citrus industry in Florida can thank Columbus for its beginnings. On his second voyage to the Americas in 1493, Columbus brought citrus seeds to the West Indies. The citrus seeds eventually made their way to Florida.

I. The Vikings Arrive in America *(pages 38–39)*

   A. Evidence shows that the first Europeans to arrive in the Americas were the Norse, or **Vikings,** a people who came from Scandinavia. In A.D. 1001, **Leif Ericsson** and 35 other Vikings explored the coast of Labrador and stayed the winter in Newfoundland.

   B. Viking attempts to settle permanently in the Americas failed, mainly because Native Americans opposed them.

✓ **Reading Check**

Answer: There is strong archaeological evidence that Vikings were the first Europeans in the Americas.

Expressing an Opinion Ask students to express their opinion about who "discovered America." Ask them if they think the term *discovered* is appropriate. **L2**

✎ **History** *Through Art*

Background: Leif Ericsson landed at L'Anse aux Meadows in Newfoundland, and built a settlement of three sod-and-timber longhouses and five smaller buildings.

Answer: Conflicts with Native Americans caused the Vikings to abandon their colony and return to Greenland.

Ask: How did the weapons of the Vikings and the Native Americans compare? *(Neither had a distinct advantage.)*

COOPERATIVE LEARNING ACTIVITY

Building a Model Have students work in small groups to create a model showing lines of longitude and latitude on a Styrofoam ball. Encourage students to use library and Internet resources to help figure out how to build the model. Remind students that degrees of longitude and latitude relate to the 360 degrees of a circle with the center of the circle located in the exact middle of the sphere. Offer students a hint: they will need to cut the Styrofoam ball into fourths in order to measure the angles. 📦

Use the rubric for a cooperative group management plan on pages 81–82 in the ***Performance Assessment Activities and Rubrics.***

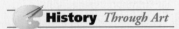
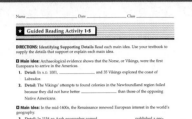
History *Through Art*

Answer: *Geography,* by Ptolemy

Ask: What Arab geographer published a geographical survey of the world known to Muslims and Europeans? *(al-Idrisi)*

you don't say...

Cartography Cartography is the science and art of making maps. A mapmaker is a cartographer.

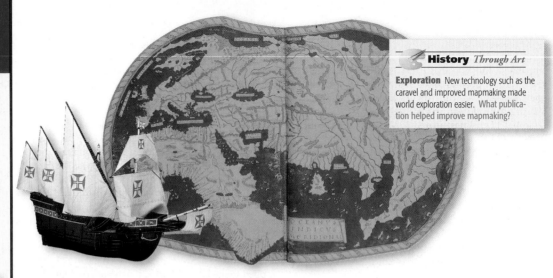

History *Through Art*

Exploration New technology such as the caravel and improved mapmaking made world exploration easier. What publication helped improve mapmaking?

For the next few years, Columbus tried to win backing from other rulers. His brother Bartholomew, a respected mapmaker in Europe, tried and failed to secure financing for Columbus's expedition from the rulers of England and France. Having no success with them, he spent six years trying to persuade King Ferdinand and Queen Isabella of Spain that his scheme would bring them wealth, empire, and converts to Catholicism. Finally, in 1492, after it became clear that Portugal was about to reach Asia by going east around Africa, Ferdinand agreed.

TURNING POINT

The First Voyage Columbus and his three ships—the *Niña,* the *Pinta,* and the *Santa Maria*—finally left Spain in August 1492. First he sailed south to the Canary Islands to take on fresh supplies. Then he embarked on the harrowing voyage westward across the mysterious and frightening Atlantic until, unaware of where he was, he reached the Caribbean and landed in the Bahamas, probably on what is today **Watling Island.** There, for the first time, he encountered the Taino people, a part of the Arawak. He called the people *Indians* because he thought he had reached the fabled Indies. Columbus noticed that some of the local people had a small piece of gold "hanging from a hole which they have in their nose." After several attempts to ask where the gold had come from, he learned that "there was a king who had large vessels of it, and possessed much gold. . . ." Columbus then headed deeper into the Caribbean, determined to find this gold he had heard about. He found the island of Cuba, and he also found Hispaniola, which today is divided into

the countries of Haiti and the Dominican Republic. Columbus mistakenly concluded that Cuba was the coast of China and that Hispaniola was Japan.

Columbus and his sailors felt equal parts admiration and curiosity toward the Native Americans that they encountered in the Bahamas and Hispaniola. Columbus wrote the following of the Arawak:

> 66[They are] artless and generous with what they have, to such a degree as no one would believe but he who had seen it. Of anything they have, if it be asked for, they never say no, but do rather invite the person to accept it, and show as much lovingness as though they would give their hearts.99

—quoted in *500 Nations*

For their part, the Arawak must have been equally curious about the white-skinned, bearded Spanish. Columbus recorded his interpretation of their reaction to him and his men:

> 66The people kept coming down to the beach, calling to us and giving thanks to God. Some brought us water, some food; others, seeing that I did not wish to go ashore, swam out to us. . . . One old man climbed into the boat, and the others, men and women, kept shouting, 'Come and see the men who have come from Heaven; bring them food and drink.'99

—quoted in *The Voyage of Christopher Columbus*

Like other Native Americans, the Arawak had an intense spiritual life. To Columbus, however, they appeared to have no religion. He predicted that "they would become Christians very easily."

MEETING SPECIAL NEEDS

Visual/Spatial To help visual learners remember the various navigators and trips discussed in the section, have them trace and label the voyages of Christopher Columbus, Amerigo Vespucci, Juan Ponce de Leon, Vasco de Balboa, and Ferdinand Magellan on a map of the world. **L1**

📂 Refer to *Inclusion for the High School Social Studies Classroom Strategies and Activities* in the TCR.

On Christmas Eve Columbus's flagship, the *Santa Maria*, struck a reef off Hispaniola and broke apart. He built a small fort called La Navidad on the island and left 40 crew members to search for gold while he headed home with his remaining ships.

In March 1493 Columbus made a triumphant return to the Spanish court with gold, parrots, spices, and Native Americans he had brought back. The king and queen awarded him the titles "Admiral of the Ocean Sea" and "Viceroy and Governor of the Indies." Ferdinand and Isabella listened closely as Columbus promised "as much gold as they want if their Highnesses will render me a little help. . . ."

Columbus's Later Voyages Less than six months after Columbus returned to Spain, he headed back across the Atlantic, this time with 17 ships and over 1,200 Spanish colonists. In November 1493 he anchored off the coast of Hispaniola, only to learn that the men he had left behind had been killed and their fort destroyed. Abandoning the ruins, Columbus founded a new colony, called Isabella.

Many of the colonists were Spanish nobles. They had come expecting to get rich, and they refused to plant crops or do other manual labor. They accused Columbus of misleading them with false promises of gold, and many of them headed back to Spain to complain to the government.

Hoping to find more gold and save his reputation, Columbus began exploring the interior of Hispaniola. There he discovered enough loose gold to make mining worthwhile. He then decided to enslave the local Taino and force them to work for the Spanish, mining gold and planting crops.

In 1496 Columbus headed back to Spain. In the meantime, his brother Bartholomew founded a new town named **Santo Domingo** on the south coast of Hispaniola closer to the gold mines. Santo Domingo became the first capital of Spain's empire in America.

Columbus made a third voyage to America in 1498. After arriving on the northern coast of South America and studying the volume of fresh water at the mouth of the Orinoco River, he wrote in his journal, "I believe that this is a very great continent, which until today has been unknown." Columbus made one final voyage in 1502. He mapped the American coastline from Guatemala to Panama before turning back.

✓ Reading Check **Describing** Describe the results of Columbus's voyages.

Spain Claims America

After Columbus had shown the way, Spanish explorers and settlers flocked to the Caribbean hoping to become wealthy through conquest and trade. By the early 1500s, the Spanish had explored the major Caribbean islands, established colonies on Hispaniola, Cuba, Jamaica, and Puerto Rico, and begun exploring the American mainland.

The Treaty of Tordesillas Before colonization could begin, however, Ferdinand and Isabella had to establish their claim to the new lands. Portugal had claimed the right to control the Atlantic route to Asia. To resolve the issue peacefully, they appealed to the pope for a decision.

Profiles IN HISTORY

Christopher Columbus
1451–1506

Christopher Columbus was born in Genoa, Italy. Growing up in a bustling seaport gave Columbus a glimpse of the wider world. Although he was the eldest son, he decided to leave his family's wool-weaving business and go to sea at the age of 14. After sailing for more than 10 years, Columbus settled in Lisbon, Portugal. His brother Bartholomew soon joined him, and the two brothers worked together as mapmakers—although Columbus continued to sail as well.

In 1479 Columbus married the sister of the governor of Porto Santo in the Madeira Islands and moved to the island to live. There he witnessed the use of enslaved Africans as forced labor on the sugar plantations. He would later introduce similar practices to America.

In the 1480s Columbus served on several Portuguese expeditions to Africa, where he schooled himself in Atlantic currents and wind patterns. In the process, he developed his theory that the easiest way to reach Asia was to sail west across the Atlantic.

Despite his achievements, Columbus remained unhappy. A devout Christian, he believed God had destined him to find the western route to Asia and spread the Christian faith. He died in 1506, frustrated that he had not found Asia nor been given the honors and recognition that he felt he deserved.

CHAPTER 1 Converging Cultures **41**

INTERDISCIPLINARY CONNECTIONS ACTIVITY

Mathematics Have students use library and Internet resources to learn more about the mathematics behind latitude and longitude. Have students prepare an explanation for why the circles that make up the lines of latitude do not intersect with each other and the lines of longitude appear to radiate from the North and South Poles. **L2**

📁 Use *Interpreting Political Cartoons,* Cartoon 2.

Why It Matters

Food production increased on both sides of the ocean as a direct result of the exchange of cultivated plants and livestock. Increased food production led to population growth in Europe and among European colonists in America. One of the reasons food production increased in Europe, and later in Asia, was the introduction of crops from America that flourished where traditional European crops could not. For example, the climate, topography, and soil conditions in Ireland were not conducive to growing wheat or rice, but white potatoes from America thrived. The introduction of livestock and poultry from Europe, Africa, and Asia provided new sources of nourishment for Native Americans and colonists living in America. In addition to using animals as sources of food, they were used to help plow fields and provide fertilizer.

In 1493, to prevent a war between the two rival Catholic nations, **Pope Alexander VI** established a line of demarcation, an imaginary north-to-south line running down the middle of the Atlantic. This line granted Spain control of everything west of the line and Portugal control of everything east. King John II of Portugal accepted the idea of division, but he asked for the line to be moved farther west.

The following year the two countries resolved their differences over the dividing line in the **Treaty of Tordesillas,** named for a town northwest of the Spanish capital, Madrid. The treaty moved the line almost 1,000 miles (1,609 km) to the west.

The Treaty of Tordesillas did two things. It confirmed Portugal's right to control the route around Africa to India, and it also confirmed Spain's claim to the new lands of America. Unknowingly, however, the line had been drawn so far west that it cut through part of South America, giving much of the land that is now Brazil to Portugal.

Naming America Interestingly enough, Columbus did not give his name to the new land he had encountered while trying to reach Asia. In 1499 an Italian named **Amerigo Vespucci,** sailing under the Spanish flag, repeated Columbus's initial attempt to sail west to Asia. Exploring part of the coast of South America, Vespucci, like Columbus, assumed that he had reached Asia.

Vespucci made his next voyage in 1501, this time commissioned by Portugal. He sailed far south along the coast of South America, and he eventually came to the conclusion that this large land mass could not be part of Asia. Vespucci's descriptions of America were published and widely read in Europe. In 1507 a German scholar named Martin Waldseemüller published a study in which he proposed that the new continent be named America for "Amerigo the discoverer."

Continuing Spanish Expeditions Even though Europe now knew that the Americas were not a part of Asia, explorers continued to chart the region. In 1513 the Spanish governor of Puerto Rico, **Juan Ponce de Leon,** sailed north. According to a traditional story, he was searching for a wondrous fountain that was said to magically restore youth, although historians have disputed whether or not

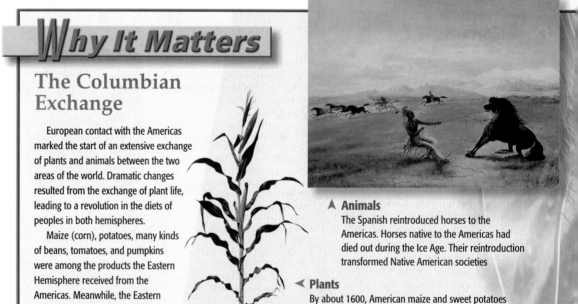

Why It Matters

The Columbian Exchange

European contact with the Americas marked the start of an extensive exchange of plants and animals between the two areas of the world. Dramatic changes resulted from the exchange of plant life, leading to a revolution in the diets of peoples in both hemispheres.

Maize (corn), potatoes, many kinds of beans, tomatoes, and pumpkins were among the products the Eastern Hemisphere received from the Americas. Meanwhile, the Eastern Hemisphere introduced rice, wheat, barley, oats, melons, coffee, bananas, and many other plants to the Western Hemisphere.

▲ **Animals**
The Spanish reintroduced horses to the Americas. Horses native to the Americas had died out during the Ice Age. Their reintroduction transformed Native American societies

◀ **Plants**
By about 1600, American maize and sweet potatoes were staple crops in China. They contributed to a worldwide population explosion beginning in this period.

42 CHAPTER 1   Converging Cultures

CRITICAL THINKING ACTIVITY

Examining Organize the class into groups of four students. Have the groups conduct research to learn about how Christopher and Bartholomew Columbus sought to convince the Portuguese and the Spanish to provide funding for the voyage across the Atlantic. Have each group select either the failed attempt to convince the Portuguese or the successful effort to gain the financial backing of King Ferdinand and Queen Isabella. Tell the groups to write a dialogue between the Columbus brothers and the potential financial backers. Have group members present their dialogues to the class. **L3**

this was really his motivation. In any event, De Leon did discover a land full of blooming wildflowers and fragrant plants. Before leaving, he gave it the name **Florida,** which means "land of flowers."

Spanish explorers continued to search for a passage to China and India by sailing west. In 1510 **Vasco de Balboa,** a planter from Hispaniola trying to escape his creditors, stowed away on a ship heading to the American mainland. There he founded a colony on the Isthmus of Panama. After hearing tales from Native Americans of a "south sea" that led to an empire of gold, Balboa hacked his way across steamy, disease-ridden jungles and swamps until he reached the opposite coast. There, in 1513, Balboa became the first European to reach the Pacific coast of America.

In 1520 **Ferdinand Magellan,** a Portuguese mariner working for Spain, discovered the strait later named for him at the southernmost tip of South America. After navigating its stormy narrows, he sailed into the ocean Balboa had seen. Its waters seemed so peaceful, or *pacific,* that Magellan gave the new ocean that name. Although Magellan died in the Philippine Islands, his crew continued west, arriving in Spain in 1522. They became the first known people to *circumnavigate,* or sail around, the globe.

✔**Reading Check** **Analyzing** Why was the Treaty of Tordesillas important?

The Columbian Exchange

The arrival of European colonists in the Americas set in motion a series of complex interactions between peoples and environments. These interactions, called the Columbian Exchange, permanently altered the world's ecosystems and changed nearly every culture around the world.

From America to Europe Native Americans taught the Europeans local farming methods and introduced them to new crops. Corn, which colonists soon adopted as a basic food, traveled back to Spain on Columbus's very first journey and then spread to the rest of Europe. Other American foods, such as squash, pumpkins, beans, sweet potatoes, tomatoes, chili peppers, peanuts, chocolate, and potatoes also made their way to Europe, as did tobacco and chewing gum.

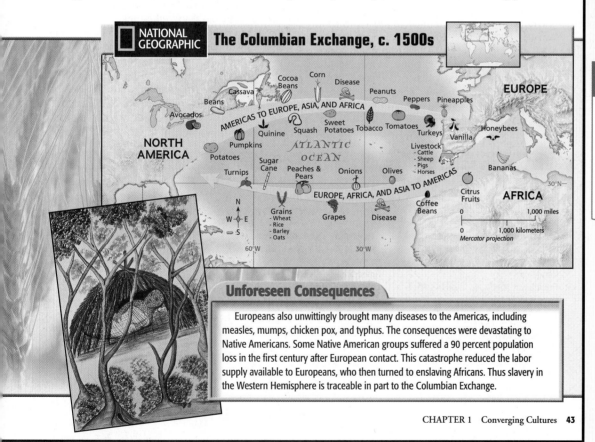

NATIONAL GEOGRAPHIC **The Columbian Exchange, c. 1500s**

AMERICAS TO EUROPE, ASIA, AND AFRICA

Cocoa Beans · Corn · Disease · Cassava · Beans · Avocados · Pumpkins · Potatoes · Quinine · Sweet Potatoes · Squash · Tobacco · Tomatoes · Peanuts · Peppers · Pineapples · Turkeys · Vanilla · Turnips · Sugar Cane · Peaches & Pears · Onions · Olives

NORTH AMERICA · ATLANTIC OCEAN · EUROPE · AFRICA

EUROPE, AFRICA, AND ASIA TO AMERICAS

Livestock - Cattle - Sheep - Pigs - Horses · Honeybees · Bananas · Citrus Fruits · Coffee Beans · Grains - Wheat - Rice - Barley - Oats · Grapes · Disease

N W E S

0 1,000 miles
0 1,000 kilometers
Mercator projection

30°N
60°W   30°W

Unforeseen Consequences

Europeans also unwittingly brought many diseases to the Americas, including measles, mumps, chicken pox, and typhus. The consequences were devastating to Native Americans. Some Native American groups suffered a 90 percent population loss in the first century after European contact. This catastrophe reduced the labor supply available to Europeans, who then turned to enslaving Africans. Thus slavery in the Western Hemisphere is traceable in part to the Columbian Exchange.

CHAPTER 1 Converging Cultures **43**

EXTENDING THE CONTENT

Brazilwood Another adventurer, Pedro Álvares Cabral, seeking a route to India, ended up landing along the coast of South America in present-day Brazil. One of the plants he transported back to Portugal was a hardwood tree known as brazilwood. The core of the tree produced a bright red dye used by clothmakers. The color became favored among the wealthiest Europeans. The French especially valued the dye and French traders were soon competing with the Portuguese to supply the demand. Largely due to the brazilwood trade, the Portuguese government established permanent settlements in present-day Brazil to deter the French from making claims on the land.

✔**Reading Check**

Answer: The treaty confirmed the Portuguese right to control the route around Africa to India and confirmed Spain's claim to lands in America. It also gave much of present-day Brazil to Portugal.

3 ASSESS

Assign Section 5 Assessment as homework or as an in-class activity.

💿 Have students use the **Interactive Tutor Self-Assessment CD-ROM.**

Reading Essentials and Study Guide 1–5

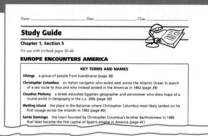

Name ___ Date ___ Class ___

Study Guide

Chapter 1, Section 5
For use with textbook pages 38–44

EUROPE ENCOUNTERS AMERICA

KEY TERMS AND NAMES

Vikings a group of people from Scandinavia *(page 38)*

Christopher Columbus an Italian navigator who sailed west across the Atlantic Ocean in search of a sea route to Asia and who instead landed in the Americas in 1492 *(page 39)*

Claudius Ptolemy a Greek-educated Egyptian geographer and astronomer who drew maps of a round world in Geography in the A.D. 200s *(page 39)*

Watling Island the place in the Bahamas where Christopher Columbus most likely landed on his first voyage across the Atlantic in 1492 *(page 40)*

Santo Domingo the town founded by Christopher Columbus's brother Bartholomew in 1496 that later became the first capital of Spain's empire in America *(page 41)*

Section Quiz 1–5

Name ___ Date ___ Class ___

★ **Chapter 1** Score ___

Section Quiz 1-5

DIRECTIONS: Matching Match each item in Column A with the items in Column B. Write the correct letters in the blanks. *(10 points each)*

Column A	Column B
___ 1. the first capital of Spain's empire in America	A. Florida
___ 2. imaginary north-to-south line running down the middle of the Atlantic Ocean	B. Santo Domingo
___ 3. "land of flowers"	C. Vikings
___ 4. complex interactions between peoples and environments started by European colonists in the Americas	D. line of demarcation
___ 5. people who came from Scandinavia	E. Columbian Exchange

DIRECTIONS: Multiple Choice In the blank at the left, write the letter of the choice that best completes the statement or answers the question. *(10 points each)*

Creating a Display Have students create a display of the food component of the Columbian Exchange. Have students use actual foods or pictures of foods to show both sides of the exchange. **L1** ELL

📂 Use the rubric for creating a map, display, or chart on pages 77–78 in the *Performance Assessment Activities and Rubrics.*

Fact | Fiction | Folklore

The current Spanish flag incorporates the coat of arms that includes the castle and lion symbols.

Reteach
Have students create a time line of events mentioned in this section starting with 1406.

Enrich
Have students investigate the long-term impact of the line of demarcation established by Pope Alexander VI and the Treaty of Tordesillas. Have students write an essay describing the impact today of the pope's decision.

4 CLOSE

Have students summarize Columbus's journeys by preparing a two-column chart. In one column students should list the effects on Native Americans; in the other column students should list the effects on Europeans.

✔ Reading Check

Answer: Europeans carried bacteria and viruses that had the potential for causing diseases such as chickenpox, influenza, measles, mumps, and typhus. Exposure to these organisms led to epidemics among the Native Americans.

Fact | Fiction | Folklore

Spain, 1492 Christopher Columbus proudly carried the Spanish banner of Castile and Leon to the shores of the Bahamas. The flag's castle represented Queen Isabella. The lion symbolized her husband, King Ferdinand.

Perhaps the most important discovery for Europeans was the potato. European farmers learned that if they planted potatoes instead of rye, about four times as many people could live off the same amount of land. Europeans also adopted many devices invented by Native Americans, including the canoe, the snowshoe, the hammock, the poncho, the toboggan, and the parka.

From Europe to America The Europeans introduced Native Americans to wheat, oats, barley, rye, rice, coffee, dandelions, onions, bananas, and oranges and other new citrus fruits, none of which existed in America. Europeans also brought over domestic livestock such as chickens, cattle, pigs, sheep, and horses. In addition, they introduced Native Americans to a range of technologies, including new types of metalworking, new techniques of shipbuilding, and new forms of weapons, including firearms.

No beneficial European import, however, could ever offset the dreadful effects of an invisible one—the bacteria and viruses that caused such diseases as influenza, measles, chicken pox, mumps, typhus, and smallpox. Native Americans had never experienced these diseases and had no immunity. Exposure led to catastrophic epidemics in which millions of Native Americans died.

The movement of disease, however, was not one-way. Native American illnesses made their way to Europe as well, where they infected millions of people. Unlike European diseases, Native American illnesses did not lead to a catastrophic collapse of the European population.

No one in Columbus's time could have imagined the course of events in the Americas that have led to the present day. Some people feel that the tragic epidemics and military conquests that devastated the Native Americans and the subsequent introduction of slavery overshadow the positive effects of the exchange Columbus initiated. The human drama that unfolded over the next few centuries, however, also led ultimately to the founding of the United States. Despite tragic events along the way, the people of the United States managed to build a nation that honors the worth of the individual and protects the rights and freedoms of its citizens and others around the globe. This too is one of the legacies of Christopher Columbus.

✔ Reading Check **Describing** Why did millions of Native Americans die as a result of contact with Europeans?

SECTION 5 ASSESSMENT

Checking for Understanding
1. **Define:** line of demarcation, circumnavigate, Columbian Exchange.
2. **Identify:** Vikings, Christopher Columbus, Claudius Ptolemy, Watling Island, Santo Domingo, Pope Alexander VI, Amerigo Vespucci, Florida.
3. **Explain** why the Vikings failed to settle in Newfoundland.

Reviewing Themes
4. **Global Connections** How did the maps drawn by Ptolemy and al-Idrisi revolutionize European sea exploration?

Critical Thinking
5. **Analyzing** Why did the king and queen of Spain agree to Columbus's second voyage?
6. **Categorizing** Use a graphic organizer similar to the one below to list the exchanges between the Native Americans and the Europeans in the Columbian Exchange.

Columbian Exchange

Europeans Received	Native Americans Received

Analyzing Visuals
7. **Examining Images** Study the images on pages 42 and 43 illustrating the importance of the Columbian Exchange. Do you think the positive effects of the exchange outweigh the negative effects? Explain your answer.

Writing About History
8. **Descriptive Writing** Take on the role of a sailor on Columbus's first voyage to the Americas. Write a journal entry about the Caribbean islands you encounter.

44   CHAPTER 1   Converging Cultures

SECTION 5 ASSESSMENT ANSWERS

1. Terms are in blue.
2. Vikings (p. 38), Christopher Columbus (p. 39), Claudius Ptolemy (p. 39), Watling Island (p. 40), Santo Domingo (p. 41), Pope Alexander VI (p. 42), Amerigo Vespucci (p. 42), Florida (p. 43)
3. The Vikings were outnumbered by hostile Native Americans.
4. Their maps were more accurate than others and more appropriate for navigation.
5. Columbus promised them enormous quantities of gold.
6. Students' answers should include foods, technologies, and sicknesses as discussed in the section.
7. Students' answers will vary but should recognize both the positive and negative impact on all involved.
8. Students' journal entries will vary but should include a thoughtful discussion of what Columbus might have seen.

Social Studies
SKILLBUILDER

Reading a Time Line

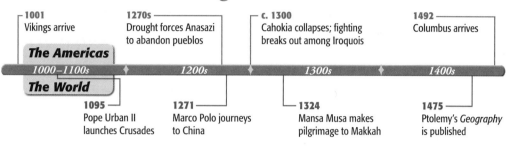

1001	1270s	c. 1300	1492
Vikings arrive	Drought forces Anasazi to abandon pueblos	Cahokia collapses; fighting breaks out among Iroquois	Columbus arrives

The Americas

1000–1100s | 1200s | 1300s | 1400s

The World

1095	1271	1324	1475
Pope Urban II launches Crusades	Marco Polo journeys to China	Mansa Musa makes pilgrimage to Makkah	Ptolemy's *Geography* is published

Why Learn This Skill?

When you read a time line, you see not only when an event took place but also what events took place before and after it. A time line can help you develop the skill of **chronological thinking.** Developing a strong sense of chronology—when events took place and in what order they took place—will help you examine relationships among the events. It will also help you understand what events caused or were the result of other events.

Learning the Skill

A **time line** is a kind of chart that lists events that occurred between specific dates. The number of years between these dates is called the **time span.** For example, a time line that begins in 1400 and ends in 1500 would have a time span of 100 years. A time line that begins in 1490 and ends in 1500 would have a 10-year time span.

Time lines are usually divided into smaller segments, or **time intervals.** If you look at the two time lines below, you will see that the first time line has a 30-year time span divided into 10-year time intervals, and the second time line has a 6-year time span divided into 2-year time intervals.

1400	1410	1420	1430

1490	1492	1494	1496

Practicing the Skill

Sometimes a time line shows events that occurred during the same time period but in two different parts of the world. The time line above shows some events in the Americas and in the rest of the world during the same time span. Study the time line, and then answer the questions.

❶ What time span and intervals appear on this time line?

❷ What two important events took place around A.D. 1300 in North America?

❸ How many years before Ptolemy's *Geography* was published did the Vikings reach North America?

❹ When did Pope Urban II begin the Crusades?

Skills Assessment

Complete the Practicing Skills questions on page 47 and the Chapter 1 Skill Reinforcement Activity to assess your mastery of this skill.

Applying the Skill

Reading a Time Line Extend the time line on this page to include at least five additional events that took place in North America between A.D. 500 and 1000.

 Glencoe's **Skillbuilder Interactive Workbook CD-ROM, Level 2,** provides instruction and practice in key social studies skills.

45

TEACH

Reading a Time Line This skill emphasizes the importance of chronological thinking to the study of history. By learning to put things in chronological order, students gain an appreciation for relationships among the events.

Have students choose an event that occurred in the 1200s. Ask them to identify all the events shown on the time line that occurred in the 1200s and indicate if they happened before or after the first event mentioned.

Additional Practice

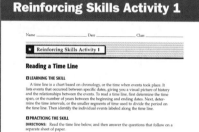

Reinforcing Skills Activity 1

Name _____ Date _____ Class _____

★ Reinforcing Skills Activity 1

Reading a Time Line

☐ LEARNING THE SKILL

A time line is a chart based on chronology, or the time when events took place. It lists events that occurred between specific dates, giving you a visual picture of history and the relationships between the events. To read a time line, first determine the time span, or the number of years between the beginning and ending dates. Next, determine the time intervals, or the smaller segments of time used to divide the period on the time line. Then identify the individual events labeled along the time line.

☐ PRACTICING THE SKILL

DIRECTIONS: Read the time line below, and then answer the questions that follow on a separate sheet of paper.

GLENCOE
TECHNOLOGY

 CD-ROM
Glencoe Skillbuilder Interactive Workbook CD-ROM, Level 2

This interactive CD-ROM reinforces student mastery of essential social studies skills.

ANSWERS TO PRACTICING THE SKILL

❶ A.D. 1000 to A.D. 1500; 100-year intervals

❷ Cahokia collapses and fighting breaks out among the Iroquois

❸ Ptolemy's *Geography* was published in western Europe 474 years after the Vikings reached North America.

❹ 1095

Applying the Skill
Students' answers will vary. Ask students to provide a page reference for each selected event.

GLENCOE TECHNOLOGY

MindJogger Videoquiz
Use the **MindJogger Videoquiz** to review Chapter 1 content.

 Available in VHS

Reviewing Key Terms

Students' answers will vary. The pages where the words appear in the text are shown in parentheses.

1. radiocarbon dating (p. 13);
2. Ice Age (p. 13); **3. glacier** (p. 13);
4. nomad (p. 13); **5. agricultural revolution** (p. 13); **6. maize** (p. 14);
7. civilization (p. 14); **8. obsidian** (p. 14); **9. kiva** (p. 16); **10. pueblo** (p. 16); **11. kachina** (p. 21); **12. slash-and-burn agriculture** (p. 23);
13. longhouses (p. 23); **14. wigwams** (p. 23); **15. kinship group** (p. 23);
16. savannah (p. 27); **17. mosque** (p. 28); **18. matrilineal** (p. 30);
19. feudalism (p. 33); **20. manorialism** (p. 33); **21. serf** (p. 33); **22. Renaissance** (p. 36); **23. astrolabe** (p. 36);
24. caravel (p. 37); **25. line of demarcation** (p. 42); **26. circumnavigate** (p. 43); **27. Columbian Exchange** (p. 43)

Reviewing Key Facts

28. Dekanawidah (p. 24), Hiawatha (p. 24), Henry the Navigator (p. 37), Bartolomeu Dias (p. 37), Vasco de Gama (p. 37), Christopher Columbus (p. 39), Claudius Ptolemy (p. 39), Pope Alexander VI (p. 42), Amerigo Vespucci (p. 42)

29. Asians came to America by crossing Beringia on foot or hugging the Beringian coast in boats. Scientists believe they migrated in search of food by following animal herds.

30. They use radiocarbon dating.

31. Native American peoples who engaged in farming were less likely to be nomadic than those who moved around following animal herds.

Reviewing Key Terms
On a sheet of paper, use each of these terms in a sentence.

1. radiocarbon dating
2. Ice Age
3. glacier
4. nomad
5. agricultural revolution
6. maize
7. civilization
8. obsidian
9. kiva
10. pueblo
11. kachina
12. slash-and-burn agriculture
13. longhouse
14. wigwam
15. kinship group
16. savannah
17. mosque
18. matrilineal
19. feudalism
20. manorialism
21. serf
22. Renaissance
23. astrolabe
24. caravel
25. line of demarcation
26. circumnavigate
27. Columbian Exchange

Reviewing Key Facts

28. Identify: Dekanawidah, Hiawatha, Henry the Navigator, Bartolomeu Dias, Vasco da Gama, Christopher Columbus, Claudius Ptolemy, Pope Alexander VI, Amerigo Vespucci.

29. How and why did Asians migrate to the Americas during the Ice Age?

30. How do scientists determine the age of ancient artifacts?

31. Why did some Native American groups settle in villages while other Native Americans groups were nomads?

32. How and why did the arrival of camels affect the trans-Saharan trade in West Africa?

33. How did the religion of Islam spread throughout West Africa?

34. What were four major factors that encouraged European exploration in the 1400s and 1500s?

35. Why were Europeans searching for a sea route to Asia?

36. What new inventions increased agricultural yields in Europe in the Middle Ages?

Chapter Summary

Europe
- **A.D. 1095–late 1400s:** The Crusades, the emergence of strong states, the Renaissance, and new technology lead to European exploration of Africa and North America.
- **1400s:** European explorers discover gold and sugarcane, which leads to the first enslavement of African peoples by Europeans.
- **Late 1400s:** Europeans encounter the Americas and later colonize the area, leading to the expansion of the slave trade.

North America
- **About 30,000 years ago:** Asians begin migrating to North America.
- **Between 9,000 and 10,000 years ago:** Agricultural revolution begins.
- **A.D. 200–late 1500s:** Various Native American culture groups shaped by the environment develop.
- **1500s:** Native American groups begin to be affected by European diseases and military conquests.
- **1565–early 1600s:** Spanish and French establish towns in St. Augustine, Quebec, and Santa Fe.

Africa
- **A.D. 400–1450:** Various African groups with different cultures shaped by the environment developed in West, Central, and Southern Africa.
- **1300s and 1400s:** The arrival of Arabs and Europeans leads to the beginning of the slave trade; many cultures are destroyed by the demand for enslaved Africans.

32. The introduction of camels revolutionized trans-Saharan trade because the camels could carry more weight and walk longer distances in a day than oxen and horses. Camels easily withstood the desert climate and could go for days without water.

33. It spread along the African trade routes using armed conquest and a sense of religious solidarity.

34. The four main factors were the Renaissance, new technology, desire for luxury goods from Asia, and advances in their understanding of world geography.

35. The collapse of the Mongol empire resulted in reduced trade with Asia while the demand for Asian luxury goods remained high. Europeans thought a sea route to Asia would increase trade.

Self-Check Quiz

Visit the *American Vision* Web site at tav.glencoe.com and click on *Self-Check Quizzes—Chapter 1* to assess your knowledge of chapter content.

Critical Thinking

37. Analyzing Themes: Cultures and Traditions How did environment, climate, and food supplies influence the lifestyles of early peoples in the Americas?

38. Forming an Opinion If you had been King Ferdinand or Queen Isabella, would you have agreed to support Christopher Columbus on his voyages to the Americas? Why or why not?

39. Sequencing Use a graphic organizer similar to the one below to list some major events in the early history of the Americas.

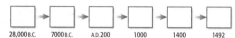

28,000 B.C.   7000 B.C.   A.D. 200   1000   1400   1492

Practicing Skills

40. Reading a Time Line Refer to the time line at the top of page 45. Then answer the following questions.
  a. Interpreting Time Lines What is the time span on this time line?
  b. Synthesizing Information How much time elapsed between the publication of Ptolemy's *Geography* and Columbus's landing in America?

Chapter Activities

41. Technology Activity: Using a Database Search a library or the Internet to find information about the early civilizations in the Americas and in Africa that were discussed in this chapter. Build a database collecting information about the cultures of these early civilizations. Include information about religious customs and traditions, ways of making a living, government, and housing. Include a map showing the locations of these civilizations.

42. American History Primary Source Document Library CD-ROM Read "Letter From Christopher Columbus" under *Exploring the Americas*. Work with a few of your classmates to describe how Columbus mapped the region he visited.

Writing Activity

43. Portfolio Writing Choose an early civilization described in the chapter and write a script for a scene in a documentary featuring this civilization. Describe the location of the scene, what the scene would be like, and what the people in the scene would be doing. Place the script in your portfolio.

NATIONAL GEOGRAPHIC

The Crusades, 1095–1204

Christian world
Islamic world
← 1st Crusade
← 2nd Crusade
⋯ 3rd Crusade
← 4th Crusade

ATLANTIC OCEAN
BRITISH ISLES
North Sea
Dartmouth
Bruges   Cologne
Paris   Mainz
    Regensburg
Lyon
Venice
IBERIAN PENINSULA
Genoa   Pisa
Lisbon   Rome
    Black Sea
    Constantinople
SICILY
Mediterranean Sea
    Acre
    Jerusalem

500 miles
500 kilometers
Azimuthal Equidistant projection

Geography and History

44. The map above shows the routes of the Crusades. Study the map and answer the questions below.
  a. Interpreting Maps Which Crusade ended at Constantinople?
  b. Applying Geography Skills Which Crusade traveled almost exclusively by land?

The Princeton Review

Standardized Test Practice

Directions: Choose the best answer to the following question.

As part of the Columbian Exchange, Spanish explorers brought such things as chocolate and tobacco from the Americas to Europe. What is one thing they brought from Europe to the Americas?

A Hieroglyphic writing

B Democratic government

C Horses

D Corn

Test-Taking Tip: Eliminate answers that don't make sense. For instance, the Spanish had a monarchy, not a democracy. Therefore, it would be illogical for them to bring democratic government to the Americas.

CHAPTER 1   Converging Cultures   **47**

Have students visit the Web site at tav.glencoe.com to review Chapter 1 and take the Self-Check Quiz.

Chapter Activities

41. Encourage students to create fields for each category of information such as religious customs and ways of gathering food. Have students use their databases as a study tool.

42. Have several groups share their findings with the class and discuss ways that maps are made today.

Writing Activity

43. Provide samples of scripts for students to critique. Have students share their scripts with a classmate for review. Encourage students to make revisions based on the feedback they receive.

Geography and History

44. a. 4th Crusade; **b.** 1st Crusade

The Princeton Review

Standardized Test Practice

Answer: C
Test-Taking Tip: Encourage students to attach an approximate date or culture to each answer. For example, hieroglyphic writing was prevalent in ancient America and Native American peoples of Mesoamerica were cultivating maize (corn) long before Spanish explorers arrived. Therefore, you can rule out A and D.

---

36. Inventions included the horse collar and a better plow.

Critical Thinking

37. In dry areas the Native Americans found crops that would grow in the dry soil or they moved from place to place looking for food. In the damp coastal areas that did not support farming, the Native Americans became expert fishers. In mild climates where wildlife was plentiful, they hunted and trapped animals.

38. Students' opinions will vary. Students should be able to clearly defend their positions.

39. Students' time lines will vary. Students should be able to provide a reference for each of their time line entries.

Practicing Skills

40. a. 500 years; **b.** about 17 years (1475–1492)

Bonus Question ?

Ask: What role did the Roman Catholic Church play in Europe in the Middle Ages? *(It promoted stability and order by having its own laws regarding marriage and morals.)*

Timesaving Tools

TeacherWorks™ All-In-One Planner and Resource Center

- **Interactive Teacher Edition** Access your Teacher Wraparound Edition and your classroom resources with a few easy clicks.
- **Interactive Lesson Planner** Planning has never been easier! Organize your week, month, semester, or year with all the lesson helps you need to make teaching creative, timely, and relevant.

Use Glencoe's **Presentation Plus!** multimedia teacher tool to easily present dynamic lessons that visually excite your students. Using Microsoft PowerPoint® you can customize the presentations to create your own personalized lessons.

TEACHING TRANSPARENCIES

Graphic Organizer 2

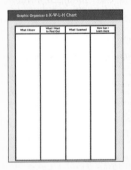

Why It Matters Chapter Transparency 2

APPLICATION AND ENRICHMENT

Linking Past and Present Activity 2

Enrichment Activity 2

Primary Source Reading 2

REVIEW AND REINFORCEMENT

Reteaching Activity 2

Vocabulary Activity 2

Time Line Activity 2

Critical Thinking Skills Activity 2

Meeting NCSS Standards

The following standards are highlighted in Chapter 2:

Section 1   IX   Global Connections: A, B, D, E
Section 2   III   People, Places, and Environments: B, G, H
Section 3   I   Culture: A, C, D
Section 4   IX   Global Connections: A, B

Local Standards

Chapter 2 Resources

ASSESSMENT AND EVALUATION

Chapter 2 Test Form A

Chapter 2 Test Form B

Standardized Test Skills Practice Workbook Activity 2

Performance Assessment Activities and Rubrics 2

ExamView® Pro Testmaker CD-ROM

MULTIMEDIA

- Vocabulary PuzzleMaker CD-ROM
- Interactive Tutor Self-Assessment CD-ROM
- ExamView® Pro Testmaker CD-ROM
- Audio Program
- American History Primary Source Documents Library CD-ROM
- MindJogger Videoquiz
- Presentation Plus! CD-ROM
- TeacherWorks™ CD-ROM
- Interactive Student Edition CD-ROM
- Glencoe Skillbuilder Interactive Workbook CD-ROM, Level 2
- The *American Vision* Video Program
- American Music: Hits Through History
- American Music: Cultural Traditions

SPANISH RESOURCES

The following Spanish language materials are available in the Spanish Resources Binder:

- Spanish Guided Reading Activities
- Spanish Reteaching Activities
- Spanish Quizzes and Tests
- Spanish Vocabulary Activities
- Spanish Summaries
- The Declaration of Independence and United States Constitution Spanish Translation

---

THE HISTORY CHANNEL®

The following videotape program is available from Glencoe as a supplement to Chapter 2:

- **Pocahontas: Her True Story** (ISBN 1-56-501555-X)

To order, call Glencoe at 1-800-334-7344. To find classroom resources to accompany many of these videos, check the following home pages:
A&E Television: www.aande.com
The History Channel: www.historychannel.com

HISTORY *Online*

Use our Web site for additional resources. All essential content is covered in the Student Edition.

You and your students can visit tav.glencoe.com, the Web site companion to the **American Vision.** This innovative integration of electronic and print media offers your students a wealth of opportunities. The student text directs students to the Web site for the following options:

- **Chapter Overviews**
- **Self-Check Quizzes**
- **Student Web Activities**
- **Textbook Updates**

Answers to the student Web activities are provided for you in the **Web Activity Lesson Plans.** Additional Web resources and Interactive Tutor Puzzles are also available.

Chapter 2 Resources

SECTION RESOURCES

Daily Objectives	Reproducible Resources	Multimedia Resources
SECTION 1 **The Spanish and French Build Empires** 1. Explain the early Spanish settlement of North America. 2. Describe the colonial society in New France.	📁 Reproducible Lesson Plan 2–1 📁 Daily Lecture and Discussion Notes 2–1 📁 Guided Reading Activity 2–1* 📁 Section Quiz 2–1* 📁 Reading Essentials and Study Guide 2–1 📁 Performance Assessment Activities and Rubrics	🖼 Daily Focus Skills Transparency 2–1 🖼 American Art & Architecture 💿 Interactive Tutor Self-Assessment CD-ROM 💿 ExamView® Pro Testmaker CD-ROM 💿 Presentation Plus! CD-ROM 💿 TeacherWorks™ CD-ROM 🎧 Audio Program 🎵 American Music: Cultural Traditions 📼 ABCNews Interactive™ Historic America Electronic Field Trips
SECTION 2 **English Colonies in America** 1. Explain the religious and economic reasons why England became interested in America. 2. Describe the founding of Jamestown and explain why it succeeded.	📁 Reproducible Lesson Plan 2–2 📁 Daily Lecture and Discussion Notes 2–2 📁 Guided Reading Activity 2–2* 📁 Section Quiz 2–2* 📁 Reading Essentials and Study Guide 2–2 📁 Performance Assessment Activities and Rubrics	🖼 Daily Focus Skills Transparency 2–2 💿 Interactive Tutor Self-Assessment CD-ROM 💿 ExamView® Pro Testmaker CD-ROM 💿 Presentation Plus! CD-ROM 💿 Skillbuilder Interactive Workbook, Level 2 💿 TeacherWorks™ CD-ROM 🎧 Audio Program
SECTION 3 **New England** 1. Discuss why John Winthrop founded Massachusetts and describe the kind of society the Puritans built there. 2. Describe why Roger Williams and Anne Hutchinson left the Massachusetts colony.	📁 Reproducible Lesson Plan 2–3 📁 Daily Lecture and Discussion Notes 2–3 📁 Guided Reading Activity 2–3* 📁 Section Quiz 2–3* 📁 Reading Essentials and Study Guide 2–3 📁 Performance Assessment Activities and Rubrics	🖼 Daily Focus Skills Transparency 2–3 🖼 American Art & Architecture 💿 Interactive Tutor Self-Assessment CD-ROM 💿 ExamView® Pro Testmaker CD-ROM 💿 Presentation Plus! CD-ROM 💿 TeacherWorks™ CD-ROM 🎧 Audio Program 🎵 American Music: Cultural Traditions
SECTION 4 **The Middle and Southern Colonies** 1. Discuss the ideas of William Penn and the Quakers, and describe the founding of Pennsylvania and Delaware. 2. Summarize why the English colonies succeeded.	📁 Reproducible Lesson Plan 2–4 📁 Daily Lecture and Discussion Notes 2–4 📁 Guided Reading Activity 2–4* 📁 Section Quiz 2–4* 📁 Reading Essentials and Study Guide 2–4 📁 Performance Assessment Activities and Rubrics	🖼 Daily Focus Skills Transparency 2–4 🖼 American Art & Architecture 💿 Interactive Tutor Self-Assessment CD-ROM 💿 ExamView® Pro Testmaker CD-ROM 💿 Presentation Plus! CD-ROM 💿 TeacherWorks™ CD-ROM 💿 Vocabulary PuzzleMaker CD-ROM 🎧 Audio Program

0:00 OUT OF TIME?
Assign the Chapter 2 **Reading Essentials and Study Guide.** 📁

*Also Available in Spanish

📁 Blackline Master 🖼 Transparency 💿 CD-ROM 💿 DVD

📕 Poster 🎵 Music Program 🎧 Audio Program 📼 Videocassette

NATIONAL GEOGRAPHIC Teacher's Corner

INDEX TO NATIONAL GEOGRAPHIC MAGAZINE

The following articles relate to this chapter.

- "The Cajuns: Still Loving Life," October 1990
- "La Salle's Last Voyage," May 1997
- "The Millennium Series Exploration," February 1998
- "New Face for a Desert Mission," December 1995
- "Pizarro, Conqueror of the Inca," February 1992
- "Search for Columbus," January 1992

NATIONAL GEOGRAPHIC SOCIETY PRODUCTS AVAILABLE FROM GLENCOE

To order the following products for use with this chapter, contact your local Glencoe sales representative, or call Glencoe at 1-800-334-7344:

- *PicturePack: The Age of Exploration* (Transparencies)
- *PicturePack: Ancient Civilizations: Middle America* (Transparencies)
- *PicturePack: Ancient Civilizations: South America* (Transparencies)
- *PictureShow: The Age of Exploration 1 & 2* (CD-ROM)
- *PictureShow: Ancient Civilizations: Middle and America* (CD-ROM)

ADDITIONAL NATIONAL GEOGRAPHIC SOCIETY PRODUCTS

To order the following, call National Geographic at 1-800-368-2728:

- *Millennium in Maps Series: Colonization and Trade in the Americas*
- *Millennium in Maps Series: Exploration*

NGS ONLINE

Access National Geographic's Web site for current events, atlas updates, activities, links, interactive features, and archives.

www.nationalgeographic.com

KEY TO ABILITY LEVELS

Teaching strategies have been coded.

L1 BASIC activities for all students
L2 AVERAGE activities for average to above-average students
L3 CHALLENGING activities for above-average students
ELL ENGLISH LANGUAGE LEARNER activities

From the Classroom of...

Lindsay Vardalos
Powell Junior High
Mesa, AZ

Colonizing America Timeline

The time line is a great study tool and helps students to see the connections between events, especially when a chapter does not go in chronological order. This can be applied to any period of time. This activity helps students become familiar with events in this time period. Ask students to put the following events in chronological order and place them on a time line. Have students include a sentence or two about each event.

- *Mayflower* arrives at Plymouth Rock
- King Philip's War begins
- Jamestown colony is founded
- Spanish troops enter Aztec capital of Tenochtitlán
- Martin Luther publishes Ninety-five Theses
- La Salle voyages to mouth of Mississippi River
- William Penn builds Philadelphia, capital of his colony
- Jacques Cartier discovers St. Lawrence River
- Pizarro lands in Peru

ADDITIONAL RESOURCES FROM GLENCOE

- American Music: Cultural Traditions
- American Art & Architecture
- Outline Map Resource Book
- U.S. Desk Map
- Building Geography Skills for Life
- Inclusion for the High School Social Studies Classroom Strategies and Activities
- Teaching Strategies for the American History Classroom (Including Block Scheduling Pacing Guides)

Block Schedule

Activities that are suited to use within the block scheduling framework are identified by:

Why It Matters Activity

Ask students to name some of the core values that they believe all Americans share and explain how they think colonists shaped these values. Students should evaluate their answers after they have completed the chapter.

GLENCOE
TECHNOLOGY

The *American Vision* Video Program
To learn more about America from 1519 to 1733, have students view the Chapter 2 video, "Early Explorers," from the *American Vision* Video Program.

 Available in DVD and VHS

MindJogger Videoquiz
Use the **MindJogger Videoquiz** to preview Chapter 2 content.

Available in VHS

CHAPTER

2 Colonizing America *1519–1733*

Why It Matters

Spanish, French, and English colonists came to North America. The colonies they founded often reflected the values and traditions of their homelands. These values and traditions helped shape core beliefs that most Americans share today.

The Impact Today

Several developments of the early colonial period are evident in the nation today.
- *The language and culture of the southwestern United States reflect the influence of the early Spanish settlers.*
- *Religious conflicts convinced the colonists of the importance of toleration and freedom of religion, values important to Americans today.*
- *The democratic traditions and institutions of the modern United States originated during colonial times.*

The **American Vision** *Video The Chapter 2 video, "Early Explorers," chronicles the voyages of some of the early European explorers.*

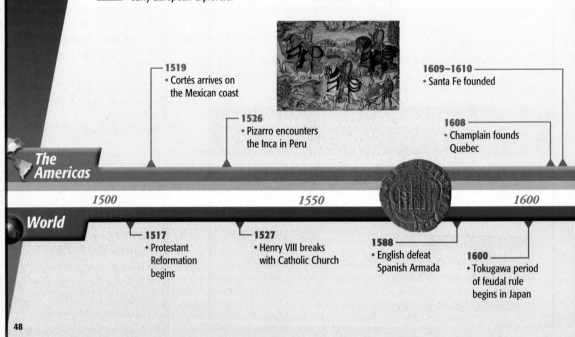

The Americas

1519
• Cortés arrives on the Mexican coast

1526
• Pizarro encounters the Inca in Peru

1608
• Champlain founds Quebec

1609–1610
• Santa Fe founded

1500   1550   1600

World

1517
• Protestant Reformation begins

1527
• Henry VIII breaks with Catholic Church

1588
• English defeat Spanish Armada

1600
• Tokugawa period of feudal rule begins in Japan

48

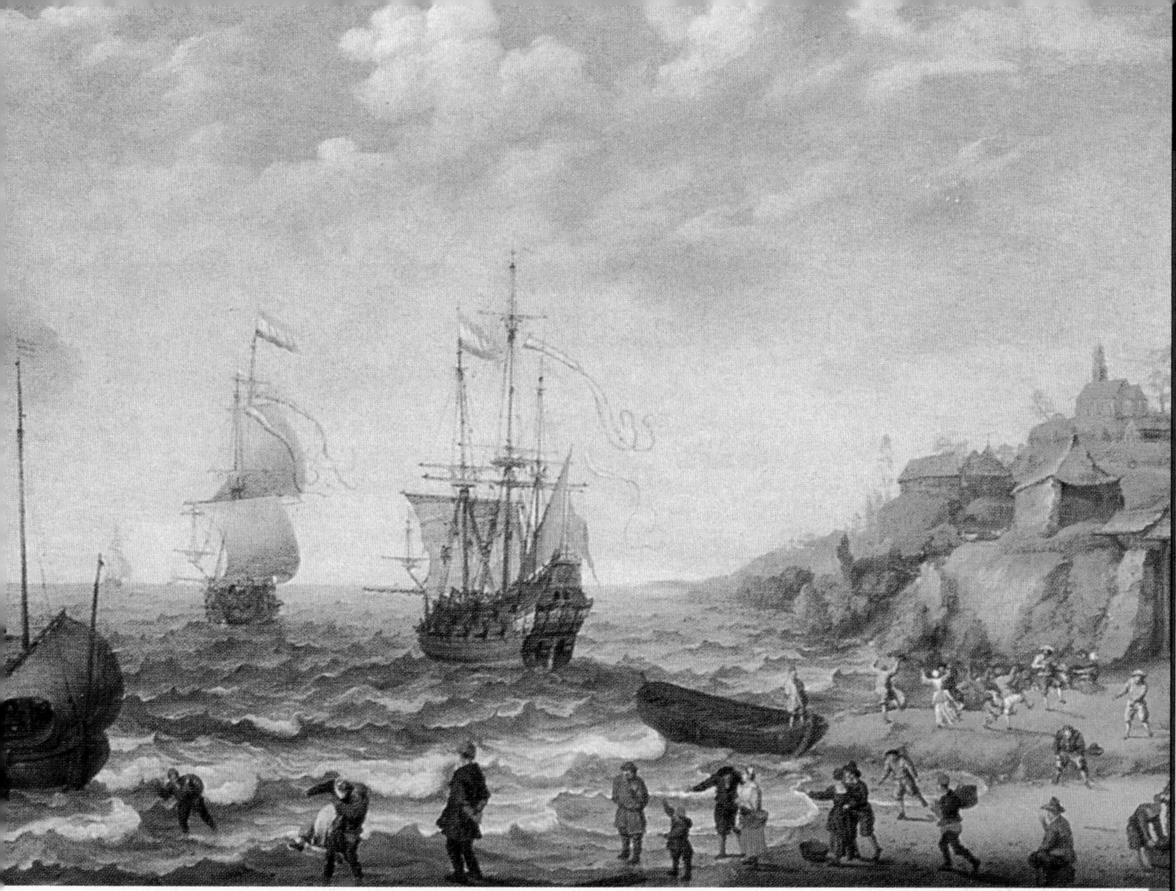

This 1638 painting by Dutch artist Adam Willaerts is believed to depict the Plymouth colony.

1619
- First meeting of Virginia House of Burgesses

1630
- Massachusetts Bay Colony established

1642
- English Civil War begins

1680
- Popé leads Native American rebellion in New Mexico

1681
- William Penn's charter for Pennsylvania granted

1688
- Glorious Revolution establishes limited monarchy in England

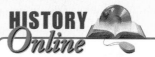

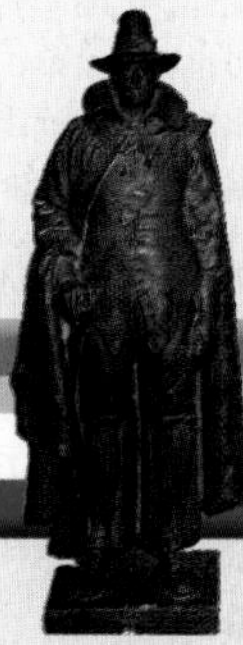

1650 — *1700*

HISTORY Online

Chapter Overview
Visit the *American Vision* Web site at tav.glencoe.com and click on ***Chapter Overviews—Chapter 2*** to preview chapter information.

Introducing CHAPTER 2

HISTORY Online

Introduce students to chapter content and key terms by having them access the **Chapter 2 Overview** at tav.glencoe.com.

More About the Art

Ask: What seems to be the reaction of the colonists to the arrival of the sailing ships? *(They appear to be excited or anxious about the ships' arrival.)*

TIME LINE ACTIVITY

Have students select a world event from the time line and learn more about it. From their research have them write a brief description of the impact the event had on American history.

GRAPHIC ORGANIZER ACTIVITY

Organizing Information Have students indicate the names and approximate founding dates of colonies mentioned in this chapter using a table similar to the one shown.

England		France	Spain
Roanoke, 1587	*New Jersey, 1664*	*Biloxi, New France, 1698*	*Mexico, New Spain, 1521*
Jamestown, 1607	*New York, 1664*		*Santa Fe, New Mexico, 1609*
Plymouth, 1620	*South Carolina, 1670*		*St. Augustine, Florida, 1565*
Massachusetts, 1630	*New Hampshire, 1677*		*Eastern Texas, 1690*
Maryland, 1634	*North Carolina, c. 1700*		

1 FOCUS

Section Overview

This section describes how life for European settlers was shaped by the values they brought with them and the geography of the regions where they settled.

BELLRINGER
Skillbuilder Activity

 Project transparency and have students answer the question.

Available as a blackline master.

Daily Focus Skills Transparency 2–1

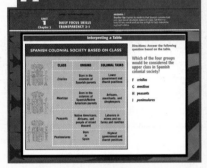

Guide to Reading

Answers to Graphic:
I. The Conquest of Mexico
   A. The Spanish Encounter the Aztec
   B. The Invasion Begins
   C. Cortés Defeats the Aztec
II. New Spain Expands
   A. Pizarro Conquers the Inca
   B. Searching for Cities of Gold
   C. The Spanish Settle the Southwest

Students should complete the outline by including all heads in the section.

Preteaching Vocabulary
Have students look up the pronunciation and practice saying the seven Key Terms that are derived from French and Spanish.

SECTION 1 The Spanish and French Build Empires

Guide to Reading

Main Idea
The Spanish and French colonies in America reflected the values of European society and the geography of the regions in which they settled.

Key Terms and Names
conquistador, Francisco Pizarro, presidio, Popé, *hidalgo, encomienda,* hacienda, vaquero, Northwest Passage, coureur de bois

Reading Strategy
Taking Notes As you read about the Spanish and French colonies in America, use the section headings to create an outline similar to the one below.

The Spanish and French Build Empires
I. The Conquest of Mexico
   A.
   B.
II.
   A.
   B.
   C.

Reading Objectives
• **Explain** the early Spanish settlement of North America.
• **Describe** the colonial society in New France.

Section Theme
Global Connections European colonizers shaped the new cultures of North America.

Preview of Events

| ♦1500 | ♦1550 | ♦1600 | ♦1650 |

| 1519 | 1532 | 1565 | 1608 | 1609–1610 |
| Cortés lands on Mexican coast | Pizarro invades Incan empire | St. Augustine, Florida, established | City of Quebec founded | Santa Fe, New Mexico, founded |

Aztec depiction of Montezuma viewing ominous omens of invaders

★ An American Story ★

In the spring of 1519, a courier arrived in Tenochtitlán, capital of the Aztec empire. He had news for the emperor, Montezuma II. Bearded white men bearing crosses were encamped on the eastern shores of the emperor's realm.

Montezuma was worried. For several years he had heard reports of strange men with "very light skin" operating in the Caribbean. His subjects had also seen "towers or small mountains floating on the waves of the sea." Now these strange white men had come to his lands, and Montezuma did not know what to do.

The men on the coast were Spanish soldiers. As they watched the soldiers, the people of eastern Mexico felt both fear and awe. One Aztec later recalled:

❝They came in battle array, as conquerors . . . their spears glinted in the sun, and their pennons fluttered like bats. They made a loud clamor as they marched, for their coats of mail and their weapons clashed and rattled. . . . They terrified everyone who saw them.❞

—quoted in *The Broken Spears: The Aztec Account of the Conquest of Mexico*

The Conquest of Mexico

Leading the Spanish march into the Aztec empire was a 34-year-old Spaniard named **Hernán Cortés.** At age 19, Cortés had boarded a ship bound for the Spanish Indies determined to make his fortune. He had no idea then that 15 years later he would overturn a civilization and change the lives of millions of people.

50 CHAPTER 2 Colonizing America

SECTION RESOURCES

Reproducible Masters
• Reproducible Lesson Plan 2–1
• Daily Lecture and Discussion Notes 2–1
• Guided Reading Activity 2–1
• Section Quiz 2–1
• Reading Essentials and Study Guide 2–1

Transparencies
• Daily Focus Skills Transparency 2–1

• American Art & Architecture

Multimedia
🕮 Interactive Tutor Self-Assessment CD-ROM
🕮 ExamView® Pro Testmaker CD-ROM
🕮 Presentation Plus! CD-ROM
🕮 TeacherWorks™ CD-ROM
🕮 Audio Program
🕮 American Music: Cultural Traditions

The Spanish Encounter the Aztec In 1511 Spanish troops, led by **Diego Velázquez,** conquered Cuba. Cortés took part in the invasion, and his courage impressed Velázquez. He rewarded Cortés by giving him control of several Native American villages.

Six years later, smallpox swept across Cuba, killing thousands of Native Americans. Without Native American labor, the farms and mines the Spanish had built in Cuba could not function. Velázquez asked Cortés to lead an expedition to the Yucatán Peninsula to find new peoples who could be forced to work for the Spanish. He also wanted to investigate reports of a wealthy civilization there. On February 18, 1519, Cortés set sail for Mexico. He had 11 ships, 550 men, and 16 horses.

The Invasion Begins After crossing the Gulf of Mexico, Cortés landed in the Yucatán Peninsula. There he found a shipwrecked sailor—Jerónimo de Aguilar—who spoke the local language and could act as translator. Despite this advantage, Cortés could not prevent an attack by thousands of warriors from a nearby city. The battle showed that the Spanish had a technological advantage over the local people. Spanish swords, crossbows, guns, and cannons quickly killed more than 200 warriors. As a peace offering, the leaders of the city gave Cortés 20 young women. Cortés then continued up the coast.

The people farther up the coast spoke a language Aguilar did not know, but among the 20 women traveling with the Spanish was **Malinche,** a woman who knew the language. She translated for Aguilar and he translated the words into Spanish for Cortés. Malinche impressed Cortés. He had her baptized, giving her the name Marina. He called her Doña Marina, and she became one of his closest advisers.

From his talks with local rulers, Cortés learned that the Aztec had conquered many peoples in the region and were at war with others, including the powerful Tlaxcalan people. He realized that if he acted carefully, he might convince the Tlaxcalan to join him against the Aztec.

As Cortés marched inland to Tlaxcala, his army's physical appearance helped him gain allies. The local people had never seen horses before. Their foaming

muzzles and the glistening armor they wore were astonishing and terrifying, and when they charged it seemed to one Aztec chronicler "as if stones were raining on the earth." Equally terrifying were the "shooting sparks" of the Spanish cannons. After several encounters that displayed Spanish power, the Tlaxcalan agreed to join with Cortés.

Two hundred miles away, Montezuma had to decide how to respond to the Spanish. He believed in a prophecy that said that the god **Quetzalcoatl**—a fair-skinned, bearded deity—would someday return from the east to conquer the Aztec. Montezuma did not know if Cortés was Quetzalcoatl, but he did not want to attack him until he knew for sure.

When he learned Cortés was negotiating with the Tlaxcalan, Montezuma sent envoys to meet the Spanish leader. The envoys promised Cortés that Montezuma would pay a yearly tribute to the king of Spain if Cortés halted his advance. To further appease the Spanish, the envoys sacrificed several captives and gave their blood to the Spanish to drink. The act horrified the Spanish and alarmed Montezuma, since he knew that Quetzalcoatl also hated human sacrifice.

With a joint Spanish-Tlaxcalan force heading toward him, Montezuma decided to ambush Cortés at the city of Cholula. Warned of the ambush by Doña Marina, the Spanish attacked first, killing over 6,000 Cholulans. Montezuma now believed Cortés could not be stopped. On November 8, 1519, Spanish troops peacefully entered the Aztec capital of Tenochtitlán.

TURNING POINT

Cortés Defeats the Aztec Sitting on an island in the center of a lake, the city of Tenochtitlán astonished the Spanish. It was larger than most European cities. The central plaza had a huge double pyramid, and canoes carried people along stone canals around the city.

Spanish suit of armor, helmet, and pistols

COOPERATIVE LEARNING ACTIVITY

Teaching Your Classmates Organize students into home teams of five and assign each member of the team a number from 1 to 5. Divide the section into five parts and number the parts. Have everyone with the number 1 meet to study and discuss part 1 of the section. Do the same for each of the other parts. Reunite the home teams and have each member of the team share his or her knowledge about this section. 📖

Use the rubric for a cooperative group management plan on pages 81–82 in the *Performance Assessment Activities and Rubrics.*

---

2 TEACH

Daily Lecture and Discussion Notes 2–1

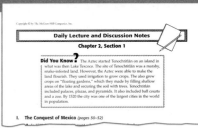

Copyright © by The McGraw-Hill Companies, Inc.

Daily Lecture and Discussion Notes

Chapter 2, Section 1

Did You Know? The Aztec started Tenochtitlán on an island in what was then Lake Texcoco. The site of Tenochtitlán was a marshy, snake-infested land. However, the Aztec were able to make the land flourish. They used irrigation to grow crops. The also grew crops on "floating gardens," which they made by filling shallow areas of the lake and securing the soil with trees. Tenochtitlán included palaces, plazas, and pyramids. It also included ball courts and a zoo. By 1520 the city was one of the largest cities in the world in population.

I.   The Conquest of Mexico *(pages 50–52)*

Discussing a Concept Ask students to discuss the concept of colonization. Encourage students to explore the reasons why European governments wanted to establish colonies, why people were willing to move to the colonies, and why Native Americans were adversely affected by colonization. At the end of the discussion, ask one or two students to summarize the discussion. **L2**

FYI

Most Mexicans agree that Doña Marina played a significant role in history. Some view her as a traitor, while others believe that her ability to negotiate spared many Aztecs from death at the hands of the Spanish. In addition to her role as Cortés's translator and negotiator, Doña Marina was his mistress and the mother of one of his sons.

you don't say...

Malinchista In Mexico the term *malinchista* means love of foreigners or traitor. This derogatory word is derived from Doña Marina's Aztec name, Malinche, and reflects the belief that she was a traitor.

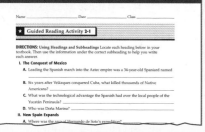
Creating a Map Have students create a map that illustrates the extent of the Inca Empire in 1500 including the cities of Cajamarca and Cuzco, as well as the present-day country borders of South America. The map should include appropriate labels. **L2**

📁 Use the rubric for creating a map, display, or chart on pages 77–78 in the *Performance Assessment Activities and Rubrics.*

History *and the* Humanities

🏴 American Music: Cultural Traditions: "Ay como flecha"
🖋 American Art & Architecture: Mission San Xavier del Bac

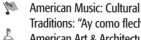
Reading Check

Answer: Cortés's expedition set out to find people to work the farms and mines the Spanish had built in Cuba and to investigate reports of a wealthy civilization.

Different Viewpoints

The Spanish in Mexico

Historians are still not sure exactly what took place when Hernán Cortés arrived in Tenochtitlán in 1519. The Aztec version of events was recorded in artists' sketches and passed down verbally for centuries, while Cortés and others, seeking to justify what they had done, wrote the original Spanish reports. To determine what actually took place, historians must compare the stories and other evidence and draw their own conclusions.

Conquistador's sword

The battle in Tenochtitlán

> **Cortés describes events to Spanish Emperor Charles V:**
>
> "I asked [Montezuma] to send some of his own men, to whom I would add an equal number of Spaniards, to the estates and houses of those nobles who had publicly offered themselves as vassals of your Majesty, asking them to do your Majesty some service with what riches they might possess. . . . With my men he sent his own, ordering them to visit the rulers of those cities and to require of each one of them in my name a certain measure of gold. And so it came about that each one of those lords to whom he sent gave very freely when he was asked, whether jewels, small bars and plates of gold and silver, or other valuables which he possessed; of all this treasure gathered together the fifth due to your Majesty amounted to over two thousand four hundred *pesos* of gold. . . ."
>
> —quoted in *Five Letters of Cortés to the Emperor*

Some of what the Spanish saw here horrified them as well. The central plaza, for example, contained the *tzompantli*—a huge rack displaying thousands of human skulls—and the Aztec priests wore their long hair matted down with dried human blood.

Surrounded by thousands of Aztec, Cortés decided to take Montezuma hostage. Montezuma, resigned to his fate, did not resist. Under instructions from Cortés, he stopped all human sacrifice and ordered the statues of the gods to be replaced with Christian crosses and images of the Virgin Mary.

Enraged at their loss of power, the Aztec priests organized a rebellion in the spring of 1520. The battle raged for days. Spanish cannons and crossbows killed thousands of Aztec. While trying to stop the fighting, Montezuma was hit by stones and later died. Realizing they would soon be overrun, the Spanish fought their way out of the city. Over 450 Spaniards died in the battle, as did more than 4,000 Aztec, in what became known as *Noche Triste*—the "Sad Night."

Although he had been driven from the city, Cortés refused to give up. He and his men took refuge with the Tlaxcalan and began building boats to attack the Aztec capital by water. At the same time, smallpox erupted in the region. Tens of thousands of Native Americans died. As one Aztec recorded, the disease devastated the defenders of Tenochtitlán:

> 66While the Spaniards were in Tlaxcala, a great plague broke out here in Tenochtitlán. . . . Sores erupted on our faces, our breasts, our bellies; we were covered with agonizing sores from head to foot. The illness was so dreadful that no one could walk or move. . . . If they did move their bodies, they screamed with pain.99
>
> —quoted in *The Broken Spears: The Aztec Account of the Conquest of Mexico*

Finally, in May 1521, Cortés launched his attack against the greatly weakened Aztec forces. His fleet sank the Aztec canoes and landed troops in the city. By August 1521, Cortés had won.

✔ Reading Check **Examining** What was the purpose of Hernán Cortés's expedition to Mexico?

New Spain Expands

After defeating the Aztec, Cortés ordered a new city to be built on the ruins of Tenochtitlán. The city, named Mexico, became the capital of the new

---

MEETING SPECIAL NEEDS

Visual/Spatial Have students create a pyramid-shaped diagram to help them understand the structure of society in New Spain. The diagram should be divided into sections to illustrate the hierarchy of the societal groups. Ask students to label the diagram using the appropriate Spanish words along with a brief description of what kind of people were included in each group. **L1**

📁 Refer to *Inclusion for the High School Social Studies Classroom Strategies and Activities* in the TCR.

The Aztec view of the Spanish actions:

"When the Spaniards were installed in the palace, they asked Motecuhzoma [Montezuma] about the city's resources and reserves. . . . They questioned him closely and then demanded gold. Motecuhzoma guided them to it. . . . When they arrived at the treasure house called Teucalco, the riches of gold and feathers were brought out to them. . . . Next they went to Motecuhzoma's storehouse, in the place called Totocalco [Palace of the Birds], where his personal treasures were kept. The Spaniards grinned like little beasts and patted each other with delight. When they entered the hall of treasures, it was as if they had arrived in Paradise. They searched everywhere and coveted everything; they were slaves to their own greed. . . . They seized these treasures as if they were their own, as if this plunder were merely a stroke of good luck."

Aztec war club

—quoted in *The Broken Spears: The Aztec Account of the Conquest of Mexico*

Learning From History

1. How would you describe the different tones and attitudes in each account?
2. What factors should you consider when evaluating why these passages present different versions of the same events?

Spanish colony of **New Spain.** Cortés then sent several expeditions to conquer the rest of the region. The men who led these expeditions became known as conquistadors, or "conquerors."

Pizarro Conquers the Inca While the Spanish were fighting for control of Central America, a Spanish army captain named **Francisco Pizarro** began exploring South America's west coast. In 1526 he landed in Peru and encountered the Inca empire. After the Spanish king granted him permission to conquer the Inca, Pizarro returned to Peru in 1531 with a small force. When he later marched inland in the spring of 1532, he learned that a powerful emperor named Atahualpa governed the Inca. After reaching the Incan town of Cajamarca, Pizarro sent his brother to find Atahualpa and invite him to Cajamarca.

While waiting for the emperor to arrive, Pizarro hid cavalry and cannons around the town square. If Atahualpa refused to submit to Spain, Pizarro intended to kidnap him. When Atahualpa arrived, he entered the square backed by some 6,000 of his followers. Pizarro sent a priest to meet Atahualpa first. When the priest gave a Bible to Atahualpa, the emperor

threw it to the ground. This rejection of Christianity was enough for Pizarro, who ordered the cannons to fire and the cavalry to charge. He and 20 soldiers then rushed the emperor and took him prisoner.

Pizarro tried to rule Peru by keeping Atahualpa as a hostage. Less than a year later, however, he executed the Incan emperor and installed a series of figurehead emperors who ruled in name only and had to follow his orders. Although many people accepted the new system created by Pizarro, others fled to the mountains and continued to fight the Spanish conquistadors until 1572.

Searching for Cities of Gold Pizarro's success in finding Peru fueled rumors of other wealthy cities. In 1528, Pánfilo de Narváez searched northern Florida for a fabled city of gold. Finding nothing and having lost contact with his ships, Narváez and his men built rafts and tried to sail to Mexico by following the coastline. They made it to what is today Texas, although most of the men, including Narváez, died in the attempt. The survivors, led by **Álvar Núñez Cabeza de Vaca** and an enslaved man named Estéban, wandered across Texas and New Mexico before reaching New Spain in 1536.

Many conquistadors had also heard tales of the Seven Golden Cities of Cibola rumored to exist north of New Spain. Hoping to find Cibola, the Spanish sent a large expedition northward in 1540 under the command of **Francisco Vásquez de Coronado.** For several months Coronado wandered through the southwestern area of what is today the United States. Members of his expedition traveled west to the Colorado River and east into territory that today belongs to Kansas. Finding nothing but wind-swept plains and strange "shaggy cows" (buffalo), Coronado returned to Mexico.

While Coronado explored the southwestern region of North America, **Hernando de Soto** took a large expedition into the region north of Florida. De Soto's expedition explored parts of what are today North Carolina, Tennessee, Alabama, Arkansas, and Texas. As they crisscrossed the region, the Spanish killed many Native Americans and raided their villages for supplies. After more than four years of wandering, the expedition returned to New Spain, but without De Soto, who had become sick and died. His men buried him in the Mississippi River.

The Spanish Settle the Southwest The failure of explorers to find gold or other wealth north of New Spain slowed Spanish settlement of the region. It

Different Viewpoints

Have students perform a dramatic reading of the two accounts of what happened when Cortés arrived in Tenochtitlán in 1519.
Answers:
1. Students' answers will vary. Students should describe how the Spanish account treats the Spanish very favorably, while the Aztec account does not.
2. Students' answers will vary. For example, some students might say that the Spanish account is more accurate because it was written down shortly after the event and the Aztec account is based on interpretations of sketches and storytelling.

you don't say...

Inca Inca is the name the Spanish gave to the Quechuan-speaking people of South America. In Quechuan, the word *inka* means prince or king, and there is only one Inca.

FYI

The Inca Empire included parts of present-day Argentina, Bolivia, Chile, Colombia, Ecuador, and Peru. The capital of the Inca Empire was Cuzco. Located in southern Peru, Cuzco is near the remains of the ancient city of Machu Picchu.

INTERDISCIPLINARY CONNECTIONS ACTIVITY

Visual Arts To help students understand what life was like in America between 1500 and 1650, have them create a visual history using drawings similar to the illustration on page 52. Have students select one of the topics shown below. **L2**

Living along El Camino Real
Living in New France
Living on an hacienda
Searching for cities of gold

Settling Louisiana
Traveling with Cortés
Traveling with Joliet and Marquette
Traveling with La Salle

Practicing Map Skills Have students use a map to trace the routes explorers followed in New Spain and New France. Ask students to label their maps with appropriate names and dates. **L1**

VIDEOCASSETTE
Historic America Electronic Field Trips

View **Tape 1, Chapter 4:** "St. Augustine."

Picturing **History**

Answer: Spain used missions as the primary method of colonizing the New World. They spread the Catholic faith through the native population and blocked exploration by other countries.
Ask: Why did Spain base its efforts to control the Southwest on converting the Native Americans already there? *(few Spaniards wanted to migrate to the New World because of the harsh conditions)*

---

was not until 1598 that settlers, led by Juan de Oñate, migrated north of the Rio Grande. Oñate's expedition almost perished while crossing northern Mexico. When they finally reached the Rio Grande, the survivors organized a feast to give thanks. This "Spanish Thanksgiving" is celebrated each April in El Paso, Texas.

The Spanish gave the name **New Mexico** to the territory north of New Spain. Pedro de Peralta, the first governor of New Mexico, founded the capital city of Santa Fe in 1609 or 1610. The Spanish also built forts called presidios throughout the region to protect settlers and to serve as trading posts. Despite these efforts, few Spaniards migrated to the harsh region. Instead, the Catholic Church became the primary force for colonizing the Southwest.

Throughout the seventeenth and eighteenth centuries, Spanish priests built missions and spread the Christian faith among the Navaho and Pueblo peoples of New Mexico. Beginning in 1769, Spanish missionaries led by the Franciscan priest **Junipero Serra** took control of California by establishing a chain of missions from San Diego to San Francisco. A road called **El Camino Real**—or the Royal Highway—linked the missions together.

The priests and missionaries in California and those in New Mexico took different approaches to their work. In California, they forced the mostly nomadic Native Americans to live in villages near the missions. In New Mexico, on the other hand, the priests and missionaries adapted their efforts to fit into the lifestyle of the Pueblo people. They built churches near where the Pueblo people lived and farmed, and tried to teach them Catholic ideas and European culture.

Picturing **History**

Mission Life The oldest surviving mission in Santa Fe, the Chapel of San Miguel, is a reminder of Spanish colonial rule. What role did missions play in Spanish rule?

The Spanish priests tried to end traditional Pueblo religious practices that conflicted with Catholic beliefs. Some priests beat and whipped Native Americans who defied them. In response, a Native American religious leader named **Popé** organized an uprising against the Spanish in 1680. Some 17,000 warriors destroyed most of the missions in New Mexico. It took the Spanish more than a decade to regain control of the region.

✓**Reading Check** **Identifying** Where did most people who colonized the southwest part of North America come from?

Spanish American Society

The society that developed in New Spain was a product of the Spanish conquest. The conquistadors were adventurers. Most were low-ranking nobles, called *hidalgos,* or working-class tradespeople. They had come to the colonies in America in search of wealth and prestige. The society they built in America reflected those goals.

The *Encomienda* System After defeating the Aztec, Cortés rewarded his men by giving each of them control over some of the towns in the Aztec empire. This was called the *encomienda* system. Each Spaniard deserving a reward was made an *encomendero,* or commissioner, and was given control over a group of Native American villages. The villagers had to pay their *encomendero* a share of the products they harvested or produced.

Under this system, the *encomendero* had obligations too. He was supposed to protect the Native Americans and work to convert them to Christianity. Unfortunately, many *encomenderos* abused their power. Native Americans were frequently overworked, and many died.

A Society Based on Class The people of Spain's colonies in the Americas formed a highly structured society. Birth, income, and education determined a person's position. At the top were *peninsulares*—people who had been born in Spain and who were appointed to most of the higher government and church positions. Below the *peninsulares* were *criollos* (kree·OH·yohs)—those born in the colonies of Spanish parents. Many *criollos* were wealthy, but high colonial positions were reserved only for *peninsulares.*

Mestizos made up the next level of society. They were of mixed Spanish and Native American parentage. Since many Spanish immigrants married Native

---

CRITICAL THINKING ACTIVITY

Comparing Have students use library and Internet resources to research the different approaches that missionaries used in their dealings with Native Americans. Have students prepare a one-page report that answers the following question: **How did their treatment by missionaries influence Native Americans? L2**

Americans, there were many *mestizos,* and their social status varied greatly. A few were accepted at the top of society. Others worked as artisans, merchants, and shopkeepers. Most, however, were poor and lived at the lowest level of society. The lowest level also included Native Americans, Africans, and people of mixed Spanish and African or African and Native American ancestry. These people provided most of the labor for New Spain's farms, mines, and ranches.

To govern this vast, diverse empire in America, the Spanish king created the **Council of the Indies.** The Council advised the king and watched over all colonial activities. To manage local affairs, the king created a special court in Mexico known as the *audiencia.* The *audiencia's* members were not only judges but also administrators and lawmakers. To ensure that his interests were represented, the king divided his American empire into regions called viceroyalties. He then appointed a viceroy to rule each region as his representative.

Mining and Ranching When the Spanish realized that most Native American cities did not have much gold, they set up mines and used Native American labor to extract minerals from the ground. Ultimately, however, it was not gold that enriched Spain, but silver. The Spanish discovered huge deposits of silver ore in the 1540s and set up mining camps all across northern Mexico, transforming the economy. The work in the dark, damp mineshafts was very difficult. Many miners were killed by explosions and cave-ins. Others died from exhaustion.

Many of the silver mines were located in the arid lands of the north. The land could not grow crops, but it could feed vast herds of cattle and sheep. To feed the miners, Spaniards created large cattle ranches in northern Mexico. These huge ranches covering thousands of acres were called haciendas. The men who herded the cattle were called vaqueros, and cowhands in the United States later adopted their lifestyle. The words *lasso* and *corral* are Spanish words that originated with the vaqueros.

✓ **Reading Check** **Describing** Why did the Spaniards set up mines and cattle ranches in northern Mexico?

Profiles IN HISTORY

Bartolomé de Las Casas
1474–1566

In the years following the Spanish conquest, many people began to protest against the abuses of the *encomienda* system. One prominent advocate for the Native Americans was Bartolomé de Las Casas, Bishop of Chiapas. As a young man, Las Casas traveled to Hispaniola in 1502. He soon became horrified by what he saw. The Spanish settlers tortured, burned, and cut off the hands and noses of Native Americans to force them to obey.

Las Casas maintained that the Church and the king had a duty to protect Native Americans. In this view, he had the support of the pope. "The said Indians," declared Pope Paul III, "are by no means to be deprived of their liberty or the possessions of their property . . . nor should they in any way be enslaved."

Las Casas published several books describing the destruction of the Native Americans. His books were read throughout Europe, creating pressure on the Spanish to change their policies.

In response, the Spanish government stopped granting *encomiendas* and banned Native American slavery. Slowly, as *encomenderos* died without heirs, the *encomienda* system came to an end. Las Casas died in 1566, still outraged at the treatment of the Native Americans. "Surely," he wrote in his will, "God will wreak his fury and anger against Spain some day for the unjust wars waged against the American Indians."

The French Empire in America

In 1524, three years after Cortés conquered the Aztec, King Francis I of France sent **Giovanni da Verrazano** to map North America's coastline. Francis wanted to find the Northwest Passage—the northern route through North America to the Pacific Ocean. Verrazano mapped the coastline from North Carolina to Newfoundland, but he found no sign of a passage through the continent. Ten years later, as he watched Spain's powerful empire grow stronger, Francis sent another explorer named **Jacques Cartier** to North America.

France Explores America On his first two trips to North America, Cartier discovered and mapped the St. Lawrence River. He then returned a third time in 1541 intending to found a colony, but the harsh winter convinced him to return to France. In the decades after Cartier's last voyage, fighting between Catholics and Protestants tore apart France. For the next 60 years, the French government made no further attempt to colonize North America. In the early 1600s, however, the French government's interest revived.

CHAPTER 2 Colonizing America **55**

Profiles
IN HISTORY

Have students explain how the *encomienda* system led to abuse of Native Americans and why the Spanish government felt that discontinuation of the system would reduce or eliminate the abuse.

FYI

Twenty-one missions were established along El Camino Real between 1769 and 1823. Junipero Serra founded seven of the first nine missions. The 21 missions in order of their founding are: (1) San Diego de Alcalá, (2) San Carlos Borromeo de Carmelo, (3) San Antonio de Padua, (4) San Gabriel Arcángel, (5) San Luis Obispo de Tolosa, (6) San Francisco de Asís (Mission Delores), (7) San Juan Capistrano, (8) Santa Clara de Asís, (9) San Buenaventura, (10) Santa Bárbara, (11) La Purísima Concepción, (12) Santa Cruz, (13) Nuestra Señora de la Soledad, (14) San José, (15) San Juan Bautista, (16) San Miguel Arcángel, (17) San Fernando Rey de España, (18) San Luis Rey de Francia, (19) Santa Inés, (20) San Rafael Arcángel, and (21) San Francisco Solano.

✓ **Reading Check**

Answer: After discovering huge deposits of silver ore in northern Mexico, the Spaniards set up mines. Cattle ranches were established to feed the miners.

EXTENDING THE CONTENT

New Sweden There was only one Swedish colony in America. The New Sweden Company established New Sweden in 1638. The first settlement, named Fort Christina in honor of Sweden's queen, was founded on the site of what is now Wilmington, Delaware. Additional settlements were founded during the next several years, but tensions grew between the Swedes and Dutch. In 1655 the Dutch captured Fort Christina and Sweden surrendered. Even though the colony was no longer under Swedish rule, the colonists were allowed to stay.

Linking Past & Present

Ask students to share their personal knowledge about a person or group of persons involved in refugee migration. Encourage students to talk about the immigration of their own families, their ancestors, acquaintances, or ancestors of acquaintances. Ask students to explain the reason why these people fled their homeland and came to America. *(Students' answers will vary. Encourage students to think about the reasons behind the immigration.)*

✓ Reading Check

Answer: These explorers were sent by the king to search for a northern route through North America to the Pacific Ocean—the Northwest Passage.

3 ASSESS

Assign Section 1 Assessment as homework or as an in-class activity.

🔘 Have students use the **Interactive Tutor Self-Assessment CD-ROM.**

Reading Essentials and Study Guide 2–1

Name _____ Date _____ Class _____

Study Guide

Chapter 2, Section 1
For use with textbook pages 50–57

THE SPANISH AND FRENCH BUILD EMPIRES

KEY TERMS AND NAMES

conquistador a Spanish explorer in the Americas *(page 53)*
Francisco Pizarro Spanish army captain who conquered the Inca empire *(page 53)*
presidio a Spanish fort *(page 54)*
Popé Native American religious leader who organized an uprising against the Spanish *(page 54)*
hidalgos low-ranking nobles *(page 54)*
encomienda a system of rewarding conquistadors by giving them control of Native American villages *(page 54)*
hacienda a huge ranch in New Spain *(page 55)*

New France Is Founded In the 1500s, the French began to fish near North America. The fishing crews often went ashore to trade their goods for furs from the Native Americans. By 1600 fur—particularly beaver fur—had become very fashionable in Europe. As the demand for fur increased, French merchants became interested in expanding the fur trade. In 1602 King Henry IV of France authorized a group of French merchants to create colonies in North America.

The merchants hired the royal geographer, **Samuel de Champlain,** to help them colonize North America. In 1605 Champlain helped establish a French colony in Acadia, what is today Nova Scotia. The site was attractive because of the many rivers that flowed to Acadia's eastern seaboard. In 1608 he founded Quebec, which became the capital of the new colony of **New France.**

Linking Past & Present

Refugee Migration to America

Past: The Huguenots
French Protestants, known as Huguenots, migrated to America in large numbers during the late 1600s. Violent persecutions under King Louis XIV caused around one million people to leave France. Many settled in South Carolina, while others found sanctuary in Rhode Island, New York, and Virginia.

Present: Jewish Immigration
Following the tragic events of World War II, thousands of homeless European Jews came to the United States. Many Eastern Jews, particularly from Iran and Syria, soon followed. With the collapse of the Soviet Union in 1991, many Russian Jews migrated to America. Unlike the Russian immigrants of the 1800s, these Jews had little opportunity to maintain Jewish customs or to study Hebrew.

56 CHAPTER 2 Colonizing America

Life in New France The company that founded New France wanted to make money from the fur trade, and so they did not need settlers to clear the land and build farms. As a result the colony grew slowly, and by 1663 it had just over 3,000 people. Most of the fur traders did not even live in the colony. Known as **coureurs de bois** (ku·RUHR·duh·BWAH), or "runners of the woods," the fur traders lived among the Native Americans with whom they traded. They learned their languages and customs and often married Native American women.

The fur traders were not the only ones who traveled into the woods to live with the Native Americans. Soon after the founding of Quebec, Jesuit missionaries arrived intending to convert the Native Americans to Christianity. Known as "black robes" to the Native Americans, the Jesuits tried to live among the local people and teach them the Catholic faith.

✓ Reading Check

Explaining Why did King Francis I of France send Verrazano and Cartier to America?

New France Expands

The slow growth of New France worried the French as they watched the Spanish and English build prosperous colonies farther south. Finally, in 1663, France's king Louis XIV seized control of New France and made it a royal colony. His government then launched a series of projects to expand the colony's population.

The French government began by shipping over 4,000 immigrants to New France. It then sent over 900 young women to provide wives for the many single men in the colony. If a woman under 16 or a man under 20 married, they received a royal wedding gift. Parents who had more than 10 children received financial bonuses. Fathers whose children did not get married early were fined. By the 1670s the population was nearly 7,000, and by 1760 it was over 60,000.

Exploring the Mississippi In addition to promoting immigration to New France, the French government began exploring North America. In 1673 a fur trader named **Louis Joliet** and a Jesuit priest named **Jacques Marquette** set off in search of a waterway the Algonquian people called the "big river"—the Mississippi. Canoeing along inland lakes and rivers, the two men finally found the Mississippi River and followed it as far south as the Arkansas River. In 1682 **René-Robert Cavelier de La Salle** (known as Lord La Salle) followed the Mississippi all the way to the Gulf of Mexico, becoming the first European to do so.

CRITICAL THINKING ACTIVITY

Researching Have students work in groups to research one of the 21 missions or four presidios linked by El Camino Real. Request that students use a variety of resources including books, magazines, travel brochures, and the Internet to collect facts, figures, illustrations, and photographs. Using the results of their research, have students create a multimedia presentation about the mission or presidio they selected. Encourage students to use a variety of presentation tools including oral presentations, electronic slide shows, displays, and models. **L2**

La Salle then claimed the region for France, and he named the entire territory Louisiana in honor of King Louis XIV.

GEOGRAPHY

Settling Louisiana **Count Frontenac,** the governor of New France, hoped to ship furs to France by way of the Mississippi River and the Gulf of Mexico. Unfortunately, settling the lower Mississippi proved to be very difficult. The coastline had no good harbors, and shifting sandbars made navigation dangerous. The oppressive heat caused food to spoil quickly. The swamps were breeding grounds for mosquitoes that spread yellow fever and malaria.

The French did not permanently settle the region until 1698, when Lord d'Iberville founded Biloxi, in what is today Mississippi. Over the next few decades, more French settlements appeared in Louisiana, including Mobile and New Orleans. Farther upriver, the French built several forts, including Fort St. Louis and Fort Detroit, to ensure control of the Mississippi River.

The French settlers in southern Louisiana realized that the crops that could be grown there, such as sugar, rice, tobacco, and indigo, required hard manual labor. Few settlers were willing to do that kind of labor unless they were paid extremely well. Enslaved people, on the other hand, could be compelled to do the work. By 1721 the French in Louisiana had imported over 1,800 enslaved Africans to work on their plantations.

Rivalry With Spain The Spanish had always been concerned about the French colonies in North America. Indeed, they had founded the town of St. Augustine, Florida, in 1565 to protect their claim

Fact Fiction Folklore

Flag of New France Settlers in New France often flew this flag of the French Royal Navy. They also flew the French Royal Banner, which was blue instead of white.

to the region after the French had tried to settle what is today the Carolinas. St. Augustine prospered and became the first permanent town established by Europeans in what is today the United States. The arrival of the French at the mouth of the Mississippi spurred the Spanish into action once again. In 1690 they established their first mission in what is today eastern Texas. In 1716 the first Spanish settlers arrived in eastern Texas to secure the Spanish claim and to block French expansion into the region. The French and Spanish empires in North America now bordered each other. Neither empire, however, posed a serious threat to the other's position in North America. The real challenge to French and Spanish domination of North America would come from another quarter. While Spain focused its colonies primarily in the Southwest and France along the Mississippi River, England began settling numerous colonies along a narrow strip of the Atlantic coast.

✓ **Reading Check** **Explaining** Why did the French establish forts and settlements along the Mississippi?

SECTION 1 ASSESSMENT

Checking for Understanding
1. **Define:** conquistador, presidio, *hidalgo, encomienda,* hacienda, vaquero, Northwest Passage, coureur de bois.
2. **Identify:** Francisco Pizarro, Popé.
3. **Explain** how the fur trade contributed to the slow growth of New France.

Reviewing Themes
4. **Global Connections** The king of Spain created a scheme to oversee his empire in America. What system did he use to govern the distant colonies?

Critical Thinking
5. **Synthesizing** Why did the various groups of Spaniards come to North America?
6. **Analyzing** Were the French or Spanish colonies more successful? Why?
7. **Categorizing** Use a graphic organizer similar to the one below to list the social classes that developed in New Spain.

Highest _____
_____
_____
Lowest _____

Analyzing Visuals
8. **Analyzing Photographs** Study the photograph of the Chapel of San Miguel on page 54. How did the Catholic Church contribute to the Spanish settlement of the New Mexico territory?

Writing About History
9. **Persuasive Writing** Imagine you are an officeholder for the French king and want to support his policies. Write an advertisement for a French newspaper to encourage people to settle in New France.

CHAPTER 2   Colonizing America   **57**

SECTION 1 ASSESSMENT ANSWERS

1. Terms are in blue.
2. Francisco Pizarro *(p. 53),* Popé *(p. 54)*
3. New France was founded to make money from the fur trade through nomadic hunters, not settlers.
4. He created the Council of the Indies to watch over colonial activity, a law court called the *audiencia* that also

administered laws, and viceroyalties.
5. for slaves and/or gold or other wealth, or to spread Catholicism
6. Students' answers will vary but should explain the purpose of the colonies and their successes.
7. *peninsulares; criollos; mestizos;* Native Americans, Africans, and

people of mixed descent
8. In New Mexico, missions were located near where the Native Americans lived and farmed to teach them Catholic ideas and European culture.
9. Students' advertisements will vary but should encourage people to leave France for America.

Section Quiz 2–1

Name _____ Date _____ Class _____

★ Chapter 2   Score _____

Section Quiz 2-1

DIRECTIONS: **Matching** Match each item in Column A with the items in Column B. Write the correct letters in the blanks. *(10 points each)*

Column A

_____ 1. a road that linked missions from San Diego to San Francisco

_____ 2. created by the Spanish king to govern the empire in America

_____ 3. low-ranking Spanish nobles

_____ 4. Spanish army captain who explored South America's west coast

_____ 5. the northern route through North America to the Pacific Ocean

Column B

A. Northwest Passage

B. Council of the Indies

C. El Camino Real

D. hidalgo

E. Francisco Pizarro

Fact Fiction Folklore

Today the flag of France consists of three vertical panels of equal size. The left panel is blue, the center panel is white, and the right panel is red. Sometimes called the Tricolor, the French flag has remained the same since 1848.

Reteach
Have students review the time line on page 50 and explain the significance of the events shown.

Enrich
Have students research one of the individuals mentioned in this section and prepare a short biography of the person.

✓ **Reading Check**

Answer: to ensure control of the river

4 CLOSE

Ask students to speculate about how their lives might be different if Europeans had not colonized America. Have them speculate about how colonization by people from Africa, the Middle East, or Asia might have shaped America.

57

1 FOCUS

Section Overview

This section explains that the English established colonies along the eastern coast of North America because of religious, economic, and political changes in England.

BELLRINGER
Skillbuilder Activity

Project transparency and have students answer the question.

Available as a blackline master.

Daily Focus Skills Transparency 2–2

Guide to Reading

Answers to Graphic: Jamestown's troubles included: food shortages, lawlessness, and sickness. These were caused by the low, swampy location of the colony; colonists who did not know how to hunt, fish, or farm; gentlemen who refused to do manual labor; and a governing council that argued constantly and could not make decisions.

Preteaching Vocabulary
Have students look up the meaning of each of the Key Terms and use each word in a sentence.

SECTION 2
English Colonies in America

Guide to Reading

Main Idea
Religious, economic, and political changes in England led the English to establish colonies along the eastern coast of North America.

Key Terms and Names
John Cabot, Puritan, joint-stock company, privateer, Walter Raleigh, Powhatan Confederacy, burgesses, headright, proprietary colony

Reading Strategy
Organizing As you read about the early troubles of the Jamestown colony, complete a graphic organizer similar to the one below by listing the problems that faced the colonists.

Jamestown's Troubles

Reading Objectives
• **Explain** the religious and economic reasons why England became interested in America.
• **Describe** the founding of Jamestown and explain why it succeeded.

Section Theme
Geography and History The headright system provided settlers with new ways to acquire more land.

Preview of Events

♦1500	♦1550	♦1600	♦1650

1497
John Cabot explores North America's coastline for England

1587
Roanoke colony founded

1607
Jamestown founded

1619
House of Burgesses meets for the first time

1634
Maryland founded

Virginia House of Burgesses

★ An American Story ★

On July 30, 1619, the first elected assembly in the English colonies met in Jamestown, Virginia. Two delegates from each of the 10 Virginia settlements, along with the governor and his 6 councilors, met in the choir of the Jamestown church. This governing body became known as the House of Burgesses.

When Governor Sir George Yeardley had arrived in Jamestown in April 1619, he carried instructions to call an assembly so that the settlers could "make and ordain whatsoever laws and orders should by them be thought good and profitable." The House of Burgesses met for five days, "sweating and stewing, and battling flies and mosquitoes." It passed strict laws against swearing, gambling, drunkenness, and excess in dress. It also made church attendance compulsory and passed laws against injuring the Native Americans.

The House of Burgesses meeting marked the first time colonists had been given a voice in their colonial government. They believed that right was now irrevocable.

—adapted from *Jamestown, 1544–1699*

England Takes Interest in America

The Jamestown colony was England's first permanent settlement in North America, but it was established more than 100 years after the first English explorers arrived. In May 1497, **John Cabot** headed west across the Atlantic. King Henry VII of England had sent Cabot to

---

SECTION RESOURCES

📁 Reproducible Masters
• Reproducible Lesson Plan 2–2
• Daily Lecture and Discussion Notes 2–2
• Guided Reading Activity 2–2
• Section Quiz 2–2
• Reading Essentials and Study Guide 2–2
• Performance Assessment Activities and Rubrics

📊 Transparencies
• Daily Focus Skills Transparency 2–2

Multimedia
💿 Interactive Tutor Self-Assessment CD-ROM
💿 ExamView® Pro Testmaker CD-ROM
💿 Presentation Plus! CD-ROM
💿 TeacherWorks™ CD-ROM
🎧 Audio Program

"discover and find, whatsoever isles, countries, regions or provinces . . . which before this time have been unknown to all Christians." Cabot, an Italian navigator, had long hoped to find a western route to Asia. He wanted, he said, to reach "the lands from which Oriental caravans brought their goods. . . ."

Cabot landed somewhere near Nova Scotia, then sailed southward along the "barren shores" and "wooded coasts" of America. While he did not see any people, he did see "notched trees, snares for game, and needles for making nets." Back in England, King Henry granted Cabot a pension and bonus for finding what the king called the "new found land."

The next year, Cabot sailed west on a second expedition to America. He was never seen again.

Although John Cabot arrived in America less than five years after Columbus, the English did not try to colonize America for the next 80 years. The English government had little money, and Cabot had found no gold or other wealth. There was also no compelling reason for anyone in England to migrate to America. Furthermore, the Spanish had already claimed America, and their claim had been upheld by the pope. In 1497 Spain and England were both Catholic countries and allies against France. Any English attempt to settle America would have

Daily Lecture and Discussion Notes 2–2

Creating a Chart Have students create a chart showing English explorations and settlements of North America between 1497 and 1682. The chart should include names, locations, and dates, along with the main purpose of the exploration or settlement. **L1**

 Use the rubric for creating a map, display, or chart on pages 77–78 in the *Performance Assessment Activities and Rubrics.*

NATIONAL GEOGRAPHIC — European Explorations and Settlements, 1497–1682

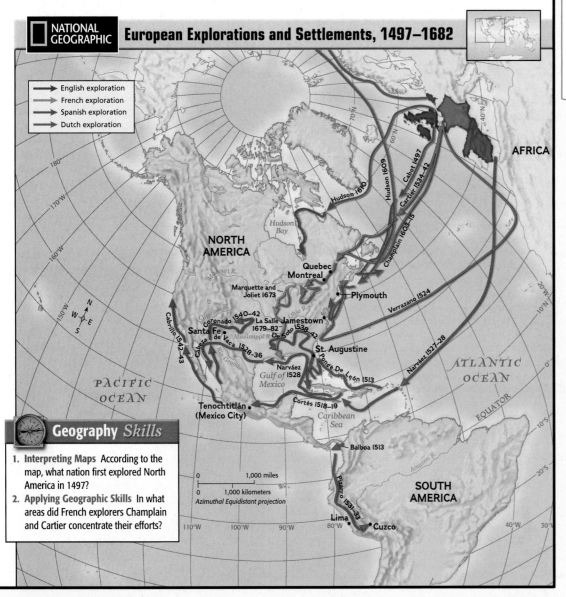

- → English exploration
- → French exploration
- → Spanish exploration
- → Dutch exploration

AFRICA

Hudson 1610
Hudson 1609
Cabot 1497
Cartier 1534–42
Champlain 1603–15

NORTH AMERICA

Hudson Bay

Missouri R.

Quebec
Montreal

Marquette and Joliet 1673

Columbia R.
Coronado 1540–42
Cabrillo 1542–43
Santa Fe
de Vaca
Cabeza
Rio Grande
Cabeza de Vaca 1528–36
La Salle 1679–82
Jamestown
De Soto 1539–42
Ohio R.
Mississippi R.

Plymouth

Verrazano 1524

St. Augustine
Ponce De León 1513
Narváez 1527–28

ATLANTIC OCEAN

PACIFIC OCEAN

Narváez 1528
Gulf of Mexico

Cortés 1518–19

Tenochtitlán (Mexico City)

Caribbean Sea

Balboa 1513

EQUATOR

Amazon R.

SOUTH AMERICA

Pizarro 1531–33

Lima
Cuzco

0 ___ 1,000 miles
0 ___ 1,000 kilometers
Azimuthal Equidistant projection

Geography Skills

1. **Interpreting Maps** According to the map, what nation first explored North America in 1497?
2. **Applying Geographic Skills** In what areas did French explorers Champlain and Cartier concentrate their efforts?

Geography Skills

Answers:
1. England
2. Cartier and Champlain concentrated their explorations in present-day Canada, near its eastern shores, and down the St. Lawrence River and Great Lakes.

Geography Skills Practice
Ask: What means do you think La Salle used to reach the Gulf of Mexico? *(He traveled by boat, following the present-day Mississippi River.)*

COOPERATIVE LEARNING ACTIVITY

Creating a Pamphlet Pamphlets were commonly used for communication in colonial America. Have students work in small groups to create a pamphlet that expresses the views of one of the religious groups mentioned in this section. Encourage students to use library and Internet resources to learn more about the views of the group they select.

Use the rubric for a cooperative group management plan on pages 81–82 in the *Performance Assessment Activities and Rubrics.*

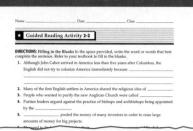
Creating a Diagram Have students create a diagram of the English monarchy starting with Henry VIII and continuing through the reign of James I. The diagram should include information about spouses and the political motivation of the marriages. **L2**

📁 Use the rubric for creating a map, display, or chart on pages 77–78 in the *Performance Assessment Activities and Rubrics.*

FYI

Henry VIII had six wives: Catherine of Aragon, Anne Boleyn, Jane Seymour, Anne of Cleves, Catherine Howard, and Catherine Parr. He had six children with his first wife, but only one girl, Mary, lived beyond infancy. Henry VIII also had a daughter, Elizabeth, with Anne Boleyn. Jane Seymour died shortly after giving birth to Henry's only male heir, Edward.

---

angered the Spanish and upset the alliance. During the late 1500s, however, a series of dramatic religious, economic, and political changes occurred that led to the founding of the first English colonies in America.

TURNING POINT

The Reformation Divides Europe At the time Cabot sailed to America, virtually all of western Europe was Catholic. This unity began to break apart in 1517, when a German monk named **Martin Luther** published an attack on the Church, accusing it of corruption. Luther's attack marked the beginning of the **Protestant Reformation.** In 1520 Luther was expelled from the Catholic Church, but his ideas continued to spread rapidly across western Europe. Luther himself went on to found the German Protestant Church, now called the Lutheran Church.

As the Reformation spread, an important development occurred in Switzerland when **John Calvin** suggested that neither kings nor bishops should control the Church. Calvin argued that congregations should choose their own elders and ministers to run the Church for them. Calvin's ideas had a profound impact on England, and ultimately America, because many of the first English settlers in America shared Calvin's ideas.

The Reformation Changes England In contrast to the theological debate sweeping Europe, the Reformation in England began with a simple disagreement between the king and the pope. In 1527 King Henry VIII asked the pope to annul his marriage to Catherine of Aragon. It was not unusual for the pope to grant a divorce to a king, but in this case the pope hesitated. Catherine was the king of Spain's aunt, and the pope did not want to anger the Spanish king.

The pope's delay infuriated Henry. He broke with the Catholic Church, declared that he was now the head of England's church, and arranged for the divorce himself. The Catholic Church in England became the **Anglican Church,** but because Henry agreed with Catholic doctrine, the Anglican Church kept the organization and most of the rituals of the Catholic Church.

Following Henry's break with the Catholic Church, those who wanted to keep the Catholic organization of the Anglican Church began to struggle with those who wanted to "purify" it of all Catholic elements. People who wanted to purify the Church became known as Puritans.

Under the reign of Henry's daughter, **Queen Elizabeth I,** many Puritan ideas such as the supreme authority of the Bible gained acceptance within the Anglican Church. Still, many Catholic rituals

remained unchanged. Although the Puritans objected to the Catholic rituals, the most important issue was who controlled the Church. John Calvin's ideas had influenced many Puritan leaders. They argued that every congregation should elect its own ministers and elders to control the Church instead of having bishops and archbishops appointed by the monarch.

The Puritan cause suffered a serious setback in 1603, when James I became king. Although King James was Protestant, he refused to tolerate any changes in the structure of the Anglican Church. Since the king headed the Church and appointed its leaders, the Puritan idea of electing ministers was a direct challenge to royal authority. James's refusal to reform the Church made many Puritans willing to leave England. Ultimately, many would choose America as their refuge.

Economic Changes in England At the same time that the Reformation was transforming the English Church, a revolution in trade and agriculture was changing English society. At the beginning of the 1500s, much of England's land was divided into large estates. The nobles who owned these estates rented their land to tenant farmers. In the 1500s, Europeans

History *Through Art*

Warring Empires In 1588 the Spanish Armada, depicted in this painting, set out with a huge fleet to settle scores with England. Spain was defeated, but if it had won, England might have become Catholic again. Why did England become more strongly Protestant after this event?

MEETING SPECIAL NEEDS

Verbal/Linguistic Have students prepare a speech that a recruiter working in an English town could use to recruit women for life in one of the American colonies. The speech should incorporate details about life in America including information about the geography and climate. **L2**

📁 Refer to *Inclusion for the High School Social Studies Classroom Strategies and Activities* in the TCR.

began to buy large quantities of English wool. As the demand for wool increased, many English landowners realized they could make more money by raising sheep than by renting their land.

The landowners converted their estates into sheep farms by enclosing their land and evicting the tenants. This became known as the **enclosure movement.** It created thousands of poor, unemployed beggars who wandered from town to town looking for work. For these people, leaving England for a chance at a better life in America was appealing.

By 1550 England was producing more wool than Europeans would buy, and the price fell. England's merchants needed to find new markets to sell their surplus wool, and they began organizing joint-stock companies to find those new markets.

Joint-stock companies pooled the money of many investors. This enabled the company to raise large amounts of money for big projects. The development of joint-stock companies meant that English merchants could afford to trade with, and colonize, other parts of the world without government financing.

✓ Reading Check **Explaining** Why did many Puritans become willing to leave England?

England Returns to America

The need to find new markets for their wool convinced English merchants to begin searching for a northern water route through North America to Asia.

In 1576 an Englishman named Martin Frobisher took three ships to America to search for a northwest passage. He made two more trips by 1578, but he did not find the passage. Although he failed, Frobisher's voyages were important. For the first time since Cabot's voyages in 1497, the English had returned to America.

England's new interest in America contributed to its growing rivalry with Spain. The Reformation had changed Europe's balance of power. England had become the leading Protestant power, while Spain remained a staunch defender of Catholicism. The former allies were now enemies.

After the Reformation, England not only had new enemies, it had new allies as well. By the 1560s, most Dutch people had become Protestant despite being part of the Spanish empire. When the Spanish tried to suppress Protestantism in the Netherlands, the Dutch rebelled. To help the Dutch revolt, Queen Elizabeth allowed English privateers to attack Spanish ships. Privateers are privately owned ships licensed by the government to attack ships of other countries.

Gilbert and Raleigh English privateers found it difficult to attack Spanish ships in the Caribbean because England had no bases in the region. This led many of Queen Elizabeth's advisers to recommend that England establish outposts in America to support naval operations against Spain.

The first attempts at colonization were not promising. In 1578 Sir Humphrey Gilbert, a well-known English soldier, received a charter from Queen Elizabeth to create a colony in America. Gilbert made two attempts to colonize America. Both failed, and Gilbert himself died at sea.

Gilbert's half-brother, **Walter Raleigh,** persuaded Queen Elizabeth to renew Gilbert's charter in his own name. He then sent two ships to scout the American coastline. The ships passed through the Outer Banks along what is today North Carolina and landed on an island the Native Americans called **Roanoke.** Impressed by the discovery, Queen Elizabeth knighted Raleigh, and he in turn named the land Virginia—in honor of Elizabeth, who was known as "the Virgin Queen."

The Lost Colony of Roanoke In 1585 Raleigh sent about 100 men to settle on Roanoke. After a hard winter, the unhappy colonists returned to England.

Raleigh tried again in 1587. He sent 91 men, 17 women, and 9 children to Roanoke. A month later Roanoke's governor, John White, headed back to England for more supplies. War erupted between

Writing a Letter Have students assume the role of a Puritan who has decided to move to America. Ask students to write a letter to a friend or relative explaining his or her decision and his or her thoughts and feelings upon landing in America. Encourage students to put a date on the letter and to consider how the season of arrival might have affected his or her reaction to arriving in America. **L2**

 Use the rubric for a diary, short story, memorandum, or letter on pages 79–80 in the *Performance Assessment Activities and Rubrics.*

✓ Reading Check

Answer: King James refused to reform the Anglican Church to allow for Puritan ideas such as electing ministers.

Defender of the Faith Before breaking with the Catholic Church, Henry VIII was a strong champion of the Catholic faith. In 1521 Henry was given the title "Defender of the Faith" by Pope Leo X for a treatise against Martin Luther, "In Defence of the Seven Sacraments."

FYI

Before its mysterious ending, the Lost Colony of Roanoke had the distinction of being the birthplace of Virginia Dare, granddaughter of Governor John White. Born on August 18, 1587, Virginia was the first child of English parents to be born on American soil.

INTERDISCIPLINARY CONNECTIONS ACTIVITY

Visual Arts Have students create a set of fashion sketches for the typical wardrobe of one of the groups mentioned in this section. Each set of sketches should include at least one ensemble for a woman and one ensemble for a man. Encourage students to use library and Internet resources to learn more about clothing and fashion in colonial times. **L2**

you don't say...

Pocahontas Rebecca Rolfe started life with the name Matoaka. Her nickname, Pocahontas, has been translated to mean "playful one" or "favorite daughter."

FYI

Among the artifacts found in Jamestown is a goffering iron. These tapered cylinders were used to crimp or frill the neck ruff that was fashionable for English gentlemen to wear. The person making the ruff first added starch for stiffness. Then the person heated the goffering iron by putting a smaller, hot iron inside the tube. Finally, the ruff was shaped with the hot goffering iron.

Profiles IN HISTORY

Have students use library and Internet resources to learn more about Pocahontas and explore the significance of her marriage to John Rolfe.

England and Spain while White was in England, and he was not able to return until 1590. When he finally returned, the colony was gone. There were no bodies, only empty houses and the letters "CRO" carved on a post, possibly referring to the Croatoan—a Native American group who lived nearby. No one knows what happened, and the fate of the "Lost Colony" of Roanoke remains a mystery today.

✓ Reading Check **Summarizing** Why did England want to establish outposts in America?

Jamestown Is Founded

Shortly after the war with Spain ended in 1604, a group of English investors petitioned the new king of England, James I, for a charter to plant colonies in Virginia. In 1606 James granted the charter. Their new company was named the **Virginia Company.**

Profiles IN HISTORY

Pocahontas 1596–1617

In 1623 Captain John Smith told a remarkable tale to a British commission investigating the Virginia Company. In 1607 Native Americans had captured him and prepared, as he said, to "beate out his braines." Just then, Pocahontas, the 11-year-old daughter of Chief Powhatan, "got his head in her armes, and laid her owne upon his to save him from death."

Although her father watched the English with concern, Pocahontas continued to interact with the people in the Jamestown settlement. Unfortunately, her friendliness and curiosity were not kindly repaid. While visiting a nearby Native American settlement in 1613, Pocahontas was abducted by Captain Samuel Argall, a Jamestown resident. Pocahontas was supposedly being held as ransom for the lives of English prisoners and for arms, tools, and food. After the Native Americans gave what they could, however, the English still refused to return Pocahontas.

The following year, a battle seemed imminent when the two sides met, but two of Pocahontas's brothers were so excited to see her that they agreed to work out a truce. Soon thereafter, a member of the Virginia Company

named John Rolfe announced to the colonial administrator that he and Pocahontas had fallen in love, and he asked to marry her.

After hearing the proposal, Chief Powhatan gave his consent, and the couple soon married. Eventually, Pocahontas bore one son, whom they named Thomas. In 1616 Pocahontas traveled with her husband and son to England to search for investors for the Virginia Company. Unfortunately, Pocahontas grew ill in 1617, just before the family was due to return to America, and she died of pneumonia or smallpox.

On December 20, 1606, the Virginia Company sent three small ships—the *Susan Constant,* the *Godspeed,* and the *Discovery*—and 144 men to Virginia. After a difficult trip, the ships arrived off the coast of North America, and the colonists founded a settlement on the banks of a river. In honor of their king, they named the river the James River and their settlement **Jamestown.** Unfortunately, the colonists' site turned out to be too close to the sea. The land they selected was swampy and swarming with malaria-carrying mosquitoes. The location was just the beginning of Jamestown's problems.

Early Troubles Most of Jamestown's colonists were townspeople. They knew little about living in the woods and could not make use of the abundant fish and game around them. Even worse, none of the colonists knew how to raise livestock or cultivate crops. Additional problems occurred when the upperclass "gentlemen" among the colonists refused to do manual labor. Making matters worse, Jamestown's governing council argued constantly and could not make decisions. The results of all of these problems were nearly catastrophic. Lawlessness, sickness, and food shortages all took their toll. Although 190 new settlers arrived in 1608, only 53 colonists were still alive by the end of the year. All of the remaining colonists may have died as well, in fact, had it not been for two men— Captain **John Smith** and Chief **Powhatan.**

Captain John Smith, a member of the colony's governing council, emerged as Jamestown's only strong leader. Born into a poor family, Smith had left home as a young man to become a soldier of fortune. In late 1607, with winter approaching and the colony short of food, Smith explored the region around Jamestown and began trading with the local Native Americans—a group called the **Powhatan Confederacy,** led by Chief Powhatan. It was this trade that helped the colony get through its first two winters.

Frustrated by events in Jamestown, the Virginia Company appointed a new governor with absolute authority, Thomas West, Lord De La Warr. To entice settlers, the company offered land to anyone who worked for the colony for seven years. The offer produced results. In August 1609, 400 new settlers arrived in Jamestown.

The arrival of so many settlers late in the summer created a crisis. There was not enough food, nor could enough be grown before winter. Governor De La Warr had not arrived yet, and John Smith had suffered a gunpowder burn and returned to England. Without strong leadership, the colony rapidly deteriorated. As winter neared, the settlers began to steal food from the Native Americans. In response, Native American warriors attacked the settlers.

The winter of 1609 and 1610 became known as the "starving time." The colonists at Jamestown ate "dogs, rats, snakes, toadstools, [and] horsehides," and a few settlers even engaged in cannibalism, digging up corpses from graves and eating them.

By the spring of 1610, only 60 settlers were still alive. They abandoned Jamestown and headed downriver. On the way, they met three English ships heading for the colony. On board were supplies, 150 more settlers, and the colony's governor, Lord De La Warr. De La Warr convinced the settlers to stay. Instead of returning to Jamestown, however, many decided to establish other towns along the James River. By 1618 there were several towns in Virginia.

De La Warr's deputy, Thomas Dale, then drafted a harsh code of laws for Jamestown. Settlers were organized into work gangs and required to work at least six hours per day. Dale's discipline saved the colony, but Jamestown still did not thrive. In 1614 Dale decided to permit private cultivation. Settlers could acquire three acres of land if they gave the colony one month of work and 2½ barrels of corn. Whatever else they produced, they could keep. According to one colonist, Ralph Hamor, the new system dramatically increased production:

66When our people were fed out of the common store and labored jointly . . . glad was the man that could slip from his labor . . . presuming that howsoever the harvest prospered, the general store must maintain them, by which means we reaped not so much corn for the labors of 30 men, as three men have done for themselves.99

—quoted in *Colonial America*

The new policy ensured Jamestown's survival, but the colony still had to find a product to sell for profit

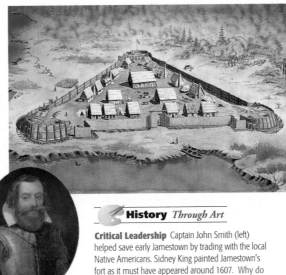

History *Through Art*

Critical Leadership Captain John Smith (left) helped save early Jamestown by trading with the local Native Americans. Sidney King painted Jamestown's fort as it must have appeared around 1607. Why do you think the fort was set up with only three sides?

in England. The solution was a product King James had already condemned as a "vile weed [of] black stinking fumes [that were] baleful to the nose, harmful to the brain, and dangerous to the lungs"—tobacco.

Tobacco Saves the Colony Well before the founding of Jamestown, the Spanish began shipping tobacco from their Caribbean colonies to Europe. Smoking tobacco became very popular in Europe in the early 1600s. The Jamestown settlers had tried growing tobacco, but the local variety was too bitter.

One colonist named **John Rolfe** continued to experiment, using seeds imported from Trinidad. He developed a new curing method, and in 1614 he shipped about 2,600 pounds (1,180 kg) to England. Rolfe's tobacco was not as good as Spanish tobacco, but it sold for a good price, and the settlers soon began planting large quantities of it.

The First Assembly In 1618 the new head of the Virginia Company in London, Edwin Sandys, introduced major reforms to attract settlers. The first reform gave the colony the right to elect its own assembly to propose laws. The first general assembly met in the Jamestown church on July 30, 1619. The new Virginia government included a governor, 6 councilors, and 20 representatives, 2 from each of the colony's 10 towns. The representatives were called burgesses, and the assembly was called the House of Burgesses.

CHAPTER 2   Colonizing America   **63**

History *Through Art*

Answer: Possible answer: It was easier to protect and defend three sides than four, and it required less space and building material.
Ask: Of what material was the fort constructed? *(wood)*

you don't say...

Burgess In the 1600s, *burgess* was the term used by the English for a member of Parliament who represented a town or borough.

FYI

Jamestown was founded on May 14, 1607, more than forty years after Pedro Menéndez de Avilés founded St. Augustine in 1565. The Spanish explorer and his expedition arrived in Florida on August 28, the feast of St. Augustine.

3 ASSESS

Assign Section 2 Assessment as homework or as an in-class activity.

Have students use the **Interactive Tutor Self-Assessment CD-ROM.**

Reading Essentials and Study Guide 2–2

Name _____ Date _____ Class _____

Study Guide
Chapter 2, Section 2
For use with textbook pages 58–64
ENGLISH COLONIES IN AMERICA

KEY TERMS AND NAMES

John Cabot Englishman who explored North America for England *(page 58)*
Puritans people who wanted to purify the Anglican Church of all Catholic elements *(page 60)*
joint-stock company company that pooled the money of many investors for big projects *(page 61)*
privateer privately owned ships licensed by the government to attack ships of other countries *(page 61)*
Walter Raleigh Englishman who sent an expedition that established a colony in Roanoke *(page 61)*
Powhatan Confederacy Native American group that lived in the area of Jamestown *(page 62)*

EXTENDING THE CONTENT

Remains of Jamestown's Fort Until 1996 the exact location of Jamestown's fort was not known. From the written descriptions, archaeologists knew that the fort lay along the James River, but they did not know its precise location. The only drawing of the fort that existed was a rough ink sketch made in 1608 by Pedro Zuniga, a Spanish spy. Researchers believed that the remains of the fort had been destroyed by erosion along the banks of the James River. However, in 1996, archaeologists finally discovered evidence of a fortification that matched the historical descriptions of the fort.

Section Quiz 2–2

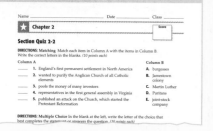

✓ Reading Check

Answer: Captain John Smith started trading with the Powhatan Confederacy. This trade helped the colony get through the first two winters.

Reteach

Have students discuss how economic, religious, and political events in England all played a significant role in the establishment of English colonies in America.

Enrich

Have students use library and Internet resources to research one of the colonies mentioned in this section and write a report about colonial life.

✓ Reading Check

Answer: to provide a refuge for English Catholics to freely practice their religion

4 CLOSE

Ask students to explain the roles religion and economics played in the colonists' decisions to move to America.

Headrights Lure Settlers To entice new settlers to Virginia, the company also introduced the system of headrights, in which new settlers who bought a share in the company or paid for their passage were granted 50 acres of land. They were given 50 more acres for each family member over 15 years of age and for each servant they transported to Virginia.

Up to that point, Jamestown had been a colony made up mostly of men. In 1619, to help ensure that male colonists stayed, the Virginia Company sent about 90 women to the colony. The first Africans also arrived in 1619 when a slave ship stopped to trade. The settlers purchased 20 Africans as "Christian servants," not enslaved people. The Africans had been baptized, and at that time English law said that Christians could not be enslaved.

Virginia Becomes a Royal Colony The new policies triggered a wave of immigration. By 1622 more than 4,500 settlers had arrived in Virginia. The dramatic increase in settlers alarmed the Native Americans. In March 1622, they attacked Jamestown, burning homes and killing nearly 350 settlers. The settlers eventually put an end to the uprising, but the colony was devastated. The uprising was the final straw for King James. An English court revoked the company's charter, and Virginia became a royal colony run by a governor appointed by the king.

> ✓ **Reading Check** **Describing** How did Captain John Smith and the Powhatan Confederacy save Jamestown?

Maryland Is Founded

A joint-stock company had founded Virginia, but the colony north of it resulted from the aspirations of one man, George Calvert, **Lord Baltimore.** Lord

Baltimore had been a member of the English Parliament until he converted to Catholicism. This decision ruined his career, but he remained a good friend of King James I and his son, Charles I.

Catholics were opposed in England for much the same reason as Puritans. Catholics did not accept the king as head of the Church, nor did they accept the authority of Anglican bishops and priests. They were viewed as potential traitors who might help Catholic countries overthrow the English king. Consequently, they were forbidden to practice law or teach school.

As he watched the persecution of his fellow Catholics, Lord Baltimore decided to found a colony where Catholics could practice their religion. In 1632 King Charles granted him a large area of land northeast of Virginia. Baltimore named the new colony Maryland, either in honor of the king's wife, or for the Virgin Mary.

Baltimore owned Maryland, making it England's first proprietary colony. The proprietor, or owner, could govern the colony any way he wished. He could appoint officials, coin money, impose taxes, establish courts, grant lands, and create towns. In most respects, he had a king's powers.

Lord Baltimore died shortly before settlers arrived in his colony. In 1634, 20 gentlemen, mostly Catholic, and 200 servants and artisans, mostly Protestant, arrived in Maryland. Despite Baltimore's hope that Maryland would become a Catholic refuge, most of its settlers were Protestant, although the government officials and most large estate owners were Catholic. The friction between the two groups plagued the colony for many years.

> ✓ **Reading Check** **Analyzing** Why did Lord Baltimore found Maryland?

SECTION 2 ASSESSMENT

Checking for Understanding

1. **Define:** Puritan, joint-stock company, privateer, burgesses, headright, proprietary colony.
2. **Identify:** John Cabot, Walter Raleigh, Powhatan Confederacy.
3. **Explain** how tobacco saved Jamestown.

Reviewing Themes

4. **Geography and History** How did the enclosure movement change England's society?

Critical Thinking

5. **Interpreting** What caused friction in the Maryland colony?
6. **Categorizing** Use a graphic organizer similar to the one below to list three ways the Virginia Company tried to attract settlers to the Jamestown colony.

Ways to Attract Settlers

Analyzing Visuals

7. **Analyzing Art** Examine the painting on pages 60 and 61. What factors contributed to the growing rivalry between Spain and England?

Writing About History

8. **Persuasive Writing** Take on the role of Captain John Smith of Jamestown. You must convince your fellow colonists that trading with the Powhatan Confederacy is a good survival strategy. Write a town circular explaining why such trade is a good idea.

SECTION 2 ASSESSMENT ANSWERS

1. Terms are in blue.
2. John Cabot (p. 58), Walter Raleigh (p. 61), Powhatan Confederacy (p. 62)
3. The colony was able to trade tobacco with England, ensuring the colony's value.
4. It created many unemployed beggars in England who hoped to get a better life in America.
5. The government officials and large estate owners were Catholic and most of the settlers were Protestant.
6. (1) granting the colony the right to elect its own general assembly to propose laws, (2) introducing the system of headrights, (3) providing opportunities for marriage
7. the English Reformation and colonization in America
8. Students' circulars will vary. Circulars should include valid reasons for trading with the Powhatan Confederacy.

Understanding the Parts of a Map

Why Learn This Skill?

Maps can direct you down the street or around the world. There are as many different kinds of maps as there are uses for them. Being able to read a map begins with learning about its parts.

Learning the Skill

Maps usually include a key, a compass rose, and a scale bar. The map key explains the meaning of special colors, symbols, and lines used on the map. On a road map, for example, the key tells what map lines stand for paved roads, dirt roads, and interstate highways.

After reading the map key, look for the compass rose. It is the direction marker that shows the cardinal directions of north, south, east, and west. A measuring line, often called a scale bar, helps you estimate distance on a map. The map's scale tells you what distance on the earth is represented by the measurement on the scale bar. For example, 1 inch (2.54 cm) on the map may represent 100 miles (160.9 km) on the earth. Knowing the scale allows you to visualize the extent of an area and to measure distances.

Practicing the Skill

The map on this page shows the early English colonization of the eastern coast of North America. Look at the parts of the map, and then answer the questions.

❶ What information is given in the key?

❷ What body of water serves as the eastern border for the colonies?

❸ What color represents the Middle Colonies?

❹ What is the approximate distance, in miles, between the settlements of Charles Town and Jamestown?

❺ What is the approximate distance, in kilometers, between the northernmost and southernmost settlements?

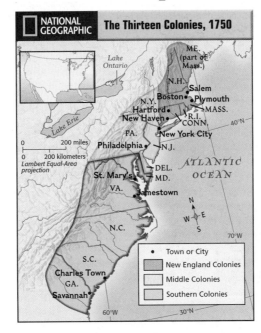

NATIONAL GEOGRAPHIC — The Thirteen Colonies, 1750

Skills Assessment

Complete the Practicing Skills questions on page 81 and the Chapter 2 Skill Reinforcement Activity to assess your mastery of this skill.

Applying the Skill

Understanding the Parts of a Map Study the map of European Explorations and Settlements on page 59. Use the map to answer the following questions.

1. When did Marquette and Joliet explore the Mississippi River?

2. What English explorer arrived in North America at the end of the 1400s?

3. Which explorer traveled the farthest north?

 Glencoe's **Skillbuilder Interactive Workbook CD-ROM, Level 2,** provides instruction and practice in key social studies skills.

65

TEACH

Understanding the Parts of a Map Looking at a map allows the user to see the big picture, including the physical relationship of the various areas depicted. To take advantage of seeing the big picture it is important for students to understand the parts of the map.

Have students identify the towns and cities that lie between 30°N and 40°N latitude. *(Savannah, Charles Town, Jamestown, St. Mary's, Philadelphia)*

Additional Practice

Reinforcing Skills Activity 2

GLENCOE
TECHNOLOGY

CD-ROM
Glencoe Skillbuilder Interactive Workbook CD-ROM, Level 2

This interactive CD-ROM reinforces student mastery of essential social studies skills.

ANSWERS TO PRACTICING THE SKILL

❶ color of regions, symbol for towns or cities
❷ Atlantic Ocean
❸ yellow
❹ approximately 400 miles
❺ approximately 900 kilometers

Applying the Skill
1. 1763
2. John Cabot
3. Henry Hudson

1 FOCUS

Section Overview

This section examines the settlement of New England.

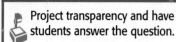

BELLRINGER
Skillbuilder Activity

📣 Project transparency and have students answer the question.

📁 Available as a blackline master.

Daily Focus Skills Transparency 2–3

Guide to Reading

Answers to Graphic: (1) the decline in fur trade minimized need for settlers to get along with Native Americans, (2) the colonial government's demand that Native Americans follow English law and customs threatened the Native American way of life, (3) the arrest and execution of three Wampanoag on murder charges, (4) retaliatory attack on the town of Swansea by the Wampanoag

Preteaching Vocabulary
Have students write four sentences, using words from the Key Terms and Names list in each sentence.

SECTION 3 New England

Guide to Reading

Main Idea
In the 1600s, English Puritans fleeing religious persecution and economic difficulties founded several colonies in New England.

Key Terms and Names
Separatist, Pilgrim, William Bradford, Squanto, John Winthrop, Massachusetts Bay Company, Great Migration, heretic, Roger Williams, Anne Hutchinson

Reading Strategy
Organizing As you read about the founding of colonies in New England, complete a graphic organizer similar to the one below by listing the causes of King Philip's War.

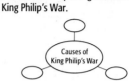

Reading Objectives
• **Discuss** why John Winthrop founded Massachusetts and describe the kind of society the Puritans built there.
• **Describe** why Roger Williams and Anne Hutchinson left the Massachusetts colony.

Section Theme
Culture and Traditions Puritan religious beliefs shaped the cultural history of New England.

Preview of Events

◆1620	◆1640	◆1660	◆1680

1620 Pilgrims arrive in Massachusetts

1630 Massachusetts Bay Colony established

1636 Roger Williams founds Providence

1639 Fundamental Orders of Connecticut introduced

1675 King Philip's War begins

⋆ An American Story ⋆

The Mayflower, *anchored in Plymouth harbor*

On a bleak November day in 1620, a tiny three-masted English ship named the *Mayflower* dropped anchor off the coast of Cape Cod. The eyes of all those aboard, 101 English men, women, and children, focused on the low strip of land before them. They were not where they were supposed to be. They had a patent for land in Virginia, but the land on the horizon was clearly not Virginia. If they went ashore, they would be on land to which they had no title in a territory where no English government existed.

On November 11, 1620, 41 adult men met in the ship's cabin to sign a document later known as the Mayflower Compact. In it they declared their intention to create a government and obey its laws. They agreed to "solemnly and mutually in the presence of God and one of another, covenant and combine ourselves together in a civil body politic, for our better ordering and preservation," and to "frame such just and equal laws, ordinances, acts, constitutions and officers, from time to time, as shall be thought most meet and convenient for the general good of the Colony, unto which we promise all due submission and obedience."

—adapted from *Basic Documents in American History*

The Pilgrims Land at Plymouth

The events that led to the arrival of the *Mayflower* off the coast of New England began several years earlier in England. A group of Puritans, called Separatists, broke away from the Anglican Church to form their own congregations. King James I viewed this

66 CHAPTER 2 Colonizing America

SECTION RESOURCES

📁 **Reproducible Masters**
• Reproducible Lesson Plan 2–3
• Daily Lecture and Discussion Notes 2–3
• Guided Reading Activity 2–3
• Section Quiz 2–3
• Reading Essentials and Study Guide 2–3

📘 **Transparencies**
• Daily Focus Skills Transparency 2–3

• American Art & Architecture

Multimedia
💿 Interactive Tutor Self-Assessment CD-ROM
💿 ExamView® Pro Testmaker CD-ROM
💿 Presentation Plus! CD-ROM
💿 TeacherWorks™ CD-ROM
🎧 Audio Program
🎵 American Music: Cultural Traditions

action as a challenge to his authority, and he imprisoned Separatist leaders. To escape this persecution, one group fled to Holland in 1608. These Separatists, who came to be known as the **Pilgrims,** found it difficult to live in Holland. They also worried that their children were losing their English heritage. In early 1617, the congregation decided to sail to America.

The *Mayflower* Arrives in America Before setting sail for America, the Pilgrims first returned to England, where they joined another group of Separatists aboard the *Mayflower.* In September 1620, 102 passengers set off on the journey across the Atlantic. The trip took 65 days. Most of the food ran out, many passengers became ill, and one died. Making matters worse, a severe storm blew the small ship off course. Finally, in early November, the Pilgrims sighted Cape Cod and tried to follow the coastline south. After encountering rough weather, they turned back.

Although they were not where they expected, the Pilgrims were not completely lost. In 1614 the Virginia Company had hired Captain John Smith to explore the region. The Pilgrims had a copy of Smith's "Map of New England," and they decided to move across Massachusetts Bay to the area Smith had labeled "Plymouth" on his map. 📖 *(See page 1061 for an excerpt from the Mayflower Compact.)*

Plymouth Colony According to **William Bradford,** one of the colony's leaders, the Pilgrims went to work as soon as they arrived at Plymouth. After constructing a "common house," the settlers built modest homes of frame construction and thatched roofs. Soon, however, a plague swept through the colony, sparing only 50 settlers.

Even the surviving Pilgrims might have perished were it not for the help of **Squanto,** a Native American man who taught them about their new environment. Bradford wrote that Squanto "directed them how to set their corn, where to take fish and [how] to procure other commodities." Squanto also helped the Pilgrims negotiate a peace treaty with the Wampanoag people who lived nearby. The following autumn, the Pilgrims joined the Wampanoag in a three-day festival to celebrate the harvest and give thanks to God for their good fortune. This celebration later became the basis for the Thanksgiving holiday.

✓ **Reading Check** **Summarizing** How did Squanto help the Pilgrims?

The Puritans Found Massachusetts

Although many Puritans in England shared the frustrations that had driven the Pilgrims to leave the country, most worked for reform within the Anglican Church. After King Charles took the throne in 1625, opposition to the Puritans began to increase, and many Puritans became willing to leave England.

A City on a Hill At about this time, a depression struck England's wool industry, which caused high unemployment, particularly in England's southeastern counties where many Puritans lived. As he watched his fellow Puritans suffering religious and economic hardship, **John Winthrop,** a wealthy attorney, wrote despairingly to his wife: "I am verily persuaded God will bring some heavy affliction upon this land, and that speedily."

Winthrop and several other wealthy Puritans were stockholders in the **Massachusetts Bay Company.** The company had already received a royal charter in March 1629 to create a colony in New England. Convinced that there was no future for Puritans in England, Winthrop decided to change what had been merely a business investment into a refuge for Puritans in America. Other Puritans embraced the idea, and in March 1630, eleven ships carrying about 900 settlers set sail. As they headed to America, John Winthrop delivered a sermon entitled "A Model of

🎨 **History** *Through Art*

Solemn Signing Tompkins Matteson, a nineteenth-century artist, painted his vision of the signing of the Mayflower Compact. By signing this document, the Pilgrims wanted to set up a legal basis for their new colony. How did the artist try to suggest the seriousness of the occasion in this painting?

2 TEACH

Creating a Thematic Map
Have students use a blank map showing the borders of the New England states to mark the colonies presented in this section. **L1**

📁 Use the rubric for creating a map, display, or chart on pages 77–78 in the *Performance Assessment Activities and Rubrics.*

✓ **Reading Check**

Answer: Squanto taught the Pilgrims about their new environment. He helped them with farming, fishing, hunting, and gathering. He also helped them negotiate peace with the Wampanoag.

🎨 **History** *Through Art*

Answer: dark clothing and surrounding except for the Compact; faces are serious and intent on the speaker
Ask: How does the portrait of John Winthrop indicate his status in the community? *(possible answer: His more formal dress and well groomed hair and beard show that he is wealthy.)*

COOPERATIVE LEARNING ACTIVITY

Creating a Table Have students work in small groups to create a three-column table to illustrate the role that ten significant people mentioned in the section played in colonial America. The table should include the colony where the person had the greatest impact. 👐

Use the rubric for a cooperative group management plan on pages 81–82 in the *Performance Assessment Activities and Rubrics.*

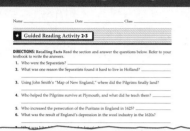

Guided Reading Activity 2-3

Name _____ Date _____ Class _____

★ Guided Reading Activity 2-3

DIRECTIONS: Recalling Facts Read the section and answer the questions below. Refer to your textbook to write the answers.

1. Who were the Separatists?
2. What was one reason the Separatists found it hard to live in Holland?
3. Using John Smith's "Map of New England," where did the Pilgrims finally land?
4. Who helped the Pilgrims survive at Plymouth, and what did he teach them?
5. Who increased the persecution of the Puritans in England in 1625?
6. What was the result of England's depression in the wool industry in the 1620s?

Geography *Skills*

Answers:

1. Chesapeake Colonies: 5,000; New England: 20,000

2. approximately 4,500 miles

Geography Skills Practice
Ask: What were the Chesapeake Colonies? *(Maryland and Virginia)*

Writing Journal Entries Have students assume the role of one of the passengers traveling on the *Mayflower* and founding Plymouth Colony. Ask students to write four brief journal entries describing their activities or feelings. The dates for the journal entries are summer 1620, autumn 1620, winter 1621, and autumn 1621. **L2**

📁 Use the rubric for a diary, short story, memorandum, or letter on pages 79–80 in the *Performance Assessment Activities and Rubrics.*

Pilgrim The term *pilgrim* refers to someone who travels to a shrine or sacred place. It can also mean a traveler. It seems appropriate that William Bradford would describe the group that arrived on the *Mayflower* as Pilgrims.

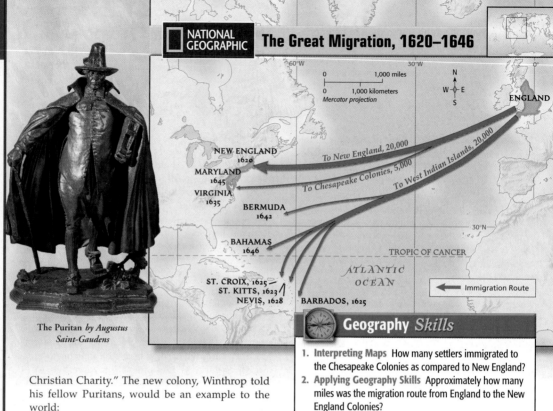

NATIONAL GEOGRAPHIC   The Great Migration, 1620–1646

The Puritan *by Augustus Saint-Gaudens*

Geography *Skills*

1. **Interpreting Maps** How many settlers immigrated to the Chesapeake Colonies as compared to New England?
2. **Applying Geography Skills** Approximately how many miles was the migration route from England to the New England Colonies?

Christian Charity." The new colony, Winthrop told his fellow Puritans, would be an example to the world:

> 66 The Lord will make our name a praise and glory, so that men shall say of succeeding plantations: 'The Lord make it like that of New England.' For we must consider that we shall be like a City upon a Hill; the eyes of all people are on us. 99

By the end of the year, 17 ships had brought another 1,000 settlers, and Massachusetts rapidly expanded. Several towns were founded, including Boston, which became the colony's capital. As conditions in England grew worse, many people began to leave the country in what was later called the **Great Migration.** By 1643 an estimated 20,000 settlers had arrived in New England.

Church and State The charter of the Massachusetts Bay Company defined the colony's government. People who owned stock in the company were called "freemen." All of the freemen together were called the **General Court.** The General Court made the laws and elected the governor.

John Winthrop had been chosen to be the first governor. To ensure that the colony became the kind of society he wanted, Winthrop ignored the charter and told the settlers that only the governor and his assistants could make laws for the colony. No one knew that these rules were not in the charter because Winthrop kept the charter locked in a chest.

Winthrop managed to restrict the freemens' power for four years, but eventually the settlers grew frustrated with how little voice they had in governing the colony. In 1634 town representatives demanded to see the charter, and Winthrop had no basis to refuse the request. As they read the charter, the representatives realized that the General Court was supposed to make the laws. When the General Court assembled in May 1634, they reorganized the government. The General Court became a representative assembly. They decided that elections would be held each year, and the freemen of each town would elect up to three deputies to send to the General Court.

John Winthrop believed that each congregation should control its own church, but he also believed that the government should help the church. Laws were passed requiring everyone to attend church. The government collected taxes to support the church and also regulated behavior. Gambling,

MEETING SPECIAL NEEDS

Logical/Mathematical Use a map to locate two points: the original destination of the *Mayflower* and the area where the *Mayflower* actually docked. Identify the latitude and longitude of these two locations. Calculate the approximate distance between the two locations. **L1**

📁 Refer to *Inclusion for the High School Social Studies Classroom Strategies and Activities* in the TCR.

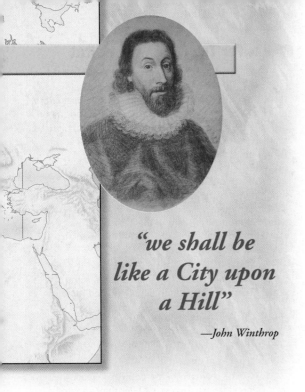

"we shall be like a City upon a Hill"

—*John Winthrop*

blasphemy, adultery, and drunkenness were all illegal and punished severely, often by flogging.

The leaders of the Massachusetts Bay Colony tried to prevent religious ideas that differed from Puritan beliefs. If settlers publicly challenged Puritan ideas, they could be charged with heresy and banished from the colony. Heretics—people whose religious beliefs differ from those accepted by the majority—were considered a threat to the community.

✓ **Reading Check** **Analyzing** How did John Winthrop's religious beliefs affect the way the Massachusetts Bay Colony was governed?

Rhode Island and Religious Dissent

Puritan efforts to suppress other religious beliefs inevitably led to conflict with those who disagreed with them. Eventually, just as Anglican intolerance of the Puritans led to the founding of Massachusetts, Puritan intolerance led to the founding of other colonies in New England.

Roger Williams Founds Providence In 1631 a young minister named **Roger Williams** arrived in Boston. When the Boston congregation offered him a teaching position, Williams refused, saying he

"[would] not officiate to an unseparated people." Williams was a strict Separatist. He believed Puritans corrupted themselves by remaining as part of the Anglican Church.

Williams became a teacher in Salem, where Separatist ideas were more accepted, but his continuing condemnation of the Puritan churches angered many people. As pressure against him mounted, Williams decided to move to Plymouth Colony. While in Plymouth, he declared that the land belonged to the Native Americans and that the king did not have the right to give it away.

Williams's ideas greatly alarmed John Winthrop. If the king heard that Puritans in Massachusetts were denying the king's authority, he might revoke the charter and impose a royal government. Winthrop feared that if that happened, the Puritans would lose control of their churches.

When Williams returned to Massachusetts in 1633, he continued to challenge Puritan authority. In October 1635, the General Court ordered him to leave the colony. Williams then headed south to found his own colony. He purchased land from the Narragansett people and founded the town of Providence. In Providence, the government had no authority in religious matters. Different religious beliefs were tolerated rather than suppressed.

Anne Hutchinson Is Banished In the midst of the uproar over Roger Williams, a woman named **Anne Hutchinson** arrived in Boston. Hutchinson was intelligent, charismatic, and widely admired. A devout Puritan, Hutchinson began to hold prayer meetings in her home. Her groups discussed sermons and compared ministers.

As Hutchinson's following grew, she began to claim to know which ministers had salvation from God and which did not. This created a problem for Puritan leaders. Hutchinson was attacking the authority of ministers. If people believed her, they would stop listening to the ministers she had condemned. In late 1637, the General Court called Hutchinson before them to answer to charges of heresy.

When questioned by the court, Hutchinson did not confess or repent. She said that God "hath let me see which was the clear [correct] ministry and which the wrong. . . ." When asked how God let her know, she replied that God spoke to her "by an immediate revelation." By claiming God spoke to her directly, Hutchinson contradicted the Puritan belief that God only spoke through the Bible. The General Court immediately banished her for heresy. Hutchinson and

Expanding a Time Line Have students use the time line on page 66 as a starting point for creating a more comprehensive time line using dates presented in this section. Then have students use library and Internet resources to add at least two events from this period of history not mentioned in the text. **L2**

✓ **Reading Check**

Answer: John Winthrop believed that each congregation should control its own church and that the government should help the church. He helped to pass laws that required church attendance and the collection of taxes to support the church.

The State of Rhode Island and Providence Plantations is the official name of what many people refer to as Rhode Island. Despite its name, this New England state is not an island. In addition to the area bordered by Connecticut and Massachusetts, there are several islands, including one named Rhode Island, that are part of the state.

History *and the* Humanities

🎵 American Music: Cultural Traditions: "Ainsworth Psalm 100," "Standish"

🖊 American Art & Architecture: Brewster-type Chair

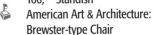

INTERDISCIPLINARY CONNECTIONS ACTIVITY

Science Invite someone from a historical society or museum to visit your class to talk about the importance of preserving historical documents. Ask the speaker to give a short history on how documents have been preserved in the past and to explain the scientific innovations that are currently used in preservation. Encourage students to ask questions at the end of the presentation to learn more about the role that science plays in preserving important historical documents. Have students write a paragraph summarizing what they learn. **L1**

Geography *Skills*

Answers:
1. 10 years
2. Hartford

Geography Skills Practice
Ask: What body of water was Hartford built beside? *(Connecticut River)* Why was it important to be close to a body of water? *(for drinking water and as a source of transportation)*

3 ASSESS

Assign Section 3 Assessment as homework or as an in-class activity.

💿 Have students use the **Interactive Tutor Self-Assessment CD-ROM.**

✓ Reading Check

Answer: They challenged Puritan authority. Williams also challenged the authority of the king. Hutchinson was considered a heretic because of her claim that God spoke directly to her. This claim contradicted the Puritan belief that God spoke only through the Bible.

Reading Essentials and Study Guide 2–3

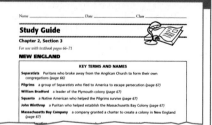

NATIONAL GEOGRAPHIC New England Colonies

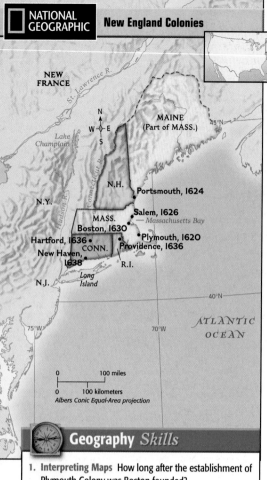

NEW FRANCE

Lake Champlain

MAINE (Part of MASS.)

N.H.

N.Y.

Portsmouth, 1624

Salem, 1626
MASS.
Boston, 1630 — *Massachusetts Bay*
Hartford, 1636
New Haven, 1638 CONN.
Plymouth, 1620
Providence, 1636

R.I.

N.J.

Long Island

ATLANTIC OCEAN

75°W 70°W 40°N 45°N

0   100 miles
0   100 kilometers
Albers Conic Equal-Area projection

Geography *Skills*

1. **Interpreting Maps** How long after the establishment of Plymouth Colony was Boston founded?
2. **Applying Geography Skills** Which English settlement was not located directly on the coast?

---

several of her followers headed south. They settled on an island and founded the town of Pocasset, later known as Portsmouth.

The Colony of Rhode Island Over the next few years, Massachusetts banished other dissenting Puritans. They too headed south and founded two more towns—Newport in 1639 and Warwick in 1643. In 1644 these two towns joined together with Portsmouth and Providence to become the colony of Rhode Island and Providence Plantations. Religious freedom, with a total separation of church and state, was a key part of the colony's charter.

✓ **Reading Check** **Explaining** Why were Roger Williams and Anne Hutchinson banished from Massachusetts?

The River Towns of Connecticut

In 1636 the Reverend **Thomas Hooker** asked the General Court of Massachusetts for permission to move his entire congregation to the Connecticut River valley. His congregation wanted to migrate because they did not have enough land near their town to raise cattle. Hooker also had his own reasons for leaving. Unlike Roger Williams, Hooker was an orthodox Puritan, but like Williams, he was frustrated by the Massachusetts political system. He thought that everyone should be allowed to vote, not just church members. Hooker argued that "the foundation of authority is laid in the consent of the governed," and that "the choice of the magistrate belongs to the people."

The General Court allowed Hooker and his congregation to migrate. A few months later, some 100 settlers headed to the Connecticut River and founded the town of Hartford. Hooker's congregation was not alone in the Connecticut River valley. Trading posts had been established in the region in 1633, and two other congregations had founded the towns of Windsor and Wethersfield in 1634.

In 1637 the towns joined together to create their own General Court. Two years later they adopted a constitution known as the **Fundamental Orders of Connecticut**—the first written constitution of the American colonies. Their government was similar to that of Massachusetts, but it had one major exception: it allowed all adult men, not just church members, to elect the governor and the General Court. 📖 *(See page 1062 for the text of the Fundamental Orders of Connecticut.)*

East of the Connecticut River lived the Pequot people, who considered the valley part of their territory. The Pequot chief Sassacus, who ruled both the Pequot and the Mohegan peoples, tolerated the English settlers at first because he needed allies against the Narraganset in Rhode Island. In 1636, however, two Massachusetts traders were killed in Pequot territory. When Massachusetts sent troops to retaliate, the Pequot War erupted. The Pequot began raiding towns along the Connecticut River. In April 1637, they surprised the town of Wethersfield and killed nine people. Furious, the Connecticut settlers assembled an army under the command of Captain John Mason. Seizing the opportunity to free themselves, the Mohegan rebelled against the Pequot and sent warriors to fight alongside Mason's troops. The Narraganset, bitter rivals of the Pequot, also joined in the attack.

Mason's troops and their Native American allies set fire to the main Pequot fort near Mystic Harbor.

CRITICAL THINKING ACTIVITY

Assessing Have students use library and Internet resources to locate five biographical references for one of the persons mentioned in this section. Provide students with guidelines for writing a reference citation and ask them to write a citation for each reference. Instruct students to evaluate each of their sources for reliability and rank them on a scale of 1 to 5 where 1 means not reliable and 5 means extremely reliable. Have students write a one-sentence explanation for each of their rankings. **L2**

When the Pequot tried to surrender, the troops opened fire, killing about 400 people, including women and children. The Connecticut General Court then put a bounty on the surviving Pequot. Many were captured and sold into slavery, while others were given to the Narraganset and Mohegan as war prizes. The Pequot were treated so poorly by the other Native Americans that in 1655, the Connecticut government resettled the survivors in two villages near the Mystic River.

✓ **Reading Check** **Contrasting** How did the Connecticut and Massachusetts constitutions differ?

New Hampshire and Maine

Not all of the settlers who left Massachusetts headed for Rhode Island or Connecticut. Although Anne Hutchinson had moved south, 36 of her followers headed north and founded the town of Exeter. During the 1640s, several other towns were also established north of Massachusetts. Many of the settlers in these towns were fishers and fur traders.

Much of the territory north of Massachusetts had been granted to two men, Sir Fernando Gorges and Captain John Mason who split the grant in half. Mason took the southern part and named it New Hampshire, while Gorges's territory in the north came to be called Maine. The government of Massachusetts claimed both New Hampshire and Maine and challenged the claims of Mason and Gorges in court. In 1677 an English court ruled against Massachusetts. Two years later, New Hampshire became a royal colony. Massachusetts, however, bought Maine from Gorges's heirs, and Maine remained part of Massachusetts until 1820.

✓ **Reading Check** **Identifying** What two colonies were established north of Massachusetts?

TURNING POINT
King Philip's War

For almost 40 years after the Pequot War, the New England settlers and Native Americans had good relations. The fur trade, in particular, facilitated peace. It enabled Native Americans to acquire tools, guns, metal, and other European products in exchange for furs. By the 1670s, however, the fur trade was in decline. At the same time, colonial governments began to demand that Native Americans follow English laws and customs. Such demands angered Native Americans, who felt that the English were trying to destroy their way of life.

Tensions peaked in 1675 when Plymouth Colony arrested, tried, and executed three Wampanoag for a murder. Angry and frustrated, Wampanoag warriors attacked the town of Swansea. This marked the beginning of what came to be called **King Philip's War,** after the Wampanoag leader **Metacomet,** whom the settlers called King Philip. Metacomet was killed in 1676, but fighting continued in Maine and New Hampshire. The war, which the settlers won in 1678, was a turning point. Afterward, few Native Americans remained in New England, and those who survived were scattered. New England now belonged to the English settlers.

✓ **Reading Check** **Analyzing** In what way was King Philip's War a turning point for Native Americans and settlers in New England?

SECTION 3 ASSESSMENT

Checking for Understanding
1. **Define:** Separatist, Pilgrim, heretic.
2. **Identify:** William Bradford, Squanto, John Winthrop, Massachusetts Bay Company, Great Migration, Roger Williams, Anne Hutchinson.
3. **Explain** Why was John Winthrop concerned about the ideas of Roger Williams?

Reviewing Themes
4. **Culture and Traditions** How did Thomas Hooker's beliefs promote the idea of separation of church and state?

Critical Thinking
5. **Comparing** In what ways were the causes and effects of the Pequot War and King Philip's War similar?
6. **Categorizing** Use a graphic organizer similar to the one below to list the New England colonies and the reasons for their founding.

Colony	Reasons Founded

Analyzing Visuals
7. **Analyzing Art** Study the painting of the signing of the Mayflower Compact on page 62. Why did the Pilgrims feel it was necessary to create their own government?

Writing About History
8. **Descriptive Writing** Imagine you are a Pilgrim in Plymouth colony. Write a letter to your friends in Europe describing your first few weeks in the new land. Explain what you hope your life will be like here.

SECTION 3 ASSESSMENT ANSWERS

1. Terms are in blue.
2. William Bradford (*p. 67*), Squanto (*p. 67*), John Winthrop (*p. 67*), Massachusetts Bay Company (*p. 67*), Great Migration (*p. 68*), Roger Williams (*p. 69*), Anne Hutchinson (*p. 69*)
3. Winthrop feared that Williams's ideas would cause the king to revoke the colony's charter.
4. Thomas Hooker thought that everyone should be allowed to vote, not just church members.
5. In both cases individuals from one side were killed by members of the other side and in both cases this led to retaliation.
6. Students' charts should list each colony mentioned.
7. to avoid religious persecution
8. Students' letters will vary. The letters should include plausible details about colonial life.

Section Quiz 2–3

Name _____ Date _____ Class _____

★ **Chapter 2** Score ____

Section Quiz 2-3

DIRECTIONS: Matching Match each item in Column A with the items in Column B. Write the correct letters in the blanks. (10 points each)

Column A	Column B
___ 1. Puritans who broke away from the Anglican Church	**A.** Squanto
___ 2. received a charter from King Charles to create a colony in New England	**B.** Heretic
___ 3. person whose religious beliefs differ from those accepted by the majority	**C.** Separatists
___ 4. Native American man who taught the Pilgrims about their new environment	**D.** Massachusetts Bay Company
___ 5. people who owned stock in the Massachusetts Bay Company	**E.** freemen

✓ **Reading Check**

Answer: The Fundamental Orders of Connecticut granted the right to vote to all adult men. Massachusetts limited the right to vote to adult men who were church members.

✓ **Reading Check**

Answer: New Hampshire and Maine

Reteach
Ask students to name the historical figures mentioned in this section and explain the role each played in colonizing America.

Enrich
Have students write a one-page description of what they think life in the colonies would have been like if the settlers and Native Americans had collaborated more effectively.

✓ **Reading Check**

Answer: King Philip's War was a turning point because so many Native Americans died and the few that survived were scattered. After the war, New England belonged to the English settlers.

4 CLOSE

Ask students to explain how the core beliefs shared by most Americans can be traced to colonial times.

1 FOCUS

Section Overview

This section discusses the resurgence in English colonization following the English Civil War and the growth of the Middle and Southern Colonies.

BELLRINGER
Skillbuilder Activity

 Project transparency and have students answer the question.

📂 Available as a blackline master.

Daily Focus Skills Transparency 2–4

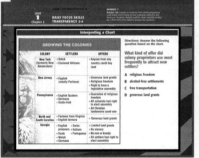

Guide to Reading

Answers to Graphic: The proprietors of the Middle and Southern Colonies attracted people to settle in the colonies by offering generous land grants, religious freedom, and the right to elect a legislative assembly.

Preteaching Vocabulary
Have students make a two-column list. Instruct them to write the Key Terms and Names in the left column and in the right column write the name of the colony most closely associated with the term or name.

The Middle and Southern Colonies

Guide to Reading

Main Idea
After the English Civil War, economic, strategic, and religious factors led to the founding of seven new English colonies along the Atlantic seaboard.

Key Terms and Names
English Civil War, Oliver Cromwell, Maryland Toleration Act, Restoration, Henry Hudson, William Penn, pacifism, James Oglethorpe

Reading Strategy
Organizing As you read about the colonization of the Middle and Southern Colonies, complete a graphic organizer similar to the one below by listing ways that proprietors attracted people to settle in the colonies.

Ways to Attract Settlers

Reading Objectives
• **Discuss** the ideas of William Penn and the Quakers, and describe the founding of Pennsylvania and Delaware.
• **Summarize** why the English colonies succeeded.

Section Theme
Global Connections After the English Civil War, England resumed colonizing America, eventually establishing seven new colonies.

Preview of Events

♦1650	♦1675	♦1700	♦1725

1642
English Civil War begins

1660
English monarchy restored

1664
English capture New Amsterdam

1681
William Penn receives charter for Pennsylvania

1733
First English settlers arrive in Georgia

★ An American Story ★

Peter Stuyvesant

On August 26, 1664, an English fleet arrived near the Dutch town of New Amsterdam. Its commander sent a note to Governor Peter Stuyvesant of New Netherland, demanding that the town surrender. Stuyvesant bellowed that he would rather "be carried out dead in his coffin." Badly outnumbered, however, leading Dutch citizens petitioned the governor to surrender:

❝We, your sorrowful community and subjects, [believe] that we cannot conscientiously foresee that anything else is to be expected . . . than misery, sorrow, conflagration, the dishonor of women . . . and, in a word, the absolute ruin and destruction of about fifteen hundred innocent souls, only two hundred and fifty of whom are capable of bearing arms. . . .❞

Two days later, Stuyvesant watched two English warships approach. Beside him stood a gunner, ready to fire. The minister at New Amsterdam talked urgently to the governor, then led him away. On September 8, the Dutch surrendered, and New Amsterdam became New York.

—adapted from *A New World* and *Colonial New York*

The English Civil War and the Colonies

The fall of New Amsterdam and the founding of New York in 1664 marked the beginning of a new wave of English colonization. For more than 20 years, no new English colonies had been founded in America because the struggle between the Puritans and the English king had finally led to war.

72 CHAPTER 2 Colonizing America

SECTION RESOURCES

📂 **Reproducible Masters**
• Reproducible Lesson Plan 2–4
• Daily Lecture and Discussion Notes 2–4
• Guided Reading Activity 2–4
• Section Quiz 2–4
• Reading Essentials and Study Guide 2–4
• Performance Assessment Activities and Rubrics

📊 **Transparencies**
• Daily Focus Skills Transparency 2–4
• American Art & Architecture

Multimedia
💿 Interactive Tutor Self-Assessment CD-ROM
💿 ExamView® Pro Testmaker CD-ROM
💿 Presentation Plus! CD-ROM
💿 TeacherWorks™ CD-ROM
🎵 Audio Program

The **English Civil War** began in 1642, when King Charles I sent troops into the English Parliament to arrest several Puritan leaders. Parliament, which was dominated by Puritans, responded by organizing its own army, and a civil war began. In 1646 Parliament's army defeated the king's troops and captured King Charles. Two and a half years later, a Parliamentary court tried King Charles and condemned him to death. **Oliver Cromwell,** the commander of Parliament's army, then dissolved Parliament and seized power, giving himself the title "Lord Protector of England."

The Colonies Choose Sides Once the English Civil War began, England's colonies had to decide whether to support the king or Parliament. In Virginia, the governor and the House of Burgesses supported the king until 1652, when a fleet sent by Parliament forced them to change sides.

Across Chesapeake Bay from Virginia, Maryland experienced its own civil war. Lord Baltimore, Maryland's proprietor, had supported the king against Parliament, as had Maryland's governor. In 1644 Protestants in Maryland rebelled. To calm things down, Lord Baltimore appointed a Protestant as governor and introduced the **Maryland Toleration Act** in 1649. The act granted religious toleration to all Christians in Maryland and was intended to protect the Catholic minority from the Protestants.

In New England, the English Civil War was a time for rejoicing. The Puritan colonies backed Parliament, and their populations fell as settlers headed home to fight in the war.

Colonization Resumes After nearly 20 years of turmoil, England's leaders longed for stability. When Cromwell died in 1658, no strong leader stepped forward to replace him. England's leaders decided to restore the monarchy that had been abruptly ended with the execution of King Charles I. In the spring of 1660, Parliament invited Charles's son, Charles II, to take the throne. This became known as the **Restoration.**

With the king back on the throne, a new round of colonization began in America. From this point forward, the English government took the lead in promoting colonization. Colonies were no longer seen as risky business ventures. English leaders now viewed them as vital sources of raw materials and as markets for manufactured goods.

✓ **Reading Check** **Examining** What started the English Civil War?

Puritan General Oliver Cromwell directed Parliament's troops in the English Civil War. What in his appearance suggests that he was a Puritan?

New Netherland Becomes New York

As King Charles II and his advisers studied the situation in North America, two regions attracted their interest. The first region was south of Virginia, and the second was located between Maryland and Connecticut. Taking control of the latter area would link Virginia and Maryland to New England. Unfortunately, the Dutch had already claimed much of that land. If the English wanted the region, they would have to take it from the Dutch.

The History of New Netherland In 1609 the Dutch East India Company hired an English navigator named **Henry Hudson** to find a route through North America to the Pacific. Hudson found a wide river, today known as the Hudson River. His report convinced many Dutch merchants that the Hudson River valley was rich in fur-bearing animals. They claimed the region, calling it New Netherland, and they established fur-trading posts there in 1614.

The Dutch located their major settlement, New Amsterdam, on Manhattan Island. According to tradition, the Dutch bought Manhattan Island from the local people for 60 florins (about 24 dollars) worth of goods. As in New France, the emphasis on the fur trade kept the Dutch colony from growing quickly. As late as 1646, New Netherland had only 1,500 people, compared to 25,000 in New England.

CHAPTER 2 Colonizing America **73**

---

2 TEACH

Daily Lecture and Discussion Notes 2–4

Copyright © by The McGraw-Hill Companies, Inc.

Daily Lecture and Discussion Notes
Chapter 2, Section 4

Did You Know? Quakers were members of the religious group known as the Society of Friends. The group grew into an important force in England in large part through the preachings of George Fox. The term *Quaker* was originally meant as an insult to Fox, who had told a judge to "tremble at the name of the Lord." In response, the judge called Fox a quaker.

I. The English Civil War and the Colonies *(pages 72–73)*

A. Conflicts between Charles I and the English Parliament intensified when the king sent troops into Parliament to arrest several Puritan leaders. Parliament, with mostly Puritan members, then organized its own army, and the **English Civil War** began. The

Background: In the conflict, both sides had popular names. The Parliamentary supporters were called Roundheads due to their severe haircuts. Loyalists were called Cavaliers, from the French word for knight, *chevalier.*
Answer: possible answers: dark, somber clothing, plain white collar, simple hairstyle

Creating a Chart Have students create a chart using some of the population data presented in the passage entitled "New Netherland becomes New York" starting on this page. Allow students to select the type of chart they feel is most appropriate for the data being charted. **L2**

📁 Use the rubric for creating a map, display, or chart on pages 77–78 in the *Performance Assessment Activities and Rubrics.*

✓ **Reading Check**

Answer: The English Civil War began in 1642 when King Charles I sent troops into Parliament to arrest several Puritan leaders. In response, the Puritan-dominated Parliament organized its own army and fighting ensued.

COOPERATIVE LEARNING ACTIVITY

Designing a Flag Have students work in small groups to design a flag for one of the colonies mentioned in this section. Have students prepare a drawing of their flag and determine the actual dimensions for the flag. Then have the groups prepare a brief written explanation of the colors and symbols used in the flag. Display the flags and explanations around the class. 📦

Use the rubric for a cooperative group management plan on pages 81–82 in the *Performance Assessment Activities and Rubrics.*

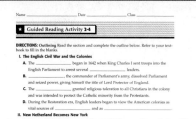

Reading Check

Answer: He wanted to seize New Netherland in order to link the English colonies of Virginia and Maryland to New England.

you don't say...

Yankees The word "Yankees" may originate from the tense relations between the English settlers in Connecticut and the Dutch settlers in New Netherland. Some scholars think that the Dutch insulted the English by calling them "Jan Kaese" or "John Cheese" and the nickname stuck.

History *Through Art*

Answer: cloth and other goods
Ask: How did Penn's Quaker beliefs affect the structure of Pennsylvania? *(Possible answers include political freedom which led to a directly elected legislature and less restrictive suffrage requirements; religious freedom which led to no state-mandated religion; opposition to violence and respect for individuals which was the basis of friendly relations with Native Americans.)*

To increase the colony's size, the Dutch allowed anyone to buy land in the colony. Soon settlers from many countries began to move to New Netherland. By 1664 the colony had over 10,000 people. Settlers came from France, Germany, Poland, Spain, Italy, and other parts of Europe. A group of Portuguese Jews moved to New Amsterdam and founded one of the first synagogues in North America.

The need for labor brought unwilling immigrants to the colony as well, when Dutch merchants entered the slave trade. The first enslaved Africans arrived in New Netherland in the 1620s. By 1664 Africans made up 10 percent of the population.

New York and New Jersey By the time King Charles II took the throne in 1660, the Dutch controlled a large portion of the fur trade. They also had begun helping English colonists smuggle tobacco to Europe and illegally import European products. In 1663 King Charles decided that the time had come to seize New Netherland. In March 1664, Charles granted all the land from Delaware Bay to the Connecticut River to his brother James, the Duke of York. James was lord high admiral for

the king, and he quickly dispatched four warships to seize New Netherland from the Dutch.

After seizing New Netherland, now named New York, James granted a large portion of his land to two of the king's closest advisers, Sir George Carteret and Lord John Berkeley. James named the new colony New Jersey, in honor of Sir George Carteret, who was from the island of Jersey. To attract settlers, the proprietors offered generous land grants, religious freedom, and the right to elect a legislative assembly. These terms convinced a large number of settlers, many of them Puritans, to head to New Jersey.

Reading Check   **Summarizing** Why did King Charles II want to seize New Netherland from the Dutch?

Pennsylvania and Delaware

Admiral William Penn was another close friend of King Charles. Penn had loaned ships and money to King Charles but died before the king could pay back the money he owed him.

Admiral Penn's son, who was also named **William Penn,** inherited his father's estate, including the

History *Through Art*

The Beginnings of Pennsylvania William Penn began his colony by signing a treaty with Native Americans who lived in the region. Penn also granted parts of his land to other settlers, as seen in this formal land deed (right). In the painting, what are the colonists giving the Native Americans in return for their land?

74 CHAPTER 2   Colonizing America

MEETING SPECIAL NEEDS

Kinesthetic Divide the textbook section into smaller parts using the headings in the text. Organize the class in small groups and assign one of the parts to each group. Have the groups read the part and prepare a short reenactment of the events described. Have the groups present their reenactments to the rest of the class. **L2**

Refer to *Inclusion for the High School Social Studies Classroom Strategies and Activities* in the TCR.

money the king owed his father. In 1680 William Penn petitioned the king for a grant of land between New York and Maryland to settle the debt. The request put the king in a dilemma. Although granting a colony was a cheap way to pay off the debt, the young man belonged to a religious group Charles had banned and persecuted. William Penn was a Quaker.

The Quakers Quakers believed that everyone had their own "inner light" from God. There was no need for a church or ministers. Even the Bible had less authority than a person's inner light. Quakers objected to all political and religious authority, including forcing people to pay taxes or serve in the military. They advocated pacifism—opposition to war or violence as a means to settle disputes.

Quaker beliefs put them into conflict with the government as well as other religions. To escape opposition, many Quakers fled to America, but they were persecuted in almost every colony. This convinced the Quakers that they needed their own colony, but they probably would never have been granted one had it not been for William Penn.

The "Holy Experiment" William Penn was one of the few wealthy Quakers and a good friend of King Charles. Penn became involved in Quaker attempts to create a colony in the 1670s, when he and other Quakers bought New Jersey from Berkeley and Carteret. Many Quakers moved to New Jersey, but Penn did not think it was the best solution since the Puritan settlers there were hostile to Quakers. In 1680 Penn asked King Charles for his own colony across the Delaware River from New Jersey. Charles agreed but insisted that the new colony be called Pennsylvania (or Penn's Woods) in honor of William Penn's father.

Penn regarded Pennsylvania as a "holy experiment" where complete political and religious freedom would be practiced. He also believed that Native Americans had been treated unjustly in other colonies, and he resolved to win the friendship of those who lived in Pennsylvania.

In late 1682, Penn made good on his word when he signed the Treaty of Shackamaxon, in which the Lenni Lenape, a Native American group, ceded land to the colonists. The treaty marked the beginning of over 70 years of peace in Pennsylvania between the European settlers and the Native Americans. On the land ceded by the Lenni Lenape, Penn built the capital of his new colony and named it Philadelphia, or "the city of brotherly love."

Penn also prepared a constitution, or "frame of government," for his colony. His initial constitution

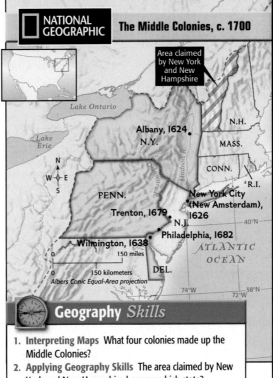

Area claimed by New York and New Hampshire

Lake Ontario
Lake Erie
N.H.
Albany, 1624
N.Y.
MASS.
CONN.
R.I.
PENN.
New York City (New Amsterdam), 1626
Trenton, 1679
N.J.
40°N
Wilmington, 1638
Philadelphia, 1682
ATLANTIC OCEAN
DEL.
0   150 miles
0 150 kilometers
Albers Conic Equal-Area projection
74°W
72°38'N

Geography *Skills*

1. **Interpreting Maps** What four colonies made up the Middle Colonies?
2. **Applying Geography Skills** The area claimed by New York and New Hampshire became which state?

allowed anyone who owned land or paid taxes to vote, but it was confusing in structure. After several confrontations with settlers over the government's structure, Penn issued a new charter establishing a legislative assembly elected directly by the voters. The proprietor appointed the governor. The charter gave the right to vote to all colonists who owned 50 acres of land and professed a faith in Jesus Christ. Despite this example of discrimination against non-Christians, the charter guaranteed all Pennsylvanians the right to practice their religion without interference.

Penn also made land readily available to settlers, a practice that attracted thousands of colonists. Many were English Quakers, but large numbers of Germans and Scots-Irish migrated to the colony as well. By 1684 Pennsylvania had over 7,000 colonists, and by 1700 Philadelphia rivaled Boston and New York City as a center for trade and commerce.

HISTORY *Online*

Student Web Activity Visit the *American Vision* Web site at tav.glencoe.com and click on *Student Web Activities— Chapter 2* for an activity on the founding of Pennsylvania.

Geography *Skills*

Answers:
1. Delaware, Pennsylvania, New Jersey, New York
2. Vermont

Geography Skills Practice
Ask: What was New York City called in 1626? *(New Amsterdam)*

Writing a Report Have students write a two-page report about Dutch colonization of America. Encourage students to use library and Internet resources for their research. Tell students that the report should include at least one table, chart, graph, or other visual representation that supports the text of the report. **L2**

HISTORY *Online*

Objectives and answers to the student activity can be found in the **Web Activity Lesson Plan** at tav.glencoe.com.

History *and the* **Humanities**

American Art & Architecture: *Penn's Treaty With the Indians*

INTERDISCIPLINARY CONNECTIONS ACTIVITY

Language Arts Have students use library and Internet resources to locate the original text of the Mayflower Compact. Have students rewrite the document in their own words using correct spelling, punctuation, and grammar. Have students answer the following question: What provisions of the Mayflower Compact are still evident in the political and social structure of the United States? **L2**

75

Reading Check

Answer: Unlike other English colonies, Pennsylvania would allow settlers complete political and religious freedom. William Penn also resolved to win the friendship of the Native Americans who lived in Pennsylvania.

Geography *Skills*

Answers:

1. Georgia, South Carolina, North Carolina, Virginia, Maryland
2. Appalachian Mountains

Geography Skills Practice
Ask: What was the southern boundary of these colonies?
(Altamaha River)

3 ASSESS

Assign Section 4 Assessment as homework or as an in-class activity.

🔘 Have students use the **Interactive Tutor Self-Assessment CD-ROM.**

Reading Essentials and Study Guide 2–4

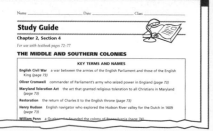

Name _____ Date _____ Class _____

Study Guide

Chapter 2, Section 4

For use with textbook pages 72–77

THE MIDDLE AND SOUTHERN COLONIES

KEY TERMS AND NAMES

English Civil War a war between the armies of the English Parliament and those of the English King *(page 73)*

Oliver Cromwell commander of Parliament's army who seized power in England *(page 73)*

Maryland Toleration Act the act that granted religious toleration to all Christians in Maryland *(page 73)*

Restoration the return of Charles II to the English throne *(page 73)*

Henry Hudson English navigator who explored the Hudson River valley for the Dutch in 1609 *(page 73)*

William Penn a Quaker who founded the colony of Pennsylvania *(page 74)*

In 1682, as Penn began to build his colony, he bought three counties south of Pennsylvania from the Duke of York. These "lower counties" later became the colony of Delaware.

Reading Check **Evaluating** Why did William Penn regard Pennsylvania as a "holy experiment"?

New Southern Colonies

King Charles and his advisers were very interested in the land south of Virginia. The year before he granted New York to his brother James, Charles II awarded a vast territory south of Virginia to eight other friends and political allies. The land was named Carolina, from the Latin version of "Charles."

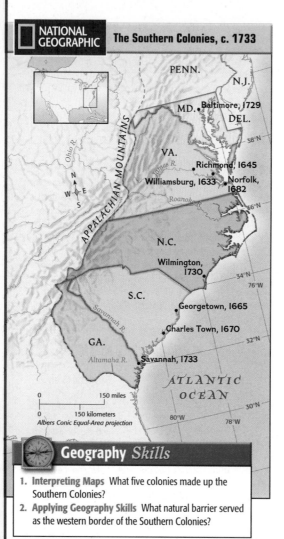

NATIONAL GEOGRAPHIC **The Southern Colonies, c. 1733**

PENN.
N.J.
MD. • Baltimore, 1729
DEL.
APPALACHIAN MOUNTAINS
Ohio R.
38°N
VA.
James R. • Richmond, 1645
Williamsburg, 1633 • Norfolk, 1682
Roanoke
36°N
N.C.
Wilmington, 1730
34°N
76°W
S.C.
Savannah R. • Georgetown, 1665
Charles Town, 1670
32°N
GA.
Altamaha R. • Savannah, 1733
ATLANTIC OCEAN
0   150 miles
0   150 kilometers
Albers Conic Equal-Area projection
80°W   78°W   30°N

Geography *Skills*

1. **Interpreting Maps** What five colonies made up the Southern Colonies?
2. **Applying Geography Skills** What natural barrier served as the western border of the Southern Colonies?

North Carolina From the beginning, Carolina developed as two separate regions. North Carolina was home to a small and scattered population. Most of the settlers were farmers who began drifting into the region from Virginia in the 1650s.

North Carolina did not have a good harbor, and the coastline, protected by the Outer Banks, was very hard for ships to reach. As a result, the colony grew very slowly, and by 1700 only 3,000 people lived in the region. Eventually North Carolina farmers began growing tobacco. They also began to export naval supplies such as tar, pitch, and turpentine.

South Carolina The proprietors who had been granted Carolina were never interested in the northern part of the colony. South Carolina, on the other hand, was believed to be suitable for growing sugarcane. The first settlers arrived in South Carolina in 1670. They named their settlement Charles Town (today called Charleston), after King Charles.

Sugarcane, it turned out, did not grow well in this region. The first product South Carolina exported in large quantity was deerskin, which had become popular for leather in England. The colony also began to capture Native Americans and ship them to the Caribbean, where the demand for enslaved workers was high.

The Georgia Experiment In the 1720s, General **James Oglethorpe,** a wealthy member of Parliament, was appalled to find that many people in England were in prison simply because they could not pay their debts. He asked King George II for a colony south of Carolina where the poor could start over.

The English government saw advantages to a new southern colony. It might help England's poor, and it would provide a strategic buffer between South Carolina and Spanish Florida. King George granted Oglethorpe and 19 other trustees permission in 1732 to settle a region between the Savannah and Altamaha Rivers. The new colony was named Georgia, in honor of the king. Oglethorpe led the first settlers to the mouth of the Savannah River in 1733.

The Georgia trustees banned slavery, rum, and brandy in the new colony and limited land grants to 500 acres. The colony attracted settlers from all over Europe, including Scots, Welsh, Germans, Swiss, Italians, and a few Portuguese Jews.

Increasingly the settlers objected to the colony's rules. In the 1740s, the trustees lifted restrictions on brandy, rum, and slavery; in 1750 they granted the settlers an elected assembly. In 1751 Georgia became a royal colony.

CRITICAL THINKING ACTIVITY

Analyzing Have students write an editorial supporting James Oglethorpe's point of view with regard to imprisonment of debtors. Encourage students to look at editorials in newspapers to see examples of editorials that support a point of view. **L2**

Comparing European Colonies in the Americas, c. 1700

Colony	Early Settlement	Population	Areas Where Concentrated	Political and Economic Organization	Economic Focus
Spanish					
	1490s–early 1500s	Between 5–7 million (including conquered Native Americans)	Mexico, Florida, Texas, Central America, the Caribbean, California, New Mexico, north and west coast of South America	Governors with strong links to Spain; large bureaucracy; *encomiendas* and haciendas	Gold, silver mining; ranching
English					
	1490s–early explorers; early 1600s–permanent settlements	250,000	Eastern seaboard of North America	Governors with weak links to English Crown; elected assemblies; small farms; plantations; private merchants	Trade and farming
French					
	1535–early explorers; 1670s–permanent settlements	15,000	St. Lawrence River; Louisiana territory; outposts on Great Lakes and Mississippi River	Strong governors; large estates	Exporting furs

Chart Skills

1. **Interpreting Charts** Which set of colonies had the narrowest economic focus? Explain your answer.
2. **Making Inferences** Which set of colonies seemed best equipped to settle the Americas most effectively?

England's American Colonies By 1775 England's colonies in North America were home to a growing population of roughly 2.5 million people. Despite the stumbling start in Jamestown, the English had succeeded in building a large and prosperous society on the east coast of North America. England's success, however, proved to be its own undoing. The English government had permitted new patterns of land ownership, new types of worship, and new kinds of government in its colonies. Once established, however, these practices became fixed principles. The colonists became used to self-government and gradually came to think of it as their right. Inadvertently, the English government had planted the seeds of rebellion and laid the foundation for what would eventually become the United States of America.

✓ **Reading Check** **Explaining** Why were South Carolina and Georgia settled?

SECTION 4 ASSESSMENT

Checking for Understanding
1. **Define:** pacifism.
2. **Identify:** English Civil War, Maryland Toleration Act, Restoration, William Penn, James Oglethorpe.

Reviewing Themes
3. **Global Connections** After the Restoration, why did the English government openly work to promote additional colonization in North America?

Critical Thinking
4. **Analyzing** How did the English Civil War affect the English colonies in America?
5. **Categorizing** Use a graphic organizer similar to the one below to list the reasons the colonies discussed in this section were founded.

Colony	Reasons Founded
New York	
New Jersey	
Pennsylvania	

Analyzing Visuals
6. **Analyzing Art** Study the painting of Oliver Cromwell on page 73. What events led to Cromwell's rise to power in England?

Writing About History
7. **Persuasive Writing** Imagine that you have been hired by the proprietors of New Jersey to persuade settlers to come there. Write an editorial for a newspaper in England to convince people to settle in New Jersey.

SECTION 4 ASSESSMENT ANSWERS

1. Terms are in blue.
2. English Civil War *(p. 73)*, Maryland Toleration Act *(p. 73)*, Restoration *(p. 73)*, William Penn *(p. 74)*, James Oglethorpe *(p. 76)*
3. because the colonies were valuable sources of raw materials and markets for manufactured goods
4. The English Civil War disrupted the founding of new colonies for approximately 20 years.
5. Students' organizers should include all of the colonies discussed in the section and list important reasons.
6. During the English Civil War, the king was put to death, then Parliament was dissolved. Cromwell then seized power.
7. Editorials should express opinions that reflect favorably on New Jersey.

Section Quiz 2–4

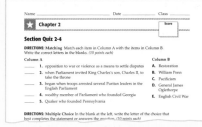

Chart Skills

Answer:
1. The French colonies focused solely on exporting furs.
2. the English colonies

Chart Skills Practice
Ask: Which colonies had the strongest links to their sponsoring country? *(Spanish colonies)*

Reteach
Ask students to identify the seven new colonies established after the English Civil War.

Enrich
Have students prepare a two-minute oral presentation about one of the colonies mentioned in this section.

✓ **Reading Check**

Answer: South Carolina: to grow sugar cane; Georgia: as a buffer against Spain

4 CLOSE

Ask students to explain the significance of the English Civil War with regard to the colonization of America.

TIME NOTEBOOK

TIME
NOTEBOOK

TEACH

Verbatim

Have students review the quotes in the Verbatim section and discuss each item as it relates to the people and themes found in their textbooks. Have students research a current social issue. Have them create a list of quotations about the issue along with a brief statement explaining the quote, identifying the person quoted, and how the quote relates to the issue. Ask students to share their lists in a class discussion.

Profile

Have students use library and Internet resources to identify the possible meaning of the letters *CRO*. Also have students identify the sign that John White had instructed the colonists to leave if they were being forcibly removed from the colony. Have students write a one-page summary of their research.

Visit the TIME Web site at www.time.com for up-to-date news, weekly magazine articles, editorials, online polls, and an archive of past magazine and Web articles.

BROWN BROTHERS

Profile

JOHN WHITE, *leader of the English settlers at Roanoke Island, returned to England for supplies in the colony's first year, leaving his family behind. With the war against Spain being fought at home, it was three years before he found passage back to Virginia. His ship was caught in a Nor'easter trying to reach the shore.*

At daybreak, we landed and we . . . proceeded to walk along the shore, rounding the northern part of the island, until we came to the place where we left our colony in the year 1586. . . . As we went inshore up the sandy bank we saw a tree on the brow of a cliff curiously carved with the clear Roman letters *CRO.*

We knew at once that these letters indicated the place to which the planters had gone. Before I left them we had agreed on a secret token. They were to write or carve on trees or doorposts the name of the place where they had settled. . . .

The weather grew fouler and fouler. Our food supply was diminishing, and we had lost our cask of fresh water. We therefore decided to go . . . visit our countrymen in Virginia on the return trip.

VERBATIM

"First, make thy will."
> ANONYMOUS,
> *opening of an "official" guide to voyagers to the Americas in the late sixteenth century*

"If I had thought you would insult my gods, I would not have shown them to you."
> AZTEC RULER MONTEZUMA TO CORTÉS,
> *after the Spanish erected a cross in one of his temples*

"[We] were entertained with all love and kindness, and with as much bounty, after their manner, as they could possibly devise. We found the people most gentle, loving and faithful, void of all guile and treason, and such as lived after the manner of the Golden Age."
> COMMANDER ARTHUR BARLOW,
> *describing the people of Roanoke Island*

"Once it happened that [the Spaniards] used 800 of the Indians instead of a team to draw their carriages, as if they had been mere beasts."
> BARTOLOMÉ DE LAS CASAS,
> *Spanish landowner and priest who argued against slavery and in favor of fairness for Native Americans in his book,* The Tears of the Indians

"Forced worship stinks in God's nostrils."
> ROGER WILLIAMS,
> *founder of Rhode Island, 1638*

IT'S THE LAW

JAMESTOWN, 1619. All colonists are required to attend two divine services every Sunday, and they must bring along "their pieces, swords, powder and shot."

PLYMOUTH, MASSACHUSETTS, 1639. The General Court of Massachusetts prohibits the drinking of toasts. "The common custom of drinking to one another is a mere useless ceremony and draweth on the abominable practice of drinking healths."

NEW AMSTERDAM, 1658. Governor Peter Stuyvesant has prohibited tennis during the time of divine services.

COOPERATIVE LEARNING ACTIVITY

Writing an Editorial Organize the class into small groups. Have each group research a law or ordinance in their local community with which they disagree. Have students learn why the law or ordinance was passed and who are its proponents and opponents. Then have the groups write an editorial to persuade lawmakers to change the law or ordinance. Encourage students to use information from their research in making their arguments. Have the groups present their letters to the class and have the class decide which letters should be sent to the local newspaper for possible publication.

Use the rubric for a cooperative group management plan on pages 81–82 in the *Performance Assessment Activities and Rubrics.*

Banned in Boston

Among the crimes for which colonists were punished in 1655 and 1656 were:

eavesdropping	pulling hair	drinking
scolding	profane dancing	tobacco smoking
neglect of work	uncharitableness	playing cards
meddling	bad grinding at a mill	delivering naughty speeches
pushing one's wife		

Milestones

FORMED, 1570. THE IROQUOIS LEAGUE, an alliance among the Cayuga, Oneida, Seneca, Mohawk, and Onandage tribes. The goal is to avoid war by settling differences in tribal councils. *Ohwichiras,* women heads of families, choose male delegates to the League.

INTRODUCED, 1630. THE FORK, by John Winthrop, who brought the utensil to America in a leather case with a bodkin (dagger) and knife. Queen Elizabeth made use of the fork popular in England despite the condemnation of the practice by many clergy.

MISSING, 1687. THE CONNECTICUT CHARTER, a document establishing greater self-governance for the colony. Its principles are opposed by Sir Edmund Andros, governor of the Dominion of New England, who demanded the charter be surrendered. When the Connecticut assembly reluctantly displayed the document, the candles mysteriously blew out, and the charter vanished. Informed sources hint it may be found in the hollow of an oak tree.

BETTMANN/CORBIS

SET SAIL, 1715. FIRST WHALING EXPEDITION from Nantucket, Massachusetts. Spurred on by the capture of the first sperm whale in 1711, the six sloops returned home with cargo yielding 600 barrels of oil and 11,000 pounds of bone.

CONSECRATED, 1730. FIRST JEWISH SYNAGOGUE, in New York. A group of Sephardic Jews who had fled the Inquisition in Portuguese Brazil established the congregation in New Amsterdam in 1655.

NUMBERS

10 million
Subjects of Montezuma II, the Aztec ruler in 1519

100 Rooms in Montezuma's palace

100 Baths in Montezuma's palace

200,000 Soldiers in Montezuma's army

550 Soldiers in the army of Hernán Cortés

1 year
Elapsed time between Cortés's arrival in Mexico and his conquest of the Aztec

25.2 million
Estimated population of Mexico in 1518

NORTH WIND PICTURES

Montezuma

CHAPTER 2 Colonizing America **79**

Portfolio Writing Project

Have students research the whaling industry in North America. Based on their research, have students prepare a research report that includes at least one graph, table, chart, or time line.

Comparing and Contrasting
Have students compare the purpose and structure of the Iroquois League with other confederations or leagues that formed in the Americas during the period of European exploration. Have students rate the effectiveness of each confederation or league researched.

CLOSE

Have students create a list of activities that they believe should be banned today. As students compare lists, discuss the difficulty in enforcing certain types of bans. For example, how could you prove someone is eavesdropping?

EXTENDING THE CONTENT

Sephardic Jews *Sefarad* is a Hebrew word meaning Spain. Originally, Sephardic Jews were Jews who came from Spain and Portugal. Today, however, the Sephardim include most Jews who are not Ashkenazim. The Ashkenazim are German, Eastern European, and Russian Jews. The largest difference between these two groups revolves around their traditions and languages. They also use different pronunciation guides for Hebrew.

Reviewing Key Terms

Students' answers will vary. The pages where the words appear in the text are shown in parentheses.

1. **conquistador** (p. 53)
2. **presidio** (p. 54)
3. **hidalgo** (p. 54)
4. **encomienda** (p. 54)
5. **hacienda** (p. 55)
6. **vaquero** (p. 55)
7. **Northwest Passage** (p. 55)
8. **coureurs de bois** (p. 56)
9. **Puritan** (p. 60)
10. **joint-stock company** (p. 61)
11. **privateer** (p. 61)
12. **burgesses** (p. 63)
13. **headright** (p. 64)
14. **proprietary colony** (p. 64)
15. **Separatist** (p. 66)
16. **Pilgrim** (p. 67)
17. **heretic** (p. 69)
18. **pacifism** (p. 75)

Reviewing Key Facts

19. Francisco Pizarro (p. 53), John Cabot (p. 58), Walter Raleigh (p. 61), William Bradford (p. 67), Squanto (p. 67), John Winthrop (p. 67), Roger Williams (p. 69), Anne Hutchinson (p. 69), Oliver Cromwell (p. 73), Henry Hudson (p. 73), William Penn (p. 74), James Oglethorpe (p. 76)

20. Their technologically superior weapons gave the Spanish the advantage they needed to defeat the Aztec and the Inca.

21. Social class in Spanish colonial society was determined by place of birth, income, and education.

Reviewing Key Terms
On a sheet of paper, use each of these terms in a sentence.

1. conquistador
2. presidio
3. *hidalgo*
4. *encomienda*
5. hacienda
6. vaquero
7. Northwest Passage
8. coureurs de bois
9. Puritan
10. joint-stock company
11. privateer
12. burgesses
13. headright
14. proprietary colony
15. Separatist
16. Pilgrim
17. heretic
18. pacifism

Reviewing Key Facts

19. **Identify:** Francisco Pizarro, John Cabot, Walter Raleigh, William Bradford, Squanto, John Winthrop, Roger Williams, Anne Hutchinson, Oliver Cromwell, Henry Hudson, William Penn, James Oglethorpe.

20. Why were the Spanish able to defeat the Aztec and the Inca?

21. What factors determined social class in the Spanish colonies?

22. What was the purpose of the Council of the Indies?

23. What role did Bartolomé de Las Casas play in reforming Spain's policies toward Native Americans?

24. How did the French treat the Native Americans?

25. How did joint-stock companies help colonize North America?

26. How did tobacco save the Jamestown colony?

27. What caused Roger Williams to leave Massachusetts and found the town of Providence?

28. Why was Georgia founded?

Critical Thinking

29. **Analyzing Themes: Cultures and Traditions** How did the relationships between Native Americans and the Spanish differ from those between Native Americans and the French?

30. **Evaluating** How were England's royal colonies and proprietary colonies governed?

31. **Identifying Cause and Effect** How did the English Civil War affect the English colonies in North America?

Chapter Summary

French Colonies
- Established to expand fur trade
- Colonization effort grew slowly
- Population of New France increased by promotion of immigration
- Enslaved Africans imported to work plantations in Louisiana

British Colonies
- Established as places to earn profits and to practice religion freely
- Provided a place for the poor to start a new life
- Offered right to elect legislative assembly
- Used as sources of raw materials and markets for British goods

Spanish Colonies
- Established to gain wealth and spread Christianity and European culture
- Structured society based on birth, income, and education
- Economy dominated by mining and ranching

Dutch Colonies
- Founded to make money in fur trade
- Settlers from many countries populated New Netherland
- Need for laborers led to Dutch involvement in slave trade
- Territory eventually surrendered to Britain

Mercator projection

22. The Council of the Indies was created to help the king of Spain govern his vast empire.

23. Bartolomé de Las Casas raised European awareness of the mistreatment of Native Americans and interceded with the pope and the king of Spain on behalf of the Native Americans.

24. Rather than force the Native Americans to change their culture, the French lived and worked among them, learning the language and culture; some of the Frenchmen married Native American women.

25. Joint-stock companies pooled the money of multiple investors in order to raise large sums of money for large projects. This meant that English merchants could afford to trade with and colonize other parts of the world without government financing.

26. Tobacco provided Jamestown with a cash crop, ensuring the colony's value to England.

27. Roger Williams left Massachusetts because he believed the Puritans were corrupting themselves by continuing to be part of the Anglican Church.

32. Categorizing Use a graphic organizer like this one to list the reasons for English colonization in North America.

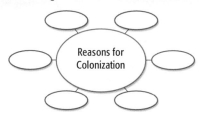

Reasons for Colonization

Practicing Skills

33. Understanding the Parts of a Map Study the map of the Great Migration on page 68. Then use the skills described on that page to answer the following questions.
   a. In what directions did English Puritans travel when they migrated to New England and to the Bahamas?
   b. Using the map labels, estimate the total number of Puritan immigrants to the New World between the 1620s and the 1640s.

Chapter Activity

34. American History Primary Source Document Library CD-ROM Read "The German Settlements in Pennsylvania" by Francis D. Pastorius, under *Colonial America.* Work with a small group of your classmates to draw a plan of Germantown based on Pastorius's description.

Writing Activity

35. Descriptive Writing The English colonies were founded for various reasons. New governments in each of these colonies offered incentives to new settlers. Pretend you have decided to move from England to America. Write a letter to your family and friends explaining why you have chosen to settle in a particular colony.

Geography and History

36. The map on this page shows English colonial settlements. Study the map and answer the questions below.
   a. Interpreting Maps Which colonies had the most territory by 1660?
   b. Applying Geography Skills Along which natural features had most of the colonies settled by 1700?

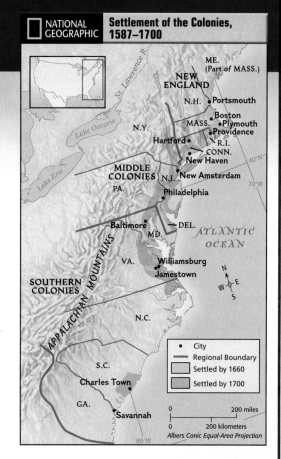

NATIONAL GEOGRAPHIC
Settlement of the Colonies, 1587–1700

ME. (Part of MASS.)
NEW ENGLAND
N.H. • Portsmouth
• Boston
MASS. • Plymouth
• Providence
N.Y. Hartford • • R.I.
• CONN.
• New Haven
MIDDLE COLONIES N.J. • New Amsterdam
PA.
• Philadelphia
• Baltimore
MD. — DEL.
ATLANTIC OCEAN
VA. • Williamsburg
• Jamestown
SOUTHERN COLONIES
N.C.
S.C.
• Charles Town
GA.
• Savannah

APPALACHIAN MOUNTAINS

• City
— Regional Boundary
☐ Settled by 1660
☐ Settled by 1700

0   200 miles
0   200 kilometers
Albers Conic Equal-Area Projection

The Princeton Review

Standardized Test Practice

Directions: Choose the best answer to the following question.

Which of the following is true about the early colonies of Jamestown and Plymouth?

A Both colonies were started by people interested in establishing a new nation.

B Food shortages caused loss of life in both colonies.

C The primary source of income for both colonies was tobacco.

D Both colonies were started by religious separatists.

Test-Taking Tip: The important word in this question is *and.* Look for an answer that applies to both colonies. For example, while it is true that the Pilgrims founded Plymouth Colony for religious reasons, the Jamestown founders were primarily looking for gold and adventure.

HISTORY
Online

Have students visit the Web site at tav.glencoe.com to review Chapter 2 and take the Self-Check Quiz.

Practicing Skills
33. a. southwest; **b.** 45,000

Chapter Activity
34. Students' plans will vary but should be based on the primary source.

Writing Activity
35. Students' answers will vary but should include an identification of the different social or political reasons a particular colony was founded and a correlation with the letter's author.

Geography and History
36. a. New England colonies; **b.** By 1700 most colonies had settled along rivers or harbors.

The Princeton Review

Standardized Test Practice

Answer: B
Test-Taking Tip: Since the question asks for the true statement, have students identify and eliminate any answers that they know are false. For example, the primary source of income for Jamestown was tobacco, but there is no evidence that the Pilgrims grew tobacco. Therefore, students can rule out C.

---

28. Georgia was founded as a way to reduce the prison population in England by allowing debtors to start over.

Critical Thinking

29. The relationship between Native Americans and the Spanish was antagonistic while the relationship between the Native Americans and the French was cooperative.

30. The king governed the royal colonies and the owners of proprietary colonies governed their own colonies.

31. The English Civil War forced the colonies to choose sides between the king and Parliament. The war limited trade and all but stopped the immigration of new settlers. The end of the war and the Restoration brought renewed efforts to colonize America.

32. Reasons for English colonial settlement in North America include: pursuing of religious freedom; providing debtors with a place to start over; searching for wealth; finding raw materials; and developing markets for manufactured goods.

Bonus Question ?

Ask: Why did the English wait almost 80 years to begin colonizing the Americas after John Cabot made his original expedition? *(The English government had little money and Cabot had found no wealth or gold.)*

Timesaving Tools

TeacherWorks™ All-In-One Planner and Resource Center

- **Interactive Teacher Edition** Access your Teacher Wraparound Edition and your classroom resources with a few easy clicks.
- **Interactive Lesson Planner** Planning has never been easier! Organize your week, month, semester, or year with all the lesson helps you need to make teaching creative, timely, and relevant.

Use Glencoe's **Presentation Plus!** multimedia teacher tool to easily present dynamic lessons that visually excite your students. Using Microsoft PowerPoint® you can customize the presentations to create your own personalized lessons.

TEACHING TRANSPARENCIES

Graphic Organizer 3

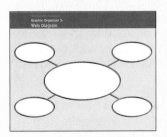

Why It Matters Chapter Transparency 3

APPLICATION AND ENRICHMENT

Linking Past and Present Activity 3

Enrichment Activity 3

Primary Source Reading 3

REVIEW AND REINFORCEMENT

Reteaching Activity 3

Vocabulary Activity 3

Time Line Activity 3

Critical Thinking Skills Activity 3

🌐 Meeting NCSS Standards

Local Standards

The following standards are highlighted in Chapter 3:

Section 1	III	People, Places, and Environments: E, G, H
Section 2	I	Culture: A, D
Section 3	IV	Individual Development and Identity: C, E, G
Section 4	IX	Global Connections: A, F

Chapter 3 Resources

ASSESSMENT AND EVALUATION

**Chapter 3 Test
Form A**

**Chapter 3 Test
Form B**

**Standardized Test Skills
Practice Workbook Activity 3**

**Performance Assessment
Activities and Rubrics 3**

**ExamView® Pro
Testmaker CD-ROM**

MULTIMEDIA

- **Vocabulary PuzzleMaker CD-ROM**
- **Interactive Tutor Self-Assessment CD-ROM**
- **ExamView® Pro Testmaker CD-ROM**
- **Audio Program**
- **American History Primary Source Documents Library CD-ROM**
- **MindJogger Videoquiz**
- **Presentation Plus! CD-ROM**
- **TeacherWorks™ CD-ROM**
- **Interactive Student Edition CD-ROM**
- **Glencoe Skillbuilder Interactive Workbook CD-ROM, Level 2**
- **The *American Vision* Video Program**
- **American Music: Hits Through History**
- **American Music: Cultural Traditions**

SPANISH RESOURCES

The following Spanish language materials are available in the Spanish Resources Binder:

- **Spanish Guided Reading Activities**
- **Spanish Reteaching Activities**
- **Spanish Quizzes and Tests**
- **Spanish Vocabulary Activities**
- **Spanish Summaries**
- **The Declaration of Independence and United States Constitution Spanish Translation**

THE HISTORY CHANNEL.

The following videotape program is available from Glencoe as a supplement to Chapter 3:

- **Benjamin Franklin: Citizen of the World** (ISBN 1-56-501426-X)

To order, call Glencoe at 1-800-334-7344. To find classroom resources to accompany many of these videos, check the following home pages:
A&E Television: www.aande.com
The History Channel: www.historychannel.com

Use our Web site for additional resources. All essential content is covered in the Student Edition.

You and your students can visit tav.glencoe.com, the Web site companion to the ***American Vision.*** This innovative integration of electronic and print media offers your students a wealth of opportunities. The student text directs students to the Web site for the following options:

- **Chapter Overviews**   • **Student Web Activities**
- **Self-Check Quizzes**   • **Textbook Updates**

Answers to the student Web activities are provided for you in the **Web Activity Lesson Plans.** Additional Web resources and Interactive Tutor Puzzles are also available.

SECTION RESOURCES

Daily Objectives	Reproducible Resources	Multimedia Resources
SECTION 1 **The Southern Colonies** 1. Describe the Southern economy and the plantation system. 2. Outline the development of slavery in the South.	Reproducible Lesson Plan 3–1 Daily Lecture and Discussion Notes 3–1 Guided Reading Activity 3–1* Section Quiz 3–1* Reading Essentials and Study Guide 3–1 Performance Assessment Activities and Rubrics	Daily Focus Skills Transparency 3–1 Interactive Tutor Self-Assessment CD-ROM ExamView® Pro Testmaker CD-ROM Presentation Plus! CD-ROM TeacherWorks™ CD-ROM Audio Program
SECTION 2 **New England and the Middle Colonies** 1. List the geographical conditions that determined the economy of the New England Colonies. 2. Summarize how life in the Middle Colonies differed from life in the New England Colonies.	Reproducible Lesson Plan 3–2 Daily Lecture and Discussion Notes 3–2 Guided Reading Activity 3–2* Section Quiz 3–2* Reading Essentials and Study Guide 3–2 Performance Assessment Activities and Rubrics	Daily Focus Skills Transparency 3–2 Interactive Tutor Self-Assessment CD-ROM ExamView® Pro Testmaker CD-ROM Presentation Plus! CD-ROM TeacherWorks™ CD-ROM Audio Program American Music: Hits Through History
SECTION 3 **The Imperial System** 1. Describe mercantilism and its effect on the relationship between the colonies and England. 2. Explain how the Glorious Revolution in England affected the colonies.	Reproducible Lesson Plan 3–3 Daily Lecture and Discussion Notes 3–3 Guided Reading Activity 3–3* Section Quiz 3–3* Reading Essentials and Study Guide 3–3 Performance Assessment Activities and Rubrics	Daily Focus Skills Transparency 3–3 Interactive Tutor Self-Assessment CD-ROM ExamView® Pro Testmaker CD-ROM Presentation Plus! CD-ROM Skillbuilder Interactive Workbook, Level 2 TeacherWorks™ CD-ROM Audio Program
SECTION 4 **A Diverse Society** 1. Summarize the plight of enslaved Africans and explain their methods of resistance. 2. Explain how the Enlightenment and the Great Awakening affected the colonies.	Reproducible Lesson Plan 3–4 Daily Lecture and Discussion Notes 3–4 Guided Reading Activity 3–4* Section Quiz 3–4* Reading Essentials and Study Guide 3–4 Performance Assessment Activities and Rubrics	Daily Focus Skills Transparency 3–4 Interactive Tutor Self-Assessment CD-ROM ExamView® Pro Testmaker CD-ROM Presentation Plus! CD-ROM TeacherWorks™ CD-ROM Vocabulary PuzzleMaker CD-ROM Audio Program

0:00 OUT OF TIME?
Assign the Chapter 3 **Reading Essentials and Study Guide.**

*Also Available in Spanish

 Blackline Master    Transparency   CD-ROM   DVD

Poster   Music Program   Audio Program   Videocassette

NATIONAL GEOGRAPHIC Teacher's Corner

INDEX TO NATIONAL GEOGRAPHIC MAGAZINE

The following articles relate to this chapter.

- "The Cruelest Commerce: African Slave Trade," September 1992
- "David Thompson," May 1996
- "Portugal's Sea Road to the East," November 1992
- "Treasure from the Silver Bank," July 1996

NATIONAL GEOGRAPHIC SOCIETY PRODUCTS AVAILABLE FROM GLENCOE

To order the following products for use with this chapter, contact your local Glencoe sales representative, or call Glencoe at 1-800-334-7344:

- *PicturePack: Colonial America* (Transparencies)
- *PictureShow: Colonial America* (CD-ROM)

ADDITIONAL NATIONAL GEOGRAPHIC SOCIETY PRODUCTS

To order the following, call National Geographic at 1-800-368-2728:

- *Millennium in Maps Series: Colonization and Trade in the Americas*

NGS ONLINE

Access National Geographic's Web site for current events, atlas updates, activities, links, interactive features, and archives.
www.nationalgeographic.com

From the Classroom of...

Erin Barrett
Lexington High School
Lexington, MA

Enlightenment Thinkers

Ask students to come up with a list of grievances about the school. With the students, weed out any illegal issues or silly grievances. Combine similar complaints into one.

Then ask the class to agree on one issue that needs to be changed. Allow for ample time for them to debate and discuss together. Tell them that the issue they agree on must be within the control of the principal to change. Once they agree on an issue, work through the process of their choosing a representative to take the issue to the school principal.

Next create a hypothetical scenario in which the student representatives present their issue calmly and thoroughly, but the principal disdainfully dismisses their complaints. Explain that their feelings of being unfairly dismissed stem from their living in a country that is built on Enlightenment principles. Discuss those principles.

ADDITIONAL RESOURCES FROM GLENCOE

- American Music: Cultural Traditions
- American Art & Architecture
- Outline Map Resource Book
- U.S. Desk Map
- Building Geography Skills for Life
- Inclusion for the High School Social Studies Classroom Strategies and Activities
- Teaching Strategies for the American History Classroom (Including Block Scheduling Pacing Guides)

KEY TO ABILITY LEVELS

Teaching strategies have been coded.

L1 BASIC activities for all students

L2 AVERAGE activities for average to above-average students

L3 CHALLENGING activities for above-average students

ELL ENGLISH LANGUAGE LEARNER activities

 Block Schedule

Activities that are suited to use within the block scheduling framework are identified by:

✓ **Performance Assessment**

Refer to Activity 3 in the Performance Assessment Activities and Rubrics booklet.

W*hy It Matters Activity*

Ask students why commerce took hold in the North and not in the South. Students should evaluate their answers after they have completed the chapter.

GLENCOE
TECHNOLOGY

The *American Vision* Video Program

To learn more about America from 1607 to 1763, have students view the Chapter 3 video, "The Middle Passage," from the ***American Vision* Video Program.**

Available in DVD and VHS

MindJogger Videoquiz

Use the **MindJogger Videoquiz** to preview Chapter 3 content.

Available in VHS

82

CHAPTER

3 Colonial Ways of Life *1607–1763*

Why It Matters

An agricultural society developed in the American colonies. In the South, a large number of Africans were enslaved for plantation labor. In the North, commerce took hold, and England's trade policies proved cause for concern. High birth rates and immigration expanded the population as American society began to take shape.

The Impact Today

Key developments in this period have influenced American society.
- *The northern United States is still more urban than much of the South.*
- *The United States remains a nation made up of immigrants from many countries.*

The American Vision Video *The Chapter 3 video, "The Middle Passage," chronicles the journey enslaved Africans endured when they were forcibly brought to the colonies.*

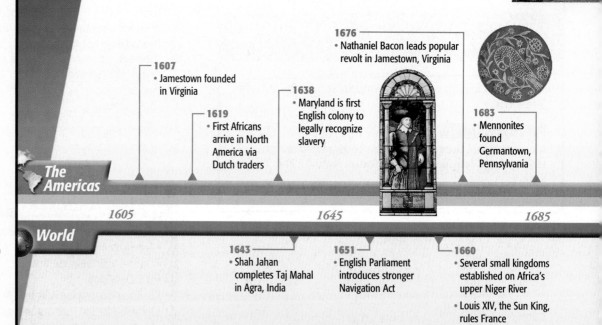

The Americas

1607
- Jamestown founded in Virginia

1619
- First Africans arrive in North America via Dutch traders

1638
- Maryland is first English colony to legally recognize slavery

1676
- Nathaniel Bacon leads popular revolt in Jamestown, Virginia

1683
- Mennonites found Germantown, Pennsylvania

1605   *1645*   *1685*

World

1643
- Shah Jahan completes Taj Mahal in Agra, India

1651
- English Parliament introduces stronger Navigation Act

1660
- Several small kingdoms established on Africa's upper Niger River
- Louis XIV, the Sun King, rules France

82

TWO-MINUTE LESSON LAUNCHER

For many people the image of colonial America is centered around the New England Colonies in the period immediately preceding the American Revolution. Ask students to share their ideas about life in colonial America. Remind students that the colonial period lasted more than 150 years. Also point out that the colonies stretched along the Atlantic coastline and included more than the colonies in New England.

HISTORY
Online

Introduce students to chapter content and key terms by having them access the **Chapter 3 Overview** at tav.glencoe.com.

Colonial Wedding by Edward Lamson Henry, 1911

More About the Art

Ask students to compare and contrast the scene pictured with modern wedding events. *(Students may point out differences in dress and manner of transportation. Similarities may include people coming to wish the couple well and the festive nature of the occasion.)* Point out that the painter, Edward Lamson Henry, lived from 1841 to 1919, long after the event depicted. He is best known for his paintings of American colonial life, but he also painted wedding scenes from other eras.

1686
• Dominion of New England established

1734
• Libel trial of newspaper publisher John Peter Zenger helps establish free press tradition

1692
• Salem witchcraft trials begin

1705
• Virginia's slave code formally regulates slavery

1727
• Coffee first planted in Brazil

1763
• French and Indian War ends in North America

1725

1765

HISTORY
Online

Chapter Overview
Visit the *American Vision* Web site at tav.glencoe.com and click on *Chapter Overviews—Chapter 3* to preview chapter information.

1688
• Power of English king restricted as Parliament awards William and Mary the throne in Glorious Revolution

1725
• Russian czar Peter the Great dies

1707
• Act of Union creates United Kingdom

1742
• Handel's "Messiah" debuts in Dublin, Ireland

TIME LINE ACTIVITY

Have students create a time line that incorporates the Americas portion of the chapter time line and all the events shown on the section time lines on pages 84, 91, 98, and 104.

83

GRAPHIC ORGANIZER ACTIVITY

Organizing Information Have students use a graphic organizer similar to the one at right to identify world events and movements that contributed to the development of the American colonies.

A. *The Enlightenment*
B. *European population explosion (wheat boom)*
C. *Glorious Revolution*
D. *Great Awakening*
E. *Mercantilism*
F. *Religious intolerance*

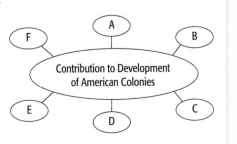

83

1 FOCUS

Section Overview

This section focuses on the development of an agricultural economy in the Southern Colonies.

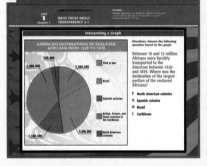
Guide to Reading

Answers to Graphic: From top to bottom, the social order of Southern society included: the planter elite, backcountry farmers, landless tenant farmers, servants, and enslaved Africans.

Preteaching Vocabulary
Have students write a paragraph using at least four of the Key Terms and Names.

SECTION 1 The Southern Colonies

Guide to Reading

Main Idea
The Southern Colonies developed labor-intensive agricultural economies that relied heavily upon enslaved labor.

Key Terms and Names
cash crop, plantation, indentured servant, Eliza Lucas, gentry, subsistence farming, William Berkeley, Royal African Company, Middle Passage, slave code

Reading Strategy
Organizing As you read about the development of Southern society, complete a graphic organizer similar to the one shown here describing the social order in the South.

Planter Elite

Reading Objectives
• **Describe** the Southern economy and the plantation system.
• **Outline** the development of slavery in the South.

Section Theme
Geography and History Patterns of land use affected the history of Virginia's colonial government.

Preview of Events

♦1620	♦1660	♦1700	♦1740
1619 First Africans arrive in North America	**1676** Bacon's Rebellion	**1705** Virginia creates slave code	**1740s** Indigo first cultivated in South Carolina

★ An American Story ★

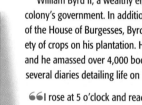

William Byrd's Westover plantation

William Byrd II, a wealthy eighteenth-century Virginia planter, played a central role in his colony's government. In addition to serving as colonel of the county militia and as a member of the House of Burgesses, Byrd founded the city of Richmond and experimented with a variety of crops on his plantation. His wealth gave him the leisure to pursue cultural interests, and he amassed over 4,000 books—the biggest private library in the colonies. He left behind several diaries detailing life on Southern plantations. On January 27, 1711, he noted:

❝I rose at 5 o'clock and read two chapters in Hebrew and some Greek in Lucian. I said my prayers and ate boiled milk for breakfast. . . . I settled several accounts; then I read some English which gave me great light into the nature of spirit. . . . In the afternoon my wife and I took a little walk and then danced together. Then I read some more English. At night I read some Italian and then played at piquet [a card game] with my wife. . . . I said my prayers and had good health, good thoughts, and good humor, thank God Almighty.❞

—quoted in *The Growth of the American Republic*

The Southern Economy

The wealth of Westover, Byrd's plantation, was built in large part on the labor of enslaved Africans. In Byrd's Virginia, a class of wealthy planters stood on society's top rung, while enslaved Africans were at the bottom. In between were many farmers who owned small farms and held few or no slaves.

From the earliest days of settlement, the Southern Colonies developed an economy based on commercial agriculture. A few years after the founding of Jamestown, tobacco

---

SECTION RESOURCES

📂 **Reproducible Masters**
• Reproducible Lesson Plan 3–1
• Daily Lecture and Discussion Notes 3–1
• Guided Reading Activity 3–1
• Section Quiz 3–1
• Reading Essentials and Study Guide 3–1
• Performance Assessment Activities and Rubrics

🔖 **Transparencies**
• Daily Focus Skills Transparency 3–1

Multimedia
🖸 Interactive Tutor Self-Assessment CD-ROM
🖸 ExamView® Pro Testmaker CD-ROM
🖸 Presentation Plus! CD-ROM
🖸 TeacherWorks™ CD-ROM
🎧 Audio Program

became the South's first successful cash crop, or crop grown primarily for market. Tobacco became the main cash crop grown in Virginia and Maryland and, to a lesser extent, North Carolina. Rice and indigo became the main cash crops in South Carolina. These cash crops needed the right kind of climate and techniques to be cultivated. These requirements led to the rise of plantations, or large commercial estates where many laborers lived on the land and cultivated the crops for the landowner.

GEOGRAPHY

Tobacco and the Chesapeake Between 1620 and 1660, the demand for tobacco in Europe was greater than the supply. This kept the price high, ensuring that most tobacco planters could make money even if they grew only a small amount. Those who could grow and harvest a large quantity of tobacco could become wealthy.

Growing tobacco required intensive manual labor. Each plant had to be carefully nurtured before being cut and hung up to cure. After curing, the leaves were packed into hogsheads—huge wooden barrels—that, once filled and sealed, often weighed close to 1,000 pounds (454 kg). The amount of labor needed to grow tobacco meant that to become wealthy, a tobacco farmer needed a large work force to cultivate a large crop.

The geography of the Chesapeake Bay region was perfectly suited to tobacco farming. The bay acted like a wide road. Numerous inlets and navigable rivers connected to the bay. If tobacco farmers located their farms next to a river, they could ship their crop from their own wharves. The colonists built very few roads or towns because they had no need to move goods overland. Instead, merchant ships made their way up the rivers from farm to farm, picking up tobacco and selling supplies.

Daily Lecture and Discussion Notes 3–1

Discussing a Concept Lead students in a discussion of supply and demand. Have students explain how supply and demand influence price. Ask them to give examples from their own experience. Then discuss how fluctuations in the prices of crops affected the economy of the Southern Colonies.
L1

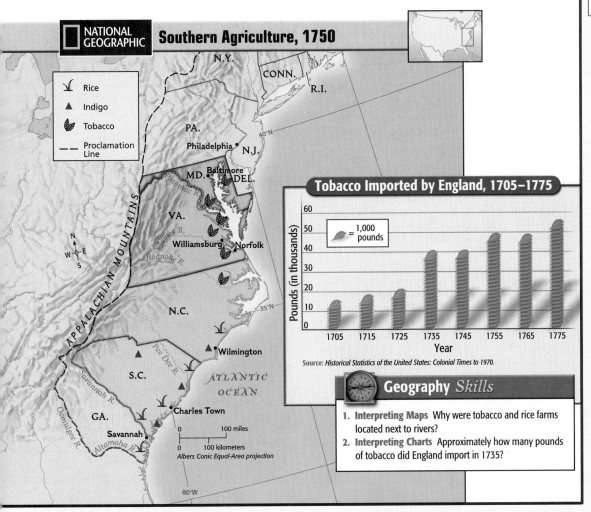

Southern Agriculture, 1750

Rice
Indigo
Tobacco
Proclamation Line

Tobacco Imported by England, 1705–1775

 = 1,000 pounds

Source: Historical Statistics of the United States: Colonial Times to 1970.

Geography Skills

1. **Interpreting Maps** Why were tobacco and rice farms located next to rivers?
2. **Interpreting Charts** Approximately how many pounds of tobacco did England import in 1735?

Geography Skills

Answers:
1. to provide water for irrigation and transportation
2. 40,000 pounds

Geography Skills Practice
Ask: Which colony produced rice, indigo, and tobacco? *(North Carolina)*

Making Contracts The contract of an indentured servant was indented (folded) and torn along the indenture. Each party to the contract kept half.

COOPERATIVE LEARNING ACTIVITY

Building a Model Plantations in the Southern Colonies functioned as self-contained communities. Have students work in small groups to build a model of a typical plantation in the late 1600s. Encourage students to use library and Internet resources to learn about plantations including the types of buildings, the layout of the plantations, and the structures that were typically built on a plantation. Display models in the classroom.

Use the rubric for a cooperative group management plan on pages 81–82 in the *Performance Assessment Activities and Rubrics.*

History *Through Art*

Answer: The cash crops of the South required the right kind of conditions and techniques to be cultivated. As large landowners gained more land and many laborers on their estates, plantations came into being.

Ask: What differences do you note between the family home and the support houses? *(Students should note differences in size and style.)*

✓ Reading Check

Answer: Early settlers did not know how to properly harvest the crop.

Writing an Advertisement

Have students write an advertisement for recruiting indentured servants. The advertisement should include information about what the landowner is willing to provide, what the servant must agree to do, and the length of service required. **L2**

📁 Use the rubric for a magazine/newspaper/Web site article or help-wanted ad on pages 85–86 in the *Performance Assessment Activities and Rubrics.*

🖋 History *Through Art*

The Ideal Plantation This painting depicts the well-structured plantation as a world unto itself. Centered around the family home, the plantation's fields, support houses, and merchant ships unite to serve the needs of the plantation. Why did plantations develop in the South?

Indentured Servants In the early days of Virginia and Maryland, there was plenty of land for tobacco farmers but not enough labor to work it. England had the opposite problem. Many poor tenant farmers had been forced off the land during the enclosure movement, creating high unemployment and a large number of people willing to sell their labor for a chance to come to America and acquire their own land. To pay for their passage, these people agreed to become indentured servants.

In this system, colonists in America agreed to pay the cost of transporting the servants to the colonies and promised to provide food, clothing, and shelter to them until their indentures, or labor contracts, expired. In exchange, the servants agreed to work for the owner of their contract for a specific number of years. These contracts usually specified four years, but some were for seven years or even more if the indentured servant arrived as a child.

For much of the 1600s, indentured servitude was a very good system for tobacco planters. Indentured servants could produce five times the price of their contracts in tobacco in the first year alone. Under the headright system, every indentured servant transported to America also earned the landowner another 50 acres of land. As large numbers of indentured servants arrived in Virginia and Maryland, tobacco production rose steadily.

Rice and Indigo in South Carolina South of Virginia, the proprietors of South Carolina had hoped their colony's warm climate would permit the cultivation of sugarcane as a cash crop. When sugarcane failed, the settlers also tried and failed to cultivate rice. This venture also failed, because the settlers did not know how to properly harvest rice. In addition, the extreme humidity, swamps, mosquitoes, and muddy fields of the lowlands where rice had to be planted discouraged cultivation.

In the 1690s, a new type of rice was introduced, and the planters—many of whom had come from Barbados and Jamaica where slavery was common—decided to import enslaved Africans to cultivate it. West Africans had cultivated rice for centuries. Although their techniques were very labor-intensive, they knew how to harvest rice and remove the hull. Rice rapidly became a major cash crop in South Carolina and, to a lesser extent, in Georgia.

In the early 1740s, South Carolina began to develop another cash crop called indigo. Indigo was used to make blue dye for cloth—a dye much in demand in Europe. Previously, planters in South Carolina had tried to grow indigo without much success. Then, in the early 1740s, 17-year-old **Eliza Lucas,** began experimenting with the plant. Lucas discovered that indigo needed high ground and sandy soil, not the wetlands that suited rice.

Indigo was a good second crop for the rice plantations. It could be grown on land unsuitable for rice, and it required care and harvesting only in seasons when the enslaved workers were not busy with rice.

✓ Reading Check ▶ **Describing** Why did attempts to grow rice in South Carolina fail at first?

Southern Society

Although many immigrants to the Southern Colonies hoped to become wealthy, very few did. The nature of the plantation system tended to create a society with distinct social classes. Planters who could afford to bring in many slaves or indentured servants received much larger land grants. With their large labor force and land area, they could produce a much larger crop. The money they earned enabled them to acquire still more workers and to extend their estates up and down the rivers of a region. The result was a society where a wealthy elite controlled most of the land and relied upon the labor of others to work it for them.

The Planter Elite The wealthy landowners, sometimes referred to as the Southern gentry or the planter elite, enjoyed enormous economic and political influence. They represented their communities in the governing councils and assemblies, commanded the local militias, and served as county judges.

MEETING SPECIAL NEEDS

Auditory Divide this section of the chapter into four parts using the primary headings as a guide. Assign each section to at least one student. Have students read their section and become familiar with the content. Invite students to present an oral summary of their section to the class. **L1**

📁 Refer to *Inclusion for the High School Social Studies Classroom Strategies and Activities* in the TCR.

With few towns or roads in the region, the plantations of the Southern gentry had to function as self-contained communities. The residents lived near each other in a group of buildings, including the planter's great house, stables and barns, and the workers' cabins. Plantations often had other facilities such as schools and chapels, and workshops for blacksmiths, carpenters, weavers, coopers (barrel makers), and leather workers.

In the 1600s, most plantations were small, rough estates. In many cases, they were little more than stump-filled clearings where the planters and their indentured servants worked side-by-side under very difficult conditions. Many became sick and died. Even in the late 1600s, plantation workforces rarely exceeded 30 people. The great houses on most of these early plantations were small, with only four to seven rooms.

In the early 1700s, as wealthier planters in Virginia and Maryland switched from indentured to slave labor, the size of their plantations began to grow. As their wealth and property increased, the gentry began to build large brick mansions with imposing steps and doorways and elaborate gardens. They also tried to copy the fashions and lifestyle of England's upper class. No longer did they labor in the fields with their workers. Instead, the gentry hired overseers to manage the enslaved Africans, while they looked after accounts and other business matters on the plantation.

As the wealth of the planter elite increased, so too did their leisure time. The gentry often amused themselves by hunting and fishing, and by gambling on horse races, cards, and dice. Some, like William Byrd, enjoyed intellectual pursuits such as reading or practicing music.

Backcountry Farmers Close to half the indentured servants who came to the Chesapeake region in the 1600s died before gaining their freedom. Of those who became free, less than half acquired their own land. Although land itself was very easy to acquire, settlers had to pay for the deed and land survey and also had to pay for tools, seeds, and livestock. Many could not afford these costs, and instead they became tenant farmers, working lands that they rented from the planter elite.

Despite such difficulties, some former indentured servants did acquire their own land. Although wealthy planters owned most of the land along the rivers, most landowners in the colonial South were actually small farmers living in the "backcountry" farther inland. These farmers are sometimes referred to as **yeomen,** to distinguish them from the gentry.

The backcountry farmers worked small plots of land and lived in tiny one- or two-room houses with few furnishings. Although these farmers grew some tobacco, they also practiced subsistence farming, or farming only enough crops to feed their own families. Subsistence crops included corn, beans, potatoes, barley, and rye. Hogs and other livestock were allowed to run wild until needed for meat.

By the 1670s, the colonial South was a sharply divided society, with a small group of wealthy planters at the top and many poor backcountry farmers, landless tenant farmers, servants, and enslaved Africans at the bottom. Eventually, this uneven distribution of wealth and power led to rebellion.

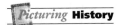 **Reading Check** **Discussing** What led to the rise of the planter elite in colonial Southern society?

Bacon's Rebellion

By the 1660s, wealthy planters led by the governor, **Sir William Berkeley,** dominated Virginia's society. Berkeley controlled the legislature through his

Picturing **History**

Bacon's Rebellion This uprising pitted backcountry farmers against Virginia's ruling gentry. Was Nathaniel Bacon a backcountry farmer? How would you describe his depiction in this engraving?

CHAPTER 3 Colonial Ways of Life **87**

Objectives and answers to the student activity can be found in the **Web Activity Lesson Plan** at tav.glencoe.com.

Writing an Article Have students imagine that they are reporters for an English magazine. Ask them to write an informative article for the magazine explaining the causes and results of Bacon's Rebellion. Tell them to be sure to include enough information that readers in England will clearly understand the situation in Virginia. Encourage students to share their articles with the rest of the class. **L2**

Use the rubric for a magazine/newspaper/Web site article or help-wanted ad on pages 85–86 in the *Performance Assessment Activities and Rubrics.*

Before Nathaniel Bacon's sudden death, he burned the estates of his rivals and controlled most of Virginia.

Student Web Activity Visit the *American Vision* Web site at tav.glencoe.com and click on *Student Web Activities— Chapter 3* for an activity on the colonial life of the English settlers.

appointments to the colony's governing council and gifts of land to members of the House of Burgesses.

Once Governor Berkeley had assembled a majority of supporters in the House of Burgesses, he exempted himself and his councilors from taxation. Convinced that voting should be reserved for the wealthy, Berkeley also arranged for the House of Burgesses to restrict the vote to people who owned property, cutting the number of voters in Virginia in half. All of these developments angered the backcountry and tenant farmers. Ultimately, however, it was the governor's Native American policies that sparked a revolt.

Crisis Over Land The most important issue for most Virginia colonists in the 1600s was their ability to acquire land. Many indentured servants and tenant farmers wanted to own their own farms eventually. Backcountry farmers who already owned a few acres wanted to expand their holdings. By the 1670s, the only land left was in the backcountry in territory Native Americans claimed.

Most wealthy planters lived near the coast in the region known as the **Tidewater.** They had no interest in the backcountry and did not want to endanger their plantations by risking war with the Native Americans. Therefore, they opposed expanding the colony into Native American lands. This stand angered the backcountry farmers.

In 1675 war erupted between backcountry settlers and the Susquehannock people of the region. Governor Berkeley tried to calm things down. He refused to sanction any further military action against the Native Americans. Instead he asked the House of Burgesses for money to build new forts along the frontier—the westernmost point of colonial settlement.

Nathaniel Bacon Leads a Revolt In April 1676, a group of backcountry farmers met to discuss the situation. At the meeting was a well-to-do planter named Nathaniel Bacon, who had recently purchased a large tract of land near the frontier. Although he was a member of the governor's council, Bacon took up the cause of the backcountry farmers. Native Americans had recently attacked his plantation, and he wanted to do something.

Bacon organized his own militia and attacked the Native Americans. Governor Berkeley decided to call new elections. He needed an assembly supported by the voters to calm the situation. The newly elected House of Burgesses authorized Bacon to raise a force

African Culture Crosses the Ocean: A Woman's Song

On a steamy March day in 1997, in the tiny town of Senehun Ngola in Sierra Leone, West Africa, Mary Moran, an African American from Georgia, first met Baindu Jabati, a Sierra Leonean. The two women had something amazing in common: a song each woman had known all her life.

In an emotional meeting, Moran and Jabati shared the song that the female ancestors of each of them had passed down for more than 200 years. Although the melody of the American version had changed, the words of this song in the Mende language of Sierra Leone probably came to America's South on the slave ships that sailed from West Africa in the 1700s.

Mary Moran (center) at a Sierra Leone market

The women in Mary Moran's family had passed the song down through the generations. Over time, the true origin of the song was lost. Although she had sung the song all her life, Moran never knew what its words meant. She imagined that it was an old African song.

Wanting to trace her family's history, Moran consulted with ethnomusicologists, who study folk music. Moran discovered that her family's song came from southern Sierra Leone and that it was traditionally sung at funerals. Jabati, who had inherited the traditional duty to sing at funerals, said that meeting Moran would have been better only if her ancestors could have been there also for the joyous occasion.

CRITICAL THINKING ACTIVITY

Comparing To help students understand the significance of geography and economics in history, have them focus their attention on agriculture in the Southern Colonies. Have students create a table to compare and contrast commercial agriculture and subsistence farming. The table should include information about crops, land use, transportation, and labor. **L2**

of 1,000 troops to attack the Native Americans. The assembly then restored the vote to all free men and took away the tax exemptions Berkeley had granted to his supporters.

Despite these reforms, Bacon was not satisfied. In July 1676 he returned to Jamestown with several hundred armed men and seized power, charging Berkeley with corruption. Berkeley fled Jamestown and raised his own army. The two sides battled until October 1676, when Bacon, hiding in a swamp, became sick and died. Without his leadership, his army rapidly disintegrated.

Slavery Increases in Virginia Bacon's Rebellion convinced many wealthy planters that the best way to keep Virginian society stable was to have land available for the backcountry farmers. From the 1680s onward, Virginia's government generally supported expanding the colony westward, regardless of the impact on Native Americans.

Bacon's Rebellion also accelerated an existing trend in Virginia—the use of enslaved Africans instead of indentured servants to work the fields. In the 1680s, after the rebellion, the number of Africans brought to the colony increased dramatically.

Planters began to switch to enslaved Africans for several reasons. Enslaved workers, unlike indentured servants, did not have to be freed and therefore would never need their own land. In addition, when

cheap land became available in the 1680s in the new colony of Pennsylvania, fewer English settlers were willing to become indentured servants.

At the same time, the English government adopted policies that encouraged slavery. English law limited trade between the English colonies and other countries. Before the 1670s, if settlers wanted to acquire enslaved Africans, they had to buy them from the Dutch or Portuguese, which was difficult to arrange. In 1672, however, King Charles II granted a charter to the **Royal African Company** to engage in the slave trade. With an English company in the slave trade, it became much easier to acquire enslaved people.

✓ Reading Check **Examining** What government policies caused some backcountry farmers to rebel?

Slavery in the Colonies

For enslaved Africans, the voyage to America usually began with a march to a European fort on the West African coast. Tied together with ropes around their necks and hands, they were traded to Europeans, branded, and forced aboard a ship. Historians estimate that between 10 and 12 million Africans were forcibly transported to the Americas between 1450 and 1870. Of those 10 to 12 million, roughly 2 million died at sea.

Olaudah Equiano, also known as Gustavus Vassa, was kidnapped from his West African home by other Africans in the 1760s. He was then traded to Europeans and shipped to America. Years later, after winning his freedom, he wrote a memoir. In it, he described the terrible journey across the Atlantic, known to Europeans as the Middle Passage:

> ❝At last, when the ship we were in had got in all her cargo, . . . we were all put under deck. . . . The closeness of the place, and heat of the climate, added to the number in the ship, which was so crowded that each had scarcely room to turn himself, almost suffocated us. . . . [This] brought on a sickness among the slaves, of which many died. . . . The shrieks of the women, and the groans of the dying, rendered the whole scene of horror almost inconceivable. . . .❞
>
> —from *The Interesting Narrative of the Life of Olaudah Equiano, or Gustavus Vassa the African*

Chained and crammed into the ships' filthy holds for more than a month, prisoners like Equiano could hardly sit or stand and were given minimal food and drink. Africans who died or became sick were thrown overboard. Those who refused to eat were whipped.

Elmire Castle, a Portuguese-built fort on the coast of Ghana, was a holding area for slaves who would soon travel across the Atlantic Ocean in the hold of crowded slave ships (depicted below).

CHAPTER 3 Colonial Ways of Life **89**

3 ASSESS

Assign Section 1 Assessment as homework or as an in-class activity.

🔘 Have students use the **Interactive Tutor Self-Assessment CD-ROM.**

Reading Essentials and Study Guide 3–1

✓ Reading Check

Answer: The government opposed expanding the colonies into Native American lands and refused to sanction military action against the Native Americans.

FYI

The Interesting Narrative of the Life of Olaudah Equiano, or Gustav Vassa the African was first published in 1789.

Section Quiz 3–1

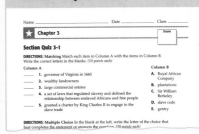

EXTENDING THE CONTENT

Indentured Servants In 1750 Gottlieb Mittelberger traveled to Pennsylvania as an indentured servant. He later wrote about his experiences in an essay entitled *On the Misfortune of Indentured Servants*. He noted that if a child's parents died during the voyage, the child had to serve long enough to pay for both his or her voyage, as well as the parents' voyage. When they finally paid off their voyages and finished their service, indentured servants were to be given a new suit of clothes. Depending on the terms of service, some male servants also received a horse, while female servants received a cow.

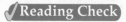
Picturing **History**

Answer: He was kidnapped by other Africans, then traded to Europeans and then shipped to America.

Ask: How did Bacon's Rebellion contribute to the use of enslaved persons in the colonies? *(Bacon's Rebellion signaled elite Virginia landowners that indentured servants were a problem: They had to be replaced periodically, and once they were independent farmers, they might challenge elite rule. Thus, well-to-do landowners increasingly relied on enslaved Africans.)*

✔ **Reading Check**

Answer: It changed from a status similar to indentured servitude, to enslavement of non-Christians, to enslavement by race based on a hereditary system, and finally to a system operating under a slave code.

Reteach
Have students create an outline using section headings.

Enrich
Use library and Internet resources to locate and read two book reviews of *The Interesting Life of Olaudah Equiano, or Gustav Vassa the African*.

4 CLOSE
Ask students to summarize why the status of Africans in Virginia and Maryland gradually changed from indentured servants to enslaved persons.

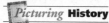
Picturing **History**

Olaudah Equiano Fortunate to eventually win his own freedom, Equiano still suffered the brutal journey to the American colonies and years of slavery. *How did Equiano end up on a slave ship bound for the United States?*

Of the 8 to 10 million Africans who reached the Americas, approximately 3.5 million went to Brazil, and another 1.5 million went to the Spanish colonies. The British, French, and Dutch colonies in the Caribbean imported nearly 4 million others to work on their sugar plantations. Approximately 500,000 Africans were transported to North America before the slave trade ended in the 1800s.

When the first Africans arrived in Virginia in 1619, English law did not recognize chattel slavery, where one human being is said to be owned by another. As a result, slavery developed slowly in the Chesapeake colonies. The first Africans brought to Virginia and Maryland were treated in a manner similar to indentured servants, and children born to Africans were not always considered enslaved.

Some of the first enslaved Africans obtained their freedom by converting to Christianity. To many English settlers in the early 1600s, enslaving Africans was acceptable not because of their race, but because they were not Christians. As the number of Africans increased in Virginia and Maryland, their status changed. In 1638 Maryland became the first British colony to formally recognize slavery when it denied Africans the same rights as English citizens. Beginning in the 1660s, new laws in Virginia and Maryland gradually lowered the status of all Africans, regardless of their religion, and changed slavery into a hereditary system based on race.

Finally, in 1705, Virginia pulled all of these different laws together into a slave code—a set of laws that formally regulated slavery and defined the relationship between enslaved Africans and free people. Other colonies created their own slave codes. Over time slave codes became increasingly strict. Africans were denied the right to own property or to testify against a white person in court. Their movements were regulated, and they were often forbidden to assemble in large numbers. By the early 1700s, slavery had become a recognized and generally accepted institution in colonial society, particularly in the Southern Colonies, where the labor of hundreds of thousands of enslaved Africans played a vital role in the growth of the plantation economy.

✔ **Reading Check** **Explaining** How did the concept of slavery in the Southern Colonies change over time?

SECTION 1 ASSESSMENT

Checking for Understanding
1. **Define:** cash crop, plantation, indentured servant, gentry, subsistence farming, Middle Passage, slave code.
2. **Identify:** Eliza Lucas, William Berkeley, Royal African Company.
3. **Explain** why South Carolina began producing indigo.

Reviewing Themes
4. **Geography and History** How did the geography of the Chesapeake region affect its economic development?

Critical Thinking
5. **Contrasting** How did the economies of the Chesapeake region and South Carolina differ?
6. **Analyzing** How did the slave trade develop in the Americas?
7. **Categorizing** Use a graphic organizer similar to the one below to list the causes of Bacon's Rebellion.

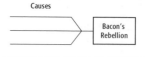
Causes → Bacon's Rebellion

Analyzing Visuals
8. **Analyzing Art** Study the painting on page 87 depicting Bacon's Rebellion. What motivated Nathaniel Bacon to lead his rebellion against the Virginia gentry?

Writing About History
9. **Descriptive Writing** Imagine you are a backcountry farmer in Virginia. Write a letter to your local newspaper describing how you feel about Sir William Berkeley and the policies he instituted.

SECTION 1 ASSESSMENT ANSWERS

1. Terms are in blue.
2. Eliza Lucas (p. 86), William Berkeley (p. 87), Royal African Company (p. 89)
3. Indigo was in demand in Europe and it was a good companion crop to rice.
4. The geography of the Chesapeake Bay was perfect for tobacco farming, which became its primary crop.
5. the Chesapeake: tobacco, indentured servants, and headrights; South Carolina: rice, indigo, and slave labor
6. Students should discuss the rise of plantations and need for labor.
7. rulers were not taxed; the restriction of voting rights; the government's unwillingness to fight Native Americans; backcountry farmers' desire for land
8. Possible answers: sympathy to the situation of backcountry farmers; anger towards Native Americans
9. Students' letters will vary. Letters should clearly express the writers' feelings about Berkely's policies.

Guide to Reading

Main Idea
In New England and the Middle Colonies, a diverse economy supported many large port cities.

Key Terms and Names
Grand Banks, fall line, town meeting, selectmen, meetinghouse, bill of exchange, triangular trade, artisan, entrepreneur, capitalist

Reading Strategy
Categorizing As you read about New England and the Middle Colonies, complete a chart similar to the one below describing how resources affected economic development.

Resources	Industries
Sea	

Reading Objectives
- **List** the geographical conditions that determined the economy of the New England Colonies.
- **Summarize** how life in the Middle Colonies differed from life in the New England Colonies.

Section Theme
Culture and Traditions The culture of the New England Colonies developed differently from that of the Southern Colonies.

Preview of Events

1630	1650	1670	1690

1630
Massachusetts Bay Colony is founded

1635
First New England sawmill built

1681
City of Philadelphia first laid out by William Markham

1692
Salem witchcraft trials take place in Massachusetts

1 FOCUS

Section Overview
This section describes the growth of the economy in New England and the Middle Colonies.

BELLRINGER
Skillbuilder Activity

Project transparency and have students answer the question.

Available as a blackline master.

Daily Focus Skills Transparency 3–2

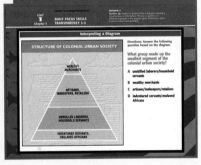

★ An American Story ★

New England's soil was thin and rocky, and from the earliest days, many settlers knew they would have to depend on the sea for their livelihood. Although some people back in England believed New England offered only a meager existence, the Reverend Francis Higginson learned otherwise. One of New England's earliest settlers, Higginson here describes the rich fishing off the coast of New England:

❝I saw great store of whales and grampuses, and such abundance of mackerels that it would astonish one to behold. . . . There is a fish called a bass, a most sweet and wholesome fish as ever I did eat. . . . Of this fish our fishers may take many hundreds together, which I have seen lying on the shore, to my admiration. Yea, their nets ordinarily take more than they are able to haul to land. . . . And besides bass, we take plenty of skate and thornback, and abundance of lobsters; and the least boy in the plantation may both catch and eat what he will of them.❞

—from "On the Riches of New England," *The Annals of America*

New England port

New England's Economy

Although the fishing industry made few New Englanders rich, it did provide a living for many settlers who built ships or engaged in foreign trade. Farther inland, numerous small farms, sawmills, and other industries helped to create a very diverse economy in New England.

CHAPTER 3 Colonial Ways of Life **91**

Guide to Reading

Answers to Graphic: Sea: fishing and whaling; Forest and waterfalls: lumber and shipbuilding; Poor farmland: subsistence farming of corn, vegetables, orchards, livestock

Preteaching Vocabulary
Have students write three questions that can be answered using the Key Terms and Names.

SECTION RESOURCES

Reproducible Masters
- Reproducible Lesson Plan 3–2
- Daily Lecture and Discussion Notes 3–2
- Guided Reading Activity 3–2
- Section Quiz 3–2
- Reading Essentials and Study Guide 3–2

Transparencies
- Daily Focus Skills Transparency 3–2

Multimedia
- Interactive Tutor Self-Assessment CD-ROM
- ExamView® Pro Testmaker CD-ROM
- Presentation Plus! CD-ROM
- TeacherWorks™ CD-ROM
- Audio Program
- American Music: Hits Through History

2 TEACH

Daily Lecture and Discussion Notes 3–2

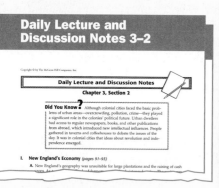

Writing a Diary Entry Ask students to imagine that they are a member of a family living in one of the New England Colonies. Have students decide how their family makes a living. Then have them write a diary entry for a typical day describing the family's activities. **L1**

 Use the rubric for a diary, short story, memorandum, or letter on pages 79–80 in the *Performance Assessment Activities and Rubrics.*

Geography *Skills*

Answers:
1. cattle, lumber, grain, rum, iron
2. It was easier to transport iron by water than by land.

Geography Skills Practice
Ask: Which products of the colonies were finished products, and which were resources shipped back to England to be converted into finished products? *(Ships, rum, fish, and some cattle products such as beef were finished products. The others were used in creating finished products.)*

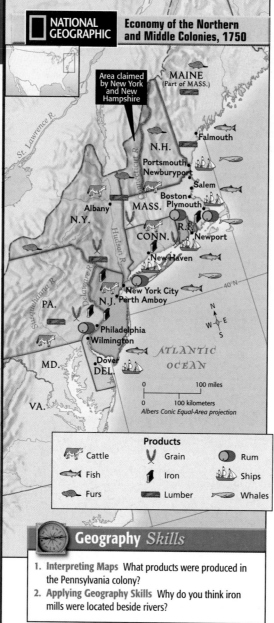

NATIONAL GEOGRAPHIC
Economy of the Northern and Middle Colonies, 1750

Products
- Cattle
- Fish
- Furs
- Grain
- Iron
- Lumber
- Rum
- Ships
- Whales

Geography *Skills*

1. **Interpreting Maps** What products were produced in the Pennsylvania colony?
2. **Applying Geography Skills** Why do you think iron mills were located beside rivers?

None of the crops that could be grown in New England were in great demand elsewhere. The region's unsuitability for cash crops prevented the development of large plantations. Instead, on small farms that dotted the New England landscape from Connecticut to Maine, New England farmers practiced subsistence farming, using nearly everything they produced.

92 CHAPTER 3 Colonial Ways of Life

Although New England farmers tried to grow wheat, in most places the soil was too poor, and the presence of a fungus called black rust prevented any real success during the colonial era. As a result, the main crop grown in colonial New England was corn.

Corn had a short growing season, and its long taproot allowed it to grow well even in New England's rocky soil. As New England became more settled, farmers began to grow barley, oats, and rye, as well as many types of vegetables, including beans, peas, pumpkins, squash, and turnips. Most farms also included orchards. Apple trees were common because apples could be used for cider or dried to feed livestock in the winter. Farmers also made use of berries, particularly cranberries, blackberries, and strawberries, which grew wild throughout New England.

New England farmers also raised livestock. They used oxen to pull plows and wagons and used horses for travel. Dairy cattle provided milk for butter and cheese, and sheep provided wool. Pigs supplied meat, and salted pork was a common source of protein during the long winter months.

GEOGRAPHY

Fishing and Whaling The geography of New England almost guaranteed that fishing would become a major industry in the region. Northeast of New England lay the **Grand Banks,** a shallow region in the Atlantic Ocean where the mixing of the warm Gulf Stream and the cold North Atlantic produced an environment favorable to plankton—an important food supply for many types of fish and whales. In the colonial era the Grand Banks teemed with fish, including cod, mackerel, halibut, and herring.

At the same time, New England's coastline had many good harbors and plenty of timber for building fishing boats. There was a great demand for fish, as it was an important source of nutrition in the colonies, southern Europe, and the Caribbean. Fishing, more than any other industry, brought prosperity to New England. Nearly every coastal town had a fishing fleet. In the early 1700s, an estimated 4,000 to 5,000 people in New England made their living by fishing.

Whaling also played a major role in New England's economy, especially for people living on Nantucket Island and in Provincetown at the end of Cape Cod. Whalers sought their prey for its blubber, used for making candles and lamp oil; ambergris, a waxy intestinal substance used to make perfume; and bones, used for buttons and combs and as supports in women's clothing.

COOPERATIVE LEARNING ACTIVITY

Presenting a Skit Organize students into groups of four or five. Have each group select an aspect of life in New England or the Middle Colonies and create a five-minute skit. Encourage students to add authenticity to their productions by using appropriate props and costumes. Encourage students to use library and Internet resources to learn more about colonial life. Have students perform their skits for each other during class.

Use the rubric for a cooperative group management plan on pages 81–82 in the *Performance Assessment Activities and Rubrics.*

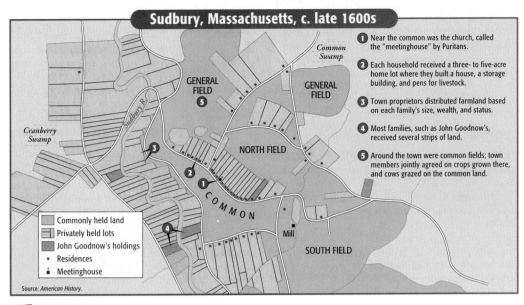

Sudbury, Massachusetts, c. late 1600s

Common Swamp

GENERAL FIELD **5**

GENERAL FIELD

Cranberry Swamp

NORTH FIELD

3

2

1

C O M M O N

Mill

4

SOUTH FIELD

1. Near the common was the church, called the "meetinghouse" by Puritans.

2. Each household received a three- to five-acre home lot where they built a house, a storage building, and pens for livestock.

3. Town proprietors distributed farmland based on each family's size, wealth, and status.

4. Most families, such as John Goodnow's, received several strips of land.

5. Around the town were common fields; town members jointly agreed on crops grown there, and cows grazed on the common land.

Legend:
- Commonly held land
- Privately held lots
- John Goodnow's holdings
- Residences
- Meetinghouse

Source: *American History.*

Picturing **History**

Sudbury, Massachusetts The town was the basic unit of community life in New England in the 1600s. Houses were laid out around a central pasture called a common. In this map, the holdings of one man, John Goodnow, are highlighted in purple to show the way each person's land holdings could be scattered about the town. Who decided how much land each person received?

Lumbering and Shipbuilding

Dense forest covered much of North America's eastern coastline in the 1600s. Although settlers relied on wood from these forests in every colony, New England's geography—particularly in Maine and New Hampshire—provided the conditions necessary for the development of a lumber industry.

In New England the **fall line**—the area where rivers descend from a high elevation to a lower one, causing waterfalls—is near the coast. Waterfalls were used to power sawmills. The first sawmill in the colonies was probably built in New Hampshire in 1635. Others soon followed. Lumber cut at these sawmills could easily be transported downriver to the coast and shipped to other colonies or to England.

Every colony needed lumber. Colonists wanted walnut, maple, and sycamore wood for furniture. They used cedar for doorframes and windowsills. Maple was made into spinning wheels. Oak and pine provided materials for boards, shingles, and barrel staves. Barrel making was a very important industry in the colonies because barrels were used to store and ship almost everything. Coopers in the colonial era made between 300,000 and 400,000 barrels per year. The lumber industry also made possible another important industry in New England—shipbuilding.

With forests and sawmills close to the coast, ships could be built quickly and cheaply. The large fishing industry and the growing trade between New England and the other colonies created a steady demand for ships. English merchants purchased many ships from the colonies because the ships could be built for 30 to 50 percent less in America than in England. By the 1770s, one out of every three English ships had been built in America.

Reading Check **Summarizing** How did geography shape New England's industries?

Life in New England's Towns

If self-sufficient plantations defined the social organization in the South, Puritan New England's social life centered on the town. Puritans believed that God had entered into a covenant—or solemn contract—with human beings that enabled them to obtain salvation. As a result they also believed that groups of Christians should come together to form church covenants—voluntary agreements to worship together.

The commitment to church covenants encouraged the development of towns. Instead of granting land to individuals, the general courts in the New

CHAPTER 3 Colonial Ways of Life **93**

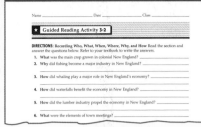

Guided Reading Activity 3–2

Name _____ Date _____ Class _____

★ **Guided Reading Activity 3-2**

DIRECTIONS: Recording Who, What, When, Where, Why, and How Read the section and answer the questions below. Refer to your textbook to write the answers.

1. What was the main crop grown in colonial New England? _____
2. Why did fishing become a major industry in New England? _____
3. How did whaling play a major role in New England's economy? _____
4. How did waterfalls benefit the economy in New England? _____
5. How did the lumber industry propel the economy in New England? _____
6. What were the elements of town meetings? _____

Picturing **History**

Answer: Town proprietors decided what each family received.

Ask: Why do you think the meetinghouse was situated near the center of the town? *(to be accessible to all members of the community, and to be the focus of community life)*

✓**Reading Check**

Answer: Thin, rocky soil limited agriculture to subsistence farming, while the ocean supported the fishing and whaling industries. Waterfalls were used to power sawmills and extensive woodlands supported lumber and shipbuilding industries.

Building a Model Have students build a model of a water-powered sawmill. Have students share their models with the class as they demonstrate how water was used to provide power. Ask students how we use water power today. **L3**

MEETING SPECIAL NEEDS

Visual/Spatial Have students create a pyramid-shaped diagram to help them understand the structure of society in the Middle Colonies in the mid-1700s. The diagram should be divided into sections to illustrate the hierarchy of social groups. Ask students to label the diagram using a brief description of what kind of people were included in each, with the most powerful group occupying the smallest and highest segment of the pyramid. **L1**

📩 Refer to *Inclusion for the High School Social Studies Classroom Strategies and Activities* in the TCR.

FYI

Puritans placed a premium on literacy. Similar to members of some other religious groups, they were particularly interested in making sure that people could read the Bible.

you don't say...

Witch-hunt The term *witch-hunt* is commonly used to describe an investigation used to harass people who hold different views from the investigators'.

CURRICULUM CONNECTION

Performing Arts Arthur Miller's 1953 play *The Crucible* is a work of fiction about the Salem witchcraft trials. Although the play is set in 1692, it reflects Miller's concern about the U.S. government's investigations of subversive activities during the 1950s.

England Colonies granted land to groups of people, who then became the town proprietors. The town proprietors were usually prominent members of a congregation that wanted to establish a new community. The town became the heart of New England society. It determined how the land was settled and how the people were governed.

GOVERNMENT

Town Meetings Town residents met to discuss local problems and issues. Free men in the towns elected leaders and chose deputies to go to the General Court of their colony. These town meetings developed into the local town government. Although anyone in the town could attend a town meeting and express an opinion, voting was limited to men who had been granted land by the town. As town meetings became more frequent, the men began to pass laws for the town and to elect officials.

The men chosen to manage the town's affairs were called selectmen, and they were elected annually. The selectmen appointed any other officials the town needed, such as clerks, constables, and justices of the peace. Town meetings were very important. Unlike farmers in England, the settlers in New England were allowed to directly participate in their own local government. They developed a strong belief that they had the right to govern themselves. Town meetings helped set the stage for the American Revolution and the emergence of democratic government.

Puritan Society The Puritans' houses were located close to the church, or **meetinghouse,** and so they could never claim distance as an excuse to miss Sunday worship, sermons, and Thursday night religious lectures. These sermons and lectures reinforced the Puritans' obedience to strict rules regulating most activities of daily life. Puritan law banned "Those infamous Games of Cards and Dice because of the lottery which is in them." Puritans also frowned upon "Stage-Players and Mixed Dancing."

Puritans also felt a sense of responsibility for the moral welfare of their neighbors. Watching over their neighbors' behavior was elevated to a religious duty, which Puritans termed "Holy Watching," or "doing the Lord's work."

Although the Puritans have acquired a reputation for being intolerant and rigidly moral, they were not opposed to everything that was fun and pleasurable. Puritans drank rum, enjoyed music, and liked to wear brightly colored clothing that indicated their wealth and social position. They worked hard, and Puritan artisans and architects produced beautiful and elegant works. In the Puritan view, God had made the world, and the things in it were to be enjoyed by people. As one colonist wrote at the time, "In New England . . . the farmers live in the midst of a

The Salem witchcraft trials (below) led to several executions (right).

Salem and Witchcraft

Devout Puritans in the late 1600s firmly believed that Satan used witches to work evil in the world. In 1692 accusations of witchcraft resulted in the execution of 20 residents of Salem, Massachusetts.

Salem's witch trials began when a group of teenage girls accused an African servant of being a witch. Their accusations soon grew to include others, including some prominent people in town. Accused witches were often spared if they confessed, especially if they pointed a finger at other community members.

Some people who denied being witches were hanged. Only after the Salem witchcraft trials ended in 1692 did the original accusers admit that they had made up the entire story. The incident may have reflected community strains and resentments. The accusers tended to be less successful people who clung to Salem's agricultural roots. Many of those accused of witchcraft were prosperous and associated with the town's seaport.

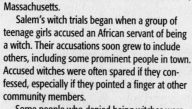

plenty of the necessaries of life; they do not acquire wealth, but they have comforts in abundance."

✔ **Reading Check** **Synthesizing** How did New England town meetings prepare the colonists for the future?

Trade and the Rise of Cities

In the early colonial era, New England produced few goods or crops that England wanted, but England produced many items that settlers wanted. Such items included hardware and various mechanical instruments, as well as fine cloth, linens, ceramic plates, and other luxury items. This situation, combined with New England's shipbuilding industry and good ports, encouraged some settlers to become merchants. The growth of trade in New England, in turn, led to the rise of cities along the coast.

Triangular Trade The only way colonial merchants could acquire the English goods that settlers wanted was to sell New England's products somewhere else in exchange for goods that England wanted. Fortunately, the sugar plantations in the Caribbean wanted to buy New England's fish, lumber, and meat.

To pay for the food and lumber from New England, Caribbean sugar planters would either trade raw sugar to the New England merchants or give them bills of exchange. Bills of exchange were credit slips English merchants gave the planters in exchange for their sugar. These bills worked as a kind of money. New England merchants would take the bills, as well as any sugar they had acquired, back home to New England and use them to buy English manufactured goods.

New England's trade with the sugar plantations of the Caribbean made many merchants very wealthy and led to new industries in New England. Using their new wealth, merchants in Northern cities built factories to refine raw sugar and distilleries to turn molasses into rum. Merchants also began trading with the Southern Colonies, exchanging Northern fish, rum, and grain for Southern rice, tobacco, and indigo.

The three-way trade New England merchants established with the Caribbean colonies and England is an example of triangular trade. Other three-way trade systems also existed. For example, New England merchants would trade rum to British merchants in exchange for British goods. British merchants then traded the rum to West Africans in exchange for enslaved Africans, who were then transported across the Atlantic to the Caribbean and traded for sugar.

A New Urban Society The rise of trade in the colonies caused several ports to grow rapidly into colonial America's first cities. By 1760 Philadelphia had over 23,000 people, making it the largest colonial city. Charles Town, South Carolina, with 8,000 people, was the largest city in the South. Within these cities and others, a new society developed with distinct social classes.

At the top of society were a small group of wealthy merchants who controlled the city's trade. The merchants in the coastal cities, in many ways similar to the planter elite in the South, patterned themselves after the British upper class. They wore elegant imported clothing, built luxurious mansions surrounded by gardens and maintained by servants, and rode through the crowded city streets in fancy carriages.

Although the merchants were the wealthiest people living in colonial cities, they were only a tiny minority. Artisans and their families made up nearly half of the urban population in colonial America. Artisans were skilled workers who knew how to manufacture various goods. They included carpenters, masons, coopers, iron and silversmiths, glassmakers, bakers, seamstresses, shoemakers, and many other tradespeople. Some artisans owned their own tools and shops, but most were employed in shops other people owned. Equal to the artisans in social status were innkeepers and retailers who owned their own places of business.

At the bottom of urban colonial society were the people without skills or property. Many of these people were employed at the harbor, where they loaded and serviced ships. Others worked as servants, washing clothes, grooming horses, cleaning houses, hauling garbage, and sweeping streets. These people made up about 30 percent of urban society during the colonial period. Below them in status were indentured servants and enslaved Africans. Enslaved Africans composed between 10 and 20 percent of the urban population. They too served as manual laborers and servants for the city's wealthier inhabitants.

The rapid development of cities created many problems, including overcrowding, crime, pollution, and epidemics. To deal with these problems, city governments established specific departments and offices. Constables' offices provided residents with some protection from crime. Charities began to address the problems of the urban poor, whose numbers swelled whenever a recession caused trade to decline.

✔ **Reading Check** **Examining** What new social classes developed in the Northern Colonies, and what contributed to their development?

CHAPTER 3 Colonial Ways of Life **95**

✔ **Reading Check**

Answer: Town meetings developed into the local town government. As the town meetings became more frequent, town leaders began to pass laws and elect officials. Through participating in their own local government, the settlers developed a strong belief in a right to self-government.

Creating a Poster Have students create a poster to explain triangular trade as described on this page. **L2**

📂 Use the rubric for creating a map, display, or chart on pages 77–78 in the *Performance Assessment Activities and Rubrics.*

History *and the* Humanities

🏴 American Music: Hits Through History: "Love in a Village/Love Forever," "Rufty Tufty," "Reel de Dennis McGee"

✔ **Reading Check**

Answer: Triangular trade resulted in merchants rising to the top of society. The rise of cities led to the development of a social class made up of artisans, innkeepers, and retailers. This group fell directly below the merchants.

CRITICAL THINKING ACTIVITY

Identifying Cause and Effect For each of the following causes related to the structure of New England society, have students list the effects. Cause: Town meetings were held to discuss local problems and issues. *(Possible effects: development of local town governments, development of elected officials, growth of belief that individuals had the right to govern themselves)* Cause: Puritan dwellings were built near their meetinghouses. *(Possible effects: Attendance at worship and meetings was expected. Puritans felt a heightened responsibility to watch over the moral lives of their neighbors.)* **L2**

Geography Skills

Answers:

1. rum

2. Caribbean colonies traded molasses to the Northern colonies where it was made into rum. Northern colonies traded the rum to British merchants in exchange for finished goods. These merchants then exchanged rum with West African traders for enslaved persons, who were then traded for sugar.

Geography Skills Practice
Ask: What exports to Great Britain were returned in a different form to the colonies? *(possible answer: the profit from lumber and furs was used to buy furniture and clothing)*

Between the time Charles II issued the charter for Pennsylvania in April of 1681 and William Penn's arrival in 1682, Penn sent his cousin William Markham to claim the land. Penn also sent along his plans for central Philadelphia, which specified the layout of streets in a grid pattern. The grid pattern, which was new to the colonies, can still be seen in downtown Philadelphia.

3 ASSESS

Assign Section 2 Assessment as homework or as an in-class activity.

⚙ Have students use the **Interactive Tutor Self-Assessment CD-ROM.**

Reading Essentials and Study Guide 3–2

Name _____ Date _____ Class _____

Study Guide
Chapter 3, Section 2
For use with textbook pages 91–97

NEW ENGLAND AND THE MIDDLE COLONIES

KEY TERMS AND NAMES

Grand Banks a shallow region in the Atlantic Ocean teeming with fish *(page 92)*
fall line the area where rivers descend from a high elevation to a lower one, causing waterfalls *(page 93)*
town meetings meetings in New England in which town residents met to discuss problems and issues *(page 94)*
selectmen men chosen to manage the affairs of New England towns *(page 94)*
meetinghouse the name given to Puritan churches *(page 94)*
bills of exchange credit slips used by New England and English merchants *(page 95)*

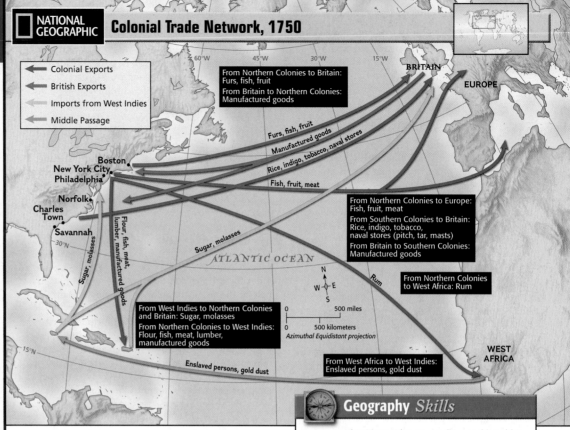

NATIONAL GEOGRAPHIC **Colonial Trade Network, 1750**

Colonial Exports
British Exports
Imports from West Indies
Middle Passage

From Northern Colonies to Britain: Furs, fish, fruit
From Britain to Northern Colonies: Manufactured goods

Furs, fish, fruit
Manufactured goods
Rice, indigo, tobacco, naval stores
Fish, fruit, meat

From Northern Colonies to Europe: Fish, fruit, meat
From Southern Colonies to Britain: Rice, indigo, tobacco, naval stores (pitch, tar, masts)
From Britain to Southern Colonies: Manufactured goods

From Northern Colonies to West Africa: Rum

Boston
New York City
Philadelphia
Norfolk
Charles Town
Savannah

Flour, fish, meat, lumber, manufactured goods
Sugar, molasses

ATLANTIC OCEAN

From West Indies to Northern Colonies and Britain: Sugar, molasses
From Northern Colonies to West Indies: Flour, fish, meat, lumber, manufactured goods

0 500 miles
0 500 kilometers
Azimuthal Equidistant projection

Enslaved persons, gold dust

From West Africa to West Indies: Enslaved persons, gold dust

BRITAIN
EUROPE
WEST AFRICA

Geography Skills

1. **Interpreting Maps** What commodity was shipped from the colonies to West Africa?
2. **Applying Geography Skills** In what sequence was rum produced and shipped to markets?

Society in the Middle Colonies

The Middle Colonies—Pennsylvania, New York, New Jersey, and Delaware—contained some of the most fertile farmland in North America. Unlike the subsistence farmers in New England, most farmers in the Middle Colonies were able to produce a surplus that they could sell. The rich soil of the region crumbled easily under their plows, and the longer growing season enabled them to bring forth bumper crops of rye, oats, barley, and potatoes. The most important crop, however, was wheat, which quickly became the region's main cash crop.

The Growth of the Middle Colonies Merchants based in the Middle Colonies rapidly duplicated the success of the New England merchants and began selling wheat and flour to the colonies in the Caribbean. The Middle Colonies also benefited from their geography. Unlike New England, the Middle Colonies had three wide rivers—the Hudson, the Delaware, and the Susquehanna—that ran deep into the interior. These rivers made it easy for farmers

to move their goods to the coast for shipping to markets elsewhere in America and Europe.

Hundreds of small ships sailed up and down the region's rivers, exchanging European goods for barrels of wheat and flour. At the same time, thousands of wagons moved goods overland from interior farms to river towns, where they could be loaded on ships and moved downriver. As might be expected, towns located where the rivers emptied into the Atlantic Ocean rapidly grew into major cities. The prosperity of the Middle Colonies enabled New York City and Philadelphia to become the two largest cities in the British colonies.

The Wheat Boom In the early 1700s, Europe's climate began to get warmer just as the diseases there began to decline. The result was a population explosion and a flood of new immigrants into

---

EXTENDING THE CONTENT

Harvard College Founded The Great and General Court of the Massachusetts Bay Colony founded Harvard College in 1636. The college was named for its first benefactor, John Harvard, a minister from Charlestown. Many of Harvard's early graduates became ministers, but the college was never affiliated with a specific denomination. The curriculum of the college was patterned after the model used by colleges and universities in England with an emphasis on prevailing Puritan beliefs. Harvard, now known as Harvard University, is the oldest institution of higher education in the United States.

America—particularly into the Middle Colonies, where land was still available. At the same time, this population explosion created a huge demand for wheat to feed the soaring number of people in Europe. Between 1720 and 1770, wheat prices more than doubled in the colonies. This brought a surge of prosperity to the Middle Colonies.

The rapid rise of the wheat trade and the arrival of so many new settlers changed the society of the Middle Colonies. Some farmers became very wealthy by hiring poor immigrants to work on their farms for wages. This enabled them to raise large amounts of wheat for sale. Other colonists became wealthy as entrepreneurs, or businesspeople who risked their money by buying land, equipment, and supplies and then selling them to the new immigrants for a profit.

One of the reasons the American colonies had few industries and had to import so many manufactured goods from England was that the British government limited manufacturing in the colonies. Money to invest in factories was also scarce. The wheat boom created a new group of capitalists, people who had money to invest in new businesses. Industry did not develop on a large scale during the colonial era, but these early capitalists did build large gristmills near New York and Philadelphia that produced tens of thousands of barrels of flour for export. Other early entrepreneurs in the Middle Colonies established glass and pottery works.

Although many farmers prospered from growing wheat, very few became wealthy, primarily because of the limited technology of the time. There were no mechanical harvesters, so all of the wheat had to be cut by hand using a sickle. Threshing, or separating the grain from the chaff, also had to be done by hand

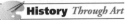

History *Through Art*

Bethlehem, Pennsylvania This painting of a town in the Middle Colonies represents a typical layout of that region of colonial America. What was the main cash crop in the Middle Colonies?

by beating the grain with a wooden flail. Using sickles, most farm families could harvest no more than 15 acres of wheat in a season. This was enough to produce a small surplus, but not enough to make most farmers rich. Only those farmers who were able to hire workers or who had extra land that they could rent to tenant farmers became wealthy.

As a result, distinct classes developed in the Middle Colonies, as they did in the other regions. At the top were wealthy entrepreneurs who owned large farms and other businesses. In the middle were many farmers who owned only a few acres and could generate a small surplus from their land. At the bottom of society were landless workers, who either rented land from large landowners or worked for wages.

✓ **Reading Check** **Explaining** Why did the colonies experience a population boom in the early 1700s?

SECTION 2 ASSESSMENT

Checking for Understanding

1. **Define:** town meeting, selectmen, bill of exchange, triangular trade, artisan, entrepreneur, capitalist.

2. **Identify:** Grand Banks, fall line, meetinghouse.

3. **Describe** the different social classes in New England and the Middle Colonies.

Reviewing Themes

4. **Culture and Traditions** How did Puritanism affect the development of New England society and government?

Critical Thinking

5. **Understanding Cause and Effect** How did the geography of the New England and Middle Colonies contribute to their economic development?

6. **Categorizing** Use a graphic organizer similar to the one below to show the effects of wheat farming on the Middle Colonies.

Effects
Wheat Farming

Analyzing Visuals

7. **Examining Maps** Study the map of a New England town on page 93. Would the practice of "Holy Watching" have been easy to do in this town? Why or why not?

Writing About History

8. **Descriptive Writing** Imagine that you are barrel maker in the New England Colonies. Write a letter to a government official stating the problems you have that you want the government to address.

SECTION 2 ASSESSMENT ANSWERS

1. Terms are in blue.

2. Grand Banks (p. 92), fall line (p. 93), meetinghouse (p. 94)

3. In urban societies the class structure included wealthy merchants, artisans, innkeepers and retailers, and people without skills or property.

4. Puritans believed that people should worship together. This led to towns and town meetings and finally local government.

5. The New England economy developed around water; the Middle Colonies' economy was based on good soil and access to waterways.

6. prosperity, capitalists with money to invest, distinct social classes

7. Yes; houses were clustered around the common

8. Letters should clearly present the barrel maker's point of view.

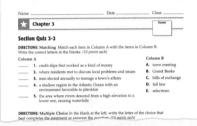

History *Through Art*

Answer: wheat
Ask: Why were the Middle Colonies able to produce greater agricultural yields than the New England Colonies? *(richer soil and longer growing season)*

Section Quiz 3–2

Name _____ Date _____ Class _____

⭐ **Chapter 3** Score _____

Section Quiz 3-2

DIRECTIONS: Matching Match each item in Column A with the items in Column B. Write the correct letters in the blanks. *(10 points each)*

Column A
____ 1. credit slips that worked as a kind of money
____ 2. where residents met to discuss local problems and issues
____ 3. men elected annually to manage a town's affairs
____ 4. a shallow region in the Atlantic Ocean with an environment favorable to plankton
____ 5. the area where rivers descend from a high elevation to a lower one, causing waterfalls

Column B
A. town meeting
B. Grand Banks
C. bills of exchange
D. fall line
E. selectmen

DIRECTIONS: Multiple Choice In the blank at the left, write the letter of the choice that best completes the statement or answers the question. *(10 points each)*

Reteach

Have students list the geographic conditions that affected the economy of the New England and Middle Colonies.

Enrich

Have students research the history of one of the towns in the New England or Middle Colonies.

4 CLOSE

Have students draw simple diagrams showing the triangular trade patterns that existed in colonial times.

✓ **Reading Check**

Answer: A population explosion in Europe resulted in more Europeans immigrating to the colonies where land was still available and opportunities seemed abundant.

1 FOCUS

Section Overview

This section explains how England's control of trade with the American colonies increased profits for the British.

BELLRINGER
Skillbuilder Activity

Project transparency and have students answer the question.

Available as a blackline master.

Daily Focus Skills Transparency 3–3

Guide to Reading

Answers to Graphic: 1684: Charles II declares Massachusetts a royal colony because the colonial government refuses to enforce the Navigation Acts. 1686: James II allows the Commissioners of Trade and Plantations to revoke the charters of Connecticut and Rhode Island and merge them with Massachusetts and Plymouth to create a new royal province, the Dominion of New England. 1691: William and Mary issue a charter establishing the royal colony of Massachusetts that incorporated Massachusetts Bay, Plymouth, and Maine.

Preteaching Vocabulary
Have students write a one-sentence definition for each of the Key Terms.

SECTION 3 The Imperial System

Guide to Reading

Main Idea
During the 1600s, England adopted several measures to make its trade with the American colonies more profitable.

Key Terms and Names
mercantilism, Charles II, James II, Dominion of New England, Glorious Revolution, natural rights

Reading Strategy
Sequencing As you read about England's trade relationship with the American colonies, complete a graphic organizer similar to the one below by describing English attempts at various times to control the colonies.

1684 → 1686 → 1691

Reading Objectives
• **Describe** mercantilism and its effect on the relationship between the colonies and England.
• **Explain** how the Glorious Revolution in England affected the colonies.

Section Theme
Individual Action Individual colonists reacted differently to the political turmoil in England.

Preview of Events

♦1684   ♦1687   ♦1690

1685
James II succeeds Charles II as English monarch

1686
Dominion of New England established

1688
Glorious Revolution in England

1690
John Locke publishes *Two Treatises of Government*

★ An American Story ★

In the later 1600s and early 1700s, Parliament passed a series of laws that restricted and controlled colonial manufacturing. One of these laws affected the hat industry, and another affected the iron industry. These laws annoyed many colonists, including Benjamin Franklin, who argued:

66 The hatters of England have prevailed to obtain an act in their own favor restraining that manufacture in America. . . . In the same manner have a few nail makers and a still smaller body of steelmakers (perhaps there are not half a dozen of these in England) prevailed totally to forbid by an act of Parliament the erecting of slitting mills or steel furnaces in America; that Americans may be obliged to take all their nails for their buildings and steel for their tools from these artificers [craft workers]. 99

An article in the *Boston Gazette* also complained:

66 A colonist cannot make a button, a horseshoe, nor a hobnail, but some sooty ironmonger or respectable buttonmaker of Britain shall bawl and squall that his honor's worship is . . . maltreated, injured, cheated, and robbed by the rascally American republicans. 99

—adapted from *The Rise of American Civilization*

Colonial spinning wheel

Mercantilism

Mercantilism is a set of ideas about the world economy and how it works. These ideas were popular in the 1600s and 1700s. Mercantilists believed that to become wealthy and powerful, a country had to accumulate gold and silver. A country could do

---

SECTION RESOURCES

Reproducible Masters
• Reproducible Lesson Plan 3–3
• Daily Lecture and Discussion Notes 3–3
• Guided Reading Activity 3–3
• Section Quiz 3–3
• Reading Essentials and Study Guide 3–3
• Performance Assessment Activities and Rubrics

Transparencies
• Daily Focus Skills Transparency 3–3

Multimedia
- Interactive Tutor Self-Assessment CD-ROM
- ExamView® Pro Testmaker CD-ROM
- Presentation Plus! CD-ROM
- TeacherWorks™ CD-ROM
- Audio Program

this by selling more goods to other countries than it bought from them, causing more gold and silver to flow into the country than what was flowing out to pay for products from other countries.

Mercantilists also argued that a country should be self-sufficient in raw materials. If it had to buy raw materials from another country, gold and silver would flow out to pay for those materials. In order to be self-sufficient, a country should establish colonies where raw materials were available. The home country would then buy the raw materials from its colonies and, in turn, sell them manufactured goods.

Mercantilism did provide some benefits to colonies. It gave them a reliable market for some of their raw materials and an eager supplier of the manufactured goods they needed. This system also had drawbacks, however. It prevented colonies from selling goods to other nations, even if they could get a better price. Also, if a colony produced nothing the home country needed, the colony could not acquire gold or silver to buy manufactured goods. This was a serious problem in New England, and it explains in part why New England merchants turned to triangular trade and smuggling. These methods were the only way for the colonies to get the gold and silver they needed.

The Navigation Acts During the first half of the 1600s, England's mercantilist policy was very simple. The government tried to encourage exports and restrict imports. Other than some attempts to regulate the tobacco trade from Virginia, little attention was paid to the colonies and how they fit into England's economic system.

When **Charles II** assumed the throne in 1660, however, he and his advisers were determined to generate wealth for England by regulating trade and expanding the colonies in America. In 1660 Charles asked Parliament to pass a navigation act. The act required all goods imported or exported from the colonies to be carried on English ships, and stated that at least three-fourths of the crew on each ship had to be English. The act also listed specific raw materials that could be sold only to England or other English colonies. The list included sugar, tobacco, lumber, cotton, wool, and indigo—the major products that earned money for the colonies. Many colonists, especially tobacco planters, complained about the

act. They argued that it forced them to deal with English merchants who charged such high prices for shipping that the planters were robbed of their profit.

Three years later, in 1663, Parliament passed another navigation act called the **Staple Act.** This act required everything the colonies imported to come through England. All merchants bringing European goods to the colonies had to stop in England, pay taxes, and then ship the goods out again on English ships. This generated money for England but also increased the price of goods in the colonies.

Frustration with these acts encouraged colonial merchants to break the new laws. To enforce the acts in the colonies Parliament authorized the appointment of customs inspectors, who would report directly to the English government. As a colonial power, England had the authority to enact and enforce the Navigation Acts. Problems arose, however, when it tried to do so.

Problems With Enforcement In 1675 King Charles II appointed a committee called the Lords Commissioners of Trade and Plantations to oversee colonial trade and advise him about problems. It was soon discovered that Dutch and other foreign ships crowded Boston Harbor and that the merchants of Massachusetts routinely ignored the Navigation Acts and smuggled goods to Europe, the Caribbean, and Africa. Massachusetts's governor, John Laverett, wasted no time in informing England that

Port of Boston As one of the main points of entry for goods entering and leaving the colonies, Boston was sensitive to the effects of the Navigation Acts. *What was the main goal of the Navigation Acts?*

2 TEACH

Daily Lecture and Discussion Notes 3–3

Creating a Chart Have students work in small groups to create a chart describing the advantages and disadvantages of mercantilism to (1) the home country and (2) to a colony. Use the charts to discuss why the colonists often felt unfairly treated by England's king and Parliament. L1

📁 Use the rubric for creating a map, display, or chart on pages 77–78 in the *Performance Assessment Activities and Rubrics.*

Picturing **History**

Answer: The Navigation Acts supported England's mercantilist policy of encouraging English exports and restricting imports. Mercantilism also emphasized the use of the colonies as sources of raw materials and markets for manufactured goods.
Ask: Why did Massachusetts resist the Navigation Acts more strongly than the other colonies? *(They suffered the most since they had many of the major ports.)*

COOPERATIVE LEARNING ACTIVITY

Conducting a Debate Organize the class into two debate teams. Have one team take the position of Sir Edmond Andros and the other take the position of John Wise. Have the groups research and then debate the following: "Be it resolved that all public gatherings and town meetings will be illegal and participants of such gatherings will be arrested and fined." 📁

Use the rubric for a cooperative group management plan on pages 81–82 in the *Performance Assessment Activities and Rubrics.*

Guided Reading Activity 3–3

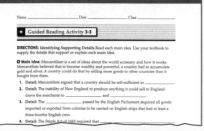

Writing a Letter Have students compose a letter from Sir Edmund Andros to James II explaining the steps he is taking to keep the Dominion of New England loyal to the king. **L2**

Use the rubric for a diary, short story, memorandum, or letter on pages 79–80 in the *Performance Assessment Activities and Rubrics.*

✓ Reading Check

Answer: The Navigation Acts regulated the shipping of goods to and from the colonies, restricted the sale of specific raw materials, and increased the cost of imported goods.

Chart *Skills*

Answers:
1. Colonists resented the Navigation Acts because they restricted how and to whom the colonists could export their goods, and increased the cost of imported goods.

2. The colonists argued they could not make a fair profit because of high shipping prices charged by English merchants.

Chart Skills Practice

Ask: How did the Navigation Act of 1673 differ from earlier acts? *(It attempted to regulate trade among the American colonies.)*

Massachusetts was not required to obey laws made by Parliament unless it was in the interest of Massachusetts to do so.

For the next few years, Massachusetts refused to answer the charges that had been brought against it. Finally, in 1684, King Charles II responded to this defiance by depriving Massachusetts of its charter and declaring it to be a royal colony.

The Dominion of New England **James II,** who succeeded his brother Charles to the English throne in 1685, went even further in asserting royal authority and punishing the merchants of New England for their defiance. In 1686 the English government merged Massachusetts, Plymouth, and Rhode Island together to create a new royal province called the **Dominion of New England.** The following year Connecticut and New Jersey were forced to join the Dominion, and by the spring of 1688, New York had been added as well.

The Dominion was to be run by a governor-general and councilors appointed directly by the king. All colonial assemblies were abolished. The governor-general and his council would have the power to make laws, impose taxes, administer justice, and confirm or deny all existing land grants.

King James II appointed **Sir Edmund Andros** to be the first governor-general. Andros, a former soldier and governor of New York, was loyal to the king. His contempt for the Puritan religion and his determination to overturn the systems of government in the colonies heightened tensions there.

Andros declared all deeds and land titles issued under the Massachusetts charter to be worthless, and he insisted that anyone who wanted a new deed would have to pay an annual tax to the government.

Working closely with English soldiers and the Royal Navy, he also rigorously enforced the Navigation Acts.

Equally disturbing to Puritans were the governor-general's efforts to undermine the Puritan Church. Andros declared that only marriages performed in Anglican churches were legal, and he demanded that Puritan meeting halls be made available for Anglican services every other Sunday. He also declared that no one was to teach school, a traditional function of Church leaders in New England, without permission.

Andros had managed to anger nearly everyone in New England society—landowners, church leaders, and merchants. Fortunately, just as tensions were peaking in New England, a peaceful revolution took place back in England, preempting violence in the colonies.

✓ Reading Check **Examining** In what ways did the Navigation Acts affect trade in the colonies?

The Glorious Revolution of 1688

While the colonists in New England raged at the actions of Governor-General Andros, the people of England were growing suspicious of their new king, James II. James insisted upon his divine right to rule, and he frequently rejected the advice of Parliament. He had revoked the charters of many English towns and corporations and offended many English people by openly practicing Catholicism. He had also prosecuted Anglican bishops for defying his wishes concerning appointments in the Anglican Church. Many members of Parliament worried that if James continued to act in this manner, he might lead the country into another civil war.

Major Navigation Acts

Year	Act
1651	Colonial trade was to be carried in English ships
1660	Tightened earlier restrictions; certain items, including tobacco, to be sold only to England or its colonies
1663	Colonial goods sold to Europe had to pass through English ports first to be taxed
1673	Duties imposed on trade *between* American colonies
1696	Gave customs officials the power to use general search warrants; Board of Trade created to oversee colonial economic activity

Chart *Skills*

1. **Evaluating** Why did the colonists resent the Navigation Acts?
2. **Determining Cause and Effect** What effect did the 1651 act have on colonial shipping?

MEETING SPECIAL NEEDS

Learning Disabled Many unfamiliar names are introduced in this section. Have students make a fact sheet for each of the following people: Charles II, Sir Edmond Andros, James II, William and Mary, and John Locke. Have students make a numbered list of the facts they learn about each person as they read and review the section. **L1** ELL

Refer to *Inclusion for the High School Social Studies Classroom Strategies and Activities* in the TCR.

A Bloodless Revolution Most of the English people and members of Parliament were willing to tolerate James because they expected his Protestant daughter Mary and her Dutch husband, William of Orange, to succeed James to the throne. These hopes were shattered in June 1688, when James's second wife gave birth to a son. The son was now the heir to the throne and would be raised Catholic.

News of the birth triggered protests. Unwilling to risk a Catholic dynasty on the throne of England, Parliament invited William and Mary to take the throne of England. When William arrived, James fled, and William became the new king of England. This bloodless change of power became known as the **Glorious Revolution.**

Before assuming the throne, William and Mary were required to swear that they would obey the laws of Parliament. In 1689 Parliament read a bill of rights to William and Mary, outlining what would be required of them. The **English Bill of Rights** abolished the king's absolute power to suspend laws and create his own courts. It also made it illegal for the king to impose taxes or raise an army without the consent of Parliament. The Bill of Rights also guaranteed freedom of speech within Parliament and banned excessive bail and cruel and unusual punishments. Every English subject was guaranteed the right to petition the king and the right to a fair and impartial jury in legal cases. Later that same year, Parliament passed the **Toleration Act,** granting freedom of worship to nearly all Protestants but not to Catholics and Jews. 📖 *(See page 1063 for an excerpt from the English Bill of Rights).*

The changes the Glorious Revolution brought to England contributed significantly to the colonists' ideas of government. Eventually the ideas found in the English Bill of Rights and the Toleration Act would be expanded and incorporated into the American Bill of Rights. At the time, however, England's Glorious Revolution offered colonists a justification to revolt against Governor-General Andros.

The Glorious Revolution in America As soon as word reached Massachusetts that Parliament had dethroned James II, an uprising occurred in Boston. Andros and his councilors were seized and imprisoned. They were later returned to England. Although

---

Profiles IN HISTORY

Anne Bradstreet
c. 1612–1672

Anne Dudley was born about 1612 in Northampton, England. At the age of 16 she married Simon Bradstreet, and two years later she accompanied her husband on board the *Arabella* to America. The Bradstreets, traveling with John Winthrop's party, were among the first settlers of the Massachusetts Bay Colony.

In America Anne Bradstreet faced the difficult task of building a home in the wilderness. Despite the hard work of raising eight children, she found time to write poetry. In 1650 the first edition of her poetry was published in England as *The Tenth Muse Lately Sprung Up in America.* Bradstreet had not anticipated this recognition. Her brother-in-law had secretly taken a copy of her manuscript to a London publisher.

Anne Bradstreet was a devoted supporter of her husband, who became a leading political figure in Massachusetts, serving two terms as governor. During the period of the Dominion of New England, he spoke out against the harsh rule of Edmund Andros. In a poem, *To My Dear Loving Husband,* published after her death, Anne described their relationship:

If ever two were one, then surely we.
If ever man were loved by wife, then thee;
If ever wife was happy in a man,
Compare with me ye women if you can.

William and Mary let the hated Dominion of New England die quietly, they did not completely restore the old system. They permitted Rhode Island and Connecticut to resume their previous forms of government, but they were unwilling to surrender all control over Massachusetts. Instead they issued a new charter in 1691. The new charter combined the Massachusetts Bay Colony, Plymouth colony, and Maine into the royal colony of Massachusetts.

Under the new charter, the people of Massachusetts were given the right to elect an assembly. The assembly, in turn, was given the right to elect the governor's councilors, but King William insisted that the governor had to be appointed by the king. The new charter also changed who could vote. Under the new system, voters had to own property, but they did not have to be members of a Puritan congregation. The new charter also granted freedom of worship to Anglicans living in Massachusetts.

GOVERNMENT

The Legacy of John Locke The Glorious Revolution of 1688 also set a very important precedent. It showed that there were times when revolution against the king was justified. During this turmoil, a political philosopher named John Locke wrote a book entitled *Two Treatises of Government,* in which he

---

Profiles IN HISTORY

Have students use library and Internet resources to locate and read a poem written by Anne Bradstreet. Have students write a paragraph describing their reaction to the poem.

3 ASSESS

Assign Section 3 Assessment as homework or as an in-class activity.

⬤ Have students use the **Interactive Tutor Self-Assessment CD-ROM.**

Reading Essentials and Study Guide 3–3

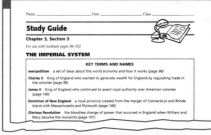

Section Quiz 3–3

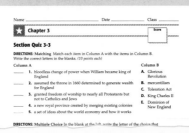

INTERDISCIPLINARY CONNECTIONS ACTIVITY

Government Have a government or political science teacher come and discuss the development of legal documents from the colonial period that affected United States history. After the presentation, have students discuss how these documents may have contributed to the American Revolution.

Fact	Fiction	Folklore

Prior to his association with the Earl of Shaftsbury, John Locke pursued his interest in experimental science. Robert Boyle, who is considered one of the founders of modern chemistry, was one of Locke's friends.

Reteach

Ask students to explain the role of mercantilism in the creation of the Dominion of New England.

Enrich

Have student research the Navigation Acts and create a table similar to the one on page 100. Students' tables should include detail that is not included in the text.

4 CLOSE

Have students discuss the following question: Does the United States government today protect the natural rights of its citizens? Why or why not?

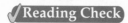

Reading Check

Answer: William and Mary swore to obey the laws of Parliament.

Fact	Fiction	Folklore

John Locke John Locke is best known for his writings on the philosophy of government. He did, however, have other talents. Though he never completed a degree in medicine, Locke was known as "Dr. Locke" in some circles. In 1666 he successfully performed an operation on the Earl of Shaftsbury to clean out an abscess in the chest. In return the earl allowed Locke to live at his home and devote his time to philosophical writings.

explained the basis of political obligation and justified revolution. 📖 *(See page 1064 for an excerpt of Locke's Two Treatises of Government.)*

Locke argued that a monarch's right to rule came from the people. He asserted that all people were born with certain natural rights, including the right to life, liberty, and property. Before governments were created, Locke said, people lived in a "state of nature" where their rights were not safe. To protect their rights, people had come together and mutually agreed to create a government. In effect the people had formed a contract. They had agreed to obey the government's laws, and the government agreed to uphold their rights in return. Locke claimed that monarchs were parties to this contract, and if they violated the people's rights, the people were justified in overthrowing the monarch and changing their system of government.

Locke's ideas had a profound influence on American colonists. The colonists understood Locke's "natural rights" to be the specific rights of English citizens that had developed over the centuries in England and were referred to in documents such as the Magna Carta and the English Bill of Rights. Furthermore, Locke seemed to be describing the colonial experience. Settlers had arrived in America in a state of nature and then built governments based on contractual arrangements. The Mayflower Compact, the Fundamental Orders of Connecticut, and the various colonial charters were all agreements between the people and their government.

Others in England and America reinforced and repeated Locke's ideas in the decades that followed the Glorious Revolution. In January 1750, for example, Jonathan Mayhew, pastor of Boston's West Church, preached:

> ❝If we calmly consider the nature of the thing itself, nothing can well be imagined more directly contrary to common sense than to suppose that millions of people should be subjected to the arbitrary, precarious pleasure of one single man—who has naturally no superiority over them in point of authority. . . . What unprejudiced man can think that God made *all* to be thus subservient to the lawless pleasure and fancy of one so that it shall always be a sin to resist him?❞

—quoted in *The Making of American Democracy*

Only a few years later, the American colonies would put these ideas into practice when they launched their own revolution against Britain.

✓ **Reading Check** **Summarizing** What actions did William and Mary take upon becoming the English monarchs?

SECTION 3 ASSESSMENT

Checking for Understanding

1. **Define:** mercantilism, natural rights.
2. **Identify:** Charles II, James II, Dominion of New England, Glorious Revolution.
3. **Discuss** how England's Glorious Revolution influenced the American colonies.

Reviewing Themes

4. **Individual Action** How did Governor-General Andros's attempt to weaken colonial resolve increase colonists' anger towards England?

Critical Thinking

5. **Predicting Consequences** How did the ideas of the philosopher John Locke contribute to revolutionary ideas in the American colonies?
6. **Categorizing** Use a graphic organizer similar to the one below to fill in the benefits of mercantilism.

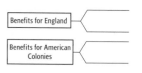

Benefits for England

Benefits for American Colonies

Analyzing Visuals

7. **Examining Art** Study the picture of Boston on page 99. Why do you think colonial merchant shippers were angry about the Navigation Acts?

Writing About History

8. **Expository Writing** Take on the role of a colonial merchant. Write a letter to a relative in England explaining how the Navigation Acts have affected your business.

102   CHAPTER 3   Colonial Ways of Life

SECTION 3 ASSESSMENT ANSWERS

1. Terms are in blue.
2. Charles II *(p. 99)*, James II *(p. 100)*, Dominion of New England *(p. 100)*, Glorious Revolution *(p. 101)*
3. The Glorious Revolution encouraged colonists to revolt against Andros, reestablished colonial control of some colonies, and fostered ideas about rights.

4. Andros' attempts to weaken colonial resolve angered nearly everyone in New England.
5. Locke's ideas about a contract between government and people, justifiable revolution, and natural rights inspired American colonists.
6. Students' answers should reflect information from the text.

7. The Navigation Acts required imports to and exports from the colonies to be sent on English merchant ships only.
8. Students' letters will vary. Letters should include references to shipping, raw materials, and the high cost of imported goods.

Social Studies
SKILLBUILDER

Reading a Bar Graph

Why Learn This Skill?

Graphs are a way of displaying numbers or statistics in a clear, easy-to-read way. Learning to read graphs will help you understand and compare statistical data. One type of graph often used to compare statistics is a bar graph.

Learning the Skill

A bar graph provides information along two sides, or axes, of a graph. The **horizontal axis** is the line across the bottom of the graph. The **vertical axis** is the line along the side. Both have labels to tell you what kind of information they are showing. Bars on the graph run horizontally or vertically along these axes. A double bar graph, such as the one on this page, shows a comparison of information. A key tells you what each bar represents.

Practicing the Skill

The bar graph above shows the population of six English colonies in 1700. Study the graph and then answer the questions.

① What two kinds of populations are shown on this graph?

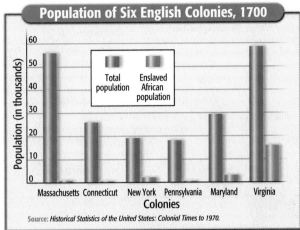

Population of Six English Colonies, 1700

Population (in thousands) — Total population, Enslaved African population

Colonies: Massachusetts, Connecticut, New York, Pennsylvania, Maryland, Virginia

Source: *Historical Statistics of the United States: Colonial Times to 1970.*

② Which colony had the highest total population in 1700? The lowest?

③ Which colony had the largest enslaved African population? The lowest? How do you account for the difference?

④ Approximately what percentage of Maryland's total population was enslaved Africans?

Skills Assessment

Complete the Practicing Skills questions on page 111 and the Chapter 3 Skill Reinforcement Activity to assess your mastery of this skill.

1750 tapestry of Beacon Hill and Boston Common

Applying the Skill

Reading a Bar Graph Gather information about the number of students in each of your classes. Create a bar graph comparing the total number of students with the number involved in after-school clubs or sports. Be sure to include a title for your graph.

  Glencoe's **Skillbuilder Interactive Workbook CD-ROM, Level 2,** provides instruction and practice in key social studies skills.

TEACH

Reading a Bar Graph A horizontal bar graph displays the data categories along the vertical axis and plots the values along the horizontal axis. When the categories are displayed along the horizontal axis and the data is plotted along the vertical axis, the result is a vertical bar graph. A vertical bar graph is sometimes called a column graph.

Have students use an almanac or other reference source to determine the male and female population of their state and four nearby states. Have students use this information to create a bar graph.

Additional Practice

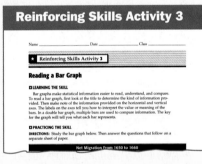

Reinforcing Skills Activity 3

Name _____ Date _____ Class _____

★ Reinforcing Skills Activity 3

Reading a Bar Graph

☐ LEARNING THE SKILL

Bar graphs make statistical information easier to read, understand, and compare. To read a bar graph, first look at the title to determine the kind of information provided. Then make note of the information provided on the horizontal and vertical axes. The labels on the axes tell you how to interpret the value or meaning of the bars. In a double bar graph, multiple bars are used to compare information. The key for the graph will tell you what each bar represents.

☐ PRACTICING THE SKILL

DIRECTIONS: Study the bar graph below. Then answer the questions that follow on a separate sheet of paper.

Net Migration From 1650 to 1660

GLENCOE
TECHNOLOGY

CD-ROM
Glencoe Skillbuilder Interactive Workbook CD-ROM, Level 2

This interactive CD-ROM reinforces student mastery of essential social studies skills.

ANSWERS TO PRACTICING THE SKILL

① total population and enslaved African population

② highest: Virginia; lowest: Pennsylvania

③ highest: Virginia; lowest: Pennsylvania; Virginia plantations required intense manual labor

④ approximately 10 percent

Applying the Skill
Graphs should include realistic data and a key or a legend.

1 FOCUS

Section Overview

This section explores the diversity of American society in the 1700s.

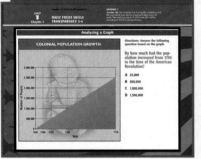
Guide to Reading

Answers to Graphic: Quakers settled in Pennsylvania to pursue religious freedom. Germans settled in Pennsylvania, Virginia, and the Carolinas to pursue religious freedom and escape religious wars. Scotch-Irish settled in Pennsylvania, the western frontier, and the backcountry South to escape rising taxes, poor harvests, and religious discrimination. Jews settled in New York, Philadelphia, Charles Town, and Savannah to pursue religious freedom.

Preteaching Vocabulary

Assign one of the Key Terms and Names to each student. Have the students prepare 30-second oral presentations related to their terms and names.

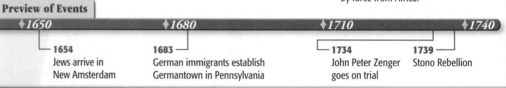

SECTION 4 A Diverse Society

Guide to Reading

Main Idea
America in the 1700s matured into a rich and diverse society.

Key Terms and Names
Cotton Mather, Pennsylvania Dutch, Stono Rebellion, Enlightenment, Great Awakening, rationalism, John Locke, Montesquieu, pietism, revival, Jonathan Edwards, George Whitefield

Reading Strategy
Categorizing As you read about colonial society in the 1700s, complete a graphic organizer similar to the one below by identifying why immigrants settled in the colonies.

Group	Where They Settled	Reasons for Immigrating
Germans		
Scotch-Irish		
Jews		

Reading Objectives
- **Summarize** the plight of enslaved Africans and explain their methods of resistance.
- **Explain** how the Enlightenment and the Great Awakening affected the colonies.

Section Theme
Global Connections Immigrants to the American colonies in the 1700s came from all across Europe or were brought by force from Africa.

Preview of Events

♦1650   ♦1680   ♦1710   ♦1740

1654
Jews arrive in New Amsterdam

1683
German immigrants establish Germantown in Pennsylvania

1734
John Peter Zenger goes on trial

1739
Stono Rebellion

Benjamin Franklin

★ An American Story ★

Early on Sunday morning, October 6, 1723, a 16-year-old boy from Boston stepped off a boat onto Philadelphia's Market Street wharf. Within just a few years, Benjamin Franklin would stride into American history. That day, however, he simply wanted to find breakfast:

❝I was in my working dress, my best clothes being to come round by sea. I was dirty from my journey . . . and I knew no soul nor where to look for lodging. I was fatigued with traveling, rowing, and want of rest; I was very hungry; and my whole stock of cash consisted of a Dutch dollar and about a shilling in copper.❞

With some of his money Franklin bought "three great puffy rolls . . . and, having no room in my pockets, walked off with a roll under each arm, and eating the other . . . I made . . . a most awkward, ridiculous appearance."

Franklin's passion for books and writing led him to Philadelphia, where he achieved success as a printer, writer, scientist, and philosopher. By the time he was 42, the man who popularized the proverb "Time is money" could afford to retire and devote himself to public life.

—adapted from *Colonial Pennsylvania: A History*

Family Life in Colonial America

Benjamin Franklin's meteoric rise from poverty to riches was extraordinary. However, his huge family—Franklin was 1 of 17 children—was not unusual in America in the 1700s. The population of the American colonies was in a period of explosive growth, partly because people were having large families, and partly because immigrants—some willing, some forced—were flooding into the colonies from Europe and Africa.

SECTION RESOURCES

📁 Reproducible Masters
- Reproducible Lesson Plan 3–4
- Daily Lecture and Discussion Notes 3–4
- Guided Reading Activity 3–4
- Section Quiz 3–4
- Reading Essentials and Study Guide 3–4
- Performance Assessment Activities and Rubrics

🖥 Transparencies
- Daily Focus Skills Transparency 3–4

Multimedia
- Interactive Tutor Self-Assessment CD-ROM
- ExamView® Pro Testmaker CD-ROM
- Presentation Plus! CD-ROM
- TeacherWorks™ CD-ROM
- Audio Program

Population Growth The birthrate in the American colonies was high in the 1700s. Most women married in their early twenties, typically to men in their early to mid-twenties. On average, colonial women gave birth to seven children, although giving birth to twice that number of children was not uncommon.

Between 1640 and 1700, the population of the American colonies increased from 25,000 to more than 250,000. In the 1700s, the population more than doubled every 25 years. More than 1 million colonists lived in America in the 1750s, and by the time of the American Revolution, the population had reached roughly 2.5 million people.

Women in Colonial Society In the American colonies, as in Europe, law and custom gave men greater authority and importance than women—in politics and in the household. In the early colonial era, married women had no legal status. A married woman could not own anything, and all of the property she brought into the marriage became her husband's. In most colonies, a married woman could not make a contract, be party to a lawsuit, or make a will. Husbands were the sole guardians of the children and were allowed to physically discipline both their wives and their children. Single women and widows, on the other hand, had considerably more rights. They could own and manage property, file lawsuits, and run businesses.

In the 1700s, the status of married women improved considerably. In most colonies, for example, husbands could not sell or mortgage their land without their wife's signature on the contract. Also, in several colonies, married women began engaging in business as well. Despite the legal limitations, many colonial women worked outside of their homes. Women operated taverns and shops, managed plantations, ran print shops, and published newspapers.

Health and Disease Improvements in housing and sanitation helped American colonists resist some diseases. Still, they frequently suffered from typhoid fever, tuberculosis, cholera, diphtheria, "fluxes" (diarrhea), "malignant fever" (influenza), typhus, and scarlet fever.

These diseases ravaged residents in colonial cities. When an epidemic of deadly smallpox swept through Boston in 1721, the scientific interests

Pennsylvania Dutch decorated pie dish

of a minister and the knowledge of enslaved Africans combined to save hundreds of lives. Reverend **Cotton Mather**, a Puritan leader, had read that the Turks had successfully developed an inoculation for smallpox. Making inquiries among enslaved Africans, Mather discovered that they also knew this technique. At Mather's urging, Dr. Zabdiel Boylston, a Boston physician and friend, inoculated willing Bostonians against the disease. Despite furious opposition, Mather and Boylston persisted in their experiment. In July 1721, Mather wrote:

❝I have instructed our Physicians in the new Method used by the Africans and Asiaticks, to prevent and abate the Dangers of the Small-Pox, and infallibly to save the Lives of those that have it wisely managed upon them. The Destroyer, being enraged at the Proposal of any Thing, that may rescue the Lives of our poor People from him, has taken a strange Possession of the People on this Occasion. They rave, they rail, they blaspheme; they talk not only like Ideots but also like Franticks, . . . I also am an Object of their Fury. . . .❞

—quoted in *The Colonial Image*

The daring experiment proved to be a great success. Of the 6,000 people who were not inoculated and caught smallpox, about 900, or 15 percent, died. In stark contrast, only 6 of the 241 inoculated people, or less than 3 percent, died of the disease.

✓ **Reading Check** **Summarizing** What rights did colonial law deny women?

Immigrants in Colonial America

The American colonies grew rapidly due to immigration and a high birthrate. Hundreds of thousands of free white immigrants arrived between 1700 and 1775, settling throughout the colonies. At the same time, traders brought large numbers of enslaved Africans to America, mostly to the Southern Colonies.

German Immigrants Arrive in Pennsylvania America's first large group of German immigrants came to Pennsylvania looking for religious freedom. First to arrive were a group of Mennonites who founded Germantown in 1683. Large-scale

2 TEACH

Daily Lecture and Discussion Notes 3–4

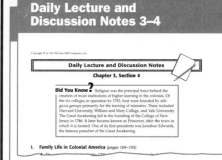

Creating a Graph Have students use the population data on this page to create a line graph. Use the graphs to discuss the population trend in the American colonies between 1640 and 1750. **L1** ELL

📁 Use the rubric for creating a map, display, or chart on pages 77–78 in the *Performance Assessment Activities and Rubrics.*

✓ **Reading Check**

Answer: Married women could not own property, make contracts, be party to a lawsuit, or make a will. Single and widowed women could own land, file lawsuits, and run businesses.

Sybilla Masters, wife of a Philadelphia merchant, invented a corn mill for producing hominy meal from Indian maize. As a woman, she could not own a patent; therefore she filed the patent application for her mill under her husband's name.

COOPERATIVE LEARNING ACTIVITY

Making Oral Presentations Organize the students into groups of four or five. Assign each group one of the immigrant groups listed in this section. Have the groups research the immigrant group to discover the reasons why they immigrated to the colonies, where they settled, how they maintained their cultural identity, and how they participated in colonial society. Have the groups present their findings in an oral presentation to the class. 🗂

Use the rubric for a cooperative group management plan on pages 81–82 in the *Performance Assessment Activities and Rubrics.*

Guided Reading Activity 3-4

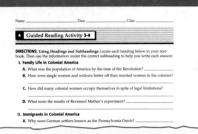

✔ Reading Check

Answer: Germans settled in Pennsylvania to pursue religious freedom and escape religious wars.

Creating Circle Graphs Have students create a pair of circle charts using the data about smallpox on page 105. The charts should compare the death rates of those who were inoculated to those who were not inoculated. **L2**

📁 Use the rubric for creating a map, display, or chart on pages 77–78 in the *Performance Assessment Activities and Rubrics.*

Profiles IN HISTORY

In 1736 Zenger published his account of the events surrounding his arrest and trial in *A Brief Narrative of the Case and Tryal of John Peter Zenger.* Although Zenger's acquittal did not change the libel laws, it set a political precedent that would be revisited when the Bill of Rights was drafted.

Word Origins The origin of several English words such as *goober, gumbo,* and *juke,* can be traced to the Gullah language.

German immigration to Pennsylvania started in the early 1700s. By 1775, more than 100,000 Germans had arrived in the colony, where they made up about one-third of the population. Known as the **Pennsylvania Dutch** (from their own word *Deutsche,* meaning "German"), these settlers became some of the colony's most prosperous farmers. They introduced the Conestoga wagon, which later generations would adapt for use in crossing the country. As early as the 1720s, many Germans also headed south along the Great Philadelphia Wagon Road to the Shenandoah River valley of Virginia. From there they spread throughout the backcountry of Virginia and the Carolinas.

The Scotch-Irish Head West The Scotch-Irish were descendants of the Scots who had helped England claim control of Northern Ireland. Beginning in 1717, rising taxes, poor harvests, and religious discrimination convinced many Scotch-Irish to flee Ireland. An estimated 150,000 Scotch-Irish immigrated to the American colonies between 1717 and 1776.

Although the Scotch-Irish settled in many colonies, most headed to Pennsylvania. Unwilling and often unable to purchase land, many migrated west to the frontier, where they occupied vacant land. Many

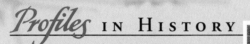

Profiles IN HISTORY

John Peter Zenger *1697–1746*

In 1710 Britain had paid for German families to immigrate to the American colonies. In time, one of these immigrants, 13-year-old John Peter Zenger, would help change colonial society.

By 1726 Zenger was running a failing printing business in New York. His only successful venture to this point had been to print the colonies' first arithmetic text.

In 1732 Zenger's luck changed when an unpopular royal governor dismissed New York's chief justice from office. The chief justice hired Zenger to publish an anti-government newspaper. In 1734 Zenger's paper called the royal governor's supporters "the dregs and scandal of human nature."

Zenger was arrested and charged for printing libel, or slanderous information. Indeed, according to British law, criticizing the royal governor—even if the criticisms were true—was a grave offense. For the eight months he spent in prison, a defiant Zenger continued to edit his newspaper through a hole in his cell door.

Zenger's attorney, Andrew Hamilton, the colonies' most famous lawyer, called Zenger's cause "the cause of liberty." Only a press free to criticize the government could prevent that government from abusing its power, Hamilton argued. The jury took only a few minutes to reach its verdict. They found Zenger not guilty. Zenger's trial helped establish the American commitment to freedom of the press.

Scotch-Irish also followed the Great Philadelphia Wagon Road south into the backcountry of the Southern Colonies.

Colonial America's Jewish Community A small group of Jews, fleeing from the Portuguese in Brazil and seeking an opportunity to practice their religion, first arrived in the colonies in New Amsterdam (later called New York City) in 1654. By 1776 approximately 2,500 Jews lived in the colonies. Most lived in the cities of New York, Philadelphia, Charles Town, Savannah, and Newport, where they were allowed to worship as they pleased. They made their living as artisans and merchants. Unlike in western Europe, where Jews could not own property or participate in professions, colonial Jews lived and worked alongside Christians.

✔ Reading Check **Explaining** Why did many Germans immigrate to Pennsylvania in the 1700s?

Africans in Colonial America

Africans arrived in the colonies from many different regions of West Africa. In the colonies, they tried to maintain their specific languages and traditions even though white planters intentionally bought slaves from different regions who spoke different languages to make it difficult for them to plot rebellion.

Africans Build a New Culture In South Carolina, where rice cultivation required a large, coordinated workforce, Africans worked and lived in larger groups than in other Southern Colonies. Their isolation from the white planters resulted in a more independent African culture, which developed its own language called Gullah. Gullah combined English and African words, and it allowed Africans from a variety of homelands to converse. In the Chesapeake region, where more of the enslaved population had been born in America, Africans spoke English.

Using a common language helped Africans from diverse backgrounds develop a new culture in America. African traditional religious beliefs became mixed with the practices of the Christian faith. African rhythms became a part of new musical forms. The fear of being sold and separated

---

MEETING SPECIAL NEEDS

Interpersonal Have students list the objections that Cotton Mather may have encountered as he tried to convince his fellow citizens in Boston to be inoculated against smallpox. Using the list of objections, have students write a script that Cotton Mather could have used to convince friends and fellow citizens to be inoculated. **L3**

📁 Refer to *Inclusion for the High School Social Studies Classroom Strategies and Activities* in the TCR.

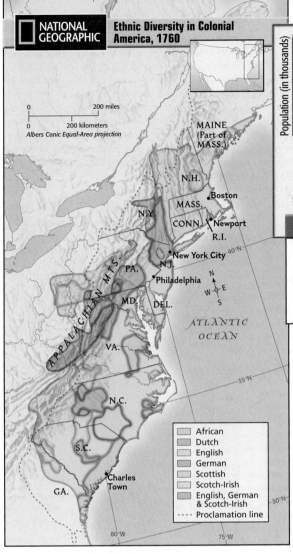

Ethnic Diversity in Colonial America, 1760

NATIONAL GEOGRAPHIC

Major Cities, c. 1760

Source: *Colonial America to 1763.*

Geography *Skills*

1. **Interpreting Maps** Where were the majority of Dutch settlers located in colonial America?
2. **Interpreting Graphs** According to the map, which of the cities listed on the graph had a predominantly African population?

from one's family, however, was always present. Despite these conditions, many Africans managed to pass on their family names and cultural traditions.

Oppression and Resistance In South Carolina, where often as few as 5 whites would oversee roughly 100 enslaved Africans, authority was maintained through harsh means. Whippings and beatings were common. Disobedient workers were branded, and some planters would slit noses or amputate fingers and toes as punishment and to terrify other workers into obeying orders. Africans in South Carolina needed passes to leave their plantations, and planters organized regular night patrols to watch for rebellion and runaways.

Planters in Virginia also whipped, branded, and mutilated Africans to force them to obey. Here, however, the enslaved population was smaller relative to the white population, and the work was not quite as exhausting and difficult. Therefore, authority was often maintained through manipulation and persuasion. Planters and overseers would bargain with the enslaved workers, promising extra rations or days off work if the workers completed a particular task.

While slaveholders tried to force enslaved Africans to obey, Africans themselves developed many different ways to fight against slavery. Some Africans resisted by running away. Many others responded with passive resistance. They would refuse to work hard, stage deliberate work slowdowns, or lose or break tools.

Occasionally groups of slaves banded together to resist the slaveholders. In the late 1730s, the governor of Spanish Florida, in an attempt to weaken South Carolina, promised freedom and land to any enslaved Africans who fled south to Florida. In 1739, 75 Africans gathered near the Stono River, attacked their white overseers, stole their guns, and raced south toward Florida, attacking whites as they traveled. The local militia eventually ended the **Stono Rebellion,** killing between 30 and 40 of the Africans.

✓**Reading Check** **Summarizing** In what ways did Africans resist their enslavement?

CHAPTER 3   Colonial Ways of Life   **107**

INTERDISCIPLINARY CONNECTIONS ACTIVITY

Music Invite a music teacher or a musician to speak to your class about the influences of African music on music around the world. Ask the speaker to include live or recorded music in the presentation. Have students answer the following question. **How do you feel your life has been enriched by African music? L1**

3 ASSESS

Assign Section 4 Assessment as homework or as an in-class activity.

🌐 Have students use the **Interactive Tutor Self-Assessment CD-ROM.**

Reading Essentials and Study Guide 3–4

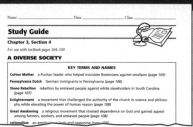

FYI

George Whitefield began preaching outdoors in England when some Anglican ministers refused to let him preach in their churches. He continued this practice when he arrived in America.

Fact	Fiction	Folklore

Saint George is the patron saint of England. His precise origins are unknown, but it is believed that he was a Roman citizen who was beheaded by Diocletian for protesting against his persecution of Christians. Saint Andrew is the patron saint of Scotland. He was one of Jesus' original followers and by church tradition is thought to have been crucified by the Romans.

The Enlightenment and the Great Awakening

Ideas as well as people made their way to the English colonies. During the 1700s, America came under the influence of two great European cultural movements. One movement, the Enlightenment, challenged the authority of the church in science and philosophy while elevating the power of human reason. In contrast, a religious movement, later known in America as the Great Awakening, stressed dependence on God and gained wide appeal among farmers, workers, and enslaved people.

The Enlightenment Enlightenment thinkers believed that natural laws applied to social, political, and economic relationships, and that people could figure out these natural laws if they employed reason. This emphasis on logic and reasoning was known as rationalism.

One of the earliest and most influential Enlightenment writers was **John Locke.** His contract theory of government and natural rights is a good example of the way Enlightenment thinkers attempted to use reason to discover natural laws that applied to politics and society.

Even more significant in some ways was Locke's *Essay on Human Understanding*. In this work, Locke argued that contrary to what the Church taught, people were not born sinful. Instead their minds were blank slates that society could shape. Locke believed that society and education could make people better. These ideas that all people have rights and that society can be improved became core beliefs in American society.

Another influential Enlightenment writer was **Baron Montesquieu.** In his work *Spirit of the Laws*,

Fact	Fiction	Folklore

English Flag This flag flew over the English settlements throughout the colonial period. First used in 1606, the flag displays the red cross of England (cross of St. George) superimposed on the white cross of Scotland (cross of St. Andrew), on the blue background field of Scotland. This "Union Flag," as it was called, remained in use until January 1, 1801.

published in 1748, Montesquieu suggested that there were three types of political power—executive, legislative, and judicial. Montesquieu argued that these powers should be separated into different branches of the government to protect the liberty of the people. The different branches would provide checks and balances against each other and prevent the government from abusing its authority. Montesquieu's idea of the separation of powers shaped the thinking of many American leaders who later helped design the American Constitution.

The Great Awakening While some Americans turned away from a religious worldview in the 1700s, others enthusiastically renewed their Christian faith. Many Americans embraced a European religious movement called pietism, which stressed an individual's piety (devoutness) and an emotional union with God.

Throughout the colonies, ministers spread the message of pietism through revivals—large public meetings for preaching and prayer. This revival of religious feeling is known as the Great Awakening.

In New England the Great Awakening was, in part, a response to declining religious fervor and a reaction to the ideas of the Enlightenment. In 1734 a Massachusetts preacher and philosopher named **Jonathan Edwards** aimed to restore New England's spiritual intensity after experiencing his own conversion. His terrifying sermons pictured humanity dangling on the brink of damnation, suspended only by the "forbearance of an incensed [angry] God." Edwards argued that a person had to repent and convert, to be "born again." This idea of having an internal emotional experience that brings a person to God became a central idea of the Great Awakening.

The Great Awakening began in earnest when the Anglican minister **George Whitefield** arrived in Philadelphia in 1739. The ideas of John Wesley, the founder of Methodism, influenced Whitefield, and both had an impact on America. Whitefield was a powerful, emotional speaker, and he attracted large crowds everywhere he preached.

Whitefield also warned of the dangers of listening to ministers who had not been born again. This challenge to the authority of other ministers created tensions within colonial congregations. During the Great Awakening, nearly all New England churches split into factions called the New Lights and the Old Lights, or the New Side and the Old Side. Many ministers found themselves dismissed by their congregations depending on which side they took. Those

CRITICAL THINKING ACTIVITY

Identifying Both the Enlightenment and the Great Awakening had a dramatic impact on life in Colonial America. The influences of these cultural movements can still be seen in America today. Have students identify the main idea presented in the passages in the text about these movements and discuss their significance. **L2**

churches that embraced the new ideas—including the Baptists, some Presbyterians and Congregationalists, and the new group called the Methodists—experienced a surge in membership, while other churches' memberships declined.

The Great Awakening also had a profound effect in the South, where the emotion and energy of Baptist preaching won converts among poor tenant and backcountry farmers. Baptists also welcomed enslaved Africans at their revivals and condemned the brutality of slavery. Hundreds of Africans joined Baptist congregations and listened to sermons that taught that all people were equal before God.

The Baptist effort to preach to the enslaved Africans provoked a violent response from the planters, who feared losing control of their workforce. Sheriffs and justices of the peace organized armed groups of planters to break up Baptist meetings by force. Despite the violence, by 1775, 20 percent of Virginia's whites and thousands of enslaved Africans had joined Baptist congregations. Within the enslaved community, converts spread the word even further, creating a separate African Christian culture on the plantations.

The Great Awakening was one of the last major cultural developments in America before the American Revolution. Like the Enlightenment, it implanted ideas that are still a very powerful part of American society.

The Enlightenment and the Great Awakening had different origins and directions. Both movements, however, served to emphasize an individualism that supported America's political independence. The

History *Through Art*

The Great Awakening George Whitefield was one of the most famous ministers of this period of intense religious revival in the colonies. How did Whitefield's emphasis on being "born again" affect churches?

Enlightenment provided arguments against British rule. The Great Awakening undermined allegiance to traditional authority.

Reading Check **Describing** How did the Great Awakening affect New England churches?

Section Quiz 3–4

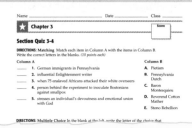

DIRECTIONS: Matching Match each item in Column A with the items in Column B. Write the correct letters in the blanks. (10 points each)

Column A
1. German immigrants in Pennsylvania
2. influential Enlightenment writer
3. when 75 enslaved Africans attacked their white overseers
4. person behind the experiment to inoculate Bostonians against smallpox
5. stresses an individual's devoutness and emotional union with God

Column B
A. Pietism
B. Pennsylvania Dutch
C. Baron Montesquieu
D. Reverend Cotton Mather
E. Stono Rebellion

DIRECTIONS: Multiple Choice In the blank at the left, write the letter of the choice that

History *Through Art*

Answer: It challenged ministers' authority and created tensions in congregations. Ministers were dismissed or retained according to their stance on the necessity of being born again.

Reading Check

Answer: It split churches into various factions, with some rapidly expanding and others declining.

Reteach

Have students compose a review question for each page of this section. Ask students to take turns asking their questions until the important points of the section are covered.

Enrich

Have students select an event from this section and write an essay about its continuing influence.

SECTION 4 ASSESSMENT

Checking for Understanding
1. **Define:** Enlightenment, Great Awakening, rationalism, pietism, revival.
2. **Identify:** Cotton Mather, Pennsylvania Dutch, Stono Rebellion, John Locke, Montesquieu, Jonathan Edwards, George Whitefield.
3. **Explain** how the Enlightenment and the Great Awakening influenced the American colonies.

Reviewing Themes
4. **Global Connections** What factors and motivations drove immigration to the American colonies in the 1700s?

Critical Thinking
5. **Making Comparisons** In what ways did enslaved Africans develop their own culture in the American colonies?
6. **Organizing** Use a graphic organizer similar to the one below to explain the reasons for the population increase in the colonies in the 1700s.

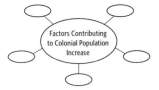
Factors Contributing to Colonial Population Increase

Analyzing Visuals
7. **Studying Paintings** Examine the painting of George Whitefield on this page. How does the imagery of the painting suggest the emotionalism that Whitefield was known for during the Great Awakening?

Writing About History
8. **Persuasive Writing** Imagine that you are a German immigrant to the colonies in 1725. Write a letter to your relatives explaining what your life in the colonies is like and encouraging them to join you in America.

CHAPTER 3 Colonial Ways of Life **109**

SECTION 4 ASSESSMENT ANSWERS

1. Terms are in blue.
2. Cotton Mather *(p. 105)*, Pennsylvania Dutch *(p. 106)*, Stono Rebellion *(p. 107)*, John Locke *(p. 108)*, Montesquieu *(p. 108)*, Jonathan Edwards *(p. 108)*, George Whitefield *(p. 108)*
3. Both movements emphasized an individualism that supported

America's political independence.
4. pursuit of religious freedom; to escape religious wars, rising taxes, and poor harvests; slavery
5. by developing their own language, by mixing traditional African religious beliefs with the Christian faith, and new musical forms
6. enslavement of Africans, immigra-

tion, improved housing and sanitation, smallpox inoculation, higher birthrate
7. Whitefield has his hands raised and his listeners look almost entranced by him.
8. Letters should include descriptive language of daily life and issue a clear invitation.

4 CLOSE

Have students compare and contrast the Enlightenment and the Great Awakening.

GLENCOE TECHNOLOGY

MindJogger Videoquiz
Use the **MindJogger Videoquiz** to review Chapter 3 content.

 Available in VHS

Reviewing Key Terms

Students' answers will vary. The pages where the words appear in the text are shown in parentheses.

1. **cash crop** (p. 85)
2. **plantation** (p. 85)
3. **indentured servant** (p. 86)
4. **gentry** (p. 86)
5. **subsistence farming** (p. 87)
6. **Middle Passage** (p. 89)
7. **slave code** (p. 90)
8. **town meeting** (p. 94)
9. **selectmen** (p. 94)
10. **bill of exchange** (p. 95)
11. **triangular trade** (p. 95)
12. **artisan** (p. 95)
13. **entrepreneur** (p. 97)
14. **capitalist** (p. 97)
15. **mercantilism** (p. 98)
16. **natural rights** (p. 102)
17. **Enlightenment** (p. 108)
18. **Great Awakening** (p. 108)
19. **rationalism** (p. 108)
20. **pietism** (p. 108)
21. **revival** (p. 108)

Reviewing Key Facts

22. William Berkeley (p. 87), Royal African Company (p. 89), Charles II (p. 99), James II (p. 100), Pennsylvania Dutch (p. 106), John Locke (p. 108), Montesquieu (p. 108), Jonathan Edwards (p. 108), George Whitefield (p. 108)

23. The Southern Colonies depended on tobacco, rice, and indigo.

24. The crops grown in the Southern Colonies required intense manual labor. Southern planters could not afford to pay wages to workers, but

Reviewing Key Terms

On a sheet of paper, use the following terms in a sentence.

1. cash crop
2. plantation
3. indentured servant
4. gentry
5. subsistence farming
6. Middle Passage
7. slave code
8. town meeting
9. selectmen
10. bill of exchange
11. triangular trade
12. artisan
13. entrepreneur
14. capitalist
15. mercantilism
16. natural rights
17. Enlightenment
18. Great awakening
19. rationalism
20. pietism
21. revival

Reviewing Key Facts

22. **Identify:** William Berkeley, Royal African Company, Charles II, James II, Pennsylvania Dutch, John Locke, Montesquieu, Jonathan Edwards, George Whitefield.

23. What crops did the economy of the Southern Colonies depend on?

24. Why did Southern planters come to rely on enslaved labor?

25. How did trade affect the economy of the Northern Colonies?

26. Why did England pass the Navigation Acts?

27. Why was the creation of the Dominion of New England unpopular in the English Colonies?

28. Why did Africans in South Carolina develop a more independent slave culture than Africans in other Southern Colonies?

29. How did the Great Awakening influence the American colonies?

Chapter Summary

The American Colonies

Region	Geography	Economy	People and Society
New England Colonies	Coastal areas with good natural harbors; inland areas with dense forests; poor rocky soil and short growing season	Small farms, lumber mills, fishing, shipbuilding, and trade flourished; cities developed along coast.	Most people organized as congregations lived on farms; in the cities merchants controlled trade, artisans made goods, unskilled workers and enslaved Africans provided labor.
Middle Colonies	Fertile soil and long growing season; rivers ran into backcountry	Colonies grew large amounts of rye, oats, barley, potatoes, and wheat as cash crops to sell; cities developed on the coast.	Wealthiest people owned large farms and other businesses. Most farmers produced a small surplus. Tenant farmers rented land from large landowners or worked for wages.
Southern Colonies	Favorable climate and soil for agriculture; wide rivers made cities unnecessary	Tobacco, rice, and indigo grown on large plantations emerged as cash crops.	Wealthy elite controlled most of the land. Cash crops required a large amount of labor, which was supplied on large farms by indentured servants and enslaved Africans.

with slave labor they could make a living from their agricultural endeavors.

25. Trade gave rise to cities and wealthy merchants in New England.

26. The Navigation Acts were passed to support England's mercantilist policy of encouraging English exports and restricting imports. Mercantilism also emphasized the use of the colonies as sources of raw materials and markets for manufactured goods.

27. The reorganization of the Dominion of New England

was unpopular because it overturned the existing systems of government and tried to undermine the Puritan church.

28. In South Carolina Africans worked in larger groups and were more isolated from the planters than in other regions. This led to a more independent culture.

29. The Great Awakening emphasized an individualism that supported America's political independence. It also undermined allegiance to traditional authority.

Self-Check Quiz

Visit the *American Vision* Web site at tav.glencoe.com and click on *Self-Check Quizzes—Chapter 3* to assess your knowledge of chapter content.

Critical Thinking

30. **Analyzing Themes: Global Connections** How did events and movements in the world contribute to the development of the American colonies?

31. **Evaluating** Do you think Nathaniel Bacon was justified in staging a revolt against Virginia's government?

32. **Forming an Opinion** Do you think slavery would have become entrenched in the South if the region's economy had not depended on cash crops and a large labor force? Why or why not?

33. **Categorizing** Use a graphic organizer similar to the one below to compare the economies of the New England, Middle, and Southern Colonies.

New England Colonies	Middle Colonies	Southern Colonies

Practicing Skills

34. **Reading a Bar Graph** Study the graph of tobacco imports on page 85. Then use the steps you learned about reading a bar graph on page 103 to answer the following questions.
   a. **Interpreting Graphs** In which year did imports reach the highest level?
   b. **Synthesizing Information** Which region would benefit most by the rise in tobacco imports from 1725 to 1735?

Geography and History

35. The map on this page shows colonization and exports in the Americas in 1750. Study the map and answer the following questions.
   a. **Interpreting Maps** Which region produced diamonds?
   b. **Applying Geography Skills** Which European country controlled the most territory in the Americas? Which controlled the least?

Writing Activity

36. **Writing a Magazine Article** Find out about slavery throughout history in various cultural and geographic areas of the world. Choose one area and compare slavery there with the slavery of Africans in the American colonies. Present your findings in a magazine article and place it in your portfolio.

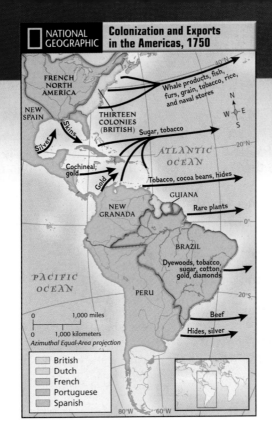

NATIONAL GEOGRAPHIC

Colonization and Exports in the Americas, 1750

FRENCH NORTH AMERICA

NEW SPAIN

THIRTEEN COLONIES (BRITISH)

Whale products, fish, furs, grain, tobacco, rice, and naval stores

Skins

Silver

Sugar, tobacco

ATLANTIC OCEAN

Cochineal, gold

Gold

Tobacco, cocoa beans, hides

GUIANA

NEW GRANADA

Rare plants

BRAZIL

Dyewoods, tobacco, sugar, cotton, gold, diamonds

PACIFIC OCEAN

PERU

Beef

Hides, silver

0   1,000 miles

0   1,000 kilometers
Azimuthal Equal-Area projection

☐ British
☐ Dutch
☐ French
☐ Portuguese
☐ Spanish

Chapter Activity

37. **Technology Activity: Using the Internet** Search the Internet for sites that describe what life was like for colonists in America in the 1700s. Create a travel brochure titled "Visit Colonial America."

Have students visit the Web site at tav.glencoe.com to review Chapter 3 and take the Self-Check Quiz.

Geography and History

35. a. Brazil; **b.** Spain controlled the most territory. The Dutch controlled the least.

Writing Activity

36. Students' magazine articles should compare and contrast slavery in the American colonies with slavery elsewhere in the world using specific details.

Chapter Activity

37. Students' travel brochures will vary but should highlight various destinations that relate to Colonial America.

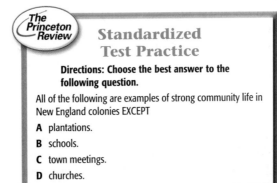

The Princeton Review

Standardized Test Practice

Directions: Choose the best answer to the following question.

All of the following are examples of strong community life in New England colonies EXCEPT

A plantations.

B schools.

C town meetings.

D churches.

Test-Taking Tip: Think about New England's geography and society. Which of the answers does not describe New England's society?

The Princeton Review

Standardized Test Practice

Answer: A

Test-Taking Tip: Encourage students to underline the key words in the question stem. In this case the key words are community life and New England.

Bonus Question ?

Ask: What was the name of the Puritan group that separated from the Anglican Church and fled to Holland? *(Pilgrims)*

Critical Thinking

30. Students' answers will vary but should include important events and movements such as the Glorious Revolution and the Enlightenment.

31. Students' answers will vary. Answers should support the stated point of view.

32. Students' answers will vary. Answers should support the stated point of view.

33. New England Colonies: based on subsistence farming; diverse economic base included livestock, fishing, shipbuilding; Middle Colonies: urban trade centers led to entrepreneurs; fertile farmland supported many crops; Southern Colonies: based on commercial agriculture; main cash crops were tobacco, rice, and indigo

Practicing Skills

34. a. 1775; **b.** Virginia

Unit 2 Resources

SUGGESTED PACING CHART

Unit 2 (1 Day)	Chapter 4 (5 Days)	Chapter 5 (4 Days)	Chapter 6 (5 Days)	Unit 2 (2 Days)
Day 1 Introduction	**Day 1** Chapter 4 Intro, Section 1	**Day 1** Chapter 5 Intro, Section 1	**Day 1** Chapter 6 Intro, Section 1	**Day 1** Wrap-Up/Project
	Day 2 Section 2	**Day 2** Section 2	**Day 2** Section 2	**Day 2** Unit 2 Assessment
	Day 3 Section 3	**Day 3** Section 3	**Day 3** Section 3	
	Day 4 Section 4	**Day 4** Chapter 5 Assessment	**Day 4** Section 4	
	Day 5 Chapter 4 Assessment		**Day 5** Chapter 6 Assessment	

Use the following tools to easily assess student learning in a variety of ways:

- Performance Assessment Activities and Rubrics
- Chapter and Unit Tests
- Section Quizzes
- Standardized Test Skills Practice Workbook

- tav.glencoe.com
- Interactive Tutor Self-Assessment CD-ROM
- MindJogger Videoquiz
- ExamView® Pro Testmaker CD-ROM
- SAT I/II Test Practice

TEACHING TRANSPARENCIES

Unit 2 Map Overlay Transparencies

Cause-and-Effect Transparency 2

*inter*NET RESOURCES

- tav.glencoe.com

The American Vision

Visit the *American Vision* Web site for history overviews, activities, assessments, and updated charts and graphs.

- www.socialstudies.glencoe.com

Glencoe Social Studies

Visit the Glencoe Web site for social studies activities, updates, and links to other sites.

- www.teachingtoday.glencoe.com

Glencoe Teaching Today

Visit the new Glencoe Web site for teacher development information, teaching tips, Web resources, and educational news.

- www.time.com

TIME Online

Visit the TIME Web site for up-to-date news and special reports.

Unit 2 Resources

ASSESSMENT

Unit 2 Pretests

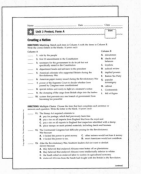

Unit 2 Posttests

APPLICATION AND ENRICHMENT

American Biography 2

History Simulation and Problem Solving 2

GEOGRAPHY

Geography and History Activity 2

INTERDISCIPLINARY ACTIVITIES

American Literature Reading 2

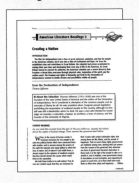

Economics and History Activity 2

Team-Teaching Interdisciplinary Strategies and Activities 2

BIBLIOGRAPHY

Readings for the Student

Thompson, Edmund, ed. *Secret New England, Spies of the American Revolution.* Provincial Press, 2001.

Readings for the Teacher

Rhodehamel, John, ed. *The American Revolution: Writings from the War of Independence.* Library of America, 2001.

Multimedia Resources

Videocassette. *To Keep Our Liberty.* National Park Service. (23 minutes)

Additional Glencoe Resources for This Unit:

- Glencoe Skillbuilder Interactive Workbook CD-ROM, Level 2
- Social Studies Guide to Using the Internet
- Writer's Guidebook for High School
- Living Constitution
- American Art Prints Strategies and Activities

0:00 Out of Time?

If time does not permit teaching each chapter in this unit, you may want to use the **Reading Essentials and Study Guide** summaries.

Unit Overview

Unit 2 explores how the nation was created and how it developed during the period from 1754 to 1816. **Chapter 4** covers the causes and events of the American Revolution, 1754–1783. **Chapter 5** focuses on the efforts to create the Constitution, 1781–1789. **Chapter 3** explores the political debate between the Federalists and Republicans about the structure and purpose of the federal government, 1789–1816.

Unit Objectives

After studying this unit, students will be able to:
1. Summarize events that fueled colonial discontent.
2. Describe the issues at stake during the Constitutional Convention.
3. Discuss the growing tensions between the nation's political parties.

Why It Matters Activity

Discuss how the unique vision of the nation's founders created a distinctive form of government. Draw conclusions about how life would have been different had the colonies remained a part of Great Britain.

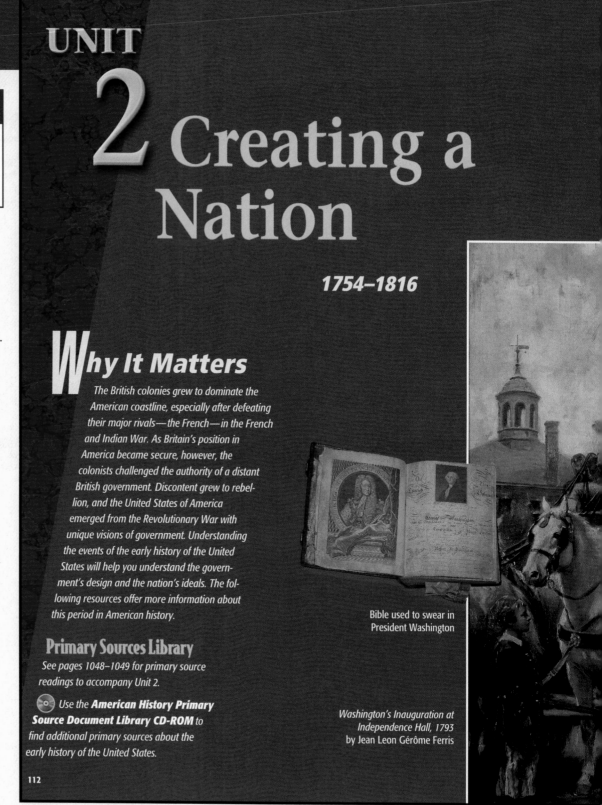

UNIT
2 Creating a Nation
1754–1816

Why It Matters

The British colonies grew to dominate the American coastline, especially after defeating their major rivals—the French—in the French and Indian War. As Britain's position in America became secure, however, the colonists challenged the authority of a distant British government. Discontent grew to rebellion, and the United States of America emerged from the Revolutionary War with unique visions of government. Understanding the events of the early history of the United States will help you understand the government's design and the nation's ideals. The following resources offer more information about this period in American history.

Primary Sources Library

See pages 1048–1049 for primary source readings to accompany Unit 2.

Use the **American History Primary Source Document Library CD-ROM** to find additional primary sources about the early history of the United States.

112

Bible used to swear in President Washington

Washington's Inauguration at Independence Hall, 1793 by Jean Leon Gérôme Ferris

TEAM TEACHING ACTIVITY

Civics Have the civics teacher discuss why citizen participation was a topic of debate among the nation's founders. Have the teacher review the ways in which citizens can participate in government in the United States. Then have groups of students create a 10-question citizenship quiz based on what they have learned. Have the groups give the quiz to a variety of people they know and chart the accuracy of the responses. Based on these responses, have students draw conclusions about how much today's society knows about participating in government.

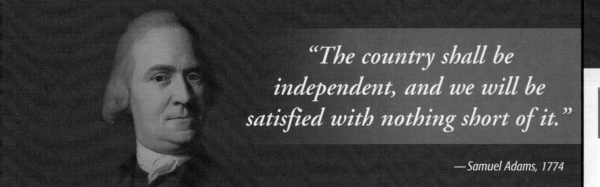

"*The country shall be independent, and we will be satisfied with nothing short of it.*"

—*Samuel Adams, 1774*

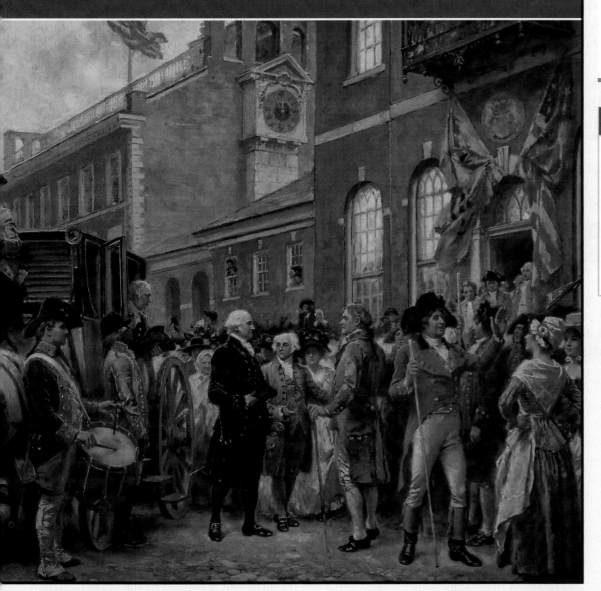

GLENCOE
TECHNOLOGY

CD-ROM
American History
Primary Source
Document Library
CD-ROM
Use the **American History Primary Source Document Library CD-ROM** to access primary source documents related to this period in history.

More About the Art

Washington's first inauguration took place in New York City on the balcony of Federal Hall. The second inauguration occurred at Congress Hall in Philadelphia, Pennsylvania. The cupola of Congress Hall can be seen on the far left side of the painting. Philadelphia served as the nation's capital from 1790 to 1800.

SERVICE-LEARNING PROJECT

Organize students into small groups. Have groups identify aspects of American life that they believe are unfair and need to be changed. Have the groups decide on a plan of action that would correct those problems. Have the groups write letters to the appropriate governmental authorities explaining their concerns and stating the plans they have developed to resolve them. Have the groups share the responses they receive with the class.

Refer to **Building Bridges: Connecting Classroom and Community through Service-Learning in Social Studies** from the National Council for the Social Studies for information about service-learning.

Timesaving Tools

TeacherWorks™ All-In-One Planner and Resource Center

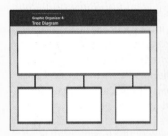

- **Interactive Teacher Edition** Access your Teacher Wraparound Edition and your classroom resources with a few easy clicks.
- **Interactive Lesson Planner** Planning has never been easier! Organize your week, month, semester, or year with all the lesson helps you need to make teaching creative, timely, and relevant.

Use Glencoe's **Presentation Plus!** multimedia teacher tool to easily present dynamic lessons that visually excite your students. Using Microsoft PowerPoint® you can customize the presentations to create your own personalized lessons.

TEACHING TRANSPARENCIES

Graphic Organizer 4

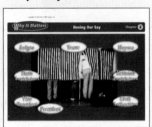

Why It Matters Chapter Transparency 4

APPLICATION AND ENRICHMENT

Linking Past and Present Activity 4

Enrichment Activity 4

Primary Source Reading 4

REVIEW AND REINFORCEMENT

Reteaching Activity 4

Vocabulary Activity 4

Time Line Activity 4

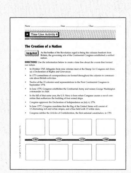

Critical Thinking Skills Activity 4

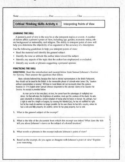

Meeting NCSS Standards

The following standards are highlighted in Chapter 4:

Section 1	X	Civic Ideals and Practices: A, B, E, F, G, I
Section 2	VI	Power, Authority, and Governance: A, C, F, H
Section 3	IX	Global Connections: B, E
Section 4	I	Culture: A, C

Local Standards

_____

_____

_____

_____

_____

**Chapter 4 Test
Form A**

**Chapter 4 Test
Form B**

**Standardized Test Skills
Practice Workbook Activity 4**

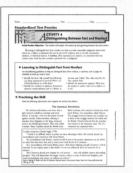

**Performance Assessment
Activities and Rubrics 4**

**ExamView® Pro
Testmaker CD-ROM**

MULTIMEDIA

- Vocabulary PuzzleMaker CD-ROM
- Interactive Tutor Self-Assessment CD-ROM
- ExamView® Pro Testmaker CD-ROM
- Audio Program
- American History Primary Source Documents
  Library CD-ROM
- MindJogger Videoquiz
- Presentation Plus! CD-ROM
- TeacherWorks™ CD-ROM
- Interactive Student Edition CD-ROM
- Glencoe Skillbuilder Interactive Workbook
  CD-ROM, Level 2
- The *American Vision* Video Program
- American Music: Hits Through History
- American Music: Cultural Traditions

THE HISTORY CHANNEL.

The following videotape programs are available
from Glencoe as supplements to Chapter 4:

- **Paul Revere: The Midnight Rider** (ISBN 1-56-501596-7)
- **Thomas Jefferson: Philosopher of Freedom** (ISBN 1-56-501502-9)
- **Benedict Arnold** (ISBN 1-56-501594-0)

To order, call Glencoe at 1-800-334-7344. To find classroom resources to
accompany many of these videos, check the following home pages:
A&E Television: www.aande.com
The History Channel: www.historychannel.com

SPANISH RESOURCES

**The following Spanish language materials are
available in the Spanish Resources Binder:**

- Spanish Guided Reading Activities
- Spanish Reteaching Activities
- Spanish Quizzes and Tests
- Spanish Vocabulary Activities
- Spanish Summaries
- The Declaration of Independence and United States Constitution
  Spanish Translation

HISTORY
Online

Use our Web site for additional resources. All essential content is covered in the Student Edition.

You and your students can visit tav.glencoe.com, the Web site companion to the *American Vision.* This innovative integration of electronic
and print media offers your students a wealth of opportunities. The
student text directs students to the Web site for the following options:

- **Chapter Overviews**   • **Student Web Activities**
- **Self-Check Quizzes**   • **Textbook Updates**

Answers to the student Web activities are provided for you in the **Web
Activity Lesson Plans.** Additional Web resources and Interactive Tutor
Puzzles are also available.

Chapter 4 Resources

SECTION RESOURCES

Daily Objectives	Reproducible Resources	Multimedia Resources
SECTION 1 **The Colonies Fight for Their Rights** 1. Summarize events that fueled colonial discontent. 2. Explain how the Stamp Act affected the relationship between Britain and the colonies.	Reproducible Lesson Plan 4–1 Daily Lecture and Discussion Notes 4–1 Guided Reading Activity 4–1* Section Quiz 4–1* Reading Essentials and Study Guide 4–1 Performance Assessment Activities and Rubrics	Daily Focus Skills Transparency 4–1 Interactive Tutor Self-Assessment CD-ROM ExamView® Pro Testmaker CD-ROM Presentation Plus! CD-ROM TeacherWorks™ CD-ROM Audio Program American Music: Cultural Traditions
SECTION 2 **The Revolution Begins** 1. Describe ways in which Massachusetts continued to defy Britain after the repeal of the Townshend Acts. 2. Summarize the first battles between Britain and the colonies.	Reproducible Lesson Plan 4–2 Daily Lecture and Discussion Notes 4–2 Guided Reading Activity 4–2* Section Quiz 4–2* Reading Essentials and Study Guide 4–2 Performance Assessment Activities and Rubrics Interpreting Political Cartoons	Daily Focus Skills Transparency 4–2 American Art & Architecture Interactive Tutor Self-Assessment CD-ROM ExamView® Pro Testmaker CD-ROM Presentation Plus! CD-ROM TeacherWorks™ CD-ROM Audio Program ABCNews Interactive™ Historic America Electronic Field Trips
SECTION 3 **The War for Independence** 1. Describe the strategies behind the Northern Campaign. 2. Summarize the scope of the war at sea.	Reproducible Lesson Plan 4–3 Daily Lecture and Discussion Notes 4–3 Guided Reading Activity 4–3* Section Quiz 4–3* Reading Essentials and Study Guide 4–3 Performance Assessment Activities and Rubrics Interpreting Political Cartoons	Daily Focus Skills Transparency 4–3 American Art & Architecture Interactive Tutor Self-Assessment CD-ROM ExamView® Pro Testmaker CD-ROM Presentation Plus! CD-ROM Skillbuilder Interactive Workbook, Level 2 TeacherWorks™ CD-ROM Audio Program American Music: Hits Through History American Music: Cultural Traditions
SECTION 4 **The War Changes American Society** 1. Describe the features of the political system of the United States set up after the Revolutionary War. 2. Explain the position of women and African Americans in the new political system.	Reproducible Lesson Plan 4–4 Daily Lecture and Discussion Notes 4–4 Guided Reading Activity 4–4* Section Quiz 4–4* Reading Essentials and Study Guide 4–4 Performance Assessment Activities and Rubrics	Daily Focus Skills Transparency 4–4 Interactive Tutor Self-Assessment CD-ROM ExamView® Pro Testmaker CD-ROM Presentation Plus! CD-ROM TeacherWorks™ CD-ROM Vocabulary PuzzleMaker CD-ROM Audio Program

0:00 OUT OF TIME?
Assign the Chapter 4 **Reading Essentials and Study Guide.**

*Also Available in Spanish

 Blackline Master   Transparency   CD-ROM   DVD

Poster   Music Program   Audio Program   Videocassette

NATIONAL GEOGRAPHIC — Teacher's Corner

INDEX TO NATIONAL GEOGRAPHIC MAGAZINE

The following articles relate to this chapter.

- "Phip's Fleet," August 2000
- "Thomas Jefferson: Architect of Freedom," February 1976
- "Two Revolutions," July 1989
- "Yorktown Shipwreck," June 1988

NATIONAL GEOGRAPHIC SOCIETY PRODUCTS AVAILABLE FROM GLENCOE

To order the following products for use with this chapter, contact your local Glencoe sales representative, or call Glencoe at 1-800-334-7344:

- *PicturePack: The American Revolution* (Transparencies)
- *PictureShow: The American Revolution* (CD-ROM)
- *PictureShow: The Story of America* (CD-ROM)

ADDITIONAL NATIONAL GEOGRAPHIC SOCIETY PRODUCTS

To order the following, call National Geographic at 1-800-368-2728:

- *Branches of Government Series* (Video)
- *The Complete National Geographic: 109 Years of National Geographic Magazine* (CD-ROM)
- *Democratic Government Series, "The United States"* (Video)

NGS ONLINE

Access National Geographic's Web site for current events, atlas updates, activities, links, interactive features, and archives.
www.nationalgeographic.com

From the Classroom of...

Mike Midler
Elsik High School
Houston, TX

King Eggbert of Eggtonia

King Eggbert is an absolute monarch in the Kingdom of Eggtonia. Many subjects wish to see major changes. Some of the more radical subjects want to secede entirely and start a new country.

Create a list of ten restrictive rules, such as: an 8 P.M. curfew; the king assigns all jobs; all subjects must belong to the Eggtonian Church; no more than three people can gather together at once; tax rate of 75%; no one may leave Eggtonia; and all subjects must carry ID papers to present to authorities on demand. Present the list to the students.

Each student role-plays one of King Eggbert's subjects who wants to bring reform or start a new nation. They write a one-page letter to the king discussing five specific grievances to which they object and justifying their solutions.

Students must decorate a cover sheet to depict what King Eggbert or his kingdom might look like. (Use a sheet of 12 × 18 paper folded over with the art on the cover and the letter pasted inside.)

ADDITIONAL RESOURCES FROM GLENCOE

- American Music: Cultural Traditions
- American Art & Architecture
- Outline Map Resource Book
- U.S. Desk Map
- Building Geography Skills for Life
- Inclusion for the High School Social Studies Classroom Strategies and Activities
- Teaching Strategies for the American History Classroom (Including Block Scheduling Pacing Guides)

KEY TO ABILITY LEVELS

Teaching strategies have been coded.

- **L1** BASIC activities for all students
- **L2** AVERAGE activities for average to above-average students
- **L3** CHALLENGING activities for above-average students
- **ELL** ENGLISH LANGUAGE LEARNER activities

Block Schedule

Activities that are suited to use within the block scheduling framework are identified by:

Why It Matters Activity

Ask students what the colonists were fighting for during the American Revolution. Students should evaluate their answers after they have completed the chapter.

CHAPTER

4 The American Revolution *1754–1783*

Why It Matters

In the early colonial period, the colonies grew accustomed to running their own affairs. When Britain tried to reestablish control, tensions mounted over taxes and basic rights. In 1775 these tensions led to battle, and in 1776 the colonists declared their independence from Britain. With the help of France and Spain, the colonists defeated the British in 1781. The Treaty of Paris in 1783 formally ended the war.

The Impact Today

The Revolutionary War experience had important results.
* *Common political traditions of our nation were born under the pressures of war.*
* *Americans value and protect local liberties and the right to representation in government.*

The American Vision *Video* *The Chapter 4 video, "Women of the Revolution," chronicles the lives of women during the Revolutionary era.*

1754
• French and Indian War begins

1765
• Parliament passes the Stamp Act, triggering protests throughout the colonies

North America

1745   *1755*   *1765*

World

1748
• Montesquieu's *Spirit of the Laws* published

1751
• Chinese invade Tibet and control succession to the throne

1755
• Samuel Johnson's *Dictionary of the English Language* published

114

TWO-MINUTE LESSON LAUNCHER

Ask students to share their ideas about why the colonists declared their independence from Britain. Make a list of the reasons suggested by students and have students edit the list as the lesson is presented.

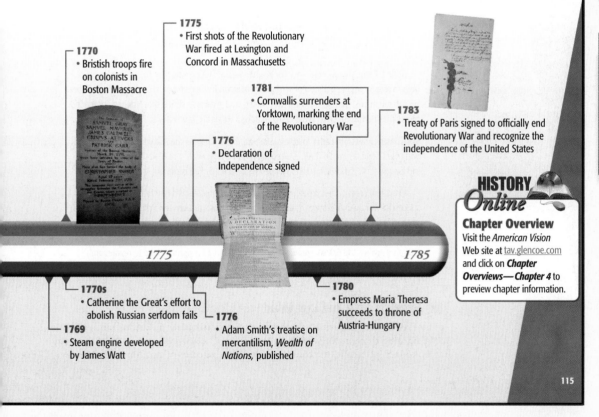

Washington Crossing the Delaware by Emanuel Gottlieb Leutze, 1851

1775
• First shots of the Revolutionary War fired at Lexington and Concord in Massachusetts

1770
• Bristish troops fire on colonists in Boston Massacre

1781
• Cornwallis surrenders at Yorktown, marking the end of the Revolutionary War

1776
• Declaration of Independence signed

1783
• Treaty of Paris signed to officially end Revolutionary War and recognize the independence of the United States

1775

1785

1770s
• Catherine the Great's effort to abolish Russian serfdom fails

1769
• Steam engine developed by James Watt

1776
• Adam Smith's treatise on mercantilism, *Wealth of Nations,* published

1780
• Empress Maria Theresa succeeds to throne of Austria-Hungary

HISTORY
Online

Chapter Overview
Visit the *American Vision* Web site at tav.glencoe.com and click on *Chapter Overviews—Chapter 4* to preview chapter information.

115

More About the Art

Ask: What techniques does the artist use to communicate the season? *(possible answers: floating ice on the water, the flag is being held against a strong wind, and people bundled up)*

TIME LINE
ACTIVITY

Have students use the chapter and section time lines to create a single time line that incorporates all of the significant dates related to the American Revolution.

GRAPHIC ORGANIZER ACTIVITY

Organizing Information Have students use a graphic organizer similar to the one shown below to keep track of the people who are mentioned in this chapter. Students' organizers will include more names than shown here.

Name	Significance
Marquise Duquesne	Governor of New France who built a chain of forts from Lake Ontario to the Ohio River
Robert Dinwiddie	Governor of Virginia who asked Washington to raise a force and expel the French from Fort Duquesne
George Washington	Young officer in the Virginia militia
Benjamin Franklin	Led the committee that developed the Albany Plan of Union

1 FOCUS

Section Overview

This section focuses on Britain's attempts to control the American colonies and the colonists' growing discontent.

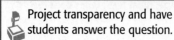

BELLRINGER
Skillbuilder Activity

Project transparency and have students answer the question.

Available as a blackline master.

Daily Focus Skills Transparency 4–1

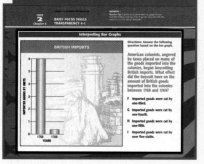

Guide to Reading

Answers to Graphic: dispute over control of the Ohio River valley and building of French forts from Lake Ontario to the Ohio River

Preteaching Vocabulary
Have students skim the section to preview each of the Key Terms and Names.

SECTION 1 The Colonies Fight for Their Rights

Guide to Reading

Main Idea
Tensions between Britain and its American colonies grew as British leaders sought greater control over their North American empire.

Key Terms and Names
Albany Plan of Union, French and Indian War, Treaty of Paris, customs duty, inflation, Quartering Act, nonimportation agreement, writ of assistance

Reading Strategy
Organizing As you read about the growing tensions between Britain and the American colonies, complete a graphic organizer like the one below by listing the causes of the French and Indian War.

Reading Objectives
- **Summarize** events that fueled colonial discontent.
- **Explain** how the Stamp Act affected the relationship between Britain and the colonies.

Section Theme
Civic Rights and Responsibilities The colonies used economic protest to fight Parliamentary power.

Preview of Events

♦1754 — ♦1758 — ♦1762 — ♦1766

1754
French and Indian War begins; Albany Conference meets

1763
Treaty of Paris ends French and Indian War

1764
Sugar Act passed

1765
Stamp Act passed

1767
Townshend Acts passed

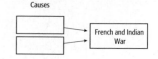

★ **An American Story** ★

At first, Pennsylvania colonist John Hughes was delighted when his friend Ben Franklin helped him to get the position of stamp tax collector. By September 1765, however, he feared his job might cost him his life. Anti-tax protests had grown so strong that Hughes barricaded himself inside his house to avoid being attacked. He wrote frantically to Franklin in London:

British revenue stamp

❝You are now from Letter to Letter to suppose each may be the last you will receive from your old Friend, as the Spirit of . . . Rebellion is to a high Pitch. . . . Madness has got hold of the people. . . . I fancy some Lives will be lost before this Fire is put out. . . .❞

Just a few years earlier, British soldiers and American colonists had fought side by side in a successful war against France. After the war ended, tensions between Britain and its colonies grew. Britain wanted the colonies to help pay for the war, while the colonists questioned Britain's authority to make them do so. Misunderstanding and distrust slowly turned many colonists against the British, creating situations that would eventually lead to revolution.

—**adapted from** *What They Didn't Teach You About the American Revolution*

The French and Indian War

The French and English had been vying for dominance in Europe since the late 1600s, fighting three major wars between 1689 and 1748. Although most of the fighting took place in Europe, the conflict eventually spilled over into America. Whenever

---

SECTION RESOURCES

Reproducible Masters
- Reproducible Lesson Plan 4–1
- Daily Lecture and Discussion Notes 4–1
- Guided Reading Activity 4–1
- Section Quiz 4–1
- Reading Essentials and Study Guide 4–1

Transparencies
- Daily Focus Skills Transparency 4–1

Multimedia
- Interactive Tutor Self-Assessment CD-ROM
- ExamView® Pro Testmaker CD-ROM
- Presentation Plus! CD-ROM
- TeacherWorks™ CD-ROM
- Audio Program
- American Music: Cultural Traditions

France and England were at war, their colonies went to war as well. In 1754 a fourth struggle began.

The First Skirmish In the 1740s, the British and French both became interested in the Ohio River valley. The French had discovered that they could cross from Lake Ontario to the Ohio River in western Pennsylvania and follow the river south to the Mississippi. This allowed the French to travel from New France to Louisiana easily. At the same time, British fur traders entered the region, and land speculators—people who bought empty land hoping to sell it to settlers for a profit—became interested in the Ohio River valley.

To block British claims in the region, New France's governor, the Marquis Duquesne, ordered a chain of French forts to be built from Lake Ontario to the Ohio River. Duquesne's actions prompted Robert Dinwiddie, the governor of Virginia, to order a British fort built in western Pennsylvania. Before the British fort was completed, the French seized it and built Fort Duquesne at the site. Dinwiddie then asked George Washington, a young officer in the Virginia militia, to raise a force and expel the French.

As Washington's troops marched toward the Ohio River in the spring of 1754, they encountered a small French force near Great Meadows. After a brief battle, Washington retreated and built a stockade named Fort Necessity. A little over a month later, a large French force arrived and forced Washington to surrender. After being released, Washington returned to Virginia, leaving the French in control of the Ohio River valley. As the fighting between France and Britain expanded into a world war, the 22-year-old Washington became a hero in the colonies for his courageous attempt to resist the French.

The Albany Conference Even before fighting started in the Ohio River valley, the British government urged its colonies to work together to prepare for the coming war. The government also suggested that the colonies negotiate an alliance with the Iroquois. The Iroquois controlled western New York—territory the French had to pass through to reach the Ohio River. In response, 7 colonies sent representatives to meet with 150 Iroquois leaders at Albany, New York, in June 1754. This meeting became known as the Albany Conference.

The Albany Conference achieved several things. Although the Iroquois refused an alliance with the British, they did agree to

remain neutral. The colonies also agreed that Britain should appoint one supreme commander of all British troops in the colonies. Finally, the conference issued the **Albany Plan of Union,** a scheme developed by a committee led by Benjamin Franklin. The Plan of Union proposed that the colonies unite to form a federal government. Although the colonies rejected the Plan of Union, the effort showed that many colonial leaders had begun to think about joining their colonies together for their common defense.

The British Triumph In 1755 the new British commander in chief, General Edward Braddock, arrived in Virginia with 1,400 British troops. He linked up with 450 local militia troops and appointed Lieutenant Colonel George Washington to serve as his aide. Braddock then headed west intending to attack Fort Duquesne. The general was not worried about being ambushed by the Native American allies of the French. "These savages may indeed be a formidable enemy to your raw American militia," he told Benjamin Franklin. "Upon the King's regular and disciplined troops, it is impossible they should make any impression."

Seven miles from Fort Duquesne, French and Native American forces did ambush Braddock's troops. Braddock was shot and later died. His inexperienced troops panicked. Only George Washington's leadership saved the British from disaster. As shots whizzed past him—four holes were later found in his

Analyzing *Political Cartoons*

Appeal for Unity In 1754, as French and Native American forces were threatening the colonies, Ben Franklin drew this cartoon urging colonists to stand together. A popular legend at the time said a snake could put itself back together and live if it did so before sunset. Why did Franklin's use of the serpent legend make his appeal for unity seem urgent?

2 *TEACH*

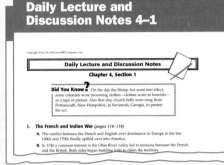

Daily Lecture and Discussion Notes 4–1

Copyright © by The McGraw-Hill Companies, Inc.

Daily Lecture and Discussion Notes
Chapter 4, Section 1

Did You Know ? On the day the Stamp Act went into effect, some colonists wore mourning clothes—clothes worn to funerals—as a sign of protest. Also that day, church bells were rung from Portsmouth, New Hampshire, to Savannah, Georgia, to protest the act.

I. **The French and Indian War** (pages 116–119)

  A. The conflict between the French and English over dominance in Europe in the late 1600s and 1700s finally spilled over into America.

  B. In 1740 a common interest in the Ohio River valley led to tensions between the French and the British. Both sides began building forts to claim the territory.

Discussing a Topic As a class, discuss the advantages and disadvantages of the Albany Plan of Union. Then extend the discussion to encourage students to consider how United States history might have been different if if the colonies had adopted the plan. **L1**

you don't say...

Fort Pitt In 1758 the French abandoned and burned Fort Duquesne. The English rebuilt it and named it Fort Pitt. The nearby town was named Pittsburgh.

Analyzing *Political Cartoons*

Answer: He wanted colonists to act before it was too late.

Ask: What is the significance of the initials along the serpent's body? *(abbreviations for the names of some of the colonies)*

COOPERATIVE LEARNING ACTIVITY

Conducting Interviews Organize students into groups of three. One student is to be an interviewer; the second, a colonial farmer or merchant; the third, a British counterpart. The interviewer, in turn, asks each of the other two to respond to one of the various trade and navigation acts imposed by the British to control the American colonies. After conducting the interview, each interviewer summarizes the two responses for the entire class.

Use the rubric for a cooperative group management plan on pages 81–82 in the ***Performance Assessment Activities and Rubrics.***

Guided Reading Activity 4–1

Creating a Thematic Map Have students create a thematic map showing the area controlled by France in 1754 and after the Treaty of Paris was signed in 1763. Remind students to include an appropriate title and legend for the map. **L2**

 Use the rubric for creating a map, display, or chart on pages 77–78 in the *Performance Assessment Activities and Rubrics.*

FYI

Just 20 years after the Treaty of Paris ended the Seven Years' War, the Paris Peace Treaty of 1783 was signed, formally ending the American Revolution. The Treaty of Paris of 1898 was signed to mark the end of the Spanish-American War.

History *Through Art*

Answer: New France became part of the British Empire.

Ask: How did control of the St. Lawrence River affect the outcome of the Battle of Quebec? *(The British cut off the flow of supplies and extra troops to help the French. This greatly weakened the French.)*

hat and clothes—Washington rallied the troops and organized a retreat. The ambush had further consequences. Having seen that the British could be beaten, the Delaware people of western Pennsylvania began attacking British settlers in their territory.

For the next two years, the **French and Indian War** raged along the frontier, as both sides raided each other's territory. Then, in 1756, the fighting between Britain and France spread to Europe, where it later became known as the Seven Years' War. While Britain's allies fought the French in Europe, British Prime Minister William Pitt decided to send most of Britain's troops and fleet to North America and India to attack the French and seize their empire.

The British fleet quickly cut off the flow of supplies and reinforcements France had been sending to North America. In the meantime, the Iroquois, realizing the tide had turned in favor of the British, pressured the Delaware to end their attacks. With their Native American allies giving up the battle, the French found themselves badly outnumbered.

In 1758 General John Forbes, the new British commander in the colonies, sent troops to attack Fort Duquesne. Realizing they were outnumbered, the French burned the fort and retreated. The British built Fort Pitt, named after the prime minister, on the same site. Fort Pitt eventually became the city of Pittsburgh.

In 1759 a British fleet commanded by General James Wolfe sailed up the St. Lawrence River to Quebec City. Wolfe discovered a path from the river up the steep cliffs that protected the city. On September 12, 1759, as his troops marched onto the Plains of Abraham near the city, the French under General Louis Joseph Montcalm attacked. Both Wolfe and Montcalm were killed, and the British won the battle. Fighting continued elsewhere in the world until 1763, but the British victory at Quebec was the turning point in North America.

After Spain entered the war in 1761 on the side of France, Britain seized Spain's colonies in Cuba and the Philippines. The **Treaty of Paris** finally ended the war in 1763. Except for a few offshore islands, the treaty eliminated French power in North America. New France became part of the British Empire, as did all of Louisiana east of the Mississippi except for

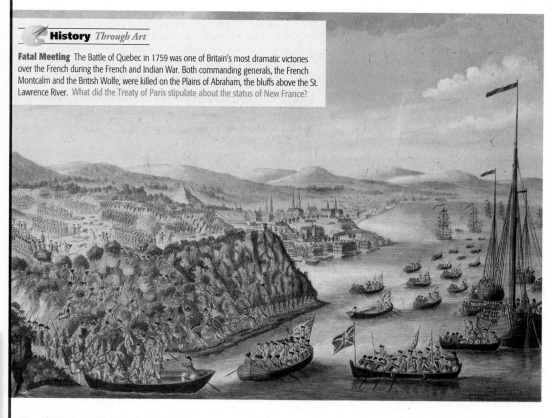

History *Through Art*

Fatal Meeting The Battle of Quebec in 1759 was one of Britain's most dramatic victories over the French during the French and Indian War. Both commanding generals, the French Montcalm and the British Wolfe, were killed on the Plains of Abraham, the bluffs above the St. Lawrence River. What did the Treaty of Paris stipulate about the status of New France?

118 CHAPTER 4 The American Revolution

MEETING SPECIAL NEEDS

Logical/Mathematical Have students identify examples of Britain's mercantile policies described in the section. Ask them to write a paragraph explaining why colonists might oppose these policies and draw conclusions about the probable outcome of Britain's continued enforcement of these policies. **L2**

 Refer to *Inclusion for the High School Social Studies Classroom Strategies and Activities* in the TCR.

New Orleans. To get Cuba and the Philippines back, Spain gave Florida to Britain. To compensate Spain for its losses, the French signed a separate treaty giving Spain control of New Orleans and all of Louisiana west of the Mississippi.

✓ **Reading Check** **Examining** Why were the French and the British interested in the Ohio River valley?

The Colonies Grow Discontented

To achieve its victory in 1763, the British government had borrowed an enormous amount of money to pay for the war and was now deeply in debt. Many British officials thought that the colonies should pay for part of the war, especially the cost of stationing British troops in the colonies. The policies Britain adopted to solve its financial problems angered the colonists and set the two sides on a course to confrontation.

The Proclamation Act of 1763 In the spring of 1763, a Native American religious leader known as the Delaware Prophet convinced **Pontiac,** chief of the Ottawa people, to go to war against the British. After uniting several Native American groups, including the Ottawa, Delaware, Shawnee, and Seneca peoples, Pontiac's forces attacked forts along the frontier and burned down several towns before British troops stopped them.

Pontiac's war did not surprise British officials. They had been expecting trouble since 1758, when reports first indicated that settlers were moving into western Pennsylvania in defiance of the colony's treaty with the region's Native Americans. British officials did not want to bear the cost of another war. Many officials also owned shares in fur trading companies operating in the region and did not want to disrupt the fur trade. They decided that the best solution was to limit western settlement until new treaties could be negotiated.

In early October, King George issued the **Royal Proclamation of 1763.** The Proclamation drew a line from north to south along the Appalachian Mountains and declared that colonists could not settle west of the line without the British government's permission. This enraged many farmers and land speculators, who wanted access to the land.

Customs Reform At the same time the Royal Proclamation Act was angering western farmers, new British tax policies were disturbing eastern merchants. In 1763 **George Grenville** became prime minister and

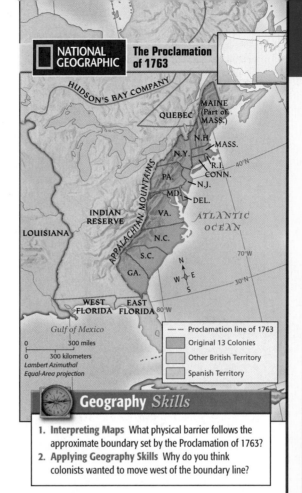

NATIONAL GEOGRAPHIC — **The Proclamation of 1763**

HUDSON'S BAY COMPANY

MAINE (Part of MASS.)
QUEBEC
N.H.
MASS.
N.Y.
R.I.
CONN.
PA.
N.J.
MD.
DEL.
VA.
INDIAN RESERVE
LOUISIANA
APPALACHIAN MOUNTAINS
ATLANTIC OCEAN
N.C.
S.C.
GA.
WEST FLORIDA
EAST FLORIDA
Gulf of Mexico

0 — 300 miles
0 — 300 kilometers
Lambert Azimuthal Equal-Area projection

- - - Proclamation line of 1763
Original 13 Colonies
Other British Territory
Spanish Territory

 Geography *Skills*

1. **Interpreting Maps** What physical barrier follows the approximate boundary set by the Proclamation of 1763?
2. **Applying Geography Skills** Why do you think colonists wanted to move west of the boundary line?

first lord of the Treasury. Grenville had to find a way to reduce Britain's debt and pay for the 10,000 British troops now stationed in North America. New tax policies emerged from his efforts.

Grenville discovered that British customs agents in America were collecting very little money. Obviously, merchants were smuggling goods into and out of the colonies without paying customs duties—taxes on imports and exports. Grenville convinced Parliament to pass a law allowing customs agents to send smugglers to a new vice-admiralty court in Halifax, Nova Scotia. Unlike colonial courts, where the juries were often sympathetic to smugglers, vice-admiralty courts were run by naval officers. These courts had no juries and did not follow British common law, a violation of the traditional English right to a jury of one's peers. Transporting colonists to distant Nova Scotia also violated their right to a speedy trial.

CHAPTER 4   The American Revolution   **119**

✓ **Reading Check**

Answer: The French used the Ohio River to travel from the region of Lake Ontario to the Mississippi River. The Ohio River thus helped to connect New France to Louisiana. The British were interested in the Ohio River valley for fur trade and land speculation.

Geography *Skills*

Answers:
1. Appalachian Mountains
2. Farmers and land speculators wanted to profit from access to more land.

Geography Skills Practice
Ask: What is the approximate length of the Ohio River measured in miles and kilometers? *(981 miles and 1579 kilometers; students' answers will not be precise)*

Drawing a Political Cartoon
Have students select an event in this section and draw a political cartoon that expresses a strongly held opinion of the day. **L2**

▭ Use the rubric for a political cartoon, pamphlet, or handbill on pages 87–88 in the *Performance Assessment Activities and Rubrics.*

History *and the* **Humanities**

🏴 American Music: Cultural Traditions: "Junto Song," "British Grenadiers"

INTERDISCIPLINARY CONNECTIONS ACTIVITY

Economics Have students use library and Internet resources to learn more about the economic contributions of the Ohio River during the time of the war for independence. In addition, have students research how the Ohio River currently contributes to the economy of the Ohio River valley. Instruct students to illustrate these contributions using a thematic map or model. **L2**

Graphic Organizer → Skills

Answer: Answers will vary but could include support for colonists' actions as the best ways to get Britain to respond to their demands for representation. Other students might remain loyal to Britain, expressing confidence in the actions and motives of Parliament.

Graphic Organizer Skills Practice
Ask: How did the Boston Tea Party boost colonists' confidence in their cause? *(Their actions showed that they could successfully stand up to the British.)*

Discussing a Topic Ask students to identify the rights that were denied colonists by the various laws enacted by the British Parliament. Then explain how people today react when they feel their rights have been denied. **L2**

✓ Reading Check

Answer: The British hoped to solve their financial problems by strictly enforcing custom duties; raising taxes on sugar and molasses; and placing new taxes on silk, wine, coffee, pimento, and indigo.

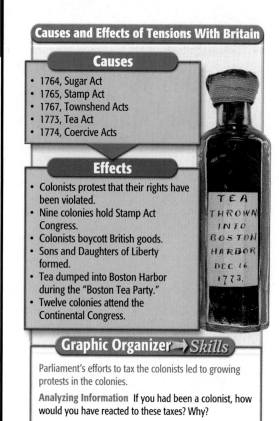

Causes and Effects of Tensions With Britain

Causes

- 1764, Sugar Act
- 1765, Stamp Act
- 1767, Townshend Acts
- 1773, Tea Act
- 1774, Coercive Acts

Effects

- Colonists protest that their rights have been violated.
- Nine colonies hold Stamp Act Congress.
- Colonists boycott British goods.
- Sons and Daughters of Liberty formed.
- Tea dumped into Boston Harbor during the "Boston Tea Party."
- Twelve colonies attend the Continental Congress.

TEA THROWN INTO BOSTON HARBOR DEC 16 1773.

Graphic Organizer → Skills

Parliament's efforts to tax the colonists led to growing protests in the colonies.

Analyzing Information If you had been a colonist, how would you have reacted to these taxes? Why?

Among those arrested for smuggling and tried by the vice-admiralty court was **John Hancock.** Hancock had made a fortune in the sugar trade, smuggling molasses from French colonies in the Caribbean. Defending Hancock was a young lawyer named **John Adams.** Adams argued that the use of vice-admiralty courts denied colonists their rights as British citizens:

> ❝Here is the contrast that stares us in the face. The Parliament in one clause guarding the people of the realm, and securing to them the benefit of tryal by the law of the land, and by the next clause depriving all Americans of that privilege. . . . Is there not in this clause a brand of infamy, or degradation or disgrace, fixed upon every American?❞
>
> —quoted in *America's History*

The Sugar Act In addition to strictly enforcing customs duties, Grenville also introduced the American Revenue Act of 1764, better known as the **Sugar Act.**

The act changed the tax rates levied on raw sugar and molasses imported from foreign colonies. It also placed new taxes on silk, wine, coffee, pimento, and indigo.

Merchants throughout the colonies complained to Parliament that the Sugar Act hurt trade. Many were also furious that the act violated several traditional English rights. The act specified that merchants accused of smuggling were presumed guilty until proven innocent. The Sugar Act also allowed British officials to seize goods without **due process,** or proper court procedures, in some circumstances, and prevented lawsuits by merchants whose goods had been improperly seized. Parliament, however, ignored the protests of the merchants.

In many colonial cities, pamphlets soon circulated condemning the Sugar Act. One pamphlet, written by **James Otis,** argued that because the colonists had no representatives in Parliament, they could not be taxed for the purpose of raising money. Parliament had the right to control trade, but taxing Americans to pay for British programs was different. Otis's arguments gave rise to the popular expression, "No taxation without representation."

Despite the protests, the Sugar Act remained in force, and Grenville pressed ahead with other new policies. To slow inflation, which happens when money loses its value over time, Parliament passed the **Currency Act of 1764.** This act banned the use of paper money in the colonies, because it tended to lose its value very quickly. The act angered colonial farmers and artisans. They liked paper money precisely because it lost value quickly. They could use paper money to pay back loans, and since the money was not worth as much as when they borrowed it, the loans were easier to pay back.

✓ Reading Check
Summarizing How did the British government hope to solve its financial problems caused by the cost of the French and Indian War?

The Stamp Act Crisis

Although the Sugar Act began to bring in money for Britain, Grenville did not believe it would raise enough to pay all of the government's expenses in America. To raise more money, he asked Parliament to introduce a stamp tax in the American colonies. The **Stamp Act** passed Parliament in March 1765.

The Stamp Act required stamps to be placed on most printed materials, including newspapers, pamphlets, posters, wills, mortgages, deeds, licenses, and even diplomas, dice, and playing cards. The

CRITICAL THINKING ACTIVITY

Comparing Remind students that General Braddock underestimated the fighting ability of his enemy, the Native Americans. Ask students to give examples of other times in history when underestimating the enemy has led to dire consequences. *(Answers will vary. Students may suggest that the United States underestimated the abilities of the guerrillas of North Vietnam, that Saddam Hussein underestimated the abilities of the United Nations forces in the Persian Gulf War, or that the Japanese underestimated the resolve of the Americans when attacking Pearl Harbor.)* **L2**

stamp tax was different from other taxes the colonies had paid to Britain. Parliament had imposed many taxes on trade, but the stamp tax was the first direct tax Britain had ever placed on the colonists.

With the Stamp Act set to take effect on November 1, 1765, Parliament passed one more law. The **Quartering Act** forced the colonies to pay more for their own defense. If the colonies did not provide barracks for British troops, the act stated that troops could stay in taverns, inns, vacant buildings, and barns, and the colonies had to pay the rent.

As word of the Stamp Act spread through the colonies in the spring of 1765, a huge debate began. A flood of editorials, pamphlets, speeches, and resolutions against the tax swept through the colonies. In Virginia, the House of Burgesses passed a series of resolutions declaring that Virginians were entitled to the rights of British people and could only be taxed by their own representatives. Other colonial assemblies passed similar statements.

By the summer of 1765, huge mass meetings and demonstrations were taking place. In Connecticut, a merchant named Isaac Sears organized a group called the **Sons of Liberty.** The organization grew quickly throughout the colonies. The Sons of Liberty organized outdoor meetings and demonstrations. They also intimidated stamp distributors. In August 1765, for example, a Boston mob hung an effigy of the city's new stamp distributor from a tree, then pulled his house apart and burned the wood. In Newport, Rhode Island, the wife of a pro-British merchant described a similar protest:

❝In the morning . . . a mob assembled and erected a gallows near the town house and then dispers'd, and about ten a clock reassembled and took the effigy's of [several] men and the Stamp Master . . . to said gallows where they was hung up by the neck. . . . And about five a clock in the afternoon they made a fire under the gallows which consumed the effigy's, gallows and all. . . . About dusk they all muster'd out again, and . . . broke every window in his house, frames and all, likewise chairs, tables, pictures and everything they cou'd come across.❞

—quoted in *Eyewitness Accounts of the American Revolution*

In October 1765, representatives from nine colonies met for what became known as the **Stamp Act Congress.** Together they issued the Declaration of Rights and Grievances. Drafted by a wealthy farmer from Pennsylvania named John Dickinson,

the declaration argued that only the colonists' political representatives and not Parliament had the right to tax them. The congress then sent a petition to King George asking for relief and to the British Parliament asking for the repeal of the Stamp Act.

On November 1 the Stamp Act took effect, but the colonists ignored it. Throughout the colonies, a movement began to boycott all British goods. People substituted sage and sassafras for imported tea. They stopped buying British cloth. In New York, 200 merchants signed a nonimportation agreement, pledging not to buy any British goods until Parliament repealed the Stamp Act.

The boycott had a very powerful effect on Britain. Thousands of workers lost their jobs as orders from the colonies were cancelled. British merchants could not collect money the colonies owed them. "The avenues of trade are all shut up," complained one merchant. "We have no remittances and are at our wits end for want of money. . . ."

Popular Protest

Past: Colonial Protests

In the 1770s, colonial women entered into the spirit of protest, too. They stopped

drinking British tea and substituted chocolate or coffee. Sometimes they even gave up buying the ribbons they used to trim their bonnets. The British cartoon above made fun of women protesters in Edenton, North Carolina.

Present: World Trade

In late 1999, protesters gathered in Seattle, Washington, to protest the World Trade Organization meeting. Established in 1995, the WTO handles trade disputes and enforces agreements on international trade. Protesters objected that large corporations had too much influence in the WTO. They also objected to WTO meetings being held in closed session. Farmers, environmentalists, and labor groups were among the protesters.

Explaining a Quote Ask students to rewrite the quote that appears on this page to make it easier to understand. **L2**

CURRICULUM CONNECTION

Performing Arts Dancing masters taught wealthy colonists the latest dance steps. A line dance called the reel was popular during colonial times. The cotillion, imported from the courts of France, was also popular. The cotillion is a forerunner of the square dance. Four couples formed a group and danced at the directions of the "caller."

Linking Past & Present

Have students interview an adult acquaintance or family member to learn more about someone's personal experience with a popular protest. Instruct students to use library and Internet resources to locate and read at least two news stories related to the protest. Direct students to write a short summary describing the protest and prepare a bibliographic citation for each of their sources.

EXTENDING THE CONTENT

Proper Role of Britain In 1774 Samuel Johnson wrote the following: "He that accepts protection, stipulates obedience. We have always protected the Americans. We may, therefore, subject them to government." Samuel Johnson, a widely respected literary figure in Britain, believed that government's role was to protect the weak. Imposing taxes was one way to ensure that government could operate to that end.

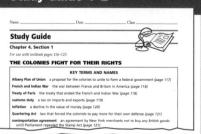

Samuel Adams wrote a pamphlet entitled "The Rights of the Colonists." In the pamphlet he explores three themes: the rights of the colonists as men, the rights of the colonists as Christians, and the rights of the colonists as subjects. In the pamphlet he argues for rights that will later be incorporated into the founding documents of the nation. Among these are the rights of life, liberty, private property, and the free exercise of religion.

✓ **Reading Check**

Answer: It was the first direct tax on colonists.

3 ASSESS

Assign Section 1 Assessment as homework or as an in-class activity.

◉ Have students use the **Interactive Tutor Self-Assessment CD-ROM.**

Reading Essentials and Study Guide 4–1

Name _____ Date _____ Class _____

Study Guide
Chapter 4, Section 1
For use with textbook pages 116–123
THE COLONIES FIGHT FOR THEIR RIGHTS

KEY TERMS AND NAMES

Albany Plan of Union a proposal for the colonies to unite to form a federal government *(page 117)*
French and Indian War the war between France and Britain in America *(page 118)*
Treaty of Paris the treaty that ended the French and Indian War *(page 118)*
customs duty a tax on imports and exports *(page 119)*
inflation a decline in the value of money *(page 120)*
Quartering Act law that forced the colonists to pay more for their own defense *(page 121)*
nonimportation agreement an agreement by New York merchants not to buy any British goods until Parliament repealed the Stamp Act *(page 121)*

Profiles IN HISTORY

Sam Adams
1722–1803

A passionate defender of colonial rights, Boston's Sam Adams was either a saint or a scoundrel—depending on who was describing him. His second cousin, John Adams, who would become the nation's second president, portrayed Sam as a "plain, simple, decent citizen of middling stature, dress, and manners." Sam's enemies, however, saw him quite differently. The royal governor of the colony called him "the most dangerous man in Massachusetts." Adams enjoyed his reputation as a fiery agitator. "Where there is a spark of patriotic fire," he once declared, "we will enkindle it."

Born in Boston, Adams graduated from Harvard College in 1740. He briefly studied law, worked as a clerk and merchant, and managed a brewery before being elected tax collector for Boston. As tensions with Great Britain increased, Adams, who had a passion for political issues, discovered his true talents: speaking out against British tax laws and organizing resistance against them. He helped organize the Boston

chapter of the Sons of Liberty and wrote several political pamphlets that encouraged Americans to rebel against the Bristish.

Adams showed particular skill in uniting Bostonians of different social classes. He forged an anti-British alliance of merchants, lawyers, and other members of the social elite with artisans, shopkeepers, and common laborers, all of whom worked together to protest British tax policies.

With protests against the Stamp Act mounting in both Britain and America, British lawmakers repealed the act in 1766. To demonstrate its authority over the colonies, however, Parliament also passed the **Declaratory Act.** This act asserted that Parliament had the power to make laws for the colonies.

✓ **Reading Check** **Evaluating** How was the Stamp Act different from other taxes Britain imposed on the colonies?

The Townshend Acts

During the Stamp Act crisis, the financial problems facing the British government had worsened. Protests in Britain had forced Parliament to lower property taxes there, which caused a further drop in revenue. As a result, **Charles Townshend,** the new Chancellor of the Exchequer, introduced a series of new regulations and taxes in 1767. These came to be called the **Townshend Acts.**

One of the Townshend Acts was the **Revenue Act of 1767.** This act put new customs duties on glass, lead,

paper, paint, and tea imported into the colonies. Violators of the Revenue Act had to face trial in vice-admiralty courts, where they were presumed guilty unless they could prove their innocence. The Townshend Acts, like the Sugar Act, allowed officials to seize private property under certain circumstances without following due process.

To assist customs officers in arresting smugglers, the Revenue Act legalized the use of writs of assistance. The writs were general search warrants that enabled customs officers to enter any location to look for evidence of smuggling. Writs had been used before, but in 1760 James Otis had argued in court that they were "instruments of slavery" that violated people's rights. The issue remained unresolved until the Revenue Act of 1767 declared writs of assistance to be legal.

Action and Reaction Not surprisingly, the Townshend Acts infuriated many colonists. During the winter of 1767 and 1768, John Dickinson published a series of essays entitled *Letters From a Pennsylvania Farmer.* In these essays, Dickinson reasserted that only assemblies elected by the colonists had the right to tax them. In addition, he called on the colonies to become "firmly bound together" to "form one body politic" to resist the Townshend Acts.

Less than a month after Dickinson's first letter appeared, the Massachusetts assembly began organizing resistance against Britain. Among the leaders of this resistance was **Sam Adams,** cousin of John Adams. In February 1768, Sam Adams, with the help of James Otis, drafted a "circular letter" for the Massachusetts assembly to pass and circulate to other colonies. In the letter, the men pointed out that Townshend's taxes would be used to pay the salaries of government officials, a power the colonial assemblies then held. By taking this power away, the Townshend Acts would weaken the assemblies, which the colonists elected to control officials appointed by the king.

British officials ordered the Massachusetts assembly to withdraw the letter. The assembly refused. Furious, the British government ordered the Massachusetts assembly dissolved. In August 1768, the merchants of Boston and New York responded by signing nonimportation agreements, promising not to

122 CHAPTER 4 The American Revolution

---

import any goods from Britain. Philadelphia's merchants joined the boycott in March 1769.

In May 1769, Virginia's House of Burgesses passed the **Virginia Resolves,** stating that only the House had the right to tax Virginians. Under orders from Britain, Virginia's governor dissolved the House of Burgesses. In response, the leaders of the House of Burgesses—including George Washington, Patrick Henry, and Thomas Jefferson—immediately called the members to a convention. This convention then passed a nonimportation law, blocking the sale of British goods in Virginia.

As the boycott spread through the colonies, Americans again stopped drinking British tea or buying British cloth. Women's groups, calling themselves the **Daughters of Liberty,** began spinning their own rough cloth, called "homespun." Wearing homespun became a sign of patriotism. Throughout the colonies, the Sons of Liberty encouraged people to support the boycotts. In 1769 colonial imports from Britain declined sharply from what they had been in 1768.

The Boston Massacre In the fall of 1768, as violence against customs officers in Boston increased, Britain dispatched roughly 1,000 troops to the city to maintain order. Bostonians referred to the British troops stationed there as "lobster backs" due to the red coats they wore. Crowds constantly heckled and harassed the troops. On March 5, 1770, a crowd of colonists began taunting and throwing snowballs at a British soldier guarding a customs house. His call for help brought Captain Thomas Preston and a squad of soldiers.

In the midst of the tumult, the troops began firing into the crowd. According to accounts, the first colonist to die was a man of African and Native

History *Through Art*

American Mockery In this cartoon, a funeral procession mourns the repeal of the Stamp Act. Third in line is "Mr. George Stamp, full of grief and despair," carrying a coffin of his "favorite child, Miss America Stamp," who "died hard in 1766." Who do you think George Stamp is supposed to represent?

American descent known as both Michael Johnson and Crispus Attucks. When the smoke cleared, three people lay dead, two more would die later, and six others were wounded. The shootings became known as the **Boston Massacre.** Colonial newspapers portrayed the British as tyrants who were willing to kill people who stood up for their rights.

News of the Boston Massacre raced like lightning across the colonies. It might have set off a revolution then and there, but only a few weeks later, news arrived that the British had repealed almost all of the Townshend Acts. Parliament kept one tax—a tax on tea—to uphold its right to tax the colonies. The repeal of the Townshend Acts again brought peace and stability to the colonies, but only temporarily.

✓ **Reading Check** **Examining** What was stated in the Virginia Resolves passed by Virginia's House of Burgesses?

SECTION 1 ASSESSMENT

Checking for Understanding
1. **Define:** customs duty, inflation, nonimportation agreement, writ of assistance.
2. **Identify:** Albany Plan of Union, French and Indian War, Treaty of Paris, Quartering Act.

Reviewing Themes
3. **Civic Rights and Responsibilities** What argument did the Stamp Act Congress make in protest against the British taxes?

Critical Thinking
4. **Evaluating** Why do you think the British were so willing to pass new taxes in the face of colonial opposition?
5. **Classifying** Use a graphic organizer similar to the one below to list the acts passed by the British Parliament and the colonists' reactions to the acts.

Act	Colonists' Reactions

Analyzing Visuals
6. **Examining Art** Study the painting of the Battle of the Plains of Abraham on page 118. How were the British able to move their troops up the steep cliffs near the city?

Writing About History
7. **Persuasive Writing** Imagine that you are a member of the Sons of Liberty or the Daughters of Liberty. Write a pamphlet explaining what your group does and urging colonists to join.

CHAPTER 4 The American Revolution **123**

History *Through Art*

Answer: King George III
Ask: **In what ways did the colonists show their displeasure with the Stamp Act?** *(They boycotted British goods.)*

Reteach
Ask students to summarize the events that fueled colonial discontent.

Enrich
Have students identify a law with which they disagree. Have them write an essay expressing the reasons for their disagreement and arguing for their point of view.

✓ **Reading Check**

Answer: Only the House of Burgesses had the right to tax Virginians.

4 CLOSE

Ask students to explain how the Stamp Act affected the relationship between Britain and the colonists.

SECTION 1 ASSESSMENT ANSWERS

1. Terms are in blue.
2. Albany Plan of Union *(p. 117)*, French and Indian War *(p. 118)*, Treaty of Paris *(p. 118)*, Quartering Act *(p. 121)*
3. Only the colonists' political representatives, not Parliament, had the right to tax colonists.
4. The British passed new taxes despite opposition because they needed the money.
5. Students' answers should include the most important acts listed in the section and accurately match the section's content.
6. General Wolfe discovered a path up the cliffs from the river. The French troops were not expecting an attack from this direction, so the British troops climbed the cliffs without attack.
7. Students' pamphlets will vary. Pamphlets should include information about the activities of the group and a call for colonists to join the group.

1 FOCUS

Remind students that even two people standing next to each other at an event can have different experiences. Ask students what might influence the way someone remembers an event.

2 TEACH

Researching a Topic Have students locate three articles in an encyclopedia or history book and compare the content to the first person accounts presented on pages 124 and 125. Have students write a paragraph based on their findings. Instruct students to prepare bibliographic citations for each of the articles. **L2**

FYI

Despite the rising hostility of the colonists against the British, John Adams, a lawyer, took on the task of defending the soldiers who stood trial for the Boston Massacre.

3 ASSESS

Have students answer the Understanding the Issue questions.

Answers:
1. the incident started around nine o'clock, some locals gathered in the center of town, the bells were rung, foul language was used, the locals threw snowballs at a British soldier, and British soldiers fired their weapons
2. Preston said the locals gathered intending to start trouble, the bells were rung to encourage more locals to

---

You're the Historian

The Bloody Massacre,
engraving by Paul Revere, 1770

Comparing Accounts of the Boston Massacre

On the night of March 5, 1770, Captain Thomas Preston sent British troops to protect the Customs House in Boston from a group of colonists who had gathered nearby. Twenty minutes later, the troops had killed or wounded 11 people. The tragedy became known as the Boston Massacre. What happened that night? You're the historian.

Read the two accounts of the Boston Massacre below. One is Captain Preston's report of the event. The other is a colonist's account that quotes eyewitness Samuel Drowne. After reading the accounts, answer the questions and complete the activities that follow.

From Captain Thomas Preston's account

On Monday night . . . about 9 some of the guards came to and informed me the town inhabitants were assembling to attack the troops. . . . In a few minutes after I reached the guard, about 100 people passed it and went towards the custom house where the king's money is lodged. They immediately surrounded the sentry posted there, and with clubs and other weapons threatened to execute their vengeance on him. . . .

I immediately sent a noncommissioned officer and 12 men to protect both the sentry and the king's money, and very soon followed myself to prevent, if possible, all disorder, fearing lest the officer and soldiers, by the insults and provocations of the rioters, should be thrown off their guard and commit some rash act. . . .

Nay, so far was I from intending the death of any person that I suffered the troops to go . . . without any loading in their [guns]; nor did I ever give orders for loading them. . . .

The mob still increased and were more outrageous, striking their clubs or bludgeons one against another, and calling out come on you rascals, you bloody backs, you lobster scoundrels, fire if you dare. . . .

At this time I was between the soldiers and the mob . . . endeavoring all in my power to persuade them to retire peaceably, but to no purpose. They advanced to the points of the bayonets, [and] struck some of them. . . . A general attack was made on the men by a great number of heavy clubs and snowballs being thrown at them, by which

all our lives were in imminent danger, some persons at the same time from behind calling out, damn you bloods—why don't you fire. Instantly three or four of the soldiers fired, one after another, and directly after three more in the same confusion and hurry. . . .

The whole of the melancholy affair was transacted in almost twenty minutes. On my asking the soldiers why they fired without orders, they said that they heard the word fire and supposed it came from me. This might be the case as many of the mob called out fire, fire, but I assured the men that I gave no such order; that my words were, don't fire, stop your firing. In short, it was scarcely possible for the soldiers to know who said fire, or don't fire, or stop your firing.

EXTENDING THE CONTENT

Expressing Discontent Merchants and wealthy planters opposed efforts by the British Parliament to tax colonists. Many others including shopkeepers, clerks, and laborers were also opposed to British taxes. These colonists were instrumental in the resistance efforts, using tactics such as boycotts. They were also responsible for some violence. It is likely that the British soldiers suspected any group of colonists as potential troublemakers.

Crispus Attucks, the first colonist to die in the Boston Massacre

From the colonist's account

Samuel Drowne [a witness] declares that, about nine o'clock of the evening of the fifth of March current, standing at his own door in Cornhill, he saw about fourteen or fifteen soldiers. . . . [The soldiers] came upon the inhabitants of the town, then standing or walking in Cornhill, and abused some, and violently assaulted others as they met them; most of them were without so much of a stick in their hand to defend themselves, as he clearly could discern, it being moonlight, and himself being one of the assaulted persons.

All or most of the said soldiers he saw go into King Street (some of them through Royal Exchange

The site of the Boston Massacre in present-day Boston

Land), and there followed them, and soon discovered them to be quarreling and fighting with the people whom they saw there, which he thinks were not more than a dozen. . . .

The outrageous behavior and the threats of the said party occasioned the ringing of the meeting house bell . . . which bell . . . presently brought out a number of the inhabitants, who . . . were naturally led to King Street, where [the British] had made a stop but a little while before, and where their stopping had drawn together a number of boys, round the sentry at the Custom House. . . .

There was much foul language between them, and some of them, in consequence of his pushing at them with his bayonet, threw snowballs at him, which occasioned him to knock hastily at the door of the Custom House. . . .

The officer on guard was Captain Preston, who with seven or eight soldiers, with firearms and charged bayonets, issued from the guardhouse, and in great haste posted himself and his soldiers in front of the Custom House, near the corner aforesaid. In passing to this station the soldiers pushed several persons

with their bayonets, driving through the people in . . . disturbance. This occasioned some snowballs to be thrown at them, which seems to be the only provocation that was given. . . .

Captain Preston is said to have ordered them to fire, and to have repeated the order. One gun was fired first; then others in succession, and with deliberation, till ten or a dozen guns were fired; or till that number of discharges were made from the guns that were fired. By which means eleven persons were killed and wounded.

Understanding the Issue

1. On what events of the night of March 5, 1770, do the two accounts excerpted here agree?
2. On what descriptions of the events do the two accounts differ?
3. As the historian, how do you assess the credibility of the two accounts?

Activities

1. **Investigate** What happened to Captain Preston after the events of March 5? What were the immediate results of the Boston Massacre? Check other sources, including those available on the Internet.
2. **Mock Trial** Assign class members roles in a mock trial of the Boston Massacre. Include other witnesses, a prosecutor, a defense attorney, a judge, and a jury.

gather, the group of locals swelled into a club wielding mob, Preston did not give the order to fire, and 12 locals were killed or wounded. Drowne said a dozen gentlemen were gathered with no intent to cause trouble, the bells were rung as a warning after the Redcoats attacked one of the locals, the locals were unarmed, someone gave the order to fire, and 11 locals were killed or wounded.

3. Students' answers will vary. They should be able to defend their position.

Activities:

1. Students' answers will vary. Through their research they might discover that Captain Preston and eight soldiers were tried for murder. Their defense counsel was John Adams, who would later be president of the United States. Two soldiers were convicted of manslaughter and they were allowed to claim benefit of clergy. This meant they could do penance instead of being sentenced by the court.
2. Encourage students to use library and Internet resources to learn more about the actual trial. Set up your classroom or another room to look like a courtroom. Invite others to watch the trial.

4 CLOSE

Ask students what might have affected the recollections of those who witnessed or participated in the events on the night of March 5, 1770.

PORTFOLIO ACTIVITY

Newspaper Story Write a 300-word newspaper article regarding the events of March 5, 1770. Assume that you interviewed two eyewitnesses—Preston and Drowne. Consider the printed accounts as transcripts of what Preston and Drowne told you when you asked what happened. Be sure to report both sides of the story.

1 FOCUS

Section Overview

This section focuses on the tensions immediately preceding the Revolutionary War and the beginning of the war.

BELLRINGER
Skillbuilder Activity

 Project transparency and have students answer the question.

📁 Available as a blackline master.

Daily Focus Skills Transparency 4–2

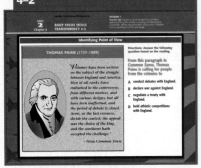

Guide to Reading

Answers to Graphic:
I. Massachusetts Defies Britain
   A. The *Gaspee* Affair
   B. The Boston Tea Party
   C. The Coercive Acts
   D. The First Continental Congress
II. The Revolution Begins
   A. Loyalists and Patriots
   B. Lexington and Concord
   C. The Second Continental Congress

Students should complete the outline by including all heads in the section.

Preteaching Vocabulary
Have students create a database of the Key Terms and Names. Instruct students to add the definition and other helpful information as they find the terms and names while reading this section.

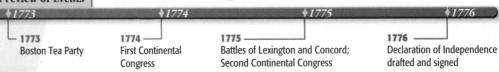

Guide to Reading

Main Idea
After years of escalating tensions and outbreaks of fighting, the colonists declared their independence from Britain on July 4, 1776.

Key Terms and Names
committee of correspondence, Boston Tea Party, Intolerable Acts, minuteman, Loyalist, Patriot, Battle of Bunker Hill, Declaration of Independence

Reading Strategy
Taking Notes As you read about the rising tensions between the colonies and Britain, use the major headings of the section to create an outline similar to the one below.

The Revolution Begins
I. Massachusetts Defies Britain
   A.
   B.
   C.
   D.
II.

Reading Objectives
• **Describe** ways in which Massachusetts continued to defy Britain after the repeal of the Townshend Acts.
• **Summarize** the first battles between Britain and the colonies.

Section Theme
Government and Democracy The First Continental Congress acted as a government during the Revolutionary crisis.

Preview of Events

♦1773	♦1774	♦1775	♦1776
1773 Boston Tea Party	**1774** First Continental Congress	**1775** Battles of Lexington and Concord; Second Continental Congress	**1776** Declaration of Independence drafted and signed

---

★ An American Story ★

On the night of December 17, 1773, a group of men secretly assembled along a Boston dock to strike a blow against Britain. One of the men was George Hewes, a struggling Boston shoemaker, who had grown to despise the British. Initially, Hewes had taken offense when British soldiers stopped and questioned him on the street and when they refused to pay him for shoes. After the Boston Massacre, which Hewes witnessed, his hatred grew deeper and more political.

So, after he "daubed his face and hands with coal dust, in the shop of a blacksmith," he gladly joined the other volunteers on that cold December night as they prepared to sneak aboard several British ships anchored in Boston Harbor and destroy the tea stored on board:

Tea chest

❝When we arrived at the wharf . . . they divided us into three parties for the purpose of boarding the three ships which contained the tea. . . . We then were ordered by our commander to open the hatches and take out all the chests of tea and throw them overboard, and we immediately proceeded to execute his orders, first cutting and splitting the chests with our tomahawks, so as thoroughly to expose them to the effects of the water. . . . In about three hours . . . we had thus broken and thrown over board every tea chest . . . in the ship.❞

—quoted in *The Spirit of 'Seventy-Six*

Massachusetts Defies Britain

Despite the tragedy of the Boston Massacre, the British decision to repeal the Townshend Acts had ended another crisis in colonial relations. For more than two years the situation remained calm. Then, in the spring of 1772, a new crisis began. Britain

---

SECTION RESOURCES

📁 **Reproducible Masters**
• Reproducible Lesson Plan 4–2
• Daily Lecture and Discussion Notes 4–2
• Guided Reading Activity 4–2
• Section Quiz 4–2
• Reading Essentials and Study Guide 4–2
• Interpreting Political Cartoons

Transparencies
• Daily Focus Skills Transparency 4–2
• American Art & Architecture

Multimedia
• Interactive Tutor Self-Assessment CD-ROM
• ExamView® Pro Testmaker CD-ROM
• Presentation Plus! CD-ROM
• TeacherWorks™ CD-ROM
• Audio Program

introduced several new policies that again ignited the flames of rebellion in the American colonies.

The *Gaspee* Affair To intercept smugglers, the British sent customs ships to patrol North American waters. One such ship was the *Gaspee*, stationed off the coast of Rhode Island. Many Rhode Islanders hated the commander of the *Gaspee* because he often searched ships without a warrant and sent his crew ashore to seize food without paying for it. In June 1772, when the *Gaspee* ran aground, some 150 colonists seized and burned the ship.

This incident outraged the British. They sent a commission to investigate and gave it authority to take suspects to England for trial. This angered the colonists, who believed it violated their right to a trial by a jury of their peers. Rhode Island's assembly then sent a letter to the other colonies asking for help.

In March 1773, Thomas Jefferson suggested that each colony create a committee of correspondence to communicate with the other colonies about British activities. The committees of correspondence helped unify the colonies and shape public opinion. They also helped colonial leaders coordinate their plans for resisting the British.

The Boston Tea Party With tensions simmering in the colonies, England's new prime minister, Lord North, made a serious mistake. In May 1773, he decided to help the **British East India Company,** which was almost bankrupt. Corrupt management and costly wars in India had put the company deeply in debt, while British taxes on tea had encouraged colonial merchants to smuggle in cheaper Dutch tea. As a result, the company had over 17 million pounds of tea in its warehouses.

To help the company sell its tea, Parliament passed the **Tea Act** of 1773. The Tea Act refunded four-fifths of the taxes the company had to pay to ship tea to the colonies, leaving only the Townshend tax. East India Company tea could now be sold at lower prices than smuggled Dutch tea. The act also allowed the East India Company to sell directly to shopkeepers, bypassing American merchants who normally distributed the tea. The Tea Act enraged the colonial merchants, who feared it was the first step by the British to squeeze them out of business.

In October 1773, the East India Company shipped 1,253 chests of tea to Boston, New York, Charles Town, and Philadelphia. The committees of correspondence rapidly alerted the colonies that the tea was on the way. The committees decided that the tea must not be allowed to land. When the first shipments arrived in

New York and Philadelphia, the colonists forced the agents for the East India Company to return home with the tea. In Charles Town, customs officers seized the tea and stored it in a local warehouse.

The most dramatic showdown occurred in December 1773, when the tea ships arrived in Boston Harbor. On the night before customs officials planned to bring the tea ashore, approximately 150 men boarded the ships. Several thousand people on shore cheered as the men dumped 342 chests of tea into the harbor. The raid came to be called the **Boston Tea Party.**

The Coercive Acts The Boston Tea Party was the last straw for the British. King George III informed Lord North that "concessions have made matters worse.

Picturing **History**

Tea Tantrum In December 1773, colonists in Boston took matters into their own hands and dumped hated imported tea into Boston Harbor. *Why did Boston tea merchants hate the Tea Act so much?*

2 TEACH

Daily Lecture and Discussion Notes 4–2

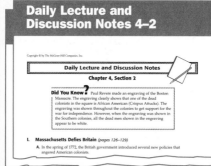

Working in a Committee
Assign students to groups representing one of the colonies. Tell the groups that they are part of that colony's committee of correspondence. Have groups research events that occurred in their colony in 1773. Then have groups compose a letter addressed to Thomas Jefferson stating events that are happening in their colony and expressing an opinion about what to do next. **L1**

📁 Use the rubric for a diary, short story, memorandum, or letter on pages 79–80 in the *Performance Assessment Activities and Rubrics.*

Picturing **History**

Background: The East India Company held a seven-year tea surplus at the time and faced financial ruin if the tea was not sold.
Answer: It took away their business.
Ask: What tactics did colonists in other places use to prevent the East India Company from selling tea in the colonies? *(In New York and Philadelphia, colonists forced agents to return home with their tea. In Charles Town customs officers seized tea and locked it up so that it could not be sold.)*

COOPERATIVE LEARNING ACTIVITY

Discussing a Topic Organize the class into groups of four or five. Then ask the following questions: **Was there ever a point during the events discussed in this section when reconciliation between the British and the colonists was possible? When? What would have been required of both parties?** After sufficient discussion time, instruct the groups to take a yes/no vote. Have one person in the group report the group's vote as well as the reasons for it. 📦

Use the rubric for a cooperative group management plan on pages 81–82 in the *Performance Assessment Activities and Rubrics.*

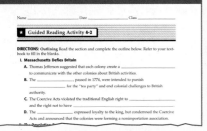
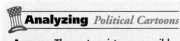
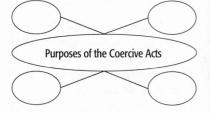

Analyzing *Political Cartoons*

Answer: The cartoonist was possibly reminding the British of previous colonial unrest.

Ask: Is this cartoon a favorable portrayal of the colonists? *(possible answer: No, because it makes the colonists look like unruly mobs.)*

Organizing Information Have students use a graphic organizer similar to the one shown below to describe the purposes of the Coercive Acts. **L1**

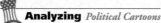

Purposes of the Coercive Acts

Creating Pamphlets Tell students to compose a pamphlet urging other students to join either the Loyalists or the Patriots. Encourage them to research the position they choose to support as well as the opposing group. Have students share their pamphlets with the class. **L2**

📁 Use the rubric for a political cartoon, pamphlet, or handbill on pages 87–88 in the *Performance Assessment Activities and Rubrics.*

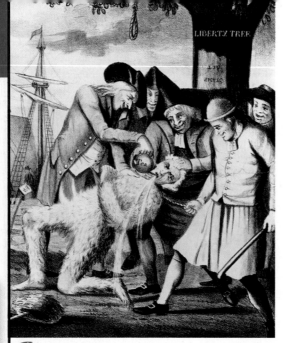

Analyzing *Political Cartoons*

Paying the Tea Tax This cartoon by a British artist shows Bostonians forcing tea down the throat of a tarred and feathered customs official. In the background, colonists dump tea in Boston Harbor. Why do you think the words "Stamp Act" are hung upside down on the Liberty Tree?

The time has come for compulsion." In the spring of 1774, Parliament passed four new laws that came to be known as the **Coercive Acts.** These laws were intended to punish Massachusetts and end colonial challenges to British authority.

The first act shut down Boston's port until the city paid for the tea that had been destroyed. The second act required all council members, judges, and sheriffs in Massachusetts to be appointed by the governor instead of being elected. This act also banned most town meetings. The third act allowed the governor to transfer trials of British soldiers and officials to England to protect them from American juries. The final act required local officials to provide lodging for British soldiers at the scene of a disturbance, in private homes if necessary. To enforce the acts, the British moved 2,000 troops to New England and appointed General Thomas Gage as the new governor of Massachusetts.

Taken together, the Coercive Acts violated several traditional English rights, including the right to trial by a jury of one's peers and the right not to have troops quartered in one's home. The king was also not supposed to maintain a standing army in peacetime

128 CHAPTER 4 The American Revolution

without the consent of Parliament. Although the British Parliament had authorized the troops, colonists believed their own local assemblies should have had to give their consent as well.

In July 1774, a month after the last Coercive Act had become law, the British introduced the **Quebec Act.** This law had nothing to do with events in the American colonies, but it angered the colonists nonetheless. The Quebec Act stated that a governor and council appointed by the king would run Quebec. The act also gave more territory to Quebec, including much of what is today Ohio, Illinois, Michigan, Indiana, and Wisconsin. If colonists moved west, they would have to live in territory where they had no elected assembly.

The Quebec Act, coming so soon after the Coercive Acts, seemed to imply that the British were trying to seize control of the colonial governments. In the colonies, the Coercive Acts and the Quebec Act together became known as the **Intolerable Acts.**

The First Continental Congress

In May 1774, the Virginia House of Burgesses declared the arrival of British troops in Boston a "military invasion" and called for colonists to observe a day of fasting and prayer. When Virginia's governor dissolved the House of Burgesses for its actions, its members adjourned to a nearby tavern and issued a resolution urging all colonies to suspend trade with Britain. They also called on the colonies to send delegates to a colonial congress to discuss what to do next.

In New York and Rhode Island, similar calls for a congress had already been made. The committees of correspondence rapidly coordinated the different proposals, and on September 5, 1774, the **First Continental Congress** met in Philadelphia.

The 55 delegates to the Congress represented 12 of Britain's North American colonies. Florida, Georgia, Nova Scotia, and Quebec did not attend. They also represented a wide range of opinion. Although opposed to the Intolerable Acts, moderate delegates believed a compromise was possible. Other more radical delegates believed the time had come to fight.

Shortly after the Congress began, the moderates, led by Joseph Galloway of Pennsylvania, put forward a compromise to end the crisis. Galloway's plan proposed a federal government for the colonies similar to the one outlined in the Albany Plan of Union. After the radicals argued that Galloway's plan would not protect American rights, the colonies voted to put off consideration of the plan.

When the Congress learned that the British had suspended the Massachusetts assembly, they responded

---

MEETING SPECIAL NEEDS

Kinesthetic Organize students into two groups. Have one group play the role of members of the British Parliament and the other group play the role of American colonial leaders. Have each group plan and present its case on imposing taxes on the colonies. Encourage students to play various historical figures as they present their arguments supporting the group's point of view. **L2**

📁 Refer to *Inclusion for the High School Social Studies Classroom Strategies and Activities* in the TCR.

with the **Declaration of Rights and Grievances.** The declaration expressed loyalty to the king but condemned the Coercive Acts. It also announced that the colonies were forming a nonimportation association. Several days later, the delegates approved the Continental Association, a plan for every county and town to form committees to enforce a boycott of British goods. The delegates then agreed to hold a second Continental Congress in May 1775 if the crisis had not been resolved.

✔ **Reading Check** **Examining** How did the British react to the Boston Tea Party?

The Revolution Begins

In October 1774, while the Continental Congress was still meeting, the Massachusetts assembly defied General Gage and organized the Massachusetts Provincial Congress. They then formed the Committee of Safety and chose John Hancock to lead it, giving him the power to call up the militia. In effect, the Provincial Congress had made Hancock a rival governor to General Gage.

A full-scale rebellion was now underway. Militias began to drill and practice shooting. The town of Concord created a special unit of men trained and ready to "stand at a minute's warning in case of alarm." These were the famous **minutemen.** All through the summer and fall of 1774, British control of the colonies weakened as colonists created provincial congresses and militias raided military depots for ammunition and gunpowder. These rebellious acts infuriated British officials.

Loyalists and Patriots British officials were not alone in their anger. Although many colonists did not agree with Parliament's policies, some still felt a strong sense of loyalty to the king and believed British law should be upheld. Americans who backed Britain came to be known as **Loyalists,** or Tories.

Loyalists came from all parts of American society. Many were government officials or Anglican ministers. Others were prominent merchants and landowners. Quite a few backcountry farmers on the frontier remained loyal as well, because they regarded the king as their protector against the planters and merchants who controlled the local governments.

On the other side were those who believed the British had become tyrants. These people were known as **Patriots,** or Whigs. Patriots also represented a wide cross section of society. They were artisans, farmers, merchants, planters, lawyers, and urban workers.

The Patriots were strong in New England and Virginia, while most of the Loyalists lived in Georgia, the Carolinas, and New York. Political differences divided communities and even split families. The American Revolution was not simply a war between the Americans and the British. It was also a civil war between Patriots and Loyalists.

Even before the Revolution, Patriot groups brutally enforced the boycott of British goods. They tarred and feathered Loyalists, and broke up Loyalist gatherings. Loyalists fought back, but they were outnumbered and not as well organized. Caught between the two groups were many Americans, possibly a majority, who did not favor either side and would support whomever won.

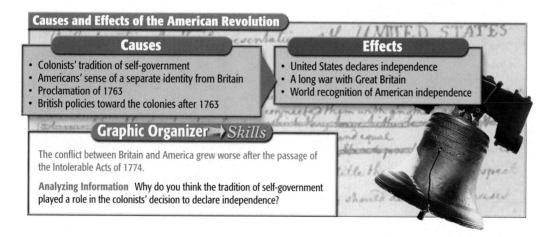

Causes and Effects of the American Revolution

Causes
- Colonists' tradition of self-government
- Americans' sense of a separate identity from Britain
- Proclamation of 1763
- British policies toward the colonies after 1763

Effects
- United States declares independence
- A long war with Great Britain
- World recognition of American independence

Graphic Organizer → Skills

The conflict between Britain and America grew worse after the passage of the Intolerable Acts of 1774.

Analyzing Information Why do you think the tradition of self-government played a role in the colonists' decision to declare independence?

CHAPTER 4 The American Revolution **129**

✔ **Reading Check**

Answer: They enacted the Coercive Acts and Quebec Act.

ABCNEWS INTERACTIVE™

 VIDEOCASSETTE
Historic America Electronic Field Trips

View **Tape 1, Chapter 6:** "Lexington and Concord."

 History *and the* **Humanities**

American Art & Architecture: Independence Hall; *The Declaration of Independence, July 4, 1776*

Graphic Organizer → Skills

Answer: It made the continual intrusion by the British into economic affairs of the colonies intolerable. Also, it gave colonists some experience in organizing and rallying around a cause.

Graphic Organizer Skills Practice Ask: When do you think the world should recognize the independence of a country? *(possible answers: after its defeated enemy recognizes it, when it forms a legitimate government, or when it seeks to participate as a member of the world community as a separate entity)*

INTERDISCIPLINARY CONNECTIONS ACTIVITY

Literature Invite students to locate and read the poem "Paul Revere's Ride" by Henry Wadsworth Longfellow. Have students compare the content of the poem with the scenario presented on page 130. Ask students to notice differences between the poem and the events recorded on the map. Ask them why they think there are differences and what effect these differences may have on our understanding of the events. **L2**

CURRICULUM CONNECTION

Role of Religion in Declaring Independence The Revolutionary War effort drew powerful support from the Congregational, Presbyterian, and other Christian churches whose clergy had no official ties with England. In contrast, the Anglican Church in America opposed the Revolution. Anglican clergy saw opposition to British rule as a danger to all authority. Their support of Britain drew widespread acceptance among colonial aristocracy, particularly in the Southern colonies.

Geography *Skills*

Answers:
1. the British
2. 15 miles

Geography Skills Practice
Ask: From what city did Paul Revere begin his journey? *(He left from Charlestown.)* Which direction were Revere, Dawes, and Prescott traveling when they left Lexington and headed for Concord? *(They were traveling west.)*

Lexington and Concord In April 1775, the British government ordered General Gage to arrest the Massachusetts Provincial Congress, even if it meant risking armed conflict. Gage did not know where the Congress was located, so he decided to seize the militia's supply depot at Concord instead. On April 18, about 700 British troops set out for Concord on a road that took them past the town of Lexington.

Patriot leaders heard about the plan and sent **Paul Revere** and **William Dawes** to spread the alarm. Revere reached Lexington by midnight and warned the people there that the British were coming. He and Dawes and a third man, **Dr. Samuel Prescott,** then set out for Concord. A British patrol stopped Revere and Dawes, but Prescott got through in time to warn Concord.

On April 19, British troops arrived in Lexington and spotted some 70 minutemen lined up on the village green. The British marched onto the field and ordered them to disperse. The minutemen had begun to back away when a shot was fired; no one is sure by whom. The British soldiers, already nervous, fired at the minutemen, killing 8 and wounding 10.

The British then headed to Concord, but when they arrived, they found that most of the military supplies had been removed. When they tried to cross the North Bridge on the far side of town, they ran into some 400 colonial militia. A fight broke out, forcing the British to retreat.

Having completed their mission, the British decided to return to Boston. Along the way, militia and farmers fired at them from behind trees, stone walls, barns, and houses. By the time the British reached Boston, they had lost 99 men, and another 174 were wounded. The colonial forces had lost 49 militia, and another 46 were wounded.

News of the fighting spread across the colonies. Militia from all over New England raced to the area to help fight the British. By May 1775, militia troops had surrounded Boston, trapping the British inside.

The Second Continental Congress Three weeks after the battles at Lexington and Concord, the Second Continental Congress met in Philadelphia. The first issue was defense. The Congress voted to "adopt" the militia army surrounding Boston, and they named it the Continental Army. On June 15, 1775, the Congress appointed George Washington as general and commander in chief of the new army.

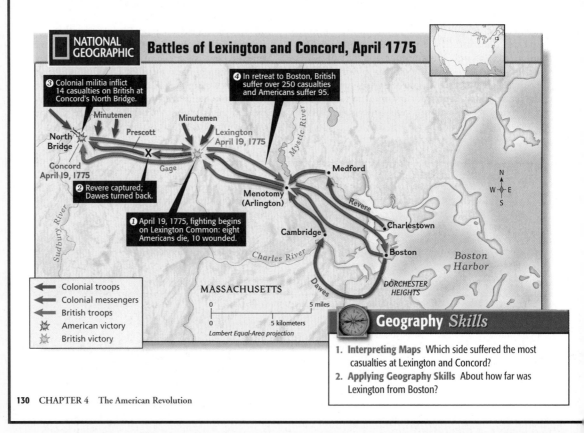

NATIONAL GEOGRAPHIC **Battles of Lexington and Concord, April 1775**

❸ Colonial militia inflict 14 casualties on British at Concord's North Bridge.

❹ In retreat to Boston, British suffer over 250 casualties and Americans suffer 95.

Minutemen — North Bridge — Prescott — Minutemen — Lexington April 19, 1775

Concord April 19, 1775 — Gage

❷ Revere captured; Dawes turned back.

❶ April 19, 1775, fighting begins on Lexington Common: eight Americans die, 10 wounded.

Medford — Menotomy (Arlington) — Revere — Charlestown — Cambridge — Boston — Dawes — Dorchester Heights — Boston Harbor

Mystic River — Charles River — Sudbury River

← Colonial troops
← Colonial messengers
← British troops
✳ American victory
✳ British victory

MASSACHUSETTS

0 ——— 5 miles
0 ——— 5 kilometers
Lambert Equal-Area projection

N W E S

Geography *Skills*

1. **Interpreting Maps** Which side suffered the most casualties at Lexington and Concord?
2. **Applying Geography Skills** About how far was Lexington from Boston?

CRITICAL THINKING ACTIVITY

Synthesizing Write the events listed below on large cards and ask students to arrange the cards in chronological order. Consider asking volunteers to hold the cards up in front of the class and ask them to move around until the class is satisfied that the cards are in the correct order. **L2**

Battle of Bunker Hill	French and Indian War
Boston Massacre	*Gaspee* Affair
Boston Tea Party	Paul Revere's ride
Declaration of Independence	Lexington and Concord
First Continental Congress	*Common Sense* published

Before Washington could get to his new command, however, the British landed reinforcements in Boston. Determined to gain control of the area, the British decided to seize the hills north of the city. Warned in advance, the militia acted first. On June 16, 1775, they dug in on Breed's Hill near Bunker Hill and began building a fort at the top.

The following day, General Gage sent 2,200 of his troops to take the hill. His soldiers, wearing heavy packs and woolen uniforms, launched an uphill, frontal attack in blistering heat. According to legend, an American commander named William Prescott told his troops, "Don't fire until you see the whites of their eyes." When the British closed to within 50 yards, the Americans took aim and fired. They turned back two British advances and were forced to retreat only after running out of ammunition.

The **Battle of Bunker Hill,** as it came to be called, helped to build American confidence. It showed that the colonial militia could stand up to one of the world's most feared armies. The British suffered more than 1,000 casualties in the fighting. Shortly afterward, General Gage resigned and was replaced by General William Howe. The situation then returned to a stalemate, with the British trapped in Boston surrounded by militia.

✓ **Reading Check** **Interpreting** Why was the Battle of Bunker Hill important to the Americans?

The Decision for Independence

Despite the onset of fighting, many colonists in the summer of 1775 were not prepared to break away from Great Britain. Most members of the Second Continental Congress wanted the right to govern themselves, but they did not want to break with the British Empire. By 1776, however, opinion had changed. Frustrated by Britain's refusal to compromise, many Patriot leaders began to call for independence.

Efforts at Peace In July 1775, as the siege of Boston continued, the Continental Congress sent a document known as the **Olive Branch Petition** to the king. John Dickinson wrote the petition. It stated that the colonies were still loyal to the king and asked George III to call off hostilities until the situation could be worked out peacefully.

In the meantime, the radical delegates of the Congress convinced the body to order an attack on the British troops based in Quebec. They hoped the attack would convince the French in Quebec to rebel

History *Through Art*

Colonial Confidence Alonzo Chappel painted *The Battle of Bunker Hill.* The battle showed the colonists they could win against the British. How does the artist portray the colonists' courage?

and join the Americans in fighting the British. The American forces captured the city of Montreal, but the French did not rebel.

The attack on Quebec convinced British officials that there was no hope of reconciliation. When the Olive Branch Petition arrived in England, King George refused to look at it. On August 22, 1775, he issued the Proclamation for Suppressing Rebellion and Sedition, stating that the colonies were now "open and avowed enemies."

With no compromise likely, the Continental Congress increasingly began to act like an independent government. It sent people to negotiate with the Native Americans, and it established a postal system and a Continental Navy and Marine Corps. It also authorized privateering. By March 1776, the Continental Navy had raided the Bahamas and begun seizing British merchant ships.

The Fighting Spreads As the revolution began, Governor Dunmore of Virginia organized two Loyalist armies to assist the British troops in

CHAPTER 4 The American Revolution **131**

History *Through Art*

Background: Alonzo Chappel combined his artistic talent and his love of history into a career of painting and drawing famous moments in American history. Although not an eyewitness to most of the events he painted, Chappel's portrayals are based on his study of history.
Answer: They look determined, fighting with whatever they can, and even the wounded fight.
Ask: Why did the colonists finally retreat from Bunker Hill? *(They ran out of ammunition.)*

✓ **Reading Check**

Answer: It helped build American confidence by showing that a largely untrained colonial militia could stand up to the British army.

Interpreting Art Have students locate a picture of Percy Moran's *Battle of Bunker Hill* or John Trumbull's *Battle of Bunker's* [sic] *Hill.* Direct students to compare and contrast the piece of art they selected with Alonzo Chappel's work that appears on this page. **L2**

FYI

Many citizens of Boston had a bird's-eye view of the Battle of Bunker Hill. Some climbed onto rooftops and church steeples to watch the fighting.

📂 Use *Interpreting Political Cartoons,* Cartoon 3.

EXTENDING THE CONTENT

The American Navy At the beginning of the Revolutionary War, the colonists had no navy, so they began to commission private ships to attack British vessels. Owners of these ships could keep half the cargo of any captured enemy vessels. This arrangement greatly aided the American cause by cutting deeply into British supply routes. One ingenious American captain, Jonathan Haraden, instructed his crew to cover the ship's gun ports with canvas to make the vessel look like a vulnerable merchant ship. When an unsuspecting British ship neared, it was met with gunfire from the disguised gun ports.

3 ASSESS

Assign Section 2 Assessment as homework or as an in-class activity.

⏺ Have students use the **Interactive Tutor Self-Assessment CD-ROM.**

Reading Essentials and Study Guide 4–2

Name _____ Date _____ Class _____

Study Guide
Chapter 4, Section 2
For use with textbook pages 126–133

THE REVOLUTION BEGINS

KEY TERMS AND NAMES

committee of correspondence committees designed to communicate with other colonies about British activities *(page 127)*

Boston Tea Party a raid by colonists on British tea ships *(page 127)*

Intolerable Acts a group of laws that led the colonists to believe that the British were trying to seize control of the colonial governments *(page 128)*

minutemen a special unit of the militia trained to fight at a minute's notice *(page 129)*

Loyalist Americans who backed Britain *(page 129)*

Patriot Americans who believed the British had become tyrants *(page 129)*

Section Quiz 4–2

Name _____ Date _____ Class _____

★ **Chapter 4** | Score

Section Quiz 4-2

DIRECTIONS: Matching Match each item in Column A with the items in Column B. Write the correct letters in the blanks. *(10 points each)*

Column A
___ 1. a special unit of militia in the town of Concord
___ 2. where a largely untrained colonial militia stood up to one of the world's most feared armies
___ 3. Americans who backed Britain
___ 4. pamphlet written by Thomas Paine that attacked the monarchy
___ 5. created by each colony to communicate with the other colonies about British activities

Column B
A. Loyalists
B. Common Sense
C. committee of correspondence
D. Battle of Bunker Hill
E. minutemen

DIRECTIONS: Multiple Choice In the blank at the left, write the letter of the choice that

HISTORY
Online

Objectives and answers to the student activity can be found in the **Web Activity Lesson Plan** at tav.glencoe.com.

What If...

The Declaration of Independence Had Condemned Slavery?

In 1776 the Continental Congress chose a committee to draft the Declaration of Independence. The committee included Thomas Jefferson, John Adams, Roger Sherman, Benjamin Franklin, and Robert Livingston. Jefferson later recalled the following in his memoirs: "[The committee members] unanimously pressed on myself alone to undertake the draught. I consented; I drew it; but before I reported it to the committee I communicated it separately to Dr. Franklin and Mr. Adams requesting their corrections. . . ."

Franklin and Adams urged Jefferson to delete his condemnation of King George's support of slavery. The two realized that the revolution needed support from all the colonies to succeed, and condemning slavery would certainly alienate pro-slavery colonists and force them to support the king. Jefferson modified the draft accordingly. If the Declaration of Independence had included Jefferson's condemnation of slavery, which is excerpted below, the history of the United States might have been very different.

❝He [King George] has waged cruel war against human nature itself, violating its most sacred rights of life and liberty in the persons of a distant people who never offended him, captivating and carrying them into slavery in another hemisphere, or to incur miserable death in their transportation thither. . . . He has [stopped] every legislative attempt to prohibit or to restrain this execrable commerce determining to keep open a market where [people] should be bought and sold. . . .❞

Virginia, one composed of white Loyalists, the other of enslaved Africans. Dunmore proclaimed that Africans enslaved by rebels would be freed if they fought for the Loyalists. The announcement convinced many Southern planters to support independence. Otherwise, they might lose their lands and labor force. They also increased their efforts to raise a large Patriot army. In December 1775, the Patriot troops attacked and defeated Dunmore's forces near Norfolk, Virginia. The British then pulled their soldiers out of Virginia, leaving the Patriots in control.

In North Carolina, Patriot troops dispersed Loyalists at the Battle of Moore's Creek in February 1776. The British then decided to seize Charles Town, South Carolina, but the Charles Town militia thwarted the British plans.

Student Web Activity Visit the *American Vision* Web site at tav.glencoe.com and click on **Student Web Activities— Chapter 4** for an activity on the American Revolution.

While fighting raged in the South, Washington ordered his troops to capture the hills south of Boston. He intended to place cannons on the hills to bombard the British. After the Americans seized the hills, however, the British Navy evacuated the British troops from Boston, leaving the Patriots in control.

Despite their defeats, it was clear that the British were not backing down. In December 1775, the king issued the Prohibitory Act, shutting down trade with the colonies and ordering a naval blockade. The British also began expanding its army by recruiting mercenaries, or soldiers for hire, from Germany. By the spring of 1776, the British had hired 30,000 German mercenaries, mostly Hessians from the region of Hesse.

Common Sense and Independence As the war dragged on, more and more Patriots began to think the time had come to declare independence, although they feared that most colonists were still loyal to the king. In January 1776, however, public opinion began to change when Thomas Paine published a lively and persuasive pamphlet called

---

CRITICAL THINKING ACTIVITY

Comparing In the 1900s, the world witnessed violent protests against totalitarian governments, such as the Tiananmen Square massacre in China. It has also seen the successful use of nonviolent action in the drive for independence in India and in the American civil rights movement. The American colonists used both violent and nonviolent protest in the period preceding the Revolutionary War. Ask students to list two examples of each type of protest and their outcomes. Then ask students which form of protest, in their opinion, was more successful. Encourage them to explain their reasoning. **L2**

What might have happened?

1. Why do you think Thomas Jefferson, who was a slave-holder, wanted to include this paragraph?

2. Would the course of American history have changed significantly if the Declaration of Independence had included Jefferson's statement? If so, how? If not, why not?

Common Sense. Until *Common Sense* appeared, nearly everyone viewed Parliament as the enemy, not the king. In *Common Sense,* Paine attacked King George III. Parliament, he wrote, did nothing without the

king's support. Paine argued that monarchies had been set up by seizing power from the people. George III was a tyrant, and it was time to declare independence:

❝Everything that is right or reasonable pleads for separation. The blood of the slain, the weeping voice of nature cries, 'Tis Time To Part. . . . Every spot of the old world is overrun with oppression. Freedom hath been hunted round the globe . . . [and] England hath given her warning to depart. Oh! Receive the fugitive, and prepare in time an asylum for mankind.❞

—from *Common Sense*

Within three months, *Common Sense* had sold 100,000 copies. George Washington wrote, "*Common Sense* is working a powerful change in the minds of men." Increasingly, many colonists were ready to declare independence. One by one the provincial congresses and assemblies told their representatives at the Continental Congress to vote for independence.

In early July a committee composed of John Adams, Benjamin Franklin, Roger Sherman, Robert Livingston, and Thomas Jefferson submitted a document Jefferson had drafted on independence. On July 4, 1776, the Continental Congress issued this **Declaration of Independence,** declaring themselves the United States of America. The American Revolution had begun.

✓ **Reading Check** **Analyzing** How did Thomas Paine help persuade colonists to declare independence?

What If...

Answers:

1. Answers may vary. Students may realize that Jefferson's rhetoric did not always match his actions.

2. Answers may vary. Possible reasons: the colonies may not have united to throw off British rule, individual colonies may have struggled for their own independence, or slavery may have ended sooner than it actually did.

✓ **Reading Check**

Answer: by publishing his pamphlet *Common Sense*

Reteach
Ask students to summarize the events that fueled colonial discontent.

Enrich
Invite students to read Thomas Paine's *Common Sense* and write a summary of the main ideas.

4 CLOSE

Ask students to explain the events that led up to the actions taken by the second Continental Congress.

SECTION 2 ASSESSMENT

Checking for Understanding

1. **Define:** committee of correspondence, minuteman, Loyalist, Patriot.

2. **Identify:** Boston Tea Party, Intolerable Acts, Second Continental Congress, Battle of Bunker Hill, Declaration of Independence.

Reviewing Themes

3. **Government and Democracy** After King George III refused to consider the Olive Branch Petition, in what ways did the Continental Congress begin to act like an independent government?

Critical Thinking

4. **Synthesizing** What role did the committees of correspondence play in the colonists' move toward independence?

5. **Organizing** Use a graphic organizer similar to the one below to indicate ways in which colonists defied Britain after the repeal of the Townshend Acts.

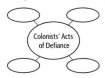

Colonists' Acts of Defiance

Analyzing Visuals

6. **Examining Maps** Study the map on page 130. Why do you think Paul Revere and William Dawes took different routes on the first leg of their journey?

Writing About History

7. **Descriptive Writing** Imagine that you were a participant in the Boston Tea Party. Write a diary entry describing the event.

SECTION 2 ASSESSMENT ANSWERS

1. Terms are in blue.

2. Boston Tea Party *(p. 127)*, Intolerable Acts *(p. 128)*, Battle of Bunker Hill *(p. 131)*, Declaration of Independence *(p. 133)*

3. It began negotiations with the Native Americans, established a postal system and a navy, and authorized privateering.

4. By communicating with other colonies about British activities, the committees helped unify colonies and shape public opinion.

5. Boston Tea Party, boycotts, burning of the *Gaspee,* formed committees of correspondence

6. Answers will vary but could include that the different routes helped

avoid capture by the British troops, that the two men started from different points, and that they wanted to alert as many people as possible.

7. Students' entries will vary. Diary entries should be written as if the students were participants.

The Declaration of Independence

1 FOCUS

Analyzing Concepts Ask students if they would risk their lives for an idea and, if so, for what idea. Remind students that the American Revolution involved great risks for the people who fought it.

Ask what ideas were being fought for in the American Revolution. (*self-government, freedom, representation, equality*) Direct students to read the first paragraph of the Declaration of Independence on this page. Ask the following questions:

- What is the tone of the document? (*possible answers: forceful, sober, respectful*)
- To whom is the document addressed? (*to the entire world; indirectly to King George III and the English Parliament*)

2 TEACH

Paraphrasing Choose a student to read aloud the first paragraph under "Declaration of Natural Rights" on this page. Discuss with students any unfamiliar terms such as *self-evident* and *inalienable*. Then have students close their textbooks and paraphrase the first paragraph in their own words. **L1** ELL

In Congress, July 4, 1776. The unanimous Declaration of the thirteen united States of America,

[Preamble]

When in the Course of human events, it becomes necessary for one people to dissolve the political bands which have connected them with another, and to assume among the Powers of the earth, the separate and equal station to which the Laws of Nature and Nature's God entitle them, a decent respect to the opinions of mankind requires that they should declare the causes which **impel** them to the separation.

[Declaration of Natural Rights]

We hold these truths to be self-evident, that all men are created equal, that they are **endowed** by their Creator with certain unalienable Rights, that among these are Life, Liberty, and the pursuit of Happiness.

That to secure these rights, Governments are instituted among Men, deriving their just powers from the consent of the governed,

That whenever any Form of Government becomes destructive of these ends, it is the Right of the People to alter or to abolish it, and to institute new Government, laying its foundation on such principles and organizing its powers in such form, as to them shall seem most likely to effect their Safety and Happiness. Prudence, indeed, will dictate that Governments long established should not be changed for light and transient causes; and accordingly all experience hath shown, that mankind are more disposed to suffer, while evils are sufferable, than to right themselves by abolishing the forms to which they are accustomed. But when a long train of abuses and usurpations, pursuing invariably the same Object evinces a design to reduce them under absolute **Despotism**, it is their right, it is their duty, to throw off such Government, and to provide new Guards for their future security.

[List of Grievances]

Such has been the patient sufferance of these Colonies; and such is now the necessity which constrains them to alter their former Systems of Government. The history of the present King of Great Britain is a history of repeated injuries and **usurpations,** all having in direct object the establishment of an absolute Tyranny over these States. To prove this, let Facts be submitted to a candid world.

He has refused his Assent to Laws, the most wholesome and necessary for the public good.

What It Means
The Preamble The Declaration of Independence has four parts. The Preamble explains why the Continental Congress drew up the Declaration.

impel *force*

What It Means
Natural Rights The second part, the Declaration of Natural Rights, states that people have certain basic rights and that government should protect those rights. John Locke's ideas strongly influenced this part. In 1690 Locke wrote that government was based on the consent of the people and that people had the right to rebel if the government did not uphold their right to life, liberty, and property.

endowed *provided*

despotism *unlimited power*

What It Means
List of Grievances The third part of the Declaration lists the colonists' complaints against the British government. Notice that King George III is singled out for blame.

usurpations *unjust uses of power*

134 The Declaration of Independence

EXTENDING THE CONTENT

Real Title Strictly speaking, the title of this famous document is not the "Declaration of Independence" but rather "The Unanimous Declaration of the Thirteen United States of America." The document was not the act by which independence was declared. That had been done on July 2, when the Continental Congress adopted Lee's resolution.

He has forbidden his Governors to pass Laws of immediate and pressing importance, unless suspended in their operation till his Assent should be obtained; and when so suspended, he has utterly neglected to attend to them.

He has refused to pass other Laws for the accommodation of large districts of people, unless those people would **relinquish** the right of Representation in the Legislature, a right **inestimable** to them and formidable to tyrants only.

He has called together legislative bodies at places unusual, uncomfortable, and distant from the depository of their Public Records, for the sole purpose of fatiguing them into compliance with his measures.

He has dissolved Representative Houses repeatedly, for opposing with manly firmness his invasions on the rights of the people.

He has refused for a long time, after such dissolutions, to cause others to be elected; whereby the Legislative Powers, incapable of **Annihilation,** have returned to the People at large for their exercise; the State remaining in the mean time exposed to all the dangers of invasion from without, and **convulsions** within.

He has endeavoured to prevent the population of these States; for that purpose obstructing the Laws for **Naturalization of Foreigners;** refusing to pass others to encourage their migrations hither, and raising the conditions of new Appropriations of Lands.

He has obstructed the Administration of Justice, by refusing his Assent to Laws for establishing Judiciary Powers.

He has made Judges dependent on his Will alone, for the **tenure** of their offices, and the amount and payment of their salaries.

He has erected a multitude of New Offices, and sent hither swarms of Officers to harass our people, and eat out their substance.

relinquish *give up*
inestimable *priceless*

annihilation *destruction*

convulsions *violent disturbances*

Naturalization of Foreigners *process by which foreign-born persons become citizens*

tenure *term*

Identifying Central Issues

Refer students to the painting on this page. Mention that the painting includes many of the delegates who also signed the Constitution. Discuss differences and similarities between this group and the current members of the United States Congress. The discussion can include observations about numbers, gender, ethnicity, age, style of dress, and so on. Conclude by pointing out that the calmness of the setting obscures the desperation of this step. In the eyes of the British government, each of these representatives was guilty of treason. For some time after, the names of the signers were kept secret, presumably to protect them from British reprisal. **L1**

Analyzing Information

Point out that the statements in the Declaration of Natural Rights voice some of the most important ideas of governments. Ask students to identify the important statements. *(Answers will vary but should include: All people are created equal; all people have certain basic rights; the purpose of government is to keep these rights safe; and the power of a government to rule comes from the people.)* **L2**

COOPERATIVE LEARNING ACTIVITY

Making Oral Presentations Tell students that the Declaration of Independence had significant influence on other independence movements. Organize the class into groups of four. Assign each group one of the following: the French Revolution, Latin American independence movements, Tiananman Square demonstrations, the breakup of the Soviet Union. Have the groups use library and Internet resources to learn about their assigned movement and the effects that the Declaration of Independence had on the movement. Have the groups prepare an oral report on their findings. **L2**

Use the rubric for a cooperative group management plan on pages 81–82 in the *Performance Assessment Activities and Rubrics.*

Determining Cause and Effect
Ask students to think about the impact of the Declaration on the colonists. Have them list as many different effects as they can resulting from news that the Congress had issued the Declaration. *(Answers will vary, but might include the following: The time for indecision was over. It forced colonists to decide whether they supported independence or the king. It rallied support and boosted morale. It also raised the conflict above the level of discontent over economic issues.)* **L2**

Researching Organize students into groups of four. Point out that the Declaration has been a force for change in the United States. People have used its words and ideas to promote such measures as the abolition of slavery and equal rights for women. Have each group do research to find three examples in which an individual or a group used the words and ideas expressed in the Declaration to promote change or reform. **L2**

He has kept among us, in times of peace, Standing Armies without the Consent of our legislature.

He has affected to render the Military independent of and superior to the Civil Power.

He has combined with others to subject us to a jurisdiction foreign to our constitution, and unacknowledged by our laws; giving his Assent to their acts of pretended legislation:

quartering *lodging*

For **quartering** large bodies of troops among us:

For protecting them, by a mock Trial, from Punishment for any Murders which they should commit on the Inhabitants of these States:

For cutting off our Trade with all parts of the world:

For imposing taxes on us without our Consent:

For depriving us in many cases, of the benefits of Trial by Jury:

For transporting us beyond Seas to be tried for pretended offences:

For abolishing the free System of English Laws in a neighbouring Province, establishing therein an Arbitrary government, and enlarging its Boundaries so as to **render** it at once an example and fit instrument for introducing the same absolute rule into these Colonies:

render *make*

For taking away our Charters, abolishing our most valuable Laws, and altering fundamentally the Forms of our Governments:

For suspending our own Legislature, and declaring themselves invested with Power to legislate for us in all cases whatsoever.

abdicated *given up*

He has **abdicated** Government here, by declaring us out of his Protection and waging War against us.

He has plundered our seas, ravaged our Coasts, burnt our towns, and destroyed the lives of our people.

He is at this time transporting large armies of foreign mercenaries to compleat the works of death, desolation and tyranny, already begun with circumstances of Cruelty & **perfidy** scarcely paralleled in the most barbarous ages, and totally unworthy the Head of a civilized nation.

perfidy *violation of trust*

He has constrained our fellow Citizens taken Captive on the high Seas to bear Arms against their Country, to become the executioners of their friends and Brethren, or to fall themselves by their Hands.

insurrections *rebellions*

He has excited domestic **insurrections** amongst us, and has endeavoured to bring on the inhabitants of our frontiers, the merciless Indian Savages, whose known rule of warfare, is an undistinguished destruction of all ages, sexes and conditions.

petitioned for redress *asked formally for a correction of wrongs*

In every stage of these Oppressions We have **Petitioned for Redress** in the most humble terms: Our repeated Petitions have been answered only by repeated injury. A Prince, whose character is thus marked by every act which may define a Tyrant, is unfit to be the ruler of a free People.

unwarrantable jurisdiction *unjustified authority*

Nor have We been wanting in attention to our British brethren. We have warned them from time to time of attempts by their legislature to extend an **unwarrantable jurisdiction** over us. We have reminded them of the circumstances of our emigration and settlement here. We have appealed to their native justice and magnanimity, and we have conjured them by the ties of our common kindred to disavow these usurpations, which, would inevitably interrupt our connections and correspondence. They too have been deaf to the voice of justice and of **consanguinity**. We must, therefore, acquiesce in the necessity, which denounces our Separation, and hold them, as we hold the rest of mankind, Enemies in War, in Peace Friends.

consanguinity *originating from the same ancestor*

136 The Declaration of Independence

MEETING SPECIAL NEEDS

Auditory/Musical Have interested students listen to the soundtrack of the Broadway play *1776*. Ask students to select one song to share with the class. Have them explain who sang the song, the historic events being portrayed, and how the lyrics and music convey the ideas of the Continental Congress. Also encourage students to point out any historical inaccuracies that they find in the song. **L2**

Refer to *Inclusion for the High School Social Studies Classroom Strategies and Activities* in the TCR.

★ ★ ★ ★ ★ ★

[Resolution of Independence by the United States]

We, therefore, the Representatives of the united States of America, in General Congress, Assembled, appealing to the Supreme Judge of the world for the **rectitude** of our intentions, do, in the Name, and by Authority of the good People of these Colonies, solemnly publish and declare, That these United Colonies are, and of Right ought to be Free and Independent States; that they are Absolved from all Allegiance to the British Crown, and that all political connection between them and the State of Great Britain, is and ought to be totally dissolved; and that as Free and Independent States, they have full Power to levy War, conclude Peace, contract Alliances, establish Commerce, and to do all other Acts and Things which Independent States may of right do.

And for the support of this Declaration, with a firm reliance on the Protection of Divine Providence, we mutually pledge to each other our Lives, our Fortunes and our sacred Honor.

What It Means
Resolution of Independence The Final section declares that the colonies are "Free and Independent States" with the full power to make war, to form alliances, and to trade with other countries.

rectitude *rightness*

What It Means
Signers of the Declaration The signers, as representatives of the American people, declared the colonies independent from Great Britain. Most members signed the document on August 2, 1776.

John Hancock
    President from
    Massachusetts

Georgia
Button Gwinnett
Lyman Hall
George Walton

North Carolina
William Hooper
Joseph Hewes
John Penn

South Carolina
Edward Rutledge
Thomas Heyward, Jr.
Thomas Lynch, Jr.
Arthur Middleton

Maryland
Samuel Chase
William Paca
Thomas Stone
Charles Carroll
    of Carrollton

Virginia
George Wythe
Richard Henry Lee
Thomas Jefferson
Benjamin Harrison
Thomas Nelson, Jr.
Francis Lightfoot Lee
Carter Braxton

Pennsylvania
Robert Morris
Benjamin Rush
Benjamin Franklin
John Morton
George Clymer
James Smith
George Taylor
James Wilson
George Ross

Delaware
Caesar Rodney
George Read
Thomas McKean

New York
William Floyd
Philip Livingston
Francis Lewis
Lewis Morris

New Jersey
Richard Stockton
John Witherspoon
Francis Hopkinson
John Hart
Abraham Clark

New Hampshire
Josiah Bartlett
William Whipple
Matthew Thornton

Massachusetts
Samuel Adams
John Adams
Robert Treat Paine
Elbridge Gerry

Rhode Island
Stephen Hopkins
William Ellery

Connecticut
Samuel Huntington
William Williams
Oliver Wolcott
Roger Sherman

The Declaration of Independence **137**

The Declaration of Independence

FYI

Roger Sherman was the only person who signed all three of the most important documents of the United States: the Declaration of Independence, the Articles of Confederation, and the Constitution.

3 ASSESS

Reteach
Ask students to identify the most important points in the Declaration of Natural Rights.

Enrich
Ask students to write a paragraph stating which idea expressed in the Declaration they think is the most important one and explaining their choice.

4 CLOSE

Have students list the powers that the new Free and Independent states planned to claim.

1 FOCUS

Section Overview
This section focuses on the fight for independence.

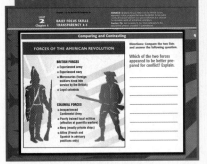
Guide to Reading

Answers to Graphic: Students should include battles for each year from 1776 to 1781. Make sure students discuss the importance and outcome of each battle.

Preteaching Vocabulary
Have students pose questions that can be answered by using the Key Terms and Names.

Guide to Reading

Main Idea
After a war lasting several years, the colonists finally won their independence from Great Britain.

Key Terms and Names
William Howe, guerrilla warfare, Nathan Hale, Valley Forge, Marquis de Lafayette, Saratoga, letters of marque, John Paul Jones, Charles Cornwallis, Battle of Kings Mountain

Reading Strategy
Sequencing As you read about the war for independence, complete a time line similar to the one below to record the major battles and their outcomes.

1776 — 1781

Reading Objectives
• **Describe** the strategies behind the Northern Campaign.
• **Summarize** the scope of the war at sea.

Section Theme
Global Connections Hostility between the French and British caused France to support the colonies.

Preview of Events

♦1775 ♦1778 ♦1781 ♦1784

1776
Battle of Trenton

1777
The British surrender at Saratoga

1777–1778
Washington camps at Valley Forge for the winter

1781
Cornwallis surrenders at Yorktown

1783
Treaty of Paris signed

★ An American Story ★

Troops at Valley Forge

Colonel Henry Beckman Livingston could only watch helplessly the suffering around him. A veteran of several military campaigns, Livingston huddled with the rest of George Washington's army at its winter quarters at Valley Forge, Pennsylvania. The winter of 1777 to 1778 was brutally cold, and the army lacked food, clothing, and other supplies. Huddled in small huts, soldiers wrapped themselves in blankets and survived on the smallest of rations. Livingston described the army's plight in a letter to his brother, Robert:

❝Our troops are in general almost naked and very often in a starveing condition. All my men except 18 are unfit for duty for want of shoes, stockings, and shirts. . . . Poor Jack has been necessitated to make up his blanket into a vest and breeches. If I did not fear starveing with cold I should be tempted to do the same.❞

—adapted from *A Salute to Courage*

The Opposing Sides
The struggle at Valley Forge was one of the darkest hours in the war for independence. No one knew if the patriots were strong enough to defeat the powerful British Empire. On the same day that the Continental Congress voted for independence, the British began landing troops in New York. By mid-August, they had assembled an estimated 32,000 men under the command of General **William Howe.** British officials did not expect the rebellion to last very long. The British troops were disciplined, well trained, and well equipped.

SECTION RESOURCES

📁 **Reproducible Masters**
• Reproducible Lesson Plan 4–3
• Daily Lecture and Discussion Notes 4–3
• Guided Reading Activity 4–3
• Section Quiz 4–3
• Reading Essentials and Study Guide 4–3

📖 **Transparencies**
• Daily Focus Skills Transparency 4–3

• American Art & Architecture
Multimedia
💿 Interactive Tutor Self-Assessment CD-ROM
💿 ExamView® Pro Testmaker CD-ROM
💿 Presentation Plus! CD-ROM
💿 TeacherWorks™ CD-ROM
🎧 Audio Program
🎵 American Music: Hits Through History
🎵 American Music: Cultural Traditions

Compared to the British troops, the Continental Army was inexperienced and poorly equipped. Throughout the war, it struggled to keep its recruits and pay their wages. Although over 230,000 men served in the Continental Army, they rarely numbered more than 20,000 at any one time. Many soldiers deserted or refused to reenlist when their term was up. Others left their posts and returned to their farms at planting or harvest time.

Paying for the war was equally difficult. Lacking the power to tax, the Continental Congress issued paper money. These "Continentals" were not backed by gold or silver and became almost worthless very quickly. Fortunately **Robert Morris,** a wealthy Pennsylvania merchant and banker, personally pledged large amounts of money for the war effort. Morris also set up an efficient method of buying rations and uniforms, arranged for foreign loans, and convinced the Congress to create the Bank of North America to finance the military.

The Continental Army was not the only force the British had to worry about. They also had to fight the local militias. The militias were poorly trained, but they fought differently. They did not always line up for battle. They hid among trees and behind walls and ambushed British troops and supply wagons, then disappeared. This kind of fighting is called guerrilla warfare, and it is very difficult to defeat.

Another problem for the British was that they were not united at home. Many merchants and members of Parliament opposed the war. The British had to win quickly and cheaply; otherwise, opinions in Parliament would shift against the war. The United States did not have to defeat Britain—it simply had to survive until the British became tired of paying for the war.

The European balance of power also hampered the British. The French, Dutch, and Spanish were all eager to exploit Britain's problems. As a result, Britain had to station much of its military elsewhere in the world to defend its empire. The European balance of power also meant that the Patriots might be able to find allies against the British.

✓ **Reading Check** **Identifying** What three major disadvantages did the British face in the American Revolution?

The Northern Campaign

The British knew that to end the war quickly, they not only had to win several battles but also had to convince the American people that their cause was hopeless. At the same time, the British had to make it safe to surrender. If the Patriots thought they would be hanged for treason, they would never surrender.

General Howe's strategy had two parts. The first part was military. He began a massive buildup in New York, hoping to intimidate the Americans and capture New York City. This would separate New

Colonial hat

Colonial rifle

The Opposing Sides

Colonial Advantages	British Advantages
Fighting on home ground	Well-trained, well-supplied army and navy
Good decisions by generals	Wealth of resources
Fighting for their rights and freedoms	Strong central government
French alliance: loans, navy, troops	
Colonial Disadvantages	**British Disadvantages**
Untrained soldiers; small army	Fighting in unfamiliar, hostile territory
Food and ammunition shortages	Fighting far away from Britain and resources
Weak and divided central government	Troops indifferent; halfhearted support at home

Chart *Skills*
1. **Interpreting Charts** Why was fighting for their rights and freedoms an advantage for the colonists?
2. **Analyzing** In what ways would a weak government be a disadvantage in war time?

2 TEACH

Daily Lecture and Discussion Notes 4–3

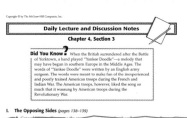

Copyright © by The McGraw-Hill Companies, Inc.

Daily Lecture and Discussion Notes
Chapter 4, Section 3

Did You Know ? When the British surrendered after the Battle of Yorktown, a band played "Yankee Doodle"—a melody that may have begun in southern Europe in the Middle Ages. The words of "Yankee Doodle" were written by an English army surgeon. The words were meant to make fun of the inexperienced and poorly trained American troops during the French and Indian War. The American troops, however, liked the song so much that it wassung by American troops during the Revolutionary War.

I. **The Opposing Sides** (pages 138–139)

Discussing an Idea Ask students to explain why the Continental army did not need to defeat the British in order to win independence. (*Many in England did not support a long, costly war.*) **L1**

✓ **Reading Check**

Answer: guerrilla warfare, opposition at home, and the European balance of power

FYI

Sometimes called the financier of the Revolutionary War, Robert Morris saw his personal wealth slip away when he got involved in land speculation. He spent more than three years in debtors' prison around the turn of the century.

Chart *Skills*

Answers:
1. It gave them a very personal, sustaining reason to fight.
2. It would not be able to formulate a central policy.

Chart Skills Practice
Ask: How do you think fighting for a cause that you believe in strongly affects the outcome of battles?
(*possible answer: will fight to the end despite all odds*)

COOPERATIVE LEARNING ACTIVITY

Building a Model Have students work in small groups to build a model depicting one of the events mentioned in this section. Encourage students to use library and Internet resources to locate descriptions and drawings to help recreate the scene. Suggest that students create a handout to accompany their model. Make arrangements to display the models at your school, the local library, or other appropriate venues.

Use the rubric for a cooperative group management plan on pages 81–82 in the *Performance Assessment Activities and Rubrics.*

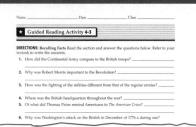
Synthesizing Information Have students view copies of paintings of the crossing of the Delaware by artists George Caleb Bingham and Thomas Sully. Ask them which one seems closest to historical accounts. **L2**

Geography *Skills*

Answers:

1. Trenton and Princeton

2. transporting troops and equipment

Geography Skills Practice
Ask: What two major cities did the British capture? *(New York and Philadelphia)*

History *and the* Humanities

🎵 American Music: Hits Through History: "General Scott's March," "The World Turned Upside Down"

🎵 American Music: Cultural Traditions: "Tunes from Colonial America," "The President's March"

🖌 American Art & Architecture: *Washington Crossing the Delaware*

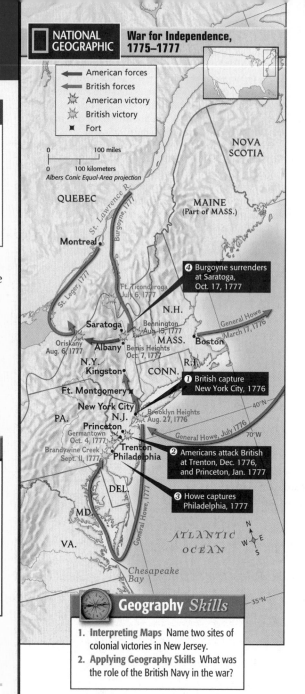

NATIONAL GEOGRAPHIC
War for Independence, 1775–1777

← American forces
← British forces
✴ American victory
✴ British victory
■ Fort

0 ___ 100 miles
0 ___ 100 kilometers
Albers Conic Equal-Area projection

NOVA SCOTIA

QUEBEC

MAINE (Part of MASS.)

Montreal

④ Burgoyne surrenders at Saratoga, Oct. 17, 1777

N.H.

Saratoga
Bennington Aug. 16, 1777
Oriskany Aug. 6, 1777
Albany
Bemis Heights Oct. 7, 1777
MASS.
Boston
General Howe March 17, 1776

N.Y.
Kingston
CONN.
R.I.

① British capture New York City, 1776

Ft. Montgomery
New York City
Brooklyn Heights Aug. 27, 1776
PA. N.J.
Princeton
Germantown Oct. 4, 1777
Brandywine Creek Sept. 11, 1777
Trenton
Philadelphia
General Howe, July 1776

② Americans attack British at Trenton, Dec. 1776, and Princeton, Jan. 1777

③ Howe captures Philadelphia, 1777

DEL.
MD.
VA.
ATLANTIC OCEAN
Chesapeake Bay

Geography *Skills*

1. **Interpreting Maps** Name two sites of colonial victories in New Jersey.
2. **Applying Geography Skills** What was the role of the British Navy in the war?

England from the Southern states and demonstrate to Americans that they could not win.

The second part of Howe's strategy was diplomatic. He invited delegates from the Continental Congress to a peace conference. The Congress sent

Benjamin Franklin, John Adams, and Edward Rutledge. Howe told them that anyone who put down their arms and swore loyalty to the king would be pardoned. The Americans quickly realized that Howe had no authority to negotiate a compromise and was only interested in talking them into surrendering. They refused to talk further, and the stage was set for the first major battle.

Opening Moves Despite the size of the British forces preparing to seize New York City, the Continental Congress asked Washington to defend the city. Congressional leaders feared that if New York fell without a fight, it would hurt American morale. Washington agreed with this assessment, and he moved much of his army to Long Island and Manhattan Island.

The inexperience of Washington's troops became obvious when British troops landed on Long Island in the summer of 1776. Many American soldiers fled, and another 1,500 became casualties. Fortunately, the British did not move quickly after their victory, and the surviving American troops escaped to Manhattan Island where they joined the remainder of Washington's army defending New York City.

Using their ships, the British could have landed troops north of New York City and surrounded the American positions, but again, they moved too slowly. Washington abandoned the city and headed to the northern end of Manhattan. The British then captured New York and used it as their headquarters for the rest of the war.

About this time, Washington sent Captain **Nathan Hale** to spy on the British. Although Hale was disguised as a Dutch schoolteacher, he was caught by the British and hanged. Brave until the end, Hale's last words were: "I only regret that I have but one life to lose for my country." Shortly afterward, Washington moved most of his troops from Manhattan to White Plains, New York, where the British once again engaged the Americans in battle.

Crossing the Delaware At the Battle of White Plains in October 1776, the British forced Washington to retreat again. Then they surprised him. Instead of coming after the Continental Army, the British troops headed toward Philadelphia, where the Continental Congress was meeting. Washington's troops received word of this new plan. They had to move fast, but they managed to get there ahead of the British.

While this march was taking place, Thomas Paine wrote another pamphlet to help boost American morale. In *The American Crisis*, he

---

MEETING SPECIAL NEEDS

Intrapersonal Have students consider what it would have been like to be one of the following people involved in the Revolutionary War: a Continental soldier, a Hessian mercenary, a wife waiting for news of her husband, a merchant smuggling supplies to the troops, or a woman spying for the Continental army. Have students write a letter about the dangers they faced and the reasons for their commitment to the cause. **L3**

📁 Refer to *Inclusion for the High School Social Studies Classroom Strategies and Activities* in the TCR.

reminded his fellow Americans that "the harder the conflict, the more glorious the triumph":

> 66 These are the times that try men's souls. The summer soldier and the sunshine patriot will in this crisis shrink from the service of their country; but he that stands it now deserves the love and thanks of man and woman. 99
>
> —from *The American Crisis*

By the time Washington reached Pennsylvania, winter had begun. The British stopped their advance and dispersed into winter quarters in New Jersey. In the 1700s, armies did not usually fight in the winter because of the weather and scarce food supplies.

At this point, Washington tried something daring and unexpected—a winter attack. On December 25, 1776, he led approximately 2,400 men across the icy Delaware River. The army then attacked a group of Hessians at Trenton in the middle of a sleet storm. They killed or captured almost 1,000 men. Several days later, at Princeton, Washington's forces scattered three British regiments. Having achieved two small victories, Washington headed into the hills of northern New Jersey for the winter.

Philadelphia Falls In March 1777, King George III approved a plan developed by General John Burgoyne to isolate New England from the other American states. Burgoyne proposed a three-pronged attack on New York. He would take a large force south into New York from Montreal. Another force would move from Montreal up the St. Lawrence River to Lake Ontario then head east into New York. A third force, led by General Howe, would march north from New York City up the Hudson River valley. The three forces would meet near Albany, then march east into New England.

Unfortunately for the British, they did not coordinate the plan. By spring 1777, General Howe had made his own plans. He loaded about 13,000 men onto ships and moved them to Maryland. From there he attacked Philadelphia from the south. Howe believed that capturing Philadelphia and the Continental Congress would cripple the Revolution.

Howe's operation was a military success but a political failure. On September 11, 1777, he defeated Washington at the Battle of Brandywine Creek and captured Philadelphia. To Howe's frustration, however, the Continental Congress escaped. Howe failed to destroy the Continental Army, which soon took up winter quarters at **Valley Forge.** There, the bitter cold and food shortages killed nearly 2,500 men.

Even amidst the harsh conditions of Valley Forge, Washington managed to secure training for his army. Joining him at Valley Forge were two European military officers, the **Marquis de Lafayette** from France and Baron Friedrich von Steuben from Prussia. These officers helped Washington improve discipline and boost morale among the weary troops.

France Enters the War General Burgoyne did not know Howe had gone south to attack Philadelphia. In June 1777, he and an estimated 8,000 troops marched south from Quebec into New York. From the eastern end of Lake Ontario, another 900 troops and over 1,000 Iroquois warriors headed east toward Albany. The Iroquois had allied with the British hoping to keep American settlers off Iroquois lands.

Despite some early victories, Burgoyne's forces were not able to defeat the Americans defending upper New York. The British troops and Iroquois marching east from Lake Ontario were ambushed by militia and then driven back by American troops under General **Benedict Arnold.** Meanwhile, Burgoyne's own troops could not drive off the militia. With his supplies dwindling, Burgoyne surrendered at Saratoga, New York. The American victory at **Saratoga** was a turning point

History *Through Art*

A Savage Winter William B.T. Trego painted *The March to Valley Forge*, depicting the difficult conditions soldiers faced during the winter of 1777 to 1778. What hardships did the troops face at Valley Forge?

Creating a Thematic Map Have students use the description on this page to create a thematic map of Burgoyne's three-pronged attack on New York. **L2**

Use the rubric for creating a map, display, or chart on pages 77–78 in the *Performance Assessment Activities and Rubrics.*

During the winter of 1777, approximately 12,000 men were quartered at Valley Forge, Pennsylvania. Although the weather is blamed for many deaths that winter, the temperatures and precipitation, including rain and snow, were typical for winter in this area of Pennsylvania. What made the winter particularly dangerous for the troops was the lack of proper housing and clothing.

History *Through Art*

This painting, like much of Trego's work, illustrates the artist's talent for showing detail. In Trego's case the talent is even more remarkable because the artist had limited use of his fingers. **Answer:** bitter cold and food shortages
Ask: How do you think Thomas Paine's words helped to boost morale? *(They reminded soldiers of the potential rewards, such as respect and honor, that would come to those who faced difficulties and stayed the course.)*

Use *Interpreting Political Cartoons,* Cartoon 4.

INTERDISCIPLINARY CONNECTIONS ACTIVITY

Visual Arts Invite an art teacher or artist to speak to your class about the artwork related to the War of Independence. Ask the speaker to give examples of works that inspired patriotism during the war and works that illustrate historical events. Encourage the speaker to talk about how artists learned about the historical events they depicted. Have students draw their own Revolutionary War scenes based on the information they have learned. **L2**

✓ Reading Check

Answer: The military strategy was to separate New England from the Southern states and demonstrate to Americans that they could not win. The diplomatic strategy included inviting delegates from the Continental Congress to a peace conference with the promise that those who put down their arms and swore loyalty to the king would be pardoned.

✓ Reading Check

Answer: It reduced the power of the Native American people.

FYI

Following their surrender at Saratoga, Burgoyne and most of his troops returned to Britain. The Saratoga Convention stipulated that the troops would be allowed to go home if they promised not to return to North America for the remainder of the war.

---

in the war. It improved American morale and also convinced France to commit troops to the American cause.

Both Spain and France had been secretly sending arms and supplies to the United States well before Saratoga. The Congress appreciated the supplies but wanted the French to send troops too. In September 1776, the Congress sent Benjamin Franklin, Arthur Lee, and Silas Deane to France to ask for troops. The French, however, were not willing to risk war until they believed the Americans could win, and the victory at Saratoga assured them. Shortly afterward, they began negotiations with the United States to create an alliance against Britain.

On February 6, 1778, the United States signed its first two treaties. In the first treaty, France became the first country to recognize the United States as an independent nation. The second treaty was an alliance between the United States and France. By June 1778, Britain and France were at war. In 1779 the Spanish entered the war as well, as an ally of France but not of the United States.

✓ Reading Check **Summarizing** What was General Howe's two-part strategy for winning the war?

The War in the West

Not all of the fighting in the Revolutionary War took place in the East. Early in 1778, Patriot **George Rogers Clark** took 175 troops down the Ohio River and captured several towns. By February 1779, the British had surrendered, giving the Americans control of the region.

While Clark fought the British in the West, Chief Joseph Brant, also known as Thayendanegea, convinced four Iroquois nations to join the British. In July 1778, British troops and Iroquois warriors attacked western Pennsylvania, burning towns and killing over 200 militia. The following summer, American troops defeated the British and Iroquois in western New York. These battles destroyed the power of the Iroquois people.

Farther south, the Cherokee people suffered a similar fate. After the Revolution began, a delegation of Shawnee, Delaware, and Mohawk convinced the Cherokee that the time had come to drive American settlers off Cherokee lands. The Cherokee attacked settlers in Virginia and North Carolina, but the American militia units were too strong. By 1780 militia units had burned down hundreds of Cherokee towns.

✓ Reading Check **Describing** What was the effect of the war on the western frontier of the United States?

The War at Sea

Americans fought the British at sea as well as on land. Instead of attacking the British fleet directly, American warships attacked British merchant ships. To further disrupt British trade, the Congress began issuing letters of marque, or licenses, to private ship owners, authorizing them to attack British merchant ships. By the end of the war, millions of dollars of cargo had been seized, seriously harming Britain's trade and economy.

Perhaps the most famous naval battle of the war involved the American naval officer, **John Paul Jones.**

The Turning Point: Saratoga

General John Burgoyne's plan to capture upper New York and seal off New England from the rest of the United States began well. His troops easily seized Fort Ticonderoga with its large store of gunpowder and supplies. In response, the Continental Congress sent in a new commander, General Horatio Gates.

After this early victory, Burgoyne's march slowed to a crawl. The Americans felled trees in front of his army and removed crops and cattle from the region to deprive his troops of food. Militia forces staged ambushes and hit-and-run raids. These tactics exasperated Burgoyne. In desperation, he retreated to Saratoga. An American army nearly three times the size of his own quickly surrounded his troops. On October 17, 1777, Burgoyne surrendered to General Gates.

CRITICAL THINKING ACTIVITY

Predicting Outcomes Have students select one of the major battles of the American Revolution. Tell them to consider what would have happened if the other side had won. Have them consider what advantage the winning side would gain and what their next likely move would be. Have students share their predictions as part of a class discussion. **L2**

Jones commanded a ship named the *Bonhomme Richard.* While sailing near Britain in September 1779, Jones encountered a group of British merchant ships protected by the warships *Serapis* and *Countess of Scarborough.* Jones attacked the *Serapis,* but the heavier guns of the British ship nearly sank the *Bonhomme Richard.* With the American ship in distress, the British commander called on Jones to surrender. Jones replied, "I have not yet begun to fight." He lashed his ship to the *Serapis* so it could not sink, then boarded the British ship. The battle lasted more than three hours before the British surrendered.

✓ Reading Check Summarizing
What was the American strategy for attacking the British at sea?

The Southern Campaign

After the British defeat at Saratoga, General Howe resigned and was replaced by Sir Henry Clinton. British officials told Clinton to begin a campaign in the southern states where the British believed they had the strongest Loyalist support. The southern states were also valuable because they produced tobacco and rice. The British hoped they could keep the South, even if they lost the northern states.

The Fall of Savannah and Charles Town In December 1778, 3,500 British troops captured Savannah, Georgia. They seized control of Georgia's backcountry and returned the British royal governor to power.

After defeating the American and French troops trying to take Savannah, General Clinton sent a massive force under the command of General **Charles Cornwallis** to capture Charles Town, South Carolina. Nearly 14,000 British troops surrounded the city, trapping the American forces. On May 8, 1780, over 5,500 American troops surrendered, the greatest American defeat in the war. The Continental Congress then sent General Horatio Gates, the hero of Saratoga, to defend the South Carolina backcountry. Gates attempted to destroy a British supply base at Camden, South Carolina, but failed.

Profiles IN HISTORY

Bernardo de Gálvez
1746–1786

Bernardo de Gálvez was born in Malaga, Spain, in 1746. Following family tradition, he joined the military, and at age 19 he traveled to America with his uncle, who had been sent by the government to inspect New Spain. In 1769 Gálvez was placed in command of Spanish forces on New Spain's northern frontier. During the next two years, he led his forces in battle against the Apache people in what is today west Texas. In 1777 he was appointed governor of Louisiana.

Even before Spain entered the Revolutionary War, Gálvez took steps to aid the United States. He exchanged letters with Patrick Henry and Thomas Jefferson, and he used his authority as governor to secure the Mississippi against the British, while allowing French, Spanish, and American ships to use the river to smuggle arms to the American forces. When Spain declared war on Britain, Gálvez raised an army, fought British troops near Baton Rouge and Natchez, and captured the British forts at Mobile and Pensacola. His campaigns were important to the U.S. victory because they tied down British troops that might otherwise have been used against the Americans farther north. The city of Galveston, Texas, is named in his honor.

TURNING POINT

The Patriots Rally After the battle of Camden, the British began subduing the Carolina backcountry. At first, everything went well for them. Many of the settlers were Loyalists and agreed to fight for Britain. Two British cavalry officers, Banastre Tarleton and Patrick Ferguson, led many of the Loyalist forces in the region. These troops became known for their brutality.

Ferguson finally went too far when he tried to subdue the people living in the Appalachian Mountains. Enraged at his tactics, the "overmountain" men, as they were known, put together a militia force. They intercepted Ferguson at Kings Mountain on October 7, 1780, and destroyed his army. The **Battle of Kings Mountain** was a turning point in the South. Southern farmers, furious with British treatment, began organizing their own forces.

The new American commander in the region, General Nathaniel Greene, hoped to wear down the British in battle while militia destroyed their supplies. Greene organized the militia into small units to carry out hit-and-run raids against British camps and supply wagons. **Francis Marion,** who was known as the "Swamp Fox," led the most famous of these units. Greene's strategy worked. By late 1781, the British

Profiles IN HISTORY

Background: During the summer of 1786, while charting the coastline of the Gulf of Mexico, Jose de Evita named Galveston Bay for Bernardo de Gálvez, the Spanish colonial governor. Gálvez died later that year having never seen the area.
Ask: What did Bernardo de Gálvez do to help the U.S. war effort before Spain declared war on Britain? *(He allowed French, Spanish, and American ships to use the Mississippi to smuggle arms to American troops.)*

✓ Reading Check

Answer: They attacked British merchant ships and hired privateers to disrupt British trade and hurt the economy.

Creating a Thematic Map Have students create a thematic map to illustrate New Spain's contributions to the American war effort. Instruct students to differentiate between the contributions made before and after Spain officially entered the war.
L2

📁 Use the rubric for creating a map, display, or chart on pages 77–78 in the *Performance Assessment Activities and Rubrics.*

EXTENDING THE CONTENT

Overmountain Men The Overmountain Victory National Historic Trail was established in 1980—two hundred years after the Battle of Kings Mountain. The 300-mile trail follows the route used by the overmountain men as they traveled from Virginia, what is now Tennessee, and North Carolina to Kings Mountain. The trail ends at the Kings Mountain National Military Park near Blacksburg, South Carolina.

Creating a Thematic Map Have students create a thematic map showing the significant battles of the Southern Campaign. **L2**

 Use the rubric for creating a map, display, or chart on pages 77–78 in the *Performance Assessment Activities and Rubrics.*

Geography *Skills*

Answers:

1. They blocked British ships.

2. Yorktown

Geography Skills Practice

Ask: What British victory was far-thest south? *(Savannah)*

✓ Reading Check

Answer: Southern farmers started to organize against the British in retaliation for British mistreatment.

3 ASSESS

Assign Section 3 Assessment as homework or as an in-class activity.

🌐 Have students use the **Interactive Tutor Self-Assessment CD-ROM.**

Reading Essentials and Study Guide 4–3

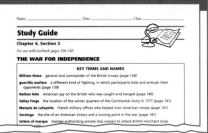

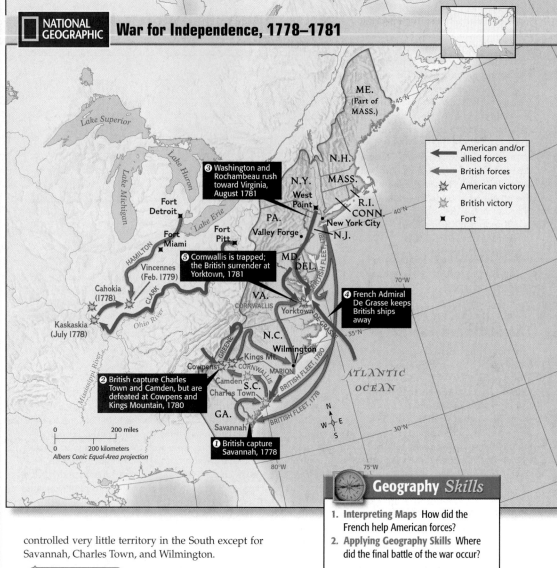

NATIONAL GEOGRAPHIC **War for Independence, 1778–1781**

- ❸ Washington and Rochambeau rush toward Virginia, August 1781
- ❺ Cornwallis is trapped; the British surrender at Yorktown, 1781
- ❹ French Admiral De Grasse keeps British ships away
- ❷ British capture Charles Town and Camden, but are defeated at Cowpens and Kings Mountain, 1780
- ❶ British capture Savannah, 1778

Vincennes (Feb. 1779)
Cahokia (1778)
Kaskaskia (July 1778)
Fort Detroit
Fort Miami
Fort Pitt
Valley Forge
West Point
New York City
Yorktown
Wilmington
Kings Mt.
Cowpens
Camden
Charles Town
Savannah

0 200 miles
0 200 kilometers
Albers Conic Equal-Area projection

Legend:
- American and/or allied forces
- British forces
- American victory
- British victory
- Fort

Geography *Skills*

1. **Interpreting Maps** How did the French help American forces?
2. **Applying Geography Skills** Where did the final battle of the war occur?

---

controlled very little territory in the South except for Savannah, Charles Town, and Wilmington.

✓ Reading Check **Explaining** Why was the Battle of Kings Mountain a turning point of the war in the South?

The War Is Won

In the spring of 1781, General Cornwallis decided to invade Virginia. As long as the Americans controlled Virginia, he believed, new troops and supplies could keep coming south. With more French troops on the way to America, the British knew they had very little time left to win the war. They had to secure Virginia.

The Battle of Yorktown In late April 1781, Cornwallis marched into Virginia, where he linked up with forces under the command of Benedict Arnold. Arnold had been an American commander early in the war but had later sold military information to the British. When his treason was discovered, Arnold fled to British-controlled New York City. There he was given command of British troops and ordered to begin raiding American positions in Virginia.

144 CHAPTER 4 The American Revolution

MEETING SPECIAL NEEDS

Kinesthetic Encourage students to work in pairs to create a design and model of an alternate American flag that would symbolize today's American ideals. Have students write a paragraph explanation of their design. Encourage the pairs to present their designs and models to the class.

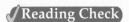 Refer to *Inclusion for the High School Social Studies Classroom Strategies and Activities* in the TCR.

After Arnold's forces joined those of Cornwallis, the British began to conquer Virginia. Their combined forces encountered very little resistance until June 1781, when a large American force led by General **Anthony Wayne** arrived in Virginia. Outnumbered and too far inland, Cornwallis retreated to the coastal town of Yorktown to protect his supplies and to maintain communications by sea.

Cornwallis's retreat created an opportunity for the Americans and their French allies. The previous year, 6,000 French troops had arrived in New England. With this support, Washington decided to march on New York City. As the troops headed to New York, the French general Rochambeau learned that a French fleet commanded by Admiral Francois de Grasse was on its way north from the Caribbean.

When he learned of the French fleet, Washington canceled the attack on New York. Instead, he and Rochambeau led their forces to Yorktown. As the American and French troops raced south, Admiral de Grasse moved into Chesapeake Bay near Yorktown. With the French fleet nearby, Cornwallis could not escape by sea or receive supplies.

On September 28, 1781, American and French forces surrounded Yorktown and began to bombard it. On October 14, Washington's aide, Alexander Hamilton, led an attack that captured key British defenses. Three days later, Cornwallis began negotiations to surrender, and on October 19, 1781, approximately 8,000 British troops marched out of Yorktown and laid down their weapons. During the surrender, a British military band played a popular nursery tune, "The World Turn'd Upside Down."

Fact · Fiction · Folklore

America's Flags On June 14, 1777, the Continental Congress declared the first Stars and Stripes the official flag. The Congress determined that "the Flag of the United States be 13 stripes, alternate red and white; that the Union be 13 stars, white in a blue field representing a new constellation." For Americans past and present, the color red symbolizes courage; white, purity of ideals; and blue, strength and unity of the states.

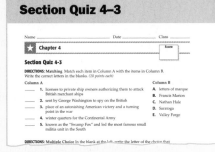

The Treaty of Paris When Lord North, the British prime minister, learned of the surrender at Yorktown, he knew the war was over. In March 1782, Parliament voted to begin peace negotiations. John Adams, Benjamin Franklin, and John Jay conducted most of the negotiations for the United States.

The final settlement, known as the **Treaty of Paris,** was signed on September 3, 1783. In this treaty, Britain recognized the United States of America as a new nation with the Mississippi River as its western border. Britain also gave Florida back to Spain. France received colonies in Africa and the Caribbean that the British had seized from them in 1763. On November 24, 1783, the last British troops left New York City. The Revolutionary War was over. The creation of a new nation was about to begin.

✓ **Reading Check** **Describing** How was the war won at Yorktown?

SECTION 3 ASSESSMENT

Checking for Understanding
1. **Define:** guerrilla warfare, letters of marque.
2. **Identify:** William Howe, Nathan Hale, Valley Forge, Marquis de Lafayette, Saratoga, John Paul Jones, Charles Cornwallis, Battle of Kings Mountain.

Reviewing Themes
3. **Global Connections** Why were the French at first reluctant to sign an alliance with the colonies?

Critical Thinking
4. **Evaluating** How did European countries aid the Americans in the war for independence?
5. **Categorizing** Use a graphic organizer similar to the one below to list the provisions of the Treaty of Paris.

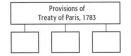

Provisions of Treaty of Paris, 1783

Analyzing Visuals
6. **Examining Art** Study the painting on page 141. How has the artist portrayed the condition of Washington's army?

Writing About History
7. **Persuasive Writing** Imagine that you are a colonist during the Revolutionary War. Write a letter to convince European nations to support the Americans in the war.

CHAPTER 4 The American Revolution **145**

SECTION 3 ASSESSMENT ANSWERS

1. Terms are in blue.
2. William Howe (*p. 138*), Nathan Hale (*p. 140*), Valley Forge (*p. 141*), Marquis de Lafayette (*p. 141*), Saratoga (*p. 141*), John Paul Jones (*p. 143*), Charles Cornwallis (*p. 143*), Battle of Kings Mountain (*p. 143*)
3. France was not willing to send

troops until they believed the Americans could win.
4. Spain and France sent arms and supplies to assist the United States. Other European nations drew part of Britain's military to other areas of the world.
5. Britain recognized the United States as a new nation; Spain

reclaimed Florida; gave France colonies in Africa and the Caribbean.
6. tired, wounded, ragged
7. Students' letters will vary. Letters should be persuasive, and include the benefits to European countries supporting the Americans.

Fact · Fiction · Folklore

Francis Hopkinson is credited with the actual design of the first Stars and Stripes. It is less clear who actually made the first flag. Historians agree that Betsy Ross made flags for the Pennsylvania navy. She may have made the first national flag.

Reteach
Ask students to describe the strategies behind the Northern Campaign.

Enrich
Invite students to locate the words and music for the song "The World Turn'd Upside Down." Ask them if the song was a good choice for the occasion.

✓ Reading Check
Answer: American and French forces surrounded Yorktown and cut off Cornwallis's access to the sea.

4 CLOSE

Ask students to explain the terms of the Treaty of Paris.

TEACH

Understanding Cause and Effect Write the following sentences on the board and ask students to identify the cause and effect in each sentence. Point out that the cause does not always precede the effect in a sentence.

- They received the award because of their leadership skills.
- Due to bad weather the game was canceled.
- As a result of an effective advertising campaign, sales increase dramatically.

Additional Practice

Reinforcing Skills Activity 4

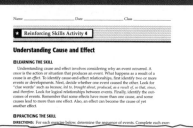

Name _____ Date _____ Class _____

★ Reinforcing Skills Activity 4

Understanding Cause and Effect

❑ LEARNING THE SKILL
Understanding cause and effect involves considering why an event occurred. A cause is the action or situation that produces an event. What happens as a result of a cause is an effect. To identify cause-and-effect relationships, first identify two or more events or developments. Next, decide whether one event caused the other. Look for "clue words" such as because, led to, brought about, produced, as a result of, so that, since, and therefore. Look for logical relationships between events. Finally, identify the outcomes of events. Remember that some effects have more than one cause, and some causes lead to more than one effect. Also, an effect can become the cause of yet another effect.

❑ PRACTICING THE SKILL
DIRECTIONS: For each exercise below, determine the sequence of events. Complete each exer-

GLENCOE
TECHNOLOGY

 CD-ROM
Glencoe Skillbuilder
Interactive Workbook
CD-ROM, Level 2

This interactive CD-ROM reinforces student mastery of essential social studies skills.

Understanding Cause and Effect

Why Learn This Skill?

To understand past events, you should look for why or how an event or a chain of events took place. This process is using the skill of understanding causes and effects.

Learning the Skill

The French and Indian War left Britain in debt. To raise money Britain introduced a stamp tax in the American colonies. The war was the *cause* that led to Britain's need for more money. The tax on the colonies was the *effect*, or result. The chart below shows how one event—the **cause**—led to another—the **effect.**

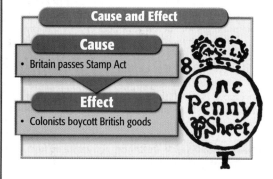

Cause and Effect

Cause
- Britain passes Stamp Act

Effect
- Colonists boycott British goods

You can often identify cause-and-effect relationships in sentences from clue words such as the following:

because	therefore	produced
due to	thus	in order to
so that	led to	as a result

In a chain of events, an effect often becomes the cause of other events. The next chart shows the chain of events in the colonial rebellion.

Practicing the Skill

Make a chart showing which events are causes and which are effects in the sentences listed in column 2.

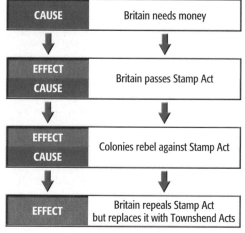

CAUSE	Britain needs money
EFFECT **CAUSE**	Britain passes Stamp Act
EFFECT **CAUSE**	Colonies rebel against Stamp Act
EFFECT	Britain repeals Stamp Act but replaces it with Townshend Acts

❶ The Treaty of Paris, which ended the French and Indian War in 1763, eliminated French power in North America.

❷ Thousands of British workers lost their jobs after the colonies cancelled orders for British goods.

❸ The British failure to listen to colonial grievances led to armed conflict.

❹ The French decided to send aid to the Americans after Burgoyne surrendered at Saratoga.

Skills Assessment

Complete the Practicing Skills questions on page 155 and the Chapter 4 Skill Reinforcement Activity to assess your mastery of this skill.

Applying the Skill

Understanding Cause and Effect Read an account of a recent event in your community in a local newspaper. Determine at least one cause and one effect of that event. Show the chain of events in a chart.

 Glencoe's **Skillbuilder Interactive Workbook CD-ROM, Level 2,** provides instruction and practice in key social studies skills.

ANSWERS TO PRACTICING THE SKILL

❶ Cause: Treaty of Paris; Effect: French power in North America is eliminated

❷ Cause: Colonies cancel orders; Effect: British workers lose their jobs

❸ Cause: British ignore grievances; Effect: Armed conflict

❹ Cause: Burgoyne surrenders at Saratoga; Effect: France aids Americans

Applying the Skill
Students' charts will vary. Charts may include instances where an effect is the cause of another effect.

The War Changes American Society

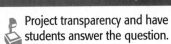

1 FOCUS

Section Overview

This section addresses the impact of the War for Independence on American society.

Guide to Reading

Main Idea

The American Revolution changed American society in a variety of ways.

Key Terms and Names

republic, Virginia Statute for Religious Freedom, Molly Pitcher, emancipation, manumission, John Trumbull, Charles Willson Peale

Reading Strategy

Organizing As you read about changes in American society after the American Revolution, complete a graphic organizer like the one below by listing the features of the U.S. political system set up after the war.

Features of New U.S. Political System

Reading Objectives

- **Describe** the features of the political system of the United States set up after the Revolutionary War.
- **Explain** the position of women and African Americans in the new political system.

Section Theme

Culture and Traditions A uniquely American culture arose as the Revolutionary War ended.

BELLRINGER
Skillbuilder Activity

Project transparency and have students answer the question.

Available as a blackline master.

Daily Focus Skills Transparency 4–4

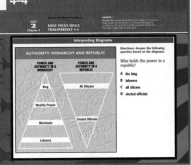

Preview of Events

1775 — 1779 — 1783 — 1787

1776
Virginia passes Declaration of Rights

1779
Judith Sargent Murray writes "On the Equality of the Sexes"

1780
New Massachusetts constitution introduced

1786
Virginia's Statute for Religious Freedom passed

Wooden statue of an African American breaking his chains

★ An American Story ★

In 1781 an enslaved Massachusetts man named Quock Walker took an extraordinary step: He took legal action against a white man who had assaulted him. Given the times, this was a bold step, but Walker believed he had the law on his side. Massachusetts's new constitution referred to the "inherent liberty" of all men. The judge, William Cushing, agreed:

❝Our Constitution [of Massachusetts] sets out with declaring that all men are born free and equal—and that every subject is entitled to liberty, and to have guarded by the laws, as well as life and property—and in short is totally repugnant to the idea of being born slaves. This being the case, I think the idea of slavery is inconsistent with our own conduct and Constitution.❞

While the Quock Walker case did not abolish slavery, it demonstrated that the Massachusetts courts would not support the institution. As a result of this ruling and various antislavery efforts, slavery ceased to exist in Massachusetts by 1790.

—adapted from *Founding the Republic*

New Political Ideas

When American leaders declared independence and founded the United States of America, they were very much aware that they were creating something new. By severing their ties to the king, they had established a republic. A republic is a form of government

---

Guide to Reading

Answers to Graphic: established a republic, elected representatives to govern according to laws or constitution, equality of all citizens under the law, voting rights expanded, freedom of religion

Preteaching Vocabulary

Have students write a sentence explaining the significance of each of the Key Names.

CHAPTER 4 The American Revolution **147**

SECTION RESOURCES

Reproducible Masters

- Reproducible Lesson Plan 4–4
- Daily Lecture and Discussion Notes 4–4
- Guided Reading Activity 4–4
- Section Quiz 4–4
- Reading Essentials and Study Guide 4–4
- Performance Assessment Activities and Rubrics

Transparencies

- Daily Focus Skills Transparency 4–4

Multimedia

- Interactive Tutor Self-Assessment CD-ROM
- ExamView® Pro Testmaker CD-ROM
- Presentation Plus! CD-ROM
- TeacherWorks™ CD-ROM
- Audio Program

2 TEACH

**Daily Lecture and
Discussion Notes 4–4**

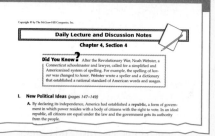

Creating a List Write the words *Monarchy* and *Republic* on the board. Have students list words that describe each of these forms of government. Review the lists and ask students to point out pairs of opposite words. **L1 ELL**

World Geography Connection

Answer: Students' answers will vary. Many students will infer that winning the war validated the American colonists.

Ask: Why do you think that many of the Latin American attempts to establish a democratic government ultimately failed, while the American efforts succeeded? *(possible answers: leadership not committed to democracy, weaknesses in countries' constitutions, lack of educated and informed citizenry)*

where power resides with a body of citizens entitled to vote. Elected representatives who are responsible to the citizens and who must govern according to laws or a constitution exercise power.

While many Europeans viewed a republic as radical and dangerous, Americans believed that a republican society could be better than other societies. In an ideal republic, all citizens are equal under the law, regardless of their wealth or social class. Americans also believed that in a republic, the government derives its authority from the people.

Such ideas conflicted with many traditional beliefs, including ideas about slavery, the idea that women should not be allowed to vote or own property, and the idea that wealthy people were "better" than others. Despite these contradictions, republican ideas helped to change American society and government in the years following the war.

New State Constitutions Events before the Revolution led many Americans to believe that each state's constitution should be written down and that it should limit the government's power over the people. The Revolutionary War and new republican ideas convinced Americans that the best form of government was a constitutional republic.

At the same time, many American leaders, including John Adams, worried that democracy could endanger a republican government. Adams argued that government needed "checks and balances" to prevent any group in society from becoming strong enough to take away the rights of the minority.

World Geography Connection

The Spread of American Democracy

While the Revolutionary War certainly transformed North America, it had a great impact on other parts of the world as well. American ideals of democracy inspired independence movements around the globe—especially in the colonies of Latin America, which overthrew their European rulers one after the other throughout the early 1800s. In Venezuela, for example, colonists developed their own "declaration of independence," in which they, like the Americans, listed their grievances with their colonial rulers, declared their desire to live free, and pledged their lives to the effort. *What may have happened to American ideals of democracy if the colonists had lost the war?*

148 CHAPTER 4 The American Revolution

A true democracy, Adams argued, would lead to a tyranny by the majority. Minority groups would not have their rights protected. For example, the poor might vote to take everything away from the rich and undermine the right to property. Instead, Adams argued, the best government was a "mixed government" with a separation of powers. The executive, legislative, and judicial branches should be separate.

Adams also argued that the legislature should have two houses: a senate to represent people of property and an assembly to protect the rights of the common people. Adams's ideas influenced several state constitutions. Virginia's constitution of 1776 and Massachusetts's constitution of 1780 established an elected governor, senate, and assembly. By the 1790s, most of the other states had created similar constitutions.

In addition to writing new constitutions, many new states began to attach a list of rights to their constitutions. This began in 1776, when George Mason drafted Virginia's Declaration of Rights. These rights guaranteed to all Virginians freedom of speech, freedom of religion, the right to bear arms, and the right to trial by jury. The declaration also proclaimed that the state could not search someone's home without a warrant, nor could it take away property without proper court proceedings. Other states followed Virginia's example and incorporated a bill of rights into their constitutions as well.

Voting Rights Expand The Revolution not only increased support for constitutional government, it also led to an expansion of voting rights. The experience of fighting side by side with people from every social class and region increased people's belief in equality, especially for white men. Everyone was fighting for the same cause and risking death for the same ideas. If everyone was equal, then everyone deserved the right to vote.

The war also weakened feelings of deference toward people in the upper classes. The Revolution had showed many farmers and artisans that they were equal to the rich planters and merchants they fought beside. While sitting in a tavern with farmers who were spitting and pulling off their muddy boots, one wealthy Virginian noted: "Every one who bore arms esteems himself upon an equal footing with his neighbors. . . . Each of these men considers himself, in every respect, my equal."

The Revolution enabled the lower classes to demand a greater role in choosing their leaders. In almost every state, the new constitutions made it easier to gain the right to vote. Many states allowed any

COOPERATIVE LEARNING ACTIVITY

Comparing Organize the students into groups of four or five. Assign each group a state close to your own state. Have groups use library and Internet resources to learn about the constitution of their assigned state. Have the groups learn when the constitution was ratified and identify its basic provisions. Conduct a class discussion comparing and contrasting the various constitutions with each other and with the Untied States Constitution.

Use the rubric for a cooperative group management plan on pages 81–82 in the *Performance Assessment Activities and Rubrics.*

white male who paid taxes to vote, whether or not he owned property.

Although voting rights expanded, people still had to own a certain amount of property to hold elective office, although usually much less than before the Revolution. The practice of paying veterans with land grants for their services during the war also increased the number of people eligible to hold office. In the North, before the Revolution, over 80 percent of the people elected were from the upper class. Ten years after the war, only a little over one-third of officeholders were wealthy. In the South, higher property qualifications kept the wealthy planters in power. Before the Revolution, almost 90 percent of people elected to office were wealthy. Afterward, the figure dropped by about 20 percent, indicating small farmers had gained some ground.

Freedom of Religion The new concern with rights led to changes in the relationship between the church and the state. Many of the Revolution's leaders opposed "ecclesiastical tyranny"—the power of a church, backed by the government, to make people worship in a certain way. After the war, the idea that government should not aid churches became more accepted.

The new push to end state funding of churches began in Virginia, where Baptists led a movement to abolish taxes collected to support the Anglican Church. In 1786 Governor Thomas Jefferson pushed the legislature to pass the **Virginia Statute for Religious Freedom.** The statute declared that Virginia no longer had an official church and that the state could not collect taxes for churches. Written by Jefferson, the statute declared:

> 66[O]ur civil rights have no dependence on our religious opinions, any more than our opinions in physics or geometry; . . . therefore . . . proscribing any citizen as unworthy the public confidence . . . unless he profess or renounce this or that religious opinion, is depriving him injuriously of those privileges and advantages to which in common with his fellow citizens he has a natural right.99

Profiles IN HISTORY

Elizabeth Freeman (Mumbet) c. 1742–1829

Elizabeth Freeman was born about 1742 to enslaved African American parents. At the age of six months she was acquired, along with her sister, by John Ashley, a wealthy Massachusetts slaveholder. She became known as "Mumbet" or "Mum Bett."

For nearly 40 years Mumbet served the Ashley family. One day, Ashley's wife tried to strike Mumbet's sister with a shovel. Mumbet intervened and took the blow instead. Furious, she stormed out of the house and refused to come back. When the Ashleys tried to make her return, Mumbet contacted a lawyer, Theodore Sedgewick. With his help, Mumbet sued for her freedom.

While serving the Ashleys, Mumbet had listened to many discussions of the new Massachusetts constitution. If the constitution said that all people were free and equal, then she thought it should apply to her. A jury agreed, and Mumbet won her freedom—the first enslaved person in Massachusetts to do so under the new constitution.

Oddly enough, after the trial, the Ashleys asked Mumbet to come back and work for them as a paid employee. She declined and instead went to work for Sedgewick. Mumbet died in 1829, but her legacy lived on in her many descendants. One of her great-grandchildren was W.E.B. DuBois, one of the founders of the NAACP, and a prominent writer and spokesperson for African American civil rights in the late 1800s and early 1900s.

Mumbet's tombstone still stands in the Massachusetts cemetery where she was buried. It reads, in part: "She was born a slave and remained a slave for nearly thirty years. She could neither read nor write, yet in her own sphere she had no superior or equal."

The idea of denying tax support to churches spread slowly throughout the newly independent nation. Massachusetts permitted Quakers and Baptists to assign their tax money to their church instead of to the congregational churches—the successors to the Puritan churches—but it did not abolish religious taxes entirely until 1833. 📖 *(See page 1065 for the text of the Virginia Statute for Religious Freedom.)*

✓ **Reading Check** **Examining** Which freedoms did Virginia's constitution guarantee in its bill of rights?

The War and American Society

The postwar notions of greater equality and liberty, as noble as they were, applied mainly to white men. For most women and African Americans, these ideals were still out of reach. Both groups participated in the Revolutionary War, and the Revolution's ideals led to some changes in the

CHAPTER 4 The American Revolution **149**

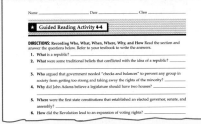

Profiles IN HISTORY

Background: Like many other African American men, Elizabeth Freeman's husband fought in the war for independence. He was killed in action.

Ask: After reading the portion of Elizabeth Freeman's epitaph that is shown on this page, what do you think it means? *(Regardless of her background, no one was better than Freeman and she was an individual.)*

Interpreting a Quote Have students write a brief explanation of the quote taken from the Virginia Statute for Religious Freedom that appears on this page. **L2**

✓ **Reading Check**

Answer: freedom of speech, freedom of religion, the right to bear arms, the right to a trial by jury, and the freedom from warrantless searches

---

MEETING SPECIAL NEEDS

Verbal/Linguistic Tell students that Josiah Tucker, an English clergyman, claimed that once the British government was gone, "the Americans will have no center of union among them, and no common interest to pursue." Ask students if they think Tucker was accurate in his description of Americans in the 1780s. Have students create an original story based on historical facts that demonstrates how difficult it was to form a union. **L3**

📂 Refer to *Inclusion for the High School Social Studies Classroom Strategies and Activities* in the TCR.

Geography Skills

Answers:
1. New Jersey in 1804
2. Six states—Connecticut, Delaware, Massachusetts, Pennsylvania, Rhode Island, and Virginia; republican ideals of liberty and equality for all

Geography Skills Practice
Ask: Which state did not formally abolish slavery? *(New Hampshire)*

Creating Circle Graphs Provide the data shown below. Ask students to select one of the states and create three circle graphs, one for each year, showing the number of enslaved persons as a segment of the total population. **L2**

Number of Enslaved Persons

	1790	1800	1810
New York	21,193	20,613	15,017
Pennsylvania	3,707	1,706	795
Rhode Island	958	380	108

Total Population

	1790	1800	1810
New York	340,241	586,182	959,049
Pennsylvania	433,611	602,365	810,019
Rhode Island	69,112	69,122	76,931

📂 Use the rubric for creating a map, display, or chart on pages 77–78 in the *Performance Assessment Activities and Rubrics.*

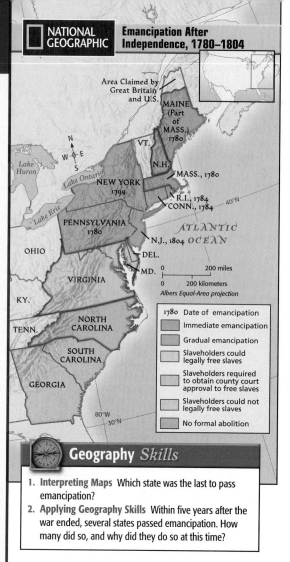

NATIONAL GEOGRAPHIC
Emancipation After Independence, 1780–1804

Area Claimed by Great Britain and U.S.

MAINE (Part of MASS.) 1780

VT.

N.H.

NEW YORK 1799

MASS., 1780

R.I., 1784
CONN., 1784

PENNSYLVANIA 1780

N.J., 1804

OHIO

DEL.

MD.

VIRGINIA

ATLANTIC OCEAN

KY.

TENN.

NORTH CAROLINA

SOUTH CAROLINA

GEORGIA

0   200 miles
0   200 kilometers
Albers Equal-Area projection

1780	Date of emancipation
	Immediate emancipation
	Gradual emancipation
	Slaveholders could legally free slaves
	Slaveholders required to obtain county court approval to free slaves
	Slaveholders could not legally free slaves
	No formal abolition

Geography Skills

1. **Interpreting Maps** Which state was the last to pass emancipation?
2. **Applying Geography Skills** Within five years after the war ended, several states passed emancipation. How many did so, and why did they do so at this time?

status of both women and African Americans in the years following the end of the conflict.

Women at War Women played a vital role in the Revolutionary War, contributing on both the home front and the battlefront. With their husbands and sons at war, some women took over running the family farm. Others traveled with the army—cooking, washing, and nursing the wounded. Women also served as spies and couriers, and a few even joined the fighting. Mary Ludwig Hays, known as **Molly Pitcher,** carried water to Patriot gunners during the Battle of Monmouth. Margaret Corbin accompanied her husband to battle, and after his death she took his place at his cannon and held the position until the battle ended.

After the war, as Americans began to think about what their revolutionary ideals implied, women made some advances. They could more easily obtain a divorce, and they gained greater access to education. In 1779 Judith Sargent Murray wrote an essay entitled "On the Equality of the Sexes." The essay argued that women were as intelligent as men but lacked the education needed to achieve more in life. After the Revolution, many schools for girls were founded, and the number of women able to read increased.

African Americans Thousands of enslaved African Americans obtained their freedom during the Revolution. In an effort to undermine the colonial economy and hurt the rebellion in the South, the British Army freed thousands of enslaved people. British officials, however, also seized thousands of African Americans and shipped them to British plantations in the Caribbean.

Many planters promised to free their slaves if the slaves fought against the British. General Washington, in order to counter the British offer to free enslaved people who joined the British, permitted African Americans to join the Continental Army. He also urged state militias to admit African Americans and to offer freedom to all who served. About 5,000 African Americans fought in the militias and the Continental Army during the Revolutionary War.

After the Revolution, more enslaved Africans gained their freedom. Many American leaders realized that enslaving people did not fit in with the new language of liberty and equality. Opposition to slavery had been growing steadily even before the Revolution, especially in the northern and middle states.

After the war began, emancipation, or freedom from enslavement, became a major issue. Many Northern states took steps to end slavery. Vermont banned slavery in 1777. In 1780 Pennsylvania freed all children born enslaved when they reached age 28. Rhode Island decreed in 1784 that enslaved men born thereafter would be free when they turned 21 and women when they turned 18. In 1799 New York freed enslaved men born that year or later when they reached age 28 and women when they reached age 25. The ending of slavery in the North was thus a gradual process that took several decades.

Discrimination did not disappear with the increase in African American freedom. While enslaved, some African Americans worked in skilled positions, such as blacksmithing. Northern whites did not want free African Americans taking these

INTERDISCIPLINARY CONNECTIONS ACTIVITY

Mathematics To illustrate the effects of Virginia's law encouraging manumission, present the data at right. Ask students to create a bar chart that illustrates the relationship between the number of enslaved persons and the total population between 1790 and 1830. Ask students if they think the law was effective. **L2**

Virginia Population Data

	Total Pop.	No. of Enslaved Persons
1790	747,550	292,627
1800	885,171	346,671
1810	974,622	392,518
1820	1,065,379	425,153
1830	1,211,405	469,757

jobs from them. African Americans often were unable to get more than menial jobs—digging, carrying, loading, or sweeping. Free African Americans also faced voting restrictions, segregation, and possible kidnapping and transportation into the South, where they would again be enslaved.

Despite the hardships, freedom offered choices. Once free, African Americans typically moved to the cities to find employment. Some found opportunities in previously barred occupations, such as artists or ministers. Often, they discarded their former names or worked for several years to purchase the freedom of friends or family members.

A small group of African Americans achieved some wealth and social status. The discrimination of Northern whites encouraged them to focus on building their own distinct culture. Religion was a strong element of that emerging culture. Now free to enter the ministry, African Americans created their own style of worship. In 1816 African American church leaders formed the first independent African American denomination, the African Methodist Episcopal (AME) Church.

The story was quite different in the South. The South relied heavily on enslaved labor to sustain its agricultural economy. As a result, Southern leaders—most of whom were slaveholders themselves—showed little interest in abolishing slavery. Only Virginia took steps toward ending the institution. In 1782 the state passed a law encouraging manumission, or the voluntary freeing of enslaved persons, especially for those who had fought in the Revolution. Through this law, about 10,000 slaves obtained their freedom, but the vast majority remained in bondage.

The Loyalists Flee Many women and African Americans found their lives little changed as a result of the Revolution, but for many Loyalists, the end of the war changed everything. Because of their support for the British, Loyalists often found themselves shunned by former friends, and state governments sometimes seized their property.

Unwilling to live under the new government and often afraid for their lives, approximately 100,000 Loyalists fled the United States after the war. Some went to England or the British West Indies, but most moved to British North America, particularly to Nova Scotia, New Brunswick, and the region near Niagara Falls. This region was part of Quebec at the time, but in 1791, Britain made it a separate colony called Upper Canada. Today it is the province of Ontario.

Americans grappled with what to do with the property and assets of Loyalists. In North Carolina, Patriots confiscated Loyalist lands outright. Officials in New York also seized Loyalist lands and goods, claiming the "sovereignty of the people of this state in respect to all property." Other public officials opposed such actions. The Massachusetts Constitution of 1780, for example, extended the rights of "life, liberty, and property" to Loyalists, and gave much of the land seized from departing Loyalists to their agents or relatives who had remained behind.

 **Reading Check** **Summarizing** How did life change for women, African Americans, and Loyalists after the Revolutionary War?

An American Culture Emerges

In the United States, victory over the British united Americans and created powerful nationalist feelings. The Revolutionary War helped this process in two ways. First, Americans in all of the states had a common enemy. Soldiers from all over the country fought side by side in each other's states. Second, the

✏️ **History** *Through Art*

Joseph Brant Gilbert Stuart painted this portrait of Joseph Brant, leader of the Mohawks, who sided with the Loyalists during the Revolution. After the Treaty of Paris, Brant led a large group of Iroquois north into British Canada. Why did Brant and other Loyalists leave the United States?

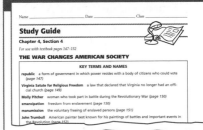

Section Quiz 4-4

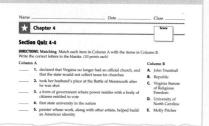

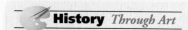

History *Through Art*

Answer: a relaxed family meal
Ask: What subjects were favored by artists such as John Trumbull and Charles Wilson Peale? *(heroic deeds and leaders of the Revolution)*

Reteach

Have students create a sentence outline for this section. Suggest that they use the headings in the textbook as a guide.

Enrich

Have students choose a country that has recently gone through a change in government such as Kosovo or Afghanistan. Have students write an open letter to the citizens of the country explaining a republican form of government and urging citizens to support such a government.

✓ Reading Check

Answer: Fighting a common enemy united the country and gave rise to patriotic symbols and common folklore.

4 CLOSE

Have students describe the major social changes that followed the War for Independence.

History *Through Art*

Family Scene Charles Willson Peale painted *The Peale Family,* showing his own family in an everyday pose. American artists favored informal scenes over the more formal European styles. What aspects of daily life does the artist show?

Revolution gave rise to many patriotic symbols and a common folklore. Stories of the Revolution and its heroes helped Americans to think of themselves as all belonging to the same group.

American Painters The Revolution sparked the creativity of American painters, including **John Trumbull** and **Charles Willson Peale.** Their work and that of other artists helped to build an American identity. Both men portrayed the heroic deeds and leaders of the Revolution. Trumbull served in the Continental Army as an aide to Washington. He is best known for his depiction of battles and important events in the Revolution. Peale fought at Trenton and Princeton and survived the winter at Valley Forge. He is best known for his portraits of Washington and other Patriot leaders.

Changes in Education As they started a new nation, American leaders considered an educated public to be critical to the republic's success. Jefferson called it the "keystone of our arch of government." Several state constitutions provided for government-funded universities. In 1795 the University of North Carolina became the first state university in the nation. At the same time, elementary education began to institute an American-centered style of teaching. Tossing out British textbooks, schools taught republican ideas and the history of the struggle for independence.

As the American people began to build a national identity, leaders of the United States turned their attention to the creation of a government that could hold the new nation together and promote the ideals and beliefs that the colonists had fought so hard to secure.

✓ Reading Check **Identifying** In what ways did the Revolutionary War help create powerful nationalist feelings in the United States?

SECTION 4 ASSESSMENT

Checking for Understanding

1. **Define:** republic, emancipation, manumission.
2. **Identify:** Virginia Statute for Religious Freedom, Molly Pitcher, John Trumbull, Charles Willson Peale.
3. **List** three features of the political system of the United States set up after the Revolutionary War.

Reviewing Themes

4. **Culture and Traditions** What new aspects of American culture emerged after the Revolutionary War?

Critical Thinking

5. **Synthesizing** Why did nationalist feelings emerge in the United States after the American Revolution?
6. **Categorizing** Use a graphic organizer similar to the one below to list the position of women, African Americans, and Loyalists in American society after the Revolution.

	Position in American Society
Women	
African Americans	
Loyalists	

Analyzing Visuals

7. **Examining Art** Study the painting by Charles Willson Peale shown above. How does this painting reveal the republican ideas of the time?

Writing About History

8. **Expository Writing** Imagine you are on a committee to write a new state constitution. List the freedoms you want attached to your state's constitution, and explain why you feel it is important to guarantee these rights.

SECTION 4 ASSESSMENT ANSWERS

1. Terms are in blue.
2. Virginia Statute for Religious Freedom *(p. 149),* Molly Pitcher *(p. 150),* John Trumbull *(p. 152),* Charles Wilson Peale *(p. 152)*
3. possible answers: government was a republic, equality of all citizens under the law, voting rights expanded, freedom of religion
4. possible answers: rise in patriotic symbols and common folklore, paintings of significant events and of everyday life, new emphasis on education
5. Fighting a common enemy united the country and gave rise to patriotic symbols and common folklore.
6. Answers should reflect the section text.
7. uncomplicated, simple style reflected the ideal republic model of common equality
8. Students' lists will vary. Each item on the list should include an explanation of its importance.

American LITERATURE

The call to arms during the Revolution was heard not only on the fields of battle but off, echoed by the leading writers of the day. Some of the most inspiring words that rang out against British tyranny were those of **Thomas Paine,** a sometime teacher, sailor, and grocer who became a journalist in his late thirties. The first essay from Paine's collection *The American Crisis,* issued in December 1776, was read by General George Washington to boost the spirits of his beleaguered troops.

Read to Discover

What language does Paine use to encourage support for the American revolutionary cause?

Reader's Dictionary

tyranny: absolute power wielded unjustly

consolation: comfort

esteem: value

impious: not respectful

from *The American Crisis, Number 1*
by Thomas Paine

These are the times that try men's souls. The summer soldier and the sunshine patriot will in this crisis, shrink from the service of his country; but he that stands it NOW deserves the love and thanks of man and woman. Tyranny, like hell, is not easily conquered; yet we have this consolation with us, that the harder the conflict, the more glorious the triumph. What we obtain too cheap, we esteem too lightly; 'tis dearness only that gives everything its value. Heaven knows how to put a proper price upon its goods and it would be strange indeed, if so celestial an article as FREEDOM should not be highly rated. Britain, with an army to enforce her tyranny, has declared that she has a right (*not only to* TAX) but "to BIND *us in* ALL CASES WHATSO-EVER," and if being *bound in that manner,* is not slavery, then is there not such a thing as slavery upon earth. Even the expression is impious, for so unlimited a power can belong only to God. . . .

. . . Let it be told to the future world that in the depth of winter, when nothing but hope and virtue could survive, that the city and the country, alarmed at one common danger, came forth to meet and to repulse it. . . . I love the man that can smile in trouble, that can gather strength from distress, and grow brave by reflection. It is the business of little minds to shrink; but he whose heart is firm, and whose conscience approves his conduct, will pursue his principles unto death.

> "These are the times that try men's souls."

Analyzing Literature

1. **Recall and Interpret** What does Paine mean by the phrase "the summer soldier and the sunshine patriot"?
2. **Evaluate and Connect** What purpose do you think essays such as this one serve in times of war and crisis?

Interdisciplinary Activity

Language Arts The language in Paine's essay may seem outdated now, but the emotions and ideas he expresses are still common. Rewrite the first paragraph of the essay, using words that a modern politician might use in a speech. Try to think of current phrases that would make sense—for example, what might we say today instead of "the summer soldier"?

Team Teaching This selection from *The America Crisis, Number 1* can be presented in a team teaching context, in conjunction with English or Language Arts.

Read to Discover
Answer: He uses words such as "firm heart" and imagery like the thanks of a loving country to encourage Patriots.

Reinforcing Vocabulary
Have students use two of the terms in a sentence. Encourage students to share their sentences with the class.

Historical Connection
Despite his popularity as a writer, Thomas Paine refused royalties for his pamphlets. By refusing royalties, he hoped to keep the cost of the pamphlets low enough that most people could afford to purchase them.

Portfolio Writing Activity
Have students locate and read another of Thomas Paine's essays. Instruct students to include in their portfolios a brief synopsis of what they have read.

HISTORY *Online*

Refer to tav.glencoe.com for additional Glencoe Literature titles, lesson plans, and study guides related to this unit.

Answers to Analyzing Literature

1. Paine is literally referring to men who were willing to fight only when the weather was pleasant. He is figuratively referring to men who were not willing to fight under adverse conditions.

2. helped to remind people why they were fighting

Interdisciplinary Activity
Paragraphs will vary. Students might substitute "fair-weather" soldier.

153

GLENCOE
TECHNOLOGY

MindJogger Videoquiz
Use the **MindJogger Videoquiz** to
review Chapter 4 content.

 Available in VHS

Reviewing Key Terms

Students' answers will vary. The pages where the words appear in the text are shown in parentheses.

1. **customs duty** (p. 119)
2. **inflation** (p. 120)
3. **nonimportation agreement** (p. 121)
4. **writ of assistance** (p. 122)
5. **committee of correspondence** (p. 127)
6. **minuteman** (p. 129)
7. **Loyalist** (p. 129)
8. **Patriot** (p. 129)
9. **guerrilla warfare** (p. 139)
10. **letters of marque** (p. 143)
11. **republic** (p. 147)
12. **emancipation** (p. 150)
13. **manumission** (p. 151)

Reviewing Key Facts

14. French and Indian War (p. 118), Boston Tea Party (p. 127), Intolerable Acts (p. 128), Battle of Bunker Hill (p. 131), Declaration of Independence (p. 133)

15. King George wanted to prevent going to war with Native Americans over the settlement of the land west of the Appalachian Mountains.

16. After the Boston Tea Party, the British Parliament enacted the Coercive Acts.

17. Winning the Battle of Saratoga improved American morale and convinced France to commit troops to the American cause.

18. In the Treaty of Paris, Britain recognized the United States as a new

---

Reviewing Key Terms

On a sheet of paper, use each of these terms in a sentence.

1. customs duty
2. inflation
3. nonimportation agreement
4. writ of assistance
5. committee of correspondence
6. minuteman
7. Loyalist
8. Patriot
9. guerilla warfare
10. letters of marque
11. republic
12. emancipation
13. manumission

Chapter Summary

1763	French and Indian War ends; Proclamation of 1763 issued
1764	Sugar Act, Currency Act passed
1765	Stamp Act passed; colonists stage protests
1766	Stamp Act repealed; Declaratory Act asserts Parliament's supremacy
1767	Townshend Acts passed
1768–1769	Colonists boycott British imports to protest Townshend Acts
1770	Boston Massacre; Townshend Acts repealed
1773	Tea Act passed; Boston Tea Party held in protest
1774	Coercive Acts passed; First Continental Congress meets
1775	Battles of Lexington and Concord; Second Continental Congress meets
1776	Declaration of Independence signed
1778	France recognizes the United States
1781	War of Independence ends when General Cornwallis surrenders at Yorktown
1783	In the Treaty of Paris, Britain recognizes the United States as a country
1786	Virginia Statute for Religious Freedom introduced

nation, gave Florida back to Spain, and gave France colonies in Africa and the Caribbean.

19. People felt a new sense of national identity and they wanted to create a culture that would support their new form of government.

Critical Thinking

20. freedom of speech, freedom of religion, the right to bear arms, the right to trial by jury, protection against searches home without a warrant, and protection

---

Reviewing Key Facts

14. **Identify:** French and Indian War, Boston Tea Party, Intolerable Acts, Battle of Bunker Hill, Declaration of Independence.

15. Why did King George III issue the Proclamation of 1763?

16. What were the effects of the Boston Tea Party?

17. Why was the Battle of Saratoga a turning point in the Revolutionary War?

18. What were the terms of the Treaty of Paris?

19. Why did a new American culture emerge after the war?

Critical Thinking

20. **Analyzing Themes: Civic Rights and Responsibilities** What rights did the colonists want from Britain?

21. **Evaluating** During the war, how did *The American Crisis, No. 1,* by Thomas Paine influence the morale of Washington's troops?

22. **Comparing and Contrasting** After the American Revolution, a new culture emerged in the United States. Compare and contrast American culture before and after the war in these areas: government, society, the arts, and education.

23. **Categorizing** Use a graphic organizer similar to the one below to list the events that led to the American Revolution.

Events That Led to the American Revolution

24. **Interpreting Primary Sources** In 1766 Benjamin Franklin testified before Parliament about the colonists' reactions to the Stamp Act. Read the excerpt from his testimony and answer the questions that follow.

Q. What is your name, and place of abode?

A. Franklin, of Philadelphia.

Q. Are not the colonies . . . very able to pay the stamp [tax]?

A. In my opinion there is not enough in the colonies to pay the stamp duty for one year.

Q. Don't you know that the money arising from the stamps was all to be laid out in America?

A. I know it is appropriated by the act to the American service; but it will be spent in the conquered colonies where the soldiers are, not in the colonies that pay it. . . .

Q. Do you think it right that America should be protected by this country and pay no part of the expense?

against the government seizing property without proper court proceedings

21. In *The American Crisis,* Paine reminded soldiers of the potential rewards such as respect and honor that would come to those who faced difficulties and stayed the course.

22. Students' answers will vary but should reflect material discussed in the chapter.

Self-Check Quiz
Visit the *American Vision* Web site at tav.glencoe.com and click on *Self-Check Quizzes—Chapter 4* to assess your knowledge of chapter content.

A. That is not the case. The colonies raised, clothed, and paid, during the last war, near 25,000 men and spent many millions.

Q. Were you not reimbursed by Parliament?

A. We were only reimbursed what, in your opinion, we had advanced beyond our proportion, or beyond what might reasonably be expected from us; and it was a very small part of what we spent. Pennsylvania, in particular, disbursed about 500,000 pounds, and the reimbursements, in the whole, did not exceed 60,000 pounds. . . .

   a. Where does Franklin say that the British will spend the money they collect from the stamp tax?

   b. Why does Franklin say that the stamp taxes are unfair?

Practicing Skills

25. Examining Cause and Effect Study the chart on page 129. Then answer the questions below.

   a. What are the four causes of the colonies' declaring independence?

   b. On page 146, the Skillbuilder lists clue words that often appear in cause-and-effect discussions. Using those clue words, write three sentences about the effects of the colonial rebellion.

Chapter Activities

26. Research Project Research some popular American painters after the Revolutionary War, such as John Trumbull and Charles Willson Peale. Write a report that explains how the themes of their paintings helped build an American identity.

27. American History Primary Source Document Library CD-ROM Read "On Liberty" by John Adams. Assuming the role of a Patriot or a Loyalist, write a letter to the editor of the *Boston Gazette* in reaction to the article.

Writing Activity

28. Descriptive Writing Imagine that you are a resident of Charles Town in 1780. The city has had to surrender, and you must face British troops wherever you go. Then you hear about Francis Marion, the "Swamp Fox," who is making hit-and-run attacks on the British. Write to a friend in New York City describing your experiences and your hopes for victory over the British.

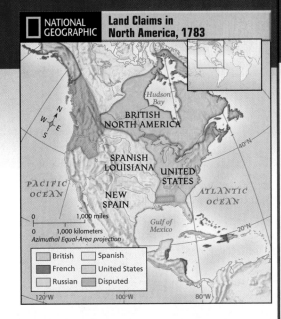

NATIONAL GEOGRAPHIC
Land Claims in North America, 1783

British   Spanish
French   United States
Russian   Disputed

Geography and History

29. The map above shows the land claims in North America as a result of the 1783 Treaty of Paris. Study the map and answer the questions below.

   a. Interpreting Maps After the Revolutionary War, what were the borders for the United States on the north? On the south? On the west?

   b. Applying Geography Skills Which countries shared a border with the United States?

Standardized Test Practice

Directions: Choose the best answer to the following question.

The colonists complained about having to pay British taxes while not being allowed to vote for members of the British Parliament. Which of the following quotations best expresses their complaint?

A "Give me liberty or give me death."

B "Taxation without representation is tyranny."

C "These are the times that try men's souls."

D "Don't fire until you see the whites of their eyes."

Test-Taking Tip: Use the process of elimination to rule out any answers that you know are wrong. For example, two of the answers suggest that the colonists and the British may already be at war, while only one answer mentions the main issue.

HISTORY Online

Have students visit the Web site at tav.glencoe.com to review Chapter 4 and take the Self-Check Quiz.

Writing Activity

28. Students' letters should show the range of emotions experienced during this period.

Geography and History

29. a. North: Hudson River and the Great Lakes; South: Gulf of Mexico; West: Mississippi River; **b.** Britain and Spain

The Princeton Review
Standardized Test Practice

Answer: B
Test-Taking Tip: Encourage students to look for the main ideas in the question. For example, this question is related to taxes and voting for representation in Parliament. Answer B is the only answer that mentions taxes and representation.

Bonus Question ?

Ask: How did *Common Sense* affect the average colonist's view of England? *(It changed people's view of the enemy from Parliament to the king.)*

---

23. possible answers: Proclamation Act of 1763, Sugar Act, Stamp Act, Quartering Act, Townshend Acts, Tea Act of 1773, Boston Tea Party, Intolerable Acts (Coercive Acts and Quebec Act), Declaration of Independence

24. a. in conquered colonies; **b.** The colonies are already paying more than their share.

Practicing Skills

25. a. Colonists' tradition of self-government; Americans' sense of separate identity from Britain; Proclamation of 1763; British policies towards the colonies after 1763.

b. Answers will vary, but should include words listed on page 146.

Chapter Activities

26. Reports will vary but should show that students examined the themes used by these artists.

27. Students' letters will vary. Students should clearly support a point of view.

Timesaving Tools

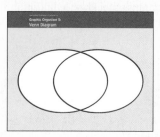

TeacherWorks™ All-In-One Planner and Resource Center

- **Interactive Teacher Edition** Access your Teacher Wraparound Edition and your classroom resources with a few easy clicks.
- **Interactive Lesson Planner** Planning has never been easier! Organize your week, month, semester, or year with all the lesson helps you need to make teaching creative, timely, and relevant.

Use Glencoe's **Presentation Plus!** multimedia teacher tool to easily present dynamic lessons that visually excite your students. Using Microsoft PowerPoint® you can customize the presentations to create your own personalized lessons.

TEACHING TRANSPARENCIES

Graphic Organizer 5

Why It Matters Chapter Transparency 5

APPLICATION AND ENRICHMENT

Linking Past and Present Activity 5

Enrichment Activity 5

Primary Source Reading 5

REVIEW AND REINFORCEMENT

Reteaching Activity 5

Vocabulary Activity 5

Time Line Activity 5

Critical Thinking Skills Activity 5

Meeting NCSS Standards

Local Standards

The following standards are highlighted in Chapter 5:

Section 1	VI	Power, Authority, and Governance: B, C, F, I
Section 2	I	Culture: B, C
Section 3	VI	Power, Authority, and Governance: B, C, D, E, F, I

ASSESSMENT AND EVALUATION

**Chapter 5 Test
Form A**

**Chapter 5 Test
Form B**

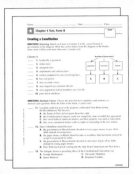

**Standardized Test Skills
Practice Workbook Activity 5**

**Performance Assessment
Activities and Rubrics 5**

**ExamView® Pro
Testmaker CD-ROM**

MULTIMEDIA

- **Vocabulary PuzzleMaker CD-ROM**
- **Interactive Tutor Self-Assessment CD-ROM**
- **ExamView® Pro Testmaker CD-ROM**
- **Audio Program**
- **American History Primary Source Documents Library CD-ROM**
- **MindJogger Videoquiz**
- **Presentation Plus! CD-ROM**
- **TeacherWorks™ CD-ROM**
- **Interactive Student Edition CD-ROM**
- **Glencoe Skillbuilder Interactive Workbook CD-ROM, Level 2**
- **The *American Vision* Video Program**
- **American Music: Hits Through History**
- **American Music: Cultural Traditions**

SPANISH RESOURCES

The following Spanish language materials are available in the Spanish Resources Binder:

- **Spanish Guided Reading Activities**
- **Spanish Reteaching Activities**
- **Spanish Quizzes and Tests**
- **Spanish Vocabulary Activities**
- **Spanish Summaries**
- **The Declaration of Independence and United States Constitution Spanish Translation**

  Biography

THE HISTORY CHANNEL®

The following videotape programs are available from Glencoe as supplements to Chapter 5:

- **Thomas Jefferson: Philosopher of Freedom** (ISBN 1-56-501502-9)
- **George Washington: Founding Father** (ISBN 1-56-501377-8)
- **Benjamin Franklin: Citizen of the World** (ISBN 1-56-501426-X)

To order, call Glencoe at 1-800-334-7344. To find classroom resources to accompany many of these videos, check the following home pages:
A&E Television: www.aande.com
The History Channel: www.historychannel.com

HISTORY Online

Use our Web site for additional resources. All essential content is covered in the Student Edition.

You and your students can visit tav.glencoe.com, the Web site companion to the ***American Vision.*** This innovative integration of electronic and print media offers your students a wealth of opportunities. The student text directs students to the Web site for the following options:

- **Chapter Overviews**
- **Student Web Activities**
- **Self-Check Quizzes**
- **Textbook Updates**

Answers to the student Web activities are provided for you in the **Web Activity Lesson Plans.** Additional Web resources and Interactive Tutor Puzzles are also available.

Chapter 5 Resources

SECTION RESOURCES

Daily Objectives	Reproducible Resources	Multimedia Resources
SECTION 1 **The Confederation** 1. List the achievements of the newly formed Confederation Congress. 2. Summarize the weaknesses of the Confederation Congress.	Reproducible Lesson Plan 5–1 Daily Lecture and Discussion Notes 5–1 Guided Reading Activity 5–1* Section Quiz 5–1* Reading Essentials and Study Guide 5–1 Performance Assessment Activities and Rubrics	Daily Focus Skills Transparency 5–1 Interactive Tutor Self-Assessment CD-ROM ExamView® Pro Testmaker CD-ROM Presentation Plus! CD-ROM Skillbuilder Interactive Workbook, Level 2 TeacherWorks™ CD-ROM Audio Program
SECTION 2 **A New Constitution** 1. Describe the issues at stake during the Constitutional Convention. 2. Discuss the compromises reached during the convention.	Reproducible Lesson Plan 5–2 Daily Lecture and Discussion Notes 5–2 Guided Reading Activity 5–2* Section Quiz 5–2* Reading Essentials and Study Guide 5–2 Performance Assessment Activities and Rubrics	Daily Focus Skills Transparency 5–2 Interactive Tutor Self-Assessment CD-ROM ExamView® Pro Testmaker CD-ROM Presentation Plus! CD-ROM TeacherWorks™ CD-ROM Audio Program
SECTION 3 **Ratification** 1. Summarize the main points in the debate between the Federalists and the Antifederalists. 2. Explain how the Constitution was finally ratified.	Reproducible Lesson Plan 5–3 Daily Lecture and Discussion Notes 5–3 Guided Reading Activity 5–3* Section Quiz 5–3* Reading Essentials and Study Guide 5–3 Performance Assessment Activities and Rubrics	Daily Focus Skills Transparency 5–3 Interactive Tutor Self-Assessment CD-ROM ExamView® Pro Testmaker CD-ROM Presentation Plus! CD-ROM TeacherWorks™ CD-ROM Vocabulary PuzzleMaker CD-ROM Audio Program ABCNews Interactive™ Historic America Electronic Field Trips

0:00 OUT OF TIME?
Assign the Chapter 5 **Reading Essentials and Study Guide.**

Also Available in Spanish

 Blackline Master   Transparency CD-ROM DVD

Poster   Music Program Audio Program Videocassette

NATIONAL GEOGRAPHIC   Teacher's Corner

INDEX TO NATIONAL GEOGRAPHIC MAGAZINE

The following articles relate to this chapter.
- "George Washington's Patowmack Canal," June 1987
- "James Madison, Architect of the Constitution," September 1987
- "L'Enfant's Washington," August 1991
- "The Peales: America's First Family of Art," December 1990

NATIONAL GEOGRAPHIC SOCIETY PRODUCTS AVAILABLE FROM GLENCOE

To order the following product for use with this chapter, contact your local Glencoe sales representative, or call Glencoe at 1-800-334-7344:
- *NGS PictureShow: Story of America, Part 1* (CD-ROM)

ADDITIONAL NATIONAL GEOGRAPHIC SOCIETY PRODUCTS

To order the following, call National Geographic at 1-800-368-2728:
- *Branches of Government Series* (Video set)
- *Democratic Government Series, "The United States"* (Video)
- *In the Eyes of the Law* (Video)
- *Star-Spangled Banner: Our Nation's Flag* (Video)
- *Wall Maps: Laminated North America Political*
- *Washington, D.C.* (Video)

NGS ONLINE

Access National Geographic's Web site for current events, atlas updates, activities, links, interactive features, and archives.
www.nationalgeographic.com

From the Classroom of...

Gary Carmichael
Whitefish High School
Whitefish, MT

Who Was the First President?

Ask students to name the first president. The students automatically say, "George Washington." You then say, "No, he wasn't the first president."

Now that you have their attention, begin a discussion of the history of the Articles of Confederation, and point out that the first president, under the Articles of Confederation, was John Hanson.

Then go through the list of presidents until you reach number 8—George Washington. The supposedly "easy" question, "Who was the first president?" and the surprising answer open the door for a great discussion starter for the Articles of Confederation and the Constitution.

Do tell the students at the end of the lesson that if they are ever stopped on the street and asked who was the first president they probably should say George Washington.

ADDITIONAL RESOURCES FROM GLENCOE

- American Music: Cultural Traditions
- American Art & Architecture
- Outline Map Resource Book
- U.S. Desk Map
- Building Geography Skills for Life
- Inclusion for the High School Social Studies Classroom Strategies and Activities
- Teaching Strategies for the American History Classroom (Including Block Scheduling Pacing Guides)

KEY TO ABILITY LEVELS

Teaching strategies have been coded.

L1 BASIC activities for all students
L2 AVERAGE activities for average to above-average students
L3 CHALLENGING activities for above-average students
ELL ENGLISH LANGUAGE LEARNER activities

 Block Schedule

Activities that are suited to use within the block scheduling framework are identified by:

Why It Matters Activity

Ask students to consider why it was so important to balance federal and state power and divide federal powers into three branches. Students should evaluate their answers after they have completed the chapter.

5 Creating a Constitution

1781–1789

Why It Matters

After the American Revolution, the new nation struggled to draw up a plan for government. Americans wanted to make sure the government did not have too much power. Eventually they came up with a way to balance federal and state power and to divide federal power into three branches. Promising to add a bill of rights helped win approval for the Constitution.

The Impact Today

The Constitution is central to American life and ideals.
• *The Constitution continually defines the rights of citizens and the limits of governmental power.*
• *The Constitution remains a model for representative government.*

 The American Vision *Video* The Chapter 5 video, "The Power of the Constitution," discusses one of the nation's most important documents.

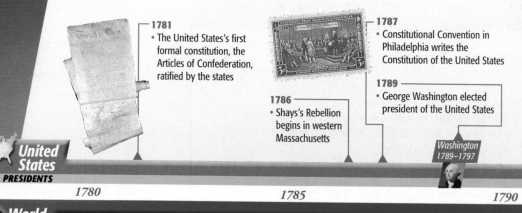

1781
• The United States's first formal constitution, the Articles of Confederation, ratified by the states

1787
• Constitutional Convention in Philadelphia writes the Constitution of the United States

1786
• Shays's Rebellion begins in western Massachusetts

1789
• George Washington elected president of the United States

Washington 1789–1797

United States
PRESIDENTS

1780   *1785*   *1790*

World

1778
• James Cook lands on Hawaii

1783
• Latin American soldier and statesman Simón Bolívar born

1787
• Sierra Leone founded by freed Africans

1789
• French Revolution begins

1790
• Lavoisier's *Table of Thirty-One Chemical Elements* published

156

TWO-MINUTE LESSON LAUNCHER

Invite a student volunteer to read the Preamble to the U.S. Constitution. (This document can be found on page 188.) Ask students how they think the members of the Constitutional Convention felt when they first heard these words. Ask them how they think ordinary citizens felt when they heard the Preamble.

"Ship of State" float parading through New York City during the 1788 ratification celebration

Introduce students to chapter content and key terms by having them access the **Chapter 5 Overview** at tav.glencoe.com.

More About the Art

In both Europe and America, artists and cartoonists often used a large sailing ship as a metaphor for government. Political leaders were portrayed as captains, and political crises were portrayed as storms that the ship of state had to weather. After New York ratified the Constitution, Federalists mounted a model ship on wheels and pulled it through New York City. Alexander Hamilton's name was painted on the platform to celebrate his role in convincing New York to ratify the Constitution.

1791
• Bill of Rights added to Constitution

1798
• Eli Whitney introduces idea of interchangeable parts in manufacturing

J. Adams
1797–1801

1795   1800

HISTORY
Online

Chapter Overview
Visit the *American Vision* Web site at tav.glencoe.com and click on *Chapter Overviews—Chapter 5* to preview chapter information.

1798
• Thomas Malthus publishes essay on population explosion

157

TIME LINE
ACTIVITY

Have students duplicate the time line that appears on pages 156–157 and add the following information to the correct positions on the timeline.

• Benjamin Franklin invents bifocals, 1784
• Congress creates U.S. Mint, 1792
• Cornwallis surrenders at Yorktown, 1781
• Louis XVI of France is beheaded by guillotine, 1793
• Rosetta Stone is found in Egypt, 1799
• Treaty of Paris signed, 1783
• Whiskey Rebellion, 1794

GRAPHIC ORGANIZER ACTIVITY

Organizing Information Have students use a graphic organizer similar to the one below to identify differences between Federalists and Antifederalists.

Federalists	Antifederalists
supported by large landowners, eastern farmers, artisans, and merchants; more educated and wealthy	supported by western farmers; less educated and less wealthy
wanted national government	did not want strong national government

1 FOCUS

Section Overview

This section examines the first attempt made at a national government for the 13 states.

Guide to Reading

Answers to Graphic: Achievements of the Confederation Congress included establishment of a system for surveying the western lands, passage of the Northwest Ordinance, and promotion of trade by signing trade treaties.

Preteaching Vocabulary

Have students create note cards with the Key Terms and Names on the front of the cards. Instruct students to use the reverse side to make notes about the term or name.

Guide to Reading

Main Idea

The 13 states ratified the Articles of Confederation, which created a national government for the new nation.

Key Terms and Names

Articles of Confederation and Perpetual Union, Northwest Ordinance, duty, recession, Shays's Rebellion

Reading Strategy

Organizing As you read about the new government created by the Articles of Confederation, complete a graphic organizer similar to the one below by listing the achievements of the Confederation Congress.

Achievements of the Confederation Congress

Reading Objectives

• **List** the achievements of the newly formed Confederation Congress.
• **Summarize** the weaknesses of the Confederation Congress.

Section Theme

Government and Democracy The Articles of Confederation provided a workable but faulty national government.

Preview of Events

| 1781 | 1783 | 1785 | 1787 |

1781 Articles of Confederation ratified

1783 Newburgh conspiracy

1784 Postwar economic recession begins

1786–1787 Shays's Rebellion

1787 Northwest Ordinance becomes law

George Washington

★ An American Story ★

On March 15, 1783, General George Washington arrived in Newburgh, New York. He had come to convince his officers—members of the so-called Newburgh conspiracy—not to rebel against the government.

Many officers were deeply in debt and angry with Congress for not giving them their back pay and pensions. Several had sent an angry letter to other officers arguing that the time had come to take action. When Washington read a copy of the letter, he called a meeting of all high-ranking officers at Newburgh and criticized their "insidious purposes" that threatened the separation between "military and civil" affairs.

Washington then said that he wished to read a different letter, and he pulled out a pair of reading glasses. No one had ever seen him wear them before. "Gentlemen," Washington began, "you must pardon me. I have grown gray in the service of my country and now feel myself growing blind." This simple statement drained the tension from the room. Some officers wept. Shortly afterward, the officers pledged their loyalty to Congress. Washington's integrity had preserved a basic principle—that the army should not interfere in politics.

—adapted from *The Forging of the Union*

The Achievements of the Confederation Congress

Even before independence was declared, Patriot leaders at the Continental Congress realized that the colonies needed to be united under some type of central government. In November 1777, the Continental Congress adopted the **Articles of Confederation and Perpetual Union**—a plan for a loose union of the states under the authority of the Congress.

SECTION RESOURCES

The Articles of Confederation The Articles of Confederation established a very weak central government. The states had spent several years fighting for independence from Britain. They did not want to give up that independence to a new central government that might become tyrannical.

Under the Articles, once a year, each state would select a delegation to send to the capital city. This group, generally referred to as the Confederation Congress, was the entire government. There were no separate executive and judicial branches.

The Confederation Congress had the right to declare war, raise armies, and sign treaties. Although these powers were significant, the Congress was not given the power to impose taxes, and it was explicitly denied the power to regulate trade.

GEOGRAPHY

Western Policies Lacking the power to tax or regulate trade, the only way for the Confederation Congress to raise money to pay its debts and finance its operations was to sell the land it controlled west of the Appalachian Mountains. To get people to buy the land and settle in the region, the Congress had to establish an orderly system for dividing and selling the land and governing the new settlements.

In 1785 the Congress established a method for surveying the western lands. It arranged the land into townships six miles square. Each township was divided into 36 sections, one mile square.

Two years later, the Congress passed the **Northwest Ordinance,** which provided the basis for governing much of the western territory. The law created a new territory north of the Ohio River and east of the Mississippi, which could eventually be divided into three to five states. Initially the Congress would choose a governor, a secretary, and three judges for the territory. When 5,000 adult male citizens had settled in a territory, they could elect a territorial legislature. When the population of a territory reached 60,000, the territory could apply to become a state "on an equal footing with the original states."

The Northwest Ordinance also guaranteed certain rights to people living in the territory. This included freedom of religion, property rights, and the right to trial by jury. The ordinance also stated that "there [would] be neither slavery nor involuntary servitude in the said territory." The exclusion of slavery from the Northwest Territory meant that as the United States expanded in future years, it would be divided between Southern slaveholding states and Northern free states.

Success in Trade In addition to organizing western settlement, the Confederation Congress tried to promote trade with other nations. After the Revolutionary War ended, the British government imposed sharp restrictions on American access to British markets. The British insisted that American goods sold to British colonies in the Caribbean had to be carried on British ships. American ships could still carry goods to Britain, but only goods from their respective states. A ship from Massachusetts, for example, could not carry goods from New York.

To overcome these problems, representatives from the Congress negotiated several trade treaties with other countries, including Holland, Prussia, and Sweden. A previous commercial treaty with France also permitted American merchants to sell goods to French colonies in the Caribbean. By 1790 the trade of the United States was greater than the trade of the American colonies before the Revolution.

✓ **Reading Check** **Describing** What were the provisions of the Northwest Ordinance of 1787?

The Congress Falters

The Confederation Congress's commercial treaties and its system of settling the west were two of its major achievements. Other problems facing the new nation were not so easily solved.

Problems With Trade During the boycotts of the 1760s and the Revolutionary War, American artisans and manufacturers had prospered by making goods that people had previously bought from the British. After the war ended, British merchants flooded the United States with inexpensive British goods, driving many American artisans out of business.

The problems facing artisans and merchants convinced many American states to fight back by restricting British imports. Unfortunately, the states did not all impose the same duties, or taxes on imported goods. The British would then land their goods at the states that had the lowest taxes or fewest restrictions. Once the British goods were in the United States, they moved overland into the states that had tried to keep them out.

Because the Confederation Congress was not allowed to regulate commerce, the states began setting up customs posts on their borders to prevent the British from exploiting the different trade laws. They also levied taxes on each other's goods to raise revenue. New York, for example, taxed firewood from Connecticut and cabbage from New Jersey.

CHAPTER 5 Creating a Constitution **159**

---

2 TEACH

Daily Lecture and Discussion Notes 5–1

Copyright © by The McGraw-Hill Companies, Inc.

Daily Lecture and Discussion Notes
Chapter 5, Section 1

Did You Know? Without money or real power over the states, the Confederation Congress got very little respect. Its members often did not bother to attend sessions.

I. **The Achievements of the Confederation Congress** (pages 158–159)

A. In November 1777, the Continental Congress adopted the **Articles of Confederation and Perpetual Union.** This was a plan for a loose union of the states under Congress.

B. The Articles of Confederation set up a weak central government. The Confederation Congress met just once a year. It had the power to declare war, raise armies, and sign treaties. It, however, did not have the power to impose taxes or regulate trade.

C. The only way the Confederation Congress had to raise money to pay its debts were to

Analyzing a Concept Have students list the ways in which the Confederation Congress could raise money. Then have students list the ways in which the federal government raises money today. Discuss the similarities and differences. **Ask:** Why is selling land not an effective long-term strategy for financing a government? **L1**

✓**Reading Check**

Answer: It created a new territory north of the Ohio River and east of the Mississippi; provided a plan for territorial legislature and application for statehood; guaranteed certain rights; banned slavery from the Northwest Territory.

FYI

The Second Continental Congress named Benjamin Franklin the postmaster general in 1775. Article IX of the Articles of Confederation gave Congress the exclusive right to establish post offices and charge postage to defray the cost of operation.

COOPERATIVE LEARNING ACTIVITY

Creating a Time Line Organize students into small groups and have them create a time line that shows the sequence of events prescribed by the Northwest Ordinance for new states to be added to the Union. Ask students to conduct research to add at least three events to the time line that are not referenced in the text.

Use the rubric for a cooperative group management plan on pages 81–82 in the *Performance Assessment Activities and Rubrics.*

Guided Reading Activity 5-1

Name _____ Date _____ Class _____

★ Guided Reading Activity 5-1

DIRECTIONS: Filling in the Blanks In the space provided, write the word or words that best complete the sentence. Refer to your textbook to fill in the blanks.

1. In November 1777, the Continental Congress adopted the _____ —a plan for a loose union of the states under the authority of the Congress.
2. The Articles of Confederation established a very weak _____.
3. The Confederation Congress had the right to _____.
4. The only way for the Confederation Congress to raise money to pay its debts and finance its operations was to _____ and _____.
5. The _____ created a new territory north of the Ohio River and east of the Mississippi.
6. When the population of a territory reached 60,000, the territory could apply to become a _____.

Using Map Skills Have students use a local road map to gain a better understanding of the size of the townships created by the Land Ordinance of 1785. Have students outline an area six miles square that includes their current location. **L1**

Why It Matters

When the Revolutionary War began, seven states claimed land west of the Appalachian Mountains. Some claims were based on their colonial charters and other claims resulted from treaties with Native Americans. These states eventually ceded the land to the Confederation. The Land Ordinance of 1785 provided the framework for surveying and selling the western lands. The land was measured and divided into townships, which were subdivided into 36 sections, each one-mile square. These sections, 640 acres, were sold at auction for at least one dollar per acre. The Northwest Ordinance of 1787 is important because it created the Northwest Territory and provided a framework for governing in the territory. The ordinance outlined the territorial government and how the territory would eventually be divided into new states. The ordinance also guaranteed certain rights to the people living in the territory and prohibited slavery.

New Jersey retaliated by charging New York for a harbor lighthouse on the New Jersey side of the Hudson River. Each state was beginning to act as an independent country, and this behavior threatened the unity of the new United States.

Problems With Diplomacy The Confederation Congress also had problems in other areas of foreign policy. The first problems surfaced immediately after the Treaty of Paris, which ended the Revolutionary War, was signed.

Before the war, many American merchants and planters had borrowed money from British lenders. In the peace treaty, the United States had agreed that the states should allow these lenders to recover their prewar debts by suing in American courts. The Congress had no power to compel the states to do this, however, and many states restricted Britain's ability to collect its debts. The United States also had agreed that the states should return the property that had been confiscated from Loyalists during the war. Again, the Congress could not compel the states to do this, which further angered the British.

In retaliation, the British refused to evacuate American soil as specified in the treaty. They continued to occupy a string of frontier posts south of the Great Lakes inside American territory. Congress had no way to resolve these problems. It did not have the power to impose taxes, so it could not raise the money to pay a financial settlement to Britain for the debts and Loyalist property. Since it could not regulate trade, it also had no way to pressure the British into a settlement.

American dealings with Spain also showed the weaknesses of the Confederation Congress. The major dispute with Spain involved the border between Spanish territory and the state of Georgia. The Spanish stopped Americans from depositing their goods on Spanish territory at the mouth of the Mississippi River. This effectively closed the river to American farmers who used it to ship their goods to market.

Again, the Confederation Congress had no leverage to pressure the Spanish, and the dispute over Georgia's border and navigation on the Mississippi remained unresolved. Once more, the limited powers of the Confederation Congress had prevented any diplomatic solution from being worked out.

The Economic Crisis While the Confederation Congress struggled with diplomatic issues, many other Americans were struggling economically. The end of the Revolutionary War and the reining in of economic activity with Britain plunged the new United States into a severe recession, or economic slowdown.

Farmers were among those most affected by the recession. Although they were not earning as much money as they once did, they had to keep borrowing to get their next crop in the ground. Many also had mortgages to pay. At the same time, the Revolutionary War had left both the Confederation Congress and many states in debt. To pay for the war, many states had issued bonds as a way to borrow money from wealthy merchants and planters. With the war over, the people holding those bonds wanted to redeem them for gold or silver.

To pay off their debts, the states could raise taxes, but farmers and other people in debt urged the state governments to issue paper money instead. They also wanted the states to make the paper money available to farmers through government loans on farm mortgages.

Since paper money would not be backed up by gold and silver, and people would not trust it, inflation—a decline in the value of money—would begin. Debtors would be able to pay their debts using paper money that was worth less than the value printed on it. This would let them pay off their debts more easily. Lenders, on the other hand, including many merchants

Why It Matters

The Northwest Ordinance

One of the major challenges facing the Confederation Congress was formulating a plan for dealing with the territory west of the Appalachian Mountains. Formerly claimed by individual states, these vast lands were now the territory of the entire United States. The Northwest Ordinance that the Congress adopted stands as one of the few successes of the Confederation.

The Ordinance provided for the survey of land west of the Appalachian Mountains, including the present-day states of Ohio, Illinois, Wisconsin, Michigan, and Indiana. It also set up a clear and orderly process by which new states were admitted on an equal basis to the Union.

MEETING SPECIAL NEEDS

Interpersonal Have students select one portion of Section 1 to teach to another student. Ask students to read the passage and then to teach it to a partner. Have the student doing the teaching ask questions about the lesson. Direct the student/teacher to review any concepts that the student/learner did not understand. **L1** ELL

📁 Refer to *Inclusion for the High School Social Studies Classroom Strategies and Activities* in the TCR.

and importers, strongly opposed paper money because they would not be receiving the true amount they were owed. Beginning in 1785, seven states began issuing paper money.

In Rhode Island, the paper money eventually became so worthless that merchants refused to accept it in payment for debts. After an angry mob rioted against the merchants, Rhode Island's assembly passed a law forcing people to accept paper money at its stated value. Those who refused could be arrested and fined.

To people with property, this signaled danger. If states were passing such laws, it was because poorer, debt-ridden citizens controlled them. With the spread of democratic ideals and a lowering of property qualifications for voting, many states had begun electing such citizens to office.

Shays's Rebellion The property owners' fears seemed justified when a full-scale rebellion, known as **Shays's Rebellion,** erupted in Massachusetts in 1786. The rebellion started when the government of Massachusetts decided to raise taxes instead of issuing paper money to pay off its debts. The taxes fell most heavily on farmers, particularly poor farmers in the western part of the state. As the recession grew worse, many found it impossible to pay their taxes as well as their mortgages and other debts. Those who could not pay often faced the loss of their farms.

Angry at the legislature's indifference to their plight, in late August 1786, farmers in western Massachusetts rebelled. They closed down several county courthouses to prevent farm foreclosures,

Creating a List Ask students to create a list of demands that Daniel Shays and other rebels might have prepared had their seizure of the state arsenal been successful. **L1**

3 ASSESS

Assign Section 1 Assessment as homework or as an in-class activity.

Have students use the **Interactive Tutor Self-Assessment CD-ROM.**

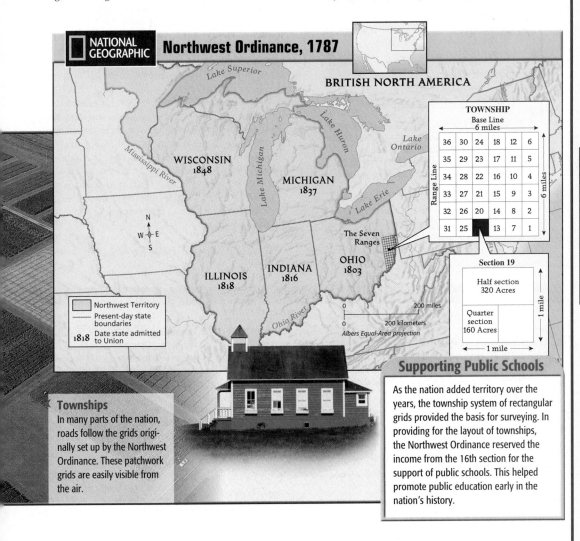

Northwest Ordinance, 1787

BRITISH NORTH AMERICA

WISCONSIN 1848

MICHIGAN 1837

ILLINOIS 1818

INDIANA 1816

OHIO 1803

Northwest Territory
Present-day state boundaries
1818 Date state admitted to Union

0   200 miles
0   200 kilometers
Albers Equal-Area projection

TOWNSHIP
Base Line
6 miles

36	30	24	18	12	6
35	29	23	17	11	5
34	28	22	16	10	4
33	27	21	15	9	3
32	26	20	14	8	2
31	25		13	7	1

Range Line   6 miles

The Seven Ranges

Section 19

Half section
320 Acres

Quarter section
160 Acres

1 mile

1 mile

Townships
In many parts of the nation, roads follow the grids originally set up by the Northwest Ordinance. These patchwork grids are easily visible from the air.

Supporting Public Schools

As the nation added territory over the years, the township system of rectangular grids provided the basis for surveying. In providing for the layout of townships, the Northwest Ordinance reserved the income from the 16th section for the support of public schools. This helped promote public education early in the nation's history.

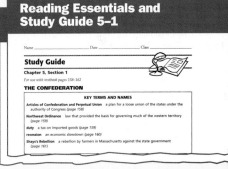

Reading Essentials and Study Guide 5–1

Name _____ Date _____ Class _____

Study Guide

Chapter 5, Section 1
For use with textbook pages 158–162

THE CONFEDERATION

KEY TERMS AND NAMES

Articles of Confederation and Perpetual Union a plan for a loose union of the states under the authority of Congress (page 158)
Northwest Ordinance law that provided the basis for governing much of the western territory (page 159)
duty a tax on imported goods (page 159)
recession an economic slowdown (page 160)
Shays's Rebellion a rebellion by farmers in Massachusetts against the state government (page 161)

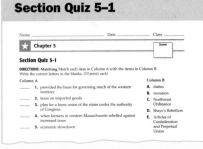

Section Quiz 5–1

Name _____ Date _____ Class _____

★ Chapter 5   Score ___

Section Quiz 5-1

DIRECTIONS: Matching Match each item in Column A with the items in Column B. Write the correct letters in the blanks. (10 points each)

Column A
___ 1. provided the basis for governing much of the western territory
___ 2. taxes on imported goods
___ 3. plan for a loose union of the states under the authority of Congress
___ 4. when farmers in western Massachusetts rebelled against increased taxes
___ 5. economic slowdown

Column B
A. duties
B. recession
C. Northwest Ordinance
D. Shays's Rebellion
E. Articles of Confederation and Perpetual Union

INTERDISCIPLINARY CONNECTIONS ACTIVITY

Economics Invite the economics teacher to discuss with the class the economic uses of taxation. Ask the teacher to compare and contrast the various forms of taxation (sales, property, and income). Have students use the information presented to create a Venn diagram of the three basic forms of taxation. **L2**

Chart *Skills*

Answer:

1. Any one state could block changes making it difficult to adapt the articles to changing conditions.

2. They feared a strong central government would become tyrannical.

Chart Skills Practice

Ask: How much respect do you think the Confederation Congress received from other countries? Explain your reasoning. *(It received little respect since it lacked power to enforce treaties.)*

Reteach

Have students create a section outline using complete sentences.

Enrich

Have interested students research a current issue that involves states' rights versus the rights of the federal government. Ask students to prepare a one-page summary of the state's position and a one-page summary of the federal government's position.

4 CLOSE

Have students list the strengths and weaknesses of the Articles of Confederation.

✓ Reading Check

Answer: When Massachusetts raised taxes to pay off debts instead of using paper money, poor farmers in the western part of the state found it impossible to pay their taxes, mortgages, and other debts.

Some Weaknesses of the Articles of Confederation

Provision	Problem Created
Congress has no power to tax	Weak currency and growing debt
	Inability to pay army leads to threats of mutiny
Congress has no power to enforce treaties	Foreign countries angry when treaties are not honored; for example, Britain keeps troops on American soil
Every state, despite size has one vote	Populous state not equally represented
Congress has no power to regulate commerce	Trade hindered by states imposing high tariffs on each other
Amendment requires unanimous vote of states	Difficult to adapt articles to changing needs

Chart *Skills*

1. **Interpreting Charts** What was the problem with requiring a unanimous vote of the states to create changes in the Articles of Confederation?
2. **Understanding Cause and Effect** Why do you think the states approved a government with so many weaknesses?

and then marched on the state supreme court. At this point, Daniel Shays, a former captain in the Continental Army who was now a bankrupt farmer, emerged as one of the rebellion's leaders.

In January 1787, Shays and about 1,200 farmers headed to a state arsenal intending to seize weapons before marching on Boston. In response, the governor sent more than 4,000 volunteers under the command of General Benjamin Lincoln to defend the arsenal. Before they arrived, Shays attacked, and the militia defending the arsenal opened fire. Four farmers died in the fighting. The rest scattered. The next day Lincoln's troops arrived and ended the rebellion. The fears the rebellion had raised, however, were harder to disperse.

A Call for Change People with greater income and social status tended to see the rebellion, as well as inflation and an unstable currency, as signs that the republic itself was at risk. They feared that as state legislatures became more democratic and responsive to poor people, they would weaken property rights and vote to take property from the wealthy. As General Henry Knox, a close aide to George Washington, concluded: "What is to afford our security against the violence of lawless men? Our government must be braced, changed, or altered to secure our lives and property."

These concerns were an important reason why many people, including merchants, artisans, and creditors, began to argue for a stronger central government, and several members of the Confederation Congress called on the states to correct "such defects as may be discovered to exist" in the present government. The Confederation's failure to deal with conditions that might lead to rebellion, as well as the problems with trade and diplomacy, only added fuel to their argument.

✓ **Reading Check** **Explaining** What caused Shays's Rebellion?

SECTION 1 ASSESSMENT

Checking for Understanding

1. **Define:** duty, recession.
2. **Identify:** Articles of Confederation and Perpetual Union, Northwest Ordinance, Shays's Rebellion.
3. **Describe** the conditions that led to Shays's Rebellion.

Reviewing Themes

4. **Government and Democracy** What do you think was the most serious flaw of the Articles of Confederation? Why do you think so?

Critical Thinking

5. **Comparing** How are the issues faced by the federal government today similar to those that were faced by the Confederation Congress?
6. **Organizing** Use a graphic organizer similar to the one below to list the weaknesses of the Confederation Congress.

Weaknesses of the Confederation Congress

Analyzing Visuals

7. **Examining Maps** Study the map of the Northwest Ordinance on page 161. What significant provision of this law would contribute to dividing the nation into competing regions?

Writing About History

8. **Persuasive Writing** Take on the role of a journalist during the time of the Confederation Congress. Write an editorial expressing your opinion of Shays's Rebellion, and suggest how the government might handle such situations better in the future.

162 CHAPTER 5 Creating a Constitution

SECTION 1 ASSESSMENT ANSWERS

1. Terms are in blue.
2. Articles of Confederation and Perpetual Union *(p. 158)*, Northwest Ordinance *(p. 159)*, Shays's Rebellion *(p. 161)*
3. When Massachusetts raised taxes to pay off debts, poor farmers in the western part of the state found it impossible to pay their taxes,

mortgages, and other debts.
4. Students' answers will vary but should state a specific flaw.
5. Students' answers will vary but should focus on specific issues.
6. no power to impose taxes, to regulate trade, to force states to abide by the peace treaty, or to regulate currency

7. The exclusion of slavery from the Northwest Territory meant that as the United States expanded, it would be divided between Southern slave-holding states and Northern free states.
8. Students' editorials will vary. Editorials should express an opinion and offer a suggestion.

Critical Thinking SKILLBUILDER

Making Comparisons

Why Learn This Skill?

Suppose you want to buy a portable compact disc (CD) player, and you must choose among three models. You would probably compare characteristics of the three models, such as price, sound quality, and size to figure out which model is best for you. In the study of American history, you often compare people or events from one time period with those from a different time period.

Learning the Skill

When making comparisons, you examine two or more groups, situations, events, or documents. Then you identify any similarities and differences. For example, the chart on this page compares two documents with regard to the powers they gave the central government. The Articles of Confederation were passed and implemented before the United States Constitution, which took their place. The chart includes a check mark in each column that applies. For example, the entry *Protect copyrights* does not have a check under *Articles of Confederation*. This shows that the government under the Articles lacked that power. The entry is checked under *United States Constitution*, showing that the government under the Constitution does have that power.

When making comparisons, you first decide what items will be compared and determine which characteristics you will use to compare them. Then you identify similarities and differences in these characteristics.

Practicing the Skill

Analyze the information on the chart on this page. Then answer the questions.

❶ What items are being compared? How are they being compared?

❷ What are the similarities and differences of the documents?

❸ Which document had the most power regarding legal matters? How can you tell?

The Articles of Confederation and the United States Constitution

Powers of the Central Government	Articles of Confederation	United States Constitution
Declare war; make peace	✔	✔
Coin money	✔	✔
Manage foreign affairs	✔	✔
Establish a postal system	✔	✔
Impose taxes		✔
Regulate trade		✔
Organize a court system		✔
Call state militia for service		✔
Protect copyrights		✔
Take other necessary actions to run the federal government		✔

❹ Which document had the most power in dealing with other nations? How can you tell?

Skills Assessment

Complete the Practicing Skills questions on page 177 and the Chapter 5 Skill Reinforcement Activity to assess your mastery of this skill.

Applying the Skill

Making Comparisons On the editorial page of your local newspaper, read two columns that express different viewpoints on the same issue. Identify the similarities and differences between the two points of view.

 Glencoe's **Skillbuilder Interactive Workbook CD-ROM, Level 2,** provides instruction and practice in key social studies skills.

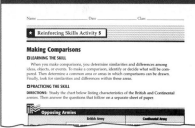

ANSWERS TO PRACTICING THE SKILL

❶ the powers of the federal government in the Articles of Confederation and United States Constitution

❷ Check marks in both columns indicate similarities. Check marks in only one column show differences.

❸ Check marks indicate that the Constitution gives the federal government more power in legal matters.

❹ Comparing powers related to other nations shows that the U.S. Constitution gives more power.

Applying the Skill
Students' answers should be presented as a table.

1 FOCUS

Section Overview

This section discusses the Constitutional Convention.

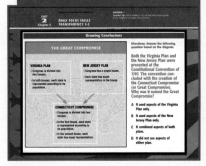

Guide to Reading

Answers to Graphic:
I. The Constitutional Convention
   A. The Founders
   B. The Virginia and New Jersey Plans
II. A Union Built on Compromise
   A. The Connecticut Compromise
   B. Compromise Over Slavery
Students should complete the outline by using all the heads in the section.

Preteaching Vocabulary
Have students make a list of the Key Terms and Names and write a helpful phrase next to each term or name. Suggest that students skip terms or names that are not familiar. Instruct students to add additional information to their list as they read the section.

Guide to Reading

Main Idea
In 1787 the Constitutional Convention set up a new government.

Key Terms and Names
Virginia Plan, New Jersey Plan, Great Compromise, Three-Fifths Compromise, popular sovereignty, federalism, separation of powers, legislative branch, executive branch, judicial branch, checks and balances, veto, impeach, amendment

Reading Strategy
Taking Notes As you read about the new government that the Constitution created, use the major headings of the section to fill in an outline similar to the one below.

A New Constitution
I. The Constitutional Convention
   A.
   B.
II.
   A.
   B.

Reading Objectives
- **Describe** the issues at stake during the Constitutional Convention.
- **Discuss** the compromises reached during the convention.

Section Theme
Culture and Traditions The new Constitution tried to uphold the principle of state authority while providing needed national authority.

Preview of Events

◆April 1787	◆June 1787	◆August 1787	◆October 1787

May 14
Constitutional Convention opens in Philadelphia

May 29
Virginia Plan introduced

June 15
New Jersey Plan introduced

July 2
Ben Franklin's committee begins seeking a compromise

September 17
Final draft of Constitution signed

Washington's chair at Constitutional Convention

★ An American Story ★

As Benjamin Franklin arrived at the Pennsylvania statehouse on September 17, 1787, he rejoiced with his colleagues about the freshness of the morning air. For 16 weeks, the 81-year-old Franklin had made the short journey from his home just off Market Street to the statehouse. There, delegates to the Constitutional Convention had exhaustively debated the future of the nation. Today, they would have a chance to sign a draft plan for the nation's new constitution.

When it came Franklin's turn to sign, the elderly leader had to be helped forward in order to write his name on the parchment. Tears streamed down his face as he signed. When the remaining delegates had finished signing, a solemn silence enveloped the hall. Franklin relieved the tension with a few well-chosen words. Pointing to the half-sun painted in gold on the back of George Washington's chair, he observed:

❝I have often . . . looked at that [sun] behind the President [of the Convention] without being able to tell whether it was rising or setting; but now, at length, I have the happiness to know it is a rising, and not a setting, Sun.❞

—quoted in *An Outline of American History*

The Constitutional Convention

The weakness of the Confederation Congress worried many American leaders, who believed that the United States would not survive without a strong central government. People who supported a stronger central government became known as "nationalists."

SECTION RESOURCES

Prominent nationalists included George Washington, John Adams, Benjamin Franklin, Alexander Hamilton, and the financier Robert Morris.

One of the most influential nationalists was **James Madison,** a member of the Virginia Assembly and head of its commerce committee. As head of the commerce committee, Madison was well aware of Virginia's trade problems with the other American states and with Britain. He firmly believed that a stronger national government was needed.

In 1786 Madison convinced Virginia's assembly to call a convention of all the states to discuss trade and taxation problems. Representatives from the states were to meet in Annapolis, Maryland, but when the convention began, delegates from only five states were present, too few to reach a final decision on the problems facing the states. Many of the delegates did discuss the weakness of the Articles of Confederation and expressed interest in modifying them.

New York delegate **Alexander Hamilton** recommended that the Congress itself call for another convention to be held in Philadelphia in May 1787. At first, the Congress was divided over whether or not to call a convention. News of Shays's Rebellion, however, and reports of unrest elsewhere convinced the Congress to call for a convention of the states "for the sole purpose of revising the Articles of Confederation."

Every state except Rhode Island sent delegates to what became known as the Constitutional Convention. In May 1787 the delegates took their places in the Pennsylvania statehouse in Philadelphia. They knew they faced a daunting task: to balance the rights and aspirations of the states with the need for a stronger national government.

The Founders The 55 delegates who attended the convention in Philadelphia included some of the shrewdest and most distinguished leaders in the United States. The majority were lawyers, and most of the others were planters and merchants. Most had experience in colonial, state, or national government. Seven had served as state governors. Thirty-nine had been members of the Confederation Congress. Eight had signed the Declaration of

Independence. In the words of Thomas Jefferson, who was unable to attend the convention because he was serving as American minister to France, the convention in Philadelphia was no less than "an assembly of demigods."

The delegates chose stern and proper George Washington of Virginia, hero of the American Revolution, as presiding officer. Benjamin Franklin was a delegate from Pennsylvania. Now 81 years old, he tired easily and had other state delegates read his speeches for him. He provided assistance to many of his younger colleagues, and his experience and good humor helped smooth the debates.

Other notable delegates included New York's Alexander Hamilton and Connecticut's Roger Sherman. Virginia sent a well-prepared delegation, including the scholarly James Madison, who kept a record of the debates. Madison's records provide the best source of information about what went on in the sessions. The meetings were closed to the public to help ensure honest and open discussion free from outside political pressures.

Profiles IN HISTORY

James Madison
1751–1836

Although many individuals contributed to the framing of the United States Constitution, the master builder was James Madison. An avid reader, the 36-year-old Virginia planter spent the better part of the year preceding the Philadelphia Convention with his nose in books. Madison read volume after volume on governments throughout history. He scoured the records of ancient Greece and Rome and delved into the administrations of Italian city-states such as Florence and Venice. He even looked at the systems used by federal alliances like Switzerland and the Netherlands. "From a spirit of industry and application," said one colleague, Madison was "the best-informed man on any point in debate."

Bringing together his research and his experience in helping to draft Virginia's constitution, Madison created the Virginia Plan. His proposal strongly influenced the final document. Perhaps Madison's greatest achievement was in defining the true source of political

power. He argued that all power, at all levels of government, flowed ultimately from the people.

At the Constitutional Convention, Madison served his nation well. The ordeal, he later said, "almost killed" him. In the years to come, though, the nation would call on him again. In 1801 he became President Thomas Jefferson's secretary of state. In 1808 he was elected the fourth president of the United States.

2 TEACH

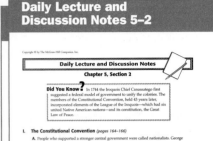
Writing a Newspaper Article
Have students choose a date from the time line on page 164 and write a newspaper article about the event. **L1**

 Use the rubric for a magazine/newspaper/Web site article or help-wanted ad on pages 85–86 in the *Performance Assessment Activities and Rubrics.*

Profiles IN HISTORY

Have students review the profile of James Madison and write down three questions about Madison's life that cannot be answered by reading the passage. Instruct students to use library and Internet resources to find the answers. Use these questions and answers as a basis for a classroom discussion about James Madison.

FYI

Although 55 delegates attended the Constitutional Convention, each state had only one vote.

COOPERATIVE LEARNING ACTIVITY

Forming a Government Organize students into small groups. Have each group act as if the members are the founders of a new country. Have them set up the legislative branch of the government using the Virginia Plan or the New Jersey Plan. Provide the following population data for the "states" involved in the new country: Anderson, 748,000; Blanchester, 85,000; Carlisle, 320,000; Destin, 60,000; Essex, 238,000; Fairmount, 142,000; Gallatin, 434,000; Henderson, 70,000; Jansen, 379,000. Have each group list reasons to support their plan.

Use the rubric for a cooperative group management plan on pages 81–82 in the *Performance Assessment Activities and Rubrics.*

Guided Reading Activity 5–2

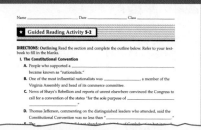

Name _____ Date _____ Class _____

★ Guided Reading Activity 5-2

DIRECTIONS: Outlining Read the section and complete the outline below. Refer to your textbook to fill in the blanks.

I. The Constitutional Convention

A. People who supported a _____ became known as "nationalists."

B. One of the most influential nationalists was _____, a member of the Virginia Assembly and head of its commerce committee.

C. News of Shays's Rebellion and reports of unrest elsewhere convinced the Congress to call for a convention of the states "for the sole purpose of _____."

D. Thomas Jefferson, commenting on the distinguished leaders who attended, said the Constitutional Convention was no less than "_____."

Making Comparisons Have students create a table to compare and contrast the basis for representation in the Virginia Plan, the New Jersey Plan, and the Connecticut Compromise. **L2**

 Use the rubric for creating a map, display, or chart on pages 77–78 in the *Performance Assessment Activities and Rubrics.*

✓Reading Check

Answer: Smaller states feared larger states would outvote them if representation was based on population.

✎ History *Through Art*

Answer: The majority were lawyers; most of the others were planters and merchants.
Ask: Why was George Washington chosen to be the presiding officer? *(He was a widely respected war hero.)*

FYI

Thomas Jefferson did not attend the Constitutional Convention. He was representing the United States in France at the time.

The Virginia and New Jersey Plans The Virginia delegation arrived at the convention with a detailed plan—mostly the work of James Madison—for a new national government. A few days after the proceedings began, the governor of Virginia, **Edmund Randolph,** introduced the plan. "A national government," declared Randolph, "ought to be established, consisting of a supreme Legislative, Executive, and Judiciary." The **Virginia Plan,** as it came to be called, proposed scrapping the Articles of Confederation entirely and creating a new national government with the power to make laws binding upon the states and to raise its own money through taxes.

The Virginia Plan proposed that the legislature be divided into two houses. The voters in each state would elect members of the first house. Members of the second house would be nominated by the state governments but actually elected by the first house. In both houses, the number of representatives for each state would reflect that state's population. The Virginia Plan, therefore, would benefit large states like Virginia, New York, and Massachusetts, which had more votes than the smaller states.

The Virginia Plan drew sharp reactions. The delegates accepted the idea of dividing the government into executive, legislative, and judicial branches, but the smaller states strongly opposed any changes that would decrease their influence by basing representation on population. They feared that the larger states would outvote them. **William Paterson,** a delegate from New Jersey, offered a counterproposal that came to be called the **New Jersey Plan.**

The New Jersey Plan did not abandon the Articles of Confederation. Instead it modified them to make the central government stronger. Under the plan, Congress would have a single house in which each state was equally represented, but it would also have the power to raise taxes and regulate trade.

If progress was to be made, the delegates had to choose one plan for further negotiation. After debating on June 19, the convention voted to proceed with the Virginia Plan. With this vote, the convention delegates decided to go beyond their original purpose of revising the Articles of Confederation. Instead, they began work on a new constitution for the United States.

✓ **Reading Check** **Explaining** Why did small states oppose the Virginia Plan?

✎ History *Through Art*

A New Government *Signing the Constitution of the United States* by Thomas Pritchard Rossiter, 1867, depicts the members of the Constitutional Convention formally endorsing their new plan of government. This silver inkwell (right) was used to sign both the Declaration of Independence and the Constitution. What were the most common professions of the Convention delegates?

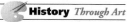

"*. . . to form a more perfect union . . .*"
—*Preamble to the Constitution*

MEETING SPECIAL NEEDS

Auditory/Musical Have students write and perform a song that will help them remember the details of one of the following: the Virginia and New Jersey Plans, the Connecticut Compromise, the system of checks and balances built into the Constitution, or the process for amending the Constitution. Encourage students to learn more about the topic to help them compose their song. **L2**

 Refer to *Inclusion for the High School Social Studies Classroom Strategies and Activities* in the TCR.

A Union Built on Compromise

As the convention hammered out the details of the new constitution, the delegates found themselves divided geographically. The small states demanded changes that would protect them against the voting power of the big states. At the same time, Northern and Southern states were divided over how to treat slavery in the new constitution. The only way to resolve these differences was through compromise.

TURNING POINT

The Connecticut Compromise After the convention voted to proceed with the Virginia Plan, tempers flared as delegates from the small states insisted that each state had to have an equal vote in Congress. The hot Philadelphia summer offered no relief, and angry delegates from the larger states threatened to walk out. By early July 1787, the convention had reached a turning point. As a delegate from North Carolina warned, "If we do not concede on both sides, our business must soon end."

In an attempt to find a solution, the convention appointed a special committee to resolve the differences between the large and small states. Delegates who were strongly committed to one side or the other were left off the committee, leaving only those who were undecided or willing to change their minds. Ben Franklin was chosen to chair the proceedings.

Throughout the proceedings, Franklin remained a calm voice of conciliation. Here, he warns the delegates about what would happen if they failed to agree:

> ❝[You will] become a reproach and by-word down to future ages. And what is worse, mankind may hereafter, from this unfortunate instance, despair of establishing governments by human wisdom, and leave it to chance, war, and conquest.❞
>
> —quoted in *Benjamin Franklin: A Biography*

The compromise that the committee worked out was based on an idea Roger Sherman of Connecticut proposed, which is why it is sometimes known as the **Connecticut Compromise.** Other historians refer to it as the **Great Compromise.**

Profiles IN HISTORY

Roger Sherman
1721–1793

Roger Sherman was born in Newton, Massachusetts, where he worked as a shoemaker as a young man. In 1743 he moved to Connecticut, where he studied law. He served in the Connecticut legislature before being appointed a superior court judge. Sherman was enormously respected for his knowledge, judgment, and integrity. He was a delegate to the Continental Congress, and he served on the special Committee of Five that drafted the Declaration of Independence. He also helped write the Articles of Confederation.

A skilled legislator and master of political compromise, Sherman was a logical choice to serve as one of Connecticut's delegates to the Constitutional Convention in 1787. There, he ably defended the interests of the smaller states, and he developed the famous compromise that saved the convention from breaking up. Following the ratification of the Constitution, Sherman was elected to the House of Representatives, where he helped prepare the Bill of Rights. He was the only person to sign the Declaration of Independence, the Articles of Confederation, *and* the Constitution—and he played an important role in drafting all three documents. Thomas Jefferson described Roger Sherman as "a man who never said a foolish thing in his life." Nathaniel Macon, a member of Congress from North Carolina, declared that Sherman "had more common sense than any man I have ever known."

Franklin's committee proposed that in one house of Congress—the House of Representatives—the states would be represented according to the size of their populations. In the other house—the Senate—each state would have equal representation. The eligible voters in each state would elect the House of Representatives, but the state legislatures would choose senators.

Compromise Over Slavery Franklin's committee also proposed that each state could elect one member to the House of Representatives for every 40,000 people in the state. This proposal caused a split between Northern and Southern delegates. Southern delegates wanted to count enslaved people when determining how many representatives they could elect. Northern delegates objected, pointing out that enslaved people could not vote.

Northern delegates also suggested that if slaves were going to be counted for representation, they should be counted for purposes of taxation as well. In the end, a solution, referred to as the **Three-Fifths Compromise,** was worked out. Every five enslaved

CHAPTER 5   Creating a Constitution   **167**

Picturing **History**

Answer: the Connecticut Compromise, the Three-Fifths Compromise, and compromises limiting the federal government's power to impose certain types of taxes and to regulate slavery

Ask: How long did the Constitutional Convention last? *(about 4 months, from May to September 1787)*

Reading Check

Answer: The South wanted each enslaved person counted in the same manner as a free person in determining a state's population.

Objectives and answers to the student activity can be found in the **Web Activity Lesson Plan** at tav.glencoe.com.

3 ASSESS

Assign Section 2 Assessment as homework or as an in-class activity.

⊙ Have students use the **Interactive Tutor Self-Assessment CD-ROM.**

Reading Essentials and Study Guide 5–2

Name _____ Date _____ Class _____

Study Guide

Chapter 5, Section 2
For use with textbook pages 164–169
A NEW CONSTITUTION

KEY TERMS AND NAMES

Virginia Plan plan of government developed by the Virginia delegates to the Constitutional Convention *(page 166)*
New Jersey Plan plan of government developed by the New Jersey delegates to the Constitutional Convention *(page 166)*
Great Compromise a compromise that solved the problem of representation in Congress *(page 167)*
Three-Fifths Compromise a compromise that solved the problem of how enslaved people were to be counted in determining representation in Congress *(page 167)*
popular sovereignty rule by the people *(page 168)*

Picturing **History**

Historic Landmark The Philadelphia Statehouse, the site of the Constitutional Convention, was later renamed Independence Hall. **What compromises were necessary to complete the Constitution?**

people in a state would count as three free persons for determining both representation and taxes.

The dispute over how to count enslaved people was not the only issue dividing the delegates. Southerners feared that a strong national government with the power to regulate trade might impose taxes on the export of farm products or ban the import of enslaved Africans. These Southern delegates insisted that the new constitution forbid interference with the slave trade and limit Congress's power to regulate trade. Northern delegates, on the other hand, knew that Northern merchants and artisans needed a government capable of controlling foreign imports into the United States.

Eventually, another compromise was worked out. The delegates agreed that the new Congress could not tax exports. They also agreed that it could not ban the slave trade until 1808 or impose high taxes on the import of enslaved persons.

The Great Compromise and the compromises between Northern and Southern delegates ended most of the major disputes between the state delegations. This enabled the convention to focus on the details of how the new government would operate.

By mid-September, the delegates had completed their task. Although everyone had had to compromise, the 39 delegates who signed the new Constitution believed it was a vast improvement over the Articles of Confederation. On September 20, they sent it to the Confederation Congress for approval. Eight days later, the Congress

HISTORY Online

Student Web Activity Visit the *American Vision* Web site at tav.glencoe.com and click on **Student Web Activities— Chapter 5** for an activity about the Constitution.

voted to submit the Constitution to the states for approval. The struggle for the Constitution now moved into a new phase. Nine of the thirteen states had to ratify the Constitution for it to take effect.

Reading Check **Describing** How did the South want to count enslaved persons when counting the population of the states?

A Framework for Limited Government

The new constitution that the states were considering was based on the principle of popular sovereignty, (SAH·vuhrn·tee) or rule by the people. Rather than a direct democracy, it created a representative system of government in which elected officials represented the voice of the people. The Constitution also created a system of government known as federalism. It divided government power between the federal, or national, government and the state governments.

The Constitution provided for a separation of powers among the three branches of the federal government. The two houses of Congress made up the legislative branch of the government. They would make the laws. The executive branch, headed by a president, would implement and enforce the laws passed by Congress. The judicial branch—a system of federal courts—would interpret federal laws and render judgment in cases involving those laws. No one serving in one branch could serve in either of the other branches at the same time.

Checks and Balances In addition to separating the powers of the government into three branches, the delegates to the convention created a system of

---

CRITICAL THINKING ACTIVITY

Drawing Conclusions Ask students why they think both the Northern states and the Southern states agreed to the Three-Fifths Compromise. *(Answers should reflect the idea that both sides benefited from the compromise. The Northern states benefited because enslaved persons would be counted for purposes of taxation, thus generating more revenue for the country. The Southern states benefited because five enslaved persons would be counted as three persons when collecting population data to be used to calculate representation. This method of calculation would increase the South's population figures and result in additional representation.)* **L2**

checks and balances to prevent any one of the three branches from becoming too powerful. Within this system, each branch of government had the ability to limit the power of the other branches.

Under the Constitution, the president—as head of the executive branch—was given far-reaching powers. The president could propose legislation, appoint judges, put down rebellions, and veto, or reject, acts of Congress. The president would also be the commander in chief of the armed forces. According to one delegate in Philadelphia, these powers might not have been so great "had not many of the members cast their eyes towards George Washington as president."

Although the president could veto acts of Congress, the legislature could override the veto with a two-thirds vote in both houses. The Senate also had to approve or reject presidential appointments to the executive branch as well as any treaties the president negotiated. Furthermore, Congress could, if necessary, impeach, or formally accuse of misconduct, and then remove the president or any other high official in the executive or judicial branch.

Members of the judicial branch of government could hear all cases arising under federal law and the Constitution. The powers of the judiciary were balanced by the other two branches. The president could nominate members of the judiciary, but the Senate had to confirm or reject such nominations. Once appointed, however, federal judges would serve for life, thus ensuring their independence from both the executive and the legislative branches.

Amending the Constitution The delegates in Philadelphia recognized that the Constitution they wrote in the summer of 1787 might need to be

amended, or changed over time. To ensure this could happen, they created a clear system for making amendments, or changes to the Constitution. To prevent the government from being changed constantly, they made it difficult for amendments to be adopted.

The delegates established a two-step process for amending the Constitution—proposal and ratification. An amendment could be proposed by a vote of two-thirds of the members of both houses of Congress. Alternatively, two-thirds of the states could call a constitutional convention to propose new amendments. To become effective, the proposed amendment then had to be ratified by three-fourths of the state legislatures or by conventions in three-fourths of the states.

The success of the Philadelphia Convention in creating a government that reflected the country's many different viewpoints was, in Washington's words, "little short of a miracle." The convention, John Adams declared, was "the single greatest effort of national deliberation that the world has ever seen."

Reading Check **Explaining** How is power divided under the system of federalism?

Fact | Fiction | Folklore

The Preamble The original draft of the Constitution's preamble began, "We the undersigned delegates of the States of New Hampshire, Massachusetts-bay. . . ." Governor Morris of Pennsylvania, a member of Benjamin Franklin's compromise committee, rewrote it to read, "We, the People of the United States. . . ."

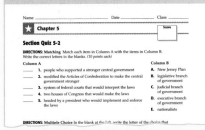

CHAPTER 5
Section 2, 164–169

Section Quiz 5–2

Name _____ Date _____ Class _____

⭐ Chapter 5   Score

Section Quiz 5-2

DIRECTIONS: Matching Match each item in Column A with the items in Column B. Write the correct letters in the blanks. *(10 points each)*

Column A
_____ 1. people who supported a stronger central government
_____ 2. modified the Articles of Confederation to make the central government stronger
_____ 3. system of federal courts that would interpret the laws
_____ 4. two houses of Congress that would make the laws
_____ 5. headed by a president who would implement and enforce the laws

Column B
A. New Jersey Plan
B. legislative branch of government
C. judicial branch of government
D. executive branch of government
E. nationalists

DIRECTIONS: Multiple Choice In the blank at the left, write the letter of the choice that

Fact | Fiction | Folklore

Although James Madison is often considered the master builder of the Constitution, a committee did the actual drafting of the document. In July 1787, a five-man Committee of Detail was charged with preparing a draft of the proceedings. A second five-man committee, the Committee of Style, was given the assignment of preparing the final draft. Governor Morris is credited with doing most of the work on the final draft.

Reading Check

Answer: Power is divided between the federal government, also known as the national government, and state governments.

Reteach
Have students review the time line on page 164 and explain the significance of each event.

Enrich
Have students create a diagram that shows the powers granted to each branch of government and how each branch can limit the power of the other two branches.

SECTION 2 ASSESSMENT

Checking for Understanding
1. **Define:** popular sovereignty, federalism, separation of powers, legislative branch, executive branch, judicial branch, checks and balances, veto, impeach, amendment.
2. **Identify:** Virginia Plan, New Jersey Plan, Great Compromise, Three-Fifths Compromise.

Reviewing Themes
3. **Culture and Traditions** Were the delegates to the Constitutional Convention representative of the American public? Why or why not?

Critical Thinking
4. **Analyzing** Do you think the Founders were right in making the amendment process difficult? Why or why not?
5. **Organizing** Use a graphic organizer similar to the one below to list the compromises that the Founders reached in creating the new Constitution.

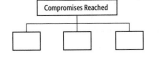
Compromises Reached

Analyzing Visuals
6. **Examining Art** Study the painting of the members of the Constitutional Convention on page 166. Why did the delegates choose to conduct the convention behind closed doors?

Writing About History
7. **Descriptive Writing** Take on the role of an observer at the Constitutional Convention. Write a journal entry describing what you witnessed. Be sure to record the arguments you heard from each side of the issues discussed, and relate your own opinion on the issues.

CHAPTER 5 Creating a Constitution **169**

SECTION 2 ASSESSMENT ANSWERS

1. Terms are in blue.
2. Virginia Plan *(p. 166)*, New Jersey Plan *(p. 166)*, Great Compromise *(p. 167)*, Three-Fifths Compromise *(p. 167)*
3. Yes and no. They were chosen by state governments elected by the

people, but they were not representative of American society.
4. Students' answers should be supported by a logical explanation.
5. Compromises reached: Connecticut or Great Compromise, Three-Fifths Compromise, compro-

mise on trade and slavery
6. Meetings were closed to ensure honest and open discussion, free from outside political pressures.
7. Students' journal entries should focus on actual events.

4 CLOSE

Ask students to explain the heading on page 167, "A Union Built on Compromise."

TIME NOTEBOOK

TEACH

Verbatim

Have students review the quotes in the Verbatim section and discuss each item as it relates to the people and themes found in their textbooks. Have students research a current political, economic, or social issue. Have them create a list of quotations about the issue along with a brief statement explaining the quote, identifying the person quoted, and describing how the quote relates to the issue. Ask students to share their lists in a class discussion.

Profile

Have students read the list of rules of civil behavior. Have students state these rules in modern language. Ask volunteers to share their versions. **Ask: Which of these rules may still be widely observed today?** *(Possible answers: to not put your hands on any part of the body that is usually covered; to stay awake while people are speaking; to not show yourself glad at another's misfortune; think before you speak)* **Why do you think some rules of civil behavior change little over time, while others change significantly?** *(Customs and manners tend to follow trends. Today's more casual society lives by different rules, but some behaviors, such as thinking before you speak, will always apply.)*

Visit the TIME Web site at www.time.com for up-to-date news, weekly magazine articles, editorials, online polls, and an archive of past magazine and Web articles.

HULTON GETTY

Profile

GEORGE WASHINGTON *At the age of 16, George Washington carefully transcribed in his own hand the* Rules of Civility and Decent Behaviour in Company and Conversation. *Among the rules our first president lived by:*

- Every action done in company ought to be with some sign of respect to those that are present.
- When in company, put not your hands to any part of the body, not usually [un]covered.
- Put not off your clothes in the presence of others, nor go out your chamber half dressed.
- Sleep not when others speak.
- Spit not in the fire, nor stoop low before it. Neither put your hands into the flames to warm them, nor set your feet upon the fire, especially if there is meat before it.
- Shake not the head, feet or legs. Roll not the eyes. Lift not one eyebrow higher than the other. Wry not the mouth, and bedew no man's face with your spittle, by approaching too near him when you speak.
- Show not yourself glad at the misfortune of another though he were your enemy.
- Be not hasty to believe flying reports to the disparagement of any.
- Think before you speak.
- Cleanse not your teeth with the Table Cloth.

VERBATIM
WAR'S END

❝I hope you will not consider yourself as commander-in-chief of your own house, but be convinced, that there is such a thing as equal command.❞

LUCY FLUCKER KNOX, *to her husband Henry Knox, upon his return as a hero from the Revolutionary War*

❝The American war is over, but this is far from being the case with the American Revolution. Nothing but the first act of the drama is closed.❞

BENJAMIN RUSH, *signer of the Declaration of Independence and member of the Constitutional Convention*

❝You could not have found a person to whom your schemes were more disagreeable.❞

GEORGE WASHINGTON, *to Colonel Lewis Nicola, in response to his letter urging Washington to seize power and proclaim himself king*

❝It appears to me, then, little short of a miracle that the delegates from so many states . . . should unite informing a system of national government.❞

GEORGE WASHINGTON, *in a letter to the Marquis de Lafayette at the close of the Constitutional Convention*

❝It astonishes me to find this system approaching to near perfection as it does; and I think it will astonish our enemies.❞

LEONARD de SELVA/CORBIS

BENJAMIN FRANKLIN, *remarking on the structure of the new United States government*

COOPERATIVE LEARNING ACTIVITY

Creating a Magazine Spread Organize the class into small groups. Assign each group one of the decades in the 1700s and ask them to create their own two-page magazine spread for the decade. Encourage students to use elements similar to those that appear in the Time Notebook but to be creative as they select information that is of particular interest. Students should look at current magazines and books for ideas about page design. This activity can be completed using desktop publishing software or the more traditional cut-and-paste method.

Use the rubric for a cooperative group management plan on pages 81–82 in the **Performance Assessment Activities and Rubrics.**

Annual Salaries

Annual federal employee salaries, 1789

President (he refused it)	$25,000
Vice President	$5,000
Secretary of State	$3,500
Chief Justice	$4,000
Senator	$6 per day
Representative	$6 per day
Army Captain	$420
Army Private	$48

CORBIS

NUMBERS

5 Number of years younger in age of average American brides compared to their European counterparts

6 Average number of children per family to survive to adulthood

7 Average number of children born per family

8 Number of Daniel Boone's surviving children

68 Number of Daniel Boone's grandchildren

$5 Average monthly wage for male agricultural laborer, 1784

$3 Average monthly wage for female agricultural laborer, 1784

PIX/FPG

Milestones

SETTLED, 1781. LOS ANGELES, by a group of 46 men and women, most of whom are of Native American and African descent.

CALLED, 1785. LEMUEL HAYNES, as minister to a church in Torrington, Connecticut. Haynes, a veteran of the Revolutionary War who fought in Lexington, is the first African American to minister to a white congregation. A parishioner insulted Haynes by refusing to remove his hat in church, but minutes into the sermon, the parishioner was so moved that the hat came off. He is now a prayerful and loyal member of the congregation.

BETTMANN/CORBIS

PUBLISHED, 1788. *THE AMERICAN SPELLING BOOK,* by Noah Webster, a 25-year-old teacher from Goshen, N.Y. The book standardizes American spelling and usage that differs from the British.

1780s WORD PLAY

Dressing the "Little Pudding Heads"

Can you match these common items of Early American clothing with their descriptions?

1. clout   **a.** a band of strong fabric wrapped around a baby to suppress the navel

2. stays   **b.** a diaper

3. surcingle   **c.** the wool cover worn over a diaper

4. pilch   **d.** a head covering for a child learning to walk to protect its brain from falls

5. pudding cap   **e.** a garment worn by children to foster good posture, made from linen and wood or baleen splints

answers: 1. b; 2. e; 3. a; 4. c; 5. d

EXTENDING THE CONTENT

American Spelling Book Noah Webster's *The American Spelling Book* was used by schoolchildren for nearly a century. It had a blue-green cover and was nicknamed "the blue-backed speller." The book contains a large collection of maxims, proverbs, fables, and some very stern views of how children should behave, including the following quote: "As for those boys and girls that mind not their books, and love not the church and school, but play with such as tell tales, tell lies, curse, swear, and steal, they will come to some bad end, and must be whipt till they mend their ways."

1 FOCUS

Section Overview

This section focuses on the differences between the Federalists and the Antifederalists.

BELLRINGER
Skillbuilder Activity

📽 Project transparency and have students answer the question.

📂 Available as a blackline master.

Daily Focus Skills Transparency 5–3

Guide to Reading

Answers to Graphic: Federalists' supporters: large landowners, merchants, artisans, and eastern farmers; goal: federal system that divided power between an effective federal government and the states. Antifederalists' supporters: western farmers; goals: national government with limited powers and a bill of rights

Preteaching Vocabulary
Have students make a two-column list with the column headings Federalists and Antifederalists. Instruct students to skim the chapter looking for names for their list.

SECTION 3 Ratification

Guide to Reading

Main Idea
Ratification of the Constitution moved to the individual states, where Federalists and Antifederalists argued their opposing views.

Key Terms and Names
Federalist, Antifederalist, John Hancock, Patrick Henry

Reading Strategy
Categorizing As you read about the efforts to ratify the Constitution, complete a graphic organizer similar to the one below by listing the supporters and goals of the Federalists and the Antifederalists.

	Federalists	Antifederalists
Source of Support		
Goals		

Reading Objectives
• **Summarize** the main points in the debate between the Federalists and Antifederalists.
• **Explain** how the Constitution was finally ratified.

Section Theme
Government and Democracy The state governments approved the Constitution through individual conventions.

Preview of Events

♦1786	♦1788	♦1790	♦1792

October 1787
First Federalist Paper published

December 1787
Delaware becomes first state to ratify the Constitution

June 21, 1788
New Hampshire ratifies the Constitution

May 1790
Rhode Island becomes last state to ratify the Constitution

December 1791
Bill of Rights added to the Constitution

★ An American Story ★

Patrick Henry

The windows of Virginia's statehouse stood open as Patrick Henry rose to speak. The man who had once declared, "Give me liberty, or give me death!" was fearful for the future of the United States. For most of June 1788, he had argued against accepting the new federal Constitution drawn up in Philadelphia the previous summer.

The afternoon of June 25 marked the final day of debate in Richmond. Henry immediately took aim at the framers of the Constitution. "What right had they to say 'We, the People?'" he demanded. "Who authorized them to speak the language of We, the People, instead of We, the States?" The future of liberty around the world was at stake, he declared. "We have it in our power to secure the happiness of one half the human race." In his closing remarks, Henry announced he would accept the will of his colleagues:

❝If I shall be in the minority, I shall have those powerful sensations which arise from a conviction of being overpowered in a good cause. Yet I will be a peaceable citizen. My head, my hand, and my heart, shall be at liberty to retrieve the loss of liberty, and remove the defects of that system in a constitutional way.❞

—quoted in *Patrick Henry: A Biography*

A Great Debate

As soon as the Philadelphia Convention closed its doors, delegates had rushed home to begin the campaign for ratification. Each state would elect a convention to vote on the new Constitution. Nine states had to vote in favor of the Constitution to put it into effect. As soon as Americans learned about the new Constitution, they began to argue over

SECTION RESOURCES

📂 **Reproducible Masters**
• Reproducible Lesson Plan 5–3
• Daily Lecture and Discussion Notes 5–3
• Guided Reading Activity 5–3
• Section Quiz 5–3
• Reading Essentials and Study Guide 5–3
• Performance Assessment Activities and Rubrics

📽 **Transparencies**
• Daily Focus Skills Transparency 5–3

Multimedia
🖥 Interactive Tutor Self-Assessment CD-ROM
🖥 ExamView® Pro Testmaker CD-ROM
🖥 Presentation Plus! CD-ROM
🖥 TeacherWorks™ CD-ROM
🔊 Audio Program

whether it should be ratified. The debate took place in state legislatures, in mass meetings, in the columns of newspapers, and in everyday conversations.

Federalists and Antifederalists Supporters of the Constitution called themselves Federalists. The name was chosen with care. It emphasized that the Constitution would create a federal system. Power would be divided between a central government and regional governments. They hoped the name would remind those Americans who feared a central government that the states would retain many of their powers.

Supporters of the Federalists and the new Constitution included large landowners who wanted the property protection a strong central government could provide. Supporters also included merchants and artisans living in large coastal cities. The inability of the Confederation Congress to regulate trade had hit these citizens hard. They believed that an effective federal government that could impose taxes on foreign goods would help their businesses.

Many farmers who lived near the coast or along rivers that led to the coast also supported the Constitution, as did farmers who shipped goods across state borders. These farmers depended on trade for their livelihood and had been frustrated by the different tariffs and duties the states imposed. They wanted a strong central government that could regulate trade consistently.

Opponents to the Constitution were called Antifederalists, a somewhat misleading name, as they were not truly against federalism. They accepted the need for a national government. The real issue, as far as they were concerned, was whether the national government or the state governments would be supreme. Prominent Antifederalists included **John Hancock, Patrick Henry,** Richard Henry Lee of Virginia, and George Clinton, governor of New York. Two members of the Constitutional Convention, Edmund Randolph and George Mason, became Antifederalists because they believed the new Constitution should have included a bill of rights. Sam Adams agreed. He opposed the Constitution because he believed it endangered the independence of the states.

Many Antifederalists were western farmers living far from the coast. These people considered themselves self-sufficient and were suspicious of the wealthy and powerful. Many of them were also deeply in debt and suspected that the new Constitution was simply a way for wealthy creditors to get rid of paper money and foreclose on their farms. One farmer named Amos Singletary wrote to the *Massachusetts Gazette* expressing views that many western farmers shared:

> ❝These lawyers and men of learning, and moneyed men, that talk so finely, and gloss over matters so smoothly, to make us poor, illiterate people swallow down the pill, expect to get into Congress themselves; they expect to be managers of this Constitution, and get all the power and all the money into their own hands, and then they will swallow up all us little folks, like the great Leviathan, Mr. President; yes, just like the whale swallowed up Jonah.❞

GOVERNMENT

The Federalist Although many influential American leaders opposed the new Constitution, several factors worked against the Antifederalists. First of all, their campaign was a negative one. The Federalists presented a definite program to meet the nation's problems. Although the Antifederalists

Analyzing *Political Cartoons*

Support for Ratification A pro-Federalist cartoon celebrates New Hampshire becoming the ninth state to ratify the Constitution in 1788. Based on the imagery of the cartoon, which state was the first to ratify the Constitution?

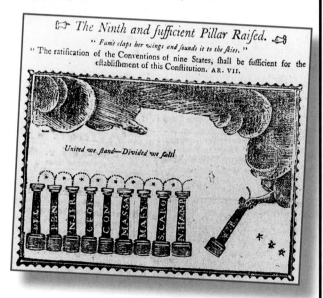

CHAPTER 5   Creating a Constitution   **173**

2 TEACH

Daily Lecture and Discussion Notes 5–3

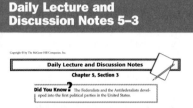

Drawing a Political Cartoon
Have students select an event or issue in this section and draw a political cartoon. Suggest that students look at examples of political cartoons in several newspapers to get ideas for their own cartoon. **L2**

Analyzing *Political Cartoons*

Answer: Delaware
Ask: When only nine states were needed to ratify the Constitution, why was the approval of Virginia and New York so important? *(They were large, powerful states needed to make the new federal government work.)*

VIDEOCASSETTE
Historic America Electronic Field Trips

View **Tape 1, Chapter 7:** "Independence Hall."

COOPERATIVE LEARNING ACTIVITY

Writing a Biography Write the following names on small slips of paper: Samuel Adams, Richard Henry Lee, George Mason, Edmund Randolph, James Madison, Alexander Hamilton, and John Jay. Repeat until you have enough slips for each student to have one. Have students draw the names without looking. Organize the class into groups according to the names the students selected. For example, all students who drew Samuel Adams are in the same group. Have each group work together to create a biography of the person whose name they selected.

Use the rubric for a cooperative group management plan on pages 81–82 in the **Performance Assessment Activities and Rubrics.**

Different Viewpoints

Should the Majority Rule?

James Madison argued persuasively for the Constitution's ratification. In *The Federalist #10*, Madison explained that the Constitution would prevent the effects of *faction*—the self-seeking party spirit of a democracy. In contrast, Thomas Jefferson argued that the will of the majority would thwart the tyranny of oppressive government.

James Madison opposes majority rule:

"When a majority is included in a faction, the form of popular government . . . enables it to sacrifice to its ruling passion or interest both the public good and the rights of other citizens.

. . . [A] pure democracy . . . can admit of no cure for the mischiefs of faction [and has always] been found incompatible with personal security or the rights of property. . . .

A republic, by which I mean a government in which the scheme of representation takes place . . . promises the cure for which we are seeking. . . . The effect of [a republic] is, on the one hand, to refine and enlarge the public views, by passing them through the medium of a chosen body of citizens, whose wisdom may best discern the true interest of their country, and whose patriotism and love of justice will be least likely to sacrifice it to temporary or partial considerations."

Thomas Jefferson defends majority rule:

"I own I am not a friend to a very energetic government. It is always oppressive. The late rebellion in Massachusetts has given more alarm than I think it should have done. Calculate that one rebellion in 13 states in the course of 11 years, is but one for each state in a century & a half. No country should be so long without one.

. . . After all, it is my principle that the will of the Majority should always prevail. If they approve the proposed [Constitution] in all its parts, I shall concur in it chearfully, in hopes that they will amend it whenever they shall find it works wrong. . . . Above all things I hope the education of the common people will be attended to; convinced that on their good sense we may rely with the most security for the preservation of a due degree of liberty."

Learning From History

1. What were the "mischiefs" that Madison believed republican government could prevent?
2. Was Jefferson correct in believing the voice of the common people would preserve liberty? Explain.

---

complained that the Constitution failed to protect basic rights, they had nothing to offer in its place.

The Federalists were also better organized than their opponents. Most of the nation's newspapers supported them. The Federalists were able to present a very convincing case in their speeches, pamphlets, and debates in state conventions.

The Federalists' arguments for ratification were summarized in *The Federalist*—a collection of 85 essays written by James Madison, Alexander Hamilton, and John Jay. Under the joint pen name of Publius, the three men published most of the essays in New York newspapers in late 1787 and early 1788 before collecting them in *The Federalist*. (*See pages 1066–1067 for examples of Federalist writings.*)

The essays explained how the new Constitution worked and why it was needed. They were very influential. Even today, judges, lawyers, legislators, and historians rely upon *The Federalist* to help them interpret the Constitution and understand what the original framers intended.

✓ **Reading Check** **Summarizing** Which groups of people tended to support the new Constitution?

The Fight for Ratification

As the ratifying conventions began to gather, the Federalists knew that they had clear majorities in some states but that the vote was going to be much closer in others, including the large and important states of Massachusetts, Virginia, and New York.

The first state conventions took place in December 1787 and January 1788. Although Delaware,

---

Different Viewpoints

Answers:

1. possible answer: the majority or a large faction making decisions in its own interest to the detriment of all others

2. Answers may vary. Some students may say the constitutional system, not the people, has preserved liberty. Others may note that slavery and civil rights issues required a struggle to achieve liberty.

Ask: Do you think that Thomas Jefferson supported Shays's Rebellion? *(He probably did not support the rebellion. Rather he supported the idea that people have the right to protest against their government or against laws that oppress them.)*

Guided Reading Activity 5–3

Name _____ Date _____ Class _____

★ Guided Reading Activity 5-3

DIRECTIONS: Recalling Facts Read the section and answer the questions below. Refer to your textbook to write the answers.

1. Where did the debate over the ratification of the new Constitution take place? _____

2. Who supported the Federalists and the Constitution? _____

3. Why were farmers who lived near the coast and farmers who shipped goods across state borders in favor of the new Constitution? _____

4. What was the real issue the Antifederalists had with the new Constitution? _____

✓ **Reading Check**

Answer: large landowners, merchants, artisans, and farmers who exported crops

3 ASSESS

Assign Section 3 Assessment as homework or as an in-class activity.

⊙ Have students use the **Interactive Tutor Self-Assessment CD-ROM.**

MEETING SPECIAL NEEDS

Learning Disability The beautifully written Preamble to the Constitution offers students an example of how the English language can be used concisely. Committing the Preamble to memory provides a useful language model for students whose spoken-language development is slow. To aid in this memory task, structure the activity by asking students to write the words *who, why,* and *what* on a piece of paper. Have students list the various phrases of the Preamble under the words to which they are most closely related. **L1** ELL

Pennsylvania, New Jersey, Georgia, and Connecticut all quickly ratified the Constitution, the most important battles still lay ahead.

Ratification in Massachusetts

In Massachusetts, opponents of the Constitution held a clear majority when the convention met in January 1788. They included the great patriot Samuel Adams. Federalists moved quickly to meet Adams's objections to the Constitution.

They promised to attach a bill of rights to the Constitution once it was ratified. They also agreed to support an amendment that would reserve for the states all powers not specifically granted to the federal government. These concessions, in combination with the fact that most artisans sided with the Federalists, persuaded Adams to vote for ratification. In the final vote, 187 members of the convention voted in favor of the Constitution while 168 voted against it.

By the end of June 1788, Maryland, South Carolina, and New Hampshire had ratified the Constitution. The Federalists had reached the minimum number of states required to put the new Constitution into effect, but Virginia and New York still had not ratified. Without the support of these two large states, many feared the new government would not succeed.

Virginia and New York

George Washington and James Madison presented strong arguments for ratification to the Virginia convention. Patrick Henry, Richard Henry Lee, and other Antifederalists made several strong arguments against it. In the end, Madison's promise to add a bill of rights won the day for the Federalists.

In New York, two-thirds of the members elected to the state convention, including Governor George Clinton, were Antifederalists. The Federalists, led by Alexander Hamilton and John Jay, managed to delay the final vote until news arrived that New Hampshire and Virginia had both ratified the Constitution and that the new federal government was now in effect. If New York refused to ratify, it would be in a very awkward position. It would have to operate independently of all of the surrounding states. This argument convinced enough Antifederalists to change sides. The vote was very close, 30 to 27, but the Federalists won.

By July 1788, all the states except Rhode Island and North Carolina had ratified the Constitution. Because ratification by nine states was all that the Constitution required, the new government could be launched without them. In mid-September 1788, the Confederation Congress established a timetable for the election of the new government. It chose March 4, 1789, as the date for the first meeting of the new Congress.

The two states that had held out finally ratified the Constitution after the new government was in place. North Carolina waited until a bill of rights had actually been proposed, then voted to ratify the Constitution in November 1789. Rhode Island, still nervous about losing its independence, did not ratify the Constitution until May 1790, and even then the vote was very close—34 to 32.

The United States now had a new government, but no one knew if the new Constitution would work any better than the Articles of Confederation. With both anticipation and nervousness, the American people waited for their new government to begin. Many expressed great confidence, because George Washington had been chosen to become the first president under the new Constitution.

☑ Reading Check **Examining** Why was it important for Virginia and New York to ratify the Constitution, even after the required nine states had done so?

SECTION 3 ASSESSMENT

Checking for Understanding

1. **Define:** Federalist, Antifederalist.
2. **Identify:** John Hancock, Patrick Henry.
3. **List** the groups of people who opposed ratification of the Constitution.
4. **Explain** why the Federalists had an advantage over the Antifederalists.

Reviewing Themes

5. **Government and Democracy** Do you think it was important for all the states to ratify the Constitution? Why or why not?

Critical Thinking

6. **Analyzing** How did the Federalists attempt to assure ratification of the Constitution?
7. **Organizing** Use a graphic organizer similar to the one below to list the factors that worked against the Antifederalists.

Factors Working Against Antifederalists

Analyzing Visuals

8. **Studying Cartoons** Examine the cartoon on page 173. Why was New Hampshire's ratification of the Constitution important?

Writing About History

9. **Persuasive Writing** Take on the role of a Federalist or an Antifederalist at a state ratifying convention. Write a speech in which you try to convince your audience to either accept or reject the new Constitution.

CHAPTER 5 Creating a Constitution **175**

SECTION 3 ASSESSMENT ANSWERS

1. Terms are in blue.
2. John Hancock *(p. 173)*, Patrick Henry *(p. 173)*
3. Ratification was opposed by western farmers, people who wanted a weak national government, and people who wanted a bill of rights.
4. Federalists had a plan while the Antifederalists did not. The

Federalists were better organized and had the support of the newspapers.

5. Students' answers should include a logical explanation.
6. Federalists gave speeches, held debates, and wrote pamphlets and articles including *The Federalist.*
7. Factors working against

Antifederalists: negative campaign, not well organized, did not have support of newspapers, were not as wealthy as the Federalists.

8. New Hampshire was the ninth state to ratify, which meant the Constitution was adopted.
9. Students' speeches will vary but should be persuasive.

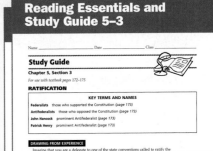

Reading Essentials and Study Guide 5–3

Study Guide
Chapter 5, Section 3
For use with textbook pages 172–175
RATIFICATION

KEY TERMS AND NAMES
Federalists those who supported the Constitution *(page 173)*
Antifederalists those who opposed the Constitution *(page 173)*
John Hancock prominent Antifederalist *(page 173)*
Patrick Henry prominent Antifederalist *(page 173)*

DRAWING FROM EXPERIENCE
Imagine that you are a delegate to one of the state conventions called to ratify the

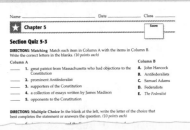

Section Quiz 5–3

★ **Chapter 5** Score

Section Quiz 5-3
DIRECTIONS: Matching Match each item in Column A with the items in Column B. Write the correct letters in the blanks. *(10 points each)*

Column A	Column B
___ 1. great patriot from Massachusetts who had objections to the Constitution	A. John Hancock
___ 2. prominent Antifederalist	B. Antifederalists
___ 3. supporters of the Constitution	C. Samuel Adams
___ 4. a collection of essays written by James Madison	D. Federalists
___ 5. opponents of the Constitution	E. *The Federalist*

DIRECTIONS: Multiple Choice In the blank at the left, write the letter of the choice that best completes the statement or answers the question. *(10 points each)*

☑ Reading Check

Answer: Without the support of these two large, influential states, many feared that the new government would not succeed.

Reteach
Have students choose sides and debate the issue of ratification.

Enrich
Have students read one of the essays from *The Federalist*. Ask them to write a short report summarizing the essay and indicating to which section of the Constitution it is related.

4 CLOSE

Ask students to speculate why a Bill of Rights was so important to many of the state conventions.

Reviewing Key Terms
Students' answers will vary. The pages where the words appear in the text are shown in parentheses.

1. **duty** (p. 159)
2. **recession** (p. 160)
3. **popular sovereignty** (p. 168)
4. **federalism** (p. 168)
5. **separation of powers** (p. 168)
6. **legislative branch** (p. 168)
7. **executive branch** (p. 168)
8. **judicial branch** (p. 168)
9. **checks and balances** (p. 169)
10. **veto** (p. 169)
11. **impeach** (p. 169)
12. **amendment** (p. 169)
13. **Federalist** (p. 173)
14. **Antifederalist** (p. 173)

Reviewing Key Facts
15. Northwest Ordinance (p. 159), Shays's Rebellion (p. 161), Three-Fifths Compromise (p. 167), John Hancock (p. 173), Patrick Henry (p. 173)

16. Shays's Rebellion focused attention on the weakness of the states in solving economic problems.

17. The separation of powers was achieved by creating three branches of government: legislative, executive, and judicial.

18. Landowners and merchants supported the Constitution because it gave the federal government the power to regulate trade.

19. The collection of 85 essays summarized the arguments for ratification of the Constitution.

Reviewing Key Terms
On a sheet of paper, use each of these terms in a sentence.

1. duty
2. recession
3. popular sovereignty
4. federalism
5. separation of powers
6. legislative branch
7. executive branch
8. judicial branch
9. checks and balances
10. veto
11. impeach
12. amendment
13. Federalist
14. Antifederalist

Reviewing Key Facts

15. **Identify:** Northwest Ordinance, Shays's Rebellion, Three-Fifths Compromise, John Hancock, Patrick Henry.

16. How did Shays's Rebellion indicate the need for a stronger national government?

17. How did the Founders provide for a separation of powers in the federal government?

18. Why did large landowners and merchants support the Constitution?

19. What was the purpose of *The Federalist*?

Critical Thinking

20. **Analyzing Themes: Government and Democracy** What do you think was the most serious flaw of the Articles of Confederation? Why do you think so?

21. **Organizing** Use a graphic organizer similar to the one below to indicate what details the Founders included in the Constitution to provide for a limited government.

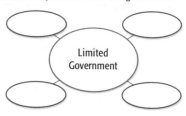

Limited Government

22. **Interpreting Primary Sources** In his 1789 textbook *The American Geography*, Reverend Jedidiah Morse discusses the defects of the Articles of Confederation. Read the excerpt and answer the questions that follow.

Chapter Summary

Problem	Solution
The newly independent colonies needed a central government.	The Articles of Confederation were adopted as the country's first constitution.
The weak central government created by the Articles led to diplomatic problems with other nations. The states began to act as independent countries to protect their trade rights.	Delegates at the Constitutional Convention adopted the Virginia Plan, which proposed the creation of a new federal government.
Opponents of the proposed new federal government feared that it would become too powerful.	The Constitution divided power between the federal government and the state governments and established three branches of power in the federal government.
Constitutional delegates feared that one branch of the federal government would become too powerful.	The Constitution gave each branch of the federal government the ability to limit the power of the other branches.
Delegates realized that the Constitution might need to be changed over time.	A system for making amendments was added, and the Constitution was ratified.

Critical Thinking
20. Students' answers will vary. Answers should focus on one of the actual flaws such as no power to impose taxes, no power to regulate trade, and no power to force states to abide by the peace treaty.

21. limited government: separation of powers, checks and balances, veto, and impeachment

22. **a.** They had no power to compel obedience. **b.** They were effective during the Revolution when states had a common goal.

Practicing Skills
23. **a.** New Jersey Plan; **b.** It gave Congress the power to raise taxes and regulate trade.

❝[The Articles of Confederation] were framed during the rage of war, when a principle of common safety supplied the place of a coercive power in government. . . .

When resolutions were passed in Congress, there was no power to compel obedience. . . . Had one state been invaded by its neighbour, the union was not constitutionally bound to assist in repelling the invasion. . . .❞

—quoted in *Readings in American History*

a. What defects in the Articles does Morse see?

b. Why does Morse think the Articles were effective during the American Revolution but not afterward?

Practicing Skills

23. **Making Comparisons** Reread the passage about the Virginia and New Jersey Plans from Chapter 5, Section 2, on page 166. Then answer the following questions.
    a. Which plan gave more power to the states?
    b. What new power did the New Jersey plan grant to Congress?

Writing Activity

24. **Portfolio Writing** Take on the role of an American living during the Constitution's ratification. Write a letter to a friend in Britain describing the form of the new government. Explain why you support or oppose ratification and what you think life will be like under the new government.

Chapter Activity

25. **Technology Activity: Sending an E-Mail** Use the Internet to find the latest bills that are pending in Congress. Choose one of these bills or choose an issue that is important to you and your community. Send an e-mail to your senator or representative, persuading him or her how to vote on the issue. Provide reasons for your position.

Geography and History

26. The map on this page shows the western land claims of the original states. Study the map and answer these questions.
    a. **Interpreting Maps** Which state had the largest land claims in the West?

 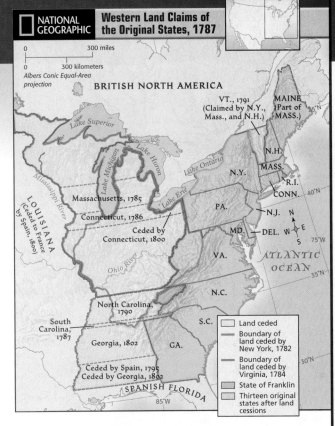

Western Land Claims of the Original States, 1787

b. **Applying Geography Skills** Why do you think the states eventually agreed to surrender their land claims to the Confederation Congress?

Standardized Test Practice

Directions: Choose the best answer to the following question.

Which of the following is an *opinion* about the Constitution?

F By 1790 all states had ratified the Constitution.

G A major concern in writing the Constitution was how many representatives each state would have.

H Under the Constitution, the federal government could raise money to operate the government.

J Because of the Constitution, the United States has a better democracy than other countries.

Test-Taking Tip: An *opinion* is not a proven fact (such as answer F). Opinions often contain subjective words, like *best.*

HISTORY Online

Have students visit the Web site at tav.glencoe.com to review Chapter 5 and take the Self-Check Quiz.

Geography and History

26. **a.** Virginia; **b.** possible answers: to support the Confederation Congress or because they thought governing the land would be too difficult

The Princeton Review

Standardized Test Practice

Answer: J

Test-Taking Tip: Since the question asks for an opinion, encourage students to look for subjective words such as better, best, worse, worst. Only J uses a subjective expression, "a better democracy."

Bonus Question ?

Ask: How did Robert Morris assist the Continental Congress? *(He personally pledged large amounts of money for the war effort, backing the worthless paper currency the Continental Congress had issued. He set up an efficient method of buying rations and uniforms, arranged for foreign loans, and convinced the Congress to create the Bank of North America to finance the military.)*

Writing Activity

24. Students' letters will vary. Students should take on a specific role such as landowner or western farmer when writing their letters. Letters should accurately reflect the sentiments that were prevalent at the time of ratification.

Chapter Activity

25. Remind students to use proper netiquette in their contacts with elected officials. Information about bills pending in Congress and contact information for representatives and senators can be found at www.house.gov and www.senate.gov.

177

The Constitution Handbook

Beginning the Handbook

Inform students that when members of the first Congress gathered in New York in 1789, a bill of rights had not been added to the Constitution. These amendments were important because a number of states made their ratification conditional on such an addition. Other states had threatened to revoke their ratification if the bill of rights proved too radical. Have students speculate why Congress moved so quickly to inaugurate the new government. *(The country was eager for a new government. Congress perhaps felt that if the process of government had begun, it would be harder for wavering states to leave the Union.)*

FYI

Constitutions vary from country to country. For example, Article XVIII of Japan's constitution guarantees academic freedom. During the era of communism, the constitution of Communist countries emphasized economic and social rights such as the right to work, the right to choose an occupation, and the right to leisure.

EXTENDING THE CONTENT

Constitutions The United States has the oldest written national constitution still in effect. Compared to other written constitutions, it might be characterized as succinct. The average federal constitution contains about 26,500 words, whereas the United States Constitution with its 27 amendments has fewer than 7,500 words.

Guide to Reading

Main Idea
The Constitution was designed to provide the United States with a stronger national government while remaining flexible enough to meet the changing circumstances of the growing nation.

Key Terms and Names
popular sovereignty, federalism, enumerated powers, reserved powers, concurrent powers, override, appropriate, impeach, constituent, bill, standing committee, select committee, joint committee, conference committee, cabinet, judicial review, due process

Reading Strategy
Taking Notes As you read about the Constitution, use the major headings of the handbook to fill in an outline similar to the one below.

I. Major Principles
   A.
   B.
   C.
   D.
   E.
   F.
   G.
II.

Reading Objectives:
- **Identify** the branches of the federal government and their separate areas of power.
- **Understand** and describe the responsibilities that American citizens share.

Section Theme
Civic Rights and Responsibilities The success of the American system of government depends on citizens being informed. An understanding of the Constitution is key to understanding how the American government operates.

Preview of Events

♦1786   ♦1787   ♦1788   ♦1789   ♦1790   ♦1791   ♦1792

September 1786
Annapolis Convention begins

May 1787
Constitutional Convention begins

September 1787
Constitution signed and Convention adjourns

June 1788
New Hampshire ratifies Constitution, making it the new form of government

December 1791
The Bill of Rights becomes part of the Constitution

Daniel Webster and George Bush

★ *An American Story* ★

In 1987 the United States began a four-year celebration commemorating the Constitution's bicentennial. In a series of ceremonies that lasted to 1991, the nation reflected on the writing and ratifying of the document providing the country's foundation of government. Proclaiming the creation of Citizenship Day and Constitution Week in August 1990, President George Bush quoted the words of Daniel Webster:

❝'We may be tossed upon an ocean where we can see no land—nor, perhaps, the sun or stars. But there is a chart and a compass for us to study, to consult, and to obey. That chart is the Constitution.'❞

Serving as the framework of national government and the source of American citizens' basic rights, the Constitution is the United States's most important document. As President Bush reminded the nation in his proclamation: "[I]f we are to continue to enjoy the blessings of freedom and self-government, each of us must understand our rights and responsibilities as citizens."

—adapted from *Proclamation of Citizenship Day* and *Constitution Week*

The Constitution Handbook **179**

BELLRINGER
Motivational Activity

Provide pairs of students with board games, such as chess or checkers. Have pairs play the game, but tell them there are no rules. They are to make up their own rules as they go along. After a few minutes, initiate a discussion about the needs for rules and organization. Conclude by asking students to consider why the Constitution might be regarded as rule book for government.

Guide to Reading

Answers to Graphic:
I. Major Principles
   A. Popular Sovereignty
   B. Republicanism
   C. Limited Government
   D. Federalism
Students should complete the outline by including all heads in the section.

Preteaching Vocabulary
Ask students to write definitions of each of the entries listed in the Key Terms. Have them check their definitions as they read the section.

FYI

Not many governments have had the stability that the United States Constitution has provided. France, for example, has had 16 constitutions since 1789. Peru, independent since 1821, has had 11.

EXTENDING THE CONTENT

Historic Building The red brick building in which the Framers met to draw up the Constitution is now known as Independence Hall. Several important events took place there, including the meetings of the First and Second Continental Congresses and Jefferson's reading of the Declaration of Independence.

2 TEACH

Discussing Precedents Have groups of students recall aspects of self-government with which American colonists had experimented. (*Answers include the Mayflower Compact, the Articles of Confederation, and organizations such as the Virginia House of Burgesses and the Continental Congress.*) Explain that this handbook will help them see how those experiments helped shape the American system of government **L1** **ELL**

Picturing **History**

Answer: the authority of the people
Ask: How is the concept of limited government a reflection of popular sovereignty? *(The central government is not all powerful, it is limited. The people give consent to be governed.)*

FYI

The power to award titles of nobility is denied to Congress. This clause was written into the Constitution to prevent the development of a noble class in the United States.

Major Principles

The principles outlined in the Constitution were the Framers' solution to the complex problems of a representative government. The Constitution rests on seven major principles of government: (1) popular sovereignty, (2) republicanism, (3) limited government, (4) federalism, (5) separation of powers, (6) checks and balances, and (7) individual rights.

Popular Sovereignty The opening words of the Constitution, "We the people," reinforce the idea of popular sovereignty, or "authority of the people." In the Constitution, the people consent to be governed and specify the powers and rules by which they shall be governed.

The Articles of Confederation form of government had few powers, and it was unable to cope with the many challenges facing the nation. The new constitutional government had greater powers and influence, but it also had specific limitations. A system of interlocking responsibilities kept any one branch of government from becoming too powerful.

Republicanism Voters hold sovereign power in a republican system. The people elect representatives and give them the responsibility to make laws and conduct government. For most Americans today, the terms *republic* and *representative democracy* mean the same thing: a system of limited government where the people are the final source of authority.

Limited Government Although the Framers agreed that the nation needed a stronger central authority, they feared misuse of power. They wanted to prevent the government from using its power to give one group special advantages or to deprive another group of its rights. By creating a limited government, they restricted the government's authority to specific powers granted by the people.

The Right to Vote The voting booth is a symbol of one of the Constitution's major principles—popular sovereignty. What does popular sovereignty mean?

The members of the Constitutional Convention wished to list the range of powers granted to the new government as specifically as possible. Their decision to write down the governmental outline also served as a clear record of what they intended. Article I of the Constitution states the powers that the government has and does not have. Other limits on government appear in the Bill of Rights, which guarantees certain rights and liberties to the people.

Federalism In establishing a strong central government, the Framers did not deprive states of all authority. The states would give up some powers to the national government while retaining others. States could no longer print their own money or tax items imported from other states, but mostly, each state continued to govern itself much as it had in the past.

This principle of shared power is federalism. Our federal government allows the people of each state to deal with their needs in their own way. At the same time, it lets the states act together to deal with matters that affect all Americans.

The Constitution defines three types of government powers. Certain powers belong only to the

The Federal System

Delegated Powers	Concurrent Powers	Reserved Powers
Powers *delegated* to national government; for example, declaring war	Powers *concurrent* to national and state governments; for example, the power to tax	Powers *reserved* for state governments; for example, setting up educational system

---

COOPERATIVE LEARNING ACTIVITY

Exploring Key Concepts Organize the class into groups of four students, one group for each of the Constitution's underlying principles: popular sovereignty, limited government, federalism, and separation of powers. Have each group define the principle and locate at least one part of the Constitution that addresses that principle. Allow time for presentations of each group's work. Follow up with a class vote about which principle they think affects their lives the most today.

Use the rubric for a cooperative group management plan on pages 81–82 in the *Performance Assessment Activities and Rubrics.*

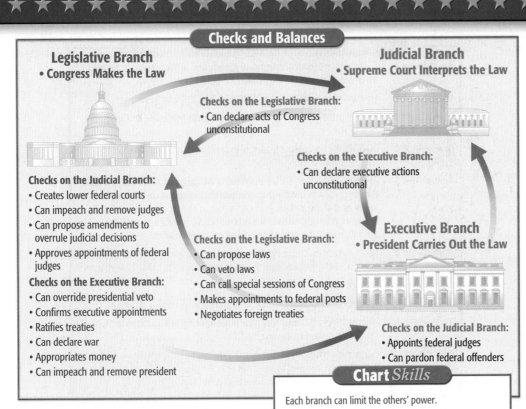

Checks and Balances

Legislative Branch
• Congress Makes the Law

Judicial Branch
• Supreme Court Interprets the Law

Checks on the Legislative Branch:
• Can declare acts of Congress unconstitutional

Checks on the Executive Branch:
• Can declare executive actions unconstitutional

Checks on the Judicial Branch:
• Creates lower federal courts
• Can impeach and remove judges
• Can propose amendments to overrule judicial decisions
• Approves appointments of federal judges

Checks on the Executive Branch:
• Can override presidential veto
• Confirms executive appointments
• Ratifies treaties
• Can declare war
• Appropriates money
• Can impeach and remove president

Checks on the Legislative Branch:
• Can propose laws
• Can veto laws
• Can call special sessions of Congress
• Makes appointments to federal posts
• Negotiates foreign treaties

Executive Branch
• President Carries Out the Law

Checks on the Judicial Branch:
• Appoints federal judges
• Can pardon federal offenders

Chart *Skills*

Each branch can limit the others' power.

Analyzing Information How can the president help control the judiciary?

---

federal government. These enumerated powers include the power to coin money, regulate interstate and foreign trade, maintain the armed forces, and create federal courts (Article I, Section 8).

The second kind of powers are those retained by the states, known as reserved powers, including the power to establish schools, pass marriage and divorce laws, and regulate trade within a state. Although specific reserved powers are not listed in the Constitution, the Tenth Amendment says that all powers not specifically granted to the federal government "are reserved to the States."

The third set of powers defined by the Constitution are concurrent powers—powers the state and federal governments share. They include the right to raise taxes, borrow money, provide for public welfare, and administer criminal justice.

Conflicts between state law and federal law must be settled in a federal court. The Constitution declares that it is "the supreme Law of the Land."

Separation of Powers To prevent any single group or institution in government from gaining too much authority, the Framers divided the federal government into three branches: legislative, executive, and judicial. Each branch has its own functions and powers. The legislative branch, Congress, makes the laws. The executive branch, headed by the president, carries out the laws. The judicial branch, consisting of the Supreme Court and other federal courts, interprets and applies the laws.

In addition to giving separate responsibility to separate branches, the membership of each branch is chosen in different ways. The president nominates federal judges and the Senate confirms the appointments. People vote for members of Congress. Voters cast ballots for president, but the method of election is indirect. On Election Day the votes in each state are counted. Whatever candidate receives a majority receives that state's electoral votes, which total the number of senators and representatives the state has in Congress. Electors from all states meet in December after the November election to formally elect a president. A candidate must receive at least 270 of 538 electoral votes to win.

Checks and Balances The Framers also established a system of checks and balances in which each branch of government can check, or limit, the

The Constitution Handbook **181**

you don't say...

Constitution A *filibuster* is an attempt to delay for as long as possible or stop altogether the passage of a bill through the Senate. A filibuster exploits the long-held tradition in the Senate of not limiting debate. A senator can hold the floor as long as he or she wants to, as long as he or she remains talking. The Senate can halt a filibuster by passing a vote of cloture to force a vote.

The Bill of Rights: The First Ten Amendments

Amendment 1	Guarantees freedom of religion, of speech, and of the press, and the right to assemble peaceably and to petition the government
Amendment 2	Guarantees the right to organize state militias and bear arms
Amendment 3	Prohibits quartering soldiers in private homes in peacetime and limits it in time of war
Amendment 4	Prohibits the unreasonable search and seizure of persons and property without a valid warrant
Amendment 5	Requires a grand jury for serious criminal charges; prohibits military trials of civilians; prohibits double jeopardy; prohibits forcing accused persons to testify against themselves; guarantees that no one may be deprived of life, liberty, or property, without due process of law; prohibits government taking private property for public use without just compensation
Amendment 6	Guarantees suspects the right to a speedy trial by jury in criminal cases; to know all charges; to question and obtain witnesses; and to have counsel
Amendment 7	Guarantees a jury trial in most civil cases
Amendment 8	Prohibits excessive bail and fines and cruel and unusual punishment
Amendment 9	Assures people that they may have other basic rights in addition to those mentioned in the Constitution
Amendment 10	Guarantees that rights not given to the federal government, nor denied to the states, are reserved to the states or to the people

power of the other branches. This system helps balance the power of the three branches. For example, imagine that Congress passes a law. Then the president can reject the law by vetoing it. However, Congress can override, or reverse, the president's veto if two-thirds of the members of both the Senate and the House of Representatives vote again to approve the law.

Individual Rights The Bill of Rights became part of the Constitution in 1791. These first 10 amendments protect basic liberties and rights that some Americans may take for granted—including freedom of speech, freedom of the press, freedom of assembly, freedom of religion, and the right to a trial by jury.

The 17 amendments that follow the Bill of Rights expand the rights of Americans and adjust certain provisions of the Constitution. Included among them are amendments that abolish slavery, define citizenship, guarantee voting rights, authorize an income tax, and set a two-term limit on the presidency.

The Legislative Branch

The legislative branch includes the two houses of Congress: the House of Representatives and the Senate. Congress's two primary roles are to make the nation's laws and to control federal spending.

The Role of Congress The government cannot spend any money unless Congress appropriates, or sets aside, funds. All tax and spending bills must originate in the House of Representatives and gain approval in both the House and the Senate before moving on to the president for signature.

Congress also monitors the executive branch and investigates possible abuses of power. The House of Representatives can impeach, or bring formal charges against, any federal official it suspects of wrongdoing or misconduct. If an official is impeached, the Senate acts as a court and tries the accused official. Officials who are found guilty may be removed from office.

182 The Constitution Handbook

INTERDISCIPLINARY CONNECTIONS ACTIVITY

Civics Federalism can be graphically illustrated in many ways. After reading the section on federalism, ask students to graphically represent federalism. Encourage them to reflect shared powers as well as independent powers in their graphics. **L1**

The Senate also holds certain special powers. Only the Senate can ratify treaties made by the president and confirm presidential appointments of federal officials such as department heads, ambassadors, and federal judges.

All members of Congress have the responsibility of representing their constituents, the people of their home states and districts. As a constituent, you can expect your senators and representative to promote national and state interests.

Congress at Work Thousands of bills—proposed laws—are introduced in Congress every year. Because individual members of Congress cannot possibly study all these bills carefully, both houses use committees of selected members to evaluate proposed legislation.

Standing committees are permanent committees in both the House and the Senate that specialize in a particular topic, such as agriculture, commerce, or veterans' affairs. These committees are usually divided into subcommittees that focus on a particular aspect of an issue.

The House and the Senate sometimes form temporary select committees to deal with issues requiring special attention. These committees meet only until they complete their task.

Occasionally the House and the Senate form joint committees with members from both houses. These committees meet to consider specific issues, such as the system of federal taxation. One type of joint committee, a conference committee, has a special function. If the House and the Senate pass different versions of the same bill, a conference committee tries to work out a compromise bill acceptable to both houses.

Once a committee in either house of Congress approves a bill, it is sent to the full Senate or House for debate. After debate the bill may be passed, rejected, or returned to the committee for further changes.

When both houses pass a bill, it goes to the president. If the president approves the bill and signs it, the bill becomes law. If the president vetoes the bill, it does not become law unless Congress overrides the veto.

The Executive Branch

The executive branch of government includes the president, the vice president, and various executive offices, departments, and agencies. The executive branch carries out the laws that Congress passes. The president plays a number of different roles in government, each of which has specific powers and responsibilities. These roles include the nation's

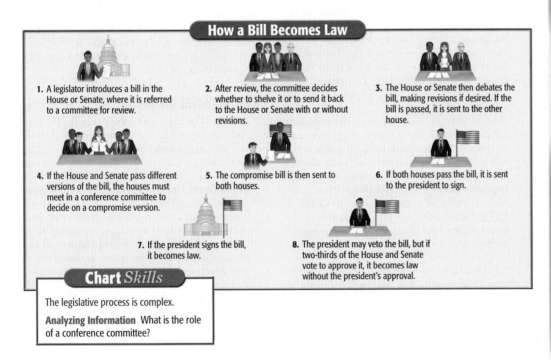

How a Bill Becomes Law

1. A legislator introduces a bill in the House or Senate, where it is referred to a committee for review.

2. After review, the committee decides whether to shelve it or to send it back to the House or Senate with or without revisions.

3. The House or Senate then debates the bill, making revisions if desired. If the bill is passed, it is sent to the other house.

4. If the House and Senate pass different versions of the bill, the houses must meet in a conference committee to decide on a compromise version.

5. The compromise bill is then sent to both houses.

6. If both houses pass the bill, it is sent to the president to sign.

7. If the president signs the bill, it becomes law.

8. The president may veto the bill, but if two-thirds of the House and Senate vote to approve it, it becomes law without the president's approval.

Chart *Skills*

The legislative process is complex.

Analyzing Information What is the role of a conference committee?

The Constitution Handbook **183**

CRITICAL THINKING ACTIVITY

Analyzing More than 9,000 amendments to the Constitution have been proposed, but only 27 have become part of the Constitution. Using this numerical information, ask students to calculate the odds of a proposed amendment being approved. Ask them to discuss the wisdom of making the amendment process so difficult. **L3**

★ ★

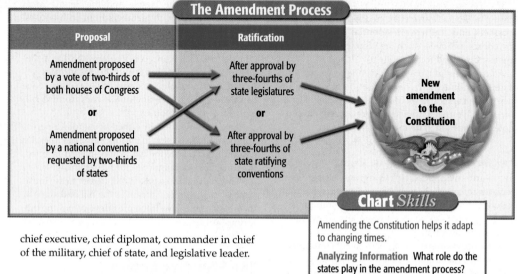

The Amendment Process

Proposal	Ratification	
Amendment proposed by a vote of two-thirds of both houses of Congress **or** Amendment proposed by a national convention requested by two-thirds of states	After approval by three-fourths of state legislatures **or** After approval by three-fourths of state ratifying conventions	New amendment to the Constitution

Chart Skills

Amending the Constitution helps it adapt to changing times.

Analyzing Information What role do the states play in the amendment process?

chief executive, chief diplomat, commander in chief of the military, chief of state, and legislative leader.

The President's Roles

- **Chief Executive and Chief Diplomat** As chief executive, the president is responsible for carrying out the nation's laws. As chief diplomat, the president directs foreign policy, appoints ambassadors, and negotiates treaties with other nations.
- **Commander in Chief** As commander in chief of the armed forces, the president can use the military to intervene or offer assistance in crises at home and around the world. The president cannot declare war; only Congress holds this power. The president can send troops to other parts of the world for up to 60 days but must notify Congress when doing so. The troops may remain longer only if Congress gives its approval or declares war.
- **Chief of State** As chief of state, the president serves a symbolic role as the representative of all Americans. The president fulfills this role when receiving foreign ambassadors or heads of state, visiting foreign nations, or honoring Americans.
- **Legislative Leader** The president serves as a legislative leader by proposing laws to Congress and working to see that they are passed. In the annual State of the Union address, the president presents goals for legislation.

The Executive Branch at Work Many executive offices, departments, and independent agencies help the president carry out and enforce the nation's laws. The Executive Office of the President (EOP) is made up of individuals and agencies that directly assist the president. Presidents rely heavily

on the EOP for advice and for gathering information needed for decision making.

The executive branch also includes 14 executive departments, each responsible for a different area of government. For example, the Department of State plans and carries out foreign policy, and the Department of the Interior manages and protects the nation's public lands and natural resources. The heads of these departments, who have the title of secretary, are members of the president's cabinet. This group helps the president make decisions and set government policy.

The Judicial Branch

Article III of the Constitution calls for the creation of a Supreme Court and "such inferior [lower] courts as Congress may from time to time ordain and establish." Today the judicial branch consists of three main categories of courts, including:

- **District Courts** United States district courts are the lowest level of the federal court system. These courts consider criminal and civil cases that come under federal authority, including such criminal offenses as kidnapping and federal tax evasion. Civil cases cover claims against the federal government and cases involving constitutional rights, such as free speech. There are 91 district courts, with at least one in every state.
- **Appellate Courts** The appellate courts, or appeals courts, consider district court decisions in which the losing side has asked for a review of the

---

EXTENDING THE CONTENT

Ambassadors As part of the duties as chief diplomat for the United States, the president appoints ambassadors who carry the title *Ambassador Extraordinary and Plenipotentiary* to foreign posts. As official representatives of the United States, ambassadors protect the political, economic, and social interests of the United States government.

verdict. If an appeals court disagrees with the lower court's decision, it can either overturn the verdict or order a retrial. There are 14 appeals courts in the United States, one for each of the 12 federal districts, a military appeals court, and an appellate court for the federal circuit.

- **The Supreme Court** The Supreme Court, the final authority in the federal court system, consists of a chief justice and eight associate justices. Most of the Supreme Court's cases come from appeals of lower court decisions. Only cases involving foreign ambassadors or disputes between states can begin in the Supreme Court.

Supreme Court Independence The Supreme Court is the least public of the government's branches. The president appoints the Court's justices for life, and the Senate confirms the appointments. The public has no input. The Framers hoped that because judges were appointed rather than elected, they would be free to evaluate the law with no consideration of pleasing a group of electors.

Judicial Review The role of the judicial branch is not described in very much detail in the Constitution, but the role of the courts has grown as powers implied in the Constitution have been put into practice. In 1803 Chief Justice John Marshall expanded the powers of the Supreme Court by striking down an act of Congress in the case of *Marbury v. Madison*. Although not mentioned in the Constitution, judicial review has become a major power of the judicial branch. Judicial review gives the Supreme Court the ultimate authority to interpret the meaning of constitutional provisions and explain how the words of this 200-year-old document apply to our modern nation. 📖 *(See page 1081 for more information on Marbury v. Madison.)*

The Rights of American Citizens

The rights of Americans fall into three broad categories: the right to be protected from unfair actions of the government, to receive equal treatment under the law, and to retain basic freedoms.

Protection from Unfair Actions Parts of the Constitution and the Bill of Rights protect all Americans from unfair treatment by the government or the law. Among these rights are the right to a lawyer when accused of a crime and the right to trial by jury when charged with a crime. In addition, the Fourth Amendment protects us from unreasonable searches and seizures. This provision requires police to have a court order before searching a person's home for criminal evidence. To obtain this, the police must have a very strong reason to suspect the person of committing a crime.

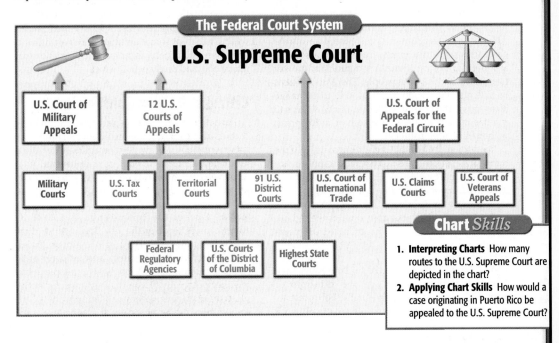

The Federal Court System

U.S. Supreme Court

- U.S. Court of Military Appeals
- 12 U.S. Courts of Appeals
- U.S. Court of Appeals for the Federal Circuit

- Military Courts
- U.S. Tax Courts
- Territorial Courts
- 91 U.S. District Courts
- U.S. Court of International Trade
- U.S. Claims Courts
- U.S. Court of Veterans Appeals

- Federal Regulatory Agencies
- U.S. Courts of the District of Columbia
- Highest State Courts

Chart *Skills*

1. **Interpreting Charts** How many routes to the U.S. Supreme Court are depicted in the chart?
2. **Applying Chart Skills** How would a case originating in Puerto Rico be appealed to the U.S. Supreme Court?

CRITICAL THINKING ACTIVITY

Analyzing Ask students to create a chart with the following presidents in the headings: Franklin D. Roosevelt, Richard M. Nixon, Harry S Truman, Ulysses S. Grant, and Ronald Reagan. Have students research the following information for each president: the total number of vetoes, the number of overturned vetoes, and the number of "pocket" vetoes. Then have students compare each president's acts and offer suggestions for them. **L2**

Discussing the Limits of Rights
The First Amendment guarantees an individual's right to free speech. The First Amendment does not, however, give individuals the right to shout "fire" in a crowded theater. Have students discuss the government's need to balance an individual's constitutional rights with society's need for order and safety. **L2**

The Eighteenth Amendment, proposed in 1919, prohibited the "manufacture, sale, or transportation of intoxicating liquors," and began what is commonly known as the era of Prohibition. The Twenty-first Amendment, ratified in 1933, repealed the Eighteenth Amendment. This is the only constitutional amendment that has been repealed.

Democracy in Action Town meetings in New England give local residents the chance to express their views. It is a responsibility of American citizens to remain informed about the actions of their local, state, and national government.

Equal Treatment All Americans, regardless of race, religion, or political beliefs, have the right to be treated the same under the law. The Fifth Amendment states that no person shall "be deprived of life, liberty, or property, without due process of law." Due process means that the government must follow procedures established by law and guaranteed by the Constitution, treating all people equally. The Fourteenth Amendment requires every state to grant its citizens "equal protection of the laws."

Basic Freedoms The basic freedoms involve the fundamental liberties outlined in the First Amendment—freedom of speech, freedom of religion, freedom of the press, freedom of assembly, and the right to petition. In a democracy, power rests in the hands of the people. Therefore, citizens in a democratic society must be able to exchange ideas freely. The First Amendment allows citizens to criticize the government, in speech or in the press, without fear of punishment.

In addition, the Ninth Amendment states that the rights of Americans are not limited to those mentioned in the Constitution. This has allowed basic freedoms to expand over the years through the passage of other amendments and laws. The Twenty-sixth Amendment, for example, extends the right to vote to American citizens who are at least 18 years of age.

Limits on Rights The rights of Americans have certain limitations, based on the principle of respecting everyone's rights equally. For example, many cities and towns require groups to obtain a permit to march on city streets. While such a law does limit free speech, it also protects the community by allowing the police to make provisions so that the march will not disturb the lives of other people. However, a law banning all marches would be unreasonable and would violate the First Amendment rights of free speech and assembly. Similarly, a law preventing only certain groups from marching would be unfair because it would not apply equally to everyone.

In this and other cases, the government balances an individual's rights, the rights of others, and the community's health and safety. Most Americans are willing to accept some limitations on their rights to gain these protections as long as the restrictions are reasonable and apply equally to all.

Citizens' Responsibilities

Participation in a democratic society involves certain duties and responsibilities. Duties are actions required by law. Responsibilities are voluntary actions. Fulfilling both your duties and your responsibilities helps ensure good government and protects your rights.

Duties One of the fundamental duties of all Americans is to obey the law. Laws serve three important functions. They help maintain order; they protect the health, safety, and property of all citizens; and they make it possible for people to live together peacefully. If you disobey laws, for example, you endanger others and interfere with the smooth functioning of society. If you believe a law

COOPERATIVE LEARNING ACTIVITY

Debating Rights Organize the class into five groups, one for each of the five rights incorporated in the First Amendment. Tell students they will have 10 minutes to prepare an outline about the right assigned to their group. Also tell them they will have five minutes to persuade the class that the right they represent is more important than the other four. Tell them to include as many factual details and real-life scenarios as possible. After each group has presented, have the class vote on which right they think is most important.

Use the rubric for a cooperative group management plan on pages 81–82 in the **Performance Assessment Activities and Rubrics.**

needs to be changed, you can work through your electoral representatives to improve it.

Americans also have a duty to pay taxes. The government uses tax money to defend the nation, provide health insurance for people over 65, and build roads and bridges. Americans benefit from services provided by the government.

Another duty of citizens is to defend the nation. All males aged 18 and older must register with the government in case the nation needs to call on them for military service. Military service is not automatic, but a war could make it necessary.

The Constitution guarantees all Americans the right to a trial by a jury of their equals. For this reason, you should be prepared for jury duty when you become eligible at the age of 18. Having a large group of jurors on hand is necessary to guarantee the right to a fair and speedy trial. You also have a duty to serve as a trial witness if called to do so.

Most states require you to attend school until a certain age. School is where you gain the knowledge and skills needed to be a good citizen. In school you learn to think more clearly, to express your opinions more accurately, and to analyze the statements and ideas of others. These skills will help you make informed choices when you vote.

Responsibilities The responsibilities of citizens are not as clear-cut as their duties. Responsibilities are as important as duties, however, because they help maintain the quality of government and society.

One important responsibility is to become well informed. You need to know what is happening in your community, your state, your country, and the world. Knowing what your government representatives are doing and expressing your feelings about their actions can help keep the government responsive to the wishes of the people.

You also need to be informed about your rights and to exercise them when necessary. Knowing your rights helps preserve them. Other responsibilities include respecting diversity, accepting responsibility for your actions, and supporting your family.

Vote, Vote, Vote! Perhaps your most important responsibility as an American citizen will be to vote when you reach the age of 18. Voting allows you to participate in government and guide its direction. When you vote for people to represent you in government, you will be exercising your right of self-government. If you disapprove of the job your representatives are doing, it will be your responsibility to help elect other people in the next election. You can also let your representatives know how you feel about issues through letters, telephone calls, and petitions and by taking part in public meetings or political rallies.

To enjoy your rights to the fullest, you must be prepared to respect the rights of others. Respecting the rights of others also means respecting the rights of people with whom you disagree. Respecting and accepting others regardless of race, religion, beliefs, or other differences is essential in a democracy.

Constitution Handbook Assessment

★ ★ ★ ★ ★ ★ ★   ★ ★ ★ ★ ★ ★ ★

Checking for Understanding

1. **Define:** popular sovereignty, federalism, enumerated powers, reserved powers, concurrent powers, override, appropriate, impeach, constituent, bill, standing committee, select committee, joint committee, conference committee, cabinet, judicial review, due process.

2. **Summarize** the provisions of the First Amendment.

Reviewing Themes

3. **Civic Rights and Responsibilities** What is the difference between a duty and a responsibility?

Critical Thinking

4. **Comparing** Some people want a limit on the number of terms one can serve in the legislature. What are some of the advantages of the present system, which does not limit the number of terms? What are some of the disadvantages? How would one make term limits an official part of the Constitution?

5. **Organizing** Use a graphic organizer like the one below to list reasons why the Framers of the Constitution provided for separation of powers.

→ Separation of Powers

Analyzing Visuals

6. **Analyzing Photographs** Study the photograph on page 122. How does the democratic voting process reflect our national identity?

Writing About History

7. **History and Government** Working with a partner, choose one of the constitutional rights listed below. Write a report that traces the right's historical development, from the time the Constitution was ratified to the present.
   suffrage
   freedom of speech
   freedom of religion
   equal protection of law

3 ASSESS

Assign the Constitution Handbook Assessment as homework or as an in-class activity.

4 CLOSE

Have students offer one-sentence definitions of the terms *legislative, executive, judicial, checks and balances,* and *amendments.*

Constitution Handbook   ASSESSMENT ANSWERS ☆ ☆ ☆ ☆ ☆ ☆

1. Terms are in blue.
2. freedom of speech, religion, and the press; right of assembly; and the right to petition
3. Duties are actions required by law; responsibilities are voluntary.
4. advantages: system functions more smoothly and efficiently with more experienced legislators; disadvantages: cronyism, willingness to stick to status quo, fewer fresh ideas; through the amendment process
5. to prevent one branch of government from becoming too powerful; to provide a system for each branch of government to check and balance the others; to protect individual rights
6. Answers will vary but should note that the ability to vote is a right shared by all citizens.
7. Reports will vary but must include the historical development of the right.

United States Constitution

FOCUS

BELLRINGER
Motivational Activity

Ask students to read the Preamble to the Constitution. Have them identify which purpose of the Constitution is most important to them personally.

FYI

The members of the Committee of Style—William Samuel Johnson, Alexander Hamilton, Gouverneur Morris, James Madison, and Rufus King—wrote the final draft of the Constitution.

you don't say...

Constitution The word *constitution* has various definitions. It can refer to the system of laws and principles that defines the right to rule and distribute power, or it can refer to the document on which those laws and principles are actually written.

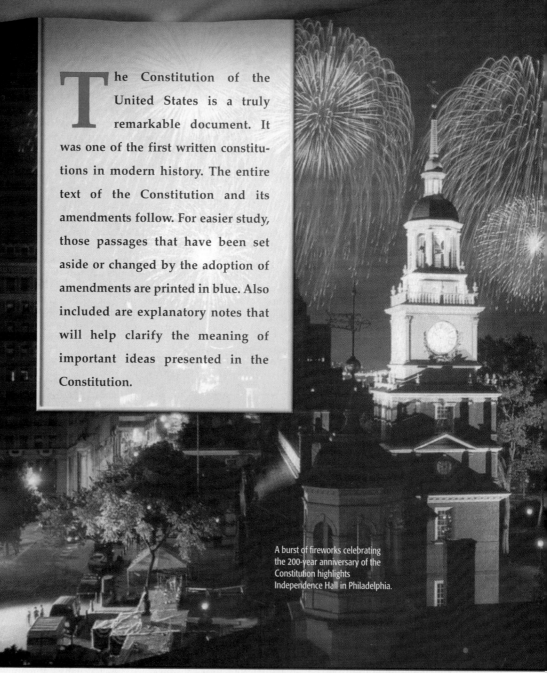

The Constitution of the United States

The Constitution of the United States is a truly remarkable document. It was one of the first written constitutions in modern history. The entire text of the Constitution and its amendments follow. For easier study, those passages that have been set aside or changed by the adoption of amendments are printed in blue. Also included are explanatory notes that will help clarify the meaning of important ideas presented in the Constitution.

A burst of fireworks celebrating the 200-year anniversary of the Constitution highlights Independence Hall in Philadelphia.

MEETING SPECIAL NEEDS

Verbal/Linguistic The Constitution, like the Declaration of Independence, is reproduced in its original language and contains a number of unfamiliar words. Point out to students that many of these words are defined in the margin notes. Suggest that students substitute the definitions for the unfamiliar words as they read through the document.

Refer to *Inclusion for the High School Social Studies Classroom Strategies and Activities* in the TCR.

[17.] To exercise exclusive Legislation in all Cases whatsoever, over such District (not exceeding ten Miles square) as may, by Cession of particular States, and the Acceptance of Congress, become the Seat of Government of the United States, and to exercise like Authority over all Places purchased by the Consent of the Legislature of the State in which the Same shall be, for the Erection of Forts, Magazines, Arsenals, dock-Yards, and other needful Buildings; And

[18.] To make all Laws which shall be necessary and proper for carrying into Execution the foregoing Powers, and all other Powers vested by this Constitution in the Government of the United States, or in any Department or Officer thereof.

Section 9

[1.] The Migration or Importation of such Persons as any of the States now existing shall think proper to admit, shall not be prohibited by the Congress prior to the Year one thousand eight hundred and eight, but a Tax or duty may be imposed on such Importation, not exceeding ten dollars for each Person.

[2.] The Privilege of the Writ of Habeas Corpus shall not be suspended, unless when in Cases of Rebellion or Invasion the public Safety may require it.

[3.] No Bill of Attainder or ex post facto Law shall be passed.

[4.] No Capitation, or other direct, Tax shall be laid, unless in Proportion to the Census or Enumeration herein before directed to be taken.

[5.] No Tax or Duty shall be laid on Articles exported from any State.

[6.] No Preference shall be given by any Regulation of Commerce or Revenue to the Ports of one State over those of another: nor shall Vessels bound to, or from, one State, be obliged to enter, clear, or pay Duties in another.

[7.] No Money shall be drawn from the Treasury, but in Consequence of Appropriations made by Law; and a regular Statement and Account of the Receipts and Expenditures of all public Money shall be published from time to time.

[8.] No Title of Nobility shall be granted by the United States:And no Person holding any Office of Profit or Trust under them, shall, without the Consent of the Congress, accept of any present, Emolument, Office, or Title, of any kind whatever, from any King, Prince, or foreign State.

Section 10

[1.] No State shall enter into any Treaty, Alliance, or Confederation; grant Letters of Marque and Reprisal; coin Money; emit Bills of Credit; make any Thing but gold and silver Coin a Tender in Payment of Debts; pass any Bill of Attainder, ex post facto Law, or Law impairing the Obligation of Contracts, or grant any Title of Nobility.

[2.] No State shall, without the Consent of the Congress, lay any Imposts or Duties on Imports or Exports, except

---

What It Means

Elastic Clause The final enumerated power is often called the "elastic clause." This clause gives Congress the right to make all laws "necessary and proper" to carry out the powers expressed in the other clauses of Article I. It is called the elastic clause because it lets Congress "stretch" its powers to meet situations the Founders could not have anticipated.

What does the phrase "necessary and proper" in the elastic clause mean? It was a subject of dispute from the beginning. The issue was whether a strict or a broad interpretation of the Constitution should be applied. The dispute was first addressed in 1819, in the case of *McCulloch* v. *Maryland,* when the Supreme Court ruled in favor of a broad interpretation. The Court supported the idea that the elastic clause gave Congress the right to make any laws necessary to carry out its other powers.

What It Means

Original Rights A writ of habeas corpus issued by a judge requires a law official to bring a prisoner to court and show cause for holding the prisoner. A bill of attainder is a bill that punishes a person without a jury trial. An "ex post facto" law is one that makes an act a crime after the act has been committed. *What does the Constitution say about bills of attainder?*

What It Means

Powers Denied to the States Section 10 lists limits on the states. These restrictions were designed, in part, to prevent an overlapping in functions and authority with the federal government.

Evaluating Issues Article I, Section 9, prohibits the suspension of the writ of habeas corpus. Discuss with students the protection this offers. Ask students if they think this is an outdated principle today or still necessary to the Constitution. *(Most students will see this as a major principle of our legal system.)* **L2**

What It Means

Answer: No bills of attainder shall be passed.

CURRICULUM CONNECTION

Civics On many occasions when the United Stated has intervened militarily, Congress has not issued a declaration of war. These "undeclared wars" of the 1900s and 2000s include the conflicts in Korea and Vietnam and the war against terrorism. All three wars were fought on the president's authority to support governments against external aggression.

EXTENDING THE CONTENT

The Capitol The interior of the Capitol is a combination of new and old. Many of the furnishings and works of art date from the mid-1800s. However, signs of modern technology are everywhere. Roll-call votes are counted electronically. In addition, members of both houses have access to computers and other electronic information services. There are even electric subways connecting many of the office buildings on Capitol Hill.

United States Constitution

FOCUS

BELLRINGER
Motivational Activity

Point out that one of the difficult questions for the Framers of the Constitution concerned the Chief Executive—exactly how much power should the president have? Have students discuss why the Framers set up an office of president with limited powers. (*Discussion should focus on the Framers' fear of a single leader with uncontrolled powers.*)

FYI

One of the most important traditional measures of public opinion of the president's performance is the Gallup presidential approval survey, or poll. Since 1945 the Gallup Organization has polled members of the public monthly—and sometimes more often—about whether they approve or disapprove of the president's handling of the job.

Article II. The Executive Branch

Article II creates an executive branch to carry out laws passed by Congress. Article II lists the powers and duties of the president, describes qualifications for office and procedures for electing the president, and provides for a vice president.

What Might Have Been
Term of Office Alexander Hamilton also provided his own governmental outline at the Constitutional Convention. Some of its most distinctive elements were that both the executive and the members of the Senate were "elected to serve during good behaviour," meaning there was no specified limit on their time in office.

What It Means
Former Method of Election In the election of 1800, the top two candidates received the same number of electoral votes, making it necessary for the House of Representatives to decide the election. To eliminate this problem, the Twelfth Amendment, added in 1804, changed the method of electing the president stated in Article II, Section 3. The Twelfth Amendment requires that the electors cast separate ballots for president and vice president.

what may be absolutely necessary for executing it's inspection Laws: and the net Produce of all Duties and Imposts, laid by any State on Imports and Exports, shall be for the Use of the Treasury of the United States; and all such Laws shall be subject to the Revision and Controul of the Congress.

[3.] No State shall, without the Consent of Congress, lay any Duty of Tonnage, keep Troops, or Ships of War in time of Peace, enter into any Agreement or Compact with another State, or with a foreign Power, or engage in War, unless actually invaded, or in such imminent Danger as will not admit of delay.

Article II
Section 1

[1.] The executive Power shall be vested in a President of the United States of America. He shall hold his Office during the Term of four Years, and, together with the Vice-President, chosen for the same Term, be elected, as follows

[2.] Each State shall appoint, in such Manner as the Legislature thereof may direct, a Number of Electors, equal to the whole Number of Senators and Representatives to which the State may be entitled in the Congress: but no Senator or Representative, or Person holding an Office of Trust or Profit under the United States, shall be appointed an Elector.

[3.] The Electors shall meet in their respective States, and vote by Ballot for two Persons, of whom one at least shall not be an Inhabitant of the same State with themselves. And they shall make a List of all the Persons voted for, and of the Number of Votes for each; which List they shall sign and certify, and transmit sealed to the Seat of the Government of the United States, directed to the President of the Senate. The President of the Senate shall, in the Presence of the Senate and House of Representatives, open all the Certificates, and the Votes shall then be counted. The Person having the greatest Number of Votes shall be the President, if such Number be a Majority of the whole Number of Electors appointed; and if there be more than one who have such Majority, and have an equal Number of Votes, then the House of Representatives shall immediately chuse by Ballot one of them for President; and if no person have a Majority, then from the five highest on the List the said House shall in like Manner chuse the president. But in chusing the President, the Votes shall be taken by States, the Representation from each State having one Vote; A quorum for this Purpose shall consist of a Member or Members from two thirds of the States, and a Majority of all the States shall be necessary to a Choice. In every Case, after the Choice of the President, the Person having the greatest Number of Votes of the Electors shall be the Vice-President. But if there should remain two or more who have equal Votes, the Senate shall chuse from them by Ballot the Vice President.

EXTENDING THE CONTENT

Two-term Limits The Constitution originally did not limit the number of terms the president could serve. George Washington set a precedent by serving only two terms. Until FDR, no president had served more than two terms. Many people opposed Roosevelt's four terms in office. This opposition eventually led to the ratification of the Twenty-second Amendment in 1951, which limited presidents to two terms.

[4.] The Congress may determine the Time of chusing the Electors, and the Day on which they shall give their Votes; which Day shall be the same throughout the United States.

[5.] No Person except a natural born Citizen, or a Citizen of the United States, at the time of the Adoption of this Constitution, shall be eligible to the Office of President; neither shall any Person be eligible to that Office who shall not have attained to the Age of thirty five Years, and been fourteen Years a Resident within the United States.

[6.] In Case of the Removal of the President from Office, or of his Death, Resignation, or Inability to discharge the Powers and Duties of the said Office, the Same shall devolve on the Vice-President, and the Congress may by Law provide for the Case of Removal, Death, Resignation or Inability, both of the President and Vice-President, declaring what Officer shall then act as President, and such Officer shall act accordingly, until the Disability be removed, or a President shall be elected.

[7.] The President shall, at stated Times, receive for his Services, a Compensation, which shall neither be encreased nor diminished during the Period for which he shall have been elected, and he shall not receive within that Period any other Emolument from the United States, or any of them.

[8.] Before he enter on the Execution of his Office, he shall take the following Oath or Affirmation—"I do solemnly swear (or affirm) that I will faithfully execute the Office of President of the United States, and will to the best of my Ability, preserve, protect and defend the Constitution of the United States."

Section 2

[1.] The President shall be Commander in Chief of the Army and Navy of the United States, and of the Militia of the several States, when called into the actual Service of the United States; he may require the Opinion, in writing, of the principal Officer in each of the executive Departments, upon any Subject relating to the Duties of their respective Offices, and he shall have Power to grant Reprieves and Pardons for Offences against the United States, except in Cases of Impeachment.

[2.] He shall have Power, by and with the Advice and Consent of the Senate, to make Treaties, provided two thirds of the Senators present concur; and he shall nominate, and by and with the Advice and Consent of the Senate, shall appoint Ambassadors, other public Ministers and Consuls, Judges of the supreme Court, and all other Officers of the United States, whose Appointments are not herein otherwise provided for, and which shall be established by Law: but the Congress may by Law vest the Appointment of such inferior Officers, as they think proper, in the President alone, in the Courts of Law, or in the Heads of Departments.

What It Means
Qualifications The president must be a citizen of the United States by birth, at least 35 years of age, and a resident of the United States for 14 years.

What Might Have Been
Qualifications At the Constitutional Convention, the New Jersey Amendments, sponsored by the smaller states, raised the possibility of making the executive a committee of people rather than a single individual. Also, executives were not allowed to run for a second term of office under this plan.

What It Means
Vacancies If the president dies, resigns, is removed from office by impeachment, or is unable to carry out the duties of the office, the vice president becomes president.

What It Means
Salary Originally, the president's salary was $25,000 per year. The president's current salary is $400,000 plus a $50,000 nontaxable expense account per year. The president also receives living accommodations in two residences—the White House and Camp David.

What It Means
Cabinet Mention of "the principal officer in each of the executive departments" is the only suggestion of the president's cabinet to be found in the Constitution. The cabinet is an advisory body, and its power depends on the president. Section 2, Clause 1 also makes the president the head of the armed forces. This established the principle of civilian control of the military.

What It Means
Treaties With Foreign Nations The president is responsible for the conduct of relations with foreign countries. *What role does the Senate have in approving treaties?*

The Constitution Handbook **195**

TEACH

Classifying Information Have students read Article II to find the powers of the president. Suggest that they classify these powers under the headings *Executive, Legislative, Diplomatic, Military,* and *Judicial.* **L1**

Making Judgments Ask students to discuss why the Framers of the Constitution made the president commander in chief of the armed forces and any state militias called to serve the United States. *(The Framers wanted to ensure civilian control of the military.)* **L2**

FYI

The electors in the Electoral College almost always vote as expected. Exceptions are rare: there have been only a small number of "faithless electors" among the more than 17,000 electors chosen since 1789. For example, in 1988 Democratic nominee Michael Dukakis was denied one of his 112 electoral votes when a West Virginia elector cast her ballot for Dukakis's running mate, Lloyd Bentsen. She gave her vice presidential vote to Dukakis.

What It Means
Answer: Two-thirds of the senators present must concur in order for a treaty to be approved.

CRITICAL THINKING ACTIVITY

Determining Cause and Effect Discuss examples showing the increase in presidential power during the 1900s and 2000s. For example, increasing globalization has expanded the president's foreign relations responsibilities, such as negotiating international treaties, military policing interventions, and waging "undeclared wars." Write the following statement on the board: "The increase in presidential power during the 1900s and 2000s was largely related to crises, whether domestic or foreign." **Ask:** Do you think this is the true cause of the increase in presidential power? Why or why not? If not, what do you think caused the increase? **L3**

United States Constitution

FOCUS

Ask students to consider the meaning of the phrase "respect for the law." Guide their discussion by asking the following questions: What is the law? How can the law affect individuals and society? Why is respect for the law necessary to good government?

FYI

In the first election, the American people had no problem selecting a president. George Washington was the unanimous choice, winning 69 electoral votes–the maximum possible in 1789. No other president has matched that feat, although Franklin D. Roosevelt came close in 1936 with 98.5 percent of the electoral vote. Most other presidential elections have been more competitive, sometimes creating issues the Founders did not foresee.

What It Means
Executive Orders An important presidential power is the ability to issue executive orders. An executive order is a rule or command the president issues that has the force of law. Only Congress can make laws under the Constitution, but executive orders are considered part of the president's duty to "take care that the laws be faithfully executed." This power is often used during emergencies. During the Civil War, for example, President Lincoln issued an order suspending writs of habeas corpus. Over time the scope of executive orders has expanded, increasing the president's power. Decisions by federal agencies and departments are also considered to be executive orders.

What It Means
Impeachment This section states the reasons for which the president and vice president may be impeached and removed from office. Only Andrew Johnson and Bill Clinton have been impeached by the House. Richard Nixon resigned before the House could vote on possible impeachment.

Article III. The Judicial Branch

The term *judicial* refers to courts. The Constitution set up only the Supreme Court but provided for the establishment of other federal courts. The judiciary of the United States has two different systems of courts. One system consists of the federal courts, whose powers derive from the Constitution and federal laws. The other includes the courts of each of the 50 states, whose powers derive from state constitutions and laws.

What It Means
Jurisdiction Federal courts deal mostly with "statute law," or laws passed by Congress, treaties, and cases involving the Constitution itself.

Vocabulary

original jurisdiction: *authority to be the first court to hear a case*

appellate jurisdiction: *authority to hear cases that have been appealed from lower courts*

What It Means
The Supreme Court A court with "original jurisdiction" has the authority to be the first court to hear a case. The Supreme Court has "appellate jurisdiction" and mostly hears cases appealed from lower courts.

[3.] The President shall have Power to fill up all Vacancies that may happen during the Recess of the Senate, by granting Commissions which shall expire at the End of their next Session.

Section 3
He shall from time to time give to the Congress Information of the State of the Union, and recommend to their Consideration such Measures as he shall judge necessary and expedient; he may, on extraordinary Occasions, convene both Houses, or either of them, and in Case of Disagreement between them, with Respect to the Time of Adjournment, he may adjourn them to such Time as he shall think proper; he shall receive Ambassadors and other public Ministers; he shall take Care that the Laws be faithfully executed, and shall Commission all the Officers of the United States.

Section 4
The President, Vice-President and all civil Officers of the United States, shall be removed from Office on Impeachment for, and Conviction of, Treason, Bribery, or other high Crimes and Misdemeanors.

Article III
Section 1
The judicial Power of the United States, shall be vested in one supreme Court, and in such inferior Courts as the Congress may from time to time ordain and establish. The Judges, both of the supreme and inferior Courts, shall hold their Offices during good Behaviour, and shall, at stated Times, receive for their Services, a Compensation, which shall not be diminished during their Continuance in Office.

Section 2
[1.] The judicial Power shall extend to all Cases, in Law and Equity, arising under this Constitution, the Laws of the United States, and Treaties made, or which shall be made, under their Authority;—to all Cases affecting Ambassadors, other public Ministers and Consuls;—to all Cases of admiralty and maritime Jurisdiction;—to Controversies to which the United States shall be a Party;—to Controversies between two or more States; —between a State and Citizens of another State;— between Citizens of different States,—between Citizens of the same State claiming Lands under Grants of different States, and between a State, or the Citizens thereof, and foreign States, Citizens or Subjects.

[2.] In all Cases affecting Ambassadors, other public Ministers and Consuls, and those in which a State shall be Party, the supreme Court shall have original Jurisdiction. In all the other Cases before mentioned, the supreme Court shall have appellate Jurisdiction, both as to Law and Fact, with such Exceptions, and under such Regulations as the Congress shall make.

EXTENDING THE CONTENT

Minorities and the Supreme Court The first African American Supreme Court justice, Thurgood Marshall, was named to the Court by President Lyndon Johnson in 1967. President Ronald Reagan nominated the first woman justice, Sandra Day O'Connor, in 1981.

[3.] The Trial of all Crimes, except in Cases of Impeachment, shall be by Jury; and such Trial shall be held in the State where the said Crimes shall have been committed; but when not committed within any State, the Trial shall be at such Place or Places as the Congress may by Law have directed.

Section 3

[1.] Treason against the United States, shall consist only in levying War against them, or in adhering to their Enemies, giving them Aid and Comfort. No Person shall be convicted of Treason unless on the Testimony of two Witnesses to the same overt Act, or on Confession in open Court.
[2.] The Congress shall have Power to declare the Punishment of Treason, but no Attainder of Treason shall work Corruption of Blood, or Forfeiture except during the Life of the Person attainted.

Article IV

Section 1

Full Faith and Credit shall be given in each State to the public Acts, Records, and judicial Proceedings of every other State. And the Congress may by general Laws prescribe the Manner in which such Acts, Records and Proceedings shall be proved, and the Effect thereof.

Section 2

[1.] The Citizens of each State shall be entitled to all Privileges and Immunities of Citizens in the several States.
[2.] A Person charged in any State with Treason, Felony, or other Crime, who shall flee from Justice, and be found in another State, shall on Demand of the executive Authority of the State from which he fled, be delivered up, to be removed to the State having Jurisdiction of the Crime.
[3.] No Person held to Service of Labour in one State, under the Laws thereof, escaping into another, shall, in Consequence of any Law or Regulation therein, be discharged from such Service or Labour, but shall be delivered up on Claim of the Party to whom such Service or Labour may be due.

Section 3

[1.] New States may be admitted by the Congress into this Union; but no new State shall be formed or erected within the Jurisdiction of any other State; nor any State be formed by the Junction of two or more States, or Parts of States, without the Consent of the Legislatures of the States concerned as well as of the Congress.
[2.] The Congress shall have Power to dispose of and make all needful Rules and Regulations respecting the Territory or other Property belonging to the United States; and nothing in this Constitution shall be so construed as to Prejudice any Claims of the United States, or of any particular State.

What It Means

Jury Trial Except in cases of impeachment, anyone accused of a crime has the right to a trial by jury. The trial must be held in the state where the crime was committed. Jury trial guarantees were strengthened in the Sixth, Seventh, Eighth, and Ninth Amendments.

Article IV. Relations Among the States

Article IV explains the relationship of the states to one another and to the national government. This article requires each state to give citizens of other states the same rights as its own citizens, addresses the admission of new states, and guarantees that the national government will protect the states.

What It Means

Official Acts This provision ensures that each state recognizes the laws, court decisions, and records of all other states. For example, a marriage license issued by one state must be accepted by all states.

Vocabulary

treason: *violation of the allegiance owed by a person to his or her own country, for example, by aiding an enemy*

What It Means

New States Congress has the power to admit new states. It also determines the basic guidelines for applying for statehood. Two states, Maine and West Virginia, were created within the boundaries of another state. In the case of West Virginia, President Lincoln recognized the West Virginia government as the legal government of Virginia during the Civil War. This allowed West Virginia to secede from Virginia without obtaining approval from the Virginia legislature.

TEACH

Analyzing Ideas Point out that federal judges are appointed for life and can be removed only by their death, resignation, or impeachment. Ask students why they think the Framers of the Constitution made judgeships lifetime appointments. (*The Framers believed that judges who felt secure in their positions would be more likely to make correct decisions, uninfluenced by public opinion.*) **L2**

Writing Reports Encourage students to listen to excerpts from "May It Please the Court," recordings of the Supreme Court in session. Have them write a brief report on the case or cases they listened to. **L2**

CURRICULUM CONNECTION

Civics The judiciary is only briefly described in the Constitution. The federal court system was established by the Judiciary Act of 1789.

CRITICAL THINKING ACTIVITY

Predicting Outcomes Have students discuss the pros and cons of federal judges being elected rather than appointed. Direct them to list the possible outcomes they foresee if the federal judiciary was subject to the electoral process. Encourage students to share and compare their lists. **L3**

FOCUS

BELLRINGER
Motivational Activity

Inform students that one political scientist has called the supremacy clause (Article VI, Section 2) "the most important single provision of the Constitution." Ask students to think about why this might be so. *(This clause made it clear that the national Constitution and laws are supreme over state constitutions.)*

TEACH

Expressing Viewpoints Have students speculate about why the Framers of the Constitution established the amendment process as they did. *(The Framers wanted to make the Constitution flexible, but not so easy to amend that it would not be respected.)*

Ask: Should the amendment process be made easier? Why or why not?

Vocabulary

amendment: *a change to the Constitution*
ratification: *process by which an amendment is approved*

Article V. The Amendment Process

Article V explains how the Constitution can be amended, or changed. All of the 27 amendments were proposed by a two-thirds vote of both houses of Congress. Only the Twenty-first Amendment was ratified by constitutional conventions of the states. All other amendments have been ratified by state legislatures. *What is an amendment?*

Article VI. National Supremacy

Article VI contains the "supremacy clause." This clause establishes that the Constitution, laws passed by Congress, and treaties of the United States "shall be the supreme Law of the Land." The "supremacy clause" recognizes the Constitution and federal laws as supreme when in conflict with those of the states.

Article VII. Ratification

Article VII addresses ratification and states that, unlike the Articles of Confederation, which required approval of all thirteen states for adoption, the Constitution would take effect after it was ratified by nine states.

Section 4

The United States shall guarantee to every State in this Union a Republican Form of Government, and shall protect each of them against Invasion; and on Application of the Legislature, or of the Executive (when the Legislature cannot be convened) against domestic Violence.

Article V

The Congress, whenever two thirds of both Houses shall deem it necessary, shall propose Amendments to this Constitution, or, on the Application of the Legislatures of two thirds of the several States, shall call a Convention for proposing Amendments, which, in either Case, shall be valid to all Intents and Purposes, as Part of this Constitution, when ratified by the Legislatures of three fourths of the several States, or by Conventions in three fourths thereof, as the one or the other Mode of Ratification may be proposed by the Congress; Provided that no Amendment which may be made prior to the Year One thousand eight hundred and eight shall in any Manner affect the first and fourth Clauses in the Ninth Section of the first Article; and that no State, without its Consent, shall be deprived of its equal Suffrage in the Senate.

Article VI

[1.] All Debts contracted and Engagements entered into, before the Adoption of this Constitution, shall be as valid against the United States under this Constitution, as under the Confederation.

[2.] This Constitution, and the Laws of the United States which shall be made in Pursuance thereof; and all Treaties made, or which shall be made, under the Authority of the United States, shall be the supreme Law of the Land; and the Judges in every State shall be bound thereby, any Thing in the Constitution or Laws of any State to the Contrary notwithstanding.

[3.] The Senators and Representatives before mentioned, and the Members of the several State Legislatures, and all executive and judicial Officers, both of the United States and of the several States, shall be bound by Oath or Affirmation, to support this Constitution; but no religious Test shall ever be required as a Qualification to any Office or public Trust under the United States.

Article VII

The Ratification of the Conventions of nine States, shall be sufficient for the Establishment of this Constitution between the States so ratifying the same.

Done in Convention by the Unanimous Consent of the States present the Seventeenth Day of September in the Year of our Lord one thousand seven hundred and Eighty seven and of the Independence of the United States of America the Twelfth. In witness whereof We have hereunto subscribed our Names,

COOPERATIVE LEARNING ACTIVITY

Writing Reports Organize students into four groups and assign to each group one of the four sections of Article I (Sections 2, 3, 4, and 9) that has been modified by amendment. Have each group research how, why, and when the amendment to its assigned section was made. Encourage groups to present their findings to the rest of the class in brief written reports.

Use the rubric for a cooperative group management plan on pages 81–82 in the *Performance Assessment Activities and Rubrics.*

Signers

George Washington,
President and Deputy
from Virginia

New Hampshire
John Langdon
Nicholas Gilman

Massachusetts
Nathaniel Gorham
Rufus King

Connecticut
William Samuel Johnson
Roger Sherman

New York
Alexander Hamilton

New Jersey
William Livingston
David Brearley
William Paterson
Jonathan Dayton

Pennsylvania
Benjamin Franklin
Thomas Mifflin
Robert Morris
George Clymer
Thomas FitzSimons
Jared Ingersoll
James Wilson
Gouverneur Morris

Delaware
George Read
Gunning Bedford, Jr.
John Dickinson
Richard Bassett
Jacob Broom

Maryland
James McHenry
Daniel of St. Thomas
Jenifer
Daniel Carroll

Virginia
John Blair
James Madison, Jr.

North Carolina
William Blount
Richard Dobbs Spaight
Hugh Williamson

South Carolina
John Rutledge
Charles Cotesworth
Pinckney
Charles Pinckney
Pierce Butler

Georgia
William Few
Abraham Baldwin

Attest:
William Jackson,
Secretary

Amendment I

Congress shall make no law respecting an establishment of religion, or prohibiting the free exercise thereof; or abridging the freedom of speech, or of the press; or the right of the people peaceably to assemble, and to petition the Government for a redress of grievances.

Amendment II

A well regulated Militia, being necessary to the security of a free State, the right of the people to keep and bear Arms, shall not be infringed.

Amendment III

No Soldier shall, in time of peace be quartered in any house, without the consent of the Owner, nor in time of war, but in a manner to be prescribed by law.

Amendment IV

The right of the people to be secure in their persons, houses, papers, and effects, against unreasonable searches and seizures, shall not be violated, and no Warrants shall issue, but upon probable cause, supported by Oath or affirmation, and particularly describing the place to be searched, and the persons or things to be seized.

Amendment V

No person shall be held to answer for a capital, or otherwise infamous crime, unless on a presentment or indictment of a Grand Jury, except in cases arising in the

The Amendments

This part of the Constitution consists of changes and additions. The Constitution has been amended 27 times throughout the nation's history.

What It Means

Bill of Rights The first 10 amendments are known as the Bill of Rights (1791). These amendments limit the powers of the federal government. The First Amendment protects the civil liberties of individuals in the United States. The amendment freedoms are not absolute, however. They are limited by the rights of other individuals. *What freedoms does the First Amendment protect?*

Vocabulary

quarter: *to provide living accommodations*
warrant: *document that gives police particular rights or powers*
probable cause: *police must have a reasonable basis to believe a person is linked to a crime*

The Constitution Handbook **199**

EXTENDING THE CONTENT

Signers of the Constitution Of the 55 delegates who attended the Constitutional Convention, only 38 signed the document. A thirty-ninth signature—that of John Dickinson—was written by George Read at Dickinson's request. Elbridge Gerry of Massachusetts and Edmund Randolph and George Mason of Virginia refused to sign, while 13 other delegates left the Convention early.

What It Means

Answer: The Grand Jury evaluates whether there is enough evidence to bring the accused person to trial.

What It Means

Answer: The requirement of a "speedy" trial ensures that an accused person will not be held in jail for a lengthy period as a means of punishing the accused without a trial.

Researching the Constitution

Encourage volunteers to research the number of amendments to the California state constitution, a relatively easy constitution to amend. Have them report to the class, using California as an example of what happens when a constitution is easily amended. Encourage students to discuss whether they think the national Constitution would work better if it were easier to amend. **L3**

What It Means

Rights of the Accused This amendment contains important protections for people accused of crimes. One of the protections is that government may not deprive any person of life, liberty, or property without due process of law. This means that the government must follow proper constitutional procedures in trials and in other actions it takes against individuals. *According to Amendment V, what is the function of a grand jury?*

What It Means

Speedy Trial A basic protection is the right to a speedy, public trial. The jury must hear witnesses and evidence on both sides before deciding the guilt or innocence of a person charged with a crime. This amendment also provides that legal counsel must be provided to a defendant. In 1963, in *Gideon* v. *Wainwright*, the Supreme Court ruled that if a defendant cannot afford a lawyer, the government must provide one to defend him or her. *Why is the right to a "speedy" trial important?*

Vocabulary

common law: *law established by previous court decisions*
bail: *money that an accused person provides to the court as a guarantee that he or she will be present for a trial*

What It Means

Powers Reserved to the People This amendment prevents government from claiming that the only rights people have are those listed in the Bill of Rights.

What It Means

Powers Reserved to the States This amendment protects the states and the people from the federal government. It establishes that powers not given to the national government—or denied to the states—by the Constitution belong to the states or to the people. These checks on the "necessary and proper" power of the federal government are provided in Article I, Section 8, Clause 18.

What It Means

Suits Against States The Eleventh Amendment (1795) provides that a lawsuit brought by a citizen of the United States or a foreign nation against a state must be tried in a state court, not in a federal court. The Supreme Court had ruled in *Chisholm* v. *Georgia* (1793) that a federal court could try a lawsuit brought by citizens of South Carolina against a citizen of Georgia.

land or naval forces, or in the Militia, when in actual service in time of War or public danger; nor shall any person be subject for the same offence to be twice put in jeopardy of life or limb; nor shall be compelled in any criminal case to be a witness against himself, nor be deprived of life, liberty, or property, without due process of law; nor shall private property be taken for public use without just compensation.

Amendment VI

In all criminal prosecutions, the accused shall enjoy the right to a speedy and public trial, by an impartial jury of the State and district wherein the crime shall have been committed, which district shall have been previously ascertained by law, and to be informed of the nature and cause of the accusation; to be confronted with the witnesses against him; to have compulsory process for obtaining Witnesses in his favor, and to have the assistance of counsel for his defence.

Amendment VII

In Suits at common law, where the value in controversy shall exceed twenty dollars, the right of trial by jury shall be preserved, and no fact tried by a jury, shall be otherwise reexamined in any Court of the United States, than according to the rules of common law.

Amendment VIII

Excessive bail shall not be required, nor excessive fines imposed, nor cruel and unusual punishments inflicted.

Amendment IX

The enumeration in the Constitution, of certain rights, shall not be construed to deny or disparage others retained by the people.

Amendment X

The powers not delegated to the United States by the Constitution, nor prohibited by it to the States, are reserved to the States respectively, or to the people.

Amendment XI

The Judicial power of the United States shall not be construed to extend to any suit in law or equity, commenced or prosecuted against one of the United States by Citizens of another State, or by Citizens or Subjects of any Foreign State.

EXTENDING THE CONTENT

The Bill of Rights Critics of the Constitution felt that it did not go far enough in protecting individual rights and liberties. To answer these objections, supporters of the Constitution promised to introduce a series of amendments listing the rights of individuals. On September 25, 1789, James Madison kept this promise by proposing 14 amendments to the Constitution, 10 of which were adopted and are now known as the Bill of Rights. One amendment not adopted concerned pay raises for members of Congress. It eventually became part of the Constitution as the Twenty-seventh Amendment.

Amendment XII

The electors shall meet in their respective states and vote by ballot for President and Vice-President, one of whom, at least, shall not be an inhabitant of the same state with themselves; they shall name in their ballots the person voted for as President, and in distinct ballots the person voted for as Vice-President, and they shall make distinct lists of all persons voted for as President, and of all persons voted for as Vice-President, and of the number of votes for each, which lists they shall sign and certify, and transmit sealed to the seat of the government of the United States, directed to the President of the Senate;—The President of the Senate shall, in the presence of the Senate and House of Representatives, open all the certificates and the votes shall then be counted;—The person having the greatest number of votes for President, shall be the President, if such number be a majority of the whole number of Electors appointed; and if no person have such majority, then from the persons having the highest numbers not exceeding three on the list of those voted for as President, the House of Representatives shall choose immediately, by ballot, the President. But in choosing the President, the votes shall be taken by states, the representation from each state having one vote; a quorum for this purpose shall consist of a member or members from two-thirds of the states, and a majority of all the states shall be necessary to a choice. And if the House of Representatives shall not choose a President whenever the right of choice shall devolve upon them, before the fourth day of March next following, then the Vice-President shall act as President, as in the case of the death or other constitutional disability of the President. The person having the greatest number of votes as Vice-President, shall be the Vice-President, if such number be a majority of the whole number of Electors appointed, and if no person have a majority, then from the two highest numbers on the list, the Senate shall choose the Vice-President; a quorum for the purpose shall consist of two-thirds of the whole number of Senators, and a majority of the whole number shall be necessary to a choice. But no person constitutionally ineligible to the office of President shall be eligible to that of Vice-President of the United States.

Amendment XIII

Section 1

Neither slavery nor involuntary servitude, except as a punishment for crime whereof the party shall have been duly convicted, shall exist within the United States, or any place subject to their jurisdiction.

> **What It Means**
> **Election Method** The Twelfth Amendment (1804) corrects a problem that had arisen in the method of electing the president and vice president, which is described in Article II, Section 1, Clause 3. This amendment provides for the Electoral College to use separate ballots in voting for president and vice president. *If no candidate receives a majority of the electoral votes, who elects the president?*

Vocabulary

majority: *more than half*

> **What It Means**
> **Abolition of Slavery** Amendments Thirteen (1865), Fourteen, and Fifteen often are called the Civil War amendments because they grew out of that conflict. The Thirteenth Amendment outlaws slavery.

The Constitution Handbook **201**

> **What It Means**
> **Answer:** the House of Representatives

CURRICULUM CONNECTION

Civics Some lawyers maintain that the mass media threaten a defendant's Sixth Amendment rights. Extensive coverage of a crime on television and in the newspapers, these lawyers argue, makes it difficult to find jurors who are truly impartial.

Analyzing Ideas Ask students to identify areas of concern that they would like to see addressed by a constitutional amendment. Write suggestions on the board and have students discuss each in terms of the following questions: **Why is an amendment needed? Would it be better for Congress to pass laws or the courts to establish precedents on this issue? L2**

CRITICAL THINKING ACTIVITY

Expressing Problems Clearly point out that the Fifth Amendment protects the right of people charged with crimes to remain silent. In some countries, however, silence is equated with an admittance of guilt. Ask students to write a paragraph that supports or challenges the following statement: The Fifth Amendment is little more than a shield for the guilty. **L3**

United States Constitution

Identifying Alternatives Point out that the Electoral College has been criticized as being obsolete, and various reforms have been suggested for changing it or abolishing it altogether. Lead a discussion about the 2000 presidential election that continued the debate over the role of the Electoral College. Ask students to research, discuss, and assess alternatives to the Electoral College. **L2**

you don't say...

Names of Political Parties The nickname of the Republican party is the GOP, which stands for the Grand Old Party. The term began to be used around the time of the 1880 Republican convention. Prime Minister William Gladstone of Great Britain was fondly referred to as the Grand Old Man, and some Republican admirers of the prime minister applied the same term of affection to their political party. Ironically, the Grand Old Party is more than a half century younger than the Democratic Party.

What It Means

Answer: Former slaveholders could not collect compensation for the loss of the people they had enslaved.

What It Means

Rights of Citizens The Fourteenth Amendment (1868) originally was intended to protect the legal rights of the freed slaves. Its interpretation has been extended to protect the rights of citizenship in general by prohibiting a state from depriving any person of life, liberty, or property without "due process of law." In addition, it states that all citizens have the right to equal protection of the laws in all states.

What It Means

Representation in Congress This section reduced the number of members a state had in the House of Representatives if it denied its citizens the right to vote. Later civil rights laws and the Twenty-fourth Amendment guaranteed the vote to African Americans.

Vocabulary

abridge: *to reduce*
insurrection: *rebellion against the government*

What It Means

Penalty The leaders of the Confederacy were barred from state or federal offices unless Congress agreed to remove this ban. By the end of Reconstruction, all but a few Confederate leaders were allowed to return to public service.

What It Means

Public Debt The public debt acquired by the federal government during the Civil War was valid and could not be questioned by the South. However, the debts of the Confederacy were declared to be illegal. *Could former slaveholders collect payment for the loss of their slaves?*

Section 2

Congress shall have power to enforce this article by appropriate legislation.

Amendment XIV

Section 1

All persons born or naturalized in the United States, and subject to the jurisdiction thereof, are citizens of the United States and of the State wherein they reside. No State shall make or enforce any law which shall abridge the privileges or immunities of citizens of the United States; nor shall any State deprive any person of life, liberty, or property, without due process of law; nor deny to any person within its jurisdiction the equal protection of the laws.

Section 2

Representatives shall be apportioned among the several States according to their respective numbers, counting the whole number of persons in each State, excluding Indians not taxed. But when the right to vote at any election for the choice of electors for President and Vice-President of the United States, Representatives in Congress, the Executive and Judicial officers of a State, or the members of the Legislature thereof, is denied to any of the male inhabitants of such State, being twenty-one years of age, and citizens of the United States, or in any way abridged, except for participation in rebellion, or other crime, the basis of representation therein shall be reduced in the proportion which the number of such male citizens shall bear to the whole number of male citizens twenty-one years of age in such State.

Section 3

No person shall be a Senator or Representative in Congress, or elector of President and Vice-President, or hold any office, civil or military, under the United States, or under any State, who, having previously taken an oath, as a member of Congress, or as an officer of the United States, or as a member of any State legislature, or as an executive or judicial officer of any State, to support the Constitution of the United States, shall have engaged in insurrection or rebellion against the same, or given aid or comfort to the enemies thereof. But Congress may by a vote of two-thirds of each House, remove such disability.

Section 4

The validity of the public debt of the United States, authorized by law, including debts incurred for payment of pensions and bounties for service, in suppressing insurrection or rebellion, shall not be questioned. But neither the United States nor any State shall assume or pay any debt or obligation incurred in aid of insurrection or rebellion against the United States, or any

---

EXTENDING THE CONTENT

Racial Discrimination and the Constitution The Thirteenth, Fourteenth, and Fifteenth Amendments represent attempts to use the Constitution to end slavery, to extend citizenship to formerly enslaved persons, and to guarantee African Americans the right to vote. Literacy tests, poll taxes, and grandfather clauses, however, continued to keep large numbers of African Americans from voting in many Southern states after Reconstruction.

claim for the loss or emancipation of any slave; but all such debts, obligations and claims shall be held illegal and void.

Section 5

The Congress shall have power to enforce, by appropriate legislation, the provisions of this article.

Amendment XV

Section 1

The right of citizens of the United States to vote shall not be denied or abridged by the United States or by any State on account of race, color, or previous condition of servitude.

Section 2

The Congress shall have power to enforce this article by appropriate legislation.

Amendment XVI

The Congress shall have power to lay and collect taxes on incomes, from whatever source derived, without apportionment among the several States and without regard to any census or enumeration.

Amendment XVII

Section 1

The Senate of the United States shall be composed of two Senators from each State, elected by the people thereof, for six years; and each Senator shall have one vote. The electors in each State shall have the qualifications requisite for electors of the most numerous branch of the State legislatures.

Section 2

When vacancies happen in the representation of any State in the Senate, the executive authority of such State shall issue writs of election to fill such vacancies: *Provided,* That the legislature of any State may empower the executive thereof to make temporary appointments until the people fill the vacancies by election as the legislature may direct.

Section 3

This amendment shall not be so construed as to affect the election or term of any Senator chosen before it becomes valid as part of the Constitution.

Amendment XVIII

Section 1

After one year from ratification of this article, the manufacture, sale, or transportation of intoxicating liquors within, the importation thereof into, or the

What It Means
Voting Rights The Fifteenth Amendment (1870) prohibits the government from denying a person's right to vote on the basis of race. Despite the law, many states denied African Americans the right to vote by such means as poll taxes, literacy tests, and white primaries.

What It Means
Income Tax The origins of the Sixteenth Amendment (1913) date back to 1895, when the Supreme Court declared a federal income tax unconstitutional. To overturn this decision, this amendment authorizes an income tax that is levied on a direct basis.

What It Means
Direct Elections The Seventeenth Amendment (1913) states that the people, instead of state legislatures, elect United States senators. *How many years are in a Senate term?*

Vocabulary

apportionment: *distribution of seats in House based on population*
vacancy: *an office or position that is unfilled or unoccupied*

What It Means
Prohibition The Eighteenth Amendment (1919) prohibited the production, sale, or transportation of alcoholic beverages in the United States. Prohibition proved to be difficult to enforce. This amendment was later repealed by the Twenty-first Amendment.

The Constitution Handbook **203**

Time Lines Have students make a time line that includes each of the amendments, the year of ratification, and significant concurrent political, economic, and social events. Encourage students to display and compare their time lines. **L2**

What It Means

Answer: 6 years

CURRICULUM CONNECTION

Civics Section 1 of the Fourteenth Amendment sets out two of the three alternative requirements of American citizenship: birth on American soil and naturalization. The third possible requirement is birth to a parent who is an American citizen.

EXTENDING THE CONTENT

Due Process of Law References to due process of law are made in the Fifth and Fourteenth Amendments. As a result of Supreme Court rulings, two types of due process have developed. Procedural due process requires that the government use fair procedures in enforcing the law. Substantive due process requires that the laws under which the government acts be fair.

Making Reasoned Judgments
Inform students that, at times, the constitutional provisions protecting personal liberties have been tested. One such test occurred during World War II, when more than 100,000 Japanese Americans were put into relocation camps. Ask students: In times of crisis, is the government justified in suspending personal liberties? Why or why not? **L2**

What It Means

Answer: January 20

FYI

Direct election of senators was one of the many political reforms advanced by the Progressive movement.

What It Means
Woman Suffrage The Nineteenth Amendment (1920) guaranteed women the right to vote. By then women had already won the right to vote in many state elections, but the amendment made their right to vote in all state and national elections constitutional.

What It Means
"Lame-Duck" The Twentieth Amendment (1933) sets new dates for Congress to begin its term and for the inauguration of the president and vice president. Under the original Constitution, elected officials who retired or who had been defeated remained in office for several months. For the outgoing president, this period ran from November until March. Such outgoing officials, referred to as "lame ducks," could accomplish little. *What date was fixed as Inauguration Day?*

What It Means
Succession This section provides that if the president-elect dies before taking office, the vice president-elect becomes president.

Vocabulary

president-elect: *individual who is elected president but has not yet begun serving his or her term*

exportation thereof from the United States and all territory subject to the jurisdiction thereof for beverage purposes is hereby prohibited.

Section 2
The Congress and the several States shall have concurrent power to enforce this article by appropriate legislation.

Section 3
This article shall be inoperative unless it shall have been ratified as an amendment to the Constitution by the legislatures of the several States, as provided in the Constitution, within seven years from the date of the submission hereof to the States by the Congress.

Amendment XIX

Section 1
The right of citizens of the United States to vote shall not be denied or abridged by the United States or by any state on account of sex.

Section 2
Congress shall have power by appropriate legislation to enforce the provisions of this article.

Amendment XX

Section 1
The terms of the President and Vice President shall end at noon on the 20th day of January, and the terms of the Senators and Representatives at noon on the 3rd day of January, of the years in which such terms would have ended if this article had not been ratified; and the terms of their successors shall then begin.

Section 2
The Congress shall assemble at least once in every year, and such meeting shall begin at noon on the 3rd day of January, unless they shall by law appoint a different day.

Section 3
If, at the time fixed for the beginning of the term of the President, the President elect shall have died, the Vice President elect shall become President. If a President shall not have been chosen before the time fixed for the beginning of his term, or if the President elect shall have failed to qualify, then the Vice President elect shall act as President until a President shall have qualified; and the Congress may by law provide for the case wherein neither a President elect nor a Vice President elect shall have qualified, declaring who shall then act as President, or the manner in which one who is to act shall be selected, and such person shall act accordingly until a President or Vice President shall have qualified.

EXTENDING THE CONTENT

The Poll Tax After the Civil War, poll taxes were levied in many Southern states. Although the poll tax kept many low-income white males from voting, its major purpose was to keep African Americans away from the polls. Not until the 1960s did Congress take firm action to enforce the Fifteenth Amendment to end this kind of racial discrimination.

Section 4

The Congress may by law provide for the case of the death of any of the persons from whom the House of Representatives may choose a President whenever the right of choice shall have devolved upon them, and for the case of the death of any of the persons from whom the Senate may choose a Vice President whenever the right of choice shall have devolved upon them.

Section 5

Sections 1 and 2 shall take effect on the 15th day of October following the ratification of this article.

Section 6

This article shall be inoperative unless it shall have been ratified as an amendment to the Constitution by the legislatures of three-fourths of the several States within seven years from the date of its submission.

Amendment XXI

Section 1

The eighteenth article of amendment to the Constitution of the United States is hereby repealed.

Section 2

The transportation or importation into any State, Territory, or possession of the United States for delivery or use therein of intoxicating liquors, in violation of the laws thereof, is hereby prohibited.

Section 3

This article shall be inoperative unless it shall have been ratified as an amendment to the Constitution by conventions in the several States, as provided in the Constitution, within seven years from the date of the submission hereof to the States by the Congress.

Amendment XXII

Section 1

No person shall be elected to the office of the President more than twice, and no person who had held the office of President, or acted as President, for more than two years of a term to which some other person was elected President shall be elected to the office of the President more than once. But this Article shall not apply to any person holding the office of President when this Article was proposed by the Congress, and shall not prevent any person who may be holding the office of President, or acting as President, during the term within which this Article becomes operative from holding the office of President or acting as President during the remainder of such term.

What It Means
Repeal of Prohibition The Twenty-first Amendment (1933) repeals the Eighteenth Amendment. It is the only amendment ever passed to overturn an earlier amendment. It is also the only amendment ratified by special state conventions instead of state legislatures.

What It Means
Presidential Term Limit The Twenty-second Amendment (1951) limits presidents to a maximum of two elected terms. The amendment wrote into the Constitution a custom started by George Washington. It was passed largely as a reaction to Franklin D. Roosevelt's election to four terms between 1933 and 1945. It also provides that anyone who succeeds to the presidency and serves for more than two years of the term may not be elected more than one more time.

Writing Reports Point out that a number of states preceded the national government in giving women the vote. Encourage students to research the fight for woman suffrage in these states. Ask them to present their findings in written reports. **L2**

CURRICULUM CONNECTION

Health Although Prohibition caused many problems, it did succeed in reducing the consumption of alcohol in the United States, thus decreasing the number of alcohol-related deaths and accidents.

CRITICAL THINKING ACTIVITY

Analyzing Make sure students understand the "lame-duck" issue by reminding them that lame ducks are presidents and members of Congress waiting to leave office after retiring or failing to gain reelection. Since lame ducks often are members of the defeated party, they are in a position to affect legislation even though they no longer speak for the majority of voters. Ask students to note how the Twentieth Amendment addressed this problem. *(It shortened the waiting period between Election Day and the beginning of a new term.)* **L1**

United States Constitution

Categorizing Information Have students categorize the amendments in a chart that contains the following headings: *Personal Freedoms, Relations Among States, Process of Government,* and *Citizenship.* They should keep in mind the substance of the amendment and its effect on American life. Remind students that some amendments might fit in more than one category. **L1**

FYI

Gerald R. Ford became the thirty-eighth president of the United States in 1974. He was the only president who was not elected either president or vice president. He replaced Spiro T. Agnew when Agnew resigned as vice president, then replaced President Richard Nixon who resigned on August 9, 1974.

you don't say...

Incapacitated Presidents The United States has had a disabled president several times in its history. In the 1880s James Garfield remained in a coma for 80 days before dying from injuries sustained by an assassin's bullet. Woodrow Wilson had a stroke and was incapacitated for the last several months of his presidency.

What It Means

Answer: the president pro tempore of the Senate (the vice president) and the Speaker of the House of Representatives

Vocabulary

District of Columbia: *site of nation's capital occupying an area between Maryland and Virginia*

What It Means
D.C. Electors The Twenty-third Amendment (1961) allows citizens living in Washington, D.C., to vote for president and vice president, a right previously denied residents of the nation's capital. The District of Columbia now has three presidential electors, the number to which it would be entitled if it were a state.

What It Means
Poll Tax The Twenty-fourth Amendment (1964) prohibits poll taxes in federal elections. Prior to the passage of this amendment, some states had used such taxes to keep low-income African Americans from voting. In 1966 the Supreme Court banned poll taxes in state elections as well.

What It Means
Presidential Disability and Succession The Twenty-fifth Amendment (1967) established a process for the vice president to take over leadership of the nation when a president is disabled. It also set procedures for filling a vacancy in the office of vice president.

This amendment was used in 1973, when Vice President Spiro Agnew resigned from office after being charged with accepting bribes. President Richard Nixon then appointed Gerald R. Ford as vice president in accordance with the provisions of the Twenty-fifth Amendment. A year later, President Nixon resigned during the Watergate scandal, and Ford became president. President Ford then had to fill the vice presidency, which he had left vacant upon assuming the presidency. He named Nelson A. Rockefeller as vice president. Thus individuals who had not been elected held both the presidency and the vice presidency. *Who does the president inform if he or she cannot carry out the duties of the office?*

Section 2
This article shall be inoperative unless it shall have been ratified as an amendment to the Constitution by the legislatures of three-fourths of the several States within seven years from the date of its submission to the States by the Congress.

Amendment XXIII
Section 1
The District constituting the seat of Government of the United States shall appoint in such manner as the Congress may direct:

A number of electors of President and Vice President equal to the whole number of Senators and Representatives in Congress to which the District would be entitled if it were a State, but in no event more than the least populous State; they shall be in addition to those appointed by the States, but they shall be considered, for the purposes of the election of President and Vice President, to be electors appointed by a State; and they shall meet in the District and perform such duties as provided by the twelfth article of amendment.

Section 2
The Congress shall have power to enforce this article by appropriate legislation.

Amendment XXIV
Section 1
The right of citizens of the United States to vote in any primary or other election for President or Vice President, for electors for President or Vice President, or for Senator or Representative in Congress, shall not be denied or abridged by the United States or any State by reason of failure to pay any poll tax or other tax.

Section 2
The Congress shall have power to enforce this article by appropriate legislation.

Amendment XXV
Section 1
In case of the removal of the President from office or his death or resignation, the Vice President shall become President.

Section 2
Whenever there is a vacancy in the office of the Vice President, the President shall nominate a Vice President who shall take the office upon confirmation by a majority vote of both Houses of Congress.

Section 3
Whenever the President transmits to the President pro tempore of the Senate and the Speaker of the House of

---

COOPERATIVE LEARNING ACTIVITY

Discussing a Concept Organize students into groups to present either the pros or cons of Prohibition. Give groups time to prepare their arguments and encourage group members to be responsible for different parts of the research. As each group presents its arguments, note major points on the board. When groups have presented their arguments, lead the class in a discussion of the following question: **Is Prohibition an issue that should have been addressed in a constitutional amendment? Why or why not?**

Use the rubric for a cooperative group management plan on pages 81–82 in the ***Performance Assessment Activities and Rubrics.***

Representatives his written declaration that he is unable to discharge the powers and duties of his office, and until he transmits to them a written declaration to the contrary, such powers and duties shall be discharged by the Vice President as Acting President.

Section 4
Whenever the Vice President and a majority of either the principal officers of the executive departments or of such other body as Congress may by law provide, transmit to the President pro tempore of the Senate and the Speaker of the House of Representatives their written declaration that the President is unable to discharge the powers and duties of his office, the Vice President shall immediately assume the power and duties of the office of Acting President.

Thereafter, when the President transmits to the President pro tempore of the Senate and the Speaker of the House of Representatives his written declaration that no inability exists, he shall resume the powers and duties of his office unless the Vice President and a majority of either the principal officers of the executive department or of such other body as Congress may by law provide, transmit within four days to the President pro tempore of the Senate and the Speaker of the House of Representatives their written declaration that the President is unable to discharge the powers and duties of his office. Thereupon Congress shall decide the issue, assembling within forty-eight hours for that purpose if not in session. If the Congress, within twenty-one days after receipt of the latter written declaration, or, if Congress is not in session, within twenty-one days after Congress is required to assemble, determines by two-thirds vote of both Houses that the President is unable to discharge the powers and duties of his office, the Vice President shall continue to discharge the same as Acting President; otherwise, the President shall resume the power and duties of his office.

Amendment XXVI

Section 1
The right of citizens of the United States, who are eighteen years of age or older, to vote shall not be denied or abridged by the United States or by any State on account of age.

Section 2
The Congress shall have power to enforce this article by appropriate legislation.

Amendment XXVII
No law, varying the compensation for the services of Senators and Representatives, shall take effect, until an election of representatives shall have intervened.

What It Means
Qualifications The Twenty-sixth Amendment (1971) lowered the voting age in both federal and state elections to 18.

What It Means
Salary Restraints The Twenty-seventh Amendment (1992) makes congressional pay raises effective during the term following their passage. James Madison offered the amendment in 1789, but it was never adopted. In 1982 Gregory Watson, then a student at the University of Texas, discovered the forgotten amendment while doing research for a school paper. Watson made the amendment's passage his crusade.

United States Constitution

Expressing Viewpoints Write the following statement on the board: "That the people of Washington, D.C., have no representation in Congress is a violation of their democratic rights." Call on volunteers to express their views on this statement. **L2**

you don't say...

The Twenty-sixth Amendment Many people used the Vietnam War to justify the adoption of the Twenty-sixth Amendment. These people argued that those old enough to fight and die for their country were also old enough to vote.

CURRICULUM CONNECTION

Civics Why do states such as Maine and Minnesota consistently turn out 60 percent of their voters in presidential elections when the national average is about 50 percent? Some states make it easy for voters to get on the election rolls. Maine, Minnesota, and Wisconsin permit registration at the voting place on Election Day. North Dakota permits citizens to vote without registering.

CRITICAL THINKING ACTIVITY

Evaluating Have students list the advantages and disadvantages of the two-term limit for presidents. Ask volunteers to present and defend their lists. Then have students discuss the following: **Should there be presidential term limits? If so, how many terms should the president be limited to? Should members of Congress have term limits? Why or why not? L2**

Timesaving Tools

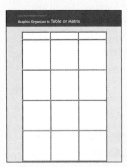

TeacherWorks™ All-In-One Planner and Resource Center

- **Interactive Teacher Edition** Access your Teacher Wraparound Edition and your classroom resources with a few easy clicks.
- **Interactive Lesson Planner** Planning has never been easier! Organize your week, month, semester, or year with all the lesson helps you need to make teaching creative, timely, and relevant.

Use Glencoe's **Presentation Plus!** multimedia teacher tool to easily present dynamic lessons that visually excite your students. Using Microsoft PowerPoint® you can customize the presentations to create your own personalized lessons.

TEACHING TRANSPARENCIES

Graphic Organizer 6

Why It Matters Chapter Transparency 6

APPLICATION AND ENRICHMENT

Linking Past and Present Activity 6

Enrichment Activity 6

Primary Source Reading 6

REVIEW AND REINFORCEMENT

Reteaching Activity 6

Vocabulary Activity 6

Time Line Activity 6

Critical Thinking Skills Activity 6

Meeting NCSS Standards

The following standards are highlighted in Chapter 6:

Section 1 | I | Culture: C, D
Section 2 | X | Civic Ideals and Practices: C, E, F, G, H
Section 3 | VI | Power, Authority, and Governance: B, C, E, I
Section 4 | IV | Individual Development and Identity: C, D, H

Local Standards

_____

_____

_____

_____

_____

Chapter 6 Resources

ASSESSMENT AND EVALUATION

**Chapter 6 Test
Form A**

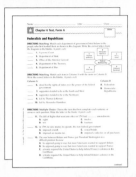

**Chapter 6 Test
Form B**

**Standardized Test Skills
Practice Workbook Activity 6**

**Performance Assessment
Activities and Rubrics 6**

**ExamView® Pro
Testmaker CD-ROM**

MULTIMEDIA

- Vocabulary PuzzleMaker CD-ROM
- Interactive Tutor Self-Assessment CD-ROM
- ExamView® Pro Testmaker CD-ROM
- Audio Program
- American History Primary Source Documents Library CD-ROM
- MindJogger Videoquiz
- Presentation Plus! CD-ROM
- TeacherWorks™ CD-ROM
- Interactive Student Edition CD-ROM
- Glencoe Skillbuilder Interactive Workbook CD-ROM, Level 2
- The *American Vision* Video Program
- American Music: Hits Through History
- American Music: Cultural Traditions

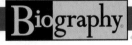

THE HISTORY CHANNEL®

The following videotape program is available from Glencoe as a supplement to Chapter 6:

- **Lewis and Clark** (ISBN 1-56-501592-4)

To order, call Glencoe at 1-800-334-7344. To find classroom resources to accompany many of these videos, check the following home pages:
A&E Television: www.aande.com
The History Channel: www.historychannel.com

SPANISH RESOURCES

The following Spanish language materials are available in the Spanish Resources Binder:

- **Spanish Guided Reading Activities**
- **Spanish Reteaching Activities**
- **Spanish Quizzes and Tests**
- **Spanish Vocabulary Activities**
- **Spanish Summaries**
- **The Declaration of Independence and United States Constitution Spanish Translation**

Use our Web site for additional resources. All essential content is covered in the Student Edition.

You and your students can visit tav.glencoe.com, the Web site companion to the ***American Vision***. This innovative integration of electronic and print media offers your students a wealth of opportunities. The student text directs students to the Web site for the following options:

- **Chapter Overviews**
- **Self-Check Quizzes**
- **Student Web Activities**
- **Textbook Updates**

Answers to the student Web activities are provided for you in the **Web Activity Lesson Plans.** Additional Web resources and Interactive Tutor Puzzles are also available.

Chapter 6 Resources

SECTION RESOURCES

Daily Objectives	Reproducible Resources	Multimedia Resources
SECTION 1 **Washington and Congress** 1. Explain Alexander Hamilton's economic initiatives. 2. Discuss the growing tensions between the nation's political parties.	Reproducible Lesson Plan 6–1 Daily Lecture and Discussion Notes 6–1 Guided Reading Activity 6–1* Section Quiz 6–1* Reading Essentials and Study Guide 6–1 Performance Assessment Activities and Rubrics	Daily Focus Skills Transparency 6–1 Interactive Tutor Self-Assessment CD-ROM ExamView® Pro Testmaker CD-ROM Presentation Plus! CD-ROM TeacherWorks™ CD-ROM Audio Program
SECTION 2 **Partisan Politics** 1. Discuss the rising tensions between Western settlers and Native Americans. 2. Explain the importance of Washington's Farewell Address.	Reproducible Lesson Plan 6–2 Daily Lecture and Discussion Notes 6–2 Guided Reading Activity 6–2* Section Quiz 6–2* Reading Essentials and Study Guide 6–2 Performance Assessment Activities and Rubrics	Daily Focus Skills Transparency 6–2 Interactive Tutor Self-Assessment CD-ROM ExamView® Pro Testmaker CD-ROM Presentation Plus! CD-ROM TeacherWorks™ CD-ROM Audio Program
SECTION 3 **Jefferson in Office** 1. Evaluate the changing role of the Supreme Court. 2. Discuss the events leading to the Louisiana Purchase.	Reproducible Lesson Plan 6–3 Daily Lecture and Discussion Notes 6–3 Guided Reading Activity 6–3* Section Quiz 6–3* Reading Essentials and Study Guide 6–3 Performance Assessment Activities and Rubrics Interpreting Political Cartoons Supreme Court Case Studies	Daily Focus Skills Transparency 6–3 American Art & Architecture Interactive Tutor Self-Assessment CD-ROM ExamView® Pro Testmaker CD-ROM Presentation Plus! CD-ROM TeacherWorks™ CD-ROM Audio Program
SECTION 4 **The War of 1812** 1. Describe why the United States declared war on Britain, and discuss the major campaigns of the war. 2. List the results of the Treaty of Ghent.	Reproducible Lesson Plan 6–4 Daily Lecture and Discussion Notes 6–4 Guided Reading Activity 6–4* Section Quiz 6–4* Reading Essentials and Study Guide 6–4 Performance Assessment Activities and Rubrics	Daily Focus Skills Transparency 6–4 Interactive Tutor Self-Assessment CD-ROM ExamView® Pro Testmaker CD-ROM Presentation Plus! CD-ROM Skillbuilder Interactive Workbook, Level 2 TeacherWorks™ CD-ROM Vocabulary PuzzleMaker CD-ROM Audio Program

0:00 OUT OF TIME?
Assign the Chapter 6 **Reading Essentials and Study Guide.**

*Also Available in Spanish

 Blackline Master   Transparency   CD-ROM   DVD

 Poster   Music Program   Audio Program   Videocassette

NATIONAL GEOGRAPHIC   Teacher's Corner

INDEX TO NATIONAL GEOGRAPHIC MAGAZINE

The following articles relate to this chapter.

- "Ghost Ships from the War of 1812: Hamilton and Scourge," March 1983
- "L'Enfant's Washington," August 1991
- "Lewis and Clark," October 1998
- "Old Ironsides," June 1997

NATIONAL GEOGRAPHIC SOCIETY PRODUCTS AVAILABLE FROM GLENCOE

To order the following products for use with this chapter, contact your local Glencoe sales representative, or call Glencoe at 1-800-334-7344:

- *PicturePack: Lewis & Clark* (Transparencies)
- *PictureShow: Lewis & Clark* (CD-ROM)

ADDITIONAL NATIONAL GEOGRAPHIC SOCIETY PRODUCTS

To order the following, call National Geographic at 1-800-368-2728:

- *1600 Pennsylvania Avenue: The White House* (Book and Video Set)
- *Wall Maps: Laminated North America Political*
- *Washington, D.C.* (Video)

NGS ONLINE

Access National Geographic's Web site for current events, atlas updates, activities, links, interactive features, and archives.

www.nationalgeographic.com

From the Classroom of...

Vince Pompo
Vernon-Verona-Sherrill
High School
Verona, NY

Influence of the American Revolution on the French Revolution: A Slideshow

This activity requires students to create a PowerPoint® slideshow that demonstrates the connection between the American and French Revolutions. The students must draw upon information from several primary sources and insert images taken from clip art, the Internet, or scanned pictures. Students can also create and insert charts, graphs, and tables.

Give them the following outline as a guide:

- 1st slide: Title slide
- 5–8 slides on causes of the French Revolution
- 4–6 slides on influence of American Revolution
- 2–4 slides on similarities and differences between revolutions
- Last slide: Summary

As a way to recognize exemplary work, award prizes for Most Accurate Slide Show, Best Use of Images, and Most Original Design.

ADDITIONAL RESOURCES FROM GLENCOE

- American Music: Cultural Traditions
- American Art & Architecture
- Outline Map Resource Book
- U.S. Desk Map
- Building Geography Skills for Life
- Inclusion for the High School Social Studies Classroom Strategies and Activities
- Teaching Strategies for the American History Classroom (Including Block Scheduling Pacing Guides)

KEY TO ABILITY LEVELS

Teaching strategies have been coded.

L1 BASIC activities for all students
L2 AVERAGE activities for average to above-average students
L3 CHALLENGING activities for above-average students
ELL ENGLISH LANGUAGE LEARNER activities

 Block Schedule

Activities that are suited to use within the block scheduling framework are identified by:

Why It Matters Activity

Have students look at the time line on pages 208 and 209 and choose the event that they think is most significant. Students should evaluate their answers after they have completed the chapter.

GLENCOE
TECHNOLOGY

The *American Vision* Video Program
To learn more about the War of 1812, have students view the Chapter 6 video, "The Battle of New Orleans," from the *American Vision* **Video Program.**

Available in DVD and VHS

MindJogger Videoquiz
Use the **MindJogger Videoquiz** to preview Chapter 6 content.

Available in VHS

CHAPTER

6 Federalists and Republicans *1789–1816*

Why It Matters

In the first government under the Constitution, important new institutions included the cabinet, a system of federal courts, and a national bank. Political parties gradually developed from the different views of citizens in the Northeast, West, and South. The new government faced special challenges in foreign affairs, including the War of 1812 with Great Britain.

The Impact Today

During this period, fundamental policies of American government came into being.
* *Politicians set important precedents for the national government and for relations between the federal and state governments. For example, the idea of a presidential cabinet originated with George Washington and has been followed by every president since that time*
* *President Washington's caution against foreign involvement powerfully influenced American foreign policy.*

The **American Vision** *Video The Chapter 6 video, "The Battle of New Orleans," focuses on this important event of the War of 1812.*

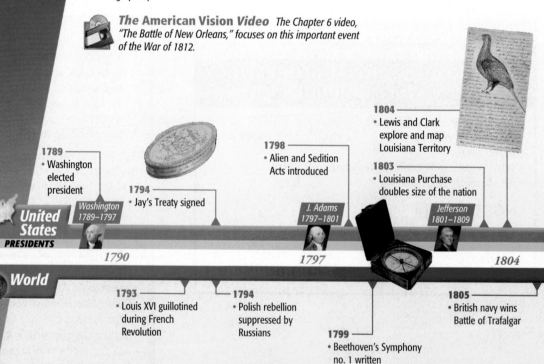

1789
• Washington elected president

1794
• Jay's Treaty signed

1798
• Alien and Sedition Acts introduced

1804
• Lewis and Clark explore and map Louisiana Territory

1803
• Louisiana Purchase doubles size of the nation

Washington 1789–1797

J. Adams 1797–1801

Jefferson 1801–1809

United States
PRESIDENTS

1790   *1797*   *1804*

World

1793
• Louis XVI guillotined during French Revolution

1794
• Polish rebellion suppressed by Russians

1799
• Beethoven's Symphony no. 1 written

1805
• British navy wins Battle of Trafalgar

208

TWO-MINUTE LESSON LAUNCHER

Ask students to share what they know about the first four presidents of the United States. Invite four students, one for each president, to record the answers using markers on large pieces of paper that can be displayed around the classroom. Encourage students to add to the lists as they study Chapter 6.

HISTORY
Online

Introduce students to chapter content and key terms by having them access the **Chapter 6 Overview** at tav.glencoe.com.

More About the Art

Images of George Washington abound. Early paintings and sculptures tended to make him a regal, unapproachable figure. As time progressed, his image was used commercially and by the mid-1800s, artists had made Washington a more human figure. Artists in the late 1800s and early 1900s returned Washington to a lofty pedestal during the Colonial Revival Movement. Artists included in the Colonial Revival Movement include J.L.G. Ferris (1863–1930), Norman Rockwell, and N.C. Wyeth.

Painter and President by J.L.G. Ferris

1807
• Embargo Act blocks American trade with Britain and France

Madison 1809–1817

1811
• Battle of Tippecanoe fought against Tecumseh and his confederacy

1812
• United States declares war on Britain

1814
• Hartford Convention meets
• Treaty of Ghent signed

1811   *1818*

1808
• Source of the Ganges River discovered

1812
• Napoleon's invasion and retreat from Russia

1816
• Argentina declares independence

HISTORY
Online

Chapter Overview
Visit the *American Vision* Web site at tav.glencoe.com and click on **Chapter Overviews—Chapter 6** to preview chapter information.

TIME LINE ACTIVITY

Have students select an event from the time lines on pages 208–209, 210, 215, 221, and 228. Ask students to read the corresponding portion of the chapter to identify the cause(s) and effect(s) of the event. Call on volunteers to create a "human" time line in the front of the class and present findings of their events.

209

GRAPHIC ORGANIZER ACTIVITY

Organizing Information Have students create a graphic organizer similar to the one shown below to explain strategies employed by the United States and Britain during the War of 1812. *(A. Invade Canada. B. Raid coastal cities. C. Isolate New England. D. Seize New Orleans)*

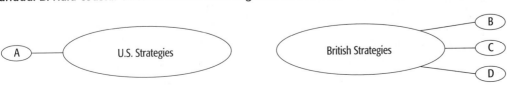

A — U.S. Strategies

British Strategies — B — C — D

209

1 FOCUS

Section Overview
This section focuses on establishing a central government for the new nation.

BELLRINGER
Skillbuilder Activity

 Project transparency and have students answer the question.

📂 Available as a blackline master.

Daily Focus Skills Transparency 6–1

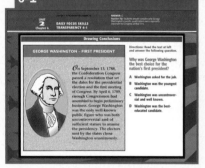

Guide to Reading

Answers to Graphic: Tasks of Congress: organized government by creating departments; organized judicial branch; adopted the Bill of Rights; financed government by imposing tariff and tonnage; created national bank; accepted debt of Confederation Congress at face value to establish ability to borrow money

Preteaching Vocabulary
Have students skim Section 1 to glean the meaning or significance of each of the Key Terms and Names.

SECTION 1 Washington and Congress

Guide to Reading

Main Idea
With the adoption of the new Constitution, Americans and their leaders had to establish a central government to deal effectively with the challenges facing the new nation.

Key Terms and Names
cabinet, Tariff of 1789, bond, speculator, enumerated powers, implied powers, Bank of the United States, Whiskey Rebellion, agrarianism

Reading Strategy
Organizing As you read about how the leaders of the United States established a central government, complete a graphic organizer similar to the one below by indicating the tasks completed by Congress.

Tasks of Congress

Reading Objectives
• **Explain** Alexander Hamilton's economic initiatives.
• **Discuss** the growing tensions between the nation's political parties.

Section Theme
Culture and Traditions George Washington helped define the office of the American presidency.

Preview of Events

♦1789 ♦1791 ♦1793 ♦1795

1789
George Washington elected president

1791
First Bank of the United States chartered

1792
Washington reelected president

1794
Whiskey Rebellion quelled in western Pennsylvania

★ *An American Story* ★

George Washington

On April 6, 1789, the ballots of the presidential electors were officially counted in the new United States Senate. As expected, George Washington became the first president of the United States under the new Constitution. Americans everywhere greeted the news with great joy, but Washington remained unexcited. Calling his election "the event which I have long dreaded," Washington described his feelings as "not unlike those of a culprit who is going to the place of his execution."

Although Washington had high hopes for the new Constitution, he did not know if it would work as intended. "I am . . . [bringing] the voice of the people and a good name of my own on this voyage; but what returns will be made of them, Heaven alone can foretell." Despite his doubts and frustrations with the "ten thousand embarrassments, perplexities and troubles of the presidency," the new president retained his faith in the American people. He explained that "nothing but harmony, honesty, industry and frugality are necessary to make us a great and happy people. . . . We are surrounded by the blessings of nature."

—adapted from *Washington: The Indispensable Man*

Creating a New Government
The Philadelphia Convention had given the nation a new Constitution. Washington's task, and the task facing the newly elected Congress, was to take the words of the Constitution and turn them into an effective government for the United States.

210 CHAPTER 6 Federalists and Republicans

📁 **SECTION RESOURCES**

📂 **Reproducible Masters**
• Reproducible Lesson Plan 6–1
• Daily Lecture and Discussion Notes 6–1
• Guided Reading Activity 6–1
• Section Quiz 6–1
• Reading Essentials and Study Guide 6–1
• Performance Assessment Activities and Rubrics

🖺 **Transparencies**
• Daily Focus Skills Transparency 6–1

Multimedia
🖸 Interactive Tutor Self-Assessment CD-ROM
🖸 ExamView® Pro Testmaker CD-ROM
🖸 Presentation Plus! CD-ROM
🖸 TeacherWorks™ CD-ROM
🎧 Audio Program

GOVERNMENT

Institutions of Power One of the first tasks of the new government was to provide the president with a bureaucracy to handle different responsibilities. In 1789 Congress created the Department of State, the Department of the Treasury, the Department of War, and the Office of the Attorney General.

To manage these departments, Washington wanted individuals who were "disposed to measure matters on a Continental Scale" instead of thinking only of their own states. He chose Thomas Jefferson as secretary of state, Alexander Hamilton for the Treasury Department, and General Henry Knox as secretary of war. For attorney general, Washington selected Edmund Randolph, the former governor of Virginia. Washington regularly met with these men to ask for their advice. The department heads came to be known as the cabinet, a group of advisers to the president.

Congress also organized the judicial branch. In the Judiciary Act of 1789, Congress established 13 district courts, 3 courts of appeal, and the Supreme Court. With the Senate's consent, Washington chose the federal judges, including John Jay as the first chief justice of the United States.

The Bill of Rights One of the most important acts of Congress was the introduction of the Bill of Rights. During the campaign to ratify the Constitution, the Federalists had promised to add such a bill. James Madison, one of the leaders in Congress, made the passage of a Bill of Rights top priority. He hoped it would demonstrate the good faith of federal leaders and build support for the new government.

In drafting the Bill of Rights, Madison relied heavily on the Virginia Declaration of Rights that George Mason had prepared in 1776 and the Virginia Statute for Religious Freedom that Thomas Jefferson had written in 1786. In late September 1789, after many debates, Congress agreed on 12 constitutional amendments. They were then sent to the states for ratification, but only 10 were approved. These 10 went into effect in 1791. They are generally referred to as the Bill of Rights, although only the first 8 protect the rights of individuals against actions of the federal government. The Ninth Amendment states that the people have other rights not listed. The Tenth Amendment states that any powers not specifically given to the federal government are reserved for the states.

✓ Reading Check **Identifying** What executive departments did Congress establish?

Financing the Government

By the end of 1789, the new federal government was up and running. The government's most pressing need now was a source of revenue. Without money, the government could not operate. James Madison and Alexander Hamilton responded to this need with different plans for financing the government.

The Tariff of 1789 James Madison suggested that the federal government raise most of its money by taxing imports from other countries. After much discussion, Congress passed the **Tariff of 1789.** This law required importers to pay a percentage of the value of their cargo when they landed it in the United States. Shippers also had to pay tonnage—a tax based on how much their ships carried.

The tariffs and tonnage rates angered many Southern planters. High tonnage rates meant they would be charged higher rates to ship their rice and

🎨 **History** *Through Art*

First Cabinet Depicted with the president (far right) are, from left, Henry Knox, Thomas Jefferson, Edmund Randolph, and Alexander Hamilton. What departments did these four cabinet members head?

2 TEACH

Daily Lecture and Discussion Notes 6-1

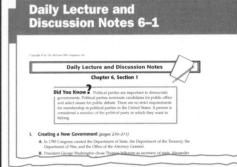

Copyright © by The McGraw-Hill Companies, Inc.

Daily Lecture and Discussion Notes
Chapter 6, Section 1

Did You Know? Political parties are important to democratic governments. Political parties nominate candidates for public office and select issues for public debate. There are no strict requirements for membership in political parties in the United States. A person is considered a member of the political party in which they want to belong.

I. Creating a New Government *(pages 210–211)*

A. In 1789 Congress created the Department of State, the Department of the Treasury, the Department of War, and the Office of the Attorney General.

B. President George Washington chose Thomas Jefferson as secretary of state, Alexander

Discussing a Topic Organize the class into 10 groups. Assign each group one of the amendments that comprise the Bill of Rights. Have each group identify a current issue that relates to their assigned amendment. Have the group present the issue to the class and lead a class discussion about it. **L1**

✓**Reading Check**

Answer: Department of State, Department of the Treasury, Department of War, Office of the Attorney General

🎨 **History** *Through Art*

Answer: Thomas Jefferson, Secretary of State; Alexander Hamilton, Secretary of the Treasury; General Henry Knox, Secretary of War; Edmund Randolph, Attorney General
Ask: Why was Thomas Jefferson a logical choice for Secretary of State? *(He had represented the colonies in France during the War for Independence.)*

COOPERATIVE LEARNING ACTIVITY

Preparing an Oral Presentation Organize the class into 10 groups. Assign each group one of the amendments included in the Bill of Rights. Have each group research their amendment and create an oral presentation answering the following question: **Why was this amendment important to citizens of the United States in 1789?**

Use the rubric for a cooperative group management plan on pages 81–82 in the *Performance Assessment Activities and Rubrics.*

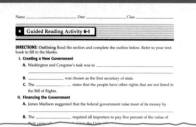
Writing a Job Description Have students write a job description for the position of President of the United States in 1789. The job descriptions should include a list of duties and qualifications. Encourage students to use help wanted ads in local newspapers or on the Internet as references. **L2**

📁 Use the rubric for a magazine/newspaper/Web site article or help-wanted ad on pages 85–86 in the *Performance Assessment Activities and Rubrics.*

History *Through Art*

Answer: It served as the nation's first capital.
Ask: Why was the capital eventually moved to the District of Columbia? *(It was part of a compromise to get Hamilton's financial program passed in Congress.)*

FYI

The founding of the Bank of the United States did not end the controversy surrounding the national bank issue. In 1811 its 20-year charter was not renewed.

---

tobacco to Europe. The new duty meant higher prices for the many goods they imported. Many Southerners began to suspect that the new federal government was opposed to their region's interests.

ECONOMICS

Hamilton's Financial Program Hamilton supported the Tariff of 1789, but he believed the government also needed the ability to borrow money. In 1790, he asked Congress to accept the debts of the Continental Congress at their full value. To fund the Revolutionary War, the Confederation Congress had issued bonds—paper notes promising to repay money after a certain length of time with interest. By 1789, the United States owed roughly $40 million to American citizens and another $11.7 million to France, Spain, and the Netherlands. Few believed the bonds would be repaid in full, and they had fallen in value to as little as 10 cents on the dollar.

History *Through Art*

First Capital Washington took his oath of office on the balcony of Federal Hall in New York City, the nation's first capital. This Amos Doolittle engraving was made from a famous painting. Why is Federal Hall identified as "the seat of Congress"?

212 CHAPTER 6 Federalists and Republicans

Hamilton believed that by accepting these debts at their full value, the wealthy creditors, bankers, and merchants who owned the bonds would have a stake in the federal government's success and enough confidence in its financial stability to loan it money in the future. Hamilton had described the importance of debt several years earlier:

❝A national debt, if it is not excessive, will be to us a national blessing; it will be a powerful cement of our new union. It will also create a necessity for keeping up taxation . . . which without being oppressive, will be a spur to industry. . . .❞

—quoted in *America, A Narrative History*

Opposition to Hamilton's Plan Led by Madison, critics argued that Hamilton's plan was unfair to the original purchasers of the bonds, many of whom were farmers and Revolutionary War veterans and their widows. These people, fearing they would never be paid, had sold their bonds at a discount to speculators—people willing to take a risk in hopes of a future financial gain. Madison was outraged that speculators who had paid as little as $10 for a $100 bond would now receive full value.

Madison and other Southerners were also upset because Northerners owned most of the bonds, while much of the tax money that would be used to pay off the bonds would come from the South. Madison also worried that creditors would eventually dominate American society and endanger liberty.

The congressional debate over Hamilton's proposals raged for months. Finally, in July 1790, Hamilton, Madison, and Jefferson struck a deal. Madison and Jefferson would use their influence to convince Southerners in Congress to vote for Hamilton's plan. In return, the capital of the United States would be moved from New York to a section of land along the Potomac River to be called the District of Columbia. Southerners believed that having the capital in the South would help to offset the strength of the Northern states in Congress.

The Bank of the United States With his system of public credit finally in place, Hamilton asked Congress to create a national bank. He argued that the government needed the bank to manage its debts and interest payments. The bank would also issue bank notes—paper money. The notes also would provide a national currency that would promote trade, encourage investment, and stimulate economic growth.

Southerners opposed the plan. They pointed out that Northern merchants would own most of the

---

MEETING SPECIAL NEEDS

Visual/Spatial Have students create a political cartoon that either supports or opposes the tariff of 1789. Encourage students to look at styles of political cartoons from the era and to use the types of tools that a satirist of the era may have used. Have students display their cartoons around the class. **L2**

📁 Refer to *Inclusion for the High School Social Studies Classroom Strategies and Activities* in the TCR.

bank's stock. Madison argued that Congress could not establish a bank because it was not among the federal government's **enumerated powers,** or powers specifically mentioned in the Constitution.

Despite Madison's objections, Congress passed the bank bill. Washington realized that his decision to sign the bill or to veto it would set an important precedent. Attorney General Randolph and Secretary of State Jefferson argued that the Constitution did not give the federal government the power to create a bank. Hamilton disagreed, pointing out that Article I, Section 8, of the Constitution gave the federal government the power "to make all laws which shall be necessary and proper" to execute its responsibilities. The "necessary and proper" clause created **implied powers**—powers not explicitly listed in the Constitution but necessary for the government to do its job.

A national bank, Hamilton argued, was necessary to collect taxes, regulate trade, and provide for the common defense. Jefferson agreed that implied powers existed, but he believed "necessary and proper" meant absolutely necessary, not simply convenient. After studying Hamilton's response, Washington agreed to sign the bill. In 1791 the **Bank of the United States** was established for a 20-year period.

The Whiskey Rebellion Hamilton believed the federal government also had to establish its right to impose direct taxes on the people. In 1791, at Hamilton's urging, Congress imposed a tax on the manufacture of whiskey. The new tax enraged Western farmers. In the Western regions of the United States, where bank notes and coins were not available in large quantities, whiskey was used as a medium of exchange. Because the Spanish had closed the Mississippi, distilling whiskey was also the easiest way for Western farmers to move their grain to Eastern markets.

Although complaints against the whiskey tax began in 1791, it was not until the summer of 1794 that a rebellion erupted. In western Pennsylvania, farmers terrorized tax collectors, stopped court proceedings, robbed the mail, and destroyed the whiskey-making stills of those who paid the tax.

Hamilton wanted to establish firmly the authority of the federal government. He urged President Washington to put down the rebellion. In August 1794 Washington sent nearly 13,000 troops to crush the **Whiskey Rebellion.** The huge army caused the rebels to disperse without a fight. The federal government's willingness to use troops against its own citizens, however, worried many people.

> ✓ **Reading Check** **Explaining** Why did Madison object to Hamilton's plan for a national bank?

The Rise of Political Parties

During Washington's first term in office, the debate over Hamilton's financial program split Congress into factions. By the mid-term elections of 1794, these factions had become the nation's first political parties. Hamilton's supporters called themselves **Federalists.** Hamilton's opponents, led by Madison and Jefferson, took the name Democratic-Republicans, although most people at the time referred to them as **Republicans.** In the 1800s, the party became known as the Democrats. Today's Republican Party is a different party.

Commander in chief reviewing the troops

HISTORY Online

Student Web Activity Visit the *American Vision* Web site at tav.glencoe.com and click on *Student Web Activities—Chapter 6* for an activity on early political parties.

CHAPTER 6 Federalists and Republicans **213**

---

3 ASSESS

Assign Section 1 Assessment as homework or as an in-class activity.

● Have students use the **Interactive Tutor Self-Assessment CD-ROM.**

Reading Essentials and Study Guide 6–1

Section Quiz 6–1

✓ Reading Check

Answer: Madison argued that Congress could not establish a bank because it was not among the federal government's enumerated powers, or powers specifically mentioned in the Constitution.

HISTORY Online

Objectives and answers to the student activity can be found in the **Web Activity Lesson Plan** at tav.glencoe.com.

INTERDISCIPLINARY CONNECTIONS ACTIVITY

Economics Have students use the Treasury Department's Web site to research the national debt for the years 1800, 1900, and 2000. Have students explain why it is not appropriate to compare these numbers directly. Encourage students to use an inflation calculator to calculate the debt figures in comparable dollars. Provide students with the Internet addresses shown below. **L2**

The Public Debt Online—http://www.publicdebt.treas.gov/opd/opd.htm

CJR Dollar Conversion Calculator—http://www.cjr.org/resources/inflater.asp

Chart Skills

Answers:
1. Federalists favored tariffs because they protected domestic industries.
2. Democratic-Republicans

Chart Skills Practice

Ask: Which party favored giving the most people a say in government? *(Democratic-Republicans)*

Reteach

For each of the major headings in this section, have students write and answer a question similar to the "Reading Check" questions. Invite students to ask their questions and call on volunteers to answer them.

Enrich

Have students use library and Internet resources to research the origins of current political parties. Ask students to write a paragraph about each of the major parties.

✓ Reading Check

Answer: Federalists favored a strong central government led by the rich and an economy based on manufacturing and trade. Democratic-Republicans favored people owning land, an economy based on agriculture, and the rights of states over the federal government.

4 CLOSE

Have students explain George Washington's role in each of the events mentioned in this section.

Competing National Visions

Hamilton and the Federalists	Jefferson and the Democratic-Republicans
National government supreme	State governments supreme
Ruling power given to wealthy, educated	Ruling power given to *all* landowners
Government should promote manufacturing	Government should promote agriculture
Loose interpretation of the Constitution	Strict interpretation of the Constitution
Protective tariffs protect domestic industries	Protective tariffs burden farmers

Chart Skills

1. **Interpreting Charts** Which party favored tariffs, and why?
2. **Drawing Conclusions** Which party do you think distrusted national government more?

Hamilton and the Federalists Hamilton favored a strong national government. He believed that democracy was dangerous to liberty and stated that "the people are turbulent and changing; they seldom judge or determine right." This distrust led him to favor putting government into the hands of the "rich, well born, and able."

Hamilton also believed that manufacturing and trade were the basis of national wealth and power. He favored policies that would support these areas of the economy. Supporters of the Federalist Party often included artisans, merchants, manufacturers, and bankers. The party also attracted urban workers and Eastern farmers who benefited from trade.

Jefferson and the Republicans Although James Madison led the opposition to Hamilton's program in Congress, Thomas Jefferson emerged as the leader of the Democratic-Republicans. Jefferson believed that the strength of the United States was its independent farmers. His ideas are sometimes referred to as agrarianism. Jefferson argued that owning land enabled people to be independent. As long as most people owned their own land, they would fight to preserve the Republic.

Jefferson feared that too much of an emphasis on commerce would lead to a society divided between the rich who owned everything and the poor who worked for wages. He also believed that the wealthy would corrupt the government and threaten the rights and liberties of ordinary people. In general, Democratic-Republicans supported agriculture over commerce and trade. They also expressed concern that Hamilton's policies tended to favor the North. Over time, the Democratic-Republicans became the party that stood for the rights of states against the power of the federal government.

The development of America's first two political parties divided the country regionally. The rural South and West tended to support the Republicans, while the more urban Northeast tended to support the Federalists. Although these parties emerged during the dispute over Hamilton's programs, events in Europe would deepen the divisions between them and create new crises for the young Republic.

✓ Reading Check **Classifying** What were the nation's first two political parties, and what issues did they favor?

SECTION 1 ASSESSMENT

Checking for Understanding
1. **Define:** cabinet, bond, speculator, enumerated powers, implied powers, agrarianism.
2. **Identify:** Tariff of 1789, Bank of the United States, Whiskey Rebellion.
3. **Describe** the intended purpose of the national bank.

Reviewing Themes
4. **Culture and Traditions** What precedent did George Washington set as president of the United States?

Critical Thinking
5. **Synthesizing** Why did Hamilton think it was important to pay the national debt, the domestic debt, and the state debts?
6. **Categorizing** Use a graphic organizer similar to the one below to list the first political parties, who their supporters were, and what issues they supported.

Political Party	Supporters	Issues Supported

Analyzing Visuals
7. **Studying Art** Examine the painting on page 211 of President Washington's first cabinet. What was the function of this group, and who served as its first members?

Writing About History
8. **Expository Writing** Imagine you are James Madison. Write a speech explaining why you are against Alexander Hamilton's financial program.

214 CHAPTER 6 Federalists and Republicans

SECTION 1 ASSESSMENT ANSWERS

1. Terms are in blue.
2. Tariff of 1789 *(p. 211)*, Bank of the United States *(p. 213)*, Whiskey Rebellion *(p. 213)*
3. It managed the government's debts and interest payments, made loans to the government and private individuals, and issued currency.
4. Washington met regularly with his cabinet.
5. Doing so would give creditors who owned bonds a stake in the federal government's success.
6. Federalist supporters included artisans, merchants, manufacturers, and bankers; issues: strong national government, manufacturing, and trade; Democratic-Republican supporters included independent farmers; issues: agriculture and states' rights
7. Students' answers should match information in the text.
8. Speeches should be based on Madison's actual beliefs.

Guide to Reading

Main Idea
The United States faced difficult foreign policy challenges during the presidencies of Washington and Adams.

Key Terms and Names
Jay's Treaty, most-favored nation, Pinckney's Treaty, Washington's Farewell Address, Quasi-War, Alien and Sedition Acts, alien, sedition, interposition, nullification

Reading Strategy
Categorizing As you read about the foreign policy challenges of the Washington and Adams presidencies, complete a graphic organizer similar to the one below by filling in the provisions of treaties made by the United States.

Treaty	Provisions
Jay's Treaty	
Pinckney's Treaty	
Convention of 1800	

Reading Objectives
• **Discuss** the rising tensions between Western settlers and Native Americans.
• **Explain** the importance of Washington's Farewell Address.

Section Theme
Civic Rights and Responsibilities Disagreements between political parties threatened citizens' rights.

Preview of Events

1795	1797	1799	1801

1794 Jay's Treaty signed with Britain

1795 Pinckney's Treaty signed with Spain; Treaty of Greenville signed with 12 Native American nations

1798 Alien and Sedition Acts introduced

1801 House of Representatives chooses Jefferson to be president

---

★ An American Story ★

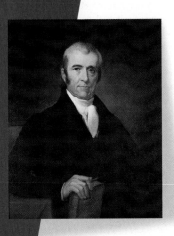

John Marshall

In 1797 Americans John Marshall, Charles Pinckney, and Elbridge Gerry went to Paris to hold talks with the French government about improving relations between the two countries. After weeks of waiting, three agents representing Charles Maurice de Talleyrand, the French minister of foreign affairs, approached the Americans. They asked for a bribe of $250,000 just to initiate talks, and they also sought an American loan of $12 million. In his journal, Marshall recounts an exchange between Pinckney and one of the agents (a "Mr. H."):

❝Mr. H. again returned to the subject of money. Said he Gentlemen you do not speak to the point—it is money—it is expected that you will offer money—Genl. Pinckney said we had spoken to that point very explicitly. . . . No said he, you have not. What is your answer? Genl. Pinckney replied it is no, no, not a sixpence.❞

When President John Adams informed Congress of the incident, he referred to the French agents as X, Y, and Z, inspiring newspapers to refer to the incident as the XYZ Affair. Newspaper writers turned Pinckney's response into the stirring Federalist slogan, "Millions for defense, but not one cent for tribute."

—adapted from *The Flavor of the Past*

Washington's Foreign Policy

Shortly after George Washington was inaugurated in 1789, the French Revolution began in Europe. At first, most Americans sympathized with the revolutionaries, who seemed to be fighting for the same rights Americans had won a few years earlier. By the

CHAPTER 6 Federalists and Republicans **215**

---

1 FOCUS

Section Overview
This section examines the challenges of the Washington and Adams presidencies.

BELLRINGER
Skillbuilder Activity

Project transparency and have students answer the question.

Available as a blackline master.

Daily Focus Skills Transparency 6–2

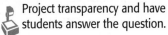

Guide to Reading

Answers to Graphic: Jay's Treaty: Britain had the right to seize cargoes bound for French ports, Britain agreed to submit the issue of compensation to American merchants for seized cargo to international arbitration, and Britain gave U.S. most-favored nation status; Pinckney's Treaty: U.S. given right to navigate Mississippi and to deposit goods at New Orleans; Convention of 1800: U.S. gave up claims against France for damage to American shipping, France released U.S. from Treaty of 1778

Preteaching Vocabulary
Have students choose one of the proper names from the list of Key Terms and Names. Ask students to skim the text to find the name and write a brief explanation of it. Ask for volunteers to share their explanations.

SECTION RESOURCES

📁 Reproducible Masters
• Reproducible Lesson Plan 6–2
• Daily Lecture and Discussion Notes 6–2
• Guided Reading Activity 6–2
• Section Quiz 6–2
• Reading Essentials and Study Guide 6–2
• Performance Assessment Activities and Rubrics

Transparencies
• Daily Focus Skills Transparency 6–2

Multimedia
• Interactive Tutor Self-Assessment CD-ROM
• ExamView® Pro Testmaker CD-ROM
• Presentation Plus! CD-ROM
• TeacherWorks™ CD-ROM
• Audio Program

215

2 TEACH

Analyzing *Political Cartoons*

Answer: the British right to seize cargo bound for France and the lack of compensation for American goods
Ask: With so much anger about the treaty, why did Washington implement it? *(to prevent a war with Great Britain and to protect the American economy)*

Writing a Report Have students use library and Internet resources to research a current issue related to most-favored nation clauses (now known as Permanent Normal Trade Relations). Then have them write a three- to five-page report on the topic. **L2**

you don't say...

The Tradition of Tribute The Romans made the countries they conquered pay tribute. The payment was seen as a sign of submission or the price of peace and protection. Tributes were also paid in feudal times. By the time of the XYZ Affair, the word *tribute* was synonymous with *bribe*.

Analyzing *Political Cartoons*

A Fiery Protest Antifederalists burned at the stake a figure representing John Jay after Jay's Treaty with England was signed in 1794. What parts of the treaty angered people such as those shown here?

spring of 1792, however, a new group of French radicals had seized control. They stripped aristocrats of their property and executed thousands of people, including the king and queen.

In 1793, eleven days after the execution of the French king, France declared war on Britain. Since both countries traded with the United States, Americans quickly found themselves embroiled in the European conflict.

The American Response Americans were divided over the French Revolution. Many Federalists, horrified by the violence and chaos, opposed it. Despite the bloodshed, many Republicans supported it, admiring the fight for liberty.

The war between Britain and France put Washington in a difficult position. The Treaty of 1778 with France required the United States to help defend France's colonies in the Caribbean. Fulfilling this agreement might mean war with Great Britain.

On April 22, 1793, Washington issued a proclamation declaring the United States to be "friendly and impartial" toward both warring powers.

Jay's Treaty Despite Washington's declaration, the British navy began intercepting all neutral ships carrying goods to French ports, including hundreds of American ships. At the same time, reports appeared that the British, operating out of forts they still occupied on American territory, were inciting Native Americans to attack western settlers. These reports, combined with British seizures of American ships, pushed Congress to the brink of war in 1794.

Desperately hoping to avoid war, Washington sent John Jay to Britain to seek a solution. The British were busy fighting France. They did not want to fight the United States, but they also knew that the United States depended on trade with Britain. They agreed to sign **Jay's Treaty**, but they drove a hard bargain.

Jay was forced to agree that Britain had the right to seize cargoes bound for French ports. He also failed to get compensation for American merchants whose goods had been seized. The British did agree, however, to submit the issue to international arbitration— a hearing by neutral third countries. In return, the British gave the United States **most-favored nation** status. This meant that American merchants would not be discriminated against when they traded with Britain. Britain also allowed limited American trade with its Caribbean colonies.

When Jay's Treaty was sent to the Senate for ratification, the senators were shocked by its terms and tried to keep them secret. Although they eventually ratified the treaty, news of its terms leaked to the public. The Republicans immediately attacked the treaty, accusing the Federalists of being pro-British. Across much of the country, public meetings were held condemning the treaty. After prolonged deliberation, Washington agreed to implement the treaty. The decision prevented war with Great Britain and protected the fragile American economy.

Pinckney's Treaty Jay's Treaty also helped the United States win concessions from Spain, which still controlled Florida and territory west of the Mississippi River. In 1795 Spain joined France in its struggle against Britain. The signing of Jay's Treaty raised fears in Spain that the British and Americans might now join forces to seize Spain's North American holdings. Spain quickly offered to negotiate all outstanding issues with the United States. Washington sent **Thomas Pinckney** from South Carolina to negotiate with Spain.

COOPERATIVE LEARNING ACTIVITY

Creating a Map Organize the class into three groups. Assign each group one of the following countries: Great Britain, Spain, or France. Have each group create a map that shows the territorial interests that each country had in the Western Hemisphere. Encourage groups also to indicate the shipping routes from Europe to the Western Hemisphere.

Use the rubric for a cooperative group management plan on pages 81–82 in the **Performance Assessment Activities and Rubrics.**

In 1795 the Spanish signed the Treaty of San Lorenzo—better known as **Pinckney's Treaty.** The treaty granted the United States the right to navigate the Mississippi and to deposit goods at the port of New Orleans. The treaty won broad acceptance, especially among western farmers who wanted to use the Mississippi to get crops to market.

✓ **Reading Check** **Summarizing** Why did President Washington choose neutrality in the war between Britain and France?

GEOGRAPHY

Westward Expansion

By 1790 the area between the Appalachian Mountains and the Mississippi River had become the most rapidly growing region in the United States. Drawn by abundant land, fertile soil, wide rivers, and a wide variety of fish and game, Americans flocked to the region. In less than a decade, Kentucky had grown from a few hundred settlers to over 70,000, and in 1792, it became a state. Four years later, Tennessee became a state as well. In the meantime, other settlers were moving steadily west from Pennsylvania and Virginia into the Northwest Territory. The rise in white settlement led to confrontations with Native Americans in the region.

In the Northwest Territory, a chief of the Miami people named **Little Turtle** had formed a confederacy of the Miami, Shawnee, Delaware, and other groups. The confederacy sought to defend its land against white settlement. In the fall of 1790, Little Turtle's warriors defeated American troops led by General Josiah Harmar. In November 1791, they ambushed another American force led by General Arthur St. Clair, killing nearly half his men.

After these disasters, Washington sent General Anthony Wayne to put down Native American resistance. In August 1794, a large force made up of Shawnee, Ottawa, Chippewa, and Potawatomi warriors, led by the Shawnee chief Blue Jacket, attacked Wayne's troops at the Battle of Fallen Timbers, near where Toledo, Ohio, is located today. This time the American troops inflicted heavy losses on the Native Americans.

Wayne's victory dealt a decisive blow to Native American resistance in the Northwest Territory. In August 1795, 12 Native American nations signed the Treaty of Greenville. (See map on page 235.) They agreed to give up part of what is today southern Ohio and Indiana in exchange for a yearly payment of $10,000 from the federal government. They also gave up land near where Chicago, Detroit, and Vincennes, Indiana, are located today. After the treaty signing, the flow of Americans into the region rapidly increased. By 1803 Ohio had enough settlers to become a state.

✓ **Reading Check** **Examining** Why did Little Turtle form a confederacy?

Washington Leaves Office

By the end of his second term in office, George Washington had grown exasperated by party politics and the attacks on his character. He decided to retire.

The Farewell Address Before leaving office, the president wrote a letter to the American people. Widely reprinted, **Washington's Farewell Address** warned Americans against sectionalism—to avoid

Picturing **History**

Battle of Fallen Timbers This monument commemorates the victory of General Anthony Wayne (left) over Blue Jacket. The Treaty of Greenville in 1795 opened the Ohio territory to American settlers. What amount did the government pay the Native Americans?

CHAPTER 6 Federalists and Republicans **217**

Guided Reading Activity 6-2

Name _____ Date _____ Class _____

★ **Guided Reading Activity 6-2**

DIRECTIONS: Recording Who, What, When, Where, Why, and How Read the section and answer the questions below. Refer to your textbook to write the answers.

1. Why did Republicans support the French Revolution? _____
2. **Where** were the colonies the United States was required to defend through the Treaty of 1778? _____
3. **How** did President Washington attempt to avoid war with Great Britain in 1793? _____
4. Why did the Republicans attack Jay's Treaty? _____
5. What benefit for the Americans came out of Pinckney's Treaty? _____

✓ **Reading Check**

Answer: to avoid breaking the treaty with France or war with Britain

✓ **Reading Check**

Answer: to defend land against white settlers

FYI

Some historians believe that the Shawnee chief Blue Jacket was Marmaduke Van Swearingen, a white teenager who was captured by the Shawnee. There is little hard evidence to substantiate this claim and DNA samples from the descendants of Blue Jacket and the Van Swearingen family indicate that the families are not related. The controversy continues because there is some dispute over whether the DNA samples were from bona fide descendants.

Picturing **History**

Answer: $10,000 annually
Ask: How did the treaty affect the region? *(It allowed for a rapid increase in the number of Americans who moved to the region and allowed Ohio to become a state in 1803.)*

MEETING SPECIAL NEEDS

Auditory/Musical Have interested students research the patriotic songs that were popular in the late 1700s. Ask students to select one of the songs and either perform it for the class or find a recording of the song to play to the class. After students have heard the song, have the presenter explain the significance of the song and any symbolism used in the song. **L2**

📁 Refer to *Inclusion for the High School Social Studies Classroom Strategies and Activities* in the TCR.

Discussing a Topic Ask students if they know of any other armed confrontations that could be labeled quasi wars. Ask students how such conflicts compare to the Quasi-War with France. **L2**

✓ Reading Check

Answer: Washington advised Americans to be cautious of political parties and to avoid permanent alliances with foreign nations.

Analyzing *Political Cartoons*

Answer: Britain
Ask: Who was president during the Quasi-War with France? *(John Adams)*

✓ Reading Check

Answer: The French were stopping American ships and seizing their cargo if they were going to Britain.

you don't say...

American Standard English Noah Webster published a work in 1789 that sought to create a noticeable difference between English spoken in Great Britain and what he termed American standard English. Some of his ideas were readily accepted, such as deleting the "u" from words like *neighbor* (*neighbour* is the British spelling).

dividing the country into North against South or East against West. Washington also cautioned Americans about political parties:

> 66 Let me now . . . warn you in the most solemn manner against the baneful effects of the spirit of party. . . . The disorders and miseries, which result, gradually incline the minds of men to seek security and repose in the absolute power of an individual. 99

Washington also warned against Americans becoming too attached to any foreign nation:

> 66 The great rule of conduct for us, in regard to foreign nations is in extending our commercial relations to have with them as little *political* connection as possible. . . . 'Tis our true policy to steer clear of permanent alliances with any portion of the foreign world. 99
>
> —from Washington's Farewell Address

📖 *(See page 1068 for a longer excerpt from Washington's Farewell Address.)*

The Election of 1796 With Washington stepping down, the United States held its first openly contested election. The Federalists rallied around John Adams for president, while the Republicans nominated Thomas Jefferson. Anger over Jay's Treaty made the election close, but when the electoral votes were tallied, John Adams edged out Jefferson 71 to 68 and became the second president of the United States.

✓ Reading Check **Describing** What advice did Washington give about political parties and alliances?

218   CHAPTER 6   Federalists and Republicans

The Quasi-War With France

President Adams faced troubled times at home and abroad. Enraged by Jay's Treaty, the French had begun stopping American ships and seizing their goods if they were going to Britain. France's actions led many Federalists to call for war against France. Although critical of the French, Adams, like Washington, was reluctant to involve the United States in a major war. Instead he sent Charles Pinckney, Elbridge Gerry, and John Marshall to negotiate with France. Americans called the French effort to get bribes before beginning negotiations the XYZ Affair (described on page 215).

Irate Americans, who had been angry with Britain a few years earlier, now called for war against France. Resolutions, mass meetings, and patriotic songs further aroused the public. In June 1798, Congress suspended trade with France and directed the navy to capture armed French ships. The two nations were soon fighting an undeclared war at sea that came to be known as the **Quasi-War.**

In the fall of 1798, France proposed new negotiations. In September 1800, the two countries signed the Convention of 1800. In this agreement, the United State gave up all claims against France for damages to American shipping. In return, France released the United States from the treaty of 1778. With the signing of the Convention of 1800, the Quasi-War came to an end.

✓ Reading Check **Explaining** What caused the Quasi-War?

Analyzing *Political Cartoons*

French Bribes Americans took a dim view of the French after the XYZ Affair. Here French leaders harass a woman who stands for the United States. On a hill in the distance, the British watch while other nations gossip over the affair. What nation was France at war with at this time?

INTERDISCIPLINARY CONNECTIONS ACTIVITY

Government Have students research theories of interposition and nullification. Ask students to discover what each theory proposed and how the states used these theories throughout American history to press their grievances against the federal government. Have students write a report based on their research. Then ask students to summarize their findings in a one-paragraph executive summary. **L2**

The War Between the Parties

The Quasi-War also affected domestic politics in the United States. Many Federalists resented the harsh criticisms printed in Republican newspapers. They remembered the angry Republican crowds that had protested Jay's Treaty. Now, the Quasi-War had reversed the situation, and Federalists in Congress decided to strike back at the Republicans.

The Alien and Sedition Acts

At the height of public anger at France in 1798, the Federalists pushed four laws through Congress. These laws became known as the **Alien and Sedition Acts.**

The first three laws were aimed at aliens—people living in the country who were not citizens. The Federalists knew that many recent immigrants had come from France and Ireland. These immigrants were often anti-British and tended to vote for the Republican Party once they became citizens. The first law required immigrants to wait 14 years before becoming citizens, thus weakening Republican support. The next two laws gave the president the power to deport without trial any alien deemed dangerous to the United States.

The fourth law was aimed at preventing sedition, or incitement to rebellion. This law made it a federal crime to utter or print anything "false, scandalous, and malicious" against the federal government or any officer of the government. In short, the act deprived citizens of their right to criticize public officials. The government indicted 15 people under this act, including several Republican newspaper editors and politicians.

The Virginia and Kentucky Resolutions

In 1798 and 1799, the Republican-controlled legislatures of Kentucky and Virginia passed resolutions, secretly written by Jefferson and Madison, criticizing the Alien and Sedition Acts. Both resolutions argued that since the states had created the Constitution, they could declare federal laws unconstitutional.

The Virginia Resolutions introduced the theory of interposition. They argued that if the federal government did something unconstitutional, the state could interpose between the federal government and the people and stop the illegal action. The Kentucky Resolutions advanced the theory of nullification. According to this theory, if the federal government passed an unconstitutional law, the states had the right to nullify the law, or declare it invalid. Although these resolutions had little effect in 1800, states used these ideas in later decades to defend their regional interests.

Analyzing *Political Cartoons*

War Between the Parties This cartoon reveals the emotions of American politics in the 1790s. Republican Matthew Lyon and Federalist Roger Griswold are shown fighting in the House of Representatives. How did Federalists respond to Republican attacks?

TURNING POINT

The Election of 1800

Although John Adams hoped to win reelection in 1800, he faced an uphill battle. The Alien and Sedition Acts had angered many people, as had a new tax the Federalists had introduced on houses, land, and enslaved Africans. The Republican nominees, Thomas Jefferson for president and Aaron Burr for vice president, campaigned against the new taxes and the national bank. They accused the Federalists of favoring monarchy and of discouraging political participation.

The election was closely contested and had an unexpected outcome, one that revealed a flaw in the system for selecting the president. The Constitution does not let citizens vote directly for the chief executive. Instead each state chooses electors—the same number as it has senators and representatives. This group, known as the Electoral College, then votes for the president.

The Constitution called for each elector in the Electoral College to vote for two people. The normal practice was for an elector to cast one vote for his party's presidential candidate and another for the vice presidential candidate. To avoid a tie between Jefferson and Burr, the Republicans had intended for one elector to refrain from voting for Burr, but the plan went awry. When the votes were counted, Jefferson and Burr each had 73. Since no candidate had a majority, the Federalist-controlled House of Representatives had to choose a president.

Many Federalists despised Jefferson and wanted to select Burr, but Alexander Hamilton preferred Jefferson. Hamilton urged his followers to support Jefferson, leading to a tie in the House of Representatives.

CHAPTER 6 **Federalists and Republicans** 219

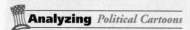

Analyzing *Political Cartoons*

Answer: pushed the Alien and Sedition Acts through Congress
Ask: How would the Alien Acts harm the Republicans? *(They targeted recent immigrants, who tended to vote Republican.)*

3 ASSESS

Assign Section 2 Assessment as homework or as an in-class activity.

⊙ Have students use the **Interactive Tutor Self-Assessment CD-ROM.**

Reading Essentials and Study Guide 6–2

Name _____ Date _____ Class _____

Study Guide
Chapter 6, Section 2
For use with textbook pages 215–220
PARTISAN POLITICS

KEY TERMS AND NAMES
Jay's Treaty a treaty signed in 1794 between the United States and Great Britain that prevented war between the two countries *(page 216)*
most-favored nation status given to a nation that guarantees no discrimination in trade with that nation *(page 216)*
Pinckney's Treaty a treaty signed in 1795 that granted the United States the right to navigate the Mississippi *(page 217)*
Washington's Farewell Address President Washington's letter to the American people in which he warned them against sectionalism *(page 217)*
Quasi-War an undeclared war at sea fought in 1798 between France and the United States

Section Quiz 6–2

Name _____ Date _____ Class _____

⭐ **Chapter 6** Score _____

Section Quiz 6-2

DIRECTIONS: Matching Match each item in Column A with the items in Column B. Write the correct letters in the blanks. *(10 points each)*

Column A	Column B
____ 1. undeclared war at sea between the United States and France	A. Quasi-War
____ 2. people living in the country who are not citizens	B. Pinckney's Treaty
____ 3. granted the United States the right to navigate the Mississippi and deposit goods at New Orleans	C. interposition
____ 4. incitement to rebellion	D. aliens
____ 5. theory that the state could interpose between the federal government and the people to stop an illegal action	E. sedition

DIRECTIONS: Multiple Choice In the blank at the left, write the letter of the choice that

CRITICAL THINKING ACTIVITY

Comparing Ask students to compare the election of 1800 with the election of 2000 by asking the following questions: What issues were similar in the two elections? What issues were different? How were the outcomes similar? Encourage students to discover more about the Electoral College, and its role in electing the president. If necessary, have students research the election of 2000. **L2**

Geography *Skills*

Answers:

1. Pennsylvania, Maryland, North Carolina

2. Northern states because of their support for trade and manufacturing

Geography Skills Practice
Ask: Which candidate did the western states favor? Why?
(Jefferson; he supported agriculture and states' rights)

Reteach

Ask students to explain the difference between state sovereignty and states' rights.

Enrich

Have students use library and Internet resources to learn more about life in the new states of Kentucky, Tennessee, and Ohio. Encourage students to present their findings in a written report.

Reading Check

Answer: limit the rights of immigrants and prevent people from criticizing the government

4 CLOSE

Ask students to explain the relationships between the following pairs: Jay's Treaty and Caribbean trade; Pinckney's Treaty and New Orleans; Little Turtle and Ohio statehood; Alien and Sedition Acts and the election of 1800.

220

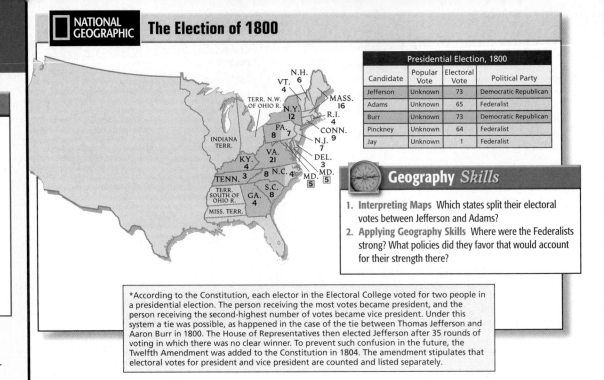

NATIONAL GEOGRAPHIC **The Election of 1800**

	Presidential Election, 1800		
Candidate	Popular Vote	Electoral Vote	Political Party
Jefferson	Unknown	73	Democratic Republican
Adams	Unknown	65	Federalist
Burr	Unknown	73	Democratic Republican
Pinckney	Unknown	64	Federalist
Jay	Unknown	1	Federalist

Geography *Skills*

1. **Interpreting Maps** Which states split their electoral votes between Jefferson and Adams?
2. **Applying Geography Skills** Where were the Federalists strong? What policies did they favor that would account for their strength there?

*According to the Constitution, each elector in the Electoral College voted for two people in a presidential election. The person receiving the most votes became president, and the person receiving the second-highest number of votes became vice president. Under this system a tie was possible, as happened in the case of the tie between Thomas Jefferson and Aaron Burr in 1800. The House of Representatives then elected Jefferson after 35 rounds of voting in which there was no clear winner. To prevent such confusion in the future, the Twelfth Amendment was added to the Constitution in 1804. The amendment stipulates that electoral votes for president and vice president are counted and listed separately.

Finally, in February 1801, Jefferson let Federalist James Bayard know that if elected, Jefferson would not fire all the Federalists in the government, nor dismantle Hamilton's financial system. These assurances convinced Bayard to cast a blank ballot, leaving Jefferson with one more vote than Burr. Jefferson became the new president.

The election of 1800 was an important turning point in American history. At the time, the Federalists controlled the army, the presidency, and the Congress. They could have refused to step down and overthrown the Constitution. Instead, they respected the people's right to choose the president. The election of 1800 demonstrated that power in the United States could be peacefully transferred despite strong disagreements between the parties.

Reading Check **Analyzing** What was the purpose of the Alien and Sedition Acts?

SECTION 2 ASSESSMENT

Checking for Understanding

1. **Define:** most-favored nation, alien, sedition, interposition, nullification.
2. **Identify:** Jay's Treaty, Pinckney's Treaty, Washington's Farewell Address, Quasi-War, Alien and Sedition Acts.

Reviewing Themes

3. **Civic Rights and Responsibilities** How did the Alien and Sedition Acts interfere with the lives of people living in the United States?

Critical Thinking

4. **Synthesizing** How did France and Great Britain test American neutrality?
5. **Organizing** Use a graphic organizer similar to the one below to list the foreign policy challenges that Washington and Adams faced during their presidencies.

Challenges Facing Washington — Challenges Facing Adams

Analyzing Visuals

6. **Analyzing Political Cartoons** Study the cartoon pictured on page 219. Why do you think the political situation of the 1790s led to fights among members of Congress?

Writing About History

7. **Expository Writing** Write an editorial that responds to George Washington's Farewell Address. Explain whether or not you think Washington was correct in warning Americans against forming political parties and permanent alliances.

220 CHAPTER 6 Federalists and Republicans

SECTION 2 ASSESSMENT ANSWERS

1. Terms are in blue.
2. Jay's Treaty (p. 216), Pinckney's Treaty (p. 217), Washington's Farewell Address (p. 217), Quasi-War (p. 218), Alien and Sedition Acts (p. 219)
3. required immigrants to wait 14 years before becoming citizens, allowed the president to deport aliens without a trial, deprived citizens of the right to criticize the government
4. Both interfered with shipping; the British incited Native Americans against settlers; the French asked for bribes before negotiating.
5. Washington: British interference with shipping, French Revolution, Spain's control of the Mississippi; Adams: XYZ Affair, Quasi-War, French interference with shipping
6. There was significant disagreement between the parties and tensions rose to the boiling point.
7. Editorials should support an opinion based on the issues.

Guide to Reading

Main Idea
As president, Jefferson worked to limit the scope of the federal government, obtain the Louisiana Territory, and keep the United States out of European wars.

Key Terms and Names
John Marshall, judicial review, Louisiana Purchase, Meriwether Lewis, William Clark, Sacagawea, Zebulon Pike, impressment, embargo

Reading Strategy
Sequencing As you read about Thomas Jefferson's administration, complete a time line similar to the one below to record the major events of Jefferson's presidency.

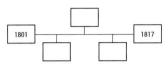

Reading Objectives
• **Evaluate** the changing role of the Supreme Court.
• **Discuss** the events leading to the Louisiana Purchase.

Section Theme
Government and Democracy An important Supreme Court decision asserted that the Court had the power to decide whether laws passed by Congress were constitutional.

Preview of Events

| ♦1800 | ♦1803 | ♦1806 | ♦1809 |

1801
Thomas Jefferson takes office

1803
Marbury v. *Madison* case decided; Louisiana Purchase expands nation

1804
Lewis and Clark head west

1807
Embargo Act passed

---

1 FOCUS

Section Overview
This section examines Jefferson's attempts to limit the scope of the federal government.

BELLRINGER
Skillbuilder Activity

Project transparency and have students answer the question.

Available as a blackline master.

Daily Focus Skills Transparency 6–3

Guide to Reading

Answers to Graphic: 1801: Jefferson elected President, Judiciary Act of 1801 repealed; 1803: Ohio becomes a state, *Marbury* v. *Madison* case decided, Louisiana Purchase expands nation; 1804: Supreme Court Justice Samuel Chase impeached, Lewis and Clark begin expedition, Burr kills Hamilton during duel; 1805: Pike maps upper Mississippi; 1806: Pike travels to Colorado, Britain issues Orders in Council; 1807: Embargo Act passed; 1809: Embargo Act repealed

Preteaching Vocabulary
Have students skim Section 3 to find time references for each of the Key Terms and Names.

★ An American Story ★

Thomas Jefferson

   March 4, 1801, was Inauguration Day in Washington, D.C. The still unfinished capital of the United States was only a tiny village. Stumps and mud holes filled Pennsylvania Avenue, and a swampy wilderness separated Capitol Hill from the president's mansion. A Washington resident described the modest inauguration ceremony:

❝The sun shone bright on that morning. . . . Mr. Jefferson had not yet arrived. He was seen walking from his lodgings, which were not far distant, attended by five or six gentlemen who were his fellow lodgers. Soon afterwards he entered . . . and bowing to the Senate, who arose to receive him, he approached a table on which the Bible lay and took the oath which was administered to him by the Chief Justice. . . . The new President walked home with two or three of the gentlemen who lodged in the same house. At dinner . . . a gentleman from Baltimore, . . . asked permission to wish him joy. 'I would advise you,' answered Mr. Jefferson smiling, 'to follow my example on nuptial occasions when I always tell the bridegroom I will wait till the end of the year before offering my congratulations.' And this was the only and solitary instance of any notice taken of the event of the morning.❞

—quoted in *The Life of Thomas Jefferson*

Thomas Jefferson Takes Office

   Thomas Jefferson privately referred to his election as the "Revolution of 1800." He believed that Washington and Adams had acted too much like royalty, and he tried to create a less formal style for the presidency. He rode horseback rather than traveling in carriages. In place of formal receptions, he entertained at more intimate dinners around

CHAPTER 6 Federalists and Republicans **221**

SECTION RESOURCES

📂 Reproducible Masters
• Reproducible Lesson Plan 6–3
• Daily Lecture and Discussion Notes 6–3
• Guided Reading Activity 6–3
• Section Quiz 6–3
• Reading Essentials and Study Guide 6–3
• Interpreting Political Cartoons
• Supreme Court Case Studies

📠 Transparencies
• Daily Focus Skills Transparency 6–3

Multimedia
🖭 Interactive Tutor Self-Assessment CD-ROM
🖭 ExamView® Pro Testmaker CD-ROM
🖭 Presentation Plus! CD-ROM
🖭 TeacherWorks™ CD-ROM
🎧 Audio Program

2 TEACH

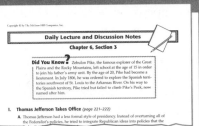

Reading Check

Answer: Jefferson was more informal. For example, he rode on horseback rather than riding in a carriage and he invited people to dinner at a round table rather than holding formal receptions.

Preparing an Oral Presentation

Have students use library and Internet resources to learn more about one of the people or events mentioned in this section. Ask students to prepare a one-minute presentation about the person or event. **L1**

Use the rubric for an oral presentation, monologue, song, or skit on pages 75–76 in the *Performance Assessment Activities and Rubrics.*

History *and the* Humanities

 American Art & Architecture: University of Virginia, Charlottesville

---

a circular table so that, as he said, "When brought together in society, all are perfectly equal." Although Jefferson set a new style for the presidency, he did not overturn all of the Federalists' policies. Instead he sought to integrate Republican ideas into the policies that the Federalists had already put in place.

A strong believer in small government, Jefferson hoped to limit the scope of federal power. He began paying off the federal debt, cut government spending, and did away with the hated whiskey tax. Instead of a standing army, he planned to rely on local militia.

Jefferson's economic ideas had worried many Federalists, who expected the new president to dismantle the national bank. Jefferson's choice of Albert Gallatin as Secretary of the Treasury reassured them. Gallatin was a skilled financier who supported Hamilton's system.

✓ Reading Check **Summarizing** What was new about Jefferson's approach to the presidency?

The Rise of the Supreme Court

Before their term expired, the Federalist majority in Congress passed the Judiciary Act of 1801. This act created 16 new federal judges. Before leaving office, President Adams appointed Federalists to these positions. These judges were nicknamed "midnight judges" because Adams supposedly signed appointments until midnight on his last day in office.

Impeaching Judges Neither Jefferson nor the Republicans in Congress were pleased that the Federalists controlled the courts. One of the first acts of Congress after Jefferson took office was to repeal the Judiciary Act of 1801, thereby doing away with the "midnight judges" by abolishing their offices.

The Republicans then tried to remove other Federalists from the judiciary by impeachment. Republican leaders believed that the impeachment power was one of the checks and balances in the Constitution. Congress could impeach and remove judges for arbitrary or unfair decisions, not just for criminal behavior.

In 1804, the House impeached Supreme Court Justice Samuel Chase. During one trial, Chase had ordered "any of those persons or creatures called democrats" removed from the jury. He had also denounced Jefferson while addressing another jury. Although these actions may have been unfair, the Senate did not convict Chase. Many senators did not think he was guilty of "treason, bribery, or other high

Birth of a Capital

To plan the new national capital, President Washington chose Pierre Charles L'Enfant. One of L'Enfant's first decisions was to place the future "Congress House" (what would become the Capitol) on high ground with a commanding view of the Potomac River. Congress House was to be the central point in a square grid of streets slashed by avenues that radiated from Capitol Hill like spokes on a wheel. At strategic spots, L'Enfant's plan called for circular intersections to join three or more avenues.

After a series of disputes with the local landowners, L'Enfant was removed from the project, taking his plans with him. Fortunately one of the surveyors, an African American named Benjamin Banneker, was able to draw the plans from memory, thus enabling the project to continue. Modern Washington, D.C., still retains many of the elements of this plan.

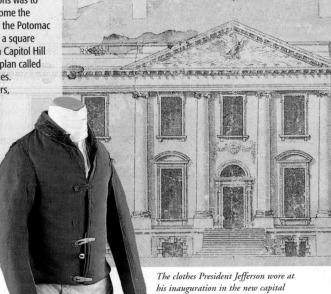

The clothes President Jefferson wore at his inauguration in the new capital

---

COOPERATIVE LEARNING ACTIVITY

Creating a Chart Organize students into small groups. Assign each group one of the states that had gained statehood by the end of 1812. You do not need to assign every state, but be sure to include some of the original 13. Have each group review a list of the counties in its assigned state and create an alphabetic list of counties that appear to be named for one of the early leaders of the United States. As a class create a chart with the states as column headings and the appropriate counties listed beneath. Have the class analyze the results.

Use the rubric for a cooperative group management plan on pages 81–82 in the *Performance Assessment Activities and Rubrics.*

crimes and misdemeanors" that the Constitution required for his removal. The impeachment of Justice Chase established that judges could only be removed for criminal behavior, not simply because Congress disagreed with their decisions.

Marbury* v. *Madison The most important judicial appointment President Adams made before leaving office was to choose **John Marshall** as Chief Justice of the United States. Marshall served as Chief Justice for 34 years. He was more responsible than any other justice for making the Supreme Court into a powerful, independent branch of the federal government.

Initially, the Supreme Court was a very minor body, but its role began to change in 1803 with the case of *Marbury* v. *Madison*. William Marbury was a Federalist who had been appointed justice of the peace in Washington, D.C., shortly before Adams left office. Although Adams had signed Marbury's appointment, the documents were not delivered before Adams left office. The new Secretary of State, James Madison, was supposed to deliver the documents, but Jefferson told him to hold them, hoping Marbury would quit and allow Jefferson to appoint a Republican to the job.

Souvenir handkerchief showing the layout of Washington, D.C.

Medallion honoring Pierre L'Enfant

Instead, Marbury asked the Supreme Court to issue a court order telling Madison to deliver the documents. Marbury based this request on the Judiciary Act of 1789, which stipulated that requests for federal court orders go directly to the Supreme Court. In *Marbury* v. *Madison*, the Supreme Court unanimously agreed with Chief Justice Marshall that the Court could not issue the order.

Marshall explained that the Court could not issue the order because it had no jurisdiction. The Constitution, Marshall pointed out, was very specific about the kind of cases that could be taken directly to the Supreme Court. A request for a court order was not one of those cases, making that section of the Judiciary Act of 1789 unconstitutional and invalid. The decision strengthened the Supreme Court because it asserted the Court's right of judicial review, the power to decide whether laws passed by Congress were constitutional and to strike down those laws that were not.

📖 *(See page 1081 for more information on Marbury v. Madison.)*

✔ **Reading Check** **Explaining** Why did Congress repeal the Judiciary Act of 1801?

The United States Expands West

One of Jefferson's strongest beliefs was that a republic could only survive if most of the people owned land. This belief led him to support the idea of expanding the country farther west.

The Louisiana Purchase In 1800 French leader Napoleon Bonaparte convinced Spain to give Louisiana back to France in exchange for helping Spain take control of part of Italy. Napoleon's deal worried Jefferson, because it gave France control of the lower Mississippi. Jefferson believed that having France back in North America would force the United States into an alliance with the British, whom Jefferson despised.

Jefferson ordered his ambassador to France, **Robert Livingston,** to try to block the deal or gain concessions for the United States. Livingston arrived in Paris in the spring of 1801, but his negotiations accomplished little until 1803.

By 1803 Napoleon had begun making plans to conquer Europe. If France resumed its war against Britain, the last thing the French wanted was an alliance between the United States and Great Britain. Furthermore, France's government was short on funds. In 1803, therefore, Napoleon offered to sell all of the Louisiana Territory, as well as New Orleans, to the United States. Livingston immediately accepted.

CHAPTER 6 Federalists and Republicans **223**

Guided Reading Activity 6–3

Name _____ Date _____ Class _____

★ Guided Reading Activity 6-3

DIRECTIONS: Identifying Supporting Details Read each main idea. Use your textbook to supply the details that support or explain each main idea.

❑ **Main Idea:** Thomas Jefferson, believing that Washington and Adams had acted too much like royalty, tried to create a less formal style for the presidency.

1. **Detail:** Instead of overturning all of the _____ policies, Jefferson sought to integrate them with his own _____ ideas.

2. **Detail:** A strong believer in _____, Jefferson hoped to limit the scope of federal power.

❑ **Main Idea:** The Supreme Court's power was strengthened during Jefferson's administration.

3. **Detail:** One of the first acts of Congress after Jefferson took office was to repeal the _____ _____, doing away with President Adams's new judges.

✔ **Reading Check**

Answer: to shift control of the judiciary away from the Federalists

Creating a Map Have students use library and Internet resources to learn about the size and location of the Louisiana Purchase. Starting with a map showing the outline of the 48 contiguous states, have students identify the states that made up the United States at the time of the Louisiana Purchase and indicate the approximate boundaries of the Louisiana Territory. Remind students that areas that are now Maine and West Virginia were parts of other states in 1803. **L2**

📁 Use the rubric for creating a map, display, or chart on pages 77–78 in the *Performance Assessment Activities and Rubrics.*

FYI

The boundaries of the Louisiana Territory were not clearly defined when the United States and France signed the treaty in May of 1803. Although the eastern and western borders were defined by the geography of the Mississippi River and the Rocky Mountains, the northern and southern borders had to be negotiated with Great Britain and Spain. The northern and southern boundaries were established in 1818 and 1819, respectively.

MEETING SPECIAL NEEDS

Intrapersonal Have interested students learn more about one of the expeditions mentioned in this section. After conducting the research, have students write a brief summary of one of the events of the expedition as though they were participants in the expedition. Encourage students to describe how they felt about the event and how they reacted to others in the expedition party. **L1**

📁 Refer to *Inclusion for the High School Social Studies Classroom Strategies and Activities* in the TCR.

✔ Reading Check

Answer: With France controlling the lower Mississippi, Jefferson was concerned that the United States would have to form an alliance with Britain. Purchasing the Louisiana Territory eliminated that concern and gave the United States control of the Mississippi.

3 ASSESS

Assign Section 3 Assessment as homework or as an in-class activity.

● Have students use the **Interactive Tutor Self-Assessment CD-ROM.**

Reading Essentials and Study Guide 6–3

Name _____ Date _____ Class _____

Study Guide
Chapter 6, Section 3
For use with textbook pages 221–225

JEFFERSON IN OFFICE

KEY TERMS AND NAMES

John Marshall Chief Justice of the Supreme Court, responsible for making the Supreme Court a powerful independent branch of the government *(page 223)*
judicial review the power of the Supreme Court to decide whether laws passed by Congress were constitutional and to strike down those laws that were not *(page 223)*
Louisiana Purchase land purchased from France in 1803 that more than doubled the size of the United States and gained U.S. control of the entire Mississippi River *(page 224)*
Meriwether Lewis Jefferson's private secretary and leader of the Corps of Discovery *(page 224)*
William Clark leader of the Corps of Discovery *(page 224)*
Sacagawea a Shoshone woman who joined the Lewis and Clark expedition of the Louisiana

📁 Use *Interpreting Political Cartoons,* Cartoon 5.

📁 Use *Supreme Court Case Study 1, Marbury* v. *Madison.*

Picturing History

Mountain Explorer Besides giving his name to Colorado's Pikes Peak, army officer Zebulon Pike led an expedition to find the Mississippi's headwaters. What skills might army officers have that would aid them in such an assignment?

On April 30, 1803, the United States bought Louisiana from France for $11.25 million. It also agreed to take on French debts owed to American citizens. These debts were worth about $3.75 million, making the total cost about $15 million. The Senate overwhelmingly ratified the **Louisiana Purchase.** As a result of the deal, the United States more than doubled its size and gained control of the entire Mississippi River.

The Lewis and Clark Expedition Even before Louisiana became a part of the United States, Jefferson asked Congress to fund a secret expedition into the Louisiana Territory to trace the Missouri River and find a route to the Pacific Ocean. After Congress approved the expedition, Jefferson chose **Meriwether Lewis,** his private secretary, and **William Clark,** the younger brother of Revolutionary War hero George Rogers Clark, to lead the expedition.

In May 1804 the "Corps of Discovery," as the expedition was called, headed west up the Missouri

224 CHAPTER 6 Federalists and Republicans

River. Along the way they met **Sacagawea,** a Shoshone woman who joined the expedition as a guide and interpreter. The expedition found a path through the Rocky Mountains and eventually traced the Columbia River to the Pacific Ocean. The expedition greatly increased American knowledge of the Louisiana Territory and also gave the United States a claim to the Oregon territory along the coast.

The Pike Expedition Lewis and Clark's expedition was not the only one exploring the Louisiana Purchase. In 1805 **Zebulon Pike** mapped much of the upper Mississippi, and in 1806 he headed west to find the headwaters of the Arkansas River. Pike traveled to Colorado, where he charted the mountain now known as Pikes Peak. He later mapped part of the Rio Grande and traveled across northern Mexico and what is now southern Texas. Pike's account of this trip gave Americans their first detailed description of the Great Plains and the Rocky Mountains.

The Essex Junto The Louisiana Purchase alarmed New England Federalists. It meant that eventually their region would lose its influence in national affairs while the South and West gained political strength through new states. In Massachusetts, a small group of Federalists known as the **Essex Junto** drafted a plan to take New England out of the Union.

Hoping to add New York to their secessionist movement, they contacted Vice President Aaron Burr, who agreed to run for governor of New York in 1804. During the campaign, Alexander Hamilton called Burr "a dangerous man, and one who ought not be trusted with the reins of government." When Hamilton's remarks were published, Burr challenged him to a duel. Hamilton accepted, but he refused to fire at Burr during the duel. Burr shot and killed Hamilton on July 11, 1804. The nation had lost one of its most brilliant leaders.

✔ Reading Check **Describing** Why did Thomas Jefferson want to purchase the Louisiana Territory?

Rising International Tensions

Burr's schemes were only a minor annoyance to President Jefferson. During his second term in office, the president was much more concerned with keeping the United States out of the war between Britain and France. A fragile peace between France and England had fallen apart in mid-1803, when Napoleon's armies surged out of France and headed east.

INTERDISCIPLINARY CONNECTIONS ACTIVITY

Geography Using a map of the 48 contiguous states, have students identify the locations mentioned in the passages about the Lewis and Clark expedition and the Pike expedition. Also, have them trace the route that Lewis and Clark took and label all the current states through which the expedition passed. Have them mount the map and display it with an appropriate title. **L2**

Economic Warfare At first, the war actually benefited American merchants. As the British seized French ships, American merchants began trading with French colonies in the Caribbean. The British left the American ships alone because the United States had proclaimed neutrality.

In 1806 Britain issued regulations known as the Orders in Council. These declared that all ships going to Europe needed British licenses and would be searched for contraband. In response, Napoleon declared that merchants who obeyed the British system would have their goods confiscated when they reached Europe. Americans were caught in the middle. No matter whom they obeyed, they were going to lose their goods.

Impressment Although British and French trade restrictions upset Americans, the British practice of stopping American ships to seize sailors angered them even more. The British navy was short of recruits because of its low pay and terrible shipboard conditions. British sailors often deserted for American vessels. Britain solved this problem by impressment, a legalized form of kidnapping that forced people into military service. Britain claimed the right to stop American ships and search for deserters. On many occasions they impressed American citizens into service as well.

In June 1807, these tensions reached the boiling point when the British warship *Leopard* stopped the American warship *Chesapeake* to search for British deserters. When the captain of the *Chesapeake* refused to comply, the *Leopard* opened fire, killing three Americans. After the Americans surrendered, the British went aboard and seized four sailors.

Economic Diplomacy Fails The attack on the *Chesapeake* enraged the public, and American newspapers clamored for war. Like Washington and Adams before him, however, President Jefferson did not want to entangle the United States in the affairs of Europe. Instead of going to war, he asked Congress to pass the Embargo Act of 1807, halting all trade between the United States and Europe.

The embargo, a government ban on trade with other countries, wound up hurting the United States more than France or Britain. In the Northeast, once-lucrative shipping businesses came to a standstill, while farmers in the South and West saw the demand for their crops plummet. In Congress, Maryland's Philip Barton Key railed against the embargo:

> 66 It has paralyzed industry. . . . Our most fertile lands are reduced to sterility. It will drive our seamen into foreign employ, and our fishermen to foreign sandbanks. . . . It has dried up our revenue. 99
>
> —quoted in *The American Spirit*

Realizing that the embargo was not working and that it was costing the Republican Party political support, Congress repealed it in March 1809, shortly before Jefferson left office.

After his second term, President Jefferson gladly retired to his estate, Monticello, in Virginia. While the embargo made Jefferson unpopular, his administration had reversed the Federalist course by limiting the power of the federal government. It had also acquired a vast new territory in the West.

✓ **Reading Check** Examining Why did Jefferson have Congress pass the Embargo Act of 1807?

SECTION 3 ASSESSMENT

Checking for Understanding

1. **Define:** judicial review, impressment, embargo.
2. **Identify:** John Marshall, Louisiana Purchase, Meriwether Lewis, William Clark, Sacagawea, Zebulon Pike.

Reviewing Themes

3. **Government and Democracy** How did the Supreme Court decision in *Marbury* v. *Madison* strengthen the federal judiciary?

Critical Thinking

4. **Comparing and Contrasting** How was Jefferson's presidency similar to and different from those of Washington and Adams in political style, goals, and foreign policy?
5. **Organizing** Use a graphic organizer similar to the one below to list the causes and effects of the Embargo Act of 1807.

Causes → Embargo Act of 1807 → Effects

Analyzing Visuals

6. **Examining Maps** Study the sketch of Washington, D.C., on page 223. Why do you think Pierre L'Enfant designed the city with wide avenues and circular intersections?

Writing About History

7. **Descriptive Writing** Imagine you are a member of the Zebulon Pike expedition in the Colorado territory. Write a journal entry describing what you have seen on the trip.

SECTION 3 ASSESSMENT ANSWERS

1. Terms are in blue.
2. John Marshall *(p. 223)*, Louisiana Purchase *(p. 224)*, Meriwether Lewis *(p. 224)*, William Clark *(p. 224)*, Sacagawea *(p. 224)*, Zebulon Pike *(p. 224)*
3. It strengthened the Supreme Court's right to judicial review.
4. Washington and Adams: formal styles; Washington: set up government; Adams: strengthened government; Jefferson: informal style and wanted to limit government; all three had foreign policies of neutrality
5. Causes: blockades and impressments; effects: halted trade between United States and Europe,

harmed U.S. shipping and farming
6. possible answer: to give the city character and make it easy for carriage travel
7. Students' journal entries will vary. Journal entries should focus on what a member of the expedition might have seen.

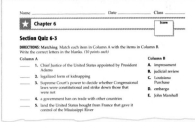
Reteach

Have students review the reading objectives on page 221.

Enrich

Have students use library and Internet resources to learn more about Thomas Jefferson's life after his presidency and write a short report on their findings.

✓ **Reading Check**

Answer: Jefferson thought that if the United States halted all trade with Europe the United States would not become entangled in European affairs.

4 CLOSE

Ask students to identify two major accomplishments of the Jefferson administration.

1 FOCUS

Tell students that the expedition traveled more than 7,600 miles to the Pacific. During the trip William Clark constructed 60 maps depicting the expedition's route. Have students identify the various landforms shown on the map, including rivers, mountains, and passes.

2 TEACH

Analyzing Information Have students study the map and read the feature. Have students create questions for a trivia game based on the information they have read. Have students pose their questions and see which student can answer them most quickly. If you choose, you can keep score and provide a small prize to the winners. **L1**

Mental Mapping Tell students to create a mental map of the route they take to school. Have students draw the map on a piece of paper. Encourage them to add appropriate details and include a legend. **L2**

FYI

Travelers' Rest is located southwest of present-day Lolo, Montana. The Lewis and Clark expedition camped there in 1805 and 1806. Native Americans also camped there while traveling to the buffalo hunting grounds of Montana. Although the name of the camp sounds inviting, the cold weather conditions made Lewis and Clark's rest quite unpleasant.

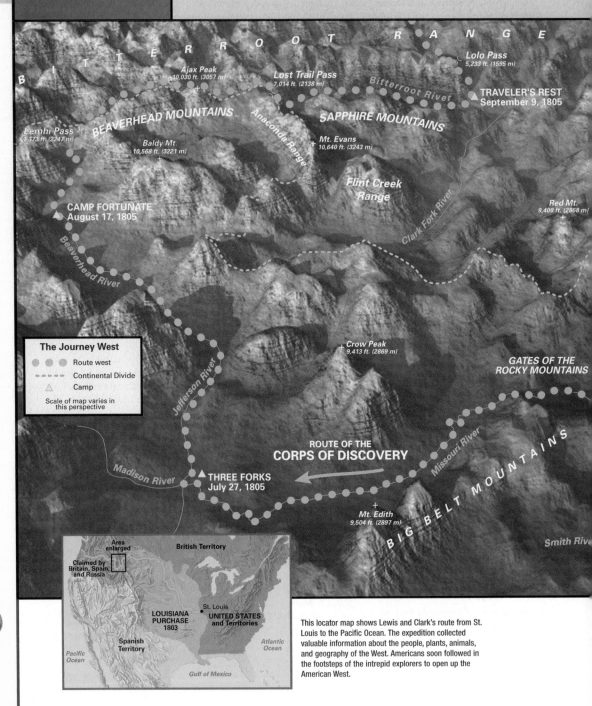

The Journey West

● ● ● Route west
‒ ‒ ‒ Continental Divide
△ Camp

Scale of map varies in this perspective

BITTERROOT RANGE

Lolo Pass
5,233 ft. (1595 m)

Ajax Peak
10,030 ft. (3057 m)

Lost Trail Pass
7,014 ft. (2138 m)

Bitterroot River

TRAVELER'S REST
September 9, 1805

BEAVERHEAD MOUNTAINS

Anaconda Range

SAPPHIRE MOUNTAINS

Lemhi Pass
7,373 ft. (2247 m)

Baldy Mt.
10,568 ft. (3221 m)

Mt. Evans
10,640 ft. (3243 m)

Flint Creek Range

Clark Fork River

Red Mt.
9,409 ft. (2868 m)

CAMP FORTUNATE
August 17, 1805

Beaverhead River

Jefferson River

Crow Peak
9,413 ft. (2869 m)

**GATES OF THE
ROCKY MOUNTAINS**

**ROUTE OF THE
CORPS OF DISCOVERY**

Missouri River

Madison River

THREE FORKS
July 27, 1805

Mt. Edith
9,504 ft. (2897 m)

BIG BELT MOUNTAINS

Smith Riv

Area enlarged

British Territory

Claimed by Britain, Spain, and Russia

LOUISIANA PURCHASE 1803

St. Louis

UNITED STATES and Territories

Spanish Territory

Pacific Ocean

Atlantic Ocean

Gulf of Mexico

This locator map shows Lewis and Clark's route from St. Louis to the Pacific Ocean. The expedition collected valuable information about the people, plants, animals, and geography of the West. Americans soon followed in the footsteps of the intrepid explorers to open up the American West.

EXTENDING THE CONTENT

Science and Nature Since many of the plants and animals that Lewis and Clark encountered were unknown to them, they collected and preserved many specimens including prairie dog, jackrabbit, black-tailed deer, pronghorn, and mountain sheep. Huge grizzly bears were a common threat to the expedition. They also found some huge bones that may have been from a dinosaur. As an avid collector of mastodon bones (the word *dinosaur* was not coined until 1840), Thomas Jefferson sent William Clark in search of more bones to add to his collection in 1807.

Westward to the Pacific

I
n May 1804, the Corps of Discovery—Meriwether Lewis, William Clark, and about 40 others—set sail up the Missouri River from their camp outside of St. Louis. Their mission was to find the so-called Northwest Passage—a water route across the continent to the Pacific Ocean. However, after crossing the Great Plains, they discovered the enormous obstacle between them and the Pacific: the Rocky Mountains. Tackling those "terrible mountains," wrote Lewis, proved "the most perilous and difficult part of our voyage" (see map at left).

One of their first challenges was to get beyond the Great Falls of the Missouri. It took them nearly a month to move their boats and supplies almost 18 miles (29 km) around the falls to a more navigable part of the river. Clear of the falls, they pressed on, up through a deep canyon known as the Gates of the Rocky Mountains —"the most remarkable cliffs that we have yet seen," recalled Lewis. From here, the Missouri River ran fast, and its current was strong. In late July 1805, the expedition arrived at Three Forks. After trekking up each fork of the river, Lewis and Clark opted for the western branch, which they named for President Thomas Jefferson. From here, progress slowed. The men often had to wade through the increasingly shallow water, drag-

ging their boats behind them. Soon they would have to abandon the boats altogether; but first they needed horses to carry their supplies over the mountains.

Lewis and three men went on ahead. On August 12 they crossed the Continental Divide at Lemhi Pass, becoming the first explorers from the United States to do so. As Lewis and his party descended the steep mountains, they encountered a band of Shoshone. Lewis convinced Cameahwait, their leader, to go back to meet the others. To everyone's astonishment, the Shoshone recognized their Native American guide, Sacagawea, as a member of their band who had been kidnapped long ago. Sacagawea suddenly realized Chief Cameahwait was her brother, and she joyfully embraced him.

With Sacagawea's help, Lewis convinced the Shoshone to sell them horses and provide a guide. The Corps crossed into the Bitterroot Range around Lost Trail Pass. After a pause at Traveler's Rest, the expedition headed over the massive peaks. They climbed the snow-covered slopes and struggled around the fallen trees, watching in horror as their horses slipped and rolled down. Game was so scarce that the famished explorers were forced to kill and eat three of their colts. Despite the hardships, the weary party trudged on until they arrived at a village of the Nez Perce, who provided food and water. The explorers finally reached a tributary of the Columbia River, built dugout boats, abandoned their horses, and floated west all the way to the Pacific Ocean.

An accomplished geographer and cartographer, William Clark compiled this detailed map of the expedition's route around the Great Falls of the Missouri River.

Area of Clark's map in log book shown above

Sun River

GREAT FALLS
June 13, 1805

Camp above the falls

Camp below the falls

On May 26, 1805, from a bluff above the Missouri River, Meriwether Lewis "beheld the Rocky Mountains for the first time."

LEARNING FROM GEOGRAPHY

1. Why were Lewis and Clark unable to complete their mission?

2. Imagine that you are a member of the expedition. Write a letter home detailing some of the sights you have seen.

227

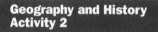

SECTION 4 The War of 1812

1 FOCUS

Section Overview

This section explores the causes and effects of the War of 1812.

BELLRINGER
Skillbuilder Activity

 Project transparency and have students answer the question.

📁 Available as a blackline master.

Daily Focus Skills Transparency 6–4

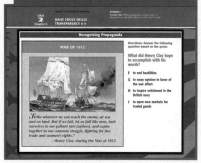

Guide to Reading

Answers to Graphic: Causes of the War of 1812: British impressment of American sailors, British seizure of American cargo, British trade restrictions angered Southern planters and frontier farmers, failure of U.S. negotiations to lift British trade restrictions, British role in Native American attacks on settlers on the frontier

Preteaching Vocabulary
Have students write a brief description of the relationship of the War of 1812 to each of the Key Terms and Names.

Guide to Reading

Main Idea
While the War of 1812 produced no clear winner, it gave Americans a strong sense of national pride.

Key Terms and Names
Non-Intercourse Act, War Hawks, Tecumseh, William Henry Harrison, Oliver Perry, Hartford Convention, nationalism, Treaty of Ghent

Reading Strategy
Organizing As you read about the War of 1812, complete a graphic organizer similar to the one below by listing the causes of the war.

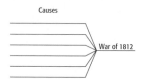

Causes ⟶ War of 1812

Reading Objectives
• **Describe** why the United States declared war on Britain, and discuss the major campaigns of the war.
• **List** the results of the Treaty of Ghent.

Section Theme
Individual Action Military leaders, including William Henry Harrison, Tecumseh, Oliver Perry, and Andrew Jackson, helped decide the outcome of the War of 1812.

Preview of Events

◆1809 — ◆1811 — ◆1813 — ◆1815

1809
Embargo Act repealed

1811
Battle of Tippecanoe

1812
United States declares war on Britain

1814
British troops burn Washington, D.C.

1815
Battle of New Orleans

★ An American Story ★

Francis Scott Key

On the night of September 13, 1814, Francis Scott Key, a young Maryland lawyer, stood on the deck of a British ship in Baltimore Harbor and watched the British bombard Fort McHenry. The shelling continued into the morning hours. Explosions lit up the night, and shells with trailing fuses streaked towards the fort. Rockets arced across the sky, as a huge American flag waved over the fort.

As the sun rose, Key strained to see if the flag still waved. To his great joy, it did. He took a letter from his pocket and began scribbling these words for a poem on the back:

❝Oh, say can you see, by the dawn's early light,
What so proudly we hailed at the twilight's last gleaming?
Whose broad stripes and bright stars, through the perilous fight,
O'er the ramparts we watched, were so gallantly streaming?
And the rockets' red glare, the bombs bursting in air,
Gave proof through the night that our flag was still there.
Oh, say does that star spangled banner yet wave,
O'er the land of the free and the home of the brave?❞

—from "The Star-Spangled Banner"

The Decision for War

After Thomas Jefferson announced that he would not run again for president in 1808, the Republican Party nominated James Madison. The Federalists nominated Charles Pinckney. Despite some lingering anger about the Embargo of 1807, Madison won the election easily.

228 CHAPTER 6 Federalists and Republicans

SECTION RESOURCES

📁 **Reproducible Masters**
• Reproducible Lesson Plan 6–4
• Daily Lecture and Discussion Notes 6–4
• Guided Reading Activity 6–4
• Section Quiz 6–4
• Reading Essentials and Study Guide 6–4
• Performance Assessment Activities and Rubrics

Transparencies
• Daily Focus Skills Transparency 6–4

Multimedia
🔘 Interactive Tutor Self-Assessment CD-ROM
🔘 ExamView® Pro Testmaker CD-ROM
🔘 Presentation Plus! CD-ROM
🔘 TeacherWorks™ CD-ROM
🔊 Audio Program

Madison assumed office in the midst of an international crisis. Tensions between the United States and Britain were rising, and it would fall to Madison to decide whether or not to lead the United States into its first full-scale war since the Revolution.

Economic Pressures Like Jefferson, Madison wanted to avoid war. To force the British to stop seizing American ships, he asked Congress to pass the **Non-Intercourse Act.** This act forbade trade with France and Britain while authorizing the president to reopen trade with whichever country removed its trade restrictions first. The idea was to play France and Britain against each other, but the plan failed.

In May 1810, Congress took a different approach with a plan drafted by Nathaniel Macon of North Carolina. The plan, called Macon's Bill Number Two, reopened trade with both Britain and France, but it stated that if either nation agreed to drop its restrictions on trade, the United States would stop importing goods from the other nation.

Soon afterward, Napoleon announced that France would no longer restrict American trade, although his statement still allowed for the seizure of American ships. Madison accepted Napoleon's statement, despite its conditions, hoping to pressure the British into dropping their trade restrictions. When the British refused, Congress passed a non-importation act against Britain in March 1811.

Madison's strategy eventually worked. By early 1812 the refusal of the United States to buy British goods had begun to hurt the British economy. British merchants and manufacturers began to pressure their government to repeal its restrictions on trade. Finally, in June 1812, Britain ended all restrictions on American trade, but it was too late. Two days later, the British learned that the United States Congress had declared war on Great Britain.

The War Hawks Although it appeared that Britain's actions against the United States had hurt mainly Eastern merchants, most members of Congress who voted for war came from the South and West. They were led by Henry Clay of Kentucky, John C. Calhoun of South Carolina, and Felix Grundy of Tennessee. Their opponents nicknamed them the War Hawks.

Americans in the South and West wanted war for two reasons. British trade restrictions hurt Southern planters and Western farmers, who earned much of their income by shipping tobacco, rice, wheat, and cotton overseas. Eastern merchants could make a profit despite British restrictions because they passed the cost of losing ships and goods onto the farmers.

Western farmers also blamed the British for clashes with Native Americans along the frontier. In the early 1800s, settlers had begun moving past the line established by the Treaty of Greenville. As clashes with Native Americans increased, many settlers accused the British in Canada of arming the Native Americans and encouraging them to attack American settlements.

Tecumseh and Tippecanoe Although Western settlers blamed the British for their problems with the Native Americans, it was the increasing demands of speculators and settlers that sparked Native American resistance. **Tecumseh,** a Shawnee leader, believed that Native Americans needed to unite to protect their lands.

While Tecumseh worked for political union, his brother Tenskwatawa (known as "the Prophet") called for a spiritual rebirth of Native American cultures. His followers lived in Prophetstown on the Tippecanoe River in Indiana, where they tried to practice traditional Native American ways of living.

Aware that Tecumseh's movement was becoming more militant, **William Henry Harrison,** governor of the Indiana territory, prepared to stamp it out. In November 1811, Harrison gathered a force and marched towards Prophetstown. Tenskwatawa decided to strike first, sending fighters to attack Harrison and his troops near the Tippecanoe River. The bloody Battle of Tippecanoe left about one-fourth of Harrison's troops dead or wounded, but its impact on the Native Americans was far greater. The clash shattered Native American confidence in the Prophet's leadership. Many, including Tecumseh, fled to Canada.

| Fact | Fiction | Folklore |

The Star-Spangled Banner, 1779–1818 The Stars and Stripes flag gained two more stars and two more stripes in 1795, after Kentucky and Vermont joined the Union. This flag flew over Fort McHenry during the War of 1812 and inspired Francis Scott Key to write "The Star-Spangled Banner."

Congress realized that the flag would become too large if a stripe were added for every new state. It decided to keep the stripes at 13—for the 13 original colonies—and to add a star for each new state.

2 TEACH

Daily Lecture and Discussion Notes 6–4

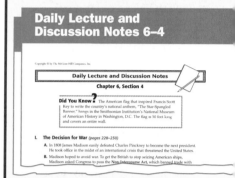

Daily Lecture and Discussion Notes
Chapter 6, Section 4

Did You Know? The American flag that inspired Francis Scott Key to write the country's national anthem, "The Star-Spangled Banner," hangs in the Smithsonian Institution's National Museum of American History in Washington, D.C. The flag is 30 feet long and covers an entire wall.

I.   The Decision for War *(pages 228–230)*

A. In 1808 James Madison easily defeated Charles Pinckney to become the next president. He took office in the midst of an international crisis that threatened the United States.

B. Madison hoped to avoid war. To get the British to stop seizing American ships, Madison asked Congress to pass the **Non-Intercourse Act,** which banned trade with

Creating a Flag Have students create a new flag for the United States and explain the significance of the elements they choose to include. **L1 ELL**

| Fact | Fiction | Folklore |

Congress approved the first official flag of the United States on June 14, 1777. It included 13 alternating red and white stripes and a blue field with 13 white stars. In 1818 Congress decided that there would always be 13 stripes, one for each of the original 13 colonies. Stars would be added on July 4 in the year following a state's admission to the Union. The exact shades of red and white were standardized in 1934.

COOPERATIVE LEARNING ACTIVITY

Creating a Profile Organize students into pairs. Assign each pair one of the prominent people who played a role in the War of 1812. The pairs will create a one-page profile of the individual assigned. Encourage students to include a picture or drawing of the person if one is available. Combine the profiles into a booklet and have the class select an appropriate title for the booklet. In addition to the people listed in the text, other important participants include John Quincy Adams, John Armstrong, Henry Bathurst, William Eustis, Isaac Chauncey, William Thornton, and James Lucas Yeo.

Use the rubric for a cooperative group management plan on pages 81–82 in the ***Performance Assessment Activities and Rubrics.***

✔ Reading Check

Answer: British trade restrictions hurt Southern planters and frontier farmers because they earned much of their income from shipping crops overseas. Western farmers also blamed the British for clashes with Native Americans along the frontier.

Profiles IN HISTORY

Background: When William Henry Harrison was serving as governor of Indiana, he told Tecumseh that only the President had the authority to return the disputed lands to the Native Americans. Tecumseh replied: "Well, as the great chief is to decide the matter, I hope the Great Spirit will put sense enough into his head to induce him to give up this land. It is true, he is so far off he will not be injured by the war; he may sit still in his town and drink his wine, while you and I will have to fight it out." Tecumseh's prediction came true.

Ask: What was Tecumseh's fear about the future of all Native Americans? *(that they would lose their hunting grounds and be pushed farther west)*

Tecumseh's flight to British-held Canada seemed to prove that the British were supporting and arming the Native Americans. Many Western farmers argued that war with Britain would enable the United States to seize Canada and end Native American attacks.

In early June 1812, President Madison gave in to the pressure and asked Congress to declare war. His war message spoke about national honor and emphasized the abuse Americans had suffered at the hands of the British:

> 66Thousands of American citizens, under the safeguard of public law and of their national flag, have been torn from . . . everything dear to them; have been dragged on board ships of a foreign nation . . . to be exiled to the most distant and deadly climes to risk their lives in battles of their oppressors.99
>
> —from Madison's
> *War Message to Congress*

In Congress, the vote split along regional lines. The South and West generally voted for war, while the Northeast did not.

✔ Reading Check **Examining** Why did Americans in the South and West favor war with Great Britain?

The Invasion of Canada

Although the Republican-led Congress had called for war, the nation was not ready to fight. The army had fewer than 7,000 troops and little equipment. The navy had only 16 ships. Also, Americans were deeply divided over the war. Many people in New York and New England called it "Mr. Madison's War," implying that it was a private fight that did not deserve the nation's support.

Paying for the war also posed a problem. The year before the war, Republicans had shut down the Bank of the United States by refusing to renew its charter. This made it difficult for the government to borrow money because most private bankers were located in the Northeast. They opposed the war and would not

Profiles IN HISTORY

Tecumseh
c. 1768–1813

Tecumseh was a Shawnee chief born near present-day Springfield, Ohio. The Shawnee had taken part in many wars in the Northwest Territory. After the Treaty of Greenville in 1795, Tecumseh and many other Shawnee moved to the Indiana territory to escape American settlers.

Tecumseh urged all Native Americans to unite. They were all one people, he said, and should cooperate in a confederacy to control their destiny. He was furious when the Delaware and Potawatomi agreed to cede about 3 million acres (1.2 million ha) to the United States. The land belonged to all Native Americans, Tecumseh argued. How could one group give it up?

In the end, Tecumseh saw no choice but to fight: "The hunting grounds are fast disappearing and they are driving the red man farther and farther to the west." Ominously, he warned, "Surely [this] will be the fate of all tribes if the power of the whites is not forever crushed. . . ."

During the War of 1812, Tecumseh allied himself with the British. A superb

commander, he met his end at the Battle of the Thames River, fought near Chatham, Ontario, in October 1813. There, 400 British troops commanded by General Henry Proctor and about 1,000 Native Americans led by Tecumseh fought some 3,000 American troops led by General William Henry Harrison. During the battle, the British broke ranks and fled, leaving Tecumseh's men to face the American forces alone. After Tecumseh's death, his confederacy collapsed, leaving the United States in firm control of the Northwest Territory.

loan money to the government. Despite the nation's military and financial weakness, President Madison ordered the military to invade Canada.

Three Strikes Against Canada American military leaders planned to attack Canada from three directions—from Detroit, from Niagara Falls, and up the Hudson River valley toward Montreal. All three attacks failed. The British navy on Lake Erie rapidly shuttled troops to Detroit and forced the American commander, General William Hull, to surrender.

Next, the British shifted their troops to Niagara Falls, where they took up positions on Queenston Heights. From there, they easily drove off some 600 American troops who had landed on the Canadian side of the Niagara River. The American force would have been larger, except that the New York militia, many of whom opposed the war, refused to cross the river. They argued that the terms of their military service did not require them to leave the country.

MEETING SPECIAL NEEDS

Visual/Spatial Have students research the types of uniforms worn by the various participants in the War of 1812. Based on their research have students create a drawing accurately portraying the military dress of the era. Have students create a legend for the drawing that explains important features of the uniforms. **L2**

📁 Refer to *Inclusion for the High School Social Studies Classroom Strategies and Activities* in the TCR.

The third American attack fared no better than the first two. General Henry Dearborn, marching up the Hudson River toward Montreal, called off the attack after the militia accompanying his troops refused to cross the border.

Perry's Victory on Lake Erie The following year, the United States had more success after Commodore **Oliver Perry** secretly arranged for the construction of a fleet on the coast of Lake Erie in Ohio. On September 10, 1813, Perry's fleet attacked the British fleet on Lake Erie near Put-in-Bay. When his own ship was no longer able to fight, Perry rowed to another vessel. After a grueling four-hour battle, the British surrendered.

Perry's victory gave the Americans control of Lake Erie. It also enabled General Harrison to recover Detroit and march into Canada, where he defeated a combined force of British troops and Native Americans at the Battle of the Thames River.

Harrison's attack from the west was supposed to meet up with American troops from Niagara Falls in the east. British troops and Canadian militia, however, stopped the American attack from the east at the Battle of Stony Creek. When Harrison learned of the defeat, he retreated to Detroit. By the end of 1813, the United States still had not conquered any territory in Canada.

✓ **Reading Check**

Explaining Why was conquering Canada an important American goal in the War of 1812?

The War Ends

In 1814, Napoleon's empire collapsed. With the war against France over, the British were able to send much of their navy and many more troops to deal with the United States. The British strategy for the war had three parts. First, the British navy would raid American cities along the coast. Second, they would march south into New York from Montreal, cutting New England off from the rest of the country. Third, they would seize New Orleans and close the Mississippi River to western farmers. The British believed this strategy would force the United States to make peace.

Raids on Washington, D.C., and Baltimore With attention focused on Canada, in August 1814 a British fleet sailed into Chesapeake Bay and landed troops within marching distance of Washington, D.C. The British easily dispersed the poorly trained militia defending the capital and entered the city unopposed. Madison and other government officials hastily fled. The British set fire to both the White House and the Capitol. They then prepared to attack Baltimore.

Unlike Washington, D.C., Baltimore was ready for the British. The city militia inflicted heavy casualties on the British troops that went ashore. After bombarding Fort McHenry throughout the night of September 13, the British abandoned their attack on the city.

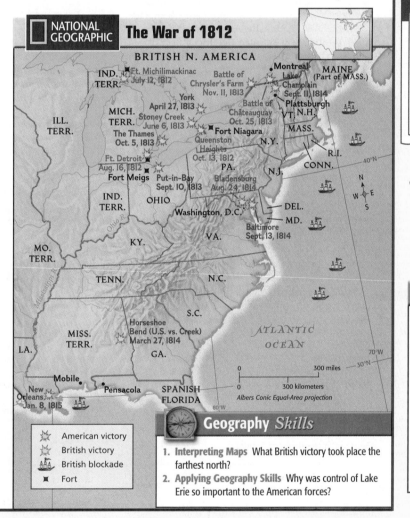

NATIONAL GEOGRAPHIC
The War of 1812

BRITISH N. AMERICA

Geography *Skills*

1. **Interpreting Maps** What British victory took place the farthest north?
2. **Applying Geography Skills** Why was control of Lake Erie so important to the American forces?

- ✳ American victory
- ✳ British victory
- ⚓ British blockade
- ✴ Fort

3 ASSESS

Assign Section 4 Assessment as homework or as an in-class activity.

🔘 Have students use the **Interactive Tutor Self-Assessment CD-ROM.**

Reading Essentials and Study Guide 6–4

Name _____ Date _____ Class _____

Study Guide

Chapter 6, Section 4
For use with textbook pages 228–232

THE WAR OF 1812

KEY TERMS AND NAMES

Non-Intercourse Act a law passed to force the British to stop seizing American ships (page 229)
War Hawks those who supported war with Britain (page 229)
Tecumseh a Shawnee leader who worked for Native American resistance against encroachment on Native American lands (page 229)
William Henry Harrison governor of the Indiana Territory (page 229)
Oliver Perry commodore whose ships attacked the British fleet on Lake Erie (page 231)
Hartford Convention a meeting that called for constitutional amendments to increase New England's political power (page 232)

✓ **Reading Check**

Answer: Western farmers thought seizing Canada would end Native American attacks.

🧭 **Geography** *Skills*

Answers:
1. Ft. Michilimackinac
2. It crippled the ability of the British to quickly move troops to meet American attacks.

Geography Skills Practice
Ask: How did Andrew Jackson defend New Orleans? *(He built a barricade of cotton bales that absorbed the British bullets.)*

INTERDISCIPLINARY CONNECTIONS ACTIVITY

Music Have students work in small groups to write a fifth verse for "The Star-Spangled Banner." The verse should be written following the same meter and rhyming pattern as the other verses. Encourage students to locate the words to all four current verses of the national anthem and listen to recordings of the song to help them understand the rhythm. Invite groups to perform their verses for the class. **L2**

Section Quiz 6–4

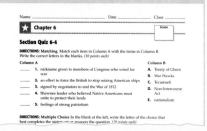

[Section Quiz 6-4 worksheet]

Name _____ Date _____ Class _____

★ **Chapter 6**   Score ☐

Section Quiz 6-4

DIRECTIONS: Matching Match each item in Column A with the items in Column B. Write the correct letters in the blanks. *(10 points each)*

Column A

___ 1. nickname given to members of Congress who voted for war

___ 2. an effort to force the British to stop seizing American ships

___ 3. signed by negotiators to end the War of 1812

___ 4. Shawnee leader who believed Native Americans must unite to protect their lands

___ 5. feelings of strong patriotism

Column B

A. Treaty of Ghent
B. War Hawks
C. Tecumseh
D. Non-Intercourse Act
E. nationalism

DIRECTIONS: Multiple Choice In the blank at the left, write the letter of the choice that best completes the statement or answers the question. *(10 points each)*

History *Through Art*

Answer: It took place two weeks after the war had officially ended.

Ask: What positive effects did the War of 1812 have? *(It increased the nation's prestige overseas and generated a new spirit of patriotism and national unity.)*

Reteach

Have students create a sentence outline using the headings in the textbook.

Enrich

Have students write an editorial in opposition to or support of the War of 1812.

Reading Check

Answer: The American victory at New Orleans made Andrew Jackson a national hero, caused nationalism to surge, and weakened the Federalist Party.

---

4 CLOSE

Have students use a map to explain the military strategies the United States and Britain used at the beginning of the War of 1812.

History *Through Art*

Battle of New Orleans This John Landis engraving depicts the triumph of Andrew Jackson (on horseback at right) over the British during the War of 1812. What was unusual about the timing of the battle?

The Battle of Lake Champlain That same month, about 15,000 well-trained British soldiers advanced southward from Montreal into New York. The key to the British advance was control of Lake Champlain. On September 11, 1814, the American naval force on the lake decisively defeated the British fleet. When the British realized that the Americans could use their control of the lake to surround the British, they abandoned the attack and retreated to Montreal.

The Hartford Convention The British offensive increased New England's opposition to the war. In December 1814, Federalists from the region met in Hartford, Connecticut, to discuss what they could do independently of the United States. Although members of the Essex Junto at the convention urged New England to secede, moderate delegates refused to support such extreme action. Instead, the **Hartford Convention** called for several constitutional amendments to increase the region's political power.

The Battle of New Orleans Less than a month after the Hartford Convention, an American victory in the South put a stop to Federalist complaints. In January 1815, a British fleet with some 7,500 men landed near New Orleans. The American commander, General Andrew Jackson, quickly improvised a defense using large cotton bales from nearby fields. The thick bales absorbed the British bullets, while the British advancing in the open provided easy targets for the American troops. The fighting ended in a decisive American victory.

The **Battle of New Orleans** made Andrew Jackson a national hero. It also helped to destroy the Federalist Party. As **nationalism,** or feelings of strong patriotism, surged, the Federalists at the Hartford Convention appeared divisive and unpatriotic. They never recovered politically, and within a few years the party ceased to exist.

The Treaty of Ghent Peace negotiations began even before the major battles of 1814. In February President Madison sent negotiators to the European city of Ghent to meet with British officials. When word arrived of the Lake Champlain victory, the British and Americans agreed to end the war.

On December 24, 1814, negotiators signed the **Treaty of Ghent,** ending the War of 1812. The treaty restored prewar boundaries but did little else. It did not mention neutral rights or impressment, and no territory changed hands. Although the War of 1812 did not have a dramatic outcome, it increased the nation's prestige overseas and generated a new spirit of patriotism and national unity.

✓ **Reading Check** **Examining** What were the effects of the Battle of New Orleans?

SECTION 4 ASSESSMENT

Checking for Understanding

1. **Define:** War Hawks, nationalism.
2. **Identify:** Non-Intercourse Act, Tecumseh, William Henry Harrison, Oliver Perry, Hartford Convention, Treaty of Ghent.
3. **Analyze** why Perry's victory on Lake Erie was important for the Americans.

Reviewing Themes

4. **Individual Action** What did Tecumseh's death signify for Native Americans of the Northwest Territory?

Critical Thinking

5. **Synthesizing** How did the War of 1812 affect the United States?
6. **Classifying** Use a graphic organizer similar to the one below to list how Americans in different sections of the country felt about war with Great Britain and why.

Section of U.S.	Position on War	Reason for War Position
West		
South		
North		

Analyzing Visuals

7. **Studying Art** Look carefully at the painting of the Battle of New Orleans pictured above. What advantage did the American forces have that helped them win the battle?

Writing About History

8. **Descriptive Writing** Think of an event that made you feel patriotic about the United States. Write a paragraph explaining why the event made you feel this way.

232 CHAPTER 6 Federalists and Republicans

SECTION 4 ASSESSMENT ANSWERS

1. Terms are in blue.
2. Non-Intercourse Act *(p. 229)*, Tecumseh *(p. 229)*, William Henry Harrison *(p. 229)*, Oliver Perry *(p. 231)*, Hartford Convention *(p. 232)*, Treaty of Ghent *(p. 232)*
3. Perry's victory led to the Americans controlling Lake Erie, recovering Detroit, and winning the Battle of the Thames River.
4. the collapse of the confederacy and loss of the Northwest Territory
5. It increased prestige and generated a new spirit of patriotism and national unity.
6. West: favored war; wanted to lift trade barriers and stop Native American attacks; South: favored war; wanted to lift trade barriers; Northeast: against war; still made money despite British restrictions
7. They were in a defensive position, protected by the bales of cotton.
8. Paragraphs should focus on feelings about the event.

Reading a Flowchart

Why Learn This Skill?

Sometimes, determining a sequence of events can be confusing, particularly when many events are occurring at the same time. Reading a flowchart can help you understand how events are related and how one event leads to others.

Learning the Skill

Flowcharts show the steps in a process or a sequence of events. A flowchart could be used to show the movement of goods through a factory, of people through a training program, or of a bill through Congress. The following steps explain how to read a flowchart:

- Read the title or caption of the flowchart to find out what you are studying.
- Read all of the labels or sentences on the flowchart.
- Look for numbers indicating sequence or arrows showing the direction of movement.
- Evaluate the information in the flowchart.

Practicing the Skill

The flowchart on this page shows a sequence of events that led to the expansion of territory within the United States. Analyze the information in the flowchart and then answer the questions.

❶ What does the flowchart show?

❷ How do you know in what sequence the events took place?

❸ What inspired Napoleon to acquire the Louisiana Territory from Spain?

❹ How did the United States react to France's acquisition of the Louisiana Territory?

❺ What additional information from the chapter could you add to the flowchart to show a further sequence of events?

Circumstances Leading to the Louisiana Purchase

French leader Napoleon plans to rebuild France's empire in North America.

Napoleon convinces Spain to give the Louisiana Territory back to France.

President Jefferson sends ambassador Robert Livingston to France to try to block the deal.

Napoleon later wants to conquer Europe, but he needs funds to carry out his plans.

President Jefferson agrees to purchase Louisiana Territory.

Skills Assessment

Complete the Practicing Skills questions on page 235 and the Chapter 6 Skill Reinforcement Activity to assess your mastery of this skill.

Applying the Skill

Making a Flowchart Gather information about the steps necessary to apply to college. Then make up a flowchart outlining the steps. Present your flowchart to the class.

Glencoe's **Skillbuilder Interactive Workbook CD-ROM, Level 2,** provides instruction and practice in key social studies skills.

233

TEACH

Reading a Flowchart Explain to students that flowcharts show connections among events. One event may be directly connected to two or three other events. By organizing the events in a flowchart, the reader can easily follow the sequence and see the connections among events.

Have students prepare flowcharts that show the steps they take to prepare for a test in their history class. Encourage students to visually chart how each step connects to the others. Have students compare their flowcharts with other students. Encourage them to revise their flowcharts based on the feedback they receive.

Additional Practice

Reinforcing Skills Activity 6

GLENCOE
TECHNOLOGY

CD-ROM
Glencoe Skillbuilder Interactive Workbook CD-ROM, Level 2

This interactive CD-ROM reinforces student mastery of essential social studies skills.

ANSWERS TO PRACTICING THE SKILL

❶ the circumstances leading to the Louisiana Purchase

❷ by the order of the boxes and the arrows indicating a top to bottom flow

❸ possible answer: a plan to rebuild the French empire in North America

❹ The United States tried to block the deal.

❺ possible answer: The Senate overwhelmingly ratified the Louisiana Purchase.

Applying the Skill
Students' flowcharts will vary. Flowcharts should include logical steps in the college application process.

GLENCOE
TECHNOLOGY

MindJogger Videoquiz
Use the **MindJogger Videoquiz** to review Chapter 6 content.

▭ Available in VHS

Reviewing Key Terms
Students' answers will vary. The pages where the words appear in the text are shown in parentheses.

1. **cabinet** (p. 211)
2. **bond** (p. 212)
3. **speculator** (p. 212)
4. **enumerated powers** (p. 213)
5. **implied powers** (p. 213)
6. **agrarianism** (p. 214)
7. **most-favored nation** (p. 216)
8. **alien** (p. 219)
9. **sedition** (p. 219)
10. **interposition** (p. 219)
11. **nullification** (p. 219)
12. **judicial review** (p. 223)
13. **impressment** (p. 225)
14. **embargo** (p. 225)
15. **War Hawks** (p. 229)
16. **nationalism** (p. 232)

Reviewing Key Facts
17. Bank of the United States (p. 213), Whiskey Rebellion (p. 213), Alien and Sedition Acts (p. 219), John Marshall (p. 223), Meriwether Lewis (p. 224), William Clark (p. 224), Sacagawea (p. 224), Tecumseh (p. 229), Treaty of Ghent (p. 232)

18. The first eight amendments offered safeguards for the rights of individuals against actions by the federal government.

19. Madison argued that the government could not establish a bank because it was not an enumerated power.

20. Tensions rose due to the increase in the number of settlers continuing to move west.

Reviewing Key Terms
On a sheet of paper, use each of these terms in a sentence.

1. cabinet
2. bond
3. speculator
4. enumerated powers
5. implied powers
6. agrarianism
7. most-favored nation
8. alien
9. sedition
10. interposition
11. nullification
12. judicial review
13. impressment
14. embargo
15. War Hawks
16. nationalism

Reviewing Key Facts

17. **Identify:** Bank of the United States, Whiskey Rebellion, Alien and Sedition Acts, John Marshall, Meriwether Lewis, William Clark, Sacagawea, Tecumseh, Treaty of Ghent.

18. What was the main focus of the first eight amendments in the Bill of Rights?

19. Why did James Madison oppose the establishment of a national bank?

20. Why did tensions between western settlers and Native Americans increase during Washington's presidency?

21. What events led to the purchase of the Louisiana Territory?

22. What events caused the United States to declare war on Great Britain in 1812?

Critical Thinking

23. **Analyzing Themes: Government and Democracy** What was the most important task for Congress after the U.S. Constitution was ratified? Explain why you think this task was important.

24. **Identifying Effects** What were the effects of the War of 1812 on the United States?

25. **Forming an Opinion** Do you think the Alien and Sedition Acts were unconstitutional? Why or why not?

26. **Classifying** Use a graphic organizer similar to the one below to list the differences between the first political parties in the United States.

Federalists	Republicans
Favored:	Favored:

27. **Interpreting Primary Sources** Many people in New England did not support the War of 1812. At a town meeting in Brewster, Massachusetts, on July 20, 1812, the residents wrote a petition to President Madison. In this petition, they stated the reasons that they opposed the war. Read the excerpt and answer the questions that follow.

❝In attending to the *reasons* for the present state of warfare as exhibited to our view by public documents, we lament that they do not furnish to our minds satisfactory evidence of its prosperity....

Chapter Summary

George Washington
- Established legitimacy of the new government
- Created executive departments
- Favored neutrality
- Used troops to stop Native American resistance in the West

Thomas Jefferson
- Republican leader; worked to limit power of national government
- Favored land ownership for all people
- Supported farmers over commerce and trade
- Negotiated purchase of the Louisiana Territory

John Adams
- Federalist leader in favor of strong national government
- Supported commerce and trade
- Favored neutrality; negotiated treaties with Britain and France to avoid war
- Angered farmer and landowners with taxes; angered political opponents with Alien and Sedition Acts

James Madison
- Republican who favored neutrality
- Asked Congress to declare war on Britain to protect trade interest in the East and farmers and settlers in the West
- Under his administration, the War of 1812 generated feelings of nationalism, and the Treaty of Ghent established fishing rights and boundaries with Canada

21. After convincing Spain to give Louisiana back to France, Napoleon Bonaparte did not want to face an alliance between Great Britain and the United States. Selling Louisiana reduced the chance of an alliance and gave the French government much-needed funds.

22. Causes of the War of 1812 include British impressment of American sailors, British seizure of American cargo, British trade restrictions on Southern planters and frontier farmers, failure of U.S. negotiations to lift British trade restrictions, and British role in Native American attacks on settlers.

Critical Thinking

23. Answers will vary. Students should defend their choice with logical reasons.

24. The War of 1812 increased American prestige overseas and generated a new spirit of patriotism and national unity.

25. Students' answers will vary. Answers should be supported by a logical explanation for the position taken.

We ask leave in conclusion to state that about three fourths of our townsmen depend on the sea for means of subsistence for themselves and families. By the recent declaration of war more than one half of that proportion is liable to fall into the hands of the enemy with a large proportion of their property, and many of their wives and children may thereby be reduced to extreme poverty. We would be permitted further to remark that out of this large proportion of [sailors] belonging to this town, we have but *four* detained by foreign nations. . . . 99

—quoted in the *Columbian Centinel,* July 20, 1812

a. What reasons do the residents give for opposing the war?

b. According to the petition, were the residents of Brewster worried more about losing townsmen and property to impressment by foreign nations or to fighting the British in the war? What reasoning do the residents use?

Practicing Skills

28. Making a Flowchart Reread the passage titled *Westward Expansion* on page 217. Then create a flowchart documenting events leading up to the end of Native American resistance in the Northwest Territory. Use the following events as the first and last items in your flowchart. Find at least four events to fit in between these first and last entries.

First event: White settlers move from Pennsylvania and Virginia into the Northwest Territory.

Last event: Treaty of Greenville is signed by 12 Native American nations in August 1795.

Writing Activity

29. Expository Writing Imagine that you are a political editor for a newspaper in 1817. You have been asked to write an article on the high and low points of the presidencies of George Washington, John Adams, Thomas Jefferson, and James Madison. Use evidence to support your ideas.

Chapter Activity

30. American History Primary Source Document Library CD-ROM Under *A New Nation,* read the "Farewell Address" by George Washington and the "First Inaugural Address" by Thomas Jefferson. Work with classmates to hold a debate about the effectiveness of today's political parties, using the opinions about parties presented by Washington and Jefferson in these primary sources.

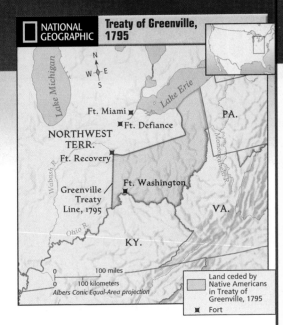

NATIONAL GEOGRAPHIC

Treaty of Greenville, 1795

Land ceded by Native Americans in Treaty of Greenville, 1795

Fort

Geography and History

31. The map above shows land ceded by Native Americans in the Treaty of Greenville. Study the map and answer the questions below.

a. Interpreting Maps The Native Americans gave up most of which present-day state in the Treaty of Greenville?

b. Applying Geography Skills Why was the land the Native Americans gave up valuable to white settlers?

Standardized Test Practice

Directions: Choose the best answer to the following question.

President Jefferson wanted to limit the power of the Federal government. Which of the following was an action he took to achieve this goal?

F He increased the size of the army.

G He proposed renewing the Alien and Sedition Acts.

H He dissolved the Republican Party to eliminate political conflict.

J He cut the federal budget.

Test-Taking Tip: Think about the word *limit.* It means to reduce or restrict. Therefore, you can eliminate answer G—it gave the government more power. You can also eliminate H because dissolving a party would not reduce governmental power.

HISTORY Online

Have students visit the Web site at tav.glencoe.com to review Chapter 6 and take the Self-Check Quiz.

Chapter Activity

30. Encourage students to prepare for the debate and to participate in their chosen position using Washington's and Jefferson's opinions.

Geography and History

31. a. Ohio; **b.** It gave them control of the Ohio River and new lands for settlement.

Standardized Test Practice

Answer: J
Test-Taking Tip: Encourage students to look for synonyms for the word *limit.* They can then look for these words to identify the correct answer.

Bonus Question ?

Ask: Who emerged as a hero of the Battle of New Orleans during the War of 1812? *(Andrew Jackson)*

---

26. Federalists favored a strong federal government and an economy based on manufacturing and trade. Republicans favored states' rights and supported agriculture.

27. a. They felt the reasons given for the war were insufficient. **b.** They were worried about impressments causing poverty due to lack of manpower because four sailors from their community were already detained by foreign nations.

Practicing Skills

28. Flowcharts will vary but should follow the pattern established in the Skillbuilder on page 233.

Writing Activity

29. Students' answers will vary. Answers should be supported by facts presented in Chapter 6.

Unit 3 Resources

SUGGESTED PACING CHART

Unit 3 (1 Day)	Chapter 7 (5 Days)	Chapter 8 (5 Days)	Chapter 9 (4 Days)	Unit 3 (2 Days)
Day 1 Introduction	**Day 1** Chapter 7 Intro, Section 1 **Day 2** Section 2 **Day 3** Section 3 **Day 4** Section 4 **Day 5** Chapter 7 Assessment	**Day 1** Chapter 8 Intro, Section 1 **Day 2** Section 2 **Day 3** Section 3 **Day 4** Section 4 **Day 5** Chapter 8 Assessment	**Day 1** Chapter 9 Intro, Section 1 **Day 2** Section 2 **Day 3** Section 3 **Day 4** Chapter 9 Assessment	**Day 1** Wrap-Up/Project **Day 2** Unit 3 Assessment

GLENCOE'S ASSESSMENT ADVANTAGE

Use the following tools to easily assess student learning in a variety of ways:

- Performance Assessment Activities and Rubrics
- Chapter and Unit Tests
- Section Quizzes
- Standardized Test Skills Practice Workbook

- tav.glencoe.com
- Interactive Tutor Self-Assessment CD-ROM
- MindJogger Videoquiz
- ExamView® Pro Testmaker CD-ROM
- SAT I/II Test Practice

TEACHING TRANSPARENCIES

Unit 3 Map Overlay Transparencies

Cause-and-Effect Transparency 3

interNET RESOURCES

- tav.glencoe.com

The American Vision
Visit the *American Vision* Web site for history overviews, activities, assessments, and updated charts and graphs.

- www.socialstudies.glencoe.com

Glencoe Social Studies
Visit the Glencoe Web site for social studies activities, updates, and links to other sites.

- www.teachingtoday.glencoe.com

Glencoe Teaching Today
Visit the new Glencoe Web site for teacher development information, teaching tips, Web resources, and educational news.

- www.time.com

TIME Online
Visit the TIME Web site for up-to-date news and special reports.

Unit 3 Resources

ASSESSMENT

Unit 3 Pretests

Unit 3 Posttests

APPLICATION AND ENRICHMENT

American Biography 3

History Simulation and Problem Solving 3

GEOGRAPHY

Geography and History Activity 3

INTERDISCIPLINARY ACTIVITIES

American Literature Reading 3

Economics and History Activity 3

Team-Teaching Interdisciplinary Strategies and Activities 3

BIBLIOGRAPHY

Readings for the Student

Worth, Richard. *Westward Expansion and Manifest Destiny in American History.* Enslow Publishers, Inc., 2001.

Readings for the Teacher

Booraem, Hendrick. *Young Hickory: The Making of Andrew Jackson.* Taylor Pub., 2001.

Multimedia Resources

Videocassette. *The Monroe Doctrine Applied: US Policy Toward Latin America.* VMA. (16 minutes)

Additional Glencoe Resources for This Unit:

- Glencoe Skillbuilder Interactive Workbook CD-ROM, Level 2
- Social Studies Guide to Using the Internet
- Writer's Guidebook for High School
- Living Constitution
- American Art Prints Strategies and Activities

236B

0:00 Out of Time?

If time does not permit teaching each chapter in this unit, you may want to use the **Reading Essentials and Study Guide** summaries.

Unit Overview

Unit 3 explores the challenges faced during the early years of the United States from 1789 to 1850. **Chapter 7** explores the growing divide between the industrial North and the agricultural South from 1816 to 1832. **Chapter 8** focuses on social and political reforms that occurred between 1828 and 1845. **Chapter 9** describes the expansion of America's borders as the concept of Manifest Destiny took hold from 1835 to 1848.

Unit Objectives

After studying this unit, students will be able to:

1. Discuss how the Industrial Revolution changed methods of production.
2. Explain the goals of different groups during the Second Great Awakening.
3. Analyze why Americans were willing to give up their lives in the East to move to the West.

Why It Matters Activity

Have students list the benefits of equality for all people in society. Then have students list barriers to achieving the goal of equality for all people that we face today. Have students suggest changes that society still needs to make to achieve the goal of equality.

UNIT 3
The Young Republic

1789–1850

Why It Matters

The United States faced many challenges in its early years. Internal improvements and industrial development began to reshape the nation, but this reshaping also highlighted the growing differences between North and South. Westward expansion generated new conflicts with Native Americans and also with Great Britain in the Northwest and Mexico in the Southwest. The push for social reforms intensified, addressing issues of education, temperance, women's rights, and slavery. Understanding these developments will help you comprehend the crises that would soon engulf the nation. The following resources offer more information about this period in American history.

Primary Sources Library

See pages 1050–1051 for primary source readings to accompany Unit 3.

Use the **American History Primary Source Document Library CD-ROM** to find additional primary sources about the young Republic.

236

Nineteenth-century water keg

New York and the Erie Canal by William Coventry Wall, 1862

TEAM TEACHING ACTIVITY

Geography Organize students into five groups. Provide each group with a large outline map of the United States that includes state boundaries. Assign each group one of the following years: 1800, 1850, 1900, 1950, and 2000. Have each group research to find out what states were part of the United States in the designated year. Have them label each state and shade the states. Tell students to include the year of the map in the map's title. Then display the maps in sequence. Pose questions about the expansion of the United States that can be answered from information contained on the maps.

"*The happy Union of these States is a wonder; their Constitution a miracle; their example the hope of Liberty throughout the world.*"

—James Madison, 1829

More About the Art

When construction began on the canal system, the United States did not have any schools of engineering. Many people ridiculed the idea since they believed that those in charge lacked the technical knowledge required to build such a massive project. Ask students to consider how people with an idea and a vision can produce results that others think are impossible. See if students can name other examples of "impossible" ideas that have become reality.

SERVICE-LEARNING PROJECT

Discuss the benefits of a good education and the importance of graduating from high school. Organize the class into small groups and have each group prepare either a poster or a script for a public service announcement that encourages high school students to stay in school and graduate. Arrange for the posters to be displayed in a public place or arrange for the public service announcements to be recorded and broadcast on local cable or radio stations.

Refer to *Building Bridges: Connecting Classroom and Community through Service-Learning in Social Studies* from the National Council for the Social Studies for information about service-learning.

Timesaving Tools

TeacherWorks™ All-In-One Planner and Resource Center

- **Interactive Teacher Edition** Access your Teacher Wraparound Edition and your classroom resources with a few easy clicks.
- **Interactive Lesson Planner** Planning has never been easier! Organize your week, month, semester, or year with all the lesson helps you need to make teaching creative, timely, and relevant.

Use Glencoe's **Presentation Plus!** multimedia teacher tool to easily present dynamic lessons that visually excite your students. Using Microsoft PowerPoint® you can customize the presentations to create your own personalized lessons.

TEACHING TRANSPARENCIES

Graphic Organizer 7

Why It Matters Chapter Transparency 7

APPLICATION AND ENRICHMENT

Linking Past and Present Activity 7

Enrichment Activity 7

Primary Source Reading 7

REVIEW AND REINFORCEMENT

Reteaching Activity 7

Vocabulary Activity 7

Time Line Activity 7

Critical Thinking Skills Activity 7

Meeting NCSS Standards

The following standards are highlighted in Chapter 7:

Section 1	II	Time, Continuity, and Change: B, C
Section 2	VIII	Science, Technology, and Society: A, B, C
Section 3	II	Time, Continuity, and Change: B, C, E, F
Section 4	V	Individuals, Groups, and Institutions: B, C, E, F

Local Standards

Chapter 7 Resources

ASSESSMENT AND EVALUATION

GLENCOE'S ASSESSMENT ADVANTAGE

Chapter 7 Test Form A

Chapter 7 Test Form B

Standardized Test Skills Practice Workbook Activity 7

Performance Assessment Activities and Rubrics 7

ExamView® Pro Testmaker CD-ROM

MULTIMEDIA

- Vocabulary PuzzleMaker CD-ROM
- Interactive Tutor Self-Assessment CD-ROM
- ExamView® Pro Testmaker CD-ROM
- Audio Program
- American History Primary Source Documents Library CD-ROM
- MindJogger Videoquiz
- Presentation Plus! CD-ROM
- TeacherWorks™ CD-ROM
- Interactive Student Edition CD-ROM
- Glencoe Skillbuilder Interactive Workbook CD-ROM, Level 2
- The *American Vision* Video Program
- American Music: Hits Through History
- American Music: Cultural Traditions

A&E HOME VIDEO. Biography® H THE HISTORY CHANNEL®

The following videotape programs are available from Glencoe as supplements to Chapter 7:

- **Railroads That Tamed the West** (ISBN 0-76-700033-1)
- **Frederick Douglass** (ISBN 0-76-700120-6)

To order, call Glencoe at 1-800-334-7344. To find classroom resources to accompany many of these videos, check the following home pages:
A&E Television: www.aande.com
The History Channel: www.historychannel.com

SPANISH RESOURCES

The following Spanish language materials are available in the Spanish Resources Binder:

- Spanish Guided Reading Activities
- Spanish Reteaching Activities
- Spanish Quizzes and Tests
- Spanish Vocabulary Activities
- Spanish Summaries
- The Declaration of Independence and United States Constitution Spanish Translation

HISTORY Online

Use our Web site for additional resources. All essential content is covered in the Student Edition.

You and your students can visit tav.glencoe.com, the Web site companion to the *American Vision.* This innovative integration of electronic and print media offers your students a wealth of opportunities. The student text directs students to the Web site for the following options:

- **Chapter Overviews**
- **Self-Check Quizzes**
- **Student Web Activities**
- **Textbook Updates**

Answers to the student Web activities are provided for you in the **Web Activity Lesson Plans.** Additional Web resources and Interactive Tutor Puzzles are also available.

Chapter 7 Resources

SECTION RESOURCES

Daily Objectives	Reproducible Resources	Multimedia Resources
SECTION 1 **American Nationalism** 1. Analyze how John Marshall strengthened the Supreme Court. 2. Evaluate how nationalism affected the nation's foreign policy after the War of 1812.	Reproducible Lesson Plan 7–1 Daily Lecture and Discussion Notes 7–1 Guided Reading Activity 7–1* Section Quiz 7–1* Reading Essentials and Study Guide 7–1 Performance Assessment Activities and Rubrics Supreme Court Case Studies	Daily Focus Skills Transparency 7–1 Interactive Tutor Self-Assessment CD-ROM ExamView® Pro Testmaker CD-ROM Presentation Plus! CD-ROM TeacherWorks™ CD-ROM Audio Program American Music: Hits Through History American Music: Cultural Traditions
SECTION 2 **Early Industry** 1. Examine the changes that took place in transportation in the early 1800s. 2. Discuss how the Industrial Revolution changed methods of production.	Reproducible Lesson Plan 7–2 Daily Lecture and Discussion Notes 7–2 Guided Reading Activity 7–2* Section Quiz 7–2* Reading Essentials and Study Guide 7–2 Performance Assessment Activities and Rubrics	Daily Focus Skills Transparency 7–2 Interactive Tutor Self-Assessment CD-ROM ExamView® Pro Testmaker CD-ROM Presentation Plus! CD-ROM TeacherWorks™ CD-ROM Audio Program ABCNews Interactive™ Historic America Electronic Field Trips
SECTION 3 **The Land of Cotton** 1. Explain why cotton dominated the Southern economy. 2. Describe the social classes in the South.	Reproducible Lesson Plan 7–3 Daily Lecture and Discussion Notes 7–3 Guided Reading Activity 7–3* Section Quiz 7–3* Reading Essentials and Study Guide 7–3 Performance Assessment Activities and Rubrics	Daily Focus Skills Transparency 7–3 Interactive Tutor Self-Assessment CD-ROM ExamView® Pro Testmaker CD-ROM Presentation Plus! CD-ROM TeacherWorks™ CD-ROM Audio Program ABCNews Interactive™ Historic America Electronic Field Trips
SECTION 4 **Growing Sectionalism** 1. List the major parts of the Missouri Compromise. 2. Describe why the election of 1824 was controversial.	Reproducible Lesson Plan 7–4 Daily Lecture and Discussion Notes 7–4 Guided Reading Activity 7–4* Section Quiz 7–4* Reading Essentials and Study Guide 7–4 Performance Assessment Activities and Rubrics	Daily Focus Skills Transparency 7–4 Interactive Tutor Self-Assessment CD-ROM ExamView® Pro Testmaker CD-ROM Presentation Plus! CD-ROM Skillbuilder Interactive Workbook, Level 2 TeacherWorks™ CD-ROM Vocabulary PuzzleMaker CD-ROM Audio Program

0:00 OUT OF TIME?
Assign the Chapter 7 **Reading Essentials and Study Guide.**

*Also Available in Spanish

Blackline Master   Transparency   CD-ROM   DVD

Poster   Music Program   Audio Program   Videocassette

NATIONAL GEOGRAPHIC   Teacher's Corner

INDEX TO NATIONAL GEOGRAPHIC MAGAZINE

The following articles relate to this chapter.

- "America's First Highway," March, 1998
- "The Cherokee," May 1995
- "Daniel Boone: First Hero of the Frontier," December 1985
- "Erie Canal: Living Link to Our Past," November 1990

NATIONAL GEOGRAPHIC SOCIETY PRODUCTS AVAILABLE FROM GLENCOE

To order the following products for use with this chapter, contact your local Glencoe sales representative, or call Glencoe at 1-800-334-7344:

- *NGS PicturePack: The Westward Movement* (Transparencies)
- *PictureShow: Native Americans, 1* (CD-ROM)
- *The Presidents: A Picture History of Our Nation* (CD-ROM)

ADDITIONAL NATIONAL GEOGRAPHIC SOCIETY PRODUCTS

To order the following, call National Geographic at 1-800-368-2728:

- *Washington, D.C.* (Video)

NGS ONLINE

Access National Geographic's Web site for current events, atlas updates, activities, links, interactive features, and archives.

www.nationalgeographic.com

From the Classroom of...

Linda J. Barth
Hillside School
Bridgewater, NJ

Canal Fever

Ask students to trace the route of the Erie Canal and the modern New York Thruway across New York State. **Ask: Why do you think that both used this particular corridor?**

The Erie Canal's success spurred canal building throughout the East. Tell the students to locate five other canals and compare them to the Erie. Indoors or out, measure and mark an area to show the width and depth of the Erie Canal.

ADDITIONAL RESOURCES FROM GLENCOE

- American Music: Cultural Traditions
- American Art & Architecture
- Outline Map Resource Book
- U.S. Desk Map
- Building Geography Skills for Life
- Inclusion for the High School Social Studies Classroom Strategies and Activities
- Teaching Strategies for the American History Classroom (Including Block Scheduling Pacing Guides)

KEY TO ABILITY LEVELS

Teaching strategies have been coded.

L1 BASIC activities for all students
L2 AVERAGE activities for average to above-average students
L3 CHALLENGING activities for above-average students
ELL ENGLISH LANGUAGE LEARNER activities

Block Schedule

Activities that are suited to use within the block scheduling framework are identified by:

Why It Matters Activity

Ask students to identify significant events that occurred between 1816 and 1832 that led to the nation's growth and to increasing divisions between North and South. Students should evaluate their answers after they have completed the chapter.

GLENCOE
TECHNOLOGY

The *American Vision* Video Program

To learn more about lifestyles of Americans in the 1800s, have students view the Chapter 7 video, "Young People of the North," from the ***American Vision* Video Program.**

 Available in DVD and VHS

MindJogger Videoquiz

Use the **MindJogger Videoquiz** to preview Chapter 7 content.

 Available in VHS

CHAPTER
7 Growth and Division *1816–1832*

Why It Matters

After the War of 1812, a new spirit of nationalism took hold in American society. A new national bank was chartered, and Supreme Court decisions strengthened the federal government. New roads and canals helped connect the country. Industry prospered in the North, while an agricultural economy dependent on slavery grew strong in the South. Regional differences began to define political life.

The Impact Today

Many developments of this period shaped our lives today.
* *Many Americans have a strong sense of national loyalty.*
* *Federal authority over interstate commerce helped create a truly national economy.*

 The American Vision Video *The Chapter 7 video, "Young People of the North," describes the lifestyle of Americans in the 1800s.*

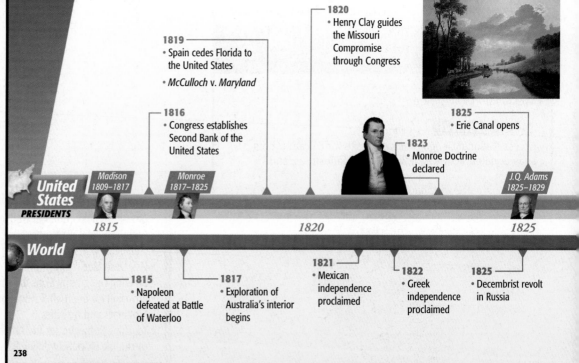

1819
* Spain cedes Florida to the United States
* *McCulloch v. Maryland*

1816
* Congress establishes Second Bank of the United States

1820
* Henry Clay guides the Missouri Compromise through Congress

1825
* Erie Canal opens

1823
* Monroe Doctrine declared

United States PRESIDENTS

Madison 1809–1817

Monroe 1817–1825

J.Q. Adams 1825–1829

1815   *1820*   *1825*

World

1815
* Napoleon defeated at Battle of Waterloo

1817
* Exploration of Australia's interior begins

1821
* Mexican independence proclaimed

1822
* Greek independence proclaimed

1825
* Decembrist revolt in Russia

238

TWO-MINUTE LESSON LAUNCHER

Ask students how the Industrial Revolution affects their lives today. Encourage students to talk about today's technology and how the Industrial Revolution made it possible. Ask students to think about where they live and how the Industrial Revolution might have played a role in the development of their community.

Election Day in Philadelphia by John L. Krimmel, 1815

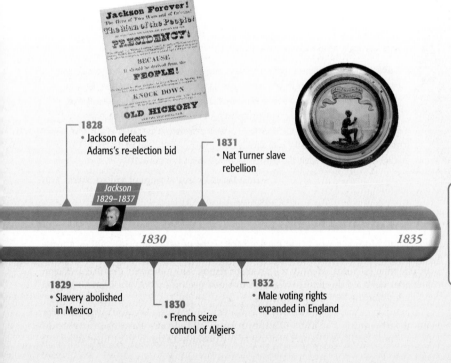

1828
• Jackson defeats Adams's re-election bid

1831
• Nat Turner slave rebellion

Jackson
1829–1837

1830   *1835*

1829
• Slavery abolished in Mexico

1830
• French seize control of Algiers

1832
• Male voting rights expanded in England

HISTORY Online

Chapter Overview
Visit the *American Vision* Web site at tav.glencoe.com and click on *Chapter Overviews—Chapter 7* to preview chapter information.

239

HISTORY Online

Introduce students to chapter content and key terms by having them access the **Chapter 7 Overview** at tav.glencoe.com.

More About the Art

John Krimmel (1789–1821) is considered one of America's first genre painters. His work expresses democratic and moralizing themes within the political and social changes affecting Philadelphia and the nation. Krimmel, born in Germany, immigrated to the United States in 1810. Much of his work, including *Election Day in Philadelphia,* contains hints of sarcasm.

TIME LINE ACTIVITY

Have students choose one of the events on the world time line and write a paragraph about how the event affected the United States. Instruct students to use library and Internet resources to learn more about the event they select.

GRAPHIC ORGANIZER ACTIVITY

Organizing Information Have students create a graphic organizer similar to the one shown below to identify states where slavery was permitted and where it was prohibited at the end of 1820.

Free States	
Connecticut	New Jersey
Illinois	New York
Indiana	Ohio
Maine	Pennsylvania
Massachusetts	Rhode Island
New Hampshire	Vermont

Slave States	
Alabama	Mississippi
Delaware	Missouri
Georgia	North Carolina
Kentucky	South Carolina
Louisiana	Tennessee
Maryland	Virginia

SECTION 1 American Nationalism

1 FOCUS

Section Overview

This section focuses on the feelings of patriotism and national pride that followed the War of 1812.

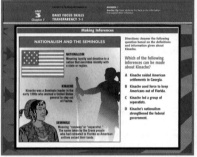
Guide to Reading

Answers to Graphic: Actions: creation of new national bank, imposition of protective tariff, decisions by Supreme Court established dominance of the nation over states, proclamation of the Monroe Doctrine

Preteaching Vocabulary
Provide the following list and have students match one of the Key Terms and Names with each item on the list. Chief Justice of the United States Supreme Court *(Marshall)*, Congressional leader *(Calhoun)*, Finalized western border of Louisiana Purchase *(Adams-Onís Treaty)*, Monroe's presidency *(Era of Good Feelings)*, Seminole leader *(Kinache)*, Tariff of 1816 *(protective tariff)*

Guide to Reading

Main Idea
Americans developed powerful feelings of patriotism and national unity after the War of 1812.

Key Terms and Names
Era of Good Feelings, John C. Calhoun, revenue tariff, protective tariff, John Marshall, Kinache, Adams-Onís Treaty, Quadruple Alliance

Reading Strategy
Organizing As you read about the United States after the War of 1812, complete a graphic organizer similar to the one below by listing actions that strengthened the federal government.

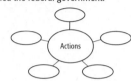

Actions

Reading Objectives
• **Analyze** how John Marshall strengthened the Supreme Court.
• **Evaluate** how nationalism affected the nation's foreign policy after the War of 1812.

Section Theme
Continuity and Change Increased national pride marked the years immediately following the War of 1812.

Preview of Events

♦1816	♦1819	♦1822	♦1825
1816 Second Bank of the United States established	**1819** Spain cedes Florida to United States; *McCulloch* v. *Maryland*	**1823** Monroe Doctrine introduced	**1824** *Gibbons* v. *Ogden*

James Monroe

★ An American Story ★

On a March day in 1817, a dignified group of Americans gathered in Washington, D.C., to witness the inauguration of the fifth president of the United States. The audience was full of hope and optimism as James Monroe delivered his inaugural address.

66 Never did a government commence under auspices so favorable. . . . If we look to the history of other nations, ancient or modern, we find no example of a growth so rapid, so gigantic, of a people so prosperous and happy. In contemplating what we have still to perform, the heart of every citizen must expand with joy when he reflects how near our Government has approached to perfection. . . . If we persevere in the career in which we have advanced so far and in the path already traced, we can not fail, under the favor of a gracious Providence, to attain the high destiny which seems to await us. 99

—from James Monroe's Inaugural Address, March 1817

The Era of Good Feelings

President Monroe's words emphasized the sense of national pride that swept the United States after the War of 1812. For a time, Americans' loyalty to the United States overrode their historical identity with state or region. The *Columbian Centinal,* a Boston newspaper, declared this time to be an **Era of Good Feelings.** The phrase has since been used to describe the Monroe presidency.

Harmony in national politics had reached a new high mostly because only one major political party—the Republicans—had any power. The Federalist Party had lost political influence and popularity, in part because of the public's disapproval of their actions at the Hartford Convention. At the same time, the War of 1812 had taught a new generation of Republican leaders that a stronger federal government was advantageous.

✓ **Reading Check** **Examining** Why is the Monroe presidency known as the Era of Good Feelings?

Economic Nationalism

American leaders prepared an ambitious program to bind the nation together. The program included creating a new national bank, protecting American manufacturers from foreign competition, and building canals and roads to improve transportation and link the country together.

ECONOMICS

The Second Bank Republicans traditionally had opposed the idea of a national bank. They had blocked the rechartering of the First Bank of the United States in 1811 and offered nothing in its place. The results were disastrous. State chartered banks and other private banks greatly expanded their lending with bank notes that were used as money. Without the regulatory presence of the national bank, prices rose rapidly during the War of 1812. When the government borrowed money to pay for the war, it had to pay high interest rates on its loans.

Because of these problems, many Republicans changed their minds after the war. In 1816 Representative **John C. Calhoun** of South Carolina introduced a bill proposing the Second Bank of the United States. With the support of **Henry Clay** of Kentucky and **Daniel Webster** of Massachusetts, the bill passed in 1816. This legislation gave the Bank power to issue notes that would serve as a national currency and to control state banks.

Tariffs and Transportation Protection of manufacturers was another example of the Republican plan. Because an embargo had prevented Americans from buying British goods during the War of 1812, American industries had increased their output to meet the demand. Once the war was over, British goods flowed into the United States at such low prices they threatened to put American companies out of business.

Congress responded with the Tariff of 1816. Unlike earlier revenue tariffs, which provided income for the federal government, this was a protective tariff, designed to nurture American manufacturers by taxing imports to drive up their prices. New England shippers and Southern farmers opposed the tariff and the higher prices it caused, but they could not block its passage.

The Republicans also wanted to improve the nation's transportation system. In 1816 Calhoun sponsored a federal internal improvement plan, but

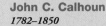

Profiles IN HISTORY

Henry Clay
1777–1852

Henry Clay was known as the Great Compromiser for his role in working out various agreements between leaders of the North and South. He served as a Kentucky state legislator, speaker of the U.S. House of Representatives, U.S. senator, and secretary of state. Although a slaveholder himself, Clay supported the gradual emancipation of enslaved persons. He later abandoned the idea, however, when it proved unpopular with his fellow Kentuckians.

Clay was a consistent champion of nationalism and devoted his career to strengthening the Union. Although nominated for president three times, the popularity of his opponents and the weakness of his political party, the Whigs, kept him from achieving his lifelong goal of winning the presidency.

John C. Calhoun
1782–1850

John C. Calhoun of South Carolina was an influential member of Congress and, at least for a time, a close friend of Henry Clay. Calhoun was a War Hawk—one who urged war with Great Britain in 1812. He was also an ardent nationalist in his early career. After the War of 1812, Calhoun helped introduce congressional bills for a new Bank of the United States, a permanent road system to connect the nation, and a tariff to protect the nation's industries.

In the 1830s Calhoun abandoned his nationalist stance in favor of states' rights and sectional interests. Fearing that the North intended to dominate the South, Calhoun spent the rest of his career trying to prevent the federal government from weakening states' rights and from interfering with the Southern way of life.

CHAPTER 7 Growth and Division **241**

---

2 TEACH

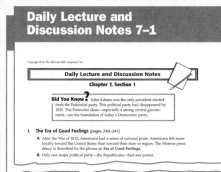

Daily Lecture and Discussion Notes 7–1

Copyright © by The McGraw-Hill Companies, Inc.

Daily Lecture and Discussion Notes
Chapter 7, Section 1

Did You Know? John Adams was the only president elected from the Federalist party. This political party had disappeared by 1820. The Federalist ideas—especially a strong central government—are the foundation of today's Democratic party.

I. The Era of Good Feelings (pages 240–241)

A. After the War of 1812, Americans had a sense of national pride. Americans felt more loyalty toward the United States than toward their state or region. The Monroe presidency is described by the phrase an Era of Good Feelings.

B. Only one major political party—the Republicans—had any power.

✓ **Reading Check**

Answer: A strong sense of national pride made Americans feel good about their country. The absence of a second political party ensured more cooperation.

Analyzing Information Have students use library and Internet resources to study the tariffs of 1807, 1812, and 1816. Have them write a short paper analyzing the effects of these tariffs. **L2**

Profiles IN HISTORY

The lives of John C. Calhoun and Henry Clay have many similarities. They devoted their lives to public service. They both served in the U.S. House of Representatives and the U.S. Senate, served as secretary of state, and aspired to the presidency. Clay was unsuccessful in his presidential bids in 1832 and 1844. Calhoun was never elected to the highest office, but he was elected vice president twice: in 1824 and in 1828.

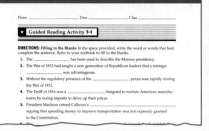
Reading Check

Answer: a national bank, protective tariffs, internal improvements

📂 Use *Supreme Court Case Study 2*, McCulloch v. Maryland.

📂 Use *Supreme Court Case Study 3*, Dartmouth College v. Woodward.

📂 Use *Supreme Court Case Study 4*, Gibbons v. Ogden.

Chart *Skills*

Answer:

1. *Marbury* v. *Madison*

2. No. In *McCulloch* v. *Maryland*, Marshall used the notion of "implied powers" to give Congress more flexibility to create institutions such as the Bank of the United States.

Chart Skills Practice
Ask: In which cases did the states lose some of their powers or rights?
(Fletcher v. Peck, Martin v. Hunter's Lessee, Cohens v. Virginia, and Gibbons v. Ogden)

President Madison vetoed it, arguing that spending money to improve transportation was not expressly granted in the Constitution. Nevertheless, road and canal construction soon began, with private businesses and state and local governments funding much of the work.

✔ **Reading Check** **Summarizing** What were three examples of economic nationalism after the War of 1812?

Judicial Nationalism

The judicial philosophy of the Chief Justice of the United States, **John Marshall**, provided another boost to the forces helping unify the nation after the war. Between 1816 and 1824, Marshall ruled in three important cases that established the dominance of the nation over the states and shaped the future of American government.

Martin v. Hunter's Lessee In 1816 the Court decided in *Martin* v. *Hunter's Lessee* that it had the authority to hear all appeals of state court decisions in cases involving federal statutes and treaties. In this case, Denny Martin, a British subject, tried to sell Virginia land inherited from his uncle, Lord Fairfax, a British Loyalist during the war. At that time, Virginia law stated that no "enemy" could inherit land. The Supreme Court upheld Martin's case, ruling that Virginia's law

John Marshall

conflicted with the 1783 Treaty of Paris, which recommended that the states restore confiscated property to Loyalists. This historic decision helped establish the Supreme Court as the nation's court of final appeal.

McCulloch v. Maryland This 1819 case concerned Maryland's attempt to tax the Second Bank of the United States. Before addressing Maryland's right to tax the national bank, the Supreme Court ruled on the federal government's right to create a national bank in the first place. In the Court's opinion, written by Marshall, the bank was constitutional, even though the Constitution did not specifically give Congress the power to create one.

Marshall observed that the Constitution gave the federal government the power to collect taxes, to borrow money, to regulate commerce, and to raise armies and navies. He noted that the national bank helped the federal government exercise these powers. He concluded that the Constitution's "necessary and proper" clause allowed the federal government to create a bank.

Opponents argued that the "necessary and proper" clause meant the government could only do things absolutely necessary, but Marshall rejected that idea. Instead, he held that "necessary and proper" meant the government could use any method that was convenient for carrying out its powers as long as the method was not expressly forbidden.

Marshall then argued that the federal government was "supreme in its own sphere of action." This meant that a state government could not interfere

Major Supreme Court Decisions, 1801–1824

Marbury v. *Madison* (1803)	Declared congressional act unconstitutional; Court asserts power of judicial review
Fletcher v. *Peck* (1810)	Protected contracts from legislative interference; Court could overturn state laws that opposed specific provisions of Constitution
Martin v. *Hunter's Lessee* (1816)	Court can accept appeals of state court decisions and review state decisions that involve federal statutes or treaties; asserted the Supreme Court's sovereignty over state courts
McCulloch v. *Maryland* (1819)	Upheld constitutionality of the Bank of the United States; doctrine of "implied powers" provided Congress more flexibility to enact legislation
Cohens v. *Virginia* (1821)	Reasserted federal judicial authority over state courts; argued that when states ratified Constitution, they gave up some sovereignty to federal courts
Gibbons v. *Ogden* (1824)	Revoked an existing state monopoly; Court gave Congress the right to regulate interstate commerce

Source: *The Oxford Companion to the Supreme Court of the United States*

Chart *Skills*

1. **Interpreting Charts** In which case did Chief Justice Marshall assert the Court's right of judicial review?

2. **Analyzing** Was Marshall a strict interpreter of the Constitution? How can you tell?

MEETING SPECIAL NEEDS

Interpersonal Have students work in pairs to recreate the arguments of one of the cases in this section. Have the pairs work together to decide which side of the issue each of them will present. Have them research the case and present a summary of the arguments to the class. Encourage the pairs to pretend that they are arguing their case before the Supreme Court. Allow the class, acting as the court, to ask questions of each person. **L3**

📂 Refer to *Inclusion for the High School Social Studies Classroom Strategies and Activities* in the TCR.

with an agency of the federal government exercising its specific constitutional powers within a state's borders. Taxing the national bank was a form of interference and therefore unconstitutional.

Gibbons v. *Ogden* This 1824 case involved a company that had a state-granted monopoly over steamboat traffic in New York waters. When the company tried to expand its monopoly to include traffic crossing the Hudson River to New Jersey, the matter went to court.

The Supreme Court declared this monopoly unconstitutional. In the Court's opinion, Marshall stated that the state legislature had overstepped its power in granting the original monopoly. The Constitution granted the federal government control over interstate commerce, which the court interpreted to include all trade along the coast or on waterways dividing the states. The state could, however, regulate commerce within its own borders.

In writing the Supreme Court's decision, Marshall defined interstate commerce in a way that went far beyond the mere exchange of goods between states. By ruling that anything crossing state boundaries came under federal control, Marshall ensured that federal law would take precedence over state law in interstate transportation.

In these cases, Marshall's nationalism strengthened the power of the federal government at the expense of the states. Although defenders of states' rights bitterly attacked Marshall's decisions, his views helped make the "necessary and proper" clause and the interstate commerce clause major vehicles for expanding federal power. 📖 *(See page 1081 for more information on Martin v. Hunter's Lessee, McCulloch v. Maryland, and Gibbons v. Ogden.)*

✓ **Reading Check** **Identifying** How did the Supreme Court establish and expand the power of the federal government over the states?

Nationalist Diplomacy

The wave of nationalism within Congress and among voters influenced the nation's foreign affairs as well. Feeling proud and confident, the United States under President Monroe expanded its borders and asserted itself on the world stage.

Jackson Invades Florida Throughout the early 1800s, Spanish-held Florida was a source of anger and frustration for Southerners. Many runaway slaves fled there, knowing that Americans could not cross the border into Spanish territory. Similarly,

Picturing **History**

Seminole Resistance Perhaps the most famous Seminole leader was Osceola, who helped lead the resistance against U.S. attempts to relocate the Seminoles to the West. He was captured by treachery while bearing a flag of truce. *From which Native American group did the Seminoles originate?*

many of the Creek people had retreated to Florida as American settlers seized their lands. These people took a new name for themselves—**Seminole,** meaning "runaway" or "separatist." The Seminoles used Florida as a base to stage raids against American settlements in Georgia. Spain was unable to control the border, causing many Americans to clamor for the United States to step in. As tensions heightened in the region, the Seminole leader **Kinache** warned a U.S. general to stay out of Florida:

> 66You charge me with killing your people, stealing your cattle and burning your houses; it is I that have cause to complain of the Americans. . . . I shall use force to stop any armed Americans from passing my towns or my lands.99
>
> —quoted in *The Seminoles of Florida*

The warning fell on deaf ears. Former representative Calhoun, now secretary of war, authorized action against the Seminoles. In 1818 he sent U.S. troops under the command of General **Andrew Jackson** into Florida. After destroying several Seminole villages, Jackson disobeyed orders and seized the Spanish settlements of St. Marks and Pensacola. He then removed the Spanish governor of Florida from power.

CHAPTER 7 Growth and Division **243**

📖 **History** *and the* **Humanities**

🏳 American Music: Hits Through History: "College Hornpipe," "Belle Catherine"

🎵 American Music: Cultural Traditions: "The Rose Tree," "Hull's Victory," "Hunters of Kentucky"

3 ASSESS

Assign Section 1 Assessment as homework or as an in-class activity.

💿 Have students use the **Interactive Tutor Self-Assessment CD-ROM.**

✓ **Reading Check**

Answer: *Martin* v. *Hunter's Lessee* established the Supreme Court as the court of final appeal. *McCulloch* v. *Maryland* prohibited states from interfering with agencies of the federal government exercising its specific constitutional powers within a state's borders. *Gibbons* v. *Ogden* defined interstate commerce broadly and granted control of it to the federal government.

Reading Essentials and Study Guide 7–1

Name _____ Date _____ Class _____

Study Guide

Chapter 7, Section 1
For use with textbook pages 240–244

AMERICAN NATIONALISM

KEY TERMS AND NAMES
Era of Good Feelings phrase used to describe James Monroe's presidency because of the harmony in national politics *(page 240)*
John C. Calhoun Republican who proposed the Second Bank of the United States and sponsored a federal internal improvement plan *(page 241)*
revenue tariff tax on goods that provides income for the federal government *(page 241)*
protective tariff tax on goods to help domestic manufacturers by taxing imports to drive up their prices *(page 241)*
John Marshall Chief Justice of the United States Supreme Court whose rulings helped establish a strong federal government *(page 242)*

INTERDISCIPLINARY CONNECTIONS ACTIVITY

Economics Have the economics teacher present a brief discussion of currency systems that have been used in the United States. Have interested students prepare a display that pictures the various coins and currency that have been used throughout the country's history. Encourage students to include brief written descriptions of the various forms of currency displayed. **L2**

Organizing Information Have students use a graphic organizer similar to the one shown below to identify the members of the Quadruple Alliance. **L1** ELL

Quadruple Alliance
- Austria
- Great Britain
- Prussia
- Russia

Reteach

Ask student to review the time line on page 240 and explain how each event reflects the spirit of nationalism.

Enrich

Invite students to choose a topic from this section and write a report. Encourage students to use library and Internet resources for their research.

4 CLOSE

Call on volunteers to offer their opinions about the development or invention that made the greatest contribution to the Industrial Revolution in the United States.

✓ **Reading Check**

Answer: invasion of Florida and the Monroe Doctrine

244

Furious Spanish officials demanded that Jackson be punished, and President Monroe sided initially with Spain. Secretary of State **John Quincy Adams** defended Jackson and argued that the true cause of the dispute lay in Spain's failure to keep order in Florida. Adams used this Florida turmoil to put pressure on Spain in ongoing border negotiations. Occupied with problems throughout its Latin American empire, Spain gave in and ceded all of Florida to the United States in the **Adams-Onís Treaty** of 1819. The treaty also finalized the western border of the Louisiana Purchase along Texas's Sabine and Red Rivers, west along the Arkansas River, and then north to the 42nd Parallel before turning west to the Pacific Ocean.

The Monroe Doctrine In 1809 rebellions began to erupt in Spain's colonies. By 1824 all of Spain's colonies on the American mainland had declared independence. Spain's once vast empire had been reduced to three islands: Cuba, Puerto Rico, and Santo Domingo.

Meanwhile a group of European countries—Great Britain, Austria, Prussia, and Russia (later joined by France)—formed the **Quadruple Alliance** in an effort to suppress movements against monarchies in Europe. Over Britain's objection, the alliance raised the possibility of helping Spain regain control of its overseas colonies in 1822.

Great Britain and the United States were not pleased. Both nations enjoyed profitable trade with Latin America and would not welcome a return of Spanish rule. In August 1823, British officials suggested that the two nations issue a joint statement supporting the independence of the new Latin American countries. Britain also wished to limit future American expansion in the hemisphere.

Russia's increasing influence on North America's Pacific Coast also worried members of Monroe's administration. Russia already claimed Alaska, and in 1821 it announced that its empire extended south into the Oregon country between Russian Alaska and the western United States.

Secretary Adams urged President Monroe to avoid working with the British when dealing with the Spanish and Russian threats. He believed it would be "more dignified to avow our principles explicitly," than to allow the United States to be looked upon as Great Britain's junior partner. Acting without the British, President Monroe declared in 1823 that the American continents were "henceforth not to be considered as subjects for future colonization by any European powers."

The president's proclamation, later called the **Monroe Doctrine,** was a bold act, because the United States might not have been able to back up its new policy if challenged. The Monroe Doctrine marked the beginning of a long-term American policy of preventing other great powers from interfering in Latin American political affairs. At the same time, by keeping the European powers out of the Americas, the Monroe Doctrine upheld Washington's policy of avoiding entanglements in European power struggles.

✓ **Reading Check** **Examining** In what ways did American foreign policy become more assertive in the early 1800s?

SECTION 1 ASSESSMENT

Checking for Understanding

1. **Define:** revenue tariff, protective tariff.
2. **Identify:** Era of Good Feelings, John C. Calhoun, John Marshall, Kinache, Adam-Onís Treaty, Quadruple Alliance.
3. **Summarize** how the Supreme Court rulings in *McCulloch* v. *Maryland* and *Gibbons* v. *Ogden* strengthened the federal government.

Reviewing Themes

4. **Continuity and Change** How did the Monroe Doctrine reinforce President Washington's foreign policy goals?

Critical Thinking

5. **Explaining** How did nationalism affect the foreign affairs of the United States?
6. **Organizing** Use a graphic organizer similar to the one below to list examples of nationalism in the United States after the War of 1812.

Examples of Nationalism		
Economic	Judicial	Diplomatic

Analyzing Visuals

7. **Examining Art** Study the painting of Osceola on page 243. What elements of this picture indicate that he was very accustomed to European culture?

Writing About History

8. **Expository Writing** Imagine you are an editor of a newspaper in Spanish-held Florida. Write an editorial in which you either attack or defend the actions of Andrew Jackson and his militia in seizing Spanish settlements in Florida.

SECTION 1 ASSESSMENT ANSWERS

1. Terms are in blue.
2. Era of Good Feelings *(p. 240),* John C. Calhoun *(p. 241),* John Marshall *(p. 242),* Kinache *(p. 243),* Adams-Onís Treaty *(p. 244),* Quadruple Alliance *(p. 244)*
3. *McCulloch* v. *Maryland* prohibited states from interfering with federal agencies exercising constitutional powers within a state's borders. *Gibbons* v. *Ogden* defined interstate commerce broadly, thereby expanding federal powers.
4. reduced the possibility of the United States becoming involved in European affairs
5. The United States invaded Florida and issued the Monroe Doctrine.
6. economic: protective tariffs; judicial: Supreme Court authority grew; diplomatic: Monroe Doctrine
7. possible answers: the ruffles on his shirt and his rifle
8. Editorials should support one side of the issue or the other.

SECTION 2 Early Industry

Guide to Reading

Main Idea
Beginning in the early 1800s, revolutions in transportation and industry brought great changes to the North.

Key Terms and Names
National Road, Robert Fulton, Industrial Revolution, Francis C. Lowell, Eli Whitney, interchangeable parts, Samuel F.B. Morse, labor union, strike

Reading Strategy
Categorizing As you read about changes that occurred in the United States in the early 1800s, complete a graphic organizer similar to the one below by filling in milestones in transportation and industrialization.

Transportation	Industrialization

Reading Objectives
• **Examine** the changes that took place in transportation in the early 1800s.
• **Discuss** how the Industrial Revolution changed methods of production.

Section Theme
Science and Technology New manufacturing techniques reshaped the organization of the American workforce.

Preview of Events

| 1800 | 1815 | 1830 | 1845 |

1807
Fulton's steamboat launched

1825
Erie Canal opens

1838
National Road reaches Vandalia, Illinois

1844
First inter-city telegraph message transmitted from Baltimore to Washington

1 FOCUS

Section Overview
This section explores the changes that resulted from the Industrial Revolution.

BELLRINGER
Skillbuilder Activity

Project transparency and have students answer the question.

Available as a blackline master.

Daily Focus Skills Transparency 7–2

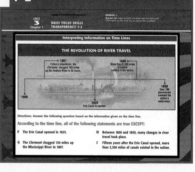

★ An American Story ★

Constructing the Erie Canal

In the summer of 1817, explosions suddenly began disturbing the peace and quiet of rural upstate New York. What had started was not a war but a great engineering challenge: a canal, 40 feet (12.2 m) wide and 4 feet (1.2 m) deep, to be built from the Hudson River at Albany to Lake Erie at Buffalo. The longest canal in the nation at that time ran almost 28 miles (45 km) . The new canal would be a colossal 363 miles (584.1 km) long.

Building the canal was difficult and dangerous. Canal beds collapsed, burying diggers. Blasting accidents killed other workers. In 1819 alone more than 1,000 men were stricken with diseases contracted in the swamps through which they dug. Here, one investor coldly complains that the number of deaths is raising costs:

❝In consequence of the sickness that prevailed in this section and its vicinity, we were under the necessity of raising wages from twelve to fourteen and some as high as seventeen dollars per month for common Labourers, and pay Physicians for atten[d]ing to the sick, purchase Coffins and grave clothes, and attend with Hands to bury the Dead.❞
—quoted in *The Artificial River*

A Revolution in Transportation

Despite the dangers they faced, the canal workers pressed on and completed the immense project in 1825. The **Erie Canal** was a striking example of a revolution in transportation that swept through the Northern states in the early 1800s. This revolution led to dramatic social and economic changes.

CHAPTER 7 Growth and Division **245**

Guide to Reading

Answers to Graphic: Transportation: 1807, *Clermont* travels between New York City and Albany; 1811, National Road begun; 1821, toll roads connect eastern cities; 1825, Erie Canal completed; **Industrialization:** 1789, Slater builds water frame in Rhode Island; 1814, Lowell opens textile mill; 1832, Morse perfects the telegraph and invents Morse code; 1844, first long distance telegraph lines connect Washington, D.C., and Baltimore

Preteaching Vocabulary
Have students make a four-column table with the column headings Transportation, Industry, Communication, and Labor. Instruct students to write each one of the Key Terms and Names in the most appropriate column.

SECTION RESOURCES

Reproducible Masters
• Reproducible Lesson Plan 7–2
• Daily Lecture and Discussion Notes 7–2
• Guided Reading Activity 7–2
• Section Quiz 7–2
• Reading Essentials and Study Guide 7–2

Transparencies
• Daily Focus Skills Transparency 7–2

Multimedia
🖰 Interactive Tutor Self-Assessment CD-ROM
🖰 ExamView® Pro Testmaker CD-ROM
🖰 Presentation Plus! CD-ROM
🖰 TeacherWorks™ CD-ROM
🎧 Audio Program
📺 ABCNews Interactive™ Historic America Electronic Field Trips

2 TEACH

Daily Lecture and Discussion Notes 7–2

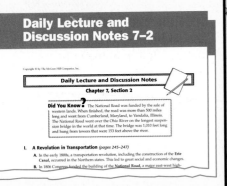

Copyright © by The McGraw-Hill Companies, Inc.

Daily Lecture and Discussion Notes

Chapter 7, Section 2

Did You Know The National Road was funded by the sale of western lands. When finished, the road was more than 500 miles long and went from Cumberland, Maryland, to Vandalia, Illinois. The National Road went over the Ohio River on the longest suspension bridge in the world at that time. The bridge was 1,010 feet long and hung from towers that were 153 feet above the river.

I. A Revolution in Transportation (pages 245–247)

A. In the early 1800s, a transportation revolution, including the construction of the **Erie Canal**, occurred in the Northern states. This led to great social and economic changes.

B. In 1806 Congress funded the building of the **National Road**, a major east-west high-

Geography *Skills*

Answers:

1. Georgia

2. The North had more industry and more money to invest in canal building.

Geography Skills Practice

Ask: What modes of transportation could you have used to travel from New York to Baltimore in 1840?

(by rail, road, or sea)

Creating a Thematic Map

Provide students an outline map of the United States without state borders. Instruct students to draw in the Ohio and Mississippi Rivers and their major tributaries. Tell students that they are planning a steamboat trip in 1850 from Wheeling, West Virginia, to New Orleans, Louisiana. Have students draw in the state borders that surround their route of travel and locate and label the major cities along the route. **L1** **ELL**

📁 Use the rubric for creating a map, display, or chart on pages 77–78 in the *Performance Assessment Activities and Rubrics.*

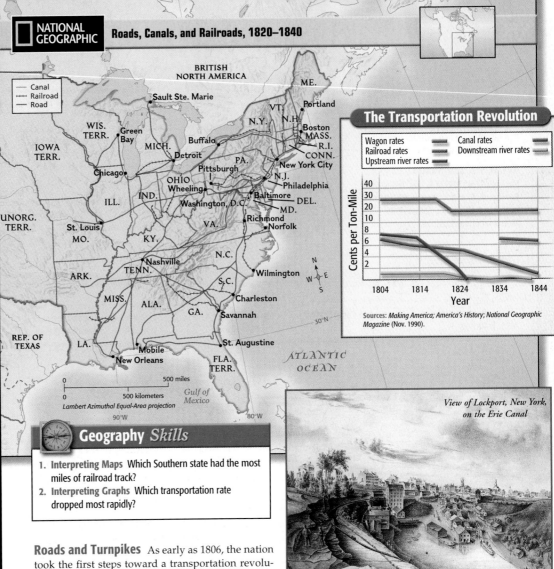

NATIONAL GEOGRAPHIC — Roads, Canals, and Railroads, 1820–1840

The Transportation Revolution

Wagon rates — Canal rates
Railroad rates — Downstream river rates
Upstream river rates

Cents per Ton-Mile

Sources: *Making America; America's History; National Geographic Magazine* (Nov. 1990).

View of Lockport, New York, on the Erie Canal

Geography *Skills*

1. **Interpreting Maps** Which Southern state had the most miles of railroad track?

2. **Interpreting Graphs** Which transportation rate dropped most rapidly?

Roads and Turnpikes As early as 1806, the nation took the first steps toward a transportation revolution when Congress funded the building of a major east–west highway, the **National Road.** In 1811 laborers started cutting the roadbed westward from the Potomac River at Cumberland, Maryland. By 1818 the roadway had reached Wheeling, Virginia (now West Virginia) on the Ohio River. Conestoga wagons drawn by teams of oxen or mules carried migrating pioneers west on this road, while livestock and wagonloads of farm produce traveled the opposite way, toward the markets of the East.

Rather than marking the start of a federal campaign to improve transportation, the National Road turned out to be the only great federally funded transportation project of its time. Jefferson and his successors believed in a strict interpretation of the Constitution and doubted that the federal government had the power to fund roads and other "internal improvements."

Instead, states, localities, and private businesses took the initiative. Private companies laid down hundreds of miles of toll roads. By 1821, some 4,000 miles (6,400 km) of toll roads had been built, mainly to connect eastern cities, where heavy traffic made the roads extremely profitable. Even so, major roads west had also been built, connecting Pittsburgh, Pennsylvania, and Buffalo, New York, to eastern markets.

246 CHAPTER 7 Growth and Division

COOPERATIVE LEARNING ACTIVITY

Writing a Script Organize students into small groups. Have the groups research the lives of children who worked in the textile mills. Based on their research, have the groups write a script of an event that might have occurred in the life of such a child. Examples include an encounter between a foreman and a worker who has fallen asleep, a dialogue with another worker as they are on their way home from a day's work, or a monologue of the child's thoughts as he or she walks to work on a hot summer day. Encourage groups to perform the script for the class.

Use the rubric for a cooperative group management plan on pages 81–82 in the *Performance Assessment Activities and Rubrics.*

Steamboats and Canals Rivers offered a far faster, more efficient, and cheaper way to move goods than did roads, which were often little more than wide paths. A barge could hold many wagonloads of grain or coal. Loaded boats and barges, however, could usually travel only downstream, as moving against the current with heavy cargoes proved difficult.

The steamboat changed all that. In 1807 **Robert Fulton** and Robert R. Livingston stunned the nation when the *Clermont* chugged 150 miles up the Hudson River from New York City to Albany in just 32 hours. The steamboat made river travel more reliable and extended the range of transportation in both directions.

Steamboats soon showed up everywhere, thrilling adults and children alike with their breathtaking power and speed, their intimidating noise, their musical whistles, and their stately appearance. They cruised in and out of the Great Lakes as well as up and down the Mississippi River and its tributaries. By 1850 over 700 steamboats, also called riverboats, traveled along the nation's waterways.

The growth of river travel—and the success of the Erie Canal—spurred a wave of canal building throughout the country. By 1840 more than 3,300 miles of canals snaked through the nation, increasing existing commerce between regions and stimulating new economic growth.

The "Iron Horse" Another mode of transportation—railroads—also appeared in the early 1800s. A wealthy, self-educated industrialist named **Peter Cooper** decided to build an American engine based on the ones originally developed in Great Britain. In 1830 Cooper's tiny but powerful locomotive *Tom Thumb* pulled the nation's first load of train passengers. Forty adventuresome men and women travelled at the then incredible speed of 10 miles per hour along 13 miles of track between Baltimore and Ellicott City, Maryland. The railroad era had dawned.

The new machines did not win universal favor. Some said they were not only dangerous and uncomfortable but dirty and ugly as well. "It is the Devil's own invention," declared one critic, "compounded of fire, smoke, soot, and dirt, spreading its infernal poison throughout the fair countryside."

Others responded to the train's awesome presence. "When I hear the iron horse make the hills echo with his snort like thunder, shaking the earth with his feet, and breathing fire and smoke from his nostrils," wrote the poet Henry David Thoreau, "it seems as if the earth had got a race now worthy to inhabit it."

The advantages of train travel soon became apparent to almost everyone. Trains traveled much faster than stagecoaches or wagons, and unlike steamboats, they could go nearly anywhere track was laid. Perhaps more than any other kind of transportation, trains helped settle the West and expand trade between the nation's different regions.

✓ **Reading Check** **Evaluating** What were two advantages of trains over other kinds of transportation in the 1800s?

A New System of Production

Along with dramatic changes in transportation, a revolution occurred in business and industry. The **Industrial Revolution**, which began in Britain in the middle 1700s, consisted of several basic developments. Manufacturing shifted from hand tools to large, complex machines. Skilled artisans gave way to workers, organized by specific tasks, and often unskilled. Factories, some housing hundreds of machines and workers, replaced home-based workshops. Manufacturers sold their wares nationwide or abroad instead of just locally.

Peter Cooper's *Tom Thumb* races a horse.

Guided Reading Activity 7-2

Name _____ Date _____ Class _____

★ **Guided Reading Activity 7-2**

DIRECTIONS: Outlining Read the section and complete the outline below. Refer to your textbook to fill in the blanks.
I. **A Revolution in Transportation**
   A. The _____ was a striking example of a revolution in transportation that swept through the Northern states in the early 1800s.
   B. Conestoga wagons carrying migrating pioneers traveled west on the _____
   C. The _____ made river travel more reliable and extended the range of transportation in both directions.
II. **A New System of Production**
   A. In the _____, manufacturing shifted from hand tools to large, complex machines, and factories replaced _____ shops.
   B. The _____ encouraged industrialization because companies in competition with each other were willing _____ with new _____

HISTORY Online

Objectives and answers to the student activity can be found in the **Web Activity Lesson Plan** at tav.glencoe.com.

✓ **Reading Check**

Answer: Trains traveled much faster than stagecoaches or wagons and could go anywhere track could be laid.

FYI

During the 1820s, William Underwood and Thomas Kensett introduced the nation to the practice of sealing food in airtight tin containers. Canning with tin containers allowed people to store or transport a wide range of foods without fear of spoilage.

Listing Cause and Effect Write the words "Industrial Revolution" on the board. Ask students to list the causes and effects of the Industrial Revolution. For example, a cause was division of labor and its effect was the rise of labor unions. Then ask students to discuss whether they think these effects would have happened without industrialization. **L2**

MEETING SPECIAL NEEDS

Kinesthetic Ask students to select one of the common means of transportation that was used in the early 1800s. Have students create a model of their choice. Encourage students to be able to explain the materials used to construct the model and how it worked. Have students share their models with the class. **L1** ELL

☛ Refer to *Inclusion for the High School Social Studies Classroom Strategies and Activities* in the TCR.

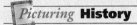
Creating a Graph Have students create a graph using the following U.S. Census Bureau data comparing the populations of the six largest cities in 1820 and 1860. **L2**

 Use the rubric for creating a map, display, or chart on pages 77–78 in the *Performance Assessment Activities and Rubrics.*

City	Pop. in 1820	Pop. in 1860
New York, NY	123,706	813,669
Philadelphia, PA	63,802	565,529
Brooklyn, NY	7,175	266,661
Baltimore, MD	62,738	212,418
Boston, MA	43,298	177,840
New Orleans, LA	27,176	168,675

ABCNEWS INTERACTIVE™

 VIDEOCASSETTE
Historic America Electronic Field Trips

View **Tape 2, Chapter 4:** "Lowell Factories."

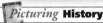

Picturing **History**

Young Mill Worker Girls like this one often worked in the textile factories that were being built in the northeastern United States during the Industrial Revolution. Why was industry initially concentrated in the Northeast?

ECONOMICS

Industrialization Sweeps the North Industry developed quickly in the United States in the early 1800s for several reasons. Perhaps the most important factor was the American system of free enterprise based on private property rights. Individuals could acquire capital and make their own choices about how to use it, without strict government controls.

The free enterprise system also encouraged industrialization because companies in competition with each other were always willing to experiment with new technologies to make goods cheaper and to transport them faster. The era's low taxes also meant that entrepreneurs had more money to invest.

Beginning in the 1830s, many states encouraged industrialization by passing general incorporation laws. These laws allowed companies to become corporations and to raise money by issuing stock without having to obtain a charter from the state legislature. These laws also limited liability. If a person bought stock in a company and it went bankrupt, the person risked losing his or her investment

but was not responsible for the company's debts. By limiting liability, the new state laws encouraged people to invest money, spurring economic growth.

Industrialization began in the Northeast, where many swift-flowing streams provided factories with waterpower. The region was also home to many entrepreneurs and merchants who were willing to invest in British industrial techniques.

At first, importing British technology was not easy. Britain had passed strict laws with harsh penalties for anyone passing on its industrial know-how to foreigners. A young English textile worker named Samuel Slater was willing to take the risk. In 1789 he moved to Rhode Island, where he reconstructed the British water frame from memory. The frame stretched and spun raw cotton fiber into cotton thread.

Taking matters a key step further was **Francis C. Lowell,** who opened a series of mills in northeastern Massachusetts beginning in 1814. Using machinery he built after touring British textile mills, Lowell introduced mass production of cotton cloth to the United States. His Boston Manufacturing Company built residences for workers in a new town named after Lowell. The company employed thousands of workers—mostly women and children, who would work for lower wages than men.

By 1840, scores of textile factories had been built in the Northeast. Industrialists soon applied factory techniques to the production of lumber, shoes, leather, wagons, and other products.

Technological Advances A wave of inventions and technological innovations spurred the nation's industrial growth. An ingenious young New Englander named **Eli Whitney** popularized the concept of interchangeable parts, transforming gunmaking from a one-by-one process into a factory process. Using this process, machines turned out large quantities of identical pieces that workers assembled into finished weapons.

Communications improved as well, particularly when American inventor **Samuel F.B. Morse** perfected the telegraph in 1832 and developed the Morse code for sending messages. In 1844 the first long-distance telegraph line connected Washington, D.C., and Baltimore. Morse publicly demonstrated the device, tapping out in code the words "What hath God wrought?" From Baltimore came a return message: "What is the news from Washington?"

Journalists saw the telegraph as a tool for speedy transmission of the news. In 1848 a group of newspapers pooled their resources to collect and share news over the wires. This organization was the Associated

---

INTERDISCIPLINARY CONNECTIONS ACTIVITY

Science Organize students into small groups. Have the groups use library and Internet resources to research how a lock in a canal works, then build a working model of a lock. Encourage students to create drawings and select appropriate materials for the model. A brief written explanation of how the model works should accompany the model. **L3**

Press. Spurred by journalists and other users of the telegraph, more than 50,000 miles of telegraph wire connected most parts of the country by 1860.

✓ **Reading Check** **Summarizing** Name two reasons the factory system began in the Northeast.

The Rise of Large Cities

The industrialization of the United States drew thousands of people from farms and villages to towns in search of factory jobs with higher wages. Many city populations doubled or tripled. In 1820 only two American cities boasted more than 100,000 residents. By 1860, eight cities had reached that size.

The growing cities provided opportunities for many different kinds of occupations. One group was printers and publishers, who shared the goal of keeping the public informed. America had always claimed a high literacy rate, and by 1840, over 75 percent of the total population and over 90 percent of the white population could read. The publishing industry arose to satisfy the growing demand for reading materials.

Many of the early writers, editors, and teachers were educated women. Sarah Buell Hale and Lydia Howard Huntley Sigourney were leading editors and literary figures of their day. Unlike women who worked in factories, women in publishing generally came from the young Republic's growing middle class.

✓ **Reading Check** **Describing** How did industrialization affect cities?

Workers Begin to Organize

The industrial boom created a new kind of laborer, the factory worker, whose ranks swelled to 1.3 million by 1860. While early factory mills stressed a paternalistic concern for their workers, the relationship between management and labor became more strained when prices slumped and wages dropped.

Eleven-year-old Lucy Larcom went to work at the Lowell Mills after her father's death left her family in financial hardship. Although at first she felt excited by the change from farm life, she soon came to dread the drudgery of her work:

❝I know that sometimes the confinement of the mill became very wearisome to me. In the sweet June weather I would lean far out of the window, and try not to hear the unceasing clash of the sound inside. Looking away to the hills, my whole stifled being would cry out, 'Oh, that I had wings!'❞

—quoted in *Ordinary Americans*

Hoping to help improve working conditions, some workers began to join together in labor unions. During the late 1820s and early 1830s about 300,000 men and women belonged to some form of union. Most of the organizations were local and focused on a single trade, such as printing or shoemaking. Although these unions worked separately, they began pushing for similar changes, such as higher wages or a shorter 10-hour workday.

During this time, unions had little success. Most employers refused to recognize or bargain with them. Unions also had little power or money to support strikes, or work stoppages, to achieve their goals.

The courts often ruled against early unions, seeing them as unlawful conspiracies that limited free enterprise. "Competition is the life of trade," a New York court declared in an 1835 case involving a union's demand that its workers be paid at least one dollar to make a pair of shoes. "If the defendants cannot make

Advances in Transportation

Past: The Steamboat
John Fitch built the first working steamboat in 1786, but his passenger and freight service from Philadelphia to New Jersey was not profitable. Robert Fulton's *Clermont* was more successful. Early steamboats were not very powerful and worked best on calm waters.

Present: The Hovercraft
Sir Christopher Cockerell invented the hovercraft, which rides above the water on a cushion of air trapped in a flexible skirt. Not used commercially until the 1950s and 1960s, hovercrafts are often seen today ferrying automobile drivers across rivers and small bodies of water.

CHAPTER 7
Section 2, 245–250

✓ **Reading Check**

Answer: The Northeast had many swift-flowing streams for water power and was home to entrepreneurs and merchants willing to invest.

3 ASSESS

Assign Section 2 Assessment as homework or as an in-class activity.

🖲 Have students use the **Interactive Tutor Self-Assessment CD-ROM.**

✓ **Reading Check**

Answer: Industrialization caused an increase in population.

Reading Essentials and Study Guide 7–2

Name _____ Date _____ Class _____

Study Guide
Chapter 7, Section 2
For use with textbook pages 245–250
EARLY INDUSTRY

KEY TERMS AND NAMES
National Road major east-west highway started in 1811 that by 1818 ran from Cumberland, Maryland, to Wheeling, Virginia (now West Virginia) *(page 246)*
Robert Fulton American inventor who designed and built the *Clermont*, the steamboat that traveled upstream on the Hudson River in 1807 *(page 247)*
Industrial Revolution time of change in business and industry in which manufacturing shifted from hand tools to large, complex machines; goods were made in factories instead of workshops in homes *(page 247)*
Francis C. Lowell industrialist who built textile machinery in the United States after touring British textile mills; opened a series of textile mills in Massachusetts; introduced mass production of cotton cloth to the U.S. *(page 248)*

Linking Past & Present

Speed and efficiency have always been concerns of transportation inventors. While the hovercraft increased the speed of travel, it cannot be used in stormy weather. For example, hovercraft cannot be used to cross the English Channel from France to Great Britain on stormy days. The traveler can either select the slower steam ferry or can travel through the Chunnel, a tunnel beneath the English Channel that connects Great Britain to the European mainland. The Chunnel opened in 1994.

CRITICAL THINKING ACTIVITY

Analyzing Tell students that America enjoyed one of the highest literacy rates in the world in the early 1800s. As a class, discuss the role that literacy played in the growth of industry and in the growth of the middle class. Have students list their ideas on the board. Then have students create a graphic organizer showing the cause-and-effect relationship between literacy and economic growth. **L2**

Section Quiz 7-2

Fact | Fiction | Folklore

Inventors attempted to apply the propulsion principles of the velocipedes to water transportation. In 1869 David Farmer patented a land and water velocipede that had removable floats and paddle wheels for moving the contraption over the water.

✓ Reading Check

Answer: Factory workers received low wages and worked more than 10 hours per day.

Reteach
Have students make a list of the major changes in transportation and industry that occurred between 1800 and 1850.

Enrich
Have students create a working model of one of the inventions mentioned in this section.

✓ Reading Check

Answer: The South had fewer cities and less industry that the North.

4 CLOSE

Ask students to discuss how the Industrial Revolution changed life in America.

250

Fact | Fiction | Folklore

Invasion of the Velocipedes Invented in France in the 1790s and later improved by Germans, bicycles—known back then as "velocipedes," or swift walkers—were introduced in the United States in 1819. The two-wheeled contraptions did not win immediate universal popularity. In August 1819, the New York City council passed a law "to prevent the use of velocipedes in the public places and on the sidewalks of the city of New York."

coarse boots for less than one dollar per pair, let them refuse to do so: but let them not directly or indirectly undertake to say that others shall not do the same work for less price."

Unions did make some gains, however. In 1840 President Martin Van Buren showed his gratitude for labor's political support by reducing the workday for federal employees to 10 hours. Two years later, in *Commonwealth* v. *Hunt*, the Massachusetts Supreme Court ruled that union strikes were legal. Still, decades would pass before organized labor achieved real influence.

✓ Reading Check **Explaining** What was life like for a factory worker in the early 1820s?

The Family Farm

Even though industry and cities expanded in the Northeast during the early 1800s, agriculture remained the country's leading economic activity. Until late in the century, farming employed more people and produced more wealth than any other kind of work.

Northern farmers produced enough to sell their surplus in eastern cities and towns. The profit was often used to buy machinery and other items. Thus, their labor not only helped feed the population but nourished the region's economy as well.

In the first half of the century, the North had more than a million farms. Northern farmers and their families worked long, hard days raising livestock and crops—mostly corn, wheat, and other grains—for the nation's growing population. A reporter traveling through Ohio in 1841 described a scene that resembled much of the North at that time:

> ❝As far as the eye can stretch in the distance nothing but corn and wheat fields are to be seen; and on some points in the Scioto Valley as high as a thousand acres of corn may be seen in adjoining fields, belonging to some eight or ten different proprietors.❞
>
> —from *A History of the United States*

Farming was even more important in the South, which had few cities and less industry. As parts of the North began concentrating on manufacturing, the South continued to tie its fortunes to agriculture—and to the institution of slavery.

✓ Reading Check **Comparing** Why was farming more important in the South than in the North?

SECTION 2 ASSESSMENT

Checking for Understanding

1. **Define:** interchangeable parts, labor union, strike.
2. **Identify:** National Road, Robert Fulton, Industrial Revolution, Francis C. Lowell, Eli Whitney, Samuel F.B. Morse.
3. **List** the changes that occurred as a result of the Industrial Revolution.
4. **Describe** advances that were made in transportation during this period.

Reviewing Themes

5. **Science and Technology** How did the concept of interchangeable parts revolutionize the manufacturing process?

Critical Thinking

6. **Synthesizing** Why did early labor unions have little success?
7. **Organizing** Use a graphic organizer similar to the one below to list the effects of some of the technological advances of the early 1800s.

Technological Advances	Effects
Steamboat →	☐
Railroad →	☐

Analyzing Visuals

8. **Analyzing Art** Study the painting of the steamboat on page 249. Why were steamboats so much more efficient than other shipping methods of the time?

Writing About History

9. **Descriptive Writing** Imagine you are a teenager working in a textile factory in the early 1800s. Write a letter to your family describing your way of life as a factory worker.

250   CHAPTER 7   Growth and Division

SECTION 2 ASSESSMENT ANSWERS

1. Terms are in blue.
2. National Road *(p. 246)*, Robert Fulton *(p. 247)*, Industrial Revolution *(p. 247)*, Francis C. Lowell *(p. 248)*, Eli Whitney *(p. 248)*, Samuel F. B. Morse *(p. 248)*
3. increased use of machine production, more use of unskilled workers, growth of national market
4. advances include canals, railroads, and steamboats
5. allowed complex products to be built in stages by unskilled workers
6. Employers refused to recognize unions. Unions had little money. Courts ruled against unions.
7. Steamboat: made river transportation reliable and extended the range of transportation in both directions; railroad: helped settle the West and expanded trade among the nation's regions
8. Steamboats could travel both up and downstream easily.
9. Students' letters will vary. Letters should be written from a teenager's point of view.

Guide to Reading

Main Idea
The South developed a social structure based largely on agriculture and the institution of slavery.

Key Terms and Names
cotton gin, planter, yeoman farmer, task system, gang system, driver, Frederick Douglass, slave code, Denmark Vesey, Nat Turner

Reading Strategy
Organizing As you read about how the South developed, complete a graphic organizer similar to the one below by listing the main categories of Southern society.

Southern Society

Highest _____

_____

_____

Lowest _____

Reading Objectives
• **Explain** why cotton dominated the Southern economy.
• **Describe** the social classes in the South.

Section Theme
Continuity and Change The invention of the cotton gin made cotton a key part of the South's economy. Cotton farming ensured that slavery continued to shape the South's society and culture.

Preview of Events

♦1790	♦1805	♦1820	♦1835

1793
Eli Whitney invents the cotton gin

1808
Congress bans international slave trade

1822
Denmark Vesey executed

1831
Nat Turner rebellion

Solomon Northup

★ An American Story ★

Solomon Northup was born free in Minerva, New York, about 1808. His parents were successful farmers. Northup, his wife, and three children also prospered in agriculture, although he supplemented his income as a violinist. In March 1841, two white men offered Northup a job as a musician in their circus. Northup accepted the job and left for Washington, D.C. Two days after arriving in the nation's capital, he was drugged, robbed of his money and papers, chained, and sold to slave traders.

For the next 12 years, Northup lived in bondage in the sugarcane and cotton regions of Louisiana. His first slaveholder, William Ford, treated him well, but Northup never stopped dreaming of freedom. In 1852 he was finally able to obtain documentation proving he was a free man.

Reflecting on his experience, Northup cut to the central cruelty of the institution of slavery:

❝There may be humane masters, as there certainly are inhumane ones; there may be slaves well-clothed, well-fed, and happy, as there surely are those half-clad, half-starved and miserable; nevertheless, the institution that tolerates such wrong and inhumanity . . . is a cruel, unjust, and barbarous one.❞

—quoted in *Twelve Years a Slave*

The Southern Economy

The South thrived on the production of several major cash crops. In the upper Southern states—Maryland, Virginia, Kentucky, and Tennessee—farmers grew tobacco. Rice paddies dominated the coastal regions of South Carolina and Georgia. In Louisiana

1 FOCUS

Section Overview
This section examines the social structure of the South, including its dependence on slavery.

BELLRINGER
Skillbuilder Activity

🖶 Project transparency and have students answer the question.

🗀 Available as a blackline master.

Daily Focus Skills Transparency 7–3

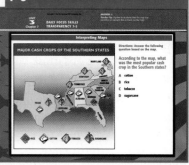

Guide to Reading

Answers to Graphic: From highest to lowest: planters, urban professionals, yeoman farmers, rural poor, enslaved African Americans

Preteaching Vocabulary
Have students look up the meaning of each of the Key Terms in the Glossary.

SECTION RESOURCES

🗀 Reproducible Masters
• Reproducible Lesson Plan 7–3
• Daily Lecture and Discussion Notes 7–3
• Guided Reading Activity 7–3
• Section Quiz 7–3
• Reading Essentials and Study Guide 7–3

🔦 Transparencies
• Daily Focus Skills Transparency 7–3

Multimedia
• Interactive Tutor Self-Assessment CD-ROM
• ExamView® Pro Testmaker CD-ROM
• Presentation Plus! CD-ROM
• TeacherWorks™ CD-ROM
• Audio Program
• ABCNews Interactive™ Historic America Electronic Field Trips

2 TEACH

Daily Lecture and Discussion Notes 7-3

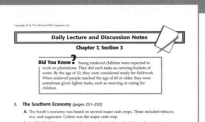

Daily Lecture and Discussion Notes
Chapter 7, Section 3

Did You Know ? Young enslaved children were expected to work on plantations. They did such tasks as carrying buckets of water. By the age of 10, they were considered ready for fieldwork. When enslaved people reached the age of 60 or older, they were sometimes given lighter tasks, such as weaving or caring for children.

I. The Southern Economy (pages 251–253)

   A. The South's economy was based on several major cash crops. These included tobacco, rice, and sugarcane. Cotton was the major cash crop.

   B. In 1793 Eli Whitney invented the cotton gin, which combed the seeds out of cotton

Creating an Annotated Map

Provide students with a map of the Southern states. Have students list the crops grown in each state. As a class, identify various regions based on the crops grown and explain the reasons that certain crops grow better in certain states. **L1**

📁 Use the rubric for creating a map, display, or chart on pages 77–78 in the *Performance Assessment Activities and Rubrics.*

TECHNOLOGY & History

Background: Eli Whitney showed mechanical skill when he built a violin at the early age of 12. He never made much money from his cotton gin. It was so easy to build that many other people were able to duplicate it.
Answer: It made the demand for slave labor skyrocket.

you don't say...

Origin of Lint The term *lint* refers to the cotton fibers. Ginning is the process that removes the lint from the seed.

---

and parts of eastern Texas, fields of sugarcane stretched for miles. No crop, however, played a greater role in the South's fortunes than cotton. This crop was grown in a wide belt stretching from inland South Carolina, west through Georgia, Alabama, and Mississippi, and into eastern Texas.

TURNING POINT

Cotton Becomes King During a visit to the South in 1793, Eli Whitney, the inventive young New Englander, noticed that removing cotton seeds by hand from the fluffy bolls was so tedious that it took a worker an entire day to separate a pound of cotton lint. An acquaintance knew of Whitney's mechanical ingenuity and suggested that he try building a machine to pick out the seeds. In only 10 days Whitney built a simple cotton gin—"gin" being short for engine—that quickly and efficiently combed the seeds out of cotton bolls.

The invention of the cotton gin happened at the same time that textile mills were expanding in Europe. Mills in England and France clamored for all the cotton they could get. In 1792, the year before Whitney invented his cotton gin, the South produced about 6,000 bales of cotton. Seven years later, annual production reached 100,000 bales.

Cotton soon dominated the region. By the late 1840s Southerners were producing more than two million bales of cotton annually, and in 1860 production reached almost four million bales. That year, Southern cotton sold for a total of $191 million in European markets—nearly two-thirds of the total export trade of the United States. Southerners began saying, rightly, "Cotton is King."

"The whole interior of the Southern states was languishing," said one Southern official in describing the region before the cotton gin. After Whitney's invention, he added, "Individuals who were depressed with poverty, and sunk with idleness, have suddenly risen to wealth and respectability. Our debts have been paid off, our capitals increased; and our lands are treble [triple] in value."

While the cotton gin made some Southern planters rich, it also strengthened the institution of slavery. The spread of cotton plantations all over the Deep

TECHNOLOGY & History

The Cotton Gin

While visiting Catherine Greene's Georgia plantation in 1793, Eli Whitney had an inspiration. He built a device that removed the seeds of the "green-seed" cotton variety that grew in abundance throughout the South. Whitney devised a "gin" (short for *engine*) that combed the seeds out of the cotton. This simple cotton gin was easy to mass produce, and it increased cotton's profitability for many Southern farmers. *How did the invention of the cotton gin affect slavery in the South?*

1 Cotton bolls are dumped into the **hopper**.

2 A crank turns the **cylinder** with wire teeth. The teeth pull the cotton past a grate.

3 Slots in the **grate** allow the cotton, but not its seeds, to pass through.

4 A second cylinder with **brushes** pulls the cotton off the toothed cylinder and sends it out of the gin.

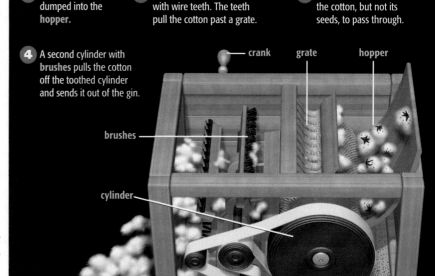

crank   grate   hopper

brushes

cylinder

COOPERATIVE LEARNING ACTIVITY

Writing a Diary Entry Organize the class into small groups. Assign each student one of the following: a planter, a yeoman farmer, an enslaved person, or a free African American. Have each student write his or her reaction to the uprising led by Nat Turner in the form of a diary entry. Then have students share their entries with the group. As a group, discuss how and why viewpoints of the uprising varied.

Use the rubric for a cooperative group management plan on pages 81–82 in the *Performance Assessment Activities and Rubrics.*

South made the demand for slave labor skyrocket. Congress had outlawed the foreign slave trade in 1808, but a high birthrate among enslaved women—encouraged by slaveholders eager to sell new laborers at high prices—kept the enslaved population growing. Between 1820 and 1860, the number of enslaved people in the South rose from 1.5 million to nearly 4 million.

Industry Lags Although the South became prosperous from agriculture, it did not industrialize as quickly as the North. For the most part, the South remained a region of rural villages and plantations, with only three large cities: Baltimore, Charleston, and New Orleans.

The South did have some industry. Coal, iron, salt, and copper mines, as well as ironworks and textile mills, could be found there. The region still relied heavily on imported goods, however, which worried some people. As one Southerner noted, "For what have we not looked to our Northern friends? From them we get not only our clothes, carriages, saddles, hats, shoes, flour, potatoes, but even our onions and horn buttons." At this time, in 1860, manufacturing in the South accounted for only 16 percent of the nation's manufacturing total. Most Southerners were content to rely on agriculture.

✓ **Reading Check** **Synthesizing** What effect did the cotton gin have on slavery in the South?

Society in the South

Social attitudes shaped Southern life and produced a definite class structure for the region. At the top were the planters, who owned the region's larger plantations. The 1850 census showed that in a Southern white population of just over 6 million, a total of 347,525 families were slaveholders. Of this number, around 37,000 were planters, defined as those who held 20 or more enslaved people. Less than 8,000 of these planters held 50 or more people in slavery, and only 11 held 500 or more.

A very small percentage of Southern slaveholders lived a life of gentility in grand mansions. Many planter mansions were little more than cottages with newly built facades. The boom in cotton production allowed some smaller-scale planters to rapidly ascend the social ladder, quickly adopting refined habits as they expanded their property. Although the wealthy planters made up a tiny group—representing less than half of one percent of white Southern families and slightly over two percent of

slaveholding families—they dominated the region's economy as well as its political and legal systems.

Ordinary farmers—who were often called yeoman farmers—and their families made up the vast majority of the white population. They may have held four or fewer enslaved persons, though most held none at all, and they worked on the land themselves. Here, writer Mark Twain gives his impressions of a typical small Southern farm in his book *Huckleberry Finn:*

> ❝A rail fence around a two-acre yard . . . big double log house for the white folks—hewed logs, with the chinks stopped up with mud or mortar . . . outside of the fence a garden; . . . then the cotton fields begin; and after the fields, the woods.❞
> —from *Huckleberry Finn*

Near the bottom of the social ladder stood the rural poor. This group, made up mostly of families living on land too barren for successful farming, scratched a meager existence from hunting and fishing, vegetable gardening, and raising a few half-wild hogs and chickens. They made up less than 10 percent of the white population.

At the bottom of society were African Americans, 93 percent of them enslaved. In 1850 nearly 3.6 million African Americans lived in the South—about 37 percent of the total Southern population.

Rounding out Southern society was a small urban class of lawyers, doctors, merchants, and other professionals. Agriculture's influence was so great that even many of these city dwellers invested in or owned farms. As one observer noted, "No matter how one might begin, as lawyer, physician, clergyman, mechanic, or merchant, he ended, if prosperous, as proprietor of a rice or cotton plantation."

✓ **Reading Check** **Identifying** What classes made up the South's social structure?

Slavery

The rice and cotton plantations depended on enslaved labor for their existence. The overwhelming majority of enslaved African Americans toiled in the South's fields. Some, however, worked in the South's few industrial plants or as skilled workers, such as blacksmiths, carpenters, and coopers. Others became house servants.

Enslaved African Americans working in the fields were organized using two basic labor systems. On farms and small plantations that held few enslaved

CHAPTER 7 Growth and Division **253**

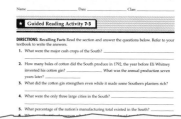

Guided Reading Activity 7-3

Name _____ Date _____ Class _____

★ **Guided Reading Activity 7-3**

DIRECTIONS: Recalling Facts Read the section and answer the questions below. Refer to your textbook to write the answers.

1. What were the major cash crops of the South? _____
2. How many bales of cotton did the South produce in 1792, the year before Eli Whitney invented his cotton gin? _____ What was the annual production seven years later? _____
3. What did the cotton gin strengthen even while it made some Southern planters rich? _____
4. What were the only three large cities in the South? _____
5. What percentage of the nation's manufacturing total existed in the South? _____

✓ **Reading Check**

Answer: Demand for slave labor skyrocketed.

Creating a Graph Provide the population data shown below and ask students to create a line graph. Ask students to explain the population trends. **L2**

Year	Total Pop. of the U.S. (in mill.)	Slave Pop. of the U.S. (in mill.)
1800	5.1	0.9
1810	6.8	1.1
1820	10.0	1.5
1830	12.8	2.0
1840	17.0	2.5
1850	23.0	3.2
1860	31.2	4.0

📁 Use the rubric for creating a map, display, or chart on pages 77–78 in the *Performance Assessment Activities and Rubrics.*

✓ **Reading Check**

Answer: planters, urban professionals, yeoman farmers, rural poor, enslaved African Americans

---

MEETING SPECIAL NEEDS

Auditory/Musical Have interested students research the music of the African Americans who lived enslaved in the South. Ask them to share examples of the music, lyrics, and tune with the class. Students may either perform the music or bring recordings. Have students explain the meaning of the lyrics of the songs they have chosen. **L1**

📁 Refer to *Inclusion for the High School Social Studies Classroom Strategies and Activities* in the TCR.

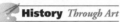

History *Through Art*

Plantation Life *The Wedding* by E.L. Henry depicts Southern gentry and their sometimes lavish lifestyle. Wealthy planters depended upon enslaved labor to work their fields, and they purchased such labor at auctions advertised in local newspapers (left). Why did such a small number of elite Southern planters have so much influence in the South?

people, the **task system** was used. Under this system workers were given a specific set of jobs to accomplish every day and worked until these were complete. After completing their tasks, the individuals were allowed to spend the remainder of the day on their own. Some enslaved people earned money through their skill as artisans. Others cultivated personal gardens or hunted for extra food.

In the 1800s, as cotton production became more common and slavery more widespread, slaveholders who owned large plantations adopted the **gang system** of labor. Under this system, enslaved persons were organized into work gangs that labored from sunup to sundown—plowing, planting, cultivating, or picking, depending on the season.

A **driver** acted as the director of a work gang. Often these individuals were enslaved people themselves, chosen for their loyalty or willingness to cooperate. They supervised the progress of the gangs, ensuring that the workers continued laboring throughout the entire day.

No matter which labor system was used, slavery was a degrading experience. **Frederick Douglass,** who rose from slavery to become a prominent leader of the anti-slavery movement, recalled how life as an enslaved person affected him:

❝My natural elasticity was crushed; my intellect languished; the disposition to read departed; the cheerful spark that lingered about my eye died out; the dark night of slavery closed in upon me, and behold a man transformed to a brute.❞

—from *Narrative of the Life of Frederick Douglass*

African Americans' Legal Status In addition to enduring a lifetime of bondage, enslaved persons had few legal rights. State slave codes forbade enslaved men and women from owning property or leaving a slaveholder's premises without permission. They could not possess firearms or testify in court against a white person. Furthermore, laws banned them from learning to read and write. Society viewed enslaved persons as property and treated them that way.

Free African Americans Although most African Americans of the time lived in slavery, some did not. By 1850 some 225,000 free African Americans resided in the South. Most lived in the towns and cities of the upper Southern states, especially Maryland and Virginia. A few were descended from Africans brought to the United States as indentured

INTERDISCIPLINARY CONNECTIONS ACTIVITY

Language Arts Mark Twain is one of America's best known authors. Have a language arts teacher discuss Twain's writing style and the subjects he chose to write about. Then have students write a short story about an adventure they have had. Encourage students to use vivid descriptions of people, places, and events. **L2**

servants in the 1700s before the slave system became universal. Some had earned their freedom fighting in the American Revolution, and still others were the half-white children of slaveholders, who had granted them freedom. There were also some former enslaved persons who had managed to purchase freedom for themselves and their families or whose slaveholders had freed them.

Free African Americans occupied an ambiguous position in Southern society. In cities like Charleston and New Orleans, some were successful enough to become slaveholders themselves. One such African American was Cecee McCarty, who amassed a fortune in New Orleans by retailing imported dry goods. McCarty dispatched a sales force of 32 enslaved Africans around the state to merchandise her highly prized wares. Still, the experiences of freed African Americans differed from state to state. In some states they had to obtain special licenses to preach or to own firearms. Like those in slavery, they always had to remember how dangerous it was to act any way but humble and subservient when dealing with white people.

Another 196,000 free African Americans lived in the North, where slavery had been outlawed, but they were not embraced there either. Samuel Ringgold Ward, who was African American, lamented that racial prejudice was "ever at my elbow":

66As a servant, it denied me a seat at the table with my white fellow servants . . . along the streets it ever pursued, ever ridiculed, ever abused me. If I sought redress, the very complexion I wore was pointed out as the best reason for my seeking it in vain; if I desired to turn to account a little learning, in the way of earning a living by it, the idea of employing a black clerk was preposterous—too absurd to be seriously entertained. . . .99

—quoted in *Long Memory: The Black Experience in America*

Still, free African Americans could organize their own churches and voluntary associations, plus earn money from the jobs they held.

An African American who not only kept his wages but also multiplied them many times over was James Forten of Philadelphia. He went to sea in his teens as a powder monkey—the person on board a warship who handled explosives—on a Revolutionary privateer. Privateers were private ships licensed to attack enemy ships. Later, he worked as a maker of sails. By the age of 32, he owned a thriving sail factory employing 40 African

American and white workers. He devoted much of his wealth to the cause of abolishing slavery.

✓**Reading Check** **Summarizing** What were some basic rights denied to enslaved persons?

Coping With Enslavement

African Americans dealt with the horrors of slavery in a variety of ways. From language to music to religion, they developed a culture that provided them with a sense of unity, pride, and mutual support.

African American Culture Songs were important to many enslaved people. Field workers often used songs to pass the long workday and to help them enjoy their scant leisure time in the evening. Some songs were more provocative than most plantation owners knew, using subtle language and secret meanings to lament the singers' bondage and express a continuing hope for freedom.

Songs also played a key role in one of the most important parts of African American culture: religion. By the early 1800s, large numbers of African Americans were Christians, though their Christianity sometimes incorporated religious traditions from Africa. The religious services enslaved persons held often centered around praying about their particular concern—their dreams of freedom or a better life in the next world.

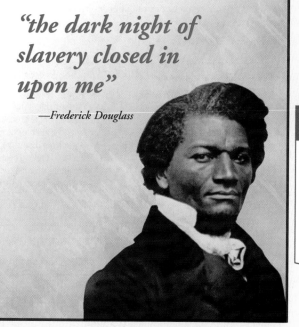

"the dark night of slavery closed in upon me"

—*Frederick Douglass*

✓**Reading Check**

Answer: Enslaved persons could not own property, leave the premises without permission, possess firearms, testify against a white person, or learn to read or write.

FYI

Work songs were used to relieve boredom but they also helped increase productivity by maintaining a regular rhythm. Workers' grunts and groans were frequently integrated into the song and the sounds made by tools were sometimes used as counterpoint.

3 ASSESS

Assign Section 3 Assessment as homework or as an in-class activity.

⬤ Have students use the **Interactive Tutor Self-Assessment CD-ROM.**

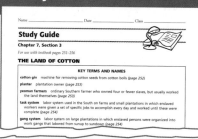
Reading Essentials and Study Guide 7–3

Name _____ Date _____ Class _____

Study Guide

Chapter 7, Section 3

For use with textbook pages 251–256

THE LAND OF COTTON

KEY TERMS AND NAMES
cotton gin machine for removing cotton seeds from cotton bolls *(page 252)*
planter plantation owner *(page 253)*
yeoman farmers ordinary Southern farmer who owned four or fewer slaves, but usually worked the land themselves *(page 253)*
task system labor system used in the South on farms and small plantations in which enslaved workers were given a set of specific jobs to accomplish every day and worked until these were complete *(page 254)*
gang system labor system on large plantations in which enslaved persons were organized into work gangs that labored from sunup to sundown *(page 254)*

CRITICAL THINKING ACTIVITY

Comparing Have students research the task system and the gang system of organizing slave labor. Have students create a chart that compares the systems from the point of view of either the landowner or the enslaved person. **L2**

Section Quiz 7-3

Profiles IN HISTORY

Ask: How did Turner's revolt affect the lives of enslaved African Americans in the short-term? *(Many states adopted even harsher restrictions on enslaved people.)* What long-term impact do you think the revolt had on the lives of enslaved people? *(possible answers: may have helped crystallize opposition to slavery, may have given enslaved people a ray of hope for the future)*

Reteach
Ask students to explain why cotton dominated the Southern economy.

Enrich
Invite students to choose a topic from this section and write a report. Encourage students to use library and Internet resources for their research.

✓ Reading Check

Answer: Most were enslaved, treated poorly, and had few legal rights.

4 CLOSE

Have students compare the task system and the gang system.

Profiles IN HISTORY

Nat Turner 1800–1831

The man who led perhaps the nation's best-known slave revolt believed from an early age—through his mother's encouragement—that he was divinely inspired. "I was intended for some great purpose," he once declared.

Although many considered Nat Turner a religious fanatic—he claimed to take his directions from mysterious voices and the movements of heavenly bodies—others knew him to have a sharp mind. "He certainly never had the advantages of education," said the man later appointed to be his lawyer, "but he can read and write . . . and for natural intelligence and quickness of apprehension is surpassed by few men I have ever seen."

As he awaited execution, Turner reportedly showed little remorse for his deeds, certain that he had acted in the name of God to free his people. "I am here loaded with chains and willing to suffer the fate that awaits me," he said.

Turner's lack of remorse chilled those around him, including his lawyer, who described the calm, deliberate composure with which Turner spoke of what he had done. "I looked on him," the lawyer wrote, "and my blood curdled in my veins."

Turner's revolt sent a wave of terror through the South and heightened fears of future uprisings. As a result, many states adopted even harsher restrictions on both enslaved and free African Americans.

Resistance and Rebellion Many enslaved men and women found ways to oppose the dreadful lifestyle forced on them. Some quietly staged work slowdowns. Others broke tools or set fire to houses and barns. Still others risked beatings or mutilations to run away.

Some enslaved persons turned to more violent means of rebellion. Despite the awful consequences they faced for doing so, some African Americans turned on their slaveholders and killed them.

On occasion, enslaved persons plotted uprisings. In 1821, for example, **Denmark Vesey,** a free African American who operated a woodworking shop in Charleston, South Carolina, was accused of planning an armed revolt to free the region's slaves. Whether or not Vesey actually planned an uprising is not known. The Charleston authorities claimed to have learned of the plot from an informer, and in 1822 Vesey was tried, convicted, and hanged.

A group of African Americans in Virginia did carry out an armed uprising during the early hours of August 22, 1831. Leading the attack was **Nat Turner,** an enslaved minister who believed God had chosen him to bring his people out of bondage. Turner and his followers killed more than 50 white men, women, and children before state and local troops put down the uprising. A court then tried Turner and sentenced him to hang.

✓ Reading Check **Describing** What was life like for African Americans in the 1800s?

SECTION 3 ASSESSMENT

Checking for Understanding
1. **Define:** cotton gin, planter, yeoman farmer, slave code.
2. **Identify:** task system, gang system, driver, Frederick Douglass, Denmark Vesey, Nat Turner.
3. **Explain** why industry lagged in the South compared to the North.

Reviewing Themes
4. **Continuity and Change** How did cotton farming change the South? What aspects of Southern life stayed the same?

Critical Thinking
5. **Synthesizing** Why was song an important part of the enslaved African American culture?
6. **Organizing** Use a graphic organizer similar to the one below to list the provisions of some slave codes for enslaved African Americans.

Slave Codes

Analyzing Visuals
7. **Examining Art** Study the painting of the Southern wedding on page 254. What elements of the painting suggest a wealthy lifestyle? Did all Southern planters live in such a lavish manner?

Writing About History
8. **Expository Writing** Imagine you are a European visitor to the South in 1830. Write a letter home explaining your impressions of life in this part of the nation.

SECTION 3 ASSESSMENT ANSWERS

1. Terms are in blue.
2. task system *(p. 254)*, gang system *(p. 254)*, driver *(p. 254)*, Frederick Douglass *(p. 254)*, Denmark Vesey *(p. 256)*, Nat Turner *(p. 256)*
3. A reliance on agriculture caused the South's population to spread out and few urban areas had the population to support industry.
4. Increased emphasis on cotton plantations meant more use of slavery. Urban growth and industrialization continued to be slow.
5. Songs helped pass time during the workday, provided enjoyment, and were used in religious services.
6. Enslaved persons could not own property, leave the premises without permission, possess firearms, testify against a white person, or learn to read or write.
7. The fine carriage and clothing suggest wealth. Many did not live in such luxury. Often the houses had impressive facades only.
8. Students' letters will vary. Letters should describe life in the South.

SECTION 4 Growing Sectionalism

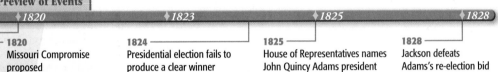
★ An American Story ★

As May approached in 1820, Thomas Jefferson should have been enjoying his retirement from public life. Instead, a bitter political controversy had him feeling deeply troubled. After more than a year of debate, Congress finally had crafted a plan to allow the Missouri Territory to enter the Union as a slave state while Maine came in as a free state. This arrangement preserved the delicate balance in the number of free and slave states. The arrangement, known as the Missouri Compromise, highlighted the growing dispute over slavery's expansion into the Western territories—a dispute that Jefferson feared could tear the nation apart:

❝This momentous question, like a firebell in the night, awakened and filled me with terror. I considered it at once as the knell [funeral bell] of the Union. It is hushed, indeed, for the moment. But this is a reprieve only, not a final sentence.❞

—quoted in *The Annals of America*

Thomas Jefferson

The Missouri Compromise

The Monroe administration's Era of Good Feelings could not ward off the nation's growing sectional disputes and the passionately differing opinions over slavery. Tensions rose to the boiling point in 1819, when Missouri's application for statehood stirred up the country's most divisive issue: whether slavery should expand westward.

In 1819 the Union consisted of 11 free and 11 slave states. While the House of Representatives already had a majority of Northerners, admitting any new state, either slave or free, would upset the balance in the Senate and touch off a bitter struggle over political power.

CHAPTER 7 Growth and Division **257**

2 TEACH

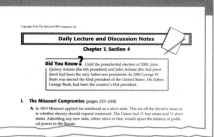
Reading Check

Answer: to keep the Senate balanced between slave and non-slave states

Creating a Table Have students create a table illustrating the four main candidates for president in 1824. Instruct students to include the candidates' names, party affiliations, home states, and positions on issues. **L1** ELL

 Use the rubric for creating a map, display, or chart on pages 77–78 in the *Performance Assessment Activities and Rubrics.*

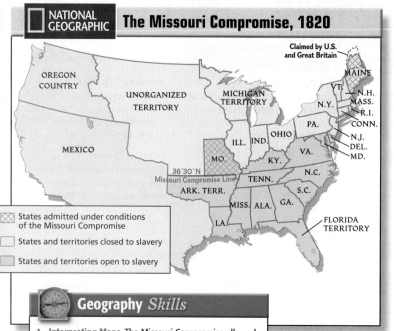

NATIONAL GEOGRAPHIC — The Missouri Compromise, 1820

Claimed by U.S. and Great Britain

- States admitted under conditions of the Missouri Compromise
- States and territories closed to slavery
- States and territories open to slavery

Geography Skills

1. **Interpreting Maps** The Missouri Compromise allowed which two states to enter the Union?
2. **Applying Geography Skills** Why did the South readily agree to making slavery illegal in the unorganized Louisiana Territory?

Missouri's territorial government requested admission into the Union as a slave state in 1819. Acting for slavery's opponents, Congressman James Tallmadge, Jr., of New York proposed a resolution that prohibited slaveholders from bringing new slaves into Missouri. The resolution also called for all enslaved children currently living in Missouri to be freed at age 25. The House accepted the proposal, but the Senate rejected it. Most Senators and members of the House of Representatives from the South voted against the ban, while most from the North voted in favor of it.

Finally, a solution emerged when Maine, which for decades had been part of Massachusetts, requested admission to the Union as a separate state. The Senate decided to combine Maine's request with Missouri's, and it voted to admit Maine as a free state and Missouri as a slave state. This solution preserved the balance in the Senate. Senator Jesse Thomas of Illinois then proposed an amendment that would prohibit slavery in the Louisiana Purchase territory north of Missouri's southern border. This would allow slavery to expand into

Arkansas territory south of Missouri, but it would keep it out of the rest of the Louisiana Purchase.

Since many people at the time thought the Great Plains area north of Missouri was not suitable for farming, it appeared that this **Missouri Compromise** benefited the South. By a very close vote, carefully managed by **Henry Clay** of Kentucky, the House of Representatives voted to accept the Compromise. The Compromise held out the hope that pairing the admission of free and slave states together would quiet the dispute over the expansion of slavery.

Once the issue was settled, however, a new problem developed. Pro-slavery members of the Missouri constitutional convention added a clause to the proposed state constitution prohibiting free African Americans from entering the state. This new controversy threatened final approval of Missouri's admission to the Union. Clay again engineered a solution by getting the Missouri legislature to state that they would not honor the spirit of the clause's wording.

Despite Clay's efforts, many leaders feared that the Missouri Compromise was only a temporary solution. "I take it for granted," John Quincy Adams wrote, "that the present question is a mere preamble—a title page to a great tragic volume."

✓ **Reading Check** **Examining** Why was the Missouri Compromise proposed?

The Election of 1824

Politics reflected the sectional tensions of the day. Although the Republicans had supporters throughout the nation, sectional differences over beliefs and policies were growing obvious. The presidential campaign of 1824 showed how splintered the party was becoming.

GOVERNMENT

A Battle of Favorite Sons Four candidates ran for president in 1824. All belonged to the Republican Party and all were "favorite sons," men who enjoyed

---

COOPERATIVE LEARNING ACTIVITY

Creating a Map Have students work in small groups to create annotated maps showing slave and free states before and after the Missouri Compromise. Have them annotate the map showing the number of seats in the House of Representatives for each state. Show the total representatives from slave and free states in a chart beside the maps.

Use the rubric for a cooperative group management plan on pages 81–82 in the *Performance Assessment Activities and Rubrics.*

the support of leaders from their own state and region. Two candidates, Henry Clay of Kentucky and Andrew Jackson of Tennessee, represented the West. John Quincy Adams, a Massachusetts man then serving as President Monroe's secretary of state, was New England's favorite son. **William Crawford** of Georgia represented the South.

Crawford ran on the original principles of Jefferson's party—states' rights and strict interpretation of the Constitution. Clay favored the national bank, the protective tariff, and nationwide internal improvements—collectively known as the **American System.** Adams was also in favor of internal improvements, but he was less enthusiastic about tariffs. Jackson steered clear of specific issues. His campaign focused on his personal heroism at the Battle of New Orleans.

On Election Day Jackson won the most popular votes, but no candidate won a majority in the Electoral College. Following constitutional procedure, the election went to the House of Representatives, whose members would select the president from the three candidates who received the highest number of electoral votes. Clay, who had placed fourth, was eliminated.

As the Speaker of the House, Henry Clay enjoyed tremendous influence there, and few doubted which candidate he would support. Clay and Jackson had been rivals for political leadership of the West and disliked each other intensely. Clay once described Jackson as "ignorant, passionate, hypocritical, [and] corrupt." Jackson referred to Clay as the "meanest scoundrel that ever disgraced the image of his god."

On a snowy February 9, 1825, the representatives met to make their choice. As expected, Clay threw his political weight behind Adams and helped him win the House election easily. Adams received 13 votes, while Jackson won 7 and Crawford won 4.

The Corrupt Bargain The hard feelings of the election campaign only intensified with Adams's victory. Andrew Jackson Donelson, Jackson's nephew, joined others in accusing Clay of arranging votes for Adams in return for a cabinet post:

> ❝It is rumored and believed by every body here that Mr. Clay will be made Secretary of State. . . . What a farce! That Mr. Adams should swear to support the constitution of the [United] States which he has purchased from Representatives who betrayed the constitution, and which he must distribute among them as rewards for the iniquity.❞
>
> —quoted in *Henry Clay*

Upon taking office, the new president did indeed name Clay as his secretary of state, and Jackson's supporters cried foul. They accused Adams and Clay of striking a "corrupt bargain."

Adams and Clay denied any wrongdoing, and no evidence of a deal ever emerged. Still, Jackson's outraged supporters came together in opposition to the Adams presidency. They took the name **Democratic-Republicans** to stress their differences with the party of John Quincy Adams—now called the **National Republicans.** Eventually the pro-Jackson party shortened the name to Democrats.

✓ **Reading Check** **Summarizing** How did John Quincy Adams win the election of 1824?

The Presidency of John Quincy Adams

John Quincy Adams, son of the second president, had earned a reputation as the greatest secretary of state in the nation's brief history. A highly intelligent and hardworking man, he intended to leave his mark on the presidency.

In his first message to Congress, Adams announced an ambitious program of nationalist legislation that exceeded even Clay's American System. Alongside standard internal improvements, Adams

John Quincy Adams

Guided Reading Activity 7–4

Name _____ Date _____ Class _____

★ Guided Reading Activity 7-4

DIRECTIONS: Recording Who, What, When, Where, Why, and How Read the section and answer the questions below. Refer to your textbook to write the answers.

1. Why did Missouri's application for statehood raise tensions to the boiling point in 1819?

2. Who proposed a resolution that prohibited slaveholders from bringing new slaves into Missouri?

3. What action in relation to the Missouri problem preserved the balance in the Senate?

4. What legislation held out the hope that pairing the admission of free and slave states together would quiet the dispute over the expansion of slavery?

5. What was the topic of the clause added by pro-slavery members of the Missouri consti-

✓**Reading Check**

Answer: When the election went to the House of Representatives, John Quincy Adams won with the help of Henry Clay's support.

3 ASSESS

Assign Section 4 Assessment as homework or as an in-class activity.

🔘 Have students use the **Interactive Tutor Self-Assessment CD-ROM.**

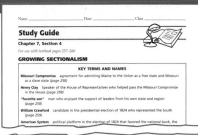

Reading Essentials and Study Guide 7–4

Name _____ Date _____ Class _____

Study Guide

Chapter 7, Section 4
For use with textbook pages 257–260

GROWING SECTIONALISM

KEY TERMS AND NAMES

Missouri Compromise agreement for admitting Maine to the Union as a free state and Missouri as a slave state (page 258)

Henry Clay Speaker of the House of Representatives who helped pass the Missouri Compromise in the House (page 258)

"favorite son" man who enjoyed the support of leaders from his own state and region (page 258)

William Crawford candidate in the presidential election of 1824 who represented the South (page 259)

American System political platform in the election of 1824 that favored the national bank, the

---

MEETING SPECIAL NEEDS

Verbal/Linguistic Have students select one of the following political figures: Henry Clay, John Quincy Adams, Andrew Jackson, or William Crawford. Have students create and present an oral biography of the political figure. Encourage students to use quotes that express their figure's political views. **L2**

📂 Refer to *Inclusion for the High School Social Studies Classroom Strategies and Activities* in the TCR.

Section Quiz 7–4

Name	Date	Class

★ **Chapter 7**   Score

Section Quiz 7-4

DIRECTIONS: Matching Match each item in Column A with the items in Column B.
Write the correct letters in the blanks. *(10 points each)*

Column A

_____ 1. Jackson's supporters who were opposed to Adams presidency

_____ 2. men who enjoyed the support of leaders from their own state and region

_____ 3. when political candidates criticize each other's personalities and morals

_____ 4. the national bank, the protective tariff, and nationwide internal improvements favored by Henry Clay

_____ 5. Andrew Jackson's nickname

Column B

A. "favorite sons"

B. "Old Hickory"

C. "American System"

D. Democratic-Republicans

E. mudslinging

✓ **Reading Check**

Answer: to build a national university and astronomical observatories, and to fund scientific research

Picturing History

Answer: the words "not barter nor bargain for the presidency" and "the purity of elections and the electors"

✓ **Reading Check**

Answer: Adams called Jackson incompetent. Jackson attacked Adams as an out-of-touch aristocrat and called him a gambler.

Reteach

Ask students to explain the significance of the Missouri Compromise.

Enrich

Encourage interested students to prepare a short oral presentation about Andrew Jackson's life before he ran for the presidency in 1824.

4 CLOSE

Ask students to explain how nationalism gave way to sectionalism.

---

urged that federal revenue also be used to build a national university and astronomical observatories, and to fund scientific research. To bar the federal government from these activities, he wrote, "would be to hide in the earth the talent committed to our change."

Adams's proposals, however, struck many legislators as a renewal of his father's Federalist principles. His opponents received the president's initiatives with scorn. It would be extravagant, they believed, to spend the taxpayers' money on such projects.

In the end, Congress granted the president funds for improving rivers and harbors and for extending the National Road westward, but this was far less than he had wanted. The repeated rebuffs he suffered in Congress set the stage for Adams's defeat in his 1828 reelection attempt.

✓ **Reading Check** **Identifying** What did John Quincy Adams hope to accomplish during his presidency?

The Election of 1828

The presidential election of 1828 pitted John Quincy Adams against Andrew Jackson. The two men waged a bitter campaign, as Jackson fought to achieve a victory that his supporters believed had been unjustly denied him four years earlier.

The campaign descended into mudslinging, in which candidates criticized each other's personalities and morals. Adams called his opponent "incompetent both by his ignorance and by the fury of his passions." Jackson portrayed himself as the candidate of the common man and attacked Adams as an out-of-touch aristocrat. Jackson's supporters also called Adams a gambler for purchasing a billiard table and chess set for the White House. Jackson also revived the

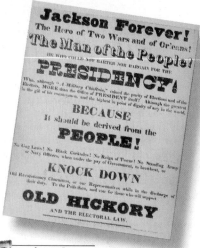

Picturing History

Stumping for Old Hickory This campaign poster for the 1828 presidential election reminds voters of Jackson's heroic military reputation and of the 1824 election. What elements in the poster refer to the "corrupt bargain?"

alleged "corrupt bargain" between Adams and Clay as evidence that the president was untrustworthy.

When the results came in, Jackson had 56 percent of the popular vote and 178 of the 261 electoral votes, a clear victory. Many of the voters who supported Jackson were from the West and South, rural and small-town men who saw Jackson as the candidate most likely to represent their interests. The man whose fiery personality had earned him the nickname "Old Hickory," after a tough, hard wood found on the frontier, finally had reached the White House.

✓ **Reading Check** **Summarizing** How did Adams and Jackson portray each other during the 1828 campaign?

SECTION 4 ASSESSMENT

Checking for Understanding

1. **Define:** "favorite son," "corrupt bargain," mudslinging.

2. **Identify:** Missouri Compromise, Henry Clay, William Crawford, American System, Democratic-Republican.

3. **Compare** the different campaign strategies of the candidates in the 1824 election.

Reviewing Themes

4. **Groups and Institutions** Why was the Democratic-Republican Party formed after the election of 1824?

Critical Thinking

5. **Synthesizing** Why do you think the candidates in the 1828 election focused on mudslinging instead of issues?

6. **Organizing** Use a graphic organizer similar to the one below to list the terms of the Missouri Compromise.

Missouri Compromise

Analyzing Visuals

7. **Examining Photographs** Study the early daguerreotype of John Quincy Adams on page 259. What characteristics of Adams shown in the image give clues as to the kind of person he was?

Writing About History

8. **Expository Writing** Imagine you are a voter in the election of 1828. Write a letter to a family member explaining which presidential candidate you will vote for and why.

SECTION 4 ASSESSMENT ANSWERS

1. Terms are in blue.

2. Missouri Compromise *(p. 258)*, Henry Clay *(p. 258)*, William Crawford *(p. 259)*, American System *(p. 259)*, Democratic-Republican *(p. 259)*

3. Crawford: states' rights and strict interpretation of the Constitution; Clay: the American System; Adams:

favored internal improvements but disliked tariffs; Jackson: his own personal heroism

4. Jackson's supporters wished to stress their differences from John Quincy Adams's supporters

5. possible answers: they disliked each other; similar opinions on issues

6. Missouri Compromise: Maine

admitted to Union as free state; Missouri admitted to Union as slave state; slavery prohibited in Louisiana Purchase above Missouri's southern border

7. possible answer: his chilly, stern manner

8. Letters should indicate the reason for voting for a specific candidate.

SKILLBUILDER

Reading a Line Graph

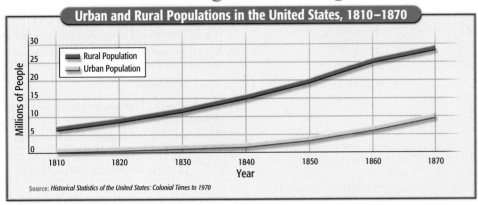

Urban and Rural Populations in the United States, 1810–1870

Source: *Historical Statistics of the United States: Colonial Times to 1970*

Why Learn This Skill?

Line graphs are a way of showing numbers visually, making them easier to read and understand. Learning to read line graphs will help you compare changes over time or differences between places, groups of people, or related events.

Learning the Skill

Line graphs are often used to show changes in number or quantity over time. They show information in two dimensions. The horizontal axis (or x-axis) is the line along the bottom of the graph. If the graph shows information over time, this axis usually shows the time period. The vertical axis (or y-axis) is the line that runs up the side of the graph. This axis usually displays the quantity, or amount, of whatever is being measured in the graph.

A double-line graph shows more than one line, recording two related quantities. For instance, you and a friend might both record your running speeds for footraces over a period of time on one graph, using a line of a different color for each of you. Before trying to understand any graph, be sure to read the labels on both axes and the key for each line.

Practicing the Skill

Study the line graph and answer the following questions.

1. What kind of information does the graph compare?
2. What are the time intervals on the horizontal axis?
3. What quantity is measured on the vertical axis?
4. What trend does the graph seem to show?
5. What two phenomena from the chapter explain the changes in the population?

Skills Assessment

Complete the Practicing Skills questions on page 263 and the Chapter 7 Skill Reinforcement Activity to assess your mastery of this skill.

Applying the Skill

Reading a Line Graph Create a line graph comparing the urban and rural population figures from 1910 to 1970. Compare your graph with the one on this page and write a summary of the differences you notice between the two.

 Glencoe's **Skillbuilder Interactive Workbook CD-ROM, Level 2,** provides instruction and practice in key social studies skills.

TEACH

Reading a Line Graph Remind students to look carefully at the graph to determine what information is being presented. Titles, labels, and legends are important parts of any graph.

Have students create a double-line graph using the data for the average height of children.

Age	Girls	Boys
6 years	46.00 in.	46.75 in.
7 years	48.00 in.	49.00 in.
8 years	50.75 in.	51.00 in.
9 years	53.25 in.	53.25 in.
10 years	55.50 in.	55.25 in.
11 years	58.50 in.	57.25 in.
12 years	60.50 in.	59.00 in.
13 years	61.25 in.	61.00 in.

Additional Practice

Reinforcing Skills Activity 7

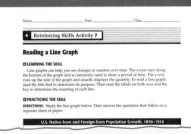

GLENCOE
TECHNOLOGY

 CD-ROM
Glencoe Skillbuilder Interactive Workbook CD-ROM, Level 2

This interactive CD-ROM reinforces student mastery of essential social studies skills.

ANSWERS TO PRACTICING THE SKILL

1. urban and rural populations
2. ten-year intervals
3. number of people
4. Increase in population is faster in rural areas.
5. immigration and high birthrate

Applying the Skill
Summaries should reflect several key points about the population between 1910 and 1970: (1) little change in rural population, (2) continual increase in urban population, and (3) urban population exceeds rural population after 1920.

CHAPTER 7 ASSESSMENT and ACTIVITIES

Reviewing Key Terms

Students' answers will vary. The pages where the words appear in the text are shown in parentheses.

1. **revenue tariff** *(p. 241)*
2. **protective tariff** *(p. 241)*
3. **interchangeable parts** *(p. 248)*
4. **labor union** *(p. 249)*
5. **strike** *(p. 249)*
6. **cotton gin** *(p. 252)*
7. **planter** *(p. 253)*
8. **yeoman farmer** *(p. 253)*
9. **slave code** *(p. 254)*
10. **"favorite son"** *(p. 258)*
11. **"corrupt bargain"** *(p. 259)*
12. **mudslinging** *(p. 260)*

Reviewing Key Facts

13. John C. Calhoun *(p. 241)*, John Marshall *(p. 242)*, Francis C. Lowell *(p. 248)*, Eli Whitney *(p. 248)*, Frederick Douglass *(p. 254)*, Denmark Vesey *(p. 256)*, Nat Turner *(p. 256)*, Henry Clay *(p. 258)*

14. The weakening of the Federalists created a one-party system in a time of nationalist pride.

15. Students' answers will vary. Answers should include three of the following: creation of new national bank, imposition of protective tariff, Supreme Court decisions established dominance of the nation over states, proclamation of the Monroe Doctrine.

16. British and American opposition to the attempts of the Quadruple Alliance to rebuild the Spanish Empire.

Reviewing Key Terms

On a sheet of paper, use each of these terms in a sentence.

1. revenue tariff
2. protective tariff
3. interchangeable parts
4. labor union
5. strike
6. cotton gin
7. planter
8. yeoman farmer
9. slave code
10. "favorite son"
11. "corrupt bargain"
12. mudslinging

Reviewing Key Facts

13. **Identify:** John C. Calhoun, John Marshall, Francis C. Lowell, Eli Whitney, Frederick Douglass, Denmark Vesey, Nat Turner, Henry Clay.

14. Why were the years following the War of 1812 known as the Era of Good Feelings?

15. What were three actions that strengthened the federal government after the War of 1812?

Chapter Summary

Nationalism in Government

- War of 1812 sparks national pride
- Second Bank of the United States and protective tariffs set up to promote nation's economy
- Supreme Court rulings give federal government power over states
- Spain cedes Florida
- Monroe Doctrine establishes foreign policy

Nationalism in Society

- Steamboats and railroads link the nation's regions
- Telegraph establishes fast, long-distance communication
- Rural farmers and immigrants come together in Northern cities to find work

Sectionalism Emerges

- South's agricultural economy relies on slavery
- Northern leaders view slavery as morally wrong
- Missouri Compromise pits Northern leaders against Southern leaders
- Disputed election of 1824 leads to return to two-party political system
- Congress votes almost strictly along sectional lines

16. What prompted the American declaration known as the Monroe Doctrine?

17. Why was agriculture, and not industry, the leading economic activity in the United States in the early 1800s?

18. How did cotton become the dominant crop in the South?

19. Why did the Republican Party split into the Democratic-Republican and the National Republican Parties?

Critical Thinking

20. **Analyzing Themes: Continuity and Change** What distinctive elements characterized enslaved African American culture?

21. **Organizing** Use a graphic organizer similar to the one below to list the effects of the Industrial Revolution.

Effects of the Industrial Revolution

22. **Interpreting Primary Sources** In *McCulloch* v. *Maryland*, the Supreme Court decided whether Congress had the power to set up the Bank of the United States. The following excerpt is from Chief Justice John Marshall's ruling. Read the excerpt and answer the questions that follow.

66The government of the United States . . . though limited in its powers, is supreme; . . . Among the enumerated powers, we do not find establishing a bank or creating a corporation. But there is no phrase [which] requires that everything granted shall be expressly and minutely described. . . . Among the enumerated powers of government . . . we find the great powers to lay and collect taxes . . . to declare war and conduct a war; . . . A government entrusted with such ample powers . . . must also be entrusted with ample means for their execution. . . . All means which are appropriate, which are plainly adapted to that end, which are not prohibited, but consist with the letter and spirit of the constitution, are constitutional. . . .99

—from *McCulloch* v. *Maryland*, 1819

a. What was Marshall's opinion about the power of the government of the United States?

b. Why do you think Marshall's ruling helped strengthen nationalist feelings in the United States?

17. Industry developed as a result of developments in transportation, passage of incorporation laws, and importation of British technology, all of which were not complete in the early 1800s.

18. The invention of the cotton gin allowed the production of cotton to soar and become more profitable.

19. anger over the outcome of the election of 1824 fueled by the belief that Andrew Jackson had been tricked out of a victory

Critical Thinking

20. The songs of enslaved African Americans often included subtle language and secret meanings to lament bondage and express hope for freedom. Christian enslaved African Americans also incorporated religious traditions from Africa.

Geography and History

23. The map on the right shows the United States in 1824. Study the map and answer the questions below.
    a. **Interpreting Maps** What international boundary was in dispute in 1824?
    b. **Applying Geography Skills** What geographic features determined the southern boundary of the Louisiana Purchase?

Practicing Skills

24. **Reading a Line Graph** The line graph below plots the number of patents issued between 1810 and 1840. Use the graph to answer the questions below.
    a. In what years did the number of patents issued drop sharply?
    b. During what time span did the number of patents issued increase the most?

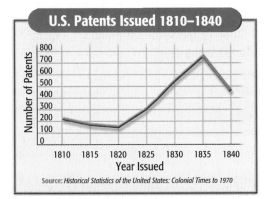

U.S. Patents Issued 1810–1840

Number of Patents / Year Issued

Source: *Historical Statistics of the United States: Colonial Times to 1970*

Writing Activity

25. **Reporting on Primary Sources** Search the Internet for a primary source (speech, letter, song, political cartoon, etc.) that describes heightened feelings of nationalism after the War of 1812. Write a brief explanation of the primary source and present your report to the class.

Chapter Activity

26. **Research Project** Research one of the technological advances made during the early 1800s. Write a description of the technological advance you have researched and create a diagram showing how it works. Place the description and the diagram in your portfolio.

The United States in 1824

OREGON COUNTRY (Occupied jointly by Britain and the United States)
British Treaty Line, 1818
Adams-Onis Treaty Line, 1819
BRITISH NORTH AMERICA
Disputed Area
ME.
N.H. MASS.
VT. N.Y. R.I.
CONN.
MICH. TERR.
PA. N.J.
UNORG. TERR.
OHIO DEL. MD.
ILL. IND.
MO. KY. VA.
N.C.
TENN.
MEXICO
ARK. TERR.
S.C.
MISS. ALA. GA.
LA.
FLA. TERR.
PACIFIC OCEAN
ATLANTIC OCEAN
Gulf of Mexico
0 300 miles
0 300 kilometers
Lambert Azimuthal Equal-Area projection

□ British Territory □ Mexico ── Louisiana Purchase □ United States

Standardized Test Practice

Directions: Read the excerpt below, taken from the Monroe Doctrine, and answer the question that follows.

The American continents, by the free and independent condition which they have assured and maintain, are hence forth not to be considered as subjects for future colonization by any European powers.

We should consider any attempt on their part to extend their system to any portion of this hemisphere as dangerous to our peace and safety.

The Monroe Doctrine sent a clear message to European powers from the United States. The Doctrine was designed to

A preserve the United States's trade routes with Europe.

B prohibit European nations from colonizing any lands in the Western Hemisphere.

C prevent Central American countries from declaring war against the United States.

D protect the United States from invasion by Central American nations.

Test-Taking Tip: Look *in the passage* to find clues to support your answer. Try not to get confused by the long sentences or old-fashioned language in this passage. Ask yourself what the *main idea* is. Then look for an answer that matches the main idea.

CHAPTER 7 Growth and Division **263**

Writing Activity

25. Students' explanations should reflect an understanding of the feelings of nationalism after the War of 1812.

Chapter Activity

26. Descriptions and diagrams will vary depending on the invention chosen.

Standardized Test Practice

Answer: B

Test-Taking Tip: Suggest that students underline the key phrases such as "free and independent" and "not . . . for future colonization" from the excerpt. This will help identify the answer.

Bonus Question ?

Ask: During the Monroe administration, what territorial claims did Russia have or make in North America? *(Russia already claimed Alaska, and in 1821 it claimed that its territory extended from Russian Alaska into the Oregon country.)*

---

21. Manufacturing shifted from hand tools to large, complex machines. Skilled artisans gave way to unskilled workers, organized by specific tasks. Factories replaced home-based workshops. Manufacturers sold their wares nationwide or abroad instead of just locally.

22. **a.** Marshall believed that the federal government was supreme. **b.** Marshall's decision confirmed that Congress could set up a national bank.

Geography and History

23. **a.** the northern boundary of Maine; **b.** the Gulf of Mexico

Practicing Skills

24. **a.** 1835–1840; **b.** 1820–1835

Chapter 8 Resources

TeacherWorks™ All-In-One Planner and Resource Center

- **Interactive Teacher Edition** Access your Teacher Wraparound Edition and your classroom resources with a few easy clicks.
- **Interactive Lesson Planner** Planning has never been easier! Organize your week, month, semester, or year with all the lesson helps you need to make teaching creative, timely, and relevant.

Use Glencoe's **Presentation Plus!** multimedia teacher tool to easily present dynamic lessons that visually excite your students. Using Microsoft PowerPoint® you can customize the presentations to create your own personalized lessons.

TEACHING TRANSPARENCIES

Graphic Organizer 8

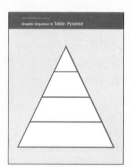

Why It Matters Chapter Transparency 8

APPLICATION AND ENRICHMENT

Linking Past and Present Activity 8

Enrichment Activity 8

Primary Source Reading 8

REVIEW AND REINFORCEMENT

Reteaching Activity 8

Vocabulary Activity 8

Time Line Activity 8

Critical Thinking Skills Activity 8

Meeting NCSS Standards

Local Standards

The following standards are highlighted in Chapter 8:

Section 1	V	Individuals, Groups, and Institutions: A, B, C, F
Section 2	V	Individuals, Groups, and Institutions: B, D, G
Section 3	II	Time, Continuity, and Change: B, C, E
Section 4	IV	Individual Development and Identity: A, F, G

Chapter 8 Resources

Chapter 8 Test Form A

Chapter 8 Test Form B

Standardized Test Skills Practice Workbook Activity 8

Performance Assessment Activities and Rubrics 8

ExamView® Pro Testmaker CD-ROM

MULTIMEDIA

- Vocabulary PuzzleMaker CD-ROM
- Interactive Tutor Self-Assessment CD-ROM
- ExamView® Pro Testmaker CD-ROM
- Audio Program
- American History Primary Source Documents Library CD-ROM
- MindJogger Videoquiz
- Presentation Plus! CD-ROM
- TeacherWorks™ CD-ROM
- Interactive Student Edition CD-ROM
- Glencoe Skillbuilder Interactive Workbook CD-ROM, Level 2
- The *American Vision* Video Program
- American Music: Hits Through History
- American Music: Cultural Traditions

SPANISH RESOURCES

The following Spanish language materials are available in the Spanish Resources Binder:

- Spanish Guided Reading Activities
- Spanish Reteaching Activities
- Spanish Quizzes and Tests
- Spanish Vocabulary Activities
- Spanish Summaries
- The Declaration of Independence and United States Constitution Spanish Translation

---

 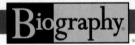

THE HISTORY CHANNEL.

The following videotape program is available from Glencoe as a supplement to Chapter 8:

- **Andrew Jackson: A Man for the People** (ISBN 1-56-501647-5)

To order, call Glencoe at 1-800-334-7344. To find classroom resources to accompany many of these videos, check the following home pages:
A&E Television: www.aande.com
The History Channel: www.historychannel.com

HISTORY Online

Use our Web site for additional resources. All essential content is covered in the Student Edition.

You and your students can visit tav.glencoe.com, the Web site companion to the *American Vision.* This innovative integration of electronic and print media offers your students a wealth of opportunities. The student text directs students to the Web site for the following options:

- **Chapter Overviews**   • **Student Web Activities**
- **Self-Check Quizzes**   • **Textbook Updates**

Answers to the student Web activities are provided for you in the **Web Activity Lesson Plans.** Additional Web resources and Interactive Tutor Puzzles are also available.

Chapter 8 Resources

SECTION RESOURCES

Daily Objectives	Reproducible Resources	Multimedia Resources
SECTION 1 **Jacksonian Era** 1. Explain how Jackson's background influenced his ideas of democratic government. 2. Describe how the nullification crisis sparked debate over states' rights.	Reproducible Lesson Plan 8–1 Daily Lecture and Discussion Notes 8–1 Guided Reading Activity 8–1* Section Quiz 8–1* Reading Essentials and Study Guide 8–1 Performance Assessment Activities and Rubrics Interpreting Political Cartoons	Daily Focus Skills Transparency 8–1 Interactive Tutor Self-Assessment CD-ROM ExamView® Pro Testmaker CD-ROM Presentation Plus! CD-ROM TeacherWorks™ CD-ROM Audio Program
SECTION 2 **A Changing Culture** 1. Explain the goals of the different groups active in the Second Great Awakening. 2. Identify the key ideas of romanticism and two important romantic thinkers or writers.	Reproducible Lesson Plan 8–2 Daily Lecture and Discussion Notes 8–2 Guided Reading Activity 8–2* Section Quiz 8–2* Reading Essentials and Study Guide 8–2 Performance Assessment Activities and Rubrics	Daily Focus Skills Transparency 8–2 American Art & Architecture Interactive Tutor Self-Assessment CD-ROM ExamView® Pro Testmaker CD-ROM Presentation Plus! CD-ROM TeacherWorks™ CD-ROM Audio Program American Music: Hits Through History American Music: Cultural Traditions
SECTION 3 **Reforming Society** 1. Analyze the connection between religious and social reform. 2. List major areas of society that reformers set out to improve.	Reproducible Lesson Plan 8–3 Daily Lecture and Discussion Notes 8–3 Guided Reading Activity 8–3* Section Quiz 8–3* Reading Essentials and Study Guide 8–3 Performance Assessment Activities and Rubrics	Daily Focus Skills Transparency 8–3 Interactive Tutor Self-Assessment CD-ROM ExamView® Pro Testmaker CD-ROM Presentation Plus! CD-ROM TeacherWorks™ CD-ROM Audio Program ABCNews Interactive™ Historic America Electronic Field Trips
SECTION 4 **The Abolitionist Movement** 1. List groups involved in the early abolitionist movement. 2. Analyze how Northerners and Southerners viewed abolitionism.	Reproducible Lesson Plan 8–4 Daily Lecture and Discussion Notes 8–4 Guided Reading Activity 8–4* Section Quiz 8–4* Reading Essentials and Study Guide 8–4 Performance Assessment Activities and Rubrics	Daily Focus Skills Transparency 8–4 Interactive Tutor Self-Assessment CD-ROM ExamView® Pro Testmaker CD-ROM Presentation Plus! CD-ROM Skillbuilder Interactive Workbook, Level 2 TeacherWorks™ CD-ROM Vocabulary PuzzleMaker CD-ROM Audio Program

0:00 OUT OF TIME?
Assign the Chapter 8 **Reading Essentials and Study Guide.**

*Also Available in Spanish

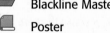 Blackline Master   Transparency   CD-ROM   DVD

Poster   Music Program   Audio Program   Videocassette

NATIONAL GEOGRAPHIC Teacher's Corner

INDEX TO NATIONAL GEOGRAPHIC MAGAZINE

The following articles relate to this chapter.
- "The Cherokee," May 1995
- "The Cruelest Commerce: African Slave Trade," September 1992
- "Erie Canal: Living Link to Our Past," November 1990

NATIONAL GEOGRAPHIC SOCIETY PRODUCTS AVAILABLE FROM GLENCOE

To order the following products for use with this chapter, contact your local Glencoe sales representative, or call Glencoe at 1-800-334-7344:
- *NGS PicturePack: Native Americans 1* (Transparencies)
- *NGS PictureShow: Story of America, Part 1*
- *PictureShow: Native Americans, 1* (CD-ROM)
- *PictureShow: The Westward Movement* (CD-ROM, Transparencies)

ADDITIONAL NATIONAL GEOGRAPHIC SOCIETY PRODUCTS

To order the following, call National Geographic at 1-800-368-2728:
- *Mark Twain: When I was a Boy* (Video)

NGS ONLINE

Access National Geographic's Web site for current events, atlas updates, activities, links, interactive features, and archives.
www.nationalgeographic.com

From the Classroom of...

John C. Horton
Covington Catholic High School
Covington, KY

Immigration: The Numbers Speak Volumes

This activity helps students understand why over 3.5 million Germans and Irish left their countries and immigrated to the U.S. between 1815 and 1860. We analyze the reasons they immigrated and where they settled once they arrived.

Organize the class into two groups and label them the German Study Group and the Irish Study Group. Give them a day to research what political, economic, religious, or social conditions caused these mass emigrations from these two countries, then ask each group to boil their research down into three basic causes.

Next give students two days to create two types of visuals. The first is a bar graph that shows immigration numbers every 10 years from 1820 to 1860 for Germans and Irish. The second is a map that shows general settlement patterns. (rural/urban)

End the unit by having each group give a ten-minute presentation and using a question-and-answer format to open up discussion.

ADDITIONAL RESOURCES FROM GLENCOE

- American Music: Cultural Traditions
- American Art & Architecture
- Outline Map Resource Book
- U.S. Desk Map
- Building Geography Skills for Life
- Inclusion for the High School Social Studies Classroom Strategies and Activities
- Teaching Strategies for the American History Classroom (Including Block Scheduling Pacing Guides)

KEY TO ABILITY LEVELS

Teaching strategies have been coded.

L1 BASIC activities for all students
L2 AVERAGE activities for average to above-average students
L3 CHALLENGING activities for above-average students
ELL ENGLISH LANGUAGE LEARNER activities

Block Schedule
Activities that are suited to use within the block scheduling framework are identified by:

Why It Matters Activity

Ask students why they think sectional rivalries grew between 1828 and 1845. Students should evaluate their answers after they have completed the chapter.

GLENCOE
TECHNOLOGY

The *American Vision* Video Program
To learn more about America between 1828 and 1845, have students view the Chapter 8 video, "The Spirit of Reform," from the *American Vision Video Program.*

 Available in DVD and VHS

MindJogger Videoquiz
Use the **MindJogger Videoquiz** to preview Chapter 8 content.

 Available in VHS

CHAPTER

8 The Spirit of Reform *1828–1845*

Why It Matters

Reform was a key theme of the 1830s and 1840s. Political reform came with the growth of popular democracy. President Jackson's election symbolized the new power of common citizens. For many Americans, social or religious reform was a goal. Some wanted to end slavery. Others wanted to expand education or women's rights. Throughout this period, sectional rivalries grew more bitter.

The Impact Today

Social and political ideals born in this period became important American values.
- *Many Americans value education highly and believe that anyone, regardless of background, might rise to a high political office if they have a good education.*
- *The desire to help others inspires many Americans.*

The American Vision Video *The Chapter 8 video, "The Spirit of Reform," chronicles important reform campaigns of this era.*

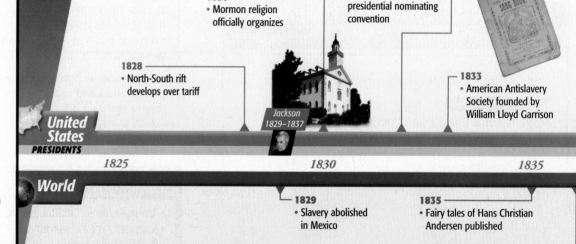

1830
- Mormon religion officially organizes

1832
- Democrats hold their first presidential nominating convention

1828
- North-South rift develops over tariff

1833
- American Antislavery Society founded by William Lloyd Garrison

Jackson 1829–1837

United States
PRESIDENTS

1825   *1830*   *1835*

World

1829
- Slavery abolished in Mexico

1835
- Fairy tales of Hans Christian Andersen published

1836
- First botany textbook published

264

The Verdict of the People by George Caleb Bingham, 1855

HISTORY Online

Introduce students to chapter content and key terms by having them access the **Chapter 8 Overview** at tav.glencoe.com.

More About the Art

George Caleb Bingham focused on two subjects in his best-known works: activity along the Mississippi River and frontier politics. During the mid-1800s, Bingham also became involved in politics. He ran for office several times and was elected to the Missouri state legislature in 1848.

TIME LINE ACTIVITY

Ask students to choose an event on the world time line and write a short report on the impact of the event on the United States. Encourage students to use library and Internet resources for their research.

1848
• Women's rights convention held at Seneca Falls, New York

1838
• Cherokee are driven from Georgia and embark on the Trail of Tears

Van Buren 1837–1841

W. Harrison 1841

Tyler 1841–1845

1840

1845

1837
• Queen Victoria ascends to English throne

1842
• China opened by force to foreign trade

1845
• Irish potato famine begins

HISTORY Online

Chapter Overview
Visit the *American Vision* Web site at tav.glencoe.com and click on *Chapter Overviews—Chapter 8* to preview chapter information.

265

GRAPHIC ORGANIZER ACTIVITY

Organizing Information Have students take notes on Chapter 8 by completing a table similar to the one shown.

Social Movement	Important Figures
Religious Revival	Charles G. Finney
Prison Reform	Dorothea Dix
Education Reform	Horace Mann, Calvin Wiley
Women's Education	Emma Willard, Mary Lyon
Women's Rights	Lucretia Mott, Elizabeth Cady Stanton
Abolitionism	William Lloyd Garrison, Frederick Douglass

265

1 FOCUS

Section Overview
This section describes the changes in politics that occurred during Andrew Jackson's two administrations.

Guide to Reading

Answers to Graphic: Calhoun's position: states had right to declare a federal law invalid; Jackson's position: states cannot nullify federal laws if the Union is to hold together

Preteaching Vocabulary
Have students use a standard dictionary to look up the words *abomination, caucus, nullification, secede,* and *spoil* to gain a better understanding of the Key Terms used in this section.

SECTION 1 Jacksonian America

Guide to Reading

Main Idea
The election of Andrew Jackson ushered in a new era of American politics.

Key Terms and Names
spoils system, caucus system, Tariff of Abominations, secede, John C. Calhoun, nullification, Daniel Webster, Force Bill, Indian Removal Act, Trail of Tears, Panic of 1837

Reading Strategy
Organizing As you read about Andrew Jackson's administration, complete a graphic organizer similar to the one below by listing the positions of Jackson and Calhoun during the nullification crisis.

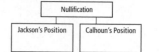

Reading Objectives
- **Explain** how Jackson's background influenced his ideas of democratic government.
- **Describe** how the nullification crisis sparked debate over states' rights.

Section Theme
Groups and Institutions The American political system became more democratic during the Jacksonian era.

Preview of Events

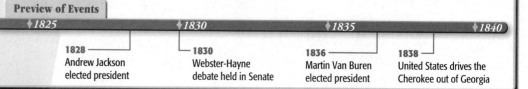

1828	1830	1836	1838
Andrew Jackson elected president	Webster-Hayne debate held in Senate	Martin Van Buren elected president	United States drives the Cherokee out of Georgia

★ An American Story ★

Hair comb worn at Jackson's Inaugural

Margaret Bayard Smith was one of the thousands of Americans who attended the presidential inauguration of Andrew Jackson in 1829. She later wrote to a friend about how much the atmosphere in Washington, D.C., impressed her. "Thousands and thousands of people, without distinction of rank, collected in an immense mass around the Capitol, silent, orderly and tranquil," she explained.

On that day, President Jackson broke a long tradition by inviting the public to his reception. When Smith later attended the White House gala, however, she quickly formed a different opinion about the crowd she had so admired just hours before. "The majesty of the people had disappeared, and a rabble, a mob, of boys, . . . women, children—[were] scrambling, fighting romping," she wrote. "The President, after having been *literally* nearly pressed to death and almost suffocated and torn to pieces by the people in their eagerness to shake hands with Old Hickory, had retreated through the back way. . . . Cut glass and china to the amount of several thousand dollars had been broken in the struggle to get refreshments. . . . Ladies and gentlemen only had been expected at this levee, not the people *en masse.* But it was the people's day, and the people's President, and the people would rule."

—adapted from *First Forty Years of Washington Society*

A New Era in Politics
The citizens who had turned the normally dignified inauguration reception into a boisterous affair represented a new class of American voters and a new era in American politics. Beginning in the early 1800s and continuing through the presidency of

The state banks, however, would often issue more paper money than they could redeem in gold or silver. This let them make more loans at lower interest rates, but it created the danger of inflation. To prevent the state banks from loaning too much money, the Bank of the United States regularly collected bank notes and asked state banks to redeem them for gold and silver. This action forced state banks to be careful about how much money they loaned, and it also limited inflation.

The Bank had done a good job stabilizing the money supply and interest rates, but many western settlers, who needed easy credit to run their farms, were unhappy with the Bank's lending policies. President Jackson also believed the Bank was unconstitutional, despite the Supreme Court's ruling in *McCulloch* v. *Maryland.* He did not believe that as president he had to accept this Supreme Court ruling.

To make the Bank an issue in the 1832 presidential campaign, Jackson's congressional opponents introduced a bill extending the Bank's charter for another 20 years. Congress passed the bill, but Jackson vetoed it. When the election was over, it was clear that most Americans supported Jackson. He easily won a second term.

Jackson took his re-election as a directive from the people to destroy the Bank at once, even though its charter did not run out until 1836. He removed the government's deposits from the Bank and placed them in state banks. The removal of the deposits forced the Bank to call in its loans and stop lending.

By putting an end to the Bank of the United States, Jackson had won a considerable political victory. Later, however, critics would charge that the end of the Bank contributed significantly to the financial woes that plagued the country in the years ahead.

✓ **Reading Check** **Examining** Why was President Jackson against the Second Bank of the United States?

A New Party Emerges

Andrew Jackson's forceful style had earned him plenty of detractors, and by the mid-1830s a new party emerged to oppose him. The group named itself the Whigs after the party in England that had worked to limit the king's power. The Whigs advocated a larger federal government, industrial and commercial development, and a centralized economy. Jackson's Democrats, on the other hand, favored a limited federal government, and they distrusted eastern merchants and business leaders.

Analyzing *Political Cartoons*

Kingly Rule? Jackson's strong-willed leadership attracted many critics. Here the cartoonist portrays Jackson as an absolute monarch. What does Jackson appear to be trampling underfoot?

The Presidency of Martin Van Buren The Whigs were united in opposing Jackson, but they were unable to settle on a leader. During the 1836 presidential election, Jackson's popularity and the nation's continuing prosperity helped Democrat Martin Van Buren defeat the Whigs, who had three candidates for president.

The new president had little time to savor his victory. Shortly after Van Buren took office, a crippling economic crisis hit the nation. During this **Panic of 1837,** as the crisis was called, many banks and businesses failed. Thousands of farmers lost their land, and unemployment soared among eastern factory workers. Van Buren, a firm believer in his party's philosophy of a limited federal government, did little to ease the crisis.

"Tippecanoe and Tyler Too" With the nation experiencing hard times, the Whigs looked forward to ousting the Democrats in the presidential election of 1840. They nominated General William Henry Harrison, who was regarded as a hero for his role in

CHAPTER 8 The Spirit of Reform **271**

3 ASSESS

Assign Section 1 Assessment as homework or as an in-class activity.

⊙ Have students use the **Interactive Tutor Self-Assessment CD-ROM.**

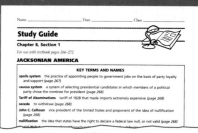

Reading Essentials and Study Guide 8–1

Name _____ Date _____ Class _____

Study Guide

Chapter 8, Section 1
For use with textbook pages 266–272

JACKSONIAN AMERICA

KEY TERMS AND NAMES

spoils system the practice of appointing people to government jobs on the basis of party loyalty and support *(page 267)*

caucus system a system of selecting presidential candidates in which members of a political party chose the nominee for president *(page 268)*

Tariff of Abominations tariff of 1828 that made imports extremely expensive *(page 268)*

secede to withdraw *(page 268)*

John C. Calhoun vice president of the United States and proponent of the idea of nullification *(page 268)*

nullification the idea that states have the right to declare a federal law null, or not valid *(page 268)*

✓ **Reading Check**

Answer: He suspiciously believed that the Bank was a financial monopoly controlled by the wealthy elite.

EXTENDING THE CONTENT

Relative and Absolute Dates The South Carolina Ordinance of Nullification was passed on November 24, 1832. The last paragraph of the ordinance recorded the date of the ordinance in two ways. First, it gave the actual date, the twenty-fourth day of November, in the year of our Lord one thousand eight hundred and thirty-two. Then it gave a relative date, the fifty-seventh year of the Declaration of the Independence of the United States of America.

Section Quiz 8–1

Name   Date   Class

★ Chapter 8   Score

Section Quiz 8-1

DIRECTIONS: Matching Match each item in Column A with the items in Column B.
Write the correct letters in the blanks. *(10 points each)*

Column A
____ 1. authorized the president to use the military to enforce acts of Congress
____ 2. a crippling economic crisis
____ 3. the vice president under Andrew Jackson and a resident of South Carolina
____ 4. idea that states had the right to declare a federal law null, or not valid
____ 5. the nominee for president would be chosen by members of a party who served in Congress

Column B
A. caucus system
B. Force Bill
C. nullification
D. John C. Calhoun
E. Panic of 1837

Graph Skills

Answers:
1. National Republican
2. since the mid-1850s

Graph Skills Practice
Ask: In what year did the Whig Party run candidates for president?
(1836)

✓ Reading Check

Answer: The Whigs won the 1840 election.

Reteach

Have students write a one-sentence description of each of these presidents: Jackson, Van Buren, Harrison, and Tyler.

Enrich

Invite students to prepare a presentation on one aspect of the Jackson presidency. Encourage students to use library and Internet resources for their research.

4 CLOSE

Ask students to explain the significance of Andrew Jackson's election to the presidency.

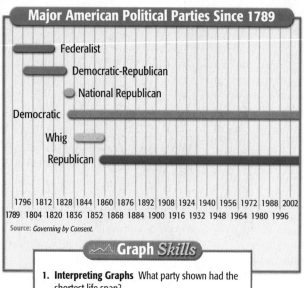

Major American Political Parties Since 1789

Federalist
Democratic-Republican
National Republican
Democratic
Whig
Republican

1789 1796 1804 1812 1820 1828 1836 1844 1852 1860 1868 1876 1884 1892 1900 1908 1916 1924 1932 1940 1948 1956 1964 1972 1980 1988 1996 2002

Source: *Governing by Consent.*

Graph Skills

1. **Interpreting Graphs** What party shown had the shortest life span?
2. **Comparing** How long have Republicans and Democrats been major political rivals?

the Battle of Tippecanoe and in the War of 1812. John Tyler, a Southerner and former Democrat who had left his party in protest over the nullification issue, joined the ticket as the vice presidential candidate. Adopting the campaign slogan "Tippecanoe and Tyler too," the Whigs blamed Van Buren for the economic depression. To attract western voters, they presented Harrison, a man born to wealth and privilege, as a simple frontiersman.

The strategy worked. Harrison won a decisive victory—234 electoral votes to 60, although the popular vote was much closer. On March 4, 1841, Harrison delivered his inauguration speech. The weather that day was bitterly cold, but Harrison insisted on delivering his nearly two-hour address without a hat or coat. He came down with pneumonia and died 32 days later, thereby serving the shortest term of any American president. Vice President John Tyler then succeeded to the presidency.

The Tyler Years Tyler's rise to the presidency shocked Whig leaders. Tyler actually opposed many Whig policies, and party leaders had placed him on the ticket mainly to attract Southern voters. Congress and the press mockingly called Tyler, "His Accidency." The Whigs in Congress tried to push through their agenda anyway, including a Third Bank of the United States and a higher tariff, but Tyler sided with the Democrats on these key issues.

Foreign relations occupied the country's attention during much of Tyler's administration, especially relations with Great Britain. Disputes over the Maine-Canadian border and other issues resulted in the 1842 **Webster-Ashburton Treaty,** which established a firm boundary between the United States and Canada from Maine to Minnesota.

By the middle of the 1800s, a wave of social change was sweeping across the nation. Americans began examining numerous aspects of their culture, from religion to literature. A social transformation soon began, which eventually led to the shaping of a uniquely American society.

✓ Reading Check
Identifying What new political party won the presidential election of 1840?

SECTION 1 ASSESSMENT

Checking for Understanding

1. **Define:** spoils system, caucus system, secede, nullification.
2. **Identify:** Tariff of Abominations, John C. Calhoun, Daniel Webster, Force Bill, Indian Removal Act, Trail of Tears, Panic of 1837.

Reviewing Themes

3. **Groups and Institutions** In what ways did the United States become more democratic during Jackson's presidency?

Critical Thinking

4. **Determining Cause and Effect** What effect did the Panic of 1837 have on the presidential election of 1840?
5. **Categorizing** Use a graphic organizer similar to the one below to list the policies of the Whigs and Jackson's Democrats.

Party	Policies
Whigs	
Democrats	

Analyzing Visuals

6. **Examining Art** Study the artwork on page 267. Some wealthy Americans claimed that President Jackson's supporters were a "mob" element in the nation. How does the artist portray Jackson's supporters? Why do you think so?

Writing About History

7. **Persuasive Writing** Imagine you are a Native American living in the United States during Andrew Jackson's presidency. Write a letter to President Jackson giving your opinion of the Indian Removal Act.

SECTION 1 ASSESSMENT ANSWERS

1. Terms are in blue.
2. Tariff of Abominations *(p. 268)*, John C. Calhoun *(p. 268)*, Daniel Webster *(p. 269)*, Force Bill *(p. 269)*, Indian Removal Act *(p. 270)*, Trail of Tears *(p. 270)*, Panic of 1837 *(p. 271)*
3. More white males participated in government through voting and government jobs.
4. President Van Buren was not reelected.
5. Whigs advocated expanding federal government, encouraging industrial and commercial development, and creating a central economy. Democrats favored limited federal government.
6. He portrays them as well-dressed, respectable citizens. The painter likely supports Jackson and wants to convey an impression that Jackson was accepted by all types of citizens.
7. Students' letters will vary. Letters should reflect the situation before the forced relocation began.

Guide to Reading

Main Idea
The United States underwent dramatic social and cultural changes during the early and mid-1800s.

Key Terms and Names
nativism, Know-Nothings, Second Great Awakening, Charles Grandison Finney, Joseph Smith, romanticism, transcendentalism, utopia

Reading Strategy
Categorizing Complete a graphic organizer similar to the one below by listing beliefs of various religious groups of the Second Great Awakening.

Religious Groups	Beliefs

Reading Objectives
• **Explain** the goals of the different groups active in the Second Great Awakening.
• **Identify** the key ideas of romanticism and two important romantic thinkers or writers.

Section Theme
Groups and Institutions The Second Great Awakening increased support for many religious groups in the United States.

Preview of Events

♦1830　　　♦1838　　　♦1846　　　♦1854

1830
Mormon religion officially organizes

1845
Potato famine strikes Ireland

1851
Whitman's *Leaves of Grass* published

1854
American Party forms

★ *An American Story* ★

By June of 1850, Daniel Guiney had made up his mind. He was going to leave his impoverished town in Ireland and move to the United States. The enthusiastic letters he had received from friends convinced him that life had to be better in the United States. Ireland was suffering a devastating famine. Tens of thousands of citizens were dying of starvation, while many more were fleeing the country.

By August 1850, Guiney and a group from his neighborhood had moved to Buffalo, New York. After settling in, Guiney wrote back home about the wondrous new land where they now resided.

Immigrant's trunk

❝We mean to let you know our situation at present. . . . We arrived here about five o'clock in the afternoon of yesterday, fourteen of us together, where we were received with the greatest kindness of respectability. . . . When we came to the house we could not state to you how we were treated. We had potatoes, meat, butter, bread, and tea for dinner. . . . If you were to see Denis Reen when Daniel Danihy dressed him with clothes suitable for this country, you would think him to be a boss or steward, so that we have scarcely words to state to you how happy we felt at present.❞

—quoted in *Out of Ireland*

The New Wave of Immigrants

Daniel Guiney was just one of the millions of immigrants who came to the United States in search of a better life in the mid-1800s. The arrival of these newcomers coincided with a time when Americans were blazing new paths in a host of cultural

CHAPTER 8　The Spirit of Reform　**273**

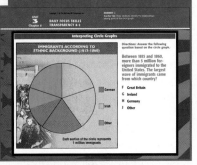

2 TEACH

Daily Lecture and Discussion Notes 8–2

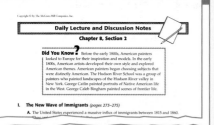

Copyright © by The McGraw-Hill Companies, Inc.

Daily Lecture and Discussion Notes
Chapter 8, Section 2

Did You Know? Before the early 1800s, American painters looked to Europe for their inspiration and models. In the early 1800s, American artists developed their own style and explored American themes. American painters began choosing subjects that were distinctly American. The Hudson River School was a group of painters who painted landscapes of the Hudson River valley in New York. George Catlin painted portraits of Native American life in the West. George Caleb Bingham painted scenes of frontier life.

I. The New Wave of Immigrants *(pages 273–275)*

A. The United States experienced a massive influx of immigrants between 1815 and 1860.

Picturing **History**

Answer: Irish and German

Ask: What was the main force behind Irish immigration during this period? *(the Irish potato famine)*

Explaining a Quote Have students explain the portion of August Blümmer's letter that is quoted on this page. Suggest that students refer to a dictionary to clarify the meanings of any unfamiliar words. *(Students' answers will vary. Answers should reflect an understanding of the meanings of the words* despotism *and* folly. *Despotism refers to a government where the ruler has absolute power. In this passage, it is likely that folly means evil, although that meaning is now considered obsolete.)* **L1**

History *and the* Humanities

🎵 American Music: Hits Through History: "Welcome Gospel Kindred," "Nabucca's Quick Step"

🎵 American Music: Cultural Traditions: "Kneebone Bend," "Come Life, Shaker Life," "The Handcart Song"

🎨 American Art & Architecture: Shaker Retiring Room

Picturing **History**

The Bay and Harbor of New York Immigrants arrive in New York City. Castle Garden, the building in the distant left, served as a processing facility for immigrants beginning in 1855. Many immigrants saw posters such as this one (left) advertising passage between Liverpool and Boston. What two nationalities made up the majority of immigrants to America during the mid-1800s?

areas, including religion, art, and literature. Together, these events helped bring great changes to American society in the years before the Civil War.

Between 1815 and 1860, the United States experienced a massive influx of immigrants. Over 5 million foreigners arrived on its shores. Many had fled violence and political turmoil at home, while others sought to escape starvation and poverty. Most of these newcomers found opportunity and a fresh start, but some also found discrimination and prejudice.

Newcomers From Ireland and Germany

The largest wave of immigrants, almost 2 million, came from Ireland. The driving force behind the massive exodus was the onset of widespread famine in 1845, when a fungus destroyed much of the nation's crop of potatoes, a mainstay of the Irish diet. Most Irish immigrants arrived in the United States with no money and few marketable skills. They generally settled in the industrialized cities of the Northeast, where many worked as unskilled laborers and servants.

Between 1815 and 1860, Germans represented the second largest group of immigrants. By 1860 over 1.5 million Germans had arrived in the United States. Most had enough money to move beyond the large

eastern cities and settle in the Midwest. There they became farmers or went into business. Like most other immigrants, Germans reveled in their new-found sense of freedom and liberty. German immigrant August Blümmer expressed this sentiment in a letter he wrote in 1838:

> 66 Over there [Germany] common sense and free speech lie in shackles. . . . I invite you to come over here, should you want to obtain a clear notion of genuine public life, freedom of people and a sense of being a nation. . . . I have never regretted that I came here, and never! never! again shall I bow my head under the yoke of despotism and folly. 99
>
> —quoted in *News from the Land of Freedom*

Nativism

While immigrants often found a new sense of freedom in the United States, some encountered discrimination. The presence of people from different cultures, with different languages and different religions, produced feelings of nativism, or hostility toward foreigners.

In the 1800s, many Americans were strongly anti-Catholic. Many prominent ministers preached

274 CHAPTER 8 The Spirit of Reform

COOPERATIVE LEARNING ACTIVITY

Making an Oral Presentation Organize the class into small groups. Have each group select one of the authors mentioned in this section. Tell the groups that they are to create an oral biography of their chosen writer. The biography should give an overview of the writer's life and include samples of his or her writing. Have the groups present their oral biographies to the class.

Use the rubric for a cooperative group management plan on pages 81–82 in the **Performance Assessment Activities and Rubrics.**

anti-Catholic sermons. Occasionally, anti-Catholic riots erupted. The arrival of millions of predominantly Catholic Irish and German immigrants led to the rise of several nativist groups, such as the Supreme Order of the Star Spangled Banner, founded in 1849. These groups pledged never to vote for a Catholic and pushed for laws banning immigrants and Catholics from holding public office. In July 1854, delegates from these groups formed the American Party. Membership in the party was secret, and those questioned were obliged to answer, "I know nothing." The **Know-Nothings,** as the party was nicknamed, built a large following in the 1850s.

✔ **Reading Check** **Analyzing** Why did nativism become so strong in the mid-1800s?

A Religious Revival

As immigrants added to the diversity of society, Americans were transforming the society in which they lived. One important change came in American religious life, where traditional Protestantism experienced a dramatic revival, and new forms of worship became prominent.

The Second Great Awakening By the end of the 1700s, many church leaders sensed that Americans' commitment to organized religion was weakening. This deterioration was due in large part to the growth of scientific knowledge and rationalism, notions that challenged the doctrine of faith. In the early 1800s, religious leaders organized to revive Americans' commitment to religion. The resulting movement came to be called the **Second Great Awakening.** It began in Kentucky, among frontier farmers, and quickly spread to the rest of the country. Leaders of the various Protestant denominations—most often Methodists, Baptists, and Presbyterians—held camp meetings that attracted thousands of followers for days of song, prayer, and emotional outpourings of faith.

The basic message of the Second Great Awakening was that individuals must readmit God and Christ into their daily lives. The new revivalism rejected the traditional Calvinist idea that only a chosen few were predestined for salvation. Instead, ministers preached that all people could attain grace through faith.

One of the most prominent advocates of this new message was a Presbyterian minister named **Charles Grandison Finney.** Finney preached that each person contained within himself or herself the capacity for spiritual rebirth and salvation. Finney helped found modern revivalism. His camp meetings were carefully planned and rehearsed to create as much emotion as possible. He compared his methods to those used by politicians and salespeople, and he used emotion to focus people's attention on his message. Finney began preaching in upstate New York, where he launched a series of revivals in towns along the Erie Canal. He then took his message to the cities of the Northeast.

Finney also served as president of Oberlin College in Ohio, the first college in the United States to admit women and African Americans. Although Oberlin became a center for social reform movements in the United States, Finney warned against using politics to change society. He believed that if Christian ideas reformed people from within, society would become better, but if people remained selfish and immoral, political reforms would not make any difference.

New Religious Groups Emerge A number of other religious groups also flourished during this period. The Unitarians and Universalists broke away from the New England Congregational Church. Unitarians reject the idea that Jesus was the son of God, arguing instead that he was a great teacher. Their name comes from the belief that God is a unity, not a trinity of Father, Son, and Holy Spirit. Universalists believe in the universal salvation of souls. They reject the idea of hell and believe God intends to save everyone.

✏ **History** *Through Art*

Religious Zeal J. Maze Burban's *Religious Camp Meeting* dramatizes religious revivalism, showing a charismatic preacher reaching many in the audience. From studying the image, can you suggest other reasons people might want to attend?

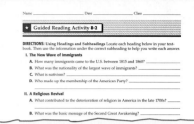

Guided Reading Activity 8-2

Name _____ Date _____ Class _____

★ Guided Reading Activity **8-2**

DIRECTIONS: Using Headings and Subheadings Locate each heading below in your textbook. Then use the information under the correct subheading to help you write each answer.

I. The New Wave of Immigrants

A. How many immigrants came to the U.S. between 1815 and 1860? _____

B. What was the nationality of the largest wave of immigrants? _____

C. What is nativism? _____

D. Who made up the membership of the American Party? _____

II. A Religious Revival

A. What contributed to the deterioration of religion in America in the late 1700s? _____

B. What was the basic message of the Second Great Awakening? _____

✔ **Reading Check**

Answer: The influx of immigrants with different religions, languages, and cultural backgrounds led to hostility toward foreigners.

Creating a Line Graph Have students use the information below to create a line graph showing the regional population increase between 1800 and 1860. **L1** ELL

	Northeast	North Central	South
1800	2,636,000	51,000	2,622,000
1810	3,487,000	292,000	3,461,000
1820	4,360,000	859,000	4,419,000
1830	5,542,000	1,610,000	5,708,000
1840	6,761,000	3,352,000	6,951,000
1850	8,627,000	5,404,000	8,983,000
1860	10,594,000	9,097,000	11,133,000

📁 Use the rubric for creating a map, display, or chart on pages 77–78 in the *Performance Assessment Activities and Rubrics.*

✏ **History** *Through Art*

Background: Camp meetings such as the one pictured were known as "revivals" because they revived people's religious zeal.
Answer: For some it was a social gathering and others wanted to observe.
Ask: What is seen in the background that helps you understand the name of these meetings? *(tents)*

MEETING SPECIAL NEEDS

Logical/Mathematical Encourage interested students to locate an example of a political speech and a sermon from the early 1800s. Have students identify ways in which emotion was used to focus attention on the point being made. Have students list the specific phrases that indicate an emotional appeal from each sample. Then have students select one of the items on the list and write a paragraph explaining what likely effect the phrase had on people who heard the message. **L3**

📁 Refer to *Inclusion for the High School Social Studies Classroom Strategies and Activities* in the TCR.

IN HISTORY

Background: In addition to arguing that women deserved equal political rights, Margaret Fuller's *Women in the Nineteenth Century* dealt with other issues facing contemporary women. She advocated education as a way for women to seek independence from home and family. She suggested that women should have career options and advocated for the reform of property laws to eliminate bias against women.

Ask: Why might Margaret Fuller have been a controversial figure during her lifetime? *(Her professional activities were unusual for a woman in the early 1800s and some of the ideas she wrote about were contrary to what was generally accepted at the time.)*

✓ Reading Check

Answer: Individuals must readmit God and Christ into their daily lives.

3 ASSESS

Assign Section 2 Assessment as homework or as an in-class activity.

🔵 Have students use the **Interactive Tutor Self-Assessment CD-ROM.**

Profiles IN HISTORY

Margaret Fuller
1810–1850

As a young woman, Margaret Fuller was a member of a group of prominent New England writers and philosophers who developed transcendentalism. In 1840, with the help of Ralph Waldo Emerson, she founded the magazine *The Dial*, which published poetry and essays of the transcendentalist movement.

Fuller also organized groups of Boston women to promote their education and intellectual development. These meetings convinced her to write the book *Women in the Nineteenth Century*, in which she argued that women deserved equal political rights.

Fuller's success in editing *The Dial* caught the eye of Horace Greeley, the famous editor of the *New York Tribune*. In 1844 Greeley hired Fuller to be the *Tribune's* literary critic. In 1846 he sent Fuller to Europe to cover European reform efforts. While visiting Italy, Fuller met and married Giovanni Angelo Ossoli, a revolutionary fighting to unite Italy into one country.

Fuller sent home reports about the Italian revolution of 1848, becoming the first American woman foreign war correspondent. In 1850, as the revolution fell apart, Fuller, Ossoli, and their young son set sail for the United States. Tragedy struck when their ship sank near Long Island, New York, and all three drowned.

Another religious group that emerged during this period was the Church of Jesus Christ of Latter-day Saints, whose followers are commonly known as Mormons. **Joseph Smith,** a New Englander living in western New York, began preaching Mormon ideas in 1830 after claiming to have been called to restore the Christian church to its original form. Smith published *The Book of Mormon* that year, saying it was a translation of words inscribed on golden plates that he had received from an angel. The text told of the coming of God and the need to build a kingdom on Earth to receive him.

After enduring continuous harassment in Ohio, Missouri, and elsewhere, Mormons from around the Midwest moved to Commerce, Illinois, in the spring of 1839. They bought the town, renamed it Nauvoo, and began building a self-contained community. The group prospered in the Midwest, with Nauvoo numbering about 15,000 in 1844. Persecution continued, however, and that same year local residents murdered Smith. After Smith's death, Brigham Young became the leader of the Church. The Mormons then left Illinois and trekked westward to the Utah territory, where they put down permanant roots.

✓ Reading Check Summarizing What was the basic message of the Second Great Awakening?

A Literary Renaissance

The optimism about human nature that influenced the Second Great Awakening also influenced philosophers and writers. Many leading thinkers of the day adopted the tenets of romanticism, a movement that began in Europe in the 1800s. Romanticism advocated feeling over reason, inner spirituality over external rules, the individual above society, and nature over environments created by humans.

One notable expression of American romanticism came from New England writers and philosophers who were known as the transcendentalists. Transcendentalism urged people to transcend, or overcome, the limits of their minds and let their souls reach out to embrace the beauty of the universe.

American Writers Emerge The most influential transcendentalist was **Ralph Waldo Emerson.** In his 1836 essay *Nature*, Emerson wrote that those who wanted fulfillment should work for communion with the natural world. Emerson influenced other writers, including **Margaret Fuller** and **Henry David Thoreau.** Thoreau believed that individuals must fight the pressure to conform. "If a man does not keep pace with his companions, perhaps it is because he hears a different drummer," he wrote. "Let him step to the music which he hears, however measured or far away."

Emerson and Thoreau were only two of many writers who set out to create uniquely American works that celebrated the people, history, and natural beauty of the United States. One writer, **James Fenimore Cooper,** romanticized Native Americans and frontier explorers in his Leatherstocking Tales, the most famous being *The Last of the Mohicans* (1826). **Nathaniel Hawthorne,** a New England customs official, wrote over 100 tales and novels. His novel *The Scarlet Letter* (1850), with its Puritan setting, explored the persecution and psychological suffering that results from sin. **Herman Melville,** another New Englander, wrote the great *Moby Dick* (1851). **Edgar Allan Poe,** a poet and short story writer, achieved fame as a writer of terror and mystery. Perhaps the most important poet of the era was **Walt Whitman,** who published a volume of poetry in 1855 called *Leaves of Grass*. Whitman loved nature,

---

INTERDISCIPLINARY CONNECTIONS ACTIVITY

Literature Invite an English teacher, librarian, or literary critic to address your class. Ask the guest to speak about the literary renaissance of the 1800s in the United States. Request that the speaker share specific examples from literature that highlight the influence of transcendentalists. As a class discuss how these examples demonstrate the influence of transcendentalists. **L2**

the common people, and American democracy, and his famous work reflects these passions. The best-remembered female poet of the era was **Emily Dickinson,** who wrote simple, personal, deeply emotional poetry.

The Penny Press Another important development of the early 1800s was the rise of the mass newspaper. Before the 1800s, most newspapers catered to well-educated readers. They were typically published once a week and cost around six cents, which was far beyond the reach of the average worker.

As more Americans learned to read and gained the right to vote, publishers began producing inexpensive newspapers, known as **penny papers,** which provided the kind of news most people liked. Reports of fires, crimes, marriages, gossip, politics, and local news made the papers an instant success.

General interest magazines that catered to a more specialized readership also emerged around this time. In 1830 Louis A. Godey founded *Godey's Lady's Book,* the first American magazine for women. The poet James Russell Lowell launched *Atlantic Monthly,* another magazine for the well-educated, in 1857, while *Harper's Weekly* covered everything from book reviews to news reports.

✓ **Reading Check** **Evaluating** What were the main themes of American writers in the early 1800s?

Utopian Communities

The ideas that drove the religious and artistic movements of the United States in the mid-1800s—optimism about human nature and a belief in people's ability to redefine their lives—also spurred the establishment of new communities. The people who formed these communities believed that society tended to corrupt human nature. They thought that the way to a better life was to separate themselves from society and form their own *utopia,* or ideal society. Cooperative living and the absence of private property characterized these communities, and dozens of them sprang up and flourished during the Jacksonian Era.

In New England, near West Roxbury, Massachusetts, transcendentalist George Ripley established a utopian community known as **Brook Farm** in 1841. The farm offered its members the chance to engage in intellectual activity while cooperatively running a farm. Ultimately, Brook Farm collapsed after a large fire left the group with huge debts.

The religious group known as the **Shakers** established small utopian communities from Maine to Kentucky. The group got its name from a ritual "shaking" dance that members performed. The Shakers reached their peak in the mid-1800s with some 6,000 members. Since they did not believe in marrying or having children, the group could only expand by making converts.

In the end, the number of Americans who chose to live in utopian communities was relatively small. Many more, inspired by a strong faith in human goodness, attempted not to escape society but to reform it.

✓ **Reading Check** **Interpreting** What spurred the establishment of utopian societies?

SECTION 2 ASSESSMENT

Checking for Understanding

1. **Define:** nativism, romanticism, transcendentalism, utopia.
2. **Identify:** Know-Nothings, Second Great Awakening, Charles Grandison Finney, Joseph Smith.
3. **Summarize** the goals of the Know-Nothings.

Reviewing Themes

4. **Groups and Institutions** What religious denominations increased their influence in the United States during the Second Great Awakening?

Critical Thinking

5. **Interpreting** How did the writers of the early to mid-1800s reflect American life?
6. **Organizing** Use a graphic organizer similar to the one below to list American cultural movements in the mid-1800s.

Movements in American Culture in the Mid-1800s

Analyzing Visuals

7. **Examining Art** Study the painting on page 275 of the camp meeting. What elements of the image suggest that the revival attracted many working-class people?

Writing About History

8. **Expository Writing** Imagine you are an Irish or German immigrant in the mid-1800s. Write an essay contrasting the United States with your homeland. Describe your new life in the United States and how you are treated.

CHAPTER 8 The Spirit of Reform **277**

SECTION 2 ASSESSMENT ANSWERS

1. Terms are in blue.
2. Know-Nothings *(p. 275),* Second Great Awakening *(p. 275),* Charles Grandison Finney *(p. 275),* Joseph Smith *(p. 276)*
3. The Know-Nothings worked to prevent Catholics from holding public office.
4. Methodists, Baptists, and Presbyterians
5. They romanticized American life.
6. nativism, revivalism, romanticism, transcendentalism, and utopian communities
7. the style of clothing worn by most people in the painting
8. Students' essays will vary. Essays should focus on the differences between life in the United States and life in either Ireland or Germany.

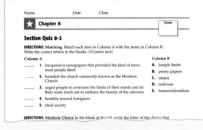

✓ **Reading Check**

Answer: Romantic writers advocated feelings over reason, inner spirituality over external rules, the individual over society, and nature over an environment created by humans. Transcendentalist writers focused on overcoming the limits of the human mind and embracing the beauty of the universe.

Reteach
Have students identify the goals of the different groups active in the Second Great Awakening.

Enrich
Have students choose a work by one of the authors mentioned in this section and write a report about the selection.

✓ **Reading Check**

Answer: optimism about human nature and a belief in people's ability to redefine their lives

4 CLOSE

Ask students to identify the key ideas of romanticism and name some of the important romantic thinkers and writers who were mentioned in this section.

1 FOCUS

Section Overview

This section explores the reform movements that occurred during the early and mid-1800s.

Guide to Reading

Answers to Graphic:
I. The Reform Spirit
  A. The Temperance Movement
  B. Prison Reform
  C. Educational Reform
  D. Women's Education
II. The Early Women's Movement
  A. "True Womanhood"
  B. Women Seek Greater Rights

Preteaching Vocabulary
Have students pair each Key Term with a name from the section and pair each Key Name with a term from the section.

SECTION 3 Reforming Society

Guide to Reading

Main Idea
Spurred on by a revival of religion and a heightened belief in the power of individuals, Americans engaged in reform efforts in the early and mid-1800s.

Key Terms and Names
Dorothea Dix, Lyman Beecher, benevolent society, temperance, penitentiary, Horace Mann, Elizabeth Cady Stanton

Reading Strategy
Taking Notes As you read about American reform efforts in the early and mid-1800s, use the section's major headings to create an outline like the one below.

Reforming Society
I. The Reform Spirit
  A.
  B.
  C.
  D.
II.

Reading Objectives
• **Analyze** the connection between religious and social reform.
• **List** major areas of society that reformers set out to improve.

Section Theme
Continuity and Change Reform movements sought to change American society, but in ways that upheld American values and ideals.

Preview of Events

♦1843   ♦1847   ♦1851   ♦1855

1843
Dorothea Dix calls for reforming care of mentally ill

1848
Seneca Falls Convention

1851
Maine passes first state law prohibiting alcohol

1852
Massachusetts passes first mandatory school attendance law

★ An American Story ★

Dorothea Dix

By 1841 Dorothea Dix had been a schoolteacher in Massachusetts for many years. That year, a clergyman asked her to lead a Sunday school class at a local prison. What Dix saw there appalled her. Mentally ill persons lay neglected in dirty, unheated rooms. Putting aside her teaching career, she began a crusade to improve prison conditions for the mentally ill and to provide them with the treatment they needed.

In 1843 Dix composed a letter to the Massachusetts legislature calling for such reforms. She pointed to the example of one local woman as evidence that more humane treatment might help many of the mentally ill. "Some may say these things cannot be remedied," she wrote. "I *know* they can. . . . A young woman, a pauper . . . was for years a raging maniac. A cage, chains, and the whip were the agents for controlling her, united with harsh tones and profane language." Dix explained that a local couple took the woman in and treated her with care and respect. "They are careful of her diet. They keep her very clean. She calls them 'father' and 'mother.' Go there now, and you will find her 'clothed,' and though not perfectly in her 'right mind,' so far restored as to be a safe and comfortable inmate."

—adapted from *Old South Leaflets*

The Reform Spirit

Largely through the efforts of **Dorothea Dix,** more than a dozen states enacted sweeping prison reforms and created special institutions for the mentally ill. As influential as she was, Dix was just one of many citizens who worked to reform various aspects of American society in the mid 1800s.

SECTION RESOURCES

Reproducible Masters
• Reproducible Lesson Plan 8–3
• Daily Lecture and Discussion Notes 8–3
• Guided Reading Activity 8–3
• Section Quiz 8–3
• Reading Essentials and Study Guide 8–3
• Performance Assessment Activities and Rubrics

Transparencies
• Daily Focus Skills Transparency 8–3

Multimedia
🎮 Interactive Tutor Self-Assessment CD-ROM
🎮 ExamView® Pro Testmaker CD-ROM
🎮 Presentation Plus! CD-ROM
🎮 TeacherWorks™ CD-ROM
🎧 Audio Program

The reform movements of the mid-1800s stemmed in large part from the revival of religious fervor. Revivalists preached the power of individuals to improve themselves and the world. **Lyman Beecher,** a prominent minister, insisted that it was the nation's citizenry more than its government that should take charge of building a better society. True reform, he said, could take place only through "the voluntary energies of the nation itself. "

Under the guidance of Beecher and other religious leaders, associations known as benevolent societies sprang up in cities and towns across the country. At first, they focused on spreading the word of God and attempting to convert nonbelievers. Soon, however, they sought to combat a number of social problems.

One striking feature of the reform effort was the overwhelming presence of women. Young women in particular had joined the revivalist movement in much larger numbers than men. One reason was that many unmarried women with uncertain futures discovered in religion a foundation on which to build their lives. As more women turned to the church, many also joined religious-based reform groups. These reform groups targeted aspects of American society they considered in dire need of change. Among these issues were excessive drinking, prisons, and education.

The Temperance Movement A number of reformers argued that no social vice caused more crime, disorder, and poverty than the excessive use of alcohol. Men who drank excessively, they argued, spent their money on liquor rather than food and other family necessities, and they sometimes abused their wives and children. While some may have disagreed with this assessment, no one could dispute the fact that alcoholism was widespread during the early 1800s. In small towns throughout the West, citizens drank to ease the isolation and loneliness of rural life, while in the pubs and saloons in eastern cities, drinking was the main leisure activity for many workers.

Although advocates of temperance, or moderation in the consumption of alcohol, had been active since the late 1700s, the new reformers energized the campaign and greatly increased its influence. Temperance groups formed across the country, preaching the evils of alcohol and persuading heavy drinkers to give up liquor. In 1833 several of these groups joined together to form the **American Temperance Union.**

Temperance societies also pushed for laws to prohibit the sale of liquor. In 1851 Maine passed the first state prohibition law, an example followed by a dozen other states by 1855. Other states passed "local option" laws, which allowed towns and villages to prohibit liquor sales within their boundaries.

Prison Reform The spirit of reform also prompted Americans to consider ways to improve the prison system. Inmates of all kinds, from violent offenders to debtors and the mentally ill, often were indiscriminately crowded together in jails and prisons, which were literally holes in the ground in some cases. One jail in Connecticut, for example, was an abandoned mineshaft. Beginning around 1816, many states began building new facilities to provide a better environment for inmates.

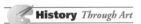

History *Through Art*

Drunkard's Progress In 1846 Nathaniel Currier made this lithograph (left), or print made by engraving on stone. It clearly lays out the path to degradation that begins in Step 1, a glass of alcohol with a friend. Some innkeepers advertised their temperance principles with a sign such as the one above. From looking at the lithograph, how can you tell that women were often temperance supporters?

CHAPTER 8 The Spirit of Reform 279

2 TEACH

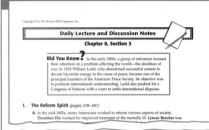

Daily Lecture and Discussion Notes 8–3

Creating a Poster Have students work in pairs to create a poster advocating reform in one of the areas mentioned in this section. Encourage students to use library and Internet resources to learn more about the reform issue. L1 ELL

Use the rubric for creating a map, display, or chart on pages 77–78 in the *Performance Assessment Activities and Rubrics.*

History *Through Art*

Background: Nathaniel Currier's brother Charles introduced him to Jim Ives. Nathaniel Currier and Jim Ives became close friends and eventually formed their well-known partnership, Currier & Ives.
Answer: A woman and child are seen weeping as the house burns.
Ask: Why did reformers consider alcohol so much of a problem? *(They argued that no other social vice caused as many problems.)*

COOPERATIVE LEARNING ACTIVITY

Creating a Display Have students work in groups to create displays similar to the "What Life Was Like" illustration on pages 280–281. Displays should feature some aspect of life in the early to mid-1800s such as school, work, home, or church. Have students contact organizations such as historical societies and public libraries for help in locating artifacts for their displays.

Use the rubric for a cooperative group management plan on pages 81–82 in the *Performance Assessment Activities and Rubrics.*

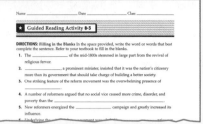
What Life Was Like...

Ask students to compare their own educational experiences with what is depicted in the illustration and the text of the "What Life Was Like" box. Invite two students to record the comparisons on the board or on flip charts.

you don't say...

On the Wagon The phrase "on the wagon," referring to a recovering alcoholic, originated during the temperance movement. To publicize their cause, reformers pulled a water wagon through the streets and urged people to climb on. Over time "going on the wagon" came to mean accepting the temperance cause and staying sober.

FYI

Horace Mann carried his ideas on education from Massachusetts to Ohio, where he became the first president of Antioch College. There he fought for equal educational opportunities for women.

What Life Was Like...

Old-Fashioned School Days

Public schools in the early to mid-1800s were rough-and-ready affairs. Students came in all ages and sizes, teachers often had little training, and books and supplies were hard to obtain.

School ink jar

• **One-Room Schoolhouse**
The painting *New England School* by Charles Frederick Bosworth tells the tale of teachers' challenges in early public schools. With a mixed-aged class, the teacher had to teach a few students at a time, leaving the others to their own education—or entertainment.

School lunch pail

Underlying the prison reform movement was a belief in rehabilitating prisoners rather than merely locking them up. Officials designed forms of rigid discipline to rid criminals of the "laxness" that had led them astray. Solitary confinement and the imposition of silence on work crews were meant to give prisoners the chance to meditate and think about their wrongdoing. Even the name of these new prisons, penitentiaries, highlighted the notion that they were places where individuals would work to achieve penitence, or remorse.

Educational Reform In the early 1800s, many reformers began to push for a system of public education—government-funded schools open to all citizens. The increase in the number of voters in the 1820s and 1830s and the arrival of millions of new immigrants convinced many people of the need for public education. Most American leaders and social reformers believed that a democratic republic could only survive if the electorate was well educated and informed.

One of the leaders of the public education movement was Massachusetts legislator **Horace Mann.** As president of the Massachusetts Senate, Mann pressed for more public education and backed a bill in 1837 creating a state board of education in Massachusetts.

He then stepped down from his elective office to serve as secretary of the new board. During his 12 years in that post he doubled teachers' salaries, opened 50 new high schools, and established schools for teacher training called "normal schools." Massachusetts quickly became the model for all other northern states. Mann's driving conviction was that a nation without an educated populace would have to struggle just to survive, much less prosper:

❝The establishment of a republican government, without well-appointed and efficient means for the universal education of the people, is the most rash and foolhardy experiment ever tried by man. . . . It may be an easy thing to make a republic, but it is a very laborious thing to make republicans; and woe to the republic that rests upon no better foundations than ignorance, selfishness and passion!❞

—from "Report of the Massachusetts Board of Education," 1848

In 1852 Massachusetts passed the first mandatory school attendance law; New York passed a similar measure the next year. In the years before the Civil War, reformers campaigned for district, or common,

280 CHAPTER 8 The Spirit of Reform

MEETING SPECIAL NEEDS

Verbal/Linguistic Have students select a reform movement mentioned in the section. Then have them create a pamphlet similar to those distributed in the early to mid-1800s encouraging people to join the cause. Tell students that they may need to research the movement in order to create the pamphlet. **L2**

📁 Refer to *Inclusion for the High School Social Studies Classroom Strategies and Activities* in the TCR.

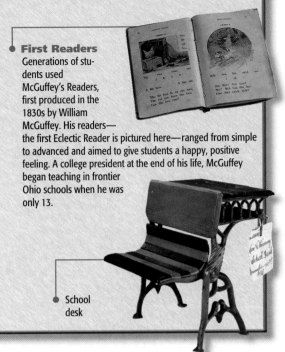

First Readers
Generations of students used McGuffey's Readers, first produced in the 1830s by William McGuffey. His readers—the first Eclectic Reader is pictured here—ranged from simple to advanced and aimed to give students a happy, positive feeling. A college president at the end of his life, McGuffey began teaching in frontier Ohio schools when he was only 13.

School desk

schools at the primary level. Reformers believed that such schools could teach all children the basics of reading, writing, and arithmetic, as well as instill a work ethic. District schools were open to all and were supported by district taxes, state funds, and tuition paid by parents.

By the 1850s, tax-supported elementary schools had gained widespread support in the northeastern states and had begun to spread to the rest of the country. Rural areas responded more slowly because children were needed to help with planting and harvesting.

In the South, a reformer named **Calvin Wiley** played a similar role in North Carolina to that of Horace Mann in Massachusetts. In 1839 North Carolina began providing support to local communities that established taxpayer-funded schools. Wiley traveled throughout the state, building support for public education. By 1860, about two-thirds of North Carolina's white children attended school part of the year. The South as a whole responded less quickly, and only about one-third of southern white children were enrolled in public schools by 1860. African American children were excluded almost entirely.

Women's Education When officials talked about educating voters, they had men in mind—women were still not allowed to cast a ballot in the 1800s. Nonetheless, a number of women took advantage

of the reform movement to create more educational opportunities for girls and women.

Emma Willard, who founded a girls' boarding school in Vermont in 1814, was an early educational pioneer. Her school covered the usual subjects for young women, such as cooking and etiquette, but it also included academic subjects like history, math, and literature, which were rarely taught to women. In 1837 another educator, **Mary Lyon,** opened the Mount Holyoke Female Seminary in South Hadley, Massachusetts, the first institution of higher education for women only.

Also in the 1800s, **Elizabeth Blackwell** became the first woman to earn a medical degree in the United States or Europe. In 1857 she founded the New York Infirmary for Women and Children, which was staffed entirely by women.

✓ **Reading Check** **Identifying** What three areas of social reform did reformers target?

The Early Women's Movement

In the early 1800s, the Industrial Revolution began to change the economic roles of men and women. In the 1700s, most economic activity took place in or near the home because most Americans lived and worked in a rural farm setting. Although husbands and wives had distinct chores, maintaining the farm was the focus of their efforts. By the mid-1800s, these circumstances had started to change, especially in the northeastern states. The development of factories and other work centers separated the home from the workplace. Men now often left home to go to work, while women tended the house and children. In time, this development led to the emergence of the first women's movement.

"True Womanhood" As the nature of work changed, many Americans began to divide life into two spheres of activity—the home and the workplace. Many believed the home to be the proper sphere for women, partly because the outside world was seen as corrupt and dangerous, and partly because of popular ideas about the family.

The Christian revivalism of the 1820s and 1830s greatly influenced the American family. For many

Student Web Activity Visit the *American Vision* Web site at tav.glencoe.com and click on *Student Web Activities— Chapter 8* for an activity on reform movements.

---

3 ASSESS

Assign Section 3 Assessment as homework or as an in-class activity.

🔵 Have students use the **Interactive Tutor Self-Assessment CD-ROM.**

Reading Essentials and Study Guide 8–3

Name _____ Date _____ Class _____

Study Guide
Chapter 8, Section 3
For use with textbook pages 278–282
REFORMING SOCIETY

KEY TERMS AND NAMES
Dorothea Dix a reformer who worked to improve conditions for the mentally ill *(page 278)*
Lyman Beecher a minister who preached the power of individuals to improve themselves and society *(page 279)*
benevolent society organization that focused on spreading God's word and solving social problems *(page 279)*
temperance moderation in the consumption of alcohol *(page 279)*
penitentiary name given to prisons during the prison reform movement *(page 280)*
Horace Mann a leader of the public education movement *(page 280)*
Elizabeth Cady Stanton woman reformer in the antislavery movement who organized the first women's rights convention *(page 282)*

✓ **Reading Check**

Answer: temperance, prison reform, and education reform

FYI

Oberlin College was the first coeducational college and one of the first to admit African American students. Among Oberlin's first African American graduates was Fannie Jackson Coppin, who had been born enslaved. She went on to have a distinguished career as a teacher and school administrator.

HISTORY *Online*

Objectives and answers to the student activity can be found in the **Web Activity Lesson Plan** at tav.glencoe.com.

INTERDISCIPLINARY CONNECTIONS ACTIVITY

Sociology Invite a professor or women's activist to speak to your class about issues that face women in today's society in the United States and in other countries. The presentation should include social and economic issues. Ask the speaker to address topics that are appropriate for the young adult audience. Have the speaker work with the students to compare today's reform movements to those in the early and mid-1800s. **L2**

Section Quiz 8-3

Section Quiz 8-3

DIRECTIONS: Matching Match each item in Column A with the items in Column B.
Write the correct letters in the blanks. (10 points each)

Column A
___ 1. opened the first institution of higher education for women only
___ 2. one of the leaders of the public education movement
___ 3. active in the antislavery and women's movements
___ 4. gathering of women reformers that marked the beginning of an organized women's movement
___ 5. abstinence from alcohol

Column B
A. Mary Lyon
B. temperance
C. Elizabeth Cady Stanton
D. Horace Mann
E. Seneca Falls Convention

DIRECTIONS: Multiple Choice In the blank at the left, write the letter of the choice that best completes the statement or answers the question. (10 points each)

ABCNEWS INTERACTIVE™

📼 VIDEOCASSETTE
Historic America Electronic Field Trips

View **Tape 2, Chapter 6:** "Seneca Falls."

✓ Reading Check

Answer: Industrial Revolution, Christian revivalism, publication of Margaret Fuller's book, and Seneca Falls

Reteach

Ask students to identify the areas of society that were targeted for reform in the early to mid-1800s.

Enrich

Invite students to make a presentation or create a display about one of the women mentioned in this section.

4 CLOSE

Ask students to explain the connection between religious and social reform.

---

parents, raising children was treated as a solemn responsibility because it prepared young people for a disciplined Christian life. Women often were viewed as more moral and charitable than men, and they were expected to be models of piety and virtue to their children and husbands.

The idea that women should be homemakers and should take responsibility for developing their children's characters evolved into a set of ideas known as "true womanhood." Magazine articles and novels aimed at women reinforced the value of their role at home. In 1841 **Catherine Beecher,** a daughter of minister and reformer Lyman Beecher, wrote a book called *A Treatise on Domestic Economy.* The popular volume argued that women could find fulfillment at home and gave instruction on childcare, cooking, and health matters.

Women Seek Greater Rights Many women did not feel the ideas of true womanhood were limiting. Instead, the new ideas implied that wives were now partners with their husbands and in some ways were morally superior to them. Women were held up as the conscience of the home and society.

The idea that women had an important role to play in building a virtuous home was soon extended to making society more virtuous. As women became involved in the great moral crusades of the era, some began to argue that they needed greater political rights to promote their ideas.

An advocate of this idea was Margaret Fuller. Fuller argued that every woman had her own relationship with God and needed "as a soul to live freely and unimpeded." She declared, "We would have every arbitrary barrier thrown down and every path laid open to women as freely as to men." Fuller believed that if men and women, whom she called the "two sides" of human nature, were treated equally, it would end injustice in society.

In 1848 **Lucretia Mott** and **Elizabeth Cady Stanton,** two women active in the antislavery movement, organized the **Seneca Falls Convention.** This gathering of women reformers marked the beginning of an organized women's movement. The convention issued a "Declaration of Sentiments and Resolutions" that began with words expanding the Declaration of Independence: "We hold these truths to be self-evident: that all men and women are created equal. . . ." Stanton shocked many of the women present by proposing that they focus on gaining the right to vote. Nevertheless, the Seneca Falls Convention is considered by many to be the unofficial beginning of the struggle for women's voting rights. 📖 *(See page 1070 for more information on the "Declaration of Sentiments and Resolutions.")*

Throughout the 1850s, women continued to organize conventions to gain greater rights for themselves. The conventions did meet with some success. By 1860, for example, reformers had convinced 15 states to pass laws permitting married women to retain their property if their husbands died. Above all, these conventions drew attention to their cause and paved the way for a stronger movement to emerge after the Civil War.

✓ Reading Check
Examining What events of the mid-1800s sparked the first women's movement?

SECTION 3 ASSESSMENT

Checking for Understanding
1. **Define:** benevolent society, temperance, penitentiary.
2. **Identify:** Dorothea Dix, Lyman Beecher, Horace Mann, Elizabeth Cady Stanton.
3. **State** the main goal of the early women's movement.

Reviewing Themes
4. **Continuity and Change** How did the Second Great Awakening affect the reform movements of the mid-1800s?

Critical Thinking
5. **Evaluating** In what ways did the new penitentiaries change the prison system?
6. **Organizing** Use a graphic organizer similar to the one below to list the major reform areas.

Analyzing Visuals
7. **Examining Art** Study the painting of the New England school on page 280. How was the room heated? What kinds of supplies did the students have?

Writing About History
8. **Expository Writing** Think of reforms you believe are needed today in the United States. Write a letter to your legislator expressing why you believe the reforms are needed. Give examples of problems in your community as evidence.

SECTION 3 ASSESSMENT ANSWERS

1. Terms are in blue.
2. Dorothea Dix (p. 278), Lyman Beecher (p. 279), Horace Mann (p. 280), Elizabeth Cady Stanton (p. 282)
3. Women wanted greater political rights.
4. It encouraged people to work for reform and brought many women into the reform movement.
5. better facilities and opportunities for rehabilitation
6. temperance movement, prison reform, education reform, women's rights
7. A fireplace provided heat. There are no individual desks, but each student has a book.
8. Students' letters will vary. Letters should focus on problems that are major issues today.

American LITERATURE

Henry David Thoreau was part of the Transcendentalist movement that started as a reform movement within the Unitarian Church. Transcendentalism stressed the connection of the soul of the individual to the soul of the world. Simply put, the Transcendentalists believed that God resided in each person. None of the works of poetry and prose during this period more fully embodied Transcendental ideals than Thoreau's *Walden*. Part journal, part social commentary, and part sermon, the work summarizes and expands Thoreau's experiences at Walden Pond, near Concord, Massachusetts, where he built a cabin and lived in relative solitude for two years.

Read to Discover
What does Thoreau say we must do to live in society?

Reader's Dictionary
swath: path
sublime: supreme; awesome
perturbation: annoyance; irritation

from Walden
by Henry David Thoreau

I went to the woods because I wished to live deliberately, to front only the essential facts of life, and see if I could not learn what it had to teach, and not, when I came to die, discover that I had not lived. I did not wish to live what was not life, living is so dear; nor did I wish to practice resignation, unless it was quite necessary. I wanted to live deep and suck out all the marrow of life, to live so sturdily and Spartan-like as to put to rout all that was not life, to cut a broad swath and shave close, to drive life into a corner, and reduce it to its lowest terms, and, if it proved to be mean, why then to get the whole and genuine meanness of it, and publish its meanness to the world; or if it were sublime, to know it by experience. . . . For most men, it appears to me, are in a strange uncertainty about it, whether it is of the devil or of God, and have *somewhat hastily* concluded that it is the chief end of man here to "glorify God and enjoy him forever."

Still we live meanly, like ants. . . . Our life is frittered away by detail. An honest man has hardly need to count more than his ten fingers. . . . Simplicity, simplicity, simplicity! I say, let your affairs be as two or three, and not a hundred or a thousand; instead of a million count half a dozen, and keep your accounts on your thumbnail. . . .

Let us spend one day as deliberately as Nature, and not be thrown off the track by every nutshell and mosquito's wing that falls on the rails. . . . Why should we knock under and go with the stream?

Analyzing Literature

1. **Recall** What motivated Thoreau to go and live alone in the wilderness?
2. **Interpret** What do you think the phrase "every nutshell and mosquito's wing" means?
3. **Evaluate and Connect** Do you think you could live alone in the woods for two years as Thoreau did? Why or why not?

Interdisciplinary Activity

Language Arts Imagine you are Thoreau at the end of your first year at Walden. Write a diary entry describing your feelings looking back on the first year and ahead to the year to come.

Read to Discover
Answer: Thoreau advocated simplifying one's life.

Reinforcing Vocabulary
Have students use the words *swath, sublime,* and *perturbation* in sentences. Instruct students to use a standard dictionary to look up the meaning of the word *rout* as it is used in the excerpt and then use it properly in a sentence. *(to drive out)* Ask students what *Spartan-like* means. *(having great courage or discipline)*

Historical Connection
During his stay at Walden, Thoreau refused to pay his taxes as a protest against the war with Mexico and slavery. Although he spent only one night in jail, he became a proponent of nonviolent protests of unfair laws. In 1849 he published the essay "Civil Disobedience." Ask students if they can think of any other famous advocates of civil disobedience. *(Mahatma Gandhi and Martin Luther King, Jr., are two examples.)*

HISTORY Online
Refer to tav.glencoe.com for additional Glencoe Literature titles, lesson plans, and study guides related to this unit.

Answers to Analyzing Literature

1. He wanted to experience the essence of life with no unnecessary interference.
2. the details, every little thing
3. Students' answers will vary. Encourage students to think of the positive and negative aspects of living alone in the woods.

Interdisciplinary Activity
Diary entries will vary. Entries should express feelings about what has already happened and what is yet to come.

1 FOCUS

Section Overview

This section describes the abolitionist movement that sought to bring an end to slavery.

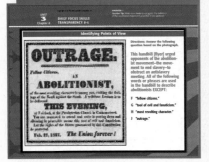
Guide to Reading

Answers to Graphic:

1790s	First antislavery societies
1816	American Colonization Society (ACS) is founded.
1821	ACS acquires land in West Africa.
1831	William Lloyd Garrison begins publishing *The Liberator.*
1832	Britain abolishes slavery; New England Antislavery Society is founded.
1833	American Antislavery Society is founded; Prudence Crandall is arrested.
1840s	Sojourner Truth's eloquent speeches draw huge crowds.

Preteaching Vocabulary
Have students use the glossary to look up the meanings of *gradualism*, *abolition*, and *emancipation*.

The Abolitionist Movement

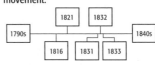

Guide to Reading

Main Idea
In the midst of the nation's reform movement, a number of citizens embarked on a crusade known as abolitionism to end slavery in the United States.

Key Terms and Names
gradualism, American Colonization Society, abolition, William Lloyd Garrison, emancipation, American Antislavery Society, Frederick Douglass

Reading Strategy
Sequencing As you read about the beginning of the abolitionist movement, complete a time line similar to the one below to record early events of this movement.

```
        1821   1832
1790s ─┐ ┌─ ──── ─┐     ┌─ 1840s
       1816  1831  1833
```

Reading Objectives
• **List** groups involved in the early abolitionist movement.
• **Analyze** how Northerners and Southerners viewed abolitionism.

Section Theme
Individual Action Abolitionist reformers challenged the morality and legality of slavery in the United States.

Preview of Events

♦1830	♦1832	♦1834	♦1836

1831
William Lloyd Garrison begins publishing the *Liberator*

1833
Prudence Crandall arrested; American Antislavery Society founded

1834
Mob attacks William Lloyd Garrison

1836
House of Representatives adopts gag rule on abolitionist petitions

---

★ An American Story ★

William Lloyd Garrison

In 1831 William Lloyd Garrison began publishing a fiery antislavery newspaper in Boston. One day in 1834, a large group gathered outside Garrison's office to express its disapproval of his views. An onlooker, Thomas Low Nichols, described what followed:

❝I was in the editorial office of Mr. Garrison when the crowd began to gather in the street below. . . . There were hundreds—then thousands. It was a mob of people dressed in black broadcloth, a mob of gentlemen—capitalists, merchants, bankers, a mob of the Stock Exchange and of the first people in Boston, which considered itself the nicest of cities, and intellectually the 'hub of the universe'. . . . There was a great howl of rage; but, a moment after, it became a yell of triumph. Garrison had been seen to go from the building into a narrow lane behind it. Pursued, he took refuge in a carpenter's shop, only to be dragged out and carried into the midst of the mob. . . . I saw him, his hat off, his bald head shining, his scanty locks flying, his face pale. . . .❞

—quoted in *Witness to America*

Early Opposition to Slavery

By the 1830s, a growing number of Americans had begun to demand an immediate end to slavery in the South. Of all the reform movements that began in the early 1800s, the movement to end slavery was the most divisive. By pitting North against South, it polarized the nation and helped bring about the Civil War.

Gradualism From the earliest days of the Republic, many Americans had opposed slavery. Many of the country's founders knew that a nation based on the principles of liberty and equality would have difficulty remaining true to its ideals if it continued to enslave human beings. Quakers and Baptists in both the North and South had long argued that slavery was a sin. After the Revolution, Baptists in Virginia called for "every legal measure to [wipe out] this horrid evil from the land."

Early antislavery societies generally supported an approach known as gradualism, or the belief that slavery had to be ended gradually. First they would stop new slaves from being brought into the country. Then they would phase out slavery in the North and the Upper South before finally ending slavery in the Lower South. Slaveholders would also be compensated for their loss. Supporters of gradualism believed it would give the South's economy time to adjust to the loss of enslaved labor.

Colonization The first antislavery societies also believed that ending slavery would not end racism in the United States. Many thought that the best solution was to send African Americans back to their ancestral homelands in Africa. In December 1816, antislavery reformers founded the **American Colonization Society** (ACS) to move African Americans to Africa. The society had the support of many prominent Americans, including James Madison, James Monroe, Henry Clay, Daniel Webster, and John Marshall.

By 1821 the ACS had acquired land in West Africa. The following year, free African Americans began boarding ships chartered by the society to take them to Africa. There they established a colony that eventually became the country of Liberia. It declared its independence as a republic in 1847 and adopted a constitution designed after the U.S. Constitution. The capital, Monrovia, was named for President Monroe.

Colonization was never a realistic solution to slavery and racism, however. The cost of transporting African Americans was high, and the ACS had to depend on donations. Moving the roughly 1.5 million African Americans who lived in the United States in 1820 to Africa was nearly impossible. Furthermore, most African Americans regarded the United States as their home and were not prepared to migrate to another continent. Only an estimated 12,000 African Americans moved to Africa between 1821 and 1860.

✔ **Reading Check** **Identifying** What two religious groups were among the first to oppose slavery?

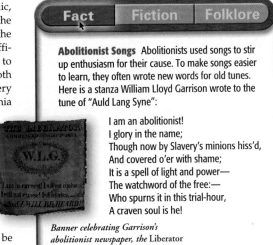

Abolitionist Songs Abolitionists used songs to stir up enthusiasm for their cause. To make songs easier to learn, they often wrote new words for old tunes. Here is a stanza William Lloyd Garrison wrote to the tune of "Auld Lang Syne":

> I am an abolitionist!
> I glory in the name;
> Though now by Slavery's minions hiss'd,
> And covered o'er with shame;
> It is a spell of light and power—
> The watchword of the free:—
> Who spurns it in this trial-hour,
> A craven soul is he!

Banner celebrating Garrison's abolitionist newspaper, the Liberator

The New Abolitionists

Gradualism and colonization remained the main goals of antislavery groups until the 1830s, when a new idea, abolition, began to gain ground. Abolitionists argued that enslaved African Americans should be freed immediately, without gradual measures or compensation to former slaveholders.

TURNING POINT

Garrison Stirs a New Movement Abolitionism began to gain support in the 1830s for several reasons. As with other reform movements of the era, it drew its strength from the Second Great Awakening, with its focus on sin and repentance. In the eyes of abolitionists, slavery was an enormous evil of which the country needed to repent.

The first well-known advocate of abolition was a free African American from North Carolina named **David Walker,** who published *Appeal to the Colored Citizens of the World.* In this pamphlet, Walker advocated violence and rebellion as the only way to end slavery. Although Walker's ideas were influential, the rapid development of a large national abolitionist movement in the 1830s was largely due to the efforts of **William Lloyd Garrison.**

In 1829 Garrison became assistant to Benjamin Lundy, the Quaker publisher of the Baltimore antislavery newspaper, *Genius of Universal Emancipation.* Garrison admired Lundy but grew impatient with his gradualist approach. In 1831 Garrison left his mentor and, with fellow abolitionist Isaac Knapp, founded Boston's antislavery newspaper, the *Liberator.*

CHAPTER 8 The Spirit of Reform **285**

---

2 TEACH

Daily Lecture and Discussion Notes 8–4

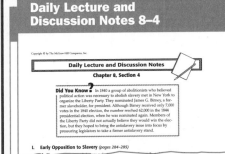

Copyright © by The McGraw-Hill Companies, Inc.

Daily Lecture and Discussion Notes
Chapter 8, Section 4

Did You Know ■ In 1840 a group of abolitionists who believed political action was necessary to abolish slavery met in New York to organize the Liberty Party. They nominated James G. Birney, a former slaveholder, for president. Although Birney received only 7,000 votes in the 1840 election, the number reached 62,000 in the 1844 presidential election, when he was nominated again. Members of the Liberty Party did not actually believe they would win the election, but they hoped to bring the antislavery issue into focus by pressuring legislators to take a firmer antislavery stand.

I. **Early Opposition to Slavery** *(pages 284–285)*

Abolitionists used a wide variety of media to generate enthusiasm for their cause. Examples were included in a 1994 exhibit at the Library of Congress—"The African-American Mosaic." At the library's Web site, you can find electronic images of abolitionists' publications including an advertisement for an antislavery fair, a page of sheet music, and a poem. The address for the Library of Congress Web site is http://www.loc.gov.

Giving an Oral Presentation
Have students prepare a short oral presentation about one of the abolitionists mentioned in this section. Encourage students to use library and Internet resources to learn more about their subjects. **L1**

🗀 Use the rubric for oral presentation, monologue, song, or skit on pages 75–76 in the *Performance Assessment Activities and Rubrics.*

✔ **Reading Check**
Answer: Quakers and Baptists

COOPERATIVE LEARNING ACTIVITY

Creating Charts Organize the class into groups of three. In each group, one person will research gradualism; one, colonization; and one, abolition. Have each student report to the group the reasons that the other group members should support his or her point of view. Have the other two students respond with reasons opposing each point of view. Based on the research and discussion, have the groups prepare a pro/con chart for each of the three proposed methods for ending slavery. 🗀

Use the rubric for a cooperative group management plan on pages 81–82 in the *Performance Assessment Activities and Rubrics.*

Profiles **IN HISTORY**

Ask students what other event in history seems remarkably similar to the incident described in the profile of Prudence Crandall. (*desegregation of schools during the 1950s and 1960s*)

Drawing Conclusions Point out to students that the Constitution allowed slavery, that it was against the law to help enslaved African Americans escape, and that the law required runaway enslaved persons to be returned to their masters. Yet many aboli-tionists broke the law. Give stu-dents five minutes to write their thoughts about the following: Are there some situations in which breaking the law is an acceptable protest? Then have students use the thoughts they have written to participate in a class discussion about whether abolitionists should have broken the law to help enslaved persons escape. You should extend the discussion to include other situa-tions in which it might be acceptable to break the law as a form of protest. **L2**

Profiles IN HISTORY

Prudence Crandall
1803–1890

In 1831 Prudence Crandall was running a successful school for girls in Canterbury, Connecticut, when Sarah Harris, the daugh-ter of a prominent African American farmer, sought admission. When Crandall agreed to let her in, local parents objected, and many withdrew their chil-dren from the school.

Rather than reverse her decision, Crandall announced that she was re-organizing her school as a teacher-training institution for African American women. The citizens of Canterbury erupted in protest. To combat Crandall's effort, the state leg-islature passed the "Black Law," which forbade Connecticut schools from admitting out-of-state African American students and severely limited the type of schools that in-state African Americans could attend. Crandall ignored the law and was arrested in August 1833.

In a highly publicized case, prosecutors con-victed her, but her convic-tion was overturned on appeal. In the wake of the trial, residents terrorized the school, dirtying its well, refusing it supplies, and creating other hardships. In 1834, Crandall closed her school.

Upon her death nearly 60 years later, a friend recalled her willingness to fight for what she believed in. "She had deep convictions of right. . . . Neither death, life, angels, principalities, things pres-ent, things to come, heights, depths, nor any other creature could keep her from following her convictions."

The paper's style was anything but moderate, as Garrison wrote caustic attacks on slavery and called for an immediate end to it. To those who objected to his fiery language, he responded that the time for moderation was over:

> ❝I am aware that many object to the severity of my language; but is there not cause for severity? I will be as harsh as truth and as uncompromising as justice. On this subject I do not wish to think, or speak, or write with moderation. No! No! Tell a man whose house is on fire to give a moderate alarm; tell him to moderately rescue his wife from the hands of the rav-isher; tell the mother to gradually [remove] her babe from the fire into which it has fallen—but urge me not to use moderation in a cause like the present. I am in earnest; I will not equivocate; I will not excuse; I will not retreat a single inch—AND I WILL BE HEARD.❞
>
> —from the *Liberator*

With his balding head, his steel-rimmed glasses, and his plain black suits, Garrison was as mild-look-ing as his words were strong. Inside this soft-spoken man, however, an intense passion burned. In his

mind, the situation was very clear: Slavery was immoral and slaveholders were evil. The only option was immediate and com-plete emancipation, or the freeing of all enslaved people.

Garrison soon attracted enough follow-ers in the North to enable him to found the New England Antislavery Society in 1832 and the **American Antislavery Society** in 1833. Membership in both organizations grew quickly. By the mid-1830s, there were hundreds of society chapters, and in 1838, there were more than 1,350 chapters with over 250,000 members.

Other Abolitionists at Work As the anti-slavery movement gained momentum, new leaders emerged from Garrison's shadow and carried on the effort. Theodore Weld, a disciple of the evangelist Charles Grandison Finney, was one of the most effective lead-ers, recruiting and training many abolition-ists for the American Antislavery Society. Arthur and Lewis Tappan, two devout and wealthy brothers from New York City, also emerged as leaders.

The orator Wendell Phillips, the poet John Greenleaf Whittier, and many others became active in the cause as well. Many women also gave their efforts to the abolitionist movement. Prudence Crandall worked as a teacher and aboli-tionist in Connecticut, and Lucretia Mott often spoke out in favor of abolitionism. Some Southern women also joined the crusade. Among the earliest were Sarah and Angelina Grimké, South Carolina sisters who moved north to work openly against slavery.

African American Abolitionists Not surprisingly, free African Americans took a prominent role in the abolitionist movement. African Americans in the North, who numbered over 190,000 by 1850, endured much prejudice, but they cherished their freedom nonetheless. When Garrison launched his newspa-per, African Americans rushed to his support, not only buying the paper but also helping to sell it. Many began writing and speaking out against slav-ery and taking part in protests and demonstrations.

One of the most prominent African American fig-ures in the movement was **Frederick Douglass,** who had escaped from slavery in Maryland. Douglass was a brilliant thinker and an electrifying speaker. "I appear before the immense assembly this evening as a thief and a robber," he told one Massachusetts

---

MEETING SPECIAL NEEDS

Auditory/Musical Have interested students work individually or in small groups to create an abo-litionist song. Encourage students to use a tune they already know and adapt the lyrics to fit the message. Have students perform their songs for the class. **L1**

☞ Refer to *Inclusion for the High School Social Studies Classroom Strategies and Activities* in the TCR.

Self-Check Quiz
Visit the *American Vision* Web site at tav.glencoe.com and click on *Self-Check Quizzes—Chapter 8* to assess your knowledge of chapter content.

now in operation are not all filled, and it is very doubtful if they are productive or of much real benefit. Would it not redound as much to the advantage of young persons, and to the honour of the State, if they should pass their days in the cotton patch, or at the plow, or in the cornfield, instead of being [confined] in a school house, where they are earning nothing?**99**

—from the *Raleigh Register,* November 9, 1829

a. What reasons does the author give for opposing free public education?

b. Are the author's reasons valid? Explain your answer.

Practicing Skills

25. Developing a Multimedia Presentation Develop a plan for a presentation on the social and cultural changes in the United States discussed in this chapter. Consider the following points to help guide you.
a. What specific examples would you use to show the different social and cultural changes taking place in the country?
b. What form of media would you use for each example?

Writing Activity

26. Portfolio Writing You read in a Boston newspaper that the Massachusetts legislature is going to hear statements from citizens concerning the care of the mentally ill. Prepare and write a paper that you can read to the committee members on this subject. In the paper, explain your ideas on caring for the mentally ill and whether or not you feel society has an obligation to do so. Save the paper in your portfolio.

Chapter Activities

27. Research Project Conduct research to learn more about one reformer discussed in the chapter. Role-play the person by introducing yourself to the class and describing your background, what you want to reform, and how you will go about making these improvements.

28. American History Primary Source Document Library CD-ROM Read "Women's Rights" by Sojourner Truth, under *The Growing Nation*. Imagine that you are a reporter for a newspaper and your assignment is to cover the Ohio Women's Convention. Write an article in which you review Truth's speech. In your article, explain her arguments for women's rights and describe how members of the convention reacted to her speech.

Voter Participation, 1824–1840

Percent of Eligible Voters Who Voted

Election Years	Percent
1824	26.9%
1828	57.6%
1832	55.4%
1836	57.8%
1840	80.2%

Source: *Historical Statistics of the United States: Colonial Times to 1970.*

Geography and History

29. The graph above shows voter participation from 1824 to 1840. Study the graph, and then answer the questions below.
a. Interpreting Graphs In which presidential election year did voter participation increase the most from the previous presidential election year?
b. Applying Graph Skills What do you think accounted for the increase in voter participation?

The Princeton Review

Standardized Test Practice

Directions: Read the passage below and answer the question that follows.

Susan B. Anthony, who was raised as a Quaker, was a powerful organizer in the women's rights movement. A dedicated reformer, she joined the temperance movement and worked for the American Antislavery Society.

Sojourner Truth, a former enslaved person, spoke out against slavery and in defense of women's rights. Truth often attended women's rights conventions to remind women that their African American sisters had a place in the movement.

Susan B. Anthony and Sojourner Truth both worked for which of the following reforms?

A Abolitionism and education

B Education and temperance

C Temperance and women's rights

D Women's rights and abolitionism

Test-Taking Tip: The important word in this question is *both*. Several reform movements are mentioned, but the question asks about the reforms *both* women supported.

Chapter Activities

27. Introductions will vary but should include specific facts from the reformer's life and an explanation of his or her point of view.

28. Articles will vary but should clearly explain her arguments and the reaction to her speech.

Geography and History

29. a. 1828; **b.** Many states had eliminated property ownership as a voting qualification.

The Princeton Review

Standardized Test Practice

Answer: D
Test-Taking Tip: Remind students to look for clues in the passage. For example, since Sojourner Truth was a former enslaved person, she likely supported abolition. Therefore, you can narrow the choices to A and D.

HISTORY Online

Have students visit the Web site at tav.glencoe.com to review Chapter 8 and take the Self-Check Quiz.

Bonus Question ?

Ask: What were the facts and the judgment in the case *Worcester* v. *Georgia*? *(The Cherokee filed suit against the government of Georgia in an attempt to stop the forced removal of the Cherokee to what is now Oklahoma. When the case reached the Supreme Court, the court ordered the state officials to respect the Native Americans' property rights. President Jackson refused to enforce the ruling, and President Van Buren sent in the army to remove the Cherokee by force.)*

Critical Thinking

21. Native Americans

22. optimism about human nature and a belief in people's ability to redefine their lives

23. religious revival, prison reform, education reform, women's education, women's rights, abolitionism

24. a. The author's reasons included scarcity of money, existence of plenty of schools, available space in existing schools, questionable benefit of schooling, and lack of earnings for children while they are in school.
b. Students' responses will vary but should express a clear point of view.

Practicing Skills

25. Students' presentations will vary but should include multiple forms of media.

Writing Activity

26. Students' papers will vary but should include a set of specific recommendations for caring for the mentally ill.

Chapter 9 Resources

Timesaving Tools

TeacherWorks™ All-In-One Planner and Resource Center

- **Interactive Teacher Edition** Access your Teacher Wraparound Edition and your classroom resources with a few easy clicks.
- **Interactive Lesson Planner** Planning has never been easier! Organize your week, month, semester, or year with all the lesson helps you need to make teaching creative, timely, and relevant.

Use Glencoe's **Presentation Plus!** multimedia teacher tool to easily present dynamic lessons that visually excite your students. Using Microsoft PowerPoint® you can customize the presentations to create your own personalized lessons.

TEACHING TRANSPARENCIES

Graphic Organizer 9

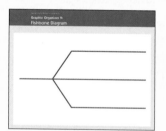

Why It Matters Chapter Transparency 9

APPLICATION AND ENRICHMENT

Linking Past and Present Activity 9

Enrichment Activity 9

Primary Source Reading 9

REVIEW AND REINFORCEMENT

Reteaching Activity 9

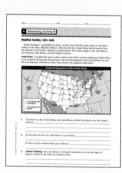

Vocabulary Activity 9

Time Line Activity 9

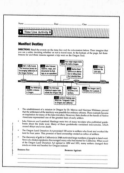

Critical Thinking Skills Activity 9

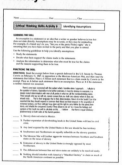

Meeting NCSS Standards

The following standards are highlighted in Chapter 9:

Section 1   VIII   Science, Technology, and Society: A, B
Section 2   V   Individuals, Groups, and Institutions: B, C, E, F
Section 3   II   Time, Continuity, and Change: B, C, D

Local Standards

Chapter 9 Resources

**Chapter 9 Test
Form A**

**Chapter 9 Test
Form B**

**Standardized Test Skills
Practice Workbook Activity 9**

**Performance Assessment
Activities and Rubrics 9**

**ExamView® Pro
Testmaker CD-ROM**

MULTIMEDIA

- 🔘 **Vocabulary PuzzleMaker CD-ROM**
- 🔘 **Interactive Tutor Self-Assessment CD-ROM**
- 🔘 **ExamView® Pro Testmaker CD-ROM**
- 🔘 **Audio Program**
- 🔘 **American History Primary Source Documents Library CD-ROM**
- 📼 **MindJogger Videoquiz**
- 🔘 **Presentation Plus! CD-ROM**
- 🔘 **TeacherWorks™ CD-ROM**
- 🔘 **Interactive Student Edition CD-ROM**
- 🔘 **Glencoe Skillbuilder Interactive Workbook CD-ROM, Level 2**
- 📼 **The *American Vision* Video Program**
- 🎵 **American Music: Hits Through History**
- 🎵 **American Music: Cultural Traditions**

SPANISH RESOURCES

The following Spanish language materials are available in the Spanish Resources Binder:

- **Spanish Guided Reading Activities**
- **Spanish Reteaching Activities**
- **Spanish Quizzes and Tests**
- **Spanish Vocabulary Activities**
- **Spanish Summaries**
- **The Declaration of Independence and United States Constitution Spanish Translation**

THE HISTORY CHANNEL®

The following videotape program is available from Glencoe as a supplement to Chapter 9:

• **The Alamo** (Two Video Set) (ISBN 1-56-501784-6)

To order, call Glencoe at 1-800-334-7344. To find classroom resources to accompany many of these videos, check the following home pages:
A&E Television: www.aande.com
The History Channel: www.historychannel.com

HISTORY Online

Use our Web site for additional resources. All essential content is covered in the Student Edition.

You and your students can visit tav.glencoe.com, the Web site companion to the ***American Vision.*** This innovative integration of electronic and print media offers your students a wealth of opportunities. The student text directs students to the Web site for the following options:

- **Chapter Overviews**
- **Student Web Activities**
- **Self-Check Quizzes**
- **Textbook Updates**

Answers to the student Web activities are provided for you in the **Web Activity Lesson Plans.** Additional Web resources and Interactive Tutor Puzzles are also available.

Chapter 9 Resources

SECTION RESOURCES

Daily Objectives	Reproducible Resources	Multimedia Resources
SECTION 1 **The Western Pioneers** 1. Discuss the inventions that made it easier to farm the plains. 2. Analyze why Americans were willing to give up their lives in the East to move to the West.	Reproducible Lesson Plan 9–1 Daily Lecture and Discussion Notes 9–1 Guided Reading Activity 9–1* Section Quiz 9–1* Reading Essentials and Study Guide 9–1 Performance Assessment Activities and Rubrics	Daily Focus Skills Transparency 9–1 American Art & Architecture Interactive Tutor Self-Assessment CD-ROM ExamView® Pro Testmaker CD-ROM Presentation Plus! CD-ROM TeacherWorks™ CD-ROM Audio Program American Music: Hits Through History
SECTION 2 **Independence for Texas** 1. Chronicle the opening of Texas to American settlers. 2. Discuss the major battles of the war against Mexico.	Reproducible Lesson Plan 9–2 Daily Lecture and Discussion Notes 9–2 Guided Reading Activity 9–2* Section Quiz 9–2* Reading Essentials and Study Guide 9–2 Performance Assessment Activities and Rubrics	Daily Focus Skills Transparency 9–2 Interactive Tutor Self-Assessment CD-ROM ExamView® Pro Testmaker CD-ROM Presentation Plus! CD-ROM Skillbuilder Interactive Workbook, Level 2 TeacherWorks™ CD-ROM Audio Program ABCNews Interactive™ Historic America Electronic Field Trip
SECTION 3 **The War with Mexico** 1. Describe the circumstances under which Texas and Oregon were admitted to the Union. 2. Discuss the major events of the war with Mexico.	Reproducible Lesson Plan 9–3 Daily Lecture and Discussion Notes 9–3 Guided Reading Activity 9–3* Section Quiz 9–3* Reading Essentials and Study Guide 9–3 Performance Assessment Activities and Rubrics	Daily Focus Skills Transparency 9–3 Interactive Tutor Self-Assessment CD-ROM ExamView® Pro Testmaker CD-ROM Presentation Plus! CD-ROM TeacherWorks™ CD-ROM Vocabulary PuzzleMaker CD-ROM Audio Program

0:00 OUT OF TIME?
Assign the Chapter 9 **Reading Essentials and Study Guide.**

*Also Available in Spanish

Blackline Master	Transparency	CD-ROM	DVD
Poster	Music Program	Audio Program	Videocassette

NATIONAL GEOGRAPHIC Teacher's Corner

INDEX TO NATIONAL GEOGRAPHIC MAGAZINE

The following articles relate to this chapter.

- "Along the Santa Fe Trail," February 1989
- "The American Prairie: Roots of the Sky," October 1993
- "The Cherokee," May 1995
- "Life and Death on the Oregon Trail: The Itch to Move West," August 1986
- "Tex-Mex Border," February 1996
- "The Way West," September 2000

NATIONAL GEOGRAPHIC SOCIETY PRODUCTS AVAILABLE FROM GLENCOE

To order the following products for use with this chapter, contact your local Glencoe sales representative, or call Glencoe at 1-800-334-7344:

- *NGS PictureShow: Story of America, Part 1*
- *PicturePack: The Westward Movement* (Transparencies)
- *PictureShow: The Westward Movement* (CD-ROM)

ADDITIONAL NATIONAL GEOGRAPHIC SOCIETY PRODUCTS

To order the following, call National Geographic at 1-800-368-2728:

- *American Indians: A Brief History* (Video)

NGS ONLINE

Access National Geographic's Web site for current events, atlas updates, activities, links, interactive features, and archives.
www.nationalgeographic.com

From the Classroom of...

Heather W. Riehl
Ewing Township Public Schools
Ewing, NJ

Manifest Destiny Debate

Organize the class into groups of three or four students. Assign members of each group the roles of Speaker, Recorder, Traveler, and Checker. Provide half of the groups this statement: "It is neither the right nor the duty of the United States to expand to the Pacific Ocean." Provide the other half of the groups this statement: "It is the right and the duty of the United States to expand to the Pacific Ocean."

Have the students brainstorm information to support their statement. The Checker should make sure each student contributes an idea; the Recorder should write down each idea.

After three minutes, send each Traveler to another group that is defending the same statement. Have him or her listen to the group's ideas and let him or her share any other ideas from his/her group. Continue moving the Travelers from group to group until they have visited all groups. Move the desks into two groups now facing each other and ask the Speakers to take turns sharing their arguments to the other side.

ADDITIONAL RESOURCES FROM GLENCOE

- American Music: Cultural Traditions
- American Art & Architecture
- Outline Map Resource Book
- U.S. Desk Map
- Building Geography Skills for Life
- Inclusion for the High School Social Studies Classroom Strategies and Activities
- Teaching Strategies for the American History Classroom (Including Block Scheduling Pacing Guides)

KEY TO ABILITY LEVELS

Teaching strategies have been coded.

L1 BASIC activities for all students
L2 AVERAGE activities for average to above-average students
L3 CHALLENGING activities for above-average students
ELL ENGLISH LANGUAGE LEARNER activities

 Block Schedule

Activities that are suited to use within the block scheduling framework are identified by:

Why It Matters Activity

Ask students to compare the locations of the large cities in the mid-1800s with the locations of today's large cities. Ask students to write a paragraph suggesting reasons for the locations of today's large cities. Students should evaluate their answers after they have completed the chapter.

GLENCOE
TECHNOLOGY

The *American Vision* Video Program

To learn more about American westward expansion, have students view the Chapter 9 video, "Manifest Destiny," from the *American Vision* **Video Program.**

 Available in DVD and VHS

MindJogger Videoquiz

Use the **MindJogger Videoquiz** to preview Chapter 9 content.

Available in VHS

CHAPTER
9 Manifest Destiny *1835–1848*

Why It Matters

In this period, Americans strove to expand the nation's boundaries. Many believed they had a "manifest destiny" to spread democratic ideals. Others simply wanted to go west to find a new and better life. In Texas, settlers came into conflict with Mexico, while those going west on the Oregon Trail came into conflict with Native Americans.

The Impact Today

Developments of the era have left a legacy for Americans.
- *The nation now stretches from the Atlantic to the Pacific Oceans.*
- *Americans remain a restless people, ready to move to pursue economic opportunity.*
- *Many Americans continue to view themselves as destined to succeed and prosper.*

 The American Vision *Video* *The Chapter 9 video, "Manifest Destiny," chronicles the war between Texas and Mexico from the Mexican point of view.*

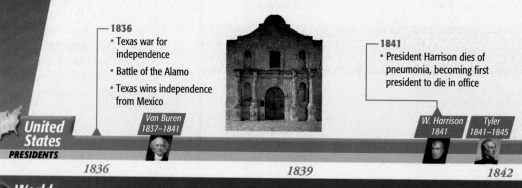

1836
- Texas war for independence
- Battle of the Alamo
- Texas wins independence from Mexico

1841
- President Harrison dies of pneumonia, becoming first president to die in office

Van Buren 1837–1841

W. Harrison 1841

Tyler 1841–1845

United States
PRESIDENTS

1836   *1839*   *1842*

World

1839
- First pedal-propelled bicycle designed by Kirkpatrick MacMillan of Scotland

1842
- China cedes Hong Kong to Britain

292

TWO-MINUTE LESSON LAUNCHER

Provide a large U.S. map and sticky notes to students. Have each student write the name of the place that they have visited that is the farthest from your current location. Have students mount their sticky notes at the approximate location of the site. Ask students to describe what they enjoyed about the location. Then ask if they would want to live in this location.

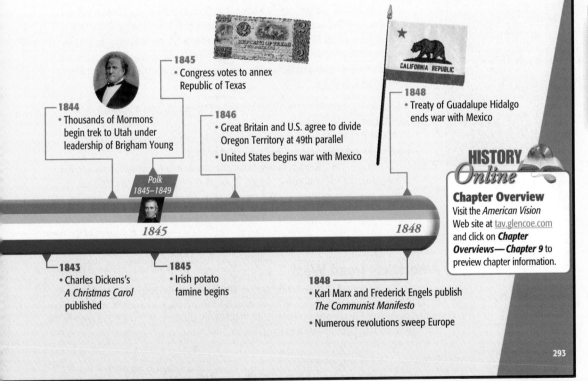

The Emigrant Train Bedding Down for the Night by Kenneth John Myers, 1867

HISTORY
Online

Introduce students to chapter content and key terms by having them access the **Chapter 9 Overview** at tav.glencoe.com.

More About the Art

Have students share travel experiences with the class. Then have them examine the picture to note similarities and differences between their travel experiences and those of the people pictured.

TIME LINE

ACTIVITY

Have students explain each event on the United States portion of the time line as it relates to Manifest Destiny.

1844
• Thousands of Mormons begin trek to Utah under leadership of Brigham Young

1845
• Congress votes to annex Republic of Texas

1846
• Great Britain and U.S. agree to divide Oregon Territory at 49th parallel
• United States begins war with Mexico

1848
• Treaty of Guadalupe Hidalgo ends war with Mexico

CALIFORNIA REPUBLIC

Polk
1845–1849

1845   *1848*

1843
• Charles Dickens's *A Christmas Carol* published

1845
• Irish potato famine begins

1848
• Karl Marx and Frederick Engels publish *The Communist Manifesto*
• Numerous revolutions sweep Europe

HISTORY
Online

Chapter Overview
Visit the *American Vision* Web site at tav.glencoe.com and click on *Chapter Overviews—Chapter 9* to preview chapter information.

293

GRAPHIC ORGANIZER ACTIVITY

Organizing Information Have students use a graphic organizer similar to the one shown below to connect military leaders with the battles for which they are best known.

Leader	Battle
William B. Travis	The Alamo
James W. Fannin	Goliad
Sam Houston	Battle of San Jacinto
John C. Frémont	California Uprising
Winfield Scott	Mexico City

293

1 FOCUS

Section Overview

This section describes the nation's westward expansion.

BELLRINGER
Skillbuilder Activity

Project transparency and have students answer the question.

Available as a blackline master.

Daily Focus Skills Transparency 9–1

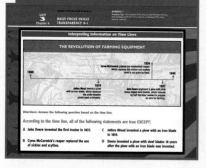

Guide to Reading

Answers to Graphic: possible answers: Oregon Trail, California Trail, Santa Fe Trail, Mormon Trail, Old Spanish Trail, Butterfield Overland Mail Trail, Pony Express Trail

Preteaching Vocabulary
Have students write short sentences to describe each of the Key Names.

SECTION 1 The Western Pioneers

Guide to Reading

Main Idea
In the 1840s, Americans headed west to the frontier states of the Midwest and the rich lands of California and Oregon.

Key Terms and Names
John Louis O'Sullivan, Manifest Destiny, squatter, Jethro Wood, John Deere, Cyrus McCormick, John Sutter, Kit Carson, Jim Bridger, overlander, Donner Party, Brigham Young

Reading Strategy
Organizing As you read about the westward movement of emigrants in the 1840s, complete a graphic organizer similar to the one below by filling in the names of the main trails they used.

Trails to the West

Reading Objectives
- **Discuss** the inventions that made it easier to farm the plains.
- **Analyze** why Americans were willing to give up their lives in the East to move to the West.

Section Theme
Science and Technology Several inventions of this period helped make settling the West possible.

Preview of Events

◆1835	◆1840	◆1845	◆1850
1834 McCormick reaper patented	**1841** Preemption Act passed	**1847** The Mormons arrive at the Great Salt Lake	**1851** Treaty of Fort Laramie signed

★ An American Story ★

Mary Richardson Walker

Mary Richardson Walker, a young woman from the East with a strong religious faith, wanted to serve God as a missionary to Native Americans. In April 1838 she and her husband started out from Missouri, bound for Oregon. After a 129-day trek along the Oregon Trail, they established a mission at Tshimakain near what is now Spokane, Washington, and began their efforts to convert the Nez Perce people to Christianity. She wrote in her diary of some of her experiences:

❝January 21, 1839. The Indians have covered our house with grass & boughs & chinked it so that we are very comfortable.

August 5, 1839. I have just been exercising some [Nez Perce] boys in adding numbers. I never could make white children understand half as quick. . . .

December 9, 1847. We were hoping to have Dr. Whitman to supper with us tonight. But about sunset, Old Solomon arrived bringing the sad intelligence that Dr. & Mrs. Whitman . . . & others have been murdered by the Indians. . . . I do not see why I should expect to be preserved when more faithful servants are cut off.❞

—quoted in *Women of the West*

Americans Head West

In 1800 only around 387,000 white settlers lived west of the Appalachian Mountains. By 1820 that number had grown to more than 2.4 million people, and the numbers continued to rise rapidly. By the time the Civil War began, more Americans lived west of the Appalachians than lived in states along the Atlantic coast.

294 CHAPTER 9 Manifest Destiny

SECTION RESOURCES

Reproducible Masters
- Reproducible Lesson Plan 9–1
- Daily Lecture and Discussion Notes 9–1
- Guided Reading Activity 9–1
- Section Quiz 9–1
- Reading Essentials and Study Guide 9–1

Transparencies
- Daily Focus Skills Transparency 9–1

- American Art & Architecture

Multimedia
- Interactive Tutor Self-Assessment CD-ROM
- ExamView® Pro Testmaker CD-ROM
- Presentation Plus! CD-ROM
- TeacherWorks™ CD-ROM
- Audio Program
- American Music: Hits Through History

Some Americans headed west for religious reasons. Others were lured by the chance to own their own farms. While most settled east of the Mississippi River, more than 250,000 Americans headed farther west, across the Great Plains and Rocky Mountains to California and the Pacific Northwest.

In 1845 a magazine editor named **John Louis O'Sullivan** declared that it was the "manifest destiny" of Americans "to overspread the continent allotted by Providence. . . ." Many Americans believed in this concept of Manifest Destiny—the idea that God had given the continent to Americans and wanted them to settle western land.

Farming the New Lands Early settlers marked out farms on the rich river bottom land. Others occupied fertile woodland soil. These pioneers became known as squatters, because they settled on lands they did not own. The federal government intended to survey the land and then sell large parcels to real estate companies, but squatters wanted to buy the land they occupied directly from the government.

Bowing to public pressure, Congress passed the Preemption Act of 1830, a renewable law made permanent in 1841. This law protected squatters by guaranteeing them the right to claim land before it was surveyed and the right to buy up to 160 acres for the government's minimum price of $1.25 per acre.

Plows and Reapers A few decades earlier, farmers had only wooden plows to break the grass cover and roots of Midwestern sod. **Jethro Wood** patented an iron-bladed plow in 1819, and in 1837, **John Deere** engineered a plow with sharp-edged steel blades that cut cleanly through the sod. This reduced by half the labor needed to prepare an acre for farming.

Midwestern agriculture also received a boost from the mechanical reaper, which **Cyrus McCormick** patented in 1834. For centuries farmers had cut grain by hand using a sickle or a scythe—time-consuming and exhausting work. Switching from a sickle to a McCormick reaper pulled by horses or mules, farmers could harvest far more grain with far less effort.

✓ **Reading Check** **Explaining** How did Congress help squatters attain land in the West?

Settling the Pacific Coast

Latecomers to the Midwest set their sights on California and Oregon. This push to the Pacific Ocean happened partly because emigrants assumed that the treeless expanse of the Great Plains, which lay just beyond the frontier, contained poor land for farming.

Dividing Oregon Other nations, as well as Native Americans, had already laid claim to parts of Oregon and California. In the case of Oregon, the United States and Great Britain competed for possession, though they had agreed in 1818 to occupy the land jointly and settle their disputes later. In the late 1830s, American missionaries began arriving in Oregon, hoping to convert Native Americans. It was these missionaries who first spread the word about Oregon, persuading many Easterners to come to the lush Willamette Valley.

Populating California In 1821, after a bloody struggle, Mexico gained its independence from Spain. The new nation controlled a vast territory, including California, but that territory lay far from the central government in Mexico City. The local California government often relied on foreign settlers because it could not attract enough emigrants from Mexico. In 1839, hoping to attract more settlers, Juan Bautista Alvarado, governor of California, granted 50,000 acres (20,250 ha) in the Sacramento Valley to **John Sutter,** a German immigrant. There Sutter built a trading post and cattle ranch. Sutter's Fort—as it was called—was often the first stopping point for Americans reaching California. By 1845 more than 200 Americans had settled in California.

GEOGRAPHY

The Trails West Much of the terrain between the frontier jumping-off points and the Pacific was difficult. A small number of trailblazers—mountain men like **Kit Carson** and **Jim Bridger**—made their living by trapping beaver and selling the furs to traders. At the same time they gained a thorough knowledge of the territory and the local Native Americans.

By the 1840s the mountain men had carved out several east-to-west passages that played a vital role in western settlement. The most popular route was the **Oregon Trail.** Others included the California Trail and the Santa Fe Trail.

Wagon Train Life Emigrants made the journey in trains of covered wagons. Before starting out, the trains

HISTORY Online

Student Web Activity Visit the *American Vision* Web site at tav.glencoe.com and click on **Student Web Activities— Chapter 9** for an activity on westward expansion.

2 TEACH

Daily Lecture and Discussion Notes 9–1

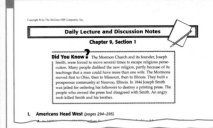

Copyright © by The McGraw-Hill Companies, Inc.

Daily Lecture and Discussion Notes

Chapter 9, Section 1

Did You Know? The Mormon Church and its founder, Joseph Smith, were forced to move several times to escape religious persecution. Many people disliked the new religion, partly because of its teachings that a man could have more than one wife. The Mormons moved first to Ohio, then to Missouri, then to Illinois. They built a prosperous community at Nauvoo, Illinois. In 1844 Joseph Smith was jailed for ordering his followers to destroy a printing press. The people who owned the press had disagreed with Smith. An angry mob killed Smith and his brother.

I. Americans Head West *(pages 294–295)*

Using a Map Have students use a current map of the United States to follow one of the trails shown on the map on page 296. Instruct students to name the current states and major geographic landmarks along the trail. L1 ELL

✓ **Reading Check**

Answer: The Preemption Act of 1830 was a renewable law that gave squatters the right to claim land before it was surveyed and buy up to 160 acres at the government's minimum price of $1.25 per acre.

HISTORY Online

Objectives and answers to the student activity can be found in the **Web Activity Lesson Plan** at tav.glencoe.com.

History *and the* Humanities

🏳️ American Music: Hits Through History: "De Boatman's Dance"

🏛️ American Art & Architecture: *The Great Blue Heron*

COOPERATIVE LEARNING ACTIVITY

Creating a Thematic Map Organize students into small groups. Have each group select one of the trails west. For the trail chosen, have students research the plant or animal life that early settlers were likely to encounter on their trip. Have students use their research to prepare a thematic map that shows where the plant or animal species was likely to be found. The group should include a picture and brief description of each plant or animal. Encourage students to include at least 12 types of plant or animal life.

Use the rubric for a cooperative group management plan on pages 81–82 in the ***Performance Assessment Activities and Rubrics.***

Guided Reading Activity 9–1

Name _____ Date _____ Class _____

★ Guided Reading Activity **9-1**

DIRECTIONS: Recalling Facts Read the section and answer the questions below. Refer to your textbook to write the answers.

1. By the time the Civil War began, where did more Americans live? _____

2. Why did Americans head west? _____

3. What was Manifest Destiny? _____

4. Who were squatters? _____

5. What was the Preemption Act of 1830? _____

6. Why did Cyrus McCormick's reaper appeal to _____

Geography *Skills*

Answers:

1. Possible answers: St. Louis, St. Joseph, and Independence

2. They assumed the land was not good for farming and they feared the Plains Indians.

Geography Skills Practice
Ask: What postal route ran from Fort Smith, Arkansas, to El Paso, Texas? *(Butterfield Overland Mail)*

3 ASSESS

Assign Section 1 Assessment as homework or as an in-class activity.

🌐 Have students use the **Interactive Tutor Self-Assessment CD-ROM.**

Reading Essentials and Study Guide 9–1

Name _____ Date _____ Class _____

Study Guide
Chapter 9, Section 1
For use with textbook pages 294–297

THE WESTERN PIONEERS

KEY TERMS AND NAMES

John Louis O'Sullivan magazine editor who declared that it was the "manifest destiny" of Americans to settle western lands *(page 295)*
Manifest Destiny idea that God had given the continent to Americans and wanted them to settle western land *(page 295)*
squatters pioneers who settled on lands they did not own *(page 295)*
Jethro Wood patented a plow with an iron blade in 1819 *(page 295)*
John Deere designed a plow with sharp-edged steel blades in 1837 *(page 295)*
Cyrus McCormick patented a mechanical reaper in 1834 *(page 295)*

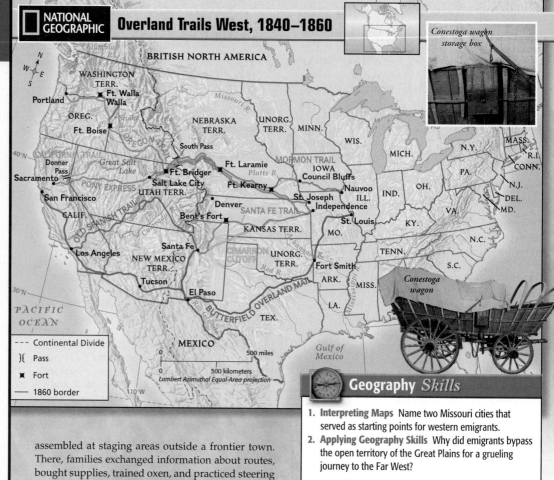

NATIONAL GEOGRAPHIC — Overland Trails West, 1840–1860

Conestoga wagon storage box

Conestoga wagon

- - - - Continental Divide
)(Pass
✖ Fort
——— 1860 border

Lambert Azimuthal Equal-Area projection

Geography *Skills*

1. **Interpreting Maps** Name two Missouri cities that served as starting points for western emigrants.
2. **Applying Geography Skills** Why did emigrants bypass the open territory of the Great Plains for a grueling journey to the Far West?

assembled at staging areas outside a frontier town. There, families exchanged information about routes, bought supplies, trained oxen, and practiced steering the cumbersome wagons, which new drivers were apt to tip over.

The first wagon trains hired mountain men to guide them. Once the trails became well worn, most of the travelers—known as overlanders—found their own way with the help of guidebooks written by earlier emigrants.

Sometimes the guidebooks were wrong, leading to tragedy. In 1846 a group of 87 overlanders, known as the **Donner Party** after the two brothers who led them, were trapped by winter snows high up in the Sierra Nevada. After 41 died of starvation, those still alive faced the choice of death or cannibalism. Many, in desperation, did resort to cannibalism in order to survive.

The typical trip west took five to six months, the wagon trains progressing about 15 miles (24 km) per day. Generally, men drove the wagons, hunted game, and bedded down the animals at night, while women looked after the children, cooked their families' food,

cleaned the camp, and laundered the clothes. As Elizabeth Geer recalls here, the journey west was exhausting and difficult:

❝I carry my babe and lead, or rather carry, another through snow, mud, and water, almost to my knees. It is the worst road. . . . [T]here was not one dry thread on one of us—not even my babe. . . . I have not told you half we suffered. I am not adequate to the task.❞

—quoted in *Women's Diaries of the Westward Journey*

Native Americans Early travelers feared attacks by Native American warriors, but such encounters were rare. By one estimate 362 emigrants died due to Native American attacks between 1840 and 1860. The same estimate calculates that emigrants killed

296 CHAPTER 9 Manifest Destiny

MEETING SPECIAL NEEDS

Intrapersonal To help students gain a better understanding of what life was like on the westward trails, have them locate and read excerpts from diaries written by people who traveled into the West between 1820 and 1860. The names of some known diarists are shown below. **L1** ELL

| James Akin, Jr. | James Madison Coon | Amelia Stewart Knight | Catherine Sager Pringle |
| William H. Ashley | Nancy Miller Coon | William Porter | Narcissa Whitman |

📂 Refer to *Inclusion for the High School Social Studies Classroom Strategies and Activities* in the TCR.

Wagon interior

Wagon wheel

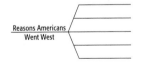

Mormons heading west

426 Native Americans. In fact, Native Americans often gave emigrants gifts of food as well as helpful information about routes, edible plants, and sources of water. They often traded fresh horses for items such as cotton clothing and ammunition.

As the overland traffic increased, Native Americans on the Great Plains became concerned and angry over the threat immigration posed to their way of life. The Sioux, Cheyenne, Arapaho, and other groups relied on the buffalo for food, shelter, clothing, tools, and countless other necessities of everyday life.

Now they feared that the increasing flow of American settlers across their hunting grounds would disrupt the age-old wanderings of the buffalo herds.

Hoping to ensure peace, the federal government negotiated the **Treaty of Fort Laramie** in 1851. Eight Native American groups agreed to specific geographic boundaries, while the United States promised that these territories would belong to the Native Americans forever.

✓ **Reading Check** **Describing** What were the difficulties facing Western settlers?

The Mormon Migration

Unlike those bound for the West Coast in search of land, the Mormons followed a deeply rooted American tradition—the quest for religious freedom. The Mormons, however, sought that freedom by leaving the United States.

In 1844, after a mob murdered Joseph Smith, the Church's leader, his successor **Brigham Young** decided to take his people west to escape further persecution. Several thousand Mormons forged their way along a path that became known as the **Mormon Trail.** Along with the Oregon Trail, it served as a valuable route into the western United States. In 1847 the Mormons stopped at the Great Salt Lake in what is now Utah. With the words "This is the place," Young declared that here the Mormons would build a new settlement. Undeterred by the wildness of the area, the Mormons staked a claim on the land they called "Deseret."

✓ **Reading Check** **Examining** Why did the Mormons emigrate to the West?

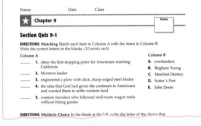

Section Quiz 9–1

Name ___ Date ___ Class ___

⭐ **Chapter 9** Score ___

Section Quiz 9-1

DIRECTIONS: Matching Match each item in Column A with the items in Column B. Write the correct letters in the blanks. *(10 points each)*

Column A
___ 1. often the first stopping point for Americans reaching California
___ 2. Mormon leader
___ 3. engineered a plow with slick, sharp-edged steel blades
___ 4. the idea that God had given the continent to Americans and wanted them to settle western land
___ 5. western travelers who followed well-worn wagon trails without hiring guides

Column B
A. overlanders
B. Brigham Young
C. Manifest Destiny
D. Sutter's Fort
E. John Deere

DIRECTIONS: Multiple Choice In the blank at the left, write the letter of the choice that

✓ **Reading Check**

Answer: difficult terrain, bad weather, and attacks by Native Americans

Reteach
Ask students to identify and explain the impact of inventions that made it easier to farm the Western plains.

Enrich
Have interested students research the development of the plow or the reaper. Have students prepare a written report or an oral presentation about how each of these inventions has evolved.

✓ **Reading Check**

Answer: to escape further religious persecution

4 CLOSE

Ask students to explain why people were willing to leave their homes in the East and head West.

SECTION 1 ASSESSMENT

Checking for Understanding

1. **Define:** Manifest Destiny, squatter, overlander.
2. **Identify:** John Louis O'Sullivan, Jethro Wood, John Deere, Cyrus McCormick, John Sutter, Kit Carson, Jim Bridger, Donner Party, Brigham Young.
3. **Evaluate** how mountain men helped settle the West.

Reviewing Themes

4. **Science and Technology** What two inventions made it easier to farm the frontier?

Critical Thinking

5. **Synthesizing** How did the United States settle its land disputes with Great Britain and the Plains Indians?
6. **Organizing** Use a graphic organizer similar to the one below to list the reasons why Americans emigrated to the West.

Reasons Americans Went West

Analyzing Visuals

7. **Examining Artifacts** Examine the feature about western migration on pages 296 and 297, especially the photo of a wagon's interior. Why would people need all of the items shown as they traveled west?

Writing About History

8. **Descriptive Writing** Imagine that you emigrated from the East and are living on a frontier farm in the West. Write a letter to a friend in the East describing your daily life.

CHAPTER 9 Manifest Destiny **297**

SECTION 1 ASSESSMENT ANSWERS

1. Terms are in blue.
2. John Louis O'Sullivan *(p. 295)*, Jethro Wood *(p. 295)*, John Deere *(p. 295)*, Cyrus McCormick *(p. 295)*, John Sutter *(p. 295)*, Kit Carson *(p. 295)*, Jim Bridger *(p. 295)*, Donner Party *(p. 296)*, Brigham Young *(p. 297)*
3. While trapping and opening trade

networks, they created trails for settlers to follow.
4. steel-blade plow and mechanical reaper
5. joint occupation
6. religious freedom, opportunity to own their own farms, to fulfill the concept of Manifest Destiny, to convert Native Americans to

Christianity, to act as trailblazers
7. Any finished goods the settlers would need in their new homes had to be carried with them because these things were not yet available in the West.
8. Students' letters will vary but should contain descriptions of everyday life in the West.

TEACH

Eulogy

Ask students the following questions after they have read the recollections of Chief Joseph.

- **What did Old Joseph say Chief Joseph's responsibility was?** *(to guide his people and to never sell or give away his land)*
- **Why do you think Old Joseph told his son to stop his ears when asked to sign a treaty?** *(Answers may vary. He suggests that the terms of the treaty might sound good and reasonable, but that his son should not even listen to the white man nor sell his father's grave.)*

Baseball

Have students compare these rules to the modern rules. **Ask:** **Which rules are still part of the game of baseball?** *(bases 90 feet apart in diamond shape; only nine players per side; at first base, a fielder can simply tag the bag to make an out)* **Which rules no longer apply? What rules have replaced them?** *(pitches will be thrown underhand replaced with pitches thrown overhand; ball caught on first bounce is an out replaced with catching the ball before it hits the ground; nine balls is a walk replaced with four balls is a walk)* **Why do you think rules of games change over time?** *(possible answers: to speed play, to reduce injuries, to make the game more challenging)*

Visit the **TIME** Web site at www.time.com for up-to-date news, weekly magazine articles, editorials, online polls, and an archive of past magazine and Web articles.

298

TIME NOTEBOOK

Eulogy

CHIEF JOSEPH *(above), a leader of the Nez Perce of the Wallowa Valley in eastern Oregon, remembers his father, Old Joseph. The Nez Perce were forced to leave the Wallowa Valley less than a decade after Old Joseph's death.*

MY FATHER SENT FOR ME. I SAW HE WAS DYING. I TOOK HIS HAND IN MINE. He said, "My son, my body is returning to my mother earth, and my spirit is going very soon to see the Great Spirit Chief. When I am gone, think of your country. You are the chief of these people. They look to you to guide them. Always remember that your father never sold his country. You must stop your ears whenever you are asked to sign a treaty selling your home. A few years more, and white men will be all around you. They have their eyes on this land. My son, never forget my dying words. This country holds your father's body. Never sell the bones of your father and your mother."

I pressed my father's hand and told him I would protect his grave with my life. My father smiled and passed to the spirit land.

I buried him in that beautiful valley of winding rivers. I love that land more than all the rest of the world. A man who would not love his father's grave is worse than a wild animal.

Baseball for Beginners

Thinking of taking up the new game of baseball? Watch out! The rules keep changing!

1845
- Canvas bases will be set 90 feet apart in a diamond shape.
- Only nine men will play on each side.
- Pitches are to be thrown underhanded.
- A ball caught on the first bounce is an out.

1846
- At first base, a fielder can tag the bag before the runner reaches it and so make an out.

1847
- Players may no longer throw the ball at a runner to put him out.

These changes may be coming:
- A poor pitch is a ball; nine balls gives the runner first base, a walk.
- A ball caught on the first bounce is no longer an out.

The New York baseball team

COOPERATIVE LEARNING ACTIVITY

Creating a Magazine Spread Organize the class into four groups. Assign each group one of the following decades: 1810–1819, 1820–1829, 1830–1839, or 1840–1849, and ask them to create their own two-page magazine spread for the decade. Encourage students to consider the Time Notebook design but to be creative as they select information that is of particular interest. Students should look at current magazines and books for design ideas. This activity can be completed using desktop publishing software or the more traditional cut-and-paste method.

Use the rubric for a cooperative group management plan on pages 81–82 in the *Performance Assessment Activities and Rubrics.*

WESTERN WORD PLAY
Word Watch

Can you talk Western? Match the word to its meaning.

1. maverick
2. Hangtown fry
3. grubstake
4. bonanza
5. palo alto
6. pard or rawwheel

a. gold rush favorite, made of eggs, bacon, and oysters

b. inexperienced '49er, Eastern type not used to wearing boots

c. a lucky discovery of gold; a source of sudden wealth

d. a style of hat worn by gold rush miners

e. a lone dissenter who takes an independent stand, from the name of a Texas cattleman who left his herd unbranded

f. food provided by an investor to a gold prospector in exchange for a share of whatever gold he finds

answers: 1.e; 2.a; 3.f; 4.c; 5.d; 6.b

Milestones

SETTLED, 1847. THE VALLEY OF THE GREAT SALT LAKE, by Brigham Young, leader of the Mormons, and a party of 143, to escape hostility toward their group in Illinois. Young plans to return to Council Bluffs, Iowa, and lead the rest of the members of his faith to a permanent home in Utah.

MOVED, 1845. HENRY DAVID THOREAU, writer, to Walden Pond, Concord, Massachusetts. Thoreau intends to build his own house on the shore of the pond and earn his living by the labor of his hands only. "Many of the so-called comforts of life," writes Thoreau, "are not only not indispensable, but positive hindrances to the elevation of mankind."

AILING, 1847. EDGAR ALLAN POE, in Baltimore, following the death of his wife, Virginia. Other than a poem on death, Poe has written little this year, devoting his dwindling energies to plagiarism suits against other authors.

Frederick Douglass

LIBRARY OF CONGRESS/CORBIS

EMIGRATED, 1845. FREDERICK DOUGLASS, former slave, author, and abolitionist leader, to England to escape the danger of re-enslavement in reaction to his autobiography, *Narrative of the Life of Frederick Douglass*. On his 1845 trip across the Atlantic, Douglass was not permitted cabin accommodations. After a lecture during the crossing, some passengers threatened to throw him overboard.

DISCOVERED, 1846. THE PLANET NEPTUNE, by German astronomer Johann Galle.

NUMBERS

18,000 Miles from New York to California by sea route around Cape Horn

90,000 People arriving in California in 1849, half by sea, half by overland route

Panning for gold

BETTMANN/CORBIS

$20 Average earned per day by California gold miners in 1849

$18 Average expenses per day for California gold miners in 1849

$390 Value of miners' average daily earnings in 2001 dollars

50 Number of years after the signing of the Declaration of Independence that Thomas Jefferson and John Adams die—within hours of each other.

17,069,453 U.S. population in 1840

55,000 Number of emigrants moving west along the Oregon Trail in 1850

 **Portfolio Writing Project**

Have students research one of the following people: Chief Joseph, Brigham Young, Henry David Thoreau, Edgar Allan Poe, Frederick Douglass, or Johann Galle. Ask students to write a one-page essay about the person's contribution to history.

Creating a Thematic Map Have students research the population of the states that were part of the United States at the end of 1850. Also have them find the population of these states using the 2000 census figures. Tell students to use an outline map of the United States to shade the states that were part of the union in 1850 and label them with the name of the state, its population in 1850, and its population in 2000.

CLOSE

Have students work in small groups to create lists of words that we associate with certain regions of the country.

EXTENDING THE CONTENT

The Pathfinder John C. Frémont was a member of the United States Corps of Topographical Engineers, an agency that surveyed and mapped the country's unorganized territories. In 1842 on his first major expedition to the West, Frémont surveyed a section of the Oregon Trail along the Platte River to the South Pass through the Rocky Mountains. During 1843 and 1844, Frémont went north along the Rocky Mountains to the South Pass, west to the Columbia River, and then south along the Cascade and Sierra Nevada mountains in California. Frémont's return journey took him across the Great Basin to the Great Salt Lake and then over the Rocky Mountains. These explorations in the West earned Frémont the nickname "The Pathfinder."

1 FOCUS

Section Overview

This sections focuses on Texas settlers' efforts to gain independence from Mexico.

BELLRINGER
Skillbuilder Activity

Project transparency and have students answer the question.

Available as a blackline master.

Daily Focus Skills Transparency 9–2

Guide to Reading

Answers to Graphic:

Major Battles	Outcomes
Gonzales	Mexicans retreat
Alamo	Texans defeated after inflicting serious losses on Mexicans
San Jacinto	Texans prevail

Preteaching Vocabulary

Have students divide the Key Terms and Names into three groups: people, places, and other.

SECTION 2 Independence for Texas

Guide to Reading

Main Idea
Settlers emigrated from the United States to Texas and fought Mexico to gain independence.

Key Terms and Names
Tejano, empresario, National Colonization Act, Washington-on-the-Brazos, Antonio López de Santa Anna, Sam Houston, Alamo, William B. Travis, annexation

Reading Strategy
Categorizing As you read about Americans settling in Texas and gaining independence, complete a graphic organizer similar to the one below by filling in the major battles of the Texas revolution and the outcome of each.

Major Battle	Outcome

Reading Objectives
• **Chronicle** the opening of Texas to American settlers.
• **Discuss** the major battles of the war against Mexico.

Section Theme
Groups and Institutions Texans hoped to transplant American institutions to their new homes.

Preview of Events

◆January, 1836	◆February, 1836	◆March, 1836	◆April, 1836

February 23, 1836
Santa Anna's troops begin arriving at San Antonio

March 2, 1836
Texas declares independence

March 6, 1836
Siege at the Alamo ends

April 21, 1836
Santa Anna's army defeated at the Battle of San Jacinto

Stephen F. Austin

★ An American Story ★

In July 1821, Stephen F. Austin set off from Louisiana for the Texas territory in the northeastern corner of Mexico. The Spanish government had promised to give his father, Moses, a huge tract of Texas land if the elder Austin settled 300 American families there. Moses died before he could fulfill his end of the deal. On his deathbed, he asked Stephen to take his place in Texas. Austin was favorably impressed with the region. As he surveyed the land grant between the Brazos and Colorado Rivers, he noted its natural abundance:

❝The Prairie comes bluff to the river . . . and affords a most beautiful situation for a Town or settlement. . . . The country . . . is as good in every respect as man could wish for, Land all first rate, plenty of timber, fine water, beautifully rolling.❞

—quoted in *Stephen F. Austin: Empresario of Texas*

Opening Texas to Americans

When Austin settled in Texas, it was not a wild and empty land. Long a part of Spain's Mexican colony, the area was under Mexican control after the country achieved independence from Spain in 1821. The Spanish-speaking inhabitants of the area, called *Tejanos,* had established such settlements as San Antonio de Bexar and Hidalgo in the southern portion of the region. Few *Tejanos* lived north of these settlements. That area was the territory of the Apache, Comanche, and other Native American groups.

SECTION RESOURCES

🗀 Reproducible Masters
• Reproducible Lesson Plan 9–2
• Daily Lecture and Discussion Notes 9–2
• Guided Reading Activity 9–2
• Section Quiz 9–2
• Reading Essentials and Study Guide 9–2
• Performance Assessment Activities and Rubrics

📄 Transparencies
• Daily Focus Skills Transparency 9–2

Multimedia
🔘 Interactive Tutor Self-Assessment CD-ROM
🔘 ExamView® Pro Testmaker CD-ROM
🔘 Presentation Plus! CD-ROM
🔘 TeacherWorks™ CD-ROM
🔘 Audio Program

Unable to persuade its own citizens to move closer to the Native American groups, Mexico decided to continue Spanish policy and invite Americans and other foreigners to settle there. Between 1823 and 1825 Mexico passed three colonization laws, which offered cheap land to nearly anyone willing to come. The last law granted new immigrants a 10-year exemption from paying taxes but required that they become Mexican citizens, live under Mexican law, and convert to Roman Catholicism.

Empresarios and Settlers Although some American emigrants headed to Texas on their own, most came at the encouragement of *empresarios,* a Spanish word meaning "agents" or "contractors." Under the **National Colonization Act,** Mexico gave 26 *empresarios* large grants of Texas land. In exchange, the *empresarios* promised to fill it with a certain number of settlers. The *empresarios* assigned a plot to each family and governed the colonies they established.

Stephen Austin was not only the first but also by far the most successful *empresario.* He founded the town of **Washington-on-the-Brazos** and, by the mid-1830s, had persuaded some 1,500 American families to immigrate.

Americanizing Texas The Americans who emigrated to Texas initially accepted Mexican citizenship as required. The government assumed they would also adopt Mexican customs and come to see Mexico as their own country, but for various reasons few did. The Spanish Catholic Church was alien to the traditions of most American settlers, and only a few bothered to learn Spanish.

Many Mexicans, in turn, distrusted the new settlers because of their American lifestyle and dismissal of Mexican ways. The Mexicans' unease increased in 1826, when *empresario* Haden Edwards's brother Benjamin led a rebellion against Mexican authority. Angry over disagreements about whether the Mexican government or the *empresario* controlled the region, Edwards declared that the settlements of Americans in Texas now constituted the independent nation of **Fredonia.** He gained few followers, however, and Stephen Austin led a contingent of troops that helped Mexico crush the revolt.

Although nearly all of the settlers ignored Edwards's call for revolution, the Mexican government feared that it signaled an American plot to acquire Texas. In 1830 Mexico closed its borders to further immigration by Americans and banned the import of enslaved labor as well. Mexico also placed taxes on goods imported from foreign countries, hoping to discourage trade with the United States.

These new laws infuriated the settlers. Without immigration their settlements could not grow. The import tax meant higher prices for goods they were accustomed to purchasing from the United States. Perhaps worst of all, the Mexican government was telling them what they could and could not do. They saw no reason to follow the orders of a government they hardly considered their own.

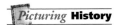 **Reading Check** **Examining** What did Mexico's colonization laws offer people willing to settle in northern Texas, and what did the laws require of these settlers?

Texas Goes to War

With tensions simmering, settlers met at two conventions in the Texas town of San Felipe in 1832 and 1833. They chose Stephen Austin as president of the first convention. The convention asked Mexico to reopen Texas to American immigrants and to loosen the taxes on imports. The second convention in 1833 was more aggressive. At that time, Texas was part of the Mexican state of Coahuila. The convention recommended separating Texas from Coahuila and creating a new Mexican state. The convention also created a constitution for the new state and designated Austin to travel to Mexico City to negotiate with the Mexican government. In the fall of 1833, the negotiations stalled, and an irritated Austin sent a letter to *Tejano* leaders in San Antonio that suggested

Picturing **History**

Land in Texas This April 1836 poster from New Orleans sought volunteers during the Texas war for independence. The offer of land also drew settlers to Texas before the war. Why do you think the sponsors offered more land to settlers who stayed longer?

TEXAS!!

Emigrants who are desirous of assisting Texas at this important crisis of her affairs may have a free passage and equipments, by applying at the **NEW-YORK and PHILADELPHIA HOTEL,** On the Old Levee, near the Blue Stores.

Now is the time to ensure a fortune in Land: To all who remain in Texas during the War will be allowed 1280 Acres. To all who remain Six Months, 640 Acres. To all who remain Three Months, 320 Acres. And as Colonists, 4600 Acres for a family and 1470 Acres for a Single Man. New Orleans, April 23d, 1836.

2 TEACH

Daily Lecture and Discussion Notes 9–2

Copyright © by The McGraw-Hill Companies, Inc.

Daily Lecture and Discussion Notes
Chapter 9, Section 2

Did You Know? Women contributed to the Texas war of independence. Many women farmed and ranched as their husbands fought in the war. Some women donated money to the Texas cause. Other women donated oxen for the Texas army. One woman served as a courier for the army.

I. Opening Texas to Americans *(pages 300–301)*

A. Texas was under Mexican control after Mexico achieved independence from Spain in 1821. *Tejanos*—the Spanish-speaking people of the area—had established settlements in the southern part of the region. Because *Tejanos* refused to move to the northern part of the region where Native American groups lived, Mexico invited Americans and

✔ **Reading Check**

Answer: cheap land and a ten-year tax exemption; required that settlers become Mexican citizens, follow Mexican law, and convert to Roman Catholicism

Calculating Value Have students create a manual or electronic worksheet to calculate the value of the land offered in the poster shown on this page. Instruct students to use the government's minimum price of $1.25 per acre when calculating value and organize their data with the values in ascending order. **L2**

Required Stay in Texas	Acres	Value per Acre	Total Value
Three months	320	1.25	$ 400
Six months	640	1.25	$ 800
Duration of the war	1,280	1.25	$1,600
Colonists, single male	1,470	1.25	$1,838
Colonists, family	4,600	1.25	$5,750

COOPERATIVE LEARNING ACTIVITY

Creating a Political Cartoon Organize students into small groups. Have each group discuss the events that led to independence for Texas and offer opinions as to whether Texas should have become an independent country or become part of the United States. Then have each group create a political cartoon that expresses the views of the group.

Use the rubric for a cooperative group management plan on pages 81–82 in the *Performance Assessment Activities and Rubrics.*

Picturing **History**

Answer: to lure those willing to make a longer commitment to the war effort and long-term settlement

Ask: Who might have placed such an ad? *(an empresario)*

Guided Reading Activity 9–2

Name _____ Date _____ Class _____

Guided Reading Activity 9-2

DIRECTIONS: Recording Who, What When, Where, Why, and How Read the section and answer the questions below. Refer to your textbook to write the answers.

1. By 1821 **where** had the Spanish-speaking inhabitants of Texas already established settlements? _____
2. **Why** did Mexico decide to invite Americans and other foreigners to settle in the Texas region? _____
3. **What** were the elements of the National Colonization Act? _____
4. **Why** did many Mexicans distrust the new settlers? _____
5. **Why** did Benjamin Edwards lead a rebellion against Mexican authority? _____

Profiles IN HISTORY

Ask: What did Santa Anna do in 1834 that might have influenced Zavala to support independence for Texas? What led to Sam Houston's removal from office? *(Santa Anna denounced Mexico's constitution and made himself a dictator. Sam Houston refused to take an oath of loyalty to the new Confederate government at the beginning of the Civil War.)*

Writing a Profile Have students choose one of the persons mentioned in this section and write a profile similar to the profiles that appear on this page. **L2**

📁 Use the rubric for a book review, research report, or position paper on pages 89–90 in the *Performance Assessment Activities and Rubrics.*

ABCNEWS
INTERACTIVE™

 VIDEOCASSETTE
Historic America Electronic Field Trips

View **Tape 1, Chapter 10:** "The Alamo."

Profiles IN HISTORY

Lorenzo de Zavala
1788–1836

Lorenzo de Zavala demonstrated his fierce support of democratic principles both in his native Mexico and as a citizen of the Republic of Texas.

Born in the Yucatán peninsula, Zavala was jailed in his youth for advocating Mexican independence from Spain. Soon after Mexico gained independence in 1821, Zavala was elected to the new national congress. Battles for political power in early Mexico were intense. Zavala was forced into exile but granted a huge tract of land in southeastern Texas.

Politics in Texas proved no less intense than in Mexico. Most Mexicans in Texas were loyal to Mexico, but Zavala's disapproval of Santa Anna's policies led him to support Texan independence. As a speaker of both Spanish and English, he helped draft the new republic's constitution and design its flag. He also served as vice president of the Republic-in-Arms until ill health forced him to resign.

Sam Houston
1793–1863

Standing over six feet tall, Sam Houston seemed larger than life. A military hero in the Creek wars, he had a brief political career in Tennessee before heading to Texas in 1832. He soon revived his military career and led the army of the Republic of Texas to victory over Mexico at the Battle of San Jacinto. Texans elected him president of the Republic and later, when Texas joined the Union, Houston served as a U.S. senator.

Despite being a slaveholder himself, Houston voted with the antislavery faction because he believed a compromise was necessary to save the Union. When the Civil War broke out, Houston refused to take an oath of loyalty to the new Southern government, and he was removed from office. In his farewell address, he declared, "Oh my fellow countrymen, the fearful conflict will fill our land with untold suffering, misfortune, and disaster." He died in July 1863 at the height of the Civil War.

Texas should start peacefully organizing its own state government. Mexican officials intercepted the letter.

After sending the letter, Austin managed to persuade President **Antonio López de Santa Anna** to agree to several demands, including lifting the hated immigration ban. On January 3, 1834, as Austin was returning home, officials arrested him for treason on the basis of the intercepted letter. The Mexican officials took Austin back to Mexico City and threw him in jail, where he languished without trial until he was released in July 1835.

Shortly after Austin was imprisoned, in April 1834, President Santa Anna abruptly denounced Mexico's Constitution of 1824 and made himself dictator. Even Austin, finally released from prison, now saw that negotiation with Santa Anna was impossible. In September 1835, he concluded that war was inevitable. He urged Texans to organize an army, which they quickly did.

The Early Battles The Texan army faced a Mexican army with serious problems. Continuing political instability in Mexico City had denied the army sound leadership, training, and support. Against this handicapped force the Texan army enjoyed its first taste of victory at the military post of **Gonzales,** about 75 miles east of San Antonio. There, Mexican soldiers ordered the Texans to surrender their arms. In response, the rebels pointed a cannon at the Mexican force and held up a cloth sign painted with the taunt,

"Come and Take It." Having no orders to attack, the Mexicans retreated to San Antonio, and the Texans followed them. The rebels, numbering only about 350, drove the much larger Mexican force out of San Antonio in December 1835.

Despite these early successes, the Texans faced tremendous difficulties of their own. Few of the men had any military training, and no one could agree at first on who should lead them. Finally a former governor of Tennessee and proven military leader named **Sam Houston** took command. In the meantime, Santa Anna organized a force of about 6,000 troops to put down the rebellion.

The Alamo When Santa Anna's forces arrived at San Antonio in February 1836, they found over 180 rebels holed up in an abandoned Spanish Catholic mission called the **Alamo.** Under the command of Lieutenant Colonel **William B. Travis,** the small force sought to delay Santa Anna and give Houston's army more time to prepare. From within the mission Travis dispatched a courier through Mexican lines with a plea to fellow Texans and U.S. citizens for help:

❝I call on you, in the name of liberty, of patriotism, and everything dear to American character, to come to our aid with all dispatch. . . . Though this call may be neglected, I am determined to sustain myself as long as possible, and die like a soldier. . . . Victory or death!❞

—quoted in *History of Texas*

MEETING SPECIAL NEEDS

Visual/Spatial Have interested students create an illustrated time line of the lives of one of the following: Stephen F. Austin, Santa Anna, or Sam Houston. Encourage students to include pictures or drawings of significant artifacts or of significant events. **L1** **ELL**

📁 Refer to *Inclusion for the High School Social Studies Classroom Strategies and Activities* in the TCR.

The call for reinforcements went almost unanswered. Only 32 settlers from Gonzales, deciding on their own to join the fight, made it into the Alamo. Running low on ammunition and gunpowder, the Texans held off Santa Anna's besieging army for 13 days. During the standoff the new Texas government met at Washington-on-the-Brazos and formally declared independence from Mexico.

On March 6, 1836, Santa Anna's army stormed the Alamo. The Texans fought off the attackers for six hours, killing or wounding about 600 before being overrun. Although the defenders of the Alamo had been defeated, they had bought Houston's army nearly two extra weeks to organize.

Goliad

Two weeks later the Mexican army overwhelmed Texan troops led by James W. Fannin at Goliad, a town southeast of San Antonio near the Gulf Coast. Fannin and his men surrendered, hoping the Mexicans would disarm them and expel them from Texas. Though the Mexican field general at Goliad wrote to Santa Anna requesting clemency, Santa Anna demanded execution. At dawn on March 27, a firing squad executed more than 300 men. The losses at the Alamo and Goliad devastated Texans but also united them behind their new country.

TURNING POINT

The Battle of San Jacinto

With the Texan army in disarray, Sam Houston desperately needed time to recruit fresh volunteers and to train the soldiers who remained. Rather than fight, he chose to retreat, heading east toward Louisiana.

Houston was biding his time. Up against a larger, more disciplined army, he decided to wait for Santa Anna to make a mistake. Such a mistake occurred on April 21, when both armies were encamped along the San Jacinto River near what is now the city of Houston. Santa Anna no longer saw Houston's army as a threat, so he allowed his men to sleep in the afternoon, confident that Houston would wait until the next day to launch an attack.

Eager for a fight, Houston's soldiers convinced the officers to launch an afternoon assault. Shielded from sight by a hill, Houston's troops crept up on Santa Anna's sleeping soldiers and charged. The surprise attack threw the Mexicans into a panic.

The Battle of San Jacinto lasted less than 20 minutes, but the killing continued for hours. Yelling "Remember the Alamo" and "Remember Goliad," Houston's men attacked the Mexican troops with guns, knives, and clubs. In addition to hundreds killed, over 700

Mosaic of the Gonzales cannon

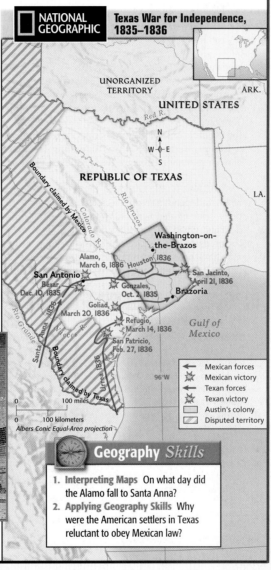

NATIONAL GEOGRAPHIC

Texas War for Independence, 1835–1836

UNORGANIZED TERRITORY
ARK.
UNITED STATES
Red R.
REPUBLIC OF TEXAS
LA.
Boundary claimed by Mexico
Colorado R.
Rio Brazos
Washington-on-the-Brazos 1836
Alamo, March 6, 1836
Houston 1836
San Antonio
Bexar Dec. 10, 1835
Gonzales, Oct. 2, 1835
San Jacinto, April 21, 1836
Brazoria
Santa Anna 1836
Goliad, March 20, 1836
Refugio, March 14, 1836
Gulf of Mexico
Rio Grande
Nueces R.
San Patricio, Feb. 27, 1836
Urrea 1836
Boundary claimed by Texas
96°W

← Mexican forces
✶ Mexican victory
← Texan forces
✶ Texan victory
☐ Austin's colony
▨ Disputed territory

0   100 miles
0   100 kilometers
Albers Conic Equal-Area projection

Geography *Skills*

1. **Interpreting Maps** On what day did the Alamo fall to Santa Anna?
2. **Applying Geography Skills** Why were the American settlers in Texas reluctant to obey Mexican law?

you don't say...

Name Origins The building that is now called "the Alamo" was originally the chapel of a Franciscan mission. How it came to be called "the Alamo" is not clear. *Alamo* is the Spanish word for cottonwood. Some historians believe there were cottonwood trees in the area, thus the name. Other historians believe the name came from a city in Mexico—Alamo de Parras, Coahuila. This was the hometown of a cavalry unit housed at the old mission in the early 1800s.

Geography *Skills*

Answers:
1. March 6, 1836
2. They did not feel a part of the Mexican culture.

Geography Skills Practice
Ask: What river did Texas claim as its boundary with Mexico? *(Rio Grande)*

3 ASSESS

Assign Section 2 Assessment as homework or as an in-class activity.

◉ Have students use the **Interactive Tutor Self-Assessment CD-ROM.**

Reading Essentials and Study Guide 9–2

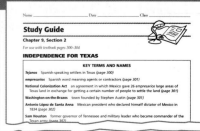

Name _____ Date _____ Class _____

Study Guide
Chapter 9, Section 2
For use with textbook pages 300–304
INDEPENDENCE FOR TEXAS

KEY TERMS AND NAMES
Tejanos Spanish-speaking settlers in Texas *(page 300)*
empresarios Spanish word meaning agents or contractors *(page 301)*
National Colonization Act an agreement in which Mexico gave 26 empresarios large areas of Texas land in exchange for getting a certain number of people to settle the land *(page 301)*
Washington-on-the-Brazos town founded by Stephen Austin *(page 301)*
Antonio López de Santa Anna Mexican president who declared himself dictator of Mexico in 1834 *(page 302)*
Sam Houston former governor of Tennessee and military leader who became commander of the Texan army *(page 303)*

INTERDISCIPLINARY CONNECTIONS ACTIVITY

Government Explain to students that Texas draws on a rich history that includes having been a part of Mexico. Have students research the various flags that have flown over Texas throughout its history. Have students prepare displays showing each flag, and explain when and why it was used. **L2**

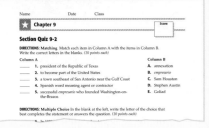

History *Through Art*

Battle of San Jacinto H.A. McArdle's painting (above) and this monument (at right) commemorate the pivotal battle of the war between Texas and Mexico. *Why were Santa Anna and his troops surprised by Houston's attack?*

members of Santa Anna's force were taken captive. The Texans suffered only 9 killed and 34 wounded.

Among the captured was Santa Anna himself. Houston forced Santa Anna to order his army out of Texas and sign a treaty recognizing independence for the Republic of Texas. The Mexican Congress refused to accept the treaty but was unwilling to launch another military campaign. Texas had won the war.

The Republic of Texas In September 1836 the newly independent republic called its citizens to the polls. They elected Sam Houston as their first president and voted 3,277 to 91 in favor of annexation, or becoming part of the United States. As proud as they may have been of the republic, even the earliest settlers still regarded themselves as Americans.

Given that Americans had enthusiastically supported the war, most Texans assumed the United States would want to annex the republic. Many Northern members of Congress, however, opposed admitting Texas as a slave state.

President Andrew Jackson did not want to increase the tensions between North and South. Nor did he want to risk a costly war with Mexico, which continued to claim ownership of Texas. Jackson made no move toward annexation, though on his last day in office he did sign a resolution officially recognizing Texas as an independent nation.

✓ **Reading Check** **Summarizing** What difficulties did the Texans face in their war against Mexico?

SECTION 2 ASSESSMENT

Checking for Understanding

1. **Define:** *Tejano, empresario, annexation.*

2. **Identify:** National Colonization Act, Washington-on-the Brazos, Antonio López de Santa Anna, Sam Houston, Alamo, William B. Travis.

3. **Explain** why Texas declared war on Mexico.

Reviewing Themes

4. **Groups and Institutions** Why did some Northern leaders oppose admitting Texas to the United States?

Critical Thinking

5. **Synthesizing** How did the Texan defeats at the Alamo and Goliad affect Texans?

6. **Categorizing** Use a graphic organizer similar to the one below to list the reasons that Texans did not wish to become Mexican citizens.

Reasons Texans Opposed Mexican Citizenship

Analyzing Visuals

7. **Examining Art** Examine the poster on page 301 advertising land to Texas settlers. How were permanent settlers and soldiers for hire rewarded differently?

8. **Examining Art** Study the painting on this page. Why do you think the artist painted the clearing blue sky in the top right of the work?

Writing About History

9. **Persuasive Writing** Imagine that you are living in Texas in the late 1830s. Write a letter to the U.S. Congress explaining why the members should or should not vote to annex Texas.

History *Through Art*

Background: The San Jacinto Monument is dedicated "to Heroes of the Battle of San Jacinto and all others who contributed to the independence of Texas." The monument is a 570-foot limestone shaft topped by a 34-foot, 220-ton star symbolizing the Lone Star Republic. The monument is located on the battlefield where Texas won its independence.
Answer: They were taking a siesta.
Ask: Why did the Mexicans panic? *(They were used to acting only on orders.)*

✓ **Reading Check**

Answer: few men had military training, there was no clear leader before Sam Houston took command, and the Texans were outnumbered

Reteach

Ask students to chronicle the American settlement of Texas.

Enrich

Have students write an essay explaining how life would be different today if Texas had remained a part of Mexico.

4 CLOSE

Have students describe the major battles of the war for the independence of Texas and explain the significance of each.

SECTION 2 ASSESSMENT ANSWERS

1. Terms are in blue.

2. National Colonization Act (p. 301), Washington-on-the-Brazos (p. 301), Antonio Lopez de Santa Anna (p. 302), Sam Houston (p. 302), Alamo (p. 302), William B. Travis (p. 302)

3. Texans felt negotiations to peacefully organize its own state government were hopeless.

4. They feared it would become a slave state.

5. The defeats united them behind their new country.

6. did not want to adopt Mexican customs, did not see Mexico as their own country, few spoke Spanish, and most found the Spanish Catholic Church alien to them

7. Permanent settlers were given more land than those who came only to fight.

8. possibly to symbolize Texas's coming victory

9. Students' letters will vary but should express appropriate reasons for or against annexation.

Understanding Latitude and Longitude

Why Learn This Skill?

Mapmakers use lines of latitude and longitude to pinpoint locations on maps and globes. Understanding these lines and what they signify will help you locate any place on a map—around the corner or around the world.

Learning the Skill

The imaginary horizontal lines that circle the globe from east to west are called lines of **latitude.** Because the distance between the lines of latitude is always the same, they are also called *parallels.* The imaginary vertical lines that intersect the parallels are lines of **longitude,** also called *meridians.*

Parallels and meridians are numbered in degrees. The **Equator,** located halfway between the North and South Poles, is at 0°. Moving north or south of the Equator, the number of degrees increases until reaching 90°N or 90°S latitude at the poles.

The **Prime Meridian** is at 0° longitude. Moving east or west of the Prime Meridian, the number of degrees east or west increases up to 180°. The 180° line of longitude is located on the opposite side of the globe from the Prime Meridian and is called the *International Date Line.*

The point at which parallels and meridians intersect is the grid address, or coordinates, of an exact location. The coordinates for Salt Lake City, for example, are 41°N latitude and 112°W longitude.

Practicing the Skill

Analyze the information on the map on this page, and then answer the questions.

❶ What are the approximate coordinates of Fort Victoria?

❷ At what line of latitude was the Oregon country divided between the United States and Britain? How many degrees south would you need to go from there to reach the South Pole?

❸ What geographic feature lies at about 42°N and 109°W?

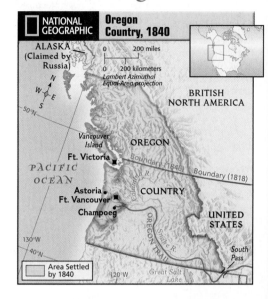

❹ The United States originally wanted Oregon's northern border to be between 54° and 55°N. Does the 1846 Boundary lie north or south of this boundary? By approximately how many degrees?

Skills Assessment

Complete the Practicing Skills questions on page 315 and the Chapter 9 Skill Reinforcement Activity to assess your mastery of this skill.

Applying the Skill

Understanding Latitude and Longitude Study the map of western trails on page 296. Use the map to answer the following questions.

1. St. Joseph is closest to which parallel?

2. Which fort is located north of 40°N latitude and east of 100°W longitude?

 Glencoe's **Skillbuilder Interactive Workbook CD-ROM, Level 2** provides instruction and practice in key social studies skills.

TEACH

Understanding Latitude and Longitude Explain that the coordinates of any given location are similar to a permanent address—the numbers never change. Remind students of the importance of including the appropriate direction when providing the coordinates for a particular location. You must always specify north or south for latitude and east or west for longitude.

Have students identify the coordinates for their hometown and several other locations of their choice.

Additional Practice

Reinforcing Skills Activity 9

Name _____ Date _____ Class _____

★ **Reinforcing Skills Activity 9**

Understanding Latitude and Longitude

◻ **LEARNING THE SKILL**

To find a location on a map, you can use the lines of *latitude* and *longitude.* Latitude lines (or parallels) are imaginary horizontal lines that circle the earth's surface east to west. Longitude lines (or meridians) are imaginary lines that run vertically from the north to the south. Latitude and longitude lines are numbered in degrees. To determine the latitude and longitude of a location on a map—also known as the grid address or coordinates—find the point where the latitude lines and longitude lines intersect.

◻ **PRACTICING THE SKILL**

DIRECTIONS: Use the map below to answer the following questions.

1. How many degrees of latitude

GLENCOE
TECHNOLOGY

CD-ROM
Glencoe Skillbuilder Interactive Workbook CD-ROM, Level 2

This interactive CD-ROM reinforces student mastery of essential social studies skills.

ANSWERS TO PRACTICING THE SKILL

❶ approximately 49°N; 123°W

❷ 49°N; 139°

❸ Great Salt Lake

❹ to the south by 6° to 7°

Applying the Skill

1. 40°N

2. Ft. Kearny

1 FOCUS

Section Overview

This section explores the war with Mexico and its outcome.

Guide to Reading

Answers to Graphic:
I. The Lingering Question of Texas
II. Texas and Oregon Enter the Union
  A. The Election of 1844
  B. The Oregon Question
  C. The Annexation of Texas
III. The War with Mexico
  A. Calling All Volunteers
  B. The Fighting Begins
  C. To Mexico City
  D. The Peace Treaty

Preteaching Vocabulary
For each of the Key Terms and Names, have students write a phrase or short sentence that will help them remember the significance of the term or name.

Guide to Reading

Main Idea
The United States clashed with Mexico in an attempt to gain new territory.

Key Terms and Names
John Tyler, James K. Polk, "Fifty-four Forty or Fight," envoy, Zachary Taylor, John C. Frémont, Bear Flag Republic, Winfield Scott, Treaty of Guadalupe Hidalgo, cede

Reading Strategy
Taking Notes As you read about the war with Mexico, use the major headings of the section to complete the outline started below.

> The War With Mexico
> I. The Lingering Question of Texas
> II.
>   A.
>   B.
>   C.

Reading Objectives
• **Describe** the circumstances under which Texas and Oregon were admitted to the Union.
• **Discuss** the major events of the war with Mexico.

Section Theme
Continuity and Change The war with Mexico brought new territories under the control of the United States.

Preview of Events

♦1845	♦1846	♦1847	♦1848
February 1845 Congress votes to annex Texas	**May 13, 1846** Congress declares war on Mexico **June 18, 1846** Oregon boundary dispute settled	**September 14, 1847** U.S. troops storm Mexico City	**February 2, 1848** Treaty of Guadalupe Hidalgo signed

---

★ An American Story ★

Mexican army shako hat

"Monterrey is ours," wrote U.S. Army lieutenant Napoleon Dana to his wife Sue in September 1846. "I can hardly describe to you with my pen what difficulties, dangers, and labors we have gone through to gain it." Lieutenant Dana had just survived four days of intense fighting as American troops captured the Mexican city of Monterrey.

66 The enemy fought very obstinately here, and we had to fight them by inches and advance upon them from house to house. . . . Soon after dark our mortar began to fire. . . . The shells all burst beautifully right in the plaza, scattering death and devastation. 99

Dana and other American troops remained in the city for two months, taking over the houses of wealthy residents. The army assigned Dana to the home of "one Don Manuel Somebody." He wrote Sue of beautiful palace grounds "such as you may have seen in pictures of Italian gardens in older times." In mid-December, the night before leaving Monterrey, he paid a farewell visit to Don Manuel, whom he now regarded as a "right good old fellow." As the elderly Mexican said goodbye, he made "a long and affecting speech . . . while his eyes filled. . . . He said that if the war continued, he foresaw nothing but the ruin of his native land."

—adapted from *Monterrey Is Ours!*

The Lingering Question of Texas

The stage had been set for war with Mexico years before. Territorial disputes between the United States and its southern neighbor began as far back as 1803, when the United States claimed Texas as part of the Louisiana Purchase. The United States renounced

---

that claim in the Adams-Onís Treaty of 1819, but the idea of Manifest Destiny and of acquiring Mexican territory had strong popular support.

Tensions grew during the administration of **John Tyler,** who hoped to bring Texas into the Union. Because Texas already possessed a significant population of Southerners who had taken enslaved African Americans into Texas, it was certain to support the cause of slavery. Antislavery leaders in Congress therefore opposed annexation. Moreover, Mexico had never recognized the independence of Texas and still considered it Mexican territory.

✔ **Reading Check** **Analyzing** Why did antislavery members of Congress oppose admitting Texas to the Union?

Texas and Oregon Enter the Union

In early 1844, after spearheading a publicity campaign in favor of annexation, President Tyler brought the matter before the Senate. He blundered, however, by including in the supporting documents a letter written by Secretary of State John C. Calhoun that contained a fierce defense of slavery. Outraged Northerners pointed to the letter as evidence that annexation was nothing but a pro-slavery plot, and by a count of 35 to 16, the Senate voted against annexation. The maneuver that Tyler believed would win him a second term instead destroyed his chances of retaining the presidency.

The Election of 1844 As the presidential race began later that year, the front-runners for the nomination were Whig senator **Henry Clay** and former Democratic president Martin Van Buren. Although politicians on both sides of the annexation issue pressed the candidates to state their positions, both responded cautiously to avoid losing supporters.

Van Buren's indecision cost him the Democratic nomination. His party instead chose **James K. Polk,** a former

Congressman and governor of Tennessee. Polk promised to annex not only Texas but also the contested Oregon territory in the Northwest. In addition, he vowed to buy California from Mexico. The ambitious platform appealed to both Northerners and Southerners because it expanded the country while promising to maintain the delicate balance between free and slave states.

The Democrats' unity on annexation caused Clay to backpedal. Reversing a statement made in the

Picturing **History**

Tensions Grow With Mexico From the time of the Louisiana Purchase in 1803, territorial tensions between the United States and Mexico threatened the possibility of war. In the late 1840s, war began between the two nations. This rare daguerreotype shows American soldiers patrolling Mexican territory. How did Texas's annexation contribute to the start of the war?

CHAPTER 9 Manifest Destiny **307**

2 *TEACH*

Daily Lecture and Discussion Notes 9–3

Copyright © by The McGraw-Hill Companies, Inc.

Daily Lecture and Discussion Notes

Chapter 9, Section 3

Did You Know? Mexicans living in the area ceded to the U.S. in the Treaty of Guadalupe Hidalgo were guaranteed all rights of U.S. citizenship, including political rights and the right to keep their lands. They were given one year to decide if they wanted to accept American citizenship.

I. **The Lingering Question of Texas** *(pages 306–307)*
   A. Territorial disputes between the United States and Mexico began in 1803, when the U.S. claimed Texas as part of the Louisiana Purchase.
   B. The idea of Manifest Destiny and of gaining Mexican territory had strong popular support.

✔ **Reading Check**

Answer: Because Texas already possessed a significant population of Southerners and enslaved persons, it was certain that Texas would join the nation as a slave state.

Fact | **Fiction** | **Folklore**

Ft. Vancouver, a British outpost established by the Hudson Bay Company, was often the final stop on the trail before emigrants reached Oregon City. Located on the northern bank of the Columbia River, Ft. Vancouver was a thriving community. John McLoughlin who, despite orders to discourage American emigrants, was known for his hospitality, welcomed tired, hungry, and often barefoot travelers.

Picturing **History**

Answer: Since Mexico had never recognized Texas's independence, annexation was seen as an act of aggression against Mexico.
Ask: How does the image in the daguerreotype differ from a photo today? *(Images are less distinct, no color is shown.)*

COOPERATIVE LEARNING ACTIVITY

Creating Historical Maps Organize the class into small groups. Provide each group with two blank outline maps of the continental United States and Mexico. Have half the groups create a map showing the United States and Mexico in 1840. Have the other half create a map showing the same area in 1850. Tell the groups to use colors to clearly label the land claimed by each country. Also have students draw in the boundaries of the states and territories in the United States. As a class, examine the maps and discuss the extent of changes that occurred in one decade. 📦

Use the rubric for a cooperative group management plan on pages 81–82 in the *Performance Assessment Activities and Rubrics.*

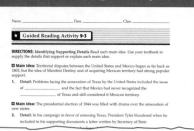
Creating a Circle Graph Have students use the data shown below to create a circle graph illustrating the presidential election results of 1844. **L2**

Candidate	Popular Vote	Electoral Vote
Polk, Dem.	1,338,464	170
Clay, Whig	1,300,097	105
Birney, Lib.	62,300	

📁 Use the rubric for creating a map, display, or chart on pages 77–78 in the *Performance Assessment Activities and Rubrics.*

FYI

If the voters in New York who cast ballots for James Birney, the Liberty Party presidential candidate in 1844, had voted for the Whig candidate, Henry Clay would have been the 11th president. With New York's 36 votes, Clay would have won the Electoral College vote 141 to 134.

✓ Reading Check

Answer: Polk promised to annex Texas and the contested Oregon territory in the Northwest.

Different Viewpoints

Did Manifest Destiny Violate American Ideals?

In the 1800s, many Americans believed the United States was destined to reach from the Atlantic Ocean to the Pacific Ocean. This national mission also implied that Americans were superior to their neighbors who also controlled territory in North America. Did this belief in American superiority contradict the spirit of equality important to so many Americans?

Public servant Albert Gallatin opposes Manifest Destiny:

At the age of 86, after a distinguished career in public service, Albert Gallatin became president of the New York Historical Society. The war against Mexico revived his interest in politics, and he wrote:

"It is said that the people of the United States have a hereditary superiority of race over the Mexicans, which gives them the right to subjugate and keep in bondage the inferior nation. . . .

Is it compatible with the principle of democracy, which rejects every hereditary claim of individuals, to admit a hereditary superiority of races? . . . Can you for a moment suppose that a very doubtful descent from men who lived 1,000 years ago has transmitted to you a superiority over your fellow men?

. . . At this time the claim is but a pretext for covering and justifying unjust usurpation and unbounded ambition.

. . . Among ourselves the most ignorant, the most inferior, either in physical or mental faculties, is recognized as having equal rights, and he has an equal vote with anyone, however superior to him in all those respects. This is founded on the immutable principle that no one man is born with the right to governing another man."

—quoted in *The Mission of the United States*

spring of 1844 against immediate annexation, Clay now supported annexation of Texas as long as it was done without causing war with Mexico. This so angered antislavery Whigs in his party that they threw their support to the Liberty Party—a small third party that supported abolition. With the Whig vote split, Polk won the election.

The Oregon Question In public, Polk took a strong stance on Oregon. Despite British claims on the region, he said that the United States had a "clear and unquestionable" right to it. His supporters cried **"Fifty-four Forty or Fight,"** declaring that they wanted all of Oregon to the line of 54° 40′ north latitude.

In private, however, Polk agreed to split the territory. In June 1846 Great Britain and the United States resolved the dispute. The United States received all of Oregon south of 49° north latitude, except for the southern tip of Vancouver Island.

The Annexation of Texas Even before Polk took office, outgoing president Tyler pushed an annexation resolution through Congress in February 1845.

The resolution succeeded because it needed only a simple majority of both houses rather than the two-thirds majority needed to ratify a treaty. Texas joined the Union in 1845. Mexico was outraged and broke diplomatic relations with the U.S. government. Matters worsened when the two countries disputed the location of Texas's southwestern border. Mexico said it was the Nueces River. Texans, and then the United States, claimed the Rio Grande, about 150 miles (240 km) farther west and south, as the boundary. The Texas-United States claim covered far more territory than the Mexican claim, including some of what is now eastern New Mexico.

Polk's intentions in California added to the growing strife. In November 1845 he sent **John Slidell** as special envoy, or representative, to Mexico City to try to purchase the territory. Mexico's new president, José Joaquín Herrera, refused even to meet with Slidell.

✓ Reading Check **Examining** What did James Polk promise to do if he was elected president?

MEETING SPECIAL NEEDS

Visual/Spatial Have interested students research the typical uniforms and gear used by soldiers during the war with Mexico. Have students prepare a display that includes drawings or pictures of the uniforms and gear used by soldiers of the era. **L1**

📁 Refer to *Inclusion for the High School Social Studies Classroom Strategies and Activities* in the TCR.

Editor John L. O'Sullivan supports Manifest Destiny:

John L. O'Sullivan first used the phrase "manifest destiny" in a July 1845 edition of the *United States Magazine and Democratic Review.* In the following article excerpt, he promotes the spread of democracy:

"Texas is now ours. Already, before these words are written, her convention has undoubtedly ratified the acceptance, by her congress, of our proffered invitation into the Union. . . . Her star and stripe may already be said to have taken their place in the glorious blazon of our common nationality. . . .

. . . The next session of Congress will see the representatives of the new young state in their places in both our halls of national legislation, side by side with those of the old Thirteen.

Why . . . [have] other nations . . . undertaken to intrude themselves into [the question of Texas]? Between us and the proper parties to the case, in a spirit of hostile interference against us, for the avowed object of thwarting our policy and hampering our power, limiting our greatness and checking the fulfillment of our manifest destiny to overspread the continent allotted by Providence for the free development of our yearly multiplying millions."

—quoted in *Annexation*

Learning From History

1. What does Albert Gallatin think is the real motivation underlying the idea of Manifest Destiny?
2. Can you find other instances in American history when Americans believed their nation had a special destiny?

The War With Mexico

Herrera's snub ended any realistic chance of a diplomatic solution. Polk ordered troops led by General **Zachary Taylor** to cross the Nueces River—in Mexico's view, an invasion of its territory. Polk wanted Mexican soldiers to fire the first shot. If he could say Mexico was the aggressor, he could more easily win popular support for a war.

Finally, on May 9, 1846, news reached him that a force of Mexicans had attacked Taylor's men. In an address to Congress, Polk declared that the United States was at war "by the act of Mexico herself." Hoping to incite the public's indignation, he added that "American blood has been shed on American soil!"

Many Whigs opposed the war as yet another plot to extend slavery. Most Washington politicians, though, recognized that however questionable Polk's

actions, the United States was committed to war. On May 13 the Senate voted 40 to 2 and the House 174 to 14 in favor of the war.

Calling All Volunteers Polk and his advisers developed a three-pronged military strategy. Taylor's troops would continue to move south, crossing the Rio Grande near the Gulf of Mexico. A separate force to the northwest would capture Santa Fe, an important trading center in what is now New Mexico, and then march west to take control of California with the help of the American navy. Finally, U.S. forces would advance to Mexico City and force Mexico to surrender.

To implement the ambitious plan, the United States needed to expand the army. Congress authorized the president to call for 50,000 volunteers, and men from all over the country rushed to enlist. Almost 73,000 answered the call.

Undisciplined and unruly, the volunteers proved to be less than ideal soldiers. As one officer observed, "They will do well enough to defend their own firesides, but they can not endure the fatigue incident to an invading army." Another bemoaned in a half-comical way their constant demands on his attention:

❝[O]ne wanted me to read a letter he had just received; another wanted me to write one for him; another wanted me to send his money home; another wanted me to keep it for him. . . . [O]ne complained that his uniform was too large, another that his was too small.❞

—from *Memoirs of a Maryland Volunteer*

The Fighting Begins In early May, several days before Polk signed the declaration of war, Taylor's troops defeated Mexican general Santa Anna, first at

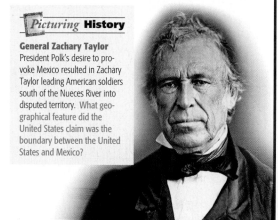

Picturing History

General Zachary Taylor
President Polk's desire to provoke Mexico resulted in Zachary Taylor leading American soldiers south of the Nueces River into disputed territory. What geographical feature did the United States claim was the boundary between the United States and Mexico?

INTERDISCIPLINARY CONNECTIONS ACTIVITY

Language Arts Have students read a biography of Santa Anna, a strong force in Mexico's politics and military. Then have students write an essay that answers the following question: **How did Santa Anna maintain power and influence for such a long period, even when he made errors or suffered defeats?** L2

3 ASSESS

Assign Section 3 Assessment as homework or as an in-class activity.

Have students use the **Interactive Tutor Self-Assessment CD-ROM.**

Reading Essentials and Study Guide 9–3

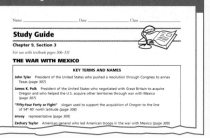

Flag's Origins When California settlers declared their independence from Mexico, they raised a flag with a white background, a single star, a red bar, and a grizzly bear. The bear flag officially became the state flag in 1911.

Geography *Skills*

Answers:
1. Sloat
2. land north of the Rio Grande and west to the Pacific Ocean

Geography Skills Practice
Ask: In what body of water did the United States set up a naval blockade? *(Gulf of Mexico)*

Palo Alto and then at Resaca de la Palma. Taylor then moved south, overcoming more enemy forces at Matamoros. By late September he had marched about 200 miles (322 km) west from the Gulf Coast and captured Monterrey.

In the meantime, Colonel Stephen W. Kearny led troops from Fort Leavenworth, west of Missouri, toward Santa Fe. The march through the dry countryside was brutal, but when Kearny's men reached the city in August, the Mexican force there had already fled. With Santa Fe secured, a small U.S. force headed on to California.

Before Kearny's force arrived and even before war with Mexico was officially declared, settlers in northern California, led by American general **John C. Frémont,** had begun an uprising. The official Mexican presence in the territory had never been strong, and the settlers had little trouble overcoming

it. On June 14, 1846, they declared California independent of Mexico and renamed the region the **Bear Flag Republic.** A few weeks later, the Bear Flag Republic came to an end when naval forces of the United States occupied San Francisco and San Diego and took possession of California for the United States.

To Mexico City The war had proceeded just as President Polk had hoped, but despite having lost vast territories, Mexico's leaders refused to surrender. Polk decided to force things to a conclusion with the third phase of his battle plan. He sent soldiers on ships to the Mexican port of Veracruz, from where they would march west and capture the Mexican capital, Mexico City.

Polk, seeing Taylor as a potential rival in the 1848 election, eased him out of the war by placing General

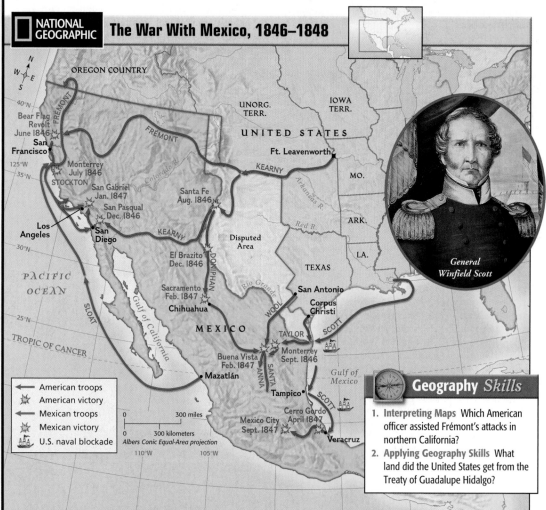

NATIONAL GEOGRAPHIC **The War With Mexico, 1846–1848**

General Winfield Scott

Geography *Skills*

1. **Interpreting Maps** Which American officer assisted Frémont's attacks in northern California?
2. **Applying Geography Skills** What land did the United States get from the Treaty of Guadalupe Hidalgo?

CRITICAL THINKING ACTIVITY

Determining Point of View Have students research historical documents and writings of the era and write a position paper defending either the United States's actions or Mexican actions during the conflict. Encourage students to take a strong stand on one side or the other of the conflict. **L3**

Winfield Scott, a member of the Whig Party, in command of this campaign. In March 1847 Scott's force landed at Veracruz. The troops headed for Mexico City, battling the enemy along the way. On September 14, after a hard fight, they finally captured the capital.

The Peace Treaty After the fall of Mexico City, Mexico's leaders could no longer hold out. On February 2, 1848, they signed the **Treaty of Guadalupe Hidalgo.** In the agreement, Mexico ceded, or gave up, more than 500,000 square miles (1,295,000 sq. km) of territory to the United States. This land is now the states of California, Utah, and Nevada, as well as most of New Mexico and Arizona and parts of Colorado and Wyoming. Mexico also accepted the Rio Grande as the southern border of Texas. In exchange, the United States paid Mexico $15 million and agreed to take over $3.25 million in debts the Mexican government owed to American citizens.

With Oregon and the former Mexican territories now under the American flag, the dream of Manifest Destiny was finally realized: the United States now stretched from ocean to ocean. Valuable ports on the west coast opened up new avenues to the Pacific nations of Asia. The question of whether the new lands should allow slavery, however, would soon lead the country into another bloody

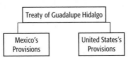

History *Through Art*

General Scott's Entrance Into Mexico This 1851 painting by Carl Nebel re-creates the scene of General Winfield Scott leading troops into Mexico City in the final phase of the war with Mexico. Scott's forces had battled their way inland to Mexico City from the coastal city of Veracruz. How do the Mexican people seem to be reacting to the arrival of the American troops?

conflict. The experience that such men as Robert E. Lee and Ulysses S. Grant gained during the war would soon be used to lead Americans against each other.

✓ **Reading Check** **Summarizing** What was President Polk's military strategy in the war with Mexico?

SECTION 3 ASSESSMENT

Checking for Understanding

1. **Define:** envoy, cede.
2. **Identify:** John Tyler, James K. Polk, "Fifty-four Forty or Fight," Zachary Taylor, John C. Frémont, Bear Flag Republic, Winfield Scott, Treaty of Guadalupe Hidalgo.
3. **Summarize** the controversy between Mexico and the United States over Texas.

Reviewing Themes

4. **Continuity and Change** The idea of Manifest Destiny was realized as a result of the war with Mexico. What new problems did this increase in land cause for the United States?

Critical Thinking

5. **Evaluating** What was the military strategy of the United States during the war with Mexico? Evaluate the success of this strategy.
6. **Organizing** Use a graphic organizer similar to the one below to list the provisions of the Treaty of Guadalupe Hidalgo.

```
        Treaty of Guadalupe Hidalgo
           /              \
   Mexico's          United States's
   Provisions         Provisions
```

Analyzing Visuals

7. **Examining Art** Study the portrait of General Winfield Scott on page 310. Why did President Taylor place Scott in charge of the invasion of Mexico City?
8. **Examining Art** Study the painting *American Progress* by John Gast on page 308. What symbols of progress are shown trailing the spirit figure heading westward?

Writing About History

9. **Expository Writing** Pretend you are James K. Polk, the Democratic candidate for president in the 1844 election. Write a speech in which you explain your platform.

CHAPTER 9 Manifest Destiny **311**

SECTION 3 ASSESSMENT ANSWERS

1. Terms are in blue.
2. John Tyler (*p. 307*), James K. Polk (*p. 307*), "Fifty-four Forty or Fight" (*p. 308*), Zachary Taylor (*p. 309*), John C. Frémont (*p. 310*), Bear Flag Republic (*p. 310*), Winfield Scott (*p. 311*), Treaty of Guadalupe Hidalgo (*p. 311*)
3. Mexico did not recognize Texas's

independence, disputed the Texas border, and was angered by the annexation of Texas.
4. expansion of slavery into new land
5. cross Rio Grande, capture Santa Fe and California, invade Mexico City; strategy succeeded
6. Mexico: ceded over 500,000 square miles of territory, accepted

Rio Grande as Texas border; United States: paid Mexico $15 million and claimed $3.25 million in Mexican debts
7. to remove him from 1848 presidential race
8. stagecoach, wagon train, train, settlers
9. Students' speeches will vary.

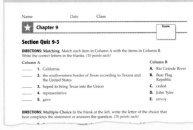

Section Quiz 9–3

Name   Date   Class

★ Chapter 9   Score

Section Quiz 9-3

DIRECTIONS: Matching Match each item in Column A with the items in Column B. Write the correct letters in the blanks. (10 points each)

Column A

___ 1. California
___ 2. the southwestern border of Texas according to Texans and the United States
___ 3. hoped to bring Texas into the Union
___ 4. representative
___ 5. gave

Column B

A. Rio Grande River
B. Bear Flag Republic
C. ceded
D. John Tyler
E. envoy

DIRECTIONS: Multiple Choice In the blank at the left, write the letter of the choice that best completes the statement or answers the question. (10 points each)

History *Through Art*

Answer: They are not resisting the Americans' arrival.
Ask: What treaty ended the war with Mexico? *(Treaty of Guadalupe Hidalgo)*

✓ **Reading Check**

Answer: Polk had a three-pronged strategy: move south across the Rio Grande, capture Santa Fe and take control of California, and invade Mexico City.

Reteach
Ask students to explain the events that led to statehood for Texas.

Enrich
Have students write a short essay on what life would be like in the southwestern United States had the land remained a part of Mexico, rather than being incorporated into the United States. Have students use the point of view of someone living in the territory.

4 CLOSE

Have students discuss the major events of the war with Mexico including names, dates, and places.

1 FOCUS

As students study the layout of a typical mission, have them determine how the following areas/groups helped the mission be self-sufficient: the tannery, the granary, the cemetery, the workshop, the pottery makers, the church, the stable, the priests, and the soldiers.

2 TEACH

Tracing a Route Have students practice their map skills by planning a trip to visit several of the missions. Tell students they will travel from Loreto to San Francisco. Have them count the number of missions that they would pass on the trip. Then have them write down the names, in order, of the missions on their journey that are labeled by name on the map. Ask students to speculate on why the route passes so many missions. (*Routes developed to connect the missions. In many places, the missions were placed a day's journey apart so that travelers could sleep in the safety of the mission walls.*) **L1**

Mental Mapping Tell students that a mental map is a person's mental image of an area. Have students draw a mental map of their neighborhood or community from an aerial perspective similar to the layout of the mission. Tell students that exact distances are not as important as the relationships among the various parts. **L2**

Spanish Missions

The Spanish settlers who came to the American Southwest had two aims: to claim the land and to convert the Native Americans to Catholicism. To achieve these aims, the Spaniards set up fortified religious settlements known as missions.

The missions reflected both the culture of Spain and the demands of life in an arid land. By the late eighteenth century, the missions were thriving, self-contained communities.

Arranged in a quadrangle around a central courtyard, the complex was a bustling world of workshops, storage areas, gardens, and living quarters. Its location was often determined by the availability of wood, water, and fields for raising crops and grazing the livestock that the Spanish brought to the Americas. The form of the mission was dictated by the building materials available. The thick walls of the one-story buildings were usually made of stone or sun-dried mud bricks known as adobe.

For security, most of the mission's residences were connected, and all windows faced inward. The entrances were locked at night. A covered arcade, or outdoor hallway, ran along the inner walls of the residences. The complex was usually dominated by a large church. Thousands of Native Americans were lured to the missions by gifts and by the prospect of finding safety and food. They were instructed in Catholicism and Spanish and put to work. Women wove cloth and cooked; men labored at handicrafts or in the fields. In addition to the native beans and corn, the converts planted crops introduced by the Spaniards such as wheat, oats, oranges, olives, and grapes.

Some of the missions would not allow the Native Americans to leave without permission once they had entered the community. Making this transition to a regimented life was difficult, and escapes were common. To enforce order and hunt down runaways, many missions had a small detachment of soldiers. The soldiers rode on horses, which the Spaniards brought to the Southwest.

The Spaniards also brought measles and smallpox—devastating diseases against which the Indians had no natural immunity. Mission cemeteries often held the bones of thousands of Native Americans who died of these European diseases.

Crops

Priests' quarters

Soldiers' barracks

Stable

Watering trough

LEARNING FROM GEOGRAPHY

1. What factors determined the selection of a mission site?

2. Why did the Spanish station troops at missions?

312 CHAPTER 9 Manifest Destiny

Spanish Missions, 1776

✝ Mission
✝ Mission & Presidio
■ Presidio

········ Present-day boundary
━━━ Road
➤ Migration

0 ___ 200 miles
0 ___ 200 kilometers

San Francisco
San Juan
SanLuis Obispo
San Juan Capistrano
San Diego
Santa Fe
Tomé
Socorro
Tubac
Tucson
El Paso
Fronteras
Horcasitas
San Antonio
San José y San Miguel de Aguayo
Loreto
Monterrey

EXTENDING THE CONTENT

Presidio of San Francisco In 1776 the Presidio of San Francisco began as the northernmost military outpost of the Spanish in North America. From 1822 to 1848, the Mexican flag flew over the presidio. When Mexico ceded California to the United States in 1848, the presidio became a U.S. Army post. During World War II, it served as the headquarters of the Western Defense Command and foxholes were dug along nearby beaches in preparation for troops to defend any attack.

The Virgin of Guadalupe adorns the church at the mission of San José y San Miguel de Aguayo.

Fruit trees

Living quarters

Gate

Oven

Workshop

Well

Pottery makers

Livestock corral

Nut trees

Garden

Fruit trees

Catholic church

Cemetery and garden

Granary

Tannery and workshops

Entrance

Soldiers

Years before the English unfurled their flag at Jamestown, Spanish missionaries and colonists from New Spain, as Mexico was known, were settling in the Southwest. The map shows their major migration routes into present-day New Mexico, Texas, and California, as well as the location of their missions and presidios, or garrisoned forts.

The Spanish built the church of San José y San Miguel de Aguayo in San Antonio, Texas, in the 1720s. Such churches were only part of much larger mission complexes. The art above shows the layout of a typical mission.

ANSWERS TO LEARNING FROM GEOGRAPHY

1. The availability of wood, water, and grazing lands determined the locations of Spanish missions.

2. The Spanish used troops to enforce order and to capture Native Americans who entered the community and then escaped.

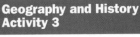

Geography and History Activity 3

Name _____ Date _____ Class _____

⊞ GEOGRAPHY AND HISTORY ACTIVITY 3

Ranches of the Southwest: A Spanish Legacy

THE SPANISH AND HISPANIC SOUTHWEST
The southwest United States was under Spanish and Hispanic rule from the time of Coronado's explorations in 1540 until the end of the Mexican-American War in 1848. During Spain's rule, the area was divided into three provinces: New Mexico, California, and Tejas (Texas). The vast province of New Mexico included what is now the state of New Mexico, most of Colorado and Arizona, and parts of Utah, Wyoming, Kansas, Oklahoma, and Texas. (See Map 1.) In 1821 Mexico won indepen-

horses. The vaqueros were the forerunners of cowhands, and the equipment and techniques they used were well suited to the open-range style of ranching. The clothing worn by cowhands, the gear for their horses, and the techniques for roping and herding cattle all originated with the Spanish.

SHEEP IN NEW MEXICO
Santa Fe, New Mexico, was founded in 1609 or 1610. It was the first permanent settlement west of the Mississippi River. Although Santa Fe was situated at a high

Making a Drawing Have students reread the feature. Then have them make a drawing from the perspective of either a Native American or a Franciscan monk about what life was like at the mission. Have volunteers share their drawings with the class. Use the drawings to discuss the different points of view of the purpose and reality of life in the mission. **L2**

3 ASSESS

Have students answer the Learning from Geography questions.

4 CLOSE

Ask students to describe what lasting influences the Spanish mission system has had on the southwestern United States.

you don't say...

Presidio The term *presidio* means fort or military post.

NGS ONLINE

Access National Geographic's Web site for current events, atlas updates, activities, links, interactive features, and archives at www.nationalgeographic.com.

CHAPTER 9 ASSESSMENT and ACTIVITIES

Reviewing Key Terms

Students' answers will vary. The pages where the words appear in the text are shown in parentheses.

1. **Manifest Destiny** *(p. 295)*
2. **squatter** *(p. 295)*
3. **overlander** *(p. 296)*
4. **Tejano** *(p. 300)*
5. **empresario** *(p. 301)*
6. **annexation** *(p. 304)*
7. **envoy** *(p. 308)*
8. **cede** *(p. 311)*

Reviewing Key Facts

9. John Louis O'Sullivan *(p. 295)*, John Sutter *(p. 295)*, Brigham Young *(p. 297)*, Antonio Lopez de Santa Anna *(p. 302)*, Sam Houston *(p. 302)*, William B. Travis *(p. 302)*, John Tyler *(p. 307)*, James K. Polk *(p. 307)*, Zachary Taylor *(p. 309)*, Winfield Scott *(p. 311)*

10. opportunity to own their own land

11. possible answers: California, Mormon, Oregon, Santa Fe, Butterfield Overland Mail, Old Spanish, Pony Express

12. wanted to better control area but Mexicans unwilling to move closer to Native Americans

13. Texans felt negotiations to peacefully organize its own state government were hopeless and felt independence was the only option.

14. The United States got over 500,000 square miles of territory and resolution of the location of the southern border of Texas.

Reviewing Key Terms

On a sheet of paper, use each of these terms in a sentence.

1. Manifest Destiny
2. squatter
3. overlander
4. *Tejano*
5. *empresario*
6. annexation
7. envoy
8. cede

Reviewing Key Facts

9. **Identify:** John Louis O'Sullivan, John Sutter, Brigham Young, Antonio López de Santa Anna, Sam Houston, William B. Travis, John Tyler, James K. Polk, Zachary Taylor, Winfield Scott.

10. Why were many Americans willing to give up their lives in the East and move to the West?

11. What were five trails that Americans followed as they emigrated west?

12. Why did the Mexican government encourage Americans to settle in northern Texas?

13. What caused settlers in Texas to declare independence from Mexico?

14. What did the United States gain from the Treaty of Guadalupe Hidalgo?

Chapter Summary

Oregon

- Great Britain and the United States claimed parts of Oregon.
- The area was almost completely British until American missionaries arrived in the 1830s.
- Large numbers of Americans sought farmland in southern Oregon in 1840.
- The two countries divided the territory without conflict.

California

- The territory was part of Mexico, although Americans still settled there.
- The local California government invited foreign settlers but was suspicious of them.
- The United States tried to purchase California from Mexico, but Mexico refused.
- An uprising overthrew the California government, and troops secured the territory during the war with Mexico.

The Midwest

- In the early 1800s, squatters settled land that they did not own in Ohio, Indiana, Illinois, Michigan, and Wisconsin.
- The Preemption Act allowed squatters to buy up to 160 acres of land.

Texas and the Southwest

- Mexico invited Americans and others to populate Texas.
- Mexico passed strict laws against American immigrants, which led to Texas's war for independence.
- Congress voted to annex Texas in 1845, and Texas also voted for annexation.
- Boundary disputes in Texas, along with the American attempt to purchase the California territory, led to the start of the war with Mexico.
- The United States won the war and gained Texas, California, and much of the territory that is now the West and Southwest.

Critical Thinking

15. **Analyzing Themes: Science and Technology** How did the inventions of Deere's steel plow and McCormick's reaper encourage the settlement of the western plains?

16. **Identifying Points of View** Why was James Polk's platform in the presidential election of 1844 popular with both Northerners and Southerners?

17. **Categorizing** Use a graphic organizer similar to the one below to list the causes and the effects of westward movement by Americans.

Americans' Westward Movement

Causes		Effects
☐	→	☐
☐	→	☐
☐	→	☐

18. **Interpreting Primary Sources** In April of 1847, Charles Sumner presented his views on the causes of the war with Mexico in his "Report on the War with Mexico" to the Commonwealth of Massachusetts. Read the excerpt and answer the questions that follow.

Critical Thinking

15. These two labor-saving inventions made it possible for farmers to plow and harvest more efficiently.

16. because it maintained the balance between slave and free states

17. some possible answers:
convert Native Americans → increased settlement in Oregon
own farms → new agricultural innovations
belief in Manifest Destiny → growing conflict with Mexico and Great Britain

18. **a.** The United States set out to acquire new lands.
b. The secretary of war gave the generals the task of making the newly acquired territories ready for new settlers, including forming civil governments.

Practicing Skills

19. **a.** between 110°W and 100°W; **b.** about 7°

HISTORY Online

Self-Check Quiz

Visit the *American Vision* Web site at tav.glencoe.com and click on *Self-Check Quizzes—Chapter 9* to assess your knowledge of chapter content.

❝It can no longer be doubted that this is a war of conquest. . . . In a letter to Commodore Sloat, . . . the Secretary [of War] says, 'You will take such measures as will render that vast region [California] a desirable place of residence for emigrants from our soil.' In a letter to Colonel Kearny . . . he says: 'Should you conquer and take possession of New Mexico and Upper California, you will establish civil governments therein. You may assure the people of these provinces that it is the wish of the United States to provide for them a free government with the least possible delay. . . .❞

—quoted in *Readings in American History*

a. According to Charles Sumner, why did the United States become involved in the war with Mexico?

b. What evidence does Sumner provide to show that this was the U.S. government's intention?

Practicing Skills

19. **Understanding Latitude and Longitude** Study the map of western trails on page 296. Then use the steps you learned on page 305 to answer the following questions.
a. The Continental Divide lies between what two lines of longitude?
b. About how many degrees of latitude are there between Salt Lake City and Los Angeles?

Writing Activity

20. **Interviewing** You and a group of your classmates should take on these roles of people in North America in the early to mid-1800s: a journalist, a British settler and an American settler in the Oregon Country, a Native American of the Great Plains, a pioneer, a Mexican official, and a farmer in the East. The journalist then interviews the people about their attitudes toward Manifest Destiny. Write summaries of each interview and place them in your portfolio.

Chapter Activity

21. **Technology Activity: Using an Electronic Card Catalog** Search your library's card catalog for books containing information about western settlement in the 1800s. Use this information to make an alphabetical directory of western trails and historic sites that tourists might like to visit. Your

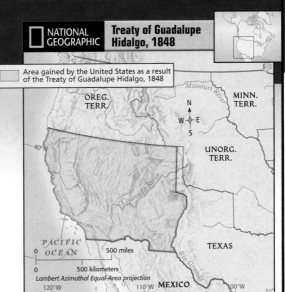

Treaty of Guadalupe Hidalgo, 1848

☐ Area gained by the United States as a result of the Treaty of Guadalupe Hidalgo, 1848

list might include cities along the trails, pioneer museums, mountain passes, and other places of interest.

Geography and History

22. The map above shows land acquired after the war with Mexico. Study the map and answer the questions below.
a. **Interpreting Maps** What seven U.S. states now hold territory acquired in the Treaty of Guadalupe Hidalgo?
b. **Applying Geography Skills** What group of immigrants who had moved outside the United States was brought back under American jurisdiction as a result of the treaty?

The Princeton Review
Standardized Test Practice

Directions: Choose the best answer to the following question.

Which of the following is NOT a condition set by Mexico for American settlers coming to live in Texas?

A They received a ten-year exemption from paying taxes.

B They could never return to live in the United States.

C They were required to become Mexican citizens.

D They were required to convert to the Roman Catholic faith.

Test-Taking Tip: Be careful—overlooking the words NOT or EXCEPT in a question is a common error. Look for the answer choice that does NOT fit the question. For example, since a tax exemption *was* a benefit for Texas newcomers, you can eliminate answer A.

HISTORY Online

Have students visit the Web site at tav.glencoe.com to review Chapter 9 and take the Self-Check Quiz.

The Princeton Review
Standardized Test Practice

Answer: B

Test-Taking Tip: Tell students to examine carefully statements that contain the words *always* and *never*. These are strong words that often give clues to the incorrect answer.

Bonus Question ?

Ask: How long did the typical wagon train trip from the staging areas in Missouri to the Pacific Coast take? *(A trip took approximately five to six months, with wagons progressing about 15 miles per day.)*

Writing Activity
20. Journalists should prepare questions to ask before conducting the interviews. Other students should consider how the person they are portraying would have felt about Manifest Destiny.

Chapter Activity
21. Lists will vary but should be in alphabetical order and follow standard guidelines for listing bibliographic material.

Geography and History
22. a. California, Utah, Nevada, most of New Mexico and Arizona, and parts of Colorado and Wyoming;
b. the Mormons

Unit 4 Resources

SUGGESTED PACING CHART

Unit 4 (1 Day)	Chapter 10 (5 Days)	Chapter 11 (6 Days)	Chapter 12 (5 Days)	Unit 4 (2 Days)
Day 1 Introduction	**Day 1** Chapter 10 Intro, Section 1	**Day 1** Chapter 11 Intro, Section 1	**Day 1** Chapter 12 Intro, Section 1	**Day 1** Wrap-Up/Project
	Day 2 Section 2	**Day 2** Section 2	**Day 2** Section 2	**Day 2** Unit 4 Assessment
	Day 3 Section 3	**Day 3** Section 3	**Day 3** Section 3	
	Day 4 Section 4	**Day 4** Section 4	**Day 4** Section 4	
	Day 5 Chapter 10 Assessment	**Day 5** Section 5	**Day 5** Chapter 12 Assessment	
		Day 6 Chapter 11 Assessment		

Use the following tools to easily assess student learning in a variety of ways:

- Performance Assessment Activities and Rubrics
- Chapter and Unit Tests
- Section Quizzes
- Standardized Test Skills Practice Workbook

- tav.glencoe.com
- Interactive Tutor Self-Assessment CD-ROM
- MindJogger Videoquiz
- ExamView® Pro Testmaker CD-ROM
- SAT I/II Test Practice

TEACHING TRANSPARENCIES

Unit 4 Map Overlay Transparencies

Cause-and-Effect Transparency 4

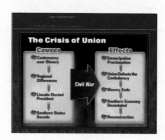

*inter*NET RESOURCES

- tav.glencoe.com
The American Vision
Visit the *American Vision* Web site for history overviews, activities, assessments, and updated charts and graphs.
- www.socialstudies.glencoe.com
Glencoe Social Studies
Visit the Glencoe Web site for social studies activities, updates, and links to other sites.
- www.teachingtoday.glencoe.com
Glencoe Teaching Today
Visit the new Glencoe Web site for teacher development information, teaching tips, Web resources, and educational news.
- www.time.com
TIME Online
Visit the TIME Web site for up-to-date news and special reports.

Unit 4 Resources

ASSESSMENT

Unit 4 Pretests

Unit 4 Posttests

APPLICATION AND ENRICHMENT

American Biography 4

History Simulation and Problem Solving 4

GEOGRAPHY

Geography and History Activity 4

INTERDISCIPLINARY ACTIVITIES

American Literature Reading 4

Economics and History Activity 4

Team-Teaching Interdisciplinary Strategies and Activities 4

BIBLIOGRAPHY

Readings for the Student

Beckett, Ian. *The American Civil War.*
Sutton Alan, 1997.

Readings for the Teacher

America Goes to War.
Fine Communications, 1997.

Multimedia Resources

Videocassette. *Living American History Series. U.S. History II: 1840–1876.* Private Learning Systems. (2 Apple diskettes, guide)

Additional Glencoe Resources for This Unit:

- Glencoe Skillbuilder Interactive Workbook CD-ROM, Level 2
- Social Studies Guide to Using the Internet
- Writer's Guidebook for High School
- Living Constitution
- American Art Prints Strategies and Activities

Unit Overview

Unit 4 describes the crises faced by the United States that resulted in the Civil War and Reconstruction from 1848 to 1877. **Chapter 10** explores the growing sectional conflicts in the United States from 1848 to 1860. **Chapter 11** describes the events of the Civil War from 1861 to 1865. **Chapter 12** discusses Reconstruction from 1865 to 1877.

Unit Objectives

After studying this unit, students will be able to:

1. Explain how the government dealt with slavery in the territories acquired after the war with Mexico.

2. Contrast the political situations of the Union and the Confederacy.

3. Contrast Lincoln's plan to reunite the nation with that of the Radical Republicans.

Why It Matters Activity

Discuss the issues of racism and civil rights in the United States today. Make generalizations about how the problems of America's past contribute to the issues faced by citizens today.

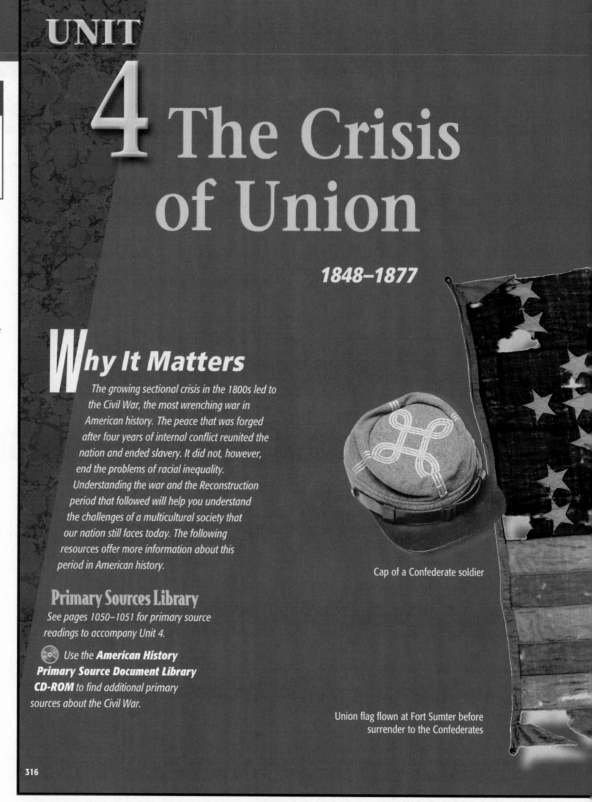

UNIT 4 The Crisis of Union

1848–1877

Why It Matters

The growing sectional crisis in the 1800s led to the Civil War, the most wrenching war in American history. The peace that was forged after four years of internal conflict reunited the nation and ended slavery. It did not, however, end the problems of racial inequality. Understanding the war and the Reconstruction period that followed will help you understand the challenges of a multicultural society that our nation still faces today. The following resources offer more information about this period in American history.

Primary Sources Library

See pages 1050–1051 for primary source readings to accompany Unit 4.

Use the **American History Primary Source Document Library CD-ROM** to find additional primary sources about the Civil War.

Cap of a Confederate soldier

Union flag flown at Fort Sumter before surrender to the Confederates

316

TEAM TEACHING ACTIVITY

Language Arts Have the language arts teacher discuss the personal accounts of the Civil War contained in letters between soldiers and their families. As a class discuss the role that bias plays in first-hand accounts of events. Have the language arts teacher point out examples of bias and personal opinions in a letter. Then have students work in groups to review other letters from the Civil War and identify bias in them.

"We shall nobly save, or meanly lose, the last best hope of earth."

—*Abraham Lincoln, 1862*

GLENCOE TECHNOLOGY

CD-ROM
American History Primary Source Document Library CD-ROM
Use the **American History Primary Source Document Library CD-ROM** to access primary source documents related to this period in history.

More About the Photo

Point out to students that over 600,000 Americans died during the Civil War, the most of any conflict involving the United States. Although the country remained united as a political entity, deep feelings of mistrust remained for a long time following the war. Ask students how unified they think the country is today and what the American flag symbolizes to them. *(Students' answers will vary. Encourage them to think about the flag as a symbol of unity.)*

SERVICE-LEARNING PROJECT

Organize students into small groups. Have each group select a civil rights issue that exists in your community today. Have students evaluate the community's response to the issue and then write an editorial supporting community efforts or suggesting constructive ways to resolve a civil rights problem. After reviewing the editorial, encourage groups to send their editorials to the local newspaper.

Refer to **Building Bridges: Connecting Classroom and Community through Service-Learning in Social Studies** from the National Council for the Social Studies for information about service-learning.

Chapter 10 Resources

Timesaving Tools

TeacherWorks™ All-In-One Planner and Resource Center

- **Interactive Teacher Edition** Access your Teacher Wraparound Edition and your classroom resources with a few easy clicks.
- **Interactive Lesson Planner** Planning has never been easier! Organize your week, month, semester, or year with all the lesson helps you need to make teaching creative, timely, and relevant.

Use Glencoe's **Presentation Plus!** multimedia teacher tool to easily present dynamic lessons that visually excite your students. Using Microsoft PowerPoint® you can customize the presentations to create your own personalized lessons.

TEACHING TRANSPARENCIES

Graphic Organizer 10

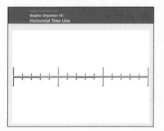

Why It Matters Chapter Transparency 10

APPLICATION AND ENRICHMENT

Linking Past and Present Activity 10

Enrichment Activity 10

Primary Source Reading 10

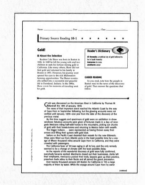

REVIEW AND REINFORCEMENT

Reteaching Activity 10

Vocabulary Activity 10

Time Line Activity 10

Critical Thinking Skills Activity 10

Meeting NCSS Standards

Local Standards

The following standards are highlighted in Chapter 10:

Section 1 III People, Places, and Environments: B, D, G, H, I
Section 2 X Civic Ideals and Practices: A, C, E, F, G, H, J
Section 3 V Individuals, Groups, and Institutions: B, C, E
Section 4 X Civic Ideals and Practices: C, E, F, G, I

ASSESSMENT AND EVALUATION

**Chapter 10 Test
Form A**

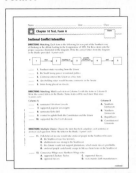

**Chapter 10 Test
Form B**

**Standardized Test Skills
Practice Workbook Activity 10**

**Performance Assessment
Activities and Rubrics 10**

**ExamView® Pro
Testmaker CD-ROM**

MULTIMEDIA

- Vocabulary PuzzleMaker CD-ROM
- Interactive Tutor Self-Assessment CD-ROM
- ExamView® Pro Testmaker CD-ROM
- Audio Program
- American History Primary Source Documents Library CD-ROM
- MindJogger Videoquiz
- Presentation Plus! CD-ROM
- TeacherWorks™ CD-ROM
- Interactive Student Edition CD-ROM
- Glencoe Skillbuilder Interactive Workbook CD-ROM, Level 2
- The *American Vision* Video Program
- American Music: Hits Through History
- American Music: Cultural Traditions

SPANISH RESOURCES

The following Spanish language materials are available in the Spanish Resources Binder:

- Spanish Guided Reading Activities
- Spanish Reteaching Activities
- Spanish Quizzes and Tests
- Spanish Vocabulary Activities
- Spanish Summaries
- The Declaration of Independence and United States Constitution Spanish Translation

---

The following videotape programs are available from Glencoe as supplements to Chapter 10:

- **Frederick Douglass** (ISBN 0-76-700120-6)
- **Underground Railroad** (ISBN 0-76-701679-3)

To order, call Glencoe at 1-800-334-7344. To find classroom resources to accompany many of these videos, check the following home pages:
A&E Television: www.aande.com
The History Channel: www.historychannel.com

Use our Web site for additional resources. All essential content is covered in the Student Edition.

You and your students can visit tav.glencoe.com, the Web site companion to the ***American Vision.*** This innovative integration of electronic and print media offers your students a wealth of opportunities. The student text directs students to the Web site for the following options:

- **Chapter Overviews**
- **Self-Check Quizzes**
- **Student Web Activities**
- **Textbook Updates**

Answers to the student Web activities are provided for you in the **Web Activity Lesson Plans.** Additional Web resources and Interactive Tutor Puzzles are also available.

Chapter 10 Resources

SECTION RESOURCES

Daily Objectives	Reproducible Resources	Multimedia Resources
SECTION 1 **Slavery and Western Expansion** 1. Explain how the government dealt with slavery in the territories acquired after the war with Mexico. 2. List the major features of the Compromise of 1850.	• Reproducible Lesson Plan 10–1 • Daily Lecture and Discussion Notes 10–1 • Guided Reading Activity 10–1* • Section Quiz 10–1* • Reading Essentials and Study Guide 10–1 • Performance Assessment Activities and Rubrics	• Daily Focus Skills Transparency 10–1 • Interactive Tutor Self-Assessment CD-ROM • ExamView® Pro Testmaker CD-ROM • Presentation Plus! CD-ROM • Skillbuilder Interactive Workbook, Level 2 • TeacherWorks™ CD-ROM • Audio Program • ABCNews Interactive™ Historic America Electronic Field Trips
SECTION 2 **Mounting Violence** 1. Evaluate how both the Fugitive Slave Act and the transcontinental railroad heightened sectional tensions. 2. Summarize the effects of the Kansas-Nebraska Act.	• Reproducible Lesson Plan 10–2 • Daily Lecture and Discussion Notes 10–2 • Guided Reading Activity 10–2* • Section Quiz 10–2* • Reading Essentials and Study Guide 10–2 • Performance Assessment Activities and Rubrics	• Daily Focus Skills Transparency 10–2 • Interactive Tutor Self-Assessment CD-ROM • ExamView® Pro Testmaker CD-ROM • Presentation Plus! CD-ROM • TeacherWorks™ CD-ROM • Audio Program • ABCNews Interactive™ Historic America Electronic Field Trips
SECTION 3 **The Crisis Deepens** 1. Analyze the events that increased sectional tensions in the late 1850s. 2. Describe the Lincoln-Douglas Senate campaign of 1858.	• Reproducible Lesson Plan 10–3 • Daily Lecture and Discussion Notes 10–3 • Guided Reading Activity 10–3* • Section Quiz 10–3* • Reading Essentials and Study Guide 10–3 • Performance Assessment Activities and Rubrics • Interpreting Political Cartoons • Supreme Court Case Studies	• Daily Focus Skills Transparency 10–3 • American Art & Architecture • Interactive Tutor Self-Assessment CD-ROM • ExamView® Pro Testmaker CD-ROM • Presentation Plus! CD-ROM • TeacherWorks™ CD-ROM • Audio Program • American Music: Hits Through History • American Music: Cultural Traditions
SECTION 4 **The Union Dissolves** 1. Describe the various attempts to find a compromise between the demands of the North and the South. 2. Explain how and why the Civil War began.	• Reproducible Lesson Plan 10–4 • Daily Lecture and Discussion Notes 10–4 • Guided Reading Activity 10–4* • Section Quiz 10–4* • Reading Essentials and Study Guide 10–4 • Performance Assessment Activities and Rubrics	• Daily Focus Skills Transparency 10–4 • Interactive Tutor Self-Assessment CD-ROM • ExamView® Pro Testmaker CD-ROM • Presentation Plus! CD-ROM • TeacherWorks™ CD-ROM • Vocabulary PuzzleMaker CD-ROM • Audio Program

0:00 OUT OF TIME?
Assign the Chapter 10 **Reading Essentials and Study Guide.**

*Also Available in Spanish

 Blackline Master   Transparency   CD-ROM   DVD

 Poster   Music Program   Audio Program   Videocassette

Chapter 10 Resources

NATIONAL GEOGRAPHIC Teacher's Corner

INDEX TO NATIONAL GEOGRAPHIC MAGAZINE

The following articles relate to this chapter.
- "America's Poet: Walt Whitman," December 1994
- "C.S.S. *Alabama*," December 1994
- "Philadelphia's African Americans," August 1990
- "The Underground Railroad," July 1984

NATIONAL GEOGRAPHIC SOCIETY PRODUCTS AVAILABLE FROM GLENCOE

To order the following products for use with this chapter, contact your local Glencoe sales representative, or call Glencoe at 1-800-334-7344:
- *PictureShow: The Civil War* (CD-ROM, Transparencies)
- *PictureShow: Story of America, Part 1 and 2*
- *PictureShow: The Westward Movement* (CD-ROM, Transparencies)

ADDITIONAL NATIONAL GEOGRAPHIC SOCIETY PRODUCTS

To order the following, call National Geographic at 1-800-368-2728:
- *Immigration: The Triumph of Hope* (Video)
- *Steal Away: The Harriet Tubman Story* (Video)

NGS ONLINE

Access National Geographic's Web site for current events, atlas updates, activities, links, interactive features, and archives.
www.nationalgeographic.com

KEY TO ABILITY LEVELS

Teaching strategies have been coded.

L1 BASIC activities for all students
L2 AVERAGE activities for average to above-average students
L3 CHALLENGING activities for above-average students
ELL ENGLISH LANGUAGE LEARNER activities

From the Classroom of...

Tim Palone
Elsik Ninth Grade Center
Alief, TX

Growing Sectionalism

For the period from 1848 to 1860, students will analyze speeches, editorials, and political cartoons found on the Internet, in local library archives, and in textbooks. Their analyses should address content and rhetorical style. Students will then present the speech, editorial, or cartoon to the class in a dramatic fashion, followed by their analysis.

In the next step the document will be placed on a time line, with students noting whether the rhetoric intensified over time.

Discuss the following questions with the class:

1. Did issues for Northerners and Southerners change over time, and if so, how?

2. Was conciliatory language ever used, and did the tone and style used change over time?

3. At what point do you feel the sides were too far apart for compromise?

ADDITIONAL RESOURCES FROM GLENCOE

- American Music: Cultural Traditions
- American Art & Architecture
- Outline Map Resource Book
- U.S. Desk Map
- Building Geography Skills for Life
- Inclusion for the High School Social Studies Classroom Strategies and Activities
- Teaching Strategies for the American History Classroom (Including Block Scheduling Pacing Guides)

 Block Schedule

Activities that are suited to use within the block scheduling framework are identified by:

318D

✓ Performance Assessment

Refer to Activity 10 in the Performance Assessment Activities and Rubrics booklet. 📦

Why It Matters Activity

Have students speculate on the causes of the Civil War. Students should evaluate their answers after they have completed the chapter.

GLENCOE
TECHNOLOGY

The *American Vision* Video Program

To learn more about the Underground Railroad, have students view the Chapter 10 video, "Tales From the Underground Railroad," from the *American Vision* Video Program.

💿 📼 Available in DVD and VHS

MindJogger Videoquiz

Use the **MindJogger Videoquiz** to preview Chapter 10 content.

📼 Available in VHS

CHAPTER

10 Sectional Conflict Intensifies *1848–1860*

Why It Matters

When the nation gained new territory, the slavery controversy intensified. Would new states be slave or free? Who would decide? States that allowed slavery were determined to prevent free states from gaining a majority in the Senate. Political compromise broke down by 1860, and when Lincoln was elected president, many Southern states decided to secede.

The Impact Today

The political and social debates of this period continue to have influence.
* *Older sectional loyalties still define some regions of the country.*
* *The modern Republican Party grew in part from opposition to slavery.*

The American Vision *Video* *The Chapter 10 video, "Tales From the Underground Railroad," features a dramatization of enslaved African Americans using the Underground Railroad to reach freedom.*

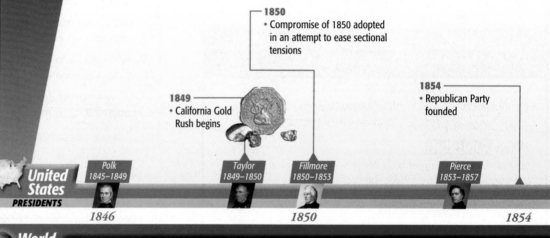

1850
* Compromise of 1850 adopted in an attempt to ease sectional tensions

1849
* California Gold Rush begins

1854
* Republican Party founded

United States PRESIDENTS

Polk 1845–1849 — Taylor 1849–1850 — Fillmore 1850–1853 — Pierce 1853–1857

1846 — *1850* — *1854*

World

1847
* Working hours limited in Britain

1848
* Serfdom abolished in Austrian Empire

1852
* Livingstone explores Africa's Zambezi River

1853
* Crimean War pitting Russia against Great Britain and Turkey begins

318

TWO-MINUTE LESSON LAUNCHER

Give students the following information. The total population of the United States increased during the 1850s by 8 million, growing from 23 to 31 million. With railroads aiding transportation to the Midwest, its population grew rapidly, and people began moving from the Midwest to the West. Ask students to speculate on what effect this westward expansion would have on the growing sectional division over the issue of slavery.

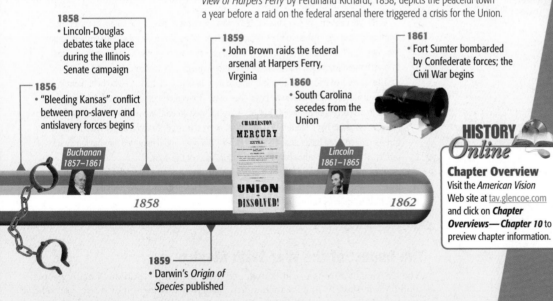

View of Harpers Ferry by Ferdinand Richardt, 1858, depicts the peaceful town a year before a raid on the federal arsenal there triggered a crisis for the Union.

HISTORY
Online

Introduce students to chapter content and key terms by having them access the **Chapter 10 Overview** at tav.glencoe.com.

More About the Art

Harpers Ferry is located at the confluence of the Potomac and Shenandoah Rivers. In addition, it is an important railroad crossing over the northern Shenandoah Valley. During the Civil War, the town changed hands eight times.

TIME LINE
ACTIVITY

Have students use the time line to determine the relative chronology of events by identifying who was president of the United States when each event occurred. Quiz the students by asking events out of order. Gold Rush begins *(Taylor)*, Compromise of 1850 *(Fillmore)*, Republican Party founded *(Pierce)*, "Bleeding Kansas" begins *(Pierce)*, Lincoln-Douglas debates *(Buchanan)*, Harpers Ferry *(Buchanan)*, South Carolina secedes *(Buchanan)*, Fort Sumter attacked *(Lincoln)*

1858
• Lincoln-Douglas debates take place during the Illinois Senate campaign

1856
• "Bleeding Kansas" conflict between pro-slavery and antislavery forces begins

1859
• John Brown raids the federal arsenal at Harpers Ferry, Virginia

1860
• South Carolina secedes from the Union

1861
• Fort Sumter bombarded by Confederate forces; the Civil War begins

Buchanan 1857–1861

CHARLESTON
MERCURY
EXTRA.

UNION
DISSOLVED!

Lincoln 1861–1865

1858

1862

HISTORY
Online

Chapter Overview
Visit the *American Vision* Web site at tav.glencoe.com and click on **Chapter Overviews—Chapter 10** to preview chapter information.

1859
• Darwin's *Origin of Species* published

319

GRAPHIC ORGANIZER ACTIVITY

Organizing Information Have students create a graphic organizer similar to the one shown below to explain the events that increased sectional tensions during the presidential administrations of Pierce and Buchanan. *(A–D: transcontinental railroad, Kansas-Nebraska Act, territorial civil war in Kansas, caning of Charles Sumner; E–F: Dred Scott decision, Kansas's Lecompton constitution)*

A
B
C
D
Franklin Pierce

E
James Buchanan
F

319

1 FOCUS

Section Overview

This section explains how the acquisition of new land heightened sectional tensions over slavery.

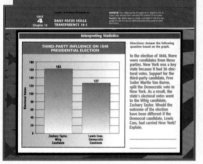
Guide to Reading

Answers to Graphic: Lewis Cass supported popular sovereignty, Martin Van Buren opposed slavery in the West, and Zachary Taylor did not express a position.

Preteaching Vocabulary
Have students create a two-column table, labeling one column North and the other South. Instruct students to place each of the Key Terms and Names in one or both columns and explain the placement.

SECTION 1 Slavery and Western Expansion

Guide to Reading

Main Idea
The question of whether to admit new states to the Union led to new tensions between the North and South over slavery.

Key Terms and Names
Wilmot Proviso, Lewis Cass, popular sovereignty, Conscience Whigs, Cotton Whigs, Free-Soil Party, "Forty-Niners," secession

Reading Strategy
Categorizing As you read about the political aftermath of the war with Mexico, complete a graphic organizer like the one below by pairing the presidential candidates of 1848 with their positions on slavery in the West.

Candidate	Position

Reading Objectives
• **Explain** how the government dealt with slavery in the territories acquired after the war with Mexico.
• **List** the major features of the Compromise of 1850.

Section Theme
Geography and History The acquisition of new lands heightened sectional tensions over slavery.

Preview of Events

♦1847　　　♦1848　　　♦1849　　　♦1850

August 1846
Wilmot Proviso presented

March 1848
Treaty of Guadalupe Hidalgo signed

August 1848
Free-Soil Party formed

1849
California Gold Rush begins

September 1850
Compromise of 1850 adopted

★ An American Story ★

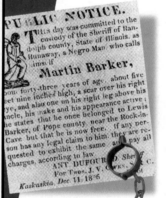

Notice of escaped enslaved person's capture

Early one cold morning in January 1847, Mrs. Crosswait woke to the sound of pistol shots. Without a word she rushed to her sleeping children, while her husband ran downstairs to bolt the door. The Crosswaits knew instantly the danger they were facing. Kidnappers had come to snatch them from their Michigan home and drag them back to Kentucky—and slavery.

The family had fled north after learning, to their horror, that the man who held them in slavery planned to sell them away from each other. They ended up in Marshall, Michigan. Home to a strong community of Quakers, Marshall welcomed them warmly.

Now, clutching her children, Mrs. Crosswait peeked fearfully from an upper window as three strangers fired bullet after bullet into their front door and demanded that the family surrender. She heard her husband pushing furniture against the door.

Then over the din came the voice of a neighbor, urging people to aid the family. Soon, friends came running. Shouting threats at the intruders, the townspeople intimidated them into leaving, thereby saving the family.

—adapted from *Black Pioneers: An Untold Story*

The Impact of the War With Mexico

The Crosswaits' struggle with kidnappers was not unique. Although many people escaped from slavery and headed north into free territory, they were not safe. Southerners believed that Article 4, Section 2, of the Constitution gave them the right to

---

SECTION RESOURCES

Reproducible Masters
• Reproducible Lesson Plan 10–1
• Daily Lecture and Discussion Notes 10–1
• Guided Reading Activity 10–1
• Section Quiz 10–1
• Reading Essentials and Study Guide 10–1
• Performance Assessment Activities and Rubrics

Transparencies
• Daily Focus Skills Transparency 10–1

Multimedia
🖲 Interactive Tutor Self-Assessment CD-ROM
🖲 ExamView® Pro Testmaker CD-ROM
🖲 Presentation Plus! CD-ROM
🖲 TeacherWorks™ CD-ROM
🎧 Audio Program

retrieve an enslaved person who fled across state lines. Some Northerners, however, held strong beliefs to the contrary and acted on those beliefs by sheltering runaways and helping them escape.

The Mexican War only heightened these opposing viewpoints and led to increasingly divisive sectional tensions. The war opened vast new lands to American settlers. This territorial expansion once again raised the divisive issue of whether slavery should be allowed to spread westward. As part of the debate over the new western territories, Southerners also demanded new laws to help them retrieve African Americans who escaped to free territory.

President Polk Sees Trouble Ahead
James K. Polk, a Southern Democrat and a slaveholder, believed any argument about slavery in the new territories acquired from Mexico was "an abstract question." No one would take enslaved African Americans to the Southwest, Polk thought, because the dry climate would not support the kinds of farming that made slavery profitable.

As an angry debate broke out in Congress, however, Polk realized that the issue of slavery in the territories was not something he could brush aside. His diary reflected his fear that the question "cannot fail to destroy the Democratic Party, if it does not ultimately threaten the Union itself."

GOVERNMENT

The Wilmot Proviso In August 1846, Representative David Wilmot, a Democrat from Pennsylvania, proposed an addition to a war appropriations bill. His amendment, known as the **Wilmot Proviso,** proposed that in any territory the United States gained from Mexico "neither slavery nor involuntary servitude shall ever exist."

Wilmot was one of a group of Northern Democrats who believed the president was "pro-Southern." Polk had supported a new tariff that helped the South at the expense of Northern manufacturers. He had then compromised with the British on Oregon, a territory where slavery was likely to be banned, but had gone to war against Mexico for land that Southerners would occupy.

Wilmot's proposal outraged Southerners. They believed that any antislavery decision about the territories would threaten slavery everywhere. Despite fierce Southern opposition, a coalition of Northern Democrats and Whigs passed the Wilmot Proviso in the House of Representatives. The Senate, however, refused to vote on it.

During the debate, Senator John C. Calhoun of South Carolina, although weak from tuberculosis, prepared a series of resolutions to counter the Wilmot Proviso. The Calhoun Resolutions never came to a vote—moderates in the Senate were unwilling to consider them—but they demonstrated the growing anger of many Southerners.

In the resolutions, Calhoun argued that the states owned the territories of the United States in common, and that Congress had no right to ban slavery in the territories. Calhoun warned somberly that "political revolution, anarchy, [and] civil war" would surely erupt if the North failed to heed Southern concerns.

Popular Sovereignty The Wilmot Proviso had stirred passions on both sides in Congress. The issue of slavery's expansion had divided the country along sectional lines, North against South. Many moderates began searching for a solution that would spare Congress from having to wrestle with the issue of slavery in the territories.

Senator **Lewis Cass** of Michigan proposed one solution. Cass suggested that the citizens of each new territory should be allowed to decide for themselves if they wanted to permit slavery or not. This idea came to be called popular sovereignty.

Popular sovereignty appealed strongly to many members of Congress because it removed the slavery issue from national politics. It also appeared

Poster calling for antislavery meeting

---

2 TEACH

Daily Lecture and Discussion Notes 10–1

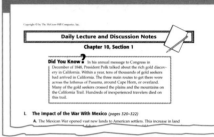

Writing an Editorial Have students write an editorial explaining why slaveholding would be the major issue of the 1848 presidential election in spite of the major parties' efforts to ignore it.

📁 Use the rubric for a magazine/newspaper/Web site article or help-wanted ad on pages 85–86 in the *Performance Assessment Activities and Rubrics.*

Predicting Civil War John C. Calhoun died on March 31, 1850. Earlier that year, he predicted the dissolution of the Union "within twelve years or three presidential terms."

Although James K. Polk saw trouble ahead, he did not live to see the trouble. Polk was only 50 years old when he was elected—the youngest man to serve as president up to that time. After finishing his one term in March of 1849, President Polk retired to his home in Nashville where he died on June 15.

COOPERATIVE LEARNING ACTIVITY

Making an Oral Presentation Organize the class into eight groups. Read the following quote made by Sidney George Fisher, a Philadelphia lawyer, in 1844: "Every day the difference between the North and the South is becoming more prominent and apparent. The difference exists in everything which forms the life of the people—in institutions, laws, opinions, manners, feelings, education, pursuits, climate and soil." Assign each group one thing which "forms the life of the people" to prepare a brief oral presentation about the growing differences between the North and South.

Use the rubric for a cooperative group management plan on pages 81–82 in the *Performance Assessment Activities and Rubrics.*

Locating Primary Sources

Have students use library and Internet resources to locate reproductions of primary sources illustrating antislavery activities. Have students prepare a short oral report about one of their findings. The Library of Congress Web site includes scanned images of documents similar to the poster that appears on page 321. The URL for the Library of Congress is www.loc.gov. **L2**

📁 Use the rubric for an oral presentation, monologue, song, or skit on pages 75–76 in the *Performance Assessment Activities and Rubrics.*

✓ Reading Check

Answer: The war opened vast new territory for settlers and raised the divisive issue of whether slavery should be allowed in the western territories.

ABCNEWS INTERACTIVE™

📼 **VIDEOCASSETTE**
Historic America Electronic Field Trips

View **Tape 1, Chapter 11:** "Sutter's Mill."

---

democratic since the settlers themselves would make the decision. Abolitionists argued that it still denied African Americans their right not to be enslaved, but many Northerners, especially in the Midwest, supported the idea because they believed Northern settlers would occupy most of the new territory and would ban slavery from their states.

The Free-Soil Party Emerges With the 1848 election approaching, the Whigs chose Zachary Taylor, hero of the war with Mexico, to run for president. The Whig Party in the North were split. Many Northern Whigs, known as **Conscience Whigs,** opposed slavery. They also opposed Taylor because they believed he wanted to expand slavery westward. Other Northern Whigs supported Taylor and voted with the Southern Whigs to nominate him. These Northern Whigs were known as **Cotton Whigs** because many of them were linked to Northern cloth manufacturers who needed Southern cotton.

The decision to nominate Taylor convinced many Conscience Whigs to quit the party. They then joined with antislavery Democrats from New York who were frustrated that their party had nominated Lewis Cass instead of Martin Van Buren. These two groups joined with members of the abolitionist Liberty Party to form the **Free-Soil Party,** which opposed slavery in the "free soil" of western territories.

Although some Free Soilers condemned slavery as immoral, most simply wanted to preserve the western territories for white farmers. They felt that allowing slavery to expand would make it difficult for free men to find work. The Free-Soil Party's slogan summed up their views: "Free soil, free speech, free labor, and free men."

The 1848 Election Candidates from three parties campaigned for the presidency in 1848. Democrat Lewis Cass of Michigan supported popular sovereignty, although this support was not mentioned in the South. His promise to veto the Wilmot Proviso, should Congress pass it, however, was often reported. Former president Martin Van Buren led the Free-Soil Party, which took a strong position against slavery in the territories and backed the Wilmot Proviso. General Zachary Taylor, the Whig candidate, avoided the whole issue.

On Election Day, support for the Free-Soilers split the Whig vote in Ohio, giving the state to Cass. More importantly, it also split the Democratic vote in New York, giving the state to Taylor. When the votes were counted, Taylor had won the election.

✓ Reading Check) Evaluating How did the war with Mexico affect the slavery debate?

The Search for Compromise

Within a year of President Taylor's inauguration, the issue of slavery once again took center stage. The discovery of gold in California had quickly led to that territory's application for statehood. The decision had to be made about whether California would enter the Union as a free state or a slave state.

The 1848 discovery of gold brought thousands to California. By the end of 1849, nearly 80,000 **"Forty-Niners"** had arrived to look for gold. Mining towns sprang up overnight, and the frenzy for gold led to chaos and violence. Needing a strong government to maintain order, Californians began to organize for statehood.

Forty-Niners Rush for Gold

In January 1848, carpenter James Marshall found traces of gold in a stream near a sawmill he was building in Sacramento. Though Marshall tried to keep his discovery a secret, word leaked out by spring, and San Franciscans rushed to the mountains in search of gold. During the summer, news of the find swept all the way to the East Coast and beyond, and the California Gold Rush was on.

Gold nuggets and $50 gold coin

Forty-niners at slush box in California

MEETING SPECIAL NEEDS

Verbal/Linguistic Sometimes inattention is caused by the difficulty of the material. Have students preview Section 1 to assess components that they might find difficult. Discuss the factors that might affect their ability to maintain attention. For example, ask the following questions: In which subsection is it easier for you to maintain attention, "Congress Struggles for a Compromise" or "The Fugitive Slave Act"? Why? **L1**

📁 Refer to *Inclusion for the High School Social Studies Classroom Strategies and Activities* in the TCR.

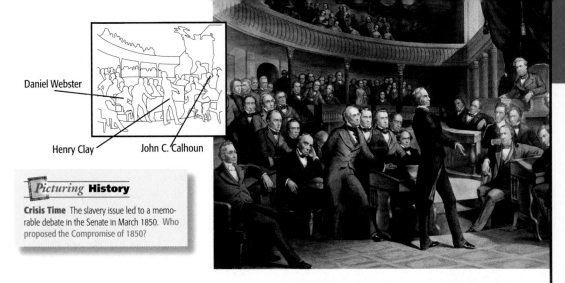

Daniel Webster

Henry Clay   John C. Calhoun

Picturing **History**

Crisis Time The slavery issue led to a memo-rable debate in the Senate in March 1850. Who proposed the Compromise of 1850?

Picturing **History**

Answer: Henry Clay
Ask: **Why was Henry Clay called the "Great Compromiser"?** *(He played significant roles in the Missouri Compromise, the tariff compromise that ended the nullification crisis in 1833, and the Compromise of 1850. These compromises aimed at balancing the rights of free and slave states.)*

3 ASSESS

Assign Section 1 Assessment as homework or as an in-class activity.

◉ Have students use the **Interactive Tutor Self-Assessment CD-ROM.**

Reading Essentials and Study Guide 10–1

Name _____ Date _____ Class _____

Study Guide

Chapter 10, Section 1
For use with textbook pages 320–324

SLAVERY AND WESTERN EXPANSION

KEY TERMS AND NAMES

Wilmot Proviso a part of a bill that proposed that slavery not be allowed in any territory gained from Mexico *(page 321)*

Lewis Cass Michigan senator who proposed that citizens of each new territory be allowed to decide whether to permit slavery in the territory *(page 321)*

popular sovereignty the idea that people living in a territory had the right to decide by voting whether to allow slavery in the territory *(page 322)*

Conscience Whigs Northern Whigs who opposed slavery *(page 322)*

Cotton Whigs Northern Whigs who supported the South and slavery *(page 322)*

Free-Soil Party a political party who opposed the spread of slavery in the western territories

Section Quiz 10–1

Name _____ Date _____ Class _____

★ **Chapter 10**   Score _____

Section Quiz 10–1

DIRECTIONS: Matching Match each item in Column A with the items in Column B. Write the correct letters in the blanks. *(10 points each)*

Column A

____ 1. opposed the spread of slavery into the western territories
____ 2. Northern Whigs opposed to slavery
____ 3. taking states out of the Union
____ 4. proposed that no slavery or involuntary servitude should exist in any territory the United States gained from Mexico
____ 5. the idea that citizens of each new territory should be allowed to decide if they wanted to permit slavery or not

Column B

A. Wilmot Proviso
B. secession
C. Free-Soil Party
D. popular sovereignty
E. Conscience Whigs

DIRECTIONS: Multiple Choice In the blank at the left, write the letter of the choice that best completes the statement or answers the question. *(10 points each)*

Before leaving office, President Polk had urged Congress to create territorial governments for California and New Mexico. Congress, bitterly divided along sectional lines, had not been able to agree on whether to allow slavery in these territories.

Although Zachary Taylor was from the South and a slaveholder, he did not think slavery's survival depended on its expansion westward. He believed that the way to avoid a fight in Congress was to have the people in California make their own decisions about slavery. California now had enough people to skip the territorial stage and come directly into the Union as a state.

With Taylor's encouragement, California applied in December 1849 for admission to the Union as a free state. Thus, the Gold Rush had forced the nation once again to confront the divisive issue of slavery.

The Great Debate Begins If California entered the Union as a free state, the slaveholding states would become a minority in the Senate. Southerners dreaded losing power in national politics, fearing it would lead to limits on slavery and states' rights. A few Southern politicians began to talk openly of secession—of taking their states out of the Union.

In early 1850, one of the most senior and influential leaders in the Senate, Henry Clay of Kentucky, tried to find a compromise that would enable California to join the Union. Clay, nicknamed "The Great Compromiser" because of his role in promoting the Missouri Compromise in 1820 and solving the nullification crisis in 1833, proposed eight resolutions to solve the crisis.

Clay grouped the resolutions in pairs, offering concessions to both sides. The first pair allowed California to come in as a free state but organized the rest of the Mexican cession without any restrictions on slavery. The second pair settled the border between New Mexico and Texas in favor of New Mexico but compensated Texas by having the federal government take on its debts. This would win Southern votes for the compromise because many Southerners held Texas bonds.

Clay's third pair of resolutions outlawed the slave trade in the District of Columbia but did not outlaw slavery itself. The final two resolutions were concessions to the South. Congress would be prohibited from interfering with the domestic slave trade and would pass a new fugitive slave act to help Southerners recover enslaved African Americans who had fled north. These concessions were necessary to assure the South that after California joined the Union, the North would not use its control of the Senate to abolish slavery.

Clay's proposal triggered a massive debate. Any such compromise would need the approval of Senator Calhoun, the great defender of the South's rights. Calhoun was too ill to address the Senate. He composed a speech in reply to Clay's proposal and then sat, hollow-eyed and shrouded in flannel blankets, as another senator read it aloud.

Calhoun's address was brutally frank. It asserted flatly that Northern agitation against slavery threatened to destroy the South. He did not think Clay's compromise would save the Union. The South needed an acceptance of its rights, the return of fugitive slaves, and a guarantee of balance between the sections. If the Southern states could not live in safety within the Union, Calhoun darkly predicted, secession was the only honorable solution.

Three days later, Senator **Daniel Webster** of Massachusetts rose to respond to Calhoun's talk of

CHAPTER 10 Sectional Conflict Intensifies **323**

INTERDISCIPLINARY CONNECTIONS ACTIVITY

Political Science Have students discuss the reasons senators from the North and South disagreed on the Compromise of 1850. List the reasons on the board under the headings North and South. Tell students that much of the reasoning was the result of differences over states' rights. Conclude by emphasizing the differences between the politics of the North and the South. **L2**

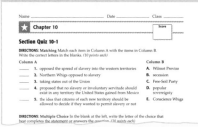

Reteach
Ask students to explain how the government dealt with slavery in the territories acquired after the war with Mexico.

Enrich
Have students create a fact or fiction game surrounding the events discussed in the section. Have other students play the game and give feedback about what they have learned.

Reading Check
Answer: California's population increased rapidly with the Gold Rush and allowed it to apply for statehood. The decision to admit California as a slave or free state created a heated Congressional debate.

4 CLOSE

Have students explain how the acquisition of new territory heightened the sectional tension over slavery.

The Compromise of 1850

Legislative Item	Victory for?
• California admitted to the Union as free state	Clear victory for the North
• Popular sovereignty to determine slavery issue in Utah and New Mexico territories	Moderate victory for both sides
• Texas border dispute with New Mexico resolved • Texas receives $10 million	Moderate Southern victories
• Slave trade, but not slavery itself, abolished in the District of Columbia	Moderate Northern victory
• Strong federal enforcement of new Fugitive Slave Act	Clear victory for the South

Chart *Skills*
1. **Interpreting Charts** Did the new Fugitive Slave Act appeal to the North or the South?
2. **Generalizing** Which side, North or South, achieved more of its goals in the Compromise of 1850?

secession. Calling on the Senate to put national unity above sectional loyalties, Webster voiced his support for Clay's plan, claiming that it was the only hope for preserving the Union. Although he sought conciliation, Senator Webster did not back away from speaking bluntly—and with chilling foresight:

❝I wish to speak to-day, not as a Massachusetts man, nor as a Northern man, but as an American. . . . I speak today for the preservation of the Union. Hear me for my cause. . . . There can be no such thing as a peaceable secession. Peaceable secession is an utter impossibility. . . . I see as plainly as I see the sun in heaven what that disruption itself must produce; I see that it must produce war, and such a war as I will not describe. . . .❞

—from the *Congressional Globe,* 31st Congress

The Compromise of 1850 In the end, Congress did not pass Clay's bill, in part because President Taylor opposed it. Then, unexpectedly, Taylor died in office that summer. Vice President Millard Fillmore succeeded him, and he quickly threw his support behind the compromise.

By the end of summer, Calhoun was dead, Webster had accepted the position of secretary of state, and Clay was exhausted, leaving leadership of the Senate to younger men. Thirty-seven-year-old Stephen A. Douglas of Illinois divided the large compromise initiative into several smaller bills. This allowed his colleagues from different sections to abstain or vote against whatever parts they disliked while supporting the rest. By fall, Congress had passed all the parts of the original proposal as Clay had envisioned it, and President Fillmore had signed them into law.

For a short time, the **Compromise of 1850** eased the tensions over slavery. In the next few years, however, the hope of a permanent solution through compromise would begin to fade.

Reading Check **Summarizing** How did the Gold Rush affect the issue of slavery?

SECTION 1 ASSESSMENT

Checking for Understanding
1. **Define:** popular sovereignty, secession.
2. **Identify:** Wilmot Proviso, Lewis Cass, Conscience Whigs, Cotton Whigs, Free-Soil Party, "Forty-Niners."
3. **Summarize** how Americans responded to the idea of popular sovereignty.

Reviewing Themes
4. **Geography and History** How did the war with Mexico and the Gold Rush affect the slavery issue in the United States?

Critical Thinking
5. **Explaining** Why did Zachary Taylor win the election of 1848?
6. **Organizing** Use a graphic organizer similar to the one below to list the main elements of the Compromise of 1850.

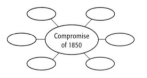

Analyzing Visuals
7. **Examining Art** Study the painting of the debate between Clay and Calhoun on page 323. What elements of the painting suggest the seriousness of the slavery issue being debated?

Writing About History
8. **Persuasive Writing** Imagine you are Henry Clay. Write a speech to present to the Senate. In your speech, try to persuade Congress to pass your compromise.

SECTION 1 ASSESSMENT ANSWERS

1. Terms are in blue.
2. Wilmot Proviso (p. 321), Lewis Cass (p. 321), Conscience Whigs (p. 322), Cotton Whigs (p. 322), Free-Soil Party (p. 322), "Forty-Niners" (p. 322)
3. Many supported the idea because it was democratic. Northerners hoped they could use it to ban slavery in new territories. Many abolitionists did not like it.
4. The victory in the war with Mexico as well as the Gold Rush resulted in large numbers of settlers in California; its application for statehood led to a debate over slavery's expansion.
5. The Democrats split their votes between Cass and Van Buren allowing Taylor to win.
6. Students' answers should match the chart on this page.
7. dignified stance of speaker, all eyes on him, gallery full
8. Speeches should address all the key elements of the compromise.

Critical Thinking SKILLBUILDER

Predicting Consequences

Why Learn This Skill?

Did you ever wish you could see into the future? Although predicting future events is very difficult, you can develop skills that will help you identify the logical consequences of decisions or actions.

Learning the Skill

Follow these steps to help you accurately predict consequences:

- Review what you already know about a situation by listing facts, events, and people's responses. The list will help you recall events and how they affected people.
- Analyze patterns. Try to determine what the patterns show.
- Use your knowledge and observations of similar situations. In other words, ask yourself, "What were the consequences of a similar decision or action that occurred in the past?"
- Analyze each of the potential consequences by asking, "How likely is it that this will occur?"
- Make a prediction.

Practicing the Skill

Candidates for public office often make campaign promises based on how they think voters will respond. Use the information in the chart on this page to help you predict what type of candidate would be elected president in 1848. Then answer the questions that follow.

❶ What event initially forced candidates to address the issue of slavery in new territories?

❷ Review the facts and events listed on the chart. Do you notice any patterns? What do the facts tell you about the 1840s?

❸ What kind of president do you think Northerners would want? Southerners?

Events of the 1840s	Results and Reactions
Victory in war with Mexico creates new territory in Southwest.	→ Americans torn over whether area should be free or slave territory.
Wilmot Proviso proposes ban on slavery in any area taken from Mexico.	→ Southerners are outraged.
Members of Congress try to avoid issue of slavery in territories.	→ Northerners and Southerners continue to angrily debate the issue.
Popular sovereignty lets settlers decide whether territories should be free or not.	→ Abolitionists argue against popular sovereignty; most Northerners support it.
Whig Party nomination of Zachary Taylor angers some party members.	→ Many Northern Whigs split and join with others to create the Free-Soil Party.

Skills Assessment

Complete the Practicing Skills questions on page 347 and the Chapter 10 Skill Reinforcement Activity to assess your mastery of this skill.

Applying the Skill

Predicting Consequences Read several newspaper articles about an event affecting your community today. Make an educated prediction about what will happen, and explain your reasoning. Write a letter to the editor, summarizing your prediction. You may want to check back at a later time to see if your prediction came true.

 Glencoe's **Skillbuilder Interactive Workbook CD-ROM, Level 2,** provides instruction and practice in key social studies skills.

TEACH

Predicting Consequences

Explain to students that predictions are not based on random guesses. Instead, they are based on extending knowledge of facts, events, reactions, patterns, and trends to new circumstances.

Ask students to offer examples of how this skill is used in business, government, and personal situations. (*Students' answers will vary. For example, a business has to predict consumer behavior before a product is launched.*)

Additional Practice

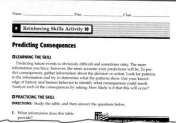

Reinforcing Skills Activity 10

Name _____ Date _____ Class _____

★ Reinforcing Skills Activity **10**

Predicting Consequences

☐ **LEARNING THE SKILL**

Predicting future events is obviously difficult and sometimes risky. The more information you have, however, the more accurate your predictions will be. To predict consequences, gather information about the decision or action. Look for patterns in the information and try to determine what the patterns show. Use your knowledge of history and human behavior to identify what consequences could result. Analyze each of the consequences by asking: How likely is it that this will occur?

☐ **PRACTICING THE SKILL**

DIRECTIONS: Study the table, and then answer the questions below.

1. What information does this table provide?

GLENCOE TECHNOLOGY

 CD-ROM
Glencoe Skillbuilder Interactive Workbook CD-ROM, Level 2

This interactive CD-ROM reinforces student mastery of essential social studies skills.

ANSWERS TO PRACTICING THE SKILL

❶ victory in the war with Mexico

❷ The slavery issue dominated the decade.

❸ Northerners: someone who would support popular sovereignty; Southerners: someone who would allow slavery in the new territories

Applying the Skill

Students' predictions will vary but should be based on reasonable assumptions based on the facts given. Have students attach their editorials to copies of the newspaper articles that they select.

1 FOCUS

Section Overview

This section focuses on the mounting violence as sectional tensions continued to rise after the Compromise of 1850.

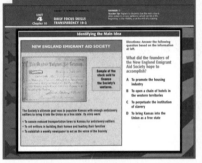
Guide to Reading

Answers to Graphic: Passage of Fugitive Slave Act, publication of *Uncle Tom's Cabin,* growth of Northern resistance to the Fugitive Slave Act, success of Underground Railroad, transcontinental railroad, Kansas-Nebraska Act

Preteaching Vocabulary
Have students make logical pairs of the Key Terms and Names and use the paired words in a sentence.

SECTION 2 Mounting Violence

Guide to Reading

Main Idea
Resentment over the Compromise of 1850 led to a further increase in sectional tensions.

Key Terms and Names
Uncle Tom's Cabin, Fugitive Slave Act, Underground Railroad, Harriet Tubman, transcontinental railroad, Gadsden Purchase, Kansas-Nebraska Act, Charles Sumner

Reading Strategy
Organizing As you read about the growing sectional conflict over slavery in the West, complete a graphic organizer similar to the one below by listing the sequence of key events leading from debate to violence.

Key Events From Debate to Violence

Reading Objectives
• **Evaluate** how both the Fugitive Slave Act and the transcontinental railroad heightened sectional tensions.
• **Summarize** the effects of the Kansas-Nebraska Act.

Section Theme
Civic Rights and Responsibilities As sectional tensions rose, some Americans openly defied laws they thought were unjust.

Preview of Events

♦1851   ♦1853   ♦1855   ♦1857

March 1852
Uncle Tom's Cabin published

May 1854
Kansas-Nebraska Act adopted

November 1855
"Bleeding Kansas" conflict begins

May 1856
Charles Sumner assaulted in the Senate

★ An American Story ★

Harriet Beecher Stowe

One evening in 1851, the comfortable, well-educated, deeply religious Stowe family sat in their parlor in Brunswick, Maine, listening to a letter being read aloud. The letter was from Harriet Beecher Stowe's sister, Isabella, in Boston.

The new Fugitive Slave Act, part of the Compromise of 1850, had gone into effect, Isabella reported, and slave-catchers prowled the streets. They pounced on African Americans without warning, breaking into their houses, destroying their shops, and carrying them off.

Isabella described daily attacks. She also told of outraged Bostonians, white and African American alike, who rallied to resist the kidnappers.

Stowe listened with growing despair. She had lived for many years in Cincinnati, across the Ohio River from the slave state of Kentucky. There she had met many runaways from slavery and heard their tragic tales. She had also visited Kentucky and witnessed slavery firsthand.

As the reading of her sister's letter continued, Stowe, who was an accomplished author, received a challenge. "Now Hattie," Isabella wrote, "if I could use a pen as you can, I would write something that would make this whole nation feel what an accursed thing slavery is." Stowe suddenly rose from her chair and announced, "I will write something. I will if I live." That year, she began writing sketches for a book called *Uncle Tom's Cabin.*

—adapted from *Harriet Beecher Stowe: A Life*

Uncle Tom's Cabin

After running as a serial in an antislavery newspaper, *Uncle Tom's Cabin* came out in book form in 1852 and sold 300,000 copies in its first year—astounding numbers for the time. Today the writing may seem overly sentimental, but to Stowe's original readers,

---

📖 SECTION RESOURCES

📁 **Reproducible Masters**
• Reproducible Lesson Plan 10–2
• Daily Lecture and Discussion Notes 10–2
• Guided Reading Activity 10–2
• Section Quiz 10–2
• Reading Essentials and Study Guide 10–2
• Performance Assessment Activities and Rubrics

🖧 **Transparencies**
• Daily Focus Skills Transparency 10–2

Multimedia
🔘 Interactive Tutor Self-Assessment CD-ROM
🔘 ExamView® Pro Testmaker CD-ROM
🔘 Presentation Plus! CD-ROM
🔘 TeacherWorks™ CD-ROM
🔘 Audio Program

mostly Northerners, it was powerful. Her depiction of the enslaved hero, Tom, and the villainous overseer, Simon Legree, changed Northern perceptions of African Americans and slavery.

Stowe presented African Americans as real people imprisoned in dreadful circumstances. Because she saw herself as a painter of slavery's horrors rather than an abstract debater, Stowe was able to evoke pity and outrage even in readers who were unmoved by rational arguments.

Southerners tried unsuccessfully to have the novel banned and strongly attacked its portrayal of slavery, accusing Stowe of writing "distortions" and "falsehoods." One Southern editor told a writer he wanted a review of *Uncle Tom's Cabin* to be "as hot as hellfire, blasting and searing the reputation of the vile wretch in petticoats."

Despite Southern outrage, the book eventually sold millions of copies. It had such a dramatic impact on public opinion that many historians consider it one of the causes of the Civil War.

✓ Reading Check **Evaluating** Why was *Uncle Tom's Cabin* so controversial?

The Fugitive Slave Act

Motivating Harriet Beecher Stowe to write *Uncle Tom's Cabin* was not the only unintended consequence of the **Fugitive Slave Act.** Although Henry Clay had conceived the law as a benefit to slaveholders, it actually hurt the Southern cause by creating active hostility toward slavery among Northerners who had previously seemed indifferent.

The Act's Inflammatory Effects Under the Fugitive Slave Act of 1850, a person claiming that an African American had escaped from slavery had only to point out that person as a runaway to take him or her into custody. The accused then would be brought before a federal commissioner. A sworn statement asserting that the captive had escaped from a slaveholder or testimony by white witnesses was all a court needed to order the person sent south. African Americans accused of being fugitives had no right to a trial and were not allowed to testify in court.

The law also included a financial incentive for the federal commissioners to find in favor of the slaveholder. The commissioner received $10 if he decided for the slaveholder but only $5 if the decision went the other way. The law also required federal marshals to help slaveholders capture African American fugitives and authorized marshals to deputize citizens on

the spot to help them capture a fugitive. Any Northerner could be compelled to help catch African Americans. A person who refused to cooperate could be jailed.

Newspaper accounts of the seizure of African Americans and descriptions of the law's injustice fueled Northern indignation. In New York, Henry Long was waiting tables at the Pacific Hotel when kidnappers seized him. Although Long had been living in New York several months before his supposed escape from a Virginia plantation, he was forced to return to the South and into slavery. The New York *Independent* publicized Long's kidnapping, noting that "almost no colored man is safe in our streets."

Northern Resistance Grows As outraged as Northerners were over such incidents, the law's requirement that ordinary citizens help capture runaways was what drove many into active defiance. Frederick Douglass emphasized this part of the law over and over again in his speeches. A powerful orator, Douglass would paint an emotional picture of an African American fleeing kidnappers. Then he would ask his audience whether they would give the runaway over to the "pursuing bloodhounds." "No!" the crowd would roar.

Antislavery activists often used the words of writer Henry David Thoreau to justify defying the Fugitive Slave Act. In his 1849 essay "Civil Disobedience," Thoreau advocated disobeying laws on moral grounds. "Unjust laws exist," he wrote. "Shall we be content to obey them, or shall we endeavor to amend them, and obey them until we have succeeded, or shall we transgress them at once?" For many Northerners the answer was to disobey them without delay.

Northern resistance became frequent, public, and sometimes violent. The violence was justified, some believed, by the violence and cruelty of the slaveholders and their hirelings. In a pamphlet, Douglass proposed "The True Remedy for the Fugitive Slave Law—A good revolver, a steady hand, and a determination to shoot down any man attempting to kidnap."

The Underground Railroad Although the Fugitive Slave Act included heavy fines and prison terms for helping a runaway, whites and free African Americans continued their work with the Underground Railroad. This informal but well-organized system, begun in the early 1830s, helped thousands of enslaved persons escape. Members, called "conductors," transported runaways north in secret, gave them shelter and food along the way, and

2 TEACH

Daily Lecture and Discussion Notes 10–2

Copyright © by The McGraw-Hill Companies, Inc.

Daily Lecture and Discussion Notes

Chapter 10, Section 2

Did You Know? Harriet Tubman helped more than 300 slaves escape to freedom on the Underground Railroad, including her own parents. Slave owners offered $40,000 for her capture. No one ever collected the money, because Tubman was never captured. During the Civil War, Tubman worked for the Union forces as a nurse, guide, and spy.

I. *Uncle Tom's Cabin* (pages 326–327)

A. *Uncle Tom's Cabin,* written by Harriet Beecher Stowe, ran as a serial in an antislavery newspaper and then came out in book form in 1852. Stowe's writings about an enslaved African American and his overseer changed Northern outlooks on African

✓ Reading Check

Answer: It changed Northerners' perceptions of African Americans and slavery. Southerners felt it included distortions and falsehoods.

Writing a Journal Entry Have students write journal entries describing the conditions in cities and towns in which escapees from slavery lived. Tell students to write either from the point of view of a federal marshal, a citizen who had just been deputized against his will to cooperate with the law, or an escapee who simply wanted to lead a normal life. **L1**

📁 Use the rubric for a diary, short story, memorandum, or letter on pages 79–80 in the *Performance Assessment Activities and Rubrics.*

FYI

In response to criticism of her work, Harriet Beecher Stowe published *A Key to Uncle Tom's Cabin* in 1853. This volume contained documents and testimonies that supported the picture of slavery she had painted in *Uncle Tom's Cabin.*

COOPERATIVE LEARNING ACTIVITY

Creating a Thematic Map Organize students into small groups to create a thematic map showing the major Underground Railroad routes. Have students use library and Internet resources to learn more about the extensive network of routes traveled by African Americans as they escaped slavery. Make arrangements to display the maps.

Use the rubric for a cooperative group management plan on pages 81–82 in the *Performance Assessment Activities and Rubrics.*

saw them to freedom in the Northern states or Canada with some money for a fresh start.

Guided Reading Activity 10–2

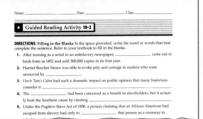

✔ Reading Check

Answer: It created active hostility toward slavery among Northerners.

Profiles
IN HISTORY

Harriet Tubman's original first name was Araminta. At some point she started calling herself Harriet, which was her mother's first name. She married John Tubman, a free man, about five years before she escaped slavery. **Ask:** What do you think Tubman meant when she wrote, "I looked at my hands to see if I was the same person"? *(Answers will vary. She may have meant that she felt freedom had transformed her as well as the world around her.)*

FYI

Slaveholders offered $40,000 for Harriet Tubman's capture. After the Civil War began, she worked as a cook, nurse, and even as a spy for the Union forces.

---

saw them to freedom in the Northern states or Canada with some money for a fresh start.

Dedicated people, many of them African Americans, made dangerous trips into the South to guide enslaved persons along the Underground Railroad to freedom. The most famous of these conductors was **Harriet Tubman,** herself a runaway. She risked many trips to the South.

In Des Moines, Iowa, Isaac Brandt used secret signals to communicate with conductors on the Underground Railroad—a hand lifted palm outwards, for example, or a certain kind of tug at the ear. "I do not know how these signs or signals originated," he later remembered, "but they had become well understood. Without them the operation of the system of running slaves into free territory would not have been possible."

Levi Coffin, a Quaker born in North Carolina, allowed escaped African Americans to stay at his home in Indiana, where three Underground Railroad routes from the South converged.

> ❝We knew not what night or what hour of the night we would be roused from slumber by a gentle rap at the door. . . . Outside in the cold or rain, there would be a two-horse wagon loaded with fugitives, perhaps the greater part of them women and children. I would invite them, in a low tone, to come in,

Profiles IN HISTORY

Harriet Tubman
c. 1820–1913

Known as "Moses" for her courage in leading enslaved persons to freedom, Harriet Tubman was a heroine of the antislavery movement. Tubman was born into slavery in Maryland and struggled early against the system's brutality. At age 13, when she tried to save another enslaved person from punishment, an overseer struck her savagely and fractured her skull. Miraculously, she recovered from the injury, but she suffered from occasional blackouts for the rest of her life.

Tubman escaped to freedom in 1849 when she was 29 years old. Upon crossing into Pennsylvania, she later wrote, "I looked at my hands to see if I was the same person. There was such a glory over everything. The sun came up

like gold through the trees, and I felt like I was in Heaven."

Her joy inspired her to help others. After Congress passed the Fugitive Slave Act, Tubman returned to the South 19 times to guide enslaved persons along the Underground Railroad to freedom.

Tubman became notorious in the eyes of slaveholders, but despite a large reward offered for her capture, no one ever betrayed her whereabouts. Furthermore, in all her rescues on the Underground Railroad, she never lost a single "passenger." Tubman's bravery and determination made her one of the most important figures in the antislavery movement.

---

and they would follow me into the darkened house without a word, for we knew not who might be watching and listening.❞

—quoted in *The Underground Railroad*

An estimated 2,000 African Americans stopped at Coffin's red brick house on their way to freedom. Coffin later moved to Cincinnati, Ohio, where he assisted another 1,300 African Americans who had crossed the river from Kentucky to freedom. A thorn in the side to slaveholders, the Underground Railroad deepened Southern mistrust of Northern intentions.

✔ **Reading Check** **Examining** What was an unintended consequence of the Fugitive Slave Act?

The Transcontinental Railroad

Sectional disagreements did not fade away when settlers left their old homes and headed west into new territories. The settlers firmly retained their identities as Northerners or Southerners. By the early 1850s, many settlers and land speculators had become interested in the fertile lands west of Missouri and Iowa. Unfortunately for the settlers, the territory was unorganized. Until the federal government organized it as a territory, it could not be surveyed and settled.

At the same time, the opening of Oregon and the admission of California to the Union had convinced Americans that a transcontinental railroad should be built to connect the West Coast to the rest of the country.

In the 1850s, getting to the West Coast of the United States required many grueling weeks of travel overland or a long sea voyage around the tip of South America. A transcontinental railroad would reduce the journey to four relatively easy days while promoting further settlement and growth in the territories along the route.

The transcontinental railroad had broad appeal, but the choice of its eastern starting point became a new element in the sectional conflict. Many Southerners preferred a southern route from New Orleans, but the geography of the Southwest required the railroad to pass through northern Mexico. Secretary of War Jefferson Davis, a strong supporter of the South's interests, sent James Gadsden,

---

MEETING SPECIAL NEEDS

Verbal/Linguistic Have students select one of the people mentioned in the section on the transcontinental railroad. Have them prepare a speech that could have been given by that person expressing his or her views on the railroad, its proposed route, and its purpose. Have students present their speeches to the class.

📁 Refer to *Inclusion for the High School Social Studies Classroom Strategies and Activities* in the TCR.

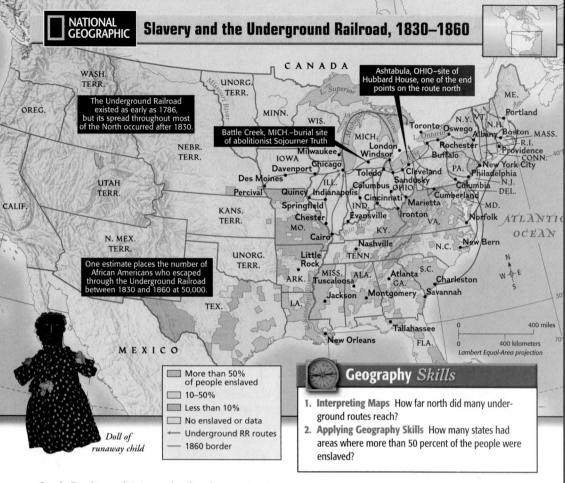

Slavery and the Underground Railroad, 1830–1860

The Underground Railroad existed as early as 1786, but its spread throughout most of the North occurred after 1830.

Battle Creek, MICH.–burial site of abolitionist Sojourner Truth

Ashtabula, OHIO–site of Hubbard House, one of the end points on the route north

One estimate places the number of African Americans who escaped through the Underground Railroad between 1830 and 1860 at 50,000.

Doll of runaway child

- More than 50% of people enslaved
- 10–50%
- Less than 10%
- No enslaved or data
- ← Underground RR routes
- — 1860 border

Geography *Skills*

1. **Interpreting Maps** How far north did many underground routes reach?
2. **Applying Geography Skills** How many states had areas where more than 50 percent of the people were enslaved?

Geography *Skills*

Answers:
1. to Canada
2. 11

Geography Skills Practice
Ask: What means of transportation was likely used to free enslaved persons from Charleston, South Carolina? *(boats or ships)*

✓ **Reading Check**

Answer: The land was needed for the transcontinental railroad.

Drawing a Thematic Map Have students use library and Internet resources to learn more about the area acquired in the Gadsden Purchase. Instruct students to create/draw a thematic map showing the Mexican border before and after the Gadsden Purchase. **L2**

📁 Use the rubric for creating a map, display, or chart on pages 77–78 in the *Performance Assessment Activities and Rubrics.*

---

a South Carolina politician and railroad promoter, to buy land from Mexico. The Mexican leader, Santa Anna, agreed to sell a 30,000-square-mile strip of land that today is part of southern Arizona and New Mexico and includes the city of Tucson. In 1853 Mexico accepted $10 million for the territory, known as the **Gadsden Purchase.**

Meanwhile in Congress, the head of the Senate committee on territories, Democratic Senator Stephen A. Douglas, had his own ideas for a transcontinental railroad. Douglas was from Illinois. He wanted the eastern terminus to be in Chicago, but he knew that any route from the north required Congress to organize the territory west of Missouri and Iowa.

In 1853 Douglas prepared a bill to organize the region into a new territory to be called Nebraska. Although the House of Representatives passed the bill quickly, Southern senators who controlled key committees refused to go along, and they prevented the bill from coming to a vote. These senators made it clear to Douglas that if he wanted Nebraska organized, he needed to repeal the Missouri Compromise and allow slavery in the new territory.

✓ **Reading Check** **Summarizing** Why did the United States make the Gadsden Purchase?

The Kansas-Nebraska Act

Stephen Douglas knew that any attempt to repeal the Missouri Compromise would divide the country. Nevertheless, he wanted to open the northern Great Plains to settlement. Douglas also believed that if he skillfully maneuvered his bill through Congress, he could split the Whig Party and quiet the slavery issue. Unfortunately, Douglas had badly misjudged the depth of antislavery feelings in the North. By persisting, he inadvertently set the country on the road to war.

CHAPTER 10 Sectional Conflict Intensifies **329**

 ABCNEWS
INTERACTIVE™

📼 **VIDEOCASSETTE**
Historic America Electronic Field Trips

View **Tape 1, Chapter 9:** "Frederick Douglass's Home."

INTERDISCIPLINARY CONNECTIONS ACTIVITY

Language Arts Jane Smiley's book *The All True Tales of Liddie Newton* is a first-person account of a Northerner moving with her husband to Kansas in order to help establish it as a non-slaveholding state. Organize the class into small groups and assign each group to read and summarize a chapter of the book. Have the groups present their summaries to the class.

Geography *Skills*

Answers:

1. 2

2. Nebraska

Geography Skills Practice

Why were there two capitals of the Kansas territory? *(Lecompton was the pro-slavery capital and Topeka was the antislavery capital.)*

Discussing a Topic Ask students to explain why slaveholders would not move to the Nebraska territory while the Missouri Compromise remained in effect. **L1**

FYI

Kansas was admitted to the Union as a free state on January 29, 1861.

3 ASSESS

Assign Section 2 Assessment as homework or as an in-class activity.

🔊 Have students use the **Interactive Tutor Self-Assessment CD-ROM.**

Reading Essentials and Study Guide 10–2

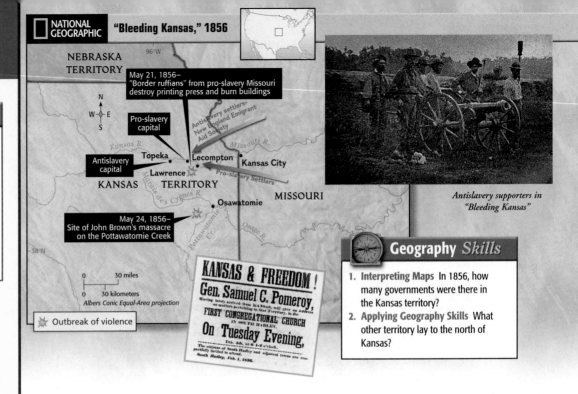

NATIONAL GEOGRAPHIC

"Bleeding Kansas," 1856

May 21, 1856—
"Border ruffians" from pro-slavery Missouri destroy printing press and burn buildings

Pro-slavery capital

Antislavery capital

Topeka · Lecompton · Kansas City

Lawrence

NEBRASKA TERRITORY

KANSAS TERRITORY

MISSOURI

Osawatomie

May 24, 1856—
Site of John Brown's massacre on the Pottawatomie Creek

New England Emigrant Aid Society

Pro-slavery Settlers

0 30 miles
0 30 kilometers
Albers Conic Equal-Area projection

⭐ Outbreak of violence

Antislavery supporters in "Bleeding Kansas"

KANSAS & FREEDOM!
Gen. Samuel C. Pomeroy,
FIRST CONGREGATIONAL CHURCH
On Tuesday Evening,

Geography *Skills*

1. **Interpreting Maps** In 1856, how many governments were there in the Kansas territory?

2. **Applying Geography Skills** What other territory lay to the north of Kansas?

Two New Territories At first, Douglas tried to dodge the issue and gain Southern support for his bill by saying that any states organized in the new Nebraska territory would be allowed to exercise popular sovereignty on slavery.

Southern leaders in the Senate were not fooled. If the Missouri Compromise remained in place while the region was settled, slaveholders would not move there. As a result, the states formed in the region would naturally become free states. Determined to get the territory organized, Douglas went a fateful step further. In his next version of the bill, he proposed to undo the Missouri Compromise and allow slavery in the region. He also proposed dividing the region into two territories. Nebraska would be on the north, adjacent to the free state of Iowa, and Kansas would be on the south, west of the slave state of Missouri. This looked like Nebraska was intended to be free territory, while Kansas was intended for slavery.

Douglas's bill outraged Northern Democrats and Whigs. Free-Soilers and antislavery Democrats called the act an "atrocious plot." They charged that abandoning the Missouri Compromise broke a solemn promise to limit the spread of slavery. Despite this opposition, the leaders of the Democrats in Congress won enough support to pass the **Kansas-Nebraska Act** in May 1854.

Bleeding Kansas Kansas became the first battleground between those favoring the extension of slavery and those opposing it. Since eastern Kansas offered the same climate and rich soil as the slave state of Missouri, settlers moving there from Missouri were likely to bring enslaved persons with them and claim Kansas for the South. Northerners responded by hurrying into the territory themselves, intent on creating an antislavery majority. Northern settlers could count on the support of the New England Emigrant Aid Society, an abolitionist group founded to recruit and outfit antislavery settlers bound for Kansas. Carrying supplies and rifles, hordes of Northerners headed for the new territory.

Pro-slavery senator David Atchison of Missouri responded by calling on men from his state to storm into Kansas. In the spring of 1855, thousands of armed Missourians—called "border ruffians" in the press—voted illegally in Kansas, helping elect a pro-slavery legislature. Furious antislavery settlers countered by holding a convention in Topeka and drafting their own constitution that excluded slavery. By March 1856, Kansas had two governments.

On May 21, 1856, border ruffians, worked up by the arrival of more Northerners, attacked the town of Lawrence, a stronghold of antislavery settlers. The

330 CHAPTER 10 Sectional Conflict Intensifies

CRITICAL THINKING ACTIVITY

Recognizing Cause and Effect Copy the following headings on the board:

CAUSES → EVENT → EFFECTS

Under Event, write Kansas-Nebraska Act, 1854. Then call on students to complete the chain by adding the causes and effects related to passage of the Kansas-Nebraska Act. *(Causes: desire to organize new territories; desire to resolve the issue of expanding slaveholding; Effects: Northern anger over spread of slavery to "free" land; outbreak of violence in Kansas)* **L2**

attackers wrecked newspaper presses, plundered shops and homes, and burned a hotel and the home of the elected free-state governor.

"Bleeding Kansas," as newspapers dubbed the territory, became the scene of a territorial civil war between pro-slavery and antislavery settlers. By the end of 1856, 200 people had died in the fighting and two million dollars' worth of property had been destroyed.

The Caning of Charles Sumner
While bullets flew and blood ran in Kansas, the Senate hotly debated the future of the Western territories. In mid-May 1856, Senator **Charles Sumner** of Massachusetts, a fiery abolitionist, delivered a speech accusing pro-slavery senators of forcing Kansas into the ranks of slave states. He singled out Senator **Andrew P. Butler** of South Carolina, saying Butler had "chosen a mistress . . . the harlot, Slavery."

Several days later, on May 22, Butler's second cousin, Representative Preston Brooks, approached Sumner at his desk in the Senate chamber. Brooks shouted that Sumner's speech had been "a libel on South Carolina, and Mr. Butler, who is a relative of mine." Before Sumner could respond, Brooks raised a gold-handled cane and beat him savagely, leaving the senator severely injured and bleeding on the floor. The growing violence over slavery had come to the very center of government.

Many Southerners considered Brooks to be a hero. Some Southerners even sent him canes

SOUTHERN CHIVALRY — ARGUMENT versus CLUB'S.

 **Analyzing** *Political Cartoons*

Violence in the Senate Representative Preston Brooks beat Senator Charles Sumner savagely for criticizing Brooks's cousin, Senator Andrew Butler. Many Southerners voiced their approval by sending Brooks canes like the one shown here. What emotions did the event stir up in the North and South?

inscribed "Hit Him Again." Shocked by the attack and outraged by the flood of Southern support for Brooks, Northerners strengthened their determination to resist the "barbarism of slavery." One New York clergyman confided in his journal that "no way is left for the North, but to strike back, or be slaves."

Reading Check **Describing** Why did Stephen Douglas propose repealing the Missouri Compromise?

SECTION 2 ASSESSMENT

Checking for Understanding
1. **Define:** Underground Railroad, transcontinental railroad.
2. **Identify:** *Uncle Tom's Cabin,* Fugitive Slave Act, Harriet Tubman, Gadsden Purchase, Kansas-Nebraska Act, Charles Sumner.
3. **Explain** how the transcontinental railroad intensified the slavery issue.

Reviewing Themes
4. **Civic Rights and Responsibilities** How did antislavery activists justify disobeying the Fugitive Slave Act?

Critical Thinking
5. **Synthesizing** What events led to "Bleeding Kansas"?
6. **Categorizing** Use a graphic organizer similar to the one below to list the effects of the Fugitive Slave Act.

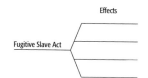

Effects

Fugitive Slave Act

Analyzing Visuals
7. **Interpreting Maps** Study the map of the Underground Railroad on page 329. Consider the entire expanse of the United States and its territories in the 1850s. If slavery failed to expand, what effect would this have on the South's influence on national policy?

Writing About History
8. **Expository Writing** Imagine you are a reporter for a Southern or Northern newspaper in the 1850s. Write an article on public reaction to *Uncle Tom's Cabin.*

CHAPTER 10 Sectional Conflict Intensifies **331**

Analyzing *Political Cartoons*

Answer: outrage in the North and gratification in the South
Ask: Which side of the issue do you think the cartoonist supports? *(The cartoonist's sarcasm about Southern chivalry leads you to conclude that he supports the Northern position.)*

Reading Check

Answer: in order to get Southern support to organize the Nebraska territory

Reteach
Ask students to summarize the effects of the Kansas-Nebraska Act.

Enrich
Have students create their own political cartoon expressing their point of view about one of the events described in this section.

4 CLOSE

Ask students to evaluate how the Fugitive Slave Act and the transcontinental railroad heightened sectional tensions.

SECTION 2 ASSESSMENT ANSWERS

1. Terms are in blue.
2. *Uncle Tom's Cabin* (p. 326), Fugitive Slave Act (p. 327), Harriet Tubman (p. 328), Gadsden Purchase (p. 329), Kansas-Nebraska Act (p. 330), Charles Sumner (p. 331)
3. The need to organize the Nebraska territory for the railroad created a debate over whether slavery would be permitted in states created from the territory.
4. They used civil disobedience.
5. Pro-slavery and antislavery settlers tried to establish a majority to ensure that they could control the future of slavery in Kansas.
6. Students' organizers should draw on information from the text.
7. The South would have lost much of its influence on national policy.
8. Students' articles should be well organized with a clear outline, introduction, body, and conclusion.

1 FOCUS

Section Overview

This section explains the breakdown of the major political parties and the growth in hostility between the North and South resulting from the issue of slavery.

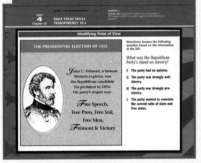
Guide to Reading

Answers to Graphic: executive: Buchanan elected in 1856; legislative: Kansas's Lecompton constitution authorized slavery in territory; judicial: *Dred Scott* decision; nongovernmental: John Brown's raid on Harpers Ferry's federal arsenal

Preteaching Vocabulary
Have students make a list of the Key Terms and Names and add a person's name, date, or phrase to help clarify the significance of the terms and names.

Guide to Reading

Main Idea
The slavery controversy accelerated both the breakdown of the major political parties and the growth of hostility between North and South.

Key Terms and Names
Republican Party, Know-Nothings, Dred Scott, referendum, Lecompton constitution, Freeport Doctrine, insurrection

Reading Strategy
Categorizing As you read about the North-South split, complete a graphic organizer like the one below to group events as executive, legislative, judicial, or nongovernmental.

Executive	
Legislative	
Judicial	
Nongovernmental	

Reading Objectives
• **Analyze** the events that increased sectional tensions in the late 1850s.
• **Describe** the Lincoln-Douglas Senate campaign of 1858.

Section Theme
Groups and Institutions Due to differing opinions within established parties, Americans forged new political alliances in the 1850s.

Preview of Events

◆1854	◆1856	◆1858	◆1860

July 1854
Republican Party founded

March 1857
Supreme Court announces *Dred Scott* decision

1857
Lecompton constitution drafted in Kansas

1858
Lincoln-Douglas debates

October 1859
John Brown and followers raid Harpers Ferry

⭐ **An American Story** ⭐

By the 1850s, feelings were running high among Northerners and Southerners over whether slavery should be allowed in new territories. These strong feelings also tore old political parties apart and created new ones. Soon after Lincoln was defeated in his race for senator from Illinois, he wrote to a Springfield friend:

❝I think I am a Whig; but others say there are not Whigs, and that I am an abolitionist. . . . I now do no more than oppose the extension of slavery. I am not a Know-Nothing. . . . How could I be? How can any one who abhors the oppression of negroes, be in favor of degrading classes of white people? . . . As a nation, we began by declaring 'all men are created equal.' We now practically read it 'all men are created equal except negroes.' When the Know-Nothings get control, it will read 'all men are created equal, except negroes, and foreigners, and catholics.' When it comes to this I should prefer emigrating to some country where they make no pretence of loving liberty—to Russia for instance. . . .❞

Abraham Lincoln

—quoted in *Abraham Lincoln*

Birth of the Republican Party

When the Kansas-Nebraska Act repealed the Missouri Compromise, it enraged many people who opposed the extension of slavery. A few of these people resorted to violence, but the effect was just as dramatic on political parties—both the Whigs and the Democrats were split. In the Whig Party, pro-slavery Southern Whigs and antislavery Northern Whigs had long battled for control of their party. With passage of the Kansas-Nebraska

---

 SECTION RESOURCES

📂 **Reproducible Masters**
• Reproducible Lesson Plan 10–3
• Daily Lecture and Discussion Notes 10–3
• Guided Reading Activity 10–3
• Section Quiz 10–3
• Reading Essentials and Study Guide 10–3
• Interpreting Political Cartoons
• Supreme Court Case Studies

📄 **Transparencies**
• Daily Focus Skills Transparency 10–3

Multimedia
🔘 Interactive Tutor Self-Assessment CD-ROM
🔘 ExamView® Pro Testmaker CD-ROM
🔘 Presentation Plus! CD-ROM
🔘 TeacherWorks™ CD-ROM
🔊 Audio Program
🎵 American Music: Cultural Traditions

<table>
<tr><td colspan="3">**1850s Political Parties**</td></tr>
<tr><td>Party</td><td>Characteristics</td><td>Major Leaders</td></tr>
<tr><td>Whig
(1834–1854)</td><td>Party strongly divided into sectional factions; united only in opposition to Democratic Party</td><td>Daniel Webster, Henry Clay</td></tr>
<tr><td>Democrat
(1828–present)</td><td>Largely controlled federal government from 1828 to 1860 but increasingly dominated by Southern Democrats after 1840</td><td>John C. Calhoun</td></tr>
<tr><td>Liberty
(1839–c. 1844)</td><td>Promoted abolition of slavery; after Liberty Party's failure, members supported Free-Soil and Republican Parties</td><td>James Birney</td></tr>
<tr><td>Free-Soil
(1848–1854)</td><td>Composed of Liberty Party members, antislavery Whigs, and antislavery New York Democrats</td><td>Martin Van Buren, Charles Francis Adams</td></tr>
<tr><td>Republican
(c. 1854–present)</td><td>Composed of Northern Whigs and Free-Soilers; opposed further expansion of slavery</td><td>Abraham Lincoln</td></tr>
<tr><td>American Party (Know-Nothings)
(1849–c. 1860)</td><td>Anti-immigrant and anti-Catholic</td><td>Millard Fillmore (former Whig)</td></tr>
</table>

Source: *Encarta Encyclopedia*

Chart *Skills*

1. **Interpreting Charts** Which party had the shortest life span?
2. **Drawing Conclusions** Does any party listed not have an obvious connection to the slavery issue?

Act, disaster was complete. Every Northern Whig in Congress had voted against the bill, while most Southern Whigs had supported it. "We Whigs of the North," wrote one member from Connecticut, "are unalterably determined never to have even the slightest political correspondence or connexion" with the Southern Whigs.

Anger over the Kansas-Nebraska Act convinced former Whigs, members of the Free-Soil Party, and a few antislavery Democrats to work together during the congressional elections of 1854. These coalitions took many different names, including the Anti-Nebraska Party, the Fusion Party, the People's Party, and the Independent Party. The most popular name for the new coalition was the **Republican Party.**

Republicans Organize At a convention in Michigan in July 1854, the Republican Party was officially organized. In choosing the same name as Jefferson's original party, the Republicans declared their intention to revive the spirit of the American Revolution. Just as Jefferson had chosen the name because he wanted to prevent the United States from becoming a monarchy, the new Republicans chose their name because they feared that the Southern planters were becoming an aristocracy that controlled the federal government.

Republicans did not agree on whether slavery should be abolished in the Southern states, but they did agree that it had to be kept out of the territories. A large majority of Northern voters seemed to agree, enabling the Republicans and the other antislavery parties to make great strides in the elections of 1854.

The Know-Nothings At the same time, public anger against the Northern Democrats also enabled the American Party—better known as the **Know-Nothings**—to make great gains as well, particularly in the Northeast. The American Party was an anti-Catholic and nativist party. It opposed immigration, particularly Catholic immigration, into the United States. Prejudice and fear that immigrants would take away jobs enabled the Know-Nothings to win many seats in Congress and the state legislatures in 1854.

Soon after the election, the Know-Nothings suffered the same fate as the Whigs. Many Know-Nothings had been elected from the Upper South, particularly Maryland, Tennessee, and Kentucky. They quickly split with Know-Nothings from the North over their support for the Kansas-Nebraska

CHAPTER 10 Sectional Conflict Intensifies **333**

2 TEACH

Daily Lecture and Discussion Notes 10–3

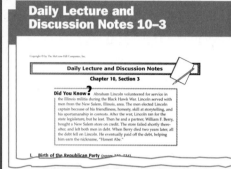

Daily Lecture and Discussion Notes
Chapter 10, Section 3

Did You Know? Abraham Lincoln volunteered for service in the Illinois militia during the Black Hawk War. Lincoln served with men from the New Salem, Illinois, area. The men elected Lincoln captain because of his friendliness, honesty, skill at storytelling, and his sportsmanship in contests. After the war, Lincoln ran for the state legislature, but lost. Then he and a partner, William F. Berry, bought a New Salem store on credit. The store failed shortly thereafter, and left both men in debt. When Berry died two years later, all the debt fell on Lincoln. He eventually paid off the debt, helping him earn the nickname, "Honest Abe."

I. **Birth of the Republican Party** (pages 332–334)

Chart *Skills*

Answer:
1. Liberty Party
2. Know-Nothings

Chart Skills Practice
Ask: Why do you think the Whigs did not last as a political party? *(They split over the Kansas–Nebraska Act, which caused such dissension among them that the party collapsed.)*

Synthesizing Information Have students reread Lincoln's statement on page 332. Discuss as a class the reasons that Lincoln could not support the Know-Nothings. **L1**

In 1852 the Whigs nominated Winfield Scott rather that the incumbent Millard Fillmore, whose strident enforcement of the Fugitive Slave Act had alienated many Northern members of the party. Fillmore sought the presidency again in 1856 as the candidate of the Know-Nothings. He finished third with about 22 percent of the popular vote.

COOPERATIVE LEARNING ACTIVITY

Forming a Hypothesis To review the *Dred Scott* decision, organize the class into groups of four. Have each student present one aspect of the event to the rest of the group. Use the following aspects: President Buchanan's reasons for not deciding on the issue, the reasons for the Supreme Court's decision, reaction in the North, and reaction in the South. Based on the discussion, have each group form a hypothesis stating what might have happened had Northerners not challenged the Court's decision.

Use the rubric for a cooperative group management plan on pages 81–82 in the ***Performance Assessment Activities and Rubrics.***

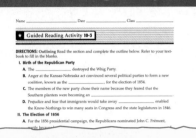
✓Reading Check

Answer: passage of the Kansas-Nebraska Act repealing the Missouri Compromise, the upcoming 1854 elections

✓Reading Check

Answer: Democrat James Buchanan

Making Predictions Ask students to predict which justices were likely to side with Dred Scott and which were not. *(Curtis and McLean dissented.)* **L2**

Justice	Home State When Appointed to the Court
John Archibald Campbell	Alabama
John Catron	Tennessee
Benjamin R. Curtis	Massachusetts
Peter Vivian Daniel	Virginia
Robert Cooper Grier	Pennsylvania
John McLean	Ohio
Samuel Nelson	New York
Roger Brooke Taney	Maryland
James Moore Wayne	Georgia

Fact | Fiction | Folklore

Many candidates for political office try to make connections with ordinary people.
Ask: How does the current president make connections with ordinary people? *(Answers will vary. Some students might identify activities such as visiting a factory or a school, attending religious services, or playing with the family pet.)*

Act. Furthermore, the violence in Kansas and the beating of Charles Sumner made slavery a far more important issue to most Americans than immigration. Eventually, the Republican Party absorbed the Northern Know-Nothings.

✓**Reading Check** **Examining** What events led to the founding of the Republican Party?

The Election of 1856

To gain the widest possible support in the 1856 campaign, the Republicans nominated **John C. Frémont,** a famous Western explorer nicknamed "The Pathfinder." Frémont had spoken in favor of Kansas becoming a free state. He had little political experience but also no embarrassing record to defend.

The Democrats nominated **James Buchanan.** Buchanan had served in Congress for 20 years and had been the American ambassador to Russia and then to Great Britain. He had been in Great Britain during the debate over the Kansas-Nebraska Act and had not taken a stand on the issue, but his record in Congress showed that he believed the best way to save the Union was to make concessions to the South.

The American Party tried to reunite its Northern and Southern members at its convention, but most of

Fact | Fiction | Folklore

"Born in a Log Cabin" The image of a "common man" president was appealing to campaign managers in the 1800s. As voting rights spread beyond landowners, the candidate with humble roots was a potent political image. Although many nineteenth-century candidates sought to appeal to the masses, only five presidents were actually born in a log home: Andrew Jackson, James K. Polk, James Buchanan, Abraham Lincoln, and James Garfield. Of these five, Jackson, Lincoln, Buchanan, and Garfield actually experienced serious poverty in childhood. William Henry Harrison campaigned with images of a log cabin childhood, but he was actually born into an elite Virginia family that was acquainted with George Washington.

the Northern delegates walked out when the party refused to call for the repeal of the Kansas-Nebraska Act. The rest of the convention then chose former president Millard Fillmore to represent the American Party, hoping to attract the vote of former Whigs.

The campaign was really two separate contests: Buchanan against Frémont in the North, and Buchanan against Fillmore in the South. Buchanan had solid support in the South and only needed his home state of Pennsylvania and one other to win the presidency. Democrats campaigned on the idea that only Buchanan could save the Union and that the election of Frémont would cause the South to secede. When the votes were counted, Buchanan had won.

✓**Reading Check** **Identifying** What political party and candidate won the presidency in 1856?

Sectional Divisions Grow

Despite Buchanan's determination to adopt policies that would calm the growing sectional strife in the country, a series of events helped drive Americans in the North and South even further apart.

The *Dred Scott* Decision In his March 1857 inaugural address, James Buchanan suggested that the nation let the Supreme Court decide the question of slavery in the territories. Most people who listened to the address did not know that Buchanan had contacted members of the Supreme Court and therefore knew that a decision was imminent.

Many Southern members of Congress had quietly pressured the Supreme Court justices to issue a ruling on slavery in the territories. They expected the Southern majority on the court to rule in favor of the South. They were not disappointed. Two days after the inauguration, the Court released its opinion in the case of *Dred Scott* v. *Sandford.* 📖 *(See page 1080 for more information on Dred Scott v. Sandford.)*

Dred Scott was an enslaved man whose Missouri slaveholder had taken him to live in free territory before returning to Missouri. Assisted by abolitionists, Scott sued to end his slavery, arguing that the time he had spent in free territory meant he was free. The case went all the way to the Supreme Court.

On March 6, 1857, Chief Justice Roger B. Taney delivered the majority opinion in the case. Taney ruled against Scott because, he claimed, African Americans were not citizens and therefore could not sue in the courts. Taney then addressed the Missouri Compromise's ban on slavery in territory north of Missouri's southern border:

MEETING SPECIAL NEEDS

Auditory/Musical Have interested students write a script for a "You Are There" radio program on the reaction to the *Dred Scott* decision. Suggest that the scripts include an introduction that provides background information and interviews with lawyers, Dred Scott, John F. A. Sandford, other eyewitnesses at the court, and various experts on the Supreme Court. Encourage students to "broadcast" their scripts for the rest of the class. **L2**

📂 Refer to **Inclusion for the High School Social Studies Classroom Strategies and Activities** in the TCR.

❝It is the opinion of the court that the Act of Congress which prohibited a citizen from holding and owning [enslaved persons] in the territory of the United States north of the line therein mentioned is not warranted by the Constitution and is therefore void.❞

—from *Dred Scott v. Sandford*

Instead of removing the issue of slavery in the territories from politics, the *Dred Scott* decision itself became a political issue that further intensified the sectional conflict. The Supreme Court had said that the federal government could not prohibit slavery in the territories. Free soil, one of the basic ideas uniting Republicans, was unconstitutional.

Democrats cheered the decision, but Republicans condemned it and claimed it was not binding. Instead they argued that it was an **obiter dictum,** an incidental opinion not called for by the circumstances of the case. Southerners, on the other hand, called on Northerners to obey the decision if they wanted the South to remain in the Union.

Many African Americans, among them Philadelphia activist Robert Purvis, publicly declared contempt for any government that could produce such an edict:

❝Mr. Chairman, look at the facts— here, in a country with a sublimity of impudence that knows no parallel, setting itself up before the world as a *free country*, a *land of liberty!*, *'the land of the free*, and the *home of the brave,'* the *'freest country in all the world'* . . . and yet here are millions of men and women . . . bought and sold, whipped, manacled, killed all the day long.❞

—quoted in *Witness for Freedom*

Kansas's Lecompton Constitution

Frustration with the government also fueled the conflict between antislavery and pro-slavery forces in "Bleeding Kansas." Hoping to end the troubles there, President Buchanan urged the territory to apply for statehood. The pro-slavery legislature scheduled an election for delegates to a constitutional convention, but antislavery Kansans boycotted it, claiming it was rigged. The resulting constitution, drafted in the town of Lecompton in 1857, legalized slavery in the territory.

Each side then held its own referendum, or popular vote, on the constitution. Antislavery forces voted down the constitution; pro-slavery forces approved it. Buchanan accepted the pro-slavery vote and asked

Picturing History

Front-Page News Chief Justice Roger B. Taney delivered the Supreme Court's ruling in the *Dred Scott* case. The decision made Scott a topic for the nation's press. What impression of Scott's family do you get from the engravings shown here?

Congress to admit Kansas as a slave state. The Senate quickly voted to accept the **Lecompton constitution,** but the House of Representatives blocked it. Many members of Congress became so angry during the debates that fistfights broke out. Southern leaders were stunned when even Stephen Douglas of Illinois refused to support them. Many had hoped that Douglas, a Northern leader and possible future president, understood the South's concerns and would make the compromise necessary to keep the South in the Union.

Finally, to get the votes they needed, President Buchanan and Southern leaders in Congress agreed to allow another referendum in Kansas on the constitution. Southern leaders expected to win this referendum. If the settlers in Kansas rejected the Lecompton constitution, they would delay statehood for Kansas for at least two more years.

CHAPTER 10 Sectional Conflict Intensifies **335**

Picturing History

Answer: They appear to be respectable people whose clothing suggests a non-slave and middle-class status.

FYI

The sons of Peter Blow, Dred Scott's original slaveholder, helped pay Scott's legal bills. Following the Supreme Court's decision, these childhood friends bought Scott and his wife Harriet and freed them. Scott died within the year.

Explaining a Quote Ask students to explain the words of Robert Purvis that are quoted on this page. Encourage students to use a dictionary to look up the meaning of unfamiliar words such as *sublimity* and *impudence.* **L2**

History *and the* Humanities

🎵 American Music: Hits Through History: "Joshua Fit the Battle of Jericho," "John Brown's Dream"
🎵 American Music: Cultural Traditions: "Hard Times Come Again No More," "Get Off the Track!"
🎨 American Art & Architecture: *John Brown Going to His Hanging*

INTERDISCIPLINARY CONNECTIONS ACTIVITY

Language Arts Encourage students to act as reporters attending the Lincoln-Douglas debates. Ask them to write a news story on the debates, detailing the major issues raised and the exchanges between Lincoln and Douglas. Recommend that students review recent news articles to help them understand the style used in good news reporting. **L2**

Reading Check

Answer: His slaveholder had taken him to live in a free territory before returning to Missouri. Scott argued that since he had spent time in a free territory, he was free.

Explaining a Quote Ask students to explain the words of Abraham Lincoln that are quoted on pages 336 and 337. Ask students to explain how Lincoln's words foreshadowed the direction the country would take by the end of his presidency. **L2**

FYI

Even though Lincoln and Douglas debated publicly, their fate was in the hands of the Illinois state legislature. Douglas was reelected to the U.S. Senate by a vote of 54 to 46. In 1913 the Seventeenth Amendment established direct election of senators.

📁 Use *Interpreting Political Cartoons,* Cartoon 8.

📁 Use *Supreme Court Case Study 5,* Dred Scott v. Sandford.

Despite these conditions, the settlers in Kansas voted overwhelmingly in 1858 to reject the Lecompton constitution. They did not want slavery in their state. As a result, Kansas did not become a state until 1861.

> ## Reading Check **Summarizing** Why did Dred Scott sue the slaveholder who held him?

Lincoln and Douglas

In 1858 Illinois Republicans chose a relative unknown named Abraham Lincoln to run for the Senate against the Democratic incumbent, Stephen A. Douglas. Lincoln launched his campaign in June with a memorable speech, in which he declared:

> ❝A house divided against itself cannot stand. I believe this Government cannot endure, permanently half *slave* and half *free.* I do not expect the Union to be *dissolved*—I do not expect the house to *fall*—but I do expect it will cease to be divided. It will become *all* one thing or *all* the other.❞
>
> —quoted in *The Civil War: An Illustrated History*

The nationally prominent Douglas, a short, stocky man nicknamed "The Little Giant," regularly drew large crowds on the campaign trail. Seeking to overcome Douglas's fame, Lincoln proposed a series of debates between the candidates, which would expose him to larger audiences than he could attract on his own. Douglas confidently accepted.

Born on the Kentucky frontier and raised in Indiana, Lincoln had experienced little more than small-town

"The right of the people to make a slave Territory or a free Territory is perfect and complete."

—*Stephen Douglas*

life. A storekeeper, mill hand, and rail-splitter during his youth, he went on to study and practice law. Later he served in the Illinois state legislature and, for a single term, in the U.S. House of Representatives as a member of the Whig Party. Despite this modest background, Lincoln proved himself a gifted debater. Both witty and logical, he regularly illuminated his points with quotations from scripture or appealing homespun stories from everyday life.

Although not an abolitionist, Lincoln believed slavery to be morally wrong and opposed its spread into western territories. Douglas, by contrast, supported popular sovereignty. During a debate in Freeport, Lincoln asked Douglas if the people of a territory could legally exclude slavery before achieving statehood? If Douglas said yes, he would appear to be supporting popular sovereignty and opposing the *Dred Scott* ruling, which would cost him Southern support. If he said no, it would make it seem as if he had abandoned popular sovereignty, the principle on which he had built his national following.

Douglas tried to avoid the dilemma, formulating an answer that became known as the **Freeport Doctrine.** He replied that he accepted the *Dred Scott* ruling, but he argued that people could still keep slavery out by refusing to pass the laws needed to

CRITICAL THINKING ACTIVITY

Analyzing Information Have students work in pairs to analyze the effects of the growth of slavery. Tell them that in 1790, there were about 698,000 enslaved persons in the United States. By 1860 there were almost 4 million enslaved persons in the South. Ask each pair to list reasons why political compromise over the slavery question might have been easier right after the American Revolution than during the 1850s. *(possible reasons: Slavery had spread throughout the South by the 1850s, the economy of the South depended on slavery, and a better political climate for compromise may have existed after the Revolution.)* Discuss student responses as a class. **L2**

regulate and enforce it. "Slavery cannot exist . . . any-where," said Douglas, "unless it is supported by local police regulations." Douglas's response pleased Illinois voters but angered Southerners.

Lincoln also attacked Douglas's claim that he "cared not" whether Kansans voted for or against slavery. Denouncing "the modern Democratic idea that slavery is as good as freedom," Lincoln called on voters to elect Republicans, "whose hearts are in the work, who *do care* for the result":

> 66Has any thing ever threatened the existence of this Union save and except this very institution of slavery? What is it that we hold most dear amongst us? Our own liberty and prosperity. What has ever threatened our liberty and prosperity save and except this institution of slavery? If this is true, how do you propose to improve the condition of things by enlarging slavery—by spreading it out and making it bigger? You may have a wen [sore] or cancer upon your person and not be able to cut it out lest you bleed to death; but surely it is no way to cure it, to engraft it and spread it over your whole body. That is no proper way of treating what you regard a wrong.99
>
> —quoted in *The Civil War: Opposing Viewpoints*

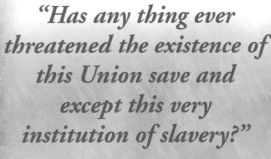

History *Through Art*

Charleston Confrontation Lincoln and Douglas matched wits seven times during the 1858 senatorial campaign. This painting by Robert Root shows them in Charleston, Illinois. How did the debates help Lincoln?

Douglas won the election, but Lincoln did not come away empty-handed. He had seized the opportunity in the debates to make clear the principles of the Republican Party. He had also established a national reputation for himself as a man of clear, insightful thinking who could argue with force and eloquence. Within a year, however, national attention shifted to another figure, a man who opposed slavery not with well-crafted phrases, but with a gun.

✓**Reading Check** **Examining** What were the positions of Stephen Douglas and Abraham Lincoln on slavery?

John Brown's Raid

John Brown was a fervent abolitionist who believed, as one minister who knew him in Kansas said, "that God had raised him up on purpose to break the jaws of the wicked." In 1859, he developed a plan to seize the federal arsenal at Harpers Ferry, Virginia (today in West Virginia), free and arm the enslaved people of the neighborhood, and begin an **insurrection**, or rebellion, against slaveholders.

On the night of October 16, 1859, Brown and 18 followers seized the arsenal. To the terrified night watchman, he announced, "I have possession now of the United States armory, and if the citizens interfere with me I must only burn the town and have blood."

Soon, however, Brown was facing a contingent of U.S. Marines, rushed to Harpers Ferry from Washington, D.C., under the command of Colonel Robert E. Lee. Just 36 hours after it had begun, Brown's attempt to start a slave insurrection ended with his capture. A Virginia court tried and

> *"Has any thing ever threatened the existence of this Union save and except this very institution of slavery?"*
>
> —*Abraham Lincoln*

CHAPTER 10 Sectional Conflict Intensifies **337**

✓**Reading Check**

Answer: Douglas supported popular sovereignty. Although Lincoln was not an abolitionist, he believed slavery to be morally wrong and opposed its spread into western territories.

3 ASSESS

Assign Section 3 Assessment as homework or as an in-class activity.

🔘 Have students use the **Interactive Tutor Self-Assessment CD-ROM.**

Reading Essentials and Study Guide 10–3

Name _____ Date _____ Class _____

Study Guide

Chapter 10, Section 3
For use with textbook pages 332–338

THE CRISIS DEEPENS

KEY TERMS AND NAMES

Republican Party a political party formed in 1854 as an antislavery party *(page 333)*
Know-Nothings an anti-catholic and nativist political party *(page 333)*
Dred Scott an enslaved man who argued that he should be free because he was taken to a free territory; his case went to the Supreme Court *(page 334)*
referendum popular vote *(page 335)*
Lecompton constitution the constitution drafted by a Kansan pro-slavery legislature that legalized slavery in Kansas *(page 335)*
Freeport Doctrine Stephen Douglas's statement that slavery could be excluded in a territory if people refused to pass the laws needed to regulate and enforce slavery *(page 335)*

History *Through Art*

Answer: He used the debates to put forth the principles of the Republican Party and to establish his reputation as a clear, insightful thinker who could argue with force and eloquence.
Ask: From the picture, what similarities and differences do you see between this debate and modern televised presidential debates? *(possible answers—similarities: both candidates well dressed, both have a glass of water available, patriotic trappings surround them; differences: today only the candidates are on the podium, no supporting signs would be displayed)*

Profiles IN HISTORY

Two of John Brown's sons participated in the raid on Harpers Ferry. Both men were killed. **Ask:** What issues today create such strong emotions that a few people believe they have the right to ignore laws and commit crimes similar to John Brown? *(Students will likely identify terrorism—by Timothy McVeigh domestically or by radical individuals based in the Middle East.)*

✓ Reading Check

Answer: Northerners: a martyr for the cause of abolition; Southerners: fear of attacks from others in the North

Reteach

Have students chronicle the Lincoln-Douglas Senate campaign of 1858.

Enrich

Have students use library and Internet resources to create a profile of one of the people mentioned in this section.

4 CLOSE

Ask students to identify and write one sentence about each of the events that increased sectional tensions in the late 1850s.

Profiles IN HISTORY

John Brown
1800–1859

John Brown, who believed he was acting with God's approval, helped to bring about the Civil War. A dedicated abolitionist, Brown initially worked with the Underground Railroad in Pennsylvania. When conflict between pro-slavery and free-soil settlers in Kansas became violent, Brown moved to Kansas to help six of his sons and other free-soil settlers in their struggle against slavery.

After pro-slavery forces from Missouri sacked the town of Lawrence, Kansas, on May 21, 1856, Brown vowed revenge. The following day, he learned of the caning of Charles Sumner in the Senate and, in the words of one witness, he "went crazy—crazy." Two days later, he abducted and murdered five pro-slavery settlers living near Pottawatomie Creek. Later he said of the deaths, "I believe that I did God service in having them killed." Brown was never arrested for the Pottawatomie Massacre, and for some Northern abolitionists he became a hero for his willingness to fight back. Three years later, he launched his raid on Harpers Ferry. Although the raid ended in disaster and Brown himself was hanged, his desperate act terrified Southerners and brought the nation another step closer to disunion and civil war.

convicted him and sentenced him to death. In his last words to the court, Brown, repenting nothing, declared:

❝I believe that to have interfered as I have done, as I have always freely admitted I have done in behalf of [God's] despised poor, I did no wrong, but right. Now if it is deemed necessary that I should forfeit my life for the furtherance of the ends of justice and mingle my blood . . . with the blood of millions in this slave country whose rights are disregarded by wicked, cruel and unjust enactments, I say, let it be done!❞

—quoted in *John Brown, 1800–1859*

On December 2, the day of his execution, Brown handed one of his jailers a prophetic note: "I, John Brown, am now quite *certain* that the crimes of this *guilty land* will never be purged *away* but with Blood. I had *as I now think vainly* flattered myself that without *very much* bloodshed it might be done."

Many Northerners viewed Brown as a martyr in a noble cause. The execution, Henry David Thoreau predicted, would strengthen abolitionist feeling in the North. "He is not old Brown any longer," Thoreau declared, "he is an angel of light."

For most Southerners, however, Brown's raid offered all the proof they needed that Northerners were actively plotting the murder of slaveholders. "Defend yourselves!" cried Georgia senator Robert Toombs. "The enemy is at your door!"

✓ Reading Check
Evaluating In what ways might a Northerner and a Southerner view John Brown's action differently?

SECTION 3 ASSESSMENT

Checking for Understanding
1. **Define:** referendum, insurrection.
2. **Identify:** Republican Party, Know-Nothings, Dred Scott, Lecompton constitution, Freeport Doctrine.
3. **List** the two rulings in *Dred Scott* v. *Sandford* that increased sectional divisiveness.

Reviewing Themes
4. **Groups and Institutions** What were the main goals of the Republican and American Parties?

Critical Thinking
5. **Synthesizing** How did Americans react to John Brown's raid?
6. **Categorizing** Use a graphic organizer similar to the one below to list causes of the growing tensions between North and South.

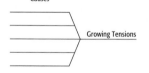

Causes → Growing Tensions

Analyzing Visuals
7. **Studying Charts** Examine the chart on page 333. Did any parties besides the Republican and Democratic survive after 1865? How does this support the idea that the 1850s and 1860s were an important transition era in the nation's history?

Writing About History
8. **Expository Writing** Imagine you have just read the Supreme Court's ruling in the *Dred Scott* case. Write a letter to the editor explaining your reaction to the decision.

338 CHAPTER 10 Sectional Conflict Intensifies

SECTION 3 ASSESSMENT ANSWERS

1. Terms are in blue.
2. Republican Party *(p. 333)*, Know-Nothings *(p. 333)*, Dred Scott *(p. 334)*, Lecompton constitution *(p. 335)*, Freeport Doctrine *(p. 336)*
3. African Americans could not sue in the courts because they were not citizens and the prohibition of slavery established by the Missouri Compromise was unconstitutional.
4. Republican Party: limit the influence of Southern planters and keep slavery out of the territories; American Party: opposed immigration
5. Northerners viewed Brown's actions as heroic. Southerners were terrified by his actions.
6. Kansas-Nebraska Act, *Dred Scott* decision, Lecompton constitution, John Brown's raid
7. No. It led to the rise of the Democratic and Republican parties as the main political parties.
8. Letters should be written in proper business letter format and express a clear point of view.

Frederick Douglass was born into slavery in Maryland in 1818. During the course of his incredible life, he escaped from slavery and eventually became renowned for eloquent lectures and writings for the causes of abolition and liberty. One of his most famous works is his autobiography about growing up under the shadow of slavery. In the following excerpt, Douglass is around eight years old, and Mrs. Auld, the wife of his slaveholder, has begun to teach him to read. Mr. Auld discovers what his wife has been doing, and his reaction causes young Frederick to decide to learn to read on his own, no matter what.

Read to Discover

Why did some slaveholders not want enslaved people to learn to read?

Reader's Dictionary

sentiments: feelings

revelation: discovery

conscious: aware

diligently: with great effort

from Narrative of the Life of Frederick Douglass

by Frederick Douglas

"Now," said [Mr. Auld], "if you teach that [boy] how to read, there would be no keeping him. It would forever unfit him to be a slave. He would at once become unmanageable, and of no value to his master. As to himself, it could do him no good, but a great deal of harm. It would make him discontented and unhappy." These words sank deep into my heart, stirred up sentiments within that lay slumbering, and called into existence an entirely new train of thought. It was a new and special revelation, explaining dark and mysterious things, with which my youthful understanding had struggled, but struggled in vain. . . . From that moment, I understood the pathway from slavery to freedom. It was just what I wanted, and I got it at a time when I least expected it. Whilst I was saddened by the thought of losing the aid of my kind mistress, I was gladdened by the invaluable instruction which, by the merest accident, I had gained from my master. Though conscious of the difficulty of learning without a teacher, I set out with high hope, and a fixed purpose, at whatever cost of trouble, to learn to read. . . . That which to [Mr. Auld] was a great evil, to be carefully shunned, was to me a great good, to be diligently sought; and the argument which he so warmly urged, against my learning to read, only served to inspire me with a desire and determination to learn. In learning to read, I owe almost as much to the bitter opposition of my master, as to the kindly aid of my mistress. I acknowledge the benefit of both.

Analyzing Literature

1. **Recall** Why did Mr. Auld oppose the idea of Douglass learning to read?
2. **Interpret** What do you think Douglass means when he speaks of "a revelation, explaining dark and mysterious things"?
3. **Evaluate and Connect** How would you feel if someone had forbidden you to learn to read?

Interdisciplinary Activity

Art Design a poster promoting literacy. Include reasons why everyone should learn to read and write and get an education.

Read to Discover
Answer: If enslaved persons could read, they would think for themselves and question their status.

Reinforcing Vocabulary
Ask students to use each of the terms in a sentence that is not related to the reading.

Historical Connection
Narrative of the Life of Frederick Douglass was the first of two volumes of Frederick Douglass's autobiography. Douglass felt the need to tell his life story because white abolitionists could never quite get a complete picture of slavery.

Portfolio Writing Activity
Ask students to write a short essay on Douglass's attitude toward education.

Refer to tav.glencoe.com for additional Glencoe Literature titles, lesson plans, and study guides related to this unit.

Answers to Analyzing Literature

1. It would make him forever unfit to be a slave.
2. possible answer: that education could be the pathway to freedom
3. possible answer: frustrated that others could do something important that you could not

Interdisciplinary Activity
Posters should support reading and education in visual and creative ways.

339

1 FOCUS

Section Overview

This section focuses on the events leading up to the attack on Fort Sumter and the secession of the Lower South.

BELLRINGER
Skillbuilder Activity

Project transparency and have students answer the question.

Available as a blackline master.

Daily Focus Skills Transparency 10–4

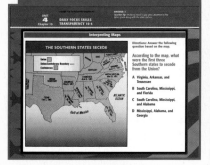

Guide to Reading

Answers to Graphic:
I. The Election of 1860
  A. The Democrats Split
  B. Lincoln Is Elected
  C. Secession
II. Compromise Fails
  A. A Last Attempt at Peace
  B. Founding the Confederacy
Students should complete the outline by including all heads in the section.

Preteaching Vocabulary
Have students scan the section and write a sentence using each of the Key Terms and Names in context.

Guide to Reading

Main Idea
Many events pushed the nation into civil war.

Key Terms and Names
John C. Breckinridge, John Bell, Crittenden's Compromise, Confederacy, Jefferson Davis, martial law

Reading Strategy
Taking Notes As you read about the downward spiral toward civil war in the United States, use the major headings of the section to create an outline similar to the one below.

The Union Dissolves
I. The Election of 1860
  A.
  B.
  C.
II.

Reading Objectives
• **Describe** the various attempts to find a compromise between the demands of the North and the South.
• **Explain** how and why the Civil War began.

Section Theme
Civic Rights and Responsibilities After Lincoln's election, many Southerners placed state loyalty above loyalty to the Republic.

Preview of Events

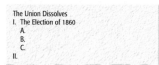

| ◆January 1861 | ◆March 1861 | ◆May 1861 |

December 20, 1860	February 8	March 4	April 12	April 17
South Carolina secedes from the Union	The Confederate States of America is formed	Lincoln inaugurated	Fort Sumter bombarded	Virginia secedes

Mary Chesnut

★ *An American Story* ★

"I do not pretend to sleep," wrote Mary Chesnut of the night of April 12, 1861. "How can I?" Hours earlier her husband, former South Carolina senator James Chesnut, had gone by rowboat to Fort Sumter, in Charleston Harbor. He was delivering an ultimatum to U.S. Army Major Robert Anderson to surrender the fort by four o'clock in the morning or be fired upon by the South Carolina militia.

Through the long night Mary Chesnut lay awake, until she heard chimes from a local church ring four times. The hour of surrender had arrived, and, she confessed, "I beg[a]n to hope." Her hopes of a peaceful outcome faded when, a half-hour later, she heard the cannons begin to boom. "I sprang out of bed. And on my knees . . . I prayed as I never prayed before."

She ran to the roof, where others had gathered to watch the bombardment of Fort Sumter. Mary Chesnut shivered and felt the first terrifying evidence of the horrors to come.

"The regular roar of the cannon—there it was. And who could tell what each volley accomplished of death and destruction."

—adapted from *Mary Chesnut's Civil War*

The Election of 1860

John Brown's raid on Harpers Ferry was a turning point for the South. The possibility of an African American uprising had long haunted many Southerners, but they were frightened and angered by the idea that Northerners would deliberately try to arm enslaved people and encourage them to rebel.

340 CHAPTER 10 Sectional Conflict Intensifies

SECTION RESOURCES

Reproducible Masters
• Reproducible Lesson Plan 10–4
• Daily Lecture and Discussion Notes 10–4
• Guided Reading Activity 10–4
• Section Quiz 10–4
• Reading Essentials and Study Guide 10–4
• Performance Assessment Activities and Rubrics

Transparencies
• Daily Focus Skills Transparency 10–4

Multimedia
- Interactive Tutor Self-Assessment CD-ROM
- ExamView® Pro Testmaker CD-ROM
- Presentation Plus! CD-ROM
- TeacherWorks™ CD-ROM
- Audio Program

Although the Republican leaders quickly denounced Brown's raid, many Southerners blamed Republicans. To them, the key point was that both the Republicans and John Brown opposed slavery. As one Atlanta newspaper noted: "We regard every man who does not boldly declare that he believes African slavery to be a social, moral, and political blessing as an enemy to the institutions of the South."

In the Senate, Robert Toombs of Georgia warned that the South would "never permit this Federal government to pass into the traitorous hands of the Black Republican party." In April 1860, with the South in an uproar, Democrats headed to Charleston, South Carolina, to choose their nominee for president.

The Democrats Split In 1860 the debate over slavery in the western territories finally tore the Democratic Party apart. Their first presidential nominating convention ended in dispute. Northern delegates wanted to support popular sovereignty, while Southern delegates wanted the party to uphold the *Dred Scott* decision and endorse a federal slave code for the territories. Stephen Douglas was not able to get the votes needed to be nominated for president, but neither could anyone else.

In June 1860, the Democrats met again, this time in Baltimore, to select their candidate. Douglas's supporters in the South had organized rival delegations to ensure Douglas's endorsement. The original Southern delegations objected to these rival delegates and again walked out. The remaining Democrats then chose Douglas as their candidate for president.

The Southern Democrats who had walked out organized their own convention and nominated the current vice president, **John C. Breckinridge** of Kentucky, for president. Breckinridge supported the *Dred Scott* decision and agreed to endorse the idea of a federal slave code for the western territories.

The split in the Democratic Party greatly improved Republican prospects, which was what some of the more radical Southern delegates had intended all along. They hoped that a Republican victory would be the final straw that would convince the Southern states to secede.

Other people, including many former Whigs, were greatly alarmed at the danger to the Union.

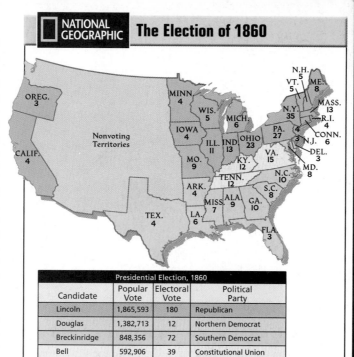

NATIONAL GEOGRAPHIC **The Election of 1860**

Presidential Election, 1860			
Candidate	Popular Vote	Electoral Vote	Political Party
Lincoln	1,865,593	180	Republican
Douglas	1,382,713	12	Northern Democrat
Breckinridge	848,356	72	Southern Democrat
Bell	592,906	39	Constitutional Union

Geography *Skills*

1. **Interpreting Maps** How does the map show that Lincoln was a sectional candidate?
2. **Applying Geography Skills** What explains the fact that Stephen Douglas won only one state, Missouri?

They created another new party, the Constitutional Union Party, and chose former Tennessee senator **John Bell** as their candidate. The Constitutional Unionists campaigned on a position of upholding both the Constitution and the Union.

TURNING POINT

Lincoln Is Elected With no possibility of winning electoral votes in the South, the Republicans needed a candidate who could sweep the North. Delegates at the Republicans' Chicago convention did not think their first choice, William Seward, had a wide enough appeal. Instead they nominated Lincoln, whose debates with Douglas had made him very popular in the North.

During the campaign, the Republicans tried to persuade voters they were more than just an antislavery party. They denounced John Brown's raid and reaffirmed the right of the Southern states to preserve

CHAPTER 10   Sectional Conflict Intensifies   **341**

2 *TEACH*

Daily Lecture and Discussion Notes 10–4

Copyright © by The McGraw-Hill Companies, Inc.

Daily Lecture and Discussion Notes

Chapter 10, Section 4

Did You Know? After Stephen A. Douglas lost the 1860 presidential election to Abraham Lincoln, he worked hard to save the Union. Douglas gave all his support to Abraham Lincoln in this endeavor. He went on an extensive speaking tour of the border and western states. He became exhausted by the travel and contracted a case of typhoid fever. He died in Chicago on June 3, 1861.

I.   The Election of 1860 (pages 340–342)

A. John Brown's raid on Harpers Ferry was a turning point for the South. Southerners feared an African American uprising and were angered that Northerners would arm them and encourage them to rebel. Republicans renounced John Brown's raid, but

Creating a Circle Graph Have students use the data shown in the 1860 election map to create a pair of circle graphs illustrating the results of the presidential election of 1860. **L1**

 Use the rubric for creating a map, display, or chart on pages 77–78 in the *Performance Assessment Activities and Rubrics.*

Geography *Skills*

Answers:

1. He won no states south of the Ohio River.

2. He lost the North to Lincoln and he was not pro-slavery enough for the South.

Geography Skills Practice
Ask: What do the election results tell you about the Northern and Southern populations in 1860? *(The North had a much larger population than the South.)*

COOPERATIVE LEARNING ACTIVITY

Creating an Election Broadcast Organize students into several groups and inform them that their task is to develop a script for an "Election Special" television broadcast on the 1860 presidential election. Suggest that group members take a number of roles: a moderator, political experts who provide analyses on the election results, reporters at the polls, and voters interviewed by the reporters. Call on groups to volunteer to "broadcast" their specials for the rest of the class.

Use the rubric for a cooperative group management plan on pages 81–82 in the *Performance Assessment Activities and Rubrics.*

FYI

In April of 1860 delegates to the Democratic convention in Charleston cast 57 ballots without selecting a candidate before they decided to adjourn. They reconvened six weeks later in Baltimore.

📋 Analyzing *Political Cartoons*

Answer: He once worked as a rail-splitter.

Ask: How does the cartoonist make Lincoln appear stronger than the others? *(He placed Lincoln in the foreground and showed him standing tall.)*

✓ Reading Check

Answer: the election of Lincoln, a Republican, as president

FYI

States seceded in this order: South Carolina, December 20, 1860; Mississippi, January 9, 1861; Florida, January 10, 1861; Alabama, January 11, 1861; Georgia, January 19, 1861; Louisiana, January 26, 1861; Texas, February 1, 1861; Virginia, April 17, 1861; Arkansas, May 6, 1861; and North Carolina, May 20, 1861. The Tennessee legislature adopted a "Declaration of Independence" on May 7, 1861–effectively breaking with the Union. Convention delegates did not formally accept secession until a referendum was passed on June 8, 1861.

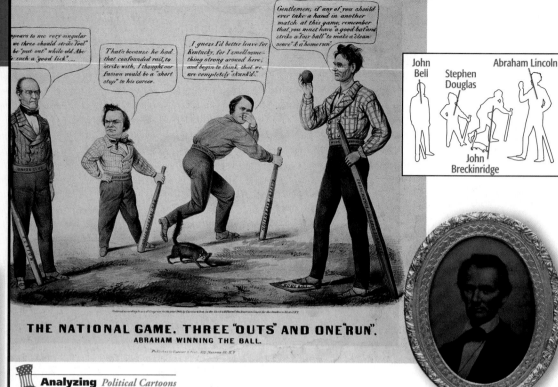

THE NATIONAL GAME. THREE "OUTS" AND ONE "RUN".
ABRAHAM WINNING THE BALL.

📋 Analyzing *Political Cartoons*

Baseball and Politics In this cartoon, baseball language is used to explain Lincoln's 1860 victory. John Bell is sad that the opponents struck out. Stephen Douglas claims Lincoln had the advantage of his "rail," and John Breckinridge admits they were "skunk'd." Why is Lincoln pictured with a rail?

slavery within their borders. They also supported higher tariffs, a new homestead law for western settlers, and a transcontinental railroad.

The Republican proposals greatly angered many Southerners. Nevertheless, with Democratic votes split between Douglas and Breckinridge, Lincoln won the election without Southern support. For the South, the election of a Republican president represented the victory of the abolitionists. The survival of Southern society and culture seemed to be at stake. For many, there was now no choice but to secede.

Secession The dissolution of the Union began with South Carolina, where anti-Northern secessionist sentiment had long been intense. Shortly after Lincoln's election, the state legislature called for a convention. Amid a frenzy of fireworks and drills, the convention unanimously voted for the Ordinance of Secession. By February 1, 1861, six more states in the Lower South—Mississippi, Florida, Alabama, Georgia, Louisiana, and Texas— had voted to secede. Many Southerners felt

secession was in the Revolutionary tradition and that they were fighting for American rights.

✓ Reading Check **Identifying** What main event triggered the secession of Southern states?

Compromise Fails

As the states of the Lower South seceded one after another, Congress tried to find a compromise to save the Union. Ignoring Congress's efforts, the secessionists seized all federal property in their states, including arsenals and forts. Only the island strongholds of Fort Sumter in Charleston Harbor and Fort Pickens in Pensacola Harbor, as well as a few other islands off the coast of Florida, remained out of Southern hands.

Although the confiscation of property horrified Northern members of Congress, they were willing to compromise. To that end, Kentucky senator John J. Crittenden proposed several amendments to the Constitution. One would guarantee slavery where it already existed. Another would also reinstate the

342 CHAPTER 10 Sectional Conflict Intensifies

MEETING SPECIAL NEEDS

Linguistic Ask students to use library and Internet resources to research information about the stated political platforms and principles of the 1854–1876 Republican Party and the Republican Party today. Based on their research, have students write a three- to five-page report comparing the party then and now. **L3**

📁 Refer to *Inclusion for the High School Social Studies Classroom Strategies and Activities* in the TCR.

Missouri Compromise line, extending it to the California border. Slavery would be prohibited north of the line and protected south of it.

Lincoln, however, asked congressional Republicans to stand firm, and **Crittenden's Compromise** did not pass.

A Last Attempt at Peace

Finally, Virginia—a slave state but still in the Union—proposed a peace conference in a last-ditch effort at peace. Delegates from 21 states attended the conference in Washington, D.C. The majority came from Northern and border states. None came from the secessionist states. The delegates met for three weeks but came up with little more than a modified version of Crittenden's Compromise. When presented to Congress, the plan went down to defeat.

Founding the Confederacy

On the same day the peace conference met, delegates from the seceding states met in Montgomery, Alabama. There, on February 8, they declared themselves to be a new nation—the Confederate States of America—or the Confederacy, as it became known.

Their convention drafted a constitution based largely on the U.S. Constitution but with some important changes. It declared that each state was independent and guaranteed the existence of slavery in Confederate territory. It also banned protective tariffs and limited the presidency to a single six-year term.

The convention then chose former Mississippi senator **Jefferson Davis** as president of the Confederacy. In his inaugural address, Davis declared, "The time for compromise has now passed. The South is determined to . . . make all who oppose her smell Southern powder and feel Southern steel."

✓ **Reading Check** **Summarizing** What did Virginia do to try to reverse secession?

The Civil War Begins

In the months before Lincoln took office, he had watched the nation fall apart. Preparing for his inauguration, he faced a splintered Union, a newly declared nation to the south, and the possibility that other states would soon secede.

Lincoln Takes Office In his inaugural speech on March 4, 1861, Lincoln addressed the seceding states directly. He repeated his commitment not to interfere with slavery where it existed but insisted that "the Union of these States is perpetual." Lincoln did not threaten the seceded states, but he said he intented to "hold, occupy, and possess" federal property in those states. Lincoln also encouraged reconciliation:

> ❝In *your* hands, my dissatisfied countrymen, and not in *mine* is the momentous issue of civil war. The government will not assail *you*. You can have no conflict, without yourselves being the aggressors. . . . We are not enemies, but friends. We must not be enemies. Though passion may have strained, it must not break our bonds of affection.❞
>
> —from Lincoln's Inaugural Address, March 4, 1861

TURNING POINT

Fort Sumter Falls In April Lincoln announced that he intended to resupply Fort Sumter. President Jefferson Davis of the Confederacy now faced a dilemma. To tolerate federal troops in the South's most vital harbor seemed unacceptable for a sovereign

"The time for compromise has now passed."
— *Jefferson Davis*

Picturing History

Southern Leader A former soldier, representative, and senator, Jefferson Davis became the first president of the Confederacy. Why did Davis give up on compromise?

Creating a Thematic Map Have students create a map that John J. Crittenden could have used as a visual aid when he presented his compromise to Congress. **L2**

📁 Use the rubric for creating a map, display, or chart on pages 77–78 in the *Performance Assessment Activities and Rubrics.*

✓ **Reading Check**

Answer: proposed a peace conference that was held in Washington, D.C., in February 1861

Picturing **History**

As Jefferson Davis left the U.S. Senate on January 21, 1861, he gave a moving farewell speech that included a plea for peace. He headed home to lead the Mississippi armed forces, but before he could take his post, he was chosen as the provisional president of the Confederacy. He was inaugurated on February 18, 1861.
Answer: He believed the time for compromise had passed.

INTERDISCIPLINARY CONNECTIONS ACTIVITY

Geography Provide students an outline map of the United States with the current state boundaries. Have students create a thematic map by first labeling and shading in one color all the states that were part of Union on June 10, 1861, then labeling and shading in another color all the states that had seceded. Finally have students shade the remaining area and label it "Territories." **L1**

3 ASSESS

Assign Section 4 Assessment as homework or as an in-class activity.

⊙ Have students use the **Interactive Tutor Self-Assessment CD-ROM.**

Reading Essentials and Study Guide 10–4

Section Quiz 10–4

nation, as the South now saw itself. After Lincoln's warning, however, firing on the supply ship would undoubtedly lead to war with the United States.

Davis decided to take Fort Sumter before the supply ship arrived. If he was successful, peace might be preserved. Confederate leaders then delivered a note to Major Robert Anderson demanding Fort Sumter's surrender by the morning of April 12, 1861.

Anderson stood fast. The fateful hour came and went, and cannon fire suddenly shook the air. Confederate forces bombarded Fort Sumter for 33 relentless hours, wrecking the fort but killing no one, until Anderson and his exhausted men finally surrendered. The Civil War had begun.

The Upper South Secedes After the fall of Fort Sumter, President Lincoln called for 75,000 volunteers to serve in the military for 90 days. The call for troops created a crisis in the Upper South. Many people there did not want to secede, but faced with the prospect of civil war, they believed they had no choice but to leave the Union. Virginia acted first,

passing an Ordinance of Secession on April 17, 1861. The Confederate Congress responded by moving the capital of the Confederacy to Richmond, Virginia. By early June of 1861, Arkansas, North Carolina, and Tennessee had also seceded.

GEOGRAPHY

Hanging on to the Border States With the Upper South gone, Lincoln was determined to keep the slaveholding border states from seceding. Delaware seemed safe, but Lincoln worried about Kentucky, Missouri, and Maryland. Virginia's secession had placed a Confederate state across the Potomac River from the nation's capital. If Maryland seceded, Washington would be surrounded by Confederate territory.

To prevent Maryland's secession, Lincoln imposed martial law in Baltimore, where angry mobs had already attacked federal troops. Under martial law, the military takes control of an area and replaces civilian authorities, and it suspends

NATIONAL GEOGRAPHIC

MOMENT in HISTORY

RUSH TO THE COLORS
In the turbulent days following the bombardment of Fort Sumter in April 1861, tens of thousands of young men in the North and South hastened to join their states' volunteer regiments. Most had no idea of the horrors that awaited them. Many saw the war as an escape from the boredom of the family farm or the misery of city tenements. Their only fear was that the fighting might end before they could take part. Here, members of the First Virginia Militia, the "Richmond Grays," pose for the camera before their first taste of battle.

344 CHAPTER 10 Sectional Conflict Intensifies

CRITICAL THINKING ACTIVITY

Analyzing Have students pick five states that seceded and research to identify the specific reasons these states gave for seceding. Have students consider what, if anything, the United States might have done to prevent their secession. **L2**

certain civil rights. Anyone supporting secession could be arrested and held without trial. Union Army officers imprisoned dozens of suspected secessionist leaders.

Lincoln knew that Kentucky was divided over whether to secede and that its control of the Ohio River's south bank was strategically important. When Kentucky declared itself neutral, Lincoln promised to leave the state alone so long as the Confederacy did the same.

Kentucky's neutrality lasted until September 1861, when Confederate forces occupied the southwest corner of the state, prompting Union troops to move in as well. The Confederate invasion angered many in the Kentucky legislature, who now voted to go to war against the Confederacy. This decision led other Kentuckians who supported the Confederacy to create a rival government and secede.

The third border state Lincoln worried about was Missouri. Although many people in the state sympathized strongly with the Confederacy, its convention voted almost unanimously against secession. A struggle then broke out between the convention and pro-secession forces led by Governor Claiborne F. Jackson. In the end, Missouri was held to the Union's cause with the support of federal forces.

From the very beginning of the Civil War, Lincoln had been willing to take political, even constitutional, risks to preserve the Union. The issue of its preservation now shifted to the battlefield.

✓ **Reading Check** **Describing** Why were the border states of Maryland and Kentucky important to the Union?

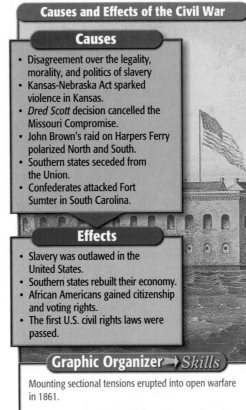

Causes and Effects of the Civil War

Causes

- Disagreement over the legality, morality, and politics of slavery
- Kansas-Nebraska Act sparked violence in Kansas.
- *Dred Scott* decision cancelled the Missouri Compromise.
- John Brown's raid on Harpers Ferry polarized North and South.
- Southern states seceded from the Union.
- Confederates attacked Fort Sumter in South Carolina.

Effects

- Slavery was outlawed in the United States.
- Southern states rebuilt their economy.
- African Americans gained citizenship and voting rights.
- The first U.S. civil rights laws were passed.

Graphic Organizer → Skills

Mounting sectional tensions erupted into open warfare in 1861.

Analyzing What do you think was the most important cause of the Civil War? Why?

✓ **Reading Check**

Answer: If Maryland seceded, Washington, D.C., would be completely surrounded by Confederate territory. Kentucky was important for its control of the southern bank of the Ohio River.

Graphic Organizer → Skills

Answer: Answers will vary, but should be supported.

Graphic Organizer Skills Practice Ask: What type of legislation resulted from the Civil War? *(civil rights laws and legislation abolishing slavery)*

Reteach
Ask students to describe the various attempts to find a compromise between the demands of the North and the South.

Enrich
Have students obtain a copy of the constitution of the Confederate States of America. Have students prepare either a chart or a written summary comparing the Confederate constitution to the U.S. Constitution.

4 CLOSE

Ask students to briefly explain how and why the Civil War began.

SECTION 4 ASSESSMENT

Checking for Understanding
1. **Define:** Confederacy, martial law.
2. **Identify:** John C. Breckinridge, John Bell, Crittenden's Compromise, Jefferson Davis.
3. **List** two provisions of Crittenden's Compromise.

Reviewing Themes
4. **Civic Rights and Responsibilities** How did Lincoln prevent Kentucky, Missouri, and Maryland from seceding? Was Lincoln justified in his actions? Why or why not?

Critical Thinking
5. **Analyzing** Why did Virginia's secession surprise Northerners?
6. **Categorizing** Use a graphic organizer similar to the one below to list the various parties' candidates and political positions in the 1860 election.

Party	Candidate	Position
Northern Democrat		
Southern Democrat		
Constitutional Unionist		
Republican		

Analyzing Visuals
7. **Analyzing Political Cartoons** Study the cartoon on page 342 about the presidential election of 1860. What does the use of a baseball comparison imply about politics?

Writing About History
8. **Persuasive Writing** Imagine you are an adviser to President Lincoln, and you have just heard about the firing on Fort Sumter. Write a brief report for the president, advising him on what steps to take next.

SECTION 4 ASSESSMENT ANSWERS

1. Terms are in blue.
2. John C. Breckinridge *(p. 341)*, John Bell *(p. 341)*, Crittenden's Compromise *(p. 343)*, Jefferson Davis *(p. 343)*
3. a constitutional amendment guaranteeing slavery where it already existed, and another reinstating and extending the Missouri

Compromise line to the California border
4. He declared martial law in Maryland, promised to leave Kentucky alone as long as the Confederacy did the same, and sent federal forces to Missouri. Students' responses should be well-thought out.

5. Students might note that Virginia had worked hard for peace.
6. Candidates' positions should match the text.
7. Both elections and baseball have winners and losers. Both might be considered a "national sport."
8. Reports should include recommendations for action.

CHAPTER 10 ASSESSMENT and ACTIVITIES

GLENCOE
TECHNOLOGY

MindJogger Videoquiz

Use the **MindJogger Videoquiz** to review Chapter 10 content.

Available in VHS

Reviewing Key Terms

Students' answers will vary. The pages where the words appear in the text are shown in parentheses.

1. **popular sovereignty** *(p. 321)*
2. **secession** *(p. 323)*
3. **Underground Railroad** *(p. 327)*
4. **transcontinental railroad** *(p. 328)*
5. **referendum** *(p. 335)*
6. **insurrection** *(p. 337)*
7. **Confederacy** *(p. 343)*
8. **martial law** *(p. 344)*

Reviewing Key Facts

9. Wilmot Proviso *(p. 321)*, Fugitive Slave Act *(p. 327)*, Harriet Tubman *(p. 328)*, Kansas-Nebraska Act *(p. 330)*, Charles Sumner *(p. 331)*, Dred Scott *(p. 334)*, John C. Breckinridge *(p. 341)*, John Bell *(p. 341)*

10. California admitted to the Union as a free state, popular sovereignty to determine the slavery issue in the Utah and New Mexico territories, Texas border dispute resolved with Mexico, slave trade but not slavery abolished in the District of Columbia, federal enforcement of the new Fugitive Slave Act, Congress not allowed to interfere with interstate slave trade

11. When California was about to enter the Union as a free state, the slave-holding states feared becoming the minority in the Senate.

12. They thought it was unjust and they were distressed by the provision that required ordinary citizens to help capture enslaved persons who had run away.

Reviewing Key Terms

On a sheet of paper, use each of these terms in a sentence.

1. popular sovereignty
2. secession
3. Underground Railroad
4. transcontinental railroad
5. referendum
6. insurrection
7. Confederacy
8. martial law

Chapter Summary

Key Events of the 1850s:

- California entered Union as a free state, giving free states a Senate majority
- Fugitive Slave Act passed to help Southerners recover enslaved people who escaped to North; act caused outrage in North
- *Uncle Tom's Cabin* published, angered many Southerners
- Kansas-Nebraska Act passed

Kansas-Nebraska Act heightened tensions:

- Angered Northerners by repealing Missouri Compromise
- Popular sovereignty regarding slavery issue led to violence in "Bleeding Kansas"
- Republican Party formed by former Whigs and members of Free-Soil Party
- *Dred Scott* decision by Southern-dominated Supreme Court angered Northerners
- Debates in Senate over Kansas led to caning of Charles Sumner
- Events in Kansas angered John Brown, who then raided Harpers Ferry

Election of 1860:

- Democratic Party split between North and South
- Republicans nominated eventual winner Abraham Lincoln
- Southern states established Confederacy in February 1861
- Fort Sumter fired upon in April 1861, starting the Civil War

346 CHAPTER 10 Sectional Conflict Intensifies

Reviewing Key Facts

9. **Identify:** Wilmot Proviso, Fugitive Slave Act, Harriet Tubman, Kansas-Nebraska Act, Charles Sumner, Dred Scott, John C. Breckinridge, John Bell.
10. What were the main elements of the Compromise of 1850?
11. Why did Southern politicians begin talking about secession?
12. Why did Northerners resist the Fugitive Slave Act?
13. How did the Republican Party try to gain Southern voters in the presidential election of 1860?
14. Why is John Brown's Harpers Ferry raid considered a turning point on the road to war?
15. What efforts were made to prevent the outbreak of war?
16. What border states did Lincoln try to keep in the Union?

Critical Thinking

17. **Analyzing Themes: Civic Rights and Responsibilities** How did the Fugitive Slave Act and the *Dred Scott* decision affect formerly enslaved African Americans living in the North?
18. **Evaluating** Why did many members of Congress support popular sovereignty?
19. **Forming an Opinion** John Brown's goal in seizing the arsenal at Harpers Ferry was to begin a rebellion against slaveholders. Do you think John Brown should have been executed for this action? Why or why not?
20. **Organizing** Use a graphic organizer similar to the one below to list the main events that pushed the nation into civil war.

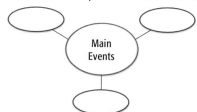

Main Events

21. **Interpreting Primary Sources** Many people have written essays on the causes of the Civil War. Edward A. Pollard of Virginia was the editor of the *Daily Richmond Examiner* during the Civil War. He wrote a book, *The Lost Cause,* about the Civil War from a Southern point of view. In the book, Pollard includes his view of the causes of the Civil War. Read the excerpt and answer the questions that follow.

❝In the ante-revolutionary period, the differences between the populations of the Northern and Southern colonies had already been strongly developed. The

13. Republicans denounced John Brown's raid and reaffirmed the rights of Southern states to preserve slavery within their borders.

14. Southerners were frightened and angry that Northerners would deliberately arm enslaved persons and encourage them to rebel.

15. Crittenden Compromise and a peace conference

16. Kentucky, Maryland, and Missouri

Critical Thinking

17. Because of the *Dred Scott* case, African Americans could not sue in the courts because they were not citizens. The prohibition of slavery established by the Missouri Compromise was declared unconstitutional. Under the Fugitive Slave Act, accused runaways were to be returned to slavery with little or no evidence and no opportunity to testify on their own behalf.

HISTORY Online

Self-Check Quiz

Visit the *American Vision* Web site at <u>tav.glencoe.com</u> and click on *Self-Check Quizzes—Chapter 10* to assess your knowledge of chapter content.

early colonists did not bear with them from the mother-country to the shores of the New World any greater degree of congeniality than existed among them at home. They had come not only from different stocks of population, but from different feuds in religion and politics. There could be no congeniality between . . . New England, and the . . . South. . . . **99**

—from *The Lost Cause*

a. According to Pollard, when did the differences between the North and South begin?

b. What did he believe caused the differences between the people of the North and the South?

Practicing Skills

22. Predicting Consequences Review the skill on predicting consequences on page 325. Then read the following statements and predict three consequences for each. Rank the three consequences in order of the one most likely to occur to the one least likely to occur.

a. A person elected to a political office does not support the issues he or she claimed to represent while campaigning.

b. Engineers develop an effective, efficient automobile powered by solar energy.

Writing Activity

23. American History Primary Source Document Library CD-ROM Read the decision in *Dred Scott* v. *Sandford* by Roger B. Taney, under *Civil War and Reconstruction*. Work with your classmates to outline the major points. Then prepare a counter-decision, addressing each major point and explaining why it could or should be overturned.

Chapter Activity

24. Technology Activity: Developing a Multimedia Presentation Use the Internet and other sources to find a map showing Underground Railroad routes, photos of conductors and fugitive slaves, and primary source documents from conductors and fugitive slaves, such as diaries or journals. Create a multimedia report about the Underground Railroad. Deliver your presentation to the class.

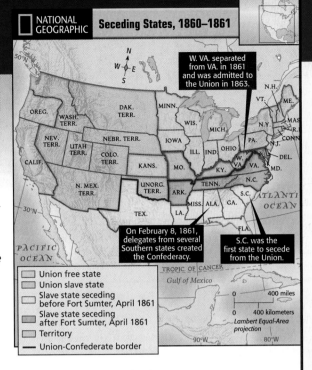

NATIONAL GEOGRAPHIC Seceding States, 1860–1861

W. VA. separated from VA. in 1861 and was admitted to the Union in 1863.

On February 8, 1861, delegates from several Southern states created the Confederacy.

S.C. was the first state to secede from the Union.

Union free state
Union slave state
Slave state seceding before Fort Sumter, April 1861
Slave state seceding after Fort Sumter, April 1861
Territory
Union-Confederate border

PACIFIC OCEAN
TROPIC OF CANCER
Gulf of Mexico

0   400 miles
0   400 kilometers
Lambert Equal-Area projection

Geography and History

25. The map above shows states that seceded from 1860 to 1861. Study the map and answer the questions below.

a. Interpreting Maps Which slave states remained in the Union after the Fort Sumter attack?

b. Applying Geography Skills Which states did not secede until after the Fort Sumter attack?

The Princeton Review

Standardized Test Practice

Directions: Choose the best answer to the following questions.

Several events in the 1850s caused anger in both North and South, making war more likely. Which of the following was not a cause of increasing tension?

A The Fugitive Slave Act

B The publication of *Uncle Tom's Cabin*

C John Brown's Harpers Ferry raid

D Crittenden's Compromise

Test-Taking Tip: Be careful—overlooking the words *not* or *except* on a question is a common error. Also, answer D refers to a compromise, which does not suggest a cause of anger.

HISTORY Online

Have students visit the Web site at <u>tav.glencoe.com</u> to review Chapter 10 and take the Self-Check Quiz.

Chapter Activity

24. Students' reports should include a variety of media, have a clear focus, and be well researched.

Geography and History

25. a. Delaware, Kentucky, Maryland, and Missouri; **b.** Virginia, Arkansas, North Carolina, and Tennessee

The Princeton Review

Standardized Test Practice

Answer: D

Test-Taking Tip: Tell students that when the question stem contains a negative, they should try to reword the sentence or phrase to make it positive. For example, which of the following was a cause of tension?

Bonus Question ?

Ask: What was the significance of choosing the name "Republican" for the new political party formed in 1854 by Northern Whigs and members of the Free-Soil Party and antislavery Democrats? *(It echoed Jefferson's original party. Jefferson had chosen the name to prevent the United States from becoming a monarchy. The new Republicans feared the Southern planter elite were becoming an aristocracy that controlled the federal government.)*

---

18. Northerners thought that people from the North would settle the territories and that they would vote to prohibit slavery. Southerners did not want an outright ban on slavery in the territories.

19. Students' answers should express a clear point of view.

20. Kansas-Nebraska Act, *Dred Scott* decision, John Brown's raid on Harpers Ferry

21. a. before settlers even arrived in the colonies; **b.** religious and political backgrounds

Practicing Skills

22. a. possible answers: 1. not re-elected; 2. people don't really object to changed point of view; 3. people support changed point of view **b.** possible answers: 1. market for cars explodes; 2. the price of gasoline goes down; 3. pollution declines

Writing Activity

23. Student's position papers should reflect each position and should include attempts to find a compromise position.

Chapter 11 Resources

Timesaving Tools

TeacherWorks™ All-In-One Planner and Resource Center

- **Interactive Teacher Edition** Access your Teacher Wraparound Edition and your classroom resources with a few easy clicks.
- **Interactive Lesson Planner** Planning has never been easier! Organize your week, month, semester, or year with all the lesson helps you need to make teaching creative, timely, and relevant.

Use Glencoe's **Presentation Plus!** multimedia teacher tool to easily present dynamic lessons that visually excite your students. Using Microsoft PowerPoint® you can customize the presentations to create your own personalized lessons.

TEACHING TRANSPARENCIES

Graphic Organizer 11

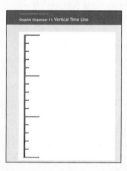

Why It Matters Chapter Transparency 11

APPLICATION AND ENRICHMENT

Linking Past and Present Activity 11

Enrichment Activity 11

Primary Source Reading 11

REVIEW AND REINFORCEMENT

Reteaching Activity 11

Vocabulary Activity 11

Time Line Activity 11

Critical Thinking Skills Activity 11

Meeting NCSS Standards

Local Standards

The following standards are highlighted in Chapter 11:

Section 1 V Individuals, Groups, and Institutions: B, C, F
Section 2 III People, Places, and Environments: A, B, E
Section 3 V Individuals, Groups, and Institutions: B, D, E, F
Section 4 III People, Places, and Environments: A, B, C, D, E
Section 5 IV Individual Development and Identity: B, C, E, F

Chapter 11 Resources

Chapter 11 Test Form A

Chapter 11 Test Form B

Standardized Test Skills Practice Workbook Activity 11

Performance Assessment Activities and Rubrics 11

ExamView® Pro Testmaker CD-ROM

MULTIMEDIA

- Vocabulary PuzzleMaker CD-ROM
- Interactive Tutor Self-Assessment CD-ROM
- ExamView® Pro Testmaker CD-ROM
- Audio Program
- American History Primary Source Documents Library CD-ROM
- MindJogger Videoquiz
- Presentation Plus! CD-ROM
- TeacherWorks™ CD-ROM
- Interactive Student Edition CD-ROM
- Glencoe Skillbuilder Interactive Workbook CD-ROM, Level 2
- The *American Vision* Video Program
- American Music: Hits Through History
- American Music: Cultural Traditions

SPANISH RESOURCES

The following Spanish language materials are available in the Spanish Resources Binder:

- Spanish Guided Reading Activities
- Spanish Reteaching Activities
- Spanish Quizzes and Tests
- Spanish Vocabulary Activities
- Spanish Summaries
- The Declaration of Independence and United States Constitution Spanish Translation

---

THE HISTORY CHANNEL®

The following videotape programs are available from Glencoe as supplements to Chapter 11:

- **American Civil War** (ISBN 0-76-700102-8)
- **Images of the Civil War** (ISBN 1-56-501171-6)

To order, call Glencoe at 1-800-334-7344. To find classroom resources to accompany many of these videos, check the following home pages:
A&E Television: www.aande.com
The History Channel: www.historychannel.com

HISTORY

Online

Use our Web site for additional resources. All essential content is covered in the Student Edition.

You and your students can visit tav.glencoe.com, the Web site companion to the *American Vision.* This innovative integration of electronic and print media offers your students a wealth of opportunities. The student text directs students to the Web site for the following options:

- **Chapter Overviews**
- **Self-Check Quizzes**
- **Student Web Activities**
- **Textbook Updates**

Answers to the student Web activities are provided for you in the **Web Activity Lesson Plans.** Additional Web resources and Interactive Tutor Puzzles are also available.

Chapter 11 Resources

SECTION RESOURCES

Daily Objectives	Reproducible Resources	Multimedia Resources
SECTION 1 **The Opposing Sides** 1. Assess the strengths and weaknesses of each region's economy. 2. Contrast the political situations of the Union and the Confederacy.	Reproducible Lesson Plan 11–1 Daily Lecture and Discussion Notes 11–1 Guided Reading Activity 11–1* Section Quiz 11–1* Reading Essentials and Study Guide 11–1 Performance Assessment Activities and Rubrics	Daily Focus Skills Transparency 11–1 Interactive Tutor Self-Assessment CD-ROM ExamView® Pro Testmaker CD-ROM Presentation Plus! CD-ROM TeacherWorks™ CD-ROM Audio Program
SECTION 2 **The Early Stages** 1. Describe the progress of war in the West. 2. Compare the eastern campaigns to those in the West.	Reproducible Lesson Plan 11–2 Daily Lecture and Discussion Notes 11–2 Guided Reading Activity 11–2* Section Quiz 11–2* Reading Essentials and Study Guide 11–2 Performance Assessment Activities and Rubrics	Daily Focus Skills Transparency 11–2 Interactive Tutor Self-Assessment CD-ROM ExamView® Pro Testmaker CD-ROM Presentation Plus! CD-ROM TeacherWorks™ CD-ROM Audio Program
SECTION 3 **Life During the War** 1. Contrast the effects of the war on regional economies. 2. Evaluate the soldiers' wartime experiences.	Reproducible Lesson Plan 11–3 Daily Lecture and Discussion Notes 11–3 Guided Reading Activity 11–3* Section Quiz 11–3* Reading Essentials and Study Guide 11–3 Performance Assessment Activities and Rubrics	Daily Focus Skills Transparency 11–3 Interactive Tutor Self-Assessment CD-ROM ExamView® Pro Testmaker CD-ROM Presentation Plus! CD-ROM TeacherWorks™ CD-ROM Audio Program
SECTION 4 **The Turning Point** 1. Evaluate the importance of events at Vicksburg and Gettysburg. 2. Describe how battles in Tennessee helped turn the war increasingly in favor of the Union.	Reproducible Lesson Plan 11–4 Daily Lecture and Discussion Notes 11–4 Guided Reading Activity 11–4* Section Quiz 11–4* Reading Essentials and Study Guide 11–4 Performance Assessment Activities and Rubrics	Daily Focus Skills Transparency 11–4 Interactive Tutor Self-Assessment CD-ROM ExamView® Pro Testmaker CD-ROM Presentation Plus! CD-ROM TeacherWorks™ CD-ROM Audio Program American Music: Cultural Traditions ABCNews Interactive™ Historic America Electronic Field Trips
SECTION 5 **The War Ends** 1. Explain the importance of Union victories in Virginia and the Deep South. 2. Discuss Lee's surrender and the events of the war's aftermath.	Reproducible Lesson Plan 11–5 Daily Lecture and Discussion Notes 11–5 Guided Reading Activity 11–5* Section Quiz 11–5* Reading Essentials and Study Guide 11–5 Performance Assessment Activities and Rubrics	Daily Focus Skills Transparency 11–5 Interactive Tutor Self-Assessment CD-ROM ExamView® Pro Testmaker CD-ROM Skillbuilder Interactive Workbook, Level 2 TeacherWorks™ CD-ROM Vocabulary PuzzleMaker CD-ROM Audio Program

0:00 OUT OF TIME?
Assign the Chapter 11 **Reading Essentials and Study Guide.**

*Also Available in Spanish

 Blackline Master   Transparency CD-ROM DVD

 Poster Music Program Audio Program Videocassette

Chapter 11 Resources

NATIONAL GEOGRAPHIC Teacher's Corner

INDEX TO NATIONAL GEOGRAPHIC MAGAZINE

The following articles relate to this chapter.

- "Colonial Florida Fort Recalls a Shining Moment in Black History," February 1997
- "The Cruelest Commerce: African Slave Trade," September 1992
- "C.S.S. *Alabama*," December 1994

NATIONAL GEOGRAPHIC SOCIETY PRODUCTS AVAILABLE FROM GLENCOE

To order the following products for use with this chapter, contact your local Glencoe sales representative, or call Glencoe at 1-800-334-7344:

- *PicturePack: The Civil War* (Transparencies)
- *PictureShow: The Civil War* (CD-ROM)

ADDITIONAL NATIONAL GEOGRAPHIC SOCIETY PRODUCTS

To order the following, call National Geographic at 1-800-368-2728:

- *The Blue and the Gray* (Book)
- *Millennium in Maps Series: Battlefields of the Civil War*

NGS ONLINE

Access National Geographic's Web site for current events, atlas updates, activities, links, interactive features, and archives.

www.nationalgeographic.com

From the Classroom of...

Mike Cobb
The Oakridge School
Arlington, TX

Civil War Letters

Tell students to imagine that they are living during the Civil War. They must write three letters: one from the start of the war, one at a turning point in the war, and one letter at the end of the war. The first letter should be written to parents; the second written to a sibling, spouse, or child; and the third letter written to a close friend who is loyal to the opposition.

To provide a sense of realism, tell the students that their letters must include:

- a location, the date, and their role in the war
- a description of living conditions
- a description of their tasks and experiences
- their thoughts and feelings about the war

Remind students that superior letters should include accurate facts and an attention to detail.

ADDITIONAL RESOURCES FROM GLENCOE

- American Music: Cultural Traditions
- American Art & Architecture
- Outline Map Resource Book
- U.S. Desk Map
- Building Geography Skills for Life
- Inclusion for the High School Social Studies Classroom Strategies and Activities
- Teaching Strategies for the American History Classroom (Including Block Scheduling Pacing Guides)

KEY TO ABILITY LEVELS

Teaching strategies have been coded.

- **L1** BASIC activities for all students
- **L2** AVERAGE activities for average to above-average students
- **L3** CHALLENGING activities for above-average students
- **ELL** ENGLISH LANGUAGE LEARNER activities

Block Schedule

Activities that are suited to use within the block scheduling framework are identified by:

Performance Assessment

Refer to Activity 11 in the Performance Assessment Activities and Rubrics booklet.

Why It Matters Activity

Have volunteers read the Thirteenth Amendment aloud. Ask students what impact they think this amendment has had on people in the United States. Students should evaluate their answers after they have completed the chapter.

GLENCOE
TECHNOLOGY

The *American Vision* Video Program

To learn more about the Civil War, have students view the Chapter 11 video, "Lincoln and the Civil War," from the *American Vision* Video Program.

 Available in DVD and VHS

MindJogger Videoquiz

Use the **MindJogger Videoquiz** to preview Chapter 11 content.

Available in VHS

CHAPTER

11 The Civil War
1861–1865

Why It Matters

The Civil War was a milestone in American history. The four-year-long struggle determined the nation's future. With the North's victory, slavery was abolished. During the war, the Northern economy grew stronger, while the Southern economy stagnated. Military innovations, including the expanded use of railroads and the telegraph, coupled with a general conscription, made the Civil War the first "modern" war.

The Impact Today

The outcome of this bloody war permanently changed the nation.
• The Thirteenth Amendment abolished slavery.
• The power of the federal government was strengthened.

The American Vision Video The Chapter 11 video, "Lincoln and the Civil War," describes the hardships and struggles that Abraham Lincoln experienced as he led the nation in this time of crisis.

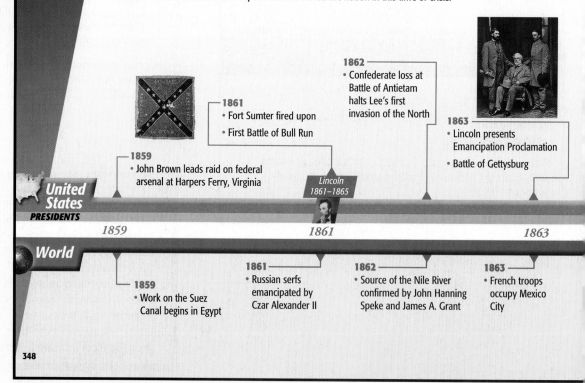

1862
• Confederate loss at Battle of Antietam halts Lee's first invasion of the North

1861
• Fort Sumter fired upon
• First Battle of Bull Run

1863
• Lincoln presents Emancipation Proclamation
• Battle of Gettysburg

1859
• John Brown leads raid on federal arsenal at Harpers Ferry, Virginia

United States
PRESIDENTS

Lincoln 1861–1865

1859   *1861*   *1863*

World

1859
• Work on the Suez Canal begins in Egypt

1861
• Russian serfs emancipated by Czar Alexander II

1862
• Source of the Nile River confirmed by John Hanning Speke and James A. Grant

1863
• French troops occupy Mexico City

348

TWO-MINUTE LESSON LAUNCHER

Present the following announcement to students:

> Wanted: Soldiers to fight for the Union! Skilled soldiers needed for the 9th Regiment of Boston. Volunteer! Sign Up Today.

Ask students whether they would enlist and have them give reasons for their decisions.

Charge by Don Troiani, 1990, depicts the advance of the Eighth Pennsylvania Cavalry during the Battle of Chancellorsville.

HISTORY Online

Introduce students to chapter content and key terms by having them access the **Chapter 11 Overview** at tav.glencoe.com.

More About the Art

Don Troiani is an artist and historian who was born in 1949 in New York City. He is well known for his realistic portrayals of Civil War and Revolutionary War scenes based on extensive research. To help him achieve his goal of presenting historical accuracy through art, Troiani maintains an extensive collection of military artifacts dating from 1754 to 1865. **Ask: How do you think the artist's research is reflected in the painting *Charge* shown on this page?** *(Students' answers will vary. Answers might focus on the detail shown in the soldiers' uniforms, weapons, and equipment.)* **What kinds of resources do you think the artist might have used in his research?** *(historical documents, letters, newspapers, and artifacts from the time period)*

TIME LINE ACTIVITY

Have students create a time line for events in the United States from 1859 through 1867 using the chapter time line and the section time lines. Instruct students to include months for all events.

1865
- Lee surrenders to Grant at Appomattox Courthouse
- Abraham Lincoln assassinated by John Wilkes Booth

1864
- Fall of Atlanta
- Sherman marches to the sea

A. Johnson 1865–1869

1865   *1867*

1864
- Karl Marx founds First International Workingmen's Association to promote socialism

1866
- Gregor Mendel publishes theory on genetic heredity

1867
- Swedish chemist Alfred Nobel invents dynamite

$100,000 REWARD!
War Department, Washington, April 20, 1865.
THE MURDERER
of our late beloved President, Abraham Lincoln,
IS STILL AT LARGE.
$50,000 REWARD
$25,000 REWARD
$25,000 REWARD

HISTORY Online

Chapter Overview
Visit the *American Vision* Web site at tav.glencoe.com and click on *Chapter Overviews—Chapter 11* to preview chapter information.

349

GRAPHIC ORGANIZER ACTIVITY

Organizing Information Have students use a graphic organizer similar to the one shown below to illustrate the sequence and results of the Civil War battles mentioned in this chapter. Students' organizers should be more extensive than what is shown here.

Date	Battle Name	Outcome
1861	Fort Sumter	War begins
	First Battle of Bull Run	Confederate victory
1862	Battle of Antietam	Union victory

1 FOCUS

Section Overview

This section outlines the specific advantages and disadvantages that the North and South had at the beginning of the Civil War.

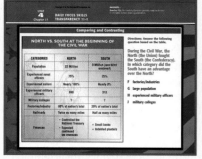
Guide to Reading

Answers to Graphic:
I. Choosing Sides
II. Advantages and Disadvantages
   A. Industry and Agriculture
   B. Financing the War
III. Party Politics in the North
IV. Weak Southern Government
V. The Diplomatic Challenge
Students should complete the outline by including all heads in the section.

Preteaching Vocabulary
Assign one of the Key Terms and Names to each student. Have the students prepare 30-second oral presentations related to their terms and names.

350

Guide to Reading

Main Idea
The North and the South each had distinct advantages and disadvantages at the beginning of the Civil War.

Key Terms and Names
Robert E. Lee, greenback, Copperheads, conscription, habeas corpus, James Mason, John Slidell, *Trent* Affair, attrition, Anaconda Plan

Reading Strategy
Taking Notes As you read about the North and South's advantages and disadvantages at the start of the Civil War, use the major headings of the section to create an outline similar to the one below.

I. Choosing Sides
II.
  A.
  B.
III.
IV.

Reading Objectives
- **Assess** the strengths and weaknesses of each region's economy.
- **Contrast** the political situations of the Union and the Confederacy.

Section Theme
Groups and Institutions The Confederacy's weak central government had difficulty coordinating the war effort.

Preview of Events

♦April 1861	♦October 1861	♦April 1862

April 1861
Robert E. Lee resigns from the U.S. Army

November 1861
Trent Affair

February 1862
Congress passes Legal Tender Act

April 1862
Confederate Congress passes conscription law

Theodore Upson

★ An American Story ★

While husking corn on his family's Indiana farm in April 1861, 16-year-old Theodore Upson heard a neighbor tell his father Jonathan that "the Rebels have fired upon and taken Fort Sumter."

"Father said little," Upson remembered. However, when the family sat down for dinner later, the boy saw that his father "looked ten years older."

Upson later recalled, "We sat down to the table. Grandma wanted to know what was the trouble. Father told her and she began to cry. 'Oh, my poor children in the South. Now they will suffer!'"

Upson's father offered to let their Southern relatives come and stay at the farm. "No, they will not do that," the grandmother replied. "There is their home. There they will stay. Oh, to think that I should have lived to see the day when Brother should rise against Brother."

—adapted from *With Sherman to the Sea*

Choosing Sides

On the same day that he learned his home state of Virginia had voted to secede from the Union, **Robert E. Lee**—one of the best senior officers in the United States Army—received an offer from General Winfield Scott to command the Union's troops. Although Lee had spoken against secession and considered slavery "a moral and political evil," he wrote, "I cannot raise my hand against my birthplace, my home, my children." Instead, he resigned from the army and offered his services to the Confederacy.

Lee was only one of hundreds of military officers who had to choose whether to support the Union or the Confederacy. Eventually 313 officers, or about one-third of the

---

SECTION RESOURCES

📁 **Reproducible Masters**
- Reproducible Lesson Plan 11–1
- Daily Lecture and Discussion Notes 11–1
- Guided Reading Activity 11–1
- Section Quiz 11–1
- Reading Essentials and Study Guide 11–1
- Performance Assessment Activities and Rubrics

🖥 **Transparencies**
- Daily Focus Skills Transparency 11–1

Multimedia
- 💿 Interactive Tutor Self-Assessment CD-ROM
- 💿 ExamView® Pro Testmaker CD-ROM
- 💿 Presentation Plus! CD-ROM
- 💿 TeacherWorks™ CD-ROM
- 🎧 Audio Program

total, resigned to join the Confederacy. These officers enabled the South to organize an effective fighting force quickly, as did the strong military tradition in the South. In 1860 the United States had eight military colleges, but seven of them were in the South. These colleges provided the South with a large number of trained officers to lead its armies.

Just as the South had a strong military tradition, the North had a strong naval tradition. More than three-quarters of the United States Navy's officers came from the North. At the same time, the crews of American merchant ships were almost entirely from the North. They provided a large pool of trained sailors for the Union navy as it expanded. Perhaps even more important, most of the navy's warships and all but one of the country's shipyards remained under Union control as well.

✓ **Reading Check** **Explaining** What advantage did the Southern army have as the war began?

Advantages and Disadvantages

Although the South had many experienced officers to lead its troops in battle, the North had several economic advantages. In 1860 the population of the North was about 22 million, while the South had about 9 million people. The North's larger population gave it a great advantage in raising an army and in supporting the war effort. Because of the smaller population in the South, about one-third of whom were enslaved, a larger percentage of its men had to fight if Southern armies were to match the Union armies in size. As a result, the South had fewer people working to support the war effort.

ECONOMICS

Industry and Agriculture The North's industries gave the region an important economic advantage over the South. In 1860 roughly 80 percent of the nation's factories were in the North. These Northern factories produced more than 90 percent of the country's clothing, boots, and shoes, and 93 percent of its pig iron (unrefined iron), essential for manufacturing weapons and equipment. Almost all of the country's firearms were manufactured in the North, and the Du Pont factories in Delaware made most of the nation's gunpowder. In contrast, the South had only one factory capable of producing cannons, the **Tredegar Iron Works** in Richmond, Virginia, and no major facilities for making gunpowder.

To remedy these deficiencies, the Confederacy's Ordnance Bureau set up armories and foundries in several Southern states, and it created a huge gunpowder mill in Augusta, Georgia. By the summer of

Picturing **History**

Brother Against Brother The Civil War divided the nation, but it also divided families. Even the First Lady, Mary Todd Lincoln, a Kentuckian, had half-brothers who fought for the Confederacy. As the nation divided, why was the Confederacy able to organize an effective army so quickly?

CHAPTER 11   The Civil War   **351**

---

2 *TEACH*

Daily Lecture and Discussion Notes 11–1

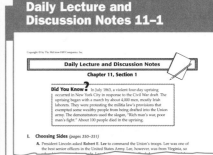

Copyright © by The McGraw-Hill Companies, Inc.

Daily Lecture and Discussion Notes
Chapter 11, Section 1

Did You Know ❓ In July 1863, a violent four-day uprising occurred in New York City in response to the Civil War draft. The uprising began with a march by about 4,000 men, mostly Irish laborers. They were protesting the militia law's provisions that exempted some wealthy people from being drafted into the Union army. The demonstrators used the slogan, "Rich man's war, poor man's fight." About 100 people died in the uprising.

I. Choosing Sides (pages 350–351)

A. President Lincoln asked **Robert E. Lee** to command the Union's troops. Lee was one of the best senior officers in the United States Army. Lee, however, was from Virginia, so

Creating a Circle Graph Have students create a circle graph showing the populations of the North and South as percentages of the U.S. population in 1860. **L1** ELL

🗂 Use the rubric for creating a map, display, or chart on pages 77–78 in the *Performance Assessment Activities and Rubrics.*

✓ **Reading Check**

Answer: strong military tradition, many trained officers who remained loyal to the South

Picturing **History**

Answer: Seven out of the nation's eight military colleges were located in the South; a third of the U.S. Army officers were from the South.
Ask: What armed force was traditionally strong in the North? How many of its members were from that region? *(The navy; three-fourths of the naval officers and almost all of the crews were from the North.)*

COOPERATIVE LEARNING ACTIVITY

Summarizing Information Organize the class into groups of four or five students. Have each group hold a roundtable discussion comparing the strengths and weaknesses of the North and of the South and explaining how their strategies were related to these strengths and weaknesses. Students should summarize their conclusions. A recorder for the group should write the summaries and another group member should present them to the class. 📦

Use the rubric for a cooperative group management plan on pages 81–82 in the *Performance Assessment Activities and Rubrics.*

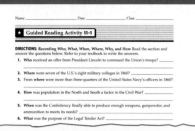

Name _____ Date _____ Class _____

★ **Guided Reading Activity 11-1**

DIRECTIONS: Recording Who, What, When, Where, Why, and How Read the section and answer the questions below. Refer to your textbook to write the answers.

1. Who received an offer from President Lincoln to command the Union's troops? _____

2. Where were seven of the U.S.'s eight military colleges in 1860? _____

3. From where were more than three-quarters of the United States Navy's officers in 1860? _____

4. How was population in the North and South a factor in the Civil War? _____

5. When was the Confederacy finally able to produce enough weapons, gunpowder, and ammunition to meets its needs? _____

6. What was the purpose of the Legal Tender Act? _____

FYI

The Bureau of Engraving and Printing was established in 1862 with six employees—two men and four women. Their main task was to separate the United States Notes, which had been printed by private companies, and affix an official seal to each note.

 Reading Check

Answer: advantage in raising an army and supporting the war effort

CURRICULUM CONNECTION

Civics Life in the northwestern counties of Virginia was very different from life in the lowland areas. Small farms, not plantations worked by enslaved persons, dominated the landscape. The northwestern Virginians did not see why they should leave the Union to protect the rights of slaveholders. In August 1861 the northwestern counties broke away to apply for statehood as West Virginia.

Linking Past & Present

While the federal income tax is the greatest source of federal government funding, state governments have the right to impose additional income taxes on citizens. Some states, such as Alaska, Florida, Nevada, South Dakota, Texas, Washington, and Wyoming, do not impose a personal income tax.

1862, the South was producing enough weapons, gunpowder, and ammunition to meet its needs.

The South also was capable of producing its own food. Although much of the South's fertile land was used for the production of cash crops such as cotton and tobacco, Southern farmers also grew rice and great quantities of corn. The problem facing the South was not its ability to produce food, but its ability to distribute it once the war began and Union troops invaded Southern soil.

The South had only half as many miles of railroad track as the North and had only one line—from Memphis to Chattanooga—connecting the western states of the Confederacy to the east. This made it much easier for Northern troops to disrupt the Southern rail system and prevent the movement of food and troops.

Financing the War Both the North and the South had to act quickly to raise money for the war. The North enjoyed several financial advantages. In addition to controlling the national treasury, the

Linking Past & Present

The Income Tax

Past: Funding the War
On July 1, 1862, a new tax law gave the United States its first federal income tax. A temporary way of funding the war debt, the tax was repealed in 1872. Another income tax passed in 1894 was challenged in court, and the Supreme Court ruled that the idea of an income tax was unconstitutional. The Sixteenth Amendment (1913) again made the income tax legal.

1860 $5 greenback

Present: The IRS Today
Today the income tax is the biggest source of federal government funding. The Internal Revenue Service (IRS) administers the tax, receiving and processing about 200 million returns every year.

Union could expect continued revenue from tariffs. Many Northern banks also held large reserves of cash, which they loaned the government by purchasing bonds.

Concern about the North's ability to win the war caused many people to withdraw gold and silver from the banks. Without gold and silver, the banks could not buy government bonds, and without the gold and silver from the sale of bonds, the government could not pay its suppliers and troops. To solve this problem, Congress passed the **Legal Tender Act** in February 1862. This act created a national currency and allowed the government to issue paper money. The paper money came to be known as **greenbacks**, because of its color.

In contrast to the Union, the Confederacy's financial situation was not good, and it became worse over time. Most Southern planters were in debt and unable to buy bonds. At the same time, Southern banks were small and had few cash reserves. They too could not buy many bonds.

The best hope for the South to raise money was by taxing trade. Shortly after the war began, however, the Union Navy blockaded Southern ports, which reduced trade and revenues. The Confederacy then resorted to direct taxation of its own people. It imposed new taxes on property and farm products, but many Southerners resented the taxes and refused to pay.

Lacking sufficient money from taxes or bonds, the Confederacy was also forced to print paper money to pay its bills. This caused rapid inflation in the South. Confederate paper money became almost worthless. By the end of the war, the South had experienced 9,000 percent inflation, compared to only 80 percent in the North.

 **Reading Check** **Examining** How was having a larger population than the South an advantage for the North?

Party Politics in the North

As the Civil War began, President Lincoln had to contend with divisions within his own party. Many members of the Republican Party were abolitionists. Lincoln's goal, however, was to preserve the Union, even if it meant allowing slavery to continue.

The president also had to contend with Democrats who challenged his policies. Northern Democrats were themselves sharply divided. One faction, called **War Democrats,** strongly supported the conflict and hoped to restore the Union to the way it was before the war. This group also opposed ending slavery.

MEETING SPECIAL NEEDS

Reading Disability Students with reading problems sometimes have difficulty locating information necessary to answer questions. Point out that some questions can be answered simply by reading the text, while other questions require the reader to synthesize information. Help students differentiate between these two question types by providing examples of them from Section 1. **L1**

📁 Refer to *Inclusion for the High School Social Studies Classroom Strategies and Activities* in the TCR.

Another faction of Northern Democrats were known as the Peace Democrats. This group opposed the war and called for reuniting the states through negotiation rather than force. Their support of this unlikely possibility angered Republicans, who saw any opposition to the war as treason. Republicans referred to Peace Democrats as **Copperheads,** after the venomous snake.

One major disagreement between Republicans and Democrats concerned civil liberties. In the summer of 1862, Congress introduced a militia law that required states to use conscription—or forcing people into military service—if this was necessary to fill their regiments. Many Democrats opposed the law, and riots erupted in several strongly Democratic districts in Indiana, Ohio, Pennsylvania, and Wisconsin.

To enforce the militia law, Lincoln suspended writs of habeas corpus. Habeas corpus refers to a person's right not to be imprisoned unless charged with a crime and given a trial. A writ of habeas corpus is a court order that requires the government to either charge an imprisoned person with a crime or let the person go free. When writs of habeas corpus are suspended, a person can be imprisoned indefinitely without trial. In this case, President Lincoln suspended the writ for anyone who openly supported the rebels or encouraged others to resist the militia draft.

Criticized for his suspension of writs of habeas corpus, Lincoln justified his actions: "Must I shoot a simple-minded soldier boy who deserts," the president asked, "while I must not touch a hair of a wily agitator who induces him to desert?"

✓**Reading Check** **Summarizing** How were Northern Democrats divided over the Civil War?

Weak Southern Government

Although the South had no organized opposition party, President Jefferson Davis still faced many political problems. The Confederate constitution emphasized states' rights and limited the central government's power. This commitment to states' rights often interfered with Davis's ability to conduct the war.

Analyzing *Political Cartoons*

Political Disagreements Northern Democrats who favored peace were mockingly called "Copperheads," after the poisonous snake, by their political opponents. How did President Lincoln deal with political criticism during the Civil War?

Although many Southern leaders supported the war, some opposed Jefferson Davis when he supported conscription and established martial law in the spring of 1862. Leaders from North Carolina and Georgia, including Davis's vice president, **Alexander Stephens,** were among those who dissented. They objected to the Confederacy forcing people to join the army and opposed Davis's decision to suspend writs of habeas corpus. The new taxes the Confederacy had imposed were another complaint.

✓**Reading Check** **Summarizing** What problems did Jefferson Davis face in governing the Confederacy?

The Diplomatic Challenge

The outbreak of the Civil War put the major governments of Europe in a difficult situation. The United States did not want the Europeans interfering in the war. In particular, it did not want the Europeans to recognize the Confederate States of America as an independent country. It also wanted the Europeans to respect the Union navy's blockade of the South.

Confederate leaders wanted the exact opposite. They wanted the Europeans, particularly the British, to recognize the South, declare the Union blockade illegal, and then use the British navy to assist the South in

CHAPTER 11 The Civil War **353**

INTERDISCIPLINARY CONNECTIONS ACTIVITY

Physics Invite a physics teacher to explain the science behind the effectiveness of the conoidal bullet. Ask the speaker to use and define scientific terminology, and to demonstrate the applicable laws of physics. **L2**

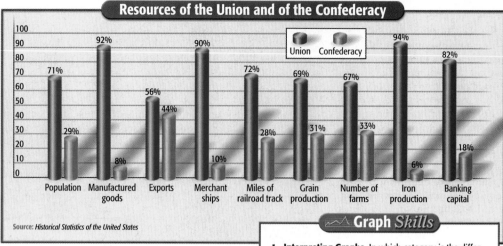

Resources of the Union and of the Confederacy

Union — Confederacy

Category	Union	Confederacy
Population	71%	29%
Manufactured goods	92%	8%
Exports	56%	44%
Merchant ships	90%	10%
Miles of railroad track	72%	28%
Grain production	69%	31%
Number of farms	67%	33%
Iron production	94%	6%
Banking capital	82%	18%

Source: *Historical Statistics of the United States*

📈 Graph *Skills*

1. **Interpreting Graphs** In which category is the difference between the resources of Union and the Confederacy the greatest?
2. **Making Inferences** What additional factors are not considered when comparing population percentages between the Union and the Confederacy?

its struggle with the North. Southern leaders knew that European textile factories, particularly in Britain and France, depended on Southern cotton. To pressure the British and French, many Southern planters voluntarily agreed not to sell their cotton in these markets until the Europeans recognized the Confederacy.

The British and French met informally with Confederate representatives in May 1861. The French promised to recognize the Confederacy if the British would do so as well. British leaders, however, did not want to risk war with the United States unless absolutely necessary. They also were not willing to recognize the Confederacy until decisive victories on the battlefield proved the South could survive and eventually win the war.

At one point, Britain and the United States did come close to war. In the autumn of 1861, the Confederacy decided to send permanent ministers to Britain and France to represent its interests. **James Mason** of Virginia was to go to Britain, and **John Slidell** of Louisiana was to go to France. Mason and Slidell slipped past the Union blockade on a Southern ship and traveled to Havana, Cuba, where they boarded the *Trent*, a British ship. When the ship left Havana, Charles Wilkes, captain of the Union warship *San Jacinto*, intercepted the *Trent* and arrested the two men.

Northerners applauded Wilkes's action. The British, however, were furious over the interference with their ship. They sent an ultimatum to the United States, demanding the release of the two Confederates. Britain sent troops to Canada to strengthen the Atlantic fleet, and war seemed imminent. After a few tense weeks, Lincoln freed Mason and Slidell, commenting, "One war at a time."

After being freed, the diplomats continued on their journey to seek Confederate allies. Although the arrest of Mason and Slidell in the so-called *Trent* Affair had excited interest worldwide, their diplomatic mission failed to gain the support the South wanted.

✓ Reading Check
Explaining Why did the Confederate States want Britain and France to recognize them?

The First "Modern" War

The economic and political situation in the North and South was very important to the outcome of the war because, in many respects, the Civil War was the first "modern" war. Unlike most of the wars fought in Europe during the previous two centuries, the Civil War was not fought by small disciplined armies with limited goals. It involved huge armies made up mostly of civilian volunteers that required vast amounts of supplies and equipment.

Military Technology and Tactics Many of the top officers who led the Union and Confederate troops had studied the campaigns of Napoleon and had themselves fought in the war with Mexico in the 1840s. They believed that the best way to win a battle was to organize the troops into tight columns and go on the offensive. Troops would march toward the enemy, firing in massed volleys. When they got close enough, they would charge the enemy and attack with **bayonets**—long knives attached to the front of their guns. These tactics were necessary earlier in the century because soldiers used smoothbore muskets loaded with round metal balls. These muskets were very inaccurate except at close range.

By the 1850s, French and American inventors had developed a new inexpensive conoidal—or cone-shaped—bullet for rifles. Rifles firing conoidal bullets were accurate at much greater ranges. This meant that troops would be fired upon several more times while charging enemy lines.

At the same time, instead of standing in a line, troops defending positions in the Civil War began to use trenches and barricades to protect themselves. The combination of rifles and trenches created a deadly situation where the attacking force often suffered very high casualties.

High casualties meant that armies had to keep replacing their soldiers. Attrition—the wearing down of one side by the other through exhaustion of soldiers and resources—played a critical role as the war dragged on. The North, with its large population, could draw on new troops for replacements, but the South had fewer men to replace soldiers who died or were wounded in battle.

Conoidal bullets

The South's Strategy Early in the war, Jefferson Davis imagined a struggle similar to the American war for independence against Britain. Like George Washington, his generals would pick their battles carefully, attacking and retreating when necessary and avoiding large battles that might risk heavy losses. In this manner, the South would wage a

What If...

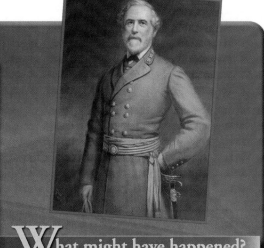

Lee Had Not Followed Virginia in Secession?

General Robert E. Lee was one of the most famous Confederate officers. The troops and the Southern population trusted his leadership and military judgment. Lee's tactical skill allowed his army to achieve many battlefield successes against difficult odds. What if, however, Lee had remained loyal to the U.S. Army at the start of the war?

U.S. General Winfield Scott met with Lee on the day after Virginia voted to break ties with the United States. Scott offered Lee the opportunity to lead the Union army into the South, hoping that a strong display of force would forestall actual warfare. The *Alexandria Gazette* also speculated about what Lee would do:

❝It is probable that the secession of Virginia will cause an immediate resignation of many officers of the Army and Navy from this State. . . . [If Lee] should resign his present position in the Army of the United States, we call the immediate attention of our State to him. . . . There is no man who would command more of the confidence of the people of Virginia, than this distinguished officer; and no one under whom the volunteers and militia would more gladly rally.❞

—from *Almost America*

What might have happened?

1. What might have happened if Lee had chosen to remain in the United States Army? If war had begun, would Lee's military skills have helped the Union defeat the Confederacy more quickly?

2. Do you believe an early show of force would have convinced the rebelling states to negotiate peace? Why or why not?

EXTENDING THE CONTENT

Military Colleges Four of the major military colleges that trained officers for the Civil War continue the tradition of military education today. Located in New York, the U.S. Military Academy, also known as West Point, was established in 1802. The Virginia Military Institute was founded in Lexington, Virginia, in 1839. Established in 1845 on ten acres in Annapolis, Maryland, the Naval School became the U.S. Naval Academy in 1850. The South Carolina Military Academy was established in 1842. Students attended The Arsenal in Columbia and The Citadel in Charleston. The Arsenal was destroyed by Sherman's troops and The Citadel suspended classes in February 1865 when Union troops entered Charleston. The college was reopened in 1882 and in 1910 the name was officially changed to The Citadel, The Military College of South Carolina.

Chart *Skills*

Answer:

1. The blockade isolated the Confederacy from European aid and trade, and cut off the flow of supplies, equipment, money, food, and cotton.

2. It would cause the least amount of bloodshed.

Chart Skills Practice

Ask: Which parts of the Anaconda Plan related to the Mississippi River? *(control the Mississippi with Union gunboats, divide the eastern part of the Confederacy from the western part, and capture New Orleans, Vicksburg, and Memphis)*

✓ Reading Check

Answer: a defensive war of attrition

Reteach

Ask students to assess the strengths and weaknesses of each region's economy.

Enrich

Invite students to prepare a two-minute oral presentation on one of the persons mentioned in this section. Have students use library and Internet resources to learn more about the person they select.

4 CLOSE

Have students contrast the political situations of the Union and the Confederacy.

The Anaconda Plan

- Blockade Southern ports on the Atlantic
- Isolate the Confederacy from European aid and trade
- Cut off flow of supplies, equipment, money, food and cotton
- Exhaust Southern resources, forcing surrender
- Control the Mississippi with Union gunboats
- Divide the eastern part of the Confederacy from the western part
- Capture New Orleans, Vicksburg, and Memphis
- Cut off shipping to and from interior

Chart *Skills*

1. **Interpreting Charts** How would a naval blockade accomplish several elements of the Anaconda Plan at once?
2. **Analyzing** Why was General Winfield Scott in favor of this plan?

defensive war of attrition, Davis believed, forcing the Union to spend its resources until it became tired of the war and agreed to negotiate.

The idea of a defensive war of attrition, however, outraged many Southerners. Believing themselves superior fighters, they scorned the idea of defensive warfare. "The idea of waiting for blows, instead of inflicting them, is altogether unsuited to the genius of our people," declared the *Richmond Examiner* in 1861.

The Southern disdain for remaining on the defensive meant that when battles occurred, Southern troops often went on the offensive, charging enemy lines and suffering enormous casualties. In 1862 and 1863, Confederate armies fought nine large battles. In six of those battles they went on the offensive, and they suffered 20,000 more casualties than the Union. These were losses the South could not afford.

The Union's Anaconda Plan Early in the war, the general in chief of the United States, **Winfield Scott,** proposed a strategy for defeating the South. Scott suggested that the Union blockade Confederate ports and send gunboats down the Mississippi to divide the Confederacy. The South, thus separated, would gradually run out of resources and surrender. The plan would take time, Scott admitted, but it would defeat the South with the least amount of bloodshed.

Many Northerners rejected the plan as too slow and indirect for certain victory, favoring instead a strong, quick invasion of the South. Northern newspapers scorned this strategy, which they called the **Anaconda Plan,** after the snake that slowly strangles its prey to death. Although Lincoln eventually agreed to implement Scott's suggestions and imposed a blockade of Southern ports, he hoped that a quick victory by Northern troops over the Southern forces massing in Virginia might discredit the secessionists and bring about a negotiated end to the crisis. Ultimately, he and other Union leaders realized that only a long war that focused on destroying the South's armies had any chance of success.

✓ Reading Check **Describing** What war strategy did Jefferson Davis develop for the South?

SECTION 1 ASSESSMENT

Checking for Understanding

1. **Define:** greenback, conscription, habeas corpus, attrition.
2. **Identify:** Robert E. Lee, Copperheads, James Mason, John Slidell, *Trent* Affair, Anaconda Plan.
3. **Explain** why the South had difficulty getting supplies from foreign nations.

Reviewing Themes

4. **Groups and Institutions** How did a belief in states' rights hamper the South during the war?

Critical Thinking

5. **Comparing** Why did the North have an economic advantage over the South?
6. **Analyzing** Why did the South resort to using paper money during the war?
7. **Organizing** Using a graphic organizer similar to the one below, list the military innovations of the Civil War era.

Military Innovations

Analyzing Visuals

8. **Examining Artifacts** Examine the conoidal bullets shown on page 355. How did conoidal bullets affect the war effort? What other innovations made the Civil War the first "modern" war?

Writing About History

9. **Descriptive Writing** Imagine that you are living in one of the border states at the beginning of the Civil War. Write a letter to a relative explaining why you are planning on joining either the Union or Confederate army.

SECTION 1 ASSESSMENT ANSWERS

1. Terms are in blue.
2. Robert E. Lee *(p. 350)*, Copperheads *(p. 353)*, James Mason *(p. 354)*, John Slidell *(p. 354)*, *Trent* Affair *(p. 354)*, Anaconda Plan *(p. 356)*
3. Foreign countries did not want to risk war with the United States.
4. The South lacked a strong central

government needed to coordinate the war effort.

5. The Union controlled the U.S. Treasury, still collected revenues from tariffs, and many northern banks had large cash reserves that they could lend to the government.
6. They needed financial resources.
7. huge armies, civilian volunteers,

conoidal bullets, trenches

8. conoidal bullets and quick-loading rifles, new defensive strategies such as trenches and barricades
9. Students' letters will vary. Letters should offer plausible scenarios about the decision to join one side or the other.

Guide to Reading

Main Idea
Union forces suffered defeat in Virginia, advanced down the Mississippi, and stopped the South's invasion of Maryland.

Key Terms and Names
"Stonewall" Jackson, Irwin McDowell, bounty, blockade runner, David G. Farragut, Ulysses S. Grant, George B. McClellan, Emancipation Proclamation

Reading Strategy
Categorizing As you read about the early battles of the war, complete a chart like the one below by filling in the results of each battle listed.

Battle	Results
First Battle of Bull Run	
Battle of Shiloh	
Battle of Murfreesboro	
Seven Days' Battle	
Second Battle of Bull Run	

Reading Objectives
• **Describe** the progress of war in the West.
• **Compare** the eastern campaigns to those in the West.

Section Theme
Geography and History The Union hoped to seize the Mississippi Valley and cut the Confederacy in two.

Preview of Events

◆1861	◆1862	◆1863
1861 Confederates defeat Union forces at First Battle of Bull Run	**1862** 20,000 casualties at the Battle of Shiloh **1862** 23,000 casualties at the Battle of Antietam	**1863** The Emancipation Proclamation takes effect

★ An American Story ★

On July 21, 1861—a hot, sultry Sunday perfect for family outings—hundreds of people from Washington, D.C., picnicked along Bull Run near Manassas Junction, Virginia. They had gathered to watch the first battle between the Union and Confederate forces.

"The spectators were all excited," wrote one reporter, "and a lady with an opera glass who was near me was quite beside herself when an unusually heavy discharge roused the current of her blood: 'That is splendid! Oh, my! Is not that first-rate?'"

The spectators who came to Bull Run expected a short, exciting fight and a quick surrender by the rebel troops. Unexpectedly, the Confederates routed the Union army. A reporter with the Boston *Journal*, Charles Coffin, described the chaos:

❝Men fall. . . . They are bleeding, torn, and mangled. . . . The trees are splintered, crushed, and broken, as if smitten by thunderbolts. . . . There is smoke, dust, wild talking, shouting; hissings, howlings, explosions. It is a new, strange, unanticipated experience to the soldiers of both armies, far different from what they thought it would be.❞

—quoted in *Voices of the Civil War*

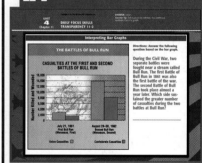

Civil War cannons near Bull Run in Manassas National Battlefield Park

Mobilizing the Troops

In the first months of the Civil War, President Lincoln was under great pressure to strike quickly against the South. Confederate troops, led by General **P.G.T. Beauregard**, were gathering 25 miles (40 km) south of Washington, D.C., near Manassas Junction, an important railroad center in northern Virginia. Lincoln approved an assault on these forces, hoping that a Union victory would lead to a quick end to the conflict.

CHAPTER 11 The Civil War **357**

 SECTION RESOURCES

Reproducible Masters
• Reproducible Lesson Plan 11–2
• Daily Lecture and Discussion Notes 11–2
• Guided Reading Activity 11–2
• Section Quiz 11–2
• Reading Essentials and Study Guide 11–2
• Performance Assessment Activities and Rubrics

Transparencies
• Daily Focus Skills Transparency 11–2

Multimedia
• Interactive Tutor Self-Assessment CD-ROM
• ExamView® Pro Testmaker CD-ROM
• Presentation Plus! CD-ROM
• TeacherWorks™ CD-ROM
• Audio Program

---

1 FOCUS

Section Overview
This section focuses on Union forces suffering defeat in Virginia, advancing down the Mississippi, and stopping the South's invasion of Maryland.

BELLRINGER
Skillbuilder Activity

🔲 Project transparency and have students answer the question.

🗂 Available as a blackline master.

Daily Focus Skills Transparency 11–2

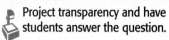

Guide to Reading

Answers to Graphic:
First Battle of Bull Run: Confederate victory; Battle of Shiloh: Union victory, both sides suffered high casualties; Battle of Murfreesboro: no decisive victory, Union retreated; Seven Days' Battle: no decisive victory, heavy casualty rate, Union forced to retreat; Second Battle of Bull Run: Confederate victory, invasion of Maryland

Preteaching Vocabulary
For each of the Key Terms and Names, have students write a phrase or short sentence that will help them remember its significance.

357

2 TEACH

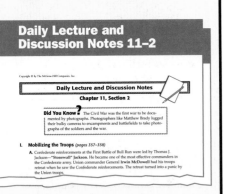

Geography *Skills*

Answers:

1. General Beauregard

2. 24 miles

Geography Skills Practice
Ask: From what point did McDowell's troops depart for the Battle of Bull Run? *(Washington, D.C.)*

✓ Reading Check

Answer: It became clear that the North would need a large, well-trained army to defeat the South.

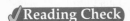

| Fact | Fiction | Folklore |

As part of the American Battlefield Protection Program, the National Park Service maintains a Web page with links to information on over 300 Civil War battles. Information about alternative names for battles is included. The address for the site is http://www2.cr.nps.gov/abpp/battles/bystate.htm.

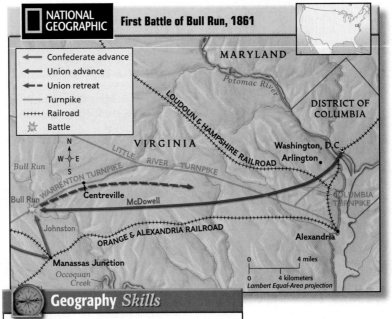

NATIONAL GEOGRAPHIC   First Battle of Bull Run, 1861

Confederate advance
Union advance
Union retreat
Turnpike
Railroad
Battle

Geography *Skills*

1. **Interpreting Maps** Who led the Confederate forces at the First Battle of Bull Run?
2. **Applying Geography Skills** How many miles from Washington, D.C., was the battlefield?

At first, the attack went well for the Union. Its forces slowly pushed the Confederates back from their positions behind a stream called Bull Run. During the fighting, Southern reinforcements from Virginia, led by Thomas J. Jackson moved into the line. As Confederate troops retreated past Jackson, their commander yelled: "There is Jackson standing like a stone wall! Rally behind the Virginians!" Afterward, Jackson became known as **"Stonewall" Jackson,** and he went on to become one of the most effective commanders in the Confederate army.

As Confederate reinforcements arrived, Union commander General **Irwin McDowell** decided to fall back. The retreat quickly turned into a panic, although the exhausted Confederate troops did not pursue the Union forces very far.

The Union defeat at the First Battle of Bull Run made it clear that the North would need a large, well-trained army to defeat the South. Lincoln had originally called for 75,000 men to serve for three months. The day after Bull Run, he signed another bill for the enlistment of 500,000 men for three years.

At first, excitement about the war inspired many Northern and Southern men to enlist, swamping recruitment offices and training camps. As the war dragged on and casualties rose, however, fewer

358 CHAPTER 11 The Civil War

young men volunteered, forcing both governments to resort to conscription. The South introduced conscription in April 1862 for all white men between the ages of 18 and 35. Exemptions were provided for key government workers, for teachers, and for planters who held at least 20 enslaved African Americans.

The North at first tried to encourage voluntary enlistment by offering a bounty—a sum of money given as a bonus—to individuals who promised three years of military service. Congress also passed the **Militia Act** in July 1862, giving Lincoln the authority to call state militias, which included drafted troops, into federal service. Finally, in 1863, Congress introduced a national draft to raise the necessary troops.

✓ **Reading Check** **Summarizing** What was the significance of the First Battle of Bull Run?

The Naval War

While the Union and Confederacy mobilized their armies, the Union navy began operations against the South. In April 1861, President Lincoln proclaimed a blockade of all Confederate ports. By the spring of 1862, the Union navy had sealed off every major Southern harbor along the Atlantic coast, except for Charleston, South Carolina and Wilmington, North Carolina. Lincoln intended to

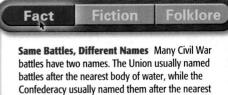

| Fact | Fiction | Folklore |

Same Battles, Different Names Many Civil War battles have two names. The Union usually named battles after the nearest body of water, while the Confederacy usually named them after the nearest settlement. Therefore, the battle known as the Battle of Bull Run (a creek) in the North was known as the Battle of Manassas (a town) in the South. Likewise, the Battle of Antietam was remembered in the South as the Battle of Sharpsburg.

COOPERATIVE LEARNING ACTIVITY

Writing a Letter Organize students into pairs. Tell the pairs that they can select one of the battles listed in the section and that one person will be a Union soldier and the other a Confederate soldier. Explain that they are to write letters to their families immediately after the battle has ended. The letters should describe what they saw, felt, and heard during the battle. Have the pairs read each other's letters and discuss how the outcome of the battle affected their attitudes as they composed their letters.

Use the rubric for a cooperative group management plan on pages 81–82 in the *Performance Assessment Activities and Rubrics.*

put as much pressure on the South's economy as possible by cutting its trade with the world.

The Blockade Although the Union blockade became increasingly effective as the war dragged on, Union vessels were thinly spread and found it difficult to stop all of the blockade runners—small, fast vessels the South used to smuggle goods past the blockade, usually under cover of night. By using blockade runners, the South could ship at least some of its cotton to Europe in exchange for shoes, rifles, and other supplies. The amount of material that made it through the blockade, however, was much less than the amount that had been shipped before the war.

At the same time, Confederate ships operating out of foreign ports attacked Northern merchant ships at sea. Two of the most famous Confederate raiders were the warships *Alabama* and *Florida*, both of which the Confederacy had built in Britain. The *Alabama* captured 64 ships before a Union warship sank it off the coast of France in 1864. The *Florida* destroyed 38 merchant ships before being captured at a harbor in Brazil.

The damage done by these two ships strained relations between the United States and Great Britain. Union officials did not think Great Britain should have allowed the ships to be built, and they demanded Britain pay damages for the losses the Union suffered.

Farragut Captures New Orleans While the Union navy fought to seal off the Confederacy's Atlantic ports, it also began preparations to seize New Orleans and gain control of the lower Mississippi River. In February 1862, **David G. Farragut** took command of a Union force composed of 42 warships and 15,000 soldiers led by General Benjamin Butler.

At the time, Farragut was 60 years old. He had gone to sea at age 9 and was a veteran of the War of 1812 and the war with Mexico. His father had moved to the United States from Spain in 1776 and had fought in the Revolutionary War and served as governor of the Mississippi Territory. Although born in the South, Farragut was a staunch supporter of the Union.

Farragut's actions at the battle for New Orleans made him a hero in the North. In early April, his fleet began bombarding Confederate forts defending the lower Mississippi River. When the attack failed to destroy the forts, Farragut made a daring decision. At 2:00 A.M. on April 24, 1862, his ships headed upriver past the forts in single file, exposing themselves to attack. The forts opened fire with more than 80 guns, while Confederate gunboats tried to ram the fleet and tugboats placed flaming rafts in front of the Union ships. Remarkably, all but four of Farragut's ships survived the battle and continued upriver.

Ironclads Clash at Sea, March 8, 1862

Southerners hoped to break the Union blockade with a secret weapon—an iron-plated ship built by covering the hull of the wooden ship *Merrimack,* a captured Union warship, with iron. The armored vessel, renamed the *Virginia,* could easily withstand Union cannon fire.

On March 8, 1862, the *Virginia* sank two Union ships guarding the James River at Hampton Roads, Virginia. In the worst day of the war for the Union navy, 240 sailors died. The next day, the Union's own ironclad ship, the newly completed *Monitor,* challenged the *Virginia.* The two ships fought for hours, but neither could deliver a decisive blow. Although the vessels never fought again, the *Monitor's* presence kept the *Virginia* from breaking the Northern blockade.

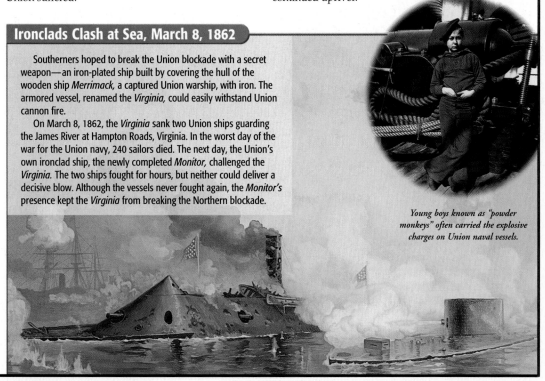

Young boys known as "powder monkeys" often carried the explosive charges on Union naval vessels.

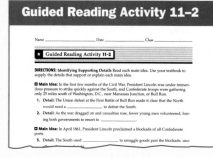

Guided Reading Activity 11–2

Name _____ Date _____ Class _____

★ Guided Reading Activity 11-2

DIRECTIONS: Identifying Supporting Details Read each main idea. Use your textbook to supply the details that support or explain each main idea.

❑ **Main Idea:** In the first few months of the Civil War, President Lincoln was under tremendous pressure to strike quickly against the South, and Confederate troops were gathering only 25 miles south of Washington, D.C., near Manassas Junction, or Bull Run.

1. **Detail:** The Union defeat at the First Battle of Bull Run made it clear that the North would need a _____ to defeat the South.

2. **Detail:** As the war dragged on and casualties rose, fewer young men volunteered, forcing both governments to resort to _____

❑ **Main Idea:** In April 1861, President Lincoln proclaimed a blockade of all Confederate ports.

3. **Detail:** The South used _____ to smuggle goods past the blockade, usually _____

Writing a Profile Have students use library and Internet resources to learn more about one of the persons mentioned in this section. Instruct students to write a profile similar to the one that appears on page 361. **L2**

FYI

Although David Glasgow Farragut was born in Tennessee, raised in Louisiana, and lived in Virginia, he was a Union hero. In 1866 he was awarded the rank of admiral—a first for the United States Navy. Farragut was touted as a possible presidential candidate in 1868, but he expressed no interest in politics. He died in 1870.

Writing a Photo Essay Have students find a photo from the Civil War. Instruct students to write a descriptive essay based on the photo. Tell students that they may use library and Internet resources to learn more about the battle or event in the picture. **L3**

📁 Use the rubric for a photo essay on pages 91–92 in the *Performance Assessment Activities and Rubrics.*

MEETING SPECIAL NEEDS

Visual/Spatial Have students create a multimedia presentation that shows Farragut's capture of New Orleans beginning with the bombardment of the Confederate forts and ending with Butler's capture of the city. Suggest that students combine drawings with captions and recorded descriptions to create an effective and informative presentation. **L2**

📁 Refer to ***Inclusion for the High School Social Studies Classroom Strategies and Activities*** in the TCR.

2 TEACH

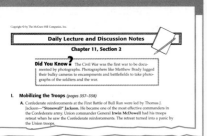
✓ Reading Check

Answer: by using small, fast vessels, known as blockade runners, to slip past the Union ships at night

Geography *Skills*

Answers:
1. Galveston
2. Tennessee

Geography Skills Practice
Which battle occurred in Union states during this period?
(*Perryville*)

CURRICULUM CONNECTION

World History The military strategy courses taught at West Point—where most of the senior officers in both armies received their training—were based on the work of Henri de Jomini. A soldier and a historian, Jomini had served on Napoleon Bonaparte's general staff. By studying Napoleon's campaigns, Jomini developed a number of rules on fighting a war: offense is better than defense, bring the greatest possible force against the weakest point of the enemy's line, and constantly harass the enemy's lines of communication. Jomini's ideas influenced the way both Union and Confederate generals fought in the early stages of the war.

On April 25, 1862, Farragut arrived at New Orleans. Six days later, General Butler's troops took control of the city. The South's largest city, and a center of the cotton trade, was now in Union hands.

✓ **Reading Check** **Explaining** How did the Confederates try to break the Union blockade?

The War in the West

In February 1862, as Farragut prepared for his attack on New Orleans, Union general **Ulysses S. Grant** began a campaign to seize control of two rivers: the Cumberland River, which flowed west past Nashville through Tennessee, and the Tennessee River, which flowed through northern Alabama and western Tennessee. Control of these rivers would cut Tennessee in two and provide the Union with a river route deep into Confederate territory.

Backed by armored gunboats, Grant first seized Fort Henry, the Confederacy's main fort on the Tennessee River. He then marched his troops east and surrounded Fort Donelson on the Cumberland River. With the fall of Fort Donelson and Fort Henry, all of Kentucky and most of western Tennessee came under Union military control.

Shiloh After Grant's victories at Fort Donelson and Fort Henry, his troops headed up the Tennessee River to attack Corinth, Mississippi. Seizing Corinth would cut the Confederacy's only rail line connecting Mississippi and western Tennessee to the east.

Early on April 6, 1862, Confederate forces launched a surprise attack on Grant's troops, who were camped about 20 miles (32 km) north of Corinth near a small church named Shiloh. Hearing the attack, Grant raced from his headquarters to the battle. Although the Union troops were forced back, Grant rushed around the battlefield and managed to assemble a defensive line that held off repeated Southern attacks.

When the first day of the battle ended, several of Grant's commanders advised him to retreat.

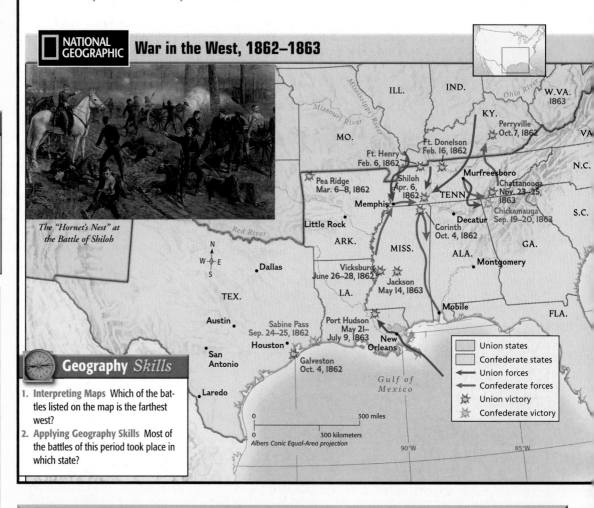

NATIONAL GEOGRAPHIC **War in the West, 1862–1863**

The "Hornet's Nest" at the Battle of Shiloh

ILL. | IND. | Ohio River | W.VA. 1863
MO. | Ft. Donelson Feb. 16, 1862 | KY. | Perryville Oct. 7, 1862 | VA.
Ft. Henry Feb. 6, 1862 | | Murfreesboro | N.C.
Pea Ridge Mar. 6–8, 1862 | Shiloh Apr. 6, 1862 | Chattanooga Nov. 23–25, 1863
Memphis | TENN. | Chickamauga Sep. 19–20, 1863 | S.C.
Little Rock | Decatur | Corinth Oct. 4, 1862
ARK. | MISS. | ALA. | GA.
Dallas | Vicksburg June 26–28, 1862 | Montgomery
Jackson May 14, 1863
TEX. | LA. | Mobile | FLA.
Austin | Sabine Pass Sep. 24–25, 1862 | Port Hudson May 21–July 9, 1863 | New Orleans
San Antonio | Houston | Galveston Oct. 4, 1862 | Gulf of Mexico
Laredo

Union states
Confederate states
← Union forces
← Confederate forces
✸ Union victory
✸ Confederate victory

0   300 miles
0   300 kilometers
Albers Conic Equal-Area projection

90°W | 85°W

Geography *Skills*

1. **Interpreting Maps** Which of the battles listed on the map is the farthest west?
2. **Applying Geography Skills** Most of the battles of this period took place in which state?

INTERDISCIPLINARY CONNECTIONS ACTIVITY

Geography Have the geography teacher help students learn about the role that geography played in Civil War battles. Have students work in groups to build a model of the Battle of Antietam. The model should focus on the landforms in the area and should show the progress of the battle. As a starting point for researching information about the battle, visit the National Park Service's Web site about the battle at http://www.nps.gov/anti/home.htm. **L2**

Knowing reinforcements were on the way, Grant replied: "Retreat? No. I propose to attack at daylight and whip them." Grant went on the offensive the next morning, surprising the Confederates and forcing General Beauregard, their commander, to order a retreat.

The Battle of Shiloh stunned people in both the North and the South. Twenty thousand troops had been killed or wounded, more than in any other battle up to that point. When newspapers demanded Grant be fired because of the high casualties, Lincoln refused, saying, "I can't spare this man; he fights."

Murfreesboro Grant's victory at Shiloh cheered Lincoln, but it was clear that the fighting was not over. Confederate troops evacuated Corinth and quickly shifted east by railroad to Chattanooga, Tennessee, where they were placed under the command of General **Braxton Bragg.**

Bragg took his troops north into Kentucky, hoping the Union armies would follow. He also hoped that his invasion of Kentucky would lead to an uprising of pro-Confederate supporters in the state. Bragg's invasion failed. Union troops led by General **Don Carlos Buell** stopped Bragg's forces at the battle of Perryville.

After Bragg retreated, General Buell was ordered to seize Chattanooga and cut the railroad lines that passed through the city. Lincoln knew that eastern Tennessee was home to many Union sympathizers, and he wanted the region under Union control. He also knew that by cutting the region's rail lines, he would deprive the Confederacy of "hogs and hominy"—vital supplies of meat and corn that the South needed.

Buell's slow advance across Tennessee frustrated Lincoln, who fired him and replaced him with General **William S. Rosecrans.** As Rosecrans's forces headed south, Bragg's forces attacked them west of the Stones River near Murfreesboro. Although the Union lines fell back before the onslaught, they did not break, and the battle ended inconclusively. Four days later, with Union reinforcements arriving from Nashville, Bragg decided to retreat.

✔ **Reading Check** **Evaluating** What was the significance of the Battle of Shiloh?

Profiles IN HISTORY

Federico Cavada
1832–1871

The Civil War introduced many innovations in warfare. One of the most striking was the use of hot-air balloons for intelligence work.

Cuban-born Federico Cavada was one of the Union soldiers sent aloft to sketch enemy positions. Cavada had enlisted in 1861 and served during the Peninsula campaign. It was during this campaign that his "balloon artistry" came in handy.

Cavada was captured at the Battle of Gettysburg and then imprisoned at Libby Prison in Richmond, Virginia. He wrote sketches, with illustrations, of prison life on any scraps of paper he could find. He hid these in his shoes and socks and got fellow prisoners to do the same. Later he wrote up an account and published it as "Libby Life."

After the war, he returned to Cuba as U.S. consul. Cavada was executed by a firing squad in July 1871 while supporting revolutionaries hoping to win Cuban independence.

The War in the East

While Union and Confederate troops were struggling for control of Tennessee and the Mississippi River, another major campaign was being waged in the east to capture Richmond, Virginia. After General McDowell's failure at the First Battle of Bull Run, President Lincoln ordered General **George B. McClellan** to lead the Union army in the east.

McClellan's Peninsula Campaign After taking several months to prepare his forces, McClellan began transporting his troops by ship to the mouth of the James River, southeast of Yorktown, Virginia. From there he intended to march up the peninsula formed by the James and York Rivers toward Richmond, only 70 miles (113 km) away.

Although popular with the troops, McClellan proved overly cautious and unwilling to attack unless he had overwhelming strength. He took 30 days to capture Yorktown, giving the Confederates time to move their troops into position near Richmond.

As McClellan advanced toward Richmond, he made another mistake. He allowed his forces to become divided by the Chickahominy River. Seizing this opportunity, the Confederate commander, General **Joseph E. Johnston,** attacked McClellan's

CHAPTER 11 The Civil War **361**

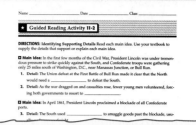

Profiles IN HISTORY

Federico Cavada was not the only person to operate a balloon during the Civil War. Others included Thaddeus Lowe and John LaMountain. In the summer of 1861, Thaddeus Lowe demonstrated aerial telegraphy for President Lincoln and LaMountain completed an aerial reconnaissance mission. The South also employed balloons for aerial observation. John Randolph Bryan drew a map of Union positions from a balloon tethered over Yorktown, Virginia, during the Peninsula Campaign in 1862.

Ask: How did Cavada's sketches help the Union? (*His sketches showed the position of more enemy troops than ground intelligence forces could provide.*)

✔ **Reading Check**

Answer: The Union cut the only railroad lines connecting Mississippi and western Tennessee; both sides suffered high casualties.

CRITICAL THINKING ACTIVITY

Analyzing Tell students that the governor of Massachusetts referred to the Emancipation Proclamation as "a poor *document,* but a mighty *act.*" Explain that his statement reflected the fact that the importance of the Emancipation Proclamation was not in the number of enslaved persons who were immediately freed, but in the fact that slavery was made the central issue of the war. Have the class make a list of the issues that divided the United States before the proclamation. Then discuss how making slavery the main issue of the war helped the Union cause. **L2**

Geography Skills

Answers:
1. Gettysburg and Antietam
2. about 100 miles

Geography Skills Practice
Ask: Which city was close to the site of the longest battle of 1862–1863? *(Richmond)*

3 ASSESS

Assign Section 2 Assessment as homework or as an in-class activity.

🌐 Have students use the **Interactive Tutor Self-Assessment CD-ROM.**

Reading Essentials and Study Guide 11–2

Section Quiz 11–2

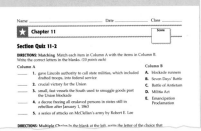

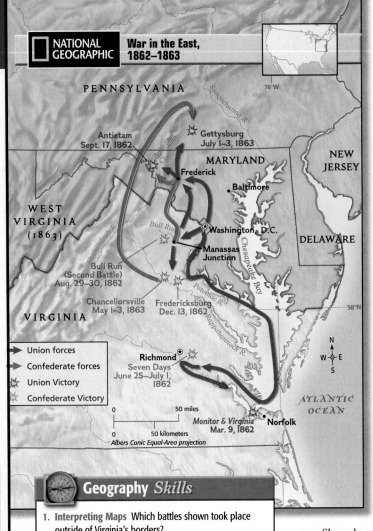

NATIONAL GEOGRAPHIC
War in the East, 1862–1863

Geography Skills

1. **Interpreting Maps** Which battles shown took place outside of Virginia's borders?
2. **Applying Geography Skills** How far apart are the two capital cities of Richmond and Washington, D.C.?

The Second Battle of Bull Run
As McClellan's troops withdrew, Lee decided to attack the Union forces defending Washington. The maneuvers by the two sides led to another battle at Bull Run, near Manassas Junction—the site of the first major battle of the war. Again, the South forced the North to retreat, leaving the Confederate forces only 20 miles (32 km) from Washington. Soon after, word arrived that Lee's forces had crossed into Maryland and begun an invasion of the North.

TURNING POINT
The Battle of Antietam Lee decided to invade Maryland for several reasons. Both he and Jefferson Davis believed that only an invasion would convince the North to accept the South's independence. They also thought that a victory on Northern soil might help the South win recognition from the British and help the Peace Democrats gain control of Congress in the upcoming midterm elections. By heading north, Lee could also feed his troops from Northern farms and draw Union troops out of Virginia during harvest season.

When he learned that McClellan had been sent after him, Lee ordered his troops to congregate near Sharpsburg, Maryland. Meanwhile, McClellan's troops took positions along Antietam (an·TEE·tuhm) Creek, east of Lee. On September 17, 1862, McClellan ordered his troops to attack.

The Battle of Antietam, the bloodiest one-day battle in the war and in American history, ended with over 6,000 men killed and another 16,000 wounded. Although McClellan did not break Lee's lines, he inflicted so many casualties that Lee decided to retreat to Virginia.

The Battle of Antietam was a crucial victory for the Union. The British government had been ready to intervene in the war as a mediator if Lee's invasion had succeeded. It had also begun making plans to recognize the Confederacy in the event the North rejected mediation. Lee's defeat at Antietam changed everything. The British decided once

army, inflicting heavy casualties. After Johnston was wounded in the battle, General Robert E. Lee was placed in command.

In late June of 1862, Lee began a series of attacks on McClellan's army that became known collectively as the **Seven Days' Battle.** Although Lee was unable to decisively defeat the Union army, he inflicted heavy casualties and forced McClellan to retreat to the James River. Together the two sides suffered over 30,000 casualties. Despite McClellan's protests, Lincoln ordered him to withdraw from the peninsula and bring his troops back to Washington.

362 CHAPTER 11 The Civil War

EXTENDING THE CONTENT

Effectiveness of the Union Blockade Estimates of the effectiveness of the Union blockade show that, in general, the blockade was a failure until the end of the war. Historians estimate that between 1861 and 1865 only one of every six blockade runners was captured. As a result, half the Southern cotton crop made it through the Union blockade after 1862.

again to wait and see how the war progressed, and with this decision the South lost its best chance at gaining international recognition and support. The South's defeat at Antietam had an even greater political impact in the United States. It convinced Lincoln that the time had come to end slavery in the South.

 **Reading Check** **Explaining** Why did President Lincoln choose General George B. McClellan after the Union's failure at the First Battle of Bull Run?

The Emancipation Proclamation

Although most Democrats opposed any move to end slavery, Republicans were divided on the issue. Many Republicans were strong abolitionists, but others, like Lincoln, did not want to endanger the loyalty of the slaveholding border states that had chosen to remain in the Union. The war's primary purpose, in their opinion, was to save the Union.

With Northern casualties rising to staggering levels, however, many Northerners began to agree that slavery had to end, in part to punish the South and in part to make the soldiers' sacrifices worthwhile. George Julian, a Republican from Indiana, summed up the argument for freeing the slaves in an important speech delivered early in 1862:

> ❝When I say that this rebellion has its source and life in slavery, I only repeat a simple truism. . . . The mere suppression of the rebellion will be an empty mockery of our sufferings and sacrifices, if slavery

shall be spared to canker the heart of the nation anew, and repeat its diabolical misdeeds.❞

—quoted in *Battle Cry of Freedom*

As Lee's forces marched toward Antietam, Lincoln said that if the Union could drive those forces from Northern soil, he would issue a proclamation ending slavery.

On September 22, 1862, encouraged by the Union victory at Antietam, Lincoln publicly announced that he would issue the **Emancipation Proclamation**—a decree freeing all enslaved persons in states still in rebellion after January 1, 1863. Because the Proclamation freed enslaved African Americans only in states at war with the Union, it did not address slavery in the border states. Short of a constitutional amendment, however, Lincoln could not end slavery in the border states, nor did he want to endanger their loyalty. 📖 *(See page 1071 for the text of the Emancipation Proclamation.)*

The Proclamation, by its very existence, transformed the conflict over preserving the Union into a war of liberation. "We shout for joy that we live to record this righteous decree," exulted Frederick Douglass. Abolitionists rejoiced at the president's announcement, and they looked forward to new energy among Union forces. "We were no longer merely the soldiers of a political controversy," recalled Union officer Regis de Trobiand. "We were now the missionaries of a great work of redemption, the armed liberators of millions."

✓ **Reading Check** **Examining** Why did Lincoln issue the Emancipation Proclamation?

SECTION 2 ASSESSMENT

Checking for Understanding

1. **Define:** bounty, blockade runner.
2. **Identify:** "Stonewall" Jackson, Irwin McDowell, David G. Farragut, Ulysses S. Grant, George B. McClellan, Emancipation Proclamation.
3. **Summarize** why David G. Farragut was considered a hero in the North.

Reviewing Themes

4. **Geography and History** Why was seizing control of the Mississippi River an important strategy of the Union navy?

Critical Thinking

5. **Forming an Opinion** Do you think the draft for military service during the Civil War violated civil liberties, or was the need for defense more important? Explain your answer.
6. **Organizing** Use a graphic organizer to explain President Lincoln's reasons for issuing the Emancipation Proclamation and the effects it had on the war.

| Reasons for | → | Emancipation Proclamation | → | Effect on War |

Analyzing Visuals

7. **Examining Art** Examine the painting of the battle between the *Monitor* and the *Virginia* on page 359. What made these vessels superior to regular warships used by the Union and the Confederacy?

Writing About History

8. **Persuasive Writing** Imagine that you are asked to advise President Lincoln about issuing the Emancipation Proclamation. Write a short paper in which you explain the reasons for the advice you give him.

SECTION 2 ASSESSMENT ANSWERS

1. Terms are in blue.
2. "Stonewall" Jackson (*p. 358*), Irwin McDowell (*p. 358*), David G. Farragut (*p. 359*), Ulysses S. Grant (*p. 360*), George B. McClellan (*p. 361*)
3. He courageously helped capture New Orleans, the South's largest city.

4. It would divide the Confederacy and hurt the cotton trade.
5. Students' answers will vary but should be supported reasonably.
6. Reasons: to help justify the war's sacrifices, to help end slavery; Effects: transformed the war from a conflict over preservation of the Union into a war of liberation

7. Ironclad vessels were resistant to regular cannon fire and less likely to burn.
8. Students' papers will vary. Papers should offer specific advice, including rationale.

✓ **Reading Check**

Answer: McClellan was chosen to replace McDowell because of McDowell's failure at the First Battle of Bull Run.

Reteach

Have students make a list comparing and contrasting the eastern and western campaigns.

Enrich

Invite students to write a short paper about public reaction to the Emancipation Proclamation. Have students use library and Internet resources to locate primary sources such as newspaper articles, journal entries, or letters written in January of 1863. Encourage them to include quotations from these primary sources in their paper.

✓ **Reading Check**

Answer: He began to believe that slavery had to be ended and to help justify the growing war casualties.

4 CLOSE

Ask students to explain the immediate impact of the Emancipation Proclamation in the North and in the South.

SECTION **3** Life During the War

1 FOCUS

Section Overview

This section presents information about military and civilian life during the Civil War.

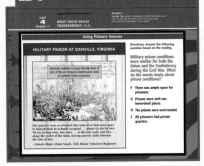
Guide to Reading

Answers to Graphic: industry supplied troops with clothes, munitions, other necessities; innovations in agriculture minimized the effect of the loss of labor as men left to fight; women filled labor shortages; new sewing machines increased productivity

Preteaching Vocabulary
Have students create a database of the Key Terms and Names. Instruct students to add the definition and other helpful information as they find the terms and names while reading this section.

Guide to Reading

Main Idea
The Civil War brought great changes to the lives of soldiers and civilians alike.

Key Terms and Names
54th Massachusetts, hardtack, Elizabeth Blackwell, United States Sanitary Commission, Clara Barton, Henry Wirz

Reading Strategy
Organizing As you read about life during the war, complete a table listing why the North experienced a wartime economic boom.

Reasons for North's Economic Boom

Reading Objectives
• **Contrast** the effects of war on regional economies.
• **Evaluate** the soldiers' wartime experiences.

Section Theme
Groups and Institutions The Civil War brought great suffering to civilians as well as soldiers on both sides of the conflict.

Preview of Events

♦January 1863	♦April 1863	♦July 1863

February 1863
54th Massachusetts regiment begins recruiting African Americans in Boston

March 1863
Congress passes the National Conscription Act

April 1863
Women lead food riots in Richmond, Virginia

July 1863
Battle of Fort Wagner

★ An American Story ★

In late December 1862, as Union and Confederate forces prepared for battle near the Virginia town of Fredericksburg, the civilian residents fled in haste. Confederate artillery operator Robert Stiles remembers seeing women and children evacuating their homes:

❝I never saw a more pitiful procession than they made trudging through the deep snow . . . little children tugging along with their doll babies . . . women so old and feeble that they could carry nothing and could barely hobble themselves. There were women carrying a baby in one arm, and its bottle, its clothes, and its covering in the other. Some had a Bible and a toothbrush in one hand, a picked chicken and a bag of flour in the other.

Most of them had to cross a creek swollen with winter rains, and deadly cold with winter ice and snow. We took the battery horses down and ferried them over, taking one child in front and two behind, and sometimes a woman or a girl on either side with her feet in stirrups, holding on by our shoulders. Where they were going we could not tell, and I doubt if they could.❞

—quoted in *Voices of the Civil War*

Battle-damaged homes in Fredericksburg

The Wartime Economies

Pressed by the costs of the war, both North and South struggled to keep their economies working. The South, with few financial resources and little industry, suffered more from wartime inflation and critical shortages. The North, supported by banks and developing industries, responded quickly to the changes brought about by the war.

Southern Shortages, Falling Morale By the end of 1862, the South's economy had begun to suffer from the war. Although many farms had converted from cotton to food crops, the collapse of the South's transportation system and the presence of Union troops in several important agricultural regions led to severe food shortages during the winter of 1862.

The food shortages hurt Southern morale, and people began to question the sacrifices they were being called upon to make—or to demand of others. Hearing of the hardships, many Confederate soldiers deserted and returned home to help their families.

In the spring of 1863, the food shortages led to riots. In several communities, mobs of women armed with knives and guns marched into shops to seize food. In Richmond, several hundred women broke into shops, yelling, "Bread, bread," and then began to loot the stores for food, clothing, shoes, and other goods. The riot finally ended when Jefferson Davis confronted the mob with a company of militia troops and ordered the rioters to disperse.

The Union's War Boom In contrast, the North experienced an economic boom because of the war. Its growing industries supplied the troops at the front with clothes, munitions, and other necessities, while innovations in agriculture helped minimize the loss of labor as men left to fight.

The expanded use of mechanized reapers and mowers made farming possible with fewer workers, many of whom were women. One traveler in Iowa in late 1862 commented that he "met more women driving teams on the road and saw more at work in the fields than men."

Women also filled labor shortages in various industries, particularly in clothing and shoemaking factories. New sewing machines greatly increased the productivity of seamstresses. As women entered the textile industry, the North produced an abundance of clothes for its soldiers, and the industry profited from government contracts.

✓ **Reading Check** **Explaining** What were the effects of food shortages on the South?

TECHNOLOGY & History

The Telegraph

Invented by Samuel Morse in 1837, the telegraph was indispensable during the Civil War. It was used to send battle orders and to verify the locations of troops. With no telegraph in the White House, President Lincoln often visited the War Department's telegraph room to receive current information. Telegraph operators sent messages by pressing a key in a pattern of short and long clicks, following Morse's alphabetic code. *In what other areas of life was the telegraph useful?*

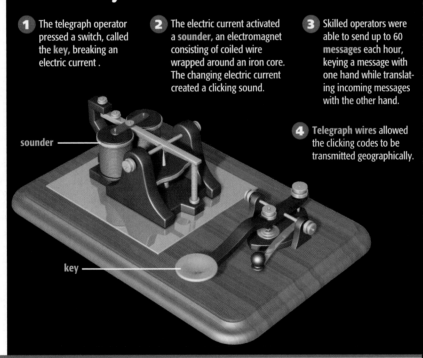

1. The telegraph operator pressed a switch, called the **key**, breaking an electric current.

2. The electric current activated a **sounder**, an electromagnet consisting of coiled wire wrapped around an iron core. The changing electric current created a clicking sound.

3. Skilled operators were able to send up to 60 **messages** each hour, keying a message with one hand while translating incoming messages with the other hand.

4. Telegraph wires allowed the clicking codes to be transmitted geographically.

sounder

key

COOPERATIVE LEARNING ACTIVITY

Comparing Organize students into small groups. Each group will write diary entries for a woman in the North who went to work to replace the labor of the men who had gone to war. Have each group select and research a potential occupation that the woman might have participated in. Then have them write a series of diary entries describing a week in the life of the woman. Remind students that they still performed most or all of the tasks that needed to be done at home, as well as working outside the home. Have groups share their entries with the class.

Use the rubric for a cooperative group management plan on pages 81–82 in the *Performance Assessment Activities and Rubrics.*

2 TEACH

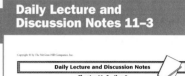

Daily Lecture and Discussion Notes 11–3

Copyright © by The McGraw-Hill Companies, Inc.

Daily Lecture and Discussion Notes

Chapter 11, Section 3

Did You Know? Clara Barton was called the "Angel of the Battlefield." She risked her life by passing through front lines to deliver supplies and to nurse wounded Union soldiers. She helped identify thousands of Union soldiers who had died in the South's Andersonville prison camp. In 1877 Barton founded the American Red Cross, which is still an important relief organization today.

I. The Wartime Economies *(pages 364–366)*

A. As a result of the collapse of the South's transportation system and the presence of Union troops in many agricultural regions, the South suffered severe food shortages by the winter of 1862. The food shortages hurt Southern morale and led to riots.

Analyzing Information Remind students that people in the South faced severe food shortages during the winter of 1862 when they could not depend on harvests for food. Ask students to answer the following questions as though they were among the people who faced these food shortages. What did you do to get food? What would you have offered to trade for food? Do you think you would have participated in a riot to seize food from shops? Why or why not? **L1**

✓ **Reading Check**

Answer: Food shortages hurt morale as people began to question the sacrifices they were being asked to make and caused desertions as soldiers returned home to help their families survive.

TECHNOLOGY & History

Background: The men who operated the telegraph were known as the signal corps. When telegraph lines could not be run, the signal corps also transmitted messages using flags during the day and torches at night. The signal corps had to memorize all the signals and codes and were not permitted to carry anything that would be useful to the enemy in case they were captured.

Answer: to transmit news, to transact business, and to communicate with distant family members

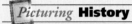

Guided Reading Activity 11-3

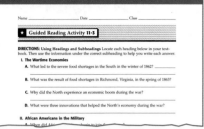

Name _____ Date _____ Class _____

★ **Guided Reading Activity 11-3**

DIRECTIONS: Using Headings and Subheadings Locate each heading below in your textbook. Then use the information under the correct subheading to help you write each answer.

I. The Wartime Economies

A. What led to the severe food shortages in the South in the winter of 1862?

B. What was the result of food shortages in Richmond, Virginia, in the spring of 1863?

C. Why did the North experience an economic boom during the war?

D. What were three innovations that helped the North's economy during the war?

II. African Americans in the Military

A. When did African Americans begin to join the...

Picturing **History**

Answer: He felt it would help them overcome discrimination.

Ask: How many African Americans served in the Union army? *(about 180,000)*

✓ Reading Check

Answer: Students' answers will vary. A possible answer is that African Americans saw volunteering to serve in the military as a way to ensure their freedom from slavery.

Interpreting a Quote Ask students how the quote from Frederick Douglass on this page relates to the *Dred Scott* decision.

you don't say...

Hardtack Army bread, also called *hardtack*, was really a quarter-inch-thick cracker made of unleavened flour. Soldiers said the crackers were so hard they would stop a bullet.

History *and the* Humanities

American Art & Architecture: *A Rainy Day in Camp*

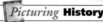

Picturing **History**

African American Soldiers Battery A of the 2nd U.S. Colored Light Artillery was only one of many groups of African Americans who fought for their own freedom. Why did Frederick Douglass favor African American enlistment?

African Americans in the Military

The Emancipation Proclamation officially permitted African Americans to enlist in the Union army and navy. Almost immediately, thousands of African Americans, including Frederick Douglass's two sons, Charles and Lewis, rushed to join the military. Douglass approved of his sons' decision. He believed that serving in the military would help African Americans overcome discrimination:

❝Once let the black man get upon his person the brass letters U.S.; let him get an eagle on his button, and a musket on his shoulder and bullets in his pocket, and there is no power on earth which can deny that he has earned the right to citizenship.❞
—quoted in *Battle Cry of Freedom*

About 180,000 African Americans served in the Union army during the Civil War, roughly 9 percent of the army's total soldiers. Another 10,000 to 15,000 served in the Union navy, making up about 10 to 12 percent of the navy's sailors.

Among the first African American regiments officially organized in the North was the **54th Massachusetts.** The regiment fought valiantly at Fort Wagner near Charleston Harbor in July 1863, losing nearly half of its soldiers in the battle. "Men all around me would fall and roll down the slope into the ditch," remembered Lewis Douglass. "Swept down like chaff, still our men went on and on."

At the end of the war, the *New York Tribune* declared that the heroism of the 54th Massachusetts

366 CHAPTER 11 The Civil War

---

regiment forever answered the question of whether African Americans could make good soldiers:

❝It is not too much to say that if this Massachusetts Fifty-Fourth had faltered when its trial came, two hundred thousand [African Americans] for whom it was a pioneer would never have been put into the field. . . . But it did not falter. It made Fort Wagner such a name to [African Americans] as Bunker Hill has been for ninety years to white Yankees.❞
—from *Like Men of War*

✓ Reading Check **Analyzing** Why do you think African Americans were so willing to volunteer to fight during the Civil War?

Military Life

Early in the war, General Irwin McDowell's troops stopped to pick berries and foolishly wasted water from their canteens to wash them. "They were not used to denying themselves much; they were not used to journeys on foot," the Union commander later reflected. Self-denial and long marches would prove to be only one of the harsh lessons of the war.

The Soldiers in the Field Union and Confederate soldiers suffered many hardships during the long days and weeks between battles. Some Southern soldiers had to sleep without blankets and tramp the roads shoeless. Union soldier Elisha Rhodes wrote home that "all that we have to eat is the cattle killed by the way. No bread or salt in the Regiment and I am most starved."

Soldiers learned to gulp down tasteless food. For the Union soldier, meals often consisted of hardtack (a hard biscuit made of wheat flour), potatoes, and beans, flavored at times with dried salt pork (pork fat cured in salty brine). Confederate soldiers had little coffee, and their bread was usually made of cornmeal. Whenever possible, soldiers on both sides supplemented their diet with fruit or vegetables seized or purchased from farms they passed.

Battlefield Medicine When Americans went to war in 1861, most were not prepared for the horrors of battle. "The sights and smells that assailed us were simply indescribable," wrote one Southern soldier. "Corpses were swollen to twice their size, some actually burst asunder. . . . The odors were so deadly that in a short time we all sickened [and] . . . most of us [were] vomiting profusely."

MEETING SPECIAL NEEDS

Verbal/Linguistic Have students write a poem that reflects experiences from one of the following points of view: an African American serving in the Union army, a nurse serving in an army hospital, a wounded soldier, or a teen-age girl facing a food shortage in the winter of 1862. **L2**

🗁 Refer to **Inclusion for the High School Social Studies Classroom Strategies and Activities** in the TCR.

The Civil War produced huge numbers of casualties, and doctors struggled to tend to the wounded. In the mid-1800s, doctors had little understanding of infectious germs. They used the same unsterilized instruments on patient after patient, and, as a result, infection spread quickly in the field hospitals.

Disease was one of the greatest threats facing Civil War soldiers. In many cases, regiments lost half their men to illness before ever going into battle. Crowded together in army camps, drinking from unsanitary water supplies, many soldiers became sick. Smallpox, when it erupted, could be deadly, as could dysentery, typhoid, and pneumonia.

Battlefield physicians also used extreme measures in treating casualties. Faced with appalling wounds, doctors often amputated arms and legs to prevent gangrene and other infections from spreading to other parts of the body. As one military officer, General Carl Schurz, commented:

66As a wounded man was lifted on the table, often shrieking with pain . . . the surgeon quickly examined the wound and resolved upon cutting off the wounded limb. Some ether was administered. . . . The surgeon snatched the knife from between his teeth, where it had been while his hands were busy, wiped it rapidly once or twice across his blood-stained apron, and the cutting began. The operation accomplished, the surgeon would look around with a deep sigh, and then— 'Next!'99

—quoted in *The Civil War*

The Role of Women in the War Women helped the war effort at home by managing family farms and businesses. On the battlefield, women made dramatic contributions to the Civil War by serving as nurses to the wounded. Before the Civil War, most army nurses were men. Inspired by the famous British nurse **Florence Nightingale,** American women took on many of the nursing tasks in army hospitals.

In 1861 **Elizabeth Blackwell,** the first female physician in the United States, started the nation's first training program for nurses. Her work led to the creation of the **United States Sanitary Commission,** an organization that provided medical assistance and supplies to army camps and hospitals. Tens of thousands of women volunteered to work for the Commission, raising money to send bandages, medicine, clothing, and food to army camps.

Not all women helping at the front lines were members of the Sanitary Commission. On her own, **Clara Barton** decided to leave her job in a patent office to nurse soldiers on the battlefield. With her face sometimes bluish with gunpowder, Barton fed the sick, bandaged the wounded, and even dug out bullets with her own small knife.

Although Southern women were encouraged to stay at home and support the troops by making bandages and other supplies, many founded small hospitals or braved the horrors of the battlefield. Kate Cumming of Mobile, Alabama, served as a nurse following the Battle of Shiloh. In her diary she vividly described a makeshift hospital:

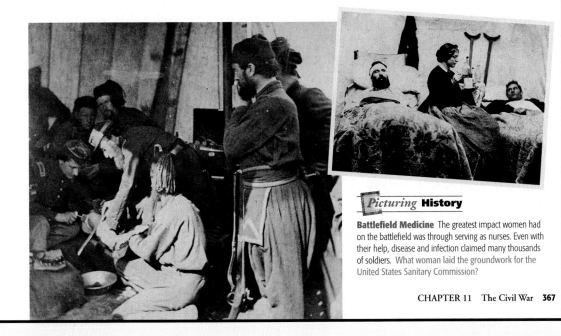

Picturing **History**

Battlefield Medicine The greatest impact women had on the battlefield was through serving as nurses. Even with their help, disease and infection claimed many thousands of soldiers. What woman laid the groundwork for the United States Sanitary Commission?

CHAPTER 11   The Civil War   **367**

3 ASSESS

Assign Section 3 Assessment as homework or as an in-class activity.

⬤ Have students use the **Interactive Tutor Self-Assessment CD-ROM.**

Reading Essentials and Study Guide 11–3

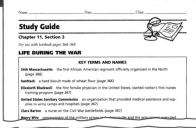

Name _____ Date _____ Class _____

Study Guide
Chapter 11, Section 3
For use with textbook pages 364–368

LIFE DURING THE WAR

KEY TERMS AND NAMES

54th Massachusetts the first African American regiment officially organized in the North (page 366)

hardtack a hard biscuit made of wheat flour (page 366)

Elizabeth Blackwell the first female physician in the United States, started nation's first nurses training program (page 367)

United States Sanitary Commission an organization that provided medical assistance and supplies to army camps and hospitals (page 367)

Clara Barton a nurse on the Civil War battlefields (page 367)

Henry Wirz commandant of the military prison at Andersonville and the only person executed

Drawing Circle Graphs Have students draw a pair of circle graphs showing the percentage of African Americans in the Union army and Union navy. **L2**

🗁 Use the rubric for creating a map, display, or chart on pages 77–78 in the *Performance Assessment Activities and Rubrics.*

Picturing **History**

Answer: Elizabeth Blackwell
Ask: What functions did battlefield nurses perform? *(They fed the sick, bandaged the wounded, gave comfort, and occasionally performed operations.)*

INTERDISCIPLINARY CONNECTIONS ACTIVITY

Health Have a health care professional speak to the class about infection prevention. Have students describe to the professional some of the unsanitary conditions that existed in battlefield hospitals during the Civil War. Then ask the health care professional to describe how modern facilities and techniques would have prevented many of the diseases and infections that occurred. **L1**

FYI

Prior to the Civil War there were only a few medical schools in the United States and they lagged behind European schools. Many doctors served only an apprenticeship and those who attended medical school trained for less than two years with little or no laboratory or clinical experience.

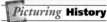
Picturing **History**

Answer: They managed farms and family businesses, supported troops by making bandages and other supplies, founded small hospitals, and nursed the sick and wounded.

Ask: What role do you think the man in the picture plays in this group? *(Students' answers will vary. A possible answer is that as a military man he trained the women to use the guns they are holding.)*

✓ **Reading Check**

Answer: infections, smallpox, dysentery, typhoid, and pneumonia

Reteach

Have students create a sentence outline using the headings in this section as a guide.

Enrich

Have students use the data on this page to create a circle graph showing the percentage of prisoners sent to Andersonville who died.

4 CLOSE

Have students contrast the effects of war on the economies of the North and the South.

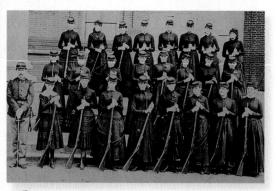

Picturing **History**

Female Volunteers Soldiers were not the only ones who experienced the Civil War. Wives, mothers, and sisters protected their homes from bands of soldiers. *How else did Southern women experience the effects of the war?*

❝Nothing that I had ever heard or read had given me the faintest idea of the horrors witnessed here. . . . The men are lying all over the house. . . . The foul air from this mass of human beings at first made me giddy and sick, but I soon got over it. . . .❞

—quoted in *Battle Cry of Freedom*

The Civil War was a turning point for the nursing profession in the United States. The courage and energy shown by women also helped to break down the belief that women were weaker than men.

Military Prisons The horrors of the battlefield and danger of disease were not the only hardships endured by soldiers during the Civil War. Prisoners of war—soldiers captured by the enemy in battle—also suffered terribly during the conflict.

Early in the war, the United States and the Confederacy held formal prisoner exchanges. After Lincoln issued the Emancipation Proclamation, however, the Confederacy announced that it would not exchange freed African Americans for Southern white prisoners. Instead, it would either re-enslave or execute all African American troops captured in battle.

In response to the South's treatment of African American troops, Lincoln stopped all prisoner exchanges. As a result, both the North and the South found themselves with large and growing numbers of prisoners of war. Taking care of them proved difficult, especially in the South. While conditions in prisons were bad in Northern prisons, the South was not able to adequately feed their prisoners because of food shortages.

The most infamous prison in the South, **Andersonville** in southwest Georgia, was an open camp with no shade or shelter for its huge population. Exposure, overcrowding, lack of food, and disease killed more than 100 men per day during the sweltering summer of 1864. In all, 13,000 of the 45,000 prisoners sent to Andersonville died in the camp. After the war, **Henry Wirz,** the commandant at Andersonville, became the only person executed for war crimes during the Civil War.

Life in the Union and Confederate armed forces during the Civil War was brutally hard. Both sides, however, were strongly committed to their cause and prepared to endure whatever hardships were necessary to achieve victory.

✓ **Reading Check** **Summarizing** What medical problems did Union and Confederate soldiers face?

SECTION 3 ASSESSMENT

Checking for Understanding

1. **Define:** hardtack.
2. **Identify:** 54th Massachusetts, Elizabeth Blackwell, United States Sanitary Commission, Clara Barton, Henry Wirz.
3. **State** the two factors that contributed to a food shortage in the South during the Civil War.

Reviewing Themes

4. **Groups and Institutions** How did the Emancipation Proclamation affect African Americans in the military?

Critical Thinking

5. **Analyzing** In what ways do you think the Civil War changed people's opinions about women's capabilities?
6. **Organizing** Complete a graphic organizer like the one below listing the contributions of women during the Civil War.

Women's Contributions to the Civil War

Analyzing Visuals

7. **Examing Photographs** Examine the photographs of battlefield hospitals on page 367. Why did infections spread so easily in hospitals, resulting in numerous deaths?

Writing About History

8. **Descriptive Writing** Imagine that you are a nurse on one of the battlefields during the Civil War. Write a journal entry describing the conditions of the soldiers and your reaction to the situation.

368 CHAPTER 11 The Civil War

SECTION 3 ASSESSMENT ANSWERS

1. Terms are in blue.
2. 54th Massachusetts *(p. 366)*, Elizabeth Blackwell *(p. 367)*, United States Sanitary Commission *(p. 367)*, Clara Barton *(p. 367)*, Henry Wirz *(p. 368)*
3. collapse of the South's transportation system and the presence of Union troops in important agricultural regions
4. It officially permitted African Americans to enlist in the Union army.
5. It helped dispel the beliefs that women were weak and unfit for some kinds of work.
6. worked as battlefield nurses, managed farms and businesses, volunteered, raised money
7. Doctors had little understanding of infectious germs and they used the same unsterilized instruments on patient after patient spreading infections.
8. Students' journal entries will vary. Journal entries should include descriptions and reactions.

Guide to Reading

Main Idea
The tide of the war turned after the North won pivotal battles in the west at Vicksburg and in the east at Gettysburg.

Key Terms and Names
Benjamin Grierson, forage, siege, Ambrose Burnside, Joseph Hooker, George Meade, Pickett's Charge, William Tecumseh Sherman

Reading Strategy
Categorizing As you read about Civil War battles that shaped the war, complete a graphic organizer listing the results of the following battles.

Battle	Results
Vicksburg	
Chancellorsville	
Gettysburg	
Chickamauga Creek	
Missionary Ridge	

Reading Objectives
- **Evaluate** the importance of events at Vicksburg and Gettysburg.
- **Describe** how battles in Tennessee helped turn the war increasingly in favor of the Union.

Section Theme
Geography and History The Union victory at Vicksburg cut the Confederacy into two parts.

Preview of Events

July 1863	November 1863	February 1864

July 1–3, 1863
Battle of Gettysburg

July 4, 1863
Vicksburg falls to Grant's soldiers

November 19, 1863
Lincoln delivers Gettysburg Address

November 24–25, 1863
Battle of Chattanooga

February 1864
Grant named general in chief

★ *An American Story* ★

At Gettysburg, Pennsylvania, in early July of 1863, Samuel Wilkeson, a reporter, sat to write his account of the battle that had raged for three days near the town. As he composed his dispatch, the body of Lieutenant Bayard Wilkeson—his son—lay dead beside him.

Wilkeson recorded the events that destroyed the peace of the Gettysburg countryside. He recalled "the singing of a bird, which had a nest in a peach tree within the tiny yard of the whitewashed cottage" that served as the Union army headquarters:

❝In the midst of its warbling a shell screamed over the house, instantly followed by another and another, and in a moment the air was full of the most complete artillery prelude to an infantry battle that was ever exhibited. Every size and form of shell known to British and to American gunnery shrieked, moaned, whirled, whistled, and wrathfully fluttered over our ground.❞

—quoted in *Eyewitness to History*

Union army headquarters at Gettysburg

Vicksburg Falls

Gettysburg was only one of a series of horrific encounters in 1863. The first battle took place farther west, where a vital part of the Union strategy involved gaining control of the Mississippi River. In April 1862, Admiral David Farragut had captured New Orleans and secured Union control of the Mississippi River delta. Later that year, Grant seized control of the river as far south as Memphis after his victory at Shiloh. If the Union could capture Vicksburg, Mississippi, the last major Confederate stronghold on the river, the North could cut the South in two.

---

1 FOCUS

Section Overview
This section describes the pivotal events of Vicksburg and Gettysburg and explains how these events turned the tide in favor of the Union.

BELLRINGER
Skillbuilder Activity

Project transparency and have students answer the question.

Available as a blackline master.

Daily Focus Skills Transparency 11–4

Guide to Reading

Answers to Graphic: Vicksburg: Union victory cut South in two; Chancellorsville: Confederate victory; Gettysburg: Union victory and turning point of war; Chickamauga Creek: Confederate victory; Missionary Ridge: Union victory, fall of Chattanooga

Preteaching Vocabulary
Have students identify the Key Terms and Names that refer to specific individuals and write a one-sentence description of each person.

SECTION RESOURCES

📂 Reproducible Masters
- Reproducible Lesson Plan 11–4
- Daily Lecture and Discussion Notes 11–4
- Guided Reading Activity 11–4
- Section Quiz 11–4
- Reading Essentials and Study Guide 11–4

♨ Transparencies
- Daily Focus Skills Transparency 11–4

Multimedia
- 💿 Interactive Tutor Self-Assessment CD-ROM
- 💿 ExamView® Pro Testmaker CD-ROM
- 💿 Presentation Plus! CD-ROM
- 💿 TeacherWorks™ CD-ROM
- 🎧 Audio Program
- 🎵 American Music: Hits Through History
- 🎵 American Music: Cultural Traditions

2 TEACH

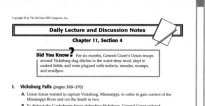
Discussing an Idea Have the class discuss the characteristics of military leaders. List the characteristics that students name on the board. Then ask: How did leadership affect the North's and the South's campaigns? *(North: Lincoln's difficulty in finding a superior general prolonged the war; Grant's determination in the West brought costly and harsh Union victories. South: Well-trained generals sustained the war at the beginning, but eventually could not overcome lack of resources.)* **L1**

Answer: to cut the South in two

Answer: more than a month

FYI

Shortly before the Confederate surrender in Vicksburg, the Union was strengthened by the addition of a new state. On June 20, 1863, West Virginia became the thirty-fifth state when the western part of Virginia broke away from Virginia.

Grierson's Raid The city of Vicksburg was located on the east bank of the Mississippi River. At first Grant tried to approach the city from the north, but the land was too swampy, and the rivers in the area were covered with vegetation and blocked by trees. To get at Vicksburg, Grant decided to move his troops across the Mississippi to the west bank and then march south. Once he was past the city, he intended to cross back to the east bank of the river and attack the city from the south.

To distract the Confederates while he carried out this difficult maneuver, Grant ordered **Benjamin Grierson** to take 1,700 troops on a cavalry raid through Mississippi. Grierson's forces traveled 600 miles (965 km) in two weeks, tearing up railroads, burning depots, and fighting skirmishes. His raid distracted the Confederate forces defending Vicksburg and enabled Grant to move his troops south of the city.

The Siege of Vicksburg After returning to the east bank of the Mississippi, Grant embarked on a daring march east, ordering his troops to live off the country. Foraging— or searching and raiding for food—as they marched, Grant's troops headed east into Mississippi. They captured the town of Jackson before turning back west toward Vicksburg. Grant's troops marched an astonishing 180 miles (290 km) in 17 days, fought 5 battles, and inflicted 7,200 casualties on the Confederates. The march ended by driving the Confederate forces back into their defenses at Vicksburg.

In May 1863, Grant launched two assaults on Vicksburg, but the city's defenders repulsed both attacks and inflicted high casualties. Grant decided

that the only way to take the city was to put it under siege—to cut off its food and supplies and bombard the city until its defenders gave up. On July 4, 1863, with his troops starving, the Confederate commander at Vicksburg surrendered. The Union victory had cut the Confederacy in two.

 **Reading Check** **Explaining** Why did President Lincoln want the Union army to capture Vicksburg?

The Road to Gettysburg

Shortly after McClellan's victory at Antietam, Lincoln became frustrated with the general. At Antietam, McClellan could have destroyed Lee's army, but he let the Confederates slip away. He then moved so slowly after the battle that Lee was able to recover from his defeat at Antietam and block McClellan's advance on Richmond. On November 7, 1862, Lincoln fired McClellan and gave command of the army to General **Ambrose Burnside.**

Lincoln wanted a general who was not intimidated by Lee's reputation. He urged Burnside to push south into Virginia and destroy Lee's army. Lincoln did not know that the turning point in the east would come not in Virginia, but far to the north in Pennsylvania.

Fredericksburg and Chancellorsville On December 13, 1862, Burnside ordered a series of bloody assaults against Lee's troops entrenched in the hills south of Fredericksburg, Virginia. The Union troops suffered more than 12,000 casualties, more than twice as many as the Confederates. Distressed by the defeat and faced with complaints about Burnside from other officers, Lincoln replaced him with General **Joseph Hooker.**

Hooker devised a plan to get at Lee's troops on the hills near Fredericksburg. First, he left a large part of his army at Fredericksburg to keep Lee's troops from moving. He then took the rest of the army

Picturing **History**

Vicksburg Besieged Union troops used this house as a headquarters during the siege of Vicksburg. Nearby are Union trenches and the opening to a tunnel being dug under Confederate lines. For how long was the city of Vicksburg under siege by Grant's Union forces?

COOPERATIVE LEARNING ACTIVITY

Sequencing Events Have students work in small groups to create a wall calendar for 1863. Suggest that students locate a perpetual calendar to correctly match dates with days of the week. Instruct students to add the events mentioned in this section to the calendar. Encourage students to use library and Internet resources to find additional information to add to the calendar. 📖

Use the rubric for a cooperative group management plan on pages 81–82 in the *Performance Assessment Activities and Rubrics.*

west to circle around behind Lee's troops and attack them from the rear. Realizing what was going on, Lee also divided his forces. He too left a small force at Fredericksburg and headed west with most of his troops to stop Hooker.

On May 2, 1863, Lee's troops attacked Hooker's forces in dense woods known as the Wilderness near the town of Chancellorsville, Virginia. Although outnumbered two to one, Lee aggressively divided his forces and repeatedly defeated the Union troops. On May 5, Hooker decided to retreat.

TURNING POINT

The Battle of Gettysburg Having weakened Union forces at Chancellorsville, Lee wanted to launch another invasion of the North. In June 1863 Lee marched into Pennsylvania, where his troops seized livestock, food, and clothing. After Hooker failed to stop Lee, Lincoln removed him from command and appointed General **George Meade** as his replacement. Meade immediately headed north to intercept Lee.

At the end of June, as Lee's army foraged in the Pennsylvania countryside, some of his troops headed into the town of Gettysburg, hoping to seize a supply of shoes. When they arrived near the town, they encountered Union cavalry. On July 1, 1863, the Confederates pushed the Union troops out of the town into the hills to the south. At the same time, the main forces of both armies hurried to the scene of the fighting. (See pages 374–375.)

On July 2 Lee attacked, but the Union troops held their ground. The following day, Lee ordered nearly 15,000 men under the command of General George E. Pickett and General A.P. Hill to make a massive assault. The attack became known as **Pickett's Charge.** As the mile-wide line of Confederate troops marched across open farmland toward Cemetery Ridge where Union forces stood, Union cannons and guns opened fire, inflicting 7,000 casualties in a less than half an hour of fighting. Soldiers like Lieutenant Jesse Bowman Young, who survived Gettysburg, later recalled the deafening gunfire and horrifying bloodshed of the final assault:

> ❝The caisson [ammunition chest] was set on fire, and in a moment with all its stock of ammunition, it exploded. . . . [T]here flashed for a single instant against the sky the sight of wheels, limbs of horses and of men, pieces of timber, and scores of exploding shells, all inextricably interwoven into a spectacle of horror. . . . Then the smoke covered the scene. . . . ❞
> —quoted in *Voices of the Civil War*

Bridging the Rappahannock Union troops build a pontoon bridge across the river in preparation for the assault on Confederate forces at Fredericksburg. The battle was a decisive Southern victory.

Aftermath of the Battle Less than 5,000 Confederate troops made it up the ridge, and Union troops overwhelmed those who did. Lee quickly rallied his troops, withdrew from Gettysburg on a rainy July 4, and retreated to Virginia. At Gettysburg the Union suffered 23,000 casualties, but the South lost an estimated 28,000 troops, over one-third of Lee's entire force.

The disaster at Gettysburg proved to be the turning point of the war. The Union's victory strengthened the Republicans politically and ensured that the British would not recognize the Confederacy. For the rest of the war, Lee's forces remained on the defensive, slowly giving ground to the Union army.

The Gettysburg Address In November 1863, Lincoln came to Gettysburg to dedicate a portion of the battlefield as a military cemetery. His speech—the Gettysburg Address—became one of the best-known orations in American history. Lincoln reminded his listeners that the nation was "conceived in liberty, and dedicated to the proposition that all men are created equal." He explained that the war was not a battle between regions but a fight for freedom:

Student Web Activity Visit the *American Vision* Web site at tav.glencoe.com and click on *Student Web Activities— Chapter 11* for an activity on the Civil War.

CHAPTER 11   The Civil War   **371**

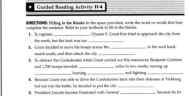

History *and the* Humanities

♫ American Music: Hits Through History: "Johnny Comes Marching Home," "The Battle Hymn of the Republic"

♫ American Music: Cultural Traditions: "Bonnie Blue Flag," "Glory! Glory! Hallelujah! (John Brown's Body)"

HISTORY *Online*

Objectives and answers to the student activity can be found in the **Web Activity Lesson Plan** at tav.glencoe.com.

ABCNEWS INTERACTIVE™

📼 **VIDEOCASSETTE**
Historic America Electronic Field Trips

View **Tape 1, Chapter 8:** "Gettysburg."

MEETING SPECIAL NEEDS

Verbal/Linguistic Have students develop a list of 10 questions to ask General Ulysses S. Grant about the victory at Vicksburg. Then have them research the types of answers that Grant might have given to their questions. Have students work in pairs to select the best of both their questions and responses and then conduct an interview for the class between a reporter and General Grant. **L2**

📖 Refer to *Inclusion for the High School Social Studies Classroom Strategies and Activities* in the TCR.

Profiles IN HISTORY

Background: On April 7, 1865, Grant wrote Lee the following: "The results of the last week must convince you of the hopelessness of further resistance. . . . I . . . regard it as my duty to shift from myself the responsibility of any further effusion of blood, by asking of you [to] surrender. . . ." Lee replied: "Though not entertaining the opinion you express on the hopelessness of further resistance . . . I reciprocate your desire to avoid useless effusion of blood, and therefore, before considering your proposition, ask the terms you will offer on condition of its surrender."

Ask: Compare these two men's military careers before the Civil War. *(Grant was undistinguished both at the military academy and as an army officer. Lee was an outstanding student and had earned praises during the war with Mexico.)*

✓ Reading Check

Answer: It failed to break Union lines and resulted in heavy Confederate casualties.

3 ASSESS

Assign Section 4 Assessment as homework or as an in-class activity.

🌐 Have students use the **Interactive Tutor Self-Assessment CD-ROM.**

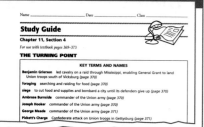

Profiles IN HISTORY

Ulysses S. Grant
1822–1885

Before his victories in Kentucky and Tennessee, Ulysses S. Grant had been a mediocre West Point cadet, a failed businessperson, and an undistinguished army officer. More than any other Union commander, however, Grant changed the strategy—and the outcome—of the Civil War. Grant's restless urge for offensive fighting and his insistence on "unconditional surrender" at Fort Donelson convinced Lincoln to place the general in command of all the Union troops in 1864. Lincoln's confidence was not misplaced. Despite mounting casualties and accusations that he was a "butcher," Grant pushed relentlessly until he finally accepted Lee's surrender at Appomattox, Virginia.

The Union's enthusiasm for its victorious general made Grant a two-term president after the war, although scandals in his administration marred his reputation. The Civil War had been the high point of Grant's life, the challenge that brought out his best qualities. More than any monument or memorial—including Grant's Tomb, in New York City—Lincoln's defense of his embattled general during the war sums up Grant's character and achievement: "I can't spare this man; he fights."

Robert E. Lee
1807–1870

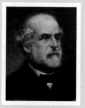

The son of a distinguished—though not wealthy—Virginia family, Robert E. Lee was raised in the socially exclusive world of the aristocratic South. From the beginning, he seemed marked by fate for brilliant success. At West Point he excelled in both his studies and his social life, impressing teachers and fellow cadets with his talent and good nature. As an army officer in the war with Mexico, he performed with brilliance and courage.

Offered command of the Union troops at the beginning of the Civil War, Lee refused, unable to oppose his fellow Virginians. He later commanded the army of Northern Virginia.

A hero to Southerners during the war, Lee felt a responsibility to set an example of Southern honor in defeat. His swearing of renewed allegiance to the United States after the war inspired thousands of former Confederate soldiers to follow his example. As president of Washington College in Virginia (later renamed Washington and Lee), Lee encouraged his students to put the war behind them and to behave as responsible citizens.

Lee died at age 63. In his last moments, he seemed to give orders to his troops, and then at last called out, "Strike the tent!"

❝It is . . . for us to be here dedicated to the great task remaining before us—that from these honored dead we take increased devotion to that cause for which they gave the last full measure of devotion; that we here highly resolve that these dead shall not have died in vain; that this nation, under God, shall have a new birth of freedom; and that the government of the people, by the people, and for the people, shall not perish from the earth.❞

—from the Gettysburg Address

📖 *(See page 1072 for more information on the Gettysburg Address.)*

✓ Reading Check **Summarizing** What was the result of Pickett's Charge?

Grant Secures Tennessee

After the Union's major victories at Vicksburg and Gettysburg, fierce fighting erupted in Tennessee near Chattanooga. Chattanooga was a vital railroad junction. Both sides knew that if the Union forces captured Chattanooga, they would control a major railroad running south to Atlanta. The way would be open for a Union advance into Georgia.

Chickamauga During the summer of 1863, Union general William Rosecrans outmaneuvered General Braxton Bragg. In early September, he forced the Confederates to evacuate Chattanooga without a fight. Bragg did not retreat far, however. When Rosecrans advanced into Georgia, Bragg launched an assault against him at Chickamauga Creek on September 19, 1863. Bragg soon smashed through part of the Union defenses, and Rosecrans ordered his troops to fall back to Chattanooga, where he found himself almost completely surrounded by Bragg's forces.

The Battle of Chattanooga In an effort to save the Union forces in Chattanooga, Lincoln decided to send some of Meade's forces to help Rosecrans. Dozens of trains were assembled, and 11 days later, 20,000 men with their artillery, horses, and equipment arrived near Chattanooga after travelling more than 1,200 miles (1,930 km).

INTERDISCIPLINARY CONNECTIONS ACTIVITY

Language Arts Tell students that Stephen Crane's novel, *The Red Badge of Courage*, presents a realistic view of the war. Have the language arts teacher select a few passages from the book that demonstrate how Crane paints a picture of the war. Then tell students that Crane did not actually fight in the Civil War. He based his book on war stories told by veterans and on the photographs taken by Mathew Brady, a famous Civil War photographer. Discuss the difference between participating in an event and having the event described by others. **L2**

Lincoln also decided to reorganize the military leadership in the west, and he placed Grant in overall command. Grant then hurried to Chattanooga to take charge of the coming battle. In late November, he ordered his troops to attack Confederate positions on Lookout Mountain. Charging uphill through swirling fog, the Union forces quickly drove the Southern troops off the mountain.

Confederates retreating from Lookout Mountain hurried to join the Southern forces at Missionary Ridge east of Chattanooga. The Confederates were outnumbered, but they awaited a Union attack, secure on a high rugged position just as the Union troops had been at Cemetery Ridge near Gettysburg.

Grant did not intend to storm Missionary Ridge. He believed an all-out assault would be suicidal. Instead he ordered General **William Tecumseh Sherman** to attack Confederate positions on the north end of the ridge. When Sherman failed to break through, Grant ordered 23,000 men under General George Thomas to launch a limited attack against the Confederates in front of Missionary Ridge as a diversion.

To Grant's astonishment, Thomas's troops overran the Confederate trenches and charged up the steep slope of Missionary Ridge itself. "They shouted 'Chickamauga,'" one Confederate remembered, "as though the word itself were a weapon." The rapid charge scattered the surprised Confederates, who retreated in panic, leaving Missionary Ridge—and Chattanooga—to the Union army.

Grant Becomes General in Chief By the spring of 1864, Grant had accomplished two crucial objectives for the Union. His capture of Vicksburg had given the Union control of the Mississippi River, while his

World History Connection

Gunpowder

The cannon and rifle fire that echoed throughout the valleys of Tennessee during Grant's campaign had become a familiar sound on the battlefields of the United States and the rest of the world by the mid-1800s. The key ingredient in these powerful weapons was gunpowder. Scholars believe that the Chinese invented this explosive mixture and were using it in fireworks and signals as early as the 900s. In 1304 the Arabs used the powder to develop the first gun. In the centuries that followed, numerous nations would develop and improve on the gun—which made all other weapons before it obsolete. *For what peaceful purposes can gunpowder be used?*

victory at Chattanooga had secured eastern Tennessee and cleared the way for an invasion of Georgia. Lincoln rewarded Grant by appointing him general in chief of the Union forces and promoting him to lieutenant general, a rank no one had held since George Washington. When the president met Grant in March 1864, he told him, "I wish to express my satisfaction with what you have done. . . . The particulars of your plan I neither know nor seek to know." The president had finally found a general he trusted to win the war.

✓ **Reading Check** **Examining** Why was capturing Chattanooga important for the Union?

SECTION 4 ASSESSMENT

Checking for Understanding
1. **Define:** forage, siege.
2. **Identify:** Benjamin Grierson, Ambrose Burnside, Joseph Hooker, George Meade, Pickett's Charge, William Tecumseh Sherman.
3. **Explain** why the Union victory at Gettysburg was so important.

Reviewing Themes
4. **Geography and History** Why was capturing Vicksburg important for the Union?

Critical Thinking
5. **Analyzing** What do you think might have been the outcome of the war if the Confederates had won the Battle of Gettysburg? Why do you think so?
6. **Organizing** Using a graphic organizer similar to the one below, list the results of the Battle of Gettysburg. Make sure you consider both the Union and the Confederacy.

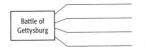

Battle of Gettysburg

Analyzing Visuals
7. **Examining Photographs** Examine the photograph on page 370 of Vicksburg, Mississippi. From looking at the picture, what do you think life was like for troops during a siege? Why do you think the troops were trying to tunnel under Confederate lines?

Writing About History
8. **Descriptive Writing** Take on the role of a Confederate soldier at the Battle of Gettysburg. Write a journal entry describing the battle and your feelings about the result of the battle.

SECTION 4 ASSESSMENT ANSWERS

1. Terms are in blue.
2. Benjamin Grierson *(p. 370)*, Ambrose Burnside *(p. 370)*, Joseph Hooker *(p. 370)*, George Meade *(p. 371)*, Pickett's Charge *(p. 371)*, William Tecumseh Sherman *(p. 373)*
3. It ensured that the British would remain out of the conflict.
4. It gave control of the Mississippi River to the Union.
5. Students might predict a Union victory but a longer war. Others might argue that it could have convinced Britain to assist the Confederacy.
6. strengthened Republicans politically, very high casualties, put

Confederacy on defensive, ended South's hope for British help
7. possible answers: dirty, uncomfortable, boring; tunnels allowed Union to sneak behind the lines and launch an attack at the front and the back of Confederate troops
8. Students' journal entries will vary.

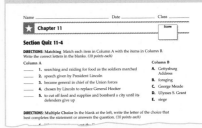

World History Connection

Students' answers will vary. Possible answers include fireworks and mining.

Section Quiz 11–4

Reteach
Have students explain how battles in Tennessee helped turn the war increasingly in favor of the Union

Enrich
Have interested students research and report on one aspect of American popular culture during the Civil War.

✓ **Reading Check**

Answer: The Union could control the major rail line running to Atlanta.

4 CLOSE

Have students describe the events of Vicksburg and Gettysburg and explain why these two battles are considered pivotal.

1 FOCUS

Tell students that Gettysburg lies about 50 miles northwest of Baltimore, Maryland. On February 11, 1895, Congress made Gettysburg a National Military Park as a memorial to the armies that fought the bloodiest battle of the Civil War.

2 TEACH

Analyzing Information Have students read Lee's quote about the defeat. Ask students why they think Lee took responsibility for the defeat. Then ask students to explain how taking responsibility was a mark of leadership. Finally, have students relate examples from their own lives that demonstrate people taking responsibility for their actions. **L1**

Comparing and Contrasting Tell students that the Union and Confederate armies were very similar. Have students use library and Internet resources to identify ways in which the armies were similar and the ways they were different. To get them started, tell students that both armies used similar weapons. You may recommend that students visit http://www.nps.gov/gett/index.htm as a starting point for their research. **L2**

FYI

The point on Cemetery Ridge that Pickett's troops reached is sometimes referred to as the Confederate "High Water Mark." Afterwards, the fortunes of the Confederacy seemed to ebb.

INVADING THE NORTH

After their victory at Chancellorsville in May 1863, the Confederates invaded the North (red arrow). Using the Blue Ridge Mountains to screen their movements, the Confederates advanced down the Shenandoah Valley, crossed the Potomac River, and pushed into Pennsylvania. The Federal army (blue arrow) placed itself between the Confederates and Washington, D.C. On July 1, the two armies met at the crossroads town of Gettysburg, Pennsylvania.

374 CHAPTER 11 The Civil War

A nurse poses with wounded soldiers outside one of the 400 tents set up as a temporary hospital at Gettysburg. During the battle, the Union army suffered 23,000 casualties, the Confederates 28,000.

EXTENDING THE CONTENT

The Hero of Little Round Top The extreme left flank of the Union lines at Gettysburg—a hill called Little Round Top—was commanded by Colonel Joshua Lawrence Chamberlain, a college professor who had taken a leave from teaching to fight in the war. Chamberlain knew that if the Confederates took Little Round Top, they would have a view of the whole Union line. Although greatly outnumbered, Chamberlain's forces withstood numerous attacks. Finally, Chamberlain led his troops in a bayonet charge that drove the Confederates from the field. Chamberlain received the Medal of Honor for his bravery at Gettysburg.

CANNON BOMBARDMENT
Pickett's Charge was preceded by a massive artillery bombardment. However, much of the Confederate artillery overshot the Federal positions on Cemetery Ridge, landing well to the rear of the frontline troops.

11th AC Hospital

Artillery Reserves

5th Corps
SYKES
9,500

6th Corps
SEDGWICK
13,600

Little Round Top

Big Round Top

Wheat Field

Devil's Den

Hood

Hood

Gettysburg Forces

	Union troops
	Confederate troops
3rd Corps	Corp
HILL	Commander
15,200	Number of troops (as of noon, July 3rd)

Scale of map varies in this perspective (distance from Gettysburg to Big Round Top 3 miles)

"It's all my fault. It is I who have lost this fight," Lee told the survivors as they struggled back after Pickett's Charge.

Gettysburg: The Final Day

The Confederate invasion of Union territory in the summer of 1863 was a bold stroke. By moving north, the Confederate commander of the Army of Northern Virginia, General Robert E. Lee, had relieved pressure on battle-ravaged Virginia. He had threatened the Federal capital of Washington, D.C., and gained access to the rich farms and other resources of Pennsylvania. Indeed, it was the prospect of finding shoes and other army supplies that lured the Confederates to Gettysburg.

By the morning of July 3, however, Lee was lamenting lost opportunities. When his troops arrived in Gettysburg on July 1, they had driven the Federals out of the town. Quickly grasping the advantages of defending the high ground, Major General George Meade had ordered his Federal Army of the Potomac to take up positions in the hills south of town. The Federal line stretched from Culp's Hill and Cemetery Hill south along Cemetery Ridge to another hill called Little Round Top. The Confederates had taken up a position along a roughly parallel ridge to the west known as Seminary Ridge. Between the two positions stretched pastureland and fields of wheat. On July 2, Lee's troops had attacked Federal positions on Culp's Hill, Cemetery Hill, and Little Round Top, but they were pushed back. Now, on the morning of July 3, Lee was determined to punch a hole in the Federal line. Among the officers preparing to attack was Major General George Pickett, who would give his name to the day's infantry charge.

At about 3:00 P.M., more than 12,000 Confederates set out from Seminary Ridge. Three-fourths of a mile away, the Federals waited atop Cemetery Ridge. Federal artillery ripped holes in the Confederate line as it advanced. When the Confederates were 200 yards from the crest of Cemetery Ridge, the Federals unleashed volley after volley. Still the Confederates pressed on. Hundreds made it all the way up the slope of the ridge, but as they did, Federal reinforcements rushed in. Firing at point-blank range, stabbing with bayonets, and striking with the ends of rifles, the Federals drove the Confederates back down the slope. Pickett's Charge had been repulsed. Lee retreated to Virginia, and the tide of war turned in favor of the North.

LEARNING FROM GEOGRAPHY

1. How did the Confederate army use the mountains of Virginia in its invasion of the North?

2. Why was the Federal army in such a strong position at Gettysburg?

Creating a Relief Map Have students work in groups to create a relief map depicting one day at Gettysburg. Each student should be assigned the role of researcher, designer, or artist. Researchers find information about the day's battles, designers create plans for the maps that the artists can use to create the maps. **L3**

3 ASSESS

Have students answer the Learning from Geography questions.

4 CLOSE

Ask students to name the landforms on the map and to explain how the armies used the landforms.

Geography and History Activity 4

Name _____ Date _____ Class _____

✦ GEOGRAPHY AND HISTORY ACTIVITY 4

Gettysburg: The Struggle for Little Round Top

THE PHYSICAL GEOGRAPHY OF GETTYSBURG

In 1863 Gettysburg, Pennsylvania, was a small town surrounded by orchards, fields, woodlands, valleys, and hills. The geography and topography of the area—the patterns and placement of the hills, ridges, boulders, woods, and open areas—influenced how the Battle of Gettysburg was fought and its eventual outcome.

The Union forces, led by Major General George Meade, were positioned just south of Gettysburg in an upside-down fishhook...

Map 1—Sites on the Gettysburg Battlefield

NGS ONLINE

Access National Geographic's Web site for current events, atlas updates, activities, links, interactive features, and archives at www.nationalgeographic.com.

ANSWERS TO LEARNING FROM GEOGRAPHY

1. They used the mountains to screen their movements as they marched north.

2. It occupied the high ground, such as Cemetery Ridge, Culp's Hill, Cemetery Hill, and Little Round Top, and would fire down on the advancing Confederate troops.

SECTION 5 The War Ends

1 FOCUS

Section Overview

This section focuses on the final year of the war, Lincoln's re-election, and his assassination.

BELLRINGER
Skillbuilder Activity

Project transparency and have students answer the question.

Available as a blackline master.

Daily Focus Skills Transparency 11–5

Guide to Reading

Answers to Graphic: May, Wilderness; June, Cold Harbor; August, Mobile; September, Fall of Atlanta; November, March to the Sea; December, Savannah

Preteaching Vocabulary
Have students make a list of the Key Terms and Names and write a helpful phrase next to each term or name. Instruct students to add additional information to their list as they read the section.

Guide to Reading

Main Idea
After four long years of fighting, the Civil War ended in 1865 in victory for the Union.

Key Terms and Names
Philip Sheridan, "Sherman neckties," March to the Sea, pillage, mandate, Thirteenth Amendment, Appomattox Courthouse, John Wilkes Booth

Reading Strategy
Sequencing As your read about the final battles of the war, complete a time line similar to the one below to record the final battles of the Civil War and their results.

1864 — May | August | November
June | September | December

Reading Objectives
• **Explain** the importance of Union victories in Virginia and the Deep South.
• **Discuss** Lee's surrender and the events of the war's aftermath.

Section Theme
Individual Action In the final year of the Civil War, General Ulysses S. Grant refused to take the pressure off of Lee's weary troops.

Preview of Events

◆September 1864 ◆November 1864 ◆January 1865 ◆April 1865

September 1864
Fall of Atlanta

November 1864
Lincoln reelected

January 1865
Thirteenth Amendment goes to states for ratification

April 9, 1865
Lee surrenders at Appomattox

April 14, 1865
Lincoln assassinated at Ford's Theater

★ An American Story ★

Ulysses S. Grant

"Why, here is General Grant," Lincoln called out at a White House reception in March 1864. "Well, this is a great pleasure, I assure you!" As guests applauded, the president reached over and shook Grant's hand. The crowd, as eager for a look at the victorious general as they were to see the president, pressed in on the pair.

At last Grant climbed up on a couch to greet the crowd, who clamored to see him. For an hour, he balanced there, exchanging greetings with his well-wishers. "For once at least," a guest recalled, "the President of the United States was not the chief figure in the picture. The little, scared-looking man who stood on a crimson-covered sofa was the idol of the hour."

—adapted from *The Civil War*

Grant Versus Lee

In the spring of 1864, the most successful general of the Union army faced the most renowned Confederate commander. Grant put his most trusted subordinate, William Sherman, in charge of Union operations in the west, then headed to Washington, D.C., to take command of the Union troops facing Lee.

From the Wilderness to Cold Harbor "Whatever happens, there will be no turning back," Grant promised Lincoln. He was determined to march southward, attacking Lee's forces relentlessly, until the South surrendered.

The first battle of Grant's campaign erupted in the Wilderness, a densely forested area near Fredericksburg, Virginia. The battle lasted two days, continuing even after the woods caught fire, blinding and choking the combatants. Despite suffering heavy casualties,

376 CHAPTER 11 The Civil War

SECTION RESOURCES

Reproducible Masters
• Reproducible Lesson Plan 11–5
• Daily Lecture and Discussion Notes 11–5
• Guided Reading Activity 11–5
• Section Quiz 11–5
• Reading Essentials and Study Guide 11–5
• Performance Assessment Activities and Rubrics

Transparencies
• Daily Focus Skills Transparency 11–5

Multimedia
◉ Interactive Tutor Self-Assessment CD-ROM
◉ ExamView® Pro Testmaker CD-ROM
◉ Presentation Plus! CD-ROM
◉ TeacherWorks™ CD-ROM
◉ Audio Program

Grant did not pause. He headed southeast toward Spotsylvania Courthouse. First in terrible heat and then in pouring rain, the two armies battled near Spotsylvania for 11 days, often in bloody hand-to-hand combat that left many traumatized.

Unlike past campaigns in which several weeks of reinforcing and resupplying followed battles, warfare now continued without pause. Savage combat, advances and retreats, and the digging of defensive trenches filled most days and nights. One Union officer noted that the men "had grown thin and haggard. The experience . . . seemed to have added twenty years to their age."

Unable to break Lee's lines at Spotsylvania, Grant headed toward Cold Harbor, a strategic crossroads northeast of Richmond. Convinced that his relentless attacks had weakened and demoralized Lee's troops, Grant decided to launch an all-out assault on Lee's forces at Cold Harbor. The attack cost his army 7,000 casualties, compared to 1,500 for the South. Grant conceded, "I regret this assault more than any one I have ever ordered."

The Siege of Petersburg Stopped by Lee at Cold Harbor, Grant tried another plan similar to the one he had used near Vicksburg. He ordered General **Philip Sheridan** to stage a cavalry raid north and west of Richmond. While Sheridan's troops distracted Lee, Grant headed southeast, crossed the James River, and then turned west toward Petersburg. Capturing Petersburg would cut the only rail line into Richmond.

When the first Union troops reached the outskirts of Petersburg, they paused. The city was defended by miles of barricades 20 feet (7 m) thick. In front of the Confederate trenches were ditches up to 15 feet (4.6 m) deep to slow down attackers. Carefully positioned cannons supported the Confederate lines.

The strength of the defenses the Confederates had erected at Petersburg intimidated the Union troops, who were already exhausted. Realizing a full-scale frontal assault would be suicidal, Grant ordered his troops to put the city under siege.

✓ **Reading Check** **Summarizing** Why did General Grant decide to capture Petersburg?

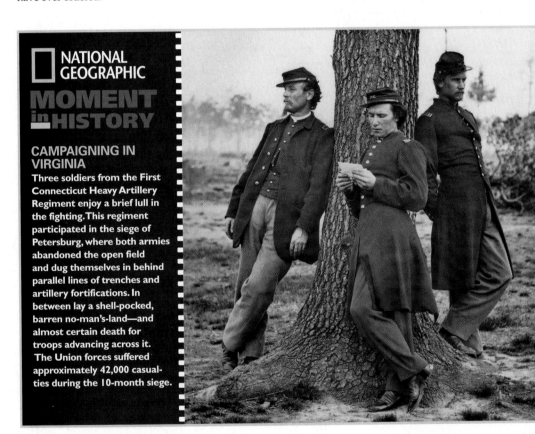

NATIONAL GEOGRAPHIC
MOMENT in HISTORY

CAMPAIGNING IN VIRGINIA

Three soldiers from the First Connecticut Heavy Artillery Regiment enjoy a brief lull in the fighting. This regiment participated in the siege of Petersburg, where both armies abandoned the open field and dug themselves in behind parallel lines of trenches and artillery fortifications. In between lay a shell-pocked, barren no-man's-land—and almost certain death for troops advancing across it. The Union forces suffered approximately 42,000 casualties during the 10-month siege.

CHAPTER 11   The Civil War   **377**

2 TEACH

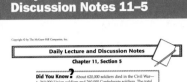

Daily Lecture and Discussion Notes 11–5

Creating a Table Have students use the data shown in the circle graph on page 378 to create a table showing American war deaths. Instruct students to organize the data in chronological order. **L1** ELL

📁 Use the rubric for creating a map, display, or chart on pages 77–78 in the *Performance Assessment Activities and Rubrics.*

✓ **Reading Check**

Answer: It would cut the only rail line into Richmond, the Confederate capital.

NATIONAL GEOGRAPHIC
MOMENT in HISTORY

The regiment is the primary means of identifying men who fought in the Civil War. Most regiments consisted of soldiers from the same state, often friends, neighbors, and relatives. Artillery regiments during the Civil War were designed to have 12 companies. The size of companies varied, but most artillery companies could have up to 150 soldiers.

COOPERATIVE LEARNING ACTIVITY

Identifying Generals Organize students into small groups. Have the groups research the generals who served in the Union and Confederate armies. Based on their research, have the groups prepare a chart listing the generals for each side, the battles they commanded, and any other pertinent information about their service.

Use the rubric for a cooperative group management plan on pages 81–82 in the *Performance Assessment Activities and Rubrics.*

Creating Circle Graphs Have students use the data presented in the bar graph on this page to create a pair of circle graphs, one for the North and one for the South, showing the percentage of battle-related and non-battle-related deaths. Ask students what conclusions can be drawn from these circle graphs. **L2**

📁 Use the rubric for creating a map, display, or chart on pages 77–78 in the *Performance Assessment Activities and Rubrics.*

3 ASSESS

Assign Section 5 Assessment as homework or as an in-class activity.

◉ Have students use the **Interactive Tutor Self-Assessment CD-ROM.**

Union Victories in the South

While Grant battled Lee in Virginia, General Sherman marched his army from Chattanooga toward Atlanta. Meanwhile, the Union navy launched an operation to close the port of Mobile, Alabama, the last major Confederate port on the Gulf of Mexico east of the Mississippi.

Farragut Attacks Mobile On August 5, 1864, David Farragut took 18 ships past the three Confederate forts defending Mobile Bay. As the fleet headed into the bay, a mine—which in the 1860s was called a torpedo—blew up a Union ship. The explosion brought the fleet to a halt, right in front of a fort's guns. "Damn the torpedoes! Full speed ahead!" cried Farragut, whose ship led the way through the minefield.

After getting past the Confederate forts, Farragut's ships destroyed a Confederate fleet defending Mobile Bay. Although Farragut did not capture Mobile, he did seal off the bay. Blockade runners moving goods in and out of the Deep South east of the Mississippi could no longer use any port on the Gulf of Mexico.

The Fall of Atlanta While Farragut had been preparing for his attack on Mobile Bay, Sherman's army pushed toward Atlanta. In late August 1864, Sherman sent his troops south around Atlanta to cut the roads and railways leading into the city. His troops destroyed the rail lines by heating the rails and twisting them into snarls of steel nicknamed **"Sherman neckties."** To avoid being trapped in the city, Confederate General John B. Hood evacuated Atlanta on September 1.

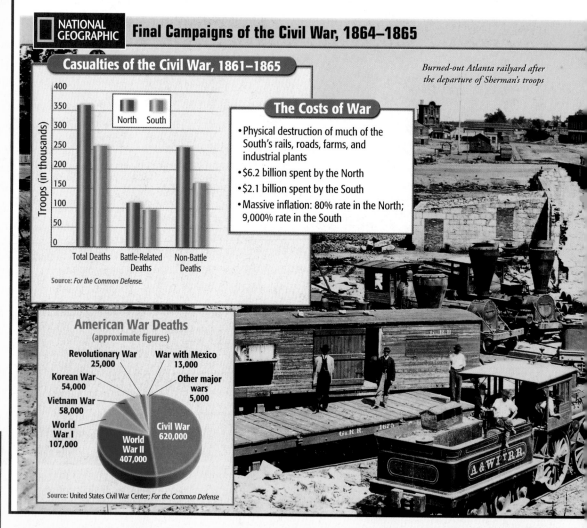

NATIONAL GEOGRAPHIC Final Campaigns of the Civil War, 1864–1865

Burned-out Atlanta railyard after the departure of Sherman's troops

Casualties of the Civil War, 1861–1865

(bar graph)
Troops (in thousands): 0 to 400
North, South
Total Deaths, Battle-Related Deaths, Non-Battle Deaths

Source: *For the Common Defense.*

The Costs of War

- Physical destruction of much of the South's rails, roads, farms, and industrial plants
- $6.2 billion spent by the North
- $2.1 billion spent by the South
- Massive inflation: 80% rate in the North; 9,000% rate in the South

American War Deaths
(approximate figures)

Revolutionary War 25,000
War with Mexico 13,000
Korean War 54,000
Other major wars 5,000
Vietnam War 58,000
World War I 107,000
World War II 407,000
Civil War 620,000

Source: United States Civil War Center; *For the Common Defense*

Sherman's March to the Sea After occupying Atlanta, Sherman proposed to march across Georgia. "I could cut a swath to the sea," he explained, "and divide the Confederacy in two." The march would be "a demonstration to the world . . . that we have a power that Davis cannot resist. I can make the march, and make Georgia howl!"

Sherman ordered all civilians to leave Atlanta. He explained to the city's mayor that he was "not only fighting hostile armies, but a hostile people." To end the war, he believed, he had no choice but to "make old and young, rich and poor, feel the hard hand of war." Sherman then ordered his troops to destroy everything in the city of military value, including railroads, warehouses, mills, factories, and machine shops. Sherman's troops set fires to destroy these structures, but the fires quickly spread, burning down more than one-third of the city.

On November 15, 1864, Sherman began his **March to the Sea.** His troops cut a path of destruction through Georgia that was in places 60 miles (97 km) wide. They ransacked houses, burned crops, and killed cattle. By December 21, 1864, they had reached the coast and seized the city of Savannah.

After reaching the sea, Sherman turned north and headed into South Carolina—the state that many people believed had started the Civil War. "The whole army," Sherman wrote, "is burning with an insatiable desire to wreak vengeance upon South Carolina." As one of Sherman's soldiers declared about South Carolina, "Here is where treason began and . . . here is where it shall end."

The troops burned and **pillaged,** or looted, nearly everything in front of them. At least 12 towns were set on fire, including Columbia, the state capital. The march demoralized Southerners. As one South Carolinian wrote, "All is gloom, despondency and inactivity. Our army is demoralized and the people panic stricken . . . to fight longer seems madness."

✓ **Reading Check** **Examining** Why did General Sherman march his army through Georgia?

The South Surrenders

When Sherman and Grant began their campaigns in the spring of 1864, Lincoln knew that his own reelection depended on their success. By summer, sensing the public's anger over the costly war, Lincoln confided to an army officer, "I am going to be beaten." He did not know that the war was rapidly approaching its conclusion. Only a few months later, the Confederacy was on the verge of collapse.

The Election of 1864 To oppose Lincoln in the 1864 election, the Democrats nominated General George McClellan, whose popularity had remained high despite his dismissal earlier in the war. Playing to the country's growing war weariness, McClellan promised to stop the hostilities and open negotiations with the South to restore the Union peaceably.

The capture of Atlanta came just in time to revitalize Northern support for the war and for Lincoln himself. The president won reelection with 55 percent of the popular vote.

Lincoln interpreted his reelection as a **mandate,** or clear sign from the voters, to end slavery permanently by amending the Constitution. To get the amendment through Congress, Republicans appealed to Democrats who were against slavery to help them. On January 31, 1865, the **Thirteenth Amendment** to the

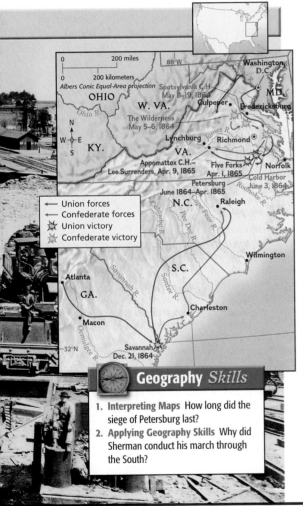

Geography Skills

1. **Interpreting Maps** How long did the siege of Petersburg last?
2. **Applying Geography Skills** Why did Sherman conduct his march through the South?

CHAPTER 11 The Civil War **379**

Section Quiz 11–5

★ Chapter 11

Section Quiz 11-5

DIRECTIONS: Matching Match each item in Column A with the items in Column B. Write the correct letters in the blanks. *(10 points each)*

Column A
1. staged a cavalry raid north and west of Richmond
2. nickname given to rail lines heated and twisted into snarls of steel by Union troops
3. banned slavery in the United States
4. when General Sherman's troops cut a swath of destruction through Georgia
5. a strategic crossroads northeast of Richmond

Column B
A. Cold Harbor
B. March to the Sea
C. Thirteenth Amendment
D. General Philip Sheridan
E. "Sherman neckties"

DIRECTIONS: Multiple Choice In the blank at the left, write the letter of the choice that

Geography *Skills*

Answers:
1. about eleven months
2. to burn and destroy Southern supplies, weaken civilian morale in the South, and to demonstrate the superior power of the Union army

✓**Reading Check**

Answer: to convince Southern civilians to give up the struggle

Creating a Circle Graph Have students use the data shown below to create a circle graph illustrating the results of the 1864 presidential election. **L2**

Candidate	Popular Vote	Electoral Vote
Lincoln, Rep.	2,206,938	212
McClellan, Dem.	1,803,787	21

 Use the rubric for creating a map, display, or chart on pages 77–78 in the *Performance Assessment Activities and Rubrics.*

FYI

Lincoln lost only three states in the 1864 election. Delaware, Kentucky, and New Jersey supported McClellan.

INTERDISCIPLINARY CONNECTIONS ACTIVITY

Government Ask students to explain the difference in the number of popular votes and electoral votes cast in the 1860 and 1864 presidential elections. *(only Northern voters participated in the 1864 election and only Northern electors cast a ballot)* **L2**

	Votes Cast in General Election	Votes Cast in Electoral College
1860	4,689,568	303
1864	4,010,725	233

✓ Reading Check

Answer: He thought that the public was growing angry over the costly war and they would show their anger at the polls.

Reteach

Ask students to explain the importance of Union victories in Virginia and the Deep South.

Enrich

Have interested students interview several people of various ages, asking them to name Lincoln's accomplishments as president. Based on the interviews, have students write a paper that begins "Abraham Lincoln's greatest impact on the United States was. . . ."

4 CLOSE

Encourage students to discuss Lee's surrender and the events of the war's aftermath.

Constitution, banning slavery in the United States, narrowly passed the House of Representatives and was sent to the states for ratification.

Surrender Meanwhile, in the trenches near Petersburg, Lee knew that time was running out. On April 1, 1865, Union troops led by Phil Sheridan cut the last rail line into Petersburg at the Battle of Five Forks. The following night, Lee's troops withdrew from their positions near the city and raced west.

Lee's desperate attempt to escape Grant's forces failed when Sheridan's cavalry got ahead of Lee's troops and blocked the road at **Appomattox Courthouse.** When his troops failed to break through, Lee sadly observed, "There is nothing left for me to do but go and see General Grant, and I would rather die a thousand deaths." With his ragged and battered troops surrounded and outnumbered, Lee surrendered to Grant on April 9, 1865.

Grant's generous terms of surrender guaranteed that the United States would not prosecute Confederate soldiers for treason. When Grant agreed to let Confederates take their horses home "to put in a crop to carry themselves and their families through the next winter," Lee thanked him, adding that the kindness would "do much toward conciliating our people." As Lee left, he shook hands with Ely Parker, a Senecan who served as Grant's secretary. "I am glad to see a real American here," Lee told the Native American. Parker replied, "We are all Americans."

Lincoln's Assassination With the war over, Lincoln described his plan to restore the Southern states to the Union, and in the speech he mentioned including African Americans in Southern state governments. One listener, the actor **John Wilkes Booth,** sneered to a friend, "That is the last speech he will ever make."

The president's advisers repeatedly warned him not to appear unescorted in public. Nevertheless, Lincoln went to Ford's Theater with his wife on the evening of April 14, 1865, to see a play. During the third act, Booth slipped quietly behind him and shot the president in the back of the head.

Lincoln's death shocked the nation. Once viewed as a rustic, unsophisticated man not suited for the presidency, Lincoln had become the Union's greatest champion. The usually stern General Grant wept openly as Lincoln's body lay in state at the White House. Tens of thousands of men, women, and children lined railroad tracks across the nation as Lincoln's body was transported back to Springfield, Illinois.

Aftermath of the Civil War The North's victory in the Civil War strengthened the power of the federal government over the states. It also transformed American society by finally ending the enslavement of millions of African Americans. At the same time, it left the South socially and economically devastated.

Following the war, many questions remained unresolved. No one yet knew how to bring the Southern states back into the Union, nor what the status of African Americans would be in Southern society. Americans from the North and the South tried to answer these questions in the years following the Civil War—an era known as Reconstruction.

✓ Reading Check **Explaining** Why did President Lincoln doubt he could win the 1864 election?

SECTION 5 ASSESSMENT

Checking for Understanding

1. **Define:** pillage, mandate.
2. **Identify:** Philip Sheridan, "Sherman neckties," March to the Sea, Thirteenth Amendment, Appomattox Courthouse, John Wilkes Booth.
3. **Describe** how General Grant conducted the Confederate surrender.

Reviewing Themes

4. **Individual Action** How did Northern military strategy change after General Ulysses S. Grant took command of the Union army?

Critical Thinking

5. **Evaluating** What was the effect of Farragut's blockade of Mobile Bay?
6. **Organizing** Complete a graphic organizer similar to the one below by listing the purpose for the Union march on Atlanta and the effects of the city's capture on the North and South.

Analyzing Visuals

7. **Examining Charts** Examine the charts of war deaths on page 378. What would account for the thousands of non-battle deaths listed in one of the charts?

Writing About History

8. **Descriptive Writing** Take on the role of a reporter living in Georgia during General Sherman's March to the Sea. Write a brief article describing the Union's actions and their effects on the people living there.

SECTION 5 ASSESSMENT ANSWERS

1. Terms are in blue.
2. Philip Sheridan *(p. 377)*, "Sherman neckties" *(p. 378)*, March to the Sea *(p. 379)*, Thirteenth Amendment *(p. 379)*, Appomattox Courthouse *(p. 380)*, John Wilkes Booth *(p. 380)*
3. Grant's generous terms allowed soldiers to go home without fear

of being prosecuted for treason.
4. It became focused on relentlessly attacking the Confederate troops.
5. It prevented Confederate blockade runners from docking at any Gulf of Mexico ports.
6. Purpose: to gain access to the heart of Southern territory and destroy Southern railroads; Effect:

crippled Southern morale and helped Lincoln win re-election in the North
7. untreated hospital and prison infections
8. Students' articles will vary. Articles should contain facts, not the reporter's opinion.

Technology SKILLBUILDER

Evaluating a Web Site

Why Learn This Skill?

The Internet has become a valuable research tool. It is convenient to use, and the information contained on the Internet is plentiful. However, some Web site information is not necessarily accurate or reliable. When using the Internet as a research tool, you will need to distinguish between quality information and inaccurate or incomplete information.

Learning the Skill

There are a number of issues to consider when evaluating a Web site. Most important is to check the accuracy of the source and content. The author and publisher or sponsor of the site should be clearly indicated, and the user must also determine the usefulness of the site. The information on the site should be current, and the design and organization of the site should be appealing and easy to navigate.

To evaluate a Web site, ask yourself the following questions:

- Are the facts on the site documented?
- Is more than one source used for background information within the site?
- Are the links within the site appropriate and up-to-date?
- Is the author clearly identified?
- Does the site contain links to other useful resources?
- Is the information easy to access? Is it properly labeled?
- Is the design appealing?

Practicing the Skill

Visit the following Web site and answer the questions that follow.

http://sunsite.utk.edu/civil-war/

❶ Who is the author or sponsor of the Web site?

❷ What links does the site contain? Are they appropriate to the topic?

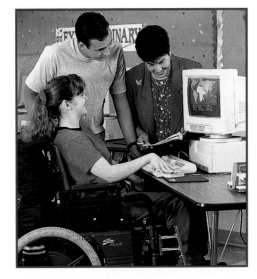

❸ What sources were used for the information contained on the site?

❹ Is the design of the site appealing? Why or why not?

❺ How is the home page organized?

Skills Assessment

Complete the Practicing Skills questions on page 383 and the Chapter 11 Skill Reinforcement Activity to assess your mastery of this skill.

Applying the Skill

Comparing Web Sites Locate two other Web sites about the Civil War. Evaluate them for accuracy and usefulness, and then compare them to the site featured above. Be certain to go through the various links that the site includes so that you can do a thorough evaluation of the site. Share your findings with the class.

 GO TO Glencoe's **Skillbuilder Interactive Workbook, CD-ROM Level 2,** provides instruction and practice in key social studies skills.

TEACH

Evaluating a Web Site Point out that virtually anyone can create and post a Web page. There are hosting sites that allow individuals to post Web pages at no charge. This means that when you search for Abraham Lincoln, it is likely that your results will include authoritative sites with content developed by historians and a site that showcases a child's third-grade homework assignment.

Ask students to search for Web sites about one of the people mentioned in the chapter. Have students find a site that they consider authoritative. Have them print the home page of the site and write a brief explanation of why they rate the site as authoritative. Then have students rate the site using the criteria listed on this page.

Additional Practice

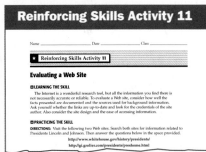

Reinforcing Skills Activity 11

Name _____ Date _____ Class _____

★ **Reinforcing Skills Activity 11**

Evaluating a Web Site

☐ **LEARNING THE SKILL**

The Internet is a wonderful research tool, but all the information you find there is not necessarily accurate or reliable. To evaluate a Web site, consider how well the facts presented are documented and the sources used for background information. Ask yourself whether the links are up-to-date and look for the credentials of the site author. Also consider the site design and the ease of accessing information.

☐ **PRACTICING THE SKILL**

DIRECTIONS: Visit the following two Web sites. Search both sites for information related to Presidents Lincoln and Johnson. Then answer the questions below in the space provided.

http://www.whitehouse.gov/history/presidents/
http://gi.grolier.com/presidents/preshome.html

GLENCOE TECHNOLOGY

 CD-ROM
Glencoe Skillbuilder Interactive Workbook CD-ROM, Level 2

This interactive CD-ROM reinforces student mastery of essential social studies skills.

ANSWERS TO PRACTICING THE SKILL

❶ Dr. George H. Hoemann

❷ primary sources, historical data and explanation; yes

❸ various university and government sites, some commercial sites, historical societies

❹ Answers may vary. The site is easy to navigate and has appealing visuals and sound.

❺ It includes a quote, photos, links to other pages, and an E-mail link to the author.

Applying the Skill

Students' evaluations will vary but should use the criteria listed in the Skillbuilder activity.

Reviewing Key Terms

Students' answers will vary. The pages where the words appear in the text are shown in parentheses.

1. **greenback** *(p. 352)*
2. **conscription** *(p. 353)*
3. **habeas corpus** *(p. 353)*
4. **attrition** *(p. 355)*
5. **bounty** *(p. 358)*
6. **blockade runner** *(p. 359)*
7. **hardtack** *(p. 366)*
8. **forage** *(p. 370)*
9. **siege** *(p. 370)*
10. **pillage** *(p. 379)*
11. **mandate** *(p. 379)*

Reviewing Key Facts

12. Robert E. Lee *(p. 350)*, Copperheads *(p. 353)*, *Trent* Affair *(p. 354)*, "Stonewall" Jackson *(p. 358)*, Irwin McDowell *(p. 358)*, Ulysses S. Grant *(p. 360)*, George B. McClellan *(p. 361)*, Emancipation Proclamation *(p. 363)*, Henry Wirz *(p. 368)*, George Meade *(p. 371)*, William Tecumseh Sherman *(p. 373)*, Thirteenth Amendment *(p. 379)*, John Wilkes Booth *(p. 380)*

13. The North had more men able to serve in the military and more people working to support the war; more resources for manufacturing clothing, weapons, and gunpowder; and more money to finance the war. The South had a large number of trained military officers and was capable of producing its own food.

14. transformed the war from a conflict over preservation of the Union into a war of liberation

Reviewing Key Terms

On a sheet of paper, use each of these terms in a sentence.

1. greenback
2. conscription
3. habeas corpus
4. attrition
5. bounty
6. blockade runner
7. hardtack
8. forage
9. siege
10. pillage
11. mandate

Reviewing Key Facts

12. **Identify:** Robert E. Lee, Copperheads, *Trent* Affair, "Stonewall" Jackson, Ulysses S. Grant, George B. McClellan, Emancipation Proclamation, 54th Massachusetts, Henry Wirz, George Meade, William Tecumseh Sherman, Thirteenth Amendment, John Wilkes Booth.

13. What were the military advantages of the North and South at the start of the Civil War?

14. What effects did the Emancipation Proclamation have on the war?

15. How did the Civil War affect the economies of the North and the South?

Critical Thinking

16. **Analyzing Themes: Civic Rights and Responsibilities** President Lincoln suspended writs of habeas corpus to prevent interference with the draft. Do you think suspending civil liberties is justified in some situations? Why or why not?

17. **Interpreting Primary Sources** At the beginning of the Civil War, Robert E. Lee wrote to his sister, Mrs. Anne Marshall, of his decision to resign from the U.S. Army. Read the excerpt and answer the questions that follow.

Chapter Summary

	1861	1862	1863	1864	1865
Military Campaigns	**July** • The Battle of Bull Run (Manassas) demonstrates that the war will not be over quickly. **September** • Grant leads troops into Kentucky and Missouri.	**March** • Two ironclad ships, the *Monitor* and the *Virginia*, battle to a draw. **April** • David Farragut captures New Orleans. **September** • The Battle of Antietam marks the bloodiest one-day battle in U.S. history. • The Battle of Shiloh makes General Grant well known.	**July** • The Battle of Gettysburg turns the tide of war in favor of the Union.	**May** • Grant and Lee battle in the Wilderness and at Spotsylvania. **June** • Grant and Lee battle at Cold Harbor. • The siege of Petersburg begins. **September** • Atlanta falls. **November** • William Sherman begins his destructive March to the Sea.	**April** • Lee surrenders to Grant at Appomattox Courthouse.
Domestic and Foreign Affairs	**April** • Elizabeth Blackwell starts the nation's first training program for nurses. • President Lincoln orders a blockade of all Confederate ports. **November** • The *Trent* Affair increases tension between Great Britain and the United States.	**April** • The South introduces conscription for military service.	**January** • Lincoln's Emancipation Proclamation goes into effect. **April** • Food shortages in the South lead to rioting. **November** • Lincoln delivers the Gettysburg Address.	**February** • Lincoln promotes Ulysses S. Grant to general-in-chief of the Union army. **November** • Lincoln is reelected.	**January** • The Thirteenth Amendment to the Constitution, banning slavery in the United States, passes the House of Representatives. **April** • John Wilkes Booth assassinates Lincoln.

15. The Northern economy was more diversified and able to adapt to wartime changes. The Southern economy suffered due to inflation and critical shortages.

Critical Thinking

16. Students' answers will vary. Answers should include a reasonable explanation of each student's point of view.

17. **a.** He could not fight a war against his own family. **b.** He did not want to stay in the Union army and have to fight against others from Virginia.

18. strengthened federal government, ended slavery, left the South socially and economically weakened, how to heal divided nation remained unclear, what to do with freed African Americans also remained unclear

Practicing Skills

19. Students' evaluations will vary depending on the sites visited. Students should use the criteria in the Skillbuilder activity to evaluate the sites.

66My Dear Sister:

. . . With all my devotion to the Union and the feeling of loyalty and duty of an American citizen, I have not been able to make up my mind to raise my hand against my relatives, my children, my home. I have, therefore, resigned my commission in the Army, and, save in defense of my native state . . . I hope I may never be called on to draw my sword. I know you will blame me; but you must think as kindly of me as you can. . . .99

—from *Personal Reminiscences, Anecdotes, and Letters of General Robert E. Lee*

a. What were Robert E. Lee's feelings about the war?

b. Why did he feel it necessary to resign from the Union army and become commander of the Virginia army?

18. Organizing Complete a graphic organizer similar to the one below by explaining the results of the Civil War on the nation.

Results of Civil War

Practicing Skills

19. Evaluating a Web Site Go through the steps described on page 381 for evaluating a Web site. Then search the Internet for Web sites that deal with prisoners of war during the Civil War. Write a report describing the best and worst sites.

Writing Activity

20. Portfolio Writing Write a newspaper article about the surrender of General Robert E. Lee. Write the article from the perspective of either a Southern or Northern reporter.

Chapter Activity

21. Technology Imagine that you are a travel agent preparing a vacation for a family interested in visiting battle sites of the Civil War and Civil War museums in the United States. Search the Internet to find such sites. Using this information, prepare a brochure on the sites.

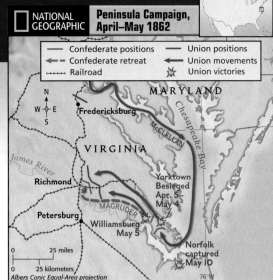

NATIONAL GEOGRAPHIC

Peninsula Campaign, April–May 1862

Confederate positions — Union positions
Confederate retreat — Union movements
Railroad — Union victories

MARYLAND
Fredericksburg
McCLELLAN
Chesapeake Bay
James River
VIRGINIA
Richmond
Yorktown Besieged Apr. 5–May 4
Petersburg
MAGRUDER
Williamsburg May 5
Norfolk captured May 10

0   25 miles
0   25 kilometers
Albers Conic Equal-Area projection
76°W

Geography and History

22. The map above shows the Peninsula Campaign of 1862. Study the map and answer the questions below.

a. Interpreting Maps How did McClellan move his troops to the southern end of the peninsula?

b. Applying Geography Skills What disadvantages did both armies face while fighting on the peninsula?

Bonus Question ?

Ask: Why did Sherman's men want to "wreak vengeance upon South Carolina" after they had marched through Georgia? *(Many people believed South Carolina had started the Civil War by seceding from the Union first and by firing the first shots of the war upon Fort Sumter.)*

Writing Activity

20. Students' points of view in their articles should clearly indicate whether they are writing from a Northern or Southern perspective.

Chapter Activity

21. Brochures should include useful information about the sites including such things as major points of interest, historical significance, and directions on how to reach the site.

Geography and History

22. a. by water; **b.** Being surrounded by water meant the troops could only advance or retreat.

Timesaving Tools

TeacherWorks™ All-In-One Planner and Resource Center

- **Interactive Teacher Edition** Access your Teacher Wraparound Edition and your classroom resources with a few easy clicks.
- **Interactive Lesson Planner** Planning has never been easier! Organize your week, month, semester, or year with all the lesson helps you need to make teaching creative, timely, and relevant.

Use Glencoe's **Presentation Plus!** multimedia teacher tool to easily present dynamic lessons that visually excite your students. Using Microsoft PowerPoint® you can customize the presentations to create your own personalized lessons.

TEACHING TRANSPARENCIES

Graphic Organizer 12

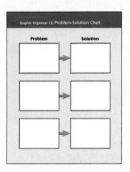

Why It Matters Chapter Transparency 12

APPLICATION AND ENRICHMENT

Linking Past and Present Activity 12

Enrichment Activity 12

Primary Source Reading 12

REVIEW AND REINFORCEMENT

Reteaching Activity 12

Vocabulary Activity 12

Time Line Activity 12

Critical Thinking Skills Activity 12

Meeting NCSS Standards

The following standards are highlighted in Chapter 12:

Section 1	V	Individuals, Groups, and Institutions: B, C, D, F
Section 2	X	Civic Ideals and Practices: A, B, C, F, H
Section 3	V	Individuals, Groups, and Institutions: A, B, C, G
Section 4	VII	Production, Distribution, and Consumption: A, D, E, F

Local Standards

_____

_____

_____

_____

Chapter 12 Test Form A

Chapter 12 Test Form B

Standardized Test Skills Practice Workbook Activity 12

Performance Assessment Activities and Rubrics 12

ExamView® Pro Testmaker CD-ROM

MULTIMEDIA

- Vocabulary PuzzleMaker CD-ROM
- Interactive Tutor Self-Assessment CD-ROM
- ExamView® Pro Testmaker CD-ROM
- Audio Program
- American History Primary Source Documents Library CD-ROM
- MindJogger Videoquiz
- Presentation Plus! CD-ROM
- TeacherWorks™ CD-ROM
- Interactive Student Edition CD-ROM
- Glencoe Skillbuilder Interactive Workbook CD-ROM, Level 2
- The *American Vision* Video Program
- American Music: Hits Through History
- American Music: Cultural Traditions

The following videotape program is available from Glencoe as a supplement to Chapter 12:

- **Ku Klux Klan: A Secret History** (ISBN 0-76-700878-2)

To order, call Glencoe at 1-800-334-7344. To find classroom resources to accompany many of these videos, check the following home pages:
A&E Television: www.aande.com
The History Channel: www.historychannel.com

SPANISH RESOURCES

The following Spanish language materials are available in the Spanish Resources Binder:

- Spanish Guided Reading Activities
- Spanish Reteaching Activities
- Spanish Quizzes and Tests
- Spanish Vocabulary Activities
- Spanish Summaries
- The Declaration of Independence and United States Constitution Spanish Translation

Use our Web site for additional resources. All essential content is covered in the Student Edition.

You and your students can visit tav.glencoe.com, the Web site companion to the *American Vision.* This innovative integration of electronic and print media offers your students a wealth of opportunities. The student text directs students to the Web site for the following options:

- **Chapter Overviews**   • **Student Web Activities**
- **Self-Check Quizzes**   • **Textbook Updates**

Answers to the student Web activities are provided for you in the **Web Activity Lesson Plans.** Additional Web resources and Interactive Tutor Puzzles are also available.

SECTION RESOURCES

Daily Objectives	Reproducible Resources	Multimedia Resources
SECTION 1 **Reconstruction Plans** 1. Contrast Lincoln's plan to reunite the nation with that of the Radical Republicans. 2. Discuss life in the South immediately after the war.	📁 Reproducible Lesson Plan 12–1 📁 Daily Lecture and Discussion Notes 12–1 📁 Guided Reading Activity 12–1* 📁 Section Quiz 12–1* 📁 Reading Essentials and Study Guide 12–1 📁 Performance Assessment Activities and Rubrics 📁 Supreme Court Case Studies	🖐 Daily Focus Skills Transparency 12–1 💿 Interactive Tutor Self-Assessment CD-ROM 💿 ExamView® Pro Testmaker CD-ROM 💿 Presentation Plus! CD-ROM 💿 TeacherWorks™ CD-ROM 💿 Skillbuilder Interactive Workbook, Level 2 🎧 Audio Program
SECTION 2 **Congressional Reconstruction** 1. Analyze the Reconstruction dispute between President Johnson and Congress. 2. Describe the major features of congressional Reconstruction.	📁 Reproducible Lesson Plan 12–2 📁 Daily Lecture and Discussion Notes 12–2 📁 Guided Reading Activity 12–2* 📁 Section Quiz 12–2* 📁 Reading Essentials and Study Guide 12–2 📁 Performance Assessment Activities and Rubrics	🖐 Daily Focus Skills Transparency 12–2 💿 Interactive Tutor Self-Assessment CD-ROM 💿 ExamView® Pro Testmaker CD-ROM 💿 Presentation Plus! CD-ROM 💿 TeacherWorks™ CD-ROM 🎧 Audio Program
SECTION 3 **Republican Rule** 1. Discuss Republican rule in the South during Reconstruction. 2. Describe how African Americans worked to improve their lives.	📁 Reproducible Lesson Plan 12–3 📁 Daily Lecture and Discussion Notes 12–3 📁 Guided Reading Activity 12–3* 📁 Section Quiz 12–3* 📁 Reading Essentials and Study Guide 12–3 📁 Performance Assessment Activities and Rubrics 📁 Interpreting Political Cartoons	🖐 Daily Focus Skills Transparency 12–3 💿 Interactive Tutor Self-Assessment CD-ROM 💿 ExamView® Pro Testmaker CD-ROM 💿 Presentation Plus! CD-ROM 💿 TeacherWorks™ CD-ROM 🎧 Audio Program 🎵 American Music: Cultural Traditions
SECTION 4 **Reconstruction Collapses** 1. Discuss the policies and problems of Grant's administration. 2. Explain how Reconstruction ended, and contrast the New South and the Old South.	📁 Reproducible Lesson Plan 12–4 📁 Daily Lecture and Discussion Notes 12–4 📁 Guided Reading Activity 12–4* 📁 Section Quiz 12–4* 📁 Reading Essentials and Study Guide 12–4 📁 Performance Assessment Activities and Rubrics	🖐 Daily Focus Skills Transparency 12–4 💿 Interactive Tutor Self-Assessment CD-ROM 💿 ExamView® Pro Testmaker CD-ROM 💿 Presentation Plus! CD-ROM 💿 TeacherWorks™ CD-ROM 💿 Vocabulary PuzzleMaker CD-ROM 🎧 Audio Program

 OUT OF TIME?
Assign the Chapter 12 **Reading Essentials and Study Guide.** 📁

*Also Available in Spanish

📁 Blackline Master   🖐 Transparency   💿 CD-ROM   💿 DVD

📕 Poster   🎵 Music Program   🎧 Audio Program   📼 Videocassette

Chapter 12 Resources

NATIONAL GEOGRAPHIC Teacher's Corner

INDEX TO NATIONAL GEOGRAPHIC MAGAZINE

The following articles relate to this chapter.
- "The Cruelest Commerce: African Slave Trade," September 1992

NATIONAL GEOGRAPHIC SOCIETY PRODUCTS AVAILABLE FROM GLENCOE

To order the following products for use with this chapter, contact your local Glencoe sales representative, or call Glencoe at 1-800-334-7344:
- *Picture Atlas of the World* (CD-ROM)
- *PicturePack: The Civil War* (Transparencies)
- *PictureShow: The Civil War* (CD-ROM)
- *PictureShow: The Westward Movement* (CD-ROM)
- *PictureShow: The Westward Movement* (Transparencies)

ADDITIONAL NATIONAL GEOGRAPHIC SOCIETY PRODUCTS

To order the following, call National Geographic at 1-800-368-2728:
- *Heritage of the Black West* (Video)

NGS ONLINE

Access National Geographic's Web site for current events, atlas updates, activities, links, interactive features, and archives.
www.nationalgeographic.com

From the Classroom of…

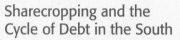

Al Cate
Central High School
Memphis, TN

Sharecropping and the Cycle of Debt in the South

To help students understand the issue of sharecropping and debt peonage in the South, tell them this story about Big Daddy and Jim Brown.

"Jim Brown and his wife bring their eight children to Cateville to sharecrop 40 acres of Big Daddy's land. Big Daddy loans Jim one mule, tools, and seed. Jim will receive one-third of the profits from the crop, and credit at Big Daddy's store. The deal sounds good so Jim puts his X on the contract.

"Because Jim Brown cannot avoid the inflated store prices and never knows what his profit from the crop will be, he goes deeper and deeper into debt. After the harvest, Brown goes to receive his money. Big Daddy merely hands Brown a bill for $100 and asks, 'How do you want to settle accounts?'"

Discuss Brown's options with students. Ask them to find the flaws in the contract between the two men.

ADDITIONAL RESOURCES FROM GLENCOE

- American Music: Cultural Traditions
- American Art & Architecture
- Outline Map Resource Book
- U.S. Desk Map
- Building Geography Skills for Life
- Inclusion for the High School Social Studies Classroom Strategies and Activities
- Teaching Strategies for the American History Classroom (Including Block Scheduling Pacing Guides)

KEY TO ABILITY LEVELS

Teaching strategies have been coded.

L1 BASIC activities for all students
L2 AVERAGE activities for average to above-average students
L3 CHALLENGING activities for above-average students
ELL ENGLISH LANGUAGE LEARNER activities

 Block Schedule

Activities that are suited to use within the block scheduling framework are identified by:

CHAPTER

12 Reconstruction
1865–1877

Why It Matters

The nation faced difficult problems after the Civil War. The first issue was how to bring the South back into the Union. Lincoln had wanted to make reunion relatively easy. After he died, Congress designed a plan that focused on punishing the South and ensuring that African Americans had the right to vote. These policies increased hostility between the regions. Pressures on the South to reform eased with the Compromise of 1877.

The Impact Today

The Reconstruction era has permanently affected American society.
- The Fourteenth and Fifteenth Amendments provide constitutional protections for all Americans.
- The Radical Republicans' rule so antagonized the South that the region remained solidly Democratic for nearly a century.

 The American Vision Video The Chapter 12 video, "The Aftermath of War," chronicles the struggles of the nation to heal itself after the Civil War.

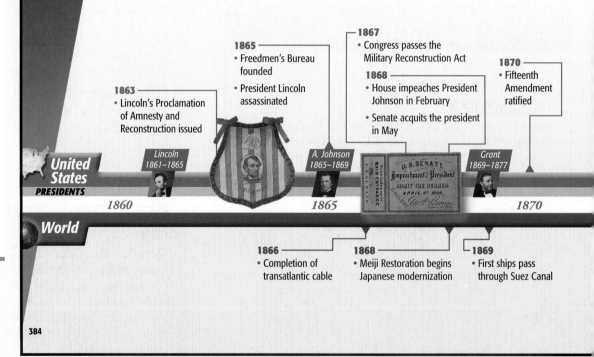

United States PRESIDENTS

1863
- Lincoln's Proclamation of Amnesty and Reconstruction issued

Lincoln 1861–1865

1865
- Freedmen's Bureau founded
- President Lincoln assassinated

A. Johnson 1865–1869

1867
- Congress passes the Military Reconstruction Act

1868
- House impeaches President Johnson in February
- Senate acquits the president in May

Grant 1869–1877

1870
- Fifteenth Amendment ratified

1860   1865   1870

World

1866
- Completion of transatlantic cable

1868
- Meiji Restoration begins Japanese modernization

1869
- First ships pass through Suez Canal

384

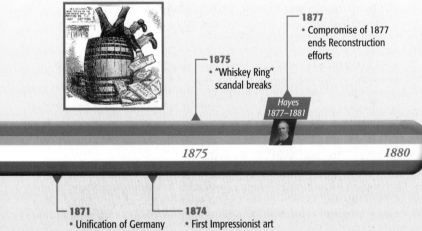

Upland Cotton by Winslow Homer shows that even after emancipation, many African Americans continued working long hours in the cotton fields.

HISTORY Online

Introduce students to chapter content and key terms by having them access the **Chapter 12 Overview** at tav.glencoe.com.

More About the Art

Background: Winslow Homer worked for *Harper's* magazine during the Civil War. He painted and sketched images of daily life in military camps in Virginia. About ten years after the war ended, the New England native returned to Virginia to study the life of rural African Americans. The result was a realistic portrayal of African Americans contrasting dramatically with the unflattering images created by many of his contemporaries.
Ask: Why do you think African Americans continued to work in cotton fields after emancipation?
(Students' answers will vary. A possible answer is that many African Americans had no other skills.)

1877
• Compromise of 1877 ends Reconstruction efforts

1875
• "Whiskey Ring" scandal breaks

Hayes 1877–1881

1875   1880

1871
• Unification of Germany completed; German Empire proclaimed

1874
• First Impressionist art exhibit opens in Paris

HISTORY Online

Chapter Overview
Visit the *American Vision* Web site at tav.glencoe.com and click on *Chapter Overviews—Chapter 12* to preview chapter information.

385

TIME LINE ACTIVITY

Have students duplicate the time line that appears on pages 384–385 and demonstrate their ability to use relative chronology by adding the following information to the time line.

• Alfred Nobel develops dynamite, 1866

• Mathematician Lewis Carroll writes *Alice's Adventures in Wonderland,* 1865

• Impressionists, including Cézanne, Degas, Monet, and Renoir, exhibit their work in Paris, 1874

• Queen Victoria becomes Empress of India, 1877

• Zanzibar closes public slave market, 1873

GRAPHIC ORGANIZER ACTIVITY

Organizing Information Have students use a graphic organizer similar to the one shown below to help them remember the various pieces of legislation related to Reconstruction. Students' organizers will be more extensive than what is shown here.

Year	Legislation	Major Provision
1866	Civil Rights Act of 1866	granted citizenship to all persons born in the U.S. except Native Americans
1867	Military Reconstruction Act	divided the former Confederacy except Tennessee into five military districts
1868	Fourteenth Amendment	granted citizenship to all persons born or naturalized in the U.S.

1 FOCUS

Section Overview

This section focuses on the plans to rebuild and reunite the nation following the Civil War.

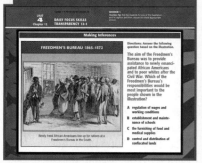
Guide to Reading

Answers to Graphic: Lincoln's plan: When 10 percent of a state's voters in the 1860 presidential election took an oath of loyalty to the United States and accepted the Union's proclamations concerning slavery, they could organize a new state government; Radical Republicans' Plan: Under the Wade-Davis Bill, a majority of white men in each Confederate state had to take a loyalty oath. Then each state had to hold a constitutional convention, abolish slavery, reject Confederate debts, and deny former Confederate leaders the right to hold office.

Preteaching Vocabulary
Have students write a brief explanation for each of the Key Terms and Names.

Guide to Reading

Main Idea
In the months after the Civil War, the nation began the effort to rebuild and reunite.

Key Terms and Names
Reconstruction, amnesty, Thaddeus Stevens, Radical Republicans, Wade-Davis Bill, pocket veto, freedmen, Freedmen's Bureau

Reading Strategy
Organizing As you read, complete a graphic organizer similar to the one below to compare plans for readmitting Southern states to the Union.

Reading Objectives
• **Contrast** Lincoln's plan to reunite the nation with that of the Radical Republicans
• **Discuss** life in the South immediately after the war.

Section Theme
Groups and Institutions Northerners disagreed on which policies would best rebuild the South and safeguard the rights of African Americans.

Preview of Events

♦1863	♦1864	♦1865	♦1866
1863 Lincoln issues Proclamation of Amnesty and Reconstruction	**1864** Congress passes Wade-Davis Bill	**March 1865** Freedmen's Bureau founded / **April 1865** Lincoln assassinated	**1866** Congress passes Fourteenth Amendment

---

★ *An American Story* ★

Artist's depiction of an emancipated African American

Houston Holloway was ready for freedom. By 1865 the 20-year-old enslaved man had toiled under three different slaveholders. President Lincoln's Emancipation Proclamation, delivered in 1863, had freed him—but only in theory. The proclamation freed enslaved persons in the Confederacy, but because the Union could not enforce its laws in Confederate territory, many African Americans in the South continued to endure a life of bondage. Holloway knew that his only hope was a Northern victory in the Civil War.

Freedom finally came in the spring of 1865 when Union troops overran his community in Georgia. Holloway rejoiced upon being freed:

❝I felt like a bird out of a cage. Amen. Amen. Amen. I could hardly ask to feel better than I did that day. . . . The week passed off in a blaze of glory.❞

—quoted in *A Short History of Reconstruction*

The Reconstruction Battle Begins

Houston Holloway and millions like him faced freedom in a devastated South. By 1865 large areas of the former Confederacy lay in ruins. A traveler on a railroad journey through the South described the region as a "desolated land," adding, "Every village and station we stopped at presented an array of ruined walls and chimneys standing useless and solitary." ·

Union troops and cannons had left few Southern cities untouched. Describing Columbia, the capital of South Carolina, a Northern reporter noted, "Two-thirds of the

---

buildings in the place were burned, including . . . everything in the business portion. Not a store, office, or shop escaped."

The devastation had left the South's economy in a state of collapse. The value of land had fallen significantly. Confederate money was worthless. Roughly two-thirds of the transportation system lay in ruins, with dozens of bridges destroyed and miles of railroad twisted and rendered useless.

Most dramatically of all, the emancipation of African Americans had thrown the agricultural system into chaos. Until the South developed a new system to replace enslaved labor, it could not maintain its agricultural output.

The president and Congress grappled with the difficult task of Reconstruction, or rebuilding after the war. They had to decide under what terms and conditions the former Confederate states would rejoin the Union.

Thaddeus Stevens

Lincoln's Plan
The problem of how to bring the Southern states back into the Union began shortly after the Civil War started. As Union forces advanced into Tennessee, Arkansas, and Louisiana in 1862, President Lincoln appointed military governors for the regions under Union control. He also began developing a plan for restoring a regular government in those states.

Lincoln wanted a moderate policy that would reconcile the South with the Union instead of punishing it for treason. In December 1863, he set forth his plan in the Proclamation of Amnesty and Reconstruction. He offered a general amnesty, or pardon, to all Southerners who took an oath of loyalty to the United States and accepted the Union's proclamations concerning slavery. When 10 percent of a state's voters in the 1860 presidential election had taken this oath, they could organize a new state government.

The Radical Republicans
Resistance to Lincoln's plan surfaced at once among the more radical Republicans in Congress. Led by Representative **Thaddeus Stevens** of Pennsylvania and Senator Charles Sumner of Massachusetts, the radicals did not want to reconcile with the South. They wanted, in Stevens's words, to "revolutionize Southern institutions, habits, and manners."

The **Radical Republicans** had three main goals. First, they wanted to prevent the leaders of the Confederacy from returning to power after the war. Second, they wanted the Republican Party to become a powerful institution in the South. Third, they wanted the federal government to help African Americans achieve political equality by guaranteeing their right to vote in the South.

Congressional Republicans knew that once the South was restored to the Union, it would gain about 15 seats in the House of Representatives. Before the Civil War, the number of Southern seats in the House was based on the Three-Fifths Compromise in the Constitution. According to this compromise, each enslaved person counted as only three-fifths of a free person. The abolition of slavery entitled the South to more seats in the House of

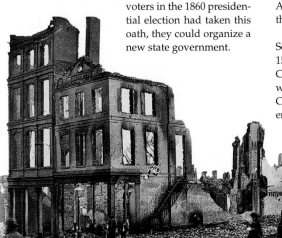

Picturing **History**

War-Shattered City The Civil War wreaked terrible devastation on Richmond, Virginia. Why do you think the women pictured here are dressed in black?

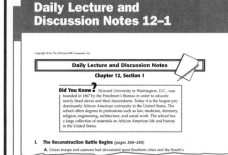
Organizing Information Have students use a graphic similar to the one shown below to identify the Radical Republicans' goals following the Civil War. **L1** ELL

Radical Republican Goals	Prevent leaders of Confederacy from returning to power
	Make Republican Party a powerful institution in the South
	Help African Americans achieve political equality

Picturing **History**

Answer: They are in mourning, perhaps for relatives who died in the war.
Ask: What do you think these citizens of Richmond may have been feeling? *(possible answers—defeated, angry, determined, hopeless)*

FYI

In addition to the devastation of Southern cities, the war brought even greater disruption to the countryside. Southern cotton production, the mainstay of the Southern economy, did not reach its 1860 levels again until 1879.

📁 Use *Supreme Court Case Study 6,* Ex Parte Milligan.

COOPERATIVE LEARNING ACTIVITY

Summarizing Information Organize the class into groups of four or five students. Have each group hold a roundtable discussion on the strengths and weaknesses of the North and of the South and how their strategies compensated for or took advantage of these strengths and weaknesses. Students should summarize their conclusions. A recorder for the group should write the summaries and present them to the class. 📓

Use the rubric for a cooperative group management plan on pages 81–82 in the *Performance Assessment Activities and Rubrics.*

NATIONAL GEOGRAPHIC
MOMENT in HISTORY

Since most formerly enslaved persons had not been allowed to learn to read or write, it was not uncommon for grandparents and parents to attend classes with their grandchildren and children so that both could learn basic literacy skills.

Guided Reading Activity 12–1

Name _____ Date _____ Class _____

★ Guided Reading Activity 12-1

DIRECTIONS: **Recalling Facts** Read the section and answer the questions below. Refer to your textbook to write the answers.

1. What was the condition of the South in 1865? _____
2. What were the elements of the economic chaos in the South after the war? _____
3. What was the purpose of Reconstruction? _____
4. When did the problem of how to bring the Southern states back into the Union begin? _____
5. How did Lincoln want the North and the South reunited? _____

Making a List Have students read the quote on this page. Then have students make a list of the things a free person can do according to Henry Wilson. Then have students add to the list other freedoms that they think freed African Americans may have valued. **Ask: If you had been enslaved, which of the freedoms on our list would you have valued most? Why? L1**

FYI

Benjamin Franklin Wade was a U.S. senator from Ohio. Henry Winter Davis was elected to the House of Representatives from Maryland.

3 ASSESS

Assign Section 1 Assessment as homework or as an in-class activity.

● Have students use the **Interactive Tutor Self-Assessment CD-ROM.**

NATIONAL GEOGRAPHIC
MOMENT in HISTORY

WINDS OF CHANGE
Two formerly enslaved women in the rural, postwar South share a treasure that was once forbidden to them—a book. Before the Civil War, it was illegal in some states to teach an enslaved person to read and write. Despite the well-intentioned efforts of some federal officials during Reconstruction, the education of African Americans continued to be an issue after the war. In 1865 only about 10 percent of African Americans could read. By 1880 more than 25 percent were considered literate and around 40 percent of African American children were enrolled in school.

Representatives. This would endanger Republican control of Congress, unless Republicans could find a way to protect African Americans' voting rights.

Although Radical Republicans knew that giving African Americans in the South the right to vote would help their party win elections, most were not acting cynically. Many had been abolitionists before the Civil War and had pushed Lincoln into making emancipation a goal of the war. They believed in a right to political equality for all Americans, regardless of their race. Senator Henry Wilson of Massachusetts summarized their position by saying:

> 66 [Congress] must see to it that the man made free by the Constitution is a freeman indeed; that he can go where he pleases, work when and for whom he pleases . . . go into schools and educate himself and his children; that the rights and guarantees of the common law are his, and that he walks the earth proud and erect in the conscious dignity of a free man. 99

388 CHAPTER 12 Reconstruction

The Wade-Davis Bill Caught between Lincoln and the Radical Republicans was a large number of moderate Republicans. The moderates thought Lincoln was being too lenient, but they also thought the radicals were going too far in their support for African Americans.

By the summer of 1864, the moderates and radicals had come up with a Reconstruction plan that they could both support as an alternative to Lincoln's and introduced it in Congress as the **Wade-Davis Bill.** This bill required the majority of the adult white men in a former Confederate state to take an oath of allegiance to the Union. The state could then hold a constitutional convention to create a new state government. Each state's convention would then have to abolish slavery, reject all debts the state had acquired as part of the Confederacy, and deprive all former Confederate government officials and military officers of the right to vote or hold office.

Although Congress passed the Wade-Davis Bill, Lincoln blocked it with a pocket veto, that is, he let the session of Congress expire without signing the

MEETING SPECIAL NEEDS

Auditory/Musical Immediately after students read this section, lead a discussion about the Reconstruction plans of President Lincoln and Congress. Tell students that you will be using some important terms from the text. Have students write each term they hear that also appeared in the text. Suggested terms include: Reconstruction, amnesty, Radical Republicans, Wade-Davis Bill, and pocket veto. **L1**

📁 Refer to *Inclusion for the High School Social Studies Classroom Strategies and Activities* in the TCR.

legislation. Although Lincoln sympathized with some of the radical goals, he felt that imposing a harsh peace would be counterproductive. The president wanted "no persecution, no bloody work."

✓ **Reading Check** **Summarizing** Why did President Lincoln favor a generous policy toward the South after the end of the Civil War?

The Freedmen's Bureau

Lincoln realized that harsh Reconstruction terms would only alienate many whites in the South. Also, the South was already in chaos. The devastation of the war and the collapse of the economy left hundreds of thousands of people unemployed, homeless, and hungry. At the same time, the victorious Union armies had to contend with the large numbers of African Americans who flocked to Union lines as the war progressed. As Sherman marched through Georgia and South Carolina, thousands of freed African Americans—now known as freedmen—began following his troops seeking food and shelter.

To help the freed people feed themselves, Sherman reserved all abandoned plantation land within 30 miles of the coast from Charleston, South Carolina, to Jacksonville, Florida, for use by freed African Americans. Over the next few months, Union troops settled more than 40,000 African Americans on roughly half a million acres of land in South Carolina and Georgia.

The refugee crisis prompted Congress to establish the Bureau of Refugees, Freedmen, and Abandoned Lands—better known as the **Freedmen's Bureau.**

The Bureau was given the task of feeding and clothing war refugees in the South using surplus army supplies. Beginning in September 1865, the Bureau issued nearly 30,000 rations a day for the next year. Its activities helped prevent mass starvation in the South.

The Bureau also helped formerly enslaved people find work on plantations. It negotiated labor contracts with planters, specifying the amount of pay workers would receive and the number of hours they had to work. It also established special courts to deal with grievances between workers and planters.

Although many people in the North applauded the Bureau's efforts, they argued those who were formerly enslaved should be given "forty acres and a mule" to support themselves. These people believed that the federal government should seize Confederate land and distribute it to emancipated African Americans. To others, however, taking land from plantation owners and giving it to freedmen seemed to violate the nation's commitment to individual property rights. Ultimately, Congress refused to support land confiscation.

Although the Freedmen's Bureau failed to provide African Americans with land to make a new start, it did make a lasting and important contribution in the field of education. The Bureau worked closely with Northern charities to educate formerly enslaved African Americans. It provided housing for schools, paid teachers, and helped to establish colleges for training African American teachers.

✓ **Reading Check** **Explaining** What were the purposes of the Freedmen's Bureau?

✓ **Reading Check**

Answer: He wanted to reconcile the South with the Union instead of punishing Southerners.

Reading Essentials and Study Guide 12–1

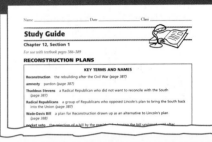

Section Quiz 12–1

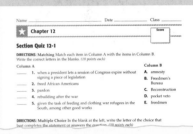

✓ **Reading Check**

Answer: to help with the refugee problem created by the war

Reteach
Contrast Lincoln's plan to reunite the nation with that of the Radical Republicans.

Enrich
Have interested students write a report about the successes and failures of the Freedmen's Bureau.

SECTION 1 ASSESSMENT

Checking for Understanding

1. **Define:** Reconstruction, amnesty, pocket veto, freedmen.
2. **Identify:** Thaddeus Stevens, Radical Republicans, Wade-Davis Bill, Freedmen's Bureau.
3. **Explain** why the efforts to provide African Americans with their own land failed.

Reviewing Themes

4. **Groups and Institutions** What services did the Freedmen's Bureau provide to Southern refugees and to newly freed people?

Critical Thinking

5. **Analyzing** What are the benefits of a compromise such as the Wade-Davis Bill to a government? What are the drawbacks?
6. **Categorizing** Use a graphic organizer similar to the one below to list the effects of the Civil War on the South.

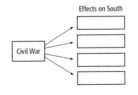

Effects on South

Civil War

Analyzing Visuals

7. **Examining Photographs** Study the National Geographic photograph of formerly enslaved women on the previous page. How would you describe the women's environment? Do you think there were other books in the house?

Writing About History

8. **Descriptive Writing** Take on the role of a Southerner after the Civil War. Write a journal entry describing the postwar South and what you hope the future will hold for the South.

CHAPTER 12   Reconstruction   389

SECTION 1 ASSESSMENT ANSWERS

1. Terms are in blue.
2. Thaddeus Stevens (p. 387), Radical Republicans (p. 387), Wade-Davis Bill (p. 388), Freedmen's Bureau (p. 389)
3. Confiscation of land violated individual property rights.
4. food, clothing, and education
5. It broke the impasse between the radicals and the moderates. However, it created a bill that Lincoln did not support and used the pocket veto to kill it.
6. Cities were in ruins; the transportation system was destroyed; money was worthless; and the agricultural system was in chaos.
7. poor, crude dwelling; probably no other books or other reading matter
8. Students' journal entries will vary. Entries should express feelings from the point of view of a Southerner.

4 CLOSE

Discuss life in the South immediately after the war.

TEACH

Interpreting Political Cartoons

Tell students that political cartoons have long been used as an effective means of expressing opinions about events, laws, and political figures.

Bring several current political cartoons from local or national newspapers to class. Ask students to identify and interpret the caricatures and symbols used in the cartoon. Have students write a sentence summarizing the point being made by each of the political cartoonists.

Additional Practice

Reinforcing Skills Activity 12

Name _____ Date _____ Class _____

| Reinforcing Skills Activity 12 |

Interpreting Political Cartoons

☐ LEARNING THE SKILL

Political cartoons reflect opinions on current events, so they are a good resource for interpreting history. Political cartoonists use caricatures and symbols to create positive or negative impressions of events and people. To interpret a political cartoon, make a note of the title and any labels or messages included. Evaluate how the cartoonist presents the characters and their relationships, and look for symbols to help determine the cartoonist's point of view.

☐ PRACTICING THE SKILL

DIRECTIONS: Study the political cartoon below, and then answer the questions that follow on a separate sheet of paper.

1. What symbols do...

GLENCOE
TECHNOLOGY

CD-ROM
Glencoe Skillbuilder Interactive Workbook CD-ROM, Level 2

This interactive CD-ROM reinforces student mastery of essential social studies skills.

Interpreting Political Cartoons

Why Learn This Skill?

Do you enjoy reading the comics section in the newspaper? Many people enjoy reading comic strips. Cartoons also appear on the editorial page. These cartoons express opinions on political issues. Political cartoons are good sources of historical information because they reflect opinions on current events.

Learning the Skill

Political cartoonists rely mostly on images to communicate a message. By using *caricatures* and *symbols*, political cartoonists help readers see relationships and draw conclusions about events. A caricature exaggerates a detail, such as a subject's features, in a drawing. Cartoonists use caricature to create a positive or negative impression of a subject. For example, if a cartoon shows one figure three times larger than another, it implies that the larger figure is more powerful than the smaller one or perhaps is a bully.

A symbol is an image or object that represents something else. For example, a cartoonist may use a crown to represent a monarch. Symbols often represent nations or political parties. The bald eagle and Uncle Sam are common symbols for the

United States, a bear often stands for Russia, and a dragon might be used to represent China.

To analyze a political cartoon, first identify the topic and main characters. Then read labels and messages and note relationships between the figures and

symbols. Review your knowledge of the cartoon's topic to determine the cartoonist's viewpoint and message.

Practicing the Skill

The political cartoon on this page, published in an 1872 newspaper, makes a statement about the Reconstruction years. After the Civil War, Southerners gave the nickname "carpetbaggers" to Northerners who moved South. Southerners claimed Northerners came with nothing but a small bag made from carpet fabric, ready to gain wealth at Southerners' expense. Study the cartoon, and then answer the following questions.

❶ The figure at the top is President Ulysses S. Grant. What symbols are surrounding him? What do these symbols represent? Why do you think Grant is placed among them?

❷ In what symbol is Grant sitting? What might this object represent?

❸ What symbols depict the North? How are they shown? What does their appearance imply about the North's feelings about Reconstruction?

❹ Summarize the cartoonist's opinion of Reconstruction and explain why you agree or disagree with this point of view.

Skills Assessment

Complete the Practicing Skills questions on page 409 and the Chapter 12 Skill Reinforcement Activity to assess your mastery of this skill.

Applying the Skill

Interpreting Political Cartoons Find a political cartoon in a newspaper or magazine. If an editorial appears with the cartoon, read that as well. Write a summary of the cartoon's message and explain whether or not you agree with this message.

 Glencoe's **Skillbuilder Interactive Workbook CD-ROM, Level 2,** provides instruction and practice in key social studies skills.

ANSWERS TO PRACTICING THE SKILL

❶ Grant is surrounded by weapons. This symbolizes military rule. Grant is among them because he is president.

❷ a carpet bag; that the North is forcing its rule on the South

❸ soldiers, weapons, carpet bag; It implies the North has conquered the South and is exploiting it.

❹ The cartoonist implies that Reconstruction hurt Southerners.

Applying the Skill

Students' answers will vary. Ask students to explain the caricatures and symbols used in the cartoon.

Guide to Reading

Main Idea
Dissatisfied with the president's lenient policies toward the South, Congress seized control of Reconstruction.

Key Terms and Names
black codes, Civil Rights Act, Fourteenth Amendment, Military Reconstruction Act, Tenure of Office Act, impeach

Reading Strategy
Categorizing As you read about Reconstruction, complete a graphic organizer like the one below to show how each piece of legislation listed affected African Americans.

Legislation	Effect
black codes	
Civil Rights Act of 1866	
Fourteenth Amendment	
Fifteenth Amendment	

Reading Objectives
• **Analyze** the Reconstruction dispute between President Johnson and Congress.
• **Describe** the major features of congressional Reconstruction.

Section Theme
Civic Rights and Responsibilities Congressional Reconstruction promoted civil rights for formerly enslaved persons.

Preview of Events

♦1866   ♦1868   ♦1870

1866
Congress passes
Fourteenth Amendment

1867
Congress passes
Reconstruction Act

1868
House impeaches President Johnson;
Senate acquits Johnson

1870
States ratify Fifteenth
Amendment

★ An American Story ★

Charles Sumner

Tensions ran high in the nation's capital as Congress reconvened in December 1865. President Andrew Johnson had implemented his Reconstruction plan, which was lenient toward the South, despite strong opposition by many members of Congress. One of the more vocal critics was Massachusetts senator Charles Sumner. Sumner advocated greater rights for formerly enslaved people and stronger punishment for the South. Just days before Christmas, Sumner expressed his distrust of the former Confederate states:

❝They will continue to assert the inferiority of the African, and they would today, if possible, precipitate the United States into a foreign war, believing that they could then reassert and obtain their independence. . . . On the whole, looking at the affair from all sides, it amounts to just this: If the Northern people are content to be ruled over by the Southerners, they will continue in the Union, if not, the first chance they get they will rise again.❞

—quoted in *Charles Sumner*

Johnson Takes Office

Lincoln's assassination dramatically changed the politics of Reconstruction. Lincoln's vice president, Andrew Johnson, now became president. Johnson had been a Democrat living in Tennessee before the Civil War. He had served as a mayor and state legislator before being elected to the United States Senate. When Tennessee seceded from the

CHAPTER 12 Reconstruction **391**

---

1 FOCUS

Section Overview
This section focuses on the Congressional plans for Reconstruction.

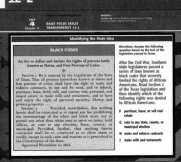
Guide to Reading

Answers to Graphic: Black codes severely limited rights of African Americans in the South; Civil Rights Act of 1866 allowed African Americans to own property, and stated that they were to be treated equally in court; Fourteenth Amendment protected due process and guaranteed all people equal protection of the laws; Fifteenth Amendment guaranteed the right to vote.

Preteaching Vocabulary
Have students make a list of the Key Terms and Names and add a person's name, date, or phrase to clarify the significance of the terms and names.

SECTION RESOURCES

📂 **Reproducible Masters**
• Reproducible Lesson Plan 12–2
• Daily Lecture and Discussion Notes 12–2
• Guided Reading Activity 12–2
• Section Quiz 12–2
• Reading Essentials and Study Guide 12–2
• Performance Assessment Activities and Rubrics

🖨 **Transparencies**
• Daily Focus Skills Transparency 12–2

Multimedia
💿 Interactive Tutor Self-Assessment CD-ROM
💿 ExamView® Pro Testmaker CD-ROM
💿 Presentation Plus! CD-ROM
💿 TeacherWorks™ CD-ROM
🎧 Audio Program

2 TEACH

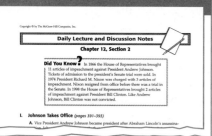
Identifying Absolute Chronology Write the title "Reconstruction During Andrew Johnson's Presidency" on the board. Below the title, draw a time line and write "1865" at one end and "1868" at the other. Call on volunteers to come to the board and enter the major events in the process of Reconstruction during these years. Ask students to use information on the time line to write a chronological summary of Reconstruction up to the presidential election of 1868. **L2**

Why It Matters

The Fourteenth Amendment was proposed on June 13, 1866. The ratification process finally was completed in July 1868. Even after the ratification process was completed, states continued to ratify the amendment. On March 18, 1976, Kentucky finally ratified the amendment 109 years after initially rejecting it.

Ask: What are the three main provisions of the Fourteenth Amendment? *(1. Grants citizenship to all persons born or naturalized in the United States. 2. Forbids states from depriving any person of life, liberty, or property without due process of law. 3. Provides equal protection of the law.)*

Why It Matters

The Fourteenth Amendment

Key provisions of the Fourteenth Amendment (1868) made all persons born in the United States citizens of both the nation and the state where they resided. States were prohibited from abridging the rights of citizenship or depriving persons of due process and equal protection of the law. The Supreme Court has often cited the Fourteenth Amendment when reviewing whether state or federal laws and actions violate the Constitution. The Court continues to do so today.

1954 — In *Brown* v. *Board of Education,* the Court found that segregated education denied minority school-children like Linda Brown (far left) the equal protection of the laws provided by the Fourteenth Amendment. This decision partially reversed *Plessy* v. *Ferguson.*

Testing the Fourteenth Amendment

♦ 1896   ♦ 1954

1896 — In *Plessy* v. *Ferguson,* the Supreme Court decided that Jim Crow laws—state-mandated segregation of public facilities such as railroad cars—did not violate the Fourteenth Amendment. The Court ruled that separate facilities could be equal and allowed segregation to continue.

FOR COLORED ONLY

Union, Johnson remained loyal and stayed in the Senate, making him a hero in the North.

As Union troops advanced into Tennessee in 1862, Lincoln appointed Johnson military governor of the state. The president then approved Johnson's nomination as vice president in 1864, hoping to convince some Democrats to vote for the Republicans. Johnson was hot-tempered and stubborn at times, but, like Lincoln, he believed that a moderate policy was needed to bring the South back into the Union and to win Southern loyalty.

Johnson's Plan In the summer of 1865, with Congress in recess, Johnson began to implement what he called his restoration program, which closely resembled Lincoln's plan. In late May 1865, he issued a new Proclamation of Amnesty to supplement the one Lincoln had issued earlier. Johnson offered to pardon all former citizens of the Confederacy who took an oath of loyalty to the Union and to return their property. He excluded from the pardon former Confederate officers and officials as well as all former Confederates who owned property worth more than $20,000. These were the people—the rich planter elite—who Johnson believed had caused the Civil War. Those who were excluded could apply to the president individually for a pardon for their acts during the war.

On the same day he issued the Proclamation of Amnesty, Johnson issued another proclamation for North Carolina. This became a model of how he wanted to restore the South to the Union. Under it, each former Confederate state had to call a constitutional convention to revoke its ordinance of secession and ratify the Thirteenth Amendment. The conventions also had to reject all Civil War debts.

The former Confederate states, for the most part, met Johnson's conditions. While the Southern states organized their new governments and elected people to Congress, Johnson began granting pardons to thousands of Southerners.

By the time Congress gathered for its next session in December 1865, Johnson's plan was well underway. Many members of Congress were astonished and angered when they realized that Southern voters had elected to Congress many former Confederate officers and political leaders, including Alexander Stephens, the former vice president of the Confederacy. Many Radical and moderate Republicans found this unacceptable and voted to reject the new Southern members of Congress.

Black Codes The election of former Confederates to Congress was not the only development that angered congressional Republicans. The new Southern state legislatures also passed a series of

392   CHAPTER 12   Reconstruction

COOPERATIVE LEARNING ACTIVITY

Writing a Skit Organize students into several groups to write short skits. Encourage groups to imagine they are members of Congress in 1864 and 1865. Some support President Lincoln's approach to Reconstruction, while others favor the Radical Republicans' approach. Have groups write skits involving a debate in Congress that might have taken place between the two factions. Then call on groups to volunteer to perform their skits for the rest of the class.

Use the rubric for a cooperative group management plan on pages 81–82 in the *Performance Assessment Activities and Rubrics.*

1963
In *Gideon* v. *Wainright,* the Supreme Court ruled that the state of Florida had violated the due process clause when it refused to appoint a lawyer to represent Clarence Gideon (right). The ruling extended the Bill of Rights to state courts.

◆ *1963*   ◆ *2000*

2000
In the disputed presidential race between George W. Bush and Al Gore, the Supreme Court decided a crucial case based on the Fourteenth Amendment. Justices argued that a lack of uniform standards for hand recounts of ballots in Florida would violate the equal protection of all the state's voters. The decision allowed Bush to claim a controversial victory.

laws known as black codes, which severely limited African Americans' rights in the South.

The black codes varied from state to state, but they all seemed intended to keep African Americans in a condition similar to slavery. African Americans were generally required to enter into annual labor contracts. African American children had to accept apprenticeships in some states and could be whipped or beaten while serving in these apprenticeships. Several state codes set specific work hours for African Americans and required them to get licenses to work in non-agricultural jobs.

The black codes enraged many Northerners. Gideon Welles, the secretary of the navy, warned, "The entire South seem to be stupid and vindictive, know not their friends, and are pursuing just the course which their opponents, the Radicals, desire."

✓ **Reading Check** **Summarizing** Who did President Johnson blame for the Civil War?

Radical Republicans Take Control

The election of former Confederates to office and the introduction of the black codes convinced many moderate Republicans to join the radicals in opposing Johnson's Reconstruction policies. In late 1865, House and Senate Republicans created the Joint Committee on Reconstruction. Their goal was to develop their own program for rebuilding the Union.

The Fourteenth Amendment In March 1866, in an effort to override the black codes, Congress passed the **Civil Rights Act** of 1866. The act granted citizenship to all persons born in the United States except Native Americans. It allowed African Americans to own property and stated that they were to be treated equally in court. It also gave the federal government the power to sue people who violated those rights.

Fearing that the Civil Rights Act might be overturned in court, the Republicans introduced the **Fourteenth Amendment** to the Constitution. This amendment granted citizenship to all persons born or naturalized in the United States and declared that no state could deprive any person of life, liberty, or property "without due process of law." It also declared that no state could deny any person "equal protection of the laws."

Increasing violence in the South convinced moderate Republicans to support the amendment. The most dramatic incident occurred in Memphis, Tennessee, in May 1866. White mobs killed 46 African Americans, and burned hundreds of black homes, churches, and schools. Congress passed the amendment in June 1866 and sent it to the states for ratification.

The Election of 1866 President Johnson attacked the Fourteenth Amendment and made it the major issue of the 1866 congressional elections. He hoped Northern voters would turn against the Radical Republicans and elect a new majority in Congress that would support his plan for Reconstruction.

As the election campaign got underway, more violence erupted in the South. In July 1866, a white mob attacked delegates to a convention in New Orleans supporting voting rights for African Americans. As Johnson attacked Radical Republicans, Republicans responded by accusing Democrats of being traitors and starting the Civil War. When the votes were counted, the Republicans achieved an overwhelming victory, winning an approximate a three-to-one majority in Congress.

HISTORY Online
Student Web Activity Visit the *American Vision* Web site at tav.glencoe.com and click on *Student Web Activities— Chapter 12* for an activity on Reconstruction.

Guided Reading Activity 12–2

Name _____ Date _____ Class _____

★ Guided Reading Activity **12-2**

DIRECTIONS: Recording Who, What, When, Where, Why, and How Read the section and answer the questions below. Refer to your textbook to write the answers.

1. When did Abraham Lincoln ask Andrew Johnson to run as vice president? _____
2. What kind of policy did Johnson have toward the South? _____
3. Who was excluded from the Proclamation of Amnesty? _____
4. Why were these people excluded? _____
5. How many members of Congress react when they realized that Southern voters had elected to Congress many former Confederate officers and political leaders? _____
6. What were the elements of the black codes? _____
7. What _____

FYI

The Republicans' three-to-one majority in Congress was significant for two reasons. The Republicans could claim that they had a mandate from the public to enact their own Reconstruction program. In addition, the Republicans could override any presidential veto if representatives voted along party lines.

you don't say...

Pocket Veto One meaning of the word *pocket* is "to set aside." With the *pocket veto,* the president simply sets aside the bill in question. Andrew Jackson was the first president to use the pocket veto.

✓ **Reading Check**

Answer: the wealthy planter aristocracy

HISTORY Online

Objectives and answers to the student activity can be found in the **Web Activity Lesson Plan** at tav.glencoe.com.

MEETING SPECIAL NEEDS

Visual/Spatial Have students research the harsh restrictions placed on African Americans by the black codes. Then have students use their research to create a political cartoon expressing their reaction to these laws. Encourage students to share their cartoons with the class and have others interpret their meaning. **L2**

📁 Refer to *Inclusion for the High School Social Studies Classroom Strategies and Activities* in the TCR.

Geography *Skills*

Answers:

1. Tennessee

2. about 5 years; Georgia was the last state readmitted, about 5 years and 3 months after the war

Geography Skills Practice

Ask: Why was Tennessee not part of a military district? *(It had already been readmitted to the Union when the districts were established.)*

Reading Essentials and Study Guide 12-2

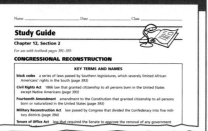

FYI

Following the Civil War the Confederate states were readmitted to the Union in the following order: Tennessee (July 24, 1866), Arkansas (June 22, 1868), Florida (June 25, 1868), North Carolina (July 4, 1868), Louisiana (July 9, 1868), South Carolina (July 9, 1868), Alabama (July 13, 1868), Virginia (January 26, 1870), Mississippi (February 23, 1870), Texas (March 30, 1870), Georgia (July 15, 1870)

3 ASSESS

Assign Section 2 Assessment as homework or as an in-class activity.

● Have students use the **Interactive Tutor Self-Assessment CD-ROM.**

NATIONAL GEOGRAPHIC

Military Districts, 1867

Military District Commander
- General John Schofield
- General Daniel Sickles
- General John Pope
- General Edward Ord
- General Philip Sheridan
- **1870** Date of readmission to union

Geography *Skills*

1. **Interpreting Maps** Only one former Confederate state was not part of a military district. What was it?
2. **Applying Geography Skills** How many years after the war was the last Southern state readmitted to the Union?

Military Reconstruction In March 1867, Congressional Republicans passed the **Military Reconstruction Act,** which essentially wiped out Johnson's programs. The act divided the former Confederacy, except for Tennessee—which had ratified the Fourteenth Amendment in 1866—into five military districts. A Union general was placed in charge of each district.

In the meantime, each former Confederate state had to hold another constitutional convention to design a constitution acceptable to Congress. The new state constitutions had to give the right to vote to all adult male citizens, regardless of their race. After a state had ratified its new constitution, it had to ratify the Fourteenth Amendment before it would be allowed to elect people to Congress.

394 CHAPTER 12 Reconstruction

With military officers supervising the registration of voters, the Southern states began holding elections and organizing constitutional conventions. By the end of 1868, six former Confederate states—North Carolina, South Carolina, Florida, Alabama, Louisiana, and Arkansas—had met all of the requirements and were readmitted to the Union.

Impeachment The Republicans knew they had the votes to override any veto of their policies, but they also knew that President Johnson could still interfere with their plans by refusing to enforce the laws they passed. Although they distrusted Johnson, Republicans in Congress knew that Secretary of War Edwin M. Stanton agreed with their program and would enforce it. They also trusted General Ulysses S. Grant, the head of the army, to support the policies of Congress.

To prevent Johnson from bypassing Grant or firing Stanton, Congress passed the Command of the Army Act and the **Tenure of Office Act.** The Command of the Army Act required all orders from the president to go through the headquarters of the general of the army—Grant's headquarters. The Tenure of Office Act required the Senate to approve the removal of any government official, including Stanton, whose appointment had required the Senate's consent.

Determined to challenge the Tenure of Office Act, Johnson fired Stanton on February 21, 1868. Stanton barricaded himself inside his office and refused to leave. Three days later, the House of Representatives voted to impeach Johnson, meaning that they charged him with "high crimes and misdemeanors" in office. The main charge against Johnson was that he had broken the law by refusing to uphold the Tenure of Office Act. Also, because Johnson had removed four commanders in the Southern military districts who supported the Republicans, the House charged him with attempting to undermine the Reconstruction program.

INTERDISCIPLINARY CONNECTIONS ACTIVITY

Civics Tell students that the Fourteenth Amendment excluded Native Americans from citizenship. Have interested students research the chronology of when Native Americans were granted rights as American citizens. Have them include in the chronology the motivating events that led to Native Americans being offered citizenship. **L2**

As provided in the Constitution, the Senate then put the president on trial. If two-thirds of the senators found the president guilty of the charges, he would be removed from office. For more than two months, amid intense public excitement, the Senate debated the president's fate. On May 16, 1868, the Senate voted 35 to 19 that Johnson was guilty of high crimes and misdemeanors—just one vote short of what was needed for conviction. Seven Republican senators joined with the Democrats in refusing to convict Johnson. These senators believed that it would set a dangerous precedent to impeach a president simply because he did not agree with congressional policies.

The Election of 1868 Although Johnson remained in office, the impeachment stripped him of what little power he had left. Demoralized, he finished his term quietly and did not run for election in 1868. The logical candidate for the Republicans was General Grant, the most popular war hero in the North. In 1868 the Republican convention unanimously nominated Grant to run for president.

During the campaign, ongoing violence in the South convinced many Northern voters that the South could not be trusted to reorganize its state governments without military supervision. At the same time, the presence of Union troops in the South enabled African Americans to vote in large numbers. As a result, Grant won six Southern states and most of the Northern states. The Republicans retained large majorities in both houses of Congress.

The Fifteenth Amendment With their majority securely established and a trusted president in office, congressional Republicans moved rapidly to continue

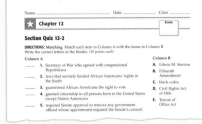

Fact Fiction Folklore

Expanding the Nation An important diplomatic achievement during President Andrew Johnson's administration was the purchase of Alaska in 1867. Secretary of State William H. Seward orchestrated the deal, buying the vast expanse of wilderness from Russia for $7.2 million. Initially, the public ridiculed the purchase. Critics labeled the newly acquired territory "Seward's Icebox." Eventually, Americans recognized the value of the region, which turned out to be rich in such resources as oil and gold.

their Reconstruction program. Recognizing the importance of African American suffrage, the Republican-led Congress passed the **Fifteenth Amendment** to the Constitution. This amendment declared that the right to vote "shall be denied . . . on account of race, color, or previous condition of servitude." By March 1870, enough states had ratified the amendment to make it part of the Constitution.

Radical Reconstruction had a dramatic impact on the South, particularly in the short term. It changed Southern politics by bringing hundreds of thousands of African Americans into the political process for the first time. It also began to change Southern society. As it did so, it angered many white Southerners, who began to fight back against the federal government's policies.

✓ **Reading Check** **Identifying** What two laws did the Radical Republicans pass to reduce presidential power?

SECTION 2 ASSESSMENT

Checking for Understanding

1. **Define:** black codes, impeach.
2. **Identify:** Civil Rights Act, Fourteenth Amendment, Military Reconstruction Act, Tenure of Office Act.
3. **Evaluate** why the congressional election of 1866 was significant to the Radical Republicans.

Reviewing Themes

4. **Civic Rights and Responsibilities** What actions by the Radical Republicans were intended to protect the civil rights of African Americans?

Critical Thinking

5. **Evaluating** Do you think Presidents Lincoln and Johnson were wise in not seeking harsh treatment of the Southern states? Why or why not?
6. **Taking Notes** Use an outline similar to the one below to list the major events of congressional Reconstruction.

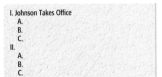

I. Johnson Takes Office
   A.
   B.
   C.
II.
   A.
   B.
   C.

Analyzing Visuals

7. **Analyzing Maps** Study the map of Military Districts on page 394. Then list the Confederate states that were readmitted to the Union in 1868, the earliest year for any such state to gain readmission.

Writing About History

8. **Persuasive Writing** Imagine that you are a citizen during Andrew Johnson's administration. Write a letter to a member of Congress urging him to vote either for or against Johnson's impeachment. Include reasons for your position.

CHAPTER 12 Reconstruction **395**

Fact Fiction Folklore

William H. Seward was the secretary of state in the Lincoln administration. On April 14, 1865, Seward was recovering from a serious carriage accident when Lewis Paine tried to assassinate him. Seward made a remarkable recovery and continued to serve in the Johnson cabinet.

FYI

The six Southern states that Grant won in 1868 were Alabama, Arkansas, Florida, North Carolina, South Carolina, and Tennessee.

✓ **Reading Check**

Answer: Command of the Army Act and Tenure of Office Act

Reteach
Analyze the Reconstruction dispute between President Johnson and Congress.

Enrich
Invite interested students to investigate who would have been president if Andrew Johnson had been removed from office.

4 CLOSE

Describe the major features of congressional Reconstruction.

SECTION 2 ASSESSMENT ANSWERS

1. Terms are in blue.
2. Civil Rights Act *(p. 393)*, Fourteenth Amendment *(p. 393)*, Military Reconstruction Act *(p. 394)*, Tenure of Office Act *(p. 394)*
3. Republicans won enough seats in Congress to have a three-to-one majority.

4. Radical Republicans introduced the Civil Rights Act of 1866, the Fourteenth Amendment, Military Reconstruction, and the Fifteenth Amendment.
5. Answers will vary.
6. I. Johnson takes office;
   A. Johnson's plan; B. Black codes;
   II. Radical Republicans take con-

trol; A. The Fourteenth Amendment; B. The election of 1866; C. Military Reconstruction; D. Impeaching Andrew Johnson; E. The election of 1868
7. Alabama, Arkansas, Florida, North Carolina, and South Carolina
8. Letters will vary but should explain the chosen position.

395

TIME NOTEBOOK

TEACH

Eyewitness

Tell students that some historians view Edmund Ross as courageous, while others view him as politically expedient. Organize the class into small groups and assign the groups to research Edmund Ross and his decision not to convict Andrew Johnson. Assign half the groups to write an editorial expressing the opinion that Ross was a courageous man. Assign the other half to write an editorial expressing the opinion that Ross was a scoundrel, using his vote for political favors. "Publish" the editorials and distribute them to the class. As a class, discuss how our understanding of events is influenced by the opinions of contemporary writers and historians.

Presidential Superlatives

Have students select one of the U.S. presidents and create a list of interesting facts and firsts about this president's term in office, or special accomplishments before taking office. Compile the various lists, placing them in sequential order, and create a display for the school.

Visit the **TIME** Web site at www.time.com for up-to-date news, weekly magazine articles, editorials, online polls, and an archive of past magazine and Web articles.

Eyewitness

WILLIAM H. CROOKE *served as a bodyguard for President Andrew Johnson and witnessed the decisive vote by Edmund Ross during the impeachment trial in the Senate on Saturday, May 16, 1868. Here, Crooke recalls the scene:*

The tension grew. There was a weary number of names before that of Ross was reached. When the clerk called it, and Ross [senator from Kansas] stood forth, the crowd held its breath.

'Not guilty,' called the senator from Kansas. It was like the babbling [sic] over of a caldron. The Radical Senators, who had been laboring with Ross only a short time before, turned to him in rage; all over the house people began to stir. The rest of the roll-call was listened to with lessened interest. . . . When it was over, and the result—35 to 19—was announced, there was a wild outburst, chiefly groans of anger and disappointment, for the friends of the president were in the minority.

It was all over in a moment, and Mr. Johnson was ordering some whiskey from the cellar. [President Johnson was not convicted.]

VERBATIM

"If the South is ever to be made a safe Republic, let her lands be cultivated by the toil of the owners, or the free labor of intelligent citizens."
THADDEUS STEVENS,
arguing for land redistribution in the South during Reconstruction

"In the South, the [Civil] war is what A.D. is elsewhere; they date from it."
MARK TWAIN,
from Life on the Mississippi

"For we colored people did not know how to be free and the white people did not know how to have a free colored person about them."
HOUSTON HARTSFIELD HOLLOWAY,
freedman, on the problem of Reconstruction

"As in the war, freedom was the keynote of victory, so now is universal suffrage the keynote of Reconstruction."
ELIZABETH CADY STANTON,
arguing for universal suffrage, 1867

"We thought we was goin' to be richer than the white folks, 'cause we was stronger and knowed how to work, and the whites didn't and they didn't have us to work for them anymore. But it didn't turn out that way. We soon found out that freedom could make folks proud but it didn't make 'em rich."
FELIX HAYWOOD,
former slave

PRESIDENTIAL SUPERLATIVES

Andrew Johnson

While he was neither "first in war, first in peace" nor "first in the hearts of his countrymen," President Andrew Johnson left his mark on history:

- First to have never attended school
- First to be impeached
- First to be elected to the Senate both before and after being president
- First to host a queen at the White House
- First tailor/president who made his own clothes
- Last not to attend successor's inauguration
- Most vetoes overridden
- Father of the Homestead Act

COOPERATIVE LEARNING ACTIVITY

Creating a Display Organize the class into groups of four or five. Have each group select one of the following time periods: 1860–1865, 1866–1870, or 1871–1877. Have each group create a display relating to the time period selected. Tell students that their displays must include a time line. Encourage students to be creative with the other elements of the display and include such items as photos, quotations from primary sources, artifacts, and drawings.

Use the rubric for a cooperative group management plan on pages 81–82 in the *Performance Assessment Activities and Rubrics.*

(Re)inventing America

Patents awarded to African American inventors during the Reconstruction period:

ALEXANDER ASHBOURNE biscuit cutter

LANDROW BELL locomotive smokestack

LEWIS HOWARD LATIMER water closets (toilets) for railway cars, electric lamp with cotton filament, dough kneader

THOMAS ELKINS refrigerator with cooling coils

THOMAS J. MARTIN fire extinguisher

ELIJAH McCOY automatic oil cup and 57 other devices and machine parts, including an ironing board and lawn sprinkler

Refrigerators keep foods cool.

Milestones

REEXAMINED. THE ROMANTIC STORY OF POCAHONTAS, based on the written account of Captain John Smith. The *London Spectator*, reporting on the work of Mr. E. Neils, debunks Smith's tale of the young Pocahontas flinging herself between him and her father's club. The young girl was captured and held prisoner on board a British ship and then forcibly married to Mr. John Rolfe. Comments *Appleton's Journal* in 1870: "All that is heroic, picturesque, or romantic in history seems to be rapidly disappearing under the microscopic scrutiny of modern critics."

FOUNDED, 1877. NICODEMUS, KANSAS, by six African American and two white Kansans. On the high, arid plains of Graham County, the founders hope to establish a community of homesteading former slaves.

TOPPED, 1875. THE ONE MILLION MARK FOR POPULATION, by New York City. New York is the ninth city in the history of the world to achieve a population level of more than one million. The first was Rome in 133 B.C.

Pocahontas

EXTINGUISHED, 1871. THE PESHTIGO FOREST FIRE in Wisconsin. The conflagration caused 2,682 deaths. The Peshtigo tragedy has been overshadowed by the Great Chicago Fire of the same year, which killed 300.

PUBLISHED, 1865. *DRUM TAPS,* by Walt Whitman. Based on his experiences as a hospital volunteer, Whitman's new poems chronicle the horrors of the Civil War.

THROWN, 1867. FIRST CURVEBALL, by William A. "Candy" Cummings of the Brooklyn Excelsiors. In a game against Harvard, pitcher Cummings put a spin on the ball to make it swerve downward. Most spectators thought the ball's curved path was an illusion.

NUMBERS

$7,200,000 Purchase price paid by U.S. to Russia for Alaska in 1867

2¢ Price paid per acre for Alaska

$30 Boarding and tuition, per quarter, at Saint Frances Academy, boarding school for African American girls in Baltimore, Maryland. Students come from states as distant as Florida and Missouri for an education "productive of the happiest effects among individuals and in society."

$5 Extra charge for instruction in embroidery

$25 Extra charge for instruction in making wax fruit

$3 Tuition, per quarter, for local "day scholars"

5,407 Number of pupils in Mississippi Freedmen's schools in 1866

50 Number of schools established for freed African Americans in Mississippi in 1866

20% Percentage of state income of Mississippi spent on artificial arms and legs for war veterans in 1866

Freedmen's classroom

Portfolio Writing Project

Have students select one of the significant events of Reconstruction. For their selected event, have them write a news article as though they were a reporter at the time the event occurred. Review with students the elements that make a good news story.

Writing a Book Review Have students read a book that was written by an American author during the 1860s or 1870s. Have students write a four- to five-page report about the book. Encourage students to include in their reports elements of the book such as characters, setting, and historical details that identify the time period in which the book was written. (Refer to the Curriculum Connection on page 404 for some popular books written during this period.)

CLOSE

Have students make a list of inventions that have improved their lives. Assign each student one invention and have them find out when it was invented and by whom.

EXTENDING THE CONTENT

Elizabeth Cady Stanton One of the founders of the National Woman Suffrage Association, Elizabeth Cady Stanton worked throughout her life to secure rights for women. She learned early in life that women did not have the same opportunities as men. She was the only girl who took the mathematics and language courses offered in her school. She was barred from attending college and practicing law simply because she was a woman. The National Woman Suffrage Association, formed in 1869, sought to gain voting rights for women. Stanton also worked to gain economic and political equality for women.

1 FOCUS

Section Overview
This section deals with life in the South during Reconstruction.

Guide to Reading

Answers to Graphic: African Americans' political roles: elected to office, encouraged other African Americans to participate in politics, chosen as delegates to state constitutional conventions, and served as administrators in state governments.

Preteaching Vocabulary
Have students choose eight words from the Key Terms and Names list that can be grouped into four logical pairs. Have students write four sentences using one of the pairs of words in each sentence.

398

SECTION 3 Republican Rule

Guide to Reading

Main Idea
Under Republican rule, the South began to rebuild. African Americans gained new opportunities, and some Southerners organized to resist the Republicans.

Key Terms and Names
carpetbagger, scalawag, Joseph Rainey, Hiram Revels, graft, Ku Klux Klan Act

Reading Strategy
Organizing As you read about Southern attempts to rebuild, complete a graphic organizer to identify how African Americans helped govern the Reconstruction South.

Reading Objectives
- **Discuss** Republican rule in the South during Reconstruction.
- **Describe** how African Americans worked to improve their lives.

Section Theme
Groups and Institutions Despite opposition, African Americans took active roles in politics during Reconstruction.

Preview of Events

◆1866	◆1868	◆1870	◆1872

1866
Ku Klux Klan formed; Fisk School, later Fisk University, founded in Tennessee

1870
First Enforcement Act passed; first African Americans elected to Congress

1871
Ku Klux Klan Act passed

Early KKK robe and hood

★ An American Story ★

On a moonlit December night in the late 1860s, Essic Harris, a formerly enslaved man, woke suddenly after hearing loud noises outside his small home in Chatham County, North Carolina. He peered out his bedroom window and a wave of terror rushed over him. Thirty men in white robes and hoods stood around the house. Many held shotguns. They were members of the Ku Klux Klan, an organization that used violence and intimidation to force African Americans and white Republicans out of Southern politics. They had come to harass Harris, who was active in local politics.

As Klan members began firing shotgun blasts at his home, Harris pushed his family into a corner and grabbed his own shotgun. He rushed to the front door and fired back, then shouted to one of his childen, "Boy, bring my five-shooter!" Harris had no such gun, but his bluff worked. The Klan members cursed Harris and rode off, but they would return. They continued harassing Harris until he abandoned his home and moved to another county.

—adapted from *The Fiery Cross*

Republican Rule in the South

By late 1870, all of the former Confederate states had rejoined the Union under the congressional Reconstruction plan. Throughout the South, the Republican Party took power and introduced several major reforms. Most white Southerners scorned the Republicans, however, partly because the party included Northerners and African Americans. Southerners also believed the Union army had forced the new Republican governments on them.

SECTION RESOURCES

📁 Reproducible Masters
- Reproducible Lesson Plan 12–3
- Daily Lecture and Discussion Notes 12–3
- Guided Reading Activity 12–3
- Section Quiz 12–3
- Reading Essentials and Study Guide 12–3

📖 Transparencies
- Daily Focus Skills Transparency 12–3

Multimedia
- 💿 Interactive Tutor Self-Assessment CD-ROM
- 💿 ExamView® Pro Testmaker CD-ROM
- 💿 Presentation Plus! CD-ROM
- 💿 TeacherWorks™ CD-ROM
- 🎧 Audio Program
- 🎵 American Music: Cultural Traditions

Carpetbaggers and Scalawags As Reconstruction began many Northerners moved to the South. Quite a few were eventually elected or appointed to positions in the South's new state governments. Southerners, particularly Democratic Party supporters, referred to these newcomers as carpetbaggers because some arrived with suitcases made of carpet fabric. Many local residents viewed the Northerners as intruders seeking to exploit the South.

Carpetbag

Some carpetbaggers did seek to take advantage of the war-torn region. Others, however, hoped to find more opportunities than existed for them in the North and West. Some simply wanted to help. Many Northern schoolteachers, for example, moved south to help educate whites and African Americans.

While many Southerners despised carpetbaggers, they also disliked white Southerners who worked with the Republicans and supported Reconstruction. They called these people scalawags—an old Scotch-Irish term for weak, underfed, worthless animals.

The scalawags were a diverse group. Some were former Whigs who had grudgingly joined the Democratic Party before the war. Many were owners of small farms who did not want the wealthy planters to regain power. Still others were business people who favored Republican plans for developing the South's economy.

African Americans Enter Politics Thousands of formerly enslaved people also took part in governing the South. Having gained the right to vote, African Americans quickly began organizing politically. "You never saw a people more excited on the subject of politics than are the [African Americans] of the South," wrote one plantation manager.

At first, African American leaders in the South came from those who had been educated before the war. These included artisans, shopkeepers, and ministers. Many had lived in the North and fought in the Union army. Helped by the Republican Party, these African Americans delivered speeches to former plantation workers, drawing them into politics.

Within a few remarkable years, African Americans went from enslaved workers to legislators and administrators on nearly all levels of government. Hundreds of formerly enslaved people served as delegates to state constitutional conventions. They also won election to numerous local offices, from mayor to police chief to school commissioner. Dozens of

---

Profiles IN HISTORY

Hiram Revels *1822–1901*

For a man reluctant to enter politics, Hiram Revels went a long way— becoming the first African American in the United States Senate. Revels was born to free parents in Fayetteville, North Carolina. In 1845 he became a minister in the African Methodist Church. Soon after, Revels settled in Baltimore, where he worked as a church pastor and as the principal of an African American school.

After the Civil War, Revels settled in Natchez, Mississippi, where he continued his religious work. At first, Revels expressed reluctance to wade too deeply into politics, but he overcame this concern and won the respect of both whites and African Americans. In 1870 Revels was elected to the Senate. The first African American senator, he served in a subdued manner, speaking much less than other African American members of Congress. Upon his retirement from the Senate, Revels served twice as president of Alcorn University, an African American college in Mississippi.

Joseph Rainey *1832–1887*

At the outbreak of the Civil War, Joseph Rainey was working as a barber in Georgetown, South Carolina. Less than 10 years later, he became the first African American elected to the U.S. House of Representatives.

Rainey was born to enslaved parents who bought their freedom in the 1840s. They opened a barbershop, where Rainey worked until the war broke out. After the war, Rainey entered politics, and in 1870 he was elected to the House of Representatives, serving in Congress until 1879.

As the body's first African American, Rainey found himself the object of intense scrutiny. During this time, he showed considerable knowledge of politics and made impressive speeches in favor of legislation to enforce the Fourteenth Amendment and the Ku Klux Klan Act. Throughout his tenure in Congress, Rainey worked tirelessly—both in and out of the House chamber—to advance African American civil rights.

CHAPTER 12 Reconstruction **399**

COOPERATIVE LEARNING ACTIVITY

Creating an Exhibit Organize the class into small groups to develop an exhibit illustrating Reconstruction. Groups may focus on aspects such as: an important person; an important event such as the impeachment of President Johnson; the culture of the period, such as hair and clothing styles, songs, and available reading material; or an important idea, such as what people expected of a Reconstruction policy. Exhibits should include illustrations, short written descriptions, and primary sources.

Use the rubric for a cooperative group management plan on pages 81–82 in the *Performance Assessment Activities and Rubrics.*

---

2 TEACH

Daily Lecture and Discussion Notes 12–3

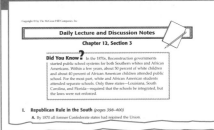

Copyright © by The McGraw-Hill Companies, Inc.

> ### Daily Lecture and Discussion Notes
> #### Chapter 12, Section 3
>
> **Did You Know?** In the 1870s, Reconstruction governments started public school systems for both Southern whites and African Americans. Within a few years, about 50 percent of white children and about 40 percent of African American children attended public school. For the most part, white and African American students attended separate schools. Only three states—Louisiana, South Carolina, and Florida—required that the schools be integrated, but the laws were not enforced.
>
> **I. Republican Rule in the South** *(pages 398–400)*
>
> **A.** By 1870 all former Confederate states had rejoined the Union.

Writing a Profile Have students research and then write a short profile of one of the following African Americans who served in the U.S. House of Representatives between 1870 and 1901: Richard H. Cain, Henry P. Cheatham, Jeremiah Haralson, John A. Hyman, John M. Langston, Jefferson F. Long, John R. Lynch, Alonzo J. Ransier. **L1**

Use the rubric for a book review, research report, or position paper, on pages 89–90 in the *Performance Assessment Activities and Rubrics.*

Profiles IN HISTORY

Hiram Revels served in the United States Senate for just over one year— February 23, 1870, to March 3, 1871. In 1875 Mississippi again elected an African American to the Senate, but not until 1967 was another African American elected to serve in the U.S. Senate. **Ask:** Why do you think African American political gains in the South were short lived? *(Reconstruction ended and many Southern states enacted laws and used force to discourage African Americans from participating in government.)*

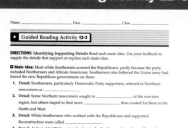

Reading Check

Answer: African Americans, carpet-baggers, and poor white farmers

Summarizing Research Have students work in groups of three to research what schools were like for the following groups during Reconstruction: African Americans, rural Southerners, and city dwellers in large Northern cities. Have each student research one of the three groups. Based on their research, have each student group create a chart that summarizes their findings. **L2**

Carpetbagger The term *carpetbagger* is currently used to describe a person who establishes residency in a community and quickly becomes involved in politics. The term is pejorative and often indicates a suspicion that a person has moved for the sole purpose of seeking elective office.

History *and the* Humanities

American Music: Cultural Traditions: "Roll, Jordan, Roll"

Use *Interpreting Political Cartoons,* Cartoons 9 and 10.

African Americans served in Southern state legislatures, while 14 were elected to the House of Representatives and 2 to the Senate.

With formerly enslaved people making such political gains, many Southerners claimed that "Black Republicanism" ruled the South. Such claims, however, were greatly exaggerated. No African American was ever elected governor. In South Carolina, where African Americans made up a majority of the population, they did achieve a majority in the legislature, but it lasted for only one legislative term. African Americans participated in government, but they did not control it.

The Republican Party took power in the South because it also had the support of a large number of white Southerners. Poor white farmers, who resented the planters and the Democratic Party that dominated the South before the Civil War, often joined with African American voters to elect Republicans.

Republican Reforms in the South The newly elected Republican governments in the South quickly instituted a number of reforms. They repealed the black codes and made many more state offices elective. They established state hospitals and institutions for orphans, the hearing and visually impaired, and the mentally ill. They rebuilt roads, railways, and bridges and provided funds for the construction of

Schools for African Americans O.O. Howard, head of the Freedmen's Bureau, is pictured here (seated, far right) with the students of a Freedmen's school.

new railroads and industries in the South. They also established a system of public schools.

The Republican reforms did not come without cost. Many state governments were forced to borrow money and to impose high property taxes to pay for the repairs and new programs. Many property owners, unable to pay these new taxes, lost their land.

Although many Republicans wanted to help the South, others were corrupt. One Republican governor admitted accepting more than $40,000 in bribes. Graft, or gaining money illegally through politics, was common in the South, just as it was in the North at the time, but it gave Southern Democrats another issue that would help them regain power in the 1870s.

✓ **Reading Check** **Summarizing** What three groups helped elect Republicans in the South during Reconstruction?

African American Communities

In addition to their efforts on the political stage, African Americans worked to improve their lives in other ways during Reconstruction. Many sought to gain an education and establish their own thriving communities.

A Desire to Learn Once they were freed, many African Americans wanted to get an education. In the first years of Reconstruction, the Freedmen's Bureau, with the help of Northern charities, established schools for African Americans across the South. By 1870 some 4,000 schools and 9,000 teachers—half of them African American—taught 200,000 formerly enslaved people of all ages. In the 1870s, Reconstruc-tion governments built a comprehensive public school system in the South, and by 1876 about 40 percent of all African American children (roughly 600,000 students) attended school in the region.

Several African American academies offering advanced education also began operating in the South. These academies grew into an important network of African American colleges and universities, including Fisk University in Tennessee and Atlanta University and Morehouse College in Georgia.

Churches and Social Organizations With the same determination they showed in pursuing an education, formerly enslaved people across the South worked to

Different Viewpoints

Carpetbaggers: Corrupt or Well-Intentioned?

According to Southerners, many carpetbaggers were corrupt Northerners who came south to get rich or to get elected. Films like *Gone with the Wind* influenced many generations to accept this view. The opposing interpretation argues that Northerners were not necessarily corrupt but often simply wanted to make new lives or aid African Americans.

In 1871 Oliver Morton, a Radical Republican senator from Indiana, defended Northerners who relocated to the South, claiming they were beneficial to that region:

"When the war ended many men who had been in the Union army remained in the South, intending to make it their home. . . . Others emigrated from the North, taking with them large capital, believing that the South presented fine prospects for business. . . . It so happened, and was, in fact, necessary, that many of these men should be elected to office. This was their right and the natural result of the circumstances by which they were surrounded. . . . Emigration is a part of the genius of the American people. . . . it is an odious and anti-American doctrine that a man has no right to be elected to an office in a State because he was not born in it. . . . What the South needs is emigrants with carpet bags well filled with capital to revive industry. . . . "

—quoted in *Reconstruction: Opposing Viewpoints*

In an 1871 question-and-answer session before Congress, William Manning Lowe, a former Confederate colonel and Alabama lawyer, criticized his state's U.S. senators, Willard Warner and George Spencer. Both were originally from Northern states:

"[A] carpet-bagger is generally understood to be a man who comes here for office sake, of an ignorant or bad character, and who seeks to array the Negroes against the whites . . . in order to get office through them. . . . (The term) does not apply to all northern men who come here. . . . We regard any republican or any man as a man of bad character, whether he is native or foreign born, who seeks to obtain office from the Negroes by exciting their passions and prejudices against the whites. We think that a very great evil—very great. We are intimately associated with the Negro race; we have a large number in the country, and we think it essential that we shall live in peace together. . . . No, sir; the term is never applied to a democrat under any circumstances. . . ."

—quoted in *Reconstruction: Opposing Viewpoints*

Learning From History

1. **Evaluating** Which of these two viewpoints most accurately describes carpetbaggers? Why?
2. **Analyzing** Choose one of the viewpoints above. Write three questions you would like to ask your chosen speaker.

Different Viewpoints

Answers:

1. Answers may vary. Students should note that Lowe's characterization seems more arbitrary and emotion-based than Morton's. That tends to make Morton's view seem more accurate.
2. Answers will vary. Possible questions include—Morton: As a Northerner, how do you know what will help the South? Lowe: Are you saying that Democrats never have the wrong motives for running for elected office?

✔ **Reading Check**

Answer: A comprehensive public school system was established for children; literacy programs and African American academies were established for higher education.

3 ASSESS

Assign Section 3 Assessment as homework or as an in-class activity.

● Have students use the **Interactive Tutor Self-Assessment CD-ROM.**

establish their own churches. Religion had long played a central role in the lives of many African Americans, and with the shackles of slavery now gone, the building of churches quickly began.

Churches served as the center of many African American communities, as they housed schools and hosted social events and political gatherings. In rural areas, church picnics, festivals, and other activities provided residents with many of their recreational and social opportunities. In many communities, churches often acted as unofficial courts by promoting social values, settling disputes among residents, and disciplining individuals for improper behavior.

African Americans also established thousands of other organizations to help and support each other. These organizations ranged from burial societies and debating clubs to drama societies and trade associations.

✔ **Reading Check** **Examining** How did education for African Americans change during Reconstruction?

Southern Resistance

At the same time these changes were taking place, African Americans faced intense resentment from many Southern whites. Many Southerners also

Reading Essentials and Study Guide 12–3

Name _____ Date _____ Class _____

Study Guide

Chapter 12, Section 3
For use with textbook pages 398–402

REPUBLICAN RULE

KEY TERMS AND NAMES

carpetbagger name given to Northern whites who moved South after the war and supported Republicans *(page 399)*

scalawag name given by former Confederates to Southern whites who supported Republican Reconstruction of the South *(page 399)*

Joseph Rainey first African American elected to the House of Representatives *(page 399)*

Hiram Revels first African American elected to the Senate *(page 399)*

graft gaining money illegally through politics *(page 400)*

Ku Klux Klan Act law that outlawed the activities of the Ku Klux Klan *(page 402)*

INTERDISCIPLINARY CONNECTIONS ACTIVITY

Sociology Have the sociology teacher discuss the importance of social organizations such as churches, clubs, trade organizations, and fraternal organizations to the transmission of culture from one generation to the next. Then have groups of students profile one of the social organizations that works actively in your community. Tell students that the profiles should include a brief history of the organization, how people become members, and the services provided or programs offered by the organization. **L2**

Picturing **History**

Answer: intimidation and violence
Ask: What actions did Congress take in response to the violence? *(It passed three Enforcement Acts which made it a federal crime to interfere with a citizen's right to vote, put federal elections under the supervision of federal marshals, and outlawed activities of the Ku Klux Klan.)*

✓ **Reading Check**

Answer: to combat violence in the South and outlaw the activities of the Ku Klux Klan

Reteach
Discuss Republican rule in the South during Reconstruction.

Enrich
Have students use historical statistical abstracts to find data on African American enrollment in schools from 1860 to 1900. Ask them to present their findings in the form of a bar graph using ten-year intervals.

4 CLOSE
Describe how African Americans worked to improve their lives after the Civil War.

despised the "Black Republican" governments, which they believed vindictive Northerners had forced upon them.

The Ku Klux Klan Unable to strike openly at the Republicans running their states, some Southerners organized secret societies. The largest of these groups was the Ku Klux Klan. Started in 1866 by former Confederate soldiers in Pulaski, Tennessee, the Klan spread rapidly throughout the South. Its goal was to drive out the Union troops and carpetbaggers and regain control of the South for the Democratic Party.

Hooded, white-robed Klan members rode in bands at night terrorizing supporters of the Republican governments. They broke up Republican meetings, drove Freedmen's Bureau officials out of their communities, burned African American homes, schools, and churches, and attempted to keep African Americans and white Republicans from voting.

Republicans and African Americans formed their own militia groups and fought back. As the violence perpetrated by both sides increased, one African American organization sent a report to the federal government asking for help:

❝We believe you are not familiar with the description of the Ku Klux Klan's riding nightly over the country, going from county to county, and in the county towns spreading terror wherever they go by robbing, whipping, ravishing, and killing our people without provocation. . . . We pray you will take some steps to remedy these evils.❞

—from the Records of the U.S. Senate, 42nd Congress

Picturing **History**

Enforcement Efforts In 1871 President Grant signed an anti–Ku Klux Klan Bill. What actions did the Klan take to interfere with African American voting rights?

The Enforcement Acts The Ku Klux Klan's activities outraged President Grant and congressional Republicans. In 1870 and 1871, Congress passed three Enforcement Acts to combat the violence in the South. The first act made it a federal crime to interfere with a citizen's right to vote. The second put federal elections under the supervision of federal marshals. The third act, also known as the **Ku Klux Klan Act,** outlawed the activities of the Klan. Local authorities and federal agents, acting under the Enforcement Acts, arrested more than 3,000 Klan members throughout the South. Southern juries, however, convicted only about 600, and fewer still served any time in prison.

✓ **Reading Check** **Describing** Why did Congress pass the Enforcement Acts?

SECTION 3 ASSESSMENT

Checking for Understanding
1. **Define:** carpetbagger, scalawag, graft.
2. **Identify:** Joseph Rainey, Hiram Revels, Ku Klux Klan Act.
3. **Describe** how some white Southerners reacted to the Republican Party gaining power in the South.

Reviewing Themes
4. **Groups and Institutions** How did the establishment of schools, churches, and social organizations benefit African Americans during Reconstruction?

Critical Thinking
5. **Analyzing** Why did white Southerners resent both carpetbaggers and scalawags?
6. **Categorizing** Use a graphic organizer similar to the one below to identify both the negative and positive aspects of carpetbag rule.

| Carpetbag Rule | |
Positives	Negatives

Analyzing Visuals
7. **Analyzing Photographs** Study the photograph of the Freedmen's school on page 400. By 1876, around how many children attended schools such as the one pictured here?

Writing About History
8. **Descriptive Writing** Imagine you are living in the postwar South. You are either a Northerner who has recently moved there or a longtime Southern resident. Write a friend and describe Southern life as you see it.

402 CHAPTER 12 Reconstruction

SECTION 3 ASSESSMENT ANSWERS

1. Terms are in blue.
2. Joseph Rainey (p. 399), Hiram Revels (p. 399), Ku Klux Klan Act (p. 402)
3. While some decided to join the Republicans, others joined the Klan and tried to prevent African Americans and white Republicans from voting.
4. Churches served as community centers and acted as unofficial courts. Social organizations helped African Americans support each other.
5. Carpetbaggers and scalawags both wanted to change the South while many Southerners wanted things to be the same as they were before the Civil War.
6. positive: provided an influx of capital and helped African Americans; negative: exploited South's postwar turmoil for personal gain
7. about 600,000 students
8. Students' letters should describe specifics of Southern life.

Guide to Reading

Main Idea
After a little more than a decade, Reconstruction ended shortly after the election of 1876.

Key Terms and Names
"sin tax," Horace Greeley, "Whiskey Ring," Panic of 1873, Compromise of 1877, tenant farmer, sharecropper, furnishing merchant, crop lien, debt peonage

Reading Strategy
Taking Notes As you read about the Grant administration and the end of Reconstruction, use the major headings of the section to create an outline similar to the one below.

I. The Grant Administration
  A.
  B.
  C.
II.
  A.
  B.

Reading Objectives
• **Discuss** the policies and problems of Grant's administration.
• **Explain** how Reconstruction ended, and contrast the New South and the Old South.

Section Theme
Economic Factors After Reconstruction the South tried to build a new economy, but many problems remained.

Preview of Events

◆1872	◆1874	◆1876	◆1878

1872
Grant reelected

1873
Jay Cooke and Company declares bankruptcy

1875
"Whiskey Ring" scandal breaks

1877
Hayes named president

★ An American Story ★

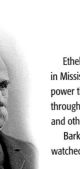

Ethelbert Barksdale

Ethelbert Barksdale could hardly contain his excitement as the 1875 election campaign in Mississippi wound down. For the past several years, Democrats had steadily regained power throughout the South, winning back various local and state offices from Republicans through political organizing and through intimidation and harassment of African Americans and other Republican supporters.

Barksdale, the editor of the *Weekly Clarion*, a Democratic Mississippi newspaper, now watched with joy and anticipation as Democrats prepared to recapture numerous political offices in his state. To Barksdale and many other white Southerners, the efforts by the Democrats to regain political control was nothing less than a revolution to free the South from despised Republican rule. "When a government is oppressed with very bad rulers, and national affairs are tending toward corruption, the people . . . bear these grievances for a long time hoping that a reformation may come," he wrote on the eve of Election Day.

—adapted from *Reconstruction and Redemption in the South*

The Grant Administration

As commander of the Union forces, Ulysses S. Grant had led the North to victory in the Civil War. His reputation had then carried him into the White House in the election of 1868. Unfortunately, Grant had little experience in politics. He believed that the

SECTION RESOURCES

Reproducible Masters
• Reproducible Lesson Plan 12–4
• Daily Lecture and Discussion Notes 12–4
• Guided Reading Activity 12–4
• Section Quiz 12–4
• Reading Essentials and Study Guide 12–4
• Performance Assessment Activities and Rubrics

Transparencies
• Daily Focus Skills Transparency 12–4

Multimedia
⊙ Interactive Tutor Self-Assessment CD-ROM
⊙ ExamView® Pro Testmaker CD-ROM
⊙ Presentation Plus! CD-ROM
⊙ TeacherWorks™ CD-ROM
⊙ Audio Program

1 FOCUS

Section Overview
This section focuses on the end of Reconstruction and the emergence of the "New South."

BELLRINGER
Skillbuilder Activity

🖎 Project transparency and have students answer the question.

🗀 Available as a blackline master.

Daily Focus Skills Transparency 12–4

Guide to Reading

Answers to Graphic:
I. The Grant Administration
  A. The Republican Split
  B. Scandals Mar Grant's Second Term
  C. The Panic of 1873
II. Reconstruction Ends
  A. Democrats "Redeem" the South
  B. The Compromise of 1877
III. A "New South" Arises
  A. New Industries
  B. Sharecropping

Preteaching Vocabulary
Have students create note cards with the Key Terms and Names on the front of the cards. Instruct students to use the reverse side to make notes about the term or name.

2 TEACH

Daily Lecture and Discussion Notes 12-4

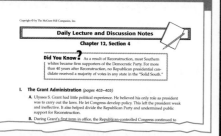

Copyright © by The McGraw-Hill Companies, Inc.

Daily Lecture and Discussion Notes

Chapter 12, Section 4

Did You Know? As a result of Reconstruction, most Southern whites became firm supporters of the Democratic Party. For more than 40 years after Reconstruction, no Republican presidential candidate received a majority of votes in any state in the "Solid South."

I. The Grant Administration (pages 403–405)

A. Ulysses S. Grant had little political experience. He believed his only role as president was to carry out the laws. He let Congress develop policy. This left the president weak and ineffective. It also helped divide the Republican Party and undermined public support for Reconstruction.

B. During Grant's first term in office, the Republican-controlled Congress continued to

Analyzing *Political Cartoons*

Answer: The cartoon implies corruption exists at all levels of government.
Ask: What administration official did some people believe was part of the "Whiskey Ring" scandal?
(Orville E. Babcock, Grant's private secretary)

Discussing a Topic Ask students to explain why taxes on alcohol and tobacco were called "sin taxes." **L1**

CURRICULUM CONNECTION

Language Arts Best-selling books during Reconstruction included Mary Mapes Dodge's *Hans Brinker and His Silver Skates* (1865); Horatio Alger's *Ragged Dick* (1867); Louisa May Alcott's *Little Women* (1868) and *Little Men* (1871); and Mark Twain's *Innocents Abroad* (1869), *Roughing It* (1872), and *Tom Sawyer* (1876).

Analyzing *Political Cartoons*

Political Corruption A cartoonist shows the Grant administration looking for those guilty of fraud in a whiskey barrel–symbol of the "Whiskey Ring." How far does the cartoonist believe the corruption goes?

president's role was to carry out the laws and leave the development of policy to Congress. This approach pleased the Radical Republicans in Congress, but it left the president weak and ineffective when dealing with other issues. Eventually, Grant's lack of political experience helped to divide the Republican Party and to undermine public support for Reconstruction.

The Republicans Split During Grant's first term in office, the Republican-controlled Congress continued to enforce Reconstruction. At the same time, Congress expanded the programs it had introduced during the Civil War to promote commerce and industry. It kept tariffs high, tightened banking regulations, promised to repay its debts with gold and not paper money, and increased federal spending on railroads, port facilities, and the national postal system.

The Republican Congress also kept in place the taxes on alcohol and tobacco that had been introduced as emergency measures during the war. These taxes, nicknamed "sin taxes," helped the government pay off the bonds that had been issued to pay for the Civil War.

Democrats attacked these Republican economic policies, arguing they benefited the wealthy, such as government bondholders, at the expense of the poor,

404 CHAPTER 12 Reconstruction

who paid most of the sin taxes. They argued that wealthy Americans were gaining too much influence in Grant's administration.

Some Republicans, known as Liberal Republicans, agreed with the Democrats. They were concerned that men who were in office to make money and sell influence were beginning to dominate the Republican Party. The Liberal Republicans tried to prevent Grant from being nominated for a second term. When that failed, they left the Republican Party in 1872 and nominated their own candidate, **Horace Greeley,** the influential newspaper publisher.

To attract Southern support, the Liberal Republicans promised to pardon nearly all former Confederates and to remove Union troops from the South. As a result, the Democratic Party, believing that only a united effort would defeat Grant, also nominated Greeley. Despite the split in his own party, Grant won the election easily.

Scandals Mar Grant's Second Term During Grant's second term, a series of scandals badly hurt his administration's reputation. In one scandal, Grant's secretary of war, **William Belknap,** was found to have accepted bribes from merchants operating at army posts in the West. He was impeached but resigned before the Senate could try him. Then, in 1875, the **"Whiskey Ring"** scandal broke. A group of government officials and distillers in St. Louis cheated the government out of millions of dollars by filing false tax reports. It was reported that Orville E. Babcock, Grant's private secretary, was in this group, although the charges were never proven.

The Panic of 1873 In addition to dealing with political scandals, Grant and the nation endured a severe economic crisis that began during Grant's second term. The turmoil started in 1873 when a series of bad railroad investments forced the powerful banking firm of Jay Cooke and Company to declare bankruptcy. A wave of fear known as the **Panic of 1873** quickly spread though the nation's financial community. The panic prompted scores of smaller banks to close and the stock market to plummet. Thousands of businesses shut down, and tens of thousands of Americans were thrown out of work.

The scandals in the Grant administration and the deepening economic depression hurt the Republicans politically. In the 1874 midterm elections, the Democrats won control of the House of Representatives and made gains in the Senate. These newly elected Democrats immediately

COOPERATIVE LEARNING ACTIVITY

Writing an Editorial Organize students into small groups. Have each group select one of the scandals of the Grant presidency to research. Based on their research, have the groups write an editorial expressing the public's opinion about the scandal. Encourage groups to review the editorial pages of newspapers to determine the style of editorial writing.

Use the rubric for a cooperative group management plan on pages 81–82 in the *Performance Assessment Activities and Rubrics.*

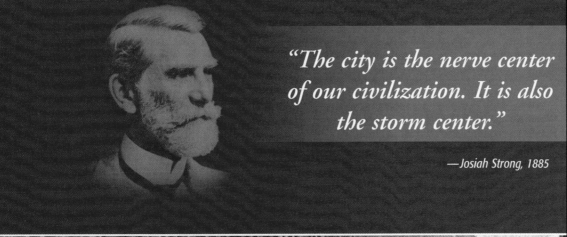

"The city is the nerve center of our civilization. It is also the storm center."

—Josiah Strong, 1885

A BUSY DAY ON DEARBORN AND RANDOLPH STREETS CHICAGO

GLENCOE
TECHNOLOGY

CD-ROM
American History Primary Source Document Library CD-ROM
Use the **American History Primary Source Document Library CD-ROM** to access primary source documents related to this period in history.

More About the Photo

Point out to students that the late 1800s and early 1900s saw significant changes in modes of transportation. Have students identify the various forms of transportation in the picture and speculate on the function and usefulness of each form. Tell students that congested streets are still a feature of most large urban areas and that pedestrians are still a major feature of large urban centers.

Glencoe Literature Library

The following novels from the *High School American History Literature Library* may be used to enrich the study of this unit:
- *The Adventures of Huckleberry Finn* by Mark Twain
- *My Ántonia* by Willa Cather
- *The Yearling* by Marjorie Rawlings

SERVICE-LEARNING PROJECT

Have a person from your local historical society describe the types of records the society keeps. Organize students into small groups. Have the groups select a significant event or period from your local history. Then have the groups work together to prepare a display about the event or period. Encourage students to contact people who remember the event and to gather and properly display historical primary source materials. If possible, have the displays set up in a public place such as a library for the community to enjoy.

Refer to **Building Bridges: Connecting Classroom and Community through Service-Learning in Social Studies** from the National Council for the Social Studies for information about service-learning.

Timesaving Tools

TeacherWorks™ All-In-One Planner and Resource Center

- **Interactive Teacher Edition** Access your Teacher Wraparound Edition and your classroom resources with a few easy clicks.
- **Interactive Lesson Planner** Planning has never been easier! Organize your week, month, semester, or year with all the lesson helps you need to make teaching creative, timely, and relevant.

Use Glencoe's **Presentation Plus!** multimedia teacher tool to easily present dynamic lessons that visually excite your students. Using Microsoft PowerPoint® you can customize the presentations to create your own personalized lessons.

TEACHING TRANSPARENCIES

Graphic Organizer 8

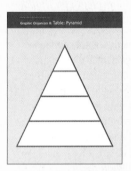

Why It Matters Chapter Transparency 13

APPLICATION AND ENRICHMENT

Linking Past and Present Activity 13

Enrichment Activity 13

Primary Source Reading 13

REVIEW AND REINFORCEMENT

Reteaching Activity 13

Vocabulary Activity 13

Time Line Activity 13

Critical Thinking Skills Activity 13

Meeting NCSS Standards

The following standards are highlighted in Chapter 13:

Section 1 VII Production, Distribution, and Consumption: B, F, I

Section 2 III People, Places, and Environments: A, B

Section 3 IV Individual Development and Identity: E, G

Local Standards

_____

_____

_____

_____

_____

_____

Chapter 13 Resources

ASSESSMENT AND EVALUATION

**Chapter 13 Test
Form A**

**Chapter 13 Test
Form B**

**Standardized Test Practice
Skills Workbook Activity 13**

**Performance Assessment
Activities and Rubrics 13**

**ExamView® Pro
Testmaker CD-ROM**

MULTIMEDIA

- Vocabulary PuzzleMaker CD-ROM
- Interactive Tutor Self-Assessment CD-ROM
- ExamView® Pro Testmaker CD-ROM
- Audio Program
- American History Primary Source Documents Library CD-ROM
- MindJogger Videoquiz
- Presentation Plus! CD-ROM
- TeacherWorks™ CD-ROM
- Interactive Student Edition CD-ROM
- Glencoe Skillbuilder Interactive Workbook CD-ROM, Level 2
- The *American Vision* Video Program
- American Music: Hits Through History
- American Music: Cultural Traditions

SPANISH RESOURCES

The following Spanish language materials are available in the Spanish Resources Binder:

- Spanish Guided Reading Activities
- Spanish Reteaching Activities
- Spanish Quizzes and Tests
- Spanish Vocabulary Activities
- Spanish Summaries
- The Declaration of Independence and United States Constitution Spanish Translation

---

The following videotape programs are available from Glencoe as supplements to Chapter 13:

- **Buffalo Bill: Showman of the West** (ISBN 1-56-501940-7)
- **Crazy Horse** (ISBN 1-56-501597-5)
- **Geronimo** (ISBN 1-56-501939-3)
- **Sitting Bull: Chief of the Lakota Nation** (ISBN 1-56-501684-X)

To order, call Glencoe at 1-800-334-7344. To find classroom resources to accompany many of these videos, check the following home pages:
A&E Television: www.aande.com
The History Channel: www.historychannel.com

Use our Web site for additional resources. All essential content is covered in the Student Edition.

You and your students can visit tav.glencoe.com, the Web site companion to the *American Vision*. This innovative integration of electronic and print media offers your students a wealth of opportunities. The student text directs students to the Web site for the following options:

- **Chapter Overviews**
- **Self-Check Quizzes**
- **Student Web Activities**
- **Textbook Updates**

Answers to the student Web activities are provided for you in the **Web Activity Lesson Plans.** Additional Web resources and Interactive Tutor Puzzles are also available.

Chapter 13 Resources

SECTION RESOURCES

Daily Objectives	Reproducible Resources	Multimedia Resources
SECTION 1 **Miners and Ranchers** 1. Trace the growth of the mining industry in the West. 2. Describe the ways that new technology changed open-range ranching.	Reproducible Lesson Plan 13–1 Daily Lecture and Discussion Notes 13–1 Guided Reading Activity 13–1* Section Quiz 13–1* Reading Essentials and Study Guide 13–1 Performance Assessment Activities and Rubrics Supreme Court Case Studies	Daily Focus Skills Transparency 13–1 American Art & Architecture Interactive Tutor Self-Assessment CD-ROM ExamView® Pro Testmaker CD-ROM Presentation Plus! CD-ROM TeacherWorks™ CD-ROM Audio Program American Music: Hits Through History
SECTION 2 **Farming the Plains** 1. Explain why and how people began settling the Plains. 2. Trace the growth of commercial farming on the Plains.	Reproducible Lesson Plan 13–2 Daily Lecture and Discussion Notes 13–2 Guided Reading Activity 13–2* Section Quiz 13–2* Reading Essentials and Study Guide 13–2 Performance Assessment Activities and Rubrics	Daily Focus Skills Transparency 13–2 Interactive Tutor Self-Assessment CD-ROM ExamView® Pro Testmaker CD-ROM Presentation Plus! CD-ROM Skillbuilder Interactive Workbook, Level 2 TeacherWorks™ CD-ROM Audio Program American Music: Cultural Traditions
SECTION 3 **Native Americans** 1. Discuss conflicts that arose between the Plains Indians and American settlers. 2. Summarize problems caused by attempts to assimilate Native Americans.	Reproducible Lesson Plan 13–3 Daily Lecture and Discussion Notes 13–3 Guided Reading Activity 13–3* Section Quiz 13–3* Reading Essentials and Study Guide 13–3 Performance Assessment Activities and Rubrics Interpreting Political Cartoons	Daily Focus Skills Transparency 13–3 American Art & Architecture Interactive Tutor Self-Assessment CD-ROM ExamView® Pro Testmaker CD-ROM Presentation Plus! CD-ROM TeacherWorks™ CD-ROM Vocabulary PuzzleMaker CD-ROM Audio Program ABCNews Interactive™ Historic America Electronic Field Trips American Music: Hits Through History

0:00 OUT OF TIME?
Assign the Chapter 13 **Reading Essentials and Study Guide.**

*Also Available in Spanish

 Blackline Master   Transparency   CD-ROM   DVD

Poster   Music Program   Audio Program   Videocassette

NATIONAL GEOGRAPHIC   Teacher's Corner

INDEX TO NATIONAL GEOGRAPHIC MAGAZINE

The following articles relate to this chapter.

- "Along the Santa Fe Trail," March 1991
- "Buffalo: Back Home on the Range," November 1994
- "Geronimo," October 1992
- "John Wesley Powell," April 1994
- "Ogallala Aquifer," March 1993
- "Wide Open Wyoming," January 1993

NATIONAL GEOGRAPHIC SOCIETY PRODUCTS AVAILABLE FROM GLENCOE

To order the following products for use with this chapter, contact your local Glencoe sales representative, or call Glencoe at 1-800-334-7344:

- *PictureShow: Native Americans, 1 and 2* (CD-ROM)
- *PictureShow: The Westward Movement* (CD-ROM)
- *PicturePack: The Westward Movement* (Transparencies)

ADDITIONAL NATIONAL GEOGRAPHIC SOCIETY PRODUCTS

To order the following, call National Geographic at 1-800-368-2728:

- *Heritage of the Black West* (Video)
- *Immigration: The Triumph of Hope* (Video)
- *The West That Was* (Video)

NGS ONLINE

Access National Geographic's Web site for current events, atlas updates, activities, links, interactive features, and archives.
www.nationalgeographic.com

From the Classroom of...

Teresa Squires Osborne
Reynolds High School
Troutdale, OR

Immigration Panel

Create a panel of students, from your class and/or from the school, made up of first and second generation immigrants to the U.S. After panel members have shown their country of origin on a map, have the student panel address the following information:

1. What is the story of your family's arrival here? Where and when did you or your parents arrive in the U.S.?
2. Why did your family choose to leave your native country?
3. What is different or similar about life in the U.S. compared to your family's native country?
4. How would your life be different if you or your parents had remained?

Have students compare the answers of the panel with the experiences of earlier immigrant groups.

ADDITIONAL RESOURCES FROM GLENCOE

- American Music: Cultural Traditions
- American Art & Architecture
- Outline Map Resource Book
- U.S. Desk Map
- Building Geography Skills for Life
- Inclusion for the High School Social Studies Classroom Strategies and Activities
- Teaching Strategies for the American History Classroom (Including Block Scheduling Pacing Guides)

KEY TO ABILITY LEVELS

Teaching strategies have been coded.

- **L1** BASIC activities for all students
- **L2** AVERAGE activities for average to above-average students
- **L3** CHALLENGING activities for above-average students
- **ELL** ENGLISH LANGUAGE LEARNER activities

Block Schedule

Activities that are suited to use within the block scheduling framework are identified by:

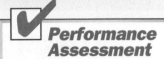
Why It Matters Activity

Ask students how the settlement of the West affects their lives today. Students should evaluate their answers after they have completed the chapter.

CHAPTER

13 Settling the West
1865–1900

Why It Matters

After the Civil War, a dynamic period in American history opened—the settlement of the West. The lives of Western miners, farmers, and ranchers were often filled with great hardships, but the wave of American settlers continued. Railroads hastened this migration. During this period, many Native Americans lost their homelands and their way of life.

The Impact Today

Developments of this period are still evident today.
* *Native American reservations still exist in the United States.*
* *The myth of the Western hero is prominent in popular culture.*

The American Vision Video The Chapter 13 video, "Life in the West," chronicles the early days of western settlement in the United States.

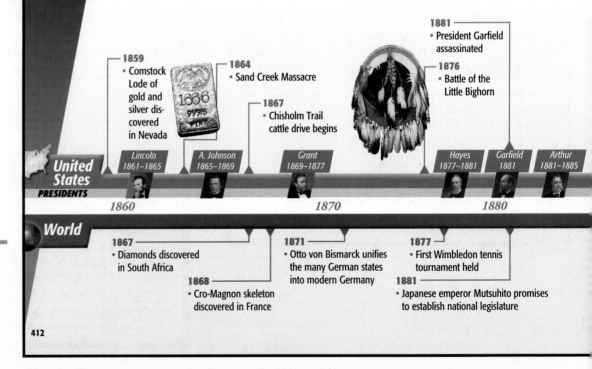

1859
* Comstock Lode of gold and silver discovered in Nevada

1864
* Sand Creek Massacre

1867
* Chisholm Trail cattle drive begins

1881
* President Garfield assassinated

1876
* Battle of the Little Bighorn

United States PRESIDENTS

| Lincoln 1861–1865 | A. Johnson 1865–1869 | Grant 1869–1877 | Hayes 1877–1881 | Garfield 1881 | Arthur 1881–1885 |

1860 *1870* *1880*

World

1867
* Diamonds discovered in South Africa

1868
* Cro-Magnon skeleton discovered in France

1871
* Otto von Bismarck unifies the many German states into modern Germany

1877
* First Wimbledon tennis tournament held

1881
* Japanese emperor Mutsuhito promises to establish national legislature

412

TWO-MINUTE LESSON LAUNCHER

Ask students what they know about the settlement of the West. Ask them how they think each of the following affected the Western settlement: government policy, railroads, investors, Native Americans, Reconstruction, natural resources, and climate.

HISTORY *Online*

Introduce students to chapter content and key terms by having them access the **Chapter 13 Overview** at tav.glencoe.com.

More About the Photo

Joseph E. Stimson was the official photographer for the Union Pacific Railroad in Cheyenne, Wyoming from 1889 to 1903. He often photographed Native Americans in Wyoming during his travels for the railroad. The mother and child who appear on page 413 stood in a field of Red Cross and Turkey Red Wheat at a U.S. experimental station at Newcastle, Wyoming.

Mother and child in a Wyoming wheat field

1885
• First skyscraper built in Chicago

1887
• Dawes Act eliminates communal ownership of Native American reservations

1896
• *Plessy* v. *Ferguson* creates "separate but equal" doctrine

Cleveland 1885–1889

B. Harrison 1889–1893

Cleveland 1893–1897

McKinley 1897–1901

1890

1900

1888
• Brazil ends slavery

1894
• China begins war against Japan

1896
• Modern Olympics begin in Athens, Greece

HISTORY *Online*

Chapter Overview
Visit the *American Vision* Web site at tav.glencoe.com and click on *Chapter Overviews—Chapter 13* to preview chapter information.

TIME LINE ACTIVITY

Have students write a short biographical profile of one of the presidents shown on the time line on pages 412 and 413. Instruct students to include information about how the president they select influenced the settlement of the West.

413

GRAPHIC ORGANIZER ACTIVITY

Organizing Information Have students create an integrated time line using the chapter and section time lines. Instruct students to use absolute chronology in placing significant events on the time line.

413

1 FOCUS

Section Overview

This section focuses on the westward migration of people searching for economic opportunities as miners and ranchers.

BELLRINGER
Skillbuilder Activity

Project transparency and have students answer the question.

Available as a blackline master.

Daily Focus Skills Transparency 13–1

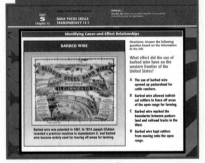

Guide to Reading

Answers to Graphic: silver in Nevada (Comstock Lode); lead and silver in Leadville, Colorado; gold in Colorado; gold in Dakota Territory; copper in Montana

Preteaching Vocabulary
Have students look up the meanings of the Key Terms and use the words in a sentence.

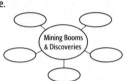

Guide to Reading

Main Idea
Miners and ranchers settled large areas of the West.

Key Terms and Names
placer mining, quartz mining, Henry Comstock, vigilance committee, open range, long drive, Chisholm Trail, maverick, barbed wire

Reading Strategy
Organizing As you read about the development of the mining industry, complete a graphic organizer listing the locations of mining booms and the discoveries made there.

Mining Booms & Discoveries

Reading Objectives
• **Trace** the growth of the mining industry in the West.
• **Describe** the ways that new technology changed open-range ranching.

Section Theme
Economic Factors People migrated to the West in search of economic opportunity.

Preview of Events

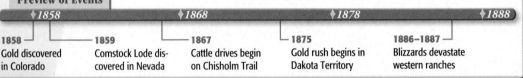

♦1858　　♦1868　　♦1878　　♦1888

1858
Gold discovered in Colorado

1859
Comstock Lode discovered in Nevada

1867
Cattle drives begin on Chisholm Trail

1875
Gold rush begins in Dakota Territory

1886–1887
Blizzards devastate western ranches

★ An American Story ★

Jacob Waldorf arrived in Virginia City, Nevada, in 1873 to seek his fortune in the fabled silver mines of the Comstock Lode. Like many others, he found work at one of the big mining companies. Seven days a week he toiled in a dangerous mine shaft, earning enough to support his family and buy a little stock in local mining companies. As his son John recalled:

❝The favorite game with our father was stocks. . . . Mother used to say to me, 'Some day we're going back east,' but for years none of the stocks in which Dad invested showed any disposition to furnish us with the price of transportation.❞

In 1877 the stock Waldorf owned skyrocketed in value. "Dad's holdings rose . . . to $10,000 and mother began to talk of buying a farm," John wrote. "The stock kept going upward. Dad was worth $15,000 for at least a minute." He waited for the stock to go even higher before selling, but instead it plummeted: "The bottom fell out of Ophi [a mining stock], and Mother's dream farm fell with it, for Dad was broke."

Jacob Waldorf overcame this financial setback. Earning the respect of his fellow workers, he headed the miners' union in 1880 and later served as a state legislator.

—adapted from *A Kid on the Comstock*

Miner working the Comstock Lode

Growth of the Mining Industry

The story of western mining is bigger than the individual stories of fortune seekers like Waldorf. The West's rich deposits of gold, silver, and copper served the needs of growing industries in the East. They also brought the first wave of settlers that populated the mountain states of the West.

SECTION RESOURCES

Reproducible Masters
• Reproducible Lesson Plan 13–1
• Daily Lecture and Discussion Notes 13–1
• Guided Reading Activity 13–1
• Section Quiz 13–1
• Reading Essentials and Study Guide 13–1

Transparencies
• Daily Focus Skills Transparency 13–1

• American Art & Architecture

Multimedia
🔘 Interactive Tutor Self-Assessment CD-ROM
🔘 ExamView® Pro Testmaker CD-ROM
🔘 Presentation Plus! CD-ROM
🔘 TeacherWorks™ CD-ROM
🎧 Audio Program
🎵 American Music: Hits Through History

News of a mineral strike in an area would start a stampede of prospectors desperately hoping to strike it rich. Early prospectors would extract the shallow deposits of ore largely by hand in a process called placer mining, using simple equipment like picks, shovels, and pans. After these surface deposits dwindled, corporations would move in to begin quartz mining, which dug deep beneath the surface. As those deposits dried up, commercial mining either disappeared or continued on a restricted basis.

ECONOMICS

The Big Strike in Nevada The story of the Comstock Lode is similar to other stories of gold, silver, and copper strikes throughout the West. In 1859 a prospector named **Henry Comstock** staked a claim in Six-Mile Canyon, Nevada. The sticky, blue-gray mud found there turned out to be nearly pure silver ore. News of the Comstock strike brought hordes of miners to Virginia City, Nevada. Almost overnight the town went from a frontier outpost to a boomtown of about 30,000, boasting an opera house, shops with furniture and fashions from Europe, several newspapers, and a six-story hotel with the West's first elevator, called a "rising room." When the silver veins were exhausted several years later, the mines closed. Without the mines, the town's economy collapsed,

and most of the townspeople moved on in search of new opportunities. This cycle of boom and bust—from boomtown to ghost town—was repeated throughout the mountainous West.

During the booms, crime posed a serious problem. Prospectors fought over claims, and thieves haunted the streets and trails. Law enforcers were scarce, and self-appointed volunteers sometimes formed **vigilance committees** to track down and punish wrongdoers. In some cases, they punished the innocent or let the guilty go free, but most people in these communities respected the law and tried to deal firmly but fairly with those accused of crimes.

Mining towns such as Virginia City at first were inhabited mostly by men, but soon they attracted more women. Some women owned property and were influential community leaders. Others worked as cooks or in laundries. Still other women worked at "hurdy-gurdy" houses (named after the mechanical musical instrument), where they danced with men for the price of a drink.

Other Bonanzas Mining also spurred the development of Colorado, the Dakota Territory, and Montana. The discovery of gold near Pikes Peak in 1858 set miners on a frantic rush. Coining the phrase "Pikes Peak

TECHNOLOGY & History

Mining Sluice

Western prospectors used sluices to search riverbeds more quickly than they could with the backbreaking panning method. A sluice diverted the current of a river into earthen or wooden trenches. The water was directed to a box with metal "riffle" bars that disturbed the current, causing heavier minerals to settle to the bottom of the box. A screen at the end of the riffle box prevented the minerals from flowing out. *Why was the sluice more efficient than panning for precious minerals?*

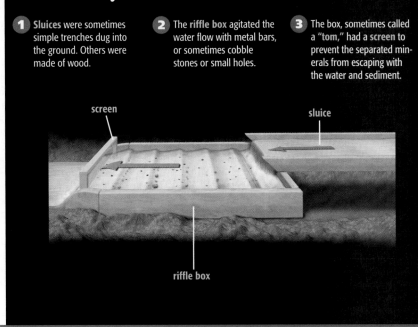

1 **Sluices** were sometimes simple trenches dug into the ground. Others were made of wood.

2 The **riffle box** agitated the water flow with metal bars, or sometimes cobble stones or small holes.

3 The box, sometimes called a **"tom,"** had a **screen** to prevent the separated minerals from escaping with the water and sediment.

screen

sluice

riffle box

2 TEACH

Daily Lecture and Discussion Notes 13–1

Copyright © The McGraw-Hill Companies, Inc.

Daily Lecture and Discussion Notes

Chapter 13, Section 1

Did You Know? Some cattle ranches in the West were enormous, covering more land than Massachusetts and Vermont put together.

I. Growth of the Mining Industry *(pages 414–416)*

A. The growing industries in the East needed the West's rich deposits of gold, silver, and copper. These deposits brought settlers to the West's mountain states.

B. Prospectors used simple equipment like picks, shovels, and pans to mine the shallow deposits of ore by hand. This process is known as **placer mining**. Corporations dug deep beneath the surface to mine the deposits of ore in a process known as **quartz mining**.

Creating a Thematic Map Have students create a thematic map showing the locations mentioned under the heading "Growth of the Mining Industry." **L1**

Use the rubric for creating a map, display, or chart on pages 77–78 in the *Performance Assessment Activities and Rubrics.*

TECHNOLOGY & History

Background: Sometimes a V-shaped cut would be made in a hill, and a system of sluice boxes would be installed to separate the material washed down the hillside. Gold and silver were separated from the worthless rock. Mounds of worthless rock still exist in some places today, lasting evidence of the miners' work.

Answer: searches for minerals went more quickly and efficiently using sluices

COOPERATIVE LEARNING ACTIVITY

Constructing a Plan Organize students into several small groups and ask groups to construct a plan for a late-1800s Western town. Suggest that groups consider the following points in preparing their plans: the buildings they will include and their location; the building materials, energy sources, and landscaping they want to use; and the public facilities they will include. Have groups draw pictorial maps of their towns and accompany them with short reports explaining the choices they made in planning.

Use the rubric for a cooperative group management plan on pages 81–82 in the *Performance Assessment Activities and Rubrics.*

Guided Reading Activity 13–1

Reading Check

Answer: The Dakota Territory was divided into the states of North Dakota, South Dakota, and Montana.

Creating a Thematic Graph

Write the following data on the board.

Population of Denver, Colorado

1870	4,759
1880	35,629
1890	106,713
1900	133,859

Ask students to create a thematic graph showing the trend of Denver's population from 1870 to 1900. **L2**

📂 Use the rubric for creating a map, display, or chart on pages 77–78 in the *Performance Assessment Activities and Rubrics.*

Linking Past & Present

The residents of Virginia City, Nevada, which was first known as Virginny Town, got some of their news from the *Territorial Enterprise*. The newspaper employed a young reporter from Hannibal, Missouri, named Sam Clemens. Most of the readers knew him by his pen name, Mark Twain.

---

or Bust," many panned for gold without success and headed home, complaining of a "Pikes Peak hoax."

In truth, there was plenty of gold and silver in the Colorado mountains, but much of it was hidden beneath the surface and hard to extract. One of the richest strikes occurred in the late 1870s in Leadville, so called for deep deposits of lead that contained large amounts of silver. By the summer of 1879, as many as 1,000 newcomers per week were pouring into Leadville, creating one of the most legendary boomtowns dotting the mining frontier.

Overall, operations at Leadville and other mining towns in Colorado yielded more than $1 billion worth of silver and gold (many billions in today's money). This bonanza spurred the building of railroads through the Rocky Mountains and transformed Denver, the supply point for the mining areas, into the second largest city in the West after San Francisco.

The discovery of gold in the Black Hills of the Dakota Territory and copper in Montana led to rapid development of the northern Great Plains. Miners flooded into the region in the 1870s. After railroads were built in the 1880s, many farmers and ranchers moved to the territory. In 1889, Congress divided the Dakota Territory and admitted North Dakota and South Dakota, as well as Montana, as new states.

✓ Reading Check **Explain** How did the creation of new states change the political boundaries of the Great Plains?

Ranching and Cattle Drives

While many Americans headed to the Rocky Mountains to mine gold and silver after the Civil War, others began building vast cattle ranches on the Great Plains. In the early 1800s, Americans did not think cattle ranches on the Great Plains were practical. Water was scarce, and cattle from the East could not survive on the tough prairie grasses. Farther south, however, in Texas, there existed a breed of cattle adapted to living on the Great Plains.

The Texas longhorn was a breed descended from Spanish cattle that had been brought to Mexico two centuries earlier. Ranchers in Mexico and Texas had allowed their cattle to run wild, and slowly a new breed—the longhorn—had emerged. Lean and rangy, the longhorn could easily survive in the harsh climate of the Plains, and by 1865, as many as 5 million of them roamed the grasslands of Texas.

Mexicans had introduced cattle ranching in New Mexico, California, and Texas before these areas became part of the United States. The industry grew in part because of the open range—a vast area of grassland owned by the government. The open range covered much of the Great Plains and provided land where ranchers could graze their herds free of charge and unrestricted by the boundaries of private farms.

Mexican cowhands developed the tools and techniques for rounding up and driving cattle. These Hispanic herders taught American cowhands their trade and enriched the English vocabulary with words of Spanish origin, including "lariat," "lasso," and "stampede."

Linking Past & Present

Virginia City

Past: Comstock Boomtown
The wealth of its silver mines turned Virginia City, Nevada, from a leaky-tent mining town into a metropolis with five newspapers and a stock exchange. Express companies carried out silver and brought in supplies for the city's 30,000 people.

Present: Tourist Center
Unlike many mining towns that became ghost towns, Virginia City still exists. The community depends on the tourist industry. Visitors can see the old school building, the opera house, and a mining museum. Virginia City is just a short drive from Carson City and Lake Tahoe.

MEETING SPECIAL NEEDS

Kinesthetic Have interested students build a model to demonstrate either the process of panning for gold and silver or using a sluice to find the minerals. Have students demonstrate the process to the class using their models. Tell students to be prepared to answer questions about their models. **L2**

📂 Refer to *Inclusion for the High School Social Studies Classroom Strategies and Activities* in the TCR.

NATIONAL GEOGRAPHIC — Mining Country and Cattle Trails, 1848–1890

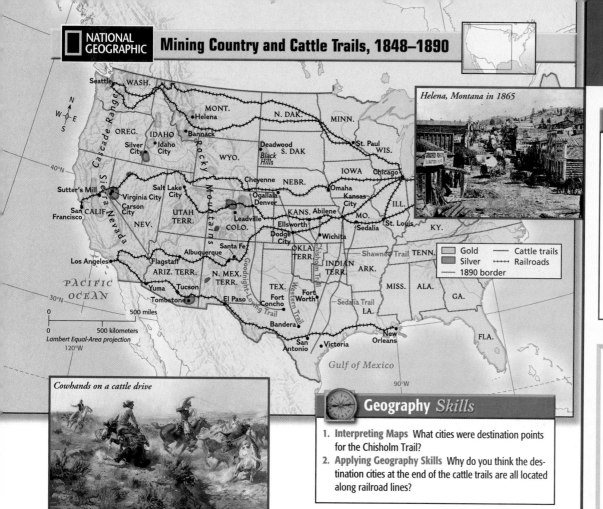

Helena, Montana in 1865

Gold | Silver | 1890 border | Cattle trails | Railroads

Cowhands on a cattle drive

Geography *Skills*

1. **Interpreting Maps** What cities were destination points for the Chisholm Trail?
2. **Applying Geography Skills** Why do you think the destination cities at the end of the cattle trails are all located along railroad lines?

Before the Civil War, ranchers had little incentive to round up the longhorns. Beef prices were low, and moving the cattle to eastern markets was not practical. Two developments changed this situation: the Civil War and the construction of the railroads. During the Civil War, eastern cattle were slaughtered in huge numbers to feed the armies of the Union and the Confederacy. After the war, beef prices soared, making it worthwhile to round up the longhorns if a way could be found to move them east.

By the 1860s, railroads had reached the Great Plains. Lines ended at Abilene and Dodge City in Kansas and at Sedalia in Missouri. Ranchers and livestock dealers realized that if the longhorns were rounded up and driven north several hundred miles to the railroad, they could be sold for a huge profit and shipped east to market.

In 1866 ranchers rounded up cattle and drove about 260,000 of them to Sedalia, Missouri. Although only a fraction of the herds survived this first long drive, the drive overall was a tremendous success, proving that cattle could be driven north to the rail lines and sold for 10 times the price they could get in Texas.

Other trails soon opened. The route to Abilene, Kansas, became the major route north. Between 1867 and 1871, cowboys drove nearly 1.5 million head of cattle up the **Chisholm Trail** to Abilene—a town that, when filled with cowboys at the end of a drive, rivaled the mining towns in terms of rowdiness. As the railroads expanded in the West, other trails reached from Texas to more towns in Kansas, Nebraska, Montana, and Wyoming.

The Long Drive A long drive was a spectacular sight. It began with the spring roundup when ranchers met with their cowboys to collect cattle from the

CHAPTER 13 Settling the West **417**

3 ASSESS

Assign Section 1 Assessment as homework or as an in-class activity.

● Have students use the **Interactive Tutor Self-Assessment CD-ROM.**

Reading Essentials and Study Guide 13–1

Name _____ Date _____ Class _____

Study Guide

Chapter 13, Section 1

For use with textbook pages 414–419

MINERS AND RANCHERS

KEY TERMS AND NAMES

placer mining the process of removing mineral ore by hand *(page 415)*

quartz mining the process of removing ore by digging deep beneath the surface *(page 415)*

Henry Comstock prospector who found huge silver strike in Nevada *(page 415)*

vigilance committee self-appointed volunteers who tracked down and punished wrongdoers *(page 416)*

open range vast areas of grassland owned by the federal government *(page 416)*

long drive cattle run in which herds were moved great distances to a rail line, where they were shipped to market *(page 417)*

Section Quiz 13–1

Name _____ Date _____ Class _____

★ **Chapter 13**   Score ____

Section Quiz 13-1

DIRECTIONS: Matching Match each item in Column A with the items in Column B. Write the correct letters in the blanks. *(10 points each)*

Column A	Column B
___ 1. the major route north to Abilene, Kansas	A. open range
___ 2. mining that dug deep beneath the surface	B. placer mining
___ 3. self-appointed volunteers to track down and punish wrongdoers	C. vigilance committees
___ 4. vast areas of grassland owned by the federal government	D. Chisolm Trail
___ 5. process of extracting shallow deposits of ore largely by hand	E. quartz mining

DIRECTIONS: Multiple Choice In the blank at the left, write the letter of the choice that best completes the statement or answers the question. *(10 points each)*

Frederic Remington statue

Picturing History

Breaking Camp This painting by Charles M. Russell captures the excitement of a long cattle drive. Ranchers hired cowboys to move thousands of cattle north to railroad towns, where the cattle were then shipped east for butchering and sale in the cities. How did the Civil War encourage the start of long cattle drives?

open range. Stock from many different owners made up these herds. Only their brands showing which rancher owned the cattle distinguished them from one another. Stray calves with no identifying symbols were called mavericks. These were divided and branded. The combined herds moving onto the trail could number anywhere from 2,000 to 5,000 cattle.

Cowboys for major ranchers went north with the herds. Most of the cowboys in the early years of the cattle drives were former Confederate army soldiers escaping the harsh life in the South during Reconstruction. A few were Hispanic, and many were African Americans such as Nat Love. Born an enslaved man in Tennessee in 1854, Love was freed at the end of the Civil War. He went west in 1869 and applied for work with a cattle-driving outfit that included several other African American cowhands:

❝After breakfast I asked the camp boss for a job as a cow boy. He asked me if I could ride a wild horse. I said 'yes sir.' He said if you can I will give you a job. So he spoke to one of the colored cow boys called Bronko Jim, and told him to go out and rope old Good Eye, saddle him and put me on his back. Bronko Jim gave me a few pointers and told me to look out for the horse was especially bad. . . . This

proved the worst horse to ride I had ever mounted in my life, but I stayed with him and the cow boys were the most surprised outfit you ever saw, as they had taken me for a tenderfoot, pure and simple. After the horse got tired and I dismounted the boss said he would give me a job and pay me $30.00 per month and more later on.❞

—quoted in *Life and Adventures of Nat Love*

Life for Love and the other cowboys on the trail demanded discipline, endurance, and courage, but those who survived the many dangers collected wages to spend in the towns at the end of the trail. Life in these towns was exciting, but many cowboys told exaggerated tales of daring that often supplied material for what were called "dime novels." These adventure books sold for a dime and helped spread the myths of the "Wild West" in eastern towns and cities.

Ranching Becomes Big Business Cowboys drove millions of cattle north from Texas to Kansas and points beyond. Some of the cattle went straight to slaughterhouses, but many were sold to ranchers who were building up herds and grazing them in Wyoming, Montana, and other territories. When sheep herders moved their flocks onto the range and when farmers settled there, blocking the trails,

418 CHAPTER 13 Settling the West

CRITICAL THINKING ACTIVITY

Analyzing Have students use the map on page 417 and the material they have learned in this section to create at least five questions that students in the class should be able to answer about railroads and cattle trails. For example, where was silver mined? Have students exchange questions with a partner. After students have answered the questions, have the class list the conclusions they can draw about the importance of railroads to the growth of the mining and cattle industries. **L1**

"range wars" broke out among competing groups. Eventually, and after considerable loss of life, the range was largely fenced off with a new invention—**barbed wire**—which enabled hundreds of square miles to be fenced off cheaply and easily.

At first, ranchers saw barbed wire as more of a threat than an opportunity. They did not want to abandon open grazing and complained when farmers put up barriers that prevented the ranchers' livestock from roaming. Soon, however, ranchers used barbed wire to shut out those competing with them for land and to keep their animals closer to sources of food and water. For cowhands, however, barbed wire ended the excitement of long cattle drives.

The fencing in of the range was not the only reason the long drives ended. Investors from the East and from Britain poured money into the booming cattle business, causing an oversupply of animals on the market. Prices dropped dramatically in the mid-1880s and many ranchers went bankrupt. Then, in the winter of 1886 to 1887, blizzards covered the ground with snow so deep that the cattle could not dig down to the grass. Temperatures fell to more than 40 degrees below zero.

The cattle industry survived this terrible blow, but it was changed forever. The day of the open range had ended. From that point on, herds were raised on fenced-in ranches. New European breeds replaced longhorns, and the cowboy became a ranch hand.

✓ **Reading Check** **Analyzing** How did heavy investment in the cattle industry affect the industry as a whole?

World Geography Connection

The Cowboys of Argentina

While cowboys are often considered a unique part of the American heritage, they also belong to the history of another nation, Argentina. Like the cowboys of the American West, this group of hardy and daring individuals made their living during the 1800s trying to tame the "pampas"—Argentina's frontier grasslands. Known as "gauchos," they rounded up wild cattle and horses on the pampas and sold their hides. Like their counterparts to the north, gauchos wore distinctive clothing—wide-brim hats, ponchos, and loose trousers tucked into low boots—and became highly romanticized and revered figures. They also went the same way as the American cowboy, eventually becoming ranch hands as big business took greater control of the cattle and herding industry. **What were the similarities between the American cowboys and the gauchos?**

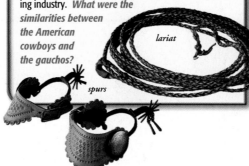
lariat

spurs

SECTION 1 ASSESSMENT

Checking for Understanding
1. **Define:** placer mining, quartz mining, open range, long drive, maverick.
2. **Identify:** Henry Comstock, vigilance committee, Chisholm Trail, barbed wire.
3. **List** the factors that contributed to the rise of the cattle industry.
4. **Explain** how cattle ranching shifted from open range to an organized business operation.

Reviewing Themes
5. **Economic Factors** What two developments in the late 1800s led to the decline of the cattle business?

Critical Thinking
6. **Evaluating** How did the mining industry contribute to the development of the West?
7. **Organizing** Use a graphic organizer similar to the one below to list the ways barbed wire was used and the result of using barbed wire on the Great Plains.

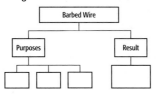

Barbed Wire

Purposes   Result

Analyzing Visuals
8. **Examining Maps** Study the map detailing the western mining country and cattle trails on page 417. Then create your own thematic map detailing either the cattle country or the mining country.

Writing About History
9. **Descriptive Writing** Write a summary for a story line for a Hollywood movie. Your script should realistically portray the lives of either a miner or rancher in the West in the mid- to late 1800s. Be sure to include descriptions of people living in a western settlement.

CHAPTER 13   Settling the West   **419**

World Geography Connection

Answer: They were hardy individuals who wore distinctive clothing and lived on the frontier.
Ask: Where did gauchos work? *(in the pampas of Argentina)*

you don't say...

Stray Cattle Unbranded animals were called mavericks after cattle rancher Samuel A. Maverick, who shunned the practice of branding. Today, the term maverick is often used to identify an independent individual.

Reteach
Have students trace the growth of the mining industry.

Enrich
Have students research the conflict among cattle ranchers, sheepherders, and farmers and write a few paragraphs on how this conflict might have been resolved without violence.

✓ **Reading Check**

Answer: It caused an oversupply of cattle, which drove prices down. Many ranchers went bankrupt.

4 CLOSE

Have students describe the ways new technology changed open-range ranching.

419

SECTION 2 Farming the Plains

1 FOCUS

Section Overview
This section focuses on the people who settled the Great Plains.

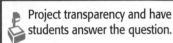

BELLRINGER
Skillbuilder Activity

Project transparency and have students answer the question.

Available as a blackline master.

Daily Focus Skills Transparency 13–2

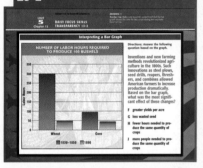

Guide to Reading

Answers to Graphic: Homestead Act, Morrill Act, and promoting railroad construction

Preteaching Vocabulary
Have students skim the section to preview each of the Key Terms and Names.

Guide to Reading

Main Idea
After 1865, settlers staked out homesteads and began farming the Great Plains.

Key Terms and Names
Great Plains, Stephen Long, Homestead Act, homestead, dry farming, sodbuster, Wheat Belt, bonanza farm

Reading Strategy
Organizing As you read about the settlement of the Great Plains, complete a graphic organizer similar to the one below listing the ways the government encouraged settlement.

Government Assistance in Settling Great Plains

Reading Objectives
• **Explain** why and how people began settling the Plains.
• **Trace** the growth of commercial farming on the Plains.

Section Theme
Science and Technology The need for new farming techniques in the West led to several technological innovations.

Preview of Events

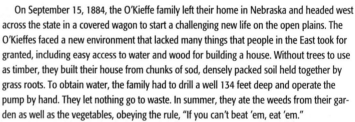

◆1860	◆1870	◆1880	◆1890

1862 — Homestead Act
1873 — Timber Culture Act
late 1870s — Bonanza farming begins on Great Plains
late 1880s — Western farmlands hit by drought

★ An American Story ★

On September 15, 1884, the O'Kieffe family left their home in Nebraska and headed west across the state in a covered wagon to start a challenging new life on the open plains. The O'Kieffes faced a new environment that lacked many things that people in the East took for granted, including easy access to water and wood for building a house. Without trees to use as timber, they built their house from chunks of sod, densely packed soil held together by grass roots. To obtain water, the family had to drill a well 134 feet deep and operate the pump by hand. They let nothing go to waste. In summer, they ate the weeds from their garden as well as the vegetables, obeying the rule, "If you can't beat 'em, eat 'em."

There were other settlers in the area, and they would gather to socialize and help each other. When disaster struck, however, each family had to be prepared to face the trouble alone. In January 1888, a three-day blizzard struck without warning. As Charley, the youngest son, reflected: "By the end of the three-day blizzard we were in fine shape to take care of our stock. Many others did not fare so well; but that's life. After all, we said to each other, this was a new country and folks had to learn how to look after themselves."

Well hand pump

—adapted from *Western Story: Recollections of Charley O'Kieffe*

Geography of the Plains

The O'Kieffes and their neighbors were early settlers in a region known today as the **Great Plains.** This region extends westward to the Rocky Mountains from around the 100th meridian—an imaginary line running north and south from the central Dakotas through western Texas. Rainfall on the Plains averages less than 20 inches per year, and trees grow

---

SECTION RESOURCES

Reproducible Masters
• Reproducible Lesson Plan 13–2
• Daily Lecture and Discussion Notes 13–2
• Guided Reading Activity 13–2
• Section Quiz 13–2
• Reading Essentials and Study Guide 13–2
• Performance Assessment Activities and Rubrics

Transparencies
• Daily Focus Skills Transparency 13–2

Multimedia
🕹 Interactive Tutor Self-Assessment CD-ROM
🕹 ExamView® Pro Testmaker CD-ROM
🕹 TeacherWorks™ CD-ROM
🎧 Audio Program
🎵 American Music: Cultural Traditions

naturally only along rivers and streams. For centuries this open country had been home to vast herds of buffalo that grazed on the prairie grasses. Nomadic Native American groups had hunted the buffalo for food and used buffalo hides for clothing and shelter.

Major **Stephen Long,** who explored the region with an army expedition in 1819, called it the "Great American Desert" and concluded that it was "almost wholly unfit for cultivation." He predicted that the scarcity of wood and water would prove to be "an insuperable obstacle in . . . settling the country."

✓ **Reading Check** **Examining** What geographic factors created challenges to the settlement of the Great Plains in the late 1800s?

The Beginnings of Settlement

During the late 1800s several factors undermined the belief that the Plains was a "Great American Desert." One important factor was the construction of the railroads, which provided easy access to the Great Plains. Railroad companies sold land along the rail lines at low prices and provided credit to prospective settlers. Railroads opened offices throughout the United States and in major cities in Europe where land was scarce. Posters and pamphlets proclaimed that booking passage to the Plains was a ticket to prosperity.

The catchy slogan "Rain follows the plow," coined by a Nebraskan to sell the idea that cultivating the Plains would increase rainfall, encouraged settlers.

As if to prove the saying correct, the weather cooperated. For more than a decade beginning in the 1870s, rainfall on the Plains was well above average. The lush green of the endless prairies contradicted the popular belief that the region was a desert.

In 1862, the government also supported settlement in the Great Plains region by passing the **Homestead Act.** For a $10 registration fee, an individual could file for a homestead—a tract of public land available for settlement. A homesteader could claim up to 160 acres of public land and could receive title to that land after living there for five years. Later government acts increased the size of the tracts available. The Homestead Act provided a legal method for settlers to acquire clear title to property in the West. With their property rights secured, settlers were more willing to move to the Plains.

When settlers arrived on the Plains, they often found life very difficult. The lack of trees and water forced them to build their first homes from sod cut from the ground and to drill wells up to 300 feet deep. Summer temperatures often soared over 100° Fahrenheit. Prairie fires were a constant danger. Sometimes swarms of grasshoppers swept over farms and destroyed the crops. In winter there were terrible blizzards and extreme cold. Despite these challenges, most homesteaders persisted and learned how to live in the harsh environment.

✓ **Reading Check** **Analyzing** What is the relationship between private property rights and the settlement of the Great Plains?

 *Picturing* **History**

Farming the Great Plains Technology made farming the vast open plains of America feasible. Here horse-drawn binders are being used to gather hay in the late 1800s. What other factors encouraged settlement on the Great Plains?

2 TEACH

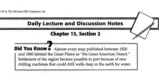

Daily Lecture and Discussion Notes 13–2

Copyright © by The McGraw-Hill Companies, Inc.

Daily Lecture and Discussion Notes
Chapter 13, Section 2

Did You Know? Almost every map published between 1820 and 1860 labeled the Great Plains as the "Great American Desert." Settlement of the region became possible in part because of new drilling machines that could drill wells deep in the earth for water.

I. Geography of the Plains (pages 420–421)

  A. The Great Plains region extends westward to the Rocky Mountains from around the 100th meridian—a line running north and south from the central Dakotas through Abilene, Texas.

  B. Rainfall on the Great Plains averages less than 20 inches per year. Trees only grow naturally along rivers and streams and on hilltops.

Summarizing Information
Have students list the problems and solutions in settling the land and in accessing transportation.
L1

✓ **Reading Check**

Answer: low rainfall and few trees

 *Picturing* **History**

Answer: Railroads sold the land along tracks cheaply; the government sold tracks at reduced prices.
Ask: How did many farmers get their land? *(They could claim 160 acres by filing for a homestead and living on the land for five years.)*

✓ **Reading Check**

Answer: The Homestead Act secured individual private property rights to settlers, which made people more willing to move there.

History *and the* **Humanities**

🎵 American Music: Cultural Traditions: "Little Old Sod Shanty"

Why It Matters

Justin Smith Morrill, a U.S. Representative from Vermont, introduced the Land-Grant College Act of 1862, also known as the Morrill Act. The Morrill Act of 1890 required states to use funds from the first Morrill Act to educate both African American and white students. The result was the establishment of 16 African American land-grant colleges across the South.

3 ASSESS

Assign Section 2 Assessment as homework or as an in-class activity.

⊕ Have students use the **Interactive Tutor Self-Assessment CD-ROM.**

Why It Matters

Land-Grant Colleges

To promote agriculture and manufacturing, the 1862 Morrill Act gave states large tracts of federal lands, with the requirement that part of the land be used to set up and maintain colleges. The colleges were required to offer programs in agriculture and engineering as well as traditional academic subjects. Military training programs were also required at these "land-grant colleges." Most state agricultural and engineering schools were established under the Morrill Act. Today every state, as well as Puerto Rico, has at least one land-grant college.

◄ 4-H Programs
Extension services associated with land-grant colleges coordinate the 4-H programs that help train future farmers. 4-H offers many programs for young people ages 5 to 19.

ROTC ►
The Reserve Officer Training Corps (ROTC) programs set up at land-grant colleges have been instrumental in providing training for the U.S. military. The program continues to provide scholarships for young Americans around the nation.

The Wheat Belt

For those who had the financial resources, farming could be very profitable on the Plains. Many inventions and new farming methods revolutionized agriculture.

One approach, called dry farming, was to plant seeds deep in the ground where there was enough moisture for them to grow. By the 1860s, farmers on the Plains were employing newly designed steel plows, seed drills, reapers, and threshing machines. The new machines made dry farming possible. Unfortunately, prairie soil often blew away, especially in a dry season. Many sodbusters, as those who plowed the soil on the Plains were called, eventually lost their homesteads through the combined effects of drought, wind erosion, and overuse of the land.

Large landholders faced similar problems, but they were able to make quick profits with the help of mechanical reapers, which speeded the harvest. Mechanical binders tied the stalks into bundles for collection. Threshing machines knocked kernels loose from the stalks. These innovations were well suited for harvesting wheat, which had the advantage of withstanding drought better than corn and some other crops. Wheat became as important to the Great Plains as cotton was to the South.

During the 1880s, many wheat farmers from Minnesota and other Midwestern states moved to the Great Plains to take advantage of the inexpensive land and the new farming technology. This productive new **Wheat Belt** began at the eastern edge of the Great Plains and encompassed much of the Dakotas and the western parts of Nebraska and Kansas.

Commercial Farming The new machines allowed a single family to bring in a substantial harvest on a wheat farm covering several hundred acres. Some wheat farms covered up to 50,000 acres. These were called bonanza farms because they often yielded big profits. Like mine owners, bonanza farmers formed companies, made large investments in property and equipment, and hired laborers as needed.

ECONOMICS

Farmers Fall on Hard Times The bountiful harvests in the Wheat Belt helped the United States become the world's leading exporter of wheat by the 1880s. American wheat growers faced rising competition, however, from other wheat-producing nations. In the 1890s, a glut of wheat on the world market caused prices to drop.

Some farmers tried to make it through lean periods by mortgaging their land—that is, they took bank loans based on the value of their property. If they failed to meet their mortgage payments, they forfeited the land to the bank and had to abandon

---

MEETING SPECIAL NEEDS

Logical/Mathematical Have students select two of the following states: Texas, Wisconsin, California, Minnesota, Oregon, Kansas, Nevada, or Nebraska. For their selected states, have students use historical data from the Census Bureau to chart their population growth from 1870 to 1890. Have the students use the charts to help them write a paragraph analyzing the Census Bureau's claim that the frontier was closing. **L2**

📁 Refer to *Inclusion for the High School Social Studies Classroom Strategies and Activities* in the TCR.

their farms or work them as tenants for the new owner. By 1900 tenants cultivated about one-third of the farms in the corn and wheat areas.

Adding to the problems of western farmers, a prolonged drought began in the late 1880s, killing crops and forcing many farmers to go back east. In Kansas, William Allen White, editor of the *Emporia Gazette,* described a disappointed farm family he saw returning from the western part of the state:

> 66There came through Emporia yesterday two old-fashioned mover wagons headed east. . . . These movers . . . had seen it stop raining for months at a time. They had heard the fury of the winter wind as it came whining across the short burned grass. . . . They have tossed through hot nights, wild with worry, and have arisen only to find their worst nightmares grazing in reality on the brown stubble in front of their sun-warped doors.99

In hard times, some homesteaders gave up and headed home, but others soon arrived to take their place.

✓ **Reading Check** **Identifying** What technological innovations helped farmers cultivate the Plains?

Closing the Frontier

In 1890 the Census Bureau reported that settlement throughout the West had been so rapid "that there can hardly be said to be a frontier line." In reality, much land was still unoccupied, and new settlement continued at a brisk pace into the 1900s. The news that the frontier was closing, however, concerned those who saw it as the end of an era. They believed that unoccupied land at the frontier had provided a "safety-valve of social discontent," the idea that Americans could always make a fresh start.

Most settlers did indeed make a fresh start, adjusting to the often hostile environment of the Plains. Water from their deep wells enabled them to plant trees and gardens. Railroads brought lumber and brick to replace sod as a building material and coal as fuel.

The O'Kieffes, who raised cattle, chickens, and a few crops, were typical of small-scale, self-sustaining homesteaders. They never got rich, but they got by. Those who struggled as the O'Keiffes did to support themselves emerged with a more realistic view of the West. It was not a land of limitless opportunity. As Charley O'Kieffe learned, the real story of the West was not about heroes who rode off into the sunset. It was about ordinary people who settled down and built homes and communities through great effort—"sterling and steady men and women whose lives were spent doing the work as it needed to be done."

✓ **Reading Check** **Examining** Why did some people feel that the closing of the frontier was the end of an era?

HISTORY Online

Student Web Activity Visit the *American Vision* Web site at tav.glencoe.com and click on *Student Web Activities— Chapter 13* for an activity on settling the West.

SECTION 2 ASSESSMENT

Checking for Understanding

1. **Define:** homestead, dry farming, sodbuster, bonanza farm.
2. **Identify:** Great Plains, Stephen Long, Homestead Act, Wheat Belt.
3. **Explain** why the Great Plains was not suitable for homesteading.

Reviewing Themes

4. **Science and Technology** How did the need for new farming techniques on the Great Plains result in technological innovations in agriculture?

Critical Thinking

5. **Analyzing** What factors contributed to the making of the Wheat Belt in the Great Plains and then to troubled times for wheat farmers in the 1890s?
6. **Categorizing** Use a graphic organizer similar to the one below to list the effects of technology on farming in the Great Plains.

Invention	Advantage for Farmers

Analyzing Visuals

7. **Examining Photographs** Study the photograph on page 421 of farmers using binding machines in western Wisconsin. Based on the terrain and the type of work they needed to do, what other types of technology would have helped farmers on the Plains?

Writing About History

8. **Persuasive Writing** Write an advertisement persuading people from the East and from Europe to establish homesteads in the Great Plains.

SECTION 2 ASSESSMENT ANSWERS

1. Terms are in blue.
2. Great Plains *(p. 420),* Stephen Long *(p. 421),* Homestead Act *(p. 421),* Wheat Belt *(p. 422)*
3. geography and climate
4. Mechanical reapers, binders, and threshing machines were all created to help farmers harvest large tracts of farmland quickly.
5. The Homestead Act, new farming techniques and equipment; good harvests, world competition caused a glut that caused prices to drop.
6. mechanical reapers: speeded harvesting; mechanical binders: tied stalks; threshing machines: knocked kernels loose
7. possible answer: windmills to supply power and irrigation
8. Advertisements will vary but should reflect information presented in the section.

Section Quiz 13–2

Name	Date _____ Class _____
⭐ **Chapter 13**	**Score**

Section Quiz 13–2

DIRECTIONS: Matching Match each item in Column A with the items in Column B. Write the correct letters in the blanks. *(10 points each)*

Column A	Column B
___ 1. a tract of public land available for settlement	**A.** bonanza farm
___ 2. often brought their owners big profits	**B.** Stephen Long
___ 3. productive farm area that began at the eastern edge of the Great Plains	**C.** Wheat Belt
___ 4. explored the Great Plains in 1819	**D.** dry farming
___ 5. planting seeds deep in the ground where there was enough moisture for them to grow	**E.** homestead

DIRECTIONS: Multiple Choice In the blank at the left, write the letter of the choice that best completes the statement or answers the question. *(10 points each)*

HISTORY Online

Objectives and answers to the student activity can be found in the **Web Activity Lesson Plan** at tav.glencoe.com.

✓ **Reading Check**

Answer: mechanical reapers, mechanical binders, threshing machines, and seed drills

Reteach
Have students explain why people settled the Plains.

Enrich
Have students research the founding of at least 10 land-grant colleges.

✓ **Reading Check**

Answer: They felt it ended the chance to make a fresh start.

4 CLOSE

Have students study commercial farming in the Plains.

TEACH

Interpreting Statistics Point out that two sets of data are not necessarily related. For example, if the local movie theater reports an increase in attendance and the local bookstore reports a dip in sales, it does not necessarily mean that people are going to the movies instead of buying books.

Assign students to find statistics related to your school and your community. Have students create a graphic or tabular display of the information. As a class, identify possible correlations and determine whether they are positive or negative.

Additional Practice

Reinforcing Skills Activity 13

Name _____ Date _____ Class _____

★ Reinforcing Skills Activity 13

Interpreting Statistics

☐ **LEARNING THE SKILL**
Statistics can help you support an opinion or make a point. Statistics are data collected and organized to help identify effects and make predictions. To interpret statistics, first read the title and any labels to get an overall idea of the information being shown. Analyze the numbers shown by looking for decreases, increases, similarities, and differences. Look for sets of numbers or data that seem to be related or that have some correlation. Draw conclusions from the information based on the relationships and trends you find.

☐ **PRACTICING THE SKILL**
DIRECTIONS: Study the statistical information, then answer the questions below on a separate sheet of paper.

GLENCOE
TECHNOLOGY

CD-ROM
Glencoe Skillbuilder Interactive Workbook CD-ROM, Level 2

This interactive CD-ROM reinforces student mastery of essential social studies skills.

Interpreting Statistics

The Railroad and Native American Population					
Year	1860	1870	1880	1890	1900
Approximate miles of railroad track in U.S.:	30,000	53,000	116,000	208,000	259,000
Approximate Native American population:	351,000	323,000	318,000	265,000	248,000

Why Learn This Skill?

Often presented in graphs and tables, statistics are collections of data that are used to support a claim or an opinion. The ability to interpret statistics allows us to understand probable effects and to make predictions.

Learning the Skill

Use the following steps to help you interpret statistical information.

- **Scan** the graph or table, reading the title and labels to get an idea of what is being shown.
- **Examine** the statistics shown, looking for increases and decreases, similarities and differences.
- **Look** for a *correlation* in the statistics. Two sets of data may be related or unrelated. If they are related, we say that there is a correlation between them. In a positive correlation, as one number rises, so does the other number. In a negative correlation, as one number rises, the other number falls. For example, there is a positive correlation between academic achievement and wages, and there is a negative correlation between smoking and life expectancy. Sometimes, statistics may try to show a correlation when none exists. For example, a report that "people who go fishing are less likely to get cancer" may be statistically true but lack any real correlation.
- **Determine** the conclusions you can draw from the statistics.

Practicing the Skill

Study the table above, and then answer the following questions.

① What claim does this set of statistics seem to support?

② Is there a correlation between miles of railroad tracks and the Native American population? Is the correlation positive or negative? Explain.

Skills Assessment

Complete the Practicing Skills questions on page 433 and the Chapter 13 Skill Reinforcement Activity to assess your mastery of this skill.

Delivering a presentation

Applying the Skill

Interpreting Statistics Create a survey with two questions for which you believe the answers will show a correlation. For example, you might ask, "How many hours of television do you watch per day?" and "How many hours of sleep do you usually get at night?" Organize your statistics in a chart or graph. Then, look for a correlation in your data and evaluate your results. Write a paragraph summarizing your evaluation.

 Glencoe's **Skillbuilder Interactive Workbook CD-ROM, Level 2,** provides instruction and practice in key social studies skills.

ANSWERS TO PRACTICING THE SKILL

① As the number of miles of railroad track increased, the Native American population declined.

② Students may see a negative correlation, but other data would be needed to support the conclusion that an increase in railroad track caused a reduction in Native American population.

Applying the Skill
Students' graphs and paragraphs will vary. Paragraphs should be supported by the data collected.

SECTION 3 Native Americans

Guide to Reading

Main Idea
The settlement of the West dramatically changed the way of life of the Plains Indians.

Key Terms and Names
nomad, annuity, Little Crow, Indian Peace Commission, George A. Custer, Ghost Dance, assimilate, allotment, Dawes Act

Reading Strategy
Sequencing As you read about the crisis facing Native Americans during the late 1800s, complete a time line to record the battles between Native Americans and the U.S. government and the results of each.

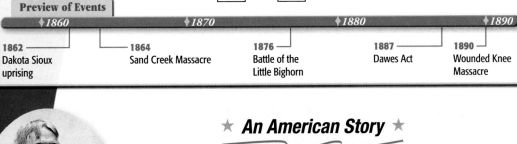

Reading Objectives
- **Discuss** conflicts that arose between the Plains Indians and American settlers.
- **Summarize** problems caused by attempts to assimilate Native Americans.

Section Theme
Individual Action Some Native American groups fought the federal government in an attempt to keep their ancestral homelands.

Preview of Events

| ♦1860 | ♦1870 | ♦1880 | ♦1890 |

1862 Dakota Sioux uprising

1864 Sand Creek Massacre

1876 Battle of the Little Bighorn

1887 Dawes Act

1890 Wounded Knee Massacre

Ten Bears

★ An American Story ★

In October 1867, a Comanche chief named Ten Bears arrived with other Native American leaders and their followers at Medicine Lodge Creek in present-day Kansas to meet with federal treaty-makers and army officers. The federal officials wanted them to sign a treaty agreeing to move to confined areas called reservations and to submit to American authority. In return, the government offered them food, housing, instruction in farming, and other assistance. After listening to the treaty-makers, Ten Bears spoke against moving to a reservation:

❝That which you say we must now live on is too small. The Texans have taken away the places where the grass grew the thickest. . . . The white man has the country which we loved, and we only wish to wander on the prairie until we die.❞

In the end, Ten Bears and the other chiefs had little choice but to sign the treaty. The army's main representative at the council, General William Tecumseh Sherman, told them bluntly that they would have to accept the deal: "You can no more stop this than you can stop the sun or moon; you must submit and do the best you can."

—adapted from *Tribes of the Southern Plains*

Culture of the Plains Indians

For centuries the Great Plains was home to many Native American nations. Some lived in communities as farmers and hunters, but most were nomads who roamed vast distances, following their main source of food—the buffalo.

Despite their differences, the groups of Plains Indians were similar in many ways. They lived in extended family networks and had a close relationship with nature. Plains

CHAPTER 13 Settling the West **425**

---

1 FOCUS

Section Overview
This section focuses on how Western settlement affected the Plains Indians.

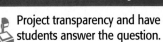

BELLRINGER
Skillbuilder Activity

Project transparency and have students answer the question.

Available as a blackline master.

Daily Focus Skills Transparency 13–3

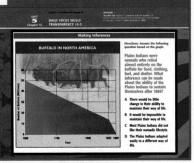

Guide to Reading

Answers to Graphic:
1862—Dakota Sioux Uprising: deaths of settlers and Native Americans; 1864—Sand Creek Massacre: formation of the Indian Peace Commission; 1866—Fetterman's Massacre: U.S. Army defeat; 1876—Battle of Little Bighorn: Native American victory; 1890—Wounded Knee: Sitting Bull killed, and about 200 Lakota died

Preteaching Vocabulary
Have students identify a person who can be tied to each of the Key Terms.

SECTION RESOURCES

📂 Reproducible Masters
- Reproducible Lesson Plan 13–3
- Daily Lecture and Discussion Notes 13–3
- Guided Reading Activity 13–3
- Section Quiz 13–3
- Reading Essentials and Study Guide 13–3
- Interpreting Political Cartoons

🎞 Transparencies
- Daily Focus Skills Transparency 13–3

Multimedia
- 💿 Interactive Tutor Self-Assessment CD-ROM
- 💿 ExamView® Pro Testmaker CD-ROM
- 💿 TeacherWorks™ CD-ROM
- 🎧 Audio Program
- 📺 ABCNews Interactive™ Historic America Electronic Field Trips

2 TEACH

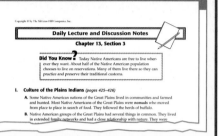
✓ **Reading Check**

Answer: They lived in extended family networks. They practiced a religion centered on the natural world. Tasks were assigned by gender.

Creating a Display Have students use library and Internet resources to create a display showcasing the history and traditions of the Plains Indians, especially those that signed the Medicine Lodge Peace Treaty in 1867—Apache, Arapaho, Cheyenne, Comanche, or Kiowa.
L1

Ask: Why did the Crow people cooperate with American settlers and soldiers? *(ancient enmity with Sioux and to secure good relations with the United States)*

Indian nations, sometimes numbering several thousand people, were divided into bands consisting of up to 500 people. A governing council headed each band, but most members participated in making decisions. Gender determined the assignment of tasks. Women generally performed domestic tasks: rearing children, cooking, and preparing hides. Men performed tasks such as hunting, trading, and supervising the military life of the band. Most Plains Indians practiced a religion based on a belief in the spiritual power of the natural world.

✓ **Reading Check** **Comparing** In what ways were different groups of Plains Indians similar?

Cultures Under Pressure

As ranchers, miners, and farmers moved onto the Plains, they deprived Native Americans of their hunting grounds, broke treaties guaranteeing certain lands to the Plains Indians, and often forced them to relocate to new territory. Native Americans resisted by attacking wagon trains, stagecoaches, and ranches. Occasionally an entire group would go to war against nearby settlers and troops. The first major clash on the Plains began in 1862, when the Sioux people in Minnesota launched a major uprising.

The Dakota Sioux Uprising The Dakota Sioux had agreed to live on a small reservation in Minnesota. In exchange for moving to the reservation, the United States government issued annuities, or payments to reservation dwellers, at least once per year. The annuities, however, amounted to only between 5 and 30 cents an acre, and much of that money ended up in the hands of American traders. These traders often made up stories about debts owed to them by the Dakota, and they took the annuities as payments.

Congress made things worse for the Dakota in 1862 by delaying annuities. By August the payments were a month late, and some of the Dakota were starving. Chief **Little Crow** asked traders to provide his people food on credit. "If they are hungry," trader Andrew Myrick replied, "let them eat grass or their

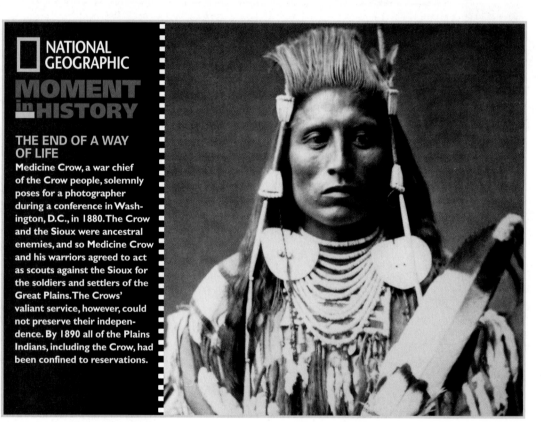

NATIONAL GEOGRAPHIC
MOMENT in HISTORY

THE END OF A WAY OF LIFE
Medicine Crow, a war chief of the Crow people, solemnly poses for a photographer during a conference in Washington, D.C., in 1880. The Crow and the Sioux were ancestral enemies, and so Medicine Crow and his warriors agreed to act as scouts against the Sioux for the soldiers and settlers of the Great Plains. The Crows' valiant service, however, could not preserve their independence. By 1890 all of the Plains Indians, including the Crow, had been confined to reservations.

426   CHAPTER 13   Settling the West

COOPERATIVE LEARNING ACTIVITY

Predicting Consequences Organize the class into small groups. Provide each group with a map showing the location of the various Native American nations. Have students compare that map with the one on page 417 that shows the railroad lines. Then ask them to decide what conflicts could have been predicted before the railroads were built. Ask each student to write a creative proposal of how to avoid conflict. Have the groups read each proposal and craft a group proposal to present to the class.

Use the rubric for a cooperative group management plan on pages 81–82 in the ***Performance Assessment Activities and Rubrics.***

own dung." Two weeks later, the Dakota rose up in arms, and Myrick was found shot to death with grass stuffed in his mouth.

Little Crow reluctantly agreed to lead this uprising. He wanted to wage war against soldiers, not civilians, but he was unable to keep angry Dakota from slaughtering settlers in the area. Hundreds died before troops arrived from St. Paul and put down the uprising.

A military tribunal sentenced 307 Dakota to death for taking part in the hostilities, but President Lincoln reviewed the evidence and reduced the number executed to 38. Many others who fled the reservation when the troops arrived became exiles in a region that bore their name—the Dakota Territory.

Lakota Sioux Defend Their Territory Following the Dakota uprising, the army sent patrols far out onto the northern Great Plains to prevent further trouble among the Sioux there. This action did more to stir up hostilities than to prevent them, for it brought troops into contact with another branch of the Sioux—the nomadic Lakota—who had offered refuge to Native Americans from Minnesota. The Lakota fought hard to keep control of their hunting grounds, which extended from the Black Hills westward to the Bighorn Mountains. They had battled rival groups for this country and did not intend to let settlers have it. Leading them were chiefs Red Cloud, Crazy Horse, and Sitting Bull.

The army suffered a stunning defeat at the hands of Red Cloud's forces in Wyoming in December 1866. Army troops were operating a fort on the Bozeman Trail, used by prospectors to reach gold mines in Montana. Crazy Horse, a religious leader as well as a war chief, lured the troops into a deadly trap. He tricked the fort's commander into sending Captain William Fetterman and about 80 soldiers out to pursue what they thought was a small raiding party. Hundreds of warriors were waiting in ambush and wiped out the entire detachment.

Sand Creek **Fetterman's Massacre,** as this battle came to be called, was just one example of the growing hostilities between settlers and Native Americans. Another incident, the **Sand Creek Massacre,** took place along Sand Creek in eastern Colorado.

In the 1860s, tensions began to rise between the Cheyenne and Arapaho peoples and the miners who had flocked to Colorado in search of gold and silver. As the number of settlers increased, bands of Native Americans began raiding wagon trains and stealing cattle and horses from ranches. By the summer of 1864, travelers heading to Denver or the mining camps were no longer safe. Trade had come to a

standstill, dozens of ranches had been burned, and an estimated 200 settlers had been killed. The territorial governor, John Evans, ordered the Native Americans to surrender at Fort Lyon, where he said they would be given food and protection. Those who failed to report would be subject to attack.

Although several hundred Native Americans surrendered at the fort, many others did not. In November 1864, Chief Black Kettle brought several hundred Cheyenne to the fort, not to surrender but to negotiate a peace deal. The fort's commander did not have the authority to negotiate, and he told Black Kettle to make camp at Sand Creek while he waited for orders. Shortly afterward, Colonel John Chivington of the Colorado Volunteers was ordered to attack the Cheyenne at Sand Creek.

When Chivington stopped at Fort Lyon, he was told that the Native Americans at Sand Creek were waiting to negotiate. Chivington replied that since the Cheyenne had been attacking settlers, including women and children, there could be no peace.

What actually happened at Sand Creek is unclear. Some witnesses stated afterward that Black Kettle had been flying both an American flag and a white flag of truce, which Chivington ignored. Others reported the American troops fired on the unsuspecting Native Americans, then brutally murdered hundreds of women and children. Still others described a savage battle in which both sides fought ferociously for two days. Fourteen soldiers died, but the number of Native Americans reported killed varied from 69 to 600, with some witnesses stating that very few

CHAPTER 13 Settling the West **427**

Fact | Fiction | Folklore

Buffalo Bill's Wild West Show Many Americans who never set foot on the Great Plains enjoyed a make-believe excursion there through a Wild West show. Various promoters staged these popular extravaganzas, but the most famous was Buffalo Bill's Wild West Show.

Members of the cast performed a mock buffalo hunt with real buffalo, and they reenacted Custer's defeat at the Little Bighorn. Among the stars of the show was Annie Oakley, a sharpshooter from Ohio who appeared in Western outfit and dazzled both the audience and her fellow performers.

BUFFALO BILL'S WILD WEST
CONGRESS, ROUGH RIDERS OF THE WORLD.

MISS ANNIE OAKLEY,
THE PEERLESS LADY WING-SHOT.

Fact | Fiction | Folklore

Annie Get Your Gun, a musical interpretation of Annie Oakley's exploits, opened on Broadway in 1946 with Ethel Merman starring as Oakley. Irving Berlin wrote the music and lyrics based on the book written by Herbert and Dorothy Fields. The musical had a long run on Broadway, was made into a movie, and is a favorite for school and community productions. Perhaps the most recognizable songs from the show are "Anything You Can Do (I can do better)" and "There's No Business Like Show Business."

Guided Reading Activity 13–3

Name _____ Date _____ Class _____

★ **Guided Reading Activity 13-3**

DIRECTIONS: Recalling Facts Read the section and answer the questions below. Refer to your textbook to write the answers.

1. How did most Native Americans of the Great Plains live? _____

2. Among most Native American groups, how were tasks assigned? _____

3. What took a serious toll on Native Americans? _____

4. What agreement did the Dakota Sioux make with the United States government? _____

5. What happened to the money the Dakota Sioux received from the government? _____

Telling a Story Ask students to develop a story describing one of the events mentioned under the heading "Cultures Under Pressure." Instruct students to develop their stories from the point of view of one of the participants. Encourage students to use library and Internet resources to learn more about the event. Invite students to tell their stories in class. **L2**

📁 Use the rubric for a diary, short story, memorandum, or letter on pages 79–80 in the *Performance Assessment Activities and Rubrics.*

MEETING SPECIAL NEEDS

Intrapersonal Have students select an event in this section and write a journal entry as if they had participated in the event. Tell students to write from the perspective of an American soldier, a Native American warrior, a settler in the region, or as a child observing the event and its results. Encourage students to describe their feelings, as well as the actions they took. **L2**

📁 Refer to *Inclusion for the High School Social Studies Classroom Strategies and Activities* in the TCR.

📂 Use *Interpreting Political Cartoons,* Cartoon 11.

History *and the* Humanities

🎵 American Music: Hits Through History: "Kiowa Hymn II"

🗿 American Art & Architecture: *The Buffalo Chase, Mouth of the Yellowstone; Merced River, Yosemite Valley; Chief Joseph*

✓ Reading Check

Answer: creation of two large reservations on the Plains: one in the Black Hills for the Sioux and the other in the Indian Territory (Oklahoma) for southern Plains Indians

Geography *Skills*

Answers:

1. at Bear Paw Mountain in Montana

2. The steady increase in white settlers and their focus on mining, cattle ranching, and buffalo hunting contributed to significant changes in the Native American way of life.

Geography Skills Practice

Ask: In what states and territories were the Native American battles fought? (*Arizona Territory, Colorado, Montana, and South Dakota*)

---

women or children died. General Nelson Miles later called Chivington's attack "the foulest and most unjustifiable crime in the annals of America," but a Senate committee investigating the incident decided that Chivington should not be charged. The truth of what really happened remains unknown.

GOVERNMENT

A Doomed Plan for Peace Fetterman's Massacre and the Sand Creek Massacre, along with several other incidents, convinced Congress that something had to be done to end the growing conflict with Native Americans on the Great Plains. In 1867 Congress formed an **Indian Peace Commission,** which proposed creating two large reservations on the Plains, one for the Sioux and another for southern Plains Indians. Agents from the federal government's Bureau of Indian Affairs would run the reservations. The army would be given authority to deal with any groups that refused to report or remain there.

This plan was doomed to failure. Pressuring Native American leaders into signing treaties, as negotiators had done at Medicine Lodge Creek in 1867, did not ensure that chiefs or their followers would abide by the terms. Those who did move to reservations faced much the same conditions that drove the Dakota Sioux to violence—poverty, despair, and the corrupt practices of American traders.

✓ **Reading Check** **Explaining** What proposal did the Indian Peace Commission present to the Plains Indians?

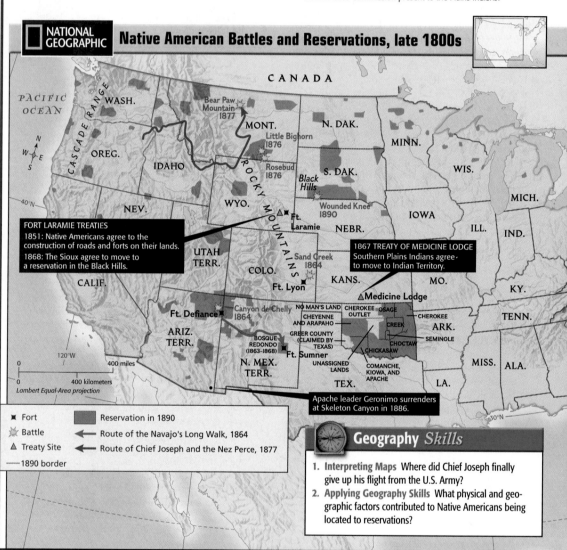

NATIONAL GEOGRAPHIC

Native American Battles and Reservations, late 1800s

FORT LARAMIE TREATIES
1851: Native Americans agree to the construction of roads and forts on their lands.
1868: The Sioux agree to move to a reservation in the Black Hills.

1867 TREATY OF MEDICINE LODGE
Southern Plains Indians agree to move to Indian Territory.

Apache leader Geronimo surrenders at Skeleton Canyon in 1886.

- ■ Fort
- ✳ Battle
- △ Treaty Site
- —— 1890 border

- Reservation in 1890
- ← Route of the Navajo's Long Walk, 1864
- ← Route of Chief Joseph and the Nez Perce, 1877

0 — 400 miles
0 — 400 kilometers
Lambert Equal-Area projection

Geography *Skills*

1. **Interpreting Maps** Where did Chief Joseph finally give up his flight from the U.S. Army?

2. **Applying Geography Skills** What physical and geographic factors contributed to Native Americans being located to reservations?

INTERDISCIPLINARY CONNECTIONS ACTIVITY

Performing Arts Have students select one of the Native American nations mentioned in the section. Tell them to use library and Internet resources to research the dances and music associated with the rituals performed by the nation. Have students create a display that shows how the dance was performed and explains what the elements mean. Encourage students to include examples of the instruments used by the Native Americans to accompany the dance. **L3**

The Last Native American Wars

By the 1870s, many Native Americans on the southern Plains had left the reservations in disgust. They preferred hunting buffalo on the open Plains, so they joined others who had also shunned the reservations. Buffalo, however, were rapidly disappearing. Beginning with the Gold Rush, migrants crossing the Plains had killed off thousands of the animals.

Following the Civil War, professional buffalo hunters invaded the area, seeking buffalo hides for markets in the East. Other hunters killed merely for sport, leaving carcasses to rot. Then railroad companies hired sharpshooters to kill large numbers of buffalo that were obstructing rail traffic. The army, determined to force Native Americans onto reservations, encouraged buffalo killing. By 1889 very few of the animals remained.

Battle of the Little Bighorn

In 1876 fortune hunters overran the Lakota Sioux reservation in South Dakota to mine gold in the Black Hills. The Lakota saw no reason why they should abide by a treaty that American settlers were violating, and many left the reservation that spring to hunt near the Bighorn Mountains in southeastern Montana.

The government responded by sending an expedition commanded by General Alfred H. Terry. Lieutenant Colonel **George A. Custer,** commander of the Seventh Cavalry, was with the expedition. An impulsive officer, Custer underestimated the fighting capabilities of the Lakota and Cheyenne.

On June 25, 1876, Custer launched a three-pronged attack in broad daylight on one of the largest groups of Native American warriors ever assembled on the Great Plains. It consisted of about 2,500 Lakota and Cheyenne warriors camped along the Little Bighorn River.

The Native American warriors first repulsed a cavalry charge from the south. Then they turned on Custer and a detachment of 210 soldiers and killed them all. One Lakota warrior recalled the scene afterward: "The soldiers were piled one on top of another, dead, with here and there, an Indian among the soldiers. Horses lay on top of men, and men on top of horses."

Profiles IN HISTORY

Sitting Bull
1831–1890

In June 1876, a showdown loomed between Custer's troops and the Lakota Sioux who had left their reservation. Lakota chief Sitting Bull sought help for his people from the supreme power they called *Wakan Tanka,* or the "Great Mystery," by performing the Sun Dance.

Before dancing, an assistant made many small cuts in the chief's arms and shoulders. Then Sitting Bull raised his bleeding arms to heaven and danced around a sacred pole with his eyes on the sun. He continued to dance through the night and into the next day, when he entered a death-like trance. When he revived, he told of a vision in which he saw white soldiers upside down. The Lakota were encouraged by Sitting Bull's dream and the sacrifice he had made for them. Many felt that his Sun Dance helped bring them victory over Custer.

Sitting Bull remained devoted to the traditional religious practices of his people even after he and his followers reluctantly returned to the reservation under pressure from the army. Federal authorities regarded ceremonies like the Sun Dance—practiced in one form or another by many Plains Indians—as heathen and subversive. In 1883 the federal government outlawed the Sun Dance and many other Native American religious rites.

Newspapers portrayed Custer as the victim of a massacre. The army stepped up its campaign against the Native Americans. Sitting Bull fled with followers to Canada, but the other Lakota were forced to return to the reservation and give up the Black Hills.

Farther west, members of the Nez Perce, led by Chief Joseph, refused to be moved to a smaller reservation in Idaho in 1877. When the army came to relocate them, they fled their homes and embarked on a flight of more than 1,300 miles. Finally, in October 1877, Chief Joseph surrendered, and his followers were exiled to Oklahoma. His speech summarized the hopelessness of the Native American cause:

> **66**Our chiefs are killed.... The little children are freezing to death. My people ... have no blankets, no food.... Hear me, my chiefs; I am tired; my heart is sick and sad. From where the sun now stands I will fight no more forever.**99**
>
> —quoted in *Bury My Heart at Wounded Knee*

Tragedy at Wounded Knee

Native American resistance to federal authority finally came to a tragic end on the Lakota Sioux reservation in 1890. Defying

Profiles IN HISTORY

For a time in the mid-1880s, Sitting Bull traveled with Buffalo Bill's Wild West Show.

Ask: Why do you think federal authorities outlawed the Sun Dance and other religious rites? *(Students might answer that federal authorities felt it would be better for everyone if Native Americans abandoned their culture and assimilated into American society as defined by white Christians.)*

ABCNEWS INTERACTIVE™

 VIDEOCASSETTE
Historic America Electronic Field Trips

View **Tape 2, Chapter 3:** "Little Bighorn."

3 ASSESS

Assign Section 3 Assessment as homework or as an in-class activity.

🌐 Have students use the **Interactive Tutor Self-Assessment CD-ROM.**

Reading Essentials and Study Guide 13–3

Name _____ Date _____ Class _____

Study Guide

Chapter 13, Section 3
For use with textbook pages 425–430
NATIVE AMERICANS

KEY TERMS AND NAMES

nomads people who roam great distances *(page 425)*
annuity payment to reservation dwellers *(page 426)*
Little Crow a Chief of the Dakota *(page 426)*
Indian Peace Commission a commission formed by Congress in 1867, which created two reservations on the Great Plains *(page 426)*
George A. Custer United States military leader in the Battle of the Little Bighorn *(page 429)*
Ghost Dance a ritual performed by the Lakota Sioux *(page 430)*
assimilate to be absorbed into *(page 430)*

CRITICAL THINKING ACTIVITY

Synthesizing Read the following statement made by Chief Joseph in an appeal to President Rutherford B. Hayes. "Let me be a free man—free to travel, free to stop, free to work, free to trade where I choose, free to choose my own teachers, free to follow the religion of my father, free to think and talk and act for myself—and I will obey every law or submit to the penalty." Ask students: **Which of the requests are guaranteed in the Bill of Rights?** *(all of them)* **How did U.S. government policies toward Native Americans deny them their rights?** *(forced them to live on reservations)* **L2**

Section Quiz 13–3

Chapter 13

Section Quiz 13-3

DIRECTIONS: Matching Match each item in Column A with the items in Column B. Write the correct letters in the blanks. *(10 points each)*

Column A
____ 1. leader of the Nez Perce people
____ 2. site of a murderous battle between U.S. soldiers and Lakota men, women, and children
____ 3. to be absorbed
____ 4. main source of food for many Native Americans
____ 5. payments to reservation dwellers

Column B
A. Chief Joseph
B. assimilate
C. annuities
D. Wounded Knee Creek
E. buffalo

DIRECTIONS: Multiple Choice In the blank at the left, write the letter of the choice that best completes the statement or answers the question. *(10 points each)*

✓ Reading Check

Answer: The U.S. Army's defeat caused it to step up its campaign which eventually forced some Lakota to the reservation.

Reteach

Have students discuss the conflicts that arose between Plains Indians and white settlers.

Enrich

Have students research life on reservations today. Suggest that they include information on the problems Native Americans face there and what economic successes they have achieved.

✓ Reading Check

Answer: Her book sparked discussions of better treatment for Native Americans.

4 CLOSE

Have students summarize problems caused by attempts to assimilate Native Americans.

---

the orders of the government agent, the Lakota continued to perform the **Ghost Dance,** a ritual that celebrated a hoped-for day of reckoning when settlers would disappear, the buffalo would return, and Native Americans would reunite with their deceased ancestors. The government agent blamed the latest defiance on Sitting Bull, who had returned to the reservation from Canada, and he sent police to arrest the chief. Sitting Bull's supporters resisted the police, and the chief himself died in an exchange of gunfire.

The participants of the Ghost Dance then fled the reservation, and U.S. troops went after them. On December 29, 1890, as troops tried to disarm the Native Americans at Wounded Knee Creek, gunfire broke out. A deadly battle ensued, costing the lives of 25 U.S. soldiers and approximately 200 Lakota men, women, and children.

✓ Reading Check **Summarizing** What was the outcome of the battle at the Little Bighorn River?

Assimilation

Some Americans had long opposed the treatment of Native Americans. Author Helen Hunt Jackson described the years of broken promises and assaults on Native Americans in her book, *A Century of Dishonor,* published in 1881. Jackson's descriptions of events such as the massacre at Sand Creek sparked discussions—even in Congress—of better treatment for Native Americans. Some people believed that the situation would improve only if Native Americans could **assimilate,** or be absorbed,

into American society as landowners and citizens. That meant breaking up reservations into individual **allotments,** where families could become self-supporting.

This policy became law in 1887 when Congress passed the **Dawes Act.** This act allotted to each head of household 160 acres of reservation land for farming; single adults received 80 acres, and 40 acres were allotted for children. The land that remained after all members had received allotments would be sold to American settlers, with the proceeds going into a trust for Native Americans.

This plan failed to achieve its goals. Some Native Americans succeeded as farmers or ranchers, but many had little training or enthusiasm for either pursuit. Like homesteaders, they often found their allotments too small to be profitable, and so they sold them. Some Native American groups had grown attached to their reservations and hated to see them transformed into homesteads for settlers as well as Native Americans.

In the end, the assimilation policy proved a dismal failure. No legislation could provide a satisfactory solution to the Native American issue, because there was no entirely satisfactory solution to be had. The Plains Indians were doomed because they were dependent on buffalo for food, clothing, fuel, and shelter. When the herds were wiped out, Native Americans on the Plains had no way to sustain their way of life, and few were willing or able to adopt American settlers' lifestyles in place of their traditional cultures.

✓ Reading Check **Cause and Effect** What effect did Helen Hunt Jackson's book *A Century of Dishonor* have?

SECTION 3 ASSESSMENT

Checking for Understanding

1. **Define:** nomad, annuity, assimilate, allotment.
2. **Identify:** Little Crow, Indian Peace Commission, George A. Custer, Ghost Dance, Dawes Act.
3. **Analyze** how Native Americans responded to land lost due to white settlement of the Great Plains.

Reviewing Themes

4. **Individual Action** How did Chief Joseph resist the government's attempts to move the Nez Perce to reservations?

Critical Thinking

5. **Analyzing** Why do you think the government's policy of assimilation of Native Americans was a failure?
6. **Organizing** Use a graphic organizer similar to the one below to list the reasons that the government's plans to move the Plains Indians onto reservations failed.

Analyzing Visuals

7. **Analyzing Maps** Examine the map of battle sites and reservations on page 428. Then, from the point of view of a historian, explain the actions taken against Native Americans within the historical context of the time.

Writing About History

8. **Descriptive Writing** Assume the role of a Plains Indian affected by the assimilation policy of the Dawes Act. Write a journal entry describing how you feel about the policy and how it has affected your life.

SECTION 3 ASSESSMENT ANSWERS

1. Terms are in blue.
2. Little Crow *(p. 426),* Indian Peace Commission *(p. 428),* George A. Custer *(p. 429),* Ghost Dance *(p. 430),* Dawes Act *(p. 430)*
3. attacked wagon trains and ranches, and killed settlers and soldiers
4. Chief Joseph and the Nez Perce fled 1,300 miles before surrendering.

5. After the buffalo herds were wiped out, Native Americans were unwilling or unable to live like American settlers.
6. Native Americans preferred life on the Plains; leaders were pressured into signing treaties; reservations were plagued by poverty, despair, and outside corruption.

7. Answers may vary. Accept different viewpoints as long as the reasoning is sound and based on facts.
8. Students' journal entries will vary. Entries should be written from the perspective of a Native American.

Gertrude Simmons Bonnin (Zitkala Sa) was a talented and educated Native American woman who spent her life fighting against prejudice toward Native American culture and women. Through her contributions in the fields of literature, music, and politics, Bonnin aimed at creating understanding between the dominant white and Native American cultures. As a woman of mixed white and Native American ancestry, she embodied the need for the two cultures to live cooperatively. In the following excerpt from her essay, *An Indian Teacher Among Indians,* she describes a reunion with her mother after being away from home teaching for several years.

Read to Discover
What evidence do you see of the "generation gap"—the differences between parents and children—in the passage?

Reader's Dictionary
position: job
steadfastly: faithfully
avenge: get even for

from An Indian Teacher Among Indians

by Gertrude Simmons Bonnin

"Mother, why is not your house cemented? Do you have no interest in a more comfortable shelter? . . ."

"You forget, my child, that I am now old, and I do not work with beads any more. Your brother Dawee, too, has lost his position, and we are left without means to buy even a morsel of food," she replied.

Dawee was a government clerk in our reservation when I last heard from him. I was surprised upon hearing what my mother said concerning his lack of employment. Seeing the puzzled expression on my face, she continued: "Dawee! Oh, has he not told you that the Great Father at Washington sent a white son to take your brother's pen from him? Since then Dawee has not been able to make use of the education the Eastern school has given him."

I found no words with which to answer satisfactorily. I found no reason with which to cool my inflamed feelings. . . .

Turning to my mother, I urged her to tell me more about Dawee's trouble, but she only said: "Well, my daughter, this village has been these many winters a refuge for white robbers. The Indian cannot complain to the Great Father in Washington without suffering outrage for it here. . . .

A Native American reservation

"My child, there is only one source of justice, and I have been praying steadfastly to the Great Spirit to avenge our wrongs," she said, seeing I did not move my lips.

My shattered energy was unable to hold longer any faith, and I cried out desperately: "Mother, don't pray again! The Great Spirit does not care if we live or die!"

Analyzing Literature

1. **Recall and Interpret** Why did Bonnin's brother lose his job?
2. **Evaluate and Connect** How does Bonnin's mother react to the injustice of the "Great Father in Washington"? How does Bonnin herself react?

Interdisciplinary Activity
Drama In small groups, assume the roles of Bonnin, her mother, and her brother, and extend the passage by imagining what might happen when Dawee returns.

Read to Discover
Answer: Zitkala Sa criticizes her mother for not keeping up her house and for praying to the Great Spirit.

Reinforcing Vocabulary
Have students look up the meaning of any other unfamiliar words, such as *morsel, inflamed,* or *refuge.*

Historical Connection
Bonnin devoted her life to working for Native Americans. In 1926 she founded the National Council of American Indians.

Portfolio Writing Activity
Have students write a short narrative about a conflict between generations of the same family.

HISTORY
Online

Refer to tav.glencoe.com for additional Glencoe Literature titles, lesson plans, and study guides related to this unit.

Answers to Analyzing Literature

1. Even though Dawee was educated in an Eastern school, he lost his job and was replaced by a white man.

2. Bonnin's mother prays for the Great Spirit to avenge wrongs. Bonnin tells her mother to stop praying because the Great Spirit does not care about them.

Interdisciplinary Activity
Students' answers will vary. Encourage students to present their role plays to the class.

CHAPTER 13 ASSESSMENT and ACTIVITIES

CHAPTER 13
Assessment and Activities

GLENCOE
TECHNOLOGY

MindJogger Videoquiz
Use the **MindJogger Videoquiz** to review Chapter 13 content.

 Available in VHS

Reviewing Key Terms

The pages where the words appear in the text are shown in parentheses.

1. **placer mining** (p. 415)
2. **quartz mining** (p. 415)
3. **open range** (p. 416)
4. **long drive** (p. 417)
5. **maverick** (p. 418)
6. **homestead** (p. 421)
7. **dry farming** (p. 422)
8. **sodbuster** (p. 422)
9. **bonanza farm** (p. 422)
10. **nomad** (p. 425)
11. **annuity** (p. 426)
12. **assimilate** (p. 430)
13. **allotment** (p. 430)

Reviewing Key Facts

14. Henry Comstock (p. 415), Great Plains (p. 420), Stephen Long (p. 421), Little Crow (p. 426), Indian Peace Commission (p. 428), George A. Custer (p. 429), Dawes Act (p. 430)

15. the discovery of copper, gold, or silver; when the lode played out, mines closed and the towns' economies collapsed

16. barbed wire

17. Railroad companies sold land along rail lines at low prices, provided credit to prospective settlers, and advertised the benefits of booking passage to the Plains.

18. Wheat could be cultivated using dry farming.

19. White settlers' moving west, railroad construction, buffalo slaughtered, and wars

Reviewing Key Terms

On a sheet of paper, use each of these terms in a sentence.

1. placer mining
2. quartz mining
3. open range
4. long drive
5. maverick
6. homestead
7. dry farming
8. sodbuster
9. bonanza farm
10. nomad
11. annuity
12. assimilate
13. allotment

Reviewing Key Facts

14. **Identify:** Henry Comstock, Great Plains, Stephen Long, Little Crow, Indian Peace Commission, George A. Custer, Dawes Act.

15. What led to the start of boomtowns, and what caused their decline?

16. What new invention finally brought an end to the open range on the Great Plains?

17. How did the railroads boost the settlement of the West?

18. Why was wheat a suitable crop to grow on the Great Plains?

19. What events brought the way of life of the Plains Indians to an end?

Critical Thinking

20. **Analyzing Themes: Economic Factors** Do you think that people moved to and settled in the West primarily for economic reasons? Why or why not?

21. **Drawing Conclusions** Why do you think that so many people were willing to give up their homes and move to mining towns and homesteads in the West?

22. **Forming an Opinion** How do you think a peaceful settlement might have been reached between the Native Americans and the U.S. government?

23. **Interpreting Primary Sources** In the late 1860s, the U.S. government adopted a policy of forcing Native Americans onto small reservations in the Black Hills of Dakota and barren regions of Oklahoma. The government forced many Native American chiefs to sign treaties and to promise to move onto the reservations. Many Native Americans, however, refused to move and fought to maintain their traditional way of life. In the excerpt that follows, Satanta, a chief of the Kiowa, responds to the government's policy. Read the excerpt and answer the questions that follow:

❝I have heard that you intend to settle us on a reservation near the mountains. I don't want to settle. I love to roam over the prairies. There I feel free and happy, but when we settle down we grow pale and die. I have laid aside my lance, bow, and shield, and yet I feel safe in your presence. I have told you the truth. I have no little lies hid about me, but I don't know how it is with the commissioners. Are they as clear as I am? A long time ago this land belonged to our fathers; but when I go up to the river I see camps of soldiers on its banks. These soldiers cut down my timber; they kill my buffalo;

Chapter Summary

Mining and Ranching

- Discovery of gold, silver, and copper attracted settlers to Colorado, the Dakota Territory, Nevada, and Montana
- Growth of cattle and sheep ranching attracted settlers to Texas, Montana, Wyoming, and other western areas

Farming

- Cheap land of Homestead Act encouraged settlement
- Farming technology and climate moderation made the Great Plains into the Wheat Belt

Native Americans

- Federal government forced Plains Indians off their lands with promise of receiving new land
- White settlers moved into lands promised to Native Americans
- Slaughter of buffalo removed a major part of Native American way of life

Role of Railroads

| Provided easy way to ship sheep and cattle to Eastern markets | Brought scarce timber and coal to the Great Plains; advertised for settlers | Helped displace Native Americans by moving settlers west, taking lands, and promoting buffalo slaughter |

Critical Thinking

20. Many did move for the hope of riches; others for adventure, freedom, or a fresh start.

21. Many settlers thought that they could prosper in the West.

22. Students' answers will vary. Discuss ideas as a class.

23. **a.** He enjoyed his nomadic life. **b.** He thinks the white man does not respect the land. He says white men kill buffalo recklessly.

24. prospects of getting rich from mining, opportunity to purchase land at a reasonable price, chance to escape the South following the Civil War

Practicing Skills

25. **a.** negative; **b.** It will continue to decline.

Writing Activity

26. Reviews should note differences between historical facts and movie portrayals of events.

and when I see that, my heart feels like bursting; I feel sorry. . . . Has the white man become a child that he should recklessly kill and not eat? When the red men slay game, they do so that they may live and not starve.**

—quoted in *Bury My Heart at Wounded Knee*

a. What reasons does Satanta give for not wanting to settle on a reservation?

b. How does Satanta view the white settlers' approach to the land and the resources on it?

24. Organizing Use a graphic organizer to list the factors that promoted the settlement of the West.

Practicing Skills

25. Interpreting Statistics Examine the chart on Native American populations displayed on this page. Then use the steps you learned about interpreting statistics to answer the following questions.

a. According to this data, is there a positive or a negative correlation between Native American population and the passage of time?

b. Based on this correlation, what conclusions can you draw about Native American population after 1900?

Writing Activity

26. Portfolio Writing Watch an older movie about the West. Look critically at the movie's depiction of cowhands and Native Americans. Write a movie review in which you assess how accurately the movie portrays the West. Place the review in your portfolio.

Chapter Activity

27. Technology: Using the Internet Search the Internet for sites about old mining towns (ghost towns) in the West. Many of these towns are tourist attractions today. Find out the location and history of a few of these towns, as well as the points of interest. Incorporate the information in a brochure for tourists interested in taking a "ghost town" vacation.

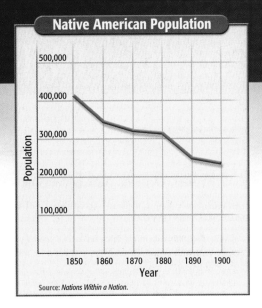

Native American Population

Source: *Nations Within a Nation.*

Geography and History

28. The graph above shows Native American population from 1850 to 1900. Study the graph and answer the questions below.

a. Interpreting Graphs What does the graph indicate about Native American populations between 1850 and 1900?

b. Understanding Cause and Effect What factor caused the Native American populations to decline sharply between 1880 and 1890?

Standardized Test Practice

Directions: Choose the best answer to the following question.

Which of the following did NOT make it easier for settlers to live and farm on the Great Plains?

A Government assistance such as the Homestead Act

B New technology such as the mechanical reaper and the combine

C New farming techniques such as dry farming

D The absence of land speculators

Test-Taking Tip: When you are not sure of an answer, it can be helpful to use the process of elimination. Eliminate the answers that you know are incorrect. For instance, machinery such as the reaper *did* make it easier for farmers to work more land at a quicker pace. Therefore, you can eliminate answer B.

Standardized Test Practice

Answer: D

Test-Taking Tip: Advise students to make sure the entire answer is true before eliminating it. For instance, the Homestead Act was a form of government assistance, and it did make it easier for settlers to live and farm on the Great Plains. Therefore, students can eliminate answer A. By using this process of elimination, students learn that D is the correct answer.

Bonus Question ?

Ask: How did dry farming damage the ecology of the prairie? (*Dry farming contributed to soil erosion and massive dust storms.*)

Chapter Activity

27. Encourage students to create an informative brochure that will interest tourists in the ghost towns.

Geography and History

28. a. They declined steadily. **b.** Students should note that Native Americans suffered high casualty rates in conflicts with white settlers.

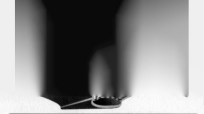

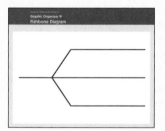

TeacherWorks™ All-In-One Planner and Resource Center

- **Interactive Teacher Edition** Access your Teacher Wraparound Edition and your classroom resources with a few easy clicks.
- **Interactive Lesson Planner** Planning has never been easier! Organize your week, month, semester, or year with all the lesson helps you need to make teaching creative, timely, and relevant.

Use Glencoe's **Presentation Plus!** multimedia teacher tool to easily present dynamic lessons that visually excite your students. Using Microsoft PowerPoint® you can customize the presentations to create your own personalized lessons.

TEACHING TRANSPARENCIES

Graphic Organizer 9

Why It Matters Chapter Transparency 14

APPLICATION AND ENRICHMENT

Linking Past and Present Activity 14

Enrichment Activity 14

Primary Source Reading 14

REVIEW AND REINFORCEMENT

Reteaching Activity 14

Vocabulary Activity 14

Time Line Activity 14

Critical Thinking Skills Activity 14

Meeting NCSS Standards

Local Standards

The following standards are highlighted in Chapter 14:

Section 1 VII Production, Distribution, and Consumption: A, B
Section 2 IV Individual Development and Identity: G
Section 3 VII Production, Distribution, and Consumption: A, B, D, E
Section 4 IV Individual Development and Identity: A, C

**Chapter 14 Test
Form A**

**Chapter 14 Test
Form B**

**Standardized Test Skills
Practice Workbook Activity 14**

**Performance Assessment
Activities and Rubrics 14**

**ExamView® Pro
Testmaker CD-ROM**

MULTIMEDIA

- Vocabulary PuzzleMaker CD-ROM
- Interactive Tutor Self-Assessment CD-ROM
- ExamView® Pro Testmaker CD-ROM
- Audio Program
- American History Primary Source Documents Library CD-ROM
- MindJogger Videoquiz
- Presentation Plus! CD-ROM
- TeacherWorks™ CD-ROM
- Interactive Student Edition CD-ROM
- Glencoe Skillbuilder Interactive Workbook CD-ROM, Level 2
- The *American Vision* Video Program
- American Music: Hits Through History
- American Music: Cultural Traditions

SPANISH RESOURCES

The following Spanish language materials are available in the Spanish Resources Binder:

- Spanish Guided Reading Activities
- Spanish Reteaching Activities
- Spanish Quizzes and Tests
- Spanish Vocabulary Activities
- Spanish Summaries
- The Declaration of Independence and United States Constitution Spanish Translation

---

THE HISTORY CHANNEL®

The following videotape programs are available from Glencoe as supplements to Chapter 14:

- **Legacy of King Coal, Empires of American Industry** (ISBN 0-76-700621-6)
- **Dow and Jones: Wizards of Wall Street** (ISBN 0-76-700203-2)

To order, call Glencoe at 1-800-334-7344. To find classroom resources to accompany many of these videos, check the following home pages:
A&E Television: www.aande.com
The History Channel: www.historychannel.com

Use our Web site for additional resources. All essential content is covered in the Student Edition.

You and your students can visit tav.glencoe.com, the Web site companion to the *American Vision.* This innovative integration of electronic and print media offers your students a wealth of opportunities. The student text directs students to the Web site for the following options:

- **Chapter Overviews**
- **Student Web Activities**
- **Self-Check Quizzes**
- **Textbook Updates**

Answers to the student Web activities are provided for you in the **Web Activity Lesson Plans.** Additional Web resources and Interactive Tutor Puzzles are also available.

SECTION RESOURCES

Daily Objectives	Reproducible Resources	Multimedia Resources
SECTION 1 **The Rise of Industry** 1. Identify the effects of expanding population on industry. 2. Explain the effects of technological innovations such as the telephone and telegraph on American development.	📁 Reproducible Lesson Plan 14–1 📁 Daily Lecture and Discussion Notes 14–1 📁 Guided Reading Activity 14–1* 📁 Section Quiz 14–1* 📁 Reading Essentials and Study Guide 14–1 📁 Performance Assessment Activities and Rubrics	🖍 Daily Focus Skills Transparency 14–1 💿 Interactive Tutor Self-Assessment CD-ROM 💿 ExamView® Pro Testmaker CD-ROM 💿 Presentation Plus! CD-ROM 💿 TeacherWorks™ CD-ROM 🎧 Audio Program 💿 Skillbuilder Interactive Workbook, Level 2 📼 ABCNews Interactive™ Historic America Electronic Field Trips
SECTION 2 **The Railroads** 1. Discuss ways in which the railroads spurred industrial growth. 2. Analyze how the railroads were financed and how they grew.	📁 Reproducible Lesson Plan 14–2 📁 Daily Lecture and Discussion Notes 14–2 📁 Guided Reading Activity 14–2* 📁 Section Quiz 14–2* 📁 Reading Essentials and Study Guide 14–2 📁 Performance Assessment Activities and Rubrics	🖍 Daily Focus Skills Transparency 14–2 💿 Interactive Tutor Self-Assessment CD-ROM 💿 ExamView® Pro Testmaker CD-ROM 💿 Presentation Plus! CD-ROM 💿 TeacherWorks™ CD-ROM 🎧 Audio Program
SECTION 3 **Big Business** 1. Analyze how large corporations came to dominate American business. 2. Evaluate how Andrew Carnegie's innovations transformed the steel industry.	📁 Reproducible Lesson Plan 14–3 📁 Daily Lecture and Discussion Notes 14–3 📁 Guided Reading Activity 14–3* 📁 Section Quiz 14–3* 📁 Reading Essentials and Study Guide 14–3 📁 Performance Assessment Activities and Rubrics 📁 Interpreting Political Cartoons	🖍 Daily Focus Skills Transparency 14–3 🖍 American Art & Architecture 💿 Interactive Tutor Self-Assessment CD-ROM 💿 ExamView® Pro Testmaker CD-ROM 💿 Presentation Plus! CD-ROM 💿 TeacherWorks™ CD-ROM 🎧 Audio Program
SECTION 4 **Unions** 1. Describe industrial working conditions in the United States in the late 1800s. 2. List the barriers to labor union growth.	📁 Reproducible Lesson Plan 14–4 📁 Daily Lecture and Discussion Notes 14–4 📁 Guided Reading Activity 14–4* 📁 Section Quiz 14–4* 📁 Reading Essentials and Study Guide 14–4 📁 Performance Assessment Activities and Rubrics	🖍 Daily Focus Skills Transparency 14–4 💿 Interactive Tutor Self-Assessment CD-ROM 💿 ExamView® Pro Testmaker CD-ROM 💿 Presentation Plus! CD-ROM 💿 TeacherWorks™ CD-ROM 💿 Vocabulary PuzzleMaker CD-ROM 🎧 Audio Program

0:00 OUT OF TIME?
Assign the Chapter 14 **Reading Essentials and Study Guide.** 📁

*Also Available in Spanish

📁 Blackline Master	🖍 Transparency	💿 CD-ROM	💿 DVD	
📕 Poster	🎵 Music Program	🎧 Audio Program	📼 Videocassette	

NATIONAL GEOGRAPHIC Teacher's Corner

INDEX TO NATIONAL GEOGRAPHIC MAGAZINE

The following articles relate to this chapter.
- "Geronimo," October 1992
- "New Life for Ellis Island," September 1990
- "Pittsburgh—Stronger than Steel," December 1991

NATIONAL GEOGRAPHIC SOCIETY PRODUCTS AVAILABLE FROM GLENCOE

To order the following products for use with this chapter, contact your local Glencoe sales representative, or call Glencoe at 1-800-334-7344:
- *PictureShow: Native Americans, 1 and 2* (CD-ROM, Transparencies)
- *PictureShow: Immigration* (CD-ROM)
- *PicturePack: Immigration* (Transparencies)

ADDITIONAL NATIONAL GEOGRAPHIC SOCIETY PRODUCTS

To order the following, call National Geographic at 1-800-368-2728:
- *Full Steam Ahead: The Race to Build a Transcontinental Railroad*
- *Immigration: The Triumph of Hope*
- *Native Americans* (Poster Set)

NGS ONLINE

Access National Geographic's Web site for current events, atlas updates, activities, links, interactive features, and archives.
www.nationalgeographic.com

From the Classroom of...

Tom Beaman
Reynolds High School
Troutdale, OR

Strategic Inventions

The rise of the United States to an industrial power started after the Civil War. The period between 1865 and 1901 saw rapid industrialization.

Give students a list of 10 to 15 items invented during this time period that contributed to the growth of industry in the United States. Consider items such as the light bulb, the elevator brake, the ice machine, the telephone, the electric streetcar, and the gasoline-powered car.

Students should research the background of one item's invention. They should then comment on how it contributed to the growth of industry.

ADDITIONAL RESOURCES FROM GLENCOE

- American Music: Cultural Traditions
- American Art & Architecture
- Outline Map Resource Book
- U.S. Desk Map
- Building Geography Skills for Life
- Inclusion for the High School Social Studies Classroom Strategies and Activities
- Teaching Strategies for the American History Classroom (Including Block Scheduling Pacing Guides)

KEY TO ABILITY LEVELS

Teaching strategies have been coded.

- **L1** BASIC activities for all students
- **L2** AVERAGE activities for average to above-average students
- **L3** CHALLENGING activities for above-average students
- **ELL** ENGLISH LANGUAGE LEARNER activities

 Block Schedule

Activities that are suited to use within the block scheduling framework are identified by:

Why It Matters Activity

Ask students to explain how the industrialization of the United States in the late 1800s affects their shopping habits in the 2000s. Students should evaluate their answers after they have completed the chapter.

GLENCOE
TECHNOLOGY

The *American Vision* Video Program
To learn more about the industrial expansion of the United States, have students view the Chapter 14 video, "Building America," from the *American Vision* Video Program.

 Available in DVD and VHS

MindJogger Videoquiz
Use the **MindJogger Videoquiz** to preview Chapter 14 content.

Available in VHS

CHAPTER
14 Industrialization
1865–1901

Why It Matters

The rise of the United States as an industrial power began after the Civil War. Many factors promoted industry, including cheap labor, new inventions and technology, and plentiful raw materials. Railroads rapidly expanded. Government policies encouraged growth, and large corporations became an important part of the economy. As industry expanded, workers tried to form unions to fight for better wages and working conditions.

The Impact Today

Trends which began in this era can still be seen today.
- *Corporations continue to play an important role.*
- *Technology continues to change American life.*
- *Unions remain powerful in many industries.*

The American Vision Video *The Chapter 14 video, "Building America," examines industrial expansion in the United States in the late 1800s.*

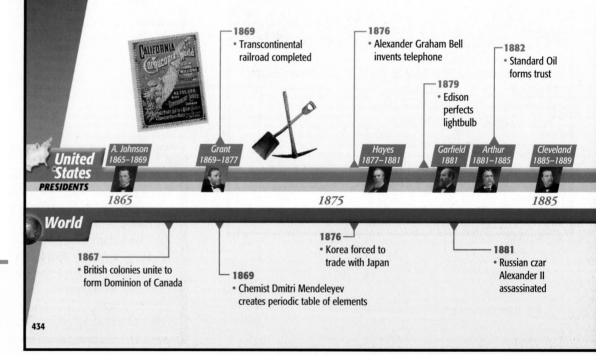

1869
- Transcontinental railroad completed

1876
- Alexander Graham Bell invents telephone

1882
- Standard Oil forms trust

1879
- Edison perfects lightbulb

United States PRESIDENTS

A. Johnson 1865–1869
Grant 1869–1877
Hayes 1877–1881
Garfield 1881
Arthur 1881–1885
Cleveland 1885–1889

1865   *1875*   *1885*

World

1867
- British colonies unite to form Dominion of Canada

1869
- Chemist Dmitri Mendeleyev creates periodic table of elements

1876
- Korea forced to trade with Japan

1881
- Russian czar Alexander II assassinated

434

TWO-MINUTE LESSON LAUNCHER

Ask students to imagine that they will be choosing outstanding modern inventions, such as machines, processes, materials, medicinal drugs, and new treatments, to exhibit at a technical fair being held in your community. Have students list the inventions that might be included in such an exhibit.

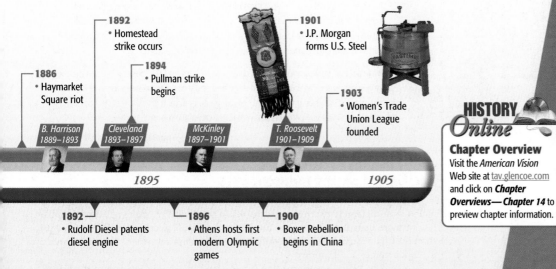

This painting by twentieth-century artist Aaron Bohrod captures the dynamism of an industrializing nation. Bohrod titled his work *The Big Blow: the Bessemer Process.*

HISTORY
Online

Introduce students to chapter content and key terms by having them access the **Chapter 14 Overview** at tav.glencoe.com.

More About the Art

Aaron Bohrod (1907–1992) was well known during his lifetime as a painter, sculptor, printmaker, ceramist, and illustrator. Many of his paintings exhibit social realism and attention to detail.

TIME LINE ACTIVITY

Have students write a paragraph about how the events listed on the time line have affected their lives within the last year. Invite students to share their experiences with the class.

1886
• Haymarket Square riot

B. Harrison 1889–1893

1892
• Homestead strike occurs

1894
• Pullman strike begins

Cleveland 1893–1897

1901
• J.P. Morgan forms U.S. Steel

1903
• Women's Trade Union League founded

McKinley 1897–1901

T. Roosevelt 1901–1909

1895

1905

1892
• Rudolf Diesel patents diesel engine

1896
• Athens hosts first modern Olympic games

1900
• Boxer Rebellion begins in China

HISTORY
Online

Chapter Overview
Visit the *American Vision* Web site at tav.glencoe.com and click on **Chapter Overviews— Chapter 14** to preview chapter information.

435

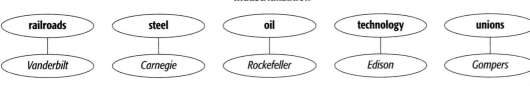

GRAPHIC ORGANIZER ACTIVITY

Organizing Information Have students use a graphic organizer similar to the one shown below to link these areas of industrialization to key names in this chapter.

Industrialization

railroads	steel	oil	technology	unions
Vanderbilt	*Carnegie*	*Rockefeller*	*Edison*	*Gompers*

435

1 FOCUS

Section Overview

This section focuses on how American industry grew and brought changes to society.

BELLRINGER
Skillbuilder Activity

 Project transparency and have students answer the question.

📁 Available as a blackline master.

Daily Focus Skills Transparency 14–1

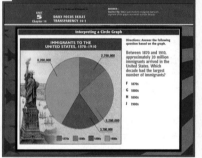

Guide to Reading

Answers to Graphic: abundance of raw materials, oil production, population increase, free enterprise system, large free trade area, new inventions

Preteaching Vocabulary
Have students scan the section and write a sentence using each of the Key Terms and Names in context.

Guide to Reading

Main Idea
American industry grew rapidly after the Civil War, bringing revolutionary changes to American society.

Key Terms and Names
gross national product, Edwin Drake, laissez-faire, entrepreneur, Morrill Tariff, Alexander Graham Bell, Thomas Alva Edison

Reading Strategy
Organizing As you read about the changes brought about by industrialization, complete a graphic organizer similar to the one below listing the causes of industrialization.

Causes

→
→ United States Becomes an Industrial Nation
→
→

Reading Objectives
- **Identify** the effects of expanding population on industry.
- **Explain** the effects of technological innovations such as the telephone and telegraph on American development.

Section Theme
Economic Factors The free enterprise system nurtured the growth of American industry.

Preview of Events

| ♦1860 | ♦1870 | ♦1880 | ♦1890 |

1859
Edwin Drake drills first oil well

1865
Thaddeus Lowe invents ice machine

1876
Alexander Graham Bell invents telephone

1879
Thomas Edison perfects lightbulb

c. 1893
Northrop automatic loom introduced

Thomas Edison

★ *An American Story* ★

On October 21, 1879, Thomas Alva Edison and his team of workers were too excited to sleep. For weeks they had worked to create an electric incandescent lamp, or lightbulb, that would burn for more than a few minutes. For much of the 1800s, inventors had struggled to develop a form of lighting that would be cheaper, safer, and brighter than traditional methods such as candles, whale oil, kerosene, and gas. If Edison and his team could do it, they would change the world. Finally, after weeks of dedicated effort, they turned night into day. Edison later recalled:

❝We sat and looked and the lamp continued to burn and the longer it burned the more fascinated we were. None of us could go to bed and there was no sleep for over 40 hours; we sat and just watched it with anxiety growing into elation. It lasted about 45 hours and then I said, 'If it will burn 40 hours now I know I can make it burn a hundred.'❞

—**quoted in** *Eyewitness to America*

The United States Industrializes

Although the Industrial Revolution began in the United States in the early 1800s, the nation was still largely a farming country when the Civil War erupted. Out of a population of more than 30 million, only 1.3 million Americans worked in industry in 1860. After the Civil War, industry rapidly expanded, and millions of Americans left their farms to work in mines and factories.

By the early 1900s, Americans had transformed the United States into the world's leading industrial nation. By 1914 the nation's **gross national product** (GNP)—the total

---

SECTION RESOURCES

📁 Reproducible Masters
- Reproducible Lesson Plan 14–1
- Daily Lecture and Discussion Notes 14–1
- Guided Reading Activity 14–1
- Section Quiz 14–1
- Reading Essentials and Study Guide 14–1

🔖 Transparencies
- Daily Focus Skills Transparency 14–1

Multimedia
- 💿 Interactive Tutor Self-Assessment CD-ROM
- 💿 ExamView® Pro Testmaker CD-ROM
- 💿 Presentation Plus! CD-ROM
- 💿 TeacherWorks™ CD-ROM
- 🎧 Audio Program
- 📼 ABCNews Interactive™ Historic America Electronic Field Trips

value of all goods and services produced by a country—was eight times greater than it had been when the Civil War ended.

Natural Resources An abundance of raw materials was one reason for the nation's industrial success. The United States contained vast natural resources upon which industry in the 1800s depended, including water, timber, coal, iron, and copper. The presence of these resources meant that American companies could obtain them cheaply and did not have to import them from other countries. Many of the nation's resources were located in the mountains of the American West. The settlement of this region after the Civil War helped to accelerate industrialization, as did the construction of the transcontinental railroad. Railroads brought settlers and miners to the region, and carried the resources back to factories in the East.

At the same time, a new resource, petroleum, began to be exploited. Even before the invention of the automobile, petroleum was in high demand because it could be turned into kerosene. Kerosene was used in lanterns and stoves. The American oil industry was built on the demand for kerosene. It began in western Pennsylvania, where residents had long noticed oil bubbling to the surface of area springs and streams. In 1859 **Edwin Drake** drilled the first oil well near Titusville, Pennsylvania. By 1900 oil fields from Pennsylvania to Texas had been opened. As oil production rose, it fueled economic expansion.

A Large Workforce The human resources available to American industry were as important as natural resources in enabling the nation to industrialize rapidly. Between 1860 and 1910, the population of the United States almost tripled. This population provided industry with a large workforce and also created greater demand for the consumer goods that factories produced.

Population growth stemmed from two causes—large families and a flood of immigrants. American industry began to grow at a time when social and economic conditions in China and eastern Europe convinced many people to leave their nations and move to the United States in search of a better life. Between 1870 and 1910, roughly 20 million immigrants arrived in the United States. These multitudes added to the growing industrial workforce, helping factories increase their production and furthering demand for industrial products.

✓ Reading Check **Explaining** How did oil production affect the American economy?

Major Industries, c. 1900

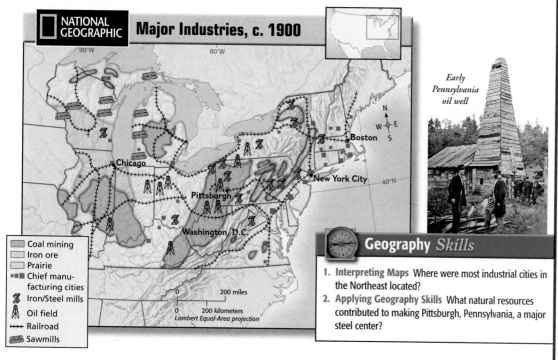

NATIONAL GEOGRAPHIC

Key:
- Coal mining
- Iron ore
- Prairie
- Chief manufacturing cities
- Iron/Steel mills
- Oil field
- Railroad
- Sawmills

Cities labeled: Chicago, Boston, New York City, Pittsburgh, Washington, D.C.

0   200 miles
0   200 kilometers
Lambert Equal-Area projection

Early Pennsylvania oil well

Geography *Skills*

1. **Interpreting Maps** Where were most industrial cities in the Northeast located?
2. **Applying Geography Skills** What natural resources contributed to making Pittsburgh, Pennsylvania, a major steel center?

CHAPTER 14   Industrialization   **437**

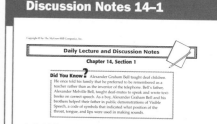

✓ Reading Check

Answer: Laissez-faire relies on supply and demand rather than the government to regulate prices and wages.

Creating a Time Line Have students research one of the inventions featured on the time line that appears on pages 438 and 439. Instruct students to create a time line for significant events related to the chosen invention. For example, a time line for the telephone might include the dates for the invention of the telephone keypad, the cordless telephone, and the cell phone. Encourage students to use library and Internet resources for this project. **L2**

📁 Use the rubric for creating a map, display, or chart on pages 77–78 in the *Performance Assessment Activities and Rubrics.*

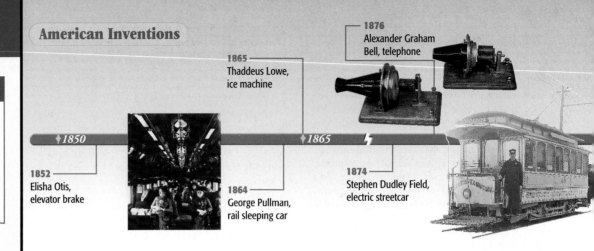

American Inventions

1876
Alexander Graham Bell, telephone

1865
Thaddeus Lowe, ice machine

◆1850

◆1865

1852
Elisha Otis, elevator brake

1864
George Pullman, rail sleeping car

1874
Stephen Dudley Field, electric streetcar

Free Enterprise

Another important factor that enabled the United States to industrialize rapidly was the free enterprise system. In the late 1800s, many Americans embraced the idea of **laissez-faire** (leh·say·FAR), literally "let do," a French phrase meaning "let people do as they choose." Supporters of laissez-faire believe the government should not interfere in the economy other than to protect private property rights and maintain peace. These supporters argue that if the government regulates the economy, it increases costs and eventually hurts society more than it helps.

Laissez-faire relies on supply and demand rather than the government to regulate prices and wages. Supporters claim that a free market with competing companies leads to greater efficiency and creates more wealth for everyone. Laissez-faire advocates also support low taxes to ensure that private individuals, not the government, will make most of the decisions about how the nation's wealth is spent. They also believe that the government's debt should be kept limited since money the government borrows from banks is not available to be loaned to individuals for their own uses.

In the United States, the profit motive attracted people of high ability and ambition into business. American **entrepreneurs**—people who risk their capital in organizing and running a business—appreciated the challenges and rewards of building a business and making profits for themselves.

In the late 1800s, the prospect of making money in manufacturing and transportation attracted many entrepreneurs. The savings that New Englanders accumulated through trade, fishing, whaling, textile mills, and shoe manufacturing helped build hundreds

of factories and thousands of miles of railroad track. An equally important source of private capital was Europe, especially Great Britain. Foreign investors saw more opportunity for profit and growth in the United States than at home, and their money also helped to fund the nation's industrial buildup.

✓ Reading Check
Explaining What does it mean when a government has a laissez-faire economic policy?

Government's Role in Industrialism

In many respects, the United States practiced laissez-faire economics in the late 1800s. State and federal governments kept taxes and spending low and did not impose costly regulations on industry. Nor did they try to control wages and prices. In other ways, the government went beyond laissez-faire and adopted policies intended to help industry, although these policies frequently produced results other than what had been intended.

Since the early 1800s, the struggle between the northeastern states and the southern states had shaped the economic debate in the United States. Northern leaders wanted high tariffs to protect American industry from foreign competition. They also sought federal subsidies for companies building roads, canals, and railroads to the west. Southern leaders opposed subsidizing internal improvements, and they favored low tariffs to promote trade and to keep the cost of imported manufactured goods low.

The Civil War ended this debate. When the South seceded, the Republicans were left in control of Congress. They quickly passed the **Morrill Tariff,**

MEETING SPECIAL NEEDS

Interpersonal Have each student list the electrical equipment he or she uses during a typical week. Then ask students to identify two adults, one between 40 and 50 years old, and a second between 60 and 70 years old. Have the adults check off the electrical appliances they used as teenagers. Have students discuss what the lists reflect about the recent explosion of inventions. **L1**

📁 Refer to *Inclusion for the High School Social Studies Classroom Strategies and Activities* in the TCR.

The railroad boom began in 1862 when President Abraham Lincoln signed the **Pacific Railway Act.** This act provided for the construction of a transcontinental railroad by two corporations, the Union Pacific and the Central Pacific railroad companies. To encourage rapid construction, the government offered each company land along its right-of-way. Feverish competition between the two companies developed, as each sought to obtain as much public land and money as possible.

The Union Pacific and Grenville Dodge Under the direction of engineer **Grenville Dodge,** a former Union general, the Union Pacific began pushing westward from Omaha, Nebraska, in 1865.

The laborers faced blizzards in the mountains, scorching heat in the desert, and sometimes angry Native Americans. Labor, money, and engineering problems plagued the supervisors of the project. As Dodge observed:

❝At one time we were using at least ten thousand animals, and most of the time from eight to ten thousand laborers. . . . To supply one mile of track with material and supplies required about forty cars. . . . Everything—rails, ties, bridging, fastenings, all

railway supplies, fuel for locomotives and trains, and supplies for men and animals on the entire work—had to be transported from the Missouri River.❞
—quoted in *The Growth of the American Republic*

The railroad workers included Civil War veterans, new immigrants from Ireland recruited especially for the task, frustrated miners and farmers, cooks, adventurers, and ex-convicts. At the height of the project, the Union Pacific employed about 10,000 workers. While most of the laborers camped along the line, about one-fourth of them slept three-deep in bunk beds on rolling boarding cars. Camp life was rough, dirty, and dangerous, with lots of gambling, hard drinking, and fighting.

The Big Four and the Central Pacific The Central Pacific Railroad began as the dream of engineer Theodore Dehone Judah, who convinced the California legislature to organize a state railroad convention to support his idea. He sold stock in his fledgling Central Pacific Railroad Company to four Sacramento merchants: grocer Leland Stanford, shop owner Charley Crocker, and hardware store owners Mark Hopkins and Collis P. Huntington.

These so-called "Big Four" eventually made huge fortunes from their investment. **Leland Stanford**

Picturing History

Engineering Victory The Union Pacific and Central Pacific were joined near Ogden, Utah. The last spike driven was made of gold. It was quickly removed and kept as a symbol. What did the event mean for the nation's commerce?

2 TEACH

Daily Lecture and Discussion Notes 14–2

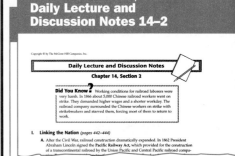

Copyright © by The McGraw-Hill Companies, Inc.

Daily Lecture and Discussion Notes

Chapter 14, Section 2

Did You Know? Working conditions for railroad laborers were very harsh. In 1866 about 5,000 Chinese railroad workers went on strike. They demanded higher wages and a shorter workday. The railroad company surrounded the Chinese workers on strike with strikebreakers and starved them, forcing most of them to return to work.

I. Linking the Nation *(pages 442–444)*

A. After the Civil War, railroad construction dramatically expanded. In 1862 President Abraham Lincoln signed the **Pacific Railway Act,** which provided for the construction of a transcontinental railroad by the Union Pacific and Central Pacific railroad compa-

Picturing History

Answer: The country now had the means to ship raw materials and finished goods coast to coast.
Ask: Who do you think the men who are shaking hands are? *(representatives of the Union Pacific and the Central Pacific railroads)*

Creating a Thematic Map Tell students that before railroads stretched across the country, communities determined their own times. Have students discuss why railroads needed to standardize times. Then have students create a time zone map of the continental United States and Canada that could be posted in a train depot. **L1**

📁 Use the rubric for creating a map, display, or chart on pages 77–78 in the *Performance Assessment Activities and Rubrics.*

COOPERATIVE LEARNING ACTIVITY

Creating a Display Organize students into small groups. Assign each group one the following topics: the development of the steam locomotive in the United States, the use of custom Pullman cars, or the architecture of railroad terminals. Have each group research its topic and prepare a display based on the research.

Use the rubric for a cooperative group management plan on pages 81–82 in the *Performance Assessment Activities and Rubrics.*

✔ Reading Check

Answer: a shortage of laborers in California

World History Connection

Background: A passenger train traveling the Trans-Siberian route takes seven days to complete the journey from Moscow to Vladivostok.

Answer: Towns would prosper during and after the construction.

Ask: How different do you think the conditions were for workers on the Trans-Siberian line compared to the transcontinental railroad in the United States? (Students' answers will vary. They might mention that weather conditions might have been worse in Siberia.)

HISTORY Online

Objectives and answers to the student activity can be found in the **Web Activity Lesson Plan** at tav.glencoe.com.

---

became governor of California and later served as a United States senator after founding Stanford University in 1885.

Because of a shortage of labor in California, the Central Pacific Railroad hired about 10,000 workers from China. All the equipment—rails, cars, locomotives, and machinery—was shipped from the East, either around Cape Horn at the tip of South America or over the Isthmus of Panama in Central America.

✔ Reading Check **Examining** Why were many workers on the Central Pacific Railroad recruited from China?

Railroads Spur Growth

The transcontinental railroad was the first of many lines that began to crisscross the nation after the Civil War. This expansion spurred American industrial growth. By linking the nation, railroads helped increase the size of markets for many products. Huge consumers themselves, the railroads also stimulated the economy by spending extraordinary amounts of money on steel, coal, timber, and other necessities.

Linking Other Lines In the early 1800s, most railroads had been built to promote specific cities or to serve local needs. By 1865 hundreds of small

World History Connection

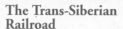

The Trans-Siberian Railroad

Nearly 50 years after Americans completed their transcontinental railroad, the Russians hammered the final spike into their own cross-country rail line. Begun in 1891 and completed in 1916, the Trans-Siberian Railroad was the longest in the world, running nearly 5,800 miles (9,330 km) from Moscow in the west to Vladivostok on the Sea of Japan in the east. Like the American railroads, the Trans-Siberian line opened up the way for trade and settlement throughout Russia's frontier—an arctic, windswept land known as Siberia. *How might the construction of a railroad affect towns along the line?*

0 1,000 miles
0 1,000 kilometers
Two-point Equidistant projection

•Moscow

RUSSIA

Vladivostok•

Trans-Siberian Railroad

---

unconnected lines existed. The challenge for eastern capitalists was to create a single rail transportation system from this maze of small companies.

Railroad consolidation proceeded rapidly from 1865 to 1900. Large rail lines took over about 400 small railroads, and by 1890 the Pennsylvania Railroad was a consolidation of 73 smaller companies. Eventually seven giant systems with terminals in major cities and scores of branches reaching into the countryside controlled most rail traffic.

One of the most famous and successful railroad consolidators was **Cornelius Vanderbilt,** a former boat captain who had built the largest steamboat fleet in America. By 1869 Vanderbilt had purchased and merged three short New York railroads to form the New York Central, running from New York City to Buffalo. Within four years he had extended his control over lines all the way to Chicago, which enabled him to offer the first direct rail service between New York City and Chicago. In 1871 Vanderbilt began construction of New York's Grand Central terminal.

The Benefits of a National System Before the 1880s each community set its clocks by the sun's position in the sky at high noon. At noon in Chicago, for example, it was 12:50 P.M. in Washington, D.C., 12:09 P.M. in Louisville, Kentucky, and 11:41 A.M. in St. Paul, Minnesota. Local time interfered with train scheduling and at times even threatened passenger safety. When two trains traveled on the same track, collisions could result from scheduling errors caused by variations in time.

To make rail service safer and more reliable, in 1883 the American Railway Association divided the country into four time zones in regions where the same time was kept. The federal government ratified this change in 1918.

Large integrated railroad systems benefited the nation. They were able to shift cars from one section of the country to another according to seasonal needs and in order to speed long-distance transportation. At the same time, new locomotive technology and the introduction of air brakes enabled railroads to put longer and heavier trains on their lines. The new rail systems, along with more powerful locomotives,

---

MEETING SPECIAL NEEDS

Kinesthetic Encourage students to use library and Internet resources to find drawings and diagrams of Edwin Drake's oil well. Then have students make a model of the well. Allow students to choose the construction material they wish to use. For students who need additional guidance, suggest making the model using 1-inch by 1-inch pinewood trim and 1.5-inch flat pine molding on a plywood base. Models should have labels explaining the parts and how they worked. **L3**

Refer to *Inclusion for the High School Social Studies Classroom Strategies and Activities* in the TCR.

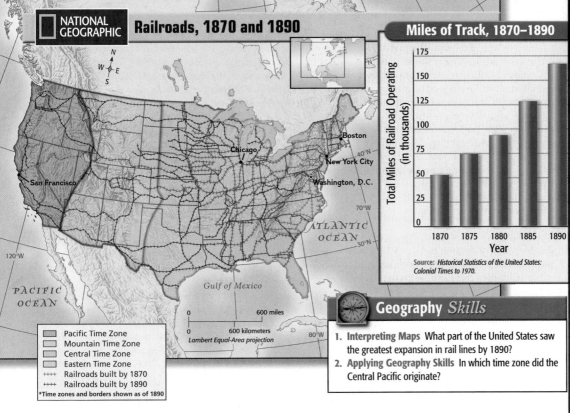

Railroads, 1870 and 1890

Boston
Chicago
New York City
Washington, D.C.
San Francisco

ATLANTIC OCEAN
PACIFIC OCEAN
Gulf of Mexico

N
W · E
S

0   600 miles
0   600 kilometers
Lambert Equal-Area projection

Pacific Time Zone
Mountain Time Zone
Central Time Zone
Eastern Time Zone
++++ Railroads built by 1870
++++ Railroads built by 1890
*Time zones and borders shown as of 1890

Miles of Track, 1870–1890

Total Miles of Railroad Operating (in thousands)

175
150
125
100
75
50
25
0

1870 1875 1880 1885 1890
Year

Source: *Historical Statistics of the United States: Colonial Times to 1970.*

Geography *Skills*

1. **Interpreting Maps** What part of the United States saw the greatest expansion in rail lines by 1890?
2. **Applying Geography Skills** In which time zone did the Central Pacific originate?

Geography *Skills*

Answers:
1. Great Plains
2. Pacific

Geography Skills Practice
Ask: What was the only California city that you could reach by train in 1870? *(San Francisco)*

✓**Reading Check**

Answer: to make rail service safer and more reliable

✓**Reading Check**

Answer: land grants

3 ASSESS

Assign Section 2 Assessment as homework or as an in-class activity.

⊕ Have students use the **Interactive Tutor Self-Assessment CD-ROM.**

made railroad operation so efficient that the average rate per mile for a ton of freight dropped from two cents in 1860 to three-fourths of a cent in 1900.

The nationwide rail network also helped unite Americans in different regions. Looking back at a quarter century of railroad travel, the *Omaha Daily Republican* observed in 1883 that railroads had "made the people of the country homogeneous, breaking through the peculiarities and provincialisms which marked separate and unmingling sections." This was, perhaps, an overstatement, but it recognized a significant contribution that railroads made to the nation.

✓**Reading Check** **Explaining** Why did the American Railway Association divide the country into four time zones?

The Land Grant System

Building and operating railroad lines, especially across the vast unsettled regions of the West, often required more money than most private investors could raise on their own. To encourage railroad construction, the federal government gave land grants to many railroad companies. Railroads would then

sell the land to settlers, real estate companies, and other businesses to raise the money they needed to build the railroad.

In the 1850s, the federal government granted individual states over 28 million acres of public lands to give to the railroads. After the Pacific Railway Acts of 1862 and 1864, the government gave the land directly to the railroad companies.

During the 1850s and 1860s, the federal land grant system awarded railroad companies over 120 million acres of land, an area larger than New England, New York, and Pennsylvania combined. Several railroad companies, including the Union Pacific and the Central Pacific, earned enough money from the government's generous land grants to cover much of the cost of building their lines.

✓**Reading Check** **Summarizing** How did the government help finance railroads?

Robber Barons

The great wealth many railroad entrepreneurs acquired in the late 1800s led to accusations that they had built their fortunes by swindling investors and

Reading Essentials and Study Guide 14–2

Name _____ Date _____ Class _____

Study Guide
Chapter 14, Section 2
For use with textbook pages 442–446
THE RAILROADS

KEY TERMS AND NAMES

Pacific Railway Act the law that provided for the construction of a transcontinental railroad *(page 443)*

Grenville Dodge engineer that helped direct the building of the Union Pacific Railroad *(page 443)*

Leland Stanford one of the "Big Four" who made a huge fortune by investing in the Central Pacific Railroad Company *(page 443)*

Cornelius Vanderbilt consolidated three railroads to form the New York Central *(page 444)*

time zone the division of the United States into regions where the same time was kept *(page 444)*

CHAPTER 14   Industrialization   **445**

INTERDISCIPLINARY CONNECTIONS ACTIVITY

Language Arts Tell students that most large industries have their own specialized terms that are used on the job. Have interested students create a lexicon of terms used by railroad workers. Tell them that the lexicon should include the term, its pronunciation, and good, working definitions. For at least two of the terms, students should also include a drawing or diagram for further explanation. **L2**

you don't say...

Time Tales Opponents of standard time called local time "God's time" because it was based on the laws of nature—the sun's position in the sky. Not until 1918 was Congress able to pass a law that standardized time zones.

Reteach

Have students analyze how the railroads were financed.

Enrich

Have students research and write a report on one of the railroad tycoons.

✓ Reading Check

Answer: shipped goods both ways, operated without aid, and was a financial success

4 CLOSE

Have students discuss ways in which the railroads spurred industrial growth.

---

taxpayers, bribing government officials, and cheating on their contracts and debts. The person with probably the worst reputation for this kind of activity was **Jay Gould,** who often practiced "insider trading." He used information he received as a railroad owner to manipulate stock prices to his benefit.

Bribery occurred frequently in this era, partly because the state and federal governments were so deeply entangled in funding the railroads. Railroad investors quickly discovered that they could make more money by acquiring government land grants than by operating the railroad. As a result, many investors bribed members of Congress and the state legislatures to vote for more grants.

The Crédit Mobilier Scandal The corruption in the railroad industry became public in 1872 when the Crédit Mobilier scandal erupted. **Crédit Mobilier** was a construction company set up by several stockholders of the Union Pacific, including Oakes Ames, a member of Congress. Acting for both the Union Pacific and Crédit Mobilier, the investors signed contracts with themselves. Crédit Mobilier greatly overcharged Union Pacific for the work it did, and since the same investors controlled both companies, the railroad agreed to pay the inflated bills.

By the time the Union Pacific railroad was completed, the investors had made several million dollars, but the railroad itself had used up its federal grants and was almost bankrupt. To convince Congress to give the railroad more grants, Ames gave other members of Congress shares in the Union Pacific at a price well below their market value.

During the election campaign of 1872, a disgruntled associate of Ames sent a letter to the *New York Sun* listing the members of Congress who had accepted shares. The scandal led to an investigation that implicated several members of Congress, including Speaker of the House James G. Blaine and James Garfield, who later became president. It also revealed that Vice President Schuyler Colfax had accepted stock from the railroad.

The Great Northern The Crédit Mobilier scandal provided sensational newspaper headlines. It created the impression that all railroad entrepreneurs were robber barons—people who loot an industry and give nothing back—but the term was not always deserved.

One railroad entrepreneur who was clearly not a robber baron was **James J. Hill.** Hill built and operated the Great Northern Railroad from St. Paul, Minnesota, to Everett, Washington, without any federal land grants or subsidies. He built the Great Northern across good land, carefully planning his route to pass by towns in the region. To increase business, he offered low fares to settlers who homesteaded along his route. He then identified American products that were in demand in China, including cotton, textiles, and flour, and arranged to haul those goods to Washington for shipment to Asia. This enabled the railroad to earn money by hauling goods both east and west, instead of simply sending lumber and farm products east and coming back empty, as many other railroads did. Operating without government subsidies or land grants, the Great Northern became the most successful transcontinental railroad and the only one that was not eventually forced into bankruptcy.

✓ Reading Check
Describing How was the Great Northern different from other railroads of the time?

SECTION 2 ASSESSMENT

Checking for Understanding

1. **Define:** time zone, land grant.
2. **Identify:** Pacific Railway Act, Grenville Dodge, Leland Stanford, Cornelius Vanderbilt, Jay Gould, Crédit Mobilier, James J. Hill.
3. **Explain** the provisions of the Pacific Railway Act.

Reviewing Themes

4. **Individual Action** How did Grenville Dodge contribute to the economic growth of the United States in the late 1800s?

Critical Thinking

5. **Synthesizing** How did railroad expansion in the United States lead to industrial growth?
6. **Organizing** Use a graphic organizer similar to the one below to list the different ways that railroads were financed.

Ways Railroads Were Financed

Analyzing Visuals

7. **Examining Maps and Graphs** Study the map and the graph on page 445. Then make up a quiz of at least five questions based on the information presented.

Writing About History
8. **Persuasive Writing** Take on the role of an employee of a major railroad corporation. Your job assignment is to write an advertisement to recruit workers for your corporation. After writing the advertisement, present it to your class.

SECTION 2 ASSESSMENT ANSWERS

1. Terms are in blue.
2. Pacific Railway Act *(p. 443),* Grenville Dodge *(p. 443),* Leland Stanford *(p. 443),* Cornelius Vanderbilt *(p. 444),* Jay Gould *(p. 446),* Crédit Mobilier *(p. 446),* James J. Hill *(p. 446)*
3. provided for the construction of the transcontinental railroad

4. supervised the Union Pacific's westward expansion
5. increased size of markets, spent great amounts of money on resources
6. land grants, private investment, gifts of public lands to railroads, money generated from running the railroads

7. Students' quizzes will vary. Students should include answers for their quiz questions.
8. Students' advertisements will vary. Advertisements should include a list of benefits.

SECTION 3 Big Business

Guide to Reading

Main Idea
After the Civil War, big business assumed a more prominent role in American life.

Key Terms and Names
corporation, stockholder, stock, economies of scale, fixed costs, operating costs, pool, Andrew Carnegie, Bessemer process, vertical integration, horizontal integration, monopoly, trust, holding company

Reading Strategy
Organizing As you read about the rise of corporations in the United States, complete a graphic organizer similar to the one below to describe the steps large business owners took to weaken or eliminate competition.

Slashed prices temporarily → ☐ → ☐ → ☐

Reading Objectives
• **Analyze** how large corporations came to dominate American business.
• **Evaluate** how Andrew Carnegie's innovations transformed the steel industry.

Section Theme
Economic Factors Large national corporations formed in the United States in the mid-1800s and contributed to greater production.

Preview of Events

♦1865	♦1875	♦1885	♦1895

1862
John D. Rockefeller buys first oil refinery

1875
Andrew Carnegie opens steel mill in Pittsburgh

1879
Woolworth's chain store opens

1882
Dow Jones & Company founded

1901
J.P. Morgan forms U.S. Steel

Cartoon of John D. Rockefeller

★ **An American Story** ★

In the 1860s, the oil industry in the United States was highly competitive. One highly efficient company was Standard Oil, owned by John D. Rockefeller and his associates. Because his company shipped so much oil, Rockefeller was able to negotiate rebates, or refunds, from railroads that wanted his business. This gave his company an advantage, and he began to pressure other oil companies to sell out to him.

Oil producer Franklin Tarbell pledged never to surrender. Tarbell's daughter Ida later recalled her father's indignation over Rockefeller's maneuvers:

❝It was as if somebody had tried to crowd me off the road. . . . There were rules, you couldn't use the road unless you obeyed those rules. . . . The railroads—so said my father—ran through the valley by the consent of the people; they had given them a right of way. The road on which I trotted was a right of way. One man had the same right as another, but the railroads had given to one something they would not give to another. . . . The strong wrested from the railroads the privilege of preying upon the weak.❞

—quoted in *All in the Day's Work*

The Rise of Big Business

Before the Civil War, the personal wealth of a few people operating in partnership financed most businesses, including many early factories. Most manufacturing enterprises were very small. By 1900 everything had changed. Big businesses dominated the economy, operating vast complexes of factories, warehouses, offices, and distribution facilities.

CHAPTER 14   Industrialization   **447**

1 FOCUS

Section Overview
This section focuses on how big business became important in American life.

BELLRINGER
Skillbuilder Activity

Project transparency and have students answer the question.

Available as a blackline master.

Daily Focus Skills Transparency 14–3

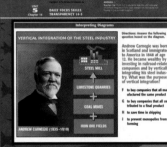

Guide to Reading

Answers to Graphic: pools, vertical and horizontal integration, holding companies, trusts

Preteaching Vocabulary
Have students use a standard dictionary to look up the Key Terms in this section to gain a better understanding of them.

SECTION RESOURCES

📖 Reproducible Masters
• Reproducible Lesson Plan 14–3
• Daily Lecture and Discussion Notes 14–3
• Guided Reading Activity 14–3
• Section Quiz 14–3
• Reading Essentials and Study Guide 14–3

📖 Transparencies
• Daily Focus Skills Transparency 14–3

• American Art & Architecture

Multimedia
🖲 Interactive Tutor Self-Assessment CD-ROM
🖲 ExamView® Pro Testmaker CD-ROM
🖲 Presentation Plus! CD-ROM
🖲 TeacherWorks™ CD-ROM
🖲 Audio Program

2 TEACH

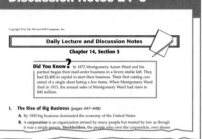

Reading Check

Answer: general incorporation laws and economies of scale

Creating a Profile Encourage students to use library and Internet resources to learn about a local philanthropist—past or present. Instruct students to prepare a short fact sheet for the person they select. **L1**

FYI

In 1898, although Carnegie Steel's output had risen threefold over the previous few years, the number of workers needed to produce the steel had decreased by 400. The use of electricity to drive automatic machinery was largely responsible for the decline in the workforce.

History and the Humanities

American Art & Architecture: Smoking Room of the John D. Rockefeller House

---

ECONOMICS

The Role of Corporations Big business would not have been possible without the corporation. A corporation is an organization owned by many people but treated by law as though it were a single person. A corporation can own property, pay taxes, make contracts, and sue and be sued. The people who own the corporation are called **stockholders** because they own shares of ownership called **stock.** Issuing stock allows a corporation to raise large amounts of money for big projects while spreading out the financial risk.

Before the 1830s, there were few corporations in the United States because entrepreneurs had to convince a state legislature to issue them a charter. Beginning in the 1830s, however, states began passing general incorporation laws, allowing companies to become corporations and issue stock without charters from the legislature.

Economies of Scale With the money they raised from the sale of stock, corporations could invest in new technologies, hire a large workforce, and purchase many machines, greatly increasing their efficiency. This enabled them to achieve what is called economies of scale, in which corporations make goods more cheaply because they produce so much so quickly using large manufacturing facilities.

All businesses have two kinds of costs, fixed costs and operating (or variable) costs. Fixed costs are costs a company has to pay, whether or not it is operating. For example, a company would have to pay its loans, mortgages, and taxes, regardless of whether it was operating. Operating costs are costs that occur when running a company, such as paying wages and shipping charges and buying raw materials and other supplies.

The small manufacturing companies that had been typical before the Civil War usually had very low fixed costs but very high operating costs. If sales dropped, it was cheaper to shut down and wait for better economic conditions. By comparison, big companies had very high fixed costs because it took so much money to build and maintain a factory. Compared to their fixed costs, big businesses had low operating costs. Wages and transportation costs were such a small part of a corporation's costs that it made sense to keep operating, even in a recession.

In these circumstances, big corporations had several advantages. They could produce goods more cheaply and efficiently. They could continue to operate in poor economic times by cutting prices to increase sales, rather than shutting down. Many were

448 CHAPTER 14 Industrialization

---

also able to negotiate rebates from the railroads, thus lowering their operating costs even further.

Small businesses with high operating costs found it difficult to compete against large corporations, and many were forced out of business. At the time, many people criticized corporations for cutting prices and negotiating rebates. They believed the corporations were behaving unethically by using their wealth to drive small companies out of business. In many cases, the changing nature of business organization and the new importance of fixed costs that caused competition to become so severe forced many small companies out of business.

Reading Check **Describing** What factors led to the rise of big business in the United States?

The Consolidation of Industry

Many corporate leaders did not like the intense competition that had been forced on them. Although falling prices benefited consumers, they cut into profits. To stop prices from falling, many companies organized pools, or agreements to maintain prices at a certain level.

American courts and legislatures were suspicious of pools because they interfered with competition and property rights. As a result, companies that formed pools had no legal protection and could not enforce their agreements in court. Pools generally did not last long. They broke apart whenever one member cut prices to steal the market share from another, which then allowed competition to resume. By the 1870s, competition had reduced many industries to a few large and highly efficient corporations.

Andrew Carnegie and Steel The remarkable life of **Andrew Carnegie** illustrates many of the different factors that led to industrialism and the rise of big business in the United States. He was born in Scotland, the son of a poor hand weaver who emigrated to the United States in 1848. At age 12, Carnegie went to work as a bobbin boy in a textile factory earning $1.20 per week. After two years, he became a messenger in a telegraph office, then served as private secretary to Thomas Scott, a superintendent and later president of the Pennsylvania Railroad. Carnegie's energy impressed Scott, and when Scott was promoted, Carnegie succeeded him as superintendent.

As a railroad supervisor, Carnegie knew that he could make a lot of money by investing in companies that served the railroad industry. He bought shares in iron mills and factories that made sleeping cars and

---

COOPERATIVE LEARNING ACTIVITY

Making a Flowchart Have students work together in small groups to make a flowchart showing how steel is made. Charts should begin with the raw materials (iron ore, limestone, and coal) and end with the finished products, such as slabs, blooms, and billets of steel, that are produced by the steel mill. Some students may do the research while others design and execute the chart. The finished charts may be displayed in your classroom or school library.

Use the rubric for a cooperative group management plan on pages 81–82 in the *Performance Assessment Activities and Rubrics.*

Vertical Integration

Purchase of Companies at All Levels of Production

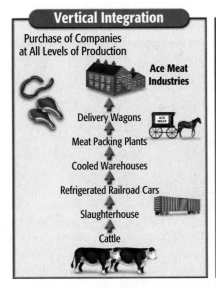

Ace Meat Industries

↑ Delivery Wagons

↑ Meat Packing Plants

↑ Cooled Warehouses

↑ Refrigerated Railroad Cars

↑ Slaughterhouse

↑ Cattle

Horizontal Integration

Purchase of Competing Companies in Same Industry

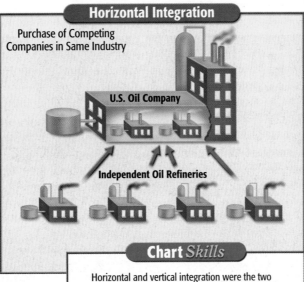

U.S. Oil Company

Independent Oil Refineries

Chart *Skills*

Horizontal and vertical integration were the two most common business combinations in the late 1800s.

Evaluating Which combination do you think would yield the most efficient business? Why?

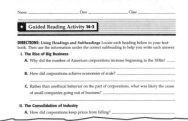

---

locomotives. He also invested in a company that built railroad bridges. In his early 30s, he was earning $50,000 per year, and he decided to quit his job with the railroad to concentrate on his own business affairs.

As part of his business activities, Carnegie frequently traveled to Europe to sell railroad bonds. On one trip, he met the English inventor, Sir Henry Bessemer, who had invented a new process for making high quality steel efficiently and cheaply. After meeting Bessemer, Carnegie decided to concentrate his investments in the steel industry. He opened a steel company in Pittsburgh in 1875 and quickly adapted his steel mills to use the **Bessemer process.** Carnegie often boasted about how cheaply he could produce steel:

❝Two pounds of iron stone mined upon Lake Superior and transported nine hundred miles to Pittsburgh; one pound and one-half of coal mined and manufactured into coke, and transported to Pittsburgh; one-half pound of lime, mined and transported to Pittsburgh; a small amount of manganese ore mined in Virginia and brought to Pittsburgh—and these four pounds of materials manufactured into one pound of steel, for which the consumer pays one cent.❞

—quoted in *The Growth of the American Republic*

Vertical and Horizontal Integration To increase manufacturing efficiency even further, Carnegie took the next step in building a big business. He did this by beginning the vertical integration of the steel industry. A vertically integrated company owns all of the different businesses on which it depends for its operation. Instead of paying companies for coal, lime, and iron, Carnegie's company bought coal mines, limestone quarries, and iron ore fields. Vertical integration saved companies money while enabling big companies to become even bigger.

Successful business leaders like Carnegie also pushed for horizontal integration, or combining many firms engaged in the same type of business into one large corporation. Horizontal integration took place frequently as companies competed. When a company began to lose market share, it would often sell out to competitors to create a larger organization. By 1880, for example, a series of buyouts had enabled Rockefeller's Standard Oil to gain control of approximately 90 percent of the oil refining industry in the United States. When a single company achieves control of an entire market, it becomes a monopoly. Many Americans feared monopolies because they believed that a company with a monopoly could charge whatever it wanted for its products. Others, however, supported monopolies. They believed that monopolies had to keep prices low because raising prices would encourage competitors to reappear and offer the products for a lower price. In some industries companies had a virtual monopoly in the United States but were competing on a global scale. Standard Oil, for example, came very close to having a monopoly in the United States, but competition with other

Chart *Skills*

Answer: Answers may vary. Both could be highly efficient if well managed. Some students may favor vertical integration since they may argue that horizontal integration reduces competition and may lead to less efficient giant business.

Chart Skills Practice
Ask: What potential problems exist if one large business buys all its competitors? (*The resulting monopoly can charge high prices; it has less reason to be highly efficient.*)

Discussing a Topic Have students compare the game of Monopoly with the monopolies built by Rockefeller and other magnates. **L1**

FYI

Today the Organization of Petroleum Exporting Countries (OPEC) tries to maintain stability in the oil industry to ensure profits. This is called a *cartel.* Since 1970 OPEC has controlled approximately one-third to one-half of the world's oil supply. In 2001 member nations included Algeria, Indonesia, Iran, Iraq, Kuwait, Libya, Nigeria, Qatar, Saudi Arabia, the United Arab Emirates, and Venezuela.

MEETING SPECIAL NEEDS

Visual/Spatial Have interested students research how by-products of oil such as kerosene, paint, or paraffin are produced. Ask students to show the process by creating a poster or flowchart that includes drawings and explanatory labels. Display the posters and flowcharts and have students answer questions about the process. **L3**

 Refer to *Inclusion for the High School Social Studies Classroom Strategies and Activities* in the TCR.

3 ASSESS

Assign Section 3 Assessment as homework or as an in-class activity.

◉ Have students use the **Interactive Tutor Self-Assessment CD-ROM.**

Reading Essentials and Study Guide 14–3

Name _____ Date _____ Class _____

Study Guide
Chapter 14, Section 3
For use with textbook pages 447–451
BIG BUSINESS

KEY TERMS AND NAMES
corporation an organization owned by many people but treated by law as though it were a single person *(page 448)*
stockholders people who own a corporation through shares of ownership *(page 448)*
stock shares of ownership *(page 448)*
economies of scale ability of large manufacturing facilities to produce more goods more cheaply *(page 448)*
fixed costs costs a company has to pay whether it is operating or not *(page 448)*
operating costs costs that occur when running a company *(page 448)*
pool agreement among companies to maintain prices at a certain level *(page 448)*

Section Quiz 14–3

Name _____ Date _____ Class _____

★ Chapter 14	Score

Section Quiz 14-3

DIRECTIONS: Matching Match each item in Column A with the items in Column B. Write the correct letters in the blanks. *(10 points each)*

Column A
____ 1. process for making high-quality steel efficiently and cheaply
____ 2. agreements to maintain prices at a certain level
____ 3. when a company owns all the different businesses on which it depends for its operation
____ 4. became one of the most successful retail chains in American history
____ 5. when a single company achieves control of an entire market

Column B
A. Woolworth's
B. pools
C. Bessemer process
D. monopoly
E. vertical integration

NATIONAL GEOGRAPHIC
MOMENT in HISTORY

Before the advent of the electric vacuum cleaner, the ritual of spring-cleaning involved moving furniture aside and taking carpets and rugs outdoors to beat the dust out of them.

✓ Reading Check

Answer: pools, vertical and horizontal integration, monopolies, trusts, and holding companies

NATIONAL GEOGRAPHIC
MOMENT in HISTORY
LABOR SAVERS

American inventiveness and the nation's growing industrial might combined to provide turn-of-the-century consumers with an ever-increasing array of products. Here, a homemaker wields an early electric vacuum cleaner. Mass-produced household devices had a tremendous impact on the lifestyles and buying habits of millions of middle-class Americans. In cities, huge shopping emporiums replaced the cozy dry goods stores of the 1800s. Even rural customers could buy an almost endless variety of merchandise from mail-order catalogues such as Sears, Roebuck and Montgomery Ward.

oil companies throughout the world forced the Standard Oil Company to keep its prices low.

Trusts By the late 1800s, many Americans had grown suspicious of large corporations and feared the power of monopolies. To preserve competition and prevent horizontal integration, many states made it illegal for one company to own stock in another without specific permission from the state legislature. In 1882 Standard Oil formed the first trust, a new way of merging businesses that did not violate the laws against owning other companies. A trust is a legal concept that allows one person to manage another person's property. The person who manages another person's property is called a trustee.

Instead of buying a company outright, which was often illegal, Standard Oil had stockholders give their stocks to a group of Standard Oil trustees. In exchange, the stockholders received shares in the trust, which entitled them to receive a portion of the trust's profits. Since the trustees did not own the stock but were merely managing it for someone else,

they were not violating the law. This arrangement enabled the trustees to control a group of companies as if they were one large merged company.

Holding Companies Beginning in 1889 the state of New Jersey further accelerated the rise of big business with a new general incorporation law. This law allowed corporations chartered in New Jersey to own stock in other businesses without any need for special legislative action. Many companies immediately used the New Jersey law to create a new organization called a holding company. A holding company does not produce anything itself. Instead, it owns the stock of companies that do produce goods. The holding company controls all of the companies it owns, effectively merging them into one large enterprise. By 1904 the United States had 318 holding companies. Together these giant corporations controlled over 5,300 factories and were worth more than $7 billion.

✓ Reading Check **Explaining** What techniques did corporations use to consolidate their industries?

INTERDISCIPLINARY CONNECTIONS ACTIVITY

Economics Invite a representative from the Small Business Administration to speak to the class about the impact of small businesses on the community. Ask the speaker to address the basics of how one goes about setting up a small business. As a class, discuss the various ways that businesses can be financed. **L2**

Selling the Product

The vast array of products that American industries churned out led retailers to look for new ways to market and sell goods. N.W. Ayer and Son of Philadelphia, for example, developed bold new formats for advertising. Large display ads with illustrations replaced the small-type line ads that had been standard in newspapers. By 1900 retailers were spending over $90 million a year on advertising, approximately 10 times what they had spent in 1865. Advertising attracted readers to the newest retail business, the department store.

In 1877 advertisements billed John Wanamaker's new Philadelphia department store, the Grand Depot, as the "largest space in the world devoted to retail selling on a single floor." When Wanamaker's opened, only a handful of department stores existed in the United States; soon hundreds sprang up. Department stores changed the idea of shopping by bringing a huge array of different products together in a large, elegant building. They created an atmosphere that made shopping seem glamorous and exciting.

Chain stores, a group of similar stores owned by the same company, first appeared in the mid-1800s. In contrast to department stores, which offered many services, chain stores focused on thrift, offering low prices instead of elaborate service and decor. Woolworth's, a chain store that opened in 1879, became one of the most successful retail chains in American history.

To reach the millions of people who lived in rural areas in the late 1800s—far from chain stores or department stores—retailers began issuing mail-order catalogs. Two of the largest mail-order retailers were Montgomery Ward and Sears, Roebuck. Their huge catalogs, widely distributed through the mail, used attractive illustrations and friendly descriptions to advertise thousands of items for sale.

Fact · Fiction · Folklore

The New York Stock Exchange In 1792 businesspeople met in New York City to establish a stock exchange—a marketplace for buying and selling stock in companies. At first, the new stock exchange was located under a buttonwood tree on Wall Street.

The organization took its present name, the New York Stock Exchange, in 1863. Huge amounts of the capital required for the nation's industrialization after the Civil War passed through the New York Stock Exchange.

As stock trading grew, investors across the nation needed financial news. In 1882 Henry Charles Dow and Edward D. Jones founded Dow Jones & Company. This new company sent bulletins on the day's business to Wall Street's financial houses. The day's last delivery contained a news sheet, which became the *Wall Street Journal* in July 1889.

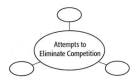

✓ **Reading Check** **Identifying** What innovations did retailers introduce in the late 1800s to sell goods to consumers?

Checking for Understanding

1. **Define:** corporation, economies of scale, fixed costs, operating costs, pool, vertical integration, horizontal integration, monopoly, trust, holding company.

2. **Identify:** stockholder, stock, Andrew Carnegie, Bessemer process.

3. **List** the new methods of advertising and selling that helped push consumer goods in the late 1800s.

Reviewing Themes

4. **Economic Factors** What factors allowed corporations to develop in the United States in the late 1800s?

Critical Thinking

5. **Forming an Opinion** Do you think an individual today can rise from "rags to riches" like Andrew Carnegie did? Why or why not?

6. **Organizing** Use a graphic organizer like the one below to list ways business leaders in the late 1800s tried to eliminate competition.

Attempts to Eliminate Competition

Analyzing Visuals

7. **Analyzing Photographs** Study the photograph on page 450 of a woman using an early electric vacuum cleaner. How would you compare this to today's vacuum cleaners? How do you think new mass-produced appliances such as this one affected the lives of women in this era?

Writing About History

8. **Expository Writing** Write a newspaper editorial in which you explain why entrepreneurs such as John D. Rockefeller and Andrew Carnegie were a positive or a negative force on the U.S. economy in the late 1800s.

CHAPTER 14 Industrialization **451**

Fact · Fiction · Folklore

Today *The Wall Street Journal* has the largest daily circulation of any newspaper in the United States.

Reteach

Have students evaluate how Andrew Carnegie's innovations transformed the steel industry.

Enrich

Ask students to create a Venn diagram comparing and contrasting the types of businesses from which people purchased goods in the 1880s and from which they purchase goods today.

✓ **Reading Check**

Answer: large display ads in newspapers, department stores, chain stores, and mail-order catalogs

4 CLOSE

Have students analyze how large corporations came to dominate American business.

---

1. Terms are in blue.
2. stockholder (*p. 448*), stock (*p. 448*), Andrew Carnegie (*p. 448*), Bessemer process (*p. 449*)
3. large display ads in newspapers, department stores, chain stores, mail-order catalogs
4. general incorporation laws
5. Students' answers will vary.
6. pools, trusts, monopolies, vertical and horizontal integration
7. today's are lighter; gave women more leisure time
8. Editorials should use clear arguments.

You're *the* Historian

1 FOCUS

In 1870 the Standard Oil Company of Ohio was one of 26 oil refineries in Cleveland. At the time of the company's creation in January of that year, Standard Oil controlled 10 percent of the nation's petroleum refining. Over the next 10 years, John D. Rockefeller gained control of over 90 percent of the oil refining in the U.S. through mergers, elimination of competition, and the use of rebates to lower shipping costs. In 1899 George Rice complained to the U.S. Industrial Commission.

2 TEACH

Discussing an Issue Ask students to look at the current economic environment and discuss the pros and cons of the chief advantages listed by John D. Rockefeller as they relate to another industry, such as the airlines, computers, cell phones, or health care. **L2**

you don't say...

Board of Trustees Even though it is now illegal to operate a business as a trust, many corporations continue to refer to the group who directs the business as the "board of trustees."

You're *the* Historian

Investigating Standard Oil

By the 1880s, the Standard Oil Company, under the direction of John D. Rockefeller and his associates, had gained control of more than 90 percent of the oil refining business in the United States. Did Standard Oil use unfair tactics? The United States Industrial Commission investigated, calling Rockefeller himself to testify. Rockefeller said his success was due to the efficiency of his company. George Rice, an independent refiner from Marietta, Ohio, told the Industrial Commission that Standard Oil's advantage was criminal collusion with the railroads. Was he right? You're the historian.

Read the following excerpts from the Industrial Commission hearings of 1899. Then complete the questions and activities on the next page.

John D. Rockefeller

From John D. Rockefeller's testimony

Standard Oil stock

Question: To what advantages, or favors, or methods of management do you ascribe chiefly the success of the Standard Oil Company?

Answer [Rockefeller]: I ascribe the success of the Standard to its consistent policy to make the volume of its business large through the merits and cheapness of its products. It has spared no expense in finding, securing, and utilizing the best and cheapest methods of manufacture. It has sought for the best superintendents and workmen and paid the best wages. It has not hesitated to sacrifice old machinery and old plants for new and better ones. It has placed its manufactories at the points where they could supply markets at the least expense. It has not only sought markets for its principal products, but for all possible by-products, sparing no expense in introducing them to the public.

It has not hesitated to invest millions of dollars in methods of cheapening the gathering and distribution of oils by pipe lines, special cars, tank steamers, and tank wagons. . . .

Question: What are, in your judgment, the chief advantages from industrial combinations—(a) financially to stockholders; (b) to the public?

Answer: All the advantages which can be derived from a cooperation of person and aggregation of capital. . . . It is too late to argue about advantages of industrial combinations. They are a necessity. And if Americans are to have the privilege of extending their business in all the States of the Union, and into foreign countries as well, they are a necessity on a large scale, and require the agency of more than one corporation. Their chief advantages are:

1. Command of necessary capital.
2. Extension of limits of business.
3. Increase the number of persons interested in the business.
4. Economy in the business.
5. Improvements and economies which are derived from knowledge of many interested persons of wide experience.
6. Power to give the public improved products at less prices and still make a profit from stockholders.
7. Permanent work and good wages for laborers.

Cartoon criticizing Standard Oil

452   CHAPTER 14   Industrialization

EXTENDING THE CONTENT

Point of View Historians disagree about some of the issues surrounding the business practices employed by John D. Rockefeller and the Standard Oil Trust. For example, while it was common practice for the railroads to offer rebates to big shippers in a variety of industries, some historical accounts indicate that in addition to rebates, Rockefeller got inside information from the railroads about the business activities of his competitors. Discrepancies can also be found in historical accounts of the business practices of George Rice. Some accounts characterize Rice as a reputable businessman, while others paint him as a charlatan and con man.

Oil derricks

From George Rice's testimony

I am a citizen of the United States. . . . Producer of petroleum for more than 30 years, and a refiner of same for 20 years, but my refinery has been shut down during the past 3 years, owing to the powerful and all-prevailing machinations of the Standard Oil Trust, in criminal collusion and conspiracy with the railroads to destroy my business of 20 years of patient industry, toil, and money in building up, wholly by and through unlawful freight discriminations. I have been driven from pillar to post, from one railway line to another, for 20 years, in the absolutely vain endeavor to get equal and just freight rates with the Standard Oil Trust, so as to be able to run my refinery at anything approaching a profit, but which I have been utterly

unable to do. I have had to consequently shut down, with my business absolutely ruined and my refinery idle. This has been a very sad, bitter, and ruinous experience for me to endure, but I have endeavored to the best of my circumstances and ability to combat it the utmost I could for many a long waiting year, expecting relief through the honest and proper execution of our laws, which have as yet, however, never come. . . .

Outside of rebates or freight discriminations I had no show with the Standard Oil trust, because of their unlawfully acquired monopoly, by which they could temporarily cut only my customers' prices, and below cost, leaving the balance of the town, nine-tenths, uncut. This they can easily do without any appreciable harm to

their general trade, and thus effectually wipe out all competition, as fully set forth. Standard Oil prices generally were so high that I could sell my goods 2 to 3 cents a gallon below their prices and make a nice profit, but these savage attacks and cuts upon my customers' goods, and their consequent loss, plainly showed them their power for evil, and the uselessness to contend against such odds, and they would buy no more of my oil. . . .

Understanding the Issue

1. What potential advantages could companies like Standard Oil offer consumers?
2. What did George Rice believe to be the reason Standard Oil was so successful?
3. How would you assess the credibility of the two accounts?

Activities

1. **Investigate** Today many industries, unions, and special interest groups lobby Congress for favorable legislation. What are the most powerful groups? How do they operate?
2. **Check the News** Are there any companies that recently have been investigated for unfair or monopolistic practices? Collect headlines and news articles and create a bulletin board display.

3 ASSESS

Have students answer the Understanding the Issue questions.

Understanding the Issue

1. According to Rockefeller's testimony, consumers would benefit from companies similar to Standard Oil because they would get a better product at a lower price. In addition, these companies claimed to offer permanent work and good wages for laborers.
2. George Rice believed that Standard Oil was successful because it paid so little to ship its oil compared to what other refiners paid for freight. He also believed that Standard Oil cut its prices drastically to entice competitors' customers so that it could later eliminate the competition.
3. Students' answers will vary. They should be able to defend their positions.

Activities

1. Students' answers will vary. You may want students to work in pairs to conduct the necessary research.
2. Students' answers will vary. Recommend that students look in financial newspapers for examples.

4 CLOSE

Ask students to explain how two people can view the same circumstances so differently.

PORTFOLIO ACTIVITY

Writing an Essay Have students write an essay expressing their point of view on the controversy described in this passage. Instruct them to include enough background information in the essay so that someone who is not familiar with this topic will be able to understand the main ideas. Students may consult one of the popular weekly newsmagazines to see examples of well-written essays. Be sure they express their opinions in the essay.

SECTION 4 Unions

1 FOCUS

Section Overview

This section focuses on the formation of labor unions during the late 1800s.

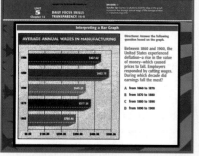
Guide to Reading

Guide to Reading

Main Idea
In an attempt to improve their working conditions, industrial workers came together to form unions in the late 1800s.

Key Terms and Names
deflation, trade union, industrial union, blacklist, lockout, Marxism, Knights of Labor, arbitration, closed shop

Reading Strategy
Sequencing As you read about the increase of American labor unions in the late 1800s, complete a time line similar to the one below by filling in the incidents of labor unrest discussed and the results of each incident.

1877 → ☐ → ☐ → ☐

Reading Objectives
• **Describe** industrial working conditions in the United States in the late 1800s.
• **List** the barriers to labor union growth.

Section Theme
Individual Action People like Samuel Gompers and Mother Jones strove to balance the power of corporations with the needs of workers.

Preview of Events

| ♦1875 | ♦1885 | ♦1895 | ♦1905 |

1877 — Great Railroad Strike

1886 — American Federation of Labor founded

1886 — Riot in Chicago's Haymarket Square

1894 — Pullman Strike

1903 — Women's Trade Union League founded

★ An American Story ★

On September 6, 1869, hundreds of miners' wives and children heard the repeated shrill blasts of the Avondale Mine's whistle, which signaled an accident. The families ran to the mine's entry and beheld a terrifying sight: hot smoke billowing from the mine shaft.

The owners of the Avondale Coal Mine in Luzerne County, Pennsylvania, had not built a second entrance to their mine. Without an escape route, the 179 miners trapped below soon died. Songs to commemorate the disaster later gave voice to the silenced victims:

66And as their souls ascended
To God who gave them breath
They plead against the company
Whose greed had caused their death99

Avondale Mine disaster

Following the deaths at Avondale, John Siney, an Irish immigrant and union leader, urged his fellow miners to unionize:

66Men, if you must die with your boots on, die for your families, your homes, your country, but do not longer consent to die like rats in a trap. . . .99

—**quoted in *Labor's Untold Story***

Working in the United States

Life for workers in industrial America was difficult. As machines replaced skilled labor, work became monotonous. Workers had to perform highly specific, repetitive tasks and could take little pride in their work. In addition, working conditions were

SECTION RESOURCES

Reproducible Masters
• Reproducible Lesson Plan 14–4
• Daily Lecture and Discussion Notes 14–4
• Guided Reading Activity 14–4
• Section Quiz 14–4
• Reading Essentials and Study Guide 14–4
• Performance Assessment Activities and Rubrics

Transparencies
• Daily Focus Skills Transparency 14–4

Multimedia
🖭 Interactive Tutor Self-Assessment CD-ROM
🖭 ExamView® Pro Testmaker CD-ROM
🖭 Presentation Plus! CD-ROM
🖭 TeacherWorks™ CD-ROM
🎧 Audio Program

often unhealthy and dangerous. Workers breathed in lint, dust, and toxic fumes. Heavy machines lacking safety devices caused a high number of injuries.

Despite the difficult working conditions, industrialism brought about a dramatic rise in the standard of living. While only a few entrepreneurs became rich, real wages earned by the average worker rose by about 50 percent between 1860 and 1890.

Despite the rise in the standard of living, the uneven division of income between the wealthy and the working class caused resentment among workers. In 1900 the average industrial worker made approximately 22¢ per hour and worked an average of 59 hours per week.

At the same time, an economic phenomenon of the late 1800s made relations between workers and employers even more difficult. Between 1865 and 1897, the United States experienced deflation, or a rise in the value of money. Throughout the late 1800s, deflation caused prices to fall, which increased the buying power of workers' wages. Although companies cut wages regularly in the late 1800s, prices fell even faster, so that wages were actually still going up in buying power. Most workers, however, believed that the companies wanted to pay them less money for the same work, and it made them angry. Eventually, many workers decided that the only way to improve their working conditions was to organize unions.

✓ **Reading Check**

Describing What aspects of industrial life caused frustration for workers in the late 1800s?

Early Unions

There were two basic types of industrial workers in the United States in the 1800s—craft workers and common laborers. Craft workers had special skills and training. They included machinists, iron molders, stonecutters, glassblowers, shoemakers, printers, carpenters, and many others. Craft workers generally received higher wages and

had more control over how they organized their time on the shop floor. Common laborers had few skills and received lower wages.

In the 1830s, as industrialism began to spread, craft workers began to form trade unions—unions limited to people with specific skills. By 1873 there were 32 national trade unions in the United States. Among the largest and most successful were the Iron Molders' International Union, the International Typographical Union, and the Knights of St. Crispin—the shoemakers' union.

Industry Opposes Unions Employers were often forced to recognize and negotiate with trade unions because they represented workers whose skills they needed. However, employers generally regarded unions as illegitimate conspiracies that interfered with their property rights. Owners of large corporations particularly opposed industrial unions, which united all craft workers and common laborers in a particular industry.

Companies used several techniques to prevent unions from forming. They required workers to take

📷 *Picturing* **History**

Unsafe Working Conditions Workers in the late 1800s often faced unsafe working conditions. Many began to join labor unions in an attempt to improve these conditions. *What unsafe conditions does this photograph of a steel mill show?*

CHAPTER 14 Industrialization **455**

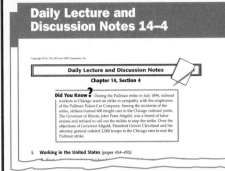

Analyzing Information Read the following quote by George Pullman: "Last year [1892], I made only 4.5 percent profit and this year it will be less than 4 percent. I am entitled to make more money than that. My workers will have to take a pay cut." **Ask:** Was Pullman justified in asking his workers to take a cut in pay and, if so, why? Discuss why present-day companies ask employees to take pay cuts. **L1**

📷 *Picturing* **History**

Answer: Workers are dangerously close to molten steel.
Ask: What problems resulted from unsafe working conditions? *(injuries, deaths, and illnesses)*

✓ **Reading Check**

Answer: working conditions, low pay, highly specific and repetitive tasks

---

COOPERATIVE LEARNING ACTIVITY

Organizing a Union Organize students into two groups. Designate one group as the employers and have them decide what they would tell their employees to keep them from joining a union. Ask the other group to be union organizers, and have them decide what they would tell workers about the advantages of joining a union. Have each group develop a list of talking points. Have several members of each group present their arguments to the class. Discuss the long-range economic and social effects of labor unions. 🖿

Use the rubric for a cooperative group management plan on pages 81–82 in the *Performance Assessment Activities and Rubrics.*

Name _____ Date _____ Class _____

★ Guided Reading Activity 14-4

DIRECTIONS: Filling in the Blanks In the space provided, write the word or words that best complete each sentence. Refer to your textbook to fill in the blanks.

1. Despite the difficult working conditions of industrial America, industrialism brought about a dramatic rise in the _____.
2. In 1900 the average industrial worker made approximately _____ an hour and worked an average of _____ a week.
3. _____ generally received higher wages and had more control over how they organized their time on the shop floor.
4. In the 1830s, craft workers began to form _____—unions limited to people with specific skills.
5. Owners of large corporations opposed _____—unions that united all craft workers and common laborers in a particular industry.
6. Workers formed _____

Profiles
IN HISTORY

Mary Harris Jones published her life story, *The Autobiography of Mother Jones*, in 1925 when she was 95 years old.

Ask: What was Mother Jones's main message? *(The only way workers could help themselves was to work together with other workers.)*

✓ **Reading Check**

Answer: They associated unions with immigrants, revolution, and anarchy.

Organizing Information Have
students create a graphic organizer similar to the one shown below to categorize the obstacles facing immigrants coming to the United States in the late 1800s. Students should include as many rows as they need. **L1**

Working Conditions	Family Life	City Life	Social Life

oaths or sign contracts promising not to join a union, and they hired detectives to go undercover and identify union organizers. Workers who tried to organize a union or strike were fired and placed on a **blacklist**—a list of "troublemakers." Once blacklisted, a laborer could get a job only by changing residence, trade, or even his or her name.

If workers formed a union, companies often used a lockout to break it. They locked workers out of the property and refused to pay them. If the union called a strike, employers would hire replacement workers, or **strikebreakers.**

Political and Social Opposition
Workers who wanted to organize a union faced several major problems. There were no laws giving workers the right to organize or requiring owners to negotiate with them. Courts frequently ruled that strikes were "conspiracies in restraint of trade," for which labor leaders might be fined or jailed.

Unions also suffered from the perception that they threatened American institutions. In the late 1800s, the ideas of Karl Marx, called Marxism, had become very influential in Europe. Marx argued that the basic force shaping capitalist society was the class struggle between workers and owners. He believed

Profiles IN HISTORY

Mother Jones 1830–1930

Mary Harris "Mother" Jones emigrated to the United States from Ireland in 1835 at the age of five. Jones became the nation's most prominent woman union leader after a tragic personal loss. In 1867 her husband George, a union organizer, and their four children died from yellow fever.

Widowed and childless, Jones moved to Chicago and opened a dressmaker's shop. From her shop window, Jones could see the effects of the economic downturn of the 1870s: "poor shivering wretches, jobless and hungry." At night she attended rallies for the Knights of Labor.

By 1890 Jones had become an organizer for the United Mine Workers. In 1897 she traveled to West Virginia. The intrepid labor organizer trudged from camp to camp along railroad tracks or rode atop farm wagons. She slept in a tent.

A journalist who followed Jones on her trip reported that Jones began her speeches slowly, encouraging her listeners to "look on yourselves, and upon each other. Let us consider this together for I am one of you, and I know what it is to suffer." Then Mother Jones would make an impassioned plea for the miners to join the union. "You pity yourselves, but you do not pity your brothers, or you would stand together to help one another."

that workers would eventually revolt, seize control of the factories, and overthrow the government.

Marxists claimed that after the revolution, the government would seize all private property and create a socialist society where wealth was evenly divided. Eventually, Marx thought, the state would wither away, leaving a Communist society where classes did not exist. Marxism strongly shaped the thinking of European unions.

While many labor supporters agreed with Marx, a few supported anarchism. Anarchists believe that society does not need any government. At the time, some believed that with only a few acts of violence, they could ignite a revolution to topple the government. In the late 1800s, anarchists assassinated government officials and set off bombs all across Europe, hoping to trigger a revolution.

As Marxist and anarchist ideas spread in Europe, tens of thousands of European immigrants began arriving in the United States. Nativism—anti-immigrant feelings—was already strong in the United States. As people began to associate immigrant workers with revolution and anarchism, they became increasingly suspicious of unions. These fears, as well as the government's duty to maintain law and order, often led officials to use the courts, the police, and even the army to crush strikes and break up unions.

✓ **Reading Check** Identifying
Why were some Americans suspicious of Unions?

The Struggle to Organize

Although workers attempted on many occasions to create large industrial unions, they rarely succeeded. In many cases the confrontations with owners and the government led to violence and bloodshed. In 1868 William Sylvis, president of the Iron Molders Union and leader of the National Labor Union, wrote to Karl Marx to encourage Marx's work and express his own hopes:

❝Our cause is a common one. . . . Go ahead in the good work that you have undertaken, until the most glorious success crowns your efforts . . . monied

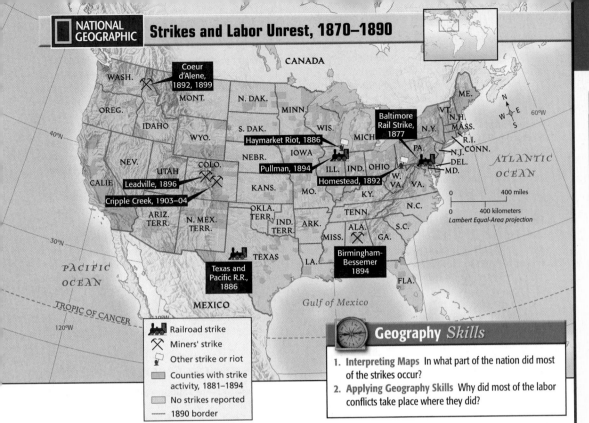

NATIONAL GEOGRAPHIC Strikes and Labor Unrest, 1870–1890

Legend:
- Railroad strike
- Miners' strike
- Other strike or riot
- Counties with strike activity, 1881–1894
- No strikes reported
- 1890 border

Geography Skills

1. **Interpreting Maps** In what part of the nation did most of the strikes occur?
2. **Applying Geography Skills** Why did most of the labor conflicts take place where they did?

power is fast eating up the substance of the people. We have made war upon it, and we mean to win it. If we can we will win through the ballot box; if not, we will resort to sterner means. A little bloodletting is sometimes necessary in desperate causes.

—quoted in *Industrialism and the American Worker*

The Great Railroad Strike of 1877 In 1873 a severe recession known as the Panic of 1873 struck the American economy and forced many companies to cut wages. In July 1877, as the recession continued, several railroads announced another round of wage cuts. This triggered the first nationwide labor protest. The day after the cuts took effect, railroad workers in Martinsburg, West Virginia, walked off the job and blocked the tracks.

As word spread, railroad workers across the country walked off the job. The strike eventually involved 80,000 railroad workers in 11 states and affected two-thirds of the nation's railways. Angry strikers smashed equipment, tore up tracks, and blocked rail service in New York, Baltimore, Pittsburgh, St. Louis,

and Chicago. The governors of several states called out their militias to stop the violence. In many places, gun battles erupted between the militia and striking workers.

Determined to stop the violence, President Hayes ordered the army to open the railroad between Philadelphia and Pittsburgh. He then sent troops to Chicago, where the strike had paralyzed the entire city. The troops restored order, but by the time the strike ended, more than 100 people lay dead, and millions of dollars of property had been destroyed.

The Knights of Labor The failure of the Great Railroad Strike convinced many labor organizers that workers across the nation needed to be better organized. By the late 1870s, enough workers had joined a new organization, the **Knights of Labor,** to make it the first nationwide industrial union.

The Knights called for an eight-hour workday and a government bureau of labor statistics. They also supported equal pay for women, the abolition of child labor, and the creation of worker-owned factories. The Knights' leaders initially opposed the use of strikes, preferring to use boycotts to pressure

CHAPTER 14 Industrialization **457**

CHAPTER 14
Section 4, 454–459

Geography Skills

Answers:
1. Northeast, Midwest, West
2. They were sites of major industrial development.

Geography Skills Practice
Ask: In which states did mining strikes occur? (*Alabama, Colorado, Idaho*)

Designing a Board Game Have students design a game based on life in the late 1800s. Invite interested students to play some of the games and explain the connections to the 1800s. **L3**

Use the rubric for creating a cooperative group management plan on pages 81–82 in the *Performance Assessment Activities and Rubrics.*

FYI

A century after the railroad strike of 1877, another group of transportation workers, air traffic controllers, went on strike demanding higher wages and fewer working hours. In August 1981, over 11,000 striking air traffic controllers were fired.

Hard Work Strict rules were enforced in the workplace in the late 1800s. Many bosses forbade singing, drinking, joking, smoking, or conversation on the job. They also denied immigrant workers time to celebrate their national holidays and holy days, and they did not accommodate workers who did not want to work on the Sabbath.

INTERDISCIPLINARY CONNECTIONS ACTIVITY

Economics Have students use magazines to create a collage of today's American workforce. Instruct students to insert text callouts to highlight how today's workforce is similar to and different from the workforce the late 1800s. **L1**

Writing a Report Have students write a report about one of the labor issues mentioned in this section. Encourage students to use library and Internet resources for their research. **L1**

3 ASSESS

Assign Section 4 Assessment as homework or as an in-class activity.

🌐 Have students use the **Interactive Tutor Self-Assessment CD-ROM.**

Reading Essentials and Study Guide 14–4

Name _____ Date _____ Class _____

Study Guide

Chapter 14, Section 4
For use with textbook pages 454–459

UNIONS

KEY TERMS AND NAMES
deflation a rise in the value of money *(page 455)*
trade unions unions that were limited to people with specific skills *(page 455)*
industrial union unions that represented all craft workers and common laborers in a particular industry *(page 455)*
blacklist a list of people who tried to organize a union or strike and were considered trouble-makers by employers *(page 456)*
lockout a method used by employers to prevent unions from forming *(page 456)*
Marxism the ideas of Karl Marx *(page 456)*

Section Quiz 14–4

Name _____ Date _____ Class _____

⭐ **Chapter 14**   Score ☐

Section Quiz 14-4

DIRECTIONS: Matching Match each item in Column A with the items in Column B. Write the correct letters in the blanks. *(10 points each)*

Column A	Column B
___ **1.** process whereby an impartial third party helps workers and management reach an agreement	**A.** Knights of Labor
___ **2.** a rise in the value of money	**B.** Women's Trade Union League
___ **3.** first national association dedicated to promoting women's labor issues	**C.** arbitration
___ **4.** unions limited to people with specific skills	**D.** deflation
___ **5.** first nationwide industrial union	**E.** trade unions

DIRECTIONS: Multiple Choice In the blank at the left, write the letter of the choice that best completes the statement or answers the question. *(10 points each)*

---

employers. They also supported arbitration, a process in which an impartial third party helps workers and management reach an agreement.

In the early 1880s, the Knights began to use strikes, and they achieved great success initially. After striking Knights convinced one of Jay Gould's railroads to reverse wage cuts in 1885, membership in the union leapt from 100,000 to 700,000 in less than a year. The following year, 1886, marked the peak of their success. In the spring of that year, an event known as the **Haymarket Riot** undermined the Knights' reputation, and the union rapidly declined.

The Haymarket Riot In the early 1880s, the movement for an eight-hour workday began to build support. In 1886 organizers called for a nationwide strike on May 1 to show support for the idea. On that date, strikes took place in many cities, including Chicago.

On May 3, a clash between strikers and police in Chicago left one striker dead. The next evening, an anarchist group organized a meeting in Chicago's Haymarket Square to protest the killing. Around 3,000 people gathered to hear the speeches. When police entered the square, someone threw a bomb. The police opened fire, and workers shot back. Seven police officers and four workers were killed.

Police arrested eight people for the bombing. Seven of those arrested were German immigrants and advocates of anarchism. The incident horrified people across the country.

No one knew who threw the bomb. Although the evidence was weak, all eight men were convicted, and four were later executed. Unfortunately for the Knights of Labor, one of the men arrested was a member of the union. The incident badly hurt the Knights' reputation, and they began to lose members rapidly.

The Pullman Strike Although the Haymarket Riot set back the drive to create industrial unions, other labor organizers continued their efforts. In 1893 railroad workers created the American Railway Union (ARU) under the leadership of Eugene V. Debs. One of the companies the ARU unionized was the Pullman Palace Car Company.

The Pullman Company was based in Illinois. It had built a town named Pullman near its factory and required its workers to live in the town and to buy goods from company stores. In 1893 a depression

struck the United States, causing the Pullman Company to slash wages. The wage cuts made it difficult for workers to pay their rent or the high prices at the company stores. In May 1894, after Pullman fired three workers who complained, a strike began. In support, the ARU stopped handling Pullman cars all across the United States.

The boycott of Pullman cars tied up railroads and threatened to paralyze the economy. Determined to break the union, railroad managers arranged for U.S. mail cars to be attached to the Pullman cars. If the strikers refused to handle the Pullman cars, they would be interfering with the U.S. mail, a violation of federal law. President Grover Cleveland then sent in troops, claiming it was his responsibility to keep the mail running. When a federal court issued an injunction ordering the union to halt the boycott, the strike at Pullman and the ARU both collapsed.

✓ Reading Check **Analyzing** Why did industrial unions frequently fail in the late 1800s?

The American Federation of Labor

Although large-scale industrial unions generally failed in the late 1800s, trade unions continued to prosper. In 1886 delegates from over 20 of the nation's trade unions organized the **American Federation of Labor** (AFL). The AFL's first leader was **Samuel Gompers.** His approach to labor relations—which he called "plain and simple" unionism—helped unions to become accepted in American society.

Gompers believed that unions should stay out of politics. He rejected socialist and communist ideas. Rather, he believed that the AFL should fight for small gains—such as higher wages and better working conditions—within the American system. He was willing to use the strike but preferred to negotiate.

Under Gompers's leadership, the AFL had three main goals. First, it tried to convince companies to recognize unions and to agree to collective bargaining. Second, it pushed for closed shops, meaning that companies could only hire union members. Third, it promoted an eight-hour workday.

Samuel Gompers

The AFL grew slowly, but by 1900 it was the biggest union in the country, with over 500,000 members. Still, at that time, the AFL represented less than 15 percent of all non-farm workers. All unions, including railroad

---

CRITICAL THINKING ACTIVITY

Synthesizing Ask students to describe stereotypes associated with unions. Have students then explain how these stereotypes were formed. Then ask students to explain the impact of these stereotypes on the efforts of organized labor. Finally, ask students to evaluate if these stereotypes about unions are still held by people today. **L1**

unions, represented only 18 percent. As the 1900s began, the vast majority of workers remained unorganized, and unions were relatively weak.

✓ **Reading Check** **Analyzing** What AFL policies contributed to its growth as a union?

Working Women

Throughout the 1800s, most wage-earning workers in the United States were men. After the Civil War, the number of women wage earners began to increase. By 1900 women made up more than 18 percent of the labor force.

The type of jobs women did outside the home in the late 1800s and early 1900s reflected society's ideas about what constituted "women's work." Roughly one-third of women worked as domestic servants. Another third worked as teachers, nurses, sales clerks, and secretaries. The remaining third were industrial workers, but they were employed in light industrial jobs that people believed appropriate to their gender. Many worked in the garment industry and food processing plants.

Regardless of their employment, women were paid less than men even when they performed the same jobs. It was assumed that a woman had a man helping to support her, either her father or her husband, and that a man needed higher wages to support a family. For this reason, most unions, including the AFL, excluded women.

In 1903 two woman labor organizers, Mary Kenney O'Sullivan and Leonora O'Reilly, decided to establish a separate union for women. With the help

Picturing **History**

Detail Work These women worked in the National Elgin Watch Company's gilding room, where they gilded metal watches with thin layers of gold. What do you notice about their working conditions?

of Jane Addams and Lillian Wald—the founders of the settlement house movement—they established the **Women's Trade Union League** (WTUL), the first national association dedicated to promoting women's labor issues. The WTUL pushed for an eight-hour day, the creation of a minimum wage, an end to evening work for women, and the abolition of child labor. The WTUL also collected funds to support women on strike.

✓ **Reading Check** **Comparing** How were female industrial workers treated differently than male workers in the late 1800s?

✓ **Reading Check**

Answer: emphasis on collective bargaining, closed shops, eight-hour workday

Picturing **History**

Answer: women workers working close together, uncomfortable chairs, dressed more formally than workers today
Ask: Why do you think this constituted women's work? (*It was light industrial work that did not involve heavy machinery.*)

Reteach
Have students list the barriers to labor union growth.

Enrich
Encourage students to write a profile of one of the leading labor unions today, such as the AFL-CIO or the Teamsters.

✓ **Reading Check**

Answer: excluded from unions, paid less than male counterparts, employed in jobs deemed appropriate for women

4 CLOSE

Have students describe industrial working conditions in the United States in the late 1800s.

SECTION 4 ASSESSMENT

Checking for Understanding
1. **Define:** deflation, trade union, industrial union, lockout, Marxism, arbitration, closed shop.
2. **Identify:** blacklist, Knights of Labor.
3. **List** the groups of workers represented by the Knights of Labor and the American Federation of Labor.

Reviewing Themes
4. **Individual Action** What political contribution did Mary Harris "Mother" Jones make to American society?

Critical Thinking
5. **Analyzing** Why did early labor unions fail?
6. **Organizing** Use a graphic organizer similar to the one below to list the factors that led to an increase in unions in the late 1800s.

Factors Contributing to Unionization

Analyzing Visuals
7. **Analyzing Photographs** Examine the photograph at the top of this page of workers in a watch factory. Most of the people in the picture are women. What do you think the jobs were of the men in the photograph?

Writing About History
8. **Persuasive Writing** Imagine that you are an American worker living in one of the nation's large cities. Write a letter to a friend explaining why you support or oppose the work of labor unions.

CHAPTER 14 Industrialization **459**

SECTION 4 ASSESSMENT ANSWERS

1. Terms are in blue.
2. blacklist (*p. 456*), Knights of Labor (*p. 457*)
3. industrial workers, trade workers
4. She became a key organizer for the United Mine Workers union.
5. confrontations led to violence, courts ruled against them, frequent strikes, fought for many things all at the same time, blacklisting
6. concern about working conditions, concern about pay, concern about job security, economic challenges such as deflation
7. managers or supervisors
8. Students' letters will vary. Letters should express a point of view.

CHAPTER 14 ASSESSMENT and ACTIVITIES

GLENCOE
TECHNOLOGY

MindJogger Videoquiz
Use the **MindJogger Videoquiz** to review Chapter 14 content.

 Available in VHS

Reviewing Key Terms

Students' answers will vary. The pages where the words appear in the text are shown in parentheses.

1. **gross national product** (p. 436)
2. **laissez-faire** (p. 438)
3. **entrepreneur** (p. 438)
4. **time zone** (p. 444)
5. **land grant** (p. 445)
6. **corporation** (p. 448)
7. **economies of scale** (p. 448)
8. **fixed costs** (p. 448)
9. **operating costs** (p. 448)
10. **pool** (p. 448)
11. **vertical integration** (p. 449)
12. **horizontal integration** (p. 449)
13. **monopoly** (p. 449)
14. **trust** (p. 450)
15. **holding company** (p. 450)
16. **deflation** (p. 455)
17. **trade union** (p. 455)
18. **industrial union** (p. 455)
19. **lockout** (p. 456)
20. **Marxism** (p. 456)
21. **arbitration** (p. 458)
22. **closed shop** (p. 458)

Reviewing Key Facts

23. Morrill Tariff (p. 438), Andrew Carnegie (p. 448)
24. iron ore, water, copper, coal, timber; large families, and floods of immigrants
25. helped increase the nation's productive capacity, improved transportation and communication

Reviewing Key Terms

On a sheet of paper, use each of these terms in a sentence.

1. gross national product
2. laissez-faire
3. entrepreneur
4. time zone
5. land grant
6. corporation
7. economies of scale
8. fixed costs
9. operating costs
10. pool
11. vertical integration
12. horizontal integration
13. monopoly
14. trust
15. holding company
16. deflation
17. trade union
18. industrial union
19. lockout
20. Marxism
21. arbitration
22. closed shop

Chapter Summary

Factors Behind Industrialization

- Abundant natural resources
- Cheap immigrant labor force
- High tariffs that reduced foreign goods
- National communication and transportation networks

Growth of Business

- Little or no government intervention
- Development of pools, trusts, holding companies, and monopolies
- Small businesses could not compete with economies–of–scale of large businesses
- Practices of some big businesses sometimes limited competition

Changing Workplace

- Rural migration and immigration created large, concentrated workforce
- In large–scale industries, low wages, long hours, and dangerous working conditions were common
- First large unions formed but had little bargaining power against large companies

---

26. by offering land grants
27. large display advertisements in newspapers, department stores, chain stores, mail-order catalogs
28. to change poor working conditions, low pay, and job security
29. craft workers and common laborers

Reviewing Key Facts

23. **Identify:** Morrill Tariff, Andrew Carnegie.
24. The United States had an advantage in industrializing due to its resources and large workforce. What resources did the nation have? Why was its workforce large?
25. How did inventions contribute to economic growth in the United States in the late 1800s?
26. How did the federal government encourage railroad companies to construct railroads?
27. What new methods of selling products were developed in the late 1800s?
28. Why did workers try to organize labor unions in the United States in the late 1800s?
29. What were the two basic types of workers in American industry at this time?

Critical Thinking

30. **Analyzing Themes: Individual Action** List the names and actions of five people who contributed to American economic growth in the late 1800s.
31. **Organizing** Use a graphic organizer similar to the one below to list the factors that led to making the United States an industrial nation.

Factors Leading to Industrialization

32. **Interpreting Primary Sources** Americans like Ida Tarbell criticized large corporations such as the Standard Oil Company. In the following excerpt from *History of the Standard Oil Company,* she warns of the results of Rockefeller's business practices on the nation's morality. Read the excerpt and answer the questions that follow:

66 Very often people who admit the facts, who are willing to see that Mr. Rockefeller has employed force and fraud to secure his ends, justify him by declaring, 'It's business.' That is, 'It's business' has come to be a legitimate excuse for hard dealing, sly tricks, special privileges. It is a common enough thing to hear men arguing that the ordinary laws of morality do not apply in business.

Critical Thinking

30. Students' answers will vary. Names may include inventors and industrialists.
31. large labor force, inventions, abundant natural resources, free enterprise system
32. **a.** force and fraud; **b.** the "it's just business" attitude that excused immoral actions

As for the ethical side, there is no cure but in an increasing scorn of unfair play. . . . When the businessman who fights to secure special privileges, to crowd his competitor off the track by other than fair competitive methods, receives the same summary disdainful ostracism by his fellows that the doctor or lawyer who is 'unprofessional,' the athlete who abuses the rules, receives, we shall have gone a long way toward making commerce a fit pursuit for our young men.**"**

—quoted in *Readings in American History*

a. According to Tarbell, what practices had Rockefeller used to establish the Standard Oil Company?

b. In what way did Tarbell believe the attitudes of the American people contributed to Rockefeller's business practices?

33. Analyzing Analyze the impact of technological innovations and industrialization on the American labor movement.

Practicing Skills

34. Making Inferences Reread the passage titled "Working in the United States" from Section 4, page 454. Then answer the following questions.

a. What facts are stated about working conditions in the United States during this time period?

b. Based on your answer to the previous question, what can you infer about the attitude of employers toward their workers during this time?

Writing Activity

35. Portfolio Writing: Persuasive Writing Think of a product that you think is essential to life today. Write an advertisement for this product that would persuade people to purchase it.

Chapter Activity

36. American History Primary Source Document Library CD-ROM Read "Driving the Golden Spike" by Alexander Toponce, under *Reshaping the Nation*. For further background, reread your textbook's coverage of the same subject on page 443. Then prepare a presentation for your classmates. In it, describe what Toponce had to say about the workers during the celebration and what Grenville Dodge

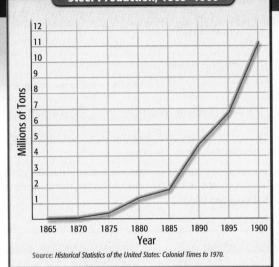

Steel Production, 1865–1900

Source: Historical Statistics of the United States: Colonial Times to 1970.

had to say about their experience during the project. What attitudes do you think each man had toward the workers?

Economics and History

37. The graph above shows steel production from 1865 to 1900. Study the graph and answer the questions below.

a. Interpreting Graphs Between what years did steel production have the greatest increase?

b. Making Inferences How did increased steel production contribute to American industrialism?

The Princeton Review

Standardized Test Practice

Directions: Choose the best answer to the following question.

Labor unions were formed for all of these reasons except:

F To improve workers' wages

G To protect factory owners from being sued

H To make factories safer

J To prevent children from working long hours

Test-Taking Tip: If a question uses the word *except*, you need to look for the answer that does not fit. Remember that unions were formed to try to help workers. Which answer is least likely to help workers?

Writing Activity

35. Advertisements should be clearly persuasive yet factually accurate.

Chapter Activity

36. Presentations should contrast the two men's views about the railroad workers.

Economics and History

37. a. 1895 and 1900; **b.** allowed railroads to be built, improving transportation and benefitting industry

The Princeton Review

Standardized Test Practice

Answer: G

Test-Taking Tip: Instruct students to add the phrase "Labor unions were formed" before each of the possible answers to help them determine which answers they should eliminate. Remind them that they are trying to eliminate answers that include reasons why unions were formed. Answers F, H, and J can be eliminated. G is the correct answer.

Bonus Question ?

Ask: What are some of the reasons the United States had become the world's leading industrial nation by the early 1900s? *(possible answers include: abundant natural resources, large workforce, free enterprise system)*

33. Inventions such as electric power and the automatic loom led to large manufacturing companies and industrialization but created a host of challenges for workers, such as harsh working conditions. This led workers to unite and join labor unions.

Practicing Skills

34. a. Working conditions were often unhealthy and dangerous. Workers breathed lint, dust, and toxic fumes. The lack of safety devices in heavy machinery caused a high number of injuries. **b.** Students' answers will vary. They might suggest that employers were not concerned with the welfare of their workers.

Timesaving Tools

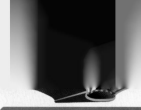

 **TeacherWorks™ All-In-One Planner and Resource Center**

- **Interactive Teacher Edition** Access your Teacher Wraparound Edition and your classroom resources with a few easy clicks.
- **Interactive Lesson Planner** Planning has never been easier! Organize your week, month, semester, or year with all the lesson helps you need to make teaching creative, timely, and relevant.

 Use Glencoe's **Presentation Plus!** multimedia teacher tool to easily present dynamic lessons that visually excite your students. Using Microsoft PowerPoint® you can customize the presentations to create your own personalized lessons.

TEACHING TRANSPARENCIES

Graphic Organizer 10

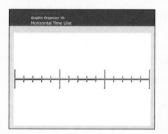

Why It Matters Chapter Transparency 15

APPLICATION AND ENRICHMENT

Linking Past and Present Activity 15

Enrichment Activity 15

Primary Source Reading 15

REVIEW AND REINFORCEMENT

Reteaching Activity 15

Vocabulary Activity 15

Time Line Activity 15

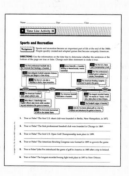

Critical Thinking Skills Activity 15

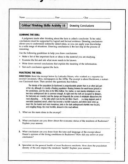

Meeting NCSS Standards

Local Standards

The following standards are highlighted in Chapter 15:

Section 1	III	People, Places, and Environments: B, C, H, I
Section 2	VI	Power, Authority, and Governance: B, C, H
Section 3	I	Culture: A, C
Section 4	IV	Individual Development and Identity: A, B, C, D

Chapter 15 Resources

**Chapter 15 Test
Form A**

**Chapter 15 Test
Form B**

**Standardized Test Skills
Practice Workbook Activity 15**

**Performance Assessment
Activities and Rubrics 15**

**ExamView® Pro
Testmaker CD-ROM**

MULTIMEDIA

- Vocabulary PuzzleMaker CD-ROM
- Interactive Tutor Self-Assessment CD-ROM
- ExamView® Pro Testmaker CD-ROM
- Audio Program
- American History Primary Source Documents Library CD-ROM
- MindJogger Videoquiz
- Presentation Plus! CD-ROM
- TeacherWorks™ CD-ROM
- Interactive Student Edition CD-ROM
- Glencoe Skillbuilder Interactive Workbook CD-ROM, Level 2
- The *American Vision* Video Program
- American Music: Hits Through History
- American Music: Cultural Traditions

SPANISH RESOURCES

The following Spanish language materials are available in the Spanish Resources Binder:

- Spanish Guided Reading Activities
- Spanish Reteaching Activities
- Spanish Quizzes and Tests
- Spanish Vocabulary Activities
- Spanish Summaries
- The Declaration of Independence and United States Constitution Spanish Translation

The following videotape programs are available from Glencoe as supplements to Chapter 15:

- **Ellis Island** (3 pack) (ISBN 0-76-700005-6)
- **Textiles: Birth of an American Industry** (ISBN 0-76-700624-0)

To order, call Glencoe at 1-800-334-7344. To find classroom resources to accompany many of these videos, check the following home pages:
A&E Television: www.aande.com
The History Channel: www.historychannel.com

HISTORY Online

Use our Web site for additional resources. All essential content is covered in the Student Edition.

You and your students can visit tav.glencoe.com, the Web site companion to the *American Vision.* This innovative integration of electronic and print media offers your students a wealth of opportunities. The student text directs students to the Web site for the following options:

- **Chapter Overviews**
- **Self-Check Quizzes**
- **Student Web Activities**
- **Textbook Updates**

Answers to the student Web activities are provided for you in the **Web Activity Lesson Plans.** Additional Web resources and Interactive Tutor Puzzles are also available.

Chapter 15 Resources

SECTION RESOURCES

Daily Objectives	Reproducible Resources	Multimedia Resources
SECTION 1 **Immigration** 1. Analyze the circumstances surrounding the great wave of immigration after the Civil War. 2. Evaluate how nativism affected immigration policies.	Reproducible Lesson Plan 15–1 Daily Lecture and Discussion Notes 15–1 Guided Reading Activity 15–1* Section Quiz 15–1* Reading Essentials and Study Guide 15–1 Performance Assessment Activities and Rubrics Interpreting Political Cartoons	Daily Focus Skills Transparency 15–1 Interactive Tutor Self-Assessment CD-ROM ExamView® Pro Testmaker CD-ROM Presentation Plus! CD-ROM TeacherWorks™ CD-ROM Audio Program American Music: Cultural Traditions ABCNews Interactive™ Historic America Electronic Field Trips
SECTION 2 **Urbanization** 1. Explain the technological developments that made the growth of cities possible. 2. Evaluate the role that political machines played in urban politics in the late 1800s.	Reproducible Lesson Plan 15–2 Daily Lecture and Discussion Notes 15–2 Guided Reading Activity 15–2* Section Quiz 15–2* Reading Essentials and Study Guide 15–2 Performance Assessment Activities and Rubrics Interpreting Political Cartoons	Daily Focus Skills Transparency 15–2 American Art & Architecture Interactive Tutor Self-Assessment CD-ROM ExamView® Pro Testmaker CD-ROM Presentation Plus! CD-ROM TeacherWorks™ CD-ROM Audio Program
SECTION 3 **The Gilded Age** 1. Evaluate the doctrine of Social Darwinism and the impact it had on American industry. 2. Explain how industrialization promoted leisure time and encouraged new forms of entertainment.	Reproducible Lesson Plan 15–3 Daily Lecture and Discussion Notes 15–3 Guided Reading Activity 15–3* Section Quiz 15–3* Reading Essentials and Study Guide 15–3 Performance Assessment Activities and Rubrics	Daily Focus Skills Transparency 15–3 American Art & Architecture Interactive Tutor Self-Assessment CD-ROM ExamView® Pro Testmaker CD-ROM Presentation Plus! CD-ROM TeacherWorks™ CD-ROM Audio Program American Music: Hits Through History American Music: Cultural Traditions
SECTION 4 **The Rebirth of Reform** 1. Explain the methods that social critics advocated to improve society. 2. Evaluate efforts to help the urban poor.	Reproducible Lesson Plan 15–4 Daily Lecture and Discussion Notes 15–4 Guided Reading Activity 15–4* Section Quiz 15–4* Reading Essentials and Study Guide 15–4 Performance Assessment Activities and Rubrics	Daily Focus Skills Transparency 15–4 Interactive Tutor Self-Assessment CD-ROM ExamView® Pro Testmaker CD-ROM Presentation Plus! CD-ROM TeacherWorks™ CD-ROM Skillbuilder Interactive Workbook, Level 2 Vocabulary PuzzleMaker CD-ROM Audio Program

0:00 OUT OF TIME?
Assign the Chapter 15 **Reading Essentials and Study Guide.**

*Also Available in Spanish

 Blackline Master   Transparency   CD-ROM   DVD

 Poster   Music Program   Audio Program   Videocassette

NATIONAL GEOGRAPHIC Teacher's Corner

INDEX TO NATIONAL GEOGRAPHIC MAGAZINE

The following articles relate to this chapter.

- "Boston's North Enders," October 2000
- "Chicago: Welcome to the Neighborhood," May 1991
- "New Life for Ellis Island," September 1990
- "New York's Chinatown," August 1998

NATIONAL GEOGRAPHIC SOCIETY PRODUCTS AVAILABLE FROM GLENCOE

To order the following products for use with this chapter, contact your local Glencoe sales representative, or call Glencoe at 1-800-334-7344:

- *PicturePack: Immigration* (Transparencies)
- *PictureShow: Immigration* (CD-ROM)

ADDITIONAL NATIONAL GEOGRAPHIC SOCIETY PRODUCTS

To order the following, call National Geographic at 1-800-368-2728:

- "Immigration: The Triumph of Hope" (Video)
- *NGS MapPack, Continents: North America*

NGS ONLINE

Access National Geographic's Web site for current events, atlas updates, activities, links, interactive features, and archives.

www.nationalgeographic.com

From the Classroom of...

Heather Pang
Castilleja School
Palo Alto, CA

Urban America

Select 10 to 15 images from Jacob Riis's *How the Other Half Lives* (available online at http://www.cis.yale.edu/amstud/inforev/riis/title.html and in most libraries). Images of children are particularly effective for this exercise. Show these pictures to the students (slides, scanned images, or photocopies).

Organize the students into small groups and assign each group one of the following roles: city police, local school board, charitable organization, philanthropic guild, schoolchildren, garment district workers, and a merchants' association. Each group should use the pictures as evidence to prepare a report titled "Poverty in the City: What Is to Be Done?" Remind the students that each of these groups will have different reactions to the Riis images depending on their own backgrounds. Each report should list the most significant problems shown in the images and provide suggestions for solutions.

It might be helpful to start the lesson with a short introduction to Riis and the tradition of muckraking journalism.

ADDITIONAL RESOURCES FROM GLENCOE

- American Music: Cultural Traditions
- American Art & Architecture
- Outline Map Resource Book
- U.S. Desk Map
- Building Geography Skills for Life
- Inclusion for the High School Social Studies Classroom Strategies and Activities
- Teaching Strategies for the American History Classroom (Including Block Scheduling Pacing Guides)

KEY TO ABILITY LEVELS

Teaching strategies have been coded.

L1 BASIC activities for all students
L2 AVERAGE activities for average to above-average students
L3 CHALLENGING activities for above-average students
ELL ENGLISH LANGUAGE LEARNER activities

Block Schedule

Activities that are suited to use within the block scheduling framework are identified by:

Performance Assessment

Refer to Activity 15 in the Performance Assessment Activities and Rubrics booklet.

Why It Matters Activity

Ask students if they think people from rural America and immigrants from other countries migrate to American cities now for the same reasons they did in the late 1800s. Students should evaluate their answers after they have completed the chapter.

GLENCOE TECHNOLOGY

The American Vision Video Program

To learn more about the problems the nation faced during this period of urbanization, have students view the Chapter 15 video, "Huddled Masses in the City," from the *American Vision Video Program.*

 Available in DVD and VHS

MindJogger Videoquiz
Use the **MindJogger Videoquiz** to preview Chapter 15 content.

 Available in VHS

CHAPTER 15
Urban America
1865–1896

Why It Matters

European and Asian immigrants arrived in the United States in great numbers during the late 1800s. Providing cheap labor, they made rapid industrial growth possible. They also helped populate the growing cities. The immigrants' presence affected both urban politics and labor unions. Reactions to immigrants and to an urban society were reflected in new political organizations and in literature and philosophy.

The Impact Today

Industrialization and urbanization permanently influenced American life.
- *The United States continues to be a magnet for immigrants seeking a better way of life.*
- *The cities of the United States continue to draw new residents in search of opportunity.*

The American Vision Video *The Chapter 15 video, "Huddled Masses in the City," depicts one of the problems the nation faced during its urbanization period.*

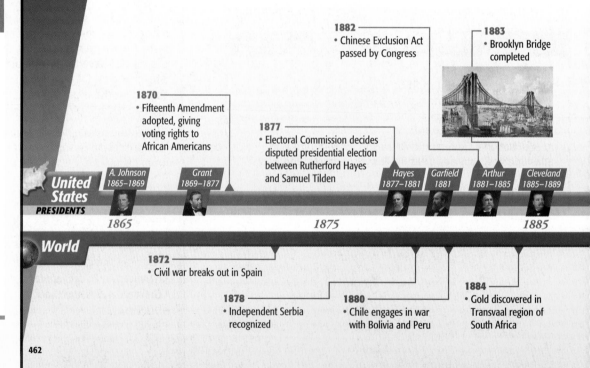

1882
- Chinese Exclusion Act passed by Congress

1883
- Brooklyn Bridge completed

1870
- Fifteenth Amendment adopted, giving voting rights to African Americans

1877
- Electoral Commission decides disputed presidential election between Rutherford Hayes and Samuel Tilden

United States PRESIDENTS

| A. Johnson 1865–1869 | Grant 1869–1877 | Hayes 1877–1881 | Garfield 1881 | Arthur 1881–1885 | Cleveland 1885–1889 |

1865   *1875*   *1885*

World

1872
- Civil war breaks out in Spain

1878
- Independent Serbia recognized

1880
- Chile engages in war with Bolivia and Peru

1884
- Gold discovered in Transvaal region of South Africa

462

TWO-MINUTE LESSON LAUNCHER

Tell students that before 1890, most immigrants to the United States were from northern and western Europe. Between 1890 and 1914, the majority came from Italy, Russia, Poland, Austria-Hungary, Greece, Romania, and Turkey. Have students locate these places on a map of the world. Ask students to speculate why the dramatic shift in immigration occurred.

Immigrants arriving at Ellis Island

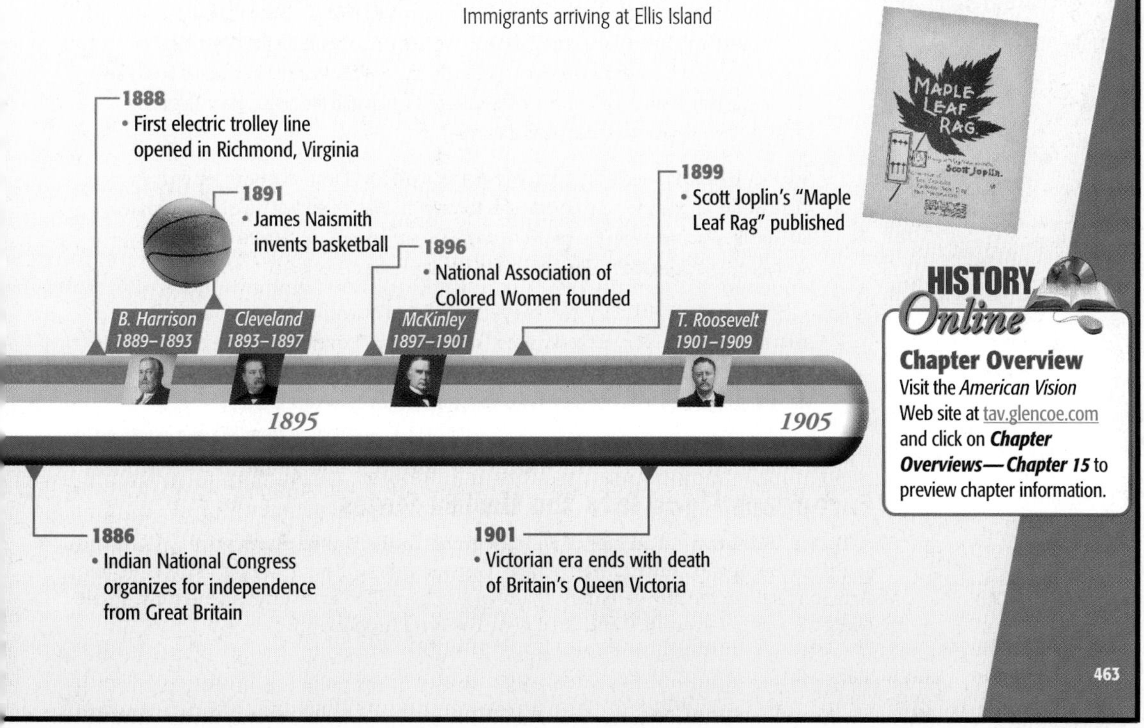

TIME LINE

1888
- First electric trolley line opened in Richmond, Virginia

1891
- James Naismith invents basketball

1896
- National Association of Colored Women founded

1899
- Scott Joplin's "Maple Leaf Rag" published

| B. Harrison 1889–1893 | Cleveland 1893–1897 | McKinley 1897–1901 | T. Roosevelt 1901–1909 |

1895   *1905*

1886
- Indian National Congress organizes for independence from Great Britain

1901
- Victorian era ends with death of Britain's Queen Victoria

HISTORY Online

Chapter Overview
Visit the *American Vision* Web site at tav.glencoe.com and click on *Chapter Overviews—Chapter 15* to preview chapter information.

463

HISTORY Online

Introduce students to chapter content and key terms by having them access the **Chapter 15 Overview** at tav.glencoe.com.

More About the Photo

Between 1892 and 1954, approximately 12 million people who entered the United States through the port of New York were legally and medically inspected at Ellis Island, a small island in New York Harbor.

TIME LINE ACTIVITY

Have students work in pairs to duplicate the United States portion of the time line. Instruct students to use absolute chronology to add the events shown on the section time lines. Suggest that students color-code the events by section to help identify the themes.

GRAPHIC ORGANIZER ACTIVITY

Organizing Information Have students use an outline map of the United States to label the cities where the various immigrant groups settled. Have students use a color code or small symbols to identify the different groups. Then ask students to use the maps to draw conclusions about immigration and its impact on urban America.

1 FOCUS

Section Overview

This section focuses on immigrants coming to the United States after the Civil War.

Guide to Reading

Answers to Graphic: Push Factors: avoid forced military service, avoid religious persecution; Pull Factors: jobs, chance to move up the social ladder

Preteaching Vocabulary
Have students skim this section to find time references for each of the Key Terms and Names.

SECTION 1 Immigration

Guide to Reading

Main Idea
After the Civil War, millions of immigrants from Europe and Asia settled in the United States.

Key Terms and Names
steerage, Ellis Island, Jacob Riis, Angel Island, nativism, Chinese Exclusion Act

Reading Strategy
Categorizing Complete a graphic organizer similar to the one below by filling in the reasons people left their homelands to immigrate to the United States.

Reasons for Immigrating	
Push Factors	Pull Factors

Reading Objectives
• **Analyze** the circumstances surrounding the great wave of immigration after the Civil War.
• **Evaluate** how nativism affected immigration policies.

Section Theme
Geography and History Immigrants from all over the world enriched the cultural life of the United States.

Preview of Events

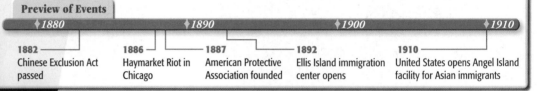

♦1880 ♦1890 ♦1900 ♦1910

1882
Chinese Exclusion Act passed

1886
Haymarket Riot in Chicago

1887
American Protective Association founded

1892
Ellis Island immigration center opens

1910
United States opens Angel Island facility for Asian immigrants

---

★ An American Story ★

Mary Antin, daughter of Hannah Hayye

In 1894, the day the steamer tickets arrived for the Hayye family, Hannah Hayye became an instant celebrity in her small village in Russian-occupied Poland. Hannah's husband had left for the United States three years earlier to prepare a new home for the Hayye family in Boston. Now that Hannah had received the tickets, she and her four children would finally be able to join him. A stream of curious visitors began to pour into the house. Hannah's daughter Mary, then 13 years old, described the crowd:

❝They wanted to handle the ticket, and mother must read them what is written on it. . . . Were we not all going to have new dresses to travel in? Was it sure that we could get kosher food on the ship? And with the questions poured in suggestions. . . . Mother mustn't carry her money in a pocketbook. She must sew it into the lining of her jacket. . . .❞

Before the family left, they gave away almost all their belongings and spent their last night at an uncle's home. "I did not really sleep," recalled Mary. "Excitement kept me awake, and my aunt snored hideously. In the morning, I was going away from Polotzk, forever and ever. I was going on a wonderful journey. I was going to America. How could I sleep?"

—adapted from *Witnessing America*

Europeans Flood Into the United States

By the 1890s, more than half of all immigrants in the United States were eastern and southern Europeans, including Italians, Greeks, Poles, Slavs, Slovaks, Russians, and Armenians. Like the Hayye family, many of the 14 million immigrants who came to the United States between 1860 and 1900 were eastern European Jews.

SECTION RESOURCES

Reproducible Masters
• Reproducible Lesson Plan 15–1
• Daily Lecture and Discussion Notes 15–1
• Guided Reading Activity 15–1
• Section Quiz 15–1
• Reading Essentials and Study Guide 15–1
• Interpreting Political Cartoons

Transparencies
• Daily Focus Skills Transparency 15–1

Multimedia
🔘 Interactive Tutor Self-Assessment CD-ROM
🔘 ExamView® Pro Testmaker CD-ROM
🔘 Presentation Plus! CD-ROM
🔘 TeacherWorks™ CD-ROM
🔊 Audio Program
🎵 American Music: Cultural Traditions

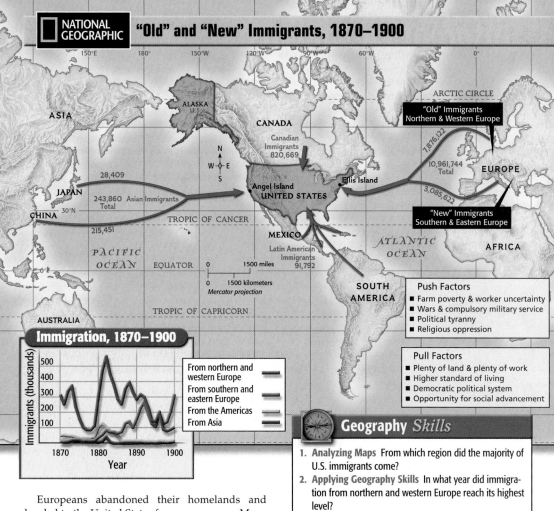

NATIONAL GEOGRAPHIC "Old" and "New" Immigrants, 1870–1900

"Old" Immigrants
Northern & Western Europe

"New" Immigrants
Southern & Eastern Europe

7,876,122
10,961,744 Total
3,085,622

Canadian Immigrants 820,669

28,409
243,860 Asian Immigrants Total
215,451

Latin American Immigrants 91,792

0   1500 miles
0   1500 kilometers
Mercator projection

Immigration, 1870–1900

Immigrants (thousands)

From northern and western Europe
From southern and eastern Europe
From the Americas
From Asia

Push Factors
■ Farm poverty & worker uncertainty
■ Wars & compulsory military service
■ Political tyranny
■ Religious oppression

Pull Factors
■ Plenty of land & plenty of work
■ Higher standard of living
■ Democratic political system
■ Opportunity for social advancement

Geography *Skills*

1. **Analyzing Maps** From which region did the majority of U.S. immigrants come?
2. **Applying Geography Skills** In what year did immigration from northern and western Europe reach its highest level?

Europeans abandoned their homelands and headed to the United States for many reasons. Many poor rural farmers came simply because the United States had plenty of jobs available and few immigration restrictions. Yet Europe in the late 1800s offered plenty of jobs in its booming industrial cities, so economic factors were not the only reason people migrated. Many moved to avoid forced military service, which in some nations could last for many years. Others, especially Jews living in Poland and Russia, fled to avoid religious persecution.

By the late 1800s, most European states had made moving to the United States easy. Immigrants were allowed to take their savings with them, and most countries had repealed old laws that had forced peasants to stay in their villages and had banned skilled workers from leaving the country. At the same time, moving to the United States offered a chance to break away from Europe's class

system and move to a democratic nation where they had a chance to move up the social ladder.

The Atlantic Voyage Getting to the United States was often very difficult. Most immigrants booked passage in steerage, the most basic and cheapest accommodations on a steamship. Edward Steiner, an Iowa clergyman who posed as an immigrant in order to write a book on immigration, described the miserable quarters:

❝Narrow, steep and slippery stairways lead to it. Crowds everywhere, ill smelling bunks, uninviting washrooms—this is steerage. The odors of scattered orange peelings, tobacco, garlic and disinfectants meeting but not blending. No lounge or chairs for

CHAPTER 15 Urban America **465**

2 TEACH

Daily Lecture and Discussion Notes 15–1

Copyright © by The McGraw-Hill Companies, Inc.

Daily Lecture and Discussion Notes

Chapter 15, Section 1

Did You Know It is estimated that the ancestors of almost one-half of all the people living in the United States today passed through Ellis Island as immigrants. Today Ellis Island is open to the public. It contains the Ellis Island Immigration Museum.

I. **Europeans Flood Into the United States** (pages 464–467)

A. By the late 1800s, most European states made it easy to move to America. By the 1890s, eastern and southern Europeans made up more than half of all immigrants. Of the 14 million immigrants who arrived between 1860 and 1900, many were European Jews. America offered immigrants employment, few immigration restrictions, avoidance of military service, religious freedom, and the chance to move up the social ladder.

Geography *Skills*

Answers:
1. Europe
2. around 1882

Geography Skills Practice
Ask: Where did most Asian immigrants arrive in the United States? *(Angel Island, California)*

Creating a Collage Have students create a collage on the origins of immigrants to the United States after 1880. Encourage students to clip photos from newsmagazines to make the collage.
L1 ELL

Guided Reading Activity 15–1

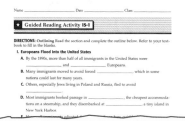

Name _____ Date _____ Class _____

★ **Guided Reading Activity 15-1**

DIRECTIONS: Outlining Read the section and complete the outline below. Refer to your textbook to fill in the blanks.

I. **Europeans Flood Into the United States**

A. By the 1890s, more than half of all immigrants in the United States were _____ and _____ Europeans.

B. Many immigrants moved to avoid forced _____, which in some nations could last for many years.

C. Others, especially Jews living in Poland and Russia, fled to avoid _____

D. Most immigrants booked passage in _____, the cheapest accommodations on a steamship, and they disembarked at _____, a tiny island in New York Harbor.

COOPERATIVE LEARNING ACTIVITY

Playing a Role Organize students into groups of three to role-play an immigrant family's arrival in America. Encourage different groups to choose different nationalities and points of entry to America. Have group members choose from the following roles: father, mother, uncle, aunt, son, or daughter. Allow groups to present their interpretations to the class. Consider live and video presentations. Then discuss specific problems different nationalities faced as they settled in America.

Use the rubric for a cooperative group management plan on pages 81–82 in the **Performance Assessment Activities and Rubrics.**

Different Viewpoints

Different Viewpoints

Answers:

1. feared anarchy, socialism, and communism

2. Students' answers will vary, but should be defended with reasons.

Creating Circle Charts Provide the census data below and have students create four circle charts to show the proportion of the U.S. population made up of persons born in the United States and persons born in foreign countries. **L2**

	U.S. Born	Foreign Born
1870	32,676,000	5,480,000
1880	42,869,000	6,499,000
1890	52,919,000	9,198,000
1900	64,344,000	10,263,000

ABCNEWS INTERACTIVE™

VIDEOCASSETTE
Historic America Electronic Field Trips

View **Tape 2, Chapter 7:** "Ellis Island."

History *and the* Humanities

American Music: Cultural Traditions: "No Irish Need Apply," "Polka Wiesniaczka"

Two Views of Immigration

The history of immigration to the United States has been both celebrated and criticized. Many millions of immigrants arrived in the United States in the late 1800s. The newcomers sought opportunity, enriched American culture, and caused concerns. Here, two political cartoons address the immigration issue.

Pro-Immigration

Uncle Sam plays the role of Noah in this cartoon. As immigrants file two by two into the safety of the ark, they leave behind the dangers of Europe that are darkening the sky. A sign lists some reasons people came to the United States to begin a new life.

Anti-Immigration

"Columbia's Unwelcome Guests" shows another view of immigration. In this 1885 cartoon, the figure of Columbia bars entry to anarchists, Socialists, and Communists who enter from the sewers of Europe's darker society. Some of the inscriptions on the column pedestal beside Columbia read "Anarchy is not liberty," and "When a Man's Rights End, His Neighbor's Begin."

Learning From History

1. According to the cartoon, why were people concerned about immigrants coming to the United States?
2. Which cartoon best expresses your own views on immigration today? Why?

---

comfort, and a continual babble of tongues—this is steerage. The food, which is miserable, is dealt out of huge kettles into the dinner pails provided by the steamship company. When it is distributed, the stronger push and crowd. . . .**"**

—quoted in *World of Our Fathers*

At the end of a 14-day journey, the passengers usually disembarked at **Ellis Island,** a tiny island in New York Harbor. There, a huge three-story building served as the processing center for many of the immigrants arriving on the East Coast after 1892.

Ellis Island Most immigrants passed through Ellis Island in about a day. They would not soon forget their hectic introduction to the United States. A medical examiner who worked there later described how "hour after hour, ship load after ship load . . . the stream of human beings with its kaleidoscopic variations

was . . . hurried through Ellis Island by the equivalent of 'step lively' in every language of the earth."

In Ellis Island's enormous hall, crowds of immigrants filed past the doctor for an initial inspection. "Whenever a case aroused suspicion," an inspector wrote, "the alien was set aside in a cage apart from the rest . . . and his coat lapel or shirt marked with colored chalk" to indicate the reason for the isolation. About one out of five newcomers was marked with an "H" for heart problems, "K" for hernias, "Sc" for scalp problems, or "X" for mental disability. Newcomers who failed the inspection might be separated from their families and returned to Europe.

GEOGRAPHY

Ethnic Cities Many of those who passed the Ellis Island inspections settled in the nation's cities. By the 1890s, immigrants made up significant percentages of

---

MEETING SPECIAL NEEDS

Verbal/Linguistic Oral histories are a good way to preserve the immigrant experience. Have students interview a person who immigrated to the United States. Their questions might include: reasons for immigrating to the United States; a description of the journey; feelings upon entering the United States; and problems faced such as finding employment or overcoming the language barrier. **L2**

📁 Refer to *Inclusion for the High School Social Studies Classroom Strategies and Activities* in the TCR.

some of the country's largest cities, including New York, Chicago, Milwaukee, and Detroit. **Jacob Riis,** a Danish-born journalist, observed in 1890 that a map of New York City, "colored to designate nationalities, would show more stripes than on the skin of a zebra."

In the cities, immigrants lived in neighborhoods that were often separated into ethnic groups, such as "Little Italy" or the Jewish "Lower East Side" in New York City. There they spoke their native languages and re-created the churches, synagogues, clubs, and newspapers of their homelands.

How well immigrants adjusted depended partly on how quickly they learned English and adapted to American culture. Immigrants also tended to adjust well if they had marketable skills or money, or if they settled among members of their own ethnic group.

As many as one in three immigrants returned to Europe shortly after coming to the United States. Some had never planned to stay and had come simply to make a little money before returning home.

✔ **Reading Check** **Explaining** How did immigration affect demographic patterns in the United States?

Asian Immigration to America

Many Chinese immigrants began crossing the Pacific to arrive in the United States in the mid-1800s. By that time, China's population had reached about 430 million, and the country was suffering from severe unemployment, poverty, and famine.

The 1848 discovery of gold in California began to lure Chinese immigrants to the United States. The following year, the Taiping Rebellion erupted in their homeland. This insurrection against the Chinese government took some 20 million lives and caused such suffering that thousands of Chinese left for the United States. In the early 1860s, as the Central Pacific Railroad began construction of its portion of the transcontinental railroad, the demand for railroad workers further increased Chinese immigration.

Chinese immigrants mainly settled in western cities, where they often worked as laborers or servants or in skilled trades. Others worked as merchants. Because native-born Americans kept them out of many businesses, some Chinese immigrants opened their own. To save enough to buy his own laundry, one immigrant, Lee Chew, had to work for two years as a servant:

❝I did not know how to do anything, and I did not understand what the lady said to me, but she showed me how to cook, wash, iron, sweep, dust, make beds, wash dishes, clean windows, paint and brass, polish the knives and forks, etc., by doing the things herself and then overseeing my efforts to imitate her.❞

—quoted in *A Sunday Between Wars*

Another group of Asians, the Japanese, also immigrated to the United States. Until 1900, however, their numbers remained small. Japanese immigration spiraled upward between 1900 and 1910 as Japan began building both an industrial economy and an empire. Both developments disrupted the economy of Japan and caused hardships for its people, thus stimulating emigration.

Until 1910 Asian immigrants arriving in San Francisco first stopped at a two-story shed at the wharf. As many as 500 people at a time were often squeezed into this structure, which Chinese immigrants from Canton called *muk uk,* or "wooden house."

In January 1910, California opened a barracks on **Angel Island** to accommodate the Asian immigrants. Most of the immigrants were young males in their teens or twenties, who nervously awaited the results of their immigration hearings in dormitories packed with double or triple tiers of bunks. This unpleasant delay could last for months. On the walls of the detention barracks, the immigrants wrote anonymous poems in pencil or ink. Some even carved their verse into the wood.

✔ **Reading Check** **Making Generalizations** Why did Chinese immigrants come to the United States?

Angel Island Over 200,000 immigrants from Japan and China arrived on the West Coast during the late 1800s.

Student Web Activity Visit the *American Vision* Web site at tav.glencoe.com and click on *Student Web Activities—Chapter 15* for an activity on immigration.

✔ **Reading Check**

Answer: larger population and a more urban population

HISTORY Online

Objectives and answers to the student activity can be found in the **Web Activity Lesson Plan** at tav.glencoe.com.

✔ **Reading Check**

Answer: high unemployment, poverty, and famine in China; Taiping Rebellion; availability of railroad jobs in the United States

📂 Use *Interpreting Political Cartoons,* Cartoon 14.

3 ASSESS

Assign Section 1 Assessment as homework or as an in-class activity.

✪ Have students use the **Interactive Tutor Self-Assessment CD-ROM.**

Reading Essentials and Study Guide 15–1

Name _____ Date _____ Class _____

Study Guide

Chapter 15, Section 1
For use with textbook pages 464–468

IMMIGRATION

KEY TERMS AND NAMES

steerage the most basic and cheapest accommodations on a steamship *(page 465)*

Ellis Island a tiny island in New York Harbor and a processing center for immigrants in the late 1800s *(page 466)*

Jacob Riis Danish-born journalist who wrote about the urban poor *(page 467)*

Angel Island a processing center in California for Asian immigrants in the late 1800s *(page 467)*

nativism an extreme dislike for foreigners by native-born people and a desire to limit immigration *(page 468)*

Chinese Exclusion Act a law that barred Chinese immigration for 10 years and prevented the Chinese already in the country from becoming citizens *(page 468)*

INTERDISCIPLINARY CONNECTIONS ACTIVITY

Sociology Write the word *Assimilation* in a circle on the board. Have students add spokes out from the circle and label each spoke with a way in which immigrants in the late 1800s and early 1900s were asked to assimilate into American culture. Repeat the process by writing *Assimilation Today* in another circle on the board. Have students add descriptive spokes to the wheel. As a class, discuss how the expectation of immigrants to assimilate has changed and how it is still the same. **L2**

Reteach

Have students analyze the circumstances surrounding the great wave of European immigration after the Civil War.

Enrich

Invite interested students to create a display that showcases a cultural tradition that immigrants brought to the United States. For example, families from the Netherlands continued the children's tradition of setting out wooden shoes in hopes that St. Nicholas would bring treats on December 6. Encourage students to share information about their own family traditions that are based on cultural heritage.

✓ Reading Check

Answer: to limit Chinese immigration; it was a reaction to the violence in California and a reflection of the era's prejudices

4 CLOSE

Have students evaluate how nativism affected immigration policies.

The Resurgence of Nativism

Eventually the wave of immigration led to increased feelings of nativism on the part of many Americans. Nativism is an extreme dislike for immigrants by native-born people and a desire to limit immigration. It had surfaced earlier in the 1800s during another large wave of immigration. In the 1840s and 1850s, it had focused primarily on Irish immigrants. Now anti-immigrant feelings focused on Asians, Jews, and eastern Europeans.

Nativists opposed immigration for many reasons. Some feared that the influx of Catholics from Ireland and southern and eastern Europe would swamp the mostly Protestant United States, giving the Catholic Church too much power in the American government. Many labor unions also opposed immigration, arguing that immigrants would work for low wages or accept work as strikebreakers, thus undermining American-born workers.

Prejudice Against Newcomers In the Northeast and Midwest, increased feelings of nativism led to the founding of two major anti-immigrant organizations. One, called the **American Protective Association**, claimed to have 500,000 members in 1887. The organization's founder, Henry Bowers, despised Catholics and foreigners and committed his group to stopping immigration. Membership peaked at about two million but declined rapidly after the economic recession of 1893 ended.

In the West, where sentiment against the Chinese was very strong, widespread racial violence erupted. Denis Kearney, himself an Irish immigrant, organized the **Workingman's Party of California** in the 1870s to fight Chinese immigration. The party won seats in California's legislature and made opposition to Chinese immigration a national issue.

Impact of the Anti-Immigrant Movement Even though several presidents vetoed other laws that would have stemmed the steady flow of new immigrants, prejudice against immigrants stimulated the passage of a new federal law. Enacted in 1882, the law banned convicts, paupers, and the mentally disabled from immigrating to the United States. The new law also placed a 50¢ head tax on each newcomer.

That same year, Congress passed the **Chinese Exclusion Act**. The law barred Chinese immigration for 10 years and prevented the Chinese already in the country from becoming citizens. The Chinese in the United States did not accept the new law quietly. They protested that white Americans did not oppose immigration by Italians, Irish, or Germans. Some Chinese organized letter-writing campaigns, petitioned the president, and even filed suit in federal court.

These efforts, however, proved fruitless. Congress renewed the Chinese Exclusion Act in 1892 and then made it permanent in 1902. In 1890 the number of Chinese living in the United States totaled 105,000. By 1900 that total had dropped to just above 74,000. In the 40 years after the passage of the act, the Chinese population in the United States continued to decrease. The act was not repealed until 1943.

✓ Reading Check **Explaining** Why did the federal government pass the Chinese Exclusion Act?

SECTION 1 ASSESSMENT

Checking for Understanding

1. **Define:** steerage, nativism.
2. **Identify:** Ellis Island, Jacob Riis, Angel Island, Chinese Exclusion Act.
3. **Describe** where most immigrants to the United States settled in the late 1800s.
4. **Explain** why nativist organizations opposed foreign immigrants.

Reviewing Themes

5. **Geography and History** What routes did European and Asian immigrants take to get to the United States?

Critical Thinking

6. **Analyzing** Why did some Americans blame immigrants for the nation's problems?
7. **Organizing** Complete a graphic organizer by listing reasons nativists opposed immigration to the United States.

Reasons Nativists Opposed Immigration

Analyzing Visuals

8. **Analyzing Political Cartoons** Compare the cartoons on page 466. What conclusions can you draw about American views on immigration in the late 1880s? Why do you think various people viewed immigration differently?

Writing About History

9. **Descriptive Writing** Imagine that you are an immigrant who arrived in the country in the 1800s. Write a letter to a relative in your home country describing your feelings during processing at either Ellis Island or Angel Island.

SECTION 1 ASSESSMENT ANSWERS

1. Terms are in blue.
2. Ellis Island *(p. 466)*, Jacob Riis *(p. 467)*, Angel Island *(p. 467)*, Chinese Exclusion Act *(p. 468)*
3. neighborhoods of large cities
4. disliked their religion; perceived to take jobs from Americans
5. Europeans generally entered through Ellis Island, New York, Asians through Angel Island, San Francisco.
6. They were blamed for economic recession and stigmatized for their religion and political beliefs.
7. influx of Catholics would give Catholic Church too much power, immigrants would weaken unions, would take jobs from Americans
8. Some Americans embraced immigrants and others were threatened by new arrivals.
9. Letters might express joy, fear, or frustration.

Guide to Reading

Main Idea
During the three decades following the Civil War, the United States transformed rapidly from a rural nation to a more urban one.

Key Terms and Names
skyscraper, Louis Sullivan, tenement, political machine, party boss, George Plunkitt, graft, William M. "Boss" Tweed

Reading Strategy
Organizing As you read about urbanization in the United States in the late 1800s, complete a graphic organizer similar to the one below by filling in the problems the nation's urban areas faced.

Reading Objectives
• **Explain** the technological developments that made the growth of cities possible.
• **Evaluate** the role that political machines played in urban politics in the late 1800s.

Section Theme
Government and Democracy Political bosses grew powerful in urban areas by helping immigrants find work and necessities.

Preview of Events

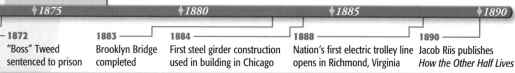

| ♦1875 | ♦1880 | ♦1885 | ♦1890 |

| **1872** | **1883** | **1884** | **1888** | **1890** |
| "Boss" Tweed sentenced to prison | Brooklyn Bridge completed | First steel girder construction used in building in Chicago | Nation's first electric trolley line opens in Richmond, Virginia | Jacob Riis publishes *How the Other Half Lives* |

★ An American Story ★

Frank Lloyd Wright

With just $3.10 in his pocket, a young man from Wisconsin named Frank Lloyd Wright wandered the streets of Chicago in the late spring of 1887. Sixteen years earlier, almost four square miles of the city had burned in the Chicago Fire of 1871. Now the rebuilt city's towering new buildings beckoned the young visitor who, within a few decades, would become one of the most famous architects in the world.

In Chicago, Wright saw electric lights and cable cars for the first time. What surprised him most about the big city, however, were the signs that seemed to be everywhere:

❝There were glaring signs on the glass shop-fronts against the lights inside, . . . HURRAH signs. STOP signs. COME ON IN signs. HELLO signs set out before the blazing windows on the sidewalks . . . food shops, barber shops, eating houses, saloons, restaurants, groceries, laundries—and [they all] became chaos in a wilderness of Italian, German, Irish, [Polish], Greek, English, Swedish, French, Chinese and Spanish names. . . .❞

—quoted in *Eyewitness to America*

Americans Migrate to the Cities

During the three decades after the Civil War, the urban population of the United States—those living in towns with a population of 2,500 or more—grew from around 10 million in 1870 to over 30 million in 1900. New York City alone, which had over 800,000 inhabitants in 1860, grew to almost 3.5 million by 1900. Frank Lloyd Wright observed Chicago during an even faster growth period. The Midwestern city swelled from 109,000 residents in 1860 to more than 1.6 million by 1900.

CHAPTER 15 Urban America **469**

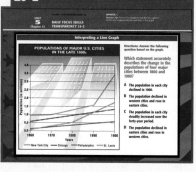

2 TEACH

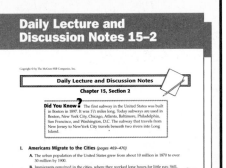

Reading Check

Answer: Cities offered more and better-paying jobs.

Creating a Postcard Have students imagine that they are immigrants living in New York City in the late 1800s. Instruct them to create a postcard that shows a scene of the city. **L1** **ELL**

📁 Use the rubric for creating a political cartoon, pamphlet, or handbill on pages 87–88 in the *Performance Assessment Activities and Rubrics.*

FYI

During the construction of the Brooklyn Bridge, John Roebling, who designed the bridge, was killed on the job. His son continued directing the work until being injured. The work was then taken over by John's wife, who completed the project with her son's direction.

History *and the* Humanities

🖋 American Art & Architecture: *Let Us Prey*, Guaranty Building, *Cliff Dwellers*

The United States had only 131 cities in 1840; by 1900 that number had risen to over 1,700.

Most of the immigrants who poured into the United States in the late 1800s lacked the money to buy farms and the education to obtain higher-paying jobs. They therefore remained in the nation's growing cities, where they toiled long hours for little pay in the rapidly expanding factories of the United States. Despite the harshness of their new lives, most immigrants found that the move had still improved their standard of living.

Many rural Americans also began moving to the cities at this time. Farmers moved to the cities because urban areas offered more and better-paying jobs than did rural areas. Cities had much to offer, too—bright lights, running water, and modern plumbing, plus many things to do and see, including museums, libraries, and theaters.

☑ **Reading Check** **Explaining** Why did rural Americans move to the cities in the late 1800s?

The New Urban Environment

As millions of people flooded into the nation's cities, engineers and architects developed new approaches to housing and transporting such a large number of people.

Skyscrapers As city populations grew, demand raised the price of land, giving owners greater incentive to grow upward rather than outward. Soon, tall steel frame buildings called skyscrapers began to appear on American skylines. Chicago's ten-story Home Insurance Building, built in 1885, was the first skyscraper, but other buildings quickly dwarfed it. New York City, with its business district on the narrow island of Manhattan, boasted more skyscrapers than any other city in the world. With limited land, New Yorkers had to build up, not out.

No one contributed more to the design of skyscrapers than Chicago's **Louis Sullivan,** whose students included Frank Lloyd Wright. "What people are within, the buildings express without," explained Sullivan, whose lofty structures featured simple lines and spacious windows using new durable plate glass.

Mass Transit Various kinds of mass transit developed in the late 1800s to move huge numbers of people around cities quickly. At first, almost all cities relied on the horsecar—a railroad car pulled by horses. In 1890 horsecars moved about 70 percent of urban traffic in the United States.

More than 20 cities, beginning with San Francisco in 1873, installed cable cars, which were pulled along tracks by underground cables. Then, in 1887, engineer **Frank J. Sprague**

The Technology of Urbanization

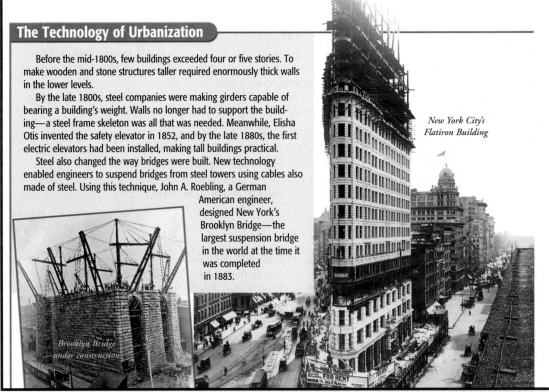

Before the mid-1800s, few buildings exceeded four or five stories. To make wooden and stone structures taller required enormously thick walls in the lower levels.

By the late 1800s, steel companies were making girders capable of bearing a building's weight. Walls no longer had to support the building—a steel frame skeleton was all that was needed. Meanwhile, Elisha Otis invented the safety elevator in 1852, and by the late 1880s, the first electric elevators had been installed, making tall buildings practical.

Steel also changed the way bridges were built. New technology enabled engineers to suspend bridges from steel towers using cables also made of steel. Using this technique, John A. Roebling, a German American engineer, designed New York's Brooklyn Bridge—the largest suspension bridge in the world at the time it was completed in 1883.

Brooklyn Bridge under construction

New York City's Flatiron Building

COOPERATIVE LEARNING ACTIVITY

Creating a Documentary Organize students into groups of five to create a videotape documentary of city life in the late 1800s. Ask group members to choose from the following topics: transportation, housing, social services, social problems, and architecture. Encourage students to scan or videotape images from their textbook and other sources as they narrate their documentary. Have students view and critique one another's documentaries. 📁

Use the rubric for a cooperative group management plan on pages 81–82 in the *Performance Assessment Activities and Rubrics.*

developed the electric trolley car. The following year, Richmond, Virginia, opened the country's first electric trolley line.

In the largest cities, congestion became so bad that engineers began looking for ways to move mass transit off the streets. Chicago responded by building an elevated railroad, while Boston, followed by New York, built the first subway systems.

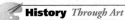 **Reading Check** **Summarizing** What new technologies helped people in the late 1800s get to and from work?

Separation by Class

In the growing cities, wealthy people and the working class lived in different parts of town. So too did the middle class. The boundaries between neighborhoods were quite definite and can still be seen in many American cities today.

High Society During the last half of the 1800s, the wealthiest families established fashionable districts in the hearts of cities. Americans with enough money could choose to construct a feudal castle, an English manor house, a French château, a Tuscan villa, or a Persian pavilion. In Chicago, merchant and real estate developer Potter Palmer chose a castle. In New York, Cornelius Vanderbilt's grandson commissioned a $3 million French château equipped with a two-story dining room, a gymnasium, and a solid marble bathroom.

Middle-Class Gentility American industrialization not only made the wealth of people like Potter Palmer possible; it also helped create a growing middle class. The nation's rising middle class included doctors, lawyers, engineers, managers, social workers, architects, and teachers. It was typical for many people in the emerging middle class to move away from the central city. Some took advantage of the new commuter rail lines to move to "streetcar suburbs."

During this period, middle-class salaries were about twice that of the average factory worker. In 1905 a college professor earned a middle-class salary of $1,100. That amount, however, still proved insufficient for one turn-of-the-century professor's wife, who complained:

❝We pay eighteen dollars a month for this poorly built, eight small-roomed house. . . . With all this straining to live comes a wish from the President and Trustees of the college that we mingle more in town society. . . . Who can afford the evening dress to go? Or the evening's sewing left undone?❞

—quoted in *A Sunday Between Wars*

History *Through Art*

The Lesson This painting by John Barnard Whittaker depicts the lifestyle of a wealthy family in the 1870s. What are several elements of this painting that show the family's wealth?

The Working Class The majority of American city dwellers at the turn of the century would have considered an eight-room house an absolute luxury. In New York, three out of four residents squeezed into tenements, dark and crowded multi-family apartments. To supplement the average industrial worker's annual income of $445, many families sent their young children to work in factories or rented precious space to a boarder. Zalmen Yoffeh, a journalist, lived in a New York tenement as a child. He recalled:

❝With . . . one dollar a day [our mother] fed and clothed an ever-growing family. She took in boarders. Sometimes this helped; at other times it added to the burden of living. Boarders were often out of work and penniless; how could one turn a hungry man out? She made all our clothes. She walked blocks to reach a place where meat was a penny cheaper, where bread was a half cent less. She collected boxes and old wood to burn in the stove. . . .❞

—quoted in *How We Lived*

 Reading Check **Explaining** What social class grew as a result of industrialization in the late 1800s?

CHAPTER 15 Urban America **471**

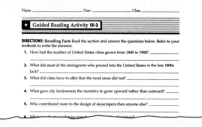
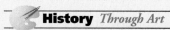
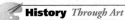 **Reading Check**

Answer: cable cars, trolleys, elevated railroads, and subway systems

History *Through Art*

Answer: expensive, formal furniture and dress
Ask: What types of architecture did wealthy people use for their homes? *(variety: feudal castle, English manor house, French château, Tuscan villa)*

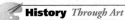 **Reading Check**

Answer: middle class

CURRICULUM CONNECTION

Economics In the 1870s people thought that typing was physically too strenuous and intellectually too complicated for women. As a result, most secretaries were men. The Young Women's Christian Association (YWCA) conducted a survey and found that stenography was a lucrative career. In order to help working-class girls who came to urban areas for jobs, the YWCA offered shorthand and typing classes for women.

MEETING SPECIAL NEEDS

Learning Disability Some students feel most comfortable when they are permitted to tape lectures and discussions. This helps bypass the writing problem but creates another problem—time needed to review the lecture. This process can be more efficient if students are cued by the teacher as to when to turn on the recorder. As you discuss the problems of urban population increases, use a prearranged cueing system to help students. **L1**

📁 Refer to ***Inclusion for the High School Social Studies Classroom Strategies and Activities*** in the TCR.

NATIONAL GEOGRAPHIC
MOMENT in HISTORY

Many tenement buildings began as tenant houses. These were often large residences of wealthy people who had moved away from the city. Real-estate agents subdivided the large rooms into smaller ones for immigrants. Agents, eager to make money, sometimes subdivided the rooms without considering lighting or ventilation.

✓ Reading Check

Answer: Sewage, street waste, smoke, soot, and ash contributed to health problems and epidemics of contagious diseases.

📁 Use *Interpreting Political Cartoons*, Cartoons 12 and 13.

3 ASSESS

Assign Section 2 Assessment as homework or as an in-class activity.

💿 Have students use the **Interactive Tutor Self-Assessment CD-ROM.**

Reading Essentials and Study Guide 15–2

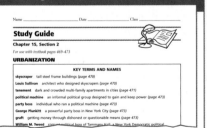

NATIONAL GEOGRAPHIC
MOMENT in HISTORY

TEEMING TENEMENTS

The swelling tide of immigration to U.S. cities in the late 1800s led to deplorable living conditions and almost unbearable congestion. By 1890, more than two-thirds of New York's 1.5 million residents lived in overcrowded apartment buildings called tenements. On the Lower East Side, one of the most densely populated areas in the world, people frequented vibrant outdoor markets such as this one on Hester Street for goods from eggs to rugs to pots and pans. Gossip, haggling, and cries of street peddlers—mostly in Yiddish in this Jewish neighborhood—echoed down the street from dawn to dusk.

Urban Problems

City living posed threats such as crime, violence, fire, disease, and pollution, especially for the working poor like Yoffeh and his family. The rapid growth of cities only made these problems worse. Minor criminals, such as pickpockets, swindlers, and thieves, thrived in crowded urban living conditions. Major crimes multiplied as well. From 1880 to 1900, the murder rate jumped sharply from 25 per million people to more than 100 per million people. In comparison, the murder rate in 1999 was 57 per million people.

Native-born Americans often blamed immigrants for the increase in crime and violence. In reality, the crime rate for immigrants was not significantly higher than that for other Americans.

Alcohol did contribute to violent crime, both inside and outside the home. Danish immigrant Jacob Riis, who documented slum life in his 1890 book *How the Other Half Lives*, accused saloons of "breeding poverty," corrupting politics, bringing suffering to the wives and children of drunkards, and fostering "the corruption of the child" by selling beer to minors.

Disease and pollution posed even bigger threats. Improper sewage disposal contaminated city drinking water and triggered epidemics of typhoid fever and cholera. Though flush toilets and sewer systems existed in the 1870s, pollution remained a severe problem as horse waste was left in the streets, smoke belched from chimneys, and soot and ash accumulated from coal and wood fires.

✓ Reading Check **Drawing Conclusions** Why were diseases and pollution big problems in American cities in the late 1800s?

Urban Politics

A new kind of political system developed to meet these urban problems. This system provided essential city services in return for political power.

INTERDISCIPLINARY CONNECTIONS ACTIVITY

Literature Have students obtain a copy of *How the Other Half Lives* by Jacob A. Riis. Have students investigate the legislation Riis advocated to improve slum conditions and research how he went about securing this legislation. Ask students to present their findings as if they were asking Congress to pass a law to protect urban dwellers. **L3**

The Political Machine and the Party Boss The political machine, an informal political group designed to gain and keep power, came about partly because cities had grown much faster than their governments. New city dwellers needed jobs, housing, food, heat, and police protection. In exchange for votes, political machines and the party bosses who ran them eagerly provided these necessities.

George Plunkitt, an Irish immigrant who rose to be one of New York City's most powerful party bosses, explained how the system worked when a fire burned a neighborhood:

❝I just get [housing] for them, buy clothes for them if their clothes were burned up, and fix them up till they get things runnin' again. It's philanthropy, but it's politics too—mighty good politics. Who can tell how many votes one of these fires bring me? The poor are the most grateful people in the world, and, let me tell you, they have more friends in their neighborhoods than the rich have in theirs.❞

—quoted in *In Search of America*

As Plunkitt observed, the payoff for party bosses came on Election Day. Urban immigrant groups, which wielded tremendous voting strength, voted in overwhelming numbers for the political machines.

Graft and Fraud The party bosses who ran the political machines also controlled the city's finances. Many machine politicians grew rich as the result of fraud or graft—getting money through dishonest or questionable means. Plunkitt defended what he called "honest graft." For example, a politician might find out in advance where a new park was to be built and buy the land near the site. The politician would then sell the land to the city for a profit. As Plunkitt stated, "I see my opportunity and I take it."

Outright fraud occurred when party bosses accepted bribes from contractors, who were supposed to compete fairly to win contracts to build streets, sewers, and buildings. Corrupt bosses also sold permits to their friends to operate public utilities, such as railroads, waterworks, and power systems.

Tammany Hall Tammany Hall, the New York Democratic political machine for which George Plunkitt performed his labors, was the most famous such organization. **William M. "Boss" Tweed** was Tammany Hall's corrupt leader during the 1860s and 1870s. Tweed was eventually arrested for corruption and sent to prison in 1872.

Other cities' machines controlled all the city services, including the police department. For example, St. Louis's boss never feared arrest when he called out to his supporters at the police-supervised voting booth, "Are there any more repeaters out here that want to vote again?" From their own base in Kansas City, Missouri, the Pendergast brothers, James and Thomas, dominated the state as well as city politics from the 1890s until the 1930s.

Despite the corruption of the system, political machines did provide necessary services, and they helped to assimilate the masses of new city dwellers.

✓**Reading Check** **Evaluating** Why did political machines help city dwellers in the late 1800s?

SECTION 2 ASSESSMENT

Checking for Understanding

1. **Define:** skyscraper, tenement, political machine, party boss, graft.
2. **Identify:** Louis Sullivan, George Plunkitt, William M. "Boss" Tweed.
3. **Explain** what two technologies made the building of skyscrapers possible in the late 1800s.

Reviewing Themes

4. **Government and Democracy** How did political machines respond to the needs of the people?

Critical Thinking

5. **Comparing** Compare the conditions under which the wealthy class, the middle class, and the working class lived in the United States in the late 1800s.
6. **Organizing** Complete a graphic organizer similar to the one below by listing the effects of many Americans moving from rural to urban areas in the late 1800s.

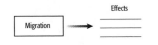

Analyzing Visuals

7. **Examining Photographs** Study the photographs on page 470 of the Brooklyn Bridge and the Flatiron Building. Why was it advantageous to construct taller buildings rather than purchase more land?

Writing About History

8. **Persuasive Writing** Take on the role of an urban planner living in one of the nation's major cities in the late 1800s. Write a letter to members of the city government listing specific reasons for the importance of setting aside city land for a park and recreational area.

CHAPTER 15 Urban America **473**

CHAPTER 15
Section 2, 469–473

Section Quiz 15–2

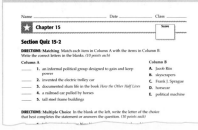

Reteach
Have students list the technological developments that made the growth of cities possible.

Enrich
Have students create a three-column table illustrating social problems, solutions, and alternatives. Instruct students to use the first column to list the social problems described in this section. In the second column, students should describe the solutions used. Students should explain their alternative solutions in the third column.

✓**Reading Check**

Answer: to gain immigrant votes and thus maintain political power

4 CLOSE

Have students evaluate the role that political machines played in urban politics in the late 1800s.

SECTION 2 ASSESSMENT ANSWERS

1. Terms are in blue.
2. Louis Sullivan *(p. 470)*, George Plunkitt *(p. 473)*, William M. ("Boss") Tweed *(p. 473)*
3. steel frames and durable plate glass
4. provided jobs, housing, food, heat, police protection
5. wealthy lived in grand homes in fashionable areas, middle class in comfortable homes in streetcar suburbs, and working class in tenements
6. new demographic patterns included more urban population and more disease; also growth of political machines
7. land was limited and expensive; allowed more people to work in the cities
8. Students' letters will vary. Letters should include specific reasons for parks and recreational areas.

1 FOCUS

Tell students that Jane Addams's efforts in Hull House were modeled on Toynbee Hall, a settlement house in England. She provided various experiences for immigrants, including visits to art galleries, classes in English, and the use of a gymnasium.

2 TEACH

Making Generalizations As a class, discuss urban living as presented in the chapter and from the students' own experiences with urban areas. Have students make generalizations about living in urban areas. Write these generalizations on the board. Allow students to refine or change their generalizations as the discussion progresses. **L1**

Analyzing Information
Organize the class into small groups and assign each group one of the immigrant groups listed on the Hull House Neighborhood inset map. Have each group research what industries or jobs were held by their assigned immigrant group. Have each group list its findings on the board. As a class, discuss how immigrant groups contributed to Chicago life. **L2**

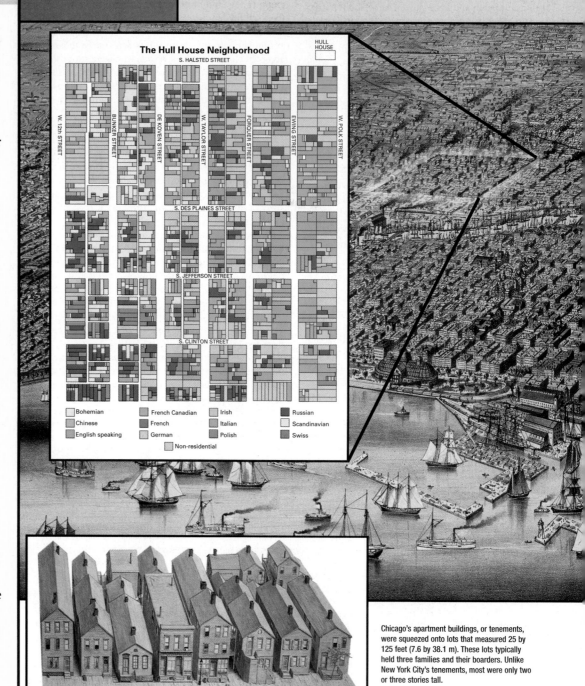

The Hull House Neighborhood

S. HALSTED STREET
HULL HOUSE

W. 12th STREET · BUNKER STREET · DE KOVEN STREET · W. TAYLOR STREET · FORQUER STREET · EWING STREET · W. POLK STREET

S. DES PLAINES STREET

S. JEFFERSON STREET

S. CLINTON STREET

☐ Bohemian   ■ French Canadian   ■ Irish   ■ Russian
☐ Chinese   ■ French   ■ Italian   ☐ Scandinavian
☐ English speaking   ☐ German   ■ Polish   ☐ Swiss
☐ Non-residential

Chicago's apartment buildings, or tenements, were squeezed onto lots that measured 25 by 125 feet (7.6 by 38.1 m). These lots typically held three families and their boarders. Unlike New York City's tenements, most were only two or three stories tall.

474 CHAPTER 15   Urban America

EXTENDING THE CONTENT

Urban Problems Urban problems are not new. Many cities in ancient times were large and crowded. Some historians place Rome's population at more than 1 million by the start of the first century A.D. Within 100 years overcrowding resulted in many of Rome's citizens living in apartment houses. Some apartments were 5 or 6 stories high and sheltered about 200 people each. Many of the city's residential structures were poorly constructed, and living conditions paralleled those in the impoverished sections of 1800s New York or Chicago.

Immigrants Arrive In Chicago

A major port and a conduit for the nation's east-west rail travel, Chicago was a booming industrial center for the lumber, grain, meatpacking, and mail-order businesses at the end of the 1800s. Since the early 1870s, more ships had been docking in Chicago than in New York, Baltimore, Philadelphia, Charleston, and San Francisco combined. The city's expansion was phenomenal. In 50 years, it grew from a modest frontier town to the second-largest city in the country.

Immigrants swarmed into Chicago seeking jobs. Poles found work slaughtering livestock; Irish laying railroads; Russian and Polish Jews making clothes; Swedes constructing buildings and Italians forging steel. Women established boardinghouses, took in sewing to do at home, and worked in factories. In most factories, the hours were long and the working conditions difficult: noisy, hot, grimy, and overcrowded. By the beginning of the 1900s, three-fourths of the people in this teeming metropolis were European immigrants and their American-born children.

Ethnic neighborhoods dotted the city, as did blocks of tenements thrown up to house the flood of newcomers. The inset map at left—an enlargement of the highlighted rectangle on the lithograph—shows the Hull House neighborhood in Chicago's West Side in 1893. Hull House was established by social reformer Jane Addams to "investigate and improve the conditions in the industrial districts of Chicago." The neighborhood was one of the city's poorest. Its tenement buildings were disease-ridden and dangerous, crowding about 270 residents into each acre. Jane Addams wrote: "The streets are inexpressibly dirty, the number of schools inadequate, sanitary legislation unenforced, the street lighting bad, the paving miserable and altogether lacking in the alleys."

The neighborhood was also one of the most ethnically diverse. As the inset shows, the bewildered new immigrants tended to settle in enclaves that had already been established by others from their homeland. They banded together as they learned about the ways of the new land. Many immigrants found comfort in social life centered on the church or synagogue. Younger immigrants were more eager to abandon their old customs. Many of them quickly adopted American clothes and manners, learned to speak English, and tried to make American friends.

A visiting nurse puts drops in an infant's eyes. Crowded conditions threatened the health of many of the immigrants in Chicago's tenements.

LEARNING FROM GEOGRAPHY

1. How did the location of Chicago influence its development?

2. Pose and answer five questions about the geographic distributions and patterns shown on this model.

CHAPTER 15 Urban America **475**

Comparing and Contrasting
Write the word *Pollution* on the board. Beneath it write *1800s Cities* and *Modern Cities*. Have students list the types of pollution for each era. **Ask:** What similarities and differences do you find? Do you think the problems of pollution can be solved? What solutions would you suggest? **L1**

3 ASSESS

Have students answer the Learning from Geography questions.

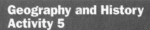

Geography and History Activity 5

Name _____ Date _____ Class _____

▣ GEOGRAPHY AND HISTORY ACTIVITY 5

Cities Within Cities: Ethnic Enclaves

FROM FARMS TO CITIES
At the time of the Civil War, most people in the United States worked on farms. As industrialization grew, people moved to the cities where new jobs were available. Just 50 years after the Civil War, more people worked in factories or in other urban workplaces than on farms. This change had begun in the northeastern United States where the first water-powered textile mills were located. Industrialization eventually spread to the Midwest, where Chicago became an important manufacturing cit

in the factories. Between 1860 and 1880, about 5 million immigrants, which included many Chinese and French Canadians, came to the United States. That figure increased to 9 million between 1880 and 1900. Many of the immigrants during those years were from Eastern Europe. (See Table 1.)

IMMIGRANT NEIGHBORHOODS
When they arrived in the United States, many immigrants settled in cities because jobs were more abundant there. Their experience in large cities such as New York

4 CLOSE

Ask students to describe what life may have been like in one of the tenement buildings pictured on page 474.

NGS ONLINE

Access National Geographic's Web site for current events, atlas updates, activities, links, interactive features, and archives at www.nationalgeographic.com.

ANSWERS TO LEARNING FROM GEOGRAPHY

1. Since it developed on the waterfront, Chicago developed both as a port city and a rail city. Ships would transport goods to the city and the goods would be shipped across the country from the rail lines.

2. Students' questions and answers will vary. You may have students trade questions and then have the pairs discuss the answers.

1 FOCUS

Section Overview

This section focuses on how American society's thinking and behavior changed in the late 1800s.

BELLRINGER
Skillbuilder Activity

Project transparency and have students answer the question.

Available as a blackline master.

Daily Focus Skills Transparency 15–3

Guide to Reading

Answers to Graphic: Social Darwinism: the theory that human society evolves through competition and natural selection—survival of the fittest; Laissez-faire: an economic doctrine that opposed government programs that interfered with business; Gospel of Wealth: the philosophy that wealthy people should give to public charity; Realism: movement in art and literature to portray people realistically

Preteaching Vocabulary
Have students write three questions that can be answered using the Key Terms and Names.

Guide to Reading

Main Idea
Industrialism and urbanization changed American society's ideas and culture in the late 1800s.

Key Terms and Names
Gilded Age, Social Darwinism, Gospel of Wealth, philanthropy, realism, vaudeville, ragtime, Scott Joplin

Reading Strategy
Categorizing Complete a graphic organizer similar to the one below by filling in the main idea of each of the theories and movements listed.

Theory or Movement	Main Idea
Social Darwinism	
Laissez-Faire	
Gospel of Wealth	
Realism	

Reading Objectives
• **Evaluate** the doctrine of Social Darwinism and the impact it had on American industry.
• **Explain** how industrialization promoted leisure time and encouraged new forms of entertainment.

Section Theme
Culture and Traditions The Gilded Age was an era of great cultural change in the United States.

Preview of Events

♦1870	♦1880	♦1890	♦1900

1869
The Cincinnati Red Stockings become the first salaried baseball team

1884
Mark Twain publishes *Huckleberry Finn*

1891
James Naismith invents basketball

1899
Scott Joplin publishes "The Maple Leaf Rag"

★ An American Story ★

William Graham Sumner

In 1872, at the age of 32, William Graham Sumner became a professor of political and social science at Yale College. Sumner's classes were very popular. One of his students, William Lyon Phelps, illustrated Sumner's tough, no-nonsense approach with this example of a class discussion:

Student: "Professor, don't you believe in any government aid to industries?"
Sumner: "No! It's root, hog, or die."
Student: "Yes, but hasn't the hog got a right to root?"
Sumner: "There are no rights. The world owes nobody a living."
Student: "You believe then, Professor, in only one system, the contract-competitive system?"
Sumner: "That's the only sound economic system. All others are fallacies."
Student: "Well, suppose some professor of political economy came along and took your job away from you. Wouldn't you be sore?"
Sumner: "Any other professor is welcome to try. If he gets my job, it is my fault. My business is to teach the subject so well that no one can take the job away from me."

—**adapted from** *Social Darwinism in American Thought*

A Changing Culture

In 1873 Mark Twain and Charles Warner wrote a novel together entitled *The Gilded Age*. Historians later adopted the term and applied it to the era in American history that begins about 1870 and ends around 1900.

476 CHAPTER 15 Urban America

SECTION RESOURCES

Reproducible Masters
• Reproducible Lesson Plan 15–3
• Daily Lecture and Discussion Notes 15–3
• Guided Reading Activity 15–3
• Section Quiz 15–3
• Reading Essentials and Study Guide 15–3

Transparencies
• Daily Focus Skills Transparency 15–3

• American Art & Architecture

Multimedia
• Interactive Tutor Self-Assessment CD-ROM
• ExamView® Pro Testmaker CD-ROM
• Presentation Plus! CD-ROM
• TeacherWorks™ CD-ROM
• Audio Program
• American Music: Hits Through History
• American Music: Cultural Traditions

This era was in many ways a time of marvels. Amazing new inventions led to rapid industrial growth. Cities expanded to sizes never seen before. Masses of workers thronged the streets. Skyscrapers reached to the sky, and electric lights banished the darkness. Newly wealthy entrepreneurs built spectacular mansions.

By calling this era the **Gilded Age,** Twain and Warner were sounding an alarm. Something is gilded if it is covered with gold on the outside but made of cheaper material inside. A gilded age might appear to sparkle, but Twain, Warner, and other writers tried to point out that beneath the surface lay corruption, poverty, crime, and great disparities in wealth between the rich and the poor.

Whether the era was golden or merely gilded, it was certainly a time of great cultural activity. Industrialism and urbanization altered the way Americans looked at themselves and their society, and these changes gave rise to new values, new art, and new forms of entertainment.

The Idea of Individualism One of the strongest beliefs of the era—and one that remains strong today—was the idea of **individualism.** Many Americans firmly believed that no matter how humble their origins, they could rise in society and go as far as their talents and commitment would take them. In 1885 the wealthy cotton manufacturer Edward Atkinson gave a speech to a group of workers at a textile factory in Rhode Island. He told them they had no reason to complain:

> 66 There is always plenty of room on the front seats in every profession, every trade, every art, every industry. . . . There are men in this audience who will fill some of those seats, but they won't be boosted into them from behind. 99
>
> —quoted in *America's History*

Horatio Alger No one expressed the idea of individualism better than Horatio Alger. A minister from Massachusetts, Alger eventually left the clergy and moved to New York. There he wrote more than 100 "rags-to-riches" novels, in which a poor person goes to the big city and becomes successful. Many young people loved reading these tales. Inspired by Alger's novels they concluded that no matter how many obstacles they faced, success was possible.

✓ **Reading Check** **Describing** What was the main idea behind individualism?

Social Darwinism

Another powerful idea of the era was Social Darwinism, which strongly reinforced the idea of individualism. English philosopher **Herbert Spencer** first proposed this idea. Historian John Fiske, political scientist William Graham Sumner, and the magazine *Popular Science Monthly* all popularized it in the United States.

Herbert Spencer Philosopher Herbert Spencer applied **Charles Darwin's** theory of evolution and natural selection to human society. In his 1859 book, *On the Origin of Species by Means of Natural Selection*, Darwin argued that plant and animal life had evolved over the years by a process he called natural selection. In this process, those species that cannot adapt to the environment in which they live gradually die out, while those that do adapt thrive and live on.

Spencer took this biological theory, intended to explain developments over millions of years, and argued that human society also evolved through competition and natural selection. He argued that society progressed and became better because only the fittest people survived.

Herbert Spencer

Spencer and others who shared his views became known as Social Darwinists, and their ideas were known as **Social Darwinism.** "Survival of the fittest" became the catchphrase of their philosophy. By 1902 over 350,000 copies of Spencer's books had been sold in the United States.

Horatio Alger novel

Daily Lecture and Discussion Notes 15–3

Copyright © by The McGraw-Hill Companies, Inc.

Daily Lecture and Discussion Notes
Chapter 15, Section 3

Did You Know *The Adventures of Tom Sawyer* was the first book that Mark Twain wrote using memories of his own childhood. The town where Tom Sawyer lives was modeled after Twain's hometown of Hannibal, Missouri. In *The Adventures of Tom Sawyer*, Huck Finn is Tom's friend. Tom Sawyer reappears in some chapters of *Adventures of Huckleberry Finn*, which was written years later.

I. A Changing Culture *(pages 476–477)*
    A. In 1873 Mark Twain and Charles Warner co-wrote the novel, *The Gilded Age*. Historians use this term to refer to the time between 1870 and 1900. The term "gilded"

✓ **Reading Check**

Answer: that regardless of background, a person could rise in society and go as far as his or her talents and commitment would take them

Creating a Profile Have students chose one of the persons mentioned in this section and write a short biographical profile emphasizing the person's connection to the Gilded Age. **L1**

📁 Use the rubric for creating a book review, research report, or handbill on pages 89–90 in the *Performance Assessment Activities and Rubrics.*

History *and the* Humanities

🎵 American Music: Hits Through History: "Maple Leaf Rag"

🎵 American Music: Cultural Traditions: "Maple Leaf Rag," "St. Louis Tickle"

🏛 American Art & Architecture: *In the Garden,* Favrile Glass Vase

---

COOPERATIVE LEARNING ACTIVITY

Creating a Magazine Organize students into groups of four to create a national magazine that would appeal to the general public in the late 1800s. Each group should choose a target market, a type of magazine, and a title. Allow group members to choose from the following roles: cover designer, advertising copywriter, fiction writer, and feature writer. Have students produce a mock-up of their magazine. 📖

Use the rubric for a cooperative group management plan on pages 81–82 in the *Performance Assessment Activities and Rubrics.*

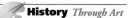
History *Through Art*

Background: Thomas Eakins was a painter, sculptor, photographer, and art teacher. Many of his portrait subjects did not appreciate his realistic approach, and his insistence on the use of nude models for teaching also presented problems. Both his realistic style and his teaching techniques achieved great acceptance after his death. Eakins's work is now exhibited in some of America's most prestigious museums, including the Art Institute of Chicago, the Metropolitan Museum of Art, and the National Gallery of Art. **Answer:** the everyday subject matter **Ask:** What artistic movement did realism follow? *(romanticism)*

✓**Reading Check**

Answer: that human society evolves through competition and natural selection—survival of the fittest

---

Social Darwinism also paralleled the economic doctrine of laissez-faire that opposed any government programs that interfered with business. Not surprisingly, industrial leaders like John D. Rockefeller heartily embraced the theory. Rockefeller maintained that survival of the fittest, as demonstrated by the growth of huge businesses like his own Standard Oil, was "merely the working out of the law of nature and the law of God."

Darwinism and the Church Rockefeller may have appreciated Spencer's interpretation of evolution, but Charles Darwin's conclusions about the origin of new species frightened and outraged many devout Christians as well as some leading scientists. They rejected the theory of evolution because they believed it contradicted the Bible's account of creation. Some American scholars and ministers, however, concluded that evolution may have been God's way of creating the world. Henry Ward Beecher of Plymouth Church in Brooklyn called himself a "cordial Christian evolutionist." Beecher accepted Spencer's ideas of Social Darwinism and championed the success of American business.

History *Through Art*

Baseball Players Practicing Thomas Eakins painted this work in 1875. A member of the Realism school of art, Eakins tried to depict everyday events in detail. What elements of this painting reflect the Realism movement?

Carnegie's Gospel of Wealth A wealthy and prominent business leader of the time, Andrew Carnegie believed wholeheartedly in Social Darwinism and laissez-faire. Speaking of the law of unregulated competition, he wrote:

❝It ensures the survival of the fittest in every department. We accept and welcome, therefore, as conditions to which we must accommodate ourselves, great inequality of environment, the concentration of business, . . . in the hands of a few, and the laws of competition . . . as being not only beneficial, but essential for the future progress of the race.❞

—quoted in *Voices from America's Past*

Believing that those who profited from society owed it something in return, Carnegie attempted to extend and soften the harsh philosophy of Social Darwinism with the **Gospel of Wealth.** This philosophy held that wealthy Americans bore the responsibility of engaging in philanthropy—using their great fortunes to further social progress. Carnegie himself, for example, donated millions of dollars as the "trustee and agent for his poorer brethren." Other industrialists also contributed to social causes. 📖 *(See page 1053 for more information on the Gospel of Wealth.)*

✓**Reading Check**

Summarizing What was the main idea of Social Darwinism?

Realism

Just as Darwin had looked at the natural world scientifically, a new movement in art and literature known as realism attempted to portray people realistically instead of idealizing them as romantic artists had done.

Realism in Art Realist painters rejected the idealistic depictions of the world of the earlier 1800s. One such painter, **Thomas Eakins** of Philadelphia, Pennsylvania, considered no day-to-day

---

MEETING SPECIAL NEEDS

Interpersonal Ask students to choose a sport that was played during the time period covered in this section. Pair students and ask them to teach one another how to play their chosen sports. Instructions should be limited to verbal cues only. As a class, discuss the problems in teaching an activity without visual aids or written directions. **L2**

📁 Refer to *Inclusion for the High School Social Studies Classroom Strategies and Activities* in the TCR.

subject beneath his interest and careful observation. On his canvases, with their realistic detail and precise lighting, young men swam, surgeons operated, and scientists experimented. Eakins even dared to paint President Hayes working in shirtsleeves instead of in more traditional formal dress.

Realism in Literature Writers also attempted to capture the world as they saw it. In several novels, **William Dean Howells** presented realistic descriptions of American life. For example, his 1885 novel *The Rise of Silas Lapham* described the attempts of a self-made businessperson to enter Boston society. Also an influential literary critic, Howells was the first to claim Mark Twain to be an American genius and hailed him as "incomparable, the Lincoln of our literature."

Twain, a Missouri native whose real name was Samuel Clemens, wrote his masterpiece, *Adventures of Huckleberry Finn,* in 1884. In this novel, the title character and his friend Jim, an escaped slave, float down the Mississippi River on a raft. Through their innocent eyes, readers gain a piercing view of American society in the pre–Civil War era. Twain wrote in local dialect with a lively sense of humor. Nevertheless, Howells realized that Twain was more than a humorist. He had written a true American novel, in which the setting, subject matter, characters, and style were unmistakably American.

Howells also recognized talent in the work of a very different writer, **Henry James,** who lived most of his adult life in England. In novels such as *Portrait of a Lady* (1881), James realistically characterized the inner lives of the upper class. Isabel Archer, the lady of the title, reflects one of the prime values of her class—the concern to maintain social position by marrying well. Ultimately Isabel's wealth interferes with her ability to pursue her own happiness.

Edith Wharton, who also concerned herself with the upper class she knew, modeled her realistic writing after those of James. She won a Pulitzer Prize for her novel *The Age of Innocence,* a stark portrait of upper-class New York society in the 1870s.

✓ **Reading Check** **Explaining** What was the significance of Mark Twain's *Adventures of Huckleberry Finn*?

Popular Culture

Popular culture changed considerably in the late 1800s. Industrialization improved the standard of living for many people, enabling them to spend money on entertainment and recreation. Increasingly, urban Americans, unlike rural people, divided their lives

| Fact | Fiction | **Folklore** |

The Seventh-Inning Stretch This baseball tradition, where fans often stand up to stretch in the middle of the seventh inning, does not have a completely reliable history. One claim is that in 1869, all the Cincinnati Red Stockings players stood during the seventh inning to seek relief from the hard wooden benches on which they were sitting. Another popular story asserts that in 1910, President William Howard Taft stood to stretch himself; thinking that the president was leaving, fans at the Washington Senators game also stood out of respect.

Moses Fleetwood Walker, early African American baseball player

into separate units—that of work and that of home. Furthermore, people began looking for things to do outside the home and began "going out" to public entertainment.

The Saloon As Frank Lloyd Wright had noted when he arrived in Chicago, the city's saloons far outnumbered its groceries and meat markets. Functioning like community centers, saloons played a major role in the life of male workers in the 1800s. They also served as political centers. Saloonkeepers often served as key figures in political machines.

Saloons offered free toilets, water for horses, and free newspapers for customers. They even offered the first "free lunch": salty food that made patrons thirsty and eager to drink more. Saloons developed loyal customers. The first workers from the night shift would stream in at 5:00 A.M., and the last would stay until late at night.

Amusement Parks and Sports While saloons catered mostly to men, working-class families or single adults who sought excitement and escape could go to amusement parks such as New York's **Coney Island.** Amusements there such as water slides and railroad rides cost only a nickel or dime.

Watching professionals box or play baseball also first became popular during the late 1800s. A game much like baseball, known as rounders and derived from the game of cricket, had enjoyed limited popularity in Great Britain in the early 1800s. Versions of the modern game of baseball began to appear in

| Fact | Fiction | **Folklore** |

Although organized baseball was played as early as the 1850s, the game really took off after the Civil War. Returning veterans helped to form teams, and by 1866 there were 202 teams in 17 states.

FYI

Football became a popular spectator sport during the Gilded Age, with college games proving to be the biggest draw. Rutgers and Princeton played in the first collegiate contest in 1869. Throughout the late 1800s, three Eastern universities–Harvard, Yale, and Princeton–dominated the sport.

✓ **Reading Check**

Answer: It was one of the first truly American novels.

3 ASSESS

Assign Section 3 Assessment as homework or as an in-class activity.

⊙ Have students use the **Interactive Tutor Self-Assessment CD-ROM.**

Reading Essentials and Study Guide 15–3

Name _____ Date _____ Class _____

Study Guide
Chapter 15, Section 3
For use with textbook pages 476–480

THE GILDED AGE

KEY TERMS AND NAMES

Gilded Age - the time period between 1870 and 1900 *(page 477)*

Social Darwinism - the idea that society progresses and becomes better because only the fittest people survive *(page 477)*

Gospel of Wealth - the philosophy that wealthy people who profited from society owed it something in return *(page 478)*

philanthropy - the using of one's wealth to further social progress *(page 478)*

realism - a movement in art and literature that attempted to portray people realistically *(page 478)*

INTERDISCIPLINARY CONNECTIONS ACTIVITY

Performing Arts Invite a performing arts teacher or artist to work with your students to produce a vaudeville-style show. Ask the guest to help students understand the kinds of acts performed in vaudeville, and offer suggestions about resources students can use to learn more about vaudeville. Arrange for students to perform for an audience. **L2**

Section Quiz 15–3

Picturing **History**

Answer: syncopated rhythms that grew out of the music of vaudeville and honky-tonk pianists and banjo players

Ask: What do you think is the role of the man wearing a business suit in the middle of the picture? *(may have been a promoter or manager)*

Reteach
Have students explain how industrialization promoted leisure time and new forms of entertainment.

Enrich
Invite interested students to learn more about popular culture in the late 1800s. Suggest that they work in pairs to create a trivia game that can be played in class.

✓ **Reading Check**

Answer: functioned as community centers and political centers for men

4 CLOSE
Have students evaluate the doctrine of Social Darwinism and its impact on industry.

the United States in the early 1800s. As the game grew in popularity, it became a source of profit. The first salaried team, the Cincinnati Red Stockings, was formed in 1869. Other cities soon fielded professional teams, and in 1903 the first modern World Series was played between the Boston Red Sox and the Pittsburgh Pirates.

The second most popular game, football, appealed first to the upper classes, in part because it began in private colleges and universities that the middle and working classes could not afford. By the late 1800s, the game had spread to public universities.

As work became less physically strenuous, many people looked for leisure activities that involved physical exercise. Lawn tennis, golf, and croquet became popular. James Naismith, a Canadian working as an athletic director for a college in Springfield, Massachusetts, invented the game of basketball in 1891.

Vaudeville and Ragtime The many people living in the cities provided large and eager markets for other types of entertainment. Adapted from French theater, vaudeville took on an American flavor in the early 1880s with its hodgepodge of animal acts, acrobats, gymnasts, and dancers. The fast-moving acts, like the tempo of big-city life, went on in continuous shows all day and night.

Picturing **History**

Ragtime Band This group of African American musicians traveled around the country playing ragtime music at motion picture shows. *What are some of the roots of ragtime music?*

Like vaudeville, ragtime music echoed the hectic pace of city life. Its syncopated rhythms grew out of the music of riverside honky-tonk, saloon pianists, and banjo players, using the patterns of African American music. **Scott Joplin,** one of the most important African American ragtime composers, became known as the "King of Ragtime." He published his signature piece, "The Maple Leaf Rag," in 1899.

✓ **Reading Check** **Describing** What importance did the saloon have in nineteenth-century life?

SECTION 3 ASSESSMENT

Checking for Understanding

1. **Define:** philanthropy, realism, vaudeville, ragtime.
2. **Identify:** Gilded Age, Social Darwinism, Gospel of Wealth, Scott Joplin.
3. **Describe** how changes in art and literature reflected the issues and characteristics of the late nineteenth century.

Reviewing Themes

4. **Culture and Traditions** What were the defining characteristics of the Gilded Age?

Critical Thinking

5. **Synthesizing** Do you think the idea of the Gospel of Wealth is still alive today? Why or why not?
6. **Organizing** Complete a graphic organizer similar to the one below by filling in new forms of entertainment that Americans turned to in the late 1800s.

New Entertainment

Analyzing Visuals

7. **Examining Photographs** Analyze the photograph at the top of this page. How does the clothing the musicians are wearing compare with the clothing worn by musicians today?

Writing About History

8. **Descriptive Writing** Imagine that you are a newspaper editor in the late 1800s. Write an editorial in which you support or oppose the philosophy of Social Darwinism. Include reasons to support your position.

480 CHAPTER 15 Urban America

SECTION 3 ASSESSMENT ANSWERS

1. Terms are in blue.
2. Gilded Age *(p. 477)*, Social Darwinism *(p. 477)*, Gospel of Wealth *(p. 478)*, Scott Joplin *(p. 480)*
3. Art and literature became more realistic as artists and writers depicted the world as they believed it to be, not as they thought it should be.
4. individualism, urbanization, new values, art, and forms of entertainment
5. Explanations will likely focus on current philanthropy of wealthy individuals.
6. saloons, sports, amusement parks, vaudeville
7. Students might mention that some groups of musicians dress alike and others do not, some wear suits and others do not, some wear clothing similar to what their audiences wear and others wear costumes.
8. Students' editorials will vary.

Guide to Reading

Main Idea
The pressing problems of the urban poor in the late 1800s and early 1900s eventually stimulated attempts to reform industrial society.

Key Terms and Names
Henry George, Lester Frank Ward, Edward Bellamy, naturalism, Jane Addams, settlement house, Americanization

Reading Strategy
Taking Notes As you read about reform movements in the United States in the late 1800s, complete an outline like the one below by listing the people whose ideas influenced the movements.

The Rebirth of Reform
I. Social Criticism
   A.
   B.
   C.
II. Naturalism in Literature

Reading Objectives
• **Explain** the methods that social critics advocated to improve society.
• **Evaluate** efforts to help the urban poor.

Section Theme
Individual Action Many middle- and upper-class individuals worked to soften social and economic inequality.

Preview of Events

♦1880	♦1885	♦1890	♦1895

1879
Henry George's *Progress and Poverty* published

1881
Booker T. Washington founds Tuskegee Institute

1889
Jane Addams founds Hull House

1893
Lester Frank Ward's *Dynamic Sociology* published

1896
National Association of Colored Women founded

★ An American Story ★

On a drizzly March morning in 1893, a nursing student named Lillian Wald was teaching a public health class to residents of New York's poor Lower East Side. Suddenly a girl broke in, disrupting the lesson. The child's mother desperately needed a nurse. The interruption changed Wald's life. She followed the girl to a squalid tenement, where she found a family of seven sharing their two rooms with boarders. The sick woman lay on a dirty bed. Wald later wrote:

❝That morning's experience was a baptism of fire. Deserted were the laboratory and the academic work of the college. I never returned to them. . . . To my inexperience it seemed certain that conditions such as these were allowed because people did not *know,* and for me there was a challenge to know and to tell. . . . If people knew things,—and "things" meant everything implied in the condition of this family,—such horrors would cease to exist. . . .❞

—**quoted in *The House on Henry Street***

Lillian Wald

In 1895 Wald and her friend Mary Brewster established the Henry Street Settlement. The young nurses offered medical care, education, labor organization, and social and cultural programs to the neighborhood residents.

Social Criticism

The tremendous changes brought about by industrialism and urbanization triggered a debate among Americans as to how best to address society's problems. While many Americans embraced the ideas of individualism and Social Darwinism, others disagreed,

CHAPTER 15   Urban America   **481**

2 TEACH

Daily Lecture and Discussion Notes 15–4

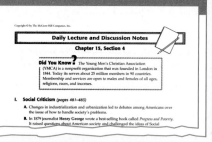

Daily Lecture and Discussion Notes

Chapter 15, Section 4

Did You Know? The Young Men's Christian Association (YMCA) is a nonprofit organization that was founded in London in 1844. Today its serves about 25 million members in 90 countries. Membership and services are open to males and females of all ages, religions, races, and incomes.

I. Social Criticism *(pages 481–483)*

  A. Changes in industrialization and urbanization led to debates among Americans over the issue of how to handle society's problems.

  B. In 1879 journalist **Henry George** wrote a best-selling book called *Progress and Poverty*. It raised questions about American society and challenged the ideas of Social

Posing and Answering Questions

Assign half the class to pose questions about Henry George's theory and the other half to pose questions about Lester Frank Ward's theory. The half of the class that is not posing questions should answer the questions based on information in the textbook or on conclusions that they have drawn. **L1**

Graph *Skills*

Answers:
1. almost 200 out of every 100,000 people
2. that conditions improved from the start to the end of the 1900s

Graph Skills Practice

Ask: Why do you think a larger percentage of students graduate from high school today than in 1900? *(possible answer: fewer have to go to work fulltime while in their teens, education is more important for the types of jobs available today)*

---

arguing that society's problems could be fixed only if Americans and their government began to take a more active role in regulating the economy and helping those in need.

Henry George on Progress and Poverty In 1879 journalist **Henry George** published *Progress and Poverty*. His book quickly became a national best-seller. "The present century has been marked by a prodigious increase in wealth-producing power," George observed, which should have made poverty "a thing of the past." Instead, he argued:

> ❝It becomes no easier for the masses of our people to make a living. On the contrary it becomes harder.... The gulf between the employed and the employer is growing wider; social contrasts are becoming sharper; as liveried carriages appear, so do barefoot children.❞
>
> —from *Progress and Poverty*

Most economists now argue that George's analysis was flawed. Industrialism did make some Americans very wealthy, but it also improved the standard of living for most other Americans as well. At the time,

however, in the midst of the poverty, crime, and harsh working conditions, many Americans did not believe things were improving.

George offered a simple solution. Land, he argued, was the basis of wealth, and people could grow wealthy just by waiting for land prices to rise. George proposed a "single tax" on this unearned wealth to replace all other taxes. He believed it would help make society more equal and also provide the government with enough money to help the poor.

Economists have since rejected George's economic theory. His real importance to American history is that he raised questions about American society and led the way in challenging the ideas of Social Darwinism and laissez-faire economics. Many future reform leaders first became interested in reform because of George's book.

Reform Darwinism Four years after Henry George challenged the ideas of Social Darwinism, **Lester Frank Ward** published *Dynamic Sociology*. Ward took the ideas of Social Darwinism and used them to reach a very different conclusion than Darwin had. He argued that human beings were different from other animals in nature because they

Social Conditions: Past and Present

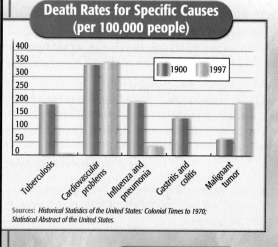

Death Rates for Specific Causes (per 100,000 people)

Legend: ▮ 1900 ▮ 1997

Y-axis: 0, 50, 100, 150, 200, 250, 300, 350, 400

Categories: Tuberculosis, Cardiovascular problems, Influenza and pneumonia, Gastritis and colitis, Malignant tumor

Sources: *Historical Statistics of the United States: Colonial Times to 1970; Statistical Abstract of the United States.*

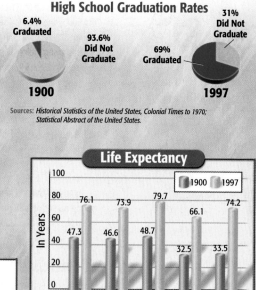

High School Graduation Rates

1900: 6.4% Graduated, 93.6% Did Not Graduate

1997: 31% Did Not Graduate, 69% Graduated

Sources: *Historical Statistics of the United States, Colonial Times to 1970; Statistical Abstract of the United States.*

Life Expectancy

Legend: ▮ 1900 ▮ 1997

Y-axis (In Years): 0, 20, 40, 60, 80, 100

	Total	White Male	White Female	African American Male	African American Female
1900	47.3	46.6	48.7	32.5	33.5
1997	76.1	73.9	79.7	66.1	74.2

Source: *Historical Statistics of the United States, Colonial Times to 1970; Statistical Abstract of the United States.*

Graph *Skills*

1. **Analyzing Graphs** How many people per 100,000 died of tuberculosis in the year 1900?
2. **Understanding Cause and Effect** Collectively, what do these graphs tell you about social conditions as the twentieth century progressed?

COOPERATIVE LEARNING ACTIVITY

Interpreting Political Cartoons Organize students into small groups. Have the groups locate political cartoons of the day showing opinions about the reform movements of this era. Have the groups determine what or who is shown in each cartoon, the message of each cartoon, and how the words or caption convey the idea. Have the groups use their research to create a political cartoon about a social problem or reform movement occurring in your local community. 📖

Use the rubric for a cooperative group management plan on pages 81–82 in the ***Performance Assessment Activities and Rubrics.***

Hypothesizing

Why Learn This Skill?

When you are reading new material, you may often encounter ideas and events that you do not immediately understand. One way to overcome this difficulty is to make educated guesses about what happened.

Learning the Skill

When you read things that you do not understand, you probably make guesses about what the material means. You may or may not have been able to prove these guesses, but you have taken a step toward deciphering the information. This step is called **hypothesizing.** When you hypothesize, you form one or more hypotheses, which are guesses that offer possible answers to a problem or provide possible explanations for an observation. When hypothesizing, follow these steps.

• Read the material carefully.

• Ask yourself what the material is actually saying. To do this, try to put the material in your own words.

• Determine what you might logically assume from your guesses. Then form one or more hypotheses.

• Test each hypothesis to determine whether or not it is correct. You can usually do this by asking yourself questions that relate to your hypothesis and then researching the answers.

• Based on your research, determine which hypothesis, if any, provides an explanation for the information that you originally read.

Hypotheses are only preliminary explanations. They must be accepted, rejected, or modified as the problem is investigated. Each hypothesis must be tested against the information gathered. Hypotheses that are supported by evidence can be accepted as explanations of the problem.

Practicing the Skill

Using the steps just discussed and what you have read in the chapter, test the following hypotheses and determine if they can be supported.

❶ Most immigrants who came to the United States came in search of work.

❷ Improved transportation led people to move to urban areas from rural areas.

❸ The general laissez-faire approach taken by the government toward growing cities was beneficial to businesses and citizens.

Students collaborating

Skills Assessment

Complete the Practicing Skills questions on page 489 and the Chapter 15 Skill Reinforcement Activity to assess your mastery of this skill.

Applying the Skill

Hypothesizing Reread the passage titled "The Resurgence of Nativism" in Section 1. Using the facts that you are given in these paragraphs, form at least two hypotheses that may explain what is being described. Test each hypothesis, then select the best one. Which hypothesis did you choose? Why?

 Glencoe's **Skillbuilder Interactive Workbook CD-ROM, Level 2,** provides instruction and practice in key social studies skills.

TEACH

Hypothesizing Remind students that it is important to test a hypothesis.

Instruct students to look at a newspaper photograph and read the caption without reading the accompanying article. Ask students to develop hypotheses based on the photo and caption. Record the hypotheses on the board. Ask students to read the newspaper article and test the hypotheses.

Additional Practice

Reinforcing Skills Activity 15

Name _____ Date _____ Class _____

★ Reinforcing Skills Activity 15

Hypothesizing

□ **LEARNING THE SKILL**

Hypotheses are guesses you may make to make sense of material you don't fully understand. When you hypothesize, you offer possible answers or explanations for a question or problem. As you read material, consider what assumptions or guesses you might be able to make. Form your hypotheses, and test them with research. When you find evidence to support a hypothesis, you have confirmed or proven your explanation.

□ **PRACTICING THE SKILL**

DIRECTIONS: The excerpt below is taken from *How the Other Half Lives*, a book written by Jacob Riis in 1890. Read the section in your text titled **Urban Problems** on page 344, and then read the excerpt below. Use both the text and the excerpt to answer the questions that follow on a separate sheet of paper.

GLENCOE
TECHNOLOGY

 CD-ROM
Glencoe Skillbuilder Interactive Workbook CD-ROM, Level 2

This interactive CD-ROM reinforces student mastery of essential social studies skills.

ANSWERS TO PRACTICING THE SKILL

❶ Students might say the hypothesis cannot be supported because there are no solid statistics in the text. They might suggest that the hypothesis could be revised to indicate that some immigrants came in search of work.

❷ Students might note that transportation is not a reason listed in the text.

❸ Students might say that the laissez-faire approach was not beneficial to all citizens.

Applying the Skill

Students' answers will vary. Students should follow the five steps outlined on this page as they complete this assignment.

Reviewing Key Terms

Students' answers will vary. The pages where the words appear in the text are shown in parentheses.

1. **steerage** (p. 465)
2. **nativism** (p. 468)
3. **skyscraper** (p. 470)
4. **tenement** (p. 471)
5. **political machine** (p. 473)
6. **party boss** (p. 473)
7. **graft** (p. 473)
8. **philanthropy** (p. 478)
9. **realism** (p. 478)
10. **vaudeville** (p. 480)
11. **ragtime** (p. 480)
12. **naturalism** (p. 483)
13. **settlement house** (p. 485)
14. **Americanization** (p. 485)

Reviewing Key Facts

15. Ellis Island (p. 466), Angel Island (p. 467), Louis Sullivan (p. 470), George Plunkitt (p. 473), William M. ("Boss") Tweed (p. 473), Gilded Age (p. 477), Herbert Spencer (p. 477), Lester Frank Ward (p. 482), Jane Addams (p. 485)

16. organized letter-writing campaigns, petitioned the president, filed suit in federal court

17. set up American Protective Association, set up Working Man's Party of California, worked to get Chinese Exclusion Act passed

18. congestion, crime, violence, fire, disease, pollution

19. the world as they saw it

20. Social Gospel, revivalism, and settlement house movement

Reviewing Key Terms

On a sheet of paper, use each of these terms in a sentence.

1. steerage
2. nativism
3. skyscraper
4. tenement
5. political machine
6. party boss
7. graft
8. philanthropy
9. realism
10. vaudeville
11. ragtime
12. naturalism
13. settlement house
14. Americanization

Reviewing Key Facts

15. **Identify:** Ellis Island, Angel Island, Louis Sullivan, George Plunkitt, William M. ("Boss") Tweed, Gilded Age, Herbert Spencer, Lester Frank Ward, Jane Addams.

16. How did the Chinese in the United States react to the Chinese Exclusion Act of 1882?

17. What attempts did nativist groups make to decrease immigration to the United States in the late 1800s?

18. What problems did cities in the United States face in the late 1800s?

19. What did realist authors such as Mark Twain and Henry James write about?

20. What movements in the late 1800s addressed urban problems?

Critical Thinking

21. **Analyzing Themes: Geography and History** What factors led so many people to immigrate to the United States in the late 1800s?

22. **Analyzing** What methods did political machines use to build support in the late 1800s?

23. **Evaluating** Recall the problems facing city dwellers in the late 1800s. What do you think is the biggest problem facing people living in large cities today? How do you think the problem should be solved?

24. **Interpreting Primary Sources** Reaction in the United States to "old" immigration was generally more favorable than reaction to "new" immigration. Some people, however, still favored all immigration. The following excerpt from an 1882 editorial in the *Commercial and Financial Chronicle* addresses the effects of immigration on the nation.

    ❝In the very act of coming and traveling to reach his destination, he [the immigrant] adds . . . to the immediate prosperity and success of certain lines of business. . . . Not only do the ocean steamers . . . get very large returns in carrying passengers of this description, but in forwarding them to the places chosen by the immigrants as their future homes the railroad companies also derive great benefit and their passenger traffic is greatly swelled. . . .

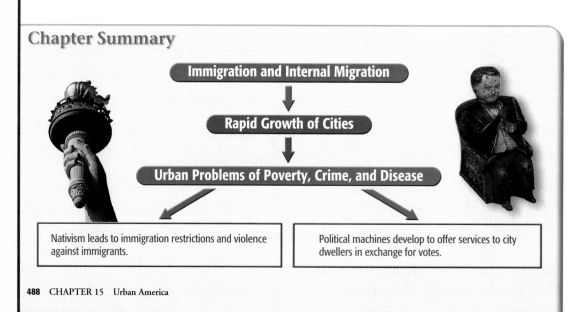

Chapter Summary

Immigration and Internal Migration
↓
Rapid Growth of Cities
↓
Urban Problems of Poverty, Crime, and Disease
↓ ↓

Nativism leads to immigration restrictions and violence against immigrants.

Political machines develop to offer services to city dwellers in exchange for votes.

488 CHAPTER 15 Urban America

Critical Thinking

21. military conscription in their homeland, religious persecution, better job opportunities in the United States

22. They provided housing, jobs, food, heat, and police protection to new immigrants unfamiliar with the United States and its culture.

23. Students' answers will vary. They should compare and contrast urban problems then and now.

24. **a.** positive; **b.** editorial viewed it positively and focused on economic benefits; nativists opposed immigration and worried about cultural and economic threats

25. skyscrapers, cable cars, elevated railroads, subway systems

HISTORY Online

Self-Check Quiz

Visit the *American Vision* Web site at tav.glencoe.com and click on *Self-Check Quizzes—Chapter 15* to assess your knowledge of chapter content.

. . . These immigrants not only produce largely, . . . but, having wants which they cannot supply themselves, create a demand for outside supplies. . . . Thus it is that the Eastern manufacturer finds the call upon him for his wares and goods growing more urgent all the time, thus the consumption of coal keeps on expanding notwithstanding the check to new railroad enterprises, and thus there is a more active and larger interchange of all commodities. . . .

a. According to the editorial, what kind of effect did immigration have on the nation's economy?

b. How is the editorial's view of the effects of immigration different from that of the nativists?

25. Organizing Complete a graphic organizer similar to the one below by listing the new technologies that contributed to urban growth in the late 1800s.

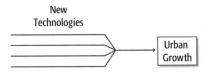

Practicing Skills

26. Hypothesizing Reread the passage titled "The Spread of Schools" from Section 4. Using the information in this passage, form a hypothesis that describes the availability of education to people during this time. Write your hypothesis down and research the topic. Then state whether or not your hypothesis was correct.

Writing Activity

27. Descriptive Writing Find out about an individual in the 1800s who experienced a "rags-to-riches" success story. You might use one of the business leaders or other individuals discussed in the chapter. Write a brief sketch of the person, describing how he or she became a success.

Chapter Activity

28. American History Primary Source Document Library CD-ROM Read the article "The Need for Public Parks" by Frederick Law Olmsted, under *Reshaping the Nation.* Then work with a partner and create a design for a park that you think would meet the recreational needs of people in your community.

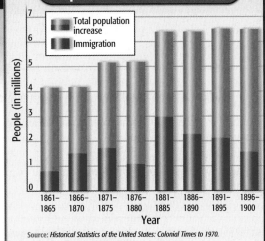

Immigration's Contribution to Population Growth, 1860–1900

Source: Historical Statistics of the United States: Colonial Times to 1970.

Geography and History

29. The graph above shows how much immigration contributed to population growth in the United States between 1860 and 1900. Study the graph and answer the questions below.

a. Interpreting Graphs By about how much did the population of the United States increase between 1861 and 1900?

b. Understanding Cause and Effect What is the relationship between immigration and population increase?

Standardized Test Practice

Directions: Choose the best answer to the following question.

Which of the following concepts is not associated with both Social Darwinism and the Gospel of Wealth?

A Survival of the fittest

B Laissez-faire

C Unregulated competition

D Philanthropy

Test-Taking Tip: Read the question carefully. From the wording of the question, you can see that Social Darwinism and the Gospel of Wealth DO have three of these concepts in common. Find the one that is part of only ONE of these philosophies.

HISTORY Online

Have students visit the Web site at tav.glencoe.com to review Chapter 15 and take the Self-Check Quiz.

Chapter Activity

28. The park designs should consider the needs of various ages and interests.

Geography and History

29. a. by about 2.5 million;
b. Immigration played a significant role, especially in the period from 1881 to 1885.

The Princeton Review
Standardized Test Practice

Answer: D
Test-Taking Tip: Teachers should tell students that if they are not sure of the answer, they should use the process of elimination. Students should ask themselves if Social Darwinism and the Gospel of Wealth are both associated with the concept of survival of the fittest. The answer is yes, so they can eliminate A. Ask the same question for each possible answer to eliminate B and C. The answer is D.

Bonus Question ?

Ask: What was the only ethnic group to be officially excluded by federal law from immigrating to the United States between 1870 and 1900? *(the Chinese)*

Practicing Skills

26. Students' answers will vary. Their hypothesis should be logical; however, it does not have to be correct. Students' research should support or refute their hypothesis.

Writing Activity

27. Students' sketches should include basic biographical facts and some insight into what enabled the person to go from rags to riches.

Timesaving Tools

TeacherWorks™ All-In-One Planner and Resource Center

- **Interactive Teacher Edition** Access your Teacher Wraparound Edition and your classroom resources with a few easy clicks.
- **Interactive Lesson Planner** Planning has never been easier! Organize your week, month, semester, or year with all the lesson helps you need to make teaching creative, timely, and relevant.

Use Glencoe's **Presentation Plus!** multimedia teacher tool to easily present dynamic lessons that visually excite your students. Using Microsoft PowerPoint® you can customize the presentations to create your own personalized lessons.

TEACHING TRANSPARENCIES

Graphic Organizer 11

Why It Matters Chapter Transparency 16

APPLICATION AND ENRICHMENT

Linking Past and Present Activity 16

Enrichment Activity 16

Primary Source Reading 16

REVIEW AND REINFORCEMENT

Reteaching Activity 16

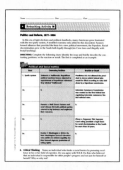

Vocabulary Activity 16

Time Line Activity 16

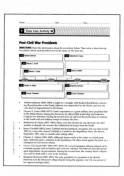

Critical Thinking Skills Activity 16

Meeting NCSS Standards

Local Standards

The following standards are highlighted in Chapter 16:

Section 1	II	Time, Continuity, and Change: A, B, D
Section 2	VII	Production, Distribution, and Consumption: B, G, I
Section 3	IV	Individual Development and Identity: A, C, E, F

Chapter 16 Resources

ASSESSMENT AND EVALUATION

**Chapter 16 Test
Form A**

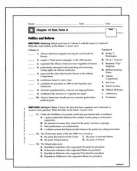

**Chapter 16 Test
Form B**

**Standardized Test Skills
Practice Workbook Activity 16**

**Performance Assessment
Activities and Rubrics 16**

**ExamView® Pro
Testmaker CD-ROM**

MULTIMEDIA

- Vocabulary PuzzleMaker CD-ROM
- Interactive Tutor Self-Assessment CD-ROM
- ExamView® Pro Testmaker CD-ROM
- Audio Program
- American History Primary Source Documents Library CD-ROM
- MindJogger Videoquiz
- Presentation Plus! CD-ROM
- TeacherWorks™ CD-ROM
- Interactive Student Edition CD-ROM
- Glencoe Skillbuilder Interactive Workbook CD-ROM, Level 2
- The *American Vision* Video Program
- American Music: Hits Through History
- American Music: Cultural Traditions

SPANISH RESOURCES

**The following Spanish language materials are
available in the Spanish Resources Binder:**

- Spanish Guided Reading Activities
- Spanish Reteaching Activities
- Spanish Quizzes and Tests
- Spanish Vocabulary Activities
- Spanish Summaries
- The Declaration of Independence and United States Constitution Spanish Translation

The following videotape programs are available
from Glencoe as supplements to Chapter 16:

- **Ku Klux Klan: A Secret History** (ISBN 0-76-700878-2)
- **J. Pierpont Morgan: Emperor of Wall Street** (ISBN 1-56-501957-1)

To order, call Glencoe at 1-800-334-7344. To find classroom resources to
accompany many of these videos, check the following home pages:
A&E Television: www.aande.com
The History Channel: www.historychannel.com

HISTORY Online

Use our Web site for additional resources. All essential content is covered in the Student Edition.

You and your students can visit tav.glencoe.com, the Web site companion to the ***American Vision.*** This innovative integration of electronic
and print media offers your students a wealth of opportunities. The
student text directs students to the Web site for the following options:

- **Chapter Overviews**
- **Self-Check Quizzes**
- **Student Web Activities**
- **Textbook Updates**

Answers to the student Web activities are provided for you in the **Web
Activity Lesson Plans.** Additional Web resources and Interactive Tutor
Puzzles are also available.

Chapter 16 Resources

Daily Objectives	Reproducible Resources	Multimedia Resources
SECTION 1 **Stalemate in Washington** 1. Explain why the Republicans and Democrats were so evenly matched during this period. 2. Cite the economic problems of the period and the basic viewpoints of each political party.	Reproducible Lesson Plan 16–1 Daily Lecture and Discussion Notes 16–1 Guided Reading Activity 16–1* Section Quiz 16–1* Reading Essentials and Study Guide 16–1 Performance Assessment Activities and Rubrics	Daily Focus Skills Transparency 16–1 Interactive Tutor Self-Assessment CD-ROM ExamView® Pro Testmaker CD-ROM Presentation Plus! CD-ROM TeacherWorks™ CD-ROM Audio Program
SECTION 2 **Populism** 1. Explain why farmers wanted a greenback currency and why the adoption of the gold standard led to the Farmers' Alliance. 2. Describe who joined the Populist Party and what the party's goals were.	Reproducible Lesson Plan 16–2 Daily Lecture and Discussion Notes 16–2 Guided Reading Activity 16–2* Section Quiz 16–2* Reading Essentials and Study Guide 16–2 Performance Assessment Activities and Rubrics	Daily Focus Skills Transparency 16–2 Interactive Tutor Self-Assessment CD-ROM ExamView® Pro Testmaker CD-ROM Presentation Plus! CD-ROM TeacherWorks™ CD-ROM Audio Program American Music: Cultural Traditions
SECTION 3 **The Rise of Segregation** 1. Discuss how African Americans in the South were disfranchised and how segregation was legalized. 2. Describe three major African American leaders' responses to discrimination.	Reproducible Lesson Plan 16–3 Daily Lecture and Discussion Notes 16–3 Guided Reading Activity 16–3* Section Quiz 16–3* Reading Essentials and Study Guide 16–3 Performance Assessment Activities and Rubrics Supreme Court Case Studies	Daily Focus Skills Transparency 16–3 Interactive Tutor Self-Assessment CD-ROM ExamView® Pro Testmaker CD-ROM Presentation Plus! CD-ROM Skillbuilder Interactive Workbook, Level 2 TeacherWorks™ CD-ROM Vocabulary PuzzleMaker CD-ROM Audio Program

0:00 OUT OF TIME?
Assign the Chapter 16 **Reading Essentials and Study Guide.**

*Also Available in Spanish

 Blackline Master   Transparency   CD-ROM   DVD

Poster   Music Program   Audio Program   Videocassette

NATIONAL GEOGRAPHIC Teacher's Corner

INDEX TO NATIONAL GEOGRAPHIC MAGAZINE

The following articles relate to this chapter.

- "Central Park: Oasis in the City," May 1993
- "Chicago: Welcome to the Neighborhood," May 1991
- "Miami," January 1992
- "New Life for Ellis Island," September 1990
- "New York's Chinatown," August 1998

NATIONAL GEOGRAPHIC SOCIETY PRODUCTS AVAILABLE FROM GLENCOE

To order the following products for use with this chapter, contact your local Glencoe sales representative, or call Glencoe at 1-800-334-7344:

- *PictureShow: Native Americans, 1 and 2* (CD-ROM)
- *PicturePack: Native Americans* (Transparencies)

ADDITIONAL NATIONAL GEOGRAPHIC SOCIETY PRODUCTS

To order the following, call National Geographic at 1-800-368-2728:

- *Immigration: The Triumph of Hope* (Video)

NGS ONLINE

Access National Geographic's Web site for current events, atlas updates, activities, links, interactive features, and archives.

www.nationalgeographic.com

From the Classroom of...

Lindsay Linoff
Mesa School District
Mesa, AZ

Political Allegory in *Wizard of Oz*

Have the students read the original version of the *Wizard of Oz.* Point out that the story can be read on several levels. For example, the yellow brick road might represent the gold standard and Dorothy's silver shoes might represent the silver standard. (For students unfamiliar with the gold and silver standards, tell them that to fully appreciate the underlying political allegory, they need to research the time period in which Baum was writing and attempt to understand what the allegory refers to.)

Ask them to find at least five items in the book that might be allegorical and research the items' symbolism in society at that time. Help them connect the history of the time to Baum's story in the *Wizard of Oz.*

Have them write a report discussing the story and the underlying political allegory they discover.

ADDITIONAL RESOURCES FROM GLENCOE

- American Music: Cultural Traditions
- American Art & Architecture
- Outline Map Resource Book
- U.S. Desk Map
- Building Geography Skills for Life
- Inclusion for the High School Social Studies Classroom Strategies and Activities
- Teaching Strategies for the American History Classroom (Including Block Scheduling Pacing Guides)

KEY TO ABILITY LEVELS

Teaching strategies have been coded.

L1 BASIC activities for all students
L2 AVERAGE activities for average to above-average students
L3 CHALLENGING activities for above-average students
ELL ENGLISH LANGUAGE LEARNER activities

Block Schedule

Activities that are suited to use within the block scheduling framework are identified by:

Performance Assessment

Refer to Activity 16 in the Performance Assessment Activities and Rubrics booklet. 📦

Why It Matters Activity

Have students discuss examples of segregation that may still remain in your community. Ask students what impact segregation has on people and on society as a whole. Students should evaluate their answers after they have completed the chapter.

GLENCOE
TECHNOLOGY

The *American Vision* Video Program

To learn more about the period in American history, have students view the Chapter 16 video, "The 1893 Chicago World's Fair," from the ***American Vision*** **Video Program.**

 Available in DVD and VHS

MindJogger Videoquiz

Use the **MindJogger Videoquiz** to preview Chapter 16 content.

 Available in VHS

CHAPTER

16 Politics and Reform *1877–1896*

Why It Matters

During this period, political parties often focused on party competition rather than on important issues. Rural Americans were suffering economically, and they began to organize to obtain relief. Many states passed laws segregating African Americans and limiting their voting rights.

The Impact Today

Events of this period remain significant today.
* *To ensure fair hiring, a federal civil service system was created.*
* *Segregation created problems that Americans are still working to overcome.*

The American Vision *Video* *The Chapter 16 video, "The 1893 Chicago World's Fair," captures the feeling of this influential age.*

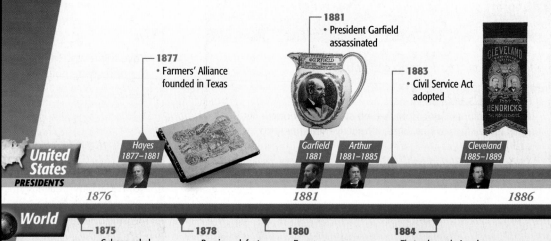

United States
PRESIDENTS

— 1877
• Farmers' Alliance founded in Texas

Hayes 1877–1881

— 1881
• President Garfield assassinated

Garfield 1881 *Arthur 1881–1885*

— 1883
• Civil Service Act adopted

Cleveland 1885–1889

1876   *1881*   *1886*

World

— 1875
• Cubans rebel against Spain

— 1878
• Russians defeat Turks in war over control of Balkans

— 1880
• France annexes Tahiti

1884 —
• First subway in London
• Last volume of Karl Marx's *Das Kapital* published

490

TWO-MINUTE LESSON LAUNCHER

Give students the following information: The center of population in 1790 was about 23 miles east of Baltimore, Maryland. In 1850 it was 23 miles southeast of Parkersburg, West Virginia. By 1900 it had moved to 6 miles southeast of Columbus, Indiana. Have students locate these cities on a map of the United States. Then ask students to speculate on the cause of this dramatic shift in population.

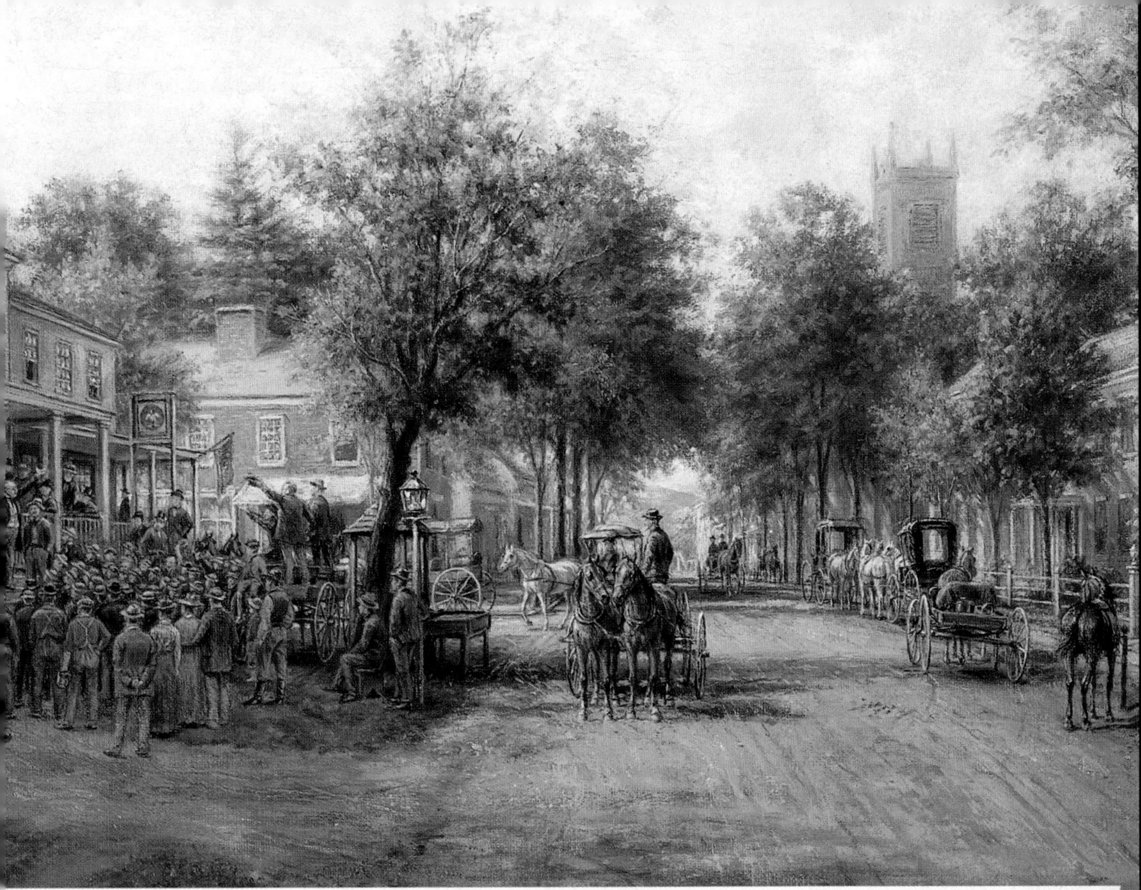

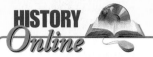

Electioneering in a Country Town by E.L. Henry

1887
- Florida initiates Jim Crow laws
- Interstate Commerce Act adopted

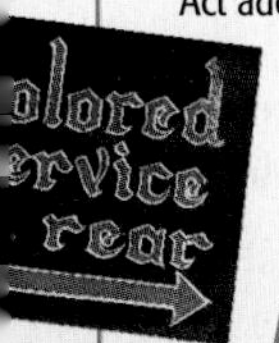

1890
- Sherman Antitrust Act passed

1895
- Booker T. Washington gives Atlanta Compromise speech

1896
- Democrats support free silver

B. Harrison 1889–1893

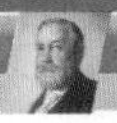

Cleveland 1893–1897

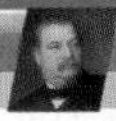

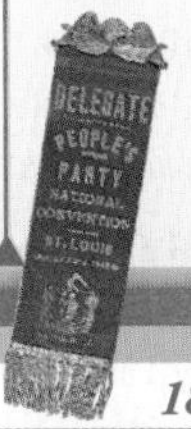

1891

1896

1893
- France acquires a protectorate over Laos

1894
- Sino-Japanese War breaks out

HISTORY Online

Chapter Overview
Visit the *American Vision* Web site at tav.glencoe.com and click on ***Chapter Overviews—Chapter 16*** to preview chapter information.

Introducing CHAPTER 16

HISTORY Online

Introduce students to chapter content and key terms by having them access the **Chapter 16 Overview** at tav.glencoe.com.

More About the Art

E.L. Henry (1841–1919) was a prolific artist who specialized in genre painting–paintings which depict everyday scenes, often in a sentimentalized or nostalgic style. He was also known for Civil War sketches in pencil and pastel crayon. Often, he sketched appealing behind-the-lines scenes of soldiers, horses, and wagons.
Ask: **From the subject portrayed, what is the artist suggesting about local elections?** *(that they are important, many are participating)*

TIME LINE ACTIVITY

Have students select one event on the time line that they would like to learn more about. Have them learn one new fact about the event to share with the class. Use the additional information to create an annotated class time line for the chapter.

GRAPHIC ORGANIZER ACTIVITY

Organizing Information Have students use a graphic organizer similar to the one shown below to identify the legislation that was passed during this period. Students' graphics will contain more lines than shown here.

Legislation	Intent
Pendleton Act	*filled federal jobs according to Civil Service Commission's rule*
McKinley Tariff	*lowered some tariffs, raised others*
Sherman Antitrust Act	*attempted to limit the power of trusts*

SECTION 1 Stalemate in Washington

1 FOCUS

Section Overview

This section focuses on political struggles between the evenly matched Democrats and Republicans.

BELLRINGER
Skillbuilder Activity

Project transparency and have students answer the question.

Available as a blackline master.

Daily Focus Skills Transparency 16–1

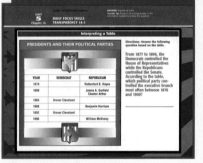

Guide to Reading

Answers to Graphic: Stalwarts supported Reconstruction; Halfbreeds supported Pendleton Act

Preteaching Vocabulary
Have students look up the meaning of each of the Key Terms in the Glossary.

Guide to Reading

Main Idea
From 1877 to 1896, the Republicans and Democrats were so evenly matched that only a few reforms were possible at the national level.

Key Terms and Names
patronage, Stalwart, Pendleton Act, rebate, Interstate Commerce Commission

Stalwarts	Halfbreeds

Reading Strategy
Organizing As you read about the electoral politics of the 1880s, complete a graphic organizer similar to the one below by filling in the ideals of each Republican Party faction listed.

Reading Objectives
• **Explain** why the Republicans and Democrats were so evenly matched during this period.
• **Cite** the economic problems of the period and the basic viewpoints of each political party.

Section Theme
Continuity and Change Political parties relied on support from different groups and regions of the country.

Preview of Events

◆1881	◆1884	◆1887	◆1890
1881 Garfield assassinated; succeeded by Chester A. Arthur	**1883** Civil Service Act adopted	**1887** Interstate Commerce Act adopted	**1890** Sherman Antitrust Act adopted

Pitcher depicting James Garfield

★ **An American Story** ★

After the election of President James A. Garfield in 1880, many of his supporters tried to claim the "spoils of office"—the government jobs that follow an election victory. One of these job-seekers was Charles Guiteau. In the spring of 1881, Guiteau made daily trips to the White House or State Department, repeatedly asking for a job. Finally, the night of May 18, he had a crazed inspiration: "[I]f the president was out of the way," he thought, "everything would go better." Unlike Garfield, Guiteau reasoned, Vice President Chester Arthur was comfortable with the old spoils system. Arthur would give him the position he deserved. On July 2, 1881, Guiteau shot President Garfield in a train station near Capitol Hill. In a note left behind, Guiteau stated:

❝The President's tragic death was a sad necessity, but it will unite the Republican party and save the Republic. . . . I had no ill-will toward the President. His death was a political necessity. I am a lawyer, theologian, and politician. I am a Stalwart of the Stalwarts. . . .❞
—quoted in *Garfield*

A Campaign to Clean Up Politics

For many, the assassination of President Garfield highlighted the need to work seriously on reforming politics. Traditionally, under the spoils system, or **patronage**, government jobs went to supporters of the winning party in an election. Many Americans believed the spoils system prevented government from addressing the nation's issues and corrupted

492 CHAPTER 16 Politics and Reform

SECTION RESOURCES

Reproducible Masters
• Reproducible Lesson Plan 16–1
• Daily Lecture and Discussion Notes 16–1
• Guided Reading Activity 16–1
• Section Quiz 16–1
• Reading Essentials and Study Guide 16–1
• Performance Assessment Activities and Rubrics

Transparencies
• Daily Focus Skills Transparency 16–1

Multimedia
⊙ Interactive Tutor Self-Assessment CD-ROM
⊙ ExamView® Pro Testmaker CD-ROM
⊙ Presentation Plus! CD-ROM
⊙ TeacherWorks™ CD-ROM
⊙ Audio Program

those who worked for the government. By the late 1870s, a movement to reform the civil service had begun to build support.

Stalwarts and Halfbreeds When Rutherford B. Hayes entered the White House in 1877, he attacked the practice of patronage by appointing reformers to his cabinet and replacing officials who owed their jobs to party bosses. His actions infuriated New York senator Roscoe Conkling, who, like other local bosses of Republican political machines, was called a **"Stalwart"** in the newspapers.

The Stalwarts were already angry with Hayes for abandoning Reconstruction, because this abandonment allowed Democrats to regain full control of the South. Conkling labeled the Republican reformers **"Halfbreeds."** He accused them of backing reform simply to create openings for their own supporters. "They are wolves in sheep's clothing," he charged. "Their real object is office and plunder."

As the presidential election of 1880 approached, Hayes announced that he did not intend to run again. The Republicans nominated a mixed ticket—a Halfbreed, James Garfield, for president, and a Stalwart, Chester A. Arthur, for vice president. Despite the party's feud, its ticket managed to win the election. A few months into his presidency, however, Garfield was assassinated.

The Pendleton Act Garfield's assassination further excited public opinion against the spoils system. In 1883 Congress responded by passing the **Pendleton Act.** This law allowed the president to decide which federal jobs would be filled according to rules laid down by a bipartisan Civil Service Commission. Candidates competed for these jobs through examinations, and appointments could be made only from the list of those who took the exams. Once appointed, a civil service official could not be removed for political reasons.

Although President Arthur was a Stalwart, he supported the Pendleton Act. He placed 14,000 jobs (about one-tenth of the total) under the control of the civil service. The federal government had finally begun to shift away from the spoils system.

✔ **Reading Check** **Explaining** Why did Garfield's assassination highlight the need for political reform?

Two Parties, Neck and Neck

Although many people thought corruption prevented the government from addressing the nation's problems, a major reason few new policies were

introduced in the 1870s and 1880s was the political system itself. The Republicans held a voting edge in New England and the upper Midwest. As the party that had preserved the Union and established pensions for Civil War veterans, the Republicans had the support of former Union soldiers and Americans who were strongly patriotic. In addition, Republicans had the support of big business and strong support among farmers on the Great Plains. The Republicans were also seen as the party of reform because they supported abolition, temperance, and other reforms. Most Republicans were Protestants who viewed their party as the defender of traditional American morals and values.

While Republicans were sometimes seen as the "party of morality," Democrats portrayed themselves as the "party of personal liberty." The Democrats dominated the South, where white voters remained anti-Republican following the Civil War and Reconstruction. The Democrats also enjoyed strong support in big cities, where large numbers of Catholics and immigrants lived.

From 1877 to 1896, these voting patterns gave the Democrats an edge in the House of Representatives, where voters in each congressional district elected

Picturing History

National Tragedy A newspaper artist captured the attack on President Garfield. Why was Charles Guiteau obsessed with the idea of killing the president?

2 TEACH

Daily Lecture and Discussion Notes 16–1

Copyright © by The McGraw-Hill Companies, Inc.

Daily Lecture and Discussion Notes
Chapter 16, Section 1

Did You Know? President James A. Garfield lived for 80 days after an assassin shot him in the arm and the back. Doctors could not find the bullet lodged in his back. Alexander Graham Bell tried to find the bullet using an electrical device, but he too failed. Garfield ended up dying from an infection. At that time, there were no X-ray machines, CAT scans, MRIs, or modern antiseptics that probably would have saved Garfield's life.

I. **A Campaign to Clean Up Politics** (pages 492–493)
  A. Under the spoils system, or **patronage**, government jobs went to supporters of the winning party in an election. By the late 1870s, many Americans believed that patron-

Drawing a Time Line Ask students to draw a time line that shows U.S. presidents from 1877 to 1896, including names, party affiliations, and why they left office. **L1**

✔ **Reading Check**

Answer: The old spoils system had led to Garfield's assassination.

Picturing History

Answer: When Guiteau did not get the government job he wanted, he decided to kill Garfield, hoping Arthur would give him a job.
Ask: Do you think this illustration accurately represents the assassination scene? *(Students' answers will vary.)*

COOPERATIVE LEARNING ACTIVITY

Assessing Campaign Tactics Organize the class into groups of five. Have the groups compose letters to either Grover Cleveland's campaign managers or James G. Blaine's campaign managers. Letters should describe how campaign tactics have changed since 1884. Suggest that the letters also include a comparison of tactics then with tactics today. Have groups select representatives to read their letters to the class.

Use the rubric for a cooperative group management plan on pages 81–82 in the *Performance Assessment Activities and Rubrics.*

Guided Reading Activity 16-1

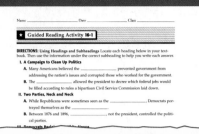

Name _____ Date _____ Class _____

★ **Guided Reading Activity 16-1**

DIRECTIONS: Using Headings and Subheadings Locate each heading below in your textbook. Then use the information under the correct subheading to help you write each answer.

I. A Campaign to Clean Up Politics

A. Many Americans believed the _____ prevented government from addressing the nation's issues and corrupted those who worked for the government.

B. The _____ allowed the president to decree which federal jobs would be filled according to rules a bipartisan Civil Service Commission laid down.

II. Two Parties, Neck and Neck

A. While Republicans were sometimes seen as the _____, Democrats portrayed themselves as the _____.

B. Between 1876 and 1896, _____, not the president, controlled the political parties.

III. Democrats Reclaim ____ House

Geography *Skills*

Answers:

1. West, Great Plains, Midwest, New England

2. New York, Pennsylvania, and Ohio; because they had the most electoral votes

Geography Skills Practice
Ask: Proportionately, was the popular vote or the Electoral College vote closer? *(the popular vote)*

✔ Reading Check

Answer: Republicans won four of the six presidential elections.

Creating Circle Graphs
Have students use the data below to make four circle graphs for the 1876 and 1888 elections. (One pair will show the electoral, and one the popular vote.) **L2**

1876 Candidate	Popular Vote	Electoral Vote
Hayes, Rep.	4,036,572	185
Tilden, Dem.	4,284,020	184

1888 Candidate	Popular Vote	Electoral Vote
Cleveland, Dem.	5,537,857	168
Harrison, Rep.	5,477,129	233

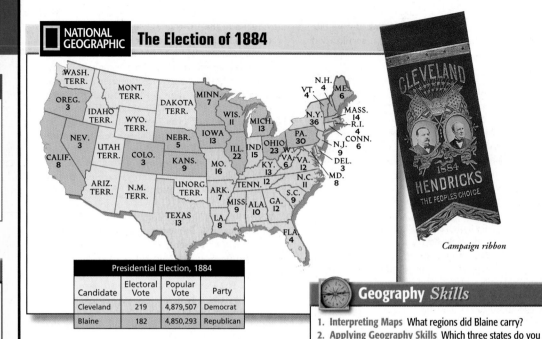

NATIONAL GEOGRAPHIC The Election of 1884

Presidential Election, 1884			
Candidate	Electoral Vote	Popular Vote	Party
Cleveland	219	4,879,507	Democrat
Blaine	182	4,850,293	Republican

Campaign ribbon

Geography *Skills*

1. **Interpreting Maps** What regions did Blaine carry?
2. **Applying Geography Skills** Which three states do you think each candidate most hoped to win? Why?

members directly. The Republicans had the upper hand in the Senate, because state legislatures chose senators and Republicans generally controlled a majority of state governments.

Both parties were well organized to turn out the vote in elections, and narrow margins decided most presidential elections between 1876 and 1896. The elections of 1880 and 1888 came down to the swing states of New York, Ohio, and Pennsylvania, with their big blocks of electoral votes. Twice during this period, in 1876 and 1888, a candidate lost the popular vote but won the election. This happened because even if candidates win several states by slim popular vote margins, they still receive all the electoral votes in those states. These narrow victories then give the candidate an Electoral College majority, regardless of the overall popular vote count.

Although the Republicans won four of the six presidential elections between 1876 and 1896, the president often had to contend with a House controlled by Democrats and a Senate dominated by Republicans who did not always agree with him on the issues. Furthermore, this was an era when local political bosses, not the president, controlled the party. The nearly even division of power produced political deadlock at the federal level.

✔ Reading Check
Summarizing What were the results of most presidential elections between 1876 and 1896?

Democrats Reclaim the White House

As the election of 1884 approached, Democrats saw their best chance to win the White House since before the Civil War. Republicans remained divided over reform, and Democrats went after the votes of pro-reform Republicans by nominating Governor Grover Cleveland of New York. Cleveland was an opponent of **Tammany Hall,** the corrupt Democratic political machine in New York City.

Cleveland's Republican opponent was James G. Blaine, a former speaker of the House of Representatives and chairman of the Maine committee of the Republican Party since 1859. Blaine was wildly popular among party workers. When his name was placed in nomination at the Republican convention in Chicago, delegates launched into a riotous celebration. The cheers "deepened into a roar fully as deafening as the voice of Niagara," a witness reported. "The air quivered, the gas lights trembled and the walls fairly shook."

The campaign was sensational and frenzied. Because so many voters believed corruption was the main problem in American government, they focused their attention on the personal morals of the

MEETING SPECIAL NEEDS

Visual/Spatial Spatial learners find it helpful to organize information with drawings and graphic organizers. Have students create a graphic organizer for each of the presidents mentioned in this section. The organizer should include their dates in office, their party affiliation, and one or two facts about their presidency. Encourage students to add other graphic organizers for other presidents and create a fact book for future reference. **L1**

📁 Refer to *Inclusion for the High School Social Studies Classroom Strategies and Activities* in the TCR.

candidates. The wild show of support for Blaine offended *New York Evening Post* editor Edwin L. Godkin, who called it a "disgrace to decency" and compared the celebration to a "mass meeting of maniacs." Godkin disliked Blaine, who had been accused during the Crédit Mobilier scandal of profiting financially from a political favor he did for the Union Pacific Railroad while serving as Speaker of the House in the 1870s.

Some Republican reformers were so unhappy with Blaine that they abandoned their party and supported Cleveland. These renegade reformers became known as **"Mugwumps,"** from an Algonquian word meaning "great man." They thought of themselves as moral leaders who were more concerned with helping the nation than with helping a particular political party. Among the leaders of the Mugwumps were Theodore Roosevelt, then a New York state legislator, and Henry Cabot Lodge, a powerful United States senator.

Cleveland, a bachelor, also faced moral criticism during the campaign when a newspaper revealed that he had fathered a child 10 years earlier. Aides asked Cleveland how they should respond to reporters seeking to know more about this story, and he replied, "Tell the truth." By admitting to the charge, Cleveland preserved his reputation for honesty and retained the support of many Mugwumps.

Blaine hoped that he could make up for the loss of the Mugwumps by persuading Roman Catholics to defect from the Democratic Party. His mother was an Irish Catholic, and there were half a million Irish Americans in New York state alone at the time. During the campaign, however, Blaine met with a Protestant minister who denounced the Democratic Party for its ties to Catholicism. Because Blaine was slow to denounce the remark, he lost most of the Irish American vote. To make matters worse for Blaine, many pro-temperance Republicans in upstate New York backed the candidate of the Prohibition Party, which was dedicated to banning the sale of alcohol. Cleveland won New York by a margin of about 1,000 votes out of more than 1,000,000 cast, and his victory there decided the election.

✓ **Reading Check** **Describing** From what sources did Grover Cleveland gain support in the 1884 presidential election?

A President Besieged by Problems

Grover Cleveland was an easy-going man who enjoyed the personal side of politics. Like his predecessors, he was shocked by the crowds that flocked to the White House seeking jobs. "This dreadful . . .

office-seeking hangs over me and surrounds me," he complained, "and makes me feel like resigning."

As the first elected Democratic president since 1856, he faced a horde of supporters who expected him to reward them with jobs. Mugwumps, on the other hand, expected him to multiply the number of positions covered under the merit system. Cleveland chose a middle course and wound up angering both sides. Economic issues, however, soon overshadowed the debate about political reform.

ECONOMICS

The Interstate Commerce Commission With greater industrialization and the growth of the labor movement, unrest among workers was mounting across the country. Many strikes occurred in this period, and police and paid guards sometimes attacked workers with clubs. This period of violence culminated in 1886 when a bomb exploded at a labor demonstration in Haymarket Square in Chicago.

The power of large corporations also concerned Americans. In particular, small businesses and farmers had become angry at the railroads. While large corporations such as Standard Oil were able to negotiate rebates—or partial refunds—and lower rates because of the volume of goods they shipped, others were forced to pay much higher rates. Although the high fixed costs and low operating costs of railroads caused much of this problem, many Americans believed railroads were gouging customers.

Neither Democrats nor Republicans moved quickly at the federal level to address these problems.

✓ **Analyzing** *Political Cartoons*

Difficult Passage In Greek mythology, Scylla and Charybdis were sea monsters who threatened the hero Odysseus from opposite sides of a narrow strait. Why do you think the artist chose this image for Grover Cleveland in 1884?

CHAPTER 16 Politics and Reform **495**

✓ **Analyzing** *Political Cartoons*

Answer: He was under pressure from both personal and political issues.
Ask: What did the Mugwumps expect? *(to add to the number of jobs under the merit system)*

Drawing a Political Cartoon
Have students choose one of the problems that President Grover Cleveland faced and create a political cartoon about it. **L3**

📁 Use the rubric for a political cartoon, pamphlet, or handbill on pages 87–88 in the *Performance Assessment Activities and Rubrics.*

Thomas Nast was responsible for creating the symbols of both the Democratic and Republican parties. To this day, the donkey symbolizes Democrats, and the elephant symbolizes Republicans.

✓**Reading Check**

Answer: Mugwumps and Irish Americans

INTERDISCIPLINARY CONNECTIONS ACTIVITY

Government Have students make a poster using newspaper and magazine ads that advertise political issues or candidates. Ask students to write a caption for each illustration that explains the message that the ad presents. Have students share their work with a partner, critiquing each other's work and making needed improvements. Display the finished products in the classroom. **L2**

3 ASSESS

Assign Section 1 Assessment as homework or as an in-class activity.

◉ Have students use the **Interactive Tutor Self-Assessment CD-ROM.**

Reading Essentials and Study Guide 16–1

Name _____ Date _____ Class _____

Study Guide

Chapter 16, Section 1

For use with textbook pages 492–497

STALEMATE IN WASHINGTON

KEY TERMS AND NAMES

patronage system in which government jobs went to supporters of the winning party in an election (page 492)

Stalwarts politicians who opposed Hayes's plan of ending patronage (page 493)

Pendleton Act a law which set up a system for filling government jobs based on passing an examination (page 493)

rebates partial refunds (page 495)

Interstate Commerce Commission a commission created to regulate interstate trade (page 496)

Section Quiz 16–1

Name _____ Date _____ Class _____

★ **Chapter 16**   Score

Section Quiz 16–1

DIRECTIONS: Matching Match each item in Column A with the items in Column B. Write the correct letters in the blanks. *(10 points each)*

Column A	Column B
___ 1. partial refunds	**A.** Mugwumps
___ 2. when government jobs go to supporters of the winning party in an election	**B.** patronage
___ 3. law that reformed civil service	**C.** Sherman Antitrust Act
___ 4. renegade reformers who thought of themselves as moral leaders, more concerned with helping the nation than a political party	**D.** rebates
___ 5. declared illegal any, "combination in the form of trust . . . or conspiracy, in restraint of trade or commerce among the several States"	**E.** Pendleton Act

---

Picturing **History**

Answer: government corruption and character of the candidates

Ask: What were the moral issues facing each of the candidates? *(Blaine had been implicated in the Crédit Mobilier scandal, and Cleveland, who was not married, had fathered a child.)*

✓ Reading Check

Answer: It had to rely on the courts to enforce its rulings.

Picturing **History**

Changing of the Guard Grover Cleveland delivers his inaugural speech in March 1885. His predecessor, Chester Arthur, is seen at left. What were the major issues of this election?

Both parties believed that government should not interfere with corporations' property rights, which courts had held to be the same as those of individuals. Many states had recently passed laws regulating railroad freight rates. In 1886, however, the Supreme Court ruled in the case of *Wabash* v. *Illinois* that the state of Illinois could not restrict the rates that the Wabash Railroad charged for traffic between states because only the federal government could regulate interstate commerce. 📖 *(See page 1083 for a summary of* Wabash v. Illinois.*)*

Public pressure forced Congress to respond to the *Wabash* ruling. In 1887 Cleveland signed a bill creating the **Interstate Commerce Commission** (ICC), the first federal law designed to regulate interstate commerce. The legislation limited railroad rates to what was "reasonable and just," forbade rebates to high-volume users, and made it illegal to charge higher rates for shorter hauls. The commission was not very effective in regulating the industry, however, because it had to rely on the courts to enforce its rulings.

Debating Tariffs Another important economic issue concerned tariffs. Although tariffs had been lowered slightly in the 1870s, they were still much higher than in the years before the Civil War. Many Democrats thought that Congress should cut tariffs

because these taxes had the effect of raising the prices of manufactured goods. While protecting weak domestic manufacturing after the Civil War may have made sense, many questioned the necessity of maintaining high tariffs in the 1880s, when large American companies were fully capable of competing internationally. High tariffs also forced other nations to respond in kind, making it difficult for farmers to export their surpluses.

In December 1887, President Cleveland proposed lowering tariffs. The House, with a Democratic majority, passed moderate tariff reductions, but the Republican-controlled Senate rejected the bill. With Congress deadlocked, tariff reduction became a major issue in the election of 1888.

✓ **Reading Check   Examining** Why was the Interstate Commerce Commission unable to carry out its goals effectively?

Republicans Regain Power

The Republicans and their presidential candidate, Benjamin Harrison, received large contributions for the 1888 campaign from industrialists who benefited from tariff protection. Cleveland and the Democrats campaigned against unnecessarily high tariff rates. In one of the closest races in American history,

496   CHAPTER 16   Politics and Reform

CRITICAL THINKING ACTIVITY

Drawing Conclusions Have interested students research the nation's budget surpluses and deficits since 1860. Based on the information, create a line graph showing the changing trends. At each point where the trend shows a change of direction, identify the events that might have brought about these changes. Have students write a paragraph stating how political leaders have contributed to surpluses and deficits and whether their decisions helped or hurt the country. **L3**

Harrison lost the popular vote but won the electoral vote with narrow victories in New York and Indiana.

The McKinley Tariff The election of 1888 gave the Republicans control of both houses of Congress as well as the White House. Using this power, the party passed legislation to address points of national concern. One major piece of legislation was McKinley's tariff bill. Representative William McKinley of Ohio pushed through a compromise tariff bill that cut rates on such items as raw sugar but raised rates on others, such as textiles, to such high levels that people stopped buying those imports.

The **McKinley Tariff** lowered federal revenue and transformed the nation's budget surplus into a budget deficit. In 1890, furthermore, Congress passed a new pension law increasing payments to veterans and the number of veterans eligible to receive them. While securing more votes for the Republicans, the new pension plan greatly worsened the federal deficit.

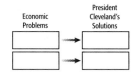

Harrison paper lantern

The Sherman Antitrust Act The Republican-controlled Congress also responded to popular pressure to do something about the power of trusts, large combinations of companies that dominated certain markets. Senator John Sherman of Ohio introduced the **Sherman Antitrust Act** of 1890, which declared illegal any "combination in the form of trust . . . or conspiracy, in restraint of trade or commerce among the several States." The courts were responsible for enforcement, however, and judges saw nothing in this vaguely worded legislation that required them to make big companies change the way they did business. In 1895, for example, the Supreme Court agreed that the American Sugar Refining Company was a trust, enjoying a nearly complete monopoly of sugar manufacturing. Nevertheless, the Court ruled that the company's actions did not violate the Sherman Antitrust Act because manufacturing was not interstate commerce. In the years following passage of the act, businesses formed trusts and combinations at a great rate. In 1899 alone there were over 1,200 recorded mergers in manufacturing and mining firms. Like the ICC, the Sherman Antitrust Act was more important for establishing a precedent than for its immediate impact.

As the midterm congressional election of 1890 approached, some Americans concluded that the two-party system was incapable of solving the nation's problems. That conviction was strongest among farmers, who felt exploited by banks and railroads and neglected by the government. They doubted that either the Democrats or the Republicans would respond to their concerns.

✓ **Reading Check** **Summarizing** What were the results of the McKinley Tariff?

SECTION 1 ASSESSMENT

Checking for Understanding

1. **Define:** patronage, rebate.
2. **Identify:** Stalwart, Halfbreed, Interstate Commerce Commission.
3. **Explain** how the Pendleton Act created civil service reform.
4. **Describe** the events leading to the establishment of the Interstate Commerce Commission.

Reviewing Themes

5. **Continuity and Change** What groups and regions were strongholds for Republicans and Democrats in the 1880s? Where is their support today?

Critical Thinking

6. **Interpreting** Why was the Sherman Antitrust Act ineffective?
7. **Organizing** Use a graphic organizer similar to the one below to list the era's economic problems and President Cleveland's proposed solutions.

Economic Problems		President Cleveland's Solutions
	→	
	→	

Analyzing Visuals

8. **Examining Photographs** Study the photograph on page 496. What similarities do you see between Cleveland's inauguration ceremony and the ones we have today? Do you see any differences between the ceremonies then and now?

Writing About History

9. **Persuasive Writing** Imagine that you are seeking a federal job in the early 1880s. Write a letter to your congressional representatives urging them to support or oppose the Pendleton Act.

The Interstate Commerce Commission no longer exists. It was terminated in 1995.

Reteach
Have students explain why the Republicans and Democrats were so evenly matched during this period.

Enrich
Have students research and report on how the Sherman Antitrust Act was used in the case to try to break up Microsoft.

✓ **Reading Check**
Answer: lowered federal revenue and transformed the nation's budget surplus into a budget deficit

4 CLOSE

Have students cite the economic problems of the period and the basic viewpoints of each political party.

SECTION 1 ASSESSMENT ANSWERS

1. Terms are in blue.
2. Stalwart *(p. 493)*, Halfbreed *(p. 493)*, Interstate Commerce Commission *(p. 496)*
3. certain federal jobs filled according to newly created Civil Service Commission rules
4. worker and consumer unrest, fear of powerful corporations and industry, anger at railroads
5. Republicans: big business, Great Plains farmers, Protestants; Midwest, South, rural areas; Democrats: Catholics and immigrants, urban areas
6. The enforcing courts judged the legislation language too vague to rule against big companies.
7. Problems: price gouging, high tariffs, trusts; Solutions: ICC, McKinley Tariff, Sherman Antitrust Act
8. similar setup; differences: clothing; more women today
9. Students' letters will vary.

TEACH

Urban Poverty

Ask students the following questions after they have read the excerpt of the exposé by Jacob Riis.

- **What problems does Riis cite in this excerpt?** (*overcrowding, filth, poor water system, and all-night parties*)

- **How does Riis view the landlords of the building?** (*They are profiting at the expense of the tenants.*)

- **What problems may children encounter in such crowded conditions?** (*possible answers: sicknesses, lack of attention, a poor night's sleep, poor nutrition*)

Livin' in the City

Have students review the family budget, identifying items that would not be included today or are not necessary today. Then tell students to assume that they are married and have two children. Both spouses work, and their combined annual salary is $48,000. Have students work in pairs to prepare a balanced budget that includes some savings. After reviewing their budgets with another pair of students, they may make any necessary adjustments. As a class, discuss why living on a budget is wise.

Visit the TIME Web site at www.time.com for up-to-date news, weekly magazine articles, editorials, online polls, and an archive of past magazine and Web articles.

Eyewitness

BROWN BROTHERS

In his exposé of urban poverty, How the Other Half Lives *(1890),* **JACOB RIIS** *documented the living conditions in New York City tenements:*

"The statement once made a sensation that between seventy and eighty children had been found in one tenement. It no longer excites even passing attention, when the sanitary police report counting 101 adults and 91 children in a Crosby Street house, one of twins, built together. The children in the others, if I am not mistaken, numbered 89, a total of 180 for two tenements! Or when midnight inspection in Mulberry Street unearths a hundred and fifty "lodgers" sleeping on filthy floors in two buildings. In spite of brown-stone fittings, plate-glass and mosaic vestibule floors, the water does not rise in summer to the second story, while the beer flows unchecked to the all-night picnics on the roof. The saloon with the side-door and the landlord divide the prosperity of the place between them, and the tenant, in sullen submission, foots the bill."

VERBATIM

❝Tell 'em quick, and tell 'em often.❞

WILLIAM WRIGLEY,
soap salesman and promoter of chewing gum,
on his marketing philosophy

❝A pushing, energetic, ingenious person, always awake and trying to get ahead of his neighbors.❞

HENRY ADAMS,
historian, describing the average New Yorker or Chicagoan

❝We cannot all live in cities, yet nearly all seem determined to do so.❞

HORACE GREELEY,
newspaper editor

INDICATORS:
Livin' in the City

Moving off the farm for a factory job? Sharpen your pencil. You'll need to budget carefully to buy all you will need.

Here are the numbers for a Georgia family of four in 1890. The husband is a textile worker, and the wife works at home. There is one child, age 4, and a boarder. They share a two-room, wood-heated, oil-lighted apartment.

INCOME: (annual)

husband's income	$312.00
boarder's rent	.10.00
TOTAL INCOME	**$322.00**

EXPENSES: (annual)

medical	$65.00
furniture	.46.90
clothing	.46.00
rent	.21.00
flour/meal	.25.00
hog products	.17.00
other meat	.13.00
vegetables	.13.00
lard	.6.50
potatoes	.6.40
butter	.5.00
sugar	.4.00
charitable donations	.6.10
vacation	.3.25
alcohol	.3.25
tobacco	.3.00
molasses	.2.00
other food	.27.80
miscellaneous	.68.20
TOTAL EXPENSES	**$382.40**

COOPERATIVE LEARNING ACTIVITY

Creating a Magazine Spread   Organize the class into four groups. Have each group identify a current social problem and write an exposé-style essay for a magazine. Groups should research the problem and use facts in the essay. Then have groups create a magazine spread for the article. Students should look at magazines for ideas about page design and photo placement. This activity can be completed using desktop publishing software or the cut-and-paste method.

Use the rubric for a cooperative group management plan on pages 81–82 in the **Performance Assessment Activities and Rubrics.**

Milestones

ON THE RUN, 1881. THE JESSE JAMES GANG, after robbing a Chicago, Rock Island, and Pacific train near Winston, Missouri, and killing the conductor and a passenger.

OVERTURNED, 1878. By the Supreme Court, a Louisiana court decision that awarded damages to an African American woman who had been refused admission to a steamship stateroom reserved for whites.

PLAGUED BY GRASSHOPPERS, 1874. THE AMERICAN GREAT PLAINS. Insect swarms a mile wide blot out the midday sun. Two inches deep on the ground, they leave "nothing but the mortgage," as one farmer put it.

CELEBRATED IN EUROPE, 1887. ANNIE OAKLEY, star of Buffalo Bill's Wild West Show. Oakley shot a cigarette from the lips of Crown Prince Wilhelm of Germany. Years later, when the U.S. goes to war against Kaiser Wilhelm, Oakley will quip: "I wish I'd missed that day!"

Jesse James

Susan B. Anthony

REMOVED, 1884. IDA B. WELLS, journalist and former slave, from a ladies coach on a train. Wells refused to move to the smoking car where African Americans were to be seated.

ESTABLISHED, 1883. STANDARD TIME. To accommodate the railroad system, noon will no longer be the moment in a given locality when the sun stands highest in the sky but, instead, will be standard across four time zones. Set your watches!

ARRESTED, 1872. SUSAN B. ANTHONY, for casting a ballot in Rochester, New York. Anthony argued that the Fourteenth and Fifteenth Amendments applied to women.

NUMBERS

1 in 12 Americans living in cities of 100,000 or more in 1865

A crowded New York City street

1 in 5 Americans living in cities in 1896

522 Inhabitants in a one-acre area in the Bowery, New York City

$2 Daily wage for a farm laborer, New York, 1869

$4 Daily wage for a plumber, New York City, 1869

50¢ Price of a pair of boy's knee pants, a parasol, button boots, or a necktie (1870s)

$8 Price of a "Fine All-Wool Suit," 1875

$3 Box seat for four at Gilmore's Concert Garden in New York City

4¢ Price for one pound of fancy white rice, 1896

25¢ Admission to "Barnum's American Museum" (featuring the smallest pair of human beings ever seen!), 1896

Portfolio Writing Project

Have students research one of the people or events listed in the Milestones. Have students write a descriptive essay about the person or event.

Using a Database Tell students to research interesting numbers from life today. They may include information on urban population, minimum wage, average wage rates or salaries for various jobs, prices of common goods and services, and prices of admission to various forms of entertainment. Have students organize the information into a database. Then have students create five questions that can be answered from the database. Have them trade databases and questions with another student and answer each other's questions.

CLOSE

As a class, discuss whether the quotes in the Verbatim section on page 498 are still valid today.

EXTENDING THE CONTENT

Urban Pollution In New York City in 1866, a report on sanitary conditions in the city listed the following problems: (1) filthy streets; (2) neglected garbage and domestic refuse; (3) obstructed and faulty sewers and drains; (4) neglected privies and stables; (5) cattle pens and large stables in the more populous districts; (6) neglected and filthy markets; (7) slaughterhouses and hide and fat depots in close proximity to populous streets; (8) droves of cattle and swine in crowded streets; (9) swill-milk stables; (10) bone boiling, fat melting . . . within the city limits; (11) . . . offensive exhalations . . . in gas manufacture; (12) . . . dumping grounds and manure yards in vicinity of populous streets; (13) . . . management of refuse and junk materials; (14) overcrowding of . . . public conveyances; (15) neglect of dead animals in the streets and gutters of the city.

1 FOCUS

Section Overview

This section focuses on the development of the Populist Party.

BELLRINGER
Skillbuilder Activity

  Project transparency and have students answer the question.

📁 Available as a blackline master.

Daily Focus Skills Transparency 16–2

Guide to Reading

Answers to Graphic:
I. Unrest in Rural America
  A. The Money Supply
  B. Deflation Hurts Farmers
  C. The Grange Takes Action
Students should complete the outline by including all heads in the section.

Preteaching Vocabulary
Have students create a simple symbol, icon, or sketch for each of the Key Terms and Names. Ask students to label each drawing.

SECTION 2 Populism

Guide to Reading

Main Idea
In the 1890s an independent political movement called populism emerged to challenge the two major parties.

Key Terms and Names
populism, greenback, inflation, deflation, Grange, cooperative, People's Party, graduated income tax, goldbug, silverite, William Jennings Bryan

Reading Strategy
Taking Notes As you read about the emergence of populism in the 1890s, use the major headings of the section to create an outline similar to the one below.

Populism
I. Unrest in Rural America
  A.
  B.
II.
  A.
  B.

Reading Objectives
• **Explain** why farmers wanted a greenback currency and why the adoption of the gold standard led to the Farmers' Alliance.
• **Describe** who joined the Populist Party and what the party's goals were.

Section Theme
Economic Factors Currency and credit problems led to the rise of the Populist movement.

Preview of Events

♦1865	♦1875	♦1885	♦1895

1867
Grange founded to aid farmers

1873
Congress adopts a gold standard for currency

1877
Farmers' Alliance founded in Texas

1890
People's Party formed in Kansas

1892
National People's Party formed

★ An American Story ★

Populist farmers gather in Dickinson County, Kansas

On July 4, 1890, Leonidas L. Polk took a political gamble. He stepped up to make a speech to a crowd of 6,000 in a small town in Kansas. Polk was a Southerner, a lifelong Democrat, and a former Confederate soldier. He was not in friendly territory.

Polk had come to Kansas because he was now involved in a different kind of battle, one that cut across the lines dividing Northerners from Southerners and Democrats from Republicans. He was calling on farmers from both parties and both regions to unite for their common good. Polk urged the crowd to reject the two-party system and join the emerging movement that became known as populism:

❝I tell you this afternoon that from New York to the Golden Gate, the farmers have risen up and have inaugurated a movement such as the world has never seen. It is a revolution of thought. . . . The farmer of North Carolina, Georgia, Texas, South Carolina is your brother. . . . Some people have stirred up sectional feelings and have kept us apart for twenty-five years. . . . They know that if we get together and shake hands . . . their doom is sealed. . . . Congress could give us a bill in forty-eight hours that would relieve us, but Wall Street says nay. . . . I believe that both of the parties are afraid of Wall Street.❞

—quoted in *Democratic Promise: The Populist Movement in America*

Unrest in Rural America

Populism was the movement to increase farmers' political power and to work for legislation in their interest. The economic crisis that drove farmers to embrace this movement had its origins in the years immediately following the Civil War. A major

500 CHAPTER 16 Politics and Reform

SECTION RESOURCES

📁 Reproducible Masters
• Reproducible Lesson Plan 16–2
• Daily Lecture and Discussion Notes 16–2
• Guided Reading Activity 16–2
• Section Quiz 16–2
• Reading Essentials and Study Guide 16–2

📖 Transparencies
• Daily Focus Skills Transparency 16–2

Multimedia
• Interactive Tutor Self-Assessment CD-ROM
• ExamView® Pro Testmaker CD-ROM
• Presentation Plus! CD-ROM
• TeacherWorks™ CD-ROM
• Audio Program
• American Music: Cultural Traditions

problem was that farm prices had dropped due to new technology. Farmers were producing more crops, and greater supply tended to lower prices. At the same time, high tariffs increased the cost of manufactured goods farmers needed and made it harder for farmers to sell their goods overseas. Farmers also felt they were victimized by large and faraway entities: the banks from which they obtained loans and the railroads that set their shipping rates. The world that farmers now dealt with was more and more one of big business, and they felt they were losing power and influence.

The Money Supply One specific problem that greatly concerned farmers was the nation's money supply. To help finance the Union war effort, the United States Treasury had greatly expanded the money supply by issuing millions of dollars in greenbacks—paper currency that could not be exchanged for gold or silver coins. This rapid increase in the money supply without an accompanying increase in goods for sale caused inflation, or a decline in the value of money. As the paper money lost value, the prices of goods soared.

After the Civil War ended, the United States had three types of currency in circulation—greenbacks, gold and silver coins, and national bank notes, such as government bonds. To get inflation under control,

the federal government stopped printing greenbacks and began paying off its bonds. In 1873 Congress also decided to stop making silver into coins.

These decisions meant that the United States did not have a large enough money supply to meet the needs of the country's growing economy. In 1865, for example, there was about $30 in circulation for each American, but by 1895 it had sunk to about $23. As the economy expanded, deflation—or an increase in the value of money and a decrease in the general level of prices—began. As money increased in value, prices began to fall.

Deflation Hurts Farmers Deflation hit farmers especially hard. Most farmers had to borrow money for seed and other supplies to plant their crops. Because money was in short supply, interest rates began to rise, which increased the amount farmers owed. For those who wanted to expand their farms, rising interest rates also made mortgages more expensive. The falling prices of the period of deflation meant the farmers sold their crops for less. Nevertheless, they still had to make the same mortgage payments to the banks.

Realizing that their problems were due to a shortage of currency, many farmers concluded that Eastern bankers had pressured Congress into reducing the money supply. Some farmers called for the

Picturing **History**

Populist Territory This farm family in Nebraska represents the kind of people who typically supported populism. Why did farmers dislike Eastern bankers?

2 TEACH

Daily Lecture and Discussion Notes 16–2

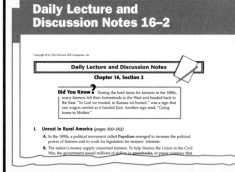

Copyright © by The McGraw-Hill Companies, Inc.

Daily Lecture and Discussion Notes

Chapter 16, Section 2

Did You Know? During the hard times for farmers in the 1880s, many farmers left their homesteads in the West and headed back to the East. "In God we trusted, in Kansas we busted," was a sign that one wagon carried as it headed East. Another sign read, "Going home to Mother."

I. **Unrest in Rural America** (pages 500–502)

A. In the 1890s, a political movement called **Populism** emerged to increase the political power of farmers and to work for legislation for farmers' interests.

B. The nation's money supply concerned farmers. To help finance the Union in the Civil War, the government issued millions of dollars in **greenbacks**, or paper currency that

Picturing **History**

Answer: Farmers thought that their problems were due to a shortage of currency and that Eastern bankers had pressured Congress into reducing the money supply.

Ask: What do you think it would be like to spend a winter in this type of dwelling? *(It would be cold and damp.)*

Drawing a Diagram Have students draw an inflation and deflation diagram. The diagram should show how the supply of money and goods and services changes under each condition, and how farmers were affected by deflation. You may want to consult the economics teacher to help review these concepts with students. **L1** ELL

COOPERATIVE LEARNING ACTIVITY

Brainstorming Organize students into groups of four or five. Give each group the topic of the Grange, the Farmers' Alliance, or the Populist Party. Using one piece of paper per group, have each student write a statement about the history of their topic during the late 1800s. Have them pass the paper around several times until they have written down all they know about their topic. Then have students review the statements and add any information that is missing. Have each group share their statements with the class.

Use the rubric for a cooperative group management plan on pages 81–82 in the *Performance Assessment Activities and Rubrics.*

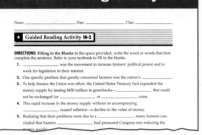

FYI

Farmers in 37 states belong to the Grange today. The organization still pursues its original goals of providing educational and social support to farmers and their families.

you don't say...

Rural Lingo Grange comes from the Middle Latin word *granica*, which is from the Latin *granum*, or "grain." At one time the grange was the farm of a monastery, where grain was stored.

CURRICULUM CONNECTION

Economics To quiet demands for a larger money supply, the government passed the Bland-Allison Act of 1878. The act authorized the U.S. Treasury to purchase silver and issue silver certificates for the first time. Silver certificates could be exchanged for silver dollars. The Treasury continued to exchange silver certificates for silver dollars until 1964. Silver certificates remain a legal form of currency in the United States.

---

printing of more greenbacks to expand the money supply. Others, particularly those living in the West where new silver mines had been found, wanted the government to begin minting silver coins. They referred to the decision to stop minting silver as **"The Crime of '73."** Increasingly, farmers realized that if they were going to convince the government to meet their demands, they needed to organize.

The Grange Takes Action In 1866 the United States Department of Agriculture sent Oliver H. Kelley to tour the rural South and report on the condition of the region's farmers. Realizing how isolated the farmers were from each other, the following year, Kelley founded the nation's first national farm organization, the Patrons of Husbandry, better known as the **Grange.**

At first Grangers got together largely for social and educational purposes. Then, in 1873, the nation plunged into a severe recession, and farm income fell sharply. Farmers looking for help joined the Grange in large numbers. By 1874 the Grange had between 800,000 and 1.5 million members.

Grangers responded to the crisis in three ways. Some pressured state legislatures to regulate railroad and warehouse rates, which they believed were too high. Others joined the Independent National Party. This new political party, nicknamed the Greenback Party, wanted the government to print more greenbacks to increase the money supply. Grangers also pooled their resources and tried to create cooperatives—marketing organizations that worked for the benefit of their members.

One of the reasons farmers could not charge higher prices for their crops was that there were so many farmers in competition. If a farmer raised prices, a buyer could always go elsewhere and pay

Farmers' Alliance This small band of farmers met in a cabin in Lampasas County, Texas, to form the Farmers' Alliance.

less. Cooperatives pooled farmers' crops and held them off the market in order to force up prices. Because a cooperative controlled a large quantity of farm products, it could also negotiate better shipping rates with the railroads.

The Grange Fails None of the strategies the Grangers employed improved farmers' economic condition. Several western states passed "Granger laws" setting maximum rates and prohibiting railroads from charging more for short hauls than for long ones. The railroads fought back by cutting services and refusing to lay new track until the laws were repealed. The 1886 Supreme Court ruling in *Wabash v. Illinois* then greatly limited the states' ability to regulate railroads by ruling that states could not regulate commerce that crossed state lines. 📖 *(See pages 496 and 1083 for more information on* Wabash v. Illinois.*)*

Meanwhile the Greenback Party failed to gain much public support. Many Americans were very suspicious of paper money. They did not believe it would hold its value, and they considered the Greenback Party's proposal to print more paper money dangerous for the economy. The Grange's cooperatives also failed, partly because they were too small to have any effect on prices, and partly because Eastern businesses and railroads considered them to be similar to unions—illegitimate conspiracies in restraint of trade—and refused to do business with them. By the late 1870s, membership in the Grange had begun to fall, as farmers moved to other organizations that they hoped would better address their problems.

The Farmers' Alliance

Even as the Grange began to fall apart, a new organization, known as the **Farmers' Alliance,** began to form. The Farmers' Alliance began in Lampasas County, Texas, in 1877. By 1885 it had built a substantial following throughout the state. The following year, Charles W. Macune became the leader of the Alliance. Macune called for the organization to begin recruiting farmers outside of Texas.

The Alliance Grows During the late 1880s, Alliance members traveled across the South and West speaking to farmers and organizing local chapters. By 1890 the Alliance had between 1.5 and 3 million members. Its support was very strong in the South and on the Great Plains, particularly in Kansas, Nebraska, and North and South Dakota.

When Macune became the leader of the Alliance, he also announced a plan to organize very large cooperatives that the Alliance called exchanges.

MEETING SPECIAL NEEDS

Verbal/Linguistic Farm families of the late 1800s bought many things through mail-order catalogs. Have pairs of students find reproductions of Sears or Montgomery Ward catalogs of the late 1800s and choose two sections for study. Have them list the types of goods sold in the sections, comparing them with current catalogs on types of items and price. Then ask students to compare the needs of families of the late 1800s with the needs of families today. **L2**

📁 Refer to *Inclusion for the High School Social Studies Classroom Strategies and Activities* in the TCR.

Picturing **History**

Hard Labor Southern farmers spent long hours working in their fields. Harvesting cotton (left) and husking corn (right) were family activities that were done by hand with no expensive mechanical equipment. What do you notice about the ages of the group husking corn?

Macune hoped these exchanges would be big enough to force farm prices up and to make loans to farmers at low interest rates. The exchanges had some success. The Texas Exchange successfully marketed cotton at prices slightly higher than those paid to individual farmers, while the Illinois Exchange negotiated slightly better railroad rates for wheat farmers.

The People's Party Despite their temporary success, the large cooperatives failed for several reasons. Many overextended themselves by loaning too much money at low interest rates that was never repaid. In many cases, wholesalers, manufacturers, railroads, and bankers discriminated against them, making it difficult for them to stay in business. The exchanges also failed because they still were too small to dramatically affect world prices for farm products.

By 1890 the failure of the Alliance to fix farmers' problems had started a power struggle within the organization. Some Alliance leaders, particularly in the Western states, wanted to form a new party and push for political reforms. Members of the Kansas Alliance formed the **People's Party,** also known as the Populists, and nominated candidates to run for Congress and the state legislature. Alliances in Nebraska, South Dakota, and Minnesota quickly followed Kansas's example.

The Subtreasury Plan Most Southern leaders of the Alliance, including Charles Macune, opposed the idea of a third party. They did not want to undermine the Democrats' control of the South. Instead, Macune suggested that the Alliance produce a list of demands and promise to vote for candidates who supported those demands. He hoped this strategy would force the Democrats to adopt the Alliance program.

As part of this strategy, Macune introduced the subtreasury plan, which called for the government to set up warehouses called subtreasuries. Farmers would store the crops in the warehouses, and the government would provide low-interest loans to the farmers. Macune believed that the plan would allow farmers to hold their crops off the market in large enough quantities to force prices up. He hoped that the Democrats would adopt the subtreasury plan and thereby win farmers' votes.

✓**Reading Check** **Explaining** How did the Farmers' Alliance try to help farmers?

The Rise of Populism

In 1890 members of the Farmers' Alliance met in Ocala, Florida, and issued what came to be known as the Ocala Demands. These demands were intended

CHAPTER 16 Politics and Reform **503**

IN HISTORY

Background: Mary Ellen Lease supported the popular election of senators, setting up postal savings banks, government control of the railroads, and federal supervision of corporations. She also spoke for woman suffrage and temperance.

Ask: What do you think critics of Mary Ellen Lease thought she should be doing rather than speaking for the People's Party? *(Some students might say that critics wanted her to behave like most other women.)*

Creating a Time Line Have students learn more about the nation's changing money supply. Have students create a time line from 1789 to the present that records significant events relating to the money supply, including the use of greenbacks and silver certificates, the use of the gold standard, and so on. **L3**

History *and the* Humanities

🏳️ American Music: Cultural Traditions: "The Farmer Is the Man That Feeds Them All"

---

to guide farmers in choosing whom to vote for in 1890. The demands called for the adoption of the sub-treasury plan, the free coinage of silver, an end to protective tariffs and national banks, tighter regulation of the railroads, and direct election of senators by voters instead of by state legislatures.

To prevent farmers from voting for Populists, the Republicans in Congress, led by Senator John Sherman, pushed through the **Sherman Silver Purchase Act of 1890.** This act authorized the United States Treasury to purchase 4.5 million ounces of silver per month. It put more money into circulation and may have reduced the deflation slightly, but it did little to help the farmers.

The midterm elections of 1890 seemed to suggest that both the Southern and Western strategies had worked for the farmers. In the South, four governors, all Democrats, were elected after promising to support the Alliance program. Several Southern legislatures now had pro-Alliance majorities, and over 40 Democrats who supported the Alliance program were elected to Congress. Meanwhile, the new People's Party did equally well in the West. Populists took control of the Kansas and Nebraska legislatures. Populists also held the balance of power in Minnesota and South Dakota. Eight Populists were elected to the U.S. House of Representatives and two to the Senate.

The South Turns to Populism At first Southern members were excited over their success in electing so many pro-Alliance Democrats to Congress and Southern state legislatures, but over the next two years, their excitement turned into frustration.

Despite their promises, few Democrats followed through by supporting the Alliance program, either at the state or the federal level.

In May 1891, Western populists met with some labor and reform groups in Cincinnati. The meeting endorsed the creation of a new national People's Party to run candidates for president. Only a few Southerners attended the convention. By the following year, however, it had become obvious to many Southern members of the Alliance that the Democrats were not going to keep their promises to the Alliance. By early 1892 many Southern farmers had reached the point where they were willing to break with the Democratic Party and join the People's Party.

A Populist for President In July 1892, the People's Party held its first national convention in Omaha, Nebraska. There, members officially organized their party and nominated **James B. Weaver** to run for president. Weaver was a former Union Army General who had run for president before as the candidate of the Greenback Party. The Omaha convention also endorsed a platform, or program, that spelled out the party's positions in strong terms. First of all, the Omaha platform denounced the government's refusal to coin silver as a "vast conspiracy against mankind." To increase the money supply, it called for a return to unlimited coinage of silver at a ratio that gave 16 ounces of silver the same value as 1 ounce of gold. Other platform planks called for federal ownership of railroads and a graduated income tax, one that taxed higher earnings more heavily.

Above all, the Populists wanted to strengthen the hand of government so that it could defend the public against what they saw as greedy and irresponsible private interests. "We believe that the powers of government—in other words, of the people—should be expanded," the platform stated, "as rapidly and as far as the good sense of an intelligent people and the teachings of experience shall justify."

Although the Populists also adopted proposals designed to appeal to organized labor, workers found it hard to identify with the rural Populists. The Populists did have close ties to the Knights of Labor, but that organization was in decline, while the fast-growing American Federation of Labor steered clear of an alliance with them. The Omaha

---

Profiles IN HISTORY

Mary Ellen Lease
1853–1933

Mary Ellen Lease, a former school-teacher and daughter of an Irish political refugee, earned a law degree while raising four children on the Kansas frontier. She was one of the most passionate speakers for the People's Party in Kansas during the 1890 election campaign. Political opponents nicknamed her "Mary Yellin" and criticized the tall and forceful Lease for acting in an "unfeminine" manner by speaking in public.

Lease's blunt style, however, appealed to Kansas farmers. "Wall Street owns the country," she declared. "It is no longer a government of the people, for the people, by the people, but a government of Wall Street, for Wall Street, and by Wall Street." Lease urged farmers to spend less time raising crops and more time campaigning against the banks and railroads.

CRITICAL THINKING ACTIVITY

Detecting Bias On the chalkboard, write the following partial quotation from a Nebraska newspaper.

"There are three great crops raised in Nebraska. One is a crop of corn, one a crop of freight rates, and one a crop of interest. One is produced by farmers, who sweat and toil on the land. The other two are produced by . . . "

Ask students to study the incomplete quotation and suggest how it might be concluded. *(possible answers: railroads and bankers)* Ask if the author of the quotation displays a bias, and if so, what is the bias. *(Yes, the author is biased in favor of farmers.)* **L2**

HARD LIFE ON THE PLAINS

English-born immigrant farmer David Hilton and his family proudly pose beside their pump organ on their home-stead in Nebraska. The organ, their prized possession, had been rescued from the Hiltons' sod-built dugout after the roof collapsed. Farm families on the sparsely-settled, treeless plains had to cope with isolation as well as a variety of natural haz-ards, including dust storms, tornadoes, erratic rainfall, and the occasional plague of destructive insects that could strip entire fields of crops in a matter of hours.

The pump organ works by pushing your foot down on the two foot ped-als, which fills the bellows with air. The ten stops each give a different sound, such as the sound of a violin or bass. This Victorian-style organ was in many households across the United States in the late 1800s.

CURRICULUM CONNECTION

Government The Populist Party had an impact on politics and gov-ernment far beyond its showing in national elections. Minor parties have often served as vehicles for reform by taking clear-cut stands on controversial issues and proposing bold and original solutions. Among the Populist proposals that were adopted and are still in place today are the federal income tax (Sixteenth Amendment, 1913), direct election of U.S. senators (Seventeenth Amendment, 1913), the secret ballot (late 1890s), and primary elections (Wisconsin, 1903).

Bimetallists People who supported using both gold and silver as currency were known as bimetallists.

---

platform took positions popular with labor, includ-ing calling for an eight-hour workday, restricting immigration, and denouncing strikebreaking, but most urban workers still preferred to remain within the Democratic Party.

Democrats retained support in Northern cities by nominating the popular New Yorker, Grover Cleveland, who was seeking to return to the White House after his close defeat in 1888. The South also remained solidly Democratic, despite determined efforts by Populists. When the votes were counted, Cleveland had won a resounding victory in the Electoral College, with 277 votes to 145 for Harrison. The Populist candidate, James Weaver, had done remarkably well, winning five states and splitting another for a total of 22 electoral votes.

The Panic of 1893 Not long after Cleveland's inau-guration in 1893, the nation plunged into the worst economic crisis it had ever experienced. The panic began in March when the Philadelphia and Reading Railroads declared bankruptcy. Many railroads had expanded too rapidly in the period before the panic and now found it hard to repay their loans. The stock

market on Wall Street crashed, and banks closed their doors. By 1894 the economy was deep in a depression. Over 500,000 workers went on strike that year, and between 2 and 3 million more were unemployed, approximately 15 to 20 percent of the workforce.

Goldbugs and Silverites The Panic of 1893 also cre-ated a crisis for the United States Treasury. Many American and European investors owned U.S. govern-ment bonds, but as the economy worsened, they began cashing in their bonds for gold. This caused gold to drain out of the U.S. Treasury and left the federal gov-ernment's gold reserves at a dangerously low level.

Although President Cleveland could not stop the flow of gold to redeem bonds, he could protect the government's reserves in another way. Gold was also being lost every time people exchanged silver for gold under the Sherman Silver Purchase Act. Unlike many Democrats, Cleveland believed the United States should use gold as the basis for its cur-rency, not silver or paper money. In June 1893, he summoned Congress into a special session and pushed through the repeal of the Sherman Silver Purchase Act.

CHAPTER 16 Politics and Reform **505**

EXTENDING THE CONTENT

Thieves on the Campaign Trail During William Jennings Bryan's presidential campaign, he was faithfully followed by a band of pickpockets. To make the point that silver was as widely accepted as gold, Bryan would first ask people who carried gold to raise their hands. He would then ask those who carried silver to do the same. The thieves, unbeknownst to Bryan, worked the packed crowd, relieving both groups of their money.

Picturing History

Background: William Jennings Bryan campaigned for the presidency in 1896, 1900, and 1908. He was unsuccessful all three times.
Answer: McKinley won
Ask: Which candidate's style is the closest to the way modern candidates campaign? *(Bryan's, because of the great distances he traveled seeking to win votes)*

✓ Reading Check

Answer: The Populist candidate, James Weaver, lost the election, but he did win 22 electoral votes.

3 ASSESS

Assign Section 2 Assessment as homework or as an in-class activity.

⊕ Have students use the **Interactive Tutor Self-Assessment CD-ROM.**

Reading Essentials and Study Guide 16–2

Picturing History

Campaigns in Contrast In 1896 Democrat William Jennings Bryan (left) ran an energetic campaign for president, traveling far and wide. Republican William McKinley (right) campaigned from the front porch of his Canton, Ohio, home. How did their campaign styles work out?

Cleveland's actions split the Democratic Party into two factions, nicknamed "goldbugs" and "silverites." The goldbugs believed the American currency should be based only on gold, while silverites believed coining silver in unlimited quantities would solve the nation's economic crisis.

✓ **Reading Check** **Summarizing** What was the main outcome of the Populist campaign in the elections of 1892?

The Election of 1896

As the election of 1896 approached, leaders of the People's Party decided to make the silver issue the focus of their campaign. They also decided to hold their convention after the Republican and Democratic conventions. They believed the Republicans would endorse a gold standard, which they did. They also expected the Democrats to compromise on the silver issue and hoped that when the People's Party strongly endorsed silver, pro-silver Democrats would abandon their party and vote for the Populists in large numbers.

Unfortunately for the Populists, their political strategy failed. The Democrats did not waffle on the silver issue. Instead, they nominated **William Jennings Bryan,** a strong supporter of silver. When the Populists gathered in St. Louis for their own convention, they faced a difficult choice: endorse Bryan and risk undermining their identity as a separate party, or nominate their own candidate and risk splitting the silver vote. They eventually decided to support Bryan.

Bryan's Campaign William Jennings Bryan, a former member of Congress from Nebraska, was only 36 years old when the Democrats and Populists nominated him for president. Bryan had served in Congress for two terms as a representative from Nebraska. He was a powerful speaker, and he won the nomination by delivering an electrifying address in defense of silver, one of the most famous in American political history. He began by telling delegates that he had come to speak "in defense of a cause as holy as the cause of liberty—the cause of humanity." With a few well-chosen words, Bryan transformed the campaign for silver into a crusade:

> 66Having behind us the producing masses of this nation and the world, supported by the commercial interests, the laboring interests and the toilers everywhere, we will answer their demand for a gold standard by saying to them: You shall not press down upon the brow of labor this crown of thorns; you shall not crucify mankind upon a cross of gold.99
>
> —quoted in *America in the Gilded Age*

Bryan waged an unusually energetic campaign for the presidency, traveling thousands of miles and making 600 speeches in 14 weeks. Some found his relentless campaigning undignified, however, and his crusade in favor of silver alienated others. Catholic immigrants and other city-dwellers cared little for the silver issue. They did not like Bryan's speaking style either. It reminded them of rural Protestant preachers, who were sometimes anti-Catholic.

Republicans knew that Bryan would be hard to beat in the South and the West. To regain the White House, they would have to sweep the Northeast and

506 CHAPTER 16 Politics and Reform

COOPERATIVE LEARNING ACTIVITY

Creating Campaign Posters Assign students to work in small groups to make campaign posters for Cleveland, Harrison, and Weaver or for Bryan and McKinley. Tell students that the posters must reflect the beliefs of the candidates and their parties. Have each group choose a member to present the poster to the class. ELL

Use the rubric for a cooperative group management plan on pages 81–82 in the *Performance Assessment Activities and Rubrics.*

the Midwest. They thought that **William McKinley** of Ohio, a former governor and member of Congress, was the candidate who could do it.

The Front Porch Campaign In sharp contrast to the hectic travels of Bryan, McKinley stayed at his home in Canton, Ohio. He conducted what the newspapers called his "Front-Porch Campaign" by meeting with various delegations that came to visit him. Meanwhile, across the Midwest and Northeast, the Republican Party launched an intensive campaign on McKinley's behalf.

The Republicans campaigned against the Democrats by blaming Cleveland's administration for the depression and promising workers that McKinley would provide a "full dinner pail." This meant a lot more to most urban workers than the issue of silver money. At the same time, most business leaders supported the Republicans, convinced that unlimited silver coinage would ruin the country. They donated huge sums of money to the Republican campaign. Many employers warned their workers that if Bryan won, businesses would fail, unemployment would rise, and wages would be cut.

McKinley's reputation for moderation on labor issues and tolerance toward different ethnic groups helped improve the Republican Party's image with urban workers and immigrants. When the votes were counted, McKinley had won a decisive victory. He captured 52 percent of the popular vote and had a winning margin of 95 electoral votes—hefty numbers in an era of tight elections. As expected, Bryan won the South and most of the West, but few of the states he carried had large populations or delivered many electoral votes. By embracing populism and its rural base, Bryan and the Democrats lost the Northern industrial areas where votes were concentrated.

Populism Declines Opposition to the gold-based currency dwindled during McKinley's time in office. The depression was over, and prospectors found gold in Alaska and Canada's Yukon territory in 1899. That wealth, combined with new gold strikes in South Africa and other parts of the world, increased the money supply without turning to silver. This meant that credit was easier to obtain and farmers were less distressed. In 1900 the United States officially adopted a gold-based currency when Congress passed the Gold Standard Act.

When the silver crusade died out, the Populists lost their momentum. Their efforts to ease the economic hardships of farmers and to regulate big business had not worked. Some of the reforms they favored, however, came about in the next century, including the graduated income tax and some governmental regulation of the economy.

✓ **Reading Check** **Evaluating** What were the results of the 1896 presidential election?

SECTION 2 ASSESSMENT

Checking for Understanding

1. **Define:** populism, greenback, inflation, deflation, cooperative, graduated income tax, goldbug, silverite.

2. **Identify:** Grange, People's Party, William Jennings Bryan.

3. **List** the issues that the Democrats endorsed in the 1896 presidential election.

Reviewing Themes

4. **Economic Factors** What economic problems caused farmers to support populism?

Critical Thinking

5. **Analyzing** How did the Farmers' Alliance contribute to the rise of a new political party?

6. **Organizing** Use a graphic organizer similar to the one below to list the factors that contributed to the Panic of 1893 and its effects on the nation.

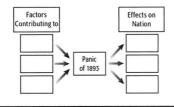

7. **Analyzing Photographs** Examine the photograph of David Hilton and his family on page 505, showing them with an organ they rescued from a collapsed sod house. Why do you think it was so important for them to rescue the organ?

Writing About History

8. **Persuasive Writing** Imagine you support the Populist Party and that you have been asked to write copy to be used in a campaign poster for your party's candidates. Include a slogan that provides reasons for people to support the Populists.

Analyzing Visuals

CHAPTER 16 Politics and Reform **507**

Section Quiz 16–2

Name _____ Date _____ Class _____

★ Chapter 16   Score _____

Section Quiz 16-2

DIRECTIONS: Matching Match each item in Column A with the items in Column B. Write the correct letters in the blanks. *(10 points each)*

Column A

___ 1. how farmers referred to the decision to stop minting silver
___ 2. nation's first national farm organization
___ 3. authorized the United States Treasury to purchase 4.5 million ounces of silver per month
___ 4. marketing organizations that worked for the benefit of their members
___ 5. a movement to increase farmers' political power and to work for legislation in their interest

Column B

A. cooperatives
B. "The Crime of '73"
C. Sherman Silver Purchase Act
D. populism
E. Grange

DIRECTIONS: Multiple Choice In the blank at the left, write the letter of the choice ...

Reteach
Have students explain why the adoption of the gold standard led to the Farmers' Alliance.

Enrich
Have students create a pair of circle graphs showing the results of the presidential election of 1896. One graph should reflect the popular vote, the other the Electoral College vote.

✓ **Reading Check**

Answer: McKinley victory, end of populism

4 CLOSE

Have students describe who joined the Populist Party and what the party's goals were.

SECTION 2 ASSESSMENT ANSWERS

1. Terms are in blue.
2. Grange *(p. 502)*, People's Party *(p. 503)*, William Jennings Bryan *(p. 506)*
3. supported farmers and silver as a monetary base
4. deflation, falling farm prices, high tariffs, high rail shipping rates
5. Some Alliance members wanted to form a new party to get their programs passed.
6. Contributing factors: widespread railroad bankruptcies, stock market crash, bank closures; effects: unemployment rose, strikes, repeal of Sherman Silver Purchase Act
7. They may recognize that the organ was one of the few sources of entertainment for the family.
8. Slogans should have a clear connection to the issues or the candidates.

1 FOCUS

Section Overview

This section focuses on how segregation grew in the late 1800s.

Guide to Reading

Answers to Graphic: poll taxes, literacy tests, Jim Crow laws, doctrine of "separate but equal," Supreme Court decision that overturned the Civil Rights Act of 1875

Preteaching Vocabulary
Have students write a paragraph using at least four of the Key Terms and Names.

Guide to Reading

Main Idea
In the late 1800s, Southern states passed laws that denied African Americans the right to vote and imposed segregation on them.

Key Terms and Names
sharecropper, poll tax, grandfather clause, segregation, Jim Crow laws, lynching, Ida B. Wells, W.E.B. Du Bois

Reading Strategy
Organizing As you read about the South in the 1890s, complete a web diagram like the one below by listing ways that states disfranchised African Americans and legalized discrimination.

Factors Contributing to Discrimination

Reading Objectives
• **Discuss** how African Americans in the South were disfranchised and how segregation was legalized.
• **Describe** three major African American leaders' responses to discrimination.

Section Theme
Individual Action African Americans stood up to fight against discrimination in the United States.

Preview of Events

♦1885	♦1890	♦1895	♦1900

1886
Colored Farmers' National Alliance formed

1887
Florida passes Jim Crow laws

1890
Mississippi introduces voting restrictions

1895
Booker T. Washington proposes Atlanta Compromise

★ An American Story ★

Tom Watson

In the fall of 1892, H.S. Doyle, a young African American preacher, defied Georgia's power structure—dominated by whites and Democrats—by giving more than 60 speeches on behalf of a white Populist, Tom Watson, who was running for Congress.

Doyle took that risk because Watson was doing something almost unbelievable for a Southern politician. He was urging poor whites and blacks to unite against the wealthy white elite. "You are kept apart that you may be separately fleeced of your earnings," Watson told a racially mixed audience at one gathering. "The accident of color can make no difference in the interests of farmers."

Shortly before the election, Doyle himself received a death threat. Watson offered the preacher refuge in his home and alerted supporters in the area. An estimated 2,000 Populists gathered there with guns in hand. The crowd then marched to the local courthouse, where Watson vowed to protect Doyle and other African American Populists. "We are determined in this free country that the humblest white or black man that wants to talk our doctrine shall do it," he declared, "and the man doesn't live who shall touch a hair of his head, without fighting every man in the People's Party."

—**adapted from** *Tom Watson: Agrarian Rebel*

Resistance and Repression

For H.S. Doyle and other African Americans, the violence of the election of 1892 was not something they could shrug off. They could see that some Southern leaders were beginning to devise ways to keep them from voting. In the end, even Watson would betray his African

---

SECTION RESOURCES

📁 Reproducible Masters
• Reproducible Lesson Plan 16–3
• Daily Lecture and Discussion Notes 16–3
• Guided Reading Activity 16–3
• Section Quiz 16–3
• Reading Essentials and Study Guide 16–3
• Performance Assessment Activities and Rubrics
• Supreme Court Case Studies

Transparencies
• Daily Focus Skills Transparency 16–3

Multimedia
🔵 Interactive Tutor Self-Assessment CD-ROM
🔵 ExamView® Pro Testmaker CD-ROM
🔵 Presentation Plus! CD-ROM
🔵 TeacherWorks™ CD-ROM
🔊 Audio Program

American supporters. He became a political boss in Georgia, cast aside his former ideals, and used crude racist rhetoric to appeal to white voters.

After Reconstruction, many African Americans in the rural South lived in conditions that were little better than slavery. They were technically free, but few escaped from grinding poverty. Most were sharecroppers, landless farmers who had to hand over to the landlord a large portion of their crops to cover the cost of rent, seed, tools, and other supplies. They were always in debt. Many eventually left farming and sought jobs in Southern towns or headed west to claim homesteads.

Exodus to Kansas In 1879, 70-year-old Benjamin "Pap" Singleton, himself formerly enslaved, took action to escape the conditions of the rural South. He organized a mass migration of thousands of African Americans from the rural South to Kansas. The newspapers called it "an Exodus," like the Hebrews' escape from Egyptian bondage. The migrants themselves came to be known as **"Exodusters."** One of them later explained why they went: "The whole South—every State in the South—had got into the hands of the very men that held us as slaves." A journalist named Henry King described the scene when the first group reached Kansas:

❝One morning in April, 1879, a Missouri steamboat arrived at Wyandotte, Kansas, and discharged a load of negro men, women and children, with . . . barrels, boxes, and bundles of household effects. . . . [T]heir garments were incredibly patched and tattered . . . and there was not probably a dollar in money in the pockets of the entire party. The wind was eager, and they stood upon the wharf shivering. . . . They looked like persons coming out of a dream. And, indeed, such they were . . . for this was the advance guard of the Exodus.❞

—quoted in *Eyewitness: The Negro in History*

Forming a Separate Alliance While some African Americans fled the South, others joined with poor white farmers who had created the Farmers' Alliance.

Alliance leaders urged African Americans to form a similar organization. In 1886 African American farmers gathered in Texas at the home of a white minister named R.M. Humphrey and formed the Colored Farmers' National Alliance. By 1890 the organization had an estimated 1.2 million members.

The **Colored Farmers' National Alliance** worked to help its members economically by setting up cooperatives. When the Populist Party formed in 1891, many African American farmers joined the new organization. They hoped that the new People's Party would unite poor whites and poor blacks to challenge the Democratic Party's power in the South.

Crushing the Populist Revolt Populism posed a new challenge to the Democratic Party in the South. If enough poor whites left the party and joined with African American Populists, the coalition might become unbeatable.

To win back the poor white vote, Democratic leaders began appealing to racism, warning whites that support for Populists or joint Republican-Populist parties would return the South to "Black Republican" rule similar to Reconstruction. In addition, although many African Americans in the South were still able to vote as of 1890, election officials began using various methods to make it harder and harder for them to do so. As one Democratic leader in the South told a reporter, "Some of our people, some editors especially, deny that [African Americans] are hindered from voting; but what is the good of lying? They are interfered with, and we are obliged to do it, and we may as well tell the truth."

✓ **Reading Check** **Examining** Who were the Exodusters, and why did they migrate to Kansas in 1879?

Picturing **History**

A Kansas Home Many African Americans left the rural South to find a new life. They usually began with very little. Why were they called Exodusters?

---

2 TEACH

Daily Lecture and Discussion Notes 16–3

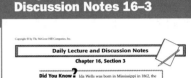

Copyright © The McGraw-Hill Companies, Inc.

Daily Lecture and Discussion Notes
Chapter 16, Section 3

Did You Know? Ida Wells was born in Mississippi in 1862, the daughter of enslaved African Americans. She was educated in a Freedmen's Bureau school. At the young age of fourteen, Wells began to teach in a rural school. In 1884 she moved to Memphis, Tennessee, where she continued teaching as well as attended Fisk University. In 1891 she lost her teaching position because she had refused to give up a seat in a "whites only" railroad car. This led to a profession in journalism in which she began a campaign against lynching.

I. Resistance and Repression *(pages 508–509)*

A. After Reconstruction, most African Americans were **sharecroppers**, or landless farmers

✓ **Reading Check**

Answer: African Americans who migrated from the rural South to Kansas in 1879; to escape discrimination

Picturing **History**

Answer: from the term *Exodus*, referring to the Hebrews' escape from Egypt
Ask: Why did the Exodusters have so little when they arrived in Kansas? *(because they were poor sharecroppers who were in debt)*

Drawing a Sketch Have students draw a sketch to accompany the Henry King quotation that appears on page 381. Then have students give an appropriate title to their drawing. Ask volunteers to display their drawings for the class. **L1** **ELL**

🗀 Use *Supreme Court Case Study 9,* Plessy v. Ferguson.

COOPERATIVE LEARNING ACTIVITY

Making a Presentation Organize the class into groups of four to create presentations on the ways in which African American rights were denied during Reconstruction. Ask groups to create a set of four transparencies, slides, or posters that can be used in sequence to illustrate the following terms: poll tax, literacy test, grandfather clause, Jim Crow laws. Invite groups to make their presentation in front of the class. 🖳

Use the rubric for a cooperative group management plan on pages 81–82 in the ***Performance Assessment Activities and Rubrics.***

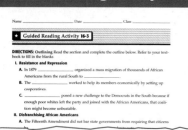

IN HISTORY

Background: Mary Church Terrell was one of the first African American women to earn a college degree. She continued her studies in Europe and became fluent in French, German, and Italian. She opposed segregation and supported woman suffrage. She was one of the founders of the National Association for the Advancement of Colored People (NAACP).

Ask: Would Mary Church Terrell's life have been different if she had chosen to stay in Europe? Why? *(Yes. She would have faced fewer racial barriers.)*

✔ **Reading Check**

Answer: poll taxes and literacy tests

Creating a Display Have students create a display of photographs and drawings that help illustrate the Fourteenth and Fifteenth Amendments. **L1**

 Use the rubric for creating a map, display, or chart on pages 77–78 in the *Performance Assessment Activities and Rubrics.*

Disfranchising African Americans

The Fifteenth Amendment prohibited states from denying citizens the right to vote on the basis of "race, color, or previous condition of servitude." However, it did not bar the governments from requiring that citizens be literate or own property in order to vote. Using this loophole, Southern states began imposing restrictions that barred nearly all African Americans from voting, even though the restrictions seemed on the surface to apply to both races.

Mississippi took this step first in 1890 by requiring that all citizens registering to vote pay a poll tax of $2, a sum beyond the means of most poor African Americans. Mississippi also instituted a literacy test, requiring that prospective voters be able to read or understand the state constitution. More than half of all African Americans who came of age in the South after the Civil War had no school to attend, and those who had grown up under slavery were largely illiterate. Even those who knew how to read often failed the literacy test because local officials deliberately picked complicated passages that few could understand.

Other Southern states later adopted similar restrictions, and the results were devastating. In Louisiana the number of African Americans registered to vote fell from about 130,000 in 1890 to around 5,300 in 1900. In Alabama the number fell from about 181,000 to around 3,700.

Election officials were far less strict in applying the poll tax and literacy requirements to whites, but the number of white voters also fell significantly. Local Democratic Party leaders were not sorry to see poor whites barred from voting, because they had helped fuel the Populist revolt. Some states gave whites a special break, however, by including a so-called grandfather clause in the restrictions. The grandfather clause in Louisiana allowed any man to vote if he had an ancestor on the voting rolls in 1867. The clause made almost all formerly enslaved Louisiana citizens ineligible to vote.

✔ **Reading Check** **Identifying** How did Southern states restrict African American voting in the 1890s?

Profiles **IN HISTORY**

Mary Church Terrell
1863–1954

Few African American women who grew up in the late 1800s had as many advantages in life as Mary Church Terrell. Her father, the son of a wealthy white man and an enslaved woman, had invested shrewdly in real estate in the South after the Civil War and became one of the nation's first African American millionaires. He spared no expense for his daughter's education. After she graduated from Oberlin College in 1884, he sent her to Europe to travel and study.

She could easily have remained in Europe where there were fewer racial barriers to overcome than in the United States, but Terrell chose to return home, she said, "to promote the welfare of my race." She taught at an African American high school in Washington, D.C., and in 1896 became the first president of the National Association of Colored Women. The organization offered day care and other services to the many African American women who worked to support their families while raising children.

Terrell continued to promote the welfare of African Americans until the last years of her life. In 1950, at the age of 86, she demanded service at a segregated restaurant in Washington, D.C. When the owner refused, she filed a lawsuit and won a ruling in the Supreme Court that desegregated restaurants in the nation's capital.

Legalizing Segregation

Discrimination in the late 1800s was not confined to the South. African Americans in the North had often been barred from many public places used by whites. In the South, segregation, or separation of the races, was different because laws enforced and perpetuated the discrimination. The statutes enforcing segregation were known as Jim Crow laws. The term probably came from the name of a character popularized by a slavery-era blackface minstrel—a white musical stage performer who darkened his face with makeup and crudely imitated supposed African American behavior.

In 1883 the Supreme Court set the stage for legalized segregation by overturning the Civil Rights Act of 1875. That law had prohibited keeping people out of public places on the basis of race, and it also prohibited racial discrimination in selecting jurors. White authorities

Segregation sign from the turn of the century

challenged the law in both the North and the South. The 1883 Supreme Court decision, however, said that the Fourteenth Amendment only provided that "no state" could deny citizens equal protection under the law. Thus, only state actions were subject to challenge. Private organizations and businesses, such as hotels, theaters, and railroads, were free to practice segregation.

Encouraged by the Supreme Court's ruling and by the decline of congressional support for civil rights, Southern states passed a series of laws that enforced segregation in virtually all public places. Southern whites and African Americans could no longer ride together in the same railroad cars, eat in the same dining halls, or even drink from the same water fountains. Restrooms, hotels, and swimming pools were all segregated.

In 1892 an African American named Homer Plessy challenged a Louisiana law that forced him to ride in a separate railroad car from whites. He was arrested for riding in a "whites-only" car and brought to trial before criminal court judge John H. Ferguson. Ferguson rejected Plessy's argument that the law was unconstitutional. In 1896 the Supreme Court, in *Plessy* v. *Ferguson,* upheld the Louisiana law and expressed a new legal doctrine endorsing "separate but equal" facilities for African Americans. 📖 *(See page 1082 for more information on* Plessy v. Ferguson.*)*

The ruling established the legal basis for discrimination in the South for more than 50 years to come. While public facilities for African Americans in the South were always separate, they were far from equal. In many cases, they were inferior.

Racial Violence Even worse than the Jim Crow laws was the brutality leveled against African Americans. In the late 1800s, mob violence increased in the United States, particularly in the South. Between 1890 and 1899, there was an average of 187 lynchings—executions without proper court proceedings—carried out by mobs each year. Over 80 percent of the lynchings occurred in the South, and nearly 70 percent of the victims were African Americans.

✓ **Reading Check** Summarizing How did the Supreme Court help to legalize segregation?

The African American Response

In 1892 **Ida B. Wells,** a fiery young African American woman from Tennessee, launched a fearless crusade against lynching. Wells pointed out that

Picturing **History**

Crusading Journalist Ida B. Wells, seen here with her son, campaigned fiercely against lynching in the 1890s. **What two factors did Wells believe to be behind lynchings?**

greed, not just racial prejudice, was often behind these brutal acts. Writing in the *Memphis Free Speech* newspaper, she reported that three African American grocers lynched in Memphis had been guilty of nothing more than competing successfully against white grocers.

A mob destroyed the press that printed the *Memphis Free Speech* and drove Wells out of town, but she settled in Chicago and continued her campaign. In 1895 she published a book denouncing mob violence against African Americans and demanding "a fair trial by law for those accused of crime, and punishment by law after honest conviction." Although Congress rejected an anti-lynching bill, the number of lynchings decreased significantly in the 1900s due in great part to the efforts of activists such as Wells.

A Call for Compromise Some African American leaders like Wells chose the path of protest, but others recommended different solutions to discrimination. One such person was the influential educator **Booker T. Washington.** He proposed that African Americans concentrate on achieving economic goals rather than legal or political ones. In 1895

CHAPTER 16 Politics and Reform **511**

✓ **Reading Check**

Answer: It upheld segregation and expressed a new legal doctrine endorsing "separate but equal" facilities for African Americans.

Picturing **History**

Background: Ida B. Wells was raised in Mississippi. She worked to put herself through college and taught school in Tennessee. In addition to being an author, Wells used her talents as a speaker to campaign against lynching. She was one of the founders of the NAACP.

Answer: greed and racial prejudice

Ask: What did Wells cite to support her opinion about the causes of the lynchings? *(the 3 African American grocers in Memphis who had successfully competed against white grocers)*

3 ASSESS

Assign Section 3 Assessment as homework or as an in-class activity.

⚙ Have students use the **Interactive Tutor Self-Assessment CD-ROM.**

Reading Essentials and Study Guide 16–3

Name _____ Date _____ Class _____

Study Guide

Chapter 16, Section 3
For use with textbook pages 508–512

THE RISE OF SEGREGATION

KEY TERMS AND NAMES

sharecropper landless farmers who had to give landlords large portions of their crops to cover rent and supplies *(page 509)*

poll tax a fee required to register to vote *(page 510)*

grandfather clause a clause that allowed people to vote if their ancestors had voted in 1867 *(page 510)*

segregation separation of the races *(page 510)*

Jim Crow laws laws that enforced segregation *(page 510)*

lynching an execution without proper court proceedings *(page 511)*

INTERDISCIPLINARY CONNECTIONS ACTIVITY

Civics Tell students that disfranchisement was the technical term for the process that removed nearly all African Americans from the voting rolls of Southern states. Organize students into small groups and assign each group one of the Southern states. Have them use library and Internet resources to identify the specific methods that various states used to restrict voting. Have each group prepare a chart that lists the state, the various provisions of its voting law, and the year that the law or state constitutional amendment was passed. Have the groups present their charts to the class. **L2**

Section Quiz 16–3

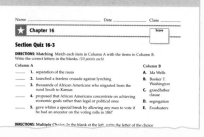

Name _____ Date _____ Class _____

⭐ **Chapter 16**   Score ____

Section Quiz 16-3

DIRECTIONS: Matching Match each item in Column A with the items in Column B.
Write the correct letters in the blanks. *(10 points each)*

Column A
_____ 1. separation of the races
_____ 2. launched a fearless crusade against lynching
_____ 3. thousands of African Americans who migrated from the rural South to Kansas
_____ 4. proposed that African Americans concentrate on achieving economic goals rather than legal or political ones
_____ 5. gave whites a special break by allowing any man to vote if he had an ancestor on the voting rolls in 1867

Column B
A. Ida Wells
B. Booker T. Washington
C. grandfather clause
D. segregation
E. Exodusters

DIRECTIONS: Multiple Choice In the blank at the left, write the letter of the choice

---

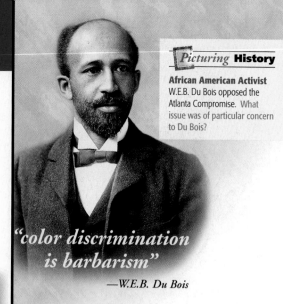

Picturing **History**

Background: W.E.B. Du Bois was educated at Harvard, where he earned three degrees—bachelor's, master's, and doctorate. He was one of the founders of the NAACP.

Answer: voting rights

Ask: Who gave the address known as the Atlanta Compromise?
(Booker T. Washington)

Reteach

Have students discuss how segregation was legalized.

Enrich

Invite interested students to learn more about Jim Crow laws and present a list of 10 examples to the other class members.

✓ Reading Check

Answer: She wrote newspaper articles and a book denouncing lynching.

4 CLOSE

Have students describe three major African American leaders' responses to discrimination.

512

Picturing **History**

African American Activist
W.E.B. Du Bois opposed the Atlanta Compromise. What issue was of particular concern to Du Bois?

"color discrimination is barbarism"
—*W.E.B. Du Bois*

he summed up his views in a speech before a mostly white audience at the Cotton States and International Exposition in Atlanta. Known as the **Atlanta Compromise,** the address came amid increasing acts of discrimination against African Americans. Washington urged his fellow African Americans to postpone the fight for civil rights and instead concentrate on preparing themselves educationally and vocationally for full equality:

❝The wisest among my race understand that the agitation of questions of social equality is the extremest folly, and that the enjoyment of all the privileges that will come to us must be the result of severe and constant struggle rather than of artificial forcing. . . . It is important and right that all privileges of the law be ours, but it is vastly more important that we be prepared for the exercise of these privileges. The opportunity to earn a dollar in a factory just now is worth infinitely more than the opportunity to spend a dollar in an opera-house.❞

–adapted from *Up From Slavery*

Voice of the Future The Atlanta Compromise speech provoked a strong challenge from **W.E.B. Du Bois,** the leader of a new generation of African American activists born after the Civil War. Du Bois pointed out in his 1903 book *The Souls of Black Folk* that white Southerners continued to strip African Americans of their civil rights. This was true in spite of the progress African Americans were making in education and vocational training. They could regain that lost ground and achieve full equality, Du Bois argued, only by demanding their rights. Du Bois was particularly concerned with protecting and exercising voting rights. "Negroes must insist continually, in season and out of season," he wrote, "that voting is necessary to proper manhood, that color discrimination is barbarism." In the years that followed, many African Americans worked to win the vote and end discrimination. The struggle, however, would prove to be a long one.

✓ Reading Check **Describing** How did Ida B. Wells attempt to stop the lynching of African Americans?

SECTION 3 ASSESSMENT

Checking for Understanding

1. **Define:** sharecropper, poll tax, grandfather clause, segregation, Jim Crow laws, lynching.
2. **Identify:** Ida B. Wells, W.E.B. Du Bois.
3. **Explain** what happened to Ida B. Wells after she began campaigning against lynching.

Reviewing Themes

4. **Individual Action** Why did Homer Plessy challenge a Louisiana law in 1892, and what was the significance of his action?

Critical Thinking

5. **Examining** After Reconstruction, why did many African Americans in the South live in conditions that were little better than slavery?
6. **Organizing** Use a graphic organizer similar to the one below to list the responses of some prominent African Americans to racial discrimination.

African American	Response to Discrimination
Ida B. Wells	
Booker T. Washington	
W.E.B. Du Bois	

Analyzing Visuals

7. **Analyzing Photographs** Examine the photograph of an "Exoduster" family on page 509. Pose questions about the photograph to your classmates in a quiz and then have them answer the questions.

Writing About History

8. **Expository Writing** Imagine that you are living in the 1890s. Write a letter to the editor of the local newspaper explaining your view of the Supreme Court ruling in *Plessy* v. *Ferguson.*

SECTION 3 ASSESSMENT ANSWERS

1. Terms are in blue.
2. Ida B. Wells *(p. 511)*, W.E.B. Du Bois *(p. 512)*
3. She was driven out of town and moved to Chicago to continue her campaign.
4. He argued that the law that forced him to ride in a separate railroad car from whites was unconstitutional; his challenge led to the "separate but equal" doctrine.
5. They owned no property and worked as sharecroppers.
6. Wells wrote against lynching. Washington urged African Americans to prepare themselves educationally and vocationally for equality. Du Bois campaigned for voting rights.
7. Students' questions will vary.
8. Students' letters will vary but their position should be based on information presented in the text.

SKILLBUILDER

Interpreting Points of View

Why Learn This Skill?

Suppose you want to see a new movie, but your friends' opinions range from "terrific" to "boring." People often have different opinions about the same people, events, or issues because they look at them from different points of view.

Learning the Skill

A point of view results from one's own beliefs and values. Many factors affect an individual's point of view, including age, gender, racial or ethnic background, economic class, and religion. To judge the accuracy or the objectivity of an argument, you must first identify the speaker's point of view.

To interpret point of view in written material, gather background information on the author that might reveal his or her point of view. Identify aspects of the topic that the author chooses to emphasize or exclude. Look for emotionally charged words such as *charming, vicious, heartwarming,* and *drastic.* Also notice metaphors and analogies that imply an opinion, such as, "If this budget can work, then pigs can fly."

Practicing the Skill

Read the following excerpts from William Jennings Bryan's "Cross of Gold" speech. Then answer the questions.

The humblest citizen in all the land, when clad in the armor of a righteous cause, is stronger than all the hosts of error. I come to speak to you in defense of a cause as holy as the cause of liberty—the cause of humanity. . . .

When you come before us and tell us that we are about to disturb your business interest, we reply that you have disturbed our business interests by your course. . . . We say not one word against those who live upon the Atlantic coast, but the hardy pioneers who have braved all the dangers of the wilderness, who have made the desert to blossom as the rose . . . it is for these that we speak. . . .

If they ask us why it is that we say more on the money question than we say upon the tariff question, I reply

that, if protection has slain its thousands, the gold standard has slain its tens of thousands. . . .

Having behind us the producing masses of this nation and the world, supported by the commercial interest, the laboring interests, and the toilers everywhere, we will answer their demand for a gold standard by saying to them: You shall not press down upon the brow of labor this crown of thorns, you shall not crucify mankind upon a cross of gold.

Cartoon portraying William Jennings Bryan

① What subject is Bryan addressing? What group is he speaking for?

② What is Bryan's point of view?

③ What emotionally charged words and phrases does Bryan use in his speech? How does this language help reveal his point of view?

Skills Assessment

Complete the Practicing Skills questions on page 515 and the Chapter 16 Skills Reinforcement Activity to assess your mastery of this skill.

Applying the Skill

Interpreting Points of View In a newspaper or magazine, find an editorial or letter to the editor that expresses a point of view on an issue. Write a paragraph analyzing the author's point of view. Compare it to your own and explain why you agree or disagree with the author.

 Glencoe's **Skillbuilder Interactive Workbook CD-ROM, Level 2,** provides instruction and practice in key social studies skills.

TEACH

Interpreting Points of View
Explain to students that this skill is particularly important when assessing Internet sources.

Bring to class two weeks' worth of newspapers for students to use and have students review the editorials. Then have them underline the specific passages in one editorial that indicate the writer's point of view.

Additional Practice

Reinforcing Skills Activity 16

Name _____ Date _____ Class _____

★ **Reinforcing Skills Activity 16**

Interpreting Points of View

☐ **LEARNING THE SKILL**

A person's point of view is affected by many factors, including racial or ethnic background, age, gender, religion, and economic class. These factors influence beliefs and values, which in turn affect a person's opinion. Before you can determine the accuracy or objectivity of a written piece, you must determine the author's point of view. To do this, first gather background information on the author. Then, as you read, look for the points of emphasis, metaphors, analogies, and words that invoke emotion or reflect opinion.

☐ **PRACTICING THE SKILL**

DIRECTIONS: The excerpt below is from a pamphlet titled *Lynch Law in Georgia,* written by Ida B. Wells-Barnett in 1899. Read the excerpt and answer the questions that follow on a separate sheet of paper.

GLENCOE
TECHNOLOGY

 CD-ROM
Glencoe Skillbuilder Interactive Workbook CD-ROM, Level 2

This interactive CD-ROM reinforces student mastery of essential social studies skills.

ANSWERS TO PRACTICING THE SKILL

① money question, farmers
② against the gold standard
③ "Hardy pioneers" expresses his view of the people for whom he speaks; references to biblical language attempt to connect his cause to righteous action.

Applying the Skill
Students' answers will vary. Paragraphs should include both an analysis of the author's point of view and a comparison to the students' own point of view.

CHAPTER 16 ASSESSMENT and ACTIVITIES

GLENCOE TECHNOLOGY

MindJogger Videoquiz

Use the **MindJogger Videoquiz** to review Chapter 16 content.

 Available in VHS

Reviewing Key Terms

Students' answers will vary. The pages where the words appear in the text are shown in parentheses.

1. **patronage** (p. 492)
2. **rebate** (p. 495)
3. **populism** (p. 500)
4. **greenback** (p. 501)
5. **inflation** (p. 501)
6. **deflation** (p. 501)
7. **cooperative** (p. 502)
8. **graduated income tax** (p. 504)
9. **goldbug** (p. 506)
10. **silverite** (p. 506)
11. **sharecropper** (p. 509)
12. **poll tax** (p. 510)
13. **grandfather clause** (p. 510)
14. **segregation** (p. 510)
15. **Jim Crow laws** (p. 510)
16. **lynching** (p. 511)

Reviewing Key Facts

17. Interstate Commerce Commission (p. 496), Sherman Antitrust Act (p. 497), Grange (p. 502), People's Party (p. 503), William Jennings Bryan (p. 506), Ida B. Wells (p. 511), W.E.B. Du Bois (p. 512)

18. There was a nearly even division of power between the Democrats and Republicans.

19. Problems included labor strikes, price gouging by railroads, and high tariffs.

Reviewing Key Terms

On a sheet of paper, use each of these terms in a sentence.

1. patronage
2. rebate
3. populism
4. greenback
5. inflation
6. deflation
7. cooperative
8. graduated income tax
9. goldbug
10. silverite
11. sharecropper
12. poll tax
13. grandfather clause
14. segregation
15. Jim Crow laws
16. lynching

Reviewing Key Facts

17. **Identify:** Interstate Commerce Commission, Sherman Antitrust Act, Grange, People's Party, William Jennings Bryan, Ida B. Wells, W.E.B. Du Bois

18. What contributed to political deadlock at the federal level between 1876 and 1896?

19. What economic problems did the United States face during the administration of President Cleveland?

20. How did the Grange attempt to solve farmers' problems in the late 1800s?

21. What was the significance of the Supreme Court's ruling in *Plessy* v. *Ferguson?*

Critical Thinking

22. **Analyzing Themes: Economic Factors** Why was the type of currency used in the United States an important issue to farmers in the late 1800s?

23. **Comparing** How did Booker T. Washington's answer to racial discrimination compare to that of W.E.B. Du Bois?

24. **Organizing** Use a graphic organizer similar to the one below to list the major reforms sought by the Populists in the 1892 presidential election.

25. **Interpreting Primary Sources** Reform movements in farming led to the organization of the Populist Party in 1891. In the following excerpt from an 1890 article, Washington Gladden, a Congregational minister, discusses the problems facing farmers in the United States.

❝The farmers of the United States are up in arms. . . . They produce the largest share of its wealth; but they are getting, they say, the smallest share for themselves. With the hardest work and with the sharpest economy, the average farmer is unable to make both ends meet;

Chapter Summary

Republican Party

- Popular in North and Midwest; appealed to rural and small town voters
- Party split over civil service reform
- Favored higher tariffs and the gold standard

Populist Party

- Sought government control over business to protect farmers
- Supported national control of railroads, increased money supply, and direct election of U.S. senators
- Support declined when gold crisis was resolved
- Lost presidential elections but inspired reforms that were later adopted

Democratic Party

- Strongly supported by Southerners, immigrants, and urban workers
- Supported civil service reform
- Supported cutting tariffs and regulating interstate commerce
- Party split over silver coinage

Political Inequality for African Americans

- Supreme Court overturned the Civil Rights Act of 1875
- Unfair voting laws disfranchised Southern African Americans
- *Plessy* v. *Ferguson* defended separate but equal public facilities

20. It pooled resources to create cooperatives, pressured legislatures to regulate railroad and warehouse rates, and encouraged the government to print more money.

21. Plessy's challenge of a state law forcing him to ride in a separate railroad car led to the Supreme Court decision establishing the "separate but equal" doctrine and continuing social segregation.

Critical Thinking

22. Without greenbacks and silver coins, the money supply could not meet the needs of the growing economy. The value of money increased, and crop prices began to fall.

23. Washington wanted to postpone the fight for voting rights and focus on educational and job training, while Du Bois pushed for voting rights.

every year closes with debt, . . . the average annual reward of the farm proprietor [of Connecticut] is $181.31, while the average annual wages of the ordinary hired man is $386.36.

    . . . [T]he root of the difficulty is overproduction; that there are too many farms . . . [but] other causes . . . should not be overlooked. The enormous tribute which the farmers of the West are paying to the moneylenders of the East is one source of their poverty. . . .

    [Farmers] believe that the miseries under which they are suffering are largely due to political causes and can be cured by legislation. . . . The prime object of the Farmers' Alliance is to better the condition of the farmers of America, mentally, morally, and financially; . . . 🙰🙰

                       —quoted in *Forum*

a. According to Gladden, why were farmers up in arms?

b. What was the main purpose of the new Farmers' Alliance?

Practicing Skills

26. Interpreting Points of View Study the American Story on page 500 that gives an excerpt of Polk's speech on July 4, 1890. Then answer these questions.

    a. How do historians analyze points of view?

    b. What emotionally charged words and phrases does Polk use? How do they reveal his point of view?

Writing Activities

27. Persuasive Writing Imagine that you are living in 1881 and have just heard about President Garfield's assassination by a disappointed office-seeker. Write to your representatives in Congress, urging them either to pass civil service reform or to keep the current "spoils system" for appointments to federal offices. Explain why you believe your recommendation is rational.

28. Chronology Quiz Absolute chronology refers to specific dates, while relative chronology looks at when something occurred with reference to when other things occurred. Memorize the unit titles and time periods in your book, then close your book. Practice relative chronology by writing the unit titles in correct order. Then apply absolute chronology by writing the unit dates.

Farm Prices, 1860–1900

Price of Crops	
$2.40	
$2.20	
$2.00	
$1.80	
$1.60	
$1.40	
$1.20	
$1.00	
$.80	
$.60	
$.40	
$.20	

Legend:
— Wheat (price per bushel)
— Corn (price per bushel)
— Cotton (price per pound)

Year: 1860 1870 1880 1890 1900

Source: *Historical Statistics of the United States: Colonial Times to 1970*

Economics and History

29. The graph above shows farm prices in the United States between 1860 and 1900. Study the graph and answer the questions below.

    a. Analyzing Graphs What happened to prices of crops between 1865 and 1895?

    b. Understanding Cause and Effect What factors might have contributed to this situation?

The Princeton Review

Standardized Test Practice

Directions: Choose the best answer to the following question.

The Sherman Antitrust Act of 1890 declared illegal "any combination . . . in restraint of trade or commerce." What *combination* was it originally intended to prevent?

A labor unions

B business mergers

C transcontinental railroads

D Farmers' Alliances

Test-Taking Tip: Make sure your answer reflects the original goal of the Antitrust Act. Only one answer reflects the reason Congress passed the law.

HISTORY
Online

Have students visit the Web site at <u>tav.glencoe.com</u> to review Chapter 16 and take the Self-Check Quiz.

Writing Activities

27. Letters should clearly state a point of view and reasons for the point of view.

28. Encourage students to review the chronologies for accuracy and to get an overview of U.S. history.

Economics and History

29. a. The trend for wheat and corn is downward. The price of cotton remained relatively constant during the period after an initial fluctuation. **b.** abundant crops, flat demand, high tariffs, or increased competition

---

The Princeton Review

Standardized Test Practice

Answer: B
Test-Taking Tip: Tell students to consider what they know about each of the choices. Which could realistically restrain trade? Labor unions and the Farmers' Alliance were combinations of workers and did not have the power to restrain trade.

Bonus Question ❓

Ask: What were some of the difficulties that settlers encountered as they settled the Great Plains? *(possible answers include: isolation, tornadoes, destructive insects, harsh weather, and dust storms)*

---

24. return to silver coinage, federal ownership of railroads, eight-hour work day, restricting immigration

25. a. because they produced so much food and got so little profit in return; **b.** better the condition of farmers mentally, morally, and financially

Practicing Skills

26. a. analyze emotionally charged words in the context of surrounding historical events; **b.** possible answers: revolution (to support farmers' fighting strength), brother (to unite all farmers), Wall Street (refers to Wall Street as a power unrestrained, even by Congress)

Unit 6 Resources

SUGGESTED PACING CHART

Unit 6 (1 Day)	Chapter 17 (4 Days)	Chapter 18 (6 Days)	Chapter 19 (5 Days)	Unit 6 (2 Days)
Day 1 Introduction	**Day 1** Chapter 17 Intro, Section 1 **Day 2** Section 2 **Day 3** Section 3 **Day 4** Chapter 17 Assessment	**Day 1** Chapter 18 Intro, Section 1 **Day 2** Section 2 **Day 3** Section 3 **Day 4** Section 4 **Day 5** Section 5 **Day 6** Chapter 18 Assessment	**Day 1** Chapter 19 Intro, Section 1 **Day 2** Section 2 **Day 3** Section 3 **Day 4** Section 4 **Day 5** Chapter 19 Assessment	**Day 1** Wrap-Up/Project **Day 2** Unit 6 Assessment

Use the following tools to easily assess student learning in a variety of ways:

- Performance Assessment Activities and Rubrics
- Chapter and Unit Tests
- Section Quizzes
- Standardized Test Skills Practice Workbook

- tav.glencoe.com
- Interactive Tutor Self-Assessment CD-ROM
- MindJogger Videoquiz
- ExamView® Pro Testmaker CD-ROM
- SAT I/II Test Practice

TEACHING TRANSPARENCIES

Unit 6 Map Overlay Transparencies

Cause-and-Effect Transparency 6

*inter*NET RESOURCES

- tav.glencoe.com

The American Vision
Visit the *American Vision* Web site for history overviews, activities, assessments, and updated charts and graphs.

- www.socialstudies.glencoe.com

Glencoe Social Studies
Visit the Glencoe Web site for social studies activities, updates, and links to other sites.

- www.teachingtoday.glencoe.com

Glencoe Teaching Today
Visit the new Glencoe Web site for teacher development information, teaching tips, Web resources, and educational news.

- www.time.com

TIME Online
Visit the TIME Web site for up-to-date news and special reports.

Unit 6 Resources

ASSESSMENT

Unit 6 Pretests

Unit 6 Posttests

APPLICATION AND ENRICHMENT

American Biography 6

History Simulation and Problem Solving 6

GEOGRAPHY

Geography and History Activity 6

INTERDISCIPLINARY ACTIVITIES

American Literature Reading 6

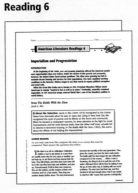

Economics and History Activity 6

Team-Teaching Interdisciplinary Strategies and Activities 6

BIBLIOGRAPHY

Readings for the Student

Chambers, John Whiteclay, III. *The Tyranny of Change: America in the Progressive Era, 1890–1920.* Rutgers University Press, 2000.

Readings for the Teacher

Keegan, John. *An Illustrated History of the First World War.* Knopf, 2001.

Multimedia Resources

Videocassette. *Mirror of America.* National Archives. (36 minutes)

Additional Glencoe Resources for This Unit:

- Glencoe Skillbuilder Interactive Workbook CD-ROM, Level 2
- Social Studies Guide to Using the Internet
- Writer's Guidebook for High School
- Living Constitution
- American Art Prints Strategies and Activities

Unit Overview

Unit 6 describes how the United States became a world power in the 1900s. **Chapter 17** explores imperialism and the Spanish-American War. **Chapter 18** focuses on the Progressive movement from 1890 to 1919. **Chapter 19** discusses World War I and its impact on America.

Unit Objectives

After studying this unit, students will be able to:
1. Analyze how a desire for more trade and markets led to political change.
2. Evaluate the legacy of the Progressive movement.
3. Analyze how the United States raised an army and won support for World War I.

*W*hy It Matters Activity

Tell students that the federal government began regulating food and drugs when the Pure Food and Drug Act was passed in 1906. Ask students what impact they think this act has on the food they eat.

UNIT
6 Imperialism and Progressivism

1890–1919

*W*hy It Matters

As the United States entered the twentieth century, it grew to become a world power. While the nation was expanding its territory into other parts of the world, conditions at home gave rise to a widespread Progressive movement. This movement worked for various reforms in government, business, and society. While Americans focused on their own country, Europe slid into a devastating world war that eventually involved the United States as well. These crucial years of domestic change and foreign conflict provided important foundations for the world you live in today. The following resources offer more information about this period in American history.

Primary Sources Library

See pages 1052–1053 for primary source readings to accompany Unit 6.

Use the **American History Primary Source Document Library CD-ROM** to find additional primary sources about imperialism and progressivism.

World War I pin

American Troops Arriving in Paris July 14, 1918 by J.F. Boucher

516

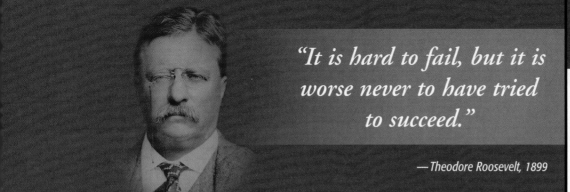

"*It is hard to fail, but it is worse never to have tried to succeed.*"

— *Theodore Roosevelt, 1899*

GLENCOE
TECHNOLOGY

 CD-ROM
**American History
Primary Source
Document Library
CD-ROM**
Use the **American History Primary Source Document Library CD-ROM** to access primary source documents related to this period in history.

More About the Art

Although the war itself was devastating to Europe, fanfare often accompanied American troops marching into large cities such as Paris. The United States's involvement in the war was brief compared to that of European powers, but the European people often viewed Americans as heroes who had saved Allied countries from complete destruction. Ask students to describe the tone and mood of the painting.

 Glencoe Literature Library

The following novel from the *High School American History Literature Library* may be used to enrich the study of this unit:
• *To Kill a Mockingbird* by Harper Lee

SERVICE-LEARNING PROJECT

Work with an elementary school to set up a mentoring or tutoring program between your students and elementary school students. Have volunteers sign up to participate in the program. Tell students that each student is to work with an elementary school student on any subject with which he or she is struggling. Arrange for all meetings to occur in a public place such as at the school or in a library. Help students develop creative ways to help mentor or tutor the younger students.

Refer to **Building Bridges: Connecting Classroom and Community through Service-Learning in Social Studies** from the National Council for the Social Studies for information about service-learning.

Timesaving Tools

TeacherWorks™ All-In-One Planner and Resource Center

- **Interactive Teacher Edition** Access your Teacher Wraparound Edition and your classroom resources with a few easy clicks.
- **Interactive Lesson Planner** Planning has never been easier! Organize your week, month, semester, or year with all the lesson helps you need to make teaching creative, timely, and relevant.

Use Glencoe's **Presentation Plus!** multimedia teacher tool to easily present dynamic lessons that visually excite your students. Using Microsoft PowerPoint® you can customize the presentations to create your own personalized lessons.

TEACHING TRANSPARENCIES

Graphic Organizer 12

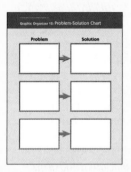

Why It Matters Chapter Transparency 17

APPLICATION AND ENRICHMENT

Linking Past and Present Activity 17

Enrichment Activity 17

Primary Source Reading 17

REVIEW AND REINFORCEMENT

Reteaching Activity 17

Vocabulary Activity 17

Time Line Activity 17

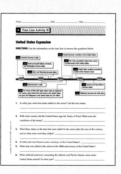

Critical Thinking Skills Activity 17

Meeting NCSS Standards

The following standards are highlighted in Chapter 17:

Section 1 **IX** Global Connections: B, C, D
Section 2 **VI** Power, Authority, and Governance: B, F, G, I
Section 3 **II** Time, Continuity, and Change: B, C, D

Local Standards

_____

_____

_____

_____

_____

GLENCOE'S ASSESSMENT ADVANTAGE

Chapter 17 Test Form A	Chapter 17 Test Form B	Standardized Test Skills Practice Workbook Activity 17	Performance Assessment Activities and Rubrics 17	ExamView® Pro Testmaker CD-ROM

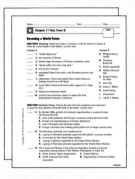
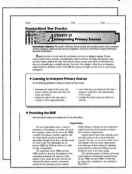

MULTIMEDIA

- Vocabulary PuzzleMaker CD-ROM
- Interactive Tutor Self-Assessment CD-ROM
- ExamView® Pro Testmaker CD-ROM
- Audio Program
- American History Primary Source Documents Library CD-ROM
- MindJogger Videoquiz
- Presentation Plus! CD-ROM
- TeacherWorks™ CD-ROM
- Interactive Student Edition CD-ROM
- Glencoe Skillbuilder Interactive Workbook CD-ROM, Level 2
- The *American Vision* Video Program
- American Music: Hits Through History
- American Music: Cultural Traditions

SPANISH RESOURCES

The following Spanish language materials are available in the Spanish Resources Binder:

- Spanish Guided Reading Activities
- Spanish Reteaching Activities
- Spanish Quizzes and Tests
- Spanish Vocabulary Activities
- Spanish Summaries
- The Declaration of Independence and United States Constitution Spanish Translation

---

The following videotape programs are available from Glencoe as supplements to Chapter 17:

- **Theodore Roosevelt: Roughrider to Rushmore** (ISBN 1-56-501806-0)
- **The Panama Canal** (ISBN 1-56-501243-7)

To order, call Glencoe at 1-800-334-7344. To find classroom resources to accompany many of these videos, check the following home pages:
A&E Television: www.aande.com
The History Channel: www.historychannel.com

HISTORY Online

Use our Web site for additional resources. All essential content is covered in the Student Edition.

You and your students can visit tav.glencoe.com, the Web site companion to the *American Vision.* This innovative integration of electronic and print media offers your students a wealth of opportunities. The student text directs students to the Web site for the following options:

- **Chapter Overviews**
- **Self-Check Quizzes**
- **Student Web Activities**
- **Textbook Updates**

Answers to the student Web activities are provided for you in the **Web Activity Lesson Plans.** Additional Web resources and Interactive Tutor Puzzles are also available.

Chapter 17 Resources

SECTION RESOURCES

Daily Objectives	Reproducible Resources	Multimedia Resources
SECTION 1 **The Imperialist Vision** 1. Analyze how a desire for more trade and markets led to political change between 1877 and 1898. 2. Cite the motivations for and methods of American expansion in the Pacific.	Reproducible Lesson Plan 17–1 Daily Lecture and Discussion Notes 17–1 Guided Reading Activity 17–1* Section Quiz 17–1* Reading Essentials and Study Guide 17–1 Performance Assessment Activities and Rubrics Interpreting Political Cartoons	Daily Focus Skills Transparency 17–1 Interactive Tutor Self-Assessment CD-ROM ExamView® Pro Testmaker CD-ROM Presentation Plus! CD-ROM TeacherWorks™ CD-ROM Skillbuilder Interactive Workbook, Level 2 Audio Program American Music: Hits Through History
SECTION 2 **The Spanish-American War** 1. Describe the circumstances that led to war between the United States and Spain in 1898. 2. Explain how the war made the United States a world power.	Reproducible Lesson Plan 17–2 Daily Lecture and Discussion Notes 17–2 Guided Reading Activity 17–2* Section Quiz 17–2* Reading Essentials and Study Guide 17–2 Performance Assessment Activities and Rubrics	Daily Focus Skills Transparency 17–2 Interactive Tutor Self-Assessment CD-ROM ExamView® Pro Testmaker CD-ROM Presentation Plus! CD-ROM TeacherWorks™ CD-ROM Audio Program American Music: Cultural Traditions
SECTION 3 **New American Diplomacy** 1. Critique Theodore Roosevelt's foreign policy as president. 2. Explain the Open Door policy and its effects on relations between the United States and Asia.	Reproducible Lesson Plan 17–3 Daily Lecture and Discussion Notes 17–3 Guided Reading Activity 17–3* Section Quiz 17–3* Reading Essentials and Study Guide 17–3 Performance Assessment Activities and Rubrics Interpreting Political Cartoons	Daily Focus Skills Transparency 17–3 Interactive Tutor Self-Assessment CD-ROM ExamView® Pro Testmaker CD-ROM Presentation Plus! CD-ROM TeacherWorks™ CD-ROM Vocabulary PuzzleMaker CD-ROM Audio Program

0:00 OUT OF TIME?
Assign the Chapter 17 **Reading Essentials and Study Guide.**

*Also Available in Spanish

Blackline Master	Transparency	CD-ROM	DVD
Poster	Music Program	Audio Program	Videocassette

NATIONAL GEOGRAPHIC Teacher's Corner

INDEX TO NATIONAL GEOGRAPHIC MAGAZINE

The following articles relate to this chapter.

- "Alone Across the Arctic Crown," April 1993
- "Kodiak, Alaska's Island Refuge," November 1993
- "Remember the *Maine*," February 1998
- "Wrangell-St. Elias: Alaska's Sky-High Wilderness," May 1994

NATIONAL GEOGRAPHIC SOCIETY PRODUCTS AVAILABLE FROM GLENCOE

To order the following products for use with this chapter, contact your local Glencoe sales representative, or call Glencoe at 1-800-334-7344:

- *NGS PictureShow: Story of America, Part 2* (CD-ROM)
- *NGS PicturePack: Story of America Library, Part 2* (Transparencies)
- *Picture Atlas of the World* (CD-ROM)

ADDITIONAL NATIONAL GEOGRAPHIC SOCIETY PRODUCTS

To order the following, call National Geographic at 1-800-368-2728:

- *Hawaii: Strangers in Paradise* (Video)

NGS ONLINE

Access National Geographic's Web site for current events, atlas updates, activities, links, interactive features, and archives.

www.nationalgeographic.com

From the Classroom of...

Richard L. Manser, Ph.D.
Upper Merion High School
King of Prussia, PA

The Change in the Paradigm

The 1890s brought a change in the diplomatic paradigm from isolation to imperialism. Using the theses of Robert Beisner in *From the Old Diplomacy to the New, 1865–1900* (1974), students will research the end of the frontier including the Turner Thesis and the 1890 census; the 1893 Depression including causes, consequences, and Cleveland's policies; agrarian unrest including the Ocala Demands and Populist Party Platform; dominant personalities including Mahan, Roosevelt, Strong, and Beveridge; and the prevailing ideologies of democracy, capitalism, white man's burden, and Social Darwinism.

Write the events on the board and invite the class to make cause-and-effect relationships between the events, characters, and attitudes. The result should be a detailed explanation of the change in paradigm that resulted in the Spanish-American War, the Open Door, and the American response to the insurrection in the Philippines.

ADDITIONAL RESOURCES FROM GLENCOE

- American Music: Cultural Traditions
- American Art & Architecture
- Outline Map Resource Book
- U.S. Desk Map
- Building Geography Skills for Life
- Inclusion for the High School Social Studies Classroom Strategies and Activities
- Teaching Strategies for the American History Classroom (Including Block Scheduling Pacing Guides)

KEY TO ABILITY LEVELS

Teaching strategies have been coded.

L1 BASIC activities for all students
L2 AVERAGE activities for average to above-average students
L3 CHALLENGING activities for above-average students
ELL ENGLISH LANGUAGE LEARNER activities

Block Schedule

Activities that are suited to use within the block scheduling framework are identified by:

Why It Matters Activity

Assign half the class to learn an interesting fact about the Panama Canal and the other half to learn an interesting fact about Puerto Rico. After students have studied the chapter, have them evaluate whether the fact they discovered relates to events that occurred in the early 1900s. If there is a connection, have them identify the connection for the class.

The *American Vision* Video Program

To learn more about how the United States became a world power, have students view the Chapter 16 video, "Teddy Roosevelt and Yellow Journalism," from the *American Vision* Video Program.

Available in DVD and VHS

MindJogger Videoquiz

Use the **MindJogger Videoquiz** to preview Chapter 17 content.

📼 Available in VHS

CHAPTER
17 Becoming a World Power
1872–1912

Why It Matters

During this era, economic and military competition from world powers convinced the United States it must be a world power. The United States became an empire when it acquired the Philippines and territory in the Caribbean. American influence in Central and South America grew as the United States took a more active role in Latin American affairs.

The Impact Today

Events of this time continue to influence American politics.
- *The United States continues to use its navy to protect its overseas interests.*
- *The Panama Canal serves as a major route for international commerce.*
- *Puerto Rico remains tied to the United States as a commonwealth.*

The American Vision *Video* The Chapter 17 video, "Teddy Roosevelt and Yellow Journalism," chronicles the events leading to the United States becoming a world power.

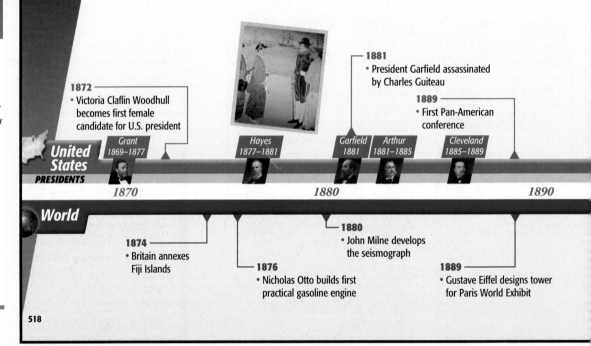

United States PRESIDENTS

1872
- Victoria Claflin Woodhull becomes first female candidate for U.S. president

1881
- President Garfield assassinated by Charles Guiteau

1889
- First Pan-American conference

Grant 1869–1877 | Hayes 1877–1881 | Garfield 1881 | Arthur 1881–1885 | Cleveland 1885–1889

1870 | *1880* | *1890*

World

1874
- Britain annexes Fiji Islands

1876
- Nicholas Otto builds first practical gasoline engine

1880
- John Milne develops the seismograph

1889
- Gustave Eiffel designs tower for Paris World Exhibit

518

TWO-MINUTE LESSON LAUNCHER

Ask students what they think it means to be a world power. List their responses on a piece of paper. Ask students what responsibilities a world power has to the world community. Again, list their answers on a piece of paper. At the end of the chapter, put the lists on the board and ask what items they would add to or remove from the lists. Also, ask if they believe that the United States lived up to its responsibilities as a world power during the early 1900s.

Theodore Roosevelt leads the charge up San Juan Hill.

HISTORY Online

Introduce students to chapter content and key terms by having them access the **Chapter 17 Overview** at tav.glencoe.com.

More About the Art

On July 1, 1898, Theodore Roosevelt and his volunteer cavalry, the Rough Riders, joined in the capture of the San Juan Hill complex. They helped secure a U.S. victory in the Battle of Santiago, the decisive battle of the brief Spanish-American War. Two days after the battle, the Spanish fleet fled the harbor at Santiago, effectively surrendering control of Cuba to the United States.

TIME LINE ACTIVITY

Have students select one of the people mentioned on the time line and prepare a brief profile of his or her life, including major accomplishments.

1893
• Americans overthrow Queen Liliuokalani of Hawaii

1898
• U.S. declares war on Spain

1899
• Hay sends Open Door notes

1901
• President McKinley assassinated

1904
• Panama Canal construction begins
• Roosevelt Corollary to Monroe Doctrine issued

SEAL OF THE CANAL ZONE ISTHMUS OF PANAMA

| B. Harrison 1889–1893 | Cleveland 1893–1897 | McKinley 1897–1901 | T. Roosevelt 1901–1909 | Taft 1909–1913 |

1900

1910

1895
• Louis and Auguste Lumière introduce motion pictures

1899
• Boer War begins between Great Britain and South African Republic

1900
• Boxer Rebellion begins in China

1904
• Russo-Japanese War begins

HISTORY Online

Chapter Overview
Visit the *American Vision* Web site at tav.glencoe.com and click on **Chapter Overviews—Chapter 17** to preview chapter information.

519

GRAPHIC ORGANIZER ACTIVITY

Organizing Information Have students use a graphic organizer similar to the one below to present the arguments for and against United States foreign expansion.

Arguments For	**Foreign Expansion**	**Arguments Against**
• *increases trade* • *helps civilize people* • *spreads American ideals*		• *too costly* • *drives down American wages* • *violates America's principles*

1 FOCUS

Section Overview

This section focuses on the United States becoming an imperialist power.

BELLRINGER
Skillbuilder Activity

Project transparency and have students answer the question.

Available as a blackline master.

Daily Focus Skills Transparency 17–1

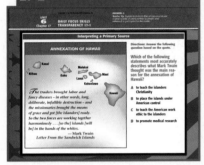

Guide to Reading

Answers to Graphic:
I. Building Support for Imperialism
   A. A Desire for New Markets
   B. A Feeling of Superiority
II. Expansion in the Pacific
   A. Perry Opens Japan
   B. Annexing Hawaii
III. Trade and Diplomacy in Latin America
IV. Building a Modern Navy

Preteaching Vocabulary
Have students look up the proper pronunciations of the Key Terms and Names.

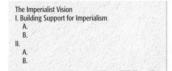

SECTION 1 The Imperialist Vision

Guide to Reading

Main Idea
In the late 1800s, many Americans wanted the United States to expand its military and economic power overseas.

Key Terms and Names
imperialism, protectorate, Anglo-Saxonism, Matthew C. Perry, Queen Liliuokalani, Pan-Americanism, Alfred T. Mahan, Henry Cabot Lodge

Reading Strategy
Organizing As you read about the development of the United States as a world power, use the major headings of the section to create an outline similar to the one below.

The Imperialist Vision
I. Building Support for Imperialism
   A.
   B.
II.
   A.
   B.

Reading Objectives:
• **Analyze** how a desire for more trade and markets led to political change between 1877 and 1898.
• **Cite** the motivations for and methods of American expansion in the Pacific.

Section Theme
Global Connections America's growing trade with the world and rivalry with European nations led to a naval buildup and a search for territory overseas.

Preview of Events

| ◆1850 | ◆1875 | ◆1900 |

1853
Commodore Perry arrives in Japan

1888
Samoan Crisis erupts

1890
Alfred T. Mahan's *Influence of Sea Power Upon History, 1660–1783* published

1893
American settlers overthrow Queen Liliuokalani of Hawaii

★ An American Story ★

John L. Stevens

On January 16, 1893, 162 United States Marines marched off the warship *Boston* and onto the shores of Oahu, one of the Hawaiian Islands. John L. Stevens, the American minister to Hawaii, had ordered the troops ashore. He claimed Hawaii's ruler, Queen Liliuokalani, had created widespread turmoil and endangered American lives and property. Stevens had other motives as well. He wanted to make Hawaii, with its profitable sugarcane plantations, part of the United States.

Stevens ordered the American troops to take up positions near Queen Liliuokalani's palace. Although the marines took no action against the Hawaiian government, their presence intimidated the queen's supporters. Within hours, the American settlers in Hawaii abolished the monarchy and set up a provisional—or temporary—government. On February 1, 1893, at the request of the provisional government, Stevens announced that Hawaii was now under American protection, and he hoisted the American flag over Hawaii's government buildings. Several weeks later, Stevens made his support for annexing Hawaii perfectly clear: "The Hawaiian pear is now fully ripe," he wrote, "and this is the golden hour for the United States to pluck it."

—adapted from *A History of the American People*

Building Support for Imperialism

John Stevens was not alone in his views. Many Americans cheered the events in Hawaii and favored expanding American power elsewhere in the world as well. The American public's enthusiasm, however, was a relatively new phenomenon. In the years

520 CHAPTER 17 Becoming a World Power

SECTION RESOURCES

Reproducible Masters
• Reproducible Lesson Plan 17–1
• Daily Lecture and Discussion Notes 17–1
• Guided Reading Activity 17–1
• Section Quiz 17–1
• Reading Essentials and Study Guide 17–1
• Interpreting Political Cartoons

Transparencies
• Daily Focus Skills Transparency 17–1

Multimedia
⊙ Interactive Tutor Self-Assessment CD-ROM
⊙ ExamView® Pro Testmaker CD-ROM
⊙ Presentation Plus! CD-ROM
⊙ TeacherWorks™ CD-ROM
⊙ Audio Program

immediately following the Civil War, most Americans showed little interest in expanding their nation's territory and international influence. Instead, they focused on reconstructing the South, building up the nation's industries, and settling the West.

Beginning in the 1880s, however, American opinion began to shift. More people wanted to make the United States a world power. Economic and military competition from other nations, as well as a growing feeling of cultural superiority, led to this shift in opinion.

ECONOMICS

A Desire for New Markets While the United States focused inward, several European nations were expanding their power overseas. This expansion became known as the New Imperialism. Imperialism is the economic and political domination of a strong nation over other weaker nations.

The Europeans embarked upon a policy of expansion and imperialism for many reasons. By the late 1800s, most industrialized countries had placed high tariffs against each other. These tariffs were intended to protect a nation's industries from foreign competition. The tariffs reduced trade between industrial countries, forcing companies to look overseas for places to sell their products.

At the same time, the growth of investment opportunities in western Europe had slowed. Most of the factories, railroads, and mines that Europe's economy needed had been built. Increasingly, Europeans began looking overseas for places to invest their capital. They began investing in industries in other countries, particularly in Africa and Asia.

To protect their investments, the European nations began exerting control over those territories where they invested their capital and sold their products. Some areas became colonies. Many others became protectorates. In a protectorate, the imperial power allowed the local rulers to stay in control and protected them against rebellions and invasion. In exchange for this protection, the local rulers usually had to accept advice from the Europeans on how to govern their countries.

The expansion of European power overseas did not go unnoticed in the United States. As the United States industrialized, many Americans took interest in the new imperialism. Until the late 1800s, the United States had always been able to expand by settling more territory in North America. Now, with settlers finally filling up the western frontier, many Americans concluded that the nation had to develop new overseas markets to keep its economy strong. "We are raising more than we can consume," declared Indiana senator Albert J. Beveridge. "We are making more than we can use. Therefore, we must find new markets for our produce, new occupation for our capital, new work for our labor."

A Feeling of Superiority In addition to economic concerns, certain other key ideas convinced many Americans to encourage their nation's expansion overseas. Many supporters of Social Darwinism argued that nations competed with each other politically, economically, and militarily, and that only the strongest would ultimately survive. They used this idea to justify expanding the power of the United States overseas.

Many Americans, such as the well-known writer and historian John Fiske, took this idea even further. Fiske argued that English-speaking nations had superior character, ideas, and systems of government, and were destined to dominate the planet:

> 66The work which the English race began when it colonized North America is destined to go on until every land . . . that is not already the seat of an old civilization shall become English in its language, in its religion, in political habits and traditions, and to a predominant extent in the blood of its people.99

> —quoted in *Expansionists of 1898*

Fiske's idea, known as **Anglo-Saxonism**, became popular in the United States because it seemed to fit with the idea of Manifest Destiny. Many Americans believed it had been the nation's destiny to expand west to the Pacific Ocean. Now they believed it was

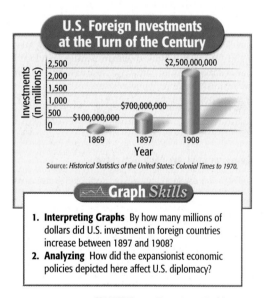

U.S. Foreign Investments at the Turn of the Century

Investments (in millions)

1869 — $100,000,000
1897 — $700,000,000
1908 — $2,500,000,000

Year

Source: *Historical Statistics of the United States: Colonial Times to 1970.*

Graph Skills

1. **Interpreting Graphs** By how many millions of dollars did U.S. investment in foreign countries increase between 1897 and 1908?
2. **Analyzing** How did the expansionist economic policies depicted here affect U.S. diplomacy?

CHAPTER 17   Becoming a World Power   **521**

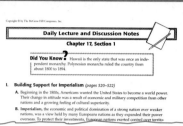

2 TEACH

Daily Lecture and Discussion Notes 17–1

Copyright © by The McGraw-Hill Companies, Inc.

Daily Lecture and Discussion Notes
Chapter 17, Section 1

Did You Know? Hawaii is the only state that was once an independent monarchy. Polynesian monarchs ruled the country from about 1800 to 1894.

I. **Building Support for Imperialism** (pages 520–522)

A. Beginning in the 1880s, Americans wanted the United States to become a world power. Their change in attitude was a result of economic and military competition from other nations and a growing feeling of cultural superiority.

B. Imperialism, the economic and political domination of a strong nation over weaker nations, was a view held by many Europeans nations as they expanded their power overseas. To protect their investments, European nations exerted control over territo-

Supporting Statements with Facts Write the following statements on the chalkboard:

1. United States emerges from isolationism.
2. United States seeks to open new markets.
3. United States changes its naval policy.
4. United States becomes a world power.

Ask students to find at least two facts in the text to support these statements. **L1** ELL

Graph *Skills*

Answers:
1. by $1,800 million
2. caused the U.S. to have greater trade and diplomatic contacts with Asia and Latin America

Graph Skills Practice
Ask: Why do you think such a dramatic increase in foreign investments made the United States feel superior? *(showed growing power of the United States around the world, opened new markets)*

COOPERATIVE LEARNING ACTIVITY

Holding a Panel Discussion Organize students into groups for a panel discussion on imperialism. Each group should choose a representative for the panel, then establish a position on the following ideas. (1) Imperialism is immoral and inhumane. (2) Imperialism leads to the problems of colonialism and militarism. (3) Imperialism aids economic expansion in underdeveloped nations. (4) Imperialism allows Americans to spread capitalism and democracy to less-developed nations. Groups should help prepare their representative.

Use the rubric for a cooperative group management plan on pages 81–82 in the ***Performance Assessment Activities and Rubrics.***

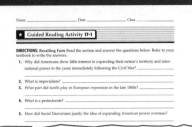

Picturing History

Answer: The Japanese realized that they could not compete against modern Western technology and weapons. They adopted Western technology, launched their own industrial revolution, and built a modern navy.
Ask: What objection did the Japanese have in the early 1850s to trading with the United States? *(The Japanese believed contact with the West would destroy their culture.)*

✓ Reading Check

Answer: More people believed it was the American destiny to spread its civilization overseas.

📁 Use *Interpreting Political Cartoons*, Cartoon 17.

History *and the* Humanities

🏳 American Music: Hits Through History: "Stars & Stripes Forever"

Picturing History

American Imperialism To open Japan to American trade, Commodore Matthew Perry led the U.S. Navy into what is now Tokyo Bay on July 8, 1853. This lithograph shows Perry's forces arriving in Yokohama in March 1854. **How did Perry's action affect Japan?**

Matthew C. Perry

the destiny of the United States to expand overseas and spread its civilization to other people.

Another influential advocate of Anglo-Saxonism was **Josiah Strong,** a popular American minister in the late 1800s. Strong linked Anglo-Saxonism to Christian missionary ideas. His ideas influenced many Americans. "The Anglo-Saxon," Strong declared, "[is] divinely commissioned to be, in a peculiar sense, his brother's keeper." By linking missionary work to Anglo-Saxonism, Strong convinced many Americans to support imperialism and an expansion of American power overseas.

✓ Reading Check

Summarizing How did Americans' opinions on overseas expansion begin to change in the 1800s?

Expansion in the Pacific

From the earliest days of the Republic, Americans had expanded their nation by moving west. When Americans began looking overseas for new markets in the 1800s, therefore, they naturally tended to look westward. Even before imperialist ideas became popular, Americans had begun expanding across the Pacific Ocean toward East Asia. By the early 1800s, dozens of ships were making the long trip to China every year.

Perry Opens Japan Many American business leaders believed that the United States would benefit from trade with Japan as well as with China. Japan's rulers, however, believed that excessive contact with the West would destroy their culture and only allowed the Chinese and Dutch to trade with their nation.

In 1852, after receiving several petitions from Congress, President Franklin Pierce decided to force Japan to trade with the United States. He ordered Commodore **Matthew C. Perry** to take a naval expedition to Japan to negotiate a trade treaty.

On July 8, 1853, four American warships under Perry's command entered Yedo Bay (today known as Tokyo Bay). The Japanese had never seen steamships before and were impressed by the display of American technology and firepower. Perry's arrival in Japan forced the Japanese to make changes internally. Realizing that they could not compete against modern Western technology and weapons, the Japanese signed a treaty opening the ports of Simoda and Hakodadi to American trade on March 31, 1854.

522 CHAPTER 17   Becoming a World Power

MEETING SPECIAL NEEDS

Auditory/Musical To focus students' attention during classroom discussion, interrupt the discussion occasionally with the announcement of a "pop listening quiz." Award "listening points" to students who can answer quiz questions correctly. For example, when the class is discussing the annexation of Hawaii, pop the question, "Who pushed for the annexation of Hawaii—President Grover Cleveland, American sugar growers, or the Hawaiian people themselves?" **L1** ELL

📁 Refer to *Inclusion for the High School Social Studies Classroom Strategies and Activities* in the TCR.

The American decision to force Japan to open trade played an important role in Japanese history. Many Japanese leaders concluded that the time had come to remake their society. In 1868, after a long internal power struggle, Japanese leaders began to Westernize their country. They adopted Western technology and launched their own industrial revolution. By the 1890s, the Japanese had built a powerful modern navy, and they set out to build their own empire in Asia.

Annexing Hawaii As trade with China and Japan grew in the 1800s, many Americans became interested in Hawaii. Ships traveling between China and the United States regularly stopped in Hawaii to allow their crews to rest and to take on supplies. In 1819 a group of missionaries from New England settled in Hawaii. At about the same time, American whaling ships operating in the North Pacific began using Hawaii as a base.

The American settlers in Hawaii quickly discovered that the climate and soil of the islands were suitable for growing sugarcane. By the mid-1800s, many sugarcane plantations had been established in the islands. In 1872 a severe recession struck Hawaii's economy. Worried that the economic crisis might force the Hawaiians to turn to the British or French for help, the United States Senate ratified a trade treaty that exempted Hawaiian sugar from tariffs. Several years later, when the treaty came up for renewal, the Senate insisted that the Hawaiians grant the United States exclusive rights to a naval base at Pearl Harbor.

The trade treaty led to a boom in the Hawaiian sugar industry and wealth for the planters. In 1887 prominent planters pressured the Hawaiian king into accepting a new constitution that limited the king's authority and increased the planters' power. These developments angered the Hawaiian people, who feared they were losing control of the country.

Tensions between the planters and the Hawaiians mounted. Congress passed the McKinley Tariff in 1890. Although the tariff eliminated all duties on sugar, it also gave subsidies to sugar producers in the United States. Hawaiian sugar was now more expensive than American sugar, despite the lack of tariffs. As sales of Hawaiian sugar declined, the islands' economy went into a tailspin.

In 1891 **Queen Liliuokalani** ascended the Hawaiian throne. Liliuokalani disliked the influence that American settlers had gained in Hawaii. In January 1893, she unsuccessfully attempted to impose a new constitution that would have reasserted her authority as ruler of the Hawaiian people.

Faced with the economic crisis and the queen's actions, the planters backed an attempt to overthrow the monarchy. Supported by the marines from the *Boston,* a group of planters forced the queen to give up power and set up a provisional government. They then requested that the United States annex Hawaii. President Cleveland strongly opposed imperialism. He refused to submit the annexation treaty to the Senate and tried to restore Liliuokalani to power. Hawaii's new leaders refused to restore Liliuokalani, and they decided to wait until a new president took office who favored annexation. Five years later, the United States annexed Hawaii. 📖 *(See page 1073 for more text on Hawaiian annexation.)*

✓ **Reading Check** **Explaining** How did the desire to expand into new markets help push the United States to become a world power?

Trade and Diplomacy in Latin America

The Pacific was not the only region where the United States sought to increase its influence in the 1800s. It also focused on Latin America. Although the United States bought raw materials from this region, Latin Americans bought most of their manufactured goods from Europe. American business leaders and government officials wanted to increase the sale of American products to the region. They also wanted the Europeans to understand that the United States was the dominant power in the region.

James G. Blaine, who served as secretary of state in two administrations in the 1880s, led early efforts

Hawaiian Queen Liliuokalani

✓ **Reading Check**

Answer: It led them to annex Hawaii and to open trade with Japan.

Creating a Thematic Map
Provide students with a map of the Pacific Ocean that includes both the West Coast of the United States and South America and the eastern coast of Asia. Have students research and map the routes taken by James Cook when he became the first European to visit the Hawaiian Islands, the trade routes used to export sugarcane, and strategic locations that allowed Hawaii to play a military role during the Spanish-American War. **L2**

📁 Use the rubric for creating a map, display, or chart on pages 77–78 in the *Performance Assessment Activities and Rubrics.*

Annex The word *annex* comes from Latin and literally means "to bind to."

In 1826, many years before the Pan-American conference was held in Washington, D.C., Simón Bolívar convened the Congress of Panama with the idea of creating an association of states in the Western Hemisphere. The OAS charter was signed in 1948. At the same conference, participants also signed the American Declaration of the Rights and Duties of Man, which was the first international statement expressing human rights principles.

INTERDISCIPLINARY CONNECTIONS ACTIVITY

World History Have interested students use library and Internet resources to learn more about how Japanese culture changed once it was forced to trade with the West. Have students use their research to write a report tracing the steps Japan took to modernize and the ways they preserved Japanese identity. **L3**

TECHNOLOGY & **History**

Background: The U.S.S. *Texas* was the first commissioned battleship in the United States fleet. It was commissioned on August 15, 1895. The battleship carried two 12-inch and six 6-inch guns and was equipped with four 14-inch torpedo tubes. The ship was protected by 12-inch-thick steel armor. For its era, it was one of the most powerful ships in the world.

Answer: Captain Alfred Mahan whose *The Influence of Sea Power Upon History, 1660–1783,* persuaded many in government that a modern navy was necessary to protect America's expanding global trade

✓ Reading Check

Answer: He wanted to create a customs union between Latin America and the United States, and he wanted to create a system for American nations to work out their disputes peacefully.

3 ASSESS

Assign Section 1 Assessment as homework or as an in-class activity.

⚙ Have students use the **Interactive Tutor Self-Assessment CD-ROM.**

Reading Essentials and Study Guide 17–1

TECHNOLOGY & History

Modern Battleships

In the late 1880s, the United States Navy modernized its fleet of battleships. Moving away from wooden ships powered by the wind, the new navy constructed steel-hulled ships with steam-powered engines. In 1889 Congress approved the construction of 18 modern battleships. Probably the most famous ship of this era was the USS *Maine* (depicted at right). It was one of the first U.S. naval vessels with electrical lighting. It had a top speed of 15 knots and a crew of 31 officers and 343 enlisted men. *Which U.S. naval officer argued for the necessity of a modern navy?*

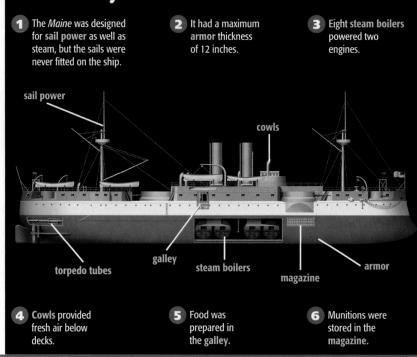

1 The *Maine* was designed for **sail power** as well as steam, but the sails were never fitted on the ship.

2 It had a maximum **armor thickness** of 12 inches.

3 Eight **steam boilers** powered two engines.

4 **Cowls** provided fresh air below decks.

5 Food was prepared in the **galley.**

6 Munitions were stored in the **magazine.**

sail power · cowls · torpedo tubes · galley · steam boilers · magazine · armor

to expand American influence in Latin America. Blaine proposed that the United States invite the Latin American nations to a conference in Washington, D.C. The conference would discuss ways in which the American nations could work together to support peace and to increase trade. The idea that the United States and Latin America should work together came to be called **Pan-Americanism.**

Blaine's idea became reality in 1889 when the Pan-American conference was held in Washington, D.C. Seventeen Latin American nations attended. Blaine had two goals for the conference. He wanted to create a customs union between Latin America and the United States, and he also wanted to create a system for American nations to work out their disputes peacefully.

A customs union would require all of the American nations to reduce their tariffs against each other and to treat each other equally in trade. Blaine hoped that a customs union would turn the Latin Americans away from European products and toward American products. He also hoped that a common system for settling disputes would keep the Europeans from meddling in American affairs.

Although the warm reception they received in the United States impressed the Latin American delegates

to the conference, they rejected both of Blaine's ideas. They did agree, however, to create the Commercial Bureau of the American Republics, an organization that worked to promote cooperation among the nations of the Western Hemisphere. This organization was later known as the Pan-American Union and is today called the **Organization of American States** (OAS).

✓ Reading Check
Summarizing How did Secretary of State Blaine attempt to increase American influence in Latin America?

Building a Modern Navy

As imperialism and Anglo-Saxonism gained support in the late 1800s, the United States became increasingly assertive in foreign affairs. Three international crises illustrated this new approach. In 1888 the country was willing to go to war to prevent Germany from taking control of the Samoa Islands in the South Pacific. Three years later, when a mob in Chile attacked American sailors in the port of Valparaíso, the United States threatened to go to war unless Chile paid reparations for the lives lost. Then, in 1895, the United States backed

CRITICAL THINKING ACTIVITY

Analyzing Pose the following question to students: **What problems arise when we view our own culture as so superior to others that we refuse to accept new ideas from other cultures?** Ask students to write their analysis in the form of a letter to the editor. If possible, have students use a personal experience of a current event as a starting point for their letter. Have students share their letters with the class. **L2**

Venezuela against Great Britain in a border dispute with the colony of British Guiana. After Britain rejected an American ultimatum to settle the dispute, many newspapers and members of Congress called for war. All three crises were eventually solved peacefully.

As both the American people and their government became more willing to risk war in defense of American interests overseas, support for building a large modern navy began to grow. Supporters argued that if the United States did not build up its navy and acquire bases overseas, it would be shut out of foreign markets by the Europeans.

Captain **Alfred T. Mahan,** an officer in the U.S. Navy who taught at the Naval War College, best expressed this argument. In 1890 Mahan published his lectures in a book called *The Influence of Sea Power Upon History, 1660–1783.* In this book Mahan pointed out that many prosperous peoples in the past, such as the British and Dutch, had built large fleets of merchant ships in order to trade with the world. He then suggested that a nation also needed a large navy to protect its merchant ships and to defend its right to trade with other countries.

After arguing that the United States needed a large navy, Mahan observed that building a modern navy meant that the United States had to acquire territory for naval bases overseas. In the 1890s, navy warships burned coal to power their engines. To operate a navy far from home, a country needed bases and coaling stations in distant regions. This would allow the ships to be resupplied en route to their destination.

Mahan's book became a best-seller, and it helped to build public support for a big navy. In Congress two powerful senators, **Henry Cabot Lodge** and Albert J. Beveridge, pushed for the construction of a new navy. In the executive branch, Benjamin Tracy, secretary of the navy under President Harrison, and John D. Long, secretary of the navy under President McKinley, strongly supported Mahan's ideas—as did future president Theodore Roosevelt, who served as an assistant secretary of the navy in the late 1890s.

By the 1890s, several different ideas had come together in the United States. Business leaders wanted new markets overseas. Anglo-Saxonism had convinced many Americans that they had a destiny to dominate the world. Growing European imperialism threatened America's security. Combined with Mahan's influence, these ideas convinced Congress to authorize the construction of a modern American navy.

By the late 1890s, the United States was well on its way to becoming one of the top naval powers in the world. Although it was not yet an imperial power, it had the power to become one if the opportunity arose. That opportunity was not long in coming. In the spring of 1898, war erupted between Spain and the United States.

✓ **Reading Check** **Explaining** Why did Alfred T. Mahan and Henry Cabot Lodge call for the building of a strong U.S. navy?

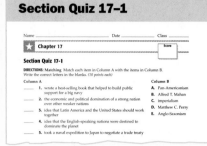

Reteach
Have students analyze how a desire for more trade and markets led to political change between 1877 and 1898.

Enrich
Have students imagine that they were living in Tokyo at the time that Matthew C. Perry steamed into Yedo Bay. Have students write a letter to a friend in another part of Japan relaying the events that transpired.

✓ **Reading Check**

Answer: to protect merchant ships and defend the nation's right to trade with other countries

4 CLOSE

Have students cite the motivations for and the methods of American expansion in the Pacific.

SECTION 1 ASSESSMENT

Checking for Understanding

1. **Define:** imperialism, protectorate.
2. **Identify:** Anglo-Saxonism, Matthew C. Perry, Queen Liliuokalani, Pan-Americanism, Alfred T. Mahan, Henry Cabot Lodge.
3. **Explain** why Secretary of State James G. Blaine convened the Pan-American conference in 1889.

Reviewing Themes

4. **Global Connections** What events in the world convinced Americans to support a large navy?

Critical Thinking

5. **Forming an Opinion** Do you think the United States should have supported the planters in their attempt to overthrow Queen Liliuokalani of Hawaii? Why or why not?
6. **Organizing** Use a graphic organizer to list the factors that led to an imperialist policy in the United States in the 1800s.

Factors Leading to U.S. Imperialist Policy

Analyzing Visuals

7. **Analyzing Art** Study the painting on page 522. How is the U.S. Navy portrayed in relation to the Japanese residents of Yokohama? Do you think the artist shows any bias in this representation? Why or why not?

Writing About History

8. **Persuasive Writing** Imagine that you are living in the United States in the 1890s. Write a letter to the president persuading him to support or oppose an imperialist policy for the United States. Be sure to use standard grammar, spelling, sentence structure, and punctuation.

SECTION 1 ASSESSMENT ANSWERS

1. Terms are in blue.
2. Anglo-Saxonism *(p. 521),* Mathew C. Perry *(p. 522),* Queen Liliuokalani *(p. 523),* Pan-Americanism *(p. 524),* Alfred T. Mahan *(p. 525),* Henry Cabot Lodge *(p. 525)*
3. He convened the conference to support peace and increase trade among the Americas.
4. Germany tried to control Samoa Islands; Chilean mob attacked American soldiers; U.S. backed Venezuela in border dispute
5. Students' answers will vary. Students should be able to defend their points of view.
6. feeling of superiority, interest in expanding trade, need for strategic military bases, European competition
7. probable bias; U.S. troops more numerous and surround Japanese representatives
8. Letters should express a clear point of view.

TEACH

Using an Electronic Spreadsheet Spreadsheets use a standard row and column format to organize information. Cells, the intersection of a row and column, may contain text, numbers, or formulas.

Give students this assignment: Assume that you are in charge of a fund-raising activity for a community event. Create a spreadsheet that you could use to track money received, expenses, and money donated.

Additional Practice

Reinforcing Skills Activity 17

Name _____ Date _____ Class _____

★ Reinforcing Skills Activity **17**

Using an Electronic Spreadsheet

☐ **LEARNING THE SKILL**

A spreadsheet is an electronic worksheet that can manage numbers quickly and easily. All spreadsheets follow a basic design of rows and columns. Each column is assigned a letter, and each row is assigned a number. Each point where a column and row intersect is called a cell. The cell's position on the spreadsheet is labeled according to its corresponding column and row, so A1 is column A, row 1. Spreadsheets use formulas to calculate column and row. To create a formula, highlight the cell you want the results in. Type an equal sign (=) and then build the formula, step by step.

☐ **PRACTICING THE SKILL**

DIRECTIONS: Use the following data to create your own spreadsheet.

Technology
SKILLBUILDER

Using an Electronic Spreadsheet

Why Learn This Skill?

Electronic spreadsheets can help people manage numbers quickly and easily. Historians use spreadsheets to easily manipulate statistical data. You can use a spreadsheet any time a problem involves numbers that can be arranged in rows and columns.

Learning the Skill

A spreadsheet is an electronic worksheet that follows a basic design of rows and columns. Each *column* (vertical) is assigned a letter or number. Each *row* (horizontal) is assigned a number. Each point where a column and row intersect is called a *cell.* The cell's position on the spreadsheet is labeled according to its column and row. Therefore, Column A, Row 1 is referred to as cell A1; Column B, Row 2 is B2, and so on.

Spreadsheets use standard formulas to calculate numbers. You create a simple mathematical equation that uses these standard formulas, and the computer does the calculations for you.

You can also create spreadsheets manually.

A1	B1	C1	D1	E1
A2	B2	C2	D2	E2
A3	B3	C3	D3	E3
A4	B4	C4	D4	E4
A5	B5	C5	D5	E5

Practicing the Skill

Use these steps to create a spreadsheet that will provide the population densities (population per square mile) of the states in the United States in 1900.

❶ In cell A1 type *State;* in cell B1 type *Population;* in cell C1 type *Land area (square miles);* in cell D1 type *Population per square mile.*

❷ In cells A2–A46, type each state's name. In cell A47, type the words *Total for the United States.*

❸ In cells B2–B46, enter the population of each of the states listed in cells A2–A46.

❹ In cells C2–C46, enter the land area (square miles) of each state shown in cells A2–A46.

❺ In cell D2, create a formula to calculate the population per square mile. The formula tells what cells (B2 ÷ C2) to divide. Copy this formula into cells D3–D46.

❻ Use the process in step 5 to create and copy a formula to calculate the nation's total population (B2 + B3 + B4 . . .) for cell B47.

❼ Use the process in step 5 to create and copy a formula to calculate the nation's population per square mile (B47 ÷ C47) for cell D47.

Skills Assessment

Complete the Practicing Skills questions on page 543 and the Chapter 17 Skill Reinforcement Activity to assess your mastery of this skill.

Applying the Skill

Using an Electronic Spreadsheet Use a spreadsheet to enter your test scores and homework grades. Following the grading period, create an equation that allows the spreadsheet to calculate your average grade.

 Glencoe's **Skillbuilder Interactive Workbook CD-ROM, Level 2,** provides instruction and practice in key social studies skills.

ANSWERS TO PRACTICING THE SKILL

Students will create a spreadsheet that gives the population density of each state. Have students use an almanac, a statistical abstract, or other reference source to obtain each state's land area and population in 1900. Remind students that Oklahoma, New Mexico, Arizona, Alaska, and Hawaii were not states in 1900.

Applying the Skill

Students' spreadsheets will vary. Rows and columns should be clearly labeled and the formula to calculate the average grade should be accurate.

1 FOCUS

Section Overview

This section focuses on how the United States became an imperialist power through going to war with Spain.

Main Idea
The United States defeated Spain in a war, acquired new overseas territories, and became an imperial power.

Key Terms and Names
José Martí, William Randolph Hearst, Joseph Pulitzer, yellow journalism, jingoism, Theodore Roosevelt, Platt Amendment

Reading Strategy
Organizing As you read about the Spanish-American War, complete a graphic organizer like the one below by listing the circumstances that contributed to war with Spain.

Factors Contributing to Declaration of War

Reading Objectives:
• **Describe** the circumstances that led to war between the United States and Spain in 1898.
• **Explain** how the war made the United States a world power.

Section Theme
Government and Democracy The United States fought Spain to help Cubans gain their independence.

BELLRINGER
Skillbuilder Activity

Project transparency and have students answer the question.

Available as a blackline master.

Daily Focus Skills Transparency 17–2

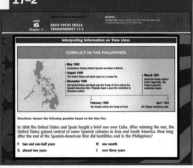

Preview of Events

◆*January 1898* ◆*May 1898* ◆*September 1898* ◆*December 1898*

February 1898
U.S.S. *Maine* explodes

April 1898
U.S. declares war on Spain

May 1898
Dewey destroys Spanish fleet in the Philippines

December 1898
Treaty of Paris ends Spanish-American War

Guide to Reading

Answers to Graphic: sinking of the *Maine,* sympathy for Cuban revolution, need to protect American investments in Cuba

Preteaching Vocabulary
Have students group Key Terms with Key Names associated with the terms.

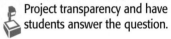

★ An American Story ★

Clara Barton

Clara Barton, the founder and first president of the American National Red Cross, was working late in her villa overlooking the harbor in Havana, Cuba, on the evening of February 15, 1898. As she and an assistant reviewed some paperwork, an enormous blast lit up the sky. She later recalled:

❝The deafening roar was such a burst of thunder as perhaps one never heard before. And off to the right, out over the bay, the air filled with a blaze of light, and this in turn filled with black specks like huge specters flying in all directions.❞

Barton quickly learned what had happened. The U.S.S. *Maine,* anchored in the Havana harbor, had exploded. Barton rushed to a nearby hospital, where she took a firsthand look at the blast's devastation. The sailors' wounds, she wrote, "were all over them—heads and faces terribly cut, internal wounds, arms, legs, feet and hands burned to the live flesh."

—adapted from *The Spanish War*

The Coming of War

Of the 354 officers and sailors aboard the *Maine* that winter night, 266 died. No one is sure why the *Maine* exploded. The size of the explosion indicates that the ship's ammunition supplies blew up. Some experts think that a fire accidentally ignited the ammunition. Others argue that a mine detonated near the ship set off the ammunition.

SECTION RESOURCES

📂 Reproducible Masters
• Reproducible Lesson Plan 17–2
• Daily Lecture and Discussion Notes 17–2
• Guided Reading Activity 17–2
• Section Quiz 17–2
• Reading Essentials and Study Guide 17–2

✒ Transparencies
• Daily Focus Skills Transparency 17–2

Multimedia
🔘 Interactive Tutor Self-Assessment CD-ROM
🔘 ExamView® Pro Testmaker CD-ROM
🔘 Presentation Plus! CD-ROM
🔘 TeacherWorks™ CD-ROM
🔈 Audio Program
🎵 American Music: Cultural Traditions

2 TEACH

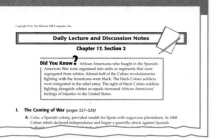
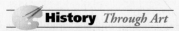

History *Through Art*

Answer: because they regarded the Spanish as tyrants

Ask: What was Cuba's main export product? *(sugarcane)*

Making a List After students have read the part of this section titled "The Coming of War" ask students what events led up to the Spanish-American War. Write their answers on the board in the order that students respond. As a class, put the list in chronological order. **L1**

you don't say...

Strong Ego William Randolph Hearst sent artist Frederic Remington to Cuba to cover events after the explosion of the *Maine.* When the expected conflict between the United States and Spain did not immediately materialize, the artist asked if he should return home. Hearst cabled back, "You furnish the pictures, I'll furnish the war."

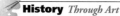
History *Through Art*

Cuban Rebellion During the Cuban Revolution in 1895, Spanish general Valeriano Weyler forced much of the Cuban population into guarded camps near military installations. Why were Americans supporting Cuba's fight against Spain?

When the explosion happened, many Americans blamed it on Spain. Cuba was a Spanish colony at the time, but it was in the midst of a revolution. The Cuban people were fighting for independence from Spain. Many Americans regarded the Spanish as tyrants and supported the Cubans in their struggle. These Americans quickly jumped to the conclusion that Spain had blown up the *Maine.* Within a matter of weeks, Spain and the United States were at war. Although the fighting only lasted a few months, the outcome dramatically altered the position of the United States on the world stage.

The Cuban Rebellion Begins Cuba was one of Spain's oldest colonies in the Americas. Its sugarcane plantations generated considerable wealth for Spain and produced nearly one-third of the world's sugar in the mid-1800s. Until Spain abolished slavery in 1886, about one-third of the Cuban population was enslaved and forced to work for wealthy landowners on the plantations.

In 1868 Cuban rebels declared independence and launched a guerrilla war against Spanish authorities. Lacking internal support, the rebellion collapsed in 1878. Many Cuban rebels then fled to the United States, where they began planning a new revolution.

528 CHAPTER 17 Becoming a World Power

One of the exiled leaders was **José Martí,** a writer and poet who was passionately committed to the cause of Cuban independence. While living in New York City in the 1880s, Martí brought together different Cuban exile groups living in the United States. The groups raised funds from sympathetic Americans, purchased weapons, and trained their troops in preparation for an invasion of Cuba.

By the early 1890s, the United States and Cuba had become closely linked economically. Cuba exported much of its sugar to the United States, and Americans had invested approximately $50 million in Cuba's mines, railroads, and sugar plantations. These economic ties created a crisis in 1894, when the United States imposed new tariffs—including a tariff on sugar—in an effort to protect its troubled economy from foreign competition. The new tariff wrecked the sale of Cuban sugar in the United States and devastated the island's economy.

With Cuba in an economic crisis, Martí's followers launched a new rebellion in February 1895. Although Martí died in battle shortly after returning to Cuba, the revolutionaries seized control of eastern Cuba, declared independence, and formally established the Republic of Cuba in September 1895.

Americans Support the Cubans When the uprising in Cuba began, President Grover Cleveland declared the United States neutral. Outside the White House, however, much of the public openly supported the rebels. Some citizens compared the Cubans' struggle to the American Revolution. A few sympathetic Americans even began smuggling guns from Florida to the Cuban rebels.

What led most Americans to support the rebels were the dramatic stories of Spanish atrocities reported in two of the nation's major newspapers, the *New York Journal* and the *New York World.* The *Journal,* owned by **William Randolph Hearst,** and the *World,* owned by **Joseph Pulitzer,** competed with each other to increase their circulation. The *Journal* reported outrageous stories of the Spanish feeding Cuban prisoners to sharks and dogs. Not to be outdone, the *World* described Cuba as a place with "blood on the roadsides, blood in the fields, blood on the doorsteps, blood, blood, blood!" This kind of sensationalist reporting, in which writers often exaggerated or even made up stories to attract readers, became known as yellow journalism.

Although the press invented sensational stories to sell more papers, there is no doubt that the Cuban people indeed suffered horribly. The Spanish dispatched nearly 200,000 troops to the island to put down

COOPERATIVE LEARNING ACTIVITY

Writing a Feature Article Organize the students into groups of four. Have each student in the group write a feature article about the causes of the Spanish-American War from one of the following points of view: a Rough Rider, a yellow journalist, a wife of a crew member of the *Maine,* or a Cuban who had been forced to live in a reconcentration camp. Have the group review and critique each feature article. Then have the groups combine the articles into a small newspaper. Have groups share their newspapers with others in the class.

Use the rubric for a cooperative group management plan on pages 81–82 in the *Performance Assessment Activities and Rubrics.*

the rebellion and appointed General Valeriano Weyler to serve as governor. Weyler's harsh policies quickly earned him the nickname *El Carnicero* ("The Butcher").

The Cuban rebels carried out a guerrilla war. They staged hit-and-run raids, burned plantations and sugar mills, tore up railroad tracks, and attacked supply depots. The rebels knew that many American businesses had invested in Cuba's railroads and plantations. They hoped that the destruction of American property would lead to American intervention in the war.

To prevent Cuban villagers from helping the rebels, Weyler herded hundreds of thousands of rural men, women, and children into "reconcentration camps," where tens of thousands died of starvation and disease. News reports of this brutal treatment of civilians enraged Americans and led to renewed calls for American intervention in the war.

Calling Out for War
In 1897 Republican William McKinley became president of the United States. The new president did not want to intervene in the war, believing it would cost too many lives and hurt the economy. In September 1897, he asked the Spanish if the United States could help negotiate an end to the conflict. He made it clear that if the war did not end soon, the United States might have to intervene.

Pressed by McKinley, the Spanish government removed Weyler from power. Spain then offered the Cubans autonomy—the right to their own government—but only if Cuba remained part of the Spanish empire. The Cuban rebels refused to negotiate. They wanted full independence.

Spain's concessions to the rebels enraged many Spanish loyalists in Cuba. In January 1898, the loyalists rioted in Havana. Worried that American citizens in Cuba might be attacked, McKinley made the fateful decision to send the battleship *Maine* to Havana in case the Americans had to be evacuated.

In February 1898, the *New York Journal* printed a private letter written by **Enrique Dupuy de Lôme,** the Spanish ambassador to the United States. A Cuban agent had intercepted the letter and delivered it to the paper. It described McKinley as "weak and a bidder for the admiration of the crowd." The nation erupted in fury over the insult.

Ambassador de Lôme resigned, but before the furor could die down, the *Maine* exploded in the Havana harbor. The press promptly blamed Spain. Rapidly responding to the hysterical anger of the American public, Congress unanimously authorized the president to spend $50 million for war preparations. Shortly afterward, on March 28, 1898, a naval

court of inquiry concluded that a mine had destroyed the *Maine*. Throughout America, people began using the slogan "Remember the *Maine!*" as a rallying cry for war. By early April, President McKinley was under tremendous pressure to go to war. American mobs were demonstrating in the streets against Spain—and against McKinley for refusing to go to war.

Within the Republican Party, jingoism, or an attitude of aggressive nationalism, was very strong, especially among younger members of the party. These members were furious at McKinley for not declaring war. Assistant Secretary of the Navy **Theodore Roosevelt,** for one, raged that McKinley had "no more backbone than a chocolate éclair." Many Democrats were also demanding war, and Republicans feared that if McKinley did not go to war, the Democrats would win the presidency in 1900. Finally, on April 11, 1898, McKinley asked Congress to authorize the use of force to end the conflict in Cuba.

On April 19, Congress declared Cuba independent, demanded that Spain withdraw from the island, and authorized the president to use armed force if necessary. In response, on April 23, Spain declared war on the United States. For the first time in 50 years, the United States was at war with another nation.

✓ **Reading Check** **Examining** What conditions led to the Cuban rebellion in 1895?

A War on Two Fronts

The Spanish in Cuba were not prepared for war. Tropical diseases and months of hard fighting had weakened their soldiers. Their warships were old and their crews poorly trained. The United States had more battleships, and both sides knew that the war ultimately would be decided at sea. If the United States could defeat Spain's fleet, the Spanish would not be able to get supplies to its troops in Cuba. Eventually, they would have to surrender.

The United States Takes the Philippines
The United States Navy was ready for war with Spain. The navy's North Atlantic Squadron blockaded Cuba, and the American fleet based in British Hong Kong was ordered to attack the Spanish fleet in the Philippines. The Philippines was a Spanish colony, and American naval planners were determined to prevent the fleet there from sailing east to attack the United States.

CHAPTER 17 Becoming a World Power **529**

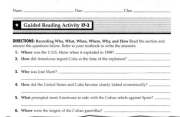

Guided Reading Activity 17-2

Name _____ Date _____ Class _____

★ **Guided Reading Activity 17-2**

DIRECTIONS: Recording Who, What, When, Where, Why, and How Read the section and answer the questions below. Refer to your textbook to write the answers.
1. Where was the U.S.S. *Maine* when it exploded in 1898? _____
2. How did Americans regard Cuba at the time of the explosion? _____
3. Who was José Martí? _____
4. How did the United States and Cuba become closely linked economically? _____
5. What prompted most Americans to side with the Cuban rebels against Spain? _____
6. Where were the targets of the Cuban guerrillas? _____

✓ **Reading Check**

Answer: Spanish oppression, Spanish economic exploitation

CURRICULUM CONNECTION

Language Arts "Yellow" journalism takes its name from the "Yellow Kid" comic strip, which featured a scrappy little bald kid in a flashy yellow nightshirt. Drawn by R.F. Outcault, the comic strip first ran in 1895 in Joseph Pulitzer's *New York World.* The bright yellow ink attracted readers. Thereafter, yellow journalism came to refer to flashy, unsubstantiated news accounts.

FYI

When President McKinley asked Congress for a declaration of war, the House of Representatives voted 311 to 6 in support of the declaration. The Senate was more evenly divided, voting 42 to 35. To appease some reluctant members of Congress, the Teller Amendment was added to the declaration. The amendment called for the United States to help Cuba become an independent country once the war had ended.

MEETING SPECIAL NEEDS

Visual/Spatial Summarizing requires students to choose key ideas or events and state them concisely. Ask students to pick one of the key events in the section and draw it. *(Most students will choose the battleship explosion.)* Then have students write a sentence that explains one event that preceded the event they drew and one event that came after it. Label the sequence 1, 2, and 3. Explain that students have used drawings and descriptions to summarize a section of text. **L1**

📁 Refer to *Inclusion for the High School Social Studies Classroom Strategies and Activities* in the TCR.

529

Geography Skills

Answers:

1. in the Caribbean and in the Philippines

2. about 320 miles (515 kilometers)

Geography Skills Practice

Ask: Who was the leader of the Spanish fleet in the Caribbean? *(Cervera)*

Creating an Absolute Chronology Have students find the dates of events in 1898 that were part of the Spanish-American War. Draw a line across the board and label it 1898. Divide the line into 12 segments to represent the months of the year. Have students enter the events in the appropriate places. Note: one source of events related to the Spanish-American War can be found at http://lcweb.loc.gov/rr/hispanic/1898/chronology.html. **L2**

The Tenth Cavalry was one of four African American units to serve in Cuba. Although their courage was highly praised, they were not considered equals. The U.S. Army did not abolish segregated units until 1948.

History *and the* Humanities

American Music: Cultural Traditions: "Battleship of Maine"

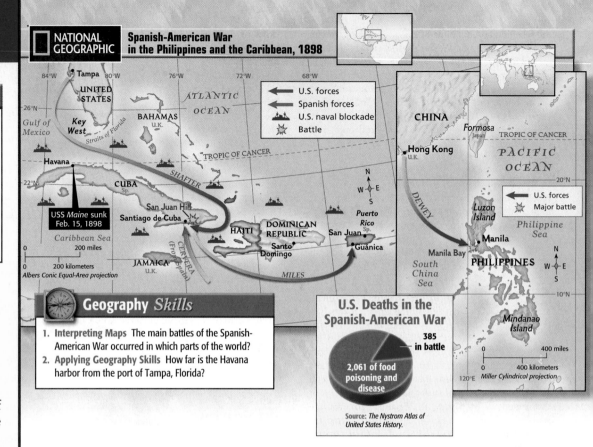

NATIONAL GEOGRAPHIC Spanish-American War in the Philippines and the Caribbean, 1898

Legend:
- U.S. forces
- Spanish forces
- U.S. naval blockade
- Battle
- U.S. forces
- Major battle

USS *Maine* sunk Feb. 15, 1898

Geography Skills

1. **Interpreting Maps** The main battles of the Spanish-American War occurred in which parts of the world?

2. **Applying Geography Skills** How far is the Havana harbor from the port of Tampa, Florida?

U.S. Deaths in the Spanish-American War

385 in battle

2,061 of food poisoning and disease

Source: *The Nystrom Atlas of United States History.*

A short time after midnight, on May 1, 1898, Commodore **George Dewey** led his squadron into Manila Bay in the Philippines. As dawn broke, Dewey's fleet opened fire and rapidly destroyed the severely outgunned Spanish warships.

Dewey's quick victory took McKinley and his advisers by surprise. The army was not yet ready to send troops to help Dewey capture the Philippines. Hastily, the army assembled 20,000 troops to sail from San Francisco to the Philippines. On the way to the Philippines, the American troops also seized the island of Guam, another Spanish possession in the Pacific.

While waiting for the American troops to arrive, Dewey contacted **Emilio Aguinaldo,** a Filipino revolutionary leader who had staged an unsuccessful uprising against the Spanish in 1896. Aguinaldo quickly launched a new guerrilla war.

At first, Aguinaldo believed the Americans were his allies, but when American troops arrived in the islands he became suspicious. The Americans quickly seized the Philippine capital of Manila from

the Spanish but refused to allow Aguinaldo's forces into the city. They also refused to recognize his rebel government. Hostility between the Filipinos and the Americans began to grow as both sides waited for the war with Spain to end.

American Forces Battle in Cuba Unlike the mobilization of the navy, which had been very efficient, the mobilization of the American army was very poorly conducted. Although volunteers flooded into army training camps, the army lacked the resources to train and equip them. In many camps, conditions were so unsanitary that epidemics broke out, and hundreds of Americans died. By the end of the war, far more Americans had died in training camps than in actual battle.

Finally, on June 14, 1898, a force of about 17,000 troops landed on the southern coast of Cuba, east of the city of Santiago. A Spanish fleet occupied Santiago Harbor, where it was well protected by powerful shore-based guns. American military planners wanted to capture those guns in order to

---

INTERDISCIPLINARY CONNECTIONS ACTIVITY

Language Arts Read the following quote from Walt Whitman, published in 1882:

"Long ere the second centennial arrives, there will be some forty to fifty great States, among them Canada and Cuba. . . . The Pacific will be ours, and the Atlantic mainly ours. There will be daily electric communication with every part of the globe. . . . The individuality of one nation must then, as always, lead the world. Can there be any doubt who the leader ought to be?" Discuss with students how Whitman expresses the expansionist views held by many Americans. **L2**

drive the Spanish fleet out of the harbor and into battle with the American fleet waiting nearby.

Among the American troops advancing toward Santiago was a volunteer cavalry unit from the American West. They were a flamboyant mix of cowboys, miners, and law officers known as the **"Rough Riders."** The commander of the Rough Riders was Colonel **Leonard Wood.** Second in command was Theodore Roosevelt, who had resigned from his post as assistant secretary of the navy to join the fight.

On July 1, American troops attacked the village of El Caney northeast of Santiago. Another force attacked the San Juan Heights, a series of hills overlooking the main road to Santiago. While one group of soldiers attacked San Juan Hill, the Rough Riders—who were on foot, not horseback—attacked Kettle Hill. After seizing Kettle Hill, Roosevelt and his men assisted in the capture of San Juan Hill.

The Rough Riders did not make their attack alone. Accompanying them up Kettle Hill were the all-black 9th and 10th Cavalry Regiments. Many African Americans had responded to the call for volunteers, and roughly one-fourth of the American troops fighting in Cuba were African American.

Four African American soldiers received the Medal of Honor for their bravery during the war.

The Spanish commander in Santiago panicked after the American victories at El Caney and the San Juan Heights. He immediately ordered the Spanish fleet in the harbor to flee. As the Spanish ships raced out of the harbor on July 3, the American warships guarding the entrance attacked them. In the ensuing battle, the American squadron sank or beached every Spanish vessel.

Spanish resistance in Cuba ended with the surrender of Santiago two weeks later. Soon after, American troops occupied the nearby Spanish colony of Puerto Rico. On August 12, 1898, Spain and the United States agreed to a cease-fire.

✓ **Reading Check** **Describing** How prepared was the U.S. Army to fight a war against Spain?

An American Empire is Born

As American and Spanish leaders met to discuss the terms for a peace treaty, Americans debated what to do about their newly acquired lands. Cuba would

NATIONAL GEOGRAPHIC
MOMENT in HISTORY

FEISTY LEADER FOR A NEW CENTURY

Theodore Roosevelt (center) embodied the spirit of the United States at the turn of the century: full of vitality, brimming with confidence, and convinced that no job was impossible, no challenge insurmountable. Whether hunting big game in Africa, roping cattle from horseback on a Dakota ranch, or leading his "Rough Riders" cavalry (right) up San Juan Hill during the Spanish-American War, Roosevelt never did anything cautiously or quietly. As president, Roosevelt guided the country into its new, unaccustomed role as a world power.

Analyzing Information Have students reexamine the painting on page 519 after they have read "American Forces Battle in Cuba." **Ask: What is the discrepancy between the painting and the facts?** *(The Rough Riders were on foot, not on horseback.)* **How do you think movies today affect the way that we view historical events?** *(Encourage students to consider how* Saving Private Ryan *and* Pearl Harbor *mix facts with fiction.)* **L1**

✓**Reading Check**

Answer: well prepared, with a plan to attack around Santiago to scare the Spanish fleet out of the harbor and into battle with the American Navy

NATIONAL GEOGRAPHIC
MOMENT in HISTORY

One of Theodore Roosevelt's greatest disappointments was President Woodrow Wilson's refusal to allow him to fight in World War I. Roosevelt was in his late 50s when the United States entered the war.

you don't say...

Literature Rudyard Kipling wrote "The White Man's Burden" in 1899 to persuade the Americans to make the Philippines a colony.

CRITICAL THINKING ACTIVITY

Synthesizing Ask students to list reasons why a nation might be justified in declaring war on another nation. Have students incorporate their reasons into a paragraph that applies them to the United States's declaration of war on Spain in 1898. Invite volunteers to share their paragraphs with the class and discuss whether these reasons are justifiable. **L2**

Interpreting Quotations Have students read the quote from McKinley on page 532. Then read the following quote from Andrew Carnegie: "You seem to have finished your work of civilizing the Filipinos; it is thought about 8,000 of them have been completely civilized and sent to heaven. I hope you like it." Ask students to interpret each quotation. **L2**

3 ASSESS

Assign Section 2 Assessment as homework or as an in-class activity.

🌐 Have students use the **Interactive Tutor Self-Assessment CD-ROM.**

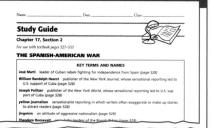
be given its freedom as promised, and Spain had agreed that the United States would annex Guam and Puerto Rico. The big question was what to do with the Philippines. The United States faced a difficult choice—remain true to its republican ideals or become an imperial power.

The Debate Over Annexation Many supporters of annexing the Philippines emphasized the economic and military benefits of taking the islands. They would provide the United States with a naval base in Asia, a stopover on the way to China, and a large market for American goods.

Other supporters believed America had a duty to teach "less civilized" peoples how to live properly. "Surely this Spanish war has not been a grab for empire," commented a New England minister, "but a heroic effort [to] free the oppressed, and to teach the millions of ignorant, debased human beings thus freed how to live."

Not all Americans supported annexation. Anti-imperialists included industrialist Andrew Carnegie, social worker Jane Addams, writer Samuel Clemens (Mark Twain), and the leader of the American Federation of Labor, Samuel Gompers. Carnegie argued that the cost of an empire far outweighed the economic benefits it provided. Gompers worried that competition from cheap Filipino labor would drive down American wages. Addams, Clemens, and others believed imperialism violated American principles.

President McKinley had to decide what to do with the Philippines. Ultimately, he decided to annex the islands. He later explained his reasoning to a group of ministers:

> 66 And one night late it came to me this way . . . (1) that we could not give them back to Spain—that would be cowardly and dishonorable; (2) that we could not turn them over to France or Germany . . . that would be bad for business and discreditable; (3) that we could not leave them to themselves—they were unfit for self-government . . . and (4) that there was nothing left for us to do but to take them all, and to educate the Filipinos, and uplift and civilize and Christianize them. 99
>
> —quoted in *A Diplomatic History of the American People*

On December 10, 1898, the United States and Spain signed the Treaty of Paris. Under the treaty, Cuba became an independent country, and the United States acquired Puerto Rico and Guam and agreed to pay Spain $20 million for the Philippines. After an intense

Picturing **History**

Building an Empire Two Filipino women nervously converse with American troops in the Philippines. Filipino civilians suffered many hardships while Filipino guerrillas fought American troops. Thousands perished from sickness, starvation, and other indirect effects of war. What American policy contributed to civilian hardships in the Philippines?

debate, the Senate ratified the treaty in February 1899. The United States had become an imperial power.

Rebellion in the Philippines The United States quickly learned that controlling its new empire would not be easy. Emilio Aguinaldo called the American decision to annex his homeland a "violent and aggressive seizure." He then ordered his troops to attack the American soldiers in the Philippines.

To fight the Filipino guerrillas, General Arthur MacArthur (the father of the future American general Douglas MacArthur) adopted many of the same policies that America had condemned Spain for using in Cuba. MacArthur set up reconcentration camps to separate guerrillas from civilians. The results were also similar to what had happened in Cuba. Thousands of Filipinos died from disease and starvation.

While MacArthur fought the guerrillas, the first U.S. civilian governor of the islands, William Howard Taft, tried to win over the Filipino people by reforming education, transportation, and health care. New railroads, bridges, and telegraph lines strengthened the economy. A public school system was set up, and new health care policies virtually eliminated severe diseases such as cholera and smallpox. These reforms slowly reduced Filipino hostility.

Emilio Aguinaldo

EXTENDING THE CONTENT

Puerto Rican Independence Eugenio María de Hostos y Bonilla championed the cause of independence for Puerto Rico. He lived and worked in New York City from 1898 to 1900 pursuing avenues to allow the people of Puerto Rico, through popular vote, to determine the future status of the island. He was a member of a delegation that delivered this demand to President McKinley. He was also a prolific writer who supported the causes of abolition and women's rights.

In March 1901, American troops captured Aguinaldo. The following month, Aguinaldo accepted American control of the islands and called on the guerrillas to surrender. By summer 1902, the United States had declared the war over. Eventually the United States allowed the Filipinos a greater role in governing their own country. By the mid-1930s, they were permitted to elect their own congress and president. Finally, in 1946, the United States granted independence to the Philippines.

GOVERNMENT

Governing Puerto Rico Another pressing question facing the United States government was how to govern Puerto Rico. In 1900 Congress passed the **Foraker Act,** making Puerto Rico an unincorporated territory. This meant that Puerto Ricans were not U.S. citizens and had no constitutional rights. The act also stated that Congress could pass whatever laws it wanted for the island.

Congress gradually allowed the inhabitants of Puerto Rico a certain degree of self-government. In 1917 the United States made Puerto Ricans citizens of the United States. In 1947 the island was allowed to elect its own governor. At this time a debate began over whether to grant Puerto Rico statehood, allow it to become an independent country, or continue it as a commonwealth of the United States. This debate over Puerto Rico's status continues today.

Cuba and the Platt Amendment After the war, the United States established a military government in Cuba. Although the United States had promised to grant Cuba its independence, President McKinley took steps to ensure that Cuba would remain tied to the United States. He allowed the Cubans to prepare a new constitution for their country, but he attached conditions. A special amendment that Senator Orville Platt attached to the 1901 army appropriations bill described those conditions.

The **Platt Amendment** specified the following: (1) Cuba could not make any treaty with another nation that would weaken its independence or allow another foreign power to gain territory in Cuba; (2) Cuba had to allow the United States to buy or lease naval stations in Cuba; (3) Cuba's debts had to be kept low to prevent foreign countries from landing troops to enforce payment; and (4) the United States would have the right to intervene to protect Cuban independence and keep order.

Although the Cubans rejected the Platt Amendment at first, they quickly realized that unless they accepted it, the United States would maintain its military government of the island. Reluctantly, they added the amendment to their constitution. The Platt Amendment governed relations between the United States and Cuba until its repeal in 1934. It effectively made Cuba an American protectorate.

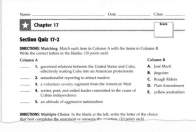

HISTORY Online

Student Web Activity Visit the *American Vision* Web site at tav.glencoe.com and click on *Student Web Activities—Chapter 17* for an activity on American imperialism.

✓ **Reading Check** **Explaining** What were the arguments for and against establishing an American empire?

SECTION 2 ASSESSMENT

Checking for Understanding

1. **Define:** yellow journalism, jingoism.
2. **Identify:** José Martí, William Randolph Hearst, Joseph Pulitzer, Theodore Roosevelt, Platt Amendment.
3. **Explain** why many Americans blamed Spain for the explosion of the U.S.S. *Maine.*

Reviewing Themes

4. **Government and Democracy** Why did many Filipinos feel betrayed by the U.S. government after the Spanish-American War?

Critical Thinking

5. **Interpreting** Do you think President McKinley could have taken a different course of action with Spain over Cuba? If so, what kind? If not, why not?
6. **Categorizing** Complete a graphic organizer by summarizing the effects of the United States annexing lands obtained after the Spanish-American War.

Lands Annexed	Effects

Analyzing Visuals

7. **Analyzing Art** Examine the painting on page 519. Considering what you have learned about the Rough Riders and this battle, what is inaccurate about the painting? What kind of bias does this misrepresentation show?

Writing About History

8. **Descriptive Writing** Imagine that you are a Filipino living during the time of the U.S. annexation of the Philippine Islands. Write a journal entry in which you describe your feelings about U.S. control of the islands.

CHAPTER 17 Becoming a World Power **533**

SECTION 2 ASSESSMENT ANSWERS

1. Terms are in blue.
2. José Martí (p. 528), William Randolph Hearst (p. 528), Joseph Pulitzer (p. 528), Theodore Roosevelt (p. 529), Platt Amendment (p. 533)
3. Cuba was fighting Spain for its independence, and many Americans saw the Spanish as tyrants.
4. The Filipinos did not want their homeland annexed.
5. Students' answers will vary.
6. Puerto Rico: U.S. control of its government, Puerto Ricans are U.S. citizens from 1917; Philippines: provide a naval base to guard U.S. trade; some improvements in Filipino schools, roads, and healthcare
7. They are on horseback in the painting; they were actually on foot. It glorifies the Rough Riders.
8. Journal entries will vary. Entries should be written from the point of view of a Filipino.

Section Quiz 17–2

Name ___ Date ___ Class ___

★ Chapter 17 — Score ___

Section Quiz 17-2

DIRECTIONS: Matching Match each item in Column A with the items in Column B. Write the correct letters in the blanks. *(10 points each)*

Column A
___ 1. governed relations between the United States and Cuba, effectively making Cuba into an American protectorate
___ 2. sensationalist reporting to attract readers
___ 3. a volunteer cavalry regiment from the American West
___ 4. writer, poet, and exiled leader committed to the cause of Cuban independence
___ 5. an attitude of aggressive nationalism

Column B
A. José Martí
B. jingoism
C. Rough Riders
D. Platt Amendment
E. yellow journalism

DIRECTIONS: Multiple Choice In the blank at the left, write the letter of the choice that best completes the statement or answers the question. *(10 points each)*

Reteach

Have students explain the significance of 1898.

Enrich

Have students write reports explaining a commonwealth government.

HISTORY Online

Objectives and answers to the student activity can be found in the **Web Activity Lesson Plan** at tav.glencoe.com.

✓ **Reading Check**

Answer: For: a naval base in Asia and a market for American goods; to teach the less fortunate. Against: cost, cheap labor might drive down American wages, competition, and violated American principles

4 CLOSE

Have students explain how the war made the United States a world power.

1 FOCUS

Remind students that improved technology can sometimes provide information about a historical event. Point out that even if we know the truth today, history was shaped by what people believed at the time.

2 TEACH

Researching a Topic Have students find a history book that was published before 1976, when Rickover's team of experts issued their conclusion. Instruct students to compare the content to what appears in this feature. Have students write a paragraph based on their findings. Instruct students to prepare a bibliographic citation for the book they use. **L2**

you don't say...

Military Hardware The word *ordnance* refers to weapons, ammunition, and military vehicles, along with the tools and equipment for maintenance.

You're the Historian

Who Sank the *Maine*?

During Cuba's revolt against Spain, the American battleship *Maine* dropped anchor in the Havana harbor to protect American interests in Cuba. On the night of February 15, 1898, the ship exploded and 266 Americans lost their lives. The United States sent a court of inquiry to Havana on February 21. Despite the lack of evidence concerning the source of the explosion, American newspapers and many public officials claimed that Spain was responsible. Pressured on all sides, President McKinley sent Spain an ultimatum that led to war. Who—or what—really sank the *Maine*?

Read the following excerpts from testimony and evidence. Then answer the questions and complete the activities that follow.

Captain Charles Sigsbee

Newspaper headline

$50,000 REWARD! WHO DESTROYED THE MAINE? $50,000 REWARD!
NEW YORK JOURNAL
AND ADVERTISER
DESTRUCTION OF THE WAR SHIP MAINE WAS THE WORK OF AN ENEMY
$50,000! | Assistant Secretary Roosevelt | $50,000!
$50,000 REWARD! | Convinced the Explosion of | $50,000 REWARD!
For the Detection of the | the War Ship Was Not | For the Detection of the
Perpetrator of | an Accident. | Perpetrator of
the Maine Outrage! | | the Maine Outrage!

From the commander and an early interview

Telegraph from the commander of the *Maine* to the secretary of the navy, February 15:

"Maine blown up in Havana harbor at nine forty to-night and destroyed. Many wounded and doubtless more killed or drowned. . . . Public opinion should be suspended until further report. . . . Many Spanish officers, including representatives of General Blanco, now with us to express sympathy."

—**Captain Charles D. Sigsbee**

The court of inquiry was interested in discovering whether the explosion had come from inside or outside the ship. If it came from inside, was it sabotage or an accident? If it came from outside, who or what caused it? Before the court met, the *Washington Evening Star* published a February 18 interview with the U.S. Navy's leading ordnance expert:

"We know of no instances where the explosion of a torpedo or mine under the ship's bottom has exploded the magazine [powder and explosives] within. It has simply torn a great hole in the side or bottom, through which water entered, and in consequence of which the ship sunk. Magazine explosions, on the contrary, produce effects exactly similar to the effects of the explosion on the *Maine*. When it comes to seeking the cause of the explosion of the *Maine's* magazine, we should naturally look not for the improbable or unusual causes. . . . The most common of these is through fires in the bunkers."

—**Philip R. Alger**

USS Maine

EXTENDING THE CONTENT

Artifacts from the *Maine* When the U.S.S. *Maine* was raised from Havana Harbor in 1911, some members of Congress wanted a piece. Frank B. Willis, a Representative from Ohio, claimed Captain Sigsbee's enameled-steel bathtub. After his hometown of Urbana turned down the gift of the bathtub, the people of Findlay, Ohio, claimed it. When the bathtub arrived in Findlay in 1913, disappointed citizens saw that the artifact was not quite the treasure they had hoped for. After being underwater for 14 years, the tub was rusted and ugly. Displayed in various places in Findlay over the years, it now resides in the Hancock Historical Museum.

Engraving of the explosion

From the inquiry and later reports

As the court of inquiry concluded its investigation, it considered reports of the divers who examined the *Maine* and evidence that suggested there had been two explosions. On March 11, 1898, Lieutenant Commander Adolph Marix, judge advocate of the court of inquiry, questioned Commander George A. Converse, who was brought in as a technical expert.

Marix: Looking at the plan of the *Maine's* forward 10-inch and 6-inch magazines, would it be possible for them to have exploded, torn out the ship's side on both sides, and leave that part of the ship forward of frame 18 so water borne as to raise the after portion of that part of the ship, drag it aft, and bring the vertical keel into the condition you see in the sketch?

Converse: It is difficult for me to realize that that effect could have been produced by an explosion of the kind supposed.

Marix: Do you think, then, necessarily, there must have been an underwater mine to produce these explosions?

Converse: Indications are that an underwater explosion produced the conditions there.

In 1911 the U.S. Navy raised the *Maine* from Havana's harbor. The navy's board of inspection reexamined the ship, and its findings were similar to those of 1898. Then, in 1976, Admiral H.G. Rickover and other naval historians gathered a team of experts to examine the official court records of 1898 and 1911. This team's conclusions were very different.

1911 board conclusion:

The board finds that the injuries to the bottom of the *Maine* above described were caused by the explosion of a charge of a low form of explosive exterior to the ship between frames 28 and 31.

H.G. Rickover team conclusion:

The general character of the overall wrecked structure of the *Maine*, with hull sides and whole deck structures peeled back, leaves no doubt that a large internal explosion occurred. . . .

The mines available in 1898 are believed to have been incapable of igniting the *Maine* magazine if they exploded on the harbor bottom or against the ship side. . . . It is most unlikely that the *Maine* explosion was indeed initiated by a mine. . . .

The available evidence is consistent with an internal explosion alone. . . . The most likely source was heat from a fire in the coal bunker adjacent to the 6-inch reserve magazine.

Mast of the Maine *at Arlington National Cemetery*

Understanding the Issue

1. Why did the original investigation's conclusion that there was an underwater explosion lead to war with Spain?
2. If there had been an underwater explosion, was it logical to conclude that a Spanish person planted the mine? Why or why not? Is this an example of a biased opinion?
3. Why did the 1976 review conclude that the explosion came from inside the *Maine*?

Activities

1. **Rewriting History** Suppose that the initial court of inquiry had concluded that an internal explosion sank the *Maine*. Write a paragraph describing an alternate course history could have taken in the following year.
2. **Oral Report** Read a biography of one of these key players in the decision of the United States to go to war: Hearst, Roosevelt, or McKinley. Write a short oral presentation on this person's perspective and influence on the war.

PORTFOLIO ACTIVITY

Creating a Brochure Give students this assignment: Create a three-panel brochure explaining the history of the sinking of the *Maine*. Use the information presented in Section 2 and in this feature, along with other information gathered from library and Internet resources. Use display type and graphics to make the brochure interesting and attractive.

SECTION 3 New American Diplomacy

1 FOCUS

Section Overview

This section focuses on how the presidency of Theodore Roosevelt helped increase America's power.

BELLRINGER
Skillbuilder Activity

Project transparency and have students answer the question.

Available as a blackline master.

Daily Focus Skills Transparency 17–3

Guide to Reading

Answers to Graphic: save time, save money, help the United States remain a world power

Preteaching Vocabulary
Have students choose one of the proper names from the list of Key Terms and Names. Ask students to find the name and write a brief description. Ask for volunteers to share their explanations.

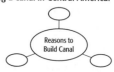

Guide to Reading

Main Idea
Under President Theodore Roosevelt, the United States increased its power on the world stage.

Key Terms and Names
sphere of influence, Open Door policy, Boxer Rebellion, "Great White Fleet," Hay-Pauncefote Treaty, Roosevelt Corollary, dollar diplomacy

Reading Strategy
Organizing As you read about the increasing presence of the United States in the world, complete a graphic organizer like the one below by listing the reasons President Roosevelt gave for wanting a canal in Central America.

Reasons to Build Canal

Reading Objectives:
• **Critique** Theodore Roosevelt's foreign policy as president.
• **Explain** the Open Door policy and its effects on relations between the United States and Asia.

Section Theme
Continuity and Change The commercial interests of the United States spurred its involvement in distant parts of the world, such as China and Latin America.

Preview of Events

| ♦1898 | ♦1900 | ♦1902 | ♦1904 |

1899
Secretary of State Hay sends Open Door notes

1900
Boxer Rebellion erupts in China

1901
McKinley assassinated; Theodore Roosevelt becomes president

1904
Construction of Panama Canal begins

★ An American Story ★

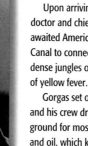

Upon arriving in Panama in 1904, Dr. William Crawford Gorgas, a U.S. Army doctor and chief sanitary officer to the Panama Canal project, quickly realized that death awaited American workers. The United States was about to begin constructing the Panama Canal to connect the Atlantic and Pacific Oceans. The task would be daunting because the dense jungles of Panama were home to swarms of mosquitoes that spread the deadly disease of yellow fever.

Gorgas set out to lessen the threat of disease by keeping mosquitoes from breeding. He and his crew drained swamps, gullies, and other sources of stagnant water, a main breeding ground for mosquitoes. On those areas of water they could not drain, they spread kerosene and oil, which killed the mosquito eggs before they hatched. They also fumigated nearly every home in the region and destroyed many buckets, pots, and other outdoor containers that local residents let fill up with rainwater. In two years Gorgas and his crew had wiped out yellow fever in the area.

—adapted from *The Strength to Move a Mountain*

Dr. William Gorgas

Theodore Roosevelt's Rise to Power

The construction of the Panama Canal might never have taken place had Theodore Roosevelt not become president. "Teddy," as the press called him, gained the presidency largely by accident. Roosevelt's exploits during the Spanish-American War had made

---

SECTION RESOURCES

Reproducible Masters
• Reproducible Lesson Plan 17–3
• Daily Lecture and Discussion Notes 17–3
• Guided Reading Activity 17–3
• Section Quiz 17–3
• Reading Essentials and Study Guide 17–3
• Interpreting Political Cartoons

Transparencies
• Daily Focus Skills Transparency 17–3

Multimedia
• Interactive Tutor Self-Assessment CD-ROM
• ExamView® Pro Testmaker CD-ROM
• Presentation Plus! CD-ROM
• TeacherWorks™ CD-ROM
• Audio Program

him famous and enabled him to win the election for governor of New York in November 1898. In 1900 President McKinley asked Roosevelt to run as his vice president. Less than a year later, a tragic turn of events thrust Roosevelt into the White House.

The Election of 1900 The election of 1900 once again pitted President McKinley against William Jennings Bryan. Bryan, an anti-imperialist, attacked the Republicans for their support of imperialism in Asia. McKinley focused on the country's increased prosperity. Employing the slogan "Four Years More of the Full Dinner Pail," the Republicans promised good times ahead if McKinley was reelected. He did indeed win the election by a wide margin, and Theodore Roosevelt became vice president.

On September 6, 1901, as President McKinley greeted the public during an appearance in Buffalo, New York, a gunman stepped from the crowd. The man was Leon Czolgosz, an avowed anarchist, who opposed all forms of government. Czolgosz fired two shots and hit the president. A few days later, McKinley died from his wounds.

Theodore Roosevelt, just 42 years old at the time, became the youngest person ever to become president. Roosevelt had been chosen as McKinley's running mate because Republican leaders knew his powerful charisma and heroic war record would be a great asset. They also hoped the relatively powerless position of vice president would quiet his reform-minded spirit. Now they cringed at the thought of a headstrong Roosevelt in the White House. Republican senator Mark Hanna exclaimed, "Now look, that . . . cowboy is president of the United States!"

Roosevelt Becomes President Roosevelt brought to the presidency an energy and enthusiasm rarely seen before in the office. Such vigor stemmed in part from his childhood. Born into a wealthy New York family, Roosevelt was a sickly child who endured a host of ailments, including poor eyesight and asthma.

Roosevelt pushed himself to overcome his frailties. He mastered marksmanship and horseback riding and could row up to 20 miles a day. He took up boxing and wrestling in college and continued with both throughout his life, practicing the belief that competition and conflict keep one healthy.

Roosevelt became a strong proponent of increasing American power on the world stage. Just as he refused to sit around idly in life, the president warned Americans not to "sit huddled" and become "an assemblage of well-to-do hucksters who care nothing for what happens beyond." Roosevelt also accepted some of the ideas of Anglo-Saxonism. He believed that the United States had a duty to shape the "less civilized" corners of the earth. The new president intended to make the country a world power.

✓ **Reading Check** **Summarizing** What was President Roosevelt's opinion on the role of the United States as a world power?

American Diplomacy in Asia

In 1899 the United States was a major power in Asia, with naval bases all across the Pacific. Operating from those bases, the United States Navy—now the third largest in the world—was capable of exerting American power anywhere in East Asia.

The nation's primary interest in Asia, however, was not conquest but commerce. Between 1895 and 1900, American exports to China increased by four times. Although China bought only about two percent of all the goods exported by the United States, the vast Chinese markets excited American business leaders, especially those in the textile, oil, and steel industries.

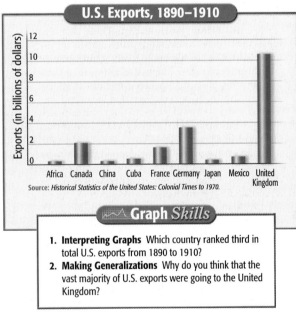

U.S. Exports, 1890–1910

Exports (in billions of dollars): vertical axis 0 to 12

Countries: Africa, Canada, China, Cuba, France, Germany, Japan, Mexico, United Kingdom

Source: *Historical Statistics of the United States: Colonial Times to 1970.*

Graph Skills

1. **Interpreting Graphs** Which country ranked third in total U.S. exports from 1890 to 1910?
2. **Making Generalizations** Why do you think that the vast majority of U.S. exports were going to the United Kingdom?

2 TEACH

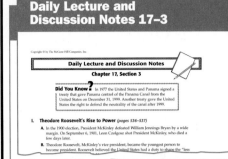

Daily Lecture and Discussion Notes 17–3

Copyright © by The McGraw-Hill Companies, Inc.

Daily Lecture and Discussion Notes
Chapter 17, Section 3

Did You Know? In 1977 the United States and Panama signed a treaty that gave Panama control of the Panama Canal from the United States on December 31, 1999. Another treaty gave the United States the right to defend the neutrality of the canal after 1999.

I. **Theodore Roosevelt's Rise to Power** *(pages 536–537)*
   A. In the 1900 election, President McKinley defeated William Jennings Bryan by a wide margin. On September 6, 1901, Leon Czolgosz shot President McKinley, who died a few days later.
   B. Theodore Roosevelt, McKinley's vice president, became the youngest person to become president. Roosevelt believed the United States had a duty to shape the "less

✓ **Reading Check**

Answer: that it should shape "less civilized" nations

Analyzing a Quote Read this statement by Theodore Roosevelt: "I wish to preach, not the doctrine of ignoble ease, but the doctrine of the strenuous life, the life of toil and effort, of labor and strife…." **Ask students:** How might Roosevelt conduct foreign affairs? (*He might try to expand the American empire, not content with American gains.*) **L1**

Graph Skills

Answers:
1. Canada
2. They had long been America's main trading partner.

Graph Skills Practice
Ask: Trade with China increased between 1895 and 1900, but how did it rank in 1910? (*at the bottom, with Africa and Japan*)

COOPERATIVE LEARNING ACTIVITY

Creating Cartoons Tell students that Theodore Roosevelt's personality and style made him a favorite with cartoonists. Organize students into groups and have each portray Roosevelt in a cartoon. Encourage students who need ideas to use library and Internet resources to locate cartoons featuring Roosevelt. Have groups share their cartoons and explain their meaning. Display cartoons in the classroom.

Use the rubric for a cooperative group management plan on pages 81–82 in the *Performance Assessment Activities and Rubrics.*

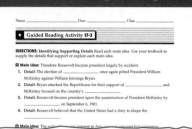
Why It Matters

In recent years, the volume of cargo passing through the Panama Canal has increased significantly with the growth of world trade.

FYI

The Boxers, also known as the Righteous and Harmonious Fists, were members of a secret society opposed to foreign influence in China. As the Boxers laid siege to the foreign legations in Beijing, diplomats, foreign civilians, and Chinese Christians were trapped behind barricades for nearly 60 days before an international rescue team ended the uprising.

you don't say...

Anti-Imperialist William Jennings Bryan was nominated for president three times. He lost in 1896, 1900, and 1908. In part his anti-imperialist stand helped defeat him. He did go on to become secretary of state under President Woodrow Wilson. In that post Bryan continued to oppose U.S. expansionist policies.

📁 Use *Interpreting Political Cartoons,* Cartoon 18.

Why It Matters

The Panama Canal

One of the most impressive feats of engineering in the world, the Panama Canal was built under a 1903 U.S. treaty with Panama. It took 10 years to build, required more than 40,000 laborers, and cost almost $390 million. The canal stretches 50 miles (80 km) across the mountainous regions of Panama. In 1977 a new treaty took effect that gave Panama control of the canal as of December 31, 1999.

A Cartoonist's View ➤
Many people criticized Roosevelt's role in building the Panama Canal. They believed that he was trying to dominate Latin America. The canal was also costly in terms of human life. Accidents and disease claimed the lives of 5,609 people, including about 4,500 Caribbean laborers.

THE MAN WHO CAN MAKE THE DIRT FLY.

▲ Trade
Nearly 13,000 oceangoing vessels pass through the canal annually. Roughly 70 percent of the cargo is coming from or going to U.S. ports. The canal's relative share of world cargo has declined somewhat, but its absolute volume has grown with the continued expansion of global trade.

The Open Door Policy In 1894 war erupted between China and Japan over Korea, which at that time was part of the Chinese empire. European and American leaders expected China, with its massive armed forces, to defeat Japan easily. These Western observers were astonished when Japan easily defeated China. In the peace treaty, China granted Korea independence. China also gave Japan territory in Manchuria that included the important city of Port Arthur. The war showed that Japan had successfully adopted Western technology and industry. It also demonstrated that China was far weaker than anyone had thought.

Japan's rising power greatly worried the Russians. They did not want Japan to acquire the territory in Manchuria, because it bordered Russia. Backed by France and Germany, Russia forced Japan to give the part of Manchuria it had acquired back to China. Then, in 1898, Russia demanded that China lease the territory to Russia instead.

Leasing a territory meant that it would still belong to China, even though a foreign government would maintain overall control. Germany and France demanded leaseholds in China, and Britain insisted on several as well. Each "leasehold"

became the center of a country's sphere of influence, an area where a foreign nation controlled economic development such as railroad construction and mining.

These events in northern China greatly worried the United States. President McKinley and Secretary of State John Hay both supported what they called an Open Door policy, in which all countries should be allowed to trade with China. In 1899 Hay sent notes to countries with leaseholds in China asking them not to discriminate against other nations that wanted to do business with the Chinese inside each leasehold. The Europeans and Japanese received the Open Door proposals coolly. Each power claimed to accept them in principle but refused to act on them unless all of the others agreed to do so as well. Hay refused to consider this a rebuff. Once he had received assurances from all of the great powers, he declared that the United States expected the other powers to abide by the plan.

The Boxer Rebellion While foreign countries debated who should control China, secret Chinese societies were organizing to get rid of foreign control. Westerners referred to one such group as the Boxers. In 1900 the group rose up to wipe out "foreign

---

MEETING SPECIAL NEEDS

Visual/Spatial Provide students with a world map. Have them trace the water route from San Francisco to New York City around Cape Horn, using the map's scale to calculate the approximate distance. *(about 13,000 miles)* Next, have students trace the route by ship from San Francisco to New York City via the Panama Canal and calculate that distance. *(about 5,200 miles)* Have students write a sentence explaining how the Panama Canal improved United States trade and business. **L2**

📁 Refer to *Inclusion for the High School Social Studies Classroom Strategies and Activities* in the TCR.

a. How does Schurz counter the argument that annexation of the Philippines was necessary to make the nation a commercial market for the United States?

b. What action other than annexation does Schurz suggest the United States could have taken to obtain the coaling stations, docks, and depots it needed for trade with Asia?

18. Organizing Using a graphic organizer similar to the one below, list ways that American imperialism affected Hawaii, Cuba, and the Philippines.

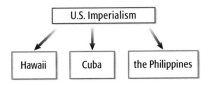

U.S. Imperialism

Hawaii · Cuba · the Philippines

Practicing Skills

19. Using an Electronic Spreadsheet Enter in a spreadsheet the land area of the territories that came under U.S. control as a result of the Spanish-American War (Puerto Rico, Guam, and the Philippines). Enter the current land area of the United States in the spreadsheet. Create an equation to calculate the percentage of land that each territory represents compared to the United States land area.

Writing Activity

20. Portfolio Writing Imagine that you are Dr. William Gorgas. You have just arrived in Havana, where you have been assigned to address the problems of workers suffering from yellow fever. Write a letter home describing some of the conditions, problems, and needs facing you as you search for a cure. Place the letter in your portfolio.

Chapter Activity

21. Evaluating the Validity of a Source Use the library or the internet to find writings by people in support of and against the Spanish-American War. Evaluate the authors' points based on the language and logic they use. Then evaluate the authors' backgrounds and experience to determine if they are reliable or objective sources.

Geography and History

22. The map on this page shows the expansion of the United States in 1900. Study the map and answer the following questions.

NATIONAL GEOGRAPHIC
U.S. Possessions in the Pacific, 1899

a. Interpreting Maps Approximately how far west is the island of Guam from the west coast of the United States?

b. Applying Geography Skills Why did the United States acquire so much island territory in the Pacific?

The Princeton Review

Standardized Test Practice

Directions: Choose the best answer to the following question.

The Platt Amendment specified all of the following conditions EXCEPT:

A Cuba could not allow another foreign power to gain territory within its borders.

B Cuba must allow the United States to buy or lease naval stations in the country.

C Cuba would be guaranteed its independence by 1915.

D The United States had the right to intervene to protect Cuban independence and to keep order.

Test-Taking Tip: Be careful—overlooking the words NOT or EXCEPT in a question is a common error. Read through all the answer choices and choose the one that does NOT fit. Also look for an answer that seems opposed to the other answers. Which of the answers above is the opposite of the rest?

HISTORY
Online

Have students visit the Web site at tav.glencoe.com to review Chapter 17 and take the Self-Check Quiz.

Chapter Activity

21. Students' evaluations should show that they can detect bias and point of view in the writings.

Geography and History

22. a. approximately 6,500 miles (10,500 kilometers); **b.** for military and trade purposes

The Princeton Review

Standardized Test Practice

Answer: C
Test-Taking Tip: Remind students that if they are unsure which answer is correct, to focus on what is known about the topic. Students might remember that the Cubans did not readily accept the Platt Amendment and that they reluctantly added it to their constitution. Now have students look at the answers and eliminate the ones that place restrictions on Cuba. The correct answer is C.

Bonus Question ?

Ask: What was the cause of the Boxer Rebellion in China? *(The fear of foreign control of China caused several secret societies to band together and attack foreign embassies.)*

them a protectorate until 1934. Philippines: U.S. controlled the Filipino government until, by the mid-1930s, Filipinos were granted some self-government. They were granted independence in 1946.

Practicing Skills

19. Spreadsheets should contain accurate data and all columns and rows should be appropriately labeled.

Writing Activity

20. The letters should describe the facts and should provide a sense of the magnitude of the problems he encountered.

543

Timesaving Tools

TeacherWorks™ All-In-One Planner and Resource Center

- **Interactive Teacher Edition** Access your Teacher Wraparound Edition and your classroom resources with a few easy clicks.
- **Interactive Lesson Planner** Planning has never been easier! Organize your week, month, semester, or year with all the lesson helps you need to make teaching creative, timely, and relevant.

Use Glencoe's **Presentation Plus!** multimedia teacher tool to easily present dynamic lessons that visually excite your students. Using Microsoft PowerPoint® you can customize the presentations to create your own personalized lessons.

TEACHING TRANSPARENCIES

Graphic Organizer 13

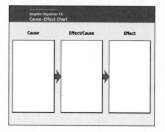

Why It Matters Chapter Transparency 18

APPLICATION AND ENRICHMENT

Linking Past and Present Activity 18

Enrichment Activity 18

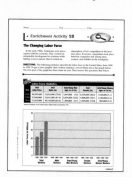

Primary Source Reading 18

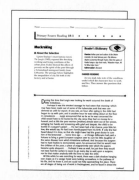

REVIEW AND REINFORCEMENT

Reteaching Activity 18

Vocabulary Activity 18

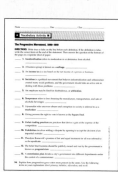

Time Line Activity 18

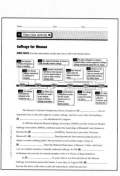

Critical Thinking Skills Activity 18

Meeting NCSS Standards

The following standards are highlighted in Chapter 18:

Section 1	VI	Power, Authority, and Governance: A, B, I
Section 2	IV	Individual Development and Identity: E, F
Section 3	II	Time, Continuity, and Change: B, C, F
Section 4	VI	Power, Authority, and Governance: A, F, I

Local Standards

_____

_____

_____

_____

_____

Chapter 18 Resources

ASSESSMENT AND EVALUATION

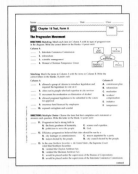

Chapter 18 Test Form A

Chapter 18 Test Form B

Standardized Test Skills Practice Workbook Activity 18

Performance Assessment Activities and Rubrics 18

ExamView® Pro Testmaker CD-ROM

MULTIMEDIA

- Vocabulary PuzzleMaker CD-ROM
- Interactive Tutor Self-Assessment CD-ROM
- ExamView® Pro Testmaker CD-ROM
- Audio Program
- American History Primary Source Documents Library CD-ROM
- MindJogger Videoquiz
- Presentation Plus! CD-ROM
- TeacherWorks™ CD-ROM
- Interactive Student Edition CD-ROM
- Glencoe Skillbuilder Interactive Workbook CD-ROM, Level 2
- The *American Vision* Video Program
- American Music: Hits Through History
- American Music: Cultural Traditions

SPANISH RESOURCES

The following Spanish language materials are available in the Spanish Resources Binder:

- Spanish Guided Reading Activities
- Spanish Reteaching Activities
- Spanish Quizzes and Tests
- Spanish Vocabulary Activities
- Spanish Summaries
- The Declaration of Independence and United States Constitution Spanish Translation

---

THE HISTORY CHANNEL®

The following videotape programs are available from Glencoe as supplements to Chapter 18:

- **Molly Brown: An American Legend** (ISBN 0-76-700767-0)
- **Susan B. Anthony: Rebel for the Cause** (ISBN 1-56-501646-7)

To order, call Glencoe at 1-800-334-7344. To find classroom resources to accompany many of these videos, check the following home pages:
A&E Television: www.aande.com
The History Channel: www.historychannel.com

HISTORY Online

Use our Web site for additional resources. All essential content is covered in the Student Edition.

You and your students can visit tav.glencoe.com, the Web site companion to the *American Vision.* This innovative integration of electronic and print media offers your students a wealth of opportunities. The student text directs students to the Web site for the following options:

- **Chapter Overviews**
- **Student Web Activities**
- **Self-Check Quizzes**
- **Textbook Updates**

Answers to the student Web activities are provided for you in the **Web Activity Lesson Plans.** Additional Web resources and Interactive Tutor Puzzles are also available.

SECTION RESOURCES

Daily Objectives	Reproducible Resources	Multimedia Resources
SECTION 1 **The Roots of Progressivism** 1. Discuss the rise of the Progressive movement. 2. Evaluate the impact of initiative, referendum, and recall, and of the Seventeenth Amendment.	Reproducible Lesson Plan 18–1 Daily Lecture and Discussion Notes 18–1 Guided Reading Activity 18–1* Section Quiz 18–1* Reading Essentials and Study Guide 18–1 Performance Assessment Activities and Rubrics Interpreting Political Cartoons	Daily Focus Skills Transparency 18–1 Interactive Tutor Self-Assessment CD-ROM ExamView® Pro Testmaker CD-ROM Presentation Plus! CD-ROM TeacherWorks™ CD-ROM Skillbuilder Interactive Workbook, Level 2 Audio Program
SECTION 2 **Roosevelt in Office** 1. Describe various efforts to regulate concentrated corporate power. 2. Discuss Theodore Roosevelt's interest in environmental conservation.	Reproducible Lesson Plan 18–2 Daily Lecture and Discussion Notes 18–2 Guided Reading Activity 18–2* Section Quiz 18–2* Reading Essentials and Study Guide 18–2 Performance Assessment Activities and Rubrics Supreme Court Case Studies	Daily Focus Skills Transparency 18–2 Interactive Tutor Self-Assessment CD-ROM ExamView® Pro Testmaker CD-ROM Presentation Plus! CD-ROM TeacherWorks™ CD-ROM Audio Program
SECTION 3 **The Taft Administration** 1. Explain how Theodore Roosevelt helped Taft get elected. 2. Discuss why progressives were disappointed with Taft as president.	Reproducible Lesson Plan 18–3 Daily Lecture and Discussion Notes 18–3 Guided Reading Activity 18–3* Section Quiz 18–3* Reading Essentials and Study Guide 18–3 Performance Assessment Activities and Rubrics	Daily Focus Skills Transparency 18–3 Interactive Tutor Self-Assessment CD-ROM ExamView® Pro Testmaker CD-ROM Presentation Plus! CD-ROM TeacherWorks™ CD-ROM Audio Program
SECTION 4 **The Wilson Years** 1. Describe Wilson's economic and social reforms. 2. Evaluate the legacy of the Progressive movement.	Reproducible Lesson Plan 18–4 Daily Lecture and Discussion Notes 18–4 Guided Reading Activity 18–4* Section Quiz 18–4* Reading Essentials and Study Guide 18–4 Performance Assessment Activities and Rubrics	Daily Focus Skills Transparency 18–4 Interactive Tutor Self-Assessment CD-ROM ExamView® Pro Testmaker CD-ROM Presentation Plus! CD-ROM TeacherWorks™ CD-ROM Vocabulary PuzzleMaker CD-ROM Audio Program

0:00 OUT OF TIME?
Assign the Chapter 18 **Reading Essentials and Study Guide.**

*Also Available in Spanish

 Blackline Master   Transparency   CD-ROM   DVD

 Poster   Music Program   Audio Program   Videocassette

NATIONAL GEOGRAPHIC Teacher's Corner

INDEX TO NATIONAL GEOGRAPHIC MAGAZINE

The following articles relate to this chapter.
- "Central Park: Oasis in the City," May 1993
- "Chicago: Welcome to the Neighborhood," May 1991
- "Miami," January 1992
- "New Life for Ellis Island," September 1990
- "New York's Chinatown," August 1998

NATIONAL GEOGRAPHIC SOCIETY PRODUCTS AVAILABLE FROM GLENCOE

To order the following products for use with this chapter, contact your local Glencoe sales representative, or call Glencoe at 1-800-334-7344:
- *PictureShow: Story of America, Part 2* (CD-ROM)
- *PicturePack: Story of America Library, Part 2* (Transparencies)
- *PictureShow: Native Americans, 1 and 2* (CD-ROM)
- *PicturePack: Native Americans* (Transparencies)

ADDITIONAL NATIONAL GEOGRAPHIC SOCIETY PRODUCTS

To order the following, call National Geographic at 1-800-368-2728:
- *Immigration: The Triumph of Hope* (Video)

NGS ONLINE

Access National Geographic's Web site for current events, atlas updates, activities, links, interactive features, and archives.
www.nationalgeographic.com

From the Classroom of...

Deborah Welch
Glade Valley High School
Glade Valley, NC

The Muckrakers

Organize the class into groups. Each will create a newspaper and divide the workload between editor and reporters. Each newspaper will then investigate a problem that reporters of the Progressive Era researched and prepare articles for inclusion in their paper. Possible topics include: workers' strikes and the courts, trust-busting, settlement houses, woman suffrage, presidential campaigns, temperance reform, and World War I and the issue of U.S. participation before 1917.

Encourage students to secure a "scoop." For example, one might create an interview with a resident of a settlement house. Another student might secure an interview with Roosevelt, Taft, or Wilson during the 1912 presidential campaign. Other interview subjects might include W.E.B. Du Bois in 1909 when the National Association for the Advancement of Colored People was formed.

Working with their editors, each group will put together their newspaper for the class to read. If time allows, the class might then debate the views presented in each newspaper.

ADDITIONAL RESOURCES FROM GLENCOE

- American Music: Cultural Traditions
- American Art & Architecture
- Outline Map Resource Book
- U.S. Desk Map
- Building Geography Skills for Life
- Inclusion for the High School Social Studies Classroom Strategies and Activities
- Teaching Strategies for the American History Classroom (Including Block Scheduling Pacing Guides)

KEY TO ABILITY LEVELS

Teaching strategies have been coded.

- **L1** BASIC activities for all students
- **L2** AVERAGE activities for average to above-average students
- **L3** CHALLENGING activities for above-average students
- **ELL** ENGLISH LANGUAGE LEARNER activities

Block Schedule

Activities that are suited to use within the block scheduling framework are identified by:

Why It Matters Activity

Have students hypothesize how direct primaries and the direct election of senators changed politics in America. Students should evaluate their answers after they have completed the chapter.

GLENCOE
TECHNOLOGY

The *American Vision* Video Program

To learn more about the meatpacking industry, have students view the Chapter 18 video, "The Stockyard Jungle," from the *American Vision* Video Program.

 Available in DVD and VHS

MindJogger Videoquiz

Use the **MindJogger Videoquiz** to preview Chapter 18 content.

Available in VHS

CHAPTER

18 The Progressive Movement *1890–1919*

Why It Matters

Industrialization changed American society. Cities were crowded with new immigrants, working conditions were often bad, and the old political system was breaking down. These conditions gave rise to the Progressive movement. Progressives campaigned for both political and social reforms for more than two decades and enjoyed significant successes at the local, state, and national levels.

The Impact Today

Many Progressive-era changes are still alive in the United States today.
- *Political parties hold direct primaries to nominate candidates for office.*
- *The Seventeenth Amendment calls for the direct election of senators.*
- *Federal regulation of food and drugs began in this period.*

The American Vision *Video* *The Chapter 18 video, "The Stockyard Jungle," portrays the horrors of the meatpacking industry first investigated by Upton Sinclair.*

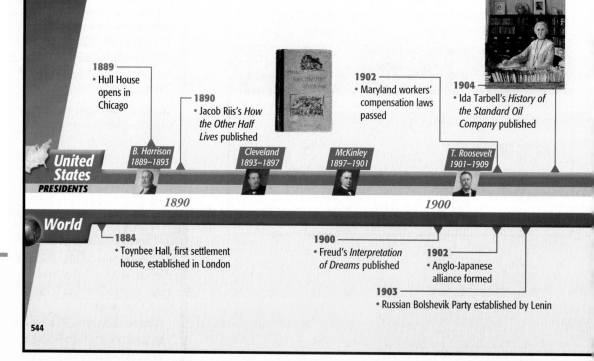

1889
- Hull House opens in Chicago

1890
- Jacob Riis's *How the Other Half Lives* published

1902
- Maryland workers' compensation laws passed

1904
- Ida Tarbell's *History of the Standard Oil Company* published

B. Harrison 1889–1893

Cleveland 1893–1897

McKinley 1897–1901

T. Roosevelt 1901–1909

United States
PRESIDENTS

1890

1900

World

1884
- Toynbee Hall, first settlement house, established in London

1900
- Freud's *Interpretation of Dreams* published

1902
- Anglo-Japanese alliance formed

1903
- Russian Bolshevik Party established by Lenin

544

TWO-MINUTE LESSON LAUNCHER

Ask if any students have ever served as volunteers in an election campaign, including for student council. Ask those who have to describe their experiences. Then ask the class to list the major elements that they believe are needed to run a successful campaign (*money, enthusiasm, a strong candidate, a good campaign staff, publicity*). Tell students that in this chapter they will meet three very different men who served as president.

HISTORY
Online

Introduce students to chapter content and key terms by having them access the **Chapter 18 Overview** at tav.glencoe.com.

More About the Photo

Demonstrations for woman suffrage were generally peaceful. However, some turned violent, and arrests were made. During World War I, militant suffragists demanded that President Wilson reverse his opposition to their cause. Some demonstrated by carrying banners comparing the president to Kaiser Wilhelm II of Germany. In the patriotic wartime climate, these banners inflamed hostility toward the protesters.

TIME LINE ACTIVITY

Have students select a world event that is shown on the time line and learn more about it. From their research, have them write a brief description of the impact the event had on American history.

Women marching for the vote in New York City, 1912

1905
• Industrial Workers of the World founded

1906
• Pure Food and Drug Act passed

1910
• Mann-Elkins Act passed

1913
• Seventeenth Amendment ratified

1920
• Nineteenth Amendment ratified, guaranteeing women's voting rights

Taft 1909–1913

Wilson 1913–1921

1910   *1920*

1910
• Mexican Revolution

1914
• World War I begins in Europe

1905
• Einstein's theory of relativity formulated

HISTORY
Online

Chapter Overview
Visit the *American Vision* Web site at tav.glencoe.com and click on *Chapter Overviews—Chapter 18* to preview chapter information.

545

GRAPHIC ORGANIZER ACTIVITY

Organizing Information Have students use a graphic organizer similar to the one shown at right to describe the details that support the main idea that progressives wanted to make government more responsive to the people. Students' details may include direct election of senators, direct primaries, legislation to protect the banking system, food supply, and so on.

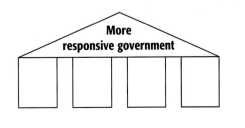

More responsive government

545

1 FOCUS

Section Overview

This section focuses on the rise of the Progressive movement.

BELLRINGER
Skillbuilder Activity

 Project transparency and have students answer the question.

📁 Available as a blackline master.

Daily Focus Skills Transparency 18–1

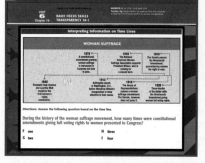

Guide to Reading

Answers to Graphic: that people could improve society if they had strong faith in science, government should play an active role in solving society's problems, government needed to be more efficient, senators should be directly elected, women should vote

Preteaching Vocabulary

Have students create a database of the Key Terms and Names. Instruct students to add the definition and other helpful information as they find the terms and names while reading this section.

Guide to Reading

Main Idea
Progressivism was a diverse response to the problems posed by industrialism and modern life.

Key Terms and Names
progressivism, muckraker, Jacob Riis, commission plan, Robert La Follette, direct primary, initiative, referendum, recall, suffrage, Alice Paul, temperance, prohibition, socialism

Reading Strategy
Organizing As you read about the beginnings of progressivism, complete a graphic organizer similar to the one below by filling in the beliefs of progressives.

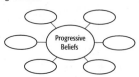
Progressive Beliefs

Reading Objectives
- **Discuss** the rise of the Progressive movement.
- **Evaluate** the impact of initiative, referendum, and recall, and of the Seventeenth Amendment.

Section Theme
Government and Democracy Progressive reformers focused on political reforms to try to keep the nation true to its democratic ideals.

Preview of Events

| ♦1890 | ♦1900 | ♦1910 | ♦1920 |

1890
Jacob Riis's *How the Other Half Lives* published

1901
Galveston, Texas, adopts commission system

1913
Seventeenth Amendment provides for direct election of senators

1920
Nineteenth Amendment gives women the vote

★ An American Story ★

A police officer arresting two suffragists in Washington, D.C.

In 1917 suffragist Rose Winslow and several other women, including Alice Paul, founder of the National Woman's Party, were arrested for obstructing traffic and blocking sidewalks. The women had been picketing the White House to draw attention to the fact that women did not yet have the right to vote in federal elections. After being sentenced to seven months in jail, Paul, Winslow, and other women prisoners went on a hunger strike. Prison authorities forced the prisoners to eat. Winslow smuggled details of their plight out to the public:

❝We have been in solitary for five weeks. . . . I have felt quite feeble the last few days—faint, so that I could hardly get my hair brushed, my arms ached so. But today I am well again. . . . [Alice Paul] dreaded forcible feeding frightfully, and I hate to think how she must be feeling. . . . I am really all right. If this continues very long I perhaps won't be. All the officers here know we are making this hunger strike [so] that women fighting for liberty may be considered political prisoners. . . . [W]e don't want women ever to have to do this over again.❞

—quoted in *Jailed for Freedom*

The Rise of Progressivism

The struggle for the right of women to vote was only one of a series of reform efforts that transformed American society in the early 1900s. Historians refer to this era in American history—from about 1890 to 1920—as the Progressive Era.

SECTION RESOURCES

📁 Reproducible Masters
- Reproducible Lesson Plan 18–1
- Daily Lecture and Discussion Notes 18–1
- Guided Reading Activity 18–1
- Section Quiz 18–1
- Reading Essentials and Study Guide 18–1
- Interpreting Political Cartoons

📀 Transparencies
- Daily Focus Skills Transparency 18–1

Multimedia
- 💿 Interactive Tutor Self-Assessment CD-ROM
- 💿 ExamView® Pro Testmaker CD-ROM
- 💿 Presentation Plus! CD-ROM
- 💿 TeacherWorks™ CD-ROM
- 🎧 Audio Program

Who Were the Progressives?

Progressivism was not a tightly organized political movement with a specific set of reforms. Instead, it was a collection of different ideas and activities. Progressives had many different views about how to fix the problems they believed existed in American society.

Progressives generally believed that industrialism and urbanization had created many social problems. Most agreed that the government should take a more active role in solving society's problems. Progressives belonged to both major political parties and usually were urban, educated middle-class Americans. Many leaders of the Progressive movement worked as journalists, social workers, educators, politicians, and members of the clergy.

Beginnings of Progressivism

Progressivism was partly a reaction against laissez-faire economics and its emphasis on an unregulated market. After seeing the poverty of the working class and the filth and crime of urban society, these reformers began to doubt the free market's ability to address those problems. At the same time, they doubted that government in its present form could fix those problems. They concluded that government had to be fixed first before it could be used to fix other problems.

One reason progressives believed people could improve society was because they had a strong faith in science and technology. The application of scientific knowledge had produced the lightbulb, the telephone, the automobile, and the airplane. It had built skyscrapers and railroads. Science and technology had benefited people; thus progressives believed using scientific principles could also produce solutions for society.

The Muckrakers

Among the first people to articulate Progressive ideas was a group of crusading journalists who investigated social conditions and political corruption. These writers became known as muckrakers after a speech by President Theodore Roosevelt:

> ❝Now, it is very necessary that we should not flinch from seeing what is vile and debasing. There is filth on the floor and it must be scraped up with the muck-rake; and there are times and places where this service is the most needed of all the services that can be performed. . . .❞
>
> —Washington, D.C., April 14, 1906

By the early 1900s, American publishers were competing to see who could expose the most corruption and scandal. A group of aggressive 10¢ and 15¢

magazines grew in popularity at this time, including *McClure's, Collier's,* and *Munsey's.*

Muckrakers uncovered corruption in many areas. Some concentrated on exposing what they considered to be the unfair practices of large American corporations. In *McClure's,* for example, **Ida Tarbell** published a series of articles critical of the Standard Oil Company. In *Everybody's Magazine,* Charles Edward Russell attacked the beef industry.

Other muckrakers targeted government. David Graham Philips described how money influenced the Senate, while **Lincoln Steffens,** another *McClure's* reporter, reported on vote stealing and other corrupt practices of urban political machines. These were later collected into a book, *The Shame of the Cities.*

Still other muckrakers concentrated on social problems. In his influential book *How the Other Half Lives,* published in 1890, **Jacob Riis** described the poverty, disease, and crime that afflicted many immigrant neighborhoods in New York City. The

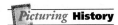
Picturing History

Muckrakers *McClure's* published Ida Tarbell's exposé on Standard Oil. What issues particularly concerned the muckrakers?

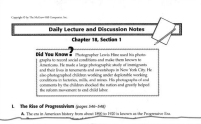
2 TEACH

Daily Lecture and Discussion Notes 18–1

Copyright © by The McGraw-Hill Companies, Inc.

Daily Lecture and Discussion Notes

Chapter 18, Section 1

Did You Know ? Photographer Lewis Hine used his photographs to record social conditions and make them known to Americans. He made a large photographic study of immigrants and their lives in tenements and sweatshops in New York City. He also photographed children working under deplorable working conditions in factories, mills, and mines. His photographs of and comments by the children shocked the nation and greatly helped the reform movement to end child labor.

I. The Rise of Progressivism (pages 546–548)

A. The era in American history from about 1890 to 1920 is known as the Progressive Era.

Listing Goals Ask students to find examples of the problems in American society that prompted Progressive objectives. Invite students to present the problems they found; have another student explain how each led to a Progressive goal. **L1**

HISTORY Online

Objectives and answers to the student activity can be found in the **Web Activity Lesson Plan** at tav.glencoe.com.

Picturing History

Answer: social conditions, political corruption, and unfair practices in industry
Ask: What company did Ida Tarbell criticize? *(Standard Oil)*

🗀 Use *Interpreting Political Cartoons,* Cartoon 19.

COOPERATIVE LEARNING ACTIVITY

Charting Reforms Organize the class into groups of five students and supply each group with a flip chart or large sheets of paper. Ask each group to make a series of charts about the reforms discussed in the chapter. Within each group, one student can record information; the others can specialize in looking for information about the following: (1) areas of reform; (2) names of reformers; (3) suggested reforms; (4) success of the suggestions. When the charts are completed, take a class vote on the reform or reformer that students consider the most important. 🗀

Use the rubric for a cooperative group management plan on pages 81–82 in the *Performance Assessment Activities and Rubrics.*

✓ **Reading Check**

Answer: They investigated social conditions, and published their findings.

A City and a Storm In addition to Galveston, two Midwestern cities saw notable reforms during this time. In Toledo, Ohio, Mayor Samuel "Golden Rule" Jones established municipal ownership of public utilities and tackled police corruption. In Detroit, Michigan, Mayor Hazen Pingree set up new schools, parks, and work programs. **Ask:** What form of local government do we have? *(Students' answers will vary depending on where they live.)* **L2**

✓ **Reading Check**

Answer: because government could not carry out reforms unless it was reformed first

---

muckrakers' articles led to a general public debate on social and economic problems and put pressure on politicians to introduce reforms.

✓ **Reading Check** **Describing** How did the muckrakers help spark the Progressive movement?

Making Government Efficient

There were many different types of progressivism. Different causes led to different approaches, and progressives even took opposing positions on how to solve some problems.

One group of progressives focused on making government more efficient. They believed that many problems in society could be solved if government worked properly. Efficiency progressives took their ideas from business. These progressives believed business had become more efficient by applying the principles of scientific management.

The ideas of scientific management had been developed in the late 1800s and were popularized by Frederick W. Taylor in his book *The Principles of Scientific Management*, published in 1911. Taylor described how a company could become more efficient by managing time, breaking tasks down into small parts, and using standardized tools.

Efficiency progressives argued that managing a modern city required experts, not politicians. They did not want more democracy in government, for they believed that the democratic process led to compromise and corruption. In most American cities, the mayor or city council chose the heads of city departments. Traditionally, these jobs went to political supporters and friends, who often knew little about city services.

Efficiency progressives wanted either a commission plan or a council-manager system. Under the **commission plan**, a city's government would be divided into several departments, which would each be placed under the control of an expert commissioner. These progressives argued that a board of commissioners or a city manager with expertise in city services should hire the specialists to run city departments. Galveston, Texas, adopted the commission system in 1901. Other cities soon followed.

✓ **Reading Check** **Explaining** Why did progressives want to reorganize city government?

A City and a Storm

On September 8, 1900, a massive hurricane devastated the city of Galveston, Texas. About 6,000 people died. When the political machine that controlled the city government proved incapable of responding to the disaster, local business leaders convinced the state to let them take control. In April 1901, Galveston introduced the commission system of government. Under this system, Galveston chose five commissioners to replace the mayor and city council.

Four commissioners were local business leaders. When the city quickly recovered, reformers in other cities were impressed. Galveston's experience seemed to prove the benefits of running a city like a business by dividing its government into departments and placing each under an expert commissioner. Many other cities soon followed, adopting either the commission plan or the council-manager system.

548 CHAPTER 18 The Progressive Movement

MEETING SPECIAL NEEDS

Visual/Spatial This activity helps to address the particular needs of visual learners. Pair students to write slogans against child labor that could have been used in the early 1900s. Slogans should be brief and clear, with emotional appeal. Then ask students to bring in contemporary magazines or books with pictures showing politicians, religious leaders, celebrities, or protesters advocating some type of political, economic, or social reform. **L1**

☞ Refer to *Inclusion for the High School Social Studies Classroom Strategies and Activities* in the TCR.

Democracy and Progressivism

Not all progressives agreed with the efficiency progressives. Many believed that society needed more democracy, not less. They wanted to make elected officials more responsive to voters.

"Laboratory of Democracy" Political reform first came to the state level when Wisconsin voters elected Republican **Robert La Follette** to be governor. La Follette used his office to attack the way political parties ran their conventions. Because party bosses controlled the selection of convention delegates, they also controlled which candidates were chosen to run for office. La Follette pressured the state legislature to require each party to hold a direct primary, in which all party members could vote for a candidate to run in the general election.

La Follette's great reform success gave Wisconsin a reputation as the "laboratory of democracy." La

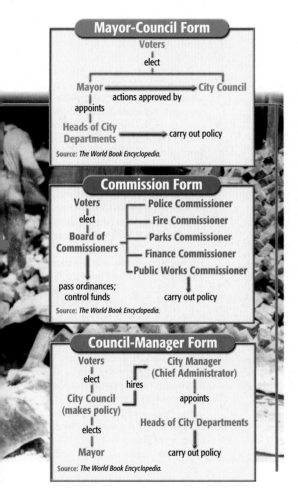

Mayor-Council Form

Voters
elect
Mayor ———————→ City Council
  actions approved by
appoints
Heads of City Departments ———→ carry out policy

Source: *The World Book Encyclopedia.*

Commission Form

Voters
elect
Board of Commissioners
— Police Commissioner
— Fire Commissioner
— Parks Commissioner
— Finance Commissioner
— Public Works Commissioner

pass ordinances; control funds   carry out policy

Source: *The World Book Encyclopedia.*

Council-Manager Form

Voters
elect
City Council (makes policy)
hires
City Manager (Chief Administrator)
appoints
Heads of City Departments
elects
Mayor   carry out policy

Source: *The World Book Encyclopedia.*

Follette claimed, "Democracy is based upon knowledge. . . . The only way to beat the boss . . . is to keep the people thoroughly informed."

Inspired by La Follette, progressives in other states pushed for similar electoral changes. To force state legislators to respond to voters, three new reforms were introduced in many states. The initiative allowed a group of citizens to introduce legislation and required the legislature to vote on it. The referendum allowed proposed legislation to be submitted to the voters for approval. The recall allowed voters to demand a special election to remove an elected official from office before his or her term had expired.

GOVERNMENT

Direct Election of Senators Another reform the progressives favored affected the federal government—the direct election of senators. As originally written, the United States Constitution directed each state legislature to elect two senators from that state. Political machines or large trusts often influenced the election of senators, who then repaid their supporters with federal contracts and jobs. By the early 1900s, muckraker Charles Edward Russell charged that the Senate had become "only a chamber of butlers for industrialists and financiers."

To counter Senate corruption, progressives called for the direct election of senators by all state voters. In 1912 Congress passed a direct-election amendment. Although the direct election of senators was intended to end corruption, it also removed one of the state legislatures' checks on federal power. In 1913 the amendment was ratified, becoming the Seventeenth Amendment to the Constitution.

✓ **Reading Check** **Evaluating** What was the impact of the Seventeenth Amendment? What problem was it intended to solve?

The Suffrage Movement

In July 1848, Elizabeth Cady Stanton and Lucretia Mott organized the first women's rights convention in Seneca Falls, New York. Stanton convinced the delegates that their first priority should be getting women the right to vote. The movement for women's voting rights became known as the suffrage movement. Suffrage is the right to vote.

Woman suffrage was an important issue for progressives. Although the suffrage movement began well before progressivism emerged, many progressives joined the movement in the late 1800s and early 1900s.

CHAPTER 18   The Progressive Movement   **549**

✓ **Reading Check**

Answer: Allowing the public to elect senators made the Senate more democratic. It was intended to end corruption but removed one of the state government's checks on federal power.

FYI

Point out that reforms often start at the local level and spread. In 1875 Nebraska established preferential primaries so voters could indicate their choices for senator. By 1912 more than one-half of the states had such primaries.

CURRICULUM CONNECTION

World History At the same time that American women were struggling for the right to vote, women in China were finally being freed from the disabling custom of foot-binding. Foot-binding had been practiced in China since the Song dynasty (A.D. 960–1279). It involved tightly wrapping strips of linen around young girls' feet to discourage growth. The practice extended to all social classes and left women throughout China virtually crippled in later life. The Chinese government officially banned the practice in 1912.

INTERDISCIPLINARY CONNECTIONS ACTIVITY

Government Invite someone from the local government to address your class about the form of government used in your community. If you live in an area where there are several kinds of governments in adjacent communities, invite representatives of each. Ask your guest(s) to prepare a short talk about the way the government operates and the kinds of services that it provides. Instruct students to prepare for the class by jotting down some questions for the speaker(s). **L2**

Background: Susan B. Anthony was the first woman depicted on a U.S. coin. Unfortunately, the Susan B. Anthony dollar was not well received by the general public. The coin is no longer minted.

Ask: How do you think employers have rationalized paying women less than their male counterparts?

(Students' answers will vary.)

Creating a Thematic Map Have students draw a map of the United States and indicate the states that allowed women to vote in 1912. **L1**

Use the rubric for creating a map, display, or chart on pages 77–78 in the *Performance Assessment Activities and Rubrics.*

FYI

Mary Church Terrell, born in 1863, was the most prominent African American in the suffrage movement, but she also led a lifelong campaign against racial injustice. Terrell encouraged picketing and sit-ins years before the civil rights movement adopted those strategies. She also was a cofounder of the NAACP. Fittingly, Terrell lived long enough to see the Supreme Court's landmark ruling in *Brown* v. *Board of Education.*

Early Problems The suffrage movement got off to a slow start. Women suffragists were accused of being unfeminine and immoral. Several were physically attacked. The movement also remained weak because many of its supporters were abolitionists as well. In the years before the Civil War, they preferred to concentrate on abolishing slavery.

After the Civil War, the Republicans in Congress introduced the Fourteenth and Fifteenth Amendments to the Constitution to protect the voting rights of African Americans. Several leaders of the woman suffrage movement had wanted these amendments worded to give women the right to vote as well. They were bitterly disappointed when Republicans refused.

The debate over the Fourteenth and Fifteenth Amendments split the suffrage movement into two groups: the National Woman Suffrage Association, led by Elizabeth Cady Stanton and Susan B. Anthony, and the American Woman Suffrage Association, led by Lucy Stone and Julia Ward Howe. The first group wanted to focus on passing a constitutional amendment allowing woman suffrage. The second group believed that the best strategy was to convince state governments to give women the right to vote before trying to amend the Constitution.

This split reduced the movement's effectiveness. In 1878 a constitutional amendment granting woman suffrage was introduced in Congress, but it failed to pass. Few state governments granted women the right to vote either. By 1900 only Wyoming, Idaho, Utah, and Colorado had granted women full voting rights.

The Movement Builds Support In 1890 the two groups united to form the **National American Woman Suffrage Association** (NAWSA). The movement still did not make significant gains, however, until about 1910. Part of the problem was convincing women to become politically active. As the Progressive movement began, however, many middle-class women concluded that they needed the vote to promote social reforms they favored. Many working-class women also wanted the vote to ensure passage of labor laws protecting women.

As the suffrage movement grew, members began lobbying lawmakers, organizing marches, and delivering speeches on street corners. By the end of 1912, Washington, Oregon, California, Arizona, and Kansas had granted women full voting rights. On March 3, 1913, the day before President Wilson's inauguration, suffragists marched in Washington, D.C., to draw attention to their cause.

Alice Paul, a Quaker social worker who headed NAWSA's congressional committee, had organized the Washington march. Paul wanted to use protests to force President Wilson to take action on suffrage. Her activities alarmed other members of NAWSA who wanted to negotiate with Wilson. Paul left NAWSA and formed the National Woman's Party. Her supporters picketed the White House, blocked sidewalks, chained themselves to lampposts, and went on hunger strikes if arrested.

In 1915 **Carrie Chapman Catt** became NAWSA's leader. Catt developed what she called her "Winning Plan" to mobilize the suffrage

Profiles IN HISTORY

Susan B. Anthony
1820–1906

Susan B. Anthony was born in Adams, Massachusetts, to Quaker parents. Quakers were generally more supportive of women's rights than some other groups, and so Anthony was able to receive a good education. She finished her schooling at the age of 17. Anthony then worked as a teacher in New York, but she was fired after protesting that her pay was one-fifth the amount of her male colleagues. She found another job, however, as a principal at New York's Canajoharie Academy. Between 1848 and 1863, Anthony was involved in both the temperance and abolitionist movements.

Her involvement in the drive for women's equality began in 1851 after she met Elizabeth Cady Stanton. Between 1854 and 1860, the duo attempted to change discriminatory laws in New York. In 1869 Anthony and Stanton organized the National Woman Suffrage Association and began promoting an amendment to grant woman suffrage. Anthony and 12 other women illegally cast votes in the presidential election of 1872. They were arrested and convicted, but the judge feared that

the jury would rule in Anthony's favor. He dismissed the jury and fined Anthony instead. She refused to pay the $100 fine, but the judge decided to let her go, afraid that appealing the case might generate sympathy for the suffrage movement.

In 1883 Anthony traveled to Europe, and she helped form the International Council of Women in 1888. This organization represented the rights of women in 48 countries. She died in Rochester, New York, in 1906. Though Anthony did not live to see her dream of woman suffrage become reality, the United States government honored her by placing her portrait on a new dollar coin in 1979.

CRITICAL THINKING ACTIVITY

Evaluating Have students research some social services available in their community. Instruct students to select a particular social issue and learn more about what services are available. Suggest that they focus on the following questions: What is the issue? What agencies or organizations provide services related to this issue? What kinds of services are provided? What impact are these services having on the community? Have students write a report answering these questions. **L2**

Guide to Reading

Main Idea
With Theodore Roosevelt's succession to the presidency in September 1901, progressivism entered national politics.

Key Terms and Names
Square Deal, Northern Securities, United Mine Workers, arbitration, Hepburn Act, Upton Sinclair

Reading Strategy
Taking Notes As you read about the administration of President Theodore Roosevelt, use the major headings of the section to create an outline similar to the one below.

Roosevelt in Office
I. Roosevelt Revives the Presidency
  A.
  B.
  C.
  D.
II.

Reading Objectives
• **Describe** various efforts to regulate concentrated corporate power.
• **Discuss** Theodore Roosevelt's interest in environmental conservation.

Section Theme
Individual Action Progressive goals were carried to the national level when Theodore Roosevelt became president.

Preview of Events

◆1900	◆1902	◆1904	◆1906

1901 Theodore Roosevelt becomes president after William McKinley's death

1902 United Mine Workers go on strike

1903 Roosevelt sets up Bureau of Corporations

1906 Upton Sinclair's *The Jungle* published

1906 Meat Inspection Act passed

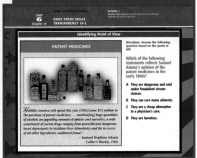

★ An American Story ★

Theodore Roosevelt

William McKinley's assassination brought Teddy Roosevelt to the presidency. Despite the tragic circumstances, he took to the office with great joy. A man who loved the outdoors and physical activity, Roosevelt impressed many people as a new kind of president. One visitor wrote that after spending time with Roosevelt, "you go home and wring the personality out of your clothes."

The famous muckraker, Lincoln Steffens, already knew Roosevelt as a fellow reformer. Steffens went to Washington to see his friend, and this is what he saw:

66His offices were crowded with people, mostly reformers, all day long. . . . He strode triumphant around among us, talking and shaking hands, dictating and signing letters, and laughing. Washington, the whole country, was in mourning, and no doubt the President felt he should hold himself down; he didn't; he tried to but his joy showed in every word and movement. . . . With his feet, his fists, his face and his free words, he laughed at his luck. . . . And he laughed with glee at the power and place that had come to him.99

—quoted in *Theodore Roosevelt, A Life*

Roosevelt Revives the Presidency

Theodore Roosevelt, better known as "Teddy," took office at age 42—the youngest person ever to serve as president. Roosevelt was intensely competitive, strong-willed, and extremely energetic. In international affairs, Roosevelt was a Social Darwinist. He believed the United States was in competition with the other nations of the world and that only the fittest would survive. Domestically, however, Roosevelt was a committed

---

2 TEACH

Drawing a Political Cartoon

Have students draw a political cartoon focusing on Roosevelt. Suggest that students use characters from contemporary culture or traditional stories such as fairy tales. **L1**

📁 Use the rubric for creating a political cartoon, pamphlet, or handbill on pages 87–88 in the *Performance Assessment Activities and Rubrics.*

FYI

On December 3, 1901, Roosevelt made his first annual address to Congress. His speech focused on the need for the federal government to restrain large corporations and trusts. During his presidency, he initiated 44 lawsuits against trusts.

progressive, who firmly believed that government should actively balance the needs of competing groups in American society.

"I shall see to it," Roosevelt declared in 1904, "that every man has a square deal, no less and no more." During his second term, his reform programs became known as the Square Deal. To Roosevelt, it was not inconsistent to believe in Social Darwinism and Progressivism at the same time. He believed the United States needed to adopt progressive reforms in order to maintain an efficient society that could compete successfully against other nations.

Roosevelt Takes on the Trusts

Although he admired competition, Roosevelt was also concerned with efficiency. He believed that trusts and other large business organizations were very efficient and part of the reason for America's prosperity. Yet Roosevelt remained concerned that in the pursuit of

Analyzing *Political Cartoons*

Corporate Giants This 1904 cartoon portrays Roosevelt as "Jack the Giant-Killer," but he actually restrained very few trusts. *Why do you think the scene is set on Wall Street?*

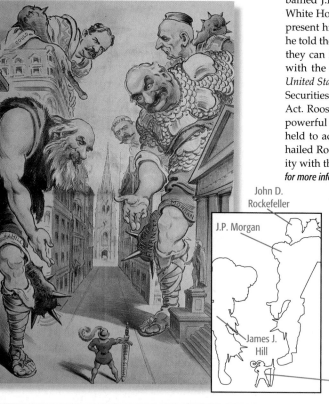

John D. Rockefeller
J.P. Morgan
James J. Hill
T. Roosevelt

their private interests, some trusts were hurting the public interest. He wanted to find a way to supervise big business without destroying its economic efficiency. When the *New York Sun* declared that Roosevelt was "bringing wealth to its knees," the president disagreed. "We draw the line against misconduct," he declared, "not against wealth."

During Roosevelt's first year in office, a fight for control of the Burlington Railroad erupted on the New York Stock Exchange. On one side was E.H. Harriman of the Union Pacific Railroad. On the other side were James J. Hill and J.P. Morgan of the Great Northern and Northern Pacific Railroads. The stock battle almost triggered a financial panic that could have plunged the nation into a recession. The three men ultimately compromised by creating a giant new holding company called **Northern Securities.**

The formation of the Northern Securities Company alarmed many Americans, including Roosevelt. The stock battle that led to its creation seemed a classic example of private interests acting in a way that threatened the nation as a whole. Roosevelt decided that the company was in violation of the Sherman Antitrust Act. In early 1902, he ordered his attorney general to file a lawsuit against Northern Securities.

Roosevelt's action pleased many progressives but baffled J.P. Morgan. He immediately traveled to the White House with two supportive senators in tow to present his case. "If we have done anything wrong," he told the president, "send your man to my man and they can fix it up." Unmoved, Roosevelt proceeded with the case. In 1904 in *Northern Securities* v. *the United States,* the Supreme Court ruled that Northern Securities had indeed violated the Sherman Antitrust Act. Roosevelt declared it a great victory. "The most powerful men in the country," he proclaimed, "were held to accountability before the law." Newspapers hailed Roosevelt as a "trustbuster," and his popularity with the American public soared. 📖 *(See page 1082 for more information on* Northern Securities v. the United States.*)*

The Coal Strike of 1902

As president, Roosevelt regarded himself as the nation's head manager. He believed it was his job to keep society operating efficiently by preventing conflict between the nation's different groups and their interests. In the fall of 1902, he put these beliefs into practice.

The previous spring, the **United Mine Workers** (UMW) union had called a strike of the miners who dug anthracite, or hard coal. Nearly 150,000 workers

COOPERATIVE LEARNING ACTIVITY

Comparing National Leaders Have students compare the power of the United States president with the power of the chief executives in other countries. Organize students into small groups, each of which should investigate another country. Groups should divide the work equally. Some students may search for information in the library, some may create outlines from their reading, others may create a written or visual presentation. 🖼

Use the rubric for a cooperative group management plan on pages 81–82 in the *Performance Assessment Activities and Rubrics.*

walked out of eastern Pennsylvania's anthracite mines demanding a pay increase, a reduction in work hours, and recognition for their union.

As the months passed and the strike continued, coal prices began to rise. To Roosevelt it was another example of groups pursuing their private interests at the expense of the nation. If the strike dragged on too long, the country would face a coal shortage that could shut down factories and leave many people's homes cold with winter fast approaching.

Roosevelt urged the union and the owners to accept arbitration—a settlement imposed by an outside party. The union agreed. The mine owners, determined to destroy the UMW, did not. One owner, George Baer, declared, "The rights and interests of the laboring man will be protected and cared for not by the labor agitators, but by the Christian men to whom God in His infinite wisdom has given the control of the property interests of the country."

The mine owners' stubbornness infuriated Roosevelt, as it did much of the public. Roosevelt threatened to order the army to run the mines. Fearful of this, the mine owners finally accepted arbitration. By intervening in the dispute, Roosevelt had taken the first step toward establishing the federal government as an honest broker between powerful groups in society.

The Bureau of Corporations Despite his lawsuit against Northern Securities and his role in the coal strike, Roosevelt was not opposed to big business. He believed most trusts benefited the economy and that breaking them up would do more harm than good. Instead, Roosevelt proposed the creation of a new federal agency to investigate corporations and publicize the results. He believed the most effective way to keep big business from abusing its power was through knowledge and publicity of the facts.

In 1903 Roosevelt convinced Congress to create the Department of Commerce and Labor. Within this department would be a division called the **Bureau of Corporations,** with the authority to investigate corporations and issue reports on their activities.

The following year, the Bureau of Corporations began investigating U.S. Steel, a gigantic holding company that had been created in 1901. Worried about a possible antitrust lawsuit, the company's leaders met privately with Roosevelt and offered a deal. They would open their account books and records to the Bureau of Corporations. In exchange, if the Bureau found anything wrong, the company would be advised privately and allowed to correct the problem without having to go to court.

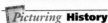

Miner's Lot In the early 1900s, miners worked under dangerous conditions for little pay. How did Roosevelt respond when they went on strike?

Roosevelt accepted this "gentlemen's agreement," as he called it. Shortly afterward he made similar deals with other companies. These arrangements gave Roosevelt the ability to regulate big business without having to sacrifice economic efficiency by breaking up the trusts.

Congress Follows In addition to creating the Department of Commerce and Labor, Congress passed the Expedition Act, which gave federal antitrust suits precedence on the dockets of circuit courts. Then, in 1906, Roosevelt pushed the **Hepburn Act** through Congress. This act was intended to strengthen the Interstate Commerce Commission (ICC). An early effort to regulate the railroad industry, the ICC had been ineffective because it lacked sufficient authority.

The Hepburn Act tried to strengthen the ICC by giving it the power to set railroad rates. The agency originally was intended to regulate rates to ensure that companies did not compete unfairly. At first, railroad companies were suspicious of the ICC and tied up its decisions by challenging them in court. Eventually, the railroads realized that they could work with the ICC to set rates and regulations that limited competition and prevented new competitors from entering the industry. Over time the ICC

Guided Reading Activity 18–2

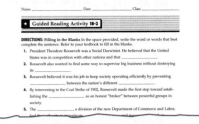

Picturing **History**

Answer: He worked to get the labor union and mine owners to accept arbitration as a way to settle the strike.
Ask: Why did mine owners finally accept arbitration as a way to settle the strike? *(Roosevelt threatened to bring in the military to run the mines.)*

Creating a Table Have students create a table to show the advantages and disadvantages of a gentlemen's agreement. **L2**

📁 Use *Supreme Court Case Study 10, Northern Securities Company* v. *United States.*

3 ASSESS

Assign Section 2 Assessment as homework or as an in-class activity.

💿 Have students use the **Interactive Tutor Self-Assessment CD-ROM.**

MEETING SPECIAL NEEDS

Reading Disability Many students with reading comprehension or attention problems have difficulty covering material in a timely fashion. To help them, set a goal and a time limit. Give students a one-minute time goal to search for the major players in the 1902 coal strike. Repeat the process. **L1**

📁 Refer to *Inclusion for the High School Social Studies Classroom Strategies and Activities* in the TCR.

✓ **Reading Check**

Answer: regulated railroad rates so that companies did not compete unfairly; not very—lacked authority

Fact | Fiction | Folklore

Michtom's wife hand stitched the first bears. After they sold quickly, Michtom sent a bear to the president and asked for permission to name the bears "Teddy." After getting a positive response, Michtom made arrangements for mass production.

✓ **Reading Check**

Answer: Meat Inspection Act and Pure Food and Drug Act

Reading Essentials and Study Guide 18–2

Name _____ Date _____ Class _____

Study Guide

Chapter 18, Section 2
For use with textbook pages 555–559

ROOSEVELT IN OFFICE

KEY TERMS AND NAMES

Square Deal the reform programs of President Roosevelt *(page 556)*
Northern Securities a giant holding company broken up by Theodore Roosevelt *(page 556)*
United Mine Workers a union for mine workers *(page 556)*
arbitration a settlement imposed by an outside party *(page 557)*
Hepburn Act a law intended to strengthen the Interstate Commerce Commission *(page 557)*
Upton Sinclair author of *The Jungle*, which described horrible conditions in the meatpacking industry *(page 558)*

Section Quiz 18–2

Name _____ Date _____ Class _____

★ **Chapter 18**   Score ___

Section Quiz 18-2

DIRECTIONS: Matching Match each item in Column A with the items in Column B. Write the correct letters in the blanks. *(10 points each)*

Column A	Column B
___ 1. wrote *The Jungle*, a book with appalling descriptions of conditions in the meatpacking industry	A. Gifford Pinchot
___ 2. had the authority to investigate corporations and issue reports on their activities	B. Square Deal
___ 3. appointed to head the United States Forest Service	C. Upton Sinclair
___ 4. a settlement imposed by an outside party	D. arbitration
___ 5. Roosevelt's reform programs	E. Bureau of Corporations

DIRECTIONS: Multiple Choice In the blank at the left, write the letter of the choice that best completes the statement or answers the question. *(10 points each)*

---

became a supporter of the railroads' interests, and by 1920 it had begun setting rates at levels intended to ensure the industry's profits.

✓ **Reading Check** **Comparing** What was the purpose of the Interstate Commerce Commission, and how successful was it?

Social Welfare Action

When Roosevelt took office, he was not greatly concerned about consumer issues, but by 1905 consumer protection had become a national issue. That year, a journalist named Samuel Hopkins Adams published a series of articles in *Collier's* magazine describing the patent medicine business.

Many companies were patenting and marketing potions they claimed would cure a variety of ills. Many patent medicines were little more than alcohol, colored water, and sugar. Others contained caffeine, opium, cocaine, and other dangerous compounds. Consumers had no way to know what they were taking, nor did they receive any assurance that the medicines worked as claimed.

Many Americans were equally concerned about the food they ate. Dr. W.H. Wiley, chief chemist at the United States Department of Agriculture, had issued reports documenting the dangerous preservatives being used in what he called "embalmed meat." Then, in 1906, **Upton Sinclair** published *The Jungle*. Based on Sinclair's close observations of the

Fact | Fiction | Folklore

The Teddy Bear The soft and cuddly teddy bear was named after the gruff and rugged Theodore ("Teddy") Roosevelt. The idea for the toy stemmed from a hunting trip Roosevelt took to Mississippi in 1902. On the trip, the president refused to kill a defenseless bear cub. Cartoonist Clifford Berryman drew a whimsical reenactment of the scene for the *Washington Post*, which in turn inspired Morris Michtom, a toy shop owner in Brooklyn, to create the "teddy bear." The toy became a runaway success in the United States and abroad.

---

slaughterhouses of Chicago, the powerful book featured appalling descriptions of conditions in the meatpacking industry:

> ❝There would come all the way back from Europe old sausage that had been rejected, and that was moldy and white—it would be dosed with borax and glycerine, and dumped into the hoppers, and made over again for home consumption. . . . There would be meat stored in great piles in rooms; and the water from leaky roofs would drip over it, and thousands of rats would race about upon it.❞
>
> —from *The Jungle*

Sinclair's book was a best-seller. It made consumers ill—and angry. Roosevelt and Congress responded with the **Meat Inspection Act.** It required federal inspection of meat sold through interstate commerce and required the Agriculture Department to set standards of cleanliness in meatpacking plants. The **Pure Food and Drug Act,** passed on the same day in 1906, prohibited the manufacture, sale, or shipment of impure or falsely labeled food and drugs.

✓ **Reading Check** **Summarizing** What two pieces of legislation were enacted due to the facts revealed in Upton Sinclair's *The Jungle*?

Conservation

Roosevelt put his stamp on the presidency most clearly in the area of environmental conservation. Realizing that the nation's bountiful natural resources were being used up at an alarming rate, Roosevelt urged Americans to conserve these resources.

An enthusiastic outdoorsman, Roosevelt valued the country's minerals, animals, and rugged terrain. He cautioned against unregulated exploitation of public lands and believed in conservation to manage the nation's resources. As president, Roosevelt eagerly assumed the role of manager. He argued that the government must distinguish "between the man who skins the land and the man who develops the country. I am going to work with, and only with, the man who develops the country."

GEOGRAPHY

Land Development in the West Roosevelt quickly applied his philosophy in the dry Western states, where farmers and city dwellers competed for scarce water. In 1902 Roosevelt supported passage of the **Newlands Reclamation Act,** authorizing the use of

---

INTERDISCIPLINARY CONNECTIONS ACTIVITY

Health Have students collect warning labels and labeling information from products and advertisements. Have students write a warning label for a product that they use or consume regularly. Have students display their labels with the appropriate product or a picture of it. **Ask:** Do you think that people read warning labels? Why is it important to have warning labels? **L2**

federal funds from public land sales to pay for irrigation and land development projects. Thus it was the federal government that began the large-scale transformation of the West's landscape and economy.

Gifford Pinchot Roosevelt also backed efforts to save the nation's forests through careful management of the timber resources of the West. He appointed his close friend Gifford Pinchot to head the United States Forest Service. "The natural resources," Pinchot said, "must be developed and preserved for the benefit of the many and not merely for the profit of a few."

As progressives, Roosevelt and Pinchot both believed that trained experts in forestry and resource management should apply the same scientific standards to the landscape that others were applying to the management of cities and industry. They rejected the laissez-faire argument that the best way to preserve public land was to sell it to lumber companies, who would then carefully conserve it because it was the source of their profits. With the president's support, Pinchot's department drew up regulations controlling lumbering on federal lands.

Roosevelt took other steps as well to conserve the nation's resources. He added over 100 million acres to the protected national forests, quadrupling their area, and established 5 new national parks and 50 federal wildlife reservations.

Roosevelt's Legacy President Roosevelt changed the role of the federal government and the nature of the presidency. Increasingly, Americans began to look to the federal government to solve the nation's economic and social problems. Under Roosevelt, the

Picturing **History**

Crowd Pleaser Teddy Roosevelt's energetic speaking style captivated audiences across the nation. *What impact did he have on the office of the presidency?*

executive branch of government had dramatically increased its power. The ICC could set rates, the Agriculture Department could inspect food, the Bureau of Corporations could monitor business, and the attorney general could rapidly bring antitrust lawsuits under the Expedition Act.

✓ **Reading Check** **Examining** How did Roosevelt's policies help the conservation of natural resources?

SECTION 2 ASSESSMENT

Checking for Understanding

1. **Define:** Square Deal, arbitration.
2. **Identify:** Northern Securities, United Mine Workers, Hepburn Act, Upton Sinclair.
3. **Explain** what was provided for in the Hepburn Act.

Reviewing Themes

4. **Individual Action** How did Upton Sinclair contribute to involving the federal government in protecting consumers?

Critical Thinking

5. **Drawing Conclusions** What impact did Roosevelt's use of the Sherman Antitrust Act have on business?
6. **Organizing** Use a graphic organizer similar to the one below to list the results of the Coal Strike of 1902.

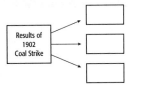

Analyzing Visuals

7. **Analyzing Political Cartoons** Look at the cartoon on page 556. Why are the giants depicted as they are? What do they represent? Roosevelt is called Jack the Giant-Killer. What fairy tale is being referred to?

Writing About History

8. **Descriptive Writing** Imagine that you are living in the early 1900s and that you have just read Upton Sinclair's *The Jungle*. Write a letter to a friend explaining what the novel is about and how it characterizes the Progressive era.

CHAPTER 18 The Progressive Movement **559**

SECTION 2 ASSESSMENT ANSWERS

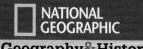

1 FOCUS

Read students the following quote from Theodore Roosevelt: "There can be nothing in the world more beautiful than the Yosemite, the groves of the giant sequoias and redwoods, the Canyon of the Colorado, the Canyon of the Yellowstone, the Three Tetons; and our people should see to it that they are pre-served for their children and their children's children forever, with their majestic beauty all unmarred."

2 TEACH

Synthesizing Information Have students look at the photograph and caption that shows Theodore Roosevelt and John Muir. Then direct students to look at the map and name the various points Roosevelt and Muir would have likely seen from their vista. (*At a minimum, they could have seen Half Dome, Sentinel Rock, Yosemite Valley, and Cloud's Rest.*) **L1**

Creating a Display Organize students into nine groups and assign each group one of the national parks shown on the map on page 432. Have the groups create a display about the park and its natural beauty. **L2**

CATHEDRAL RANGE

Clouds
9,926 ft. (3

Eagle Peak

Yosemite Point

Upper
Yosemite Falls
1,430 ft. (436 m)

El Capitan
7,569 ft. (2,307 m)

Yosemite Falls
total drop
2,425 ft. (739 m)

Royal Arches

Cathedr
Spires

Yosemite Valley
4,000 ft. (1,219 m)

Cathedral Rocks

Bridalveil Fall
620 ft. (189 m)

Merced River

Early National Parks

• Mount Rainier, 1899

• Sullys Hill, 1904

• Crater Lake, 1902

• Yellowstone, 1872

• Wind Cave, 1903

• Yosemite, 1890
• General Grant (Kings Canyon), 1890
• Sequoia, 1890

• Mesa Verde, 1906

Atlantic
Ocean

Pacific
Ocean

Gulf of Mexico

OUR GROWING HERITAGE

This map of the United States shows the national parks that existed by the end of President Theodore Roosevelt's administration. In addition to nearly doubling the number of national parks to 9, Roosevelt established 55 wildlife preserves and 150 national forests.

EXTENDING THE CONTENT

Conservationist Theodore Roosevelt first visited the Badlands in 1883. As an avid hunter, he came to hunt bison but soon learned that the animals were virtually extinct as a result of hide hunters and disease. As he spent more time in the West, Roosevelt became alarmed at the environmental damage being done to the land and the wildlife. He translated his concerns into action when he became president, creating national parks, bird and game reserves, and national forests.

The Story of Yosemite

The breathtaking beauty of the Yosemite Valley has always astounded visitors to California's High Sierra. In 1851 volunteer soldiers came upon the valley. One officer felt a "peculiar exalted sensation" as he marveled at his surroundings.

The officer's reaction was a natural one. Carved by glaciers and rivers, the seven-mile-long valley into which he and his men rode lies at an elevation of 4,000 feet (1219 m). Above them rose the near-vertical cliffs and great granite monoliths of El Capitan, Half Dome, and Cathedral Rocks. Down onto the valley floor poured the waters of Bridalveil Fall. A dozen other waterfalls spilled over sheer cliffs elsewhere in the valley, some of them— like Yosemite Falls at 2,425 feet (739 m)—among the highest on Earth. Within five years, horseback parties were coming to gaze at Bridalveil Fall and the face of El Capitan. The tourists had found Yosemite.

To guarantee that the public could continue to enjoy the beauty, in 1864 President Abraham Lincoln granted the valley to California as a wilderness preserve. In so doing, Lincoln laid the foundation for the national park system. (The first official national park, Yellowstone, was not created until eight years later.) By the late 1880s Yosemite was attracting about 5,000 visitors a year. John Muir and other conservationists were anxious to preserve the area. Muir had spent years tramping through the woods and up and down the

President Theodore Roosevelt and John Muir stand atop Glacier Point.

mountains and glaciers of the park. His compelling descriptions swayed many influential people. In 1890 Congress expanded the protected area and made Yosemite an official national park.

In many ways Yosemite established a pattern for our national park system. It started programs to teach visitors about native plants and wildlife and was the first park to build a museum to help visitors understand and enjoy the region.

In 1903 President Theodore Roosevelt visited the park with Muir. The natural beauty of the valley captivated the environmentalist president and stimulated his desire to protect vast areas of the country. "We are not building this country of ours for a day," declared Roosevelt. "It is to last through the ages." During his presidency Roosevelt enlarged Yosemite, established the U.S. Forest Service, and put millions of acres of land under federal protection. In 1916 the National Park Service was established, and today it manages more than 380 areas, including 57 national parks.

Image labels (left panel):
Half Dome 6 ft. (2,693 m)
Nevada Falls 594 ft. (181 m)
Glacier Point 7,214 ft. (2,199 m)
Sentinel Rock
Bridalveil Creek

Sightseers admire Yosemite Falls as they ride along Glacier Point Trail in 1901. Today some 3.5 million tourists visit the park each year.

LEARNING FROM GEOGRAPHY

1. How was the Yosemite Valley formed?

2. How did the establishment of the national park system help to conserve natural resources?

561

FYI

After Roosevelt left office, he continued his adventures with nature. In 1913 he participated in an expedition to the Amazon River sponsored by the American Museum of Natural History. He and his companions traveled more than 1,000 miles on the previously uncharted Rio da Duvida.

3 ASSESS

Have students answer the Learning from Geography questions.

4 CLOSE

Have students who have visited Yosemite or another national park describe how they benefited from the experience.

NGS ONLINE

Access National Geographic's Web site for current events, atlas updates, activities, links, interactive features, and archives at www.nationalgeographic.com.

ANSWERS TO LEARNING FROM GEOGRAPHY

1. Yosemite Valley was created by glaciers and rivers.

2. It protected the land by establishing ways in which the land could be used, and it established programs to teach people about the rich plant and animal life.

1 FOCUS

Section Overview

This section focuses on how Progressives were disappointed with the Taft administration.

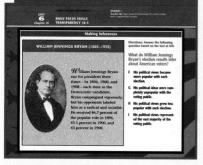

Guide to Reading

Answers to Graphic: progressives' campaign to unseat Cannon as Speaker of the House, Payne-Aldrich Tariff, Ballinger-Pinchot controversy

Preteaching Vocabulary
Have students create note cards with the Key Terms and Names on the front of the cards. Instruct students to use the reverse side to make notes about the term or name.

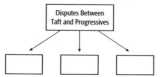

Guide to Reading

Main Idea
President Taft continued with Roosevelt's Progressive policies, but he did not live up to the expectations of many progressives.

Key Terms and Names
Joseph G. Cannon, Payne-Aldrich Tariff, Richard Ballinger, syndicate, insubordination

Reading Strategy
Organizing As you read about progressivism in this section, complete a graphic organizer similar to the one below listing Taft's conflicts with the progressives.

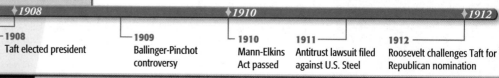

Disputes Between Taft and Progressives

Reading Objectives
• **Explain** how Theodore Roosevelt helped Taft get elected.
• **Discuss** why progressives were disappointed with Taft as president.

Section Theme
Continuity and Change Political differences with Roosevelt caused President Taft to lose Progressive support, even though he supported many Progressive policies.

Preview of Events

♦1908   ♦1910   ♦1912

1908
Taft elected president

1909
Ballinger-Pinchot controversy

1910
Mann-Elkins Act passed

1911
Antitrust lawsuit filed against U.S. Steel

1912
Roosevelt challenges Taft for Republican nomination

★ An American Story ★

William Howard Taft

One evening in January 1908, President Theodore Roosevelt sat chatting with Secretary of War William Howard Taft and his wife, Nellie, in the second-floor White House library. The mood was relaxed. Seated comfortably in his easy chair, Roosevelt was talking about a subject he had often discussed with his guests: the future role of Taft. Roosevelt toyed with a couple of options. "At one time it looks like the presidency," he mused, considering a future role for his trusted lieutenant, "then again it looks like the chief justiceship."

The Tafts knew that Roosevelt had the power to bring about either of these options. "Make it the presidency," interrupted Nellie Taft, always ambitious about her husband's career. Taft himself was less convinced that he would make a good chief executive. "Make it the chief justiceship," he uttered.

In the end, Taft bowed to the wishes of his wife and his boss. Following George Washington's example and honoring his own promise of 1904, Roosevelt decided not to seek reelection in 1908. Instead, he endorsed an experienced administrator and moderate progressive to run for president on the Republican ticket: William Howard Taft.

—adapted from *The American Heritage Pictorial History of the Presidents of the United States*

Taft Becomes President

Roosevelt loved "Smiling Bill" Taft like a brother and believed him to be the ideal person to continue his policies. He was, Roosevelt said, a leader who possessed "a scorn of all that is base and mean, a hearty sympathy with the oppressed [and a] kindly generosity of nature which makes him feel that all of his countrymen are in very truth his friends and

---

SECTION RESOURCES

Reproducible Masters
• Reproducible Lesson Plan 18–3
• Daily Lecture and Discussion Notes 18–3
• Guided Reading Activity 18–3
• Section Quiz 18–3
• Reading Essentials and Study Guide 18–3
• Performance Assessment Activities and Rubrics

Transparencies
• Daily Focus Skills Transparency 18–3

Multimedia
• Interactive Tutor Self-Assessment CD-ROM
• ExamView® Pro Testmaker CD-ROM
• Presentation Plus! CD-ROM
• TeacherWorks™ CD-ROM
• Audio Program

brothers." Taft had been Roosevelt's most trusted lieutenant. He had served as a judge, as governor of the Philippines, and as Roosevelt's secretary of war. In fact, Taft seemed acceptable to almost everyone. Thanks to Roosevelt's efforts, he easily received his party's nomination. His victory in the general election in November 1908 was a foregone conclusion. The Democratic candidate, twice-defeated William Jennings Bryan, lost once more.

Taft's Approach to Government "My dear Theodore," Taft wrote to his old friend a couple of weeks after assuming office. "When I am addressed as 'Mr. President,' I turn to see whether you are at my elbow." The comment was telling.

In that same letter, Taft admitted some of his early fears about his presidency:

> ❝I have no doubt that when you return you will find me very much under suspicion. . . . I have not the prestige which you had. . . . I am not attempting quite as much as you did . . . and so I fear that a large part of the public will feel as if I had fallen away from your ideals; but you know me better and will understand that I am still working away on the same old plan.❞
> —quoted in *The American Heritage Pictorial History of the Presidents of the United States*

Roosevelt and Taft were very different people. Roosevelt was a dynamic person who loved the spotlight and the rough-and-tumble world of politics. He had grand ideas and schemes but left the details of administering them to others. Taft was the opposite in many ways. He was a skillful administrator and judge. He disliked political maneuvering and preferred to avoid conflict with others. Unlike Roosevelt, who acted quickly and decisively on issues, Taft responded slowly, approaching problems from a legalistic point of view. "I don't like politics," he wrote, "I don't like the limelight." Although committed to many progressive ideas, Taft's personality and approach to politics quickly brought him into conflict with progressives.

Picturing **History**

Presidential Ritual In 1910 President Taft threw out the first baseball of the season at Lincoln Park in Washington, D.C., as his wife Nellie looked on. Why do you think presidents often continue this practice today?

2 TEACH

Daily Lecture and Discussion Notes 18–3

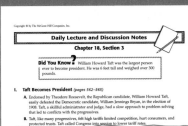

Daily Lecture and Discussion Notes
Chapter 18, Section 3

Did You Know? William Howard Taft was the largest person ever to become president. He was 6 feet tall and weighed over 300 pounds.

I. **Taft Becomes President** (pages 562–565)

A. Endorsed by Theodore Roosevelt, the Republican candidate, William Howard Taft, easily defeated the Democratic candidate, William Jennings Bryan, in the election of 1908. Taft, a skillful administrator and judge, had a slow approach to problem solving that led to conflicts with the progressives.

B. Taft, like many progressives, felt high tariffs limited competition, hurt consumers, and protected trusts. Taft called Congress into session to lower tariff rates.

Creating Circle Graphs Provide the data below and ask students to make a pair of circle graphs showing the results of the presidential election of 1908. **L1**

Candidate	Popular Vote	Electoral Vote
Taft, Rep.	7,675,320	321
Bryan, Dem.	6,412,294	162

📂 Use the rubric for creating a map, display, or chart on pages 77–78 in the *Performance Assessment Activities and Rubrics.*

Picturing **History**

Answer: Students might say it shows that the president is interested in the same things that other Americans enjoy.
Ask: What is different about the place from which Taft threw out the first pitch compared to presidents today? *(Taft was in the stands. Most dignitaries today are invited to throw out the pitch from the pitcher's mound.)*

COOPERATIVE LEARNING ACTIVITY

Holding a Presidential Debate Organize the class into two teams—one representing William Jennings Bryan's campaign staff, the other William Howard Taft's. Have the teams take on different roles as they prepare for the debate. For example, one person could take on the role of the candidate, another person could take on the role of the opponent, and others could take on the roles of campaign strategists and speechwriters. After the preparation is complete, hold a debate. 📦

Use the rubric for a cooperative group management plan on pages 81–82 in the *Performance Assessment Activities and Rubrics.*

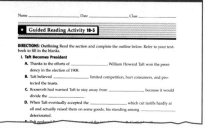

Guided Reading Activity 18–3

Name _____ Date _____ Class _____

★ Guided Reading Activity 18-3

DIRECTIONS: Outlining Read the section and complete the outline below. Refer to your text-book to fill in the blanks.

I. Taft Becomes President

A. Thanks to the efforts of _____, William Howard Taft won the presi-dency in the election of 1908.

B. Taft believed _____ limited competition, hurt consumers, and pro-tected the trusts.

C. Roosevelt had warned Taft to stay away from _____ because it would divide the _____

D. When Taft eventually accepted the _____, which cut tariffs hardly at all and actually raised them on some goods, his standing among _____ deteriorated.

E. Taft replaced _____

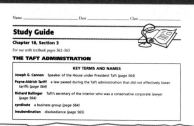

Picturing **History**

Answer: Pinchot was fired for insub-ordination, and a congressional com-mission cleared Ballinger.

Ask: How does this incident high-light Pinchot's Progressive views?
(showed he was ready to fight the president himself if he thought Progressive principles were being violated)

3 ASSESS

Assign Section 3 Assessment as homework or as an in-class activity.

🔘 Have students use the **Interactive Tutor Self-Assessment CD-ROM.**

Reading Essentials and Study Guide 18–3

Name _____ Date _____ Class _____

Study Guide

Chapter 18, Section 3

For use with textbook pages 562–565

THE TAFT ADMINISTRATION

KEY TERMS AND NAMES
Joseph G. Cannon Speaker of the House under President Taft *(page 564)*
Payne-Aldrich Tariff a law passed during the Taft administration that did not effectively lower tariffs *(page 564)*
Richard Ballinger Taft's secretary of the interior who was a conservative corporate lawyer *(page 564)*
syndicate a business group *(page 564)*
insubordination disobedience *(page 565)*

Political Uproar Taft's interior secretary, Richard Ballinger, pictured at left, ignited controversy when he made nearly one million acres of public land available for development. Progressive Gifford Pinchot, at right, leaked the story to the press. **How was the controversy resolved?**

The Payne-Aldrich Tariff Act Like many progres-sives, Taft believed high tariffs limited competition, hurt consumers, and protected trusts. Roosevelt had warned him to stay away from tariff reform because it would divide the Republican Party. Taft, however, went ahead and called Congress into special session to lower tariff rates.

To pass a new tariff, Taft needed the help of Speaker of the House **Joseph G. Cannon.** As Speaker, Cannon appointed all committees and decided which bills they handled. By exercising almost total control over debate, Cannon could push some bills through without discussion and see that others never came to a vote. Progressives, however, wanted to unseat Cannon because he often blocked their legislation.

Taft disagreed with the effort to unseat Cannon. He pressured progressive Republicans into stopping their campaign against Cannon. In exchange, Cannon quickly pushed the tariff bill through the House of Representatives. Taft's compromise angered many progressives. The following year, they defied the president by joining with House Democrats and removing Cannon from power.

Taft further alienated progressives when the tariff bill went to the Senate. The powerful head of the Senate Finance Committee, Republican Nelson Aldrich from Rhode Island, wanted to protect high tariffs, as did many other conservative senators. The result was the **Payne-Aldrich Tariff,** which cut tariffs hardly at all and actually raised them on some goods.

After discussions with Aldrich and other senators, however, Taft decided to accept the new tariff.

Progressives felt betrayed and outraged by Taft's decision: "I knew the fire had gone out of [the Progressive movement]," recalled chief forester Gifford Pinchot after Roosevelt left office. "Washington was a dead town. Its leader was gone, and in his place [was] a man whose fundamental desire was to keep out of trouble."

The Ballinger-Pinchot Controversy With Taft's standing among Republican progressives deterio-rating, a sensational controversy broke out late in 1909 that helped destroy Taft's popularity with reformers for good. Many progressives had been unhappy when Taft replaced Roosevelt's secretary of the interior, James R. Garfield, an aggressive con-servationist, with **Richard A. Ballinger,** a more con-servative corporate lawyer. Suspicion of Ballinger grew when he tried to make nearly a million acres of public forests and mineral reserves available for pri-vate development.

In the midst of this mounting concern, Gifford Pinchot charged the new secretary with having once plotted to turn over valuable public lands in Alaska to a private syndicate, or business group, for personal profit. Pinchot took the charges to the president. Taft's attorney general investigated the charges and decided they were groundless.

Still not satisfied, Pinchot leaked the story to the press and asked Congress to investigate. Taft fired

564 CHAPTER 18 The Progressive Movement

MEETING SPECIAL NEEDS

Learning Disability This activity will be particularly helpful for students needing extra work on the basic points. Ask students to bring in pictures, newspaper or magazine stories, or objects that por-tray or represent the United States president in action. Discuss the many roles of the president, such as proposing legislation, representing the United States overseas, and commanding the military. **L1** 🔲 **ELL**

📂 Refer to ***Inclusion for the High School Social Studies Classroom Strategies and Activities*** in the TCR.

Pinchot for insubordination, or disobedience. The congressional committee appointed to study the controversy cleared Ballinger.

By signing the Payne-Aldrich Tariff Act, supporting Ballinger against Pinchot, and backing Cannon, Taft gave the impression that he had "sold the Square Deal down the river." Popular indignation was so great that the congressional elections of 1910 resulted in a sweeping Democratic victory, with Democrats taking the majority in the House and Democrats and Progressive Republicans grabbing control of the Senate from the conservatives.

> **Reading Check** **Summarizing** What problems did President Taft have with progressives on tariff issues?

Taft's Progressive Reforms

Despite his political problems, Taft also had several successes. Although Roosevelt was nicknamed the "trustbuster," Taft was a strong supporter of competition and actually brought twice as many antitrust cases in four years as his predecessor had in seven.

In other areas, too, Taft was at least as strong a progressive as Roosevelt. Taft established the **Children's Bureau,** a federal agency similar to Roosevelt's Bureau of Corporations. The Children's Bureau investigated and publicized problems with child labor. Taft also supported the **Mann-Elkins Act** of 1910, which increased the regulatory powers of the ICC.

The Ballinger-Pinchot controversy aside, Taft was also a dedicated conservationist. His contributions in this area actually equaled or surpassed those of Roosevelt. He set up the Bureau of Mines to monitor the activities of mining companies, expanded the national forests, and protected waterpower sites from private development.

After Taft took office in 1909, Roosevelt left for a big-game hunt in Africa followed by a tour of Europe. He did not return to the United States until June 1910. Although disturbed by stories of Taft's "betrayal" of progressivism, Roosevelt at first refused to criticize the president.

In October 1911, Taft announced an antitrust lawsuit against U.S. Steel, claiming that the company's decision to buy the Tennessee Coal and Iron Company in 1907 had violated the Sherman Antitrust Act. The lawsuit was the final straw for Roosevelt. As president, he had approved U.S. Steel's plan to buy the company.

Roosevelt believed Taft's focus on breaking up trusts was destroying the carefully crafted system of cooperation and regulation that Roosevelt had established with big business through the Bureau of Corporations. In November 1911, Roosevelt publicly criticized Taft's decision. Roosevelt argued that the best way to deal with the trusts was to allow them to exist while at the same time increasing government's ability to regulate them.

Having broken with Taft, it was only a matter of time before progressives convinced Roosevelt to reenter politics. In late February 1912, Roosevelt announced that he would enter the presidential campaign of 1912 and attempt to replace Taft as the Republican nominee for president.

> **Reading Check** **Evaluating** How did President Taft's accomplishments regarding conservation and trustbusting compare to President Roosevelt's?

SECTION 3 ASSESSMENT

Checking for Understanding

1. **Define:** syndicate, insubordination.
2. **Identify:** Joseph G. Cannon, Payne-Aldrich Tariff, Richard Ballinger.
3. **Describe** how Taft helped conservation efforts, alleviated child labor problems, and strengthened the ICC.

Reviewing Themes

4. **Continuity and Change** How did replacing Roosevelt's secretary of the interior cause a dispute between Taft and the progressives?

Critical Thinking

5. **Comparing** What was the difference between Roosevelt and Taft regarding the relationship between the president and Congress?
6. **Organizing** Use a graphic organizer like the one below to list Taft's Progressive reforms.

Taft's Progressive Reforms

Analyzing Visuals

7. **Examining Photographs** Study the photograph on page 563. Note the formal attire of the president and his wife. How would you compare the clothes the people in the photograph are wearing with today's style of dress for leisure activities?

Writing About History

8. **Descriptive Writing** Write a magazine article in which you defend or criticize President Taft's administration in terms of its support of progressivism.

SECTION 3 ASSESSMENT ANSWERS

1. Terms are in blue.
2. Joseph G. Cannon (p. 564), Payne-Aldrich Tariff (p. 564), Richard Ballinger (p. 564)
3. expanded national forests, protected water sites, set up a commission to investigate child labor and supported the Mann-Elkins Act
4. Garfield, an aggressive conservationist, was replaced by Ballinger, a conservative corporate lawyer.
5. Roosevelt came up with great ideas and left administration up to others while Taft preferred administration.
6. Children's Bureau, Mann-Elkins Act, Bureau of Mines
7. The people in the photograph are more formally dressed than we dress today.
8. Students' articles should back up their defense or criticism with fact.

Section Quiz 18–3

Name _____ Date _____ Class _____

⭐ **Chapter 18**   Score ☐

Section Quiz 18-3

DIRECTIONS: Matching Match each item in Column A with the items in Column B. Write the correct letters in the blanks. *(10 points each)*

Column A	Column B
___ 1. disobedience	A. syndicate
___ 2. senator who wanted to protect high tariffs	B. Mann-Elkins Act
___ 3. increased the ICC's regulatory powers	C. insubordination
___ 4. business group	D. Nelson Aldrich
___ 5. Speaker of the House who appointed all committees and decided which bills they handled	E. Joseph G. Cannon

DIRECTIONS: Multiple Choice In the blank at the left, write the letter of the choice that best completes the statement or answers the question. *(10 points each)*

> **Reading Check**

Answer: Taft alienated them when he did not veto the Payne-Aldrich Tariff, which hardly cut tariffs and actually raised a few.

Reteach

Have students explain how Theodore Roosevelt helped Taft get elected.

Enrich

Invite interested students to research the conservation efforts of the Taft administration. Encourage students to use library and Internet resources for their research.

> **Reading Check**

Answer: Taft equaled or surpassed Roosevelt's actions.

4 CLOSE

Have students discuss why progressives were disappointed with Taft as president.

565

1 FOCUS

Section Overview

This section focuses on the many economic and social reforms of Wilson's Progressive agenda.

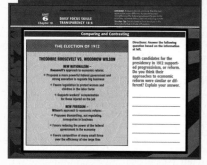
Guide to Reading

Answers to Graphic: Economic: Federal Reserve Act, Antitrust Act, Underwood Tariff, Federal Trade Commission; Social: Keating-Owen Child Labor Act, Adamson Act

Preteaching Vocabulary
Have students identify a person who can be tied to each of the Key Terms. Have them identify an event that can be tied to each of the Key Names.

Guide to Reading

Main Idea
Woodrow Wilson pursued a Progressive agenda after his 1912 election victory.

Key Terms and Names
Progressive Party, New Nationalism, New Freedom, income tax, Federal Reserve Act, Federal Trade Commission, unfair trade practices, National Association for the Advancement of Colored People

Reading Strategy
Categorizing As you read about progressivism during the Wilson administration, complete a chart similar to the one below by listing Wilson's Progressive economic and social reforms.

Economic Reforms	Social Reforms

Reading Objectives
• **Describe** Wilson's economic and social reforms.
• **Evaluate** the legacy of the Progressive movement.

Section Theme
Government and Democracy Woodrow Wilson's reforms greatly increased the federal government's role in regulating the nation's economy.

Preview of Events

| 1912 | 1914 | 1916 |

1912 Woodrow Wilson elected president
1913 Federal Reserve Act passed
1914 Federal Trade Commission Act passed
1916 Keating-Owen Child Labor Act passed

★ **An American Story** ★

FOR GOVERNOR

WOODROW WILSON

A Woodrow Wilson election poster

On September 15, 1910, in the Taylor Opera House in Trenton, New Jersey, a young progressive named Joseph Patrick Tumulty watched as a lean man with iron-gray hair made his way toward the stage. The man was Thomas Woodrow Wilson, the Democratic Party's nominee for governor.

Wilson was the choice of the party bosses. As Tumulty recalled, progressives were "feeling sullen, beaten, and hopelessly impotent." To Tumulty's astonishment, Wilson announced: "I shall enter upon the duties of the office of governor, if elected, with absolutely no pledge of any kind to prevent me from serving the people of the state with singleness of purpose."

Tumulty knew that Wilson was declaring his independence from the New Jersey political machine. It brought the progressives at the convention roaring to their feet. From one came the cry, "Thank God, at last, a leader has come!"

Two years later, Woodrow Wilson was the Democrats' nominee for the presidency, an office they had won only twice since the Civil War. This time they were confident of victory, for Wilson, a committed progressive, faced a Republican Party wracked by division.

—adapted from *Wilson: The Road to the White House*

The Election of 1912

The 1912 presidential campaign featured a current president, a former president, and an academic who had entered politics only two years earlier. The election's outcome determined the path of the Progressive movement and helped shape the nation's path in the 1900s.

SECTION RESOURCES

📁 Reproducible Masters
• Reproducible Lesson Plan 18–4
• Daily Lecture and Discussion Notes 18–4
• Guided Reading Activity 18–4
• Section Quiz 18–4
• Reading Essentials and Study Guide 18–4
• Performance Assessment Activities and Rubrics

✋ Transparencies
• Daily Focus Skills Transparency 18–4

Multimedia
🔘 Interactive Tutor Self-Assessment CD-ROM
🔘 ExamView® Pro Testmaker CD-ROM
🔘 Presentation Plus! CD-ROM
🔘 TeacherWorks™ CD-ROM
🔘 Audio Program

The Republican Party Splits Believing that President Taft had failed to live up to Progressive ideals, Theodore Roosevelt informed seven state governors that he was willing to accept the Republican nomination. "My hat is in the ring!" he declared. "The fight is on."

The struggle for control of the Republican Party reached its climax at the national convention in Chicago in June. Conservatives rallied behind Taft. Most of the progressives lined up for Roosevelt. When it became clear that Taft's delegates controlled the nomination, Roosevelt decided to leave the party and campaign as an independent. "We stand at Armageddon," he told his supporters, "and we battle for the Lord."

Declaring himself "fit as a bull moose," Roosevelt became the presidential candidate for the newly formed **Progressive Party,** nicknamed the Bull Moose Party. Because Taft had alienated so many groups, the election of 1912 became a contest between two progressives: the Bull Moose Roosevelt and the Democrat Wilson.

Wilson's Character and Background Woodrow Wilson entered politics as a firm progressive. As governor of New Jersey, he pushed one Progressive reform after another through the statehouse. He revamped election laws, established utility regulatory boards, and allowed cities to change to the commissioner form of government. In less than two years, New Jersey became a model of Progressive reform.

"New Freedom" Versus "New Nationalism" The election of 1912 was a contest between two men who supported progressivism, although they had different approaches to reform. Roosevelt accepted the economic power of the trusts as a fact of life and proposed a more powerful federal government and a strong executive to regulate them. Roosevelt also outlined a complete program of reforms. He favored legislation to protect women and children in the labor force and supported workers' compensation for those injured on the job. He also wanted a federal trade commission to regulate industry in a manner similar to the ICC's authority over railroads. Roosevelt called his program the **New Nationalism.**

Wilson countered with what he called the **New Freedom.** He criticized Roosevelt's program as one that supported "regulated monopoly." Monopolies, he believed, were evils to be destroyed, not regulated. Wilson argued that Roosevelt's approach gave the federal government too much power in the economy

and did nothing to restore competition. Freedom, in Wilson's opinion, was more important than efficiency. "The history of liberty," Wilson declared, "is the history of the limitation of governmental power. . . . If America is not to have free enterprise, then she can have freedom of no sort whatever."

Wilson Is Elected As expected, Roosevelt and Taft split the Republican voters, enabling Wilson to win the Electoral College and the election with 435 votes, even though he received less than 42 percent of the popular vote—less than Roosevelt and Taft combined. For the first time since Grover Cleveland's election in 1892, a Democrat became president of the United States.

✓ **Reading Check** **Summarizing** Who were the three major candidates in the presidential election of 1912?

Regulating the Economy

The new chief executive lost no time in embarking on his program of reform. He immediately took charge of the government. "The president is at liberty, both in law and conscience, to be as big a man as he can,"

Picturing **History**

The New Freedom Woodrow Wilson initially believed that government should break up trusts. Why did Wilson favor economic competition?

2 TEACH

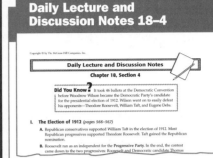

Daily Lecture and Discussion Notes 18–4

Copyright © by The McGraw-Hill Companies, Inc.

Daily Lecture and Discussion Notes

Chapter 18, Section 4

Did You Know? It took 46 ballots at the Democratic Convention before Woodrow Wilson became the Democratic Party's candidate for the presidential election of 1912. Wilson went on to easily defeat his opponents—Theodore Roosevelt, William Taft, and Eugene Debs.

I. **The Election of 1912** *(pages 566–567)*

A. Republican conservatives supported William Taft in the election of 1912. Most Republican progressives supported Theodore Roosevelt. Taft gained the Republican nomination.

B. Roosevelt ran as an independent for the **Progressive Party.** In the end, the contest came down to the two progressives: Roosevelt and Democratic candidate Thomas

Using Social Studies Terminology To make certain that students understand the business and economics terminology in this section, have them write a paragraph in which they correctly use the following terms: *antitrust, competition, tariff,* and *monopoly.* Ask for volunteers to share their paragraphs with the class. Allow students time to ask questions to further clarify the meanings of these terms. **L1**

✓ **Reading Check**

Answer: Theodore Roosevelt, William Howard Taft, and Woodrow Wilson

Picturing **History**

Answer: He believed economic freedom was more important than efficiency.
Ask: Of what state was Wilson governor? *(New Jersey)*

COOPERATIVE LEARNING ACTIVITY

Recognizing the Role of Third Parties Have students work in groups of four or five to discuss the following question: Why has it been so difficult for third parties to develop in the American political system? Suggest that students scan the index for references to third parties that have been mentioned in earlier chapters of the text. Call on students randomly to report their group's progress.

Use the rubric for a cooperative group management plan on pages 81–82 in the *Performance Assessment Activities and Rubrics.*

Guided Reading Activity 18–4

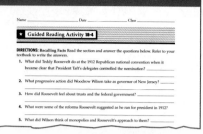

Name _____ Date _____ Class _____

★ **Guided Reading Activity 18-4**

DIRECTIONS: Recalling Facts Read the section and answer the questions below. Refer to your textbook to write the answers.

1. What did Teddy Roosevelt do at the 1912 Republican national convention when it became clear that President Taft's delegates controlled the nomination? _____

2. What progressive action did Woodrow Wilson take as governor of New Jersey? _____

3. How did Roosevelt feel about trusts and the federal government? _____

4. What were some of the reforms Roosevelt suggested as he ran for president in 1912? _____

5. What did Wilson think of monopolies and Roosevelt's approach to them? _____

Creating a Table Have students create a table showing the major legislation mentioned in this section. Instruct students to include the date and name of the act and a brief description of its intended effect. **L2**

📁 Use the rubric for creating a map, display, or chart on pages 65–66 in the *Performance Assessment Activities and Rubrics.*

Geography *Skills*

Answers:
1. Texas
2. Students' answers will vary but may include population density and size of a region's economy.

Geography Skills Practice
Ask: What is the role of the Board of Governors? *(setting the branch banks' interest rates, thereby adjusting the amount of money in circulation nationally)*

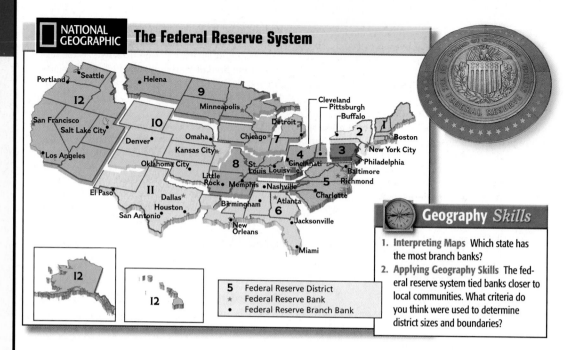

NATIONAL GEOGRAPHIC The Federal Reserve System

Geography *Skills*

1. **Interpreting Maps** Which state has the most branch banks?
2. **Applying Geography Skills** The federal reserve system tied banks closer to local communities. What criteria do you think were used to determine district sizes and boundaries?

5 Federal Reserve District
★ Federal Reserve Bank
● Federal Reserve Branch Bank

Wilson had once written. "His capacity will set the limit." During his eight years as president, Wilson demonstrated his power as he crafted reforms affecting tariffs, the banking system, trusts, and workers' rights.

Reforming Tariffs Five weeks after taking office, Wilson appeared before Congress, the first president to do so since John Adams. He had come to present his bill to reduce tariffs.

He personally lobbied members of Congress to support the tariff reduction bill. Not even Roosevelt had taken such an active role in promoting special legislation. In Wilson's message to Congress, he declared that high tariffs had "built up a set of privileges and exemptions from competition behind which it was easy . . . to organize monopoly until . . . nothing is obliged to stand the tests of efficiency and economy."

Wilson believed that the pressure of foreign competition would lead American manufacturers to improve their products and lower their prices. Lower tariff rates, he claimed, would help businesses by putting them under the "constant necessity to be efficient, economical, and enterprising."

In 1913 the Democrat-controlled Congress passed the **Underwood Tariff** and Wilson signed it into law. This piece of legislation reduced the average tariff on imported goods to about 30 percent of the value of the goods, or about half the tariff rate of the 1890s.

An important section of the Underwood Tariff Act was the provision for levying an income tax, or a direct tax on the earnings of individuals and corporations. The Constitution originally prohibited direct taxes unless they were apportioned among the states on the basis of population. In other words, the states would be paying the income tax, not individuals, and states with more people would pay more tax. Passage of the Sixteenth Amendment in 1913, however, made it legal for the federal government to tax the income of individuals directly.

ECONOMY

Reforming the Banks The United States had not had a central bank since the 1830s. During the economic depressions that hit the country periodically after that time, hundreds of small banks collapsed, wiping out the life savings of many of their customers. The most recent of these crises had been in 1907.

To restore public confidence in the banking system, Wilson supported the establishment of a Federal Reserve system. Banks would have to keep a portion of their deposits in a regional reserve bank, which would provide a financial cushion against unanticipated losses.

At the center of the Federal Reserve system would be a Board of Governors, appointed by the president. The Board could set the interest rates the reserve

568 CHAPTER 18   The Progressive Movement

MEETING SPECIAL NEEDS

Kinesthetic Bring a game of Monopoly to class. Display the board and outline the basic rules of the game if necessary. Then have volunteers, working individually or with partners, present a lesson based upon the game. For example, they might purchase houses or buy up all of the railroads to explain what trusts were, how they operated in this era, and how the president tried to prevent them. **L1** ELL

📁 Refer to *Inclusion for the High School Social Studies Classroom Strategies and Activities* in the TCR.

banks charged other banks, thereby indirectly controlling the interest rates of the entire nation and the amount of money in circulation. This gave the Board the ability to fight inflation by raising interest rates and to stimulate the economy during a recession by lowering interest rates. Congress approved the new system at the end of 1913. The **Federal Reserve Act** became one of the most significant pieces of legislation in American history.

Antitrust Action During his campaign, Wilson had promised to restore competition to the economy by breaking up big business monopolies. Roosevelt argued that Wilson's ideas were unrealistic because big business was more efficient and unlikely to be replaced by smaller, more competitive firms. Once in office, Wilson's opinion shifted, and he came to agree with Roosevelt—but progressives in Congress continued to demand action against big business.

In the summer of 1914, at Wilson's request, Congress created the **Federal Trade Commission** (FTC) to monitor American business. The FTC had the power to investigate companies and issue "cease and desist" orders against companies engaging in unfair trade practices, or those which hurt competition. The FTC could be taken to court if a business disagreed with its rulings.

Wilson did not want the FTC to break up big business. Instead, it was to work with business to limit activities that unfairly limited competition. He deliberately appointed conservative business leaders to serve as the FTC's first commissioners.

Wilson's approach did not satisfy progressives in Congress, who responded by passing the **Clayton Antitrust Act.** The act banned tying agreements, which required retailers who bought from one company to stop selling a competitor's products. It also banned price discrimination. Businesses could not charge different customers different prices. Manufacturers could no longer give discounts to chain stores and other retailers who bought a large volume of goods.

Before the act passed, labor unions lobbied Congress to exempt unions from the antitrust laws. The Clayton Antitrust Act specifically declared that unions were not unlawful combinations in restraint of trade. When the bill became law, Samuel Gompers, head of the American Federation of Labor, called the Clayton Antitrust Act the worker's "Magna Carta," because it gave unions the right to exist.

✓ **Reading Check** **Evaluating** What was the impact of the passage of the Sixteenth Amendment?

Federal Aid and Social Welfare

By the fall of 1914, Wilson believed that his New Freedom program was essentially complete. As a result, he began to retreat from activism.

The congressional elections of 1914, however, shattered the president's complacency. Democrats suffered major losses in the House of Representatives, and voters who had supported the Bull Moose Party in 1912 began returning to the Republicans. Realizing that he would not be able to rely on a divided opposition when he ran for re-election in 1916, Wilson began to support further reforms.

In 1916, for example, Wilson signed the first federal law regulating child labor. The Keating-Owen Child Labor Act prohibited the employment of children under the age of 14 in factories producing goods for interstate commerce. The Supreme Court

The NAACP

Past
Violent race riots broke out in 1908 in Springfield, Illinois, as immigrants and African Americans vied with other residents for scarce jobs. In one riot, a mob killed several African Americans and destroyed much property. Responding to the growing racial violence in the nation, an integrated group of citizens met in New York City to discuss remedies. Out of that meeting, the National Association for the Advancement of Colored People (NAACP) was born.

Present
Today the NAACP works for such causes as school desegregation, fair housing and employment, voter registration, and equal health care and income opportunity. It plays a role in establishing legal precedents to improve the quality of life for African Americans across the nation.

Linking Past & Present

The NAACP has chapters in all 50 states and the District of Columbia. It also has chapters in some foreign countries.

✓ **Reading Check**

Answer: The Sixteenth Amendment made it legal for the federal government to directly tax the income of individuals.

3 ASSESS

Assign Section 4 Assessment as homework or as an in-class activity.

💿 Have students use the **Interactive Tutor Self-Assessment CD-ROM.**

Reading Essentials and Study Guide 18–4

Name _____ Date _____ Class _____

Study Guide

Chapter 18, Section 4
For use with textbook pages 566–570

THE WILSON YEARS

KEY TERMS AND NAMES

Progressive Party newly formed political party, nicknamed the Bull Moose Party (page 567)

New Nationalism suggested reform programs of Theodore Roosevelt in the 1912 election (page 567)

New Freedom suggested reform programs of Woodrow Wilson in the 1912 election (page 567)

income tax direct tax on the earnings of individuals and corporations (page 568)

Federal Reserve Act law that set up a central banking system in 1913 (page 569)

Federal Trade Commission agency created by Congress to monitor American business (page 569)

unfair trade practices business practices that unfairly limited competition (page 569)

INTERDISCIPLINARY CONNECTIONS ACTIVITY

Literature In 1903 W.E.B. Du Bois published one of his most famous works, *The Soul of Black Folk,* a collection of 15 essays. In one essay, Du Bois spelled out his differences with and praise for Booker T. Washington. "Manly self-respect," Du Bois claimed, was "worth more than land and houses." Have students select one of the essays from *The Soul of Black Folk* and prepare a one-minute presentation about it. Presentations should include a summary of the essay and the reader's reaction. **L2**

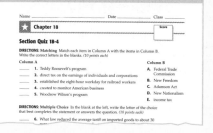
✓ Reading Check

Answer: created an eight-hour work-day for railroad workers

Reteach

Have students list Wilson's economic and social reforms.

Enrich

Invite interested students to research the early history of the NAACP and report their findings to the class. Encourage students to use library and Internet resources for their research.

✓ Reading Check

Answer: expanded democracy and raised expectations of the federal government's role in the economy and society

4 CLOSE

Have students evaluate the legacy of the Progressive movement.

---

declared the law unconstitutional on the grounds that child labor was not interstate commerce and therefore only states could regulate it. Wilson's effort, however, helped his reputation with progressive voters. Wilson also supported the Adamson Act, which established the eight-hour workday for railroad workers, and the Federal Farm Loan Act, which created 12 Federal Land Banks to provide farmers with long-term loans at low interest rates.

✓ Reading Check Examining How did the Adamson Act improve labor conditions in the United States?

The Legacy of Progressivism

During his presidency, Wilson had built upon Roosevelt's foundation. He expanded the role of the federal government and of the president.

A New Kind of Government Progressivism made important changes in the political life of the United States. Before this era, most Americans did not expect the government to pass laws protecting workers or regulating big business. In fact, many courts had previously ruled that it was unconstitutional for the government to do so.

By the end of the Progressive era, however, both legal and public opinion had shifted. Increasingly, Americans expected the government, particularly the federal government, to play a more active role in regulating the economy and solving social problems.

The Limits of Progressivism The most conspicuous limit to progressivism was its failure to address African American reform issues. African Americans themselves, however, were absorbing the reform spirit, which fueled their longstanding desire for advancement.

In 1905 W.E.B. Du Bois and 28 other African American leaders met at Niagara Falls to demand full political rights and responsibilities for African Americans. They met on the Canadian side of the falls because no hotel on the American side would accept them. There they launched what became known as the Niagara Movement. This meeting was one of many steps leading to the founding of the **National Association for the Advancement of Colored People (NAACP)** in 1909. Du Bois and other NAACP founders believed that the vote was essential to bring about an end to lynching and racial discrimination. "The power of the ballot we need in sheer self-defense," Du Bois said, "else what shall save us from a second slavery?"

Despite the failure of most progressives to focus on racial issues, Progressive reform helped change American society in many ways. Although they excluded many groups from their efforts, the progressives expanded democracy and improved the quality of life for millions of men, women, and children. As the country entered World War I, however, Americans soon turned from reforming their own society to a crusade to "make the world safe for democracy."

✓ Reading Check Evaluating How did progressivism change American beliefs about the federal government?

SECTION 4 ASSESSMENT

Checking for Understanding

1. **Define:** income tax, unfair trade practices.
2. **Identify:** Progressive Party, New Nationalism, New Freedom, Federal Reserve Act, Federal Trade Commission, National Association for the Advancement of Colored People.
3. **Explain** why President Wilson proposed the establishment of the Federal Reserve System.

Reviewing Themes

4. **Government and Democracy** What new federal agencies increased the government's power to regulate the economy?

Critical Thinking

5. **Forming an Opinion** Which of Wilson's reforms do you consider most important? Why?
6. **Organizing** Use a graphic organizer similar to the one below to list the effects progressivism had on American society.

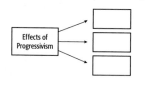

Analyzing Visuals

7. **Analyzing Photographs** Study the photograph on page 571. What details do you see in the image that might have contributed to tainted meat? When do you think the stamp above the photo began to be used?

Writing About History

8. **Expository Writing** Imagine that you are a newspaper editor during President Wilson's administration. Write an article on the shortcomings of the Progressive movement in terms of its attitudes about race. Provide ideas about how the movement might have addressed discrimination and segregation.

SECTION 4 ASSESSMENT ANSWERS

1. Terms are in blue.
2. Progressive Party (*p. 567*), New Nationalism (*p. 567*), New Freedom (*p. 567*), Federal Reserve Act (*p. 569*), Federal Trade Commission (*p. 569*), National Association for the Advancement of Colored People (*p. 570*)
3. to restore public confidence in the banking system
4. the Federal Reserve System and the Federal Trade Commission
5. Students' answers will vary but should include a reasonable argument.
6. expanded democracy, improved quality of life, expanded government role
7. condition of floors, wheelbarrow carrying meat; after 1906
8. Students' editorials will vary. Students should point out specific shortcomings and suggest ways that the progressives could have addressed these social problems.

American LITERATURE

Born in Maryland in 1878, **Upton Sinclair** spent his life writing about and trying to change what he saw as wrong in the United States. One of his most famous novels, *The Jungle*, deals with working conditions and the rights of immigrants. The novel tells the story of Jurgis Rudkus, a Lithuanian immigrant who comes to the United States with his family in the early 1900s, dreaming of wealth and freedom. What he finds is "Packingtown," the bustling, filthy stockyards of Chicago. In the following excerpt, Sinclair describes the system Jurgis comes to know after gaining his first job in a meatpacking plant.

Read to Discover
What qualities did Sinclair believe a person must have to succeed in Packingtown?

Reader's Dictionary
pitted: set against each other
caldron: a large kettle or pot for boiling
knave: a tricky, deceitful person

from The Jungle

by Upton Sinclair

After Jurgis had been there awhile he would know that the plants were simply honeycombed with rottenness . . . —the bosses grafted off the men, and they grafted off each other; and some day the superintendent would find out about the boss, and then he would graft off the boss. . . . Here was Durham's, for instance, owned by a man who was trying to make as much money out of it as he could, and did not care in the least how he did it; and underneath him . . . were managers and superintendents and foremen, each one driving the man next below him and trying to squeeze out of him as much work as possible. And all the men of the same rank were pitted against each other. . . . So from top to bottom the place was simply a seething caldron of jealousies and hatreds; there was no loyalty or decency anywhere about it, there was no place in it where a man counted for anything against a dollar. . . .

Jurgis would find these things out for himself, if he stayed there long enough; it was the men [like him] who had to do all the dirty jobs. . . . Jurgis had come there, and thought he was going to make himself useful, and rise and become a skilled man; but he would soon find out his error—for nobody rose in Packingtown by doing good work. [I]f you met a man who was rising in Packingtown, you met a knave. . . . [T]he man who minded his own business and did his work— why, they would (wear) him out, and then . . . throw him into the gutter.

Analyzing Literature

1. According to the passage, what is the plant owner's main goal?
2. What does Sinclair mean when he says, ". . . there was no place in it where a man counted for anything against a dollar. . . ."?

Interdisciplinary Activity

Government When it was published, *The Jungle* was so shocking that it launched a government investigation of the meatpacking industry. The investigation eventually led to the establishment of laws regulating the industry. Using the Internet, research these laws and read about how they are enforced today. Write a short report on your findings.

Read to Discover

Answer: greed, jealousy, and hatred

Reader's Dictionary

Have students look up words that might have a different meaning in this context, for example, *honeycombed* and *seething*.

Historical Connection

Upton Sinclair set out to expose the poor working conditions of immigrants but readers focused on how the meatpacking conditions affected *them*.

Portfolio Writing Activity

Have students write a short narrative about working conditions in a place a family member has worked.

HISTORY Online

Refer to tav.glencoe.com for additional Glencoe Literature titles, lesson plans, and study guides related to this unit.

Answers to Analyzing Literature

1. His main goal is to make money.
2. He means that making money was more important than human life.

Interdisciplinary Activity
Students' reports will vary. Remind students to include bibliographic information about the sources they use.

CHAPTER 18 ASSESSMENT and ACTIVITIES

CHAPTER
18 ASSESSMENT and ACTIVITIES

Reviewing Key Terms

Students' answers will vary. The pages where the words appear in the text are shown in parentheses.

1. **progressivism** *(p. 547)*
2. **muckraker** *(p. 547)*
3. **commission plan** *(p. 548)*
4. **direct primary** *(p. 549)*
5. **initiative** *(p. 549)*
6. **referendum** *(p. 549)*
7. **recall** *(p. 549)*
8. **suffrage** *(p. 549)*
9. **temperance** *(p. 553)*
10. **prohibition** *(p. 553)*
11. **socialism** *(p. 553)*
12. **Square Deal** *(p. 556)*
13. **arbitration** *(p. 557)*
14. **syndicate** *(p. 564)*
15. **insubordination** *(p. 565)*
16. **income tax** *(p. 568)*
17. **unfair trade practices** *(p. 569)*

Reviewing Key Facts

18. Robert La Follette *(p. 549)*, Alice Paul *(p. 550)*, Hepburn Act *(p. 557)*, Upton Sinclair *(p. 558)*, Payne-Aldrich Tariff *(p. 564)*, Federal Reserve Act *(p. 569)*, Federal Trade Commission *(p. 569)*

19. belief that people could improve society, that government should play an active role in reform

20. He threatened to send in the army to work the mines. His threat finally got the mine owners to agree to arbitration.

21. He set up the Federal Reserve System to control the circulation of money in the United States.

Reviewing Key Terms

On a sheet of paper, use each of these terms in a sentence.

1. progressivism	10. prohibition
2. muckraker	11. socialism
3. commission plan	12. Square Deal
4. direct primary	13. arbitration
5. initiative	14. syndicate
6. referendum	15. insubordination
7. recall	16. income tax
8. suffrage	17. unfair trade practices
9. temperance	

Reviewing Key Facts

18. **Identify:** Robert La Follette, Alice Paul, Hepburn Act, Upton Sinclair, Payne-Aldrich Tariff, Federal Reserve Act, Federal Trade Commission.

19. What were the characteristics of the Progressive era?

20. How did President Roosevelt influence the outcome of the 1902 coal strike?

21. How did President Wilson attempt to reform the banking industry?

Critical Thinking

22. **Analyzing Themes: Government and Democracy** How did Wisconsin governor Robert La Follette help to expand democracy in the United States?

23. **Analyzing** How did Progressive reforms strengthen the cause of woman suffrage?

24. **Evaluating** What was the impact of reform leaders such as W.E.B. Du Bois and Robert La Follette on American society?

25. **Organizing** Use a graphic organizer similar to the one below to list the economic, political, and social welfare reforms brought about during the Progressive era.

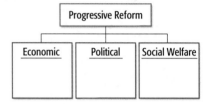

26. **Interpreting Primary Sources** Ida Husted Harper was a social reformer, a newspaper reporter, and a strong supporter of suffrage for women. In the following excerpt, she examines the attitudes of the time toward the kinds of work women should do.

Chapter Summary

Basic Beliefs of Progressives
- People could improve society by relying on science and knowledge.
- Industrialism and urbanization caused problems.
- Government should fix problems.
- To achieve reform, government itself had to be reformed.

Government Reforms
- Commission and city-manager forms of government were adopted.
- Direct primary system let citizens choose office candidates.
- Initiative, referendum, and recall were adopted.
- Seventeenth Amendment gave voters right to elect senators directly.
- Nineteenth Amendment gave women the right to vote.

Business Regulation
- Interstate Commerce Commission was strengthened.
- Consumer protection laws were passed.
- Federal Trade Commission was set up to regulate business.
- Federal Reserve System was set up to control money supply.

Social Reforms
- Zoning laws and building codes improved urban housing.
- Child labor laws were passed.
- Workers' compensation laws were passed.
- Temperance movement worked to ban alcohol.

Critical Thinking

22. pressured the state legislature to require each party to hold a direct primary, weakening the party caucus system

23. many middle class women concluded that they needed the vote to promote the social reforms they favored and to ensure the passage of labor laws to protect women

24. Du Bois helped establish the NAACP and La Follette helped create a more democratic government.

25. Economic: Federal Reserve Act, Sherman Antitrust Act, Underwood Tariff, Hepburn Act, Payne-Aldrich Tariff, Mann-Elkins Act, Newlands Reclamation Act; Political: city government structure, Nineteenth Amendment, direct primaries, direct election of senators, initiative, referendum, and recall; Social Welfare: Keating-Owen Child Labor Act, Adamson Act, Meat Inspection Act, Pure Food and Drug Act

HISTORY Online

Self-Check Quiz

Visit the *American Vision* Web site at tav.glencoe.com and click on *Self-Check Quizzes—Chapter 18* to assess your knowledge of chapter content.

66The moment we accept the theory that women must enter wage-earning occupations only when compelled to do so by poverty, that moment we degrade labor and lower the status of all women who are engaged in it. This theory prevailed throughout past ages, and it placed a stigma upon working women which is only beginning to be removed by the present generation. . . .

There is not, there never has been, an effort 'to create a sentiment that home is no place for a girl.' A good home is the one place above all others for a girl, as it is for a boy. It is her rest, her haven, her protection, but this does not necessarily imply that she must not engage in any work outside its limits. . . .

It is wholly impracticable to draw a dividing line between the employments which are suitable and those which are unsuitable for women. They have just as much right as men to decide this question for themselves. . . .

It is not intended to argue that every woman should leave the home and go into business, but only that those who wish to do so shall have the opportunity, and that men shall no longer monopolize the gainful occupations.99

—quoted in *The Independent,* 1901

a. What views does Ida Harper have on the kinds of work women should do?

b. What kinds of work-related issues do women face today?

Practicing Skills

27. **Taking Notes** Reread the subsection titled "The Coal Strike of 1902" on pages 556 and 557. Then use the steps you learned about taking notes on page 554 to take notes on the subsection.

Chapter Activities

28. **Technology** Search the Internet for an article written by a muckraker mentioned in the chapter. Using a word processor, prepare a two-page summary of the article and indicate how its contents may have sparked the demand for reform.

29. **Research Project** Worker safety was an important issue for progressives. Research three worker safety laws in your state, and describe how they benefit workers. Present your findings in a written report.

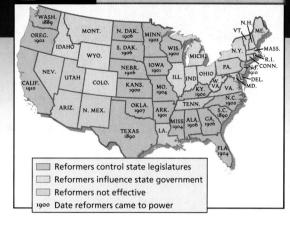

NATIONAL GEOGRAPHIC
The Progressive Movement and State Governments 1889–1912

☐ Reformers control state legislatures
☐ Reformers influence state government
☐ Reformers not effective
1900 Date reformers came to power

Writing Activity

30. **Informative Writing** Imagine you are a reporter in 1906, assigned to interview Upton Sinclair. Reread pages 558 and 571, then prepare a list of questions to ask him during the interview.

Geography and History

31. The map above shows the relationship between the Progressive movement and state governments. Study the map and answer the questions below.
    a. **Interpreting Maps** Which three states came under the control of reformers before Wisconsin did?
    b. **Applying Geography Skills** What generalization can you make about progressives in state governments?

The Princeton Review
Standardized Test Practice

Directions: Choose the best answer to the following question.

In 1920 women won an important victory when the Nineteenth Amendment was ratified. What did this amendment accomplish?

A It required colleges to accept women.

B It guaranteed child care for workers' children.

C It granted women the right to vote.

D It guaranteed equal wages for equal work.

Test-Taking Tip: Some answers can be eliminated by using your own knowledge. For example, you probably know that child care is still an issue for parents today, so it cannot be guaranteed in the Nineteenth Amendment. Therefore, you can eliminate answer B.

HISTORY Online

Have students visit the Web site at tav.glencoe.com to review Chapter 18 and take the Self-Check Quiz.

Writing Activity

30. Students' lists will vary but should show a keen understanding of the material presented on pages 558 and 571.

Geography and History

31. **a.** Texas, Washington, and South Carolina **b.** Reformers were most active in the South, Great Plains, and Far West.

The Princeton Review
Standardized Test Practice

Answer: C
Test-Taking Tip: Tell students to use the information in the stem of the question to help organize their thoughts. Most women were not worried about attending college in the 1920s, so they can eliminate A. Child care and equal wages are still issues facing women today, so they can also eliminate B and D.

Bonus Question ?

Ask: What does the term *suffrage* mean? *(the right to vote)*

---

26. **a.** She believed women could work at the same jobs as men. **b.** Possible answers: lower wages, sexual harassment, discrimination, difficulty finding child care

Practicing Skills

27. Have students trade their notes with a classmate and suggest improvements in their classmates' note-taking skills.

Chapter Activities

28. The summaries will vary but students should include an analysis of how the piece may have sparked the demand for reform.

29. The written reports should highlight the benefits of worker safety laws in your state.

Chapter 19 Resources

Timesaving Tools

TeacherWorks™ All-In-One Planner and Resource Center

- **Interactive Teacher Edition** Access your Teacher Wraparound Edition and your classroom resources with a few easy clicks.
- **Interactive Lesson Planner** Planning has never been easier! Organize your week, month, semester, or year with all the lesson helps you need to make teaching creative, timely, and relevant.

Use Glencoe's **Presentation Plus!** multimedia teacher tool to easily present dynamic lessons that visually excite your students. Using Microsoft PowerPoint® you can customize the presentations to create your own personalized lessons.

TEACHING TRANSPARENCIES

Graphic Organizer 14

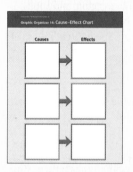

Why It Matters Chapter Transparency 19

APPLICATION AND ENRICHMENT

Linking Past and Present Activity 19

Enrichment Activity 19

Primary Source Reading 19

REVIEW AND REINFORCEMENT

Reteaching Activity 19

Vocabulary Activity 19

Time Line Activity 19

Critical Thinking Skills Activity 19

Meeting NCSS Standards

The following standards are highlighted in Chapter 19:

Section 1 | II | Time, Continuity, and Change: B, C, F
Section 2 | VI | Power, Authority, and Governance: B, C, D, I
Section 3 | IV | Individual Development and Identity: A, D, E
Section 4 | II | Time, Continuity, and Change: A, B, E

Local Standards

_____

_____

_____

_____

**Chapter 19 Test
Form A**

**Chapter 19 Test
Form B**

**Standardized Test Skills
Practice Workbook Activity 19**

**Performance Assessment
Activities and Rubrics 19**

**ExamView® Pro
Testmaker CD-ROM**

MULTIMEDIA

- Vocabulary PuzzleMaker CD-ROM
- Interactive Tutor Self-Assessment CD-ROM
- ExamView® Pro Testmaker CD-ROM
- Audio Program
- American History Primary Source Documents Library CD-ROM
- MindJogger Videoquiz
- Presentation Plus! CD-ROM
- TeacherWorks™ CD-ROM
- Interactive Student Edition CD-ROM
- Glencoe Skillbuilder Interactive Workbook CD-ROM, Level 2
- The *American Vision* Video Program
- American Music: Hits Through History
- American Music: Cultural Traditions

SPANISH RESOURCES

The following Spanish language materials are available in the Spanish Resources Binder:

- Spanish Guided Reading Activities
- Spanish Reteaching Activities
- Spanish Quizzes and Tests
- Spanish Vocabulary Activities
- Spanish Summaries
- The Declaration of Independence and United States Constitution Spanish Translation

HISTORY *Online*

Use our Web site for additional resources. All essential content is covered in the Student Edition.

You and your students can visit tav.glencoe.com, the Web site companion to the *American Vision.* This innovative integration of electronic and print media offers your students a wealth of opportunities. The student text directs students to the Web site for the following options:

- **Chapter Overviews**
- **Student Web Activities**
- **Self-Check Quizzes**
- **Textbook Updates**

Answers to the student Web activities are provided for you in the **Web Activity Lesson Plans.** Additional Web resources and Interactive Tutor Puzzles are also available.

THE HISTORY CHANNEL®

The following videotape programs are available from Glencoe as supplements to Chapter 19:

- **Woodrow Wilson: Reluctant Warrior** (ISBN 0-76-700101-X)
- **Pancho Villa: Outlaw Hero** (ISBN 0-76-700315-2)

To order, call Glencoe at 1-800-334-7344. To find classroom resources to accompany many of these videos, check the following home pages:
A&E Television: www.aande.com
The History Channel: www.historychannel.com

Chapter 19 Resources

SECTION RESOURCES

Daily Objectives	Reproducible Resources	Multimedia Resources
SECTION 1 **The United States Enters World War I** 1. Discuss the causes and results of American intervention in Mexico and the Caribbean. 2. Explain the causes of World War I and why the United States entered the war.	Reproducible Lesson Plan 19–1 Daily Lecture and Discussion Notes 19–1 Guided Reading Activity 19–1* Section Quiz 19–1* Reading Essentials and Study Guide 19–1 Performance Assessment Activities and Rubrics	Daily Focus Skills Transparency 19–1 American Art & Architecture Interactive Tutor Self-Assessment CD-ROM ExamView® Pro Testmaker CD-ROM Presentation Plus! CD-ROM TeacherWorks™ CD-ROM Audio Program American Music: Hits Through History American Music: Cultural Traditions
SECTION 2 **The Home Front** 1. Analyze how the United States raised an army and won support for World War I. 2. Explain how the economy was controlled to support the war.	Reproducible Lesson Plan 19–2 Daily Lecture and Discussion Notes 19–2 Guided Reading Activity 19–2* Section Quiz 19–2* Reading Essentials and Study Guide 19–2 Performance Assessment Activities and Rubrics Supreme Court Case Studies	Daily Focus Skills Transparency 19–2 Interactive Tutor Self-Assessment CD-ROM ExamView® Pro Testmaker CD-ROM Presentation Plus! CD-ROM TeacherWorks™ CD-ROM Audio Program
SECTION 3 **A Bloody Conflict** 1. Discuss the fighting techniques used in World War I. 2. Characterize the American response to the Treaty of Versailles.	Reproducible Lesson Plan 19–3 Daily Lecture and Discussion Notes 19–3 Guided Reading Activity 19–3* Section Quiz 19–3* Reading Essentials and Study Guide 19–3 Performance Assessment Activities and Rubrics	Daily Focus Skills Transparency 19–3 Interactive Tutor Self-Assessment CD-ROM ExamView® Pro Testmaker CD-ROM Presentation Plus! CD-ROM Skillbuilder Interactive Workbook, Level 2 TeacherWorks™ CD-ROM Audio Program
SECTION 4 **The War's Impact** 1. Describe the effects of the postwar recession on the United States. 2. Discuss the causes of and reaction to the Red Scare.	Reproducible Lesson Plan 19–4 Daily Lecture and Discussion Notes 19–4 Guided Reading Activity 19–4* Section Quiz 19–4* Reading Essentials and Study Guide 19–4 Performance Assessment Activities and Rubrics Interpreting Political Cartoons	Daily Focus Skills Transparency 19–4 American Art & Architecture Interactive Tutor Self-Assessment CD-ROM ExamView® Pro Testmaker CD-ROM Presentation Plus! CD-ROM TeacherWorks™ CD-ROM Vocabulary PuzzleMaker CD-ROM Audio Program

0:00 OUT OF TIME?
Assign the Chapter 19 **Reading Essentials and Study Guide.**

*Also Available in Spanish

 Blackline Master   Transparency CD-ROM DVD

Poster   Music Program Audio Program Videocassette

NATIONAL GEOGRAPHIC Teacher's Corner

INDEX TO NATIONAL GEOGRAPHIC MAGAZINE

The following articles relate to this chapter.

NATIONAL GEOGRAPHIC SOCIETY PRODUCTS AVAILABLE FROM GLENCOE

To order the following products for use with this chapter, contact your local Glencoe sales representative, or call Glencoe at 1-800-334-7344:

- *PictureShow: Story of America, Part 2* (CD-ROM)
- *PicturePack: Story of America Library, Part 2* (Transparencies)
- *PicturePack: World War I Era* (Transparencies)

ADDITIONAL NATIONAL GEOGRAPHIC SOCIETY PRODUCTS

To order the following, call National Geographic at 1-800-368-2728:

- *Last Voyage of the* Lusitania (Video)
- *1917: Revolution in Russia* (Video)
- *1914–1918: World War I* (Video)

NGS ONLINE

Access National Geographic's Web site for current events, atlas updates, activities, links, interactive features, and archives.

www.nationalgeographic.com

From the Classroom of...

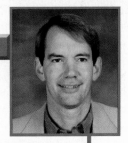

Lee Weber
Price Laboratory School
Cedar Falls, IA

U.S. Entrance into World War I

Place the following "Causes of American Entrance into World War I" on an overhead transparency:

- Loss of innocent lives
- Loss of trade
- Historical/cultural ties to British/French
- Defense of democracy against dictatorship
- Freedom of the seas
- The Zimmermann Note

Ask students to individually rank the causes from most important to least important. Then randomly group students and have them try to reach consensus. The interrelated nature of the six causes makes the task extremely difficult. If time permits, repeat the process and make a hypothetical change in the historical facts. For instance, suggest that Germany had a large surface navy and Britain developed unrestricted submarine warfare. How would U.S. policy have changed? Or, what if Germany were our major trading partner, not England and its allies?

ADDITIONAL RESOURCES FROM GLENCOE

- American Music: Cultural Traditions
- American Art & Architecture
- Outline Map Resource Book
- U.S. Desk Map
- Building Geography Skills for Life
- Inclusion for the High School Social Studies Classroom Strategies and Activities
- Teaching Strategies for the American History Classroom (Including Block Scheduling Pacing Guides)

KEY TO ABILITY LEVELS

Teaching strategies have been coded.

L1 BASIC activities for all students
L2 AVERAGE activities for average to above-average students
L3 CHALLENGING activities for above-average students
ELL ENGLISH LANGUAGE LEARNER activities

Block Schedule

Activities that are suited to use within the block scheduling framework are identified by:

✓ **Performance Assessment**

Refer to Activity 19 in the Performance Assessment Activities and Rubrics booklet.

Why It Matters Activity

Ask students how they think the United States's involvement in World War I affects their lives today. Students should evaluate their answers after they have completed the chapter.

GLENCOE TECHNOLOGY

The *American Vision* Video Program

To learn more about how royal marriages and political alliances contributed to the war in Europe, have students view the Chapter 19 video, "Cousins: royalty and World War I," from the *American Vision* Video Program.

 Available in DVD and VHS

MindJogger Videoquiz

Use the **MindJogger Videoquiz** to preview Chapter 19 content.

 Available in VHS

CHAPTER
19 World War I and Its Aftermath
1914–1920

Why It Matters

The United States reluctantly entered World War I after German submarines violated American neutrality. After the war ended, President Wilson supported the Treaty of Versailles, believing its terms would prevent another war. The U.S. Senate, however, rejected the treaty. It did not want the country to be tied to European obligations. Instead, Americans turned their attention to the difficult adjustment to peacetime.

The Impact Today

The experience of World War I had a long-term effect on American history.
• The United States continues to be involved in European affairs.
• The horrors of the conflict helped reshape how people view warfare.

 The American Vision *Video* *The Chapter 19 video, "Cousins: Royalty and World War I," explains how royal marriages and complex political alliances contributed to the outbreak of war in Europe.*

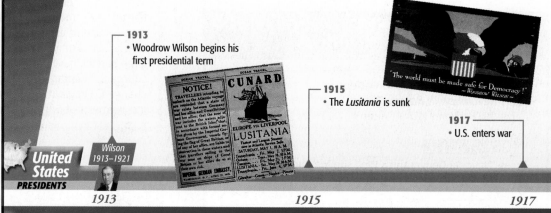

1913
• Woodrow Wilson begins his first presidential term

1915
• The *Lusitania* is sunk

1917
• U.S. enters war

"The world must be made safe for Democracy!" — WOODROW WILSON —

United States PRESIDENTS — Wilson 1913–1921

1913 — *1915* — *1917*

World

1914
• Archduke Franz Ferdinand assassinated; war begins in Europe

1915
• Italy joins Allies in war
• Japan gains rights in Chinese territory

1916
• British suppress Easter Rebellion in Ireland
• Battle of the Somme begins in July

1917
• Russian Revolution begins in October
• Balfour Declaration favors setting up a Jewish homeland in Palestine

574

TWO-MINUTE LESSON LAUNCHER

Read to students this statement from President Wilson's response to the sinking of the British passenger ship *Lusitania*: "There is such a thing as a nation being so right that it does not need to convince others by force that it is right." **Ask: What is Wilson's main point?** (*If your stand is a moral one, all nations will eventually support you.*) Tell students that despite the president's resistance, the United States eventually did enter World War I.

American soldiers in the 23rd Infantry fire on German positions in the Argonne Forest.

1918
- Congress passes Sedition Act
- Battle of Argonne Forest begins in September
- Armistice ends fighting on November 11

1919
- Race riots and strikes take place in Northern cities

1920
- Red Scare and Palmer raids target Communists in the U.S.

Harding 1921–1923

1919   *1921*

1918
- Treaty of Brest-Litovsk ends Russian-German war

1919
- Treaty of Versailles conference begins

1920
- Civil war breaks out in Ireland

1921
- Irish Free State established

HISTORY *Online*

Chapter Overview
Visit the *American Vision* Web site at tav.glencoe.com and click on **Chapter Overviews—Chapter 19** to preview chapter information.

575

HISTORY *Online*

Introduce students to chapter content and key terms by having them access the **Chapter 19 Overview** at tav.glencoe.com.

More About the Photo

Alvin C. York was one of the men on the battlefield at Argonne Forest. He is credited with almost single-handedly capturing 132 Germans. York kept a diary of the events, and his recollections of October 7, 1918, include the following description: "It was raining a little bit all day, drizzly and very damp. Lots of big shells bursting all around us. We were not up close enough for the machine guns to reach us, but airplanes were buzzing overhead most all the time, just like a lot of hornets. Lots of men were killed by the artillery fire. And lots more wounded." Ask students how the conditions of war produce heroes like York. (*Responses may typically refer to feelings for comrades.*)

TIME LINE
ACTIVITY

Have students use the chapter and section time lines to create a single time line that incorporates all of the significant dates related to World War I.

GRAPHIC ORGANIZER ACTIVITY

Organizing Information Have students create two maps of Europe, one showing Europe in 1914 and the other showing Europe after World War I. Encourage students to review these maps as they prepare for chapter assessments and to keep these maps for use with their study of World War II.

1 FOCUS

Section Overview

This section focuses on the events that led up to World War I and how the United States became involved.

Guide to Reading

Answers to Graphic: Balkan crisis, alliance system, naval race, assassination of Franz Ferdinand

Preteaching Vocabulary
For each of the Key Terms and Names, have students write a phrase or short sentence that will help them remember the significance of the term or name.

The United States Enters World War I

Guide to Reading

Main Idea
Although the United States tried to remain neutral, events soon pushed the nation into World War I.

Key Terms and Names
Pancho Villa, guerrilla, nationalism, self-determination, Franz Ferdinand, Allies, Central Powers, propaganda, contraband, U-boat, Sussex Pledge, Zimmermann telegram

Reading Strategy
Organizing As you read about the start of World War I, complete a graphic organizer similar to the one below by identifying the factors that contributed to the conflict.

(Factors Contributing to World War I)

Reading Objectives
• **Discuss** the causes and results of American intervention in Mexico and the Caribbean.
• **Explain** the causes of World War I and why the United States entered the war.

Section Theme
Continuity and Change Ties with the British influenced American leaders to enter World War I on the side of the Allies.

Preview of Events

◆1914	◆1915	◆1916	◆1917

April 1914
U.S. Marines occupy Veracruz, Mexico

June 1914
Assassination of Archduke Franz Ferdinand

July 1914
World War I begins

May 1915
Sinking of the *Lusitania*

April 1917
United States enters the war

★ An American Story ★

Edith O'Shaughnessy could not sleep on the rainy night of April 20, 1914. Living at the American embassy in Mexico City, the wife of diplomat Nelson O'Shaughnessy was well aware of the growing crisis between Mexico and the United States. Earlier that day, President Wilson had asked Congress to authorize the use of force against Mexico. In her diary, O'Shaughnessy described the tensions in the Mexican capital:

❝I can't sleep. National and personal potentialities [possibilities] are surging through my brain. Three stalwart railroad men came to the Embassy this evening. They brought reports of a plan for the massacre of Americans in the street to-night, but, strange and wonderful thing, a heavy rain is falling. . . . Rain is as potent as shell-fire in clearing the streets, and I don't think there will be any trouble.❞

The next day, O'Shaughnessy reported that the conflict had begun: "We are in Mexico, in full intervention! . . . Marines are due to-day in Vera Cruz. . . ."

Raising the flag at Veracruz

—adapted from *A Diplomat's Wife in Mexico*

Woodrow Wilson's Diplomacy

As president, Wilson resolved to "strike a new note in international affairs" and to see that "sheer honesty and even unselfishness . . . should prevail over nationalistic self-seeking in American foreign policy." Wilson strongly opposed imperialism. He also

576 CHAPTER 19 World War I and Its Aftermath

---

country from being drawn into a foreign war. "We must be impartial in thought as well as in action," Wilson stated. For many Americans, however, that proved difficult to do.

Americans Take Sides
Despite the president's plea, many Americans showed support for one side or the other. This was especially true for recent immigrants from Europe. Many of the 8 million German Americans, for example, supported their homeland. The nation's 4.5 million Irish Americans, whose homeland endured centuries of British rule, also sympathized with the Central Powers.

In general, though, American public opinion favored the Allied cause. Many Americans valued the heritage, language, and political ideals they shared with Britain. Others treasured America's historic links with France, a great friend to America during the Revolutionary War.

Pro-British Sentiment
One select group of Americans was decidedly pro-British: President Wilson's cabinet. Only Secretary of State William Jennings Bryan favored neutrality. The other cabinet members, as well as Bryan's chief adviser, Robert Lansing, and Walter Hines Page, the American ambassador to London, argued forcefully on behalf of Britain. American military leaders also backed the British. They believed that an Allied victory was the only way to preserve the international balance of power.

British officials worked diligently to win American support. One method they used was propaganda, or information designed to influence opinion. Both the Allies and the Central Powers used propaganda, but German propaganda was mostly anti-Russian and did not appeal to most Americans. British propaganda, on the other hand, was extremely skillful. Furthermore, Britain cut the transatlantic telegraph cable from Europe to the United States, limiting news about the war mainly to British reports. Stories arrived depicting numerous German war atrocities, including the charge that Germans used corpses from the battlefield to make fertilizer and soap. Although many such reports were questionable, enough Americans believed them to help sway American support in favor of the Allies.

ECONOMICS

Business Links American business interests also leaned toward the Allies. Companies in the United States, particularly on the East Coast, had strong ties with businesses in the Allied countries. As business leader Thomas W. Lamont stated, "Our firm had

never for one moment been neutral: we did not know how to be. From the very start we did everything that we could to contribute to the cause of the Allies."

Many American banks began to invest heavily in an Allied victory. American loans to the cash-hungry Allies skyrocketed. By 1917 such loans would total over $2 billion. Other American banks, particularly in the Midwest, where pro-German feelings were strongest, also lent some $27 million to Germany. Even more might have been lent, but most foreign loans required the approval of William McAdoo, the secretary of the Treasury. McAdoo was strongly pro-British and did what he could to limit loans to Germany. As a result, the country's prosperity was intertwined with the military fortunes of Britain, France, and Russia. If the Allies won, the money would be paid back; if not, the money might be lost forever.

Reading Check Evaluating How was American prosperity intertwined with the military fortunes of the Allies?

Moving Toward War

Although most Americans supported the Allies and hoped for their victory, they did not want to join the conflict. However, a series of events gradually eroded American neutrality and drew the nation into the war firmly on the side of the Allies.

The British Blockade Shortly after the war began, the British deployed their navy to blockade Germany and keep it from obtaining supplies. The British planted mines in the North Sea and forced neutral ships into port for inspections in case they were trying to transport valuable materials to Germany or its neutral neighbors. British officials also expanded their definition of contraband, or prohibited materials, to prevent neutral countries from shipping food to Germany.

The Germans knew that the Allies depended on food, equipment, and other supplies from both the United States and their overseas empires. If Germany could strangle that trade, it could starve the British and French into surrendering. To get around Britain's blockade, the Germans deployed submarines known as U-boats—from the German word *Unterseeboot* (meaning

Student Web Activity Visit the *American Vision* Web site at tav.glencoe.com and click on **Student Web Activities— Chapter 19** for an activity on World War I.

Reading Check

Answer: Many American banks invested in an Allied victory and made loans to the Allies.

Discussing a Topic Have students discuss the differences between news reporting, propaganda, and advertising. Ask students to identify the purpose of each and explain the value of each. **L2**

CURRICULUM CONNECTION

Government Concerning the Mexican Revolution, President Wilson cautioned "watchful waiting." Interventionists termed his policy "deadly drifting." One critic joked about Wilson's diplomacy by making up an ironic dance step he called the Wilson Tango. It consisted of one step forward, two steps back, one to the side, and then a hesitation.

HISTORY Online

Objectives and answers to the student activity can be found in the **Web Activity Lesson Plan** at tav.glencoe.com.

EXTENDING THE CONTENT

Distress Signals From the early days of wireless telegraphy, a distress call has had absolute priority over all other communications. In 1904 the Marconi Company directed its ships to use the letters *CQD*, popularly defined as "Come Quick—Distress" or "Come Quick—Danger." These abbreviations were adopted by the British Post Office telegraph service. Because the letters CQ were also used for general calls, confusion often developed. The distress signal, therefore, was replaced in 1912 by *SOS*, popularly defined as "Sink or Swim" or "Save Our Ship." The distress call used in radio telephony, "Mayday," is a corruption of the French phrase *M'aidez*, "Help me."

3 ASSESS

Assign Section 1 Assessment as homework or as an in-class activity.

● Have students use the **Interactive Tutor Self-Assessment CD-ROM.**

Reading Essentials and Study Guide 19–1

Name _____ Date _____ Class _____

Study Guide

Chapter 19, Section 1
For use with textbook pages 576–583

THE UNITED STATES ENTERS WORLD WAR I

KEY TERMS AND NAMES

Pancho Villa leader of a Mexican guerilla group *(page 577)*
guerrillas an armed band that carries out surprise attacks and sabotage rather than open warfare *(page 577)*
nationalism an intense pride in one's homeland *(page 578)*
self-determination the idea that people who belong to a nation should have their own country and government *(page 578)*
Franz Ferdinand the heir to the Austro-Hungarian throne *(page 578)*
Allies the alliance of France, Russia, Great Britain, and Italy in World War I *(page 580)*

Section Quiz 19–1

Name _____ Date _____ Class _____

★ **Chapter 19**   Score ____

Section Quiz 19-1

DIRECTIONS: Matching Match each item in Column A with the items in Column B. Write the correct letters in the blanks. *(10 points each)*

Column A	Column B
___ 1. information designed to influence opinion	A. Central Powers
___ 2. led a group of Mexican guerrillas that burned Columbus, New Mexico	B. U-boats
___ 3. Germany, Austria-Hungary, Ottoman Empire, and Bulgaria	C. Pancho Villa
___ 4. German submarines	D. propaganda
___ 5. Britain, France, and Russia	E. Triple Entente

DIRECTIONS: Multiple Choice In the blank at the left, write the letter of the choice that best completes the statement or answers the question. *(10 points each)*

FYI

The first German U-boat was built in 1906. During World War I, Germany was able to put several types of U-boats into service.

"underwater boat"). In February 1915, the Germans announced that they would attempt to sink without warning any ship they found in the waters around Britain.

Germany's announcement triggered outrage in the United States and elsewhere. Attacking civilian vessels without warning violated an international treaty stipulating that military vessels must reveal their intentions to merchant ships and make provisions for the safety of the targeted ship's crew and passengers before sinking it. The Germans claimed that many merchant ships were actually warships in disguise and that their U-boats would be placed at great risk if they revealed themselves before firing.

The issue reached a crisis on May 7, 1915. Despite warnings from Germany, the British passenger liner *Lusitania* entered the war zone. A submerged German submarine fired on the ship, killing nearly 1,200 passengers—including 128 Americans. Many Americans were outraged and regarded the attack as an act of terrorism, not war.

Picturing History

The Sinking of the *Lusitania* In May 1915, German U-boats sank the British passenger liner *Lusitania*. Among those who drowned were 128 Americans. Here the *Los Angeles Tribune* reports the attack, and a newspaper advertisement warns ship passengers to travel the Atlantic at their own risk. Why were the Germans sinking passenger liners?

582   CHAPTER 19   World War I and Its Aftermath

Others argued that the passengers traveling on ships of foreign nations did so at their own risk.

Wilson steered a middle course on the issue of the U-boats. He refused to take extreme measures against Germany, saying that the United States was "too proud to fight." Nevertheless, he sent several diplomatic notes to Germany insisting that its government safeguard the lives of noncombatants in the war zones.

Late in March 1916, Wilson's policy was tested when a U-boat torpedoed the French passenger ship *Sussex,* injuring several Americans on board. Although Wilson's closest advisers favored breaking off diplomatic relations with Germany immediately, the president, busy with the crisis in Mexico, chose to issue one last warning. He demanded that the German government abandon its methods of submarine warfare or risk war with the United States.

Germany did not want to strengthen the Allies by drawing the United States into the war. It promised with certain conditions to sink no more merchant ships without warning. The **Sussex Pledge,** as it was called, met the foreign-policy goals of both Germany and President Wilson by keeping the United States out of the war a little longer.

Wilson's efforts to keep American soldiers at home played an important part in his re-election bid in 1916. Campaigning as the "peace" candidate, his campaign slogan, "He kept us out of the war," helped lead Wilson to a narrow victory over the Republican nominee, Charles Evans Hughes.

The United States Declares War Following Wilson's re-election, events quickly brought the country to the brink of war. In January 1917, a German official named Arthur Zimmermann cabled the German ambassador in Mexico, instructing him to make an offer to the Mexican government. Zimmermann proposed that Mexico ally itself with Germany in the event of war between Germany and the United States. In return, Mexico would regain its "lost territory in Texas, New Mexico, and Arizona" after the war. Germany hoped Mexico would tie down the American forces and prevent them from being sent to Europe. British intelligence intercepted the **Zimmermann telegram.** Shortly afterward, it was leaked to American newspapers. Furious, many Americans now concluded war with Germany was necessary.

Then, on February 1, 1917, Germany resumed unrestricted submarine warfare. German military leaders believed that they could starve Britain into

---

CRITICAL THINKING ACTIVITY

Determining Causes Discuss with students what caused the outbreak of World War I. Aside from the assassination of Archduke Franz Ferdinand, the economic interests and military alliances of the European countries made war probable. Because of entangled treaties and continued colonial aspirations, Europe was poised for a war that could have been set off by any number of events. Ask students to explain how the Russian Revolution affected the war. *(Because of the revolution, Russia withdrew from the war. This meant Germany was free to concentrate its forces on the Western Front.)* **L2**

> ## "The world must be made safe for democracy."
>
> —*Woodrow Wilson, April 1917*

 *Picturing* **History**

Americans Go to War Congress voted heavily in favor of entering the European war. Here, excited Americans wave from an Army recruitment truck. What events pushed the United States to finally declare war?

San Francisco Examiner

HOUSE PASSES WAR RESOLUTION, 373 TO 50; 12 INTERNED GERMAN VESSELS SEIZED BY U.S.

Picturing **History**

Answer: British blockade, sinking of the *Lusitania* and other passenger liners, Germany's attempt to ally with Mexico

Ask: By looking at this picture, what might you assume about public opinion related to the U.S. government's decision to enter the war? *(that people supported the decision)*

---

submission in four to six months if their U-boats could return to a more aggressive approach of sinking all ships on sight. Although they recognized that their actions might draw the United States into the war, the Germans did not believe that the Americans could raise an army and transport it to Europe in time to prevent the Allies from collapsing.

In the first three weeks of March 1917, German U-boats sank four American merchant ships without warning. Finally roused to action, President Wilson appeared before a special session of Congress on April 2, 1917, to ask for a declaration of war against Germany.

❝It is a fearful thing to lead this great peaceful people into war. . . . But the right is more precious than peace, and we shall fight for the things which we have always carried nearest to our hearts—for democracy, for the right of those who submit to authority to have a voice in their own governments, for the rights and liberties of small nations. . . .❞

—quoted in the Congressional Record, 1917

After a spirited debate, the Senate passed the resolution on April 4 by a vote of 82 to 6. The House concurred 373 to 50 on April 6, and Wilson signed the resolution. America was now at war.

☑ **Reading Check** **Summarizing** How did Germany's use of unrestricted submarine warfare lead to American entry into World War I?

Reteach
Have students explain the causes and results of American intervention in Mexico and the Caribbean.

Enrich
Invite interested students to develop a multimedia presentation to help explain the history of the Balkans. Encourage students to use library and Internet resources for this assignment.

☑ **Reading Check**

Answer: The Germans sank civilian passenger liners and U.S. merchant ships, which outraged the Americans, who then sided with the British.

4 CLOSE

Have students discuss the causes of World War I and why the United States entered the war.

SECTION 1 ASSESSMENT

Checking for Understanding

1. **Define:** guerrilla, nationalism, self-determination, propaganda, contraband, U-boat.
2. **Identify:** Pancho Villa, Franz Ferdinand, Allies, Central Powers, Sussex Pledge, Zimmermann telegram.
3. **Name** the two alliances that Europe was divided into at the start of World War I.

Reviewing Themes

4. **Continuity and Change** Why did most of President Wilson's cabinet members support the British?

Critical Thinking

5. **Synthesizing** How did European nationalism contribute to the outbreak of World War I?
6. **Organizing** Use a graphic organizer similar to the one below to identify the events that led the United States to enter World War I.

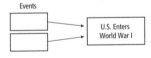

Analyzing Visuals

7. **Analyzing Time Lines** Examine the time line on page 579. How does the order in which countries declared war reflect the European alliance system?

Writing About History

8. **Expository Writing** Imagine that you are a Mexican citizen living in Mexico between 1914 and 1917. Write a script for a radio newscast in which you express your feelings about American actions in Mexico. Include reasons for your feelings.

CHAPTER 19 World War I and Its Aftermath **583**

SECTION 1 ASSESSMENT ANSWERS

1. Terms are in blue.
2. Pancho Villa *(p. 577)*, Franz Ferdinand *(p. 578)*, Allies *(p. 580)*, Central Powers *(p. 580)*, Sussex Pledge *(p. 582)*, Zimmermann telegram *(p. 582)*
3. Triple Alliance and Triple Entente
4. They believed that Allied victory was the only way to preserve the international balance of power, and they cited the close historical ties with Britain and France.
5. Each major ethnic group in European empires wanted its own country.
6. unrestricted submarine warfare;
   Germany's attempt to ally with Mexico
7. When one country declared war, its allies declared war.
8. Students' scripts will vary. Encourage students to act out their scripts as if they were actually on the radio.

1 FOCUS

Section Overview

This section focuses on the efforts undertaken at home to mobilize the nation for war.

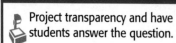
BELLRINGER
Skillbuilder Activity

Project transparency and have students answer the question.

Available as a blackline master.

Daily Focus Skills Transparency 19–2

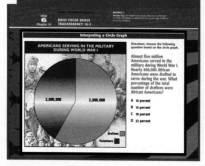

Guide to Reading

Answers to Graphic:
  I. Building Up the Military
   A. Selective Service
   B. African Americans in the War
   C. Women in the Military
  II. Organizing Industry
Students should complete the outline by including all heads in the section.

Preteaching Vocabulary
Have students create a simple symbol, icon, or sketch for each of the Key Terms and Names.

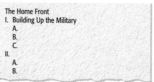
SECTION 2 The Home Front

Guide to Reading

Main Idea
To successfully fight the war, the United States had to mobilize the entire nation.

Key Terms and Names
conscription, War Industries Board, Bernard Baruch, victory garden, Liberty Bond, Victory Bond, Committee on Public Information, espionage

Reading Strategy
Taking Notes As you read about how the United States mobilized for war, use the major headings of the section to create an outline similar to the one below.

The Home Front
I. Building Up the Military
  A.
  B.
  C.
II.
  A.
  B.

Reading Objectives
• **Analyze** how the United States raised an army and won support for World War I.
• **Explain** how the economy was controlled to support the war.

Section Theme
Government and Democracy To fight the war, the federal government created new agencies to mobilize the economy, draft soldiers, and build public support.

Preview of Events

♦1917	♦1918	♦1919
1917 Selective Service Act and Espionage Act passed	**May 1918** Sedition Act passed	**September 1918** Eugene Debs imprisoned	**1919** *Schenck* v. *United States*

⋆ **An American Story** ⋆

Eugene Debs

Even as he began to address the crowd of about 1,200 people, Eugene Debs suspected he was heading for trouble with the authorities. The 62-year-old Socialist leader had traveled to Canton, Ohio, on June 16, 1918, to speak at the state's convention of the Socialist Party. The time had come, Debs decided, to condemn American participation in World War I.

"I realize that in speaking to you this afternoon," he told the crowd, "there are certain limitations placed upon the right of free speech. I must be exceedingly careful, prudent, as to what I say, and even more careful as to how I say it." Laughter came from the crowd, and then applause. "But I am not," Debs continued, "going to say anything that I do not think. I would rather a thousand times be a free soul in jail than to be a . . . coward in the streets!"

When the transcript of Debs' speech arrived at the federal office in Cleveland, a grand jury indicted him for violating the newly passed Espionage Act. The Socialist leader was arrested and imprisoned. Said Debs, "I had a hunch that speech was likely to settle the matter."

—adapted from *Echoes of Distant Thunder*

Building Up the Military

When the United States declared war against Germany in April 1917, progressives controlled the federal government. They did not abandon their ideas simply because a war had begun. Instead, they applied progressive ideas to fighting the war.

Selective Service When the United States entered the war in 1917, the army and National Guard together had slightly more than 300,000 troops. Although many men volunteered after war was declared, many felt more soldiers needed to be drafted.

SECTION RESOURCES

📂 Reproducible Masters
• Reproducible Lesson Plan 19–2
• Daily Lecture and Discussion Notes 19–2
• Guided Reading Activity 19–2
• Section Quiz 19–2
• Reading Essentials and Study Guide 19–2
• Performance Assessment Activities and Rubrics
• Supreme Court Case Studies

📑 Transparencies
• Daily Focus Skills Transparency 19–2

Multimedia
🔘 Interactive Tutor Self-Assessment CD-ROM
🔘 ExamView® Pro Testmaker CD-ROM
🔘 Presentation Plus! CD-ROM
🔘 TeacherWorks™ CD-ROM
🔘 Audio Program

Many progressives believed that conscription—forced military service—was a violation of democratic and republican principles. Realizing a draft was necessary, however, Congress, with Wilson's support, created a new conscription system called **selective service.** Instead of having the military run the draft from Washington, D.C., the Selective Service Act of 1917 required all men between 21 and 30 to register for the draft. A lottery randomly determined the order they were called before a local draft board in charge of selecting or exempting people from military service.

The thousands of local boards were the heart of the system. The members of the draft boards were civilians from local communities. Progressives believed local people, understanding community needs, would know which men to draft. Eventually about 2.8 million Americans were drafted. Approximately 2 million others volunteered for military service.

African Americans in the War Of the nearly 400,000 African Americans who were drafted, about 42,000 served overseas as combat troops. African American soldiers encountered discrimination and prejudice in the army, where they served in racially segregated units almost always under the supervision of white officers.

Despite these challenges, many African American soldiers fought with distinction in the war. For example, the African American 92nd and 93rd Infantry Divisions fought in bitter battles along the Western Front. Many of them won praise from both the French commander, Marshal Henri Pétain, and the United States commander, General John Pershing. The entire 369th Infantry Division won the highly prized French decoration, the Croix de Guerre ("war cross"), for gallantry in combat.

Women in the Military World War I was the first war in which women officially served in the armed forces, although only in noncombat positions. Women nurses had served in both the army and navy since the early 1900s, but as auxiliaries. Nurses were not assigned ranks, and the women were not technically enlisted in the army or navy.

As the military prepared for war in 1917, it faced a severe shortage of clerical workers because so many men were assigned to active duty. Early in 1917, the navy authorized the enlistment of women to meet its clerical needs. The women wore a standard uniform and were assigned the rank of yeoman. By the end of the war, over 11,000 women had served in the navy. Although most performed clerical duties, others served as radio operators, electricians, pharmacists, photographers, chemists, and torpedo assemblers.

Unlike the navy, the army refused to enlist women. Instead, it began hiring women as temporary employees to fill clerical jobs. The only women to actually serve in the army were in the **Army Nursing Corps.** Army nurses were the only women in the military to be sent overseas during the war. Over 20,000 nurses served in the army during the war, including more than 10,000 overseas.

✓ **Reading Check** **Describing** How did Congress ensure that the United States would have enough troops to serve in World War I?

Organizing Industry

The progressive emphasis on careful planning and scientific management shaped the federal government's approach to mobilizing the American war economy. To efficiently manage the relationship between the federal government and private companies, Congress created special boards to coordinate mobilization of the economy. Instead of having the government control the economy, these boards emphasized cooperation between big business and government. Business executives, professional

Picturing **History**

Women and War Although not allowed in combat, many women served in auxiliary positions, such as nursing. Here, Birmingham, Alabama, women collect money during a Red Cross parade in 1918. In what other capacities did women serve during the war?

CHAPTER 19 World War I and Its Aftermath **585**

2 TEACH

Daily Lecture and Discussion Notes 19–2

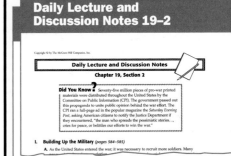

Copyright © The McGraw-Hill Companies, Inc.

Daily Lecture and Discussion Notes

Chapter 19, Section 2

Did You Know? Seventy-five million pieces of pro-war printed materials were distributed throughout the United States by the Committee on Public Information (CPI). The government passed out this propaganda to unite public opinion behind the war effort. The CPI ran a full-page ad in the popular magazine the *Saturday Evening Post*, asking American citizens to notify the Justice Department if they encountered, "the man who spreads the pessimistic stories... cries for peace, or belittles our efforts to win the war."

I. Building Up the Military *(pages 584–585)*

A. As the United States entered the war, it was necessary to recruit more soldiers. Many ...

Interpreting Quotations Have students note whether the following quotes support neutrality or war. **L1**

" . . . loans by American bankers to any foreign nation at war are inconsistent with the true spirit of neutrality."—William Jennings Bryan, 1914

"Our whole duty . . . is summed up in this motto: America first."—Woodrow Wilson, 1915

✓ **Reading Check**

Answer: The Selective Service Act of 1917 required all men ages 21 to 30 to register for the draft.

Picturing **History**

Answer: secretaries, radio operators, electricians, and pharmacists, among others
Ask: Why did the Navy finally enlist women? *(to meet its clerical needs)*

COOPERATIVE LEARNING ACTIVITY

Giving Four-Minute Speeches Four-minute speeches were one means of encouraging Americans to support the war effort. Have pairs of students write and give a four-minute speech that presents one of the following patriotic messages: buy Liberty Bonds, conserve food, don't strike, find a job (directed toward women), or come work in the North (directed toward African Americans). Students can divide writing and editing tasks. One student can give the speech while his or her partner provides music or artwork.

Use the rubric for a cooperative group management plan on pages 81–82 in the *Performance Assessment Activities and Rubrics.*

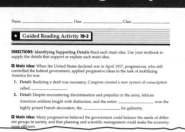
✓ Reading Check

Answer: War Industries Board, Food Administration, Fuel Administration

🗎 *Picturing* **History**

Answer: The general theme is supporting the war effort. The posters were effective in reminding people of their patriotic duty.

Ask: What was the main message of each of these posters? *(Students' answers will vary. Some ideas might include encouraging men to enlist in the armed forces, coming together at work for the war effort, patriotic messages about democracy, and encouraging victory gardens.)*

Creating a Poster Have students create a poster that might have been used by the Committee on Public Information to boost support of the war effort. Encourage students to use the posters shown on this page as models. **L2**

📁 Use *Supreme Court Case Study 12, Schenck v. United States.*

managers, and government representatives staffed the boards. Their goal was to ensure the most efficient use of national resources to further the war effort.

The War Industries Board One of the first agencies established was the **War Industries Board** (WIB). Created in July 1917, the WIB's job was to coordinate the production of war materials. At first, President Wilson was reluctant to give the WIB much authority over the economy, but by March 1918, he decided industrial production needed better coordination. The WIB was reorganized and **Bernard Baruch** was appointed to run it. Under this Wall Street stockbroker's supervision, the WIB told manufacturers what they could and could not produce. It controlled the flow of raw materials, ordered the construction of new factories, and occasionally, with the president's approval, set prices.

Food and Fuel Perhaps the most successful government agency was the Food Administration, run by Herbert Hoover. This agency was responsible for increasing food production while reducing civilian consumption. Instead of using rationing, Hoover encouraged Americans to save food on their own. Using the slogan "Food Will Win the War—Don't Waste It," the Food Administration encouraged families to "Hooverize" by "serving just enough" and by having Wheatless Mondays, Meatless Tuesdays, and Porkless Thursdays. Hoover also encouraged citizens to plant victory gardens to raise their own vegetables, leaving more for the troops.

While Hoover managed food production, the Fuel Administration, run by Harry Garfield, tried to manage the nation's use of coal and oil. To conserve energy, Garfield introduced **daylight savings time** and shortened workweeks for factories that did not make war materials. He also encouraged Americans to observe Heatless Mondays.

Paying for the War By the end of World War I, the United States was spending about $44 million a day—leading to a total expenditure of about $32 billion for the entire conflict. To fund the war effort, Congress raised income tax rates. Congress also placed new taxes on corporate profits and an extra tax on the profits of arms factories.

Taxes, however, could not cover the entire cost of the war. To raise the money it needed, the government borrowed more than $20 billion from the American people by selling **Liberty Bonds** and **Victory Bonds.** By buying the bonds, Americans were loaning the government money. The government agreed to repay the money with interest in a specified number of years. Posters, rallies, and "Liberty Loan sermons" encouraged people to buy the bonds as an act of patriotism.

✓ Reading Check **Summarizing** What federal agencies helped control American industries during the war?

🗎 *Picturing* **History**

Propaganda Posters George Creel's Committee on Public Information encouraged Americans to do all they could to support the war effort. What is the general theme of these posters? Do you think the posters were effective?

MEETING SPECIAL NEEDS

Intrapersonal Have students imagine that they are teens living in the United States when Wilson declared that the country would enter the war. Have students write a series of diary entries that describes their reactions to and feelings about entering the war and the preparations that were made on the home front as the nation geared up to fight. **L2**

📁 Refer to *Inclusion for the High School Social Studies Classroom Strategies and Activities* in the TCR.

Mobilizing the Workforce

While the WIB and other agencies tried to build cooperation between the government and business, officials knew that they also needed workers to cooperate if mobilization was to succeed. To prevent strikes from disrupting the war effort, the government established the **National War Labor Board** (NWLB) in April 1918. Chaired by William Howard Taft and Frank Walsh, a prominent labor attorney, the NWLB attempted to mediate labor disputes that might otherwise lead to strikes.

The NWLB frequently pressured industry to grant important concessions to workers, including wage increases, an eight-hour workday, and the right of unions to organize and bargain collectively. In exchange, labor leaders agreed not to disrupt war production with strikes or other disturbances. As a result, membership in unions increased by more than 1.5 million between 1917 and 1919.

Women Support Industry The war increased work opportunities for women, who filled industrial jobs vacated by men serving in the military. These included factory and manufacturing jobs and various positions in the shipping and railroad industries. War-generated changes in female employment, however, were not permanent. After the war, when the servicemen returned home, most women returned to their previous jobs or stopped working.

The Great Migration Begins With the flow of immigrants from Europe cut off and large numbers of white workers being drafted, the war also opened new doors for African Americans. Wartime job openings and high wages drew thousands of African Americans to factories producing war materials. Encouraged by recruiting agents promising high wages and plentiful work, between 300,000 and 500,000 African Americans left the South to settle in Northern cities. This became known as the "Great Migration." This massive population movement altered the racial makeup of such cities as Chicago, New York, Cleveland, and Detroit.

Mexican Americans Head North African Americans were not the only group to migrate north during the war. Continuing political turmoil in Mexico and the wartime labor shortage in the United States convinced many Mexicans to head north. Between 1917 and 1920, over 100,000 Mexicans migrated into Texas, Arizona, California, and New Mexico, providing labor for the farmers and ranchers of the Southwest.

Federal Mobilization Agencies

Agency	Purpose
War Industries Board	Organized industry to increase efficiency, maximizing production
Railroad Administration	Assumed temporary control of rail lines to modernize equipment and increase operating efficiency
Food Administration	Supervised agricultural production, promoted food conservation and rationing
Fuel Administration	Increased production of coal and oil; maintained conservation of fuel with such innovations as daylight savings time
National War Labor Board	Maintained cooperation between industry management and labor unions; acted as mediator to prevent and quickly settle disputes
Committee on Public Information	Provided propaganda to rally citizen support for all aspects of the war effort

Chart *Skills*

1. **Interpreting Charts** Which agency worked with manufacturers and labor unions?
2. **Analyzing** How did the Fuel Administration's daylight savings time plan achieve its goal?

Meanwhile, tens of thousands of Mexican Americans headed north to Chicago, St. Louis, Omaha, and other cities to take wartime factory jobs. Many Mexican Americans faced hostility and discrimination when they arrived in American cities. Like other immigrants before them, they tended to settle in their own separate neighborhoods, called **barrios,** where they could support each other.

✓ **Reading Check** **Evaluating** How permanent were women's advances in the wartime workplace?

Ensuring Public Support

Progressives in the government did not think coordinating business and labor was enough to ensure the success of the war effort. They also believed that the government should take steps to shape public opinion and build support for the war.

CHAPTER 19 World War I and Its Aftermath **587**

Chart *Skills*

Answer:
1. National War Labor Board
2. Because daylight savings time moved sunset one hour later, people used less fuel.

Chart Skills Practice
Ask: Which of the federal mobilization agencies do you think had the greatest impact on ordinary citizens? *(Many students will note that the Committee on Public Information had the broadest impact.)*

Finding an Artifact Encourage students to use library and Internet resources to find a photograph, piece of art, graph, or book about the Great Migration. Have students bring the artifacts or copies of them to class. Display them around the classroom. Then hold a class discussion on the Great Migration's impact. **L2**

✓**Reading Check**

Answer: The gains were mostly temporary.

FYI

Some of the posters printed by the United States government contained highly charged language and images. One showed two German soldiers robbing a house after shooting the owner; the soldiers were labeled "Hindenburglers." Another, entitled "Halt the Hun," showed an American soldier preventing a German soldier from bayoneting a defenseless woman and her baby.

INTERDISCIPLINARY CONNECTIONS ACTIVITY

Music Tell students that George M. Cohan wrote his most famous song, "Over There," on the day war was declared. He sat down at the piano and wrote what he said was just a bugle call. Have students research other songs of World War I and study their lyrics. Then ask: **How do the lyrics reflect the attitudes of the time? Are they idealistic, humorous, optimistic, patriotic, or sentimental? L2**

Different Viewpoints

Different Viewpoints

Answers:

1. inciting revolution

2. freedom of the press and freedom of speech

Ask: Why does Justice Holmes dissent from the majority opinion? *(He believed that the writers had constitutional protection in writing and publishing their leaflets.)*

FYI

The mass media of the World War I era consisted only of newsprint. Neither film nor radio had developed as a medium for spreading ideas. Considering these limitations, World War I propaganda was extremely effective.

3 ASSESS

Assign Section 2 Assessment as homework or as an in-class activity.

⏺ Have students use the **Interactive Tutor Self-Assessment CD-ROM.**

Reading Essentials and Study Guide 19–2

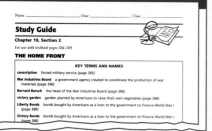

Name _____ Date _____ Class _____

Study Guide

Chapter 19, Section 2
For use with textbook pages 584–589

THE HOME FRONT

KEY TERMS AND NAMES
conscription forced military service *(page 585)*
War Industries Board a government agency created to coordinate the production of war materials *(page 586)*
Bernard Baruch the head of the War Industries Board *(page 586)*
victory garden garden planted by Americans to raise their own vegetables *(page 586)*
Liberty Bonds bonds bought by Americans as a loan to the government to finance World War I *(page 586)*
Victory Bonds bonds bought by Americans as a loan to the government to finance World War I *(page 586)*

Abrams v. United States, 1919

The Espionage Act of 1917 made it a crime to "willfully utter, print, write, or publish any disloyal, profane, scurrilous or abusive language about the government." Although the act limited First Amendment freedoms, many Americans believed winning World War I was more important. *(See page 1080 for more information on* Abrams v. the United States.*)*

Justice John H. Clarke delivered the majority opinion:

It is argued, somewhat faintly, that the acts charged against the defendants were not unlawful because within the protection of that freedom . . . of speech and of the press . . . and that the entire Espionage Act is unconstitutional. . . .

. . . the plain purpose of their propaganda was to excite, at the supreme crisis of the war, disaffection, sedition, riots, and, as they hoped, revolution, in this country for the purpose of embarrassing, and, if possible, defeating the military plans of the Government in Europe. . . . [T]he language of these circulars was obviously intended to provoke and to encourage resistance to the United States in the war, as the third count runs, and the defendants, in terms, plainly urged and advocated a resort to a general strike of workers in ammunition factories for the purpose of curtailing the production of ordnance and munitions necessary and essential to the prosecution of the war. . . . Thus, it is clear not only that some evidence, but that much persuasive evidence, was before the jury tending to prove that the defendants were guilty as charged. . . .

Justice Oliver Wendell Holmes, Jr., dissenting:

It is only the present danger of immediate evil or an intent to bring it about that warrants Congress in setting a limit to the expression of opinion where private rights are not concerned. Congress certainly cannot forbid all effort to change the mind of the country. Now nobody can suppose that the surreptitious publishing of a silly leaflet by an unknown man, without more, would present any immediate danger that its opinions would hinder the success of the government arms or have any appreciable tendency to do so.

In this case, sentences of twenty years' imprisonment have been imposed for the publishing of two leaflets that I believe the defendants had as much right to publish as the Government has to publish the Constitution of the United States now vainly invoked by them. . . . I regret that I cannot put into more impressive words my belief that, in their conviction upon this indictment, the defendants were deprived of their rights under the Constitution of the United States.

Amendment I

–Congress shall make no law respecting an establishment of religion, or prohibiting the free exercise thereof; or abridging the freedom of speech, or of the press; or the right of the people peaceably to assemble, and to petition the Government for a redress of grievances.

Learning From History

1. What were the charges against the defendants?
2. On what key point did Holmes and Clarke disagree?

Selling the War A new government agency, the **Committee on Public Information,** had the task of "selling" the war to the American people. The head of the CPI was journalist George Creel, who recruited advertising executives, commercial artists, authors, songwriters, entertainers, public speakers, and motion picture companies to help sway public opinion in favor of the war.

The CPI distributed pamphlets and arranged for thousands of short patriotic talks, called "four-minute speeches," to be delivered at movie theaters and public halls and gathering places. The Four-Minute Men urged audiences to support the war in various ways, from buying war bonds to reporting draft dodgers to the proper authorities.

Civil Liberties Curtailed In addition to using propaganda and persuasion, the government also passed legislation to fight antiwar activities or enemies at home. Espionage, or spying to acquire secret government information, was addressed in the Espionage Act of 1917, which established penalties and prison terms for anyone who gave aid to the enemy. This act also penalized disloyalty, giving false reports, or otherwise interfering with the war effort. The Post Office even hired college professors to translate foreign periodicals to find out if they contained antiwar messages.

The Sedition Act of 1918 expanded the meaning of the Espionage Act to make illegal any public expression of opposition to the war. In practice, it allowed officials to prosecute anyone who criticized

588 CHAPTER 19 World War I and Its Aftermath

CRITICAL THINKING ACTIVITY

Evaluating Ask students to identify actions the government took to organize the war effort (regulating industry, encouraging greater production, propaganda, keeping an eye on dissenters). Write the responses on the board. After students identify the actions, have them list the effects of those actions. Then discuss why the government tends to expand its control in wartime. Ask students if they think all of the government's actions on the home front in World War I were necessary. **L2**

the president or the government. Combined, these laws generated over 1,500 prosecutions and 1,000 convictions.

A Climate of Suspicion The fear of spies and emphasis on patriotism quickly led to the mistreatment and persecution of German Americans. To avoid German-sounding names, advertisers began to call sauerkraut "Liberty cabbage" and hamburger "Salisbury steak." Many schools dropped German language classes from their curricula, and orchestras stopped performing the music of Beethoven, Schubert, Wagner, and other German composers. Anti-German feelings sometimes led to violence. Some citizens beat neighbors who were German-born. In Collinsville, Illinois, a mob lynched a German-born man whom they suspected of disloyalty.

German Americans were not the only ones under suspicion. Mobs attacked labor activists, socialists, and pacifists. Newspapers ads urged Americans to monitor the activities of their fellow citizens. Americans even formed private organizations, such as the American Protective League and the Boy Spies of America, to spy on neighbors and coworkers. Secretary of War Newton Baker expressed concern about the growing intolerance:

❝There is a growing frenzy of suspicion and hostility toward disloyalty. I am afraid we are going to have a good many instances of people roughly treated on very slight evidence of disloyalty. Already a number of men and some women have been tarred and feathered, and a portion of the press is urging with great vehemence more strenuous efforts at detection and punishment.❞

—quoted in *Echoes of Distant Thunder*

The Supreme Court Limits Free Speech Despite protests against the government's tactics, however, the courts generally upheld the principle behind them. Although the First Amendment specifically states that "Congress shall make no law . . . abridging the freedom of speech, or of the press," the Supreme Court decided otherwise, departing from a strict literal interpretation of the Constitution.

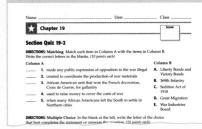

George Creel

In the landmark case of *Schenck v. the United States* (1919), the Supreme Court ruled that an individual's freedom of speech could be curbed when the words uttered constitute a "clear and present danger." The Court used as an example someone yelling "Fire!" in a crowded theater as a situation in which freedom of speech would be superseded by the theater-goers' right to safety. The Court's majority opinion stated, "When a nation is at war, many things that might be said in times of peace are such a hindrance to its effort that their utterance will not be endured so long as [soldiers] fight. . . ." 📖 *(See page 1083 for more information on* Schenck v. *the United States.)*

✓ **Reading Check** **Explaining** Why did Congress pass the Espionage Act in 1917?

SECTION 2 ASSESSMENT

Checking for Understanding

1. **Define:** conscription, victory garden, espionage.
2. **Identify:** War Industries Board, Bernard Baruch, Liberty Bond, Victory Bond, Committee on Public Information.
3. **Describe** the contributions of African Americans during the war.

Reviewing Themes

4. **Government and Democracy** How did government efforts to ensure support for the war conflict with democratic ideals?

Critical Thinking

5. **Analyzing** How did World War I cause the federal government to change its relationship with the business world?
6. **Organizing** Use a graphic organizer similar to the one below to identify the effects of the war on the American workforce.

Effects of War on U.S. Workforce

Analyzing Visuals

7. **Analyzing Posters** Examine the posters on page 586. How do these images encourage support for the war? How effective do you think they would be today?

Writing About History

8. **Persuasive Writing** Imagine that you are working for the Committee on Public Information. Write text for an advertisement or lyrics to a song in which you attempt to sway public opinion in favor of the war.

CHAPTER 19 World War I and Its Aftermath **589**

Reteach
Have students analyze how the United States raised an army and won support for World War I.

Enrich
Have students write newspaper editorials questioning the moral implications of using advertising to "sell" a war to a nation. Invite volunteers to read their editorials to the class. Then ask students what might have happened in 1917 to anyone who wrote such an editorial.

✓ **Reading Check**

Answer: to control public opinion and stop antiwar supporters

4 CLOSE

Have students explain how the economy was controlled to support the war.

SECTION 2 ASSESSMENT ANSWERS

1. Terms are in blue.
2. War Industries Board *(p. 586)*, Bernard Baruch *(p. 586)*, Liberty Bond *(p. 586)*, Victory Bond *(p. 586)*, Committee on Public Information *(p. 588)*
3. About 400,000 African Americans were drafted to serve in the war; many received high praise for their courage from French generals.
4. limited free speech and freedom of the press
5. Special boards were created that encouraged cooperation between business and government.
6. Effects should include increased job opportunities for women and African Americans.
7. Supporting the war is portrayed as good; other answers will vary.
8. Answers will vary. Invite students to display or perform their work.

TEACH

World War I Firsts

Organize students into four groups. Assign each group one of the following: aerial combat, gas attacks and gas masks, donkey's ears, or Big Bertha. Have the groups research to learn more about their assigned item. Then have students research modern warfare to find either the state of the art in their assigned category (fighter planes and gas masks) or to find corollaries in modern warfare (for example, a corollary to donkey's ears may be night vision goggles or satellite tracking information). Have the groups prepare a display to present the information they have found.

Color My World

Have interested students research nonmilitary inventions that occurred between 1914 and 1918. Have students write a report on their findings. As a class, create a time line of the various inventions.

Visit the **TIME** Web site at www.time.com for up-to-date news, weekly magazine articles, editorials, online polls, and an archive of past magazine and Web articles.

American soldiers set sail for Europe.

World War Firsts

Human ingenuity goes to work in the service of war:

AERIAL COMBAT, 1914. War takes to the air. Two Allied aircraft chase two German planes across Britain.

GAS ATTACKS, 1915. The German High Command admits to using chlorine gas bombs and shells on the field of combat. Deadly mustard gas is used in 1917.

GAS MASKS. Issued to Allied soldiers in 1915.

DONKEY'S EARS. A new trench periscope enables soldiers to observe the battleground from the relative safety of a trench without risking sniper fire.

BIG BERTHA. Enormous howitzer gun bombards Paris. "Big Bertha," named after the wife of its manufacturer, is thought to be located nearly 63 miles behind German lines. Moving at night on railroad tracks, the gun is difficult for the Allies to locate.

Color My World

Some bright spots in a dark decade:

- Color newspaper supplements (1914)
- 3-D films (1915)
- Nail polish (1916)
- Three-color traffic lights (1918)
- Color photography introduced by Eastman Kodak (1914)

One of the first color photographs

VERBATIM

"My message was one of death for young men. How odd to applaud that."
WOODROW WILSON,
on returning to the White House after asking Congress for a declaration of war, 1917

"Food is Ammunition—Don't Waste It"
POSTER FROM U.S. FOOD ADMINISTRATION,
administered by Herbert Hoover

"I have had a hard time getting over this war. My old world died."
RAY STANNARD BAKER,
journalist

"Let us, while this war lasts, forget our special grievances and close our ranks shoulder to shoulder with our own white fellow citizens and the allied nations that are fighting for democracy."
W.E.B. DU BOIS,
African American scholar and leader, 1918

"America has at one bound become a world power in a sense she never was before."
BRITISH PRIME MINISTER DAVID LLOYD GEORGE,
on the U.S. entry into World War I, 1917

"In the camps I saw barrels mounted on sticks on which zealous captains were endeavoring to teach their men how to ride a horse."
THEODORE ROOSEVELT,
on touring U.S. military training facilities, 1917

"The war was over, and it seemed as if everything in the world were possible, and everything was new, and that peace was going to be all we dreamed about."
FLORENCE HARRIMAN,
Red Cross volunteer, in Paris on Armistice Day, 1918

COOPERATIVE LEARNING ACTIVITY

Creating a Magazine Spread Organize the class into groups of four or five. Have students create a magazine spread about America's war on terrorism. Although students may use ideas from recent news magazines, encourage the groups to look for their own unique angle for the spread. Students should look at current magazines and books for ideas about page design. This activity can be completed using desktop publishing software or the more traditional cut-and-paste method.

Use the rubric for a cooperative group management plan on pages 81–82 in the **Performance Assessment Activities and Rubrics.**

How to Make a Doughboy

Take one American infantryman.

1. Arm with 107 pieces of fighting equipment, including:
   - rifle
   - rifle cartridges
   - cartridge belt
   - steel helmet
   - clubs
   - knives
   - gas mask
   - wire cutters
   - trench tool
   - bayonet and scabbard
   - grenades

2. Add 50 articles of clothing, including 3 wool blankets and a bedsack.

3. Equip with eating utensils and 11 cooking implements.

4. Train well.

TOTAL COST: $156.30

(not including training and transportation to Europe)

BROWN BROTHERS

Milestones

REPATRIATED, APRIL 10, 1917. VLADIMIR ILYICH LENIN, to Russia, after an 11-year absence. The leader of the leftist Bolshevik party hopes to reorganize his revolutionary group.

CULVER PICTURES

Vladimir Lenin

SHOT DOWN AND KILLED, APRIL 22, 1918. "THE RED BARON," Manfred von Richthofen, Germany's ace pilot. Von Richthofen destroyed more than 80 Allied aircraft. On hearing of the Red Baron's death, English fighter pilot Edward Mannock said, "I hope he roasted all the way down."

Jeannette Rankin

BROWN BROTHERS

ELECTED, MARCH 4, 1917. JEANNETTE RANKIN of Montana, to the U.S. Congress. The first woman congressional representative explained her victory by saying that women "got the vote in Montana because the spirit of pioneer days was still alive."

EXECUTED, OCTOBER 15, 1917. MATA HARI, in France, for espionage. The famous Dutch dancer was sentenced to death for spying for the Germans.

NUMBERS 1915

$1,040 Average annual income for workers in finance, insurance, and real estate

$687 Average income for industrial workers (higher for union workers, lower for nonunion workers)

$510 Average income for retail trade workers

$355 Average income for farm laborers

$342 Average income for domestic servants

$328 Average income for public school teachers

$11.95 Cost of a bicycle

BROWN BROTHERS

$1.15 Cost of a baseball

$1 Average cost of a hotel room

39¢ Cost of one dozen eggs

5¢ Cost of a glass of cola

7¢ Cost of a large roll of toilet paper

EXTENDING THE CONTENT

Stars and Stripes *Stars and Stripes,* the armed forces newspaper staffed entirely by soldiers, was first published in 1918. In addition to being a source of information and morale for soldiers, it provided many young journalists and cartoonists with their first jobs. Two well-known cartoonists whose work appeared in *Stars and Stripes* were Milt Caniff ("Terry and the Pirates") and Bill Mauldin, who would win the Pulitzer Prize in 1945 for his "Willie" and "GI Joe" cartoons.

1 FOCUS

Section Overview

This section focuses on the military aspects of World War I.

Guide to Reading

Answers to Graphic: airplanes, poison gas, machine guns, trenches, tanks

Preteaching Vocabulary
Have students identify the Key Terms and Names that refer to specific individuals and write a one-sentence description of each person.

Guide to Reading

Main Idea
After four years of fighting, the war in Europe ended in November 1918.

Key Terms and Names
"no man's land," convoy, Vladimir Lenin, Treaty of Brest-Litovsk, armistice, Fourteen Points, League of Nations, Treaty of Versailles, reparations

Reading Strategy
Organizing As you read about the battles of World War I, complete a graphic organizer similar to the one below by listing the kinds of warfare and technology used in the fighting.

Warfare and Technology Used in World War I

Reading Objectives
- **Discuss** the fighting techniques used in World War I.
- **Characterize** the American response to the Treaty of Versailles.

Section Theme
Individual Action American troops played a major role in helping end the war, while President Wilson played a major role in the peace negotiations.

Preview of Events

◆1915   ◆1917   ◆1919

July 1916
Battle of the Somme begins

November 1917
Communists seize power in Russia

March 1918
Treaty of Brest-Litovsk ends war between Russia and Germany

September 1918
Beginning of Battle of the Argonne Forest

November 1918
Armistice ends war

★ An American Story ★

John J. Pershing

General John J. Pershing, commander of the American forces in World War I, could not help but feel a sense of pride and excitement as he watched the Second Battalion of the First Division's 16th Infantry march through the streets of Paris on July 4, 1917:

66 . . . The battalion was joined by a great crowd, many women forcing their way into the ranks and swinging along arm in arm with the men. With wreaths about their necks and bouquets in their hats and rifles, the column looked like a moving flower garden. With only a semblance of military formation, the animated throng pushed its way through avenues of people to the martial strains of the French band and the still more thrilling music of cheering voices. 99

—quoted in *The Yanks Are Coming*

While his men marched through Paris, Pershing raced to Picpus Cemetery, the burial place of the Marquis de Lafayette, a French noble who had fought in the American Revolution. One of Pershing's officers, Colonel Charles E. Stanton, raised his hand in salute and acknowledged the continuing American-French relationship by proclaiming, "Lafayette, we are here!"

Combat in World War I

By the spring of 1917, World War I had devastated Europe and claimed millions of lives. Terrible destruction resulted from a combination of old-fashioned strategies and new technologies. Despite the carnage Europeans had experienced, many Americans believed their troops would make a difference and quickly bring the war to an end.

592 CHAPTER 19 World War I and Its Aftermath

SECTION RESOURCES

📂 Reproducible Masters
- Reproducible Lesson Plan 19–3
- Daily Lecture and Discussion Notes 19–3
- Guided Reading Activity 19–3
- Section Quiz 19–3
- Reading Essentials and Study Guide 19–3
- Performance Assessment Activities and Rubrics

📽 Transparencies
- Daily Focus Skills Transparency 19–3

Multimedia
- ⊙ Interactive Tutor Self-Assessment CD-ROM
- ⊙ ExamView® Pro Testmaker CD-ROM
- ⊙ Presentation Plus! CD-ROM
- ⊙ TeacherWorks™ CD-ROM
- ⊙ Audio Program

Trench Warfare The early offensives of 1914 quickly demonstrated that the nature of warfare had changed. Troops that dug themselves in and relied upon modern rifles and a new weapon—the rapid-fire machine gun—could easily hold off the attacking forces. On the Western Front, troops dug a network of trenches that stretched from the English Channel to the Swiss border. The space between the opposing trenches was known as **"no man's land,"** a rough, barren landscape pockmarked with craters from artillery fire.

To break through enemy lines, both sides began with massive artillery barrages. Then bayonet-wielding soldiers would scramble out of their trenches, race across no man's land, and hurl grenades into the enemy's trenches. The results were often disastrous. The artillery barrages rarely destroyed the enemy defenses, and troops crossing no man's land were easily stopped by enemy machine guns and rifle fire. These kind of assaults caused staggeringly high casualties. In major battles, both sides often lost several hundred thousand men.

These battles produced horrific scenes of death and destruction, as one American soldier noted in his diary:

❝Many dead Germans along the road. One heap on a manure pile . . . Devastation everywhere. Our barrage has rooted up the entire territory like a ploughed field. Dead horses galore, many of them have a hind quarter cut off—the Huns [Germans] need food. Dead men here and there.❞

—quoted in *The American Spirit*

New Technology As it became clear that charging enemy trenches could bring only limited success at great cost, both sides began to develop new technologies to help them break through enemy lines. In April 1915, the Germans first used poison gas in the Second Battle of Ypres. The fumes caused vomiting, blindness, and suffocation. Soon afterward the Allies also began using poison gas, and gas masks became a necessary part of a soldier's equipment.

In 1916 the British introduced the tank into battle. The first tanks were very slow and cumbersome, mechanically unreliable, and fairly easy to destroy. They could roll over barbed wire and trenches, but there were usually not enough of them to make a

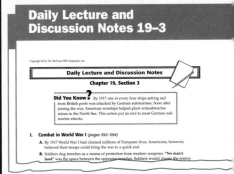

2 TEACH

Writing a Letter Have students take on the role of a young soldier leaving for war. Instruct students to write a letter to a family member or close friend. The letter should explain why the person is going to war, what he or she fears, and what the friend or relative can do to help. **L1**

📁 Use the rubric for creating a diary, short story, memorandum, or letter on pages 79–80 in the *Performance Assessment Activities and Rubrics.*

you don't say...

Stalemate A stalemate occurs in the game of chess when one player cannot make any move without putting his or her king in a position to be captured, and thus lose the game. It is an apt term for the deadlock along the Western Front.

An American Hero

Although the brutal trench warfare of World War I led to many acts of astonishing bravery, the heroism of one American, Corporal Alvin York, captured the nation's imagination. Born in 1887, York grew up poor in the mountains of Tennessee, where he learned to shoot by hunting wild game.

On October 8, 1918, during the Battle of the Argonne Forest, York's patrol lost its way and ended up behind enemy lines. When a German machine gun emplacement on a fortified hill fired on the patrol and killed nine men, York took command and charged the machine gun. Although the details of the battle are unclear, when it ended, York had killed between 9 and 25 Germans, captured the machine guns, and taken 132 prisoners. For his actions, he received the Medal of Honor and the French Croix de Guerre. After returning home, he used his fame to raise money for the Alvin York Institute—a school for underprivileged Tennessee children.

COOPERATIVE LEARNING ACTIVITY

Making a List Organize students into small groups and ask them to make a list of items an American soldier should pack in his field kit before he goes off to the trenches. Encourage students to use library and Internet resources to learn more about what a soldier actually needed. Have students compare their lists and determine which items occur most often. 📦

Use the rubric for a cooperative group management plan on pages 81–82 in the *Performance Assessment Activities and Rubrics.*

Guided Reading Activity 19-3

Name _____ Date _____ Class _____

★ Guided Reading Activity **19-3**

DIRECTIONS: Using Headings and Subheadings Locate each heading below in your textbook. Then use the information under the correct subheading to help you write each answer.

I. Combat in World War I

A. How did soldiers from both sides attempt to break through enemy lines? _____

B. What were the results of such actions? _____

C. Why did both sides begin to develop new technology? _____

D. When and where did the Germans first use poison gas? _____

E. What two military vehicles were introduced during World War I? _____

II. The Americans and Victory

✓ Reading Check

Answer: machine guns, tanks, airplanes, poison gas

Creating a Drawing Have interested students create drawings of the types of aircraft used by both the Allies and the Central Powers during World War I. Have students label and display their drawings. **L2**

FYI

Three pilots who flew bombers in World War I were among the best-known fighters of the war. American Eddie Rickenbacker shot down 22 planes during the war. Flying aces from other countries also became famous. Manfred von Richthofen of Germany, known as the "Red Baron," was credited with 80 victories, and Rene Fonck of France with 75.

you don't say...

Ace The term *ace* originally referred to a pilot who shot down five enemy planes. It later came to mean anyone who was exceptionally good at something.

NATIONAL GEOGRAPHIC   Battles of World War I, 1914–1918

6 Lusitania sunk May 7, 1915

Battles of Ypres
3 Oct.–Nov. 1914
4 Apr.–May 1915

1 Tannenberg Aug. 1914

8 Battle of the Somme July–Nov. 1916

7 Battle of Verdun Feb.–Dec. 1916

2 First Battle of the Marne Sept. 1914

9 Caporetto Oct.–Dec. 1917

5 Gallipoli Apr. 1915–Jan. 1916

Legend:
- Allied Powers
- Central Powers
- Neutral nations
- German unrestricted submarine warfare zone
- → Allied offensives
- ← Central Powers' offensives
- — Farthest advance of Central Powers
- --- Line of trench warfare, 1915–1917
- ✳ Allied victory
- ✳ Central Powers' victory
- ✳ Indecisive battle

0 500 miles
0 500 kilometers
Lambert Azimuthal Equal-Area projection

---

difference. While tanks did help troops, they did not revolutionize warfare in World War I.

World War I also saw the first use of airplanes in combat. At first, planes were used mainly to observe enemy activities. Soon, the Allies and Central Powers used them to drop small bombs. As technology advanced, they also attached machine guns to aircraft to engage in deadly air battles known as dogfights.

✓ Reading Check **Describing** What new technologies were introduced in World War I?

The Americans and Victory

Wave upon wave of American troops marched into this bloody stalemate—nearly 2 million before the war's end. These **"doughboys,"** a nickname for American soldiers, were largely inexperienced, but they were fresh, so their presence immediately boosted the morale of Allied forces.

594 CHAPTER 19 World War I and Its Aftermath

Winning the War at Sea No American troopships were sunk on their way to Europe—an accomplishment due largely to the efforts of American Admiral William S. Sims. For most of the war, the British preferred to fight German submarines by sending warships to find them. Meanwhile, merchant ships would race across the Atlantic individually. The British approach had not worked well, and submarines had inflicted heavy losses on British shipping.

Sims proposed that merchant ships and troop transports be gathered into groups, called convoys, and escorted across the Atlantic by warships. If submarines wanted to attack a convoy, they would have to get past the warships protecting it. The convoy system greatly reduced shipping losses and ensured that American troops arrived safely in Europe. They arrived during a pivotal time in late 1917.

Russia Leaves the War In March 1917, riots broke out in Russia over the government's handling of the war and over the scarcity of food and fuel. On March

---

MEETING SPECIAL NEEDS

Reading Disability To help improve reading comprehension for students with reading difficulties, help them create a list of key terms for this section. Start with the terms in the Guide to Reading. Add other names and unfamiliar words and phrases. Have students work in pairs to quiz each other on the meaning and importance of each name and term on the list. **L1** **ELL**

📁 Refer to *Inclusion for the High School Social Studies Classroom Strategies and Activities* in the TCR.

Western Front, 1914–1918

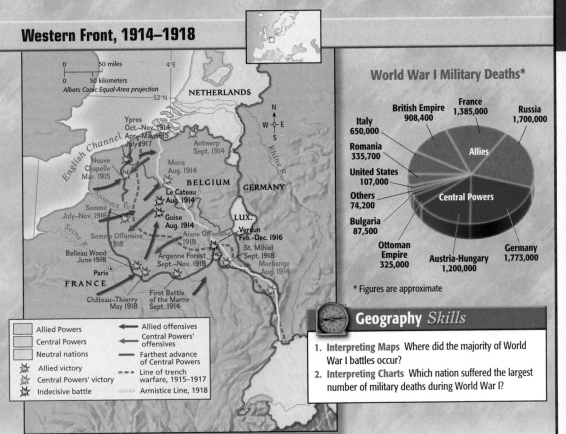

World War I Military Deaths*

British Empire 908,400
France 1,385,000
Russia 1,700,000
Italy 650,000
Romania 335,700
United States 107,000
Others 74,200
Bulgaria 87,500
Ottoman Empire 325,000
Austria-Hungary 1,200,000
Germany 1,773,000

Allies

Central Powers

* Figures are approximate

Geography *Skills*

1. **Interpreting Maps** Where did the majority of World War I battles occur?
2. **Interpreting Charts** Which nation suffered the largest number of military deaths during World War I?

Map legend:
- Allied Powers
- Central Powers
- Neutral nations
- ✹ Allied victory
- ✹ Central Powers' victory
- ✹ Indecisive battle
- ← Allied offensives
- ← Central Powers' offensives
- — Farthest advance of Central Powers
- --- Line of trench warfare, 1915–1917
- ░ Armistice Line, 1918

FYI

John Reed was an eyewitness to the 1917 revolution in Russia. Back in the United States, he wrote *Ten Days That Shook the World* and helped lead the Communist Labor Party. For his Communist activities, Reed was indicted for sedition. In 1919 he returned to Russia and was elected to the Second Congress of the Communist International.

CURRICULUM CONNECTION

Health Although the Russian people had faced war, revolution, and civil war, their greatest danger came in the form of lice. Lice carry *Rickettsia* bacteria, which causes typhus. After the revolution of 1917, Russia experienced the worst typhus epidemic in history. Between 1917 and 1921, over 2.5 million Russians died of typhus. The use of fumigants prevented a similar outbreak on the Western Front.

15, Czar Nicholas II, the leader of the Russian Empire, abdicated his throne. Political leadership in Russia passed into the hands of a provisional, or temporary, government, consisting largely of moderate representatives who supported Russia's continued participation in World War I. The government, however, was unable to adequately deal with the major problems, such as food shortages, that were afflicting the nation.

The **Bolsheviks,** a group of Communists, soon competed for power in Russia. In November 1917, **Vladimir Lenin,** the leader of the Bolshevik Party, overthrew the Russian government and established a Communist government.

Germany's military fortunes improved with the Bolshevik takeover of Russia. Lenin's first act after seizing power was to pull Russia out of the war and concentrate on establishing a Communist state. He accomplished this by agreeing to the **Treaty of Brest-Litovsk** with Germany on March 3, 1918. Under this treaty, Russia lost substantial territory, giving up Ukraine, its Polish and Baltic territories, and Finland. However, the treaty also removed the German army from the remaining Russian lands. With the Eastern Front settled, Germany was now free to concentrate its forces in the west.

The German Offensive Falters On March 21, 1918, the Germans launched a massive attack along the Western Front, beginning with gas attacks and a bombardment by over 6,000 artillery pieces. German forces, reinforced with troops transferred from the Russian front, pushed deeply into Allied lines. By late May, they were less than 40 miles (64 km) from Paris.

American troops played an important role in containing the German offensive. Seven days after the German offensive began, American troops launched their first major attack, quickly capturing the village of Cantigny. On May 31, American and French troops blocked the German drive on Paris at the town of Château-Thierry. On July 15, the Germans launched

CHAPTER 19   World War I and Its Aftermath   **595**

INTERDISCIPLINARY CONNECTIONS ACTIVITY

Literature Explain that German author Erich Maria Remarque told of life in the trenches in his novel *All Quiet on the Western Front.* Provide the quote shown below and ask students to paraphrase Remarque's words. **L2**

"The sun goes down, night comes, the shells whine, life is at an end.

"Still the little piece of convulsed earth in which we lie is held. We have yielded no more than a few hundred yards of it as a prize to the enemy. But on every yard there lies a dead man."

3 ASSESS

Assign Section 3 Assessment as homework or as an in-class activity.

⊕ Have students use the **Interactive Tutor Self-Assessment CD-ROM.**

Reading Essentials and Study Guide 19–3

Name _____ Date _____ Class _____

Study Guide

Chapter 19, Section 3
For use with textbook pages 592–597

A BLOODY CONFLICT

KEY TERMS AND NAMES

"**no man's land**" the space between opposing trenches *(page 593)*
convoys groups of merchant ships and troop transports *(page 594)*
Vladimir Lenin leader of the Bolshevik Party *(page 595)*
Treaty of Brest-Litovsk treaty between Germany and Russia that ended Russia's involvement in World War I *(page 595)*
armistice a cease-fire *(page 596)*
Fourteen Points President Wilson's plan for peace after World War I *(page 596)*
League of Nations an association of nations organized to help keep peace and prevent future

---

Section Quiz 19–3

Name _____ Date _____ Class _____

★ **Chapter 19**   Score ☐

Section Quiz 19-3

DIRECTIONS: Matching Match each item in Column A with the items in Column B. Write the correct letters in the blanks. *(10 points each)*

Column A
_____ 1. supreme commander of the Allied forces
_____ 2. a group of Communists
_____ 3. commander of the American troops
_____ 4. payments for war damages
_____ 5. the space between opposing trenches

Column B
A. General John J. Pershing
B. Marshall Ferdinand Foch
C. "no man's land"
D. Bolsheviks
E. reparations

DIRECTIONS: Multiple Choice In the blank at the left, write the letter of the choice that best completes the statement or answers the question. *(10 points each)*

---

one last massive attack in a determined attempt to take Paris, but American and French troops held their ground.

The Battle of the Argonne Forest With the German drive stalled, French Marshal Ferdinand Foch, supreme commander of the Allied forces, ordered massive counterattacks all along the front. In mid-September, American troops drove back German forces at the battle of Saint-Mihiel. The attack was a prelude to a massive American offensive in the region between the Meuse River and the Argonne Forest. General Pershing assembled over 600,000 American troops, some 40,000 tons of supplies, and roughly 4,000 artillery pieces for the most massive attack in American history.

The attack began on September 26, 1918. Slowly, one German position after another fell to the advancing American troops. The Germans inflicted heavy casualties on the American forces, but by early November, the Americans had shattered the German defenses and opened a hole in the German lines.

The War Ends While fighting raged along the Western Front, a revolution engulfed Austria-Hungary, and the Ottoman Turks surrendered. Faced with the surrender of their allies and a naval mutiny at Kiel in early November, the people of Berlin rose in rebellion on November 9 and forced the German emperor to step down. At the 11th hour on the 11th day of the 11th month, 1918, the fighting stopped. Germany had finally signed an armistice, or cease-fire, that ended the war.

✓ **Reading Check** **Explaining** What was Vladimir Lenin's first goal after controlling Russia in 1917?

Picturing **History**

American Artillery This photo shows some of the materials used to fight World War I. Artillery shells are piled at the feet of these American soldiers. What American battle demanded the largest amount of supplies and artillery pieces?

A Flawed Peace

In January 1919, a peace conference began in Paris to try to resolve the complicated issues arising from World War I. The principal figures in the negotiations were the "Big Four," the leaders of the victorious Allied nations: President Wilson of the United States, British prime minister David Lloyd George, French premier Georges Clemenceau, and Italian prime minister Vittorio Orlando. Germany was not invited to participate.

Wilson had presented his plan, known as the **Fourteen Points,** to Congress in January 1918. The Fourteen Points were based on "the principle of justice to all peoples and nationalities." In the first five points, the president proposed to eliminate the general causes of the war through free trade, disarmament, freedom of the seas, impartial adjustment of colonial claims, and open diplomacy instead of secret agreements. The next eight points addressed the right of self-determination. They also required the Central Powers to evacuate all of the countries invaded during the war, including France, Belgium, and Russia. The fourteenth point, perhaps the most important one to Wilson, called for the creation of a "general association of nations" known as the **League of Nations.** The League's member nations would help preserve peace and prevent future wars by pledging to respect and protect each other's territory and political independence. 📖 *(See page 1074 for the text of the* Fourteen Points.*)*

The Treaty of Versailles As the peace talks progressed in the Palace of Versailles (vehr·SY), it became clear that Wilson's ideas did not coincide with the interests of the other Allied governments. They criticized his plan as too lenient toward Germany.

Despite Wilson's hopes, the terms of peace were harsh. The **Treaty of Versailles,** signed by Germany on June 28, 1919, had weakened or discarded many of Wilson's proposals. Under the treaty, Germany was stripped of its armed forces and was made to pay reparations, or war damages, in the amount of $33 billion to the Allies. This sum was far beyond Germany's financial means. Perhaps most humiliating, the treaty required Germany to acknowledge guilt for the outbreak of World War I and the devastation caused by the war.

The war itself resulted in the dissolution of four empires: the Russian Empire, the Ottoman Empire, which lost territory in the war and fell to revolution in 1922, the German Empire after the abdication of the emperor and loss of territory in the treaty, and

---

CRITICAL THINKING ACTIVITY

Supporting Key Ideas Write the following statement on the board: "The peace treaty in Europe did not establish a lasting peace." Have students work in pairs to locate evidence to support this statement. *(Evidence includes Germany's severe punishment and disputed national boundaries.)*
L2

Austria-Hungary, which was split into separate countries. Furthermore, nine new countries were established in Europe, including Yugoslavia, Poland, and Czechoslovakia.

While Wilson expressed disappointment in the treaty, he found consolation in its call for the creation of his cherished League of Nations. He returned home to win approval for the treaty.

The U.S. Senate Rejects the Treaty The Treaty of Versailles, especially the League of Nations, faced immediate opposition from numerous U.S. lawmakers. A key group of senators, nicknamed "the Irreconcilables" in the press, assailed the League as the kind of "entangling alliance" that Washington, Jefferson, and Monroe had warned against. These critics feared that the League might supersede the power of Congress to declare war and thus force the United States to fight in numerous foreign conflicts.

A larger group of senators, known as the "Reservationists," was led by the powerful chairman of the Foreign Relations committee, Henry Cabot Lodge. This group supported the League but would ratify the treaty only with amendments that would preserve the nation's freedom to act independently. Wilson feared such changes would defeat the basic purpose of the League and insisted that the Senate ratify the treaty without changes.

Convinced that he could defeat his opposition by winning public support, Wilson took his case directly to the American people. Starting in Ohio in September 1919, he traveled 8,000 miles and made over 30 major speeches in three weeks. The physical strain of his tour, however, proved too great. Wilson collapsed in Colorado on September 25 and returned to the White House. There, he suffered a stroke and was bedridden for months, isolated from even his closest advisers but determined not to compromise with the Senate.

The Senate voted in November 1919 and again in March 1920, but it refused to ratify the treaty. After Wilson left office in 1921, the United States negotiated separate peace treaties with each of the Central Powers. The League of Nations, the foundation of President Wilson's plan for lasting world peace, took shape without the United States.

✓ **Reading Check** **Examining** What major issues did Wilson's Fourteen Points address?

World Geography Connection

Global War

Although World War I was fought mainly in Europe, it touched the lives of peoples throughout the world, including those in Africa and India. By the time the war broke out, both African and Indian society had been turned upside down by European imperialism. While the British controlled much of India, no less than seven European powers had divided up Africa among themselves. In addition to living under the rule of Europeans, Africans and Indians were forced to take part in their great war as well. About one million Indians fought for the British in Europe, while nearly as many Africans served in the French army. The fighting also spread to Africa, as the Allies fought to seize control of Germany's African colonies. *How do you think the average Indian or African felt about World War I?*

Answer: Possible answers: They disliked participating in a war that did not seem to involve them; they supported the efforts of their colonial rulers, hoping this might win them independence.

✓ **Reading Check**

Answer: free trade, disarmament, freedom of the seas, impartial adjustment of colonial claims, open diplomacy, self-determination, creation of the League of Nations

Reteach
Have students discuss fighting strategies of World War I.

Enrich
Invite interested students to research what happened to the League of Nations after the Treaty of Versailles.

4 CLOSE

Have students characterize the American response to the Treaty of Versailles.

SECTION 3 ASSESSMENT

Checking for Understanding
1. **Define:** convoy, armistice, reparations.
2. **Identify:** "no man's land," Vladimir Lenin, Treaty of Brest-Litovsk, Fourteen Points, League of Nations, Treaty of Versailles.
3. **List** the four nations that dominated the Paris peace conference in 1919.

Reviewing Themes
4. **Individual Action** Why did President Wilson propose his Fourteen Points?

Critical Thinking
5. **Analyzing** What impact did John J. Pershing and the Battle of the Argonne Forest have on World War I?
6. **Organizing** Use a graphic organizer to list the results of World War I.

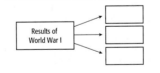

Analyzing Visuals
7. **Analyzing Maps and Charts** Examine the map and graph on page 595. Prepare a quiz with questions based on information from both. Give the quiz to some of your classmates.

Writing About History
8. **Descriptive Writing** Imagine that you are an American soldier fighting in Europe during World War I. Write a letter home describing your situation and how you feel about fighting there.

CHAPTER 19 World War I and Its Aftermath **597**

SECTION 3 ASSESSMENT ANSWERS

1. Terms are in blue.
2. "no man's land" *(p. 593)*, Vladimir Lenin *(p. 595)*, Treaty of Brest-Litovsk *(p. 595)*, Fourteen Points *(p. 596)*, League of Nations *(p. 596)*, Treaty of Versailles *(p. 596)*
3. Italy, Britain, France, United States
4. He wanted to provide justice for all peoples and nationalities.
5. It shattered German defenses and opened a hole in the German line.
6. League of Nations, dissolution of four empires, nine new European countries, Germany pays reparations
7. Instruct students to provide answers for all questions posed.
8. Letters should focus on the soldier's reaction to his situation.

TEACH

Analyzing Information Point out that reading and understanding can be enhanced by students' ability to analyze information and place it in context with other knowledge they already possess.

To help students learn the process, ask them to analyze the information in a short newspaper or magazine article on a topic of personal interest. Suggest that they choose a topic that is not related to their schoolwork. Instruct them to follow the steps outlined on page 598.

Additional Practice

Reinforcing Skills Activity 19

Name _____ Date _____ Class _____

★ **Reinforcing Skills Activity 19**

Analyzing Information

☐ LEARNING THE SKILL

Before you can make a decision or form an opinion about a subject, you must analyze information about it. As you read about a subject, first identify the topic. Next, identify the main points made by the author and summarize the information in your own words. Use this information plus your previous knowledge about the topic to form your own statement on the topic.

☐ PRACTICING THE SKILL

DIRECTIONS: Read the excerpt below from A. Mitchell Palmer's "The Case Against the Reds." Then answer the questions that follow on a separate sheet of paper.

GLENCOE
TECHNOLOGY

CD-ROM
Glencoe Skillbuilder Interactive Workbook CD-ROM, Level 2

This interactive CD-ROM reinforces student mastery of essential social studies skills.

Analyzing Information

Why Learn This Skill?

The ability to analyze information is important in deciding your position on a subject. For example, you need to analyze a political decision to determine if you should support it. You would also analyze a candidate's position statements to determine if you should vote for him or her.

Learning the Skill

To analyze information, use the following steps:

• Identify the topic that is being discussed.

• Examine how the information is organized. What are the main points?

• Summarize the information in your own words, and then make a statement of your own based on your understanding of the topic and on what you already know.

Practicing the Skill

Read the following information taken from Henry Cabot Lodge's *On the League of Nations* speech. Use the steps listed above to analyze the information and answer the questions that follow.

I am as anxious as any human being can be to have the United States render every possible service to the civilization and the peace of mankind. But I am certain that we can do it best by not putting ourselves in leading strings, or subjecting our policies and our sovereignty to other nations. The independence of the United States is not only more precious to ourselves, but to the world, than any single possession.

I will go as far as anyone in world service that the first step to world service is the maintenance of the United States. You may call me selfish if you will, conservative or reactionary, or use any other harsh adjective you see fit to apply. But an American I was born, an

American I've remained all my life. I can never be anything else but an American, and I must think of the United States first. And when I think of the United States first in an argument like this, I am thinking of what is best for the world. For if the United States fails, the best hope of mankind fails with it. I have never had but one allegiance; I cannot divide it now. I have loved but one flag and I cannot share that devotion and give affection to the mongrel banner invented for a league. Internationalism, illustrated by the Bolshevik and by the men to whom all countries are alike, provided they can make money out of them, is to me repulsive. National I must remain and in that way I, like all Americans, can render the amplest service to the world.

The United States is the world's best hope, but if you fetter her in the interest through quarrels of other nations, if you tangle her in the intrigues of Europe, you will destroy her powerful good, and endanger her very existence.

❶ What topic is being discussed?

❷ What are the main points of this excerpt from Senator Lodge's speech?

❸ Summarize the information in this excerpt, and then provide your analysis based on this information and what you know from the rest of the chapter.

Skills Assessment

Complete the Practicing Skills questions on page 605 and the Chapter 19 Skill Reinforcement Activity to assess your mastery of this skill.

Applying the Skill

Analyzing Information Find a short, informative piece of news, such as a political candidate's position paper, an editorial in a newspaper, or an explanation of a new law that will be enacted soon. Analyze the information and make a statement of your own.

GO TO Glencoe's **Skillbuilder Interactive Workbook CD-ROM, Level 2,** provides instruction and practice in key social studies skills.

ANSWERS TO PRACTICING THE SKILL

❶ League of Nations

❷ Independence of the United States is precious to us and to the world; he cannot share his devotion to the United States with the League of Nations; getting involved in the intrigues of Europe will endanger the existence of the United States.

❸ Students' answers will vary but should demonstrate an understanding of the material in the chapter.

Applying the Skill

Students should show that they used the three-step process to analyze the information.

Guide to Reading

Main Idea

As American society moved from war to peace, turmoil in the economy and fear of communism caused a series of domestic upheavals.

Key Terms and Names

cost of living, general strike, Red Scare, A. Mitchell Palmer, J. Edgar Hoover, deport

Reading Strategy

Organizing As you read about the war's aftermath, complete a graphic organizer similar to the one below to list the effects of the end of World War I on the American economy.

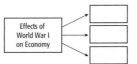

Effects of World War I on Economy →

Reading Objectives:

• **Describe** the effects of the postwar recession on the United States.
• **Discuss** the causes of and reaction to the Red Scare.

Section Theme

Continuity and Change The postwar period proved a difficult readjustment period for the United States, in part because of economic turmoil and the fear of communism.

Preview of Events

♦1917   ♦1918   ♦1919   ♦1920

1917
Riots erupt in East St. Louis, Illinois

1918
House approves Nineteenth Amendment giving women the right to vote

1919
Race riots and strikes erupt in numerous northern cities

1920
Red Scare and Palmer raids

1 FOCUS

Section Overview

This section focuses on the impact World War I had on America when the war was over.

BELLRINGER
Skillbuilder Activity

Project transparency and have students answer the question.

Available as a blackline master.

Daily Focus Skills Transparency 19–4

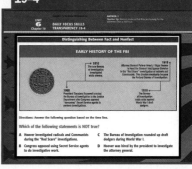

★ An American Story ★

On August 20, 1919, Mary Harris Jones, also known as "Mother" Jones, was thrown in jail in Homestead, Pennsylvania. The 89-year-old had just finished delivering a fiery, impassioned speech in an attempt to gain support for steel unions. Referring to the owners of the big steel companies, she said:

❝Our Kaisers sit up and smoke seventy-five cent cigars and have lackeys with knee pants bring them champagne while you starve, while you grow old at forty, stoking their furnaces. You pull in your belts while they banquet. They have stomachs two miles long and two miles wide and you fill them. . . . If Gary [chair of U.S. Steel] wants to work twelve hours a day, let him go in the blooming mill and work. What we want is a little leisure, time for music, playgrounds, a decent home, books, and the things that make life worthwhile.❞

—**quoted in** *Labor in Crisis*

"Mother" Jones

An Economy in Turmoil

The end of World War I brought great upheaval to American society. When the war ended, government agencies removed their controls from the American economy. This released pent-up demand in the economy. People raced to buy goods that had been rationed, while businesses rapidly raised prices they had been forced to keep low during the war. The result was rapid inflation. Through most of 1919 and 1920, prices rose at an average of more than 15 percent per year. Inflation greatly increased the cost of living— the cost of food, clothing, shelter, and other essentials that people need to survive.

CHAPTER 19   World War I and Its Aftermath   **599**

Guide to Reading

Answers to Graphic: rapid inflation, mass demand for goods, strikes

Preteaching Vocabulary
Have students scan the section and write a sentence using each of the Key Terms and Names in context.

SECTION RESOURCES

📂 Reproducible Masters
• Reproducible Lesson Plan 19–4
• Daily Lecture and Discussion Notes 19–4
• Guided Reading Activity 19–4
• Section Quiz 19–4
• Reading Essentials and Study Guide 19–4

📷 Transparencies
• Daily Focus Skills Transparency 19–4

• American Art & Architecture

Multimedia
🖰 Interactive Tutor Self-Assessment CD-ROM
🖰 ExamView® Pro Testmaker CD-ROM
🖰 Presentation Plus! CD-ROM
🖰 TeacherWorks™ CD-ROM
🎧 Audio Program

2 TEACH

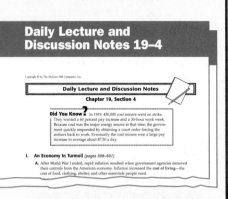

NATIONAL GEOGRAPHIC MOMENT in HISTORY

Historians believe that the bands that accompanied African American regiments introduced jazz and ragtime to Europeans.

Creating an Outline Have students use the headings in this section to create a sentence outline as a guide to reading the section. **L1** **ELL**

FYI

As fresh memories of the war, economic problems, labor unrest, and racial tension combined to create a sense of disillusionment, scandal marred a symbol of American life. In 1919 eight members of the Chicago White Sox were accused of taking mob money to lose the World Series to the Cincinnati Reds. The players, dubbed the Black Sox, were acquitted in court but were banned from professional baseball for life.

Inflation Leads to Strikes Many companies had been forced to raise wages during the war, but inflation now threatened to wipe out all the gains workers had made. While workers wanted higher wages to keep up with inflation, companies wanted to hold down wages because inflation was also driving up their operating costs.

During the war, the number of workers in unions had increased dramatically. By the time the war ended, workers were better organized and much more capable of organizing strikes than they had been before. Many business leaders, on the other hand, were determined to break the power of the unions and roll back the gains labor had made. These circumstances led to an enormous wave of strikes in 1919. By the end of the year, more than 3,600 strikes involving more than 4 million workers had taken place.

The Seattle General Strike The first major strike took place in Seattle, when some 35,000 shipyard workers walked off the job demanding higher wages and shorter hours. Soon other unions in Seattle joined the shipyard workers and organized a general strike. A general strike is a strike that involves all workers living in a certain location, not just workers in a particular industry. The Seattle general strike involved more than 60,000 people and paralyzed the city for five days. Although the strikers returned to work without making any gains, their actions worried many Americans because the general strike was a common tactic used in Europe by Communists and other radical groups.

The Boston Police Strike Perhaps the most famous strike of 1919 took place in Boston, when roughly 75 percent of the police force walked off the job. Riots and looting soon erupted in the city, forcing the governor of Massachusetts, **Calvin Coolidge,** to send in the National Guard. When the strikers tried to return to work, the police commissioner refused to accept them. He fired the strikers and hired a new police force instead.

Despite protests, Coolidge agreed the men should be fired. He declared, "There is no right to strike

NATIONAL GEOGRAPHIC MOMENT in HISTORY

HERO'S HOMECOMING
A wounded soldier of the 369th Regiment, the Harlem "Hell-Fighters," accepts congratulations during a victory parade through New York City in 1919. Facing discrimination within their own army, African American soldiers at the front received a warm reception from their French allies. "I have never before experienced what it meant really to be free, to taste real liberty," one soldier wrote home, "in a phrase, 'to be a man.'" Two African American infantry divisions suffered some 6,000 casualties, but at war's end, they still came home to a segregated American society.

600 CHAPTER 19 World War I and Its Aftermath

COOPERATIVE LEARNING ACTIVITY

Creating an Inflation Chart Organize students into groups of four. Tell the groups to find the prices of at least three goods in 1918. See the price list on page 591 for a starting point. Have students assume that inflation was 5 percent in 1918 and 15 percent during 1919 and 1920. Have students calculate and chart the prices of the goods at the end of each of those years. Then have students calculate and chart the prices of those same goods if inflation was 20 percent per year. Use the charts as a basis for a class discussion on inflation.

Use the rubric for a cooperative group management plan on pages 81–82 in the *Performance Assessment Activities and Rubrics.*

Effects of World War I on the United States

Developments in the War
- War-torn economies of Europe
- Russian Revolution
- Industrial demand of wartime
- Sacrifices of wartime; disappointment with Versailles Peace Treaty

Effects on U.S.
- Boom in U.S. economy; emergence of U.S. as world industrial leader
- "Red Scare" in postwar U.S.; suspicion of immigrants
- Internal migration in U.S., especially African American migration to Northern cities
- Failure to join League of Nations

Graphic Organizer → Skills

World War I had profound effects on the United States.

Interpreting Why did the destruction of European economies cause an industrial boom in the United States?

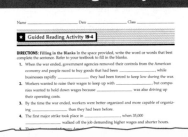

Guided Reading Activity 19–4

Name _____ Date _____ Class _____

★ Guided Reading Activity 19-4

DIRECTIONS: Filling in the Blanks In the space provided, write the word or words that best complete the sentence. Refer to your textbook to fill in the blanks.

1. When the war ended, government agencies removed their controls from the American economy and people raced to buy goods that had been _____, while businesses rapidly _____ they had been forced to keep low during the war.
2. Workers wanted to raise their wages to keep up with _____, but companies wanted to hold down wages because _____ was also driving up their operating costs.
3. By the time the war ended, workers were better organized and more capable of organizing _____ than they had been before.
4. The first major strike took place in _____, when 35,000 _____ walked off the job demanding higher wages and shorter hours.

---

against the public safety by anybody, anywhere, anytime." Coolidge's response brought him to national attention and earned him widespread public support. It also convinced the Republicans to make Coolidge their vice presidential candidate in the 1920 election.

The Steel Strike Shortly after the police strike ended, one of the largest strikes in American history began when an estimated 350,000 steelworkers went on strike for higher pay, shorter hours, and recognition of their union. **Elbert H. Gary,** the head of U.S. Steel, refused even to talk to union leaders. Instead, the company set out to break the union by using anti-immigrant feelings to divide the workers.

Many steelworkers were immigrants. The company blamed the strike on foreign radicals and called for loyal Americans to return to work. Meanwhile, the company hired African Americans and Mexicans as replacement workers and managed to keep its steel mills operating despite the strike. Clashes between company guards and strikers were frequent, and in Gary, Indiana, a riot left 18 strikers dead. In early January, the strike collapsed. The failure of the strike set back the union cause in the steel industry. Steelworkers remained unorganized until 1937.

✓Reading Check **Explaining** What caused the wave of strikes in 1919?

Racial Unrest

Adding to the nation's economic turmoil was the return of hundreds of thousands of American soldiers from Europe who needed to find employment.

Many African Americans who had moved north during the war were also competing for jobs and housing. Frustration and racism combined to produce violence. In the summer of 1919, race riots broke out in over 20 northern cities.

The worst violence occurred in Chicago. An African American teenager swimming in Lake Michigan on a hot July day happened to drift toward a beach restricted to whites. Whites on shore allegedly stoned him unconscious, and he drowned. Angry African Americans almost immediately marched into white neighborhoods to retaliate, while white mobs roamed African American neighborhoods attacking people and destroying property. For almost two weeks, Chicago was virtually at war. In the end, 38 people died—15 white and 23 black—and over 500 were injured.

✓Reading Check **Analyzing** Why did the end of the war lead to race riots?

The Red Scare

The wave of strikes in 1919 helped to fuel fears that Communists were conspiring to start a revolution in the United States. Americans had been stunned when Lenin and the Bolsheviks seized power and withdrew Russia from the war. Americans had become very anti-German as the war progressed, and when the Communists withdrew Russia from the war, they seemed to be helping Germany. American anger at Germany quickly expanded into anger at Communists as well. Americans began to associate communism with being unpatriotic and disloyal.

CHAPTER 19 World War I and Its Aftermath **601**

Graphic Organizer → Skills

Answer: American industry was undamaged by the war and was needed to help rebuild Europe.

Graphic Organizer Skills Practice Ask: What development during the war most contributed to the Red Scare? *(Russian Revolution)*

✓Reading Check

Answer: Business attempted to break the wartime gains of unions and roll back wages.

Organizing Information Have students use a graphic with columns labeled Who, Where, When, How Many, and Results to compare the three major strikes mentioned in this section. **L2**

✓Reading Check

Answer: Returning soldiers and African Americans competed for jobs.

📁 Use *Interpreting Political Cartoons,* Cartoon 20.

MEETING SPECIAL NEEDS

Visual/Spatial This activity helps to address the particular needs of visual learners. As students read this section, lead them through the photographs, charts, and other graphics as a way of informally telling the story of the section. Have students use the time lines to summarize events and to discuss absolute and relative chronology of events. Encourage students to add important dates to create a master time line in the classroom. **L1** ELL

📁 Refer to *Inclusion for the High School Social Studies Classroom Strategies and Activities* in the TCR.

Picturing History

Answer: J. Edgar Hoover

Ask: Into what federal agency did the Justice Department's General Intelligence Division evolve? *(Federal Bureau of Investigation—FBI)*

History *and the* Humanities

American Art & Architecture: *Allies Day*

FYI

During the Red Scare, many Americans believed that people who promoted radical causes should be treated without regard for their rights. Others, such as journalist William Allen White, argued that the arrests and deportation of alleged Communists gave radical causes more publicity than they deserved.

3 ASSESS

Assign Section 4 Assessment as homework or as an in-class activity.

🌐 Have students use the **Interactive Tutor Self-Assessment CD-ROM.**

Reading Essentials and Study Guide 19–4

Picturing History

Terror in the Streets After the House of Morgan–a bank in New York City–was damaged by a bomb in 1920, Attorney General A. Mitchell Palmer instituted raids on antigovernment activists and many immigrants, often violating their civil liberties in the process. Whom did Palmer appoint to coordinate these investigations?

Americans had long been suspicious of Communist ideas. Throughout the late 1800s, many Americans had accused immigrants of importing radical socialist and Communist ideas into the United States and blamed them for labor unrest and violence. Now Communists had seized control of an entire nation, and fears surged that they would try to incite revolutions elsewhere. These fears seemed to be confirmed in 1919, when the Soviet Union formed the **Communist International**—an organization for coordinating the activities of Communist parties in other countries.

The Red Scare Begins As strikes erupted across the United States in 1919, the fear that Communists, or "reds," as they were called, might seize power led to a nationwide panic known as the **Red Scare.** Seattle's mayor, Ole Hanson, spoke for others when he condemned the leaders of the Seattle general strike as revolutionaries who wanted to "take possession of our American government and try to duplicate the anarchy of Russia."

In April the postal service intercepted more than 30 parcels addressed to leading businesspeople and politicians that were triggered to explode when opened. In June eight bombs in eight cities exploded within minutes of one another, suggesting a nationwide conspiracy. One of them damaged the home of United States Attorney General **A. Mitchell Palmer** in Washington, D.C. Most people believed the bombings were the work of Communists or other revolutionaries trying to destroy the American way of life.

The Palmer Raids Declaring that a "blaze of revolution" was "burning up the foundations of society," Palmer took action. He established a special division within the Justice Department, the General Intelligence Division, headed by **J. Edgar Hoover.** This division eventually became the Federal Bureau of Investigation (FBI). From late 1919 to the spring of 1920, Palmer organized a series of raids on the headquarters of various radical organizations. Although evidence pointed to no single group as the bombers, Palmer's agents focused on foreign residents and immigrants. The authorities detained thousands of suspects and **deported,** or expelled from the country, nearly 600 of them.

602 CHAPTER 19 World War I and Its Aftermath

INTERDISCIPLINARY CONNECTIONS ACTIVITY

Music Have students work in small groups to write a song describing the turmoil of the early 1900s. Ask each group to choose an existing melody, or write their own, and then write lyrics that relate to one of these topics: fear of radicalism, racial unrest, or labor unrest. Encourage students to use the names of people, places, and events mentioned in this section. Invite students to perform their songs for the class. **L2**

Palmer's agents often disregarded the civil liberties of the suspects. Officers entered homes and offices without search warrants. People were mistreated and jailed for indefinite periods of time and were not allowed to talk to their attorneys.

For a while, Palmer was regarded as a national hero. His raids, however, failed to turn up any hard evidence of revolutionary conspiracy. When his dire prediction that violence would rock the nation on May Day 1920—a popular European celebration of workers—proved wrong, Palmer lost much of his credibility and soon faded from prominence.

The Red Scare greatly influenced people's attitudes during the 1920s. Americans often linked radicalism with immigrants, and that attitude led to a call for Congress to limit immigration.

✓ **Reading Check** **Examining** After World War I, why were Americans suspicious of some union leaders?

An End to Progressivism

Economic problems, labor unrest, and racial tensions, as well as the fresh memories of World War I, all combined to create a general sense of disillusionment in the United States. By 1920 Americans wanted an end to the upheaval. During the 1920 campaign, Ohio Governor James M. Cox and his running mate, Assistant Secretary of the Navy Franklin D. Roosevelt, ran on a platform of keeping alive Woodrow Wilson's progressive ideals. The Republican candidate, Warren G. Harding, called for a return to "normalcy." He urged that what the United States needed was a return to the simpler days before the Progressive Era reforms:

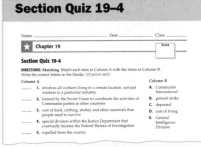

A. Mitchell Palmer and J. Edgar Hoover

❝[Our] present need is not heroics, but healing; not nostrums, but normalcy; not revolution, but restoration; not agitation, but adjustment; not surgery, but serenity; not the dramatic, but the dispassionate; . . . not submergence in internationality, but sustainment in triumphant nationality.❞

—quoted in *Portrait of a Nation*

Harding's sentiments struck a chord with voters, and he won the election by a landslide margin of over 7 million votes. Americans were weary of more crusades to reform society and the world. They hoped to put the country's racial and labor unrest and economic troubles behind them and build a more prosperous and stable society.

✓ **Reading Check** **Explaining** How was Harding able to win the presidential election of 1920?

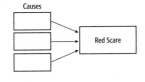
CHAPTER 19 World War I and Its Aftermath **603**

CHAPTER 19
Section 4, 599–603

Section Quiz 19–4

[Section Quiz 19-4 form]

Name ___ Date ___ Class ___

★ Chapter 19   Score ___

Section Quiz 19–4

DIRECTIONS: Matching Match each item in Column A with the items in Column B. Write the correct letters in the blanks. *(10 points each)*

Column A

___ 1. involves all workers living in a certain location, not just workers in a particular industry

___ 2. formed by the Soviet Union to coordinate the activities of Communist parties in other countries

___ 3. cost of food, clothing, shelter, and other essentials that people need to survive

___ 4. special division within the Justice Department that eventually became the Federal Bureau of Investigation

___ 5. expelled from the country

Column B

A. Communist International
B. general strike
C. deported
D. cost of living
E. General Intelligence Division

✓ **Reading Check**

Answer: They blamed union leaders for causing social unrest through strikes.

Reteach

Have students describe the effects of the postwar recession on the United States.

Enrich

Invite interested students to research one of the persons mentioned in this chapter and prepare a short biographical profile. Encourage students to use library and Internet resources for their research.

✓ **Reading Check**

Answer: by campaigning for a return to a simpler time before racial and labor unrest and economic troubles

4 CLOSE

Have students create a graphic organizer showing the causes of and the reactions to the Red Scare.

CHAPTER
19 ASSESSMENT and ACTIVITIES

GLENCOE
TECHNOLOGY

MindJogger Videoquiz
Use the **MindJogger Videoquiz** to review Chapter 19 content.

Available in VHS

Reviewing Key Terms
Students' answers will vary. The pages where the words appear in the text are shown in parentheses.

1. **guerrilla** (p. 577)
2. **nationalism** (p. 578)
3. **self-determination** (p. 578)
4. **propaganda** (p. 581)
5. **contraband** (p. 581)
6. **U-boat** (p. 581)
7. **conscription** (p. 585)
8. **victory garden** (p. 586)
9. **espionage** (p. 588)
10. **convoy** (p. 594)
11. **armistice** (p. 596)
12. **reparations** (p. 596)
13. **cost of living** (p. 599)
14. **general strike** (p. 600)
15. **deport** (p. 600)

Reviewing Key Facts
16. Pancho Villa (p. 577), Franz Ferdinand (p. 578), Zimmermann telegram (p. 582), Bernard Baruch (p. 586), Committee on Public Information (p. 588), "no man's land" (p. 593), Vladimir Lenin (p. 595), Fourteen Points (p. 596), League of Nations (p. 596), A. Mitchell Palmer (p. 602), J. Edgar Hoover (p. 602)

17. the alliance system, the naval buildup, nationalism in the Balkans, and the assassination of Archduke Franz Ferdinand

18. Women filled noncombat positions such as nurses, clerical help, and other jobs vacated by men who had become soldiers.

Reviewing Key Terms
On a sheet of paper, use each of these terms in a sentence.

1. guerrilla
2. nationalism
3. self-determination
4. propaganda
5. contraband
6. U-boat
7. conscription
8. victory garden
9. espionage
10. convoy
11. armistice
12. reparations
13. cost of living
14. general strike
15. deport

Reviewing Key Facts
16. **Identify:** Pancho Villa, Franz Ferdinand, Zimmermann telegram, Bernard Baruch, Committee on Public Information, "no man's land," Vladimir Lenin, Fourteen Points, League of Nations, A. Mitchell Palmer, J. Edgar Hoover.

17. What factors contributed to the start of World War I in Europe?

18. What role did American women play in the war effort during World War I?

19. What did the American government do to solve the problem of supplying its troops?

20. What were the provisions of the Treaty of Versailles?

21. What were the Palmer raids?

Critical Thinking

22. **Analyzing Themes: Government and Democracy** Do you think government action to suppress opposition to World War I was justified? Why or why not?

23. **Interpreting Primary Sources** On September 12, 1918, Socialist leader Eugene V. Debs was convicted of violating the Espionage Act. Debs later spoke to the court at his sentencing. Read his speech and answer the questions that follow.

❝I look upon the Espionage laws as a despotic enactment in flagrant conflict with democratic principles and with the spirit of free institutions. . . . I am opposed to the social system in which we live. . . . I believe in fundamental change, but if possible by peaceful and orderly means. . . .

I am thinking this morning of the men in the mills and factories, . . . of the women who for a paltry wage

Chapter Summary

Mobilizing for War

Armed Forces
- Congress passed Selective Service Act which required young men ages 21–30 to register for the draft
- Employed women in noncombat roles

Domestic Front
- War Industries Board controlled war materials and production
- Committee on Public Information created war propaganda
- Government worked with employers and labor to ensure production
- Congress passed Espionage and Sedition Acts to limit opposition to the war
- Congress increased taxes and sold Liberty Bonds to pay for war

Postwar Problems
- Cost of living greatly increased
- Economic problems led to racial violence and widespread strikes
- Fear of communism led to Red Scare and Palmer raids

19. A draft was initiated to alleviate the shortage of troops; convoys ensured they—and supplies—could get to Europe safely.

20. Germany was stripped of its armed forces, forced to accept guilt for the war, and made to pay reparations to the Allies.

21. raids of various radical organizations to round up suspects to deport or imprison

Critical Thinking
22. A possible positive answer is that it protected American people from Communist propaganda. A possible negative answer is that it violated civil rights and liberties.

23. **a.** Problems: low wages, child labor, love of money; change should be peaceful and orderly **b.** He calls it despotic and states that it violates the principles of democracy. Students' responses should consider the need to balance liberty and safety.

are compelled to work out their barren lives; of the little children who in this system are robbed of their childhood and . . . forced into industrial dungeons. . . . In this high noon of our twentieth century Christian civilization, money is still so much more important than the flesh and blood of childhood. In very truth, gold is god. . . . 99

—quoted in *Echoes of Distant Thunder*

a. According to Debs, what were some problems in American society at this time? How did he believe change should be brought about?

b. How did Debs seem to feel about the Espionage Act? Do you agree with him? Why or why not?

24. Organizing Use a table like the one below to list the significant events of each year from 1914 to 1918.

Year	Event	Significance
1914		
1915		
1916		
1917		
1918		

Practicing Skills

25. Analyzing Information Read the subsections titled "The Treaty of Versailles" and "The U.S. Senate Rejects the Treaty" on pages 596 and 597. Using the information on these pages, write an analysis of the effects of the treaty in the form that it was finally accepted.

Geography and History

26. The map on this page shows the geographical changes in Europe after World War I. Study the map and answer the questions below.

a. Interpreting Maps After World War I, what new countries were formed using territory that had belonged to Austria-Hungary?

b. Applying Geography Skills What countries acquired territory from the former Russian Empire?

Writing Activity

27. Persuasive Writing Take on the role of a newspaper editor in 1919. Write an editorial favoring or opposing ratification of the Treaty of Versailles.

NATIONAL GEOGRAPHIC **Europe After World War I, 1920**

Chapter Activity

28. Research Project Both the British and the American governments used propaganda to garner support for the war. Use the library and other resources to find examples of these propaganda techniques. Compile your research in an illustrated and captioned poster, and display it in the classroom.

The Princeton Review
Standardized Test Practice

Directions: Choose the best answer to the following question.

Which of the following was one of the primary causes of World War I?

F A complex set of alliances among European nations

G The exile of Mexican General Victoriano Huerta

H The dissatisfaction of Russian peasants

J The breakup of the Austro-Hungarian Empire

Test-Taking Tip: Eliminate answers you know are incorrect. For example, the breakup of Austria-Hungary took place after World War I, so you can eliminate that answer. Similarly, the exile of Huerta occurred in Mexico, which had little effect on European nations. You also can eliminate that answer.

Chapter Activity

28. Posters should reflect the types of propaganda used during World War I.

The Princeton Review
Standardized Test Practice

Answer: F

Test-Taking Tip: After students have eliminated one or two of the answers, they can concentrate on what they know about the remaining possibilities. For example, students might know that one of the results of World War I was the breakup of several empires. This makes J less likely to be the correct answer. F is the correct answer.

Bonus Question ?

Ask: What was the name of the Austrian archduke whose assassination started World War I? (*Franz Ferdinand*)

---

24. 1914: beginning of World War I; 1915: *Lusitania* sunk, Americans side with British; 1916: fighting in trenches worsens; 1917: United States commits resources and soldiers to help Allies; 1918: Americans break through German lines leading to Germany's defeat

Practicing Skills

25. Students should use the skills they learned in the Skillbuilder Activity to analyze the treaty.

Geography and History

26. a. Czechoslovakia, Austria, Hungary, Romania, and parts of Yugoslavia, Italy, and Poland; **b.** Poland, Lithuania, Latvia, Estonia, Finland, and part of Romania

Writing Activity

27. Editorials will vary. Students should clearly express an opinion about ratification of the treaty.

Unit 7 Resources

SUGGESTED PACING CHART

Unit 7 (1 Day)	Chapter 20 (4 Days)	Chapter 21 (4 Days)	Chapter 22 (4 Days)	Chapter 23 (5 Days)	Unit 7 (2 Days)
Day 1 Introduction	Day 1 Chapter 20 Intro, Section 1	Day 1 Chapter 21 Intro, Section 1	Day 1 Chapter 22 Intro, Section 1	Day 1 Chapter 23 Intro, Section 1	Day 1 Wrap-Up/Project
	Day 2 Section 2	Day 2 Section 2	Day 2 Section 2	Day 2 Section 2	Day 2 Unit 7 Assessment
	Day 3 Section 3	Day 3 Section 3	Day 3 Section 3	Day 3 Section 3	
	Day 4 Chapter 20 Assessment	Day 4 Chapter 21 Assessment	Day 4 Chapter 22 Assessment	Day 4 Section 4	
				Day 5 Chapter 23 Assessment	

GLENCOE'S ASSESSMENT ADVANTAGE

Use the following tools to easily assess student learning in a variety of ways:

- Performance Assessment Activities and Rubrics
- Chapter and Unit Tests
- Section Quizzes
- Standardized Test Skills Practice Workbook

- tav.glencoe.com
- Interactive Tutor Self-Assessment CD-ROM
- MindJogger Videoquiz
- ExamView® Pro Testmaker CD-ROM
- SAT I/II Test Practice

TEACHING TRANSPARENCIES

Unit 7 Map Overlay Transparencies

Cause-and-Effect Transparency 7

*inter*NET RESOURCES

- tav.glencoe.com

The American Vision

Visit the *American Vision* Web site for history overviews, activities, assessments, and updated charts and graphs.

- www.socialstudies.glencoe.com

Glencoe Social Studies

Visit the Glencoe Web site for social studies activities, updates, and links to other sites.

- www.teachingtoday.glencoe.com

Glencoe Teaching Today

Visit the new Glencoe Web site for teacher development information, teaching tips, Web resources, and educational news.

- www.time.com

TIME Online

Visit the TIME Web site for up-to-date news and special reports.

Unit 7 Resources

ASSESSMENT

Unit 7 Pretests

Unit 7 Posttests

APPLICATION AND ENRICHMENT

American Biography 7

History Simulation and Problem Solving 7

GEOGRAPHY

Geography and History Activity 7

INTERDISCIPLINARY ACTIVITIES

American Literature Reading 7

Economics and History Activity 7

Team-Teaching Interdisciplinary Strategies and Activities 7

BIBLIOGRAPHY

Readings for the Student

Terkel, Studs. *Hard Times: An Oral History of the Great Depression.* New Press, 2000.

Readings for the Teacher

Clements, Kendrick A. *Hoover, Conservation, and Consumerism: Engineering the Good Life.* University Press of Kansas, 2000.

Multimedia Resources

Videocassette. *Brother, Can You Spare a Dime?* History in Action. Films for the Humanities. (20 minutes)

Additional Glencoe Resources for This Unit:

- Glencoe Skillbuilder Interactive Workbook CD-ROM, Level 2
- Social Studies Guide to Using the Internet
- Writer's Guidebook for High School
- Living Constitution
- American Art Prints Strategies and Activities

0:00 Out of Time?

If time does not permit teaching each chapter in this unit, you may want to use the **Reading Essentials and Study Guide** summaries.

Unit Overview

Unit 7 describes the Boom and Bust cycles the United States experienced from 1920 to 1941. **Chapter 20** explores the jazz age and the African American cultural renaissance. **Chapter 21** focuses on the good times of the 1920s. **Chapter 22** discusses the beginning years of the Great Depression. **Chapter 23** focuses on Roosevelt and the New Deal.

Unit Objectives

After studying this unit, students will be able to:

1. Describe the clash of values in the 1920s and the changing status of women.
2. Analyze how the growing importance of the automobile and other new industries improved the U.S. standard of living.
3. Identify the causes of the Great Depression.
4. Explain the worsening situation in the U.S. banking system in the early 1930s.

Why It Matters Activity

Tell students that the economic problems that triggered the Great Depression brought a new awareness of economic cycles. Have students bring in an article to share with the class about the current state of the economy. Ask students how important they think economic news is to their daily lives.

UNIT
7 Boom and Bust *1920–1941*

Why It Matters

After World War I, the United States enjoyed a time of prosperity and confidence. The decade of the 1920s saw rising stock prices and increased consumer spending. It also witnessed cultural innovations such as jazz music and motion pictures. At the end of the 1920s, however, several economic problems combined to trigger the Great Depression that began in 1929. Understanding the events of these decades will help you understand American society today. The following resources offer more information about this period in American history.

Primary Sources Library

See pages 1054–1055 for primary source readings to accompany Unit 7.

*Use the **American History Primary Source Document Library CD-ROM** to find additional primary sources about the Roaring Twenties and the Great Depression.*

Hatbox depicting a New York street scene

Sixth Avenue Elevated at Third St. by John Sloan, 1928

606

TEAM TEACHING ACTIVITY

Art Have the art teacher explain the Art Deco style and show classic examples of the style. Then have students research your local community for examples of Art Deco architecture, art, and design. If possible, have students take photos of the examples to present to the class. Have students explain why the samples they have shown illustrate this art style.

> "I have no fears for the future of our country. It is bright with hope."
>
> —Herbert Hoover, 1929

GLENCOE
TECHNOLOGY

 CD-ROM
American History Primary Source Document Library CD-ROM

Use the **American History Primary Source Document Library CD-ROM** to access primary source documents related to this period in history.

More About the Art

Flappers such as these are iconic depictions of the 1920s. Despite the carefree attitude many had during that decadent decade, the Great Depression soon followed, bringing with it hardship. Have students discuss why they think the 1920s was a decade of great cultural change.

Glencoe Literature Library

The following novel from the *High School American History Literature Library* may be used to enrich the study of this unit:
* *Picture Bride* by Yoshiko Uchida

SERVICE-LEARNING PROJECT

Tell students that no matter what the country's economic circumstances there are always people who do not have adequate food, clothing, or shelter. Have students learn about the needs of a local food or clothing pantry. After learning about the pantry's needs, have students plan a food or clothing drive for the benefit of the pantry.

Refer to ***Building Bridges: Connecting Classroom and Community through Service-Learning in Social Studies*** from the National Council for the Social Studies for information about service-learning.

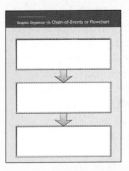
TeacherWorks™ All-In-One Planner and Resource Center

- **Interactive Teacher Edition** Access your Teacher Wraparound Edition and your classroom resources with a few easy clicks.

- **Interactive Lesson Planner** Planning has never been easier! Organize your week, month, semester, or year with all the lesson helps you need to make teaching creative, timely, and relevant.

Use Glencoe's **Presentation Plus!** multimedia teacher tool to easily present dynamic lessons that visually excite your students. Using Microsoft PowerPoint® you can customize the presentations to create your own personalized lessons.

TEACHING TRANSPARENCIES

Graphic Organizer 15

Why It Matters Chapter Transparency 20

APPLICATION AND ENRICHMENT

Linking Past and Present Activity 20

Enrichment Activity 20

Primary Source Reading 20

REVIEW AND REINFORCEMENT

Reteaching Activity 20

Vocabulary Activity 20

Time Line Activity 20

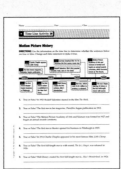

Critical Thinking Skills Activity 20

Meeting NCSS Standards

Local Standards

The following standards are highlighted in Chapter 20:

Section 1   II   Time, Continuity, and Change: B, C, E, F

Section 2   I   Culture: A, C

Section 3   V   Individuals, Groups, and Institutions: B, C, E, F

Chapter 20 Resources

GLENCOE'S
ASSESSMENT
ADVANTAGE

**Chapter 20 Test
Form A**

**Chapter 20 Test
Form B**

**Standardized Test Skills
Practice Workbook Activity 20**

**Performance Assessment
Activities and Rubrics 20**

**ExamView® Pro
Testmaker CD-ROM**

EXAMVIEW® PRO
Testmaker CD-ROM
WINDOWS/MACINTOSH

The American Vision

- QuickTest Wizard does all the work for you
- Choose ExamView tests or create your own
- Complete editing capability

MULTIMEDIA

- Vocabulary PuzzleMaker CD-ROM
- Interactive Tutor Self-Assessment CD-ROM
- ExamView® Pro Testmaker CD-ROM
- Audio Program
- American History Primary Source Documents Library CD-ROM
- MindJogger Videoquiz
- Presentation Plus! CD-ROM
- TeacherWorks™ CD-ROM
- Interactive Student Edition CD-ROM
- Glencoe Skillbuilder Interactive Workbook CD-ROM, Level 2
- The *American Vision* Video Program
- American Music: Hits Through History
- American Music: Cultural Traditions

SPANISH RESOURCES

The following Spanish language materials are available in the Spanish Resources Binder:

- Spanish Guided Reading Activities
- Spanish Reteaching Activities
- Spanish Quizzes and Tests
- Spanish Vocabulary Activities
- Spanish Summaries
- The Declaration of Independence and United States Constitution Spanish Translation

A&E HOME VIDEO
Biography
THE HISTORY CHANNEL

The following videotape programs are available from Glencoe as supplements to Chapter 20:

- **Babe Ruth: His Life** (ISBN 1-56-501422-7)
- **The Monkey Trial: In Search of History** (ISBN 0-76-700609-7)
- **The Prohibition Era** (3 pack) (ISBN 0-76-700179-6)

To order, call Glencoe at 1-800-334-7344. To find classroom resources to accompany many of these videos, check the following home pages:
A&E Television: www.aande.com
The History Channel: www.historychannel.com

HISTORY
Online

Use our Web site for additional resources. All essential content is covered in the Student Edition.

You and your students can visit tav.glencoe.com, the Web site companion to the *American Vision.* This innovative integration of electronic and print media offers your students a wealth of opportunities. The student text directs students to the Web site for the following options:

- **Chapter Overviews**
- **Self-Check Quizzes**
- **Student Web Activities**
- **Textbook Updates**

Answers to the student Web activities are provided for you in the **Web Activity Lesson Plans.** Additional Web resources and Interactive Tutor Puzzles are also available.

Chapter 20 Resources

SECTION RESOURCES

Daily Objectives	Reproducible Resources	Multimedia Resources
SECTION 1 **A Clash of Values** 1. Explain the rise in racism and nativism in the 1920s. 2. Describe the clash of values in the 1920s and the changing status of women.	Reproducible Lesson Plan 20–1 Daily Lecture and Discussion Notes 20–1 Guided Reading Activity 20–1* Section Quiz 20–1* Reading Essentials and Study Guide 20–1 Interpreting Political Cartoons Supreme Court Case Studies Performance Assessment Activities and Rubrics	Daily Focus Skills Transparency 20–1 Interactive Tutor Self-Assessment CD-ROM ExamView® Pro Testmaker CD-ROM Presentation Plus! CD-ROM TeacherWorks™ CD-ROM Skillbuilder Interactive Workbook, Level 2 Audio Program
SECTION 2 **Cultural Innovations** 1. Describe the explosion of art and literature and the disillusionment of 1920s artists. 2. Summarize the effects of sports, movies, radio, and music on popular culture.	Reproducible Lesson Plan 20–2 Daily Lecture and Discussion Notes 20–2 Guided Reading Activity 20–2* Section Quiz 20–2* Reading Essentials and Study Guide 20–2 Performance Assessment Activities and Rubrics	Daily Focus Skills Transparency 20–2 American Art & Architecture Interactive Tutor Self-Assessment CD-ROM ExamView® Pro Testmaker CD-ROM Presentation Plus! CD-ROM TeacherWorks™ CD-ROM Audio Program American Music: Hits Through History American Music: Cultural Traditions
SECTION 3 **African American Culture** 1. Describe the Harlem Renaissance and the rediscovery of African American cultural roots. 2. Explain the increase in African American political activism.	Reproducible Lesson Plan 20–3 Daily Lecture and Discussion Notes 20–3 Guided Reading Activity 20–3* Section Quiz 20–3* Reading Essentials and Study Guide 20–3 Performance Assessment Activities and Rubrics	Daily Focus Skills Transparency 20–3 Interactive Tutor Self-Assessment CD-ROM ExamView® Pro Testmaker CD-ROM Presentation Plus! CD-ROM TeacherWorks™ CD-ROM Vocabulary PuzzleMaker CD-ROM Audio Program American Music: Hits Through History American Music: Cultural Traditions

`0:00` OUT OF TIME?
Assign the Chapter 20 **Reading Essentials and Study Guide.**

*Also Available in Spanish

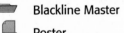 Blackline Master Transparency CD-ROM DVD

Poster Music Program Audio Program  Videocassette

NATIONAL GEOGRAPHIC Teacher's Corner

INDEX TO NATIONAL GEOGRAPHIC MAGAZINE

The following articles relate to this chapter.
- "Growing up in East Harlem," May 1990
- "Offbeat New Orleans," January 1995
- "Traveling the Blues Highway," April 1999

NATIONAL GEOGRAPHIC SOCIETY PRODUCTS AVAILABLE FROM GLENCOE

To order the following products for use with this chapter, contact your local Glencoe sales representative, or call Glencoe at 1-800-334-7344:
- *PictureShow: Story of America, Part 2* (CD-ROM)
- *PicturePack: Story of America Library, Part 2* (Transparencies)

ADDITIONAL NATIONAL GEOGRAPHIC SOCIETY PRODUCTS

To order the following, call National Geographic at 1-800-368-2728:
- *The Complete National Geographic: 109 Years of National Geographic Magazine* (CD-ROM)
- *Eyewitness to the 20th Century* (Book)

NGS ONLINE

Access National Geographic's Web site for current events, atlas updates, activities, links, interactive features, and archives.
www.nationalgeographic.com

From the Classroom of...

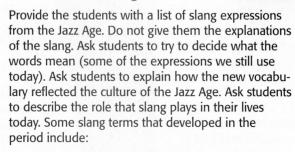

Jennifer G. Lange
Forest Hills High School
Forest Hills, NY

The Culture of Slang

Provide the students with a list of slang expressions from the Jazz Age. Do not give them the explanations of the slang. Ask students to try to decide what the words mean (some of the expressions we still use today). Ask students to explain how the new vocabulary reflected the culture of the Jazz Age. Ask students to describe the role that slang plays in their lives today. Some slang terms that developed in the period include:

- cat's meow (or cat's pajamas)—something fantastic
- crush—an infatuation with someone
- gatecrasher—someone who "crashes" a party
- blind date—dating someone you have never met
- big cheese—the boss
- bump off—murder or kill
- goofy—silly
- gams—a woman's legs
- heebie jeebies—jitters
- high hat—snub
- flapper—the "new woman" of the 1920s
- gyp—cheat
- darb—something truly wonderful
- gin mill—a speakeasy

ADDITIONAL RESOURCES FROM GLENCOE

- American Music: Cultural Traditions
- American Art & Architecture
- Outline Map Resource Book
- U.S. Desk Map
- Building Geography Skills for Life
- Inclusion for the High School Social Studies Classroom Strategies and Activities
- Teaching Strategies for the American History Classroom (Including Block Scheduling Pacing Guides)

KEY TO ABILITY LEVELS

Teaching strategies have been coded.

- **L1** BASIC activities for all students
- **L2** AVERAGE activities for average to above-average students
- **L3** CHALLENGING activities for above-average students
- **ELL** ENGLISH LANGUAGE LEARNER activities

Block Schedule

Activities that are suited to use within the block scheduling framework are identified by:

Why It Matters Activity

Read the title of Section 1 and the main idea statement from the Guide to Reading. Ask students to jot down ideas about why this time in history matters today. Repeat for Sections 2 and 3. Ask students to evaluate and revise their responses after they have completed the chapter. Invite students to share their ideas with the class.

GLENCOE
TECHNOLOGY

The *American Vision* Video Program

To learn more about Harlem's art and music, have students view the Chapter 20 video, "The Harlem Renaissance," from the *American Vision* Video Program.

 Available in DVD and VHS

MindJogger Videoquiz

Use the **MindJogger Videoquiz** to preview Chapter 20 content.

📼 Available in VHS

CHAPTER
20 The Jazz Age
1921–1929

Why It Matters

The 1920s was an era of rapid change and clashing values. Many Americans believed society was losing its traditional values, and they took action to preserve these values. Other Americans embraced new values associated with a freer lifestyle and the pursuit of individual goals. Writers and artists pursued distinctively American themes, and the Harlem Renaissance gave African Americans new pride.

The Impact Today

The 1920s left permanent legacies to American culture.
* *National celebrities in sports and film emerged.*
* *Jazz music became part of American culture.*
* *F. Scott Fitzgerald and Ernest Hemingway wrote classics of American literature.*

 The *American Vision* *Video* *The Chapter 20 video, "The Harlem Renaissance," focuses on Harlem's lively arts and music scene and the movement's contributions to American culture.*

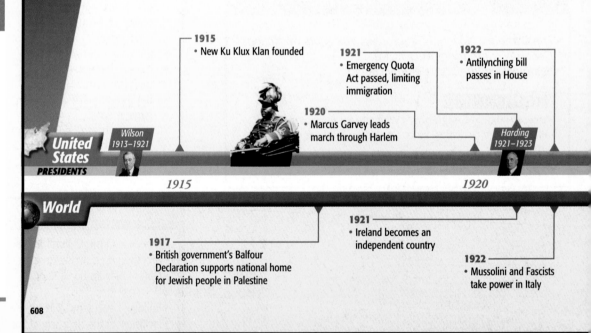

United States PRESIDENTS

1915
* New Ku Klux Klan founded

1920
* Marcus Garvey leads march through Harlem

1921
* Emergency Quota Act passed, limiting immigration

1922
* Antilynching bill passes in House

Wilson 1913–1921

Harding 1921–1923

1915   *1920*

World

1917
* British government's Balfour Declaration supports national home for Jewish people in Palestine

1921
* Ireland becomes an independent country

1922
* Mussolini and Fascists take power in Italy

608

TWO-MINUTE LESSON LAUNCHER

Bring to class a recording by a famous jazz musician, preferably one from the early era of jazz. Before you play the recording, ask students to listen for the distinctive rhythms of the music. If the piece has lyrics, also ask students to listen for the theme. After students have listened to the recording, ask how the piece made them feel, what they think the mood of the piece is, and, if there are lyrics, what the theme of the piece is. Tell students that they will learn more about jazz in this chapter.

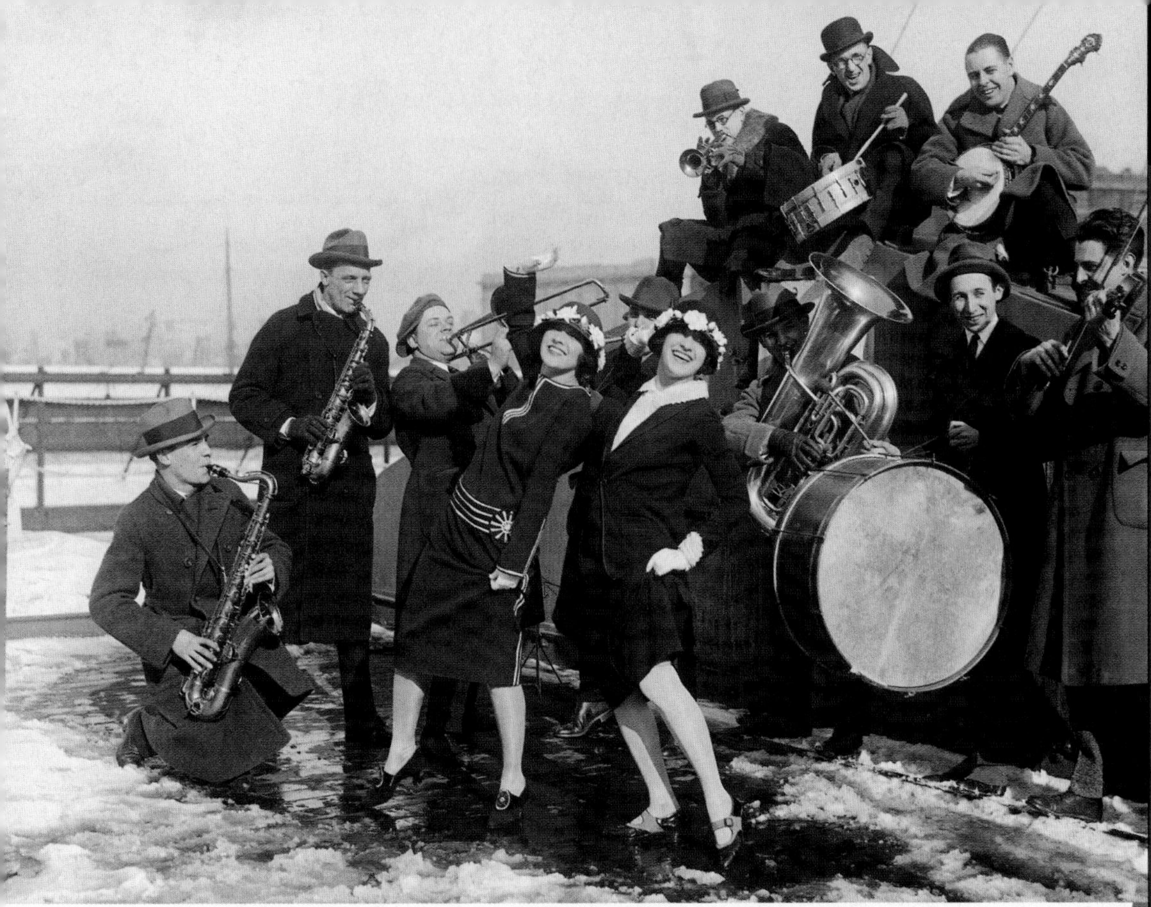

This photograph of jazz musicians captures the boisterous spirit of the 1920s.

1925
- Scopes trial begins
- F. Scott Fitzgerald's *The Great Gatsby* published

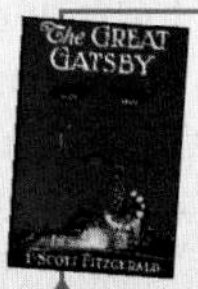

1924
- National Origins Act passed

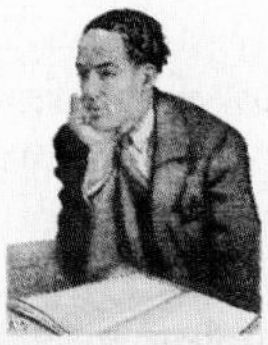

1926
- Langston Hughes's *The Weary Blues* published

1927
- First feature film with sound debuts
- Lindbergh completes first solo transatlantic flight

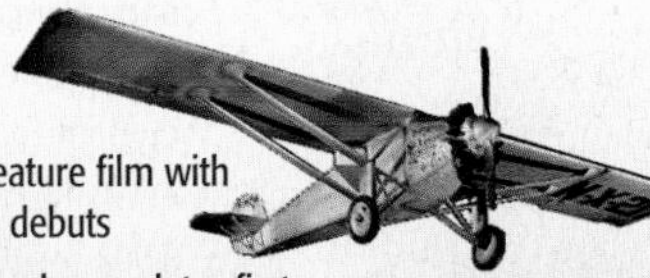

Coolidge 1923–1929

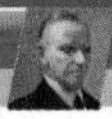

Hoover 1929–1933

1925

1930

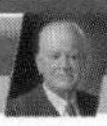

HISTORY Online

Chapter Overview
Visit the *American Vision* Web site at tav.glencoe.com and click on ***Chapter Overviews—Chapter 20*** to preview chapter information.

1924
- Britain recognizes the USSR

1926
- Pavlov's *Conditioned Reflexes* published

1923
- Turkish Republic founded

1928
- Chiang Kai-shek elected president of China

Introducing CHAPTER 20

HISTORY Online

Introduce students to chapter content and key terms by having them access the **Chapter 20 Overview** at tav.glencoe.com.

More About the Photo

Clothing styles were beginning to change before World War I. The pace of change accelerated after the war. For women, scooped necklines, knee-length hems, and sleeveless dresses departed radically from the frumpy styles of the Victorian era. Clothing styles reflected the carefree, happy-go-lucky feeling of the time.

TIME LINE ACTIVITY

Have students re-create the United States portion of the chapter time line on a separate piece of paper. Instruct students to link the Key Terms and Names from this chapter to an appropriate event on the time line. Remind students that the terms and names appear in the Guide to Reading at the beginning of each section.

GRAPHIC ORGANIZER ACTIVITY

Organizing Information Have students create a graphic organizer similar to the one shown below to explain the forms of entertainment that were popular in the 1920s and to give an example of a person or form of each. (Answers may vary from those shown here.)

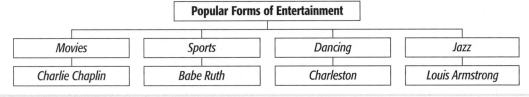

Popular Forms of Entertainment

Movies	Sports	Dancing	Jazz
Charlie Chaplin	Babe Ruth	Charleston	Louis Armstrong

1 FOCUS

Section Overview

This section focuses on the rise of racism and nativism during the 1920s.

Guide to Reading

Answers to Graphic: Causes: job competition, European immigrant influx, eugenics, economic recession; Effects: return of KKK, Sacco-Vanzetti case, governmental control of immigration

Preteaching Vocabulary
Have students look up the meaning of each of the Key Terms in the Glossary and write the definition on a sheet of paper to use while they are studying the section.

Guide to Reading

Main Idea
During the 1920s, clashes between traditional and modern values shook the United States.

Key Terms and Names
anarchist, eugenics, Ku Klux Klan, Emergency Quota Act, flapper, Fundamentalism, evolution, creationism, police powers, speakeasy

Reading Strategy
Organizing As you read about Americans' reactions to immigrants in the 1920s, complete a graphic organizer similar to the one below by filling in the causes and effects of anti-immigrant prejudices.

Causes → Anti-Immigrant Prejudices → Effects

Reading Objectives
- **Explain** the rise in racism and nativism in the 1920s.
- **Describe** the clash of values in the 1920s and the changing status of women.

Section Theme
Continuity and Change The rapid changes of the early 1900s challenged Americans who wanted to preserve traditional values.

Preview of Events

♦1919	♦1924	♦1929	♦1934
1919 Eighteenth Amendment ratified	**1921** Emergency Quota Act passed	**1924** National Origins Act passed	**1927** Sacco and Vanzetti executed	**1933** Prohibition repealed

★ An American Story ★

In 1911 Alfred Levitt left a small town in Russia to immigrate to New York City. Like many immigrants before and since, he had big ambitions, despite his poor English and lack of education. He wanted to forget his Russian heritage and become a successful American:

❝My conscious drive when I got here was to escape the rigors of poverty, to become somebody of importance. This I don't mean economically, but someone who can justify his presence on the planet. I wonder: Who am I? What am I here for? At seventeen years, the first question for me, though, was: What was I going to do? What will I become? . . . I made up my mind, as young as I was, that I'm going to amount to something in the world, and I'm not going to continue being one of those who starve.❞

—quoted in *Centenarians: The Story of the Twentieth Century by the Americans Who Lived It*

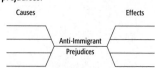

Alfred Levitt (standing)

Levitt did indeed "amount to something." A successful artist, he lived the rest of his life in New York City. Twenty of his paintings are part of the permanent collection of the city's Metropolitan Museum of Art.

Nativism Resurges

As the 1920s opened, an economic recession, an influx of immigrants, and racial and cultural tensions combined to create an atmosphere of disillusionment and intolerance. The fear and prejudice many felt toward Germans and Communists expanded to include all immigrants. This triggered a general rise in racism and in nativism, the desire to protect the interests of old-stock Americans against those of immigrants.

610 CHAPTER 20 The Jazz Age

📁 SECTION RESOURCES

📁 Reproducible Masters
- Reproducible Lesson Plan 20–1
- Daily Lecture and Discussion Notes 20–1
- Guided Reading Activity 20–1
- Section Quiz 20–1
- Reading Essentials and Study Guide 20–1
- Interpreting Political Cartoons
- Supreme Court Case Studies

Transparencies
- Daily Focus Skills Transparency 20–1

Multimedia
- Interactive Tutor Self-Assessment CD-ROM
- ExamView® Pro Testmaker CD-ROM
- Presentation Plus! CD-ROM
- TeacherWorks™ CD-ROM
- Audio Program

During World War I, immigration to the United States had dropped sharply. By 1921, however, it had returned to prewar levels, with the majority of immigrants at this time coming from southern and eastern Europe. Many Americans saw immigrants as a threat to stability and order. The arrival of millions of immigrants also seemed to pose a threat to the four million recently demobilized military men and women searching for work in an economy with soaring unemployment and rising prices.

As the new immigrants, many of whom were unskilled workers, sought to enter the workforce and establish a foothold in American life, many of them encountered ethnic and religious prejudices. The experience of two Italian immigrants, Nicola Sacco and Bartolomeo Vanzetti, exemplified the prejudices and fears of the period.

The Sacco-Vanzetti Case Shortly after 3:00 P.M. on April 15, 1920, two men shot and killed two employees of the Slater & Morrill Shoe Company in South Braintree, Massachusetts, and robbed the company of its $15,000 payroll. Police subsequently arrested Nicola Sacco, a shoemaker, and Bartolomeo Vanzetti, a fish peddler.

The **Sacco and Vanzetti case** created a furor, as newspapers around the country revealed that the two immigrants were anarchists, or people who oppose all forms of government. They also discovered that Sacco owned a gun similar to the murder weapon and that the bullets used in the murders matched those in Sacco's gun. Although no one at the time knew if Sacco and Vanzetti were guilty, many people leaped to that conclusion because the two men were Italian immigrants and anarchists. Others viewed the case as an example of prejudice against people based on their ethnic origin and political beliefs.

On July 14, 1921, a jury found Sacco and Vanzetti guilty, and the judge sentenced them to death. Many Americans, caught up in the antiforeign fever of the time, applauded the verdict and the penalty. Over the next six years, lawyers filed numerous appeals for a new trial, but all were denied. In April 1927, a special Massachusetts commission studied the case and upheld the verdict. Four months later, on August 23, 1927, Sacco and Vanzetti were executed, proclaiming their innocence all the while. 📖 *(See You're the Historian on pages 618–619 for more information on Sacco and Vanzetti.)*

Pseudo-Scientific Racism Nativist and racist feelings in the 1920s were reinforced by the beliefs of the eugenics movement. Eugenics is a pseudo-science (or false science) that deals with improving hereditary traits. Developed in Europe in the early 1900s, eugenics emphasized that human inequalities were inherited and warned against breeding the "unfit" or "inferior." Eugenics fueled the nativists' argument for the superiority of the "original" American stock—white Protestants of northern European descent. Political, intellectual, and cultural figures like Woodrow Wilson and Henry Cabot Lodge embraced eugenics. By doing so, they lent authority to racist theories, which reinvigorated the nativist argument for strict immigration control.

Return of the Ku Klux Klan At the forefront of the movement to restrict immigration was the **Ku Klux Klan,** or KKK. The old KKK had flourished in the South after the Civil War and used threats and violence to intimidate newly freed African Americans. The new Klan had other targets as well—Catholics, Jews, immigrants, and other groups believed to represent "un-American" values.

William J. Simmons founded the new Ku Klux Klan in Atlanta, Georgia, in 1915. A former circuit-riding Methodist preacher, Simmons pledged to preserve America's white, Protestant civilization. In the 1920s, Klan publicity claimed that the organization was fighting for "Americanism."

The Klan attracted few members until 1920, when Simmons hired public relations entrepreneurs Edward Young Clarke and Elizabeth Tyler, paying

🎩 **Analyzing** *Political Cartoons*

New Immigrants This cartoon portrays the feelings of many Americans who were opposed to immigration. *What comment does the cartoon make about immigrants?*

2 *TEACH*

Daily Lecture and Discussion Notes 20–1

Copyright © by The McGraw-Hill Companies, Inc.

Daily Lecture and Discussion Notes

Chapter 20, Section 1

Did You Know? During the 1920s, cosmetic sales soared as women tried to copy the look of Hollywood movie stars. The average American woman used about one pound of face powder a year.

I. **Nativism Resurges** *(pages 610–612)*

A. In the 1920s, racism and nativism increased. Immigrants and demobilized military men and women competed for the same jobs during a time of high unemployment and an increased cost of living.

B. Ethnic prejudice was the basis of the *Sacco and Vanzetti* case, in which the two immigrant men were accused of murder and theft. They were thought to be anarchists, or opposed to all forms of government. Sacco and Vanzetti were sentenced to death, and

Discussing a Topic Ask students to offer examples of how adults show bias toward teenagers. Invite students to share how they feel when they encounter bias. Have students consider reasons for the bias and discuss ways to initiate a dialogue to lessen the bias. **L1**

🎩 **Analyzing** *Political Cartoons*

Answer: It implies that other countries were sending their unwanted citizens to the United States.

Ask: Why did some people have such a strong opposition to the new wave of immigrants? *(competition for scarce jobs, fear that immigrants were anarchists and revolutionaries)*

COOPERATIVE LEARNING ACTIVITY

Creating a Cartoon Organize students into groups of four. Have the groups select one of the following topics: the Sacco-Vanzetti case, eugenics, Ku Klux Klan, or the National Origins Act of 1924. Tell the groups to create a political cartoon against the topic they have chosen. For example, those who choose the Sacco-Vanzetti case could develop a cartoon expressing the opinion that the two were not given a fair trial. 🖼️

Use the rubric for a cooperative group management plan on pages 81–82 in the ***Performance Assessment Activities and Rubrics.***

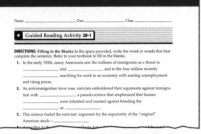
Reading Check

Answer: fear of communists, nativism, economic competition, eugenics

Interpreting Statistics Have students use library and Internet resources to locate historical immigration statistics for 1890, 1900, 1910, 1920, and 1930. Tell them to select two countries to compare, one from Western Europe and one from Eastern Europe. Have students use the data to construct an immigration chart that shows the effects of the immigration laws of 1921 and 1924. Ask students to write a brief explanation of the significance of their findings. **L2**

Reading Check

Answer: Students might suggest that Hispanics made the United States more ethnically and linguistically diverse.

them a commission of $8 of every $10 initiation fee for a new Klan recruit. Clarke and Tyler divided the nation into regions and paid more than 1,000 "salespeople" to promote the Klan. As a result of their strategy, membership in the Ku Klux Klan exploded, reaching nearly 4 million by 1924 as it spread beyond the South and into Northern cities.

The Klan began to decline in the late 1920s, however, largely as a result of scandals and power struggles involving its leaders. Membership shrank, and politicians whom the Klan supported were voted out of office. The sharp reduction in immigrants due to new immigration laws further disabled the Klan, depriving it of a major issue. The Klan never again had a major impact on politics.

✔ **Reading Check** **Explaining** Why did many Americans oppose immigration after World War I?

Controlling Immigration

After World War I, American immigration policies changed in response to the postwar recession and nativist pleas to "Keep America American." Even big business, which previously favored unrestricted immigration as a source of cheap labor, now feared the new immigrants as radicals.

In 1921 President Harding signed the **Emergency Quota Act,** which established a temporary quota system, limiting immigration. According to this act, only three percent of the total number of people in any ethnic group already living in the United States, as indicated in the 1910 census, could be admitted in a single year. This theoretically restricted the number of immigrants from all countries, but in practice it discriminated heavily against people from southern and eastern Europe. Ethnic identity and national origin thus determined admission to the United States.

Henry Curran, the commissioner of Ellis Island from 1922 to 1926, commented on the heartbreak caused by the Emergency Quota Act:

❝The hardest quota cases were those that separated families. When part of the family had been born in a country with a quota still open, while the other part had been born in a country whose quota was exhausted, the law let in the first part and deported the other part. Mothers were torn from children, husbands from wives. The law came down like a sword between them.❞

—quoted in *Ellis Island: Echoes from a Nation's Past*

GOVERNMENT

The National Origins Act of 1924 In 1924 the National Origins Act made immigrant restriction a permanent policy. The law also tightened the quota system, setting quotas at two percent of each national group residing in the country in 1890. By moving back the year to 1890, an even larger proportion of the quotas were allotted to immigrants from northwestern Europe.

A second part of the act, which took effect in 1929, replaced the 1924 quotas with a limit of 150,000 immigrants admitted per year. In addition, the percentage allotted to each nationality would now be based on the 1920 census. This resulted in northwestern European countries accounting for 87 percent of the total immigration quota.

Hispanic Immigration to the United States The immigration acts of 1921 and 1924 reduced the available labor pool in the United States. While workers and unions rejoiced at the reduction in competition for jobs, employers desperately needed laborers for agriculture, mining, and railroad work. Mexican immigrants helped to fill this need.

The first wave of Mexican immigration to the United States followed the passage of the Newlands Reclamation Act of 1902, which provided funds for irrigation projects in the arid Southwest. Factory farms soon dominated the landscape, and they needed large numbers of agricultural laborers. By 1914 more than 70,000 Mexican immigrants had poured into the United States, many of them fleeing the terror and aftermath of the Mexican Revolution of 1910.

A larger wave of immigration brought more than 600,000 Mexicans to the United States between 1914 and the end of the 1920s. The National Origins Act of 1924 exempted natives of the Western Hemisphere from the quota system. As the demand for cheap farm labor in California and the Southwest steadily increased, Mexican immigrants crossed the border in record numbers.

✔ **Reading Check** **Explaining** How did Hispanic immigrants help shape the national identity of the United States?

The New Morality

Many groups that wanted to restrict immigration also wanted to preserve what they considered to be traditional values. They feared that a "new morality" was taking over the nation. Challenging traditional

---

MEETING SPECIAL NEEDS

Reading Disability To help address the needs of students who have difficulty reading, have students create an outline using the subheadings in this section. Once they have done that, encourage them to listen to the Audio Program and highlight or circle the topics in their outline as they are discussed. **L1** ELL

☛ Refer to *Inclusion for the High School Social Studies Classroom Strategies and Activities* in the TCR.

ways of seeing and thinking, the new morality glorified youth and personal freedom and influenced various aspects of American society.

The New Morality Ideals of the loving family and personal satisfaction—views popularized in magazines and other media—influenced popular views on relationships. As the loving and emotional aspects of marriage grew in importance, the ideas of romance, pleasure, and friendship became linked to successful marriages. Advice books in the 1920s dispensed such hints as, "Have lots of pleasure that both husband and wife enjoy . . . and above all, be good friends."

Women in the workforce also began to define the new morality. Many single, working-class women held jobs simply because they needed the wages for themselves or for their families. For some young, single women, work was a way to break away from parental authority and establish a personal identity. Work also provided the wages that allowed women to participate in the consumer culture.

Women who attended college in the 1920s often found support for their emerging sense of independence. Women's colleges, in particular, encouraged their students to pursue careers and to challenge traditional ideas about the nature of women and their role in society.

The automobile also played a role in encouraging the new morality. The nation's youth loved cars because cars made them more independent and allowed them to escape the careful watch of their parents. Instead of socializing at home with the family, many youths could now use cars to seek new forms of entertainment with their friends and to find privacy.

Women in the 1920s Fashion took on a modern look during the 1920s, as women "bobbed," or shortened, their hair and wore flesh-colored silk stockings. It also emphasized the youthful appearance of

European Immigration Totals, 1890–1920

Number of People Immigrating to the United States by region, 1890–1920

488,099	2,135,312
672,223	3,060,151
1,130,656	3,695,828
1,195,628	3,859,297
—— 1914 border	

Lambert Azimuthal Equal-Area projection

Geography *Skills*

1. **Interpreting Maps** Between 1890 and 1920, what European regions sent more than three million immigrants to the United States?
2. **Applying Geography Skills** Why were so many people willing to leave their homelands to come to the United States?

glamorous stage and screen stars. In this new culture, the carefree, chic "flapper" played a prominent role.

Though hardly typical of American women at the time, the flapper—a young, dramatic, stylish, and unconventional woman—personified women's changing behavior in the 1920s. The flapper smoked cigarettes, drank prohibited liquor, and dressed in attire considered too revealing by previous generations.

While flappers pursued social freedoms, other women sought financial independence by entering the workforce, many of them as salesclerks, secretaries, or telephone operators. A few made contributions in science, medicine, law, or literature. In science, Florence Sabin's medical research led to a

Geography *Skills*

Answers:
1. Italy, Austro-Hungarian Empire and Serbia, and Russian Empire
2. They hoped to find greater opportunities.

Geography Skills Practice
Ask: From what countries did the fewest number of people emigrate? *(France, the Netherlands, Belgium, Luxembourg, and Switzerland)*

Making a Table Have students make a table showing areas where women's roles changed in the 1920s. Ask them to include visuals and examples for each area on the chart. **L1**

📁 Use the rubric for creating a map, display, or chart on pages 77–78 in the *Performance Assessment Activities and Rubrics.*

FYI

The first Miss America was crowned in 1921. It seems fitting that sixteen-year-old Margaret Gorman was from the nation's capital—Washington, D.C.

📁 Use *Interpreting Political Cartoons,* Cartoon 21.

📁 Use *Supreme Court Case Study 15,* Olmsted v. *United States.*

📁 Use *Supreme Court Case Study 16,* Near v. *Minnesota.*

INTERDISCIPLINARY CONNECTIONS ACTIVITY

Economics Have interested students research the number of women in the workforce in 1900, 1910, 1920, and 1930. Also, have them find the average annual wage that women earned in each of these years. Have students use the statistics to create a line graph showing the economic gains that women made during the early 1900s. **L2**

What Life Was Like...

Ask: How does modern clothing compare to clothing of the 1920s? *(possible answers: less formal, more synthetic fabrics; in both eras, boldly colored hats were popular and clothing expressed a person's identity with a group)*

✓ Reading Check

Answer: Some pursued social freedoms, entered the workforce, and contributed to medicine, literature, and science. Many others focused on enhancing traditional marriage relationships.

Creating a Cause-and-Effect Graphic Have students use a graphic organizer similar to the one shown below to illustrate some of the causes and effects of Prohibition. Invite students to share their graphics with the class. Create a composite graphic from the various student responses. **L2**

Prohibition

FYI

Charismatic preacher Aimee Semple McPherson gained added notoriety for a five-week disappearance she claimed was a kidnapping and for the many lawsuits filed against her in the following years, often for libel or slander.

What Life Was Like...

● **Modern Clothing**
Women's clothing changed significantly in the 1920s. Hemlines were much shorter and showed more of the body. Stylish new hats also emphasized bold colors and a freer design.

Flappers

Perhaps no other symbol of the 1920s captured the spirit of the time like the flapper. Psychologist G. Stanley Hall wrote his observation of a typical flapper:

❝She wore a knitted hat, with hardly any brim, of a flame or bonfire hue; a henna scarf; two strings of Betty beads, of different colors, twisted together; an open short coat, with ample pockets; a skirt with vertical stripes. . . . Her stockings were woolen and of brilliant hue. But most noticeable of all were her high overshoes, or galoshes. One seemed to be turned down at the top and entirely unbuckled, while the other was fastened below and flapped about her trim ankle in a way that compelled attention.❞

—quoted in *We, the American Women*

● **New Forms of Expression**
Rebelling against older, more formal dancing styles, these Charleston dancers perform steps that one observer described as "knock-kneed and pigeon-toed."

---

dramatic drop in death rates from tuberculosis. In literature, Edith Wharton received the Pulitzer Prize for her novel *The Age of Innocence*. Public health nurse Margaret Sanger, believing that the standard of living could be improved if families limited the number of children they had, founded the American Birth Control League in 1921. This organization became Planned Parenthood in the 1940s. In 1928 **Margaret Mead,** one of the first woman anthropologists, published the highly regarded study, *Coming of Age in Samoa,* which described life in a Pacific island culture.

✓ Reading Check Identifying What political, social, and economic contributions did women make to American society in the 1920s?

The Fundamentalist Movement

While many Americans embraced the new morality, millions more feared that the country was losing its traditional values. To these Americans, the modern consumer culture, relaxed ethics, and growing urbanism symbolized the nation's moral decline. Many of these people, especially those in small rural

towns, responded by joining a religious movement known as **Fundamentalism**—a name derived from a series of pamphlets titled *The Fundamentals,* published by oil millionaire Lyman Stewart.

Fundamentalist Beliefs Meant to reassert the authority of the Bible, Fundamentalism focused on defending the Protestant faith against ideas that implied that human beings derived their moral behavior from society and nature, not God. In particular, Fundamentalists rejected Charles Darwin's theory of evolution, which said that human beings had developed from lower forms of life over the course of millions of years. Instead, they believed in creationism—the belief that God created the world as described in the Bible.

Two popular evangelical preachers, **Billy Sunday** and **Aimee Semple McPherson,** stirred Fundamentalists' passions by preaching traditional religious and moral values in very nontraditional ways. A former professional baseball player, Sunday drew huge crowds with his rapid-fire sermons and on-stage showmanship. McPherson conducted her revivals and faith healings in Los Angeles in a

---

CRITICAL THINKING ACTIVITY

Making Generalizations Initiate a discussion by asking the following questions: What sorts of attempts have been made to limit alcohol consumption in recent years? *(raising the minimum legal age for alcohol purchase, restrictions on hard liquor advertisements on television, warning labels on alcohol products, high alcohol taxes, education programs, MADD, SADD)* Ask whether students think these attempts have been successful and whether other initiatives should be considered. **L2**

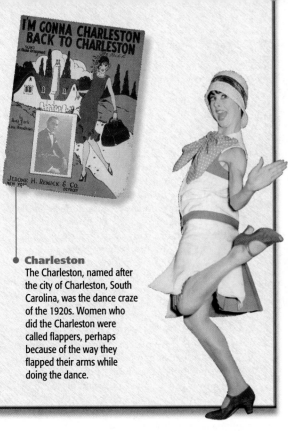

Charleston
The Charleston, named after the city of Charleston, South Carolina, was the dance craze of the 1920s. Women who did the Charleston were called flappers, perhaps because of the way they flapped their arms while doing the dance.

flamboyant theatrical style, using stage sets and costumes that expressed the themes of her highly emotional sermons.

The Scopes Trial Evolutionists and creationists eventually clashed in a historic trial. In 1925 Tennessee passed the Butler Act, which outlawed any teaching that denied "the story of the Divine Creation of man as taught in the Bible," and taught instead that "man descended from a lower order of animals." The American Civil Liberties Union (ACLU) raised money to test the new law and asked John T. Scopes, a biology teacher in Dayton, Tennessee, if he would be willing to be arrested for teaching evolution to his high school class. Scopes agreed. He taught evolution and was subsequently arrested and put on trial.

The trial took place in the summer of 1925. William Jennings Bryan, a three-time Democratic presidential candidate, was the prosecutor and represented the creationists. Clarence Darrow, one of the country's most celebrated trial lawyers, defended Scopes. After eight days of trial, Scopes was found guilty and fined $100, although the conviction was later overturned on a technicality. Parts of the trial had been broadcast over

the radio, and Darrow's blistering cross-examination of Bryan did little for the Fundamentalist cause. Increasingly, Fundamentalists found themselves isolated from mainstream Protestantism, and their commitment to political activism declined.

✓ **Reading Check** **Explaining** What were the major beliefs of Fundamentalists?

Prohibition

The movement to ban alcohol had been building throughout the late 1800s. By the early 1900s, many progressives and traditionalists supported prohibition. Many people believed the prohibition of alcohol would help reduce unemployment, domestic violence, and poverty. Their support helped pass the Eighteenth Amendment, which took effect on January 29, 1920.

To try to enforce the amendment, Congress passed the National Prohibition Act, also known as the **Volstead Act.** Enforcing Prohibition became the responsibility of the U.S. Treasury Department. Treasury agents had enforced federal tax laws for many years, but police powers—a government's power to control people and property in the interest of public safety, health, welfare, and morals—had generally been reserved for the state governments. The Eighteenth Amendment granted federal and state governments the power to enforce Prohibition, marking a dramatic increase in federal police powers.

The Treasury Department's new Prohibition Unit struggled to enforce Prohibition. During the 1920s, treasury agents made more than 540,000 arrests, but Americans persisted in blatantly ignoring the law. People flocked to secret bars called speakeasies, where they could purchase alcohol. In New York City alone, an estimated 32,000 such bars sold liquor illegally. Liquor also was readily available in rural

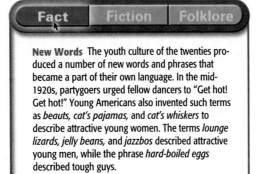

Fact Fiction Folklore

New Words The youth culture of the twenties produced a number of new words and phrases that became a part of their own language. In the mid-1920s, partygoers urged fellow dancers to "Get hot! Get hot!" Young Americans also invented such terms as *beauts, cat's pajamas,* and *cat's whiskers* to describe attractive young women. The terms *lounge lizards, jelly beans,* and *jazzbos* described attractive young men, while the phrase *hard-boiled eggs* described tough guys.

✓**Reading Check**

Answer: They believed in the authority of the Bible and creationism.

Fact Fiction Folklore

Prohibition also expanded American vocabulary. *Bootlegger, speakeasy,* and *hip flask* became part of common speech. It also gave new meaning to the words *wet* and *dry.*

FYI

Tennessee's law against teaching evolution remained on the books until 1967.

3 ASSESS

Assign Section 1 Assessment as homework or as an in-class activity.

⊙ Have students use the **Interactive Tutor Self-Assessment CD-ROM.**

Reading Essentials and Study Guide 20–1

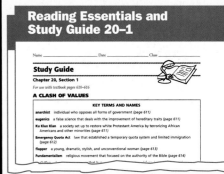

Name _____ Date _____ Class _____

Study Guide

Chapter 20, Section 1
For use with textbook pages 610–616
A CLASH OF VALUES

KEY TERMS AND NAMES

anarchist individual who opposes all forms of government (page 611)
eugenics a false science that deals with the improvement of hereditary traits (page 611)
Ku Klux Klan a society set up to restore white Protestant America by terrorizing African Americans and other minorities (page 611)
Emergency Quota Act law that established a temporary quota system and limited immigration (page 612)
flapper a young, dramatic, stylish, and unconventional woman (page 613)
Fundamentalism religious movement that focused on the authority of the Bible (page 614)

EXTENDING THE CONTENT

Agents of Prohibition Isador Einstein, known as Izzy, and his partner, Moe Smith, worked as a team to trap lawbreakers during Prohibition. Masters of disguise, they were a flamboyant pair who used any number of methods to enforce the law. Izzy was particularly adept at going through diverse neighborhoods because he spoke five languages. He once nabbed an unsuspecting speakeasy owner by disguising himself as a pickle salesman. Together Izzy and Moe made some 4,000 arrests and hauled in around $15 million worth of alcohol. Have students research Einstein and Smith to learn more about their actions during Prohibition.

Picturing History

Answer: not very successful
Ask: How did the American public respond to Prohibition? Give some examples. *(many blatantly ignored the law; speakeasies, organized crime supplied alcohol, bootlegging, smuggling)*

Reteach
Have students explain the reasons for the rise in racism and nativism in the 1920s, especially toward immigrants.

Enrich
Invite interested students to create a collage showcasing the changing role of women in the 1920s.

✓ Reading Check
Answer: Many people believed Prohibition would help reduce unemployment, domestic violence, and poverty.

4 CLOSE
Have students explain the resurgence, impact, and decline of the Ku Klux Klan.

Picturing History

Prohibition in Action Federal revenue agents carried out the laws of Prohibition by destroying barrels of alcohol. How successful were their enforcement efforts?

America, where bootlegging—the illegal production and distribution of liquor—was common.

Organized crime specialized in supplying and often running these speakeasies, which popped up all over the country. The huge profits that could be made supplying liquor encouraged some people to become smugglers, bringing liquor into the United States from Canada and the Caribbean. Smuggling and the consumption of liquor by millions helped create an illegal billion-dollar industry for gangsters. More than 70 federal agents were killed while enforcing Prohibition in the 1920s.

Crime became big business, and some gangsters had enough money to corrupt local politicians. Al Capone, one of the most successful and violent gangsters of the era, had many police officers, judges, and other officials on his payroll. Capone dominated organized crime in Chicago, where he ran bootlegging and other criminal rackets. Finally, Elliot Ness, the leader of a special Treasury Department task force, brought Capone to justice.

The battle to repeal Prohibition began almost as soon as the Eighteenth Amendment was ratified. Supporters of repeal associated Prohibition with "priggish fanaticism." The ratification of the Twenty-first Amendment in 1933 repealed the Eighteenth Amendment and ended federally-mandated Prohibition. It was a victory for the forces of modernism and a defeat for the supporters of traditional moral values.

✓ Reading Check **Analyzing** Analyze the reasons for the adoption of the Eighteenth Amendment.

SECTION 1 ASSESSMENT

Checking for Understanding
1. **Define:** anarchist, eugenics, flapper, evolution, creationism, police powers, speakeasy.
2. **Identify:** Ku Klux Klan, Emergency Quota Act, Fundamentalism.
3. **Explain** why the Eighteenth Amendment was repealed.

Reviewing Themes
4. **Continuity and Change** How did the passage of the Eighteenth Amendment and the Volstead Act change the federal government's role?

Critical Thinking
5. **Synthesizing** Why were immigrants from Mexico not included in the quota system set by the immigration acts?
6. **Categorizing** Use a graphic organizer similar to the one below to list the provisions of the immigration acts passed in the 1920s.

Act	Provisions

Analyzing Visuals
7. **Analyzing Photographs** Study the image on this page of the federal agent destroying barrels of alcohol. Why do you think the barrels were destroyed in public with a crowd watching?

Writing About History
8. **Persuasive Writing** Imagine it is the 1920s. Write a letter to your senator to persuade him or her to either continue to support Prohibition or to work for its repeal.

616 CHAPTER 20 The Jazz Age

SECTION 1 ASSESSMENT ANSWERS

1. Terms are in blue.
2. Ku Klux Klan *(p. 611)*, Emergency Quota Act *(p. 612)*, Fundamentalism *(p. 614)*
3. People recognized that Prohibition was not successful.
4. The federal government obtained police powers to enforce the law.

5. They provided cheap labor.
6. 1921 Emergency Quota Act limited the number of immigrants to 3 percent of the existing immigrant population based on the 1910 census; 1924 National Origins Act limited the number of immigrants to

2 percent of the existing immigrant population based on the 1890 census
7. to intimidate people, hoping to make them fearful and submissive in the face of federal authority
8. Letters should clearly express a point of view.

Synthesizing Information

Why Learn This Skill?

The authors of this book gathered information from many sources to present a story of how the United States came about and how the country's people lived. To combine the information into a logical story, the authors used a process called *synthesis*. Being able to synthesize information can be a useful skill for you as a student when you need to gather data from several sources for a report or a presentation.

Learning the Skill

The skill of synthesizing involves combining and analyzing information gathered from separate sources or at different times to make logical connections. Follow these steps to synthesize information:

- Select important and relevant information.
- Analyze the information and build connections.
- Reinforce or modify the connections as you acquire new information.

Suppose you need to write a research paper on the status of women in the 1920s. You would need to synthesize what you learn to inform others. You could begin by detailing the ideas and information you already have about the status of women in the 1920s. A graphic organizer such as the one on this page could help categorize the facts.

Then you could select an article about women in the 1920s, such as the following:

In 1923 the National Woman's Party first proposed an equal rights amendment to the Constitution. This amendment stated that "men and women shall have equal rights throughout the United States and every place subject to its jurisdiction." The National Woman's party pointed out that legislation discriminating against women existed in every state. . . .

Some progressive women reformers, however, opposed the goals of the National Woman's Party. These progressives favored protective legislation, which had brought shorter hours and better working conditions for many women. The efforts of the progressives helped defeat the equal rights amendment.

Women's Status in the 1920s

Economic:	Many more women worked in factories and other jobs outside the home.
Social:	Women had much more social freedom, including greater choices in clothing styles and public behavior.
Educational:	Many women had a high school education, and more than ever were attending college.

Practicing the Skill

Use the graphic organizer and the passage on this page to answer the following questions.

① What information is presented in the table?

② What is the main idea of the passage? What information does the passage add to your knowledge of this topic?

③ By synthesizing the two sources and using what you know from reading Section 1 of this chapter, what conclusions can you draw about the role of women in 1920s society?

Skills Assessment

Complete the Practicing Skills questions on page 633 and the Chapter 20 Skill Reinforcement Activity to assess your mastery of this skill.

Applying the Skill

Synthesizing Information Find two sources of information on the same topic and write a short report. In your report, answer these questions: What kinds of sources did you use—primary or secondary? What are the main ideas in these sources? How does each source add to your understanding of the topic? Do the sources support or contradict each other?

Glencoe's **Skillbuilder Interactive Workbook CD-ROM, Level 2**, provides instruction and practice in key social studies skills.

617

TEACH

Synthesizing Information Point out that synthesizing information is a skill that people use every day. To properly prepare for a test, a student would have to know what kind of information will be on the test, when the test will be, how much time the student needs to study, and when the student has available time to study.

Ask students to share some other examples of how they synthesize information in their daily lives.

Additional Practice

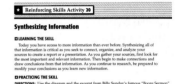

Reinforcing Skills Activity 20

Name _____ Date _____ Class _____

★ Reinforcing Skills Activity 20

Synthesizing Information

☐ **LEARNING THE SKILL**
Today you have access to more information than ever before. Synthesizing all of that information is critical as you seek to connect, organize, and analyze your sources to create a report or a presentation. As you gather your sources, first look for the most important and relevant information. Then begin to make connections and draw conclusions from that information. As you continue to research, be prepared to modify your conclusions as you learn new information.

☐ **PRACTICING THE SKILL**
DIRECTIONS: Use the diagram and the excerpt from Billy Sunday's famous "Booze Sermon" below to answer the following questions on a separate sheet of paper.

National Origins Act   Fundamentalist

GLENCOE
TECHNOLOGY

 CD-ROM
Glencoe Skillbuilder Interactive Workbook CD-ROM, Level 2

This interactive CD-ROM reinforces student mastery of essential social studies skills.

ANSWERS TO PRACTICING THE SKILL

① status of women in the 1920s

② An amendment dedicated to women's rights was proposed in 1923, but it was defeated with the help of women who opposed it.

③ Women pursued social freedom, entered the workforce, and made contributions in medicine, literature, and science.

Applying the Skill
Students' reports will vary. Students should correctly identify the sources they used as primary or secondary.

1 FOCUS

Remind students that the American criminal justice system is based on the presumption of innocence. The judge and the foreman of the jury that convicted Sacco and Vanzetti presumed that the defendants were guilty before the evidence was heard.

2 TEACH

Analyzing Information Tell students that many of the people who testified for the two defendants were Italians who spoke English poorly. Much of their testimony had to be taken in Italian and translated for the judge and jury. Ask students: **How do you think the witnesses' inability to speak English well affected their credibility?** (*Students should recognize that it should not have affected their credibility, but that bias toward immigrants might have unfairly influenced the jury.*) **Do you think people who do not speak English well face similar bias in the United States today?** (*Answers will vary. Students may note that they do not face the same degree of bias, but that bias still exists.*) **L2**

You're the Historian

Painting supporting the accused

The Sacco-Vanzetti Case

On April 15, 1920, in South Braintree, Massachusetts, armed robbers murdered two factory employees during a payroll holdup. Police arrested two Italian immigrants and anarchists—Nicola Sacco and Bartolomeo Vanzetti—as suspects. After a court found the two men guilty, defense attorneys fought for six years for a new trial. The attorneys believed the trial had shown signs of prejudice, intimidation, and dishonesty. Did Sacco and Vanzetti receive a fair trial, or were they victims of the troubled atmosphere in the United States at the time? You're the historian.

Read the following excerpts from testimony and evidence. Then complete the questions and activities that follow.

From trial testimony

The defense produced several people who supported the defendants' alibis. When arrested, Nicola Sacco had been carrying a pistol. The prosecuting attorney questioned Captain Proctor, a Massachusetts State Police ballistics expert, about the gun.

Q. Captain Proctor, have you an opinion as to whether bullet three was fired from the Colt automatic which is in evidence [Sacco's pistol]?

A. I have.

Q. And what is your opinion?

A. My opinion is that it is consistent with being fired by that pistol.

Defense experts, however, testified that in their judgment, bullet three had not been fired from Sacco's gun. The defense called on Sacco to testify, which gave the prosecution an opportunity to ask Sacco about his political beliefs.

Q. Did you say yesterday you love a free country?

A. Yes, sir.

Q. Did you love this country in the month of May 1917? [At this time, Sacco had gone to Mexico to escape military service.]

A. If you can, Mr. Katzman, if you give me that, —I could explain.

Q. There are two words you can use, Mr. Sacco, yes or no.

A. Yes.

[later]

Q. What did you mean when you said yesterday you loved a free country?

A. . . .When I came to this country I saw there was not what I was thinking before. . . . I could see the best men, intelligent, education, they been arrested and sent to prison and died in prison . . . and Debs, one of the great men in his country, he is in prison . . . because he is a socialist. He wanted the laboring class

to have better conditions . . . but they put him in prison. . . . They want the working class to be low all the times.

The jury returned a verdict of guilty. In the sentencing phase, Bartolomeo Vanzetti was asked to explain why he should not be sentenced to death.

I am suffering because I am a radical, and indeed I am a radical. I have suffered because I am an Italian, and indeed I am an Italian. I have suffered more for my family and for my beloved than for myself, but I am so convinced to be right that if you could execute me two times, and if I could be reborn two other times, I would live again to do what I have done already. . . . You know I am innocent. That is the same words I pronounced seven years ago. You condemn two innocent men.

618   CHAPTER 20   The Jazz Age

EXTENDING THE CONTENT

Due Process The Sacco-Vanzetti case influenced the Supreme Court's actions in the 1950s and 1960s under the leadership of Chief Justice Earl Warren. In more than one case, the Court ruled that the due process clause of the Bill of Rights extended to the states. This, in effect, altered the legal system in many states. Massachusetts had already changed its laws in 1939 to allow a new trial not only if the verdict violated the law, but also if it went against the evidence presented at the trial.

The Boston Daily Globe

MADEIROS, SACCO, VANZETTI DIED IN CHAIR THIS MORNING
Electrocuted in That Order Soon After Midnight—All Reject Religious Consolation to the Last—Two Make Statements

Headline announcing the execution

Comments on the case

The Sacco-Vanzetti case aroused indignation among intellectuals from the 1920s on. They generally agreed that the two were found guilty because they were Italian radicals, not because there was clear evidence against them. However, two students of the case, Robert Hanson, a local historian, and Francis Russell, who wrote two books on the case, believe Sacco and Vanzetti received a fair trial. Russell cites James Graham, an attorney for Sacco:

We spent considerable time with him [Vanzetti] at the Plymouth County Jail as the case was drawing to a close. . . . Toward the end of the discussion Mr. Vahey said to Vanzetti, in substance, "I can advise you as to what the District Attorney may inquire about the effect of your failure to take the stand, but you are the one who has to make the decision as to whether you will testify or not."

Workers showing support for Sacco (right) and Vanzetti (center)

Vanzetti replied,

I don't think I can improve on the alibi which has been established. I had better not take the stand.

Russell also reports that Carlo Tresca, an anarchist who had supported the two Italians, told friends that Sacco was guilty, Vanzetti innocent. Then Russell quotes a letter from labor writer Paul Jacobs:

. . . I had a close friend, Anthony Ramuglia. . . . One day he came to me and said he had a story he wanted me to write. . . . The story was that when he was a young man around the anarchist movement in Boston, he had been approached by one of Sacco's witnesses for his alibi in the restaurant at lunch. My friend Tony agreed, and evidently, was carefully coached in what he was to say, when suddenly he remembered that on the day in question

he had actually been in jail in St. Louis and so might obviously be found out as a perjurer. He told someone about this and was relieved of his responsibilities. . . . I asked Tony whether he thought Sacco and Vanzetti were really guilty, and he replied in much the same way as you quote Tresca. "Sacco could have done it but Vanzetti was never capable of such a thing."

Understanding the Issue

1. Why did the defense attorneys believe that the defendants were not given a fair trial?
2. Why do you think the prosecution questioned Sacco on his political beliefs?
3. After studying the historical context of the case and the frame of reference of the jury, how might a modern historian argue that Sacco and Vanzetti did not receive a fair trial?

Activities

1. **Investigate** Check your local library or the Internet and prepare a report on the latest information on the case.
2. **Create a Simulation** Recreate the trial. Research the testimony and the people involved in the case. Assign roles to class members, including witnesses, jury members, a prosecutor, a defense attorney, and a judge.

3 ASSESS

Have students answer the Understanding the Issues questions and complete the Activities.

Understanding the Issues

1. They argued that the defendants were found guilty because of their political views, not because of the evidence against them.
2. They wanted to establish that his radical views made him dangerous, regardless of whether he actually committed the crime.
3. A historian might argue that since the evidence was inconclusive, the verdict was unfounded.

Activities

1. Reports should consider the quality of the arguments presented.
2. Encourage students to prepare for their assigned roles. At the end of the trial, have the jury read its verdict, then discuss as a class the various opinions and thoughts about the event.

4 CLOSE

Ask students to explain how public opinion can affect the outcome of a trial.

PORTFOLIO ACTIVITY

Court Drawings Ask students to select one moment in the trial and create a drawing about it similar to the ones done by court artists today. Have students write a paragraph describing the scene they have drawn. **L2**

1 FOCUS

Section Overview

This section focuses on the cultural innovations of the 1920s including art, literature, mass media, music, and sports.

BELLRINGER
Skillbuilder Activity

- Project transparency and have students answer the question.

- Available as a blackline master.

Daily Focus Skills Transparency 20–2

Guide to Reading

Answers to Graphic: Art: diverse, individual expression influenced by European art movement; Literature: various styles and subject matter, themes of disillusionment and emptiness; Popular Culture: sports heroes, Hollywood allure, radio shows, jazz, and blues

Preteaching Vocabulary
Have students skim the section to preview each of the Key Terms and Names.

Guide to Reading

Main Idea
An era of exciting and innovative cultural trends, the 1920s witnessed changes in art and literature. This period also saw a dramatic increase in the country's interest in sports and other forms of popular culture.

Key Terms and Names
Bohemian, Carl Sandburg, Eugene O'Neill, Ernest Hemingway, F. Scott Fitzgerald, mass media

Reading Strategy
Organizing As you read about the 1920s, complete a graphic organizer like the one below by filling in the main characteristics of art, literature, and popular culture that reflect the era.

Cultural Movement	Main Characteristics
Art	
Literature	
Popular Culture	

Reading Objectives
- **Describe** the explosion of art and literature and the disillusionment of 1920s artists.
- **Summarize** the effects of sports, movies, radio, and music on popular culture.

Section Theme
Culture and Traditions American culture in the 1920s saw a rise in both the arts and popular entertainment.

Preview of Events

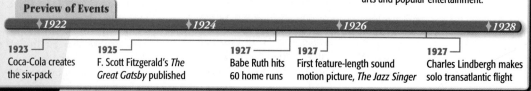

◆1922   ◆1924   ◆1926   ◆1928

1923 Coca-Cola creates the six-pack

1925 F. Scott Fitzgerald's *The Great Gatsby* published

1927 Babe Ruth hits 60 home runs

1927 First feature-length sound motion picture, *The Jazz Singer*

1927 Charles Lindbergh makes solo transatlantic flight

Charles Lindbergh and his Spirit of St. Louis

★ An American Story ★

On May 20, 1927, a lanky, sandy-haired young man named Charles Lindbergh took off from an airfield on Long Island, New York, in a small, single-engine plane called the *Spirit of St. Louis* and headed east across the Atlantic Ocean. The next evening—more than 33 hours after Lindbergh left New York—thousands of people waited anxiously at the small Le Bourget airfield outside Paris, France. Attention was riveted on the sky, and the spectators strained their eyes as they watched Lindbergh's small airplane softly slip out of the darkness. When the plane landed, the crowd ecstatically greeted the pilot, who had just completed a historic event—the first solo nonstop flight across the Atlantic Ocean.

In an era when people questioned ideals and heroes, Lindbergh's historic flight symbolized American progress in the modern age, and his solo triumph restored Americans' belief in the courageous, pioneering individual. American writer F. Scott Fitzgerald said of Lindbergh:

❝A young Minnesotan who seemed to have nothing to do with his generation did a heroic thing, and for the moment people set down their glasses in country clubs and speakeasies and thought of their old dreams.❞

—quoted in *Echoes of the Jazz Age*

Art and Literature

The modern age symbolized by Lindbergh's historic transatlantic flight was reflected strongly in American art, literature, and popular culture. During the 1920s, American artists and writers challenged traditional ideas. These artists explored what

SECTION RESOURCES

Reproducible Masters
- Reproducible Lesson Plan 20–2
- Daily Lecture and Discussion Notes 20–2
- Guided Reading Activity 20–2
- Section Quiz 20–2
- Reading Essentials and Study Guide 20–2

Transparencies
- Daily Focus Skills Transparency 20–2

Multimedia
- Interactive Tutor Self-Assessment CD-ROM
- ExamView® Pro Testmaker CD-ROM
- Presentation Plus! CD-ROM
- TeacherWorks™ CD-ROM
- Audio Program
- American Music: Hits Through History
- American Music: Cultural Traditions

it meant to be "modern," and they searched for meaning in the emerging challenges of the modern world.

Greenwich Village and the South Side
Many artists, writers, and intellectuals of the era flocked to Manhattan's Greenwich Village and Chicago's South Side. As writer Brooks Atkinson noted in a memoir,

> 66The Village was no prude . . . no matter what you did you could hardly be conspicuous. On my street the middle-aged lady in knickers who aired her cat on a pink ribbon twice a day and the rosy-cheeked damsel in overalls who split kindling wood on the side walk . . . were hardly more conspicuous than the formal citizenry. To become conspicuous you would probably have to shoot someone in the street.99
> —from *New York's Greenwich Village*

The artistic and unconventional, or Bohemian, lifestyle of these neighborhoods offered young artists and writers new lifestyles.

Modern American Art
European art movements greatly influenced the modernists of American art. Perhaps most striking was the diverse range of artistic styles, each attempting to express the individual, modern experience.

Taking his cue from the bold and colorful Impressionism of French artist Paul Cézanne, American painter John Marin drew on nature as well as the urban dynamics of New York for inspiration, explaining, "the whole city is alive; buildings, people, all are alive; and the more they move me the more I feel them to be alive." Painter Charles Scheeler applied the influences of photography and the geometric forms of Cubism to urban and rural American landscapes. **Edward Hopper** revived the visual accuracy of Realism in his haunting scenes. His paintings conveyed a modern sense of disenchantment and isolation.

Poets and Writers
Poets and writers of the 1920s varied greatly in their styles and subject matter. Chicago poet **Carl Sandburg** used common speech to glorify the Midwest and the expansive nature of American life. In Greenwich Village, Edna St.

Vincent Millay, in her poem "First Fig," expressed women's freedom and equality and praised a life intensely lived:

> 66My candle burns at both ends;
> It will not last the night;
> But ah, my foes, and oh, my friends—
> It gives a lovely light.99

Several poets of this time had an important impact on the literary culture. Gertrude Stein, for example, was supposed to have been able to make or break a writer's career with a few well-placed remarks. Poets such as Ezra Pound, Amy Lowell, and William Carlos Williams used clear, concise images to express moments in time.

Some poets concentrated on what they considered the negative effects of modernism. In his poem "The Hollow Men," for example, **T.S. Eliot** described a world filled with empty dreams and "hollow men," and he foresaw a world that would end "not with a bang but a whimper."

Among playwrights, one of the most innovative was **Eugene O'Neill.** His plays, filled with bold artistry and modern themes, portrayed realistic characters and situations, offering a vision of life that sometimes touched on the tragic.

Many novelists, affected by the experiences of World War I, wrote about disillusionment and reevaluated the myths of American heroes. They often created characters who were "heroic antiheroes"—flawed individuals who still had heroic qualities of mind and spirit. **Ernest Hemingway,** who served as an ambulance driver in Italy during World War I, was one such writer. His fiction presented a new literary style characterized by direct, simple, and concise prose, as when he wrote about war in such works as *For Whom the Bell Tolls* and *A Farewell to Arms.*

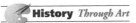
History *Through Art*

Lonely People Like many of his works, Edward Hopper's *Nighthawks* depicts isolated people. How do you think this painting reflects the experience of small-town people who moved to cities in the 1920s?

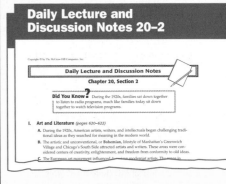
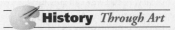
COOPERATIVE LEARNING ACTIVITY

Creating Multimedia Presentations Organize students into six groups. Divide Section 2 into six parts and assign one part to each group. Instruct members within each group to prepare a classroom presentation based on the topics covered in their part of the section. Each group should decide how to present its findings to the class. Encourage students to use a variety of media for their presentations.

Use the rubric for a cooperative group management plan on pages 81–82 in the *Performance Assessment Activities and Rubrics.*

✓ **Reading Check**

Answer: These communities offered freedom from conformity to old ideas.

NATIONAL GEOGRAPHIC

MOMENT in HISTORY

The Kelly Air Mail Act of 1925 allowed private carriers to deliver air mail. The act supported the fledgling airline industry, which was still considered by many people to be a novelty, partly because of the barnstormers.

History *and the* Humanities

🎵 American Music: Hits Through History: "Can the Circle Be Unbroken"

🎵 American Music: Cultural Traditions: "Wildwood Flower"

🎨 American Art & Architecture: *Yellow Cactus Flower*

3 ASSESS

Assign Section 2 Assessment as homework or as an in-class activity.

🖱 Have students use the **Interactive Tutor Self-Assessment CD-ROM.**

John Dos Passos, a critic of America's capitalist culture, experimented with the form of the novel in his innovative trilogy *U.S.A.,* which combined fiction, biography, news headlines, and prose poems. Sinclair Lewis wrote about the absurdities of traditional life in small-town America in his novels *Main Street* and *Babbitt.* **F. Scott Fitzgerald,** perhaps the most famous writer of the era, created colorful, glamorous characters who chased futile dreams in *The Great Gatsby,* a novel that poignantly exposed the emptiness and superficiality of much of modern society.

✓ **Reading Check** **Examining** Why did many artists, writers, and intellectuals flock to New York City's Greenwich Village and Chicago's South Side during the 1920s?

Popular Culture

The economic prosperity of the 1920s provided many Americans with more leisure time and more spending money, which they devoted to making their lives more enjoyable. Millions of Americans eagerly watched and participated in sports and enjoyed music, theater, and other forms of popular entertainment. They also fell in love with radio shows and motion pictures.

Baseball, Boxing, and Other Sports Thanks to radio and motion pictures, sports such as baseball and boxing reached new heights of popularity in the 1920s. Baseball star **Babe Ruth** became a national hero, famous for hitting hundreds of home runs. As one broadcaster later remarked, "He wasn't a baseball player. He was a worldwide celebrity, an international star, the likes of which baseball has never seen since."

Sports fans also idolized boxer Jack Dempsey. Dempsey held the title of world heavyweight champion from 1919 until 1926, when he lost it to Gene Tunney. When Dempsey attempted to win back the title in 1927, fans' enthusiasm for the rematch reached such a frenzy that one store sold $90,000 worth of radios—an incredible sum at that time—in the two weeks before the event.

NATIONAL GEOGRAPHIC

MOMENT in HISTORY

ENTERTAINMENT FOR A NEW ERA

In the 1920s, the United States developed an almost insatiable appetite for daredevils and death-defying stunts. Itinerant pilots, known as "barnstormers," crisscrossed the country offering airplane rides for a dollar and performing dangerous aerial maneuvers for delighted spectators. Some pilots banded together to form "flying circuses." Competition was fierce as these troupes dreamed up ever more complex and hair-raising stunts to thrill audiences. Here, the "Flying Black Hats" engage in an airborne tennis match.

622 CHAPTER 20 The Jazz Age

Americans eagerly followed other sports and sports figures, too. Newspaper coverage helped generate enthusiasm for college football. One of the most famous players of the 1920s was Red Grange of the University of Illinois. Grange was known as the "Galloping Ghost" because of his speed and ability to evade members of opposing teams.

Millions of sports fans also were thrilled by the achievements of Bobby Jones, the best golfer of the decade, and tennis players Bill Tilden and Helen Wills, who dominated world tennis. In 1926 Jones became the first golfer to win the U.S. Open and the British Open in the same year. In 1927 swimmer Gertrude Ederle enchanted Americans when she shattered records by swimming the English Channel in a little over 14 hours.

The Rise of Hollywood Although sports became increasingly popular in the 1920s, nothing quite matched the allure of motion pictures. Technology had not yet made sound possible in films, so theaters hired piano players to provide music during the feature, while subtitles revealed the plot. Audiences thronged to see such stars as Mary Pickford, Charlie Chaplin, Tom Mix, Douglas Fairbanks, Gloria Swanson, Rudolph Valentino, and Clara Bow. In 1927 the first "talking" picture—*The Jazz Singer*—was produced, and the golden age of Hollywood began.

Popular Radio Shows and Music Radio also enjoyed a large following during the Jazz Age. In 1920, in one of the first commercial radio broadcasts in history, listeners of station KDKA in Pittsburgh learned the news of Warren G. Harding's landslide victory in the presidential election. Within two years, Americans could turn the dial to more than 400 different radio stations around the country.

Most stations in the 1920s played the popular music of the day, such as "Yes! We Have No Bananas" and "Lover Come Back Again." Broadcasts such as *The Eveready Hour* offered everything from classical music to comedy. In one of the most popular radio shows, *Amos 'n' Andy*, the trials and tribulations of two African American characters (portrayed by white actors) captured the nation's attention every evening.

The mass media—radio, movies, newspapers, and magazines aimed at a broad audience—did more than just entertain. Their easy availability to millions helped break down patterns of provincialism, or narrow focus on local interests. They fostered a sense of shared national experience that helped unify the nation and spread the new ideas and attitudes of the time.

Babe Ruth

✓**Reading Check** **Summarizing** How did the American economy of the 1920s affect popular culture?

SECTION 2 ASSESSMENT

Checking for Understanding
1. **Define:** Bohemian, mass media.
2. **Identify:** Carl Sandburg, Eugene O'Neill, Ernest Hemingway, F. Scott Fitzgerald.
3. **Describe** the main themes of artists and writers during the 1920s.

Reviewing Themes
4. **Culture and Traditions** How did writers, artists, and popular culture of the 1920s affect traditional ideas in the United States?

Critical Thinking
5. **Synthesizing** How did World War I influence the literature written during the 1920s?
6. **Organizing** Use a graphic organizer similar to the one below to list the effects of mass media on American culture.

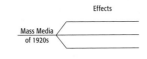

Effects

Mass Media of 1920s

Analyzing Visuals
7. **Interpreting Art** Study the Edward Hopper painting, *Nighthawks*, on page 621. How do different elements of this piece work to convey a sense of isolation?

Writing About History
8. **Descriptive Writing** Imagine that you have moved to New York's Greenwich Village in the 1920s. Write a letter to a friend describing the atmosphere in your neighborhood.

CHAPTER 20   The Jazz Age   **623**

SECTION 2 ASSESSMENT ANSWERS

1. Terms are in blue.
2. Carl Sandburg *(p. 621),* Eugene O'Neill *(p. 621),* Ernest Hemingway *(p. 621),* F. Scott Fitzgerald *(p. 622)*
3. disenchantment, isolation, disillusionment, and emptiness
4. They broke down patterns of narrow focus on local interest.
5. It led many writers to portray disillusionment and to reevaluate the myths of American heroes.
6. broke down patterns of provincialism, unified Americans through shared national experience, spread new ideas and attitudes
7. One man eats by himself, there are only three customers in the diner, there is only one person working at the diner, and there are no people on the sidewalk or in the street.
8. Letters should include words and phrases popular at the time.

Reading Essentials and Study Guide 20–2

Name _____ Date _____ Class _____

Study Guide
Chapter 20, Section 2
For use with textbook pages 620–623

CULTURAL INNOVATIONS

KEY TERMS AND NAMES

Bohemian an artistic and unconventional lifestyle *(page 621)*
Carl Sandburg a poet who used common speech to glorify the Midwest *(page 621)*
Eugene O'Neill an innovative playwright whose plays showed realistic characters and situations *(page 621)*
Ernest Hemingway a novelist who presented a new literary style characterized by direct, simple, and concise prose *(page 621)*
F. Scott Fitzgerald famous writer of the 1920s who created colorful, glamorous characters that chased futile dreams *(page 622)*
mass media radio, movies, newspapers, and magazines aimed at a broad, popular audience

---

Section Quiz 20–2

Name _____ Date _____ Class _____

⭐ **Chapter 20** | Score _____

Section Quiz 20-2

DIRECTIONS: Matching Match each item in Column A with the items in Column B. Write the correct letters in the blanks. *(10 points each)*

Column A	Column B
____ 1. a film star	A. F. Scott Fitzgerald
____ 2. Chicago poet who used common speech to glorify the Midwest	B. Bohemian
____ 3. part of Manhattan where many artists, writers, and intellectuals flocked	C. Mary Pickford
____ 4. famous writer who created colorful, glamorous characters who chased futile dreams in *The Great Gatsby*	D. Greenwich Village
____ 5. artistic and unconventional lifestyle	E. Carl Sandburg

DIRECTIONS: Multiple Choice In the blank at the left, write the letter of the choice

---

Reteach
Have students describe the disillusionment of 1920s artists.

Enrich
Invite interested students to locate and view a silent movie and prepare a brief report on how silent movies differ from movies made today.

✓**Reading Check**

Answer: Economic prosperity allowed Americans more leisure time and more spending money to pursue different kinds of popular culture.

4 CLOSE

Have students summarize the effects of sports, movies, radio, and music on popular culture.

TEACH

Appreciation

Have students work in groups to select one Louis Armstrong recording and find photos to illustrate the mood and tone of the piece. Have the groups combine the music and the photos into a multimedia tribute to the jazz legend. Have the groups share their presentations with the class and, if possible, select several of the presentations to be made to a wider audience.

Verbatim

Have students select one of the quotes and find a list of specific examples that support or refute the statement. Have students use their lists to write a letter to the person named in the quote. The letter should either offer support of their point of view or refute their statement.

Visit the TIME Web site at www.time.com for up-to-date news, weekly magazine articles, editorials, online polls, and an archive of past magazine and Web articles.

TIME NOTEBOOK

Appreciation

BETTMANN/CORBIS

LOUIS DANIEL ARMSTRONG *Writer Stanley Crouch remembers Louis Armstrong, a Jazz Age great.*

Pops. Sweet Papa Dip. Satchmo. He had perfect pitch and perfect rhythm. His improvised melodies and singing could be as lofty as a moon flight or as low-down as the blood drops of a street thug dying in the gutter. The extent of his influence across jazz and across American music continues to this day.

Not only do we hear Armstrong in trumpet players who represent the present renaissance in jazz, we can also detect his influence in certain rhythms that sweep from country-and-western music to rap.

Louis Daniel Armstrong was born in New Orleans on August 4, 1901. It was at a home for troubled kids that young Louis first put his lips to the mouthpiece of a cornet and later, a trumpet.

In 1922 Armstrong went to Chicago, where he joined King Oliver and his Creole Jazz Band. The band brought out the people and all the musicians, black and white, who wanted to know how it was truly done.

When he first played in New York City in 1924, his improvisations set the city on its head. The stiff rhythms of the time were slashed away by his combination of the percussive and the soaring. He soon returned to Chicago, perfected what he was doing, and made one record after another.

Louis Armstrong was so much, in fact, that every school of jazz since has had to address how he interpreted the basics of the idiom—swing, blues, ballads, and Afro-Hispanic rhythms. His freedom, his wit, and his discipline give his music a perpetual position in the wave of the future that is the station of all great art.

VERBATIM

❝The great creators of the government . . . thought of America as a light to the world, as created to lead the world in the assertion of the right of peoples and the rights of free nations.❞

> **WOODROW WILSON,**
> *in defense of the League of Nations, 1920*

❝We seek no part in directing the destinies of the Old World.❞

> **WARREN G. HARDING,**
> *Inaugural Address, 1921*

❝Here was a new generation, . . . dedicated more than the last to the fear of poverty and the worship of success; grown up to find . . . all wars fought, all faiths in man shaken.❞

F. Scott Fitzgerald

CULVER PICTURES

> **F. SCOTT FITZGERALD,**
> *author,* This Side of Paradise

❝There has been a change for the worse during the past year in feminine dress, dancing, manners and general moral standards. [One should] realize the serious ethical consequences of immodesty in girls' dress.❞

> *from the* **PITTSBURGH OBSERVER**

❝[In New York] I saw 7,000,000 two-legged animals penned in an evil smelling cage, . . . streets as unkempt as a Russian steppe, . . . rubbish, waste paper, cigar butts. . . . One glance and you know no master hand directs.❞

> *article in Soviet newspaper* **PRAVDA**
> *describing New York City in 1925*

624 CHAPTER 20 The Jazz Age

COOPERATIVE LEARNING ACTIVITY

Creating a Magazine Spread Organize the class into small groups. Tell the groups that they are to create a magazine spread that includes articles or items about each section of Chapter 20. Students should look at current magazines and books for ideas about page design. This activity can be completed using desktop publishing software or the more traditional cut-and-paste method.

Use the rubric for a cooperative group management plan on pages 81–82 in the *Performance Assessment Activities and Rubrics.*

THE JAZZ AGE: 1920-1929

Hide the Hooch

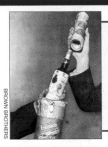

BROWN BROTHERS

Ingenious Americans are finding unusual places to store their liquor under Prohibition:

- canes
- hot water bottles
- shoe heels
- rolled newspaper
- folds of coats
- perfume bottles

Milestones

EMBARRASSED, 1920. TEXAS SENATOR MORRIS SHEPPARD, a leading proponent of the Eighteenth Amendment, when a large whiskey still is found on his farm.

ERASED, 1922. THE WORD "OBEY," from the Episcopal marriage ceremony, by a vote of American Episcopal bishops.

DIED, 1923. HOMER MOREHOUSE, 27, in the 87th hour of a record-setting 90-hour, 10-minute dance marathon.

EXONERATED, 1921. EIGHT CHICAGO WHITE SOX PLAYERS charged with taking bribes to throw the 1919 World Series. The players were found "not guilty" when grand jury testimony disappeared. Newly appointed commissioner of baseball Kenesaw Mountain Landis banned the "Black Sox" from baseball.

CULVER PICTURES

MAKING A COMEBACK. SANTA CLAUS, after falling into low favor in the last decade. Aiming at children, advertisers are marketing St. Nick heavily.

WHAT'S NEW
Invented This Decade
How did we live without . . .

- push-button elevators
- neon signs
- oven thermostats
- electric razors
- tissues
- spiral-bound notebooks
- motels
- dry ice
- zippers
- pop-up toasters
- flavored yogurt
- car radios
- adhesive tape
- food disposals
- water skiing
- automatic potato peeler
- self-winding wristwatch

BROWN BROTHERS

NUMBERS

60,000
Families with radios in 1922

9,000,000
Motor vehicles registered in U.S. in 1920

$2,467,946
Income tax paid by Henry Ford in 1924

500,000
People who wrote to Henry Ford in 1924 begging for money

33.5 Number of hours Charles Lindbergh spent in his nonstop flight from New York to Paris on May 20, 1927

1,800 Tons of ticker tape and shredded paper dropped on Charles Lindbergh in his parade in New York City

$16,000 Cost of cleaning up after the parade

7,000 Job offers received by Lindbergh

3.5 million
Number of letters received by Lindbergh

BROWN BROTHERS

Charles Lindbergh

Portfolio Writing Project
Have students research one of the inventions mentioned in the magazine spread. They should discover what preceded the invention, who invented it, and what improvements were made to the product. Students should also decide if the invention is still relevant today or has become obsolete. Based on their research, students should write a two-page report about their chosen invention.

Compare and Contrast
Have students create two political cartoons, one expressing the popular sentiment about Prohibition and one expressing the concerns over alcohol consumption today.

CLOSE

Have students select one of the numbers and find a correlating statistic for today. For example, a student could identify the number of motor vehicles registered in the United States in the current year.

EXTENDING THE CONTENT

Banned From the Game Commissioner Landis banned all White Sox players from professional baseball, saying that "regardless of the verdict of the juries, no player who throws a ball game, no player who undertakes or promises to throw a ball game, no player who sits in confidence with a bunch of crooked players and does not promptly tell his club about it, will ever play professional baseball." The ban remained in effect, and none of the players were ever allowed to participate in professional baseball again.

1 FOCUS

Section Overview

This section focuses on African American culture during the 1920s, including the Harlem Renaissance and political activism.

Guide to Reading

Answers to Graphic: Causes: Great Migration and racial pride; Effects: important African American writers, jazz, blues, theater; also sparked political change

Preteaching Vocabulary
Have students write a paragraph using at least four of the Key Terms and Names.

SECTION 3 African American Culture

Main Idea
During World War I, the prospect of employment and greater freedoms spurred the "Great Migration" of African Americans from the rural South to industrial cities in the North.

Key Terms and Names
Great Migration, Harlem Renaissance, Claude McKay, Langston Hughes, jazz, Cotton Club, blues, Marcus Garvey

Reading Strategy
Organizing As you read about the African American experience in the 1920s, complete a graphic organizer similar to the one below by filling in the causes and effects of the Harlem Renaissance.

Causes — Harlem Renaissance — Effects

Reading Objectives
• **Describe** the Harlem Renaissance and the rediscovery of African American cultural roots.
• **Explain** the increase in African American political activism.

Section Theme
Groups and Institutions African Americans played stronger political and cultural roles in the 1920s than they had in previous decades.

Preview of Events

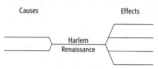

♦1922   ♦1924   ♦1926   ♦1928

1922
Antilynching bill passes in the House but not in the Senate

1924
The Negro League holds its first world series

1926
Langston Hughes's *The Weary Blues* published

1928
Claude McKay's *Home to Harlem* published

★ An American Story ★

Louis Armstrong

On August 8, 1922, a young cornet player named Louis Armstrong took the train from New Orleans to Chicago. His hero, the bandleader Joe "King" Oliver, had sent a telegram to Armstrong offering him a job. Here, Armstrong recalls his trip:

❝When I got to the station in Chicago, I couldn't see Joe Oliver anywhere . . . I'd never seen a city that big. All those tall buildings, I thought they were universities. I said, no, this is the wrong city. I was just fixing to take the next train back home . . . when a red cap [train porter] Joe had left word with came up to me. He took me to the Lincoln Gardens and when I got to the door there and heard Joe and his band wailing so good, I said to myself, 'No, I ain't supposed to be in this band. They're too good.'❞

The next night, near the end of the show, Oliver let Armstrong perform a solo. Armstrong later recalled his feelings: "I had hit the big time. I was up North with the greats. I was playing with my idol, the King, Joe Oliver. My boyhood dream had come true at last."

—quoted in *The African American Family Album*

The Harlem Renaissance

Louis Armstrong's first impressions of Chicago and his desire to fulfill a dream were probably similar to the first impressions and desires of hundreds of thousands of other African Americans who joined in what was called the **Great Migration** from the rural

---

SECTION RESOURCES

Reproducible Masters
• Reproducible Lesson Plan 20–3
• Daily Lecture and Discussion Notes 20–3
• Guided Reading Activity 20–3
• Section Quiz 20–3
• Reading Essentials and Study Guide 20–3

Transparencies
• Daily Focus Skills Transparency 20–3

Multimedia
🖰 Interactive Tutor Self-Assessment CD-ROM
🖰 ExamView® Pro Testmaker CD-ROM
🖰 Presentation Plus! CD-ROM
🖰 TeacherWorks™ CD-ROM
🎧 Audio Program
🎵 American Music: Hits Through History
🎵 American Music: Cultural Traditions

South to industrial cities in the North. By moving north, African Americans sought to escape the segregated society of the South, to find economic opportunities, and to build better lives. After World War I, black populations swelled in large northern cities. The cities were full of nightclubs and music, particularly in the New York City neighborhood of Harlem—the heart and soul of the African American renaissance. It was there that African Americans created an environment that stimulated artistic development, racial pride, a sense of community, and political organization. The result was a flowering of African American arts that became known as the **Harlem Renaissance.**

The Writers Considered the first important writer of the Harlem Renaissance, **Claude McKay** emigrated from Jamaica to New York. There, he translated the shock of American racism into *Harlem Shadows,* a collection of poetry published in 1922. In such poems as "The Lynching" and "If We Must Die," McKay's eloquent verse expressed a proud defiance and bitter contempt of racism—two striking characteristics of Harlem Renaissance writing.

One of the most prolific, original, and versatile writers of the Harlem Renaissance was **Langston Hughes.** Born in Joplin, Missouri, Hughes became a leading voice of the African American experience in the United States. *(See American Literature on page 631 for more information on Langston Hughes.)*

Harlem Renaissance authors continue to influence writers today. **Zora Neale Hurston** published her first novels, *Jonah's Gourd Vine* and *Their Eyes Were Watching God,* in the 1930s. These works influenced such contemporary authors as Ralph Ellison and Toni Morrison. Hurston's personal and spirited portrayals of rural African American culture, often set in Florida where she grew up, were also the first major stories featuring African American females as central characters. Other notable writers of the Harlem Renaissance include Countee Cullen, Alain Locke, Dorothy West, and Nella Larsen.

Jazz, Blues, and the Theater Shortly after **Louis Armstrong** arrived in Chicago from New Orleans, he introduced an improvisational, early form of jazz, a style of music influenced by Dixieland music and ragtime, with its ragged rhythms and syncopated melodies.

In 1925, three years after joining Joe "King" Oliver's band, Armstrong awed fellow musicians with a series of recordings made with his group, the "Hot Five." In these recordings, especially in the song "Cornet Chop Suey," Armstrong broke away from the New Orleans tradition of ensemble or group playing by performing highly imaginative solos. He became the first great cornet and trumpet soloist in jazz music.

Ragtime also influenced the composer, pianist, and bandleader **Duke Ellington,** who listened as a teenager to ragtime piano players in Washington, D.C. In 1923 Ellington formed a small band, moved to New York, and began playing in speakeasies and clubs. He soon created his own sound, a blend of improvisation and orchestration using different combinations of instruments. The Ellington style appeared in such hits as "Mood Indigo" and "Sophisticated Lady."

Like many other African American entertainers, Ellington got his start at the **Cotton Club,** one of the most famous Harlem nightspots. Years later, reflecting on the music of this era, Ellington said, "Everything, and I repeat, *everything* had to swing. And that was just it, those cats really had it; they had that soul. And you know you can't just play some of this music without soul. Soul is very important."

Picturing History

Renaissance Writers Claude McKay wrote about his Jamaican homeland, while Zora Neale Hurston celebrated the courage of African Americans in the rural South. How did these writers contribute to African Americans' cultural identity?

HISTORY Online

Student Web Activity Visit the *American Vision* Web site at tav.glencoe.com and click on *Student Web Activities— Chapter 20* for an activity on the Jazz Age.

HISTORY Online

Objectives and answers to the student activity can be found in the **Web Activity Lesson Plan** at tav.glencoe.com.

2 TEACH

Daily Lecture and Discussion Notes 20–3

Copyright © by The McGraw-Hill Companies, Inc.

Daily Lecture and Discussion Notes
Chapter 20, Section 3

Did You Know? Langston Hughes was a recent graduate from high school when his first poem, "The Negro Speaks of Rivers," was published. He enrolled in Columbia University in 1921, but only stayed a year. While working as a busboy in a Washington, D.C., hotel in 1925, Hughes showed some of his writings to poet Vachel Lindsay, who helped Hughes get his work published.

I.   **The Harlem Renaissance** *(pages 626–628)*

   A. The Great Migration occurred when hundreds of thousands of African Americans from the rural South headed to industrial cities in the North with the hope of a better life.

Reading Poetry Have students select a poem by an African American poet of the Harlem Renaissance and prepare to read it aloud for the class. Suggest that students work in pairs as they practice reading the poetry with the proper rhythm and intonation. **L1**

Picturing History

Answer: by writing proudly about their own experience
Ask: What two striking characteristics of Harlem Renaissance writing are evident in some of McKay's poetry? *(proud defiance and bitter contempt of racism)*

COOPERATIVE LEARNING ACTIVITY

Holding Panel Discussions Have students prepare for a panel discussion on aspects of the following general topic: The Legacy of the Harlem Renaissance. Organize students into groups which have students with varying abilities and interests. Each group should decide on a focus for its discussion. Remind students that each person should contribute to the discussion.

Use the rubric for a cooperative group management plan on pages 81–82 in the *Performance Assessment Activities and Rubrics.*

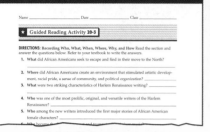
✓ Reading Check

Answer: They developed the rhythms and sound of jazz and the blues; their literature reflected the African American as a part of American life.

Picturing History

Answer: After World War I, many African Americans moved to large cities. There they found many nightclubs that welcomed them as performers. The African American community in these cities stimulated artistic development, racial pride, a sense of community, and political organization.
Ask: Although they made economic gains, what persistent problems still existed for African Americans? *(segregation and racial prejudice)*

📖 History *and the* Humanities

- 🎵 American Music: Hits Through History: "Ain't Misbehavin'," "These Foolish Things"
- 🎵 American Music: Cultural Traditions: "Muskrat Ramble," "Downhearted Blues"

Bessie Smith seemed to symbolize soul. Her emotional singing style and commanding voice earned her the title "the Empress of the Blues." Smith sang of unfulfilled love, poverty, and oppression—the classic themes of the blues, a soulful style of music that evolved from African American spirituals. Born in Tennessee, Smith started performing in tent shows, saloons, and small theaters in the South. Discovered by Ma Rainey, one of the first great blues singers, Smith later performed with many of the greatest jazz bands of the era, including those of Louis Armstrong, Fletcher Henderson, and Benny Goodman. Her first recorded song, "Down Hearted Blues," became a major hit in 1923.

While jazz and blues filled the air during the Harlem Renaissance, the theater arts were also flourishing. *Shuffle Along*, the first musical written, produced, and performed by African Americans, made its debut on Broadway in 1921. The show's success helped launch a number of careers, including those of Florence Mills and Paul Robeson.

Paul Robeson, a celebrated singer and actor, received wide acclaim in the title role of a 1924 New York production of *Emperor Jones,* a play by Eugene O'Neill. In 1928 Robeson gained fame for his work in the musical *Show Boat.* He also often appeared at the Apollo Theater, another famous entertainment club in Harlem. Robeson's fame ultimately spread to Europe, where he became well known as a singer and actor.

Perhaps the most daring performer of the era, Josephine Baker transformed a childhood knack for flamboyance into a career as a well-known singer and dancer. Baker performed on Broadway but went to Paris to dance in 1925. Baker took Paris by storm, launching an international career.

The Harlem Renaissance succeeded in bringing international fame to African American arts. It also sparked a political transformation in the United States.

✓ Reading Check
Analyzing Analyze how African Americans helped shape the national identity through the use of music.

Picturing History

Harlem Renaissance The growing fame of African American artists, who often performed (but could not be patrons) at Harlem's "Cotton Club," encouraged a flamboyant lifestyle. What conditions encouraged the growth of African American art?

MEETING SPECIAL NEEDS

Auditory/Musical Have interested students create a presentation titled "Introduction to Jazz." Encourage students to create a multimedia presentation that provides a musical overview of the musical patterns and themes common in jazz. **L2**

📂 Refer to *Inclusion for the High School Social Studies Classroom Strategies and Activities* in the TCR.

African American Politics

The racial pride that sparked the artistic achievements of the Harlem Renaissance also fueled the political and economic aspirations of many African Americans. The postwar years saw the development of new attitudes among African Americans, who forged new roles in life and in politics. For many, the sight of the 1,300 African American men of the Fifteenth Regiment of New York's National Guard, returning from the war and marching through Manhattan and home to Harlem, symbolized these aspirations. W.E.B. Du Bois, editor of *The Crisis*, captured the new sense of dignity and defiance of African Americans:

> 66We return.
> We return from fighting.
> We return fighting.
> Make way for democracy! We saved it in France, and
> by the Great Jehovah, we will save it in the United
> States of America, or know the reason why.99
>
> —from *When Harlem Was in Vogue*

The Black Vote in the North The Great Migration had a significant impact on the political power of African Americans in the North. As their numbers grew in certain city neighborhoods, African Americans became a powerful voting bloc that could sometimes sway the outcome of elections.

At election time, most African American voters in the North cast their votes for Republicans, the party of Abraham Lincoln. In 1928 African American voters in Chicago achieved a significant political breakthrough. Voting as a bloc, they helped elect **Oscar DePriest,** the first African American representative in Congress from a Northern state. During his three terms in Congress, DePriest introduced laws to provide pensions to formerly enslaved African Americans over 75 years old, to declare Lincoln's birthday a public holiday, and to fine and imprison officials who allowed lynchings of prisoners.

The NAACP Battles Lynching On the legal front, the National Association for the Advancement of Colored People (NAACP) battled valiantly but often unsuccessfully against segregation and discrimination against African Americans. Its efforts focused primarily on lobbying public officials and working through the court system.

From its beginning in 1909, the NAACP lobbied and protested against the horrors of lynching. The NAACP's persistent efforts led to the passage of anti-lynching legislation in the House of

World History Connection

Jazz's Global Roots

Jazz may be an American creation, but its roots stretch across the Atlantic Ocean to Europe and Africa. The music Louis Armstrong and Duke Ellington helped to make famous originated from the spirituals and work songs of African slaves. These songs were a blend of African rhythms and European melodies and harmonies, which African slaves encountered after arriving in North America. This music evolved into ragtime during the late 1800s and early 1900s. By the 1920s, artists had combined aspects of ragtime with the uniquely African American sounds of the blues, and thus jazz was born. *Why do you think music often spreads easily across different cultures?*

Representatives in 1922. The Senate defeated the bill, but the NAACP continued to lobby against lynching throughout the 1920s and 1930s. Its ongoing efforts kept the issue in the news and probably helped to reduce the number of lynchings that took place.

One of the NAACP's greatest political triumphs occurred in 1930 with the defeat of Judge John J. Parker's nomination to the U.S. Supreme Court. The NAACP joined with labor unions to launch a highly organized national campaign against the North Carolina judge, who allegedly was racist and anti-labor. By a narrow margin, the Senate refused to confirm Parker's nomination. His defeat demonstrated that African American voters and lobby groups had finally begun to achieve enough influence to affect national politics and change decisions in Congress.

While some people were fighting for integration and improvement in the economic and political position of African Americans, other groups began to emphasize black nationalism and black pride. Eventually, some began to call for black separation from white society.

Black Nationalism and Marcus Garvey A dynamic black leader from Jamaica, **Marcus Garvey,** captured the imagination of millions of African Americans with his call for "Negro Nationalism," which glorified the black culture and traditions of the past.

Inspired by Booker T. Washington's call for self-reliance, Garvey founded the Universal Negro Improvement Association (UNIA), an organization aimed at promoting black pride and unity. The central message of Garvey's Harlem-based movement was that African Americans could gain economic and

CHAPTER 20 The Jazz Age **629**

World History Connection

Answer: There is no language barrier; everyone can appreciate instrumental music.
Ask: What elements were blended together to create jazz? *(ragtime and blues)*

you don't say...

All That Jazz The origin of the term *jazz* is one notable dispute in American English. It may have come from the word *Chaz*, the nickname of an early ragtime drummer named Charles Washington, or from *chasse*, a kind of dance step. African and Creole sources are also possibilities.

3 ASSESS

Assign Section 3 Assessment as homework or as an in-class activity.

🖲 Have students use the **Interactive Tutor Self-Assessment CD-ROM.**

Reading Essentials and Study Guide 20–3

Name _____ Date _____ Class _____

Study Guide
Chapter 20, Section 3
For use with textbook pages 626–630
AFRICAN AMERICAN CULTURE

KEY TERMS AND NAMES

Great Migration the movement of African Americans from the rural South to the industrial North (page 626)
Harlem Renaissance the flourishing of African American arts (page 627)
Claude McKay an important writer of the Harlem Renaissance (page 627)
Langston Hughes a writer of the Harlem Renaissance and leading voice of the African American experience in the United States (page 627)
jazz a style of music influenced by Dixieland music and ragtime (page 627)
Cotton Club a famous Harlem nightspot (page 627)

INTERDISCIPLINARY CONNECTIONS ACTIVITY

Music Have students listen to recordings of jazz and blues performances by popular musicians from the 1920s, such as Duke Ellington and Bessie Smith. Instruct students to use the library, Internet, and other resources to learn more about the performer they have selected. Have students prepare a profile of the life of their chosen performer. Encourage students to include a look at their music and their personal lives. **L2**

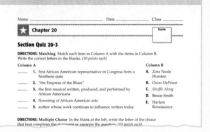
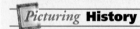

Picturing **History**

Answer: He was convicted of mail fraud and deported. His attempts to revive his movement worldwide failed.

✓ Reading Check

Answer: African Americans saw themselves as defenders of democracy and thus entitled to all the rights of citizens.

Reteach

Have students describe the rediscovery of African American cultural roots.

Enrich

Invite students to read one of the novels mentioned in the section and write a book report.

4 CLOSE

Have students explain the increase in African American political activism.

Picturing **History**

Black Nationalism Marcus Garvey's Universal Negro Improvement Association advocated African American self-reliance and separation from whites and white society. *What eventually happened to Garvey and his movement?*

Harlem in a show of support. Garvey told his followers they would never find justice or freedom in America, and he proposed to lead them to Africa.

Garvey's plan to create a settlement in the African country of Liberia alarmed France and Great Britain, which governed surrounding territories. In the United States, the emerging African American middle class and intellectuals distanced themselves from Garvey and his push for racial purity and separation. FBI officials saw UNIA as a dangerous catalyst for black uprisings in urban areas. Garvey also alienated key figures in the Harlem Renaissance by characterizing them as "weak-kneed and cringing . . . [flatterers of] the white man."

Garvey was convicted of mail fraud in 1923 and served time in prison. In 1927 President Coolidge commuted Garvey's sentence and used Garvey's immigrant status to have him deported to Jamaica. Garvey's subsequent attempts to revitalize his movement from abroad failed.

Despite Garvey's failure to keep his movement alive, he inspired millions of African Americans with a sense of pride in their heritage and hope for the future. That sense of pride and hope survived long after Garvey and his "back to Africa" movement was gone. This pride and hope reemerged strongly during the 1950s and played a vital role in the civil rights movement of the 1960s.

political power by educating themselves. Garvey also advocated separation and independence from whites.

In 1920, at the height of his power, Garvey presided over an international conference in the UNIA Liberty Hall in Harlem. After the convention, about 50,000 people, led by Garvey, marched through the streets of

✓ Reading Check **Summarizing** How did World War I change attitudes among African Americans toward themselves and their country?

SECTION 3 ASSESSMENT

Checking for Understanding

1. **Define:** jazz, blues.
2. **Identify:** Great Migration, Harlem Renaissance, Claude McKay, Langston Hughes, Cotton Club, Marcus Garvey.
3. **Explain** how Bessie Smith's blues music conveyed universal themes.
4. **Explain** the importance of the defeat of Judge John Parker's nomination to the U.S. Supreme Court.
5. **Describe** the goals of Marcus Garvey's Universal Negro Improvement Association.

Reviewing Themes

6. **Groups and Institutions** What actions did the NAACP take to expand political rights for African Americans?

Critical Thinking

7. **Synthesizing** How did the Great Migration affect the political power of African Americans in the North?
8. **Analyzing** How did Duke Ellington create a new musical style that grew out of the ragtime tradition?
9. **Organizing** Use a graphic organizer similar to the one below to describe the impact of the Harlem Renaissance on U.S. society.

Impact of Harlem Renaissance

Analyzing Visuals

10. **Examining Photographs** Study the pictures on page 628 of the Cotton Club and African Americans posing by their car. What are some elements of these pictures that show African Americans adopting parts of the 1920s social culture?

Writing About History

11. **Descriptive Writing** Imagine that you witnessed the African American men of the Fifteenth Regiment of New York's National Guard, who had come back from the war, march through Manhattan and home to Harlem. Write a paragraph describing your feelings upon seeing these men.

SECTION 3 ASSESSMENT ANSWERS

1. Terms are in blue.
2. Great Migration (p. 626), Harlem Renaissance (p. 627), Claude McKay (p. 627), Langston Hughes (p. 627), Cotton Club (p. 627), Marcus Garvey (p. 629)
3. She sang of love, poverty, and oppression.
4. showed political strength of African Americans
5. emphasized black pride and separate African American society
6. lobbied and worked through the courts
7. created a strong voting bloc
8. distinctive orchestration and improvisation
9. literature; new styles of music; theater; political influence
10. style of clothing
11. Students' paragraphs should focus on emotional responses.

American
LITERATURE

Langston Hughes was born in Joplin, Missouri, in 1902. After high school Hughes went on to Columbia University to study engineering, but he soon dropped out to pursue his first love—poetry. Hughes eventually became known as the "Poet Laureate of Harlem." The following poems are representative of Hughes's work. In "I, Too" he describes the disenfranchisement many African Americans felt in the United States in the 1920s, and their willingness to stand up and take pride in their heritage. In "The Negro Speaks of Rivers," Hughes reveals a profound love of his heritage.

Read to Discover

What is Hughes's perception of the place of African Americans in society at the time he wrote these poems?

Reader's Dictionary

Euphrates: River in the Middle East

Congo and **Nile:** Rivers in Africa

lulled: calmed; soothed

Selected Poems by Langston Hughes

The Negro Speaks of Rivers

I've known rivers:
I've known rivers ancient as the
    world and older than the
flow of human blood in human veins.

My soul has grown deep like the
    rivers.

I bathed in the Euphrates when
    dawns were young.
I built my hut near the Congo and it
    lulled me to sleep.
I looked upon the Nile and raised
    the pyramids above it.
I heard the singing of the Mississippi
    when Abe Lincoln went down to
    New Orleans, and I've seen its
    muddy bosom turn all golden in
    the sunset.

I've known rivers:
Ancient, dusky rivers

My soul has grown deep like the
    rivers.

I, Too

I, too, sing America.

I am the darker brother.
They send me to eat in the kitchen
When company comes,
But I laugh,
And eat well,
And grow strong.

Tomorrow,
I'll be at the table
When company comes.
Nobody'll dare
Say to me,
"Eat in the kitchen,"
Then.

Besides,
They'll see how beautiful I am
And be ashamed—

I, too, am America.

Analyzing Literature

1. **Recall and Interpret** How do you think Hughes's use of punctuation and line breaks helps convey his point?
2. **Evaluate and Connect** Do you think these poems convey a positive message or a negative one? Why?

Interdisciplinary Activity
Response Writing The poem "I, Too" is a response to Walt Whitman's poem, "I Hear America Singing." Using the Internet or other resources, find and read Whitman's poem. In small groups, try to figure out how Hughes's poem ties in to Whitman's. Then write your own response poem to "I Hear America Singing."

Block Schedule

Team Teaching This selection of poems by Langston Hughes can be presented in conjunction with English or Language Arts.

Read to Discover
Answer: The poem indicates that African Americans are not currently accepted in American society but they will be in the future.

Reinforcing Vocabulary
Have students locate and label the rivers on a world map.

Historical Connection
Point out that "I, too" demonstrates the racial pride that was characteristic of the Harlem Renaissance.

Portfolio Writing Activity
Have students read "The Weary Blues" and listen to a recording by blues singer Bessie Smith. Instruct students to write a short paper on the poem and blues music.

HISTORY
Online

Refer to tav.glencoe.com for additional Glencoe Literature titles, lesson plans, and study guides related to this unit.

Answers to Analyzing Literature

1. Answers will vary. The use of punctuation and line breaks forces the reader to pause and reflect on the line just read.

2. Possible response: a positive, hopeful message; the poet suggests that while things are not good now, there is hope for the future

Interdisciplinary Activity
Students' answers will vary. Encourage students to reflect on their own experiences in composing their response.

Reviewing Key Terms
Students' answers will vary. The pages where the words appear in the text are shown in parentheses.

1. **anarchist** (p. 611)
2. **eugenics** (p. 611)
3. **flapper** (p. 613)
4. **evolution** (p. 614)
5. **creationism** (p. 614)
6. **police powers** (p. 615)
7. **speakeasy** (p. 615)
8. **Bohemian** (p. 621)
9. **mass media** (p. 623)
10. **jazz** (p. 627)
11. **blues** (p. 628)

Reviewing Key Facts
12. Emergency Quota Act (p. 612), Fundamentalism (p. 614), Carl Sandburg (p. 621), Eugene O'Neill (p. 621), Ernest Hemingway (p. 621), F. Scott Fitzgerald (p. 622), Great Migration (p. 626), Harlem Renaissance (p. 627), Claude McKay (p. 627), Langston Hughes (p. 627), Marcus Garvey (p. 629)
13. influx of immigrants and a recession
14. Emergency Quota Act and National Origins Act
15. Southern and Eastern Europeans
16. allowed them to escape parents' control
17. It was a religious movement to reassert the Bible's authority in life.
18. The communities offered freedom from conformity and traditional ideas.
19. because of its large, concentrated African American population
20. Harlem Renaissance and African American experience in World War I

632

Reviewing Key Terms
On a sheet of paper, use each of these terms in a sentence.

1. anarchist
2. eugenics
3. flapper
4. evolution
5. creationism
6. police powers
7. speakeasy
8. Bohemian
9. mass media
10. jazz
11. blues

Chapter Summary

Cultural Changes
- The "new morality" emphasized youth and beauty
- Young people and women gained more independence
- The working class enjoyed more leisure time
- The mass media expanded

African American Renaissance

Harlem Renaissance
- Breakthrough period for African American arts
- Literature revealed racial pride and contempt of racism
- Jazz and blues popularized

Political Renaissance
- Great Migration created strong African American voting blocs in northern cities
- First African American elected to Congress from a northern state
- NAACP battled segregation and discrimination

Revitalized Traditional Values
- Fundamentalists preached traditional religious values
- Emphasis on family and moral values
- Traditionalists supported Prohibition

Nativism
- Nativists used eugenics as a pseudo-scientific basis for ethnic and religious prejudice
- The new Ku Klux Klan targeted African Americans, Jews, Catholics, immigrants, and other groups they considered to be "un-American"
- Congress established immigration quotas

632 CHAPTER 20 The Jazz Age

Reviewing Key Facts
12. **Identify:** Emergency Quota Act, Fundamentalism, Carl Sandburg, Eugene O'Neill, Ernest Hemingway, F. Scott Fitzgerald, Great Migration, Harlem Renaissance, Claude McKay, Langston Hughes, Marcus Garvey.
13. Why was there a rise in racism and nativism in the 1920s?
14. What actions did Congress and the president take during the first half of the 1920s to restrict immigration?
15. What national groups were affected most by the new restrictions on immigration?
16. What role did the automobile play in changing the way that young people in the United States lived and socialized?
17. What was the Fundamentalist movement?
18. Why did artists and writers move to Greenwich Village and Chicago's South Side in the 1920s?
19. Why was Harlem the center of the African American renaissance?
20. What were two reasons for the rise in African American political activism?

Critical Thinking
21. **Analyzing Themes: Groups and Institutions** In what ways did the new morality change American family life?
22. **Interpreting** Why was Charles Lindbergh a symbol of modern America?
23. **Determining Cause and Effect** Analyze the causes and effects of the changing role of women in the 1920s.
24. **Identifying** List three works of American art or literature that convey universal themes.
25. **Analyzing** Analyze the impact that Clarence Darrow and William Jennings Bryan had on American society as the lawyers in the Scopes trial.
26. **Categorizing** Use a graphic organizer similar to the one below to list the major organizations and movements of the 1920s and their goals or purposes.

Organizations/Movements	Goals/Purposes

27. **Interpreting Primary Sources** Arna Bontemps was a poet who started his writing career during the Harlem Renaissance. Read the poem and answer the questions that follow.

Critical Thinking
21. The new morality increased youth's independence and allowed women to develop a personal identity that was demonstrated in work and fashion.
22. His solo flights restored Americans' belief in the courageous, pioneering individual.
23. Causes: new morality, more education, and job experience; Effects: greater public freedom, women's contributions in new fields

24. Students' answers will vary but should include reasonable examples from the text.
25. They caused a debate over science and religion.
26. the new morality aimed to expand individual freedom; Fundamentalism aimed to restore the Bible's authority; Prohibition aimed to ban alcohol
27. **a.** He has worked hard all his life but has little to show for it. **b.** disillusionment

Self-Check Quiz

Visit the *American Vision* Web site at tav.glencoe.com and click on *Self-Check Quizzes—Chapter 20* to assess your knowledge of chapter content.

A Black Man Talks of Reaping

I have sown beside all waters in my day.
I planted deep, within my heart the fear
That wind or fowl would take the grain away.
I planted safe against this stark, lean year.

I scattered seed enough to plant the land
In rows from Canada to Mexico
But for my reaping only what the hand
Can hold at once is all that I can show.

Yet what I sowed and what the orchard yields
My brother's sons are gathering stalk and root,
Small wonder then my children glean in fields
They have not sown, and feed on bitter fruit.

a. What does Bontemps mean by "what the hand can hold at once is all that I can show" and "bitter fruit"?

b. What major theme of Harlem Renaissance writing is evident in this poem?

Practicing Skills

28. Synthesizing Information Read the subsections titled "Nativism Resurges" and "Pseudo-Scientific Racism" at the beginning of Section 1. What information is presented in the first subsection? The second? Synthesize the information in these two subsections and write a short statement that describes American attitudes toward immigrants during the 1920s.

Chapter Activities

29. Research Project Work with another student to research the art of Georgia O'Keeffe made in the 1920s. Examine how her efforts reflect the characteristics of the Jazz Age, such as experimentation and innovation. Present your findings to the class.

30. American History Primary Source Document Library CD-ROM Under *The Roaring Twenties,* read "The Movies" by Preston William Slossen. Work with a few of your classmates to write an article that compares and contrasts the motion picture industry in the 1920s with the motion picture industry today.

Writing Activity

31. Persuasive Writing Imagine that you are living during the early 1920s. Marcus Garvey is campaigning to lead African Americans to a new settlement to be founded in Liberia.

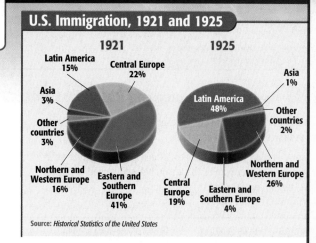

U.S. Immigration, 1921 and 1925

1921

Latin America 15%
Central Europe 22%
Asia 3%
Other countries 3%
Northern and Western Europe 16%
Eastern and Southern Europe 41%

1925

Asia 1%
Latin America 48%
Other countries 2%
Northern and Western Europe 26%
Central Europe 19%
Eastern and Southern Europe 4%

Source: *Historical Statistics of the United States*

Write a letter to a newspaper editor in which you take a position on the merits of Garvey's plan. In your letter, describe how you think this plan will affect the nation and your own community.

Geography and History

32. The circle graphs above show immigration numbers in the United States in 1921 and 1925. Study the graphs and answer the questions below.

a. Interpreting Graphs What significant changes in immigration do the circle graphs show?

b. Applying Geography Skills Why did these changes in immigration occur between 1921 and 1925?

Standardized Test Practice

Directions: Choose the best answer to the following question.

Which of the following trends of the 1920s did NOT contribute to a renewed nativist movement?

A Economic recession

B Influx of immigrants

C Fear of radicals and Communists

D Prohibition

Test-Taking Tip: First you must be clear on the meaning of nativism. Then use the process of elimination to rule out the one answer that seems the least related to the definition of nativism.

Have students visit the Web site at tav.glencoe.com to review Chapter 20 and take the Self-Check Quiz.

Writing Activity

31. Letters to the editor will vary but should express a clear point of view.

Geography and History

32. a. They show a dramatic increase in the percentage of immigrants from Latin America and a dramatic decrease in the percentage of immigrants from Eastern and Southern Europe. **b.** changes in immigration laws

Standardized Test Practice

Answer: D
Test-Taking Tip: If students know that nativism means favoring native-born people over immigrants they can infer an influx of immigrants contributed to nativism. This means students can eliminate B. Although some fundamentalists were nativists, fundamentalist beliefs were not anti-immigrant. Therefore students can infer that the correct answer is D.

Bonus Question ?

Ask: Billy Sunday and Aimee Semple McPherson are both regarded as examples of what religious movement of the 1920s? *(Fundamentalism)*

Practicing Skills

28. Students' statements will vary but should reflect the difficulties faced by immigrants during the 1920s.

Chapter Activities

29. Multimedia presentations featuring O'Keeffe and her works are ideal.

30. Students' comparisons will vary and should include specific examples.

Chapter 21 Resources

Timesaving Tools

TeacherWorks™ All-In-One Planner and Resource Center

- **Interactive Teacher Edition** Access your Teacher Wraparound Edition and your classroom resources with a few easy clicks.
- **Interactive Lesson Planner** Planning has never been easier! Organize your week, month, semester, or year with all the lesson helps you need to make teaching creative, timely, and relevant.

Use Glencoe's **Presentation Plus!** multimedia teacher tool to easily present dynamic lessons that visually excite your students. Using Microsoft PowerPoint® you can customize the presentations to create your own personalized lessons.

TEACHING TRANSPARENCIES

Graphic Organizer 1

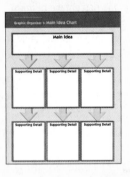

Why It Matters Chapter Transparency 21

APPLICATION AND ENRICHMENT

Linking Past and Present Activity 21

Enrichment Activity 21

Primary Source Reading 21

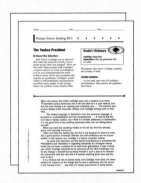

REVIEW AND REINFORCEMENT

Reteaching Activity 21

Vocabulary Activity 21

Time Line Activity 21

Critical Thinking Skills Activity 21

Meeting NCSS Standards

The following standards are highlighted in Chapter 21:

Section 1 VI Power, Authority, and Governance: B, E
Section 2 VIII Science, Technology, and Society: A, B, C
Section 3 VII Production, Distribution, and Consumption: A, D, F

Local Standards

_____

_____

_____

_____

_____

ASSESSMENT AND EVALUATION

GLENCOE'S
ASSESSMENT
ADVANTAGE

**Chapter 21 Test
Form A**

**Chapter 21 Test
Form B**

**Standardized Test Skills
Practice Workbook Activity 21**

**Performance Assessment
Activities and Rubrics 21**

**ExamView® Pro
Testmaker CD-ROM**

MULTIMEDIA

- Vocabulary PuzzleMaker CD-ROM
- Interactive Tutor Self-Assessment CD-ROM
- ExamView® Pro Testmaker CD-ROM
- Audio Program
- American History Primary Source Documents
  Library CD-ROM
- MindJogger Videoquiz
- Presentation Plus! CD-ROM
- TeacherWorks™ CD-ROM
- Interactive Student Edition CD-ROM
- Glencoe Skillbuilder Interactive Workbook
  CD-ROM, Level 2
- The *American Vision* Video Program
- American Music: Hits Through History
- American Music: Cultural Traditions

 Biography
A&E HOME VIDEO.

THE HISTORY CHANNEL®

The following videotape programs are available
from Glencoe as supplements to Chapter 21:

- **Amelia Earhart** (ISBN 1-56-501960-1)
- **Henry Ford: Tin Lizzy Tycoon** (ISBN 1-56-501380-8)
- **Radio: Out of Thin Air** (ISBN 0-76-700464-7)

To order, call Glencoe at 1-800-334-7344. To find classroom resources to
accompany many of these videos, check the following home pages:
A&E Television: www.aande.com
The History Channel: www.historychannel.com

SPANISH RESOURCES

**The following Spanish language materials are
available in the Spanish Resources Binder:**

- Spanish Guided Reading Activities
- Spanish Reteaching Activities
- Spanish Quizzes and Tests
- Spanish Vocabulary Activities
- Spanish Summaries
- The Declaration of Independence and United States Constitution
  Spanish Translation

HISTORY
Online

Use our Web site for additional resources. All essential content is covered in the Student Edition.

You and your students can visit tav.glencoe.com, the Web site companion to the *American Vision.* This innovative integration of electronic
and print media offers your students a wealth of opportunities. The
student text directs students to the Web site for the following options:

- **Chapter Overviews**   • **Student Web Activities**
- **Self-Check Quizzes**   • **Textbook Updates**

Answers to the student Web activities are provided for you in the **Web
Activity Lesson Plans.** Additional Web resources and Interactive Tutor
Puzzles are also available.

SECTION RESOURCES

Daily Objectives	Reproducible Resources	Multimedia Resources
SECTION 1 **Presidential Politics** 1. Describe the corruption that tainted the Harding administration. 2. Explain how Calvin Coolidge restored public confidence after assuming the presidency.	Reproducible Lesson Plan 21–1 Daily Lecture and Discussion Notes 21–1 Guided Reading Activity 21–1* Section Quiz 21–1* Reading Essentials and Study Guide 21–1 Performance Assessment Activities and Rubrics	Daily Focus Skills Transparency 21–1 Interactive Tutor Self-Assessment CD-ROM ExamView® Pro Testmaker CD-ROM Presentation Plus! CD-ROM TeacherWorks™ CD-ROM Audio Program
SECTION 2 **A Growing Economy** 1. Analyze how the growing importance of the automobile and other new industries improved the U.S. standard of living. 2. Analyze the growing economic crisis in farming in the 1920s.	Reproducible Lesson Plan 21–2 Daily Lecture and Discussion Notes 21–2 Guided Reading Activity 21–2* Section Quiz 21–2* Reading Essentials and Study Guide 21–2 Performance Assessment Activities and Rubrics	Daily Focus Skills Transparency 21–2 Interactive Tutor Self-Assessment CD-ROM ExamView® Pro Testmaker CD-ROM Presentation Plus! CD-ROM TeacherWorks™ CD-ROM Audio Program
SECTION 3 **The Policies of Prosperity** 1. Explain Andrew Mellon's economic strategies for maintaining prosperity. 2. Describe how the United States remained involved in world affairs without joining the League of Nations.	Reproducible Lesson Plan 21–3 Daily Lecture and Discussion Notes 21–3 Guided Reading Activity 21–3* Section Quiz 21–3* Reading Essentials and Study Guide 21–3 Performance Assessment Activities and Rubrics	Daily Focus Skills Transparency 21–3 American Art & Architecture Interactive Tutor Self-Assessment CD-ROM ExamView® Pro Testmaker CD-ROM Presentation Plus! CD-ROM Skillbuilder Interactive Workbook, Level 2 TeacherWorks™ CD-ROM Vocabulary PuzzleMaker CD-ROM Audio Program American Music: Hits Through History

0:00 OUT OF TIME?
Assign the Chapter 21 **Reading Essentials and Study Guide.**

*Also Available in Spanish

 Blackline Master   Transparency   CD-ROM   DVD

Poster   Music Program   Audio Program   Videocassette

NATIONAL GEOGRAPHIC Teacher's Corner

INDEX TO NATIONAL GEOGRAPHIC MAGAZINE

The following articles relate to this chapter.
• "Growing up in East Harlem," May 1990
• "Offbeat New Orleans," January 1995
• "Traveling the Blues Highway," April 1999

NATIONAL GEOGRAPHIC SOCIETY PRODUCTS AVAILABLE FROM GLENCOE

To order the following products for use with this chapter, contact your local Glencoe sales representative, or call Glencoe at 1-800-334-7344:
• *PictureShow: Story of America, Part 2* (CD-ROM)
• *PicturePack: Story of America Library, Part 2* (Transparencies)

ADDITIONAL NATIONAL GEOGRAPHIC SOCIETY PRODUCTS

To order the following, call National Geographic at 1-800-368-2728:
• *The Complete National Geographic: 109 Years of National Geographic Magazine* (CD-ROM)
• *Eyewitness to the 20th Century* (Book)

NGS ONLINE

Access National Geographic's Web site for current events, atlas updates, activities, links, interactive features, and archives.
www.nationalgeographic.com

From the Classroom of...

F. Rick Johnston
Shroder Paideia Academy
Cincinnati, OH

"All the News That's Fit to Print"

Introduce the activity by asking students to predict the types of news stories that will be found in a daily newspaper. Responses may include: sports; business; classified; national, international, and local news; entertainment; and editorial. List these quickly on the board.

Ask: If a current newspaper provides a good way to get a sense of national issues and concerns, could newspapers from earlier times in U.S. history reflect the issues and concerns of that era? Why or why not?

Point out that this chapter focuses on the 1920s. Introduce the era of the postwar decade. Explain that the class will be using the format of modern newspapers to create a 1920s newspaper. As the class reads the chapter, have students select "stories" to "cover." Students should label their stories according to the type of "news" it is. For example, the Scopes trial would go on the national news page. The stories should represent the social, economic, and political developments in the chapter.

ADDITIONAL RESOURCES FROM GLENCOE

• American Music: Cultural Traditions
• American Art & Architecture
• Outline Map Resource Book
• U.S. Desk Map
• Building Geography Skills for Life
• Inclusion for the High School Social Studies Classroom Strategies and Activities
• Teaching Strategies for the American History Classroom (Including Block Scheduling Pacing Guides)

KEY TO ABILITY LEVELS

Teaching strategies have been coded.

L1 BASIC activities for all students
L2 AVERAGE activities for average to above-average students
L3 CHALLENGING activities for above-average students
ELL ENGLISH LANGUAGE LEARNER activities

Block Schedule

Activities that are suited to use within the block scheduling framework are identified by:

Performance Assessment

Refer to Activity 21 in the Performance Assessment Activities and Rubrics booklet.

Why It Matters Activity

Have students interview five adults whom they know and ask them when and how they got their first automobile. After students have conducted their interviews, ask them to report their findings. Then ask students how important they think automobiles are to the American way of life. Students should evaluate their answers after they have completed the chapter.

GLENCOE
TECHNOLOGY

The *American Vision* Video Program

To learn more about the importance of the radio in American life, have students view the Chapter 21 video, "Tuning in to Radio in the 1920s," from the *American Vision* Video Program.

Available in DVD and VHS

MindJogger Videoquiz

Use the **MindJogger Videoquiz** to preview Chapter 21 content.

Available in VHS

CHAPTER
21 Normalcy and Good Times
1921–1929

Why It Matters

Prosperity was the theme of the 1920s, and national policy favored business. Although farmers were going through an economic depression, most people remained optimistic about the economy. The middle class bought on credit the many new convenience products available. One of the most popular purchases of the day was the automobile, which had a major impact on how Americans lived.

The Impact Today

Important elements of American life were first seen at this time.
• The automobile remains central to American transportation.
• Credit is a standard means for making purchases.

The American Vision *Video* The Chapter 21 video, "Tuning in to Radio in the 1920s," describes the growth of a mass media culture in the United States and the importance of the radio.

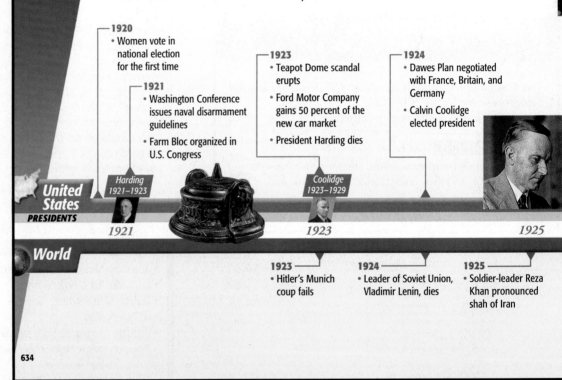

1920
• Women vote in national election for the first time

1921
• Washington Conference issues naval disarmament guidelines
• Farm Bloc organized in U.S. Congress

1923
• Teapot Dome scandal erupts
• Ford Motor Company gains 50 percent of the new car market
• President Harding dies

1924
• Dawes Plan negotiated with France, Britain, and Germany
• Calvin Coolidge elected president

United States PRESIDENTS
Harding 1921–1923
Coolidge 1923–1929

1921   1923   1925

World

1923
• Hitler's Munich coup fails

1924
• Leader of Soviet Union, Vladimir Lenin, dies

1925
• Soldier-leader Reza Khan pronounced shah of Iran

634

TWO-MINUTE LESSON LAUNCHER

Tell students that in 1920, just before he was elected president, Warren G. Harding gave a speech in which he declared, "America's present need is not heroics but healing, not nostrums but normalcy, not revolution but restoration. . . ." Ask students to put the main idea of Harding's statement in their own words. *(Americans are tired of action; they want to rest, to restore a normal life.)* Have students reassess this statement after reading the chapter and see if they agree with Harding's assessment.

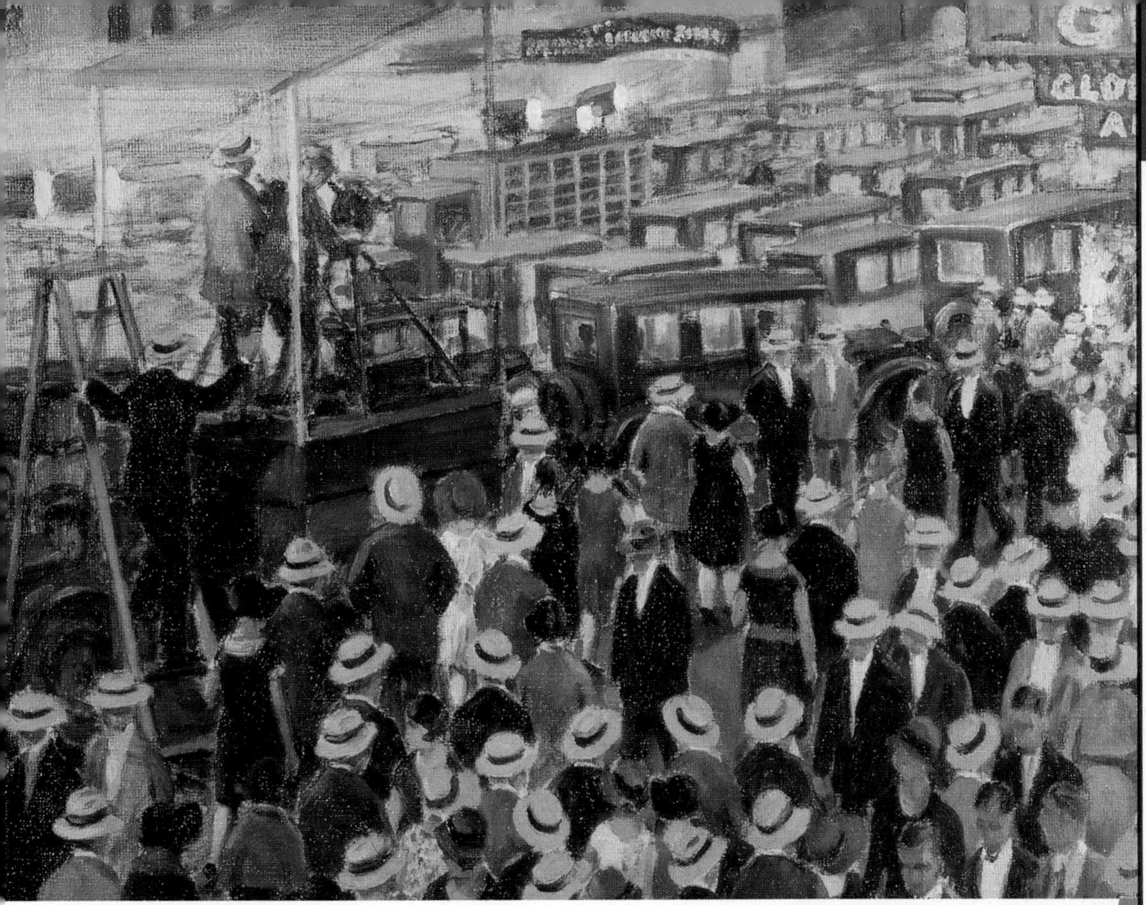

Opening Night, Ziegfeld Follies by Howard A. Thain captures the excitement surrounding the opening of a new musical revue in New York City.

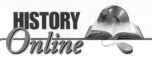

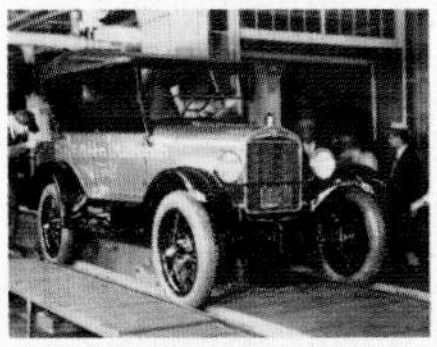

1927
• 15 millionth Model T sold

1928
• Kellogg-Briand Pact proposes an end to war

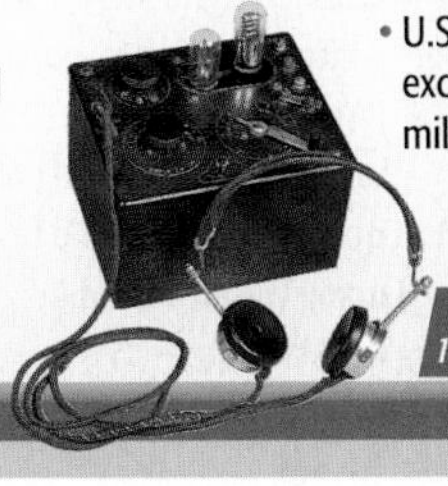

1929
• U.S. radio sales exceed $800 million

Hoover 1929–1933

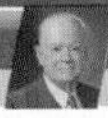

1927 *1929*

1926
• British General Strike paralyzes the British economy

1929
• Lateran Treaties with Italy make the Vatican sovereign territory

HISTORY Online

Chapter Overview
Visit the *American Vision* Web site at tav.glencoe.com and click on ***Chapter Overviews—Chapter 21*** to preview chapter information.

Introducing CHAPTER 21

HISTORY Online

Introduce students to chapter content and key terms by having them access the **Chapter 21 Overview** at tav.glencoe.com.

More About the Art

Howard A. Thain was born in Dallas, Texas. He studied art in St. Louis, Chicago, and New York City. The Impressionist influence can be seen in this oil painting celebrating the opening of Florenz Ziegfeld's "No Foolin'." In the upper right hand corner of the painting, you can see part of the Globe Theater's marquee–"No Foolin'–Globe–Glorifying the American Girl."

TIME LINE ACTIVITY

Have students select an event from the time lines on pages 634–635, 636, 640, and 647. Ask students to read the corresponding portion of the chapter to identify the cause(s) and effect(s) of the events.

GRAPHIC ORGANIZER ACTIVITY

Organizing Information Have students create a graphic organizer similar to the one below to classify members of Harding's administration as effective, ineffective, or involved in scandal.

Effective	Ineffective	Involved in Scandal
Charles Evans Hughes, Secretary of State	*Charles Sawyer, White House Physician*	*Charles R. Forbes, head of Veterans Bureau*
Herbert Hoover, Secretary of Commerce	*Daniel Crissinger, Chairman of the Federal Reserve*	*Albert B. Fall, Secretary of the Interior*

1 FOCUS

Section Overview

This section focuses on the Harding and Coolidge administrations.

BELLRINGER
Skillbuilder Activity

Project transparency and have students answer the question.

Available as a blackline master.

Daily Focus Skills Transparency 21–1

Guide to Reading

Answers to Graphic:
Presidential Politics
I. The Harding Administration
   A. A Self-Doubter in the White House
   B. The Ohio Gang
   C. The Teapot Dome Scandal
II. The Coolidge Administration
   A. "Silent Cal" Takes Over
   B. The Election of 1924

Preteaching Vocabulary
Have students list the Key Terms and Names and add information to clarify their significance.

Guide to Reading

Main Idea
Warren Harding's administration suffered from several scandals. His successor, Calvin Coolidge, promised to support business.

Key Terms and Names
normalcy, Ohio Gang, Albert B. Fall, Teapot Dome scandal, immunity, Progressive Party, Robert M. La Follette

Reading Strategy
Taking Notes As you read about Presidents Harding and Coolidge, use the major headings of the section to create an outline similar to the one below.

Presidential Politics
I. The Harding Administration
   A.
   B.
II.
   A.
   B.

Reading Objectives
• **Describe** the corruption that tainted the Harding administration.
• **Explain** how Calvin Coolidge restored public confidence after assuming the presidency.

Section Theme
Government and Democracy The "Ohio Gang" of the Harding administration created scandals and political upheaval.

Preview of Events

◆1920   ◆1922   ◆1924   ◆1926

1920
Women vote in national election for the first time; Warren G. Harding elected president

1923
Teapot Dome scandal; Harding dies; Calvin Coolidge becomes president

1924
Coolidge elected president in his own right

★ An American Story ★

Calvin Coolidge (right) being sworn in as president after his 1924 election

In August 1923, Vice President Calvin Coolidge was taking a short vacation at his family's homestead in Plymouth Notch, Vermont. The straitlaced Coolidge went to bed at 9:00 as usual on August 2, but at 2:30 A.M., his father woke him. "I noticed that his voice trembled," Coolidge said later. "I knew that something of the gravest nature had occurred." After learning that President Warren G. Harding was dead, Coolidge dressed hurriedly and went downstairs. Shortly afterward, in a small, sparsely furnished room lit by a flickering kerosene lamp, the elder Coolidge, a farmer and justice of the peace, got out the family Bible and administered the presidential oath of office to his son.

Later, while painting a portrait of the new president, artist Charles Hopkinson asked, "Mr. Coolidge, what was the first thought that came into your mind when you were told that Mr. Harding was dead and the presidency was yours?" Coolidge replied, "I thought I could swing it."

—**adapted from *Flappers, Bootleggers, "Typhoid Mary" and the Bomb***

The Harding Administration

Coolidge assumed the presidency during a time when Americans yearned to go back to simpler and steadier times after the carnage of World War I. Coolidge's predecessor, Warren G. Harding, had tailored his presidency to this goal. The oldest of eight children, Harding was born in 1865 in Corsica, Ohio. As an adult, he was active in civic and fraternal organizations, and he also published the *Marion Daily Star*. In 1899 Harding was elected to the Ohio legislature. He fit in comfortably with the powerful Ohio Republican

636 CHAPTER 21 Normalcy and Good Times

SECTION RESOURCES

📂 Reproducible Masters
• Reproducible Lesson Plan 21–1
• Daily Lecture and Discussion Notes 21–1
• Guided Reading Activity 21–1
• Section Quiz 21–1
• Reading Essentials and Study Guide 21–1
• Performance Assessment Activities and Rubrics

📖 Transparencies
• Daily Focus Skills Transparency 21–1

Multimedia
🖳 Interactive Tutor Self-Assessment CD-ROM
🖳 ExamView® Pro Testmaker CD-ROM
🖳 Presentation Plus! CD-ROM
🖳 TeacherWorks™ CD-ROM
🎧 Audio Program

The automobile was just one part of a rising standard of living that Americans experienced in the 1920s. Real per capita earnings soared 22 percent between 1923 and 1929. Meanwhile, as Americans' wages increased, their work hours decreased. In 1923 U.S. Steel cut its daily work shift from 12 hours to 8 hours. In 1926 Henry Ford cut the workweek for his employees from six days to five, and International Harvester, a maker of trucks, tractors, and other farm machinery, instituted an annual two-week paid vacation for employees.

At the same time, the rise of mass production, or large-scale product manufacturing usually done by machinery, created more supply and reduced consumer costs. This formula reshaped the American economy. Within this prosperous and productive atmosphere, innovation thrived and new industries emerged.

TECHNOLOGY

The Assembly Line Another major industrial development enormously increased manufacturing efficiency. First adopted by carmaker Henry Ford, the assembly line divided operations into simple tasks that unskilled workers could do and cut unnecessary

motion to a minimum. In 1913, Ford installed the first moving assembly line at his plant in Highland Park, Michigan. By the following year, workers were building automobiles every 93 minutes. Previously, the task had taken 12 hours. By 1925 a Ford car was rolling off the line every 10 seconds. "The way to make automobiles," Ford said, "is to make one automobile like another . . . to make them come through the factory all alike, just as one pin is like another pin when it comes from the pin factory."

Ford's assembly-line product was the **Model T**— affectionately called the "Tin Lizzie" or "Flivver." In 1908, the Model T's first year, it sold for $850. In 1914 mass production reduced the price to $490. Three years later, improved assembly-line methods and a high volume of sales brought the price down to $360. By 1924 Model Ts were selling for $295, and Ford sold millions of them. His business philosophy was simple: lower the cost per car and thereby increase the volume of sales. "Every time I reduce the charge for our car by one dollar," he boasted, "I get a thousand new buyers." In this way, Ford made the automobile available to millions of American consumers.

Ford also increased his workers' wages in 1914 to an unprecedented $5 a day and reduced the workday

2 TEACH

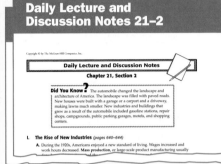

Daily Lecture and Discussion Notes 21–2

Copyright © by The McGraw-Hill Companies, Inc.

Daily Lecture and Discussion Notes
Chapter 21, Section 2

Did You Know? The automobile changed the landscape and architecture of America. The landscape was filled with paved roads. New houses were built with a garage or a carport and a driveway, making lawns much smaller. New industries and buildings that grew as a result of the automobile included gasoline stations, repair shops, campgrounds, public parking garages, motels, and shopping centers.

I. **The Rise of New Industries** (pages 640–644)
   A. During the 1920s, Americans enjoyed a new standard of living. Wages increased and work hours decreased. **Mass production,** or large-scale product manufacturing usually

Demonstrating a Concept
Have students work in small groups to demonstrate the efficiency concept behind the assembly line. Suggest that students use children's building toys for their demonstrations. **L1**

TECHNOLOGY & History

Background: Committed to large-volume production of the Model T, Henry Ford innovated mass-production techniques at his plant in Highland Park, Michigan. The plant opened in 1910, but Ford did not introduce the moving assembly line until 1913. "The step forward in assembly line," Ford said, "came when we began taking the work to the men instead of the men to the work."
Answer: The price fell as the time to manufacture the vehicle decreased.
Ask: What kind of injuries are assembly line workers prone to? *(repetitive stress injuries)*

TECHNOLOGY & History

The Assembly Line

The idea of an assembly line had existed before Henry Ford, but he helped popularize its use in manufacturing. Ford combined sub-assembly lines into one continuously moving line, which was positioned at waist level to reduce back strain. Ford's Highland Park factory featured a multistoried assembly line that reduced the construction time of a single Model T from 12 hours, 8 minutes to 1 hour, 33 minutes. *How did Ford's assembly technique affect the price of his product?*

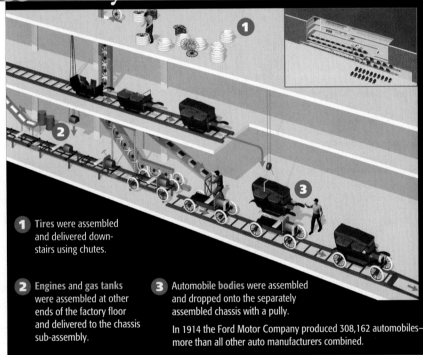

1. **Tires** were assembled and delivered downstairs using chutes.

2. **Engines and gas tanks** were assembled at other ends of the factory floor and delivered to the chassis sub-assembly.

3. Automobile **bodies** were assembled and dropped onto the separately assembled chassis with a pully.

In 1914 the Ford Motor Company produced 308,162 automobiles—more than all other auto manufacturers combined.

COOPERATIVE LEARNING ACTIVITY

Analyzing the Effects of the Automobile Organize the class into groups of five students each. Assign the following roles to one member of each group: advertising executive, assembly line worker, housewife, farmer, and union leader. Pose this question: **How has the automobile affected your life and other Americans like you?** Students should play their assigned roles when answering the question. Encourage members of the group to share information and ask questions of each other until everyone in the group has a good understanding of the effect the automobile had on society.

Use the rubric for a cooperative group management plan on pages 81–82 in the *Performance Assessment Activities and Rubrics.*

Making Comparisons Have students place images of a Model T and a popular contemporary family vehicle on a display board or large piece of paper. Ask them to compare the features of the vehicles. Suggest that students use callouts to highlight the differences and similarities. **L1**

NATIONAL GEOGRAPHIC
MOMENT in HISTORY

In 1920 there were about 8 million cars on the road but fewer than 36,000 miles of paved roads. Few roads had names, numbers, or signs to warn drivers of imminent danger. From 1920 to 1930, about 100,000 miles of road were paved—the government's second-greatest expense.

---

to eight-hour shifts. Ford took these dramatic steps to build up workers' loyalty and to undercut union organizers.

There were strings attached, however, to the wage increase. Ford created a "Sociological Department," which set requirements workers had to meet. For instance, the common practice of renting living space to nonfamily members was strictly forbidden. Investigators visited employees' homes to verify their eligibility and to see that they spent their wages in approved ways. Workers who transgressed could be disqualified from extra pay, suspended, or even fired.

The low prices made possible by Ford's mass-production methods not only created an immense market for his cars but also spawned imitators. By the mid-1920s, other car manufacturers, notably General Motors and Chrysler, competed successfully with Ford.

The auto industry spurred growth in other industries, such as rubber, plate glass, nickel, and lead. Automaking alone consumed 15 percent of the nation's steel, and the flood of cars stimulated a tremendous expansion of the petroleum industry.

The Social Impact of the Automobile Just as he had revolutionized manufacturing, Henry Ford was the force behind a social revolution related to the automobile. He almost single-handedly changed the auto from a toy of the wealthy to an affordable necessity for the middle class.

Cars revolutionized American life. Although many small businesses declined during the 1920s, the automobile created new small-business opportunities for such enterprises as garages and gas stations.

The automobile eased the isolation of rural life, putting towns within reach of many farmers and the countryside a mere ride away for city dwellers. Cars also enabled more people to live farther from work. An entirely new kind of consumer and worker, the auto commuter, appeared. Commuters lived in growing suburban communities and drove to work in the city.

The Consumer Goods Industry Many other new goods came on the market to take advantage of rising disposable income. Americans bought such innovations as electric razors, disposable facial tissues, frozen foods, and home hair dye.

NATIONAL GEOGRAPHIC
MOMENT in HISTORY

ON THE ROAD
The United States first felt the sweeping impact of the automobile during the 1920s. Mass production, pioneered by Henry Ford with his famous Model T, reduced costs and put practical, reliable cars within the reach of millions of middle-class Americans. Adventurous families—like the one shown here driving an upscale, open touring car through a giant Sequoia tree in Yosemite National Park—set out to explore the country. They used a network of roads that had been little more than rutted wagon trails two decades earlier.

642 CHAPTER 21 Normalcy and Good Times

MEETING SPECIAL NEEDS

Intrapersonal Have students make journal entries about American dependence on the automobile over a period of several days. Remind students that their experience is not limited to driving or riding in a car, but includes where they go and what they do. Instruct students to write an essay based on their journal entries. **L2**

📁 Refer to *Inclusion for the High School Social Studies Classroom Strategies and Activities* in the TCR.

Profiles IN HISTORY

Bessie Coleman c.1892–1926

Bessie Coleman was the first African American woman to receive a pilot's license and the first to become a stunt pilot. She performed in her first air show in September 1922 in Garden City, Long Island.

Coleman was born in Atlanta, Texas, to an African American mother and a Choctaw father. Too poor to attend college for more than one term, she moved to Chicago to become a pilot. No flight school she applied to, however, was willing to admit an African American. With the help of a Chicago publisher, Coleman then went to France to train. Back home, she championed the African American cause through her public statements and impressive flying feats.

Coleman's achievements inspired the founding of Chicago's Coffey School of Aeronautics. Its graduates helped train the U.S. military's first African American pilots, the Tuskegee Airmen, who served with distinction in World War II.

Amelia Earhart 1897–1937

Amelia Earhart, perhaps the world's most celebrated woman pilot, saw her first airplane at the Iowa State Fair when she was 10 years old. She was unimpressed: "It was a thing of rusty wire and wood and not at all interesting. . . ." In her early 20s, however, she attended a California "aerial meet," a fateful decision.

Known for promoting women's flying, Earhart seemed destined for celebrity from early on. By 1932 she was flying solo across the Atlantic.

Earhart's most daring flight was her last. In 1937 she set out to fly around the world with her navigator. Two-thirds of the trip was covered when their plane disappeared. On the trip, she had written her husband, "Please know I am quite aware of the hazards. . . . I want to do it because I want to do it. Women must try to do things as men have tried."

Many of the new products were created for the home. As indoor plumbing became more common, Americans' concern for hygiene spawned the development of numerous household cleaning products. By appealing to people's health concerns, advertisers were able to convince homemakers to buy cleansers to protect their families from disease.

New appliances advertised as labor-savers changed the home. Electric irons, vacuum cleaners, washing machines, and refrigerators, as well as gas stoves and improved glass cookware, changed the way people cleaned their homes and prepared meals.

Another lucrative category of consumer products focused on Americans' concerns with fashion, youthful appearance, and success in personal and business endeavors. Mouthwash, deodorants, cosmetics, and perfumes became popular products in the 1920s.

The Airline Industry Technological advances in aviation during World War I suggested the potential importance of the airplane to the transportation industry. Aviation, however, did not experience the same postwar boom as the automobile industry. In the early 1920s, most Americans still thought of airplanes as dangerous novelties. The only planes they saw were the flimsy craft that barnstorming pilots flew at air shows. Still, the opportunity to go up in the air inspired many Americans, such as Lena Stanley:

❝My first airplane ride was out at Brush Lake. . . . There was an aviator taking riders up; barnstorming, they called it. . . . So we climbed in, just went in and sat down, nothing over us, nothing to hold us down. I didn't know enough to be scared. And that pilot, he flew all around. Oh, it was beautiful, to see down on earth like we seen at that time.❞

—quoted in *Centenarians: The Story of the Twentieth Century by the Americans Who Lived It*

By the 1920s, airplanes were being used for more than just joyrides. President Wilson's postmaster general had introduced the world's first regular airmail service in 1918 by hiring pilots to fly mail between Washington, D.C., and New York. In 1919 the Post Office expanded airmail service across the continent with the aid of railroad connections. The aviation industry received an economic boost in 1925 with the passage of the Kelly Act, which authorized postal officials to contract with private airplane operators to carry mail.

In 1926 the aviation industry received another boost with the passage of the Air Commerce Act, which provided federal aid for building airports. It was the extraordinary transatlantic solo flight of former airmail pilot **Charles Lindbergh** in 1927, however, that demonstrated the possibilities of aviation

CHAPTER 21 Normalcy and Good Times **643**

✔ **Reading Check**

Answer: Technological innovations increased manufacturing efficiency and reduced the need to hire skilled workers.

Making a Collage Have students make a collage using copies of advertisements for consumer products from the 1920s paired with current advertisements for similar products. **L1**

FYI

Born in 1902, Charles Lindbergh grew up in Minnesota. After two years at the University of Wisconsin, he started flying as a stunt pilot. Lindbergh completed flight training to become an Army Air Service Reserve pilot. Later he flew mail between Chicago and St. Louis. An offer of $25,000 to become the first pilot to fly nonstop from New York to Paris inspired Lindbergh's famous flight.

HISTORY
Online

Objectives and answers to the student activity can be found in the **Web Activity Lesson Plan** at tav.glencoe.com.

Washing machine advertisement

and won popular support for commercial flight. By the end of 1928, 48 airlines were serving 355 American cities.

Advertisers praised the benefits of commercial flying for business executives, as in this 1928 ad for the Ford Motor Company's "Trimotor" plane: "When the occasion comes for your first time up, it will not be to 'joy-ride' in an antiquated and hazardous machine; but far more probably it will be to reach some distant meeting-place in advance of business competition!"

The Radio Industry In 1913 Edwin Armstrong, an American engineer, invented a special circuit that made long-range radio transmission of voice and music practical. The radio industry began a few years later. In November 1920, the Westinghouse Company broadcast the news of Harding's landslide election victory from station KDKA in Pittsburgh— one of the first public broadcasts in history. That success persuaded Westinghouse to open other stations.

In 1926 the **National Broadcasting Company**

HISTORY
Online

Student Web Activity Visit the *American Vision* Web site at tav.glencoe.com and click on **Student Web Activities— Chapter 21** for an activity on politics and economics in the 1920s.

(NBC) established a permanent network of stations to distribute daily programs. By 1927 almost 700 stations dotted the country, and the Federal Radio Commission had been established to regulate them. Sales of radio equipment skyrocketed from $12.2 million in 1921 to $842.5 million in 1929, by which time 10 million radio sets were in use in the United States.

In 1928 the **Columbia Broadcasting System** (CBS) assembled a coast-to-coast network of stations to rival NBC. The two networks sold advertising time and hired popular musicians, actors, and comedians from vaudeville, movies, and the nightclub circuit to appear on their shows. In 1928 Americans experienced complete coverage of the first presidential election campaign conducted over the airwaves, when the radio networks sold more than $1 million in advertising time to the Republican and Democratic Parties.

✔ **Reading Check** **Analyzing** How did technological innovations such as the assembly line impact the nature of work?

The Consumer Society

Higher wages and shorter workdays resulted in a decade-long buying spree that kept the economy booming. Shifting from traditional attitudes of thrift and prudence, Americans in the 1920s enthusiastically accepted their new role as consumers.

ECONOMICS

Easy Consumer Credit One notable aspect of the economic boom was the growth of individual borrowing. The prosperity of the 1920s gave many Americans the confidence to go into debt to buy new consumer goods.

Credit had been available before the boom, but most Americans had considered debt to be shameful. Now, however, American attitudes toward debt started changing as people began believing in their ability to pay their debts over time. Many listened to the sales pitch, "Buy now and pay in easy installments," and racked up debts for the family car, radio, furniture, washing machine, and vacuum cleaner. Americans bought 75 percent of their radios and 60 percent of their automobiles on the installment plan. Some started buying on credit at a faster rate than their incomes increased.

Mass Advertising When inventor Otto Rohwedder developed a commercial bread slicer in 1928, he faced a problem common to new inventions: the bread slicer was a device that made a product—sliced bread—that no one knew they needed. To create consumers for

---

CRITICAL THINKING ACTIVITY

Analyzing Write the following sentence on the board: *The business technology of the 1920s created an era of prosperity.* Have students find three facts in the section to support the generalization. Write supporting facts on the board as students state them. Then have students make a generalization about the early radio industry and find three facts to support their generalization. **L1**

their new products, manufacturers turned to advertising, another booming industry in the 1920s.

Advertisers created appealing, persuasive messages that linked their clients' products with qualities associated with the modern era, such as progress, convenience, leisure, success, fashion, and style. In a 1924 magazine advertisement for deodorant, the headline read, "Flappers they may be—but they know the art of feminine appeal!" An advertisement for a prepared spaghetti product told the busy homemaker that heating is the same as cooking: "Just one thing to do and it's ready to serve." Advertisers also preyed on consumers' fears and anxieties, whether they be jarred nerves due to the hectic pace of modern life or insecurities about one's status or weight.

The Managerial Revolution By the early 1920s, many industries had begun to create modern organizational structures. Companies were divided into divisions with different functions, such as sales, marketing, accounting, and operations. To run these divisions, businesses needed to hire managers. Managers freed executives and owners from the day-to-day business of running their companies and allowed them to develop long-range plans and goals.

The managerial revolution in companies created a new career—the professional manager—and companies began to hire large numbers of people with managerial training from business schools. The large numbers of managers helped to expand the size of the middle class, which in turn added to the nation's prosperity. Similarly, so many companies relied on new technology to drive their business that engineers were also in very high demand. They too joined the ranks of the rapidly growing middle class.

Welfare Capitalism Middle-class Americans were not the only members of the new consumer society. Industrial workers also prospered in the 1920s, partly due to rising wages and partly because many corporations introduced what came to be called welfare capitalism. Companies allowed workers to buy stock, participate in profit sharing, and receive benefits such as medical care and pensions.

Benefits programs also made unions seem unnecessary to many workers. During the 1920s, unions lost both influence and membership. Employers promoted the open shop—a workplace where employees were not required to join a union.

With benefits covering some of their basic needs, workers were able to spend more of their income. Many eagerly purchased consumer goods they previously could not afford.

✓ **Reading Check** **Analyzing Bias** How did advertisers try to convince Americans to buy their products?

The Farm Crisis Returns

American farmers did not share in the prosperity of the 1920s. As a group, they earned less than one-third of the average income for workers in the rest of the economy. Technological advances in fertilizers, pesticides, seed varieties, and farm machinery allowed them to produce more, but higher yields without a corresponding increase in demand meant that they received lower prices. Between 1920 and 1921, corn prices dropped almost 19 percent, and

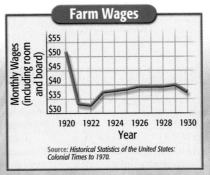

Farm Wages

Source: *Historical Statistics of the United States: Colonial Times to 1970.*

Graph Skills

1. **Interpreting Graphs** How far did farm wages fall between 1920 and 1930?
2. **Understanding Cause and Effect** What caused the decline in wages? Do you think farmers could have done anything to prevent this?

Percentage of National Income Generated by Industry, 1919–1928

Finance and Miscellaneous 16.1%
Agriculture 10.5%
Mining 2.5%
Government 9.6%
Manufacturing 21.9%
Services 11.6%
Contract Construction 4.4%
Trade 13.6%
Transportation and Other Public Utilities 9.8%

Source: *Historical Statistics of the United States: Colonial Times to 1970.*

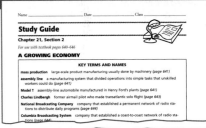

✓ **Reading Check**

Answer: preyed on consumers' fears and anxieties; linked products to progress and success

3 ASSESS

Assign Section 2 Assessment as homework or as an in-class activity.

⊙ Have students use the **Interactive Tutor Self-Assessment CD-ROM.**

Reading Essentials and Study Guide 21–2

Name _____ Date _____ Class _____

Study Guide

Chapter 21, Section 2
For use with textbook pages 640–646
A GROWING ECONOMY

KEY TERMS AND NAMES

mass production large-scale product manufacturing usually done by machinery *(page 641)*
assembly line a manufacturing system that divided operations into simple tasks that unskilled workers could do *(page 641)*
Model T assembly-line automobile manufactured in Henry Ford's plants *(page 641)*
Charles Lindbergh former airmail pilot who made transatlantic solo flight *(page 643)*
National Broadcasting Company company that established a permanent network of radio stations to distribute daily programs *(page 644)*
Columbia Broadcasting System company that established a coast-to-coast network of radio stations *(page 644)*

Graph Skills

Answers:
1. about $13 per month
2. higher production rates, increased debt, and a drop in foreign sales

Graph Skills Practice
Ask: From 1920 to 1930, when were farm wages lowest and highest?
(lowest in 1922, highest in 1920)

EXTENDING THE CONTENT

Industry Growth and Decline While the automobile helped boost some industries and activities, it led to decline or even obsolescence in other areas. Railroads, for example, declined as personal cars and the burgeoning trucking industry brought more flexibility to both personal and commercial transport. Some thriving towns on railroad lines became virtual ghost towns as railway travel fell out of favor. City streets and downtown areas also suffered. New road designs and layouts catered to auto circulation and speed; the results were rarely pedestrian-friendly. The premium on parking turned many downtown buildings into lifeless parking lots and garages.

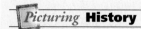
Picturing **History**

Answer: producing more; greater European competition after the war

Reteach
Have students analyze the growing importance of the automobile.

Enrich
Suggest that students work in groups to discuss the changes in people's attitudes toward big business that took place in the 1920s.

✓ Reading Check

Answer: a decline in foreign markets and increased productivity

4 CLOSE

Have students explain the growing economic crisis in farming.

Picturing **History**

Price of Progress With the help of improved technology in the 1920s, farm production went up—and farm prices and farmers' income went down. How do you explain this "quiet depression"?

wheat went from $1.83 a bushel to $1.03. The cost to farmers of the improved technology, meanwhile, continued to increase.

Changing Market Conditions Many factors contributed to this "quiet depression" in American agriculture. During the war, the government had urged farmers to produce more to meet the great need for food supplies in Europe. Many farmers borrowed heavily to buy new land (at inflated prices) and new machinery in order to raise more crops. Sales were strong, prices were high, and farmers prospered. After the war, however, European farm output rose, and the debt-ridden countries of Europe had little to spend on

American farm products. Congress had unintentionally made matters worse when it passed the Fordney-McCumber Act in 1922. This act raised tariffs dramatically in an effort to protect American industry from foreign competition. By dampening the American market for foreign goods, it provoked a reaction in foreign markets against American agricultural products. Farmers in the United States could no longer sell as much of their output overseas, and prices tumbled.

Helping Farmers Some members of Congress tried to help the farmers sell their surplus. Every year from 1924 to 1928, Senator Charles McNary of Oregon and Representative Gilbert Haugen of Iowa proposed the McNary-Haugen Bill, which called for the federal government to purchase surplus crops and sell them abroad while protecting the American market with a high tariff. McNary and Haugen argued that the plan would immediately raise the domestic price of crops, and it would aid farmers just as the Fordney-McCumber tariffs helped manufacturers.

Congress passed the bill twice, but President Coolidge vetoed it both times. He argued that with money flowing to farmers under this law, the farmers would be encouraged to produce even greater surplus volumes, which the government would be unable to sell in glutted overseas markets. American farmers remained mired in recession throughout the 1920s. Their problems would only grow worse when the Great Depression began in 1929.

✓ Reading Check **Synthesizing** What factors led to the growing economic crisis in farming in the 1920s?

SECTION 2 ASSESSMENT

Checking for Understanding

1. **Define:** mass production, assembly line, welfare capitalism, open shop.
2. **Identify:** Model T, Charles Lindbergh, National Broadcasting Company, Columbia Broadcasting System.
3. **Summarize** the factors that led to the new consumer society in the United States during the 1920s.

Reviewing Themes

4. **Science and Technology** How did the automobile impact American society?

Critical Thinking

5. **Identifying Cause and Effect** How did the United States government help spur the growth of the airline industry?
6. **Organizing** Use a graphic organizer similar to the one below to list some of the new industries that grew in importance during the 1920s.

Analyzing Visuals

7. **Analyzing Advertisements** Examine the advertisement on page 644. How did the growing consumer culture impact the nation's economy?

Writing About History

8. **Expository Writing** Write an article for a contemporary newspaper analyzing the impact of Charles Lindbergh's transatlantic flight on the development of aviation in the United States and the world.

SECTION 2 ASSESSMENT ANSWERS

1. Terms are in blue.
2. Model T *(p. 641)*, Charles Lindbergh *(p. 643)*, National Broadcasting Company *(p. 644)*, Columbia Broadcasting System *(p. 644)*
3. mass production, easy credit, mass advertisement, and economic prosperity
4. eased rural isolation, allowed workers to live farther away from work
5. governmental airmail service and funds for airports
6. airline, automobile, consumer goods, radio
7. raised standard of living, encouraged Americans to buy new goods
8. Students' articles will vary but should contain factual information.

The Policies of Prosperity

Guide to Reading

Main Idea
Economic policies of the United States government encouraged the prosperity of the 1920s.

Key Terms and Names
supply-side economics, cooperative individualism, isolationism, Charles G. Dawes, Charles Evans Hughes, moratorium, Kellogg-Briand Pact

Reading Strategy
Organizing As you read about government policies in the 1920s, complete a graphic organizer similar to the one below by filling in ways the government attempted to stimulate economic growth and prosperity.

Reading Objectives
• **Explain** Andrew Mellon's economic strategies for maintaining prosperity.
• **Describe** how the United States remained involved in world affairs without joining the League of Nations.

Section Theme
Economic Factors After World War I, the United States had to pay down a large amount of war debt while maintaining economic growth.

Preview of Events

| ♦1920 | ♦1923 | ♦1926 | ♦1929 |

1921
Washington Conference produces guidelines for naval disarmament

1922
Fordney-McCumber Act passed

1924
Dawes Plan negotiated with France, Britain, and Germany

1928
Kellogg-Briand Pact signed by 15 nations

Andrew W. Mellon

★ An American Story ★

After Election Day 1920, President-elect Harding began searching for qualified Americans for his cabinet. One of the most important posts would be secretary of the treasury. The nation faced a large national debt, and many worried that the country would not easily pull out of its postwar recession.

Harding was considering Andrew W. Mellon, a successful banker and industrialist, but he worried about Mellon's ties to industry and his relative anonymity. Harding's campaign manager, Harry Daugherty, reassured the president with a ringing endorsement of Mellon:

❝A man who can quietly make the millions this modest-looking man has gathered in is little short of a magician. If there is one thing he knows it's money. He will make for you the greatest Secretary of the Treasury since Alexander Hamilton. . . .❞

—adapted from *Mellon's Millions*

Promoting Prosperity

Harry Daugherty's confidence in Andrew Mellon proved to be well founded. Mellon became the chief architect of economic policy in the United States in the 1920s, and he served as secretary of the treasury in three successive Republican administrations. His policies encouraged growth and led to a stock market boom.

CHAPTER 21 Normalcy and Good Times **647**

1 FOCUS

Section Overview
This section focuses on the economic policies of the federal government during the 1920s.

BELLRINGER
Skillbuilder Activity

 Project transparency and have students answer the question.

 Available as a blackline master.

Daily Focus Skills Transparency 21–3

Guide to Reading

Answers to Graphic: less government regulation of business, tax cuts, refinancing of the national debt, and reduced government spending

Preteaching Vocabulary
Have students create a database of the Key Terms and Names. Instruct students to add definitions and other helpful information as they read the section.

SECTION RESOURCES

☞ **Reproducible Masters**
• Reproducible Lesson Plan 21–3
• Daily Lecture and Discussion Notes 21–3
• Guided Reading Activity 21–3
• Section Quiz 21–3
• Reading Essentials and Study Guide 21–3

📖 **Transparencies**
• Daily Focus Skills Transparency 21–3

• American Art & Architecture

Multimedia
🖸 Interactive Tutor Self-Assessment CD-ROM
🖸 ExamView® Pro Testmaker CD-ROM
🖸 Presentation Plus! CD-ROM
🖸 TeacherWorks™ CD-ROM
🎧 Audio Program
🎵 American Music: Hits Through History

2 TEACH

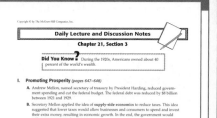
Picturing History

Answer: He cut government spending, refinanced the debt to a lower interest rate, and convinced the Federal Reserve to lower its interest rates.

Discussing a Topic Have students discuss isolationism. Ask students what types of global activities, if any, they think isolationists would support. **L1**

✓ Reading Check

Answer: tax cuts, lowering the interest rate on the national debt, lowering Federal Reserve interest rates

History *and the* Humanities

📂 American Music: Hits Through History: "Yes Sir! That's My Baby"

🖋 American Art & Architecture: Empire State Building

Picturing History

Harding's Cabinet Some members of Harding's cabinet (posing here with the president, seated center, in 1921) were effective administrators. How did Secretary of the Treasury Andrew Mellon lower the national debt between 1921 and 1929?

ECONOMICS

The Mellon Program Mellon firmly believed that the government should apply business principles to its operations. In 1921 he convinced Congress to create both the Bureau of the Budget to prepare a unified federal budget and the General Accounting Office to track government spending.

When Mellon took office, he had three major goals—to balance the budget, to reduce the government's debt, and to cut taxes. He was convinced that these policies would promote economic growth and ensure prosperity.

Mellon began by cutting government spending. The federal budget fell from $6.4 billion to less than $3 billion in seven years. One major expense was the interest on the national debt. World War I costs had raised the debt from $5.7 billion in 1917 to almost $26 billion by 1920. Mellon refinanced the debt to lower the interest on it and persuaded the Federal Reserve to lower its interest rates as well. These steps, combined with increased tax revenue from the nation's economic boom, reduced the debt by $8 billion between 1921 and 1929.

In addition to trimming government spending, Mellon focused on reducing tax rates. He believed that high taxes reduced the money available for private investment and prevented business expansion. Mellon further argued that high tax rates actually reduced the amount of tax money the government collected. If taxes were lower, businesses and consumers would spend and invest their extra money, causing the economy to grow. As the economy grew, Americans would earn more money, and the government would actually

---

collect more taxes at a lower rate than it would if it kept tax rates high. This idea is known today as supply-side economics.

At Mellon's urging, Congress dramatically reduced tax rates. When Mellon took office, most Americans paid 4 percent federal income tax, while wealthy Americans in the highest bracket paid 73 percent. By 1928 Congress had reduced the rate most Americans paid to .5 percent and cut the rate for the wealthiest Americans to 25 percent.

Hoover's Cooperative Individualism Mellon's program was only one part of the government's effort to promote economic growth. Secretary of Commerce Herbert Hoover also sought to promote economic stability in various industries. Hoover tried to balance government regulation with his own philosophy of cooperative individualism. This idea involved encouraging manufacturers and distributors to form their own trade associations, which would voluntarily share information with the federal government. Hoover believed this system would reduce costs and promote economic efficiency.

To assist American businesses, Hoover also created several other agencies. He set up the Bureau of Foreign and Domestic Commerce to find new markets and business opportunities for American companies. He also established the Bureau of Aviation to regulate and support the airline industry and the Federal Radio Commission, which set rules regarding the use of radio frequencies and the power of radio transmitters.

✓ Reading Check
Evaluating What government policies were intended to promote economic growth and improve business efficiency in the 1920s?

Trade and Arms Control

Before World War I the United States had owed billions of dollars more to foreign investors than foreigners owed to Americans. By the end of the war, the situation was reversed. Former wartime allies owed the United States more than $10 billion in war debts incurred for food and armaments. By the 1920s the United States was the dominant economic power in the world—its national income far greater than that of Britain, Germany, France, and Japan combined. This new power presented the United States with a unique diplomatic challenge.

Isolationism In his victory speech after the 1920 election, President Harding declared the issue of American involvement in the League of Nations

---

COOPERATIVE LEARNING ACTIVITY

Tracking the Stock Market Discuss the impact the stock market has on the American economy. Organize the class into groups of four and have each group pretend they have $110,000 to invest. Instruct the group to use their pretend money to purchase stocks in at least four different companies. Have the groups meet to discuss their portfolio and to track the value of their investments. After a set time, have all groups sell their investments and report how much they made or lost.

Use the rubric for a cooperative group management plan on pages 81–82 in the *Performance Assessment Activities and Rubrics.*

"deceased." The majority of Americans, tired of being entangled in the baffling, mutually hostile, and dangerous politics of Europe, favored isolationism. They simply wanted to be left alone to pursue prosperity.

The United States, however, was too powerful, too economically interconnected with other countries, and too widely involved in international affairs to retreat into isolationism. American delegations participated in many League conferences. It was United States policy to promote peace through agreements with individual countries rather than doing so through the collective efforts of the League.

The Dawes Plan The United States's former wartime allies had difficulty making the payments on their immense war debts. They claimed that high American tariffs had closed the American market to their products and hampered their economic recovery. If they could not sell their products in the United States, they could not acquire the money they needed to pay off their war debts. They also argued that the United States should be willing to bear more of the financial burden because it had suffered far fewer wartime casualties than its allies.

The United States government took the stance that American taxpayers should not be asked to assume the debts of others. American officials argued further that America's allies had gained new territory as a result of the victory over Germany, while the United States had gained nothing. These countries also were receiving reparations—huge cash payments Germany was required to make as punishment for starting the war and causing so much destruction. These payments, however, were completely crippling the German economy.

It was vital for the United States that European economies be healthy so that the Europeans could buy American exports and repay their war debts. Thus, in 1924, **Charles G. Dawes,** an American banker and diplomat, negotiated an agreement with France, Britain, and Germany by which American banks would make loans to the Germans that would enable them to meet their reparations payments. At the same time, Britain and France would accept less in reparations and pay more on their war debts.

Although well intended, the Dawes Plan did little to ease Europe's economic problems. Britain, France, and Germany went through the motions of paying what they owed while in fact going deeper into debt to American banks and corporations.

The Washington Conference Despite severe economic hardship, the major powers were involved in a costly postwar naval arms race. To help halt this arms race, the United States invited representatives from eight major countries—Great Britain, France, Italy, China, Japan, Belgium, the Netherlands, and

The Washington Conference, November 1921–February 1922

Treaty	Signers	Terms	Weaknesses
Four-Power Treaty	United States, Great Britain, France, Japan	• All agreed to respect the others' territory in the Pacific • Full and open negotiations in the event of disagreements	• Mutual defense of other co-signers not specified
Five-Power Treaty	United States, Great Britain, France, Japan, Italy	• All agreed to freeze naval production at 1921 levels and halt production of large warships for 10 years • U.S. and Great Britain would not build new naval bases in the western Pacific	• No restrictions on the construction of smaller battle craft such as submarines and naval destroyers • Did not place restrictions on the ground forces
Nine-Power Treaty	United States, Great Britain, France, Japan, Italy, Belgium, China, the Netherlands, Portugal	• All agreed to preserve equal commercial rights to China—a reassertion of the "Open Door Policy"	• No enforcement of the terms of the "Open Door Policy" specified

Chart Skills

1. **Interpreting Charts** Which countries signed the Five-Power Treaty?
2. **Analyzing** Why do you think the terms of the treaties focused on the Pacific region?

MEETING SPECIAL NEEDS

Interpersonal Have a group develop an alternative to the Dawes Plan that would have achieved the following goals: maximizing repayments of debts to the United States, encouraging economic stability in Europe, and helping Europe rebuild from the war. Encourage groups to present their ideas in the form of an economic stabilization and development plan. **L3**

☞ Refer to ***Inclusion for the High School Social Studies Classroom Strategies and Activities*** in the TCR.

Fact	Fiction	Folklore

The Tomb of the Unknown Soldier On March 4, 1921, Congress approved the burial of an unidentified World War I soldier in Arlington National Cemetery on a hill that overlooks Washington, D.C. This burial site, which was dedicated on November 11, 1921, is called the Tomb of the Unknown Soldier.

In 1958 two unknown soldiers from World War II and the Korean War were buried alongside the original unknown soldier. In 1984 a Vietnam War soldier was added.

On the side of the original tomb are inscribed the words: "Here rests in honored glory an American soldier known but to God." The Tomb is guarded year-round, day and night, regardless of weather.

Portugal—to Washington to discuss disarmament. The Washington Conference opened on November 12, 1921.

In his address to the delegates, Secretary of State **Charles Evans Hughes** proposed a 10-year moratorium—or pause—on the construction of major new warships. He also proposed a list of warships in each country's navy to be destroyed, beginning with some American battleships. The delegates cheered Hughes's speech and then entered into lengthy negotiations.

Their efforts produced three agreements. In the **Five-Power Naval Limitation Treaty,** Britain, France, Italy, Japan, and the United States essentially formalized Hughes's proposal. The **Four-Power Treaty** between the United States, Japan, France, and Britain recognized each country's island possessions in the Pacific. Finally, all the participating countries signed the **Nine-Power Treaty,** which guaranteed China's independence.

As a long-term effort to prevent war, the conference had some serious shortcomings. It did nothing to limit land forces. It also angered the Japanese because it required Japan to maintain a smaller navy than either the United States or Great Britain. It did, however, give Americans cause to look forward to a period of peace, recovery, and prosperity.

Abolishing War The apparent success of the Washington Conference boosted the belief that written agreements could end war altogether. Perhaps the highest expression of that idea occurred when U.S. Secretary of State Frank Kellogg and French Foreign Minister Aristide Briand proposed a treaty to outlaw war. On August 27, 1928, the United States and 14 other nations signed the **Kellogg-Briand Pact.** Eventually 62 nations ratified it.

Though it had no binding force, the pact was hailed as a victory for peace. It stated that all signing nations agreed to abandon war and to settle all disputes by peaceful means. The Kellogg-Briand Pact and the Dawes Plan were perhaps the most notable foreign policy achievements of the Coolidge administration.

✓ **Reading Check** **Identifying** Why did the Dawes Plan fail to ease Europe's economic problems?

Reteach
Have students explain Andrew Mellon's economic strategies for maintaining prosperity.

Enrich
Have students write a paragraph explaining why they think a written agreement to end war could or could not be an effective deterrent to war.

✓ **Reading Check**

Answer: It caused Britain, France, and Germany to go further into debt.

4 CLOSE

Have students explain how the United States remained involved in world affairs without being a League of Nations member.

Fact	Fiction	Folklore

The identities of the three other soldiers buried in the Tomb of the Unknown Soldier are, in fact, unknown. In 1998, however, DNA analysis allowed the Vietnam War soldier buried there to be identified. He is U.S. Air Force First Lieutenant Michael Joseph Blassie.

SECTION 3 ASSESSMENT

Checking for Understanding
1. **Define:** supply-side economics, cooperative individualism, isolationism, moratorium.
2. **Identify:** Charles G. Dawes, Charles Evans Hughes, Kellogg-Briand Pact.

Reviewing Themes
3. **Economic Factors** Why did Andrew Mellon work to reduce federal tax rates?

Critical Thinking
4. **Evaluating** What efforts did the United States make to promote permanent peace and worldwide economic recovery? Were these efforts successful? Explain your answer.
5. **Categorizing** Use a graphic organizer like the one below to list the major terms of the treaties resulting from the Washington Conference.

Major Terms of Treaties	

Analyzing Visuals
6. **Analyzing Photographs** Study the photograph on page 648 of President Harding's cabinet of advisers. What differences do you see between politics and the media then and now?

Writing About History
7. **Persuasive Writing** Imagine you are an American business owner or farmer in the 1920s. Write a letter to your representatives in Congress explaining why you think cutting tax rates is a good or bad idea.

SECTION 3 ASSESSMENT ANSWERS

1. Terms are in blue.
2. Charles G. Dawes *(p. 649)*, Charles Evans Hughes *(p. 650)*, Kellogg-Briand Pact *(p. 650)*
3. He believed that lowering tax rates would spur the economy by encouraging businesses and consumers to invest and spend.
4. Students' answers should reflect analysis of text information, including the Dawes Plan and the Washington Naval Conference.
5. Answers should match information in the text.
6. Students should note that media coverage in both cases is often staged. However, today there is almost instant access by the media to politicians.
7. Letters should be written from the point of view of a business owner or a farmer.

Critical Thinking SKILLBUILDER

Distinguishing Fact From Opinion

Why Learn This Skill?

Imagine that you are watching two candidates for president debate the merits of the college loan program. One candidate says, "In my view, the college loan program must be reformed. Sixty percent of students do not repay their loans on time."

The other candidate responds, "College costs are skyrocketing, but only 30 percent of students default on their loans for more than one year. I believe we should spend more money on this worthy program."

How can you tell who or what to believe? First, you must learn to distinguish a fact from an opinion. Then you will be better prepared to evaluate the statements that other people make.

Learning the Skill

A **fact** is a statement that can be proven. In the example above, the statement "Sixty percent of students do not repay their loans on time" may be a fact. By reviewing statistics on the number of student loan recipients who repay their loans, we can determine whether the statement is true or false. To identify potential facts, look for words and phrases indicating specific people, places, events, dates, amounts, or times.

An **opinion,** on the other hand, expresses a personal belief, viewpoint, or emotion. Because opinions are subjective, we cannot prove or disprove them. In the example above, most statements by the candidates are opinions. To identify opinions, look for qualifying words and phrases such as *I think, I believe, probably, seems to me, may, might, could, ought, should, in my judgment,* and *in my view.* Also, look for expressions of approval or disapproval such as *good, bad, poor,* and *satisfactory.* Be aware of superlatives such as *greatest, worst, finest,* and *best,* and notice words with negative meanings and implications such as *squander, contemptible,* and *disgrace.* Also, identify generalizations such as *none, every, always,* and *never.*

Practicing the Skill

For each pair of statements below, determine which is a fact and which is an opinion. Give a reason for each of your choices.

① **a.** President Harding was born in Ohio in 1865.

   b. Harding later became the most scandalous president in United States history.

② **a.** Harding's administration suffered numerous public scandals, including the Teapot Dome scandal.

   b. Calvin Coolidge was probably disgusted with Harding's poor performance in the White House.

③ **a.** Harding stated that the United States needed a return to normalcy, but he did not do anything to help the country.

   b. Coolidge took over the White House after Harding's death and led the nation for the next several years.

④ **a.** Henry Ford significantly lowered the price of the automobile with his mass production methods.

   b. Ford's Model T was the most significant invention of the 20th century.

Skills Assessment

Complete the Practicing Skills questions on page 653 and the Chapter 21 Skill Reinforcement Activity to assess your mastery of this skill.

> **Applying the Skill**
> **Distinguishing Fact From Opinion** In a newspaper, find a news article and an editorial on the same topic or issue. Identify five facts and five opinions from these sources.
>
> Glencoe's **Skillbuilder Interactive Workbook CD-ROM, Level 2,** provides instruction and practice in key social studies skills.

651

Critical Thinking SKILLBUILDER

TEACH

Distinguishing Fact from Opinion In a world of instant information, being able to distinguish between fact and opinion is increasingly important. As students learn to use this skill, they will be able to analyze the validity of information more effectively.

Select a news article and an editorial on the same topic and have students identify the facts and opinions. Then discuss the effectiveness of each article.

Additional Practice

> **Reinforcing Skills Activity 21**
>
> Name _____ Date _____ Class _____
>
> ★ Reinforcing Skills Activity **21**
>
> **Distinguishing Fact From Opinion**
>
> ☐ **LEARNING THE SKILL**
>
> Facts can be proven by evidence such as records or historical sources. Opinions are based on people's differing values and beliefs. To help you identify facts and opinions, read or listen to the information carefully. Identify the facts. If a statement can be proven, it is factual. Identify opinions by looking for expressions of beliefs, approval or disapproval, or superlatives such as *best* or *worst.*
>
> ☐ **PRACTICING THE SKILL**
>
> **DIRECTIONS:** Read the excerpt below about President Warren G. Harding. Then answer the questions that follow.
>
> Everyone who knows anything at all about American history believes that Warren G. Harding was our worst President–Harding, the affable tool from Marion, Ohio, who, after passing two utterly undistinguished terms as state senator and...

GLENCOE TECHNOLOGY

CD-ROM

Glencoe Skillbuilder Interactive Workbook CD-ROM, Level 2

This interactive CD-ROM reinforces student mastery of essential social studies skills.

ANSWERS TO PRACTICING THE SKILL

① **a.** fact, it can be proven; **b.** opinion, expresses a viewpoint, includes the word *most*

② **a.** fact, it can be proven; **b.** opinion, includes the word *probably*

③ **a.** opinion, expresses a viewpoint; **b.** fact, it can be proven

④ **a.** fact, it can be proven; **b.** opinion, expresses a point of view, includes the phrase *most significant*

Applying the Skill

Students' lists will vary. Students should be able to distinguish between fact and opinion.

GLENCOE TECHNOLOGY

MindJogger Videoquiz

Use the **MindJogger Videoquiz** to review Chapter 21 content.

Available in VHS

Reviewing Key Terms

Students' answers will vary. The pages where the words appear in the text are shown in parentheses.

1. **normalcy** *(p. 637)*
2. **immunity** *(p. 638)*
3. **mass production** *(p. 641)*
4. **assembly line** *(p. 641)*
5. **welfare capitalism** *(p. 645)*
6. **open shop** *(p. 645)*
7. **supply-side economics** *(p. 648)*
8. **cooperative individualism** *(p. 648)*
9. **isolationism** *(p. 649)*
10. **moratorium** *(p. 650)*

Reviewing Key Facts

11. Albert B. Fall *(p. 638)*, Teapot Dome scandal *(p. 638)*, Charles Lindbergh *(p. 643)*, Charles G. Dawes *(p. 649)*, Charles Evans Hughes *(p. 650)*, Kellogg-Briand Pact *(p. 650)*
12. Inefficiency and scandal plagued his presidency.
13. Coolidge distanced himself from the Harding administration and named the most capable individuals to his cabinet.
14. automobile-related industries such as garage and gas stations, the consumer goods, airlines, and radio industries
15. He increased workers' wages and reduced the workday, weakening the power of unions.
16. reduce taxes, reduce federal debt, balance the budget

Reviewing Key Terms

On a sheet of paper, use each of the following terms in a sentence.

1. normalcy
2. immunity
3. mass production
4. assembly line
5. welfare capitalism
6. open shop
7. supply-side economics
8. cooperative individualism
9. isolationism
10. moratorium

Reviewing Key Facts

11. **Identify:** Albert B. Fall, Teapot Dome scandal, Charles Lindbergh, Charles G. Dawes, Charles Evans Hughes, Kellogg-Briand Pact.
12. What was the presidency of Warren G. Harding like?
13. How did President Coolidge restore public confidence?
14. What were four new industries, besides the automobile industry, that grew in importance during the 1920s?
15. How did Henry Ford increase worker loyalty and impact the labor movement?
16. What were Andrew Mellon's strategies for maintaining postwar American prosperity?

Critical Thinking

17. **Analyzing Themes: Culture and Traditions** How did automobiles change the standard of living during the 1920s?

18. **Evaluating** How effective were President Coolidge's attempts to distance himself from the Harding administration? Explain your answer.
19. **Forming an Opinion** The former World War I allies felt that the United States should have borne more of the financial burden after the war. Do you agree or disagree? Explain your answer.
20. **Identifying Cause and Effect** Examine the graph on page 645. What caused the trend illustrated in this graph?
21. **Interpreting Primary Sources** In December 1928, President Coolidge delivered his annual State of the Union message to Congress. Read the excerpt and answer the questions that follow.

❝The great wealth created by our enterprise and industry, and saved by our economy, has had the widest distribution among our own people, and has gone out in a steady stream to serve the charity and the business of the world. The requirements of existence have passed beyond the standard of necessity into the region of luxury. . . . The country can regard the present with satisfaction and anticipate the future with optimism.

The main source of these unexplained blessings lies in the integrity and character of the American people. They have had great faith, which they have supplemented with mighty works. . . . Yet these remarkable powers would have been exerted almost in vain

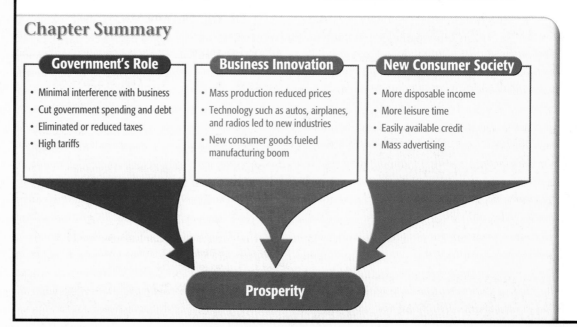

Chapter Summary

Government's Role
- Minimal interference with business
- Cut government spending and debt
- Eliminated or reduced taxes
- High tariffs

Business Innovation
- Mass production reduced prices
- Technology such as autos, airplanes, and radios led to new industries
- New consumer goods fueled manufacturing boom

New Consumer Society
- More disposable income
- More leisure time
- Easily available credit
- Mass advertising

Prosperity

Critical Thinking

17. Automobiles allowed people to travel much greater distances more quickly and allowed workers to live outside cities. Rural Americans' sense of isolation also decreased. Successful mass production resulted in new and cheaper consumer goods.

18. Coolidge was quite successful in distancing himself from Harding. He did this by choosing effective cabinet members and associating himself with prosperity and big business.
19. Opinions will vary. Students should note that the United States was not an original combatant in the war but that the United States played a major role in the war, including contributing to the destruction in Europe.

without the constant cooperation and careful adminis-tration of the Federal Government. . . . 99

—from President Coolidge's Annual Message
to Congress, December 4, 1928

a. According to Coolidge, how should Americans feel about the present economy and the future economy?

b. Whom does Coolidge credit for U.S. prosperity?

22. **Organizing** Use a graphic organizer like the one below to list the factors that helped create a new consumer society in the United States during the 1920s.

New Consumer Society

Practicing Skills

23. **Distinguishing Fact From Opinion** Read the following statements. Determine which are facts and which are opin-ions. Give a reason for each of your choices.

a. American farmers earned less than one-third the average income for workers in the rest of the economy in the 1920s.

b. President Harding's choice to appoint Colonel Charles R. Forbes to head the Veterans Bureau was his worst deci-sion in office.

c. The Kelly Act authorized postal officials to contract with private airplane operators to carry mail.

Chapter Activity

24. **American History Primary Source Document Library CD-ROM** Under *The Roaring Twenties,* read "Ford and the Model T" by Charles E. Sorenson. Work with a few of your classmates to create a diorama of the first Model T assembly line based on the information in the article.

Writing Activity

25. **Persuasive Writing** Use the Internet or other resources to research advertisements and products from the 1920s. Then, based on the style of these advertisements, create an ad for a personal-care product that became popular in the 1920s, such as mouthwash, deodorant, cosmetics, or perfume.

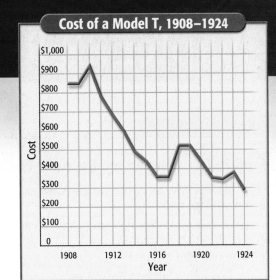

Cost of a Model T, 1908–1924

Cost (vertical axis): $1,000, $900, $800, $700, $600, $500, $400, $300, $200, $100, 0

Year (horizontal axis): 1908, 1912, 1916, 1920, 1924

Economics and History

26. The graph above shows the cost of a new Model T automo-bile between 1908 and 1924. Study the graph and answer the questions below.

a. **Interpreting Graphs** By how much did the cost of the Model T drop from 1908 to 1920?

b. **Evaluating** How was Henry Ford able to lower the price of the Model T?

Writing Activity
25. The ad should persuade consumers to purchase the product.

Economics and History
26. **a.** about $400; **b.** decreased produc-tion costs, increased productivity level and sales volume

Bonus Question ?

Ask: What was the Teapot Dome scandal? *(During the Harding admin-istration, government lands contain-ing large reserves of oil in Teapot Dome, Wyoming, were leased to private interests.)*

---

20. mass production created a large supply, rising cost of farm machinery, decrease in demand due to tariffs

21. **a.** Coolidge says they should be satisfied and optimistic. **b.** He credits the American people.

22. shorter workday, higher wages, mass production tech-niques, easy consumer credit, mass advertising, mana-gerial revolution

Practicing Skills

23. **a.** fact, it can be proven; **b.** opinion, expresses a point of view, uses the word *worst*; **c.** fact, it can be proven

Chapter Activity

24. The diorama should demonstrate the efficiency of the assembly line.

Timesaving Tools

TeacherWorks™ All-In-One Planner and Resource Center

- **Interactive Teacher Edition** Access your Teacher Wraparound Edition and your classroom resources with a few easy clicks.
- **Interactive Lesson Planner** Planning has never been easier! Organize your week, month, semester, or year with all the lesson helps you need to make teaching creative, timely, and relevant.

Use Glencoe's **Presentation Plus!** multimedia teacher tool to easily present dynamic lessons that visually excite your students. Using Microsoft PowerPoint® you can customize the presentations to create your own personalized lessons.

TEACHING TRANSPARENCIES

Graphic Organizer 2

Why It Matters Chapter Transparency 22

APPLICATION AND ENRICHMENT

Linking Past and Present Activity 22

Enrichment Activity 22

Primary Source Reading 22

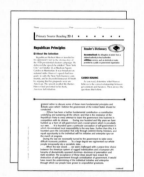

REVIEW AND REINFORCEMENT

Reteaching Activity 22

Vocabulary Activity 22

Time Line Activity 22

Critical Thinking Skills Activity 22

Meeting NCSS Standards

Local Standards

The following standards are highlighted in Chapter 22:

Section 1	VII	Production, Distribution, and Consumption: A, B, D
Section 2	I	Culture: A, C
Section 3	V	Individuals, Groups, and Institutions: B, C, F, G

Chapter 22 Resources

ASSESSMENT AND EVALUATION

GLENCOE'S
ASSESSMENT
ADVANTAGE

Chapter 22 Test Form A

Chapter 22 Test Form B

Standardized Test Skills Practice Workbook Activity 22

Performance Assessment Activities and Rubrics 22

ExamView® Pro Testmaker CD-ROM

MULTIMEDIA

- Vocabulary PuzzleMaker CD-ROM
- Interactive Tutor Self-Assessment CD-ROM
- ExamView® Pro Testmaker CD-ROM
- Audio Program
- American History Primary Source Documents Library CD-ROM
- MindJogger Videoquiz
- Presentation Plus! CD-ROM
- TeacherWorks™ CD-ROM
- Interactive Student Edition CD-ROM
- Glencoe Skillbuilder Interactive Workbook CD-ROM, Level 2
- The *American Vision* Video Program
- American Music: Hits Through History
- American Music: Cultural Traditions

The following videotape programs are available from Glencoe as supplements to Chapter 22:

- **Dow and Jones: Wizards of Wall Street** (ISBN 0-76-700203-2)
- **The Stock Exchange** (ISBN 0-76-700562-7)

To order, call Glencoe at 1-800-334-7344. To find classroom resources to accompany many of these videos, check the following home pages:
A&E Television: www.aande.com
The History Channel: www.historychannel.com

SPANISH RESOURCES

The following Spanish language materials are available in the Spanish Resources Binder:

- Spanish Guided Reading Activities
- Spanish Reteaching Activities
- Spanish Quizzes and Tests
- Spanish Vocabulary Activities
- Spanish Summaries
- The Declaration of Independence and United States Constitution Spanish Translation

HISTORY
Online

Use our Web site for additional resources. All essential content is covered in the Student Edition.

You and your students can visit tav.glencoe.com, the Web site companion to the *American Vision.* This innovative integration of electronic and print media offers your students a wealth of opportunities. The student text directs students to the Web site for the following options:

- **Chapter Overviews**
- **Self-Check Quizzes**
- **Student Web Activities**
- **Textbook Updates**

Answers to the student Web activities are provided for you in the **Web Activity Lesson Plans**. Additional Web resources and Interactive Tutor Puzzles are also available.

Chapter 22 Resources

SECTION RESOURCES

Daily Objectives	Reproducible Resources	Multimedia Resources
SECTION 1 **Causes of the Depression** 1. Describe the characteristics of the 1920s stock market. 2. Identify the causes of the Great Depression.	▸ Reproducible Lesson Plan 22–1 ▸ Daily Lecture and Discussion Notes 22–1 ▸ Guided Reading Activity 22–1* ▸ Section Quiz 22–1* ▸ Reading Essentials and Study Guide 22–1 ▸ Performance Assessment Activities and Rubrics	▸ Daily Focus Skills Transparency 22–1 ▸ Interactive Tutor Self-Assessment CD-ROM ▸ ExamView® Pro Testmaker CD-ROM ▸ Presentation Plus! CD-ROM ▸ TeacherWorks™ CD-ROM ▸ Audio Program
SECTION 2 **Life During the Depression** 1. Describe how the Great Depression affected American families. 2. Discuss how artists portrayed the effects of the Depression.	▸ Reproducible Lesson Plan 22–2 ▸ Daily Lecture and Discussion Notes 22–2 ▸ Guided Reading Activity 22–2* ▸ Section Quiz 22–2* ▸ Reading Essentials and Study Guide 22–2 ▸ Performance Assessment Activities and Rubrics ▸ Interpreting Political Cartoons	▸ Daily Focus Skills Transparency 22–2 ▸ American Art & Architecture ▸ Interactive Tutor Self-Assessment CD-ROM ▸ ExamView® Pro Testmaker CD-ROM ▸ Presentation Plus! CD-ROM ▸ TeacherWorks™ CD-ROM ▸ Audio Program ▸ American Music: Hits Through History ▸ American Music: Cultural Traditions
SECTION 3 **Hoover Responds** 1. Evaluate President Hoover's attempts to revive the economy. 2. Analyze the limitations of Hoover's recovery plans.	▸ Reproducible Lesson Plan 22–3 ▸ Daily Lecture and Discussion Notes 22–3 ▸ Guided Reading Activity 22–3* ▸ Section Quiz 22–3* ▸ Reading Essentials and Study Guide 22–3 ▸ Performance Assessment Activities and Rubrics	▸ Daily Focus Skills Transparency 22–3 ▸ Interactive Tutor Self-Assessment CD-ROM ▸ ExamView® Pro Testmaker CD-ROM ▸ Presentation Plus! CD-ROM ▸ Skillbuilder Interactive Workbook, Level 2 ▸ TeacherWorks™ CD-ROM ▸ Vocabulary PuzzleMaker CD-ROM ▸ Audio Program

0:00 OUT OF TIME?
Assign the Chapter 22 **Reading Essentials and Study Guide.**

*Also Available in Spanish

 Blackline Master   Transparency   CD-ROM   DVD

 Poster   Music Program   Audio Program   ▐▌ Videocassette

NATIONAL GEOGRAPHIC Teacher's Corner

INDEX TO NATIONAL GEOGRAPHIC MAGAZINE

The following articles relate to this chapter.
• "The Okies—Beyond the Great Depression," September 1984

ADDITIONAL NATIONAL GEOGRAPHIC SOCIETY PRODUCTS

To order the following, call National Geographic at 1-800-368-2728:
• *1929–1941: The Great Depression* (Video)
• *The Complete National Geographic: 109 Years of National Geographic Magazine* (CD-ROM)
• *National Geographic World Atlas for Young Explorers—Classroom Library Edition* (Teacher's Guide, Transparencies, Resource Masters)

NGS ONLINE

Access National Geographic's Web site for current events, atlas updates, activities, links, interactive features, and archives.
www.nationalgeographic.com

From the Classroom of...

Jon Lever
Green River High School
Green River, WY

Beginning of the Great Depression: 1929–1932

As a class, read from the text or other source about life in the early part of the Depression. Focus on the lifestyle changes that occurred as a result of the deepening Depression. This provides the background for the activity.

Once the students show an understanding of the changes in life during the Depression, have the students visit the American Memories Web site, located at memory.loc.gov and find three different pictures of the time period from three different regions. Once the students have found their pictures, they are to write a short story describing the background of that picture based on the life changes in America.

ADDITIONAL RESOURCES FROM GLENCOE

• American Music: Cultural Traditions
• American Art & Architecture
• Outline Map Resource Book
• U.S. Desk Map
• Building Geography Skills for Life
• Inclusion for the High School Social Studies Classroom Strategies and Activities
• Teaching Strategies for the American History Classroom (Including Block Scheduling Pacing Guides)

KEY TO ABILITY LEVELS

Teaching strategies have been coded.

L1 BASIC activities for all students
L2 AVERAGE activities for average to above-average students
L3 CHALLENGING activities for above-average students
ELL ENGLISH LANGUAGE LEARNER activities

Block Schedule

Activities that are suited to use within the block scheduling framework are identified by:

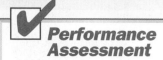
✔ Performance Assessment

Refer to Activity 22 in the Performance Assessment Activities and Rubrics booklet. 📀

Why It Matters Activity

Ask students to describe how they think businesses and government cooperate today. Then ask if they think this cooperation helps workers and consumers. Students should evaluate their answers after they have completed the chapter.

GLENCOE
TECHNOLOGY

The American Vision Video Program

To learn more about life during the Great Depression, have students view the Chapter 22 video, "Brother, Can You Spare a Dime?" from the *American Vision* Video Program.

Available in DVD and VHS

MindJogger Videoquiz
Use the **MindJogger Videoquiz** to preview Chapter 22 content.

Available in VHS

CHAPTER
22 The Great Depression Begins
1929–1932

Why It Matters

Prosperity in the United States seemed limitless before the Great Depression struck. Overproduction and agricultural problems contributed to the economic catastrophe. President Hoover looked to voluntary business action and limited government relief as solutions, but these efforts failed. Meanwhile, millions of Americans lost their jobs and life savings. Artists and writers depicted this suffering, and many people turned to lighthearted films to escape their difficult lives.

The Impact Today

Events of this period remain important.
• Hoover's model of business-government cooperation is still influential.
• John Steinbeck's novel The Grapes of Wrath and Grant Wood's painting American Gothic are permanent artistic legacies.

The American Vision Video The Chapter 22 video, "Brother, Can You Spare a Dime?" chronicles Depression-era life in the United States.

October 29, 1929
• Stock market crashes on Black Tuesday

1930
• Grant Wood paints *American Gothic*

June 1930
• Hawley-Smoot Tariff passed

THIS IS A HOOVER HOUSE
SERVICE • ACHIEVEMENT • VISION
• INTEGRITY •

United States
PRESIDENTS

Hoover 1929–1933

1929　　　　　*1930*　　　　　*1931*

World

1929
• Remarque's *All Quiet on the Western Front* published

1930
• Ras Tafari becomes Emperor Haile Selassie of Ethiopia

1931
• Gandhi released from prison in India, ending second passive resistance campaign against British rule

654

TWO-MINUTE LESSON LAUNCHER

Write the term *economic depression* on the board. Ask for volunteers to define the term. Write their definitions on the board. Discuss the term with students and as a class come up with a one-sentence definition. Tell students that in this chapter they will explore both the causes and effects of the Great Depression.

HISTORY *Online*

Introduce students to chapter content and key terms by having them access the **Chapter 22 Overview** at tav.glencoe.com.

More About the Photo

Lawrence Svobida, an eyewitness to the Dust Bowl days, remembers, ". . . With the gales came the dust. Sometimes it was so thick that it completely hid the sun. Visibility ranged from nothing to fifty feet, the former when the eyes were filled with dirt which could not be avoided, even with goggles."

Girls pump for water during a dust storm in Springfield, Colorado.

TIME LINE ACTIVITY

Ask students to select one of the political or economic events on the United States portion of the time line and identify at least one cause and one effect of the event.

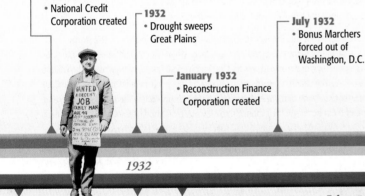

October 1931
• National Credit Corporation created

1932
• Drought sweeps Great Plains

July 1932
• Bonus Marchers forced out of Washington, D.C.

January 1932
• Reconstruction Finance Corporation created

F. Roosevelt 1933–1945

1932   *1933*

September 21, 1931
• Britain abandons gold standard

1932
• Salazar becomes premier of Portugal

February 1932
• Japan sets up puppet government in Manchukuo in northern China

HISTORY *Online*

Chapter Overview
Visit the *American Vision* Web site at tav.glencoe.com and click on **Chapter Overviews—Chapter 22** to preview chapter information.

655

GRAPHIC ORGANIZER ACTIVITY

Organizing Information Have students use a graphic organizer similar to the one below to help them identify the chains of events that led to the Great Depression.

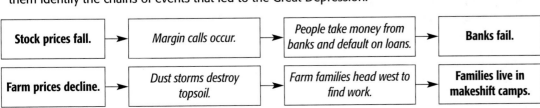

| Stock prices fall. | → | Margin calls occur. | → | People take money from banks and default on loans. | → | Banks fail. |

| Farm prices decline. | → | Dust storms destroy topsoil. | → | Farm families head west to find work. | → | Families live in makeshift camps. |

1 FOCUS

Section Overview

This section focuses on the stock market crash of 1929 and the causes of the Great Depression.

BELLRINGER
Skillbuilder Activity

Project transparency and have students answer the question.

Available as a blackline master.

Daily Focus Skills Transparency 22–1

Guide to Reading

Answers to Graphic: Hoover: Republican, Quaker, engineer, eight years as Secretary of Commerce, favored Prohibition; Smith: Democrat, Catholic, four-time governor of New York, opposed Prohibition

Preteaching Vocabulary
Have students write a paragraph using at least five of the Key Terms and Names.

SECTION 1 Causes of the Depression

Guide to Reading

Main Idea
Inflated stock prices, overproduction, high tariffs, and mistakes by the Federal Reserve led to the Great Depression.

Key Terms and Names
Alfred E. Smith, stock market, bull market, margin, margin call, speculation, Black Tuesday, installment, Hawley-Smoot Tariff

Reading Strategy
Categorizing As you read about the election of 1928, complete a graphic organizer similar to the one below comparing the backgrounds and issues of the presidential candidates.

1928 Presidential Campaign		
Candidate	Background	Issues

Reading Objectives
• **Describe** the characteristics of the 1920s stock market.
• **Identify** the causes of the Great Depression.

Section Theme
Economic Factors The Great Depression was caused by a combination of various economic problems and government policies.

Preview of Events

◆November 1928	◆September 1929	◆July 1930

November 1928
Herbert Hoover elected president

October 24, 1929
Stocks fall during Black Thursday

October 29, 1929
Black Tuesday stock market crash

June 1930
Congress passes Hawley-Smoot Tariff

★ An American Story ★

Bank run

In the years just after the 1929 stock market crash, Annetta Gibson taught English in a Rockford, Illinois, grade school. As a teacher, Gibson was lucky because she was at least able to keep her job, unlike many other American workers.

❝Everyone knew that the teachers' salaries were being held up. . . . The stores charged anything we wanted, and we'd pay them when we got paid, so it wasn't too bad.

The one thing that was bad was that we had worked hard at school to get the children to save. . . . The children would bring, oh, maybe just a few pennies that they would put in their banks. Some of them had nice little bank accounts when the Depression hit, and some of them never got their money back. It wasn't too good a lesson . . . because they thought they might as well spend their money as save it and then have it gone.❞

—quoted in *Centenarians: The Story of the Twentieth Century by the Americans Who Lived It*

The Election of 1928

The economic collapse that began in 1929 had seemed unimaginable only a year earlier. In the election of 1928, the presidential candidates vied with each other to paint a rosy picture of the future. Republican Herbert Hoover declared, "We are nearer to the final triumph over poverty than ever before in the history of any land."

SECTION RESOURCES

📁 Reproducible Masters
• Reproducible Lesson Plan 22–1
• Daily Lecture and Discussion Notes 22–1
• Guided Reading Activity 22–1
• Section Quiz 22–1
• Reading Essentials and Study Guide 22–1
• Performance Assessment Activities and Rubrics

📄 Transparencies
• Daily Focus Skills Transparency 22–1

Multimedia
🖭 Interactive Tutor Self-Assessment CD-ROM
🖭 ExamView® Pro Testmaker CD-ROM
🖭 Presentation Plus! CD-ROM
🖭 TeacherWorks™ CD-ROM
🔊 Audio Program

The Candidates When Calvin Coolidge decided not to run for president in 1928, he cleared the way for Herbert Hoover to head the Republican ticket. A successful engineer and former head of the Food Administration during World War I, Hoover had spent eight years as secretary of commerce in the Harding and Coolidge administrations. The Democrats chose **Alfred E. Smith,** four-time governor of New York. Smith was an Irish American from New York's Lower East Side and the first Roman Catholic ever nominated to run for president.

Campaign Issues By 1928 Prohibition had become a major issue among voters. Because he favored the ban on liquor sales, Hoover was considered a "dry" in the popular language of the day. Smith, who disliked the ban, was a "wet."

The candidates' religious differences sparked a smear campaign against Smith. Many Protestants were willing to believe that the Catholic Church financed the Democratic Party and would rule the United States if Smith got into the White House. These slurs embarrassed Hoover, a Quaker, and he tried to quash them, but the charges seriously damaged Smith's candidacy.

Smith's biggest problem, however, was the prosperity of the 1920s, for which the Republicans took full credit. Republican candidates promised to continue the trend with such slogans as "two cars in every garage." Hoover received over 6 million more votes than Smith and won the Electoral College in a landslide, 444 to 87.

On March 4, 1929, an audience of 50,000 stood in the rain to hear Hoover's inaugural speech. Sound movie cameras covered the inauguration for the first time and radios broadcast the address worldwide. "I have no fears for the future of our country," Hoover said. "It is bright with hope."

> ✓ **Reading Check** **Examining** What campaign issues led to Herbert Hoover's election to the presidency?

The Long Bull Market

The wave of optimism that swept Hoover into the White House also drove stock prices to new highs. The stock market was established as a system for buying and selling shares of companies. Sometimes circumstances in the stock market lead to a long period of rising stock prices, which is known as a bull market. In the late 1920s a prolonged bull market convinced many Americans to invest heavily in stocks. By 1929 between 3 and 4 million Americans, or roughly 10 percent of households, owned stocks.

As the market continued to soar, many investors began buying stocks on margin, meaning they made only a small cash down payment—as low as 10 percent of the price. With $1,000 an investor could buy $10,000 worth of stock. The other $9,000 would come as a loan from a stockbroker, who earned both a commission on the sale and interest on the loan. The broker held the stock as collateral.

As long as stock prices kept rising, buying on margin was safe. For example, an investor who borrowed money to buy $10,000 worth of stocks had to wait only a short time for them to rise to $11,000 in value. The investor could then sell the stock, repay the loan, and make $1,000 in profit. The problem came if the stock price began to fall. To protect the loan, a broker could issue a margin call, demanding the investor repay the loan at once. As a result, many investors were very sensitive to any fall in stock prices. If prices fell, they had to sell quickly, or they might not be able to repay their loans.

Before the late 1920s, the prices investors paid for stocks had generally reflected the stocks' true value. If a company made a profit or had good future sales prospects, its stock price rose, while a drop in earnings or an aging product line could send the price down. In the late 1920s, however, hordes of new investors bid prices up without regard to a company's earnings and profits. Buyers, hoping to make a fortune overnight, engaged in speculation. Instead of investing in the future of the companies whose shares they bought,

Picturing **History**

Herbert Hoover The nation and its new president felt confident about the future in early 1929. Why were Americans so optimistic?

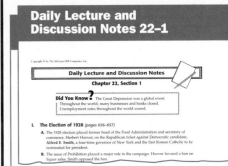
Making Comparisons Write on the board the three Ps that guided the outcome of the 1928 presidential election: prosperity, Prohibition, and Protestantism. Ask students to write on a piece of paper one example for each, showing how it worked for Hoover and against Smith. Have volunteers share their answers with the class. **L1**

> ✓ **Reading Check**
> **Answer:** Prohibition, religious values, economic prosperity

Picturing **History**

Background: Herbert Hoover was born in Iowa, grew up in Oregon, and graduated from Stanford University.
Answer: The economy and stock market were growing.
Ask: What campaign slogan did Hoover use to assure Americans of continuing prosperity? *(two cars in every garage)*

COOPERATIVE LEARNING ACTIVITY

Coping with a Crisis Organize students into groups of four and have them discuss how they would economize if their families' incomes were drastically reduced and there was no aid available. **Ask:** What would you give up first? How would you cut back? How would you help your family?

Use the rubric for a cooperative group management plan on pages 81–82 in the *Performance Assessment Activities and Rubrics.*

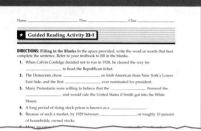
Graph Skills

Answers:

1. 1924

2. It resulted in falling demand for textiles, oil, steel, and rubber. Businesses in these industries laid off workers.

Graph Skills Practice

Ask: How did tariffs affect the Great Depression? *(High tariffs reduced foreign demand for American goods.)*

✓ Reading Check

Answer: bull market, a long period of rising stock prices

CURRICULUM CONNECTION

Economics The growing gap between the rich and poor in the 1920s reveals that many business leaders had forgotten Henry Ford's insight into the importance of paying workers enough so that they could buy the products they were making.

The Great Depression

Causes

- Overproduction and low demand leads to employee layoffs
- Low wages reduce consumer buying power
- High tariffs restrict foreign demand for American goods
- Unemployment reduces buying power further

Cyclical Effect

Automobile sales declined. This loss of demand meant less demand for:

Textiles
Oil
Steel
Rubber

Which helped contribute further to . . .

Unemployment

Lower wages

Industry slowed, which caused:

Stock Prices, 1920–1932

— Annual high
— Annual low

Price per Share: $350, $300, $250, $200, $150, $100, $50, 0

1920 1922 1924 1926 1928 1930 1932
Dow-Jones Industrial Averages

Source: Standard and Poor's *Security Price Index Record.*

Graph Skills

1. **Interpreting Graphs** Stock prices peaked in 1929. Before this peak, when did they begin to rise sharply?
2. **Making Generalizations** How did the decline in auto sales affect many other industries?

speculators took risks, betting that the market would continue to climb, thus enabling them to sell the stock and make money quickly.

✓ Reading Check **Summarizing** What was the stock market like in the 1920s?

The Great Crash

The bull market lasted only as long as investors continued putting new money into it. By the latter half of 1929, the market was running out of new customers. In September professional investors sensed danger and began to sell off their holdings. Prices slipped. Other investors sold shares to pay the interest on their brokerage loans. Prices fell further.

TURNING POINT

Crash! On Monday, October 21, Groucho Marx, the comic star of stage and screen, was awakened by a telephone call from his broker. "You'd better get

down here with some cash to cover your margin," the broker said. The stock market had plunged. The dazed comedian had to pay back the money he had borrowed to buy stocks, which were now selling for far less than he had paid.

Other brokers made similar margin calls. Frightened customers put their stocks up for sale at a frenzied pace, driving the market into a tailspin. When Marx arrived at the brokerage, he found ticker tape "knee-deep on the floor." He further recalled, "People were shouting orders to sell and others were frantically scribbling checks in vain efforts to save their original investments."

On October 24, a day that came to be called Black Thursday, the market plummeted further. Marx was wiped out. He had earned a small fortune from plays and films, and now it was gone in the blink of an eye. Like many other investors, he was deeply in debt. Arthur Marx recalled his father's final visit to the brokerage, as Groucho looked around and spotted his broker:

❝He was sitting in front of the now-stilled ticker-tape machine, with his head buried in his hands. Ticker tape was strewn around him on the floor, and

MEETING SPECIAL NEEDS

Reading Disability For students who have reading difficulties, you may wish to have them outline this rather complex section. Ask them to copy the main ideas and subheads in their notebooks, leaving plenty of space after each head for their notes about key events and concepts. Remind students to use the chapter and section time lines to preview the events that they will read about. **L1**

☞ Refer to *Inclusion for the High School Social Studies Classroom Strategies and Activities* in the TCR.

the place . . . looked as if it hadn't been swept out in a week. Groucho tapped [him] on the shoulder and said, 'Aren't you the fellow who said nothing could go wrong?' 'I guess I made a mistake,' the broker wearily replied. 'No, I'm the one who made a mistake,' snapped Groucho. 'I listened to you.' 99

—quoted in *1929: The Year of the Great Crash*

The following week, on October 29, a day later dubbed **Black Tuesday,** prices took the steepest dive yet. That day stocks lost $10 to $15 billion in value.

By mid-November stock prices had dropped by over one-third. Some $30 billion was lost, a sum roughly equal to the total wages earned by Americans in 1929. The stock market crash was not the major cause of the Great Depression, but it undermined the economy's ability to hold out against its other weaknesses.

Banks in a Tailspin The market crash severely weakened the nation's banks in two ways. First, many banks had lent money to stock speculators. Second, many banks had invested depositors' money in the stock market, hoping for higher returns than they could get by using the money for conventional loans.

When stock values collapsed, the banks lost money on their investments, and the speculators defaulted on their loans. Having suffered serious losses, many banks cut back drastically on the loans they made. With less credit available, consumers and businesses were unable to borrow as much money as they had previously. This helped to put the economy into a recession.

For some banks, the losses they suffered in the crash were more than they could absorb, and they were forced to close. At that time, the government did not insure bank deposits; therefore, if a bank collapsed, customers lost their savings. The bank failures in 1929 and early 1930 triggered a crisis of confidence in the banking system.

News of bank failures worried many Americans. They began to make runs on the nation's banks, causing the banks to collapse. A bank run takes place when many depositors decide to withdraw their money at one time, usually for fear the bank is going to collapse.

Most banks make a profit by lending money received from depositors and collecting interest on the loans. The bank holds on to only a fraction of the depositors' money to cover everyday business, such as occasional withdrawals. Ordinarily that reserve is enough to meet the bank's needs, but if too many people withdraw their money, the bank will eventually collapse. During the first two years

of the Depression, more than 3,000 banks—over 10 percent of the nation's total—were forced to close.

✓ **Reading Check** **Evaluating** How did bank failures contribute to the Great Depression?

The Roots of the Great Depression

The stock market crash helped put the economy into a recession. Yet the crash would not have led to a long-lasting depression if other forces had not been at work. The roots of the Great Depression were deeply entangled in the economy of the 1920s.

The Uneven Distribution of Income Most economists agree that overproduction was a key cause of the Depression. More efficient machinery increased the production capacity of both factories and farms.

Most Americans did not earn enough to buy up the flood of goods they helped produce. While manufacturing output per person-hour rose 32 percent, the average worker's wage increased only 8 percent. In 1929 the top 5 percent of all American households earned 30 percent of the nation's income. By contrast, about two-thirds of families earned less than $2,500 a year, leaving them little expendable income.

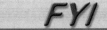

Picturing **History**

Wall Street Panic This painting shows the confusion and chaos surrounding the American financial industry in October 1929. How does the artist depict a sense of disorder?

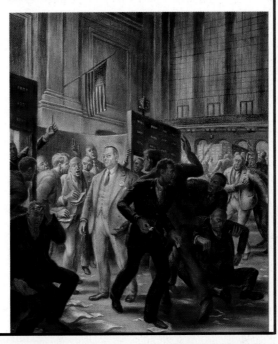

CHAPTER 22
Section 1, 656–660

✓ **Reading Check**

Answer: The bank failures triggered a crisis of confidence in the banking system. Many people made runs on the banks, causing them to collapse.

Picturing **History**

Answer: the urgent sense of movement; the paper littered on the floor; the shocked look of several figures

Ask: What occurred on Black Tuesday? (*Stocks lost $10 to $15 billion in value in their steepest drop.*)

FYI

By 1932 the nation's manufacturing output stood at 47 percent of its 1929 level.

3 ASSESS

Assign Section 1 Assessment as homework or as an in-class activity.

◉ Have students use the **Interactive Tutor Self-Assessment CD-ROM.**

Reading Essentials and Study Guide 22–1

Name _____ Date _____ Class _____

Study Guide

Chapter 22, Section 1

For use with textbook pages 656–660

CAUSES OF THE DEPRESSION

KEY TERMS AND NAMES

Alfred E. Smith the Democratic nominee in the 1928 presidential election *(page 657)*

stock market a system for buying and selling shares of companies *(page 657)*

bull market a long period of rising stock prices *(page 657)*

margin a way of buying stocks by paying only a small percent of the price of the stock and taking a loan from a stockbroker to pay the rest *(page 657)*

margin call a demand by a broker for the investor to repay the loan at once *(page 657)*

speculation buying shares, betting that the stock market would continue to climb, and then selling the stock to make money quickly *(page 657)*

INTERDISCIPLINARY CONNECTIONS ACTIVITY

Economics Invite an economist or an economics teacher to speak to the class about the safeguards that are now in place to help prevent a depression as serious as the Great Depression. Ask the speaker to look at other drops in the stock market and how these safeguards have worked at these times. Ask the speaker to provide an activity or pretest that students can complete in advance of the presentation. **L2**

FYI

Some of the country's leading financiers had tried to avert the crash by pumping money into the market, but others wanted to profit from the panic. The president of Chase National Bank sold 42,506 shares of his own bank's stock, bought them back later in the year at a lower price, and made a profit of $4 million.

Reteach

Have students describe the characteristics of the 1920s stock market.

Enrich

Ask students to hypothesize how the crash might have affected the business of a toy company and the business of a dairy company.

✓ Reading Check

Answer: Tariffs damaged American sales abroad and discouraged imports.

4 CLOSE

Have students list the causes of the Great Depression.

Newspaper headline the day after Black Tuesday

During the 1920s many Americans bought high-cost items, such as refrigerators and cars, on the installment plan, under which they would make a small down payment and pay the rest in monthly installments. Some buyers reached a point where paying off their debts forced them to reduce other purchases. This low consumption then led manufacturers to cut production and lay off employees.

The slowdown in retail manufacturing had repercussions throughout the economy. When radio sales slumped, for example, makers cut back on their orders for copper wire, wood cabinets, and glass radio tubes. Montana copper miners, Minnesota lumberjacks, and Ohio glassworkers, in turn, lost their jobs. Jobless workers had to cut back purchases, further reducing sales. This kind of chain reaction put more and more Americans out of work.

The Loss of Export Sales Many jobs might have been saved if American manufacturers had sold more goods abroad. As the bull market of the 1920s accelerated, U.S. banks made high-interest loans to stock speculators instead of lending money to foreign companies. Without these loans from U.S. banks, foreign companies purchased fewer products from American manufacturers.

Matters grew worse after June 1930, when Congress passed the **Hawley-Smoot Tariff** raising the average tariff rate to the highest level in American history. Rates went up on more than 900 manufactured items. The Hawley-Smoot Tariff aimed to protect American manufacturers from foreign competition, but it damaged American sales abroad. Because imports now cost much more, Americans bought fewer of them. When foreign countries did not sell products in the United States, they had neither the money nor the inclination to buy American exports. In 1932 U.S. exports fell to about one-fifth of what they had been in 1929, which hurt both American companies and farmers.

Mistakes by the Federal Reserve Just as consumers were able to buy more goods on credit, access to easy money propelled the stock market. Instead of raising interest rates to curb excessive speculation, the Federal Reserve Board kept its rates very low throughout the 1920s.

The Board's failure to raise interest rates significantly helped cause the Depression in two ways. First, by keeping rates low, it encouraged member banks to make risky loans. Second, its low interest rates led business leaders to think the economy was still expanding. As a result, they borrowed more money to expand production, a serious mistake because it led to overproduction when sales were falling. When the Depression finally hit, companies had to lay off workers to cut costs. Then the Fed made another mistake. It raised interest rates, tightening credit. The economy continued to spiral downward.

✓ Reading Check **Examining** How did the decline in worldwide trade contribute to the Depression?

SECTION 1 ASSESSMENT

Checking for Understanding

1. **Define:** stock market, bull market, margin, margin call, speculation, installment.

2. **Identify:** Alfred E. Smith, Black Tuesday, Hawley-Smoot Tariff.

3. **Explain** the significance of the year 1929.

Reviewing Themes

4. **Economic Factors** How did the practices of buying on margin and speculation cause the stock market to rise?

Critical Thinking

5. **Determining Cause and Effect** Why did the stock market crash cause banks to fail?

6. **Organizing** Use a graphic organizer similar to the one below to list the causes of the Great Depression.

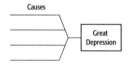

Analyzing Visuals

7. **Analyzing Graphs** Study the graphs on page 658. Note that decreased demand for automobiles ultimately led to layoffs. These layoffs further decreased the demand for automobiles. What do you think might have ended this cycle?

Writing About History

8. **Expository Writing** Write an article for a financial magazine explaining the rapid decline of the stock market in 1929 and the reasons for the Black Tuesday crash.

SECTION 1 ASSESSMENT ANSWERS

1. Terms are in blue.
2. Alfred E. Smith *(p. 657)*, Black Tuesday *(p. 659)*, Hawley-Smoot Tariff *(p. 660)*
3. The Great Depression began.
4. Speculation drove up market prices beyond the stock's value.

5. Banks had lent money to stock speculators and had invested depositors' money in stocks.
6. uneven distribution of wealth, decline in sales, mistakes by the Federal Reserve
7. Answers will vary. Students may

suggest that businesses could have avoided layoffs or that the government could have intervened.
8. Students' articles will vary but should include appropriate vocabulary.

Guide to Reading

Main Idea

Many people were impoverished during the Great Depression, but some found ways to cope with the hard times.

Key Terms and Names

bailiff, shantytown, Hooverville, hobo, Dust Bowl, Walt Disney, soap opera, Grant Wood, John Steinbeck, William Faulkner

Reading Strategy

Taking Notes As you read about life in the United States during the Great Depression, use the major headings of the section to create an outline similar to the one below.

Life During the Depression
I. The Depression Worsens
   A.
   B.
   C.
II.

Reading Objectives

• **Describe** how the Great Depression affected American families.
• **Discuss** how artists portrayed the effects of the Depression.

Section Theme

Culture and Traditions Radio and motion pictures provided ways to escape the worries that plagued people during the Depression's early years.

Preview of Events

♦1930   ♦1935   ♦1940

1930
Grant Wood paints *American Gothic*

1932
Drought sweeps Great Plains

1934
Dust storms destroy 300 million acres

1937
Walt Disney releases *Snow White and the Seven Dwarfs*

1939
Popular musical *The Wizard of Oz* released

★ An American Story ★

A young girl with the unusual name of Dynamite Garland was living with her family in Cleveland, Ohio, in the 1930s when her father, a railroad worker, lost his job. Unable to afford rent, they gave up their home and moved into a two-car garage.

The hardest aspect of living in a garage was getting through the frigid winters. "We would sleep with rugs and blankets over the top of us," Garland later recalled. "In the morning we'd . . . get some snow and put it on the stove and melt it and wash 'round our faces." When Garland's father found a part-time job in a Chinese restaurant, the family "lived on those fried noodles."

On Sundays the family looked at houses for sale. "That was a recreation during the Depression," said Garland. "You'd go and see where you'd put this and where you could put that, and this is gonna be my room." In this way, the family tried to focus on better times. Movies and radio programs also provided a brief escape from their troubles, but the struggle to survive left little room for pleasure.

—adapted from *Hard Times*

An unemployed man advertising his skills

The Depression Worsens

In 1930, 1,352 banks suspended operations across the nation, more than twice the number of bank failures in 1929. The Depression grew steadily worse during Hoover's administration. By 1933 more than 9,000 banks had failed. In 1932 alone some 30,000 companies

CHAPTER 22   The Great Depression Begins   **661**

---

1 FOCUS

Section Overview

This section focuses on life during the Great Depression, including the hardships and the diversions.

BELLRINGER
Skillbuilder Activity

Project transparency and have students answer the question.

Available as a blackline master.

Daily Focus Skills Transparency 22–2

Guide to Reading

Answers to Graphic:
I. The Depression Worsens
   A. Lining up at Soup Kitchens
   B. Living in Makeshift Villages
   C. The Dust Bowl
II. Escaping the Depression
   A. The Hollywood Fantasy Factory
   B. On the Air
III. The Depression in Art

Preteaching Vocabulary

Have students create a simple symbol, icon, or sketch for each of the Key Terms and Names.

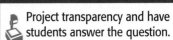

SECTION RESOURCES

Reproducible Masters
• Reproducible Lesson Plan 22–2
• Daily Lecture and Discussion Notes 22–2
• Guided Reading Activity 22–2
• Section Quiz 22–2
• Reading Essentials and Study Guide 22–2

Transparencies
• Daily Focus Skills Transparency 22–2

Multimedia
• Interactive Tutor Self-Assessment CD-ROM
• ExamView® Pro Testmaker CD-ROM
• Presentation Plus! CD-ROM
• TeacherWorks™ CD-ROM
• Audio Program
• American Music: Hits Through History
• American Music: Cultural Traditions

2 TEACH

Daily Lecture and Discussion Notes 22–2

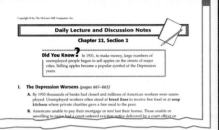

Copyright © by The McGraw-Hill Companies, Inc.

Daily Lecture and Discussion Notes

Chapter 22, Section 2

Did You Know? In 1931, to make money, large numbers of unemployed people began to sell apples on the streets of major cities. Selling apples became a popular symbol of the Depression years.

I. The Depression Worsens *(pages 661–663)*

A. By 1933 thousands of banks had closed and millions of American workers were unemployed. Unemployed workers often stood at **bread lines** to receive free food or at **soup kitchens** where private charities gave a free meal to the poor.

B. Americans unable to pay their mortgage or rent lost their homes. Those unable or unwilling to move had a court-ordered eviction notice delivered by a court officer or

Discussing a Topic Ask students to consider both negative and positive emotions and activities a major depression might cause in a nation. **L1**

During the 1930s, the Resettlement Administration trained recreational leaders by having them gather the folk music of many immigrant groups. Today the Library of Congress has the song sheets from this project.

History *and the* Humanities

- American Music: Hits Through History: "Brother, Can You Spare a Dime?" "Flores Negras"
- American Music: Cultural Traditions: "Talking Dust Bowl"
- American Art & Architecture: "Migrant Mother"

IMAGE OF AN ERA

Lasting a decade, the Great Depression deprived many Americans of jobs, land, and livelihoods. Plummeting crop prices and farms withering under drought and dust clouds forced many families to take to the road in search of work, often with little success. Dismayed by scenes of destitution and homelessness, photographer Dorothea Lange joined the Resettlement Administration in 1935. In 1936 in rural Nipomo, California, Lange photographed this "Migrant Mother," a 32-year-old woman with seven children. She had just sold her car tires to buy food.

went out of business. By 1933 more than 12 million workers were unemployed—about one-fourth of the workforce. Average family income dropped from $2,300 in 1929 to $1,600 just three years later.

Lining Up at Soup Kitchens People without jobs often went hungry. Whenever possible they joined **bread lines** to receive a free handout of food or lined up outside **soup kitchens,** which private charities set up to give poor people a meal.

Peggy Terry, a young girl in Oklahoma City during the Depression, later told an interviewer how each day after school, her mother sent her to the soup kitchen:

> ❝If you happened to be one of the first ones in line, you didn't get anything but water that was on top. So we'd ask the guy that was ladling out soup into the buckets—everybody had to bring their own bucket to get the soup—he'd dip the greasy, watery stuff off the top. So we'd ask him to please dip down to get some meat and potatoes from the bottom of the kettle. But he wouldn't do it.❞
>
> —quoted in *Hard Times*

662 CHAPTER 22 The Great Depression Begins

Living in Makeshift Villages Families or individuals who could not pay their rent or mortgage lost their homes. Some of them, paralyzed by fear and humiliation over their sudden misfortune, simply would not or could not move. Their landlord would then ask the court for an eviction notice. Court officers called **bailiffs** then ejected the nonpaying tenants, piling their belongings in the street.

Throughout the country, newly homeless people put up shacks on unused or public lands, forming communities called **shantytowns.** Blaming the president for their plight, people referred to such places as **Hoovervilles.**

In search of work or a better life, many homeless and unemployed Americans began to wander around the country, walking, hitchhiking, or, most often, "riding the rails." These wanderers, called **hobos,** would sneak past railroad police to slip into open boxcars on freight trains for a ride to somewhere else. They camped in "hobo jungles," usually situated near rail yards. Hundreds of thousands of people, mostly boys and young men, wandered from place to place in this fashion.

COOPERATIVE LEARNING ACTIVITY

Posing Interview Questions Have students work in pairs and ask each other interview questions that a journalist might have asked someone during the Great Depression. The questions should concern the government's responses to the Depression and the interviewee's opinions about the response, either pro or con.

Use the rubric for a cooperative group management plan on pages 81–82 in the ***Performance Assessment Activities and Rubrics.***

Hoover Dam

American farmers and settlers in the low-lying valleys of southern California and southwestern Arizona have been tapping the waters of the Colorado River for more than a century. Thanks to irrigation canals, the parched desert valleys became year-round gardens that provided fruit and vegetables for the nation. At times, however, the unpredictable river would decrease to a trickle. Other times, it became a raging torrent, destroying all in its path. The federal government decided to dam the Colorado to control it. In 1931 construction began in Black Canyon, whose high rock walls made it an ideal site. Here, on the border between Arizona and Nevada, would rise one of the most ambitious engineering projects the world had ever seen: the Hoover Dam.

Named after President Herbert Hoover, the dam was built in the middle of a forbidding desert. Everything had to be imported, including labor. There was no shortage of candidates. The country was in the grips of the Great Depression; thousands of unemployed workers flocked to the remote canyon. To accommodate them, an entire town was built—Boulder City, Nevada.

The new arrivals faced brutal conditions. Men worked in three shifts around the clock. Summer temperatures climbed higher than 120 degrees in the canyon, and even those who worked at night had to endure temperatures of more than 85 degrees. Still, the project was completed in less than five years. Lake Mead, the 115-mile-long reservoir created by the dam, is large enough to hold two years' worth of the average flow of the Colorado River—enough to cover the entire state of New York with one foot of water. The benefits to the Southwest were immense. Hoover Dam created much-needed employment. It also provided a regular supply of water, irrigating over a million acres of rich agricultural land and producing hydroelectric power, which has allowed Southwestern cities to grow.

McCullough Range

Henderson

River Mountains

to Las Vegas

Aqueduct

Saddle Island

MEAD

Las Vegas Bay

Swallow Bay

Hoover Dam and Environs
- ········· State boundary
- – – – Aqueduct
- —— Road
- ✶—✶ Power line
- ▨ Urban area

Scale varies in this perspective

Suspended on ropes, "high scalers" armed with dynamite and jackhammers prepare the walls of Black Canyon to take the concrete of Hoover Dam. Such work was hazardous. Twenty-four workers fell to their deaths during construction of the dam.

Hoover Dam, a major supplier of hydroelectric power, is more than 700 feet (213 m) tall and contains about 4,360,000 cubic yards of concrete—enough for a two-lane highway from Los Angeles to Boston.

LEARNING FROM GEOGRAPHY

1. Why did the federal government decide to dam the Colorado River?

2. Why did engineers choose the Black Canyon site?

667

ANSWERS TO LEARNING FROM GEOGRAPHY

1. The river was dammed to control its unpredictable flow.

2. The high rock walls made Black Canyon the preferred site for the dam.

1 FOCUS

Section Overview

This section focuses on Hoover's responses to the Depression.

Guide to Reading

Answers to Graphic: Industry was to keep factories open and stop slashing wages, but business leaders did not follow through; to increase public works, but this had little effect; to pump money into the economy, but this was too limited and could not reverse the accelerating collapse.

Preteaching Vocabulary
Have students make a list of the Key Terms and Names and write a helpful phrase next to each term or name.

Guide to Reading

Main Idea
President Hoover's philosophy of government guided his response to the Depression.

Key Terms and Names
public works, Reconstruction Finance Corporation, relief, foreclose, Bonus Army

Reading Strategy
Categorizing As you read about Hoover's response to the Depression, complete a graphic organizer by listing his major initiatives and their results.

Reading Objectives
• **Evaluate** President Hoover's attempts to revive the economy.
• **Analyze** the limitations of Hoover's recovery plans.

Section Theme
Groups and Institutions President Hoover began using new government agencies to improve the nation's slumping economy.

Preview of Events

◆1931	◆1932	◆1933

October 1931
National Credit Corporation created

January 1932
Congress approves Reconstruction Finance Corporation

July 1932
Congress passes Emergency Relief and Construction Act; soldiers rout the Bonus Marchers

---

★ An American Story ★

Joseph Heffernan

In December 1929, Mayor Joseph Heffernan of Youngstown, Ohio, listened impatiently to fellow public officials assembled in the Cleveland Chamber of Commerce hall. He had been called to one of a series of conferences on unemployment that President Hoover had arranged. At the conference, Heffernan grew restless as he listened to the other speakers. He felt that it would take too long to pass their confident proposals for ending unemployment, and by that time, it would be too late to prevent a depression. He asked the other conference members, "Why not tell people the truth?"

Youngstown business leaders criticized Heffernan for trying to tell his constituents how bad the economic outlook was. Heffernan later recalled that one of them said to him, "Don't emphasize hard times and everything will be all right."

The man who rebuked Mayor Heffernan expressed what many, including President Hoover himself, believed in late 1929: The country merely needed to regain its confidence. As the crisis worsened, Hoover took steps to help the economy recover, but only within the limits of his philosophy of government.

—adapted from *The Great Depression*

Promoting Recovery

On Friday, October 25, the day after Black Thursday, President Hoover issued a statement assuring the nation that industry was "on a sound and prosperous basis." In March 1930 he told the public that "the worst effects of the crash . . . will have passed during the next 60 days." Critics derided his optimism as conditions worsened. Hoover,

---

SECTION RESOURCES

📁 **Reproducible Masters**
• Reproducible Lesson Plan 22–3
• Daily Lecture and Discussion Notes 22–3
• Guided Reading Activity 22–3
• Section Quiz 22–3
• Reading Essentials and Study Guide 22–3
• Performance Assessment Activities and Rubrics

🖥 **Transparencies**
• Daily Focus Skills Transparency 22–3

Multimedia
🔘 Interactive Tutor Self-Assessment CD-ROM
🔘 ExamView® Pro Testmaker CD-ROM
🔘 Presentation Plus! CD-ROM
🔘 TeacherWorks™ CD-ROM
🔘 Audio Program

however, hoped to downplay the public's fears. He wanted to avoid more bank runs and layoffs by urging consumers and business leaders to become more rational in their decision making.

Voluntary Efforts and Public Works Despite his soothing words, Hoover was seriously worried about the economy. He organized a series of conferences, bringing together the heads of banks, railroads, and other big businesses, as well as labor and government officials.

He won a pledge from industry to keep factories open and to stop slashing wages. By 1931, however, business leaders had abandoned those pledges. Hoover's next step was to increase public works—government-financed building projects. The resulting construction jobs could replace some of those lost

in the private sector. He urged governors and mayors throughout the nation to increase public works spending.

Hoover's actions did spur construction increases, but the effort made up for only a small fraction of the jobs lost in the private sector. The only way the government could create enough new jobs would be to massively increase government spending, which Hoover refused to do.

The problem was that someone had to pay for public works projects. If the government raised taxes to pay for them, it would take money away from consumers and hurt businesses that were already struggling. If the government decided to keep taxes low and run a budget deficit instead—spending more money than it collected in taxes—it would have to borrow the money from banks. If the government did this, less

2 TEACH

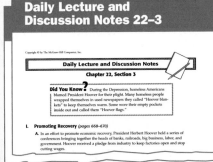

Daily Lecture and Discussion Notes 22–3

Discussing a Concept Conduct a class discussion about the role of government in the economy by asking students what the government should do to help those who are unemployed and what responsibility the government has to keep the economy healthy. **L1**

Different Viewpoints

What Should the Government's Role in the Economy Be?

The government's role in the economy was an important issue in the 1932 presidential election, when the country was in the throes of the Depression. President Herbert Hoover explained, in a 1928 speech why a limited government role was best, while President Franklin Roosevelt argued in his inaugural address in 1933 that an expanded government role was necessary.

from Hoover's Madison Square Garden Address, 1928

"During one hundred and fifty years we have built up a form of self-government and a social system which is peculiarly our own. . . . It is founded upon a particular conception of self-government in which decentralized local responsibility is the very base. . . .

During the war we necessarily turned to the government to solve every difficult economic problem. . . . However justified in time of war, if continued in peacetime it would destroy . . . our progress and freedom. . . . The acceptance of these ideas would have meant the destruction of self-government through centralization of government. It would have meant the undermining of the individual initiative and enterprise through which our people have grown to unparalleled greatness."

from Roosevelt's Inaugural Address, 1933

"Our greatest primary task is to put people to work. This is no unsolvable problem if we face it wisely and courageously. It can be accomplished in part by direct recruiting by the Government itself, treating the task as we would treat the emergency of a war, but at the same time, through this employment, accomplishing greatly needed projects to stimulate and reorganize the use of our natural resources.

. . . The task can be helped . . . by national planning for and supervision of all forms of transportation and of communications and other utilities which have a definitely public character. There are many ways in which it can be helped, but it can never be helped merely by talking about it. We must act and act quickly.

. . . We now realize as we have never realized before our interdependence on each other; . . . that if we are to go forward, we must move as a trained and loyal army willing to sacrifice for the good of a common discipline."

Learning From History

1. **Analyzing Arguments** What did Hoover fear would happen if government programs started during World War I were continued after the war?
2. **Making Inferences** Do you think Roosevelt would have agreed with Hoover's assessment of the government's role during World War I? Why or why not?

Different Viewpoints

Answers:
1. It would destroy freedom and initiative.
2. Yes, because during a national emergency—whether World War I or the Great Depression—Roosevelt believed the government should take more responsibility for the economy

Ask: Do you think that Hoover might have changed his mind by the time Roosevelt was inaugurated? *(Students' answers will vary.)*

COOPERATIVE LEARNING ACTIVITY

Analyzing Ideas Remind students that Herbert Hoover was a Quaker, a member of a religious group that believes in pacifism. Organize students into small groups and ask them to research the beliefs of Quakers and write a paragraph analyzing the difficulty of following pacifist beliefs. Encourage students to explore how Hoover's Quaker beliefs may have affected his policies.

Use the rubric for a cooperative group management plan on pages 81–82 in the ***Performance Assessment Activities and Rubrics.***

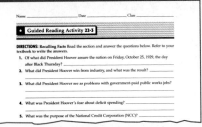
✓ Reading Check

Answer: He believed it would delay an economic recovery.

CURRICULUM CONNECTION

Music The music of Woody Guthrie gave an uplifting voice to people who struggled through the Depression. Unlike swing or big-band songs, Guthrie's lyrics told of rough living and fighting back. The guitarist drew upon the traditional tunes of farmers and workers to write workers' anthems for decades to come.

✓ Reading Check

Answer: He felt that only state and city governments should give out relief.

FYI

Ironically the board game Monopoly was invented during the Depression. Charles Darrow was an unemployed Pennsylvania engineer when he designed the famous game in the early 1930s.

---

money would be available for businesses that wanted to expand and for consumers who wanted mortgages or other loans. Hoover feared that deficit spending would actually delay an economic recovery.

The Midterm Election As the congressional elections of 1930 approached, most Americans felt that worsening unemployment posed a grave threat to their well-being. Citizens blamed the party in power for the stumbling economy. The Republicans lost 49 seats and their majority in the House of Representatives; they held on to the Senate by a single vote.

✓ **Reading Check** **Examining** Why did Hoover oppose deficit spending?

Pumping Money Into the Economy

Hoover soon turned his attention to the problem of money. There was very little in the economy now that so many banks had collapsed. The government, he believed, had to make sure that banks could make loans to corporations so they could expand production and rehire workers.

White Angel Breadline In 1932 a wealthy woman nicknamed the "White Angel" set up a breadline in San Francisco. Dorothea Lange captured the hopelessness of the Depression in this famous photograph of the breadline.

GOVERNMENT

Trying to Rescue the Banks The president asked the Federal Reserve Board to put more currency into circulation, but the Board refused. In an attempt to ease the money shortage, Hoover set up the National Credit Corporation (NCC) in October 1931. The NCC created a pool of money to enable troubled banks to continue lending money in their communities. Hoover then persuaded a number of New York bankers to contribute to the NCC. Their contributions, however, did not meet the nation's needs.

By 1932 Hoover concluded that the only way to provide funding for borrowers was for the government to do the lending. He requested that Congress set up the **Reconstruction Finance Corporation (RFC)** to make loans to banks, railroads, and agricultural institutions. By early 1932, the RFC had lent about $238 million to approximately 160 banks, 60 railroads, and 18 building-and-loan organizations. The RFC was overly cautious, however. It failed to increase its loans in sufficient amounts to meet the need, and the economy continued its decline.

Direct Help for Citizens From the start, Hoover strongly opposed the federal government's participation in relief—money that went directly to impoverished families. He believed that only state and city governments should dole out relief. By the spring of 1932, however, they were running out of money.

In 1932 political support was building for a relief measure, and Congress passed the Emergency Relief and Construction Act. Although reluctant, Hoover signed the bill on July 21. The new act called for $1.5 billion for public works and $300 million in loans to the states for direct relief. By this time, however, the new program could not reverse the accelerating collapse.

✓ **Reading Check** **Summarizing** Why did Hoover oppose the federal government's participation in relief programs?

In an Angry Mood

In the months after the Wall Street crash, Americans had seemed resigned to bad economic news. By 1931, however, they were growing increasingly discontented, and open acts of revolt began to occur.

Hunger Marches In January 1931, around 500 men and women in Oklahoma City, shouting angrily about hunger and joblessness, broke into a grocery store and looted it. Crowds began showing

---

MEETING SPECIAL NEEDS

Logical/Mathematical Tell students that library use surged during the 1930s; one Indiana town, for example, found that the circulation of books rose 145 percent between 1929 and 1933. Ask students to identify the relationship between the economic circumstances of the day and the increased reading of books. Ask them to suggest the types of books people would logically choose. **L2**

☞ Refer to *Inclusion for the High School Social Studies Classroom Strategies and Activities* in the TCR.

Picturing **History**

Poverty and Plenty Spattered with milk, dairy farmers are shown here destroying their product in a vain effort to drive up prices. For the hungry and unemployed, like the families at left, the farmers' actions were unthinkable. Why did the farmers think their actions would drive up prices?

up at rallies and "hunger marches" held by the American Communist Party, which was eager to take advantage of national problems to change the American form of government. On December 5, 1932, a freezing day in the nation's capital, around 1,200 hunger marchers assembled and chanted, "Feed the hungry, tax the rich." Police herded them into a blocked-off area, where they had to spend the night sleeping on the sidewalk or in trucks. The police denied them food, water, and medical treatment until some members of Congress insisted on the marchers' right to petition their government. They were then released and permitted to march to Capitol Hill.

Farmers Revolt In the summer of 1932, farmers also took matters into their own hands. Beginning in the boom days of World War I, many farmers had heavily mortgaged their land to pay for seed, feed, and equipment. After the war, prices sank so low that farmers could not even earn back their costs, let alone make a profit. Between 1930 and 1934 creditors foreclosed on nearly one million farms, taking possession of them and evicting the families.

Some farmers began destroying their crops in a desperate attempt to raise crop prices by reducing the supply. In Nebraska grain growers burned corn

to heat their homes in the winter. In Iowa food growers forcibly prevented the delivery of vegetables to distributors. Georgia dairy farmers blocked highways and stopped milk trucks, emptying the milk cans into ditches.

The Bonus Marchers In appreciation of the World War I service of American soldiers and sailors, Congress in 1924 had enacted a $1,000 bonus for each veteran, to be distributed in 1945. The economic crisis, however, made the wait more difficult. In 1931 Texas congressman Wright Patman introduced a bill in the House of Representatives that authorized early payment of the veterans' bonuses. The bill later passed the House and moved to the Senate for debate.

In May 1932 several hundred Portland, Oregon, veterans set off on a month-long march to Washington to lobby Congress to pass the legislation. As they moved east, other veterans joined them until they numbered about 1,000. Wearing ragged military uniforms, they trudged along the highways or rode the rails, singing old war songs and reminiscing about army days. The press termed the marchers the **"Bonus Army."**

Once in Washington, the marchers camped in Hoovervilles. As weeks went by, additional veterans joined them, until the Bonus Army swelled to

CHAPTER 22 The Great Depression Begins **671**

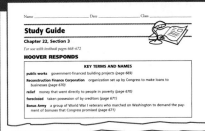

INTERDISCIPLINARY CONNECTIONS ACTIVITY

Sociology Point out to students that acting selflessly is a survival mechanism for groups as a whole. Often the most selfless people are those who have the least. Tell students that in *The Grapes of Wrath,* Ma Joad says, "If you're in trouble or hurt or need—go to poor people. They're the only ones that'll help." Ask students to analyze this statement and then write a paragraph that discusses why they feel that acting selflessly might be a group survival mechanism. Have students use examples to support their analysis. **L2**

Picturing History

Answer: They had a negative reaction toward Hoover.
Ask: What alternatives do you think the government had? *(Students' answers will vary.)*

FYI

In 1931 a Christmas tree was placed amid the rubble from some demolished buildings. Workers who still had jobs decorated the tree with tin cans and paper. A few years later at the same site, the official Rockefeller Center tree tradition was inaugurated.

Reteach

Have students evaluate President Hoover's attempts to invigorate the economy.

Enrich

Invite interested students to interview someone who lived during the Depression. Suggest that they pose questions to learn about housing, food, clothing, entertainment, and emotions during the era.

Reading Check

Answer: Reactions included hunger marches, farmers' revolts, and the Bonus Army march.

4 CLOSE

Have students analyze the limitations of Hoover's recovery plans.

Picturing History

Clearing Out the Bonus Marchers Fierce battles resulted when President Hoover ordered the Washington, D.C., police to evict the Bonus Army from public buildings and land they had been occupying. How did the public feel when they saw or heard about this event?

15,000. President Hoover acknowledged the veterans' petition rights but refused to meet with them.

When the Senate voted the new bonus bill down, veterans waiting outside the Capitol began to grumble, until one of their leaders started them singing "America." Gradually their anger cooled, and many returned home. A significant number of the marchers, however, stayed on since they had no job prospects. Some moved from the camps to unoccupied buildings downtown.

In late July, Hoover ordered the buildings cleared. The police made the first try, but one of them panicked and fired into a crowd, killing two veterans. The Washington, D.C., government then called in the army. Army chief of staff Douglas MacArthur gave

the veterans one hour to gather their possessions and go home. MacArthur deployed cavalry troops, infantry, and tanks to enforce the order.

A Federal Trade Commission member, A. Everette McIntyre, watched as the infantry "fixed their bayonets and also fixed their gas masks over their faces. At orders they brought their bayonets at thrust and moved in. The bayonets were used to jab people to make them move." Soon unarmed veterans were on the run with 700 soldiers at their heels. The soldiers tear-gassed stragglers and burned the shacks. Tear gas killed a baby boy.

The nationwide press coverage and newsreel images of veterans under assault by troops presented an ugly picture to the public. The routing of the veterans hounded the president throughout his 1932 re-election campaign.

Hoover failed to resolve the crisis of the Depression, but he did more to expand the economic role of the federal government than any previous president. The Reconstruction Finance Corporation marked the first time the federal government had established a federal agency to stimulate the economy during peacetime. It was the image of the routed Bonus Marchers and the lingering Depression, however, that shaped the public's perception of President Hoover.

Reading Check **Evaluating** How did Americans react as the Depression continued?

SECTION 3 ASSESSMENT

Checking for Understanding

1. **Define:** public works, relief, foreclose.
2. **Identify:** Reconstruction Finance Corporation, Bonus Army.
3. **Summarize** three major initiatives taken by Hoover to improve the economy and the results of each.

Reviewing Themes

4. **Groups and Institutions** What did business leaders promise Hoover they would do to help the economy? Did they keep their promises?

Critical Thinking

5. **Interpreting** How did President Hoover's philosophy of government guide his response to the Depression?
6. **Organizing** Use a graphic organizer similar to the one below to list American reactions to the Depression.

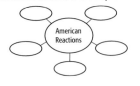

American Reactions

Analyzing Visuals

7. **Picturing History** Study the photographs on page 671. The farmers shown would rather dump their milk than sell it. What did they hope to achieve by their actions?

Writing About History

8. **Persuasive Writing** Imagine that you are a veteran of World War I. Write a letter to members of Congress explaining your circumstances and asking them to give you your bonus early.

SECTION 3 ASSESSMENT ANSWERS

1. Terms are in blue.
2. Reconstruction Finance Corporation (p. 670), Bonus Army (p. 671)
3. Funding from the National Credit Corporation and the Reconstruction Finance Corporation were insufficient; Emergency Relief and Construction funds came too late
4. They promised to keep factories open and stop slashing wages; no.
5. Belief in volunteerism and loans, rather than direct relief, restricted his actions.
6. bonus marchers, discontent, farmers' revolts, hunger strikes, squatting
7. They hoped to drive up prices by limiting supply.
8. Students' letters will vary. Letters should be written from the perspective of a World War I veteran.

Technology SKILLBUILDER

Building a Database

Why Learn This Skill?

Do you have a collection of sports cards, CDs, or DVDs? Have you ever kept a list of the names, addresses, and phone numbers of friends and relatives? If you have collected information and kept it in a list or file, then you have created a database.

Learning the Skill

An electronic database is a collection of facts that are stored in a file on a computer. The information is organized in fields.

A database can be organized and reorganized in any way that is useful to you. By using a database management system (DBMS)—special software developed for record keeping—you can easily add, delete, change, or update information. You give commands to the computer that tell it what to do with the information, and it follows these commands. When you want to retrieve information, the computer searches through the file, finds the information, and displays it on the screen.

Practicing the Skill

The Great Depression is a well-known period in American history. Follow these steps to build a database containing the events that led to the Great Depression and its effects on the country.

1. Determine what facts you want to include in your database.

2. Follow instructions to set up fields in the DBMS that you are using. Then enter each item of data in its assigned field.

3. Determine how you want to organize the facts in the database—chronologically by the date of the event, or alphabetically by the name of the event.

4. Follow the instructions in your computer program to place the information in the order you selected.

Skills Assessment

Complete the Practicing Skills questions on page 675 and the Chapter 22 Skill Reinforcement Activity to assess your mastery of this skill.

Applying the Skill

Building a Database Bring current newspapers or news magazines to class. Using the steps just described, build a database of current political events in the United States. Include a brief explanation of why the database is organized the way it is and how it might be used in class.

 Glencoe's **Skillbuilder Interactive Workbook CD-ROM, Level 2,** provides instruction and practice in key social studies skills.

673

Technology SKILLBUILDER

TEACH

Building a Database Remind students that a database is a way to organize information. Explain that database management systems allow people to organize large amounts of information according to selected categories; they can then search for specific data or manipulate the categories to draw conclusions.

Additional Practice

Reinforcing Skills Activity 22

Name _____ Date _____ Class _____

★ Reinforcing Skills Activity 22

Building a Database

☐ LEARNING THE SKILL

An electronic database is a collection of data—names, facts, and statistics—that are stored in a file on the computer. People use databases to organize large amounts of information. The database organizes information into categories call *fields*, such as Name, Event, or Date. A database management system (DBMS) will electronically store, sort, and display information from your database on screen.

☐ PRACTICING THE SKILL

DIRECTIONS: Use the information from Section 2 of your text to create a database containing Depression Era artists and entertainers. Use resources from your library or the Internet to add fields with additional information as your teacher directs.

1. Using the fields listed below as your categories, build your database by filling in as much information as you are able to locate.

GLENCOE TECHNOLOGY

 CD-ROM
Glencoe Skillbuilder Interactive Workbook CD-ROM, Level 2

This interactive CD-ROM reinforces student mastery of essential social studies skills.

ANSWERS TO PRACTICING THE SKILL

1. Facts should surround the events of the Great Depression.

2. Encourage students to identify fields that will fit with the facts they have gathered.

3. and 4. Explain to students that data can be sorted in various ways. Encourage students to experiment with different choices.

Applying the Skill

Students' databases and explanations will vary. The explanations should readily help a person understand the information contained in the database.

CHAPTER

22 ASSESSMENT and ACTIVITIES

Reviewing Key Terms

Students' answers will vary. The pages where the words appear in the text are shown in parentheses.

1. **stock market** *(p. 657)*
2. **bull market** *(p. 657)*
3. **margin** *(p. 657)*
4. **margin call** *(p. 657)*
5. **speculation** *(p. 657)*
6. **installment** *(p. 660)*
7. **bailiff** *(p. 662)*
8. **shantytown** *(p. 662)*
9. **Hooverville** *(p. 662)*
10. **hobo** *(p. 662)*
11. **Dust Bowl** *(p. 663)*
12. **soap opera** *(p. 664)*
13. **public works** *(p. 669)*
14. **relief** *(p. 670)*
15. **foreclose** *(p. 671)*

Reviewing Key Facts

16. Black Tuesday *(p. 659)*, Hawley-Smoot Tariff *(p. 660)*, Walt Disney *(p. 664)*, Grant Wood *(p. 664)*, John Steinbeck *(p. 665)*, Reconstruction Finance Corporation *(p. 670)*, Bonus Army *(p. 671)*

17. It was a bull market that crashed because stocks were overvalued and many people had purchased stocks on margin.

18. They focused on pictures and stories of the homeless and unemployed.

19. They migrated searching for work. Many ended up working as homeless migrant laborers.

Reviewing Key Terms

On a sheet of paper, use each of these terms in a sentence.

1. stock market
2. bull market
3. margin
4. margin call
5. speculation
6. installment
7. bailiff
8. shantytown
9. Hooverville
10. hobo
11. Dust Bowl
12. soap opera
13. public works
14. relief
15. foreclose

Reviewing Key Facts

16. **Identify:** Black Tuesday, Hawley-Smoot Tariff, Walt Disney, Grant Wood, John Steinbeck, Reconstruction Finance Corporation, Bonus Army.

17. What was the character of the stock market in the late 1920s, and what caused it to crash?

18. How did artists and writers capture the effects of the Great Depression?

19. Why did "Okies" migrate to California during the Great Depression, and what happened to them once they got there?

20. What three major initiatives did President Hoover take to try to help the economy of the United States?

21. What did World War I veterans do to try to get their service bonuses early?

Critical Thinking

22. **Analyzing Themes: Culture and Traditions** Many people in the United States were impoverished during the Depression, yet 60 to 90 million weekly viewers paid to see movies. Why do you think movies were so popular?

23. **Evaluating** Do you think President Hoover could have done more to end the Great Depression? Why or why not?

24. **Identifying** What approaches were used in literature and photography to highlight social problems during the Depression?

25. **Categorizing** Use a graphic organizer similar to the one below to list the causes and effects of the Great Depression.

Causes	Effects

26. **Interpreting Primary Sources** E.Y. Harburg lived during the Great Depression. After he lost his business, he became a poet and lyricist. He wrote the lyrics to one of the most famous songs of the time, "Brother, Can You Spare a Dime?" Read an excerpt of the lyrics to this song and answer the questions that follow.

❝They used to tell me I was building a dream
With peace and glory ahead—
Why should I be standing on line
Just waiting for bread?

Chapter Summary

Stock Market Helps Trigger Depression
• Bull market encouraged widespread speculation.
• Many investors bought stocks on margin.
• Sharp drop in market prices left investors in debt.
• Bank closings left many in debt.

Underlying Causes of Great Depression
• Overproduction and low interest rates
• Uneven distribution of income, which led to low demand
• Depressed farm sector
• Weak international market with high tariffs

Downward Momentum of the Great Depression

Low Sales → Job Layoffs → Less Income → Fewer Purchases → Lower Sales → More Job Layoffs

---

20. National Credit Corporation, Reconstruction Finance Corporation, Emergency Relief and Construction Act

21. They marched to Washington to petition Congress and then became squatters in unoccupied buildings.

Critical Thinking

22. Movies gave people an escape from their own lives.

23. Students' answers will vary. Possible explanations: Yes, the government should have gotten more involved in relief efforts. No, the problems were so great that there was nothing more the government could do.

24. Writing and visual styles evoked sympathy for the homeless and unemployed. Stream-of-consciousness writing illuminated peoples' thoughts and emotions.

Once I built a railroad, made it run,
Made it run against time.
Once I built a railroad,
Now it's done—
Brother, can you spare a dime?

Once I built a tower to the sun.
Brick and rivet and lime,
Once I built a tower,
Now it's done—
Brother, can you spare a dime?**"**

a. How was the narrator's life different before the Great Depression than it was during it?

b. During the 1932 presidential campaign, the Republicans tried to discourage the radio networks from playing this song. Why do you think they did that?

Practicing Skills

27. **Building a Database** Use the business section of your local newspaper to prepare a database that lists the prices of three different stocks for one week. Use the following information in your database:
- Stock symbol
- Date
- Stock price at the end of each day (closing price)

Be sure to follow these steps to build your database:

a. Follow instructions in the DBMS that you are using. Then enter each item in its assigned field.

b. Determine how you want to organize the information in the database.

c. Place the information in the order you choose (by date, alphabetically by symbol, by price, etc.).

d. Check the accuracy of the information. Make necessary changes.

Writing Activity

28. **Creating a Dictionary** Create a dictionary of words and phrases that grew out of the Great Depression. If possible, include pictures or photographs that illustrate the entries.

Chapter Activity

29. **Creating Presentations** Analyze the statistical information you gathered in building the computer database in

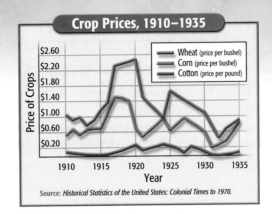
Crop Prices, 1910–1935

Legend:
— Wheat (price per bushel)
— Corn (price per bushel)
— Cotton (price per pound)

Y-axis: Price of Crops ($0.20 to $2.60)
X-axis: Year (1910 to 1935)

Source: *Historical Statistics of the United States: Colonial Times to 1970.*

question 27. Write a short report describing the progress of the stocks you followed. Create a chart and a graph as a visual aid to present your findings to the class.

Economics and History

30. The graph above shows changes in crop prices from 1910 to 1935. Study the graph and answer the questions below.

a. **Interpreting Graphs** What trend does this graph show about wheat and corn prices in the 1930s?

b. **Analyzing** Between which 10-year span did the greatest increase and decrease in farm prices occur?

The Princeton Review

Standardized Test Practice

Directions: Choose the phrase that best completes the following sentence.

A major reason for the collapse of the American economy after 1929 was

A high interest rates.

B decreased farm production.

C low tariffs at home and abroad.

D overproduction of consumer goods.

Test-Taking Tip: If you are not sure of the answer, use the process of elimination. For example, farmers were not prosperous in the 1920s because their huge crops forced down agricultural prices. Therefore, answer B is incorrect.

Chapter Activity

29. Students' reports should accurately summarize the information in the database.

Economics and History

30. **a.** They declined sharply in the early 1930s, then rose steadily.
b. For the most *volatile* ten-year period, students will choose 1915 to 1925 when graph lines rise and plummet dramatically; for the ten-year period in which there was the *greatest overall difference* in farm prices, students should add the price points of all three crops and figure the difference, yielding the answer *between 1910 and 1920*.

The Princeton Review

Standardized Test Practice

Answer: D

Test-Taking Tip: The Hawley-Smoot Tariff, passed in 1930, was the highest tariff ever. This means you can eliminate C. Because interest rates were low, business leaders continued to overproduce. This means you can eliminate answer A. The correct answer is D.

Bonus Question **?**

Ask: What does the phrase "Dust Bowl" refer to? *(Starting in 1932, a prolonged drought caused great clouds of dust to blanket the region from Texas to the Dakotas.)*

---

25. Causes: overproduction, uneven distribution of wealth, decline in exports and sales, mistakes by the Federal Reserve, stock market crash; Effects: unemployment, poverty, migration, government programs to influence the economy

26. **a.** He was a productive worker, now is unemployed.
b. Students might say that hearing the song suggested criticism of society and discouraged the unemployed.

Practicing Skills

27. Databases should reflect accurate information about the three stocks.

Writing Activity

28. Dictionaries will vary. Encourage students to check standard dictionary entries as they write their own dictionaries.

Timesaving Tools

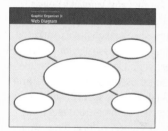

TeacherWorks™ All-In-One Planner and Resource Center

- **Interactive Teacher Edition** Access your Teacher Wraparound Edition and your classroom resources with a few easy clicks.
- **Interactive Lesson Planner** Planning has never been easier! Organize your week, month, semester, or year with all the lesson helps you need to make teaching creative, timely, and relevant.

Use Glencoe's **Presentation Plus!** multimedia teacher tool to easily present dynamic lessons that visually excite your students. Using Microsoft PowerPoint® you can customize the presentations to create your own personalized lessons.

TEACHING TRANSPARENCIES

Graphic Organizer 3

Why It Matters Chapter Transparency 23

APPLICATION AND ENRICHMENT

Linking Past and Present Activity 23

Enrichment Activity 23

Primary Source Reading 23

REVIEW AND REINFORCEMENT

Reteaching Activity 23

Vocabulary Activity 23

Time Line Activity 23

Critical Thinking Skills Activity 23

Meeting NCSS Standards

The following standards are highlighted in Chapter 23:

Section 1   IV   Individual Development and Identity: D, F, H
Section 2   V   Individuals, Groups, and Institutions: B, C, F, G
Section 3   VI   Power, Authority, and Governance: A, B, C, H, I
Section 4   V   Individuals, Groups, and Institutions: A, B, E

Local Standards

_____

_____

_____

_____

Chapter 23 Resources

ASSESSMENT AND EVALUATION

**Chapter 23 Test
Form A**

**Chapter 23 Test
Form B**

**Standardized Test Skills
Practice Workbook Activity 23**

**Performance Assessment
Activities and Rubrics 23**

**ExamView® Pro
Testmaker CD-ROM**

MULTIMEDIA

- Vocabulary PuzzleMaker CD-ROM
- Interactive Tutor Self-Assessment CD-ROM
- ExamView® Pro Testmaker CD-ROM
- Audio Program
- American History Primary Source Documents Library CD-ROM
- MindJogger Videoquiz
- Presentation Plus! CD-ROM
- TeacherWorks™ CD-ROM
- Interactive Student Edition CD-ROM
- Glencoe Skillbuilder Interactive Workbook CD-ROM, Level 2
- The *American Vision* Video Program
- American Music: Hits Through History
- American Music: Cultural Traditions

SPANISH RESOURCES

The following Spanish language materials are available in the Spanish Resources Binder:

- Spanish Guided Reading Activities
- Spanish Reteaching Activities
- Spanish Quizzes and Tests
- Spanish Vocabulary Activities
- Spanish Summaries
- The Declaration of Independence and United States Constitution Spanish Translation

THE HISTORY CHANNEL.

The following videotape programs are available from Glencoe as supplements to Chapter 23:

- **FDR: The Years of Crisis** (ISBN 1-56-501511-8)
- **Eleanor Roosevelt: A Restless Spirit** (ISBN 1-56-501405-7)
- **The Great Depression** (ISBN 0-76-700859-6)

To order, call Glencoe at 1-800-334-7344. To find classroom resources to accompany many of these videos, check the following home pages:
A&E Television: www.aande.com
The History Channel: www.historychannel.com

HISTORY Online

Use our Web site for additional resources. All essential content is covered in the Student Edition.

You and your students can visit tav.glencoe.com, the Web site companion to the *American Vision*. This innovative integration of electronic and print media offers your students a wealth of opportunities. The student text directs students to the Web site for the following options:

- **Chapter Overviews**
- **Self-Check Quizzes**
- **Student Web Activities**
- **Textbook Updates**

Answers to the student Web activities are provided for you in the **Web Activity Lesson Plans.** Additional Web resources and Interactive Tutor Puzzles are also available.

Chapter 23 Resources

SECTION RESOURCES

Daily Objectives	Reproducible Resources	Multimedia Resources
SECTION 1 **Roosevelt Takes Office** 1. Discuss Franklin Roosevelt's early political career. 2. Explain the worsening situation in the U.S. banking system in the early 1930s.	Reproducible Lesson Plan 23–1 Daily Lecture and Discussion Notes 23–1 Guided Reading Activity 23–1* Section Quiz 23–1* Reading Essentials and Study Guide 23–1 Performance Assessment Activities and Rubrics	Daily Focus Skills Transparency 23–1 American Art & Architecture Interactive Tutor Self-Assessment CD-ROM ExamView® Pro Testmaker CD-ROM Presentation Plus! CD-ROM TeacherWorks™ CD-ROM Audio Program American Music: Cultural Traditions
SECTION 2 **The First New Deal** 1. List three programs of the First New Deal that provided jobs for the unemployed. 2. Discuss why New Dealers believed that sometimes the government needs to regulate industry and labor.	Reproducible Lesson Plan 23–2 Daily Lecture and Discussion Notes 23–2 Guided Reading Activity 23–2* Section Quiz 23–2* Reading Essentials and Study Guide 23–2 Performance Assessment Activities and Rubrics Interpreting Political Cartoons	Daily Focus Skills Transparency 23–2 Interactive Tutor Self-Assessment CD-ROM ExamView® Pro Testmaker CD-ROM Presentation Plus! CD-ROM Skillbuilder Interactive Workbook, Level 2 TeacherWorks™ CD-ROM Audio Program
SECTION 3 **The Second New Deal** 1. Describe the political challenges Roosevelt faced in the mid-1930s. 2. Explain why the Social Security Act is still regarded as an important piece of legislation.	Reproducible Lesson Plan 23–3 Daily Lecture and Discussion Notes 23–3 Guided Reading Activity 23–3* Section Quiz 23–3* Reading Essentials and Study Guide 23–3 Performance Assessment Activities and Rubrics Supreme Court Case Studies	Daily Focus Skills Transparency 23–3 Interactive Tutor Self-Assessment CD-ROM ExamView® Pro Testmaker CD-ROM Presentation Plus! CD-ROM TeacherWorks™ CD-ROM Audio Program
SECTION 4 **The New Deal Coalition** 1. Explain the achievements and the defeats of Roosevelt's second term. 2. Analyze how the New Deal affected Americans' sense of security and their attitude toward the role of government.	Reproducible Lesson Plan 23–4 Daily Lecture and Discussion Notes 23–4 Guided Reading Activity 23–4* Section Quiz 23–4* Reading Essentials and Study Guide 23–4 Performance Assessment Activities and Rubrics	Daily Focus Skills Transparency 23–4 Interactive Tutor Self-Assessment CD-ROM ExamView® Pro Testmaker CD-ROM Presentation Plus! CD-ROM TeacherWorks™ CD-ROM Vocabulary PuzzleMaker CD-ROM Audio Program

0:00 OUT OF TIME?
Assign the Chapter 23 **Reading Essentials and Study Guide.**

*Also Available in Spanish

 Blackline Master    Transparency   CD-ROM   DVD

 Poster   Music Program   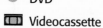 Audio Program   Videocassette

NATIONAL GEOGRAPHIC Teacher's Corner

INDEX TO NATIONAL GEOGRAPHIC MAGAZINE

The following articles relate to this chapter.

• "The Okies—Beyond the Great Depression," September 1984

ADDITIONAL NATIONAL GEOGRAPHIC SOCIETY PRODUCTS

To order the following, call National Geographic at 1-800-368-2728:

• *The Complete National Geographic: 109 Years of National Geographic Magazine* (CD-ROM)
• *Eyewitness to the 20th Century* (Book)
• *1929–1941: The Great Depression* (Video)
• *National Geographic World Atlas for Young Explorers—Classroom Library Edition* (Teacher's Guide, Transparencies, Resource Masters)

NGS ONLINE

Access National Geographic's Web site for current events, atlas updates, activities, links, interactive features, and archives.
www.nationalgeographic.com

From the Classroom of...

Rick Harris
Cincinnati Public Schools
Cincinnati, OH

Understanding the TVA

The Tennessee Valley Authority (TVA) demonstrates the profound effects of the New Deal on the United States. After introducing the unit, I give the groups two research days, one day to prepare, and a day to present. I assign groups one of the following areas:

• **Map:** This group creates a map showing all areas shaped by the TVA, including the states affected, the dams and reservoirs created, reforested areas, and diverted roads and rail lines.

• **Time Line:** Students create a detailed time line that shows the major milestones of the TVA.

• **Budget:** This group creates graphs to show the TVA's original budget, its final budget, and its budget in modern dollars. Students should show how specific congressional appropriations provided TVA funding.

• **Long-term Impact:** Students present a photographic essay of the long-term impact of the TVA. Examples include before and after shots of areas where dams created reservoirs and recreational areas.

ADDITIONAL RESOURCES FROM GLENCOE

• American Music: Cultural Traditions
• American Art & Architecture
• Outline Map Resource Book
• U.S. Desk Map
• Building Geography Skills for Life
• Inclusion for the High School Social Studies Classroom Strategies and Activities
• Teaching Strategies for the American History Classroom (Including Block Scheduling Pacing Guides)

KEY TO ABILITY LEVELS

Teaching strategies have been coded.

L1 BASIC activities for all students
L2 AVERAGE activities for average to above-average students
L3 CHALLENGING activities for above-average students
ELL ENGLISH LANGUAGE LEARNER activities

 Block Schedule

Activities that are suited to use within the block scheduling framework are identified by:

Why It Matters Activity

Ask students how they think Social Security benefits people today. **Ask:** Is Social Security used in the ways in which it was originally intended? Students should evaluate their answers after they have completed the chapter.

GLENCOE
TECHNOLOGY

The *American Vision* Video Program

To learn more about the personal and political challenges FDR faced as president, have students view the Chapter 23 video, "Franklin Roosevelt and the New Deal," from the *American Vision* Video Program.

 Available in DVD and VHS

MindJogger Videoquiz

Use the **MindJogger Videoquiz** to preview Chapter 23 content.

 Available in VHS

CHAPTER
23 Roosevelt and the New Deal
1933–1939

Why It Matters

Unlike Herbert Hoover, Franklin Delano Roosevelt was willing to employ deficit spending and greater federal regulation to revive the depressed economy. In response to his requests, Congress passed a host of new programs. Millions of people received relief to alleviate their suffering, but the New Deal did not really end the Depression. It did, however, permanently expand the federal government's role in providing basic security for citizens.

The Impact Today

Certain New Deal legislation still carries great importance in American social policy.
- *The Social Security Act still provides retirement benefits, aid to needy groups, and unemployment and disability insurance.*
- *The National Labor Relations Act still protects the right of workers to unionize.*
- *Safeguards were instituted to help prevent another devastating stock market crash.*
- *The Federal Deposit Insurance Corporation still protects bank deposits.*

The American Vision Video The Chapter 23 video, "Franklin Roosevelt and the New Deal," describes the personal and political challenges Franklin Roosevelt faced as president.

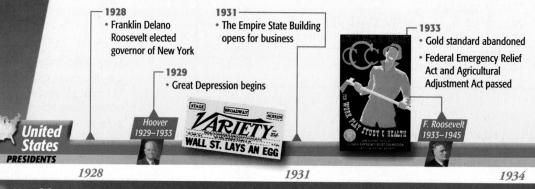

1928
- Franklin Delano Roosevelt elected governor of New York

1929
- Great Depression begins

1931
- The Empire State Building opens for business

1933
- Gold standard abandoned
- Federal Emergency Relief Act and Agricultural Adjustment Act passed

United States PRESIDENTS

Hoover 1929–1933

F. Roosevelt 1933–1945

1928   *1931*   *1934*

World

1928
- Alexander Fleming discovers penicillin

1930
- Germany's Nazi Party wins 107 seats in Reichstag

1931
- German unemployment reaches 5.6 million
- Surrealist artist Salvador Dali paints *Persistence of Memory*

1933
- Adolf Hitler appointed German chancellor
- Japan withdraws from League of Nations

676

TWO-MINUTE LESSON LAUNCHER

Have the class consider what programs or actions taken by the government, businesses, and banks might have helped ease the devastating effects of the Depression. Have students categorize the actions or programs as government, business, or banking. Reexamine the list at the end of the chapter to compare their lists with the actions actually taken by the government, businesses, and banks during the 1930s.

In this Ben Shahn mural detail, New Deal planners (at right) design the town of Jersey Homesteads as a home for impoverished immigrants.

Time Line

1935
- Supreme Court strikes down NIRA
- Social Security Act passed

1937
- Court-packing bill defeated
- "Roosevelt recession" begins

1938
- Fair Labor Standards Act passed

1937   *1940*

1936
- Civil War erupts in Spain

1938
- Hitler annexes Austria

1939
- World War II begins

HISTORY Online

Chapter Overview
Visit the *American Vision* Web site at tav.glencoe.com and click on *Chapter Overviews—Chapter 23* to preview chapter information.

HISTORY Online

Introduce students to chapter content and key terms by having them access the **Chapter 23 Overview** at tav.glencoe.com.

More About the Art

Born in Lithuania, Ben Shahn immigrated to the United States in 1906. During the Depression, he enlisted in one of Roosevelt's New Deal programs for the arts. The program provided funds for the production of public murals. The Resettlement Administration built the town of Jersey Homesteads depicted in this fresco to house Jewish garment workers from New York City.

TIME LINE ACTIVITY

Have students select and research a world event from the time line. Then have them write a brief description of the impact the event had on American history.

677

GRAPHIC ORGANIZER ACTIVITY

Organizing Information Have students create a time line of New Deal legislation. Ask them to include the years 1933 to 1938. Have students identify the significant legislation passed in each of these years and the purpose of the legislation.

1 FOCUS

Section Overview

This section focuses on Franklin Delano Roosevelt's early life and election as president.

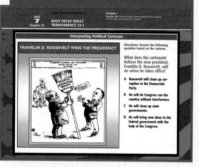
Guide to Reading

Answers to Graphic: love of the outdoors, polio, assistant secretary of the navy, governor of New York

Preteaching Vocabulary
Have students skim this section to glean the meaning or significance of each of the Key Terms and Names.

SECTION 1 Roosevelt Takes Office

Guide to Reading

Main Idea
Franklin Delano Roosevelt's character and experiences prepared him for the presidency of a nation in crisis.

Key Terms and Names
New Deal, polio, gold standard, bank holiday

Reading Strategy
Organizing As you read about Franklin Roosevelt's background, complete a graphic organizer similar to the one below by listing the early influences and experiences that helped shape Roosevelt as a politician.

Influences and Experiences

Reading Objectives
• **Discuss** Franklin Roosevelt's early political career.
• **Explain** the worsening situation in the U.S. banking system in the early 1930s.

Section Theme
Individual Action Franklin Roosevelt's optimism, determination, and outgoing personality shaped his approach to politics.

Preview of Events

1905	1915	1925	1935

1905 Franklin Roosevelt and Eleanor Roosevelt marry

1910 Roosevelt elected to New York State Senate

1921 Roosevelt stricken with polio

1928 Roosevelt elected governor of New York

★ An American Story ★

Franklin D. Roosevelt as a young man

When Louis Howe was a child in Saratoga Springs, New York, a bicycle accident left his face scarred. As an adult and a reporter for his father's newspaper, he cheerfully described himself as "one of the four ugliest men in the state of New York." Howe dressed sloppily, perhaps to demonstrate how little importance he attached to appearance. He worked hard, however, and was respected for his reporting.

In the winter of 1911, Howe traveled to Albany to interview a Democratic state senator, Franklin Delano Roosevelt—or FDR, as he was called. Howe found himself fascinated by the tall, intense young man with the gold-rimmed glasses who paced back and forth in front of him, earnestly answering his questions. He admired the dashing appearance Roosevelt made.

During the interview Roosevelt declared his intention to challenge the party bosses. The usually skeptical Howe found himself believing the young legislator.
"I made up my mind," Howe later recalled, "that nothing but an accident could keep him from becoming president."

—**adapted from *The Crisis of the Old Order***

Roosevelt's Rise to Power

In mid-June 1932, with the country deep in the Depression, Republicans gathered in Chicago and nominated Herbert Hoover to run for a second term as president. The mood at the convention was somber. Delegates knew the Depression had turned many voters against Hoover.

SECTION RESOURCES

📁 **Reproducible Masters**
• Reproducible Lesson Plan 23–1
• Daily Lecture and Discussion Notes 23–1
• Guided Reading Activity 23–1
• Section Quiz 23–1
• Reading Essentials and Study Guide 23–1

📄 **Transparencies**
• Daily Focus Skills Transparency 23–1

• American Art & Architecture

Multimedia
🔘 Interactive Tutor Self-Assessment CD-ROM
🔘 ExamView® Pro Testmaker CD-ROM
🔘 Presentation Plus! CD-ROM
🔘 TeacherWorks™ CD-ROM
🔘 Audio Program
🔘 American Music: Cultural Traditions

Later that month, the Democrats also met in Chicago to choose their own candidate for president. It took four ballots and a great deal of negotiating, but the party eventually chose the popular governor of New York, Franklin Delano Roosevelt. When he won the nomination, Roosevelt broke with tradition by flying to Chicago to deliver the first acceptance speech ever made to a nominating convention. Roosevelt's speech set the tone for his campaign:

> ❝The appearance before a National Convention of its nominee for President . . . is unprecedented and unusual, but these are unprecedented and unusual times. . . . Let it also be symbolic that in so doing I broke traditions. Let it be from now on the task of our Party to break foolish traditions. . . . It is inevitable that the main issue of this campaign should revolve about . . . a depression so deep that it is without precedent. . . . Republican leaders not only have failed in material things, they have failed in national vision, because in disaster they have held out no hope. . . . I pledge you, I pledge myself, to a new deal for the American people.❞
>
> —quoted in *The Public Papers and Addresses of Franklin D. Roosevelt*

The next day, a cartoonist used the words "new deal" to stand for Roosevelt's program. From that point forward, Roosevelt's policies for ending the Depression became known as the **New Deal.** Roosevelt's confidence that he could make things better contrasted sharply with Hoover's apparent failure to do anything effective. On Election Day, Roosevelt won the Electoral College in a landslide, 472 votes to 59, and he received nearly 23 million votes to slightly less than 16 million for Hoover in the general election.

Picturing **History**

The Young Roosevelts Franklin Roosevelt and Eleanor Roosevelt were married in 1905. They were distantly related through former president Theodore Roosevelt—her uncle and his cousin. What sort of childhood did Franklin Roosevelt have growing up in Hyde Park, New York?

Roosevelt's Background Franklin Roosevelt—a distant cousin of President Theodore Roosevelt—was born in 1882 to a wealthy New York family. Roosevelt grew up on his family's estate at Hyde Park on the Hudson River. There, Roosevelt learned to hunt, fish, ride horses, and sail, and he developed his lifelong commitment to conservation and a love of rural America. Roosevelt was educated at Harvard and Columbia Law School. While at Harvard, he became friends with Theodore Roosevelt's niece, Eleanor. Soon afterward, they were married.

Roosevelt was intensely competitive. He enjoyed winning and liked to be in control. He also liked being around people. His charming personality, deep rich voice, and wide smile expressed confidence and optimism. He could also be very persuasive. Overall, FDR's personality seemed made for a life in politics.

FDR's Early Political Career Shortly after leaving law school, Roosevelt plunged into politics. In 1910 he won a seat in the New York State Senate, where he earned a reputation as a progressive reformer willing to stand up to the party bosses. Roosevelt strongly supported Woodrow Wilson's presidential campaign in 1912. After winning the election, Wilson rewarded Roosevelt by appointing him assistant secretary of the navy, a position he held through World War I.

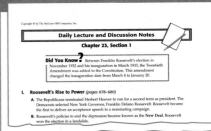

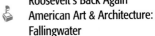

2 *TEACH*

Daily Lecture and Discussion Notes 23–1

Copyright © by The McGraw-Hill Companies, Inc.

Daily Lecture and Discussion Notes
Chapter 23, Section 1

Did You Know? Between Franklin Roosevelt's election in November 1932 and his inauguration in March 1933, the Twentieth Amendment was added to the Constitution. This amendment changed the inauguration date from March 4 to January 20.

I. Roosevelt's Rise to Power (pages 678–680)

A. The Republicans nominated Herbert Hoover to run for a second term as president. The Democrats selected New York Governor, Franklin Delano Roosevelt. Roosevelt became the first to deliver an acceptance speech to a nominating campaign.

B. Roosevelt's policies to end the depression became known as the **New Deal.** Roosevelt won the election in a landslide.

Creating Circle Graphs Provide the data below and ask students to make a pair of circle graphs showing the results of the presidential election of 1932. **L2**

Candidate	Popular Vote	Electoral Vote
Roosevelt, Dem.	22,809,638	472
Hoover, Rep.	15,758,901	59
Thomas, Social.	881,951	0

Picturing **History**

Answer: life of privilege, wealth, education
Ask: How would you describe Franklin Roosevelt's personality? (*possible answers: competitive, confident, optimistic, persuasive*)

History *and the* Humanities

🎵 American Music: Cultural Traditions: "Franklin D. Roosevelt's Back Again"
🏛 American Art & Architecture: Fallingwater

COOPERATIVE LEARNING ACTIVITY

Creating a Visual Aid Organize the class into small groups and ask them to create a visual aid about the life of Franklin Delano Roosevelt. Each team member should concentrate on one of the following tasks: collecting images, creating a list of accomplishments, choosing excerpts from speeches, creating a time line, or collecting anecdotes. The group should work together to organize the information into an effective visual aid, such as a poster, display, or multimedia presentation.

Use the rubric for a cooperative group management plan on pages 81–82 in the *Performance Assessment Activities and Rubrics.*

Linking Past & Present

A twentieth-century vaccine was developed not only for polio but also for smallpox. By 1980 the disease had been eradicated except for small samples kept for research.

✓ Reading Check

Answer: privileged upbringing, love of the outdoors, polio, service in political office

3 ASSESS

Assign Section 1 Assessment as homework or as an in-class activity.

◉ Have students use the **Interactive Tutor Self-Assessment CD-ROM.**

In 1920, hoping his name would win votes, the Democrats nominated Roosevelt as their candidate for vice president. After losing the election, Roosevelt temporarily withdrew from politics. The next year he came down with a fever and soon felt numbness in both legs. He had caught the dreaded and paralyzing disease known as **polio.** Although there was no cure, Roosevelt refused to give in. He began a vigorous exercise program to restore muscle control. Eventually, by wearing heavy steel braces on his legs, he was able to appear to walk by leaning on a cane and someone's arm and swinging his legs forward by moving his hips.

While recovering from polio, Roosevelt depended on his wife to keep his name prominent in the New York Democratic Party. Although shy, Eleanor Roosevelt became an effective public speaker. Her efforts during this time kept her husband's political career alive.

Linking Past & Present

Roosevelt Dime

Past: Search for a Cure
In 1921 Franklin Roosevelt contracted polio, a disease that paralyzed his legs. Few people knew of his physical limitations when he became president. His only freedom from braces came when he swam.

After Roosevelt established a foundation for polio victims at Warm Springs, Georgia, entertainer Eddie Cantor suggested that everyone in the country send a dime for polio research to the president. This campaign, which became known as the March of Dimes, produced 150,000 letters a day. In 1945 Congress voted to honor Roosevelt by placing his image on the dime.

Present: A Threat Eliminated
In the early 1950s, Dr. Jonas Salk discovered the polio vaccine. Today polio is no longer the threat to health that it once was.

Governor of New York By the mid-1920s, Roosevelt was again active in the Democratic Party. He became a strong supporter of New York's governor, Alfred E. Smith. When the Democratic Party nominated Smith for president in 1928, Smith urged Roosevelt to run for governor of New York. Roosevelt campaigned hard to demonstrate that his illness had not slowed him down, and he narrowly won the election.

Roosevelt's policies as governor made him very popular. He cut taxes for farmers and worked to reduce the rates charged by public utilities. In 1931, as the Depression worsened, Roosevelt convinced the New York legislature to set up a new state agency to help unemployed New Yorkers. The agency distributed over $25 million in aid that provided relief to about 10 percent of New York's families.

Roosevelt's popularity in New York paved the way for his presidential nomination in 1932. Many Americans applauded his use of the government's power to help people in economic distress. Others believed that his struggle against polio had given him a better understanding of their hardships.

Perhaps most important, Americans saw in Roosevelt an energy and optimism that gave them hope despite the tough economic times. After Roosevelt became president, his serenity and confidence amazed many people. When one aide commented on his attitude, Roosevelt replied, "If you had spent two years in bed, trying to wiggle your big toe, after that anything else would seem easy."

✓ Reading Check **Interpreting** What events in Roosevelt's life shaped his ideas and character?

Roosevelt Is Inaugurated

Although Roosevelt won the presidency in November 1932, the country's unemployed and homeless had to endure one more winter as they waited for his inauguration on March 4, 1933. All through the winter, unemployment continued to rise. Theater director Harold Clurman later wrote about the fear:

❝Yes, we could smell the depression in the air, that historically cruel winter of 1932–33, which chilled so many of us like a world's end. . . . It was like a raw wind; the very houses we lived in seemed to be shrinking, hopeless of real comfort.❞

—quoted in *Franklin Roosevelt and the New Deal*

MEETING SPECIAL NEEDS

Verbal/Linguistic Remind students of the hardships faced by many Americans during the early years of the Depression. Then have students read the quote by Franklin Roosevelt on page 554. Based on what they have learned about the Depression, have students compose a poem about the winter of 1932 as though they were either an unemployed factory worker, a banker whose bank has just collapsed, or a farmer who has lost his land. **L2**

📂 Refer to **Inclusion for the High School Social Studies Classroom Strategies and Activities** in the TCR.

*". . . the only thing we have
to fear is fear itself . . ."*

—Franklin D. Roosevelt

Picturing History

Inspiring Words President Roosevelt used his first Inaugural Address of March 1933 to rally the nation's spirits. What problems had made the nation anxious and fearful?

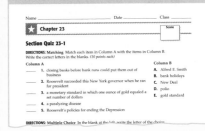
Picturing History

Answer: high unemployment, massive bank failures, and the weak economy

Meanwhile, bank runs greatly increased, further threatening the nation's banking system. Some of the bank runs occurred because people feared Roosevelt would abandon the gold standard and reduce the value of the dollar in order to fight the Depression. Under the gold standard, one ounce of gold equaled a set number of dollars. To reduce the value of the dollar, the United States would have to stop exchanging dollars for gold. Many Americans, and many foreign investors with deposits in American banks, decided to take their money out of the banks and convert it to gold before it lost its value.

Across the nation, people stood in long lines with paper bags and suitcases, waiting to withdraw their money from banks. By March 1933, over 4,000 banks had collapsed, wiping out 9 million savings accounts. In 38 states, governors declared **bank holidays**—closing the remaining banks before bank runs could put them out of business.

By the day of Roosevelt's inauguration, most of the nation's banks were closed. One in four workers was unemployed. The economy seemed paralyzed. Roosevelt knew he had to restore the nation's confidence. "First of all," the president declared in his Inaugural Address, "let me assert my firm belief that the only thing we have to fear is fear itself. . . . This nation asks for action, and action now!"

Reading Check **Summarizing** What was the nation's condition when Roosevelt took office?

Reteach

Have students discuss Franklin Roosevelt's early political career.

Enrich

Have students write a summary of Roosevelt's first inaugural address.

Reading Check

Answer: 25% unemployment, many bank failures

4 CLOSE

Have students discuss America's banking system in the early 1930s.

SECTION 1 ASSESSMENT

Checking for Understanding

1. **Define:** gold standard.
2. **Identify:** New Deal, polio, bank holiday.
3. **Describe** the ways in which early influences and experiences shaped Roosevelt as a politician.

Reviewing Themes

4. **Individual Action** Why did Roosevelt's election lead to an increase in bank runs?

Critical Thinking

5. **Explaining** How did FDR's experiences as governor of New York prepare him for the presidency?
6. **Organizing** Use a graphic organizer like the one below to list early influences on Roosevelt's political career.

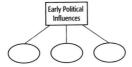

Analyzing Visuals

7. **Analyzing Photographs** Study the photograph on this page. What did the president mean when he said "the only thing we have to fear is fear itself"?

Writing About History

8. **Persuasive Writing** Imagine you are living during the Depression. In your hometown, there has been a run on the bank. Write a letter to the president describing this event. In your letter, ask him to take steps to cure the bank crisis.

SECTION 1 ASSESSMENT ANSWERS

1. Term is in blue.
2. New Deal *(p. 679)*, polio *(p. 680)*, bank holiday *(p. 681)*
3. Roosevelt was influenced by his experience with polio, his competitive nature, and his support for Wilson's presidency.
4. People feared that Roosevelt would take the United States off the gold standard, and that their paper money would become worthless.
5. He used government's power to help New Yorkers in economic distress.
6. family, love of outdoors, political service
7. Fear would drive people to stop trying to get the economy out of its tailspin. If people could avoid fearing the future, they would be able to improve conditions.
8. Letters should express a point of view.

1 FOCUS

Section Overview

This section focuses on the first 100 days of Roosevelt's presidency.

Guide to Reading

Answers to Graphic: Problems addressed include: bank runs, unprotected bank deposits, stock fraud, and the plight of farmers.

Preteaching Vocabulary
Provide the following list and have students match one of the Key Terms and Names with each item on the list: new laws, radio, stocks, banks, farms, and forests.

Guide to Reading

Main Idea
In the first 100 days of Roosevelt's presidency, his team initiated a series of laws that transformed the United States.

Key Terms and Names
Hundred Days, fireside chats, Securities and Exchange Commission, Federal Deposit Insurance Corporation, Agricultural Adjustment Administration, Civilian Conservation Corps

Reading Strategy
Sequencing As you read about President Roosevelt's first three months in office, complete a time line similar to the one below to record the major problems he addressed during this time.

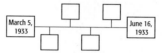

Reading Objectives
- **List** three programs of the First New Deal that provided jobs for the unemployed.
- **Discuss** why New Dealers believed that sometimes the government needs to regulate industry and labor.

Section Theme
Groups and Institutions FDR's attempts to end the Depression resulted in many new government agencies.

Preview of Events

♦ *March 1933*   ♦ *May 1933*   ♦ *July 1933*

March 4, 1933 — FDR inaugurated

March 31, 1933 — Civilian Conservation Corps created

May 12, 1933 — Federal Emergency Relief Act; Agricultural Adjustment Act

June 16, 1933 — National Industrial Recovery Act; Glass-Steagall Banking Act; Farm Credit Act

Will Rogers

★ An American Story ★

In the 1920s, cowboy and comedian Will Rogers said that his life's work was "to rescue the country from the hands of the politicians." He used his sharp wit to go after these public figures. A friend of presidents and politicians of both parties, Rogers nevertheless satirized them mercilessly in public appearances and on the radio.

With FDR, however, Rogers changed his tune: "President Roosevelt closed the banks before lunch and called Congress into session while he was having dessert. . . . The whole country is with him. . . . Even if he does what is wrong they are with him, just so he does something. . . . If he burned down the Capitol, we would cheer and say, 'Well, we at least got a fire started anyhow.'"

As Roosevelt's New Deal gained momentum, Rogers praised the resulting flurry of legislation: "Mr. Roosevelt just makes out a little list of things every morning that he wants [Congress] to do . . . and the whole country is better off."

—adapted from *Will Rogers: A Biography*

The Hundred Days Begins

Roosevelt and his advisers came into office bursting with ideas for recovery from the Depression. Roosevelt had no clear agenda. The previous spring, during his campaign for the presidential nomination, Roosevelt had revealed the approach he would take as president. "The country needs," Roosevelt explained, "bold, persistent experimentation. . . . Above all, try something."

The new president began to send bill after bill to Congress. Between March 9 and June 16, 1933—which came to be called the **Hundred Days**—Congress passed 15 major acts to

---

SECTION RESOURCES

Reproducible Masters
- Reproducible Lesson Plan 23–2
- Daily Lecture and Discussion Notes 23–2
- Guided Reading Activity 23–2
- Section Quiz 23–2
- Reading Essentials and Study Guide 23–2
- Interpreting Political Cartoons

Transparencies
- Daily Focus Skills Transparency 23–2

Multimedia
- Interactive Tutor Self-Assessment CD-ROM
- ExamView® Pro Testmaker CD-ROM
- Presentation Plus! CD-ROM
- TeacherWorks™ CD-ROM
- Audio Program

meet the economic crisis, setting a pace for new legislation that has never been equaled. Together, these programs made up what would later be called the First New Deal.

Origins of the New Deal The New Deal was not based on a clear strategy shaped by a single philosophy. Roosevelt was not an intellectual, nor did he have a strong political ideology. He was a practical politician. FDR was willing to try a variety of approaches both to see whether they worked and whether they were helping or hurting him politically.

To generate new ideas and programs, Roosevelt sought advice from a wide range of advisers with experience in academia, business, agriculture, government, law, and social work. The president deliberately chose advisers who disagreed with each other. He wanted to hear many different points of view, and by setting his advisers against one another, Roosevelt ensured that he alone made the final decision on what policies to pursue.

A Divided Administration Roosevelt's advisers were divided roughly into three main groups. Despite their disagreements, most of the advisers had grown up in the Progressive Era, and their approaches reflected progressive ideas. They generally favored some form of government intervention in the economy—although they disagreed over what the government's role should be.

One group that was very influential during the early years of Roosevelt's administration supported the "New Nationalism" of Theodore Roosevelt. These advisers believed that business and government should work together to manage the economy. They had been very impressed by business-government cooperation on the War Industries Board during World War I. They believed that if government agencies worked with businesses to regulate wages, prices, and production, they could lift the economy out of the Depression.

A second group of advisers in the Roosevelt administration went even further. They distrusted big business and blamed business leaders for causing the Depression. These advisers wanted government planners to run key parts of the economy.

A third group in Roosevelt's administration supported the "New Freedom" of Woodrow Wilson. They too blamed large trusts for the Depression, but they believed the government had to restore competition to the economy. These advisers wanted Roosevelt to support "trust busting" by breaking up big companies and allowing competition to set wages, prices, and production levels. They also thought the government should impose regulations on the economy to keep competition fair.

✓ **Reading Check** **Summarizing** What ideas did Roosevelt's advisers support?

Fixing the Banks and the Stock Market

As the debate over policies and programs swirled around him, President Roosevelt took office with one thing clear in his mind. Very few of the proposed solutions would work as long as the nation's banks remained closed. The first thing he had to do was restore confidence in the banking system.

The Emergency Banking Relief Act On his very first night in office, Roosevelt told Secretary of the Treasury William H. Woodin he wanted an emergency banking bill ready for Congress in less than five days. The following afternoon, Roosevelt declared a national bank holiday, temporarily closing all banks, and called Congress into a special session scheduled to begin on March 9, 1933.

On the day Congress convened, the House of Representatives unanimously passed the Emergency Banking Relief Act after only 38 minutes of debate.

Picturing **History**

Presidential Assurances President Roosevelt often used radio addresses to calm the public's fears during the Great Depression. At the beginning of his first term, he encouraged Americans to put their money back in federally inspected banks. *Why do you think the president declared a bank holiday?*

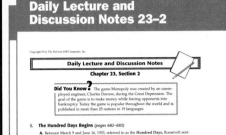
✓ **Reading Check**

Answer: One group wanted joint government-business cooperation; another wanted government control of business; another wanted more competition.

Discussing a Topic Ask students to comment on the following statement: "The New Deal was a continuation of the Progressive era." Have students who agree with the statement list specific ways in which the New Deal resembled the Progressive era. Have those who disagree point out the differences between the New Deal and Progressivism. **L1**

Picturing **History**

Answer: It would provide a brief interval during which depositors could not withdraw money. Roosevelt hoped to restore confidence in the banking system.

Ask: How many people listened to Roosevelt's fireside chat on March 12, 1933? *(60 million)*

COOPERATIVE LEARNING ACTIVITY

Creating a Plan Before students learn about actual New Deal programs, organize them into groups of four or five. Ask each student to design his or her own "new deal" program. Each student in the group should tackle a different issue, such as creating jobs, providing emergency relief, bolstering business, or safeguarding bank deposits. Have members of the groups review and refine each other's proposals. Have the groups present their ideas to the class.

Use the rubric for a cooperative group management plan on pages 81–82 in the *Performance Assessment Activities and Rubrics.*

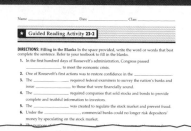
Why It Matters

Background: The TVA's original mission focused on making the Tennessee River navigable and controlling floods. In addition, reforestation and land reclamation were part of the mission. The agency was also charged with the responsibility of generating electrical power and assisting with industrial and agricultural development. Today the TVA's mission focuses on the sustained, integrated development of the region. Supplying reliable, economical power, supporting the river system, and stimulating economic growth are key to the mission.

Ask: Which seven states are directly affected by the TVA?
(Alabama, Georgia, Kentucky, Mississippi, North Carolina, Tennessee, and Virginia)

you don't say...

FDIC Since 1933 the Federal Deposit Insurance Corporation (FDIC) has insured bank deposits. Originally the FDIC insured each bank account for up to $5,000. Today accounts are insured up to $100,000.

Why It Matters

The TVA

Perhaps no New Deal program produced as many visible benefits as the Tennessee Valley Authority (TVA). This dam-building project was a bold venture to control floods, conserve forestlands, and bring electricity to rural America. The TVA created a comprehensive plan for developing a vast seven-state region drained by the Tennessee and Cumberland Rivers and populated mainly by poor farmers working worn-out land. The TVA erected 20 dams, employing up to 40,000 workers at a time. The agency also reforested millions of acres, built fertilizer factories and power plants, and strung thousands of miles of wire to bring electricity to rural families for the first time.

◄ Recreation
Millions of people each year fish, swim, ski, white-water raft, or go boating on the reservoirs. Sometimes the reservoir system is referred to as the "Great Lakes of the South."

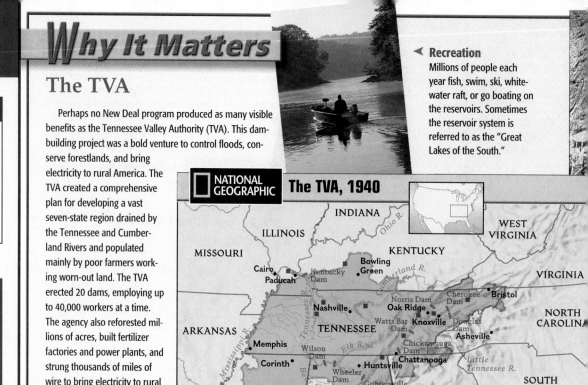

NATIONAL GEOGRAPHIC — The TVA, 1940

Area supplied with power from the TVA
Dam
Steam power plant

The Senate approved the bill that evening, and Roosevelt signed it into law shortly afterward. The new law required federal examiners to survey the nation's banks and issue Treasury Department licenses to those that were financially sound.

On March 12, President Roosevelt addressed the nation by radio. Sixty million people listened to this first of many "fireside chats," direct talks FDR held with the American people to let them know what he was trying to accomplish. He told the people that their money would now be secure if they put it back into the banks. "I assure you that it is safer to keep your money in a reopened bank than under the mattress." When banks opened the day after the speech, deposits far outweighed withdrawals. The banking crisis was over.

Regulating Banks and Brokers Although President Roosevelt had restored confidence in the banking system, many of his advisers who favored trust-busting and fair competition urged him to go further. They pushed for new regulations for both banks and the stock market. Roosevelt agreed with their ideas and threw his support behind the Securities Act of 1933 and the Glass-Steagall Banking Act.

The Securities Act required companies that sold stocks and bonds to provide complete and truthful information to investors. The following year Congress created an independent agency, the **Securities and Exchange Commission** (SEC), to regulate the stock market and prevent fraud.

The Glass-Steagall Act separated commercial banking from investment banking. Commercial banks handle everyday transactions. They take deposits, pay interest, cash checks, and loan money for mortgages and other business activities. Under the Glass-Steagall Act, these banks were no longer permitted to risk depositors' money by using it to speculate on the stock market.

To further protect depositors, the Glass-Steagall Act also created the **Federal Deposit Insurance Corporation** (FDIC) to provide government insurance

MEETING SPECIAL NEEDS

Visual/Linguistic Have students work in pairs to create a diagram showing how the banking system worked before and after the Glass-Steagall Act and the creation of the Federal Deposit Insurance Corporation. Suggest that students use visuals, such as play money, to make their diagrams interesting. **L2**

Refer to *Inclusion for the High School Social Studies Classroom Strategies and Activities* in the TCR.

◄ Flood Control
In spring 1984, torrential rains would have brought the Tennessee River crest to almost 20 feet (6 m) above flood level. However, by storing water in reservoirs behind dams such as Dawson Dam and releasing it slowly, the TVA prevented most potential flooding.

The TVA Today

The TVA's power facilities include 29 hydroelectric dams, 11 fossil-fuel plants, 3 nuclear power plants, 4 combustion-turbine plants, a pumped-storage facility, and 17,000 miles of transmission lines. These facilities provide power to nearly 8 million people in the seven-state region.

for bank deposits up to a certain amount. By protecting depositors in this way, the FDIC greatly increased public confidence in the banking system.

✓ **Reading Check** **Explaining** How did the government restore confidence in the banking system?

Managing Farms and Industry

Many of Roosevelt's advisers believed that both farmers and businesses were suffering because prices were too low and production too high. Several advisers believed competition was inefficient and bad for the economy. They wanted business and government to work together and favored the creation of federal agencies to manage the economy.

The Agricultural Adjustment Administration

The nation's farmers had been hit hard by the Depression. One week after calling Congress into special session, Roosevelt announced plans for a new farm program. Working closely with the leaders of the nation's farm organizations, Secretary of Agriculture Henry Wallace raced to complete a new farm bill before planting season began.

The Agricultural Adjustment Act that Roosevelt asked Congress to pass was based on a simple idea—that prices for farm goods were low because farmers grew too much food. Under Roosevelt's program, the government would pay farmers *not* to raise certain livestock, such as hogs, and *not* to grow certain crops, such as cotton, corn, wheat, and tobacco. The farm program was administered by the **Agricultural Adjustment Administration** (AAA).

By the time the AAA was organized, however, farmers had already planted their crops for the year and begun raising the season's livestock. To prevent cotton—which was already at a very low price—from reaching the market, the AAA paid cotton farmers about $100 million to plow under about 25 percent of their crop. Similarly, hog producers slaughtered 6 million piglets instead of fattening them for market.

Over the next two years, farmers withdrew millions of acres from production and received more than $1 billion in support payments. The program accomplished its goal: The farm surplus fell greatly by 1936. Food prices then rose, as did total farm income, which quickly increased by more than 50 percent.

In a nation caught in a Depression, however, raising food prices drew harsh criticism. Furthermore, not all farmers benefited. Large commercial farmers, who concentrated on one crop, profited more than smaller farmers who raised several products. Worse, thousands of poor tenant farmers—many of them African Americans—became homeless and jobless when landlords chose their fields to be taken out of production.

A Blueprint for Industrial Recovery The government turned its attention from farming to manufacturing in June 1933, when Roosevelt and Congress enacted the **National Industrial Recovery Act** (NIRA). The NIRA suspended the antitrust laws and allowed business, labor, and government to cooperate in setting up voluntary rules for each industry.

These rules were known as codes of fair competition. Some codes set prices, established minimum wages, and limited factories to two shifts per day so production could be spread to as many firms as possible. Other codes shortened workers' hours with the goal of creating additional jobs. Another provision in the law guaranteed workers the right to form unions.

Under the leadership of Hugh Johnson, the **National Recovery Administration** (NRA) ran the entire program. Business owners who signed code agreements received signs displaying the NRA's symbol—a blue eagle—and the slogan, "We do our part." Since the NRA had limited power to enforce the

✓**Reading Check**

Answer: Roosevelt ordered a bank holiday, signed the Emergency Banking Relief Act into law, and addressed the nation in a "fireside chat." He also supported the Glass-Steagall Act, which created the FDIC to provide government insurance for bank deposits.

Drawing Conclusions Ask students to discuss whether it is a citizen's duty to follow the suggestion of a president such as Roosevelt's to redeposit money in a bank. Ask students if a president has made a similar request during their lifetime. Then ask how citizens responded to the request. (If students cannot identify a similar request, direct the discussion towards likely reactions from citizens to such requests.) **L1**

FYI

Throughout his presidency Franklin Roosevelt averaged two press conferences a week. These were informal affairs, with as many as 200 reporters cramming into the Oval Office to hear Roosevelt's pronouncements. He answered questions off the cuff and seemed to know each reporter by name.

📁 Use *Interpreting Political Cartoons,* Cartoon 24.

INTERDISCIPLINARY CONNECTIONS ACTIVITY

Language Arts Have students write a persuasive speech that Franklin Roosevelt could have used during the Hundred Days to promote his solutions to the banking crisis or to defend his emergency relief measures. Students may want to study transcripts or recordings of some of Roosevelt's speeches to get a sense of his speaking style. Students should also identify characteristics of the audience and write a speech targeted to those characteristics. **L2**

✓ **Reading Check**

Answer: The AAA paid farmers to limit production. The NIRA set prices, established minimum wages, limited shifts, shortened work hours, and guaranteed workers the right to form unions.

Creating a Chart Have students create a chart similar to the one on page 687 that explores the current status of each of the agencies listed. The columns should include Agency, Established, Original Function, and Current Function. For any agency that no longer exists, have students use the Current Function column to state when the agency ceased its function. **L2**

📁 Use the rubric for a map, display, or chart on pages 77–78 in the *Performance Assessment Activities and Rubrics.*

✓ **Reading Check**

Answer: Home Owners' Loan Corporation and Farm Credit Administration

---

📷 *Picturing* **History**

Background: Even though the Supreme Court declared the NRA unconstitutional, many of its labor provisions were reenacted in later legislation.

Answer: The NRA failed to accomplish many of its goals.

Ask: What was the slogan of the NRA? *(We do our part.)*

---

codes, it used public opinion to pressure companies into going along. It urged consumers to buy goods only from companies that displayed the blue eagle.

The NRA did produce a revival of a few industries, but the gains proved short-lived. Small companies complained, justifiably, that large corporations wrote the codes to favor themselves. More efficient companies disliked price fixing, which limited competition and made it hard for them to increase their market share by cutting prices. Employers disliked codes that gave workers the right to form unions and bargain collectively over wages and hours. They also argued that paying high minimum wages forced them to charge higher prices to cover their costs.

The codes were also very difficult to administer, and business leaders often ignored them. It became obvious that the NRA was failing when industrial production actually fell after the organization was established. By the time the Supreme Court declared the NRA to be unconstitutional in 1935, it had already lost much of its political support.

✓ **Reading Check** **Examining** What were the provisions of the Agricultural Adjustment Act and the National Industrial Recovery Act?

Providing Debt Relief

While some of Roosevelt's advisers believed low prices had caused the Depression, others believed that debt was the main obstacle to economic recovery. With incomes falling, people had to use most of their money to pay their debts and had little left over to buy goods or pay for services. Many Americans, terrified of losing their homes and farms, deliberately cut back on their spending to make sure they could pay their mortgages. President Roosevelt responded to the crisis by introducing several policies intended to assist Americans with their debts.

The Home Owners' Loan Corporation To help homeowners pay their mortgages, Roosevelt asked Congress to establish the Home Owners' Loan Corporation (HOLC). The HOLC bought the mortgages of many homeowners who were behind in their payments. It then restructured them with longer terms of repayment and lower interest rates. Roughly 10 percent of the nation's homeowners received HOLC loans.

The HOLC did not help everyone. It only made loans to homeowners who were still employed. When people lost their jobs and could no longer pay their mortgages, the HOLC foreclosed on their property, just as a bank would have done. By 1938

686 CHAPTER 23 Roosevelt and the New Deal

the HOLC had foreclosed on more than 100,000 mortgages. Despite these failures, the HOLC helped refinance one out of every five mortgages on private homes in the United States.

The Farm Credit Administration Three days after Congress authorized the creation of the HOLC, it authorized the Farm Credit Administration (FCA) to begin helping farmers refinance their mortgages. Over the next seven months, the FCA lent four times as much money to farmers as the entire banking system had done the year before. It was also able to push interest rates substantially lower. "I would be without a roof over my head if it hadn't been for the government loan," wrote one of the millions of farmers who were saved by FCA loans.

Although FCA loans helped many farmers in the short term, their long-term value can be questioned. FCA loans helped less efficient farmers keep their land, but giving loans to poor farmers meant that the money was not available to loan to more efficient businesses in the economy. Although FCA loans may have slowed the overall economic recovery, they did help many desperate and impoverished people hold onto their land.

✓ **Reading Check** **Identifying** What New Deal programs helped farmers and homeowners?

Spending and Relief Programs

While many of Roosevelt's advisers emphasized tinkering with prices and providing debt relief in order to cure the Depression, others maintained that the fundamental cause of the Depression was low consumption. People were simply not buying enough products to keep the economy going. The fastest way out of the Depression, these advisers asserted, was to get money directly into the hands of needy individuals.

Neither President Roosevelt nor his advisers wanted simply to give money to the unemployed. They argued that recipients were more likely to maintain work skills and self-respect if they earned their

📷 *Picturing* **History**

The NRA Eagle As a symbol of the National Recovery Administration, this eagle informed consumers about industries that were meeting the standards of the National Industrial Recovery Act. How successful was the NRA?

Townsend's proposal attracted millions of supporters, especially among the elderly, who mobilized as a political force for the first time in American history. Townsend's program was particularly popular in the West. When combined with Long's support in the Midwest and South and Coughlin's support among urban Catholics in the Northeast, there was a real possibility of a coalition that would draw enough votes away from Roosevelt to prevent his re-election in 1936.

Reading Check **Examining** What groups of people challenged Roosevelt and the New Deal? What concerns did they have?

Launching the Second New Deal

Although he remained tremendously popular with the American people, Roosevelt realized that his political support could be undermined by the attacks from left and right. He was also disturbed by the failure of the New Deal to generate a rapid economic recovery. In 1935 he launched what came to be called the Second New Deal—another series of programs and reforms that he hoped would speed up the

nation's recovery, provide economic security to every American, and ensure his re-election in 1936.

The WPA In January 1935, Roosevelt began by asking Congress for nearly $5 billion "for work relief and to increase employment by providing useful projects." Much of the money would be given to the **Works Progress Administration** (WPA), a new federal agency headed by Harry Hopkins. "The big boss is ready to go places in a big way," Hopkins told a colleague.

Over the next several years, the WPA spent $11 billion. Its 8.5 million workers constructed about 650,000 miles of highways, roads, and streets, 125,000 public buildings, and more than 8,000 parks. It built or improved more than 124,000 bridges and 853 airports.

The WPA's most controversial program was "Federal Number One," a section of the Professional Projects Division that offered work to artists, musicians, theater people, and writers. "They've got to eat just like other people," Hopkins commented to critics of the program. The artists created thousands of murals and sculptural works to beautify the walls and halls of public buildings. Musicians established

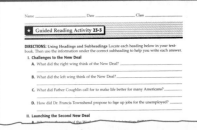

Guided Reading Activity 23–3

Name _____ Date _____ Class _____

★ Guided Reading Activity 23-3

DIRECTIONS: Using Headings and Subheadings Locate each heading below in your textbook. Then use the information under the correct subheading to help you write each answer.

I. Challenges to the New Deal

A. What did the right wing think of the New Deal? _____

B. What did the left wing think of the New Deal? _____

C. What did Father Coughlin call for to make life better for many Americans? _____

D. How did Dr. Francis Townsend propose to free up jobs for the unemployed? _____

II. Launching the Second New Deal

Reading Check

Answer: Right: American Liberty League (business leaders and anti-New Deal politicians)—organize opposition and teach necessity of respect for rights of person and property; Left: Democrats (Huey Long)—share wealth with all; National Union for Social Justice (Fr. Charles Coughlin)—heavy taxes on rich and nationalization of banks; Townsend Plan (Dr. Francis Townsend)—universal pension

NATIONAL GEOGRAPHIC

MOMENT in HISTORY

BRIEF RESPITE FOR FDR

Enjoying a short break from the pressures of dealing with the country's economic woes, President Franklin D. Roosevelt holds his beloved dog Fala while chatting with the granddaughter of the family gardener at his Hyde Park, New York, estate. The president and his staff, with the help of the press, took great pains to conceal his polio-induced paralysis. He was never filmed or photographed being wheeled or carried from place to place. This rare snapshot is one of the few known to exist that shows Roosevelt seated in his wheelchair.

NATIONAL GEOGRAPHIC

MOMENT in HISTORY

This is one of only two photographs that show Roosevelt seated in a wheelchair. In January 2001 a new portion of the Roosevelt Memorial in Washington, D.C., was unveiled. The statue shows Roosevelt seated in a wheelchair. After initial resistance, his family now supports the addition of the statue. His grandson David Roosevelt said, "I hope that when young people—a young person who goes to visit the FDR Memorial who perhaps is in a wheelchair herself or himself—when they first see the entrance and when they see FDR in a wheelchair, they will say, 'I can do that, too.'"

MEETING SPECIAL NEEDS

Visual/Spatial To help students with reading disabilities, have them list the headings of the section. Then have them scan the information under each heading to find out what sector of society leveled certain criticisms at Roosevelt and how Roosevelt reacted. Ask students to list this information under each heading on their list to make an outline for studying. **L1** **ELL**

📁 Refer to *Inclusion for the High School Social Studies Classroom Strategies and Activities* in the TCR.

The Second New Deal, 1935

Agency/Legislation	Function
Works Progress Administration (WPA)	Combated unemployment; created jobs throughout economy
Rural Electrification Administration (REA)	Brought electricity to isolated agricultural areas
Social Security Act	Created unemployment system, disability insurance, old-age pension, and child welfare benefits
Public Utility Holding Company Act	Eliminated unfair practices and abuses of utility companies
Banking Act	Strengthened the Federal Reserve
Resettlement Act	Assisted poor families and sharecroppers in beginning new farms or purchasing land

Chart *Skills*

1. **Interpreting Charts** What did the Resettlement Act try to accomplish?
2. **Understanding Cause and Effect** How did these acts create a safety net for American citizens?

30 city symphony orchestras, as well as hundreds of smaller musical groups. The Federal Theater Project financed playwrights, actors, and directors. The program also funded historians who interviewed former slaves to document American history.

The Supreme Court's Role When Roosevelt asked Congress to fund the WPA in January 1935, he had expected quick action on the bill. He quickly discovered that opposition to his programs was growing in Congress. The bill creating the WPA did not pass until April 1935. By late May, Congress was preparing to adjourn for the summer, leaving Roosevelt with very few accomplishments.

Suddenly, the political situation shifted. On May 27, 1935, the Supreme Court unanimously struck down the National Industrial Recovery Act in *Schechter* v. *United States*. The Schechter brothers, who had a poultry business in Brooklyn, New York, had been convicted in 1933 of violating the NIRA's Live Poultry Code. They had sold diseased chickens and violated the code's wage-and-hour provisions. 📖 *(See page 1082 for more about Schechter v. United States.)*

In what became known as the "sick chicken case," the Court ruled that the Constitution did not allow Congress to delegate its powers to the executive branch. Thus it considered the NIRA codes unconstitutional. The decision worried Roosevelt. The ruling suggested that the Court could soon strike down the rest of the New Deal as well.

Shortly after the Schechter decision, Roosevelt sprang into action. With the Court threatening to strike down the New Deal and with growing challenges from the left and right, the president knew he needed a new series of programs to keep voters' support. He called congressional leaders to a White House conference. Pounding his desk, he thundered that Congress could not go home until it passed his new bills. That summer, Congress began what the press nicknamed the "second hundred days" and worked feverishly to pass Roosevelt's programs.

✓**Reading Check** **Examining** How did the Supreme Court's ruling affect the New Deal?

The Rise of Industrial Unions

When the Supreme Court ruled against the NIRA, it also struck down the section of the law that established labor's right to organize. President Roosevelt and the Democrats in Congress knew that the working-class vote was very important in winning re-election in 1936. They also believed that unions could help end the Depression. They thought that high union wages would let workers spend more money, thereby boosting the economy. Opponents disagreed, arguing that high wages forced companies to charge higher prices and to hire fewer people. Despite these concerns, Congress pushed ahead with new labor legislation.

The National Labor Relations Act In July 1935, Congress passed the National Labor Relations Act, also called the Wagner Act after its author, Democratic senator Robert Wagner of New York. The act guaranteed workers the right to organize unions without interference from employers and to bargain collectively. The law set up the **National Labor Relations Board** (NLRB), which organized factory elections by secret ballot to determine whether workers wanted a union. The NLRB then certified the successful unions.

The new law also set up a process whereby dissatisfied union members could take their complaints to binding arbitration, in which a neutral party would listen to both sides and decide the issues. The NLRB was authorized to investigate the

---

INTERDISCIPLINARY CONNECTIONS ACTIVITY

Performing and Visual Arts Invite an actor, director, or drama teacher to speak to your class about the role government has played in the past and currently plays in funding and encouraging the performing arts. After hearing the presentation, have students write a position paper explaining their support for or opposition to government funding for the arts. Encourage students to use reasoned arguments to support their positions. **L3**

actions of employers and had the power to issue "cease and desist" orders against unfair practices.

The CIO The Wagner Act stimulated a burst of labor activity. In the mid-1930s, the United Mine Workers union, led by John L. Lewis, began working with several other unions to organize workers in industries where unions did not yet exist. To coordinate their efforts, they formed the **Committee for Industrial Organization** (CIO) in 1935.

The CIO set out to organize industrial unions, or unions that included all workers in a particular industry, skilled and unskilled. The CIO began by focusing on the automobile and steel industries—two of the largest industries in America where workers were not yet organized into unions.

Sit-Down Strikes In late December 1936, officials at the General Motors auto-body plant in Cleveland, Ohio, demoted two union men. In an unplanned protest, a shift of 135 workers sat down and launched an unprecedented kind of strike. They stopped working but refused to leave the factory. A few days later, the workers at the company's plant in Flint, Michigan, launched their own sit-down strike,

as the press quickly dubbed it. Workers at other plants followed suit or carried out traditional strikes.

Bruce Bliven, editor of *The New Republic* magazine, was among the few journalists allowed into the plant. Regarding the condition of the strike, he reported:

> 66 The place was remarkably neat and tidy, at least as clean as it is under normal conditions. Beds were made up on the floor of each car, the seats being removed if necessary. . . . I could not see—and I looked for it carefully—the slightest damage done anywhere to the General Motors Corporation. The nearly completed car bodies, for example, were as clean as they would be in the salesroom, their glass and metal shining. 99
>
> —quoted in *The Great Depression*

Violence broke out in Flint when police launched a tear gas assault on one of the smaller plants. The strikers turned back the attack with whatever was at hand—door hinges, bottles, stones, and balls of ice. The police wounded 13 strikers and two bystanders with gunfire, but the strike held. On February 11, 1937, the company gave in and recognized the CIO's

Graph Skills

Answers:
1. approximately 4 million
2. Union membership increased as a result of passage of the Wagner Act.

Graph Skills Practice
Ask: What was the approximate increase in labor membership between 1933 and 1943? *(approximately 10 million)*

3 ASSESS

Assign Section 3 Assessment as homework or as an in-class activity.

🔵 Have students use the **Interactive Tutor Self-Assessment CD-ROM.**

Reading Essentials and Study Guide 23–3

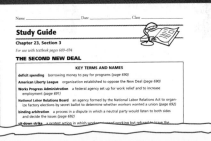

Name _____ Date _____ Class _____

Study Guide
Chapter 23, Section 3
For use with textbook pages 689–694
THE SECOND NEW DEAL

KEY TERMS AND NAMES

deficit spending borrowing money to pay for programs *(page 690)*
American Liberty League organization established to oppose the New Deal *(page 690)*
Works Progress Administration a federal agency set up for work relief and to increase employment *(page 691)*
National Labor Relations Board an agency formed by the National Labor Relations Act to organize factory elections by secret ballot to determine whether workers wanted a union *(page 692)*
binding arbitration a process in which a dispute in which a neutral party would listen to both sides and decide the issues *(page 692)*
sit-down strike a protest action in which workers stopped working but refused to leave the

Trying to Improve Working Conditions

Autoworkers stage a sit-down strike in 1937 in Flint, Michigan.

Union Membership, 1933–1943

Members (in millions)

Year: 1933, 1934, 1935, 1936, 1937, 1938, 1939, 1940, 1941, 1942, 1943

Source: *Historical Statistics of the United States: Colonial Times to 1970.*

Graph Skills

1. **Interpreting Graphs** Approximately how many people were union members in 1936?
2. **Understanding Cause and Effect** Why did union membership increase steadily after 1936?

CRITICAL THINKING ACTIVITY

Analyzing Although President Roosevelt did not fully support the Wagner Act, he believed that the Supreme Court's invalidation of the National Industrial Recovery Act made it imperative to restore labor's rights. The National Labor Relations Board, which the Wagner Act established, supported the right of workers to organize unions. Organize students into two groups, with one developing arguments for unionization, and the other developing arguments against unionization. Ask each group to present its view. **L2**

✓ Reading Check

Answer: the right to organize unions without interference, and collective bargaining

Reteach

Have students describe the kinds of political challenges Roosevelt faced in the mid-1930s.

Enrich

Remind students that Roosevelt's goals when he took office were relief, recovery, and reform. Ask students to write an essay that evaluates his success in achieving these goals.

✓ Reading Check

Answer: It provided temporary income to unemployed workers looking for new jobs and provided a small pension for retired workers.

4 CLOSE

Have students explain why the Social Security Act is still regarded as an important piece of legislation.

United Auto Workers (UAW) as its employees' sole bargaining agent. The UAW quickly became one of the most powerful unions in the United States.

The United States Steel Corporation, the nation's largest steel producer, decided it did not want to repeat the General Motors experience. The company recognized the CIO's United Steelworkers of America, which won a 40-hour workweek and a 10-percent pay raise. Smaller steel producers did not initially recognize unions, and strikes broke out around the country. By 1941, however, the steelworkers' union had contracts with the entire industry.

In the late 1930s, workers in other industries also sat down at their jobs to gain union recognition. In only six years, total union membership tripled from roughly 3 million in 1933 to about 9 million in 1939. In 1938 the CIO changed its name to the Congress of Industrial Organizations and became a federation of industrial unions.

✓ Reading Check **Examining** What provisions did the National Labor Relations Act establish?

The Social Security Act

After passing the Wagner Act, Congress began work on a bill that ranks as one of the most important pieces of legislation in American history. This was the Social Security Act, which became law in August 1935. Its major goal was to provide some security for the elderly and for unemployed workers.

With the support of Secretary of Labor Frances Perkins, Roosevelt and his team spent months preparing the bill. The framers viewed it primarily as

an insurance bill. Workers earned the right to receive benefits because they paid premiums. The legislation also provided modest welfare payments to other needy people, including those with disabilities and poor families with young dependent children.

The core of Social Security was the monthly retirement benefit, which people could collect when they stopped working at age 65. Another important benefit, unemployment insurance, supplied a temporary income to unemployed workers looking for new jobs. Some critics did not like the fact that the money came from payroll taxes imposed on workers and employers, but to Roosevelt these taxes were crucial: "We put those payroll contributions there so as to give the contributors a legal, moral, and political right to collect their pensions and the unemployment benefits."

Since the people receiving benefits had already paid for them, he explained, "no politician can ever scrap my social security program." What Roosevelt did not anticipate was that in the future, Congress would borrow money from the Social Security fund to pay for other programs while failing to raise payroll deductions enough to pay for the benefits.

Social Security helped many people, but initially it left out many of the neediest members of society—farm and domestic workers. Some 65 percent of all African American workers in the 1930s fell into these two categories. Nevertheless, Social Security established the principle that the federal government should be responsible for those who, through no fault of their own, were unable to work.

✓ Reading Check **Explaining** How did the Social Security Act protect workers?

SECTION 3 ASSESSMENT

Checking for Understanding

1. **Define:** deficit spending, binding arbitration, sit-down strike, Social Security Act.
2. **Identify:** American Liberty League, Works Progress Administration, National Labor Relations Board.
3. **Contrast** the ideas of Father Charles Coughlin, Senator Huey Long, and Dr. Francis Townsend.

Reviewing Themes

4. **Government and Democracy** How did the New Deal contribute to the growth of industrial unions?

Critical Thinking

5. **Analyzing** Why is the Social Security Act an important piece of legislation?
6. **Organizing** Use a graphic organizer similar to the one below to list the political challenges Roosevelt faced in his first term.

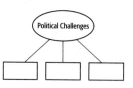

Political Challenges

Analyzing Visuals

7. **Analyzing Graphs** Examine the photo and graph on page 693. How did successful strikes such as the sit-down strike shown in the photograph lead to a rise in union membership?

Writing About History

8. **Descriptive Writing** Imagine you are either a General Motors worker or a member of management during the sit-down strike in Flint, Michigan. Write a letter to your local newspaper describing the strike and explaining your actions during it.

694 CHAPTER 23 Roosevelt and the New Deal

SECTION 3 ASSESSMENT ANSWERS

1. Terms are in blue.
2. American Liberty League *(p. 690)*, Works Progress Administration *(p. 691)*, National Labor Relations Board *(p. 692)*
3. Coughlin: tax the rich and nationalize the banking system; Long: share the wealth; Townsend: pen-

sions for the elderly
4. Legislation such as the Wagner Act encouraged workers to organize unions where none existed and set up a process to protect unions as they developed.
5. It forced the government to protect the unemployed.

6. American Liberty League, left-wing Democrats, urban Catholics
7. As workers saw that unions helped them, more workers supported and joined unions.
8. Letters should clearly express a point of view.

Guide to Reading

Main Idea
Backed by a new coalition of voters, Roosevelt easily won a second term, but the opposition of conservatives weakened his ability to achieve additional reforms.

Key Terms and Names
Frances Perkins, court-packing, Henry Morgenthau, John Maynard Keynes, broker state, safety net

Reading Strategy
Taking Notes As you read about the New Deal coalition, use the major headings of the section to create an outline similar to the one below.

The New Deal Coalition
I. Roosevelt's Second Term
   A.
   B.
   C.
II.
   A.
   B.

Reading Objectives
• **Explain** the achievements and the defeats of Roosevelt's second term.
• **Analyze** how the New Deal affected Americans' sense of security and their attitude toward the role of government.

Section Theme
Groups and Institutions The Democratic Party's victory in 1936 resulted from a new alignment in politics that lasted for several decades.

Preview of Events

| ◆1936 | ◆1937 | ◆1938 |

1936
FDR reelected

1937
Court-packing bill defeated; Farm Tenant Act; National Housing Act

1937
Roosevelt Recession begins

1938
Fair Labor Standards Act passed

★ An American Story ★

Robert Vann

One day in 1932, Emma Guffey Miller, the sister of Democratic senator Joseph Guffey, was having her nails done at a salon in Pittsburgh. Her manicurist mentioned that Robert Vann, publisher of the *Pittsburgh Courier,* a leading African American newspaper, wanted to see the senator. When Senator Guffey met Vann, Vann told him that the Democrats could win most of the 280,000 African American votes in Pennsylvania if they made the effort.

Since the Civil War, most African Americans had voted for the Republicans. Now times had changed. The Depression had hit the African American community very hard, and Republicans had done little to help. In talks to African American voters, Vann often said, "My friends, go home and turn Lincoln's picture to the wall. That debt has been paid in full."

Guffey was impressed. He persuaded party leaders to appoint Vann to lead "the first really effective Negro division a Democratic campaign committee ever had." By 1936 the majority of African American voters had switched their support to the Democratic Party.

—**adapted from** *The Politics of Upheaval*

Roosevelt's Second Term

The dramatic shift in party allegiance by African Americans was part of a historic political realignment triggered by FDR's New Deal. As the election of 1936 approached, millions of voters owed their jobs, mortgages, or salvaged bank accounts to the New Deal, and they knew it.

CHAPTER 23   Roosevelt and the New Deal   **695**

1 FOCUS

Section Overview
This section focuses on Roosevelt's second term as president.

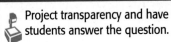

BELLRINGER
Skillbuilder Activity

👆 Project transparency and have students answer the question.

📁 Available as a blackline master.

Daily Focus Skills Transparency 23–4

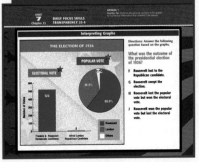

Guide to Reading

Answers to Graphic:
I. Roosevelt's Second Term
   A. The Election of 1936
   B. The Court-Packing Plan
   C. The Roosevelt Recession
II. The Last New Deal Reforms
   A. The National Housing Act
   B. The Farm Security Administration
   C. The Fair Labor Standards Act
III. The Legacy of The New Deal
   A. The Broker State
   B. Government's New Role

Preteaching Vocabulary
Have students identify the Key Terms and Names that refer to specific individuals and write a one-sentence description of each person.

SECTION RESOURCES

📁 **Reproducible Masters**
• Reproducible Lesson Plan 23–4
• Daily Lecture and Discussion Notes 23–4
• Guided Reading Activity 23–4
• Section Quiz 23–4
• Reading Essentials and Study Guide 23–4
• Performance Assessment Activities and Rubrics

📖 **Transparencies**
• Daily Focus Skills Transparency 23–4

Multimedia
🔵 Interactive Tutor Self-Assessment CD-ROM
🔵 ExamView® Pro Testmaker CD-ROM
🔵 Presentation Plus! CD-ROM
🔵 TeacherWorks™ CD-ROM
🔵 Audio Program

2 TEACH

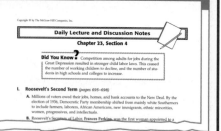
Profiles
IN HISTORY

Background: Bethune started her school with $1.50 and five students. Today Bethune-Cookman College in Daytona Beach, Florida, has more than 2,500 students and an endowment worth more than $25 million.

Ask: How did Bethune and Perkins help today's working women? (*Answers will vary.*)

Creating Circle Graphs Provide the data below and ask students to make a pair of circle graphs showing the results of the presidential election of 1936. **L1**

Candidate	Popular Vote	Electoral Vote
Roosevelt, Dem.	27,752,869	523
Landon, Rep.	16,674,665	8
Lemke, Union	882,479	0

📁 Use the rubric for a map, display, or chart on pages 77–78 in the *Performance Assessment Activities and Rubrics.*

Profiles IN HISTORY

Mary McLeod Bethune
1875–1955

Mary McLeod Bethune was born into a poor South Carolina family, the 15th of 17 children. Although she worked from a young age picking cotton and washing clothes, Bethune was determined to get an education. She won a scholarship to a seminary in North Carolina and later graduated from the Moody Bible Institute in Chicago. Bethune then began teaching at the Haines Institute. In 1904 she founded a school in Florida for the children of African American railroad workers. "I rang doorbells," she later recalled. "I wrote articles . . . distributed leaflets, [and] invaded churches, clubs, lodges, [and] chambers of commerce." Gradually she raised enough money to found the Daytona Normal and Industrial School, later known as Bethune College.

Bethune's efforts gained her a national reputation. In the 1920s, she visited the White House to discuss African American affairs. She also became a good friend of Eleanor Roosevelt. In 1936 FDR appointed her director of the Negro Division of the National Youth Administration (NYA), which provided job training for young people. Bethune also founded the National Council of Negro Women to support civil rights. In later years, she advised Presidents Truman and Eisenhower.

Frances Perkins
1882–1965

From the moment she became FDR's secretary of labor at the age of 50, Frances Perkins confronted the challenge of being the first female cabinet member in the nation's history.

Perkins studied social work at Columbia University. Early in her career, she assisted Jane Addams at Hull House and worked with Florence Kelley of the Consumers' League. From her lobbying efforts there, Perkins learned how to deal with politicians.

Perkins first met Roosevelt when she worked for the New York Committee on Safety, lobbying state legislators to limit the workweek for women to 54 hours. When Roosevelt became governor in 1928, he appointed Perkins state industrial commissioner.

After Roosevelt won the presidency in 1932, he asked Perkins to head the Department of Labor. Upon taking the job, Perkins found many areas that needed improvement: offices that were run down, disorganized files, and lax work schedules, conditions she quickly remedied.

Given her background, it was fitting that one of Perkins's major tasks was to head the team that designed the Social Security program. She also supervised implementation of the Fair Labor Standards Act and built up the Bureau of Labor Statistics.

The white South, which had been the core of the Democratic Party, now became just one part of a new coalition that included farmers, laborers, African Americans, new immigrants, ethnic minorities, women, progressives, and intellectuals. First Lady Eleanor Roosevelt helped bring about the change in the African American and women's vote. She had demonstrated strong sympathies toward these groups, with whom she spoke in her many tours of the country. She recounted her experiences to her husband and persuaded him to address at least some of their problems in his New Deal programs.

African Americans and women made some modest gains during the New Deal. For example, the president appointed a number of African Americans to positions in his administration; informally, they became known as the Black Cabinet. Roosevelt also tried to see that New Deal relief programs did not exclude African Americans.

A similar approach guided New Deal policies toward women. Roosevelt appointed the first woman to a cabinet post, Secretary of Labor **Frances Perkins,** and assigned many women to lower-level jobs in the

federal bureaucracy. Even so, the general view was that women did not need federal government action to ensure equal treatment, but rather to provide certain protections for them.

The Election of 1936 To oppose Roosevelt, the Republicans nominated Kansas Governor Alfred Landon. Although Landon favored some New Deal policies, he declared it was time "to unshackle initiative and free the spirit of American enterprise." As the election neared, Landon became more aggressive. The New Deal "violates the basic ideals of the American system," he declared. "If we are to preserve our American form of government, this administration must be defeated."

Despite Landon's attacks, Roosevelt and the New Deal remained overwhelmingly popular with the American people. The challenge from left-wing radicals also proved much weaker than expected—primarily because Huey Long had been assassinated in Louisiana in September of 1935. Long's supporters joined with those of Father Coughlin and Francis Townsend in the summer of 1936 to form a new

---

COOPERATIVE LEARNING ACTIVITY

Researching Women's Wages Mention that in 1937 the U.S. Supreme Court upheld a minimum wage law for women in the decision of *West Coast Hotel* v. *Parrish*. This judgment reversed a 1923 ruling. Organize students into two groups. Have the members of one group work together to research the cases dealing with women's wages that the Supreme Court reviewed during the New Deal years. Ask the other group to research how women's wages changed during the New Deal. Have the two groups share their findings. 👥

Use the rubric for a cooperative group management plan on pages 81–82 in the *Performance Assessment Activities and Rubrics.*

political movement called the **Union Party,** but without a strong leader, the party had no chance. On Election Day, Roosevelt swept to victory in one of the largest landslides in American history. He won more than 60 percent of the popular vote and carried every state except Maine and Vermont.

The Court-Packing Plan Although popular opinion supported most of the president's programs, the Supreme Court saw things differently. In January 1936, the Court declared the Agricultural Adjustment Act to be unconstitutional. With cases pending on Social Security and the Wagner Act, it seemed likely the Court would strike down nearly all of the major New Deal programs.

Roosevelt was furious that a handful of jurists, "nine old men" as he called them, were blocking the wishes of a majority of the people. After winning re-election, he decided to try to change the political balance on the Supreme Court. Claiming that the Court was overburdened with work, Roosevelt sent Congress a bill to increase the number of justices: If any justice had served for 10 years and did not retire within six months after reaching the age of 70, the president could appoint an additional justice to the Court. Since four justices were in their 70s and two more were in their late 60s, the bill, if passed, would allow Roosevelt to quickly appoint as many as six new justices.

The **court-packing** plan, as the press called it, was Roosevelt's first serious political mistake as president. Although Congress had the power to change the size of the Court, the scheme created the impression that the president was trying to interfere with the Constitution's separation of powers and undermine the Court's independence.

The issue split the Democratic Party. Many Southern Democrats feared Roosevelt's plan would put justices on the Court who would overturn segregation. At the same time, African American leaders worried that once Roosevelt set the precedent of changing the Court's makeup, a future president might pack the Court with justices opposed to civil rights. Many Americans believed the plan would give the president too much power.

Despite the uproar over the scheme, Roosevelt's actions appeared to force the Supreme Court to back down. In April 1937, the Court upheld the Wagner Act, and in May it declared the Social Security Act to be constitutional. Shortly afterward, one of the more conservative judges resigned, enabling Roosevelt to appoint a supporter of the New Deal to the Court.

In mid-July, the Senate quietly killed the court-packing bill without bringing it to a vote. Although Roosevelt had achieved his goal of changing the Court's view of the New Deal, the fight over the plan had hurt his reputation with the American people and encouraged conservative Democrats in Congress to work with Republicans to oppose further New Deal proposals.

ECONOMICS

The Roosevelt Recession In late 1937, Roosevelt's reputation suffered another blow when unemployment suddenly surged. Earlier in the year, the economy had seemed to be on the verge of full recovery. Industrial output was almost back to the level it had reached before the Depression began, and many people believed the worst was over.

Although unemployment remained high, Roosevelt decided it was time to balance the budget. Concerned about the dangers of too much debt, Roosevelt ordered the WPA and the PWA to be cut significantly. Unfortunately, Roosevelt cut spending just as the first Social Security payroll taxes removed $2 billion from the economy. Almost immediately the economy plummeted. By the end of 1937, about two million people had been thrown out of work.

The recession of 1937 led to a debate inside Roosevelt's administration over what to do. Treasury Secretary **Henry Morgenthau** favored balancing the

Picturing **History**

Campaigning in 1936 During the 1936 election, FDR's Democratic Party brought together farmers, like this North Dakotan, and many other groups of Americans to form a new coalition of political supporters. This coalition helped give Roosevelt a strong re-election victory. *What different groups made up this coalition?*

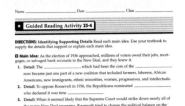
Writing a Biographical Profile
Have students write a short biographical profile of one of the people mentioned in this section. Encourage them to select the person whose actions they most admire. **L2**

FYI

As part of the New Deal, the WPA produced posters publicizing a variety of programs and events. Over 2,000 of these graphically diverse posters are known to exist today. The Library of Congress has more than 900 of the them.

Picturing **History**

Answer: farmers, union members, African Americans, new immigrants, ethnic minorities, women, intellectuals, progressives
Ask: Why do you think so many different groups supported Roosevelt's bid for re-election? *(Many people were benefiting from the initiatives of his first term in office.)*

MEETING SPECIAL NEEDS

Kinesthetic Have interested students play the role of the Supreme Court justices at the time that Roosevelt sent his court plan to Congress. First have students conduct biographical research on the justices. Then have the students create a dramatic reenactment of the justices' first meeting after the plan was announced. Encourage students to rehearse their roles and present their reenactment to the class. **L2**

☞ Refer to *Inclusion for the High School Social Studies Classroom Strategies and Activities* in the TCR.

Making Predictions Have students make a two-column list. Instruct them to list the reasons why they think Roosevelt might be reelected in 1940 in column one and the reasons he might not be reelected in column two. Instruct students to review their lists and predict the outcome of the 1940 presidential race. **L2**

CURRICULUM CONNECTION

Economics FDR favored a stronger role for federal government in improving the lives of all Americans. These improvements cost money. Under FDR the public debt increased more than it had in the nation's history, reaching $43 billion in 1940 compared with $16.2 billion in 1930.

What Life Was Like...

1930s Entertainment

During the Depression, people needed entertainment more than ever. Movies topped the list of ways to escape everyday hardship, but music and dance were popular as well. For really cheap entertainment, one could stay at home and play cards or board games.

● **Movie Escapism**
Movies cost less than 25¢ in many places, so children could afford to go, too. These children display door prizes handed out during a matinee in California.

● **Dance Craze**
Dance marathons got their start in the manic 1920s, but they gained wide popularity in the 1930s. Couples might dance hundreds of hours, until they were exhausted. The last couple standing could win substantial prize money.

---

budget and cutting spending. This would reassure business leaders and encourage them to invest in the economy. Harry Hopkins, head of the WPA, and **Harold Ickes,** head of the PWA, both disagreed with Morgenthau and pushed for more government spending. They pointed to a new theory called "Keynesianism" to support their arguments.

Keynesianism was based on the theories of an influential British economist named **John Maynard Keynes.** In 1936 Keynes published a book that discussed the causes of recessions. He argued that the government should spend heavily during a recession, even if it had to run a deficit, in order to jumpstart the economy.

According to Keynesian economics, Roosevelt had done exactly the wrong thing when he cut back programs in 1937. At first Roosevelt was reluctant to begin deficit spending again. Many critics of his policies had argued that the recession proved the American people were becoming too dependent on government spending, and Roosevelt worried they might be right. Finally, in the spring of 1938, with no recovery in sight, he asked Congress for $3.75 billion for the PWA, the WPA, and other programs.

✓ **Reading Check** **Summarizing** What events weakened Roosevelt's reputation in 1937?

The Last New Deal Reforms

In his second inaugural speech, Roosevelt had pointed out that despite the nation's progress in climbing out of the Depression, many Americans still endured crippling poverty:

> ❝In this nation I see tens of millions of its citizens—a substantial part of its whole population—who at this very moment are denied the greater part of what the very lowest standards of today call the necessities of life. . . . I see one-third of a nation ill-housed, ill-clad, ill-nourished. . . . The test of our progress is not whether we add more to the abundance of those who have much; it is whether we provide enough for those who have too little.❞
>
> —quoted in *Public Papers and Addresses of Franklin D. Roosevelt*

Despite the president's idealistic goals, the fight over the court-packing scheme and the recession of 1937 had weakened Roosevelt politically. Although he pushed ahead with a new series of New Deal programs, his successes were far more limited than they had been in previous years.

INTERDISCIPLINARY CONNECTIONS ACTIVITY

Civics Organize the class into groups of three. Have each member of the groups prepare to debate the issue of adding additional members to the Supreme Court. All three members of the group should be prepared to debate either side of the issue. Invite groups to debate in front of the class. Assign the sides randomly and ask the third member of the group to be the moderator. **L2**

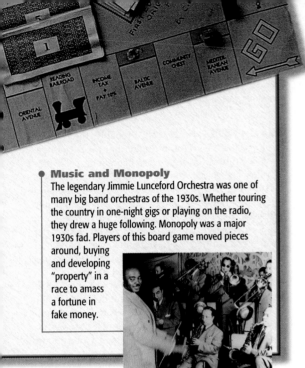

● **Music and Monopoly**
The legendary Jimmie Lunceford Orchestra was one of many big band orchestras of the 1930s. Whether touring the country in one-night gigs or playing on the radio, they drew a huge following. Monopoly was a major 1930s fad. Players of this board game moved pieces around, buying and developing "property" in a race to amass a fortune in fake money.

The National Housing Act One of the president's goals for his second term was to provide better housing for the nation's poor. The Home Owners Loan Corporation had helped many middle-class citizens, but it had not provided housing for those who could not afford a mortgage. Eleanor Roosevelt, who had toured poverty-stricken regions of Appalachia and the Deep South, was among those urging the president to do something.

Senator Wagner, who shared the First Lady's concerns, prepared a new housing bill with Roosevelt's full support. The 1937 National Housing Act established the United States Housing Authority, which received $500 million to subsidize loans for builders willing to buy blocks of slums and build low-cost housing.

The Farm Security Administration Before the Supreme Court struck it down, the Agricultural Adjustment Administration had paid many farmers to take land out of production to force food prices to rise. The price-support program raised farm income, but it badly hurt tenant farmers. Landowners often expelled tenants from the land in order to take it out of production. About 150,000 white and 195,000 African American tenants left farming during the 1930s for this reason.

To stop this trend, the Farm Security Administration was created in 1937 to give loans to tenants so they could purchase farms. Over the next four years it extended loans of about $1 billion. Members of Congress, many of whom believed the program made agricultural problems worse by increasing farm production and driving down prices, kept its appropriations at a low level.

The Fair Labor Standards Act In 1938 New Dealers were still trying to reinstate important pro-labor regulations to make up for the Supreme Court's dismantling of the NIRA in 1935. The Fair Labor Standards Act of 1938 provided more protection for workers, abolished child labor, and established a 40-hour workweek for many workers to come into effect within three years.

Congress, however, was beginning to turn against the New Deal. The recession of 1937 enabled the Republicans to win many seats in Congress in the midterm elections of 1938. Together with conservative Southern Democrats, they began blocking further New Deal legislation. Roosevelt, meanwhile, became increasingly preoccupied with the growing international threat posed by Germany and Japan. By 1939 the New Deal era had come to an end.

✔ **Reading Check** **Examining** What groups did Roosevelt's last New Deal programs try to help?

The Legacy of the New Deal

In terms of its main goal of ending the Depression, the New Deal was only a limited success. Unemployment remained high, and economic recovery was not complete until after World War II. Even so, the New Deal gave many Americans a stronger sense of security and stability.

The Broker State As a whole, the New Deal tended to operate so that it balanced competing economic interests. Business leaders, farmers, workers, consumers, homeowners, and others now looked to government to protect their interests.

The federal government's ability to take on this new role was enhanced by two important Supreme Court decisions. In 1937, in *NLRB* v. *Jones and Laughlin Steel,* the Court ruled that the federal government had the constitutional authority, under the interstate commerce clause, to regulate production within a state. In 1942, in *Wickard* v. *Filburn,* the Court used a similar argument to allow the federal government to regulate consumption in the states. These

What *Life* **Was Like...**

Ask students to compare and contrast 1930s entertainment with today's entertainment. **L2**

Creating a Display Have students research one aspect of entertainment in the 1930s, such as dancing, movies, or board games. Have students create displays based on their research.

✔ **Reading Check**

Answer: farmers, the poor, workers, and children

3 ASSESS

Assign Section 4 Assessment as homework or as an in-class activity.

◉ Have students use the **Interactive Tutor Self-Assessment CD-ROM.**

Reading Essentials and Study Guide 23–4

Name _____ Date _____ Class _____

Study Guide

Chapter 23, Section 4
For use with textbook pages 695–700

THE NEW DEAL COALITION

KEY TERMS AND NAMES

Frances Perkins the Secretary of Labor under President Roosevelt, the first woman appointed to a cabinet post *(page 696)*

court-packing Roosevelt's plan to add justices to the Supreme Court *(page 697)*

Henry Morgenthau Secretary of the Treasury under President Roosevelt *(page 697)*

John Maynard Keynes influential British economist *(page 698)*

broker state a government whose role includes mediating between competing groups *(page 700)*

safety net safeguards and relief programs that protected Americans against economic disasters *(page 700)*

CRITICAL THINKING ACTIVITY

Comparing and Contrasting Tell students that in 1936 about 38 percent of the families in the United States had annual incomes of less than $1,000. The poverty line at that time was $1,330. Ask students to use sources such as the *Statistical Abstract of the United States* to find the most recent poverty figures. Have students compare the poverty situation today to that of the mid-1930s. Then ask them to discuss the following question: **What changes made in the 1930s may help us deal with poverty today? L2**

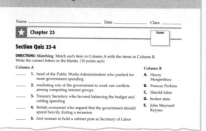
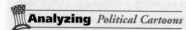
Analyzing *Political Cartoons*

Answer: Many people came to view government as the provider of a safety net for Americans.

Ask: Why do you think wealthy Americans believed that FDR had turned his back on his upbringing? *(They believed that his programs took money from wealthier groups and gave it to lower-income people.)*

Reteach
Have students explain the achievements and the defeats of Roosevelt's second term.

Enrich
Have students select one segment of the American population, such as women, Native Americans, African Americans, or farmers. Have them research how their chosen group fared under the New Deal programs and write a one-page analysis of the group's gains or losses during the 1930s.

Reading Check

Answer: The New Deal increased the government's role and fostered the attitude that the government was responsible for providing a safety net.

4 CLOSE

Have students analyze how the New Deal affected Americans' sense of security and their attitude toward the role of government.

"Come along. We're going to the Trans-Lux to hiss Roosevelt."

Analyzing *Political Cartoons*

Traitor to His Class By 1936 many wealthy Americans believed that FDR had turned his back on his own upbringing, and they actively worked to prevent his re-election. How did the New Deal change the way many people view government?

decisions increased federal power over the economy and allowed it to mediate between competing groups. 📖 *(See page 1082 and 1083 for more information on these Supreme Court cases.)*

In taking on this mediating role, the New Deal established what some have called the broker state, working out conflicts among different interests. This broker role has continued under the administrations of both parties ever since.

Government's New Role Probably the biggest change the New Deal brought about was the new public attitude toward government. Roosevelt's programs had succeeded in creating something of a safety net for average Americans—safeguards and relief programs that protected them against economic disaster. By the time the Roosevelt years were over, the American people felt that the government had a duty to maintain this safety net even though it required a larger, more expensive federal government than at any time in American history.

Critics continued to argue that the New Deal made the government too powerful. Another legacy of the New Deal, therefore, is a debate that has continued to the present over how much the government should intervene in the economy or support the disadvantaged.

Throughout the hard times of the Depression, most Americans maintained a surprising degree of confidence in the American system. Journalist Dorothy Thompson expressed this feeling in 1940:

> 66We have behind us eight terrible years of a crisis. . . . Here we are, and our basic institutions are still intact, our people relatively prosperous and most important of all, our society relatively affectionate. . . . No country is so well off.99

✓ **Reading Check** **Summarizing** What was the legacy of Roosevelt's New Deal?

SECTION 4 ASSESSMENT

Checking for Understanding
1. **Define:** broker state, safety net.
2. **Identify:** Frances Perkins, court-packing, Henry Morgenthau, John Maynard Keynes.
3. **Explain** Roosevelt's court-packing plan and how it was received.

Reviewing Themes
4. **Groups and Institutions** What groups made up the New Deal coalition?

Critical Thinking
5. **Interpreting** How did the New Deal change attitudes toward government?
6. **Categorizing** Use a chart like the one below to list the achievements and defeats of Roosevelt's second term.

Achievements	Defeats

Analyzing Visuals
7. **Analyzing Photographs** Study the photograph on page 697. What does it suggest about Roosevelt's method of campaigning?

Writing About History
8. **Persuasive Writing** Write an essay evaluating the effectiveness of New Deal measures in ending the Depression.

SECTION 4 ASSESSMENT ANSWERS

1. Terms are in blue.
2. Frances Perkins *(p. 696)*, court-packing *(p. 697)*, Henry Morgenthau *(p. 697)*, John Maynard Keynes *(p. 698)*
3. wanted to change the political balance of the Supreme Court; seen as interfering with separation of powers
4. African Americans, farmers, labor, minorities, new immigrants, women, intellectuals, and progressives
5. Americans felt government had a duty to maintain a safety net.
6. Achievements: Social Security, Wagner Act, Fair Labor Standards Act; Defeats: AAA, WPA/PWA, court-packing plan
7. shows he went directly to the people
8. Essays should reflect that the New Deal was a mixed success.

Study and Writing SKILLBUILDER

Outlining

Why Learn This Skill?

To draw a scene, first you would sketch the rough shape, or outline, of the picture. Then you would fill in this rough shape with details. Outlining written material is a similar process. You begin with the rough shape of the material and gradually fill in the details.

Learning the Skill

When studying written material, outlining helps you identify main ideas and group together related facts. In writing, it helps you put information in a logical order.

There are two kinds of outlines—*formal* and *informal*. An informal outline is similar to taking notes. You write only words and phrases needed to remember ideas. Under the main ideas, jot down related but less important details. This kind of outline is useful for reviewing material before a test.

A formal outline has a standard format. In a formal outline, label main heads with Roman numerals, subheads with capital letters, and details with Arabic numerals. Each level must have at least two entries and should be indented from the previous level. All entries use the same grammatical form. For example, if one entry is a complete sentence, all other entries at that level must also be complete sentences.

When outlining written material, first read the material to identify the main ideas. In textbooks, section heads provide clues to main topics. Next, identify the subheads. List details that support or explain subheads underneath the appropriate subhead.

Practicing the Skill

Study the outline on this page on Roosevelt's New Deal. Then answer the following questions.

❶ Is this an example of a formal or an informal outline?

❷ What are the main headings?

❸ How do the subheads under "Managing Farm and Industry" relate to the main idea?

❹ Give two examples of grammatical inconsistency in this outline:

I. The Hundred Days Begins
　A. Origins of the New Deal
　B. A Divided Administration
　　1. Some advisers wanted government and business cooperation.
　　2. Others wanted government to run the economy or regulate competition.

II. Fixing the Banks and Stock Market
　A. The Emergency Banking Relief Act
　　1. All banks closed temporarily.
　　2. The banks reopened and were monitored by federal examiners.
　B. Regulating Banks and Brokers
　　1. The Securities Act ensured complete and truthful investment information.
　　2. The Glass-Steagall Act separated commercial banking from investment banking.

III. Managing Farms and Industry
　A. The Agricultural Adjustment Administration
　　1. Addressed the oversupply of farm products
　　2. Increased farm income
　B. A Blueprint for Industrial Recovery
　　1. The National Recovery Administration established "fair competition" for industry.
　　2. Set minimum wages for employees
　　3. The codes were difficult to administer and gains were short-lived.

Skills Assessment

Complete the Practicing Skills questions on page 703 and the Chapter 23 Skill Reinforcement Activity to assess your mastery of this skill.

Applying the Skill

Outlining Write a formal or informal outline for Section 4 of this chapter.

 Glencoe's **Skillbuilder Interactive Workbook CD-ROM, Level 2,** provides instruction and practice in key social studies skills.

701

CHAPTER 23 ASSESSMENT and ACTIVITIES

MindJogger Videoquiz

Use the **MindJogger Videoquiz** to review Chapter 23 content.

 Available in VHS

Reviewing Key Terms

Students' answers will vary. The pages where the words appear in the text are shown in parentheses.

1. **gold standard** *(p. 681)*
2. **fireside chats** *(p. 684)*
3. **deficit spending** *(p. 690)*
4. **binding arbitration** *(p. 692)*
5. **sit-down strike** *(p. 693)*
6. **Social Security Act** *(p. 694)*
7. **broker state** *(p. 700)*
8. **safety net** *(p. 700)*

Reviewing Key Facts

9. New Deal *(p. 679)*, bank holiday *(p. 681)*, Hundred Days *(p. 682)*, Securities and Exchange Commission *(p. 684)*, Federal Deposit Insurance Corporation *(p. 684)*, Agricultural Adjustment Administration *(p. 685)*, Works Progress Administration *(p. 691)*, National Labor Relations Board *(p. 692)*, Frances Perkins *(p. 696)*, court-packing *(p. 697)*, John Maynard Keynes *(p. 698)*

10. He was concerned about too much debt and its repercussions, especially on the business community.

11. The programs were designed to speed up economic recovery by providing income to American workers.

12. The Supreme Court overturned some of the New Deal legislation by declaring it unconstitutional.

13. The Wagner Act gave workers the right to organize without interference and forced companies to recognize unions as bargaining agents.

14. He was frustrated with the defeats he had suffered and wanted to change the makeup of the Supreme Court.

Reviewing Key Terms

On a sheet of paper, use each of these terms in a sentence.

1. gold standard
2. fireside chats
3. deficit spending
4. binding arbitration
5. sit-down strike
6. Social Security Act
7. broker state
8. safety net

Reviewing Key Facts

9. **Identify:** New Deal, bank holiday, Hundred Days, Securities and Exchange Commission, Federal Deposit Insurance Corporation, Agricultural Adjustment Administration, Works Progress Administration, National Labor Relations Board, Frances Perkins, court-packing, John Maynard Keynes.

10. Why was President Roosevelt reluctant to use deficit spending to help the American economy recover from the Great Depression?

11. Why did the federal government create work programs during the Depression?

12. How did the Supreme Court challenge the New Deal?

13. How did the Wagner Act contribute to the growth of unions?

14. Why did President Roosevelt devise the court-packing plan?

15. What impact did New Deal legislation have on the role of the federal government in state commerce?

Critical Thinking

16. **Analyzing Themes: Economic Factors** What caused the recession in 1937, and how did Keynesian economics explain this recession?

17. **Analyzing** Choose one of the New Deal programs. Describe its goals and evaluate its success.

18. **Forming an Opinion** Which method should be used to settle differences between unions and companies—binding arbitration or sit-down strikes? Explain your answer.

19. **Interpreting Primary Sources** In her autobiography, Eleanor Roosevelt wrote about discussions she had with people across the country. Read the excerpt and answer the questions that follow.

❝This trip to the mining areas was my first contact with the work being done by the Quakers. I liked the idea of trying to put people to work to help themselves. The men were started on projects and taught to use their abilities to develop new skills. The women were encouraged to revive any household arts they might once have known but which they had neglected in the drab life of the mining village.

This was only the first of many trips into the mining districts but it was the one that started the homestead

Chapter Summary

Major New Deal Programs

Financial and Debt

- Emergency Banking Relief Act regulated banks.
- Federal Deposit Insurance Corporation insured bank deposits.
- Farm Credit Administration refinanced farm mortgages.
- Home Owners' Loan Corporation financed homeowners' mortgages.

Work and Relief

- Civilian Conservation Corps created forestry jobs for young men.
- Federal Emergency Relief Administration funded city and state relief programs.
- Public Works Administration created work programs to build public projects, such as roads, bridges, and schools.

Agriculture and Industry

- Agricultural Adjustment Administration paid farmers to limit surplus production.
- National Industrial Recovery Act limited industrial production and set prices.
- National Labor Relations Act gave workers the right to organize unions and bargain collectively.
- Tennessee Valley Authority financed rural electrification and helped develop the economy of a seven-state region.

Social "Safety Net"

- Social Security Act provided:
  – income for elderly, handicapped, and unemployed.
  – monthly retirement benefit for people over 65

702 CHAPTER 23 Roosevelt and the New Deal

15. *NLRB* v. *Jones and Laughlin Steel* gave the federal government power to regulate production in a state.

Critical Thinking

16. A reduction in government spending at the same time that the payroll tax went into effect was the main cause of the recession. Keynesian economics argued that government should increase spending during a recession.

17. Students' answers will vary. They should realistically evaluate the program's successes and failures.

18. Binding arbitration is a fair compromise because a neutral party listens to both sides and decides issues. Sit-down strikes might be used where employers are resisting negotiation.

idea [placing people in planned communities with homes, farms, and jobs]. . . . It was all experimental work, but it was designed to get people off relief, to put them to work building their own homes and to give them enough land to start growing food. 99

a. Why did Eleanor Roosevelt like the Quaker project?

b. Based on this excerpt, do you think that Eleanor Roosevelt supported her husband's New Deal programs? Explain your answer.

20. Categorizing Use a graphic organizer like the one below to list groups of people helped by each program.

New Deal Agencies	Whom It Helped
NRA →	[ ]
AAA →	[ ]
FDIC →	[ ]
HOLC →	[ ]
CCC →	[ ]

Practicing Skills

21. Outlining Study the subheads of Section 3, "The Second New Deal," and Section 4, "The New Deal Coalition," to review the sections. Then do the following exercises.

a. Make a formal outline of Section 3. Pay special attention to forming complete sentences.

b. Make an informal outline of Section 4.

Writing Activity

22. Expository Writing Under *Economic Crisis and the New Deal* on the American History Primary Source Document Library CD-ROM, read Roosevelt's First Inaugural Address. Work with another student to write a commentary on the address and then present it as a radio broadcast to the class. Your commentary should include opinions about Roosevelt's economic ideas.

Chapter Activity

23. Technology Activity: Researching the Internet Use the Internet to research two New Deal agencies: the FDIC and

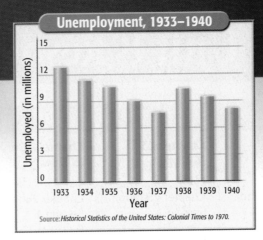

Unemployment, 1933–1940

Source: *Historical Statistics of the United States: Colonial Times to 1970.*

the SEC. Write a short report explaining how they continue to affect the lives of U.S. citizens and the U.S. economy today.

Economics and History

24. Examine the graph above showing unemployment figures, and then answer the questions below.

a. Interpreting Graphs What was the difference in unemployment between 1937 and 1938?

b. Analyzing Why did unemployment decline between 1933 and 1937? Why did it increase in 1938?

Standardized Test Practice

Directions: Choose the best answer to the following question.

Each of the following is true of the bills passed during the first Hundred Days of Roosevelt's presidency EXCEPT:

F They were intended to provide immediate relief to American citizens.

G They were known as the New Deal.

H They were designed as temporary measures to restart the economy.

J They were the subject of divisive and protracted debate in Congress.

Test-Taking Tip: Remember, this question asks for the *exception.* Read through each answer carefully to see if it is true of FDR's first Hundred Days. You are looking for the answer that is false. For example, you probably remember that these bills were intended to combat the effects of the Great Depression. Therefore, answer F is true, so it is not the correct answer.

Chapter Activity

23. Reports will vary but should be based on solid sources and contain appropriate bibliographic references.

Economics and History

24. a. It increased from approximately 8 million to 10.5 million. **b.** It declined due to the New Deal programs and an improving economy. It increased in 1938 as a result of recession and reduced funding for some New Deal programs.

Standardized Test Practice

Answer: J

Test-Taking Tip: Have students look for information in the question stem that will help them find the correct answer. For example, 100 days is less than four months. It does not seem likely that much could have been accomplished if Congress was involved in divisive and protracted debate. Remind students that they are looking for the answer that is the exception. The correct answer is J.

Bonus Question ?

Ask: What board game became a national fad during the 1930s? *(Monopoly)*

19. a. It emphasized individual initiative in improving the lives of miners. **b.** She did support his New Deal programs and often advised him on people's needs.

20. NRA: industrial workers; AAA: farmers; FDIC: bank depositors; HOLC: middle-class homeowners; CCC: single men ages 18–25

Practicing Skills

21. Students' outlines should follow rules for formal and informal outline techniques and be based on the content of the two sections.

Writing Activity

22. Allow time for students to present their radio broadcasts. Students could place the script or recording in their portfolios.

703

SUGGESTED PACING CHART

Unit 8 (1 Day)	Chapter 24 (5 Days)	Chapter 25 (6 Days)	Chapter 26 (5 Days)	Chapter 27 (5 Days)	Unit 8 (2 Days)
Day 1 Introduction	**Day 1** Chapter 24 Intro, Section 1	**Day 1** Chapter 25 Intro, Section 1	**Day 1** Chapter 26 Intro, Section 1	**Day 1** Chapter 27 Intro, Section 1	**Day 1** Wrap-Up/Project **Day 2** Unit 8 Assessment
	Day 2 Section 2	**Day 2** Section 2	**Day 2** Section 2	**Day 2** Section 2	
	Day 3 Section 3	**Day 3** Section 3	**Day 3** Section 3	**Day 3** Section 3	
	Day 4 Section 4	**Day 4** Section 4	**Day 4** Section 4	**Day 4** Section 4	
	Day 5 Chapter 24 Assessment	**Day 5** Section 5	**Day 5** Chapter 26 Assessment	**Day 5** Chapter 27 Assessment	
		Day 6 Chapter 25 Assessment			

Use the following tools to easily assess student learning in a variety of ways:

- Performance Assessment Activities and Rubrics
- Chapter and Unit Tests
- Section Quizzes
- Standardized Test Skills Practice Workbook

- tav.glencoe.com
- Interactive Tutor Self-Assessment CD-ROM
- MindJogger Videoquiz
- ExamView® Pro Testmaker CD-ROM
- SAT I/II Test Practice

TEACHING TRANSPARENCIES

Unit 8 Map Overlay Transparencies

Cause-and-Effect Transparency 8

interNET RESOURCES

- tav.glencoe.com

The American Vision
Visit the *American Vision* Web site for history overviews, activities, assessments, and updated charts and graphs.

- www.socialstudies.glencoe.com

Glencoe Social Studies
Visit the Glencoe Web site for social studies activities, updates, and links to other sites.

- www.teachingtoday.glencoe.com

Glencoe Teaching Today
Visit the new Glencoe Web site for teacher development information, teaching tips, Web resources, and educational news.

- www.time.com

TIME Online
Visit the TIME Web site for up-to-date news and special reports.

Unit 8 Resources

ASSESSMENT

Unit 8 Pretests

Unit 8 Posttests

APPLICATION AND ENRICHMENT

American Biography 8

History Simulation and Problem Solving 8

GEOGRAPHY

Geography and History Activity 8

INTERDISCIPLINARY ACTIVITIES

American Literature Reading 8

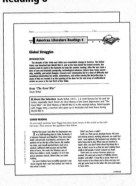

Economics and History Activity 8

Team-Teaching Interdisciplinary Strategies and Activities 8

BIBLIOGRAPHY

Readings for the Student

Drez, Ronald J. and Stephen E. Ambrose. *Twenty-Five Yards of War: The Extraordinary Courage of Ordinary Men in World War II.* Hyperion, 2001.

Readings for the Teacher

Yancey, Diane. *Life in a Japanese American Internment Camp.* Lucent Books, 1998.

Multimedia Resources

Videocassette. *December 7th.* National Archives. (34 minutes)

Additional Glencoe Resources for This Unit:

- Glencoe Skillbuilder Interactive Workbook CD-ROM, Level 2
- Social Studies Guide to Using the Internet
- Writer's Guidebook for High School
- Living Constitution
- American Art Prints Strategies and Activities

`0:00` **Out of Time?**

If time does not permit teaching each chapter in this unit, you may want to use the **Reading Essentials and Study Guide** summaries.

Unit Overview

Unit 8 explores the global struggles faced by the United States between 1931 and 1960. **Chapter 24** covers the 10 years leading up to World War II, 1931–1941. **Chapter 25** focuses on America and World War II, 1941–1945. **Chapter 26** details the beginning of the Cold War, 1945–1960. **Chapter 27** focuses on postwar America, 1945–1960.

Unit Objectives

After studying this unit, students will be able to:

1. Identify events leading up to World War II.
2. Detail the major battles and strategies of World War II.
3. Explain how the Cold War began.
4. Describe life in postwar America.

Why It Matters Activity

Discuss the reasons countries become involved in wars. Ask students to identify places where wars or armed conflicts are currently taking place. Ask students if they think another world war is possible.

UNIT
8 Global Struggles

1931–1960

Why It Matters

The rise of dictatorships in the 1930s led to World War II, the most destructive war in the history of the world. After the war, the fragile alliance between the United States and the Soviet Union collapsed into the Cold War—a period of intense political, economic, and military competition. Learning about the events of this crucial period in our nation's history will help you understand the events occurring in the nation and around the world today. The following resources offer more information about this period in American history.

Primary Sources Library

See pages 1054–1055 for primary source readings to accompany Unit 8.

Use the **American History Primary Source Document Library CD-ROM** to find additional primary sources about global struggles.

Dog tags

American soldier in World War II

704

TEAM TEACHING ACTIVITY

Economics The booming postwar economy affected millions of Americans during 1945–1960 and the effects are still felt today. Cold War military spending, new home construction, and demand for consumer goods all played a role in the healthy economy. Work with the economics teacher to coordinate the study of the economic trends of postwar America.

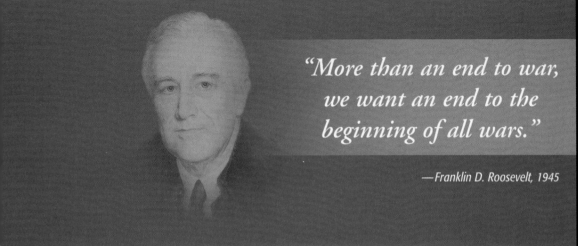

"More than an end to war, we want an end to the beginning of all wars."

—Franklin D. Roosevelt, 1945

GLENCOE TECHNOLOGY

CD-ROM
American History Primary Source Document Library CD-ROM

Use the **American History Primary Source Document Library CD-ROM** to access primary source documents related to this period in history.

More About the Photo

Point out to students that over 400,000 Americans died in World War II. Most Americans personally knew someone who died or was injured during the war—a friend, relative, or neighbor. Have students describe what they see in the photograph and ask them what sacrifices were made by American soldiers. *(Students' answers will vary. They might mention the physical surroundings of the soldier shown in the photograph, time away from family, and the threat of injury or death.)*

Glencoe Literature Library

The following novels from the *High School American History Literature Library* may be used to enrich the study of this unit:

- *And the Earth Did Not Devour Him* by Tomás Rivera
- *A Separate Peace* by John Knowles

SERVICE-LEARNING PROJECT

Organize students into small groups. Have each group use music from the 1930s and 1940s to prepare an "Evening of Musical Entertainment." Arrange for each group to share its program at a local assisted living or nursing home facility. Encourage students to be creative in their presentations. Have each group member write a few paragraphs about his or her experience.

Refer to **Building Bridges: Connecting Classroom and Community through Service-Learning in Social Studies** from the National Council for the Social Studies for information about service-learning.

Timesaving Tools

TeacherWorks™ All-In-One Planner and Resource Center

- **Interactive Teacher Edition** Access your Teacher Wraparound Edition and your classroom resources with a few easy clicks.
- **Interactive Lesson Planner** Planning has never been easier! Organize your week, month, semester, or year with all the lesson helps you need to make teaching creative, timely, and relevant.

Use Glencoe's **Presentation Plus!** multimedia teacher tool to easily present dynamic lessons that visually excite your students. Using Microsoft PowerPoint® you can customize the presentations to create your own personalized lessons.

TEACHING TRANSPARENCIES

Graphic Organizer 4

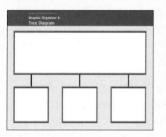

Why It Matters Chapter Transparency 24

APPLICATION AND ENRICHMENT

Linking Past and Present Activity 24

Enrichment Activity 24

Primary Source Reading 24

REVIEW AND REINFORCEMENT

Reteaching Activity 24

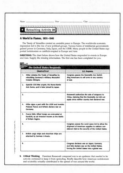

Vocabulary Activity 24

Time Line Activity 24

Critical Thinking Skills Activity 24

Meeting NCSS Standards

The following standards are highlighted in Chapter 24:

Section 1	IX	Global Connections: B, E, F
Section 2	II	Time, Continuity, and Change: B, C
Section 3	X	Civic Ideals and Practices: B, F, G, J
Section 4	IV	Individual Development and Identity: A, C, F

Local Standards

Chapter 24 Resources

ASSESSMENT AND EVALUATION

**Chapter 24 Test
Form A**

**Chapter 24 Test
Form B**

**Standardized Test Skills
Practice Workbook Activity 24**

**Performance Assessment
Activities and Rubrics 24**

**ExamView® Pro
Testmaker CD-ROM**

MULTIMEDIA

- Vocabulary PuzzleMaker CD-ROM
- Interactive Tutor Self-Assessment CD-ROM
- ExamView® Pro Testmaker CD-ROM
- Audio Program
- American History Primary Source Documents Library CD-ROM
- MindJogger Videoquiz
- Presentation Plus! CD-ROM
- TeacherWorks™ CD-ROM
- Interactive Student Edition CD-ROM
- Glencoe Skillbuilder Interactive Workbook CD-ROM, Level 2
- The *American Vision* Video Program
- American Music: Hits Through History
- American Music: Cultural Traditions

SPANISH RESOURCES

The following Spanish language materials are available in the Spanish Resources Binder:

- Spanish Guided Reading Activities
- Spanish Reteaching Activities
- Spanish Quizzes and Tests
- Spanish Vocabulary Activities
- Spanish Summaries
- The Declaration of Independence and United States Constitution Spanish Translation

THE HISTORY CHANNEL®

The following videotape program is available from Glencoe as a supplement to Chapter 24:

- **The War in Europe** (ISBN 1-56-501993-8)

To order, call Glencoe at 1-800-334-7344. To find classroom resources to accompany this video, check the following home pages:
A&E Television: www.aande.com
The History Channel: www.historychannel.com

Use our Web site for additional resources. All essential content is covered in the Student Edition.

You and your students can visit tav.glencoe.com, the Web site companion to the *American Vision.* This innovative integration of electronic and print media offers your students a wealth of opportunities. The student text directs students to the Web site for the following options:

- **Chapter Overviews**
- **Self-Check Quizzes**
- **Student Web Activities**
- **Textbook Updates**

Answers to the student Web activities are provided for you in the **Web Activity Lesson Plans.** Additional Web resources and Interactive Tutor Puzzles are also available.

Chapter 24 Resources

SECTION RESOURCES

Daily Objectives	Reproducible Resources	Multimedia Resources
SECTION 1 **America and the World** 1. Describe how postwar conditions contributed to the rise of antidemocratic governments in Europe. 2. Explain why many Americans supported a policy of isolationism in the 1930s.	Reproducible Lesson Plan 24–1 Daily Lecture and Discussion Notes 24–1 Guided Reading Activity 24–1* Section Quiz 24–1* Reading Essentials and Study Guide 24–1 Performance Assessment Activities and Rubrics Supreme Court Case Studies	Daily Focus Skills Transparency 24–1 Interactive Tutor Self-Assessment CD-ROM ExamView® Pro Testmaker CD-ROM Presentation Plus! CD-ROM TeacherWorks™ CD-ROM Audio Program
SECTION 2 **World War II Begins** 1. Explain why Hitler was able to take over Austria and Czechoslovakia. 2. Describe the early events of the war and why Britain was able to resist the Nazis.	Reproducible Lesson Plan 24–2 Daily Lecture and Discussion Notes 24–2 Guided Reading Activity 24–2* Section Quiz 24–2* Reading Essentials and Study Guide 24–2 Performance Assessment Activities and Rubrics	Daily Focus Skills Transparency 24–2 Interactive Tutor Self-Assessment CD-ROM ExamView® Pro Testmaker CD-ROM Presentation Plus! CD-ROM TeacherWorks™ CD-ROM Audio Program
SECTION 3 **The Holocaust** 1. Describe Nazi prejudices against Jews and early persecution of German Jews. 2. Explain the methods Hitler used to try to exterminate Europe's Jewish population.	Reproducible Lesson Plan 24–3 Daily Lecture and Discussion Notes 24–3 Guided Reading Activity 24–3* Section Quiz 24–3* Reading Essentials and Study Guide 24–3 Performance Assessment Activities and Rubrics	Daily Focus Skills Transparency 24–3 Interactive Tutor Self-Assessment CD-ROM ExamView® Pro Testmaker CD-ROM Presentation Plus! CD-ROM TeacherWorks™ CD-ROM Audio Program ABCNews Interactive™ Historic America Electronic Field Trips
SECTION 4 **America Enters the War** 1. Explain how Roosevelt helped Britain while maintaining official neutrality. 2. Trace the events that led to increasing tensions, and ultimately war, between the United States and Japan.	Reproducible Lesson Plan 24–4 Daily Lecture and Discussion Notes 24–4 Guided Reading Activity 24–4* Section Quiz 24–4* Reading Essentials and Study Guide 24–4 Performance Assessment Activities and Rubrics Interpreting Political Cartoons	Daily Focus Skills Transparency 24–4 Interactive Tutor Self-Assessment CD-ROM ExamView® Pro Testmaker CD-ROM Presentation Plus! CD-ROM Skillbuilder Interactive Workbook, Level 2 TeacherWorks™ CD-ROM Vocabulary PuzzleMaker CD-ROM Audio Program ABCNews Interactive™ Historic America Electronic Field Trips

0:00 OUT OF TIME?
Assign the Chapter 24 **Reading Essentials and Study Guide.**

*Also Available in Spanish

 Blackline Master   Transparency   CD-ROM   DVD

Poster   Music Program   Audio Program   Videocassette

NATIONAL GEOGRAPHIC Teacher's Corner

INDEX TO NATIONAL GEOGRAPHIC MAGAZINE

The following articles relate to this chapter.

- "The Bismarck Found," November 1989
- "Blueprints for Victory," May 1995
- "Douglas MacArthur: An American Soldier," March 1992
- "Pearl Harbor: A Return to the Day of Infamy," December 1991
- "Remembering the Blitz," July 1991

NATIONAL GEOGRAPHIC SOCIETY PRODUCTS AVAILABLE FROM GLENCOE

To order the following products for use with this chapter, contact your local Glencoe sales representative, or call Glencoe at 1-800-334-7344:

- *PictureShow: Story of America, Part 2* (CD-ROM)
- *PicturePack: Story of America Library, Part 2* (Transparencies)

ADDITIONAL NATIONAL GEOGRAPHIC SOCIETY PRODUCTS

To order the following, call National Geographic at 1-800-368-2728:

- *Eyewitness to the 20th Century* (Book)
- *Lost Fleet of Guadalcanal* (Video)

NGS ONLINE

Access National Geographic's Web site for current events, atlas updates, activities, links, interactive features, and archives.
www.nationalgeographic.com

From the Classroom of...

Wendy FitzHenry
Trinity Lutheran School
Bend, OR

Pre-World War II German Family Dilemma

Organize students into "families" with each student assigned a role such as mom, dad, and oldest son. Describe the following scenario to them:

It is 1938. You are a German family who has become close friends with the Jewish family next door. In the past few years, Jewish citizens have had to abide by nightly curfews and have often been the victims of violence. One night, the family asks you if they can hide in your basement.

Discuss their request as a family. Remember, if caught, all of you would be subjected to the same punishment as your Jewish neighbors.

Make a list of difficulties your family would face if you say yes. How would you keep their existence a secret? What about food and clothing? What if you are inspected by German soldiers?

You must make a final decision either yes or no. The dad has the final say. Justify your reason.

ADDITIONAL RESOURCES FROM GLENCOE

- American Music: Cultural Traditions
- American Art & Architecture
- Outline Map Resource Book
- U.S. Desk Map
- Building Geography Skills for Life
- Inclusion for the High School Social Studies Classroom Strategies and Activities
- Teaching Strategies for the American History Classroom (Including Block Scheduling Pacing Guides)

KEY TO ABILITY LEVELS

Teaching strategies have been coded.

L1 BASIC activities for all students
L2 AVERAGE activities for average to above-average students
L3 CHALLENGING activities for above-average students
ELL ENGLISH LANGUAGE LEARNER activities

Block Schedule

Activities that are suited to use within the block scheduling framework are identified by:

Performance Assessment

Refer to Activity 24 in the Performance Assessment Activities and Rubrics booklet.

Why It Matters Activity

Ask students if they would support or oppose U.S. involvement in a conflict between other countries if it might result in a world war. *(Students should give reasons for their positions.)* Point out that the issue of involvement was very important before the onset of World War II.

GLENCOE
TECHNOLOGY

The *American Vision* Video Program

To learn more about this period in U.S. history, have students view the Chapter 24 video, "Holocaust Stories," from the *American Vision* Video Program.

 Available in DVD and VHS

MindJogger Videoquiz

Use the **MindJogger Videoquiz** to preview Chapter 24 content.

 Available in VHS

CHAPTER

24 A World in Flames *1931–1941*

Why It Matters

After World War I, Europe was unstable. Fascists led by Benito Mussolini seized power in Italy, and Adolf Hitler and the Nazis took control of Germany. Meanwhile, Japan expanded its territory in Asia. As the Nazis gained power, they began a campaign of violence against Jews. When Germany attacked Poland, World War II began. The United States clung to neutrality until Japan attacked Pearl Harbor.

The Impact Today

European events of this time serve as lessons for American leaders.
- The danger of ethnic and religious prejudice is more readily recognized than it was before.
- Many American leaders believe that international aggression cannot be ignored.

 The American Vision *Video* The Chapter 24 video, "Holocaust Stories," presents firsthand accounts from survivors of the Holocaust.

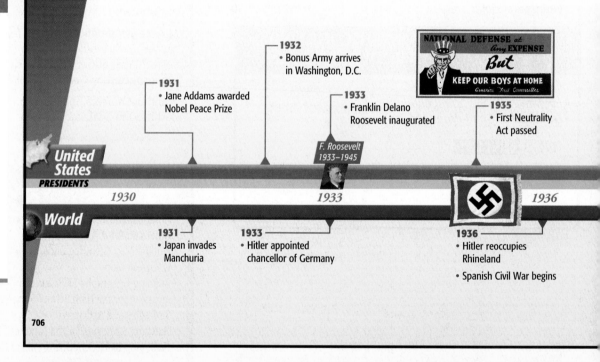

United States PRESIDENTS

1930 — 1933 — 1936

- 1931 • Jane Addams awarded Nobel Peace Prize
- 1932 • Bonus Army arrives in Washington, D.C.
- 1933 • Franklin Delano Roosevelt inaugurated

F. Roosevelt 1933–1945

- 1935 • First Neutrality Act passed

NATIONAL DEFENSE at any EXPENSE But KEEP OUR BOYS AT HOME *America First Committee*

World

- 1931 • Japan invades Manchuria
- 1933 • Hitler appointed chancellor of Germany
- 1936 • Hitler reoccupies Rhineland
  • Spanish Civil War begins

706

TWO-MINUTE LESSON LAUNCHER

Ask students to make a list of the major combatants in World War II—Germany, Japan, and Italy on the Axis side, and Britain, France, the United States, and the Soviet Union on the Allied side. Then use a large world map to have students point out these countries.

German chancellor Adolf Hitler reviews a parade of Nazi troops.

HISTORY
Online

Introduce students to chapter content and key terms by having them access the **Chapter 24 Overview** at tav.glencoe.com.

More About the Photo

Ask students what symbols they see in the photo that are traditionally associated with Hitler or the Third Reich. *(swastika and Hitler's salute)* The swastika, a symbol in the form of a Greek cross with the ends of the arms extended, was used in ancient times to symbolize prosperity and as a good luck symbol. The Nazi Party adopted it as a symbol of its goals of German expansionism and anti-Semitism.

TIME LINE
ACTIVITY

Have students select an event shown on the time line and research more about it. From their research have them write a brief description of the event and the impact it had on American history.

1937
• Neutrality Act bans sale of arms to nations at war

1938
• Munich Conference appeases Hitler

1939
• SS *St. Louis* denied permission to dock in United States

1939
• World War II begins with Hitler's attack on Poland

1940
• Roosevelt makes "destroyers-for-bases" deal with Britain

1940
• France falls to the Nazis

1941
• Roosevelt and Churchill coauthor Atlantic Charter

December 7, 1941
• Japan attacks Pearl Harbor

1939   *1942*

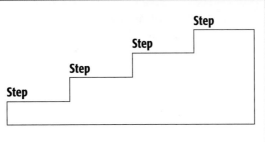

HISTORY
Online

Chapter Overview
Visit the *American Vision* Web site at tav.glencoe.com and click on **Chapter Overviews—Chapter 24** to preview chapter information.

707

GRAPHIC ORGANIZER ACTIVITY

Organizing Information Have students use a graphic organizer like the one shown at right to help them identify the steps that Roosevelt took to aid the Allied cause.

Step

Step

Step

Step

1 FOCUS

Section Overview

This section examines how anti-democratic governments came to power in Europe and Asia.

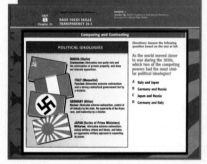
Guide to Reading

Answers to Graphic:

America and the World
I. The Rise of Dictators
   A. Mussolini and Fascism in Italy
   B. Stalin Takes Over the USSR
   C. Hitler and Nazism in Germany
   D. Militarists Gain Control of Japan
II. America Turns to Neutrality

Preteaching Vocabulary

Have students write a paragraph using at least three of the Key Terms and Names.

Guide to Reading

Main Idea
In the years following World War I, aggressive and expansionist governments took power in both Europe and Asia.

Key Terms and Names
Benito Mussolini, fascism, Vladimir Lenin, Joseph Stalin, Adolf Hitler, Manchuria, Neutrality Act of 1935, internationalism

Reading Strategy
Taking Notes As you read about the events in Europe and Asia after World War I, use the major headings of the section to create an outline similar to the one below.

America and the World
I. The Rise of Dictators
   A.
   B.
   C.
   D.
II.

Reading Objectives
• **Describe** how postwar conditions contributed to the rise of antidemocratic governments in Europe.
• **Explain** why many Americans supported a policy of isolationism in the 1930s.

Section Theme
Global Connections German and Japanese actions in the 1930s led President Roosevelt to work to prevent aggression.

Preview of Events

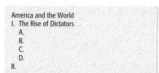

♦1922	♦1927	♦1932	♦1937

1922	1931	1933	1935	1937
Fascist Party takes power in Italy; USSR established	Japan takes control of Manchuria	Hitler takes power in Germany	Congress passes first Neutrality Act	Japan attacks China

★ An American Story ★

Dorothy Thompson

In August 1934, American journalist Dorothy Thompson received an urgent call from the porter at her Berlin hotel. A member of Germany's secret state police wanted to talk to her. Thompson had been reporting on Adolf Hitler's rise to power, and she had written various anti-Nazi articles for the American press. In one she described the beautiful singing she had heard at a Hitler youth camp, where thousands of boys ages 10 to 16 marched and sang. The boys' lovely voices echoing across the hills stirred Thompson, but the words on an enormous banner hanging across one hillside chilled her:

❝It was so prominent that every child could see it many times a day. It was white, and there was a swastika painted on it, and besides that only seven words, seven immense black words: YOU WERE BORN TO DIE FOR GERMANY.❞

When Thompson met with the police, they ordered her to leave Germany immediately. "I, fortunately, am an American," Thompson observed, "so I was merely sent to Paris. Worse things can happen to one."

—quoted in *The Women Who Wrote the War*

The Rise of Dictators

Less than 20 years before the dictatorial German government expelled Dorothy Thompson, the future of democracy in Europe seemed bright. When World War I ended in 1918, President Woodrow Wilson had announced, "Everything for which America fought has been accomplished." Wilson had hoped that the United States could "aid in

708 CHAPTER 24 A World in Flames

SECTION RESOURCES

Reproducible Masters
• Reproducible Lesson Plan 24–1
• Daily Lecture and Discussion Notes 24–1
• Guided Reading Activity 24–1
• Section Quiz 24–1
• Reading Essentials and Study Guide 24–1
• Supreme Court Case Studies

Transparencies
• Daily Focus Skills Transparency 24–1

Multimedia
• Interactive Tutor Self-Assessment CD-ROM
• ExamView® Pro Testmaker CD-ROM
• Presentation Plus! CD-ROM
• TeacherWorks™ CD-ROM
• Audio Program

the establishment of just democracy throughout the world." Instead, the treaty that ended the war, along with the economic depression that followed, contributed to the rise of antidemocratic governments in both Europe and Asia.

Mussolini and Fascism in Italy

One of Europe's first major dictatorships arose in Italy. There, a former schoolmaster and journalist named **Benito Mussolini** returned from World War I convinced that his country needed a strong leader.

In 1919 Mussolini founded Italy's Fascist Party. Fascism was a kind of aggressive nationalism. Fascists believed that the nation was more important than the individual. They argued that individualism made countries weak and that a strong government led by a dictator was needed to impose order on society. Fascists believed a nation became great by expanding its territory and building up its military.

Fascism was also strongly anticommunist. After the Communist revolution in Russia, many Europeans feared that Communists, allied with labor unions, were trying to bring down their governments. Mussolini exploited these fears by portraying fascism as a bulwark against the Communists. Fascism began to stand for the protection of private property and of the middle class. Mussolini also offered the working class full employment and social security. He stressed national prestige, pledging to return Italy to the glories of the Roman Empire.

Backed by the Fascist militia known as the Blackshirts, Mussolini threatened to march on Rome in 1922, claiming he was coming to defend Italy against a Communist revolution. Liberal members of the Italian parliament insisted that the king declare martial law. When he refused, the cabinet resigned. Conservative advisers then persuaded the king to appoint Mussolini as the premier.

Once in office, Mussolini worked quickly to destroy democracy and set up a dictatorship. Weary of strikes and riots, many Italians welcomed Mussolini's leadership. With the support of industrialists, landowners, and the Roman Catholic Church, Mussolini—who took the title of *Il Duce*, or "The Leader"—embarked on an ambitious program of bringing order to Italy.

Stalin Takes Over the USSR

The Communists were a much larger force in Russia than in Italy. After the Russian Revolution began in 1917, the Bolshevik Party, led by **Vladimir Lenin,** established Communist governments throughout the Russian empire. In 1922 they renamed these territories the Union of Soviet Socialist Republics (USSR). They then proceeded to establish control over these territories. To

do this, the Communists instituted one-party rule, suppressed individual liberties, and punished opponents. After Lenin died in 1924, a power struggle began. By 1926, **Joseph Stalin** had become the new Soviet dictator. In 1928 Stalin began a massive effort to industrialize his country. Tolerating no opposition, the effort brought about the deaths of 8 to 10 million peasants who resisted the Communist policies.

Hitler and Nazism in Germany

Adolf Hitler was a fervent anticommunist and an admirer of Mussolini. Hitler had fought for Germany in World War I. Germany's surrender and the subsequent Versailles Treaty left him and many other Germans with a smoldering hatred for the victorious Allies and for the German government that had accepted the peace terms.

The political and economic chaos in postwar Germany led to the rise of new political parties. One of these was the National Socialist German Workers' Party, or the **Nazi Party.** The party did not represent the working class, as its name suggested, but was nationalistic and anticommunist. Adolf Hitler was one of the party's first recruits.

In November 1923, the Nazis tried to seize power by marching on city hall in Munich, Germany. Hitler intended to seize power locally

Picturing History

Supreme Soviets Joseph Stalin (right) took over control of the Soviet Union after Lenin's death in 1924. He was determined to modernize and industrialize his nation. **How many people died while opposing Stalin's leadership?**

2 TEACH

Daily Lecture and Discussion Notes 24–1

Copyright © by The McGraw-Hill Companies, Inc.

Daily Lecture and Discussion Notes

Chapter 24, Section 1

Did You Know? After World War I, money in Germany became nearly worthless because of high inflation. Some Germans burned money for fuel to symbolize the little value of German money.

I. The Rise of Dictators (pages 708–710)

A. The treaty that ended World War I and the economic depression that followed contributed to the rise of dictatorships in Europe and Asia.

B. Italy developed the first major dictatorship in Europe. In 1919 Benito Mussolini founded Italy's Fascist Party. Fascism was a kind of aggressive nationalism. Fascists believed that the nation was more important than the individual, and that a nation became great by expanding its territory and building up its military. Fascists were

Comparing Have students compare the goals of Mussolini and Hitler. Ask students: **What objectives did the two leaders have in common?** (desire for a totalitarian state, building up the military, and territorial expansion) **L1**

Political Symbols The word *fascist* comes from the Latin word *fasces,* or the rods and axes that Roman officials carried in ancient times to represent their authority.

Picturing History

Answer: 8 to 10 million people
Ask: How did the Bolsheviks establish control over the territories of the former Russian Empire? *(They established Communist governments, instituted one-party rule, suppressed individual liberties, and punished opponents.)*

 Use *Supreme Court Case Study 15, DeJonge* v. *Oregon.*

COOPERATIVE LEARNING ACTIVITY

Identifying Central Issues Organize students into groups of three. Ask each student to play one of the following: Tojo, Hitler, or Mussolini. Have each group discuss the growth of dictatorships in Japan, Germany, and Italy, listing reasons for aggressive policies in the early to mid-1930s. During class discussion, have one person from each group share his or her list.

Use the rubric for a cooperative group management plan on pages 81–82 in the **Performance Assessment Activities and Rubrics.**

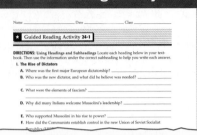
Writing an Editorial Tell students to choose an internationalist or isolationist point of view. Have students write a newspaper editorial expressing their point of view while trying to convince readers to join with them. Have students present their editorials to the class. **L2**

FYI

A section of Amy Tan's popular novel *The Joy Luck Club* was set during the troubles between China and Japan during the 1930s.

Picturing History

Answer: Both were extreme nationalists who wanted to expand their territories and build up their military.

✓ Reading Check

Answer: Political inequities caused by the Versailles Treaty ending World War I fueled nationalism. Widespread economic depression and social unrest created desperation among the people for new, stronger leadership. Dictators were able to capitalize on these feelings to seize control of governments.

and then march on Berlin, the German capital, but the plan failed and Hitler was arrested.

While in prison, Hitler wrote his autobiography, titled *Mein Kampf* ("My Struggle"). In the book, Hitler called for the unification of all Germans under one government. He claimed that Germans, particularly blond, blue-eyed Germans, belonged to a "master race" called Aryans. He argued that Germans needed more lebensraum, or living space, and called for Germany to expand east into Poland and Russia. According to Hitler, the Slavic people of Eastern Europe belonged to an inferior race, which Germans should enslave. Hitler's racism was strongest, however, toward Jews. He believed that Jews were responsible for many of the world's problems, especially for Germany's defeat in World War I.

After his release from prison, Hitler changed his tactics. Instead of trying to seize power violently, he focused on getting Nazis elected to the Reichstag, the lower house of the German parliament. When the Great Depression struck Germany, many desperate Germans began to vote for radical parties, including the Nazis and Communists. By 1932 the Nazis were the largest party in the Reichstag.

Many traditional German leaders supported Hitler's nationalism. They believed that if they helped Hitler become leader of Germany legally, they could control him. In 1933 the German president appointed Hitler as chancellor, or prime minister.

After taking office, Hitler called for new elections. He then ordered the police to crack down on the Socialist and Communist Parties. Storm Troopers, as

Picturing History

Meeting of Minds Mussolini and Hitler are shown here meeting in October 1940. *What beliefs did they share?*

the Nazi paramilitary units were called, began intimidating voters. After the election, the Reichstag, dominated by the Nazis and other right-wing parties, voted to give Hitler dictatorial powers. In 1934 Hitler became president, which gave him control of the army. He then gave himself the new title of führer, or "leader." The following year, he began to rebuild Germany's military, in violation of the Treaty of Versailles.

Militarists Gain Control of Japan In Japan, as in Germany, difficult economic times helped undermine the political system. Japanese industries had to import nearly all of the resources they needed to produce goods. During the 1920s, Japan did not earn enough money from its exports to pay for its imports, which limited economic growth and increased unemployment. When the Depression struck, other countries raised their tariffs. This made the situation even worse.

Many Japanese military officers blamed the country's problems on corrupt politicians. Most officers believed that Japan was destined to dominate East Asia. Many also believed that democracy was "un-Japanese" and bad for the country.

Japanese military leaders and the civilians who supported them argued that the only way for Japan to get needed resources was to seize territory. They targeted the resource-rich province of **Manchuria** in northern China as the perfect place to conquer.

A group of Japanese officers decided to act without the government's permission. In September 1931, the Japanese army invaded Manchuria. After the invasion began, the Japanese government tried to end the war, but when the Japanese prime minister began negotiations, officers assassinated him. From that point forward, the military was effectively in control. Although Japan still had a civilian government, it now supported the nationalist policy of expanding the empire, and it appointed several military officers to serve as prime minister.

✓ Reading Check

Examining How did postwar conditions contribute to the rise of dictatorships in Europe?

MEETING SPECIAL NEEDS

Visual/Spatial Have students create a thematic map of Europe that shows the territorial changes included in the Treaty of Versailles. Include new countries created, land gained by Italy, France, Belgium, and Denmark, and demilitarized areas. Have students use their maps to explain why Germany felt slighted by the treaty and how that affected later events. **L2**

📁 Refer to *Inclusion for the High School Social Studies Classroom Strategies and Activities* in the TCR.

America Turns to Neutrality

The rise of dictatorships and militarism after World War I discouraged many Americans. The sacrifices they had made during the war seemed pointless. Once again, Americans began to support isolationism, or the belief that the United States should avoid international commitments that might drag the nation into another war.

The Nye Committee Isolationist ideas became even stronger in the early 1930s for two reasons. When the Depression began, many European nations found it difficult to repay money they had borrowed during World War I. In June 1934, all of the debtor nations except Finland announced they would no longer repay their war debts.

At about the same time, dozens of books and articles appeared arguing that arms manufacturers had tricked the United States into entering World War I. In 1934 Senator Gerald P. Nye of North Dakota held hearings to investigate the country's involvement in World War I. The **Nye Committee** documented the huge profits that arms factories had made during the war. The report created the impression that these businesses influenced the United States to go to war. The European refusal to repay their loans and the Nye Committee's findings turned even more Americans toward isolationism.

Legislating Neutrality Worried that growing German and Italian aggression might lead to war, Congress passed the **Neutrality Act of 1935.** Based on the belief that arms sales had helped bring the United States into World War I, the act made it illegal for Americans to sell arms to any country at war.

In 1936 a rebellion erupted in Spain after a coalition of Republicans, Socialists, and Communists was elected. General **Francisco Franco** led the rebellion. Franco was backed by the Falangists, or Spanish Fascists, army officers, landowners, and Catholic Church leaders.

The revolt quickly became a civil war and attracted worldwide attention. The Soviet Union provided arms and advisers to the government forces, while Germany and Italy sent tanks, airplanes, and soldiers to help Franco. To keep the United States neutral, Congress passed another neutrality act, banning the sale of arms to either side in a civil war.

Shortly after the **Spanish Civil War** began in 1936, Hitler and Mussolini signed an agreement pledging to cooperate on several international issues. Mussolini referred to this new relationship with Germany as the Rome-Berlin Axis. The following month, Japan aligned itself with Germany and Italy when it signed the **Anti-Comintern Pact** with Germany. The pact required the two countries to exchange information about Communist groups. Together Germany, Italy, and Japan became known as the **Axis Powers,** although they did not formally become allies until September 1940.

With the situation in Europe getting worse, Congress passed the Neutrality Act of 1937. This act continued the ban on selling arms to nations at war, but it also required warring countries to buy nonmilitary supplies from the United States on a "cash-and-carry" basis. If a country at war wanted goods from the United States, it had to send its own ships to pick up the goods, and it had to pay cash. Loans were not allowed. Isolationists knew that attacks on neutral American ships carrying supplies to Europe had helped bring the country into World War I. They were determined to prevent it from happening again.

LA GARRA DEL INVASOR ITALIANO PRETENDE ESCLAVIZARNOS

Picturing History

Anti-Fascist Propaganda Spanish general Francisco Franco led the Fascist rebellion that received support from Hitler and Mussolini. This poster translates to "The claw of the Italian invader intends to make slaves of us." How did the United States respond to these events?

Picturing History

Answer: Congress passed another neutrality act, extending the ban on selling arms to countries at war to include both sides of a civil war.
Ask: How did the Soviet Communists and Italian and German Fascists support similar groups in Spain during the Spanish Civil War? *(The Soviet Union provided arms and advisers to the republican government forces; Germany and Italy sent tanks, airplanes, and soldiers to help Franco and the Fascists.)*

3 ASSESS

Assign Section 1 Assessment as homework or as an in-class activity.

Have students use the **Interactive Tutor Self-Assessment CD-ROM.**

Reading Essentials and Study Guide 24–1

Name _____ Date _____ Class _____

Study Guide

Chapter 24, Section 1

For use with textbook pages 708–712

AMERICA AND THE WORLD

KEY TERMS AND NAMES

Benito Mussolini Fascist dictator of Italy (page 709)
fascism a kind of aggressive nationalism (page 709)
Vladimir Lenin leader of the Bolshevik Party in Russia (page 709)
Joseph Stalin dictator of the Soviet Union (page 709)
Adolf Hitler Nazi leader of Germany (page 709)
Manchuria province in northern China (page 710)
Neutrality Act of 1935 law that made it illegal for Americans to sell arms to any country at war (page 711)

Section Quiz 24–1

Name _____ Date _____ Class _____

★ **Chapter 24** Score ____

Section Quiz 24–1

DIRECTIONS: Matching Match each item in Column A with the items in Column B. Write the correct letters in the blanks. *(10 points each)*

Column A
___ 1. Germany, Italy, and Japan
___ 2. idea that a country should focus on its own problems and avoid international commitments
___ 3. Adolph Hitler's autobiography written while he was in prison
___ 4. a kind of aggressive nationalism
___ 5. resource-rich province of China invaded by the Japanese army

Column B
A. isolationism
B. Axis Powers
C. fascism
D. Mein Kampf
E. Manchuria

DIRECTIONS: Multiple Choice In the blank at the left, write the letter of the choice

INTERDISCIPLINARY CONNECTIONS ACTIVITY

Life Skills Have students choose a leader from this period and create a résumé that includes pertinent details of the leader's education, career experience, political offices held, and major events in which the person participated. Also have them include any skills, activities, and memberships that might present a fuller picture of the person. Possible subjects include Adolf Hitler, Benito Mussolini, Joseph Stalin, Hideki Tojo, Winston Churchill, and Franklin Roosevelt. **L2**

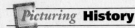
Reteach

Ask students to summarize how postwar conditions affected the rise of dictatorships in Europe.

Enrich

Have students borrow or rent the video *For Whom the Bell Tolls.* Have them write a few paragraphs related to the film on the themes of isolationism and neutrality. Discuss these themes in class and how they relate to the period between World War I and World War II.

Reading Check

Answer: They felt remaining apart from European conflicts would avoid another war.

4 CLOSE

Have students draw a political cartoon that expresses the feelings of internationalists or isolationists.

GOVERNMENT

Roosevelt and Internationalism When he took office in 1933, President Roosevelt declared that "our international relations, though vastly important, are in point of time and necessity secondary to the establishment of a sound national economy." Roosevelt knew that ending the Depression was his first priority, but he was not an isolationist. He supported internationalism, the idea that trade between nations creates prosperity and helps to prevent war. Internationalists also believed the United States should try to preserve peace in the world.

Roosevelt supported internationalism but knew that the public wanted neutrality. He warned that the neutrality acts "might drag us into war instead of keeping us out," but he did not veto the bills. Isolationism was too strong to resist.

In July 1937, Japanese forces in Manchuria launched a full-scale attack on China. Roosevelt decided to help the Chinese. Since neither China nor Japan had actually declared war, Roosevelt claimed the Neutrality Act of 1937 did not apply, and he authorized the sale of weapons to China. He warned that the nation should not stand by and let an "epidemic of lawlessness" infect the world:

66When an epidemic of physical disease starts to spread, the community . . . joins in a quarantine of the patients in order to protect the health of the community against the spread of the disease. . . . War is a contagion, whether it be declared or undeclared. . . . There is no escape through mere isolation or neutrality. . . .99

—quoted in *Freedom from Fear*

 *Picturing* **History**

Imperial Expansion In 1931 Japan occupied the northeast Chinese province of Manchuria. In 1937 the Japanese invaded all of China, prompting FDR to authorize the sale of arms to the Chinese Army. How did Roosevelt justify his actions in light of the Neutrality Act?

Despite Roosevelt's words, Americans were still not willing to risk another war to stop aggression overseas. "It is a terrible thing," the president said, "to look over your shoulder when you are trying to lead—and find no one there."

Reading Check **Evaluating** Why did many Americans support isolationism?

SECTION 1 ASSESSMENT

Checking for Understanding
1. **Define:** fascism, internationalism.
2. **Identify:** Benito Mussolini, Vladimir Lenin, Joseph Stalin, Adolf Hitler, Manchuria, Neutrality Act of 1935.
3. **Explain** why isolationism was strong in the United States in the early 1930s.

Reviewing Themes
4. **Global Connections** What events caused President Roosevelt to become more of an internationalist?

Critical Thinking
5. **Interpreting** Why did antidemocratic governments rise to power in postwar Europe and Asia?
6. **Categorizing** Use a graphic organizer similar to the one below to compare the antidemocratic governments that arose in Europe and Asia.

Country	Dictator	Ideology

Analyzing Visuals
7. **Analyzing Art** Study the Spanish Civil War era propaganda poster reproduced on page 711. Without being told the phrase, how would you be able to discover the poster's meaning?

Writing About History
8. **Persuasive Writing** Write a newspaper editorial urging fellow citizens to embrace either isolationism or internationalism after World War I. Be certain to include reasons your readers should back a specific position.

SECTION 1 ASSESSMENT ANSWERS

1. Terms are in blue.
2. Benito Mussolini (*p. 709*), Vladimir Lenin (*p. 709*), Joseph Stalin (*p. 709*), Adolf Hitler (*p. 709*), Manchuria (*p. 710*), Neutrality Act of 1935 (*p. 711*)
3. unpaid European war debts; belief that arms manufacturers influenced U.S. to enter World War I
4. Japanese invasion of China
5. unhappiness with Treaty of Versailles terms; worldwide economic depression
6. Italy: Mussolini, Fascism; USSR: Stalin, Communism; Germany: Hitler, Nazism; Japan: Japanese military, militarism
7. a cruel claw-like hand is trying to grasp the country; colors of Italian flag superimposed on hand
8. Answers will vary but should include text material.

Guide to Reading

Main Idea
World War II officially began with the Nazi invasion of Poland and the French and British declaration of war on Germany in September 1939.

Key Terms and Names
Anschluss, appeasement, blitzkrieg, Maginot Line, Winston Churchill, Battle of Britain

Reading Strategy
Sequencing As you read about the events leading up to the beginning of World War II, record them by completing a time line similar to the one below.

| 1937 | March 1938 | Oct. 1938 | Aug. 1939 | Sept. 1939 |
| Feb. 1938 | Sept. 1938 | March 1939 | | |

Reading Objectives
• **Explain** why Hitler was able to take over Austria and Czechoslovakia.
• **Describe** the early events of the war and why Britain was able to resist the Nazis.

Section Theme
Continuity and Change The desire of the French and British to avoid another war helped encourage Hitler's aggression in Europe.

Preview of Events

| ♦1938 | ♦1939 | ♦1940 | ♦1941 |

March 1938
Hitler announces German-Austrian unification

August 1939
Hitler and Stalin sign Nazi-Soviet pact

September 1939
World War II begins

June 1940
France surrenders to Germany

August 1940
Battle of Britain begins

 ★ *An American Story* ★

In February 1940, President Franklin Roosevelt sent Undersecretary of State Sumner Welles to Europe to report on the political situation. A few months earlier, Germany had invaded Poland, and Roosevelt hoped to negotiate peace before wider hostilities erupted.

In Italy Welles found Mussolini intent on war and judged that "there was not the slightest chance of any successful negotiation." In Paris Welles glumly noted the "sullen apathy" in people's faces and concluded that France had little will to resist a German onslaught. After speaking to Hitler, Welles concluded that a negotiated peace settlement was impossible: "It was only too tragically plain that all decisions had already been made." In London, Welles did not feel the sense of doom he had in Paris. The British, he reported, would "fight to the very last ditch." Welles later reflected on his mission:

Sumner Welles

66Only one thing could have deflected Hitler from his purpose: the sure knowledge that the power of the United States would be directed against him if he attempted to carry out his intention of conquering the world by force. . . . At that time no representative of this government could have been authorized to intimate any such thing. . . . My mission, therefore, was a forlorn hope.99

—quoted in *Roosevelt and Churchill*

"Peace in Our Time"

Whether or not the United States could have forced Hitler to negotiate is uncertain. By 1940 the German army had been rebuilt, and Hitler was bent on conquest. What is known is that in the years before Welles visited Europe, when the Nazi regime was

CHAPTER 24 A World in Flames **713**

---

1 FOCUS

Section Overview
This section focuses on the beginning of World War II in Europe.

BELLRINGER
Skillbuilder Activity

Project transparency and have students answer the question.

Available as a blackline master.

Daily Focus Skills Transparency 24–2

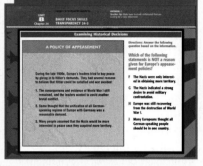

Guide to Reading

Answers to Graphic: Hitler calls for German unity; Hitler threatens to invade Austria; the *Anschluss*; Germany claims Sudetenland; Germany demands return of Danzig; Germany annexes Czechoslovakia; Nazi-Soviet Nonaggression Pact; Germany invades Poland

Preteaching Vocabulary
Assign one of the Key Terms and Names to each student. Have each student prepare a 30-second oral presentation related to the selected term or name.

SECTION RESOURCES

📁 Reproducible Masters
• Reproducible Lesson Plan 24–2
• Daily Lecture and Discussion Notes 24–2
• Guided Reading Activity 24–2
• Section Quiz 24–2
• Reading Essentials and Study Guide 24–2
• Performance Assessment Activities and Rubrics

📽 Transparencies
• Daily Focus Skills Transparency 24–2

Multimedia
🔘 Interactive Tutor Self-Assessment CD-ROM
🔘 ExamView® Pro Testmaker CD-ROM
🔘 Presentation Plus! CD-ROM
🔘 TeacherWorks™ CD-ROM
🔘 Audio Program

2 TEACH

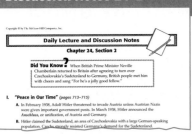
Organizing Information Have the students make a list of the regions or countries that Germany annexed or invaded between 1935 and 1941. *(Rhineland, Austria, Sudetenland, Czechoslovakia, Polish Corridor, Poland, Norway, Denmark, the Netherlands, Belgium, Luxembourg, France)* Ask students what some of the motivations were for expanding the territory. *(Answers will vary but should include the unification of German-speaking peoples, lebensraum, and access to more natural resources.)* **L1**

The Baltic city of Gdansk (Danzig in German) has alternated through its history between being a politically free city, or part of Poland or German-speaking Prussia. It was a part of Prussia until the Treaty of Versailles, when it became a free city again. Identification with Germany has been strong however. In the 1930s, Nazi officials were voted into the majority of the city assembly. Gunter Grass writes of this era in his book *The Tin Drum.*

Appeasement in Action At Munich in September 1938, Mussolini (second from left), Britain's Neville Chamberlain (left), and Hitler (second from right) were among those deciding Czechoslovakia's fate.

much weaker, European leaders did not try to stop Hitler. Instead, they vainly tried to buy peace by giving in to his demands.

Europe's leaders had several reasons for believing—or wanting to believe—that Hitler could be satisfied and war avoided. First, the shadow of World War I loomed large, making many leaders fearful of another bloody conflict. Second, some thought Hitler's demand that all German-speaking regions of Europe be united with Germany was reasonable. Third, many people assumed that the Nazis would be more interested in peace once they gained more territory.

The Austrian *Anschluss* Hitler's first demands concerned Austria and Czechoslovakia. In late 1937 Hitler stepped up his call for the unification of all German-speaking people, including those in Austria and Czechoslovakia. Seizing Austria and Czechoslovakia would also gain food supplies, defensible frontiers, and soldiers for Germany. Hitler believed that Germany could only expand its territory by "resort[ing] to force with its attendant risks."

In February 1938 Hitler threatened to invade German-speaking Austria, his native land, unless Austrian Nazis were given important government posts. Austria's chancellor quickly gave in to this demand. Several weeks later, the chancellor tried to put the matter of unification with Germany to a democratic vote. Fearing the outcome, Hitler sent troops into Austria in March and announced the *Anschluss,* or unification, of Austria and Germany.

The Munich Crisis and Appeasement Shortly after Germany annexed Austria, Hitler announced German claims to the Sudetenland, an area of Czechoslovakia with a large German-speaking

population. Since Austrians shared a common culture and language with Germany, many people had accepted the *Anschluss.* In Czechoslovakia, on the other hand, people spoke several different languages. In addition, while Austria had an authoritarian government, Czechoslovakia was a democracy. Furthermore, Austria had no allies to help it defend itself, but Czechoslovakia was allied with France and the Soviet Union.

The Czechs strongly resisted Germany's demands for the Sudetenland. France threatened to fight if Germany attacked, and the Soviet Union also promised assistance. British prime minister **Neville Chamberlain** publicly promised to support France, Britain's ally.

To prevent another war, representatives of Britain, France, Italy, and Germany agreed to meet in Munich to decide Czechoslovakia's fate. At the Munich Conference on September 29, 1938, Britain and France agreed to Hitler's demands, a policy that came to be known as appeasement. Appeasement is the policy of giving concessions in exchange for peace. Supporters of appeasement mistakenly believed that Hitler had a few limited demands. They felt that if they gave Hitler what he wanted, he would be satisfied and war would be avoided. Czechoslovakia was informed that it must give up the Sudetenland or fight Germany on its own.

Chamberlain had gambled that sacrificing part of Czechoslovakia would satisfy Hitler. He also knew that Britain's military was not ready for war, so he was buying time. When Chamberlain returned home he promised "a peace with honor . . . peace in our time," but he also began to speed up British rearmament.

The following March, in brazen violation of the Munich agreement, Germany sent troops into Czechoslovakia and broke up the country. Slovakia became independent in name, but it was actually a satellite state under German control. The Czech lands became a German protectorate.

Danzig and the Polish Corridor After the Munich conference, Hitler turned his sights on Poland. In October 1938 he demanded the return of Danzig, a Baltic Sea port with strong German roots, to German control. Although Danzig was more than 90 percent German, it had been separated from Germany at the end of World War I to give Poland access to the sea. Hitler also requested a highway and railroad across the Polish Corridor, which separated western Germany from the German state of East Prussia.

Hitler's demands on Poland convinced the British and French that appeasement had failed. On March 31,

COOPERATIVE LEARNING ACTIVITY

Preparing a News Broadcast Organize the class into small groups. Assign one of the following to each group: the Austrian *Anschluss,* the Munich Conference, the Nazi-Soviet Nonaggression Pact, the invasion of Poland, the invasion of France, and the evacuation of Dunkirk. Have each group create a brief television news broadcast covering that event. If possible allow the students to videotape the stories in chronological order and play the videotape for the class.

Use the rubric for a cooperative group management plan on pages 81–82 in the *Performance Assessment Activities and Rubrics.*

1939, the British announced that if Poland went to war to defend its territory, Britain and France would come to its aid. This encouraged the Polish government to refuse Hitler's demands.

In May 1939, Hitler ordered the German army to prepare to invade Poland. He also ordered his foreign minister to begin negotiations with the USSR. If Germany was going to fight Britain and France, Hitler did not want to have to fight the Soviets too.

The Nazi-Soviet Nonaggression Pact When German officials proposed a nonaggression treaty to the Soviets, Stalin agreed. He believed the best way to protect the USSR was to turn the capitalist nations against each other. If the treaty worked, Germany would go to war against Britain and France, and the USSR would be safe.

On August 23, 1939, Germany and the USSR signed the nonaggression pact. The Nazi-Soviet pact shocked the world. Communism and Nazism were supposed to be totally opposed to each other. Leaders in Britain and France understood, however,

that Hitler had made the deal to free himself for war against their countries and Poland. What they did not know was that the treaty also contained a secret deal between Germany and the Soviet Union to divide Poland between them.

✓ **Reading Check** **Explaining** What were three reasons European leaders agreed to a policy of appeasement?

The War Begins

On September 1, 1939, Germany invaded Poland from the west, and soon after the Soviets invaded from the east. On September 3, Britain and France declared war on Germany, marking the start of World War II.

Blitzkrieg in Poland Poland bravely resisted Germany's onslaught, but to no avail. The Germans used a new type of warfare called blitzkrieg, or lightning war. Blitzkrieg used large numbers of massed tanks to break through and rapidly encircle enemy

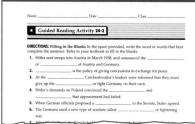

Guided Reading Activity 24–2

Name _____ Date _____ Class _____

★ **Guided Reading Activity 24-2**

DIRECTIONS: Filling in the Blanks In the space provided, write the word or words that best complete the sentence. Refer to your textbook to fill in the blanks.

1. Hitler sent troops into Austria in March 1938, and announced the _____ or _____ of Austria and Germany.
2. _____ is the policy of giving concessions in exchange for peace.
3. At the _____, Czechoslovakia's leaders were informed that they must give up the _____ or fight Germany on their own.
4. Hitler's demands on Poland convinced the _____ and _____ that appeasement had failed.
5. When German officials proposed a _____ to the Soviets, Stalin agreed.
6. The Germans used a new type of warfare called _____, or lightening war.
7. After World War I, the French had _____

✓ **Reading Check**

Answer: wished to avoid war; the goal of unifying German-speaking regions seemed reasonable; thought the Nazis would be more interested in peace once they acquired more territory

Expressing an Opinion Ask students to reread this section and assess whether appeasement was justified. **L2**

Geography Skills

Answers:
1. Vichy
2. It was nearly surrounded by Germany and German-controlled Austria.

Geography Skills Practice
Ask: Why was Hitler interested in negotiating the nonaggression pact with the USSR before invading Poland? *(Germany did not want to fight a war on its eastern and western fronts simultaneously.)*

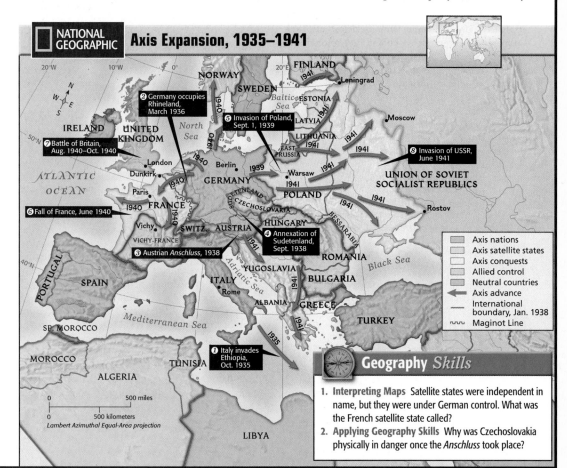

NATIONAL GEOGRAPHIC — **Axis Expansion, 1935–1941**

- ② Germany occupies Rhineland, March 1936
- ⑤ Invasion of Poland, Sept. 1, 1939
- ⑦ Battle of Britain, Aug. 1940–Oct. 1940
- ⑧ Invasion of USSR, June 1941
- ⑥ Fall of France, June 1940
- ④ Annexation of Sudetenland, Sept. 1938
- ③ Austrian *Anschluss*, 1938
- ① Italy invades Ethiopia, Oct. 1935

Legend:
- Axis nations
- Axis satellite states
- Axis conquests
- Allied control
- Neutral countries
- → Axis advance
- International boundary, Jan. 1938
- ∿∿∿ Maginot Line

0 — 500 miles
0 — 500 kilometers
Lambert Azimuthal Equal-Area projection

Geography Skills

1. **Interpreting Maps** Satellite states were independent in name, but they were under German control. What was the French satellite state called?
2. **Applying Geography Skills** Why was Czechoslovakia physically in danger once the *Anschluss* took place?

MEETING SPECIAL NEEDS

Verbal/Linguistic Have students imagine that they are newspaper editors in London at the time of the Munich crisis. Have students write an editorial supporting or opposing Neville Chamberlain's actions, especially his agreement to the policy of appeasement. Have students review newspaper editorials for proper style. **L2**

📁 Refer to *Inclusion for the High School Social Studies Classroom Strategies and Activities* in the TCR.

Creating a Thematic Map Have students research and map the Maginot Line and the Siegfried Line. During World War II the Siegfried Line was a defensive line in western Germany along the border between Germany and France. Ask the students to discover when the plan was put forward and by whom, what was proposed, why more of the planned fortifications were not built, and why, ultimately, the line did not achieve its purpose.

 Use the rubric for creating a map, display, or chart on pages 77–78 in the *Performance Assessment Activities and Rubrics.*

FYI

At the time of the invasion, the Polish military consisted of outdated infantry and horse cavalry. They were ineffectual against the 1,500 planes, including *Stuka* dive bombers, and the panzers, or German tanks. Also, they were not prepared for their invaders, whom Hitler had instructed to "close their hearts to pity."

Fact	Fiction	Folklore

Despite the success of the evacuation of Dunkirk, Churchill warned Parliament, "Wars are not won by evacuations."

---

positions. Supporting the tanks were waves of aircraft that bombed enemy positions and dropped paratroopers to cut their supply lines. Blitzkrieg depended on radios to coordinate the tanks and aircraft. The Polish army was unable to cope with the German attack. On September 27, the Polish capital of Warsaw fell to the Germans. By October 5, 1939, the Polish army had been defeated.

GEOGRAPHY

The Fall of France In contrast to the war in Poland, western Europe remained eerily quiet. The Germans referred to this situation as the *sitzkrieg,* or sitting war. The British called it the "Bore War," while American newspapers nicknamed it the "Phony War." The British had sent troops to France, but both countries remained on the defensive, waiting for the Germans to attack.

After World War I, the French had built a line of concrete bunkers and fortifications called the **Maginot Line** along the German border. Rather than risk their troops by attacking, the French preferred to wait behind the Maginot Line for the Germans to approach. Unfortunately, this decision allowed Germany to concentrate on Poland first before turning west to face the British and French.

After taking Poland, Hitler and his generals decided to attack Norway and Denmark before invading France. Germany's industry depended on iron ore from Sweden that had to be shipped down Norway's coast part of the year. If the British sent

Fact	Fiction	Folklore

The Battle of Dunkirk Hitler's invasion of Poland fueled the fears of Americans who preferred not to become involved in Europe's conflict. In contrast, the evacuation from Dunkirk less than a year later generated very different reactions. For example, soon after the evacuation, the *New York Times* wrote:

> ❝So long as the English tongue survives, the word Dunkirk will be spoken with reverence. For in that harbor, in such a hell as never blazed on earth before, at the end of a lost battle, the rages and blemishes that have hidden the soul of democracy fell away. There, beaten but unconquered, in shining splendor, she faced the enemy.❞

Indeed, the Battle of Dunkirk would soon help to lift the United States out of its isolationism.

---

troops to Norway, they could block the iron shipments. On April 9, 1940, the attack began, and within a month, Germany controlled both countries.

With his northern flank secure, Hitler turned his attention to France. Hitler planned to go around the Maginot Line, which protected France's border with Germany but not France's border with Belgium and Luxembourg. To get around the Maginot Line, the Germans would have to invade the Netherlands, Belgium, and Luxembourg first—which is exactly what they did. On May 10, Hitler launched a new blitzkrieg in the west. While German troops parachuted into the Netherlands, an army of tanks rolled into Belgium and Luxembourg.

The British and French had expected the German attack. As soon as it began, British and French forces raced north into Belgium. This was a mistake. Instead of sending their tanks through the open countryside of central Belgium, the Germans sent their main force through the Ardennes Mountains of Luxembourg and eastern Belgium. The French did not think that large numbers of tanks could move through the mountains, and they had left only a few troops to defend that part of the border. The Germans easily smashed through the French lines, then raced west across northern France to the English Channel. The British and French armies were still in Belgium and could not move back into France quickly enough. They were now trapped in Belgium.

The Miracle at Dunkirk After trapping the Allied forces in Belgium, the Germans began to drive them toward the English Channel. The only hope for Britain and France was to evacuate their surviving troops by sea, but the Germans had captured all but one port, **Dunkirk,** a small town in northern France near the Belgian border.

As German forces closed in on Dunkirk, Hitler suddenly ordered them to stop. No one is sure why he gave this order. Historians know that Hitler was nervous about risking his tank forces, and he wanted to wait until more infantry arrived. Hermann Goering, the head of the German air force, was also assuring Hitler that aircraft alone could destroy the trapped soldiers. There is also some evidence that Hitler thought that the British would be more willing to accept peace if the Germans did not humiliate them by destroying their forces at Dunkirk.

Whatever Hitler's reasons, his order provided a three-day delay. This gave the British time to strengthen their lines and begin the evacuation. Some 850 ships of all sizes, from navy warships to small sailboats operated by civilian volunteers, headed to

---

INTERDISCIPLINARY CONNECTIONS ACTIVITY

Literature Locate a copy of Paul Gallico's short story *The Snow Goose.* The story describes how a disabled man in England was able to help with the evacuation of Dunkirk. Read the story to the students. Ask them to prepare a written response describing how the story made them feel and why they think that so many citizens wanted to find a way to contribute to the war effort. **L3**

NATIONAL GEOGRAPHIC
MOMENT in HISTORY

NEVER GIVE IN

Few photographs capture the British resolve to keep a stiff upper lip better than this one. Night after night between September 1940 and May 1941, German warplanes rained bombs on London, Coventry, and other British cities. The attacks were intended to destroy British morale and war production, but Royal Air Force pilots shot down bombers faster than Germany could replace them. Plucky British civilians, like this milkman making his rounds through a debris-strewn London street, remained determined to carry on as usual each morning.

NATIONAL GEOGRAPHIC
MOMENT in HISTORY

Ask: What does this picture symbolize? (*British determination to live their usual lives despite the war*)

3 ASSESS

Assign Section 2 Assessment as homework or as an in-class activity.

⬤ Have students use the **Interactive Tutor Self-Assessment CD-ROM.**

Reading Essentials and Study Guide 24–2

Name _____ Date _____ Class _____

Study Guide

Chapter 24, Section 2
For use with textbook pages 713–718

WORLD WAR II BEGINS

KEY TERMS AND NAMES

Anschluss the unification of Austria and Germany *(page 714)*
appeasement giving concessions in exchange for peace *(page 714)*
blitzkrieg lightning war *(page 715)*
Maginot Line a line of bunkers and fortifications built by the French along the German border *(page 716)*
Winston Churchill prime minister of Great Britain *(page 717)*
Battle of Britain an all-out German air attack against the British Royal Air Force *(page 718)*

Section Quiz 24–2

Name _____ Date _____ Class _____

⭐ **Chapter 24** | Score ___

Section Quiz 24-2

DIRECTIONS: Matching Match each item in Column A with the items in Column B. Write the correct letters in the blanks. *(10 points each)*

Column A	Column B
___ 1. lightning war; use of tanks massed together to break through and rapidly encircle enemy positions	A. blitzkrieg
___ 2. unification	B. Danzig
___ 3. a line of concrete bunkers and fortifications built by the French along the German border	C. Maginot Line
___ 4. the policy of giving concessions in exchange for peace	D. appeasement
___ 5. a Polish port with strong German roots	E. Anschlass

DIRECTIONS: Multiple Choice In the blank at the left, write the letter of the choice that best completes the statement or answers the question. *(10 points each)*

Dunkirk from England. The British had hoped to rescue about 45,000 troops. Instead, when the evacuation ended on June 4, an estimated 338,000 British and French troops had been saved. This stunning success led British newspapers to refer to the evacuation as the "Miracle at Dunkirk."

The evacuation had its price, however. Almost all of the British army's equipment remained at Dunkirk—90,000 rifles, 7,000 tons of ammunition, and 120,000 vehicles. If Hitler invaded Britain, it would be almost impossible to stop him from conquering the country.

Three weeks later, on June 22, 1940, Hitler accepted the French surrender in the same railway car in which the Germans had surrendered at the end of World War I. Germany now occupied much of northern France and its Atlantic coastline. To govern the rest of the country, Germany installed a puppet government at the town of Vichy and made Marshal Philippe Pétain the new government's figurehead leader. Pétain predicted that Britain "will have her neck wrung like a chicken."

✓ Reading Check **Summarizing** Why was Germany able to overtake Poland?

Britain Remains Defiant

Neither Pétain nor Adolf Hitler anticipated the bravery of the British people or the spirit of their leader, **Winston Churchill,** who had replaced Neville Chamberlain as prime minister. Hitler fully expected the British to negotiate peace after France surrendered. For Winston Churchill, however, peace was not an option. The war was a fight to defend civilization. On June 4, 1940, Churchill delivered a defiant speech in Parliament, intended not only to rally the British people but to alert the isolationist United States to Britain's plight:

❝Even though large tracts of Europe have fallen . . . we shall not flag or fail. . . . We shall defend our island, whatever the cost may be, we shall fight on the beaches, we shall fight on the landing grounds, we shall fight in the fields and in the streets, we shall fight in the hills; we shall never surrender.❞

—quoted in *Freedom from Fear*

When Hitler realized that Britain would not surrender, he ordered his commanders to prepare to invade. Only the choppy waters of the narrow

CHAPTER 24 A World in Flames **717**

✓ Reading Check

Answer: Germans used a new type of warfare, the *blitzkrieg,* that used large numbers of tanks, infantry, and air power in a coordinated attack.

CRITICAL THINKING ACTIVITY

Analyzing Consequences Have students reexamine the photo on this page. Ask students to explain what the German goal was in bombing civilian targets. *(to demoralize resistance)* Then ask students to explain why they think British resolve was actually strengthened as a result of the bombings. Ask students to suggest other factors that might influence a population's response to aerial attacks on civilians. **L2**

FYI

During the bombing of Great Britain from August 1940 to May 1941, large areas of London and the entire city of Coventry were reduced to rubble.

Reteach

Have students explain why Hitler was able to take over Austria and Czechoslovakia.

Enrich

Invite interested students to create a model depicting the evacuation of Dunkirk. Encourage students to use library and Internet resources for this project.

Reading Check

Answer: Germany had few transport ships to send troops across the English Channel; the British had developed radar.

4 CLOSE

Summarize with the class the content of the section by creating a time line of the major events.

Picturing **History**

Never Surrender Hitler ordered Nazi aircraft to bomb British cities, intending to weaken the people's will. Though shaken, the British, like the dome of St. Paul's Cathedral (right), stood firm. What technology allowed the outnumbered Royal Air Force to resist the German *Luftwaffe?*

English Channel separated Britain from Germany's powerful army, but getting across the Channel posed a major challenge. Germany had few transport ships, and the British air force would sink them if they tried to land troops in England. To invade, therefore, Germany first had to defeat the British air force.

In June 1940, the German air force, called the *Luftwaffe,* began to attack British shipping in the English Channel. Then, in mid-August, the *Luftwaffe* launched an all-out air battle to destroy the British Royal Air Force. This air battle, which lasted into the fall of 1940, became known as the **Battle of Britain.**

On August 23, German bombers accidentally bombed London, the British capital. This attack on civilians enraged the British, who responded by bombing Berlin the following night. For the first time in the war, bombs fell on the German capital. Infuriated, Hitler ordered the *Luftwaffe* to stop its attacks on British military targets and to concentrate on bombing London.

Hitler's goal now was to terrorize the British people into surrendering. The British people endured, however, hiding out in the city's subway tunnels whenever German bombers appeared.

Although the Royal Air Force was greatly outnumbered, the British had one major advantage. They had developed a new technology called radar. Using radar stations placed along their coast, the British were able to detect incoming German aircraft and direct British fighters to intercept them.

Day after day, the British fighters inflicted more losses on the Germans than they suffered. The skill of a few hundred pilots saved Britain from invasion. Praising the pilots, Churchill told Parliament, "Never in the field of human conflict was so much owed by so many to so few." On October 12, 1940, Hitler cancelled the invasion of Britain.

Reading Check   **Evaluating** Why was Britain able to resist Hitler and the Nazis?

SECTION 2 ASSESSMENT

Checking for Understanding

1. **Define:** appeasement, blitzkrieg.
2. **Identify:** *Anschluss,* Maginot Line, Winston Churchill, Battle of Britain.
3. **Explain** why Hitler was able to take over Austria and Czechoslovakia.

Reviewing Themes

4. **Continuity and Change** How did the policy of appeasement affect France and Great Britain?

Critical Thinking

5. **Evaluating** Why were the British able to prevent the Germans from invading their country?
6. **Organizing** Use a graphic organizer similar to the one below to list the early events of the war in Poland and western Europe.

Events

Analyzing Visuals

7. **Analyzing Photographs** Study the photographs on pages 717 and 718. How do they reflect the British resolve to "never surrender"?

Writing About History

8. **Expository Writing** Using library or Internet resources, find more information on the German annexation of Czechoslovakia. Use the information to write a report detailing the events leading up to and including the annexation. Share your report with the class.

SECTION 2 ASSESSMENT ANSWERS

1. Terms are in blue.
2. *Anschluss (p. 714),* Maginot Line *(p. 716),* Winston Churchill *(p. 717),* Battle of Britain *(p. 718)*
3. Britain and France gave in to Hitler's demands.
4. France was not prepared for German attack; Britain left to fight alone
5. Britain was an island, with a strong air force, navy, and radar stations.
6. Germany and Soviets invade Poland; Britain and France enter the war; Germany invades Norway, Denmark, Belgium, the Netherlands, Luxembourg, and France
7. shows British desire to continue with their daily routines and activities in spite of devastation
8. Reports should include details about the political and social structure of Czechoslovakia before the annexation.

Guide to Reading

Main Idea
The Nazis believed Jews to be subhuman. They steadily increased their persecution of Jews and eventually set up death camps and tried to kill all the Jews in Europe.

Key Terms and Names
Holocaust, Shoah, Nuremberg Laws, Wannsee Conference, concentration camp, extermination camp

Reading Strategy
Organizing As you read about the Holocaust, complete a graphic organizer similar to the one below by listing examples of Nazi persecution of German Jews.

Examples of Persecution

Reading Objectives
• **Describe** Nazi prejudices against Jews and early persecution of German Jews.
• **Explain** the methods Hitler used to try to exterminate Europe's Jewish population.

Section Theme
Civic Rights and Responsibilities The Nazis systematically deprived Jews of their rights, while other nations refused to accept many Jewish refugees.

Preview of Events

♦1933	♦1936	♦1939	♦1942

Autumn 1935
Nuremberg Laws deprive German Jews of citizenship

November 1938
Anti-Jewish violence erupts during *Kristallnacht*

June 1939
SS *St. Louis* denied permission to dock in the United States

January 1942
Nazis' Wannsee Conference determines "final solution" for Jews

---

★ An American Story ★

Mira Ryczke was born in 1923 to a middle-class Jewish family in Danzig, Poland, a port on the Baltic Sea. After World War II broke out in September 1939, the Nazis expelled Danzig's Jews to Warsaw, where they were forced to live in deplorable conditions in a special area known as the Warsaw ghetto. In 1943 the Nazis emptied the Warsaw ghetto. The Ryczkes had to ride for three days in a suffocating cattle car headed for Auschwitz, the infamous Nazi death camp, and its neighboring camp of Birkenau.

After arriving at the camps, the terrified newcomers learned that a selection was to take place. When 20-year-old Mira asked what the selection was for, an old-time prisoner pointed to chimneys on top of a building and replied, "Selected for the gas chambers to go up in smoke." Mira later wrote:

Mira Ryczke

> ❝[W]e were told by the old-timers to try to look strong, healthy, and to walk in an upright position when our turn came. . . . Because the women I was with were young, only a few were taken out. Their numbers, tattooed on their left arms, were written down by the SS, and after a few days during roll call, their tattoo numbers were called out and these women were marched to the gas chamber.❞
>
> —quoted in *Echoes from the Holocaust*

Nazi Persecution of the Jews

Mira Ryczke and her family were only a few of the millions of Jews who suffered terrible persecution before and during World War II. During the Holocaust, the catastrophe that ravaged Europe's Jews, the Nazis killed nearly 6 million Jews. The Nazis also killed

---

1 FOCUS

Section Overview
This section focuses on the Holocaust.

BELLRINGER
Skillbuilder Activity

Project transparency and have students answer the question.

Available as a blackline master.

Daily Focus Skills Transparency 24–3

Guide to Reading

Answers to Graphic: Segregated from the rest of the population, lost their jobs, stripped of citizenship, prohibited from voting or holding office, had identifying mark put in passport, confined to concentration camps, killed at extermination camps

Preteaching Vocabulary
Have students look up the proper pronunciations of the Key Names.

SECTION RESOURCES

📁 Reproducible Masters
• Reproducible Lesson Plan 24–3
• Daily Lecture and Discussion Notes 24–3
• Guided Reading Activity 24–3
• Section Quiz 24–3
• Reading Essentials and Study Guide 24–3

📊 Transparencies
• Daily Focus Skills Transparency 24–3

Multimedia
🖲 Interactive Tutor Self-Assessment CD-ROM
🖲 ExamView® Pro Testmaker CD-ROM
🖲 Presentation Plus! CD-ROM
🖲 TeacherWorks™ CD-ROM
🖲 Audio Program
📺 ABCNews Interactive™ Historic America Electronic Field Trips

2 TEACH

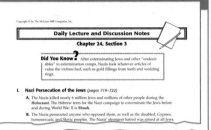

Profiles IN HISTORY

Background: Because they were persecuted in Germany, a number of brilliant
Jewish German scientists immigrated to
the United States in the 1930s.

Ask: When and why did Einstein
leave Germany? *(in 1933 when Hitler
became chancellor; Hitler's policies
were anti-Semitic)*

Discussing a Topic Ask students to discuss how a dictator
acquires and maintains power,
for example, by promising security and threatening violence. **L1**

VIDEOCASSETTE
**Historic America Electronic
Field Trips**

View **Tape 2, Chapter 9:** "The
Holocaust Museum."

Profiles IN HISTORY

Albert Einstein
1879–1955

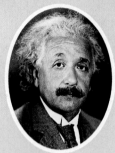

Among the Jews who left Nazi
Germany in the early 1930s was Albert
Einstein, whose brilliant scientific theories revolutionized physics. Einstein
gained international fame in 1919
when the Royal Society of London
announced that calculations had supported his general theory of relativity.
Einstein's fame increased after he won
the Nobel Prize for Physics in 1921.
Lecture invitations poured in from
around the world.

Einstein never actively practiced
Judaism, but he did proudly identify
himself as a Jew. As anti-Semitism
took hold in Germany, Einstein's
worldwide fame contrasted with the
insults he faced in Berlin for practicing
"Bolshevism [Communism] in physics."
His public support for Zionism, the
right of Jews to settle in Palestine
(later Israel), aroused further anger
among Nazis.

Soon after Hitler became Germany's
chancellor in 1933, Einstein renounced
his citizenship and left Germany for
Belgium. Fears for his life prompted
friends to take him secretly by private

yacht to England. He later settled in
Princeton, New Jersey.

A pacifist who had opposed World
War I, Einstein ironically saw his scientific ideas applied to the creation of a
powerful and destructive weapon, the
atomic bomb. After the United States
detonated the first atomic bomb in
combat over Hiroshima, Japan, in
1945, Einstein devoted his final years
to promoting pacifism. The scientist's
greatest legacy, however, would be
the revolutionary scientific discoveries
he had made in the early 1900s. As
Einstein himself had observed,
"Politics are for the moment. An
equation is for eternity."

---

millions of people from other groups they considered
inferior. The Hebrew term for the Holocaust is **Shoah,**
meaning "catastrophe," but it is often used specifically to refer to the Nazi campaign to exterminate the
Jews during World War II.

Nazi Ideology Once the Nazis took power in
Germany, they acted swiftly to implement the political racial policies Hitler had outlined in *Mein
Kampf.* Although the Nazis persecuted anyone who
dared oppose them, as well as the disabled,
Gypsies, homosexuals, and Slavic peoples, they
reserved their strongest hatred for the Jews. This
loathing went far beyond the European anti-
Semitism common at the time. Over the centuries,
people who were prejudiced against Jews had put
down Jewish religious practices and discriminated
against Jews in many ways. For example, Jews were
sometimes segregated in ghettos or prohibited from
owning land. For the Nazis, however, all Jewish

people were evil no matter what their
religion, occupation, or education.

The Nuremberg Laws After the
Nazis took power, they quickly moved
to deprive German Jews of many
rights that all citizens had long taken
for granted. In September 1935 the
Nuremberg Laws took citizenship
away from Jewish Germans and
banned marriage between Jews and
other Germans. Two months later,
another decree defined a Jew as a
person with at least one Jewish grand-
parent and prohibited Jews from holding public office or voting. Other laws
forbade Jews from employing female
German servants under age 35
and compelled Jews with German-
sounding names to adopt "Jewish"
names. Soon the passports of Jews
were marked with a red "J" to clearly
identify them as Jewish.

By the summer of 1936, at least half
of Germany's Jews were jobless, having lost the right to work as civil servants, journalists, farmers, teachers,
and actors. In 1938 the Nazis also
banned Jews from practicing law and
medicine and from operating businesses. With no source of income, life
became very difficult.

Despite worsening conditions, many
Jews chose to remain in Germany during the early
years of Nazi rule. Well integrated into German society
before this time, they were reluctant to leave and give
up the lives they had built there. Many also thought
that conditions would surely improve after a time. In
fact, they soon became worse.

Kristallnacht On November 7, 1938, a young
Jewish refugee named Herschel Grynszpan shot and
killed a German diplomat in Paris. Grynszpan's
father and 10,000 other Jews had been deported from
Germany to Poland, and the distraught young man
was seeking revenge for this act and for the persecution of the Jews in general.

In retaliation for the killing, an infuriated Hitler
ordered his minister of propaganda, Joseph
Goebbels, to stage attacks against the Jews that
would appear to be a spontaneous popular reaction
to news of the murder. On the night of November 9,
this plan played out in a spree of destruction.

COOPERATIVE LEARNING ACTIVITY

Analyzing Concepts Organize students into small groups and have them research one of the following topics: *Kristallnacht,* the Warsaw ghetto, German use of slave labor, artwork stolen from
occupied countries by Germany. Have each group present their findings to the class as a panel.
Each member of the group should present one aspect of the topic. When the panel is finished,
they should field questions from other members of the class.

Use the rubric for a cooperative group management plan on pages 81–82 in the *Performance
Assessment Activities and Rubrics.*

In Vienna a Jewish child named Frederick Morton watched in terror that night as 10 young Nazi Storm Troopers broke into his family's apartment:

> ❝They yanked out every drawer in every one of our chests and cupboards, and tossed each in the air. They let the cutlery jangle across the floor, the clothes scatter, and stepped over the mess to fling the next drawer. . . . 'We might be back,' the leader said. On the way out he threw our mother-of-pearl ashtray over his shoulder, like confetti. We did not speak or move or breathe until we heard their boots against the pavement.❞
>
> —quoted in *Facing History and Ourselves*

The anti-Jewish violence that erupted throughout Germany and Austria that night came to be called *Kristallnacht*, or "night of broken glass," because broken glass littered the streets afterward. When daylight came, more than 90 Jews lay dead, hundreds were badly injured, and thousands more were terrorized. The Nazis had forbidden police to interfere while roving bands of thugs destroyed 7,500 Jewish businesses and wrecked nearly 180 synagogues.

The lawlessness of *Kristallnacht* did not end with the dawn. Following that night of violence, the **Gestapo,** the government's secret police, arrested around 30,000 wealthy Jews, releasing them only if they agreed to emigrate and surrender all their possessions. The state also confiscated insurance payments owed to Jewish owners of ruined businesses.

The week after *Kristallnacht,* Nazi interior minister Hermann Goering added insult to injury by fining the Jewish community to pay for the damage. "German Jewry," he proclaimed "shall, as punishment for their abominable crimes . . . have to make a contribution for one billion marks. . . . I would like to say that I would not like to be a Jew in Germany."

Jewish Refugees Try to Flee *Kristallnacht* and its aftermath marked a significant escalation in the Nazi policy of persecution against the Jews. Many Jews, including Frederick Morton's family, decided that it was time to leave and fled to the United States. Between 1933, when Hitler took power, and the start of World War II in 1939, some 350,000 Jews escaped Nazi-controlled Germany. These emigrants included prominent scientists such as Albert Einstein and businesspeople like Otto Frank, who resettled his family in Amsterdam in 1933. Otto's daughter **Anne Frank** would later keep a diary of her family's life in hiding after the Nazis overran the Netherlands.

By 1938 the American consulate in Stuttgart, Germany, had a backlog of over 100,000 visa applications from Jews trying to leave Germany and come to the United States. Following the Nazi *Anschluss,* 3,000 Austrian Jews each day applied for American visas. Many never received visas to the United States

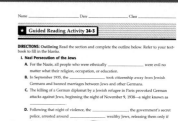

Name _____ Date _____ Class _____

★ **Guided Reading Activity 24-3**

DIRECTIONS: Outlining Read the section and complete the outline below. Refer to your textbook to fill in the blanks.

I. **Nazi Persecution of the Jews**

   A. For the Nazis, all people who were ethnically _____ were evil no matter what their religion, occupation, or education.

   B. In September 1935, the _____ took citizenship away from Jewish Germans and banned marriages between Jews and other Germans.

   C. The killing of a German diplomat by a Jewish refugee in Paris provoked German attacks against Jews, beginning the night of November 9, 1938—a night known as _____

   D. Following that night of violence, the _____, the government's secret police, arrested around _____ wealthy Jews, releasing them only if _____

Creating a Thematic Chart
Have students use the information presented in this section, including the maps, to create a chart to illustrate the following: the number of Jews who fled Germany from 1933 to 1939, the number of immigrants allowed to enter the U.S. each year, the number of Jews killed at Auschwitz, and the number of Jews killed in Europe. Encourage students to create visuals that reflect the statistics for the map. **L2**

📁 Use the rubric for creating a map, display, or chart on pages 77–78 in the *Performance Assessment Activities and Rubrics.*

you don't say...

Complete Destruction *Holocaust* means a sacrifice consumed by fire, especially a complete or thorough sacrifice or destruction.

The Final Solution

Before the war, a Jewish family in Germany poses for a photograph during a family outing. Few members of this family would survive the war.

On *Kristallnacht,* roaming bands of thugs destroyed Jewish property and menaced Jewish families throughout Germany.

MEETING SPECIAL NEEDS

Logical/Mathematical Have students examine the effects of propaganda by selecting a major war in American history and examining the positive and negative roles of propaganda. To report their findings, have students create a chart that shows benefits and drawbacks of propaganda, listing examples of each classification. **L28**

📁 Refer to **Inclusion for the High School Social Studies Classroom Strategies and Activities** in the TCR.

Creating a Chart Have students work in pairs to prepare a chart that compares the United States Bill of Rights and the rights that Nazis denied the Jews. Use the charts as a basis for a class discussion about the effects of Nazi rule on the Jews. **L2**

 Use the rubric for creating a map, display, or chart on pages 77–78 in the *Performance Assessment Activities and Rubrics.*

CURRICULUM CONNECTION

World History In addition to the Jews, millions of others were exterminated by the Nazis. To learn more about how the Poles were treated by the Nazis, read *Forgotten Holocaust: The Poles Under German Occupation, 1934–1944,* by R. C. Lukas (Lexington, Kentucky, 1986).

✓ Reading Check

Answer: Jews remained because of restrictions on immigration to other countries, because they thought conditions would improve, because Germany was their home, or because they either had no money or their savings would be lost if they emigrated.

or to the other countries where they applied. As a result, millions of Jews remained trapped in Nazi-dominated Europe.

Several factors limited Jewish immigration to the United States. First, Nazi orders prohibited Jews from taking more than about four dollars out of Germany. Second, many countries refused to accept Jewish immigrants. In the United States, laws restricted granting a visa to anyone "likely to become a public charge." American customs officials tended to assume that this applied to Jews since Germany had forced them to leave any wealth behind. High unemployment rates in the 1930s also made immigration politically unpopular. Few Americans wanted to raise immigration quotas, even to accommodate European refugees. The existing immigration policy allowed only a total of 150,000 immigrants annually, with a fixed quota from each country. The law permitted no exceptions for refugees or victims of persecution.

At an international conference on refugees in 1938, several European countries, the United States, and Latin America stated their regret that they could not take in more of Germany's Jews without raising their immigration quotas. Meanwhile, Nazi propaganda chief Joseph Goebbels announced that "if there is any country that believes it has not enough Jews, I shall gladly turn over to it all our Jews." Hitler also declared himself "ready to put all these criminals at the disposal of these countries . . . even on luxury ships."

As war loomed in 1939, many ships departed from Germany crammed with Jews desperate to escape. Some of their visas, however, had been forged or sold illegally, and Mexico, Paraguay, Argentina, and Costa Rica all denied access to Jews with such documents. So too did the United States.

On May 27, 1939, the **SS *St. Louis*** entered the harbor in Havana, Cuba, with 930 Jewish refugees on board. Most of these passengers hoped to go to the United States eventually, but they had certificates improperly issued by Cuba's director of immigration giving them permission to land in Cuba. When the ships arrived in Havana, the Cuban government, partly in response to anti-Semitic sentiment stirred up by Nazi propaganda, revoked the certificates and refused to let the refugees come ashore. For several days, the ship's captain steered his ship in circles off the coast of Florida, awaiting official permission to dock at a United States port. Denied such permission, the ship turned back toward Europe on June 6. The forlorn passengers finally disembarked in France, Holland, Belgium, and Great Britain. Within two years, the first three of these countries fell under Nazi domination. Many of the refugees brought to these countries aboard the SS *St. Louis* perished in the Nazis' "final solution."

✓ Reading Check **Analyzing** Why did many Jews remain in Germany even though they were persecuted?

The Final Solution

After the war broke out, the Nazis methodically deprived Jews of their rights, confining many to overcrowded ghettos. After weeks of fierce resistance, Jews in the Warsaw ghetto were rounded up for deportation to concentration camps in May 1943.

INTERDISCIPLINARY CONNECTIONS ACTIVITY

Current Events Journalist C.L. Sulzberger reported that after General Eisenhower first visited a concentration camp, "He cabled Washington and London to send journalists and members of Congress and Parliament to Germany as soon as possible." Eisenhower wanted no one to doubt the extent of the atrocities that had been committed. His fears have been partly justified, for today some individuals insist that the Holocaust did not take place. Have students research who has tried to deny the Holocaust and how their denials have been received. Urge students to describe the kinds of evidence that are available to determine what actually happened in the camps. **L3**

The Final Solution

On January 20, 1942, 15 Nazi leaders met at the **Wannsee Conference,** held in a Berlin suburb, to determine the "final solution of the Jewish question." Previous "solutions" had included rounding up Jews, Gypsies, and Slavs from conquered areas, shooting them, and piling them into mass graves. Another method required forcing Jews and other "undesirables" into trucks and then piping in exhaust fumes to kill them. These methods, however, had proven too slow and inefficient for the Nazis.

At Wannsee, the Nazis made plans to round up Jews from the vast areas of Nazi-controlled Europe and take them to detention centers known as concentration camps. There, healthy individuals would work as slave laborers until they dropped dead of exhaustion, disease, or malnutrition. Most others, including the elderly, the infirm, and young children, would be sent to extermination camps, attached to many of the concentration camps, to be executed in massive gas chambers.

Concentration Camps The Nazis had established their first concentration camps in 1933 to jail political opponents. After the war began, the Nazis built concentration camps throughout Europe.

Buchenwald, one of the first and largest concentration camps, was built near the town of Weimar in Germany in 1937. During the war it held about 20,000 prisoners, who worked 12-hour shifts as slave laborers in nearby factories. Though Buchenwald had no gas chambers, hundreds of prisoners died there every month as a result of exhaustion and the horrible living conditions.

Leon Bass, a young American soldier, described viewing a barracks in Buchenwald at the end of the war. Built to hold 50 people, the room had housed more than 150, with bunks built almost to the ceiling. Bass recalled:

> ❝I looked at a bottom bunk and there I saw one man. He was too weak to get up; he could just barely turn his head. He was skin and bones. He looked like a skeleton; and his eyes were deep set. He didn't utter a sound; he just looked at me with those eyes, and they still haunt me today.❞

—quoted in *Facing History and Ourselves*

Extermination Camps After the Wannsee Conference, the Nazis built extermination facilities in a number of the concentration camps, mostly in Poland, to kill Jews more efficiently. At these camps, including the infamous Treblinka and Auschwitz, Jews were the Nazis' main victims. **Auschwitz** alone housed about 100,000 people in 300 prison barracks. Its gas chambers, built to kill 2,000 people at a time, sometimes gassed 12,000 people in a day. Of the

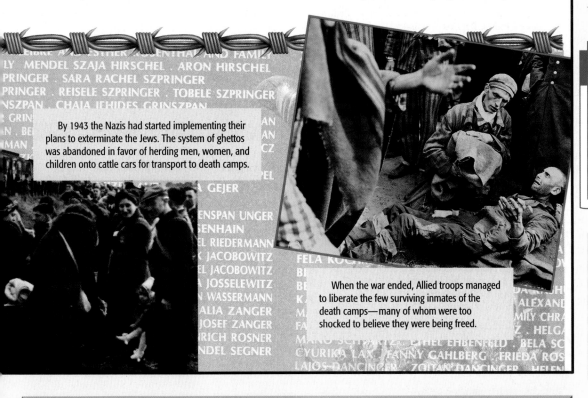

By 1943 the Nazis had started implementing their plans to exterminate the Jews. The system of ghettos was abandoned in favor of herding men, women, and children onto cattle cars for transport to death camps.

When the war ended, Allied troops managed to liberate the few surviving inmates of the death camps—many of whom were too shocked to believe they were being freed.

CHAPTER 24
Section 3, 719–794

Interpreting a Map Have students locate the major concentration and extermination camps and calculate the distance of each from the nearest large city. Then ask students to discuss how residents of the cities must have reacted, what they must have known, and why they did not act to rescue the people in the camps. **L2**

3 ASSESS

Assign Section 3 Assessment as homework or as an in-class activity.

🖥 Have students use the **Interactive Tutor Self-Assessment CD-ROM.**

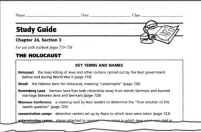

Reading Essentials and Study Guide 24–3

Name _____ Date _____ Class _____

Study Guide

Chapter 24, Section 3
For use with textbook pages 719–724

THE HOLOCAUST

KEY TERMS AND NAMES

Holocaust the mass killing of Jews and other civilians carried out by the Nazi government before and during World War II (page 719)

Shoah the Hebrew term for Holocaust, meaning "catastrophe" (page 720)

Nuremberg Laws German laws that took citizenship away from Jewish Germans and banned marriage between Jews and Germans (page 720)

Wannsee Conference a meeting held by Nazi leaders to determine the "final solution of the Jewish question" (page 723)

concentration camps detention centers set up by Nazis to which Jews were taken (page 723)

extermination camps places attached to concentration camps in which Jews were executed in

Section Quiz 24–3

Name _____ Date _____ Class _____

⭐ **Chapter 24**   Score _____

Section Quiz 24-3

DIRECTIONS: Matching Match each item in Column A with the items in Column B. Write the correct letters in the blanks. *(10 points each)*

Column A	Column B
___ 1. Hebrew for "catastrophe" and used specifically to refer to the Holocaust	A. Nuremberg Laws
___ 2. girl who kept a diary of her life in hiding from the Nazis	B. Auschwitz
___ 3. extermination camp where 1,600,000 people died	C. Anne Frank
___ 4. German government's secret police	D. Shoah
___ 5. took citizenship away from Jewish Germans and banned marriage between Jews and other Germans	E. Gestapo

DIRECTIONS: Multiple Choice In the blank at the left, write the letter of the choice that best completes the statement or answers the question. *(10 points each)*

CRITICAL THINKING ACTIVITY

Analyzing Information Tell students that wars have always involved the killing of innocent civilians. Ask students to explain what made the killing of the Jewish people by the Nazis in World War II different. Based on the class discussion, have students write a descriptive essay that compares and contrasts the collateral killing of civilians during a war with the intentional killing of people in concentration and execution camps. **L2**

Geography Skills

Answers:

1. Poland (3 million)

2. Fascists were not as anti-Semitic as the Nazis.

Geography Skills Practice

Ask: Which of the Soviet Socialist Republics had the smallest percentage of their Jewish population killed under the Nazis? *(Russian S.S.R.)*

Reteach

Have students describe Nazi prejudice against Jews and early persecution of German Jews.

Enrich

Invite interested students to read, or reread, an excerpt from Anne Frank's diary. Ask students to share their feelings about what they read.

✓ Reading Check

Answer: Some died of exhaustion, disease, or malnutrition in concentration camps. Others were executed in gas chambers at extermination camps.

4 CLOSE

Have students summarize the gradually intensifying steps of Hitler's campaign against the Jews.

NATIONAL GEOGRAPHIC Jewish Losses, 1939–1945

DENMARK 500

BALTIC STATES 228,000

RUSSIAN S.S.R. 107,000

BYELORUSSIAN S.S.R. 245,000

NETHERLANDS 105,000

GERMANY AND AUSTRIA 210,000

POLAND 3,000,000

BELGIUM 40,000

UKRAINIAN S.S.R. 900,000

CZECHOSLOVAKIA 155,000

FRANCE 90,000

HUNGARY 450,000

ITALY 8,000

ROMANIA 300,000

YUGOSLAVIA 26,000

BULGARIA 14,000

GREECE 54,000

Percentage of Jewish Population Annihilated
- 83–90
- 65–77
- 50–60
- 11–26

FRANCE 90,000 Number of Jews killed under Nazi racial policies

200 miles

200 kilometers

Lambert Azimuthal Equal-Area projection

Geography Skills

1. **Interpreting Maps** What country had the highest number of Jews in its population killed?

2. **Applying Geography Skills** A relatively low percentage of Italy's Jewish population died in the Holocaust. From this information, how would you compare Fascists and Nazis in terms of their Jewish policies?

estimated 1,600,000 people who died at Auschwitz, about 1,300,000 were Jews. The other 300,000 were Poles, Soviet prisoners-of-war, and Gypsies.

Upon arrival at Auschwitz, healthy prisoners such as Mira Ryczke were selected for slave labor. Elderly or disabled people, the sick, and mothers and children went immediately to the gas chambers, after which their bodies were burned in giant crematoriums. In her memoirs, Ryczke described "columns of people marching slowly toward the gas chambers" and "the horrible stench in the air—the smell of burning human flesh. I have never forgotten that smell."

In only a few years, Jewish culture, which had existed in Europe for over 1,000 years, had been virtually obliterated by the Nazis in the lands they conquered. Despite exhaustive debate, there is still great controversy about why and how an event so horrifying as the Holocaust could have occurred. No consensus has been reached, but most historians point to a number of factors: the German people's sense of injury after World War I; severe economic problems; Hitler's control over the German nation; the lack of a strong tradition of representative government in Germany; German fear of Hitler's secret police; and a long history of anti-Jewish prejudice and discrimination in Europe.

✓ Reading Check Summarizing What methods did Hitler use to try to exterminate Europe's Jewish population?

SECTION 3 ASSESSMENT

Checking for Understanding

1. **Define:** Holocaust, concentration camp, extermination camp.

2. **Identify:** Shoah, Nuremberg Laws, Wannsee Conference.

3. **List** the groups of people who were persecuted by the Nazis.

Reviewing Themes

4. **Civic Rights and Responsibilities** Do you think the German people or other nations could have prevented the Holocaust? Why or why not?

Critical Thinking

5. **Analyzing** What are some factors that attempt to explain the Holocaust?

6. **Organizing** Use a graphic organizer similar to the one below to list the methods used to try to exterminate Europe's Jewish population.

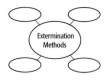

Extermination Methods

Analyzing Visuals

7. **Analyzing Photographs** Study the photographs of the Final Solution on pages 721–723. How do the photographs show the systematic destruction of Jewish life?

Writing About History

8. **Descriptive Writing** Take on the role of a person living in Germany during *Kristallnacht.* Write a diary entry describing the events of that night. Include a description of the events during the days following *Kristallnacht* as well.

SECTION 3 ASSESSMENT ANSWERS

1. Terms are in blue.
2. Shoah *(p. 720)*, Nuremberg Laws *(p. 720)*, Wannsee Conference *(p. 723)*
3. Jews, disabled, Gypsies, homosexuals, Slavic peoples
4. Students' answers will vary but should be based on reasoned argument.
5. Hitler's dictatorship, European anti-Semitism, propaganda, fear
6. gas chambers, malnutrition, untreated disease, worked to death
7. shows stages of Hitler's campaign, from civil discrimination and violence to deportation to camps
8. Students' diary entries should focus on events surrounding *Kristallnacht,* as told from a Jewish perspective.

Guide to Reading

Main Idea
After World War II began, the United States attempted to continue its prewar policy of neutrality.

Key Terms and Names
America First Committee, Lend-Lease Act, hemispheric defense zone, Atlantic Charter, strategic materials

Reading Strategy
Organizing As you read about the efforts of the United States to stay neutral in the war, complete a graphic organizer similar to the one below by naming two events that shifted American opinion toward helping the Allies.

Events That Shifted American Opinion

Reading Objectives
• **Explain** how Roosevelt helped Britain while maintaining official neutrality.
• **Trace** the events that led to increasing tensions, and ultimately war, between the United States and Japan.

Section Theme
Individual Action Even while the United States was officially neutral, President Roosevelt found ways to help the British fight Germany.

Preview of Events

♦September 1940	♦March 1941	♦August 1941	♦December 1941

September 1940
FDR makes destroyers-for-bases deal with Britain

March 1941
Congress passes Lend-Lease Act

August 1941
Roosevelt and Churchill sign Atlantic Charter

October 1941
Germans sink *Reuben James*

December 7, 1941
Japan attacks Pearl Harbor

★ An American Story ★

Daniel Inouye after joining the U.S. Army's 442nd Infantry

December 7, 1941, dawned like any other Sunday in Hawaii, where teenager Daniel Inouye lived with his family. Like other Americans who lived through the experience, Inouye would never forget what he was doing the moment American isolationism ended:

❝As soon as I finished brushing my teeth and pulled on my trousers, I automatically clicked on the little radio that stood on the shelf above my bed. I remember that I was buttoning my shirt and looking out the window . . . when the hum of the warming set gave way to a frenzied voice. 'This is no test,' the voice cried out. 'Pearl Harbor is being bombed by the Japanese!'❞

The Inouye family ran outside and gazed toward the naval base at Pearl Harbor:

❝And then we saw the planes. They came zooming up out of that sea of gray smoke, flying north toward where we stood and climbing into the bluest part of the sky, and they came in twos and threes, in neat formations, and if it hadn't been for that red ball on their wings, the rising sun of the Japanese Empire, you could easily believe that they were Americans, flying over in precise military salute.❞

—quoted in *Eyewitness to America*

FDR Supports England

The Japanese attack surprised many Americans. Most people had believed that Germany posed the greatest danger. What Americans did not realize was that the causes of the Japanese attack could be traced back more than two years to President Roosevelt's policies for helping Britain against Germany.

CHAPTER 24 A World in Flames **725**

1 FOCUS

Section Overview
This section focuses on the events that led to the United States entering World War II.

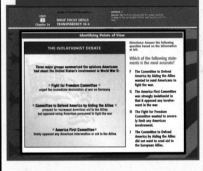
Guide to Reading

Answers to Graphic: Britain's struggle with Germany, Japan's attack on Pearl Harbor

Preteaching Vocabulary
Have students write a sentence explaining the significance of each of the Key Names.

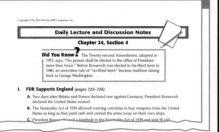

Analyzing Political Cartoons

Answer: instituted a cash-and-carry policy for arms sales to France and Britain; Roosevelt's destroyers-for-bases deal

✓ Reading Check

Answer: They were adjusted to allow the United States to sell arms to warring countries as long as they paid cash and carried the goods away on their own ships.

Expressing Points of View

Organize the class into three groups representing the views in the isolationist debate. Assign one group to be the Fight for Freedom Committee, one to be the Committee to Defend America by Aiding the Allies, and one to be the America First Committee. Have each group develop a one-paragraph position statement and present it to the class. Discuss the reasons for the varying opinions as a class. **L1**

✓ Analyzing *Political Cartoons*

Peace Above All Many Americans were willing to help European democracies but did not want to sell them arms. In what ways did the United States assist these nations?

The Neutrality Act of 1939 President Roosevelt officially proclaimed the United States neutral two days after Britain and France declared war on Germany. Despite this declaration, he was determined to do all he could to help the two countries in their struggle against Hitler. Soon after the war began, Roosevelt called Congress into a special session to revise the neutrality laws. He asked Congress to replace the ban on arms sales to nations at war with a cash-and-carry provision. Public opinion strongly supported the president. Despite isolationist opposition, Congress passed the new law. Under the Neutrality Act of 1939, warring nations could buy weapons from the United States if they paid cash and carried the arms on their own ships.

Destroyers-for-Bases Deal In the spring of 1940, the United States faced its first test in remaining neutral. In June British Prime Minister Winston Churchill began asking Roosevelt to transfer old American destroyers to Britain. Britain had lost nearly half its destroyers and needed more to protect its cargo ships from German submarines and to block any German attempt to invade Britain.

Determined to give Churchill the destroyers, Roosevelt used a loophole in the provision of the Neutrality Act that required cash for purchases. In exchange for the right to build American bases on British-controlled Newfoundland, Bermuda, and islands in the Caribbean, Roosevelt sent 50 old American destroyers to Britain. Since the deal did not involve an actual sale, the Neutrality Act did not apply. On September 3, 1940, he announced his action to an astonished press.

✓ Reading Check **Examining** How were the Neutrality Acts revised?

The Isolationist Debate

Widespread public acceptance of the destroyers-for-bases deal demonstrated a marked change in American public opinion. The shift began after the German invasion of France and the rescue of Allied forces at Dunkirk. By July 1940 most Americans favored offering limited aid to the Allies.

The Range of Opinion American opinion was hardly unanimous. In fact, beginning in the spring of 1940, a spirited debate took place between people who wanted greater American involvement in World War II and those who felt that the United States should remain neutral.

At one extreme was the Fight for Freedom Committee, a group which urged the immediate declaration of war on Germany. Closer to the center, the Committee to Defend America by Aiding the Allies, headed by journalist William Allen White, pressed for increased American aid to the Allies but opposed armed intervention.

Roosevelt's destroyers-for-bases deal led to the founding of the **America First Committee,** a staunchly isolationist group that firmly opposed any American intervention or aid to the Allies. The group had many famous members, including aviator Charles Lindbergh, Senator Gerald Nye, and former president Herbert Hoover.

The Election of 1940 The heated debate over neutrality took place in the midst of the 1940 presidential election campaign. For months Americans had wondered whether President Roosevelt would follow long-standing tradition by retiring at the end of his second term. With the United States in a precarious position, a change of leaders might not be in the country's best interest. Roosevelt decided to run for an unprecedented third term.

COOPERATIVE LEARNING ACTIVITY

Analyzing Propaganda Organize the class into groups of three. Have each group analyze the propaganda used by both the Axis powers and the Allied powers during World War II. Assign each member of the group one of the following tasks: researching the information, writing descriptions of the information, or analyzing the propaganda. Have group members combine their efforts to make an in-class presentation.

Use the rubric for a cooperative group management plan on pages 81–82 in the *Performance Assessment Activities and Rubrics.*

During the campaign, FDR steered a careful course between neutrality and intervention. The Republican nominee, Wendell Willkie, did the same, promising that he too would stay out of the war but assist the Allies. The voters re-elected Roosevelt by a wide margin, preferring to stick with a president they knew during this crisis period.

✓ **Reading Check** **Analyzing** Why did Roosevelt win an unprecedented third term in office?

Edging Toward War

With the election safely over, Roosevelt expanded the nation's role in the war. Britain was fighting for democracy, he said, and the United States had to help. Speaking to Congress, he listed the "Four Freedoms" for which both the United States and Great Britain stood: freedom of speech, freedom of worship, freedom from want, and freedom from fear. 📖 *(See page 1075 for an excerpt from this speech.)*

The Lend-Lease Act By December 1940, Great Britain had run out of funds to wage its war against Germany. President Roosevelt came up with a way to remove the cash requirement of the Neutrality Act. With the **Lend-Lease Act,** the United States would be able to lend or lease arms to any country considered "vital to the defense of the United States." This act meant that the United States could send weapons to Britain if Britain promised to return or pay rent for them after the war.

The president warned that if Britain fell, an "unholy alliance" of Germany, Japan, and Italy would keep trying to conquer the world, and then "all of us in all the Americas would be living at the point of a gun." The president argued that the United States should become the "great arsenal of democracy" to keep the British fighting and make it unnecessary for Americans to go to war.

The America First Committee disagreed, but Congress passed the Lend-Lease Act by a wide margin. By the time the program ended, the United States had contributed more than $50 billion in weapons, vehicles, and other supplies to the Allied war effort.

While shipments of supplies to Britain began at once, lend-lease aid eventually went to the Soviet Union as well. After calling off the invasion of Britain, Hitler returned to his original goal of carving out lebensraum for Germany in eastern Europe. In June 1941, in violation of the Nazi-Soviet pact, Hitler launched a massive invasion of the Soviet Union. Although Churchill detested communism and

considered Stalin a harsh dictator, he vowed that any person or state "who fights against Nazism will have our aid." Roosevelt, too, supported this policy.

The Hemispheric Defense Zone Congressional approval of the Lend-Lease Act did not solve the problem of how to get American arms and supplies to Britain. German submarines patrolling the Atlantic Ocean were sinking hundreds of thousands of tons of shipping each month, and the British navy simply did not have enough ships in the Atlantic to stop them.

Roosevelt could not simply order the U.S. Navy to protect British cargo ships, since the United States was still technically neutral. Instead, he developed the idea of a hemispheric defense zone. Roosevelt declared that the entire western half of the Atlantic was part of the Western Hemisphere and therefore neutral. He then ordered the U.S. Navy to patrol the western Atlantic and reveal the location of German submarines to the British.

The Atlantic Charter In August 1941 Roosevelt and Churchill met face-to-face on board American and British warships anchored near Newfoundland. During these meetings, the two men agreed on the text of the **Atlantic Charter.** It committed the two

Picturing **History**

Neutrality Debate The America First Committee strongly opposed the increasingly weak neutrality of the United States. Here an American soldier confronts an isolationist marching outside the White House. How did the Lend-Lease Act further weaken the nation's official neutrality?

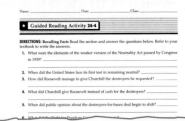

Guided Reading Activity 24-4

Name _____ Date _____ Class _____

◆ Guided Reading Activity 24-4

DIRECTIONS: Recalling Facts Read the section and answer the questions below. Refer to your textbook to write the answers.

1. What were the elements of the weaker version of the Neutrality Act passed by Congress in 1939? _____

2. When did the United States face its first test in remaining neutral? _____

3. How did Roosevelt manage to give Churchill the destroyers he requested? _____

4. What did Churchill give Roosevelt instead of cash for the destroyers? _____

5. When did public opinion about the destroyers-for-bases deal begin to shift? _____

6. What did the Fight for Freedom Committee encourage? _____

✓**Reading Check**

Answer: Americans wanted to stay with a president that they knew during this period of unrest.

Organizing Information Have students create a graphic to illustrate the ways America edged toward war economically and militarily. **L1**

FYI

Isolationist sentiment in the United States arose in part from the fact that the nation was an ocean away from the conflict in Europe and Asia.

Picturing **History**

Answer: It involved the United States in the war by lending or leasing arms to any country fighting Hitler.
Ask: What messages were protesters trying to convey? *(support for the country but not for the war)*

📁 Use *Interpreting Political Cartoons,* Cartoon 25.

MEETING SPECIAL NEEDS

Reading Disability Help students organize events by having them make four columns on a sheet of paper and labeling them Allied Powers, Axis Powers, Axis-controlled Countries, and Neutral Countries. Students should then use the text, including maps, to identify and list the countries under the appropriate headings. **L1** **ELL**

📁 Refer to *Inclusion for the High School Social Studies Classroom Strategies and Activities* in the TCR.

✓ Reading Check

Answer: by getting arms to the Allies

Organizing Information Have students outline the ways Roosevelt discouraged Japan from attacking the British Empire. **L2**

CURRICULUM CONNECTION

Geography To gain direct access to natural resources, Japanese military leaders aimed to build an empire in the Pacific. The U.S. Pacific Fleet was headquartered at Oahu island in Hawaii—approximately 70 warships, including 8 battleships and 24 auxiliary vessels, were stationed at Pearl Harbor on the island. Thus, Japanese military leaders saw the fleet as an obstacle that had to be destroyed if they were to achieve their goals.

---

leaders to a postwar world of democracy, non-aggression, free trade, economic advancement, and freedom of the seas. Churchill later said that FDR pledged to "force an 'incident' . . . which would justify him in opening hostilities" with Germany.

An incident quickly presented itself. In early September a German U-boat fired on the American destroyer *Greer,* which had been radioing the U-boat's position to the British. Roosevelt promptly responded by ordering American ships to follow a "shoot-on-sight" policy toward German submarines.

The Germans escalated hostilities the following month, targeting two American destroyers. One of them, the *Reuben James,* broke in two after being torpedoed. It sank into the frigid waters of the North Atlantic, where 115 sailors died. As the end of 1941 grew near, Germany and the United States continued a tense standoff in the North Atlantic.

✓ Reading Check **Evaluating** How did the Lend-Lease Act help the Allied war effort?

Japan Attacks the United States

Despite the growing tensions in the Atlantic, the Japanese attack on Pearl Harbor was what finally brought the United States into World War II. Ironically, Japan's decision to attack the United States was a direct result of Roosevelt's efforts to help Britain in its war against Germany.

America Embargoes Japan Between August 1939 and December 1941, Roosevelt's primary goal was to help Britain and its allies defeat Germany. He knew that one of the problems Britain faced was the need to keep much of its navy in Asia to protect British territories there from Japanese attack. As German submarines began sinking British shipping, the British began moving warships from Southeast Asia to the Atlantic, leaving their empire vulnerable. In response, Roosevelt introduced policies to discourage the Japanese from attacking the British Empire.

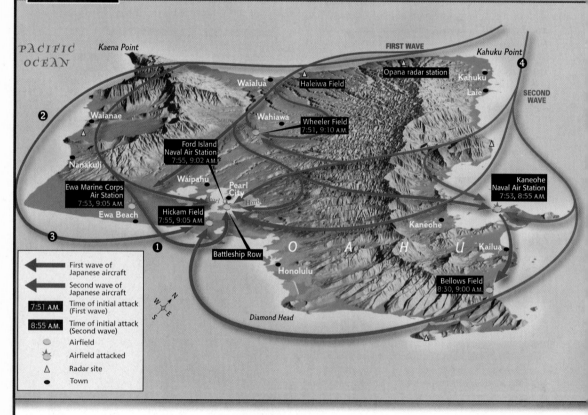

NATIONAL GEOGRAPHIC **Pearl Harbor, Hawaii, December 7, 1941**

INTERDISCIPLINARY CONNECTIONS ACTIVITY

Communication Many Americans who were alive on December 7, 1941, remember the attack on Pearl Harbor. Have students interview three residents of the community who remember the day of the attack. Encourage students to work in pairs to prepare sample interview questions, such as what people were doing when they heard about the attack, how they reacted, and how the attack affected them. Have students write a newspaper article based on their interviews. If possible, students should include an appropriate photograph with their article. **L2**

Roosevelt began by putting economic pressure on Japan. Japan depended on the United States for many key materials, including scrap iron, steel, and especially oil. Approximately 80 percent of Japan's oil came from the United States. In July 1940, Congress passed the Export Control Act, giving Roosevelt the power to restrict the sale of strategic materials (materials important for fighting a war) to other nations. Roosevelt immediately blocked the sale of airplane fuel and scrap iron to Japan. Furious, the Japanese signed an alliance with Germany and Italy, formally becoming a member of the Axis.

In 1941 Roosevelt began sending lend-lease aid to China. Japan had invaded China in 1937, and by 1941, it controlled much of the Chinese coast. Roosevelt hoped that lend-lease aid would enable the Chinese to tie down the Japanese and prevent them from attacking elsewhere. The strategy failed. By July 1941, the Japanese had sent troops into southern Indochina, posing a direct threat to the British Empire. Japanese aircraft were now in position to strike British shipping in the Strait of Malacca and bomb Hong Kong and Singapore.

Roosevelt responded very quickly to the Japanese threat. He froze all Japanese assets in the United States, reduced the amount of oil being shipped to Japan, and sent General Douglas MacArthur to the Philippines to build up American defenses there.

Roosevelt made it clear that he would lift the oil embargo only if Japan withdrew from Indochina and made peace with China. With the war against China now in jeopardy because of a lack of oil and other resources, the Japanese military began making plans to attack the resource-rich British and Dutch colonies in Southeast Asia. They also decided to seize the Philippines and to attack the American fleet at Pearl Harbor. They could not risk leaving the United States with a navy in the Pacific to oppose their plans. While the Japanese prepared for war, negotiations with the United States continued, but neither side would back down. On November 26, 1941, six Japanese aircraft carriers, two battleships, and several other warships set sail for Hawaii.

Japan Attacks Pearl Harbor The Japanese government appeared to be continuing negotiations with the United States in good faith. American intelligence, however, had decoded Japanese communications that made it clear that Japan was preparing to go to war against the United States.

On November 27, American commanders at the Pearl Harbor naval base received a war warning from Washington, but Hawaii was not mentioned as a possible target. It was a great distance from Japan to Hawaii, and Washington officials doubted Japan would try to launch such a long-range attack.

The failure to collect sufficient information and the failure of the branches of the U.S. military to share the information available left Pearl Harbor an open target. The result was devastating. Japan's surprise attack on December 7, 1941, sank or damaged 21 ships of the U.S. Pacific Fleet, including 8 battleships, 3 cruisers, 4 destroyers, and

❶ 6:45 A.M.: The destroyer *Ward* sinks a Japanese midget submarine near the entrance to Pearl Harbor.

❷ 7:02 to 7:39 A.M.: Army radar at Opana tracks a cloud of aircraft approaching from the north. An officer at Fort Shafter concludes it is a flight of B-17s due in from California.

❸ 7:49 A.M.: The first wave of 183 Japanese planes is ordered to attack. The force includes 40 torpedo bombers and 49 high-altitude bombers—each armed with a single projectile—bound for Battleship Row. Other bombers and Zero fighters attack airfields.

❹ 8:55 A.M.: The second wave of 167 planes renews the attack on airfields and ships. Oil tanks and most ship-repair facilities are ignored, an omission the Japanese later regret.

Dorie Miller, World War II's first recognized African American hero, won the Navy Cross for bravery for defending a battleship during the Japanese attack at Pearl Harbor.

Student Web Activity Visit the *American Vision* Web site at tav.glencoe.com and click on *Student Web Activities— Chapter 24* for an activity on Pearl Harbor.

Objectives and answers to the student activity can be found in the **Web Activity Lesson Plan** at tav.glencoe.com.

Interpreting a Map To help students understand how geography affected the war, have them calculate the distance between each of these locations and Washington, D.C.: Hawaii, Tokyo, and San Francisco. Ask students what they notice about the distances. **L1**

3 ASSESS

Assign Section 4 Assessment as homework or as an in-class activity.

Have students use the **Interactive Tutor Self-Assessment CD-ROM.**

Reading Essentials and Study Guide 24–4

Name _____ Date _____ Class _____

Study Guide

Chapter 24, Section 4
For use with textbook pages 725–730

AMERICA ENTERS THE WAR

KEY TERMS AND NAMES

America First Committee   an isolationist group that firmly opposed any American intervention or aid to the Allies *(page 726)*

Lend-Lease Act   a law that would allow the United States to lend or lease arms to any country considered vital to the defense of the United States *(page 727)*

hemispheric defense zone   the western half of the Atlantic which was declared part of the Western Hemisphere and therefore neutral *(page 727)*

Atlantic Charter   an agreement between the United States and Britain to a postwar world of democracy, nonaggression, free trade, economic advancement and freedom of the seas *(page 727)*

CRITICAL THINKING ACTIVITY

Comparing Remind students of the embargo cutting off exports of scrap metal to Japan ordered by Roosevelt in 1940. The embargo was later extended to other products with military uses. Discuss the embargoes imposed against Iraq in 1990 and Haiti in 1993. Ask students to write their opinions on whether embargoes are successful in preventing war or accomplishing the goals established by the nations who impose them. **L3**

Section Quiz 24–4

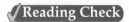

Name _____ Date _____ Class _____

★ **Chapter 24** | Score

Section Quiz 24-4

DIRECTIONS: Matching Match each item in Column A with the items in Column B. Write the correct letters in the blanks. *(10 points each)*

Column A	Column B
___ 1. materials important for fighting a war	A. Lend-Lease Act
___ 2. revised to allow warring countries to buy arms from the United States on a cash-and-carry basis	B. hemispheric defense zone
___ 3. American destroyer torpedoed and sank by a German submarine	C. Neutrality Act of 1939
___ 4. stated the United States could lend or lease arms to any country considered "vital to the defense of the United States"	D. strategic materials
___ 5. the entire western half of the Atlantic Ocean that Roosevelt declared as neutral territory	E. Reuben James

World Geography Connection

Answer: Since much of East-West trade went through the strait, its control would allow the Japanese to keep other powers out of the region.

Reteach

Have students explain how Roosevelt helped Britain under a neutrality policy.

Enrich

Invite students to write a report on the accuracy of a World War II film.

✓ Reading Check

Answer: attack on Pearl Harbor

4 CLOSE

Have students create a relative chronology explaining the events that eventually led to war between the United States and Japan.

World Geography Connection

Geography and War

Throughout history, geography has played a key role in wars. In 1941, for example, Japan attacked Malaya and Indonesia to gain access to oil and rubber. It also wanted control of the Strait of Malacca, an important waterway linking the Indian Ocean with the South China Sea. Geography can also influence a war's outcome, as it did in the Vietnam War. There, miles of dense jungle allowed guerrillas to wage war first against French troops and then against American forces. *Why do you think the Strait of Malacca was so important?*

6 other vessels. The attack also destroyed 188 airplanes and killed 2,403 Americans. Another 1,178 were injured.

On the night of the attack, a gray-faced Roosevelt met with his cabinet to tell them the country now faced the most serious crisis since the outbreak of the Civil War. The next day, the president asked Congress to declare war:

❝Yesterday, December 7, 1941—a date which will live in infamy—the United States of America was suddenly and deliberately attacked by the naval and air forces of Japan. . . . I believe I interpret the will of the Congress and of the people when I assert that we will not only defend ourselves to the uttermost, but we will make very certain that this form of treachery shall never endanger us again. . . . No matter how long it may take us . . . the American people in their righteous might will win through to absolute victory.❞

—quoted in *Franklin D. Roosevelt: A Rendezvous with Destiny*

Following the president's speech, the Senate voted 82 to 0 and the House 388 to 1 to declare war on Japan.

Germany Declares War Although Japan was now at war with the United States, Hitler did not have to declare war on the Americans. The terms of the alliance with Japan specified that Germany only had to come to Japan's aid if Japan was attacked, not if Japan attacked another country. Hitler, however, had grown frustrated with the American navy's attacks on German submarines, and he believed the time had come to declare war.

Hitler greatly underestimated the strength of the United States, and he expected the Japanese to easily defeat the Americans in the Pacific. He hoped that by helping Japan now, he could count on Japanese support against the Soviet Union once the Americans had been beaten. On December 11, Germany and Italy both declared war on the United States.

✓ Reading Check | **Examining** What finally caused the United States to become involved in World War II?

SECTION 4 ASSESSMENT

Checking for Understanding

1. **Define:** hemispheric defense zone, strategic materials.
2. **Identify:** America First Committee, Lend-Lease Act, Atlantic Charter.

Reviewing Themes

3. **Individual Action** After Roosevelt made the destroyers-for-bases deal with Britain, some Americans called him a dictator. Do you think Roosevelt was right or wrong in his actions? Explain your answer.

Critical Thinking

4. **Interpreting** Why was the United States unprepared for Japan's attack on Pearl Harbor?
5. **Organizing** Use a graphic organizer to list how Roosevelt helped Britain while maintaining official neutrality.

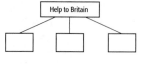

Analyzing Visuals

6. **Analyzing Maps** Study the map on pages 728–729. Based on the geography of Oahu, why was the location of Pearl Harbor perfect for a naval base?

Writing About History

7. **Persuasive Writing** Take on the role of an American in 1940. Write a letter to the editor of your newspaper explaining why you think the United States should either remain neutral or become involved in World War II.

SECTION 4 ASSESSMENT ANSWERS

1. Terms are in blue.
2. America First Committee *(p. 726)*, Lend-Lease Act *(p. 727)*, Atlantic Charter *(p. 727)*
3. Some may say it was important to stop Germany; others that Roosevelt violated the Neutrality Act.
4. The United States was still negotiating with Japan and had failed to collect sufficient information. The U.S. military had not shared information among the various branches.
5. destroyers for bases, Lend-Lease Act, hemispheric defense zone
6. It was sheltered and provided easy access to the ocean.
7. Students' letters will vary but should express a clear and reasoned opinion.

Critical Thinking SKILLBUILDER

Making Generalizations

Why Learn This Skill?

Have you heard statements such as "Only tall people play basketball well," or "Dogs make better pets than cats"? Do you accept these statements at face value, or do you stop and consider whether or not they are valid?

Learning the Skill

The statements listed above are called *generalizations*, which are broad statements about a topic. To be valid, a generalization must be based on accurate information.

Let's examine the generalization, "Only tall people play basketball well." We can find many examples of tall basketball players, but there are also many shorter players who excel at this sport.

In this case, we began with a generalization and looked for facts to support or disprove it. In other cases, you will start with a group of facts about a topic and then make a generalization from these facts. To make a valid generalization, first collect information relevant to the topic. This information must consist of accurate facts, not opinions.

Suppose that you want to make a generalization about the relative danger of airplane travel compared to automobile travel. First, you would collect accident statistics involving airplanes and cars. Your next step would be to classify the information into categories. Then you would look for relationships between these categories. For example, you might put the airplane and automobile statistics in separate categories. You might also categorize the number of accidents and the number of fatalities. Finally, you should make a generalization that is consistent with most of the facts you gathered.

Practicing the Skill

Reread the passage about the Austrian *Anschluss* on page 714, and then answer these questions.

❶ What facts about the *Anschluss* are presented?

❷ Organize these facts into categories.

❸ How does the vote held in Austria relate to the other facts?

❹ What generalization can you make about Austria regarding the *Anschluss*?

Skills Assessment

Complete the Practicing Skills questions on page 733 and the Chapter 24 Skill Reinforcement Activity to assess your mastery of this skill.

Applying the Skill

Making Generalizations Review the information in the chapter about appeasement as it related to the countries of Czechoslovakia, France, and Britain. Write a generalization about Czechoslovakia's role in the appeasement policy. Support your generalization with at least five facts.

 Glencoe's **Skillbuilder Interactive Workbook CD-ROM, Level 2,** provides instruction and practice in key social studies skills.

731

ANSWERS TO PRACTICING THE SKILL

❶ Hitler demanded *Anschluss* on the basis of common language. He wanted to expand German territory and resources. He used threats and force to achieve it.

❷ Possible categories: Hitler's actions, Austria's response

❸ The vote was held after Hitler's troops were already in Austria.

❹ Possible answers: Austrians could not have prevented the *Anschluss*; Austrians shared language and culture with Germans.

Applying the Skill
Students' answers should support the generalization.

Reviewing Key Terms

Students' answers will vary. The pages where the words appear in the text are shown in parentheses.

1. **fascism** *(p. 709)*
2. **internationalism** *(p. 712)*
3. **appeasement** *(p. 714)*
4. **blitzkrieg** *(p. 715)*
5. **Holocaust** *(p. 719)*
6. **concentration camp** *(p. 723)*
7. **extermination camp** *(p. 723)*
8. **hemispheric defense zone** *(p. 727)*
9. **strategic materials** *(p. 729)*

Reviewing Key Facts

10. Benito Mussolini *(p. 709)*, Vladimir Lenin *(p. 709)*, Adolf Hitler *(p. 709)*
11. Germany, Italy, USSR, Japan
12. Austrians spoke German and had an authoritarian government. Czechoslovakians spoke several languages and had a democratic government and allies.
13. Nazis took away their civil liberties, seized their property, imprisoned them, and killed them.
14. Roosevelt made a destroyers-for-bases deal, got Congress to pass the Lend-Lease Act, and developed the hemispheric defense zone strategy.

Critical Thinking

15. Answers will vary. A possible reason for a positive answer is that the attack on Pearl Harbor was the result of the United States's efforts to help Britain in the war against Germany. A possible reason for a negative answer is that Hitler seemed bent on world domination so that U.S. interests would eventually have needed protection.

Reviewing Key Terms

On a sheet of paper, use each of these terms in a sentence.

1. fascism
2. internationalism
3. appeasement
4. blitzkrieg
5. Holocaust
6. concentration camp
7. extermination camp
8. hemispheric defense zone
9. strategic materials

Reviewing Key Facts

10. **Identify:** Benito Mussolini, Vladimir Lenin, Adolf Hitler.
11. Where did antidemocratic governments arise in Europe and Asia after World War I?
12. Why was Austria easier for Hitler to annex than Czechoslovakia?
13. What were four ways that Nazis persecuted Jews?
14. In what three ways did Roosevelt help Britain while maintaining an American policy of neutrality?

Critical Thinking

15. **Analyzing Themes: Global Connections** If Roosevelt's internationalist policy had been fully pursued, do you think it could have prevented World War II?
16. **Evaluating** Why were the British able to stop the German invasion of their country?
17. **Determining Cause and Effect** How did the rise of dictatorships and the attack on Pearl Harbor cause the United States to become involved in World War II?
18. **Organizing** Use a graphic organizer similar to the one below to list countries that Hitler and the Nazis seized during the early years of World War II.

Countries Seized by Hitler and the Nazis

Chapter Summary

Axis

Italy
- Mussolini's Fascist Party believed in supreme power of the state
- Cooperated with Germany from 1936 onward

Germany
- Hitler's Nazi Party believed in all-powerful state, territorial expansion, and ethnic purity
- Invaded Poland in 1939, France in 1940, and the USSR in 1941

Japan
- Military leaders pushed for territorial expansion
- Attacked Manchuria in 1931
- Invaded China in 1937
- Attacked Pearl Harbor in 1941

Allies

United States
- Passed Neutrality Acts in 1935, 1937, and 1939
- Gave lend-lease aid to Britain, China, and the USSR
- Declared war on Japan in 1941

Great Britain
- Tried to appease Hitler by allowing territorial growth
- Declared war on Germany in 1939
- Resisted German attack in 1940
- Received U.S. aid through lend-lease program and cash-and-carry provision

France
- Along with Great Britain, tried to appease Hitler
- Declared war on Germany in 1939 after Poland was invaded
- Occupied by Nazis in 1940

USSR
- Communists, led by harsh dictator Joseph Stalin, created industrial power
- Signed non-aggression pact with Germany in 1939
- Received U.S. aid; eventually fought with Allies to defeat Germany

16. the British use of radar; skill of British air force
17. The United States sided with democratically-based governments, particularly after Nazi Germany attacked France and Britain; Pearl Harbor was an outright attack on the United States.
18. Austria, Czechoslovakia, Poland, Denmark, Belgium, France, Luxembourg, the Netherlands, Norway
19. **a.** Lindbergh believed that many Americans were against entering the war and that in a democratic nation, their wishes should be listened to. **b.** Students' answers will vary. It might not have changed his mind; he believed we needed to protect ourselves.

19. Interpreting Primary Sources The America First Committee tried to prevent American involvement in World War II. On April 24, 1941, aviator Charles Lindbergh spoke in New York on behalf of this committee. Read the excerpt from his speech and answer the questions that follow.

War is not inevitable for this country. Such a claim is defeatism in the true sense. No one can make us fight abroad unless we ourselves are willing to do so. No one will attempt to fight us here if we arm ourselves as a great nation should be armed. Over a hundred million people in this nation are opposed to entering the war. If the principles of democracy mean anything at all, that is reason enough for us to stay out. If we are forced into war against the wishes of an overwhelming majority of our people, we will have proved democracy such a failure at home that there will be little use fighting for it abroad.

—quoted in *Readings In American History*

a. Why did Lindbergh favor isolationism?

b. How do you think Lindbergh might have felt about isolationism after the attack on Pearl Harbor?

Practicing Skills

20. Making Generalizations Read the passage below and answer the questions that follow.

Hitler and the Nazis believed the Germanic people to be superior to all others. . . . The groups the Nazis held in low regard included homosexuals, the disabled, Gypsies, and Slavic peoples. The Nazis reserved their most virulent hatred for the Jews, however. . . . For the Nazis, all people who were ethnically Jewish were completely evil no matter what their religion, occupation, or education.

a. What facts are presented about the attitude of Hitler and the Nazis toward Germans and Jews?

b. What generalization can be made from these facts?

Geography and History

21. The map on this page shows Nazi concentration and extermination camps. Study it and answer these questions.
   a. Interpreting Maps In which two countries were most of the concentration and extermination camps located?

NATIONAL GEOGRAPHIC

Nazi Concentration and Extermination Camps, 1933–1945

- ⊛ Capital city
- ■ Nazi concentration camp/ death camp

0   200 miles
0   200 kilometers
Lambert Azimuthal Equal-Area projection

   b. Applying Geography Skills What can you conclude about the extent of the Nazis' "final solution"?

Chapter Activity

22. Research Project Research and write a short biography of Winston Churchill. Then describe his career, involvement in World War II, and beliefs to the class.

Writing Activity

23. Descriptive Writing Using the Internet and the library, find firsthand accounts of Holocaust survivors. Create a report on these survivors, and present the report to your classmates.

The Princeton Review
Standardized Test Practice

Directions: Choose the phrase that best completes the following statement.

When Roosevelt signed the Lend-Lease Act in 1941, he said that the United States must become the "arsenal of democracy" in order to

A end the Depression.

B help the Axis powers.

C remain neutral.

D help Great Britain and France.

Test-Taking Tip: An *arsenal* is a stockpile or storehouse of weapons. Eliminate any answer that does not relate to using weapons to protect democracy.

The Princeton Review
Standardized Test Practice

Answer: D

Test-Taking Tip: Instruct students to ask themselves what they know about the timing of the event. This will help them rule out A since the Depression was largely over by this time. Then have them ask themselves who the Axis powers were. Once they realize that Germany, Italy, and Japan were not democratic countries, they can rule out B. Finally, ask if supplying aid to one side is likely to allow the country to remain neutral. By ruling out C, they are left with the answer D.

Bonus Question ❓

Ask: What is the name of the German-born Nobel prize-winning physicist whose scientific theories revolutionized modern physics? *(Albert Einstein)*

Practicing Skills
20. a. Hitler believed in faulty concepts of race, that Germans were a superior race, and that Jews were an evil race. **b.** Hitler and the Nazis were racists.

Geography and History
21. a. Germany and Poland; **b.** The Nazis applied the "Final Solution" in Germany and in all the countries he conquered.

Chapter Activity
22. Students' biographies of Churchill will vary. The biographies should focus on his career, his involvement in the war, and his beliefs.

Writing Activity
23. Reports will vary depending on the research. All should include accounts of survivors' experiences and will to live.

Chapter 25 Resources

Timesaving Tools

TeacherWorks™ All-In-One Planner and Resource Center

- **Interactive Teacher Edition** Access your Teacher Wraparound Edition and your classroom resources with a few easy clicks.
- **Interactive Lesson Planner** Planning has never been easier! Organize your week, month, semester, or year with all the lesson helps you need to make teaching creative, timely, and relevant.

Use Glencoe's **Presentation Plus!** multimedia teacher tool to easily present dynamic lessons that visually excite your students. Using Microsoft PowerPoint® you can customize the presentations to create your own personalized lessons.

TEACHING TRANSPARENCIES

Graphic Organizer 5

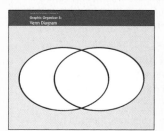

Why It Matters Chapter Transparency 25

APPLICATION AND ENRICHMENT

Linking Past and Present Activity 25

Enrichment Activity 25

Primary Source Reading 25

REVIEW AND REINFORCEMENT

Reteaching Activity 25

Vocabulary Activity 25

Time Line Activity 25

Critical Thinking Skills Activity 25

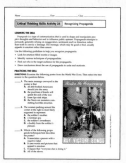

Meeting NCSS Standards

The following standards are highlighted in Chapter 25:

Section 1	V	Individuals, Groups, and Institutions: B, D, E
Section 2	I	Culture: A, B, D
Section 3	II	Time, Continuity, and Change: B, C, F
Section 4	III	People, Places, and Environments: A, F, H
Section 5	VII	Production, Distribution, and Consumption: A, F

Local Standards

Chapter 25 Resources

ASSESSMENT AND EVALUATION

**Chapter 25 Test
Form A**

**Chapter 25 Test
Form B**

**Standardized Test Skills
Practice Workbook Activity 25**

**Performance Assessment
Activities and Rubrics 25**

**ExamView® Pro
Testmaker CD-ROM**

MULTIMEDIA

- Vocabulary PuzzleMaker CD-ROM
- Interactive Tutor Self-Assessment CD-ROM
- ExamView® Pro Testmaker CD-ROM
- Audio Program
- American History Primary Source Documents
  Library CD-ROM
- MindJogger Videoquiz
- Presentation Plus! CD-ROM
- TeacherWorks™ CD-ROM
- Interactive Student Edition CD-ROM
- Glencoe Skillbuilder Interactive Workbook
  CD-ROM, Level 2
- The *American Vision* Video Program
- American Music: Hits Through History
- American Music: Cultural Traditions

SPANISH RESOURCES

**The following Spanish language materials are
available in the Spanish Resources Binder:**

- Spanish Guided Reading Activities
- Spanish Reteaching Activities
- Spanish Quizzes and Tests
- Spanish Vocabulary Activities
- Spanish Summaries
- The Declaration of Independence and United States Constitution
  Spanish Translation

THE HISTORY CHANNEL.

The following videotape programs are available
from Glencoe as supplements to Chapter 25:

- **FDR: The War Years** (1-56-501458-8)
- **The Best Kept Secret: D Day** (0-76-700680-1)
- **Propaganda Wars: Japan and the U.S.** (1-56-501320-4)
- **The War in the Pacific** (1-56-501994-6)

To order, call Glencoe at 1-800-334-7344. To find classroom resources to
accompany many of these videos, check the following home pages:
A&E Television: www.aande.com
The History Channel: www.historychannel.com

HISTORY
Online

Use our Web site for additional resources. All essential content is covered in the Student Edition.

You and your students can visit tav.glencoe.com, the Web site companion to the *American Vision.* This innovative integration of electronic
and print media offers your students a wealth of opportunities. The
student text directs students to the Web site for the following options:

- **Chapter Overviews**
- **Self-Check Quizzes**
- **Student Web Activities**
- **Textbook Updates**

Answers to the student Web activities are provided for you in the **Web
Activity Lesson Plans.** Additional Web resources and Interactive Tutor
Puzzles are also available.

SECTION RESOURCES

Daily Objectives	Reproducible Resources	Multimedia Resources
SECTION 1 **Mobilizing for War** 1. Explain how the United States mobilized its economy. 2. Describe the issues involved in raising an American army.	Reproducible Lesson Plan 25–1 Daily Lecture and Discussion Notes 25–1 Guided Reading Activity 25–1* Section Quiz 25–1* Reading Essentials and Study Guide 25–1 Performance Assessment Activities and Rubrics	Daily Focus Skills Transparency 25–1 Interactive Tutor Self-Assessment CD-ROM ExamView® Pro Testmaker CD-ROM Presentation Plus! CD-ROM TeacherWorks™ CD-ROM Audio Program
SECTION 2 **The Early Battles** 1. Analyze how the Allies were able to fight a war on two fronts and turn the war against the Axis in the Pacific, Russia, and North Atlantic. 2. Explain why Stalingrad is considered a major turning point of World War II.	Reproducible Lesson Plan 25–2 Daily Lecture and Discussion Notes 25–2 Guided Reading Activity 25–2* Section Quiz 25–2* Reading Essentials and Study Guide 25–2 Performance Assessment Activities and Rubrics	Daily Focus Skills Transparency 25–2 Interactive Tutor Self-Assessment CD-ROM ExamView® Pro Testmaker CD-ROM Presentation Plus! CD-ROM Skillbuilder Interactive Workbook, Level 2 TeacherWorks™ CD-ROM Audio Program
SECTION 3 **Life on the Home Front** 1. Describe how the wartime economy created opportunities for women and minorities. 2. Discuss how Americans coped with shortages and rapidly rising prices.	Reproducible Lesson Plan 25–3 Daily Lecture and Discussion Notes 25–3 Guided Reading Activity 25–3* Section Quiz 25–3* Reading Essentials and Study Guide 25–3 Supreme Court Case Studies	Daily Focus Skills Transparency 25–3 American Art & Architecture Interactive Tutor Self-Assessment CD-ROM ExamView® Pro Testmaker CD-ROM Presentation Plus! CD-ROM American Music: Cultural Traditions
SECTION 4 **Pushing the Axis Back** 1. Describe the goals of the two major offensives the Allies launched in Europe in 1943. 2. Explain the American strategy for pushing the Japanese back in the Pacific.	Reproducible Lesson Plan 25–4 Daily Lecture and Discussion Notes 25–4 Guided Reading Activity 25–4* Section Quiz 25–4* Reading Essentials and Study Guide 25–4 Performance Assessment Activities and Rubrics	Daily Focus Skills Transparency 25–4 Interactive Tutor Self-Assessment CD-ROM ExamView® Pro Testmaker CD-ROM Presentation Plus! CD-ROM TeacherWorks™ CD-ROM Audio Program
SECTION 5 **The War Ends** 1. Explain the tactics the Allies used to invade Germany and to defeat Japan. 2. Outline the reasons the Allies created the United Nations and held war crimes trials.	Reproducible Lesson Plan 25–5 Daily Lecture and Discussion Notes 25–5 Guided Reading Activity 25–5* Section Quiz 25–5* Reading Essentials and Study Guide 25–5 Performance Assessment Activities and Rubrics	Daily Focus Skills Transparency 25–5 Interactive Tutor Self-Assessment CD-ROM ExamView® Pro Testmaker CD-ROM Presentation Plus! CD-ROM TeacherWorks™ CD-ROM Vocabulary PuzzleMaker CD-ROM Audio Program American Music: Cultural Traditions

0:00 OUT OF TIME?
Assign the Chapter 25 **Reading Essentials and Study Guide.**

*Also Available in Spanish

Blackline Master	Transparency	CD-ROM	DVD
Poster	Music Program	Audio Program	Videocassette

NATIONAL GEOGRAPHIC Teacher's Corner

INDEX TO NATIONAL GEOGRAPHIC MAGAZINE

NATIONAL GEOGRAPHIC SOCIETY PRODUCTS AVAILABLE FROM GLENCOE

To order the following products for use with this chapter, contact your local Glencoe sales representative, or call Glencoe at 1-800-334-7344:

• *PictureShow: Story of America, Part 2* (CD-ROM)
• *PicturePack: Story of America Library, Part 2* (Transparencies)
• *PicturePack: World War II Era* (Transparencies)
• *PictureShow: World War II Era* (CD-ROM)

ADDITIONAL NATIONAL GEOGRAPHIC SOCIETY PRODUCTS

To order the following, call National Geographic at 1-800-368-2728:

• *Eyewitness to the 20th Century* (Book)
• *Lost Fleet of Guadalcanal* (Video)

NGS ONLINE

Access National Geographic's Web site for current events, atlas updates, activities, links, interactive features, and archives.
www.nationalgeographic.com

KEY TO ABILITY LEVELS

Teaching strategies have been coded.

L1 BASIC activities for all students
L2 AVERAGE activities for average to above-average students
L3 CHALLENGING activities for above-average students
ELL ENGLISH LANGUAGE LEARNER activities

From the Classroom of...

Ellen Closs
Okemos Public Schools
Okemos, MI

Reporters and the Times

Ask students to try to adopt the point of view of someone living in the 1940s. Organize the class into groups of 3 people each (reporter, soldier, and someone on the home front). Instruct the reporter to interview both the soldier and the person on the home front about how America's role in the war has changed their lives. How have they themselves changed as people? Has the war changed their view of the American government or the world? If possible, give them primary resources, such as letters and autobiographies from the time to help them prepare their questions.

Have them present their interviews to the class, acting as people who are living during World War II.

ADDITIONAL RESOURCES FROM GLENCOE

• American Music: Cultural Traditions
• American Art & Architecture
• Outline Map Resource Book
• U.S. Desk Map
• Building Geography Skills for Life
• Inclusion for the High School Social Studies Classroom Strategies and Activities
• Teaching Strategies for the American History Classroom (Including Block Scheduling Pacing Guides)

 Block Schedule

Activities that are suited to use within the block scheduling framework are identified by:

Performance Assessment

Refer to Activity 25 in the Performance Assessment Activities and Rubrics booklet. 📦

Why It Matters Activity

Have students explain how they think World War II continues to have an impact on the lives of Americans. Students should evaluate their answers after they have completed the chapter.

GLENCOE
TECHNOLOGY

The *American Vision* Video Program
To learn more about America's role in World War II, have students view the Chapter 25 video, "Japanese American Internment Camps," from the ***American Vision* Video Program.**

💿 📼 Available in DVD and VHS

MindJogger Videoquiz
Use the **MindJogger Videoquiz** to preview Chapter 25 content.

📼 Available in VHS

CHAPTER 25 America and World War II
1941–1945

Why It Matters

The United States entered World War II unwillingly and largely unprepared. The American people, however, quickly banded together to transform the American economy into the most productive and efficient war-making machine in the world. American forces turned the tide in Europe and the Pacific, and they played a crucial role in the defeat of Germany, Italy, and Japan.

The Impact Today

Many changes that began in World War II are still shaping our lives today.
- *The United Nations was founded.*
- *Nuclear weapons were invented.*
- *The United States became the most powerful nation in the world.*

 **The American Vision Video** *The Chapter 25 video, "Japanese American Internment Camps," chronicles the treatment of Japanese Americans during World War II.*

1943
- Detroit race riots
- Zoot suit riots in Los Angeles

1941
- President Roosevelt forbids racial discrimination in defense industries
- United States enters World War II

1942
- Women's Army Auxiliary Corps established
- Japanese American relocation ordered

 F. Roosevelt 1933–1945

United States **PRESIDENTS**

1941   *1942*   *1943*

World

1941
- Japan attacks Pearl Harbor and the Philippines

1942
- Japan takes Philippines; MacArthur vows: "I shall return."
- Americans turn the tide in the Pacific at the Battle of Midway

1943
- Battle of Tarawa
- Germans defeated at Stalingrad
- Allied forces land in Italy

734

TWO-MINUTE LESSON LAUNCHER

Before the Japanese attack on Pearl Harbor, most Americans were aware of the war in Europe but held fast to their beliefs that the United States should not become involved. Ask students if they would support or oppose American involvement in a conflict between other countries if that involvement might result in a world war.

Introduce students to chapter content and key terms by having them access the **Chapter 25 Overview** at tav.glencoe.com.

More About the Photo

Landing craft were used to transport troops and equipment on D-Day. Have students imagine that they are one of these soldiers. Ask them what they were experiencing as their landing craft's ramp was lowered. *(Students may describe the physical conditions such as the cold, salty water or the emotions that the soldiers likely experienced such as determination or fear.)*

TIME LINE
ACTIVITY

Have students use a globe or world map to identify the approximate location where the world events on the time line occurred.

Allied soldiers landing at Omaha Beach in Normandy on D-Day—June 6, 1944

1945
• Franklin Roosevelt dies in office; Harry S Truman becomes president

1944
• Supreme Court rules in *Korematsu* v. *the United States* that Japanese American relocation is constitutional

Truman 1945–1953

HISTORY Online
Chapter Overview
Visit the *American Vision* Web site at tav.glencoe.com and click on *Chapter Overviews—Chapter 25* to preview chapter information.

1944

1945

1944
• Eisenhower leads D-Day invasion
• Battle of Leyte Gulf

1945
• United States drops atomic bomb on Japan
• World War II ends

735

GRAPHIC ORGANIZER ACTIVITY

Organizing Information Have students take notes on Chapter 25 by completing a table similar to the one shown below. Students' notes should be concise, addressing the concepts or themes found in the chapter.

Allied Power	Axis Power
Britain	Germany
Russia	Italy
United States	Japan

1 FOCUS

Section Overview

This section describes the preparations the U.S. made in anticipation of entering the war.

Guide to Reading

Answers to Graphic: A restructured Reconstruction Finance Corporation, War Production Board, Office of War Mobilization, draft board (under Selective Service and Training Act)

Preteaching Vocabulary
Have students write two questions that can be answered using the Key Terms.

Mobilizing for War

Guide to Reading

Main Idea
The United States quickly mobilized its economy and armed forces to fight World War II.

Key Terms and Names
cost-plus, Reconstruction Finance Corporation, Liberty ship, War Production Board, Selective Service and Training Act, disfranchise

Reading Strategy
Organizing As you read about American mobilization for World War II, complete a graphic organizer like the one below by filling in the agencies the U.S. government created to mobilize the nation's economy for war.

Government Agencies Created to Mobilize the Economy

Reading Objectives
- **Explain** how the United States mobilized its economy.
- **Describe** the issues involved in raising an American army.

Section Theme
Individual Action The success of the United States in mobilizing for war was due largely to the cooperation of individual American citizens.

Preview of Events

♦1940	♦1941	♦1942	♦1943
1940 Fall of France; Selective Service Act	**December 7, 1941** Japan attacks Pearl Harbor	**1942** Women's Army Auxiliary Corps (WAAC) established	**1943** Office of War Mobilization (OWM) established

★ An American Story ★

Franklin D. Roosevelt

Shortly after 1:30 P.M. on December 7, 1941, Secretary of the Navy Frank Knox phoned President Roosevelt at the White House. "Mr. President," Knox said, "it looks like the Japanese have attacked Pearl Harbor." A few minutes later, Admiral Harold Stark, chief of naval operations, phoned and confirmed the attack.

As Eleanor Roosevelt passed by the president's study, she knew immediately something very bad had happened:

"All the secretaries were there, two telephones were in use, the senior military aides were on their way with messages." Eleanor also noticed that President Roosevelt remained calm: "His reaction to any event was always to be calm. If it was something that was bad, he just became almost like an iceberg, and there was never the slightest emotion that was allowed to show."

Turning to his wife, President Roosevelt expressed anger at the Japanese: "I never wanted to have to fight this war on two fronts. We haven't got the Navy to fight in both the Atlantic and Pacific. . . . We will have to build up the Navy and the Air Force and that will mean we will have to take a good many defeats before we can have a victory."

—**adapted from *No Ordinary Time***

Converting the Economy

Although the difficulties of fighting a global war troubled the president, British Prime Minister Winston Churchill was not worried. Churchill knew that victory in modern war depended on a nation's industrial power. He compared the American economy

---

to a gigantic boiler: "Once the fire is lighted under it there is no limit to the power it can generate."

Churchill was right. The industrial output of the United States during the war astounded the rest of the world. American workers were twice as productive as German workers and five times more productive than Japanese workers. American war production turned the tide in favor of the Allies. In less than four years, the United States achieved what no other nation had ever done—it fought and won a two-front war against two powerful military empires, forcing each to surrender unconditionally.

The United States was able to expand its war production so rapidly after the attack on Pearl Harbor in part because the government had begun to mobilize the economy before the country entered the war. When the German blitzkrieg swept into France in May 1940, President Roosevelt declared a national emergency and announced a plan to build 50,000 warplanes a year. Shocked by the success of the German attack, many Americans were willing to build up the country's defenses.

Roosevelt and his advisers believed that the best way to rapidly mobilize the economy was to give industry an incentive to move quickly. As Henry Stimson, the new secretary of war, wrote in his diary: "If you are going to try and go to war, or to prepare for war, in a capitalist country, you have got to let business make money out of the process or business won't work."

Normally when the government needed military equipment, it would ask companies to bid for the contract, but that system was too slow in wartime. Instead of asking for bids, the government signed cost-plus contracts. The government agreed to pay a company whatever it cost to make a product plus a guaranteed percentage of the costs as profit. Under the cost-plus system, the more a company produced and the faster it did the work, the more money it would make. The system was not cheap, but it did get war materials produced quickly and in quantity.

Although cost-plus convinced many companies to convert to war production, others could not afford to reequip their factories to make military goods. To convince more companies to convert, Congress gave new authority to the **Reconstruction Finance Corporation** (RFC). The RFC, a government agency set up during the Depression, was now permitted to make loans to companies to help them cover the cost of converting to war production.

✔ **Reading Check** Analyzing What government policies helped American industry to produce large quantities of war materials?

American Industry Gets the Job Done

By the fall of 1941, much had already been done to prepare the economy for war, but it was still only partially mobilized. Although many companies were producing military equipment, most still preferred to make consumer goods. The Depression was ending and sales were rising. The Japanese attack on Pearl Harbor, however, changed everything. By the summer of 1942, almost all major industries and some 200,000 companies had converted to war production. Together they made the nation's wartime "miracle" possible.

ECONOMICS

Tanks Replace Cars The automobile industry was uniquely suited to the mass production of military equipment. Automobile factories began to produce trucks, jeeps, and tanks. This was critical in modern warfare because the country that could move troops and supplies most quickly usually

✦ **History** *Through Art*

WW II Posters War posters were designed to help encourage and inform the American public. How would you have felt to see a poster such as this one?

CHAPTER 25 America and World War II **737**

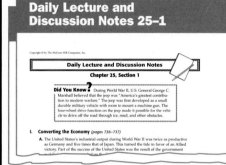
Designing a Bulletin Board
Have students create a bulletin board on one of the topics in this section. Students should focus on either industry or government as the nation prepared for war. L1 ELL

📁 Use the rubric for creating a map, display, or chart on pages 77–78 in the *Performance Assessment Activities and Rubrics.*

✔ **Reading Check**

Answer: The cost-plus program encouraged companies to produce many products quickly and in quantity. The RFC made loans to help companies convert to war production.

✦ **History** *Through Art*

Answer: Students may say it would have encouraged them to consider the threats to American freedom.

COOPERATIVE LEARNING ACTIVITY

Creating a Plan Arrange the class into four groups and assign each group one of these industries: cellular telephones, computer software, agriculture, and construction. Have each group develop a plan for converting their industry to wartime production. Have each group share their plan with the class. Encourage students to offer constructive criticism of each group's plan.

Use the rubric for a cooperative group management plan on pages 81–82 in the *Performance Assessment Activities and Rubrics.*

Analyzing Information Have students look carefully at the photograph and graphs on pages 738–739. Using what they see in the photo and graphs, along with the content of this section, have students write a paragraph describing what they think was happening when the photograph was taken. **L2**

〰 Graph *Skills*

Answers:

1. As the production of cars decreases, the production of tanks increases. When tank production is at its highest, auto production is at its lowest. When the production of tanks decreases the production of autos increases.

2. The graphs show that producing tanks to help win the war took precedence over producing automobiles.

Graph Skills Practice
Ask: Why does the production of tanks jump so sharply between 1941 and 1942? *(U.S. entered the war at the end of 1941.)*

---

won the battle. As General George C. Marshall, chief of staff for the United States Army, observed:

❝The greatest advantage the United States enjoyed on the ground in the fighting was . . . the jeep and the two-and-a-half ton truck. These are the instruments that moved and supplied United States troops in battle, while the German army . . . depended on animal transport. . . . The United States, profiting from the mass production achievements of its automotive industry . . . had mobility that completely outclassed the enemy.❞

—quoted in *Miracle of World War II*

Automobile factories did not just produce vehicles. They also built artillery, rifles, mines, helmets, pontoon bridges, cooking pots, and dozens of other pieces of military equipment. Henry Ford launched one of the most ambitious projects when he created an assembly line for the enormous B-24 bomber known as "the Liberator" at Willow Run Airport near Detroit. By the end of the war, the factory had built over 8,600 aircraft. Overall, the automobile industry produced nearly one-third of the military equipment manufactured during the war.

Building the Liberty Ships Henry Kaiser's shipyards more than matched Ford's achievement in aircraft production. Kaiser's shipyards built many ships, but they were best known for their production of Liberty ships. The Liberty ship was the basic cargo ship used during the war. Most Liberty ships were welded instead of riveted. Welded ships were cheap, easy to build, and very hard to sink compared to riveted ships.

When a riveted ship was hit, the rivets often came loose, causing the ship to fall apart and sink. A welded ship's hull was fused into one solid piece of steel. A torpedo might blow a hole in it, but the hull would not come apart. A damaged Liberty ship could often get back to port, make repairs, and return to service.

The War Production Board As American companies converted to war production, many business leaders became frustrated with the mobilization process. Government agencies argued constantly about supplies and contracts and whose orders had the highest priority.

After Pearl Harbor, President Roosevelt tried to improve the system by creating the **War Production Board** (WPB). He gave the WPB the authority to set

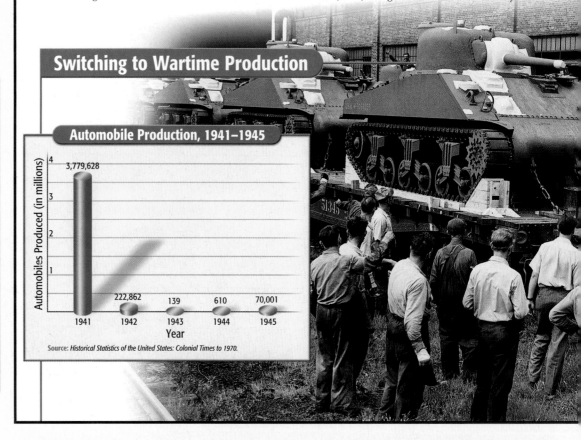

Switching to Wartime Production

Automobile Production, 1941–1945

Automobiles Produced (in millions)

- 1941: 3,779,628
- 1942: 222,862
- 1943: 139
- 1944: 610
- 1945: 70,001

Year

Source: *Historical Statistics of the United States: Colonial Times to 1970.*

MEETING SPECIAL NEEDS

Learning Disability Students with language-based learning disabilities often know a variety of strategies for studying text, but they sometimes forget to employ these strategies appropriately. Ask students to preview Section 1 to determine the topics presented. List the topics on the board and ask students to think of strategies and skills they have employed throughout the text that might help in learning the information in this section. **L1** ELL

📁 Refer to *Inclusion for the High School Social Studies Classroom Strategies and Activities* in the TCR.

priorities and production goals and to control the distribution of raw materials and supplies. Almost immediately, the WPB clashed with the military. Military agencies continued to sign contracts without consulting with the WPB. Finally, in 1943, Roosevelt established the **Office of War Mobilization** (OWM) to settle arguments between the different agencies.

✔ **Reading Check** **Explaining** What military need led to the production of Liberty ships?

Building an Army

Converting factories to war production was only part of the mobilization process. If the United States was actually going to fight and win the war, the country also needed to build up its armed forces.

Creating an Army Within days of Germany's attack on Poland, President Roosevelt expanded the army to 210,000 soldiers. After France surrendered to Germany in June 1940, two members of Congress introduced the **Selective Service and Training Act,** a plan for the first peacetime draft in American history. Before the spring of 1940, college students, labor unions, isolationists, and most members of Congress had opposed a peacetime draft. Opinions changed after Germany defeated France. In August Congress approved the draft by a wide margin.

You're in the Army Now At first the flood of draftees overwhelmed the army's training facilities. Many recruits had to live in tents and use temporary facilities. The army also endured equipment shortages. Troops carried sticks representing guns, threw stones simulating grenades, and practiced maneuvers with trucks carrying signs that read "TANK."

New draftees were initially sent to a reception center, where they were given physical exams and injections against smallpox and typhoid. The draftees were then issued uniforms, boots, and whatever equipment was available. The clothing bore the label "G.I.," meaning "Government Issue," which is why American soldiers were called "GIs."

After taking aptitude tests, recruits were sent to basic training for eight weeks. They learned how to handle weapons, load backpacks, read maps, pitch tents, and dig trenches. Trainees drilled and exercised constantly and learned how to work as a team.

After the war, many veterans complained that basic training had been useless. Soldiers were rushed through too quickly, and the physical training left them too tired to learn the skills they needed. A sergeant in Italy told a reporter for *Yank* magazine that during a recent battle, a new soldier had held up his rifle and yelled, "How do I load this thing?"

Despite its problems, basic training helped to break down barriers between soldiers. Recruits came from all over the country, and training together made them into a unit. Training created a "special sense of kinship," one soldier noted. "The reason you storm the beaches is not patriotism or bravery. It's that sense of not wanting to fail your buddies."

A Segregated Army Although basic training promoted unity, most recruits did not encounter Americans from every part of society. At the start of the war, the U.S. military was completely segregated. White recruits did not train alongside African Americans. African Americans had separate barracks, latrines, mess halls, and recreational facilities.

Tank Production, 1941–1945

Year	Tanks Produced (in thousands)
1941	4,203
1942	23,884
1943	29,497
1944	17,565
1945	11,184

Source: *Historical Statistics of the United States: Colonial Times to 1970.*

📉 Graph *Skills*

1. **Interpreting Graphs** How does the number of tanks produced relate to the number of automobiles produced in the previous graph?
2. **Making Generalizations** How do these two graphs illustrate the commitment of the United States to winning the war?

CHAPTER 25 America and World War II **739**

✔ **Reading Check**

Answer: the need to have ships that were cheap, easy to build, and hard to sink

Creating a Chart Have students use the data in the chart that appears on this page to create a circle graph showing what proportion of all tanks made between 1941–1945 were made in each of the years. Tell them to use different color slices for each year and to prepare a legend to correlate the colors with the years. **L3**

you don't say...

World War II Terms A term commonly used by GIs during World War II was *O-dark-30.* The expression means *early in the morning* and refers to military time of 30 minutes past midnight.

FYI

From 1948 until 1973, during both peacetime and periods of conflict, men were drafted to fill vacancies in the armed forces which could not be filled through voluntary means. The draft ended in 1973 and the U.S. converted to an all-volunteer military.

INTERDISCIPLINARY CONNECTIONS ACTIVITY

Government Ask students to discuss current U.S. policy regarding readiness for a draft. Ask the following questions: **Do you think that current policy would allow the government to mobilize effectively? How do you feel about requiring persons of specific ages, gender, and citizenship status to register? Do you think that women should be required to register? Why or why not?** The Selective Service System Web site at www.sss.gov provides information about current policy and answers to frequently asked questions. **L2**

3 ASSESS

Assign Section 1 Assessment as homework or as an in-class activity.

🔵 Have students use the **Interactive Tutor Self-Assessment CD-ROM.**

Reading Essentials and Study Guide 25–1

Name _____ Date _____ Class _____

Study Guide

Chapter 25, Section 1
For use with textbook pages 736–741

MOBILIZING FOR WAR

KEY TERMS AND NAMES

cost-plus type of government contract in which the government agreed to pay a company whatever it cost to make a product plus a guaranteed percentage of the costs as profit (page 737)

Reconstruction Finance Corporation a government agency that made loans to companies to help cover the cost of converting to war production (page 737)

War Production Board a government agency with the authority to set priorities and production goals and to control the distribution of raw materials and supplies (page 738)

Selective Service and Training Act a plan for the first peacetime draft in American history

---

Section Quiz 25–1

Name _____ Date _____ Class _____

★ **Chapter 25**   Score _____

Section Quiz 25–1

DIRECTIONS: Matching Match each item in Column A with the items in Column B. Write the correct letters in the blanks. (10 points each)

Column A

_____ 1. government agreed to pay a company whatever it cost to make a product plus a guaranteed percentage of the costs as profit

_____ 2. an African American unit, the 99th Pursuit Squadron, that played an important role during the Battle of Anzio

_____ 3. nickname for American soldiers because their clothing was labeled "Government Issue"

_____ 4. first regular army corps for women

_____ 5. basic cargo ship used during the war

Column B

A. Women's Army Corps

B. cost-plus contracts

C. GIs

D. Liberty ship

E. Tuskegee Airmen

Once trained, African Americans were organized into their own military units, but white officers were generally in command of them. Most military leaders also wanted to keep African American soldiers out of combat and assigned them to construction and supply units.

Pushing for "Double V" Some African Americans did not want to support the war. As one student at a black college noted: "The Army Jim Crows us. . . . Employers and labor unions shut us out. Lynchings continue. We are disenfranchised . . . and spat upon. What more could Hitler do to us than that?" By disfranchised, the student meant that African Americans were often denied their right to vote. Despite the bitterness, most African Americans agreed with African American writer Saunders Redding that they should support their country:

> ❝There are many things about this war I do not like . . . yet I believe in the war. . . . We know that whatever the mad logic of [Hitler's] New Order there is no hope for us under it. The ethnic theories of the Hitler 'master folk' admit of no chance of freedom. . . . This is a war to keep [people] free. The struggle to broaden and lengthen the road of freedom—our own private and important war to enlarge freedom here in America—will come later. . . . I believe in this war because I believe in America. I believe in what America professes to stand for. . . . ❞
>
> —quoted in *America at War*

Picturing **History**

Tuskegee Airmen The Tuskegee Airmen distinguished themselves in combat, yet they were not allowed to serve in integrated units. In what theater of the war did the Tuskegee Airmen serve?

Benjamin O. Davis

Many African American leaders combined patriotism with protest. In 1941 the National Urban League set two goals for its members: "(1) To promote effective participation of [African Americans] in all phases of the war effort. . . . (2) To formulate plans for building the kind of United States in which we wish to live after the war is over. . . ."

The *Pittsburgh Courier,* a leading African American newspaper, embraced these ideas and launched what it called the **"Double V" campaign.** African Americans, the paper argued, should join the war effort in order to achieve a double victory—a victory over Hitler's racism abroad and a victory over racism at home. If the United States wanted to portray itself as a defender of democracy, Americans might be willing to end discrimination in their own country.

President Roosevelt knew that African American voters had played an important role in his election victories. Under pressure from African American leaders, he ordered the army air force, navy, and marines to begin recruiting African Americans, and he directed the army to put African Americans into combat. He also appointed Colonel **Benjamin O. Davis,** the highest-ranking African American officer in the U.S. Army, to the rank of brigadier general.

African Americans in Combat In response to the president's order, the army air force created the 99th Pursuit Squadron, an African American unit that trained in Tuskegee, Alabama. These African American fighter pilots became known as the **Tuskegee Airmen.** After General Davis urged the military to put African Americans into combat, the 99th Pursuit Squadron was sent to the Mediterranean in April 1943. The squadron played an important role during the Battle of Anzio in Italy.

African Americans also performed well in the army. The all-African American 761st Tank Battalion was commended for its service during the Battle of the Bulge. Fighting in northwest Europe, African Americans in the 614th Tank Destroyer Battalion won 8 Silver Stars for distinguished service, 28 Bronze Stars, and 79 Purple Hearts.

Although the military did not end all segregation during the war, it did integrate military bases in 1943 and steadily expanded the role of African Americans within the armed forces. These successes paved the way for President Truman's decision to fully integrate the military in 1948.

CRITICAL THINKING ACTIVITY

Analyzing Events World War II resulted in the devastation of lives and property. Ask students the following questions: Could World War II have been avoided? Why or why not? *(Answers will vary. Some students might say that it could have been avoided if the Allies had not used the policy of appeasement with Hitler in the late 1930s. They might also indicate that it could have been avoided if the League of Nations had been given greater power after World War I. Other students might say that a war could not have been avoided, because force was the only way to stop the military aggression of Germany and Japan.)* **L2**

Women Join the Armed Forces As in World War I, women joined the armed forces. The army enlisted women for the first time, although they were barred from combat. Instead, as the army's recruiting slogan suggested, women were needed to "release a man for combat." Many jobs in the army were administrative and clerical. By assigning women to these jobs, more men would be available for combat.

Congress first allowed women in the military in May 1942, when it established the **Women's Army Auxiliary Corps** (WAAC) and appointed **Oveta Culp Hobby,** an official with the War Department, to serve as its first director. Although pleased about the establishment of the WAAC, many women were unhappy that it was an auxiliary corps and not part of the regular army. A little over a year later, the army replaced the WAAC with the **Women's Army Corps** (WAC). Director Hobby was assigned the rank of colonel. "You have a debt and a date," Hobby explained to those training to be the nation's first women officers. "A debt to democracy, a date with destiny." The Coast Guard, the navy, and the marines quickly followed the army and set up their own women's units. In addition to serving in these new organizations, another 64,000 women served as nurses in the army and navy.

Americans Go to War The Americans who went to war in 1941 were not well trained. Most of the troops had no previous military experience. Most of the officers had never led men in combat. The armed forces mirrored many of the tensions and prejudices of American society. Despite these challenges, the United States armed forces performed well in battle.

Picturing **History**

Women Pilots General Barney M. Giles inspects the guard of honor of the Women Air Service Pilots (WASPS) at Avenger Field in Sweetwater, Texas. Many pilots wore Filfinella patches (right) for good luck. *Why do you think the army refused to allow women to fly in combat?*

Of all the major powers involved in the war, the United States suffered the fewest casualties in combat.

American troops never adopted the spit-and-polish style of the Europeans. When they arrived at the front, Americans' uniforms were usually a mess, and they rarely marched in step. When one Czechoslovakian was asked what he thought of the sloppy, unprofessional American soldiers, he commented, "They walk like free men."

✓ **Reading Check** **Summarizing** How did the status of women and African Americans in the armed forces change during the war?

Reteach
Have students create a two-column chart. In one column, have them list the industries affected by the war mobilization effort. In the other column, have students list how the industries were affected.

Enrich
Have students research one of the persons or organizations mentioned in this section using library and Internet resources to write a one-page paper about the topic.

✓ **Reading Check**

Answer: African Americans had several units that gave distinguished service. Women were allowed to serve in non-combat units.

4 CLOSE

Ask students to speculate on how their lives might be different if the U.S. had not begun to prepare for war when it did.

SECTION **1** ASSESSMENT

Checking for Understanding
1. **Define:** cost-plus, Liberty ship, disfranchise.
2. **Identify:** Reconstruction Finance Corporation, War Production Board, Selective Service and Training Act.
3. **Describe** the role of the OWM in the war production effort.

Reviewing Themes
4. **Individual Action** Why do you think African Americans were willing to fight in the war even though they suffered discrimination in American society?

Critical Thinking
5. **Evaluating** How effectively did American industry rally behind the war effort? Give examples to support your opinion.
6. **Categorizing** Use a graphic organizer like the one below to list the challenges facing the United States as it mobilized for war.

Challenges to Mobilization

Analyzing Visuals
7. **Analyzing Graphs** Study the graphs of automobile and tank production on pages 738 and 739. Why did automobile production decrease while tank production increased?

Writing About History
8. **Descriptive Writing** Take on the role of a draftee who has just completed the first week of basic training. Write a letter to your parents telling them about basic training and what you hope to accomplish once the training is over.

SECTION **1** ASSESSMENT ANSWERS

1. Terms are in blue.
2. Reconstruction Finance Corporation *(p. 737),* War Production Board *(p. 738),* Selective Service and Training Act *(p. 739)*
3. The OWM resolved conflicts among mobilization agencies.
4. They opposed Hitler's ethnic theories, believed America should wage this war, and demonstrated their support for democracy and equality at home and overseas.
5. By 1942, almost all major industries were producing trucks, jeeps, and tanks.
6. converting to wartime economy, building an army, training troops
7. Auto manufacturers were producing tanks rather than cars.
8. Answers should be in the form of a letter.

SECTION 2 The Early Battles

1 FOCUS

Section Overview

This section describes the early battles of World War II.

BELLRINGER
Skillbuilder Activity

Project transparency and have students answer the question.

Available as a blackline master.

Daily Focus Skills Transparency 25–2

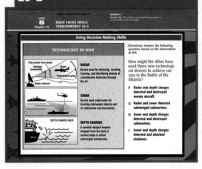

Guide to Reading

Answers to Graphic: April 1942, Doolittle Raid, Allies; May 1942, Philippines, Axis; May 1942, Coral Sea, Allies; June 1942, Midway, Allies; November 1942, Stalingrad, Allies; May 1943, North Africa, Allies

Preteaching Vocabulary
Have students write a paragraph containing at least four of the Key Terms and Names introduced in this section.

Guide to Reading

Main Idea
By late 1942, the Allies had stopped the German and Japanese advance.

Key Terms and Names
Chester Nimitz, Douglas MacArthur, James Doolittle, periphery, George Patton, convoy system

Reading Strategy
Sequencing As you read about the military campaigns of 1942, complete a time line similar to the one below to record the major battles discussed and the victor in each.

Reading Objectives
• **Analyze** how the Allies were able to fight a war on two fronts and turn the war against the Axis in the Pacific, Russia, and the North Atlantic.
• **Explain** why Stalingrad is considered a major turning point of the war.

Section Theme
Individual Action Many American soldiers made heroic sacrifices in order to turn the tide against the Axis Powers.

Preview of Events

♦1942	♦1943	♦1944

May 1942
Fall of the Philippines; Battle of the Coral Sea

June 1942
Battle of Midway

February 1943
Germans defeated at Stalingrad

May 1943
Germans driven out of North Africa

⭐ *An American Story* ⭐

James S. Thach

On June 4, 1942, Lieutenant Commander James Thach climbed into his F4F Wildcat fighter plane. Thach knew that the Japanese Zero fighter planes were better than his Wildcat. To improve his chances against them, he had developed a new tactic he called the "Thach weave." At the Battle of Midway, he had his first chance to try it:

❝So we boarded our planes. All of us were highly excited and admittedly nervous. . . . A very short time after, Zero fighters came down on us—I figured there were twenty. . . . The air was just like a beehive, and I wasn't sure that anything would work. And then my weave began to work! I got a good shot at two Zeros and burned them . . . then Ram, my wingman, radioed: 'There's a Zero on my tail.' . . . I was really angry then. I was mad because my poor little wingman had never been in combat before [and] this Zero was about to chew him to pieces. I probably should have ducked under the Zero, but I lost my temper and decided to keep my fire going into him so he'd pull out. He did, and I just missed him by a few feet. I saw flames coming out of his airplane. This was like playing chicken on the highway with two automobiles headed for each other, except we were shooting at each other as well.❞

—**quoted in *The Pacific War Remembered***

Holding the Line Against Japan

While officers like James Thach developed new tactics to fight the Japanese, the commander of the United States Navy in the Pacific, Admiral **Chester Nimitz,** began planning operations against the Japanese navy. Although the Japanese had badly damaged the American fleet at Pearl Harbor, they had missed the American aircraft carriers,

SECTION RESOURCES

Reproducible Masters
• Reproducible Lesson Plan 25–2
• Daily Lecture and Discussion Notes 25–2
• Guided Reading Activity 25–2
• Section Quiz 25–2
• Reading Essentials and Study Guide 25–2
• Performance Assessment Activities and Rubrics

Transparencies
• Daily Focus Skills Transparency 25–2

Multimedia
🔘 Interactive Tutor Self-Assessment CD-ROM
🔘 ExamView® Pro Testmaker CD-ROM
🔘 Presentation Plus! CD-ROM
🔘 TeacherWorks™ CD-ROM
🔘 Audio Program

which were at sea on a mission. The United States had several carriers in the Pacific, and Nimitz was determined to use them. In the days just after Pearl Harbor, however, he could do little to stop Japan's advance into Southeast Asia.

The Fall of the Philippines A few hours after they bombed Pearl Harbor, the Japanese attacked American airfields in the Philippines. Two days later, Japanese troops landed in the islands. The American and Filipino forces defending the Philippines were badly outnumbered. Their commander, General **Douglas MacArthur,** decided to retreat to the Bataan Peninsula. Using the peninsula's rugged terrain, MacArthur's troops held out for more than three months. Gradually, the lack of supplies along with diseases such as malaria, scurvy, and dysentery took their toll. Realizing MacArthur's capture would demoralize the American people, President Roosevelt ordered the general to evacuate to Australia. In Australia MacArthur made a promise: "I came through, and I shall return."

On April 9, 1942, the weary defenders of Bataan finally surrendered. Nearly 78,000 prisoners of war were forced to march—sick, exhausted, and starving—65 miles (105 km) to a Japanese prison camp. Thousands died on this march, which came to be known as the **Bataan Death March.** Here one captured American, Leon Beck, recalls the nightmare:

66 They'd halt us in front of these big artesian wells . . . so we could see the water and they wouldn't let us have any. Anyone who would make a break for water would be shot or bayoneted. Then they were left there. Finally, it got so bad further along the road that you never got away from the stench of death. There were bodies laying all along the road in various degrees of decomposition—swollen, burst open, maggots crawling by the thousands. . . . 99
—quoted in *Death March: The Survivors of Bataan*

Although the troops in the Bataan Peninsula surrendered, a small force held out on the island of **Corregidor** in Manila Bay. Finally, in May 1942, Corregidor surrendered. The Philippines had fallen.

The Doolittle Raid Even before the fall of the Philippines, President Roosevelt was searching for a way to raise the morale of the American people. He wanted to bomb Tokyo, but American planes could reach Tokyo only if an aircraft carrier brought them close enough. Unfortunately, Japanese ships in the North Pacific prevented carriers from getting close enough to Japan to launch their short-range bombers.

In early 1942, a military planner suggested replacing the carrier's usual short-range bombers with long-range B-25 bombers that could attack from farther away. Although B-25s could take off from a carrier, they could not land on its short deck. After attacking Japan, they would have to land in China.

President Roosevelt put Lieutenant Colonel **James Doolittle** in command of the mission. At the end of March, a crane loaded sixteen B-25s onto the aircraft carrier *Hornet.* The next day the *Hornet* headed west across the Pacific. On April 18, American bombs fell on Japan for the first time.

Striking Back: The Doolittle Raid, April 18, 1942

The plan for the Doolittle raid was to launch B-25 bombers from aircraft carriers between 450 and 650 miles from Japan. The planes would bomb selected targets, and fly another 1,200 miles to airfields in China.

All went well until the Japanese discovered the carriers more than 150 miles from the proposed launch site. Instead of canceling the mission, the bombers took off early. The planes reached Japan and dropped their bombs, but they did not have enough fuel to reach the friendly airfields in China. The crews were forced to bail out or crash-land, and only 71 of the 80 crew members survived. Nevertheless, the raid provided an instant boost to sagging American morale.

Planes arrive in China
Carriers launch B-25s
Tokyo is bombed

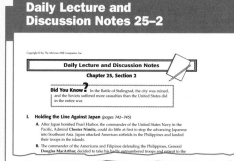

CHAPTER 25
Section 2, 742–747

2 TEACH

Daily Lecture and Discussion Notes 25–2

Copyright © by The McGraw-Hill Companies, Inc.

Daily Lecture and Discussion Notes

Chapter 25, Section 2

Did You Know? In the Battle of Stalingrad, the city was ruined, and the Soviets suffered more casualties than the United States did in the entire war.

I. Holding the Line Against Japan *(pages 742–745)*

A. After Japan bombed Pearl Harbor, the commander of the United States Navy in the Pacific, Admiral **Chester Nimitz,** could do little at first to stop the advancing Japanese into Southeast Asia. Japan attacked American airfields in the Philippines and landed their troops in the islands.

B. The commander of the Americans and Filipinos defending the Philippines, General **Douglas MacArthur,** decided to take his badly outnumbered troops and retreat to the

Writing a Press Release

Organize the class into two groups. Have one group represent Roosevelt. Have the other group represent the Japanese leaders. As you review each of the major battles in the Pacific front discussed in this section, have each group write a press release intended for publication to their people the day after the battle. **L1**

More About the Photo

In addition to the B-25, the U.S. used B-24 and B-29 bombers. Fighter planes included the P-38 and P-40. Ask students why they think American leaders decided not to cancel the mission. *(Because the Japanese had bombed American soil and captured U.S. forces, American leaders felt that bombing Japan would raise American morale.)*

COOPERATIVE LEARNING ACTIVITY

Questioning Isolationism Organize students into small groups. Ask the groups: What influenced the shift in American public opinion away from isolation? Have the groups discuss and prepare a written response to the question and share their responses with the class. As a class, discuss the ideas presented by the groups. *(Students might say that the fall of France and the threat to Britain changed Americans' belief that events outside the Western Hemisphere were none of their business.)*

Use the rubric for a cooperative group management plan on pages 81–82 in the *Performance Assessment Activities and Rubrics.*

Geography *Skills*

Background: Before World War II, few of the indigenous peoples of the islands of the South Pacific had encountered people from other parts of the world.

Answers:

1. June 4, 1942, 4:30 A.M.

2. Aircraft carriers reduced the distance planes had to fly and the amount of fuel they consumed.

Geography Skills Practice
Ask: What general direction did the *Enterprise* and *Hornet* take? *(southwest)*

Writing a Report Ask students to prepare a one-page report on the career of a World War II military leader. The report should address how the leader contributed to the war effort and what the leader did earlier or later in his career. **L2**

📁 Use the rubric for creating a book review, research report, or position paper on pages 89–90 in the *Performance Assessment Activities and Rubrics.*

Guided Reading Activity 25–2

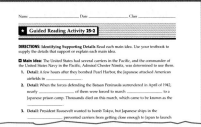

Name _____ Date _____ Class _____

★ **Guided Reading Activity 25-2**

DIRECTIONS: Identifying Supporting Details Read each main idea. Use your textbook to supply the details that support or explain each main idea.

☐ **Main Idea:** The United States had several carriers in the Pacific, and the commander of the United States Navy in the Pacific, Admiral Chester Nimitz, was determined to use them.

1. **Detail:** A few hours after they bombed Pearl Harbor, the Japanese attacked American airfields in _____.

2. **Detail:** When the forces defending the Bataan Peninsula surrendered in April of 1942, nearly _____ of them were forced to march _____ to a Japanese prison camp. Thousands died on this march, which came to be known as the _____.

3. **Detail:** President Roosevelt wanted to bomb Tokyo, but Japanese ships in the _____ prevented carriers from getting close enough to Japan to launch

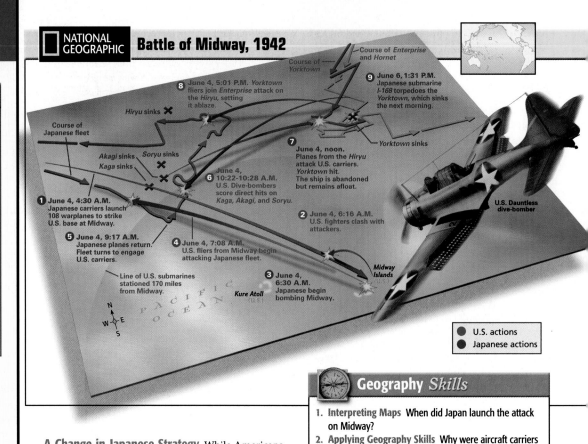

NATIONAL GEOGRAPHIC **Battle of Midway, 1942**

Course of *Enterprise* and *Hornet*

Course of *Yorktown*

8 June 4, 5:01 P.M. *Yorktown* fliers join *Enterprise* attack on the *Hiryu*, setting it ablaze.

9 June 6, 1:31 P.M. Japanese submarine *I-168* torpedoes the *Yorktown*, which sinks the next morning.

Hiryu sinks ✖

Course of Japanese fleet

Yorktown sinks

7 June 4, noon. Planes from the *Hiryu* attack U.S. carriers. *Yorktown* hit. The ship is abandoned but remains afloat.

Akagi sinks ✖   *Soryu* sinks ✖
Kaga sinks ✖

1 June 4, 4:30 A.M. Japanese carriers launch 108 warplanes to strike U.S. base at Midway.

6 June 4, 10:22-10:28 A.M. U.S. Dive-bombers score direct hits on *Kaga*, *Akagi*, and *Soryu*.

2 June 4, 6:16 A.M. U.S. fighters clash with attackers.

U.S. Dauntless dive-bomber

5 June 4, 9:17 A.M. Japanese planes return. Fleet turns to engage U.S. carriers.

4 June 4, 7:08 A.M. U.S. fliers from Midway begin attacking Japanese fleet.

Line of U.S. submarines stationed 170 miles from Midway.

3 June 4, 6:30 A.M. Japanese begin bombing Midway.

Kure Atoll (U.S.)

Midway Islands (U.S.)

PACIFIC OCEAN

N W E S

● U.S. actions
● Japanese actions

Geography *Skills*

1. **Interpreting Maps** When did Japan launch the attack on Midway?
2. **Applying Geography Skills** Why were aircraft carriers so vital to the war in the Pacific?

A Change in Japanese Strategy While Americans were overjoyed that the air force had finally struck back, Japanese leaders were aghast. Doolittle's bombs could have killed the emperor. The Doolittle raid convinced Japanese leaders to change their strategy.

Before the raid, the Japanese Navy had been arguing about what to do next. The officers in charge of the navy's planning wanted to cut American supply lines to Australia by capturing the south coast of New Guinea. The commander of the fleet, Admiral Yamamoto, wanted to attack Midway Island—the last American base in the North Pacific west of Hawaii. Yamamoto believed that attacking Midway would lure the American fleet into battle and enable his fleet to destroy it.

After Doolittle's raid, the planners dropped their opposition to Yamamoto's plan. The American fleet had to be destroyed in order to protect Tokyo from bombing. The attack on New Guinea would still go ahead, but only three aircraft carriers were assigned to the mission. All of the other carriers were ordered to prepare for an assault on Midway.

The Battle of the Coral Sea The Japanese believed that they could proceed with two different attacks. They thought the United States was unaware of Japan's activity and would not be able to respond in time. Japan did not know that an American team of code breakers, based in Hawaii, had already broken the Japanese Navy's secret code for conducting operations.

In March 1942, decoded Japanese messages alerted the United States to the Japanese attack on New Guinea. In response, Admiral Nimitz sent two carriers, the *Yorktown* and the *Lexington*, to intercept the Japanese in the Coral Sea. There, in early May, carriers from both sides launched all-out airstrikes against each other. Although the Japanese sank the *Lexington* and badly damaged the *Yorktown*, the American attacks forced the Japanese to call off their landing on the south coast of New Guinea. The American supply lines to Australia stayed open.

MEETING SPECIAL NEEDS

Interpersonal Have students select one portion of Section 2 to teach to another student. Ask students to read the passage and then to teach it to a partner. Have the student doing the teaching ask questions about what has been taught. Direct the teaching student to review any concepts that the learner did not understand. **L1** **ELL**

📁 Refer to *Inclusion for the High School Social Studies Classroom Strategies and Activities* in the TCR.

JAPANESE FORCES To destroy the U.S. Pacific Fleet, crippled by the 1941 attack on Pearl Harbor, Japan plots an occupation of two Aleutian islands and an invasion of Midway. Strategists believe that the twin actions will lure U.S. carriers to their doom. Two Japanese carriers and 58 other ships sail for the Aleutians. For Midway, Japan commits 4 large carriers, 2 light carriers, 280 planes, 7 battleships, 14 cruisers, 15 submarines, 42 destroyers, and more than 30 supporting ships. These include transports carrying 5,000 troops to take Midway.

U.S. FORCES No battleships guard U.S. carriers sent to Midway to engage the enemy fleet. Into combat go 3 carriers, including battle-damaged Yorktown. Protecting them are 8 cruisers and 16 destroyers. The U.S. has a total of 360 aircraft, including 234 carrier-based fighters and small bombers. Based on Midway are 28 fighters, 46 small bombers, 31 PBY Catalina scout planes, 4 Marauder medium bombers, and 17 Flying Fortresses. Most pilots on Midway have never flown in combat.

TURNING POINT

The Battle of Midway Back at Pearl Harbor, the code-breaking team that had alerted Nimitz to the attack on New Guinea now learned of the plan to attack Midway. With so many ships at sea, Admiral Yamamoto transmitted the plans for the Midway attack by radio, using the same code the Americans had already cracked.

Admiral Nimitz had been waiting for the opportunity to ambush the Japanese fleet. He immediately ordered carriers to take up positions near Midway. Unaware they were heading into an ambush, the Japanese launched their aircraft against Midway on June 4, 1942. The island was ready. The Japanese planes ran into a blizzard of antiaircraft fire, and 38 of them were shot down.

As the Japanese prepared a second wave to attack Midway, aircraft from the American carriers *Hornet*, *Yorktown*, and *Enterprise* launched a counterattack. The American planes caught the Japanese carriers with fuel, bombs, and aircraft exposed on their flight decks. Within minutes three Japanese carriers were reduced to burning wrecks. A fourth was sunk a few hours later. By nightfall it was apparent that the Americans had

dealt the Japanese navy a deadly blow. Admiral Yamamoto ordered his remaining ships to retreat.

The Battle of Midway was a turning point in the war. The Japanese Navy lost four of its largest carriers—the heart of its fleet. Just six months after Pearl Harbor, the United States had stopped the Japanese advance in the Pacific. As Admiral Ernest King, the commander in chief of the U.S. Navy, later observed, Midway "put an end to the long period of Japanese offensive action." The victory was not without cost, however. The battle killed 362 Americans and 3,057 Japanese. Afterward, one naval officer wrote to his wife: "Let no one tell you or let you believe that this war is anything other than a grim, terrible business."

✓ **Reading Check** **Explaining** Why was the Battle of Midway considered a turning point?

Turning Back the German Army

In 1942 Allied forces began to win victories in Europe as well. Almost from the moment the United States entered the war, Joseph Stalin, the leader of the Soviet Union, urged President Roosevelt to open a second front in Europe. Stalin appreciated the Lend-Lease supplies that the United States had sent, but the Soviet people were still doing most of the fighting. If British and American troops opened a second front by attacking Germany from the west, it would take pressure off the Soviet Union.

Roosevelt wanted to get American troops into battle in Europe, but Prime Minister Churchill urged caution. He did not believe the United States and Great Britain were ready to launch a full-scale invasion of Europe. Instead Churchill wanted to attack the periphery, or edges, of the German empire. Roosevelt agreed, and in July 1942 he ordered the invasion of Morocco and Algeria—two French territories indirectly under German control.

The Struggle for North Africa

Roosevelt decided to invade Morocco and Algeria for two reasons. First, the invasion would give the army some experience without requiring a lot of troops. More importantly, once American troops were in North Africa, they would be able to help British troops fighting the Germans in Egypt.

Student Web Activity Visit the *American Vision* Web site at tav.glencoe.com and click on *Student Web Activities—Chapter 25* for an activity on America and World War II.

Creating a Thematic Map Have students create a map of the Pacific region with labels for major landforms and bodies of water. Students should also label the countries to show whether they were an Allied nation, a neutral nation, or part of the Japanese Empire. **L2**

📁 Use the rubric for creating a map, display, or chart on pages 77–78 in the *Performance Assessment Activities and Rubrics.*

✓ **Reading Check**

Answer: The Japanese lost four large carriers and their initiative.

FYI

The Japanese flag shown on this page is the regimental flag for the Japanese cavalry and infantry. The national flag of Japan since 1870 has consisted of a white background with a red circle in the middle. The red circle is said to symbolize the rising sun.

HISTORY Online

Objectives and answers to the student activity can be found in the **Web Activity Lesson Plan** at tav.glencoe.com.

INTERDISCIPLINARY CONNECTIONS ACTIVITY

Visual Arts Have students work in groups to research and report on the military vessels and planes used in World War II. Ask students to organize their research to show the development of the vessels during the course of the war. Have students illustrate their work with photos, drawings, and models. Create a display area to showcase students' work. **L2**

IN HISTORY

Use a Venn diagram to compare and contrast the lives and military careers of Nimitz and Yamamoto.

3 ASSESS

Assign Section 2 Assessment as homework or as an in-class activity.

● Have students use the **Interactive Tutor Self-Assessment CD-ROM.**

Reading Essentials and Study Guide 25–2

Name _____ Date _____ Class _____

Study Guide

Chapter 25, Section 2

For use with textbook pages 742–747

THE EARLY BATTLES

KEY TERMS AND NAMES

Chester Nimitz the commander of the United States Navy in the Pacific *(page 742)*

Douglas MacArthur the commander of the American and Filipino forces in the Philippines *(page 743)*

James Doolittle lieutenant colonel and head of the mission to bomb Tokyo *(page 743)*

periphery the edges *(page 745)*

George Patton commander of the American forces in Morocco during the American invasion of North Africa *(page 746)*

convoy system a system in which cargo ships traveled in groups and were escorted by navy warships *(page 746)*

Section Quiz 25–2

Name _____ Date _____ Class _____

★ **Chapter 25** ___ Score ___

Section Quiz 25-2

DIRECTIONS: Matching Match each item in Column A with the items in Column B.
Write the correct letters in the blanks. *(10 points each)*

Column A

___ 1. cargo ships traveled in groups and were escorted by navy warships

___ 2. turning point in the war that put the Germans on the offensive

___ 3. edges

___ 4. turning point in the war that stopped the Japanese advance in the Pacific

___ 5. when 78,000 prisoners of war were forced to march 65 miles to a Japanese prison camp

Column B

A. Battle of Midway

B. Battle of Stalingrad

C. Bataan Death March

D. convoy system

E. periphery

Profiles IN HISTORY

Fleet Admiral Chester W. Nimitz 1885–1966

Taking command of the Pacific Fleet after the bombing of Pearl Harbor, Admiral Chester Nimitz did not view the Japanese attack as a complete disaster. The United States still had its aircraft carriers, and base facilities were in good repair. Even though the battle fleet was at the bottom of the harbor, most of the ships could be retrieved and repaired. If the Japanese had attacked the fleet at sea, nothing would have been salvageable.

Nimitz believed that the only way to win the war was to keep constant pressure on the Japanese. He ordered attacks in early 1942 and firmly backed the Doolittle raid. Nimitz planned the American campaigns that turned the tide of war at Midway and Guadalcanal. Nimitz kept the pressure on the Japanese throughout the war, and he signed the Japanese surrender document as the official representative of the United States government in 1945. In less than four years, he had taken a badly damaged fleet and made it victorious throughout the Pacific.

Admiral Isoroku Yamamoto 1884–1943

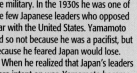

The son of a schoolmaster, Isoroku Yamamoto spent his entire adult life in the military. In the 1930s he was one of the few Japanese leaders who opposed war with the United States. Yamamoto did so not because he was a pacifist, but because he feared Japan would lose.

When he realized that Japan's leaders were intent on war, Yamamoto became convinced that Japan's only hope lay in launching a surprise attack that would destroy the American Pacific Fleet. Although some officers opposed his plan, Yamamoto won out, and he planned and implemented the attack on Pearl Harbor. During the first years of the war, he enjoyed tremendous prestige because of Japanese victories he helped engineer.

In April 1943 the admiral took an inspection flight of several islands. Having already broken the Japanese codes, the Americans knew of the flight. On April 18, American fighters shot down Yamamoto's plane in the South Pacific, and the admiral was killed in the attack.

Egypt was very important to Britain because of the Suez Canal. Most of Britain's empire, including India, Hong Kong, Singapore, Malaya, and Australia, used the canal to send supplies to Britain. The German forces in the area, known as the "Afrika Korps," were commanded by General Erwin Rommel—a brilliant leader whose success earned him the nickname "Desert Fox."

The British forced Rommel to retreat at the battle of El Alamein, but his forces remained a serious threat. On November 8, 1942, the American invasion of North Africa began under the command of General Dwight D. Eisenhower. The American forces in Morocco, led by General **George Patton,** quickly captured the city of Casablanca, while those in Algeria seized the cities of Oran and Algiers. The Americans then headed east into Tunisia, while British forces headed west into Libya. The plan was to trap Rommel between the two Allied forces.

When the American troops advanced into the mountains of western Tunisia, they had to fight the German army for the first time. They did not do well. At the **Battle of Kasserine Pass,** the Americans were outmaneuvered and outfought. They suffered roughly 7,000 casualties and lost nearly 200 tanks. Eisenhower fired the general who led the attack and put Patton in

command. Together, the American and British forces finally pushed the Germans back. On May 13, 1943, the last German forces in North Africa surrendered.

The Battle of the Atlantic As American and British troops fought the German army in North Africa, the war against German submarines in the Atlantic Ocean continued to intensify. After Germany declared war on the United States, German submarines entered American coastal waters. They found American cargo ships to be easy targets, especially at night when the glow from the cities in the night sky silhouetted the vessels. To protect the ships, cities on the East Coast dimmed their lights every evening. People also put up special "blackout curtains" and drove with their headlights off.

By August 1942, German submarines had sunk about 360 American ships along the American coast. So many oil tankers were sunk that gasoline and fuel oil had to be rationed. To keep oil flowing, the government built the first long-distance oil pipeline, stretching some 1,250 miles (2,010 km) from the Texas oil fields to Pennsylvania.

The loss of so many ships convinced the U.S. Navy to set up a convoy system. Under this system, cargo ships traveled in groups and were escorted by navy warships. The convoy system improved the

746 CHAPTER 25 America and World War II

CRITICAL THINKING ACTIVITY

Comparing and Contrasting Have students work in small groups to compare and contrast the early battles that the Allies fought against the Japanese and the Germans. Ask each group to prepare a chart showing the similarities and differences that they discover. Have the groups post their charts in the class. Give time for the groups to review the charts. Then hold a class discussion about the similarities and differences that they discovered. **L1**

situation dramatically. It made it much harder for a submarine to torpedo a cargo ship and escape without being attacked.

The spring of 1942 marked the high point of the German submarine campaign. In May and June alone, over 1.2 million tons of shipping were sunk. Yet in those same two months, American and British shipyards built over 1.1 million tons of new shipping. From July 1942 onward, American shipyards produced more ships than German submarines managed to sink. At the same time, American airplanes and warships began to use new technology, including radar, sonar, and depth charges, to locate and attack submarines. As the new technology began to take its toll on German submarines, the Battle of the Atlantic slowly turned in favor of the Allies.

TURNING POINT

Stalingrad In the spring of 1942, before the Battle of the Atlantic turned against Germany, Adolf Hitler was very confident he would win the war. Rommel's troops were pushing the British back in Egypt. German submarines were sinking American ships rapidly, and the German army was ready to launch a new offensive to knock the Soviets out of the war.

Hitler was convinced that the only way to defeat the Soviet Union was to destroy its economy. In May 1942, he ordered his army to capture strategic oil fields, industries, and farmlands in southern Russia and Ukraine. The key to the attack was the city of Stalingrad. The city controlled the Volga River and was a major railroad junction. If the German army captured Stalingrad, the Soviets would be cut off from the resources they needed to stay in the war.

When German troops entered Stalingrad in mid-September, Stalin ordered his troops to hold the city

Picturing **History**

Halting the German Advance Soviet troops assault German positions in Stalingrad in November 1942. Why did the Soviet army need to hold on to the city of Stalingrad?

at all cost. Retreat was forbidden. The Germans were forced to fight from house to house, losing thousands of soldiers in the process.

On November 23, Soviet reinforcements arrived and surrounded Stalingrad, trapping almost 250,000 German troops. When the battle ended, 91,000 Germans had surrendered, although only 5,000 of them survived the Soviet prison camps and returned home after the war. The Battle of Stalingrad was a major turning point in the war. Just as the Battle of Midway put the Japanese on the defensive for the rest of the war, the Battle of Stalingrad put the Germans on the defensive as well.

☑ **Reading Check** **Evaluating** What did the Allies do to win the Battle of the Atlantic?

SECTION 2 ASSESSMENT

Checking for Understanding

1. **Define:** periphery, convoy system.
2. **Identify:** Chester Nimitz, Douglas MacArthur, James Doolittle, George Patton.
3. **Explain** the American strategy in North Africa.

Reviewing Themes

4. **Individual Action** How did the Doolittle raid help boost American morale?

Critical Thinking

5. **Analyzing** How did code breakers help stop Japanese advances?
6. **Evaluating** How were the Americans able to win the Battle of the Atlantic?
7. **Organizing** Use a graphic organizer like the one below to list the reasons the Battle of Midway was a major turning point in the war.

Battle of Midway

Analyzing Visuals

8. **Examining Maps** Study the map of Midway on page 744. Why do you think the Japanese forces attacked when they did?

Writing About History

9. **Descriptive Writing** Take on the role of an American soldier fighting in the Pacific in World War II. Write a letter to your family explaining what conditions are like for you and what you hope to accomplish during the war.

CHAPTER 25 America and World War II **747**

SECTION 2 ASSESSMENT ANSWERS

1. Terms are in blue.
2. Chester Nimitz *(p. 742)*, Douglas MacArthur *(p. 743)*, James Doolittle *(p. 743)*, George Patton *(p. 746)*
3. The North African campaign gave the army some experience and helped the British in Egypt.
4. Americans felt they had avenged Pearl Harbor by attacking Japanese soil.
5. They alerted the U.S. to the imminent attacks on New Guinea and Midway.
6. the convoy system protected cargo ships; radar, sonar, and depth charges located and damaged German submarines
7. Japanese navy lost four carriers; stopped the Japanese advance in the Pacific; ended Japanese offensive
8. Answers may note that early morning attacks held an element of surprise.
9. Letters should focus on soldiers' emotions and activities.

747

TEACH

Reading a Thematic Map This skill emphasizes the importance of maps to understanding many historical events. By learning to read military maps using the legends, map scale, and other visuals, students gain an appreciation for the influence of geography on history.

Have students trace the troop movements of the Japanese and U.S. forces. Ask students to identify the main battles that occurred on the Bataan Peninsula.

Additional Practice

Reinforcing Skills Activity 25

Name _____ Date _____ Class _____
★ **Reinforcing Skills Activity 25**
Reading a Thematic Map
▢ **LEARNING THE SKILL**
Thematic maps focus on a specific subject or theme. To read a thematic map, (1) read the title of the map; (2) find the map's scale to determine the general size of the area you are looking at; (3) read the compass rose to determine north, south, east, and west; (4) read the map key; and (5) analyze the areas on the map that are highlighted in the key. Look for patterns.
▢ **PRACTICING THE SKILL**
DIRECTIONS: Analyze the map below, and then answer the following questions on a separate sheet of paper.
Invasion of Normandy

GLENCOE
TECHNOLOGY

CD-ROM
Glencoe Skillbuilder Interactive Workbook CD-ROM, Level 2

This interactive CD-ROM reinforces student mastery of essential social studies skills.

Social Studies
SKILLBUILDER

Reading a Thematic Map

Why Learn This Skill?

In your study of American history, you will often encounter thematic maps. Knowing how to read a thematic map will help you get more out of it.

Learning the Skill

Military maps use colors, symbols, and arrows to show major battles, troop movements, and defensive positions during a particular battle or over a period of time. When reading a military map, follow these steps:

- **Read the map title.** This will indicate the location and time period covered on the map.
- **Read the map key.** This tells what the symbols on the map represent. For example, battle sites may be indicated by crossed swords or burst shells.
- **Study the map itself.** This will reveal the actual event or sequence of events that took place. Notice the geography of the area, and try to determine how it could affect military strategy.
- **Use the map to draw conclusions.**

Practicing the Skill

The map on this page shows troop movements in the Philippines from December 1941 to May 1942. Analyze the information on the map, then answer the following questions.

1. What part of the world does the map show?
2. When did MacArthur leave for Australia? What information on the map shows you this?
3. Where did the Japanese imprison the survivors of the Bataan Death March?
4. What geographic features did the Japanese encounter on the Bataan Peninsula?

Skills Assessment

Complete the Practicing Skills questions on page 775 and the Chapter 25 Skill Reinforcement Activity to assess your mastery of this skill.

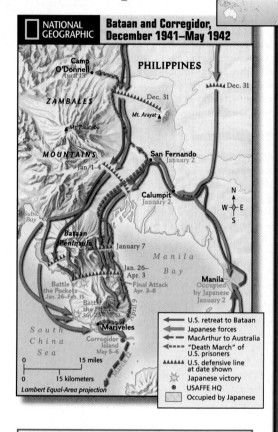

NATIONAL GEOGRAPHIC | **Bataan and Corregidor, December 1941–May 1942**

Legend:
- ← U.S. retreat to Bataan
- ← Japanese forces
- ◄--- MacArthur to Australia
- ◄---- "Death March" of U.S. prisoners
- ▲▲▲▲ U.S. defensive line at date shown
- ✳ Japanese victory
- ⊛ USAFFE HQ
- ▢ Occupied by Japanese

0 ___ 15 miles
0 ___ 15 kilometers
Lambert Equal-Area projection

Applying the Skill

Reading a Thematic Map Study the map of the Battle of Midway on pages 744–745. Use the information on the map to answer the following questions.

1. When was the battle fought?
2. What American aircraft carriers took part in the battle?
3. What was the fate of the *Hiryu*?

 Glencoe's **Skillbuilder Interactive Workbook CD-ROM, Level 2,** provides instruction and practice in key social studies skills.

748

ANSWERS TO PRACTICING THE SKILL

1. Bataan and Corregidor, in Southeast Asia
2. March 12, the date beside the troop movement arrow
3. Camp O'Donnell
4. mountainous terrain

Applying the Skill
1. June 4–6, 1942
2. *Enterprise, Hornet,* and *Yorktown*
3. It sank.

Guide to Reading

Main Idea
World War II placed tremendous demands on Americans at home and led to new challenges for all Americans.

Key Terms and Names
Rosie the Riveter, A. Philip Randolph, Sunbelt, zoot suit, rationing, victory garden, E bond

Reading Strategy
Categorizing As you read about the challenges facing Americans on the home front, complete a graphic organizer listing opportunities for women and African Americans before and after the war. Also evaluate what progress still needed to be made after the war.

Opportunities			
	Before War	After War	Still Needed
Women			
African Americans			

Reading Objectives
• **Describe** how the wartime economy created opportunities for women and minorities.
• **Discuss** how Americans coped with shortages and rapidly rising prices.

Section Theme
Civic Rights and Responsibilities To win the war, American citizens at home made countless changes in work patterns and lifestyles.

Preview of Events

1941	1942	1943	1944

June 1941
Executive Order 8802 forbids race discrimination in industries with government contracts

August 1941
Roosevelt creates the Office of Price Administration

February 1942
Japanese American relocation ordered

June 1943
Race riots in Detroit; zoot suit riots in Los Angeles

★ An American Story ★

Laura Briggs was a young woman living on a farm in Idaho when World War II began. As with many other Americans, the war completely changed her outlook on life:

❝When I was growing up, it was very much depression times. . . . As farm prices [during the war] began to get better and better, farm times became good times. . . . We and most other farmers went from a tarpaper shack to a new frame house with indoor plumbing. Now we had an electric stove instead of a wood-burning one, and running water at the sink. . . . The war made many changes in our town. I think the most important is that aspirations changed. People suddenly had the idea, 'Hey I can reach that. I can have that. I can do that. I could even send my kid to college if I wanted to.'❞

—quoted in *Wartime America: The World War II Home Front*

"Rosie the Riveter" symbolized new roles for women

Women and Minorities Gain Ground

As American troops fought their first battles against the Germans and Japanese, the war began to dramatically change American society at home. In contrast to the devastation the war brought to large parts of Europe and Asia, World War II had a positive effect on American society. The war finally put an end to the Great Depression. Mobilizing the economy created almost 19 million new jobs and nearly doubled the average family's income.

When the war began, American defense factories wanted to hire white men. With so many men in the military, there simply were not enough white men to fill all of the jobs. Under pressure to produce, employers began to recruit women and minorities.

CHAPTER 25 America and World War II **749**

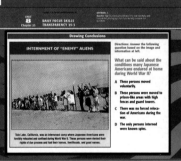

Daily Lecture and Discussion Notes 25-3

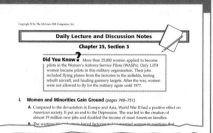

Copyright © by The McGraw-Hill Companies, Inc.

Daily Lecture and Discussion Notes
Chapter 25, Section 3

Did You Know? More than 25,000 women applied to become pilots in the Women's Airforce Service Pilots (WASPs). Only 1,074 women became pilots in this military organization. Their jobs included flying planes from the factories to the airfields, testing rebuilt aircraft, and hauling gunnery targets. After the war, women were not allowed to fly for the military again until 1977.

I. Women and Minorities Gain Ground *(pages 749–751)*

A. Compared to the devastation in Europe and Asia, World War II had a positive effect on American society. It put an end to the Depression. The war led to the creation of almost 19 million new jobs and doubled the income of most American families.

B. The wartime labor shortage forced factories to hire married women in positions that

Writing a Letter Have students take on the role of a young woman who just took a job working in a defense factory during the war and is writing to her grandmother about her first few days on the job. **L1**

📁 Use the rubric for creating a diary, short story, memorandum, or letter on pages 79–80 in the *Performance Assessment Activities and Rubrics.*

Profiles
IN HISTORY

One of the advantages of using Navajo code talkers was that a three-line English message could be encoded, transmitted, and decoded in about 20 seconds. Code machines in use at the time took at least 30 minutes to perform the same task. **Ask:** What is the significance of the Navajo language being a "hidden language"? *(Because the language has no written alphabet and was known only to a few people, it was a very secure code.)*

Women in the Defense Plants During the Depression, many people believed married women should not work outside the home, especially if it meant taking jobs away from men trying to support their families. Most women who did work were young, single, and employed in traditional female jobs. The wartime labor shortage, however, forced factories to recruit married women to do industrial jobs that traditionally had been reserved for men.

Although the government hired nearly 4 million women for mostly clerical jobs, it was the women in the factories who captured the public's imagination. The great symbol of the campaign to hire women was **"Rosie the Riveter,"** a character from a popular song by the Four Vagabonds. The lyrics told of Rosie, who worked in a factory while her boyfriend served in the marines. Images of Rosie appeared on posters, in newspapers, and in magazines. Eventually 2.5 million women went to work in shipyards, aircraft factories, and other manufacturing plants. For many older middle-class women like Inez Sauer, working in a factory changed their perspective:

Profiles IN HISTORY

The Navajo Code Talkers
1942–1945

When American marines stormed an enemy beach, they used radios to communicate. Using radios, however, meant that the Japanese could intercept and translate the messages. In the midst of the battle, however, there was no time to use a code machine. Acting upon the suggestion of Philip Johnston, an engineer who had lived on a Navajo reservation as a child, the marines recruited Navajos to serve as "code talkers."

The Navajo language was a "hidden language"—it had no written alphabet and was known only to the Navajo and a few missionaries and anthropologists. The Navajo recruits developed a code using words from their own language to represent military terms. For example, the Navajo word *jay-sho,* or "buzzard," was code for bomber; *lotso,* or "whale," meant battleship; and *na-ma-si,* or "potatoes," stood for grenades.

Code talkers proved invaluable in combat. They could relay a message in

minutes that would have taken a code machine operator hours to encipher and transmit. At the battle of Iwo Jima, code talkers transmitted more than 800 messages during the first 48 hours as the marines struggled to get ashore under intense bombardment.

Over 400 Navajo served in the marine corps as code talkers. Sworn to secrecy, their mission was not revealed until many years after the war. In 2001 Congress awarded the code talkers the Congressional Gold Medal to recognize their unique contribution to the war effort.

750 CHAPTER 25 America and World War II

❝I learned that just because you're a woman and have never worked is no reason you can't learn. The job really broadened me. . . . I had always been in a shell; I'd always been protected. But at Boeing I found a freedom and an independence I had never known. After the war I could never go back to playing bridge again, being a clubwoman. . . . when I knew there were things you could use your mind for. The war changed my life completely.❞

—quoted in *Eyewitness to World War II*

Although most women left the factories after the war, their success permanently changed American attitudes about women in the workplace.

African Americans Demand War Work Although factories were hiring women, they resisted hiring African Americans. Frustrated by the situation, **A. Philip Randolph,** the head of the Brotherhood of Sleeping Car Porters—a major union for African American railroad workers—decided to take action.

He informed President Roosevelt that he was organizing "from ten to fifty thousand [African Americans] to march on Washington in the interest of securing jobs . . . in national defense and . . . integration into the military and naval forces."

In response, Roosevelt issued Executive Order 8802, on June 25, 1941. The order declared, "there shall be no discrimination in the employment of workers in defense industries or government because of race, creed, color or national origin." To enforce the order, the president created the Fair Employment Practices Commission—the first civil rights agency established by the federal government since the Reconstruction era.

Mexicans Become Farmworkers The wartime economy needed workers in many different areas. To help farmers in the Southwest overcome the labor shortage, the government introduced the **Bracero Program** in 1942. *Bracero* is Spanish for worker. The federal government arranged for Mexican farmworkers to help in the harvest. Over 200,000 Mexicans came to the United States to help harvest

COOPERATIVE LEARNING ACTIVITY

Creating a Display Have students work in small groups to create a display about the home front during World War II. Encourage students to use such items as photographs and memorabilia. Encourage students to ask older family members and acquaintances about wartime sacrifices. Even if these adults have no personal experiences, they might remember stories of sacrifice from their own parents or grandparents. All students in the group should contribute to the display in a specific way. 📁

Use the rubric for a cooperative group management plan on pages 81–82 in the *Performance Assessment Activities and Rubrics.*

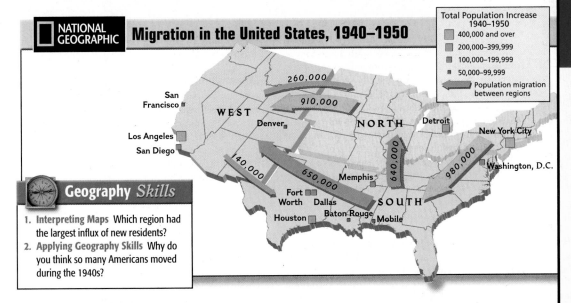

NATIONAL GEOGRAPHIC **Migration in the United States, 1940–1950**

Total Population Increase
1940–1950
- 400,000 and over
- 200,000–399,999
- 100,000–199,999
- 50,000–99,999
- Population migration between regions

WEST · NORTH · SOUTH

San Francisco · Los Angeles · San Diego · Denver · Detroit · New York City · Washington, D.C. · Memphis · Fort Worth · Dallas · Houston · Baton Rouge · Mobile

260,000 · 910,000 · 140,000 · 650,000 · 640,000 · 980,000

Geography *Skills*

1. **Interpreting Maps** Which region had the largest influx of new residents?
2. **Applying Geography Skills** Why do you think so many Americans moved during the 1940s?

fruit and vegetables in the Southwest. Many also helped to build and maintain railroads. The Bracero Program continued until 1964. Migrant farmworkers became an important part of the Southwest's agricultural system.

✓ **Reading Check** **Describing** How did mobilizing the economy help end the Depression?

A Nation on the Move

The wartime economy created millions of new jobs, but the Americans who wanted these jobs did not always live nearby. To get to the jobs, 15 million Americans moved during the war. Although the assembly plants of the Midwest and the shipyards of the Northeast attracted many workers, most Americans headed west and south in search of jobs.

Taken together, the growth of southern California and the expansion of cities in the Deep South created a new industrial region—the Sunbelt. For the first time since the Industrial Revolution began in the United States, the South and West led the way in manufacturing and urbanization.

The Housing Crisis Perhaps the most difficult task facing cities with war industries was deciding where to put the thousands of new workers. Many people had to live in tents and tiny trailers. To help solve the housing crisis, the federal government allocated over $1.2 billion to build public housing, schools, and community centers during the war.

Although prefabricated government housing had tiny rooms, thin walls, poor heating, and

almost no privacy, it was better than no housing at all. Nearly two million people lived in government-built housing during the war.

Racism Explodes Into Violence African Americans began to leave the South in great numbers during World War I, but this **"Great Migration,"** as historians refer to it, slowed during the Depression. When jobs in war factories opened up for African Americans during World War II, the Great Migration resumed. When African Americans arrived in the crowded cities of the North and West, however, they were often met with suspicion and intolerance. Sometimes these attitudes led to violence.

The worst racial violence of the war erupted in Detroit on Sunday, June 20, 1943. The weather that day was sweltering. To cool off, nearly 100,000 people crowded into Belle Isle, a park on the Detroit River. Fights erupted between gangs of white and African American teenage girls. These fights triggered others, and a full-scale riot erupted across the city. By the time the violence ended, 25 African Americans and 9 whites had been killed. Despite the appalling violence in Detroit, African American leaders remained committed to their Double V campaign.

The Zoot Suit Riots Wartime prejudice erupted elsewhere as well. In southern California, racial tensions became entangled with juvenile delinquency. Across the nation, crimes committed by young people rose dramatically. In Los Angeles, racism against Mexican Americans and the fear of juvenile crime became linked because of the "zoot suit."

CHAPTER 25 America and World War II **751**

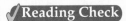

Geography *Skills*

Background: Remind students that during World War II the United States consisted of only 48 states. Alaska and Hawaii had not yet become states.
Answers:
1. the West, with 1,560,000 (650,000 from the South and 910,000 from the North)
2. job opportunities

Geography Skills Practice
Give students a list of the 48 states and ask them to use the map to classify the states by region.

✓ **Reading Check**

Answer: Mobilizing the economy for war production created nearly 19 million new jobs and nearly doubled the average family's income.

Guided Reading Activity 25–3

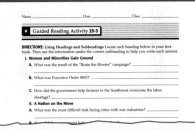

History *and the* Humanities

🎵 American Music: Cultural Traditions: "Take Me Back to Tulsa," "Boogie Woogie Bugle Boy"

🖌 American Art & Architecture: *The Red Stairway*

MEETING SPECIAL NEEDS

Kinesthetic Have students work in small groups to create a short play about daily life in the United States during the war. Encourage students to use props and costumes that represent the period. Have the groups present their plays to the rest of the class. As a class, discuss what students have learned about the daily lives of people in the United States during World War II. **L1** ELL

📂 Refer to *Inclusion for the High School Social Studies Classroom Strategies and Activities* in the TCR.

Expressing an Opinion Provide the following information: In March 1942, United States General John DeWitt, acting under War Department orders, began the evacuation of all persons of Japanese descent from the western half of Washington, Oregon, and California, and from southern Arizona. Most of the evacuees were American citizens. DeWitt explained the evacuation by saying, "It makes no difference whether a Japanese is theoretically a citizen. He is still Japanese . . ." Organize the class into groups and have each group draft a response to DeWitt's statement. **L2**

📁 Use *Supreme Court Case Study 23, Endo* v. *United States.*

📁 Use *Supreme Court Case Study 24, Korematsu* v. *United States.*

NATIONAL GEOGRAPHIC
MOMENT in HISTORY

List the names and locations of the following camps on the board and have students use a map to point out the general locations of the camps: Amache, Colorado; Gila River, Arizona; Heart Mountain, Wyoming; Jerome, Arkansas; Manzanar, California; Minidoka, Idaho; Poston, Arizona; Rohwer, Arkansas; Topaz, Utah; and Tule Lake, California. Ask students to look at the picture and describe the emotions that these young boys are probably feeling.

A **zoot suit** had very baggy, pleated pants and an overstuffed, knee-length jacket with wide lapels. Accessories included a wide-brimmed hat and a long key chain. Zoot-suit wearers usually wore their hair long, gathered into a ducktail. The zoot suit angered many Americans. In order to save fabric for the war, most men wore a **"victory suit"**—a suit with no vest, no cuffs, a short jacket, and narrow lapels. By comparison, the zoot suit seemed unpatriotic.

In California, Mexican American teenagers adopted the zoot suit. In June 1943, after hearing rumors that zoot suiters had attacked several sailors, 2,500 soldiers and sailors stormed into Mexican American neighborhoods in Los Angeles. They attacked Mexican American teenagers, cut their hair, and tore off their zoot suits. The police did not intervene, and the violence continued for several days. The city of Los Angeles responded by banning the zoot suit.

Racial hostility against Mexican Americans did not deter them from joining the war effort. Approximately 500,000 Hispanic Americans served in the armed forces during the war. Most—about 400,000—were Mexican American. Another 65,000 were from Puerto Rico. They fought in Europe, North Africa, and the Pacific, and by the end of the war, 17 Mexican Americans had received the Medal of Honor.

Japanese American Relocation When Japan attacked Pearl Harbor, many West Coast Americans turned their anger against Japanese Americans. Mobs attacked Japanese American businesses and homes. Banks would not cash their checks, and grocers refused to sell them food.

Newspapers printed rumors about Japanese spies in the Japanese American community. Members of Congress, mayors, and many business and labor leaders demanded that all people of Japanese ancestry be removed from the West Coast. They did not believe that Japanese Americans would remain loyal to the United States in the face of war with Japan.

On February 19, 1942, President Roosevelt gave in to pressure and signed an order allowing the War Department to declare any part of the United States to be a military zone and to remove anybody they wanted from that zone. Secretary of War Henry Stimson declared most of the West Coast a military zone and ordered all people of Japanese ancestry to evacuate to 10 internment camps.

NATIONAL GEOGRAPHIC
MOMENT in HISTORY

BEHIND BARBED WIRE
As wartime hysteria mounted, the U.S. government rounded up 120,000 people of Japanese ancestry—77,000 of whom were American citizens—and forced them into internment camps in early 1942. Given just days to sell their homes, businesses, and personal property, whole families were marched under military guard to rail depots, then sent to remote, inhospitable sites where they lived in cramped barracks surrounded by barbed wire and watchtowers. By 1945, with the tide of war turned, most had been released, but they did not get an official apology or financial compensation until 1988.

INTERDISCIPLINARY CONNECTIONS ACTIVITY

Economics Have students work in small groups to explore the effects of inflation on consumer prices. Ask the groups to research the way in which inflation is measured, especially the makeup of the Consumer Price Index (CPI). Ask the groups to prepare tabletop displays showing the effects of inflation from 1900 to 1999. Encourage groups to link the periods of high or low inflation to political and social events. **L3**

Not all Japanese Americans accepted the relocation without protest. Fred Korematsu argued that his rights had been violated and took his case to the Supreme Court. In December 1944, in *Korematsu v. the United States*, the Supreme Court ruled that the relocation was constitutional because it was based not on race, but on "military urgency." Shortly afterward, the Court did rule in *Ex Parte Endo* that loyal American citizens could not be held against their will. In early 1945, therefore, the government began to release the Japanese Americans from the camps. 📖 *(See page 1081 for more information on Korematsu v. the United States.)*

Despite the fears and rumors, no Japanese American was ever tried for espionage or sabotage. Japanese Americans served as translators for the army during the war in the Pacific. The all-Japanese 100th Battalion, later integrated into the **442nd Regimental Combat Team,** was the most highly decorated unit in World War II.

After the war, the **Japanese American Citizens League** (JACL) tried to help Japanese Americans who had lost property during the relocation. In 1988 President Reagan apologized to Japanese Americans on behalf of the U.S. government and signed legislation granting $20,000 to each surviving Japanese American who had been interned.

✔ **Reading Check** **Comparing** Why did racism lead to violence in Detroit and Los Angeles in 1943?

Daily Life in Wartime America

Housing problems and racial tensions were serious difficulties during the war, but mobilization strained society in many other ways as well. Prices rose, materials were in short supply, and the question of how to pay for it all loomed ominously over the entire war effort.

ECONOMICS

Wage and Price Controls As the economy mobilized, the president worried about inflation. Both wages and prices began to rise quickly during the war because of the high demand for workers and raw materials. To stabilize both wages and prices, Roosevelt created the **Office of Price Administration** (OPA) and the Office of Economic Stabilization (OES). The OES regulated wages and the price of farm products. The OPA regulated all other prices. Despite some problems with labor unions, the OPA and OES were able to keep inflation under control.

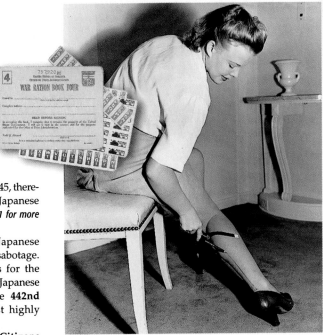

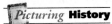
Picturing **History**

Rationing Products War rationing affected everyone. Women painted seams on their legs to make it appear they were wearing stockings, because silk was needed to make parachutes instead of stockings. Why was rationing so vital to the war effort?

While the OPA and OES worked to control inflation, the War Labor Board (WLB) tried to prevent strikes that might endanger the war effort. In support, most American unions issued a "no strike pledge," and instead of striking, asked the WLB to serve as a mediator in wage disputes. By the end of the war, the WLB had helped to settle 20,000 disputes involving 20 million workers.

Blue Points, Red Points The demand for raw materials and supplies created shortages. The OPA began rationing, or limiting the availability of, many products to make sure enough were available for military use. Meat and sugar were rationed to provide enough for the army. To save gasoline and rubber, gasoline was rationed, driving was restricted, and the speed limit was set at 35 miles per hour.

Every month each household would pick up a book of ration coupons. Blue coupons, called blue points, controlled processed foods. Red coupons, or red points, controlled meats, fats, and oils. Other coupons controlled items such as coffee and sugar. When people bought food, they also had to give enough coupon points to cover their purchases.

Picturing **History**

Answer: It allowed enough goods to be available for the war effort.
Ask: What types of goods were rationed? *(silk, meat, sugar, gasoline, processed foods, fats, and oils)*

✔ **Reading Check**

Answer: African Americans who migrated to Detroit were often met with suspicion and intolerance. In Los Angeles, racism against Mexican Americans and fear of juvenile crime became linked because of zoot suits. These attitudes sometimes led to violence.

3 ASSESS

Assign Section 3 Assessment as homework or as an in-class activity.

💿 Have students use the **Interactive Tutor Self-Assessment CD-ROM.**

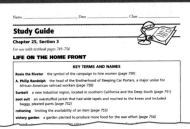

Reading Essentials and Study Guide 25–3

Name _____ Date _____ Class _____

Study Guide

Chapter 25, Section 3
For use with textbook pages 749–754

LIFE ON THE HOME FRONT

KEY TERMS AND NAMES

Rosie the Riveter the symbol of the campaign to hire women *(page 750)*
A. Philip Randolph the head of the Brotherhood of Sleeping Car Porters, a major union for African American railroad workers *(page 750)*
Sunbelt a new industrial region, located in southern California and the Deep South *(page 751)*
zoot suit an overstuffed jacket that had wide lapels and reached to the knees and included baggy, pleated pants *(page 752)*
rationing limiting the availability of an item *(page 753)*
victory garden a garden planted to produce more food for the war effort *(page 754)*

CRITICAL THINKING ACTIVITY

Evaluating Decisions In 1942 the U.S. government removed more than 100,000 people of Japanese birth and ancestry from their homes on the Pacific Coast to relocation centers. Ask students the following question: **Do you think the government ever has the right to relocate or keep a group in detention? Why or why not?** *(Answers will vary. Students who oppose the relocation policy might suggest that it was a violation of civil rights; those who agree with the policy might indicate that sometimes the country's security takes precedence over the issue of a group's rights.)* **L2**

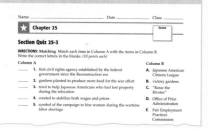

Analyzing *Political Cartoons*

Answer: to be conscious of the dangers their city lights pose to American sailors

Reteach

Have students create a poster encouraging efforts such as rationing, victory gardens, or war bonds.

Enrich

Have students prepare a two-minute oral presentation on the way rationing would affect their lives today if it was implemented.

Reading Check

Answer: Rationing limited access to common products, but allowed people to purchase necessities.

4 CLOSE

As a class, discuss the effects of prejudice in society by focusing on groups discriminated against in the 1940s and today.

Illumination for the Shooting Gallery

Analyzing *Political Cartoons*

Turning Off the Lights Early in the war, lights from eastern cities silhouetted ships along the east coast, making them easy targets for German submarines. Americans were asked to turn out lights or put up dark curtains. What point is the cartoon making to Americans?

Victory Gardens and Scrap Drives

Americans also planted gardens to produce more food for the war effort. Any area of land might become a garden—backyards, schoolyards, city parks, and empty lots. The government encouraged victory gardens by praising them in film reels, pamphlets, and official statements.

Certain raw materials were so vital to the war effort that the government organized scrap drives. Americans collected spare rubber, tin, aluminum, and steel. They donated pots, tires, tin cans, car bumpers, broken radiators, and rusting bicycles. Oils and fats were so important to the production of explosives that the WPB set up fat-collecting stations. Americans would exchange bacon grease and meat drippings for extra ration coupons. The scrap drives were very successful and one more reason for the success of American industry during the war.

Paying for the War The United States had to pay for all of the equipment and supplies it needed. The federal government spent more than $300 billion during World War II—more money than it had spent from Washington's administration to the end of Franklin Roosevelt's second term.

To raise money, the government raised taxes. Because most Americans opposed large tax increases, Congress refused to raise taxes as high as Roosevelt requested. As a result, the extra taxes collected covered only 45 percent of the cost of the war.

To raise the rest of the money, the government issued war bonds. When Americans bought bonds, they were loaning money to the government. In exchange for the money, the government promised that the bonds could be cashed in at some future date for the purchase price plus interest. The most common bonds were **E bonds,** which sold for $18.75 and could be redeemed for $25.00 after 10 years. Individual Americans bought nearly $50 billion worth of war bonds. Banks, insurance companies, and other financial institutions bought the rest—over $100 billion worth of bonds.

"V" for Victory Despite the hardships, the overwhelming majority of Americans believed the war had to be fought. Although the war brought many changes to the United States, most Americans remained united behind one goal—winning the war.

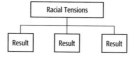

Reading Check **Evaluating** How did rationing affect daily life in the United States? How did it affect the economy?

SECTION 3 ASSESSMENT

Checking for Understanding

1. **Define:** Sunbelt, rationing, victory garden.
2. **Identify:** Rosie the Riveter, A. Philip Randolph, zoot suit, E bond.
3. **Explain** how the federal government expanded during the war.

Reviewing Themes

4. **Civic Rights and Responsibilities** What changes did American citizens and industry have to make to adapt to the war?

Critical Thinking

5. **Evaluating** If you had been a government official during the war, how would you have proposed paying for the war?
6. **Categorizing** Use a graphic organizer like the one below to list the results of increased racial tensions during the war.

```
         Racial Tensions
      ┌───────┼───────┐
   Result   Result   Result
```

Analyzing Visuals

7. **Examining Maps** Study the map on page 751. Which cities had populations over 400,000?
8. **Analyzing Photographs** Study the photograph on page 752. Why were Japanese Americans interned?

Writing About History

9. **Persuasive Writing** Write a newspaper editorial urging fellow citizens to conserve resources so that these resources can be diverted to the war effort.

SECTION 3 ASSESSMENT ANSWERS

1. Terms are in blue.
2. Rosie the Riveter *(p. 750)*, A. Philip Randolph *(p. 750)*, zoot suit *(p. 752)*, E bond *(p. 754)*
3. New government agencies controlled the economy, raised taxes, and issued war bonds.
4. Industry and workers accepted wage and price controls and agreed to settle wage disputes by using WLB mediators. Citizens accepted rationing, planted victory gardens, recycled, and purchased war bonds.
5. Students' answers should include a rationale for their plan.
6. racial violence in Detroit, juvenile delinquency, Japanese internment
7. Los Angeles, Houston, New York
8. Many believed that they would not remain loyal to the United States.
9. Students' editorials should follow the style of a newspaper editorial.

Guide to Reading

Main Idea
The Allies slowly pushed back the German and Japanese forces in 1943 and 1944.

Key Terms and Names
Casablanca Conference, Operation Overlord, D-Day, Omar Bradley, amphtrac, Guadalcanal, kamikaze

Reading Strategy
Organizing As you read about the major battles of 1943 and 1944, complete a graphic organizer similar to the one below by filling in the names of the battles fought. Indicate whether each battle was an Allied or an Axis victory.

Pacific — Major Battles 1943–1944 — Europe

Reading Objectives
• **Describe** the goals of the two major offensives the Allies launched in Europe in 1943.
• **Explain** the American strategy for pushing the Japanese back in the Pacific.

Section Theme
Geography and History The United States fought the war by landing troops in Italy and France and island-hopping across the Pacific toward Japan.

Preview of Events

◆1943   ◆1944   ◆1945

January 1943
Casablanca Conference

July 1943
The Allies invade Italy

November 1943
Roosevelt, Churchill, and Stalin meet at Tehran

June 6, 1944
D-Day invasion begins

October 20, 1944
MacArthur returns to the Philippines

★ An American Story ★

Men board a landing craft on D-Day

On the morning of June 6, 1944, Lieutenant John Bentz Carroll of the 16th Infantry Regiment scrambled down a net ladder from his troop ship to a small landing craft tossing in the waves 30 feet (9 m) below. The invasion of France had begun. Carroll's platoon would be among the first Americans to land in Normandy. Their objective was a beach, code-named "Omaha":

❝Two hundred yards out, we took a direct hit. . . . [A machine gun] was shooting a rat-tat-tat on the front of the boat. Somehow or other, the ramp door opened up . . . and the men in front were being struck by machine gun fire. Everyone started to jump off into the water. They were being hit as they jumped, the machine gun fire was so heavy. . . . The tide was moving us so rapidly. . . . We would grab out on some of those underwater obstructions and mines built on telephone poles and girders, and hang on. We'd take cover, then make a dash through the surf to the next one, fifty feet beyond. The men would line up behind those poles. They'd say, 'You go—you go—you go,' and then it got so bad everyone just had to go anyway, because the waves were hitting with such intensity on these things.❞

—quoted in *D-Day: Piercing the Atlantic Wall*

Striking Back at the Third Reich

As Lieutenant Carroll's experience shows, storming a beach under enemy control can be a terrifying ordeal. There is no cover on a beach, no place to hide, and no way to turn back. Launching an invasion from the sea is very risky. Unfortunately, the Allies had no choice. If they were going to win the war, they had to land their troops in Europe and on islands in the Pacific.

CHAPTER 25 America and World War II **755**

1 FOCUS

Section Overview

This section describes the Allied strategies and the battles of the later years of World War II.

BELLRINGER
Skillbuilder Activity

 Project transparency and have students answer the question.

📁 Available as a blackline master.

Daily Focus Skills Transparency 25–4

Guide to Reading

Answers to Graphic: Pacific—Tarawa Atoll, Gilbert Islands, 1943, Allies; Guam, August 1944, Allies; Europe—Sicily, July–August 1943, Allies; D-Day, June 1944, Allies

Preteaching Vocabulary
Have students write three questions that can be answered using the Key Terms and Names. Remind them to use all the terms and names.

SECTION RESOURCES

📁 Reproducible Masters
• Reproducible Lesson Plan 25–4
• Daily Lecture and Discussion Notes 25–4
• Guided Reading Activity 25–4
• Section Quiz 25–4
• Reading Essentials and Study Guide 25–4
• Performance Assessment Activities and Rubrics

🖥 Transparencies
• Daily Focus Skills Transparency 25–4

Multimedia
• Interactive Tutor Self-Assessment CD-ROM
• ExamView® Pro Testmaker CD-ROM
• Presentation Plus! CD-ROM
• TeacherWorks™ CD-ROM
• Audio Program

2 TEACH

Daily Lecture and Discussion Notes 25–4

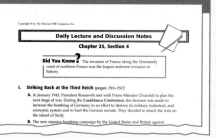

Creating a Database Have students create a database of the battles presented in this section. The database should include such information as site, dates, results, and casualties. Encourage students to conduct independent research to fill in any missing fields in the database. Have students use the database to pose and answer questions about the battles fought in Europe.

Picturing **History**

Background: Being in the infantry meant working as a team. Each soldier had a specific role, and the team counted on each member to perform that role efficiently.

Answer: The Allies thought that the Italians would quit the war if their territory was invaded.

Ask: Who led the Allied forces on the ground during the invasion of Sicily? (*General Patton for the United States and General Montgomery for the British*)

The first large Allied invasion of the war—the attack on North Africa in November 1942—had shown that the Allies could mount a large-scale invasion from the sea. The success of the landings convinced Roosevelt that it was again time to meet with Churchill to plan the next stage of the war. In January 1943, the president headed to Casablanca, Morocco, to meet the prime minister.

At the **Casablanca Conference,** Roosevelt and Churchill agreed to step up the bombing of Germany. The goal of this new campaign was "the progressive destruction of the German military, industrial, and economic system, and the undermining of the morale of the German people." The Allies also agreed to attack the Axis on the island of Sicily. Churchill called Italy the "soft underbelly" of Europe and was convinced that the Italians would quit the war if the Allies invaded their homeland.

Strategic Bombing The Allies had been bombing Germany even before the Casablanca Conference. Britain's Royal Air Force had dropped an average of 2,300 tons (2,093 t) of explosives on Germany every month for over three years. The United States Eighth Army Air Force had joined the campaign in the summer of 1942, and they had dropped an additional 1,500 tons (1,365 t) of bombs by the end of the year.

These numbers were tiny, however, compared to the massive new campaign. Between January 1943 and May 1945, the Royal Air Force and the United States Eighth Army Air Force dropped approximately 53,000 tons (48,230 t) of explosives on Germany every month.

Picturing **History**

Softening the Gustav Line Infantrymen fire an 81-millimeter mortar to soften the German Gustav Line near the Rapido River. *Why do you think the Allies decided to attack first in Italy rather than in France?*

The bombing campaign did not destroy Germany's economy or undermine German morale, but it did cause a severe oil shortage and wrecked the railroad system. It also destroyed so many aircraft factories that Germany's air force could not replace its combat losses. By the time the Allies landed in France, they had total control of the air, ensuring that their troops would not be bombed.

Striking at the Soft Underbelly As the bombing campaign against Germany intensified, the plan for the invasion of Sicily moved ahead as well. General Dwight D. Eisenhower was placed in overall command of the invasion. General Patton and the British General Bernard Montgomery were put in charge of the actual forces on the ground. The invasion began before dawn on July 10, 1943. Despite bad weather, the Allied troops made it ashore with few casualties. A new vehicle, the **DUKW**—an amphibious truck—proved very effective in bringing supplies and artillery to the soldiers on the beach.

Nine days after the troops came ashore, American tanks led by General Patton smashed through enemy lines and captured the western half of the island. After capturing western Sicily, Patton's troops headed east, staging a series of daring end-runs around the German positions, while the British, under Montgomery, attacked from the south. By August 18, the Germans had evacuated the island.

The attack on Sicily created a crisis within the Italian government. The king of Italy, Victor Emmanuel, and a group of Italian generals decided that it was time to get rid of Mussolini. On July 25, 1943, the king invited the dictator to his palace. "My dear Duce," the king began, "it's no longer any good. Italy has gone to bits. The soldiers don't want to fight anymore. At this moment, you are the most hated man in Italy." The king then placed Mussolini under arrest, and the new Italian government began secretly negotiating with the Allies for Italy's surrender.

On September 8, 1943, the Italian government publicly announced Italy's surrender. The following day, American troops landed at Salerno. Although stunned by the surrender, Hitler was not about to lose Italy to the Allies. German troops went into action at once. They seized control of northern Italy, including Rome, attacked the Americans at Salerno, and put Mussolini back in power.

To stop the Allied advance, the German army took up positions near the heavily

---

EXTENDING THE CONTENT

American POWs Approximately 130,000 Americans were held as prisoners-of-war (POWs) during World War II. The largest number were airmen, captured after being shot down during the strategic bombing campaign. Most nations that took POWs had signed the Geneva Convention of 1929. Under the Geneva Convention, POWs were to be given adequate medical care, shelter, and food, and were allowed to correspond with their family. Japan and the Soviet Union were the only two major powers that had not signed the agreement when World War II began. Germany generally upheld the Geneva Convention when holding American or British POWs, but treated Soviet POWs brutally. The Japanese provided minimum food and shelter to POWs and worked the prisoners hard. Approximately 14,000 American POWs died while imprisoned during World War II.

Guided Reading Activity 25–4

Name _____ Date _____ Class _____

★ Guided Reading Activity 25–4

DIRECTIONS: Filling in the Blanks In the space provided, write the word or words that best complete the sentence. Refer to your textbook to fill in the blanks.

1. The first large Allied invasion of the war was the attack on _____.
2. Among the agreements reached at the _____ was the decision to step up the bombing of Germany.
3. Winston Churchill called Italy the _____ of Europe and was convinced that Italians would quit the war if the Allies invaded their homeland.
4. The _____ was one of the bloodiest in the war, costing the Allies more than 300,000 casualties.
5. At the Tehran, Iran, meeting with Churchill and Roosevelt, Stalin promised to launch a _____ against the Germans when the Allies invaded France in 1944.
6. Stalin also promised that once Germany was beaten, the Soviet Union would help

The Big Three Stalin, Roosevelt, and Churchill meet at Tehran.

fortified town of Cassino. The terrain near Cassino was steep, barren, and rocky. Instead of attacking such difficult terrain, the Allies chose to land at Anzio, behind German lines. They hoped the maneuver would force the Germans to retreat. Instead of retreating, however, the Germans surrounded the Allied troops near Anzio.

It took the Allies five months to break through the German lines at **Cassino** and **Anzio.** Finally, in late May 1944, the Germans were forced to retreat. Less than two weeks later, the Allies captured Rome. Fighting in Italy continued, however, until May 2, 1945. The Italian campaign was one of the bloodiest in the war. It cost the Allies more than 300,000 casualties.

Roosevelt Meets Stalin at Tehran

Roosevelt wanted to meet with Stalin before the Allies launched the invasion of France. In late 1943 Stalin agreed, and he proposed that Roosevelt and Churchill meet him in Tehran, Iran.

The leaders reached several agreements. Stalin promised to launch a full-scale offensive against the Germans when the Allies invaded France in 1944. Roosevelt and Stalin then agreed to break up Germany after the war so that it would never again threaten world peace. Stalin also promised that once Germany was beaten, the Soviet Union would help the United States defeat Japan. He also accepted Roosevelt's proposal to create an international organization to help keep the peace after the war.

✓ Reading Check **Explaining** What two major decisions did the Allies make at Casablanca?

Landing in France

After the conference in Tehran, Roosevelt headed to Cairo, Egypt, where he and Churchill continued planning the invasion of France. One major decision still had to be made. The president had to choose the commander for **Operation Overlord**—the code name for the planned invasion. Roosevelt wanted to appoint General George C. Marshall, Chief of Staff for the United States Army, but he depended on Marshall for military advice and did not want to send him to Europe. Instead, the president selected General Eisenhower to command the invasion.

Planning Operation Overlord Knowing that the Allies would eventually invade France, Hitler had fortified the coast. Although these defenses were formidable, the Allies did have one advantage—the element of surprise. The Germans did not know when or where the Allies would land. They believed that the Allies would land in Pas-de-Calais—the area of France closest to Britain. To convince the Germans they were right, the Allies placed inflated rubber tanks, empty tents, and dummy landing craft along the coast across from Calais. To German spy planes, the decoys looked real, and they succeeded in fooling the Germans. The real target was not Pas-de-Calais, but Normandy.

By the spring of 1944, everything was ready. Over 1.5 million American soldiers, 12,000 airplanes, and more than 5 million tons (4.6 million t) of equipment had been sent to England. Only one

CHAPTER 25 America and World War II **757**

More About the Photo

Background: Tehran is the capital of Iran. Tehran was an ideal location for the meeting because it was not a combat area and not a home to any of the big three Allied powers.

Discussing a Topic As a class, discuss how each of the following influenced Operation Overlord: the weather, the decoys placed along the coast opposite Calais, and the choice of five beaches for landing the troops. L1 ELL

The Women's Airforce Service Pilots tested new and rebuilt fighter planes and flew military aircraft from factories to bases in the United States and Europe. Despite their outstanding service, they did not receive recognition or veterans benefits until 1977.

✓ Reading Check

Answer: to step up the bombing of Germany and attack the Axis at Sicily

MEETING SPECIAL NEEDS

Visual/Spatial Ask interested students to sketch the typical battle gear of Allied soldiers. Students should include the standard weapons used by the infantry. Have students write a paragraph to accompany each sketch that describes the item and how it was used. L1 ELL

📂 Refer to **Inclusion for the High School Social Studies Classroom Strategies and Activities** in the TCR.

Creating a Table Have students create a table to illustrate these four important conferences: Arcadia, Casablanca, Tehran, and Yalta. The table should include the dates, the city and country where the conference was held, which world leaders attended, and the outcomes. Have students use their tables to pose and answer questions about the purposes and results of the various conferences. **L2**

What If...

A good way to help students understand the importance of historical events is to have them think about what might have happened if things had turned out differently. Have students read the passage and answer the questions on their own. Organize students into small groups and have them discuss their answers.

Answers:

1. Students' answers will vary. Likely answers will focus on how fog and rain would have hindered visibility for landing craft crews, troops approaching the beach, and pilots.

2. Students' answers will vary. Likely answers will focus on the potential casualties of the war if the Germans had known about the attack.

---

thing was left to do—pick the date and give the command to go. The invasion had to begin at night to hide the ships crossing the English Channel. The ships had to arrive at low tide so that they could see the beach obstacles. The low tide had to come at dawn so that gunners bombarding the coast could see their targets. Before the main landing on the beaches, paratroopers would be dropped behind enemy lines. They required a moonlit night in order to see where to land. Perhaps most important of all, the weather had to be good. A storm would ground the airplanes, and high waves would swamp the landing craft.

Given all these conditions, there were only a few days each month when the invasion could begin. The first opportunity would last from June 5 to 7, 1944. Eisenhower's planning staff referred to the day any operation began by the letter D. The date for the invasion, therefore, came to be known as **D-Day.** Heavy cloud cover, strong winds, and high waves made it impossible to land on June 5. A day later the weather briefly improved. The Channel was still rough, but the landing ships and aircraft could operate. It was a difficult decision. Eisenhower's advisers were split on what to do. After looking at weather forecasts one

last time, shortly after midnight on June 6, 1944, Eisenhower gave the final order: "OK, we'll go."

The Longest Day Nearly 7,000 ships carrying more than 100,000 soldiers set sail for the coast of Normandy on June 6, 1944. At the same time, 23,000 paratroopers were dropped inland, east and west of the beaches. Allied fighter-bombers raced up and down the coast, hitting bridges, bunkers, and radar sites. As dawn broke, the warships in the Allied fleet let loose with a tremendous barrage of fire. Thousands of shells rained down on the beaches, code-named "Utah," "Omaha," "Gold," "Sword," and "Juno."

The American landing at Utah Beach went very well. The German defenses were weak, and in less than three hours American troops had captured the beach and moved inland, suffering less than 200 casualties in the process. On the eastern flank, the British and Canadian landings also went well. By the end of the day, British and Canadian forces were several miles inland.

Omaha Beach, however, was a different story. Under intense German fire, the American assault almost disintegrated. As General **Omar Bradley,** the commander of the American forces landing at Omaha

What If...

Operation Overlord Had Failed?

In what some historians believe was the most important weather prediction in military history, Group Captain James Stagg, chief meteorologist for the Royal Air Force, predicted gradual clearing for Normandy, France, on June 6, 1944. The prediction was critical for General Dwight D. Eisenhower, Supreme Commander of the Allied Expeditionary Forces. He had already delayed Operation Overlord once. The invasion forces of Operation Overlord were assembled and ready to go at a moment's notice. Everything depended upon a break in the bad weather so that the assault would take the Germans by surprise. Eisenhower trusted the weather prediction and believed in the battle plan. The day before the invasion, however, he wrote the following note on a small piece of paper—a message he would deliver in the event the invasion failed. He mistakenly jotted "July 5" on the bottom and stuck the note in his wallet.

❝Our landings in the Cherbourg-Havre area have failed to gain a satisfactory foothold and I have withdrawn the troops. My decision to attack at this time and place was based upon the best information available. The troops, the air and the Navy did all that Bravery and devotion to duty could do. If any blame or fault attaches to the attempt it is mine alone.❞

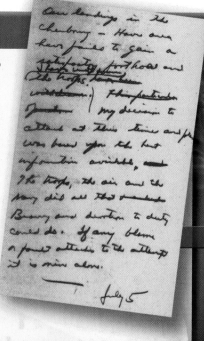

INTERDISCIPLINARY CONNECTIONS ACTIVITY

Performing Arts Have students work in teams to research popular songs and films from this period to determine if the war had an impact on these arts. Have students prepare a short written report along with in-class presentations of their findings. Encourage them to integrate performances into their presentations. Costumes, singing, lip-synching to recorded music, dancing, and skits are all appropriate. **L1** ELL

and Utah, grimly watched the carnage, he began making plans to evacuate Omaha. Slowly, however, the American troops began to knock out the German defenses. More landing craft arrived, ramming their way through the obstacles to get to the beach. Nearly 2,500 Americans were either killed or wounded on Omaha, but by early afternoon Bradley received this message: "Troops formerly pinned down on beaches . . . [are] advancing up heights behind beaches." By the end of the day, nearly 35,000 American troops had landed at Omaha, and another 23,000 had landed at Utah. Over 75,000 British and Canadian troops were on shore as well. The invasion had succeeded.

✔ **Reading Check** **Summarizing** What conditions had to be met before Eisenhower could order D-Day to begin?

Driving the Japanese Back

While the buildup for the invasion of France was taking place in Britain, American military leaders were also developing a strategy to defeat Japan. The American plan called for a two-pronged attack. The Pacific Fleet, commanded by Admiral Nimitz, would

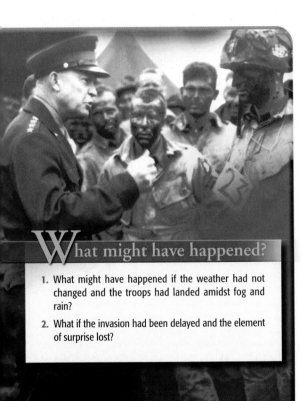

W̅hat might have happened?

1. What might have happened if the weather had not changed and the troops had landed amidst fog and rain?

2. What if the invasion had been delayed and the element of surprise lost?

advance through the central Pacific by hopping from one island to the next, closer and closer to Japan. Meanwhile, General MacArthur's troops would advance through the Solomon Islands, capture the north coast of New Guinea, and then launch an invasion to retake the Philippines.

GEOGRAPHY

Island-Hopping in the Pacific By the fall of 1943, the navy was ready to launch its island-hopping campaign, but the geography of the central Pacific posed a problem. Many of the islands were coral reef atolls. The water over the coral reef was not always deep enough to allow landing craft to get to the shore. If the landing craft ran aground on the reef, the troops would have to wade to the beach. As some 5,000 United States Marines learned at Tarawa Atoll, wading ashore could cause very high casualties.

Tarawa, part of the Gilbert Islands, was the Navy's first objective in the Pacific. When the landing craft hit the reef, at least 20 ships ran aground. The marines had to plunge into shoulder-high water and wade several hundred yards to the beach. Raked by Japanese fire, only one marine in three made it ashore. Once the marines reached the beach the battle was still far from over. As reporter Robert Sherrod wrote, the marines faced savage hand-to-hand fighting:

> ❝A Marine jumped over the seawall and began throwing blocks of fused TNT into a coconut-log pillbox. . . . Two more Marines scaled the seawall, one of them carrying a twin-cylindered tank strapped to their shoulders, the other holding the nozzle of the flame thrower. As another charge of TNT boomed inside the pillbox, causing smoke and dust to billow out, a khaki-clad figure ran out the side entrance. The flame thrower, waiting for him, caught him in its withering stream of intense fire. As soon as it touched him, the [Japanese soldier] flared up like a piece of celluloid. He was dead instantly . . . charred almost to nothingness.❞
>
> —from *Tarawa: The Story of a Battle*

Over 1,000 marines died on Tarawa. Photos of bodies lying crumpled next to burning landing craft shocked Americans back home. Many people began to wonder how many lives it would cost to defeat Japan.

Although many troops died wading ashore, one vehicle had been able to cross the reef and deliver its troops onto the beaches. The vehicle was the LVT—a boat with tank tracks. Nicknamed the "Alligator," the

CHAPTER 25 America and World War II **759**

✔ **Reading Check**

Answer: The invasion had to begin at night, the ships had to arrive at low tide, and the weather had to be relatively good.

you don't say...

Banzai On the final night of the battle of Tarawa, the Japanese made a last desperate charge against the American lines. This type of suicidal charge became known as a *banzai* attack, because the Japanese would yell, "Tenno heika banzai!" (Long Live the Emperor!)

Creating a Drawing Have interested students use the quote on this page as the basis for a pencil or chalk drawing that might have accompanied a news story filed by Robert Sherrod. Have students include the quote at the bottom of the drawing so that people viewing the drawing will have a frame of reference. **L3**

CURRICULUM CONNECTION

Science American soldiers carried a first aid pouch attached to their waist belt. The pouch contained a package of sulfa powder and a bandage to dress wounds. The use of the sulfa drug Sulfanilamide significantly reduced the mortality rate during World War II, because the sulfa powder immediately went to work to fight bacterial infections. Sulfa drugs are still in use today.

CRITICAL THINKING ACTIVITY

Synthesizing Information Have students explain the significance of the promises that Stalin made at the Tehran Conference. *(By agreeing to launch a full-scale offensive against the Germans when the Allies invaded France, Stalin guaranteed that Germany would be defending itself on two fronts. Stalin's promise to declare war on Japan as soon as Germany was beaten meant that the Japanese would be fighting on two fronts.)* **L2**

3 ASSESS

Assign Section 4 Assessment as homework or as an in-class activity.

◉ Have students use the **Interactive Tutor Self-Assessment CD-ROM.**

Reading Essentials and Study Guide 25–4

Name _____ Date _____ Class _____

Study Guide

Chapter 25, Section 4
For use with textbook pages 755–761

PUSHING THE AXIS BACK

KEY TERMS AND NAMES

Casablanca Conference a meeting between Roosevelt and Churchill in which they agreed to increase the bombing of Germany and to invade Sicily *(page 756)*

Operation Overlord the code name for the planned invasion of France *(page 757)*

D-Day the day the invasion of France began *(page 758)*

Omar Bradley the commander of the American forces at Utah and Omaha Beaches in Normandy *(page 758)*

amphtrac an amphibious tractor *(page 760)*

Guadalcanal an island in the southwest Pacific and the first to be invaded by MacArthur's troops in the plan to defeat Japan *(page 760)*

Section Quiz 25–4

Name _____ Date _____ Class _____

★ **Chapter 25**   Score ____

Section Quiz 25-4

DIRECTIONS: Matching Match each item in Column A with the items in Column B. Write the correct letters in the blanks. *(10 points each)*

Column A

____ 1. an amphibious tractor invented in the late 1930s to rescue people in Florida swamps

____ 2. when Japanese pilots would deliberately crash their planes into American ships, killing themselves but also inflicting severe damage

____ 3. an amphibious truck

____ 4. code name for the invasion of France

____ 5. the date for the invasion of France

Column B

A. D-Day
B. amphtrac
C. kamikaze attacks
D. DUKW
E. Operation Overlord

DIRECTIONS: Multiple Choice In the blank at the left, write the letter of the choice

NATIONAL GEOGRAPHIC   **Island-Hopping in the Pacific, 1942–1945**

Geography *Skills*

1. **Interpreting Maps** Where did the first major battle between the American and Japanese forces in the Philippines take place?
2. **Applying Geography Skills** Why do you think Americans adopted the policy of island-hopping?

amphibious tractor, or amphtrac, had been invented in the late 1930s to rescue people in Florida swamps. It had never been used in combat, and not until 1941 did the navy decide to buy 200 of them. Had more been available at Tarawa, the number of American casualties probably would have been much lower.

The assault on the next major objective—Kwajalein Atoll in the Marshall Islands—went much more smoothly. This time all of the troops went ashore in amphtracs. Although the Japanese resisted fiercely, the marines captured Kwajalein and nearby Eniwetok with far fewer casualties.

After the Marshall Islands, the navy targeted the Mariana Islands. American military planners wanted to use the Marianas as a base for a new heavy bomber, the B-29 Superfortress. The B-29 could fly farther than any other plane in the world. From airfields in the

Marianas, B-29s could bomb Japan. Admiral Nimitz decided to invade three of the Mariana Islands: Saipan, Tinian, and Guam. Despite strong Japanese resistance, American troops captured all three by August 1944. A few months later, B-29 bombers began bombing Japan.

MacArthur Returns to the Philippines As the forces under Admiral Nimitz hopped across the central Pacific, General MacArthur's troops began their own campaign in the southwest Pacific. The campaign began with the invasion of **Guadalcanal** in August 1942. It continued until early 1944, when MacArthur's troops finally captured enough islands to surround Rabaul, the main Japanese base in the region. In response the Japanese withdrew their ships and aircraft from the base, although they left 100,000 troops behind to hold the island.

Worried that the navy's advance across the central Pacific was leaving him behind, MacArthur ordered his forces to leap nearly 600 miles (966 km) past Rabaul to capture the Japanese base at Hollandia on

EXTENDING THE CONTENT

Clare Boothe Luce Although women did not participate in combat during World War II, some were assigned to cover the fighting as journalists, broadcasters, or photographers. Before she became well-known as a member of Congress (1942–1946), ambassador, and playwright, Clare Boothe Luce (1903–1987) worked for *Life* magazine during World War II. She endured battle experiences ranging from bombing raids in Europe and the Pacific to arrest in Trinidad by British customs officials who were upset by her accurate article about poor military preparedness in Libya. As a result of her article, Luce's longtime friend Winston Churchill changed Great Britain's Middle Eastern military policy.

the north coast of New Guinea. Shortly after securing New Guinea, MacArthur's troops seized the island of Morotai—the last stop before the Philippines.

To take back the Philippines, the United States assembled an enormous invasion force. In October 1944, more than 700 ships carrying over 160,000 troops sailed for Leyte Gulf in the Philippines. On October 20, the troops began to land on Leyte, an island on the eastern side of the Philippines. A few hours after the invasion began, MacArthur headed to the beach. Upon reaching the shore, he strode to a radio and spoke into the microphone: "People of the Philippines, I have returned. By the grace of Almighty God, our forces stand again on Philippine soil."

To stop the American invasion, the Japanese sent four aircraft carriers toward the Philippines from the north and secretly dispatched another fleet to the west. Believing the Japanese carriers were leading the main attack, most of the American carriers protecting the invasion left Leyte Gulf and headed north to stop them. Seizing their chance, the Japanese warships to the west raced through the Philippine Islands into Leyte Gulf and ambushed the remaining American ships.

The Battle of Leyte Gulf was the largest naval battle in history. It was also the first time that the Japanese used kamikaze attacks. *Kamikaze* means "divine wind" in Japanese. It refers to the great storm that destroyed the Mongol fleet during its invasion of Japan in the thirteenth century. Kamikaze pilots would deliberately crash their planes into American ships, killing themselves but also inflicting severe damage. Luckily for the Americans, just as their situation was becoming

A Triumphant Return In October 1944, Douglas MacArthur fulfilled his promise and returned to the Philippines.

desperate, the Japanese commander, believing more American ships were on the way, ordered a retreat.

Although the Japanese fleet had retreated, the campaign to recapture the Philippines from the Japanese was long and grueling. Over 80,000 Japanese were killed; less than 1,000 surrendered. MacArthur's troops did not capture Manila until March 1945. The battle left the city in ruins and over 100,000 Filipino civilians dead. The remaining Japanese retreated into the rugged terrain north of Manila, and they were still fighting when word came in August 1945 that Japan had surrendered.

✓ **Reading Check** **Describing** What strategy did the United States Navy use to advance across the Pacific?

More About the Photo

Writing about his return to the Philippines, MacArthur said, "It took me only 30 or 40 strides to reach dry land, but that was one of the most meaningful walks I ever took."

Reteach

Write the years 1941–1945 on the board. Have students list important events that occurred during these years and explain how they affected U.S. foreign and domestic policy.

Enrich

In addition to the 6 major powers, over 50 other nations were at war during World War II. Some countries entered the war as early as 1939, while others did not make a commitment until 1945. Have students work in pairs to research the roles five other countries played in World War II.

✓ **Reading Check**

Answer: They moved from island to island, advancing slowly toward Japan.

4 CLOSE

Ask students to discuss why they think it was so important for the Allies to recapture the Philippines.

SECTION 4 ASSESSMENT

Checking for Understanding

1. **Define:** amphtrac, kamikaze.
2. **Identify:** Casablanca Conference, Operation Overlord, D-Day, Omar Bradley, Guadalcanal.
3. **Explain** why D-Day's success was so vital to an Allied victory.

Reviewing Themes

4. **Geography and History** How did the geography of the Pacific affect American strategy?

Critical Thinking

5. **Analyzing** What made the invasion of Normandy so important?
6. **Organizing** Use a graphic organizer to explain the significance of each leader listed below.

Leader	Significance
Dwight Eisenhower	
George Patton	
George Marshall	
Omar Bradley	
Douglas MacArthur	

Analyzing Visuals

7. **Examining Photographs** Study the photograph on this page. What effect do you think MacArthur's return had on Philippine morale?

Writing About History

8. **Expository Writing** Using library or Internet resources, find more information on one of the battles discussed in this section. Use the information to write a report detailing the importance of the battle. Share your report with the class.

SECTION 4 ASSESSMENT ANSWERS

1. Terms are in blue.
2. Casablanca Conference *(p. 756)*, Operation Overlord *(p. 757)*, D-Day *(p. 758)*, Omar Bradley *(p. 758)*, Guadalcanal *(p. 760)*
3. It would force the Germans to fight on two fronts.
4. Coral reefs around some of the atolls made landing craft hard to maneuver. They began using amphtracs to land the soldiers.
5. The Germans now had to fight a two-front war, which stretched their resources even further. The Soviet Union had promised help in defeating the Japanese once the Germans were defeated.
6. Answers should match chapter content.
7. Answers may vary. They welcomed him because they had been treated harshly by the Japanese.
8. Reports should include details that do not appear in the student text.

NATIONAL GEOGRAPHIC

Geography&History

1 FOCUS

Have students consider the obstacles faced by an invading army. **Ask:** What kinds of landing sites were the Allies looking for when they were planning to invade Europe in 1944? *(a sheltered coastline somewhere between Denmark and Portugal with flat, firm beaches and within range of fighter planes based in England)*

2 TEACH

Writing a Narrative Have students choose one of the groups that landed at Omaha Beach and describe their journey after reaching the beach. Include information about the distance and direction traveled, the geography traversed, and German defenses encountered. **L1**

Practicing Map Skills Have students calculate the approximate distances Canadian, British, and U.S. troops traveled from England to France on D-Day. Have students use a table to report the starting point, distance traveled, landing site, and nationality of troops for each of the five beaches along the coast of Normandy. **L2**

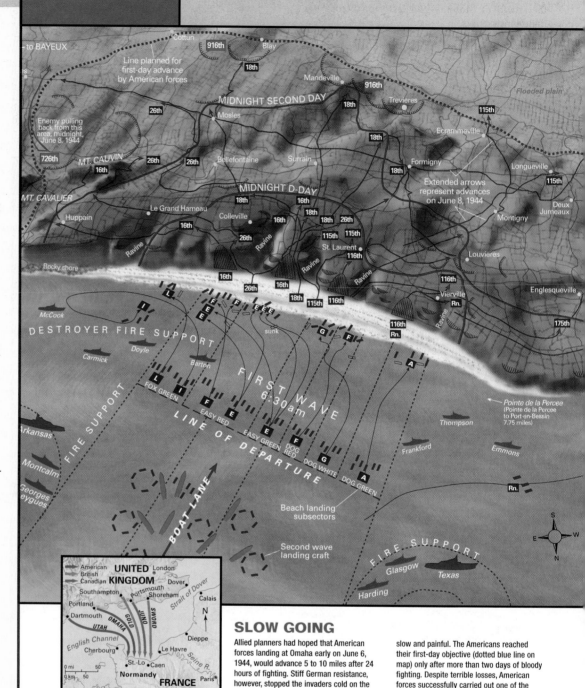

SLOW GOING

Allied planners had hoped that American forces landing at Omaha early on June 6, 1944, would advance 5 to 10 miles after 24 hours of fighting. Stiff German resistance, however, stopped the invaders cold on the beach. Progress inland was excruciatingly slow and painful. The Americans reached their first-day objective (dotted blue line on map) only after more than two days of bloody fighting. Despite terrible losses, American forces successfully carried out one of the most crucial missions of the war.

762 CHAPTER 25 America and World War II

EXTENDING THE CONTENT

Military Inventions For centuries French farmers had erected high banks of earth around every small field to fence in livestock and protect crops from coastal winds. These natural barriers, known as hedgerows, grew thick with the roots of shrubs and trees. Although Allied tanks could ride up over these hedgerows, they exposed their undersides to antitank fire. The enemy was able to attack the tanks at their most vulnerable point. A creative sergeant solved the problem by adding tusks to the fronts of the tanks. The tusks would get caught in the underbrush and hold the tank in place as the engine propelled it forward through the mound of dirt.

Nightmare at Omaha

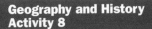

The selection of a site for the largest amphibious landing in history was one of the biggest decisions of World War II. Allied planners considered coastlines from Denmark to Portugal in search of a sheltered location with flat, firm beaches and within range of friendly fighter planes based in England.

There had to be enough roads and paths to move jeeps and trucks off the beaches and to accommodate the hundreds of thousands of American, Canadian, and British troops set to stream ashore following the invasion. An airfield and a seaport that the Allies could use were also needed. Most important was a reasonable expectation of achieving the element of surprise.

Five beaches on the northern coast of Normandy, France, met all the criteria and were chosen as invasion sites. On D-Day the attack on four beaches—Utah in the west and Gold, Juno, and Sword in the east (inset, opposite page) went according to plan. But at Omaha Beach (map), between Utah and Gold, the landing of the U.S. 1st Infantry Division threatened to turn into what American general Omar Bradley feared was an "irreversible catastrophe."

Surrounded at both ends by cliffs that rose wall-like from the sea, Omaha was only four miles long. It was the only sand beach in the area, however, and thus the only place for a landing. Unless the Allies were to leave a 20-mile gap between Utah

Troops crowd into a landing craft to head across the English Channel to Omaha Beach.

and Gold, they would have to come ashore at Omaha Beach.

To repel the Allies at the water's edge, the Germans built a fortress atop the cliffs at Pointe du Hoc overlooking Omaha from the west. They dug trenches and guns into the 150-foot bluffs lining the beach and along five ravines leading off it (see map).

Wading into the surf, the Americans advanced toward Omaha Beach, which had been divided into sectors with code names such as Dog Red and Easy Green. Many men were cut down as the doors of their landing craft opened. The survivors had to cross more than 300 yards across a tidal flat strewn with man-made obstacles. Winds and a current pushed landing craft into clumps as the men moved ashore. As a result, soldiers ran onto the beach in groups and became easy targets. Many died. Of the more than 9,000 Allied casualties on D-Day, Omaha accounted for about one-third.

D-Day Forces

A-L	U.S. Company — 200 men
116th	U.S. Battalion — 900 men
Rn.	U.S. Rangers
916th	German infantry — forces associated with German battalion
German resistance point	Battleship
German coastal defense	Cruiser
U.S. stronghold	Transport
Landing craft	Hedgerows
Landing craft — sunk	Town

Scale varies in this perspective

Bandaged and shell-shocked, infantrymen from the American 1st Division wait to be evacuated after landing on Omaha Beach.

LEARNING FROM GEOGRAPHY

1. Why did the Allies choose Normandy as the site of the invasion?

2. Why was the landing at Omaha Beach so much more difficult than U.S. leaders expected?

763

ANSWERS TO LEARNING FROM GEOGRAPHY

1. The Allies chose Normandy because it was a sheltered location with flat, firm beaches and was within range of friendly fighter planes based in England. There were roads or paths to lead jeeps, trucks, and troops off the beaches. There was an airfield and a seaport that could be used by the Allies. There was a reasonable expectation of achieving the element of surprise.

2. Winds and steady currents pushed landing craft into clumps as the men moved to shore. As groups of soldiers ran onto the beach they became easy targets for the Germans who had built strong defenses atop the cliffs overlooking Omaha Beach.

SECTION 5 The War Ends

1 FOCUS

Section Overview

This section describes the end of World War II, including the dropping of the atomic bomb.

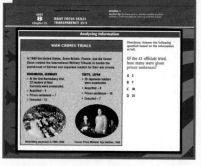
Guide to Reading

Answers to Graphic:
The War Ends
I. The Third Reich Collapses
  A. The Battle of the Bulge
  B. V-E Day: War Ends in Europe
II. Japan Is Defeated
  A. Uncommon Valor on Iwo Jima
Students should complete the outline by including all heads in the section.

Preteaching Vocabulary
Organize the class into eight groups. Assign each group one of the Key Terms and Names. Have each group prepare a brief presentation for its assigned term.

Guide to Reading

The Main Idea
The ferocious military campaigns of 1945 finally convinced the Axis powers to surrender and the Allies to set up organizations to prevent another global war.

Key Terms and Names
hedgerow, Battle of the Bulge, V-E Day, Harry S Truman, Curtis LeMay, napalm, Manhattan Project, V-J Day, United Nations, charter

Reading Strategy
Taking Notes As you read about the end of World War II and the organizations set up to maintain global peace, use the major headings of the section to create an outline similar to the one below.

The War Ends
I. The Third Reich Collapses
  A.
  B.
II.
  A.
  B.

Reading Objectives
• **Explain** the tactics the Allies used to invade Germany and to defeat Japan.
• **Outline** the reasons the Allies created the United Nations and held war crimes trials.

Section Theme
Groups and Institutions Allied leaders forged plans for an international organization to prevent future wars.

Preview of Events

| ♦1944 | ♦1945 | ♦1946 |

December 16, 1944
Battle of the Bulge begins

February 19, 1945
American troops invade Iwo Jima

April 12, 1945
Franklin Roosevelt dies; Harry Truman becomes president

May 7, 1945
Germany surrenders

August 15, 1945
V-J Day, Japan surrenders

★ An American Story ★

Jewish prisoners at a German concentration camp

In 1945 Captain Luther Fletcher entered the German concentration camp at Buchenwald with a group of Germans who were being forced to see what their country had done. In his diary Fletcher described what they witnessed:

❝They saw blackened skeletons and skulls in the ovens of the crematorium. In the yard outside, they saw a heap of white human ashes and bones. . . . [The] dead were stripped of their clothing and lay naked, many stacked like cordwood waiting to be burned at the crematory. At one time 5,000 had been stacked on the vacant lot next to the crematory. . . . At headquarters of the SS troops who ran the place were lamp shades made from human skin. . . . Often, the guide said, the SS wished to make an example of someone in killing him. . . . They used what I call hay hooks, catching him under the chin and the other in the back of the neck. He hung in this manner until he died.❞

—quoted in *World War II: From the Battle Front to the Home Front*

The Third Reich Collapses

Well before the war ended, President Roosevelt and other Allied leaders were aware that the Nazis were committing atrocities. In 1943 the Allies officially declared that they would punish the Nazis for their crimes after the war. Meanwhile, Roosevelt was convinced that the best way to put an end to the concentration camps was to destroy the Nazi regime. To do that, he believed the Allies had to dedicate their resources to breaking out of Normandy, liberating France, and conquering Germany.

764 CHAPTER 25 America and World War II

The bombing stunned the Japanese. Three days later, on August 9, the Soviet Union declared war on Japan. Later that same day, the United States dropped another atomic bomb, code-named "Fat Man," on the city of Nagasaki, killing between 35,000 and 74,000 people.

Faced with such massive destruction and the shock of the Soviets joining the war, the Japanese emperor ordered his government to surrender. On August 15, 1945—**V-J Day**—Japan surrendered. On the other side of the world, Americans celebrated. For American soldiers the news was especially good. As one veteran recalled: "We would not be obliged to run up the beaches near Tokyo assault firing while being mortared and shelled. For all the fake manliness of our facades, we cried with relief and joy. We were going to live. We were going to grow up to adulthood after all." The long war was finally over.

✓ **Reading Check** **Analyzing** What arguments did Truman consider when deciding whether to use the atomic bomb?

A historian defends Truman's decision:

Historian Herbert Feis argues that Truman's desire to avoid an invasion of Japan, thus saving thousands of lives on both sides, motivated his decision to drop the bomb.

"Our right, legal and historical, to use the bomb may thus well be defended; but those who made the decision to use it were not much concerned over these considerations, taking them for granted. Their thoughts about its employment were governed by one reason which was deemed imperative: that by using the bomb, the agony of war might be ended more quickly.

The primary and sustaining aim from the start of the great exertion to make the bomb was military, and the impelling reason for the decision to use it was military—to end the war victoriously as soon as possible."

—quoted in *Japan Subdued: The Atomic Bomb and the End of the War in the Pacific*

Learning From History

1. Which of the above interpretations do you think is the most valid? Why?
2. Using the internet or other resources, find an account of the bombing from the point of a Japanese citizen. How does it differ from the accounts above, and why?

Fact **Fiction** **Folklore**

Family Sacrifices Millions of American homes proudly displayed banners such as these during the war. The blue star on the flag indicated that a family member was serving in the military. A gold star proclaimed that an individual had been killed. Many homes displayed banners with several stars, indicating the family had sent many members off to war.

Building a New World

Well before the war ended, President Roosevelt had begun to think about what the world would be like after the war. The president had wanted to ensure that war would never again engulf the world.

Creating the United Nations President Roosevelt believed that a new international political organization could prevent another world war. In 1944, at the Dumbarton Oaks Estate in Washington, D.C., delegates from 39 countries met to discuss the new organization, which was to be called the **United Nations** (UN).

The delegates at the conference agreed that the UN would have a General Assembly, where every member nation in the world would have one vote. The UN would also have a Security Council with 11 members. Five countries would be permanent members of the Security Council: Britain, France, China, the Soviet Union, and the United States—the five big powers that had led the fight against the Axis. These five permanent members would each have veto power.

On April 25, 1945, representatives from 50 countries came to San Francisco to officially organize the United Nations and design its charter, or constitution. The General Assembly was given the power to vote on resolutions, to choose the non-permanent members of the Security Council, and to vote on the UN budget. The Security Council was responsible for international peace and security. It could investigate any international problem and propose settlements to countries that had disputes with each other. It could also take action to preserve the peace, including asking its members to use military force to uphold a UN resolution.

CHAPTER 25 America and World War II **771**

✓ **Reading Check**

Answer: the potentially massive casualties involved in a ground invasion of Japan and his duty to save American lives

Fact **Fiction** **Folklore**

It is not uncommon for Americans to display symbols to signify their support for family and friends who serve in the military. Point out that during the Persian Gulf War in 1991, many Americans tied yellow ribbons on trees and poles to show their support for the American troops.

Different Viewpoints

Organize the students into small groups to research Truman's decision to use the atomic bomb. Ask them to debate the following: Truman's decision to drop the atomic bomb was or was not morally and ethically justified. **Answers:**

1. Answers will vary but should focus on the use of evidence and potential bias.
2. Answers will vary but should include details from the selected narrative.

INTERDISCIPLINARY CONNECTIONS ACTIVITY

Government Organize the class into small groups. Assign each group one of the following topics related to the United Nations: how it is funded, what it has accomplished, what types of humanitarian aid it provides, what influence it has today, and how the leader is chosen. Have each group prepare an oral presentation of their findings. Encourage groups to use charts, pictures, tables, and other visual aids during their presentations. **L2**

Reteach

Have students select a significant date mentioned in this section to write a newspaper headline for the day.

Enrich

Read students the following quotation by President Truman announcing the use of the atomic bomb: "[The Japanese] may expect a rain from the air, the like of which has never been seen on this earth." Ask them to discuss the ways in which the atomic bomb altered international politics.

Reading Check

Answer: a General Assembly of all member nations and an 11-member Security Council with five permanent members each of whom has veto power over UN actions

4 CLOSE

Ask students if they think the Allies would have indicted Adolph Hitler had he not committed suicide. Also ask if they think that an indictment of Hitler would have influenced the Allied decision about indicting Emperor Hirohito.

Picturing History

V-J Day Photographer Alfred Eisenstaedt captured this image in Times Square during the victory celebration on V-J Day. No one knows the identities of the sailor and the nurse in the photo. *Why did this photograph become so famous?*

Putting the Enemy on Trial Although the Allies had declared their intention to punish German and Japanese leaders for their war crimes, they did not work out the details until the summer of 1945. In early August, the United States, Britain, France, and the Soviet Union created the **International Military**

Tribunal (IMT). At the **Nuremberg trials** in Nuremberg, Germany, the IMT tried German leaders suspected of committing war crimes.

Twenty-two leaders of Nazi Germany were prosecuted at Nuremberg. Three were acquitted and another seven were given prison sentences. The remaining 12 were sentenced to death by hanging. Trials of lower-ranking government officials and military officers continued until April 1949. Those trials led to the execution of 24 more German leaders. Another 107 were given prison sentences.

Similar trials were held in Tokyo for the leaders of wartime Japan. The IMT for the Far East charged 25 Japanese leaders with a variety of war crimes. Significantly, the Allies did not indict the Japanese emperor. They feared that any attempt to put him on trial would lead to an uprising by the Japanese people. Eighteen Japanese defendants were sentenced to prison. The rest were sentenced to death by hanging.

The war crimes trials punished many of the people responsible for World War II and the Holocaust, but they were also part of the American plan for building a better world. As Robert Jackson, chief counsel for the United States at Nuremberg, observed in his opening statement to the court: "The wrongs we seek to condemn and punish have been so calculated, so malignant and so devastating, that civilization cannot tolerate their being ignored because it cannot survive their being repeated."

Reading Check **Describing** How is the United Nations organized?

SECTION 5 ASSESSMENT

Checking for Understanding

1. **Define:** hedgerow, napalm, charter.
2. **Identify:** Battle of the Bulge, V-E Day, Harry S Truman, Curtis LeMay, Manhattan Project, V-J Day, United Nations.
3. **List** the major campaigns on the European and Pacific fronts in 1945.
4. **Explain** how the United States developed the atomic bomb.
5. **Describe** the war crimes trials.

Reviewing Themes

6. **Continuity and Change** Why do you think the goal of world peace has yet to be achieved?

Critical Thinking

7. **Analyzing** If you had been an adviser to President Truman, what advice would you have given him about dropping the atomic bomb? Give reasons why you would have given this advice.
8. **Categorizing** Using a graphic organizer like the one below, fill in the structure of the United Nations.

```
            United Nations
             /         \
        Branch        Branch
           |             |
    Responsibilities  Responsibilities
```

Analyzing Visuals

9. **Examining Photographs** Study the photograph on page 770 of Hiroshima after the atomic bomb was dropped. What effect do you think this photograph may have had on the American public? Why?

Writing About History

10. **Descriptive Writing** Imagine you are on the staff of the International Military Tribunal in Nuremberg after the war. Write a letter to a family member in the United States explaining why the tribunal is conducting trials and what you hope the trials will accomplish.

772 CHAPTER 25 America and World War II

SECTION 5 ASSESSMENT ANSWERS

1. Terms are in blue.
2. Battle of the Bulge *(p. 765)*, V-E Day *(p. 766)*, Harry S Truman *(p. 766)*, Curtis LeMay *(p. 768)*, Manhattan Project *(p. 769)*, V-J Day *(p. 771)*, United Nations *(p. 771)*
3. Battle of the Bulge, Iwo Jima, Okinawa
4. secretly in New Mexico
5. 3 Nazis acquitted, 7 imprisoned, 12 executed; 18 Japanese imprisoned, 7 executed
6. Answers will vary.
7. Answers will vary but should be defensible.
8. General Assembly: voting body; Security Council: international security
9. Answers will vary. Many would have been shocked by the devastation.
10. Students' letters should include a description of what the tribunal will accomplish.

American LITERATURE

Jeanne Wakatsuki Houston was born in Inglewood, California. In 1942, when she was seven years old, her family was uprooted from their home and sent to live at the Manzanar internment camp in California. The detainees had committed no crimes. They were detained simply because of their heritage.

Farewell to Manzanar is the story of the Wakatsuki family's attempt to survive the indignities of forced detention and living behind barbed wire in the United States.

Read to Discover

How does Jeanne Wakatsuki Houston describe the internment camp that is to be her new home? What does her description remind you of?

Reader's Dictionary

barracks: plain and barren lodgings usually used to house soldiers

milling: wandering

savory: seasoned with spices

from Farewell to Manzanar

by Jeanne Wakatsuki Houston *and* James D. Houston

The following excerpt describes Jeanne Wakatsuki's first impressions as she and her family arrived at the internment camp.

We drove past a barbed-wire fence, through a gate, and into an open space where trunks and sacks and packages had been dumped from the baggage trucks that drove out ahead of us. I could see a few tents set up, the first rows of black barracks, and beyond them . . . rows of barracks that seemed to spread for miles across the plain. People were sitting on cartons or milling around . . . waiting to see which friends or relatives might be on this bus. . . .

We had pulled up just in time for dinner. The mess halls weren't completed yet. . . . They issued us army mess kits, the round metal kind that fold over, and plopped in scoops of canned Vienna sausage, canned string beans, steamed rice that had been cooked too long, and on top of the rice a serving of canned apricots. The caucasian servers were thinking that the fruit poured over rice would make a dessert. Among the Japanese, of course, rice is never eaten with sweet foods, only with salty or savory foods. . . .

After dinner we were taken to Block 16, a cluster of fifteen barracks. . . . The shacks were built of one thickness of pine planking covered with tarpaper. . . . We were assigned two of these for the twelve

people in our family group; and our official family "number" was enlarged by three digits—16 plus the number of this barracks. We were issued steel army cots, two brown army blankets, each, and some mattress covers, which my brothers stuffed with straw.

Analyzing Literature

1. **Recall and Interpret** How did the food served at the camp show a lack of understanding of Japanese culture?
2. **Evaluate and Connect** Why do you think the families in the camps were assigned numbers?

Interdisciplinary Activity

Art and Architecture Draw plans for a community memorial for remembering Japanese Americans who were treated unfairly during World War II.

Block Schedule

Team Teaching This selection from *Farewell to Manzanar* can be presented in a team teaching context, in conjunction with English or Language Arts.

Read to Discover

Answer: The barracks are crudely built and unfinished. Students may see a parallel between these camps and the Nazi camps built in Europe.

Reinforcing Vocabulary

Ask students to use each of the terms in a sentence that is not related to the reading.

Historical Connection

In 1983 the Commission of Wartime Relocation and Internment of Civilians reported in *Personal Justice Denied* that there was no military necessity for internment.

Portfolio Writing Activity

Ask students to interview an older family member, neighbor, or friend. Ask them to describe how the most important historical event of his or her lifetime affected them. Write the results of the interview in a question-and-answer format.

HISTORY Online

Refer to tav.glencoe.com for additional Glencoe Literature titles, lesson plans, and study guides related to this unit.

Answers to Analyzing Literature

1. Students' answers will vary depending on their understanding of Japanese culture. Answers should mention that rice is never eaten with sweet foods.

2. Students' answers will vary. Camp officials likely chose to use numbers because they found Japanese names difficult to spell and pronounce.

Interdisciplinary Activity

The plans for the memorial should show details including the size and shape of the memorial. The plans should emphasize how community members might interact with the memorial.

Reviewing Key Terms
Students' answers will vary. The pages where the words appear in the text appear below.

1. cost-plus *(p. 737)*; **2. Liberty ship** *(p. 738)*; **3. disfranchise** *(p. 740)*; **4. periphery** *(p. 745)*; **5. convoy system** *(p. 746)*; **6. Sunbelt** *(p. 751)*; **7. rationing** *(p. 753)*; **8. victory garden** *(p. 754)*; **9. amphtrac** *(p. 760)*; **10. kamikaze** *(p. 761)*; **11. hedgerow** *(p. 765)*; **12. napalm** *(p. 768)*; **13. charter** *(p. 771)*

Reviewing Key Facts
14. Selective Service and Training Act *(p. 739)*, Chester Nimitz *(p. 742)*, Douglas MacArthur *(p. 743)*, George Patton *(p. 746)*, E bond *(p. 754)*, Casablanca Conference *(p. 756)*, D-Day *(p. 758)*, Manhattan Project *(p. 769)*, United Nations *(p. 771)*

15. It was a campaign to enlist support in the African American community for the war effort. Double V stood for double victory—victory over Hitler's racism and victory over racism in the United States.

16. 15 million Americans moved during the war, usually for work opportunities; some moved to the northeast, but most moved to the Sunbelt.

17. Women and African Americans were able to get jobs not normally available to them. The gains were short lived.

18. It boosted America's morale by striking on Japanese soil.

19. They used rationing, encouraged victory gardens, and controlled wages and prices.

20. It was a way to efficiently move materials and troops closer to Japan.

21. The United States committed its manpower and economic resources to fight in World War II.

22. It gave Americans landing areas within striking distance of Japan.

23. The Nuremberg trials and trials of the Japanese leaders convicted many of the Axis leaders of war crimes, imprisoned some and executed others, but spared the emperor of Japan.

Reviewing Key Terms
On a sheet of paper, use each of these terms in a sentence.

1. cost-plus
2. Liberty ship
3. disfranchise
4. periphery
5. convoy system
6. Sunbelt
7. rationing
8. victory garden
9. amphtrac
10. kamikaze
11. hedgerow
12. napalm
13. charter

Reviewing Key Facts
14. **Identify:** Selective Service and Training Act, Chester Nimitz, Douglas MacArthur, George Patton, E bond, Casablanca Conference, D-Day, Manhattan Project, United Nations.

15. What was the "Double V" campaign?

16. How did the war change patterns of population movement and settlement in the United States?

17. How did the war effort change employment opportunities for women and African Americans?

18. Why was the Doolittle raid so important to Americans?

19. How did the American government ensure that there were enough necessities to supply the war effort?

20. Why did the United States adopt a policy of island-hopping in the Pacific?

21. What was problematic about the Allied invasion at Omaha Beach?

22. Why were the victories on Iwo Jima and Okinawa so vital to the Allies?

23. What did the Allies do to punish Axis leaders after the war?

Critical Thinking
24. **Interpreting Primary Sources** Many historians believe that the civil rights movement of the 1950s and 1960s had its roots in the Double V campaign and the March on Washington. Alexander Allen, a member of the Urban League during the war, believed that World War II was a turning point for African Americans. Read the excerpt and answer the questions that follow.

❝Up to that point the doors to industrial and economic opportunity were largely closed. Under the pressure of war, the pressures of government policy, the pressures of world opinion, the pressures of blacks themselves and their allies, all this began to change. . . . The war forced the federal government to take a stronger position with reference to discrimination, and things began to change as a result. There was a tremendous attitudinal change that grew out of the war. There had been a new experience for blacks, and many weren't willing to go back to the way it was before. ❞

—quoted in *Wartime America*

a. How did the war change the status of African Americans in American society?

b. Why do you think the war forced the government to take a stronger position on discrimination in the workplace?

25. **Analyzing Themes: Global Connections** How did World War II underscore the importance of an international organization such as the United Nations?

Chapter Summary

	1941	1942	1943	1944	1945
The Pacific	Japan attacks Pearl Harbor on December 7.	The United States defeats Japan in the Battles of the Coral Sea and Midway.	The United States launches its island-hopping campaign.	The United States retakes the Philippines.	The United States drops atomic bombs; Japan surrenders on August 15.
Europe and North Africa		The Allies turn the tide in the Battle of the Atlantic.	The Allies invade Italy; Germans surrender at Stalingrad.	The Allies invade Normandy on June 6.	Germany surrenders unconditionally on May 7.
The Home Front	President Roosevelt forbids race discrimination in defense industries.	WAAC is established; Japanese American relocation is ordered.	OWM is established; Detroit and Zoot Suit Riots occur.	The case of *Korematsu* v. *United States* is decided.	The UN charter is signed.

Critical Thinking
24. **a.** It allowed many to work in industry and benefit from such work for the first time. Most were not willing to return to the way things had been. **b.** Possible answers: the war effort demanded a large domestic workforce; wished to avoid work stoppages

25. It pointed out the need to investigate and propose settlements to international disputes before war erupted.

Self-Check Quiz

Visit the *American Vision* Web site at tav.glencoe.com and click on *Self-Check Quizzes—Chapter 25* to assess your knowledge of chapter content.

26. **Analyzing Effects** Do you think the opportunities that opened up for women during World War II would have developed if the United States had stayed out of the war? Explain your answer.

27. **Synthesizing** Why do you think the United States was able to successfully fight a war on multiple fronts?

28. **Categorizing** Use a concept web similar to the one below to list the major campaigns in the Pacific and in Europe.

Practicing Skills

29. **Reading a Thematic Map** Study the map of migration patterns on page 751. Then use the steps you learned about reading thematic maps on page 748 to answer the following questions.
    a. **Interpreting Maps** Which regions had a net loss of residents to other regions during this period?
    b. **Synthesizing Information** How were the locations of the four fastest growing cities similar?

Chapter Activities

30. **Research Project** Use library or Internet resources to find information on the United Nations today. Use what you find to design an illustrated brochure highlighting the organization's work.

31. **Analyzing Geographic Patterns and Distributions** Look at the chart on Military and Civilian Deaths in World War II found on page 767. Create a thematic map indicating each country and the deaths that occurred there. Then write a quiz based on the chart about the distribution of casualties around the world and the patterns this suggests.

Writing Activity

32. **Persuasive Writing** Assume the role of an immigrant who fled Fascist Europe in 1933 and who has become a U.S. citizen. You have just read about the proposed United Nations, and you want to write your senator to urge that the United States join the organization or boycott it. Choose which position you support, and write a letter trying to convince the senator to support your position.

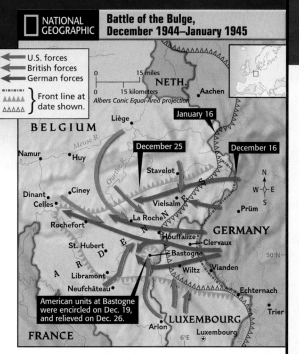

NATIONAL GEOGRAPHIC **Battle of the Bulge, December 1944–January 1945**

⬅ U.S. forces
⬅ British forces
⬅ German forces

} Front line at date shown.

Albers Conic Equal-Area projection

American units at Bastogne were encircled on Dec. 19, and relieved on Dec. 26.

Geography and History

33. The map above shows troop movements at the Battle of the Bulge. Study the map and answer the questions below.
    a. **Interpreting Maps** At what location did the Germans surround American forces on December 25?
    b. **Applying Geography Skills** What geographic features did the Germans encounter as they attacked? What information on the map shows you this?

Standardized Test Practice

Directions: Choose the best answer to the following question.

Why did Britain and France finally declare war in 1939?

A Because Germany annexed part of Czechoslovakia

B Because Germany invaded Poland

C Because Italy invaded France

D Because of the non-aggression pact between Russia and Germany

Test-Taking Tip: Use the process of elimination to rule out answers you know are wrong. For example, it is unlikely that a non-aggression pact between Russia and Germany would cause Britain and France to declare war, so this answer can be eliminated.

Have students visit the Web site at tav.glencoe.com to review Chapter 25 and take the Self-Check Quiz.

31. Maps should reflect data in charts and quizzes should be based on the maps.

Writing Activity

32. Letters should express a clear and reasoned opinion using standard grammar, spelling, sentence structure, and punctuation.

Geography and History

33. **a.** Bastogne; **b.** rivers and mountainous terrain; the dark shading in the south, as opposed to flatter northern areas

Standardized Test Practice

Answer: B
Test-Taking Tip: Ask students to use the process of elimination to rule out answers they know are wrong. For example, it is unlikely that a nonaggression pact between Russia and Germany would cause Britain and France to declare war.

Bonus Question ?

Ask: Why was the Battle of Midway so crucial to the war in the Pacific? *(Losing four carriers gutted the heart of the Japanese fleet and stopped Japan's ability to advance in the Pacific.)*

26. Answers may vary. Students should use knowledge of women's past experiences as part of their answer.

27. Answers will vary. Students should note that most industrial production was geared to supporting both fronts and that the United States had personnel available to wage both fronts of the war.

28. Pacific: Battle of Coral Sea, Battle of Midway, Guadalcanal, Iwo Jima, Okinawa; Europe: North African campaign, Battle of the Atlantic, Stalingrad, D-Day, Battle of the Bulge

Practicing Skills

29. **a.** Northeast and South; **b.** They were all located on large bodies of water.

Chapter Activities

30. Brochures should reflect current information about the United Nations.

Chapter 26 Resources

TEACHING TRANSPARENCIES

Graphic Organizer 6

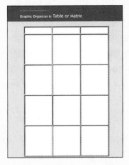

Why It Matters Chapter Transparency 26

APPLICATION AND ENRICHMENT

Linking Past and Present Activity 26

Enrichment Activity 26

Primary Source Reading 26

REVIEW AND REINFORCEMENT

Reteaching Activity 26

Vocabulary Activity 26

Time Line Activity 26

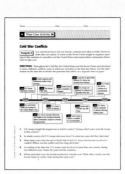

Critical Thinking Skills Activity 26

Meeting NCSS Standards

The following standards are highlighted in Chapter 26:

Section 1	IX	Global Connections: B, D, E, G
Section 2	IX	Global Connections: B, C, D, E, G
Section 3	X	Civic Ideals and Practices: C, F
Section 4	VIII	Science, Technology, and Society: B, C

Local Standards

_____

_____

_____

_____

_____

Chapter 26 Resources

ASSESSMENT AND EVALUATION

Chapter 26 Test Form A

Chapter 26 Test Form B

Standardized Test Skills Practice Workbook Activity 26

Performance Assessment Activities and Rubrics 26

ExamView® Pro Testmaker CD-ROM

MULTIMEDIA

- Vocabulary PuzzleMaker CD-ROM
- Interactive Tutor Self-Assessment CD-ROM
- ExamView® Pro Testmaker CD-ROM
- Audio Program
- American History Primary Source Documents Library CD-ROM
- MindJogger Videoquiz
- Presentation Plus! CD-ROM
- TeacherWorks™ CD-ROM
- Interactive Student Edition CD-ROM
- Glencoe Skillbuilder Interactive Workbook CD-ROM, Level 2
- The *American Vision* Video Program
- American Music: Hits Through History
- American Music: Cultural Traditions

SPANISH RESOURCES

The following Spanish language materials are available in the Spanish Resources Binder:

- Spanish Guided Reading Activities
- Spanish Reteaching Activities
- Spanish Quizzes and Tests
- Spanish Vocabulary Activities
- Spanish Summaries
- The Declaration of Independence and United States Constitution Spanish Translation

The following videotape programs are available from Glencoe as supplements to Chapter 26:

- **Dwight D. Eisenhower: Commander-in-Chief** (1-56-501807-9)
- **Senator Joseph McCarthy: An American Inquisitor** (1-56-501610-6)
- **The Rosenbergs** (0-76-700193-1)
- **Harry S Truman: A New View** (1-56-501449-9)

To order, call Glencoe at 1-800-334-7344. To find classroom resources to accompany many of these videos, check the following home pages:
A&E Television: www.aande.com
The History Channel: www.historychannel.com

HISTORY Online

Use our Web site for additional resources. All essential content is covered in the Student Edition.

You and your students can visit tav.glencoe.com, the Web site companion to the *American Vision.* This innovative integration of electronic and print media offers your students a wealth of opportunities. The student text directs students to the Web site for the following options:

- **Chapter Overviews**
- **Student Web Activities**
- **Self-Check Quizzes**
- **Textbook Updates**

Answers to the student Web activities are provided for you in the **Web Activity Lesson Plans.** Additional Web resources and Interactive Tutor Puzzles are also available.

Chapter 26 Resources

SECTION RESOURCES

Daily Objectives	Reproducible Resources	Multimedia Resources
SECTION 1 **Origins of the Cold War** 1. Explain the growing tensions between the United States and the Soviet Union at the end of World War II. 2. Identify the goals of Stalin's foreign policy immediately after the war.	Reproducible Lesson Plan 26–1 Daily Lecture and Discussion Notes 26–1 Guided Reading Activity 26–1* Section Quiz 26–1* Reading Essentials and Study Guide 26–1 Performance Assessment Activities and Rubrics	Daily Focus Skills Transparency 26–1 Interactive Tutor Self-Assessment CD-ROM ExamView® Pro Testmaker CD-ROM Presentation Plus! CD-ROM TeacherWorks™ CD-ROM Audio Program American Music: Cultural Traditions
SECTION 2 **The Early Cold War Years** 1. Describe the American view of the Soviet Union and the policy of containment. 2. Explain the causes of the Korean War.	Reproducible Lesson Plan 26–2 Daily Lecture and Discussion Notes 26–2 Guided Reading Activity 26–2* Section Quiz 26–2* Reading Essentials and Study Guide 26–2 Performance Assessment Activities and Rubrics Supreme Court Case Studies	Daily Focus Skills Transparency 26–2 Interactive Tutor Self-Assessment CD-ROM ExamView® Pro Testmaker CD-ROM Presentation Plus! CD-ROM TeacherWorks™ CD-ROM Audio Program
SECTION 3 **The Cold War and American Society** 1. Describe the new Red Scare. 2. Discuss how American society reflected fears of the nuclear age.	Reproducible Lesson Plan 26–3 Daily Lecture and Discussion Notes 26–3 Guided Reading Activity 26–3* Section Quiz 26–3* Reading Essentials and Study Guide 26–3 Performance Assessment Activities and Rubrics Interpreting Political Cartoons	Daily Focus Skills Transparency 26–3 Interactive Tutor Self-Assessment CD-ROM ExamView® Pro Testmaker CD-ROM Presentation Plus! CD-ROM TeacherWorks™ CD-ROM Audio Program
SECTION 4 **Eisenhower's Policies** 1. Evaluate Eisenhower's military policy known as the "New Look." 2. Debate the effectiveness of Eisenhower's foreign policy.	Reproducible Lesson Plan 26–4 Daily Lecture and Discussion Notes 26–4 Guided Reading Activity 26–4* Section Quiz 26–4* Reading Essentials and Study Guide 26–4 Performance Assessment Activities and Rubrics	Daily Focus Skills Transparency 26–4 Interactive Tutor Self-Assessment CD-ROM ExamView® Pro Testmaker CD-ROM Presentation Plus! CD-ROM Skillbuilder Interactive Workbook, Level 2 TeacherWorks™ CD-ROM Vocabulary PuzzleMaker CD-ROM Audio Program

0:00 OUT OF TIME?
Assign the Chapter 26 **Reading Essentials and Study Guide.**

*Also Available in Spanish

 Blackline Master   Transparency   CD-ROM   DVD

 Poster   Music Program   Audio Program   Videocassette

Chapter 26 Resources

NATIONAL GEOGRAPHIC | Teacher's Corner

INDEX TO NATIONAL GEOGRAPHIC MAGAZINE

The following articles relate to this chapter.
- "Bikini's Nuclear Graveyard," June 1992
- "Douglas MacArthur: An American Soldier," March 1992

ADDITIONAL NATIONAL GEOGRAPHIC SOCIETY PRODUCTS

To order the following, call National Geographic at 1-800-368-2728:
- *1945–1989: The Cold War* (Video)
- *The Complete National Geographic: 109 Years of National Geographic Magazine* (CD-ROM)
- *National Geographic World Atlas For Young Explorers—Classroom Library Edition* (Teacher's Guide, Transparencies, Resource Masters)
- *The Rise and Fall of the Soviet Union* (Video)

NGS ONLINE

Access National Geographic's Web site for current events, atlas updates, activities, links, interactive features, and archives.
www.nationalgeographic.com

From the Classroom of...

Tricia Hock
Heritage Academy
Fort Walton Beach, FL

Cold War Interviews

Students work in groups, pairs, or individually to conduct interviews with persons who were alive during the Cold War. Interviews can be with people of different ages, but similar questions can be asked, such as:

- What year were you born? How old were you when you realized the United States was in a "Cold War"?

- If you were in school during the Cold War years, did your school conduct air raid drills? How were they conducted?

- Were you afraid the United States would be the target of bombs or missiles? Who did you think would fire them?

- Did anyone you know have a bomb shelter? Did you ever see one? If so, what was it like?

- Did TV, books, or the media heighten the fear of nuclear attack? How?

- When did you realize that the Cold War was over, or coming to an end?

Students should report their findings to the class.

ADDITIONAL RESOURCES FROM GLENCOE

- American Music: Cultural Traditions
- American Art & Architecture
- Outline Map Resource Book
- U.S. Desk Map
- Building Geography Skills for Life
- Inclusion for the High School Social Studies Classroom Strategies and Activities
- Teaching Strategies for the American History Classroom (Including Block Scheduling Pacing Guides)

KEY TO ABILITY LEVELS

Teaching strategies have been coded.

L1   BASIC activities for all students
L2   AVERAGE activities for average to above-average students
L3   CHALLENGING activities for above-average students
ELL   ENGLISH LANGUAGE LEARNER activities

 Block Schedule

Activities that are suited to use within the block scheduling framework are identified by:

Performance Assessment

Refer to Activity 26 in the Performance Assessment Activities and Rubrics booklet.

Why It Matters Activity

Ask students how they think the Cold War and the fear of communism might have affected life in the 1950s. Students should evaluate their answers after they have completed the chapter.

GLENCOE TECHNOLOGY

The *American Vision* Video Program

To learn more about the Cold War, have students view the Chapter 26 video, "Symbols of the Cold War," from the *American Vision* **Video Program.**

Available in DVD and VHS

MindJogger Videoquiz

Use the **MindJogger Videoquiz** to preview Chapter 26 content.

Available in VHS

CHAPTER

26 The Cold War Begins *1945–1960*

Why It Matters

After World War II, an intense rivalry developed between the United States and the Soviet Union—two superpowers with very different political and economic systems. This rivalry, known as the Cold War, led to a massive buildup of military weapons on both sides. The determination of American leaders to contain communism also led to the Korean War, in which over 54,000 Americans died.

The Impact Today

The effects of Cold War events are still evident today.
- The NATO alliance works to guarantee the security of many democratic countries.
- The math and science training important to the space race remains an educational priority.

The American Vision *Video* The Chapter 26 video, "Symbols of the Cold War," examines the era by focusing on the crisis of the Berlin airlift.

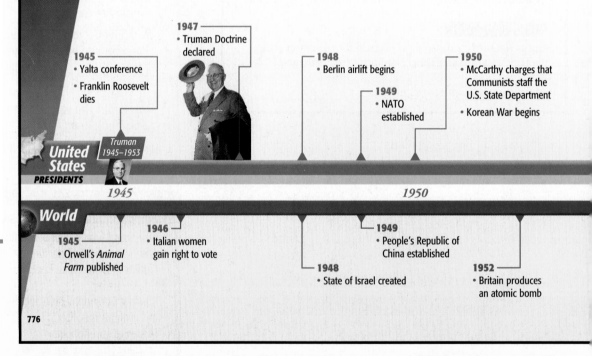

United States PRESIDENTS

Truman 1945–1953

1945
- Yalta conference
- Franklin Roosevelt dies

1947
- Truman Doctrine declared

1948
- Berlin airlift begins

1949
- NATO established

1950
- McCarthy charges that Communists staff the U.S. State Department
- Korean War begins

1945

1950

World

1945
- Orwell's *Animal Farm* published

1946
- Italian women gain right to vote

1948
- State of Israel created

1949
- People's Republic of China established

1952
- Britain produces an atomic bomb

776

TWO-MINUTE LESSON LAUNCHER

Ask students to identify some of the issues facing the United States today in terms of its relationships with other nations. Then discuss with students how many of these events, such as the political and economic changes in the countries of the former Soviet Union and the continuing unrest in Southwest Asia, are responses to situations that originated during the post-World War II era.

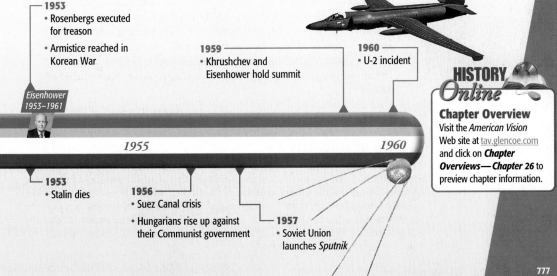

During Nixon's 1959 visit to Moscow, the vice president exchanged angry words with Soviet leader Nikita Khrushchev during the "kitchen" debate at an exhibit at the U.S. Trade and Cultural Fair.

1953
- Rosenbergs executed for treason
- Armistice reached in Korean War

Eisenhower 1953–1961

1959
- Khrushchev and Eisenhower hold summit

1960
- U-2 incident

1953
- Stalin dies

1955

1956
- Suez Canal crisis
- Hungarians rise up against their Communist government

1957
- Soviet Union launches *Sputnik*

1960

HISTORY *Online*

Chapter Overview
Visit the *American Vision* Web site at tav.glencoe.com and click on **Chapter Overviews—Chapter 26** to preview chapter information.

777

HISTORY *Online*

Introduce students to chapter content and key terms by having them access the **Chapter 26 Overview** at tav.glencoe.com.

More About the Photo

The day after this meeting, *The New York Times* published a transcript of the exchange between Nixon and Khrushchev. After asking Nixon how long America had existed, Khrushchev is reported to have said, "One hundred and fifty years? Well then we will say America has been in existence for 150 years and this is the level she has reached. We have existed not quite 42 years and in another seven years we will be on the same level as America. . . . Plainly speaking, if you want capitalism you can live that way. That is your own affair and doesn't concern us. We can still feel sorry for you, but since you don't understand us—live as you do understand."

TIME LINE
ACTIVITY

Have students create a time line for events in the United States spanning 1945 through 1960 using the chapter time line and the section time lines. Instruct students to include months for all events.

GRAPHIC ORGANIZER ACTIVITY

Organizing Information Have students compare the Soviet and American views of world affairs that led to the Cold War by completing the following graphic organizer. Students' answers will vary but should show the vastly different approaches taken by the two powers.

Soviet Views → **World Affairs** ← American Views

1 FOCUS

Section Overview

This section focuses on the growing tensions between the United States and the Soviet Union at the end of World War II.

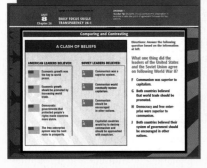
Guide to Reading

Answers to Graphic: Yalta: Poland's government recognized, Poland to have free elections, Declaration of Liberated Europe, Germany divided into four zones, terms of German reparations set; Potsdam: New border established between Germany and Poland, Germany's reparations to the Soviet Union restructured

Preteaching Vocabulary
Have students write a paragraph using all the Key Terms and Names.

Guide to Reading

Main Idea
The detonation of the atomic bomb and the end of World War II led to disagreements among the "Big Three" wartime Allies and a shift in American attitudes toward the Soviet Union.

Key Terms and Names
Cold War, Potsdam, satellite nation, iron curtain

Reading Strategy
Categorizing As you read about the origins of the Cold War, complete a graphic organizer similar to the one below by filling in the names of the conferences held among the "Big Three" Allies and the outcomes of each.

Conferences	Outcomes

Reading Objectives
- **Explain** the growing tensions between the United States and the Soviet Union at the end of World War II.
- **Identify** the goals of Stalin's foreign policy immediately after the war.

Section Theme
Global Connections As World War II was ending, the United States and the Soviet Union began to negotiate to influence the shape of the postwar world.

Preview of Events

◆February 1945	◆July 1945	◆December 1945	◆May 1946

February 1945
Yalta conference held in the USSR

April 1945
President Roosevelt dies

July 1945
Potsdam conference convenes in Germany

March 1946
Churchill delivers "iron curtain" speech

★ An American Story ★

Harry S Truman

On April 23, 1945, President Harry S Truman welcomed Soviet Foreign Minister Vyacheslav Molotov into the Oval Office of the White House. Truman had been president for less than two weeks, but he was determined to get tough with Molotov.

Truman told the Soviet diplomat how disgusted he was with Moscow's refusal to permit free elections in Poland, expressing his "deep disappointment" that the Soviet Union was not carrying out its agreements. Bluntly, he warned Molotov that Soviet defiance would seriously shake the confidence of the United States and Great Britain in their wartime ally.

Molotov began to explain the Soviet position, but Truman interrupted again and again, repeating his demand that Stalin "carry out that agreement in accordance with his word." Astonished, Molotov blurted out, "I have never been talked to like that in my life!"

"Carry out your agreements," the president snapped back, "and you won't get talked to like that!"

—adapted from *The Cold War: A History*

A Clash of Interests

Even before World War II ended, the wartime alliance between the United States and the Soviet Union had begun to show signs of strain. President Roosevelt had hoped that a victory over the Axis and the creation of the United Nations would lead to a more peaceful world. Instead, the United States and the Soviet Union became increasingly hostile toward each other after the war. This led to an era of confrontation and competition between the United States and the Soviet Union that lasted from about 1946 to 1990. This era became known as the Cold War.

Soviet Security Concerns Tensions between the United States and the Soviet Union began to increase because the two sides had different goals. As the war ended, Soviet leaders became concerned about security. Germany had invaded Russia twice in less than 30 years. The Soviets wanted to keep Germany weak and make sure that the countries between Germany and the Soviet Union were under Soviet control.

Although security concerns influenced their thinking, Soviet leaders were also Communists. They believed that communism was a superior economic system that would eventually replace capitalism and that the Soviet Union should encourage communism in other nations. Soviet leaders also accepted Lenin's theory that capitalist countries eventually would try to destroy communism. This made Soviet leaders suspicious of capitalist nations.

American Economic Concerns While Soviet leaders focused on securing their borders, American leaders focused on economic problems. Many American officials believed that the Depression had caused World War II. Without it, Hitler would never have come to power, and Japan would not have wanted to expand its empire.

American advisers also thought the Depression had been overly severe because countries cut back on trade. They believed that when nations seal themselves off economically, it forces them to go to war to get the resources they need. By 1945 President Roosevelt and his advisers were convinced that economic growth was the key to world peace. They wanted to promote economic growth by increasing world trade.

Similar reasoning convinced American leaders to promote democracy and free enterprise. They believed that democratic government with protections for people's rights made countries more stable and peaceful. They also thought that the free enterprise system, with private property rights and limited government intervention in the economy, was the best route to prosperity.

✓ **Reading Check**

Describing Why did U.S. leaders promote both international trade and free enterprise?

The Yalta Conference

In February 1945, with the war in Europe almost over, Roosevelt, Churchill, and Stalin met at **Yalta**—a Soviet resort on the Black Sea—to plan the postwar world. Although the conference seemed to go well, several agreements reached at Yalta later played an important role in causing the Cold War.

Poland The first issue discussed at Yalta was what to do about Poland. Shortly after the Germans invaded Poland, the Polish government leaders had fled to Britain. In 1944, however, Soviet troops drove back the Germans and entered Poland. As they liberated Poland from German control, the Soviets encouraged Polish Communists to set up a new government. This meant there were now two governments claiming the right to govern Poland, one Communist and one non-Communist.

President Roosevelt and Prime Minister Churchill both argued that the Poles should be free to choose their own government. "This is what we went to war against Germany for," Churchill explained, "that Poland should be free and sovereign."

Stalin quickly responded to Churchill's comments. According to Stalin, the Polish government had to be friendly to the Soviet Union. It was a matter of "life and death." Eventually, the three leaders compromised. Roosevelt and Churchill agreed to recognize the Polish government set up by the Soviets. Stalin agreed that the government would include members

Germany in Ruins World War II devastated many German cities. Here a woman sits among the ruins of Cologne, a northern city on the Rhine River.

2 TEACH

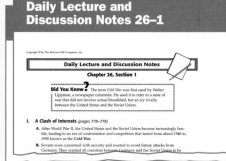

Daily Lecture and Discussion Notes 26–1

Copyright © by The McGraw-Hill Companies, Inc.

Daily Lecture and Discussion Notes

Chapter 26, Section 1

Did You Know? The term *Cold War* was first used by Walter Lippman, a newspaper columnist. He used it to refer to a state of war that did not involve actual bloodshed, but an icy rivalry between the United States and the Soviet Union.

I. A Clash of Interests (pages 778–779)

A. After World War II, the United States and the Soviet Union became increasingly hostile, leading to an era of confrontation and competition that lasted from about 1946 to 1990 known as the Cold War.

B. Soviets were concerned with security and wanted to avoid future attacks from Germany. They wanted all countries between Germany and the Soviet Union to be

Reading Check

Answer: in hopes that trade and free enterprise would increase prosperity and peace

Organizing Information Have students make a two-column list showing the postwar concerns of the Soviet Union and the United States. Use them to guide a class discussion on mounting tensions. **L1** ELL

FYI

The only two superpowers left after World War II were the United States and the Soviet Union; they had as much productive capacity between them as the rest of the world combined.

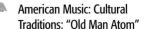

History *and the* Humanities

American Music: Cultural Traditions: "Old Man Atom"

COOPERATIVE LEARNING ACTIVITY

Researching Topics Organize the class into two groups and assign one of the topics below to each group. Have group members answer the question corresponding to their topic and explain their answer to the other group. **East-West Suspicions—Ask:** What was the main reason the alliance between the United States and the Soviet Union began to shatter after the war? **The Strength of Communism—Ask:** Why was communism appealing after the war?

Use the rubric for a cooperative group management plan on pages 81–82 in the *Performance Assessment Activities and Rubrics.*

NATIONAL GEOGRAPHIC
MOMENT in HISTORY

As a neutral country, Switzerland accepted refugees from the war, although it did close its borders during part of the war. Those who were able to support themselves were allowed to live and work freely in Switzerland. Those who could not support themselves lived in work camps run by the Swiss police.

Creating a Thematic Map Have students create a thematic map that shows the countries affected by Yalta. Instruct students to indicate where the Soviets did not abide by the Yalta agreement. **L2**

 Use the rubric for creating a map, display, or chart on pages 77–78 in the *Performance Assessment Activities and Rubrics.*

FYI

Over 750 years old, Berlin has been a major European cultural center since the 1700s. Following the reunification of Germany in 1990, Berlin was reestablished as the capital in 1991.

of the prewar Polish government and that free elections would be held as soon as possible.

Declaration of Liberated Europe After reaching a compromise on Poland, Roosevelt, Churchill, and Stalin agreed to issue the **Declaration of Liberated Europe.** The declaration asserted "the right of all people to choose the form of government under which they will live."

The Allies promised that the people of Europe would be allowed "to create democratic institutions of their own choice." They also promised to create temporary governments that represented "all democratic elements" and pledged "the earliest possible establishment through free elections of governments responsive to the will of the people."

Dividing Germany After agreeing to a set of principles for liberating Europe, the conference focused on Germany. Roosevelt, Churchill, and Stalin agreed to divide Germany into four zones. Great Britain, the United States, the Soviet Union, and France would each control one zone. The same four countries would also divide the city of Berlin, even though it was in the Soviet zone.

Although pleased with the decision to divide Germany, Stalin also wanted to weaken the country economically. He demanded that Germany pay heavy reparations for the war damage it caused. Roosevelt agreed, but he insisted reparations be based on Germany's ability to pay. He also suggested, and Stalin agreed, that Germany pay reparations with trade goods and products instead of cash. The Allies would also be allowed to remove industrial machinery, railroad cars, and other equipment from Germany as reparations.

This decision did not resolve the issue. Over the next few years, arguments about reparations and economic policy in Germany increased tensions between the United States and the Soviet Union. These arguments became one of the major causes of the Cold War.

Tensions Begin to Rise The Yalta decisions shaped the expectations of the United States. Two weeks after Yalta, the Soviets pressured the King of Romania into

NATIONAL GEOGRAPHIC
MOMENT in HISTORY

AID FOR WAR'S YOUNGEST VICTIMS

The gift of a new pair of shoes from the American Red Cross lights up the face of a young Austrian refugee. Millions of people across Europe were uprooted by almost six years of fighting that seldom distinguished between combatants and civilians. Millions more fled as victorious Soviet troops advanced through Eastern Europe into Germany at the end of World War II. The fate of the refugees became enmeshed in the growing power struggle between the United States and the Soviet Union, which turned the former allies into Cold War enemies.

MEETING SPECIAL NEEDS

Verbal/Linguistic Winston Churchill's metaphor of an iron curtain to describe Soviet control in Eastern Europe is very evocative. Have students work individually or with partners to come up with words and images they associate with the words *iron* (for example, strength, its use in the making of weapons) and *curtain* (for example, its ability to cut off contact with others or to hide what lies behind it). Allow students to draw as well as list the images that come to mind. **L1**

 Refer to *Inclusion for the High School Social Studies Classroom Strategies and Activities* in the TCR.

The Truman Doctrine Frustrated in Iran, Stalin turned to Turkey. There the straits of the Dardanelles were a vital route from Soviet Black Sea ports to the Mediterranean. For centuries Russia had wanted to control this strategic route. In August 1946, Stalin demanded joint control of the Dardanelles with Turkey. Presidential adviser **Dean Acheson** saw this move as the first step in a Soviet plan to control the Mideast, and he advised Truman to make a show of force. The president declared, "We might as well find out whether the Russians are bent on world conquest." He then ordered the new aircraft carrier *Franklin D. Roosevelt* to join the *Missouri* in protecting Turkey and the eastern Mediterranean.

While the United States supported Turkey, Britain tried to help Greece. In August 1946, Greek Communists launched a guerrilla war against the Greek government. For about six months, British troops helped the Greeks fight the guerrillas. The effort strained Britain's economy, which was still weak from World War II. In February 1947, Britain informed the United States that it could no longer afford to help Greece.

On March 12, 1947, Truman went before Congress to ask for $400 million to fight Soviet aggression in Greece and Turkey. His speech outlined a policy which became known as the **Truman Doctrine.** Its goal was to aid "free peoples who are resisting attempted subjugation by armed minorities or by outside pressures." Its immediate effects were to stabilize the Greek government and ease Soviet demands in Turkey. In the long run, it pledged the United States to fight communism worldwide. 📖 *(See page 1076 for more on the Truman Doctrine.)*

ECONOMICS

The Marshall Plan Meanwhile, postwar Western Europe faced grave problems. Economies were in ruin, people were near starvation, and political chaos was at hand. The terrible winter of 1946 made things worse.

In June 1947, Secretary of State George C. Marshall proposed the European Recovery Program, or **Marshall Plan,** which would give European nations American aid to rebuild their economies. Truman saw the Marshall Plan and the Truman Doctrine as "two halves of the same walnut," both essential

George Marshall

for containment. Marshall offered help to all nations planning a recovery program:

❝Our policy is not directed against any country or doctrine, but against hunger, poverty, desperation and chaos. Its purpose should be the revival of a working economy in the world so as to permit the emergence of political and social conditions in which free institutions can exist. . . .❞

—quoted in *Marshall: A Hero for Our Times*

The Soviet Union and its satellite nations in Eastern Europe rejected the offer. Instead, the Soviets developed their own economic program. This action further separated Europe into competing regions. The Marshall Plan pumped billions of dollars worth of supplies, machinery, and food into Western Europe. Western Europe's recovery weakened the appeal of communism and opened new markets for trade.

✓ **Reading Check** **Summarizing** What were the goals of the Truman Doctrine and the Marshall Plan?

The Berlin Crisis

The Marshall Plan was only one part of the American strategy for rebuilding Europe. President Truman and his advisers believed that Western Europe's prosperity depended on Germany's recovery. The Soviets, however, still wanted Germany to pay reparations to the Soviet Union. Eventually, the dispute over Germany brought the United States and the Soviet Union to the brink of war.

West Germany Is Founded By early 1948, U.S. officials had concluded that the Soviets were deliberately trying to undermine Germany's economy. In response, the United States, Great Britain, and France announced that they were merging their zones in Germany and allowing the Germans to have their own government. They also agreed to merge their zones in Berlin and to make West Berlin part of the new German republic.

The new nation was officially called the Federal Republic of Germany, but it became known as West Germany. West Germany's economy was completely separate from the Soviet zone, which eventually became known as East Germany. West Germany was not allowed to have a military, but in most respects, it was independent.

Guided Reading Activity 26–2

✓ Reading Check

Answer: fight Soviet aggression in Greece and Turkey, stabilize Europe's economy to defeat communism

Creating a Chart Have students create a chart showing examples of Truman's containment policies in Iran, Turkey, Greece, Germany, and China. **L2**

📁 Use the rubric for creating a map, display, or chart on pages 77–78 in the *Performance Assessment Activities and Rubrics.*

you don't say...

Marshall Opposition Senator Robert A. Taft opposed the Marshall Plan, calling it a "global give-away program." He was concerned that the plan would bankrupt the United States.

📁 Use *Supreme Court Case Study 27, Dennis* v. *United States.*

MEETING SPECIAL NEEDS

Verbal/Linguistic It is often difficult for students with poor vocabularies to understand the emotional impact of words and how these words shape our feelings about events. Have students examine the quote on this page and make a list of words they believe have an emotional impact. Then ask what emotions these words held for people in the United States and for people who lived in postwar Europe. **L1** ELL

📁 Refer to *Inclusion for the High School Social Studies Classroom Strategies and Activities* in the TCR.

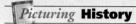

Reading Check

Answer: Soviet blockade of West Berlin

Creating a Map On an outline map of Europe, have students show the division between East and West by shading the European countries that made up the NATO alliance in 1949 in one color and those that made up the Warsaw Pact in 1955 in another color. **L1**

📁 Use the rubric for creating a map, display, or chart on pages 77–78 in the *Performance Assessment Activities and Rubrics.*

FYI

During the Berlin airlift, a plane flew into the city every three minutes. Without the supplies those planes carried, West Berliners would have had to back down.

Picturing History

Bucking the Blockade The Berlin airlift became a symbol of American determination to resist the Soviet Union's effort to control Berlin. *For how many months did American pilots supply Berlin with food and supplies?*

The Berlin Airlift The decision to create West Germany convinced the Soviets that they would never get the reparations they wanted. In late June 1948, Soviet troops cut all road and rail traffic to West Berlin. The blockade provoked a crisis. President Truman sent long-range bombers with atomic weapons to bases in Britain. General Lucius Clay, the American commander in Germany, warned that if Berlin fell, West Germany would be next. "If we mean to hold Europe against communism, then we must not budge," he said.

The challenge was to keep West Berlin alive without provoking war with the Soviets. In June 1948, Truman ordered the **Berlin airlift** to begin. For 11 months, cargo planes supplied Berliners with food, medicine, and coal. The airlift continued through the spring of 1949, bringing in over 2 million tons of supplies. Stalin finally lifted the blockade on May 12. The Berlin airlift became a symbol of American determination to stand by the divided city.

NATO The Berlin blockade convinced many Americans that the Soviets were bent on conquest. Both the public and Congress began to support a military alliance with Western Europe. By April 1949, an agreement had been reached to create the North Atlantic Treaty Organization (NATO)—a mutual defense alliance.

NATO initially included 12 countries: the United States, Canada, Britain, France, Italy, Belgium, Denmark, Portugal, the Netherlands, Norway, Luxembourg , and Iceland. NATO members agreed to come to the aid of any member who was attacked. For the first time in its history, the United States had committed itself to maintaining peace in Europe. Six years later, the United States and its allies decided to allow West Germany to rearm and join NATO. This decision alarmed Soviet leaders. They responded by organizing a military alliance in Eastern Europe, which became known as the **Warsaw Pact.**

Reading Check **Evaluating** What triggered the beginning of the Berlin airlift?

The Cold War Spreads to East Asia

The Cold War eventually spread beyond Europe. Conflicts also emerged in Asia, where events in China and Korea brought about a new attitude toward Japan.

Civil War and Revolution in China In China, Communist forces led by **Mao Zedong** had been struggling against the Nationalist government led by Chiang Kai-shek since the late 1920s. During World War II, the two sides suspended their war to resist Japanese occupation. With the end of World War II, however, civil war broke out again. Although Mao made great gains, neither side could win, and neither would accept a compromise.

To prevent a Communist revolution in Asia, the United States sent the Nationalist government $2 billion in aid beginning in the mid-1940s, but it squandered this advantage with poor military planning and corruption. By 1949 the Communists had captured the Chinese capital of Beijing and moved southward, while support for the Nationalists declined.

In August 1949, the State Department discontinued aid to the Chinese Nationalists. The defeated Nationalists then fled the Chinese mainland for the small island of Taiwan (Formosa). The victorious Communists established the People's Republic of China in October 1949.

After the Fall China's fall to communism shocked Americans. To make matters worse, in September 1949 the Soviet Union announced that it had successfully

INTERDISCIPLINARY CONNECTIONS ACTIVITY

Government Berlin remained a focal point throughout the Cold War. In 1961 the government of East Germany built the Berlin Wall to prevent its people from moving to West Germany. The dismantling of the Berlin Wall in 1989 foreshadowed the end of the Communist domination of Eastern Europe. Encourage students to use library and Internet resources to learn more about the reunification of Germany and the reestablishment of Berlin as Germany's capital.

tested its first atomic weapon. Then, early in 1950, the People's Republic of China and the Soviet Union signed a treaty of friendship and alliance. Many Western leaders feared that China and the Soviet Union would support Communist revolutions in other nations.

The United States kept formal diplomatic relations with only the Nationalists in Taiwan. It used its veto power in the UN Security Council to keep representatives of the new Communist China out of the UN, allowing the Nationalists to retain their seat.

The Chinese revolution brought about a significant change in American policy toward Japan. At the end of World War II, General Douglas MacArthur had taken charge of occupied Japan. His mission was to introduce democracy and keep Japan from

threatening war again. Once the United States lost China as its chief ally in Asia, it adopted policies to encourage the rapid recovery of Japan's industrial economy. Just as the United States viewed West Germany as the key to defending all of Europe against communism, it saw Japan as the key to defending Asia.

Reading Check **Analyzing** How did the revolution in China affect American foreign policy with Japan?

The Korean War

At the end of World War II, American and Soviet forces entered Korea to disarm the Japanese troops stationed there. The Allies divided Korea at the 38th

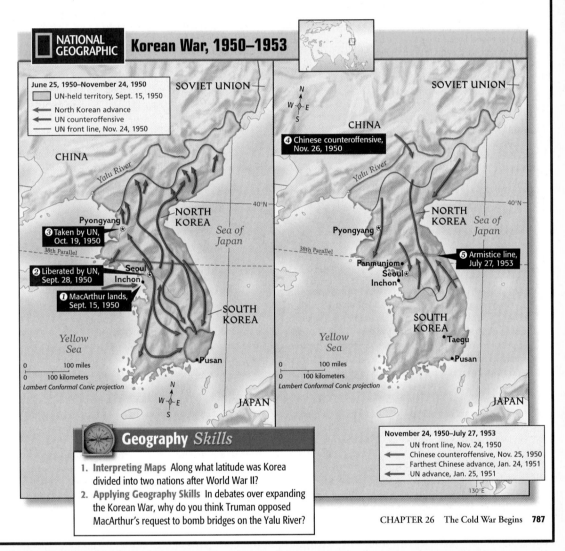

NATIONAL GEOGRAPHIC **Korean War, 1950–1953**

June 25, 1950–November 24, 1950
☐ UN-held territory, Sept. 15, 1950
← North Korean advance
← UN counteroffensive
— UN front line, Nov. 24, 1950

SOVIET UNION

CHINA

Yalu River

40°N

❸ Taken by UN, Oct. 19, 1950
NORTH KOREA
Pyongyang ⊛
Sea of Japan
38th Parallel

❷ Liberated by UN, Sept. 28, 1950
Seoul
Inchon ⊛

❶ MacArthur lands, Sept. 15, 1950

SOUTH KOREA

Yellow Sea
0   100 miles
0   100 kilometers
Lambert Conformal Conic projection

•Pusan

N W E S

JAPAN

SOVIET UNION

CHINA

❹ Chinese counteroffensive, Nov. 26, 1950

Yalu River

40°N

NORTH KOREA
Pyongyang ⊛
Sea of Japan
38th Parallel

❺ Armistice line, July 27, 1953

Panmunjom•
Seoul ⊛
Inchon ⊛

SOUTH KOREA

•Taegu

Yellow Sea
0   100 miles
0   100 kilometers
Lambert Conformal Conic projection

•Pusan

JAPAN

130°E

November 24, 1950–July 27, 1953
— UN front line, Nov. 24, 1950
← Chinese counteroffensive, Nov. 25, 1950
— Farthest Chinese advance, Jan. 24, 1951
← UN advance, Jan. 25, 1951

Geography *Skills*

1. **Interpreting Maps** Along what latitude was Korea divided into two nations after World War II?
2. **Applying Geography Skills** In debates over expanding the Korean War, why do you think Truman opposed MacArthur's request to bomb bridges on the Yalu River?

CHAPTER 26   The Cold War Begins   **787**

Reading Check

Answer: The United States adopted policies to encourage the rapid recovery of Japan's industrial economy.

 Geography *Skills*

Answers:
1. 38°N
2. Truman did not want to risk bringing the Chinese into the war, or to use the atomic bomb.

Geography Skills Practice
Ask: What was the importance of the Yalu River in the Korean War? *(It was the boundary between China and North Korea.)*

 you don't say...

Chinese Changes In October 2000 the Library of Congress and other U.S. libraries joined the international community and began using the Pinyin standard to convert Chinese characters. Pinyin has been widely used since 1979. In the older Wade-Giles system, it was Mao Tse-tung. In the Pinyin system, it is Mao Zedong.

 *FYI*

Douglas MacArthur and his father are the only father and son to have both received the Medal of Honor for people who perform extraordinary acts of heroism.

CRITICAL THINKING ACTIVITY

Making Judgments The Truman administration's policy toward China was met with criticism. Have students answer the following questions: **Could the United States have saved China from Communist domination? If so, how? If not, why not?** *(Students' answers will vary. Some might suggest that the United States should have given the Nationalists more military and economic aid. Other students might suggest that the conflict in China was a civil war and thus beyond the control of the U.S. government.)* **L2**

Different Viewpoints

Learning from History
Answers:
1. MacArthur believed Truman's policy would lead to war later. Truman did not want to widen the conflict, or lose allies.
2. The president is commander in chief.

Creating a Time Line Have students create a time line for the Korean War. Suggest that they use the time lines in this chapter as a reference. Encourage them to illustrate the time line with drawings or photographs. **L2**

3 ASSESS

Assign Section 2 Assessment as homework or as an in-class activity.

⊙ Have students use the **Interactive Tutor Self-Assessment CD-ROM.**

Reading Essentials and Study Guide 26–2

Name _____ Date _____ Class _____

Study Guide
Chapter 26, Section 2
For use with textbook pages 783–789

THE EARLY COLD WAR YEARS

KEY TERMS AND NAMES

George Kennan American diplomat who explained Soviet goals *(page 784)*
containment the policy of keeping communism within its present territory through the use of diplomatic, economic, and military actions *(page 784)*
Marshall Plan an economic recovery plan in which the United States provided aid to European nations to rebuild their economies *(page 785)*
NATO a military alliance made up of the United States, Canada, and several Western European nations *(page 786)*
limited war a war fought to achieve a limited objective such as containing communism *(page 789)*

Different Viewpoints

Should the War in Korea Be Expanded?

A controversy between President Harry S Truman and General Douglas MacArthur began shortly after the outbreak of the Korean War. It reached a climax when the president relieved MacArthur of his command. Truman believed in a limited war in Korea, while MacArthur wanted total victory.

President Harry S Truman defends limited war:

The Kremlin [Soviet Union] is trying, and has been trying for a long time, to drive a wedge between us and the other nations. It wants to see us isolated. It wants to see us distrusted. It wants to see us feared and hated by our allies. Our allies agree with us in the course we are following. They do not believe that we should take the initiative to widen the conflict in the Far East. If the United States were to widen the conflict, we might well have to go it alone.

If we go it alone in Asia, we may destroy the unity of the free nations against aggression. Our European allies are nearer to Russia than we are. They are in far greater danger. . . . Going it alone brought the world to the disaster of World War II. . . .

I do not propose to strip this country of its allies in the face of Soviet danger. The path of collective security is our only sure defense against the dangers that threaten us.

General Douglas MacArthur addresses Congress, April 19, 1951:

History teaches with unmistakable emphasis that appeasement but begets new and bloodier war. . . . Like blackmail, it lays the basis for new and successively greater demands, until, as in blackmail, violence becomes the only other alternative. Why, my soldiers asked of me, surrender military advantage to an enemy in the field? I could not answer.

It was my constant effort to preserve them and end this savage conflict honorably and with the least loss of time and minimum sacrifice of life.

I am closing 52 years of military service. . . . But I still remember the refrain of one of the most popular barrack ballads of that day which proclaimed most proudly that—

"Old soldiers never die, they just fade away." And like the old soldier of that ballad, I now close my military career and just fade away—an old soldier who tried to do his duty as God gave him the light to see that duty. Good-by.

Learning From History

1. **Identifying Central Issues** How did MacArthur view Truman's decision to fight a limited war in Korea? How did Truman see it?
2. **Making Inferences** On the basis of what authority did Truman fire MacArthur?

---

parallel of latitude. Soviet troops controlled the north, while American troops controlled the south.

As the Cold War began, talks to reunify Korea broke down. A Communist Korean government was organized in the north, while an American-backed government controlled the south. Both governments claimed authority over all of Korea, and border clashes were common. The Soviet Union provided extensive military aid to the North Koreans, who quickly built up a large, well-equipped army. On June 25, 1950, North Korean troops invaded into the south, rapidly driving back the poorly equipped South Korean forces.

The UN Intervenes Truman saw the Communist invasion of South Korea as a test of the containment policy and ordered United States naval and airpower into action. He then called on the United Nations to act. Truman succeeded because the Soviet delegate was boycotting the Security Council over its China policy and was not present to veto the American proposal. With the pledge of UN troops, Truman ordered General MacArthur to send American troops from Japan to the Korean peninsula.

The American and South Korean troops were driven back into a small pocket of territory near the port of Pusan. Inside the "Pusan perimeter," as it came to be called, the troops stubbornly resisted the North Korean onslaught, buying time for MacArthur to organize reinforcements.

EXTENDING THE CONTENT

Chinese Civil War The civil war between the Chinese Nationalists and the Chinese Communists might have been avoided had the Nationalists kept their promises to the people. By denying peasants the land they were promised, by forcing friendly Communists out of the government, and by ignoring corruption, the Nationalists practically guaranteed their unpopularity and the struggle for power with the Communists.

On September 15, MacArthur ordered a daring invasion behind enemy lines at the port of Inchon. The Inchon landing took the North Koreans by surprise. Within weeks they were in full retreat back across the 38th parallel. Truman then gave the order to pursue the North Koreans beyond the 38th parallel. MacArthur pushed the North Koreans north to the Yalu River, the border with China.

China Enters the War The Communist Chinese government saw the advancing UN troops as a threat and warned the forces to halt their advance. When those warnings were ignored, China launched a massive attack across the Yalu River in November. Hundreds of thousands of Chinese troops flooded across the border, driving the UN forces back across the 38th parallel.

As his troops fell back, an angry MacArthur demanded approval to expand the war against China. He asked for a blockade of Chinese ports, the use of Chiang Kai-shek's Nationalist forces, and the bombing of Chinese cities with atomic weapons.

Truman Fires MacArthur President Truman refused MacArthur's demands because he did not want to expand the war into China or to use the atomic bomb. MacArthur persisted. He publicly criticized the president, saying, "There is no substitute for victory."

Determined to maintain control of policy and show that the president commanded the military, an exasperated Truman fired MacArthur for insubordination in April 1951. MacArthur, who remained popular despite being fired, returned home to parades and a hero's welcome. Despite criticism, Truman remained

committed to limited war— a war fought to achieve a limited objective, such as containing communism.

Changes in Policy Truman chose General Matthew Ridgway to replace MacArthur. By mid-1951, the UN forces had pushed the Chinese and North Korean forces back across the 38th parallel. The war then settled down into a series of relatively small battles over hills and other local objectives. In November 1951, peace negotiations began, but an armistice would not be signed until July 1953. More than 33,600 American soldiers died in action in the Korean War, and more than 20,600 died from accidents or from disease.

The Korean War marked an important turning point in the Cold War. Until 1950 the United States had preferred to use political pressure and economic aid to contain communism. After the Korean War began, the United States embarked on a major military buildup.

The Korean War also helped expand the Cold War to Asia. Before 1950 the United States had focused on Europe as the most important area in which to contain communism. After the Korean War began, the United States became more militarily involved in Asia. Defense agreements were signed with Japan, South Korea, Taiwan, the Philippines, and Australia. American aid also began to flow to the French forces fighting Communist guerrillas in Vietnam.

✓ **Reading Check** **Analyzing** How did President Truman view the Communist invasion of South Korea?

HISTORY Online

Student Web Activity Visit the *American Vision* Web site at tav.glencoe.com and click on *Student Web Activities— Chapter 26* for an activity on the Cold War.

SECTION 2 ASSESSMENT

Checking for Understanding
1. **Define:** containment, limited war.
2. **Identify:** George Kennan, Marshall Plan, NATO.
3. **Review Facts** How did the Truman Doctrine and the Marshall Plan address the spread of communism?

Reviewing Themes
4. **Global Connections** What long-term Cold War strategy did the United States follow?

Critical Thinking
5. **Evaluating** How did the Long Telegram influence American policy?
6. **Categorizing** Use a graphic organizer similar to the one below to list early conflicts between the USSR and the U.S.

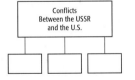

Conflicts Between the USSR and the U.S.

Analyzing Visuals
7. **Analyzing Maps** Study the maps of the Korean War on page 787. When did the United Nations control the most territory in Korea? When did both sides finally agree upon an armistice line?

Writing About History
8. **Persuasive Writing** Write a letter to the editor of a newspaper explaining whether you agree or disagree with President Truman's firing of General MacArthur.

SECTION 2 ASSESSMENT ANSWERS

1. Terms are in blue.
2. George Kennan (p. 784), Marshall Plan (p. 785), NATO (p. 786)
3. They would help any country fight against communism and they would help rebuild economies to strengthen the resistance to communism.
4. the policy of containing communism through international aid, diplomacy, and a strong military
5. It recommended patient but firm and vigilant containment of Russian expansion.
6. crisis in Iran, Berlin crisis, Korean War
7. November 1950; July 27, 1953
8. Students' letters will vary. Letters should express a point of view based on facts.

Section Quiz 26–2

Name _____ Date _____ Class _____

⭐ Chapter 26   Score ___

Section Quiz 26-2

DIRECTIONS: Matching Match each item in Column A with the items in Column B. Write the correct letters in the blanks. *(10 points each)*

Column A
___ 1. keeping communism within its present territory through the use of diplomatic, economic, and military actions
___ 2. the Soviet zone of Germany
___ 3. a war fought to achieve a limited objective such as containing communism
___ 4. gave European nations American aid to rebuild their economies
___ 5. when cargo planes supplied Berliners with food, medicine, and coal

Column B
A. East Germany
B. limited war
C. containment
D. Berlin airlift
E. Marshall Plan

HISTORY Online

Objectives and answers to the student activity can be found in the **Web Activity Lesson Plan** at tav.glencoe.com.

✓ **Reading Check**

Answer: Truman viewed it as a test of the United States containment policy.

Reteach
Have students describe the American view of the Soviet Union and containment.

Enrich
Invite interested students to write an editorial expressing an opinion about when, if ever, it is appropriate for a military leader to override a president's decision.

4 CLOSE

Have students create a cause-and-effect organizer for the Korean War.

1 FOCUS

Section Overview

This section focuses on the impact of the Cold War on American society.

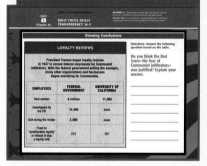
Guide to Reading

Answers to Graphic:
The Cold War and American Society
I. The New Red Scare
   A. The Loyalty Review Program
   B. HUAC
   C. Alger Hiss
   D. The Rosenbergs
   E. Project Venona
   F. The Red Scare Spreads
Students should complete the outline by including all heads in the section.

Preteaching Vocabulary
Have students create a study card for each Key Term and Name with the term on one side and a definition or description on the other side.

SECTION 3 — The Cold War and American Society

Guide to Reading

Main Idea
The Cold War heightened Americans' fears of Communist infiltration and atomic attack.

Key Terms and Names
subversion, loyalty review program, Alger Hiss, perjury, McCarran Act, McCarthyism, censure, fallout, fallout shelter

Reading Strategy
Taking Notes As you read about American reaction to the Cold War, use the major headings of the section to create an outline similar to the one below.

> The Cold War and American Society
> I. A New Red Scare
>   A. The Loyalty Review Program
>   B.
>   C.
>   D.

Reading Objectives
• **Describe** the new Red Scare.
• **Discuss** how American society reflected fears of the nuclear age.

Section Theme
Civic Rights and Responsibilities In the early part of the Cold War, the fear of communism led to a hunt for spies and to intolerance and suspicion of people with radical ideas in the United States.

Preview of Events

| ♦1947 | ♦1950 | ♦1953 |

March 1947 — Loyalty Review Board established

February 1950 — McCarthy claims to have a list of Communists in the State Department

September 1950 — McCarran Act passed

June 1953 — Rosenbergs executed

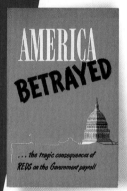

Book produced during the Red Scare of the 1950s

★ An American Story ★

In the 1940s, Ruth Goldberg belonged to the Parent-Teacher Association in Queens, New York. In 1947 she agreed to run for PTA president, but the campaign turned nasty. Because Goldberg had associated with people with left-wing interests, a rumor spread through the neighborhood that she was a Communist. Suddenly Goldberg's quiet life became terrifying. Callers threatened her, and the local priest denounced her in his sermons. One afternoon, Goldberg's eight-year-old son came home in tears. A playmate had told him, "You know, your mother's a Red. She should be put up against a wall and shot."

Looking back much later, Goldberg saw the PTA campaign as part of a bigger and more complex pattern of distrust and hatred. "It was a small thing, but it was an indication of what had happened with the Cold War, with this Red specter—that somebody like me could be a danger to a community."

—**adapted from** *Red Scare*

A New Red Scare

During the 1950s, thousands of ordinary people—from teachers to autoworkers to high government officials—shared Ruth Goldberg's disturbing experience. Rumors and accusations of Communists in the United States and of Communist infiltration of the government tapped into fears that the Communists were trying to take over the world.

SECTION RESOURCES

📁 Reproducible Masters
• Reproducible Lesson Plan 26–3
• Daily Lecture and Discussion Notes 26–3
• Guided Reading Activity 26–3
• Section Quiz 26–3
• Reading Essentials and Study Guide 26–3
• Interpreting Political Cartoons

🖎 Transparencies
• Daily Focus Skills Transparency 26–3

Multimedia
🖥 Interactive Tutor Self-Assessment CD-ROM
🖥 ExamView® Pro Testmaker CD-ROM
🖥 Presentation Plus! CD-ROM
🖥 TeacherWorks™ CD-ROM
🔊 Audio Program

The Red Scare began in September 1945, when a clerk named Igor Gouzenko walked out of the Soviet Embassy in Ottawa, Canada, and defected. Gouzenko carried documents revealing a massive effort by the Soviet Union to infiltrate organizations and government agencies in Canada and the United States with the specific goal of obtaining information about the atomic bomb.

The Gouzenko case stunned Americans. It implied that spies had infiltrated the American government. Soon, however, the search for spies escalated into a general fear of Communist subversion. Subversion is the effort to secretly weaken a society and overthrow its government. As the Cold War intensified in 1946 and early 1947, Americans began to fear that Communists were secretly working to subvert the American government.

GOVERNMENT

The Loyalty Review Program In early 1947, just nine days after his powerful speech announcing the Truman Doctrine, the president established a **loyalty review program** to screen all federal employees. Rather than calm public suspicion, Truman's action seemed to confirm fears that Communists had infiltrated the government and helped increase the fear of communism sweeping the nation.

Between 1947 and 1951, over 6 million federal employees were screened for their loyalty—a term difficult to define. A person might become a suspect for reading certain books, belonging to various groups, traveling overseas, or even seeing certain foreign films. About 14,000 employees were subject to intensive scrutiny from the Federal Bureau of Investigation (FBI). Some 2,000 employees quit their jobs during the check, many under pressure. Another 212 were fired for "questionable loyalty," though no actual evidence against them was uncovered.

HUAC Although the FBI helped screen federal employees, FBI Director **J. Edgar Hoover** was not satisfied. In 1947 Hoover went before the House Un-American Activities Committee (HUAC). Formed in 1938 to investigate both Communist and Fascist activities in the United States, HUAC was a relatively minor committee until Hoover catapulted it to prominence.

Hoover urged HUAC to hold public hearings on Communist subversion. The committee, Hoover said, could reveal "the diabolic machinations of sinister figures engaged in un-American activities." Once Communists were identified, he explained, the public would isolate them and end their influence. Hoover's aim was to expose not just Communists but also "Communist sympathizers" and "fellow travelers." Under Hoover's leadership, the FBI sent agents to infiltrate groups suspected of subversion and wiretapped thousands of telephones.

Alger Hiss In 1948 HUAC heard startling revelations from **Whittaker Chambers**, a *Time* magazine editor. Chambers admitted that he had been a Communist courier between 1934 and 1937, and he claimed that several government officials had been Communists or spies at that time.

The most prominent among these was **Alger Hiss**, a lawyer and diplomat who had served in Roosevelt's administration, attended the Yalta conference, and taken part in organizing the United Nations. Chambers claimed that in 1937 and 1938, Hiss had given him secret documents from the State Department. Hiss denied being a member of the Communist Party and also denied ever knowing Chambers.

The committee was ready to drop the investigation until Representative Richard Nixon of California convinced his colleagues to continue the hearings to determine whether Hiss or Chambers had lied. As the committee continued to question Hiss, he admitted that he had indeed met Chambers in the 1930s. When Chambers continued to claim that Hiss was a Communist, Hiss sued him, claiming that his accusations were unfounded and malicious.

To defend himself, Chambers produced copies of secret documents along with microfilm that he had hidden in a hollow pumpkin on his farm. These "pumpkin papers," Chambers claimed, proved that

Picturing History

Convicted of Conspiracy Ethel and Julius Rosenberg were convicted of transmitting atomic secrets to Soviet Russia. What sentence did they receive?

2 TEACH

Daily Lecture and Discussion Notes 26–3

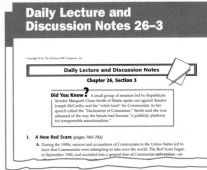

Copyright © by The McGraw-Hill Companies, Inc.

Daily Lecture and Discussion Notes

Chapter 26, Section 3

Did You Know? A small group of senators led by Republican Senator Margaret Chase Smith of Maine spoke out against Senator Joseph McCarthy and his "witch hunt" for Communists. In her speech called the "Declaration of Conscience," Smith said she was ashamed of the way the Senate had become "a publicity platform for irresponsible sensationalism."

I. A New Red Scare *(pages 790–792)*

A. During the 1950s, rumors and accusations of Communists in the Unites States led to fears that Communists were attempting to take over the world. The Red Scare began in September 1945, and escalated into a general fear of Communist subversion—an

Organizing Information Have students create a chart of the major players in the new Red Scare. Instruct students to include the names of the persons involved, a description of their involvement, and an explanation of the outcome of their involvement. **L1** ELL

📁 Use the rubric for creating a map, display, or chart on pages 77–78 in the *Performance Assessment Activities and Rubrics.*

Picturing History

Answer: condemned to death for espionage

Ask: Do you think the Soviet Union could have produced an atomic bomb without help? Why or why not? *(Most students will likely note that it probably would have taken the Soviet Union longer without help.)*

COOPERATIVE LEARNING ACTIVITY

Role-playing To dramatize the Cold War fears, have students act out scenes that might have occurred during this period. Groups might present a skit based on one of the situations below. Each group should choose a director, a scriptwriter, and actors. 🗂

A history teacher finding out that the FBI is investigating her
A blacklisted actor at an audition
Coworkers in an office discussing the Hiss or Rosenberg cases
A family talking about building a fallout shelter

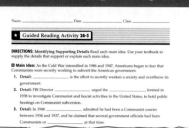
✓ **Reading Check**

Answer: to check for Communists who might have infiltrated the government of the United States

Writing an Article Have students write an article for a history journal about the impact of accusations of disloyalty. For example, anyone accused of disloyalty had a very difficult time finding a job. Encourage students to use library and Internet resources. **L2**

📁 Use the rubric for creating a magazine/newspaper/Web site article or help-wanted ad on pages 85–86 in the *Performance Assessment Activities and Rubrics.*

FYI

Many people, including Albert Einstein and Pope Pius XII, urged clemency for the Rosenbergs. Files released after the fall of the Soviet Union seem to indicate that the Rosenbergs were guilty. However, information based on a 1996 interview with David Greenglass, Ethel Rosenberg's brother, puts Ethel's guilt in doubt.

---

he was telling the truth. A jury agreed and convicted Hiss of perjury, or lying under oath.

The Rosenbergs Another sensational spy case centered around accusations that American Communists had sold the secrets of the atomic bomb. Many people did not believe that the Soviet Union could have produced an atomic bomb in 1949 without help. This belief intensified the hunt for spies.

In 1950 the hunt led to Klaus Fuchs, a British scientist who admitted sending information to the Soviet Union. His testimony led the FBI to arrest **Julius and Ethel Rosenberg,** a New York couple who were members of the Communist Party. The government charged them with heading a Soviet spy ring.

The Rosenbergs denied the charges but were condemned to death for espionage. Many people believed that they were not leaders or spies, but victims caught up in the wave of anti-Communist frenzy. Appeals, public expressions of support, and pleas for clemency failed, however, and the couple was executed in June 1953.

Project Venona The American public hotly debated the guilt or innocence of individuals like the Rosenbergs who were accused as spies. There was, however, solid evidence of Soviet espionage, although very few Americans knew it at the time. In 1946 American cryptographers working for a project code-named "Venona" cracked the Soviet spy code of the time, enabling them to read approximately 3,000

messages between Moscow and the United States collected during the Cold War. The messages confirmed extensive Soviet spying and sent federal investigators on a massive hunt. To keep the Soviets from learning how thoroughly the United States had penetrated their codes, authorities chose not to make the intercepted messages public. Not until 1995 did the government reveal **Project Venona's** existence. The Venona documents provided strong evidence that the Rosenbergs were guilty.

The Red Scare Spreads Following the federal government's example, many state and local governments, universities, businesses, unions, and churches began their own efforts to find Communists. The University of California required its 11,000 faculty members to take loyalty oaths and fired 157 who refused to do so. Many Catholic groups became strongly anticommunist and urged their members to identify Communists within the church.

The Taft-Hartley Act required union leaders to take oaths that they were not Communists, but many union leaders did not object. Instead they launched their own efforts to purge Communists from their organizations. The president of the CIO called Communist sympathizers "skulking cowards" and "apostles of hate." The CIO eventually expelled 11 unions that refused to remove Communist leaders from their organization.

✓ **Reading Check** **Explaining** What was the purpose of the loyalty review boards and HUAC?

Hollywood on Trial

One of HUAC's first hearings focused on the film industry as a powerful cultural force that Communists might use and manipulate. Its interviews routinely began, "Are you now, or have you ever been, a member of the Communist Party?" As fear of Communists in Hollywood spread, producers then drew up a blacklist and agreed not to hire anyone in the film industry who was believed to be a Communist or who refused to cooperate with the committee. The blacklist created an atmosphere of distrust and fear. People could be blacklisted for making chance remarks, criticizing HUAC, or knowing a suspected Communist.

Ronald Reagan, head of the Screen Actors Guild at the time, testified that there were Communists in Hollywood.

Ten screenwriters, known as the "Hollywood Ten" (shown here with their lawyers) used their Fifth Amendment right to protect themselves from self-incrimination and refused to testify before HUAC.

MEETING SPECIAL NEEDS

Interpersonal To help demonstrate the impact of McCarthyism, invite two volunteers to portray a HUAC member and someone called to testify before the committee. Have the HUAC member question the witness for several minutes about Communist influence in his or her workplace and among his or her friends and family. Afterward, ask participants and listeners to share their reactions. **L2**

📁 Refer to ***Inclusion for the High School Social Studies Classroom Strategies and Activities*** in the TCR.

"A Conspiracy So Immense"

In 1949 the Red Scare intensified even further. That year, the Soviet Union successfully tested an atomic bomb, and China fell to communism. To many Americans these events seemed to prove that the United States was losing the Cold War. Deeply concerned, they wanted an explanation as to why their government was failing. As a result, many continued to believe that Communists had infiltrated the government and remained undetected.

In February 1950, soon after Alger Hiss's perjury conviction, a little-known Wisconsin senator gave a political speech to a Republican women's group in West Virginia. Halfway through his speech, Senator **Joseph R. McCarthy** made a surprising statement:

> ❝While I cannot take the time to name all the men in the State Department who have been named as members of the Communist Party and members of a spy ring, I have here in my hand a list of 205 that were known to the Secretary of State as being members of the Communist Party and who nevertheless are still working and shaping the policy of the State Department.❞
>
> —quoted in *The Fifties*

By the next day, the Associated Press had picked up the statement and sent it to papers all over the country. When McCarthy arrived at the Denver airport, reporters crowded around him and asked to see his list of Communists in the state department. McCarthy replied that he would be happy to show them the list, but unfortunately, it was packed in his bag on the plane. In fact, the list never appeared. McCarthy, however, continued to make charges and draw attention.

McCarthy's Charges Born in 1908 near Appleton, Wisconsin, Joseph R. McCarthy studied law and served in World War II before his first run for the Senate. McCarthy's 1946 political campaign sounded the keynote of his career. Without making any specific charges or offering any proof, McCarthy accused his opponent, Robert M. La Follette, Jr., of being "communistically inclined." Fear of communism, plus McCarthy's intense speeches, won him the election.

After becoming a senator, McCarthy continued to proclaim that Communists were a danger both at home and abroad. To some of his audiences, he distributed a booklet called "The Party of Betrayal," which accused Democratic Party leaders of corruption and of protecting Communists. Secretary of State Dean Acheson was a frequent target. According to McCarthy, Acheson was incompetent and a tool of Stalin. He wildly accused George C. Marshall, the former army chief of staff and secretary of state, of disloyalty as a member of "a conspiracy so immense as to dwarf any previous such ventures in the history of man."

Red Channels, published in 1950, was prepared by three ex-FBI agents. The booklet claimed to identify 151 subversive entertainers in radio and television.

A number of well-known Hollywood celebrities, including actors Humphrey Bogart and Lauren Bacall (front row), went to Washington to protest HUAC's investigation of alleged Communists.

Drawing a Political Cartoon
Have students draw a political cartoon on the effect Senator Joseph McCarthy had on the American people. The cartoon should express a clear opinion about McCarthy's tactics. **L2**

 Use the rubric for creating a political cartoon, pamphlet, or handbill on pages 87–88 in the *Performance Assessment Activities and Rubrics.*

 CURRICULUM CONNECTION

Literature In his 1953 play, *The Crucible,* playwright Arthur Miller wrote about the witch trials in Salem, Massachusetts, in the 1600s. Despite the setting, Miller made it clear that the play was referring to the McCarthy era.

FYI

Of the film industry people investigated by HUAC, ten went to prison. This group, often referred to as "The Hollywood Ten," consisted of Alvah Bessie, Herbert J. Biberman, Lester Cole, Edward Dmytryk, Ring Lardner, Jr., John Howard Lawson, Albert Maltz, Samuel Ornitz, Adrian Scott, and Dalton Trumbo.

INTERDISCIPLINARY CONNECTIONS ACTIVITY

Psychology Have students use library and Internet resources to learn how mass hysteria contributed to the hunt for Communists in the United States in the 1950s. Ask students to write a report that answers the following questions: What fears did people have that made them so worried about Communist infiltration? How did media and government actions fuel these fears? **L2**

793

Creating Relative Chronology
Have students chronicle the major events of the McCarthy era by creating a chart listing significant events in the order they occurred. Encourage students to use library and Internet resources to learn more about the events of the McCarthy era. **L2**

 Use the rubric for creating a map, display, or chart on pages 77–78 in the *Performance Assessment Activities and Rubrics.*

FYI

Many Americans were afraid to challenge McCarthy. Even Dwight D. Eisenhower, running for president in 1952, did not speak out against him, though Eisenhower disliked McCarthy's tactics. Once he was elected president, he worked with congressional leaders to undermine McCarthy's authority.

 Use *Interpreting Political Cartoons,* Cartoon 26.

Picturing **History**
McCarthy Goes Too Far Army lawyer Joseph Welch listens to Senator McCarthy during the televised Army-McCarthy hearings. How did televising the hearings affect McCarthyism?

McCarthy was not alone in making such charges. In the prevailing mood of anxiety about communism, many Americans were ready to believe them.

The McCarran Internal Security Act In 1950, with the Korean War underway and McCarthy and others arousing fears of Communist spies, Congress passed the Internal Security Act, usually called the **McCarran Act.** Declaring that "world Communism has as its sole purpose the establishment of a totalitarian dictatorship in America," Senator Pat McCarran of Nevada offered a way to fight "treachery, infiltration, sabotage, and terrorism." The act made it illegal to "combine, conspire, or agree with any other person to perform any act which would substantially contribute to . . . the establishment of a totalitarian government." The law required all Communist Party and "Communist-front" organizations to register with the United States attorney general and publish their records. The act also created other restrictions for Communists. For example, they could not get passports to travel abroad.

The McCarran Act did not stop there. In case of a national emergency, it allowed the arrest and detention of Communists and Communist sympathizers. Unwilling to punish people for their opinions, Truman vetoed the bill, but Congress easily passed it

over his veto in 1950. Later Supreme Court cases, however, ensured that the McCarran Act would never be very effective.

McCarthy's Tactics After the 1952 election gave the Republicans control of Congress, McCarthy became chairman of the Senate subcommittee on investigations. Using the power of his committee to force government officials to testify about alleged Communist influences, McCarthy turned the investigation into a witch hunt—a search for disloyalty based on flimsy evidence and irrational fears. His tactic of damaging reputations with vague and unfounded charges became known as **McCarthyism.**

McCarthy's theatrics and sensational accusations drew the attention of the press, which put him in the headlines and quoted him widely. When he questioned witnesses, McCarthy would badger them and then refuse to accept their answers. His tactics left a cloud of suspicion that McCarthy and others interpreted as guilt. Furthermore, people were afraid to challenge him for fear of becoming targets themselves.

McCarthy's Downfall In 1954 McCarthy began to look for Soviet spies in the United States Army. Alerted to his intentions, the army conducted its

794 CHAPTER 26 The Cold War Begins

CRITICAL THINKING ACTIVITY

Assessing Outcomes The McCarthy era officially ended with McCarthy's death in 1957. In the end few spies were purged from the United States government. Yet for many people, the impact of McCarthy was felt for a lifetime. During the 1950s, many workers in a variety of industries lost their jobs because they were accused of having Communist sympathies. Although some of those accused probably were Communists, many others were not. **Ask:** Why do you think that fellow workers might have been afraid to stand up for their friends? *(for fear of being attacked themselves)* **L2**

own internal investigation and found no spies or any suspicion of espionage. Furious at the denial, McCarthy took his investigation onto television. He questioned and challenged officers in a harsh voice, harassing them about trivial details and accusing them of misconduct.

During weeks of televised **Army-McCarthy hearings** in the spring of 1954, millions of Americans watched McCarthy bully witnesses. His popular support started to fade. Finally, to strike back at the army lawyer, Joseph Welch, McCarthy brought up the past of a young lawyer in Welch's firm who had been a member of a Communist-front organization during his law school years. Welch, who was fully aware of the young man's past, now exploded at McCarthy for possibly ruining the young man's career: "Until this moment, I think I never really gauged your cruelty or your reckless-ness. . . . You have done enough. Have you no sense of decency, sir, at long last? Have you left no sense of decency?"

Spectators cheered. Welch had said aloud what many Americans had been thinking. One senator on the committee, Stuart Symington of Missouri, was also repelled: "The American people have had a look at you for six weeks. You are not fooling anyone." McCarthy had lost the power to arouse fear. Newspaper head-lines repeated, "Have you no sense of decency?"

Later that year, the Senate passed a vote of censure, or formal disapproval, against McCarthy—one of the most serious criticisms it can level against a member. His influence gone, McCarthy faded from public view. Although he remained in the Senate, he had little influence. He died in 1957, a broken and embittered man.

✓**Reading Check** **Evaluating** What were the effects of McCarthyism?

Life During the Early Cold War

The Red Scare and the spread of nuclear weapons had a profound impact on life in the 1950s. Fear of communism and of nuclear war dominated life for ordinary Americans as well as for government lead-ers throughout the era.

Facing the Bomb Already upset by the first Soviet atomic test in 1949, Americans were shocked when the USSR again successfully tested the much more powerful hydrogen bomb, or H-bomb, in 1953. This was less than a year after the United States had tested its own H-bomb.

Americans prepared for a surprise Soviet attack. Schools set aside special areas as bomb shelters. In bomb drills, students learned to duck under their

Picturing **History**

Signs of the Times During the Cold War, the media often gave survival tips for the nuclear holocaust many saw just around the corner. At right, a California resident works on his fallout shelter. How did such fears affect American politics?

✓**Reading Check**

Answer: It ruined many careers, colored political life, and influenced popular culture.

Picturing **History**

Answer: led to HUAC, the McCarran Act, and increased concern with national defense
Ask: What kinds of things were in the "survival kit" that is displayed in this illustration? *(bottled water, first aid kit, flashlights, canned food)*

Discussing a Topic Have stu-dents discuss how effective they think fallout shelters would have been during and after a nuclear attack. Ask what they think sur-vivors would have faced when they came out of the shelter. **L2**

3 ASSESS

Assign Section 3 Assessment as homework or as an in-class activity.

⊙ Have students use the **Interactive Tutor Self-Assessment CD-ROM.**

Reading Essentials and Study Guide 26–3

Name _____ Date _____ Class _____

Study Guide

Chapter 26, Section 3
For use with textbook pages 790–796

THE COLD WAR AND AMERICAN SOCIETY

KEY TERMS AND NAMES

subversion an effort to secretly weaken a society and overthrow its government (page 791)
loyalty review program a screening process of federal employees set up by President Truman in 1947 (page 791)
Alger Hiss a government official accused of being a Communist spy (page 791)
perjury lying under oath (page 792)
McCarran Act a law passed by Congress that required Communist organizations to provide the government with their records (page 794)
McCarthyism Senator McCarthy's method of destroying reputations with weak evidence and unfounded charges of Communist activity (page 794)

EXTENDING THE CONTENT

Nuclear Powers In 1945 the United States exploded the first atomic bomb in New Mexico. The Soviet Union tested its first atomic bomb in 1949. China, France, Great Britain, India, and Pakistan have also exploded nuclear weapons. In addition to the countries that have tested nuclear weapons, there are several countries believed to possess nuclear capabilities. **L2**

Section Quiz 26–3

Name _____ Date _____ Class _____

★ **Chapter 26**   Score ☐

Section Quiz 26–3

DIRECTIONS: Matching Match each item in Column A with the items in Column B.
Write the correct letters in the blanks. *(10 points each)*

Column A

_____ **1.** formal disapproval

_____ **2.** the effort to secretly weaken a society and overthrow its government

_____ **3.** blackening reputations with vague and unfounded charges

_____ **4.** built to protect people from the radiation left over after a nuclear blast

_____ **5.** lying under oath

Column B

A. fallout shelters
B. McCarthyism
C. subversion
D. perjury
E. censure

DIRECTIONS: Multiple Choice In the blank at the left, write the letter of the choice that best completes the statement or answers the question. *(10 points each)*

Fact | Fiction | Folklore

The Cold War inspired the marketing of Nuclear Attack Survival Kit Water, which was bottled water claiming to be "impervious to nuclear fallout."

✓ Reading Check

Answer: Americans prepared for a surprise Soviet attack, worried about a nuclear war, and watched films and read books about Communist infiltration of the United States.

Reteach

Have students describe the new Red Scare.

Enrich

Have interested students make a poster using headlines and sayings from the McCarthy era.

4 CLOSE

Have students discuss how American society reflected fears of the nuclear age.

Fact | Fiction | Folklore

Cold War Words The development of nuclear weapons and artificial satellites created not only new anxieties but also new words and expressions.

"*Sputnik,*" the name of the Soviet satellite, started its own language trend, as words gained a *-nik* ending for a foreign-sounding effect. One new word, *beatnik,* described a young person influenced by the style of Beat writers such as Jack Kerouac and Allen Ginsberg. Another word, *peacenik,* was used to describe a peace activist.

The atomic bomb test on Bikini Atoll gave the Nuclear Age two new words: *fallout,* the term for the harmful radiation left over after an atomic blast, and *bikini,* a skimpy swimsuit that French designers promised would produce an "explosion" on the beach.

---

desks, turn away from the windows, and cover their heads with their hands. These "duck-and-cover" actions were supposed to protect them from a nuclear bomb blast.

"Duck-and-cover" might have made people feel safe, but it would not have protected them from deadly nuclear radiation. According to experts, for every person killed outright by a nuclear blast, four more would die later from fallout, the radiation left over after a blast. To protect themselves, some families built backyard fallout shelters and stocked them with canned food.

Popular Culture in the Cold War Worries about nuclear war and Communist infiltration filled people's imaginations. Cold War nightmares soon appeared in films and popular fiction.

Matt Cvetic was an FBI undercover informant who secretly infiltrated the Communist Party in Pittsburgh. His story captivated magazine readers in the *Saturday Evening Post* in 1950 and came to the screen the next year as *I Was a Communist for the FBI*. Another suspense film, *Walk East on Beacon* (1951), features the FBI's activities in an espionage case. In 1953 television took up the theme with a series about an undercover FBI counterspy who was also a Communist Party official. Each week, *I Led Three Lives* kept television viewers on edge.

In 1954 author Philip Wylie published *Tomorrow!* This novel describes the horrific effects of nuclear war on an unprepared American city. As an adviser on civil defense, Wylie had failed to convince the federal government to play a strong role in building bomb shelters. Frustrated, he wrote this novel to educate the public about the horrors of atomic war.

At the same time these fears were haunting Americans, the country was enjoying postwar prosperity and optimism. That spirit, combined with McCarthyism, witch hunts, fears of Communist infiltration, and the threat of atomic attack, made the early 1950s a time of contrasts. As the 1952 election approached, Americans were looking for someone or something that would make them feel secure.

✓ Reading Check **Describing** How did the Cold War affect life in the 1950s?

SECTION 3 ASSESSMENT

Checking for Understanding

1. **Define:** subversion, perjury, censure, fallout, fallout shelter.
2. **Identify:** loyalty review program, Alger Hiss, McCarran Act, McCarthyism.
3. **Explain** the goals of Project Venona.
4. **Review Facts** What did the McCarran Act propose to do?

Reviewing Themes

5. **Civic Rights and Responsibilities** How did McCarthyism and the Red Scare change American society and government?

Critical Thinking

6. **Interpreting** Why did McCarthy initially receive a lot of support for his efforts to expose Communists?
7. **Organizing** Use a graphic organizer to list the causes and effects of the new Red Scare.

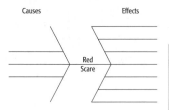

Causes | Effects

Red Scare

Analyzing Visuals

8. **Analyzing Photographs** Study the photograph on page 794 of the Army-McCarthy hearings. From their postures, how would you describe the attitude of army lawyer Joseph Welch toward Senator Joseph McCarthy? Do you think Welch respects McCarthy's presentation?

Writing About History

9. **Persuasive Writing** Imagine you are a newspaper editor during the McCarthy hearings. Write an editorial supporting or condemning Senator McCarthy. Defend your position.

796 CHAPTER 26   The Cold War Begins

SECTION 3 ASSESSMENT ANSWERS

1. Terms are in blue.
2. loyalty review program *(p. 791)*, Alger Hiss *(p. 791)*, McCarran Act *(p. 794)*, McCarthyism *(p. 794)*
3. to crack the Soviet spy code, and confirm Soviet spying
4. to make it illegal to associate with or be a Communist
5. While people were enjoying postwar prosperity and optimism, they feared communism and an atomic attack.
6. People feared communism.
7. Causes: Gouzenko case, Alger Hiss trial, Rosenbergs, Russia's successful test of an atomic bomb; Effects: Loyalty Review Program, HUAC, McCarran Act, McCarthyism, fallout shelters
8. Students might suggest disgust or annoyance.
9. Students' editorials will vary. Editorials should address the tactics McCarthy used and express a clear point of view.

fellows start something, we may have to hit them—and if necessary, with everything in the bucket."

Under strong American pressure, the British and French called off their invasion. The Soviet Union had won a major diplomatic victory, however, by supporting Egypt. Soon afterward, other Arab nations began accepting Soviet aid as well.

✓ **Reading Check** **Identifying** What was brinkmanship?

Fighting Communism Covertly

President Eisenhower relied on brinkmanship on several occasions, but he knew it could not work in all situations. It could prevent war, but it could not, for example, prevent Communists from staging revolutions within countries. To prevent Communist uprisings in other countries, Eisenhower decided to use covert, or hidden, operations conducted by the **Central Intelligence Agency** (CIA).

Containment in Developing Nations Many of the CIA's operations took place in developing nations—nations with primarily agricultural economies. Many of these countries blamed European imperialism and American capitalism for their problems. Their leaders looked to the Soviet Union as a model of how to industrialize their countries. They often threatened to nationalize, or put under government control, foreign businesses operating in their countries.

American officials feared that these leaders might align their nations with the Soviet Union or even stage a Communist revolution. One way to stop developing nations from moving into the Communist camp was to provide them with financial aid, as Eisenhower had tried to do in Egypt. In some cases, however, where the threat of communism seemed stronger, the CIA staged covert operations to overthrow anti-American leaders and replace them with pro-American leaders.

Iran and Guatemala Two examples of covert operations that achieved American objectives took place in Iran and Guatemala. By 1953 Iranian prime minister Mohammed Mossadegh had already nationalized the Anglo-Iranian Oil Company. He seemed ready to make an oil deal with the Soviet Union. In 1953 Mossadegh moved against the pro-American Shah of Iran, who was temporarily forced into exile. Dulles quickly sent agents to organize street riots and arrange a coup that ousted Mossadegh, and the Shah returned to power.

Picturing **History**

Distinguished Brothers John Foster Dulles (right) became secretary of state under Eisenhower; his brother Allen Dulles (center) was director of the CIA in the 1950s. With what policy is John Foster Dulles associated?

The following year, the CIA acted to protect American-owned property in Guatemala. In 1951 Jacobo Arbenz Guzmán won election as president of Guatemala with Communist support. His land reform program took over large estates, including those of the American-owned United Fruit Company. In May 1954, Communist Czechoslovakia delivered arms to Guatemala. The CIA responded by arming the Guatemalan opposition and training them at secret camps in Nicaragua and Honduras. Shortly after these CIA-trained forces invaded Guatemala, Arbenz Guzmán left office.

Uprising in Hungary Covert operations did not always work as Eisenhower hoped. In 1953 Stalin died, and a power struggle began in the Soviet Union. By 1956 **Nikita Khrushchev** had emerged as the leader of the Soviet Union. That year, Khrushchev delivered a secret speech to Soviet leaders. He attacked Stalin's policies and insisted there were

CHAPTER 26 The Cold War Begins **801**

✓ **Reading Check**
Answer: Brinkmanship is the willingness to go to the brink of war to force the other side to back down.

Picturing **History**
Answer: brinkmanship
Ask: Who coined the term brinkmanship? *(critics of Eisenhower's willingness to threaten nuclear war to get the other side to back down)*

FYI

Many people in Iran resented the Shah's close ties with the West. Their anger at the Shah's attachment to Western ideas and customs helped fuel the 1979 revolt against him. Mohammed Reza Shah Pahlavi died in exile in 1980.

3 ASSESS

Assign Section 4 Assessment as homework or as an in-class activity.

● Have students use the **Interactive Tutor Self-Assessment CD-ROM.**

Reading Essentials and Study Guide 26–4

Study Guide
Chapter 26, Section 4
For use with textbook pages 797–802
EISENHOWER'S POLICIES

KEY TERMS AND NAMES
massive retaliation the policy of threatening Communist states with nuclear war if the state tried to take territory by force *(page 798)*
Sputnik developed by the Soviet Union, the first artificial satellite to orbit the earth *(page 799)*
brinkmanship the willingness to go to the brink of war to force the other side to back down *(page 799)*
covert hidden *(page 801)*
Central Intelligence Agency an agency that conducted covert operations *(page 801)*
developing nation nation with a primarily agricultural economy *(page 801)*

CRITICAL THINKING ACTIVITY

Evaluating Action The overthrow of the leftist Guatemalan government was made possible by the activities of the Central Intelligence Agency. Ask students the following questions: **Is secret aggression, such as that by the CIA, justifiable? Why or why not? What events in your lifetime have helped shape your opinion? L2**

✓ Reading Check

Answer: He used covert actions to secretly help countries fight communism and overthrow anti-American leaders.

✓ Reading Check

Answer: He thought that a military-industrial complex could threaten democracy.

Reteach

Have students rate the changes Eisenhower brought to the White House as positive or negative.

Enrich

Have interested students research the social, cultural, and historical factors that affected the Hungarians' reaction to Communist control. Encourage students to use library and Internet resources.

4 CLOSE

Have students debate the effectiveness of Eisenhower's foreign policy.

---

many ways to build a Communist society. Although the speech was secret, the CIA obtained a copy. With Eisenhower's permission, the CIA arranged for it to be broadcast to Eastern Europe.

Many Eastern Europeans had long been frustrated with Communist rule. Hearing Khrushchev's speech further discredited communism. In June 1956, riots erupted in Eastern Europe. By late October, a full-scale uprising had begun in Hungary. Although Khrushchev was willing to tolerate greater freedom in Eastern Europe, he had never meant to imply that the Soviets would tolerate an end to communism in Eastern Europe. Soon after the uprising began, Soviet tanks rolled into Budapest, the capital of Hungary, and crushed the rebellion.

✓ **Reading Check** **Explaining** Why did Eisenhower use covert operations?

Continuing Tensions

The uprising in Hungary forced Khrushchev to reassert Soviet power and the superiority of communism. Previously, he had supported "peaceful coexistence" with capitalism. Now he accused the "capitalist countries" of starting a "feverish arms race." In 1957, after the launch of Sputnik, Khrushchev boasted, "We will bury capitalism. . . . Your grandchildren will live under communism."

In late 1958 Khrushchev demanded that the United States, Great Britain, and France withdraw their troops from West Berlin. Secretary of State Dulles rejected Khrushchev's demands. If the Soviets threatened

Berlin, Dulles announced, NATO would respond, "if need be by military force." Brinkmanship worked again, and Khrushchev backed down.

To try to improve relations, Eisenhower invited Khrushchev to visit the United States in late 1959. The visit went well, and the two leaders agreed to hold a summit in Paris in 1960. A **summit** is a formal face-to-face meeting of leaders from different countries to discuss important issues.

Shortly before the summit was to begin, the Soviet Union shot down the American U-2 spy plane piloted by **Francis Gary Powers.** At first, Eisenhower claimed that the aircraft was a weather plane that had strayed off course. Then Khrushchev dramatically produced the pilot. Eisenhower refused to apologize, saying the flights had protected American security. In response, Khrushchev broke up the summit.

In this climate of heightened tension, President Eisenhower prepared to leave office. In January 1961, he delivered a farewell address to the nation. In the address, he pointed out that a new relationship had developed between the military establishment and the defense industry. He warned Americans to be on guard against the immense influence of this military-industrial complex in a democracy. Although he had avoided war and kept communism contained, Eisenhower admitted to some frustration: "I confess I lay down my official responsibility in this field with a definite sense of disappointment. . . . I wish I could say that a lasting peace is in sight."

✓ **Reading Check** **Evaluating** Why did Eisenhower warn Americans about the military-industrial complex?

SECTION 4 ASSESSMENT

Checking for Understanding

1. **Define:** massive retaliation, brinkmanship, covert, developing nation, military-industrial complex.

2. **Identify:** *Sputnik,* Central Intelligence Agency.

3. **Reviewing Facts** What was the significance of the Soviet Union's launching of *Sputnik* in 1957?

Reviewing Themes

4. **Science and Technology** How did technology shape Eisenhower's military policy?

Critical Thinking

5. **Interpreting** Do you think Eisenhower's foreign policy was successful? Why or why not?

6. **Organizing** Use a graphic organizer similar to the one below to list Eisenhower's strategies for containing Communism.

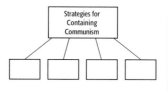

Strategies for Containing Communism

Analyzing Visuals

7. **Analyzing Maps** Study the map on page 800. How many nations belonged to NATO? How many nations belonged to the Warsaw Pact? Which nations did not belong to either NATO or the Warsaw Pact?

Writing About History

8. **Persuasive Writing** Imagine you are a member of Eisenhower's cabinet. Defend or attack brinkmanship as a foreign policy tactic. Be sure to provide specific reasons for your point of view.

802 CHAPTER 26 The Cold War Begins

SECTION 4 ASSESSMENT ANSWERS

1. Terms are in blue.

2. *Sputnik (p. 799),* Central Intelligence Agency *(p. 801)*

3. It stunned Americans and led to the creation of NASA and the passage of the NDEA.

4. It allowed him to pursue the policy of brinkmanship since the nuclear

arsenal was a real threat. It also allowed covert operations in Iran and Guatemala.

5. Students' answers will vary. Students should cite specific events to support their conclusion.

6. strong economy, nuclear weapons for massive retaliation, brinkman-

ship, covert operations

7. 12 NATO on map (Iceland also a member, but not shown on map); 8 Warsaw Pact; 7 did not belong to NATO or the Warsaw Pact

8. Students' answers should express a point of view supporting or opposing brinkmanship.

Making Decisions

Why Learn This Skill?

Suppose you have been given the choice of taking an art class or a music class during your free period during school. How will you decide which class to take?

Learning the Skill

When you make a decision, you are making a choice between alternatives. In order to make that choice, you must be informed and aware. There are five key steps you should follow that will help you through the process of making decisions.

- Identify the problem. What are you being asked to choose between?
- Gather information to identify and consider various alternatives that are possible.
- Determine the consequences for each alternative. Identify both positive and negative consequences.
- Evaluate the consequences. Consider both the positive and negative consequences for each alternative.
- Determine which alternative seems to have more positive than negative consequences. Then make your decision.

Practicing the Skill

Decisions throughout history have affected the outcome of events and defined history as we know it today. Identify the alternatives and describe their consequences for each of the following events that occurred after World War II. Each of these events took place as a result of a decision made by a person or a group of people.

❶ Britain and the United States recognize the Soviet-backed government that takes control in Poland.

❷ The United States orchestrates the Berlin airlift to assist residents of West Berlin after Stalin cuts off surface transportation bringing supplies from the West.

President Truman and Dean Acheson

❸ The Marshall Plan for rebuilding war-torn Western Europe is approved.

❹ President Truman relieves General Douglas MacArthur of his command because of insubordination.

Skills Assessment

Complete the Practicing Skills questions on page 805 and the Chapter 26 Skill Reinforcement Activity to assess your mastery of this skill.

Applying the Skill

Making Decisions Use a newspaper or magazine to find a current issue that directly affects your life. Identify the issue, and then review the facts and what you already know about the issue. Identify various alternatives and determine the consequences for each. Use this information to evaluate both positive and negative consequences. Make a sound decision about which alternative would be best for you, and write a paragraph defending your decision.

Glencoe's **Skillbuilder Interactive Workbook CD-ROM, Level 2,** provides instruction and practice in key social studies skills.

803

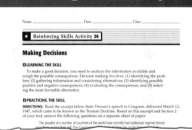

ANSWERS TO PRACTICING THE SKILL

❶ Nonrecognition leads to tension and possible war.

❷ No airlift makes Berlin residents suffer and the United States look weak.

❸ No Marshall Plan hurts Europe's economy and its political stability.

❹ Leaving MacArthur in command might lead to war with China and greater American involvement in Asia.

Applying the Skill
Students' reasoning should be clearly evident.

GLENCOE
TECHNOLOGY

MindJogger Videoquiz
Use the **MindJogger Videoquiz** to review Chapter 26 content.

Available in VHS

Reviewing Key Terms
Students' answers will vary. The pages where the words appear in the text are shown in parentheses.

1. **Cold War** (p. 778)
2. **iron curtain** (p. 782)
3. **containment** (p. 784)
4. **limited war** (p. 789)
5. **subversion** (p. 791)
6. **perjury** (p. 792)
7. **censure** (p. 795)
8. **fallout** (p. 796)
9. **fallout shelter** (p. 796))
10. **massive retaliation** (p. 798)
11. **brinkmanship** (p. 799)
12. **covert** (p. 801)
13. **developing nation** (p. 801)
14. **military-industrial complex** (p. 802)

Reviewing Key Facts
15. Potsdam (p. 781), Marshall Plan (p. 785), NATO (p. 786), McCarthyism (p. 794)

16. Stalin's push for German reparations and for a Communist government in Poland conflicted with United States desire for democracy in Poland and economic recovery for Germany.

17. NATO was formed to maintain peace and freedom for European nations and the Warsaw Pact was formed to achieve Soviet foreign policy goals.

18. The long-term strategy was to fight the spread of communism worldwide.

19. Federal employees faced stricter screening and termination if they were suspected of being disloyal.

Reviewing Key Terms
On a sheet of paper, use each of these terms in a sentence.

1. Cold War
2. iron curtain
3. containment
4. limited war
5. subversion
6. perjury
7. censure
8. fallout
9. fallout shelter
10. massive retaliation
11. brinkmanship
12. covert
13. developing nation
14. military-industrial complex

Reviewing Key Facts
15. **Identify:** Potsdam, Marshall Plan, NATO, McCarthyism.

16. How did Stalin's postwar foreign policy goals add to the growing tensions between the United States and the USSR?

17. Why were NATO and the Warsaw Pact formed?

18. What was the long-term strategy of the United States during the Cold War?

19. What were the effects of the new Red Scare on federal employees?

20. What was President Eisenhower's "new look" for the military?

Critical Thinking
21. **Analyzing Themes: Global Connections** How did the Truman Doctrine and the Marshall Plan cause the United States to change its foreign policy goal of isolationism?

22. **Evaluating** How did the Korean War affect American domestic and international policy?

23. **Organizing** Use a graphic organizer similar to the one below to list the causes of the Cold War.

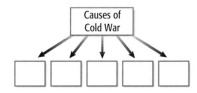

24. **Interpreting Primary Sources** Margaret Chase Smith, a Republican from Maine, was elected to the Senate in 1948. As a newcomer and the only woman in the Senate, she had very little power. Smith was upset by Joseph McCarthy's accusations, but she hoped her senior colleagues would reprimand him. When they failed to do so, Smith made her "Declaration of Conscience" speech. Read the excerpt and answer the questions that follow.

Chapter Summary

The Cold War

Soviet Union		Western Allies
• To create a protective sphere of Communist countries along European border • To promote the spread of communism	**General Goals**	• To contain the spread of communism by supporting capitalist democratic governments
• Occupied Eastern European nations and saw that Communist governments were established	**In Europe**	• Expected free elections to occur in Soviet-controlled Eastern Europe
• Sought access to oil in Iran • Aided Communists in Greece and pressured Turkey for access to the Mediterranean	**In the Middle East**	• Forced Soviet withdrawal from Iran • Pledged aid to halt Soviet threats to Turkey and Greece
• Communists seize power in China in 1949 • China and Soviet Union signed treaty of friendship and alliance • Communist North Korea invaded South Korea to start Korean War • Chinese troops fought for North Korea	**In Asia**	• Aided China's Nationalist government • Dedicated money and troops to establish democratic stronghold in Japan • United Nations troops sent to fight for South Korea in Korean War
• Promoted development of high-technology weapons and surveillance	**At Home**	• Focused on the development of advanced technology weapons

20. Eisenhower favored the use of atomic weapons, instead of maintaining a large and expensive army.

Critical Thinking
21. They highlighted the possibility of Communist influence in Turkey, Greece, and Europe, resulting in the containment policy and increased foreign aid.

22. domestic: reinforced the idea of containment and greater military readiness; international: brought the Cold War to Asia, and led to United States defense agreements with Asian countries

HISTORY
Online

Self-Check Quiz

Visit the *American Vision* Web site at tav.glencoe.com and click on *Self-Check Quizzes—Chapter 26* to assess your knowledge of chapter content.

66As a United States Senator, I am not proud of the way in which the Senate has been made a publicity platform for irresponsible sensationalism. I am not proud of the reckless abandon in which unproved charges have been hurled from this side of the aisle. I am not proud of the obviously staged, undignified countercharges that have been attempted in retaliation from the other side of the aisle. . . . I am not proud of the way we smear outsiders from the Floor of the Senate and hide behind the cloak of congressional immunity. . . .

As an American, I am shocked at the way Republicans and Democrats alike are playing directly into the Communist design of 'confuse, divide, and conquer'. . . . I want to see our nation recapture the strength and unity it once had when we fought the enemy instead of ourselves.99

—from *Declaration of Conscience*

a. With whom is Smith angry, and why?

b. According to Smith, who is really dividing the nation?

Practicing Skills

25. Making Decisions Study the text on the Truman Doctrine on page 785. Then use the steps you learned about making decisions on page 803 to identify the alternatives the president had in making a decision to ask for aid to fight Soviet aggression in Turkey and Greece. Create a graphic organizer to list the alternatives you have identified.

Chapter Activity

26. Technology Activity: Developing a Multimedia Presentation Use the Internet and other resources to find out more about American popular culture during the Cold War. Then create a multimedia report about popular culture at this time, and present your report to the class. Your report could discuss films, books, and magazine articles.

Writing Activity

27. Persuasive Writing Imagine that you have witnessed the crowds giving General MacArthur a hero's welcome. Write an opinion piece for a magazine justifying his reception or criticizing it because of his disagreement with Truman.

NATIONAL GEOGRAPHIC

The Occupation of Berlin After World War II, 1945

Tegel

EAST GERMANY

Brandenburg Gate

West Berlin

Gatow

East Berlin

Tempelhof

Legend:
- ✈ Airports
- American sector
- British sector
- French sector
- Soviet sector

0 5 miles
0 5 kilometers
Albers Conic Equal-Area projection

Geography and History

28. The map above shows the occupation of Berlin after World War II. Study the map and answer the questions below.

a. Interpreting Maps How was West Berlin's location a disadvantage? How did Stalin use this disadvantage against the Western Allies?

b. Applying Geography Skills What transportation advantage did West Berlin have over East Berlin? How did the United States use this advantage when West Berlin was stranded?

The Princeton Review

Standardized Test Practice

Directions: Choose the phrase that best completes the following sentence.

One historical lesson from the McCarthy era is the realization that

A loyalty oaths prevent spying.

B communism is influential in prosperous times.

C Communist agents had infiltrated all levels of the U.S. government.

D public fear of traitors can lead to intolerance and discrimination.

Test-Taking Tip: Think about the definition of McCarthyism, the use of unsubstantiated accusations to discredit people. Which of the answers relates best to this definition?

HISTORY
Online

Have students visit the Web site at tav.glencoe.com to review Chapter 26 and take the Self-Check Quiz.

Chapter Activity

26. Multimedia reports will vary but should reflect elements of popular culture from the 1950s.

Writing Activity

27. Students' opinion pieces will vary but should clearly express a reasoned opinion supporting or opposing MacArthur's reception.

Geography and History

28. a. It was completely surrounded by East Germany; blockaded it; **b.** It had three airports that were used to shuttle food and supplies to the Berliners.

The Princeton Review

Standardized Test Practice

Answer: D

Test-Taking Tip: Tell students to try using the process of elimination to help rule out answers that cannot possibly be correct. For example, if a student knows that communism often takes hold in poor countries, he or she can eliminate B.

Bonus Question ?

Ask: How long did the era called the Cold War last? *(from 1946 to 1991)*

---

23. Soviet-U.S. conflict over Soviet control of Eastern Europe and Soviet reparations demands from Germany; U.S. fear of Communist influence or control in the Middle East and Asia

24. a. with the Senate because of its behavior in pursuing suspected Communists; **b.** believed the Republicans and Democrats were dividing the nation

Practicing Skills

25. Problem: USSR demanded control of Dardanelles and Greek Communists began guerrilla warfare; alternatives: allow USSR and Communists to control and expand or stand up to the USSR in Turkey and support the Greek government; consequences: further expansion of communism, fewer overseas entanglements, and less spending overseas, or increased overseas involvement, more security for United States, and halt the spread of communism

Timesaving Tools

TeacherWorks™ All-In-One Planner and Resource Center

- **Interactive Teacher Edition** Access your Teacher Wraparound Edition and your classroom resources with a few easy clicks.
- **Interactive Lesson Planner** Planning has never been easier! Organize your week, month, semester, or year with all the lesson helps you need to make teaching creative, timely, and relevant.

Use Glencoe's **Presentation Plus!** multimedia teacher tool to easily present dynamic lessons that visually excite your students. Using Microsoft PowerPoint® you can customize the presentations to create your own personalized lessons.

TEACHING TRANSPARENCIES

Graphic Organizer 7

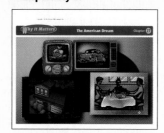

Why It Matters Chapter Transparency 27

APPLICATION AND ENRICHMENT

Linking Past and Present Activity 27

Enrichment Activity 27

Primary Source Reading 27

REVIEW AND REINFORCEMENT

Reteaching Activity 27

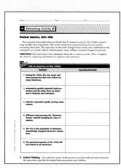

Vocabulary Activity 27

Time Line Activity 27

Critical Thinking Skills Activity 27

Meeting NCSS Standards

Local Standards

The following standards are highlighted in Chapter 27:

Section 1	VII	Production, Distribution, and Consumption: A, B, D, F
Section 2	II	Time, Continuity, and Change: C, E
Section 3	I	Culture: A, C
Section 4	II	Time, Continuity, and Change: B, E

ASSESSMENT AND EVALUATION

Chapter 27 Test Form A

Chapter 27 Test Form B

Standardized Test Skills Practice Workbook Activity 27

Performance Assessment Activities and Rubrics 27

ExamView® Pro Testmaker CD-ROM

MULTIMEDIA

- Vocabulary PuzzleMaker CD-ROM
- Interactive Tutor Self-Assessment CD-ROM
- ExamView® Pro Testmaker CD-ROM
- Audio Program
- American History Primary Source Documents Library CD-ROM
- MindJogger Videoquiz
- Presentation Plus! CD-ROM
- TeacherWorks™ CD-ROM
- Interactive Student Edition CD-ROM
- Glencoe Skillbuilder Interactive Workbook CD-ROM, Level 2
- The *American Vision* Video Program
- American Music: Hits Through History
- American Music: Cultural Traditions

SPANISH RESOURCES

The following Spanish language materials are available in the Spanish Resources Binder:

- Spanish Guided Reading Activities
- Spanish Reteaching Activities
- Spanish Quizzes and Tests
- Spanish Vocabulary Activities
- Spanish Summaries
- The Declaration of Independence and United States Constitution Spanish Translation

 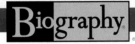

THE HISTORY CHANNEL®

The following videotape programs are available from Glencoe as supplements to Chapter 27:

- **Harry S Truman: A New View** (ISBN 1-56-501449-9)
- **Dwight D. Eisenhower: Commander-in-Chief** (ISBN 1-56-501807-9)
- **The Television: Window to the World** (ISBN 0-76-700137-0)

To order, call Glencoe at 1-800-334-7344. To find classroom resources to accompany many of these videos, check the following home pages:
A&E Television: www.aande.com
The History Channel: www.historychannel.com

Use our Web site for additional resources. All essential content is covered in the Student Edition.

You and your students can visit tav.glencoe.com, the Web site companion to the **American Vision.** This innovative integration of electronic and print media offers your students a wealth of opportunities. The student text directs students to the Web site for the following options:

- **Chapter Overviews**
- **Student Web Activities**
- **Self-Check Quizzes**
- **Textbook Updates**

Answers to the student Web activities are provided for you in the **Web Activity Lesson Plans.** Additional Web resources and Interactive Tutor Puzzles are also available.

Chapter 27 Resources

SECTION RESOURCES

Daily Objectives	Reproducible Resources	Multimedia Resources
SECTION 1 **Truman and Eisenhower** 1. Explain the Truman administration's efforts on the domestic front. 2. Describe President Eisenhower's domestic agenda.	Reproducible Lesson Plan 27–1 Daily Lecture and Discussion Notes 27–1 Guided Reading Activity 27–1* Section Quiz 27–1* Reading Essentials and Study Guide 27–1 Performance Assessment Activities and Rubrics	Daily Focus Skills Transparency 27–1 Interactive Tutor Self-Assessment CD-ROM ExamView® Pro Testmaker CD-ROM Presentation Plus! CD-ROM TeacherWorks™ CD-ROM Audio Program
SECTION 2 **The Affluent Society** 1. Explain the reasons for and the effects of the nation's economic boom. 2. Describe changes to the American family that took place during the 1950s.	Reproducible Lesson Plan 27–2 Daily Lecture and Discussion Notes 27–2 Guided Reading Activity 27–2* Section Quiz 27–2* Reading Essentials and Study Guide 27–2 Performance Assessment Activities and Rubrics	Daily Focus Skills Transparency 27–2 Interactive Tutor Self-Assessment CD-ROM ExamView® Pro Testmaker CD-ROM Presentation Plus! CD-ROM TeacherWorks™ CD-ROM Audio Program
SECTION 3 **Popular Culture of the 1950s** 1. Explain the characteristics of the new youth culture. 2. Discuss the contributions of African Americans to 1950s culture.	Reproducible Lesson Plan 27–3 Daily Lecture and Discussion Notes 27–3 Guided Reading Activity 27–3* Section Quiz 27–3* Reading Essentials and Study Guide 27–3 Performance Assessment Activities and Rubrics	Daily Focus Skills Transparency 27–3 American Art & Architecture Interactive Tutor Self-Assessment CD-ROM ExamView® Pro Testmaker CD-ROM Presentation Plus! CD-ROM TeacherWorks™ CD-ROM Audio Program American Music: Hits Through History American Music: Cultural Traditions
SECTION 4 **The Other Side of American Life** 1. Identify those groups that found themselves left out of the American economic boom following World War II. 2. Explain the factors that contributed to the poverty among various groups.	Reproducible Lesson Plan 27–4 Daily Lecture and Discussion Notes 27–4 Guided Reading Activity 27–4* Section Quiz 27–4* Reading Essentials and Study Guide 27–4 Performance Assessment Activities and Rubrics	Daily Focus Skills Transparency 27–4 Interactive Tutor Self-Assessment CD-ROM ExamView® Pro Testmaker CD-ROM Presentation Plus! CD-ROM Skillbuilder Interactive Workbook, Level 2 TeacherWorks™ CD-ROM Vocabulary PuzzleMaker CD-ROM Audio Program

0:00 OUT OF TIME?
Assign the Chapter 27 **Reading Essentials and Study Guide.**

*Also Available in Spanish

 Blackline Master Transparency CD-ROM DVD

 Poster Music Program Audio Program  Videocassette

Chapter 27 Resources

NATIONAL GEOGRAPHIC Teacher's Corner

INDEX TO NATIONAL GEOGRAPHIC MAGAZINE

The following articles relate to this chapter.

- "Alone Across the Arctic Crown," April 1993
- "Kodiak, Alaska's Island Refuge," November 1993
- "Wrangell-St. Elias: Alaska's Sky-High Wilderness," May 1994

ADDITIONAL NATIONAL GEOGRAPHIC SOCIETY PRODUCTS

To order the following, call National Geographic at 1-800-368-2728:

- *1945–1989: The Cold War* (Video)
- *The Complete National Geographic: 109 Years of National Geographic Magazine* (CD-ROM)
- *Eyewitness to the 20th Century* (Book)
- *Hawaii: Strangers in Paradise* (Video)
- *National Geographic World Atlas for Young Explorers— Classroom Library Edition* (Guide, Transparencies, Resource Masters)

NGS ONLINE

Access National Geographic's Web site for current events, atlas updates, activities, links, interactive features, and archives.

www.nationalgeographic.com

From the Classroom of...

Dr. Jerry A. Micelle
Calcasieu Career Center
Lake Charles, LA

American History Journal

Ask students to find and analyze five pictures that span the time period from 1945 to 1960. Consider the following questions and others that come to mind.

- Where is the photograph taken?
- What is occurring? What are the expressions on the subjects' faces, and why might that be important?
- What types of objects are being held or used?
- What might that tell you?
- What does the photograph tell you about the level of science and technology during the era?
- What does the photograph tell you about clothing styles and fashion?

Next, have students find quotations they can relate to each picture. Finally, have them write reports on their five pictures.

ADDITIONAL RESOURCES FROM GLENCOE

- American Music: Cultural Traditions
- American Art & Architecture
- Outline Map Resource Book
- U.S. Desk Map
- Building Geography Skills for Life
- Inclusion for the High School Social Studies Classroom Strategies and Activities
- Teaching Strategies for the American History Classroom (Including Block Scheduling Pacing Guides)

KEY TO ABILITY LEVELS

Teaching strategies have been coded.

L1 BASIC activities for all students
L2 AVERAGE activities for average to above-average students
L3 CHALLENGING activities for above-average students
ELL ENGLISH LANGUAGE LEARNER activities

Block Schedule

Activities that are suited to use within the block scheduling framework are identified by:

Why It Matters Activity

Ask students to conduct brief interviews with five adults. Tell them to ask each one the following questions about his or her childhood: favorite television programs, number of televisions at home, and times television was watched. Based on their brief interviews, have students draw conclusions about the influence of television in America. Students should evaluate their answers after they have completed the chapter.

CHAPTER 27

Postwar America
1945–1960

Why It Matters

After World War II, the country enjoyed a period of economic prosperity. Many more Americans could now aspire to a middle-class lifestyle, with a house in the suburbs and more leisure time. Television became a favorite form of entertainment. This general prosperity, however, did not extend to many Hispanics, African Americans, Native Americans, or people in Appalachia.

The Impact Today

The effects of this era can still be seen.
- The middle class represents a large segment of the American population.
- Television is a popular form of entertainment for many Americans.

The American Vision *Video* The Chapter 27 video, "America Takes to the Roads," describes the cultural impact of the automobile and its importance to the growing baby boom generation.

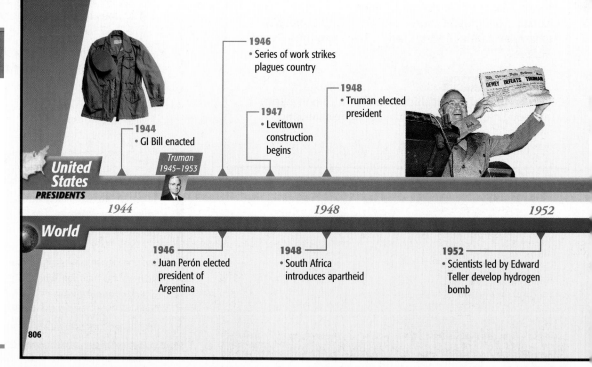

1944
• GI Bill enacted

Truman 1945–1953

1946
• Series of work strikes plagues country

1947
• Levittown construction begins

1948
• Truman elected president

United States PRESIDENTS

1944   *1948*   *1952*

World

1946
• Juan Perón elected president of Argentina

1948
• South Africa introduces apartheid

1952
• Scientists led by Edward Teller develop hydrogen bomb

806

TWO-MINUTE LESSON LAUNCHER

Ask students how shifting from war to peace might affect the economy, the movement of people from place to place, and the kinds of technology developed. List student responses on the board, then tell students to add items to these lists as they study the chapter.

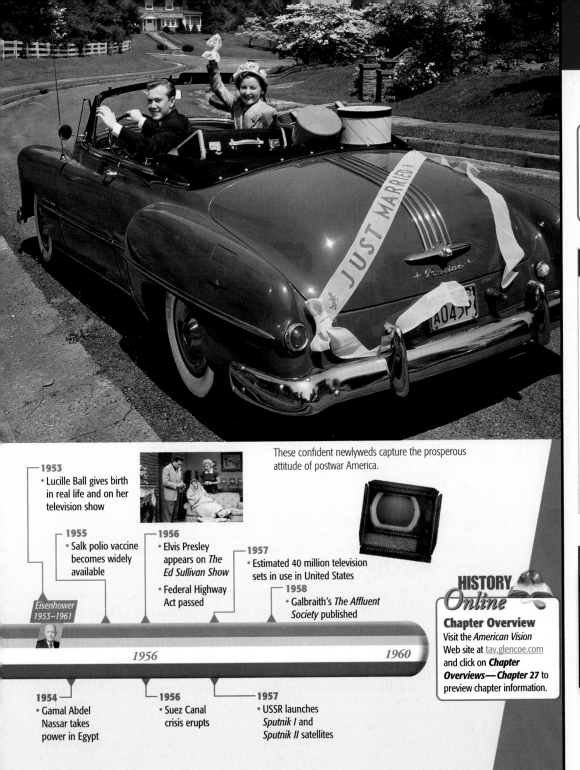

These confident newlyweds capture the prosperous attitude of postwar America.

1953
• Lucille Ball gives birth in real life and on her television show

1955
• Salk polio vaccine becomes widely available

1956
• Elvis Presley appears on *The Ed Sullivan Show*
• Federal Highway Act passed

1957
• Estimated 40 million television sets in use in United States

1958
• Galbraith's *The Affluent Society* published

Eisenhower 1953–1961

1956   *1960*

1954
• Gamal Abdel Nassar takes power in Egypt

1956
• Suez Canal crisis erupts

1957
• USSR launches *Sputnik I* and *Sputnik II* satellites

HISTORY Online

Chapter Overview
Visit the *American Vision* Web site at tav.glencoe.com and click on **Chapter Overviews—Chapter 27** to preview chapter information.

807

HISTORY Online

Introduce students to chapter content and key terms by having them access the **Chapter 27 Overview** at tav.glencoe.com.

More About the Photo

Tell students that the life of middle-class citizens in the United States was very different from that of the poor. Middle-class families in the suburbs could afford newer automobiles. Family vacations often revolved around driving to national parks or amusement centers across the country. Many poor, on the other hand, had to rely on public transportation. This often meant that poor workers had limited access to jobs. Ask students to explain how they think automobiles affected the growth of suburbs.

TIME LINE ACTIVITY

Have students select one of the people listed on the time line to research. Have students make a bulleted list of the person's achievements and honors received.

GRAPHIC ORGANIZER ACTIVITY

Organizing Information Have students create web diagrams similar to the ones below to show the experiences of the middle class and the poor during the 1950s. Have students list at least four characteristics for each group.

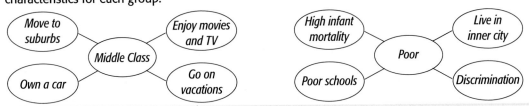

807

1 FOCUS

Section Overview

This section focuses on the post-war administrations of Truman and Eisenhower.

BELLRINGER
Skillbuilder Activity

Project transparency and have students answer the question.

Available as a blackline master.

Daily Focus Skills Transparency 27–1

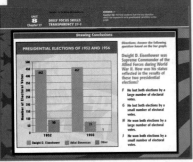

Guide to Reading

Answers to Graphic: increased consumer spending, higher prices, rising inflation, labor unrest

Preteaching Vocabulary
Have students make a two-column list with the headings Truman and Eisenhower and write the Key Terms and Names in the appropriate columns.

Truman and Eisenhower

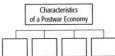

Guide to Reading

Main Idea
After World War II, the Truman and Eisenhower administrations set out to help the nation adjust to peacetime.

Key Terms and Names
GI Bill, closed shop, right-to-work law, union shop, featherbedding, "Do-Nothing Congress," Fair Deal, dynamic conservatism, Federal Highway Act

Reading Strategy
Categorizing As you read about the Truman and Eisenhower administrations, complete a graphic organizer similar to the one below by listing the characteristics of the postwar economy of the United States.

Characteristics of a Postwar Economy

Reading Objectives
• **Explain** the Truman administration's efforts on the domestic front.
• **Describe** President Eisenhower's domestic agenda.

Section Theme
Economic Factors Following World War II, the federal government supported programs that helped the economy make the transition to peacetime production.

Preview of Events

♦1944	♦1947	♦1950	♦1953

1944
Congress passes GI Bill

1946
Strikes take place across the country

1948
Harry S Truman wins presidential election

1952
Dwight D. Eisenhower wins presidential election

★ An American Story ★

As World War II ended, Robert Eubanks was worried as he prepared for his discharge from the army. He had joined the army because, as an African American, it was hard for him to find a job that paid well. Then he heard about something known as the GI Bill, a government program that paid veterans' tuition for college and provided a living allowance.

Eubanks took advantage of the program and enrolled at the Illinois Institute of Technology. He earned three degrees on the GI Bill and eventually became a professor at the University of Illinois.

Years later Eubanks recalled how his life was changed by the bill. "It's very hard to explain how things were during the 1940s," he said. "The restrictions on blacks then were rough. The GI Bill gave me my start on being a professional instead of a stock clerk."

—**adapted from** *When Dreams Came True*

Army fatigues and college diploma

Return to a Peacetime Economy

After the war many Americans feared the return to a peacetime economy. They worried that after military production halted and millions of former soldiers glutted the labor market, unemployment and recession might sweep the country.

Despite such worries, the economy continued to grow after the war as increased consumer spending helped ward off a recession. After 17 years of economic depression and wartime shortages, Americans rushed out to buy the luxury goods they had long desired.

SECTION RESOURCES

Reproducible Masters
• Reproducible Lesson Plan 27–1
• Daily Lecture and Discussion Notes 27–1
• Guided Reading Activity 27–1
• Section Quiz 27–1
• Reading Essentials and Study Guide 27–1
• Performance Assessment Activities and Rubrics

Transparencies
• Daily Focus Skills Transparency 27–1

Multimedia
⦿ Interactive Tutor Self-Assessment CD-ROM
⦿ ExamView® Pro Testmaker CD-ROM
⦿ Presentation Plus! CD-ROM
⦿ TeacherWorks™ CD-ROM
⦿ Audio Program

The Servicemen's Readjustment Act, popularly called the **GI Bill,** further boosted the economy. The act provided generous loans to veterans to help them establish businesses, buy homes, and attend college.

Inflation and Strikes The postwar economy was not without its problems. A greater demand for goods led to higher prices, and this rising inflation soon triggered labor unrest. As the cost of living rose, workers across the country went on strike for better pay. Work stoppages soon affected the automobile, electrical, steel, and mining industries.

Afraid that the nation's energy supply would be drastically reduced because of the striking miners, President Truman forced the miners to return to work after one strike that had lasted over a month. Truman ordered government seizure of the mines while pressuring mine owners to grant the union most of its demands. The president also halted a strike that shut down the nation's railroads by threatening to use the army to run the trains.

Republican Victory Labor unrest and high prices prompted many Americans to call for a change. The Republicans seized upon these sentiments during the 1946 congressional elections, winning control of both houses of Congress for the first time since 1930.

Disgusted with the rash of strikes that was crippling the nation, the new conservative Congress quickly set out to curb the power of organized labor. Legislators proposed a measure known as the **Taft-Hartley Act,** which outlawed the closed shop, or the practice of forcing business owners to hire only union members. Under the law, states could pass right-to-work laws, which outlawed union shops (shops in which new workers were required to join the union). The measure also prohibited featherbedding, the practice of limiting work output in order to create more jobs. Furthermore, the bill forbade unions from using their money to support political campaigns. When the bill reached Truman, however, he vetoed it, arguing:

> 66 . . . [It would] reverse the basic direction of our national labor policy, inject the government into private economic affairs on an unprecedented scale, and conflict with important principles of our democratic society. Its provisions would cause more strikes, not fewer. 99
>
> —quoted in *The Growth of the American Republic*

The president's concerns did little to sway Congress, which passed the Taft-Hartley Act in 1947 over Truman's veto. Its supporters claimed the law held irresponsible unions in check just as the Wagner Act of 1935 had restrained anti-union activities and employers. Labor leaders called the act a "slave labor" law and insisted that it erased many of the gains that unions had made since 1933.

✓ **Reading Check**

Explaining Why did Truman veto the Taft-Hartley Act?

Truman's Domestic Program

The Democratic Party's loss of members in the 1946 elections did not dampen President Truman's spirits or his plans. Shortly after taking office, Truman had proposed a series of domestic measures that sought to continue the work done as part of Franklin Roosevelt's New Deal. During his tenure in office, Truman worked to push this agenda through Congress.

Truman's Legislative Agenda Truman's proposals included the expansion of Social Security benefits; the raising of the legal minimum wage from 40¢ to 65¢ an hour; a program to ensure full employment through aggressive use of federal spending and investment; public housing and slum clearance; long-range environmental and public works planning; and a system of national health insurance.

Truman also boldly asked Congress in February 1948 to pass a broad civil rights bill that would

The GI Bill African American soldiers review the benefits of the GI Bill, which included loans to attend college and to buy homes.

CHAPTER 27 Postwar America **809**

2 TEACH

Daily Lecture and Discussion Notes 27–1

Daily Lecture and Discussion Notes

Chapter 27, Section 1

Did You Know? The play *The Crucible*, written by Arthur Miller in 1953, is about the Salem witch trials of 1662. Miller wrote the play in reaction to the treatment of people in America who were suspected of being Communists.

I. Return to a Peacetime Economy *(pages 808–809)*

  A. The U.S. economy continued to grow after World War II because of increased consumer spending.

  B. The Servicemen's Readjustment Act, also called the GI Bill, helped the economy by providing loans to veterans to attend college, set up businesses, and buy homes.

  C. Increased spending led to higher prices for goods, which then led to rising inflation.

HISTORY Online

Objectives and answers to the student activity can be found in the **Web Activity Lesson Plan** at tav.glencoe.com.

✓ **Reading Check**

Answer: He felt it brought the government into private economic affairs on an unprecedented scale and would cause more strikes without contributing to economic stability and progress.

Discussing a Concept Explain that President Truman favored an increase in the minimum wage, and Congress supported him. In 1949 the minimum wage went from 40 cents to 75 cents per hour; in 1955 the hourly rate reached $1. Have students discuss the positive and negative results of raising the minimum wage. **L1** ELL

COOPERATIVE LEARNING ACTIVITY

Debating an Issue Organize the class into two teams. Ask both teams to imagine themselves as workers considering Harry S Truman as a presidential candidate in 1948. Have teams prepare and present a debate. One team should support Truman's labor reforms; the other team should criticize his interference with organized labor and blame him for the nation's economic problems. Assign some team members to research, others to prepare key statements, and others to defend the team's position in the debate.

Use the rubric for a cooperative group management plan on pages 81–82 in the *Performance Assessment Activities and Rubrics.*

Making a Comparison Have students research the cost of a modest suburban home built in their community during the 1950s and the cost of the same home today. Instruct students to include an exterior sketch or photograph, a floor plan, and a description of special features such as a patio or garage. Encourage students to use library and Internet resources to locate real estate records. Use the reports as a starting point for a discussion about the affordability of housing in the 1950s and today. **L2**

FYI

In addition to providing low interest loans to help veterans buy homes and farms, the GI Bill provided unemployment benefits for veterans who could not find jobs.

---

protect African Americans' right to vote, abolish poll taxes, and make lynching a federal crime. He also issued an executive order barring discrimination in federal employment, and he ended segregation in the armed forces.

Most of Truman's legislative efforts, however, met with little success, as a coalition of Republicans and conservative Southern Democrats defeated many of his proposals. While these defeats angered Truman, the president soon had to worry about other matters.

The Election of 1948 As the presidential election of 1948 approached, most observers gave Truman little chance of winning. Some Americans still believed that he lacked the stature for the job, and they viewed his administration as weak and inept.

Divisions within the Democratic Party also seemed to spell disaster for Truman. At the Democratic Convention that summer, two factions abandoned the party altogether. Reacting angrily to Truman's support of civil rights, a group of Southern Democrats formed the States' Rights, or Dixiecrat, Party and nominated South Carolina governor **Strom Thurmond** for president. At the same time, the party's more liberal members were frustrated by Truman's ineffective domestic policies and critical of his anti-Soviet foreign policy. They formed a new Progressive Party, with Henry A. Wallace as their presidential candidate. In addition, the president's Republican opponent was New York governor Thomas Dewey, a dignified and popular candidate who seemed unbeatable. After polling 50 political writers, *Newsweek* magazine declared three weeks before the election, "The landslide for Dewey will sweep the country."

Picturing History

African Americans Rally for Truman During the 1948 election, President Truman spoke at many rallies similar to this one in New York City. What legislative proposals by President Truman built African American political support?

Perhaps the only one who gave Truman a chance to win was Truman himself. "I know every one of those 50 fellows," he declared about the writers polled in *Newsweek*. "There isn't one of them has enough sense to pound sand in a rat hole." Ignoring the polls, the feisty president poured his efforts into an energetic campaign. He traveled more than 20,000 miles by train and made more than 350 speeches. Along the way, Truman attacked the majority Republican Congress as "do-nothing, good-for-nothing" for refusing to enact his legislative agenda.

Truman's attacks on the **"Do-Nothing Congress"** did not mention that both he and Congress had been very busy dealing with foreign policy matters. Congress had passed the Truman Doctrine's aid program to Greece and Turkey, as well as the Marshall Plan. It had also created the Department of Defense and the CIA and established the Joint Chiefs of Staff as a permanent organization. The 80th Congress, therefore, did not "do nothing" as Truman charged, but its accomplishments were in areas that did not affect most Americans directly. As a result, Truman's charges began to stick, and to the surprise of almost everyone, his efforts paid off.

With a great deal of support from laborers, African Americans, and farmers, Truman won a narrow but stunning victory over Dewey. Perhaps just as remarkable as the president's victory was the resurgence of the Democratic Party. When the dust had cleared after Election Day, Democrats had regained control of both houses of Congress.

GOVERNMENT

The Fair Deal Truman's State of the Union message to the new Congress repeated the domestic agenda he had put forth previously. "Every segment of our population and every individual," he declared, "has a right to expect from . . . government a fair deal." Whether intentional or not, the president had coined a name—the **Fair Deal**—to set his program apart from the New Deal.

The 81st Congress did not completely embrace Truman's Fair Deal. Legislators did raise the legal minimum wage to 75¢ an hour. They also approved an important expansion of the Social Security system, increasing benefits by 75 percent and extending them to 10 million additional people. Congress also passed the National Housing Act of 1949, which provided for the construction of more than 800,000 units of low-income housing, accompanied by long-term rent subsidies.

Congress refused, however, to pass national health insurance or to provide subsidies for farmers or

---

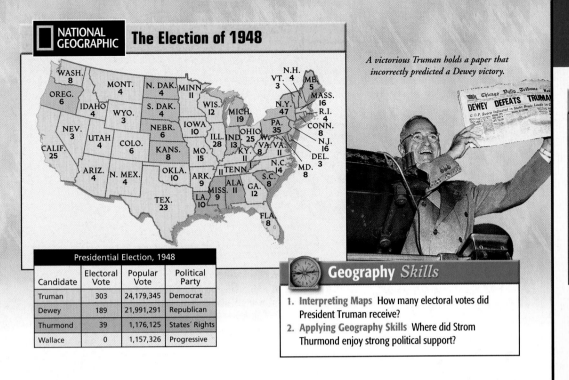

NATIONAL GEOGRAPHIC — The Election of 1948

A victorious Truman holds a paper that incorrectly predicted a Dewey victory.

Presidential Election, 1948			
Candidate	Electoral Vote	Popular Vote	Political Party
Truman	303	24,179,345	Democrat
Dewey	189	21,991,291	Republican
Thurmond	39	1,176,125	States' Rights
Wallace	0	1,157,326	Progressive

Geography *Skills*

1. **Interpreting Maps** How many electoral votes did President Truman receive?
2. **Applying Geography Skills** Where did Strom Thurmond enjoy strong political support?

federal aid for schools. In addition, legislators opposed Truman's efforts to enact civil rights legislation.

Reading Check **Summarizing** What was the outcome of Truman's proposed legislative agenda?

The Eisenhower Years

In 1950 the United States went to war in Korea. The war consumed the nation's attention and resources and basically ended Truman's Fair Deal. By 1952, with the war a bloody stalemate and his approval rating dropping quickly, Truman declined to run again for the presidency. With no Democratic incumbent to face, Republicans pinned their hopes of regaining the White House on a popular World War II hero.

The Election of 1952 Dwight Eisenhower decided to run as the Republican nominee for president in 1952. His running mate was a young California senator, Richard Nixon. The Democrats nominated Illinois governor Adlai Stevenson, a witty and eloquent speaker who had the support of leading liberals and organized labor.

The Republicans adopted the slogan: "It's time for a change!" The warm and friendly Eisenhower, known as "Ike," promised to end the war in Korea. "I like Ike" became the Republican rallying cry.

Eisenhower's campaign soon came under fire as reports surfaced that Richard Nixon had received gifts from California business leaders totaling $18,000 while he was a senator. For a while, it looked as if Nixon might be dropped from the ticket. In a nationwide speech broadcast on radio and television, Nixon insisted the funds had been used for legitimate political purposes. He did admit that his family had kept one gift, a cocker spaniel puppy named "Checkers." He declared, "The kids love the dog, [and] regardless about what they say about it, we're going to keep it." This so-called "Checkers speech" won praise from much of the public and kept Nixon on the ticket.

Eisenhower won the election by a landslide, carrying the Electoral College 442 votes to 89. The Republicans also gained an eight-seat majority in the House, while the Senate became evenly divided between Democrats and Republicans.

Ike as President President Eisenhower had two favorite phrases. "Middle of the road" described his political beliefs, which fell midway between conservative and liberal. He also referred to the notion of "dynamic conservatism," which meant balancing economic conservatism with some activism.

CHAPTER 27 Postwar America **811**

INTERDISCIPLINARY CONNECTIONS ACTIVITY

Government Have students illustrate how Truman's Fair Deal fared in Congress. **L2**

Fair Deal Legislation	Fair Deal Programs Not Enacted
increase in minimum wage	*national health insurance*
expansion of the Social Security system	*farm subsidies*
National Housing Act	*federal aid to schools*
	civil rights legislation

Why It Matters

Background: The numbering system for interstate highways is a good example of effective planning. One- and two-digit numbers designate all major routes. The north-south routes use odd numbers while the east-west routes use even numbers. East-west routes begin with the lowest numbers along the southern border of the United States and north-south routes begin with the lowest numbers along the West Coast.

Ask: Assuming that you drive 10 hours a day for 4.5 days, what is your average speed in traveling the 2,800 miles across the country? *(10 hrs. × 4.5 days = 45 hours of driving time; 2,800 ÷ 45 = 62.2 miles per hour)* Have students compare their result to the average speed of Eisenhower's convoy.

3 ASSESS

Assign Section 1 Assessment as homework or as an in-class activity.

🔘 Have students use the **Interactive Tutor Self-Assessment CD-ROM.**

Reading Essentials and Study Guide 27–1

Name _____ Date _____ Class _____

Study Guide

Chapter 27, Section 1
For use with textbook pages 808–813
TRUMAN AND EISENHOWER

KEY TERMS AND NAMES

GI Bill   a bill that provided loans to veterans to help them start businesses, buy homes, and attend college *(page 809)*

closed shop   the practice of forcing business owners to hire only union members *(page 809)*

right-to-work laws   laws which outlawed union shops *(page 809)*

union shop   shops in which new workers were required to join the union *(page 809)*

featherbedding   the practice of limiting work output in order to create more jobs *(page 809)*

"Do-Nothing Congress"   the name President Truman gave to the Republican Congress *(page 810)*

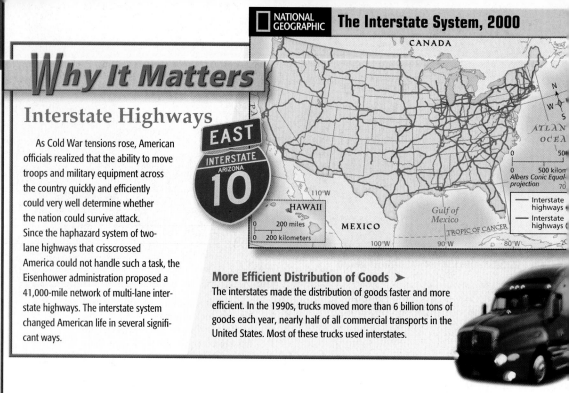

NATIONAL GEOGRAPHIC **The Interstate System, 2000**

Why It Matters

Interstate Highways

As Cold War tensions rose, American officials realized that the ability to move troops and military equipment across the country quickly and efficiently could very well determine whether the nation could survive attack. Since the haphazard system of two-lane highways that crisscrossed America could not handle such a task, the Eisenhower administration proposed a 41,000-mile network of multi-lane interstate highways. The interstate system changed American life in several significant ways.

More Efficient Distribution of Goods ➤
The interstates made the distribution of goods faster and more efficient. In the 1990s, trucks moved more than 6 billion tons of goods each year, nearly half of all commercial transports in the United States. Most of these trucks used interstates.

Eisenhower wasted little time in showing his conservative side. The new president's cabinet appointments included several business leaders. Under their guidance, Eisenhower ended government price and rent controls, which many conservatives had viewed as unnecessary federal control over the business community. The Eisenhower administration viewed business growth as vital to the nation. The president's secretary of defense, formerly the president of General Motors, declared to the Senate that "what is good for our country is good for General Motors, and vice versa."

Eisenhower's conservatism showed itself in other ways as well. In an attempt to curb the federal budget, the president vetoed a school construction bill and agreed to slash government aid to public housing. Along with these cuts, he supported some modest tax reductions.

Eisenhower also targeted the federal government's continuing aid to businesses, or what he termed "creeping socialism." Shortly after taking office, the president abolished the Reconstruction Finance Corporation (RFC), which since 1932 had lent money to banks, railroads, and other large institutions in financial trouble. Another Depression-era agency, the Tennessee Valley Authority (TVA), also came under Eisenhower's economic scrutiny.

During his presidency, appropriations for the TVA fell from $185 million to $12 million.

In some areas, President Eisenhower took an activist role. For example, he advocated the passage of two large government projects. During the 1950s, as the number of Americans who owned cars increased, so too did the need for greater and more efficient travel routes. In 1956 Congress responded to this growing need by passing the **Federal Highway Act,** the largest public works program in American history. The act appropriated $25 billion for a 10-year effort to construct more than 40,000 miles (64,400 km) of interstate highways. Congress also authorized construction of the Great Lakes-St. Lawrence Seaway to connect the Great Lakes with the Atlantic Ocean through a series of locks on the St. Lawrence River. Three previous presidents had been unable to reach agreements with Canada to build this waterway to aid international shipping. Through Eisenhower's efforts, the two nations finally agreed on a plan to complete the project.

Extending the New Deal Although President Eisenhower cut federal spending and worked to limit the federal government's role in the nation's economy, he also agreed to extend the Social Security system to an additional 10 million people. He also extended unemployment compensation to an

---

CRITICAL THINKING ACTIVITY

Determining a Point of View The Taft-Hartley Act created controversy for the Truman administration. Have students determine their position on the following statement: The president should have the right to enact a "cooling off" period to stop economically damaging strikes. Students should provide reasons for their positions. *(Students' answers will vary but their positions need to be substantiated with specific reasons.)* **L2**

◄ **Suburbanization and Urban Sprawl**
The interstate system contributed to the growth of suburban communities and the eventual geographic spread of center-less cities. Using the interstates, suburbanites could commute to their jobs miles away.

A New Road Culture ➤
The interstates created an automobile society. In 1997, $687 billion were spent on private automobiles compared to $22.8 billion for public transit. Additionally, chains of fast food restaurants and motels replaced independent operators across the country.

Speed of Travel

The interstate highways drastically decreased the time it took to travel across the continent. In 1919 a young Dwight D. Eisenhower joined 294 other members of the army to travel the 2,800 miles from Washington, D.C., to San Francisco. They made the trip in 62 days, averaging 5 miles per hour. During World War II, General Eisenhower was impressed with the modern design of Germany's freeway system, the Autobahn. "The old convoy," he said, "had started me thinking about good, two-lane highways, but Germany had made me see the wisdom of broader ribbons across the land." Wide lanes and controlled entrance and exit points allowed cars to travel at much higher speeds. Using the interstate highways, Eisenhower's trip would now take 4½ days.

Travel Times: Washington, D.C., to San Francisco

■ 2,800 mile trip took 62 days in 1919
■ 2,800 mile trip takes 4 ½ days today

additional 4 million citizens and agreed to increase the minimum hourly wage from 75¢ to $1 and to continue to provide some government aid to farmers.

By the time Eisenhower ran for a second term in 1956—a race he won easily—the nation had successfully completed the transition from a wartime to a peacetime economy. The battles between liberals and conservatives over whether to continue New Deal policies would continue. In the meantime, however, most Americans focused their energy on enjoying what had become a decade of tremendous prosperity.

✓ **Reading Check** **Evaluating** What conservative and activist measures did Eisenhower take during his administration?

SECTION 1 ASSESSMENT

Checking for Understanding
1. **Define:** closed shop, right-to-work law, union shop, featherbedding, dynamic conservatism.
2. **Identify:** GI Bill, "Do-Nothing Congress," Fair Deal, Federal Highway Act.

Reviewing Themes
3. **Economic Factors** How did President Eisenhower aid international shipping during his administration?

Critical Thinking
4. **Interpreting** In what ways did the Taft-Hartley Act hurt labor unions?
5. **Categorizing** Use a graphic organizer to compare the agendas of the Truman and Eisenhower administrations.

```
        Agendas
         /    \
   Truman    Eisenhower
     □          □
```

Analyzing Visuals
6. **Analyzing Maps** Study the map on page 811. Which parts of the country did Dewey win? Why do you think he did so well in these areas?

Writing About History
7. **Persuasive Writing** Take on the role of a member of Congress during the Truman administration. Write a speech in which you try to persuade the 81st Congress to either pass or defeat Truman's Fair Deal measures.

SECTION 1 ASSESSMENT ANSWERS

1. Terms are in blue.
2. GI Bill *(p. 809)*, "Do-Nothing Congress" *(p. 810)*, Fair Deal *(p. 810)*, Federal Highway Act *(p. 812)*
3. He authorized the Great Lakes-St. Lawrence Seaway, which connected the Great Lakes with the Atlantic Ocean.
4. It outlawed closed shops, allowed states to outlaw union shops, and prohibited featherbedding.
5. Truman: increase government involvement in business, expand federal spending; Eisenhower: limit government involvement in business, curb federal spending
6. Northeast, Great Plains; governor of New York, strong in traditional Republican areas
7. Students' speeches will vary. Speeches should focus on several components of the Fair Deal.

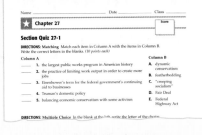

FYI

In the fall of 1955, President Eisenhower had a heart attack. The problem of presidential incapacity was not new. In 1881 James Garfield lingered for over two months before he died from an assassin's bullet. In 1919 Woodrow Wilson's stroke rendered him unable to participate in final treaty negotiations.

✓ **Reading Check**

Answer: reduced government control over business, cut spending on public housing, passed the Federal Highway Act, extended the Social Security System, and increased the minimum wage

Reteach
Have students explain Truman's domestic policy.

Enrich
Invite interested students to write and deliver the opening paragraph of a speech that a presidential candidate could have used in 1948, 1952, or 1956.

4 CLOSE

Have students describe President Eisenhower's domestic agenda.

813

1 FOCUS

Section Overview

This section focuses on the postwar economic boom in the United States.

BELLRINGER
Skillbuilder Activity

Project transparency and have students answer the question.

Available as a blackline master.

Daily Focus Skills Transparency 27–2

Guide to Reading

Answers to Graphic: 1946, earliest computer; 1947, transistor developed; 1955, polio vaccine injection developed; 1958, U.S. satellite launched

Preteaching Vocabulary
Have students write a word or phrase next to each of the Key Terms and Names to help clarify their meanings.

Guide to Reading

Main Idea
The postwar economic boom brought great changes to society, including the ways many Americans worked and lived.

Key Terms and Names
John Kenneth Galbraith, white-collar, blue-collar, multinational corporation, franchise, David Riesman, Levittown, baby boom, Jonas Salk

Reading Strategy
Sequencing As you read about American society in the 1950s, complete a time line similar to the one below by recording the scientific and technological breakthroughs of the time.

1946 — 1958

Reading Objectives
• **Explain** the reasons for and the effects of the nation's economic boom.
• **Describe** changes to the American family that took place during the 1950s.

Section Theme
Continuity and Change Americans became avid consumers in the atmosphere of postwar abundance.

Preview of Events

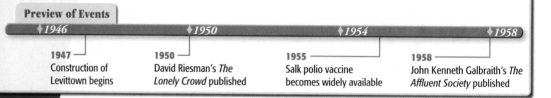

♦1946 ───── ♦1950 ───── ♦1954 ───── ♦1958

1947 — Construction of Levittown begins
1950 — David Riesman's *The Lonely Crowd* published
1955 — Salk polio vaccine becomes widely available
1958 — John Kenneth Galbraith's *The Affluent Society* published

---

★ An American Story ★

Kemmons Wilson on magazine cover

In the summer of 1951, Kemmons Wilson traveled with his family from Memphis, Tennessee, to Washington, D.C. He noticed that some of the motels they stayed in were terrible. Each added a $2 charge per child to the standard room price, and many were located far from restaurants, forcing travelers back into their cars to search for meals.

Frustrated, Wilson decided to build a motel chain that would provide interstate travelers with comfortable lodgings. They would be located near good family restaurants and allow kids to stay free. Together with a group of investors, Wilson began building the Holiday Inn motel chain. Families loved his motels, and soon Holiday Inns were sprouting up all over the country.

Wilson said he never doubted the success of his endeavor. "I like to think that I'm so . . . normal that anything I like, everybody else is going to like too," he said. "The idea that my instincts are out of line just doesn't occur to me." His prosperity mirrored a growing affluence in the nation. This time of prosperity made the shortages of the Great Depression and World War II a distant memory.

—adapted from *The Fifties*

American Abundance

Wilson's motel chain proved successful largely because the 1950s was a decade of incredible prosperity. In 1958 economist **John Kenneth Galbraith** published *The Affluent Society,* in which he claimed that the nation's postwar prosperity was a new phenomenon. In the past, Galbraith said, all societies had an "economy of scarcity,"

SECTION RESOURCES

Reproducible Masters
• Reproducible Lesson Plan 27–2
• Daily Lecture and Discussion Notes 27–2
• Guided Reading Activity 27–2
• Section Quiz 27–2
• Reading Essentials and Study Guide 27–2
• Performance Assessment Activities and Rubrics

Transparencies
• Daily Focus Skills Transparency 27–2

Multimedia
• Interactive Tutor Self-Assessment CD-ROM
• ExamView® Pro Testmaker CD-ROM
• Presentation Plus! CD-ROM
• TeacherWorks™ CD-ROM
• Audio Program

meaning that a lack of resources and overpopulation had limited economic productivity. Now, the United States and a few other industrialized nations had created what Galbraith called an "economy of abundance." New business techniques and improved technology enabled these nations to produce an abundance of goods and services for their people—all of which allowed many of them to enjoy a standard of living never before thought possible.

The Spread of Wealth Some critics accused Galbraith of overstating the situation, but the facts and figures seemed to support his theory. Between 1940 and 1955, the average income of American families roughly tripled. Americans in all income brackets—poor, middle-class, and wealthy—experienced this rapid rise in income. The dramatic rise in home ownership also showed that the income of average families had risen significantly. Between 1940 and 1960, the number of Americans owning their own homes rose from about 41 to about 61 percent.

Accompanying the country's economic growth were dramatic changes in work environments. Mechanization in farms and factories meant that fewer farmers and laborers were needed to provide the public with food and goods. As a result, more Americans began working in what are called white-collar jobs, such as those in sales and management. In 1956, for the first time, white-collar workers outnumbered blue-collar workers, or people who perform physical labor in industry.

Multinationals and Franchises Many white-collar employees worked for large corporations. As these businesses competed with each other, some expanded overseas. These multinational corporations located themselves closer to important raw materials and benefited from a cheaper labor pool, which made them more competitive.

The 1950s also witnessed the rise of franchises, in which a person owns and runs one or several stores of a chain operation. Because many business leaders believed that consumers valued dependability and familiarity, the owners of chain operations often demanded that their franchises present a uniform look and style.

The Organization Man Like franchise owners, many corporate leaders also expected their employees to conform to company standards. In general, corporations did not desire free-thinking individuals or people who might speak out or criticize the company.

Some social observers recognized this phenomenon and disapproved of it. In his 1950 book, *The Lonely Crowd,* sociologist **David Riesman** argued that this conformity was changing people. Formerly, he claimed, people were "inner-directed," judging themselves on the basis of their own values and the esteem of their families. Now, however, people were becoming "other-directed," concerning themselves with winning the approval of the corporation or community.

In his 1956 book *The Organization Man,* writer **William H. Whyte, Jr.,** assailed the similarity many business organizations cultivated in order to keep any individual from dominating. "In group doctrine," Whyte wrote, "the strong personality is viewed with overwhelming suspicion," and the person with ideas is considered "a threat."

The New Consumerism The conformity of the 1950s included people's desires to own the same new products as their neighbors. With more disposable income, Americans bought more luxury items, such as refrigerators, washing machines, vacuum cleaners, and air conditioners. Americans also bought a variety of labor-saving machines. As *House and Garden* magazine boasted in a 1954 article, coffeemakers, blenders, and lawn trimmers "[replaced] the talents of caretaker, gardener, cook, [and] maid."

"He never wastes a minute, J.P.—that's his lunch."

Analyzing *Political Cartoons*

The Organization Man In the 1950s, more and more people worked in white-collar corporate jobs. Some social critics worried that this development emphasized conformity. In what other ways did society encourage people to conform?

2 TEACH

Daily Lecture and Discussion Notes 27–2

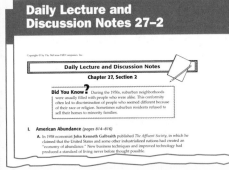

Copyright © by The McGraw-Hill Companies, Inc.

Daily Lecture and Discussion Notes

Chapter 27, Section 2

Did You Know? During the 1950s, suburban neighborhoods were usually filled with people who were alike. This conformity often led to discrimination of people who seemed different because of their race or religion. Sometimes suburban residents refused to sell their homes to minority families.

I. American Abundance *(pages 814–816)*

A. In 1958 economist John Kenneth Galbraith published *The Affluent Society,* in which he claimed that the United States and some other industrialized nations had created an "economy of abundance." New business techniques and improved technology had produced a standard of living never before thought possible.

Discussing a Concept Have students discuss how lifestyles have changed since World War II. Ask them to consider the number of entertainment items their family owns, from televisions to computers, CD players, and sports equipment. Ask them to suggest the kind of leisure-related possessions families probably owned in the 1920s and 1930s. **L2**

Analyzing *Political Cartoons*

Answer: social pressure to purchase similar consumer goods and homes, pressure to "keep up with the Joneses"

Ask: What distinguishes a white-collar job from a blue-collar job? *(White-collar workers are employed in sales and management positions, while blue-collar workers perform physical labor in industry.)*

COOPERATIVE LEARNING ACTIVITY

Creating a Display Organize students into groups of five or six and ask each group to prepare a display on the lives of suburban families in the United States during the 1950s. The reports should include both written material and visuals. Before they begin the project, instruct the groups to divide the tasks among the members of the group. Some students may do research, others may write text, while others may prepare visuals or collect memorabilia from the 1950s.

Use the rubric for a cooperative group management plan on pages 81–82 in the *Performance Assessment Activities and Rubrics.*

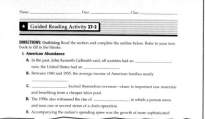

Guided Reading Activity 27–2

Name _____ Date _____ Class _____

★ **Guided Reading Activity 27-2**

DIRECTIONS: Outlining Read the section and complete the outline below. Refer to your text-book to fill in the blanks.

I. American Abundance

A. In the past, John Kenneth Galbraith said, all societies had an _____; now, the United States had an _____.

B. Between 1940 and 1955, the average income of American families nearly _____.

C. _____ located themselves overseas—closer to important raw materials and benefiting from a cheaper labor pool.

D. The 1950s also witnessed the rise of _____, in which a person owns and runs one or several stores of a chain operation.

E. Accompanying the nation's spending spree was the growth of more sophisticated _____.

Graph Skills

Answers:

1. about 1947

2. Couples had delayed marriage until after the war and could now afford a family, and popular culture celebrated pregnancy, parenthood, and large families.

Graph Skills Practice

Ask: What do you suppose caused the birth rate to rise again in the late 1960s? *(The first baby boomers were having children of their own.)*

✔ Reading Check

Answer: causes: new business methods and improved manufacturing technology; effects: average family income tripled, increase in white-collar employment

CURRICULUM CONNECTION

Geography Three Levittowns were built, the first on Long Island, the second in Bucks County, Pennsylvania, and the third in Willingboro, New Jersey. These planned communities allowed people to live in smaller communities but commute to larger cities.

The Baby Boom

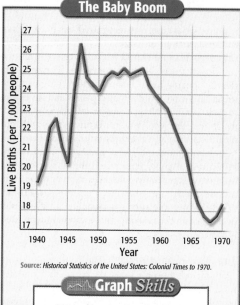

Source: *Historical Statistics of the United States: Colonial Times to 1970.*

Graph Skills

1. **Interpreting Graphs** When did the rapid rise in population shown here reach its peak?
2. **Analyzing Cause and Effect** What factors contributed to this rapid rise in births?

Accompanying the nation's spending spree was the growth of more sophisticated advertising. Advertising became the fastest-growing industry in the United States, as manufacturers employed new marketing techniques to sell their products. These techniques were carefully planned to whet the consumer's appetite. The purpose of these advertisers was to influence choices among brands of goods that were essentially the same. According to the elaborate advertising campaigns of the time, a freezer became a promise of plenty, a second car became a symbol of status, and a mouthwash became the key to immediate success.

The Growth of Suburbia Advertisers targeted their ads to consumers who had money to spend. Many of these consumers lived in the nation's growing suburbs that grew up around cities.

Levittown, New York, was one of the earliest of the new suburbs. The driving force behind this planned residential community was Bill Levitt, who mass-produced hundreds of simple and similar-looking homes in a potato field 10 miles east of New York City. Between 1947 and 1951, thousands of families rushed to buy the inexpensive homes, and

soon other communities similar to Levittown sprang up throughout the United States.

Suburbs became increasingly popular throughout the 1950s, accounting for about 85 percent of new home construction. The number of suburban dwellers doubled, while the population of cities themselves rose only 10 percent. Reasons for the rapid growth of suburbia varied. Some people wanted to escape the crime and congestion of city neighborhoods. Others viewed life in the suburbs as a move up to a better life for themselves and their children. In contrast to city life, suburbia offered a more picturesque environment. As developers in earlier periods had done, the developers of the 1950s attracted home buyers with promises of fresh air, green lawns, and trees.

Affordability became a key factor in attracting home buyers to the suburbs. Because the GI Bill offered low-interest loans, new housing was more affordable during the postwar period than at any other time in American history. Equally attractive was the government's offer of income tax deductions for home mortgage interest payments and property taxes. For millions of Americans, the suburbs came to symbolize the American dream. They owned their homes, sent their children to good schools, lived in safe communities, and enjoyed economic security.

Nevertheless, some observers viewed the growth of such plain and identical-looking communities as another sign of Americans' tendency toward conformity. "You too can find a box of your own," one sarcastic critic wrote about Levittown, "inhabited by people whose age, income, number of children, problems, habits, conversations, dress, possessions, perhaps even blood types are almost precisely like yours."

✔ Reading Check
Interpreting What were two causes and effects of the economic boom of the 1950s?

The 1950s Family

In addition to all the other transformations taking place in the nation during the 1950s, the American family also was changing. Across the country, many families grew larger, and more married women entered the workforce.

The Baby Boom The American birthrate exploded after World War II. From 1945 to 1961, a period known as the baby boom, more than 65 million children were born in the United States. At the height of the baby boom, a child was born every seven seconds.

Several factors contributed to the baby boom. First, young couples who had delayed marriage during

---

MEETING SPECIAL NEEDS

Visual/Spatial To address the needs of visual learners, have students work with a map of a large metropolitan area. Have them identify the suburbs and the city center. Also, have students label or identify the major shopping malls around the city. Discuss how suburbs changed the landscape and the lifestyles of people in the 1950s. **L1**

📂 Refer to *Inclusion for the High School Social Studies Classroom Strategies and Activities* in the TCR.

World War II and the Korean War could now marry, buy homes, and begin their families. In addition, the government encouraged the growth of families by offering generous GI benefits for home purchases. Finally, on television and in magazines, popular culture celebrated pregnancy, parenthood, and large families.

Women in the Fifties Many women focused on their traditional role of homemaker during the 1950s. Even though 8 million American women had gone to work during the war, the new postwar emphasis on having babies and establishing families now discouraged women from seeking employment. Many Americans assumed that a good mother should stay home to take care of her children.

"Let's face it, girls," declared one female writer in *Better Homes and Gardens* in April 1955, "that wonderful guy in your house—and in mine—is building your house, your happiness and the opportunities that will come to your children." The magazine advised stay-at-home wives to "set their sights on a happy home, a host of friends and a bright future through success in HIS job."

Despite the popular emphasis on homemaking, however, the number of women who held jobs outside the home actually increased during the 1950s. Most women who went to work did so in order to help their families maintain their comfortable lifestyles. By 1960 nearly one-third of all married women were part of the paid workforce.

✓ **Reading Check** **Evaluating** What were three factors that contributed to the baby boom?

Technological Breakthroughs

As the United States underwent many social changes during the postwar era, the nation also witnessed several important scientific advances. In medicine, space exploration, and electronics, American scientists broke new ground during the 1950s.

Advances in Electronics The electronics industry made rapid advances after World War II. In 1947 three American physicists—John Bardeen, Walter H. Brittain, and William Shockley—developed the transistor, a tiny device that generated electric signals and made it possible to miniaturize radios and calculators.

The age of computers also dawned in the postwar era. In 1946 scientists working under a U.S. Army contract developed one of the nation's earliest

computers—known as ENIAC (Electronic Numerical Integrator and Computer)—to make military calculations. Several years later, a newer model called UNIVAC (Universal Automatic Computer) would handle business data and launch the computer revolution. The computer, along with changes and improvements in communication and transportation systems, allowed many Americans to work more quickly and efficiently. As a result, families in the 1950s had more free time, and new forms of leisure activity became popular.

Medical Miracles The medical breakthroughs of the 1950s included the development of powerful antibiotics to fight infection; the introduction of new drugs to combat arthritis, diabetes, cancer, and heart

The Incredible Shrinking Computer

Past: The First Computer
ENIAC (Electronic Numerical Integrator and Computer) was the first large-scale digital computer. Operating from 1946 to 1955, its primary function was to provide data for the military. It weighed more than 30 tons and took up 1,800 square feet—more than some houses!

Present: Modern Marvels
Modern computers are very small and very fast. Many personal computers now fit easily in a briefcase or backpack. They are also more efficient. While the ENIAC could perform approximately 5,000 calculations per second, the typical home computer performs about 70 million calculations per second—14,000 times faster!

INTERDISCIPLINARY CONNECTIONS ACTIVITY

Science Have students research one of the technological or medical advances discussed in this section. Have them identify the inventor or researcher who discovered and developed the advance, the way in which it changed American society, and whether it is still in use today. If the advance has become obsolete, have students identify its replacement. Students should present their findings in an illustrated report. **L2**

FYI

Parents of baby boomers seized the opportunity to give their children what they themselves never had. Memories of rationing and limited supplies during the Great Depression and World War II often fueled their enthusiasm for activities such as music lessons and Little League.

3 ASSESS

Assign Section 2 Assessment as homework or as an in-class activity.

⊙ Have students use the **Interactive Tutor Self-Assessment CD-ROM.**

Reading Essentials and Study Guide 27–2

Name _____ Date _____ Class _____

Study Guide

Chapter 27, Section 2

For use with textbook pages 814–819

THE AFFLUENT SOCIETY

KEY TERMS AND NAMES

John Kenneth Galbraith economist who published *The Affluent Society* (page 814)

white-collar kind of jobs that do not involve physical labor in industry (page 815)

blue-collar kind of jobs that involve physical labor (page 815)

multinational corporation large corporations that expanded overseas (page 815)

franchise a business in which a person owns and runs one or several stores of a chain operation (page 815)

David Riesman sociologist who wrote *The Lonely Crowd* (page 815)

Levittown one of the earliest suburbs in the United States (page 816)

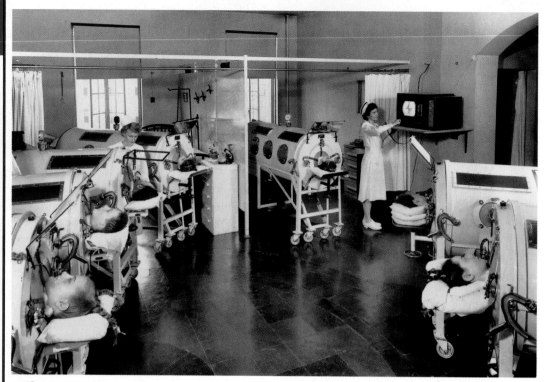

Picturing **History**

Polio Epidemic In the 1940s and 1950s, Americans were very concerned about the wave of polio cases that struck so many young children. Here, devices known as iron lungs help polio patients breathe. How did people try to safeguard against the spread of the disease?

disease; and groundbreaking advances in surgical techniques. Polio, however, continued to baffle the medical profession.

Periodic polio epidemics had been occurring in the United States since 1916. The disease had even struck the young Franklin Roosevelt and forced him to use a wheelchair. In the 1940s and 1950s, however, polio struck the nation in epidemic proportions. Officially known as infantile paralysis because it generally targeted the young, the disease brought a wave of terror to the country. No one knew where or when polio would strike, but an epidemic broke out in some area of the country each summer, crippling and killing its victims. People watched helplessly while neighbors fell sick. Many died, and those who did not were often confined to iron lungs—large metal tanks with pumps that helped patients breathe. If they eventually recovered, they were often paralyzed for the rest of their lives.

Because no one knew what caused the disease, parents searched for ways to safeguard their families each summer. Some sent their children to the country to avoid excessive contact with others. Public swimming pools and beaches were closed. Parks and playgrounds across the country stood deserted. Nevertheless, the disease continued to strike. In 1952 a record 58,000 new cases were reported.

Finally, a research scientist named **Jonas Salk** developed an injectable vaccine that prevented polio. Salk first tested the vaccine on himself, his wife, and his three sons. It was then tested on 2 million schoolchildren. In 1955 the vaccine was declared safe and effective and became available to the general public. The results were spectacular. New cases of polio fell to 5,700 in 1958 and then to 3,277 in 1960. American scientist Albert Sabin then developed an oral vaccine for polio. Because it was safer and more convenient than Salk's injection vaccine, the Sabin vaccine became the most common form of treatment against the disease. In the years to come, the threat of polio would almost completely disappear.

Conquering Space After the Soviet Union launched *Sputnik,* the world's first space satellite, in October 1957, the United States hastened to catch up with its

818 CHAPTER 27 Postwar America

CRITICAL THINKING ACTIVITY

Analyzing During the 1950s, American economic production was quite high. To ensure that people bought enough to match the output, business and government often followed certain policies or practices: (1) emphasizing yearly style changes encouraged built-in obsolescence and made consumers feel the need to stay current; (2) advertising to create new demand; and (3) the shipping of excess food and technology to less-advantaged nations. Ask students to discuss what would happen if an oversupply of goods vanished. How would these policies change in an economy of scarcity? **L1**

Cold War rival. Less than four months later, on January 31, 1958, the United States launched its own satellite from Cape Canaveral, Florida. Reporter Milton Bracker described the jubilant scene:

66As the firing command neared, a deadly silence fell on those who were watching. In the glare of the searchlights, a stream of liquid oxygen could be seen venting like a lavender cloud from the side of the seventy-foot rocket. . . . At fourteen and one-half seconds after time zero . . . the main stage engine came to life with an immeasurable thrust of flame in all directions. . . . With thousands of eyes following it, the rocket dug into the night and accelerated as its sound loudened. Spectators on near-by beaches pointed and craned their necks and cried, 'There it is!' and began to cheer.99

—quoted in *Voices from America's Past*

Meanwhile, engineers were building smoother and faster commercial planes. Poet Carl Sandburg wrote about taking the first American jet flight from New York to Los Angeles. The trip took only five and a half hours. "You search for words to describe the speed of this flight," wrote an amazed Sandburg.

Profiles IN HISTORY

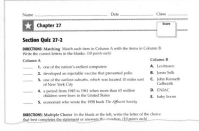

Dr. Jonas Salk
1914–1995

The man who developed the vaccine for one of the nation's most feared diseases almost did not go into medicine. Jonas Salk enrolled in college as a pre-law student but soon changed his mind. "My mother didn't think I would make a very good lawyer," Salk said, "probably because I could never win an argument with her." Salk switched his major to premed and went on to become a research scientist.

Salk initially directed the search for a cure to the dreaded ailment of polio at the University of Pittsburgh's Virus Research Laboratory. Every so often, Salk would make rounds in the overcrowded polio wards of nearby Municipal Hospital, where nurses described their feelings of pity and helpless rage as paralyzed children cried for water. As one nurse said, "I can remember how the staff used to kid Dr. Salk—kidding in earnest—telling him to hurry up and do something."

Salk became famous for his breakthrough vaccine. The shy doctor, however, did not desire fame. About his becoming a celebrity, Salk observed that it was "a transitory thing and you wait till it blows over. Eventually people will start thinking, 'That poor guy,' and leave me alone. Then I'll be able to get back to my laboratory."

"You are whisked . . . from an ocean on one side of the continent to an ocean on the opposite side in less time than it takes the sun to trace a 90-degree arc across the sky."

✓ **Reading Check** **Examining** What medical and technological advances met specific needs in the late 1940s and 1950s?

SECTION 2 ASSESSMENT

Checking for Understanding

1. **Define:** white-collar, blue-collar, multinational corporation, franchise, baby boom.
2. **Identify:** John Kenneth Galbraith, David Riesman, Levittown, Jonas Salk.
3. **Describe** how and why the suburbs became popular places to live.

Reviewing Themes

4. **Continuity and Change** How was the affluent society of the United States in the 1950s different from previous decades?

Critical Thinking

5. **Interpreting** What caused the advertising industry boom in the 1950s?
6. **Organizing** Use a graphic organizer similar to the one below to list the causes and effects of the economic boom of the 1950s.

Analyzing Visuals

7. **Analyzing Photographs** Study the photograph on page 818 of children suffering from polio. What do you think it was like to live in such an environment? Do Americans today face similar medical fears?

Writing About History

8. **Descriptive Writing** Write an article for a magazine such as *Better Homes and Gardens* describing changes the American family underwent during the 1950s.

CHAPTER 27 Postwar America **819**

Profiles IN HISTORY

Jonas Salk attended medical school at New York University, where he received his medical degree in 1939.

✓ **Reading Check**

Answer: antibiotics; drugs for arthritis, diabetes, cancer, and heart disease; new surgical techniques; polio vaccine

Reteach
Have students explain the effects the nation's economic boom had on American society.

Enrich
Invite interested students to research technological and medical advances not mentioned in the section and report their findings to the class.

4 CLOSE

Have students describe changes in the American family that took place during the 1950s.

SECTION 2 ASSESSMENT ANSWERS

1. Terms are in blue.
2. John Kenneth Galbraith (*p. 814*), David Riesman (*p. 815*), Levittown (*p. 816*), Jonas Salk (*p. 818*)
3. government programs made homeownership more affordable and improved construction made houses cheaper; people moved to suburbs to escape urban problems

or improve their standard of living
4. all segments of American society showed measurable economic improvement
5. increased product mass production generated new emphasis on higher sales of consumer goods
6. Causes: new business techniques, improved technology; effects:

answers may include consumerism and suburban growth
7. Descriptions will vary. It must have been depressing and frustrating both for the patients and the people treating them.
8. Articles should use realistic examples and offer explanations for the changes.

1 FOCUS

Section Overview
This section focuses on the popular culture that grew out of postwar prosperity.

BELLRINGER
Skillbuilder Activity

 Project transparency and have students answer the question.

📂 Available as a blackline master.

Daily Focus Skills Transparency 27–3

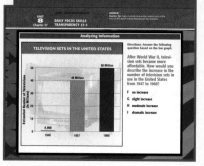

Guide to Reading

Answers to Graphic: Television: action shows, game shows, situation comedies, variety shows; radio: recorded music, news, weather, talk shows; cinema: cinemascope, 3-D movies; music: rock 'n' roll; literature: the beat movement

Preteaching Vocabulary
Have students create a database for the Key Terms and Names in this section.

SECTION 3 Popular Culture of the 1950s

Guide to Reading

Main Idea
During the carefree and prosperous 1950s, Americans turned to television, new forms of music, cinema, and literature to entertain themselves.

Key Terms and Names
Ed Sullivan, Alan Freed, Elvis Presley, generation gap, Jack Kerouac, Little Richard

Reading Strategy
Categorizing As you read about the popular culture of the 1950s, complete a graphic organizer similar to the one below comparing new forms of mass media during the 1950s.

New Forms of Mass Media	Description

Reading Objectives
- **Explain** the characteristics of the new youth culture.
- **Discuss** the contributions of African Americans to 1950s culture.

Section Theme
Culture and Traditions The 1950s added such elements as rock 'n' roll music and sitcom television to modern culture.

Preview of Events

◆1955	◆1956	◆1957	◆1958

1955
The quiz show *The $64,000 Question* debuts

1956
Elvis Presley appears on the *Ed Sullivan Show*; Allen Ginsburg's "Howl" published

1957
40 million television sets in use in the United States

1958
TV quiz show scandals begin to surface

Lucille Ball and Desi Arnez

★ An American Story ★

In 1953 Lucille Ball and her real-life husband, Desi Arnez, were starring in one of the most popular shows on American television, *I Love Lucy.* In January, Ball had a baby—both in real life and on her show. Her pregnancy and the birth of her baby became a national event that captivated her audience. A pre-filmed segment of the show showed Lucy and her husband going to the hospital to have the baby, and the show was broadcast only a few hours after the real birth. More than two-thirds of the nation's television sets tuned in, an audience of around 44 million viewers. Far fewer people watched the next day when television broadcast a presidential inauguration for the first time.

I Love Lucy was so popular that some people actually set up their work schedules around the show. Marshall Field's, which had previously held sales on the same night the show was on, eventually switched its sales to a different night. A sign on its shop window explained, "We love Lucy too, so we're closing on Monday nights." A relatively new medium, television had swept the nation by the mid-1950s.

—adapted from *Watching TV: Four Decades of American Television*

The New Mass Media

Although regular television broadcasts had begun in the early 1940s, there were few stations, and sets were expensive. By the end of the 1950s, however, the small, black-and-white-screened sets sat in living rooms across the country. Television's popularity

820 CHAPTER 27 Postwar America

📖 **SECTION RESOURCES**

📂 **Reproducible Masters**
- Reproducible Lesson Plan 27–3
- Daily Lecture and Discussion Notes 27–3
- Guided Reading Activity 27–3
- Section Quiz 27–3
- Reading Essentials and Study Guide 27–3

📇 **Transparencies**
- Daily Focus Skills Transparency 27–3

Multimedia
- 💿 Interactive Tutor Self-Assessment CD-ROM
- 💿 ExamView® Pro Testmaker CD-ROM
- 💿 Presentation Plus! CD-ROM
- 💿 TeacherWorks™ CD-ROM
- 🎧 Audio Program
- 🎵 American Music: Hits Through History
- 🎵 American Music: Cultural Traditions

forced the other forms of mass media—namely motion pictures and radio—to innovate in order to keep their audiences.

The Rise of Television Popularity During World War II, televisions became more affordable for consumers. In 1946 it is estimated there were between 7,000 and 8,000 sets in the entire United States. By 1957 there were 40 million television sets in use. Over 80 percent of families had televisions.

By the late 1950s, television news had become an important vehicle for information. Television advertising spawned a growing market for many new products. Advertising, after all, provided television with the money that allowed it to flourish. As one critic concluded, "Programs on television are simply a device to keep the advertisements and commercials from bumping loudly together." Televised athletic events gradually made professional and college sports one of the most prominent sources of entertainment.

Comedy, Action, and Games Early television programs fell into several main categories including comedy, action and adventure, and variety-style entertainment. Laughter proved popular in other formats besides the half-hour situation comedy. Many of the early television comedy shows, such as those starring Bob Hope and Jack Benny, were adapted from popular old radio shows. Benny enjoyed considerable television success with his routines of bad violin playing and stingy behavior.

Television watchers in the 1950s also relished action shows. Westerns such as *Hopalong Cassidy, The Lone Ranger,* and *Gunsmoke* grew quickly in popularity. Viewers also enjoyed police programs such as *Dragnet,* a hugely successful show featuring Joe Friday and his partner hunting down a new criminal each week.

Variety shows such as **Ed Sullivan's** *Toast of the Town* provided a mix of comedy, opera, popular song, dance, acrobatics, and juggling. Quiz shows attracted large audiences, too, after the 1955 debut of *The $64,000 Question.* In this show and its many imitators, two contestants tried to answer questions from separate glass-encased booths. The questions, stored between shows in a bank vault, arrived at the studio at airtime in the hands of a stern-faced bank executive flanked by two armed guards. The contestants competed head-to-head, with the winner returning the following week to face a new challenger.

TV Nation

Television programming depicted a narrow view of American culture in the 1950s. Most television shows during these years centered around a common image of American life—an image that was predominantly white, middle-class, and suburban, epitomized by the popular situation comedy *The Adventures of Ozzie and Harriet.* Such shows also reinforced traditional gender roles, showing fathers working and mothers staying home to raise children and take care of the house.

Westerns were also popular at the time, especially *The Lone Ranger,* in which a mysterious masked man helped people in distress. *The Howdy Doody Show,* which featured Buffalo Bob and his freckle-faced marionette, was the first network kids' show to run five days a week, the first television show ever broadcast in color, and the first show ever to air more than 1,000 continuous episodes.

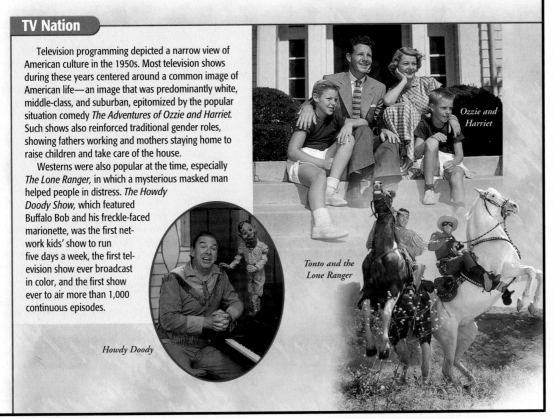

Ozzie and Harriet

Tonto and the Lone Ranger

Howdy Doody

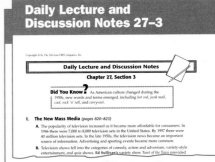

Fact	Fiction	Folklore

The Swanson Company created its first frozen meals in 1952 and started using the name "Swanson TV Dinner" in 1954. Swanson sold 10 million TV dinners the first year they were distributed nationally. By the time the TV dinner celebrated its 45th birthday, Americans were buying 3 million a week. The famous compartmentalized aluminum tray was retired in 1986 and replaced with microwave-safe packaging.

Creating a Culture Dictionary

Have students select a movie video that depicts the 1950s, such as *Back to the Future*, *American Graffiti*, or *Grease* or watch a rerun of a television program that depicts or was popular during the 1950s such as *I Love Lucy*, *Laverne and Shirley*, or *The Many Loves of Dobie Gillis*. Tell them to make a list of the styles, slang expressions, attitudes, and behaviors that are different from those of today. Discuss the lists and then compile them into a 1950s culture dictionary. **L2**

Fact	Fiction	Folklore

Quick and Easy Eats Along with the television came . . . TV dinners! Capitalizing on the television boom of the 1950s, these frozen individual meals offered an entrée, a side dish or two, and a dessert, all on an aluminum tray divided into compartments.

Not everyone actually ate TV dinners in front of the television, but the meals were popular because they offered convenience. Noted one food industry executive of the time, "When Mary Smith rushes home from work late in the afternoon, she wants to buy food that not only will look pretty on the table but is something she can get ready in the half hour before her husband comes home for dinner."

In 1956 the quiz show *Twenty-One* caused an uproar across the nation after **Charles Van Doren,** a young assistant professor with a modest income, won $129,000 during his weeks on the program. The viewing public soon learned, however, that Van Doren and many of the other contestants had received the answers to the questions in advance. Before a congressional committee in 1959, Van Doren admitted his role in the scandal and apologized to his many fans, saying, "I was involved, deeply involved, in a deception." In the wake of the *Twenty-One* fraud, many quiz shows went off the air.

Hollywood Adapts to the Times As the popularity of television grew, movies lost viewers. "Hollywood's like Egypt," lamented producer David Selznick in 1951. "Full of crumbling pyramids." While the film business may not have been collapsing, it certainly did suffer after the war. Attendance dropped from 82 million in 1946 to 36 million by 1950. By 1960, when some 50 million Americans owned a television, one-fifth of the nation's movie theaters had closed.

Throughout the decade, Hollywood struggled mightily to recapture its audience. "Don't be a 'Living Room Captive,'" one industry ad pleaded. "Step out and see a great movie!" When contests, door prizes, and an advertising campaign announcing that "Movies Are Better Than Ever" failed to lure people out of their homes, Hollywood began to try to make films more exciting. Between 1952 and 1954, audiences of 3-D films received special

glasses that gave the impression that a monster or a knife was lunging directly at them from off the screen. Viewers, however, soon tired of both the glasses and the often ridiculous plots of 3-D movies.

Cinemascope, movies shown on large, panoramic screens, finally gave Hollywood a reliable lure. Wide-screen spectacles like *The Robe*, *The Ten Commandments,* and *Around the World in 80 Days* cost a great deal of money to produce. These blockbusters, however, made up for their cost by attracting huge audiences and netting large profits. The movie industry also made progress by taking the "if you can't beat 'em, join 'em" approach. Hollywood eventually began to film programs especially for television and also sold old movies, which could be rebroadcast cheaply, to the networks.

Like television, the films of the fifties for the most part adhered to the conformity of the times. Roles for single women who did not want families were few and far between. For example, each of Marilyn Monroe's film roles featured the blond movie star as married, soon to be married, or unhappy that she was not married.

Movies with African Americans routinely portrayed them in stereotypical roles, such as maids, servants, or sidekicks for white heroes. Even when African Americans took leading roles, they were often one-dimensional characters who rarely showed human emotions or characteristics. African American actor Sidney Poitier resented having to play such parts:

> 66 The black characters usually come out on the screen as saints, as the other-cheek-turners, as people who are not really people: who are so nice and good. . . . As a matter of fact, I'm just dying to play villains. 99
>
> —quoted in *The Fifties: The Way We Really Were*

Radio Draws Them In Television also lured away radio listeners and forced the radio industry, like Hollywood, to develop new ways to win back audiences. After television took over many of radio's concepts of comedies, dramas, and soap operas, for example, many radio stations began to specialize in presenting recorded music, news, talk shows, weather, public-service programming, and shows for specific audiences.

As a result of this targeted programming, radio stations survived and even flourished. Their numbers more than doubled between 1948, when 1,680 stations were broadcasting to the nation, and 1957, when more than 3,600 stations filled the airwaves.

✔ **Reading Check** **Identifying** How did the television industry affect the U.S. economy?

The New Youth Culture

While Americans of all ages embraced the new mass media, some of the nation's youth rebelled against such a message. During the 1950s, a number of young Americans turned their backs on the conformist ideals adult society promoted. Although these youths were a small minority, their actions brought them widespread attention. In general, these young people longed for greater excitement and freedom, and they found an outlet for such feelings of restlessness in new and controversial styles of music and literature.

Rock 'n' Roll In the early 1950s, rock 'n' roll emerged as the distinctive music of the new generation. In 1951 at a record store in downtown Cleveland,

Ohio, radio disc jockey **Alan Freed** noticed white teenagers buying African American rhythm and blues records and dancing to the music in the store. A week later, Freed won permission from his station manager to play the music on the air. Just as the disc jockey had suspected, the listeners went crazy for it. Soon, white artists began making music that stemmed from these African American rhythms and sounds, and a new form of music, **rock 'n' roll,** had been born.

With a loud and heavy beat that made it ideal for dancing along with lyrics about romance, cars, and other themes that spoke to young people, rock 'n' roll grew wildly popular among the nation's teens. Before long boys and girls around the country were rushing out to buy the latest hits from such artists as Buddy Holly, Chuck Berry, and Bill Haley and the Comets. In 1956 teenagers found their first rock 'n' roll hero in **Elvis Presley.** Presley, who had been born in rural Mississippi and grown up poor in Memphis, Tennessee, eventually claimed the title of "King of Rock 'n' Roll."

While in high school, Presley had learned to play guitar and sing by imitating the rhythm and blues

✔ **Reading Check**

Answer: Television spawned a growing market for many new products through advertising and weakened the movie industry until it adapted.

Elvis Presley's leather jacket and ducktail haircut became standard dress for young men in the 1950s.

History *and the* Humanities

- American Music: Hits Through History: "Chances Are," "Little Joe Cook and The Thrillers," "Jet Song," "I'll Fly Away," "I Walk the Line"
- American Music: Cultural Traditions: "Rocket 88," "Rock Around the Clock"
- American Art & Architecture: *Finny Fish,* Rock and Roll Hall of Fame Museum

NATIONAL GEOGRAPHIC
MOMENT in HISTORY

THE KING OF ROCK
Elvis Presley, shown here signing autographs after a performance in Houston, took American youth in the 1950s by storm. Parents, on the other hand, were less than thrilled with his music—a blend of African American-inspired rhythm and blues and early rock 'n' roll—and his hip-swiveling gyrations on stage. For Presley's first appearance on The Ed Sullivan Show, the host insisted that cameras show him only from the waist up. Elvis added to his fame by starring in a string of films that audiences loved but critics panned.

NATIONAL GEOGRAPHIC
MOMENT in HISTORY

Dancing became extremely popular among teenagers in the 1950s. Teenagers continued to dance the jitterbug that their parents had originated, in addition to their own creations such as line dances, the twist, the bop, the Watusi, the stroll, the slide, the pony, and the monkey.

CHAPTER 27 Postwar America **823**

INTERDISCIPLINARY CONNECTIONS ACTIVITY

Music One way to trace the beginnings of the generation gap is to review the top-selling records during the 1950s. In 1952, for example, such hits as "Blue Tango" and "I Saw Mommy Kissing Santa Claus" dominated the pop charts. By 1956 Doris Day's "Whatever Will Be, Will Be (Que Sera Sera)" competed with Elvis Presley's "Hound Dog." By 1959 rock 'n' roll was pushing for evergreater dominance on the charts. Ask students to discuss how the music reflected a changing American society. Consider playing music from the 1950s during the discussion. **L2**

3 ASSESS

Assign Section 3 Assessment as homework or as an in-class activity.

🔵 Have students use the **Interactive Tutor Self-Assessment CD-ROM.**

Reading Essentials and Study Guide 27-3

Name _____ Date _____ Class _____

Study Guide

Chapter 27, Section 3

For use with textbook pages 820–825

POPULAR CULTURE OF THE 1950S

KEY TERMS AND NAMES

Ed Sullivan host of a variety show (page 821)

Alan Freed a radio disc jockey who introduced African American rhythm and blues records to white radio stations (page 823)

Elvis Presley the first rock 'n' roll hero (page 823)

generation gap a cultural separation between children and their parents (page 824)

Jack Kerouac a beat writer (page 824)

Little Richard African American rock 'n' roll singer (page 824)

✔Reading Check

Answer: It generated musical disagreement between children and parents and created a bond among the younger generation.

Section Quiz 27-3

Name _____ Date _____ Class _____

⭐ **Chapter 27** Score ___

Section Quiz 27-3

DIRECTIONS: Matching Match each item in Column A with the items in Column B. Write the correct letters in the blanks. *(10 points each)*

Column A

___ 1. cultural separation between children and their parents

___ 2. movies shown on large, panoramic screens

___ 3. group of mostly white artists who sought to live unconventional lives as fugitives from a culture they despised

___ 4. enjoyed television success with routines of bad violin playing and stingy behavior

___ 5. beat member who published *On the Road* in 1957

Column B

A. cinemascope

B. Jack Kerouac

C. generation gap

D. beats

E. Jack Benny

DIRECTIONS: Multiple Choice In the blank at the left, write the letter of the choice

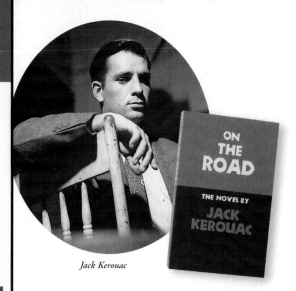

Jack Kerouac

music he heard on the radio. By 1956 Elvis had a record deal with RCA Victor, a movie contract, and public appearances on several television shows. At first the popular television variety show host Ed Sullivan refused to invite Presley on, insisting that the rock 'n' roll music was not fit for a family-oriented show. When a competing show featuring Presley upset his own high ratings, however, Sullivan relented. He ended up paying Presley $50,000 per performance for three appearances, more than triple the amount he had paid any other performer.

The dark-haired and handsome Presley owed his wild popularity as much to his moves as to his music. During his performances he would gyrate his hips and dance in other suggestive ways that shocked many in the audience. Presley himself admitted the importance of this part of his act:

❝I'm not kidding myself. My voice alone is just an ordinary voice. What people come to see is how I use it. If I stand still while I'm singing, I'm dead, man. I might as well go back to driving a truck.❞

—quoted in *God's Country: America in the Fifties*

Not surprisingly, parents—many of whom listened to Frank Sinatra and other more mellow and mainstream artists—condemned rock 'n' roll as loud, mindless, and dangerous. The city council of San Antonio, Texas, actually banned rock 'n' roll from the jukeboxes at public swimming pools. The music, the council declared, "attracted undesirable elements given to practicing their gyrations in abbreviated bathing suits." A minister in Boston complained that "rock and roll inflames and excites youth."

The rock 'n' roll hits that teens bought in record numbers united them in a world their parents did not share. Thus in the 1950s rock 'n' roll helped to create what became known as the generation gap, or the cultural separation between children and their parents.

The Beat Movement If rock 'n' roll helped to create a generation gap, a group of mostly white artists who called themselves the **beats** highlighted a values gap in the 1950s United States. The term *beat* may have come from the feeling among group members of being "beaten down" by American culture, or from jazz musicians who would say, "I'm beat right down to my socks."

The beats sought to live unconventional lives as fugitives from a culture they despised. Beat poets, writers, and artists harshly criticized what they considered the sterility and conformity of American life, the meaninglessness of American politics, and the emptiness of popular culture.

In 1956, 29-year-old beat poet **Allen Ginsburg** published a long poem called "Howl," which blasted modern American life. Another beat member, **Jack Kerouac,** published *On the Road* in 1957. Although Kerouac's book about his freewheeling adventures with a car thief and con artist shocked some readers, the book went on to become a classic in modern American literature.

✔**Reading Check** **Summarizing** How did rock 'n' roll help create the generation gap?

African American Entertainers

While artists such as Jack Kerouac rejected American culture, African American entertainers struggled to find acceptance in a country that often treated them as second-class citizens. With a few notable exceptions, television tended to shut out African Americans. In 1958, for example, a popular African American singer named Nat King Cole had been slated to host a musical variety show. When the network failed to secure a sponsor willing to back an African American star, however, Cole's show was canceled.

African American rock 'n' roll singers had more luck gaining acceptance. The talented African American singers and groups who recorded hit songs in the fifties included **Chuck Berry, Ray Charles, Little Richard,** and the **Drifters.** The latter years of the 1950s also saw the rise of several African American women's groups, including the

---

CRITICAL THINKING ACTIVITY

Analyzing Increased spending and the use of consumer credit are trends of the 1950s that imply two assumptions—that Americans believed they deserved the latest and best products and that the economy would continue to prosper. Ask students to review Section 3 and identify other assumptions they can link with specific trends and developments. **L2**

Little Richard

Fats Domino

Picturing **History**

African American Entertainers Rhythm and blues music provided the roots of the 1950s rock 'n' roll sound. Did African American rock 'n' roll artists experience the same acceptance as artists like Elvis Presley? Why or why not?

Picturing **History**

Answer: No. Television tended to shut them out, and they often were treated as second-class citizens.
Ask: Why was Nat King Cole's television show canceled before it aired? *(The network was unable to find a sponsor willing to back an African American performer.)*

Crystals, the **Chiffons,** the **Shirelles,** and the **Ronettes.** With their catchy, popular sound, these groups became the musical ancestors of the famous late 1960s groups **Martha and the Vandellas** and the **Supremes.**

Over time, the music of the early rock 'n' roll artists had a profound influence on music throughout the world. Little Richard and Chuck Berry, for example, provided inspiration for the Beatles, whose music swept Britain and the world in the 1960s. Elvis's music transformed generations of rock 'n' roll bands that were to follow him and other pioneers of rock.

Despite the innovations in music and the economic boom of the 1950s, not all Americans were part of the affluent society. For much of the country's minorities and rural poor, the American dream remained well out of reach.

Reading Check **Evaluating** What impact did American rock 'n' roll artists have on the rest of the world?

Reading Check

Answer: They influenced music throughout the world and inspired such bands as the Beatles.

Reteach
Have students present a skit, complete with costumes and props, to highlight the characteristics of the new youth culture.

Enrich
Encourage interested students to interview someone who was a teenager or young adult during the 1950s and write a magazine-style article about what life was like.

4 CLOSE

Have students pose a series of questions that can be used to stimulate discussion about the contributions of African Americans to 1950s culture.

SECTION 3 ASSESSMENT

Checking for Understanding
1. **Define:** generation gap.
2. **Identify:** Ed Sullivan, Alan Freed, Elvis Presley, Jack Kerouac, Little Richard.
3. **Explain** what happened to motion pictures and radio when television became popular.

Reviewing Themes
4. **Culture and Traditions** What roles did African Americans play in television and rock 'n' roll?

Critical Thinking
5. **Comparing** How did the themes of television shows of the 1950s differ from the themes of the literature of the beat movement?
6. **Organizing** Use a graphic organizer similar to the one below to list the styles of music and literature that made up the new youth culture of the 1950s.

New Youth Culture

Analyzing Visuals
7. **Analyzing Photographs** Study the photographs on pages 820 and 821. Many people have criticized these television programs for presenting a one-sided view of American life. Do you agree with this criticism? Why or why not?

Writing About History
8. **Expository Writing** Imagine you are a beat writer in the 1950s. Explain to your readers how the themes you write about are universal themes that could apply to everyone.

CHAPTER 27 Postwar America **825**

SECTION 3 ASSESSMENT ANSWERS

1. Terms are in blue.
2. Ed Sullivan *(p. 821)*, Alan Freed *(p. 823)*, Elvis Presley *(p. 823)*, Jack Kerouac *(p. 824)*, Little Richard *(p. 824)*
3. Motion picture attendance and radio listenership dropped for a while.
4. They had limited opportunities on television but more success in the music industry.
5. Television shows depicted middle-class values, endorsing mainstream American society; beat literature depicted it as meaningless and sterile.
6. rock 'n' roll and beat literature
7. Students' answers will vary. Most will likely agree that the view was somewhat one-sided due to an emphasis on white, middle-class experiences.
8. Students' papers will vary. Papers should describe beat themes as being applicable to more than just American culture.

TEACH

Verbatim
Have students review the quotes in the Verbatim section and discuss each item as it relates to the people and themes found in the textbook. Have students research a current political, economic, or social issue. Have them find quotations about the issue and create a brief statement explaining the quotes, identifying the people quoted, and describing how the quotes relate to the issue. Ask students to share their lists in a class discussion.

American Scene
Have students look at the graph on page 827 and explain the differences between 1950 and 1960. **Ask:** Why is there an increase in each category? (*As the number of children grew, so did the number participating in sports and recreation.*)

Be Prepared
Have students review the information about bomb shelters. **Ask:** Have you experienced or heard about any similar kind of preparedness effort? (*Answers will vary, but many students will have had personal experience with preparations for Y2K or for natural disasters such as tornadoes.*)

Translation, Please
Have students interview friends and relatives who were teenagers in the 1950s to learn about more teenage lingo. Make a list of all the words and definitions that students bring in.

Numbers 1957
Have students research the current numbers for each item on the list and create a table to show the dollar amounts in 1957 and today.

TIME NOTEBOOK

BETTMANN/CORBIS

Profile

JAMES DEAN *had a brief but spectacular career as a film star. His role in* Rebel Without a Cause *made him an icon for American youth in the mid-50s. In 1955 Dean was killed in a car crash. He was 24.*

"I guess I have as good an insight into this rising generation as any other young man my age. Therefore, when I do play a youth, I try to imitate life. *Rebel Without a Cause* deals with the problems of modern youth. . . . If you want the kids to come and see the picture, you've got to try to reach them on their own grounds. If a picture is psychologically motivated, if there is truth in the relationships in it, then I think that picture will do good."

—*from an interview for* Rebel Without a Cause

WINNERS & LOSERS

ARCHIVE PHOTOS

Poodle Cut

POODLE CUTS
Short, curly hairstyle gains wide popularity and acceptance

TV GUIDE
New weekly magazine achieves circulation of 6.5 million by 1959

PALMER PAINT COMPANY OF DETROIT
Sells 12 million paint-by-number kits ranging from simple landscapes and portraits to Leonardo da Vinci's *The Last Supper*

THE DUCKTAIL
Banned in several Massachusetts schools in 1957

COLLIER'S
The respected magazine loses circulation, publishes its final edition on January 4, 1957

LEONARDO DA VINCI'S
THE LAST SUPPER
Now everyone can paint their own copy to hang in their homes

The Ducktail

SUPER STOCK

826   CHAPTER 27   Postwar America

VERBATIM

❝It will make a wonderful place for the children to play in, and it will be a good storehouse, too.❞
MRS. RUTH CALHOUN,
mother of three, on her backyard fallout shelter, 1951

❝Riddle: What's college? That's where girls who are above cooking and sewing go to meet a man they can spend their lives cooking and sewing for.❞
ad for Gimbel's department store campus clothes, 1952

❝Radioactive poisoning of the atmosphere and hence annihilation of any life on Earth has been brought within the range of technical possibilities.❞
ALBERT EINSTEIN,
physicist, 1950

❝If the television craze continues with the present level of programs, we are destined to have a nation of morons.❞
DANIEL MARSH,
President of Boston University, 1950

❝Every time the Russians throw an American in jail, the House Un-American Activities Committee throws an American in jail to get even.❞
MORT SAHL,
comedian, 1950s

COOPERATIVE LEARNING ACTIVITY

Creating a Magazine Spread Organize the class into small groups and ask them to create their own two-page magazine spread for one year between 1950 and 1960. Encourage students to use elements similar to those that appear in the text but to be creative as they select information. Students should look at current magazines and books for ideas about page design. This activity can be completed using desktop publishing software or the more traditional cut-and-paste method.

Use the rubric for a cooperative group management plan on pages 81–82 in the ***Performance Assessment Activities and Rubrics.***

1950s WORD PLAY
Translation, Please!

Match the word to its meaning.

Teen-Age Lingo

1. cool
2. hang loose
3. hairy
4. yo-yo

a. a dull person, an outsider
b. worthy of approval
c. formidable
d. don't worry

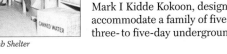

answers: 1. b; 2. d; 3. c; 4. a

Bomb Shelter

BETTMANN/CORBIS

Be Prepared

"Know the Bomb's True Dangers. Know the Steps You Can Take to Escape Them!—You Can Survive."
Government pamphlet, 1950

DIGGING YOUR OWN BOMB SHELTER? Better go shopping. Below is a list of items included with the $3,000 Mark I Kidde Kokoon, designed to accommodate a family of five for a three- to five-day underground stay.

- air blower
- radiation detector
- protective apparel suit
- face respirator
- radiation charts (4)
- hand shovel combination (for digging out after the blast)
- gasoline driven generator
- gasoline (10 gallons)

- chemical toilet
- toilet chemicals (2 gallons)
- bunks (5)
- mattresses and blankets (5)
- air pump (for blowing up mattresses)
- incandescent bulbs (2) 40 watts
- fuses (2) 5 amperes
- clock—non-electric

- first aid kit
- waterless hand cleaner
- sterno stove
- canned water (10 gallons)
- canned food (meat, powdered milk, cereal, sugar, etc.)
- paper products

NUMBERS 1957

3¢ Cost of first-class postage stamp

19¢ Cost of loaf of bread

25¢ Cost of issue of *Sports Illustrated*

35¢ Cost of movie ticket

50¢ Cost of gallon of milk (delivered)

$2.05 Average hourly wage

$2,845 Cost of new car

POPPERFOTO/ARCHIVE PHOTO

$5,234 Median income for a family of four

$19,500 Median price to buy a home

American Scene, 1950–1960
(MILLIONS)

	1950	1960
Children 5–14	24.3	35.5
Girl Scouts & Brownies	1.8	4.0
Bicycle Production	2.0	3.8
National Forest Campers	1.5	6.6
Outboard Motors in Use	2.8	5.8

Portfolio Writing Project

Have students research a social phenomenon of the 1950s and write an essay about its impact now and then. Suggest that students review popular magazines from the time period to generate topic ideas. Provide a list of appropriate magazines such as *Look, Life, Saturday Evening Post, Time, Newsweek.*

FYI

The race to build bombs even more powerful than the atomic bombs dropped on Hiroshima and Nagasaki marked the 1950s. President Dwight D. Eisenhower was a strong supporter of the effort to stockpile large numbers of hydrogen bombs. He believed that the bombs would provide U.S. security at an affordable price. However, by 1960 he had realized the potential horrors of a war of hydrogen bombs and reported to the National Security Council that "war no longer has any logic whatsoever."

CLOSE

Ask: What does the photo at the bottom of the numbers list reflect about what was happening in the 1950s? (*Home ownership and the use of the automobile increased dramatically during the 1950s.*)

Visit the TIME Web site at www.time.com for up-to-date news, weekly magazine articles, editorials, online polls, and an archive of past magazine and Web articles.

EXTENDING THE CONTENT

Music Popular music in the 1950s included doo-wop. Groups named for birds such as Flamingos and Cardinals, cars such as Cadillacs and El Dorados, or household items such as Coasters or Cufflinks appeared on stage dressed in perfectly matched suits. One member of the group sang falsetto, while the others chimed in with complicated harmonies and syncopated rhythms. Nonsense syllables such as "oooh, oo-wee-oooh" were repeated by the bass singer. Fans loved the romantic, moving sounds and the rhythms. Doo-wop remained at the top of pop music charts until it was displaced by Beatles hits in the early 1960s.

1 FOCUS

Section Overview

This section focuses on the difficulties faced by those who were not included in the postwar economic boom.

BELLRINGER
Skillbuilder Activity

📽 Project transparency and have students answer the question.

🗂 Available as a blackline master.

Daily Focus Skills Transparency 27–4

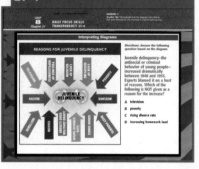

Guide to Reading

Answers to Graphic:
The Other Side of American Life
I. Poverty Amidst Prosperity
  A. The Decline of the Inner City
  B. African Americans
  C. Hispanics
  D. Native Americans
  E. Appalachia
II. Juvenile Delinquency

Preteaching Vocabulary
Have students write a short paragraph using at least three of the Key Names or Terms.

SECTION 4 The Other Side of American Life

Guide to Reading

Main Idea
Not everyone in the United States prospered during the nation's postwar boom, as millions of minorities and rural whites struggled daily with poverty.

Key Terms and Names
poverty line, Michael Harrington, urban renewal, Bracero program, termination policy, juvenile delinquency

Reading Strategy
Taking Notes As you read about social problems in the United States in the 1950s, use the major headings of the section to create an outline similar to the one below.

The Other Side of American Life
I. Poverty Amidst Prosperity
  A.
  B.
  C.
  D.
  E.
II.

Reading Objectives
• **Identify** those groups that found themselves left out of the American economic boom following World War II.
• **Explain** the factors that contributed to the poverty among various groups.

Section Theme
Continuity and Change For some groups, poverty continued during the apparent abundance of the 1950s.

Preview of Events

◆1953	◆1956	◆1959	◆1962

1953
Federal government institutes termination policy directed at Native Americans

1955
Rudolf Flesch's *Why Johnny Can't Read* published

1959
A Raisin in the Sun opens on Broadway

1962
Michael Harrington's *The Other America* published

★ An American Story ★

Lorraine Hansberry

In 1959 Lorraine Hansberry's play, *A Raisin in the Sun,* opened on Broadway. The play told the story of a working-class African American family struggling against poverty and racism. The title referred to a Langston Hughes poem that wonders what happens to an unrealized dream: "Does it dry up like a raisin in the sun?" Hansberry's play won the New York Drama Critics Circle Award for the best play of the year. Reflecting later upon the play's theme, she wrote:

66Vulgarity, blind conformity, and mass lethargy need not triumph in the land of Lincoln and Frederick Douglass. . . . There is simply no reason why dreams should dry up like raisins or prunes or anything else in the United States. . . . I believe that we can impose beauty on our future.99

Postwar prosperity had bypassed many segments of the population. Minorities and the poor wondered when they could seize their own piece of the American dream.

—adapted from *To Be Young, Gifted, and Black*

Poverty Amidst Prosperity

Although the 1950s saw a tremendous expansion of the middle class, at least 1 in 5 Americans, or about 30 million people, lived below the poverty line, a figure the government set to reflect the minimum income required to support a family. Such poverty

---

SECTION RESOURCES

🗂 **Reproducible Masters**
• Reproducible Lesson Plan 27–4
• Daily Lecture and Discussion Notes 27–4
• Guided Reading Activity 27–4
• Section Quiz 27–4
• Reading Essentials and Study Guide 27–4
• Performance Assessment Activities and Rubrics

💿 **Transparencies**
• Daily Focus Skills Transparency 27–4

Multimedia
💿 Interactive Tutor Self-Assessment CD-ROM
💿 ExamView® Pro Testmaker CD-ROM
💿 Presentation Plus! CD-ROM
💿 TeacherWorks™ CD-ROM
💿 Audio Program

remained invisible to most Americans, who assumed that the country's general prosperity had provided everyone with a comfortable existence. The writer **Michael Harrington,** however, made no such assumptions. During the 1950s, Harrington set out to chronicle poverty in the United States. In his book, *The Other America,* published in 1962, he alerted those in the mainstream to what he saw in the run-down and hidden communities of the country:

❝Tens of millions of Americans are, at this very moment, maimed in body and spirit, existing at levels beneath those necessary for human decency. If these people are not starving, they are hungry, and sometimes fat with hunger, for that is what cheap foods do. They are without adequate housing and education and medical care.❞

—from *The Other America*

The poor included single mothers and the elderly; minority immigrants such as Puerto Ricans and Mexicans; rural Americans, black and white; and inner city residents, who remained stuck in crowded slums as wealthier citizens fled to the suburbs. Poverty also gripped many Americans in the nation's Appalachian region, which stretches from Pennsylvania to Georgia, as well as Native Americans, many of whom endured grinding poverty whether they stayed on reservations or migrated to cities.

ECONOMICS

The Decline of the Inner City The poverty in the 1950s was most apparent in the nation's urban centers. As white families moved to the suburbs, many inner cities became home to poorer, less educated minority groups. The centers of many cities deteriorated, because as the middle class moved out, their tax money went with them. This deprived inner cities of the tax dollars necessary to provide adequate public transportation, housing, and other services.

When government tried to help inner city residents, it often made matters worse. During the 1950s, for example, urban renewal programs tried to eliminate poverty by tearing down slums and erecting new high-rise buildings for poor residents. The crowded, anonymous conditions of these high-rise projects, however, often created an atmosphere of violence. The government also unwittingly encouraged the residents of public housing to remain poor by evicting them as soon as they began to earn any money.

In the end, urban renewal programs actually destroyed more housing space than they created. Too

often in the name of urban improvement, the wrecking ball destroyed poor people's homes to make way for roadways, parks, universities, tree-lined boulevards, or shopping centers.

African Americans Many of the citizens left behind in the cities as families fled to the suburbs were African American. The large number of African American inner city residents resulted largely from the migration of more than 3 million African Americans from the South to the North between 1940 and 1960.

Many African Americans had migrated in the hopes of finding greater economic opportunity and escaping violence and racial intimidation. For many of these migrants, however, life proved to be little better in Northern cities. Fewer and fewer jobs were available as numerous factories and mills left the cities for suburbs and smaller towns in order to cut their costs. Long-standing patterns of racial discrimination in schools, housing, hiring, and salaries in the North kept inner-city African Americans poor. The last hired and the first fired for good jobs, they often remained stuck in the worst-paying occupations. In 1958 African American salaries, on average, equaled only 51 percent of what whites earned.

Picturing History

Inner-City Poverty This young African American girl in Chicago's inner city struggles to fill a bowl with water that has frozen due to lack of heat. Why did the numbers of poor in the country's inner cities grow in the 1950s?

2 TEACH

Daily Lecture and Discussion Notes 27–4

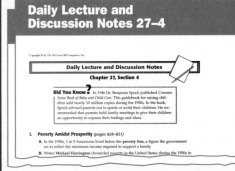

Copyright © by The McGraw-Hill Companies, Inc.

Daily Lecture and Discussion Notes

Chapter 27, Section 4

Did You Know? In 1946 Dr. Benjamin Spock published *Common Sense Book of Baby and Child Care.* This guidebook for raising children sold nearly 10 million copies during the 1950s. In the book, Spock advised parents not to spank or scold their children. He recommended that parents hold family meetings to give their children an opportunity to express their feelings and ideas.

I.   Poverty Amidst Prosperity *(pages 828–831)*

   A. In the 1950s, 1 in 5 Americans lived below the **poverty line,** a figure the government set to reflect the minimum income required to support a family.

   B. Writer **Michael Harrington** chronicled poverty in the United States during the 1950s in

Brainstorming Explain that between 1941 and 1945, one out of every five Americans moved from one area of the country to another. During that time, more than 700,000 African Americans left the South for the North and the West. Ask students to consider what kinds of problems such migration presented for individuals and communities. **L1**

Picturing History

Answer: Poor immigrants as well as African Americans from the South moved to the cities.
Ask: How did government programs make things worse for the urban poor? *(Urban renewal replaced slums with high-rise buildings that were plagued by violence. The government unwittingly contributed to poverty by evicting the poor from government housing when they earned too much money.)*

COOPERATIVE LEARNING ACTIVITY

Writing a Report Organize the class into groups of five. Have each group report on attitudes toward children and child-rearing practices in the United States from colonial times to the present. The reports should include illustrations, drawings, or charts. Groups may explore such topics as Puritan child-rearing practices and child labor during the 1800s. Each group should assign a specific responsibility to each member in the group, such as research, writing, or graphic presentation. Have each group present its report to the rest of the class.

Use the rubric for a cooperative group management plan on pages 81–82 in the *Performance Assessment Activities and Rubrics.*

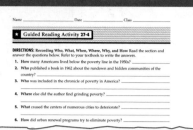
Picturing History

Answer: The government intended to raise their standard of living by integrating them into American society.

Ask: What was the termination policy? (It removed all official recognition of Native American groups as legal entities, making Native Americans subject to the same laws as white citizens.)

Predicting Consequences

Remind students that the life of the poor in the 1950s was very different from the life that middle-class Americans were enjoying. Have students discuss the differences that existed among the classes in the United States. Then ask students to predict the problems that were likely to result from these differences. **L2**

FYI

Lorraine Hansberry achieved another first on April 7, 1959, when she became the first African American, and only the fifth woman, to win the prestigious New York Drama Critics Circle Award for her first play, *A Raisin in the Sun.*

Poverty and racial discrimination also deprived many African Americans of other benefits, such as decent medical care. Responding to a correspondent who had seen *A Raisin in the Sun,* Lorraine Hansberry wrote, "The ghettos are killing us; not only our dreams . . . but our very bodies. It is not an abstraction to us that the average [African American] has a life expectancy of five to ten years less than the average white."

Several African American groups, such as the NAACP and the Congress of Racial Equality (CORE), pressed for greater economic opportunity for African Americans. In general, however, these organizations met with little success.

Hispanics African Americans were not the only minority group that struggled with poverty. Much of the nation's Hispanic population faced the same problems. During the 1940s and 1950s, the country witnessed a sharp rise in the number of Hispanic residents, as nearly 5 million Mexicans immigrated to the United States. They came to help fill the country's agricultural labor needs through what was known as the **Bracero program.**

These laborers, who worked on large farms throughout the country, lived a life of extreme poverty and hardship. They toiled long hours for little pay in conditions that were often unbearable. As Michael Harrington noted, "[The nation's migrant

Picturing History

Vocational Training Native American Franklin Beaver learns to become a stone mason at this vocational school sponsored by the U.S. Indian Bureau. Why was the government trying to bring Native Americans into mainstream society?

laborers] work ten-eleven-twelve hour days in temperatures over one hundred degrees. Sometimes there is no drinking water. . . . Women and children work on ladders and with hazardous machinery. Babies are brought to the field and are placed in 'cradles' of wood boxes."

Away from the fields, many Mexican families lived in small, crudely built shacks, while some did not even have a roof over their heads. "They sleep where they can, some in the open," Harrington noted about one group of migrant workers. "They eat when they can (and sometimes what they can)." The nation would pay little attention to the plight of Mexican farm laborers until the 1960s, when the workers began to organize for greater rights.

Native Americans Native Americans also faced challenges throughout the postwar era of prosperity. By the middle of the 1900s, Native Americans—who made up less than one percent of the population—were the poorest group in the nation. Average annual family income for Native American families, for example, was $1,000 less than that for African Americans.

After World War II, during which many Native American soldiers had served with distinction, the U.S. government launched a program to bring Native Americans into mainstream society—whether they wanted to assimilate or not. Under the plan, which became known as the termination policy, the federal government withdrew all official recognition of the Native American groups as legal entities and made them subject to the same laws as white citizens. At the same time, the government encouraged Native Americans to blend in to larger society by helping them move off the reservations to cities such as Minneapolis, Minnesota.

Although the idea of integrating Native Americans into mainstream society began with good intentions, some of its supporters had more selfish goals. Speculators and developers sometimes gained rich farmland at the expense of destitute Native American groups.

Most Native Americans found termination a disastrous policy that only deepened their poverty. In the mid-1950s, for example, the Welfare Council of Minneapolis described Native American living conditions in that city as miserable. "One Indian family of five or six, living in two rooms, will take in relatives and friends who come from the reservations seeking jobs until perhaps fifteen people will be crowded into the space," the council reported. During the 1950s, Native Americans in Minneapolis could expect to live only 37 years, compared to 46

MEETING SPECIAL NEEDS

Auditory/Musical Tell students that music has long been a way for people to express their emotions, whether they are joyful or sad. Challenge interested students to take the impressions that they have gained while reading the chapter to compose and perform a song expressing the plight of one of the ethnic groups mentioned in this section. **L3**

Refer to ***Inclusion for the High School Social Studies Classroom Strategies and Activities*** in the TCR.

Picturing **History**

Poverty in Appalachia This mining family lived in the kind of extreme poverty that was often overlooked in the 1950s. Eight people lived in this three-room house lined with newspaper. *Why was infant mortality so high in Appalachia?*

years for all Minnesota Native Americans and 68 years for other Minneapolis residents. Benjamin Reifel, a Sioux, described the widespread despair that the termination policy produced:

66 The Indians believed that when the dark clouds of war passed from the skies overhead, their rising tide of expectations, though temporarily stalled, would again reappear. Instead they were threatened by termination. . . . Soaring expectations began to plunge. Termination took on the connotation of extermination for many. 99

—quoted in *The Earth Shall Weep*

Appalachia The nation's minorities were not the only people dealing with poverty. The picturesque streams and mountains of Appalachia hid the ruined mines, scarred hills, and abandoned farms of impoverished families who had dwelled in these hills for generations.

During the 1950s, 1.5 million people abandoned Appalachia to seek a better life in the nation's cities. They left behind elderly and other less mobile residents. "Whole counties," wrote one reporter who visited the region, "are precariously held together by a

flour-and-dried-milk paste of surplus foods. . . . The men who are no longer needed in the mines and the farmers who cannot compete . . . have themselves become surplus commodities in the mountains."

A host of statistics spoke to Appalachia's misery. Studies revealed high rates of nutritional deficiency and infant mortality. Appalachia had fewer doctors per thousand people than the rest of the country, and the doctors it did have were older than their counterparts in other areas. In addition, schooling in the region was considered even worse than in inner city slums.

✓ **Reading Check** **Identifying** Which groups of people were left out of the country's economic boom of the 1950s?

Juvenile Delinquency

During the 1950s, many middle-class white Americans found it easy to ignore the poverty and racism that afflicted many of the nation's minorities, since they themselves were removed from it. Some social problems, however, became impossible to ignore.

One problem at this time was a rise in, or at least a rise in the reporting of, juvenile delinquency—antisocial or criminal behavior of young people. Between 1948 and 1953, the United States saw a 45 percent rise in juvenile crime rates. A popular 1954 book titled *1,000,000 Delinquents* correctly calculated that in the following year, about 1 million young people would get into some kind of criminal trouble. Car thefts topped the list of juvenile crimes, but people were

Picturing **History**

Answer: nutritional deficiencies, few doctors, and poor living conditions
Ask: Why do you think newspapers cover the walls in this house? *(to provide some insulation, to keep out cold drafts and insects)*

✓ **Reading Check**

Answer: African Americans, Hispanics, Native Americans, people in Appalachia

FYI

James Baldwin created a vivid description of African American life in the postwar years in his novel *Go Tell It on the Mountain*. The novel describes a day in the lives of members of a church in Harlem, and, through flashbacks, their ancestors. Baldwin was recognized as a leading African American novelist noted for his powerful treatment of bigotry and oppression in American society.

3 ASSESS

Assign Section 4 Assessment as homework or as an in-class activity.

⬤ Have students use the **Interactive Tutor Self-Assessment CD-ROM.**

Reading Essentials and Study Guide 27–4

Name _____ Date _____ Class _____

Study Guide

Chapter 27, Section 4
For use with textbook pages 828–832

THE OTHER SIDE OF AMERICAN LIFE

KEY TERMS AND NAMES

poverty line a figure the government set to reflect the minimum income required to support a family (page 828)

Michael Harrington author who wrote *The Other America*, which reported on poverty in the United States (page 829)

urban renewal type of program that tried to eliminate poverty by tearing down slums and building high-rise buildings for poor residents (page 829)

Bracero program a program that brought millions of Mexicans to the United States to help fill the nation's farm labor needs (page 830)

termination policy government plan that withdrew all official recognition of the Native

INTERDISCIPLINARY CONNECTIONS ACTIVITY

Performing Arts Organize students into small groups and have them discuss what life was like in the 1950s for one of the groups mentioned in this section. Have students produce a skit depicting one aspect of life for the group they selected. Encourage students to use appropriate music to set the tone for their skits. Make arrangements for students to perform for their classmates. **L2**

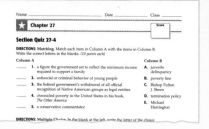
Discussing a Topic Have students discuss the causes of juvenile delinquency. Ask if they think the same conditions exist today. Explore the similarities and differences that they note. **L2**

✔ Reading Check

Answer: The educational system could not keep up with population growth and there was a lack of scientific and technical education.

Reteach

Identify those groups that found themselves left out of the American economic boom following World War II.

Enrich

Invite interested students to research the life of migrant workers today and compare today's situation to the situation in the 1950s.

4 CLOSE

Explain the factors that contributed to the poverty among various groups.

Rebelling Against Conformity This biker, one of the Louisville "Outlaws," fits the stereotype of the 1950s juvenile delinquent.

also alarmed at the behavior of young people who belonged to street gangs and committed muggings, rape, and even murder.

Americans could not agree on what had triggered the rise in delinquency. Experts blamed it on a host of reasons, including poverty, lack of religion, television, movies, comic books, racism, busy parents, a rising divorce rate, and anxiety over the military draft. Some cultural critics claimed that young people were rebelling against the hypocrisy and conformity of their parents. Conservative commentators pinned the blame on a lack of discipline. Doting parents, complained Bishop Fulton J. Sheen, had raised bored children who sought new thrills, such as "alcohol, marijuana, even murder." Liberal observers preferred to pinpoint social causes, blaming teen violence on poverty and feelings of hopelessness among underprivileged youths. Delinquency in the 1950s, however, cut across class and racial lines—the majority of car thieves, for example, had grown up in middle-class homes.

Most teens, of course, steered clear of gangs, drugs, and crime. Nonetheless, the public tended to stereotype young people as juvenile delinquents, especially those teens who favored unconventional clothing, long hair, or street slang.

Many parents were also growing concerned over the nation's educational system. As baby boomers began entering the school system, they ignited a spurt in school construction. During the 1950s, school enrollments increased by 13 million. School districts struggled to erect new buildings and hire new teachers. Nevertheless, shortages sprang up in both buildings and the people to staff them.

Americans' education worries only intensified in 1957 after the Soviet Union launched the world's first space satellites, *Sputnik I* and *Sputnik II*. Many Americans felt they had fallen behind their Cold War enemy and blamed what they felt was a lack of technical education in the nation's schools. *Life* magazine proclaimed a "Crisis in Education," and offered a grim warning: "What has long been an ignored national problem, *Sputnik* has made a recognized crisis." In the wake of the *Sputnik* launches, efforts began to improve math and science education in the schools. Profound fears about the country's young people, it seemed, dominated the end of a decade that had brought great progress for many Americans.

✔ Reading Check
Evaluating How did many Americans feel about the education system of the 1950s?

SECTION 4 ASSESSMENT

Checking for Understanding

1. **Define:** poverty line, urban renewal, termination policy, juvenile delinquency.
2. **Identify:** Michael Harrington, Bracero program.
3. **Evaluate** how the federal government's termination policy affected Native Americans.

Reviewing Themes

4. **Continuity and Change** Why did urban renewal fail the poor of the inner cities?

Critical Thinking

5. **Interpreting** What were some possible reasons for a dramatic rise in juvenile delinquency in the 1950s?
6. **Organizing** Use a graphic organizer similar to the one below to list the groups of Americans who were left out of the country's postwar economic boom.

Groups of Low-Income Americans

Analyzing Visuals

7. **Analyzing Photographs** Study the photograph on this page. What in the photograph might attract young people to this type of life? Why would others oppose such a life?

Writing About History

8. **Expository Writing** Using library or Internet resources, find information about juvenile delinquency in the United States today to write a report. Compare today's problems with those of the 1950s. Share your report with the class.

832 CHAPTER 27 Postwar America

SECTION 4 ASSESSMENT ANSWERS

1. Terms are in blue.
2. Michael Harrington (*p. 829*), Bracero program (*p. 830*)
3. The policy deepened their poverty.
4. The high-rise buildings were too crowded, destroyed more housing than they created, and created an atmosphere of violence.
5. Reasons offered included poverty, lack of supervision, media influences, racism, lack of discipline or of religion.
6. single mothers, elderly, minority immigrants, rural Americans, inner city residents, people in Appalachia
7. Shows a lone cyclist crossing a bridge, unconventional clothes, chance to rebel; many would oppose it because it suggests a rejection of many traditional values
8. Students' reports will vary but should define the problem of juvenile delinquency in the context of the changing times.

Writing a Journal

Why Learn This Skill?

Journal writing is personal writing with a casual style. The style in which you write is not as important as what you write about—your experiences, interests, and feelings. Journal writing can help you generate new ideas, and it can also give you a clearer picture of your thoughts and help you put them in order.

Learning the Skill

A journal is a written account that records what you have learned or experienced. In a journal you can express your feelings about a subject, summarize key topics, describe difficulties or successes in solving particular problems, and draw maps or other visuals. To help you get started writing in your journal, follow these steps.

• Jot down notes or questions about a specific topic or event as you read your textbook. Then look for details and answers about it as you continue reading.

• Describe your feelings as you read a selection or look at a photograph. Are you angry, happy, frustrated, or sad? Explain why you are reacting in this way.

• Ask yourself if drawing a map or flowchart would help you understand an event better. If so, draw in your journal.

Practicing the Skill

The following excerpt is a journal entry describing the launching of the nation's first satellite in 1958. Read the excerpt, and then use the following questions to help you write entries in your own journal.

"As the firing command neared, a deadly silence fell on those who were watching. . . . At fourteen and one-half seconds after time zero, after the priming fuel had ignited almost invisibly, the main stage engine came to life with an immeasurable thrust of flame in all directions. . . . With

thousands of eyes following it, the rocket dug into the night and accelerated as its sound loudened. Spectators on nearby beaches pointed and craned their necks and cried, 'There it is!' and began to cheer."

❶ What is particularly interesting about this description?

❷ What are your feelings as you read the excerpt?

❸ Note the descriptive phrases and details that make the event come to life. Try to use similar techniques when writing in your journal.

❹ Draw a map or other visual to help you understand the situation described here.

Cover from a World War II journal

Skills Assessment

Complete the Practicing Skills questions on page 835 and the Chapter 27 Skill Reinforcement Activity to assess your mastery of this skill.

Applying the Skill

Writing a Journal Imagine that you have had the chance to take part in a great adventure—for instance, serving in the armed forces during a war overseas or participating in a spaceflight. Make notes for a journal entry describing what you have done and seen.

 GO TO Glencoe's **Skillbuilder Interactive Workbook CD-ROM, Level 2,** provides instruction and practice in key social studies skills.

TEACH

Journal Writing Tell students that journal writing can help with generating ideas, with placing events or reactions in context, and with being able to put their thoughts in order.

Encourage students to keep a journal about their lives and experiences for a week. Ask volunteers to share one thing that they learned about themselves or their experiences in the process.

Additional Practice

Reinforcing Skills Activity 27

Name _____ Date _____ Class _____

★ **Reinforcing Skills Activity 27**

Writing a Journal

☐ **LEARNING THE SKILL**

Journals contain personal accounts, feelings, and reflections on experiences. Writing in a journal can help you express your thoughts, gain understanding, and think creatively. A journal might include maps or other visuals, as well as personal writing. To write a journal entry in response to your reading, begin by writing questions or thoughts about the subject matter, and then look for answers or related material as you read. Describe your reactions and feelings as you read. Consider drawing visuals such as a flowchart to help you understand the material better.

☐ **PRACTICING THE SKILL**

DIRECTIONS: Read the excerpt below from Robert Friedman's "The Baby Boom Turns 50." On a separate sheet of paper, use the questions that follow to help you write journal entries in response to the reading.

GLENCOE TECHNOLOGY

CD-ROM
Glencoe Skillbuilder Interactive Workbook CD-ROM, Level 2

This interactive CD-ROM reinforces student mastery of essential social studies skills.

ANSWERS TO PRACTICING THE SKILL

Possible answers:

❶ the precision and moment-by-moment quality of the description

❷ suspense, excitement

❸ Answers will vary.

❹ Visual representations will vary. Have students share them with the class.

Applying the Skill
Journal entries will vary. Encourage students to use the techniques learned in this Skillbuilder activity.

CHAPTER 27
ASSESSMENT and ACTIVITIES

Reviewing Key Terms

Students' answers will vary. The pages where the words appear in the text are shown in parentheses.

1. **closed shop** (p. 809)
2. **right-to-work law** (p. 809)
3. **union shop** (p. 809)
4. **featherbedding** (p. 809)
5. **dynamic conservatism** (p. 811)
6. **white-collar** (p. 815)
7. **blue-collar** (p. 815)
8. **multinational corporation** (p. 815)
9. **franchise** (p. 815)
10. **baby boom** (p. 816)
11. **generation gap** (p. 824)
12. **poverty line** (p. 828)
13. **urban renewal** (p. 829)
14. **termination policy** (p. 830)
15. **juvenile delinquency** (p. 831)

Reviewing Key Facts

16. GI Bill (p. 809), Fair Deal (p. 810), John Kenneth Galbraith (p. 814), David Riesman (p. 815), Ed Sullivan (p. 821), Alan Freed (p. 823), Elvis Presley (p. 823), Jack Kerouac (p. 824), Michael Harrington (p. 829)

17. The three characteristics of the postwar economy were abundant goods, low unemployment, and a housing boom.

18. The economic boom was the result of consumerism and the GI Bill.

19. They wanted to escape urban crime and make a better life for their families. They had automobiles to transport them to and from work.

Reviewing Key Terms

On a sheet of paper, use each of these terms in a sentence.

1. closed shop
2. right-to-work law
3. union shop
4. featherbedding
5. dynamic conservatism
6. white-collar
7. blue-collar
8. multinational corporation
9. franchise
10. baby boom
11. generation gap
12. poverty line
13. urban renewal
14. termination policy
15. juvenile delinquency

Reviewing Key Facts

16. **Identify:** GI Bill, Fair Deal, John Kenneth Galbraith, David Riesman, Ed Sullivan, Alan Freed, Elvis Presley, Jack Kerouac, Michael Harrington.

17. What were three characteristics of the economy of the United States after World War II?

18. What were two reasons for the economic boom of the 1950s?

19. What caused many Americans to move to the suburbs in the 1950s?

20. How did the scientific discovery of the transistor affect communications?

21. Which groups of Americans found themselves left out of the postwar economic boom?

Critical Thinking

22. **Analyzing Themes: Continuity and Change** How has mass media changed since the 1950s?

23. **Evaluating** What factors led to a rise in juvenile delinquency in the United States during the 1950s?

24. **Comparing and Contrasting** Harry S Truman was a Democrat, and Dwight D. Eisenhower was a Republican. How were the domestic agendas of these two presidents different? How were they similar?

25. **Interpreting Primary Sources** George Gallup, one of the nation's first pollsters, spoke at the University of Iowa in 1953 about the importance of mass media in the United States. Read the excerpt and answer the questions that follow.

❝One of the real threats to America's future place in the world is a citizenry which duly elects to be entertained and not informed. From the time the typical citizen arises and looks at his morning newspaper until he turns off his radio or television set before going to bed,

Chapter Summary

	Signs of Prosperity	**Signs of Inequality**
Economy	• The GI Bill provided loans to millions of war veterans. • Consumer spending increased rapidly. • More Americans owned homes than ever before.	• Workers went on strike for higher wages. • Truman's civil rights bill did not pass. • Eisenhower cut back New Deal programs.
Population Patterns	• The U.S. population grew dramatically. • The number of working women increased.	• Financially able people moved from crowded cities to new suburbs. • Many poor people remained in cities that now faced major economic and social problems.
Science, Technology, and Medicine	• Medical breakthroughs included the polio vaccine, antibiotics, and treatments for heart disease, arthritis, cancer, and diabetes. • Improvements in communication, transportation, and electronics allowed Americans to work more efficiently.	• Many poor people in inner cities and rural areas had limited access to health care.
Popular Culture	• Popular culture included new forms of music, radio, cinema, and literature. • Television replaced radio as the nation's newest form of mass media.	• African Americans and other minorities were, for the most part, not depicted on television. • Many television programs promoted stereotypical gender roles.

20. The transistor made the miniaturization of radios and calculators possible and resulted in improvements in communication and transportation.

21. Single mothers, the elderly, minority immigrants, rural Americans, inner-city residents, African Americans, Hispanics, Native Americans, and people in Appalachia were left out of the postwar economic boom.

Critical Thinking

22. Mass media has become more pervasive. Hundreds of radio and television stations, as well as the Internet, are available 24 hours a day, 7 days a week.

23. Different reasons were suggested, including poverty, lack of supervision, media influences, racism, lack of discipline or of religion.

HISTORY Online

Self-Check Quiz

Visit the *American Vision* Web site at tav.glencoe.com and click on *Self-Check Quizzes—Chapter 27* to assess your knowledge of chapter content.

he has unwittingly cast his vote a hundred times for entertainment or for education. Without his knowing it, he has helped to determine the very character of our three most important media of communication—the press, radio, and television. . . .**99**

—quoted in *Vital Speeches of the Day*

a. According to Gallup, what is a threat to the future of the United States in the world?

b. How do American citizens determine what is read, seen, and heard in the mass media?

26. **Organizing** Use a graphic organizer similar to the one below to list the changes to the American family during the 1950s.

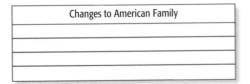

Changes to American Family

Practicing Skills

27. **Writing a Journal** Imagine that you are Dr. Jonas Salk, and you realize that you have just discovered the world's first successful polio vaccine. Write a journal entry that describes how you feel about this accomplishment and what impact it will have on the world.

Writing Activity

28. **Writing a Book Report** Read one of the books about American society in the 1950s, such as *Why Johnny Can't Read* or *The Other America*. Write a book report explaining the main concepts of the book and whether or not the issues are similar to or different from the main issues in American society today.

Chapter Activities

29. **American History Primary Source Document Library CD-ROM** Read the speech "On Television" by Newton Minow, under *The Postwar World*. Working with a few of your classmates, evaluate whether television has improved since Minow's critical assessment. Has television content changed since the 1950s? If so, how? Present your findings and comparisons to your class.

Suburban Dwellers, 1910–1980

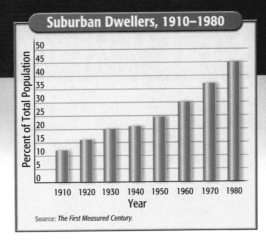

Source: *The First Measured Century.*

30. **Research Project** Work with a small group to research advertisements from the 1950s. Write a report comparing and contrasting advertisements from that decade with advertisements today. Present one or more of the advertisements along with your comparisons to your class.

Geography and History

31. The graph above shows the number of suburban dwellers in the United States as a percentage of the total population. Study the data displayed in the graph and answer the questions below.

a. Interpreting Graphs What trend in the percentage of suburban dwellers does this graph show?

b. Understanding Cause and Effect How might the trend of suburban dwellers shown on this graph have affected life in suburbs and cities?

 Standardized Test Practice

Directions: Choose the phrase that best completes the following statement.

The Eisenhower administration worked to achieve all of the following EXCEPT

F ending wage and price controls.

G winning passage for the Federal Highway Act.

H repealing right-to-work laws.

J extending the Social Security system.

Test-Taking Tip: Pay careful attention to the wording of the question. Note here that *EXCEPT* means that three of the four choices were part of Eisenhower's programs.

HISTORY Online

Have students visit the Web site at tav.glencoe.com to review Chapter 27 and take the Self-Check Quiz.

Writing Activity

28. Students' reports will vary. Be sure students include some comparison to problems in society today.

Chapter Activities

29. Students' findings should point out differences and similarities in content. Their assessments of television should reflect a critical look at available programs.

30. Students' comparisons will vary. Encourage students to share their findings with the class.

Geography and History

31. **a.** rising; **b.** caused urban life to decline and suburban life to become the ideal

 Standardized Test Practice

Answer: H
Test-Taking Tip: Encourage students to consider the goals of dynamic conservatism. **Ask:** Which answers are most consistent with those goals? Tell students they can eliminate those answers.

Bonus Question ?

Ask: What does the term *Baby Boom* refer to? *(a 16-year period from 1945 to 1961 when 65 million children were born in the United States)*

---

24. Differences: Truman's policies included aggressive federal spending, the creation of public housing, and a system of national health insurance. Eisenhower's policies included curbing federal spending, ending government price and rent controls, and cutting aid to public housing and businesses. Similarities: Both presidents expanded Social Security and raised the minimum wage.

25. **a.** He feared a citizenry that chose to be entertained and not informed. **b.** They do it by the choices they make in forms of entertainment.

26. the move to suburbs, travel by automobile, growing gap between generations

Practicing Skills

27. Journal entries should reflect what the students know about Salk, such as the fact that he preferred research to celebrity.

Unit 9 Resources

SUGGESTED PACING CHART

Unit 9 (1 Day)	Chapter 28 (4 Days)	Chapter 29 (4 Days)	Chapter 30 (5 Days)	Chapter 31 (5 Days)	Unit 9 (2 Days)
Day 1 Introduction	**Day 1** Chapter 28 Intro, Section 1 **Day 2** Section 2 **Day 3** Section 3 **Day 4** Chapter 28 Assessment	**Day 1** Chapter 29 Intro, Section 1 **Day 2** Section 2 **Day 3** Section 3 **Day 4** Chapter 29 Assessment	**Day 1** Chapter 30 Intro, Section 1 **Day 2** Section 2 **Day 3** Section 3 **Day 4** Section 4 **Day 5** Chapter 30 Assessment	**Day 1** Chapter 31 Intro, Section 1 **Day 2** Section 2 **Day 3** Section 3 **Day 4** Section 4 **Day 5** Chapter 31 Assessment	**Day 1** Wrap-Up/Project **Day 2** Unit 9 Assessment

GLENCOE'S ASSESSMENT ADVANTAGE

Use the following tools to easily assess student learning in a variety of ways:

- Performance Assessment Activities and Rubrics
- Chapter and Unit Tests
- Section Quizzes
- Standardized Test Skills Practice Workbook

- tav.glencoe.com
- Interactive Tutor Self-Assessment CD-ROM
- MindJogger Videoquiz
- ExamView® Pro Testmaker CD-ROM
- SAT I/II Test Practice

TEACHING TRANSPARENCIES

Unit 9 Map Overlay Transparencies

Cause-and-Effect Transparency 9

*inter*NET RESOURCES

- tav.glencoe.com

The American Vision
Visit the *American Vision* Web site for history overviews, activities, assessments, and updated charts and graphs.
- www.socialstudies.glencoe.com

Glencoe Social Studies
Visit the Glencoe Web site for social studies activities, updates, and links to other sites.
- www.teachingtoday.glencoe.com

Glencoe Teaching Today
Visit the new Glencoe Web site for teacher development information, teaching tips, Web resources, and educational news.
- www.time.com

TIME Online
Visit the TIME Web site for up-to-date news and special reports.

Unit 9 Resources

ASSESSMENT

Unit 9 Pretests

Unit 9 Posttests

APPLICATION AND ENRICHMENT

American Biography 9

History Simulation and Problem Solving 9

GEOGRAPHY

Geography and History Activity 9

INTERDISCIPLINARY ACTIVITIES

American Literature Reading 9

Economics and History Activity 9

Team-Teaching Interdisciplinary Strategies and Activities 9

BIBLIOGRAPHY

Readings for the Student

Sturkey, Marion F. *Bonnie-Sue: A Marine Corps Helicopter Squadron in Vietnam.* Heritage Press International, 2000.

Readings for the Teacher

Polsgrove, Carol. *Divided Minds: Intellectuals and the Civil Rights Movement.* W.W. Norton & Company, 2001.

Multimedia Resources

Videocassette. *America and the World Since World War II, 1961–1975, Volume III.* ABC News. (52 minutes)

Additional Glencoe Resources for This Unit:

- Glencoe Skillbuilder Interactive Workbook CD-ROM, Level 2
- Social Studies Guide to Using the Internet
- Writer's Guidebook for High School
- Living Constitution
- American Art Prints Strategies and Activities

0:00 Out of Time?

If time does not permit teaching each chapter in this unit, you may want to use the **Reading Essentials and Study Guide** summaries.

Unit Overview

Unit 9 describes the upheavals that occurred from 1954 to 1980. **Chapter 28** explores the New Frontier and the Great Society. **Chapter 29** focuses on the civil rights movement. **Chapter 30** explores the Vietnam War. **Chapter 31** discusses the politics of protest.

Unit Objectives

After studying this unit, students will be able to:

1. Summarize Kennedy's economic policies.
2. Discuss the changing role of the federal government in civil rights enforcement.
3. Describe how President Johnson deepened American involvement in Vietnam.
4. Describe the workplace concerns that fueled the growth of the women's movement.

Why It Matters Activity

Have students interview someone who was growing up or an adult in the late 1960s and the 1970s. Interviews should center around finding out how this era influenced the United States today. Students should prepare a transcript of the interview. Ask for volunteers to share insightful portions of their transcripts as you discuss the importance of this era to life in America today.

UNIT 9
A Time of Upheaval 1954–1980

Why It Matters

From a presidential assassination to massive governmental programs, from the Vietnam War to the civil rights movement, the post–World War II decades immensely affected the lives of Americans. The nation struggled to put its social and political ideals into practice while fighting military wars overseas and social wars at home. Understanding how these events unfolded provides a window to the world you live in today. The following resources offer more information about this period in American history.

Primary Sources Library

See pages 1056–1057 to find additional primary source readings to accompany Unit 9.

Use the **American History Primary Source Document Library CD-ROM** to find additional primary sources about this eventful era.

Poster from the March on Washington

Mural on building in Davenport, Iowa

836

TEAM TEACHING ACTIVITY

Music Have the music teacher share classic examples of the protest music that was popular in the 1960s and 1970s. Have students examine the lyrics and pose questions to the teacher about what particular phrases mean. Have students compile a database of the new words they learn, along with their meanings. Encourage students to add to this database as they study this unit.

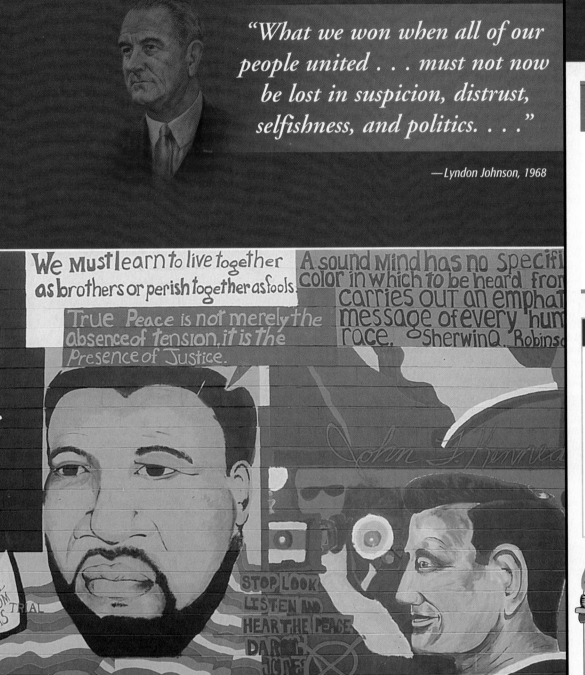

"What we won when all of our people united . . . must not now be lost in suspicion, distrust, selfishness, and politics. . . ."

— Lyndon Johnson, 1968

We Must learn to live together as brothers or perish together as fools.

True Peace is not merely the absence of tension, it is the Presence of Justice.

A sound Mind has no specifi color in which to be heard fror carries out an emphati message of every 'hum race. Sherwin Q. Robins

STOP LOOK
LISTEN AND
HEAR THE PEACE

NELSON MANDELA

GLENCOE
TECHNOLOGY

CD-ROM
American History Primary Source Document Library CD-ROM

Use the **American History Primary Source Document Library CD-ROM** to access primary source documents related to this period in history.

More About the Photo

The social movements of the late 1960s and the 1970s encouraged many artists to paint murals on buildings, usually in inner-city neighborhoods and near freeways. African Americans and Hispanics created many of the murals that can be seen in cities across the nation. With several thousand murals on city walls, Los Angeles may be the "mural capital" of the United States.

Glencoe Literature Library

The following novel from the *High School American History Literature Library* may be used to enrich the study of this unit:
• *And the Earth Did Not Devour Him* by Tomás Rivera

SERVICE-LEARNING PROJECT

Tell students that many Vietnam War veterans felt abandoned by American society. Unlike veterans of other wars, many Vietnam veterans did not return to a heroes' welcome. They often took protests about the war to mean that their country did not value their sacrifices or that they had done something wrong by serving. Have the class prepare a display honoring the Vietnam veterans living in the local community. Arrange to have the display exhibited in a public location for the community to enjoy.

Refer to **Building Bridges: Connecting Classroom and Community through Service-Learning in Social Studies** from the National Council for the Social Studies for information about service-learning.

Timesaving Tools

TeacherWorks™ All-In-One Planner and Resource Center

- **Interactive Teacher Edition** Access your Teacher Wraparound Edition and your classroom resources with a few easy clicks.
- **Interactive Lesson Planner** Planning has never been easier! Organize your week, month, semester, or year with all the lesson helps you need to make teaching creative, timely, and relevant.

Use Glencoe's **Presentation Plus!** multimedia teacher tool to easily present dynamic lessons that visually excite your students. Using Microsoft PowerPoint® you can customize the presentations to create your own personalized lessons.

TEACHING TRANSPARENCIES

Graphic Organizer 8

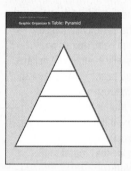

Why It Matters Chapter Transparency 28

APPLICATION AND ENRICHMENT

Linking Past and Present Activity 28

Enrichment Activity 28

Primary Source Reading 28

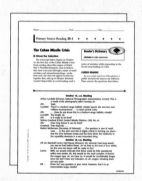

REVIEW AND REINFORCEMENT

Reteaching Activity 28

Vocabulary Activity 28

Time Line Activity 28

Critical Thinking Skills Activity 28

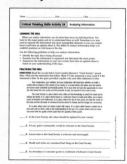

Meeting NCSS Standards

The following standards are highlighted in Chapter 28:

Section 1	X	Civic Ideals and Practices: A, C, F
Section 2	VIII	Science, Technology, and Society: A, B, C
Section 3	VI	Power, Authority, and Governance: A, B, C, H, I

Local Standards

_____

_____

_____

_____

_____

ASSESSMENT AND EVALUATION

GLENCOE'S
ASSESSMENT
ADVANTAGE

**Chapter 28 Test
Form A**

**Chapter 28 Test
Form B**

**Standardized Test Skills
Practice Workbook Activity 28**

**Performance Assessment
Activities and Rubrics 28**

**ExamView® Pro
Testmaker CD-ROM**

EXAMVIEW® PRO
Testmaker CD-ROM

WINDOWS/MACINTOSH

The American Vision

• QuickTest Wizard does all the work for you
• Choose ExamView tests or create your own
• Complete editing capability

MULTIMEDIA

- Vocabulary PuzzleMaker CD-ROM
- Interactive Tutor Self-Assessment CD-ROM
- ExamView® Pro Testmaker CD-ROM
- Audio Program
- American History Primary Source Documents Library CD-ROM
- MindJogger Videoquiz
- Presentation Plus! CD-ROM
- TeacherWorks™ CD-ROM
- Interactive Student Edition CD-ROM
- Glencoe Skillbuilder Interactive Workbook CD-ROM, Level 2
- The *American Vision* Video Program
- American Music: Hits Through History
- American Music: Cultural Traditions

SPANISH RESOURCES

The following Spanish language materials are available in the Spanish Resources Binder:

- Spanish Guided Reading Activities
- Spanish Reteaching Activities
- Spanish Quizzes and Tests
- Spanish Vocabulary Activities
- Spanish Summaries
- The Declaration of Independence and United States Constitution Spanish Translation

HISTORY Online

Use our Web site for additional resources. All essential content is covered in the Student Edition.

You and your students can visit tav.glencoe.com, the Web site companion to the *American Vision.* This innovative integration of electronic and print media offers your students a wealth of opportunities. The student text directs students to the Web site for the following options:

- **Chapter Overviews**
- **Self-Check Quizzes**
- **Student Web Activities**
- **Textbook Updates**

Answers to the student Web activities are provided for you in the **Web Activity Lesson Plans.** Additional Web resources and Interactive Tutor Puzzles are also available.

THE HISTORY CHANNEL®

The following videotape programs are available from Glencoe as supplements to Chapter 28:

- **John F. Kennedy: A Personal Story** (ISBN 0-76-700010-2)
- **Lyndon Johnson: Triumph and Tragedy** (ISBN 0-76-700109-5)
- **Bay of Pigs Cuban Missile Crisis** (ISBN 0-76-701199-6)
- **Malcolm X: A Search for Identity** (ISBN 1-56-501674-2)

To order, call Glencoe at 1-800-334-7344. To find classroom resources to accompany many of these videos, check the following home pages:
A&E Television: www.aande.com
The History Channel: www.historychannel.com

Chapter 28 Resources

SECTION RESOURCES

Daily Objectives	Reproducible Resources	Multimedia Resources
SECTION 1 **The New Frontier** 1. Summarize Kennedy's economic policies. 2. Explain why Congress often did not support Kennedy's proposals.	Reproducible Lesson Plan 28–1 Daily Lecture and Discussion Notes 28–1 Guided Reading Activity 28–1* Section Quiz 28–1* Reading Essentials and Study Guide 28–1 Performance Assessment Activities and Rubrics Supreme Court Case Studies	Daily Focus Skills Transparency 28–1 Interactive Tutor Self-Assessment CD-ROM ExamView® Pro Testmaker CD-ROM Presentation Plus! CD-ROM TeacherWorks™ CD-ROM Audio Program
SECTION 2 **JFK and the Cold War** 1. Describe Kennedy's plan for the armed forces. 2. Explain how the Cold War influenced foreign aid and the space program.	Reproducible Lesson Plan 28–2 Daily Lecture and Discussion Notes 28–2 Guided Reading Activity 28–2* Section Quiz 28–2* Reading Essentials and Study Guide 28–2 Performance Assessment Activities and Rubrics Interpreting Political Cartoons	Daily Focus Skills Transparency 28–2 Interactive Tutor Self-Assessment CD-ROM ExamView® Pro Testmaker CD-ROM Presentation Plus! CD-ROM TeacherWorks™ CD-ROM Audio Program
SECTION 3 **The Great Society** 1. Explain what inspired Johnson's Great Society programs. 2. Identify several specific health and employment programs of the Johnson administration.	Reproducible Lesson Plan 28–3 Daily Lecture and Discussion Notes 28–3 Guided Reading Activity 28–3* Section Quiz 28–3* Reading Essentials and Study Guide 28–3 Performance Assessment Activities and Rubrics	Daily Focus Skills Transparency 28–3 Interactive Tutor Self-Assessment CD-ROM ExamView® Pro Testmaker CD-ROM Presentation Plus! CD-ROM Skillbuilder Interactive Workbook, Level 2 TeacherWorks™ CD-ROM Vocabulary PuzzleMaker CD-ROM Audio Program

`0:00` OUT OF TIME?
Assign the Chapter 28 **Reading Essentials and Study Guide.**

*Also Available in Spanish

 Blackline Master   Transparency   CD-ROM   DVD

Poster Music Program 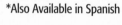 Audio Program Videocassette

NATIONAL GEOGRAPHIC Teacher's Corner

INDEX TO NATIONAL GEOGRAPHIC MAGAZINE

The following articles relate to this chapter.

- "I Dream a World: America's Black Women," August 1989
- "National Trail to Recall Civil Rights Marches," March 1994
- "Philadelphia's African Americans," August 1990
- "Selma to Montgomery: The Road to Equality," February 2000

NATIONAL GEOGRAPHIC SOCIETY PRODUCTS AVAILABLE FROM GLENCOE

To order the following products for use with this chapter, contact your local Glencoe sales representative, or call Glencoe at 1-800-334-7344:

- *PictureShow: Civil Rights* (CD-ROM)
- *PicturePack: Civil Rights* (Transparencies)

ADDITIONAL NATIONAL GEOGRAPHIC SOCIETY PRODUCTS

To order the following, call National Geographic at 1-800-368-2728:

- *NGS PictureShow: Civil Rights* (CD-ROM, Transparencies)

NGS ONLINE

Access National Geographic's Web site for current events, atlas updates, activities, links, interactive features, and archives.
www.nationalgeographic.com

From the Classroom of...

Joe Naumann
Ferguson-Florissant
School District
St. Louis, MO

**U.S. Foreign Policy:
Cold War Map and Time Line**

Select 10 to 15 events that the U.S. reacted to or was involved in during the Cold War. Give students the list of events and a blank map of the world or a part of the world if the events relate to only one region. If students' map skills are weak, draw arrows to the places on the map and have the students write the place-names next to the appropriate arrows. If you do not supply the dates of the events, students could research that information.

Tell the students to arrange the list of events on a time line, allowing students to see the geographical dimensions of the events as well as the sequence of events.

Consider expanding the project with a written assignment where students explain the connections among events or why the United States got involved in some places while choosing not to get involved in others at that time.

ADDITIONAL RESOURCES FROM GLENCOE

- American Music: Cultural Traditions
- American Art & Architecture
- Outline Map Resource Book
- U.S. Desk Map
- Building Geography Skills for Life
- Inclusion for the High School Social Studies Classroom Strategies and Activities
- Teaching Strategies for the American History Classroom (Including Block Scheduling Pacing Guides)

KEY TO ABILITY LEVELS

Teaching strategies have been coded.

L1 BASIC activities for all students
L2 AVERAGE activities for average to above-average students
L3 CHALLENGING activities for above-average students
ELL ENGLISH LANGUAGE LEARNER activities

 **Block Schedule**

Activities that are suited to use within the block scheduling framework are identified by:

Why It Matters Activity

Contact your local Social Security Administration office to obtain brochures describing the Medicaid and Medicare programs and benefits. Have students review these brochures and provide a brief overview of these programs. Ask students why they think these programs were instituted. Students should evaluate their answers after they have completed the chapter.

GLENCOE **TECHNOLOGY**

The *American Vision* Video Program

To learn more about the American space program, have students view the Chapter 28 video, "A New Frontier: The Space Race," from the *American Vision* Video Program.

 Available in DVD and VHS

MindJogger Videoquiz

Use the **MindJogger Videoquiz** to preview Chapter 28 content.

📼 Available in VHS

CHAPTER

28 The New Frontier and the Great Society
1961–1968

Why It Matters

President John F. Kennedy urged Americans to work for progress and to stand firm against the Soviets. Cold War tensions and the threat of nuclear war peaked during the Cuban missile crisis. Kennedy's assassination changed the nation's mood, but President Lyndon Johnson embraced ambitious goals, including working toward the passage of major civil rights legislation and eradicating poverty.

The Impact Today

Initiatives introduced in this era remain a part of American society.
• Medicaid and Medicare legislation provides major health benefits for elderly and low-income people.
• The Head Start program provides early educational opportunities for disadvantaged children.

The American Vision Video The Chapter 28 video, "A New Frontier: The Space Race," explores the dramatic history of the American space program.

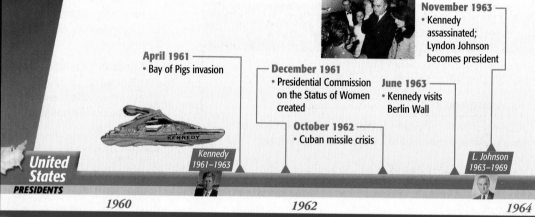

April 1961
• Bay of Pigs invasion

December 1961
• Presidential Commission on the Status of Women created

October 1962
• Cuban missile crisis

June 1963
• Kennedy visits Berlin Wall

November 1963
• Kennedy assassinated; Lyndon Johnson becomes president

United States
PRESIDENTS

Kennedy 1961–1963

L. Johnson 1963–1969

1960   *1962*   *1964*

World

1959
• Cuban revolution brings Castro to power

April 1961
• Eichmann goes on trial for crimes against Jews

August 1961
• Construction of Berlin Wall begins

1964
• South Africa's Nelson Mandela sentenced to life in prison

838

TWO-MINUTE LESSON LAUNCHER

Read aloud the following excerpt from President Kennedy's Inaugural Address: "Let the word go forth from this time and place, to friend and foe alike, that the torch has been passed to a new generation of Americans born in this century, tempered by war, disciplined by a cold and bitter peace." Ask students to identify who the nation's foes were at this time (*primarily the Soviet Union*), what war had influenced this generation (*World War II*), and what the "cold and bitter peace" referred to (*the Cold War*).

HISTORY
Online

Introduce students to chapter content and key terms by having them access the **Chapter 28 Overview** at tav.glencoe.com.

More About the Photo

Tell students that to many Americans and people around the world, John and Jacqueline Kennedy represented a complete change in American politics. The charismatic Kennedy was young and energetic, and he was the first Catholic to be elected president. Ask students what other qualities attracted people to the Kennedys.

President John F. Kennedy at his inaugural ball in 1961

TIME LINE ACTIVITY

Ask students to select one of the items on the United States time line to learn more about. Have students write one paragraph summarizing the event. Invite students to share their paragraphs with the class.

July 1965
- Congress establishes Medicare and Medicaid programs

October 1966
- Fair Packaging and Labeling Act passed

March 1968
- Lyndon Johnson announces that he will not run for re-election

1966

1968

1966
- Indira Gandhi becomes prime minister of India

1968
- Student riots paralyze France

HISTORY
Online

Chapter Overview
Visit the *American Vision* Web site at tav.glencoe.com and click on *Chapter Overviews—Chapter 28* to preview chapter information.

839

GRAPHIC ORGANIZER ACTIVITY

Organizing Information Have students identify the important legislation and government programs passed during the Kennedy and Johnson administrations by completing a graphic organizer similar to the one below.

Legislation and Government Programs	
Kennedy	**Johnson**
increase in minimum wage	*Economic Opportunity Act*
Area Redevelopment Act	*VISTA*
Housing Act	*Medicare and Medicaid*

1 FOCUS

Section Overview
This section focuses on the domestic aspects of the Kennedy administration.

BELLRINGER
Skillbuilder Activity

 Project transparency and have students answer the question.

📂 Available as a blackline master.

Daily Focus Skills Transparency 28–1

Guide to Reading

Answers to Graphic: Successes: more funds in defense and space exploration, some advance in women's rights, economic improvement; Setbacks: health insurance for the elderly, a Department of Urban Affairs, federal aid to education, aid for migrant workers

Preteaching Vocabulary
Have students define the Key Terms in their own words.

Guide to Reading

Main Idea
John F. Kennedy encountered both success and setbacks on the domestic front.

Key Terms and Names
missile gap, New Frontier, Earl Warren, reapportionment, due process

Reading Strategy
Categorizing As you read about the presidency of John F. Kennedy, complete a graphic organizer similar to the one below by filling in the domestic successes and setbacks of Kennedy's administration.

Successes	Setbacks

Reading Objectives
- **Summarize** Kennedy's economic policies.
- **Explain** why Congress often did not support Kennedy's proposals.

Section Theme
Civic Rights and Responsibilities The Supreme Court made decisions that protected individual rights, including the "one man, one vote" decision.

Preview of Events

♦1960   ♦1961   ♦1962   ♦1963

1960 — John Kennedy defeats Richard Nixon for the presidency

1961 — Kennedy creates Presidential Commission on the Status of Women

1962 — Supreme Court issues *Baker* v. *Carr* ruling

1963 — Kennedy signs Equal Pay Act for women

★ An American Story ★

John F. Kennedy and Richard Nixon in the 1960 debate

On September 26, 1960, at 9:30 P.M. eastern standard time, streets all across the United States grew strangely still. An estimated 75 million people sat indoors, focused on their television sets, where they saw two men standing behind lecterns. One was John F. Kennedy, and the other was Richard M. Nixon.

For the first time, thanks to the wonders of television, two presidential candidates were coming right into the nation's living rooms to debate. Americans were enthralled: "You hear each man directly," observed one. "There's nothing between you and what he says," added another. "You can see which man gets rattled easily."

The man who seemed to get rattled easily was Nixon. Kennedy, the Democratic nominee, looked healthy, strong, and confident. Nixon, the Republicans' choice, came across as tired and frazzled. "He appeared ill," one viewer commented. In fact, Nixon had been ill recently. Kennedy had a glowing tan, while Nixon's face was pale and drawn, shadowed by the stubble of a beard. As one observer noted, "Nixon's eyes darted around, perspiration was clearly noticeable on his chin, and with the tight shots . . . these things were more obvious."

—adapted from *The Great Debate*

The Election of 1960

The television debates of the 1960 presidential election had enormous impact. Following the first debate, the media focused more strongly on the appearance of the candidates. Suddenly the whole country seemed to have become experts on makeup and

---

SECTION RESOURCES

📂 **Reproducible Masters**
- Reproducible Lesson Plan 28–1
- Daily Lecture and Discussion Notes 28–1
- Guided Reading Activity 28–1
- Section Quiz 28–1
- Reading Essentials and Study Guide 28–1
- Performance Assessment Activities and Rubrics
- Supreme Court Case Studies

Transparencies
- Daily Focus Skills Transparency 28–1

Multimedia
- Interactive Tutor Self-Assessment CD-ROM
- ExamView® Pro Testmaker CD-ROM
- Presentation Plus! CD-ROM
- TeacherWorks™ CD-ROM
- Audio Program

television lighting. One Republican leader even wondered if the Democrats had supplied Nixon's makeup.

With that debate, the era of television politics had begun. Though television had been used in campaigns as early as 1948, it was not until the 1960 election that a large majority of voters used the medium as a voting tool. The nation itself seemed on the brink of a new age. Having lived through a decade of unprecedented prosperity and the onset of the Cold War and the atomic age, Americans looked to the future with excitement and anxiety.

Both candidates shared the desire to lead the nation through the challenges of a new decade, but they differed in many ways. Kennedy, a Catholic, came from a wealthy and influential Massachusetts family. Nixon, a Quaker, was a Californian from a financially struggling family. Kennedy seemed outgoing and relaxed, while Nixon struck many as formal and even stiff in manner.

A New Kind of Campaign Compared to earlier campaigns, the 1960 presidential race made new use of television, with both major parties spending substantial amounts of money on television ads. The Democrats spent over $6 million in television and radio spots, while the Republicans spent more than $7.5 million.

Not everyone was happy with this new emphasis on image. Television news commentator Eric Sevareid complained that the candidates had become "packaged products," and he stated that "the Processed Politician has finally arrived."

The Main Issues The campaign centered on the economy and the Cold War. Although the candidates presented different styles, they differed little on these two issues. Both promised to boost the economy, and both portrayed themselves as "Cold Warriors" determined to stop the forces of communism.

Kennedy argued that the nation faced serious threats from the Soviets. In Cuba, Fidel Castro was allying himself with the Soviet Union. At home, many people lived in fear of a Soviet nuclear attack. Kennedy voiced his concern about a suspected "missile gap," in which the United States lagged behind the Soviets in weaponry. (Decades later, Americans learned that, in fact, the only area where the Soviet Union was briefly ahead was in rocketry). The nation, Kennedy argued, had grown complacent and aimless. "It is time to get this country moving again."

Nixon countered that the United States was on the right track under the current administration. "I'm tired of hearing our opponents downgrade the United States," the vice president said. Nixon also warned that the Democrats' fiscal policies would boost inflation, and that only he had the necessary foreign policy experience to guide the nation.

Kennedy came under scrutiny about his religion. The United States had never had a Catholic president, and many Protestants had concerns about Kennedy. Kennedy decided to confront this issue openly in a speech. "I believe in an America where the separation of the church and state is absolute," he said, "where no Catholic prelate would tell the president, should he be a Catholic, how to act."

The four televised debates strongly influenced the outcome of the election, one of the closest in American history. Kennedy won the popular vote by 118,000 out of 68 million votes cast and the Electoral College by 303 votes to 219. In several states only a few thousand votes could have swung the Electoral College numbers the other way.

✓ **Reading Check** **Identifying** What were two main issues of the 1960 presidential election?

The Kennedy Mystique

Despite his narrow victory, John F. Kennedy, commonly referred to as JFK, captured the imagination of the American public as few presidents before him had. During the campaign, many had been taken with Kennedy's youth and optimism. The new president strongly reinforced this impression when he gave his Inaugural Address.

Inauguration Day, January 20, 1961, was crisp and cold in Washington, D.C. At the site of the ceremony, a crowd gathered, wrapped in coats and blankets. As Kennedy rose to take the oath of office, he wore neither a coat nor a hat. During his speech, the new president declared, "The torch has been passed to a new generation," and he called on his fellow citizens to take a more active role in making the United States a better place. "My fellow Americans," he exclaimed, "ask not what your country can do for you—ask what you can do for your country."

Kennedy, his wife Jacqueline, their children Caroline and John, and their large extended family seemed to have been created for media coverage. Reporters followed the family everywhere.

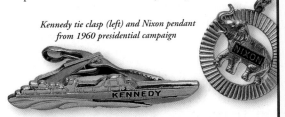

Kennedy tie clasp (left) and Nixon pendant from 1960 presidential campaign

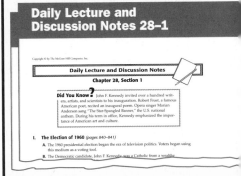

2 TEACH

Daily Lecture and Discussion Notes 28–1

> **Daily Lecture and Discussion Notes**
> **Chapter 28, Section 1**
>
> **Did You Know** John F. Kennedy invited over a hundred writers, artists, and scientists to his inauguration. Robert Frost, a famous American poet, recited an inaugural poem. Opera singer Marian Anderson sang "The Star-Spangled Banner," the U.S. national anthem. During his term in office, Kennedy emphasized the importance of American art and culture.
>
> **I. The Election of 1960** (pages 840–841)
>   **A.** The 1960 presidential election began the era of television politics. Voters began using this medium as a voting tool.
>   **B.** The Democratic candidate, John F. Kennedy, was a Catholic from a wealthy

Identifying a Strategy Organize the class into two groups. Have one group represent Nixon's staff and the other represent Kennedy's staff. After students have read this page, have each group identify the campaign strategies that each should use to overcome their weaknesses, to explain their goals for the country, and to encourage undecided voters to vote for them. Have each group present their strategies. As a class, discuss why the election results were so close. **L1**

✓ **Reading Check**

Answer: The issues were the economy and the Cold War.

The 1960 vote was so close that Nixon considered demanding a recount, but then decided against it. He explained that if there were a recount, "the organization of the new administration and the orderly transfer of responsibility from the old to the new might be delayed for months. The situation within the entire federal government would be chaotic."

COOPERATIVE LEARNING ACTIVITY

Researching the Candidates Organize the class into six groups. Assign each group one of the following topics: Kennedy's childhood and family background, Kennedy's college years and military service, Kennedy's political background, Nixon's childhood and family background, Nixon's college years and military service, or Nixon's political background. Have the groups research their topic. Then have the Kennedy groups and the Nixon groups work together to prepare a display providing a portrait of the two men.

Use the rubric for a cooperative group management plan on pages 81–82 in the *Performance Assessment Activities and Rubrics.*

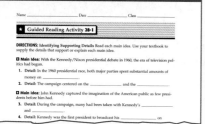

Picturing History

Background: In 2001 the Metropolitan Museum of Art and the John F. Kennedy Library organized an exhibit of clothing worn by Jacqueline Kennedy while she was First Lady.
Answer: Students' answers will vary. Students might suggest that the young family provided good stories for the media, and the family encouraged the attention.
Ask: What technology helped make scrutiny of the Kennedys possible? *(television)*

✓ Reading Check

Answer: Kennedy inspired the nation with his optimism, his youth, and his ability to handle the media.

FYI

John Kennedy, his wife, and their two small children were the youngest family to live in the White House since Theodore Roosevelt's days.

Picturing History

The Kennedy White House Jacqueline Kennedy (center right) brought youthful elegance and style to the White House. Why do you think the media scrutinized the First Family so much?

Kennedy himself was a master of the media, particularly television. He was the first to broadcast his press conferences live on television.

The Kennedy charisma inspired many of his staff members. His press secretary, Pierre Salinger, put this feeling into words:

> ❝None of us will ever have a better job as long as we live. . . . The big *plus*—the fringe benefit that made it all worthwhile—was JFK himself. . . . Our faith in him and in what he was trying to do was absolute, and he could impart to our work together a sense of challenge and adventure—a feeling that he was moving, and the world with him, toward a better time.❞
>
> —quoted in *With Kennedy*

✓ Reading Check
Summarizing In what ways did John F. Kennedy inspire the nation?

Success and Setback on the Domestic Front

Not everyone in the nation fell for the Kennedy mystique. His high culture, elite Northeast upbringing, and Catholicism irritated some Americans. Congress also was less than taken with the new president. Upon entering office, President Kennedy set out to implement a legislative agenda, which became known as the **New Frontier.** He hoped to increase aid to education, provide health insurance to the elderly, create a Department of Urban Affairs, and help migrant workers. He

would soon find that transforming lofty ideals into real legislation was no easy task on Capitol Hill.

Kennedy Struggles With Congress Although the Democratic Party enjoyed large majorities in both houses of Congress, Kennedy was unable to push through many of his domestic programs. Kennedy had trailed Nixon in many Democratic districts and had not helped many Democrats get elected. Those who did win, therefore, did not feel they owed him anything. As one Democrat in Congress told *U.S. News & World Report*, "A good many [congressional representatives] were elected in 1960 in spite of his presence on the ticket rather than because his name was there." As a result, legislators found it easy to follow their own interests rather than those of the president.

In addition, Republicans as well as conservative Southern Democrats—who were responsible for holding the Democratic majority in Congress—viewed the New Frontier as too big and too costly. Senator Everett Dirksen, Republican minority leader from Illinois, claimed that Kennedy's efforts to increase the power and reach of the federal government would push the nation down an ominous path.

In the end, Congress defeated a number of JFK's proposals, including health insurance for the elderly, a Department of Urban Affairs, and federal aid to education. The president often resisted calls to push harder for his agenda. He decided not to fight every battle on Capitol Hill and preferred to reserve his bargaining power for issues that were both truly important and winnable.

ECONOMICS

Strengthening the Economy Kennedy did achieve some victories in Congress, particularly in his efforts to improve the nation's economy. The American economy, which had soared through much of the 1950s, had slowed by the end of the decade. From 1960 to 1961, the growth rate of the gross national product was only 2 percent, while the unemployment rate hovered near 7 percent of the workforce, the second-highest figure since World War II.

In an effort to increase growth and create more jobs, Kennedy advocated the New Deal strategy of deficit spending, first implemented during Franklin Roosevelt's presidency. The new president convinced Congress to invest more funds in defense and in space exploration. Such spending did indeed create more jobs and stimulate economic growth. Reluctant to rely too heavily on deficit spending, which tends to cause inflation, Kennedy also sought to boost the economy by increasing business production and efficiency. In

---

MEETING SPECIAL NEEDS

Kinesthetic Arrange to videotape students as you conduct mock debates on topics of interest to students. As a class watch the videotapes and have students select which debaters look comfortable and which look uncomfortable. Have students note particular mannerisms or actions that make people look comfortable in front of the camera. **L1**

📁 Refer to ***Inclusion for the High School Social Studies Classroom Strategies and Activities*** in the TCR.

addition, his administration asked businesses to hold down prices and labor leaders to hold down pay increases.

Prodded by Secretary of Labor Arthur Goldberg, labor unions in the steel industry agreed to reduce their demands for higher wages. In 1962, however, several steel companies raised prices sharply.

The president threatened to have the Department of Defense buy cheaper steel from foreign companies and instructed the Justice Department to investigate whether the steel industry was guilty of price-fixing. In response to Kennedy's tactics, the steel companies backed down and cut their prices. To achieve this victory, however, the president had strained his relations with the nation's business community.

In an effort to get the economy moving, Kennedy also adopted supply-side ideas and pushed for a cut in tax rates. When opponents argued that a tax cut would only help the wealthy, Kennedy asserted that lower taxes meant businesses would have more money to expand, which would create new jobs and benefit everybody. "A rising tide lifts all boats," Kennedy explained, as a way to illustrate how tax cuts would stimulate the economy and help all Americans.

Kennedy also convinced Congress to increase the minimum hourly wage to $1.25. In addition, he provided more than $400 million in aid to distressed areas under the Area Redevelopment Act. Meanwhile, the administration's Housing Act created an extensive home-building and slum clearance program as well as thousands of construction jobs.

Women's Rights Kennedy also helped women make strides during the 1960s. Although Kennedy never appointed a woman to his cabinet, a number of women worked in prominent positions in his administration, including **Esther Peterson,** assistant secretary of labor and director of the Women's Bureau of the Department of Labor.

Kennedy advanced women's rights in other ways as well. In 1961 he created the **Presidential Commission on the Status of Women.** The commission called for federal action against gender discrimination and affirmed the right of women to equally paid employment. Kennedy responded by issuing an executive order ending gender discrimination in the federal civil service, and in 1963 he signed the Equal Pay Act for women. The commission also sparked the creation of similar groups on the state level and inspired many women to work together to further their interests.

✓ **Reading Check** **Evaluating** Why did Kennedy have difficulty getting his New Frontier legislation passed?

Warren Court Reforms

During the Kennedy years, the Supreme Court also took an active role in social issues. In 1953 President Eisenhower had nominated **Earl Warren,** the popular Republican governor of California, to become Chief Justice of the United States. More so than previous courts, the Warren Court took an activist stance, helping to shape national policy by taking a forceful stand on a number of key issues of the day.

GOVERNMENT

"One Man, One Vote" One of the Warren Court's more notable decisions had a powerful impact on who would hold political power in the United States. This decision concerned reapportionment, or the way in which states draw up political districts based on changes in population. By 1960 many more Americans resided in cities and suburbs than in rural areas. Yet many states had failed to restructure their electoral districts to reflect that change.

In Tennessee, for example, a rural county with only 2,340 voters had 1 representative in the state assembly, while an urban county with 133 times more voters had only 7. The vote of a city dweller counted for less than the vote of a rural resident. Some Tennessee voters took the matter to court.

The *Baker* v. *Carr* case reached the Supreme Court after a federal court ruled that the issue should be

Fact	Fiction	Folklore

Camelot In December 1960, *Camelot,* a musical starring Richard Burton and Julie Andrews, opened on Broadway in New York City. The Kennedys attended the show, which told the legend of the heroism of King Arthur and the Knights of the Round Table, and so enjoyed it that they listened to the music often. The president's favorite song included the lines: "Don't let it be forgot, that once there was a spot, for one brief shining moment that was known as Camelot."

In later years, the Kennedy presidency became known as "Camelot," largely because of Mrs. Kennedy. Shortly after the president's death in 1963, she told a journalist that all she could think about was the president's favorite line. She went on to say: "There'll be great presidents again, . . . but there'll never be another Camelot again." Journalist Theodore H. White later wrote that "all she could repeat was, 'Tell people there will never be that Camelot again.'"

CHAPTER 28   The New Frontier and the Great Society   **843**

Making a Collage Have students make a collage using images of important events in the Kennedy administration. Invite students to post their collages and explain any unique elements that they included. **L1**

CURRICULUM CONNECTION

Civics Tell students that Eleanor Roosevelt had remained a popular and active political figure after her husband's death. During the 1960 presidential campaign, she appeared in a television commercial urging people to vote for Kennedy because he was the man to improve human rights. Her appearance indicated to traditional Democrats and women that Kennedy was the man for the job.

Fact	Fiction	Folklore

In the legendary Camelot, leaders sat at a round table. With no head of the table, it was implied that rule was by all, not just by one.

📁 Use *Supreme Court Case Study 33, Baker* v. *Carr.*

✓ **Reading Check**

Answer: The legislation was perceived as too expensive and too broad in scope.

INTERDISCIPLINARY CONNECTIONS ACTIVITY

Language Arts Tell students that John F. Kennedy won a Pulitzer Prize in biography for his book, *Profiles in Courage.* Encourage students to find the book in the library, read one of the profiles, and write a report on the person profiled. Have volunteers share their reports with the class. Then as a class, discuss the virtue of courage and how the people Kennedy selected represented it. **L2**

Major Decisions of the Warren Court, 1954–1967

Civil Rights	
Brown v. Board of Education (1954)	Segregation in public schools unconstitutional
Baker v. Carr (1962)	Established that federal courts can hear lawsuits seeking to force state authorities to redraw electoral districts
Reynolds v. Sims (1964)	Congressional districts should be equal in population
Heart of Atlanta Motel v. United States (1964)	Desegregation of public accommodations established in the Civil Rights Act of 1964 is legal
Loving v. Virginia (1967)	States may not ban interracial marriage
Due Process	
Mapp v. Ohio (1961)	Unlawfully seized evidence is inadmissible at trial
Gideon v. Wainwright (1963)	Suspects are entitled to court-appointed attorney if unable to afford one on their own
Escobedo v. Illinois (1964)	Accused has the right to an attorney during police questioning
Miranda v. Arizona (1966)	Police must inform suspects of their rights during the arrest process
Freedom of Religion and Freedom of Speech	
Engel v. Vitale (1962)	Nondenominational prayer in school banned
Abington School District v. Schempp (1963)	Daily Bible reading in school banned
New York Times v. Sullivan (1964)	Celebrities may sue the media for libel only in certain circumstances

Chart *Skills*

Answers:
1. Students should discuss school integration and reapportionment.
2. It affected civil rights, due process, and freedom of religion and speech.

Chart Skills Practice
Ask: Which cases are related to the separation of church and state?
(Engel *v.* Vitale *and* Abington School District *v.* Schempp)

📂 Use *Supreme Court Case Study 32,* Mapp v. Ohio; *34,* Engel v. Vitale; *35,* Abington School District v. Schempp; *36,* Gideon v. Wainwright; *37,* Escobedo v. Illinois; *38,* Reynolds v. Sims; *41,* Miranda v. Arizona.

3 ASSESS

Assign Section 1 Assessment as homework or as an in-class activity.

🔘 Have students use the **Interactive Tutor Self-Assessment CD-ROM.**

Reading Essentials and Study Guide 28–1

Name _____ Date _____ Class _____

Study Guide
Chapter 28, Section 1
For use with textbook pages 840–845

THE NEW FRONTIER

KEY TERMS AND NAMES

missile gap the United States's lag behind the Soviet Union in weaponry *(page 841)*
New Frontier President Kennedy's domestic programs *(page 842)*
Earl Warren Chief Justice of the United States, starting in the Eisenhower administration *(page 843)*
reapportionment the way in which states draw up political districts based on changes in population *(page 843)*
due process the idea that the law may not treat individuals unfairly or unreasonably and that courts must follow proper procedures when trying cases *(page 844)*

---

solved by legislation. The Fourteenth Amendment specifically gives Congress authority to enforce voting rights. In 1962 the Supreme Court ruled that the federal courts did have jurisdiction and sent the matter back to the lower courts. 📖 *(See page 1080 for more information on* Baker v. Carr*.)*

Two years later, in June 1964, the Supreme Court ruled in *Reynolds* v. *Sims* that the current apportionment system in most states was indeed unconstitutional. In a decision that helped to promote the principle of "one man, one vote," the Warren Court required state legislatures to reapportion electoral districts so that all citizens' votes would have equal weight. The Court's decision was a momentous one, for it shifted political power throughout the country from rural and often conservative areas to urban areas, where more liberal voters resided. The Court's decision also boosted the political power of African Americans and Hispanics, who typically lived in cities. 📖 *(See page 1082 for more information on* Reynolds v. Sims*.)*

Extending Due Process In a series of historic rulings in the 1960s, the U.S. Supreme Court began to use the Fourteenth Amendment to apply the Bill of Rights to the states. Originally, the Bill of Rights

Chart *Skills*

1. **Interpreting Charts** Analyze the effects *Brown v. Board of Education* and *Reynolds* v. *Sims* had on the nation.
2. **Summarizing** What three major areas of policy did the Warren Court's decisions affect?

applied only to the federal government. Many states had their own bill of rights, but some federal rights did not exist at the state level. The Fourteenth Amendment specifically stated that "no state shall . . . deprive any person of life, liberty, or property without due process of law." Due process means that the law may not treat individuals unfairly, arbitrarily, or unreasonably, and that courts must follow proper procedures and rules when trying cases. Due process ensures that all people are treated the same by the court system. In the 1960s, the Supreme Court ruled in several cases that upholding due process meant applying the federal bill of rights to the states.

In 1961 the Supreme Court ruled in *Mapp* v. *Ohio* that state courts could not consider evidence obtained in violation of the federal Constitution. In *Gideon* v. *Wainwright* (1963), the Court ruled that a defendant in a state court had the right to a lawyer, regardless of his or her ability to pay. The following year, in *Escobedo* v. *Illinois,* the justices ruled that a

CRITICAL THINKING ACTIVITY

Analyzing a Concept Ask students the meaning of the word *frontier*. As a class, discuss both the denotation of the word (what the word means) and the connotation (what the word suggests beyond the literal meaning). Then ask students why they think Kennedy named his program the New Frontier. **L2**

suspect must be allowed access to a lawyer and must be informed of his or her right to remain silent before being questioned by the police. *Miranda* v. *Arizona* (1966) went even further, requiring that authorities immediately give suspects a fourfold warning. The warning consisted of informing suspects that they have the right to remain silent, that anything they say can and will be used against them in court, that they have a right to a lawyer while being questioned, and that if they cannot afford a lawyer, the court will appoint one for them. Today these warnings are known as the Miranda rights. 📖 *(See pages 1081–1082 for more information on* Mapp *v.* Ohio, Gideon *v.* Wainwright, Escobedo *v.* Illinois, *and* Miranda *v.* Arizona.*)*

Many citizens and police departments and even some of the Supreme Court justices accused the Warren Court of favoring criminals. Others cheered the decisions, seeing them as promoting the rights of all citizens, even the less privileged.

Prayer and Privacy The Supreme Court also handed down decisions that reaffirmed the separation of church and state. The Court applied the First Amendment to the states in *Engel* v. *Vitale* (1962). In this ruling, the Court decided that states could not compose official prayers and require those prayers to be recited in state public schools. The following year, in *Abington School District* v. *Schempp,* it ruled against daily Bible readings in public schools. Weighing in on another controversial issue, the Court ruled in *Griswold* v. *Connecticut* (1965) that prohibiting the sale and use of birth control devices violated citizens' constitutional right to privacy. 📖 *(See pages 1080–1081 for more information on these Supreme Court cases.)*

Activist Court The Warren Court poses for its official portrait in 1962, with Chief Justice Earl Warren front and center.

As with most rulings of the Warren Court, these decisions delighted some and deeply disturbed others. What most people did agree upon, however, was the Court's pivotal role in shaping national policy. The Warren Court, wrote *New York Times* columnist Anthony Lewis, "has brought about more social change than most Congresses and most Presidents."

From the political arena to the legal system to people's everyday lives, the Warren Court indeed left its imprint on the nation. Meanwhile, away from the domestic arena, President Kennedy worked to make his mark on the country's foreign affairs during a time of rising Cold War tensions.

✓ **Reading Check** **Examining** What was the significance of the Warren Court's "One Man, One Vote" ruling?

SECTION 1 ASSESSMENT

Checking for Understanding

1. **Define:** missile gap, reapportionment, due process.
2. **Identify:** New Frontier, Earl Warren.
3. **Summarize** the progress made for women's rights during Kennedy's administration.

Reviewing Themes

4. **Civic Rights and Responsibilities** Name three decisions of the Warren Court that protected civil rights.

Critical Thinking

5. **Interpreting** In what way was the 1960 presidential election a turning point in campaign history?
6. **Organizing** Use a graphic organizer similar to the one below to list the economic policies of the Kennedy administration.

Economic Policies

Analyzing Visuals

7. **Analyzing Charts** Study the chart of Warren Court decisions on page 844. How did the Court expand the rights of the accused? Were these sound decisions? Why or why not?

Writing About History

8. **Expository Writing** In his Inaugural Address, President Kennedy asked his fellow Americans to "Ask what you can do for your country." Respond to this statement in an essay.

SECTION 1 ASSESSMENT ANSWERS

1. Terms are in blue.
2. New Frontier *(p. 842)*, Earl Warren *(p. 843)*
3. Presidential Commission on the Status of Women, ending gender discrimination in federal civil service, and the Equal Pay Act
4. Answers should include any of the civil rights decisions listed on page 844.
5. Television played a more influential role.
6. a cut in tax rates, an increase in funds for defense and space exploration, an increase in the minimum wage, housing and redevelopment
7. Students should summarize the chart's due process decisions and weigh individual rights against police concerns.
8. Students' essays will vary but should focus on the meaning of Kennedy's statement.

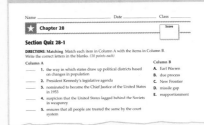
More About the Photo

In 1962 the members of the Warren Court included two members appointed by Franklin Delano Roosevelt, one appointed by Harry S Truman, four appointed by Eisenhower, and two appointed by John F. Kennedy.

Reteach

Have students summarize Kennedy's economic policies.

Enrich

Invite interested students to learn more about the life and career of one of the justices who served on the Warren Court. Encourage students to use library and Internet resources.

✓ **Reading Check**

Answer: All citizens' votes would have equal weight regardless of where they lived.

4 CLOSE

Have students explain why Congress often did not support Kennedy's proposals.

1 FOCUS

Section Overview

This section focuses on the Cold War during the Kennedy administration.

Guide to Reading

Answers to Graphic: January 1959, Castro's overthrow of Batista; April 17, 1961, Bay of Pigs; June 1961, Kennedy and Khrushchev meet in Vienna; October 1962, Cuban missile crisis; October 1962, Soviets agree to remove missiles from Cuba

Preteaching Vocabulary
Have students select one of the Key Terms and Names and write several questions about the term or name. Then have students work in pairs to answer the questions.

Guide to Reading

Main Idea
As president, John F. Kennedy had to confront the challenges and fears of the Cold War.

Key Terms and Names
flexible response, Peace Corps, space race, Berlin Wall, Warren Commission

Reading Strategy
Sequencing As you read about the crises of the Cold War, complete a time line similar to the one below to record the major events of the Cold War in the late 1950s and early 1960s.

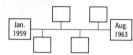

Reading Objectives
- **Describe** Kennedy's plan for the armed forces.
- **Explain** how the Cold War influenced foreign aid and the space program.

Section Theme
Science and Technology During the Cold War, the nation devoted much of its scientific and technological resources to competing with the Soviet Union, especially in getting to the moon.

Preview of Events

◆1961	◆1962	◆1963	◆1964

April 1961
Bay of Pigs invasion

May 1961
Kennedy informs Congress of moon expedition goal

October 1962
Cuban missile crisis

September 1963
Senate ratifies Limited Test Ban Treaty

November 22, 1963
Kennedy assassinated

★ An American Story ★

Like millions of other Americans in late October 1962, Tami Gold was having trouble concentrating on anything. For several tension-filled days that fall, the world seemed headed for nuclear destruction. U.S. officials had discovered that the Soviet Union had placed missiles in Cuba—a mere 90 miles (145 km) from the shores of the United States. When the Soviets refused to remove the weapons, a bitter weeklong standoff ensued in which the two superpowers hurled threats and warnings at each other and moved to the brink of nuclear war. Gold, then a seventh-grade student in Long Island, New York, recalled the events of one particular day:

Emergency water supplied by Department of Defense

❝I remember I was in the bathroom of the school . . . when they had said over the loud speaker . . . that everyone had to return to their homerooms immediately and get instruction from their homeroom teacher. And it was probably one of the scariest moments of my life, it was like the sensation that our country could go to war and I didn't understand at all what it was about, but the fact that the country could go to war at any moment was really really present. . . . It was chilling, it was scary, it was really nauseating. . . .❞

—quoted in *Collective Memories of the Cuban Missile Crisis*

Kennedy Confronts Global Challenges

The Cuban missile crisis, as the standoff came to be called, may have been the most dramatic foreign policy episode Kennedy faced. It was not the only one, however. As Kennedy entered the White House, the nation's dangerous rivalry with the Soviet Union continued to intensify. As a result, the new president had to devote much of

846 CHAPTER 28 The New Frontier and the Great Society

📁 SECTION RESOURCES

📁 Reproducible Masters
- Reproducible Lesson Plan 28–2
- Daily Lecture and Discussion Notes 28–2
- Guided Reading Activity 28–2
- Section Quiz 28–2
- Reading Essentials and Study Guide 28–2
- Interpreting Political Cartoons

📄 Transparencies
- Daily Focus Skills Transparency 28–2

Multimedia
- 💿 Interactive Tutor Self-Assessment CD-ROM
- 💿 ExamView® Pro Testmaker CD-ROM
- 💿 Presentation Plus! CD-ROM
- 💿 TeacherWorks™ CD-ROM
- 🔊 Audio Program

his energy in foreign policy matters to guiding the nation through the deepening Cold War.

Kennedy appeared ready to stand up to the Soviets. Upon taking the oath of office, the new president devoted much of his Inaugural Address to the role of the United States in a divided world:

> ❝Let the word go forth from this time and place . . . that the torch has been passed to a new generation of Americans—born in this century, tempered by war, disciplined by a hard and bitter peace, proud of our ancient heritage—and unwilling to witness or permit the slow undoing of those human rights to which this nation has always been committed. . . . Let every nation know, whether it wishes us well or ill, that we shall pay any price, bear any burden, meet any hardship, support any friend, oppose any foe, to assure the survival and the success of liberty.❞
>
> —quoted in *Let the Word Go Forth*

Kennedy attempted to reduce the threat of nuclear war and to stop the spread of communism with a range of programs. These included a conventional weaponry program, economic aid, and the Peace Corps.

A More Flexible Response Kennedy took office at a time of growing global instability. Nationalism was exploding throughout the developing world, and the Soviet Union actively supported "wars of national liberation." *Newsweek* magazine wrote that the "greatest single problem that faces John Kennedy is how to meet the aggressive power of the Communist bloc."

Kennedy felt that Eisenhower had relied too heavily on nuclear weapons, which could only be used in extreme situations. To allow for a "flexible response" if nations needed help against Communist movements, the president pushed for a buildup of conventional troops and weapons. Although costly, a flexible response plan would allow the United States to fight a limited style of warfare.

In adopting this plan, Kennedy supported the Special Forces, a small army unit created in the 1950s to wage guerrilla warfare in limited conflicts. Kennedy expanded it and allowed the soldiers to wear their distinctive "Green Beret" headgear.

Aid to Other Countries One area of the world where Kennedy wanted to renew diplomatic focus was Latin America. Conditions in much of Latin American society were not good: Governments were often in the hands of the wealthy few and many of their citizens lived in extreme poverty. In some Latin American countries, these conditions spurred the growth of left-wing movements aimed at overthrowing their governments. When the United States was involved in Latin America, it was usually to help existing governments stay in power in order to prevent Communist movements from flourishing. Poor Latin Americans resented this intrusion, just as they resented American corporations that had business operations in their countries, a presence that was seen as a kind of imperialism.

To improve relations between the United States and Latin America, President Kennedy proposed an **Alliance for Progress,** a series of cooperative aid projects with Latin American governments. The alliance was designed to create a "free and prosperous Latin America" that would be less likely to support Communist-inspired revolutions.

Over a 10-year period, the United States pledged $20 billion to help Latin American countries establish better schools, housing, health care, and fairer land distribution. The results were mixed. In some countries—notably Chile, Colombia, Venezuela, and the Central American republics—the alliance did promote real reform. In others, governing rulers used the money to keep themselves in power.

The Peace Corps Another program aimed at helping less developed nations fight poverty was the **Peace Corps,** an organization that sent young Americans to perform humanitarian services in these countries.

After rigorous training, volunteers spent two years in countries that had requested assistance. They laid out sewage systems in Bolivia and trained medical technicians in Chad. Others taught English or helped to build roads. By late 1963 thousands of Peace Corps volunteers were serving in over 30 countries. Today, the Peace Corps is still active and remains one of Kennedy's most enduring legacies.

TECHNOLOGY

The Cold War Moves Into Space President Kennedy sought to increase the country's presence not only around the world but also in space. With Cold War tensions continuing to rise, the United States and the Soviet Union engaged in a space race—vying for dominance of the heavens to enhance their competitive positions on Earth.

Student Web Activity Visit the *American Vision* Web site at tav.glencoe.com and click on *Student Web Activities— Chapter 28* for an activity on the New Frontier.

2 TEACH

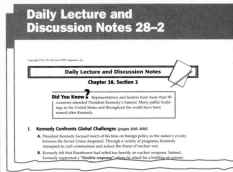

Daily Lecture and Discussion Notes 28–2

Copyright © by The McGraw-Hill Companies, Inc.

Daily Lecture and Discussion Notes

Chapter 28, Section 2

Did You Know? Representatives and leaders from more than 90 countries attended President Kennedy's funeral. Many public buildings in the United States and throughout the world have been named after Kennedy.

I. Kennedy Confronts Global Challenges *(pages 846–848)*

   A. President Kennedy focused much of his time on foreign policy as the nation's rivalry between the Soviet Union deepened. Through a variety of programs, Kennedy attempted to curb communism and reduce the threat of nuclear war.

   B. Kennedy felt that Eisenhower had relied too heavily on nuclear weapons. Instead, Kennedy supported a **"flexible response"** where he asked for a buildup of conven-

Discussing a Topic Have students discuss how President Kennedy's plans for space exploration reflected the Cold War.
L1 ELL

Since the Peace Corps was established in 1961, over 160,000 volunteers have served in 135 countries. Volunteer sectors include education, environment, health, business, and agriculture. In 2001 there were 7,300 Peace Corps volunteers serving in 72 countries.

Objectives and answers to the student activity can be found in the **Web Activity Lesson Plan** at tav.glencoe.com.

COOPERATIVE LEARNING ACTIVITY

Reviewing the Kennedy Assassination Help students assess the effect of President Kennedy's death. Organize them into three groups with one of the following tasks: locating images of the assassination, outlining various conspiracy theories, or interviewing people for personal recollections of the event. When these tasks are completed, form new groups with membership covering all three tasks. Have members share their information. 🖳

Use the rubric for a cooperative group management plan on pages 81–82 in the ***Performance Assessment Activities and Rubrics.***

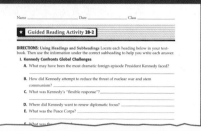
Why It Matters

Background: When the Soviets launched *Sputnik I* on October 4, 1957, American scientists were concerned about the military implications. The launching of *Sputnik II* a month later caused even more concern. Much larger than its predecessor and carrying a passenger–a dog named Laika–*Sputnik II* was propelled into space by an incredibly powerful rocket, which might, it seemed, be modified to carry missiles against the United States.

✔ Reading Check

Answer: the spread of communism, the Cuban missile crisis, Latin American relations, and reducing the threat of nuclear war

FYI

The names of the early manned space programs, Mercury, Gemini, and Apollo, were based on mythology. In Roman mythology, for example, Mercury was the messenger of the gods. In Greek mythology, Apollo carried the sun across the sky in his chariot each day.

Why It Matters
The Space Program

The space program expanded significantly when President Kennedy announced his determination to beat the Soviets to the moon. By the time Neil Armstrong and Edwin ("Buzz") Aldrin walked on the moon in 1969, the National Aeronautics and Space Administration (NASA) had spent over $33 billion. Since that time, NASA expenditures have affected far more than space missions. NASA research findings have advanced knowledge of the nature of the universe, and people have applied them to many technical fields and manufacturing processes.

▼ Moon boot material developed for the space program is used in many running shoes. It has improved shock absorption and provides superior stability and motion control.

Kennedy was determined that the first humans to reach the moon would be Americans, not Russians. In 1961 he recommended to Congress that "this nation should commit itself to achieving the goal, before this decade is out, of landing a man on the moon." Kennedy's dream was realized in July 1969, during Richard Nixon's first administration, when astronaut Neil Armstrong became the first person to set foot on the moon.

✔ Reading Check **Examining** What global challenges did Kennedy face during his presidency?

Crises of the Cold War

President Kennedy's efforts to combat Communist influence in other countries led to some of the most intense crises of the Cold War. At times these crises left Americans and people in many other nations wondering whether the world would survive.

The Bay of Pigs The first crisis occurred in Cuba, only 90 miles (145 km) from American shores. There, Fidel Castro had overthrown the corrupt Cuban dictator Fulgencio Batista in 1959. Almost immediately, Castro established ties with the Soviet Union, instituted drastic land reforms, and seized foreign-owned businesses, many of them American. Cuba's alliance with the Soviets worried many Americans. The Communists were now too close for comfort, and Soviet Premier Nikita Khrushchev was also expressing his intent to strengthen Cuba militarily.

Fearing that the Communists would use Cuba as a base from which to spread revolution throughout the Western Hemisphere, President Eisenhower had authorized the Central Intelligence Agency (CIA) to secretly train and arm Cuban exiles, known as La Brigada, to invade the island. The invasion was intended to touch off a popular uprising against Castro.

When Kennedy became president, his advisers approved the plan. In office fewer than three months and trusting his experts, Kennedy agreed to the operation with some changes. On April 17, 1961, 1,400 armed Cuban exiles landed at the **Bay of Pigs** on the south coast of Cuba. The invasion was a disaster. La Brigada's boats ran aground on coral reefs, Kennedy cancelled their air support to keep United States involvement a secret, and the

848 CHAPTER 28 The New Frontier and the Great Society

MEETING SPECIAL NEEDS

Visual/Spatial Many Americans found inspiration in Kennedy's idealism, grieved at his death, and recaptured some hope for their country in President Johnson's determination. Ask students to create a poster that they feel captures the essence of President Kennedy's "New Frontier" or of his handling of international issues. **L1**

📂 Refer to *Inclusion for the High School Social Studies Classroom Strategies and Activities* in the TCR.

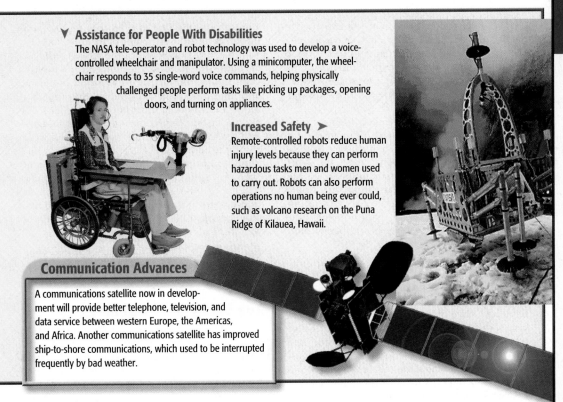

▼ **Assistance for People With Disabilities**
The NASA tele-operator and robot technology was used to develop a voice-controlled wheelchair and manipulator. Using a minicomputer, the wheelchair responds to 35 single-word voice commands, helping physically challenged people perform tasks like picking up packages, opening doors, and turning on appliances.

Increased Safety ➤
Remote-controlled robots reduce human injury levels because they can perform hazardous tasks men and women used to carry out. Robots can also perform operations no human being ever could, such as volcano research on the Puna Ridge of Kilauea, Hawaii.

Communication Advances

A communications satellite now in development will provide better telephone, television, and data service between western Europe, the Americas, and Africa. Another communications satellite has improved ship-to-shore communications, which used to be interrupted frequently by bad weather.

Writing a Speech Have students write speeches that President Kennedy might have given during the Cuban missile crisis. Ask volunteers to present their speeches to the class. **L3**

 Use the rubric for an oral presentation, monologue, song, or skit on pages 75–76 in the *Performance Assessment Activities and Rubrics*.

you don't say...

Proud Words Almost two years after the Berlin Wall was built, President Kennedy paid tribute to the spirit of Berliners when he spoke to a crowd gathered near the wall. He said, "All free men, wherever they may live, are citizens of Berlin. And, therefore, as a free man, I take pride in the words 'Ich bin ein Berliner' (I am a Berliner)."

FYI

Although the city of Berlin had been divided into East Berlin and West Berlin since the end of World War II, in August 1961 an actual wall of concrete, barbed wire, and stone was erected.

Use *Interpreting Political Cartoons*, Cartoon 27.

expected popular uprising never happened. Within two days, Castro's forces killed or captured almost all the members of La Brigada.

The Bay of Pigs was a dark moment for the Kennedy administration. The action exposed an American plot to overthrow a neighbor's government, and the outcome made the United States look weak and disorganized.

The Berlin Wall Goes Up Still reeling from the Bay of Pigs fiasco, Kennedy faced another foreign policy challenge beginning in June 1961 when he met with Khrushchev in Vienna, Austria. The Soviet leader was determined to test the resolve of the young president. Khrushchev also wanted to stop the flood of Germans pouring out of Communist East Germany into West Berlin. He demanded that the Western powers recognize East Germany and that the United States, Great Britain, and France withdraw from Berlin, a city lying completely within East Germany. Kennedy refused and reaffirmed the West's commitment to West Berlin.

Khrushchev retaliated by building a wall through Berlin, blocking movement between the Soviet sector

and the rest of the city. Guards posted along the wall shot at many of those attempting to escape from the East. For nearly 30 years afterward, the **Berlin Wall** stood as a visible symbol of the Cold War division between East and West.

The Cuban Missile Crisis By far the most terrifying crisis of the Kennedy era occurred the next year. Once again, the crisis dealt with Cuba. Over the summer of 1962, American intelligence agencies learned that Soviet technicians and equipment had arrived in Cuba and that military construction was in progress. Then, on October 22, President Kennedy announced on television that American spy planes had taken aerial photographs showing that the Soviet Union had placed long-range missiles in Cuba. Enemy missiles stationed so close to the United States posed a dangerous threat.

Kennedy ordered a naval blockade to stop the Soviets from delivering more missiles, demanded that they dismantle existing missile sites, and warned that if any weapons were launched against the United States, he would respond fully against the Soviet Union. Still, work on the missile sites continued. Nuclear holocaust seemed imminent.

CHAPTER 28 The New Frontier and the Great Society **849**

INTERDISCIPLINARY CONNECTIONS ACTIVITY

Language Arts Tell students that through the Peace Corps, American volunteers offer help to developing nations around the world. Ask students to imagine that they want to join the Peace Corps today. Have them research the process and write a short report about what they learn. Encourage students to use library and Internet resources for their research. Remind students that they are to gather information. They should not actually submit an application to the Peace Corps. The Internet address for the Peace Corps is www.peacecorps.gov. **L2**

✓ **Reading Check**

Answer: It was resolved through negotiations. The Soviet Union agreed to remove the missiles and Kennedy publicly agreed not to invade Cuba. Privately, Kennedy agreed to remove missiles from Turkey.

Picturing **History**

Answer: He announced the existence of the missiles, ordered a naval blockade, demanded the dismantling of the sites, warned that the U.S. was ready to respond with force to any attack, and negotiated a settlement with the Soviet Union.

3 ASSESS

Assign Section 2 Assessment as homework or as an in-class activity.

⊕ Have students use the **Interactive Tutor Self-Assessment CD-ROM.**

Reading Essentials and Study Guide 28–2

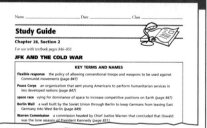

Then, after a flurry of secret negotiations, the Soviet Union offered a deal. It would remove the missiles if the United States promised not to invade Cuba and to remove its missiles from Turkey near the Soviet border. As American officials considered the offer, letters and cables flew between the two leaders and their chief advisers.

The reality was that neither Kennedy nor Khrushchev wanted nuclear war. "Only lunatics . . . who themselves want to perish and before they die destroy the world, could do this," wrote the Soviet leader. Still, the dangerous standoff persisted. On October 28, the leaders reached an agreement. Kennedy publicly agreed not to invade Cuba and privately agreed to remove the Turkish missiles; the Soviets agreed to remove their missiles from Cuba. The world could breathe again.

The Impact of the Cuban Missile Crisis The Cuban missile crisis brought the world closer to nuclear war than at any time since World War II. Both the United States and the Soviet Union had been forced to consider the consequences of such a war. In the following months, each country seemed ready to work to lessen world tensions. In August 1963, the United States and the Soviet Union concluded years of negotiation by agreeing to a treaty to ban the testing of nuclear weapons in the atmosphere—the first step toward mutual arms reduction since the beginning of the Cold War.

In the long run, however, the missile crisis had ominous consequences. The humiliating retreat the United States forced upon the Soviet leadership undermined the position of Nikita Khrushchev and contributed to his fall from power a year later. The new leadership was less interested in reaching agreements with the West. Perhaps more important, the crisis gave the Soviets evidence of their military inferiority and helped produce a dramatic Soviet arms buildup over the next two decades. This buildup contributed to a comparable military increase in the United States in the early 1980s. For a time, the arms race undermined American support for negotiating with the Soviets.

✓ **Reading Check** **Summarizing** How was the Cuban missile crisis resolved?

The Death of a President

Soon after the Senate ratified the test ban treaty, John F. Kennedy's presidency came to a shocking and tragic end. On November 22, 1963, Kennedy and his wife traveled to Texas with Vice President Lyndon Johnson for a series of political appearances. As the presidential motorcade rode slowly through the

Picturing **History**

Cold War Peak Fears of communism peaked during the Cuban missile crisis. Routine reconnaissance flights over Cuba revealed the construction of missile sites, fueling facilities, and launch pads. **What steps did Kennedy take to deal with the crisis?**

CRITICAL THINKING ACTIVITY

Comparing Most people in the United States alive at the time of President Kennedy's assassination remember what they were doing when they heard the news. Ask students to compare the impact of the assassination on the lives of Americans to the impact of the events of September 11, 2001. In small groups have students compare the two tragedies in terms of their impact on the lives of Americans. **L2**

crowded streets of Dallas, gunfire rang out. Someone had shot the president twice—once in the throat and once in the head. Horrified government officials sped Kennedy to a nearby hospital, where he was pronounced dead moments later.

Lee Harvey Oswald, the man accused of killing Kennedy, appeared to be a confused and embittered Marxist who had spent time in the Soviet Union. He himself was shot to death while in police custody two days after the assassination. The bizarre situation led some to speculate that the second gunman, local nightclub owner Jack Ruby, killed Oswald to protect others involved in the crime. In 1964 a national commission headed by Chief Justice Warren concluded that Oswald was the lone assassin. The report of the **Warren Commission** left some questions unanswered, and theories about a conspiracy to kill the president have persisted, though none has gained wide acceptance.

In the wake of the assassination, the United States and the world went into mourning. Americans across the land sobbed in public. Thousands traveled to Washington, D.C., and waited in a line that stretched for several miles outside the Capitol in order to walk silently past the president's flag-draped casket. Millions of others spent hours in front of their televisions, simply watching people file past the casket. In Rome, Italy, people brought flowers to the American embassy. In the streets of New Delhi, India, crowds wept. In Africa, the president of Guinea said, "I have lost my only true friend in the outside world."

John F. Kennedy served as president for little more than 1,000 days. Yet his powerful personality and active approach to the presidency made a profound impression on most Americans. Aided by the tidal

Picturing History

A Final Salute John F. Kennedy, Jr. (right) bravely salutes his father's coffin during the state funeral. How did people around the world react to JFK's assassination?

wave of emotion that followed the president's death, his successor, Lyndon Baines Johnson, would set out to promote many of the programs that Kennedy left behind.

✓ **Reading Check** Evaluating How did Kennedy's presidency end?

SECTION 2 ASSESSMENT

Checking for Understanding

1. **Define:** flexible response, space race.
2. **Identify:** Peace Corps, Berlin Wall, Warren Commission.
3. **Explain** the goals of the Alliance for Progress.

Reviewing Themes

4. **Science and Technology** What was Kennedy's goal for the United States in the space race?

Critical Thinking

5. **Interpreting** What was the role of foreign aid in the relations between the United States and Latin America?
6. **Organizing** Use a graphic organizer similar to the one below to list the programs that Kennedy used to reduce the threat of nuclear war and to try to stem communism.

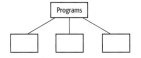

Analyzing Visuals

7. **Analyzing Photographs** Study the photographs on pages 848–849. Explain how space exploration has led to other innovations that have affected our daily lives and standard of living.

Writing About History

8. **Descriptive Writing** Take on the role of an American citizen during the Cuban missile crisis. Write a journal entry describing the mood of the country during that time.

CHAPTER 28 The New Frontier and the Great Society **851**

SECTION 2 ASSESSMENT ANSWERS

1. Terms are in blue.
2. Peace Corps *(p. 847)*, Berlin Wall *(p. 849)*, Warren Commission *(p. 851)*
3. The goals were to create cooperative aid projects that helped establish better schools, improve housing, distribute land more equitably, and improve health care.
4. to beat the Soviets to the moon
5. to help governments stay in power and prevent Communist revolutions
6. conventional weaponry program, aid to foreign governments, the Peace Corps
7. Space discoveries have provided new solutions to problems faced by the disabled as well as scientists.
8. Journal entries will vary but should focus on emotions.

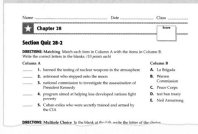
Picturing **History**

Answer: People brought flowers to American embassies or wept.
Ask: When was President Kennedy assassinated? *(November 22, 1963)*

Reteach
Have students describe Kennedy's plan for the armed forces.

Enrich
Invite interested students to create a video history of how Americans remember the assassination of President Kennedy. Suggest that students work in pairs to videotape interviews with people about where they were, how they felt, and what they remember about the day of the assassination and the days leading up to and including the funeral.

✓ **Reading Check**
Answer: He was assassinated.

4 CLOSE
Have students explain how the Cold War influenced foreign aid and the space program.

TEACH

Eyewitness

Tell students that President Johnson delivered his speech six months after Kennedy's assassination. His words set a clear agenda for the nation. Ask students to identify the particular phrases that they found inspiring. Then ask why they think this speech was important both for the president and for the American public. Have interested students use library and Internet resources to read Johnson's entire speech.

Verbatim

Have students review the quotes in the Verbatim section and discuss each item as it related to the people and themes found in their textbook. Have students research a current political, economic, or social issue. Have them create a list of quotations about the issue along with a brief statement explaining the quote, identifying the person quoted, and how the quote relates to the issue. Ask students to share their lists in a class discussion.

What Is a Pip, Anyway?

Have students work in pairs to create a matching game that lists popular groups today in one column and the lead singer(s) in the other column. Have students see how other students, their parents or guardians, or their younger siblings do on the quiz.

Visit the **TIME** Web site at www.time.com for up-to-date news, weekly magazine articles, editorials, online polls, and an archive of past magazine and Web articles.

852

TIME NOTEBOOK

Eyewitness

BETTMANN/CORBIS

On May 22, 1964, **PRESIDENT LYNDON JOHNSON** *delivered a speech in Ann Arbor, Michigan, outlining his domestic agenda that would become known as "The Great Society." Speechwriter and policy adviser Richard Goodwin watched the speech on videotape the next morning back in Washington. He recalls his reaction:*

Then, with the cheers, at first muted as if the audience were surprised at their own response, then mounting toward unrestrained, accepting delight, Johnson concluded: "There are those timid souls who say . . . we are condemned to a soulless wealth. I do not agree. We have the power to shape civilization. . . . But we need your will, your labor, your hearts. . . . So let us from this moment begin our work, so that in the future men will look back and say: It was then, after a long and weary way, that man turned the exploits of his genius to the full enrichment of his life."

Watching the film in the White House basement, almost involuntarily I added my applause to the tumultuous acclaim coming from the sound track. . . . I clapped for the President, and for our country.

WHAT IS A PIP, ANYWAY?

Match these rock 'n' roll headliners with their supporting acts.

1. Paul Revere and
2. Martha and
3. Gary Puckett and
4. Gladys Knight and
5. Smokey Robinson and
6. Diana Ross and

a. the Union Gap
b. the Supremes
c. the Miracles
d. the Vandellas
e. the Raiders
f. the Pips

answers: 1. e; 2. d; 3. a; 4. f; 5. c; 6. b

VERBATIM

❝Is there any place we can catch them? What can we do? Are we working 24 hours a day? Can we go around the moon before them?❞

PRESIDENT JOHN F. KENNEDY,
to Lyndon B. Johnson, after hearing that Soviet cosmonaut Yuri Gagarin had orbited the earth, 1961

❝It was quite a day. I don't know what you can say about a day when you see four beautiful sunsets. . . . This is a little unusual, I think.❞
COLONEL JOHN GLENN,
in orbit, 1962

❝There are tens of millions of Americans who are beyond the welfare state. Taken as a whole there is a culture of poverty . . . bad health, poor housing, low levels of aspiration and high levels of mental distress. Twenty percent of a nation, some 32,000,000.❞
MICHAEL HARRINGTON,
The Culture of Poverty, 1962

❝I have a dream.❞
MARTIN LUTHER KING,
1963

❝I don't see an American dream; . . . I see an American nightmare . . . Three hundred and ten years we worked in this country without a dime in return.❞
MALCOLM X,
1964

❝The Great Society rests on abundance and liberty for all. It demands an end to poverty and racial injustice.❞
LYNDON B. JOHNSON,
1964

❝In 1962, the starving residents of an isolated Indian village received 1 plow and 1,700 pounds of seeds. They ate the seeds.❞
PEACE CORPS AD,
1965

COOPERATIVE LEARNING ACTIVITY

Creating a Magazine Spread Organize the class into small groups. Assign each group one of the years in the 1960s and ask them to create their own two-page magazine spread for the year. Encourage students to use elements similar to those that appear in the Time Notebook, but to be creative as they select information that is of particular interest. Students should look at current magazines and books for ideas about page design. This activity can be completed using desktop publishing software or the more traditional cut-and-paste method.

Use the rubric for a cooperative group management plan on pages 81–82 in the *Performance Assessment Activities and Rubrics.*

Space Race

Want to capture some of the glamour and excitement of space exploration? Create a new nickname for your city. You won't be the first.

CITY	NICKNAME
Danbury, CT	Space Age City
Muscle Shoals, AL	Space Age City
Houston, TX	Space City, USA
Galveston, TX	Space Port, USA
Cape Kennedy, FL	Spaceport, USA
Blacksburg, VA	Space Age Community
Huntsville, AL	~~Rocket City, USA~~
	~~Space City, USA~~
	~~Space Capital of the Nation~~
	Space Capital of the World

RALPH MORSE/TIMEPIX

John Glenn, first American to orbit Earth

Milestones

PERFORMED IN ENGLISH, 1962. THE CATHOLIC MASS, following Pope John XXIII's Second Vatican Council. "Vatican II" allows the Latin mass to be translated into local languages around the world.

ENROLLED, 1962. JAMES MEREDITH, at the University of Mississippi, following a Supreme Court ruling that ordered his admission to the previously segregated school. Rioting and a showdown with state officials who wished to bar his enrollment preceded Meredith's entrance to classes.

BROKEN, 1965. 25-DAY FAST BY CÉSAR CHÁVEZ, labor organizer. His protest convinced others to join his nonviolent strike against the grape growers; shoppers boycotted table grapes in sympathy.

STRIPPED, 1967. MUHAMMAD ALI, of his heavyweight champion title, after refusing induction into the army following a rejection of his application for conscientious objector status. The boxer was arrested, given a five-year sentence, and fined $10,000.

PICKETED, 1968. The Miss America Pageant in Atlantic City, by protesters who believe the contest's emphasis on women's physical beauty is degrading and minimizes the importance of women's intellect.

AP

REMOVED, 1968. TOY GUNS, from the Sears, Roebuck Christmas catalog after the assassinations of Martin Luther King, Jr., and Robert Kennedy.

NUMBERS

7% of African American adults registered to vote in Mississippi in 1964 before passage of the Voting Rights Act of 1965

67% of African American adults in Mississippi registered to vote in 1969

70% of white adults registered to vote in 1964, nationwide

90% of white adults registered to vote nationwide in 1969

57 Number of days senators filibustered to hold up passage of the Civil Rights Bill in 1964

14½ Hours duration of all-night speech delivered by Senator Robert Byrd before a cloture vote stopped the filibuster

72% of elementary and high school teachers approve of corporal punishment as a disciplinary measure in 1961

HULTON-DEUTSCH COLLECTION/CORBIS

$80–90 Weekly pay for a clerk/typist in New York in 1965

$200 Rent for a two-bedroom apartment at Broadway and 72nd Street on New York City's Upper West Side in 1965

Portfolio Writing Project

Have students research one of the following people: John Glenn, Pope John XXIII, James Meredith, César Chávez, Muhammad Ali, Martin Luther King, Jr., or Robert Kennedy. Ask students to write a one-page essay about the person's contributions to history.

Creating a Nickname Have students research whether their city or county has a nickname, and what local history might have led to it. Then have students work in small groups to find a new nickname based on contemporary events, products, or reputation. Encourage students to be creative, but to select something that positively characterizes the area. List the groups' ideas on ballots. Have students vote for their top three choices. Tally the responses and identify the new nickname for the area. Have students give their suggested nickname to a local political leader.

CLOSE

Have students find out the number of registered voters who voted in the last presidential election. Students may focus on either national results or those from their own state or community.

EXTENDING THE CONTENT

Popular Culture In 1963 the top 10 television programs were: 1. *The Beverly Hillbillies,* 2. *Bonanza,* 3. *The Dick Van Dyke Show,* 4. *Petticoat Junction,* 5. *The Andy Griffith Show,* 6. *The Lucy Show,* 7. *Candid Camera,* 8. *The Ed Sullivan Show,* 9. *The Danny Thomas Show,* and 10. *My Favorite Martian.* The Limbo Rock, introduced by Chubby Checker, was the popular dance craze. The Beach Boys, with their melodic songs about hot rods and surfing, had five hit songs in 1963. *Cleopatra,* a film starring Elizabeth Taylor and Richard Burton, opened and was the most expensive film ever made to that date.

SECTION 3 The Great Society

Section Overview

This section focuses on the Johnson administration.

BELLRINGER
Skillbuilder Activity

Project transparency and have students answer the question.

Available as a blackline master.

Daily Focus Skills Transparency 28–3

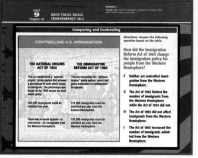

Guide to Reading

Answers to Graphic: Programs include Higher Education Act, HUD, Job Corps, Medicaid, Medicare, Project Head Start. (See chart, page 858 for summary.)

Preteaching Vocabulary
Have students create a database of the Key Terms and Names that includes a definition and other important facts.

Guide to Reading

Main Idea
Lyndon Johnson succeeded John F. Kennedy as president and greatly expanded Kennedy's agenda with far-reaching programs in many areas.

Key Terms and Names
consensus, war on poverty, VISTA, Great Society, Medicare, Medicaid, Head Start, Robert Weaver

Reading Strategy
Organizing As you read about Lyndon Johnson's presidency, complete a graphic organizer similar to the one below to list the social and economic programs started during his administration.

Reading Objectives
- **Explain** what inspired Johnson's Great Society programs.
- **Identify** several specific health and employment programs of the Johnson administration.

Section Theme
Government and Democracy In a time of prosperity, President Johnson won support for extending government aid to the poor and elderly.

Preview of Events

| ♦November 1963 | ♦June 1964 | ♦January 1965 | ♦August 1965 |

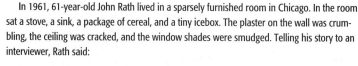

November 1963
Johnson becomes president upon Kennedy's death

August 1964
Congress enacts Economic Opportunity Act

November 1964
Johnson wins election as president

July 1965
Congress passes Medical Care Act, establishing Medicare and Medicaid

★ An American Story ★

In 1961, 61-year-old John Rath lived in a sparsely furnished room in Chicago. In the room sat a stove, a sink, a package of cereal, and a tiny icebox. The plaster on the wall was crumbling, the ceiling was cracked, and the window shades were smudged. Telling his story to an interviewer, Rath said:

Urban poverty in Chicago

I come home to an empty room. I don't even have a dog. No, this is not the kind of life I would choose. If a man had a little piece of land or something, a farm, or well . . . anyway, you've got to have something. You sit down in a place like this, you grit your teeth, you follow me? So many of them are doing that, they sit down, they don't know what to do, they go out. I see 'em in the middle of the night, they take a walk. Don't know what to do. Have no home environment, don't have a dog, don't have nothing . . . just a big zero.💬

—quoted in *Division Street: America*

Johnson Takes the Reins

John Rath's life was not the image that many Americans had of their country in the mid-1960s. The United States that President Lyndon Johnson inherited from John F. Kennedy appeared to be a booming, bustling place. From new shopping malls to new roads with new cars to fill them, everything in the country seemed to shout prosperity. Away from the nation's affluent suburbs, however, was another country, one inhabited by the poor, the ill-fed, the ill-housed, and the ill-educated. Writer Michael Harrington examined the nation's impoverished areas in his 1962 book, *The Other America.* Harrington claimed that while the truly poor numbered almost 50 million, they remained largely

SECTION RESOURCES

Reproducible Masters
- Reproducible Lesson Plan 28–3
- Daily Lecture and Discussion Notes 28–3
- Guided Reading Activity 28–3
- Section Quiz 28–3
- Reading Essentials and Study Guide 28–3
- Performance Assessment Activities and Rubrics

Transparencies
- Daily Focus Skills Transparency 28–3

Multimedia
- Interactive Tutor Self-Assessment CD-ROM
- ExamView® Pro Testmaker CD-ROM
- Presentation Plus! CD-ROM
- TeacherWorks™ CD-ROM
- Audio Program

hidden in city slums, in rural areas, in the Deep South, and on Native American reservations.

Harrington's book moved many Americans and inspired both President Kennedy and his successor, Lyndon Johnson, to make the elimination of poverty a major policy goal. The nation was prosperous, and many leaders had come to believe that the economy could be managed so that prosperity would be permanent. Thus it would be immoral not to devote national resources to reducing human suffering.

Lyndon Johnson invoked these ideals during the first dramatic days of his presidency. Immediately after President Kennedy was pronounced dead, officials whisked Johnson to the airport. At 2:38 P.M. on November 22, 1963, he stood in the cabin of Air Force One, the president's plane, with Jacqueline Kennedy on one side of him and his wife, Lady Bird, on the other. Johnson raised his right hand, placed his left hand on a Bible, and took the oath of office.

Johnson knew that he had to assure a stunned public that he could hold the nation together, that he was a leader. He later recalled the urgency with which he had to act:

❝A nation stunned, shaken to its very heart, had to be reassured that the government was not in a state of paralysis . . . that the business of the United States would proceed. I knew that not only the nation but the whole world would be anxiously following every move I made—watching, judging, weighing, balancing. . . . It was imperative that I grasp the reins of power and do so without delay. Any hesitation or wavering, any false step, any sign of self-doubt, could have been disastrous.❞

—quoted in *Lyndon Johnson and the American Dream*

Days after the assassination, Johnson appeared before Congress and urged the nation to move on. "The ideas and ideals which [Kennedy] so nobly represented must and will be translated into effective action," he stated. "John Kennedy's death commands what his life conveyed—that America must move forward."

Johnson's Leadership Style Lyndon Baines Johnson was born and raised in the "hill country" of central Texas, near the banks of the Pedernales River. He remained a Texan in his heart and in his life.

Johnson's style posed a striking contrast with Kennedy's. He was a man of impressive stature who spoke directly, convincingly, and even roughly at times. His style was more that of a persuasive and personable politician than of the elegant society man. Finding it difficult to gain acceptance from the Eastern establishment in the nation's capital, he often reveled in his rough image.

Johnson had honed his style in long years of public service. By the time he became president at age 55, he already had 26 years of congressional experience behind him. He had been a congressional staffer, a member of the U.S. House of Representatives, a U.S. senator, Senate majority leader, and vice president.

As he moved up the political ladder, Johnson developed a reputation as a man who got things done. He did favors, twisted arms, bargained, flattered, and threatened. The tactics he used to persuade others became known throughout Washington as the "Johnson treatment." Several writers described this often overpowering and intimidating style:

❝The Treatment could last ten minutes or four hours. . . . Its tone could be supplication, accusation, cajolery, exuberance, scorn, tears, complaint, the hint of threat. It was all these together. . . . Interjections from the target were rare. Johnson anticipated them

Picturing **History**

Home on the Range Born and raised in Texas, President Johnson loved to get back to his ranch in the Texas hill country. How does this image contrast with those of his predecessors?

2 TEACH

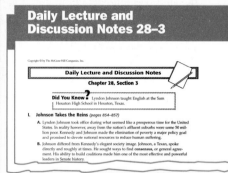

Daily Lecture and Discussion Notes 28–3

Copyright © by The McGraw-Hill Companies, Inc.

Daily Lecture and Discussion Notes
Chapter 28, Section 3

Did You Know? Lyndon Johnson taught English at the Sam Houston High School in Houston, Texas.

I. **Johnson Takes the Reins** *(pages 854–857)*

A. Lyndon Johnson took office during what seemed like a prosperous time for the United States. In reality however, away from the nation's affluent suburbs were some 50 million poor. Kennedy and Johnson made the elimination of poverty a major policy goal and promised to devote national resources to reduce human suffering.

B. Johnson differed from Kennedy's elegant society image. Johnson, a Texan, spoke directly and roughly at times. He sought ways to find consensus, or general agreement. His ability to build coalitions made him one of the most effective and powerful leaders in Senate history.

Creating a Poster Have students create a poster that illustrates one of the Great Society initiatives. Encourage students to use a before-and-after technique in which the poster shows both the need for the initiative and the proposed result of the program. **L1** ELL

you don't say...

What's in a Name? Lyndon Baines Johnson was the second man named Johnson to assume the mantle of the presidency after an assassination. Andrew Johnson became president after President Lincoln was killed.

Picturing **History**

Answer: Students should recognize that Johnson's image was considered rough compared to Kennedy's.
Ask: Where was Johnson born? *(Texas)*

COOPERATIVE LEARNING ACTIVITY

Identifying Influences Students will understand President Johnson better if they know something about his early years. Organize the class into small groups. Have the groups assign various topics to group members. Topics may include Johnson's hometown, home life, family social position, family members, favorite sports and hobbies, and schooling. The groups will meet to assemble a word portrait of President Johnson based on the information each group member finds. Have the groups share their word portraits with the class.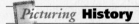

Use the rubric for a cooperative group management plan on pages 81–82 in the *Performance Assessment Activities and Rubrics.*

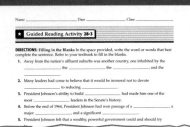
Writing a Letter Have students play the role of a member of one of the groups that had not experienced economic prosperity after World War II. From the point of view of the person they are playing, have students write a letter to President Johnson explaining what life is like and asking him to help. **L2**

📁 Use the rubric for a diary, short story, memorandum, or letter on pages 79–80 in the *Performance Assessment Activities and Rubrics.*

Picturing **History**

Background: The images in this picture present a sharp contrast to the prosperity many Americans had experienced in the years after World War II.
Answer: He had known hard times and felt a wealthy nation should try to improve living standards for all.
Ask: What was the name of Johnson's antipoverty program? *(the war on poverty)*

---

before they could be spoken. He moved in close, his face a scant millimeter from his target, his eyes widening and narrowing, his eyebrows rising and falling. From his pocket poured clippings, memos, statistics. Mimicry, humor, and the genius of analogy made The Treatment an almost hypnotic experience and rendered the target stunned and helpless. 99

—from *Lyndon Johnson: The Exercise of Power*

With every technique he could think of, Johnson sought to find consensus, or general agreement. His ability to build coalitions had made him one of the most effective and powerful leaders in the Senate's history.

A War on Poverty As president, Johnson used his considerable talents to push through a number of Kennedy's initiatives. Before the end of 1964, he won passage of a tax cut, a major civil rights bill, and a significant anti-poverty program.

Why was this powerful man so concerned about poor people? Johnson liked to exaggerate the poor conditions of his childhood for dramatic effect, but he had in fact known hard times. He had also seen extreme poverty firsthand in a brief career as a teacher in a low-income area. Johnson understood suffering, and he believed deeply in social action. He felt that a wealthy, powerful government could and should try to improve the lives of its citizens. Kennedy himself had said of Johnson, "He really cares about this nation." Finally, there was Johnson's ambition. He wanted to achieve great things so that history would record him as a great president. Attacking poverty was a good place to begin.

Plans for an anti-poverty program were already in place when Johnson took office, and he knew that he would be able to command strong support for any program that could be linked to Kennedy. In his State of the Union address to Congress in 1964, barely seven weeks after taking office, President Johnson told his audience: "Unfortunately, many Americans live on the outskirts of hope, some because of their poverty and some because of their color and all too many because of both." Johnson concluded his speech by announcing that his administration was declaring an "unconditional war on poverty in America."

Picturing **History**

Rural Poverty Photographs such as this one of Alice Mae Wyatt and her children—6-year-old Sally and 17-month-old Henry—shocked many Americans and won support for Johnson's programs. Why was the president so concerned about poverty?

" . . . *many Americans live on the outskirts of hope . . .*"
—*Lyndon Johnson*

MEETING SPECIAL NEEDS

Visual/Spatial Have interested students examine the photograph on this page and then research other scenes of poverty from the 1960s. Based on their research, have students draw or paint a scene depicting the reality of poverty. Encourage students to focus on the expressions of the people living in poverty. **L2**

📁 Refer to *Inclusion for the High School Social Studies Classroom Strategies and Activities* in the TCR.

By the summer of 1964, Johnson had convinced Congress to pass the Economic Opportunity Act. The act established a wide range of programs aimed at creating jobs and fighting poverty. It also created a new government agency, the Office of Economic Opportunity (OEO) to coordinate the new programs. Many of the new programs were directed at young Americans living in the inner city. The Neighborhood Youth Corps provided work-study programs to help underprivileged young men and women earn a high school diploma or college degree. The Job Corps tried to help young unemployed people find jobs. One of the more dramatic programs introduced was **VISTA** (Volunteers in Service to America), which was essentially a domestic Peace Corps. VISTA put young people with skills and community-minded ideals to work in poor neighborhoods and rural areas to help people overcome poverty.

The Election of 1964 As early as April 1964, *Fortune* magazine declared, "Lyndon Johnson has achieved a breadth of public approval few observers would have believed possible when he took office." Johnson had little time to enjoy such praise, for he was soon to run for the office he had first gained through a tragic event.

Johnson's Republican opponent in the 1964 presidential election was **Barry Goldwater** of Arizona, a senator known for his outspoken conservatism. He set the tone for his campaign when he accepted his party's nomination, declaring, "Extremism in the defense of liberty is no vice! And let me remind you also that moderation in the pursuit of justice is no virtue!"

Few Americans were ready to embrace Goldwater's message, which was too aggressive for a nation nervous about nuclear war. On Election Day, Johnson won in a landslide, winning all but five southern states and Arizona. "For the first time in my life," he said later, "I truly felt loved by the American people."

✓ **Reading Check** **Examining** What inspired the war on poverty?

The Great Society

After his election, Johnson began working with Congress to create the "Great Society" he had promised during his campaign. In this same period, major goals of the civil rights movement were achieved with the passage of the Civil Rights Act of 1964, which barred discrimination of many kinds, and the Voting Rights Act of 1965, which ensured African Americans' right to vote.

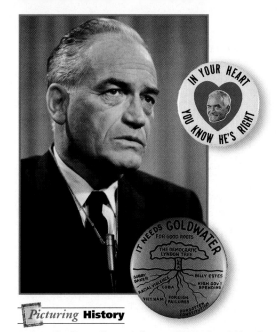

Picturing **History**

Conservative Stance The extreme language of Senator Barry Goldwater's campaign posed little challenge to President Johnson. How many states did Goldwater win?

The **Great Society** was Johnson's vision of the more perfect and equitable society the United States could and should become. According to Bill Moyers, who served as Johnson's press secretary, Johnson admired Franklin Roosevelt and wanted to fulfill FDR's mission. To do that would require a program that would be on the same large scale as the New Deal.

Johnson's goals were consistent with the times for several reasons. The civil rights movement had brought the grievances of African Americans to the forefront, reminding many that greater equality of opportunity had yet to be realized. Economics also supported Johnson's goal. The economy was strong, and many believed it would remain so indefinitely. There was no reason, therefore, that poverty could not be significantly reduced—especially when some had so much and others had so little.

Johnson first elaborated on the goals of the Great Society during a speech at the University of Michigan. It was clear that the president did not intend only to expand relief to the poor or to confine government efforts to material things. The president wanted, he said, to build a better society for all, a society "where leisure is a welcome chance to build and reflect, . . . where the city of man serves not only the needs of the body and the demands of commerce but the desire for beauty and the hunger for community. . . ."

CHAPTER 28 The New Frontier and the Great Society **857**

Creating Circle Graphs Provide the data below and ask students to make a pair of circle graphs showing the results of the presidential election of 1964. **L2**

Candidate	Popular Vote	Electoral Vote
Goldwater, Rep.	27,178,188	52
Johnson, Dem.	43,129,566	486

 Use the rubric for creating a map, display, or chart on pages 77–78 in the *Performance Assessment Activities and Rubrics.*

✓ **Reading Check**

Answer: the existence of pockets of extreme poverty in a generally prosperous society

FYI

When Head Start began, it was a summer program, but by 1970 most programs were year round. In 1999 Head Start enrollment was over 800,000 and cost an average of $5,400 per child.

INTERDISCIPLINARY CONNECTIONS ACTIVITY

Economics Ask the economics teacher to discuss with your class transfer payments by which the government transfers money from taxpaying citizens to needy people. Have the teacher provide statistics on transfer payments and discuss why Americans accept transfer payments as a way to deal with the problems of poverty. As a class, discuss the reasons that Americans approve of this role of the federal government. **L3**

Explaining Symbolism
President Johnson signed the Elementary and Secondary Education Act at his one-room schoolhouse, the Voting Rights Act in the room where Abraham Lincoln signed the Emancipation Proclamation, and the Immigration Act in the shadow of the Statue of Liberty. Ask students to explain the symbolism of each of these locations. **L2**

Chart *Skills*

Answers:
1. The Office of Economic Opportunity oversaw many inner-city programs.
2. Students' answers will vary but they should be able to explain how their chosen programs changed society.

Chart Skills Practice
Ask: How did health and welfare programs promote education?
(Child nutrition made students better able to learn from the educational programs offered.)

This ambitious vision encompassed a multitude of programs. In the three years between 1965 and 1968, more than 60 programs were passed. Among the most significant programs were **Medicare** and **Medicaid.** Health care reform had been a major issue since the days of Harry Truman. By the 1960s, public support for better health care benefits had solidified. Medicare had especially strong support since it was directed at the entire elderly population—in 1965, around half of those over the age of 65 had no health insurance.

Johnson convinced Congress to set up Medicare as a health insurance program funded through the Social Security system. Medicare's twin program, Medicaid, financed health care for welfare recipients, those who were living below the poverty line. Like the New Deal's Social Security program, both programs created what have been called "entitlements," that is, they entitle certain categories of Americans to benefits. Today, the cost of these programs has become a permanent part of the U.S. budget.

Great Society programs also strongly supported education. For Johnson, who had taught school when he was a young man, education was a personal passion. Vice President Hubert Humphrey once said that Johnson "was a nut on education. . . . [He] believed in it, just like some people believe in miracle cures."

The Elementary and Secondary Education Act of 1965 granted millions of dollars to public and private schools for textbooks, library materials, and special education programs. Efforts to improve education also extended to preschoolers, where Project **Head Start,** administered by the Office of Economic Opportunity, was directed at disadvantaged children who had "never looked at a picture book or scribbled with a crayon." Another program, Upward Bound, was designed to provide college preparation for low-income teenagers.

Improvements in health and education were only the beginning of the Great Society programs. Because of the deterioration of inner cities, Johnson told Congress that "America's cities are in crisis." Conditions in the cities—poor schools, crime, slum housing, poverty, and pollution—blighted the lives of those who lived there. Johnson urged Congress to act on several pieces of legislation addressing this issue.

Major Great Society Programs

Health and Welfare	Education	The "War on Poverty"	Consumer and Environmental Protection
Medicare (1965) established a comprehensive health insurance program for all elderly people; financed through the Social Security system.	**The Elementary and Secondary Education Act** (1965) targeted aid to students and funded related activities such as adult education and education counseling.	**The Office of Economic Opportunity** (1964) oversaw many programs to improve life in inner cities, including Job Corps, an education and job training program for at-risk youth.	**The Water Quality Act and Clean Air Acts** (1965) supported development of standards and goals for water and air quality.
Medicaid (1965) funded by federal and state governments, provided health and medical assistance to low-income families.	**Higher Education Act** (1965) supported college tuition scholarships, student loans, and work-study programs for low- and middle-income students.	**Housing and Urban Development Act** (1965) established new housing subsidy programs and made federal loans and public housing grants easier to obtain.	**The Highway Safety Act** (1966) supported highway safety by improving federal, state, and local coordination and by creating training standards for emergency medical technicians.
Child Nutrition Act (1966) established a school breakfast program and expanded the school lunch program and milk program to improve poor children's nutrition.	**Project Head Start** (1965) funded a preschool program for the disadvantaged.	**Demonstration Cities and Metropolitan Development Act** (1966) helped revitalize urban areas through a variety of social and economic programs.	**The Fair Packaging and Labeling Act** (1966) required all consumer products to have true and informative labels.

Chart *Skills*

1. **Interpreting Charts** What was the purpose of the Office of Economic Opportunity?
2. **Evaluating** Which Great Society program do you think had the most impact on American society? Why?

CRITICAL THINKING ACTIVITY

Evaluating Policies Tell students that Franklin Roosevelt appointed 27-year-old Lyndon Baines Johnson to serve as the national youth administrator for the state of Texas. Under Johnson's leadership, thousands of young people returned to high school, and thousands found work on government or private projects. Ask students how Johnson's early experience under Franklin Roosevelt's New Deal influenced his Great Society legislation in the 1960s. **L2**

NATIONAL GEOGRAPHIC
MOMENT in HISTORY

YOUTH'S HELPING HAND
In 1965 VISTA (Volunteers in Service to America) was created as part of President Johnson's war on poverty. Roused by the social consciousness of the early 1960s, thousands of students and young people focused their energy into working with local agencies in low-income communities around the nation. One of VISTA's basic themes was to help local communities mobilize their own resources. Since 1993 VISTA has been a part of the AmeriCorps network of service programs.

NATIONAL GEOGRAPHIC
MOMENT in HISTORY

Ask: How do you think programs such as VISTA brought out the positive, giving side of Americans? *(It allowed them to help people who were less fortunate.)*

✓ **Reading Check**

Answer: They included health, housing, job, and education programs.

3 ASSESS

Assign Section 3 Assessment as homework or as an in-class activity.

🖒 Have students use the **Interactive Tutor Self-Assessment CD-ROM.**

Reading Essentials and Study Guide 28–3

Name _____ Date _____ Class _____

Study Guide

Chapter 28, Section 3
For use with textbook pages 854–860

THE GREAT SOCIETY

KEY TERMS AND NAMES

consensus general agreement *(page 856)*
war on poverty a program announced by President Johnson to fight poverty in the United States *(page 856)*
VISTA a Great Society program in which young people were put to work in poor school districts *(page 857)*
Great Society the domestic programs and goals of President Johnson's administration *(page 857)*
Medicare a government health insurance program for the elderly *(page 858)*
Medicaid a government health care program that financed health care for people on welfare

One created a new cabinet agency, the Department of Housing and Urban Development, in 1965. Its first secretary, **Robert Weaver,** was the first African American to serve in a cabinet. A broad-based program informally called "Model Cities" authorized federal subsidies to many cities nationwide. The funds, matched by local and state contributions, supported an array of programs, including transportation, health care, housing, and policing. Since many depressed urban areas lacked sufficient or affordable housing, legislation also authorized about $8 billion to build houses for low- and middle-income people.

One notable Great Society measure changed the composition of the American population: the Immigration Reform Act of 1965. For a brief time, this act maintained a strict limit on the number of immigrants admitted to the United States each year: 170,000 from the Eastern Hemisphere and 120,000 from the Western Hemisphere. It did, however, eliminate the national origins system established in the 1920s, which had given preference to northern European immigrants. The new measure opened wider the door of the United States to newcomers from all parts of Europe, as well as from Asia and Africa.

✓ **Reading Check** **Summarizing** What were the Great Society programs?

Legacy of the Great Society

The Great Society programs touched nearly every aspect of American life and improved thousands if not millions of lives. In the years since President Johnson left office, however, debate has continued over whether or not the Great Society was truly a success.

In many ways, the impact of the Great Society was limited. In his rush to get as much done as he could, Johnson did not calculate exactly how his programs might work. As a result, some of them did not work as well as people had hoped. Furthermore, the programs grew so quickly they were often unmanageable and difficult to evaluate.

Cities, states, and groups eligible for aid began to expect immediate and life-changing benefits. These

CHAPTER 28 The New Frontier and the Great Society **859**

EXTENDING THE CONTENT

Social Security Administration The Social Security Administration has many service facilities around the country, employing thousands. In Johnson's Great Society, it participated in community projects to identify, train, and motivate unemployed and underemployed people. It worked with college placement officers, especially in African American colleges, to communicate information about government careers. It also worked with local community groups such as the Opportunities Industrialization Center, Metropolitan Employment Councils, and Equal Opportunity Commissions to reach the chronically unemployed.

Section Quiz 28–3

Profiles IN HISTORY

Ask: For what causes did Esther Peterson fight? (*women's rights, trade unions, and consumer rights*)

Reteach
Have students explain what inspired the Great Society programs.

Enrich
Have interested students research LBJ's plan for Model Cities and write a report on the plans and how they were later modified.

✓ Reading Check

Answer: It improved millions of lives and reshaped government.

4 CLOSE

Have students identify several specific health and employment programs of the Johnson era.

Profiles IN HISTORY

Esther Peterson
1906–1997

In the 1930s, Boston employers asked women who sewed aprons for them to switch from square pockets to a more difficult heart-shaped pocket, but they did not offer any increase in pay. Esther Peterson, a local teacher and outspoken advocate for women's rights, led the workers in a strike for more money. The women won their pay raise. For 60 years, Esther Peterson continued to use her tact and will to fight for women's rights, trade unions, and consumers.

Born in Provo, Utah, as Esther Eggertsen, Peterson became a teacher in the 1930s. She taught milliners, telephone operators, and garment workers at the innovative Bryn Mawr Summer School for Women Workers in Industry. In 1961 President Kennedy selected her to serve as Assistant Secretary of Labor and Director of the Women's Bureau.

Peterson then encouraged Kennedy to create a Presidential Commission on the Status of Women to focus attention on working women.

Under President Johnson, Peterson served as Special Assistant for Consumer Affairs, where she worked on consumer concerns. Lynda Johnson Robb, daughter of President Johnson, described Peterson this way: "She had a velvet hammer and talked people into doing what was right, even if we didn't know it at the time." Peterson continued to use her "velvet hammer" for the public good throughout her long life. At the time of her death at the age of 91, she was actively promoting senior citizens' health issues.

expectations often left many feeling frustrated and angry. Other Americans opposed the massive growth of federal programs and criticized the Great Society for intruding too much into their lives.

A lack of funds also hurt the effectiveness of Great Society programs. The programs themselves were expensive enough. When Johnson attempted to fund both his grand domestic agenda and the increasingly costly war in Vietnam, the Great Society eventually suffered. Some Great Society initiatives have survived

to the present, however. These include Medicare and Medicaid, two cabinet agencies—the Department of Transportation and the Department of Housing and Urban Development (HUD)—and Project Head Start. Overall, the programs provided some important benefits to poorer communities and gave political and administrative experience to minority groups.

An important legacy of the Great Society was the questions it produced, questions Americans continue to consider. How can the federal government help its disadvantaged citizens? How much government help can a society have without weakening the private sector? How much help can its people receive without losing motivation to fight against hardships on their own?

Lyndon Johnson came into office determined to change the United States in a way few other presidents had attempted. If he fell short, it was perhaps that the goals he set were so high. In evaluating the administration's efforts, the *New York Times* wrote, "The walls of the ghettos are not going to topple overnight, nor is it possible to wipe out the heritage of generations of social, economic, and educational deprivation by the stroke of a Presidential pen."

✓ Reading Check
Evaluating What was the impact of the Great Society?

SECTION 3 ASSESSMENT

Checking for Understanding
1. **Define:** consensus, war on poverty.
2. **Identify:** VISTA, Great Society, Medicare, Medicaid, Head Start, Robert Weaver.
3. **Describe** how the Great Society programs were inspired.

Reviewing Themes
4. **Government and Democracy** How did Johnson's war on poverty strive to ensure greater fairness in American society?

Critical Thinking
5. **Interpreting** What were three legacies of the Great Society?
6. **Organizing** Use a graphic organizer similar to the one below to list five of the Great Society initiatives that have survived to the present.

Great Society Initiatives

Analyzing Visuals
7. **Photographs** Study the photograph on page 856. Why do you think pictures such as this one would help build support for the war on poverty?

Writing About History
8. **Descriptive Writing** Take on the role of a biographer. Write a chapter in a biography of Lyndon Johnson in which you compare and contrast his leadership style to that of John Kennedy.

860 CHAPTER 28   The New Frontier and the Great Society

SECTION 3 ASSESSMENT ANSWERS

1. Terms are in blue.
2. VISTA (*p. 857*), Great Society (*p. 857*), Medicare (*p. 858*), Medicaid (*p. 858*), Head Start (*p. 858*), Robert Weaver (*p. 859*)
3. Johnson wanted to fulfill FDR's mission for a nation of equal opportunity.
4. by offering the less fortunate education, training, and access to jobs
5. Answers should reflect text, for example, Medicare and Medicaid, political experience for minorities, Head Start.
6. Medicare, Medicaid, Department of Transportation, Department of Housing and Urban Development, Project Head Start
7. Answers will vary. Students should describe the emotions evoked by such photographs.
8. Chapters should include specific information about the leadership styles of the two men.

Critical Thinking SKILLBUILDER

Problem Solving

Why Learn This Skill?

Imagine you have just done poorly on a chemistry exam. You wonder why you cannot do better since you always go to class, take notes, and study for exams. In order to improve your grades, you need to identify the specific problem and then take actions to solve it.

Learning the Skill

There are six key steps you should follow that will help you through the problem-solving process.

- Identify the problem. In the case listed above, you know that you are not doing well on chemistry exams.

- Gather information. You know that you always go to class and take notes. You study by yourself for about two hours each day for two or three days before the exam. You also know that you sometimes forget details or get confused about things as you are taking the exam.

- List and consider possible solutions. For example, instead of studying by yourself, you might try studying with a friend or a group. You might also study for shorter timespans to avoid overloading yourself with information.

- Consider the advantages and disadvantages of each solution.

- Now that you have listed and considered the possible options, you need to choose the best solution to your problem. Choose what you think is the right solution, and carry it out.

- Evaluate the effectiveness of the solution. This will help you determine if you have solved the problem. If you earn better scores on the next few chemistry tests, you will know that you have solved your problem.

Practicing the Skill

Reread the material in Section 1 on page 842 under the heading "Kennedy Struggles with Congress." Use that information and the steps listed on this page to answer the following questions.

1. What problem did Kennedy encounter as he tried to pass domestic policy legislation through Congress?

2. What options were available to the president in facing this opposition? What were the advantages and disadvantages?

3. Explain the solution Kennedy implemented to solve his problem.

4. Evaluate the effectiveness of Kennedy's solution. Was it successful? How do you determine this?

Skills Assessment

Complete the Practicing Skills questions on page 863 and the Chapter 28 Skill Reinforcement Activity to assess your mastery of this skill.

Applying the Skill

Problem Solving The conservation club at your school has no money to continue its recycling project. The school district allocated money to the club at the beginning of the year, but that money has been spent. As a member of the club, you have been asked to join a committee to save the conservation club and its projects. Write an essay describing the problem, the list of options and their advantages and disadvantages, a solution, and an evaluation of the chosen solution.

 Glencoe's **Skillbuilder Interactive Workbook CD-ROM, Level 2,** provides instruction and practice in key social studies skills.

861

TEACH

Problem Solving Tell students that when they encounter problems the first step is identifying the problem.

As a class, students should select a problem that the community is facing. Have students work in pairs to use the problem-solving process to identify the best solution. Have the class reach a consensus on the best solution. Submit the class's suggestion to local political leaders or other decision makers who may be working on the problem.

Additional Practice

Reinforcing Skills Activity 28

Name _____ Date _____ Class _____

★ Reinforcing Skills Activity 28

Problem Solving

❏ **LEARNING THE SKILL**
The first step in identifying a problem is clearly defining it. After you have identified a problem, begin to gather information about it. Then consider possible solutions to the problem, and weigh the advantages and disadvantages of each solution you have identified. Use your list of positives and negatives to pick the best solution. As you begin to put your solution into action, monitor the results. Has your solution been effective in solving your problem? If not, make adjustments to your solution as necessary.

❏ **PRACTICING THE SKILL**
DIRECTIONS: Read the excerpt below from page 847 of your text. Then answer the questions that follow on a separate sheet of paper.

GLENCOE TECHNOLOGY

 CD-ROM
Glencoe Skillbuilder Interactive Workbook CD-ROM, Level 2

This interactive CD-ROM reinforces student mastery of essential social studies skills.

ANSWERS TO PRACTICING THE SKILL

1. congressional resistance
2. He could push harder for all aspects of his agenda or reserve his bargaining power for only the issues that were truly important and winnable.
3. He chose to reserve his bargaining power.
4. Students' answers will vary. Students might mention

that many of JFK's proposals were defeated, or that he lacked political leverage no matter what strategy he used.

Applying the Skill
Students' essays will vary. Encourage students to use the steps on this page as they plan their essays.

CHAPTER 28 ASSESSMENT and ACTIVITIES

Reviewing Key Terms

Students' answers will vary. The pages where the words appear in the text are shown in parentheses.

1. **missile gap** *(p. 841)*
2. **reapportionment** *(p. 843)*
3. **due process** *(p. 844)*
4. **flexible response** *(p. 847)*
5. **space race** *(p. 847)*
6. **consensus** *(p. 856)*
7. **war on poverty** *(p. 856)*

Reviewing Key Facts

8. New Frontier *(p. 842)*, Earl Warren *(p. 843)*, Peace Corps *(p. 847)*, Warren Commission *(p. 851)*, Great Society *(p. 857)*, Head Start *(p. 858)*

9. The campaign marked the first time that television played a major role, including the televised debate between Kennedy and Nixon.

10. They focused on the economy and the Cold War.

11. Kennedy won the popular vote by only 118,000, with 68 million votes cast. In the Electoral College, the margin was greater: 303 to 219.

12. He threatened to buy steel from foreign companies and investigated price fixing.

13. He used deficit spending, invested in space exploration and defense to create jobs, and asked businesses to hold down prices and labor leaders to hold down pay increase requests.

14. conventional weaponry program, foreign aid, the Peace Corps

15. Johnson's personal experiences and the nation's ability to finance programs

Reviewing Key Terms

On a sheet of paper, use each of these terms in a sentence.

1. missile gap
2. reapportionment
3. due process
4. flexible response
5. space race
6. consensus
7. war on poverty

Reviewing Key Facts

8. **Identify:** New Frontier, Earl Warren, Peace Corps, Warren Commission, Great Society, Head Start.

9. How was the 1960 presidential election a new kind of campaign?

10. What main issues did Nixon and Kennedy discuss in their televised debate?

11. How close was the outcome of the 1960 presidential election between Nixon and Kennedy?

12. What was Kennedy's response to the steel industry's decision to raise prices sharply?

13. What were three measures Kennedy took to strengthen the economy?

14. What were three programs set up by Kennedy to reduce the threat of nuclear war and to try to stem communism?

15. What inspired President Johnson's war on poverty?

16. What was the purpose of Medicare, passed during Johnson's administration?

17. Which Great Society initiatives are still in effect today?

Critical Thinking

18. **Analyzing Themes: Government and Democracy** Why were Medicare and Medicaid landmark pieces of legislation in American history?

19. **Evaluating** In the 1960 presidential debate, most radio listeners thought Nixon had won, while most television viewers thought Kennedy had. Why do you think this was so?

20. **Drawing Conclusions** How did Kennedy help prevent Communist movements from flourishing in Latin America?

21. **Analyzing** President Kennedy was unable to pass civil rights legislation. What were some of the factors that allowed President Johnson to push civil rights forward after Kennedy's assassination?

22. **Organizing** Use a graphic organizer similar to the one below to list the crises of the Cold War during the Kennedy administration.

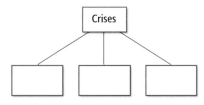

23. **Evaluating** How did the Warren Court decisions in *Baker* v. *Carr* and *Reynolds* v. *Sims* affect voting power in the nation?

24. **Interpreting Primary Sources** Although the standard of living for most Americans rose dramatically throughout the

Chapter Summary

The New Frontier and the Great Society

Domestic Programs
- Office of Economic Opportunity fights illiteracy, unemployment, and disease.
- Civil Rights Act of 1964 prohibits race discrimination and social segregation.
- Voting Rights Act protects the right to vote.
- Medicare and Medicaid Acts provide federal medical aid to the elderly and poor.
- Elementary and Secondary Education Act increases aid for public schools.

Foreign Policy
- "Flexible response" policy maintains opposition to communism.
- U.S. pledges aid to struggling Latin American nations.
- Peace Corps offers humanitarian aid in poor countries.
- Nuclear Test Ban Treaty with the Soviet Union eases Cold War tensions.

Supreme Court Cases
- *Reynolds* v. *Sims* boosts voting power of urban dwellers, including many minorities.
- Extension of due process gives more protection to people accused of crimes.
- Court rules that states could not require prayer and Bible readings in public schools.

16. Medicare was designed as a health insurance program for the elderly.

17. Among programs or agencies still in effect are Medicare, Medicaid, Head Start, Department of Transportation, and Department of Housing and Urban Development.

Critical Thinking

18. They represented the first time that the U.S. government had funded health care on a large scale.

19. Kennedy's physical appearance and demeanor made a positive impact on the television audience. Their reaction to Nixon's appearance and demeanor was negative. Because they could only hear the candidates, radio listeners had a different reaction.

1960s, some Americans remained mired in poverty. Reread the excerpt on page 854 in which John Rath discusses his personal experiences with coping with poverty in his sparsely furnished room in Chicago. Then answer the following questions.

a. What does Rath think might help him to have some purpose in his life?

b. What does Rath mean when he says: "You sit down in a place like this, you grit your teeth. . . ."?

Practicing Skills

25. Problem Solving Reread the passage on pages 849–850 titled "The Cuban Missile Crisis." Use that information to answer the following questions.

a. What problem did Kennedy encounter in Cuba?

b. What options were available to the president in this situation? What were the advantages and disadvantages of each option?

c. Explain the solution Kennedy used to resolve the Cuban missile crisis.

d. Was Kennedy's solution successful? Why or why not?

Chapter Activity

26. Technology Activity: Using the Internet Search the Internet to check the status of Great Society programs today. Find out how these programs have changed since they were initiated. Make a chart showing the provisions of the programs in the 1960s compared to the provisions of the programs today.

Writing Activity

27. Expository Writing Assume the role of a historian. Evaluate the effectiveness of Kennedy's New Frontier and Johnson's Great Society programs. Write an article for a historical journal explaining the successes and setbacks of each president's policy agendas.

Geography and History

28. The map on this page shows the results of the presidential election of 1960. Study the map and answer the questions below.

a. Interpreting Maps Which regions of the country supported Kennedy? Which regions supported Nixon?

b. Applying Geography Skills What would have happened if Kennedy had lost New York to Nixon?

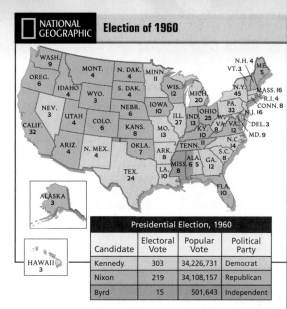

NATIONAL GEOGRAPHIC **Election of 1960**

Presidential Election, 1960			
Candidate	Electoral Vote	Popular Vote	Political Party
Kennedy	303	34,226,731	Democrat
Nixon	219	34,108,157	Republican
Byrd	15	501,643	Independent

The Princeton Review

Standardized Test Practice

Directions: Choose the best answer to the following question.

All of the following were effects of rulings by the Warren Court EXCEPT:

A Involved federal courts in the reapportionment of state election districts

B Extended rights for people accused of crimes

C Protected religious minorities through greater separation of church and state

D Increased state authority at the expense of federal authority

Test-Taking Tip: This question calls for an answer that does NOT accurately complete the statement. The Warren Court expanded individual civil liberties and the power of the judicial branch. Eliminate answers that had either of those effects.

CHAPTER 28   The New Frontier and the Great Society   **863**

Chapter Activity

26. Students' charts will vary. You may want to have students work in pairs on this activity.

Writing Activity

27. Students' articles will vary but should use the perspective of history to evaluate the successes and failures of the programs.

Geography and History

28. a. Nixon: Midwest, West; Kennedy: Northeast, some Southern and Midwestern states; **b.** Nixon would have won the election by six electoral votes.

The Princeton Review

Standardized Test Practice

Answer: D

Test-Taking Tip: Even if students do not know all the rulings of the Warren Court, they can eliminate some of the answers by applying the knowledge they do have. For example, if students know that the decision of one case banned prayer in public schools, they can eliminate answer C because one of the effects of the Warren Court protected religious minorities through greater separation of church and state. The correct answer is D.

---

20. He provided aid to Latin America so that countries would be less likely to support communist-inspired revolutions.

21. the civil rights movement, Kennedy's death, Johnson's style of leadership

22. Bay of Pigs, Berlin Wall, Cuban missile crisis

23. In *Baker* v. *Carr,* the court ruled that the federal government has the right to enforce voting rights in the states. In *Reynolds* v. *Sims,* the court ruled that many states' apportionment plans were unconstitutional.

24. a. owning his home; **b.** The statement shows helplessness, desperation, and frustration.

Practicing Skills

25. a. long-range missiles; **b.** acceptance of the missiles (unacceptable for national security); threats to use nuclear weapons (nuclear devastation); negotiation backed by threat of force (actual choice); **c.** negotiations; **d.** solution was successful for the immediate problem but it led to arms buildup

Bonus Question ?

Ask: Which president started the Peace Corps? *(Kennedy)*

Chapter 29 Resources

TeacherWorks™ All-In-One Planner and Resource Center

- **Interactive Teacher Edition** Access your Teacher Wraparound Edition and your classroom resources with a few easy clicks.
- **Interactive Lesson Planner** Planning has never been easier! Organize your week, month, semester, or year with all the lesson helps you need to make teaching creative, timely, and relevant.

Use Glencoe's **Presentation Plus!** multimedia teacher tool to easily present dynamic lessons that visually excite your students. Using Microsoft PowerPoint® you can customize the presentations to create your own personalized lessons.

TEACHING TRANSPARENCIES

Graphic Organizer 9

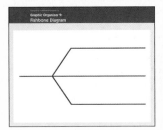

Why It Matters Chapter Transparency 29

APPLICATION AND ENRICHMENT

Linking Past and Present Activity 29

Enrichment Activity 29

Primary Source Reading 29

REVIEW AND REINFORCEMENT

Reteaching Activity 29

Vocabulary Activity 29

Time Line Activity 29

Critical Thinking Skills Activity 29

Meeting NCSS Standards

The following standards are highlighted in Chapter 29:

Section 1 Ⅵ Power, Authority, and Governance: A, C, D, F, H, I
Section 2 Ⅷ Science, Technology, and Society: A, B, C
Section 3 Ⅹ Civic Ideals and Practices: A, C, E, F, G, J

Local Standards

Chapter 29 Resources

ASSESSMENT AND EVALUATION

Chapter 29 Test Form A

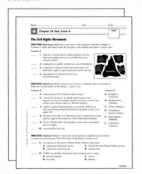

Chapter 29 Test Form B

Standardized Test Skills Practice Workbook Activity 29

Performance Assessment Activities and Rubrics 29

ExamView® Pro Testmaker CD-ROM

MULTIMEDIA

- Vocabulary PuzzleMaker CD-ROM
- Interactive Tutor Self-Assessment CD-ROM
- ExamView® Pro Testmaker CD-ROM
- Audio Program
- American History Primary Source Documents Library CD-ROM
- MindJogger Videoquiz
- Presentation Plus! CD-ROM
- TeacherWorks™ CD-ROM
- Interactive Student Edition CD-ROM
- Glencoe Skillbuilder Interactive Workbook CD-ROM, Level 2
- The *American Vision* Video Program
- American Music: Hits Through History
- American Music: Cultural Traditions

SPANISH RESOURCES

The following Spanish language materials are available in the Spanish Resources Binder:

- Spanish Guided Reading Activities
- Spanish Reteaching Activities
- Spanish Quizzes and Tests
- Spanish Vocabulary Activities
- Spanish Summaries
- The Declaration of Independence and United States Constitution Spanish Translation

---

The following videotape programs are available from Glencoe as supplements to Chapter 29:

- **Martin Luther King, Jr.: The Man and the Dream** (ISBN 0-76-701057-4)
- **Thurgood Marshall: Justice for All** (ISBN 0-76-700121-4)
- **Malcolm X: A Search for Identity** (ISBN 1-56-501674-2)

To order, call Glencoe at 1-800-334-7344. To find classroom resources to accompany many of these videos, check the following home pages:
A&E Television: www.aande.com
The History Channel: www.historychannel.com

Use our Web site for additional resources. All essential content is covered in the Student Edition.

You and your students can visit tav.glencoe.com, the Web site companion to the *American Vision*. This innovative integration of electronic and print media offers your students a wealth of opportunities. The student text directs students to the Web site for the following options:

- **Chapter Overviews**
- **Self-Check Quizzes**
- **Student Web Activities**
- **Textbook Updates**

Answers to the student Web activities are provided for you in the **Web Activity Lesson Plans.** Additional Web resources and Interactive Tutor Puzzles are also available.

Chapter 29 Resources

SECTION RESOURCES

Daily Objectives	Reproducible Resources	Multimedia Resources
SECTION 1 **The Movement Begins** 1. Explain the origin of the Southern Christian Leadership Conference. 2. Discuss the changing role of the federal government in civil rights enforcement.	Reproducible Lesson Plan 29–1 Daily Lecture and Discussion Notes 29–1 Guided Reading Activity 29–1* Section Quiz 29–1* Reading Essentials and Study Guide 29–1 Performance Assessment Activities and Rubrics Supreme Court Case Studies	Daily Focus Skills Transparency 29–1 Interactive Tutor Self-Assessment CD-ROM ExamView® Pro Testmaker CD-ROM Presentation Plus! CD-ROM TeacherWorks™ CD-ROM Audio Program
SECTION 2 **Challenging Segregation** 1. Evaluate the Civil Rights Act of 1964. 2. Summarize the efforts to establish voting rights for African Americans.	Reproducible Lesson Plan 29–2 Daily Lecture and Discussion Notes 29–2 Guided Reading Activity 29–2* Section Quiz 29–2* Reading Essentials and Study Guide 29–2 Performance Assessment Activities and Rubrics	Daily Focus Skills Transparency 29–2 Interactive Tutor Self-Assessment CD-ROM ExamView® Pro Testmaker CD-ROM Presentation Plus! CD-ROM TeacherWorks™ CD-ROM Audio Program American Music: Hits Through History American Music: Cultural Traditions
SECTION 3 **New Issues** 1. Describe the division between Dr. Martin Luther King, Jr., and the black power movement. 2. Discuss the direction and progress of the civil rights movement after 1968.	Reproducible Lesson Plan 29–3 Daily Lecture and Discussion Notes 29–3 Guided Reading Activity 29–3* Section Quiz 29–3* Reading Essentials and Study Guide 29–3 Performance Assessment Activities and Rubrics Supreme Court Case Studies	Daily Focus Skills Transparency 29–3 Interactive Tutor Self-Assessment CD-ROM ExamView® Pro Testmaker CD-ROM Presentation Plus! CD-ROM Skillbuilder Interactive Workbook, Level 2 TeacherWorks™ CD-ROM Vocabulary PuzzleMaker CD-ROM Audio Program

`0:00` OUT OF TIME?
Assign the Chapter 29 **Reading Essentials and Study Guide.**

*Also Available in Spanish

 Blackline Master Transparency CD-ROM DVD

 Poster Music Program Audio Program Videocassette

NATIONAL GEOGRAPHIC | **Teacher's Corner**

INDEX TO NATIONAL GEOGRAPHIC MAGAZINE

The following articles relate to this chapter.
- "I Dream a World: America's Black Women," August 1989
- "National Trail to Recall Civil Rights Marches," March 1994
- "Philadelphia's African Americans," August 1990
- "Selma to Montgomery: The Road to Equality," February 2000

NATIONAL GEOGRAPHIC SOCIETY PRODUCTS AVAILABLE FROM GLENCOE

To order the following products for use with this chapter, contact your local Glencoe sales representative, or call Glencoe at 1-800-334-7344:
- *PictureShow: Civil Rights* (CD-ROM)
- *PicturePack: Civil Rights* (Transparencies)

ADDITIONAL NATIONAL GEOGRAPHIC SOCIETY PRODUCTS

To order the following, call National Geographic at 1-800-368-2728:
- *NGS PictureShow: Civil Rights* (CD-ROM, Transparencies)

NGS ONLINE

Access National Geographic's Web site for current events, atlas updates, activities, links, interactive features, and archives.

www.nationalgeographic.com

From the Classroom of...

Jason Follett
Malcolm Price Laboratory School
Cedar Falls, IA

Birmingham's 16th Street Baptist Church Bombing Lesson Plan

This activity helps students understand how the civil rights movement in the United States affected students their own age.

First, read and discuss literature that focuses on the tensions in Birmingham in 1963. Present Associated Press file photos of the era and discuss the Robert Chambliss trial. Then watch, discuss, and take notes on Spike Lee's documentary *4 Little Girls*. To end this section, have students read the latest news surrounding this event.

Students should build a story map with the climax and resolution clearly identified. Using the story map, students create a hand-drawn or computer-drawn comic book of the bombing and a student guide to drawing a comic book. Examples of non-humor comic books can be obtained through the Federal Reserve System. The best way to evaluate these comic books is to use a rubric.

ADDITIONAL RESOURCES FROM GLENCOE

- American Music: Cultural Traditions
- American Art & Architecture
- Outline Map Resource Book
- U.S. Desk Map
- Building Geography Skills for Life
- Inclusion for the High School Social Studies Classroom Strategies and Activities
- Teaching Strategies for the American History Classroom (Including Block Scheduling Pacing Guides)

KEY TO ABILITY LEVELS

Teaching strategies have been coded.

L1 BASIC activities for all students

L2 AVERAGE activities for average to above-average students

L3 CHALLENGING activities for above-average students

ELL ENGLISH LANGUAGE LEARNER activities

 Block Schedule

Activities that are suited to use within the block scheduling framework are identified by:

Why It Matters Activity

Ask students what kind of an impact they think the civil rights movement had on their communities. Students should evaluate their answers after they have completed the chapter.

864

CHAPTER
29 The Civil Rights Movement *1954–1968*

Why It Matters

During the 1960s, African Americans made major strides. They began by challenging segregation in the South. With the Montgomery bus boycott, Martin Luther King, Jr., achieved national and worldwide recognition. His peaceful resistance inspired many, especially students. After King's assassination, the civil rights movement became more assertive. Many people in the movement began to see economic opportunity as the key to equality.

The Impact Today

Changes brought about by the civil rights movement are still with us.
- Civil rights legislation provides protection against discrimination for all citizens.
- Economic programs for inner-city residents by government and social service agencies continue.

The American Vision *Video* The Chapter 29 video, "The Civil Rights Movement," chronicles the milestones of the movement to win rights for African Americans.

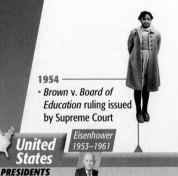

1954
- *Brown* v. *Board of Education* ruling issued by Supreme Court

1955
- Rosa Parks refuses to give up bus seat; Montgomery bus boycott begins in Alabama

1957
- Eisenhower sends troops to a Little Rock, Arkansas, high school to ensure integration

1960
- Sit-in protests begin

United States PRESIDENTS

Eisenhower 1953–1961

Kennedy 1961–1963

1953　　　　*1957*　　　　*1961*

World

1955
- West Germany admitted to NATO

1958
- Pasternak's *Dr. Zhivago* awarded Nobel Prize for Literature

1959
- Mary Leakey discovers 1.7 million-year-old hominid skull fragment in Tanzania

1960
- France successfully tests nuclear weapons

864

TWO-MINUTE LESSON LAUNCHER

Bring to class books or magazines that show pictures from the civil rights movement. Invite students to examine the photos without reading the captions. Ask students to look closely at the facial expressions and body language of the participants. Ask students what they can learn about the civil rights movement simply from looking at these photos.

Americans march from Selma, Alabama, to Montgomery in support of the civil rights movement.

HISTORY *Online*

Introduce students to chapter content and key terms by having them access the **Chapter 29 Overview** at tav.glencoe.com.

More About the Photo

Tell students that in 1963, Selma, Alabama, was a small town of about 30,000 people. At the time only about 1 percent of the African Americans eligible to vote in Dallas County, where Selma is located, was registered. The system there strongly discouraged African Americans from registering to vote. Ask students how they think the civil rights movement showed both how far African Americans had come and how far they still had to go to obtain full rights as citizens of the United States.

1963
• Over 200,000 civil rights supporters march on Washington, D.C.

Johnson 1963–1969

1965
• Malcolm X assassinated
• Race riots erupt in Los Angeles neighborhood of Watts

1968
• Civil Rights Act of 1968 passed
• Martin Luther King, Jr., assassinated

1965   *1969*

1963
• Organization of African Unity formed
• Kenya becomes an independent nation

1965
• China's Cultural Revolution begins

1967
• Arab-Israeli War brings many Palestinians under Israeli rule

HISTORY *Online*

Chapter Overview
Visit the *American Vision* Web site at tav.glencoe.com and click on *Chapter Overviews—Chapter 29* to preview chapter information.

TIME LINE ACTIVITY

Have students write a paragraph about how the events listed on the time line have affected their lives within the last year. Invite students to share their paragraphs with the class.

GRAPHIC ORGANIZER ACTIVITY

Organizing Information Have students complete a graphic organizer similar to the one below to help them focus on the results of various events in the civil rights movement. Student answers will vary but should include: the Montgomery bus boycott; challenging segregation at the voting booths and in public transportation, housing, and facilities; the sit-in movement; the formation of SNCC; the registration of African American voters; and the challenge to segregation in the Democratic party.

Civil Rights Confrontation	Reactions and Results

865

SECTION 1 The Movement Begins

1 FOCUS

Section Overview

This section focuses on the beginning of the civil rights movement.

BELLRINGER
Skillbuilder Activity

Project transparency and have students answer the question.

Available as a blackline master.

Daily Focus Skills Transparency 29–1

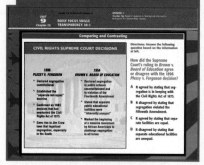

Guide to Reading

Answers to Graphic: segregation, lack of voting rights, African American experiences in World War II

Preteaching Vocabulary
Have students create a database using the Key Terms and Names. Have them add facts as they learn more about each term, person, event, or group.

Guide to Reading

Main Idea
After World War II, African Americans and other supporters of civil rights challenged segregation in the United States.

Key Terms and Names
separate-but-equal, de facto segregation, NAACP, sit-in, Thurgood Marshall, Linda Brown, Dr. Martin Luther King, Jr., Southern Christian Leadership Conference

Reading Strategy
Organizing As you read about the birth of the civil rights movement, complete a graphic organizer similar to the one below by filling in the causes of the civil rights movement.

Civil Rights Movement

Reading Objectives
• **Explain** the origin of the Southern Christian Leadership Conference.
• **Discuss** the changing role of the federal government in civil rights enforcement.

Section Theme
Government and Democracy In the 1950s, African Americans began a movement to win greater social equality.

Preview of Events

◆1954	◆1955	◆1956	◆1957
1954 Brown v. Board of Education of Topeka, Kansas, decision	**1955** Rosa Parks refuses to give up bus seat in Montgomery, Alabama	**1956** Group of 101 Southern members of Congress sign Southern Manifesto	**1957** Southern Christian Leadership Conference formed

Rosa Parks

★ An American Story ★

On December 1, 1955, Rosa Parks left her job as a seamstress in Montgomery, Alabama, and boarded a bus to go home. In 1955 buses in Montgomery reserved seats in the front for whites and seats in the rear for African Americans. Seats in the middle were open to African Americans, but only if there were few whites on the bus.

Rosa Parks took a seat just behind the white section. Soon all of the seats on the bus were filled. When the bus driver noticed a white man standing at the front of the bus, he told Parks and three other African Americans in her row to get up and let the white man sit down. Nobody moved. The driver cautioned, "Y'all better make it light on yourselves and let me have those seats." The other three African Americans rose, but Rosa Parks did not. The driver then called the Montgomery police, who took Parks into custody.

News of the arrest soon reached E.D. Nixon, a former president of the local chapter of the National Association for the Advancement of Colored People (NAACP). Nixon wanted to challenge bus segregation in court, and he told Parks, "With your permission we can break down segregation on the bus with your case." Parks told Nixon, "If you think it will mean something to Montgomery and do some good, I'll be happy to go along with it."

—adapted from *Parting the Waters: America in the King Years*

The Origins of the Movement

When Rosa Parks agreed to challenge segregation in court, she did not know that her decision would launch the modern civil rights movement. Within days of her arrest, African Americans in Montgomery had organized a boycott of the bus system. Mass

---

SECTION RESOURCES

Reproducible Masters
• Reproducible Lesson Plan 29–1
• Daily Lecture and Discussion Notes 29–1
• Guided Reading Activity 29–1
• Section Quiz 29–1
• Reading Essentials and Study Guide 29–1
• Supreme Court Case Studies

Transparencies
• Daily Focus Skills Transparency 29–1

Multimedia
• Interactive Tutor Self-Assessment CD-ROM
• ExamView® Pro Testmaker CD-ROM
• Presentation Plus! CD-ROM
• TeacherWorks™ CD-ROM
• Audio Program

protests began across the nation. After decades of segregation and inequality, many African Americans had decided the time had come to demand equal rights.

The struggle would not be easy. The Supreme Court had declared segregation to be constitutional in *Plessy v. Ferguson* in 1896. The ruling had established the "separate-but-equal" doctrine. Laws segregating African Americans were permitted as long as equal facilities were provided for them.

After the *Plessy* decision, laws segregating African Americans and whites spread quickly. These laws, nicknamed "Jim Crow" laws, segregated buses and trains, schools, restaurants, swimming pools, parks, and other public facilities. Jim Crow laws were common throughout the South, but segregation existed in other states as well. Often it was left up to each local community to decide whether to pass segregation laws. Areas without laws requiring segregation often had de facto segregation—segregation by custom and tradition. 📖 *(See page 1082 for more information on* Plessy v. Ferguson.*)*

Court Challenges Begin

The civil rights movement had been building for a long time. Since 1909, the **National Association for the Advancement of Colored People** (NAACP) had supported court cases intended to overturn segregation. Over the years, the NAACP achieved some victories. In 1935, for example, the Supreme Court ruled in *Norris* v. *Alabama* that Alabama's exclusion of African Americans from juries violated their right to equal protection under the law. In 1946 the Court ruled in *Morgan* v. *Virginia* that segregation on interstate buses was unconstitutional. In 1950 it ruled in *Sweatt* v. *Painter* that state law schools had to admit qualified African American applicants, even if parallel black law schools existed. 📖 *(See pages 1082–1083 for more information on these cases.)*

Student Web Activity Visit the *American Vision* Web site at tav.glencoe.com and click on *Student Web Activities— Chapter 29* for an activity on the civil rights movement.

NATIONAL GEOGRAPHIC

MOMENT in HISTORY

AMERICAN SEGREGATION

In an Oklahoma City streetcar station in 1939, a man takes a drink from a water cooler labeled "COLORED." Racially segregated facilities—waiting rooms, railroad cars, lavatories, and drinking fountains—were prevalent all across the South. Under the so-called Jim Crow system, African Americans were legally entitled to "separate-but-equal" education, housing, and social services. In practice, however, only a small percentage of public funds earmarked for schools, streets, police, and other expenses found its way to African American neighborhoods.

Objectives and answers to the student activity can be found in the **Web Activity Lesson Plan** at tav.glencoe.com.

2 TEACH

Daily Lecture and Discussion Notes 29–1

Daily Lecture and Discussion Notes
Chapter 29, Section 1

Did You Know? Long before being arrested for refusing to give up her seat on a bus to a white man, Rosa Parks had protested segregation through her daily activities. She refused to drink out of the drinking fountains labeled "Colored Only." When possible, she refused to ride in segregated elevators and walked up the stairs instead.

I. **The Origins of the Movement** *(pages 866–868)*

   A. The African American civil rights movement began after Rosa Parks refused to give up her seat on a bus to a white man. An organized boycott of the bus system was just the beginning as African Americans demanded equal rights.

Discussing a Topic To help students identify with Linda Brown and James Meredith, give them a few minutes to write diary notes about how it might have felt to attend a school where he or she was unwanted. **L1** ELL

NATIONAL GEOGRAPHIC

MOMENT in HISTORY

Ask: How did the disparity between white and "colored" facilities indicate that America had not changed its views on race? *(It showed that African Americans were still being treated as second-class citizens.)*

COOPERATIVE LEARNING ACTIVITY

Creating a Documentary Have students work in small groups to produce a documentary of the civil rights movement during the 1950s. Each group should write a script that covers the main events described in the section. Ask students to reenact interviews with on-the-scene participants such as Linda Brown, Rosa Parks, and Martin Luther King, Jr. The scripts should conclude with speculation about the potential gains of the civil rights movement and future challenges. One student in each group might act as a narrator to present the script to the class for discussion.

Use the rubric for a cooperative group management plan on pages 81–82 in the *Performance Assessment Activities and Rubrics.*

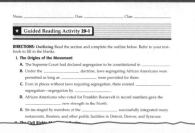
Analyzing a Decision Have interested students research the NAACP's strategy of ending school segregation. Ask students to report their findings to the class. As a class, analyze why the NAACP might have chosen to challenge school segregation rather than segregation in other areas of American life. **Ask: What do you think would have happened if the NAACP had lost in the Supreme Court? L2**

Rosa Parks and her husband both lost their jobs as a result of taking part in the bus boycott.

📁 Use *Supreme Court Case Study 29*, *Brown v. Board of Education of Topeka, Kansas.*

✓ Reading Check

Answer: The ruling said the segregation was constitutional as long as equal facilities were provided for African Americans.

New Political Power In addition to a string of court victories, African Americans enjoyed increased political power. Before World War I, most African Americans lived in the South, where they were largely excluded from voting. During the Great Migration, many moved to Northern cities, where they were allowed to vote. Increasingly, Northern politicians sought their votes and listened to their concerns.

During the 1930s, many African Americans benefited from FDR's New Deal programs. Thus they began supporting the Democratic Party, giving it new strength in the North. This wing of the party was now able to counter Southern Democrats, who often supported segregation.

The Push for Desegregation During World War II, African American leaders began to use their new political power to demand more rights. Their efforts helped end discrimination in factories that held government contracts and increased opportunities for African Americans in the military.

In Chicago in 1942, James Farmer and George Houser founded the **Congress of Racial Equality** (CORE). CORE began using sit-ins, a form of protest first used by union workers in the 1930s. In 1943 CORE attempted to desegregate restaurants that refused to serve African Americans. Using the sit-in strategy, members of CORE went to segregated restaurants. If they were denied service, they sat down and refused to leave. The sit-ins were intended to shame restaurant managers into integrating their restaurants. Using these protests, CORE successfully integrated many restaurants, theaters, and other public facilities in Chicago, Detroit, Denver, and Syracuse.

✓ Reading Check

Examining How had the ruling in *Plessy* v. *Ferguson* contributed to segregation?

Separate but Unequal Linda Brown's court case ended decades of official segregation in the South.

The Civil Rights Movement Begins

When World War II ended, many African American soldiers returned home optimistic that their country would appreciate their loyalty and sacrifice. In the 1950s, when change did not come as quickly as hoped, their determination to change prejudices in the United States led to protests and marches—and to the emergence of the civil rights movement.

Brown v. Board of Education After World War II, the NAACP continued to challenge segregation in the courts. From 1939 to 1961, the NAACP's chief counsel and director of its Legal Defense and Education Fund was the brilliant African American attorney **Thurgood Marshall**. After World War II, Marshall focused his efforts on ending segregation in public schools.

In 1954 the Supreme Court decided to combine several different cases and issue a general ruling on segregation in schools. One of the cases involved a young African American girl named **Linda Brown**, who was denied admission to her neighborhood school in Topeka, Kansas, because of her race. She was told to attend an all-black school across town. With the help of the NAACP, her parents then sued the Topeka school board.

On May 17, 1954, the Supreme Court ruled unanimously in the case of *Brown* v. *Board of Education of Topeka, Kansas,* that segregation in public schools was unconstitutional and violated the equal protection clause of the Fourteenth Amendment. Chief Justice Earl Warren summed up the Court's decision when he wrote: "In the field of public education, the doctrine of separate but equal has no place. Separate educational facilities are inherently unequal." 📖 *(See pages 1077 and 1080 for information on* Brown v. *Board of Education.)*

The Southern Manifesto The Brown decision marked a dramatic reversal of the ideas expressed in the *Plessy* v. *Ferguson* case. *Brown* v. *Board of Education* applied only to public schools, but the ruling threatened the entire system of segregation. Although it convinced many African Americans that the time had come to challenge other forms of segregation, it also angered many white Southerners, who became even more determined to defend segregation, regardless of what the Supreme Court ruled.

Although some school districts in border states integrated their schools in compliance with the Court's ruling, anger and opposition was a far more common reaction. In Washington, D.C., Senator Harry F. Byrd of Virginia called on Southerners to

---

EXTENDING THE CONTENT

Oliver Hill The famous civil rights case of *Brown* v. *Board of Education* actually combined several cases involving more than 100 parents and children in different school districts. One of those cases was *Davis* v. *Prince Edward County Schools.* The lawyer representing the plaintiffs in that case was Oliver Hill—the famous Virginia civil rights lawyer. Hill was born in Richmond, Virginia, and graduated from Howard Law School in 1933, second in his class behind his friend, Thurgood Marshall. Hill worked on several landmark cases including the desegregation of buses and trains, and the right of black citizens to serve on juries and participate in primary elections. He served as director of the Virginia chapter of the NAACP for 20 years. During that time, he and a team of 13 lawyers filed more civil rights cases in Virginia than were filed in any other Southern state.

ELPOSEY. PARKING LOT

Picturing **History**

Car Pool Pick-Up Station During the months of the Montgomery bus boycott, African Americans walked or volunteered their own cars as free taxis for other protesters. Why did African Americans choose to boycott the city bus system?

you don't say...

Independent Spirit Supreme Court Justice Thurgood Marshall, the great-grandson of an enslaved person "of independent spirit," served with the NAACP for 25 years, argued 32 major cases for the organization, and won 29 of them.

Picturing **History**

Answer: They were protesting Rosa Parks's arrest and segregation.
Ask: How much of a sacrifice do you think African Americans made by boycotting public buses?
(Students' answers will vary. Students should recognize that buses were the only means of transportation that many African Americans could afford.)

adopt "massive resistance" against the ruling. Across the South, hundreds of thousands of white Americans joined citizens' councils to pressure their local governments and school boards into defying the Supreme Court. Many states adopted pupil assignment laws. These laws created an elaborate set of requirements other than race that schools could use to prevent African Americans from attending white schools.

The Supreme Court inadvertently encouraged white resistance when it followed up its decision in *Brown* v. *Board* a year later. The Court ordered school districts to proceed "with all deliberate speed" to end school segregation. The wording was vague enough that many districts were able to keep their schools segregated for many more years.

Massive resistance also appeared in the halls of Congress. In 1956 a group of 101 Southern members of Congress signed the **Southern Manifesto,** which denounced the Supreme Court's ruling as "a clear abuse of judicial power" and pledged to use "all lawful means" to reverse the decision. Although the Southern

Manifesto had no legal standing, the statement encouraged white Southerners to defy the Supreme Court.

The Montgomery Bus Boycott In the midst of the uproar over the *Brown* v. *Board of Education* case, Rosa Parks made her decision to challenge segregation of public transportation. Outraged by Parks's arrest, Jo Ann Robinson, head of a local organization called the Women's Political Council, called on African Americans to boycott Montgomery's buses on the day Rosa Parks appeared in court.

The boycott was a dramatic success. That afternoon, several African American leaders formed the Montgomery Improvement Association to run the boycott and to negotiate with city leaders for an end to segregation. They elected a 26-year-old pastor named **Martin Luther King, Jr.,** to lead them.

On the evening of December 5, 1955, a meeting was held at Dexter Avenue Baptist Church, where Dr. King was pastor. In the deep, resonant tones and powerful phrases that characterized his speaking style, King encouraged the people to continue their

CURRICULUM CONNECTION

Language Arts African American authors wrote about their experiences during the civil rights movement. James Baldwin's *Notes of a Native Son* is a classic example of such literature.

FYI

Hattie McDaniel was the first African American woman to sing on American radio. In the 1930s and 1940s, she appeared in many films, generally in the role of a maid. She won an Academy Award for her role in the movie *Gone with the Wind.*

CHAPTER 29   The Civil Rights Movement   **869**

INTERDISCIPLINARY CONNECTIONS ACTIVITY

Communication Invite a journalist who covered events in your community during the civil rights movement to address your class about his or her experiences and perceptions of how minorities are portrayed in the media. Ask the speaker to suggest an activity that students can do to prepare for the presentation, such as reading an article or researching a topic. **L2**

IN HISTORY

✔ Reading Check

Answer: Public school segregation was ruled unconstitutional because it violated the Fourteenth Amendment.

Creating a Display Have students base a display on African Americans who broke racial barriers. Ask each student to bring an image and a caption to contribute to the display. Encourage students to search a variety of fields, including entertainment, sports, sciences, and arts. **L2**

📁 Use the rubric for creating a map, display, or chart on pages 77–78 in the *Performance Assessment Activities and Rubrics.*

protest. "There comes a time, my friends," he said, "when people get tired of being thrown into the abyss of humiliation, where they experience the bleakness of nagging despair." He explained, however, that the protest had to be peaceful:

> ❝Now let us say that we are not advocating violence. . . . The only weapon we have in our hands this evening is the weapon of protest. If we were incarcerated behind the iron curtains of a communistic nation—we couldn't do this. If we were trapped in the dungeon of a totalitarian regime—we couldn't do this. But the great glory of American democracy is the right to protest for right!❞
>
> —quoted in *Parting the Waters: America in the King Years*

King had earned a Ph.D. in theology from Boston University. He believed that the only moral way to end segregation and racism was through nonviolent passive resistance. He told his followers, "We must use the weapon of love. We must realize that so many people are taught to hate us that they are not totally responsible for their hate." African Americans, he urged, must say to racists and segregationists: "We will soon wear you down by our capacity to suffer, and in winning our freedom we will so appeal to your heart and conscience that we will win you in the process."

King drew upon the philosophy and techniques of Indian leader Mohandas Gandhi, who had used nonviolent resistance effectively against British rule in India. Like Gandhi, King encouraged his followers to disobey unjust laws. Believing in people's ability to transform themselves, King was certain that public opinion would eventually force the government to end segregation.

Stirred by King's powerful words, African Americans in Montgomery continued their boycott for over a year. Instead of riding the bus, they organized car pools or walked to work. They refused to be intimidated, yet they avoided violence. Meanwhile Rosa Parks's legal challenge to bus segregation worked its way through the courts. Finally, in December 1956, the Supreme Court

Profiles IN HISTORY

Thurgood Marshall
1908–1993

Over his long lifetime, Thurgood Marshall made many contributions to the civil rights movement. Perhaps his most famous accomplishment was representing the NAACP in the *Brown* v. *Board of Education* case.

Marshall's speaking style was both simple and direct. During the *Brown* case, Justice Frankfurter asked Marshall for a definition of equal. "Equal means getting the same thing, at the same time and in the same place," Marshall answered.

Born into a middle-class Baltimore family in 1908, Marshall earned a law degree from Howard University Law School. The school's dean, Charles Hamilton Houston, enlisted Marshall to work for the NAACP. Together the two laid out the legal strategy for challenging discrimination in many arenas of American life.

Marshall became the first African American on the Supreme Court when President Lyndon Johnson appointed him in 1967. On the Court, he remained a voice for civil rights. In his view, the Constitution was not perfect because it had accepted slavery. Its ideas of liberty, justice, and equality had to be refined. "The true miracle of the Constitution," he once wrote, "was not the birth of the Constitution, but its life."

affirmed the decision of a special three-judge panel declaring Alabama's laws requiring segregation on buses to be unconstitutional.

✔ Reading Check **Describing** What was the ruling in *Brown* v. *Board of Education*?

African American Churches

Martin Luther King, Jr., was not the only prominent minister in the bus boycott. Many of the other leaders were African American ministers. The boycott could not have succeeded without the support of the African American churches in the city. As the civil rights movement gained momentum, African American churches continued to play a critical role. They served as forums for many of the protests and planning meetings, and they also mobilized many of the volunteers for specific civil rights campaigns.

After the Montgomery bus boycott demonstrated that nonviolent protest could be successful, African American ministers led by King established the **Southern Christian Leadership Conference (SCLC)** in 1957. The SCLC set out to eliminate segregation from American society and to encourage

---

CRITICAL THINKING ACTIVITY

Comparing Philosophies Martin Luther King, Jr., took many of his nonviolent ideas from those of Mohandas K. Gandhi, leader of India's nationalist movement against Britain. Ask students to research Gandhi's philosophy and his work. Have them compare each man's philosophy. **Ask: How are they similar? How are they different? What impact did each leader have on his nation? How successful was each in reaching his goals?** Have students present their findings orally for class discussion. **L2**

African Americans to register to vote. Dr. King served as the SCLC's first president. Under his leadership, the organization challenged segregation at the voting booths and in public transportation, housing, and public accommodations.

✓ **Reading Check** **Summarizing** What role did African American churches play in the civil rights movement?

Eisenhower and Civil Rights

President Eisenhower sympathized with the goals of the civil rights movement, and he personally disagreed with segregation. Following the precedent set by President Truman, he ordered navy shipyards and veterans' hospitals to be desegregated.

At the same time, however, Eisenhower disagreed with those who wanted to roll back segregation through protests and court rulings. He believed that people had to allow segregation and racism to end gradually as values changed. With the nation in the midst of the Cold War, he worried that challenging white Southerners on segregation might divide the nation and lead to violence at a time when the country

had to pull together. Publicly, he refused to endorse the *Brown* v. *Board of Education* decision. Privately, he remarked, "I don't believe you can change the hearts of men with laws or decisions."

Despite his belief that the *Brown* v. *Board of Education* decision was wrong, Eisenhower felt he had to uphold the authority of the federal government, including its court system. As a result, he became the first president since Reconstruction to send federal troops into the South to protect the constitutional rights of African Americans.

Crisis in Little Rock In September 1957, the school board in Little Rock, Arkansas, won a court order to admit nine African American students to Central High, a school with 2,000 white students. Little Rock was a racially moderate Southern city, as was most of the state of Arkansas. A number of Arkansas communities, as well as the state university, had already begun to desegregate their schools.

The governor of Arkansas, Orval Faubus, was believed to be a moderate on racial issues, unlike many other Southern politicians. Faubus was determined to win re-election, however, and so he began to campaign

Picturing History

Crisis in Little Rock Fifteen-year-old Elizabeth Echford (in sunglasses at right) braves an angry crowd of Central High School students in Arkansas. How did Governor Orval Faubus react to attempts to integrate the high school?

EXTENDING THE CONTENT

Sports In 1947 Jackie Robinson became the first African American to play major-league baseball. Other professional sports integrated at different times. African American prizefighters and jockeys had been successful even before 1904 when Charles W. Follis became the first African American professional football player. It was not until 1950 that the Boston Celtics of the National Basketball Association signed Charles "Chuck" Cooper to be the first African American player in the league.

Section Quiz 29–1

Name _____ Date _____ Class _____

★ **Chapter 29** _____ Score

Section Quiz 29-1

DIRECTIONS: Matching Match each item in Column A with the items in Column B.
Write the correct letters in the blanks. (10 points each)

Column A

_____ 1. governor who ordered troops from the Arkansas National
Guard to prevent African American students from entering
school

_____ 2. set out to eliminate segregation from American society and
to encourage African Americans to register to vote

_____ 3. segregation by custom and tradition

_____ 4. challenged segregation in court and launched the modern
civil rights movement

_____ 5. African American attorney who was the NAACP's chief
counsel

Column B

A. Thurgood
Marshall

B. Southern
Christian
Leadership
Conference

C. Orval Faubus

D. Rosa Parks

E. de facto
segregation

Reteach

Have students explain the origin of the Southern Christian Leadership Conference.

Enrich

Invite interested students to prepare a presentation about one of the persons mentioned in this section. Encourage students to use library and Internet resources.

✓ Reading Check

Answer: He intervened because the governor of Arkansas had used armed forces to oppose the authority of the federal government. After the governor withdrew the National Guard troops, Eisenhower used federal troops to stop the violence and enforce the law.

4 CLOSE

Have students discuss the changing role of the federal government in civil rights enforcement.

---

as a defender of white supremacy. He ordered troops from the Arkansas National Guard to prevent the nine African American students from entering the school. The next day, as the National Guard troops surrounded the school, an angry white mob joined the troops to protest the integration plan and to intimidate the African American students trying to register.

Television coverage of this episode placed Little Rock at the center of national attention. Faubus had used the armed forces of a state to oppose the authority of the federal government—the first such challenge to the Constitution since the Civil War. Eisenhower knew that he could not allow Faubus to defy the federal government. After a conference between Eisenhower and Faubus proved fruitless, the district court ordered the governor to remove the troops. Instead of ending the crisis, however, Faubus simply left the school to the mob. After the African American students entered the school, angry whites beat at least two African American reporters and broke many of the school's windows. The mob came so close to capturing the terrified African American students that the police had to take them away to safety.

The mob violence finally pushed President Eisenhower's patience to the breaking point. Federal authority had to be upheld. He immediately ordered the U.S. Army to send troops to Little Rock. By nightfall 1,000 soldiers of the elite 101st Airborne Division had arrived. By 5:00 A.M. the troops had encircled the school, bayonets ready. A few hours later, the nine African American students arrived in an army station wagon, and they walked into the high school. The law had been upheld, but the troops were forced to remain in Little Rock for the rest of the school year.

New Civil Rights Legislation The same year that the Little Rock crisis began, Congress passed the first civil rights law since Reconstruction. The **Civil Rights Act of 1957** was intended to protect the right of African Americans to vote. Eisenhower believed firmly in the right to vote, and he viewed it as his responsibility to protect voting rights. He also knew that if he sent a civil rights bill to Congress, conservative Southern Democrats would try to block the legislation. In 1956 he did send the bill to Congress, hoping not only to split the Democratic Party but also to convince more African Americans to vote Republican.

Several Southern senators did try to stop the Civil Rights Act of 1957, but the Senate majority leader, Democrat Lyndon Johnson, put together a compromise that enabled the act to pass. Although its final form was much weaker than originally intended, the act still brought the power of the federal government into the civil rights debate. The act created a civil rights division within the Department of Justice and gave it the authority to seek court injunctions against anyone interfering with the right to vote. It also created the United States Commission on Civil Rights to investigate allegations of denial of voting rights. After the bill passed, the SCLC announced a campaign to register 2 million new African American voters.

✓ Reading Check **Explaining** Why did President Eisenhower intervene in the civil rights controversy?

SECTION 1 ASSESSMENT

Checking for Understanding

1. **Define:** separate-but-equal, de facto segregation, sit-in.
2. **Identify:** NAACP, Thurgood Marshall, Linda Brown, Martin Luther King, Jr., Southern Christian Leadership Conference.
3. **State** the outcome of the *Brown* v. *Board of Education* case.

Reviewing Themes

4. **Government and Democracy** Why did the role of the federal government in civil rights enforcement change?

Critical Thinking

5. **Interpreting** Do you think the civil rights movement would have been successful in gaining civil rights for African Americans without the help of the NAACP and the SCLC? Explain.
6. **Organizing** Use a graphic organizer similar to the one below to list the efforts made to end segregation.

Efforts to End Segregation

Analyzing Visuals

7. **Examining Photographs** Study the photograph of Central High School students on page 871. How would you describe Elizabeth Echford's demeanor compared to those around her? What might this tell you about her character?

Writing About History

8. **Expository Writing** Take on the role of an African American soldier returning to the United States after fighting in World War II. Write a letter to the editor of your local newspaper describing your expectations of civil rights as an American citizen.

872 CHAPTER 29 The Civil Rights Movement

SECTION 1 ASSESSMENT ANSWERS

1. Terms are in blue.
2. NAACP *(p. 867)*, Thurgood Marshall *(p. 868)*, Linda Brown *(p. 868)*, Martin Luther King, Jr. *(p. 869)*, Southern Christian Leadership Conference *(p. 870)*
3. Segregation in public schools is unconstitutional.
4. because its authority and decisions were challenged by individual states
5. Students should recognize that the NAACP and the SCLC provided financial support, leadership, and organization to the civil rights movement.
6. founding of CORE, NAACP court challenges, bus boycott, voter registration movement
7. Students' answers will vary but should recognize her courage.
8. Letters should include specific expectations.

Guide to Reading

Main Idea
African American citizens and white supporters created organizations that directed protests, targeted specific inequalities, and attracted the attention of the mass media and the government.

Key Terms and Names
Jesse Jackson, Ella Baker, Freedom Riders, filibuster, cloture, Civil Rights Act of 1964, poll tax

Reading Strategy
Organizing As you read about challenges to segregation in the South, complete a cause/effect chart like the one below.

Cause	Effect
Sit-In Movement	
Freedom Riders	
	African American support of Kennedy
	African American voter registration

Reading Objectives
• **Evaluate** the Civil Rights Act of 1964.
• **Summarize** the efforts to establish voting rights for African Americans.

Section Theme
Science and Technology The civil rights movement gained momentum in the early 1960s due to national television coverage.

Preview of Events

◆1960	◆1962	◆1964	◆1966

May 1961
Freedom Riders attempt to desegregate interstate buses in the South

Spring 1963
Martin Luther King, Jr., jailed in Birmingham

August 28, 1963
March on Washington

July 1964
President Johnson signs Civil Rights Act of 1964

1965
Voting Rights Act passed

1 FOCUS

Section Overview
This section focuses on the efforts made to challenge segregation.

BELLRINGER
Skillbuilder Activity

Project transparency and have students answer the question.

Available as a blackline master.

Daily Focus Skills Transparency 29–2

Guide to Reading

Answers to Graphic: *Cause:* sit-in movement, *Effect:* brought attention to the civil rights movement; *Cause:* Freedom Riders, *Effect:* Kennedy's decision to control violence; *Cause:* King's release from jail, *Effect:* African American support for Kennedy; *Cause:* Selma march, *Effect:* African American voter registration

Preteaching Vocabulary
Have students look up the words *filibuster* and *cloture* in the glossary. Then have them write the definitions in their own words.

★ An American Story ★

In the fall of 1959, four young African Americans—Joseph McNeil, Ezell Blair, Jr., David Richmond, and Franklin McCain—enrolled at North Carolina Agricultural and Technical College in Greensboro. The four freshmen became close friends and spent evenings talking about the civil rights movement. In January 1960, McNeil told his friends that he thought the time had come to take action, and he suggested a sit-in at the whites-only lunch counter in the nearby Woolworth's department store.

"All of us were afraid," Richmond later recalled, "but we went and did it." On February 1, 1960, the four friends entered the Woolworth's. They purchased school supplies and then sat at the lunch counter and ordered coffee. When they were refused service, Blair said, "I beg your pardon, but you just served us at [the checkout] counter. Why can't we be served at the counter here?" The students stayed at the counter until it closed, then announced that they would sit at the counter every day until they were given the same service as white customers.

As they left the store, the four were excited. McNeil recalled, "I just felt I had powers within me, a superhuman strength that would come forward." McCain was also energized, saying, "I probably felt better that day than I've ever felt in my life."

—adapted from *Civilities and Civil Rights*

Four North Carolina College students after they participated in a lunch counter sit-in.

The Sit-In Movement

News of the daring sit-in at the Woolworth's store spread quickly across Greensboro. The following day, 29 African American students arrived at Woolworth's determined to sit at the counter until served. By the end of the week, over 300 students were taking part.

CHAPTER 29 The Civil Rights Movement **873**

SECTION RESOURCES

📁 Reproducible Masters
• Reproducible Lesson Plan 29–2
• Daily Lecture and Discussion Notes 29–2
• Guided Reading Activity 29–2
• Section Quiz 29–2
• Reading Essentials and Study Guide 29–2

📠 Transparencies
• Daily Focus Skills Transparency 29–2

Multimedia
• Interactive Tutor Self-Assessment CD-ROM
• ExamView® Pro Testmaker CD-ROM
• Presentation Plus! CD-ROM
• TeacherWorks™ CD-ROM
• Audio Program
• American Music: Hits Through History
• American Music: Cultural Traditions

2 TEACH

Daily Lecture and Discussion Notes 29–2

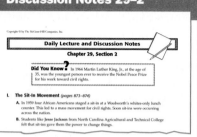

Copyright © by The McGraw-Hill Companies, Inc.

Daily Lecture and Discussion Notes
Chapter 29, Section 2

Did You Know? In 1964 Martin Luther King, Jr., at the age of 35, was the youngest person ever to receive the Nobel Peace Prize for his work toward civil rights.

I. The Sit-In Movement *(pages 873–874)*

A. In 1959 four African Americans staged a sit-in at a Woolworth's whites-only lunch counter. This led to a mass movement for civil rights. Soon sit-ins were occurring across the nation.

B. Students like Jesse Jackson from North Carolina Agricultural and Technical College felt that sit-ins gave them the power to change things.

Creating a Chart Have students create a chart similar to the one shown below to illustrate the activities of the persons mentioned in this section. **L1** **ELL**

Working for Civil Rights	
Name	Involvement

Working to Maintain Segregation	
Name	Involvement

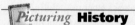
Reading Check

Answer: It got the nation's attention and gave people a way to get involved in the civil rights movement.

Picturing **History**

Answer: They were nervous.
Ask: How did young people staging sit-ins generally behave? *(They were nonviolent.)*

Reading Check

Answer: She urged students to create SNCC.

Starting with just four students, a new mass movement for civil rights had begun. Within two months, sit-ins had spread to 54 cities in 9 states. Sit-ins were staged at segregated stores, restaurants, hotels, movie theaters, and swimming pools. By 1961 sit-ins had been held in more than 100 cities.

The sit-in movement brought large numbers of idealistic and energized college students into the civil rights struggle. Many African American students had become discouraged by the slow pace of desegregation. Students like **Jesse Jackson,** a student leader at North Carolina Agricultural and Technical College, wanted to see things change. The sit-in offered them a way to take matters into their own hands.

At first the leaders of the NAACP and the SCLC were nervous about the sit-in movement. They feared that students did not have the discipline to remain nonviolent if they were provoked enough. For the most part, the students proved them wrong. Those conducting sit-ins were heckled by bystanders, punched, kicked, beaten with clubs, and burned with cigarettes, hot coffee, and acid—but most did not fight back. They remained peaceful, and their heroic behavior grabbed the nation's attention.

✓ **Reading Check** **Examining** What were the effects of the sit-in movement?

SNCC

As the sit-ins spread, student leaders in different states realized that they needed to coordinate their efforts. The person who brought them together was **Ella Baker,** the 55-year-old executive director of the SCLC. In April 1960, Baker invited student leaders to

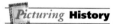
Picturing **History**

Sit-Ins Fight Segregation African American students challenged Southern segregation laws by demanding equal service at lunch counters. How did the NAACP initially feel about the sit-in movement?

attend a convention at Shaw University in Raleigh, North Carolina. At the convention, Baker urged students to create their own organization instead of joining the NAACP or the SCLC. Students, she said, had "the right to direct their own affairs and even make their own mistakes."

The students agreed with Baker and established the **Student Nonviolent Coordinating Committee** (SNCC). They then chose **Marion Barry,** a student leader from Nashville who later served as mayor of Washington, D.C., to be SNCC's first chairperson. African American college students from all across the South made up the majority of SNCC's members, although many whites also joined.

Between 1960 and 1965, SNCC played a key role in desegregating public facilities in dozens of Southern communities. SNCC also began sending volunteers into rural areas of the Deep South to register African Americans to vote. The idea for what came to be called the Voter Education Project began with Robert Moses, an SNCC volunteer from New York. Moses pointed out that the civil rights movement tended to focus on urban areas. He urged SNCC to fill in the gap by helping rural African Americans. Moses himself went to rural Mississippi, where African Americans who tried to register to vote frequently met with violence.

Despite the danger, many SNCC volunteers headed to Mississippi and other parts of the Deep South. Several had their lives threatened, and others were beaten. In 1964 local officials in Mississippi brutally murdered three SNCC workers as the workers attempted to register African American voters.

One SNCC organizer, a former sharecropper named **Fannie Lou Hamer,** had been evicted from her farm after registering to vote. She was then arrested in Mississippi for urging other African Americans to register, and she was severely beaten by the police while in jail. She then helped organize the Mississippi Freedom Democratic Party, and she challenged the legality of the segregated Democratic Party at the 1964 Democratic National Convention.

✓ **Reading Check** **Explaining** What role did Ella Baker play in forming SNCC?

The Freedom Riders

Despite rulings outlawing segregation in interstate bus service, bus travel remained segregated in much of the South. In 1961 CORE leader James Farmer asked teams of African Americans and whites to travel into the South to draw attention to

---

COOPERATIVE LEARNING ACTIVITY

Registering to Vote Organize the class into two groups to research the ease or difficulty of registering to vote in the 1960s versus today. One group can research the tactics used before 1965 to keep African Americans from registering to vote. Students should look for examples of actions taken in the North as well as the South. The other group can contact the local election board to find out how to register to vote in their community. Have students make a display showing the process, including options such as registering in person, by mail, or online.

Use the rubric for a cooperative group management plan on pages 81–82 in the *Performance Assessment Activities and Rubrics.*

the South's refusal to integrate bus terminals. The teams became known as the Freedom Riders.

In early May 1961, the first Freedom Riders boarded several southbound interstate buses. When the buses carrying them arrived in Anniston, Birmingham, and Montgomery, Alabama, angry white mobs attacked them. The mobs slit the bus tires and threw rocks at the windows. In Anniston, someone threw a firebomb into one bus, although fortunately no one was killed.

In Birmingham the riders emerged from a bus to face a gang of young men armed with baseball bats, chains, and lead pipes. They beat the riders viciously. One witness later reported, "You couldn't see their faces through the blood." The head of the police in Birmingham, Public Safety Commissioner Theophilus Eugene ("Bull") Connor, explained that there had been no police at the bus station because it was Mother's Day, and he had given many of his officers the day off. FBI evidence later showed that Connor had contacted the local Ku Klux Klan and told them he wanted the Freedom Riders beaten until "it looked like a bulldog got a hold of them."

The violence in Alabama made national news, shocking many Americans. The attack on the Freedom Riders came less than four months after President John F. Kennedy took office. The new president felt compelled to do something to get the violence under control.

 **Reading Check** **Summarizing** What was the goal of the Freedom Riders?

John F. Kennedy and Civil Rights

While campaigning for the presidency in 1960, John F. Kennedy promised to actively support the civil rights movement if elected. His brother, Robert F. Kennedy, had used his influence to get Dr. King released from jail after a demonstration in Georgia. African Americans responded by voting overwhelmingly for Kennedy. Their votes helped him narrowly win several key states, including Illinois, which Kennedy carried by only 9,000 votes. Once in office, however, Kennedy at first seemed as cautious as Eisenhower on civil rights, which disappointed many African Americans. Kennedy knew that he needed the support of many Southern senators to get

Picturing **History**

Riding Into Danger On May 14, 1961, Freedom Riders were driven from their bus outside of Anniston, Alabama, when angry townspeople set the bus on fire. Which civil rights protest organization coordinated the Freedom Riders?

other programs he wanted through Congress, and that any attempt to push through new civil rights legislation would anger them.

Kennedy did, however, name approximately 40 African Americans to high-level positions in the federal government. He also appointed Thurgood Marshall to a judgeship on the Second Circuit Appeals Court in New York—one level below the Supreme Court and the highest judicial position an African American had attained to that point. Kennedy also created the **Committee on Equal Employment Opportunity** (CEEO) to stop the federal bureaucracy from discriminating against African Americans when hiring and promoting people.

The Justice Department Takes Action Although President Kennedy was unwilling to challenge Southern Democrats in Congress, he allowed the Justice Department, run by his brother Robert, to actively support the civil rights movement. Robert Kennedy tried to help African Americans register to vote by having the civil rights division of the Justice Department file lawsuits throughout the South.

When violence erupted against the Freedom Riders, the Kennedys came to their aid as well, although not at first. At the time the Freedom Riders took action, President Kennedy was preparing for a meeting with Nikita Khrushchev, the leader of the Soviet Union. Kennedy did not want violence in the South to disrupt the meeting by giving the impression that his country was weak and divided.

After the Freedom Riders were attacked in Montgomery, the Kennedys publicly urged them to

CHAPTER 29 The Civil Rights Movement **875**

Guided Reading Activity 29–2

Name _____ Date _____ Class _____

★ **Guided Reading Activity 29-2**

DIRECTIONS: Recalling Facts Read the section and answer the questions below. Refer to your textbook to write the answers.

1. Who organized a convention at Shaw University and urged students to create the Student Nonviolent Coordinating Committee (SNCC)?
2. Who, as an SNCC volunteer from New York, urged the SNCC to help rural African Americans register to vote?
3. Who helped organize the Mississippi Freedom Democratic Party, and then challenged the legality of the segregated Democratic Party at the 1964 Democratic National Convention?
4. Why did President Kennedy seem cautious at first on civil rights?
5. What was the purpose of the Committee on Equal Employment Opportunity?

Picturing **History**

Answer: CORE (Congress of Racial Equality)
Ask: Who was responsible for the violence against the Freedom Riders in Birmingham, Alabama? (*Ku Klux Klan*)

 Reading Check

Answer: CORE wanted to draw attention to segregation in Southern bus terminals.

FYI

Presidential aide John Siegenthaler recounted the mob scene at the bus terminal: "The Freedom Riders emerging from the bus were being mauled. It looked like two hundred, three hundred people all over them. There were screams and shouts...." The one white man aboard the bus, Jim Zwerg, was viciously attacked—as if the mob was furious that he would side with African Americans.

History *and the* **Humanities**

♪ American Music: Hits Through History: "Why? (Am I Treated So Bad)"
♪ American Music: Cultural Traditions: "We Shall Not Be Moved"

MEETING SPECIAL NEEDS

Auditory/Musical Ask students to listen to an audio recording of the "I Have a Dream" speech delivered by Martin Luther King, Jr., at the 1963 March on Washington. Instruct students not to take notes. After listening to the speech have the students jot down their impressions. Play the recording again and allow students to take notes. Discuss the speech elements that make it powerful, such as word choice, delivery, and timing. **L2**

📁 Refer to *Inclusion for the High School Social Studies Classroom Strategies and Activities* in the TCR.

Creating a Brochure Have students create a brochure encouraging people to register to vote. Suggest that they contact the local board of elections and organizations that encourage voting, such as the League of Women Voters, to get examples of actual brochures. **L2**

Use the rubric for creating a political cartoon, pamphlet, or handbill on pages 87–88 in the *Performance Assessment Activities and Rubrics.*

CURRICULUM CONNECTION

Government Like many leading political figures in Southern states, George Wallace opposed integration. Elected in 1962 as the governor of Alabama, his actions and words, such as his statement, "segregation now, segregation tomorrow, segregation forever," openly defied the federal government's efforts. So strong was Southern anger over the segregation issue that Wallace would garner much support in his 1968 and 1972 presidential bids. Wallace eventually apologized for his racist beliefs.

---

stop the rides and give everybody a "cooling off" period. James Farmer replied that African Americans "have been cooling off now for 350 years. If we cool off anymore, we'll be in a deep freeze." Instead he announced that the Freedom Riders planned to head into Mississippi on their next trip.

To stop the violence, President Kennedy made a deal with Senator James Eastland of Mississippi, a strong supporter of segregation. If Eastland would use his influence in Mississippi to prevent violence, Kennedy would not object if the Mississippi police arrested the Freedom Riders. Eastland kept the deal. No violence occurred when the buses arrived in Jackson, Mississippi, but the riders were arrested.

The cost of bailing the Freedom Riders out of jail used up most of CORE's funds, which meant that the rides would have to end unless more money could be found. When Thurgood Marshall learned of the situation, he offered James Farmer the use of the NAACP's Legal Defense Fund's huge bail bond account to keep the rides going.

When President Kennedy returned from his meeting with Khrushchev and found that the Freedom Riders were still active, he changed his position and ordered the Interstate Commerce Commission to tighten its regulations against segregated bus terminals. In the meantime, Robert Kennedy ordered the Justice Department to take legal action against Southern cities that were maintaining segregated bus terminals. The continuing pressure of CORE and the actions of the ICC and the Justice Department finally produced results. By late 1962, segregation in interstate travel had come to an end.

James Meredith As the Freedom Riders were trying to desegregate bus terminals, efforts continued to integrate Southern schools. On the very day John F. Kennedy was inaugurated, an African American air force veteran named **James Meredith** applied for a transfer to the University of Mississippi. Up to that point, the university had avoided complying with the Supreme Court ruling ending segregated education.

In September 1962, Meredith tried to register at the university's admissions office, only to find Ross Barnett, the governor of Mississippi, blocking his path. Although Meredith had a court order directing the university to register him, Governor Barnett stated emphatically, "Never! We will never surrender to the evil and illegal forces of tyranny."

Frustrated, President Kennedy dispatched 500 federal marshals to escort Meredith to the campus. Shortly after Meredith and the marshals arrived, an

angry white mob attacked the campus, and a full-scale riot erupted. The mob hurled rocks, bottles, bricks, and acid at the marshals. Some people fired shotguns at them. The marshals responded with tear gas, but they were under orders not to fire.

The fighting continued all night. By morning, 160 marshals had been wounded. Reluctantly Kennedy ordered the army to send several thousand troops to the campus. For the rest of the year, Meredith attended classes at the University of Mississippi under federal guard. He graduated the following August.

Violence in Birmingham The events in Mississippi frustrated Martin Luther King, Jr., and other civil rights leaders. Although they were pleased that Kennedy had intervened to protect Meredith's rights, they were disappointed that the president had not seized the moment to push for a new civil rights law. When the Cuban missile crisis began the following month, civil rights issues dropped out of the news, and for the next several months, foreign policy became the main priority at the White House.

Reflecting on the problem, Dr. King came to a difficult decision. It seemed to him that only when violence and disorder got out of hand would the federal government intervene. "We've got to have a crisis to bargain with," one of his advisers observed. King agreed. In the spring of 1963, he decided to launch demonstrations in Birmingham, Alabama, knowing they would probably provoke a violent response. He believed it was the only way to get President Kennedy to actively support civil rights.

The situation in Birmingham was volatile. Public Safety Commissioner Bull Connor, who had arranged for the attack on the Freedom Riders, was now running for mayor. Eight days after the protests began, King was arrested and held for a time in solitary confinement. While in prison, King began writing on scraps of paper that had been smuggled into his cell. The "Letter From a Birmingham Jail" that he produced is one of the most eloquent defenses of nonviolent protest ever written.

In his letter, King explained that although the protesters were breaking the law, they were following a higher moral law based on divine justice. To the charge that the protests created racial tensions, King argued that the protests "merely bring to the surface the hidden tension that is already alive." Injustice, he insisted, had to be exposed "to the light of human conscience and the air of national opinion before it can be cured." *(See page 1056 for more on "Letter From a Birmingham Jail.")*

876 CHAPTER 29 The Civil Rights Movement

INTERDISCIPLINARY CONNECTIONS ACTIVITY

Civics Tell students that protests have always been a part of the American tradition and that many protests have involved demonstrations in Washington, D.C. Have students research and write a report about one of the marches or rallies in Washington that occurred between 1960 and 1980. Examples of appropriate subjects for research are the Poor People's Campaign, 1968; ERA, 1978; Earth Day, 1970; or antinuclear protests, 1980. **L2**

After King was released, the protests, which had been dwindling, began to grow again. Bull Connor responded with force, ordering the police to use clubs, police dogs, and high-pressure fire hoses on the demonstrators, including women and children. Millions of people across the nation watched the graphic violence on television. Outraged by the brutality and worried that the government was losing control, Kennedy ordered his aides to prepare a new civil rights bill.

✓**Reading Check** Evaluating How did President Kennedy help the civil rights movement?

The Civil Rights Act of 1964

Determined to introduce a civil rights bill, Kennedy now waited for a dramatic opportunity to address the nation on the issue. Shortly after the violence in Birmingham had shocked the nation, Alabama's governor, George Wallace, gave the president his chance. Wallace was committed to segregation. At his inauguration, he had stated, "I draw a line in the dust . . . and I say, Segregation now! Segregation tomorrow! Segregation forever!" On June 11, 1963, Wallace personally stood in front of the University of Alabama's admissions office to block the enrollment of two African Americans. He stayed until federal marshals ordered him to stand aside.

President Kennedy seized the moment to announce his civil rights bill. That evening, he went on television to speak to the American people about a "moral issue . . . as old as the scriptures and as clear as the American Constitution":

66The heart of the question is whether . . . we are going to treat our fellow Americans as we want to be treated. If an American, because his skin is dark, cannot eat lunch in a restaurant open to the public, if he cannot send his children to the best public school available, if he cannot vote for the public officials who will represent him . . . then who among us would be content to have the color of his skin changed and stand in his place?

One hundred years of delay have passed since President Lincoln freed the slaves, yet their heirs, their grandsons, are not fully free. . . . And this nation, for all its hopes and all its boasts, will not be fully free until all its citizens are free. . . . Now the time has come for this nation to fulfill its promise.99

—from Kennedy's White House Address, June 11, 1963

TURNING POINT

The March on Washington Dr. King realized that Kennedy would have a very difficult time pushing his civil rights bill through Congress. Therefore, he searched for a way to lobby Congress and to build more public support. When A. Philip Randolph suggested a march on Washington, King agreed.

On August 28, 1963, more than 200,000 demonstrators of all races flocked to the nation's capital. The audience heard speeches and sang hymns and songs as they gathered peacefully near the Lincoln Memorial. Dr. King then delivered a powerful speech outlining his dream of freedom and equality for all Americans:

Picturing **History**

Forcing Change Birmingham police used high-pressure hoses to force civil rights protesters to stop their marches. Why did King's followers offer no resistance?

CRITICAL THINKING ACTIVITY

Analyzing Gains Although African Americans have gained many rights and opportunities as a result of the civil rights movement, much remains to be done. Ask students to identify areas where they think more could be done to ensure that all Americans have equal rights. Have students write their ideas in the form of a letter to their representative in Congress. Invite students to read their letters aloud to the class. **L2**

Analyzing Decisions Explain to students that President Kennedy decided to support the civil rights movement in the summer of 1963. The country had watched with revulsion as the drama in Birmingham played itself out. Tell them that the mood of the country was changing and that Kennedy was working to get out in front of a movement that was gaining momentum. Discuss with students their opinions about Kennedy's decision and its timing in light of the March on Washington and his political strength in Congress. **L2**

FYI

In 1989 the Southern Poverty Law Center dedicated the Civil Rights Memorial to those who died during the struggle for civil rights in the South. Located in Montgomery, Alabama–the scene of so many of the events in that cause–the memorial serves to inform and educate young people about the civil rights movement. Maya Lin, the creator of the Vietnam Veterans Memorial in Washington, D.C., designed the monument.

"I have a dream"

—*Martin Luther King, Jr.*

Picturing **History**

A Dream Deferred The 1963 March on Washington was the emotional high point of the civil rights movement. Its nonviolent atmosphere and Dr. King's eloquent speech made it one of the most momentous American events of the twentieth century. What significant legislation resulted from the March on Washington?

> ❝I have a dream that one day this nation will rise up and live out the true meaning of its creed . . . that all men are created equal. . . . I have a dream that one day . . . the sons of former slaves and the sons of former slave owners will be able to sit together at the table of brotherhood. . . . I have a dream that my four little children will one day live in a nation where they will not be judged by the color of their skin but by the content of their character. I have a dream . . . when all of God's children, black men and white men, Jews and Gentiles, Protestants and Catholics, will be able to join hands and sing . . . 'Free at last, Free at last, Thank God Almighty, we are free at last.'❞
>
> —quoted in *Freedom Bound: A History of America's Civil Rights Movement*

King's speech and the peacefulness and dignity of the March on Washington had built momentum for the civil rights bill. Opponents in Congress, however, continued to do what they could to slow the bill down, dragging out their committee investigations and using procedural rules to delay votes. 📖 *(See page 1078 for an excerpt from Dr. King's "I Have a Dream" speech.)*

The Civil Rights Bill Becomes Law Although the civil rights bill was likely to pass the House of Representatives, where a majority of Republicans and Northern Democrats supported the measure, it faced a much more difficult time in the Senate. There, a small group of determined senators would try to block the bill indefinitely.

In the U.S. Senate, senators are allowed to speak for as long as they like when a bill is being debated. The Senate cannot vote on a bill until all senators have finished speaking. A filibuster occurs when a small group of senators take turns speaking and refuse to stop the debate and allow a bill to come to a vote. Today a filibuster can be stopped if at least 60 senators vote for cloture, a motion which cuts off debate and forces a vote. In the 1960s, however, 67

878 CHAPTER 29 The Civil Rights Movement

EXTENDING THE CONTENT

Commitment to Nonviolence Ralph Abernathy's church and home were bombed shortly after Martin Luther King, Jr., had organized the Atlanta conference in January 1957. In the face of this and many other acts of violence, King and his followers stuck to their commitment to nonviolence.

senators had to vote for cloture to stop a filibuster. This meant that a minority of senators opposed to civil rights could easily prevent the majority from enacting new civil rights laws.

Worried the bill would never pass, many African Americans became even more disheartened. Then President Kennedy was assassinated in Dallas, Texas, on November 22, 1963, and his vice president, Lyndon Johnson, became president. Johnson was from Texas and had been the leader of the Senate Democrats before becoming vice president. Although he had helped push the Civil Rights Acts of 1957 and 1960 through the Senate, he had done so by weakening their provisions and by compromising with other Southern senators.

To the surprise of the civil rights movement, Johnson committed himself wholeheartedly to getting Kennedy's program, including the civil rights bill, through Congress. Unlike Kennedy, Johnson was very familiar with how Congress operated, having served there for many years. He knew how to build public support, how to put pressure on members of Congress, and how to use the rules and procedures to get what he wanted.

In February 1964, President Johnson's leadership began to produce results. The civil rights bill passed the House of Representatives by a majority of 290 to 130. The debate then moved to the Senate. In June, after 87 days of filibuster, the Senate finally voted to end debate by a margin of 71 to 29—four votes over the two-thirds needed for cloture. On July 2, 1964, President Johnson signed the **Civil Rights Act of 1964** into law.

The Civil Rights Act of 1964 was the most comprehensive civil rights law Congress had ever enacted. It gave the federal government broad power to prevent racial discrimination in a number of areas. The law made segregation illegal in most places of public accommodation, and it gave citizens of all races and nationalities equal access to such facilities as restaurants, parks, libraries, and theaters. The law gave the attorney general more power to bring lawsuits to force school desegregation, and it required private employers to end discrimination in the workplace. It also established the **Equal Employment Opportunity Commission** (EEOC) as a permanent agency in the federal government. This commission monitors the ban on job discrimination by race, religion, gender, and national origin.

✓ **Reading Check** **Examining** How did Dr. King lobby Congress to expand the right to participate in the democratic process?

The Struggle for Voting Rights

Even after the Civil Rights Act of 1964 was passed, voting rights were far from secure. The act had focused on segregation and job discrimination, and it did little to address voting issues. The Twenty-fourth Amendment, ratified in 1964, helped somewhat by eliminating poll taxes, or fees paid in order to vote, in federal (but not state) elections. African Americans still faced hurdles, however, when they tried to vote. As the SCLC and SNCC stepped up their voter registration efforts in the South, their members were often attacked and beaten, and several were murdered.

Across the South, bombs exploded in African American businesses and churches. Between June and October 1964, arson and bombs destroyed 24 African American churches in Mississippi alone. Convinced that a new law was needed to protect African American voting rights, Dr. King decided to stage another dramatic protest.

The Selma March In January 1965, the SCLC and Dr. King selected Selma, Alabama, as the focal point for their campaign for voting rights. Although African Americans made up a majority of Selma's

Voting Rights In the early 1960s, African Americans focused on increasing their political power.

CHAPTER 29 The Civil Rights Movement **879**

CHAPTER 29
Section 2, 873–880

Creating a Poster Have students create a poster highlighting one of the struggles of the civil rights movement. Have students decide on the message they want to convey and then select images and words that convey the message. **L2**

✓ **Reading Check**

Answer: with the March on Washington and his speech at the Lincoln Memorial

3 ASSESS

Assign Section 2 Assessment as homework or as an in-class activity.

🖥 Have students use the **Interactive Tutor Self-Assessment CD-ROM.**

Reading Essentials and Study Guide 29–2

Name _____ Date _____ Class _____

Study Guide
Chapter 29, Section 2
For use with textbook pages 873–880

CHALLENGING SEGREGATION

KEY TERMS AND NAMES

Jesse Jackson student leader in the sit-in movement to end segregation *(page 874)*

Ella Baker executive director of the SCLC, who urged African American students to start their own organization *(page 874)*

Freedom Riders teams of African Americans and white Americans who traveled through the South to draw attention to the South's refusal to integrate bus terminals *(page 875)*

filibuster a tactic in which senators take turns speaking and refuse to stop the debate and allow a bill to come to a vote *(page 878)*

cloture a motion which cuts off debate and forces a vote *(page 878)*

Civil Rights Act of 1964 law that made segregation illegal in most public places *(page 879)*

COOPERATIVE LEARNING ACTIVITY

Analyzing Nonviolent Resistance Organize students into small groups and discuss the major events of the civil rights movement during the Kennedy and Johnson administrations. Ask if they think the nonviolent aspect of the movement helped or hindered success. In their analyses, have each group compare the results of early actions of the movement to those taken as the movement progressed. Have each group present its analysis to the class. To conclude, have the class as a whole come to a consensus on the effectiveness of nonviolent resistance. 🖥

Use the rubric for a cooperative group management plan on pages 81–82 in the *Performance Assessment Activities and Rubrics.*

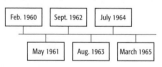

Section Quiz 29-2

DIRECTIONS: Matching Match each item in Column A with the items in Column B. Write the correct letters in the blanks. *(10 points each)*

Column A

___ 1. when a small group of senators take turns speaking and refuse to stop the debate and allow a bill to come to vote

___ 2. teams of African Americans and white Americans who traveled into the South to draw attention to the South's refusal to integrate bus terminals

___ 3. African American air force veteran who applied for a transfer to the University of Mississippi

___ 4. former sharecropper and Student Nonviolent Coordinating Committee organizer

___ 5. a march from Selma to Montgomery, Alabama, organized by Dr. King and SNCC

Column B

A. Fannie Lou Hamer
B. filibuster
C. "march for freedom"
D. James Meredith
E. Freedom Riders

Reteach

Have students summarize the efforts to establish voting rights for African Americans.

Enrich

Invite interested students to locate photographs and artifacts from your community that illustrate "separate but equal." Encourage students to use museum, library, and Internet resources.

✓ Reading Check

Answer: It eliminated poll taxes in federal elections.

4 CLOSE

Have students evaluate the Civil Rights Act of 1964.

880

---

population, they comprised only 3 percent of registered voters. To prevent African Americans from registering to vote, Sheriff Jim Clark had deputized and armed dozens of white citizens. His posse terrorized African Americans and frequently attacked demonstrators with clubs and electric cattle prods.

Just weeks after receiving the Nobel Peace Prize in Oslo, Norway, for his work in the civil rights movement, Dr. King stated, "We are not asking, we are demanding the ballot." King's demonstrations in Selma led to more than 2,000 African Americans, including schoolchildren, being arrested by Sheriff Clark. Clark's men attacked and beat many of the demonstrators, and Selma quickly became a major story in the national news.

To keep pressure on the president and Congress to act, Dr. King joined with SNCC activists and organized a "march for freedom" from Selma to the state capitol in Montgomery, a distance of about 50 miles (80 km). On Sunday, March 7, 1965, the march began. The SCLC's Hosea Williams and SNCC's John Lewis led 500 protesters toward U.S. Highway 80, the route that marchers had planned to follow to Montgomery.

As the protesters approached the Edmund Pettus Bridge, which led out of Selma, Sheriff Clark ordered them to disperse. While the marchers kneeled in prayer, more than 200 state troopers and deputized citizens rushed the demonstrators. Many were beaten in full view of television cameras. This brutal attack, known later as "Bloody Sunday," left 50 African Americans hospitalized and many more injured.

The nation was stunned as it viewed the shocking footage of law enforcement officers beating peaceful demonstrators. Watching the events from the White House, President Johnson became furious. Eight days later, he appeared before a nationally televised joint session of the legislature to propose a new voting rights law.

The Voting Rights Act of 1965 On August 1, 1965, the House of Representatives passed the voting rights bill by a wide margin. The following day, the Senate also passed the bill. The **Voting Rights Act of 1965** authorized the attorney general to send federal examiners to register qualified voters, bypassing local officials who often refused to register African Americans. The law also suspended discriminatory devices such as literacy tests in counties where less than half of all adults had been allowed to vote.

The results were dramatic. By the end of the year, almost 250,000 African Americans had registered as new voters. The number of African American elected officials in the South also increased, from about 100 in 1965 to more than 5,000 in 1990.

The passage of the Voting Rights Act of 1965 marked a turning point in the civil rights movement. The movement had now achieved its two major legislative goals. Segregation had been outlawed, and new federal laws were in place to prevent discrimination and protect voting rights.

After 1965 the movement began to shift its focus. It began to pay more attention to the problem of achieving full social and economic equality for African Americans. As part of that effort, the movement turned its attention to the problems of African Americans trapped in poverty and living in ghettos in many of the nation's major cities.

✓ Reading Check
Summarizing How did the Twenty-fourth Amendment affect African American voting rights?

SECTION 2 ASSESSMENT

Checking for Understanding

1. **Define:** Freedom Riders, filibuster, cloture, poll tax.
2. **Identify:** Jesse Jackson, Ella Baker, Civil Rights Act of 1964.
3. **Describe** the provisions of the Civil Rights Act of 1964 aimed at ending segregation and racial discrimination.

Reviewing Themes

4. **Science and Technology** How did television help the civil rights movement?

Critical Thinking

5. **Evaluating** How did protesting and lobbying lead to the passage of the Voting Rights Act of 1965?
6. **Sequencing** Use a time line like the one below to show relative chronology of events in the civil rights movement.

| Feb. 1960 | Sept. 1962 | July 1964 |
| May 1961 | Aug. 1963 | March 1965 |

Analyzing Visuals

7. **Examining Photographs** Study the photographs in this section. What elements of the photographs show the sacrifices African Americans made in the civil rights movement?

Writing About History

8. **Descriptive Writing** Take on the role of a journalist for the student newspaper of a college in 1960. Write an article for the newspaper describing the sit-in movement taking place across the country.

SECTION 2 ASSESSMENT ANSWERS

1. Terms are in blue.
2. Jesse Jackson *(p. 874)*, Ella Baker *(p. 874)*, Civil Rights Act of 1964 *(p. 879)*
3. The act gave the federal government broad powers to prevent racial discrimination in a number of areas.

4. Television brought national attention to the civil rights movement.
5. Police resistance to peaceful protests, seen on TV, raised sympathy for the civil rights cause.
6. 1960: sit-ins in Greensboro; 1961: Freedom Riders; 1962: James

Meredith enters the University of Mississippi; 1963: March on Washington; 1964: Civil Rights Act; 1965: Selma march
7. Photographs show the humiliations African Americans endured.
8. Students' articles will vary but must be historically accurate.

SECTION 3 New Issues

Guide to Reading

Main Idea
In the mid-1960s, civil rights leaders began to understand that merely winning political rights for African Americans would not address the problem of African Americans' economic status.

Key Terms and Names
racism, Chicago Movement, Richard Daley, black power, Stokely Carmichael, Malcolm X, Black Panthers

Reading Strategy
Organizing As you read about the changing focus of the civil rights movement, complete a chart similar to the one below. Fill in five major violent events and their results.

Event	Result

Reading Objectives
- **Describe** the division between Dr. Martin Luther King, Jr., and the black power movement.
- **Discuss** the direction and progress of the civil rights movement after 1968.

Section Theme
Civic Rights and Responsibilities In the late 1960s, the civil rights movement tried to address the persistent economic inequality of African Americans.

Preview of Events

◆1965	◆1966	◆1967	◆1968
1965 Watts riots break out in Los Angeles; Malcolm X assassinated	**1966** Chicago Movement fails	**1967** Kerner Commission studies problems of inner cities	**1968** Dr. Martin Luther King, Jr., assassinated

★ An American Story ★

Thursday, July 12, 1965, was hot and humid in Chicago. That evening Dessie Mae Williams, a 23-year-old African American woman, stood on the corner near the firehouse at 4000 West Wilcox Street. A firetruck sped out of the firehouse, and the driver lost control. The truck smashed into a stop sign near Williams, and the sign struck and killed her.

African Americans had already picketed this firehouse because it was not integrated. Hearing of Williams's death, 200 neighborhood young people streamed into the street, surrounding the firehouse. For two nights, rioting and disorder reigned. Angry youths threw bricks and bottles at the firehouse and nearby windows. Shouting gangs pelted police with rocks and accosted whites and beat them. Approximately 75 people were injured.

African American detectives, clergy, and National Guard members eventually restored order. Mayor Richard Daley then summoned both white and black leaders to discuss the area's problems. An 18-year-old man who had been in the riot admitted that he had lost his head. "We're sorry about the bricks and bottles," he said, "but when you get pushed, you shove back. Man, you don't like to stand on a corner and be told to get off it when you got nowhere else to go."

—adapted from *Anyplace But Here*

Dr. Martin Luther King, Jr., marching with protesters in Chicago.

Problems Facing Urban African Americans

Civil rights leaders had made great progress in the decade following the Montgomery bus boycott, but full equality still eluded many African Americans. Until 1965 the civil rights movement had focused on ending segregation and restoring the voting rights of

CHAPTER 29 The Civil Rights Movement **881**

SECTION RESOURCES

☞ Reproducible Masters
- Reproducible Lesson Plan 29–3
- Daily Lecture and Discussion Notes 29–3
- Guided Reading Activity 29–3
- Section Quiz 29–3
- Reading Essentials and Study Guide 29–3
- Supreme Court Case Studies

♨ Transparencies
- Daily Focus Skills Transparency 29–3

Multimedia
- Interactive Tutor Self-Assessment CD-ROM
- ExamView® Pro Testmaker CD-ROM
- Presentation Plus! CD-ROM
- TeacherWorks™ CD-ROM
- Audio Program

1 FOCUS

Section Overview
This section focuses on the attention paid by African American leaders to improving the economic status of African Americans.

BELLRINGER
Skillbuilder Activity

 Project transparency and have students answer the question.

☞ Available as a blackline master.

Daily Focus Skills Transparency 29–3

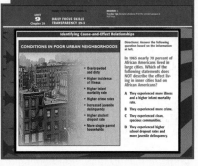

Guide to Reading

Answers to Graphic: *Event:* Dessie Mae Williams is killed, *Result:* riots; *Event:* Watts Riot, *Result:* Kerner Commission report on urban riots; *Event:* Malcolm X breaks with the Nation of Islam, *Result:* Malcolm X assassinated; *Event:* King supports strike by African American sanitation workers in Memphis, *Result:* King assassinated

Preteaching Vocabulary
Have students scan the section to preview the Key Terms and Names.

2 TEACH

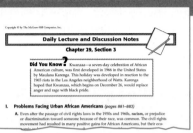

**Daily Lecture and
Discussion Notes 29-3**

Copyright © by The McGraw-Hill Companies, Inc.

Daily Lecture and Discussion Notes
Chapter 29, Section 3

Did You Know? Kwanzaa—a seven-day celebration of African American culture, was first developed in 1966 in the United States by Maulana Karenga. This holiday was developed in reaction to the 1965 riots in the Los Angeles neighborhood of Watts. Karenga hoped that Kwanzaa, which begins on December 26, would replace anger and rage with black pride.

I. Problems Facing Urban African Americans (pages 881–883)

  A. Even after the passage of civil rights laws in the 1950s and 1960s, racism, or prejudice or discrimination toward someone because of their race, was common. The civil rights movement had resulted in many positive gains for African Americans, but their eco-

Summarizing Concepts Discuss with students the discontent among many African Americans. Then have them summarize in a list the tactics used by groups such as SNCC, CORE, and the Black Panthers. Discuss as a class the effect of these tactics on the attitudes of white Americans.
L1 ELL

CURRICULUM CONNECTION

Art Many African American artists used African motifs in their creations, which often expressed outrage with society or portrayed scenes from African American history. An example is *Wall of Love* by William Walker.

Analyzing *Political Cartoons*

Answer: Allegations of police brutality sparked the riots.
Ask: What symbol does the cartoon use to highlight the problems of riots, tension, and racial violence in cities? *(mines)*

African Americans in the South. These were goals that could be achieved through court decisions and by convincing Congress to pass new laws.

Despite the passage of several civil rights laws in the 1950s and 1960s, racism—prejudice or discrimination toward someone because of his or her race—was still common in American society. Changing the law could not change people's attitudes immediately, nor could it help those African Americans trapped in poverty in the nation's big cities.

In 1965 nearly 70 percent of African Americans lived in large cities. Many had moved from the South to the big cities of the North and West during the Great Migration of the 1920s and 1940s. There, they often found the same prejudice and discrimination that had plagued them in the South. Many whites refused to live with African Americans in the same neighborhood. When African Americans moved into a neighborhood, whites often moved out. Real estate agents and landlords in white neighborhoods refused to rent or sell to African Americans, who often found it difficult to arrange for mortgages at local banks.

Even if African Americans had been allowed to move into white neighborhoods, poverty trapped many of them in inner cities while whites moved to the suburbs. Many African Americans found themselves channeled into low-paying jobs. They served as custodians and maids, porters and dock workers, with little chance of advancement. Those who did better typically found employment as blue-collar workers in factories, but very few advanced beyond that. In 1965 only 15 percent of African Americans held professional, managerial, or clerical jobs, compared to 44 percent of whites. Half of all African American families lived in poverty, and the average income of an African American family was half that of the average white family. Unemployment among African Americans was typically twice that among whites.

Poor neighborhoods in the nation's major cities were overcrowded and dirty, leading to higher rates of illness and infant mortality. At the same time, the crime rate increased in the 1960s, particularly in low-income neighborhoods. Incidents of juvenile delinquency rose, as did the rate of young people dropping out of school. Complicating matters even more was a rise in the number of single-parent households. All poor neighborhoods suffered from these problems, but because more African Americans lived in poverty, their communities were disproportionately affected.

Many African Americans living in urban poverty knew the civil rights movement had made enormous gains, but when they looked at their own circumstances, nothing seemed to be changing. The movement had raised their hopes, but their everyday problems were economic and social, and therefore harder to address. As a result, their anger and frustration at their situation began to rise—until it finally erupted.

The Watts Riot Just five days after President Johnson signed the Voting Rights Act, a race riot broke out in Watts, an African American neighborhood in Los Angeles. Allegations of police brutality had served as the catalyst of this uprising, which lasted for six days and required over 14,000 members of the National Guard and 1,500 law officers to restore order. Rioters burned and looted entire neighborhoods and destroyed nearly $30 million in property. They killed 34 people, and about 900 suffered injuries.

More rioting was yet to come. Race riots broke out in dozens of American cities between 1965 and 1968. It seemed that they could explode at any place and at any time. The worst riot took place in Detroit in 1967. Burning, looting, and skirmishes with police and National Guard members resulted in 43 deaths and over 1,000 wounded. Eventually the U.S. Army sent in tanks and soldiers armed with machine guns to get control of the situation. Nearly 4,000 fires destroyed

Analyzing *Political Cartoons*

"Perilous Going" This political cartoon highlights the problems that American cities were experiencing in the mid-1960s. Why did riots break out in the Los Angeles neighborhood of Watts?

882 CHAPTER 29 The Civil Rights Movement

COOPERATIVE LEARNING ACTIVITY

Discussing Forms of Protest To review the civil rights movement as it progressed in the 1960s, ask students to count off from 1 to 5 to determine which of the following topic groups they will join: (1) student sit-ins; (2) SCLC marches; (3) speeches by Stokely Carmichael; (4) Freedom Rides; (5) speeches by Malcolm X. Within each group, ask volunteers to take on the tasks of explaining the form of protest, why it was chosen, where it was used, and what results it produced. Have each group prepare a presentation for the entire class.

Use the rubric for a cooperative group management plan on pages 81–82 in the *Performance Assessment Activities and Rubrics.*

1,300 buildings, and the damage in property loss was estimated at $250 million. The governor of Michigan, who viewed the smoldering city from a helicopter, remarked that Detroit looked like "a city that had been bombed."

GOVERNMENT

The Kerner Commission In 1967 President Johnson appointed the National Advisory Commission on Civil Disorders, headed by Governor Otto Kerner of Illinois, to study the causes of the urban riots and to make recommendations to prevent them from happening again in the future. The **Kerner Commission,** as it became known, conducted a detailed study of the problem. The commission blamed white society and white racism for the majority of the problems in the inner city. "Our nation is moving toward two societies, one black, one white—separate and unequal," it concluded.

The commission recommended the creation of 2 million new jobs in the inner city, the construction of 6 million new units of public housing, and a renewed federal commitment to fight de facto segregation. President Johnson's war on poverty, however, which addressed some of the same concerns for inner-city jobs and housing, was already underway. Saddled with massive spending for the Vietnam War, however, President Johnson never endorsed the recommendations of the commission.

✓ **Reading Check** **Explaining** What was the federal government's response to the race riots in Los Angeles and Detroit?

The Shift to Economic Rights

By the mid-1960s, a number of African American leaders were becoming increasingly critical of Martin Luther King's nonviolent strategy. They felt it had failed to improve the economic position of African Americans. What good was the right to dine at restaurants or stay at hotels if most African Americans could not afford these services anyway? Dr. King became sensitive to this criticism, and in 1965 he began to focus on economic issues.

In 1966 the Reverend Albert Raby, president of a council of community organizations that worked to

Picturing History

Anger in Chicago When Dr. King refocused the civil rights movement on the North, some white Americans protested. What did King do to draw attention to slum conditions in Chicago?

improve conditions for Chicago's poor, invited Dr. King to visit the city. Dr. King and his staff had never conducted a civil rights campaign in the North. By focusing on the problems that African Americans faced in Chicago, Dr. King believed he could call greater attention to poverty and other racial problems that lay beneath the urban race riots.

To call attention to the deplorable housing conditions that many African American families faced, Dr. King and his wife Coretta moved into a slum apartment in an African American neighborhood in Chicago. Dr. King and the SCLC hoped to work with local leaders to improve the economic status of African Americans in Chicago's poor neighborhoods.

The **Chicago Movement,** however, made little headway. When Dr. King led a march through the all-white suburb of Cicero to demonstrate the need for open housing, he was met by angry white mobs similar to those in Birmingham and Selma. Mayor **Richard Daley** ordered the Chicago police to protect the marchers, but he wanted to avoid any repeat of the violence. He met with Dr. King and proposed a new program to clean up the slums. Associations of realtors and bankers also agreed to promote open housing. In theory, mortgages and rental property would be available to everyone, regardless of race. In practice, very little changed.

✓ **Reading Check** **Describing** How did Dr. King and SCLC leaders hope to address economic concerns?

CHAPTER 29 The Civil Rights Movement **883**

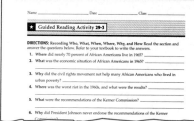

Guided Reading Activity 29–3

Name _____ Date _____ Class _____

★ Guided Reading Activity 29-3

DIRECTIONS: Recording Who, What, When, Where, Why, and How Read the section and answer the questions below. Refer to your textbook to write the answers.
1. Where did nearly 70 percent of African Americans live in 1965?
2. What was the economic situation of African Americans in 1965?
3. Why did the civil rights movement not help many African Americans who lived in urban poverty?
4. Where was the worst riot in the 1960s, and what were the results?
5. What were the recommendations of the Kerner Commission?
6. Why did President Johnson never endorse the recommendations of the Kerner Commission?

✓ **Reading Check**

Answer: United States Army troops were deployed, and the Kerner Commission recommended reforms to prevent further riots.

Picturing History

Answer: King and his wife moved into a slum apartment in Chicago.
Ask: Why did whites protest when the civil rights movement moved to the North? *(There was prejudice and racism in the North.)*

✓ **Reading Check**

Answer: by meeting with local leaders to discuss housing and economic reforms

Writing an Article Have students research the Watts riot using library and Internet resources. Then have them write a headline and a brief newspaper article describing the riot.

📁 Use the rubric for a magazine/newspaper/Web site article or help-wanted ad on pages 85–86 in the *Performance Assessment Activities and Rubrics.*

MEETING SPECIAL NEEDS

Linguistic/Verbal Form volunteers into two groups to conduct a debate. Ask one group to present arguments supporting African American nationalism, the other opposing it. Give students time to consider their arguments. Have each side present its views to the class. Make sure each side presents evidence to support its views. As the students discuss the pros and cons of African American nationalism, encourage the class to reach a consensus. **L2**

📁 Refer to *Inclusion for the High School Social Studies Classroom Strategies and Activities* in the TCR.

Conducting an Interview Have students draw up questions in order to conduct an interview with someone who lived through or participated in the civil rights movement. Help students prepare questions that will get the interviewee to tell how his or her life changed as a result of the civil rights movement. Have students conduct the interviews and then present their findings to the class. Discuss how the interviews add to the information in the text. **L3**

☞ Use the rubric for an interview on pages 93–94 in the *Performance Assessment Activities and Rubrics.*

☞ Use *Supreme Court Case Study 30, Yates v. United States.*

Picturing History

Background: Because they were treated as property, very few enslaved people had last names. If they did have a last name, it was often the name of their slaveholder. Members of the Nation of Islam adopted the "X" to eliminate the historical ties to their enslaved past.

Answer: The X was a symbol for the family name of his African ancestors.

Ask: What belief did Malcolm X share with Marcus Garvey? *(Both believed that African Americans should form their own self-governing communities; Malcolm X later abandoned separatism.)*

Black Power

Dr. King's failure in Chicago seemed to show that nonviolent protests could do little to change economic problems. After 1965 many African Americans, especially young people living in cities, began to turn away from King. Some leaders called for more aggressive forms of protest. Their new strategies ranged from armed self-defense to the suggestion that the government set aside a number of states where African Americans could live free from the presence of whites.

As African Americans became more assertive, they placed less emphasis on cooperation with sympathetic whites in the civil rights movement. Some African American organizations, including CORE and SNCC, voted to expel all whites from leadership positions within their organizations, believing that African Americans alone should determine the course and direction of their struggle.

Many young African Americans called for black power, a term that had many different meanings. A few interpreted black power to mean that physical self-defense and even violence were acceptable in defense of one's freedom—a clear rejection of Dr. King's philosophy. To most, including **Stokely Carmichael,** the leader of SNCC in 1966, the term meant that African Americans should control the social, political, and economic direction of their struggle:

❝This is the significance of black power as a slogan. For once, black people are going to use the words they want to use—not just the words whites want to hear. . . . The need for psychological equality is the reason why SNCC today believes that blacks must organize in the black community. Only black people can . . . create in the community an aroused and continuing black consciousness. . . . Black people must do things for themselves; they must get . . . money they will control and spend themselves; they must conduct tutorial programs themselves so that black children can identify with black people.❞

—from the *New York Review of Books,*
September 1966

Black power also stressed pride in the African American cultural group. It emphasized racial distinctiveness rather than **cultural assimilation**—the process by which minority groups adapt to the dominant culture in a society. African Americans showed pride in their racial heritage by adopting new Afro hairstyles and African-style clothing. Many also took on African names. In universities, students demanded that African and African American Studies courses be adopted as part of the standard school curriculum. Dr. King and some other leaders criticized black power as a philosophy of hopelessness and despair. The idea was very popular, however, in the poor urban neighborhoods where many African Americans resided.

Malcolm X and the Nation of Islam By the early 1960s, a man named **Malcolm X** had become a symbol of the black power movement that was sweeping the nation. Born Malcolm Little in Omaha, Nebraska, he experienced a difficult childhood and adolescence. He drifted into a life of crime, and in 1946, he was convicted of burglary and sent to prison for six years.

Prison transformed Malcolm. He began to educate himself, and he played an active role in the prison debate society. Eventually he joined the **Nation of Islam,** commonly known as the Black Muslims, who were led by Elijah Muhammad. Despite their name, the Black Muslims do not hold the same beliefs as mainstream Muslims. The Nation of Islam preached black nationalism. Like Marcus Garvey in the 1920s, Black Muslims believed that African Americans should separate themselves from whites and form their own self-governing communities.

Shortly after joining the Nation of Islam, Malcolm Little changed his name to Malcolm X. The "X" stood as a symbol for the family name of his African ancestors who had been enslaved. Malcolm argued that his true family name had been stolen from him by slavery, and he did not intend to use the name white society had given him.

The Black Muslims viewed themselves as their own nation and attempted to make themselves as economically self-sufficient as possible. They ran their own businesses, organized their own schools, established

Picturing History

Malcolm X Makes His Point Once the most visible spokesperson for the Nation of Islam, Malcolm X originally disagreed with Dr. King's passive protest tactics. What did the "X" in his name symbolize?

INTERDISCIPLINARY CONNECTIONS ACTIVITY

Citizenship Have students work in pairs to read about and find photo images of one of the radical African American groups such as the Black Panther Party or the Nation of Islam. Have the pairs create a photo essay of their chosen group. Tell students that the essay should involve photos and descriptive captions that give readers insight into the goals of the organization and motives for specific actions. **L2**

their own weekly newspaper (*Muhammad Speaks*), and encouraged their members to respect each other and to strengthen their families. Although the Black Muslims did not advocate violence, they did advocate self-defense. Malcolm X was a powerful and charismatic speaker, and his criticisms of white society and the mainstream civil rights movement gained national attention for the Nation of Islam.

By 1964 Malcolm X had broken with the Black Muslims. Discouraged by scandals involving the Nation of Islam's leader, he went to the Muslim holy city of Makkah (also called Mecca) in Saudi Arabia. After seeing Muslims from many different races worshipping together, he concluded that an integrated society was possible. In a revealing letter describing his pilgrimage to Makkah, he stated that many whites that he met during the pilgrimage displayed a spirit of brotherhood that gave him a new, positive insight into race relations.

After Malcolm X broke with the Nation of Islam, he continued to criticize the organization and its leader, Elijah Muhammad. Because of this, three organization members shot and killed him in February 1965 while he was giving a speech in New York. Although Malcolm X left the Nation of Islam before his death, his speeches and ideas from those years with the Black Muslims are those for which he is most remembered. In Malcolm's view, African Americans may have been victims in the past, but they did not have to allow racism to victimize them in the present. His ideas have influenced African Americans to take pride in their own culture and to believe in their ability to make their way in the world.

The Black Panthers Malcolm X's ideas influenced a new generation of militant African American leaders who also preached black power, black nationalism, and economic self-sufficiency. In 1966 in Oakland, California, Huey Newton, Bobby Seale, and Eldridge Cleaver organized the Black Panther Party for Self-Defense, or the **Black Panthers,** as they were known. They considered themselves the heirs of Malcolm X, and they recruited most of their members from poor urban communities across the nation.

The Black Panthers believed that a revolution was necessary in the United States, and they urged African Americans to arm themselves and confront white society in order to force whites to grant them equal rights. Black Panther leaders adopted a "Ten-Point Program," which called for black empowerment, an end to racial oppression, and control of major institutions and services in the African American community, such as schools, law enforcement, housing, and medical

 **Picturing History**

Black Power U.S. athletes Tommie Smith and John Carlos give the black power salute during the medal ceremony at the 1968 Olympic Games in Mexico City. How did black power supporters demonstrate their belief in the movement?

facilities. **Eldridge Cleaver,** who served as the minister of culture, articulated many of the organization's objectives in his 1967 best-selling book, *Soul on Ice.*

 **Reading Check** **Describing** What caused a division between Dr. Martin Luther King, Jr., and the black power movement?

The Assassination of Martin Luther King, Jr.

By the late 1960s, the civil rights movement had fragmented into dozens of competing organizations with philosophies for reaching equality. At the same time, the emergence of black power and the call by some African Americans for violent action angered many white civil rights supporters. This made further legislation to help blacks economically less likely.

In this atmosphere, Dr. King went to Memphis, Tennessee, to support a strike of African American sanitation workers in March 1968. At the time, the SCLC had been planning a national "Poor People's Campaign" to promote economic advancement for

CHAPTER 29 The Civil Rights Movement **885**

 **Picturing History**

Answer: They gave this same black power salute by raising a clenched fist.

 **Reading Check**

Answer: King was nonviolent; the black power movement advocated aggressive self-defense, even violence.

Understanding Relative Chronology Have students create a fact sheet tracing the changing tactics of the civil rights movement. L2

3 ASSESS

Assign Section 3 Assessment as homework or as an in-class activity.

⬥ Have students use the **Interactive Tutor Self-Assessment CD-ROM.**

Reading Essentials and Study Guide 29–3

Name _____ Date _____ Class _____

Study Guide

Chapter 29, Section 3
For use with textbook pages 881–886

NEW ISSUES

KEY TERMS AND NAMES

racism prejudice or discrimination toward someone because of his or her race *(page 882)*
Chicago Movement a plan by Martin Luther King, Jr., and other civil rights leaders to improve the economic conditions of African Americans in Chicago's poor neighborhoods *(page 883)*
Richard Daley the mayor of Chicago *(page 883)*
black power a movement that called for African American control of the social, political, and economic direction of the struggle for equality and stressed pride in the African American cultural group *(page 884)*
Stokely Carmichael the leader of the SNCC in 1966 *(page 884)*
Malcolm X the most visible spokesperson of the black power movement *(page 884)*

CRITICAL THINKING ACTIVITY

Analyzing Concepts Ask students to consider the following questions and write their thoughts and responses on a sheet of paper. **Is violence in self-defense, or in response to violence, justifiable? Is nonviolent civil disobedience an effective strategy for attaining full equality?** After students have had a chance to write down their thoughts, conduct a class discussion about the differences between violent and nonviolent protests. Encourage students to share differing views as they explore these complex concepts. **L2**

Section Quiz 29–3

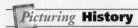

Picturing **History**

Answer: to support a strike by African American sanitation workers

Reteach

Have students describe the division between Dr. Martin Luther King, Jr., and the black power movement.

Enrich

Have interested students write a paragraph explaining why the Kerner Commission was largely ignored.

☑ **Reading Check**

Answer: The Poor People's Campaign promoted economic advancement for all impoverished Americans.

4 CLOSE

Have students discuss the direction and progress of the civil rights movement after 1968.

Picturing **History**

Atlanta Mourns Martin Luther King, Jr. The nation joined Coretta Scott King (right) in sorrow following the assassination of her husband in 1968. Why was King in Memphis at the time of his death?

there with you, but I want you to know tonight that we as a people will get to the Promised Land."

Dr. King's assassination touched off both national mourning and riots in more than 100 cities, including Washington, D.C. The Reverend **Ralph Abernathy,** who had served as a trusted assistant to Dr. King for many years, led the Poor People's Campaign in King's absence. The demonstration, however, did not achieve any of the major objectives that either King or the SCLC had hoped it would.

In the wake of Dr. King's death, Congress passed the Civil Rights Act of 1968. The act contained a fair housing provision outlawing discrimination in housing sales and rentals and gave the Justice Department authority to bring suits against such discrimination.

Dr. King's death marked the end of an era in American history. Although the civil rights movement continued, it lacked the unity of purpose and vision that Dr. King had given it. Under his leadership, and with the help of tens of thousands of dedicated African Americans, many of whom were students, the civil rights movement transformed American society. Although many problems remain to be resolved, the achievements of the civil rights movement in the 1950s and 1960s dramatically improved life for African Americans, creating new opportunities where none had existed before.

all impoverished Americans. The purpose of this campaign, the most ambitious one that Dr. King would ever lead, was to lobby the federal government to commit billions of dollars to end poverty and unemployment in the United States. People of all races and nationalities were to converge on the nation's capital, as they had in 1963 during the March on Washington, where they would camp out until both Congress and President Johnson agreed to pass the requested legislation to fund the proposal.

On the evening of April 4, 1968, as he stood on his hotel balcony in Memphis, Dr. King was assassinated by a sniper. Ironically, he had told a gathering at a local African American church just the previous night, "I've been to the mountaintop. . . . I've looked over and I've seen the Promised Land. I may not get

☑ **Reading Check** **Summarizing** What were the goals of the Poor People's Campaign?

SECTION *3* ASSESSMENT

Checking for Understanding

1. **Define:** racism, black power.
2. **Identify:** Chicago Movement, Richard Daley, Stokely Carmichael, Malcolm X, Black Panthers.
3. **Explain** the goals of the Nation of Islam in the 1960s.
4. **Summarize** the findings of the Kerner Commission.

Reviewing Themes

5. **Civic Rights and Responsibilities** How was the Civil Rights Act of 1968 designed to help end discrimination?

Critical Thinking

6. **Identifying Cause and Effect** What were the effects of the assassination of Dr. Martin Luther King, Jr.?
7. **Categorizing** Using a graphic organizer like the one below, list the main views of the three leaders listed.

Leader	Views
Dr. Martin Luther King, Jr.	
Malcolm X	
Eldridge Cleaver	

Analyzing Visuals

8. **Analyzing Political Cartoons** The cartoon on page 882 suggests that the violence of the mid-1960s was as bad as the violence of the Vietnam War going on at the same time. What images does the cartoonist use to compare violence at home with the violence of the war?

Writing About History

9. **Expository Writing** Take on the role of a reporter in the late 1960s. Imagine you have interviewed a follower of Dr. King and a Black Panther member. Write out a transcript of each interview.

SECTION *3* ASSESSMENT ANSWERS

1. Terms are in blue.
2. Chicago Movement *(p. 883),* Richard Daley *(p. 883),* Stokely Carmichael *(p. 884),* Malcolm X *(p. 884),* Black Panthers *(p. 885)*
3. It wanted separate self-governing communities for African Americans.
4. It blamed racism for inner-city problems and urged job and housing programs.
5. by outlawing housing discrimination
6. It touched off both national mourning and riots; the Civil Rights Act of 1968 was passed.
7. King: nonviolent protest; Malcolm X: self-defense and separatism; Cleaver: revolution
8. the ocean ships, floating mines
9. Students' articles will vary but should be written as if a reporter were describing an interview.

Study and Writing SKILLBUILDER

Preparing a Bibliography

Why Learn This Skill?

When you write research reports, you should include a list of the sources used to find your information. This list, called a *bibliography*, allows you to credit the sources you cited and supports the report's accuracy.

Learning the Skill

A bibliography is a list of sources used in a research report. These sources include books; articles from newspapers, magazines, and journals; interviews; and other sources.

There are two main reasons to write a bibliography. First, those who read your report may want to learn more about the topic. Second, a bibliography supports the reliability of your report.

A bibliography follows an established format. The entry for each source contains all the information needed to find that source, including the author, title, page numbers, publisher information, and publication date. You should document this information as you carry out your research. If you neglect this step early in your research, you must locate your sources again in order to credit them in your report.

You should arrange bibliographic entries alphabetically by the author's last name. The following are acceptable formats, followed by sample entries. Note that all lines after the first line are indented.

Books:

Author's last name, first name. *Full Title.* Place of publication: publisher, copyright date.

Hay, Peter. *Ordinary Heroes: The Life and Death of Chana Szenes, Israel's National Heroine.* New York: Paragon House, 1986.

Articles:

Author's last name, first name. "Title of Article." *Name of Periodical* in which article appears, volume number (date of issue): page numbers.

Watson, Bruce. "The New Peace Corps in the New Kazakhstan." *Smithsonian,* Vol. 25 (August 1994): pp. 26–35.

Other Sources:

For other kinds of sources, adapt the format for book entries as needed.

Practicing the Skill

Review the sample bibliography below from a report on Martin Luther King, Jr. Then answer the questions that follow.

Patrick, Diane. *Martin Luther King, Jr.* New York: Franklin Watts, 1990.

Franklin, John H. "Jim Crow Goes to School: The Genesis of Legal Segregation in Southern Schools." *South Atlantic Quarterly,* 57 (1956): pp. 225–235.

Washington, James Melvin, ed. *A Testament of Hope: The Essential Writings of Martin Luther King, Jr.* San Francisco: Harper & Row.

King, Jr., Martin Luther. Time for Freedom has Come. *New York Times Magazine* (Sept. 10, 1961).

❶ Are the bibliography entries in the correct order? Why or why not?

❷ What is missing from the second book listing?

❸ What features are missing from the second article listing?

Skills Assessment

Complete the Practicing Skills questions on page 889 and the Chapter 29 Skill Reinforcement Activity to assess your mastery of this skill.

Applying the Skill

Preparing a Bibliography Put together a bibliography of at least five sources that you could use for a report on the civil rights movement. Include books, periodicals, and any other sources you wish.

 Glencoe's **Skillbuilder Interactive Workbook CD-ROM, Level 2,** provides instruction and practice in key social studies skills.

TEACH

Preparing a Bibliography
Provide students with information about acceptable styles for a bibliography for this class. Point out that while there is more than one acceptable format, a teacher, department, or school often selects one style to be used by all students. This is also common at the college level and in the business world.

Additional Practice

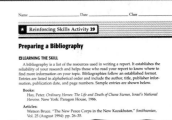

Reinforcing Skills Activity 29

Name _____ Date _____ Class _____

★ Reinforcing Skills Activity 29

Preparing a Bibliography

◻ LEARNING THE SKILL
A bibliography is a list of the resources used in writing a report. It establishes the reliability of your research and helps those who read your report to know where to find more information on your topic. Bibliographies follow an established format. Entries are listed in alphabetical order and include the author, title, publisher information, publication date, and page numbers. Sample entries are shown below.

Books:
Hay, Peter. *Ordinary Heroes: The Life and Death of Chana Szenes, Israel's National Heroine.* New York: Paragon House, 1986.
Articles:
Watson Bruce. "The New Peace Corps in the New Kazakhstan." *Smithsonian,* Vol. 25 (August 1994): pp. 26–35.

GLENCOE
TECHNOLOGY

 CD-ROM
Glencoe Skillbuilder Interactive Workbook CD-ROM, Level 2

This interactive CD-ROM reinforces student mastery of essential social studies skills.

ANSWERS TO PRACTICING THE SKILL

❶ No, they should be in alphabetical order using the last name of each author.

❷ publication date

❸ quotes around the title of the article, and italics for the *New York Times Magazine*

Applying the Skill
Students' bibliographies will vary. Students should follow the guidelines on this page or other guidelines you provide.

GLENCOE
TECHNOLOGY

MindJogger Videoquiz
Use the **MindJogger Videoquiz** to review Chapter 29 content.

📼 Available in VHS

Reviewing Key Terms

Students' answers will vary. The pages where the words appear in the text are shown in parentheses.

1. **separate-but-equal** *(p. 867)*
2. **de facto segregation** *(p. 867)*
3. **sit-in** *(p. 868)*
4. **Freedom Riders** *(p. 875)*
5. **filibuster** *(p. 878)*
6. **cloture** *(p. 878)*
7. **poll tax** *(p. 879)*
8. **racism** *(p. 882)*
9. **black power** *(p. 884)*

Reviewing Key Facts

10. NAACP *(p. 867)*, Thurgood Marshall *(p. 868)*, Linda Brown *(p. 868)*, Martin Luther King, Jr. *(p. 869)*, Southern Christian Leadership Conference *(p. 870)*, Jesse Jackson *(p. 874)*, Chicago Movement *(p. 883)*, Stokely Carmichael *(p. 884)*, Malcolm X *(p. 884)*

11. Rosa Parks's arrest led to the bus boycott.

12. It was the first case in which the Court found segregation to be unconstitutional.

13. It worked for desegregation of public facilities and voter registration.

14. It sent in National Guard and U.S. Army troops, and appointed the Kerner Commission.

15. It moved from focusing on ending segregation to focusing on full social and economic equality. It also moved from nonviolent resistance to militancy.

Reviewing Key Terms

On a sheet of paper, use each of these terms in a sentence.

1. separate-but-equal
2. de facto segregation
3. sit-in
4. Freedom Riders
5. filibuster
6. cloture
7. poll tax
8. racism
9. black power

Reviewing Key Facts

10. **Identify:** NAACP, Thurgood Marshall, Linda Brown, Martin Luther King, Jr., Southern Christian Leadership Conference, Jesse Jackson, Chicago Movement, Stokely Carmichael, Malcolm X.

11. What event led to the bus boycott in Montgomery, Alabama?

12. Why was the decision in *Brown* v. *Board of Education* a significant step toward ending segregation?

13. What was the role of SNCC in the civil rights movement?

14. How did the government react to race riots in cities such as Los Angeles and Detroit?

15. What were two changes in the focus of the civil rights movement in the mid-1960s?

Critical Thinking

16. **Analyzing Themes: Civic Rights and Responsibilities** Do you agree with the viewpoint of Dr. Martin Luther King, Jr., or with that of the Black Panthers concerning the civil rights movement? Explain your answer.

17. **Evaluating** Why did the civil rights movement make fewer gains after 1968?

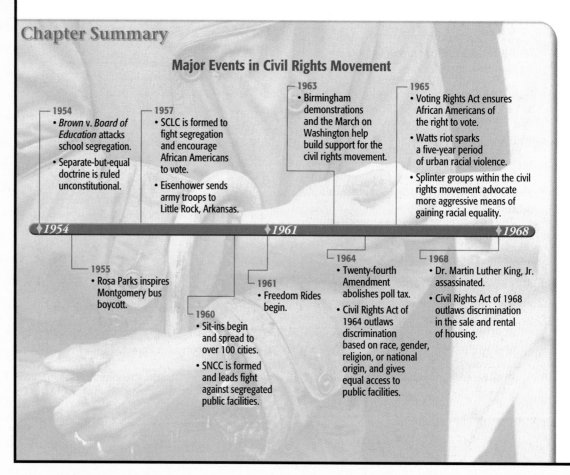

Chapter Summary

Major Events in Civil Rights Movement

1954
- *Brown* v. *Board of Education* attacks school segregation.
- Separate-but-equal doctrine is ruled unconstitutional.

1957
- SCLC is formed to fight segregation and encourage African Americans to vote.
- Eisenhower sends army troops to Little Rock, Arkansas.

1963
- Birmingham demonstrations and the March on Washington help build support for the civil rights movement.

1965
- Voting Rights Act ensures African Americans of the right to vote.
- Watts riot sparks a five-year period of urban racial violence.
- Splinter groups within the civil rights movement advocate more aggressive means of gaining racial equality.

◆1954   **◆1961**   **◆1968**

1955
- Rosa Parks inspires Montgomery bus boycott.

1960
- Sit-ins begin and spread to over 100 cities.
- SNCC is formed and leads fight against segregated public facilities.

1961
- Freedom Rides begin.

1964
- Twenty-fourth Amendment abolishes poll tax.
- Civil Rights Act of 1964 outlaws discrimination based on race, gender, religion, or national origin, and gives equal access to public facilities.

1968
- Dr. Martin Luther King, Jr. assassinated.
- Civil Rights Act of 1968 outlaws discrimination in the sale and rental of housing.

Critical Thinking

16. Students' answers will vary. Students should refer to the results and reactions in this chapter in discussing their opinions.

17. After Martin Luther King, Jr., was assassinated, the movement fragmented; also, economic gains were harder to win.

18. It was a nonviolent protest that offered immediate results and gained sympathy from many people in the nation.

19. Civil Rights Act of 1957: created the civil rights division of the Department of Justice to support the right to vote, created the United States Commission of Civil Rights; Twenty-Fourth Amendment: ended poll taxes; Voting Rights Act: authorized the attorney general to send federal examiners to register qualified voters;

HISTORY Online

Self-Check Quiz

Visit the *American Vision* Web site at tav.glencoe.com and click on *Self-Check Quizzes—Chapter 29* to assess your knowledge of chapter content.

18. **Making Generalizations** Why was the sit-in movement considered a major turning point in the civil rights movement?

19. **Organizing** Use a graphic organizer similar to the one below to compare examples of civil rights legislation.

Civil Rights Legislation	Provisions
Civil Rights Act 1957	
Twenty-Fourth Amendment	
Voting Rights Act	
Civil Rights Act of 1964	
Civil Rights Act of 1968	

Practicing Skills

20. **Preparing a Bibliography** Review the following bibliography for a report on the civil rights movement. Then answer the questions that follow.

Fairclough, Adam. Martin Luther King, Jr. Athens and London: University of Georgia Press, 1995.

Juan Williams. Eyes on the Prize. New York: Viking Penguin, Inc., 1987.

Patterson, James T. Grand Expectations, The United States, 1945–1974. New York: Oxford University Press, 1996.

Bontemps, Arna, and Jack Conroy. Anyplace but Here. Columbia: University of Missouri Press. (NO PUB DATE)

a. The entries presented above are not listed in the correct order. Using just the names of the authors, put them in the correct order.

b. What is incorrect in the Patterson listing?

c. Rewrite the Juan Williams listing correctly.

Geography and History

21. The map on this page shows routes of Freedom Riders. Study the map and answer the questions below.
    a. Interpreting Maps Which states did the Freedom Riders travel through? What was their final destination?
    b. Applying Geography Skills Why do you think the Freedom Riders faced protests during this trip?

Writing Activity

22. **Writing a Script** Work in small groups to write a script for a documentary on the civil rights movement in the 1950s

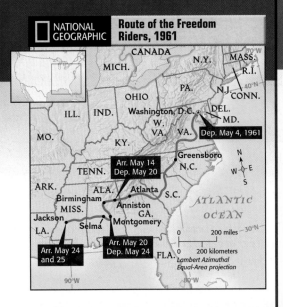

Route of the Freedom Riders, 1961

and 1960s. Your group should choose a specific topic, movement leader, or time period to write about. Use your script to produce a documentary to present to the other groups in your class.

Chapter Activity

23. **Examining Interviews** Work with a classmate to research interviews with Martin Luther King, Jr., and Malcolm X. Take notes on the different points of view of these civil rights leaders, and then prepare a chart illustrating similarities, differences, and any bias which shapes their beliefs.

The Princeton Review

Standardized Test Practice

Directions: Choose the phrase that best completes the following statement.

One difference between the strategies of Dr. Martin Luther King, Jr., and some later civil rights groups was that King was committed to

A ending discrimination in housing and unemployment.

B using only nonviolent forms of protest.

C demanding equal rights for African Americans.

D gaining improvements in living conditions for African Americans.

Test-Taking Tip: If you read this question carefully, you will notice that it asks for one *difference* in civil rights strategies. Three of the answer choices will represent *common goals*. Be careful to read through all the choices to find the one that represents a *different* type of strategy.

HISTORY Online

Have students visit the Web site at tav.glencoe.com to review Chapter 29 and take the Self-Check Quiz.

Writing Activity

22. Documentaries should indicate a clear understanding of events and should express the emotions of the times.

Chapter Activity

23. Charts should show the similarities and differences between the two leaders.

The Princeton Review

Standardized Test Practice

Answer: B

Test-Taking Tip: Tell students to think about what some of the later civil rights groups advocated. The one issue on this list that some of the later groups did not support was nonviolence. The correct answer is B.

Bonus Question ?

Ask: What was the purpose of the March on Washington? *(to build public support for passage of the Civil Rights Act of 1964)*

Civil Rights Act of 1964: gave the federal government broad powers to prevent racial discrimination, required equal access to public facilities for citizens of all races, established the EEOC, required private employers to end workplace discrimination, gave the attorney general power to bring lawsuits to force school desegregation; Civil Rights Act of 1968: outlawed discrimination in housing

Practicing Skills

20. **a.** The author order should be Bontemps, Fairclough, Patterson, and Williams. **b.** The author, not the title, is underlined. **c.** Williams, Juan. *Eyes on the Prize.* New York: Viking Penguin, Inc., 1987.

Geography and History

21. **a.** Maryland, Virginia, North Carolina, South Carolina, Georgia, Alabama; final destination: Jackson, Mississippi; **b.** because they wanted to desegregate society

Chapter 30 Resources

Timesaving Tools

TeacherWorks™ All-In-One Planner and Resource Center

- **Interactive Teacher Edition** Access your Teacher Wraparound Edition and your classroom resources with a few easy clicks.
- **Interactive Lesson Planner** Planning has never been easier! Organize your week, month, semester, or year with all the lesson helps you need to make teaching creative, timely, and relevant.

Use Glencoe's **Presentation Plus!** multimedia teacher tool to easily present dynamic lessons that visually excite your students. Using Microsoft PowerPoint® you can customize the presentations to create your own personalized lessons.

TEACHING TRANSPARENCIES

Graphic Organizer 10

Why It Matters Chapter Transparency 30

APPLICATION AND ENRICHMENT

Linking Past and Present Activity 30

Enrichment Activity 30

Primary Source Reading 30

REVIEW AND REINFORCEMENT

Reteaching Activity 30

Vocabulary Activity 30

Time Line Activity 30

Critical Thinking Skills Activity 30

Meeting NCSS Standards

The following standards are highlighted in Chapter 30:

Section 1	VI	Power, Authority, and Governance: B, C, F, I
Section 2	VIII	Science, Technology, and Society: A, C
Section 3	X	Civic Ideals and Practices: C, D, E, F, G, H
Section 4	VI	Power, Authority, and Governance: B, C, F

Local Standards

Chapter 30 Resources

ASSESSMENT AND EVALUATION

Chapter 30 Test Form A

Chapter 30 Test Form B

Standardized Test Skills Practice Workbook Activity 30

Performance Assessment Activities and Rubrics 30

ExamView® Pro Testmaker CD-ROM

MULTIMEDIA

- Vocabulary PuzzleMaker CD-ROM
- Interactive Tutor Self-Assessment CD-ROM
- ExamView® Pro Testmaker CD-ROM
- Audio Program
- American History Primary Source Documents Library CD-ROM
- MindJogger Videoquiz
- Presentation Plus! CD-ROM
- TeacherWorks™ CD-ROM
- Interactive Student Edition CD-ROM
- Glencoe Skillbuilder Interactive Workbook CD-ROM, Level 2
- The *American Vision* Video Program
- American Music: Hits Through History
- American Music: Cultural Traditions

SPANISH RESOURCES

The following Spanish language materials are available in the Spanish Resources Binder:

- Spanish Guided Reading Activities
- Spanish Reteaching Activities
- Spanish Quizzes and Tests
- Spanish Vocabulary Activities
- Spanish Summaries
- The Declaration of Independence and United States Constitution Spanish Translation

The following videotape programs are available from Glencoe as supplements to Chapter 30:

- **Vietnam: A Soldier's Story** (ISBN 0-76-700772-7)
- **Richard M. Nixon: Man and President** (ISBN 1-56-501742-0)

To order, call Glencoe at 1-800-334-7344. To find classroom resources to accompany many of these videos, check the following home pages:
A&E Television: www.aande.com
The History Channel: www.historychannel.com

Use our Web site for additional resources. All essential content is covered in the Student Edition.

You and your students can visit tav.glencoe.com, the Web site companion to the *American Vision.* This innovative integration of electronic and print media offers your students a wealth of opportunities. The student text directs students to the Web site for the following options:

- **Chapter Overviews**
- **Self-Check Quizzes**
- **Student Web Activities**
- **Textbook Updates**

Answers to the student Web activities are provided for you in the **Web Activity Lesson Plans.** Additional Web resources and Interactive Tutor Puzzles are also available.

Chapter 30 Resources

SECTION RESOURCES

Daily Objectives	Reproducible Resources	Multimedia Resources
SECTION 1 **The United States Focuses on Vietnam** 1. Describe the nationalist motives of Vietnamese leader Ho Chi Minh. 2. Explain the origins of American involvement in Vietnam during the 1950s.	Reproducible Lesson Plan 30–1 Daily Lecture and Discussion Notes 30–1 Guided Reading Activity 30–1* Section Quiz 30–1* Reading Essentials and Study Guide 30–1 Performance Assessment Activities and Rubrics	Daily Focus Skills Transparency 30–1 Interactive Tutor Self-Assessment CD-ROM ExamView® Pro Testmaker CD-ROM Presentation Plus! CD-ROM TeacherWorks™ CD-ROM Audio Program
SECTION 2 **Going to War in Vietnam** 1. Describe how President Johnson deepened American involvement in Vietnam. 2. Discuss how the Vietcong and the North Vietnamese were able to frustrate the American military.	Reproducible Lesson Plan 30–2 Daily Lecture and Discussion Notes 30–2 Guided Reading Activity 30–2* Section Quiz 30–2* Reading Essentials and Study Guide 30–2 Performance Assessment Activities and Rubrics Interpreting Political Cartoons	Daily Focus Skills Transparency 30–2 Interactive Tutor Self-Assessment CD-ROM ExamView® Pro Testmaker CD-ROM Presentation Plus! CD-ROM TeacherWorks™ CD-ROM Audio Program
SECTION 3 **Vietnam Divides the Nation** 1. Analyze why support for the war began to weaken. 2. Describe the motives of those in the antiwar movement.	Reproducible Lesson Plan 30–3 Daily Lecture and Discussion Notes 30–3 Guided Reading Activity 30–3* Section Quiz 30–3* Reading Essentials and Study Guide 30–3 Performance Assessment Activities and Rubrics	Daily Focus Skills Transparency 30–3 Interactive Tutor Self-Assessment CD-ROM ExamView® Pro Testmaker CD-ROM Presentation Plus! CD-ROM TeacherWorks™ CD-ROM Audio Program American Music: Cultural Traditions
SECTION 4 **The War Winds Down** 1. Explain the events of Nixon's first administration that inspired more antiwar protests. 2. Summarize the major lessons the United States learned from the Vietnam War experience.	Reproducible Lesson Plan 30–4 Daily Lecture and Discussion Notes 30–4 Guided Reading Activity 30–4* Section Quiz 30–4* Reading Essentials and Study Guide 30–4 Performance Assessment Activities and Rubrics Supreme Court Case Studies	Daily Focus Skills Transparency 30–4 American Art & Architecture Interactive Tutor Self-Assessment CD-ROM ExamView® Pro Testmaker CD-ROM Presentation Plus! CD-ROM Skillbuilder Interactive Workbook, Level 2 TeacherWorks™ CD-ROM Vocabulary PuzzleMaker CD-ROM Audio Program ABCNews Interactive™ Historic America Electronic Field Trips

0:00 OUT OF TIME?
Assign the Chapter 30 **Reading Essentials and Study Guide.**

*Also Available in Spanish

 Blackline Master   Transparency   CD-ROM   DVD
Poster   Music Program   Audio Program   Videocassette

NATIONAL GEOGRAPHIC Teacher's Corner

INDEX TO NATIONAL GEOGRAPHIC MAGAZINE

The following articles relate to this chapter.
- "Hong-Kong—Plight of the Boat People," February 1991
- "The Mekong," February 1993
- "The New Saigon," April 1995
- "Vietnam Memorial: To Heal a Nation," May 1985
- "Vietnam: The Hard Road to Peace," November 1989

NATIONAL GEOGRAPHIC SOCIETY PRODUCTS AVAILABLE FROM GLENCOE

To order the following product for use with this chapter, contact your local Glencoe sales representative, or call Glencoe at 1-800-334-7344:
- *Picture Atlas of the World* (CD-ROM)

ADDITIONAL NATIONAL GEOGRAPHIC SOCIETY PRODUCTS

To order the following, call National Geographic at 1-800-368-2728:
- *Historical Atlas of the World* (Atlas)

NGS ONLINE

Access National Geographic's Web site for current events, atlas updates, activities, links, interactive features, and archives.

www.nationalgeographic.com

From the Classroom of...

Joseph Anastasio
Academy of the Holy Names
Albany, NY

The Vietnam War: A Musical History

The Vietnam War is still controversial, but few debates consider the soldiers' experiences. The following activity allows the class to analyze the experiences of the soldiers during and after the war.

To introduce the lesson, students should discuss their impressions of the war. Then, play a video of the dedication ceremony of the Vietnam Veterans Memorial. Play Billy Joel's "Goodnight Saigon" while the video is playing. Discuss and analyze the song.

Finally, ask students to write an essay that compares the soldiers' experiences in Vietnam to that of their counterparts in World War II.

ADDITIONAL RESOURCES FROM GLENCOE

- American Music: Cultural Traditions
- American Art & Architecture
- Outline Map Resource Book
- U.S. Desk Map
- Building Geography Skills for Life
- Inclusion for the High School Social Studies Classroom Strategies and Activities
- Teaching Strategies for the American History Classroom (Including Block Scheduling Pacing Guides)

KEY TO ABILITY LEVELS

Teaching strategies have been coded.

L1 BASIC activities for all students
L2 AVERAGE activities for average to above-average students
L3 CHALLENGING activities for above-average students
ELL ENGLISH LANGUAGE LEARNER activities

Block Schedule

Activities that are suited to use within the block scheduling framework are identified by:

Why It Matters Activity

Have students list the places where American troops have been sent since the Vietnam War and the results of those efforts. Ask students how they think the Vietnam experience has influenced these decisions. Students should evaluate their answers after they have completed the chapter.

CHAPTER
30 The Vietnam War
1954–1975

Why It Matters

The Vietnam War created very bitter divisions within the United States. Supporters argued that patriotism demanded that communism be halted. Opponents argued that intervening in Vietnam was immoral. Many young people protested or resisted the draft. Victory was not achieved, although more than 58,000 American soldiers died. After the war, the nation had many wounds to heal.

The Impact Today

Changes brought about by the war are still evident in the United States today.
- *The nation is reluctant to commit troops overseas.*
- *The War Powers Act limits a president's power to involve the nation in war.*

The American Vision *Video* The Chapter 30 video, "Vietnam: A Different War," explores the causes and the impact of this longest war in American history.

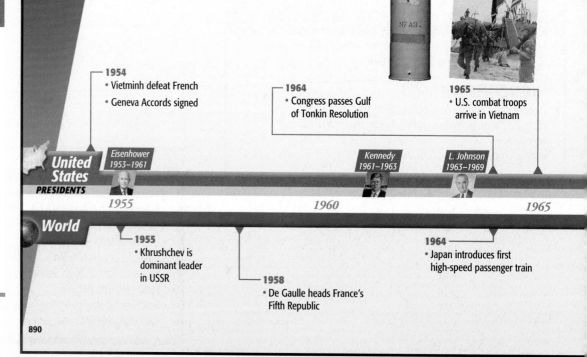

1954
- Vietminh defeat French
- Geneva Accords signed

1964
- Congress passes Gulf of Tonkin Resolution

1965
- U.S. combat troops arrive in Vietnam

United States PRESIDENTS

Eisenhower 1953–1961

Kennedy 1961–1963

L. Johnson 1963–1969

1955   *1960*   *1965*

World

1955
- Khrushchev is dominant leader in USSR

1958
- De Gaulle heads France's Fifth Republic

1964
- Japan introduces first high-speed passenger train

890

TWO-MINUTE LESSON LAUNCHER

Make a line of dominoes standing on end. Knock the first one over so that the rest fall in turn. After the demonstration, ask students what they think the domino theory meant in relation to Southeast Asia. Then ask: **How did the domino theory influence Americans?** *(It created fear.)*

HISTORY
Online

Introduce students to chapter content and key terms by having them access the **Chapter 30 Overview** at tav.glencoe.com.

More About the Photo

The Vietnam Veterans Memorial is made of black granite panels that carry the names of the approximately 58,000 Americans who died or remain missing in action in Vietnam. Visitors often touch the names of those they knew and can make a rubbing of the soldier's name. Ask students why they think the memorial has helped the nation come to terms with the Vietnam War. *(It has brought a sense of closure and acknowledgment that those who died served their country well.)*

The dedication ceremony for the Vietnam Veterans Memorial in Washington, D.C., November 13, 1982

1967
• March on the Pentagon takes place

1968
• Tet offensive
• Students protest at Democratic National Convention in Chicago

1970
• National Guard troops kill students at Kent State University

1973
• Cease-fire signed with North Vietnam

1975
• Evacuation of last Americans from Vietnam

Nixon
1969–1974

Ford
1974–1977

1970   *1975*

1967
• First heart transplant performed

1968
• Soviets repress Czechoslovakia's rebellion

1971
• Pakistani civil war leads to independent Bangladesh

1975
• Civil war breaks out in Angola

HISTORY
Online

Chapter Overview
Visit the *American Vision* Web site at tav.glencoe.com and click on **Chapter Overviews— Chapter 30** to preview chapter information.

TIME LINE
ACTIVITY

Have students select one of the events on the time line and conduct a brief interview with someone who was a teenager or adult at the time. Encourage students to learn what the interviewee remembers about the event and what impact the event had on his or her life. Invite students to share what they learned with the class.

891

GRAPHIC ORGANIZER ACTIVITY

Organizing Information Have students complete the following graphic organizer to make a generalization about how media coverage and student protests affected public opinion of the war. A sample generalization may be that the media coverage and protests helped force a shift in U.S. policies. Details should support the generalization made.

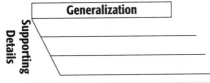

Generalization

Supporting Details

1 FOCUS

Section Overview

This section focuses on the events that led to the United States fighting the Vietnam War.

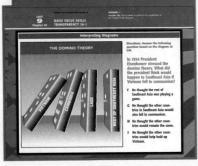

Guide to Reading

Answers to Graphic: fall of China to communism and the outbreak of the Korean War

Preteaching Vocabulary
Have students use a standard dictionary or online resource to learn the correct pronunciation of the Key Terms and Names. For example, some dictionary sites have an audio feature where the user can hear words pronounced correctly.

SECTION 1 The United States Focuses on Vietnam

Guide to Reading

Main Idea
American efforts to stop the spread of communism led to U.S. involvement in the affairs of Vietnam.

Key Terms and Names
Ho Chi Minh, domino theory, guerrilla, Dien Bien Phu, Ngo Dinh Diem

Reading Strategy
Organizing As you read about the increasing involvement of the United States in Vietnam, complete a graphic organizer similar to the one below by providing reasons that the United States aided France in Vietnam.

```
Reasons for U.S.  →  [  ]
Support of France
                  →  [  ]
```

Reading Objectives
• **Describe** the nationalist motives of Vietnamese leader Ho Chi Minh.
• **Explain** the origins of American involvement in Vietnam during the 1950s.

Section Theme
Government and Democracy American involvement in Vietnam was a reflection of Cold War strategy.

Preview of Events

◆1946 ◆1950 ◆1954 ◆1958

1946
French-Vietminh War begins

1950
The United States supplies military aid to France

1954
Vietminh defeat French at Dien Bien Phu; Geneva Accords signed in Paris

1956
Ngo Dinh Diem refuses to participate in nationwide elections in Vietnam

---

★ An American Story ★

Major Allison Thomas

On July 16, 1945, as World War II continued to rage in the Pacific, a small military force that included Major Allison Thomas parachuted into a jungle clearing of Vietnam. Their mission was to gather information on the Japanese, who had controlled Vietnam since 1941.

Shortly after landing, Thomas's team encountered a group of Vietnamese independence fighters. Led by Ho Chi Minh, they were fighting to free Vietnam from Japanese rule. The guerrillas quickly escorted the team to their encampment, where the team learned that Ho Chi Minh had fallen ill. The team's medic, Paul Hoagland, treated Ho for dysentery and malaria and most likely saved his life. Thomas later recalled his first night at Ho's camp.

❝They [Ho Chi Minh's forces] had built for us a special bamboo shelter, consisting of a bamboo floor a few feet off the ground and a roof of palm leaves. We then had supper consisting of beer, rice, bamboo sprouts and barbecued steaks. They freshly slaughtered a cow in our honor.❞

—quoted in *The Perfect War*

Early American Involvement in Vietnam

In the late 1940s and early 1950s, most Americans knew little about Vietnam. During this time, however, American officials came to view the nation as increasingly important in the campaign to halt the spread of communism.

SECTION RESOURCES

📂 **Reproducible Masters**
• Reproducible Lesson Plan 30–1
• Daily Lecture and Discussion Notes 30–1
• Guided Reading Activity 30–1
• Section Quiz 30–1
• Reading Essentials and Study Guide 30–1
• Performance Assessment Activities and Rubrics

🖎 **Transparencies**
• Daily Focus Skills Transparency 30–1

Multimedia
💿 Interactive Tutor Self-Assessment CD-ROM
💿 ExamView® Pro Testmaker CD-ROM
💿 Presentation Plus! CD-ROM
💿 TeacherWorks™ CD-ROM
🎧 Audio Program

The Growth of Vietnamese Nationalism When the Japanese seized power in Vietnam during World War II, it was one more example of foreigners ruling the Vietnamese people. China had controlled the region off and on for hundreds of years. From the late 1800s until World War II, France ruled Vietnam and neighboring Laos and Cambodia—a region known collectively as French Indochina.

By the early 1900s, nationalism had become a powerful force in Vietnam. The Vietnamese formed several political parties to push for independence or reform of the French colonial government. One of the leaders of the nationalist movement was Nguyen Tat Thanh—better known by his alias, **Ho Chi Minh,** or "Bringer of Light." He was born in 1890 in central Vietnam. As a young man, Ho Chi Minh taught at a village school. At the age of 21, he sailed for Europe on a French freighter, paying his passage by working in the galley. During his travels abroad, including a stay in the Soviet Union, Ho Chi Minh became an advocate of communism. In 1930 he returned to Southeast Asia, where he helped found the Indochinese Communist Party and worked to overthrow French rule.

Ho Chi Minh's activities made him a wanted man. He fled Indochina and spent several years in exile in the Soviet Union and China. In 1941 he returned to Vietnam. By then Japan had seized control of the country. Ho Chi Minh organized a nationalist group called the **Vietminh.** The group united both Communists and non-Communists in the struggle to

Picturing History

Rural Economy Most of Vietnam's people live in the country's low-lying fertile lands near the Red River delta in the north and the Mekong River delta in the south. *What does the image below suggest about the use of human labor in the country's agricultural economy?*

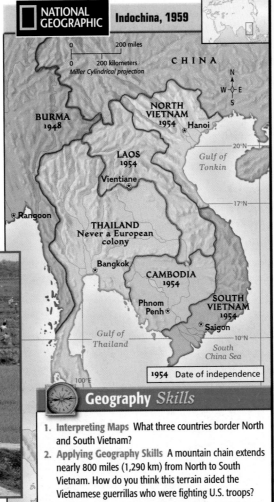

expel the Japanese forces. Soon afterward, the United States began sending military aid to the Vietminh.

The United States Supports the French With the Allies' victory over Japan in August 1945, the Japanese surrendered control of Indochina. Ho Chi Minh and his forces quickly announced that Vietnam was an independent nation. He even crafted a Vietnam Declaration of Independence. Archimedes Patti, an American officer stationed in Vietnam at the time, helped the rebel leader write the document. When a translator read aloud the opening—"All men are created equal; they are endowed by their Creator with certain inalienable rights; among these are liberty, life, and the pursuit of happiness"—Patti suddenly sat up, startled, recognizing the words as very similar to the American Declaration of Independence.

NATIONAL GEOGRAPHIC **Indochina, 1959**

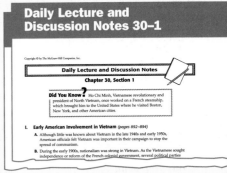

CHINA

0   200 miles
0   200 kilometers
Miller Cylindrical projection

N
W   E
S

BURMA
1948

NORTH
VIETNAM
1954   ⊛ Hanoi

20°N

LAOS
1954
Vientiane

Gulf of Tonkin

17°N

⊛ Rangoon

THAILAND
Never a European
colony

Bangkok

CAMBODIA
1954

Phnom
Penh

SOUTH
VIETNAM
1954

⊛ Saigon

Gulf of Thailand

10°N

South China Sea

100°E

1954   Date of independence

Geography Skills

1. **Interpreting Maps** What three countries border North and South Vietnam?
2. **Applying Geography Skills** A mountain chain extends nearly 800 miles (1,290 km) from North to South Vietnam. How do you think this terrain aided the Vietnamese guerrillas who were fighting U.S. troops?

2 TEACH

Daily Lecture and Discussion Notes 30–1

Copyright © by The McGraw-Hill Companies, Inc.

Daily Lecture and Discussion Notes

Chapter 30, Section 1

Did You Know ? Ho Chi Minh, Vietnamese revolutionary and president of North Vietnam, once worked on a French steamship, which brought him to the United States where he visited Boston, New York, and other American cities.

I.   **Early American Involvement in Vietnam** *(pages 892–894)*

A. Although little was known about Vietnam in the late 1940s and early 1950s, American officials felt Vietnam was important in their campaign to stop the spread of communism.

B. During the early 1900s, nationalism was strong in Vietnam. As the Vietnamese sought independence or reform of the French colonial government, several political parties

Creating a Mental Map Have students draw and label a map of the Indochina peninsula.
L1 ELL

Picturing History

Answer: that it is labor intensive

Geography Skills

Answers:

1. Cambodia, China, and Laos
2. They used it to their advantage to launch hit-and-run and ambush attacks.

**Geography Skills Practice
Ask:** What bodies of water form the east coast of Vietnam? *(Gulf of Tonkin and the South China Sea)*

COOPERATIVE LEARNING ACTIVITY

Conducting a Peace Conference Organize the class into eight groups. Inform the groups that they are to represent countries that met in Geneva in 1954 to draft a peace agreement between the French and the Vietminh. One group should represent each of the following: Great Britain, the United States, France, the Soviet Union, China, Laos, Cambodia, and the Vietminh. Have each group research its position. Groups should present their findings as if they were at the peace conference.

Use the rubric for a cooperative group management plan on pages 81–82 in the *Performance Assessment Activities and Rubrics.*

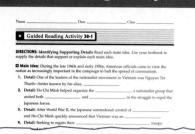
Picturing History

Answer: France

Ask: What countries made up French Indochina? *(Cambodia, Laos, and Vietnam)*

✓ Reading Check

Answer: He sought independence for Vietnam.

3 ASSESS

Assign Section 1 Assessment as homework or as an in-class activity.

🌐 Have students use the **Interactive Tutor Self-Assessment CD-ROM.**

Reading Essentials and Study Guide 30–1

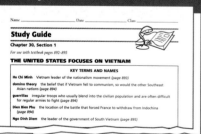

❝I stopped him and turned to Ho in amazement and asked if he really intended to use it in his declaration. . . . Ho sat back in his chair, his palms together with fingertips touching his lips ever so lightly, as though meditating. Then, with a gentle smile he asked softly, 'Should I not use it?' I felt sheepish and embarrassed. Of course, I answered, why should he not?❞

—quoted in *The Perfect War*

France, however, had no intention of seeing Vietnam become independent. Seeking to regain their colonial empire in Southeast Asia, French troops returned to Vietnam in 1946 and drove the Vietminh forces into hiding in the countryside. By 1949 French officials had set up a new government in Vietnam.

The Vietminh fought back against the French-dominated regime and slowly increased their control over large areas of the countryside. As fighting between the two sides escalated, France appealed to the United States for help.

The request put American officials in a difficult position. The United States opposed colonialism. It had pressured the Dutch to give up their empire in Indonesia, and it supported the British decision to give India independence in 1947. In Vietnam, however, the independence movement had become entangled with the Communist movement. American officials did not think France should control Vietnam, but they did not want Vietnam to be Communist either.

Picturing History

Nationalist Leader Ho Chi Minh was already involved in fighting for Vietnam's independence when this photograph was taken in 1946. *What foreign country was he opposing at that time?*

Two events convinced the Truman administration to help France—the fall of China to communism, and the outbreak of the Korean War. Korea, in particular, convinced American officials that the Soviet Union had begun a major push to impose communism on East Asia. Shortly after the Korean War began, Truman authorized a massive program of military aid to French forces fighting in Vietnam.

On taking office in 1953, President Eisenhower continued to support the French military campaign against the Vietminh. By 1954 the United States was paying roughly three-fourths of France's war costs. During a news conference that year, Eisenhower defended United States policy in Vietnam by stressing what became known as the domino theory—the belief that if Vietnam fell to communism, so too would the other nations of Southeast Asia:

❝You have a row of dominoes set up, you knock over the first one, and what will happen to the last one is the certainty that it will go over very quickly. . . . Asia, after all, has already lost 450 million of its peoples to the Communist dictatorship, and we simply can't afford greater losses. . . .❞

—quoted in *America in Vietnam*

✓ Reading Check

Summarizing Why did Ho Chi Minh lead a resistance movement against France?

The Vietminh Drive Out the French

Despite significant amounts of aid from the United States, the French struggled against the Vietminh, who consistently frustrated the French with hit-and-run and ambush tactics. These are the tactics of guerrillas, irregular troops who usually blend into the civilian population and are often difficult for regular armies to fight. The mounting casualties and the inability of the French to defeat the Vietminh made the war very unpopular in France. Finally, in 1954, the struggle reached a turning point.

TURNING POINT

Defeat at Dien Bien Phu In 1954 the French commander ordered his forces to occupy the mountain town of **Dien Bien Phu.** Seizing the town would interfere with the Vietminh's supply lines and force them into open battle.

Soon afterward, a huge Vietminh force surrounded Dien Bien Phu and began bombarding the town. "Shells rained down on us without stopping like a hailstorm on a fall evening," recalled one

---

MEETING SPECIAL NEEDS

Visual/Spatial Have students examine each of the photographs in this section. Then have them write a one-sentence caption explaining what they learned about Vietnam and its people from observing the photographs. Encourage students to pay particular attention to people's activities and their facial expressions. **L1** ELL

📂 Refer to *Inclusion for the High School Social Studies Classroom Strategies and Activities* in the TCR.

French soldier. "Bunker after bunker, trench after trench collapsed, burying under them men and weapons." On May 7, 1954, the French force at Dien Bien Phu fell to the Vietminh. The defeat convinced the French to make peace and withdraw from Indochina.

Geneva Accords Negotiations to end the conflict were held in Geneva, Switzerland. The **Geneva Accords** divided French Indochina into three nations—Vietnam, Laos, and Cambodia. The agreement also temporarily divided Vietnam along the 17th parallel, with Ho Chi Minh and the Vietminh in control of North Vietnam and a pro-Western regime in control of the South. In 1956 elections were to be held to reunite the country under a single government.

Shortly after the Geneva Accords partitioned Vietnam, the French finally left. The United States almost immediately stepped in and became the principal protector of the new government in the South, led by a nationalist leader named **Ngo Dinh Diem** (NOH DIHN deh·EHM). Like Ho Chi Minh, Diem had been educated abroad, but unlike the North Vietnamese leader, Diem was pro-Western and fiercely anti-Communist. A Catholic, he welcomed the roughly one million North Vietnamese Catholics who migrated south to escape Ho Chi Minh's rule.

When the time came in 1956 to hold countrywide elections, as called for by the Geneva Accords, Diem refused. He knew that the Communist-controlled

Picturing **History**

Last Stand French troops assemble a tank near the Dien Bien Phu airfield shortly before their defeat by the Vietminh. How did this defeat influence French policy in Indochina?

north would not allow genuinely free elections, and that Ho Chi Minh would almost certainly have won as a result. Eisenhower supported Diem and increased American military and economic aid to South Vietnam. In the wake of Diem's actions, tensions between the North and South intensified. The nation seemed headed toward civil war, with the United States caught in the middle of it.

✓ **Reading Check** **Examining** What was the effect of the French defeat at Dien Bien Phu?

SECTION 1 ASSESSMENT

Checking for Understanding
1. **Define:** domino theory, guerrilla.
2. **Identify:** Ho Chi Minh, Dien Bien Phu, Ngo Dinh Diem.
3. **Explain** the goals of the Vietminh.

Reviewing Themes
4. **Government and Democracy** Why did Ngo Dinh Diem refuse to hold countrywide elections in Vietnam in 1956?

Critical Thinking
5. **Interpreting** Why do you think the United States supported the government of Ngo Dinh Diem?
6. **Organizing** Use a graphic organizer like the one below to list provisions of the Geneva Accords.

Geneva Accords Provisions

Analyzing Visuals
7. **Analyzing Photographs** Study the Vietnam scene on page 893. How would you describe the contrast between American and Vietnamese societies? How do you think this contrast influenced American thinking toward the war?

Writing About History
8. **Descriptive Writing** Take on the role of a Vietnamese peasant in the 1940s. Write a journal entry on your feelings toward the French.

CHAPTER 30   The Vietnam War   **895**

Section Quiz 30–1

Name _____ Date _____ Class _____

★ Chapter 30   Score [   ]

Section Quiz 30-1

DIRECTIONS: Matching Match each item in Column A with the items in Column B. Write the correct letters in the blanks. *(10 points each)*

Column A
___ 1. nationalist leader in the South after the Geneva Accords
___ 2. nationalist group organized by Ho Chi Minh
___ 3. belief that if Vietnam fell to communism, so too would the other nations of Southeast Asia
___ 4. founder of the Indochinese Communist Party
___ 5. Vietnam, Laos, and Cambodia when under French rule

Column B
A. Ho Chi Minh
B. Ngo Dinh Diem
C. domino theory
D. French Indochina
E. Vietminh

DIRECTIONS: Multiple Choice In the blank at the left, write the letter of the choice that best completes the statement or answers the question. *(10 points each)*

Picturing **History**

Answer: It convinced the French to make peace and withdraw from Indochina.
Ask: Where were the negotiations held to end the conflict? *(Geneva, Switzerland)*

✓ **Reading Check**

Answer: The defeat at Dien Bien Phu caused the French to withdraw and led to the Geneva Accords.

Reteach
Have students describe the nationalist motives of Vietnamese leader Ho Chi Minh.

Enrich
Invite interested students to research French rule in Indochina and its impact on the culture of Vietnam. Have them report their results in the form of a descriptive essay.

4 CLOSE

Have students explain the origins of American involvement in Vietnam during the 1950s.

SECTION 1 ASSESSMENT ANSWERS

1. Terms are in blue.
2. Ho Chi Minh *(p. 893)*, Dien Bien Phu *(p. 894)*, Ngo Dinh Diem *(p. 895)*
3. The Vietminh fought for independence first from Japan, then from France.
4. He feared he would lose to the Vietnamese Communist party.
5. because he was pro-Western and anti-Communist
6. divided Vietnam; set countrywide elections for 1956; divided French Indochina into Cambodia, Laos, and Vietnam
7. Since Vietnam appeared to be less prosperous than the United States, it was easy to believe the United States could defeat the Vietnamese.
8. Students' journal entries should be written from a peasant's perspective.

1 FOCUS

Section Overview

This section focuses on the commitment to send United States troops to Vietnam.

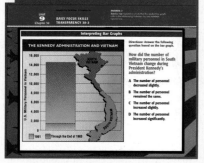

Guide to Reading

Answers to Graphic:
Going to War in Vietnam
I. American Involvement Deepens
  A. Kennedy Takes Over
  B. The Overthrow of Diem
II. Johnson and Vietnam
  A. The Gulf of Tonkin Resolution
  B. The United States Sends in Troops
III. A Bloody Stalemate Emerges
  A. Frustrating Warfare
  B. A Determined Enemy

Preteaching Vocabulary
Have students look up the Key Terms and Names in the glossary. Then have them write a description or definition of each in their own words.

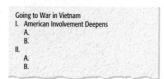

Guide to Reading

Main Idea
After providing South Vietnam with much aid and support, the United States finally sent in troops to fight as well.

Key Terms and Names
Vietcong, Gulf of Tonkin Resolution, napalm, Agent Orange, Ho Chi Minh trail

Reading Strategy
Taking Notes As you read about the beginnings of the Vietnam War, use the major headings of the section to create an outline similar to the one below.

Going to War in Vietnam
I. American Involvement Deepens
  A.
  B.
II.
  A.
  B.

Reading Objectives
• **Describe** how President Johnson deepened American involvement in Vietnam.
• **Discuss** how the Vietcong and the North Vietnamese were able to frustrate the American military.

Section Theme
Science and Technology American military procedures differed significantly from those of the Vietcong troops.

Preview of Events

♦1963 ♦1964 ♦1965 ♦1966

1963 —
Number of American military advisers in South Vietnam reaches around 15,000

1964 —
Congress passes Gulf of Tonkin Resolution

1965 —
The United States begins bombing North Vietnam; first American combat troops arrive in Vietnam

---

★ An American Story ★

Marlene Kramel

Marlene Kramel joined the Army Nurse Corps in 1965 when she was 21, and she went to Vietnam the following year. She was working in a makeshift hospital on what was a particularly quiet night. Most of the patients who filled the beds that evening were suffering from malaria.

Suddenly, a row of helicopters roared in from over the horizon, carrying wounded from a nearby battle. As the casualties came in on stretchers, the hospital turned chaotic. Doctors ran about the facility screaming orders and frantically trying to treat patients.

The only nurse on duty at the time, Kramel felt overwhelmed by the confusion. "Every one of the doctors is yelling for me," she recalled. "I didn't know what to do next. 'Start this. Do that.' Everybody's yelling at me. I couldn't do enough." Things happened so quickly that night, she insisted, that she could not remember most of it. "I can't remember blood, even. I can only remember, 'What am I going to do?' And the doctors moving at tremendous speed. And I'm there. And I'm not able to move fast enough. . . . That's all I remember."

—adapted from *The Living and the Dead*

American Involvement Deepens

The steps that led to the chaos and casualties Marlene Kramel experienced in 1966 began in the mid-1950s when American officials decided to support the government of South Vietnam in its struggle against North Vietnam. After Ngo Dinh Diem refused to

---

hold national elections, Ho Chi Minh and his followers began an armed struggle to reunify the nation. They organized a new guerrilla army, which became known as the Vietcong. As fighting began between the Vietcong and South Vietnam's forces, President Eisenhower increased American aid, and sent hundreds of military advisers to train South Vietnam's army.

Despite the American assistance, the Vietcong continued to grow more powerful, in part because many Vietnamese opposed Diem's government, and in part because of the Vietcong's use of terror. By 1961 the Vietcong had assassinated thousands of government officials and established control over much of the countryside. In response Diem looked increasingly to the United States to keep South Vietnam from collapsing.

Kennedy Takes Over On taking office in 1961, President Kennedy continued the nation's policy of support for South Vietnam. Like presidents Truman and Eisenhower before him, Kennedy saw the Southeast Asian country as vitally important in the battle against communism.

In political terms, Kennedy needed to appear tough on communism, since Republicans often accused Democrats of having lost China to communism during the Truman administration. Kennedy's administration sharply increased military aid and sent more advisers to Vietnam. From 1961 to late 1963, the number of American military personnel in South Vietnam jumped from 1,364 to around 15,000.

American officials believed the Vietcong continued to grow because Diem's government was unpopular and corrupt. They urged him to create a more democratic government and to introduce reforms to help Vietnam's peasants. Diem introduced some limited reforms, but they had little effect.

One program Diem introduced, at the urging of American advisers, made the situation worse. The South Vietnamese created special fortified villages, known as **strategic hamlets.** These villages were protected by machine guns, bunkers, trenches, and barbed wire. Vietnamese officials then moved villagers to the

Picturing **History**

Self-Immolation On June 11, 1963, flames erupted around a Buddhist monk as he set himself on fire to protest government religious policies. What policies did Ngo Dinh Diem take toward Buddhism?

strategic hamlets, partly to protect them from the Vietcong, and partly to prevent them from giving aid to the Vietcong. The program proved to be extremely unpopular. Many peasants resented being uprooted from their villages, where they had worked to build farms and where many of their ancestors lay buried.

The Overthrow of Diem Diem made himself even more unpopular by discriminating against Buddhism, one of the country's most widely practiced religions. In the spring of 1963, Diem, a Catholic, banned the traditional religious flags for Buddha's birthday. When Buddhists took to the streets in protest, Diem's police killed 9 people and injured 14 others. In the demonstrations that followed, a Buddhist monk set himself on fire, the first of several to do so. The photograph of his self-destruction appeared on television and on the front pages of newspapers around the world. It was a stark symbol of the opposition to Diem.

In August 1963, American ambassador Henry Cabot Lodge arrived in Vietnam. He quickly learned that Diem's unpopularity had so alarmed several Vietnamese generals that they were plotting to overthrow him. When Lodge expressed American sympathy for their cause, the generals launched a military coup. They seized power on November 1, 1963, and executed Diem shortly afterward.

Diem's overthrow only made matters worse. Despite his unpopularity with some Vietnamese, Diem had been a respected nationalist and a capable administrator. After his death, South Vietnam's

CHAPTER 30 The Vietnam War **897**

2 TEACH

Daily Lecture and Discussion Notes 30–2

Copyright © by The McGraw-Hill Companies, Inc.

Daily Lecture and Discussion Notes

Chapter 30, Section 2

Did You Know? The Vietnam War posed problems never before encountered by American troops. They had difficulty figuring out the terrain of Vietnam and difficulty in locating and identifying the enemy.

I. **American Involvement Deepens** *(pages 896–898)*

A. After Ngo Dinh Diem refused to hold national elections, Ho Chi Minh and his followers created a new guerrilla army known as the **Vietcong**. Their goal was to reunify North and South Vietnam.

B. The United States continued to send aid to South Vietnam. The Vietcong's power, however, continued to grow because many Vietnamese opposed Diem's government.

Expressing an Opinion Have students write a letter to the editor about the Diem regime and U.S. support for it. Remind students that their editorials should support or oppose the U.S. position. **L1**

Picturing **History**

Answer: Diem discriminated against Buddhism by doing such things as banning the traditional religious flags used to celebrate the birthday of Buddha.

Ask: What message was the monk trying to send when he set himself on fire? *(He wanted to draw attention to opposition to Diem.)*

COOPERATIVE LEARNING ACTIVITY

Creating Headlines Students can trace the events in Section 2 by writing headlines that would have been appropriate for the events mentioned in the section. Organize the class into two teams. On each team, have one or two students examine the headline style of current newspapers. Half the students on each team should outline the events discussed in this section. The remaining students should write several headlines for each event, with the team as a whole choosing the headline they prefer.

Use the rubric for a cooperative group management plan on pages 81–82 in the *Performance Assessment Activities and Rubrics.*

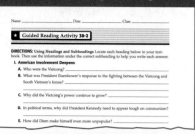
✓ Reading Check

Answer: The Vietcong wanted to reunify Vietnam.

Creating Circle Graphs Provide the data below and ask students to make a pair of circle graphs showing the results of the presidential election of 1964. **L2**

Candidate	Popular Vote	Electoral Vote
Goldwater, Rep.	27,178,188	52
Johnson, Dem.	43,129,566	486

📁 Use the rubric for creating a map, display, or chart on pages 77–78 in the *Performance Assessment Activities and Rubrics.*

you don't say...

Helicopters GI slang referred to helicopters as TWA—teenie-weenie airlines. They were used on a massive scale during the Vietnam War. With gas turbines replacing piston engines, the helicopters had remarkable range and maneuverability.

---

government grew increasingly weak and unstable. The United States became even more deeply involved in order to prop up the weak South Vietnamese government. Coincidentally, three weeks after Diem's death, President Kennedy was also assassinated. The presidency, as well as the growing problem of Vietnam, now belonged to Kennedy's vice president, Lyndon Johnson.

✓ Reading Check
Examining What was the main goal of the Vietcong?

Johnson and Vietnam

Initially President Johnson exercised caution and restraint regarding the conflict in Vietnam. "We seek no wider war," he repeatedly promised. At the same time, Johnson was determined to prevent South Vietnam from becoming Communist. "The battle against communism," he declared shortly before becoming president, "must be joined . . . with strength and determination."

Politics also played a role in Johnson's Vietnam policy. Like Kennedy, Johnson remembered that many Republicans blamed the Truman administration for the fall of China to communism in 1949. Should the Democrats also "lose" Vietnam, Johnson feared, it might cause a "mean and destructive debate that would shatter my Presidency, kill my administration, and damage our democracy."

TURNING POINT

The Gulf of Tonkin Resolution On August 2, 1964, President Johnson announced that North Vietnamese torpedo boats had fired on two American destroyers in the Gulf of Tonkin. Two days later, the president reported that another similar attack had taken place. Johnson was campaigning for the presidency and was very sensitive to accusations of being soft on communism. He insisted that North Vietnam's attacks were unprovoked and immediately ordered American aircraft to attack North Vietnamese ships and naval facilities. Johnson

Different Viewpoints

The Vietnam War

As the war in Vietnam dragged on, a clear division of American opinion emerged. In January 1966, George W. Ball, undersecretary of state to President Johnson, delivered an address to indicate "how we got [to Vietnam] and why we must stay." George F. Kennan, former ambassador to Russia, testified before the Senate Foreign Relations Committee that same year, arguing that American involvement in Vietnam was "something we would not choose deliberately if the choice were ours to make all over again today."

George W. Ball:

"[T]he conflict in Vietnam is a product of the great shifts and changes triggered by the Second World War. Out of the war, two continent-wide powers emerged—the United States and the Soviet Union. The colonial systems through which the nations of Western Europe had governed more than a third of the people of the world were, one by one, dismantled.

. . . [E]ven while the new national boundaries were still being marked on the map, the Soviet Union under Stalin exploited the confusion to push out the perimeter of its power and influence in an effort to extend the outer limits of Communist domination by force or the threat of force.

The bloody encounters in [Vietnam] are thus in a real sense battles and skirmishes in a continuing war to prevent one Communist power after another from violating internationally recognized boundary lines fixing the outer limits of Communist dominion.

. . . The evidence shows clearly enough that, at the time of French withdrawal . . . the Communist regime in Hanoi never intended that South Vietnam should develop in freedom.

. . . In the long run our hopes for the people of South Vietnam reflect our hopes for people everywhere. What we seek is a world living in peace and freedom."

MEETING SPECIAL NEEDS

Intrapersonal The increased military commitment to Vietnam touched virtually every neighborhood in the United States. As a result, almost every American was challenged to consider American actions in Vietnam. Ask students to imagine that they have just been drafted for military service in Vietnam. Have them write diary entries or letters in which they share their fears, hopes, and questions about being drafted. Invite students to share their writing with classmates. **L2**

📁 Refer to *Inclusion for the High School Social Studies Classroom Strategies and Activities* in the TCR.

did not reveal that the American warships had been helping the South Vietnamese conduct electronic spying and commando raids against North Vietnam.

Johnson then asked Congress to authorize the use of force to defend American forces. Congress agreed to Johnson's request with little debate. Most members of Congress agreed with Republican Representative Ross Adair of Indiana, who defiantly declared, "The American flag has been fired upon. We will not and cannot tolerate such things."

On August 7, 1964, the Senate and House passed the **Gulf of Tonkin Resolution,** authorizing the president to "take all necessary measures to repel any armed attack against the forces of the United States and to prevent further aggression." With only two dissenting votes, Congress had, in effect, handed its war powers over to the president. 📖 *(See page 1079 for more on the Gulf of Tonkin Resolution.)*

The United States Sends in Troops Shortly after Congress passed the Gulf of Tonkin Resolution, the Vietcong began to attack bases where American advisers were stationed in South Vietnam. The attacks began in the fall of 1964 and continued to escalate. After a Vietcong attack on a base at Pleiku in February 1965 left 7 Americans dead and more than 100 wounded, President Johnson decided to respond. Less than 14 hours after the attack, some 132 American aircraft struck North Vietnam.

After the airstrikes, one poll showed that Johnson's approval rating on his handling of Vietnam jumped from 41 percent to 60 percent. The president's actions also met with strong approval from his closest advisers, including Secretary of Defense **Robert McNamara** and National Security Adviser **McGeorge Bundy.**

There were some dissenters in the White House, chief among them Undersecretary of State George Ball, who had earlier supported the president. He warned that if the United States got too deeply involved in Vietnam, it might become difficult to get out. "Once on the tiger's back," he warned, "we cannot be sure of picking the place to dismount."

Most of the advisers who surrounded Johnson, however, firmly believed the nation had a duty to halt communism in Vietnam, both to maintain stability in Southeast Asia and to ensure the United States's continuing power and prestige in the world. In a memo to the president, Bundy argued:

> ❝The stakes in Vietnam are extremely high. The American investment is very large, and American responsibility is a fact of life which is palpable in the atmosphere of Asia, and even elsewhere. The international prestige of the U.S. and a substantial part of our influence are directly at risk in Vietnam.❞
>
> —quoted in *The Best and the Brightest*

In March 1965, Johnson expanded American involvement by shifting his policy to a sustained bombing campaign against North Vietnam. The campaign was named **Operation Rolling Thunder.** That month the president also ordered the first combat troops into Vietnam. American soldiers were now fighting alongside the South Vietnamese troops against the Vietcong.

✓**Reading Check** **Describing** How did politics play a role in President Johnson's Vietnam policy?

A Bloody Stalemate Emerges

By the end of 1965, more than 180,000 American combat troops were fighting in Vietnam. In 1966 that number doubled. Since the American military was

George F. Kennan:

"Vietnam is not a region of major military and industrial importance. It is difficult to believe that any decisive developments of the world situation would be determined in normal circumstances by what happens on that territory. . . . Even a situation in which South Vietnam was controlled exclusively by the Vietcong, while regrettable . . . would not, in my opinion, present dangers great enough to justify our direct military intervention.

. . . To attempt to crush North Vietnamese strength to a point where [it] could no longer give any support for Vietcong political activity in the South, would . . . have the effect of bringing in Chinese forces at some point.

. . . Our motives are widely misinterpreted, and the spectacle emphasized and reproduced in thousands of press photographs and stories . . . produces reactions among millions of people throughout the world profoundly detrimental to the image we would like them to hold of this country."

Learning From History

1. **Recognizing Ideologies** How do the two speakers assess the value of Vietnam and its people to the United States?

2. **Making Inferences** Why does George Kennan believe that the United States government got involved in Vietnam when it did? How does he feel about this involvement?

Different Viewpoints

Learning from History Answers:

1. Ball argues that the United States is committed to the people of Vietnam and wants to protect them from communism. Kennan argues that Vietnam has no particular significance to the United States, and while it would be unfortunate if the Vietcong took over, it would not present a danger great enough for the United States to take military action.

2. He believes that the United States was misguided in entering the war, that it has hurt the national image.

✓**Reading Check**

Answer: Johnson thought his presidency would be ruined and democracy damaged if the Democrats lost Vietnam to communism.

CHAPTER 30   The Vietnam War   **899**

INTERDISCIPLINARY CONNECTIONS ACTIVITY

Art Tell students that Maya Lin's design for the Vietnam Veterans Memorial was praised as having an "extraordinary sense of dignity and nobility." It was also condemned as being "unheroic" and "a black gash of shame." Construction did not begin until it was agreed that a statue of three servicemen and a flagpole would be added. Nevertheless, many visitors to the monument are quite moved by what they see. Discuss with students what makes a monument moving and memorable. Extend the discussion by inviting interested students to submit sketches for a memorial to a person or cause that they consider noteworthy. **L2**

Lucy, Andy Griffith, and Gomer Pyle were mainstays on American television in 1968. The images of the Vietnam War were a sharp contrast.

3 ASSESS

Assign Section 2 Assessment as homework or as an in-class activity.

⊙ Have students use the **Interactive Tutor Self-Assessment CD-ROM.**

Reading Essentials and Study Guide 30–2

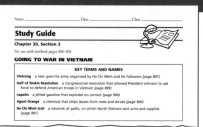

NATIONAL GEOGRAPHIC
MOMENT in HISTORY

AMERICA'S LONGEST WAR

Clinging to his M-16 rifle, a wounded American Marine is shown after being pulled to safety by a fellow soldier. In the late 1950s, American military advisers were sent to help the South Vietnamese army fight guerrillas known as the Vietcong, who were receiving weapons, supplies, and training from Communist North Vietnam. The dense jungles of Vietnam made fighting the guerrillas very difficult. By 1968 about 500,000 U.S. troops were fighting in the increasingly unpopular war. American forces finally withdrew in March 1973.

---

extremely strong, it marched into Vietnam with great confidence. "America seemed omnipotent then," said Philip Caputo, one of the first marines to arrive. "We saw ourselves as the champions of a 'cause that was destined to triumph.'"

Frustrating Warfare Lacking the firepower of the Americans, the Vietcong used ambushes, booby traps, and guerrilla tactics. Ronald J. Glasser, an American army doctor, described the devastating effects of one booby trap:

❝Three quarters of the way through the tangle, a trooper brushed against a two-inch vine, and a grenade slung at chest high went off, shattering the right side of his head and body. . . . Nearby troopers took hold of the unconscious soldier and, half carrying, half dragging him, pulled him the rest of the way through the tangle.❞

—quoted in *Vietnam, A History*

The Vietcong also frustrated American troops by blending in with the general population in the cities and the countryside and then quickly vanishing. "It

was a sheer physical impossibility to keep the enemy from slipping away whenever he wished," one American general said. Journalist Linda Martin noted, "It's a war where nothing is ever quite certain and nowhere is ever quite safe."

To counter the Vietcong's tactics, American troops went on "search and destroy" missions. They tried to find enemy troops, bomb their positions, destroy their supply lines, and force them out into the open for combat.

American forces also sought to take away the Vietcong's ability to hide in the thick jungles by literally destroying the landscape. American planes dropped napalm, a jellied gasoline that explodes on contact. They also used **Agent Orange,** a chemical that strips leaves from trees and shrubs, turning farmland and forest into wasteland.

A Determined Enemy United States military leaders underestimated the Vietcong's strength. They also misjudged the enemy's stamina. American generals believed that continuously bombing and killing large numbers of Vietcong would destroy the enemy's morale and force them to give up. The guerrillas,

900 CHAPTER 30 The Vietnam War

CRITICAL THINKING ACTIVITY

Identifying Assumptions In a guerrilla war, the mobility of a single soldier is as important as the mobility of an army. The United States mistakenly assumed that it could fight the Vietcong in the rice fields and jungles of Vietnam with troops trained to fight on the battlefields of Western Europe. Discuss with students other assumptions of American leaders that proved to be incorrect. **L2**

however, had no intention of surrendering, and they were willing to accept huge losses in human lives.

In the Vietcong's war effort, North Vietnamese support was a major factor. Although the Vietcong forces were made up of many South Vietnamese, North Vietnam provided arms, advisers, and significant leadership. Later in the war, as Vietcong casualties mounted, North Vietnam began sending regular North Vietnamese Army units to fight in South Vietnam.

North Vietnam sent arms and supplies south by way of a network of jungle paths known as the **Ho Chi Minh trail.** The trail wound through the countries of Cambodia and Laos, bypassing the border between North and South Vietnam. Because the trail passed through countries not directly involved in the war, President Johnson refused to allow a full-scale attack on the trail to shut it down.

North Vietnam itself received military weapons and other support from the Soviet Union and China. One of the main reasons President Johnson refused to order a full-scale invasion of North Vietnam was his fear that such an attack would bring China into the war, as had happened in Korea. By placing limits on the war, however, Johnson made it very difficult to win. Instead of conquering enemy territory, American troops were forced to fight a war of attrition—a strategy of defeating the enemy forces by slowly wearing them down. This strategy led troops to conduct grisly body counts after battles to determine how many enemy soldiers had been killed.

Bombing from American planes killed about 179,000 Vietnamese between 1965 and 1967. Nevertheless, the Vietcong and North Vietnamese troops showed no sign of surrendering. Meanwhile, American casualties

continued to mount. By the spring of 1966, more than 4,000 American soldiers had been killed.

As the number of Americans killed and wounded continued to grow, the notion of a quick and decisive victory grew increasingly remote. As a result, many citizens back home began to question the nation's involvement in the war.

☑ **Reading Check** **Describing** What tactics did the United States adopt to fight the Vietcong?

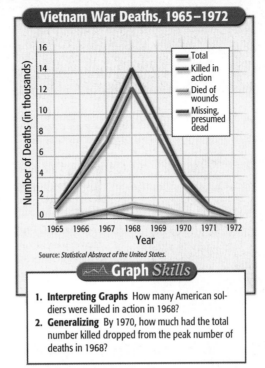

Vietnam War Deaths, 1965–1972

Number of Deaths (in thousands)

- Total
- Killed in action
- Died of wounds
- Missing, presumed dead

Source: *Statistical Abstract of the United States.*

Graph Skills

1. **Interpreting Graphs** How many American soldiers were killed in action in 1968?
2. **Generalizing** By 1970, how much had the total number killed dropped from the peak number of deaths in 1968?

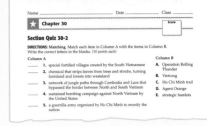

Section Quiz 30–2

Name _____ Date _____ Class _____

★ Chapter 30   Score ____

Section Quiz 30-2

DIRECTIONS: Matching Match each item in Column A with the items in Column B. Write the correct letters in the blanks. *(10 points each)*

Column A
___ 1. special fortified villages created by the South Vietnamese
___ 2. chemical that strips leaves from trees and shrubs, turning farmland and forests into wasteland
___ 3. network of jungle paths through Cambodia and Laos that bypassed the border between North and South Vietnam
___ 4. sustained bombing campaign against North Vietnam by the United States
___ 5. a guerrilla army organized by Ho Chi Minh to reunify the nation

Column B
A. Operation Rolling Thunder
B. Vietcong
C. Ho Chi Minh trail
D. Agent Orange
E. strategic hamlets

Graph Skills

Answers:
1. about 12,000
2. by about 10,000

Graph Skills Practice
Ask: How many American military personnel were killed in action in 1967? *(about 7,000)*

☑ **Reading Check**

Answer: search and destroy missions, bombing, the use of napalm and Agent Orange

Reteach
Have students describe President Johnson's Vietnam policy.

Enrich
Have interested students research the plight of the Vietnamese "boat people."

4 CLOSE

Have students discuss Vietcong tactics.

SECTION 2 ASSESSMENT

Checking for Understanding

1. **Define:** Vietcong, napalm.
2. **Identify:** Gulf of Tonkin Resolution, Agent Orange, Ho Chi Minh trail.
3. **Explain** how the Gulf of Tonkin Resolution affected the powers of Congress and the presidency.

Reviewing Themes

4. **Science and Technology** Why did the United States use napalm and Agent Orange in its fight against the Vietcong?

Critical Thinking

5. **Analyzing** Why did fighting in Vietnam turn into a stalemate by the mid-1960s?
6. **Sequencing** Complete a time line similar to the one below to fill in events leading to American involvement in Vietnam.

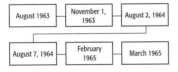

| August 1963 | → | November 1, 1963 | → | August 2, 1964 |

| August 7, 1964 | → | February 1965 | → | March 1965 |

Analyzing Visuals

7. **Analyzing Photographs** Look closely at the photograph on page 897 of Buddhist monk Reverend Quang Duc. What in the photograph suggests that this event was planned by Buddhists to protest their treatment in South Vietnam?

Writing About History

8. **Persuasive Writing** Imagine that you are a member of Congress in August 1964. Write a statement supporting or opposing the Gulf of Tonkin Resolution.

CHAPTER 30   The Vietnam War   **901**

SECTION 2 ASSESSMENT ANSWERS

1. Terms are in blue.
2. Gulf of Tonkin Resolution *(p. 899)*, Agent Orange *(p. 900)*, Ho Chi Minh trail *(p. 901)*
3. It gave congressional war powers to the president.
4. to destroy the landscape so the Vietcong could not hide in the jungle
5. The Vietcong showed no signs of surrendering and Johnson refused to order a full-scale invasion.
6. August 1963, Henry Cabot Lodge arrives in Vietnam; November 1, 1963, Diem is overthrown; August 2, 1964, Gulf of Tonkin incident; August 7, 1964, Gulf of Tonkin Resolution; February 1965, attack on Pleiku base; March 1965, Johnson expands bombing campaign
7. The presence of the Buddhist onlookers suggests a planned event.
8. Students' statements should express a point of view.

1 FOCUS

Remind students that President Johnson was facing a re-election campaign in which he did not want to appear as though he was weak or soft on communism.

2 TEACH

Understanding the Gulf of Tonkin Incident To help students better understand the events, assign various students to research the following topics: foreign involvement in Indochina, rise of communism in Indochina, events that triggered the initial U.S. involvement in Vietnam, and public opinion in the United States about the events in Vietnam. Tell students that the research should extend beyond what is presented in the text. Have students make oral presentations about their topics. Then have a class discussion about the Gulf of Tonkin incident and its handling by the Johnson administration. Have students identify the points of view of Johnson, his advisers, and members of Congress. **L2**

FYI

In addition to the human cost of the Vietnam War, economists estimate that the cost to the United States of the war was at least $200 billion.

You're the Historian

Incident in the Gulf of Tonkin

President Lyndon Johnson

In 1963 the Vietcong in South Vietnam were trying to topple the government and unite the country under communism. To prevent this, the United States had already committed money, supplies, and advisers. President Johnson asked Congress to authorize using force after reports that North Vietnam had made unprovoked attacks on U.S. warships in the Gulf of Tonkin. Congress responded with the Gulf of Tonkin Resolution. Had the warship USS *Maddox* provoked the attack? Was Johnson fully informed of events in the Gulf? You're the historian.

Read the following excerpts, then answer the questions and complete the activities that follow.

From accounts of an unprovoked attack

The sources advising President Johnson on the Gulf of Tonkin incident included the navy and the Defense Department. These excerpts suggest how difficult it was to know what had happened—and also how tension influenced the American interpretation.

U.S. Navy Commander John Herrick of the USS *Maddox*:
I am being approached by high-speed craft with apparent intention of torpedo attack. I intend to open fire in self-defense if necessary.

—**from a cable of August 2, 1964**

U.S. Defense Department:
While on routine patrol in international waters . . . the U.S. destroyer *Maddox* underwent an unprovoked attack by three PT-type boats in . . . the Tonkin Gulf.

The attacking boats launched three torpedoes and used 37-millimeter gunfire. The *Maddox* answered with 5-inch gunfire. . . . The PT boats were driven off, with one seen to be badly damaged and not moving. . . .

No casualties or damage were sustained by the *Maddox* or the aircraft.

—**from a press release of August 2, 1964**

National Security Council Meeting:
Secretary McNamara: The North Vietnamese PT boats have continued their attacks on the two U.S. destroyers in international waters in the Gulf of Tonkin. . . .

Secretary Rusk: An immediate and direct action by us is necessary. The unprovoked attack on the high seas is an act of war for all practical purposes. . . .

CIA Director McCone: The proposed U.S. reprisals will result in sharp North Vietnamese military action, but such actions would not represent a deliberate decision to provoke or accept a major escalation of the Vietnamese war.

President Johnson: Do they want a war by attacking our ships in the middle of the Gulf of Tonkin?

U.S. Intelligence Agency Director Rowan: Do we know for a fact that the North Vietnamese provocation took place?

Secretary McNamara: We will know definitely in the morning.

—**August 2, 1964**

Secretary Rusk:
We believe that present OPLAN 34-A activities are beginning to rattle Hanoi [capital of North Vietnam], and the *Maddox* incident is directly related to their effort to resist these activities. We have no intention of yielding to pressure.

—**from a top secret telegram to Ambassador Maxwell Taylor (South Vietnam), August 3, 1964**

EXTENDING THE CONTENT

Boat People Tell students that many Vietnamese fled by boat to escape political tensions. Unfortunately, some "boat people" found themselves caught in racial tensions. For example, in 1979 Vietnamese "boat people" who were mostly ethnic Chinese arrived in Malaysia, already an ethnically diverse country. So intense was the fear that the arrival of the Vietnamese would upset the country's ethnic balance that, instead of welcoming the newcomers, the Malaysian government issued orders to shoot any "boat person" found landing on Malaysian shores.

Secretary McNamara

From accounts of a possible mistake

Two days after the alleged attack, the Turner Joy joined the Maddox in the Gulf. On the night of August 4, 1964, the two destroyers experienced a series of events they interpreted as a second attack. However, Commander Herrick later revised this report. President Johnson referred to the "repeated" attacks later when he asked Congress for war powers.

Commander Herrick:
Review of action makes many contacts and torpedoes fired appear doubtful. Freak weather effects on radar and overeager sonarmen may have accounted for many reports. No actual visual sightings by *Maddox*. Suggest complete evaluation before any further action. . . .

Turner Joy also reports no actual visual sightings or wake. . . . Entire action leaves many doubts except for apparent attempt to ambush at beginning.

—from two cables of
August 4, 1964

President Johnson:
The initial attack on the destroyer *Maddox*, on August 2, was repeated today by a number of hostile vessels attacking two U.S. destroyers with torpedoes. The destroyers and supporting aircraft acted at once on the orders I gave after the initial act of aggression. . . . Repeated acts of violence against the Armed Forces of the United States must be met not only with alert defense, but with positive reply.

—in a television and radio
address, August 4, 1964

In 1968 Senator William Fulbright opened an investigation into the 1964 Gulf of Tonkin incident. The following exchange took place between Senator Fulbright and Secretary McNamara.

Secretary McNamara: I don't believe Commander Herrick in his cable stated that he had doubt that the attack took place. He questioned certain details of the attack. . . . Secondly, his doubts were resolved that afternoon before the retaliatory action was taken.

Senator Fulbright: I think he went further than that. He advised you not to do anything until it had been reevaluated. . . . It is a very strong statement.

Vietcong guerrillas

Secretary McNamara: Nothing was done until it was reevaluated.

Senator Fulbright: He says "Suggest complete reevaluation before any further action." Now that is a very strong recommendation from a man on the scene in charge of the operation. . . . Both committees, except for the Senator from Oregon [Morse], unanimously accepted your testimony then as the whole story, and I must say this raises very serious questions about how you make decisions to go to war.

Understanding the Issue
1. What statement by Rusk suggests the United States may have provoked the attack on the *Maddox?*
2. Do you think President Johnson was misled by his advisers? Explain.
3. How soon after the alleged attacks did the president address the American people? Did the United States rush to judgment in this case? Explain.

Activities
1. **Investigate** What were the conclusions of the Fulbright investigations into the Gulf of Tonkin incident? Check sources, including the Internet.
2. **Discuss** Research and review American decisions to go to war in 1898, 1917, and 1941. What were the concerns? Do you think the nation made the right decisions?

CHAPTER 30   The Vietnam War   **903**

3 ASSESS

Have students answer the Understanding the Issue questions and complete the Activities.

Understanding the Issue
1. He named a plan of activity, the OPLAN 34-A, which implies that the United States had some type of operation underway.
2. Students' answers will vary. Students should support their points of view with facts and clear observations.
3. Two days. Students may say that the cables Commander Herrick sent on August 4 suggest more time was needed to verify the facts.

Activities
1. Answers may vary depending on the research undertaken. Students should learn that although Fulbright originally supported the administration, he came to believe that Congress had been deceived.
2. You may elect to assign this activity to be done in groups with each group member researching one of the wars. Students' conclusions will vary.

4 CLOSE

Ask students to consider how decision makers decide what information to supply to the public and how this information shapes the public's impressions.

PORTFOLIO ACTIVITY

Newspaper Story Ask students to write a newspaper editorial focusing on the effects of misinformation on Congress. Have students predict how the Gulf of Tonkin Resolution might affect the future of U.S. involvement in Vietnam. Tell them to conclude their editorial with recommendations that the president or Congress might take to prevent similar incidents. **L2**

1 FOCUS

Section Overview

This section focuses on the escalation of military action in Vietnam and the division between those who supported the war and those who did not.

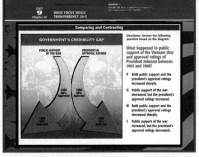
Guide to Reading

Answers to Graphic: Reasons for opposition to Vietnam War: credibility gap, unfair draft system, immorality of defending a corrupt dictatorship in South Vietnam, and belief that it was a civil war in which the United States had no business

Preteaching Vocabulary
Have students scan the section to learn the meanings of the Key Terms and Names.

Vietnam Divides the Nation

Guide to Reading

Main Idea
The experience of Vietnam produced sharp divisions between Americans who supported the war and those who did not.

Key Terms and Names
William Westmoreland, credibility gap, teach-in, dove, hawk, Tet offensive

Reading Strategy
Organizing As you read about Americans' reactions to the Vietnam War, complete a graphic organizer like the one below to list the reasons for opposition to the war.

> Reasons for Opposition to Vietnam War

Reading Objective
• **Analyze** why support for the war began to weaken.
• **Describe** the motives of those in the antiwar movement.

Section Theme
Civic Rights and Responsibilities Many Americans protested their country's involvement in the Vietnam War.

Preview of Events

♦1965   ♦1966   ♦1967   ♦1968

1965
Teach-ins on college campuses begin

1966
Senate Foreign Relations Committee begins Vietnam hearings

1967
March on the Pentagon

January 1968
Tet offensive

★ An American Story ★

Antiwar activists burning draft cards at the Pentagon in 1972

Martin Jezer, a 27-year-old copywriter living in New York City, had never considered himself a radical. "I campaigned for Lyndon Johnson in 1964," he recalled. As his opposition to the war in Vietnam grew, however, Jezer decided to stage a public protest.

On April 15, 1967, he and dozens of other young men gathered with their military draft cards in New York's Central Park. Before an audience of reporters, photographers, FBI officials, and citizens, the men pulled out matches and lighters and burned the cards.

❝We began singing freedom songs and chanting, 'Resist! Resist!' and 'Burn Draft Cards, Not People'. . . . People in the audience were applauding us, shouting encouragement. Then some guys began to come out of the audience with draft cards in hand. They burned them. Alone, in pairs, by threes they came. Each flaming draft card brought renewed cheering and more people out of the crowd. . . . Some of the draft card burners were girls, wives, or girlfriends of male card burners. . . . It lasted this way for about half an hour.❞

—quoted in *The Vietnam War: Opposing Viewpoints*

A Growing Credibility Gap

Jezer's protest was just one of many, as American opposition to the Vietnam War grew in the late 1960s. When American troops first entered the Vietnam War in the spring of 1965, many Americans had supported the military effort. A Gallup poll

---

SECTION RESOURCES

📁 Reproducible Masters
• Reproducible Lesson Plan 30–3
• Daily Lecture and Discussion Notes 30–3
• Guided Reading Activity 30–3
• Section Quiz 30–3
• Reading Essentials and Study Guide 30–3

🖐 Transparencies
• Daily Focus Skills Transparency 30–3

Multimedia
💿 Interactive Tutor Self-Assessment CD-ROM
💿 ExamView® Pro Testmaker CD-ROM
💿 Presentation Plus! CD-ROM
💿 TeacherWorks™ CD-ROM
🎧 Audio Program
🎵 American Music: Cultural Traditions

published around that time showed that 66 percent of Americans approved of the policy in Vietnam. As the war dragged on, however, public support began to drop. Suspicion of the government's truthfulness about the war was a significant reason. Throughout the early years of the war, the American commander in South Vietnam, General **William Westmoreland,** reported that the enemy was on the brink of defeat. In 1967 he confidently declared that the "enemy's hopes are bankrupt" and added, "we have reached an important point where the end begins to come into view."

Contradicting such reports were less optimistic media accounts, especially on television. Vietnam was the first "television war," with footage of combat appearing nightly on the evening news. Day after day, millions of people saw images of wounded and dead Americans and began to doubt government reports. In the view of many, a credibility gap had developed, meaning it was hard to believe what the Johnson administration said about the war.

Congress, which had given the president a nearly free hand in Vietnam, soon grew uncertain about the war. Beginning in January 1966, the Senate Foreign Relations Committee held "educational" hearings on Vietnam, calling in Secretary of State **Dean Rusk** and other policy makers to explain the administration's war program. The committee also listened to critics such as American diplomat George Kennan. Although Kennan had helped create the policy of containment, he argued that Vietnam was not strategically important to the United States.

✓ **Reading Check** **Explaining** Why was the Vietnam War the first "television war"?

An Antiwar Movement Emerges

As casualties mounted in Vietnam, many people began to protest publicly against the war and to demand that the United States pull out. Although many other Americans supported the war, opponents of the conflict received the most attention.

Teach-Ins Begin In March 1965, a group of faculty members and students at the University of Michigan abandoned their classes and joined together in a teach-in. Here, they informally discussed the issues surrounding the war and reaffirmed their reasons for opposing it. The gathering inspired teach-ins at many campuses. In May 1965, 122 colleges held a "National Teach-In" by radio for more than 100,000 antiwar demonstrators.

People who opposed the war did so for different reasons. Some saw the conflict as a civil war in which the United States had no business. Others viewed South Vietnam as a corrupt dictatorship and insisted that defending that country was immoral and unjust.

Anger at the Draft Young protesters especially focused on what they saw as an unfair draft system. At the beginning of the war, a college student was often able to defer military service until after graduation. By contrast, young people from low-income families were more likely to be sent to Vietnam because they were unable to afford college. This meant minorities, particularly African Americans, made up a disproportionately large number of the soldiers in Vietnam. By 1967, for example, African Americans accounted for about 20 percent of American combat deaths—about twice their proportion of the population within the United States. That number would decline to roughly match their population proportion by the war's end.

Analyzing *Political Cartoons*

Dark Passage One particular phrase came to represent the government's claims that it was on the verge of ending the Vietnam War: "the light at the end of the tunnel." Why did many people become skeptical about such government claims?

2 *TEACH*

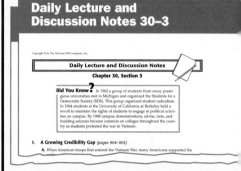

Daily Lecture and Discussion Notes 30–3

Making Comparisons Have students create a chart to show a comparison between the civil rights protests and the Vietnam War protests. **L1** **ELL**

📁 Use the rubric for creating a map, display, or chart on pages 77–78 in the *Performance Assessment Activities and Rubrics.*

✓ **Reading Check**

Answer: Combat footage appeared nightly on the evening news.

🇺🇸 **Analyzing** *Political Cartoons*

Answer: Television news reports were different from what military leaders were reporting.
Ask: What are the people in the cartoon doing? *(They are feeling their way along a dark tunnel because there is no "light at the end of the tunnel.")*

COOPERATIVE LEARNING ACTIVITY

Symbolizing a Campaign A wide variety of hopefuls sought the presidency in 1968. To illustrate their differences, organize students into five groups, one each for Eugene McCarthy, Robert F. Kennedy, Hubert H. Humphrey, George Wallace, and Richard Nixon. Have members of each group write three words that describe their candidate and one sentence about their candidate's political views. They should then work together to create a campaign button, banner, or logo for their candidate. Have groups share and discuss their ideas. 📦

Use the rubric for a cooperative group management plan on pages 81–82 in the *Performance Assessment Activities and Rubrics.*

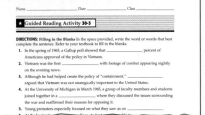

Guided Reading Activity 30–3

Name _____ Date _____ Class _____

★ Guided Reading Activity 30-3

DIRECTIONS: Filling in the Blanks In the space provided, write the word or words that best complete the sentence. Refer to your textbook to fill in the blanks.

1. In the spring of 1965, a Gallup poll showed that _____ percent of Americans approved of the policy in Vietnam.
2. Vietnam was the first _____ with footage of combat appearing nightly on the evening news.
3. Although he had helped create the policy of "containment," _____ argued that Vietnam was not strategically important to the United States.
4. At the University of Michigan in March 1965, a group of faculty members and students joined together in a _____, where they discussed the issues surrounding the war and reaffirmed their reasons for opposing it.
5. Young protesters especially focused on what they saw as an _____.
6. At the beginning, _____ college student _____

Picturing **History**

Answer: People opposed the war because of the credibility gap, the unfair draft system, the corrupt government of South Vietnam, and the belief that it was a civil war in which the United States had no business.

Ask: Why do you think the young man in the photograph is putting flowers in the barrels of the weapons? *(Students will recognize the symbolism—flowers for the peace movement.)*

Making a Poster Have students make a poster that would have been appropriate for people marching in support of or opposition to the Vietnam War. **L2**

History *and the* Humanities

American Music: Cultural Traditions: "The Big Muddy," "Okie From Muskogee"

Picturing **History**

Flower Power Student antiwar protests ranged from violent confrontation to this peaceful but dramatic demonstration near the Pentagon in Washington, D.C. What were some reasons many people opposed the war?

The high number of African Americans and poor Americans dying in Vietnam angered African American leaders, including Dr. Martin Luther King, Jr. Early on, King had refrained from speaking out against the war for fear that it would draw attention from the civil rights movement. In April 1967, however, he broke his silence and publicly condemned the conflict:

> 66 Somehow this madness must cease. I speak as a child of God and brother to the suffering poor of Vietnam and the poor of America who are paying the double price of smashed hopes at home and death and corruption in Vietnam. I speak as a citizen of the world, for the world as it stands aghast at the path we have taken. I speak as an American to the leader of my own nation. The great initiative in this war is ours. The initiative to stop must be ours. 99
>
> —quoted in *A Testament of Hope*

As the war escalated, American officials increased the draft call, putting many college students at risk. An estimated 500,000 draftees refused to go. Many publicly burned their draft cards or simply did not report when called for induction. Some fled the country, moving to Canada, Sweden, or other nations. Others stayed and went to prison rather than fight in a war they opposed.

Between 1965 and 1968, officials prosecuted more than 3,300 Americans for refusing to serve. The draft became less of an issue in 1969 when the government introduced a lottery system, in which only those with low lottery numbers were subject to the draft.

Protests against the war were not confined to college campuses. Demonstrators held public rallies and marches in towns across the country. In April 1965, Students for a Democratic Society (SDS), a left-wing student organization, organized a march on Washington, D.C., that drew more than 20,000 participants. Two years later, in October 1967, a rally at Washington's Lincoln Memorial drew tens of thousands of protesters as well.

Anger over the draft also fueled discussions of voting age. Many draftees argued that if they were old enough to fight, they were old enough to vote. In 1971, Congress ratified the new voting age of 18 with the passage of the Twenty-sixth Amendment to the Constitution.

906 CHAPTER 30 The Vietnam War

MEETING SPECIAL NEEDS

Interpersonal The 1968 Democratic National Convention illustrates the divided nation of the late 1960s. Ask students with strong interpersonal skills to review the text's coverage of this event and write a paragraph explaining the divided feelings. Conclude with this comment from Robert McNamara's *In Retrospect: The Tragedy and Lesson of Vietnam:* "A nation's deepest strength lies not in its military process but rather in the unity of its people." **L2**

Refer to **Inclusion for the High School Social Studies Classroom Strategies and Activities** in the TCR.

Hawks and Doves In the face of growing opposition to the war, President Johnson remained determined to continue fighting. He assailed his critics in Congress as "selfish men who want to advance their own interests." As for the college protesters, Johnson viewed them as naive and unable to appreciate the importance of resisting communism.

The president was not alone in his views. Although the antiwar protesters became a vocal group, they did not represent majority opinion on Vietnam. In a poll taken in early 1968, 53 percent of the respondents favored stronger military action in Vietnam, compared to only 24 percent who wanted an end to the war. Of those Americans who supported the policy in Vietnam, many openly criticized the protesters for a lack of patriotism.

By 1968 the nation seemed to be divided into two camps. Those who wanted the United States to withdraw from Vietnam were known as **doves.** Those who insisted that the United States stay and fight came to be known as **hawks.** As the two groups debated, the war took a dramatic turn for the worse, and the nation endured a year of shock and crisis.

✓ **Reading Check** **Explaining** What led to the passage of the Twenty-sixth Amendment?

1968: The Pivotal Year

The most turbulent year of the chaotic 1960s was 1968. The year saw a shocking political announcement, a pair of traumatic assassinations, and a violent political convention. First, however, the nation endured a surprise attack in Vietnam.

TURNING POINT

The Tet Offensive On January 30, 1968, during Tet, the Vietnamese New Year, the Vietcong and North Vietnamese launched a massive surprise attack. In this **Tet offensive,** the guerrilla fighters attacked virtually all American airbases in South Vietnam and most of the South's major cities and provincial capitals. Vietcong commandos even blasted their way into the American embassy in Saigon.

Militarily, Tet turned out to be a disaster for the Communist forces. After about a month of fighting, the American and South Vietnamese soldiers repelled the enemy troops, inflicting heavy losses on them. General Westmoreland boasted that the Communists' "well-laid plans went afoul," while President Johnson triumphantly added that the enemy's effort had ended in "complete failure."

In fact, the North Vietnamese had scored a major political victory. The American people were shocked that an enemy supposedly on the verge of defeat could launch such a large-scale attack. When General Westmoreland requested 209,000 troops in addition to the 500,000 already in Vietnam, it seemed to be an admission that the United States could not win the war.

To make matters worse, the mainstream media, which had tried to remain balanced in their war coverage, now openly criticized the effort. "The American people should be getting ready to accept, if they haven't already, the prospect that the whole Vietnam effort may be doomed," the *Wall Street Journal* declared. Walter Cronkite, then the nation's most respected television newscaster, announced after Tet that it seemed "more certain than ever that the bloody experience in Vietnam is to end in a stalemate."

Public opinion no longer favored the president. In the weeks following the Tet offensive, the president's approval rating plummeted to a dismal 35 percent, while support for his handling of the war fell even lower, to 26 percent. The administration's credibility gap now seemed too wide to repair.

Johnson Leaves the Presidential Race With the war growing increasingly unpopular and Johnson's credibility all but gone, some Democrats began looking for an alternative candidate to nominate for president in 1968. In November 1967, even before the Tet disaster, a little-known liberal senator from Minnesota, Eugene McCarthy, became the first dove to announce his candidacy against Johnson. In March 1968, McCarthy stunned the nation by winning more than 40 percent of the votes in the New Hampshire primary

Fact	Fiction	Folklore

The Peace Symbol This familiar symbol of the 1960s was originally designed to stand for the fight for nuclear disarmament. Created by British artist Gerald Holtom in 1958, the symbol was first used at a British demonstration against a research center for the development of nuclear weapons. It combined the semaphore for the letters "N" and "D," standing for nuclear disarmament. Semaphore is a system of visual signaling using two flags, one held in each hand. N is two flags held in an upside-down V, and D is one flag pointed straight up and the other pointed straight down.

Creating a Headline Have students write a headline that might have appeared in a January 1969 newspaper summing up the mood of the country after surviving the turmoil of 1968. **L1**

✓ **Reading Check**

Answer: Protests over the draft led to discussion about the right of draft-age citizens to vote and the passage of the Twenty-sixth Amendment.

FYI

The Tet offensive caught the United States military completely off guard. In the words of a West Point textbook published after the war, Tet was an "intelligence failure ranking with Pearl Harbor."

Fact	Fiction	Folklore

In the early 1970s another sign of the growing concern over the Vietnam War was the proliferation of POW/MIA bracelets. Each bracelet was engraved with the name of someone who was a prisoner of war or missing in action, as well as the date the person was lost. Most people who wore the bracelets continued to wear them until they learned the fate of the person named on their bracelet. As the war ended and service personnel came home, the bracelets were sent to the returning veterans, or, in many cases, the veteran's family.

INTERDISCIPLINARY CONNECTIONS ACTIVITY

Technology The United States used a variety of strategies in its attempt to cut off North Vietnamese supply routes and locate the ground units of the North Vietnamese and Vietcong. Ask students to research and report on some of these strategies, including saturation bombing and the use of napalm and chemical defoliants. Have students explain how each strategy worked and the kind of damage it did. As students present their information, discuss why such firepower failed to bring the Communist forces to a point of surrender. **L2**

Geography Skills

Answers:

1. Laos and Cambodia

2. Attacks were on almost all U.S. bases and major South Vietnam cities. It showed that the United States did not have the level of control its generals were portraying.

Geography Skills Practice

Ask: Why was the Ho Chi Minh trail located outside of Vietnam? (because the U.S. was not at war with Laos or Cambodia)

3 ASSESS

Assign Section 3 Assessment as homework or as an in-class activity.

🔘 Have students use the **Interactive Tutor Self-Assessment CD-ROM.**

Reading Essentials and Study Guide 30–3

NATIONAL GEOGRAPHIC **The Tet Offensive, 1968**

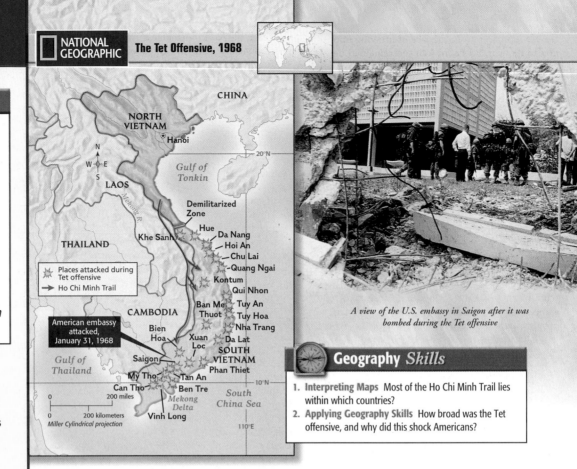

A view of the U.S. embassy in Saigon after it was bombed during the Tet offensive

Geography Skills

1. **Interpreting Maps** Most of the Ho Chi Minh Trail lies within which countries?
2. **Applying Geography Skills** How broad was the Tet offensive, and why did this shock Americans?

and almost defeating the president. Realizing that Johnson was vulnerable, Senator Robert Kennedy, who also opposed the war, quickly entered the race for the Democratic nomination.

With the division in the country and within his own party growing, Johnson addressed the public on television on March 31, 1968. He stunned viewers by stating, "I have concluded that I should not permit the presidency to become involved in the partisan divisions that are developing in this political year. Accordingly, I shall not seek, and I will not accept, the nomination of my party for another term as your President."

A Season of Violence Following Johnson's announcement, the nation endured even more shocking events. In April James Earl Ray was arrested for killing Dr. Martin Luther King, Jr., an event which led to riots in several major cities. Just two months later, another assassination rocked the country—that of Robert Kennedy. Kennedy, who appeared to be on his way to winning the Democratic nomination, was

gunned down on June 5 in a California hotel just after winning the state's Democratic primary. The assassin was Sirhan Sirhan, an Arab nationalist apparently angry over the candidate's pro-Israeli remarks a few nights before.

The violence that seemed to plague the country at every turn in 1968 culminated with a chaotic and well-publicized clash between protesters and police at the Democratic National Convention in Chicago. Thousands of protesters descended on the August convention, demanding that the Democrats adopt an antiwar platform.

On the third day of the convention, the delegates chose Hubert Humphrey, President Johnson's vice president, as their presidential nominee. Meanwhile, in a park not far from the convention hall, the protesters and police began fighting. A full-scale riot soon engulfed the streets of downtown Chicago. As officers tried to disperse demonstrators with tear gas and billy clubs, demonstrators taunted the authorities with the chant, "The whole world is watching!"

908 CHAPTER 30 The Vietnam War

CRITICAL THINKING ACTIVITY

Analyzing Tell students that in 1964 the Vietnam War was not a national issue. Two factors, however, would soon bring it to national attention. The first was the controversy surrounding the Gulf of Tonkin incident. The second was campaign speeches in which Johnson pledged he would not "send American boys halfway around the world to do a job that Asian boys ought to be doing for themselves." Have students analyze how both events became crucial issues by 1967 and 1968. **L2**

Nixon Wins the Presidency The violence and chaos now associated with the Democratic Party benefited the 1968 Republican presidential candidate, Richard Nixon. Although defeated in the 1960 election, Nixon had remained active in national politics. A third candidate, Governor George Wallace of Alabama, also decided to run in 1968 as an independent. Wallace, an outspoken segregationist, sought to attract those Americans who felt threatened by the civil rights movement and urban social unrest.

Public opinion polls gave Nixon a wide lead over Humphrey and Wallace. Nixon's campaign promise to unify the nation and restore law and order appealed to Americans who feared their country was spinning out of control. Nixon also declared that he had a plan for ending the war in Vietnam, although he did not specify how the plan would work.

At first Humphrey's support of President Johnson's Vietnam policies hurt his campaign. After Humphrey broke with the president and called for a complete end to the bombing of North Vietnam, he began to move up in the polls. A week before the election, President Johnson helped Humphrey by announcing that the bombing of North Vietnam had halted and that a cease-fire would follow.

Johnson's announcement had come too late. In the end, Nixon's promises to end the war and restore order at home were enough to sway the American people. On Election Day, Nixon defeated Humphrey by more than 100 electoral votes, although he won the popular vote by a slim margin of 43 percent to 42. Wallace helped account for the razor-thin margin by winning 46 electoral votes and more than 13 percent of the popular vote.

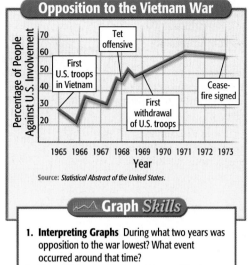

Opposition to the Vietnam War

Source: *Statistical Abstract of the United States.*

Graph Skills

1. **Interpreting Graphs** During what two years was opposition to the war lowest? What event occurred around that time?
2. **Generalizing** In what year did opposition to the Vietnam War peak? How was this sentiment logically related to the withdrawal of American troops?

Speaking to reporters after his election, Nixon recalled seeing a young girl carrying a sign at one of his rallies that said: "Bring Us Together." This, he promised, would be his chief goal as president. Nixon also vowed to implement his plan to end the Vietnam War.

✓ **Reading Check** **Explaining** Why did President Johnson not run for re-election in 1968?

SECTION 3 ASSESSMENT

Checking for Understanding

1. **Define:** credibility gap, teach-in, dove, hawk.
2. **Identify:** William Westmoreland, Tet offensive.
3. **Summarize** three important events that occurred in 1968.

Reviewing Themes

4. **Civic Rights and Responsibilities** Why did many people believe that the Vietnam War reflected racial and economic injustices in the United States?

Critical Thinking

5. **Synthesizing** Why did support of the Vietnam War begin to dwindle by the late 1960s?
6. **Organizing** Use a graphic organizer similar to the one below to list the effects of the Tet offensive.

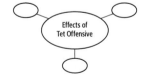

Effects of Tet Offensive

Analyzing Visuals

7. **Analyzing Photographs** Study the photograph on page 906. The phrase "flower power" was a slogan of the hippie movement. Explain what you think the phrase meant to hippies and how the slogan was used to express opposition to the war.

Writing About History

8. **Expository Writing** Imagine that you are living in 1968. Write a paragraph for the local newspaper in which you explain your reasons for either supporting or opposing the Vietnam War.

CHAPTER 30 The Vietnam War **909**

SECTION 3 ASSESSMENT ANSWERS

1. Terms are in blue.
2. William Westmoreland (p. 905), Tet offensive (p. 907)
3. any three of the following: Tet offensive, Johnson's not running, Democratic National Convention, King and Kennedy assassinations
4. Poorer men, including a high proportion of minorities, who were unable to afford college were more likely to be drafted than those who could afford college.
5. Media coverage of the mounting casualties fueled anger and distrust of government officials' reports, and many were angry over the draft.
6. support for war dropped, the

media became critical of the war effort, and the president's approval rating plummeted
7. Flowers represented the growing peace movement.
8. Students' paragraph should express a clear point of view.

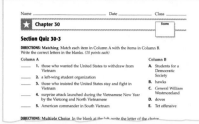

Section Quiz 30–3

Graph Skills

Answers:
1. 1965, 1966; first U.S. troops arrive
2. 1971; Withdrawal showed government did not believe the war could be won.

Graph Skills Practice
Ask: When was the cease-fire signed? *(1973)*

✓**Reading Check**

Answer: He did not want the presidency to become involved in partisan division.

Reteach
Have students describe the antiwar movement.

Enrich
Have interested students write antiwar slogans for the 1968 presidential campaign.

4 CLOSE

Have students describe the motives of those in the antiwar movement.

1 FOCUS

Section Overview
This section focuses on the withdrawal of United States forces and the war's impact at home.

BELLRINGER
Skillbuilder Activity

Project transparency and have students answer the question.

Available as a blackline master.

Daily Focus Skills Transparency 30–4

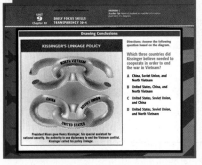

Guide to Reading

Answers to Graphic: Kissinger appointment, linkage policy, Vietnamization, bombing campaign, Cambodian invasion

Preteaching Vocabulary
Have students look up the Key Terms and Names in the glossary. Then have them use two of the terms in a sentence.

Guide to Reading

Main Idea
After nearly eight years of fighting in Vietnam, the United States withdrew its forces.

Key Terms and Names
Henry Kissinger, linkage, Vietnamization, Pentagon Papers, War Powers Act

Reading Strategy
Organizing As you read about the end of the Vietnam War, complete a graphic organizer similar to the one below by listing the steps that President Nixon took to end American involvement in Vietnam.

Steps Nixon Took

Reading Objectives
• **Explain** the events of Nixon's first administration that inspired more antiwar protests.
• **Summarize** the major lessons the United States learned from the Vietnam War experience.

Section Theme
Government and Democracy The Vietnam War led to changes in the way the U.S. military is deployed.

Preview of Events

♦1969	♦1971	♦1973	♦1975

1969
Secret peace negotiations between the U.S. and North Vietnam begin

1972
Nixon initiates Christmas bombings

1973
Cease-fire signed

1975
Evacuation of the last Americans from Vietnam

★ An American Story ★

Frank Snepp

On the evening of April 29, 1975, Frank Snepp, a young CIA officer, scrambled up to the American embassy rooftop to catch one of the last helicopters out of Saigon. Throughout that day, Snepp had witnessed the desperation of the South Vietnamese people as they besieged the embassy grounds in an to effort escape the approaching Communist army. Now he was leaving. Later, he recalled the scene:

66The roof of the Embassy was a vision out of a nightmare. In the center of the dimly lit helo-pad a CH-47 was already waiting for us, its engines setting up a roar like a primeval scream. The crew and controllers all wore what looked like oversized football helmets, and in the blinking under-light of the landing signals they reminded me of grotesque insects rearing on their hindquarters. Out beyond the edge of the building a Phantom jet streaked across the horizon as tracers darted up here and there into the night sky.99

—quoted in *Decent Interval*

Nixon Moves to End the War

Frank Snepp was one of the last Americans to leave Vietnam. Shortly after taking office, President Nixon had taken steps to end the nation's involvement in the war, but the final years of the conflict would yield much more bloodshed and turmoil.

As a first step, Nixon appointed Harvard professor **Henry Kissinger** as special assistant for national security affairs and gave him wide authority to use diplomacy to end the conflict. Kissinger embarked upon a policy he called linkage, which meant improving

---

SECTION RESOURCES

Reproducible Masters
• Reproducible Lesson Plan 30–4
• Daily Lecture and Discussion Notes 30–4
• Guided Reading Activity 30–4
• Section Quiz 30–4
• Reading Essentials and Study Guide 30–4

Transparencies
• Daily Focus Skills Transparency 30–4

Multimedia
🔘 Interactive Tutor Self-Assessment CD-ROM
🔘 ExamView® Pro Testmaker CD-ROM
🔘 Presentation Plus! CD-ROM
🔘 TeacherWorks™ CD-ROM
🎧 Audio Program
📺 ABCNews Interactive™ Historic America Electronic Field Trips

relations with the Soviet Union and China—suppliers of aid to North Vietnam—so he could persuade them to cut back on their aid.

Kissinger also rekindled peace talks with the North Vietnamese. In August 1969, Kissinger entered into secret negotiations with North Vietnam's negotiator, Le Duc Tho. In their talks, which dragged on for four years, Kissinger and Le Duc Tho argued over a possible cease-fire, the return of American prisoners of war, and the ultimate fate of South Vietnam.

Meanwhile, Nixon cut back the number of American troops in Vietnam. Known as Vietnamization, this process involved the gradual withdrawal of U.S. troops while South Vietnam assumed more of the fighting. On June 8, 1969, Nixon announced the withdrawal of 25,000 soldiers. Nixon refused to view this troop withdrawal as a form of surrender. He was determined to maintain a strong American presence in Vietnam to ensure bargaining power during peace negotiations. In support of that goal, the president increased air strikes against North Vietnam and began bombing Vietcong sanctuaries in neighboring Cambodia.

✓ **Reading Check** **Identifying** When did secret negotiations with the North Vietnamese begin?

Turmoil at Home Continues

Even though the United States had begun scaling back its involvement in Vietnam, the American home front remained divided and volatile as Nixon's war policies stirred up new waves of protest.

Massacre at My Lai In November 1969, Americans learned of a horrifying event. That month, the media reported that in the spring of 1968, an American platoon under the command of Lieutenant William Calley had massacred possibly more than 200 unarmed South Vietnamese civilians in the hamlet of **My Lai.** Most of the victims were old men, women, and children. Calley eventually went to prison for his role in the killings.

Most American soldiers acted responsibly and honorably throughout the war. The actions of one soldier, however, increased the feeling among many citizens that this was a brutal and senseless conflict. Jan Barry, a founder of the Vietnam Veterans Against the War, viewed the massacre at My Lai as a symbol of the dilemma his generation faced in the conflict:

> ❝To kill on military orders and be a criminal, or to refuse to kill and be a criminal is the moral agony of America's Vietnam war generation. It is what has forced upward of sixty thousand young Americans, draft resisters and deserters to Canada, and created one hundred thousand military deserters a year in this country and abroad.❞
>
> —quoted in *Who Spoke Up?*

The Invasion of Cambodia Sparks Protest

Americans heard more startling news when Nixon announced in April 1970 that American troops had invaded Cambodia. The troops wanted to destroy Vietcong military bases there.

Many viewed the Cambodian invasion as a widening of the war, and it set off many protests. At **Kent State University** on May 4, 1970, Ohio National Guard soldiers, armed with tear gas and rifles, fired on demonstrators without an order to do so. The soldiers killed four students and wounded at least nine others. Ten days later, police killed two African American students during a demonstration at Jackson State University in Mississippi.

Picturing **History**

National Trauma When members of the Ohio National Guard fired on Kent State University demonstrators, the event triggered a nationwide student strike that forced hundreds of colleges and universities to close. How does this image connect with the phrase "the war at home"?

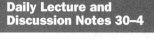

2 TEACH

✓ **Reading Check**

Answer: August 1969

Picturing **History**

Answer: Americans were being shot at by United States soldiers.

Designing a Memorial Have students sketch a design for a memorial to the students who died at Kent State or Jackson State. L1 ELL

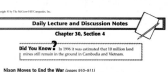
ABCNEWS INTERACTIVE™

 VIDEOCASSETTE
Historic America Electronic Field Trips

View **Tape 2, Chapter 10:** "The Vietnam Veterans Memorial."

COOPERATIVE LEARNING ACTIVITY

Summarizing Information Organize the class into groups of five to seven students each. Have the groups consider this fill-in-the-blank statement: The war in Vietnam was tragic because _____. Ask everyone in the group to provide at least one original answer. Have a representative of each group present the responses to the class. As a class, look for common elements in the responses.

Use the rubric for a cooperative group management plan on pages 81–82 in the *Performance Assessment Activities and Rubrics.*

IN HISTORY

Have students make a list of the qualities essential to a hero.

📁 Use **Supreme Court Case Study 45,** New York Times v. United States.

✓ Reading Check

Answer: that the government had not been honest with them about Vietnam

3 ASSESS

Assign Section 4 Assessment as homework or as an in-class activity.

💿 Have students use the **Interactive Tutor Self-Assessment CD-ROM.**

The Pentagon Papers In addition to sparking violence on campuses, the invasion of Cambodia cost Nixon significant congressional support. Numerous legislators expressed outrage over the president's failure to notify them of the action. In December 1970, an angry Congress repealed the Gulf of Tonkin Resolution, which had given the president near complete power in directing the war in Vietnam.

Support for the war weakened further in 1971 when Daniel Ellsberg, a disillusioned former Defense Department worker, leaked what became known as the **Pentagon Papers** to the New York Times. The documents revealed that many government officials during the Johnson administration privately questioned the war while publicly defending it.

The documents contained details of decisions that were made by the presidents and their advisers without the consent of Congress. They also showed how the various administrations acted to deceive Congress, the press, and the public about the situation in Vietnam. The Pentagon Papers confirmed what many Americans had long believed: The government had not been honest with them.

✓ Reading Check **Evaluating** What did the Pentagon Papers confirm for many Americans?

The United States Pulls Out of Vietnam

By 1971 polls showed that nearly two-thirds of Americans wanted to end the Vietnam War as quickly as possible. In April 1972, President Nixon dropped his longtime insistence that North Vietnamese troops had to withdraw from South Vietnam before any peace treaty could be signed. In October, less than a month before the 1972 presidential election, Henry Kissinger emerged from his secret talks with Le Duc Tho to announce that "peace is at hand."

A month later, Americans went to the polls to decide on a president. Senator George McGovern, the

---

Profiles IN HISTORY

Roy P. Benavidez

1935–

Roy P. Benavidez received the Medal of Honor, the nation's highest award for heroism, for his actions in the Vietnam War. Growing up, Benavidez worked on the streets selling empty soda bottles and cleaning a local stockyard. His father's family had been *vaqueros* (cowboys from Mexico), immigrating in the 1830s during the Texas War for Independence. His mother, a Yaqui Native American, was born in northern Mexico. Both parents died by the time Benavidez was seven, and

he was raised by his uncle.

A tough life made Benavidez a fighter. In May 1968 while fighting in Vietnam, Benavidez rescued members of his Special Forces group who were surrounded by the enemy. Wounded three times while getting to the men by helicopter, he stayed with them some eight hours, preparing an evacuation. Then while carrying the men to the rescue helicopters, he was attacked from behind but managed to kill his attacker. Only after loading all the dead and wounded did Benavidez himself board a helicopter.

Democratic candidate, was an outspoken critic of the war. He did not appeal to many middle-class Americans, however, who were tired of antiwar protesters. When the votes were cast, Nixon won re-election in a landslide.

The Two Sides Reach Peace Just weeks after the presidential election, the peace negotiations broke down. South Vietnam's president, **Nguyen Van Thieu,** refused to agree to any plan that left North Vietnamese troops in the South. Kissinger tried to win additional concessions from the Communists, but talks broke off on December 16, 1972.

The next day, to force North Vietnam to resume negotiations, the Nixon administration began the most destructive air raids of the entire war. In what became known as the "Christmas bombings," American B-52s dropped thousands of tons of bombs on North Vietnamese targets for 11 straight days, pausing only on Christmas day.

In the wake of the bombing campaign, the United States and North Vietnam returned to the bargaining table. Thieu finally gave in to American pressure and allowed North Vietnamese troops to remain in the South. On January 27, 1973, the warring sides signed an agreement "ending the war and restoring the peace in Vietnam."

MEETING SPECIAL NEEDS

Auditory/Musical Bring to class a recording of Bob Dylan's song "Blowin' in the Wind." As you play the recording, have students summarize what the lyrics are saying. Then have them write why the music helps convey the message of the lyrics. Finally, have students write a poem or song highlighting the fact that more than 58,000 Americans died or went missing in action in Vietnam. **L2**

📁 Refer to **Inclusion for the High School Social Studies Classroom Strategies and Activities** in the TCR.

The United States promised to withdraw the rest of its troops, and both sides agreed to an exchange of prisoners of war. The parties did not resolve the issue of South Vietnam's future, however. After almost eight years of war—the longest war in American history—the nation ended its direct involvement in Vietnam.

South Vietnam Falls

The United States had barely pulled out its last troops from Vietnam when the peace agreement collapsed. In March 1975, the North Vietnamese army launched a full-scale invasion of the South. Thieu desperately appealed to Washington, D.C., for help.

President Nixon had assured Thieu during the peace negotiations that the United States "[would] respond with full force should the settlement be violated by North Vietnam." Nixon, however, had resigned under pressure following the Watergate scandal. The new president, Gerald Ford, asked for funds to aid the South Vietnamese, but Congress refused.

On April 30, the North Vietnamese captured Saigon, South Vietnam's capital, and united Vietnam under Communist rule. They then renamed Saigon Ho Chi Minh City.

✔ **Reading Check** Explaining Why did the peace talks break down in December 1972?

The Legacy of Vietnam

"The lessons of the past in Vietnam," President Ford declared in 1975, "have already been learned—learned by Presidents, learned by Congress, learned by the American people—and we should have our focus on the future." Although Americans tried to put the war behind them, Vietnam left a deep and lasting impact on American society.

The War's Human Toll The United States paid a heavy price for its involvement in Vietnam. The war had cost the nation almost $150 billion in direct costs and much more in indirect economic expenses. More significantly, it had resulted in the deaths of approximately 58,000 young Americans and the injury of more than 300,000. In Vietnam, around one million North and South Vietnamese soldiers died in the conflict, as did countless civilians.

Even after they returned home from fighting, some American veterans, as in other wars, found it hard to escape the war's psychological impact. Army Specialist Doug Johnson recalled the problems he faced on returning home:

66It took a while for me to recognize that I did suffer some psychological problems in trying to deal with my experience in Vietnam. The first recollection I have of the effect took place shortly after I arrived back in the States. One evening . . . I went to see a movie on post. I don't recall the name of the movie or what it was about, but I remember there was a sad part, and that I started crying uncontrollably. It hadn't dawned on me before this episode that I had . . . succeeded in burying my emotions. 99

—quoted in *Touched by the Dragon*

One reason it may have been harder for some Vietnam veterans to readjust to civilian life was that many considered the war a defeat. Many Americans wanted to forget the war. Thus, the sacrifices of many veterans often went unrecognized. There were relatively few welcome-home parades and celebrations after the war.

The war also lingered for the American families whose relatives and friends were classified as

Picturing **History**

Desperate Pleas When President Ford ordered all Americans to leave Vietnam immediately in April 1975, many Saigon residents stormed the U.S. embassy pleading for rescue. When did the North Vietnamese take control of Saigon?

Reading Essentials and Study Guide 30–4

Name _____ Date _____ Class _____

Study Guide
Chapter 30, Section 4
For use with textbook pages 910–914

THE WAR WINDS DOWN

KEY TERMS AND NAMES

Henry Kissinger special assistant for national security affairs under President Nixon (page 910)
linkage the policy of improving relations with the Soviet Union and China to persuade them to reduce their assistance to North Vietnam (page 910)
Vietnamization a plan for a gradual withdrawal of American troops and for the South Vietnamese army to take over more of the fighting in Vietnam (page 911)
Pentagon Papers documents that revealed that various administrations had deceived Congress and the people about the situation in Vietnam (page 912)
War Powers Act a law that required the president to inform Congress of any troop commitment within 48 hours and to withdraw the troops in 60 days unless Congress approved the troop

Section Quiz 30–4

Name _____ Date _____ Class _____

★ **Chapter 30** Score

Section Quiz 30–4

DIRECTIONS: Matching Match each item in Column A with the items in Column B. Write the correct letters in the blanks. *(10 points each)*

Column A
___ 1. reestablished some limits on executive power
___ 2. the most destructive air raids of the entire Vietnam War
___ 3. special assistant for national security affairs
___ 4. a plan calling for the gradual withdrawal of American troops and for the South Vietnamese army to assume more of the fighting
___ 5. Democratic candidate for president in 1972

Column B
A. Vietnamization
B. "Christmas bombings"
C. Henry Kissinger
D. War Powers Act
E. George McGovern

DIRECTIONS: Multiple Choice In the blank at the left, write the letter of the choice that best completes the statement or answers the question. *(10 points each)*

✔ **Reading Check**

Answer: Kissinger tried to win additional concessions.

Picturing **History**

Answer: April 30, 1975

FYI

Ho Chi Minh City (formerly Saigon) proclaimed 1990 its "Year of Tourism." The tunnels once used for the Vietcong guerrillas—a network of 200 miles—were one of the featured tourist attractions.

History *and the* Humanities

American Art & Architecture: Vietnam Veterans Memorial

INTERDISCIPLINARY CONNECTIONS ACTIVITY

Language Arts Have students write a newspaper or magazine article based on an interview with someone in their community who was a young adult at the time of the Vietnam War. To prepare for the interview, encourage students to use library and Internet resources to learn more about what was going on in their community at the time of the war. Have interested students combine the articles into a publication. **L2**

HISTORY Online

Objectives and answers to the student activity can be found in the **Web Activity Lesson Plan** at tav.glencoe.com.

World Geography Connection

Answer: Many Americans felt responsible for the refugees' plight.

✓**Reading Check**

Answer: became more reluctant to intervene in other countries' affairs

Reteach

Have students explain the events of Nixon's first administration.

Enrich

Have students tell the story of the Vietnam War by reading articles on the war using library and Internet resources.

4 CLOSE

Have students summarize the lessons of the Vietnam War.

---

prisoners of war (POWs) or missing in action (MIA). Despite many official investigations, these families were not convinced that the government had told the truth about POW/MIA policies in the last years of the war.

The nation finally began to come to terms with the war almost a decade later. In 1982 the nation dedicated the National Vietnam Veterans Memorial in Washington, D.C., a large black stone wall inscribed with the names of those killed and missing in action in the war. "It's a first step to remind America of what we did," veteran Larry Cox of Virginia said at the dedication of the monument.

GOVERNMENT

The War's Impact on the Nation The war also left its mark on the nation as a whole. In 1973 Congress passed the **War Powers Act** as a way to reestablish some limits on executive power. The act required the president to inform Congress of any commitment of troops abroad within 48 hours and to withdraw them in 60 days unless Congress explicitly approved the troop commitment.

HISTORY Online

Student Web Activity Visit the *American Vision* Web site at tav.glencoe.com and click on *Student Web Activities— Chapter 30* for an activity on the Vietnam War.

The legislation addresses the struggle between the executive and legislative branches over what checks and balances are proper in matters of war and foreign policy. No president has recognized this limitation, and the courts have tended to avoid the issue as a strictly political question. In general, the war shook the nation's confidence and led some to embrace a new kind of isolationism. In the years after the war, many Americans became more reluctant to intervene in the affairs of other nations.

On the domestic front, the Vietnam War increased Americans' cynicism about their government. Many felt the nation's leaders had misled them. Together with Watergate, a scandal that broke as the war was winding down, Vietnam made Americans more wary of their leaders.

✓**Reading Check** **Describing** How did the Vietnam War affect Americans' attitudes toward international conflicts?

World Geography Connection

The War's Refugees

Another of the Vietnam War's enduring legacies was the wave of human migration and resettlement it prompted. From the mid-1970s through the 1980s, between 1.5 and 2 million people fled the newly installed Communist regimes in Vietnam, Cambodia, and Laos. These men, women, and children became known as "boat people" because their main route of escape was by sea. More than half of these refugees came to the United States. Between 1980 and 1990, the Vietnamese population of the United States more than doubled from about 245,000 to almost 615,000. *Why do you think the United States was willing to accept so many refugees from the Vietnam War?*

SECTION 4 ASSESSMENT

Checking for Understanding

1. **Define:** linkage, Vietnamization.
2. **Identify:** Henry Kissinger, Pentagon Papers, War Powers Act.
3. **Describe** what happened in Vietnam in 1975 after the United States withdrew.

Reviewing Themes

4. **Government and Democracy** Why did Congress pass the War Powers Act? How did this act reflect a struggle between the legislative and executive branches?

Critical Thinking

5. **Analyzing** Why did the invasion of Cambodia cost President Nixon congressional support?
6. **Organizing** Use a graphic organizer similar to the one below to list the effects of the Vietnam War on the nation.

Effects of Vietnam War

Analyzing Visuals

7. **Analyzing Photographs** Study the photograph on page 913 of South Vietnamese citizens attempting to enter the U.S. embassy. How do you think this image affected American attitudes toward the war? Why do you think so?

Writing About History

8. **Descriptive Writing** Imagine that you are a college student in 1970. Write a journal entry expressing your feelings about the events at Kent State and Jackson State Universities.

SECTION 4 ASSESSMENT ANSWERS

1. Terms are in blue.
2. Kissinger *(p. 910)*, Pentagon Papers *(p. 912)*, War Powers Act *(p. 914)*
3. North Vietnam took control of South Vietnam, uniting the two countries under Communist rule.
4. to limit executive power; reflected the struggle over checks and balances in war and foreign policy between the executive and legislative branches
5. Nixon failed to notify Congress of this action in advance, costing him congressional support.
6. American cynicism toward government, war dead and casualties, cost, and War Powers Act
7. Answers will vary. Responses could include relief at getting out of the war or guilt for leaving allies behind.
8. Journal entries should focus on feelings.

Conducting an Interview

Why Learn This Skill?

Suppose that your friends went to see a concert, but you were unable to attend. How would you find out how the show was?

Learning the Skill

You probably would not normally think of asking your friends questions about a concert as conducting an interview, but that is exactly what you are doing. Interviews are an excellent way of collecting important facts and opinions from people. Interviews allow you to gather information from people who witnessed or participated in an event firsthand. For example, William Prochnau interviewed many different people and used the results to write his book *Once Upon a Distant War*, which examines the way the press covered the Vietnam War. To conduct an interview with someone, follow these steps.

- **Make an appointment.** Contact the person and explain why you want to conduct the interview, what kinds of things you hope to learn, and how you will use the information. Discuss where and when you will conduct the interview, and ask if you may use a tape recorder.

- **Gather background information.** Find out about the education, career, and other accomplishments of the person you want to interview. Research the topics you wish to discuss.

- **Prepare questions.** Group questions into subject categories. Begin each category with general questions and move toward more specific questions. Formulate each question carefully. If the answer could be simply yes or no, rephrase the question.

- **Conduct the interview.** Introduce yourself and restate the purpose of the interview. Ask questions and record responses accurately. Ask follow-up questions to fill gaps in information.

- **Transcribe the interview.** Convert your written or tape-recorded notes into a *transcript*, a written record of the interview presented in a question-and-answer format.

Practicing the Skill

Imagine you are assigned to interview someone who participated in or is old enough to remember the events that occurred during the Vietnam War.

1. What kind of background information might you gather?

2. What are some broad categories of questions you might ask based on what you know about the person you are interviewing and what you know about the war?

3. What are some general questions you might want to ask within these broad categories? Consider the responses you might get to these general questions, and formulate follow-up questions for each.

Skills Assessment

Complete the Practicing Skills questions on page 917 and the Chapter 30 Skill Reinforcement Activity to assess your mastery of this skill.

Applying the Skill

Conducting an Interview The Vietnam War probably included some people you know—your parents, grandparents, aunts, uncles, or neighbors. Even if they were not directly involved with the conflict, they probably remember what the United States was like during the war. Use the questions you developed above to interview one or more of these people. Ask about their experiences regarding Vietnam, including their attitudes toward the war and its many related issues, past and present. Summarize your findings in a short report or in a comparison chart.

 Glencoe's **Skillbuilder Interactive Workbook CD-ROM, Level 2,** provides instruction and practice in key social studies skills.

TEACH

Conducting an Interview
Review the steps students will use to conduct successful interviews. Remind students that interviews become primary sources.

Encourage students to use the list of steps to create an interview checklist that they can use for each interview they conduct.

Additional Practice

Reinforcing Skills Activity 30

Name _____ Date _____ Class _____

★ Reinforcing Skills Activity 30

Conducting an Interview

☐ LEARNING THE SKILL
An interview can provide firsthand and personal information you may not be able to find in a book or magazine. To begin the interview process, first contact the person you want to interview. Let them know about the purpose of the interview, and make arrangements for your meeting. Before you meet, find out as much as you can about the interviewee and about the topics you plan to discuss. Also prepare and organize your questions. As you begin your interview, introduce yourself. Listen carefully, ask additional questions for detail, and record responses. After the interview, convert your notes into a transcript.

☐ PRACTICING THE SKILL
DIRECTIONS: Select a person from the Vietnam War era to research. Imagine that you have the opportunity to interview this person.

GLENCOE
TECHNOLOGY

 CD-ROM
Glencoe Skillbuilder Interactive Workbook CD-ROM, Level 2

This interactive CD-ROM reinforces student mastery of essential social studies skills.

ANSWERS TO PRACTICING THE SKILL

Students should review information on the war. Questions might be: for 2, what subjects did during the war, their attitude to the war; for 3, what factors influenced their attitude, if the war affected their friends or family, how they now see the war.

Applying the Skill
Students' reports will vary depending on the people interviewed and their recollections of the war. Remind students that their reports are to summarize their findings, not merely to present a transcript of the interview.

GLENCOE
TECHNOLOGY

GLENCOE
TECHNOLOGY

MindJogger Videoquiz
Use the **MindJogger Videoquiz** to review Chapter 30 content.

 Available in VHS

Reviewing Key Terms

Students' answers will vary. The pages where the words appear in the text are shown in parentheses.

1. **domino theory** (p. 894)
2. **guerrilla** (p. 894)
3. **Vietcong** (p. 897)
4. **napalm** (p. 900)
5. **credibility gap** (p. 905)
6. **teach-in** (p. 905)
7. **dove** (p. 907)
8. **hawk** (p. 907)
9. **linkage** (p. 910)
10. **Vietnamization** (p. 911)

Reviewing Key Facts

11. Ho Chi Minh (p. 893), Tet offensive (p. 907)

12. President Eisenhower defended involvement in Vietnam by stressing the domino theory and the need to stop the spread of communism.

13. The number of military personnel began to increase significantly in 1963 during the Kennedy administration.

14. The peasants resented being uprooted from their villages and family farms and resettled in strategic hamlets.

15. Ngo Dinh Diem was unpopular due to the strategic hamlet policy and his discrimination against Buddhism.

16. The Tet offensive began to turn American public opinion against the war. Mainstream media began to criticize the war and Johnson decided not to run for another term as president.

Reviewing Key Terms

On a sheet of paper, use each of these terms in a sentence.

1. domino theory
2. guerrilla
3. Vietcong
4. napalm
5. credibility gap
6. teach-in
7. dove
8. hawk
9. linkage
10. Vietnamization

Chapter Summary

American Involvement in Vietnam

Roots of the Conflict

- Eisenhower financially supported French war against Vietnam
- Geneva Accords established North and South Vietnam
- U.S.-backed leader of South Vietnam refused national elections, fearing defeat by Communist opponent
- Kennedy sharply increased military aid and presence in South Vietnam
- Johnson escalated U.S. involvement and gained war powers after the incident in the Gulf of Tonkin

Full-Scale War

- President Johnson responded to a Vietcong attack with aggressive air strikes; American people applauded his actions
- U.S. committed 360,000 ground troops to fighting in Vietnam by 1966

Opposition to the War

- American people questioned the government's honesty about the war, creating the so-called "credibility gap"
- Wartime economy hurt domestic spending efforts
- President Nixon was elected largely on promises to end the war and unite the divided country

The End of the War

- Nixon withdrew troops but increased air strikes
- American troops pulled out after a 1973 peace agreement
- Congress passed the War Powers Act to limit the power of the president during times of war

Reviewing Key Facts

11. **Identify:** Ho Chi Minh, Tet offensive.
12. How did President Eisenhower defend American policy in Vietnam?
13. When did the number of American military personnel begin to increase in Vietnam?
14. How did Vietnamese peasants respond to the strategic hamlets program?
15. What actions made Ngo Dinh Diem an unpopular leader in South Vietnam?
16. What was the effect of the Tet offensive on Americans?
17. How did Richard Nixon benefit from the chaos in the nation in 1968?
18. What did the Pentagon Papers reveal?

Critical Thinking

19. **Analyzing Themes: Civic Rights and Responsibilities** How did Americans show their frustration with the direction the country was taking in 1968?

20. **Analyzing** How do you think the use of chemicals such as Agent Orange and napalm by the United States affected Vietnamese feelings toward Americans and the war?

21. **Organizing** Use a graphic organizer to list the reasons the United States became involved in Vietnam and the effects the war had on the nation.

22. **Interpreting Primary Sources** In the 1960s many young Americans enlisted or were drafted for military service. Some believed they had a duty to serve their country. Many had no clear idea of what they were doing or why. In the following excerpt, a young man interviewed for Mark Baker's book *Nam* presents his thoughts about going to war.

   ❝I read a lot of pacifist literature to determine whether or not I was a conscientious objector. I finally concluded that I wasn't. . . .

   The one clear decision I made in 1968 about me and the war was that if I was going to get out of it, I was going to get out in a legal way. I was not going to defraud the system in order to beat the system. I wasn't going to leave the country, because the odds of coming back looked real slim. . . .

17. Violence and chaos associated with the Democratic National Convention in the 1968 election benefited Republican candidate Richard Nixon.

18. The Pentagon Papers revealed that U.S. government officials had not been honest about the war's progress.

Critical Thinking

19. They elected Nixon, participated in violence, and protested.

20. Since the chemicals turned farmland and forest into wasteland, it made the Vietnamese more anti-American.

HISTORY Online

Self-Check Quiz

Visit the *American Vision* Web site at tav.glencoe.com and click on *Self-Check Quizzes—Chapter 30* to assess your knowledge of chapter content.

With all my terror of going into the Army . . . there was something seductive about it, too. I was seduced by World War II and John Wayne movies. . . . I had been, as we all were, victimized by a romantic, truly uninformed view of war.

—quoted in *Nam*

a. What options did the young man have regarding going to war?

b. Do you think World War II movies gave him a realistic view of what fighting in Vietnam would be like?

Practicing Skills

23. Conducting an Interview Review the material on page 915 about interviewing. Then follow these steps to prepare for an interview with President Johnson on his Vietnam policies.

a. Study Section 2 of this chapter on the president's Vietnam policies and conduct library or Internet research on this subject.

b. Prepare a list of 10 questions to ask the president.

Geography and History

24. The map on this page shows supply routes and troop movements during the Vietnam War. Study the map and answer the questions below.

a. Interpreting Maps What nations besides North and South Vietnam were the sites of battles or invasions?

b. Analyzing Why did the Ho Chi Minh Trail pass through Laos and Cambodia instead of South Vietnam?

Chapter Activity

25. Evaluating Bias A person's life experiences often influence his or her arguments one way or another, creating a biased opinion. Reread the speeches in Different Viewpoints on pages 898–899. What might have influenced the points of view of George Ball and George Kennan? Create a cause-and-effect chart showing possible reasons for their biases and effects their experiences have had on their political opinions.

Writing Activity

26. Portfolio Writing Many songs and pieces of literature have been written on the Vietnam War. Find examples of these. Then write an original poem or song lyrics in which you present antiwar or pro-war sentiments about the Vietnam War. Include your work in your portfolio.

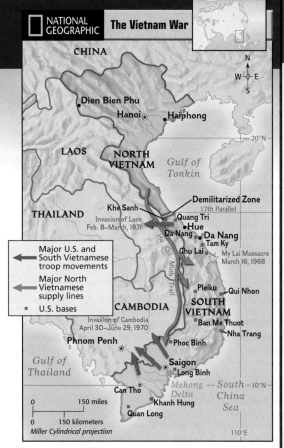

NATIONAL GEOGRAPHIC **The Vietnam War**

The Princeton Review
Standardized Test Practice

Directions: Choose the phrase that best completes the following statement.

The purpose of the War Powers Act was to ensure that the president would

A have greater authority over the military.

B consult Congress before committing troops to extended conflicts.

C have the authority to sign treaties without Senate approval.

D have a freer hand in fighting the spread of communism.

Test-Taking Tip: After Vietnam and Watergate, Congress wanted legislation to limit the president's power during wartime. Three of the answers actually do the opposite, giving the president *more* power. You can eliminate these three answers.

HISTORY Online

Have students visit the Web site at tav.glencoe.com to review Chapter 30 and take the Self-Check Quiz.

Chapter Activity

25. Students' charts will vary. Students should focus on the official positions of Ball and Kennan as part of the causes for their bias.

Writing Activity

26. Students' poems or songs will vary. Encourage students to write from the perspective of a young person living during the Vietnam War era.

The Princeton Review
Standardized Test Practice

Answer: B
Test-Taking Tip: Encourage students to consider which answers would give the president more power by looking for comparative adjectives. For example, answer C mentions "greater authority" and answer D states "freer hand." The correct answer is B.

Bonus Question ?

Ask: What is the name of the university in Ohio where four students were killed by National Guard troops? *(Kent State University)*

---

21. causes: fall of China to communism and the outbreak of the Korean War; effects: cynicism toward government, casualties and war dead, cost, protests, War Powers Act

22. a. He could declare he was a conscientious objector, he could avoid service in a legal way, he could leave the country, or he could fight. **b.** No, he realized that the view of war presented in movies had been romanticized.

Practicing Skills

23. Students' lists of questions will vary but should focus on the president's policies.

Geography and History

24. a. Laos and Cambodia were also invaded. **b.** The Ho Chi Minh trail passed through Laos and Cambodia to avoid discovery and capture of troops and supplies passing along the trail.

917

Chapter 31 Resources

Timesaving Tools

TeacherWorks™ All-In-One Planner and Resource Center

- **Interactive Teacher Edition** Access your Teacher Wraparound Edition and your classroom resources with a few easy clicks.
- **Interactive Lesson Planner** Planning has never been easier! Organize your week, month, semester, or year with all the lesson helps you need to make teaching creative, timely, and relevant.

Use Glencoe's **Presentation Plus!** multimedia teacher tool to easily present dynamic lessons that visually excite your students. Using Microsoft PowerPoint® you can customize the presentations to create your own personalized lessons.

TEACHING TRANSPARENCIES

Graphic Organizer 11

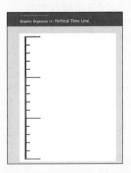

Why It Matters Chapter Transparency 31

APPLICATION AND ENRICHMENT

Linking Past and Present Activity 31

Enrichment Activity 31

Primary Source Reading 31

REVIEW AND REINFORCEMENT

Reteaching Activity 31

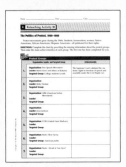

Vocabulary Activity 31

Time Line Activity 31

Critical Thinking Skills Activity 31

Meeting NCSS Standards

Local Standards

The following standards are highlighted in Chapter 31:

Section 1	VI	Power, Authority, and Governance: A, D, F, H
Section 2	X	Civic Ideals and Practices: A, D, E, F, G, I
Section 3	X	Civic Ideals and Practices: A, D, E, F, G, I
Section 4	V	Individuals, Groups, and Institutions: B, E, F, G

Chapter 31 Resources

Chapter 31 Test Form A

Chapter 31 Test Form B

Standardized Test Skills Practice Workbook Activity 31

Performance Assessment Activities and Rubrics 31

ExamView® Pro Testmaker CD-ROM

MULTIMEDIA

- Vocabulary PuzzleMaker CD-ROM
- Interactive Tutor Self-Assessment CD-ROM
- ExamView® Pro Testmaker CD-ROM
- Audio Program
- American History Primary Source Documents Library CD-ROM
- MindJogger Videoquiz
- Presentation Plus! CD-ROM
- TeacherWorks™ CD-ROM
- Interactive Student Edition CD-ROM
- Glencoe Skillbuilder Interactive Workbook CD-ROM, Level 2
- The *American Vision* Video Program
- American Music: Hits Through History
- American Music: Cultural Traditions

The following videotape program is available from Glencoe as a supplement to Chapter 31:

- **Gloria Steinem: Ms. America** (ISBN 1-56-501518-5)

To order, call Glencoe at 1-800-334-7344. To find classroom resources to accompany many of these videos, check the following home pages:
A&E Television: www.aande.com
The History Channel: www.historychannel.com

SPANISH RESOURCES

The following Spanish language materials are available in the Spanish Resources Binder:

- Spanish Guided Reading Activities
- Spanish Reteaching Activities
- Spanish Quizzes and Tests
- Spanish Vocabulary Activities
- Spanish Summaries
- The Declaration of Independence and United States Constitution Spanish Translation

Use our Web site for additional resources. All essential content is covered in the Student Edition.

You and your students can visit tav.glencoe.com, the Web site companion to the *American Vision.* This innovative integration of electronic and print media offers your students a wealth of opportunities. The student text directs students to the Web site for the following options:

- **Chapter Overviews**
- **Student Web Activities**
- **Self-Check Quizzes**
- **Textbook Updates**

Answers to the student Web activities are provided for you in the **Web Activity Lesson Plans.** Additional Web resources and Interactive Tutor Puzzles are also available.

Chapter 31 Resources

SECTION RESOURCES

Daily Objectives	Reproducible Resources	Multimedia Resources
SECTION 1 **The Student Movement and the Counterculture** 1. Explain the origins of the nation's youth movement. 2. Define the goals of serious members of the counterculture.	Reproducible Lesson Plan 31–1 Daily Lecture and Discussion Notes 31–1 Guided Reading Activity 31–1* Section Quiz 31–1* Reading Essentials and Study Guide 31–1 Performance Assessment Activities and Rubrics	Daily Focus Skills Transparency 31–1 American Art & Architecture Interactive Tutor Self-Assessment CD-ROM ExamView® Pro Testmaker CD-ROM Presentation Plus! CD-ROM TeacherWorks™ CD-ROM Audio Program American Music: Hits Through History
SECTION 2 **The Feminist Movement** 1. Describe the workplace concerns that fueled the growth of the women's movement. 2. Identify major achievements of the women's movement.	Reproducible Lesson Plan 31–2 Daily Lecture and Discussion Notes 31–2 Guided Reading Activity 31–2* Section Quiz 31–2* Reading Essentials and Study Guide 31–2 Performance Assessment Activities and Rubrics Interpreting Political Cartoons Supreme Court Case Studies	Daily Focus Skills Transparency 31–2 Interactive Tutor Self-Assessment CD-ROM ExamView® Pro Testmaker CD-ROM Presentation Plus! CD-ROM TeacherWorks™ CD-ROM Audio Program
SECTION 3 **New Approaches to Civil Rights** 1. Describe the goal of affirmative action policies. 2. Analyze the rise of Hispanic and Native American protests.	Reproducible Lesson Plan 31–3 Daily Lecture and Discussion Notes 31–3 Guided Reading Activity 31–3* Section Quiz 31–3* Reading Essentials and Study Guide 31–3 Performance Assessment Activities and Rubrics Interpreting Political Cartoons Supreme Court Case Studies	Daily Focus Skills Transparency 31–3 Interactive Tutor Self-Assessment CD-ROM ExamView® Pro Testmaker CD-ROM Presentation Plus! CD-ROM Skillbuilder Interactive Workbook, Level 2 TeacherWorks™ CD-ROM Audio Program
SECTION 4 **Saving the Earth** 1. Explain the origins of the environmental movement. 2. Identify the significant measures taken to combat environmental problems.	Reproducible Lesson Plan 31–4 Daily Lecture and Discussion Notes 31–4 Guided Reading Activity 31–4* Section Quiz 31–4* Reading Essentials and Study Guide 31–4 Performance Assessment Activities and Rubrics Interpreting Political Cartoons	Daily Focus Skills Transparency 31–4 American Art & Architecture Interactive Tutor Self-Assessment CD-ROM ExamView® Pro Testmaker CD-ROM Presentation Plus! CD-ROM TeacherWorks™ CD-ROM Vocabulary PuzzleMaker CD-ROM Audio Program American Music: Hits Through History American Music: Cultural Traditions

0:00 OUT OF TIME?
Assign the Chapter 31 **Reading Essentials and Study Guide.**

*Also Available in Spanish

 Blackline Master   Transparency   CD-ROM   DVD

 Poster   Music Program   Audio Program   Videocassette

918C

NATIONAL GEOGRAPHIC Teacher's Corner

INDEX TO NATIONAL GEOGRAPHIC MAGAZINE

The following articles relate to this chapter.

ADDITIONAL NATIONAL GEOGRAPHIC SOCIETY PRODUCTS

To order the following, call National Geographic at 1-800-368-2728:

- *Branches of Government Series* (Video)
- *The Complete National Geographic: 109 Years of National Geographic Magazine* (CD-ROM)
- *Democratic Government Series: The United States* (Video)
- *National Geographic World Atlas for Young Explorers— Classroom Library Edition* (Guide, Transparencies, Resource Masters)

NGS ONLINE

Access National Geographic's Web site for current events, atlas updates, activities, links, interactive features, and archives.
www.nationalgeographic.com

From the Classroom of...

Daniel Levinson Wilk
District 78, New York City
Board of Education
New York, NY

Setting Goals

In preparation, have students read about social movements of the late 1960s and early 1970s. Assign each student a person from the reading and ask them to come to class in character. There should be a variety of characters: conservatives, liberals, and radicals.

In class, ask students to put on name tags and introduce themselves, each saying their name and describing their positions on major issues of the day. Then give them these directions: "Stand up, mill around, and talk to the other characters in the room. Decide whom you think you could build a political movement with. Sit down with them and build a set of goals for your movement and a strategy to achieve them." Allow at least 20 minutes for this.

Then call the students back into a larger group. Have one member of each movement present their goals and strategy, and allow other students (in character) to question the members of that movement. For the last few minutes of class, have students step out of character to discuss the exercise.

ADDITIONAL RESOURCES FROM GLENCOE

- American Music: Cultural Traditions
- American Art & Architecture
- Outline Map Resource Book
- U.S. Desk Map
- Building Geography Skills for Life
- Inclusion for the High School Social Studies Classroom Strategies and Activities
- Teaching Strategies for the American History Classroom (Including Block Scheduling Pacing Guides)

KEY TO ABILITY LEVELS

Teaching strategies have been coded.

- **L1** BASIC activities for all students
- **L2** AVERAGE activities for average to above-average students
- **L3** CHALLENGING activities for above-average students
- **ELL** ENGLISH LANGUAGE LEARNER activities

 ### Block Schedule

Activities that are suited to use within the block scheduling framework are identified by:

Performance Assessment

Refer to Activity 31 in the Performance Assessment Activities and Rubrics booklet.

Why It Matters Activity

Have students make a prediction about how the efforts of the protesters in the 1960s and 1970s continue to influence the workplace and economic opportunities of women and ethnic groups today. Students should evaluate their answers after they have completed the chapter.

GLENCOE
TECHNOLOGY

The *American Vision* Video Program

To learn more about César Chávez, have students view the Chapter 31 video, "Behind the Scenes with César," from the *American Vision* Video Program.

Available in DVD and VHS

MindJogger Videoquiz

Use the **MindJogger Videoquiz** to preview Chapter 31 content.

 Available in VHS

31 The Politics of Protest *1960–1980*

Why It Matters

Protest characterized the 1960s. Young people often led the civil rights and antiwar movements. Some of them wanted to change the entire society and urged more communal, less materialistic values. Young people were not the only protesters, however. Using the civil rights movement as a model, women, Hispanic Americans, and Native Americans also organized to gain greater recognition and equality.

The Impact Today

Changes of the 1960s still affect our lives today.
- *Women are visible in many more leadership roles in government and business.*
- *Hispanic political organizations represent a growing segment of the population.*
- *The cultural traditions of Native Americans receive greater recognition.*

The American Vision Video The Chapter 31 video, "Behind the Scenes with César," profiles the role that César Chávez played in the United Farm Workers organization.

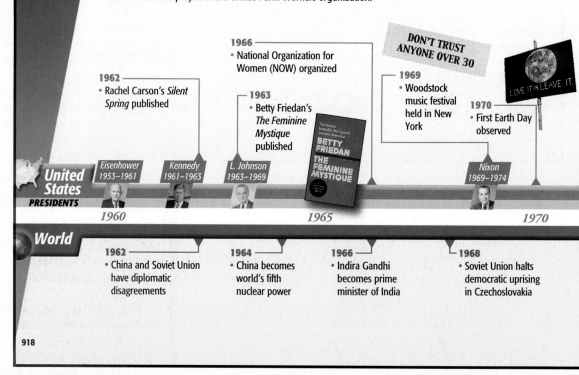

1962
- Rachel Carson's *Silent Spring* published

1966
- National Organization for Women (NOW) organized

1963
- Betty Friedan's *The Feminine Mystique* published

1969
- Woodstock music festival held in New York

1970
- First Earth Day observed

DON'T TRUST ANYONE OVER 30

LOVE IT OR LEAVE IT.

United States PRESIDENTS

Eisenhower 1953–1961

Kennedy 1961–1963

L. Johnson 1963–1969

Nixon 1969–1974

1960 · 1965 · 1970

World

1962
- China and Soviet Union have diplomatic disagreements

1964
- China becomes world's fifth nuclear power

1966
- Indira Gandhi becomes prime minister of India

1968
- Soviet Union halts democratic uprising in Czechoslovakia

918

TWO-MINUTE LESSON LAUNCHER

Have students work as a group to come up with a list of the qualities of a leader. Record their responses on the board. Tell students that in this chapter, various groups began to reevaluate the limits that American society placed on them. Some strong leaders emerged to organize the resulting protest efforts. Have students modify their lists as they read the chapter and learn about these leaders.

Labor leader César Chávez meeting with farmworkers

HISTORY Online

Introduce students to chapter content and key terms by having them access the **Chapter 31 Overview** at tav.glencoe.com.

More About the Photo

César Chávez was born in 1927, on a small farm near Yuma, Arizona. When his father lost his land during the Depression, Chávez began working as a migrant farmworker to help support the family. After serving in the navy during World War II, he returned to farm labor. Soon he became committed to improving the lives of farmworkers. For his leadership, he received the Presidential Medal of Freedom.

1972
• Use of pesticide DDT banned

1973
• Supreme Court issues *Roe* v. *Wade* ruling
• AIM and government clash at Wounded Knee, South Dakota

1979
• Nuclear accident at Three Mile Island

Ford 1974–1977
Carter 1977–1981

1975   *1980*

1972
• Britain imposes direct rule on Northern Ireland

1975
• End of the Portuguese empires in Africa

1979
• Ayatollah Khomeini leads Islamic overthrow of Iran

HISTORY Online

Chapter Overview
Visit the *American Vision* Web site at tav.glencoe.com and click on *Chapter Overviews—Chapter 31* to preview chapter information.

TIME LINE ACTIVITY

Have students classify each of the relevant events on the United States portion of the time line as connected with the efforts of one of the following groups: Hispanics, women, environmentalists, or Native Americans.

919

GRAPHIC ORGANIZER ACTIVITY

Organizing Information Have students use graphic organizers similar to the one below to identify the causes and effects of each of the major movements discussed in the chapter.

Cause	Native American Rights Movement	Effect
• *threats to cultural identity* • *joblessness* • *discrimination*	→	• *Indian Civil Rights Act* • *Indian Self-Determination and Educational Assistance Act* • *increased land and water rights*

1 FOCUS

Section Overview

This section focuses on student protests in the 1960s.

 Project transparency and have students answer the question.

Available as a blackline master.

Daily Focus Skills Transparency 31–1

Guide to Reading

Answers to Graphic:
I. The Growth of the Youth Movement
   A. The Roots of the Movement
   B. Students for a Democratic Society
   C. The Free Speech Movement
II. The Counterculture
   A. Hippie Culture
   B. New Religious Movements
   C. The Counterculture Declines
III. Impact of the Counterculture
   A. Fashion
   B. Art
   C. Music and Dance

Preteaching Vocabulary
Have students write short sentences to describe each of the Key Terms and Names.

The Student Movement and the Counterculture

Guide to Reading

Main Idea
During the 1960s, many of the country's young people raised their voices in protest against numerous aspects of American society.

Key Terms and Names
Port Huron Statement, Tom Hayden, counterculture, commune, Haight-Ashbury district, Jimi Hendrix

Reading Strategy
Taking Notes As you read about the student movement and culture of the 1960s, use the major headings of the section to create an outline similar to the one below.

The Student Movement and the Counterculture
I. The Growth of the Youth Movement
   A.
   B.
   C.
II.
   A.
   B.

Reading Objectives
• **Explain** the origins of the nation's youth movement.
• **Define** the goals of serious members of the counterculture.

Section Theme
Government and Democracy Although protest movements often challenged the opinions and values of many Americans, the courts protected the protesters' rights of self-expression under the Constitution.

Preview of Events

| 1961 | 1964 | 1967 | 1970 |

1962
Students for a Democratic Society deliver Port Huron Statement

1964
Free Speech Movement begins; the Beatles embark on their first U.S. tour

August, 1969
400,000 young people gather at Woodstock music festival

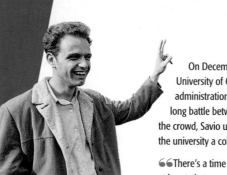

★ **An American Story** ★

On December 2, 1964, Mario Savio, a 20-year-old philosophy student at the University of California at Berkeley, stood before a supportive crowd at the school's administration building. The massive "sit-in" demonstration was the climax of a month-long battle between school officials and students over unpopular campus policies. Facing the crowd, Savio urged them to continue pressuring school officials. In his speech he called the university a cold and heartless "machine" that deserved to be shut down.

❝There's a time when the operation of the machine becomes so odious, makes you so sick at heart, that you . . . can't even tacitly take part," he declared. "And you've got to put your bodies upon the gears and upon the wheels . . . you've got to make it stop. And you've got to indicate to the people who run it, to the people who own it, that unless you're free the machine will be prevented from working at all.❞

Mario Savio

—quoted in *Decade of Shocks*

The Growth of the Youth Movement

The 1960s was one of the most tumultuous and chaotic decades in United States history. The decade also gave birth to a conspicuous youth movement, which challenged the American political and social system and conventional middle-class values. Perhaps no other time in the nation's history witnessed such protest.

920 CHAPTER 31 The Politics of Protest

SECTION RESOURCES

Reproducible Masters
• Reproducible Lesson Plan 31–1
• Daily Lecture and Discussion Notes 31–1
• Guided Reading Activity 31–1
• Section Quiz 31–1
• Reading Essentials and Study Guide 31–1
• Performance Assessment Activities and Rubrics

Transparencies
• Daily Focus Skills Transparency 31–1

Multimedia
◉ Interactive Tutor Self-Assessment CD-ROM
◉ ExamView® Pro Testmaker CD-ROM
◉ Presentation Plus! CD-ROM
◉ TeacherWorks™ CD-ROM
◉ Audio Program

The Roots of the Movement The roots of the 1960s youth movement stretched back to the 1950s. In the decade after World War II, the nation's economy boomed, and much of the country enjoyed a time of peace and prosperity. Prosperity did not extend to all, however, and some, especially the artists and writers of the "beat" movement, had openly criticized American society. They believed it valued conformity over independence and financial gain over spiritual and social advancement. Meanwhile, such events as the growing nuclear arms race between the United States and the Soviet Union made many more of the nation's youth uneasy about their future. Writer Todd Gitlin, who was a senior at the Bronx High School of Science in 1959, recalls the warning that the editors of his student yearbook delivered.

> ❝In today's atomic age . . . the flames of war would write *finis* not only to our civilization, but to our very existence. Mankind may find itself unable to rise again should it be consumed in a nuclear pyre of its own making. In the years to come, members of this class will bear an ever-increasing responsibility for the preservation of the heritage given us.❞
> —from *The Sixties*

Concern about the future led many young people to become more active in social causes, from the civil rights movement to President Kennedy's Peace Corps. The emergence of the youth movement grew out of the huge numbers of people of the postwar "baby boom" generation. By 1970, 58.4 percent of the American population was 34 years old or younger. (By comparison, those 34 or younger in 2000 represented an estimated 48.9 percent.)

The early 1960s saw another phenomenon that fueled the youth movement—the rapid increase in enrollment at colleges throughout the nation. The economic boom of the 1950s led to a boom in higher education, since more families could afford to send their children to college. Between 1960 and 1966, enrollment in 4-year institutions rose from 3.1 million to almost 5 million

students. College life empowered young people with a newfound sense of freedom and independence. It also allowed them to meet and bond with others who shared their feelings about society and fears about the future. It was on college campuses across the nation where the protest movements would rage the loudest.

Students for a Democratic Society Some youths were concerned most about the injustices they saw in the country's political and social system. In their view, a few wealthy elites controlled politics, and wealth itself was unfairly divided. These young people formed what came to be known as the New Left. (The "new" left differed from the "old" left of the 1930s, which had advocated socialism and communism.) A prominent organization of this group was the **Students for a Democratic Society** (SDS). It defined its views in a 1962 declaration known as the **Port Huron Statement.** Written largely by **Tom Hayden,** editor of the University of Michigan's student newspaper, the declaration called for an end to apathy and urged citizens to stop accepting a country run by big corporations and big government.

SDS groups focused on protesting the Vietnam War, but they also addressed such issues as poverty, campus regulations, nuclear power, and racism.

DON'T TRUST ANYONE OVER 30

Picturing **History**

Youth Movement The Students for a Democratic Society (SDS) worked to address many of the problems they saw in the 1960s. Made up primarily of college students, the group was suspicious of the motives of adults. Where did the SDS begin its reform crusade?

CHAPTER 31   The Politics of Protest   **921**

2 TEACH

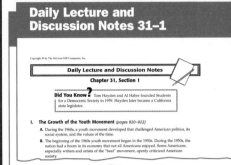

Daily Lecture and Discussion Notes 31–1

Copyright © The McGraw-Hill Companies, Inc.

Daily Lecture and Discussion Notes

Chapter 31, Section 1

Did You Know? Tom Hayden and Al Haber founded Students for a Democratic Society in 1959. Hayden later became a California state legislator.

I. The Growth of the Youth Movement *(pages 920–922)*

  A. During the 1960s, a youth movement developed that challenged American politics, its social system, and the values of the time.

  B. The beginning of the 1960s youth movement began in the 1950s. During the 1950s, the nation had a boom in economy that not all Americans enjoyed. Some Americans, especially writers and artists of the "beat" movement, openly criticized American society.

Discussing a Topic Have students discuss the causes of the 1960s generation gap and whether there is a generation gap today. If they believe there is, ask them to identify its causes. **L1**

Picturing **History**

Answer: University of Michigan

CURRICULUM CONNECTION

Mathematics In 1955 young people ages 15 to 19 made up 7 percent of the population—11,185,000 out of a total population of 165,248,000. By 1965 the percentage had increased to 9 percent—17,052,000 out of a total population of 194,583,000. The increase reflects the years when baby boomers were teenagers.

COOPERATIVE LEARNING ACTIVITY

Researching a Topic Organize the class into small research groups to investigate student protests on college campuses during 1968. Groups should choose a particular incident to study and report their findings to the class. Students should include what the protest was about, how many people took part, and any reform that resulted from it.

Use the rubric for a cooperative group management plan on pages 81–82 in the *Performance Assessment Activities and Rubrics.*

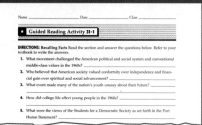
Organizing Information Have students create a chart illustrating the similarities and differences between the hippie culture of the 1960s and current countercultures. Suggest that they focus on these questions: What is the issue? What is the goal? What are the outward signs of the movement? **L2**

Use the rubric for creating a map, display, or chart on pages 77–78 in the *Performance Assessment Activities and Rubrics.*

Picturing History

Answer: San Francisco, California
Ask: What were some of the outward signs that defined the hippie movement? *(Students' answers will vary. They might mention long hair, headbands, cowboy boots, long dresses, shabby jeans, and drug use.)*

Reading Check

Answer: concern about future, increased college enrollment, injustices in the political and social system

---

Picturing History

The Counterculture Commonly known as "hippies," members of the counterculture separated themselves from society in the 1960s by trying to create their own culture of love and tolerance. What western city was a focal point of the hippie culture?

In 1968, for example, SDS leaders assisted in an eight-day occupation of several buildings at Columbia University in New York City to protest the administration's plan to build a new gym in an area that served as a neighborhood park near Harlem.

The Free Speech Movement Another group of protesters who captured the nation's attention were members of the Free Speech Movement, led by **Mario Savio** and others at the University of California at Berkeley. The issue that sparked the movement was the university's decision in the fall of 1964 to restrict students' rights to distribute literature and to recruit volunteers for political causes on campus. The protesters, however, quickly targeted more general campus matters and drew in more and more supporters.

Like many college students, those at Berkeley were disgruntled with the practices at their university. Officials divided huge classes into sections taught by graduate students, while many professors claimed they were too busy with research to meet with students. Faceless administrators made rules that were not always easy to obey and imposed punishments for violations. Isolated in this impersonal environment, many Berkeley students found a purpose in the Free Speech Movement.

The struggle between school administrators and students peaked on December 2, 1964, with the sit-in and Savio's famous speech at the administration

building. Early the next morning, California Governor Pat Brown sent in 600 police officers to break up the demonstration. Police arrested more than 700 protesters.

The arrests set off a new and even larger protest movement. Within a few days, thousands of Berkeley students participated in a campus-wide strike, stopping classes for two days. Much of the faculty also voiced its support for the Free Speech Movement. In the face of this growing opposition, the administration gave in to the students' demands shortly before the Christmas recess.

The following week, the Supreme Court validated the students' First Amendment rights to freedom of speech and assembly on campus. In a unanimous vote, the Court upheld the section of the Civil Rights Act assuring these rights in places offering public accommodations, which, by definition, included college campuses. The Berkeley revolt was one of the earliest outbursts in a decade of campus turmoil. The tactics the protesters used there—abandoning classes and occupying buildings—would serve as a model for college demonstrators across the country.

Reading Check

Synthesizing What were three reasons for the growth of the youth movement of the 1960s?

The Counterculture

While a number of young Americans in the 1960s sought to challenge the system, others wanted to leave it and build their own society. Throughout the decade, thousands of mostly white youths turned away from their middle- and upper-class existence and created a new lifestyle—one that promoted the virtues of flamboyant dress, rock music, drug use, and free and independent living. With their alternative ways of life, these young men and women formed what became known as the counterculture and were commonly called "hippies."

Hippie Culture Originally, hippie culture represented a rebellion against the dominant culture in the United States. This included a rejection of Western civilization, of rationality, order, and the traditional values of the middle class. At its core, the counterculture held up a utopian ideal: the ideal of a society that was freer, closer to nature, and full of love, empathy, tolerance, and cooperation. Much of this was in reaction to the 1950s American stereotype of the man in the gray flannel suit who led a constricted and colorless life.

MEETING SPECIAL NEEDS

Visual/Spatial Help students who are visual learners determine the main idea of the section by having them look at and think about all the visuals. They should consider the overall impression and then study the details. In pairs, students can discuss what the visuals tell them about the counterculture. Encourage students to use drawings and symbols in their notebooks to help them when they study for a quiz or test. **L1**

Refer to *Inclusion for the High School Social Studies Classroom Strategies and Activities* in the TCR.

When the movement grew larger, many of the newcomers did not always understand these original ideas of the counterculture. For them, what mattered were the outward signs that defined the movement—long hair, Native American headbands, cowboy boots, long dresses, shabby jeans, and the use of drugs such as marijuana and LSD. Drug use, especially, came to be associated with the hippie culture.

Many hippies desired to literally drop out of society by leaving home and living together with other youths in communes—group living arrangements in which members shared everything and worked together. A number of hippies established communes in small and rural communities, while others lived together in parks or crowded apartments in the nation's large cities. One of the most popular hippie destinations became San Francisco's **Haight-Ashbury district.** By the mid-1960s, thousands of hippies had flocked there.

New Religious Movements In their rejection of materialism, many members of the counterculture embraced spirituality. This included a broad range of beliefs, from astrology and magic to Eastern religions and new forms of Christianity.

Many of the religious groups centered around authoritarian leaders. In these groups, the leader dominated others and controlled their lives, sometimes to the point of arranging marriages between members. Religion became the central experience in the believer's life. The authoritarian figure was a sort of parent figure, and believers formed an extended family that took the place of the family into which a member had been born. This could lead to painful conflicts. Some parents accused religious sects of using mind-control methods; some attempted to recapture and "deprogram" their children.

Two new religious groups that attracted considerable attention beginning in the 1960s were the **Unification Church** and the **Hare Krishna** movement. Both were offshoots of established religions, and both came from abroad. Members of the Unification Church were popularly known as "Moonies," after their Korean-born founder, the Reverend Sun Myung Moon. He claimed to have had a vision in which Jesus told Moon that he was the next messiah and was charged with restoring the Kingdom of God on Earth. The Hare Krishnas traced their spiritual lineage to a Hindu sect that began in India in the 1400s and worshiped the god Krishna. In dress, diet, worship, and general style of living, Hare Krishnas tried to emulate these Hindu practitioners of another time and place.

The Counterculture Declines After a few years, the counterculture movement began to deteriorate. Some hippie communities in the cities soon turned into seedy and dangerous places where muggings and other criminal activity became all too frequent. The glamour and excitement of drug use soon waned, especially as more and more young people became addicted or died from overdoses. In addition, a number of the people involved in the movement had gotten older and moved on in life. Upon witnessing the decline of Haight-Ashbury, one writer dismissed the one-time booming urban commune as "the desperate attempt of a handful of pathetically unequipped children to create a community out of a social vacuum." In the end, most of the young men and women of the counterculture, unable to establish an ideal community and unable to support themselves, gradually returned to mainstream society.

✓ **Reading Check** **Summarizing** What were the core ideals of members of the counterculture?

Impact of the Counterculture

In the long run, the counterculture did change American life in some ways. Over time, mainstream America accepted many of these changes.

Fashion The counterculture generation, as one observer of the 1960s noted, dressed in costumes rather than in occupational or class uniforms. The colorful, beaded, braided, patched, and fringed garments that both men and women wore turned the fashion industry upside down. The international fashion world took its cues from young men and

Fact	Fiction	Folklore

New 1960s Words During the 1960s, Americans coined a host of new words and phrases. The word *hippie*, used to describe members of the counterculture, probably originated from the 1930s term *hep*, for "those in the know." Other people believe *hippie* may have evolved from the 1950s word *hipster*, which referred to members of the beatnik movement.

Hippies themselves introduced a few terms to the country. They often uttered the phrase *far out* to indicate anything that was very good or very bad. Individuals who rejected the free-living counterculture lifestyle were considered *straight* or *square.*

CHAPTER 31   The Politics of Protest   **923**

FYI

Moonies were married in mass wedding ceremonies known as "Blessings." Rev. Moon and his wife presided over the ceremonies. Moonies believed that blessed couples would have sinless children.

✓**Reading Check**

Answer: a society that was freer, closer to nature, and full of love, empathy, tolerance, and cooperation

Fact	Fiction	Folklore

In addition to the language of the counterculture, there was a look. Counterculture youth liked to borrow clothing styles from other cultures, especially from cultures that were less involved with mass industry than the United States. Popular styles were colorful patterned pullover shirts, or dashikis from Africa, and paisley designs from India and Persia.

History *and the* Humanities

🎵 American Music: Hits Through History: "Blowin' in the Wind," "Turn, Turn, Turn"

🖼 American Art & Architecture: *Map*

INTERDISCIPLINARY CONNECTIONS ACTIVITY

Performing Arts Organize the class into three or four groups and have each prepare a skit on one of the situations below. Encourage all students to participate and have each group present their skit to the rest of the class. **L2**

• A group of friends deciding whether to participate in an antiwar or a pro-war rally
• A member of the SDS speaking at a meeting of university officials
• A college student trying to explain the counterculture to his or her parents

3 ASSESS

Assign Section 1 Assessment as homework or as an in-class activity.

🌐 Have students use the **Interactive Tutor Self-Assessment CD-ROM.**

Reading Essentials and Study Guide 31–1

Name _____ Date _____ Class _____

Study Guide

Chapter 31, Section 1
For use with textbook pages 920–925

THE STUDENT MOVEMENT AND THE COUNTERCULTURE

KEY TERMS AND NAMES

Port Huron Statement declaration by the Students for a Democratic Society that called for citizens to stop accepting a country run by big corporations and big government *(page 921)*

Tom Hayden author of the Port Huron Statement *(page 921)*

counterculture youth who adopted alternative ways of life *(page 922)*

communes group living arrangements in which members shared everything and worked together *(page 923)*

Haight-Ashbury district a popular hippie destination in San Francisco *(page 923)*

Jimi Hendrix musician who was a master at the electrically amplified guitar *(page 925)*

Section Quiz 31–1

Name _____ Date _____ Class _____

⭐ **Chapter 31** | Score _____

Section Quiz 31–1

DIRECTIONS: Matching Match each item in Column A with the items in Column B. Write the correct letters in the blanks. *(10 points each)*

Column A

____ 1. one of the most famous rock 'n' roll groups

____ 2. derived its subject matter from elements of the popular culture

____ 3. defined the views of the Students for a Democratic Society

____ 4. group living arrangements in which members shared everything and worked together

____ 5. young men and women with alternative ways of life, commonly called "hippies"

Column B

A. counterculture

B. Port Huron Statement

C. pop art

D. The Beatles

E. communes

DIRECTIONS: Multiple Choice In the blank at the left, write the letter of the choice

NATIONAL GEOGRAPHIC MOMENT in HISTORY

Most Woodstock festival-goers were white, middle- or upper-class, and between 16 and 30 years of age.

---

women on the street. As a result, men's clothing became more colorful, and women's clothing became more comfortable.

Protesters often expressed themselves with their clothing. The counterculture adopted military surplus attire not only because it was inexpensive, but also because it expressed rejection of materialist values and blurred the lines of social class. For the same reasons, clothing of another age was recycled, and worn-out clothing was repaired with patches. Ethnic clothing was popular for similar reasons. Beads and fringes imitated Native American costumes, while tie-dyed shirts borrowed techniques from India and Africa.

Perhaps the most potent symbol of the era was hair. A popular 1967 musical about the period was titled, fittingly, *Hair.* Long hair on a young man was the ultimate symbol of defiance. Slogans appeared, such as "Make America beautiful—give a hippie a haircut." School officials debated the acceptable length of a student's hair—could it curl over the collar or not? Once the initial shock wore off, however, longer hair on men and more individual clothing for both genders became generally accepted. What was once clothing of defiance was now mainstream.

Art During the 1960s, one art critic observed, the distinctions between traditional art and popular art, or **pop art,** dissolved. Pop art derived its subject matter from elements of popular culture, such as photographs, comic books, advertisements, and brandname products. Artist **Andy Warhol,** for example, used images of famous people, such as Marilyn Monroe and Elizabeth Taylor, and repeated them over and over. Warhol also reproduced items such as cans of soup, making the pictures as realistic as possible. Roy Lichtenstein used frames from comic strips as his inspirations. He employed the bold primary colors of red, yellow, and black, and put words like *blam* and *pow* into his paintings in comic book fashion.

Pop artists expected these symbols of popular culture to carry some of the same meaning as they did in their original form. The artists sometimes referred to themselves as only the "agents" of the art and said it

NATIONAL GEOGRAPHIC
MOMENT in HISTORY

WOODSTOCK NATION

In August 1969, more than 400,000 young people descended on a 600-acre farm in upstate New York for what was billed as "three days of peace and music." Organizers of the Woodstock Music and Art Fair were overwhelmed by the turnout. Massive traffic jams, supply shortages, inadequate first aid and sanitation facilities, and torrential rainfall did not dampen the joyous spirit of the crowd. People shared their food and blankets, bathed in the rain, and listened to an amazing collection of some of the greatest musicians of the 1960s.

924   CHAPTER 31   The Politics of Protest

CRITICAL THINKING ACTIVITY

Comparing Ask students to discuss today's hairstyles, fashions, and music. **Ask:** Do they reflect any of the trends of the 1960s? What messages do today's styles send? Ask students to speculate why some members of the 1960s counterculture are now part of mainstream society. **L2**

was up to the observer to give meaning to the work and thus become part of it.

Music and Dance Counterculture musicians hoped that their music, rock 'n' roll, would be the means of toppling the establishment and reforming society. This did not happen because rock music was absorbed into the mainstream, where it brought material success worth billions of dollars to performers, promoters, and record companies.

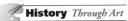
History *Through Art*

Pop Art Artists like Roy Lichtenstein mocked certain aspects of American life by using common examples of commercial art, such as comics and advertisements. What statement is this piece of art making?

One of the most famous rock groups, the **Beatles,** took the country by storm in 1964. "Beatlemania" later swept the country, inspiring hundreds of other rock 'n' roll groups both in Great Britain and the United States.

Many of the new groups combined rock 'n' roll rhythms with lyrics that expressed the fears and hopes of the new generation and the widening rift between them and their parents. **Bob Dylan** provided these lyrics, as did the Beatles and many other musicians, while spirited performers like Janis Joplin made the songs come alive.

The use of electrically amplified instruments also drastically changed the sound and feel of the new music. One master of this new sound was **Jimi Hendrix,** a guitarist from Seattle. Hendrix lived overseas and achieved stardom only after returning to the United States with the influx of musicians from Great Britain. His innovative guitar playing continues to influence musicians today.

At festivals such as **Woodstock,** in upstate New York in August 1969, and Altamont, California, later that year, hundreds of thousands of people got together to celebrate the new music. Though the fast-paced, energetic beat of rock 'n' roll was made for dancing, the style of dancing had changed dramatically. Each person danced without a partner, surrounded by others who also danced alone—a perfect metaphor for the counterculture, which stressed individuality within the group.

Headline-grabbing events such as Woodstock made it difficult for the nation to ignore the youth movement. By this time, however, other groups in society were also raising their voices in protest. For example, many women began renewing their generations-old efforts for equality, hoping to expand upon the successes gained during the early 1900s.

Reading Check **Evaluating** What lasting impact did the counterculture have on the nation?

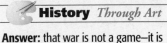
History *Through Art*

Answer: that war is not a game—it is destructive and dangerous
Ask: What characterized pop art? *(It used popular culture for its subject matter, and it expected the symbols of popular culture to carry the same meaning as they did in their original form. They encouraged the observer to become part of the art through their interpretation of it.)*

Reading Check

Answer: changes in fashion, music, dance, and the idea that alternatives to mainstream culture were possible

Reteach
Have students explain the origins of the nation's youth movement.

Enrich
Invite interested students to use library and Internet resources to learn more about the health food movement that began in the 1960s.

4 CLOSE

Have students define the goals of serious members of the counterculture.

SECTION 1 ASSESSMENT

Checking for Understanding
1. **Define:** counterculture, commune.
2. **Identify:** Port Huron Statement, Tom Hayden, Haight-Ashbury district, Jimi Hendrix.
3. **Summarize** two legacies of the counterculture movement.

Reviewing Themes
4. **Government and Democracy** How did the U.S. Supreme Court validate the actions of the members of the Free Speech Movement?

Critical Thinking
5. **Contrasting** How were hippies different from members of the New Left?
6. **Analyzing** Why did the counterculture movement decline?
7. **Organizing** Use a graphic organizer similar to the one below to list the causes of the youth movement.

Causes → Youth Movement

Analyzing Visuals
8. **Analyzing Photographs** Look closely at the photograph of a group of hippies and their bus on page 922. How does the bus itself represent values of the counterculture?

Writing About History
9. **Descriptive Writing** Imagine you are a journalist in the 1960s. Write an article in which you visit a commune and describe the hippie culture you see.

SECTION 1 ASSESSMENT ANSWERS

1. Terms are in blue.
2. Port Huron Statement *(p. 921)*, Tom Hayden *(p. 921)*, Haight-Ashbury district *(p. 923)*, Jimi Hendrix *(p. 925)*
3. It contributed new styles of popular culture and encouraged greater self-expression.
4. It upheld the right to freedom of speech and assembly on campus.
5. Hippies were more interested in creating a utopian lifestyle than in political protest.
6. Many participants were unable to establish an ideal community or support themselves.
7. concern about the future; "baby boom"; social injustice
8. colorful, individualized appearance, communal transport
9. Students' articles will vary. Articles should include descriptions of what a journalist might have seen.

SECTION 2 The Feminist Movement

Guide to Reading

Main Idea
During the 1960s and 1970s, a large number of American women organized to push for greater rights and opportunities in society.

Key Terms and Names
feminism, Equal Pay Act, Equal Employment Opportunity Commission, Betty Friedan, National Organization for Women, Title IX, Phyllis Schlafly

Reading Strategy
Categorizing As you read about the women's movement, use a graphic organizer similar to the one below to compare the ideas of the two organizations that formed when the women's movement split.

Organization	Ideas

Reading Objectives
- **Describe** the workplace concerns that fueled the growth of the women's movement.
- **Identify** major achievements of the women's movement.

Section Theme
Civic Rights and Responsibilities
Women organized to claim their rights and responsibilities as citizens and employees.

Preview of Events

| 1963 | 1970 | 1977 | 1984 |

1963
Betty Friedan's *The Feminine Mystique* published

1966
Women activists form NOW

1973
Roe v. *Wade* decision ensures abortion rights

1982
Equal Rights Amendment fails

---

1 FOCUS

Section Overview
This section focuses on the push for greater rights and opportunities for American women.

BELLRINGER
Skillbuilder Activity

Project transparency and have students answer the question.

Available as a blackline master.

Daily Focus Skills Transparency 31–2

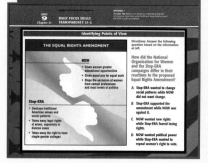

Guide to Reading

Answers to Graphic: League of Women Voters: promoted laws to protect women and children; National Woman's Party: opposed protective legislation

Preteaching Vocabulary
Have students write three questions that can be answered using the Key Terms and Names.

A 1960s-era women's magazine

★ An American Story ★

In 1960 the housewife-oriented magazine *Redbook* asked readers to send examples of "Why Young Mothers Feel Trapped." Some 24,000 women responded. One of them was Herma Snider, a housewife and mother of three in Nevada. Snider wrote that as a high school and college student, she had dreamed of a career in journalism. After getting married and having three children, that dream died.

"Cemented to my house by three young children," she wrote, "there were days in which I saw no adult human being except the milkman as he made his deliveries and spoke to no one from the time my husband left in the morning until he returned at night." She added, "Each night as I tucked my sons into bed, I thanked God that they would grow up to be *men*, that they would able to teach, write, heal, advise, travel, or do anything else they chose."

Desperate for greater fulfillment in her life, Snider eventually took a job as a part-time hotel clerk. About this decision, she said:

❝My cashier's job is not the glamorous career I once dreamed of. And I know that it can be said that my solution is not a solution at all, merely an escape. But it seems to me that when the demands of children and household threaten to suffocate you, an escape *is* a solution.❞

—quoted in *The Female Experience: An American Documentary*

A Weakened Women's Movement

Herma Snider was not alone. Although many women were content to be homemakers, by the early 1960s scores of them had grown dissatisfied with their roles. At the same time, those who worked outside the home were recognizing their unequal status

---

SECTION RESOURCES

📁 Reproducible Masters
- Reproducible Lesson Plan 31–2
- Daily Lecture and Discussion Notes 31–2
- Guided Reading Activity 31–2
- Section Quiz 31–2
- Reading Essentials and Study Guide 31–2
- Performance Assessment Activities and Rubrics

Transparencies
- Daily Focus Skills Transparency 31–2

Multimedia
- Interactive Tutor Self-Assessment CD-ROM
- ExamView® Pro Testmaker CD-ROM
- Presentation Plus! CD-ROM
- TeacherWorks™ CD-ROM
- Audio Program

as reflected in lower pay and fewer opportunities. These developments led to the rise of a new feminist movement in the 1960s.

Feminism, the belief that men and women should be equal politically, economically, and socially, had been a weak and often embattled force since the adoption of the Nineteenth Amendment guaranteeing women's voting rights in 1920. Soon after the amendment's passage, the women's movement split into two camps. One group, the League of Women Voters, tended to promote laws to protect women and children, such as limiting the hours they could work. The National Woman's Party (NWP), on the other hand, opposed protective legislation for women. The NWP believed it reinforced workplace discrimination. In 1923 the NWP persuaded members of Congress to introduce the first Equal Rights Amendment aimed at forbidding federal, state, and local laws from discriminating on the basis of gender. Since the women's movement was divided, however, Congress could afford to ignore the amendment.

The onset of World War II provided women with greater opportunity, at least temporarily. With many men enlisted in the army, women became an integral part of the nation's workforce. When the war ended, however, many women lost their jobs to the returning men.

Despite having to return to their domestic work, many women gradually reentered the labor market. By 1960 they made up almost one-third of the nation's workforce. Yet many people continued to believe that women, even college-educated women, could better serve society by remaining in the home to influence the next generation of men.

 **Reading Check** **Examining** How did World War II affect women?

The Women's Movement Reawakens

By the early 1960s, many women were increasingly resentful of a world where newspaper ads separated jobs by gender, clubs refused them memberships, banks denied them credit, and, worst of all, they often were paid less for the same work. Generally, women found themselves shut out of higher-paying and prestigious professions such as law, medicine, and finance. Although about 47 percent of American women were in the workforce in the 1960s, three-fourths of them worked in lower paying and routine clerical, sales, or factory jobs, or

as cleaning women and hospital attendants. As more women entered the workforce, the protest against inequities grew louder.

Women had also gained a better understanding of their inequality in society from their experiences in the civil rights and antiwar movements. Often they were restricted to menial tasks and rarely had a say in any policy decisions. From the broader perspective, the women's movement was part of the 1960s quest for rights.

GOVERNMENT

Fighting for Workplace Rights Two forces helped bring the women's movement to life again. One was the mass protest of ordinary women. The second was a government initiative: the **President's Commission on the Status of Women,** established by President Kennedy and headed by Eleanor Roosevelt. The commission's report highlighted the problems of women in the workplace and helped create networks of feminist activists, who lobbied Congress for women's legislation. In 1963, with the support of labor, they won passage of the **Equal Pay Act,** which in most cases outlawed paying men more than women for the same job.

Congress gave women another boost by including them in the 1964 Civil Rights Act, a measure originally designed to fight racial bias. **Title VII** of the act outlawed job discrimination by private employers not only on the basis of race, color, religion, and

Perfect Home, Perfect Wife This image of a proud wife in her spotless kitchen reflects some of the traditional ideas of the 1950s and 1960s. *What did the women's movement criticize about these ideas?*

2 TEACH

Daily Lecture and Discussion Notes 31–2

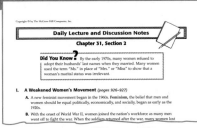

Daily Lecture and Discussion Notes
Chapter 31, Section 2

Did You Know? By the early 1970s, many women refused to adopt their husbands' last names when they married. Many women used the term "Ms." in place of "Mrs." or "Miss" to show that a woman's marital status was irrelevant.

I. A Weakened Women's Movement (pages 926–927)

  A. A new feminist movement began in the 1960s. Feminism, the belief that men and women should be equal politically, economically, and socially, began as early as the 1920s.

  B. With the onset of World War II, women joined the nation's workforce as many men went off to fight the war. When the soldiers returned after the war, many women lost

Discussing a Topic Have students discuss women's career choices today. Ask them if parents, teachers, counselors, and others steer women toward some careers and away from others. **L1**

 Reading Check

Answer: Many took jobs outside the home.

Picturing **History**

Answer: the idea that a woman's place was in the home

Use *Interpreting Political Cartoons,* Cartoon 30.

FYI

In the past many people lumped women together with minority groups, using references such as "women and other minorities." In fact, since 1950, women in the United States make up a little more than half the population.

COOPERATIVE LEARNING ACTIVITY

Analyzing Salary Differences Between Men and Women Organize the class into small groups of three or four students. Ask each group to choose a profession or line of work in which they think men and women earn equal pay. Ask them to research and graph the average salaries for male and female workers in that profession in five-year increments since 1955. Encourage students to use library and Internet resources. Have groups compare their graphs and discuss their findings.

Use the rubric for a cooperative group management plan on pages 81–82 in the *Performance Assessment Activities and Rubrics.*

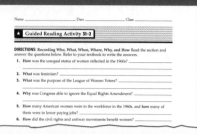
Picturing **History**

Answer: NOW (National Organization for Women)

Ask: Some people wrongly assumed that Friedan and other feminists were antifamily. How does this photo portray Friedan? *(as a caring mother)*

Creating a Chart Have students learn more about the roles of women in other cultures and countries in the 1960s and 1970s. Instruct students to create a chart to compare and contrast the roles of women in the country they have chosen with American women. **L2**

📁 Use the rubric for creating a map, display, or chart on pages 77–78 in the *Performance Assessment Activities and Rubrics.*

📁 Use *Supreme Court Case Study 46, Reed* v. *Reed.*

✓ Reading Check

Answer: the mass protest of ordinary women, and the President's Commission on the Status of Women

Picturing **History**

The Feminine Mystique Betty Friedan's best-selling book (right) exposed a sense of dissatisfaction that many women experienced but were reluctant to speak about openly. *What political organization stemmed from women's growing sense of unfulfillment?*

national origin, but also of gender. This measure became decisive legal basis for advances made by the women's movement.

Given prevailing attitudes about what kind of work was proper for women, change took time. Even the federal agency charged with administering the new law, the **Equal Employment Opportunity Commission** (EEOC), still held to the idea that jobs should be distinguished by gender. In August 1965, for example, the commission ruled that gender-segregated help-wanted ads were legal.

The Feminine Mystique Many date the women's movement from the publication of **Betty Friedan's** *The Feminine Mystique* in 1963. Friedan had traveled around the country interviewing the women who had graduated with her from Smith College in 1942. She found that while most of these women reported having everything they could want in life, they still felt unfulfilled. Friedan described these feelings in her book:

> ❝The problem lay buried, unspoken, for many years in the minds of American women. . . . Each suburban wife struggled with it alone. As she made the beds, shopped for groceries . . . chauffeured Cub Scouts and Brownies . . . she was afraid to ask even of herself the silent question—'Is this all?'❞
>
> —from *The Feminine Mystique*

928 CHAPTER 31 The Politics of Protest

Friedan's book became a best-seller. Many women soon began reaching out to one another, pouring out their anger and sadness in what came to be known as consciousness-raising sessions. While they talked informally about their unhappiness, they were building the base for a nationwide movement.

The Time Is NOW In June 1966, Friedan returned to a thought that she and others had been considering, the need for women to form a national organization. On the back of a napkin, she scribbled down her intentions "to take the actions needed to bring women into the mainstream of American society, now . . . in fully equal partnership with men." Friedan and others then set out to form the **National Organization for Women** (NOW).

NOW soon leapt off the napkin and into the headlines. In October 1966, a group of about 300 women and men held the founding conference of NOW. "The time has come," its founders declared, "to confront with concrete action the conditions which now prevent women from enjoying the equality of opportunity and freedom of choice which is their right as individual Americans and as human beings."

The new organization responded to frustrated housewives by demanding greater educational opportunities for women. The group also focused much of its energy on aiding women in the workplace. NOW leaders denounced the exclusion of women from certain professions and from most levels of politics. They lashed out against the practice of paying women less than men for equal work, a practice the Equal Pay Act had not eliminated.

The efforts to pass the Equal Rights Amendment pushed the organization's membership over 200,000. By July 1972, the movement even had a magazine of its own, *Ms.,* which kept readers informed on women's issues. The editor of the new magazine was **Gloria Steinem,** an author and public figure who was one of the movement's leading figures.

✓ Reading Check **Identifying** What two forces helped bring the women's movement to life again?

Successes and Failures

During the late 1960s and early 1970s, the women's movement fought to enforce Title VII of the Civil Rights Act, lobbied to repeal laws against abortion,

---

MEETING SPECIAL NEEDS

Learning Disability To help students with learning disabilities, pick out the most important points of this section, and then have students use the heads of the section to create a study outline. As they complete each subhead, have them write notes about the important points. Then encourage them to discuss their outlines with a partner and make any modifications that would improve the outline. **L1**

📁 Refer to *Inclusion for the High School Social Studies Classroom Strategies and Activities* in the TCR.

and worked for legislation against gender discrimination in employment, housing, and education. Along the way, it experienced success as well as failure.

Striving for Equality in Education One of the movement's notable achievements was in education. Kathy Striebel's story highlighted the discrimination female students often faced in the early 1970s. In 1971, Striebel, a high school junior in St. Paul, Minnesota, wanted to compete for her school's swim team, but the school did not allow girls to join. Kathy's mother, Charlotte, was a member of the local NOW chapter. Through it, she learned that St. Paul had recently passed an ordinance prohibiting gender discrimination in education. She filed a grievance with the city's human rights department, and officials required the school to allow Kathy to swim.

Shortly after joining the team, Kathy beat out one of the boys and earned a spot at a meet. As she stood on the block waiting to swim, the opposing coach declared that she was ineligible to compete because the meet was outside St. Paul and thus beyond the jurisdiction of its laws. "They pulled that little girl right off the block," Charlotte Striebel recalled angrily.

Recognizing the problem, leaders of the movement pushed lawmakers to enact federal legislation banning gender discrimination in education. In 1972 Congress responded by passing a law known collectively as the Educational Amendments. One section, Title IX, prohibited federally funded schools from discriminating against girls and young women in nearly all aspects of its operations, from admissions to athletics. Many schools implemented this new law slowly or not at all, but women now had federal law on their side.

Roe* v. *Wade One of the most important goals for many women activists was the repeal of laws against abortion. Until 1973, the right to regulate abortion was reserved to the states. This was in keeping with the original plan of the Constitution, which reserved all police power—the power to control people and property in the interest of safety, health, welfare, and morals—to the state. Early in the country's history, some abortion was

permitted in the early stages of pregnancy, but after the middle of the 1800s, when states adopted statutory law, abortion was prohibited except to save the life of the mother. Women who chose to have an abortion faced criminal prosecution.

In the late 1960s, some states began adopting more liberal abortion laws. For example, several states allowed abortion if carrying a baby to term might endanger the woman's mental health or if she was a victim of rape or incest. The big change came with the 1973 Supreme Court decision in *Roe* v. *Wade.* The Supreme Court ruled that state governments could not regulate abortion during the first three months of pregnancy, a time that was interpreted as being within a woman's constitutional right to privacy. During the second three months of pregnancy, states could regulate abortions on the basis of the health of the mother. States could ban abortion in the final three months except in cases of a medical emergency.

Those in favor of protecting abortion rights cheered *Roe* v. *Wade* as a victory, but the issue was far

Profiles IN HISTORY

Shirley Chisholm
1924–

Shirley Chisholm once remarked, "Of my two 'handicaps,' being female put more obstacles in my path than being black." Her attempts to overcome these obstacles propelled the Brooklyn, New York, native into the national spotlight and provided encouragement for other women and African Americans attempting to overcome discrimination.

Chisholm first gained national prominence when she defeated two other candidates for Congress from New York's 12th District in 1968. Upon her swearing in, she became the first African American woman to serve in the United States Congress.

In Congress Chisholm became an ardent defender of several causes. An opponent of the seniority system, she protested the ways that party leaders assigned House members to committees and was instrumental in changing them. Chisholm was an early opponent of arms sales to South Africa's racist regime. She also worked on education issues and to increase day care

programs, and she cosponsored a bill to guarantee an annual income to families.

In 1972 Chisholm ran for the Democratic nomination for president. She campaigned extensively and entered primaries in 12 states, winning 28 delegates and receiving 152 first ballot votes at the convention.

She returned to Congress after the convention and continued her crusade to help women and minorities for several more terms. She declined to run for re-election in 1982, citing the difficulties of campaigning for liberal issues in an increasingly conservative political atmosphere.

📁 Use *Supreme Court Case Study 48,* *Roe* v. *Wade.*

FYI

Bella Abzug served in the United States House of Representatives from 1971 to 1977. A strong supporter of women's rights, in the 1960s she also helped establish Women Strike for Peace, an organization for worldwide nuclear disarmament.

3 ASSESS

Assign Section 2 Assessment as homework or as an in-class activity.

💿 Have students use the **Interactive Tutor Self-Assessment CD-ROM.**

Reading Essentials and Study Guide 31–2

Name _____ Date _____ Class _____

Study Guide
Chapter 31, Section 2
For use with textbook pages 926–930
THE FEMINIST MOVEMENT

KEY TERMS AND NAMES

feminism the belief that men and women should be equal politically, economically, and socially (page 927)
Equal Pay Act a law that outlawed paying men more than women for the same job (page 927)
Equal Employment Opportunity Commission federal agency in charge of administering the new legislation for women (page 928)
Betty Friedan writer who wrote *The Feminine Mystique* (page 928)
National Organization for Women the national women's organization started in the mid-1960s (page 928)
Title IX part of a law that prohibited federally funded schools from discriminating against girls

Profiles IN HISTORY

Ask: What were the two handicaps Shirley Chisholm faced and which did she find more difficult to overcome? *(She thought that being a woman had put more obstacles in her way than being African American.)*

INTERDISCIPLINARY CONNECTIONS ACTIVITY

Visual Arts Have students create three sketches of typical women's fashions from the 1960s and 1970s. Sketches should include clothing for several occasions. For example, students might choose to include a sketch of an outfit worn by a college student, a homemaker, and an office worker. Formal wear for special occasions such as weddings and proms could also be included. Encourage students to use library and Internet resources to locate fashion images to help them with their sketches. **L2**

Picturing History

Answer: 35

Reteach

Have students explain the workplace issues for many women.

Enrich

Have interested students research the impact of Title IX.

✓ Reading Check

Answer: Successes: the Educational Amendments, abortion rights, and improved working conditions; Failures: not passing the ERA, lingering income gap, women still mostly in low-paying jobs

4 CLOSE

Have students identify achievements of the women's movement.

Picturing History

Opposing Viewpoints The Equal Rights Amendment had strong support, but it also had strong opposition, led by Phyllis Schlafly (right). How many states ratified the ERA?

from settled. The decision gave rise to the right-to-life movement, whose members consider abortion morally wrong and advocate its total ban. After the *Roe* v. *Wade* ruling, the two sides began an impassioned battle that continues today. 📖 *(For more information on* Roe v. Wade, *see page 1082.)*

The Equal Rights Amendment In 1972 Congress passed the Equal Rights Amendment (ERA). To become part of the Constitution, this amendment to protect women against discrimination had to be ratified by 38 states. Many states did so—35 by 1979—but there was significant opposition to the amendment as well. Some people feared the ERA would take away

some traditional rights, such as the right to alimony in divorce cases or the right to have single-gender colleges. One outspoken opponent was **Phyllis Schlafly,** who organized the Stop-ERA campaign. The Equal Rights Amendment finally failed in 1982.

The Impact of the Women's Movement Despite the failure of the ERA, the women's movement would ultimately bring about profound changes in society. Since the 1970s, many more women have pursued college degrees and careers outside of the home than did so in previous decades. Since the women's movement began, two-career families are much more common than they were in the 1950s and 1960s, although a need for greater family income may also be a factor. Employers began to offer employees options to help make work more compatible with family life, including flexible hours, on-site child care, and job-sharing.

Even though the women's movement helped change social attitudes toward women, a significant income gap between men and women still exists. A major reason for the income gap is that most working women still hold lower-paying jobs such as bank tellers, administrative assistants, cashiers, schoolteachers, and nurses. It is in professional jobs that women have made the most dramatic gains since the 1970s. By the end of the 1900s, women made up roughly one-fourth of the nation's doctors and lawyers.

✓ **Reading Check** **Summarizing** What successes and failures did the women's movement experience during the late 1960s and early 1970s?

SECTION 2 ASSESSMENT

Checking for Understanding

1. **Define:** feminism, Title IX.
2. **Identify:** Equal Pay Act, Equal Employment Opportunity Commission, Betty Friedan, National Organization for Women, Phyllis Schlafly.
3. **Summarize** Shirley Chisholm's political contributions.

Reviewing Themes

4. **Civic Rights and Responsibilities** How have women's rights improved since the 1960s?

Critical Thinking

5. **Synthesizing** What two events weakened the women's movement after 1920?
6. **Organizing** Use a graphic organizer similar to the one below to list the major achievements of the women's movement.

Achievements

Analyzing Visuals

7. **Analyzing Photographs** Study the photograph on page 927 of a housewife in her kitchen. Think about depictions of housewives in modern television or magazine advertisements you have seen. How would you compare the photograph on page 927 with today's images?

Writing About History

8. **Persuasive Writing** Take on the role of a supporter or opponent of the ERA. Write a letter to the editor of your local newspaper to persuade people to support your position.

SECTION 2 ASSESSMENT ANSWERS

1. Terms are in blue.
2. Equal Pay Act (p. 927), Equal Employment Opportunity Commission (p. 928), Betty Friedan (p. 928), National Organization for Women (p. 928), Phyllis Schlafly (p. 930)
3. The first African American woman in Congress, she helped reform the House committee appointment system, and worked on education and day care.
4. More women have achieved equal pay for the same job, more career choices, and more political power.
5. division within the women's movement and World War II
6. Equal Pay Act; inclusion in Title VII of the 1964 Civil Rights Act; Title IX; *Roe* v. *Wade;* more career possibilities
7. Answers will vary. Answers could mention that current depictions are realistic.
8. Students' letters will vary.

American LITERATURE

Charlotte Perkins Gilman was a prominent American social critic and feminist writer in the late 1800s and early 1900s. In her most famous work, *The Yellow Wallpaper* (1899), she presents the story of a woman diagnosed with hysteria, for whom a doctor has prescribed total rest. Cut off from any intellectual activity, the woman is slowly driven mad by her "cure."

In this work, Gilman makes a statement against a common belief of the time—that women were generally unfit for scholarship. The story remained obscure for almost 50 years but was rediscovered in the 1970s. It has become a staple of many college literary courses.

Read to Discover

How does the narrator feel about her "illness"? How does her opinion differ from that of her physician and her family?

Reader's Dictionary

scoff: make fun of

phosphates: a carbonated drink, often used as medicine in the 1800s and early 1900s

congenial: agreeable; pleasant

---

from The Yellow Wallpaper
by Charlotte Perkins Gilman

In the following excerpt, the narrator of the story, writing in a secret journal, is describing her "illness" and how her husband John and others feel about it.

John is practical in the extreme. He has no patience with faith, an intense horror of superstition, and he scoffs openly at any talk of things not to be felt and seen and put down in figures.

John is a physician, and *perhaps*—(I would not say it to a living soul, of course, but this is dead paper and a great relief to my mind)—*perhaps* that is one reason I do not get well faster.

You see he does not believe I am sick!

And what can one do?

If a physician of high standing, and one's own husband, assures friends and relatives that there is really nothing the matter with one but temporary nervous depression—a slight hysterical tendency—what is one to do?

My brother is also a physician, and also of high standing, and he says the same thing.

So I take phosphates or phospites—whichever it is, and tonics, and journeys, and air, and exercise, and am absolutely forbidden to "work" until I am well again.

Personally, I disagree with their ideas.

Personally, I believe that congenial work, with excitement and change, would do me good.

But what is one to do?

I did write for a while in spite of them; but it *does* exhaust me a good deal—having to be so sly about it, or else meet with heavy opposition.

Analyzing Literature

1. What is the main idea in this passage? How does it support the author's point?

2. Does the narrator think this remedy will help her? Why or why not? What clues can you find about how the narrator feels about her illness?

Interdisciplinary Activity

Science Using the Internet and other resources, research some ways that diseases and illnesses were treated in the 1800s and 1900s. Do we still use these treatments today? Create a chart showing the progression of treatment for some of the illnesses you researched.

American LITERATURE

Block Schedule

Team Teaching This selection from *The Yellow Wallpaper* can be presented in conjunction with English or Language Arts.

Read to Discover

Answer: The narrator feels that doing something other than resting would improve her health. Her family does not believe she is sick.

Reinforcing Vocabulary

Ask students to use each of the terms in a sentence that is not related to the reading.

Historical Connection

Charlotte Perkins Gilman drew on her own experience after the birth of her first child in writing *The Yellow Wallpaper*. The great-niece of Harriet Beecher Stowe, she wrote novels, poems, and magazine articles on a variety of subjects.

Portfolio Writing Activity

Have students write a narrative essay about a time when they were not believed. Encourage students to describe the circumstances and explore how the incident made them feel.

HISTORY *Online*

Refer to tav.glencoe.com for additional Glencoe Literature titles, lesson plans, and study guides related to this unit.

Answers to Analyzing Literature

1. This passage contrasts what her doctors think and what she thinks. Her weak and timid disagreement emphasizes the strength and power of her male doctors' opinions. phrase "what is one to do?" and tentative word choices such as *relief, perhaps,* and *exhaust.*

Interdisciplinary Activity
Charts should show the progress in diagnosing and treating selected illnesses and diseases.

2. No, she wants congenial work, excitement, and change. Her passivity shows in repetitions of the

931

1 FOCUS

Section Overview

This section focuses on the efforts by minority groups to improve their status.

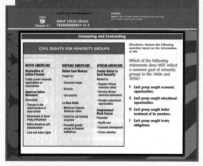
Guide to Reading

Answers to Graphic: 1966: UFW pushed for better wages and working conditions; 1968: AIM protested Native American conditions; 1969: *La Raza Unida* organized Mexican Americans for job training and access to financial institutions; 1971: PUSH organized voter registration, developed African American businesses, and broadened educational opportunities; CBC focused on African American interests in Congress

Preteaching Vocabulary
Have students group the Key Terms and Names into logical categories.

Guide to Reading

Main Idea
Throughout the 1960s and 1970s, minority groups developed new ways to improve their status in the United States.

Key Terms and Names
affirmative action, Allan Bakke, busing, Jesse Jackson, Congressional Black Caucus, César Chávez, *La Raza Unida*, bilingualism, American Indian Movement

Reading Strategy
Sequencing As you read about the civil rights movement's new approaches, complete a time line similar to the one below to record new groups and their actions.

Reading Objectives
• **Describe** the goal of affirmative action policies.
• **Analyze** the rise of Hispanic and Native American protests.

Section Theme
Civic Rights and Responsibilities African Americans, Hispanics, and Native Americans organized to fight discrimination and to gain access to better education and jobs.

Preview of Events

♦1965	♦1969	♦1973

1966
Hispanic Americans form United Farm Workers of America

1968
Kerner Commission reports on racism in the United States

1969
Hispanic leaders form *La Raza Unida*

1973
Native Americans and government clash in South Dakota

★ An American Story ★

Vernon Bellecourt

In 1968 Vernon and Clyde Bellecourt, along with other Native Americans in Minneapolis, were struggling to earn a living. The Bellecourts decided to take a stand against their conditions. Spurred by the 1960s protest movements and by reawakened pride in their culture, the brothers helped organize the American Indian Movement (AIM). AIM's goal was to combat discrimination and brutality by the local police. Vernon recalled how AIM worked:

❝They got a small grant from the Urban League of Minneapolis to put two-way radios in their cars and to get tape recorders and cameras. They would listen to the police calls, and when they heard . . . that police were being dispatched to a certain community or bar, they'd show up with cameras and take pictures of the police using more than normal restraint on people. . . . AIM would show up and have attorneys ready. Often they would beat the police back to the station. They would have a bondsman there, and they'd start filing lawsuits against the police department.❞

—quoted in *Native American Testimony*

Fighting for Greater Opportunity

At a time of heightened protest in the United States, Native Americans began raising their voices for reform and change. Other groups did as well. During the 1960s and early 1970s, Hispanic Americans organized to improve their status in society. In the wake of the

---

assassination of Dr. Martin Luther King, Jr., African Americans continued their fight for greater civil rights, now focusing more on access to jobs.

Affirmative Action By the end of the 1960s, many African American leaders expressed a growing sense of frustration. Although most legal forms of racial discrimination had been dismantled, many African Americans felt there had been little improvement in their daily lives. In the eyes of leading civil rights activists, the problems facing most African Americans lay in their lack of access to good jobs and adequate schooling. As a result, leaders of the civil rights movement began to focus their energies on these problems.

As part of their effort, civil rights leaders looked to an initiative known as affirmative action. Enforced through executive orders and federal policies, affirmative action called for companies and institutions doing business with the federal government to actively recruit African American employees with the hope that this would lead to improved social and economic status. Officials later expanded affirmative action to include other minority groups and women.

Supporters of the policy argued that because so few companies hired from these groups in the past, they had had little chance to develop necessary job skills. If businesses opened their doors wider to minorities, more of them could begin building better lives.

In one example of affirmative action's impact, Atlanta witnessed a significant increase in minority job opportunities shortly after **Maynard Jackson** became its first African American mayor in 1973. When Jackson took office, less than one percent of all city contracts went to African Americans, even

Picturing **History**

Equal Opportunity Allan Bakke graduated from medical school after the Supreme Court overturned the University of California's use of specific racial quotas. *How did the Bakke case affect affirmative action?*

though they made up about half of Atlanta's population. Jackson used the expansion of the city's airport to redress this imbalance by opening the bidding process for airport contracts more widely to minority firms. Through his efforts, small companies and minority firms took on 25 percent of all airport construction work, earning them some $125 million in contracts.

Challenges to Affirmative Action Affirmative action programs did not go unchallenged. Critics viewed them as a form of "reverse discrimination." They claimed that qualified white workers were kept from jobs, promotions, and a place in schools because a certain number of such positions had been set aside for minorities or women.

One of the more notable attacks on affirmative action came in 1974, after officials at the University of California Medical School at Davis turned down the admission of a white applicant named **Allan Bakke** for a second time. When Bakke learned that slots had been set aside for minorities, he sued the school. Bakke argued that by admitting minority applicants, some of whom had scored lower than Bakke on their exams, the school had discriminated against him due to his race.

In 1978, in *University of California Regents* v. *Bakke*, the Supreme Court, in a 5 to 4 ruling, declared that the university had indeed violated Bakke's rights. On the other hand, it ruled that schools could use racial criteria as part of their admissions process so long as they did not use "fixed quotas." While *Bakke* was not a strong and definitive ruling, the Court had nevertheless supported affirmative action programs as constitutional. 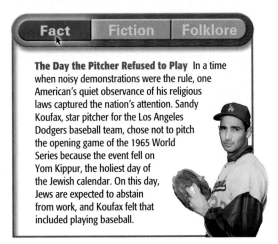 *(See page 1082 for more information on University of California Regents* v. *Bakke.)*

CHAPTER 31 The Politics of Protest 933

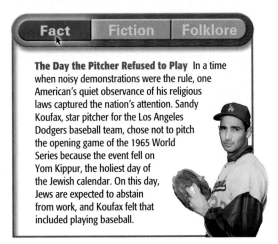

| Fact | Fiction | Folklore |

The Day the Pitcher Refused to Play In a time when noisy demonstrations were the rule, one American's quiet observance of his religious laws captured the nation's attention. Sandy Koufax, star pitcher for the Los Angeles Dodgers baseball team, chose not to pitch the opening game of the 1965 World Series because the event fell on Yom Kippur, the holiest day of the Jewish calendar. On this day, Jews are expected to abstain from work, and Koufax felt that included playing baseball.

---

2 *TEACH*

Daily Lecture and Discussion Notes 31–3

Daily Lecture and Discussion Notes
Chapter 31, Section 3

Did You Know When Hispanic civil rights worker, César Chávez was a teenager, he went to see a movie, but found out that the theater was segregated. Whites sat on one side of the aisle, while Mexicans had to sit on the other side. Chávez sat down in the whites-only section where he was later arrested by the local police.

I.   Fighting for Greater Opportunity *(pages 932–935)*

A. During the 1960s and early 1970s, Native Americans, Hispanic Americans, and African Americans organized to improve their position within society.

B. African American leaders looked to **affirmative action** to gain good jobs and adequate housing. This initiative, enforced through executive orders and federal policies, called

Discussing a Topic Have students consider how members of minority groups are portrayed in film and television today. Have them speculate on how the civil rights movement influenced these media. **L1**

Picturing **History**

Answer: supported affirmative action but ruled against fixed quotas

| Fact | Fiction | Folklore |

During the 1924 Olympic Games in Paris, Eric Liddell of Scotland refused to run in a qualifying heat because it was scheduled on a Sunday. The movie *Chariots of Fire* is based on the experiences of Liddell and his teammate, Harold Abrahams.

Use *Supreme Court Case Study 51, Regents of the University of California* v. *Bakke.*

COOPERATIVE LEARNING ACTIVITY

Conducting a Debate Organize the class into two groups. Tell the groups that they are to prepare for a debate about bilingual education. Assign one group to concentrate on the pros of bilingual education; the other group should concentrate on the cons. Tell the groups to conduct research to identify facts and theories to support their assigned point of view. Conduct an informal debate in which each side presents its case and rebuts the point of view of the other side. Encourage all students to participate.

Use the rubric for a cooperative group management plan on pages 81–82 in the *Performance Assessment Activities and Rubrics.*

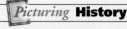

Guided Reading Activity 31-3

Guided Reading Activity 31-3

Name _____ Date _____ Class _____

DIRECTIONS: Identifying Supporting Details Read each main idea. Use your textbook to supply the details that support or explain each main idea.

☐ **Main Idea:** During the 1960s and early 1970s, African Americans continued their fight for greater civil rights in the wake of the assassination of Dr. Martin Luther King, Jr.

1. **Detail:** In the eyes of leading civil rights activists, the problems facing most African Americans lay in their lack of access to _____ and _____

2. **Detail:** _____ called for companies and institutions doing business with the federal government to actively recruit _____

3. **Detail:** _____ is the claim that qualified white workers are kept from jobs, promotions, and a place in schools because a certain number of such positions are set aside for minorities or women.

4. **Detail:** An activist in the civil rights movement, _____ sought the _____

Picturing **History**

Answer: Congressional Black Caucus

Ask: What organization did Jesse Jackson found? *(People United to Save Humanity—PUSH)*

 Use *Interpreting Political Cartoons,* Cartoon 29.

FYI

Stokely Carmichael turned down scholarships to other colleges in order to attend Howard University, a historically African American university. Following graduation from Howard, he again turned down scholarships, this time for graduate studies, and went to work for SNCC.

Analyzing Points of View

Review with students the issue of school desegregation. Have students explain why some thought that busing would be a good solution to the problem. Then have students explain why many people came to believe that busing caused more problems than it solved. **L2**

Picturing **History**

New African American Leadership Andrew Young and Jesse Jackson both worked with Dr. Martin Luther King, Jr., in the civil rights movement. Young went on to become the first African American ambassador to the United Nations, while Jackson has become a prominent member of the Democratic Party. What group of African American members of Congress became influential in the 1970s?

Equal Access to Education By the early 1970s, African American leaders also had begun to push harder for educational improvements. In the 1954 case of *Brown* v. *Board of Education of Topeka, Kansas,* the Supreme Court had ordered an end to segregated public schools. In the 1960s, however, many schools remained segregated as local communities moved slowly to comply with the Court. Since children normally went to neighborhood public schools, segregation in schooling reflected the race segregation of neighborhoods. White schools were usually far superior to African American schools, as Ruth Baston of the NAACP noted in 1965 after visiting Boston schools:

❝When we would go to white schools, we'd see these lovely classrooms with a small number of children in each class. The teachers were permanent. We'd see wonderful materials. When we'd go to our schools, we'd see overcrowded classrooms, children sitting out in the corridors. And so then we decided that where there were a large number of white students, that's where the care went. That's where the books went. That's where the money went.❞

—quoted in *Freedom Bound*

934   CHAPTER 31   The Politics of Protest

To ensure desegregated schools, local governments resorted to a policy known as busing, transporting children to schools outside their neighborhoods to achieve greater racial balance. The Supreme Court upheld the constitutionality of busing in the 1971 case, *Swann* v. *Charlotte-Mecklenburg Board of Education.* 📖 *(See page 1083 for more information on* Swann *v.* Charlotte-Mecklenburg Board of Education.)

Many whites responded to busing by taking their children out of public schools. Nearly 20,000 white students left Boston's public system for parochial and private schools. By late 1976, African Americans, Hispanics, and other minorities made up the majority of Boston's public school students. This "white flight" also occurred in other cities.

New Political Leaders In their struggle for equal opportunity, African Americans found new political leaders in people such as **Jesse Jackson.** In 1971 Jackson founded People United to Save Humanity, or PUSH, a group aimed at registering voters, developing African American businesses, and broadening educational opportunities. In 1984 and 1988, Jackson sought the Democratic presidential

---

MEETING SPECIAL NEEDS

Logical/Mathematical To help students understand the attitudes behind passage of the Equal Pay Act and the Indian Civil Rights Act, have students analyze the following questions. **L2**

• In a company, who benefits if women are paid less than men?

• On a Native American reservation, who benefits from limited Native American government?

Refer to ***Inclusion for the High School Social Studies Classroom Strategies and Activities*** in the TCR.

Self-Check Quiz

Visit the *American Vision* Web site at <u>tav.glencoe.com</u> and click on *Self-Check Quizzes—Chapter 31* to assess your knowledge of chapter content.

18. **Evaluating** In what ways did the counterculture movement change American society?

19. **Drawing Conclusions** Why do you think so many protest movements emerged in the United States during the 1960s and 1970s?

Practicing Skills

20. **Analyzing Primary Sources** Reread "An American Story" at the beginning of Section 2 on page 926. Then answer the questions below.
   a. Whose opinion is expressed in this letter?
   b. When was this letter written? In what publication did it appear?
   c. What role in society is the writer discussing? What is her opinion of this role?

Chapter Activities

21. **American History Primary Source Document Library CD-ROM** Under *Struggle for Civil Rights,* read "Delano Grape Workers, A Proclamation" by the Delano Grape Workers. Using information from the grape workers' proclamation, work with a few of your classmates to create a two-minute television advertisement to persuade all Americans to join the grape boycott. In your advertisement, you should use facts you learned about the grape boycott and also appeal to people's emotions.

22. **Creating a Database, Thematic Model, and Quiz** Use the Internet and other resources to research student protests in the 1960s and 1970s. Create a database of these protests that clearly depicts where, when, and why the protests took place. Then create a thematic model of this information by labeling the locations of the protests on a map of the United States. Finally, create a quiz for your classmates by writing five questions about the geographic distribution of the protests and the patterns this might suggest.

Writing Activity

23. **Persuasive Writing** Use library and Internet resources to learn about the predictions scientists are making on how future population growth and distribution will affect the physical environment. Pay special attention to the evidence that these scientists use and the types of predictions that each makes. Is there agreement or disagreement in the scientific community about population growth and its environmental effects? Present the findings of your research in a written report.

ERA Ratification, 1972–1982

Date Ratified:
- 1972
- 1973
- 1974
- 1975
- 1977
- Did not ratify

Albers Conic Equal-Area projection

Geography and History

24. The map above shows the states that ratified the Equal Rights Amendment between 1972 and 1982. Study the map and answer the questions below.
   a. **Interpreting Maps** How many states had ratified the Equal Rights Amendment by 1977?
   b. **Applying Geography Skills** What conclusion can you draw about the distribution of states that did not approve the ERA?

Standardized Test Practice

Directions: Choose the phrase that best completes the following sentence.

Women faced all of the following kinds of discrimination in the 1960s EXCEPT

F unequal pay for performing the same tasks as men.

G being prohibited from attending certain universities.

H being denied the right to vote.

J the inability to obtain loans and credit.

Test-Taking Tip: This question is looking for the *exception*. Three of the answer choices describe types of discrimination that women faced *in the 1960s*. Women gained the right to vote in 1920, when the Nineteenth Amendment was signed into law.

HISTORY Online

Have students visit the Web site at <u>tav.glencoe.com</u> to review Chapter 31 and take the Self-Check Quiz.

Geography and History

24. **a.** 35 states had ratified the ERA by 1977. **b.** States that did not ratify the ERA tended to be in the more socially conservative and rural areas of the country.

Standardized Test Practice

Answer: H
Test-Taking Tip: Tell students that even if they do not remember when women got the right to vote, they may be able to eliminate some of the answers. For example, they may know that unequal pay for women performing the same task as men is still an issue today. The correct answer is H.

Bonus Question ?

Ask: Who was the first African American woman to serve in Congress? *(Shirley Chisholm)*

19. Answers will vary. Students should note the relative prosperity of many Americans and the growing sense of disillusionment on the part of groups left out of social, economic, and political life.

Practicing Skills

20. **a.** Herma Snider, a young mother; **b.** 1960; *Redbook* magazine; **c.** the roles of wife, mother, and homemaker; feeling of needing more in her life beyond these roles

Chapter Activities

21. Students' projects will vary. Advertisements should be factual and persuasive.

22. Answers will vary. Encourage students to trade their quizzes and see how their classmates do.

Writing Activity

23. Answers will vary. Reports should reflect findings grounded in scientific evidence.

SUGGESTED PACING CHART

Unit 10 (1 Day)	Chapter 32 (5 Days)	Chapter 33 (5 Days)	Chapter 34 (6 Days)	Unit 10 (2 Days)
Day 1 Introduction	**Day 1** Chapter 32 Intro, Section 1	**Day 1** Chapter 33 Intro, Section 1	**Day 1** Chapter 34 Intro, Section 1	**Day 1** Wrap-Up/Project
	Day 2 Section 2	**Day 2** Section 2	**Day 2** Section 2	**Day 2** Unit 10 Assessment
	Day 3 Section 3	**Day 3** Section 3	**Day 3** Section 3	
	Day 4 Section 4	**Day 4** Section 4	**Day 4** Section 4	
	Day 5 Chapter 32 Assessment	**Day 5** Chapter 33 Assessment	**Day 5** Section 5	
			Day 6 Chapter 34 Assessment	

GLENCOE'S
ASSESSMENT
ADVANTAGE

Use the following tools to easily assess student learning in a variety of ways:

- Performance Assessment Activities and Rubrics
- Chapter and Unit Tests
- Section Quizzes
- Standardized Test Skills Practice Workbook

- tav.glencoe.com
- Interactive Tutor Self-Assessment CD-ROM
- MindJogger Videoquiz
- ExamView® Pro Testmaker CD-ROM
- SAT I/II Test Practice

TEACHING TRANSPARENCIES

Unit 10 Map Overlay Transparencies

Cause-and-Effect Transparency 10

*inter*NET RESOURCES

- tav.glencoe.com

The American Vision

Visit the *American Vision* Web site for history overviews, activities, assessments, and updated charts and graphs.

- www.socialstudies.glencoe.com

Glencoe Social Studies

Visit the Glencoe Web site for social studies activities, updates, and links to other sites.

- www.teachingtoday.glencoe.com

Glencoe Teaching Today

Visit the new Glencoe Web site for teacher development information, teaching tips, Web resources, and educational news.

- www.time.com

TIME Online

Visit the TIME Web site for up-to-date news and special reports.

Unit 10 Resources

ASSESSMENT

Unit 10 Pretests

Unit 10 Posttests

APPLICATION AND ENRICHMENT

American Biography 10

History Simulation and Problem Solving 10

GEOGRAPHY

Geography and History Activity 10

INTERDISCIPLINARY ACTIVITIES

American Literature Reading 10

Economics and History Activity 10

Team-Teaching Interdisciplinary Strategies and Activities 10

BIBLIOGRAPHY

Readings for the Student

Reeves, Richard. *President Nixon: Alone in the White House.* Simon & Schuster, 2001.

Readings for the Teacher

Time-Life Books, ed. *Pride and Prosperity: The 80s (Our American Century).* Time Life, 1999.

Multimedia Resources

Videocassette. *Watergate Hearings: Summer of Judgment.* WETA. (120 minutes)

Videocassette. *Spaceship Earth: Our Global Environment.* WORLDLINK. (25 minutes)

Additional Glencoe Resources for This Unit:

- Glencoe Skillbuilder Interactive Workbook CD-ROM, Level 2
- Social Studies Guide to Using the Internet
- Writer's Guidebook for High School
- Living Constitution
- American Art Prints Strategies and Activities

Unit Overview

Unit 10 describes the changing society from 1968 to the present. **Chapter 32** explores the politics and economics of the Nixon, Ford, and Carter years. **Chapter 33** focuses on the resurgence of conservatism from 1980 to 1992. **Chapter 34** describes recent events in American history including the Clinton presidency, the election of 2000, and the terrorist attacks on the World Trade Center and the Pentagon.

Unit Objectives

After studying this unit, students will be able to:
1. Describe Nixon's foreign policy achievements.
2. Explain President Reagan's economic recovery plans.
3. Describe the ways in which technology has affected American business and communications.

Why It Matters Activity

Have students write down one fact they know or opinion they have about the following presidents: President Reagan, President George H. W. Bush, President Clinton, and President George W. Bush. Have volunteers share their statements with the class, having the class identify the statement as fact or opinion.

UNIT
10 A Changing Society

1968–Present

Why It Matters

A reassessment of postwar developments marked the last three decades of the twentieth century. The Cold War ended and political boundaries were redrawn. The United States remained a global force, but the role of the federal government was diminished in the wake of scandal and a renewed conservatism. As the United States entered a new century, the nation continued to redefine itself. The country's social diversity posed new challenges and provided new strength to the nation. Understanding the shifts of this period will help prepare you for your future. The following resources offer more information about this time in American history.

Primary Sources Library

See pages 1056–1057 for primary source readings to accompany Unit 10.

*Use the **American History Primary Source Document Library CD-ROM** to find additional primary sources about the changes in recent years of American history.*

Handheld computer and stylus

New Yorkers celebrate the millennium, January 1, 2000

948

TEAM TEACHING ACTIVITY

Microchips Invite the science or technology teacher to share with students the basic makeup of a microchip and explain how we use microchips in a variety of products daily. As part of the discussion, have the class create a list of all the products they use that include microchip technology. Encourage class members to add to the list as they study this unit.

"*I was not elected to serve one party, but to serve one nation.*"

—*George W. Bush, 2001*

GLENCOE
TECHNOLOGY

 CD-ROM
American History
Primary Source
Document Library
CD-ROM
Use the **American History Primary Source Document Library CD-ROM** to access primary source documents related to this period in history.

More About the Photo

Tell students that watching the famous ball drop from One Times Square signaling the arrival of the new year has been a New York tradition since 1906. Ask students how they celebrated the millennium's arrival.

SERVICE-LEARNING PROJECT

Have students learn more about Habitat for Humanity. You may suggest that students visit www.habitat.org as a starting point for finding information. Identify a Habitat for Humanity house project that is planned for your community, or in a nearby community. Contact the Habitat affiliate nearest you to find out about opportunities for your students to participate in some phase of the program. Encourage students to record their experiences either in pictures or in words.

Refer to ***Building Bridges: Connecting Classroom and Community through Service-Learning in Social Studies*** from the National Council for the Social Studies for information about service-learning.

Timesaving Tools

 **TeacherWorks™** All-In-One Planner and Resource Center

- **Interactive Teacher Edition** Access your Teacher Wraparound Edition and your classroom resources with a few easy clicks.
- **Interactive Lesson Planner** Planning has never been easier! Organize your week, month, semester, or year with all the lesson helps you need to make teaching creative, timely, and relevant.

 Use Glencoe's **Presentation Plus!** multimedia teacher tool to easily present dynamic lessons that visually excite your students. Using Microsoft PowerPoint® you can customize the presentations to create your own personalized lessons.

TEACHING TRANSPARENCIES

Graphic Organizer 12

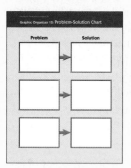

Why It Matters Chapter Transparency 32

APPLICATION AND ENRICHMENT

Linking Past and Present Activity 32

Enrichment Activity 32

Primary Source Reading 32

REVIEW AND REINFORCEMENT

Reteaching Activity 32

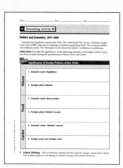

Vocabulary Activity 32

Time Line Activity 32

Critical Thinking Skills Activity 32

Meeting NCSS Standards

The following standards are highlighted in Chapter 32:

Section		
Section 1	IX	Global Connections: B, D
Section 2	VI	Power, Authority, and Governance: B, C, E, F
Section 3	VII	Production, Distribution, and Consumption: A, B
Section 4	I	Culture: A, C, E

Local Standards

Chapter 32 Resources

ASSESSMENT AND EVALUATION

**Chapter 32 Test
Form A**

**Chapter 32 Test
Form B**

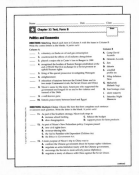

**Standardized Test Skills
Practice Workbook Activity 32**

**Performance Assessment
Activities and Rubrics 32**

**ExamView® Pro
Testmaker CD-ROM**

MULTIMEDIA

- Vocabulary PuzzleMaker CD-ROM
- Interactive Tutor Self-Assessment CD-ROM
- ExamView® Pro Testmaker CD-ROM
- Audio Program
- American History Primary Source Documents Library CD-ROM
- MindJogger Videoquiz
- Presentation Plus! CD-ROM
- TeacherWorks™ CD-ROM
- Interactive Student Edition CD-ROM
- Glencoe Skillbuilder Interactive Workbook CD-ROM, Level 2
- The *American Vision* Video Program
- American Music: Hits Through History
- American Music: Cultural Traditions

The following videotape programs are available
from Glencoe as supplements to Chapter 32:

- **Richard M. Nixon: Man and President** (ISBN 1-56-501742-0)
- **The Secret Service** (Four-video Set) (ISBN 1-56-501521-5)
- **Jimmy Carter** (ISBN 1-56-501530-4)

To order, call Glencoe at 1-800-334-7344. To find classroom resources to
accompany many of these videos, check the following home pages:
A&E Television: www.aande.com
The History Channel: www.historychannel.com

SPANISH RESOURCES

**The following Spanish language materials are
available in the Spanish Resources Binder:**

- Spanish Guided Reading Activities
- Spanish Reteaching Activities
- Spanish Quizzes and Tests
- Spanish Vocabulary Activities
- Spanish Summaries
- The Declaration of Independence and United States Constitution Spanish Translation

Use our Web site for additional resources. All essential content is covered in the Student Edition.

You and your students can visit tav.glencoe.com, the Web site companion to the *American Vision.* This innovative integration of electronic
and print media offers your students a wealth of opportunities. The
student text directs students to the Web site for the following options:

- **Chapter Overviews**
- **Self-Check Quizzes**
- **Student Web Activities**
- **Textbook Updates**

Answers to the student Web activities are provided for you in the **Web
Activity Lesson Plans.** Additional Web resources and Interactive Tutor
Puzzles are also available.

Chapter 32 Resources

SECTION RESOURCES

Daily Objectives	Reproducible Resources	Multimedia Resources
SECTION 1 **The Nixon Administration** 1. Describe Nixon's domestic agenda. 2. Discuss Nixon's foreign policy achievements.	Reproducible Lesson Plan 32–1 Daily Lecture and Discussion Notes 32–1 Guided Reading Activity 32–1* Section Quiz 32–1* Reading Essentials and Study Guide 32–1 Performance Assessment Activities and Rubrics	Daily Focus Skills Transparency 32–1 Interactive Tutor Self-Assessment CD-ROM ExamView® Pro Testmaker CD-ROM Presentation Plus! CD-ROM TeacherWorks™ CD-ROM Audio Program
SECTION 2 **The Watergate Scandal** 1. Describe the character of Richard Nixon and the attitude of his White House. 2. Explain the Watergate scandal and discuss its effects.	Reproducible Lesson Plan 32–2 Daily Lecture and Discussion Notes 32–2 Guided Reading Activity 32–2* Section Quiz 32–2* Reading Essentials and Study Guide 32–2 Performance Assessment Activities and Rubrics Supreme Court Case Studies	Daily Focus Skills Transparency 32–2 Interactive Tutor Self-Assessment CD-ROM ExamView® Pro Testmaker CD-ROM Presentation Plus! CD-ROM TeacherWorks™ CD-ROM Audio Program
SECTION 3 **Ford and Carter** 1. Explain the reasons for economic troubles in the United States during the 1970s. 2. Discuss Jimmy Carter's domestic and foreign policies.	Reproducible Lesson Plan 32–3 Daily Lecture and Discussion Notes 32–3 Guided Reading Activity 32–3* Section Quiz 32–3* Reading Essentials and Study Guide 32–3 Performance Assessment Activities and Rubrics	Daily Focus Skills Transparency 32–3 Interactive Tutor Self-Assessment CD-ROM ExamView® Pro Testmaker CD-ROM Presentation Plus! CD-ROM TeacherWorks™ CD-ROM Audio Program
SECTION 4 **The "Me" Decade: Life in the 1970s** 1. Explain the emergence of new spiritual movements and religions. 2. Discuss the disappearance of some traditional values during the 1970s.	Reproducible Lesson Plan 32–4 Daily Lecture and Discussion Notes 32–4 Guided Reading Activity 32–4* Section Quiz 32–4* Reading Essentials and Study Guide 32–4 Performance Assessment Activities and Rubrics Interpreting Political Cartoons	Daily Focus Skills Transparency 32–4 Interactive Tutor Self-Assessment CD-ROM ExamView® Pro Testmaker CD-ROM Presentation Plus! CD-ROM Skillbuilder Interactive Workbook, Level 2 TeacherWorks™ CD-ROM Vocabulary PuzzleMaker CD-ROM Audio Program American Music: Hits Through History American Music: Cultural Traditions

0:00 OUT OF TIME?
Assign the Chapter 32 **Reading Essentials and Study Guide.**

*Also Available in Spanish

 Blackline Master   Transparency   CD-ROM   DVD

 Poster   Music Program   Audio Program   Videocassette

NATIONAL GEOGRAPHIC Teacher's Corner

INDEX TO NATIONAL GEOGRAPHIC MAGAZINE

The following articles relate to this chapter.

- "Great Lakes: Troubled Water," July 1987
- "Our Polluted Runoff," February 1996
- "Tex-Mex Border," February 1996

ADDITIONAL NATIONAL GEOGRAPHIC SOCIETY PRODUCTS

To order the following, call National Geographic at 1-800-368-2728:

- *Branches of Government Series* (Video)
- *The Complete National Geographic: 109 Years of National Geographic Magazine* (CD-ROM)
- *Democratic Government Series: The United States* (Video)
- *National Geographic World Atlas for Young Explorers—Classroom Library Edition* (Guide, Transparencies, Resource Masters)

NGS ONLINE

Access National Geographic's Web site for current events, atlas updates, activities, links, interactive features, and archives.

www.nationalgeographic.com

From the Classroom of...

Mary Jo Dudek
Erie 1 Board of Cooperative
Educational Services
West Seneca, NY

1776 or 1976?

Have students imagine that either George Washington, Thomas Jefferson, or James Madison had traveled from 1776 to 1976. **Ask: What do you think their impressions of our country's political system would be?**

After the class has discussed the topic, have students write either a journal entry or letter from the point of view of one of these former presidents as they view the United States at its bicentennial. Journal entries and letters should address whether these presidents would be proud or ashamed of what they saw. Encourage students to explain why the presidents feel the way they do.

ADDITIONAL RESOURCES FROM GLENCOE

- American Music: Cultural Traditions
- American Art & Architecture
- Outline Map Resource Book
- U.S. Desk Map
- Building Geography Skills for Life
- Inclusion for the High School Social Studies Classroom Strategies and Activities
- Teaching Strategies for the American History Classroom (Including Block Scheduling Pacing Guides)

KEY TO ABILITY LEVELS

Teaching strategies have been coded.

- **L1** BASIC activities for all students
- **L2** AVERAGE activities for average to above-average students
- **L3** CHALLENGING activities for above-average students
- **ELL** ENGLISH LANGUAGE LEARNER activities

Block Schedule

Activities that are suited to use within the block scheduling framework are identified by:

Why It Matters Activity

Have each student ask an adult what impact he or she thinks Watergate had on politics in America. Have students share their observations. Have students reevaluate their observations after they have completed the chapter.

GLENCOE
TECHNOLOGY

The *American Vision* Video Program

To learn more about the circumstances surrounding the Watergate scandal, have students view the Chapter 32 video, "The Watergate Break-In," from the *American Vision* Video Program.

💿 Available in
DVD and VHS

MindJogger Videoquiz

Use the **MindJogger Videoquiz** to preview Chapter 32 content.

📼 Available in VHS

CHAPTER
32 Politics and Economics *1971–1980*

Why It Matters

The protests of the 1960s were passionate and sometimes violent. The nation elected President Nixon on a promise to uphold the values of what Nixon called "Middle America." In foreign policy, Nixon charted a new path with a historic visit to China. At home he introduced "New Federalism." In 1974 the Watergate scandal forced Nixon to resign. Presidents Ford and Carter faced an economic downturn and a major energy crisis.

The Impact Today

Experiences of the 1970s have had an impact today.
• The Watergate scandal has left many Americans less confident in political leaders.
• The Department of Energy, created by President Carter, still exists as a cabinet-level agency.

 The American Vision *Video* The Chapter 32 video, "The Watergate Break-In," examines the circumstances surrounding this scandal.

United States PRESIDENTS

Nixon 1969–1974

1972
• Nixon visits China and the Soviet Union
• Watergate burglars arrested at Democratic National Committee headquarters

1973
• *Roe* v. *Wade* Supreme Court decision legalizes abortion
• Senate Watergate investigations begin
• OPEC oil embargo leads to fuel shortages

1974
• Nixon resigns
• Gerald Ford becomes president

Ford 1974–1977

1971   *1974*

World

1971
• People's Republic of China admitted to UN

1973
• Britain, Ireland, and Denmark join Common Market

1974
• India becomes world's sixth nuclear power

950

TWO-MINUTE LESSON LAUNCHER

Ask students what they know about President Nixon, his administration, and the Watergate scandal. Write students' impressions on the board. Remind students that it is important to understand the details of these subjects in order to understand fully the history of those years.

HISTORY *Online*

Introduce students to chapter content and key terms by having them access the **Chapter 32 Overview** at tav.glencoe.com.

More About the Photo

Point out to students that Nixon's visit to China in 1972 was historic because the United States had refused to recognize the Communist Chinese government since 1949. Ask students to consider how the meeting shown here would help ease tensions between the two countries. *(possible answers include: the leaders appear friendly, at ease, willing to negotiate)*

President Nixon with Chinese premier Zhou Enlai (on Nixon's right) during Nixon's historic visit to China in 1972

TIME LINE ACTIVITY

Have students select one of the events on the world time line and identify the continent on which the event occurred. Have students speculate on the significance of the event to events happening in the United States at the time.

1975
• President Ford signs Helsinki Accords

1976
• Jimmy Carter elected president

Carter 1977–1981

1979
• Iranian revolutionaries seize U.S. embassy in Tehran

1977   *1980*

1976
• Mao Zedong dies

1977
• Human rights manifesto signed by 241 Czech activists and intellectuals

1979
• Sandinista guerrillas overthrow dictatorship of Somoza
• Margaret Thatcher becomes prime minister of Great Britain

HISTORY *Online*

Chapter Overview
Visit the *American Vision* Web site at tav.glencoe.com and click on **Chapter Overviews—Chapter 32** to preview chapter information.

951

GRAPHIC ORGANIZER ACTIVITY

Organizing Information Have students use a graphic organizer similar to the one below to indicate the domestic and foreign policy challenges Nixon, Ford, and Carter faced. *(Answers will vary, but domestic challenges may include the Watergate scandal for Nixon, the pardoning of Nixon for Ford, and stagflation for Carter. Foreign challenges should include détente for Nixon, problems in Southeast Asia for Ford, and the Iranian hostage crisis for Carter.)*

Challenges	Nixon	Ford	Carter
Domestic			
Foreign			

1 FOCUS

Section Overview

This section focuses on the events of the Nixon presidency.

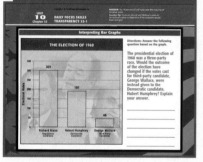
Guide to Reading

Answers to Graphic:
Nixon Administration

Domestic policy	Foreign policy
New Federalism	Détente

Preteaching Vocabulary
Have students look up the meanings of the Key Terms and Names and use the words in a sentence.

The Nixon Administration

Guide to Reading

Main Idea
President Nixon sought to restore law and order and traditional values at home and to ease Cold War tensions abroad.

Key Terms and Names
Southern strategy, revenue sharing, impound, Henry Kissinger, détente, summit

Reading Strategy
Organizing As you read about President Nixon's administration, complete a graphic organizer by listing his domestic and foreign policies.

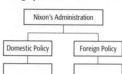

Reading Objectives
• **Describe** Nixon's domestic agenda.
• **Discuss** Nixon's foreign policy achievements.

Section Theme
Global Connections One of President Nixon's most dramatic accomplishments was changing the relationship between the United States, Communist China, and the Soviet Union.

Preview of Events

◆1968	◆1970	◆1972	◆1974
1968 Nixon wins presidential election	**1969** Nixon proposes Family Assistance Plan	**February 1972** Nixon visits China	**May 1972** Moscow hosts American-Soviet summit

Students and police clash at the 1968 Democratic National Convention

★ An American Story ★

Millions of Americans saw police and demonstrators clash on the streets of Chicago at the Democratic National Convention in late August 1968. Many television viewers were outraged at the police tactics they saw. G.L. Halbert, however, was not one of them. To make his support of police efforts public, Halbert wrote a letter to *Newsweek* magazine:

❝Congratulations to Mayor Daley and the Chicago police on their tough handling of the yippies, Vietniks, and newsmen. If more mayors and police departments had the courage to crack down on those who carry only the flags of our enemies and newsmen who consistently slant their coverage of events in favor of those who would undermine and disrupt our country, there would be greater freedom for the majority of Americans rather than greater lawlessness for the few. It is a tragedy that such individuals are allowed to cringe behind our constitutional guarantees after they have wreaked destruction by their agitation.❞

—quoted in *Newsweek*, September 16, 1968

Appealing to Middle America

The views expressed by G.L. Halbert were not unusual. While they did not shout as loudly as the protesters, many Americans supported the government and longed for an end to the violence and turmoil that seemed to plague the nation in the 1960s. The presidential candidate in 1968 who appealed to many of these frustrated citizens was

---

SECTION RESOURCES

Reproducible Masters
• Reproducible Lesson Plan 32–1
• Daily Lecture and Discussion Notes 32–1
• Guided Reading Activity 32–1
• Section Quiz 32–1
• Reading Essentials and Study Guide 32–1
• Performance Assessment Activities and Rubrics

Transparencies
• Daily Focus Skills Transparency 32–1

Multimedia
🖲 Interactive Tutor Self-Assessment CD-ROM
🖲 ExamView® Pro Testmaker CD-ROM
🖲 Presentation Plus! CD-ROM
🖲 TeacherWorks™ CD-ROM
🎧 Audio Program

Richard Nixon, a Republican. Nixon aimed many of his campaign messages at these Americans, whom he referred to as "Middle America" and the "silent majority." He promised them "peace with honor" in Vietnam, law and order, a streamlined government, and a return to more traditional values at home.

The Election of 1968 Nixon's principal opponent in the 1968 presidential election was Democrat **Hubert Humphrey,** who had served as vice president under Lyndon Johnson. Nixon also had to wage his campaign against a strong third-party candidate, **George Wallace,** an experienced Southern politician and avowed supporter of segregation. In a 1964 bid for the Democratic presidential nomination, the former Alabama governor had attracted considerable support.

On Election Day, Wallace captured an impressive 13.5 percent of the popular vote, the best showing of a third-party candidate since 1924. Nixon managed a victory, however, receiving 43.4 percent of the popular vote to Humphrey's 42.7 and 301 electoral votes to Humphrey's 191.

The Southern Strategy One of the keys to Nixon's victory was his surprisingly strong showing in the South. Even though the South had long been a Democratic stronghold, Nixon had refused to concede the region. To gain Southern support, Nixon had met with powerful South Carolina senator Strom Thurmond and won his backing by promising several things: to appoint only conservatives to the federal courts, to name a Southerner to the Supreme Court, to oppose court-ordered busing, and to choose a vice presidential candidate acceptable to the South. (Nixon ultimately chose Spiro Agnew, governor of the border state of Maryland.)

Nixon's efforts paid off on Election Day. Large numbers of white Southerners deserted the Democratic Party, granting Humphrey only one victory in that region—in Lyndon Johnson's home state of Texas. While Wallace claimed most of the states in the Deep South, Nixon captured Virginia, Tennessee, Kentucky, and North Carolina. Senator Strom Thurmond's support delivered his state of South Carolina for the Republicans as well.

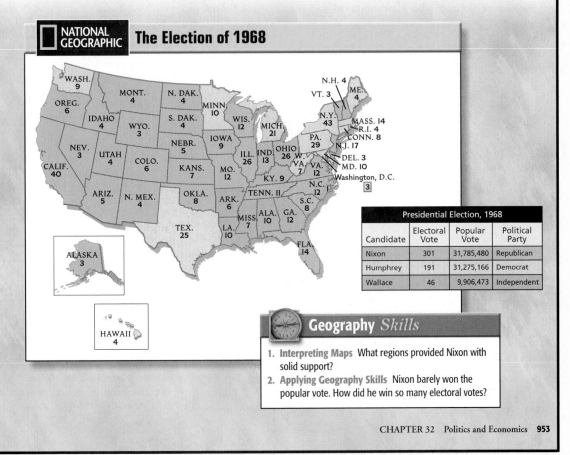

The Election of 1968

Presidential Election, 1968			
Candidate	Electoral Vote	Popular Vote	Political Party
Nixon	301	31,785,480	Republican
Humphrey	191	31,275,166	Democrat
Wallace	46	9,906,473	Independent

Geography *Skills*

1. **Interpreting Maps** What regions provided Nixon with solid support?
2. **Applying Geography Skills** Nixon barely won the popular vote. How did he win so many electoral votes?

2 TEACH

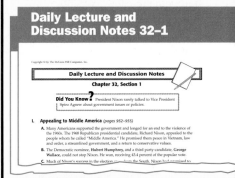

Daily Lecture and Discussion Notes 32–1

Creating Circle Graphs Provide the data below and ask students to make a pair of circle graphs showing the results of the 1968 presidential election. **L1**

Candidate	Popular Vote	Electoral Vote
Nixon, Rep.	31,785,480	301
Humphrey, Dem.	31,275,166	191
Wallace, Ind.	9,906,473	46

Use the rubric for creating a map, display, or chart on pages 77–78 in the *Performance Assessment Activities and Rubrics.*

Geography *Skills*

Answers:
1. Midwest and West
2. If a candidate has only a bare majority in a state's popular vote, he or she still receives all of its electoral votes.

Geography Skills Practice
Which New England states voted for Nixon? *(New Hampshire and Vermont)* Which Western state voted for Humphrey? *(Washington)*

COOPERATIVE LEARNING ACTIVITY

Creating a Chart Organize the class into small groups of three or four students. Have the members of each group create individual charts showing the successes and failures of the Nixon administration. Have the groups compare their charts and create a composite for the class.
Use the rubric for a cooperative group management plan on pages 81–82 in the *Performance Assessment Activities and Rubrics.*

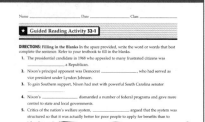

Profiles IN HISTORY

Ask: What were some of the accomplishments of Romana Acosta Bañuelos before being named U.S. Treasurer? *(She started her own business that grew into a multimillion-dollar enterprise, and she helped found the Pan-American National Bank.)*

Writing a Research Report

Have students write a research report describing the ways in which the Burger Court disappointed conservatives. Remind students to include bibliographic references and footnotes in proper style. **L3**

📁 Use the rubric for a book review, research report, or position paper on pages 89–90 in the *Performance Assessment Activities and Rubrics.*

Following his victory, Nixon set out to attract even more Southerners to the Republican Party, an effort that became known as the **Southern strategy.** Toward this end, the president fulfilled his agreements with Thurmond and took steps to slow desegregation. During his tenure, Nixon worked to overturn several civil rights policies. He reversed a Johnson administration policy, for example, that had cut off federal funds for racially segregated schools.

A Law-and-Order President Having also won the presidency with a promise of law and order, Nixon immediately set out to battle crime in America. His administration specifically targeted the nation's antiwar protesters. Attorney General John Mitchell declared that he stood ready to prosecute "hard-line militants" who crossed state lines to stir up riots. Mitchell's deputy, Richard Kleindienst, went even further with the boast, "We're going to enforce the law against draft evaders, against radical students, against deserters, against civil disorders, against organized crime, and against street crime."

Nixon also went on the attack against the recent Supreme Court rulings that expanded the rights of

Profiles IN HISTORY

Romana Acosta Bañuelos 1925–

On her first day of business in downtown Los Angeles, California, Romana Acosta Bañuelos made $36 selling tortillas. That was in 1949. She made great strides after that, becoming a successful businessperson and serving as U.S. treasurer in the 1970s.

Born in 1925 in a small town in Arizona to Mexican American immigrants, Bañuelos spent part of her childhood on a relative's small ranch in Mexico. Rising early, she tended the crops and helped her mother make empanadas (Mexican turnovers) to sell to local restaurants. "My mother was the type of woman that taught us how to live in any place and work with what we have."

That lesson inspired Bañuelos to start her own business when she returned to the United States at the age of 19. Gradually her business grew, and by the mid-1960s, it was thriving. In 1979 Romana's Mexican Food Products

employed about 400 people and had sales of some $12 million annually.

Bañuelos worked at more than accumulating wealth. She contributed to scholarships for Mexican American students, especially those interested in business, which Bañuelos believes is an important path to political influence. With a number of partners, she also founded the Pan-American National Bank. It too was successful.

Bañuelos' success and community leadership led to President Nixon's appointing her as U.S. treasurer in 1971.

954 CHAPTER 32 Politics and Economics

---

accused criminals. Nixon openly criticized the Court and its chief justice, Earl Warren. The president promised to fill vacancies on the Supreme Court with judges who would support the rights of law enforcement over the rights of suspected criminals.

When Chief Justice Warren retired shortly after Nixon took office, the president replaced him with **Warren Burger,** a respected conservative judge. He also placed three other conservative justices on the Court, including one from the South. The Burger Court did not reverse Warren Court rulings on the rights of criminal suspects. It did, however, refuse to expand those rights further. For example, in *Stone* v. *Powell* (1976), it agreed to limits on the rights of defendants to appeal state convictions to the federal judiciary. The Court also continued to uphold capital punishment as constitutional. 📖 *(See page 1083 for more information on* Stone v. Powell.*)*

The New Federalism President Nixon's Republican constituency also favored dismantling a number of federal programs and giving more control to state and local governments. Nixon called this **New Federalism.** He argued that it would provide the government agencies that were closest to the citizens the opportunity to address more of their issues.

"I reject the patronizing idea that government in Washington, D.C., is inevitably more wise and more efficient than government at the state or local level," Nixon declared. "The idea that a bureaucratic elite in Washington knows what's best for people . . . is really a contention that people cannot govern themselves." Under the New Federalism program, Congress passed a series of revenue-sharing bills that granted federal funds to state and local agencies to use.

Although **revenue sharing** was intended to give state and local agencies more power, over time it gave the federal government new power. As states came to depend on federal funds, the federal government could impose conditions on the states. Unless they met those conditions, their funds would be cut off.

While he worked to limit federal government responsibilities, Nixon also sought to increase the power of the executive branch. Nixon did not

---

MEETING SPECIAL NEEDS

Visual/Spatial Have students draw a picture or icon to illustrate the Key Terms and Names for this section. Have students use at least one of their drawings in a political cartoon to illustrate an event, concept, or issue presented in this section. **L1** ELL

📁 Refer to *Inclusion for the High School Social Studies Classroom Strategies and Activities* in the TCR.

build many strong relationships in Congress. His lack of camaraderie with lawmakers and the fact that the Republican Party controlled neither house led to struggles with the legislative branch. Nixon often responded by trying to work around Congress and use greater executive authority. For instance, when Congress appropriated money for programs he opposed, Nixon **impounded**, or refused to release, the funds. The Supreme Court eventually declared the practice of impoundment unconstitutional.

The Family Assistance Plan One federal program Nixon sought to reform was the nation's welfare system—**Aid to Families with Dependent Children** (AFDC). The program had many critics, Republican and Democratic alike. They argued that AFDC was structured so that it was actually better for poor people to apply for benefits than to take a low-paying job. A mother who had such a job, for example, would then have to pay for child care, sometimes leaving her with less income than she had on welfare. There was also great inequity among states since each was allowed to develop its own guidelines.

In 1969 Nixon proposed replacing the AFDC with the Family Assistance Plan. The plan called for providing needy families a guaranteed yearly grant of $1,600, which could be supplemented by outside earnings. Many liberals applauded the plan as a significant step toward expanding federal responsibility for the poor. Nixon, however, presented the program in a conservative light, arguing it would reduce federal supervision and encourage welfare recipients to become more responsible.

Although the program won approval in the House in 1970, it soon came under harsh attack. Welfare recipients complained that the federal grant was too low, while conservatives, who disapproved of guaranteed income, also criticized the plan. Such opposition led to the program's defeat in the Senate.

✓ **Reading Check** **Evaluating** What impact did third party candidate George Wallace have on the 1968 election?

Nixon's Foreign Policy

Despite Nixon's domestic initiatives, a State Department official later recalled that the president had a "monumental disinterest in domestic policies." Nixon once expressed his hope that a "competent cabinet" of advisers could run the country. This would allow him to focus his energies on the subject that truly fascinated him, foreign affairs. Embarking on an ambitious foreign policy agenda

---

Fact | Fiction | Folklore

"Ping-Pong Diplomacy" In April 1971, nearly a year before President Nixon made his historic trip there, Communist China welcomed a different kind of U.S. delegation—the American ping-pong team. When the team received their surprise invitation, *Time* magazine called it "the ping heard round the world." The nine players, four officials, and two spouses who arrived on the Chinese mainland were the first Americans to enter China since the Communist takeover in 1949.

---

that included historic encounters with both China and the Soviet Union, Nixon set out to leave his mark on the world stage.

Nixon and Kissinger In a move that would greatly influence his foreign policy, Nixon chose as his national security adviser **Henry Kissinger,** a former Harvard professor. As a teenager Kissinger had fled to the United States from Germany with his family in 1938 to escape Nazi persecution of Jews. He had served as a foreign policy consultant for Presidents Kennedy and Johnson. Though Secretary of State William Rogers technically outranked him, Kissinger soon took the lead in helping shape Nixon's foreign policy.

Nixon and Kissinger shared views on many issues. Both believed simply abandoning the war in Vietnam would damage the United States's position in the world. Thus they worked toward a gradual withdrawal. Nixon and Kissinger also believed in shaping a foreign policy rooted in practical approaches rather than ideologies. They felt the nation's decades-long anticommunist crusade had created a foreign policy that was too rigid and often worked against the nation's interests. While both leaders wanted to continue to contain communism, they believed that engagement and negotiation with Communists offered a better way for the United States to achieve its international goals. As a surprised nation watched, Nixon and Kissinger put their philosophy into practice by forging friendlier relations with the Soviet Union and China.

CHAPTER 32 Politics and Economics **955**

Fact | Fiction | Folklore

In another example of the continuing efforts to normalize relations with China, Ling-Ling and Hsing-Hsing arrived at the National Zoo in 1972. A gift from China, the rare giant pandas attracted visitors and volunteers. In addition, the pair provided a wealth of scientific knowledge about the endangered panda. Following the deaths of Ling-Ling and Hsing-Hsing in 1992 and 1999, the National Zoo made arrangements to borrow two new pandas from China. Tian-Tian and Mei Xiang arrived in December 2000.

FYI

Henry Kissinger and his family fled Nazi Germany in 1938. He studied at Harvard and later became a professor there. In 1973 he shared the Nobel Peace Prize with North Vietnamese leader Le Duc Tho.

✓ **Reading Check**

Answer: Wallace garnered enough conservative votes to make the popular vote totals for Nixon and Humphrey very close.

INTERDISCIPLINARY CONNECTIONS ACTIVITY

Government Have students research the order of succession for the president and the process for replacing a vice president who leaves office during his or her term. Have students create a poster showing the steps prescribed by the Twenty-fifth Amendment to the Constitution. Then discuss as a class why it is important to have an established procedure for replacing national leaders. **L2**

Writing a Press Release Have students write a press release detailing the strategic goals of Nixon's visit to China. Tell students that a good press release uses an inverted pyramid format with the most important information in the first sentence of the release. **L2**

3 ASSESS

Assign Section 1 Assessment as homework or as an in-class activity.

◉ Have students use the **Interactive Tutor Self-Assessment CD-ROM.**

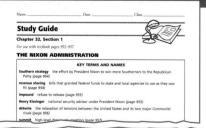

Analyzing *Political Cartoons*

Arms Buildup Anxiety The urgent need to negotiate a reduction in nuclear arms is demonstrated in this 1970 cartoon. When was the SALT I agreement finally signed?

The Establishment of Détente The Soviet Union was not initially pleased when Nixon, a man with a history of outspoken anticommunist actions, became president. The Washington correspondent for the Soviet newspaper *Izvestia*, Yuri Barsukov, had called the election "unwelcome news for Moscow" and predicted that Soviet leaders "would have to deal with a very stubborn president."

Things did not turn out that way, however. Nixon was still a staunch anticommunist, but he came to reject the notion of a bipolar world in which the superpowers of the United States and the Soviet Union confronted one another. He believed the United States needed to understand the growing role that China, Japan, and Western Europe would soon

play. This "multipolar" world of the future demanded a different approach to American foreign policy.

With Kissinger's help, Nixon fashioned an approach called **détente,** or relaxation of tensions, between the United States and its two major Communist rivals, the Soviet Union and China. In explaining détente to the American people, Nixon said that the United States had to build a better relationship with its main rivals in the interests of world peace:

> ❝We must understand that détente is not a love fest. It is an understanding between nations that have opposite purposes, but which share common interests, including the avoidance of a nuclear war. Such an understanding can work—that is, restrain aggression and deter war—only as long as the potential aggressor is made to recognize that neither aggression nor war will be profitable.❞
>
> —quoted in *The Limits of Power*

Nixon Visits China Détente began with an effort to improve American-Chinese relations. Since 1949, when a Communist government came to power in China, the United States had refused to recognize the Communists as the legitimate rulers. Instead, the American government recognized the exiled regime on the island of Taiwan as the Chinese government. Having long supported this policy, Nixon now set out to reverse it. He began by lifting trade and travel restrictions and withdrawing the Seventh Fleet from defending Taiwan.

After a series of highly secret negotiations between Kissinger and Chinese leaders, Nixon announced that he would visit China in February 1972. During the historic trip, the leaders of both nations agreed to establish "more normal" relations between their countries. In a statement that epitomized the notion of détente, Nixon told his Chinese hosts during a banquet toast, "Let us start a long march together, not in lockstep, but on different roads leading to the same goal, the goal of building a world structure of peace and justice."

In taking this trip, Nixon hoped not only to strengthen ties with the Chinese, but also to encourage the Soviets to more actively pursue diplomacy. Since the 1960s, a rift had developed between the Communist governments of the Soviet Union and China. Troops of the two nations occasionally clashed along their borders. Nixon believed détente with China would encourage Soviet premier Leonid Brezhnev to be more accommodating with the United States.

CRITICAL THINKING ACTIVITY

Synthesizing Information As a class, have students identify the links between anti-Communist thinking and Cold War policies. Ask students to explain how President Nixon's policy of détente represented a shift from past United States foreign policy, especially in dealing with Communist nations such as China. **L2**

U.S.-Soviet Tensions Ease Nixon's feelings about the Soviets proved correct. Shortly after the public learned of U.S. negotiations with China, the Soviets proposed an American-Soviet **summit**, or high-level diplomatic meeting, to be held in May 1972. On May 22, President Nixon flew to Moscow for a weeklong summit. Thus, he became the first American president ever to visit the Soviet Union.

Before Nixon's visit, Secretary of Commerce Maurice Stans spent 11 days in the Soviet Union. In his visits to a tractor plant, a steel mill, and an oil field, Stans recalled, "It was as friendly a meeting as if I were representing California and negotiating with the state of Arizona." Before leaving, however, Stans requested a favor from his Soviet host, Alexei Kosygin:

66 'There is one thing I hope you will take care of: on the highway into Moscow there is a great big billboard with the United States pictured as a vicious killer, with a sword in one hand and a gun in the other, killing people all over the world. I don't think that will be a good entrance for President Nixon, and the sign ought to come down.' He said, 'It will.' 99

—quoted in *Nixon: An Oral History of His Presidency*

During the historic Moscow summit, the two superpowers signed the first **Strategic Arms Limitation Treaty,** or SALT I, a plan to limit nuclear arms the two nations had been working on for years. Nixon and Brezhnev also agreed to increase trade and the exchange of scientific information.

Détente profoundly eased tensions between the Soviet Union and the United States. By the end of Nixon's presidency, one Soviet official admitted that

Picturing **History**

Détente Discussion Soviet premier Leonid Brezhnev listens to President Nixon during Brezhnev's June 1973 visit to Washington, D.C. On June 22 the two signed an agreement on the prevention of nuclear war. What does the word détente mean?

"the United States and the Soviet Union had their best relationship of the whole Cold War period." President Nixon indeed had made his mark on the world stage. As he basked in the glow of his 1972 foreign policy triumphs, however, trouble was brewing on the home front. A scandal was about to engulf his presidency and plunge the nation into one of its greatest constitutional crises.

✓ **Reading Check** **Summarizing** What were the results of the 1972 American-Soviet summit?

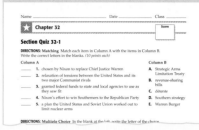
Picturing **History**

Answer: relaxation of tensions
Ask: Who prepared the way for Nixon's visit to the Soviet Union? (*Secretary of Commerce Maurice Stans*)

✓ **Reading Check**

Answer: signed SALT I, agreed to increase trade and exchange scientific information

Reteach
Have students describe Nixon's domestic agenda.

Enrich
Have students use library and Internet resources to research the basic provisions of the SALT I and SALT II treaties. Based on their research, have students create a chart showing the provisions of each treaty.

4 CLOSE

Have students discuss Nixon's foreign policy achievements.

SECTION 1 ASSESSMENT

Checking for Understanding
1. **Define:** impound, détente, summit.
2. **Identify:** Southern strategy, revenue sharing, Henry Kissinger.
3. **Describe** Nixon's New Federalism policy.

Reviewing Themes
4. **Global Connections** What were the results of Nixon's policy of détente?

Critical Thinking
5. **Evaluating** How did Nixon's China visit affect Soviet relations?
6. **Categorizing** Use a graphic organizer similar to the one below to describe how President Nixon established détente in the countries listed.

| China | |
| Soviet Union | |

Analyzing Visuals
7. **Analyzing Political Cartoons** Study the cartoon on page 956. What is the artist's message about the impact of the arms buildup on the average citizen in both the Soviet Union and the United States?

Writing About History
8. **Expository Writing** Take on the role of a member of President Nixon's staff. Write a press release explaining Nixon's domestic and foreign policies.

SECTION 1 ASSESSMENT ANSWERS

1. Terms are in blue.
2. Southern strategy *(p. 954)*, revenue sharing *(p. 954)*, Henry Kissinger *(p. 955)*
3. He granted federal funds to state and local agencies.
4. Détente eased tensions between the United States and the Soviet Union and led to more normal relations between the U.S. and China.
5. The Soviet Union became more accommodating to the United States.
6. China: lifted trade and travel restrictions, withdrew Seventh Fleet from Taiwan; Soviet Union: increased trade, signed SALT I, exchanged scientific information
7. The arms race burdened citizens.
8. Students' press releases will vary. Students should be instructed on the proper format for a news release.

1 FOCUS

Section Overview

This section focuses on Nixon's re-election, the Watergate scandal, and the president's resignation.

Guide to Reading

Answers to Graphic:
I. The Roots of Watergate
  A. Nixon and His "Enemies"
  B. Mounting a Re-election Fight
  C. The Cover-Up Begins
II. The Cover-Up Unravels
  A. The First Cracks Show
  B. A Summer of Shocking Testimony
  C. The Case of the Tapes
  D. Nixon Resigns
III. The Impact of Watergate

Preteaching Vocabulary
Have students write a short summary of the Watergate scandal using all of the Key Terms and Names.

Guide to Reading

Main Idea
During his second term, President Nixon became embroiled in a scandal that ultimately forced him to resign.

Key Terms and Names
Sam J. Ervin, John Dean, executive privilege, impeach, Federal Campaign Act Amendments

Reading Strategy
Taking Notes As you read about the Watergate scandal, use the major headings of the section to create an outline similar to the one below.

The Watergate Scandal
I. The Roots of Watergate
  A.
  B.
  C.
II.
  A.
  B.

Reading Objectives
• **Describe** the character of Richard Nixon and the attitude of his White House.
• **Explain** the Watergate scandal and discuss its effects.

Section Theme
Government and Democracy The Watergate scandal intensified the lingering distrust of government that had grown in the United States during the Vietnam War.

Preview of Events

| ♦June 1972 | ♦March 1973 | ♦December 1973 | ♦September 1974 |

June 1972 —
Burglars arrested in Democratic National Committee headquarters at Watergate complex

May 1973
Senate begins Watergate investigation

October 1973
Battle over White House tapes leads to "Saturday Night Massacre"

August 1974
Nixon resigns

★ An American Story ★

As Bob Woodward, a young reporter for the *Washington Post,* sat in a Washington, D.C., courtroom on the morning of June 17, 1972, he was in a rather foul mood. His editor had ruined his Saturday by calling him in to cover a seemingly insignificant but bizarre incident. In the early hours of that morning, five men had broken into the Democratic National Committee (DNC) headquarters in the city's Watergate apartment-office complex.

Woodward sat toward the back of the courtroom listening to the bail proceedings for the five defendants. At one point, the judge asked each man his occupation. One of the men, James McCord, answered that he was retired from government service.

"Where in government?" asked the judge.

"CIA," McCord whispered.

Woodward sprang to attention. Why was a former member of the Central Intelligence Agency involved in what seemed to be nothing more than a burglary?

Over the next two years, Woodward and another reporter, Carl Bernstein, would investigate this question. In so doing they uncovered a scandal that helped bring about a grave constitutional crisis and eventually forced the president to resign.

—adapted from *All the President's Men*

Reporters Bob Woodward and Carl Bernstein

The Roots of Watergate

The scandal known as **Watergate** originated from the Nixon administration's attempts to cover up its involvement in the break-in at the Democratic National Committee (DNC) headquarters, along with other illegal actions committed during

---

Nixon's re-election campaign. While the affair began with the burglary at the Watergate complex, a number of scholars attribute the scandal in large part to the character of Richard Nixon and the atmosphere that he and his advisers created in the White House.

Nixon and His "Enemies" Richard Nixon had fought hard to become president. He had battled back from numerous political defeats, including a loss to John Kennedy in the 1960 presidential election, to win the presidency in 1968. Along the way, however, Nixon had grown defensive, secretive, and often resentful of his critics.

In addition, Nixon had become president during a time when the United States was still very much at war with itself. Race riots and protests over the Vietnam War continued to consume the country. In Nixon's view, these protesters and other "radicals" were out to bring down his administration. Nixon was so consumed with his opponents that he compiled an "enemies list" filled with people—from politicians to members of the media—whom he considered a threat to his presidency.

Mounting a Re-election Fight As Nixon's re-election campaign got underway in 1972, many in his administration expressed optimism about winning a second term. The president had just finished triumphant trips to China and the Soviet Union. In May, former Alabama governor George Wallace, who had mounted a strong third-party campaign in 1968, had dropped his bid for another run at the White House after an assassin's bullet paralyzed him. Meanwhile, Nixon's Democratic

opponent, South Dakota senator George McGovern, was viewed as too liberal on many issues.

At the same time, Nixon's hold on the presidency was uncertain. Despite the high approval ratings for the president's summit meetings in Beijing and Moscow, the unpopular Vietnam War still raged. Nixon staffers also remembered how close the margin of Nixon's 1968 victory had been. Seeking to gain an edge in every way they could, Nixon's team engaged in a host of subversive tactics, from spying on opposition rallies to spreading rumors and false reports.

These tactics included an effort to steal information from the Democratic Party's headquarters. In the early hours of June 17, 1972, five Nixon supporters broke into the party's office at the Watergate complex in Washington, D.C. They had intended to obtain any sensitive campaign information and to place wiretaps on the office telephones. While the burglars were at work, a security guard making his rounds spotted a piece of tape holding a door lock. The guard ripped off the tape, but when he passed the door later, he noticed that it had been replaced. He quickly called police, who arrived shortly and arrested the men.

The Cover-Up Begins In the wake of the Watergate break-in, the media discovered that one of the burglars, James McCord, was not only an ex-CIA official but also a member of the Committee for the Re-election of the President (CRP). Reports soon surfaced that the burglars had been paid to execute the break-in from a secret CRP fund controlled by the White House.

2 TEACH

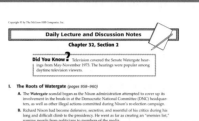

Daily Lecture and Discussion Notes 32–2

Daily Lecture and Discussion Notes
Chapter 32, Section 2

Did You Know? Television covered the Senate Watergate hearings from May–November 1973. The hearings were popular among daytime television viewers.

I. The Roots of Watergate (pages 958–960)
  A. The Watergate scandal began as the Nixon administration attempted to cover up its involvement in the break-in at the Democratic National Committee (DNC) headquarters, as well as other illegal actions committed during Nixon's re-election campaign.
  B. Richard Nixon had become defensive, secretive, and resentful of his critics during his long and difficult climb to the presidency. He went as far as creating an "enemies list," naming people from politicians to members of the media.

Using Relative Chronology
Have students create a graphic showing the relative chronology of the Watergate scandal starting with the break-in and ending with Nixon's resignation. Encourage students to use drawings, symbols, and colors to illustrate the events. **L1**

Objectives and answers to the student activity can be found in the **Web Activity Lesson Plan** at tav.glencoe.com.

Watergate Hotel The hotel gave its name to the scandal that brought down President Nixon. Hotel guard Frank Willis, pictured here, reported to police the evidence of a break-in at the Democratic National Committee headquarters there. *What was Nixon's response to the break-in?*

Picturing **History**

Answer: He denied any involvement and asked the CIA to intervene to stop the FBI from investigating the source for the money paid to the burglars. **Ask:** What was the source of the financial support for the burglary at Watergate? *(The burglars were paid from a secret CRP fund.)*

COOPERATIVE LEARNING ACTIVITY

Creating Campaign Materials Organize students into groups to create campaign materials for the 1972 presidential election. Have each group choose one of the presidential candidates and develop a campaign platform and slogan. Allow group members to choose which of the following they would like to create: bumper sticker, placard, button, or hat. Ask groups to present their platform, slogan, and campaign materials to the class.

Use the rubric for a cooperative group management plan on pages 81–82 in the *Performance Assessment Activities and Rubrics.*

Guided Reading Activity 32–2

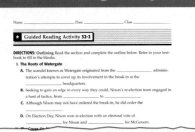

Name _____ Date _____ Class _____

★ **Guided Reading Activity 32-2**

DIRECTIONS: Outlining Read the section and complete the outline below. Refer to your textbook to fill in the blanks.

I. The Roots of Watergate

A. The scandal known as Watergate originated from the _____ administration's attempts to cover up its involvement in the break-in at the
_____ headquarters.

B. Seeking to gain an edge in every way they could, Nixon's re-election team engaged in
a host of tactics, from _____ to _____.

C. Although Nixon may not have ordered the break-in, he did order the _____

D. On Election Day, Nixon won re-election with an electoral vote of
_____ for Nixon and _____ for McGovern.

Picturing History

Answer: The committee voted to
recommend three articles of
impeachment.

Ask: What charges did the committee make? (*Nixon had obstructed justice, misused federal agencies to
violate the rights of citizens, and
defied the authority of Congress by
refusing to deliver tapes and other
evidence.*)

Predicting Outcomes Ask students to consider how the presidential election of 1972 might
have been different had the
information about the Watergate
scandal been uncovered and
reported the week before the
election. Have students give reasons for their responses. **L2**

📁 Use *Supreme Court Case
Study 49*, *United States* v. *Nixon*.

As questions swirled about a possible White
House connection to the burglary, the cover-up
began. Administration officials destroyed incriminat-
ing documents and provided false testimony to
investigators. Meanwhile, President Nixon stepped
in. While the president may not have ordered the
break-in, he did order a cover-up. With Nixon's consent, administration officials asked the CIA to intervene and stop the FBI from inquiring into the source
of the money paid to the burglars. Their justification
was that such an investigation would threaten
national security.

All the while, the White House strongly denied
any involvement in the break-in. Nixon's press secretary dismissed the incident as a "third-rate burglary
attempt," while the president himself told the
American public, "The White House has had no
involvement whatever in this particular incident."

The strategy worked. Most Americans believed
President Nixon. Despite efforts by the media, in particular the *Washington Post*, to keep the story alive,
few people paid much attention to the Watergate
affair during the 1972 presidential campaign. On
Election Day, Nixon won re-election by one of the

Picturing History

Sitting in Judgment Representative Barbara Jordan from Texas was an outspoken member of the House Judiciary Committee. *What was this committee's
role in the impeachment process?*

largest margins in history with nearly 61 percent of
the popular vote compared to 37.5 percent for George
McGovern. The electoral vote was 520 votes for
Nixon and 17 for McGovern.

✓ **Reading Check** **Examining** Why did members of
the CRP break into the Democratic National Committee
headquarters?

The Cover-Up Unravels

Shortly after his triumphant re-election, an exu-
berant and confident Nixon told his cabinet and staff
that 1973 "can be and should be the best year ever."
In a matter of months, however, the Watergate affair
would erupt, and the coming year would be one of
the president's worst.

The First Cracks Show In 1973 the Watergate burglars went on trial. Under relentless prodding from
federal judge John J. Sirica, McCord agreed to cooperate with both a grand jury investigation and with
the Senate's Select Committee on Presidential
Campaign Activities, which had been recently established under Senator **Sam J. Ervin** of North Carolina.
McCord's testimony opened a floodgate of confes-
sions, and a parade of White House and campaign
officials exposed one illegality after another over the
next several months. Foremost among the officials
was counsel to the president **John Dean,** a member of
the inner circle of the White House who leveled allegations against Nixon himself.

A Summer of Shocking Testimony In June 1973,
John Dean testified before Senator Ervin's committee
that former Attorney General John Mitchell had
ordered the Watergate break-in and that Nixon had
played an active role in attempting to cover up any
White House involvement. As a shocked nation
absorbed Dean's testimony, the Nixon administration strongly denied the charges.

A standoff ensued for the next month, as the
Senate committee attempted to determine who was
telling the truth. Then, on July 16, the answer
appeared unexpectedly. On that day, White House
aide Alexander Butterfield testified that Nixon had
ordered a taping system installed in the White
House to record all conversations. The president
had done so, Butterfield said, to help him write his
memoirs after he left office. For members of the
committee, however, the tapes would tell them
exactly what the president knew and when he
knew it.

MEETING SPECIAL NEEDS

Visual/Spatial Have students create a photo essay about the Watergate scandal. Encourage students to use photographs and captions to tell how the Watergate scandal started, who was
involved, when it happened, and how it concluded. **L2** **ELL**

📁 Refer to *Inclusion for the High School Social Studies Classroom Strategies and
Activities* in the TCR.

Picturing History

High Political Drama After resigning his office on August 9, 1974, President Nixon and his family say goodbye to aides and friends on the White House lawn. On the capital's streets, a reader takes in the news in the *Washington Post,* the newspaper that started the Watergate investigation. Who replaced Nixon as president?

The Case of the Tapes All the groups investigating the scandal sought access to the tapes. Nixon refused, pleading executive privilege—the principle that White House conversations should remain confidential to protect national security. A special prosecutor appointed by the president to handle the Watergate cases, Archibald Cox, took Nixon to court in October 1973 to force him to give up the recordings. Nixon, clearly growing desperate, ordered Attorney General Elliot Richardson, and then Richardson's deputy, to fire Cox. Both men refused and resigned in protest. Solicitor General Robert Bork finally fired Cox, but the incident, nicknamed the "Saturday Night Massacre" in the press, badly damaged Nixon's reputation with the public.

The fall of 1973 proved to be a disastrous time for Nixon for other reasons as well. His vice president, Spiro Agnew, was forced to resign in disgrace. Investigators had discovered that Agnew had taken bribes from state contractors while he was governor of Maryland and that he had continued to accept bribes while serving in Washington. Gerald Ford, the Republican leader of the House of Representatives, became the new vice president. Nixon then had to defend himself against allegations about his own past financial dealings.

GOVERNMENT

Nixon Resigns In an effort to quiet the growing outrage over his actions, President Nixon appointed a new special prosecutor, Texas lawyer Leon Jaworski, who proved no less determined than Cox to obtain the president's tapes. In April 1974, Nixon released edited transcripts of the tapes, claiming that they proved his innocence. Investigators felt otherwise and went to court again to force Nixon to turn over the unedited tapes. In July the Supreme Court ruled that the president had to turn over the tapes themselves, not just the transcripts. With nowhere else to appeal, Nixon handed over the tapes.

Several days later, the House Judiciary Committee voted to impeach Nixon, or officially charge him of presidential misconduct. The committee charged that Nixon had obstructed justice in the Watergate cover-up; misused federal agencies to violate the rights of citizens; and defied the authority of Congress by refusing to deliver tapes and other materials that the committee had requested. The next step was for the entire House of Representatives to vote whether or not to impeach the president.

As the nation held its collective breath in anticipation, investigators finally found indisputable

CHAPTER 32 Politics and Economics **961**

INTERDISCIPLINARY CONNECTIONS ACTIVITY

Communication Have students find articles in newspapers from the Watergate era that reported on the events surrounding Watergate. Select one group of three or four students to research polling data showing Nixon's popularity from 1971 until his resignation and to create a chart reporting this data. Have volunteers provide a summary of their articles to the class and then have the group who prepared the chart show their findings. Discuss as a class the power of the press to influence public opinion. **L2**

Name _____ Date _____ Class _____

⭐ **Chapter 32**   Score ____

Section Quiz 32-2

DIRECTIONS: Matching Match each item in Column A with the items in Column B.
Write the correct letters in the blanks. (10 points each)

Column A

____ 1. principle that White House conversations should remain confidential to protect national security
____ 2. member of Nixon's inner circle who leveled allegations against Nixon
____ 3. limited campaign contributions and established an independent agency to administer stricter election laws
____ 4. appointed by President Nixon to handle the Watergate cases and eventually fired at Nixon's request
____ 5. senator from North Carolina and head of the Senate's Select Committee on Presidential Campaign Activities

Column B

A. John Dean
B. Federal Campaign Act Amendments
C. Sam J. Ervin
D. executive privilege
E. Archibald Cox

✔ Reading Check

Answer: Dean testified that former Attorney General John Mitchell had ordered the Watergate break-in and that Nixon had played an active role in attempting to cover up any White House involvement. This shocked the nation and led to further investigation.

Reteach

Have students describe the character of Richard Nixon and the attitude of his White House.

Enrich

Invite interested students to read and report on *All the President's Men* by Carl Bernstein and Bob Woodward.

✔ Reading Check

Answer: Congress wanted to reestablish the balance of power between the branches of government.

4 CLOSE

Have students explain the Watergate scandal and discuss its effects.

---

evidence against the president. One of the unedited tapes revealed that on June 23, 1972, just six days after the Watergate burglary, Nixon had ordered the CIA to stop the FBI's investigation of the break-in. With this news, even the president's strongest supporters conceded that impeachment and conviction in the Senate now seemed inevitable. On August 9, 1974, Nixon resigned his office in disgrace. Gerald Ford took the oath of office and became the nation's 38th president.

✔ **Reading Check** **Explaining** What was the significance of John Dean's testimony before the Senate committee?

The Impact of Watergate

Upon taking office, President Ford urged Americans to put the Watergate affair behind them and move on. "Our long national nightmare is over," he declared. The effects of the scandal, however, endured long after Richard Nixon's resignation.

The Watergate crisis prompted a series of new laws intended to limit the power of the executive branch. In the 1970s Congress passed a number of laws aimed at reestablishing a greater balance of power in government. The **Federal Campaign Act Amendments** limited campaign contributions and established an independent agency to administer stricter election laws. The Ethics in Government Act required financial disclosure by high government officials in all three branches of government. The FBI Domestic Security Investigation Guidelines restricted the bureau's political intelligence-gathering activities. After Watergate, Congress also established a means for appointing an independent counsel to investigate and prosecute wrongdoing by high government officials.

Despite these efforts, Watergate left many Americans with a deep distrust of their public officials. Speaking some 20 years after the Watergate affair, Alexander Haig, a former high-level Nixon aide, said the scandal had produced, "a fundamental discrediting of respect for the presidency . . . [and] a new skepticism about politics, in general, which every American feels to this day." On the other hand, some Americans saw the Watergate affair as proof that in the United States, no person is above the law. As Bob Woodward observed:

❝Watergate was probably a good thing for the country; it was a good, sobering lesson. Accountability to the law applies to everyone. The problem with kings and prime ministers and presidents is that they think that they are above it, and there is no accountability, and that they have some special rights, and privileges, and status. And a process that says: No. We have our laws and believe them, and they apply to everyone, is a very good thing.❞

—quoted in *Nixon: An Oral History of His Presidency*

After the ordeal of Watergate, most Americans attempted to put the affair behind them. In the years ahead, however, the nation encountered a host of new troubles, from a stubborn economic recession to a heart-wrenching hostage crisis overseas.

✔ **Reading Check** **Evaluating** Why did Congress pass new laws after the Watergate scandal?

SECTION 2 ASSESSMENT

Checking for Understanding

1. **Define:** executive privilege, impeach.
2. **Identify:** Sam J. Ervin, John Dean, Federal Campaign Act Amendments.
3. **Evaluate** the effects of the Watergate scandal on the way American citizens viewed the federal government.

Reviewing Themes

4. **Government and Democracy** How did the Watergate scandal alter the balance of power between the executive and legislative branches of government?

Critical Thinking

5. **Evaluating** How did the discovery of the White House tapes change the Watergate cover-up investigation?
6. **Organizing** Using a graphic organizer similar to the one below, fill in the effects of the Watergate scandal.

Effects of Watergate Scandal

Analyzing Visuals

7. **Analyzing Photographs** Study the photograph on page 961. How would you describe the scene of Nixon's leave-taking? What in the photo suggests that this is a formal occasion? Why do you think this ceremony might be important for the nation?

Writing About History

8. **Descriptive Writing** Take on the role of a television news analyst. Write a script in which you explain the Watergate scandal and analyze the factors that led to the scandal.

962 CHAPTER 32 Politics and Economics

SECTION 2 ASSESSMENT ANSWERS

1. Terms are in blue.
2. Sam J. Ervin *(p. 960)*, John Dean *(p. 960)*, Federal Campaign Act Amendments *(p. 962)*
3. Many citizens distrusted the federal government, especially the presidency, while some saw the events as proof that no one is above the law.
4. It led to laws that limit the power of the executive branch.
5. It led to an abuse of executive privilege, but resulted in proof of Nixon's guilt.
6. Nixon's resignation, Federal Campaign Act Amendments, Ethics in Government Act, FBI Domestic Security Investigation Guidelines
7. Students' answers should thoughtfully consider the photograph.
8. Students' scripts will vary. Scripts should include suggested visuals.

Guide to Reading

Main Idea
During the 1970s, Presidents Gerald Ford and Jimmy Carter attempted to lead the United States through both domestic and foreign crises.

Key Terms and Names
inflation, embargo, stagflation, Helsinki Accords, Department of Energy

Reading Strategy
Organizing As you read about the administrations of Presidents Ford and Carter, complete a graphic organizer listing the causes of economic problems in the 1970s.

Causes

Economic
Problems
in the 1970s

Reading Objectives
• **Explain** the reasons for economic troubles in the United States during the 1970s.
• **Discuss** Jimmy Carter's domestic and foreign policies.

Section Theme
Economic Factors A weakening economy and growing energy crisis marred the terms of Ford and Carter.

Preview of Events

♦1973   ♦1975   ♦1977   ♦1979

1973
OPEC oil embargo leads to fuel shortage in the United States

1974
President Ford pardons Richard Nixon

1976
Jimmy Carter wins presidential election

1979
Iranian revolutionaries seize U.S. embassy in Iran

★ An American Story ★

*Lines of jobseekers at
an unemployment office*

On a sunny February day in 1977, Ellen Griffith and her fiancé, Roger Everson, both of Nashville, Tennessee, sat together in a place where neither of them dreamed they would be—the state unemployment office. Just a month before, Griffith, a 20-year-old salesclerk in a shopping center, and Everson, 21, had been excitedly making wedding plans. Now, with Everson laid off and Griffith on a reduced work schedule, the young couple had decided to put their future plans on hold. "It cost something to get married, you know," said Everson.

What had landed the two in this predicament was a one-two punch of a particularly bitter winter and an energy shortage that had gone on for much of the decade. The brutally cold weather in the Midwest and East had increased the demand for oil and fuel, already in short supply throughout the country. In response, the government had asked numerous companies and shops to conserve energy by cutting back on their business hours. As a result, Griffith saw her work schedule slashed from 40 hours per week to 20 hours.

As the couple sat stoically in the unemployment office waiting for their names to be called, Griffith wondered how she would pay her bills on her reduced salary and whatever she might be able to get from the state. "I just feel like we've been rained on," she said glumly.

—**adapted from the** *New York Times,* **February 3, 1977**

The Economic Crisis of the 1970s

Since the end of World War II, the American economy had been the envy of the world. During the 1950s and 1960s, many Americans enjoyed remarkable prosperity and had come to assume it was the norm. This prosperity rested in large part on easy access to

---

1 FOCUS

Section Overview

This section focuses on the Ford and Carter administrations and the domestic and foreign crises these presidents faced.

BELLRINGER
Skillbuilder Activity

 Project transparency and have students answer the question.

Available as a blackline master.

Daily Focus Skills Transparency 32–3

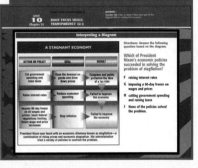

Guide to Reading

Answers to Graphic: rising cost of raw materials and rising cost of fossil fuel, increased international competition, insufficient training for new jobs

Preteaching Vocabulary
Have students use a standard dictionary to look up the words *inflation, embargo,* and *stagflation* to gain a better understanding of the Key Terms and Names used in this section.

SECTION RESOURCES

📁 Reproducible Masters
• Reproducible Lesson Plan 32–3
• Daily Lecture and Discussion Notes 32–3
• Guided Reading Activity 32–3
• Section Quiz 32–3
• Reading Essentials and Study Guide 32–3
• Performance Assessment Activities and Rubrics

🖐 Transparencies
• Daily Focus Skills Transparency 32–3

Multimedia
• Interactive Tutor Self-Assessment CD-ROM
• ExamView® Pro Testmaker CD-ROM
• Presentation Plus! CD-ROM
• TeacherWorks™ CD-ROM
• Audio Program

2 TEACH

Daily Lecture and Discussion Notes 32–3

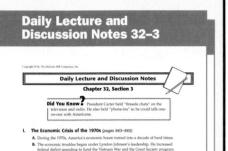

Copyright © by The McGraw-Hill Companies, Inc.

Daily Lecture and Discussion Notes

Chapter 32, Section 3

Did You Know? President Carter held "fireside chats" on the television and radio. He also held "phone-ins" so he could talk one-on-one with Americans.

I. **The Economic Crisis of the 1970s** (pages 963–965)

  A. During the 1970s, America's economic boom turned into a decade of hard times.

  B. The economic troubles began under Lyndon Johnson's leadership. He increased federal deficit spending to fund the Vietnam War and the Great Society program without raising taxes. Pumping large amounts of money into the economy created inflation, or a rise in the cost of goods.

  C. In 1973 the Organization of Petroleum Exporting Countries (OPEC) announced an

Creating a Thematic Map Have students draw a map showing the countries that currently belong to OPEC. Have them use the map to identify the regions of the world in which a large percentage of the world's oil reserves are found. **L1**

 Use the rubric for creating a map, display, or chart on pages 77–78 in the *Performance Assessment Activities and Rubrics.*

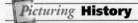

Picturing **History**

Answer: because the United States supported Israel in the Yom Kippur War

Ask: Before the 1973 OPEC embargo, what was the price of a barrel of crude oil? ($3)

FYI

OPEC is responsible for approximately 40 percent of the world's oil production and controls 75 percent of the world's proven oil reserves.

---

raw materials around the world and a strong manufacturing industry at home. By the 1970s, however, both conditions began to disappear. The nation's boom years gave way to a decade of hard times.

A Mighty Economic Machine Slows The nation's economic troubles began to take shape as early as the mid-1960s during the administration of Lyndon Johnson. Johnson significantly increased federal deficit spending when he attempted to fund both the Vietnam War and his ambitious Great Society program without raising taxes. This pumped large amounts of money into the economy, which spurred inflation, or a rise in the cost of goods.

Rising costs of raw materials due to greater competition for them was another cause of inflation. In particular, the rising cost of oil dealt a strong blow to the nation's economy. More than any other nation, the United States based its economy on the easy availability of cheap and plentiful fossil fuels. With the highest volume of oil consumption in the world, the nation had become heavily dependent on imports from the Middle East and Africa.

For years, the **Organization of Petroleum Exporting Countries** (OPEC) sold oil for its member countries. Prices remained low until the early 1970s, when OPEC decided to use oil as a political and economic weapon. In 1973 the Yom Kippur War was raging between Israel and its Arab neighbors. Tension had existed between Israel and the Arab world ever since the founding of modern Israel in 1948. Since most Arab states did not recognize

Picturing **History**

A Scarce Commodity Americans had to schedule their lives around the availability of gasoline during the OPEC oil embargo. **Why did OPEC institute the embargo?**

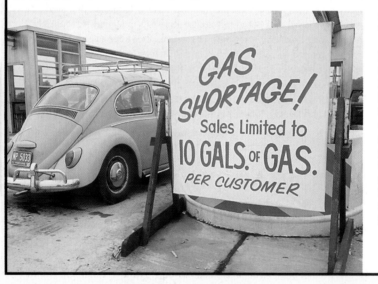

Israel's right to exist, U.S. support of Israel made American relations with Arab states uneasy.

Now OPEC announced that its members would embargo, or stop shipping, petroleum to countries that supported Israel, namely the United States and some Western European nations. OPEC also raised the price of crude oil by 70 percent, and then by another 130 percent a few months later. As a result, the United States suffered its first fuel shortage since World War II.

Although the embargo ended a few months after it began, oil prices continued to rise. OPEC raised prices three more times in the 1970s and again in 1980. By that time, the price of a barrel of crude oil had risen from $3 in 1973 to $30 in 1980. The dramatic increase helped accelerate inflation throughout the American economy. High prices for gasoline and home heating oil meant that Americans had less money to spend on other goods, which helped send the economy into a recession.

ECONOMICS

A Stagnant Economy Another economic problem was the decline of the manufacturing sector. In the years following World War II, the United States had dominated international trade, but by the 1970s, it faced increased international competition. Many manufacturing plants were now decades old and less efficient than the newer plants that Japan and European industrial nations built after the war.

These factors forced many factories to close, and millions of workers lost their jobs. Although new jobs were available in the growing information and service-oriented sector, many industrial workers were poorly equipped for them. The result was a growing pool of unemployed and underemployed workers.

Thus in the early 1970s President Nixon faced a new and puzzling economic dilemma that came to be known as "stagflation," a combination of rising prices and economic stagnation. Economists who emphasized the demand side of economic theory, including supporters of Keynesianism, did not think that inflation and recession could occur at the same time. They believed that demand drives prices and that inflation would only occur in a booming economy when

---

COOPERATIVE LEARNING ACTIVITY

Role-Playing Organize students into groups of five. Have groups role-play a meeting among representatives from OPEC, Israel, the United States, Japan, and West Germany to discuss economic concerns. Assign students to groups composed of individuals with varying abilities. Have each group prepare and stage a meeting for the class.

Use the rubric for a cooperative group management plan on pages 81–82 in the *Performance Assessment Activities and Rubrics.*

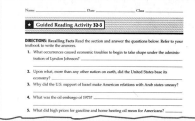

Guided Reading Activity 32–3

Name _____ Date _____ Class _____

★ Guided Reading Activity 32-3

DIRECTIONS: Recalling Facts Read the section and answer the questions below. Refer to your textbook to write the answers.

1. What occurrences caused economic troubles to begin to take shape under the administration of Lyndon Johnson?

2. Upon what, more than any other nation on earth, did the United States base its economy?

3. Why did the U.S. support of Israel make American relations with Arab states uneasy?

4. What was the oil embargo of 1973?

5. What did high prices for gasoline and home heating oil mean for Americans?

Analyzing *Political Cartoons*

Coping With Shortages Cartoonist Brant Parker reflected the public's frustration over the oil shortages of the 1970s. What message does the cartoonist convey with the statement "the figs are next"?

demand for goods was high. As a result, they did not know what fiscal policy the government should pursue. Increased spending might help end the recession, but it would increase inflation. Raising taxes might slow inflation, but it would also keep the economy in recession.

Nixon decided to focus on controlling inflation. The government moved first to cut spending and raise taxes. The president hoped that higher taxes would prompt Americans to spend less, which would ease the demand on goods and drive down prices. Congress and much of the public, however, protested the idea of a tax hike. Nixon then tried to reduce consumer spending by getting the Federal Reserve Board to raise interest rates. When this failed, the president tried to stop inflation by imposing a 90-day freeze on wages and prices and then issuing federal regulations limiting future wage and price increases. This too met with little success.

When Nixon resigned in 1974, the nation's inflation rate was still high, despite many efforts to reduce prices. Meanwhile, the unemployment rate was over five percent. It would now be up to Gerald Ford to confront stagflation.

✓ **Reading Check** **Explaining** How did President Nixon attempt to stop stagflation?

Ford Takes Over

Most Americans considered Gerald Ford a decent and honest if not particularly dynamic leader. When he became vice president, Ford had readily acknowledged his bland personality. "I'm a Ford, not a Lincoln," he said. Still, the new president boasted excellent credentials, including a degree from Yale

Law School, naval service during World War II, and service in the House of Representatives since 1949. His fellow Republicans had elected him as minority leader in 1965. Ford would need to draw on all his experience during his time in office.

Ford Pardons Nixon Ford was in the White House just a month when his efforts to restore faith in the nation's leadership suffered a serious setback. On September 8, 1974, Ford announced that he would grant a "full, free, and absolute pardon" to Richard Nixon for any crimes he "committed or may have committed or taken part in" while president. "This is an American tragedy in which we all have played a part," he told the nation. "It could go on and on and on, or someone must write the end to it."

Ford insisted he was acting not out of sympathy for Nixon, but in the public interest. Ford's position was that he wanted to avoid the division that charges against Nixon and a public trial would create. Nonetheless, the pardon aroused fierce criticism. Ford's approval ratings soon plunged from 71 percent to 50 percent.

Ford Tries to "Whip" Inflation By 1975 the American economy was in its worst recession since the Great Depression, with unemployment at nearly nine percent. Rejecting the notion of mandatory wage and price controls to reduce inflation, Ford requested voluntary controls. Under a plan known as WIN—Whip Inflation Now—he urged Americans to cut back on their oil and gas consumption and to undertake other energy-conserving measures. The plan stirred up little enthusiasm and eventually failed. The president then turned to cutting government spending and advocating higher interest rates to curb inflation. This too failed.

CHAPTER 32 Politics and Economics **965**

Analyzing *Political Cartoons*

Answer: Because of American dependence on foreign oil, the cartoonist implies that OPEC countries could dictate to the U.S. government.

✓ **Reading Check**

Answer: The government cut spending and raised taxes, the Federal Reserve raised interest rates, and the president imposed a 90-day freeze on wages and prices and issued regulations to limit future wage and price increases.

Creating a Graph Provide the data below and have students create a graph showing the average price of a gallon of gasoline in the United States between 1973 and 1980. **L2**

Year	Price	Year	Price
1973	$ .39	1977	$ .64
1974	.53	1978	.65
1975	.57	1979	.88
1976	.60	1980	1.22

MEETING SPECIAL NEEDS

Learning Disability Pair students with different abilities and have them work together to create a study outline for this section. Encourage students to use the section headings as a guide for structuring their outlines. They can also use the section and chapter time lines to help sequence information. **L1**

👉 Refer to *Inclusion for the High School Social Studies Classroom Strategies and Activities* in the TCR.

Creating a Chart Have students refer to the chapter on the Great Depression and compare the unemployment rates then with those during the years 1974–1975. Have students create a chart showing the comparison.

📁 Use the rubric for creating a map, display, or chart on pages 77–78 in the *Performance Assessment Activities and Rubrics.*

✓ Reading Check

Answer: Ford urged Americans to cut back on gas and oil consumption and undertake other energy-conserving measures; he cut government spending and advocated higher interest rates; he attempted to limit federal authority, balance the budget, and keep taxes low.

Picturing **History**

Answer: He suggested voluntary measures to cut back on energy use and governmental solutions, such as cutting back on spending and advocating higher interest rates.
Ask: What kind of garden was the predecessor of the WIN garden?
(the Victory Gardens of World War II)

Picturing **History**

Reassuring Presence After the turmoil of Watergate, President Gerald Ford, shown here with First Lady Betty Ford, was a comforting leader, but he was unable to solve the problem of inflation. Through what methods did Ford try to "whip inflation now"?

As Ford attempted to revive the economy, he also attempted to limit federal authority, balance the budget, and keep taxes low. Ford vetoed more than 50 bills that the Democratic-led Congress passed during the first two years of his administration.

Ford's Foreign Policy In foreign policy, Ford continued Nixon's general strategy. Ford kept Kissinger on as secretary of state and continued to pursue détente with the Soviets and the Chinese. In August 1975 he met with leaders of NATO and the Warsaw Pact to sign the **Helsinki Accords.** Under the accords, the parties recognized the borders of Eastern Europe established at the end of World War II. The Soviets in return promised to uphold certain basic human rights, including the right to move across national borders. The subsequent Soviet failure to uphold these basic rights turned many Americans against détente.

Ford also encountered problems in Southeast Asia. In May 1975, Cambodia seized the *Mayaguez,* an American cargo ship traveling near its shores, claiming that it had been on an intelligence-gathering mission. Calling the ship's seizure an "act of piracy," Ford dispatched U.S. Marines to retrieve it. Cambodia released the crew before the marines arrived.

The Election of 1976 As the 1976 presidential election approached, Americans were pessimistic and unsure of the future. With rising inflation and unemployment, many citizens were undergoing an adverse change of lifestyle. There were equally serious problems in foreign affairs. Political turmoil in developing nations threatened world stability, while the Soviet Union was pursuing an aggressive foreign policy. Americans therefore looked to elect a man who could meet these challenges.

The presidential race pitted Gerald Ford against James Earl Carter, Jr., or Jimmy Carter, as he liked to be called. Carter was somewhat of a political outsider. A former governor of Georgia, Carter had no national political experience. Nonetheless, he had won the Democratic primary with an inspiring and well-organized campaign. Carter sought to take advantage of his outsider image, promising to restore morality and honesty to the federal government. He also promised new programs for energy development, tax reform, welfare reform, and national medical care.

More than the programs he proposed, it was Carter's image as a moral and upstanding individual that attracted most supporters. Ford meanwhile characterized Carter as a liberal whose social program spending would produce higher rates of inflation and require tax increases.

In the end, Carter edged Ford with 50.1 percent of the popular vote to Ford's 47.9 percent, while capturing 297 electoral votes to Ford's 240. On Inauguration Day, to demonstrate his man-of-the-people style, Carter declined the traditional limousine ride and walked from the Capitol to the White House.

✓ Reading Check
Examining What steps did President Ford take to try to control inflation?

Carter Battles the Economic Crisis

Carter devoted much of his domestic agenda to trying to fix the economy. At first he tried to end the recession and reduce unemployment by increasing government spending and cutting taxes. When inflation surged in 1978, he changed his mind. He delayed the tax cuts and vetoed the spending programs he had himself proposed to Congress. He then tried to ease inflation by reducing the money supply and raising interest rates. His main focus, however, was on the energy crisis. In the end, none of his efforts succeeded.

INTERDISCIPLINARY CONNECTIONS ACTIVITY

Economics Have the economics teacher present an explanation of cartels, including the fact that OPEC is the most long-lived cartel in history. Then have students research other cartels, either past or present. Have students determine the purpose of cartels, what holds cartels together, and what types of problems bring an end to cartels. Have students report their findings in a research report. **L2**

A "War" Against Consumption Carter felt that the nation's most serious problem was its dependence on foreign oil. In one of his first national addresses, he tried to rally Americans to support what he termed a "war" against rising energy consumption. "Our decision about energy will test the character of the American people and the ability of the President and Congress to govern this nation," Carter stated.

Carter proposed a national energy program to conserve oil and to promote the use of coal and renewable energy sources such as solar power. He persuaded Congress to create a **Department of Energy** and also asked Americans to make personal sacrifices to reduce their energy consumption. Most of the public complied as best they could, although many ignored the president's suggestion.

At the same time, many business leaders and economists urged the president and Congress to deregulate the oil industry. The regulations, first imposed as part of President Nixon's price control plan, limited the ability of oil companies to pass on OPEC price increases to American consumers. As a result, oil companies found it difficult to make a profit, and they lacked the capital to invest in new domestic oil wells. These regulations, combined with OPEC price increases, helped create the energy crisis of the 1970s. Carter agreed to support deregulation but insisted on a "windfall profits tax" to prevent oil companies from overcharging consumers. The tax, however, conflicted with the basic idea of deregulation, which was to free up corporate capital for use in searching for new sources of oil. In the end, Carter's contradictory plan did not solve the country's energy crisis.

In the summer of 1979, instability in the Middle East produced a second major fuel shortage and deepened the nation's economic problems. Under increasing pressure to act, Carter made several proposals in a television address. The speech was notable for Carter's bleak assessment of the national condition. He complained about a "crisis of confidence" that had struck "at the very heart and soul of our national will." The address became known as the "malaise" speech, although Carter had not specifically used that word. Many Americans interpreted the speech not as a timely warning but as Carter blaming the people for his failures.

Carter's Leadership Problems In retrospect, President Carter's difficulties in solving the nation's economic problems lay in his inexperience and inability to work with Congress. Carter, who was proud of his outsider status, made little effort to reach out to Washington's legislative leaders. As a result, Congress blocked many of his energy proposals.

Carter also failed to translate his ideas into a concrete set of goals to inspire the nation. He offered no unifying theme for his administration, but instead followed a cautious middle course that left people confused. By 1979 public opinion polls showed that Carter's popularity had dropped lower than President Nixon's during Watergate.

 **Reading Check** **Summarizing** To what did President Carter devote much of his domestic agenda?

Carter's Foreign Policy

In contrast to his uncertain leadership at home, Carter's foreign policy was more clearly defined. A man of strong religious beliefs, Carter argued that the United States must try to be "right and honest and truthful and decent" in dealing with other nations. Yet it was on the international front that President Carter suffered one of his most devastating defeats.

Picturing **History**

Change of Pace Jimmy Carter underscored his campaign image of being a new kind of politician by walking to the White House after his inauguration. What about Carter's image in 1976 might have been appealing to the public?

Reading Check

Answer: His main focus was the energy crisis.

Picturing **History**

Answer: He had a down-to-earth image that appealed to people after the less accessible personalities of Nixon and Ford.
Ask: Why did Carter face leadership problems? *(He was inexperienced, he failed to work with Congress, and he did not translate his ideas into concrete goals.)*

FYI

After his inauguration, Jimmy Carter and his family chose to walk up Pennsylvania Avenue from the Capitol to the White House instead of riding in the traditional limousine. The gesture symbolized Carter's desire to lead a simple life even while in the White House.

Recognizing Ideologies Have students create a list of President Carter's foreign policy decisions that reflected his belief in human rights. Then have students select a decision and defend or reject its human rights basis. **L2**

CRITICAL THINKING ACTIVITY

Expressing an Opinion Tell students that government officials, such as state governors and the president, can grant reprieves and pardons to individuals convicted of offenses except in impeachment cases. A pardon releases the individual from any punishment due for a crime committed, but does not free the person from any implied guilt. President Ford's pardon of Richard Nixon was one of the most controversial pardons in American history. Ask students if they think President Ford did the right thing. Ask them to explain their opinions. **L2**

NATIONAL GEOGRAPHIC
MOMENT in HISTORY

For over 14 months, the hostage crisis dominated the news. Some television stations opened or closed their newscasts with statements such as, "Good evening on day 334 of the Iranian hostage crisis." Thus, the crisis stayed at the forefront of public attention. Many people hung yellow ribbons around trees as a constant reminder of the hostages' plight.

3 ASSESS

Assign Section 3 Assessment as homework or as an in-class activity.

⬤ Have students use the **Interactive Tutor Self-Assessment CD-ROM.**

Reading Essentials and Study Guide 32–3

Name _____ Date _____ Class _____

Study Guide

Chapter 32, Section 3

For use with textbook pages 963–969

FORD AND CARTER

KEY TERMS AND NAMES

inflation a rise in the cost of goods *(page 964)*

embargo a stoppage of shipping *(page 964)*

stagflation a combination of rising prices and economic stagnation *(page 964)*

Helsinki Accords agreement signed in 1975 between the United States and the leaders of NATO and the Warsaw Pact *(page 966)*

Department of Energy an executive department set up to deal with the nation's energy problems *(page 967)*

NATIONAL GEOGRAPHIC
MOMENT in HISTORY

HOSTAGE TO TERROR
Bound and blindfolded, American diplomat Jerry Miele is led out of the U.S. embassy in Tehran, Iran, after militants stormed the building on November 4, 1979. Ten months earlier, an Islamic fundamentalist revolution had overthrown the Shah of Iran, a staunch American ally. President Carter's decision to allow the ailing Shah to seek medical treatment in the United States led to the embassy takeover. Of the Americans taken captive, 52 were held for more than a year. The crisis contributed to Carter's defeat in the presidential election in 1980.

Morality in Foreign Policy Carter had set the tone for his foreign policy in his inaugural speech, when he announced, "Our commitment to human rights must be absolute. . . . The powerful must not persecute the weak, and human dignity must be enhanced." With the help of his foreign policy team—including **Andrew Young,** the first African American ambassador to the United Nations—Carter strove to achieve these goals.

The president put his principles into practice in Latin America. To remove a major symbol of U.S. interventionism in the region, he moved to give the Panamanians control of the Panama Canal. The United States had built and run the canal since 1903. In 1978 the president won Senate ratification of two Panama Canal treaties, which transferred control of the canal to Panama on December 31, 1999.

Most dramatically, Carter singled out the Soviet Union as a violator of human rights. He strongly condemned, for example, the Soviet practice of imprisoning people who protested against the government. Relations between the two superpowers suffered a further setback when Soviet troops invaded the Central

Asian nation of Afghanistan in December 1979. Carter responded by imposing an embargo on the sale of grain to the Soviet Union and boycotting the 1980 Summer Olympic Games in Moscow. Under the Carter administration, détente virtually collapsed.

Triumph and Failure in the Middle East It was in the volatile Middle East that President Carter met his greatest foreign policy triumph and his greatest failure. In 1978 Carter helped broker a historic peace treaty, known as the **Camp David Accords,** between Israel and Egypt, two nations that had been bitter enemies for decades. The treaty was formally signed in 1979. Most other Arab nations in the region opposed the treaty, but it marked a first step to achieving peace in the Middle East.

Just months after the Camp David Accords, Carter encountered a crisis in Iran. The United States had long supported Iran's monarch, the Shah, because Iran was a major oil supplier and a buffer against Soviet expansion in the Middle East. The Shah, however, had grown increasingly unpopular in Iran. He was a repressive ruler and had

968 CHAPTER 32 Politics and Economics

EXTENDING THE CONTENT

Habitat for Humanity The Carters have had a long-standing relationship with Habitat for Humanity, an organization promoting affordable housing in the United States and around the world. The organization builds thousands of houses for low-income families. Each house is built by volunteers, with the families themselves working alongside volunteers to build the homes. Many of the building supplies are donated or are purchased at cost. **L2**

introduced Westernizing reforms to Iranian society. The Islamic clergy fiercely opposed the Shah's reforms. Opposition to the Shah grew, and in January 1979 protesters forced him to flee. An Islamic republic was then declared.

The new regime, headed by religious leader Ayatollah Khomeini, distrusted the United States because of its ties to the Shah. In November 1979, revolutionaries stormed the American embassy in Tehran and took 52 Americans hostage. The militants threatened to kill the hostages or try them as spies.

The Carter administration tried unsuccessfully to negotiate for the hostages' release. In April 1980, as pressure mounted, Carter approved a daring rescue attempt. To the nation's dismay, the rescue mission failed when several helicopters malfunctioned and one crashed in the desert. Eight servicemen died in the accident. Hamilton Jordan, President Carter's chief of staff, described the gloomy atmosphere in the White House the day after the crash:

❝I arrived at the White House a few minutes before the President went on television to tell the nation about the catastrophe. He looked exhausted and careworn. . . . The mood at the senior staff meeting was somber and awkward. I sensed that we were all uncomfortable, like when a loved one dies and friends don't quite know what to say. . . . After the meeting, I wandered around the White House. . . . My thoughts kept returning to the bodies [of the servicemen] in the desert.❞

—quoted in *Crisis: The Last Year of the Carter Presidency*

World Geography Connection

The Islamic State

In establishing an Islamic republic, the Ayatollah Khomeini created a state in which the codes and beliefs of Islam guide politics and thus direct nearly every aspect of life. Mullahs, or Islamic religious leaders, became political leaders as well, which allowed them to impose Islamic codes on Iranian citizens. In a religious state, religious practices are not a matter of choice but the law of the land. Politics and religion have joined forces in other parts of the Islamic world as well. In 1996 a group known as the Taliban transformed Afghanistan into an Islamic state. From insisting that men grow beards to forbidding women to work outside the home, Afghanistan's leaders enforced a social order based on an interpretation of Islam. *What long-held American principle does the creation of a religious state violate?*

The crisis continued into the fall of 1980. Every night, news programs reminded viewers how many days the hostages had been held. The president's inability to free the hostages cost him support in the 1980 presidential election. Negotiations with Iran continued right up to Carter's last day in office. Ironically, on January 20, 1981, the day Carter left office, Iran released the Americans, ending their 444 days in captivity.

✓ **Reading Check** **Summarizing** What was President Carter's main foreign policy theme?

SECTION 3 ASSESSMENT

Checking for Understanding

1. **Define:** inflation, embargo, stagflation.
2. **Identify:** Helsinki Accords, Department of Energy.
3. **Identify** the achievement and failure President Carter experienced in the Middle East during his administration.

Reviewing Themes

4. **Economic Factors** How did President Carter attempt to deal with the nation's energy crisis?

Critical Thinking

5. **Evaluating** Do you think President Ford should have pardoned Richard Nixon? Why or why not?
6. **Organizing** Complete a graphic organizer similar to the one below by listing the ways that President Carter applied his human rights ideas to his foreign policy.

Carter's Human Rights Foreign Policy

Analyzing Visuals

7. **Analyzing Photographs** Study the photograph on page 968. What effect do you think images such as this one had on Americans who were living or traveling in other countries?

Writing About History

8. **Expository Writing** Write an essay identifying what you believe to be President Carter's most important foreign policy achievement. Explain your choice.

CHAPTER 32   Politics and Economics   **969**

SECTION 3 ASSESSMENT ANSWERS

1. Terms are in blue.
2. Helsinki Accords *(p. 966)*, Department of Energy *(p. 967)*
3. the Camp David Accords and the hostage crisis in Iran
4. Carter proposed a national energy program to conserve oil and promote the use of renewable energy sources, created the Department of Energy, and deregulated the oil industry.
5. Students' answers will vary. Some students may say the pardon saved the nation from witnessing a divisive trial. Others may say that Nixon escaped punishment.
6. Answers should reflect text information, particularly about the Soviet Union and Panama on page 968.
7. They would fear attacks on themselves.
8. Students' essays will vary. Essays should include facts to support the position taken.

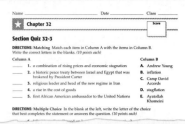

World Geography Connection

Answer: Creation of a religious state violates the American principle of separation of church and state.

✓ **Reading Check**

Answer: the need to be honest, truthful, and decent in foreign relations

Reteach

Have students explain the reasons for economic trouble in the United States during the 1970s.

Enrich

Have students explain whether they agree or disagree with the 1980 Olympic boycott.

4 CLOSE

Have students discuss Jimmy Carter's domestic and foreign policies.

1 FOCUS

Section Overview

This section focuses on the popular culture of the 1970s.

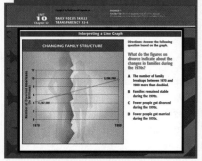
Guide to Reading

Answers to Graphic: birth rate dropped, divorce rate doubled, parents and children spent less time together, and women were active outside the home

Preteaching Vocabulary
Have students write three questions that can be answered using the Key Terms and Names.

The "Me" Decade: Life in the 1970s

Guide to Reading

Main Idea
In the midst of widespread cynicism about their leaders and concerns about the economy, Americans sought fulfillment and escape during the 1970s.

Key Terms and Names
New Age movement, guru, transcendental meditation, *All in the Family*, disco

Reading Strategy
Categorizing As you read about life in the United States in the 1970s, complete a graphic organizer similar to the one below by listing the changes that occurred in family life during that time.

Changes in Family Life

Reading Objectives
- **Explain** the emergence of new spiritual movements and religions.
- **Discuss** social changes of the 1970s.

Section Theme
Culture and Traditions Even after the turbulent 1960s, American culture continued changing to reflect new trends and ideas.

Preview of Events

◆1970	◆1973	◆1976	◆1979

1971 — *All in the Family* debuts

1974 — *Good Times* debuts

1977 — Disco mania peaks with release of *Saturday Night Fever; The Complete Book of Running* published

---

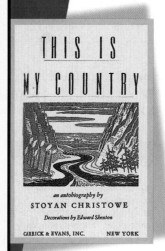

Cover of Stoyan Christowe's book

★ *An American Story* ★

As the United States prepared to celebrate its bicentennial on July 4, 1976, a reporter asked Stoyan Christowe for his views on the state of the nation on the eve of its 200th birthday. The 77-year-old Vermont resident acknowledged that the United States was "in pretty bad shape," but added that the country would turn around—as it always had.

❝I believe in this country. I've always believed in it. There is a quotation by Benjamin Franklin, in a letter to George Washington during the Revolutionary War. Franklin talked of a cornfield during a drought, and how the cornstalks have shriveled and curled, and it was a sad sight. And then, he said a thunderstorm came along, spilling rain, and a day or two after, the sun came out, and the corn came to life, and it was a delight. . . . I know we're going through a kind of turmoil now, but the country is okay. . . . My faith in this country was never shaken. Like that cornfield—the sun will shine again, and the rains will come, and brother, those cornstalks will revive, and it will be a beautiful sight.❞

—quoted in *Newsweek*, July 4, 1976

The Search for Fulfillment

Like Stoyan Christowe, many Americans in the 1970s believed that the United States would eventually move beyond the Watergate scandal, the Vietnam War, and the country's nagging economic problems. In the meantime, some Americans sought ways to get

---

SECTION RESOURCES

Reproducible Masters
- Reproducible Lesson Plan 32–4
- Daily Lecture and Discussion Notes 32–4
- Guided Reading Activity 32–4
- Section Quiz 32–4
- Reading Essentials and Study Guide 32–4

Transparencies
- Daily Focus Skills Transparency 32–4

Multimedia
- Interactive Tutor Self-Assessment CD-ROM
- ExamView® Pro Testmaker CD-ROM
- Presentation Plus! CD-ROM
- TeacherWorks™ CD-ROM
- Audio Program
- American Music: Hits Through History
- American Music: Cultural Traditions

on with their daily lives. As a way of coping with anxious times, they sought escape, laughter, and fulfillment in a wide range of fads, entertainment, and spiritual movements.

Writer Tom Wolfe labeled the 1970s the "me decade," referring to the idea that many Americans grew more self-obsessed in this decade as they strove for greater individual satisfaction. Indeed, the most popular books of the period included such titles as *I'm OK, You're OK; How to Be Your Own Best Friend;* and *Looking Out for Number One.* Journalist Richard Michael Levine argued that in light of the growing feelings of despair and cynicism about American society, it was little wonder that many people turned inward. "In the damp, late autumn of 1973, it did not take a religious fanatic in a tattered overcoat to sense that the real Kingdom lay within, things being as rotten as they were without," he wrote. In their quest for self-improvement, many Americans were willing to embrace new movements.

The New Age Movement Disenchanted with the conventional religions of their parents, some young men and women sought fulfillment through the host of secular movements and activities that made up the **New Age movement.** New Age enthusiasts embraced the idea that people were responsible for and capable of everything from self-healing to creating the world. They believed spiritual enlightenment could be found in common practices, not just in traditional churchgoing. They tried activities such as yoga, martial arts, and chanting to achieve fuller spiritual awareness. Kathy Smith, a college student during the 1970s, recalled how she and others claimed to find "Zen," or enlightenment, in running and other physical activities:

> 66They were beginning to understand how exercise affects your soul, how it affects your being. People started getting in the 'Zen' of things: the Zen of tennis, the Zen of working out, the Zen of motorcycle repair, the Zen of running. I, like many others, started connecting physical activity to the spiritual side. People also started looking at yoga and tai chi, and not only the stretching aspects of these disciplines but the mental aspects. Now they were working the body, the mind, and the spirit.99
>
> —quoted in *The Century*

The New Age movement took many different paths to transform individuals and society. Some New Agers extolled the power of crystals and gemstones to improve life; others touted astrology. Some were inspired by the Eastern belief in reincarnation, which taught that people could be reborn many times until reaching perfection. Awareness of former lives was supposed to bring knowledge of the true inner self.

Transcendental Meditation Many Americans who were dissatisfied with established religions sought new religions. A number of these new religions originated in Asia and centered on the teachings of **gurus,** or mystical leaders. One of the more well-known gurus was Maharishi Mahesh Yogi. A native of India, Maharishi moved to the United States in 1959, where he led a spiritual movement known as **transcendental meditation.** Maharishi worked in relative obscurity until 1967, when the wildly popular rock group the Beatles began to explore his teachings. Their attention brought an American following. Transcendental meditation suggested daily meditation and the silent repetition of spiritual mantras as a way of achieving peak intelligence, harmony, and health. If all the people on Earth practiced transcendental meditation, its advocates believed, the world would enjoy peace.

Changing Families The search for fulfillment had an impact on many American families. The campaigns of the era, especially the women's movement, began to change how many women viewed their roles as wives and mothers. By 1970, 60 percent of women between the ages of 16 and 24 had joined the

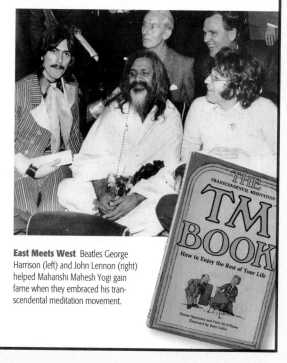

East Meets West Beatles George Harrison (left) and John Lennon (right) helped Maharishi Mahesh Yogi gain fame when they embraced his transcendental meditation movement.

2 TEACH

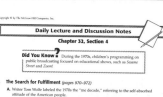

Daily Lecture and Discussion Notes 32–4

Copyright © by The McGraw-Hill Companies, Inc.

> **Daily Lecture and Discussion Notes**
>
> **Chapter 32, Section 4**
>
> **Did You Know?** During the 1970s, children's programming on public broadcasting focused on educational shows, such as *Sesame Street* and *Zoom!*
>
> **I. The Search for Fulfillment** (pages 970–972)
>
> **A.** Writer Tom Wolfe labeled the 1970s the "me decade," referring to the self-absorbed attitude of the American people.
>
> **B.** Some young Americans looked for fulfillment through an array of secular movements and activities that made up the **New Age movement.** Believers in the movement felt that people were responsible for and capable of everything. They believed spiritual enlightenment could be found in common practices.

Writing a Script Organize students into small groups to write a scene, set in the 1970s, involving conversations among an American homemaker, a manager of an automobile factory, a young unemployed worker, a college student, and a newspaper reporter. Each person should express his or her reasons why they lack confidence in the country's future. *(Reasons may include the energy crisis, foreign competition, rising inflation and unemployment rates, and social and economic inequality).* Have each group present their scripts in dramatic fashion. **L1**

Use the rubric for an oral presentation, monologue, song, or skit on pages 75–76 in the *Performance Assessment Activities and Rubrics.*

you don't say...

Fads Popular fashion fads of the 1970s included platform shoes for men, leisure suits, tank tops, and Farrah Fawcett hairdos.

COOPERATIVE LEARNING ACTIVITY

Creating a Display Organize students into small groups. Have each group review the section and select the topic that most interests them. Have the groups prepare a display on the topic they have chosen. Suggested topics include the New Age movement, transcendental meditation, fashion, popular television shows, popular musical groups, and disco.

Use the rubric for a cooperative group management plan on pages 81–82 in the *Performance Assessment Activities and Rubrics.*

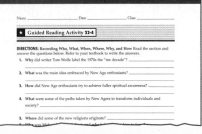

Reading Check

Answer: New Age enthusiasts embraced the idea that people were responsible for and capable of almost anything. They believed spiritual enlightenment could be found in many different ways, not just traditional churchgoing.

What *Life* Was Like...

Organize students into groups to conduct research on either fashion, disco, or movies popular in the 1970s. Then hold a class discussion asking a representative of each group to report to the class what they learned.

History *and the* Humanities

🎵 American Music: Hits Through History: "Shining Star," "Oye Como Va," "Boogie Nights," "Lean on Me"

🎵 American Music: Cultural Traditions: "Me and Bobby McGee"

📂 Use *Interpreting Political Cartoons*, Cartoon 31.

What *Life* Was Like...

Disco

The counterculture of the 1960s provided music designed to raise people's consciousness of social issues. The disco music of the 1970s, with its simple lyrics and intense beats, was designed simply to entertain. By the end of the decade, millions of people throughout the nation and the world were dancing under flashing disco lights.

● **Bee Gees**
Disco fans around the country and the world danced to the sounds of the Australian group the Bee Gees. The movie *Saturday Night Fever* featured their music and catapulted them into the limelight.

● **Fashion**
New styles of clothing, first associated with disco patrons, became common for everyone. Men wore brightly patterned synthetic shirts, bell-bottom pants, and platform shoes or boots. Women wore wildly patterned dresses or jumpsuits with high heels or boots.

labor force. Between 1970 and 1980, women aged 25 to 34 had the largest annual percentage growth in the workforce.

These changes in turn led to changes in family life. With women increasingly active outside the home, smaller families became the norm. The birthrate fell to an all-time low in 1976, and parents and their children began spending less time together. A greater number of families also split apart, as the divorce rate doubled from 2.5 divorces per thousand people in 1966 to 5 per thousand 10 years later.

✓ **Reading Check** **Summarizing** What were the basic beliefs of the New Age movement?

Cultural Trends in the 1970s

Popular culture in the 1970s reflected many of the changes taking place in society. Television now sometimes portrayed women in independent roles or took on formerly taboo subjects such as racism, poverty, and abortion. Meanwhile, Americans listened and danced to new forms of music and sought fun and escape in a variety of new fads.

TURNING POINT

Television in the 1970s The decade opened with a revolutionary new situation comedy on Saturday nights. Unlike earlier sitcoms, *The Mary Tyler Moore Show* featured an unmarried woman with a

meaningful career at its center. Actress Mary Tyler Moore played the main character, Mary Richards, who had left a small town for a big-city job as a television news producer. Mary sparred with her gruff but caring boss, despaired over the shallowness of the blow-dried news announcer, and had adventures with friends. Mary also went on dates but never got around to marrying.

The debut of the sitcom *All in the Family* in January 1971 marked an even bigger turning point in television programming. The show took risks by confronting potentially volatile social issues and by featuring a controversial hero, the blue-collar and bigoted Archie Bunker. Archie called his wife Edith "Dingbat" and his liberal son-in-law "Meathead." He also mocked his feminist daughter and various ethnic groups. Though Archie prided himself on being the man of the house, he never won any arguments with his liberal family or his African American neighbors.

By carefully mixing humor and sensitive issues and by not preaching to its audience, *All in the Family* provided viewers with a way to examine their own feelings about issues such as racism. Producer Norman Lear claimed that the show "holds a mirror up to our prejudices. . . . We laugh now, swallowing just the littlest bit of truth about ourselves. . . ."

Several years later, Archie Bunker's African American neighbors became the stars of another television series, *The Jeffersons.* George Jefferson, like Archie, was opinionated and prejudiced but

---

MEETING SPECIAL NEEDS

Visual/Spatial Have students videotape five minutes of a television show that originally aired in the 1970s. Have students prepare a summary of how their chosen clip demonstrates life in the 1970s. Have students show their clips and present their summaries to the class. **L1**

📂 Refer to *Inclusion for the High School Social Studies Classroom Strategies and Activities* in the TCR.

Saturday Night Fever
John Travolta played the role of Tony Manero in this 1977 film. By day Tony worked as a clerk in a Brooklyn store. At night, however, he transformed himself into a disco star. A popular success, the film showed Tony as a young working-class kid with a dream to escape his ordinary existence. Life at the disco provided a road to that escape.

ultimately likable. *The Jeffersons* portrayed African Americans in a new light: as successful and respected. *Maude,* another spin-off from *All in the Family,* featured Edith Bunker's feminist cousin, who had recently remarried after her third divorce. The strong-willed Maude did not need to depend on her new husband, Walter. This popular program drew intense controversy in 1972 when Maude made the difficult decision to have an abortion.

Maude's African American maid, Florida, generated another series in 1974. Starring Esther Rolle as Florida, *Good Times* portrayed an African American family struggling to raise three children in a low-income housing development in Chicago.

Music of the 1970s The music of this period reflected the end of the 1960s youth and protest movements. The hard-driving rock of the tumultuous 1960s gave way to softer sounds. "The fading out of ear-numbing, mind-blowing acid rock," *Time* commented in 1971, "is related to the softening of the youth revolution." The music became more reflective and less political, reflecting a desire to seek fulfillment from within. "These days, nobody wants to hear songs that have a message," said a member of the rock group Chicago. Popular entertainers in tune with the new meditative atmosphere included singers Barry Manilow and John Denver and the bands ABBA and the Eagles.

The 1970s also saw the rise of disco music. The disco craze of the later 1970s began in African

American and Latin nightclubs. There, disc jockeys played recorded dance music with a loud and persistent beat. The fast pace and easy rhythm attracted fans, but disco also seemed well suited for the "me generation." Unlike rock 'n' roll, disco allowed the people dancing to it to assume greater prominence than the music. As the co-owner of a popular discotheque in New York described the phenomena, "Everybody secretly likes to be on center stage and here we give them a huge space to do it all on."

Gus Rodriguez, who had moved with his family from Puerto Rico to Brooklyn 20 years earlier, recalled going to discos with his friends in the mid-1970s:

66We would go to the discos several times a week, but the weekends were always the best. Getting ready to go out was sort of a ritual, especially on Saturdays. During the day you would go buy that shirt, or that belt, or those platform shoes, all of which seemed incredibly important at the time. You had to have a particular type of look. And we all dressed the same way. We would call each other up to coordinate what color suits everybody was wearing—who's wearing the powder-blue suit, who's wearing the white suit, who's wearing this, who's wearing that. And then we would carefully iron everything so it was just so.99

—quoted in *The Century*

Disco mania reached its peak after the 1977 movie, *Saturday Night Fever.* In the film, a middle-class

All in the Family Many Americans saw a little of themselves in the characters of this popular sitcom.

CHAPTER 32
Section 4, 970–974

The two *Viking* spacecraft landed on Mars in July and September of 1976. They transmitted more than 52,000 pictures back to Earth, giving people their first close-up look at the planet.

3 ASSESS

Assign Section 4 Assessment as homework or as an in-class activity.

● Have students use the **Interactive Tutor Self-Assessment CD-ROM.**

Reading Essentials and Study Guide 32–4

Name _____ Date _____ Class _____

Study Guide

Chapter 32, Section 4
For use with textbook pages 970–974

THE "ME" DECADE: LIFE IN THE 1970S

KEY TERMS AND NAMES

New Age movement secular movement of the 1970s *(page 971)*

gurus mystical leaders *(page 971)*

transcendental meditation a religious movement started by Maharishi Mahesh Yogi that suggested daily meditation and the silent repetition of spiritual mantras *(page 971)*

All in the Family a situation comedy of the 1970s that confronted uncomfortable social issues *(page 972)*

disco dance music with a loud and persistent beat that became popular in the 1970s *(page 973)*

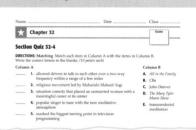

Section Quiz 32–4

Name _____ Date _____ Class _____

★ Chapter 32   Score ____

Section Quiz 32-4

DIRECTIONS: Matching Match each item in Column A with the items in Column B. Write the correct letters in the blanks. *(10 points each)*

Column A

____ 1. allowed drivers to talk to each other over a two-way frequency within a range of a few miles

____ 2. religious movement led by Maharishi Mahesh Yogi

____ 3. situation comedy that placed an unmarried woman with a meaningful career at its center

____ 4. popular singer in tune with the new meditative atmosphere

____ 5. marked the biggest turning point in television programming

Column B

A. *All in the Family*
B. CBs
C. John Denver
D. *The Mary Tyler Moore Show*
E. transcendental meditation

INTERDISCIPLINARY CONNECTIONS ACTIVITY

Science Tell students that the 1970s witnessed many scientific and technological firsts including the first CAT scan, the first test-tube baby, the first home computer, and the first portable tape players. Have students select one of these "firsts" or another invention or advance from the 1970s to research. Have students prepare a three-to-five minute oral presentation based on their research. Ask them to consider how the invention or discovery affected the development of the country, the standard of living, the nature of work, and what need it met, as well as any subsequent innovations or discoveries. **L2**

| Fact | Fiction | Folklore |

In the late 1990s the United States Postal Service issued a series of stamps depicting the twentieth century. The "Celebrate the Century" series featured 15 stamps for each decade. The ubiquitous smiley face was one of the images selected for the 1970s series. Two other stamps, one depicting disco and the other featuring 1970s fashion, also commemorated the 1970s.

✓ Reading Check

Answer: Millions of records were sold, and it spurred the opening of discos.

Reteach

Have students explain the emergence of new spiritual movements and religions.

Enrich

Have students create a time line of popular culture that includes the items mentioned here and other relevant events. Encourage students to illustrate some or all of the entries.

4 CLOSE

Have students discuss whether some traditional values became weaker during the 1970s.

| Fact | Fiction | Folklore |

Put on a Happy Face Throughout the 1960s and 1970s, the nation experienced a "button craze" as people expressed themselves by pinning buttons with slogans to their clothing. The most popular button actually said nothing at all. In 1971 Americans began buying a yellow button with a simple smile on it. By the fall of 1971, marketers estimated that more than 20 million smile buttons had been sold, making it the most popular fad item since the hula hoop.

Italian American teenager played by John Travolta transformed himself into a white-suited disco king each Saturday night. The movie's soundtrack sold millions of copies and spurred a wave of disco openings across the country and around the world.

Fads and Fashions In addition to disco, the nation embraced many other fads during the 1970s. Americans by the millions bought T-shirts that bore personalized messages, while teenagers flew down suburban and city streets on skateboards. Obsessed with self-discovery, a number of Americans slipped mood rings on their fingers to get in touch with their innermost feelings. Supposedly, the ring's color changed to match the wearer's ever-changing mood. Blue, for example, signaled happiness and bliss, while gray denoted nervousness and anxiety.

Meanwhile, millions of drivers bought citizens band ("CB") radios for their vehicles. This radio system allowed drivers to talk to each other over a two-way frequency within a range of a few miles. Many truck drivers installed the radios in an effort to warn each other of police and speed traps. Soon, however, average drivers had purchased them, mostly for entertainment purposes. Drivers adopted their own CB name, or "handle," and talked to each other using CB jargon and code words.

Fitness was another trend during the "me decade," as many Americans turned to exercise to improve the way they felt and looked. One popular type of exercise in the 1970s was aerobics. Physician Kenneth H. Cooper popularized the exercise concept in his 1968 book *Aerobics*. It was a way to achieve cardiovascular fitness without the drudgery and isolation that often accompanies physical exercise. This new way to stay fit while having fun and interacting socially with others quickly gained popularity. By the mid-1970s, men and women were dancing in gyms across the country. Running also attracted a wide following, as scores of Americans began pounding the pavement to stay fit and trim. In a testament to the popularity of running, athlete Jim Fixx's work *The Complete Book of Running* was a bestseller following its publication in 1977.

By the end of the 1970s, a number of these fads and trends began to fade. A decade in which Americans came to recognize their country's vulnerability and its limits had ended. As the new decade dawned, Americans looked forward to regaining confidence in their country and optimism in their own futures.

✓ Reading Check **Examining** What was the impact of disco music on American society?

SECTION 4 ASSESSMENT

Checking for Understanding

1. **Define:** guru, transcendental meditation, disco.
2. **Identify:** New Age movement, *All in the Family*.
3. **Summarize** the basic beliefs of followers of transcendental meditation.

Reviewing Themes

4. **Culture and Traditions** What new cultural trends affected American society in the 1970s?

Critical Thinking

5. **Analyzing** How did television in the 1970s reflect society at that time?
6. **Organizing** Complete a graphic organizer similar to the one below by listing the cultural trends of the 1970s.

Cultural Trends of the 1970s

Analyzing Visuals

7. **Analyzing Photographs** Study the photographs in the "What Life Was Like" feature on pages 972–973. How has popular music and fashion changed since the 1970s?

Writing About History

8. **Descriptive Writing** View a television program that was popular in the 1970s. Write a description of the program and explain how it reflected society at that time.

SECTION 4 ASSESSMENT ANSWERS

1. Terms are in blue.
2. New Age movement *(p. 971)*, *All in the Family (p. 972)*
3. daily meditation and mantras as a way of achieving peak intelligence, harmony, and health
4. television dealt with controversial issues; transcendental meditation; disco and new fashion developed; fitness became a craze
5. Television portrayed characters in situations similar to what viewers were experiencing.
6. Disco music, CBs, fitness, social issues on television, T-shirts with messages, mood rings
7. Dance music has become more varied; fashions less tailored and more casual
8. Students' descriptions will vary. Encourage students to comment on the content, music, wardrobe, language, and settings used in the television program.

Analyzing Secondary Sources

Why Learn This Skill?

This textbook, like many other history books, is a secondary source. Secondary sources draw from primary sources to explain a topic. The value of a secondary source depends on how its author uses primary sources. Learning to analyze secondary sources will help you figure out whether those sources are presenting a complete and accurate picture of a topic or event.

Learning the Skill

To determine whether an author uses primary sources effectively, ask these questions:

- Are there references to primary sources in the text, footnotes, or acknowledgments?
- Who are the authors of the primary sources? What insights or biases might these people have?
- Is the information from the primary sources interwoven effectively to support or describe an event?
- Are different kinds of primary sources considered? Do they represent varied testimony?
- Is the interpretation of the primary sources sound and logical?

Practicing the Skill

In the following excerpt from *The Cold War, 1945–1987*, author Ralph B. Levering discusses President Carter's China policy. Carter sent his national security adviser, Zbigniew Brzezinski, to China to encourage better relations and thus put pressure on the Soviets. As you read, identify the primary sources Levering uses to make his argument.

During his trip to Peking, Brzezinski did everything he could to please the Chinese leaders. . . . He stressed repeatedly the evil nature of the Soviet Union. . . . Upon his return, Brzezinski told a New York Times *reporter that the trip was intended to "underline the long-term strategic nature of the United States' relationship to China."*

. . . Soviet leaders were deeply concerned. An editorial in Pravda *on May 30, 1978, stated that Brzezinski "stands before the world as an enemy of détente."*

President Nixon and First Lady Pat Nixon visiting the Great Wall of China during their historic 1972 trip.

Pravda *also blamed China, stating on June 17 that "Soviet-American confrontation . . . is the cherished dream of Peking." On the whole, U.S. officials were not displeased by the Kremlin's anger and concern: perhaps it would make Soviet leaders more anxious to conclude the SALT negotiations and more inclined to show restraint in the Third World.*

1. What kind of primary source does Levering use twice in this passage?
2. Do you think this kind of primary source has any possible weaknesses?
3. Would the use of government documents strengthen the author's argument? Why or why not?

Skills Assessment

Complete the Practicing Skills questions on page 977 and the Chapter 32 Skill Reinforcement Activity to assess your mastery of this skill.

Applying the Skill

Analyzing Secondary Sources Find and read an in-depth article in a newspaper. Then list the primary sources the article uses and analyze how reliable you think they are.

 Glencoe's **Skillbuilder Interactive Workbook CD-ROM, Level 2,** provides instruction and practice in key social studies skills.

975

TEACH

Analyzing Secondary Sources

When researching a topic, recommend that students use several secondary sources in order to evaluate all aspects of the topic and to identify various writers' points of view.

Assign students various passages from the *An American Story* features in this book. Have students identify which portions of the information are primary sources and which are secondary sources. Have volunteers share their findings with the class.

Additional Practice

Reinforcing Skills Activity 32

Name _____ Date _____ Class _____

★ Reinforcing Skills Activity 32

Analyzing Secondary Sources

□ **LEARNING THE SKILL**

Secondary source documents, such as your textbook, weave together a variety of primary sources. To judge the quality and reliability of a secondary source document, you need to analyze the primary sources cited by the author. As you read from a secondary source, look for references in the text such as footnotes or acknowledgments. Consider the authorship of the primary sources used. What biases might they have? Ask yourself how well the primary source material supports the information provided. Does the author use a variety of well-balanced sources? Does the author's interpretation make sense in light of the source documents used?

□ **PRACTICING THE SKILL**

DIRECTIONS: Read the excerpt below from Kenneth E. Morris's biography of President Jimmy Carter titled *Jimmy Carter: American Moralist.* Then answer the questions that follow.

GLENCOE
TECHNOLOGY

 CD-ROM
Glencoe Skillbuilder Interactive Workbook CD-ROM, Level 2

This interactive CD-ROM reinforces student mastery of essential social studies skills.

ANSWERS TO PRACTICING THE SKILL

1. an editorial in a newspaper
2. The reporter could be using the quote out of context. The *Pravda* editorials, as all editorials, are opinions. Since the Soviet state ran *Pravda,* articles and editorials uniformly reflected government policy.
3. Students' answers will vary.

Applying the Skill
Students' answers will vary. Encourage students to attach the article to their analysis.

CHAPTER
32 ASSESSMENT and ACTIVITIES

Reviewing Key Terms

Students' answers will vary. The pages where the words appear in the text are shown in parentheses.

1. **impound** (p. 955)

2. **détente** (p. 956)

3. **summit** (p. 957)

4. **executive privilege** (p. 961)

5. **impeach** (p. 961)

6. **inflation** (p. 964)

7 **embargo** (p. 964)

8. **stagflation** (p. 964)

9. **guru** (p. 971)

10. **transcendental meditation** (p. 971)

11. **disco** (p. 973)

Reviewing Key Facts

12. Southern strategy (p. 954), Sam J. Ervin (p. 960), OPEC (p. 964), New Age movement (p. 971)

13. Nixon's domestic policy focused on the New Federalism and his foreign policy focused on détente.

14. Most Americans lost trust in public officials.

15. President Nixon believed wage and price freezes would stop stagflation, a combination of rising prices and economic stagnation.

16. rising oil prices, increased international competition, low job training for new jobs, and a decline in manufacturing

17. Changes in family life included smaller families, more divorces, parents and children spending less time together, and women becoming more active in the workplace and outside the home.

Reviewing Key Terms

On a sheet of paper, use each of these terms in a sentence.

1. impound
2. détente
3. summit
4. executive privilege
5. impeach
6. inflation
7. embargo
8. stagflation
9. guru
10. transcendental meditation
11. disco

Reviewing Key Facts

12. **Identify:** Southern strategy, Sam J. Ervin, OPEC, New Age movement.

13. What were the main aspects of President Nixon's domestic and foreign policies?

14. What was the impact of the Watergate scandal on the American people?

15. Why did President Nixon freeze wages and prices in the early 1970s?

16. What factors caused economic problems in the United States in the 1970s?

17. What changes in family life occurred in the United States in the 1970s?

Critical Thinking

18. **Analyzing Themes: Government and Democracy** How did the Watergate scandal affect the relationship among the three branches of government?

19. **Evaluating** What impact did cultural phenomena such as disco music, the use of CB radios, and exercise trends have on the U.S. economy?

20. **Forming an Opinion** Alexander Haig stated that the Watergate scandal led to "a fundamental discrediting of respect for the presidency . . . [and] a new skepticism about politics, in general, which every American feels to this day." Do you agree with his statement? Why or why not?

21. **Interpreting Primary Sources** When the Arab-Israeli War of 1973 developed into a stalemate, the Arab nations imposed an oil embargo on the United States, the chief supporter of Israel. Because Arab countries supplied much of the oil used in the United States, the embargo created an energy crisis. The excerpt below is taken from an article in the December 3, 1973, issue of *U.S. News & World Report.* It details the growing energy problems that the United States was facing at that time. Read the excerpt and answer the questions that follow.

❝Evidence of the full dimensions of the energy crisis in this country is becoming more clear each day.

- Electric-power brownouts, even blackouts, are predicted for many parts of the U.S. before the end of the year.

- Voltage reduction of 5 percent from 4 P.M. to 8 P.M. each day was ordered starting November 26 in all six New England States, where fuel shortages threaten homes, schools, factories. . . .

- As a first step to cut gasoline use, President Nixon was reportedly ready to order closing of service stations nationwide from 9 P.M. Saturday to midnight Sunday on weekends. . . .

Chapter Summary

Uniting a Divided Country

- Nixon's conservative politics appeal to "Middle America."
- Nixon begins pulling ground troops out of Vietnam.
- Tensions with Soviet Union and China ease.
- Nixon signs treaty limiting nuclear arms.

Scandal and Economic Turmoil

- Watergate scandal brings down Nixon.
- Congress enacts new laws to limit presidential power.
- Inflation, energy crisis, and foreign competition cause economic slowdown.
- Ford and Carter fail to revive economy.

Challenging Traditional Values

- New Age movement advocates self-fulfillment.
- More women join the workforce.
- Television shows prominently feature African Americans and independent women; address sensitive issues such as racism and abortion.

Critical Thinking

18. The Supreme Court forced the president to yield presidential privilege, thus decreasing the power of the executive branch. Congress passed laws establishing a greater balance of power, requiring financial disclosure from all branches of government, and establishing independent counsel to investigate wrongdoings of government officials.

19. Disco music led to the opening of dance clubs; millions of people bought CB radios; and exercise clubs opened throughout the country. Each helped the economy expand.

20. Students' answers will vary but should carefully consider current feelings toward the government.

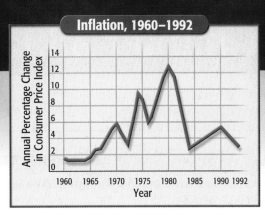

Inflation, 1960–1992

- Immediate rationing of gasoline and fuel oil is being urged on the President by top oil-industry executives. . . .

  One major piece of legislation . . . directs the President to take measures necessary to reduce the nation's energy demands by 25 percent within four weeks.

  Speed limits would be cut nationally; lighting and heating of public and commercial buildings would be curtailed; home-owners would be given tax deductions to winterize their homes. . . .

  Other pending measures would impose year-round daylight saving time and would open naval oil reserves for intensive exploration. . . .**99**

  a. What proposals did the U.S. government make to deal with the energy crisis?

  b. What lessons do you think the United States might have learned from the crisis?

22. **Categorizing** Complete a chart similar to the one below by listing the attempts each president made to strengthen the nation's economy.

President	Attempts to Strengthen Economy
Nixon	
Ford	
Carter	

Practicing Skills

23. **Analyzing Secondary Sources** Examine the Bob Woodward quotation on Watergate's impact on page 962. Then use the steps you learned on the subject of analyzing secondary sources on page 975 to answer the following questions.

   a. Who is Bob Woodward, and how was he related to the Watergate scandal?

   b. How knowledgeable or reliable do you think Woodward is as a source? Why do you think so?

Chapter Activity

24. **Researching Artifacts** One useful way of learning about cultures of different periods is by examining artifacts from the era. Many of these artifacts can be found in museums and art galleries, while others may be found in your own home. What sorts of artifacts could you find about the 1970s? What would they tell you about the culture and lifestyle of that era? Create a chart listing possible artifacts and how they represent the 1970s.

Writing Activity

25. **Persuasive Writing** Imagine you are an aide to President Nixon during the early 1970s. Nixon has just returned from his historic mission to China to establish diplomatic relations with the Communist nation. Write a press release on the president's trip for reporters, explaining the reasons Nixon reversed American policy and the expected benefits from doing so.

Economics and History

26. The graph above shows inflation rates in the United States from 1960 to 1992. Study the graph and answer the questions below.

   a. **Interpreting Graphs** How did the nation's inflation rate change between 1965 and 1980?

   b. **Determining Cause and Effect** What factor was most important in causing this change?

Standardized Test Practice

Directions: Choose the phrase that best completes the following sentence.

As a political conservative, President Nixon wanted to

A increase federal spending on welfare programs.

B take more aggressive federal action to speed desegregation.

C return power to state governments.

D appoint activist-minded justices to the Supreme Court.

Test-Taking Tip: Think of the meaning of *political conservative:* someone who believes that the federal government's role in society should be limited. Choose the answer that best reflects this meaning.

Have students visit the Web site at tav.glencoe.com to review Chapter 32 and take the Self-Check Quiz.

Chapter Activity

24. Students' charts will vary but should include analysis of 1970s artifacts.

Writing Activity

25. Students' press releases will vary but should discuss Nixon's goals.

Economics and History

26. **a.** The inflation rate increased from under 2 percent in 1965 to over 12 percent in 1980. **b.** The rise in the price of crude oil was the biggest factor for the ballooning rate of inflation.

Standardized Test Practice

Answer: C

Test-Taking Tip: Have students look at each answer to determine if it limits or increases the government's role. For example, students can eliminate answer A because of the phrase "increase federal spending." They can eliminate answer B because it says "more aggressive federal action."

Bonus Question ?

Ask: What did the impeachment process test? *(the system of checks and balances)*

---

21. **a.** Proposals included cutting speed limits, curtailing heat and lighting in public buildings, giving tax deductions for homeowners to winterize their homes, imposing year-round daylight savings time, and opening the naval oil reserves for exploration. **b.** Students' answers will vary.

22. Nixon: cut spending, raised taxes, raised interest rates, and froze wages and prices; Ford: urged Americans to cut back on gas and oil consumption and undertake other energy-conserving measures; cut government spending and advocated higher interest rates, attempted to limit federal authority, balance the budget, and keep taxes low; Carter: increased government spending, cut taxes, reduced the money supply, and raised interest rates

Practicing Skills

23. **a.** Woodward was a reporter for the *Washington Post* and he, along with Carl Bernstein, broke the story that uncovered the Watergate scandal. **b.** Students' answers will vary.

977

Timesaving Tools

TeacherWorks™ All-In-One Planner and Resource Center

- **Interactive Teacher Edition** Access your Teacher Wraparound Edition and your classroom resources with a few easy clicks.
- **Interactive Lesson Planner** Planning has never been easier! Organize your week, month, semester, or year with all the lesson helps you need to make teaching creative, timely, and relevant.

Use Glencoe's **Presentation Plus!** multimedia teacher tool to easily present dynamic lessons that visually excite your students. Using Microsoft PowerPoint® you can customize the presentations to create your own personalized lessons.

TEACHING TRANSPARENCIES

Graphic Organizer 13

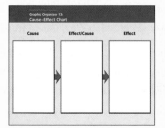

Why It Matters Chapter Transparency 33

APPLICATION AND ENRICHMENT

Linking Past and Present Activity 33

Enrichment Activity 33

Primary Source Reading 33

REVIEW AND REINFORCEMENT

Reteaching Activity 33

Vocabulary Activity 33

Time Line Activity 33

Critical Thinking Skills Activity 33

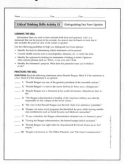

Meeting NCSS Standards

The following standards are highlighted in Chapter 33:

Section 1   VII   Production, Distribution, and Consumption: F
Section 2   IX   Global Connections: B, C, D
Section 3   VIII   Science, Technology, and Society: A, B
Section 4   VII   Production, Distribution, and Consumption: F

Local Standards

_____

_____

_____

_____

_____

Chapter 33 Resources

ASSESSMENT AND EVALUATION

**Chapter 33 Test
Form A**

**Chapter 33 Test
Form B**

**Standardized Test Skills
Practice Workbook Activity 33**

**Performance Assessment
Activities and Rubrics 33**

**ExamView® Pro
Testmaker CD-ROM**

MULTIMEDIA

- **Vocabulary PuzzleMaker CD-ROM**
- **Interactive Tutor Self-Assessment CD-ROM**
- **ExamView® Pro Testmaker CD-ROM**
- **Audio Program**
- **American History Primary Source Documents Library CD-ROM**
- **MindJogger Videoquiz**
- **Presentation Plus! CD-ROM**
- **TeacherWorks™ CD-ROM**
- **Interactive Student Edition CD-ROM**
- **Glencoe Skillbuilder Interactive Workbook CD-ROM, Level 2**
- **The *American Vision* Video Program**
- **American Music: Hits Through History**
- **American Music: Cultural Traditions**

SPANISH RESOURCES

The following Spanish language materials are available in the Spanish Resources Binder:

- **Spanish Guided Reading Activities**
- **Spanish Reteaching Activities**
- **Spanish Quizzes and Tests**
- **Spanish Vocabulary Activities**
- **Spanish Summaries**
- **The Declaration of Independence and United States Constitution Spanish Translation**

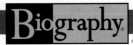

THE HISTORY CHANNEL®

The following videotape programs are available from Glencoe as supplements to Chapter 33:

- **Ronald Reagan: The Many Lives** (ISBN 1-56-501099-X)
- **Ronald Reagan: The Role of a Lifetime** (ISBN 1-56-501808-7)
- **George Bush: A Sense of Duty** (ISBN 1-56-501809-5)

To order, call Glencoe at 1-800-334-7344. To find classroom resources to accompany many of these videos, check the following home pages:
A&E Television: www.aande.com
The History Channel: www.historychannel.com

Use our Web site for additional resources. All essential content is covered in the Student Edition.

You and your students can visit tav.glencoe.com, the Web site companion to the *American Vision.* This innovative integration of electronic and print media offers your students a wealth of opportunities. The student text directs students to the Web site for the following options:

- **Chapter Overviews**
- **Self-Check Quizzes**
- **Student Web Activities**
- **Textbook Updates**

Answers to the student Web activities are provided for you in the **Web Activity Lesson Plans.** Additional Web resources and Interactive Tutor Puzzles are also available.

Chapter 33 Resources

SECTION RESOURCES

Daily Objectives	Reproducible Resources	Multimedia Resources
SECTION 1 **The New Conservatism** 1. Explain how discontent with government led to a conservative shift in Americans' political convictions. 2. Describe how the nation's population shifts led to a change in voting patterns.	📁 Reproducible Lesson Plan 33–1 📁 Daily Lecture and Discussion Notes 33–1 📁 Guided Reading Activity 33–1* 📁 Section Quiz 33–1* 📁 Reading Essentials and Study Guide 33–1 📁 Performance Assessment Activities and Rubrics	🖼 Daily Focus Skills Transparency 33–1 💿 Interactive Tutor Self-Assessment CD-ROM 💿 ExamView® Pro Testmaker CD-ROM 💿 Presentation Plus! CD-ROM 💿 TeacherWorks™ CD-ROM 🎧 Audio Program
SECTION 2 **The Reagan Years** 1. Explain President Reagan's economic recovery plan. 2. Discuss Reagan's policies toward the Soviet Union.	📁 Reproducible Lesson Plan 33–2 📁 Daily Lecture and Discussion Notes 33–2 📁 Guided Reading Activity 33–2* 📁 Section Quiz 33–2* 📁 Reading Essentials and Study Guide 33–2 📁 Performance Assessment Activities and Rubrics 📁 Interpreting Political Cartoons	🖼 Daily Focus Skills Transparency 33–2 💿 Interactive Tutor Self-Assessment CD-ROM 💿 ExamView® Pro Testmaker CD-ROM 💿 Presentation Plus! CD-ROM 💿 TeacherWorks™ CD-ROM 🎧 Audio Program
SECTION 3 **Life in the 1980s** 1. Discuss the importance of money to the culture of the 1980s. 2. Explain the growth in social activism during the decade.	📁 Reproducible Lesson Plan 33–3 📁 Daily Lecture and Discussion Notes 33–3 📁 Guided Reading Activity 33–3* 📁 Section Quiz 33–3* 📁 Reading Essentials and Study Guide 33–3 📁 Performance Assessment Activities and Rubrics	🖼 Daily Focus Skills Transparency 33–3 🖼 American Art & Architecture 💿 Interactive Tutor Self-Assessment CD-ROM 💿 ExamView® Pro Testmaker CD-ROM 💿 Presentation Plus! CD-ROM 💿 Skillbuilder Interactive Workbook, Level 2 💿 TeacherWorks™ CD-ROM 🎧 Audio Program 🎵 American Music: Hits Through History 🎵 American Music: Cultural Traditions
SECTION 4 **The End of the Cold War** 1. Identify the events that brought an end to the Cold War. 2. Explain the domestic challenges facing the Bush administration.	📁 Reproducible Lesson Plan 33–4 📁 Daily Lecture and Discussion Notes 33–4 📁 Guided Reading Activity 33–4* 📁 Section Quiz 33–4* 📁 Reading Essentials and Study Guide 33–4 📁 Performance Assessment Activities and Rubrics 📁 Interpreting Political Cartoons	🖼 Daily Focus Skills Transparency 33–4 💿 Interactive Tutor Self-Assessment CD-ROM 💿 ExamView® Pro Testmaker CD-ROM 💿 Presentation Plus! CD-ROM 💿 TeacherWorks™ CD-ROM 💿 Vocabulary PuzzleMaker CD-ROM

`0:00` **OUT OF TIME?**
Assign the Chapter 33 **Reading Essentials and Study Guide.**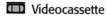

*Also Available in Spanish

 Blackline Master   Transparency 💿 CD-ROM 💿 DVD

📕 Poster 🎵 Music Program 🎧 Audio Program 📼 Videocassette

NATIONAL GEOGRAPHIC Teacher's Corner

INDEX TO NATIONAL GEOGRAPHIC MAGAZINE

The following articles relate to this chapter.
- "Alcohol, the Legal Drug," February 1992
- "A Broken Empire," March 1993
- "Persian Gulf Pollution," February 1992

ADDITIONAL NATIONAL GEOGRAPHIC SOCIETY PRODUCTS

To order the following, call National Geographic at 1-800-368-2728:
- *Branches of Government Series* (Video)
- *The Complete National Geographic: 109 Years of National Geographic Magazine* (CD-ROM)
- *Democratic Government Series: The United States* (Video)
- *National Geographic World Atlas for Young Explorers– Classroom Library Edition* (Guide, Transparencies, Resource Masters)

NGS ONLINE

Access National Geographic's Web site for current events, atlas updates, activities, links, interactive features, and archives.
www.nationalgeographic.com

From the Classroom of...

Linda Kelley
Connally High School
Waco, TX

Honing Research Skills

This activity helps students understand some of the significant events at the end of the twentieth century and reviews how to find relevant information using library and Internet resources.

List 10 to 15 significant events discussed in Chapter 33. Students, working alone or in pairs, will choose one event and create either a Web page or a PowerPoint® presentation. Before beginning research, walk students through the library's reference materials. The reference librarian can help students learn how to research on the Internet and with other online resources.

The final PowerPoint® presentation or Web page is turned in as a computer file to the teacher. The teacher can then use the presentation with other classes or allow the student to make the presentation.

ADDITIONAL RESOURCES FROM GLENCOE

- American Music: Cultural Traditions
- American Art & Architecture
- Outline Map Resource Book
- U.S. Desk Map
- Building Geography Skills for Life
- Inclusion for the High School Social Studies Classroom Strategies and Activities
- Teaching Strategies for the American History Classroom (Including Block Scheduling Pacing Guides)

KEY TO ABILITY LEVELS

Teaching strategies have been coded.

- **L1** BASIC activities for all students
- **L2** AVERAGE activities for average to above-average students
- **L3** CHALLENGING activities for above-average students
- **ELL** ENGLISH LANGUAGE LEARNER activities

Block Schedule

Activities that are suited to use within the block scheduling framework are identified by:

Introducing
CHAPTER 33

Performance Assessment

Refer to Activity 33 in the Performance Assessment Activities and Rubrics booklet.

Why It Matters Activity

Have students use recent newspapers to find an article related to one of the items listed under *The Impact Today*. Have volunteers share their articles with the class. You may want to have some students share their articles at the end of your study of this chapter, encouraging them to discuss what they have learned about the topic while studying the chapter.

GLENCOE
TECHNOLOGY

The *American Vision* Video Program

To learn more about the history of the Berlin Wall, have students view the Chapter 33 video, "Tear Down This Wall!" from the *American Vision* **Video Program.**

 Available in DVD and VHS

MindJogger Videoquiz
Use the **MindJogger Videoquiz** to preview Chapter 33 content.

 Available in VHS

CHAPTER
33 Resurgence of Conservatism
1980–1992

Why It Matters

The 1980s saw the rise of a new conservatism. President Reagan, standing for traditional values and smaller government, symbolized this movement. While tax cuts and new technologies fueled an economic boom, Reagan embarked on a massive military buildup and expanded efforts to contain communism. During President George Bush's term, the United States fought the Persian Gulf War, and the Cold War came to a dramatic end with the fall of the Soviet Union.

The Impact Today

Developments of the Reagan era are still visible today.
• The struggle between conservative and liberal ideas often defines American politics.
• Foreign policy has greatly changed because of the fall of the Soviet Union.
• The Americans with Disabilities Act has opened up doors for disabled citizens.

The American Vision *Video* The Chapter 33 video, "Tear Down This Wall!" describes the history of the Berlin Wall, one of the Cold War's most powerful symbols.

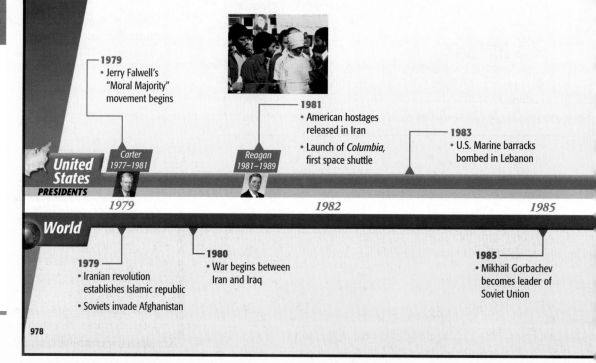

1979
• Jerry Falwell's "Moral Majority" movement begins

1981
• American hostages released in Iran
• Launch of *Columbia,* first space shuttle

1983
• U.S. Marine barracks bombed in Lebanon

United States PRESIDENTS

Carter 1977–1981

Reagan 1981–1989

1979   *1982*   *1985*

World

1979
• Iranian revolution establishes Islamic republic
• Soviets invade Afghanistan

1980
• War begins between Iran and Iraq

1985
• Mikhail Gorbachev becomes leader of Soviet Union

978

TWO-MINUTE LESSON LAUNCHER

Tell students that Ronald Reagan was an extremely popular president. Ask students to identify reasons for his widespread appeal. Encourage students as they read the chapter to look for confirmation of their reasons or to identify additional reasons for Reagan's popularity and consider how his image matched his presidency.

HISTORY
Online

Introduce students to chapter content and key terms by having them access the **Chapter 33 Overview** at tav.glencoe.com.

More About the Photo

Remind students that the Communists erected the Berlin Wall in 1961 to prevent East Germans from fleeing to the West. Ask students to explain the symbolism of the Berlin Wall and President Reagan's challenge to Mikhail Gorbachev to tear it down.

TIME LINE
ACTIVITY

Have students select one event on the United States time line and one on the world time line. For their chosen events have students write newspaper headlines that capture the emotion of the event.

President Reagan at the Berlin Wall in 1987

1986
• Iran-Contra scandal enters the news

1987
• INF Treaty between U.S. and USSR reduces land-based intermediate-range nuclear missiles

1988
• More than 35,000 cases of AIDS diagnosed for the year

G. Bush 1989–1993

1991
• Persian Gulf War occurs between Iraq and UN coalition

1988

1991

1986
• Dictatorship of Ferdinand Marcos overthrown in the Philippines

1989
• Tiananmen Square protests for democracy break out in China
• Several Communist governments in Eastern Europe collapse

1990
• Germany reunified into one nation

1991
• Soviet Union dissolves

HISTORY
Online

Chapter Overview
Visit the *American Vision* Web site at tav.glencoe.com and click on *Chapter Overviews—Chapter 33* to preview chapter information.

979

GRAPHIC ORGANIZER ACTIVITY

Organizing Information Have students complete the following graphic organizer to analyze the issues facing world leaders and U.S. policymakers before and after the collapse of communism in the Soviet Union. *Issues before* may include military buildup and Cold War threats. *Issues after* may include economic stability, the future of various countries in the Communist bloc, and the role of the United States in world affairs.

Issues Before → Collapse of Communism → Issues After

SECTION 1 The New Conservatism

1 FOCUS

Section Overview

This section focuses on the rise of a new conservative coalition.

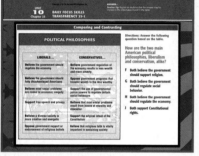
Guide to Reading

Answers to Graphic:
The New Conservatism
I. Conservatism and Liberalism
   A. Liberalism
   B. Conservatism
II. Conservatism Revives
   A. Conservatism and the Cold War
   B. Conservatives Organize
III. Conservatism Gains Support
Students should complete the outline by including all heads in the section.

Preteaching Vocabulary
Have students make a list of the Key Terms and Names and add a symbol, name, or phrase to help them remember their meanings.

Guide to Reading

Main Idea
In the 1980s, discontent with government and changes in society resulted in the rise of a new conservative coalition.

Key Terms and Names
liberal, conservative, William F. Buckley, Sunbelt, Billy Graham, televangelist, Moral Majority

Reading Strategy
Taking Notes As you read about the rise of a new conservative coalition in the United States, use the major headings of the section to create an outline similar to the one below.

The New Conservatism
I. Conservatism and Liberalism
   A.
   B.
II.
   A.

Reading Objectives
• **Explain** how discontent with government led to a conservative shift in Americans' political convictions.
• **Describe** how the nation's population shifts led to a change in voting patterns.

Section Theme
Economic Factors High taxes as well as economic and moral concerns led the country toward a new conservatism.

Preview of Events

✦1965	✦1970	✦1975	✦1980
1964 Conservative Barry Goldwater is defeated for presidency	**1972** Nixon wins re-election	**1976** Reagan challenges Ford for nomination	**1979** Jerry Falwell's "Moral Majority" movement begins	**1980** Reagan wins presidential election

★ An American Story ★

Midge Decter

Midge Decter, a New Yorker and a writer for the conservative publication *Commentary*, was appalled at the terror that hit her city on a hot July night in 1977. On the night of July 13, the power failed in New York City. Street lights went dark. Elevators, subways, and air conditioners stopped running. The blackout left millions of people in darkness, and looting and arson rocked the city.

City officials and the media blamed the lawlessness on the anger and despair of youth in neglected areas. "They were just waiting for something like this so they could go berserk," said Lydia Rivers, a Brooklyn resident. Decter, however, had other ideas about who was to blame for the terror in her city:

❝The answer is that all those young men went on their spree of looting because they had been given permission to do so. They had been given permission to do so by all the papers and magazines, movies and documentaries—all the outlets for the purveying of enlightened liberal attitude and progressive liberal policy—which had for years and years been proclaiming that race and poverty were sufficient excuses for lawlessness. . . .❞

—quoted in *Commentary*, **September 1977**

Conservatism and Liberalism

Midge Decter's article blaming liberalism for the riots in New York during the 1977 blackout exemplifies a debate in American politics that continues to the present day. On one side of the debate are people who call themselves liberals; on the other side are those who identify themselves as conservatives. Liberal ideas generally dominated American

politics for much of the 1900s, but conservative ideas gained significant support among Americans in the 1970s. In 1980 Ronald Reagan, a strong conservative, was elected president.

Liberalism In American politics today, people who call themselves liberals believe several basic ideas. In general, liberals believe that the government should regulate the economy to protect people from the power of large corporations and wealthy elites. Liberals also believe that the government, particularly the federal government, should play an active role in helping disadvantaged Americans, partly through social programs and partly by putting more of society's tax burden on wealthier people.

Although liberals favor government intervention in the economy, they are suspicious of any attempt by the government to regulate social behavior. They are strong supporters of free speech and privacy, and they are opposed to the government supporting or endorsing religious beliefs, no matter how indirectly. They believe that a diverse society made up of many different races, cultures, and ethnic groups tends to be more creative and energetic.

Liberals often support high taxes on the wealthy, partly because they believe taxes weaken the power of the rich and partly because the government can transfer the wealth to other Americans to keep society more equal. They believe that most social problems have their roots in economic inequality.

Conservatism Unlike liberals, conservatives generally have a fundamental distrust of the power of government, particularly the federal government. They support the original intent of the Constitution and believe that governmental power should be divided into different branches and split between the state and federal levels to limit its ability to intrude into people's lives.

Conservatives believe that if the government regulates the economy, it makes the economy less efficient, resulting in less wealth and more poverty. They believe that the free enterprise system is the best way to organize society. They often argue that if people and businesses are free to make their own economic choices, there will be more wealth and a higher standard of living for everyone.

For this reason, conservatives generally oppose high taxes and government programs that transfer wealth from the rich to those who are less wealthy. They believe that taxes and government programs discourage investment, take away people's incentive to work hard, and reduce the amount of freedom in society.

The more the government regulates the economy, conservatives argue, the more it will have to regulate every aspect of people's behavior. Ultimately, conservatives fear, the government will so restrict people's economic freedom that Americans will no longer be able to improve their standard of living and get ahead in life.

Many conservatives believe that religious faith is vitally important in sustaining society. They believe most social problems result from issues of morality and character—issues, they argue, that are best addressed through commitment to a religious faith and through the private efforts of individuals and communities helping those in need. Despite this general belief, conservatives do support the use of the governmental police powers to regulate social behavior in some instances.

✓ **Reading Check** **Contrasting** How do liberal and conservative opinions about government differ?

Conservatism Revives

During the New Deal era of the 1930s, conservative ideas had lost much of their influence in national politics. In the years following World War II, however, conservatism began to revive.

Conservatism and the Cold War Support for conservative ideas began to revive for two major reasons, both related to the Cold War. First, the struggle against communism revived the debate about the role of the government in the economy. Some Americans believed that liberal economic ideas were slowly leading the United States toward communism and became determined to stop this trend. They also thought the United States had failed to stop the spread of Soviet power because liberals did not fully understand the need for a strong anticommunist foreign policy.

At the same time, many Americans viewed the Cold War in religious terms. Communism rejected religion and emphasized the material side of life. To Americans with a deep religious faith, the struggle against communism was a struggle between good and evil. Liberalism, which emphasizes economic welfare, gradually lost the support of many religious Americans, who increasingly turned to conservatism.

Conservatives Organize In 1955 a young conservative named **William F. Buckley** founded a new conservative magazine called *National Review.* Buckley's magazine helped to revive conservative ideas in the United States. Buckley debated in front

2 *TEACH*

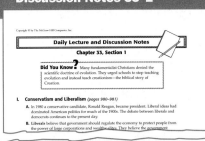

Daily Lecture and Discussion Notes 33–1

Copyright © by The McGraw-Hill Companies, Inc.

Daily Lecture and Discussion Notes

Chapter 33, Section 1

Did You Know? Many fundamentalist Christians denied the scientific doctrine of evolution. They urged schools to stop teaching evolution and instead teach creationism—the biblical story of Creation.

I. **Conservatism and Liberalism** *(pages 980–981)*

  A. In 1980 a conservative candidate, Ronald Reagan, became president. Liberal ideas had dominated American politics for much of the 1900s. The debate between liberals and democrats continues to the present day.

  B. Liberals believe that government should regulate the economy to protect people from the power of large corporations and wealthy elites. They believe the government

✓ **Reading Check**

Answer: Liberals tend to believe in government's duty to help the poor and disadvantaged and to regulate the economy in the interests of the general public. Conservatives tend to distrust the federal government, and dislike both government regulation of the economy and government programs to transfer wealth to lower-income people.

Making a List Have students use the information presented in the text to create a list of the differences between liberalism and conservatism. For each item on the list, have students provide one example. **L1**

COOPERATIVE LEARNING ACTIVITY

Creating a Time Capsule Organize students into groups of three and tell them their task is to create a time capsule that will inform people of the future about the Soviet economic system. Suggest that students search for photographs or other illustrations, written materials such as books, pamphlets, slogans, or artifacts that illustrate some aspect of Soviet government. Have students display the materials they locate. Then ask the class as a whole to select the best materials for inclusion in the time capsule.

Use the rubric for a cooperative group management plan on pages 81–82 in the *Performance Assessment Activities and Rubrics.*

✓ Reading Check

Answer: Because some feared that liberal ideas would lead to a Communist-style government; some also feared that any Communist influence would threaten religion.

Creating a Spreadsheet
Provide the population data for the United States and selected Sunbelt states as shown below. Explain that although you can see the population of these states increased between 1950 and 1980, the real significance can be seen when you express each state's population as a percentage of the country's total population. Have students calculate each state's population, in the selected years, as a percentage of the total U.S. population. **L2**

	1950	1960
U.S. Total	151,868,000	179,975,000
Arizona	750,000	1,302,000
California	10,586,000	15,717,000
Florida	2,771,000	4,952,000
Texas	7,712,000	9,580,000

	1970	1980
U.S. Total	203,302,000	226,546,000
Arizona	1,775,000	2,718,000
California	19,971,000	23,668,000
Florida	6,791,000	9,746,000
Texas	11,199,000	14,229,000

of college students and appeared on radio and tele-vision shows, spreading conservative ideas to an even wider audience.

Within the Republican Party, conservatives, particularly young conservatives, began to push their ideas and demand a greater role in party decision-making. In 1960 some 90 young conservative leaders met at Buckley's family estate and founded Young Americans for Freedom (YAF), an independent conservative group, to push their ideas and to support conser-vative candidates.

By 1964 the new conservative move-ment had achieved enough influence with-in the Republican Party to enable the conservative **Barry Goldwater** to win the nomination for president. To the dismay of the conservatives, however, President Johnson easily defeated Goldwater and won the election in a landslide.

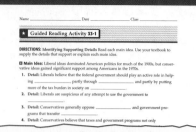
William F. Buckley

✓ Reading Check
Explaining Why did conservatism revive in the 1950s?

Conservatism Gains Support

Conservatism could not have become a mass movement if Americans had not responded to conser-vative ideas. The events of the late 1960s and 1970s played an important role in convincing Americans to support conservatism. After Goldwater's huge loss in 1964, American society moved decisively in a conser-vative direction.

GEOGRAPHY

The Rise of the Sunbelt One of the problems fac-ing conservatives in the 1950s and early 1960s was that they generally split their votes between the Republicans and the Democrats. Two regions of the country, the South and the West, were more conser-vative than other areas. Southern conservatives, however, generally voted for the Democrats, while conservatives in the West voted Republican. This meant that the party that won the heavily populated Northeast would win the election. Since the Northeast strongly supported liberal ideas, both par-ties were pulled toward liberal policies.

This pattern began to change during World War II, when large numbers of Americans moved south and west to take jobs in the war factories. The movement to the South and West—together known as the **Sunbelt**—continued after the war. As the Sunbelt's

economy expanded, Americans living in those regions began to view the federal government differ-ently from people living in the Northeast.

Sunbelt Conservatism Industry in the Northeast was in decline, leading to the region's nickname—the **Rust Belt.** This region had more unemployed people than any other, and its cities were often congested and polluted. These problems prompted Americans in the Northeast to look to the federal government for pro-grams and regulations that would help them solve their problems.

In contrast, Americans in the Sunbelt opposed high taxes and federal regulations that threatened to interfere with their region's growth. Many white Southerners were also angry with the Democrats for supporting civil rights, which they interpreted as an effort by the federal gov-ernment to impose its policies on the South.

When Barry Goldwater argued in 1964 that the federal government was becoming too strong, many Southerners agreed. For the first time since Reconstruction, they began voting Republican in large numbers. Although Goldwater lost the elec-tion, his candidacy showed Republicans that the best way to attract Southern votes was to support conser-vative policies.

Americans living in the West also responded to conservative attacks on the size and power of the fed-eral government. Westerners were proud of their frontier heritage and spirit of "rugged individual-ism." They resented federal environmental regula-tions that limited ranching, controlled water use, and restricted the development of the region's natural resources. Western anger over such policies inspired the "Sagebrush Rebellion" of the early 1970s—a widespread protest led by conservatives against fed-eral laws hindering the region's development.

By 1980 the population of the Sunbelt had surpassed the Northeast. This gave the conservative regions of the country more electoral votes and therefore more influence in shaping party policies. With Southerners shifting their votes to the Republican Party, conserva-tives could now build a coalition to elect a president.

Suburban Conservatism As riots erupted and crime soared during the 1960s and 1970s, many Americans moved to suburbs to escape the chaos of the cities. Even there, however, they found the quiet middle-class lifestyle they desired to be in danger. The rapid inflation of the 1970s had caused the

---

MEETING SPECIAL NEEDS

Logical/Mathematical Have students create a chart similar to the one below. **L1**

	Conservative	Moderate	Liberal
Social Policy			
Foreign Policy			
Economic Policy			

Refer to ***Inclusion for the High School Social Studies Classroom Strategies and Activities*** in the TCR.

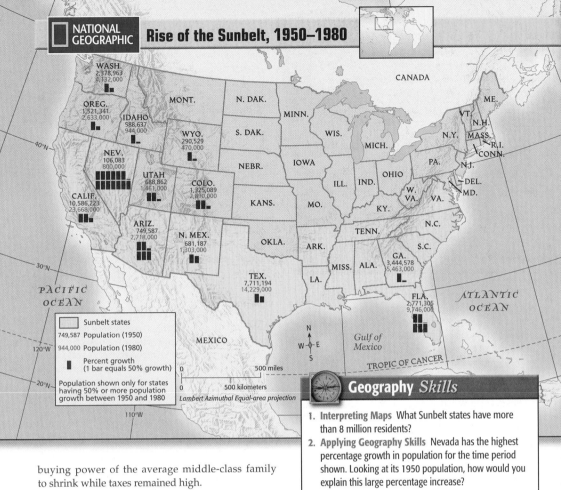

NATIONAL GEOGRAPHIC **Rise of the Sunbelt, 1950–1980**

CANADA

WASH.
2,378,963
4,132,000

OREG.
1,521,341
2,633,000

IDAHO
588,637
944,000

MONT.

N. DAK.

MINN.

ME.

VT.
N.H.
MASS.
R.I.
CONN.

WYO.
290,529
470,000

S. DAK.

WIS.

MICH.

N.Y.

PA.

NJ.

NEV.
106,083
800,000

NEBR.

IOWA

OHIO

W.
VA.

DEL.
MD.

UTAH
688,862
1,461,000

COLO.
1,325,089
2,890,000

ILL.

IND.

VA.

CALIF.
10,586,223
23,668,000

KANS.

MO.

KY.

ARIZ.
749,587
2,718,000

N. MEX.
681,187
1,303,000

OKLA.

TENN.

N.C.

S.C.

ARK.

GA.
3,444,578
5,463,000

PACIFIC
OCEAN

TEX.
7,711,194
14,229,000

MISS.

ALA.

LA.

FLA.
2,771,305
9,746,000

ATLANTIC
OCEAN

Legend
- Sunbelt states
- 749,587 Population (1950)
- 944,000 Population (1980)
- Percent growth (1 bar equals 50% growth)
- Population shown only for states having 50% or more population growth between 1950 and 1980

MEXICO

Gulf of Mexico

TROPIC OF CANCER

N
W E
S

0 ___ 500 miles
0 ___ 500 kilometers
Lambert Azimuthal Equal-area projection

40°N
30°N
120°W
20°N
110°W

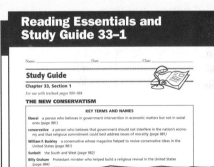

Geography *Skills*

Answers:
1. California, Texas, and Florida
2. Nevada had the smallest state population in 1950. Since the percentage growth is based on the population in 1950, a state with a small population will likely have a large percentage growth.

Geography Skills Practice
Ask: Where do you think the Sunbelt got its name? *(from its sunny climate)*

3 ASSESS

Assign Section 1 Assessment as homework or as an in-class activity.

● Have students use the **Interactive Tutor Self-Assessment CD-ROM.**

Reading Essentials and Study Guide 33–1

Name _____ Date _____ Class _____

Study Guide
Chapter 33, Section 1
For use with textbook pages 980–984
THE NEW CONSERVATISM

KEY TERMS AND NAMES

liberal a person who believes in government intervention in economic matters but not in social ones *(page 981)*
conservative a person who believes that government should not interfere in the nation's economy and that religious commitment could best address issues of morality *(page 981)*
William F. Buckley a conservative whose magazine helped to revive conservative ideas in the United States *(page 982)*
Sunbelt the South and West *(page 982)*
Billy Graham Protestant minister who helped build a religious revival in the United States *(page 984)*

buying power of the average middle-class family to shrink while taxes remained high.

Many Americans resented the taxes they had to pay for New Deal and Great Society programs when they themselves were losing ground economically. By the late 1970s, Americans had begun to rebel against these high taxes. In 1978 Howard Jarvis, a conservative activist, launched the first successful tax revolt in California with **Proposition 13**, a referendum on the state ballot that greatly reduced property taxes.

Soon afterward anti-tax movements appeared in other states, and tax cuts quickly became a national issue. For many Americans, the conservative argument that the government had become too big meant simply that taxes were too high. As conservatives began to call for tax cuts, middle-class Americans flocked to their cause.

The Religious Right While many Americans turned to conservatism for economic reasons, others were drawn to it because they feared American society had lost touch with its traditional values. For many

Americans of deep religious faith, the events of the 1960s and 1970s were shocking. The Supreme Court decision in *Roe v. Wade,* which established abortion as a constitutional right, greatly concerned them. Other Supreme Court decisions that limited prayer in public schools and expanded the rights of people accused of crimes also drew criticism from religious groups. *(See page 1083 for more information on* Roe v. Wade.)

The feminist movement and the push for the Equal Rights Amendment (ERA) further alarmed religious Americans because it seemed to represent an assault on the traditional family. Many religious people were also shocked by the behavior of some university students in the 1960s, whose contempt for authority seemed to indicate a general breakdown in American values and morality. These concerns helped expand the conservative cause into a mass movement.

INTERDISCIPLINARY CONNECTIONS ACTIVITY

Civics Have interested students examine the income, property, and sales tax rate structure in their state. Have students prepare a visual display of the rates to use during a brief oral presentation in which they either support the state's current tax policies or propose a plan to raise or lower taxes. **L3**

Section Quiz 33–1

Name _____ Date _____ Class _____

⭐ Chapter 33   Score ___

Section Quiz 33-1

DIRECTIONS: Matching Match each item in Column A with the items in Column B. Write the correct letters in the blanks. *(10 points each)*

Column A

____ **1.** a movement founded by Jerry Falwell that built up a network of ministers to register new voters who backed conservative candidates and issues

____ **2.** a referendum question on the state ballot in California that greatly reduced property taxes

____ **3.** the South and West

____ **4.** conservative Republican nominee for president in 1964

____ **5.** Protestant minister with a national following

Column B

A. Sunbelt
B. Billy Graham
C. Moral Majority
D. Proposition 13
E. Barry Goldwater

DIRECTIONS: Multiple Choice In the blank at the left, write the letter of the choice

Creating a Poster Have students create a poster that expresses one of the conservative views held by a group mentioned in this section. Display their posters around the class. **L2**

Reteach

Have students explain the conservative shift in Americans' political convictions.

Enrich

Have interested students investigate how migration to the Sunbelt changed the composition of Congress.

✓ Reading Check

Answer: They thought it would improve the economy, and they wanted to return to traditional values.

4 CLOSE

Have students describe how the nation's population shifts changed voting patterns.

Jerry Falwell (below) and Pat Robertson (right)

Although religious conservatives included people of many different faiths, the largest group within the social conservative movement was evangelical Protestant Christians. Evangelicals believe they are saved from their sins through conversion (which they refer to as being "born again") and a personal commitment to follow Jesus Christ, whose death and resurrection reconciles them to God.

After World War II, a religious revival began in the United States. Protestant ministers such as **Billy Graham** and Oral Roberts built national followings. By the late 1970s, about 70 million Americans described themselves as "born again." Christian evangelicals owned their own newspapers, magazines, radio stations, and television networks.

Television in particular allowed evangelical ministers to reach a large nationwide audience. These "televangelists," as they were nicknamed, included Marion "Pat" Robertson, who founded the Christian Broadcasting Network, and Jerry Falwell, who used his television show *The Old-Time Gospel Hour* to found a movement that he called the **"Moral Majority."** Using television and mail campaigns, the Moral Majority built up a network of ministers to register new voters who backed conservative candidates and issues. Falwell later claimed to have brought in 2 million new voters by 1980.

A New Coalition By the end of the 1970s, the new conservative coalition of voters had begun to come together in the United States. Although the members of this coalition were concerned with many different issues, they were held together by a common belief that American society had somehow lost its way.

The Watergate scandal, high taxes, and special interest politics had undermined many Americans' faith in their government. Rising unemployment, rapid inflation, and the energy crisis had shaken their confidence in the economy. Riots, crime, and drug abuse suggested that society itself was falling apart. The retreat from Vietnam, the hostage crisis in Iran, and the Soviet invasion of Afghanistan made the nation look weak and helpless internationally. Many Americans were tired of change and upheaval. They wanted stability and a return to what they remembered as a better time. For some, the new conservatism and its most prominent spokesperson, Ronald Reagan, offered hope to a nation in distress.

✓ **Reading Check** **Summarizing** Why did many Americans begin to support the conservative movement?

SECTION 1 ASSESSMENT

Checking for Understanding

1. **Define:** liberal, conservative, televangelist.
2. **Identify:** William F. Buckley, Sunbelt, Billy Graham, Moral Majority.
3. **Explain** why evangelical Protestant Christians began to support conservative issues.

Reviewing Themes

4. **Economic Factors** What kind of economy did conservatives want?

Critical Thinking

5. **Analyzing** How did Christian evangelicals contribute to a growing conservative national identity?
6. **Organizing** Use a graphic organizer similar to the one below to list conservative beliefs.

Conservative Beliefs

Analyzing Visuals

7. **Analyzing Maps** Study the map of the Sunbelt on page 983. What impact would the migration patterns shown have on representation in the U.S. House of Representatives?

Writing About History

8. **Persuasive Writing** Many conservatives believe that "government that governs least, governs best." Write a paragraph supporting or opposing this statement.

984 CHAPTER 33 Resurgence of Conservatism

SECTION 1 ASSESSMENT ANSWERS

1. Terms are in blue.
2. William F. Buckley *(p. 981),* Sunbelt *(p. 982),* Billy Graham *(p. 984),* Moral Majority *(p. 984)*
3. because they feared American society had lost touch with its traditional values

4. Conservatives wanted to strengthen the free enterprise system.
5. Their media supported conservative candidates.
6. free enterprise, emphasis on religious values, little government regulation of the economy

7. The population increase would give the Sunbelt more seats in the House of Representatives, and conservatives would likely be elected to fill those seats.
8. Students' paragraphs should express a clear point of view.

SECTION 2 The Reagan Years

Guide to Reading

Main Idea
The presidency of Ronald Reagan brought a new conservative attitude to government.

Key Terms and Names
supply-side economics, Reaganomics, budget deficit, Sandra Day O'Connor, William Rehnquist, Geraldine Ferraro, contra, Iran-Contra scandal, Oliver North, Mikhail Gorbachev

Reading Strategy
Organizing As you read about the Reagan presidency, complete the graphic organizer below by filling in the major points of the supply-side theory of economics.

Supply-Side Theory

Reading Objectives
- **Explain** President Reagan's economic recovery plan.
- **Discuss** Reagan's policies toward the Soviet Union.

Section Theme
Global Connections President Reagan believed the United States should take strong action to resist Communist influence overseas.

Preview of Events

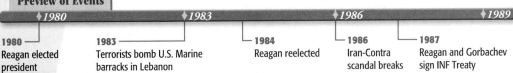

| 1980 | 1983 | 1986 | 1989 |

1980 Reagan elected president

1983 Terrorists bomb U.S. Marine barracks in Lebanon

1984 Reagan reelected

1986 Iran-Contra scandal breaks

1987 Reagan and Gorbachev sign INF Treaty

★ An American Story ★

In 1926 when he was 15 years old, Ronald Reagan earned $15 a week as a lifeguard at Lowell Park on the Rock River in Illinois. Being a lifeguard, Reagan later wrote, taught him quite a bit about human nature:

❝Lifeguarding provides one of the best vantage points in the world to learn about people. During my career at the park, I saved seventy-seven people. I guarantee you they needed saving—no lifeguard gets wet without good reason. . . . Not many thanked me, much less gave me a reward, and being a little money-hungry, I'd done a little daydreaming about this. They felt insulted. I got to recognize that people hate to be saved. . . .❞

—quoted in *Where's the Rest of Me?*

The belief that people did not really want to be saved by someone else was one of the ideas that Ronald Reagan took with him to the White House. It fit with his philosophy of self-reliance and independence.

A young Ronald Reagan

The Road to the White House

Ronald Reagan grew up in Dixon, Illinois, the son of an Irish American shoe salesman. After graduating from Eureka College in 1932, Reagan worked as a sports broadcaster at an Iowa radio station. In 1937 he took a Hollywood screen test and won a contract from a movie studio. Over the next 25 years, he made over 50 movies. As a broadcaster and actor, Reagan learned how to speak publicly and how to project an image, skills that proved invaluable when he entered politics.

CHAPTER 33 Resurgence of Conservatism **985**

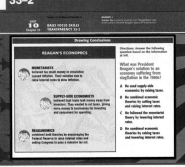

SECTION RESOURCES

📁 Reproducible Masters
- Reproducible Lesson Plan 33–2
- Daily Lecture and Discussion Notes 33–2
- Guided Reading Activity 33–2
- Section Quiz 33–2
- Reading Essentials and Study Guide 33–2
- Interpreting Political Cartoons

🎞 Transparencies
- Daily Focus Skills Transparency 33–2

Multimedia
- 💿 Interactive Tutor Self-Assessment CD-ROM
- 💿 ExamView® Pro Testmaker CD-ROM
- 💿 Presentation Plus! CD-ROM
- 💿 TeacherWorks™ CD-ROM
- 🎧 Audio Program

2 TEACH

Daily Lecture and Discussion Notes 33–2

Daily Lecture and Discussion Notes

Chapter 33, Section 2

Did You Know? In March 1981, President Reagan was shot by a man trying to assassinate him. In the operating room, as surgeons prepared to remove the bullet, Reagan told the surgeons, "I hope you fellas are Republicans." Reagan quickly recovered from his wound. His sense of humor and actions following the assassination attempt increased his popularity with Americans.

I. The Road to the White House *(pages 985–987)*

A. Ronald Reagan had worked as a broadcaster and actor, which helped him with public speaking and his image.

B. Reagan had been a Democrat and a supporter of the New Deal, but during his time as

Different Viewpoints

Answers:

1. Carter felt Americans should make sacrifices so government could solve problems. Reagan felt Americans should solve problems themselves.

2. Students' answers will vary but students should support their choices with clear reasoning.

Ask: What words does Carter use to point the finger at Reagan's background as an actor? *(world of tinsel and make-believe)*

Discussing Public Opinion Tell students that Carter was the first incumbent president to lose a re-election bid since Herbert Hoover. As a class, discuss the events that contributed to his defeat. **L1**

Different Viewpoints

Carter and Reagan on Government

As President Carter sought re-election in 1980, he had to deal with inflation, unemployment, and an energy crisis. He urged Americans to make sacrifices so that the government could solve these problems. His opponent, Ronald Reagan, disagreed. Reagan argued that Americans should trust themselves, not the government, to solve their problems.

President Jimmy Carter:

"[A] president cannot yield to the shortsighted demands, no matter how rich or powerful the special interests might be that make those demands. And that is why the president cannot bend to the passions of the moment, however popular they might be. And that is why the president must sometimes ask for sacrifice when his listeners would rather hear the promise of comfort.

. . . The only way to build a better future is to start with realities of the present. But while we Democrats grapple with the real challenges of a real world, others talk of a world of tinsel and make-believe.

. . . A world of good guys and bad guys, where some politicians shoot first and ask questions later. No hard choices. No sacrifice. No tough decisions. It sounds too good to be true—and it is."

—*from his acceptance speech at the Democratic National Convention, August 14, 1980*

California governor Ronald Reagan:

"The American people, the most generous people on earth, who created the highest standard of living, are not going to accept the notion that we can only make a better world for others by moving backwards ourselves. Those who believe we *can* have no business leading the nation.

I will not stand by and watch this great country destroy itself under mediocre leadership that drifts from one crisis to the next, eroding our national will and purpose.

"Trust me" government asks that we concentrate our hopes and dreams on one man; that we trust him to do what's best for us. My view of government places trust not in one person or one party, but in those values that transcend persons and parties. The trust is where it belongs—in the people."

—*from his acceptance speech at the Republican National Convention, July 17, 1980*

Learning From History

1. **Recognizing Ideologies** How do the two candidates differ regarding the role of government in solving the nation's problems?
2. **Making Inferences** Ronald Reagan won the election of 1980. What part of his speech do you think may have had the most influence on voters? Why?

Moving to Conservatism In 1947 Reagan became president of the **Screen Actors Guild**—the actors' union. As head of the union, he testified about communism in Hollywood before the House Un-American Activities Committee. Reagan had been a staunch Democrat and supporter of the New Deal, but his experience in dealing with Communists in the union began shifting him toward conservative ideas.

In 1954 Reagan became the host of a television program called *General Electric Theater* and agreed to be a motivational speaker for the company. As he traveled around the country speaking to workers, secretaries, and managers, he became increasingly conservative. Over and over again, Reagan said later, he heard stories from average Americans about how high taxes and government regulations made it impossible for them to get ahead.

By 1964 Reagan had become such a popular national speaker that Barry Goldwater asked him to make a televised speech on behalf of Goldwater's presidential campaign. Reagan's speech greatly impressed several wealthy entrepreneurs in California. They convinced Reagan to run for governor of California in 1966 and helped finance his campaign. Reagan won the election and was reelected in 1970. Ten years later, he won the Republican presidential nomination.

986 CHAPTER 33 Resurgence of Conservatism

COOPERATIVE LEARNING ACTIVITY

Evaluating Policies Have students reread the passage about supply-side economics in this section. Then organize the class into three groups and ask group members to work together to write letters to President Reagan regarding the impact of his economic polices. One group should represent business owners, another should represent workers in manufacturing industries, and the third should represent people on fixed incomes, such as senior citizens or welfare recipients. Have each group select a representative to read the group's letter to the rest of the class.

Use the rubric for a cooperative group management plan on pages 81–82 in the *Performance Assessment Activities and Rubrics.*

The Election of 1980 Reagan's campaign appealed to Americans who were frustrated with the economy and worried that the United States had become weak internationally. Reagan promised to cut taxes and increase defense spending. He won the support of social conservatives by calling for a constitutional amendment banning abortion. During one debate with Carter, Reagan asked voters, "Are you better off than you were four years ago?" On Election Day, the voters answered "No." Reagan won nearly 51 percent of the popular vote and 489 electoral votes, easily defeating Carter in the Electoral College. For the first time since 1954, Republicans also gained control of the Senate.

✓ **Reading Check** **Describing** What event jump-started Ronald Reagan's political career as a conservative leader?

Reagan's Domestic Policies

Ronald Reagan believed the key to restoring the economy and overcoming problems in society was to get Americans to believe in themselves again. He expressed this idea in his Inaugural Address:

> ❝We have every right to dream heroic dreams. . . . You can see heroes every day going in and out of factory gates. Others, a handful in number, produce enough food to feed all of us. . . . You meet heroes across a counter. . . . There are entrepreneurs with faith in themselves and faith in an idea who create new jobs, new wealth and opportunity. . . . Their patriotism is quiet but deep. Their values sustain our national life.❞
>
> —from Reagan's First Inaugural Address

Reagan also explained that Americans should not look to Washington for answers: "In this present crisis, government is not the solution to our problem. Government is the problem."

ECONOMICS

Reaganomics Reagan's first priority was the economy, which was suffering from stagflation—a combination of high unemployment and high inflation. According to most economists, the way to fight unemployment was to increase government spending. Increasing spending, however, made inflation worse. Stagflation puzzled many economists, who did not expect inflation and high unemployment to occur at the same time.

Conservative economists offered two competing ideas for fixing the economy. One group, known as **monetarists**, argued that inflation was caused by too much money in circulation. They believed the best solution was to raise interest rates. Another group supported supply-side economics. They argued that the economy was weak because taxes were too high.

Supply-side economists believed that high taxes took too much money away from investors. If taxes were cut, businesses and investors could use their extra capital to make new investments, and businesses could expand and create new jobs. The result would be a larger supply of goods for consumers, who would now have more money to spend because of the tax cuts.

Reagan combined monetarism and supply-side economics. He encouraged the Federal Reserve to keep interest rates high, and asked Congress to pass a massive tax cut. Critics called his approach **Reaganomics** or "trickle-down economics." They believed Reagan's policy would help corporations and wealthy Americans, while only a little bit of the wealth would "trickle down" to average Americans.

Reagan made deals with conservative Democrats in the House and moderate Republicans in the Senate. Eventually Congress passed a 25 percent tax rate cut.

Cutting Programs Cutting tax rates meant the government would receive less money. This would increase the budget deficit—the amount by which expenditures exceed income. To keep the deficit under control, Reagan proposed cuts to social programs. Welfare benefits, including the food stamp program and the school lunch program, were cut back. Medicare payments, student loans, housing subsidies, and unemployment compensation were also reduced.

After a struggle, Congress passed most of these cuts. The fight convinced Reagan that he would never get Congress to cut spending enough to balance the budget. He decided that cutting taxes and building up the military were more important than balancing the budget. He accepted the high deficit as the price of getting his other programs passed.

Deregulation Reagan believed that burdensome government regulations were another cause of the economy's problems. His first act as president was to sign an executive order eliminating price controls on oil and gasoline. Critics argued that getting rid of controls would

Student Web Activity Visit the *American Vision* Web site at tav.glencoe.com and click on *Student Web Activities— Chapter 33* for an activity on the 1980s.

Guided Reading Activity 33–2

✓ **Reading Check**

Answer: A televised speech on behalf of Barry Goldwater's presidential campaign aided his political career as a conservative leader.

FYI

Ronald Reagan used his experience as an actor for his life in public office. Just as he had rehearsed his lines as an actor, he spent hours fine-tuning the wording and delivery of his speeches.

HISTORY Online

Objectives and answers to the student activity can be found in the **Web Activity Lesson Plan** at tav.glencoe.com.

📁 Use *Interpreting Political Cartoons*, Cartoon 32.

MEETING SPECIAL NEEDS

Visual/Spatial Ask students to research the events that took place in El Salvador, Grenada, and Nicaragua during the Reagan administration. Have students examine the major factions in each country, their relationships with the United States, the major events, and the important leaders. Have students present their findings in chart form, accompanied by a thematic map showing all four countries. **L1**

📁 Refer to *Inclusion for the High School Social Studies Classroom Strategies and Activities* in the TCR.

you don't say...

Television In contrast to Ronald Reagan, who was at home in front of the television camera, Walter Mondale appeared awkward and uncomfortable. After losing the 1984 election, Mondale commented on the role of television. "Modern politics today requires a mastery of television," he said. "I've never really warmed up to television and, in fairness to television, it's never warmed up to me."

✓ **Reading Check**

Answer: Supply-side economics proposes low taxes as an incentive to generate more investment in business. In theory, this leads to new and larger businesses and more jobs. Under this theory more workers would have income with which to purchase the expanded production.

drive prices up, but in fact, they began to fall. The falling energy prices freed up money for businesses and consumers to spend elsewhere, helping the economy to recover.

Other deregulation soon followed. The National Highway Traffic and Safety Administration reduced its demand for air bags and higher fuel efficiency for cars. The Federal Communications Commission abandoned efforts to regulate the new cable television industry. Carter had already begun deregulating the airline industry, and Reagan encouraged the process, which led to price wars, cheaper fares, and the founding of new airlines.

Reagan's Secretary of the Interior, **James Watt,** increased the amount of public land corporations could use for oil drilling, mining, and logging. Watt's decisions angered environmentalists, as did the Environmental Protection Agency's decisions to ease regulations on pollution control equipment and to reduce safety checks on chemicals and pesticides.

The Economy Booms In 1983 the economy finally began to recover. By 1984 the United States had begun the biggest economic expansion in its history up to that time. The median income of American families climbed steadily, rising 15 percent by 1989. Sales of goods and services shot upward. Five million new businesses and 20 million new jobs were created. By 1988 unemployment had fallen to about 5.5 percent, the lowest in 14 years.

Shifting the Judicial Balance Reagan did not apply his conservative ideas only to the economy. He also tried to bring a strict constructionist outlook to the federal judiciary. Reagan wanted judges who followed the original intent and wording of the Constitution rather than those who interpreted and expanded its meaning. He also changed the face of the Supreme

Court by nominating **Sandra Day O'Connor** to be the first woman on the Supreme Court.

In 1986 Chief Justice Warren Burger retired. Reagan chose the most conservative associate justice, **William Rehnquist,** to succeed him. He then named **Antonin Scalia,** also a conservative, to fill the vacancy left by Rehnquist. In 1987 Reagan's nomination of Robert Bork to the Court led to a bitter confirmation fight in the Senate. Liberals argued that Bork's opinions on issues were too extreme, and they managed to block his confirmation. **Anthony Kennedy,** a moderate, ultimately became the new associate justice.

Reagan Wins Re-election As the 1984 election approached, the growing economy made Reagan very popular. Democrats nominated Jimmy Carter's vice president, **Walter Mondale.** He chose as his running mate Representative **Geraldine Ferraro,** the first woman to run for vice president for a major party.

Instead of arguing issues with his opponent, Reagan emphasized the good economy. In an overwhelming landslide, he won about 59 percent of the popular vote and all the electoral votes except those from Mondale's home state of Minnesota and the District of Columbia.

✓ **Reading Check** **Explaining** What is supply-side economics?

Reagan Builds Up the Military

Reagan did not limit his reforms to the domestic scene. He adopted a new Cold War foreign policy that rejected both containment and détente. Reagan called the Soviet Union "the focus of evil in the modern world" and "an evil empire." In his view, the United States should not negotiate with or try to contain evil. It should try to defeat it.

The Attempt to Kill the President, March 30, 1981

Barely two months after the inauguration, on March 30, 1981, John Hinckley tried to kill President Reagan in a misguided attempt to impress actress Jodie Foster. Hinckley fired six shots as Reagan left a hotel in Washington, D.C. One bullet bounced off the president's rib and lodged near his heart. Another bullet seriously wounded press secretary Jim Brady. Reagan's recovery was long, but he stayed upbeat. His jaunty reply to his wife, "Honey, I forgot to duck," won the affection of many.

John Hinckley (center)

SECTION 4 The End of the Cold War

Guide to Reading

Main Idea
President George Bush's foreign policy commanded broad support, but his domestic agenda did not.

Key Terms and Names
perestroika, glasnost, Boris Yeltsin, Tiananmen Square, Saddam Hussein, downsizing, capital gains tax, H. Ross Perot, grassroots movement

Reading Strategy
Categorizing As you read about the administration of President Bush, complete a chart similar to the one below by describing U.S. foreign policy in each of the places listed on the chart.

Place	Foreign Policy
Soviet Union	
China	
Panama	
Middle East	

Reading Objectives
• **Identify** the events that brought an end to the Cold War.
• **Explain** the domestic challenges facing the Bush administration.

Section Theme
Economic Factors The deficit and an economic slowdown hurt George Bush's attempt to win re-election in 1992.

Preview of Events

1989	1990	1991	1992

May, 1989
Tiananmen Square protests begin

November, 1989
Berlin Wall falls

August, 1990
Iraq invades Kuwait

January, 1991
Persian Gulf War begins

December, 1991
Soviet Union collapses

★ *An American Story* ★

Colin Powell

On October 31, 1990, General Colin Powell, who was the chairman of the Joint Chiefs of Staff, Secretary of Defense Dick Cheney, and other high-ranking officials met with President George Bush. In August the country of Iraq had invaded neighboring Kuwait. American troops had been rushed to the Middle East in response. Now the president had to decide whether to go to war.

General Brent Scrowcroft, a close adviser to Bush, began the meeting: "Mr. President, we are at a Y in the road. Down one branch we can continue sanctions. . . . Down the other branch we . . . go on the attack." Powell then presented the plan for attacking Iraq. Several advisers gasped at the numbers, which called for over 500,000 American troops. "Mr. President," Powell began, "I wish . . . that I could assure you that air power alone could do it but you can't take that chance. We've gotta take the initiative out of the enemy's hands if we're going to go to war." Cheney later recalled that Bush "never hesitated." He looked up from the plans and said simply, "Do it."

—adapted from *Triumph Without Victory* and *PBS Frontline Gulf War Interviews*

George Bush Takes Office

The war in the Persian Gulf was only one of many international crises that confronted President George Bush after his election in 1988. Fortunately, Bush's strength was in foreign policy. In the 1970s, he had served as ambassador to the UN and as the nation's first

---

1 FOCUS

Section Overview
This section focuses on the foreign policy successes and domestic problems during the presidency of George Bush.

BELLRINGER
Skillbuilder Activity

 Project transparency and have students answer the question.

📂 Available as a blackline master.

Daily Focus Skills Transparency 33–4

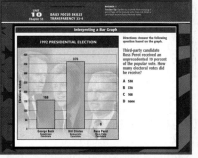

Guide to Reading

Answers to Graphic: Soviet Union: cooperated with reform leader Gorbachev; China: halted arms sales and reduced diplomatic contact; Panama: invaded and seized dictator to help people hold elections and organize a new government; Middle East: imposed economic sanctions against Iraq and carried out Operation Desert Storm

Preteaching Vocabulary
For each of the Key Terms and Names, have students write a phrase or short sentence that will help them remember the significance of the term or name.

SECTION RESOURCES

📂 **Reproducible Masters**
• Reproducible Lesson Plan 33-4
• Daily Lecture and Discussion Notes 33-4
• Guided Reading Activity 33-4
• Section Quiz 33-4
• Reading Essentials and Study Guide 33-4
• Interpreting Political Cartoons

🎞 **Transparencies**
• Daily Focus Skills Transparency 33-4

Multimedia
🖥 Interactive Tutor Self-Assessment CD-ROM
🖥 ExamView® Pro Testmaker CD-ROM
🖥 Presentation Plus! CD-ROM
🖥 TeacherWorks™ CD-ROM
🎧 Audio Program

2 TEACH

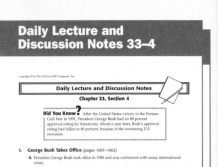

Geography *Skills*

Answers:

1. Poland, Hungary, Bulgaria, and Romania

2. It was particularly significant because it meant that Germany could be reunified.

Geography Skills Practice
Ask: What happened to Czechoslovakia? (*In 1993 it was divided into two countries: the Czech Republic and Slovakia.*)

✓ Reading Check

Answer: He promised no new taxes and to continue Ronald Reagan's domestic policies.

Analyzing a Point of View
Review with students what they know about the Communist government in the Soviet Union. Then ask students to defend or refute the following statement: "The collapse of the Soviet Union was inevitable." Encourage students to use reasoned arguments to support their point of view. **L1**

1002

NATIONAL GEOGRAPHIC
Revolution in Eastern Europe, 1989–1993

⑤ Baltic States became independent, 1991
④ Germany reunited, 1990
① Democratic elections, 1989
③ Berlin Wall torn down, Nov. 1989
⑥ Czechoslovakia separated, 1993
② Non-Communist governments created, 1989

Lambert Azimuthal Equal-Area projection

Geography *Skills*

1. **Interpreting Maps** Which Eastern European countries abandoned communism first?
2. **Applying Geography Skills** Why was the fall of communism in East Germany significant?

diplomatic envoy to the People's Republic of China. He then headed the CIA from 1976 to 1977 before becoming vice president in 1981.

When Ronald Reagan left office, few Americans were thinking about foreign policy. They generally wanted a continuation of Reagan's domestic policies—low taxes and less government action. When Bush accepted the Republican nomination in 1988, he tried to reassure Americans by making a promise: "Read my lips: No new taxes."

The Democrats hoped to regain the White House in 1988 by promising to help working-class Americans, minorities, and the poor. One candidate for the nomination, civil rights leader Jesse Jackson, tried to create a "rainbow coalition"—a broad group of minorities and the poor—by speaking about homelessness and unemployment. Jackson finished second in the primaries, the first African American to make a serious run for the nomination.

The Democrats' final choice was Massachusetts governor Michael Dukakis. The Bush campaign

1002 CHAPTER 33 Resurgence of Conservatism

portrayed him as too liberal, unpatriotic, and "soft on crime." The Democrats questioned Bush's leadership abilities, but Bush had Reagan's endorsement, and with the economy still doing well, few Americans wanted to switch parties. Bush won 54 percent of the popular vote and defeated Dukakis 426 to 111 in the Electoral College. Democrats, however, kept control of Congress.

✓ Reading Check

Describing What kind of strategy did the Bush campaign use in the 1988 election?

The Cold War Ends
Almost immediately after taking office, President Bush had to draw on his foreign policy experience. With the help of Secretary of State James Baker, the president steered the United States through an era of sweeping change that resulted from the sudden end of the Cold War.

Gorbachev's Reforms As president, Bush continued Reagan's policy of cooperation with Soviet leader Mikhail Gorbachev. By the late 1980s, the Soviet economy was suffering from years of inefficient central planning and huge expenditures on the arms race. To save the economy, Gorbachev instituted *perestroika,* or "restructuring," and allowed some private enterprise and profit-making.

The other principle of Gorbachev's plan was *glasnost,* or "openness." It allowed more freedom of religion and speech, allowing people to discuss politics openly.

Revolution in Eastern Europe With Gorbachev's support, *glasnost* spread to Eastern Europe. In 1989 peaceful revolutions replaced Communist rulers with democratic governments in Poland, Hungary, Czechoslovakia, Romania, and Bulgaria. The spreading revolution soon reached East Germany, and at midnight on November 9, 1989, guards at the Berlin Wall opened the gates. Within days, bulldozers leveled the hated symbol of Communist repression. Within a year, East and West Germany had reunited.

COOPERATIVE LEARNING ACTIVITY

Creating a Thematic Map Organize students into groups of four or five and have each group create a large thematic map showing the countries that were once Soviet republics. Encourage students to use library and Internet resources to find out what has happened to those nations and place an important fact in a balloon caption for each country. Groups can also make an illustrated time line of important events to accompany the map. Work should be divided evenly among all group members.

Use the rubric for a cooperative group management plan on pages 81–82 in the ***Performance Assessment Activities and Rubrics.***

The Soviet Union Collapses As Eastern Europe abandoned communism, Gorbachev faced mounting criticism from opponents at home. In August 1991, a group of Communist officials and army officers staged a coup—an overthrow of the government. They arrested Gorbachev and sent troops into Moscow.

In Moscow, Russian president **Boris Yeltsin** defied the coup leaders from his offices in the Russian Parliament. About 50,000 people surrounded the Russian Parliament to protect it from troops. President Bush telephoned Yeltsin to express the support of the United States. Soon afterward, the coup collapsed, and Gorbachev returned to Moscow.

The defeat of the coup brought change swiftly. All 15 Soviet republics declared their independence from the Soviet Union. Yeltsin outlawed the Communist Party in Russia. In late December 1991, Gorbachev announced the end of the Soviet Union. Most of the former Soviet republics then joined in a federation called the Commonwealth of Independent States.

✓ **Reading Check** **Explaining** Why did Mikhail Gorbachev institute the policy of *perestroika*?

The "New World Order"

After the Cold War, the world became increasingly unpredictable. In a phrase made popular by President Bush, a "new world order" was developing. While trying to redefine American foreign policy, Bush faced crises in China, Panama, and the Middle East.

Tragedy in Tiananmen Square Despite the collapse of communism in Eastern Europe and the Soviet Union, China's Communist leaders were determined to stay in power. China's government had relaxed controls on the economy, but it continued to repress political speech and dissent. In May 1989, Chinese students and workers held demonstrations for democracy. In early June, government tanks and soldiers crushed their protests in **Tiananmen Square** in Beijing—China's capital. Many people were killed and hundreds of pro-democracy activists were arrested. Many were later sentenced to death.

These events shocked the world. The United States and several European countries halted arms sales and reduced their diplomatic contacts with China. The World Bank suspended loans. Some congressional

NATIONAL GEOGRAPHIC

MOMENT in HISTORY

A CITY REUNITED

Built in 1961, the Berlin Wall served to stem the mounting tide of immigration from Communist East Germany into the democratic western sector of the city. The wall also stood as a symbol of Cold War tensions between the world's superpowers. As reforms sparked by Mikhail Gorbachev swept through Eastern Europe, however, East German citizens began pressuring their government to open its borders. On November 9, 1989, the gates were thrown open, and East and West Berliners finally mingled freely. With great enthusiasm, they took hammers and chisels to the wall and tore down the hated symbol of division.

Guided Reading Activity 33–4

✦ Guided Reading Activity **33-4**

DIRECTIONS: Outlining Read the section and complete the outline below. Refer to your textbook to fill in the blanks.

I. George Bush Takes Office

A. When Ronald Reagan left office in 1988, Americans wanted a continuation of his domestic policies— _____ and _____

B. George Bush won _____ percent of the popular vote and defeated Michael Dukakis in the Electoral College, _____ to _____

II. The Cold War Ends

A. To save his country's economy, Soviet leader Gorbachev instituted _____ or "restructuring" and allowed some _____

B. He also instituted _____ or "openness," which allowed more freedom _____

✓ **Reading Check**

Answer: *Perestroika* was intended to save the Soviet economy by allowing some private enterprise and profit-making.

NATIONAL GEOGRAPHIC

MOMENT in HISTORY

The following events immediately preceded the wall's destruction: In October, East Germany celebrated its fortieth anniversary with a two-day visit by Mikhail Gorbachev. After Gorbachev left, the government arrested demonstrators who were protesting economic problems and the lack of democratic freedoms. Continued unrest forced President Erich Honecker, a hard-line Communist who had ruled East Germany since its inception, to resign. In November, the government opened its borders in an attempt to turn the tide of escaping citizens and convince them that leaving the country was unnecessary.

📁 Use *Interpreting Political Cartoons,* Cartoons 34 and 35.

MEETING SPECIAL NEEDS

Visual/Spatial To help students understand the impact of the Berlin Wall coming down, use a large map of your community and draw a line down the center of it. Ask students to look at the map closely and make a list of all the aspects of their lives that would be affected if they could not cross "the wall." Invite students to share some of the entries on their lists. **L2**

📁 Refer to *Inclusion for the High School Social Studies Classroom Strategies and Activities* in the TCR.

Creating a Circle Graph Have students use the information presented in the graph that appears at the top of this page to create a circle graph showing the proportional contribution of each region to the total oil production for these regions in 2000. **L2**

Use the rubric for creating a map, display, or chart on pages 77–78 in the *Performance Assessment Activities and Rubrics.*

you don't say...

Saddam Iraqi leader Saddam Hussein likes to be called by his first name. When pronounced correctly, with the emphasis on the second syllable, Saddam means "leader" or "learned one." During the Persian Gulf War, President Bush insisted on pronouncing the name with the emphasis on the first syllable. Pronounced this way, Saddam means "a boy who fixes or cleans shoes."

Why It Matters

Strait of Hormuz

The Strait of Hormuz is a narrow shipping lane between the Persian Gulf, the Gulf of Oman, and the Arabian Sea. Most of the crude oil produced in the Middle East passes through the Strait of Hormuz. In 1997 about 14 million barrels of crude oil passed through the Strait every day. Since the waterway is only about 40 miles (64 km) across at its widest point, it is possible that a country might block or hamper passage of ships. During the 1980s, the United States began escorting oil tankers through the Strait to protect them from Iranian attacks. If the passage were ever closed, oil would have to be shipped overland by pipeline—a much more expensive option.

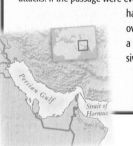

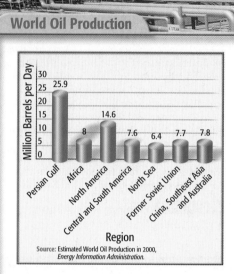

World Oil Production

Million Barrels per Day

Region	
Persian Gulf	25.9
Africa	8
North America	14.6
Central and South America	7.6
North Sea	6.4
Former Soviet Union	7.7
China, Southeast Asia and Australia	7.8

Source: Estimated World Oil Production in 2000, *Energy Information Administration.*

The Persian Gulf countries consist of Saudi Arabia, Iran, Iraq, Kuwait, Qatar, and the United Arab Emirates. They may hold as much as 70 percent of the world's proven oil reserves.

leaders urged even stronger sanctions, but President Bush resisted these harsher measures, believing that trade and diplomacy would eventually moderate China's behavior.

Panama While President Bush struggled to deal with global events elsewhere, a crisis developed in Panama. In 1978 the United States had agreed to give Panama control over the Panama Canal by the year 2000. Because of the canal's importance, American officials wanted to make sure Panama's government was both stable and pro-American.

By 1989 Panama's dictator, General Manuel Noriega, had stopped cooperating with the United States. He also aided drug traffickers, cracked down on opponents, and harassed American military personnel defending the canal. In December 1989, Bush ordered American troops to invade Panama. The troops seized Noriega, who was sent to the United States to stand trial on drug charges. The troops then helped the Panamanians hold elections and organize a new government.

The Persian Gulf War President Bush faced perhaps his most serious crisis in the Middle East. In August 1990, Iraq's dictator, **Saddam Hussein,** sent his army to invade oil-rich Kuwait. American officials feared the invasion was only the first step and that Iraq's ultimate goal was to capture Saudi Arabia and its vast oil reserves.

President Bush persuaded other UN member countries to join a coalition to stop Iraq. Led by the United States, the United Nations first imposed economic sanctions on Iraq and demanded the Iraqis withdraw. The coalition forces included troops from the United States, Canada, Europe, and Arab nations. The UN set a deadline for the Iraqi withdrawal, or the coalition would use force to remove them. Congress also voted to authorize the use of force if Iraq did not withdraw.

Iraq refused to comply with the UN deadline, and on January 16, 1991, the coalition forces launched **Operation Desert Storm.** Dozens of cruise

1004 CHAPTER 33 Resurgence of Conservatism

INTERDISCIPLINARY CONNECTIONS ACTIVITY

Economics Tell students that the 1992 defense budget of the United States was close to $300 billion. Some have suggested that instead of producing costly weapons, regardless of the need, the government should support research and put off producing weapons until a need becomes clear and cost controls are assured. Others argue that when orders to a defense plant decrease, it affects the local economy. The plant orders fewer raw materials from suppliers, the truckers who deliver goods lose business, and individual workers get laid off or work fewer hours. Discuss with students the pros and cons of decreasing or increasing defense spending for the American economy. **L2**

War in the Persian Gulf, 1991

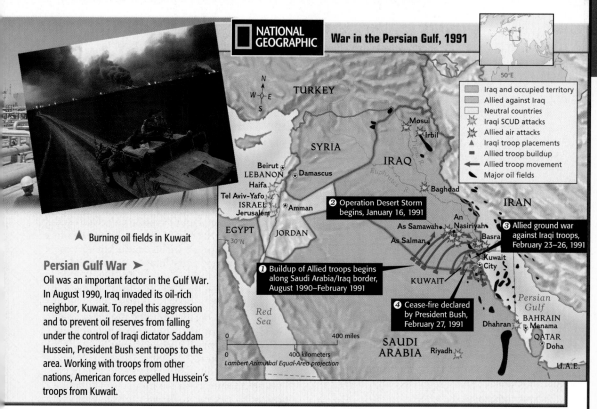

Legend:
- Iraq and occupied territory
- Allied against Iraq
- Neutral countries
- Iraqi SCUD attacks
- Allied air attacks
- Iraqi troop placements
- Allied troop buildup
- Allied troop movement
- Major oil fields

❷ Operation Desert Storm begins, January 16, 1991

❸ Allied ground war against Iraqi troops, February 23–26, 1991

❶ Buildup of Allied troops begins along Saudi Arabia/Iraq border, August 1990–February 1991

❹ Cease-fire declared by President Bush, February 27, 1991

▲ Burning oil fields in Kuwait

Persian Gulf War ➤
Oil was an important factor in the Gulf War. In August 1990, Iraq invaded its oil-rich neighbor, Kuwait. To repel this aggression and to prevent oil reserves from falling under the control of Iraqi dictator Saddam Hussein, President Bush sent troops to the area. Working with troops from other nations, American forces expelled Hussein's troops from Kuwait.

missiles and thousands of laser-guided bombs fell on Iraq, destroying its air defenses, bridges, artillery, and other military targets. After about six weeks of bombardment, the coalition launched a massive ground attack. Waves of tanks and troop carriers smashed through Iraqi lines and encircled the Iraqi forces defending Kuwait.

The attack killed thousands of Iraqi soldiers. Hundreds of thousands more surrendered. Less than 300 coalition troops were killed. Just 100 hours after the ground war began President Bush declared victory. "Kuwait is liberated," he announced. Iraq accepted the coalition's cease-fire terms. American troops returned home to cheering crowds celebrating the U.S. victory in the first large-scale war since Vietnam.

✓ **Reading Check** **Examining** Why did President Bush take action when Iraqi troops invaded Kuwait?

Domestic Challenges

President Bush spent much of his time dealing with foreign policy, but he could not ignore domestic issues. He inherited a growing deficit and a slowing

economy. As the Persian Gulf crisis began, the economy plunged into a recession and unemployment rose rapidly.

ECONOMICS

The Economy Slows The recession that began in 1990 was partly caused by the end of the Cold War. As the Soviet threat faded, the United States began reducing its armed forces and canceling orders for military equipment. Thousands of soldiers and defense industry workers were laid off.

Across the nation, other companies also began downsizing—laying off workers and managers to become more efficient. The nation's high level of debt made the recession worse. Americans had borrowed heavily during the 1980s and now faced paying off large debts.

In addition, the huge federal deficit forced the government to borrow money to pay for its programs. This borrowing kept money from being available to expanding businesses. The government also had to pay interest on its debt, money that might otherwise have been used to fund programs or jump-start the economy.

CHAPTER 33 Resurgence of Conservatism **1005**

you don't say...

Downsizing Some companies chose to use the term *downsizing* rather than *layoff* because *layoff* sounded too negative. After several years of downsizing, some companies started to use the term *right-sizing* to infer that cuts were being made to adjust the workforce to the correct size.

✓ **Reading Check**

Answer: American officials feared the invasion was only the first step and that Iraq's ultimate goal was to capture Saudi Arabia and its vast oil reserves.

3 ASSESS

Assign Section 4 Assessment as homework or as an in-class activity.

🖰 Have students use the **Interactive Tutor Self-Assessment CD-ROM.**

Reading Essentials and Study Guide 33–4

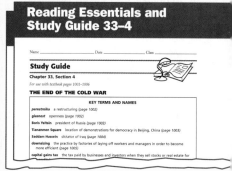

Study Guide
Chapter 33, Section 4
For use with textbook pages 1001–1006

THE END OF THE COLD WAR

KEY TERMS AND NAMES
perestroika a restructuring (page 1002)
glasnost openness (page 1002)
Boris Yeltsin president of Russia (page 1003)
Tiananmen Square location of demonstrations for democracy in Beijing, China (page 1003)
Saddam Hussein dictator of Iraq (page 1004)
downsizing the practice by factories of laying off workers and managers in order to become more efficient (page 1005)
capital gains tax the tax paid by businesses and investors when they sell stocks or real estate for

---

CRITICAL THINKING ACTIVITY

Synthesizing Information In the debate over whether to use force against Saddam Hussein, some who favored military action used the example of Hitler to justify their stance. Those who opposed action used the example of Vietnam. Have students explain whether each of these examples applied to the situation in Kuwait and decide whether the outcome of the war meant that one historical example was more fitting than the other. **L3**

Section Quiz 33–4

✓ Reading Check

Answer: Bush broke his promise that there would be no new taxes.

Reteach

Have students identify the events that ended the Cold War.

Enrich

Have interested students create a narrative history of America's involvement in the crises in China, the Middle East, or Panama during George H.W. Bush's presidency.

✓ Reading Check

Answer: They did not like either Bush or Clinton. Perot had the best showing of a third-party candidate since 1912.

4 CLOSE

Have students explain the domestic challenges facing the Bush administration between 1989 and 1992.

Gridlock in Government Shortly after taking office, Bush tried to improve the economy. He called for a cut in the capital gains tax—the tax paid by businesses and investors when they sell stocks or real estate for a profit. Bush believed the tax cut would encourage businesses to expand. Calling the idea a tax break for the rich, Democrats in Congress defeated it.

Aware that the growing federal deficit was hurting the economy, Bush broke his "no new taxes" campaign pledge. After meeting with congressional leaders, he agreed to a tax increase in exchange for cuts in spending. This decision turned many voters against Bush. They blamed him both for the tax increase and for trying to cut social programs.

Extending Rights Although President Bush and Democrats in Congress disagreed on economic issues, they cooperated on other legislation. One example was the Americans with Disabilities Act (ADA), signed by Bush in 1990. The legislation forbade discrimination in workplaces and public places against people who were physically or mentally challenged. The law had widespread effect. Access ramps were added to buildings, closed-captioned television became more commonplace, and wheelchair lifts were installed on city buses.

✓ **Reading Check** **Summarizing** Why did President Bush lose popularity as the 1992 election approached?

The 1992 Election

Although the recession had weakened his popularity, Bush won the Republican nomination. Bush promised to address voters' economic concerns, and he blamed congressional Democrats for the gridlock that seemingly paralyzed the nation's government.

The Democrats nominated Arkansas governor Bill Clinton, despite stories that questioned his character and his failure to serve in Vietnam. Calling himself a "New Democrat" to separate himself from more liberal Democrats, Clinton promised to cut middle-class taxes and spending and to reform the nation's health care and welfare programs. His campaign repeatedly blamed Bush for the recession.

Many Americans were not happy with either Bush or Clinton. This enabled an independent candidate, billionaire Texas businessman **H. Ross Perot,** to make a strong challenge. Perot stressed the need to end deficit spending. His no-nonsense style appealed to many Americans. A grassroots movement—groups of people organizing at the local level—put Perot on the ballot in all 50 states.

Bill Clinton won the election with 43 percent of the popular vote and 370 electoral votes. The Democrats also retained control of Congress. Bush won 38 percent of the popular vote, while Perot received 19 percent—the best showing for a third-party candidate since 1912—but no electoral votes.

As the first president born after World War II, the 46-year-old Clinton was the first person from the "baby boom" generation to enter the White House. It was his task to revive the economy and guide the United States in a rapidly changing and increasingly technological world.

✓ **Reading Check** **Evaluating** Why did some people vote for H. Ross Perot in 1992? How successful was his election campaign as a third-party candidate?

SECTION 4 ASSESSMENT

Checking for Understanding

1. **Define:** *perestroika, glasnost,* downsizing, capital gains tax, grassroots movement.
2. **Identify:** Boris Yeltsin, Tiananmen Square, Saddam Hussein, H. Ross Perot.
3. **Describe** how Mikhail Gorbachev tried to reform the Soviet government.

Reviewing Themes

4. **Economic Factors** How did the economy affect the 1992 election?

Critical Thinking

5. **Analyzing** How did the United States and its Western allies finally achieve victory in the Cold War?
6. **Organizing** Use a graphic organizer similar to the one below to list the causes of the recession of the early 1990s.

Budget Problems	Economic Problems	Foreign Developments

Analyzing Visuals

7. **Studying Maps** Examine the map on page 1005. Which nations have significant oil resources?

Writing About History

8. **Descriptive Writing** Imagine that you are traveling in West Germany in 1989 when the Berlin Wall is being torn down. Write a letter back home to describe the event and the feelings of the German people. Also include your reaction to the situation and how you think it will affect the United States.

SECTION 4 ASSESSMENT ANSWERS

1. Terms are in blue.
2. Boris Yeltsin (p. 1003), Tiananmen Square (p. 1003), Saddam Hussein (p. 1004), H. Ross Perot (p. 1006)
3. Gorbachev wanted to allow some private enterprise and profit-making, and to allow more freedom of speech and religion.
4. The recession hurt Bush's efforts to get reelected.
5. The West forced the Soviets to engage in an arms race they could not afford; Western powers also supported Gorbachev's reform ideas.
6. budget problems: tax increase; economic problems: recession, high consumer debt, federal deficit; foreign developments: fall of the Soviet Union, Persian Gulf War
7. Saudi Arabia, Kuwait, Iraq, and Iran
8. Students' letters will vary but should be descriptive and use standard grammar and punctuation.

American LITERATURE

Richard Rodriguez

Hispanic Americans are the fastest-growing minority in the United States. Hispanics cherish their heritage, and many speak only Spanish among their friends and family. Most of their children's teachers, however, speak only English. As a result, Hispanic students often find school confusing and humiliating. Hispanic American Richard Rodriguez describes his struggle to become educated in his autobiography, *Hunger of Memory.*

In this excerpt, Rodriguez describes the difficulties he encountered at home after he became comfortable speaking English at school.

Read to Discover

What is the reaction of Richard's relatives to his reluctance to speak Spanish to them?

Reader's Dictionary

reticent: reluctant

anglicized: made to sound English

diminutive: shorter or more affectionate version

from Hunger of Memory

by Richard Rodriguez

I grew up victim to a disabling confusion. As I grew fluent in English, I no longer could speak Spanish with confidence. I continued to understand spoken Spanish. And in high school, I learned how to read and write Spanish. But for many years I could not pronounce it. A powerful guilt blocked my spoken words; an essential glue was missing whenever I'd try to connect words to form sentences. . . .

When relatives and Spanish-speaking friends of my parents came to the house, my brother and sisters seemed reticent to use Spanish, but at least they managed to say a few necessary words before being excused. . . . I was cursed with guilt. Each time I'd hear myself addressed in Spanish, I would be unable to respond with any success. I'd know the words I wanted to say, but I couldn't manage to say them. I would try to speak, but everything I said seemed to me horribly anglicized. My mouth would not form the words right. . . .

It surprised my listeners to hear me. They'd lower their heads, better to grasp what I was trying to say. They would repeat their questions in gentle, affectionate voices. But by then I would answer in English. No, no, they would say, we want you to speak to us in

Spanish. . . . But I couldn't do it. *Pocho* then they called me. Sometimes playfully, teasingly, using the tender diminutive—*mi pochito.* Sometimes not so playfully, mockingly, *Pocho.* (A Spanish dictionary defines that word as an adjective meaning "colorless" or "bland." But I heard it as a noun, naming the Mexican-American who, in becoming an American, forgets his native society. . . .)

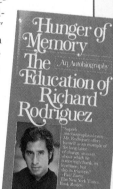

Analyzing Literature

1. **Recall and Interpret** What do you think Richard meant when he said that "an essential glue was missing" whenever he tried to speak Spanish?

2. **Evaluate and Connect** Why did Richard's relatives nickname him *Pocho?*

Interdisciplinary Activity

Journalism Interview a bilingual friend, relative, or classmate about when and where they use each of the languages they speak. Write a transcript of the interview.

Team Teaching This selection from *Hunger of Memory* can be presented in conjunction with English or Language Arts.

Read to Discover

Answer: They teased him.

Reinforcing Vocabulary

Encourage students to look up the meaning of unfamiliar words such as *diminutive.*

Historical Connection

Richard Rodriguez knew only 50 words of English when he started school in Sacramento, California. He attended Stanford University and the University of California at Berkeley where he earned a doctorate in English Renaissance Literature.

Portfolio Writing Activity

Have students write a short essay about a time when they encountered a language barrier. Encourage students to describe how they overcame the difficulty of communicating with a person who spoke another language.

HISTORY *Online*

Refer to tav.glencoe.com for additional Glencoe Literature titles, lesson plans, and study guides related to this unit.

Answers to Analyzing Literature

1. Even though he knew vocabulary, he could not connect words to have a conversation in Spanish.

2. They gave him the nickname because he would not speak to them in Spanish.

Interdisciplinary Activity

Transcripts will vary but should describe the experiences of a bilingual friend or relative, and perhaps his or her ideas of bilingual education.

GLENCOE TECHNOLOGY

MindJogger Videoquiz

Use the **MindJogger Videoquiz** to review Chapter 33 content.

 Available in VHS

Reviewing Key Terms

Students' answers will vary. The pages where the words appear in the text are shown in parentheses.

1. **liberal** *(p. 981)*
2. **conservative** *(p. 981)*
3. **televangelist** *(p. 984)*
4. **supply-side economics** *(p. 987)*
5. **budget deficit** *(p. 987)*
6. **contra** *(p. 990)*
7. **yuppie** *(p. 995)*
8. **space shuttle** *(p. 998)*
9. **space station** *(p. 999)*
10. **perestroika** *(p. 1002)*
11. **glasnost** *(p. 1002)*
12. **downsizing** *(p. 1005)*
13. **capital gains tax** *(p. 1006)*
14. **grassroots movement** *(p. 1006)*

Reviewing Key Facts

15. William F. Buckley *(p. 981)*, William Rehnquist *(p. 988)*, Mikhail Gorbachev *(p. 990)*, AIDS *(p. 996)*, Boris Yeltsin *(p. 1003)*, Saddam Hussein *(p. 1004)*, H. Ross Perot *(p. 1006)*

16. Their economy was expanding and they did not want the government to interfere with their region's growth.

17. Reaganomics, cutting programs, and deregulation

18. Social issues facing the United States included AIDS, alcohol abuse, crime, drug abuse, homelessness, and Social Security.

19. Iraq's invasion of Kuwait and subsequent refusal to withdraw

20. George Bush faced the economic problems of recession, high consumer debt, and the federal deficit.

Reviewing Key Terms

On a sheet of paper, use each of these terms in a sentence.

1. liberal	8. space shuttle
2. conservative	9. space station
3. televangelist	10. *perestroika*
4. supply-side economics	11. *glasnost*
5. budget deficit	12. downsizing
6. contra	13. capital gains tax
7. yuppie	14. grassroots movement

Reviewing Key Facts

15. **Identify:** William F. Buckley, William Rehnquist, Mikhail Gorbachev, AIDS, Boris Yeltsin, Saddam Hussein, H. Ross Perot.

16. Why did people in the Sunbelt tend to be conservative?

17. What three steps did President Reagan take to improve the economy?

18. What social issues did the United States face in the 1980s?

19. What event triggered the Persian Gulf War?

20. What economic problems did President George Bush face during his administration?

Critical Thinking

21. **Analyzing Themes: Global Connections** What event brought an end to the Cold War in the 1980s? What effect did that have on U.S. policies and on the U.S. economy?

22. **Synthesizing** How did conservatives gain political power in the 1980s?

23. **Forming an Opinion** On what part of the liberal-conservative spectrum would you place yourself? Why?

24. **Interpreting Primary Sources** President Ronald Reagan addressed the American people for the last time at the end of his presidency in 1988. The following is an excerpt from that address:

❝It's been quite a journey this decade, and we held together through some stormy seas. And at the end, together, we are reaching our destination. . . . The way I see it, there were two great triumphs, two things that I'm proudest of. One is the economic recovery, in which the people of America created—and filled—19 million new jobs. The other is the recovery of our morale. America is respected again in the world and looked to for leadership. . . .

Common sense told us that when you put a big tax on something, the people will produce less of it. So, we cut the people's tax rates, and the people produced more than ever before. The economy bloomed. . . . Common sense told us that to preserve the peace, we'd have to become strong again after years of weakness and confusion. So, we rebuilt our defenses, and this New Year we toasted the new peacefulness around the globe. . . .

Countries across the globe are turning to free markets and free speech and turning away from the ideologies of the past. . . .

Chapter Summary

Resurgence of Conservative Politics

- The Cold War promotes a strong foreign policy and an emphasis on minimal government intervention in economics.
- Cold War fears of communism encourage religious Americans to turn to conservative ideas.
- Barry Goldwater wins the 1964 Republican presidential nomination.
- The growth of the Sunbelt increases conservative support.

Reagan's Agenda

- Supply-side economics emphasizes large tax cuts.
- Reagan's administration takes a strong anti-Communist stance in Latin America, the Caribbean, and the Middle East.
- Reagan and Gorbachev begin new nuclear arms reductions.
- Military spending drives the growing budget deficit to record levels.

The Bush Years

- Communism collapses in Eastern Europe and the Soviet Union.
- The uncertainty of a "New World Order" replaces the dualism of the Cold War.
- The Persian Gulf War drives Bush's popularity to its highest level.
- A domestic economic recession weakens Bush's re-election campaign.

Critical Thinking

21. Signing of the INF treaty in 1987 triggered a reduction in Soviet military spending and the beginning of Gorbachev's reforms; U.S. economy slowed as a result of reductions in military spending.

22. They elected two presidents who reinforced conservative values and economic policies.

23. Students' answers will vary. Answers should reflect an understanding of liberal and conservative beliefs.

24. **a.** Reagan was most proud of the economic recovery and the recovery of morale. **b.** Reagan thought attention to American history and to civic ritual would promote patriotism. Students' answers will vary.

[O]ne of the things I'm proudest of in the past eight years [is] the resurgence of national pride that I called the new patriotism. This national feeling is good, but it won't count for much, and it won't last unless it's grounded in thoughtfulness and knowledge. . . .

An informed patriotism is what we want. . . . Let's start with some basics: more attention to American history and greater emphasis on civic ritual. . . .**99**

—from *Speaking My Mind*

a. What did Reagan believe were his greatest accomplishments as president?

b. What did Reagan believe would promote patriotism in the nation? Do you agree with his belief? Why or why not?

25. Organizing Use a graphic organizer similar to the one below to list the domestic and foreign issues that the Reagan and Bush administrations faced in the 1980s.

Issues	Reagan Administration	Bush Administration
Domestic		
Foreign		

Practicing Skills

26. Analyzing News Media Choose one current issue or event and compare its coverage in two different media. Which medium supplies the most facts? Is the coverage that is provided by both media consistent? What are the advantages and disadvantages of each medium? Write a two-page analysis comparing the two media, including a conclusion about which one is better.

Writing Activity

27. Writing a Report Research the status today of the independent republics formed from the Soviet Union. Find out about their political, social, and economic situations. Present your findings in a written report.

Chapter Activity

28. Creating a Thematic Graph Using a scale of 1 to 10, evaluate how successful each president was in dealing with the issues you listed in question 25. Create a thematic graph depicting each president's success rate per issue.

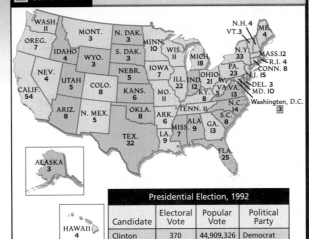

NATIONAL GEOGRAPHIC **The Election of 1992**

Presidential Election, 1992			
Candidate	Electoral Vote	Popular Vote	Political Party
Clinton	370	44,909,326	Democrat
Bush	168	39,103,882	Republican
Perot	0	19,741,657	Independent

Geography and History

29. The map above shows the results of the 1992 presidential election. Study the map and answer the questions below.
  a. Interpreting Maps How far short did President Bush fall in the race for Electoral College votes?
  b. Applying Geography Skills Bill Clinton won his strongest support in which region of the nation?

The Princeton Review

Standardized Test Practice

Directions: Choose the phrase that best completes the following sentence.

The Strategic Defense Initiative (SDI) was proposed to strengthen the military by

A preventing the expansion of Communist countries.

B reemphasizing the use of infantry troops in future wars.

C developing weapons that would intercept and destroy incoming nuclear missles.

D severely reducing the number of American troops stationed worldwide.

Test-Taking Tip: Eliminate answers that do not make sense. Reducing the number of American troops (answer D), for example, probably would not strengthen the military.

HISTORY
Online

Have students visit the Web site at tav.glencoe.com to review Chapter 33 and take the Self-Check Quiz.

Chapter Activity

28. Graphs will vary. Students should be able to back up their ratings with logical reasoning.

Geography and History

29. a. 102 votes of the 270 needed in the Electoral College; **b.** Northeast and Pacific coast

The Princeton Review

Standardized Test Practice

Answer: C
Test-Taking Tip: Remind students that another name for the Strategic Defense Initiative is Star Wars. That should lead them to the fact that the initiative is probably technologically advanced. Answer C seems to be the answer that is most focused on technology. The correct answer is C.

Bonus Question **?**

What industries were deregulated during the Reagan years? *(oil and gas, automobile, cable television, and airline)*

25.

Issues	Reagan Administration	Bush Administration
Domestic	stagflation growing deficit	recession unemployment growing deficit
Foreign	Soviet invasion of Afghanistan Grenada Iran-Contra scandal	Eastern Europe collapse of Soviet Union Tiananmen Square

Practicing Skills

26. Comparisons will help students analyze various media sources.

Writing Activity

27. Reports will vary but should include information about political, social, and economic conditions in the chosen country.

Timesaving Tools

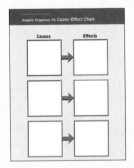

TeacherWorks™ All-In-One Planner and Resource Center

- **Interactive Teacher Edition** Access your Teacher Wraparound Edition and your classroom resources with a few easy clicks.
- **Interactive Lesson Planner** Planning has never been easier! Organize your week, month, semester, or year with all the lesson helps you need to make teaching creative, timely, and relevant.

Use Glencoe's **Presentation Plus!** multimedia teacher tool to easily present dynamic lessons that visually excite your students. Using Microsoft PowerPoint® you can customize the presentations to create your own personalized lessons.

TEACHING TRANSPARENCIES

Graphic Organizer 14

Why It Matters Chapter Transparency 34

APPLICATION AND ENRICHMENT

Linking Past and Present Activity 34

Enrichment Activity 34

Primary Source Reading 34

REVIEW AND REINFORCEMENT

Reteaching Activity 34

Vocabulary Activity 34

Time Line Activity 34

Critical Thinking Skills Activity 34

Meeting NCSS Standards

Local Standards

The following standards are highlighted in Chapter 34:

Section 1	VII	Production, Distribution, and Consumption: D, F
Section 2	VII	Production, Distribution, and Consumption: A, C, F
Section 3	IX	Global Connections: B, C, D, E
Section 4	VI	Power, Authority, and Governance: B, C, E, G
Section 5	IX	Global Connections: A, B, D, G

Chapter 34 Resources

Chapter 34 Test Form A

Chapter 34 Test Form B

Standardized Test Skills Practice Workbook Activity 34

Performance Assessment Activities and Rubrics 34

ExamView® Pro Testmaker CD-ROM

MULTIMEDIA

- Vocabulary PuzzleMaker CD-ROM
- Interactive Tutor Self-Assessment CD-ROM
- ExamView® Pro Testmaker CD-ROM
- Audio Program
- American History Primary Source Documents Library CD-ROM
- MindJogger Videoquiz
- Presentation Plus! CD-ROM
- TeacherWorks™ CD-ROM
- Interactive Student Edition CD-ROM
- Glencoe Skillbuilder Interactive Workbook CD-ROM, Level 2
- The *American Vision* Video Program
- American Music: Hits Through History
- American Music: Cultural Traditions

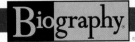

The following videotape programs are available from Glencoe as supplements to Chapter 34:

- **Bill Clinton: In the Running** (ISBN 1-56-501824-9)
- **Hillary Rodham Clinton** (ISBN 1-56-501371-9)
- **Colin Powell: A Soldier's Campaign** (ISBN 1-56-501701-3)

To order, call Glencoe at 1-800-334-7344. To find classroom resources to accompany many of these videos, check the following home pages:
A&E Television: www.aande.com
The History Channel: www.historychannel.com

SPANISH RESOURCES

The following Spanish language materials are available in the Spanish Resources Binder:

- Spanish Guided Reading Activities
- Spanish Reteaching Activities
- Spanish Quizzes and Tests
- Spanish Vocabulary Activities
- Spanish Summaries
- The Declaration of Independence and United States Constitution Spanish Translation

HISTORY Online

Use our Web site for additional resources. All essential content is covered in the Student Edition.

You and your students can visit tav.glencoe.com, the Web site companion to the *American Vision*. This innovative integration of electronic and print media offers your students a wealth of opportunities. The student text directs students to the Web site for the following options:

- **Chapter Overviews**
- **Self-Check Quizzes**
- **Student Web Activities**
- **Textbook Updates**

Answers to the student Web activities are provided for you in the **Web Activity Lesson Plans.** Additional Web resources and Interactive Tutor Puzzles are also available.

Chapter 34 Resources

SECTION RESOURCES

Daily Objectives	Reproducible Resources	Multimedia Resources
SECTION 1 **The Technological Revolution** 1. Describe the evolution of the computer from scientific tool to household appliance. 2. Evaluate how the computer has revolutionized science, medicine, and communications.	Reproducible Lesson Plan 34–1 Daily Lecture and Discussion Notes 34–1 Guided Reading Activity 34–1* Section Quiz 34–1* Reading Essentials and Study Guide 34–1 Performance Assessment Activities and Rubrics	Daily Focus Skills Transparency 34–1 Interactive Tutor Self-Assessment CD-ROM ExamView® Pro Testmaker CD-ROM Presentation Plus! CD-ROM TeacherWorks™ CD-ROM Audio Program
SECTION 2 **The Clinton Years** 1. Describe the difficulties and successes of Bill Clinton's two terms as president. 2. Discuss the nation's involvement in world affairs during the Clinton presidency.	Reproducible Lesson Plan 34–2 Daily Lecture and Discussion Notes 34–2 Guided Reading Activity 34–2* Section Quiz 34–2* Reading Essentials and Study Guide 34–2 Performance Assessment Activities and Rubrics	Daily Focus Skills Transparency 34–2 Interactive Tutor Self-Assessment CD-ROM ExamView® Pro Testmaker CD-ROM Presentation Plus! CD-ROM TeacherWorks™ CD-ROM Audio Program American Music: Hits Through History
SECTION 3 **An Interdependent World** 1. Explain the development of regional economic blocs around the world. 2. Assess environmental issues that have become important internationally.	Reproducible Lesson Plan 34–3 Daily Lecture and Discussion Notes 34–3 Guided Reading Activity 34–3* Section Quiz 34–3* Reading Essentials and Study Guide 34–3 Performance Assessment Activities and Rubrics	Daily Focus Skills Transparency 34–3 Interactive Tutor Self-Assessment CD-ROM ExamView® Pro Testmaker CD-ROM Presentation Plus! CD-ROM TeacherWorks™ CD-ROM Audio Program
SECTION 4 **America Enters a New Century** 1. Describe the unusual circumstances surrounding the outcome of the 2000 presidential election. 2. Evaluate the programs President George W. Bush initiated.	Reproducible Lesson Plan 34–4 Daily Lecture and Discussion Notes 34–4 Guided Reading Activity 34–4* Section Quiz 34–4* Reading Essentials and Study Guide 34–4 Performance Assessment Activities and Rubrics Interpreting Political Cartoons	Daily Focus Skills Transparency 34–4 Interactive Tutor Self-Assessment CD-ROM ExamView® Pro Testmaker CD-ROM Presentation Plus! CD-ROM Skillbuilder Interactive Workbook, Level 2 TeacherWorks™ CD-ROM Audio Program
SECTION 5 **The War on Terrorism** 1. Describe the development of Middle East terrorism. 2. Explain the response of the United States to the terrorist attacks on the World Trade Center and the Pentagon.	Reproducible Lesson Plan 34–5 Daily Lecture and Discussion Notes 34–5 Guided Reading Activity 34–5* Section Quiz 34–5* Reading Essentials and Study Guide 34–5 Performance Assessment Activities and Rubrics	Daily Focus Skills Transparency 34–5 Interactive Tutor Self-Assessment CD-ROM ExamView® Pro Testmaker CD-ROM Presentation Plus! CD-ROM TeacherWorks™ CD-ROM Vocabulary PuzzleMaker CD-ROM Audio Program

0:00 OUT OF TIME?
Assign the Chapter 34 **Reading Essentials and Study Guide.**

*Also Available in Spanish

 Blackline Master   Transparency   CD-ROM   DVD

 Poster   Music Program   Audio Program   Videocassette

NATIONAL GEOGRAPHIC Teacher's Corner

INDEX TO NATIONAL GEOGRAPHIC MAGAZINE

The following articles relate to this chapter.

- "Grand Staircase Escalante," July 1999
- "Rediscovering America," January 2000
- "Robot Revolution," July 1997
- "Unveiling the Universe," October 1999

ADDITIONAL NATIONAL GEOGRAPHIC SOCIETY PRODUCTS

To order the following, call National Geographic at 1-800-368-2728:

- *Branches of Government Series* (Video)
- *The Complete National Geographic: 109 Years of National Geographic Magazine* (CD-ROM)
- *Democratic Government Series: The United States* (Video)
- *National Geographic World Atlas for Young Explorers–Classroom Library Edition* (Guide, Transparencies, Resource Masters)

NGS ONLINE

Access National Geographic's Web site for current events, atlas updates, activities, links, interactive features, and archives.

www.nationalgeographic.com

From the Classroom of...

Philip Prale
Oak Park and River Forest
High School
Oak Park, IL

Into the New Century–The Keeper's Project

The purpose of this project is to analyze developments of the 1900s and explain why they are worth keeping in this new century.

Construct a list of five to ten items that are Twentieth Century Keepers. Variations include:

1. Draw keepers from specific categories—Political, Economic, Social, Cultural, Religious, or Environmental.

2. Add one item that you would want to eliminate in this new century.

3. For each item write a description of the item and how it fits into the category.

4. Write an introductory paragraph explaining the general connection, besides time, of the keepers. What is the theme or central idea?

5. Make a poster with images or produce a PowerPoint® presentation of the material.

ADDITIONAL RESOURCES FROM GLENCOE

- American Music: Cultural Traditions
- American Art & Architecture
- Outline Map Resource Book
- U.S. Desk Map
- Building Geography Skills for Life
- Inclusion for the High School Social Studies Classroom Strategies and Activities
- Teaching Strategies for the American History Classroom (Including Block Scheduling Pacing Guides)

KEY TO ABILITY LEVELS

Teaching strategies have been coded.

L1 BASIC activities for all students
L2 AVERAGE activities for average to above-average students
L3 CHALLENGING activities for above-average students
ELL ENGLISH LANGUAGE LEARNER activities

Block Schedule

Activities that are suited to use within the block scheduling framework are identified by:

☑ ***Performance Assessment***

Refer to Activity 34 in the Performance Assessment Activities and Rubrics booklet.

W*hy It Matters Activity*

As a class, have students list the ways in which businesses, schools, governments, and individuals use the Internet. **Ask: How important has the Internet become to everyday life in the United States?** Students should evaluate their answers after they have completed the chapter.

GLENCOE
TECHNOLOGY

The *American Vision* Video Program
To learn more about how the American public dealt with the attacks of September 11, 2001, have students view the Chapter 34 video, "America's Response to Terrorism," from the ***American Vision* Video Program.**

 Available in DVD and VHS

MindJogger Videoquiz
Use the **MindJogger Videoquiz** to preview Chapter 34 content.

 Available in VHS

Why It Matters

During the 1990s, a technological revolution transformed society. President Clinton pushed for budget cuts, health care and welfare reforms, and global trade. He also worked for peace in the Middle East and the Balkans. In 2000 George W. Bush won the presidency. He supported tax cuts, a new energy program, increased trade, and a missile defense system. After terrorists killed thousands of people in the United States, the new president launched a war on terrorism.

The Impact Today

Major developments of the era continue to influence modern society.
• The use of the Internet is widespread in commerce, schools, and government.
• The North American Free Trade Agreement (NAFTA) continues to shape economic relations between the United States, Canada, and Mexico.
• The debate between conservatives and liberals continues in the United States.

The American Vision Video The Chapter 34 video, "America's Response to Terrorism," examines how ordinary Americans responded to the terrorist attacks in New York City and Washington, D.C.

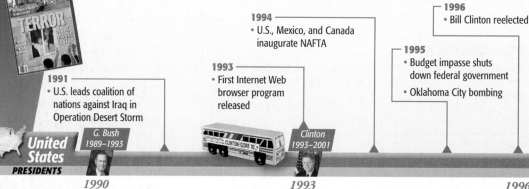

1991
• U.S. leads coalition of nations against Iraq in Operation Desert Storm

1993
• First Internet Web browser program released

1994
• U.S., Mexico, and Canada inaugurate NAFTA

1995
• Budget impasse shuts down federal government
• Oklahoma City bombing

1996
• Bill Clinton reelected

United States PRESIDENTS

G. Bush 1989–1993

Clinton 1993–2001

1990   *1993*   *1996*

World

1991
• Bosnian war begins in Eastern Europe

1992
• Earth Day summit held in Rio de Janeiro, Brazil

1993
• Israeli-Palestinian peace accord signed
• European Union launched

1994
• Multiracial elections held in South Africa; Nelson Mandela elected president

1995
• Cease-fire signed in Bosnian war

1010

TWO-MINUTE LESSON LAUNCHER

Have students list their impressions of Bill Clinton and George W. Bush. Then ask students to describe how they formed their opinions of these two leaders. Have students identify the sources of most of the information they have about these two presidents. Ask students which sources they think are most influential in shaping the public's opinion of a president.

January 20, 2001: George W. Bush is inaugurated as the nation's 43rd president.

HISTORY *Online*

Introduce students to chapter content and key terms by having them access the **Chapter 34 Overview** at tav.glencoe.com.

More About the Photo

Ask students who is administering the oath of office to George W. Bush. *(Chief Justice of the United States William Rehnquist)* Ask students to identify other government leaders pictured here. *(possible answers: Senator Mitch McConnell, Speaker of the House Dennis Hastert, Vice President Dick Cheney [who is only partially visible])*

1998
• House of Representatives impeaches President Clinton

1999
• Senate acquits Clinton

2000
• Electoral crisis delays naming of 43rd president

2001
• First map of the human genome completed
• Terrorist attacks destroy World Trade Center and damage Pentagon

2002
• Winter Olympics held in Salt Lake City, Utah

G.W. Bush 2001–

1999

2002

1997
• Britain returns control of Hong Kong to China

2000
• Mexico's election of Vicente Fox ends 71 years of single-party rule

2001
• China chosen to be site of 2008 Olympic Games

HISTORY *Online*

Chapter Overview
Visit the *American Vision* Web site at tav.glencoe.com and click on **Chapter Overviews—Chapter 34** to preview chapter information.

TIME LINE
ACTIVITY

Have students review the items on the time line and classify each as something they knew about or something they did not know about. Have students select one of the items about which they know little or nothing and research it to learn at least one fact related to the event.

1011

GRAPHIC ORGANIZER ACTIVITY

Organizing Information Have students use a graphic organizer similar to the one at right to identify changes that have occurred in the United States since 1992. *(Answers may include the rise of the compact computer, the telecommunications revolution, the rise of the Internet, welfare reform, the growth of global economy, and the increase in terrorism.)*

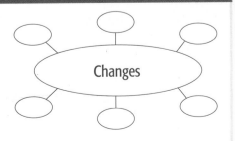

Changes

1 FOCUS

Section Overview

This section focuses on the history of the technology revolution.

BELLRINGER
Skillbuilder Activity

Project transparency and have students answer the question.

Available as a blackline master.

Daily Focus Skills Transparency 34–1

Guide to Reading

Answers to Graphic:
Microprocessors: reduced computers' size, increased their speed, and expanded their function; Apple II: first practical and affordable computer; Macintosh: popularized mouse and graphic icons; Windows: made Macintosh innovations widespread

Preteaching Vocabulary
Have students choose one of the proper names from the list of Key Terms and Names. Ask students to skim the text to find the name and write a brief explanation.

SECTION 1

The Technological Revolution

Guide to Reading

Main Idea
The introduction of the first electronic digital computer in 1946 launched a technological revolution.

Key Terms and Names
ENIAC, integrated circuit, Silicon Valley, microprocessor, Bill Gates, software, telecommute, Internet, biotechnology, James Watson, Francis Crick, DNA

Reading Strategy
Categorizing As you read about the computer age, complete a chart similar to the one below to describe products that revolutionized the computer industry.

	How It Revolutionized Computer Industry
Microprocessors	
Apple II	
Macintosh	
Windows	

Reading Objectives
• **Describe** the evolution of the computer from scientific tool to household appliance.
• **Evaluate** how the computer has revolutionized science, medicine, and communications.

Section Theme
Economic Factors The computer has helped reshape the nation's economy.

Preview of Events

♦1993	♦1996	♦1999	♦2002

1993
First Web browser introduced

1996
Congress deregulates telephone companies

1999
Over 86 million Americans own cell phones

2001
Human Genome Project maps the human genome

★ *An American Story* ★

Michael Kinsley

After years as a magazine editor and television news commentator, Michael Kinsley jumped into the new technology of the Internet in 1996, by agreeing to edit an online magazine called *Slate*. "I was determined," Kinsley said, "to be on the next train to pull out of the station no matter where it was going—provided that I was the engineer."

Soon newspaper and print magazines were also developing Web resources. Television stations also used the Internet to update news stories, allowing consumers to access news when and how they wanted. As Kinsley explained:

❝Web readers *surf*. They go quickly from site to site. If they really like a particular site, they may visit it often, but they are unlikely to devote a continuous half-hour or more to any one site. . . . This appears to be in the nature of the Web and not something that is likely to change.❞

—from "Slate Goes Free," *Slate*, February 13, 1999

The Rise of the Compact Computer

The development of a computer capable of supporting publications such as *Slate* began at the end of World War II. The world's first electronic digital computer, called **ENIAC** (Electronic Numerical Integrator and Computer), went into operation in

---

SECTION RESOURCES

📂 Reproducible Masters
• Reproducible Lesson Plan 34–1
• Daily Lecture and Discussion Notes 34–1
• Guided Reading Activity 34–1
• Section Quiz 34–1
• Reading Essentials and Study Guide 34–1
• Performance Assessment Activities and Rubrics

📄 Transparencies
• Daily Focus Skills Transparency 34–1

Multimedia
🖥 Interactive Tutor Self-Assessment CD-ROM
🖥 ExamView® Pro Testmaker CD-ROM
🖥 Presentation Plus! CD-ROM
🖥 TeacherWorks™ CD-ROM
🎧 Audio Program

February 1946. ENIAC weighed over 30 tons and took up as much floor space as a medium-sized house. In 1957 Gordon Moore, Robert Noyce, and other young scientists and engineers developed the first **integrated circuit**—a complete electronic circuit on a single chip of the element silicon—which made circuits vastly easier to manufacture. Other electronics companies sprang up south of San Francisco, an area soon nicknamed **Silicon Valley.**

In 1968 Moore and Noyce formed Intel, for "Integrated Electronics," a company that revolutionized computers by combining on a single chip several integrated circuits containing both memory and computing functions. Called microprocessors, these new chips further reduced the size of computers, increased their speed, and expanded their functions.

Computers for Everyone Using microprocessor technology, Stephen Wozniak and his 20-year-old friend Steven Jobs set out to build a small computer suitable for personal use. In 1976 they founded Apple Computer and completed the Apple I. The following year they introduced the Apple II, the first practical and affordable home computer.

Apple's success sparked intense competition in the computer industry. In 1981 International Business Machines (IBM) introduced its own compact machine, which it called the **"Personal Computer"** (PC). Apple responded in 1984 with the revolutionary **Macintosh,** a new model featuring a simplified operating system using on-screen graphic symbols called icons, which users could manipulate with a hand-operated device called a mouse.

Bill Gates and Microsoft As Jobs and Wozniak were creating Apple, 19-year-old Harvard dropout **Bill Gates** co-founded Microsoft to design PC software, the instructions used to program computers to perform desired tasks. In 1980 IBM hired Microsoft to develop an operating system for its new PC. Gates quickly paid a Seattle programmer $50,000 for the rights to his software, and with some refinements, it became MS-DOS (Microsoft Disk Operating System).

In 1985 Microsoft introduced the "Windows" operating system, which enabled PCs to use the mouse-activated, on-screen graphic icons that the Macintosh had popularized. Soaring sales and rising Microsoft stock values made Gates a billionaire at the age of 31.

Compact computers soon transformed the workplace, linking employees within an office or among office branches. They became essential tools in virtually every kind of business. By the late 1990s, many workers used home computers and electronic mail to "telecommute," or do their jobs via computer without having to go to the office.

✓ **Reading Check** **Describing** How was Microsoft different from other computer companies?

The Telecommunications Revolution

A parallel revolution in communications coincided with the growing impact of computers. In the 1970s, 1980s, and 1990s, the government loosened telecommunications regulations, allowing more companies to compete in the telephone and television industries. In 1996 Congress passed the Telecommunications Act. This act allowed telephone companies to compete with each other and to send television signals, but it also permitted cable television companies to offer telephone service. Such developments spurred the creation of new

Picturing **History**

Apple Founders In 1984 Apple president John Sculley (center), along with Steve Jobs (left) and Steve Wozniak, show off their new briefcase-sized Apple IIc computer. *On what basic technology do personal computers rely?*

2 TEACH

Daily Lecture and Discussion Notes 34–1

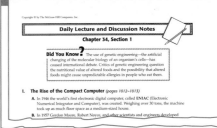

Copyright © by The McGraw-Hill Companies, Inc.

Daily Lecture and Discussion Notes

Chapter 34, Section 1

Did You Know ? The use of genetic engineering—the artificial changing of the molecular biology of an organism's cells—has caused international debate. Critics of genetic engineering question the nutritional value of altered foods and the possibility that altered foods might cause unpredictable allergies in people who eat them.

I. **The Rise of the Compact Computer** *(pages 1012–1013)*

A. In 1946 the world's first electronic digital computer, called **ENIAC** (Electronic Numerical Integrator and Computer), was created. Weighing over 30 tons, the machine took up as much floor space as a medium-sized house.

B. In 1957 Gordon Moore, Robert Noyce, and other scientists and engineers developed

HISTORY *Online*

Objectives and answers to the student activity can be found in the **Web Activity Lesson Plan** at tav.glencoe.com.

Creating an Outline Have students create an outline for this section. Suggest that they use the headings as a starting point. **L1** **ELL**

✓ **Reading Check**

Answer: The company purchased its original software rather than creating it from scratch.

Picturing **History**

Answer: microprocessor technology
Ask: How did Intel revolutionize computers? *(Intel combined several integrated circuits on a single chip containing both memory and computing functions.)*

HISTORY *Online*
Student Web Activity Visit the *American Vision* Web site tav.glencoe.com and click on **Student Web Activities— Chapter 34** for an activity on the technological revolution.

COOPERATIVE LEARNING ACTIVITY

Creating a Time Line Organize students into small groups and have them create a time line illustrating advances in computer technology during their lifetimes. Instruct students to start their time line with the year the first member of the group was born and try to find a significant event or milestone for each year up until the present time. As a class, have students review the time lines from each group and make a composite time line.

Use the rubric for a cooperative group management plan on pages 81–82 in the *Performance Assessment Activities and Rubrics.*

technologies such as Web-enabled cellular phones and other mixing of data-platforms.

✓ **Reading Check** **Explaining** How did deregulation affect the telecommunications industry?

The Rise of the Internet

Digital electronics also made possible a new worldwide communications system. The Internet let computer users post and receive information and communicate with each other. It had its roots in a computer networking system that the U.S. Defense Department's Advanced Research Project Agency established in 1969. Known as ARPANET, this system linked government agencies, defense contractors, and scientists at various universities, enabling them to communicate with each other by electronic mail. In 1985 the National Science Foundation funded several supercomputer centers across the country. This paved the way for the Internet, a global information system that operated commercially rather than through the government.

At first, Internet users employed different types of information. With the development of the hypertext transport protocol (http) and new software known as Web browsers, the Internet rapidly expanded. Users could now click on Internet links using their computer mouse and easily jump from Web site to Web site. Internet use expanded by almost 300 percent between 1997 and 2000.

The Internet also spawned a "dot-com" economy (from the common practice of using a business name as a World Wide Web address, followed by ".com"). Seemingly rich with promise, a wide variety of dot.com companies made millions of dollars for stock investors without ever earning actual profit from operations. Internet-related stocks helped fuel the prosperity of the 1990s but dropped dramatically in 2000, raising questions about the ultimate profitability of online companies.

✓ **Reading Check** **Explaining** How did the Internet expand business opportunities?

Breakthroughs in Biotechnology

Computers greatly assisted scientists engaged in **biotechnology**—the managing of biological systems to improve human life. Computers made it possible to study and manipulate genes and cells at the molecular level. Through biotechnology, researchers developed new medicines, animal growth hormones, genetically engineered plants, and industrial chemicals.

TECHNOLOGY & History

Magnetic Resonance Imaging

One extension of computer technology is magnetic resonance imaging (MRI). An MRI allows physicians to diagnose certain diseases, abnormalities, and injuries without resorting to x-rays or surgery. An MRI unit is made up of a large cylindrical magnet, devices for transmitting and receiving radio signals, and a computer. **Why do you think physicians prefer MRIs over x-rays and surgery?**

1. A large cylindrical magnet with a magnetic field 30,000 times stronger than the earth's magnetic field surrounds the patient.

2. Radio signals are transmitted within the machine and pass through the patient's body.

3. A computer converts the radio signals into precise images of the body's internal structure.

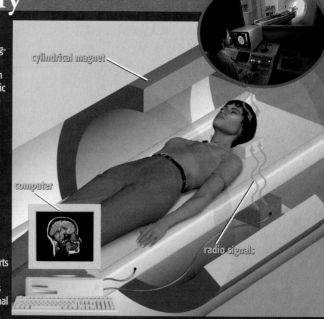

cylindrical magnet

computer

radio signals

Unraveling the Secrets of Life The first steps toward biotechnology came in 1953, when American molecular biologist **James Watson** and his British colleague, **Francis Crick,** deciphered the structure of deoxyribonucleic acid (DNA). **DNA** is the genetic material in cells that determine all forms of life.

Once scientists learned how to read the message of DNA, their new knowledge improved medical research and provided law enforcement with new methods of identification. Further research in biotechnology created artificial genes and assisted genetic engineering for plants, animals, and humans.

The Human Genome Project For years scientists talked of mapping out the human genome by recording the DNA sequence of the human species. With the development of supercomputers, the Human Genome Project began in earnest at the National Institutes of Health (NIH) in 1990. NIH decided to place all of the Human Genome Project's data on the Internet to make it available to scientists all over the world, free of charge. Researchers hoped to prevent any single nation or private laboratory from controlling the outcome and limiting the use of genome findings. In February 2001, the project completed its first map of

the human genome. Medical researchers expected that this information would help them determine which genes made people more susceptible to disease, thereby improving medical diagnoses and preventive medication and assisting in finding cures.

✓ **Reading Check** **Explaining** How did computers assist the development of biotechnology?

Profiles IN HISTORY

Jerry Yang
1968–

Jerry Yang was born in Taiwan in 1968 and immigrated with his family to San Jose, California, when he was 10 years old. Yang is a cofounder of Yahoo!, one of the world's best-known gateways to information and consumer goods on the Web. It is estimated that by the late 1990s, around 40 million people were visiting the Yahoo! Web site every month.

The company developed out of Yang's desire to be able to find good Web sites quickly. At Stanford University, he and cofounder David Filo were doctoral students sharing office space in a trailer. They also shared information on their favorite Web sites, and Yang began compiling a list of

them. He nicknamed the list "Jerry's Guide to the World Wide Web," and he posted it on the Internet.

Inquiries to the site boomed, and Yang and Filo concluded that they had found an untapped market. With the help of a loan from an imaginative venture capitalist, Yahoo! was born. Yang says they chose the name because it suggested the sort of "Wild West" character of the Internet. The mission for Yahoo! was not just to collect Web sites but to organize them into convenient categories, such as news, sports, games, and weather. Yahoo! became a popular gateway, or "portal," to the Web.

SECTION 1 ASSESSMENT

Checking for Understanding
1. **Define:** microprocessor, software, telecommute, Internet, DNA.
2. **Identify:** ENIAC, integrated circuit, Silicon Valley, Bill Gates, biotechnology, James Watson, Francis Crick.
3. **Explain** how scientific discoveries in biotechnology have improved people's lives.

Reviewing Themes
4. **Economic Factors** How have personal computers transformed the workplace?

Critical Thinking
5. **Analyzing** How have advances in telecommunications and the rise of the Internet affected the standard of living in the United States?
6. **Organizing** Complete a graphic organizer similar to the one below by listing developments that led to the technological revolution.

Analyzing Visuals
7. **Analyzing Photographs** Study the crowd in the photograph of George W. Bush's inauguration on page 1011. How would you describe the attitudes reflected in the faces of the people photographed?

Writing About History
8. **Descriptive Writing** Write two paragraphs describing the ways that you and your family use the Internet and how your way of life would be different without it.

Profiles IN HISTORY

Ask: Before naming it Yahoo!, what did Yang call his site? *(Jerry's Guide to the World Wide Web)*

Reteach
Have students describe the evolution of the computer from scientific tool to household appliance.

Enrich
Have students prepare a demonstration of how they use the Internet for a specific purpose.

✓ **Reading Check**

Answer: Computers made it possible to study and manipulate genes and cells at the molecular level.

4 CLOSE

Ask: How has the computer revolutionized daily life? *(Students' answers should reflect section content.)*

SECTION 1 ASSESSMENT ANSWERS

1. Terms are in blue.
2. ENIAC *(p. 1012)*, integrated circuit *(p. 1013)*, Silicon Valley *(p. 1013)*, Bill Gates *(p. 1013)*, biotechnology *(p. 1014)*, James Watson *(p. 1015)*, Francis Crick *(p. 1015)*
3. led to the development of artificial genes and assisted genetic engineering of plants, animals, and humans
4. linked employees, became essential in all kinds of business, and allowed people to telecommute
5. New technology, such as Web-enabled cell phones and the Internet, made a new communications system possible

and spawned the "dot.com" economy.
6. deregulation of telecommunications industry, microprocessors, Internet, personal computers, wireless technology
7. most look happy; the Bush family looks proud
8. Students' paragraphs will vary.

1 FOCUS

Section Overview

This section focuses on the Clinton administration.

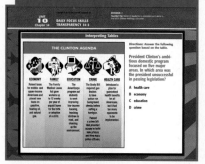

SECTION 2 The Clinton Years

Guide to Reading

Main Idea
Although President Clinton struggled with Republicans in Congress and faced impeachment, several major economic and social reforms were achieved during his presidency.

Key Terms and Names
AmeriCorps, Contract with America, Kenneth Starr, perjury, ethnic cleansing, Dayton Accords

Reading Strategy
Taking Notes As you read about the administration of President Clinton, use the major headings of the section to create an outline similar to the one below.

The Clinton Years
I. Clinton's Agenda
   A.
   B.
   C.
   D.
II.

Reading Objectives
• **Describe** the difficulties and successes of Bill Clinton's two terms as president.
• **Discuss** the nation's involvement in world affairs during the Clinton presidency.

Section Theme
Economic Factors The United States, along with much of the industrialized world, experienced economic prosperity in the 1990s.

Preview of Events

◆1993	◆1995	◆1997	◆1999

1993
Israeli-Palestinian peace accord

1994
Republicans win both houses of Congress

1995
Federal government shuts down during budget impasse

1998
House impeaches Clinton; NATO aircraft bomb Serbia

1999
Senate acquits Clinton

★ *An American Story* ★

George Stephanopoulos

Bill Clinton was the third-youngest person ever to serve as president and the first of the "baby boom" generation to reach the Oval Office. Clinton brought with him a team of young energetic advisers. In the early weeks of the administration, Clinton's team spent many hours at the White House adjusting to their new life. In early 1993, they began discussing plans for Clinton's new economic strategy for paying down the deficit and reducing interest rates. George Stephanopoulos, an aide to the president, remembers their inexperienced beginnings:

66The president presided over the rolling Roosevelt Room meetings in shirtsleeves, with glasses sliding down the end of his nose. . . . Clinton let everyone have a say, played us off against one another, asked pointed questions, and took indecipherable notes. But the reminders of who we were and what we were doing was never far away. Late one night, we ordered pizzas. When they arrived, the president grabbed a slice with the rest of us . . . [b]ut just before he took his first bite, [a secret service] agent placed a hand on his shoulder and told him to put it down. The pie hadn't been screened. . . .99

—quoted in *All Too Human*

Clinton's Agenda

Clinton's first years in office were filled with grandiose plans and the difficult realities of politics. The new president put forth an ambitious domestic program focusing on five major areas: the economy, the family, education, crime, and health care.

1016 CHAPTER 34 Into a New Century

SECTION RESOURCES

Raising Taxes, Cutting Spending As he had promised in his election campaign, Clinton focused first on the economy. The problem, in the president's view, was the federal deficit. Under Reagan and Bush, the deficit had nearly quadrupled, adding billions of dollars annually to the national debt. High deficits forced the government to borrow large sums of money to pay for its programs and helped to drive up interest rates.

Clinton believed that the key to economic growth was to lower interest rates. Low interest rates would enable businesses to borrow more money to expand and create more jobs. Low rates would also make it easier for consumers to borrow money for mortgages, car loans, and other items, which in turn would promote economic growth.

One way to bring interest rates down was to reduce the federal deficit. In early 1993, Clinton sent Congress a deficit reduction plan. In trying to cut the deficit, however, Clinton faced a serious problem. About half of all government spending went to entitlement programs, such as Social Security, Medicare, and veterans' benefits. Entitlement programs are very hard to cut because so many Americans depend on them.

Faced with these constraints, Clinton decided to raise taxes, even though he had promised to cut taxes during his campaign. Clinton's plan raised tax rates for middle- and upper-income Americans and placed new taxes on gasoline, heating oil, and natural gas. The tax increases were very unpopular, and Republicans in Congress refused to support them. Clinton pressured Democrats, and after many amendments, a modified version of Clinton's plan narrowly passed.

Stumbling on Health Care During his campaign, Clinton had promised to reform the U.S. health care system. An estimated 40 million Americans, or roughly 15 percent of the nation, did not have private health insurance. The president appointed a task force headed by his wife, **Hillary Rodham Clinton**—an unprecedented role for a first lady. The task force developed a plan that guaranteed health benefits for all Americans, but it put much of the burden of payment of these benefits on employers. Small-business owners feared they could not afford it. The insurance industry and doctors' organizations also opposed the plan.

Republicans opposed the plan as being complicated, costly, and reliant on government control. Congressional Democrats were divided. Some supported alternative plans, but no plan had enough support to pass. Faced with public opposition, Clinton's plan died without ever coming to a vote.

Families and Education Clinton did manage to push several major pieces of legislation through Congress. During his campaign, he had stressed the need to help American families. His first success was the **Family Medical Leave Act.** This law gave workers up to 12 weeks per year of unpaid family leave for the birth or adoption of a child or for the illness of a family member.

Clinton also persuaded Congress to create the **AmeriCorps** program. This program put students to work improving low-income housing, teaching children to read, and cleaning up the environment. AmeriCorps volunteers earned a salary and were awarded a scholarship to continue their education.

Crime and Gun Control Clinton had also promised to get tough on crime during his campaign, and he strongly endorsed new gun-control laws. Despite strong opposition from many Republicans and the **National Rifle Association** (NRA), the Democrats in Congress passed a gun-control law known as the **Brady Bill.** The bill imposed a waiting period before people could buy handguns. It also required gun dealers to have police run a background check on a person's criminal record before selling them a handgun. The following year, Clinton introduced another crime bill. The bill provided states with extra funds to build new prisons and put 100,000 more police officers on the streets.

✓ **Reading Check** **Explaining** Why did President Clinton's proposed health care plan fail?

Picturing **History**

High Hopes The Clintons entered the White House in 1993 determined to change the United States for the better. It took time for them to adjust to life in Washington, and many of their ambitious plans were defeated in Congress. What legislative proposal was given to the First Lady to oversee?

Creating a Chart Have students create a chart similar to the one shown below to illustrate some of Clinton's domestic agenda. **L1**

	Issue	Action
Taxes		
Health Care		
Families		
Education		
Crime		
Gun Control		

📁 Use the rubric for creating a map, display, or chart on pages 77–78 in the *Performance Assessment Activities and Rubrics.*

✓ **Reading Check**

Answer: Republicans said it was too costly and relied on federal control. Public opposition was also strong.

Picturing **History**

Answer: health care reform
Ask: What happened to health care reform? *(The plan died before a congressional vote.)*

COOPERATIVE LEARNING ACTIVITY

Understanding Elections Organize students into cooperative groups. Remind them that as a result of the 1992 elections, almost one-fourth of the members of Congress were newly elected. The numbers of minorities and women increased significantly. Have groups research reasons for the dramatic changes. Ask groups to investigate how scandals, voter registration and turnout, and prevailing economic conditions may have contributed to the changes. Allow the groups to decide how the research is to be done and how the findings will be presented.

Use the rubric for a cooperative group management plan on pages 81–82 in the *Performance Assessment Activities and Rubrics.*

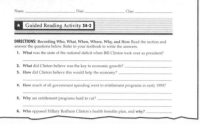

Picturing **History**

Answer: The Senate defeated several proposals, including the balanced budget amendment, while the president vetoed others.

Ask: Who was the leader of the Republicans who created the Contract with America? *(Newt Gingrich)*

✓ **Reading Check**

Answer: They agreed on health insurance portability and welfare reform.

FYI

William Jefferson Blythe IV was born in Hope, Arkansas, three months after his father died in a traffic accident. While in high school, Blythe took his stepfather's last name of Clinton. Bill Clinton graduated from Georgetown University and won a Rhodes Scholarship to Oxford University. At Yale University, he earned a law degree and met his future wife, law school classmate Hillary Rodham. After serving as the attorney general and governor of Arkansas, Clinton ran for president. His 1992 campaign video was titled "A Man from Hope."

Picturing **History**

Republicans Triumphant As a result of the 1994 midterm congressional elections, the Republican Party gained control of the House and the Senate for the first time since the 1950s. Newt Gingrich (at podium) helped lead a group of young GOP congressional representatives in passing the Contract with America legislation. How successful was the Contract with America legislation? Explain.

The Republicans Gain Control of Congress

Despite his successes, Clinton was very unpopular by late 1994. Instead of cutting taxes, he had raised them, and he had not fixed health care. Although the economy was improving, many companies were still downsizing. Several personal issues involving President Clinton further weakened public confidence in him. These factors convinced many Americans to vote Republican in 1994.

The Contract With America As the 1994 midterm elections neared, congressional Republicans, led by Newt Gingrich of Georgia, created the **Contract with America.** This program proposed 10 major changes, including lower taxes, welfare reform, tougher anti-crime laws, term limits for members of Congress, and a balanced budget amendment. Republicans won a stunning victory—for the first time in 40 years, they had a majority in both houses of Congress.

In their first 100 days in office, House Republicans passed almost the entire Contract with America, but they soon ran into trouble. The Senate defeated several proposals, including the balanced budget amendment, while the president vetoed others.

The Budget Battle In 1995 the Republicans lost more momentum when they clashed with the president over the new federal budget. Clinton vetoed several

Republican budget proposals, claiming they cut into social programs too much. Gingrich believed that if Republicans stood firm, the president would back down and approve the budget. Otherwise, the entire federal government would shut down for lack of funds. Clinton, however, refused to budge, and allowed the federal government to close.

By standing firm against Republican budget proposals and allowing the government to shut down, Clinton regained much of the support he had lost in 1994. The Republicans in Congress realized they needed to work with the president to pass legislation. Soon afterward, they reached an agreement with Clinton to balance the budget.

In the months before the 1996 election, the president and the Republicans worked together to pass new legislation. In August Congress passed the Health Insurance Portability Act. This act improved coverage for people who changed jobs and reduced discrimination against people with preexisting illnesses.

Later that month, Congress passed the **Welfare Reform Act,** which limited people to no more than two consecutive years on welfare and required them to work to receive welfare benefits. The law also increased childcare spending and gave tax breaks to companies that hired new employees who had been on welfare.

✓ **Reading Check** **Identifying** What two reforms did Clinton and Congress agree to support?

The 1996 Election

As the 1996 campaign began, Clinton took credit for the economy. The economic boom of the 1990s was the longest sustained period of growth in American history. Unemployment and inflation fell to their lowest levels in 40 years. The stock market soared, wages rose, crime rates fell, and the number of people on welfare declined. With the economy booming, Clinton's popularity climbed rapidly.

The Republican Party nominated Senator **Bob Dole** of Kansas, the Republican leader in the Senate, to run against Clinton. Dole chose as his running

MEETING SPECIAL NEEDS

Reading Disability Have students with reading comprehension difficulties complete a chart similar to the one shown below. List ideas and laws from the section and each person's position. Students should fill in the resolutions column after reading the section. **L1** ELL

Issues	Bill Clinton	Newt Gingrich	Bob Dole	Resolution

☞ Refer to *Inclusion for the High School Social Studies Classroom Strategies and Activities* in the TCR.

mate Jack Kemp, a popular conservative and former member of Congress from New York. Dole promised a 15 percent tax cut if elected and tried to portray Clinton as a tax-and-spend liberal.

H. Ross Perot also ran again as a candidate. This time he ran as the candidate of the Reform Party, which he had created. Once again Perot made the deficit the main campaign issue.

President Clinton won re-election, winning a little more than 49 percent of the popular vote and 379 electoral votes. Dole received slightly less than 41 percent and 159 electoral votes. Perot won about 8.4 percent of the vote—less than half of what he had received in 1992. Despite Clinton's victory, Republicans retained control of Congress.

✓ **Reading Check** **Explaining** Why do you think President Clinton won re-election in 1996?

Clinton's Second Term

During Clinton's second term, the economy continued its expansion. As people's incomes rose, so too did the amount of taxes they paid. At the same time, despite their differences, the president and Congress continued to shrink the deficit. In 1997, for the first time in 24 years, the president was able to submit a balanced budget to Congress. Beginning in

1998, the government began to run a surplus—that is, it collected more money than it spent.

Despite these achievements, Clinton's domestic agenda was less aggressive in his second term. Much of his time was spent on foreign policy and in struggling against a personal scandal.

Putting Children First During his second term, Clinton's domestic agenda shifted toward helping the nation's children. He began by asking Congress to pass a $500 per child tax credit. He also signed the Adoption and Safe Families Act and asked Congress to ban cigarette advertising aimed at children. In August 1997, Clinton signed the Children's Health Insurance Program—a plan to provide health insurance for children whose parents could not afford it.

Clinton also continued his efforts to help students. "I come from a family where nobody had ever gone to college before," Clinton said. "When I became president, I was determined to do what I could to give every student that chance." To help students, he asked for a tax credit, a large increase in student grants, and an expansion of the Head Start program for preschoolers.

Clinton Is Impeached The robust economy and his high standing in the polls allowed Clinton to regain the initiative in dealing with Congress. By 1998, however,

Impeaching the President

Chief Justice William Rehnquist being sworn in for the impeachment trial in the Senate

The Constitution gives Congress the power to remove a president from office "upon impeachment for and Conviction of, Treason, Bribery, or other High Crimes and Misdemeanors." The House of Representatives has the sole power over impeachment—the formal accusation of wrongdoing in office. If the majority of the House votes to impeach the president, the Senate conducts a trial. A two-thirds vote of those present is needed for conviction. When the impeachment proceeding involves a president, the chief justice of the United States presides.

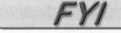

A somber President and Mrs. Clinton after the decision for impeachment was reached

Creating Circle Graphs Provide the data below and ask students to create a pair of circle graphs showing the results of the presidential election of 1996. **L1**

Candidate	Popular Vote	Electoral Vote
Clinton, Dem.	47,402,357	379
Dole, Rep.	39,198,755	159
Perot, Rfm.	8,085,402	0

🗁 Use the rubric for creating a map, display, or chart on pages 77–78 in the *Performance Assessment Activities and Rubrics.*

✓ **Reading Check**

Answer: One possible answer: Clinton was reelected because the economy was booming.

History *and the* Humanities

🎵 American Music: Hits Through History: "Little Miss Can't Be Wrong"

FYI

Madeleine Albright, appointed by President Clinton, was the first woman to serve as secretary of state. This appointment made her the highest-ranking woman ever to serve in the federal government—fourth in line for presidential succession. Interestingly, she would not have been able to assume the presidency because she was not born a citizen of the United States.

INTERDISCIPLINARY CONNECTIONS ACTIVITY

Poetry Tell students that on January 20, 1961, Robert Frost recited one of his poems at President Kennedy's inauguration. He had written a poem for the occasion, but the glare of the sunny day made it impossible for him to read his notes. He recited "The Gift Outright" from memory. Thirty-two years later, Maya Angelou recited her poem, "On the Pulse of Morning," written for the occasion, at President Clinton's 1993 inauguration. Have students read both poems and write a short comparative analysis. **L2**

3 ASSESS

Assign Section 2 Assessment as homework or as an in-class activity.

🔘 Have students use the **Interactive Tutor Self-Assessment CD-ROM.**

✔ Reading Check

Answer: allegations that Clinton had arranged illegal loans while he was governor of Arkansas; also allegations that he had perjured himself while testifying about his relationship with a White House intern

---

he had become entangled in a serious scandal that threatened to undermine his presidency.

The scandal began in Clinton's first term, when he was accused of arranging illegal loans for Whitewater Development—an Arkansas real estate company—while he was governor of that state. Attorney General **Janet Reno** decided that an independent counsel should investigate the president. A special three-judge panel appointed **Kenneth Starr,** a former federal judge, to this position.

In early 1998, a new scandal emerged involving a personal relationship between the president and a White House intern. Some evidence suggested that the president had committed perjury, or had lied under oath, about the relationship. The three-judge panel directed Starr to investigate this scandal as well. In September 1998, after examining the evidence, Starr sent his report to the Judiciary Committee of the House of Representatives. Starr argued that Clinton had obstructed justice, abused his power as president, and committed perjury.

After the 1998 elections, the House began impeachment hearings. Clinton's supporters charged that Starr's investigation was politically motivated. Clinton's accusers argued that the president was accountable if his actions were illegal.

On December 19, 1998, the House of Representatives passed two articles of impeachment, one for perjury and one for obstruction of justice. The vote split almost evenly along party lines, and the case moved to the Senate for trial. On February 12, 1999, the senators cast their votes. The vote was 55 to 45 that Clinton was not guilty of perjury, and 50–50 on the charge of obstruction of justice. Although both votes were well short of the two-thirds needed to remove the president from office, Clinton's reputation had suffered.

✔ **Reading Check** **Examining** What events led to the impeachment of President Clinton?

Clinton's Foreign Policy

While attracting worldwide attention, the impeachment drama did not affect world affairs. The collapse of the Soviet Union virtually ended the struggle between communism and democracy, but small bloody wars continued to erupt around the world. On several occasions President Clinton used force to bring an end to regional conflicts.

The Haitian Intervention In 1991 military leaders in Haiti overthrew Jean-Bertrand Aristide, the country's first democratically elected president in many decades. Aristide sought refuge in the United States. The new rulers of Haiti used violence, even murder, to suppress the opposition. Seeking to restore democracy, the Clinton administration convinced the United Nations to impose a trade embargo on Haiti. The embargo created a severe economic crisis in that country. Thousands of Haitian refugees fled to the United States in small boats, and many died at sea.

Determined to put an end to the crisis, Clinton ordered an invasion of Haiti. Before the troops arrived, however, former president Jimmy Carter convinced Haiti's rulers to step aside.

Peacekeeping in Bosnia and Kosovo The United States also was concerned about mounting tensions in southeastern Europe. During the Cold War, Yugoslavia had been a single federated nation made up of many different ethnic groups under a strong Communist government. In 1991, after the collapse of communism, Yugoslavia split apart.

In Bosnia, one of the former Yugoslav republics, a vicious three-way civil war erupted between Orthodox Christian Serbs, Catholic Croatians, and Bosnian Muslims. Despite international pressure, the fighting continued until 1995. The Serbs began what they called ethnic cleansing—the brutal expulsion of an ethnic group from a geographic area. In some cases, Serbian troops slaughtered the Muslims instead of moving them.

The United States convinced its NATO allies that military action was necessary. NATO warplanes attacked the Serbs in Bosnia, forcing them to negotiate. The Clinton administration then arranged peace talks in Dayton, Ohio. The participants signed a peace plan known as the **Dayton Accords.** In 1996 some 60,000 NATO troops, including 20,000 Americans, entered Bosnia to enforce the plan.

In 1998 another war erupted, this time within the Serbian province of Kosovo. Kosovo has two major ethnic groups—Serbs and Albanians. Many of the Albanians wanted Kosovo to separate from Serbia. To keep Kosovo in Serbia, Serbian leader **Slobodan Milosevic** ordered a crackdown. The Albanians then organized their own army to fight back. Worried by reports of Serbian violence against Albanian civilians, President Clinton convinced European leaders that NATO should again use force to stop the fighting. In March 1999, NATO began bombing Serbia. The bombing convinced Serbia to pull its troops out of Kosovo.

CRITICAL THINKING ACTIVITY

Analyzing Early presidents were able to oversee all the daily activities of the executive office and still have time for leisurely pursuits. Today the president's schedule is packed with meetings, reports, decisions, and ceremonial duties. With all this activity, a president is not able to keep up with every decision of hundreds of executive agencies and offices. Ask students what part, if any, of the president's responsibilities should be delegated to another person or agency. Have students explain their responses. **L2**

Peacemaking in the Middle East Despite the overwhelming defeat Iraq suffered in the Persian Gulf War, Iraqi President Saddam Hussein remained in power and continued to make threats against Iraq's neighbors. In 1996 Iraq attacked the Kurds, an ethnic group whose homeland lies in northern Iraq. To stop the attacks, the United States fired cruise missiles at Iraqi military targets.

Relations between Israel and the Palestinians were even more volatile. In 1993 Israeli Prime Minister **Yitzhak Rabin** and Palestine Liberation Organization leader **Yasir Arafat** reached an agreement. The PLO recognized Israel's right to exist, and Israel recognized the PLO as the representative of the Palestinians. President Clinton then invited Arafat and Rabin to the White House, where they signed the Declaration of Principles—a plan for creating a Palestinian government.

Opposition to the peace plan emerged on both sides. Radical Palestinians exploded bombs in Israel and in 1995 a right-wing Israeli assassinated Prime Minister Rabin.

In 1998 Israeli and Palestinian leaders met with President Clinton at the Wye River plantation in Maryland to work out details of the withdrawal of Israeli troops from the West Bank and the Gaza Strip. This agreement, however, failed to settle the status of Jerusalem, which both sides claimed.

In July 2000, President Clinton invited Arafat and Israeli Prime Minister Ehud Barak to reach an agreement, but these talks failed. Beginning in October, violence started to break out between Palestinians and Israeli soldiers. The region was as far from peace as ever.

Picturing **History**

Middle East Conflict The struggle over control of the Israeli/Palestinian areas intensified in the 1990s. Although President Clinton directed many negotiations to attempt to resolve the conflict, the region remained a very dangerous place. Which leaders agreed to a framework for peace in 1993?

Clinton Leaves Office As he prepared to leave office, President Clinton's legacy was uncertain. He had balanced the budget and presided over the greatest period of economic growth in American history. Clinton's presidency was marred, however, by the impeachment trial, which had divided the nation and widened the divide between liberals and conservatives. In the election of 2000, that division would lead to the closest election in American history.

✓ **Reading Check** **Identifying** In what three regions of the world did Clinton use force to support his foreign policy?

Picturing **History**

Answer: Yitzhak Rabin and Yasir Arafat
Ask: What did the Declaration of Principles accomplish? *(It created a plan for a Palestinian government.)*

Reteach
Have students describe the difficulties and successes of Bill Clinton's two terms as president.

Enrich
Have interested students research the current state of affairs in the Middle East by summarizing appropriate magazine and newspaper articles.

✓ **Reading Check**
Answer: in southeastern Europe (Bosnia and Kosovo); in the Middle East (Iraq); was prepared to use force in Latin America (Haiti) but the crisis ended peacefully

4 CLOSE

Have students discuss the nation's involvement in world affairs during the Clinton administration.

SECTION 2 ASSESSMENT

Checking for Understanding
1. **Define:** perjury, ethnic cleansing.
2. **Identify:** AmeriCorps, Contract with America, Kenneth Starr, Dayton Accords.
3. **Explain** why the federal government shut down in 1995.

Reviewing Themes
4. **Economic Factors** What government policies helped create the U.S. prosperity of the 1990s?

Critical Thinking
5. **Analyzing** Why was President Clinton able to win re-election in 1996?
6. **Categorizing** Complete a chart similar to the one below by explaining the foreign policy issues facing President Clinton in each of the areas listed.

Region	Issue
Latin America	
Southeastern Europe	
Middle East	

Analyzing Visuals
7. **Analyzing Photographs** Study the photographs on page 1019 of Clinton's impeachment trial. What elements in the photograph reflect the seriousness of the occasion?

Writing About History
8. **Persuasive Writing** Take on the role of a member of Congress. Write a letter in which you attempt to persuade other lawmakers to vote either for or against the impeachment of President Clinton. Provide reasons for your position.

CHAPTER 34   Into a New Century   **1021**

SECTION 2 ASSESSMENT ANSWERS

1. Terms are in blue.
2. AmeriCorps *(p. 1017)*, Contract with America *(p. 1018)*, Kenneth Starr *(p. 1020)*, Dayton Accords *(p. 1020)*, Yasir Arafat *(p. 1021)*
3. A budget impasse between Congress and Clinton led to a government shutdown.

4. a reduced federal deficit and lower interest rates
5. Americans' desire to encourage the continuation of the economic boom
6. Latin America: Haiti's democratically elected president overthrown; southeastern Europe: ethnic cleansing in Bosnia and Kosovo;

Middle East: tension between Israel and the Palestinians, and Iraqi attacks on Kurds
7. Possible answers: people's somber expressions, Clinton's bowed head
8. Students' letters will vary. Letters should express a clear point of view.

1 FOCUS

Section Overview

This section focuses on the advantages and disadvantages of economic globalization and global environmental issues.

BELLRINGER
Skillbuilder Activity

Project transparency and have students answer the question.

Available as a blackline master.

Daily Focus Skills Transparency 34–3

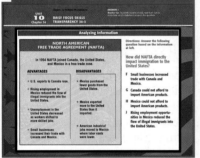

Guide to Reading

Answers to Graphic: global warming, international trade, nuclear proliferation, terrorism, world economy

Preteaching Vocabulary
Have students create a database for the Key Terms and Names. Encourage them to enter additional words, terms, and names as they read this section.

SECTION 3 An Interdependent World

 An American Story

Madeleine Albright

It was an important breakthrough when President Clinton appointed Madeleine Albright in 1996 to be the first woman to serve as secretary of state. Born in Czechoslovakia, Albright immigrated to the United States as a young girl. She earned a Ph.D. in Russian studies from Columbia University. Her tough-talking approach as U.S. ambassador to the United Nations earned her the nation's top foreign policy job.

As secretary of state, Albright dealt with everything from peace negotiations in the Middle East to improving trade relations with China. She also championed women's rights in developing countries. Here, she expresses her views on women's rights:

❝[Halting violence against women] is a goal of American foreign policy around the world, where abuses range from domestic violence . . . to forcing young girls into prostitution. Some say all this is cultural, and there's nothing we can do about it. I say it's criminal, and we each have a responsibility to stop it.❞

—quoted in *Madeleine Albright and the New American Diplomacy*

The New Global Economy

In the latter part of the 1900s, American leaders became more concerned with many global issues. Economies around the world had become much more interdependent. Computer technology and the Internet played a big role in forging a global economy.

SECTION RESOURCES

Reproducible Masters
• Reproducible Lesson Plan 34–3
• Daily Lecture and Discussion Notes 34–3
• Guided Reading Activity 34–3
• Section Quiz 34–3
• Reading Essentials and Study Guide 34–3
• Performance Assessment Activities and Rubrics

Transparencies
• Daily Focus Skills Transparency 34–3

Multimedia
• Interactive Tutor Self-Assessment CD-ROM
• ExamView® Pro Testmaker CD-ROM
• Presentation Plus! CD-ROM
• TeacherWorks™ CD-ROM
• Audio Program

Selling American-made goods abroad had long been important to American prosperity. By the 1970s, however, serious trade deficits had mounted—Americans purchased more from foreign nations than American industry and agriculture sold abroad. The United States found it necessary to compete harder in the global marketplace by streamlining industry, using new technology, and opening new markets.

From World War II to the present, Republican and Democratic administrations have both tried to lower barriers to international trade. They reasoned that the U.S. economy benefited from the sale of American exports, and that the purchase of imports would keep consumer prices, inflation, and interest rates low for Americans. Opponents warned that the global economy might cost the United States industrial jobs as manufacturing shifted to lesser-developed nations with few environmental regulations and cheap labor. By the 1990s, the debate between supporters of free trade and those who wanted to limit trade to protect industries had become an important part of American politics.

Regional Blocs One means of increasing international trade was to create regional trade pacts. In 1994 the **North American Free Trade Agreement** (NAFTA) joined Canada, the United States, and Mexico in a free-trade zone. With NAFTA in operation, exports of American goods to both Canada and Mexico rose dramatically. From 1993 to 2000, it is estimated that combined exports to those two countries rose from $142 to $290 billion, an increase of 105 percent.

One concern of many Americans was that industrial jobs would go to Mexico, where labor costs were lower. Although some jobs were lost to Mexico, unemployment rates in the United States fell during this period and wages rose. Many American businesses upgraded their technology, and workers shifted to more skilled jobs or to the service industry.

NAFTA faced competing regional trade blocs in Europe and Asia. In 1993 the **European Union** (EU) was created to promote economic and political cooperation among many European nations. The EU created a common bank and the euro, a common currency for member nations. The organization also removed trade barriers between its members and set policies on imports from nations outside the community.

EU rules tended to favor imports from the European nations' former colonies in Asia, Africa, and the Pacific over competing products from the United States. The EU also banned scientifically modified food, such as hormone-treated beef from the United States. American exporters argued that hormones were a safe way to accelerate livestock growth rates and produce leaner meat. They protested that European fears lacked a scientific basis.

The **Asia Pacific Economic Cooperation** (APEC) was an attempt to create a Pacific trade community to rival the European Union. APEC represented the fastest-growing region in the world and controlled 43 percent of global trade in 1999. APEC began as a

Picturing **History**

A Busy Border NAFTA greatly increased trade across the Texas-Mexico border (below). It also led to the building of foreign-owned factories, known as *maquiladoras*, in Mexico near the American border to take advantage of low Mexican wages. The *maquiladora* pictured at right is located in Tijuana. How did NAFTA affect both the United States and Mexico?

CHAPTER 34   Into a New Century   **1023**

2 TEACH

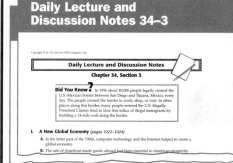
Creating a Thematic Map Have students create a thematic world map showing the countries that have nuclear weapons. Have students use the maps to discuss present dangers related to nuclear weapons. **L1**

Use the rubric for creating a map, display, or chart on pages 77–78 in the *Performance Assessment Activities and Rubrics.*

Picturing **History**

Answer: U.S. unemployment fell and wages rose as workers shifted to more skilled jobs or to the service industry. U.S. exports to Mexico rose and Mexico gained jobs.
Ask: Why did Americans fear losing jobs to Mexico rather than to Canada? (*Possible answers: wages and Mexico's standard of living were lower; workers feared that their jobs would be lost to low-wage workers in Mexico*)

COOPERATIVE LEARNING ACTIVITY

Assessing Policy Organize students into seven groups. Assign one of the following areas to each group: South Africa, China, Japan, Western Europe, Eastern Europe, Latin America, and the Middle East. Have each group present a report on American policy today toward its assigned area. Have students from each group take on specific tasks such as obtaining resources, researching, writing, and presenting. Have the spokesperson for each group present a five-minute report, then open the topic for class discussion.

Use the rubric for a cooperative group management plan on pages 81–82 in the *Performance Assessment Activities and Rubrics.*

NATIONAL GEOGRAPHIC
MOMENT in HISTORY

The Oklahoma City National Memorial includes 168 chairs, one for each victim, in 9 rows, one for each floor of the destroyed building. Each chair is made of bronze and stone and is on a lighted glass base etched with a victim's name.

✓ Reading Check

Answer: to promote economic and political cooperation in Europe

3 ASSESS

Assign Section 3 Assessment as homework or as an in-class activity.

🌑 Have students use the **Interactive Tutor Self-Assessment CD-ROM.**

NATIONAL GEOGRAPHIC
MOMENT in HISTORY

TERRORISM IN THE HEARTLAND

A couple comforts each other after placing flowers on one of the 168 chairs that form part of the Oklahoma City National Memorial. The site was dedicated on April 19, 2000—five years to the day after Timothy McVeigh detonated a massive bomb outside the Alfred P. Murrah Federal Building in downtown Oklahoma City. Most of the 168 killed and hundreds injured were government employees, but 19 children attending a day-care facility in the building also died in the blast. A jury found McVeigh guilty, and he was executed in 2001.

forum to promote economic cooperation and lower trade barriers, but major political differences kept its members from acting together.

The World Trade Organization Central to the effort to promote a global economy was the **World Trade Organization** (WTO). The WTO administered international trade agreements and helped settle trade disputes. American supporters of the WTO cited benefits for U.S. consumers, including cheaper imports, new markets, and copyright protection for the American entertainment industry. On the other hand, the United States had no veto power in the WTO and poorer nations could outvote it.

Trade With China China played an increasingly important role in world trade. Its huge population offered vast potential as a market for American goods. Many Americans, however, had strong reservations about China's record on human rights, and they worried about its threats to invade Taiwan. Despite these concerns, President Clinton argued that regularizing trade with China would help bring it into the world community.

After negotiating a new trade agreement, Clinton pressed Congress to grant China permanent normal trade relation status. Those opposing the bill were an unusual coalition. Labor unions were concerned that inexpensive Chinese goods would flood U.S. markets; conservatives objected to China's military ambitions; and environmentalists worried about pollution from Chinese factories. Despite their opposition, the bill passed in late 2000.

✓ Reading Check **Explaining** Why was the European Union (EU) created in 1993?

Issues of Global Concern

Although the end of the Cold War had reduced the threat of nuclear war between the United States and the Soviet Union, it also increased fears that nuclear weapons might fall into the wrong hands. Equally worrisome were efforts by several nations, including Pakistan, North Korea, and Iraq, to acquire nuclear weapons and long-range missiles. Beginning in the 1980s, nations also began to be concerned about the environment.

MEETING SPECIAL NEEDS

Interpersonal Have small groups of students consider possible approaches to resolving one of the global concerns mentioned in this section. After students list their ideas, discuss them and develop a proposed solution. Prepare a letter to the United Nations explaining the issue and the group's proposed solution. **L2**

📁 Refer to *Inclusion for the High School Social Studies Classroom Strategies and Activities* in the TCR.

TECHNOLOGY

Nuclear Proliferation During the Cold War, only a few nations had possessed nuclear weapons, and they tried to restrict the spread of nuclear technology to other countries. When Russia agreed to reduce its nuclear arsenal, concerns arose that some of its nuclear weapons or radioactive material could be lost, stolen, or sold on the black market. In response, the United States provided funds to Russia to assist in the reduction of its nuclear stockpile.

Other measures followed to reduce the threat of nuclear proliferation, or the spread of nuclear weapons to new nations. Congress passed legislation that cut aid and imposed sanctions on nations seeking to acquire nuclear weapons. In 1996 President Clinton also signed the Comprehensive Nuclear Test Ban Treaty, but the U.S. Senate refused to ratify it fearing it would limit American nuclear research.

Concern About Ozone In the 1980s, scientists discovered that chemicals called chlorofluorocarbons (CFCs) had the potential to deplete the earth's atmosphere of ozone. Ozone is a gas in the atmosphere that protects life on Earth from the cancer-causing ultraviolet rays of the sun. At that time, CFCs were widely used in air conditioners and refrigerators. Many environmental activists began to push for a ban on CFC production. In the late 1980s, public awareness of the ozone issue increased dramatically when stories appeared documenting a large ozone "hole" over Antarctica. In 1987 the United States and 22 other nations agreed to phase out the production of CFCs and other chemicals that might be weakening the ozone layer.

Global Warming In the early 1990s, another global environmental issue developed when some scientists found evidence of global warming—an increase in average world temperatures over time. Such a rise in temperature could eventually lead to more droughts and other forms of extreme weather. A furious debate is now underway among scientists over how to measure changes in the earth's temperature and what the results mean.

Many experts believe carbon dioxide emissions from factories and power plants caused global warming, but others disagree. Some question whether global warming even exists. The issue is very controversial because the cost of controlling emissions would affect the global economy. Industries would have to pay the cost of further reducing emissions, and those costs would eventually be passed on to consumers. Developing nations trying to industrialize would be hurt the most, but economic growth in wealthier nations would be hurt, too.

Concern about global warming led to an international conference in Kyoto, Japan, in 1997. Thirty-nine nations signed the **Kyoto Protocol** promising to reduce emissions, but very few put it into effect. President Clinton did not submit the Kyoto Protocol to the Senate for ratification because most senators were opposed to it. In 2001 President George W. Bush withdrew the United States from the Kyoto Protocol, citing flaws in the treaty. As the 2000s began, Americans struggled to balance economic progress with environmental concerns.

Reading Check **Identifying** What is the ozone layer, and why is it important?

SECTION 3 ASSESSMENT

Checking for Understanding

1. **Define:** trade deficit, euro, nuclear proliferation, global warming.
2. **Identify:** North American Free Trade Agreement, Kyoto Protocol.
3. **Describe** the international response to concerns about global warming.

Reviewing Themes

4. **Global Connections** Why was China an important factor in world trade?

Critical Thinking

5. **Analyzing** Do you think the new global economy has helped or hurt the United States?
6. **Organizing** Complete a graphic organizer similar to the one below by listing and describing the regional trade blocs that formed in the 1990s.

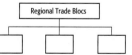

Regional Trade Blocs

Analyzing Visuals

7. **Analyzing Photographs** Study the photograph on page 1024 of the Oklahoma City National Memorial. What do the empty chairs represent? How has the memorial helped relatives of the victims?

Writing About History

8. **Expository Writing** Decide which issue of global concern today is the most serious. In an essay, explain why you think it is the most serious problem, and provide some possible solutions.

CHAPTER 34 Into a New Century **1025**

SECTION 3 ASSESSMENT ANSWERS

1. Terms are in blue.
2. North American Free Trade Agreement *(p. 1023),* Kyoto Protocol *(p. 1025)*
3. The Kyoto Protocol pledged to reduce emissions, but the United States did not sign it. Few of the 39 countries that signed it have implemented any plans.
4. China's large population provides a huge market for imported goods.
5. Students' answers will vary. Encourage students to provide reasons for their opinions.
6. NAFTA increased trade between Canada, Mexico, and the United States. EU promoted economic and political cooperation among European nations. APEC created a Pacific trade bloc.
7. bombing victims; answers should focus on the need to remember
8. Students' essays should clearly identify the issue.

1025

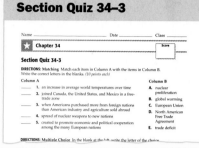

Reteach

Have students explain the development of regional economic blocs around the world.

Enrich

Invite interested students to investigate the cultural diversity of their own community and report their findings in an oral report to the class.

Reading Check

Answer: The ozone layer is a layer of gas in the atmosphere that protects life on Earth from the cancer-causing ultraviolet rays of the sun.

4 CLOSE

Have students list the environmental issues that have become important internationally.

1 FOCUS

Section Overview

This section focuses on the controversy surrounding the election of George W. Bush and the beginning of his presidency.

BELLRINGER
Skillbuilder Activity

 Project transparency and have students answer the question.

Available as a blackline master.

Daily Focus Skills Transparency 34–4

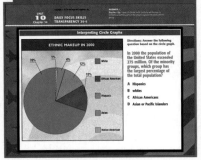

Guide to Reading

Answers to Graphic: Recounts begin in Florida; Florida Supreme Court extends deadline for recount; U.S. Supreme Court rules in *Bush* v. *Gore* that recount in Florida is unconstitutional.

Preteaching Vocabulary
Have students prepare a set of study cards with each Key Term or Name on one side and significant facts or definitions on the other.

America Enters a New Century

Guide to Reading

Main Idea
The closest presidential election in American history served as the prelude to the new century. The new president initiated an ambitious program.

Key Terms and Names
Al Gore, George W. Bush, Ralph Nader, chad, strategic defense

Reading Strategy
Organizing As you read about the 2000 presidential election, complete a graphic organizer similar to the one below by charting the key post-election events culminating in George W. Bush's victory.

☐ → ☐ → ☐ → Bush's Victory

Reading Objectives
- **Describe** the unusual circumstances surrounding the outcome of the 2000 presidential election.
- **Evaluate** the programs President George W. Bush initiated.

Section Theme
Government and Democracy The 2000 presidential election was very close, and the outcome was controversial.

Preview of Events

| ♦Aug. 2000 | ♦Dec. 2000 | ♦Mar. 2001 | ♦June 2001 |

August 2000
Republicans nominate Bush; Democrats nominate Gore

November 2000
Election takes place; recounts begin in Florida

December 2000
Gore concedes election to Bush

January 2001
George W. Bush inaugurated as president

June 2001
Bush signs tax cut bill into law

★ An American Story ★

May Akabogu-Collins

The 2000 presidential election was very close. Two candidates battled over the Electoral College votes of one state—Florida. The election remained undecided for more than a month. Though this election was a spectacle of demonstrations and detailed ballot evaluations, some people tried to put it all in perspective. May Akabogu-Collins, an American citizen originally from Nigeria, contrasted the "turmoil" and "chaos" of the election with the transfer of power in other parts of the world:

❝America should be grateful that this election was as wild as it gets. Some of us originally came from places where heads would have rolled during a similar crisis. So far, not a gunshot has been heard on account of the balloting, and you call this 'wild'? An election held in Nigeria in 1993 led to the President-elect's being thrown in jail for trying to assume office and ultimately to his mysterious death. Going to court to decide who won this contest is, in my opinion, as civilized as it gets.❞

—quoted in *Time,* December 11, 2000

A New President for a New Century

The close election of 2000 was, in some ways, another legacy of Bill Clinton's years in power. Clinton's presidency had left the country deeply divided. Many people were pleased with the economy but disappointed with the president's personal behavior. As

1026 CHAPTER 34 Into a New Century

SECTION RESOURCES

Reproducible Masters
- Reproducible Lesson Plan 34–4
- Daily Lecture and Discussion Notes 34–4
- Guided Reading Activity 34–4
- Section Quiz 34–4
- Reading Essentials and Study Guide 34–4
- Interpreting Political Cartoons

Transparencies
- Daily Focus Skills Transparency 34–4

Multimedia
- Interactive Tutor Self-Assessment CD-ROM
- ExamView® Pro Testmaker CD-ROM
- Presentation Plus! CD-ROM
- TeacherWorks™ CD-ROM
- Audio Program

the election approached, the Republicans and the Democrats both tried to find candidates who would appeal to a broad cross-section of society.

The Candidates Are Chosen The Democrats nominated Vice President **Al Gore** for president in 2000. As his running mate, Gore chose Senator Joseph Lieberman from Connecticut, the first Jewish American ever to run for vice president on a major party ticket.

The Republican contest for the presidential nomination came down to two men: Governor **George W. Bush** of Texas, son of former president George Bush, and Senator John McCain of Arizona, a former navy pilot and prisoner of war in North Vietnam. Most Republican leaders endorsed Bush, who was also popular with conservative Republicans. He easily won the nomination, despite some early McCain victories in the primaries. Bush chose former defense secretary Richard Cheney as his vice presidential running mate.

The 2000 Campaign The election campaign revolved around the question of what to do with surplus tax revenues. Both Bush and Gore agreed that Social Security needed reform, but they disagreed on the details. Both promised to cut taxes, although Bush proposed a much larger tax cut than Gore. Both men also promised to improve public education and to support plans to help seniors pay for prescription drugs.

The healthy economy helped Gore, who stressed that the Clinton-Gore administration had brought prosperity to the nation. Many voters, however, were concerned with what they perceived as a decline in moral values among the nation's leaders. Bush promised to restore dignity to the White House.

Frustrated by the similarities between Bush and Gore, well-known consumer advocate **Ralph Nader** entered the race as the nominee of the Green Party. Nader was known for his strong environmentalist views and his criticism of the power of large corporations. Nader argued that both Bush and Gore were

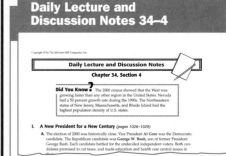

2 TEACH

Daily Lecture and Discussion Notes 34–4

Discussing a Topic Have students discuss the ramifications of the media projecting election results. Ask students what, if any, restrictions should be put on news organizations. **L1** ELL

Picturing **History**

Answer: Florida

Ask: Approximately how large was Bush's lead at midnight? *(about 130,000 votes)*

Name Game Traditionally former presidents retain the title of "president." George W. Bush and his father, however, are both called President Bush. Some Bush family members affectionately call the men "41" and "43," because George Bush was the forty-first president elected and George W. Bush was the forty-third.

Use *Interpreting Political Cartoons,* Cartoon 36.

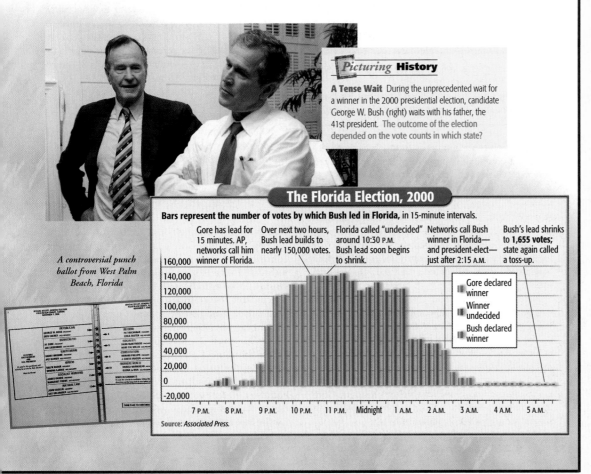

Picturing **History**

A Tense Wait During the unprecedented wait for a winner in the 2000 presidential election, candidate George W. Bush (right) waits with his father, the 41st president. The outcome of the election depended on the vote counts in which state?

A controversial punch ballot from West Palm Beach, Florida

The Florida Election, 2000

Bars represent the number of votes by which Bush led in Florida, in 15-minute intervals.

Gore has lead for 15 minutes. AP, networks call him winner of Florida.

Over next two hours, Bush lead builds to nearly 150,000 votes.

Florida called "undecided" around 10:30 P.M. Bush lead soon begins to shrink.

Networks call Bush winner in Florida— and president-elect— just after 2:15 A.M.

Bush's lead shrinks to **1,655 votes**; state again called a toss-up.

Legend:
- Gore declared winner
- Winner undecided
- Bush declared winner

Source: *Associated Press.*

COOPERATIVE LEARNING ACTIVITY

Researching Voting Statistics During the 1970s, 1980s, and 1990s, about 53 percent of all qualified voters voted in presidential elections. More women voted than men, and there were more voters in the 55–75 age range than in any other age group. Organize students into cooperative groups and have them research why some groups of people vote more than others. Ask them to discuss how being from a group that is likely to vote affects a person's clout with politicians. Allow students to choose how they will organize the work among group members and how they will report their findings.

Use the rubric for a cooperative group management plan on pages 81–82 in the ***Performance Assessment Activities and Rubrics.***

Guided Reading Activity 34-4

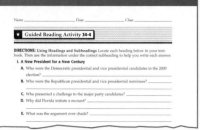

★ Guided Reading Activity **34-4**

Name _____ Date _____ Class _____

DIRECTIONS: Using Headings and Subheadings Locate each heading below in your text-book. Then use the information under the correct subheading to help you write each answer.

I. A New President for a New Century

A. Who were the Democratic presidential and vice presidential candidates in the 2000 election? _____

B. Who were the Republican presidential and vice presidential nominees? _____

C. Who presented a challenge to the major party candidates? _____

D. Why did Florida initiate a recount? _____

E. What was the argument over chads? _____

Geography *Skills*

Answers:

1. New Hampshire

2. There were a large number of electoral votes in the states Gore won.

Geography Skills Practice

Ask: Which candidate won the popular and electoral votes in Bush's home state of Texas and Gore's home state of Tennessee? *(Bush won both states.)*

3 ASSESS

Assign Section 4 Assessment as homework or as an in-class activity.

🌐 Have students use the **Interactive Tutor Self-Assessment CD-ROM.**

Reading Essentials and Study Guide 34-4

Name _____ Date _____ Class _____

Study Guide

Chapter 34, Section 4

For use with textbook pages 1026–1029

AMERICA ENTERS A NEW CENTURY

KEY TERMS AND NAMES

Al Gore the Democratic nominee for president in 2000 *(page 1027)*

George W. Bush the Republican nominee for president in 2000 *(page 1027)*

Ralph Nader consumer advocate who was the presidential nominee of the Green Party in 2000 *(page 1027)*

chad the piece of cardboard punched out of a ballot *(page 1028)*

strategic defense a military program to develop missiles and other devices that can shoot down nuclear missiles before they hit the United States *(page 1029)*

NATIONAL GEOGRAPHIC The Election of 2000

Presidential Election, 2000			
Candidate	Electoral Vote	Popular Vote	Political Party
Bush	271	50,455,156	Republican
Gore	266	50,992,335	Democrat

* 1 elector from Washington, D.C., abstained.

Geography *Skills*

1. **Interpreting Maps** Which single New England state did George W. Bush win in the election?
2. **Applying Geography Skills** Though Gore won less than half of the states, the election was extremely close. Why?

dependent on campaign funds from large companies and were unwilling to support policies that favored American workers and the environment.

A Close Vote The 2000 election was one of the closest in American history. Gore narrowly won the popular vote. He received 48.4 percent of the vote to 47.9 for Bush. To win the presidency, however, candidates have to win a majority of state electoral votes, not the overall popular vote.

Neither candidate had the 270 electoral votes needed to win. The election came down to the Florida vote—both men needed its 25 electoral votes.

The results in Florida were so close that state law required a recount of the ballots using vote-counting machines. There were, however, thousands of ballots that had been thrown out because the counting machines could not discern a vote for president. Gore immediately asked for a hand recount of ballots in several strongly Democratic counties.

After the machine recount showed Bush still ahead, a battle began over the manual recounts. Most Florida ballots required voters to punch a hole. The little piece of cardboard punched out of the ballot is called a chad. The problem for vote counters was how to count a ballot when the chad was still partially attached. On some, the chad was still in place, and the voter had left only a dimple on the surface of the ballot. When looking at the ballots, vote counters had to determine what the voter intended—and different counties used different standards.

Under state law, Florida officials had to certify the results by a certain date. When it became clear that not all of the recounts could be finished in time, Gore went to court to overturn the deadline. The Florida Supreme Court agreed to set a new deadline. At Bush's request, the United States Supreme Court then intervened in the case to decide whether the Florida Supreme Court had acted unconstitutionally.

While lawyers for Bush and Gore prepared their arguments for the Supreme Court, the hand recounts continued. Despite having more time, not all of the counties where Gore wanted recounts were able to meet the new deadline. On November 27, Florida officials certified Bush the winner by 537 votes.

Bush v. ***Gore*** Although Bush had been declared the winner in Florida, Gore's lawyers headed back to court arguing that thousands of ballots were still uncounted. The Florida Supreme Court ordered all Florida counties to begin a hand recount of ballots rejected by the counting machines. As counting began, the United States Supreme Court ordered the recount to stop until it had issued its ruling.

On December 12, in ***Bush*** v. ***Gore,*** the United States Supreme Court ruled 7–2 that the hand recounts in Florida violated the equal protection clause of the Constitution. The Court argued that because different vote counters used different standards, the recount did not treat all voters equally. 📖 *(See page 1080 for more information on* Bush v. Gore.*)*

MEETING SPECIAL NEEDS

Visual/Spatial Have students examine the map on this page. Ask students to identify what each color on the map stands for and then have them explain how many electoral votes each candidate received. Ask them to identify regions of the country where each candidate won support. Then ask them to explain what these voting patterns tell us about the United States. **L1**

📁 Refer to ***Inclusion for the High School Social Studies Classroom Strategies and Activities*** in the TCR.

Both federal law and the Constitution require the electoral votes for president to be cast on a certain day. If Florida missed that deadline, its electoral votes would not count. The Court ruled 5–4 that there was not enough time left to conduct a manual recount that would pass constitutional standards. This ruling left Bush the certified winner in Florida. In a televised speech the next day, Gore conceded the election. Bush responded with a message intended to unite Americans after the bitter election battle:

> ❝I have faith that . . . together we will create an America that is open . . . an America that is united in our diversity and our shared American values that are larger than race or party. I was not elected to serve one party, but to serve one nation.❞
>
> —George W. Bush, televised statement, December 13, 2000

✓ **Reading Check** **Analyzing** Why did the U.S. Supreme Court stop the manual recounts in Florida?

Bush Becomes President

On January 20, 2001, George W. Bush became the 43rd president of the United States. In his inaugural address, Bush promised to improve the nation's public schools, to cut taxes, to reform Social Security and Medicare, and to build up the nation's defenses.

After taking office, the president's first priority was to cut taxes to try to boost the economy. During the election campaign, the economy had begun to slow. The stock market dropped sharply, and many new Internet-based companies went out of business. Many other businesses laid off thousands of workers. Despite opposition from some Democrats, Congress passed a large $1.35 trillion tax cut to be phased in over 10 years. In the summer of 2001, Americans began receiving tax rebate checks that put about $40 billion back into the economy in an effort to prevent a recession.

Soon after Congress passed the tax cut plan, President Bush proposed two major reforms in education. He wanted public schools to hold annual standardized tests, and he wanted to allow parents to use federal funds to pay for private schools if their public schools were doing a poor job. Although Congress refused to give federal funds to private schools, it did vote in favor of annual reading and math tests in public schools for grades 3–8.

Shortly after taking office, President Bush asked Secretary of Defense Donald Rumsfeld to conduct a comprehensive review of the nation's military. The president wanted to increase military spending, but he also wanted new military programs designed to meet the needs of the post–Cold War world.

One military program Bush strongly favored was strategic defense—the effort to develop missiles and other devices that could shoot down nuclear missiles. Bush argued that missile defense was needed because many unfriendly nations were developing the technology to build nuclear missiles.

As the debate about the nation's military programs continued in the summer of 2001, a horrific event changed everything. On September 11, 2001, terrorists crashed passenger jets into the World Trade Center and the Pentagon. A new war had begun.

✓ **Reading Check** **Explaining** What was President George W. Bush's first priority when he took office?

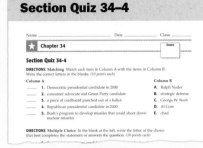

Section Quiz 34–4

SECTION 4 ASSESSMENT

Checking for Understanding
1. **Define:** chad, strategic defense.
2. **Identify:** Al Gore, George W. Bush, Ralph Nader.
3. **Reviewing Facts** What did the Supreme Court decide in *Bush* v. *Gore?*

Reviewing Themes
4. **Government and Democracy** What caused the vote-count controversy in Florida in the 2000 election?

Critical Thinking
5. **Forming an Opinion** Do you think the 2000 presidential election was decided fairly? Why or why not?
6. **Organizing** Complete a graphic organizer similar to the one below by listing President Bush's goals when he took office.

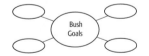

Bush Goals

Analyzing Visuals
7. **Interpreting Graphs** Study the graph on page 1027. By how many votes was Gore leading when news networks declared him the winner in Florida? What was Bush's lead when networks declared him to be the winner?

Writing About History
8. **Persuasive Writing** Take on the role of a Supreme Court justice. Write a statement explaining how you voted in *Bush* v. *Gore.*

CHAPTER 34 Into a New Century **1029**

SECTION 4 ASSESSMENT ANSWERS

1. Terms are in blue.
2. Al Gore *(p. 1027)*, George W. Bush *(p. 1027)*, Ralph Nader *(p. 1027)*
3. There was not enough time to conduct a manual recount that passed constitutional standards, ensuring Bush's victory.
4. confusing ballot designs and unclear voting results; different standards used to manually recount ballots
5. Students' answers will vary. Students should be encouraged to present reasoned arguments for their points of view.
6. tax cuts and rebates, new energy plan, public school reform, federal funding for faith-based groups to run social service programs, and strategic defense
7. about 3,000 votes; about 45,000 votes
8. Students' statements will vary but should express a clear, reasoned opinion based on existing law.

TEACH

Reading a Cartogram Tell students that a cartogram shows a proportional representation of land areas, population numbers, or other types of information.

Suggest that students imagine they are members of a city school board charged with the responsibility of planning where the city needs new schools. The standard city map shows the various residential areas and the borders of school districts. Ask students to consider what type of a cartogram would help them. Have students suggest other situations in which a cartogram would be helpful.

Additional Practice

Reinforcing Skills Activity 34

Name _____ Date _____ Class _____

★ **Reinforcing Skills Activity 34**

Reading a Cartogram

☐ **LEARNING THE SKILL**
Cartograms are maps that distort boundaries to show a value—other than land area—for a particular region. Because the size of a country or region is based on a specific value such as population, cartograms are excellent tools for making comparisons. To read a cartogram, begin with the title and key. These elements tell you the value used to render the cartogram. Look at the sizes of the countries or regions featured. Then compare the cartogram with a conventional map so you can see the variations in size.

☐ **PRACTICING THE SKILL**
DIRECTIONS: Analyze the thematic map and cartogram below. Then answer the questions that follow on a separate sheet of paper.

GLENCOE
TECHNOLOGY

CD-ROM
Glencoe Skillbuilder Interactive Workbook CD-ROM, Level 2

This interactive CD-ROM reinforces student mastery of essential social studies skills.

Reading a Cartogram

Why Learn This Skill?

On most maps, land areas are drawn in proportion to their actual surface areas on the earth. On some maps, however, a small country may appear much larger than usual, and a large country may look much smaller. The shapes of the countries may also look different.

Learning the Skill

Maps that distort country size and shape are called **cartograms.** In a cartogram, country size reflects some value *other* than land area, such as population or gross national product. For example, on a conventional map, Canada appears much larger than India. In a cartogram showing world population, however, India would appear larger than Canada because it has a much larger population. The cartogram is a tool for making visual comparisons. At a glance, you can see how each country or region compares with another in a particular value.

To use a cartogram, first read the title and key to identify what value the cartogram illustrates. Then examine the cartogram to see which countries or regions appear. Find the largest and smallest countries. Compare the cartogram with a conventional land-area map to determine the degree of distortion of particular countries. Finally, draw conclusions about the topic.

Practicing the Skill

Study the cartogram shown on this page, and then answer these questions.

❶ What is the subject of the cartogram?

❷ Which region appears largest on the cartogram? Which appears smallest?

❸ Compare the cartogram to the map of the United States found in the Atlas. Which region is the most distorted in size compared to a land-area map?

❹ Provide a brief explanation for this distortion.

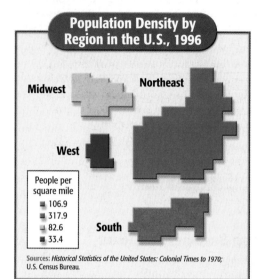

Population Density by Region in the U.S., 1996

Midwest
Northeast
West
South

People per square mile
■ 106.9
■ 317.9
■ 82.6
■ 33.4

Sources: *Historical Statistics of the United States: Colonial Times to 1970;* U.S. Census Bureau.

Skills Assessment

Complete the Practicing Skills questions on page 1039 and the Chapter 34 Skill Reinforcement Activity to assess your mastery of this skill.

Applying the Skill

Reading a Cartogram Find statistics that compare some value for different states or countries. For example, you might compare the number of farms in each state or the annual oil consumption of countries on one continent. Be creative in your choice. Convert these statistics into a simple cartogram. Determine the relative size of each country or state according to the chosen value. For example, if the United States consumes five times more oil than Canada, then the United States should appear five times larger.

 Glencoe's **Skillbuilder Interactive Workbook CD-ROM, Level 2,** provides instruction and practice in key social studies skills.

ANSWERS TO PRACTICING THE SKILL

❶ population density

❷ Northeast appears largest and West appears smallest.

❸ West

❹ Population density is low in much of the West.

Applying the Skill
Students' cartograms will vary depending on the statistic chosen. Encourage students to use graph paper to construct the cartogram showing correct proportions.

Main Idea
After suffering the worst terrorist attack in its history when airplanes crashed into the Pentagon and the World Trade Center, the United States launched a massive effort to end international terrorism.

Key Terms and Names
terrorism, state-sponsored terrorism, Osama bin Laden, al-Qaeda, anthrax

Reading Strategy
As you read about America's war on terrorism, complete a graphic organizer similar to the one below to show the different reasons terrorists attack Americans.

Causes of Terrorism

Reading Objectives
• **Describe** the development of Middle East terrorism.
• **Explain** the response of the United States to the terrorist attacks on the World Trade Center and the Pentagon.

Section Theme
Global Connections International terrorists targeted Americans in order to coerce the United States.

Preview of Events

◆1980		◆1990		◆2000

1979
Soviet Union invades Afghanistan

1988
Al-Qaeda is organized

1998
Bombs explode at U.S. embassies in Kenya and Tanzania

2001
Attacks on the Pentagon and World Trade Center

★ An American Story ★

Petra Bartosiewicz

At 8:45 A.M. Eastern Daylight Time on September 11, 2001, a Boeing 767 passenger jet slammed into the North Tower of the World Trade Center in New York City. As people below gazed in horror, a second plane collided with the South Tower. Soon afterward, a third plane crashed into the Pentagon in Washington, D.C. At 9:50 A.M., the South Tower collapsed in a billowing cloud of dust and debris. The North Tower fell about 40 minutes later. The collapsing towers killed thousands of people, burying them beneath a vast mound of rubble. The next day, journalist Petra Bartosiewicz filed a report from New York City:

❝I am at the foot of the smoking wreck. . . . Buildings on either side rise silent and black, their windows shattered. . . . Everywhere is frantic activity. . . . Firefighters fan out in teams, sliding across the girders and beams, prodding the ground, looking for bodies, guided only by the smell of death. But the odor is everywhere, and there are many false alarms—"Got one here, chief!"—a team descends, search dogs are brought in, a frantic digging ensues, yielding nothing, a scrap of skin, a leg. . . . Many firefighters have succumbed to exhaustion and lie sprawled on makeshift cots. . . . I, too, am tired . . . [and] my bones feel ground, my nose numb from dust and asbestos.❞

—**quoted in** *The Atlantic Online,* **September 19, 2001**

September 11, 2001

The airplanes that hit the World Trade Center and the Pentagon did not do so accidentally. Hijackers deliberately crashed them into the buildings. Hijackers also seized a fourth airplane, but some of the passengers heroically resisted the hijacking, causing the plane to crash in western Pennsylvania.

1 FOCUS

Section Overview
This section focuses on the U.S. effort to end international terrorism.

BELLRINGER
Skillbuilder Activity

Project transparency and have students answer the question.

Available as a blackline master.

Daily Focus Skills Transparency 34–5

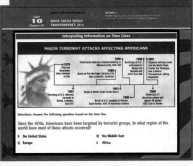

Guide to Reading

Answers to Graphic: U.S. support of wealthy countries and families that control Middle Eastern oil; the belief that Western influence undermines Islamic values and beliefs; new strict fundamentalist religious movements that hope to establish a pure Islamic society; American support for Israel

Preteaching Vocabulary
Have students write a short paragraph using all of the Key Terms and Names.

SECTION RESOURCES

Reproducible Masters
• Reproducible Lesson Plan 34–5
• Daily Lecture and Discussion Notes 34–5
• Guided Reading Activity 34–5
• Section Quiz 34–5
• Reading Essentials and Study Guide 34–5
• Performance Assessment Activities and Rubrics

Transparencies
• Daily Focus Skills Transparency 34–5

Multimedia
 Interactive Tutor Self-Assessment CD-ROM
 ExamView® Pro Testmaker CD-ROM
 Presentation Plus! CD-ROM
 TeacherWorks™ CD-ROM
 Audio Program

2 TEACH

Daily Lecture and Discussion Notes 34–5

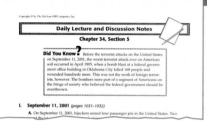

Interpreting a Photograph

Show students a picture of the flag raising at Iwo Jima and ask them how it compares to the picture of firefighters raising the flag at the site of the World Trade Center attack. **L1**

Picturing **History**

Answer: September 11, 2001

Ask: Why do you think terrorists chose the World Trade Center and the Pentagon as targets? *(Students' answers will vary. Students should recognize that the World Trade Center was a symbol of American economic power and the Pentagon is a symbol of U.S. military power.)*

✓ Reading Check

Answer: to instill fear in people and to frighten their governments into changing their policies

Construction on the Pentagon began on September 11, 1941, exactly 60 years before terrorists attacked.

Picturing **History**

Transcending Tragedy Although the destruction of the World Trade Center (lower right) and the attack on the Pentagon (right) shocked Americans, people responded rapidly to the crisis. Across the nation, images such as that of firefighters raising a flag in the ruins of the World Trade Center (left) inspired Americans. Many lined up to donate blood. Others raised money and collected food, blankets, and other supplies for the victims and rescue workers. On what date did the attacks occur?

All 266 passengers and crew members on the four planes were killed. Another 125 people died in the Pentagon. In New York City, thousands of people died or could not be located amid the massive piles of rubble. More Americans were killed in the attacks than died at Pearl Harbor or on D-Day in World War II.

The attacks on the World Trade Center and the Pentagon were acts of terrorism. **Terrorism** is the use of violence by nongovernmental groups against civilians to achieve a political goal. Terrorist acts are intended to instill fear in people and to frighten their governments into changing their policies.

✓ Reading Check ▸ Summarizing What is the goal of terrorism?

Middle East Terrorism and the United States

Although there have been many incidents of terrorism in American history, most terrorist attacks on Americans since World War II have been carried out by Middle Eastern groups. The reason Middle Eastern terrorists have targeted Americans can be traced back to events early in the twentieth century.

As oil became important to the American economy in the 1920s, the United States invested heavily in the Middle East oil industry. This industry brought great wealth to the ruling families in some Middle Eastern kingdoms, but it left most of the people poor. Some became angry at the United States for supporting the wealthy kingdoms and families.

The growth of the oil industry increased the Middle East's contact with Western society. As Western ideas spread through the region, many devout Muslims—followers of the region's dominant religion—feared that their traditional values and beliefs were being weakened.

Throughout the Middle East, new movements arose calling for a strict interpretation of the Quran—the Muslim holy book—and a return to traditional Muslim religious laws. These movements sought to overthrow pro-Western governments in the Middle East and hoped to establish a pure Islamic society. Muslims who support these movements are referred to as fundamentalist militants. Although the vast majority of Muslims believe terrorism is contrary to their faith, militants began using terrorism to achieve their goals.

American support of Israel also angered many in the Middle East. In 1947 the UN divided British-controlled Palestine into two territories to provide a home for Jews. One part became Israel. The other part was to become a Palestinian state, but fighting between Israel and the Arab states in 1948 left this territory under the control of Israel, Jordan, and Egypt.

The Palestinians wanted their own nation. In the 1950s, they began staging guerrilla raids and terrorist attacks against Israel. Since the United States gave military and economic aid to Israel, it became the target of Muslim hostility. In the 1970s, several Middle Eastern nations realized they could fight Israel and the United States without going to war by providing terrorist groups with money, weapons, and training. When a government secretly supports terrorism, this is called

---

COOPERATIVE LEARNING ACTIVITY

Creating a Photo Essay Organize students into small groups. Have students use a variety of magazine and newspaper resources to find images of the effects of terrorism, either in the United States or abroad. Have the groups create a photo essay using these images and sentence captions to tell the story of terrorism today.

Use the rubric for a cooperative group management plan on pages 81–82 in the ***Performance Assessment Activities and Rubrics.***

state-sponsored terrorism. The governments of Libya, Syria, Iraq, and Iran have all sponsored terrorists.

✓ **Reading Check** **Explaining** What are the three main reasons certain Muslims became angry with the United States?

A New Terrorist Threat

In 1979 the Soviet Union invaded Afghanistan. Young Muslims from across the Middle East flocked to Afghanistan to join the struggle against the Soviets. Among them was a 22-year-old Muslim named **Osama bin Laden.**

Osama bin Laden came from one of Saudi Arabia's wealthiest families. He used his wealth to support the Afghan resistance. In 1988 he founded an organization called **al-Qaeda** (al KY·duh), or "the Base." Al-Qaeda recruited Muslims to fight in Afghanistan and channeled money and arms to the Afghan resistance.

Bin Laden's experience in Afghanistan convinced him that superpowers could be beaten. He also believed that Western ideas had contaminated Muslim society. He was outraged when Saudi Arabia allowed American troops on Saudi soil after Iraq invaded Kuwait. He transformed al-Qaeda into a terrorist organization and launched a series of attacks against Americans.

Operating first from Sudan and then from Afghanistan—now under the control of Muslim fundamentalists known as the Taliban—bin Laden dedicated himself and al-Qaeda to driving Westerners, and especially Americans, out of the Middle East. In 1998 he issued a statement calling on Muslims to kill Americans. Soon afterward, bin Laden's followers set off bombs at the American embassies in Kenya and Tanzania.

Shortly after these bombings, President Clinton ordered cruise missiles launched at terrorist facilities in Afghanistan and Sudan. Undeterred, bin Laden continued to target Americans. In late 1999, terrorists linked to al-Qaeda were arrested trying to smuggle explosives into the United States in an attempt to bomb Seattle, Washington. In October 2000, al-Qaeda terrorists crashed a boat loaded with explosives into the USS *Cole,* an American warship, while it was docked in the Middle Eastern country of Yemen.

✓ **Reading Check** **Explaining** Why was Osama bin Laden able to create a terrorist organization?

America Unites

The attack on the *Cole* and the attempted bombing of Seattle were overshadowed by the close presidential election of 2000 and the policies of President Bush's new administration. Then, on September 11, 2001, terrorists struck again, hijacking four American passenger planes and executing the most devastating terrorist attack in history.

Citizens Respond to the Crisis The attacks on the World Trade Center and the Pentagon shocked Americans, but they responded rapidly to the crisis. Firefighters and medical workers from other cities headed to New York to help. Across the nation, Americans lined up to donate blood. Others raised

A Nation Mourns In Las Vegas, Nevada (below), and across the nation, Americans gathered at candlelight vigils to remember the victims of the terrorist attacks of September 11, 2001, and to pray for their families.

Guided Reading Activity 34–5

Name _____ Date _____ Class _____

★ **Guided Reading Activity 34-5**

DIRECTIONS: Recalling Facts Read the section and answer the questions below. Refer to your textbook to write the answers.

1. What did hijackers do on September 11, 2001? _____

2. What is terrorism? _____

3. What role did America's need for oil play in Middle Eastern terrorism? _____

4. What do fundamentalist militant Muslims seek? _____

✓ **Reading Check**

Answer: U.S. support of wealthy countries and families, Western influence undermining traditional values and beliefs, and American support for Israel

Designing a Memorial Have students work in pairs to design a memorial to the victims and heroes of the September 11, 2001, terrorist attacks. Encourage students to use library and Internet resources to learn about the designs of other memorials. Have students note how symbolism is used in the design of many memorials. Have the pairs write a paragraph explaining the symbolism they chose for their memorial. **L2**

✓ **Reading Check**

Answer: He was wealthy and found a government willing to allow him to train his terrorists.

MEETING SPECIAL NEEDS

Visual/Spatial Have students create an illustrated time line of the terrorist attacks mentioned in this section. Instruct students to use illustrations and photographs from magazines and other sources to depict each event on the time line. Encourage students to add other related events. **L1** **ELL**

📂 Refer to *Inclusion for the High School Social Studies Classroom Strategies and Activities* in the TCR.

FYI

The American Red Cross, one of the leading relief agencies assisting victims of the terrorist attacks, came under fire when it announced that some of the money donated to the Liberty Fund would not be used for the relief effort surrounding the 2001 terrorist attacks. Criticized for misleading the public, the Red Cross launched a public relations campaign to reassure the public that all the money donated to the Liberty Fund would be used to help victims of the September 11 attacks.

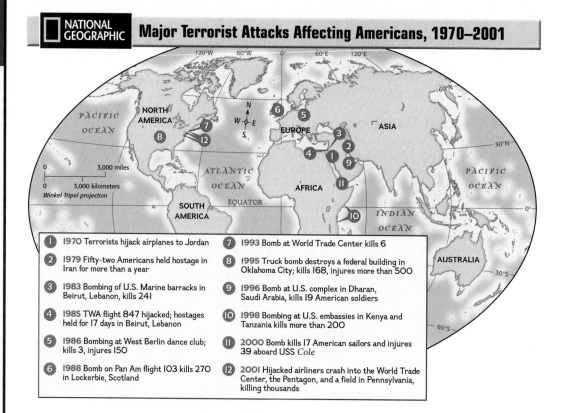

NATIONAL GEOGRAPHIC Major Terrorist Attacks Affecting Americans, 1970–2001

1. 1970 Terrorists hijack airplanes to Jordan
2. 1979 Fifty-two Americans held hostage in Iran for more than a year
3. 1983 Bombing of U.S. Marine barracks in Beirut, Lebanon, kills 241
4. 1985 TWA flight 847 hijacked; hostages held for 17 days in Beirut, Lebanon
5. 1986 Bombing at West Berlin dance club; kills 3, injures 150
6. 1988 Bomb on Pan Am flight 103 kills 270 in Lockerbie, Scotland
7. 1993 Bomb at World Trade Center kills 6
8. 1995 Truck bomb destroys a federal building in Oklahoma City; kills 168, injures more than 500
9. 1996 Bomb at U.S. complex in Dharan, Saudi Arabia, kills 19 American soldiers
10. 1998 Bombing at U.S. embassies in Kenya and Tanzania kills more than 200
11. 2000 Bomb kills 17 American sailors and injures 39 aboard USS *Cole*
12. 2001 Hijacked airliners crash into the World Trade Center, the Pentagon, and a field in Pennsylvania, killing thousands

money and collected food, blankets, and other supplies for victims and rescue workers. Businesses and charities donated millions of dollars, and popular American celebrities organized a telethon to raise funds. Within weeks, Americans donated over one billion dollars.

Everywhere across the nation, Americans put up flags to show their unity and resolve. They held candlelight vigils and prayer services as they searched for ways to help. Citizens in Atlanta provided lodging to people stranded at the airport. A marching band from Alabama drove to New York to play inspirational music for rescue workers. Cheerleaders in Virginia organized car washes to raise money for the Red Cross. An 11-year-old in Massachusetts baked nearly 1,500 cookies for firefighters and police officers. With all aircraft grounded, two medical workers in Dallas, Texas, drove all through the night to bring huge containers loaded with 70 square feet of human skin to burn victims in Washington, D.C.

If the terrorists had hoped the attacks would divide Americans, they were wrong. As the Reverend Billy Graham noted at a memorial service: "A tragedy like this could have torn our country apart. But instead it has united us and we have become a family."

A National Emergency The American government also responded quickly to the crisis. All civilian airliners were grounded. The armed forces were put on high alert. Fighter aircraft began patrolling the skies over major American cities. National Guard troops were deployed to airports to strengthen security, and the FBI began a massive investigation.

On September 14, President Bush declared a national emergency, and Congress voted nearly unanimously to authorize the use of force to fight the terrorists. Congress then approved a $40 billion emergency aid package for rescue and repair work and increased security measures.

While Congress worked on legislation to help the country recover, President Bush focused on responding to the attacks. Intelligence sources and FBI investigators quickly identified the attacks as the work of Osama bin Laden and the al-Qaeda network.

The government began planning a massive and comprehensive response to the terrorist attacks. The devastation in New York had alerted Americans to the grave danger terrorism posed. It had also shocked other nations, many of whom had also lost citizens in the World Trade Center. From all around the world came expressions of sympathy and support.

1034 CHAPTER 34 Into a New Century

INTERDISCIPLINARY CONNECTIONS ACTIVITY

Geography Provide students an outline map of Afghanistan. Have students create a series of maps showing the progress of Northern Alliance forces against the Taliban forces. Each map should show major cities and major physical features of the country. The maps should indicate the approximate areas controlled by the opposing sides on each date chosen. Encourage students to create a minimum of five maps, using October 7, 2001, as the date of the first map. Have students display the completed maps in time line fashion. **L2**

President Bush decided the time had come to end the threat of terrorism in the world. While Secretary of State Colin Powell began building an international coalition to support the United States, Secretary of Defense Donald Rumsfeld began deploying troops, aircraft, and warships to the Middle East.

The president then issued an ultimatum to the Taliban regime in Afghanistan, demanding they turn over bin Laden and his supporters and close all terrorist camps. The president also made it clear that although the war on terrorism would start by targeting al-Qaeda, it would not stop there. "It will not end," the president announced, "until every terrorist group of global reach has been found, stopped, and defeated."

The president also announced that the United States would no longer tolerate states that aided terrorists. "From this day forward," the president proclaimed, "any nation that continues to harbor or support terrorism will be regarded by the United States as a hostile regime." The war, President Bush warned Americans, would not end quickly and would cost more American lives, but it was a war Americans were now called to fight:

❛❛Great harm has been done to us. We have suffered great loss. And in our grief and anger we have found our mission and our moment. . . . Our Nation—this generation—will lift a dark threat of violence from our people and our future. . . .❝❝

—President George W. Bush, Address to Joint Session of Congress, September 20, 2001

✓ **Reading Check** **Explaining** How did American citizens respond to the terrorist attacks?

A New War Begins

Several major challenges confronted the United States as it began its war against terrorism. In a letter to the *New York Times,* Secretary of Defense Rumsfeld warned Americans that "this will be a war like none other our nation has faced." The enemy, he explained, "is a global network of terrorist organizations and their state sponsors, committed to denying free people the opportunity to live as they choose." Fighting terrorism would not be as simple as fighting the armies of an enemy nation. Military force would be used, but terrorism would be fought by other means as well.

Cutting Terrorist Funding One important way to fight terrorist organizations is to cut off their funding. On September 24, President Bush issued an executive order freezing the financial assets of several individuals and organizations suspected of terrorism. As information about terrorist groups increased, more names and organizations were added to the list.

Depriving terrorists of their funding, however, requires the cooperation of financial institutions in other countries. President Bush asked other nations to cooperate, but he also gave the Treasury Department the authority to freeze all assets and transactions in the United States of foreign banks that refused to cooperate. Within weeks, some 80 nations had issued orders freezing the assets of the organizations and individuals on the American list.

Fighting Terrorism At Home As part of his effort to protect the American people from further terrorist attacks, President Bush announced the creation of a

Writing an Essay Have students write a descriptive essay explaining how they think the terrorist attacks united Americans and brought a great sense of patriotism to the country. Then have them consider the many acts of heroism and sacrifice that followed the attacks. Have volunteers read their essays to the class. **L2**

✓ **Reading Check**

Answer: Americans were shocked by the attacks, but quickly responded by volunteering as relief workers, donating blood, and collecting supplies for victims and rescue workers. Within a few weeks of the attacks, Americans had raised more than one billion dollars toward the relief effort. Patriotism flourished and emotional support and encouragement were offered to victims and rescue workers.

you don't say...

Taliban The Taliban claimed to be Allah's followers desiring to bring pure Islamic government to Afghanistan. Some of their earlier successes in ending corruption and in dealing with cruel warlords won them much support in Afghanistan. However, as their control of the country became more complete, their repressive regime greatly burdened the people of Afghanistan, who were already weary from nearly 20 years of war.

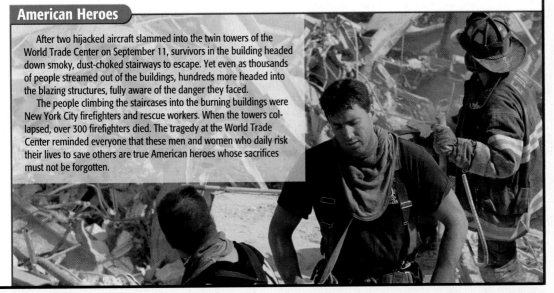

American Heroes

After two hijacked aircraft slammed into the twin towers of the World Trade Center on September 11, survivors in the building headed down smoky, dust-choked stairways to escape. Yet even as thousands of people streamed out of the buildings, hundreds more headed into the blazing structures, fully aware of the danger they faced.

The people climbing the staircases into the burning buildings were New York City firefighters and rescue workers. When the towers collapsed, over 300 firefighters died. The tragedy at the World Trade Center reminded everyone that these men and women who daily risk their lives to save others are true American heroes whose sacrifices must not be forgotten.

CRITICAL THINKING ACTIVITY

Analyzing Have students find and bring to class an example of an article that uses both primary and secondary sources to tell the story of the September 11, 2001, terrorist attacks or of the massive relief effort that followed. Have students write a one-page summary of their article identifying the various points of view and explaining how the writer used a variety of source material to paint a picture of the events. As a class, discuss the importance of both types of sources in explaining historical events. **L2**

Creating a Fact Sheet Have small groups of students create fact sheets about bioterrorism, including information about possible threats, known treatments, and common sense precautions recommended to Americans to reduce the threat of a biological attack. Encourage students to include statistics about the risks. Remind the groups that they should use good sources for their information. Have students submit a separate bibliography citing sources used. **L2**

3 ASSESS

Assign Section 5 Assessment as homework or as an in-class activity.

🖸 Have students use the **Interactive Tutor Self-Assessment CD-ROM.**

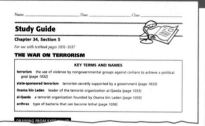
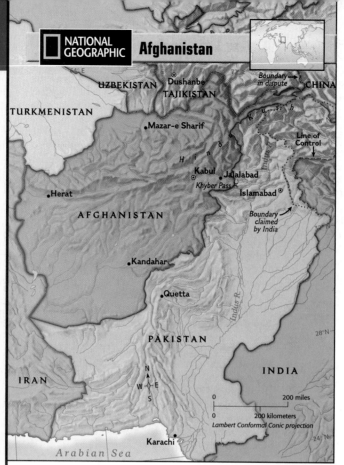

NATIONAL GEOGRAPHIC **Afghanistan**

Map labels: TURKMENISTAN, UZBEKISTAN, Dushanbe, TAJIKISTAN, CHINA, Boundary in dispute, Mazar-e Sharif, Line of Control, Herat, Kabul, Jalalabad, Khyber Pass, Islamabad, AFGHANISTAN, Boundary claimed by India, Kandahar, Quetta, PAKISTAN, IRAN, INDIA, 28°N, Indus R., Karachi, Arabian Sea, 24°N

0 — 200 miles / 0 — 200 kilometers / Lambert Conformal Conic projection

new federal agency—the Office of Homeland Security. The agency's mission was to centralize and coordinate the dozens of federal agencies and departments working to prevent terrorism. He then appointed Pennsylvania governor Tom Ridge to serve as the agency's director.

The president also asked Congress to pass legislation to help law enforcement agencies track down terrorist suspects. Drafting the legislation took time, as Congress struggled over how to balance Americans' Fourth Amendment protections against unreasonable search and seizure with the need to increase security.

President Bush signed the new antiterrorist bill into law in late October 2001. In cases involving terrorism, the new law permitted secret searches to avoid tipping off suspects and allowed authorities to obtain a single nationwide search warrant that could be used in any jurisdiction. The law also made it easier to wiretap suspects and allowed authorities to track Internet communications and seize voice mail.

Bioterrorism Strikes America As the nation struggled to cope with the attacks on the Pentagon and the World Trade Center, another attack began. On October 5, 2001, an editor at the *Sun* newspaper in Boca Raton, Florida, died after being infected with anthrax.

Anthrax is a type of bacteria. It grows in soil and often infects sheep, cows, and horses. In its natural form, it is very difficult for people to contract. It can be cured with antibiotics, but if left undetected, it can become lethal.

During the Cold War, the United States and the Soviet Union used anthrax to create biological weapons. When combined with other chemicals, anthrax can be made into tiny spores that float in the air and are easy to inhale. In the 1980s, the Iraqi government also developed weapons using anthrax. As the technology spread, fears grew that terrorist groups were also trying to make or acquire anthrax.

At first authorities thought the anthrax case in Florida was an isolated incident. Soon afterward, however, anthrax was discovered at the network news offices of NBC, CBS, and ABC, and at the *New York Post.* In Washington, a letter containing anthrax spores arrived at Senate majority leader Tom Daschle's office. It was now clear that terrorists were using the mail to spread anthrax.

Traces of anthrax were soon discovered at the Supreme Court, the CIA, and buildings used by the Senate and the House of Representatives. Several post offices also tested positive for anthrax. A number of postal workers contracted the disease, and two died.

The discovery of bioterrorism in the United States alarmed Americans. Across the country, people reported any suspicious substance they encountered. Special **hazmat**—hazardous materials—teams worked around the clock in biohazard suits and gas masks to check the reports. Although most Americans did not panic, some bought gas masks, pressured their doctors for antibiotics, and took precautions when opening their mail. Meanwhile, the FBI and intelligence agencies continued to investigate who had made and distributed the anthrax.

War in Afghanistan On October 7, 2001, the United States launched the first military operation of the war on terrorism. Warplanes began bombing targets in Afghanistan. In a televised address to the nation, President Bush explained that he had ordered the military to attack al-Qaeda's camps and the Taliban's military forces. He explained that Islam and the

EXTENDING THE CONTENT

Women's Rights On November 17, 2001, First Lady Laura Bush used the president's weekly radio address to deliver a message of support and hope for the women and children of Afghanistan. In the address she said: ". . . Fighting brutality against women and children is not the expression of a specific culture; it is the acceptance of our common humanity—a commitment shared by people of good will on every continent. . . . The fight against terrorism is also a fight for the rights and dignity of women."

Afghan people were not the enemy, and he announced that the United States would begin dropping food, medicine, and other supplies to Afghan refugees.

While American warplanes bombed the Taliban's forces, the United States began sending military aid to a coalition of Afghan groups known as the Northern Alliance, or the United Front. The Northern Alliance had been fighting a civil war with the Taliban for several years. American special forces also entered Afghanistan to advise the Northern Alliance and identify targets for American aircraft.

The American bombing campaign quickly shattered the Taliban's defenses. The Northern Alliance then launched a massive attack on Taliban lines. By early December, the Taliban government had collapsed, and surviving Taliban and al-Qaeda forces had fled to the mountains of Afghanistan.

After the Taliban fled, the United States and its allies worked with Afghan leaders to create an interim, or temporary, government to run the country. Nations around the world pledged more than $4 billion to help Afghanistan. Thousands of American and allied troops began arriving in Afghanistan to act as peacekeepers and to hunt for al-Qaeda terrorists.

American officials had expected al-Qaeda to hide in the caves that honeycomb Afghanistan's mountains. President Bush promised "sustained, comprehensive and relentless operations to drive them out and bring them to justice." Meanwhile, other American troops headed to the Philippines, Yemen, and the republic of Georgia to train local forces to fight terrorists hiding in

Patriotism Surges Across the United States, many Americans, like these preschoolers in Avon, Colorado, expressed their love of country in the wake of the terrorist attacks on New York City and Washington, D.C.

these countries. As the president had warned earlier, the war against terrorism was only beginning.

> 66 Today we focus on Afghanistan, but the battle is broader. Every nation has a choice to make. In this conflict, there is no neutral ground. If any government sponsors the outlaws and killers of innocents, they have become outlaws and murderers, themselves. And they will take that lonely path at their own peril. . . . The battle is now joined on many fronts. We will not waver; we will not tire; we will not falter; and we will not fail. Peace and freedom will prevail. Thank you. May God continue to bless America. 99

— President George W. Bush, Address to the Nation, October 7, 2001

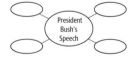 **Reading Check** **Outlining** What steps did the president take in response to the terrorist attacks?

SECTION 5 ASSESSMENT

Checking for Understanding
1. **Define:** terrorism, state-sponsored terrorism.
2. **Identify:** Osama bin Laden, al-Qaeda, anthrax.
3. **Explain** how the United States responded to the attacks on New York City and Washington, D.C.

Reviewing Themes
4. **Global Connections** Why does American foreign policy anger Islamic fundamentalists in the Middle East?

Critical Thinking
5. **Interpreting** What factors have contributed to the rise of Middle Eastern terrorist groups?
6. **Organizing** Use a graphic organizer similar to the one below to list the main ideas of President Bush's address to Congress on the terrorist attacks.

President Bush's Speech

Analyzing Visuals
7. **Examining Maps** Study the map of Afghanistan on page 1036. Why do you think al-Qaeda used Afghanistan as a base?

Writing About History
8. **Persuasive Writing** The attacks on New York City and Washington, D.C., convinced many Americans that more security was needed, even if it meant giving up some freedoms. Write a letter to a newspaper explaining why you are for or against increased security.

Reteach
Have students describe the development of Middle East terrorism.

Enrich
Invite interested students to report on the U.S. efforts to end international terrorism. Have students share successes, failures, and ongoing challenges.

✔ Reading Check
Answer: He declared a national emergency; requested a $40 billion emergency aid package; formed an international coalition against terrorism; deployed American troops; and issued an ultimatum against terrorism and states sponsoring or aiding terrorists.

4 CLOSE
Have students explain America's response to the terrorist attacks on New York and the Pentagon.

SECTION 5 ASSESSMENT ANSWERS

1. Terms are in blue.
2. Osama bin Laden (p. 1033), al-Qaeda (p. 1033), anthrax (p. 1036)
3. citizens donated money and supplies; the government vowed to end terrorism and targeted al-Qaeda and the Taliban regime in Afghanistan

4. U.S. support for Israel and for wealthy ruling families in some Middle Eastern countries angers Islamic fundamentalists.
5. increased contact with Western society, the growth of Islamic fundamentalism, and countries that provide terrorists with money, weapons, and training

6. war on terrorism, target governments that support or harbor terrorists, war is a long-term commitment and a national priority
7. Osama bin Laden founded al-Qaeda in Afghanistan. Its mountainous terrain has many caves from which to operate.
8. Students' letters will vary.

CHAPTER 34 ASSESSMENT and ACTIVITIES

Reviewing Key Terms
Students' answers will vary. The pages where the words appear in the text are shown in parentheses.

1. **microprocessor** (p. 1013)
2. **software** (p. 1013)
3. **telecommute** (p. 1013)
4. **Internet** (p. 1014)
5. **perjury** (p. 1020)
6. **ethnic cleansing** (p. 1020)
7. **trade deficit** (p. 1023)
8. **euro** (p. 1023)
9. **nuclear proliferation** (p. 1025)
10. **global warming** (p. 1025)
11. **chad** (p. 1028)
12. **strategic defense** (p. 1029)
13. **terrorism** (p. 1032)
14. **state-sponsored terrorism** (p. 1033)

Reviewing Key Facts
15. ENIAC (p. 1012), Silicon Valley (p. 1013), AmeriCorps (p. 1017), Contract with America (p. 1018), Kenneth Starr (p. 1020), North American Free Trade Agreement (p. 1023), Kyoto Protocol (p. 1025), Al Gore (p. 1027), George W. Bush (p. 1027), Ralph Nader (p. 1027), Osama bin Laden (p. 1033), al-Qaeda (p. 1033)
16. connected employees in offices together, modernized record-keeping, increased productivity, and streamlined research avenues
17. The mapping of the human genome made it possible to study and manipulate genes and cells at the molecular level. Other advances resulted in new medicines, animal growth hormones, new industrial chemicals, and genetically engineered plants.

Reviewing Key Terms
On a sheet of paper, use each of these terms in a sentence.

1. microprocessor
2. software
3. telecommute
4. Internet
5. perjury
6. ethnic cleansing
7. trade deficit

8. euro
9. nuclear proliferation
10. global warming
11. chad
12. strategic defense
13. terrorism
14. state-sponsored terrorism

Reviewing Key Facts

15. **Identify:** ENIAC, Silicon Valley, AmeriCorps, Contract with America, Kenneth Starr, NAFTA, Kyoto Protocol, Al Gore, George W. Bush, Ralph Nader, Osama bin Laden, al-Qaeda.
16. How did compact computers transform the workplace?
17. What advances in biotechnology occurred in the 1990s?
18. After his election in 1992, how did President Clinton propose to strengthen the nation's economy?
19. What regional trade blocs were formed in the 1990s to increase international trade?
20. Which state was significant in the 2000 presidential election?

Critical Thinking

21. **Analyzing Themes: Global Connections** What foreign-policy challenges did President Clinton face? Do you think he handled the situations effectively? Why or why not?

22. **Evaluating** What developments in the Middle East explain the rise of terrorist groups that want to attack Americans?
23. **Analyzing Points of View** Read the excerpt below about global warming, and then answer the questions that follow.

66 The world is getting warmer, and by the end of the 21st century could warm by another 6 degrees Celsius (10.8 degrees Fahrenheit). . . . And climate scientists at the heart of the research are now convinced that human action is to blame for some or most of this warming. . . .

Everywhere climatologists look—at tree-ring patterns, fossil successions in rock strata, ocean-floor corings . . . they see evidence of dramatic shifts from cold to hot to cold again. . . . None of these ancient shifts can be blamed on humans. . . . There is still room for argument about the precise role of the sun or other natural cycles in the contribution to global warming. . . . Richard S. Lindzen, a leading meteorologist at the Massachusetts Institute of Technology said . . . the picture of a consensus about global warming was 'misleading to the public and even to scientists. . . .' But most climate scientists . . . now believe that the climate is being influenced by human beings. 99

—from *World Press Review*, February 2001

a. According to the article, what two points of view exist about global warming?
b. Why is the debate on global warming important?

Chapter Summary

The Technological Revolution
- Personal computers grow faster and more powerful.
- Communications deregulation expands cellular phone usage.
- The Internet provides a worldwide network of information.
- Biotechnology research increases knowledge of human genetics.

The Clinton Years
- A new global economy emerges based on regional trade blocs.
- The ozone layer and global warming become major environmental issues.
- Clinton and Congress cut spending; reform welfare and health care.
- U.S. economy grows rapidly; federal budget is balanced.
- U.S. tries to end violence in Haiti, the Middle East, and the Balkans.
- Scandal and impeachment tarnish the Clinton administration.

Bush Takes Office
- 2000 election results disputed in Florida; Supreme Court resolves dispute; George W. Bush becomes president.
- Bush focuses on cutting taxes, reforming education, and working on energy problems.
- Terrorists destroy the World Trade Center and attack the Pentagon.
- Bush organizes a global coalition and launches a new war on terrorism.

18. by lowering interest rates and reducing federal deficits
19. North American Free Trade Agreement, European Union, Asia Pacific Economic Cooperation
20. The outcome in Florida determined the winner of the election of 2000.

Critical Thinking
21. Foreign policy challenges included restoring Haiti's president, ethnic cleansing in Bosnia and Kosovo, and

ongoing tensions in the Middle East. Students' evaluations of Clinton's effectiveness should be supported with examples and sound reasoning.

22. American support for Israel; American investment in the oil industry in the Middle East; belief of some Muslims that American support of wealthy oil-producing countries increased Western influence and undermined traditional values and beliefs

24. Categorizing Complete the graphic organizer below by listing changes in communications, politics, the economy, and population that occurred in the United States by the end of the 1900s.

	Change
Communications	
Politics	
Economy	
Population	

Practicing Skills

25. Reading a Cartogram Create a cartogram that reflects the importance of each state in the Electoral College. Research the number of votes held by each state, and alter the size of each state to roughly show that state's number of available votes. Create questions that refer to the information you present in your cartogram.

Chapter Activities

26. Applying Chronology Skills Absolute chronology refers to specific dates, while relative chronology looks at when something occurred with reference to when other things occurred. Practice relative chronology by listing the presidents of the twentieth century in the order they served as president. Then practice absolute chronology by giving the dates of their terms in office.

27. Researching Election Results Study the 2000 election map and chart on page 1028. Then use library or Internet resources to research statistics on the 1996 presidential election. Using the 2000 election map and chart as a guide, create a similar thematic map and chart of the 1996 election. Create questions about your map and chart that would help a classmate understand the data you have compiled.

Writing Activity

28. Informative Writing Research the changing roles of the federal and state governments as a result of recent legislative reforms, including gun control and welfare reforms. Based on your research, write a short paper predicting how the role of the federal government and the state governments might change in order to implement the legislative programs. Present your predictions to the class.

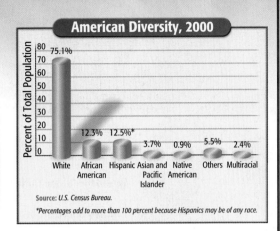

American Diversity, 2000

Percent of Total Population

- White: 75.1%
- African American: 12.3%
- Hispanic: 12.5%*
- Asian and Pacific Islander: 3.7%
- Native American: 0.9%
- Others: 5.5%
- Multiracial: 2.4%

Source: *U.S. Census Bureau.*

*Percentages add to more than 100 percent because Hispanics may be of any race.

Geography and History

29. The graph above shows the diverse population of the United States at the beginning of the new century. Study the graph and answer the questions below.

a. Interpreting Graphs Why is getting accurate data on the Hispanic population difficult?

b. Making Generalizations How will population diversity affect government in the future?

The Princeton Review

Standardized Test Practice

Directions: Choose the phrase that best completes the following sentence.

The Contract with America involved

F a commitment by Russia to eliminate land-based nuclear weapons.

G a campaign promise by President Clinton to create a national health care system for all Americans.

H a legislative agenda promoted by the Republican Party in 1994.

J programs intended to increase the size and readiness of the military.

Test-Taking Tip: This question requires that you remember details of a specific program. Use the process of elimination if you are unsure. Does the Contract with America sound like a foreign policy agreement between two countries?

HISTORY Online

Have students visit the Web site at tav.glencoe.com to review Chapter 34 and take the Self-Check Quiz.

27. Students' maps and questions will vary. Encourage students to work with a partner to share their maps and questions.

Writing Activity

28. Students' reports should include specific predictions about the federal and state legislative programs.

Geography and History

29. a. Students should note that some Hispanics would classify themselves in the Other or Multiracial categories. **b.** Students' answers will vary. Encourage students to give reasons for their answers.

The Princeton Review

Standardized Test Practice

Answer: H
Test-Taking Tip: Encourage students to put a face with the Contract with America. Even if they cannot remember Newt Gingrich's name they might remember that it was not a Clinton initiative and therefore they can eliminate answer G. The correct answer is H.

Bonus Question ?

Ask: Who were the Democratic and Republican presidential and vice presidential candidates in 2000? *(Democratic: Al Gore and Joseph Lieberman; Republican: George W. Bush and Richard Cheney)*

23. a. Some scientists believe human activity causes global warming. Others think natural factors may be involved. **b.** Global warming may alter the climate. If human activity is causing global warming, we may be able to stop it.

24. communications: Internet, wireless technology; politics: government shutdowns, impeachment; economy: global economic blocs, Internet, and world economy; population: racial diversity, aging, immigration

Practicing Skills

25. Cartograms will vary but should reflect the number of electoral votes in each state.

Chapter Activities

26. Students may present their lists in the form of a chart that contains the presidents' names in order in one column and their terms in a second column.

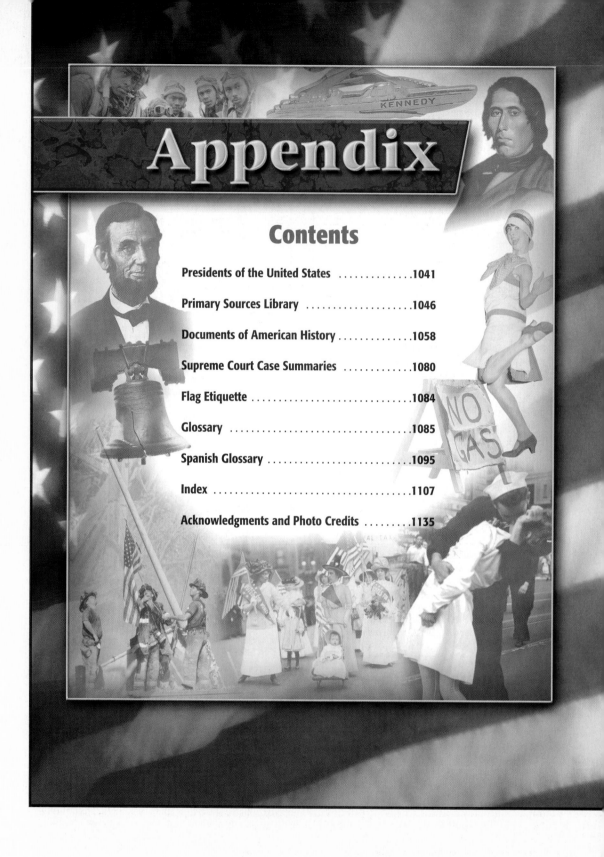

Appendix

Contents

Presidents of the United States

In this resource you will find portraits of the individuals who served as presidents of the United States, along with their occupations, political party affiliations, and other interesting facts.

**The Republican Party during this period developed into today's Democratic Party. Today's Republican Party originated in 1854.

1 George Washington

Presidential term: 1789–1797
Lived: 1732–1799
Born in: Virginia
Elected from: Virginia
Occupations: Soldier, Planter
Party: None
Vice President: John Adams

2 John Adams

Presidential term: 1797–1801
Lived: 1735–1826
Born in: Massachusetts
Elected from: Massachusetts
Occupations: Teacher, Lawyer
Party: Federalist
Vice President: Thomas Jefferson

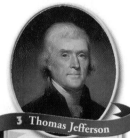

3 Thomas Jefferson

Presidential term: 1801–1809
Lived: 1743–1826
Born in: Virginia
Elected from: Virginia
Occupations: Planter, Lawyer
Party: Republican**
Vice Presidents: Aaron Burr, George Clinton

4 James Madison

Presidential term: 1809–1817
Lived: 1751–1836
Born in: Virginia
Elected from: Virginia
Occupation: Planter
Party: Republican**
Vice Presidents: George Clinton, Elbridge Gerry

5 James Monroe

Presidential term: 1817–1825
Lived: 1758–1831
Born in: Virginia
Elected from: Virginia
Occupation: Lawyer
Party: Republican**
Vice President: Daniel D. Tompkins

6 John Quincy Adams

Presidential term: 1825–1829
Lived: 1767–1848
Born in: Massachusetts
Elected from: Massachusetts
Occupation: Lawyer
Party: Republican**
Vice President: John C. Calhoun

7 Andrew Jackson

Presidential term: 1829–1837
Lived: 1767–1845
Born in: South Carolina
Elected from: Tennessee
Occupations: Lawyer, Soldier
Party: Democratic
Vice Presidents: John C. Calhoun, Martin Van Buren

8 Martin Van Buren

Presidential term: 1837–1841
Lived: 1782–1862
Born in: New York
Elected from: New York
Occupation: Lawyer
Party: Democratic
Vice President: Richard M. Johnson

9 William H. Harrison

Presidential term: 1841
Lived: 1773–1841
Born in: Virginia
Elected from: Ohio
Occupations: Soldier, Planter
Party: Whig
Vice President: John Tyler

10 John Tyler

Presidential term: 1841–1845
Lived: 1790–1862
Born in: Virginia
Elected as V.P. from: Virginia
Succeeded Harrison
Occupation: Lawyer
Party: Whig
Vice President: None

11 James K. Polk

Presidential term: 1845–1849
Lived: 1795–1849
Born in: North Carolina
Elected from: Tennessee
Occupation: Lawyer
Party: Democratic
Vice President: George M. Dallas

12 Zachary Taylor

Presidential term: 1849–1850
Lived: 1784–1850
Born in: Virginia
Elected from: Louisiana
Occupation: Soldier
Party: Whig
Vice President: Millard Fillmore

13 Millard Fillmore

Presidential term: 1850–1853
Lived: 1800–1874
Born in: New York
Elected as V.P. from: New York
Succeeded Taylor
Occupation: Lawyer
Party: Whig
Vice President: None

14 Franklin Pierce

Presidential term: 1853–1857
Lived: 1804–1869
Born in: New Hampshire
Elected from: New Hampshire
Occupation: Lawyer
Party: Democratic
Vice President: William R. King

15 James Buchanan

Presidential term: 1857–1861
Lived: 1791–1868
Born in: Pennsylvania
Elected from: Pennsylvania
Occupation: Lawyer
Party: Democratic
Vice President: John C. Breckinridge

16 Abraham Lincoln

Presidential term: 1861–1865
Lived: 1809–1865
Born in: Kentucky
Elected from: Illinois
Occupation: Lawyer
Party: Republican
Vice Presidents: Hannibal Hamlin, Andrew Johnson

17 Andrew Johnson

Presidential term: 1865–1869
Lived: 1808–1875
Born in: North Carolina
Elected as V.P. from: Tennessee
Succeeded Lincoln
Occupation: Tailor
Party: Republican
Vice President: None

18 Ulysses S. Grant

Presidential term: 1869–1877
Lived: 1822–1885
Born in: Ohio
Elected from: Illinois
Occupations: Farmer, Soldier
Party: Republican
Vice Presidents: Schuyler Colfax,
Henry Wilson

19 Rutherford B. Hayes

Presidential term: 1877–1881
Lived: 1822–1893
Born in: Ohio
Elected from: Ohio
Occupation: Lawyer
Party: Republican
Vice President: William A.
Wheeler

20 James A. Garfield

Presidential term: 1881
Lived: 1831–1881
Born in: Ohio
Elected from: Ohio
Occupations: Laborer, Professor
Party: Republican
Vice President: Chester A.
Arthur

21 Chester A. Arthur

Presidential term: 1881–1885
Lived: 1830–1886
Born in: Vermont
Elected as V.P. from: New York
Succeeded Garfield
Occupations: Teacher, Lawyer
Party: Republican
Vice President: None

22 Grover Cleveland

Presidential term: 1885–1889
Lived: 1837–1908
Born in: New Jersey
Elected from: New York
Occupation: Lawyer
Party: Democratic
Vice President: Thomas A.
Hendricks

23 Benjamin Harrison

Presidential term: 1889–1893
Lived: 1833–1901
Born in: Ohio
Elected from: Indiana
Occupation: Lawyer
Party: Republican
Vice President: Levi P. Morton

24 Grover Cleveland

Presidential term: 1893–1897
Lived: 1837–1908
Born in: New Jersey
Elected from: New York
Occupation: Lawyer
Party: Democratic
Vice Presidents: Adlai E.
Stevenson

25 William McKinley

Presidential term: 1897–1901
Lived: 1843–1901
Born in: Ohio
Elected from: Ohio
Occupations: Teacher, Lawyer
Party: Republican
Vice Presidents: Garret Hobart,
Theodore Roosevelt

26 Theodore Roosevelt

Presidential term: 1901–1909
Lived: 1858–1919
Born in: New York
Elected as V.P. from: New York
Succeeded McKinley
Occupations: Historian, Rancher
Party: Republican
Vice President: Charles W.
  Fairbanks

27 William H. Taft

Presidential term: 1909–1913
Lived: 1857–1930
Born in: Ohio
Elected from: Ohio
Occupation: Lawyer
Party: Republican
Vice President: James S.
  Sherman

28 Woodrow Wilson

Presidential term: 1913–1921
Lived: 1856–1924
Born in: Virginia
Elected from: New Jersey
Occupation: College Professor
Party: Democratic
Vice President: Thomas R.
  Marshall

29 Warren G. Harding

Presidential term: 1921–1923
Lived: 1865–1923
Born in: Ohio
Elected from: Ohio
Occupations: Newspaper Editor,
  Publisher
Party: Republican
Vice President: Calvin Coolidge

30 Calvin Coolidge

Presidential term: 1923–1929
Lived: 1872–1933
Born in: Vermont
Elected as V.P. from:
  Massachusetts
Succeeded Harding
Occupation: Lawyer
Party: Republican
Vice President: Charles G. Dawes

31 Herbert C. Hoover

Presidential term: 1929–1933
Lived: 1874–1964
Born in: Iowa
Elected from: California
Occupation: Engineer
Party: Republican
Vice President: Charles Curtis

32 Franklin D. Roosevelt

Presidential term: 1933–1945
Lived: 1882–1945
Born in: New York
Elected from: New York
Occupation: Lawyer
Party: Democratic
Vice Presidents: John N. Garner,
  Henry A. Wallace, Harry S
  Truman

33 Harry S Truman

Presidential term: 1945–1953
Lived: 1884–1972
Born in: Missouri
Elected as V.P. from: Missouri
Succeeded Roosevelt
Occupations: Clerk, Farmer
Party: Democratic
Vice President: Alben W.
  Barkley

34 Dwight D. Eisenhower

Presidential term: 1953–1961
Lived: 1890–1969
Born in: Texas
Elected from: New York
Occupation: Soldier
Party: Republican
Vice President: Richard M.
  Nixon

35 John F. Kennedy

Presidential term: 1961–1963
Lived: 1917–1963
Born in: Massachusetts
Elected from: Massachusetts
Occupations: Author, Reporter
Party: Democratic
Vice President: Lyndon B. Johnson

36 Lyndon B. Johnson

Presidential term: 1963–1969
Lived: 1908–1973
Born in: Texas
Elected as V.P. from: Texas Succeeded Kennedy
Occupation: Teacher
Party: Democratic
Vice President: Hubert H. Humphrey

37 Richard M. Nixon

Presidential term: 1969–1974
Lived: 1913–1994
Born in: California
Elected from: New York
Occupation: Lawyer
Party: Republican
Vice Presidents: Spiro T. Agnew, Gerald R. Ford

38 Gerald R. Ford

Presidential term: 1974–1977
Lived: 1913–
Born in: Nebraska
Appointed as V.P. upon Agnew's resignation; succeeded Nixon
Occupation: Lawyer
Party: Republican
Vice President: Nelson A. Rockefeller

39 James E. Carter, Jr.

Presidential term: 1977–1981
Lived: 1924–
Born in: Georgia
Elected from: Georgia
Occupations: Business, Farmer
Party: Democratic
Vice President: Walter F. Mondale

40 Ronald W. Reagan

Presidential term: 1981–1989
Lived: 1911–
Born in: Illinois
Elected from: California
Occupations: Actor, Lecturer
Party: Republican
Vice President: George H.W. Bush

41 George H.W. Bush

Presidential term: 1989–1993
Lived: 1924–
Born in: Massachusetts
Elected from: Texas
Occupation: Business
Party: Republican
Vice President: J. Danforth Quayle

42 William J. Clinton

Presidential term: 1993–2001
Lived: 1946–
Born in: Arkansas
Elected from: Arkansas
Occupation: Lawyer
Party: Democratic
Vice President: Albert Gore, Jr.

43 George W. Bush

Presidential term: 2001–
Lived: 1946–
Born in: Connecticut
Elected from: Texas
Occupation: Business
Party: Republican
Vice President: Richard B. Cheney

Introduction

Have students complete the activities that follow to familiarize themselves with the types of primary sources.

Printed Publications

To help students analyze printed publications, instruct students to read the first two paragraphs under "Declaration of Natural Rights" in the Declaration of Independence (page 134). Discuss this passage in class, using questions such as: Is this a primary or secondary source? What is the main idea of the passage? What do you think this passage means?

Oral Histories

Work together with an English or Language Arts teacher to help students complete the following oral history activity. Interview a relative or friend who is much older than you to see how his or her life was different from yours when he or she was a teenager. Create a list of interview questions such as: What regular chores did you have to do? What did you and your friends talk about? What were your classes like in school?

Ask students to provide a transcript, or written record, of the interview and discuss their findings with the class.

Primary Sources Library

TABLE OF CONTENTS

Using Primary Sources

Primary sources are written or artistic testimony to an era in history or to an important development. They can also be objects of daily life, reflecting how people lived and thought at a certain time. Perhaps a primary source represents the ideas of an industrial leader like Andrew Carnegie, who helped shape the American economy. Perhaps the source is a soldier's poem or the autobiography of a migrant worker.

Reading primary sources is important because it is an excellent way to understand how and why people believed and acted as they did in the past. While many people might have written down their stories or beliefs, the sources chosen here are from witnesses who were close to events or especially sensitive to them.

Opera glasses, late 1800s

1046

Checking Your Sources

When you read primary or secondary sources, you should analyze them to figure out if they are dependable or reliable. Historians usually prefer primary sources to secondary sources, but both can be reliable or unreliable, depending on the following factors.

Time Span

With primary sources, it is important to consider how long after the event occurred the primary source was written. Generally, the longer the time span between the event and the account, the less reliable the account. As time passes, people often forget details and fill in gaps with events that never took place. Although we like to think we remember things exactly as they happened, the fact is we often remember them as we wanted them to occur.

Reliability

Another factor to consider when evaluating a primary source is the writer's background and reliability. First, try to determine how this person knows about what he or she is writing. How much does he or she know? Is the writer being truthful? Is the account convincing?

Teacher Notes

After studying the introduction to the Primary Sources Library, students should be able to meet the following objectives:

- explain how to interpret primary sources.
- explain the difference between primary sources and secondary sources.
- identify the different types of primary sources.
- understand that primary sources offer a unique view of people and events in a particular era.

Opinions

When evaluating a primary source, you should also decide whether the account has been influenced by emotion, opinion, or exaggeration. Writers can have reasons to distort the truth to suit their personal purposes. Ask yourself: Why did the person write the account? Do any key words or expressions reveal the author's emotions or opinions? You may wish to compare the account with one written by another witness to the event. If the two accounts differ, ask yourself why.

Interpreting Primary Sources

To help you analyze a primary source, use the following steps:

- **Examine the origins of the document.**
  You need to determine if it is a primary source.

- **Find the main ideas.**
  Read the document and summarize the main ideas in your own words. These ideas may be fairly easy to identify in newspapers and journals, for example, but are much more difficult to find in poetry.

- **Reread the document.**
  Difficult ideas are not always easily understood on the first reading.

- **Use a variety of resources.**
  Form the habit of using dictionaries, encyclopedias, and maps. These resources are tools to help you discover new ideas and knowledge, and they can be used to check the validity of various sources.

Log book from Lewis and Clark expedition

Classifying Primary Sources

Primary sources fall into different categories:

 **Printed Publications**

Printed publications include books such as biographies and autobiographies. Printed publications also include newspapers and magazines.

 **Songs & Poems**

Songs and poems include works that express personal thoughts and feelings or political or religious beliefs of the writer, often using rhyming and rhythmic language.

 **Visual Materials**

Visual materials include a wide range of forms: original paintings, drawings, and sculpture; photographs; film; and maps.

 **Oral Histories**

Oral histories are chronicles, memoirs, myths, and legends that are passed along from one generation to another by word of mouth. Interviews are another form of oral history.

 **Personal Records**

Personal records are accounts of events kept by an individual who is a participant in or witness to these events. Personal records include diaries, journals, and letters.

 Artifacts

Artifacts are objects such as tools or ornaments. Artifacts present information about a particular culture or a stage of technological development.

 **Songs & Poems**

Ask students to write a poem about a happy event in their lives. Suggest that the poem be in a standard form such as a limerick, haiku, or sonnet.

Personal Records

Ask students to describe what it might be like to witness an important public event. Provide the following guidelines: Write a journal entry describing the event. Begin by giving an overview of the event, including some objective facts. Then make the event personal by focusing on your own opinions or feelings.

Visual Materials

Help students create a poster showing how your community or state changed during the 1900s. Students may use photographs or original drawings.

Artifacts

To help students analyze artifacts, provide the following instructions: Find a primary source from your past such as a photograph, a report card, or a letter. Bring this source to class and explain what it shows about the time from which it comes.

Teacher Notes

Through the study of the selections in the Primary Sources Library and their accompanying questions, students should be able to:

- find main ideas in the selections.

- analyze information in a variety of written texts in order to make inferences and generalizations.

- provide an interpretation of the material in their own words.

Unit Link

Use the primary source selections on pages 1048–1049 to accompany Unit 1, "Three Worlds Meet," and Unit 2, "Creating a Nation."

Reinforcing Vocabulary

Review the **Reader's Dictionary** on this page with students to be sure they understand any unfamiliar terms. Write *lamentable* on the board. Ask students to use the term in a sentence.

Background Information

Purpose Explain that purpose is the intent to explain, persuade, or inform. An author may have more than one purpose. Have students read the Letter of Don Antonio de Otermin on Popé's revolt in 1680. **Ask:** What do you think the purpose of the letter is? (*Answers may vary. The letter attempts to explain why the Spaniards retreated in face of the revolt.*)

For use with Unit 1, "Three Worlds Meet," and Unit 2, "Creating a Nation"

From the Beginnings to American Nationhood

Europeans arriving in the Americas fought with Native Americans for control of the continent, just as British colonists later fought against the British government for their rights.

The first excerpt tells the story of the Pueblo people's revolt against their colonial Spanish rulers in what is today the American Southwest. Catholic missionaries had been trying to suppress the Pueblo religion. In 1680 a religious leader named Popé led a revolt which drove the Spanish from the region for a dozen years. The letter from the colonial governor asks for relief forces to be sent.

The second excerpt is from a speech of Patrick Henry (1736–1799). A lawyer by profession, Henry was already known for his eloquence from speeches in the Virginia House of Burgesses. He delivered this passionate plea at the second Virginia convention during a debate over whether to resist the British by force of arms.

Reader's Dictionary

don: honorary title for Spanish nobleman or gentleman

lamentable: sad; tragic

comport: to behave in a proper way

extenuate: to make excuses for or try to justify

Letter of Don Antonio de Otermin on Popé's revolt in 1680

Personal Records

My very reverend Father, Sir, and friend, most beloved Fray Francisco de Ayeta:

The time has come when, with tears in my eyes and deep sorrow in my heart, I commence to give an account of the lamentable tragedy, such as has never before happened in the world. . . .

On Tuesday, the 13th of the said month, at about nine o'clock in the morning, there came in sight of us in the suburb of Analco . . . all the Indians of the Tanos and Pecos nations and the Queres of San Marcos, armed and giving war whoops. As I learned that one of the Indians who was leading them was from the villa and had gone to join them shortly before, I sent some soldiers to summon him and tell him on my behalf that he could come to see me in entire safety, so that I might ascertain from him the purpose for which they were coming. Upon receiving this message he came to where I was, and . . . I asked him how it was that he had gone crazy too— being an Indian who spoke our language, was so intelligent, and had lived all his life in the villa among the Spaniards, where I had placed such confidence in him—and was now coming as a leader of the Indian rebels. He replied to me that they had elected him as their captain, and that they were carrying two banners, one white and the other red, and that the white one signified peace and the red one war. Thus if we wished to choose the white it must be upon our agreeing to leave the country, and if we chose the red, we must perish, because the rebels were numerous and we were very few;

Stone cross

EXTENDING THE CONTENT

Honoring Popé Statuary Hall in the U.S. Capitol's Old Hall of the House of Representatives contains statues of famous people from American history. According to a law which took effect on July 2, 1864, states may contribute up to two bronze or marble statues of citizens from their states known for their civic or military service. In 1999 New Mexico decided to honor Popé and his role as leader of the Pueblo peoples by commissioning a statue for Statuary Hall. It will be New Mexico's second, and final, contribution to Statuary Hall. The other New Mexican citizen accorded this honor is the late Senator Dennis Chavez.

Patrick Henry giving his speech in 1775

"Give Me Liberty or Give Me Death" by Patrick Henry (1775)

 Printed Publications

there was no alternative, inasmuch as they had killed so many religious and Spaniards.

On hearing this reply, I spoke to him very persuasively, to the effect that he and the rest of his followers were Catholic Christians, asking how they expected to live without the religious; and said that even though they had committed so many atrocities, still there was a remedy, for if they would return to obedience to his Majesty they would be pardoned; and that thus he should go back to this people and tell them in my name all that had been said to him, and persuade them to agree to it and to withdraw from where they were; and that he was to advise me of what they might reply. He came back . . . after a short time, saying that his people asked that all classes of Indians who were in our power be given up to them, both those in the service of the Spaniards and those of the Mexican nation of that suburb of Analco. He demanded also that his wife and children be given up to him, and likewise that all the Apache men and women whom the Spaniards had captured in war be turned over to them, inasmuch as some Apaches who were among them were asking for them. If these things were not done they would declare war immediately, and they were unwilling to leave the place where they were because they were awaiting the Taos, Percuries, and Teguas nations, with whose aid they would destroy us. . . .

The question before the House is one of awful moment to this country. For my own part, I consider it as nothing less than a question of freedom or slavery. . . . Mr. President, it is natural to man to indulge in the illusions of hope. We are apt to shut our eyes against a painful truth. . . .

I have but one lamp by which my feet are guided, and that is the lamp of experience. . . . And judging by the past, I wish to know what there has been in the conduct of the British ministry for the last ten years to justify those hopes with which gentlemen have been pleased to solace themselves and the House. . . . Ask yourselves how this gracious reception of our petition comports with those warlike preparations which cover our waters and darken our land. Are fleets and armies necessary to a work of love and reconciliation? . . . They are meant for us: they can be meant for no other. . . . And what have we to oppose to them? Shall we try argument? Sir, we have been trying that for the last ten years. . . . We must fight! . . .

They tell us, sir, that we are weak; unable to cope with so formidable an adversary. But when shall we be stronger? Will it be the next week, or the next year? Will it be when we are totally disarmed? . . . It is in vain, sir, to extenuate the matter. Gentlemen may cry, Peace, Peace—but there is no peace. . . . I know not what course others may take; but as for me, give me liberty or give me death!

 Analyzing Primary Sources

1. What Spanish actions triggered Popé's revolt?
2. Why does Don Otermin write that Popé has "gone crazy"?
3. What does Patrick Henry use to judge British intentions?
4. Why does Henry say it is foolish to wait longer before resisting?

Analyzing Primary Sources

1. Spanish missionaries had been trying to suppress the Pueblo religion.
2. because Popé left his life in the villa to become the captain of the Indian forces opposing the Spanish
3. He judges them based on British action over the previous ten years.
4. He argues that waiting longer will not improve their situation and implies that waiting will weaken them.

Team Teaching These selections may be implemented in a team-teaching context, in conjunction with English/Language Arts.

Unit Link

Use the primary source selections on pages 1050–1051 to accompany study of Unit 3, "The Young Republic," and Unit 4, "The Crisis of Union."

Reinforcing Vocabulary

Review the **Reader's Dictionary** on this page with students to be sure they understand any unfamiliar terms. Write *intrude* on the board. Ask students to use the term in a sentence.

Background Information

Persuasion Point out that persuasive writing attempts to sway the reader to think or act in a particular way. Ask students to identify the course of action promoted in each of the selections. Then ask: Which selection is the most persuasive? Why?

For use with Unit 3, "The Young Republic," and Unit 4, "The Crisis of Union"

From Dynamic Nationalism to Civil War

During the first half of the 19th century, the United States expanded its population and its borders. At the same time, the North and the South were developing their own identities. Each viewed the growing power of the federal government differently. Many Southerners believed increased federal power posed a threat to slavery.

The first excerpt is by New York City journalist John L. O'Sullivan. In 1845, in an article on Texas annexation, O'Sullivan coined the phrase "Manifest Destiny" to sum up his feelings about territorial expansion.

Northerner George F. Root wrote the "Battle Cry of Freedom," but the tune was so popular a Confederate version was written, too. Both versions are shown against the background of an Augustus Saint-Gaudens sculpture. The sculpture honors the 54th regiment of African American soldiers under the command of Robert Gould Shaw. The memorial is in Boston, Massachusetts, Shaw's hometown. The regiment's story was the subject of the movie Glory.

Reader's Dictionary

intrude: to force in or upon something without permission

Anglo-Saxon: term loosely used for any native whites in English-speaking countries

Dixie: nickname for the South, popularized in Daniel Emmett's song, "Land of Dixie"; term may derive from the French *dix* for "ten," referring to Louisiana ten-dollar bank notes

bonnie: fine, attractive, or fair

"Annexation" by John L. O'Sullivan (1845)

Printed Publications

It is time now for opposition to the Annexation of Texas to cease.... Texas is now ours.... Why, were other reasoning wanting in favor of ... the reception of Texas into the Union ..., it surely is to be found ... in the manner in which other nations have undertaken to intrude themselves into it ... for the avowed object of ... limiting our greatness and checking the fulfilment of our manifest destiny to overspread the continent allotted by Providence for the free development of our yearly multiplying millions.

... Texas has been absorbed into the Union in the inevitable fulfilment of the general law which is rolling our population westward; the connexion of which with that ratio of growth in population ... is too evident to leave us in doubt of the manifest design of Providence in regard to the occupation of this continent.

... Already the advance guard of the irresistible army of Anglo-Saxon emigration has begun to pour down upon (California), armed with the plough and the rifle, and marking its trail with schools and colleges, courts and representative halls, mills and meeting-houses.... The day is not distant when the Empires of the Atlantic and Pacific would again flow together into one.... The day cannot be distant which shall witness the conveyance of the representatives from Oregon and California to Washington within less time than a few years ago was devoted to a similar journey by those from Ohio....

The Origin of "Dixie" The well-known Confederate anthem "Dixie" is attributed to Daniel Emmett, of Knox County, Ohio, a musician who first played it in New York in 1859. However, there is evidence tracing it to the African American Snowden family, also of Knox County, who made their living by farming, but were best known as the "Snowden Family Band." The Snowdens were talented musicians and composers who performed popular songs throughout rural central Ohio from the 1850s to the early 1900s. The mother, Ellen Cooper Snowden, had been born into slavery in Maryland, moved to Ohio, and married, gaining her freedom. The lyrics can be read to reflect her experiences, moving from the "land of cotton" to a difficult life in the North. On the Snowden family gravestone is inscribed "They taught 'Dixie' to Dan Emmett."

"Battle Cry of Freedom"

BATTLE CRY OF FREEDOM

VERSE 3

Union: We will wel-come to our num-bers the loy-al, true and brave,
Confederate: They have laid down their — lives on the blood-y bat-tle field,

Shout-ing the bat-tle cry of Free-dom, And al-though he may be poor Not a
Shout, shout the bat-tle cry of Free-dom, Their_ mot-to is re-sis-tance, To

man shall be a slave, Shout-ing the bat-tle cry of Free-dom
ty-rants we'll not yield! Shout, shout the bat-tle cry of Free-dom

CHORUS

The Un-ion for-ev-er, Hur-rah, boys, Hur-rah!
Our Dix-ie for-ev-er, she's never at a loss

Down with the trai-tor, up with the star; While we ral-ly 'round the flag boys,
Down with the eag-le, up with the cross. We'll_ ral-ly 'round the bonnie flag,

ral-ly once a-gain Shout-ing the bat-tle cry of Free-dom.
we'll rally once a-gain Shout, shout the bat-tle cry of Free-dom.

Analyzing Primary Sources

1. What is O'Sullivan's main argument in favor of annexation?
2. How did white settlers justify their claim to the California territory?
3. What is the main theme of the Union lyrics to "Battle Cry"?
4. In the Confederate lyrics to "Battle Cry," how are Northerners portrayed?

Alternative Assessment

Organize students into pairs within groups of four. Have students identify a local issue in their school or community newspaper and work together to write a short editorial article representing each side of the issue. Have them concentrate on presenting persuasive arguments to convince others and change minds.

GLENCOE
TECHNOLOGY

CD-ROM
American History Primary Source Document Library CD-ROM

Use the **American History Primary Source Document Library CD-ROM** to access other primary source documents related to nationalism.

History *and the* Humanities

American Music: Hits Through History: "Johnny Comes Marching Home," "The Battle Hymn of the Republic"

American Music: Cultural Traditions: "Bonnie Blue Flag," "Glory! Glory! Hallelujah (John Brown's Body)"

Analyzing Primary Sources

1. He argues it is the destiny of the United States to control the continent from east to west.
2. by working the land, erecting buildings such as schools, colleges, courts, mills, and meeting-houses
3. The Union will rally and fight to free enslaved persons.
4. They are named as tyrants.

1051

Block Schedule

Team Teaching These selections may be implemented in a team-teaching context, in conjunction with English/Language Arts.

Unit Link

Use the primary source selections on pages 1052–1053 to accompany study of Unit 5, "The Birth of Modern America," and Unit 6, "Imperialism and Progressivism."

Reinforcing Vocabulary

Review the **Reader's Dictionary** on this page with students to be sure they understand any unfamiliar terms. Write *antidote* on the board. Ask students to use the term in a sentence.

Background Information

Tone Explain that *tone* in writing uses carefully chosen words to help the author express two messages—the facts, and the author's or character's feelings underneath those facts. Have students identify the tone in these selections, and support this with words in the text. *(Students' answers will vary but should compare content with word choice. For example, the flatness of the land is underscored by the flat, lifeless description of Jim's journey and arrival ["what would be would be"]. The title of Carnegie's article, "The Gospel of Wealth," and his dictatorial style emphasizes his directions on how people should spend their money.)*

For use with Unit 5, "The Birth of Modern America," and Unit 6, "Imperialism and Progressivism"

From Settling the West to Becoming a World Power

In the latter part of the 19th century, immigrants flocked to the United States to settle on farms or to work in newly industrializing cities. The experience transformed both the immigrants and the still-youthful nation. Change created many political and social problems, and Progressivism tried to solve them. New challenges arose in foreign affairs as well, as the nation began to wield the influence that came with an expanding economy.

In the first excerpt, the 1918 novel My Ántonia *by Willa Cather provides us with a glimpse of the life of Easterners and immigrants who moved west. Cather drew on her own experiences to create her characters. Her fiction has a strong sense of place, as can be seen in this passage where Jim Burden gets his first sight of the Nebraska prairie.*

In the second excerpt, Andrew Carnegie presents his personal solution to the problem of a nation with both rich and poor citizens, a solution termed the "Gospel of Wealth." An immigrant himself, Carnegie became one of the nation's wealthiest industrialists. His charitable donations of about $350 million supported more than 2,800 libraries and other institutions.

Reader's Dictionary

plush: a luxurious fabric

surplus wealth: in a capitalist system, the wealth remaining after labor and other costs are met

antidote: a remedy for a poison; something that prevents or relieves a problem

unostentatious: plain, not flashy or showy

My Ántonia by Willa Cather

 **Printed Publications**

I do not remember crossing the Missouri River, or anything about the long day's journey through Nebraska. Probably by that time I had crossed so many rivers that I was dull to them. The only thing very noticeable about Nebraska was that it was still, all day long, Nebraska.

I had been sleeping, curled up in a red plush seat, for a long while when we reached Black Hawk. . . . We stumbled down from the train to a wooden siding, where men were running about with lanterns. I couldn't see any town, or even distant lights; we were surrounded by utter darkness. . . .

Another lantern came along. A bantering voice called out: "Hello, are you Mr. Burden's folks? If you are, it's me you're looking for. I'm Otto Fuchs. I'm Mr.

Carnegie Library, Shelbyville, Ind.

EXTENDING THE CONTENT

Willa Cather Willa Cather was born in wooded, mountainous Virginia, and moved to the dry, flat plains of Nebraska in 1893, when she was nine. After graduating from the University of Nebraska, she moved to Pittsburgh, and then to New York, where she had a successful career as a magazine editor and journalist. Friends encouraged her to leave journalism and devote herself to fiction, suggesting she use the land in which she had lived to ground her work. Several novels, such as *My Ántonia, Song of the Lark,* and *O Pioneers!,* are set in Nebraska in detail if not in name. Many of her books deal with the tension of not fitting in with one's community, of growing up and moving away, and the pull that home will always exert.

Burden's hired man, and I'm to drive you out. Hello, Jimmy, ain't you scared to come so far west?"

... He told us we had a long night drive ahead of us, and had better be on the hike. He led us to a hitching-bar where two farm-wagons were tied. ... I rode on the straw in the bottom of the wagon-box, covered up with a buffalo hide. ...

I tried to go to sleep, but the jolting made me bite my tongue, and I soon began to ache all over. When the straw settled down, I had a hard bed. Cautiously I slipped from under the buffalo hide, got up on my knees and peered over the side of the wagon. There seemed to be nothing to see; no fences, no creeks or trees, no hills or fields. If there was a road, I could not make it out in the faint starlight. There was nothing but land: not a country at all, but the material out of which countries are made. ... I had the feeling that the world was left behind, that we had got over the edge of it, and were outside man's jurisdiction. I had never before looked up at the sky when there was not a familiar mountain ridge against it. But this was the complete dome of heaven, all there was of it. I did not believe that my dead father and mother were watching me from up there; they would still be looking for me at the sheep-fold down by the creek, or along the white road that led to the mountain pastures. I had left even their spirits behind me. The wagon jolted on, carrying me I knew not whither. I don't think I was homesick. If we never arrived anywhere, it did not matter. Between that earth and that sky I felt erased, blotted out. I did not say my prayers that night: here, I felt, what would be would be.

"Gospel of Wealth" by Andrew Carnegie (1889)

 Printed Publications

We start, then, with a condition of affairs under which the best interests of the race are promoted, but which inevitably gives wealth to the few. ...

There are but three modes in which surplus wealth can be disposed of. It can be left to the families of the decedents; or it can be bequeathed for public purposes; or, finally, it can be administered during their lives by its possessors. ...

The growing disposition to tax more and more heavily large estates left at death is a cheering indication of the growth of a salutary change in public opinion. ... Of all forms of taxation, this seems the wisest. ...

There remains, then, only one mode of using great fortunes: but in this way we have the true antidote for the temporary unequal distribution of wealth, the reconciliation of the rich and the poor. . . . Even the poorest can be made to ... agree that great sums ... gathered by some of their fellow-citizens and spent for public purposes, from which the masses reap the principal benefit, are more valuable to them than if scattered among them through the course of many years in trifling amounts.

This, then, is held to be the duty of the man of Wealth: First, to set an example of modest, unostentatious living, ... ; to provide moderately for the legitimate wants of those dependent upon him; and ... to consider all surplus revenues which come to him simply as trust funds ... the man of wealth thus becoming the ... trustee for his poorer brethren, ... doing for them better than they would or could do for themselves.

Analyzing Primary Sources

1. Is Willa Cather giving an objective description of the landscape, or do her feelings color her description? Why do you think so?
2. How does Willa Cather convey a sense of endless space?
3. What does Carnegie believe wealthy people should do with their excess money?
4. How does Carnegie think wealthy people should live? What are their other responsibilities?

Analyzing Primary Sources

1. Her feelings shape her words. Answers should recognize words such as *surrounded* and *blotted out* that convey emotional and factual meaning.
2. Burden had been crossing Nebraska all day; there was no changing scenery, only sky.
3. spend large amounts of it on public projects before their death
4. modestly, providing for the needs of those who depend on him, and spending the remainder for the good of the less fortunate

Unit Link

Use the primary source selections on pages 1054–1055 to accompany study of Unit 7, "Boom and Bust," and Unit 8, "Global Struggles."

Reinforcing Vocabulary

Review the **Reader's Dictionary** on this page with students to be sure they understand any unfamiliar terms. Write *scuttle* on the board. Ask students to use the term in a sentence.

Background Information

Imagery Point out that Steinbeck and Murphy create pictures with words, while O'Keeffe creates pictures with paint and canvas. Have students find examples of visual images in the works by Steinbeck and Murphy, and discuss other interpretations of the painting by O'Keeffe. *(Students' answers will vary but could include families' reactions to a baby's birth in Steinbeck's piece, or the dead sleeping on the field or marching on in Murphy's.)*

For use with Unit 7, "Boom and Bust," and Unit 8, "Global Struggles"

From Prosperity, through the Depression, to World War

Many artists and writers blossomed in the 1920s when the freer values of modern society took hold. Artists no longer tried to copy European models so much but instead created thoroughly American works. Art flourished during the Depression as well; at that time it often focused on the sorrows and hopes of the common people. Artists of the World War II era produced many works on themes of heroism and death.

Georgia O'Keeffe (1887–1986) created some of the most original images in the history of American art. A 1929 New Mexico trip powerfully influenced her style. Known for her strong sense of color, her most famous works are of single flowers.

John Steinbeck (1902–1968) is best known for his 1940 novel, The Grapes of Wrath. *It describes the Joad family's effort to find a new life in California after they have lost their Oklahoma farm. On the trip west, the Joads and thousands of others find solace at the makeshift camps they create along the way.*

The sacrifices that come with struggle are expressed in Audie Murphy's poetry on World War II. The son of a poor Texas sharecropper, Murphy is the most decorated U.S. combat soldier of that war.

Reader's Dictionary

scuttle: to run with short, shuffling steps

biomorphic: resembling or suggesting the forms of living organisms

---

The Grapes of Wrath
by John Steinbeck (1940)

Printed Publications

The cars of the migrant people crawled out of the side roads onto the great cross-country highway, and they took the migrant way to the West. In the daylight they scuttled like bugs to the westward; and as the dark caught them, they clustered like bugs near to shelter and to water. And because they were lonely and perplexed, because they had all come from a place of sadness and worry and defeat, and because they were all going to a new mysterious place, they huddled together; they talked together; they shared their lives, their food, and the things they hoped for in the new country. Thus it might be that one family camped near a spring, and another camped for the spring and for company, and a third because two families had pioneered the place and found it good. And when the sun went down, perhaps twenty families and twenty cars were there.

In the evening a strange thing happened: the twenty families became one family, the children were the children of all. The loss of home became one loss, and the golden time in the West was one dream. And it might be that a sick child threw despair into the hearts of twenty families, of a hundred people; that a birth there in a tent kept a hundred people quiet and awestruck through the night and filled a hundred people with birth-joy in the morning. A family which the night before had been lost and fearful might search its goods to find a present for a new baby. In the evening, sitting about the fires, the twenty were one. They grew to be units of the camps, units of the evenings and the nights. A guitar unwrapped from a blanket and tuned— and the songs, which were all of the people, were sung in the nights. Men sang the words, and women hummed the tunes.

John Steinbeck

EXTENDING THE CONTENT

Audie Murphy While serving in the 3rd Infantry Division, Audie Murphy received 33 decorations, including the Medal of Honor and 5 decorations from France and Belgium. He was wounded three times. After the war, Murphy became a film star and appeared in 44 movies, many of them westerns. He also wrote poetry and became a successful songwriter. Many performers, including Dean Martin, Eddy Arnold, Charley Pride, and Roy Clark, recorded Murphy's songs. Audie Murphy also suffered from post-traumatic stress disorder. He publicly called for the government to study the emotional impact of war and to extend health-care benefits to veterans suffering from war-related mental health problems. Murphy died in a plane crash in 1971. He is buried at Arlington National Cemetery. In 1996 Texas designated his birthday, June 20th, as Audie Murphy Day.

Georgia O'Keeffe's *Oriental Poppies* (1927)

Visual Materials

Georgia O'Keeffe's paintings of biomorphic flowers, rocks, and skulls are *abstract* paintings, meaning that they symbolize things other than what they actually are. *Oriental Poppies*, for example, could be seen as representing a cave-like enclosure.

Georgia O'Keeffe

"Alone and Far Removed" by Audie Murphy

Songs & Poems

Alone and far removed from earthly care
The noble ruins of men lie buried here.
You were strong men, good men
Endowed with youth and much the will to live
I hear no protest from the mute lips of the dead.
They rest; there is no more to give.

So long my comrades,
Sleep ye where you fell upon the field.
But tread softly please
March o'er my heart with ease
March on and on,
But to God alone we kneel.

Audie Murphy

Analyzing Primary Sources

1. Why does Steinbeck compare the migrant camps to a circus?
2. How do you think Steinbeck feels about the migrants?
3. What is an abstract painting? How is it different from other paintings?
4. What is the main mood of Murphy's poem?

Analyzing Primary Sources

1. They are like a circus because they exist only for a night and then are disassembled in the morning.
2. Although the migrants are struggling and desperate, Steinbeck sees them as extraordinarily human, showing a full range of human emotions.
3. Abstract paintings are of items that symbolize things other than what they actually show. Many other paintings are realistic, showing people and places as they are.
4. He feels sadness for friends and comrades that were young and strong but have died, leaving him behind.

Unit Link

Use the primary source selections on pages 1056–1057 to accompany study of Unit 9, "A Time of Upheaval," and Unit 10, "A Changing Society."

Reinforcing Vocabulary

Review the **Reader's Dictionary** on this page with students to be sure they understand any unfamiliar terms. Write *civil disobedience* on the board with additional space between the words. Have students discuss a list of synonyms for each word and write the synonyms under the appropriate word. Ask the students what it means when two such different words are joined together.

Background Information

The Literary Letter Explain to students that what Martin Luther King, Jr., wrote in *Letter from a Birmingham Jail* was a literary letter, addressed to a specific group of clergymen but intended for a wider audience. Ask the students: If Martin Luther King, Jr., came to your school, what might he say about the state of race relations in your town?

For use with Unit 9, "A Time of Upheaval," and Unit 10, "A Changing Society"

From Divisiveness to Diversity

American society took a sharp turn in the 1960s as a new generation sought to change some American values. Change became the challenge throughout the century as many new immigrants came to the United States to make it their home. By the year 2000, the nation was much more diverse. Hispanic Americans alone made up 12.5 percent of the population, approximately the same percentage as African Americans.

The 1960s were a breakthrough time for African Americans. Martin Luther King, Jr., persuaded many white Americans to acknowledge the need for more just laws for minorities. His "Letter from a Birmingham Jail" of April 16, 1963, makes the case that nonviolent resistance is not only moral, but is as American as the Boston Tea Party.

Elva Trevino Hart, born in southern Texas to Mexican immigrants, has a story that mirrors that of many immigrants. A migrant worker as a child, Hart eventually earned a master's degree from Stanford University. In this excerpt, she describes her father and his reaction to her graduation from high school.

Reader's Dictionary

conversely: reversed in order or action

civil disobedience: peaceful refusal to obey government demands as a means of forcing government concessions or changes in the law

admonish: to warn or express disapproval

macho: a strong sense of masculine pride

1056 Primary Sources Library

Letter from a Birmingham Jail by Martin Luther King, Jr. (1963)

Personal Records

My dear fellow clergymen: . . . Birmingham is probably the most thoroughly segregated city in the United States. On the basis of these conditions, Negro leaders sought to negotiate with the city fathers. . . . As in so many past experiences, our hopes had been blasted. . . . We had no alternative except to prepare for direct action, whereby we would present our very bodies as a means of laying our case before the conscience of the local and the national community. . . .

You may well ask: . . . Why sit-ins, marches and so forth? Isn't negotiation a better path?" . . . Indeed, this is the very purpose of direct action. Nonviolent direct action seeks to create such a crisis . . . that a community . . . is forced to confront the issue. . . .

. . . For years now I have heard the word "Wait!" It rings in the ear of every Negro with piercing familiarity. This "Wait" has almost always meant "Never." We must come to see, with one of our distinguished

Martin Luther King, Jr., (right) and Ralph Abernathy in Birmingham, Alabama

---

EXTENDING THE CONTENT

Letter from a Birmingham Jail In retrospect, it is easy to think that in a successful movement the ideas and methods were always recognized as right. This letter came early in the fight for civil rights. In it King struggles to answer his own supporters and friends who are cautioning him against going too far too fast. At that point, even people committed to achieving equal civil rights were not sure that King's new style of mass symbolic action was the best way to achieve change. They felt it might be better to continue individual negotiations to improve conditions in specific situations. The letter's title echoes the well-known folk song, "Birmingham Jail."

jurists, that "justice too long delayed is justice denied." . . . Perhaps it is easy for those who have never felt the stinging dark of segregation to say, "Wait." . . .

You express a great deal of anxiety over our willingness to break laws. . . . One may . . . ask: "How can you advocate breaking some laws and obeying others?" The answer lies in the fact that there are two types of laws: just and unjust. . . . One has not only a legal but a moral responsibility to obey just laws. Conversely, one has a moral responsibility to disobey unjust laws. . . .

Of course, there is nothing new about this kind of civil disobedience. . . . It was practiced superbly by the early Christians, who were willing to face hungry lions . . . rather than submit to certain unjust laws of the Roman Empire. . . . In our own nation, the Boston Tea Party represented a massive act of civil disobedience. . . .

. . . We will have to repent in this generation not merely for the hateful words and actions of the bad people but for the appalling silence of the good people. Human progress never rolls in on wheels of inevitability; it comes through the tireless efforts of men willing to be co-workers with God. . . .

I have heard numerous Southern religious leaders admonish their worshipers to comply with a desegregation decision because it is the law, but I have longed to hear white ministers declare: "Follow this decree because integration is morally right and because the Negro is your brother." . . . But even if the church does not come to the aid of justice, I have no despair about the future. . . . We will reach the goal of freedom . . . all over the nation, because the goal of America is freedom. . . . We will win our freedom because the sacred heritage of our nation and the eternal will of God are embodied in our echoing demands. . . .

Barefoot Heart
by Elva Trevino Hart

Printed Publications

"To get ahead, hijos (children). That's why we go a los trabajos (to work). When I first came from Mexico, I got paid dos reales al dia (two Spanish coins a day). I worked at building the railroad, . . . clearing land. . . . The only thing I would never do is strap on the contraption to burn brush with liquid fuel. Too dangerous. . . ."

I fingered the nickels in the pocket of my sun dress and tried to imagine Apa (Daddy) working for fifty cents a day. And I felt I understood why we had to go to Minnesota. Our family could make more money in the migrant fields than anywhere else. . . .

* * *

Barefoot Heart
Stories of a Migrant Child

Elva Treviño Hart

(My father) had only gone as far as the fourth grade in Mexico. . . . When I was in the fourth grade, I told my father that I wanted to go to college. . . .

On (high school) graduation night I delivered the valedictory speech, entitled "He Conquers who Conquers Himself." I wish now I had said "she," but it has remained the theme of my life nevertheless. Apa came up to me afterwards with big macho tears in his eyes. I had never seen him even close to crying before.

He pressed two thousand dollars in cash into my hand. "I have been saving this for you, mija (my daughter). It's your money to go to college." . . . I knew that this money would only be enough for about one semester, but I didn't tell him. Instead I hugged him, crying violently.

Analyzing Primary Sources

1. Why does King say African Americans should not wait longer for change?
2. Who in ancient history practiced nonviolent resistance?
3. Why did Hart's father take his family so far to work in the summers?

Alternative Assessment

Using library and Internet resources, research one of the following organizations: SNCC, CORE, NAACP, or SCLC. Write a brief paragraph describing its leaders, actions, and contribution to the civil rights movement.

GLENCOE
TECHNOLOGY

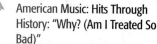

CD-ROM
American History Primary Source Document Library CD-ROM

Use the **American History Primary Source Document Library CD-ROM** to access other primary source documents related to minorities' struggles for equality.

History *and the* Humanities

- American Music: Hits Through History: "Why? (Am I Treated So Bad)"
- American Music: Cultural Traditions: "We Shall Not Be Moved"

Analyzing Primary Sources

1. In the past, waiting for change often meant change never came.
2. Christian opposition to the Roman Empire was an early example of nonviolent resistance.
3. He could make more money working in the migrant fields than anywhere else.

1057

Documents of American History

TABLE OF CONTENTS

(above) Notes for Washington's Farewell Address

(right) Lincoln's drafts of the Gettysburg Address

Magna Carta

Why They Matter

Documents are often public statements by a president or an official body, such as a legislature, on an important issue. They have become documents because they define a particular issue so well that Americans continue to refer to them. Many documents here address fundamental American beliefs, such as the rights of the individual and the proper limits of government. Other documents, such as the Monroe Doctrine or the Truman Doctrine, address the nation's position and responsibilities in the world.

Documents matter because they are guides to American government and values. Sometimes people study them to learn how Americans came to believe in certain principles. Other times people read documents simply because these writings express certain principles passionately.

Signing the Mayflower Compact

Founding Documents of the American Republic

The first seven documents in this collection represent some of the founding documents of American democracy. Each contributed an essential building block for American political principles. Ultimately these principles were embodied in the Declaration of Independence, the Bill of Rights, and the Constitution.

DOCUMENT	WHY IT MATTERS
The Magna Carta In signing this charter in 1215, King John of England granted his subjects certain permanent liberties or rights, such as the right to a fair trial by a jury of their peers.	Over the centuries, English people believed that the Magna Carta gave them certain rights. They took this idea with them when they settled the American colonies. Some provisions of the Bill of Rights reflect ancient Magna Carta liberties.
The Mayflower Compact In 1620 the Pilgrims signed a compact while still aboard the *Mayflower.* This document laid out a plan for self-government the Pilgrims would use once they landed in America.	This document is the first plan for self-government put into effect in the English colonies. It reflected the idea that government should be based on a consensus of the entire community.
The Fundamental Orders of Connecticut Connecticut settlers agreed they would be governed according to a certain set of laws and through certain institutions. All citizens, not only those of a certain religion, could vote.	This document, the first written constitution drawn up in America, strengthened the colonists' beliefs about governing themselves.
The English Bill of Rights In 1689, after the Glorious Revolution, Parliament forced the king to accept this Bill of Rights guaranteeing basic civil rights.	This document clearly established that English subjects had certain rights and that the king could be removed from power for violating those rights.
Second Treatise of Government English philosopher John Locke wrote this document during the 1680s. One of his basic arguments was that government should be based on a contract between a ruler and those who are ruled. Rebellion is justified if a ruler violates the contract.	During the American Revolution, the colonists drew from Locke's theories of government and especially his ideas about the right to rebel.
The Virginia Statute for Religious Freedom This 1786 statute declared that the state of Virginia should not support Anglicanism or any other religious denomination.	The religious clauses of the Bill of Rights protecting the free exercise of religion and prohibiting an official religion were based on this statute.
The Federalist No. 10 In 1787 James Madison wrote this paper, one of a series arguing for stronger central government as reflected in the new Constitution.	The framework for American government today— a representative government with a strong federal government—was laid out in the Federalist Papers.

Use the ***American History Primary Source Document Library CD-ROM*** *to find additional primary sources about American heritage.*

The Magna Carta

The Magna Carta, signed by King John of England in 1215, marked a decisive step forward in the development of English constitutional government. Later it served as a model for the colonists, who carried the Magna Carta's guarantees of political rights to America.

John, by the grace of God, king of England, lord of Ireland, duke of Normandy and Aquitaine, and count of Anjou: to the archbishops, bishops, abbots, earls, barons, justiciaries, foresters, sheriffs, reeves, ministers, and all bailiffs and others his faithful subjects, greeting. . . .

1. We have, in the first place, granted to God, and by this our present charter, confirmed for us and our heirs forever that the English church shall be free. . . .

9. Neither we nor our bailiffs shall seize any land or rent for any debt so long as the debtor's chattels are sufficient to discharge the same. . . .

12. No scutage [tax] or aid shall be imposed in our kingdom unless by the common counsel thereof. . . .

14. For obtaining the common counsel of the kingdom concerning the assessment of aids. . . or of scutage, we will cause to be summoned, severally by our letters, the archbishops, bishops, abbots, earls, and great barons; we will also cause to be summoned generally, by our sheriffs and bailiffs, all those who hold lands directly of us, to meet on a fixed day . . . and at a fixed place. . . .

20. A free man shall be amerced [punished] for a small fault only according to the measure thereof, and for a great crime according to its magnitude. . . . None of these amercements shall be imposed except by the oath of honest men of the neighborhood.

21. Earls and barons shall be amerced only by their peers, and only in proportion to the measure of the offense. . . .

38. In the future no bailiff shall upon his own unsupported accusation put any man to trial without producing credible witnesses to the truth of the accusation.

39. No free man shall be taken, imprisoned, disseised [seized], outlawed, banished, or in any way destroyed, nor will we proceed against or prosecute him, except by the lawful judgment of his peers and by the law of the land.

40. To no one will we sell, to none will we deny or delay, right or justice. . . .

42. In the future it shall be lawful . . . for anyone to leave and return to our kingdom safely and securely by land and water, saving his fealty to us. Excepted are those who have been imprisoned or outlawed according to the law of the land. . . .

61. Whereas we, for the honor of God and the amendment of our realm, and in order the better to allay the discord arisen between us and our barons, have granted all these things aforesaid. . . .

63. Wherefore we will, and firmly charge . . . that all men in our kingdom shall have and hold all the aforesaid liberties, rights, and concessions . . . fully, and wholly to them and their heirs . . . in all things and places forever. . . . It is moreover sworn, as well on our part as on the part of the barons, that all these matters aforesaid will be kept in good faith and without deceit. Witness the above named and many others. Given by our hand in the meadow which is called Runnymede. . . .

The Mayflower Compact

On November 21, 1620, 41 colonists drafted the Mayflower Compact while still aboard the **Mayflower.** *It was the first self-government plan ever put into effect in the English colonies. The compact was drawn up under these circumstances, as described by Governor William Bradford:*

"This day, before we came to harbor, observing some not well affected to unity and concord, but gave some appearance of faction, it was thought good there should be an association and agreement that we should combine together in one body, and to submit to such government and governors as we should by common consent agree to make and choose, and set our hands to this that follows word for word."

In the Name of God, Amen. We, whose names are underwritten, the Loyal Subjects of our dread Sovereign Lord King James, by the Grace of God, of Great Britain, France, and Ireland, King, Defender of the Faith, etc.

Having undertaken for the Glory of God, and Advancement of the Christian Faith, and the honor of our King and Country, a Voyage to plant the first Colony in the northern Parts of Virginia, Do by these Presents, solemnly and mutually, in the Presence of God and one another, covenant and combine ourselves together into a civil Body Politick, for our better Ordering and Preservation, and Furtherance of the Ends aforesaid; And by Virtue hereof do enact, constitute, and frame, such just and equal Laws, Ordinances, Acts, Constitutions, and Offices, from time to time, as shall be thought most meet and convenient for the general Good of the Colony; unto which we promise all due Submission and Obedience. In Witness whereof we have hereunder subscribed our names at Cape Cod the eleventh of November, in the Reign of our Sovereign Lord King James of England, France, and Ireland, the eighteenth and of Scotland, the fifty-fourth. Anno Domini, 1620.

Signing of the Mayflower Compact

The Fundamental Orders of Connecticut

In January 1639, settlers in Connecticut, led by Thomas Hooker, drew up the Fundamental Orders of Connecticut—America's first written constitution. It is essentially a body of laws and a compact among the settlers.

Forasmuch as it has pleased the Almighty God by the wise disposition of His Divine Providence so to order and dispose of things that we, the inhabitants and residents of Windsor, Hartford, and Wethersfield are now cohabiting and dwelling in and upon the river of Conectecotte and the lands thereunto adjoining; and well knowing where a people are gathered together the Word of God requires that, to maintain the peace and union of such a people, there should be an orderly and decent government established according to God, . . . do therefore associate and conjoin ourselves to be as one public state or commonwealth. . . . As also in our civil affairs to be guided and governed according to such laws, rules, orders, and decrees as shall be made, ordered, and decreed, as follows:

1. It is ordered . . . that there shall be yearly two general assemblies or courts; . . . The first shall be called the Court of Election, wherein shall be yearly chosen . . . so many magistrates and other public officers as shall be found requisite. Whereof one to be chosen governor . . . and no other magistrate to be chosen for more than one year; provided aways there be six chosen besides the governor . . . by all that are admitted freemen and have taken the oath of fidelity, and do cohabit within this jurisdiction. . . .

4. It is ordered . . . that no person be chosen governor above once in two years, and that the governor be always a member of some approved congregation, and formerly of the magistracy within this jurisdiction; and all the magistrates freemen of this Commonwealth. . . .

5. It is ordered . . . that to the aforesaid Court of Election the several towns shall send their deputies. . . . Also, the other General Court . . . shall be for making of laws, and any other public occasion which concerns the good of the Commonwealth. . . .

7. It is ordered . . . that . . . the constable or constables of each town shall forthwith give notice distinctly to the inhabitants of the same . . . that . . . they meet and assemble themselves together to elect and choose certain deputies to be at the General Court then following to [manage] the affairs of the Commonwealth; . . .

10. It is ordered . . . that every General Court . . . shall consist of the governor, or someone chosen to moderate the Court, and four other magistrates, at least, with the major part of the deputies of the several towns legally chosen. . . . In which said General Courts shall consist the supreme power of the Commonwealth, and they only shall have power to make laws or repeal them, to grant levies, to admit of freemen, dispose of lands undisposed of to several towns or person, and also shall have power to call either Court or magistrate or any other person whatsoever into question for any misdemeanor. . . .

Connecticut settlers on their way to Hartford

The English Bill of Rights

In 1689 William of Orange (pictured at right) and his wife Mary became joint rulers of England after accepting a list of conditions that later became known as the English Bill of Rights. This document assured the English people of certain basic civil rights and limited the power of the English monarchy.

An act declaring the rights and liberties of the subject and settling the succession of the crown. Whereas the lords spiritual and temporal and commons assembled at Westminster lawfully fully and freely representing all the estates of the people of this realm did upon the thirteenth day of February in the year of our Seal of William and Mary Lord one thousand six hundred eighty-eight [-nine] present unto their majesties . . . William and Mary prince and princess of Orange . . . a certain declaration in writing made by the said lords and commons in the words following viz [namely]

Whereas the late king James the second, by the assistance of divers evil counsellors, judges, and ministers employed by him did endeavor to subvert and extirpate the protestant religion and the laws and liberties of this kingdom.

By assuming and exercising a power of dispensing with and suspending of laws and the execution of laws without consent of parliament. . . .

By levying money for and to the use of the crown by pretence of prerogative for other time and in other manner than the same was granted by parliament.

By raising and keeping a standing army within this kingdom in time of peace without consent of parliament and quartering soldiers contrary to law. . . .

By violating the freedom of election of members to serve in parliament. . . .

And excessive bail hath been required of persons committed in criminal cases to elude the benefit of the laws made for the liberty of the subjects.

And excessive fines have been imposed.

And illegal and cruel punishments inflicted. . . .

And thereupon the said lords spiritual and temporal and commons . . . do . . . declare that the pretended power of suspending of laws or the execution of laws by regal authority without consent of parliament is illegal. . . .

That levying money for or to the use of the crown . . . without grant of parliament for longer time or in other manner than the same is or shall be granted is illegal.

That it is the right of the subjects to petition the king and all commitments and prosecutions for such petitioning are illegal.

That the raising or keeping a standing army within the kingdom in time of peace unless it be with consent of parliament is against law. . . .

That election of members of parliament ought to be free. . . .

That excessive bail ought not to be required nor excessive fines imposed nor cruel and unusual punishments inflicted. . . .

The said lords . . . do resolve that William and Mary, prince and princess of Orange, be declared king and queen of England, France, and Ireland. . . .

Second Treatise of Government

English philosopher John Locke (above) wrote "Two Treatises of Government" in the early 1680s. Published in 1690, the "Second Treatise of Government" argues that government should be based on an agreement between the people and their ruler, and that if the ruler violates the agreement, a rebellion by the people may be justified.

Of the State of Nature

To understand Political Power right, and to derive it from its Original, we must consider what State all Men are naturally in, and that is, a State of perfect Freedom to order their Actions, and dispose of their Possessions, and Persons as they think fit, within the bounds of the Law of Nature, without asking leave, or depending upon the Will of any other Man. . . .

Of the Beginning of Political Societies

Men being, as has been said, by Nature, all free, equal and independent, no one can be put out of this Estate, and subjected to the Political Power of another, without his own Consent.

The only way whereby any one divests himself of his Natural Liberty, and puts on the bonds of Civil Society is by agreeing with other Men to joyn and unite into a Community, for their comfortable, safe, and peaceable living one amongst another, in a secure Enjoyment of their properties, and a greater Security against any that are not of it. This any number of Men may do, because it injures not the Freedom of the rest; they are left as they were in the Liberty of the State of Nature. . . .

Whosoever therefore out of a state of Nature unite into a Community, must be understood to give up all the power, necessary to the ends for which they unite into Society, to the majority of the Community. . . .

Of the Dissolution of Government

Governments are dissolved from within . . . when the Legislative is altered. . . . First, that when such a single Person or Prince sets up his own Arbitrary Will in place of the Laws, which are the Will of the Society, declared by the Legislative, then the Legislative is changed. . . . Secondly, when the Prince hinders the legislative from . . . acting freely, pursuant to those ends, for which it was Constituted, the Legislative is altered. . . . Thirdly, When by the Arbitrary Power of the Prince, the Electors, or ways of Election are altered, without the Consent, and contrary to the common Interest of the People, there also the Legislative is altered. . . .

In these and the like Cases, when the Government is dissolved, the People are at liberty to provide for themselves, by erecting a new Legislative, differing from the other, by the change of Persons, or Form, or both as they shall find it most for their safety and good. For the Society can never, by the fault of another, lose the Native and Original Right it has to preserve itself. . . .

The Virginia Statute for Religious Freedom

This statute, excerpted below, was the basis for the religion clauses in the Bill of Rights. Thomas Jefferson drafted the statute, and James Madison guided it through the Virginia legislature in 1786. The issue it addresses arose when the new state considered whether citizens should continue to support the Anglican Church, as they had in colonial times, or whether they should support any or all other denominations.

Whereas Almighty God hath created the mind free; that all attempts to influence it by temporal punishments . . . tend only to beget habits of hypocrisy and meanness, and are a departure from the plan of the Holy author of our religion; . . . that the impious presumption of legislators and rulers, civil as well as ecclesiastical, who being themselves but fallible and uninspired men, have assumed dominion over the faith of others, setting up their own opinions and modes of thinking as the only true and infallible, and as such endeavouring to impose them on others, hath established and maintained false religions over the greatest part of the world, and through all time; . . . that to compel a man to furnish contributions of money for the propagation of opinions which he disbelieves, is sinful and tyrannical; . . . that our civil rights have no dependence on our religious opinions, any more than our opinions in physics or geometry; that therefore the proscribing any citizen as unworthy the public confidence by laying upon him an incapacity of being called to offices of trust . . . unless he profess or renounce this or that religious opinion, is depriving him injuriously of those privileges and advantages to which in common with his fellow-citizens he has a natural right; that it tends only to corrupt the principles of that religion it is meant to encourage, by bribing with a monopoly of worldly honours and emoluments, those who will externally profess and conform to it . . . :

Be it enacted by the General Assembly, That no man shall be compelled to frequent or support any religious worship, place, or ministry whatsoever, nor shall be enforced, restrained, molested, or burthened in his body or goods, nor shall otherwise suffer on account of his religious opinions or belief; but that all men shall be free to profess, and by argument to maintain, their opinion in matters of religion, and that the same shall in no wise diminish enlarge, or affect their civil capacities. . . .

Thomas Jefferson

The Federalist No. 10

James Madison (pictured at right) wrote several articles for a New York newspaper supporting ratification of the Constitution. In the excerpt below, he argues for the idea of a federal republic as a guard against factions, or overzealous parties, in governing the nation.

The latent causes of faction are thus sown in the nature of man; and we see them everywhere. . . . A zeal for different opinions concerning religion, concerning government, and many other points; . . . an attachment to different leaders ambitiously contending for pre-eminence and power . . . have, in turn, divided mankind into parties . . . disposed to vex and oppress each other than to cooperate for their common good. . . . But the most common and durable source of factions has been the various and unequal distribution of property. Those who hold and those who are without property have ever formed distinct interests in society. Those who are creditors, and those who are debtors, fall under a like discrimination. A landed interest, a manufacturing interest, a mercantile interest, a moneyed interest, with many lesser interests, grow up of necessity in civilized nations, and divide them into different classes, actuated by different sentiments and views. The regulation of these various and interfering interests forms the principal task of modern legislation and involves the spirit of party and faction in the necessary and ordinary operations of government. . . .

The inference to which we are brought is that the causes of faction cannot be removed and relief is only to be sought in the means of controlling its effects. . . .

By what means is this object attainable? Evidently by one of two only. Either the existence of the same passion or interest in a majority at the same time must be prevented, or the majority, having such coexistent passion or interest, must be rendered, by their number and local situation, unable to concert and carry into effect schemes of oppression. . . .

From this . . . it may be concluded that a pure democracy, by which I mean a society consisting of a small number of citizens, who assemble and administer the government in person, can admit of no cure for the mischiefs of faction. A common passion or interest will, in almost every case, be felt by a majority of the whole; a communication and concert results from the form of government itself; and there is nothing to check the inducements to sacrifice the weaker party or an obnoxious individual. Hence it is that such democracies have ever been spectacles of turbulence and contention. . . .

A republic, by which I mean a government in which the scheme of representation takes place, opens a different prospect and promises the cure for which we are seeking. . . .

The two great points of difference between a democracy and a republic are: first, the delegation of the government in the latter to a small number of citizens elected by the rest; secondly, the greater number of citizens and great sphere of country over which the latter may be extended.

The Federalist No. 51

The author of this Federalist paper is not known. It may have been either James Madison or Alexander Hamilton. The author argues that the Constitution's federal system and separation of powers will protect the rights of the people.

In order to lay a due foundation for that separate and distinct exercise of the different powers of government, which to a certain extent is admitted on all hands to be essential to the preservation of liberty, it is evident that. . . the great security against a gradual concentration of the several powers in the same department, consists in giving to those who administer each department the necessary constitutional means and personal motives to resist encroachments of the others. . . .

Ambition must be made to counteract ambition. . . . A dependence on the people is, no doubt, the primary control on the government; but experience has taught mankind the necessity of auxiliary precautions. . . . The constant aim is to divide and arrange the several offices in such a manner as that each may be a check on the other. . . . In the compound republic of America, the power surrendered by the people is first divided between two distinct governments, and then the portion allotted to each subdivided among distinct and separate departments. . . .

In a free government the security for civil rights must be the same as that for religious rights. It consists in the one case in the multiplicity of interests, and in the other in the multiplicity of sects. . . . In the extended republic of the United States, and among the great variety of interests, parties, and sects which it embraces, a coalition of a majority of the whole society could seldom take place on any other principles than those of justice and the general good. . . . It is no less certain than it is important . . . that the larger the society, provided it lie within a practical sphere, the more duly capable it will be of self-government.

The Federalist No. 59

In this Federalist paper, Alexander Hamilton explains why Congress, and not the states, should have the final say in how federal elections are conducted.

The natural order of the subject leads us to consider . . . that provision of the Constitution which authorizes the national legislature to regulate, in the last resort, the election of its own members. . . . Its propriety rests upon the evidence of this plain proposition, that every government ought to contain in itself the means of its own preservation. . . . Nothing can be more evident, than that an exclusive power of regulating elections for the national government, in the hands of the state legislatures, would leave the existence of the union entirely at their mercy. They could at any moment annihilate it, by neglecting to provide for the choice of persons to administer its affairs. . . .

It is certainly true that the state legislatures, by forbearing the appointment of senators, may destroy the national government. But it will not follow that, because they have a power to do this in one instance, they ought to have it in every other. . . . It is an evil; but it is an evil which could not have been avoided without excluding the states . . . from a place in the organization of the national government. If this had been done, it would doubtless have been interpreted into an entire dereliction of the federal principle; and would certainly have deprived the state governments of that absolute safeguard which they will enjoy under this provision. . . .

Washington's Farewell Address

Washington never orally delivered his Farewell Address. Instead, he arranged to have it printed in a Philadelphia newspaper on September 19, 1796. Designed in part to remove him from consideration for a third presidential term, the address also warned about dangers the new nation was facing, especially the dangers of political parties and sectionalism.

Washington preparing to leave office

Friends and Fellow Citizens:

The period for a new election of a citizen to administer the executive government of the United States being not far distant . . . I should now apprise you of the resolution I have formed to decline being considered. . . .

The unity of government which constitutes you one people is . . . a main pillar in the edifice of your real independence; the support of your tranquility at home, your peace abroad; of your safety; of your prosperity in every shape; of that very liberty which you so highly prize. But as it is easy to foresee that, from different causes and from different quarters, much pains will be taken, many artifices employed to weaken in your minds the conviction of this truth. . . .

The name of American, which belongs to you, in your national capacity, must always exalt the just pride of patriotism more than any appellation derived from local discriminations. . . .

In contemplating the causes which may disturb our Union, it occurs as matter of serious concern that any ground should have been furnished for characterizing parties by geographical discriminations: Northern and Southern; Atlantic and Western; whence designing men may endeavor to excite a belief that there is a real difference of local interests and views. . . .

Let me now take a more comprehensive view and warn you in the most solemn manner against the baneful effects of the spirit of party generally. . . .

The alternate domination of one faction over another, sharpened by the spirit of revenge natural to party dissension . . . is itself a frightful despotism. . . .

Of all the dispositions and habits which lead to political prosperity, religion and morality are indispensable supports. . . . A volume could not trace all their connections with private and public felicity. Let it simply be asked where is the security for property, for reputation, for life, if the sense of religious obligation desert the oaths, which are the instruments of investigation in courts of justice? And let us with caution indulge the supposition, that morality can be maintained without religion. Whatever may be conceded to the influence of refined education on minds of peculiar structure—reason and experience both forbid us to expect that national morality can prevail in exclusion of religious principle.

The great rule of conduct for us, in regard to foreign nations, is in extending our commercial relations to have with them as little political connection as possible. . . .

In offering you, my countrymen, these counsels of an old and affectionate friend, I dare not hope that they will make the strong and lasting impression I could wish. . . . But if I may even flatter myself that they may be productive of some partial benefit. . . .

The Kentucky Resolution

The Alien and Sedition Acts of 1798 made it easier for the government to suppress criticism and to arrest political enemies. This Federalist legislation inspired fierce opposition among Republicans, who looked to the state governments to reverse the acts. Two states, Kentucky and Virginia, passed resolutions stating their right to, in effect, disregard federal legislation. The resolutions laid the groundwork for the states' rights often cited during the Civil War. Thomas Jefferson wrote the Kentucky Resolution, excerpted below, which was adopted in 1799.

RESOLVED, . . . that if those who administer the general government be permitted to transgress the limits fixed by that compact, by a total disregard to the special delegations of power therein contained, annihilation of the state governments, and the erection upon their ruins, of a general consolidated government, will be the inevitable consequence; that the principle and construction contended for by sundry of the state legislatures, that the general government is the exclusive judge of the extent of the powers delegated to it, stop nothing short of despotism; . . . that the several states who formed that instrument, being sovereign and independent, have the unquestionable right to judge of its infraction; and that a nullification, by those sovereignties, of all unauthorized acts done under colour of that instrument, is the rightful remedy; . . .

"The Star-Spangled Banner"

Francis Scott Key

During the British bombardment of Fort McHenry during the War of 1812, a young Baltimore lawyer named Francis Scott Key was inspired to write the words to "The Star-Spangled Banner." Although it became popular immediately, it was not until 1931 that Congress officially declared "The Star-Spangled Banner" as the national anthem of the United States.

O! say can you see, by the dawn's early light,

What so proudly we hail'd at the twilight's last gleaming,

Whose broad stripes and bright stars through the perilous fight,

O'er the ramparts we watch'd, were so gallantly streaming?

And the Rockets' red glare, the Bombs bursting in air,

Gave proof through the night that our Flag was still there;

O! say, does that star-spangled Banner yet wave,

O'er the Land of the free, and the home of the brave!

Fort McHenry flag

The Monroe Doctrine

When Spain's power in South America began to weaken, other European nations seemed ready to step in. The United States was developing trade and diplomatic relations with South America, and it wanted to curb European influence there. The following is a statement President Monroe made on the subject in his annual message to Congress on December 2, 1823.

The occasion has been judged proper for asserting, as a principle in which the rights and interests of the United States are involved, that the American continents, by the free and independent condition which they have assumed and maintain, are henceforth not to be considered as subjects for future colonization by any European powers. . . .

. . . We owe it, therefore, to candor and to the amicable relations existing between the United States and those [European] powers to declare that we should consider any attempt on their part to extend their system to any portion of this hemisphere as dangerous to our peace and safety. With the existing colonies or dependencies of any European power we have not interfered and shall not interfere. But with the Governments who have declared their independence and maintain it, and whose independence we have, on great consideration and on just principles, acknowledged, we could not view any interposition for the purpose of oppressing them, or controlling in any other manner their destiny, by any European power in any other light than as the manifestation of an unfriendly disposition toward the United States. . . .

Our policy in regard to Europe, which was adopted at an early stage of the wars which have so long agitated that quarter of the globe, nevertheless remains the same, which is, not to interfere in the internal concerns of any of its powers; to consider the government de facto as the legitimate government for us; to cultivate friendly relations with it, and to preserve those relations by a frank, firm, and manly policy, meeting in all instances the just claims of every power, submitting to injuries from none.

The Seneca Falls Declaration

One of the first documents to call for equal rights for women was the Declaration of Sentiments and Resolutions, issued in 1848 at the Seneca Falls Convention in Seneca Falls, New York. Led by Lucretia Mott and Elizabeth Cady Stanton, the delegates at the convention used the language of the Bill of Rights to call for women's rights.

We hold these truths to be self-evident: that all men and women are created equal; that they are endowed by their Creator with certain inalienable rights; that among these are life, liberty, and the pursuit of happiness; that to secure these rights governments are instituted, deriving their just powers from the consent of the governed. Whenever any form of government becomes destructive of these ends, it is the right of those who suffer from it to refuse allegiance to it, and to insist upon the institution of a new government. . . .

The history of mankind is a history of repeated injuries and usurpations on the part of man toward woman, having in direct object the establishment of an absolute tyranny over her.

Now, in view of this entire disfranchisement . . . we insist that they have immediate admission to all the rights and privileges which belong to them as citizens of the United States. . . .

Lucretia Mott

The Emancipation Proclamation

On January 1, 1863, President Abraham Lincoln issued the Emancipation Proclamation, which freed all enslaved persons in states under Confederate control. The Proclamation was a significant step toward the passage of the Thirteenth Amendment (1865), which ended slavery in the United States.

Whereas, on the 22nd day of September, in the year of our Lord 1862, a proclamation was issued by the President of the United States, containing, among other things, the following, to wit:

That on the 1st day of January, in the year of our Lord 1863, all persons held as slaves within any state or designated part of a state, the people whereof shall then be in rebellion against the United States, shall be then, thenceforward, and forever free; and the executive government of the United States, including the military and naval authority thereof, will recognize and maintain the freedom of such persons and will do no act or acts to repress such persons, or any of them, in any efforts they may make for their actual freedom.

That the executive will, on the 1st day January aforesaid, by proclamation, designate the states and parts of states, if any, in which the people thereof, respectively, shall then be in rebellion against the United States; and the fact that any state or the people thereof shall on that day be in good faith represented in the Congress of the United States by members chosen thereto at elections wherein a majority of the qualified voters of such states shall have participated shall, in the absence of strong countervailing testimony, be deemed conclusive evidence that such state and the people thereof are not then in rebellion against the United States.

Now, therefore, I, Abraham Lincoln, President of the United States, by virtue of the power in me vested as commander in chief of the Army and Navy of the United States, in time of actual armed rebellion against the authority and government of the United States, and as a fit and necessary war measure for suppressing said rebellion, do, on this 1st day of January, in the year of our Lord 1863, and in accordance with my purpose so to do, publicly proclaimed for the full period of 100 days from the day first above mentioned, order, and designate as the states and parts of states wherein the people thereof, respectively, are this day in rebellion against the United States. . . .

And, by virtue of the power and for the purpose aforesaid, I do order and declare that all persons held as slaves within said designated states and parts of states are, and henceforward shall be, free; and that the executive government of the United States, including the military and naval authorities thereof, will recognize and maintain the freedom of said persons. . . .

And upon this act, sincerely believed to be an act of justice, warranted by the Constitution upon military necessity, I invoke the considerate judgment of mankind and the gracious favor of Almighty God. . . .

Abraham Lincoln

The Gettysburg Address

*National monument
at Gettysburg*

President Abraham Lincoln delivered the Gettysburg Address on November 19, 1863, during the dedication of the Gettysburg National Cemetery. The dedication was in honor of the more than 7,000 Union and Confederate soldiers who died in the Battle of Gettysburg earlier that year. Lincoln's brief speech is often recognized as one of the finest speeches in the English language. It is also one of the most moving speeches in the nation's history.

There are five known manuscript copies of the address, two of which are in the Library of Congress. Scholars debate about which, if any, of the existing manuscripts comes closest to Lincoln's actual words that day.

Four score and seven years ago our fathers brought forth on this continent a new nation, conceived in liberty and dedicated to the proposition that all men are created equal.

Now we are engaged in a great civil war, testing whether that nation or any nation so conceived and so dedicated can long endure. We are met on a great battlefield of that war. We have come to dedicate a portion of that field as a final resting-place for those who here gave their lives that that nation might live. It is altogether fitting and proper that we should do this.

But in a larger sense, we cannot dedicate, we cannot consecrate, we cannot hallow this ground. The brave men, living and dead who struggled here have consecrated it far above our poor power to add or detract. The world will little note nor long remember what we say here, but it can never forget what they did here. It is for us the living rather to be dedicated here to the unfinished work which they who fought here have thus far so nobly advanced. It is rather for us to be here dedicated to the great task remaining before us—that from these honored dead we take increased devotion to that cause for which they gave the last full measure of devotion—that we here highly resolve that these dead shall not have died in vain, that this nation under God shall have a new birth of freedom, and that government of the people, by the people, for the people shall not perish from the earth.

The Pledge of Allegiance

*Students in a New York City school
reciting the Pledge of Allegiance*

In 1892 the nation celebrated the 400th anniversary of Columbus's landing in America. In connection with this celebration, Francis Bellamy, a magazine editor, wrote and published the Pledge of Allegiance. The words "under God" were added by Congress in 1954 at the urging of President Dwight D. Eisenhower.

I pledge allegiance to the Flag of the United States of America and to the Republic for which it stands, one Nation under God, indivisible, with liberty and justice for all.

President Harrison on Hawaiian Annexation

An early expression of American imperialism came in the annexation of Hawaii. With the support of the American government, a small number of American troops overthrew the Hawaiian monarchy in January 1893. The excerpt below is from President Benjamin Harrison's written message to Congress. He sent the message along with the treaty for annexation to Congress on February 15, 1893.

I do not deem it necessary to discuss at any length the conditions which have resulted in this decisive action. It has been the policy of the administration not only to respect but to encourage the continuance of an independent government in the Hawaiian Islands so long as it afforded suitable guarantees for the protection of life and property and maintained a stability and strength that gave adequate security against the domination of any other power. . . .

The overthrow of the monarchy was not in any way promoted by this government, but had its origin in what seems to have been a reactionary and revolutionary policy on the part of Queen Liliuokalani, which put in serious peril not only the large and preponderating interests of the United States . . . but all foreign interests. . . . It is quite evident that the monarchy had become effete and the queen's government is weak and inadequate as to be the prey of designing and unscrupulous persons. The restoration of Queen Liliuokalani . . . is undesirable . . . and unless actively supported by the United States would be accompanied by serious disaster and the disorganization of all business interests. The influence and interest of the United States in the islands must be increased and not diminished.

Only two courses are now open—one the establishment of a protectorate by the United States, and the other annexation, full and complete. I think the latter course, which has been adopted in the treaty, will be highly promotive of the best interest of the Hawaiian people and is the only one that will adequately secure the interests of the United States. These interests are not wholly selfish. It is essential that none of the other great powers shall secure these islands. Such a possession would not consist with our safety and with the peace of the world. This view of the situation is so apparent and conclusive that no protest has been heard from any government against proceedings looking to annexation.

The American's Creed

In the patriotic fervor of World War I, national leaders sponsored a contest in which writers submitted ideas for a national creed that would be a brief summary of American beliefs. Of the 3,000 entries, the judges selected that of William Tyler Page as the winner. In a 1918 ceremony in the House of Representatives, the Speaker of the House accepted the creed for the United States.

I believe in the United States of America as a Government of the people, by the people, for the people, whose just powers are derived from the consent of the governed; a democracy in a republic; a sovereign Nation of many sovereign States; a perfect union, one and inseparable; established upon those principles of freedom, equality, justice, and humanity for which American patriots sacrificed their lives and fortunes.

I therefore believe it is my duty to my Country to love it; to support its Constitution; to obey its laws; to respect its flag, and to defend it against all enemies.

The Fourteen Points

On January 8, 1918, President Woodrow Wilson went before Congress to offer a statement of war aims called the Fourteen Points. They reflected Wilson's belief that if the international community accepted certain basic principles of conduct and set up institutions to carry them out, there would be peace in the world.

We entered this war because violations of right had occurred. . . . What we demand in this war, therefore, is . . . that the world be made fit and safe to live in. . . .

The only possible programme, as we see it, is this:

I. Open covenants of peace, openly arrived at, after which there shall be no private international understandings of any kind but diplomacy shall proceed always frankly and in the public view.

II. Absolute freedom of navigation upon the seas, outside territorial waters, alike in peace and in war. . . .

III. The removal, so far as possible, of all economic barriers and the establishment of an equality of trade conditions among all the nations. . . .

IV. Adequate guarantees given and taken that national armaments will be reduced to the lowest point consistent with domestic safety.

V. A free, open-minded, and absolutely impartial adjustment of all colonial claims, based upon a strict observance of the principle that in determining all such questions of sovereignty the interests of the populations concerned must have equal weight with the equitable claims of the government whose title is to be determined.

VI. The evacuation of all Russian territory and . . . opportunity for the independent determination of her own political development and national polity. . . .

VII. Belgium . . . must be evacuated and restored. . . .

VIII. All French territory should be freed and the invaded portions restored, and the wrong done to France by Prussia in 1871 in the matter of Alsace-Lorraine should be righted. . . .

IX. A readjustment of the frontiers of Italy should be effected along clearly recognizable lines of nationality.

X. The peoples of Austria-Hungary . . . should be accorded the freest opportunity of autonomous development.

XI. Rumania, Serbia, and Montenegro should be evacuated; occupied territories restored . . . the relations of the several Balkan states to one another determined by friendly counsel along historically established lines of allegiance and nationality. . . .

XII. The Turkish portions of the present Ottoman Empire should be assured a secure sovereignty. . . .

XIII. An independent Polish state should be erected which should include the territories inhabited by indisputably Polish populations. . . .

XIV. A general association of nations must be formed under specific covenants for the purpose of affording mutual guarantees of political independence and territorial integrity. . . .

Discussion of the Fourteen Points at the Versailles peace conference

The Four Freedoms

President Franklin D. Roosevelt delivered this address on January 6, 1941, in his annual message to Congress. In it, Roosevelt called for a world founded on "four essential human freedoms": freedom of speech and expression, freedom of worship, freedom from want, and freedom from fear.

Just as our national policy in internal affairs has been based upon a decent respect for the rights and dignity of all our fellow men within our gates, so our national policy in foreign affairs has been based on a decent respect for the rights and dignity of all nations, large and small. And the justice of morality must and will win in the end.

Our national policy is this:

First, by an impressive expression of the public will and without regard to partisanship, we are committed to all-inclusive national defense.

Second, by an impressive expression of the public will and without regard to partisanship, we are committed to full support of all those resolute peoples, everywhere, who are resisting aggression and are thereby keeping war away from our Hemisphere. . . .

Third . . . we are committed to the proposition that principles of morality and considerations for our own security will never permit us to acquiesce in a peace dictated by aggressors. . . .

Let us say to the democracies, "We Americans are vitally concerned in your defense of freedom. We are putting forth our energies, our resources, and our organizing powers to give you the strength to regain and maintain a free world. We shall send you, in ever increasing numbers, ships, planes, tanks, guns. This is our purpose and our pledge." In fulfillment of this purpose we will not be intimidated by the threats of dictators that they will regard as a breach of international law and as an act of war our aid to the democracies which dare to resist their aggression. . . .

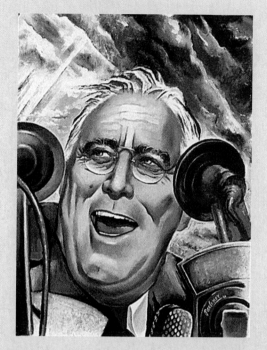

Caricature of President Roosevelt

In the future days, which we seek to make secure, we look forward to a world founded upon four essential human freedoms.

The first is freedom of speech and expression everywhere in the world.

The second is freedom of every person to worship God in his own way everywhere in the world.

The third is freedom from want, which, translated into world terms, means economic understandings which will secure to every nation a healthy peacetime life for its inhabitants everywhere in the world.

The fourth is freedom from fear—which, translated into world terms, means a worldwide reduction of armaments to such a point and in such a thorough fashion that no nation will be in a position to commit an act of physical aggression against any neighbor—anywhere in the world. . . .

The Truman Doctrine

President Harry S Truman addressed a joint session of Congress on March 12, 1947, to request aid to fight Communist influence in Greece and Turkey. His message that communism had to be contained represents the central idea of American foreign policy during the Cold War.

The United States has received from the Greek Government an urgent appeal for financial and economic assistance. . . .

When forces of liberation entered Greece they found that the retreating Germans had destroyed virtually all the railways, roads, port facilities, communications, and merchant marine. More than a thousand villages had been burned. Eighty-five percent of the children were tubercular. Livestock, poultry, and draft animals had almost disappeared. Inflation had wiped out practically all savings. As a result of these tragic conditions, a militant minority, exploiting human want and misery, was able to create political chaos which, until now, has made economic recovery impossible.

Greece is today without funds to finance the importation of those goods which are essential to bare subsistence. Under these circumstances the people of Greece cannot make progress in solving their problems of reconstruction. Greece is in desperate need of financial and economic assistance to enable it to resume purchases of food, clothing, fuel and seeds. These are indispensable for the subsistence of its people and are obtainable only from abroad. Greece must have help to import the goods necessary to restore internal order and security, so essential for economic and political recovery. . . .

Meanwhile, the Greek Government is unable to cope with the situation. The Greek army is small and poorly equipped. It needs supplies and equipment if it is to restore the authority of the government throughout Greek territory. Greece must have assistance if it is to become a self-supporting and self-respecting democracy.

The United States must supply that assistance. We have already extended to Greece certain types of relief and economic aid but these are inadequate. There is no other country to which democratic Greece can turn. . . .

No government is perfect. One of the chief virtues of a democracy, however, is that its defects are always visible and under democratic processes can be pointed out and corrected. The Government of Greece is not perfect. Nevertheless it represents eighty-five percent of the members of the Greek Parliament who were chosen in an election last year. . . .

Greece's neighbor, Turkey, also deserves our attention. The future of Turkey as an independent and economically sound state is clearly no less important to the freedom-loving peoples of the world than the future of Greece. The circumstances in which Turkey finds itself today are considerably different from those of Greece. Turkey has been spared the disasters that have beset Greece. And during the war, the United States and Great Britain furnished Turkey with material aid. Nevertheless, Turkey now needs our support.

. . . To ensure the peaceful development of nations, free from coercion, the United States has taken a leading part in establishing the United Nations. The United Nations is designed to make possible lasting freedom and independence for all its members. We shall not realize our objectives, however, unless we are willing to help free peoples to maintain their free institutions . . . against aggressive movements that seek to impose upon them totalitarian regimes. . . .

This is an investment in world freedom and world peace. . . . The seeds of totalitarian regimes are nurtured by misery and want. They spread and grow in the evil soil of poverty and strife. They reach their full growth when the hope of a people for a better life has died. We must keep that hope alive. . . . If we falter in our leadership, we may endanger the peace of the world—and we shall surely endanger the welfare of our own nation.

Brown v. Board of Education

On May 17, 1954, the Supreme Court ruled in **Brown** *v.* **Board of Education of Topeka, Kansas,** *that racial segregation in public schools was unconstitutional. This decision provided the legal basis for court challenges to segregation in every aspect of American life.*

These cases come to us from the States of Kansas, South Carolina, Virginia, and Delaware. They are premised on different facts and different local conditions, but a common legal question justifies their consideration together in this consolidated opinion.

In each of the cases, minors of the Negro race, through their legal representatives, seek the aid of the courts in obtaining admission to the public schools of their community on a nonsegregated basis. In each instance, they had been denied admission to schools attended by white children under laws requiring or permitting segregation according to race. This segregation was alleged to deprive the plaintiffs of the equal protection of the laws under the Fourteenth Amendment.

The plaintiffs contend that segregated public schools are not "equal" and cannot be made "equal," and that hence they are deprived of the equal protection of the laws. Because of the obvious importance of the question presented, the Court took jurisdiction. . . .

. . . Our decision . . . cannot turn on merely a comparison of these tangible factors in the Negro and white schools involved in each of the cases. We must look instead to the effect of segregation itself on public education.

In approaching this problem, we cannot turn the clock back to 1868 when the Amendment was adopted, or even to 1896 when *Plessy* v. *Ferguson* was written. We must consider public education in the light of its full development and its present place in American life throughout the nation. Only in this

way can it be determined if segregation in public schools deprives these plaintiffs of the equal protection of the laws.

Today, education is perhaps the most important function of state and local governments. Compulsory school attendance laws and the great expenditures for education both demonstrate our recognition of the importance of education to our democratic society. . . . In these days, it is doubtful that any child may reasonably be expected to succeed in life if he is denied the opportunity of an education. Such an opportunity, where the state has undertaken to provide it, is a right which must be made available to all on equal terms.

We come then to the question presented: Does segregation of children in public schools solely on the basis of race, even though the physical facilities and other "tangible" factors may be equal, deprive the children of the minority group of equal educational opportunities? We believe that it does.

. . . We conclude that, in the field of public education, the doctrine of "separate but equal" has no place. Separate educational facilities are inherently unequal. Therefore, we hold that the plaintiff and others similarly situated for whom the actions have been brought are, by reason of the segregation complained of, deprived of the equal protection of the laws guaranteed by the Fourteenth Amendment. . . .

Linda Brown

"I Have a Dream"

On August 28, 1963, while Congress was debating broad civil rights legislation, Martin Luther King, Jr., led more than 200,000 people in a march on Washington, D.C. On the steps of the Lincoln Memorial, King gave a stirring speech in which he eloquently spoke of his dreams for African Americans and for the United States.

Martin Luther King, Jr., speaking at the march

Five score years ago, a great American, in whose symbolic shadow we stand, signed the Emancipation Proclamation. This momentous decree came as a great beacon light of hope to millions of Negro slaves who had been seared in the flames of withering injustice. It came as a joyous daybreak to end the long night of captivity.

But one hundred years later, we must face the tragic fact that the Negro is still not free. One hundred years later, the life of the Negro is still sadly crippled by the manacles of segregation and the chains of discrimination. . . .

There are those who are asking the devotees of civil rights, "When will you be satisfied?"

We can never be satisfied as long as the Negro is the victim of the unspeakable horrors of police brutality.

We can never be satisfied as long as our bodies, heavy with the fatigue of travel, cannot gain lodging in the motels of the highways and the hotels of the cities.

We cannot be satisfied as long as the Negro's basic mobility is from a smaller ghetto to a larger one.

We can never be satisfied as long as a Negro in Mississippi cannot vote and a Negro in New York believes he has nothing for which to vote.

No, no, we are not satisfied, and we will not be satisfied until justice rolls down like waters and righteousness like a mighty stream. . . .

I say to you today, my friends, that in spite of the difficulties and frustrations of the moment I still have a dream. It is a dream deeply rooted in the American dream.

I have a dream that one day this nation will rise up and live out the true meaning of its creed: "We hold these truths to be self-evident; that all men are created equal. "

I have a dream that one day on the red hills of Georgia the sons of former slaves and the sons of former slaveowners will be able to sit down together at the table of brotherhood.

I have a dream that one day even the state of Mississippi, a desert state sweltering with the heat of injustice and oppression, will be transformed into an oasis of freedom and justice.

I have a dream that my four little children will one day live in a nation where they will not be judged by the color of their skin but by the content of their character. . . .

When we let freedom ring, when we let it ring from every village and every hamlet, from every state and every city, we will be able to speed up that day when all of God's children, black men and white men, Jews and Gentiles, Protestants and Catholics, will be able to join hands and sing in the words of the old Negro spiritual, "Free at last! Free at last! Thank God Almighty, we are free at last!"

Gulf of Tonkin Resolution

On August 7, 1964, Congress passed the Gulf of Tonkin Resolution, which stood as the legal basis for the Vietnam War.

Resolved by the Senate and House of Representatives of the United States of America in Congress assembled,

That the Congress approves and supports the determination of the President, as Commander in Chief, to take all necessary measures to repel any armed attack against the forces of the United States and to prevent further aggression.

Section 2. The United States regards as vital to its national interest and to world peace the maintenance of international peace and security in southeast Asia. Consonant with the Constitution of the United States and the Charter of the United Nations and in accordance with its obligations under the Southeast Asia Collective Defense Treaty, the United States is, therefore, prepared, as the President determines, to take all necessary steps, including the use of armed force, to assist any member or protocol state of the Southeast Asia Collective Defense Treaty requesting assistance in defense of its freedom.

President Bush's Address to Joint Session of Congress, September 20, 2001

On September 11, 2001, terrorists crashed airplanes into the World Trade Center in New York City and the Pentagon in Washington, D.C. Thousands of people were killed. In his address, President George W. Bush announced a new kind of war against terrorism.

. . . On September the eleventh, enemies of freedom committed an act of war against our country. . . . Americans have known surprise attacks—but never before on thousands of civilians. All of this was brought upon us in a single day—and night fell on a different world, a world where freedom itself is under attack. . . .

The evidence we have gathered all points to a collection of loosely affiliated terrorist organizations known as al-Qaeda. . . . Our war on terror begins with al-Qaeda, but it does not end there. It will not end until every terrorist group of global reach has been found, stopped, and defeated.

Americans are asking: Why do they hate us? They hate what we see right here in this chamber—a democratically elected government. Their leaders are self-appointed. They hate our freedoms. . . . By sacrificing human life to serve their radical visions—by abandoning every value except the will to power—they follow in the path of fascism, and Nazism, and totalitarianism. And they will follow that path all the way, to where it ends: in history's unmarked grave of discarded lies.

. . . We will direct every resource at our command—every means of diplomacy, every tool of intelligence, every instrument of law enforcement, every financial influence, and every necessary weapon of war—to the disruption and defeat of the global terror network. . . .

I know there are struggles ahead, and dangers to face. But this country will define our times, not be defined by them. . . . Great harm has been done to us. We have suffered great loss. And in our grief and anger we have found our mission and our moment. . . . Our Nation—this generation—will lift a dark threat of violence from our people and our future. We will rally the world to this cause, by our efforts and by our courage. We will not tire, we will not falter, and we will not fail.

Supreme Court Case Summaries

The following case summaries explain the significance of major Supreme Court cases mentioned in the text.

Abington School District v. Schempp (1963) struck down a Pennsylvania statute requiring public schools in the state to begin each school day with Bible readings and a recitation of the Lord's Prayer. The Court held that the Constitution's establishment clause leaves religious beliefs and religious practices to each individual's choice and expressly commands that government not intrude into this decision-making process.

Abrams v. United States (1919) upheld a conviction under the Sedition Act and Espionage Act of 1917. The Court ruled that freedom of speech could be limited if there was a threat to the country.

Baker v. Carr (1962) established that federal courts can hear suits seeking to force state authorities to redraw electoral districts. In this case, the plaintiff wanted the population of each district to be roughly equal to the population in all other districts. The plaintiff claimed that the votes of voters in the least populous districts counted as much as the votes of voters in the most populous districts.

Brown v. Board of Education (1954) overruled *Plessy* v. *Ferguson* (1896) and abandoned the separate-but-equal doctrine in the context of public schools. In deciding this case, the Supreme Court rejected the idea that equivalent but separate schools for African Americans and white students would be constitutional. The Court stated that the Fourteenth Amendment's command that all persons be accorded the equal protection of the law (U.S. Const. amend. XIV, sec. 1) is not satisfied by ensuring that African American and white schools "have been equalized, or are being equalized, with respect to buildings, curricula, qualifications, and salaries, and other tangible factors."

The Court then held that racial segregation in public schools violates the equal protection clause because it is inherently unequal. In other words, the separation of schools by race marks the separate race as inferior. The ruling in this case has been extended beyond public education to virtually all public accommodations and activities.

Bush v. Gore (2000) found that a manual recount of disputed presidential ballots in Florida lacked a uniform standard of judging a voter's intent, thus violating the equal protection clause of the Constitution. The Court also ruled that there was not enough time to conduct a new manual recount that would meet constitutional standards. The case arose when Republican candidate George W. Bush asked the Court to stop a hand recount. This decision ensured that Bush would receive Florida's electoral votes and win the election.

Chisholm v. Georgia (1793) stripped the immunity of the states to lawsuits in federal court. The Supreme Court held that a citizen of one state could sue another state in federal court without that state consenting to the suit. The Court's decision created a furor and led to the adoption of the Eleventh Amendment, which protects states from federal court suits by citizens of other states.

Dred Scott v. Sandford (1857) was decided before the Fourteenth Amendment. The Fourteenth Amendment provides that anyone born or naturalized in the United States is a citizen of the nation and of his or her state. In this case, the Supreme Court held that a slave was property, not a citizen, and thus had no rights under the Constitution. The decision was a prime factor leading to the Civil War.

Engel v. Vitale (1962) held that the establishment clause (U.S. Const. amend. I, cl. 1) was violated by a public school district's practice of starting each school day with a prayer which began, "Almighty God, we acknowledge our dependence upon Thee." The Supreme Court ruled that religion is a personal matter and that government should not align itself with a particular religion in order to prevent religious persecution.

***Escobedo* v. *Illinois* (1964)** held that Danny Escobedo's right to counsel, as provided by the Sixth Amendment, had been violated. Throughout police questioning, Escobedo asked repeatedly, but unsuccessfully, to see his attorney. The Supreme Court reversed Escobedo's murder conviction, holding that an attorney could have assisted Escobedo in invoking his Fifth Amendment right against self-incrimination. This case served as a forerunner to *Miranda* v. *Arizona.*

***Gibbons* v. *Ogden* (1824)** made it clear that the authority of Congress to regulate interstate commerce (U.S. Const. art. I, sec. 8, cl. 3) includes the authority to regulate intrastate commercial activity that relates to interstate commerce. Before this case, it was thought that the Constitution would allow a state to close its borders to interstate commercial activity. This ruling says that a state can only regulate internal commercial activity, but Congress can regulate commercial activity that has both intrastate and interstate dimensions.

***Gideon* v. *Wainwright* (1963)** ruled that poor defendants in criminal cases have the right to a state-paid attorney under the Sixth Amendment. The ruling in this case has been refined to apply only when the defendant, if convicted, can be sentenced to more than six months in jail.

***Griswold* v. *Connecticut* (1965)** overturned the conviction of two Planned Parenthood employees charged with violating an 1879 state law banning the use of contraceptives. In deciding this case, the Court went beyond the actual words of the Constitution to protect a right—the right to privacy—which is not listed in the Constitution. The case also served as a forerunner to the *Roe* v. *Wade* decision that legalized abortion on the same basis.

***Heart of Atlanta Motel, Inc.* v. *United States* (1964)** upheld the Civil Rights Act of 1964, which prohibits racial discrimination by those who provide goods, services, and facilities to the public. The Georgia motel in the case drew its business from other states but refused to rent rooms to African Americans. The Supreme Court explained that Congress had the authority to prohibit such discrimination under both the equal protection clause (U.S. Const. amend. XIV, sec. 1) and the commerce clause (art. I, sec. 8, cl. 3). With respect to the commerce clause, the Court explained that Congress had ample evidence to conclude that racial discrimination by hotels and motels impedes interstate commerce.

***Korematsu* v. *United States* (1944)** allowed the federal government's authority to exclude Japanese Americans, many of whom were citizens, from designated military areas that included almost the entire West Coast. The government defended the orders as a necessary response to Japan's attack on Pearl Harbor. Yet, in upholding the orders, the Court established that government actions that discriminate on the basis of race would be subject to strict scrutiny.

***Loving* v. *Virginia* (1967)** ruled that state laws that outlaw interracial marriages are unconstitutional under the Fourteenth Amendment. The Court explained that such laws violated the equal protection clause and deprived "citizens of liberty without due process of law." The Court went on to say, "Marriage is one of the basic civil rights of man, fundamental to our very existence and survival."

***Mapp* v. *Ohio* (1961)** established that evidence seized in violation of the Fourth Amendment could not be used by the prosecution as evidence of a defendant's guilt at the federal, state, or local level.

***Marbury* v. *Madison* (1803)** established one of the most important principles of American constitutional law. The Supreme Court held that the Court itself has the final say on what the Constitution means. It is also the Supreme Court that has the final say whether or not an act of government—legislative or executive at the federal, state, or local level—violates the Constitution.

***Martin* v. *Hunter's Lessee* (1816)** affirmed that the Supreme Court has the authority to review state court decisions and is the nation's final court of appeal. The Supreme Court ruled that section 25 of the Judiciary Act of 1789 was constitutional. This section granted the Supreme Court appellate jurisdiction over state courts in certain situations, such as a state court denying the authority of federal law.

***McCulloch* v. *Maryland* (1819)** established the basis for the expansive authority of Congress. The Supreme Court held that the necessary and proper clause (U.S. Const. art. I, sec. 8, cl. 18) allows Congress to do more than the Constitution specifically authorizes it to do. This case holds that Congress can enact almost any law that will help it achieve the ends established by Article I, Section 8 of the Constitution. For example, Congress has the power to regulate interstate commerce; the necessary and proper clause permits Congress to do so in ways not specified in the Constitution.

***Miranda* v. *Arizona* (1966)** held that a person in police custody may not be held unless reminded of his or her rights. These rights include: 1) the right to remain silent, 2) the right to an attorney (at government expense if the person is unable to pay), and 3) that anything the person says after acknowledging that he or she understands these rights can be used as evidence of guilt at a trial.

The Supreme Court explained that a person alone in police custody may not understand, even if told, that he or she can remain silent and thus might be misled into answering questions. The presence of an attorney is essential.

***Morgan* v. *Virginia* (1946)** challenged racial segregation in the South. Irene Morgan was convicted for refusing to give up her seat on an interstate bus bound from Virginia to Maryland. The Court ruled that the Virginia law posed an undue burden on interstate commerce and struck down the statute. However, segregation on southern buses continued on an informal basis.

***National Labor Relations Board* v. *Jones and Laughlin Steel Corp.* (1937)** upheld President Franklin Roosevelt's New Deal legislation, the National Labor Relations Act, which allowed workers to organize unions in businesses operating or affecting interstate commerce. Employers were prohibited from discriminating against their employees because of union membership. Prior to this case, the Supreme Court had ruled much New Deal legislation unconstitutional. This ruling came less than a week after Roosevelt's proposed court-packing plan. The president intended on "packing" the Supreme Court with additional justices in order to obtain a pro–New Deal majority on the Court.

***New York Times Co.* v. *Sullivan* (1964)** extended the protections afforded to the press by the free press clause (U.S. Const. amend. I). In this case, the Supreme Court held that a public official or public figure suing a publisher for libel (i.e., defamation) must prove that the publisher published a story that he or she knew was false or published the story in "reckless disregard of its truth or falsity," which means that the publisher did not take professionally adequate steps to determine the story's truth or falsity.

***Norris* v. *Alabama* (1935)** overturned the conviction of Clarence Norris, an African American sentenced to death for a crime in Alabama. The Supreme Court held that the grand jury and trial jury had systematically eliminated African American jurors. Thus, the Court reversed the conviction because it violated the equal protection clause of the Fourteenth Amendment.

***Northern Securities Company* v. *United States* (1904)** dealt with the application of congressional antitrust legislation. The party involved held

three-fourths of the stock in two parallel railroad lines. By a narrow 5–4 decision, the Court upheld the application of the Sherman Antitrust Act. The Court ruled that the holding company clearly intended to eliminate competition between the two railroads, violating the constitutional right of Congress to regulate interstate commerce.

***Plessy* v. *Ferguson* (1896)** upheld the separate-but-equal doctrine used by Southern states to perpetuate segregation after the Civil War officially ended law-mandated segregation. The decision upheld a Louisiana law requiring passenger trains to have "equal but separated accommodations for the white and colored races." The Court held that the Fourteenth Amendment's equal protection clause required only equal public facilities for the two races, not equal access. This case was overruled by *Brown* v. *Board of Education* (1954).

***Regents of the University of California* v. *Bakke* (1978)** was the first Supreme Court decision to suggest that an affirmative action program could be justified on the basis of diversity. The Court explained that racial quotas were not permissible under the equal protection clause of the Fourteenth Amendment. However, the justices ruled that the diversity rationale was a legitimate interest that would allow a state medical school to consider an applicant's race in evaluating his or her application for admission. (Recent Supreme Court cases suggest that the diversity rationale is no longer enough to defend an affirmative action program.)

***Reynolds* v. *Sims* (1964)** extended the one-person, one-vote doctrine announced in *Wesberry* v. *Sanders* to state legislative elections. The Court held that the inequality of representation in the Alabama legislature violated the equal protection clause of the Fourteenth Amendment.

***Roe* v. *Wade* (1973)** held that women have the right under various provisions of the Constitution—most notably, the due process clause of the Fourteenth Amendment—to decide whether or not to terminate a pregnancy. The Court's ruling in this case was the most significant in a long line of decisions over a period of 50 years that recognized a constitutional right of privacy, even though the word *privacy* is not found in the Constitution.

***Schechter Poultry Corporation* v. *United States* (1935)** overturned the conviction of the employers, who were charged with violating the wage and hour limitations of a law adopted under the authority of the

National Industrial Recovery Act. The Court held that because the defendants did not sell poultry in interstate commerce, they were not subject to federal regulations on wages and hours.

Schenck v. United States (1919) upheld convictions under the Federal Espionage Act. The defendants were charged under the act with distributing leaflets aimed at inciting draft resistance during World War I; their defense was that antidraft speech was protected under the First Amendment.

The Supreme Court unanimously rejected the defense, explaining that whether or not speech is protected depends on the context in which it occurs. Because the defendants' antidraft rhetoric created a "clear and present danger" to the success of the war effort, it was not protected.

Stone v. Powell (1976) reversed a Court of Appeals decision that evidence was seized illegally and should therefore be excluded. The Court ruled that the defendant was provided a fair and legal opportunity to claim a Fourth Amendment violation before a trial jury. The trial jury found that the search was constitutional and the evidence should not be excluded. The Court stated, "Where the state has provided an opportunity for full and fair litigation of a Fourth Amendment claim, a state prisoner may not be granted federal habeas corpus relief."

Swann v. Charlotte-Mecklenburg Board of Education (1971) established a new plan to ensure that public schools were not segregated. Many school systems were slow to desegregate after *Brown* v. *Board of Education* and used various tactics to appear to be resolving the problem. This case ordered that busing students, reorganizing school boundaries, and racial ratios all be used as methods to obtain desegregated public school systems.

Sweatt v. Painter (1950) held that it was unconstitutional for African Americans to be denied admission to the University of Texas Law School based on race. An inferior law school established for African Americans did not give the state justification to deny admission to the main school. This act was a violation of the Fourteenth Amendment.

Wabash v. Illinois (1886) held that states have no authority to regulate railroad rates for interstate commerce. The Supreme Court held that the commerce clause (U.S. Const. art. I, sec. 8, cl. 3) allowed states to enforce "indirect" but not "direct" burdens on interstate commerce. State railroad rates were ruled "direct" burdens and therefore could not be enforced by states. The decision created a precedent by establishing rate regulation of interstate commerce as an exclusive federal power.

Wickard v. Filburn (1942) indicated how far the Supreme Court had come in complying with President Franklin Roosevelt's economic philosophies. The Court upheld specific parts of the Second Agricultural Adjustment Act. In its ruling, the Supreme Court held that marketing quotas could be applied to wheat that never left the farm. Using the commerce clause (U.S. Const. art. I, sec. 8, cl. 3) as the basis for its decision, the Court ruled that wheat that never left the farm still had an effect on interstate commerce. Farmers growing their own grain depressed the overall demand and market price of wheat. The decision further extended the power of the commerce clause.

Worcester v. Georgia (1832) overturned the conviction of Samuel A. Worcester, a missionary among the Cherokee. Worcester was imprisoned under a Georgia law forbidding whites to reside in Cherokee country without taking an oath of allegiance to the state and obtaining a permit. The Supreme Court voided the state law, ruling that the Cherokee were an independent nation based on a federal treaty and free from the jurisdiction of the state. Georgia ignored the decision, and President Jackson refused to enforce it, instead supporting the removal of the Cherokee to the Indian Territory.

Flag Etiquette

For Americans, the flag has always had a special meaning.
It is a symbol of our nation's freedom and democracy.

Rules and Customs

Over the years, Americans have developed rules and customs concerning the use and display of the flag. One of the most important things every American should remember is to treat the flag with respect.

- The flag should be raised and lowered by hand and displayed only from sunrise to sunset. On special occasions, the flag may be displayed at night, but it should be illuminated.

- The flag may be displayed on all days, weather permitting, particularly on national and state holidays and on historic and special occasions.

- No flag may be flown above the American flag or to the right of it at the same height.

- The flag should never touch the ground or floor beneath it.

- The flag may be flown at half-staff by order of the president, usually to mourn the death of a public official.

- The flag may be flown upside down only to signal distress.

- When the flag becomes old and tattered, it should be destroyed by burning. According to an approved custom, the Union (stars on blue field) is first cut from the flag; then the two pieces, which no longer form a flag, are burned.

Continental Colors
1775-1777

First Stars and Stripes
1777-1795

Betsy Ross Flag
c. 1790

15-Star Flag
1795-1818

20-Star Flag
1818

Great Star Flag
1818

35-Star Flag
1863-1865

38-Star Flag
1877-1890

48-Star Flag
1912-1959

50-Star Flag
1960

Glossary

A

abolition the immediate ending of slavery (p. 285)

affirmative action an active effort to improve employment or educational opportunities for minorities (p. 933)

agrarianism philosophy that agriculture and owning land is the backbone of the economy (p. 214)

agricultural revolution period when early Americans learned how to plant and raise crops (p. 13)

alien a person living in a country who is not a citizen of that country (p. 219)

allotment a plot of land assigned to an individual or family for cultivation (p. 430)

amendment a change to the Constitution (p. 169)

Americanization causing someone to acquire American traits and characteristics (p. 485)

amnesty the act of granting a pardon to a large group of people (p. 387)

amphtrac an amphibious tractor used to move troops from ships to shore (p. 760)

anarchist person who believes that there should be no government (p. 611)

annexation incorporating a territory within the domain of a country (p. 304)

annuity money paid by contract on regular intervals (p. 426)

Antifederalist an opponent of the Constitution (p. 173)

appeasement accepting demands in order to avoid conflict (p. 714)

appropriate to allocate funds for spending (p. 183)

arbitration settling a dispute by agreeing to accept the decision of an impartial outsider (pp. 458, 557)

armistice a temporary agreement to end fighting (p. 596)

artisan a skilled worker who practices a trade or handicraft (p. 95)

assembly line a production system with machines and workers arranged so that each person performs an assigned task again and again as the item passes before him or her (p. 641)

assimilate to absorb a group into the culture of a larger population (p. 430)

astrolabe device used to determine direction, latitude, and local time (p. 36)

attrition the act of wearing down by constant harassment or attack (p. 355)

B

baby boom a marked rise in birthrate, such as occurred in the United States following World War II (p. 816)

bailiff minor officer of the courts (p. 662)

benevolent society an association focusing on spreading the word of God and combating social problems (p. 279)

bilingualism the practice of teaching immigrant students in their own language (p. 935)

bill a proposed law (p. 183)

bill of exchange credit slip given by English merchants to planters in exchange for sugar or other goods (p. 95)

binding arbitration process whereby a neutral party hears arguments from two opposing sides and makes a decision that both must accept (p. 692)

black codes laws passed in the South just after the Civil War aimed at controlling freedmen and enabling plantation owners to exploit African American workers (p. 393)

black power the mobilization of the political and economic power of African Americans, especially to compel respect for their rights and to improve their condition (p. 884)

blitzkrieg name given to sudden violent offensive attacks the Germans used during World War II; "lightning war" (p. 715)

blockade runner ship that runs through a blockade, usually to smuggle goods through a protected area (p. 359)

blue-collar jobs in the manual labor field, particularly those requiring protective clothing (p. 815)

blues style of music evolving from African American spirituals and noted for its melancholy sound (p. 628)

Bohemian a person (as an artist or writer) leading an unconventional lifestyle (p. 621)

bonanza farm a large, highly-profitable wheat farm (p. 422)

bond a note issued by the government which promises to pay off a loan with interest (p. 212)

bounty money given as a reward, as to encourage enlistment in the army (p. 358)

brinkmanship the willingness to go to the brink of war to force an opponent to back down (p. 799)

broker state role of the government to work out conflicts among competing interest groups (p. 700)

budget deficit the amount by which expenses exceed income (p. 987)

bull market a long period of rising stock prices (p. 657)

burgesses representatives to the general assembly of the Virginia colony (p. 64)

busing a policy of transporting children to schools outside their neighborhoods to achieve greater racial balance (p. 934)

C

cabinet a group of advisers to the president (pp. 184, 211)

capital gains tax a federal tax paid by businesses and investors when they sell stocks or real estate (p. 1006)

capitalist person who invests wealth, particularly money, in a business (p. 97)

caravel sailing ship capable of long-distance exploration (p. 37)

carpetbagger name given to many Northerners who moved to the South after the Civil War and supported the Republicans (p. 399)

cash crop a crop grown primarily for profit (p. 85)

caucus system a system in which members of a political party meet to choose their party's candidate for president or decide policy (p. 268)

cede to give up by treaty (p. 311)

censure to express a formal disapproval of an action (p. 795)

chad a small piece of cardboard produced by punching a data card (p. 1028)

charter a constitution (p. 771)

checks and balances the system in which each branch of government has the ability to limit the power of the other branches to prevent any from becoming too powerful (p. 168)

circumnavigate to sail around (p. 43)

civilization a highly organized society marked by knowledge of trade, government, the arts, science, and, often, written language (p. 14)

closed shop an agreement in which a company agrees to hire only union members (pp. 458, 809)

cloture a motion which ends debate and calls for an immediate vote, possible in the U.S. Senate by a vote of 60 senators (p. 878)

Cold War the ideological and often confrontational conflict between the United States and the Soviet Union between 1946 and 1990 (p. 778)

Columbian Exchange series of complex societal and environmental interactions between Europe and the Americas begun with Columbus's first voyage (p. 43)

commission plan a plan in which a city's government is divided into different departments with different functions, each placed under the control of a commissioner (p. 548)

committee of correspondence committee organized in each colony to communicate with and unify the colonies (p. 127)

commune a group living arrangement in which members share everything and work together (p. 923)

concentration camp a camp where persons are detained or confined (p. 723)

concurrent powers those powers which the state and federal governments share (p. 181)

Confederacy nation declared to have been formed by the southern states that seceded from the Union in 1860–1861 (p. 343)

conference committee a special joint committee organized to help the House and Senate work on a compromise bill acceptable to both houses (p. 183)

conquistador Spanish for conqueror, the men who led the expeditions to conquer the Americas (p. 52)

conscription requiring people to enter military service (pp. 353, 585)

consensus general agreement (p. 856)

conservative a person who believes government power, particularly in the economy, should be limited in order to maximize individual freedom (p. 981)

constituent a resident of an electoral district (p. 183)

containment the policy or process of preventing the expansion of a hostile power (p. 784)

contra Spanish for counterrevolutionary, an anti-Sandinista guerrilla force in Nicaragua (p. 990)

contraband goods whose importation, exportation, or possession is illegal (p. 581)

convoy a group that travels with something, such as a ship, to protect it (p. 594)

convoy system a system in which merchant ships travel with naval vessels for protection (p. 746)

cooperative store where farmers bought products from each other; an enterprise owned and operated by those who use its services (p. 502)

cooperative individualism President Hoover's policy of encouraging manufacturers and distributors to form their own organizations and volunteer information to the federal government in an effort to stimulate the economy (p. 648)

corporation an organization that is authorized by law to carry on an activity but treated as though it were a single person (p. 448)

"corrupt bargain" an illegitimate agreement between politicians (p. 259)

cost of living the cost of purchasing goods and services essential for survival (p. 599)

cost-plus a government contract to pay a manufacturer the cost to produce an item plus a guaranteed percentage (p. 737)

cotton gin a machine that removed seeds from cotton fiber (p. 252)

counterculture a culture with values and beliefs different than the mainstream (p. 922)

coureur de bois French fur traders who lived among the Native Americans (p. 56)

covert not openly shown or engaged in (p. 801)

creationism the belief that God created the world and everything in it, usually in the way described in Genesis (p. 614)

credibility gap lack of trust or believability (p. 905)

crop lien obligation placed on a farmer to repay a debt with crops (p. 407)

customs duty a tax on imports and exports (p. 119)

D

de facto segregation segregation by custom and tradition (p. 867)

debt peonage condition of sharecroppers who could not pay off their debts and therefore could not leave the property they worked (p. 407)

deficit spending government practice of spending borrowed money rather than raising taxes, usually an attempt to boost the economy (p. 690)

deflation a decline in the volume of available money or credit that results in lower prices, and, therefore, increases the buying power of money (pp. 455, 501)

deport to expel individuals from the country (p. 602)

détente a policy which attempts to relax or ease tensions between nations (p. 956)

developing nation a nation whose economy is primarily agricultural (p. 801)

direct primary a vote held by all members of a political party to decide their candidate for public office (p. 549)

disco popular dance music characterized by hypnotic rhythm, repetitive lyrics, and electronically produced sounds (p. 973)

disfranchise to deprive of the right to vote (p. 740)

DNA the genetic material in cells that determines all forms of life (p. 1015)

dollar diplomacy a policy of joining the business interests of a country with its diplomatic interests abroad (p. 541)

domino theory the belief that if one nation in Asia fell to the Communists, neighboring countries would follow (p. 894)

dove a person in favor of the United States withdrawing from the Vietnam War (p. 907)

downsizing reducing a company in size by laying off workers and managers to become more efficient (p. 1005)

dry farming a way of farming dry land in which seeds are planted deep in the ground where there is some moisture (p. 422)

due process a judicial requirement that laws may not treat individuals unfairly, arbitrarily, or unreasonably, and that courts must follow proper procedures and rules when trying cases (pp. 186, 844)

Dust Bowl name given to the area of the southern Great Plains severely damaged by droughts and dust storms during the 1930s (p. 663)

duty a tax on imports (p. 159)

dynamic conservatism policy of balancing economic conservatism with some activism (p. 811)

E

economies of scale the reduction in the cost of a good brought about especially by increased production at a given facility (p. 448)

emancipation the act or process of freeing enslaved persons (pp. 150, 286)

embargo a government ban on trade with other countries (pp. 225, 964)

empresario a person who arranged for the settlement of Texas in the 1800s (p. 301)

encomienda system of rewarding conquistadors tracts of land, including the right to tax and exact labor from Native Americans (p. 54)

Enlightenment movement during the 1700s that promoted science, knowledge, and reason (p. 108)

entrepreneur one who organizes, manages, and assumes the risks of a business or enterprise (pp. 97, 438)

enumerated powers powers listed in the Constitution as belonging to the federal government (pp. 181, 213)

envoy a person delegated to represent one country to another (p. 309)

espionage spying, especially to gain government secrets (p. 588)

ethnic cleansing the expulsion, imprisonment, or killing of ethnic minorities by a dominant majority group (p. 1020)

eugenics a pseudo-science that deals with the improvement of hereditary qualities of a race or breed (p. 611)

euro the basic currency shared by the countries of the European Union since 1999 (p. 1023)

evolution the scientific theory that humans and other forms of life have evolved over time (p. 614)

executive branch branch of government that implements and enforces laws (p. 168)

executive privilege principle stating that communications of the executive branch should remain confidential to protect national security (p. 961)

extermination camp a camp where prisoners were sent to be executed (p. 723)

F

fallout radioactive particles dispersed by a nuclear explosion (p. 796)

fallout shelter a shelter built with the intent to house and protect people from nuclear fallout (p. 796)

fascism a political system headed by a dictator that calls for extreme nationalism and racism and no tolerance of opposition (p. 709)

"favorite son" men who enjoyed the support of leaders from their own state and region (p. 259)

featherbedding practice of limiting work output in order to create more jobs (p. 809)

federalism political system in which power is divided between the national and state governments (pp. 168, 181)

Federalist a supporter of the Constitution (p. 173)

feminism the belief that men and women should be equal politically, economically, and socially (p. 927)

Glossary

feudalism political system in which powerful leaders gave land to nobles in exchange for pledges of loyalty and service (p. 33)

filibuster an attempt to kill a bill by having a group of senators take turns speaking continuously so that a vote cannot take place (p. 878)

fireside chats radio broadcasts made by FDR to the American people to explain his initiatives (p. 684)

fixed costs costs a company must pay regardless of whether or not it is operating (p. 448)

flapper a young woman of the 1920s who showed freedom from convention, especially in dress (p. 613)

flexible response the buildup of conventional troops and weapons to allow a nation to fight a limited war without using nuclear weapons (p. 847)

forage to search or raid for food (p. 370)

foreclose to take possession of a property from a mortgagor because of defaults on payments (p. 671)

fossil fuel a fuel formed in the earth from decayed plant or animal remains (p. 942)

franchise the right or license to market a company's goods or services in an area, such as a store of a chain operation (p. 815)

freedmen persons freed from slavery (p. 389)

Freedom Riders name given to a group of people who traveled to the South in 1961 to protest the South's refusal to integrate bus terminals (p. 875)

fundamentalist a Protestant evangelical Christian who believes in being saved from sins by being born again and making a personal commitment to follow Jesus Christ (p. 614)

furnishing merchant merchant who provides sharecroppers with supplies on credit at high interest rates (p. 407)

G

general strike a strike involving all the workers in a particular geographic location (p. 600)

generation gap a cultural separation between parents and their children (p. 824)

gentry wealthy landowners in the South, also called the planter elite (p. 86)

glacier a huge ice sheet (p. 13)

glasnost a Soviet policy permitting open discussion of political and social issues and freer dissemination of news and information (p. 1002)

global warming an increase in average world temperatures over time (p. 1025)

gold standard a monetary standard in which one ounce of gold equaled a set number of dollars (p. 681)

goldbug a person who believes that American currency should be based on a gold standard (p. 506)

gradualism theory that slavery should be ended gradually (p. 285)

graduated income tax tax based on the net income of an individual or business and which taxes different income levels at different rates (p. 504)

graft the acquisition of money in dishonest ways, as in bribing a politician (pp. 400, 473)

grandfather clause a clause that allowed individuals who did not pass the literacy test to vote if their fathers or grandfathers had voted before Reconstruction began; an exception to a law based on preexisting circumstances (p. 510)

grassroots movement a group of people organizing at the local or community level, away from political or cultural centers (p. 1006)

Great Awakening movement during the 1700s that stressed dependence on God (p. 108)

greenback a piece of U.S. paper money first issued by the North during the Civil War (pp. 352, 501)

gross national product the total value of goods and services produced by a country during a year (p. 436)

guerrilla member of an armed band that carries out surprise attacks and sabotage rather than open warfare (pp. 577, 894)

guerrilla warfare a hit-and-run technique used in fighting a war; fighting by small bands of warriors using tactics such as sudden ambushes (p. 139)

guru a person with knowledge or expertise, especially a religious teacher and spiritual guide in Hinduism (p. 971)

H

habeas corpus a legal order for an inquiry to determine whether a person has been lawfully imprisoned (p. 353)

hacienda a huge ranch (p. 55)

hardtack a hard biscuit made of wheat flour (p. 366)

hawk someone who believed the United States should continue its military efforts in Vietnam (p. 907)

headright system in which settlers were granted land in exchange for settling in Virginia (p. 64)

hedgerow row of shrubs or trees surrounding a field, often on a dirt wall (p. 765)

hemispheric defense zone national policy during World War II that declared the Western Hemisphere to be neutral and that the United States would patrol this region against German submarines (p. 727)

heretic a dissenter from established church beliefs (p. 69)

hidalgo low-ranking nobles who came to America as conquistadors (p. 54)

hobo a homeless and usually penniless wanderer (p. 662)

holding company a company whose primary business is owning a controlling share of stock in other companies (p. 450)

Holocaust name given to the mass slaughter of Jews and other groups by the Nazis during World War II (p. 719)

homestead method of acquiring a piece of U.S. public land by living on and cultivating it (p. 421)

Hooverville nickname given to shantytowns in the United States during the Depression (p. 662)

horizontal integration the combining of competing firms into one corporation (p. 449)

I

Ice Age a period of extremely cold temperatures when part of the planet's surface was covered with massive ice sheets (p. 13)

immunity freedom from prosecution (p. 638)

impeach to formally charge a public official with misconduct in office (pp. 169, 183, 394, 961)

imperialism the actions used by one nation to exercise political or economic control over a smaller or weaker nation (p. 521)

implied powers powers not specifically listed in the Constitution but claimed by the federal government (p. 213)

impound to take possession of (p. 955)

impressment a kind of legalized kidnapping in which people are forced into military service (p. 225)

income tax a tax based on the net income of a person or business (p. 568)

indentured servant an individual who contracts to work for a colonist for a specified number of years in exchange for transportation to the colonies, food, clothing, and shelter (p. 86)

industrial union an organization of common laborers and craft workers in a particular industry (p. 455)

inflation the loss of value of money (pp. 120, 501, 844)

initiative the right of citizens to place a measure or issue before the voters or the legislature for approval (p. 549)

installment buying an item on credit with a monthly plan to pay off the value of the good (p. 662)

insubordination disobedience (p. 565)

insurrection an act of rebellion against the established government (p. 337)

interchangeable parts uniform pieces that can be made in large quantities to replace other identical pieces (p. 248)

internationalism a national policy of actively trading with foreign countries to foster peace and prosperity (p. 712)

Internet an electronic communications network that connects computer networks and organizational computer facilities around the world (p. 1014)

interposition theory that a state should be able to intervene between the federal government and the people to stop an illegal action (p. 220)

iron curtain the political and military barrier that isolated Soviet-controlled countries of Eastern Europe after World War II (p. 782)

isolationism a national policy of avoiding involvement in world affairs (pp. 649, 711)

J

jazz American style of music that developed from ragtime and blues and which uses syncopated rhythms and melodies (p. 627)

Jim Crow laws statutes or laws created to enforce segregation (p. 510)

jingoism extreme nationalism marked by aggressive foreign policy (p. 529)

joint committee a committee organized with members from both the House and Senate to work on specific issues (p. 183)

joint-stock company form of business organization in which many investors pool funds to raise large amounts of money for large projects (p. 61)

judicial branch branch of government that interprets laws and renders judgment in cases involving those laws (p. 168)

judicial review power of the Supreme Court to determine whether laws of Congress are constitutional and to strike down those that are not (pp. 185, 223)

juvenile delinquency antisocial or criminal behavior of young people (p. 831)

K

kachina a good spirit that the Pueblo people believed brought messages from the gods to their town each year (p. 21)

kamikaze during World War II, a Japanese suicide pilot whose mission was to crash into his target (p. 761)

kinship group large group of extended families (p. 23)

kiva circular ceremonial room built by the Anasazi (p. 16)

L

labor union an organization of workers formed for the purpose of advancing its members' interests (p. 249)

laissez-faire policy that government should interfere as little as possible in the nation's economy (p. 438)

land grant a grant of land by the federal government especially for roads, railroads, or agricultural colleges (p. 445)

legislative branch a branch of government that makes the nation's laws (p. 168)

letters of marque licenses issued by Congress to private ship owners authorizing them to attack British merchant ships (p. 143)

Glossary

liberal a person who generally believes the government should take an active role in the economy and in social programs but should not dictate social behavior (p. 981)

Liberty ship basic cargo ship used by the United States during World War II (p. 738)

limited war a war fought with limited commitment of resources to achieve a limited objective, such as containing communism (p. 789)

line of demarcation north-south line of longitude through the Atlantic Ocean dividing lands in the Americas claimed by Spain and Portugal (p. 42)

linkage policy of improving relations with the Soviet Union and China in hopes of persuading them to cut back their aid to North Vietnam (p. 910)

lockout a company tool to fight union demands by refusing to allow employees to enter its facilities to work (p. 456)

longhouse large, rectangular building with barrel-shaped roofs covered in bark, used by some Native Americans (p. 23)

long drive driving cattle long distances to a railroad depot for fast transport and great profit (p. 417)

Loyalist American colonists who supported Britain and opposed the War for Independence (p. 129)

lynching an execution performed without lawful approval (p. 511)

M

maize one of the first crops grown by early Americans, known today as corn (p. 14)

mandate authorization to act given to a representative (p. 378)

Manifest Destiny idea popular in the United States during the 1800s that the country must expand its boundaries to the Pacific Ocean (p. 295)

manorialism economic system in which peasants provide services to a feudal lord in exchange for protection (p. 33)

manumission the voluntary freeing of enslaved persons (p. 151)

margin buying a stock by paying only a fraction of the stock price and borrowing the rest (p. 657)

margin call demand by a broker that investors pay back loans made for stocks purchased on margin (p. 657)

martial law the law administered by military forces that is invoked by a government in an emergency (p. 345)

Marxism theory of socialism in which a class struggle would exist until the workers were finally victorious, creating a classless society (p. 456)

mass media a medium of communication (as in television and radio) intended to reach a wide audience (p. 623)

mass production the production of large quantities of goods using machinery and often an assembly line (p. 641)

massive retaliation a policy of threatening a massive response, including the use of nuclear weapons, against a Communist state trying to seize a peaceful state by force (p. 798)

matrilineal relating to, based on, or tracing descent through the maternal line (p. 30)

maverick a stray calf with no identifying symbol (p. 418)

mercantilism the theory that a state's power depends on its wealth (p. 98)

microprocessor a computer processor containing both memory and computing functions on a single chip (p. 1013)

Middle Passage the difficult journey slaves endured in crossing the Atlantic Ocean to the Americas (p. 89)

military-industrial complex an informal relationship that some people believe exists between the military and the defense industry to promote greater military spending and influence government policy (p. 802)

minutemen companies of civilian soldiers who boasted they were ready to fight on a minute's notice (p. 129)

missile gap belief that the Soviet Union had more nuclear weapons than the United States (p. 841)

monopoly total control of a type of industry by one person or one company (p. 449)

moratorium a suspension of activity (p. 650)

mosque Muslim place of worship (p. 28)

most-favored nation a policy between countries ensuring fair trading practices (p. 216)

muckraker a journalist who uncovers abuses and corruption in a society (p. 547)

mudslinging attempt to ruin an opponent's reputation with insults (p. 260)

multinational corporation large corporations with overseas investments (p. 815)

N

napalm a jellied gasoline used for bombs (pp. 768, 900)

nationalism loyalty and devotion to a nation (pp. 232, 578)

nativism hostility toward immigrants (pp. 274, 468)

natural rights fundamental rights all people are born possessing, including the right to life, liberty, and property (p. 102)

naturalism a philosophy and approach to art and literature in which nature is treated realistically, can be understood through scientific observation, and that society will function best with some governmental regulation (p. 483)

nomad a person who continually moves from place to place, usually in search of food (pp. 13, 425)

nonimportation agreement a pledge by merchants not to buy imported goods from a particular source (p. 121)

normalcy the state or fact of being normal (p. 637)

Northwest Passage the mythical northern water route through North America to the Pacific Ocean (p. 55)

nuclear proliferation the spread of nuclear weapons to new nations (p. 1025)

nullification theory that states have the right to declare a federal law invalid (pp. 220, 268)

O

---

obsidian a dark glass formed by the cooling of molten lava (p. 14)

Open Door policy a policy that allowed each foreign nation in China to trade freely in the other nations' spheres of influence (p. 538)

open range vast areas of grassland owned by the federal government (p. 416)

open shop a workplace where workers are not required to join a union (p. 645)

operating costs costs that occur while running a company (p. 448)

overlander someone who travels overland to the West (p. 296)

override ability of Congress to reverse a presidential veto by a two-thirds majority vote (p. 182)

P

---

pacifism opposition to war or violence as a means of settling disputes (p. 75)

party boss the person in control of a political machine (p. 473)

Patriot American colonist who supported the War for Independence (p. 129)

patronage another name for the spoils system, in which government jobs or favors are given out to political allies and friends (p. 492)

penitentiary prison whose purpose is to reform prisoners (p. 280)

perestroika a policy of economic and government restructuring instituted by Mikhail Gorbachev in the Soviet Union in the 1980s (p. 1002)

periphery the outer boundary of something (p. 745)

perjury lying when one has sworn under oath to tell the truth (pp. 792, 1020)

philanthropy providing money to support humanitarian or social goals (p. 478)

pietism movement in the 1700s that stressed an individual's piety and an emotional union with God (p. 108)

Pilgrim a Separatist who journeyed to the American colonies in the 1600s for religious freedom (p. 67)

pillage to loot or plunder (p. 379)

placer mining method of extracting mineral ore by hand using simple tools like picks, shovels, and pans (p. 415)

plantation a large, commercial, agricultural estate (p. 85)

planter plantation owners who held 20 or more enslaved people (p. 253)

pocket veto indirectly vetoing a bill by letting a session of Congress expire without signing the bill (p. 388)

police powers a government's power to control people and property in the interest of public safety, health, welfare, and morals (p. 615)

political machine an organization linked to a political party that often controlled local government (p. 473)

poll tax a tax of a fixed amount per person that had to be paid before the person could vote (pp. 510, 879)

pool a group sharing in some activity; for example, among railroad owners who made secret agreements and set rates among themselves (p. 448)

popular sovereignty government subject to the will of the people (p. 168); before the Civil War, the idea that people living in a territory had the right to decide by voting if slavery would be allowed there (pp. 180, 321)

populism political movement founded in the 1890s representing mainly farmers, favoring free coinage of silver and government control of railroads and other large industries (p. 500)

poverty line a level of personal or family income below which one is classified as poor by the federal government (p. 828)

presidio fort built by the Spanish in the Americas (p. 54)

privateer privately owned ship licensed by the government to attack ships of other countries (p. 61)

progressivism a political movement that crossed party lines which believed that industrialism and urbanization had created many social problems and that government should take a more active role in dealing with these problems (p. 547)

prohibition laws banning the manufacture, transportation, and sale of alcoholic beverages (p. 553)

propaganda the spreading of ideas about an institution or individual for the purpose of influencing opinion (p. 581)

proprietary colony a colony owned by an individual (p. 64)

protective tariff tax on imports designed to protect American manufacturers (p. 241)

protectorate a country that is technically independent but is actually under the control of another country (p. 521)

public works projects such as highways, parks, and libraries built with public funds for public use (p. 669)

pueblo Spanish for village, term used by early Spanish explorers to denote large housing structures built by the Anasazi (p. 16)

Puritan someone who wanted to purify the Anglican Church during the 1500s and 1600s (p. 60)

Q

---

quartz mining method of extracting minerals involving digging beneath the surface (p. 415)

Glossary

R

racism prejudice or discrimination against someone because of his or her race (p. 882)

radiocarbon dating method of determining how old biological objects are by measuring the radioactivity left in a special type of carbon (p. 13)

ragtime a type of music with a strong rhythm and a lively melody with accented notes (p. 480)

rationalism philosophy that emphasizes the role of logic and reason in gaining knowledge (p. 108)

rationing the giving out of scarce items on a limited basis (p. 753)

realism an approach to literature, art, and theater that attempts to accurately portray things as they really are and holds that society will function best if left to itself (p. 478)

reapportionment the method states use to draw up political districts based on changes in population (p. 843)

rebate a partial refund to lower the rate of a good or commodity (p. 495)

recall the right that enables voters to remove unsatisfactory elected officials from office (p. 549)

recession an economic slowdown (p. 160)

Reconstruction the reorganization and rebuilding of the former Confederate states after the Civil War (p. 387)

referendum the practice of letting voters accept or reject measures proposed by the legislature (pp. 335, 549)

relief aid for the needy, welfare (p. 670)

Renaissance French for rebirth, a period in Europe from 1350 to 1600 during which a rebirth of interest in the culture of ancient Greece and Rome occurred (p. 36)

reparations payment by the losing country in a war to the winner for the damages caused by the war (p. 596)

republic form of government in which power resides in a body of citizens entitled to vote (p. 147)

reserved powers those powers which, according to the Constitution, are retained by the states (p. 181)

Restoration term used to describe when the English Parliament decided to put the monarchy back into place in 1660 (p. 73)

revenue tariff tax on imports for the purpose of raising money (p. 241)

revival large public meeting for preaching and prayer (p. 108)

right-to-work law a law making it illegal to require employees to join a union (p. 809)

romanticism a literary, artistic, and philosophical movement in the 1700s emphasizing the imagination and the emotions, advocating feeling over reason, inner spirituality over external rules, the individual above society, and nature over environments created by humans (p. 276)

S

safety net something that provides security against misfortune; specifically, government relief programs intended to protect against economic disaster (p. 700)

savannah a rolling grassland (p. 27)

scalawag name given to Southerners who supported Republican Reconstruction of the South (p. 399)

secede to leave or withdraw (p. 268)

secession withdrawal from the Union (p. 323)

sedition incitement to rebellion (p. 219)

segregation the separation or isolation of a race, class, or group (p. 510)

select committee a committee organized in the House or Senate to complete a specific task (p. 183)

selectmen men chosen to manage a town's affairs (p. 94)

self-determination belief that people in a territory should have the ability to choose their own government (p. 578)

separate-but-equal doctrine established by the 1896 Supreme Court case *Plessy* v. *Ferguson* that permitted laws segregating African Americans as long as equal facilities were provided (p. 867)

separation of powers government principle in which power is divided among different branches (p. 168)

Separatist a Puritan who broke away from the Anglican Church (p. 66)

serf person bound to a manor (p. 33)

settlement house institution located in a poor neighborhood that provided numerous community services such as medical care, child care, libraries, and classes in English (p. 485)

shantytown an economically depressed section of town consisting of crudely built dwellings usually made of wood (p. 662)

sharecropper farmer who works land for an owner who provides equipment and seed and receives a share of the crop (pp. 407, 509)

siege a military blockade of a city or fortified place to force it to surrender (p. 370)

silverite person who believes that coining silver currency in unlimited quantities will eliminate economic crisis (p. 506)

sin tax federal tax on alcohol and tobacco (p. 404)

sit-down strike method of boycotting work by sitting down at work and refusing to leave the establishment (p. 693)

sit-in a form of protest involving occupying seats or sitting down on the floor of an establishment (p. 868)

skyscraper a very tall building (p. 470)

slash-and-burn agriculture farming technique in which land is cleared and made fertile by cutting down and burning forests (p. 23)

slave code a set of laws that formally regulated slavery and defined the relationship between enslaved Africans and free people (pp. 90, 254)

smog fog made heavier and darker by smoke and chemical fumes (p. 940)

soap opera a serial drama on television or radio using melodramatic situations (p. 664)

Social Security Act a law requiring workers and employers to pay a tax; the money provides a monthly stipend for retired people (p. 694)

socialism belief that business should be publicly owned and run by the government (p. 553)

sodbuster a name given to Great Plains farmers (p. 422)

software a computer program (p. 1013)

space race refers to the Cold War competition over dominance of space exploration capability (p. 847)

space shuttle a reusable spacecraft designed to transport people and cargo between Earth and space (p. 998)

space station a large satellite designed to be occupied for long periods and to serve as a base for operations in space (p. 999)

speakeasy a place where alcoholic beverages are sold illegally (p. 615)

speculation act of buying stocks at great risk with the anticipation that the price will rise (p. 657)

speculator person who risks money in hopes of a financial profit (p. 212)

sphere of influence section of a country where one foreign nation enjoys special rights and powers (p. 538)

spoils system practice of handing out government jobs to supporters; replacing government employees with the winning candidate's supporters (p. 267)

Square Deal Theodore Roosevelt's promise of fair and equal treatment for all (p. 556)

squatter someone who settles on public land under government regulation with the hopes of acquiring the title to the land (p. 295)

stagflation persistent inflation combined with stagnant consumer demand and relatively high unemployment (p. 964)

standing committee a permanent committee in the House or Senate organized for a specific area of focus (p. 183)

state-sponsored terrorism violent acts against civilians that are secretly supported by a government in order to attack other nations without going to war (p. 1033)

steerage cramped quarters on a ship's lower decks for passengers paying the lowest fares (p. 465)

stock market a system for buying and selling stocks in corporations (p. 657)

strategic defense a plan to develop missiles and other devices that can shoot down nuclear missiles before they hit the United States (p. 1029)

strategic materials materials needed for fighting a war (p. 729)

strike work stoppage by workers to force an employer to meet demands (p. 249)

subsistence farming farming only enough food to feed one's family (p. 87)

subversion a systematic attempt to overthrow a government by using persons working secretly from within (p. 791)

suffrage the right to vote (p. 549)

summit a meeting of heads of government (p. 957)

Sunbelt a new industrial region in southern California and the Deep South developing during World War II (p. 751)

supply-side economics economic theory that lower taxes will boost the economy as businesses and individuals invest their money, thereby creating higher tax revenue (pp. 648, 987)

syndicate a business group (p. 564)

teach-in an extended meeting or class held to discuss a social or political issue (p. 905)

Tejano Spanish-speaking inhabitants of Texas (p. 300)

telecommute to work at home by means of an electronic linkup with a central office (p. 1013)

televangelist an evangelist who conducts regularly televised religious programs (p. 984)

temperance moderation in or abstinence from alcohol (pp. 279, 553)

tenant farmer farmer who works land owned by another and pays rent either in cash or crops (p. 407)

tenement multi-family apartments, usually dark, crowded, and barely meeting minimum living standards (p. 471)

termination policy a government policy to bring Native Americans into mainstream society by withdrawing recognition of Native American groups as legal entities (p. 830)

terrorism the use of violence by non-governmental groups against civilians to achieve a political goal by instilling fear and frightening governments into changing policies (p. 1032)

time zone a geographical region in which the same standard time is kept (p. 444)

Title IX section of the 1972 Educational Amendments prohibiting federally funded schools from discriminating against girls and young women in nearly all aspects of their operations (p. 929)

town meeting a gathering of free men in a New England town to elect leaders which developed into the local town government (p. 94)

trade deficit the difference between the value of a country's imports versus its exports (p. 1023)

trade union an organization of workers with the same trade or skill (p. 455)

Glossary

Glossary

transcendental meditation a technique of meditation in which a mantra is chanted as a way of achieving peak intelligence, harmony, and health (p. 971)

transcendentalism a philosophy stressing the relationship between human beings and nature, spiritual things over material things, and the importance of the individual conscience (p. 276)

transcontinental railroad a railway system extending across the continent (p. 328)

triangular trade a three-way trade route that exchanged goods between the American colonies and two other trading partners (p. 95)

trust a combination of firms or corporations formed by a legal agreement, especially to reduce competition (p. 450)

U-boat German submarine, term means *Unterseeboot* (undersea boat) (p. 581)

Underground Railroad a system that helped enslaved African Americans follow a network of escape routes out of the South to freedom in the North (p. 327)

unfair trade practices trading practices which derive a gain at the expense of the competition (p. 569)

union shop a business that requires employees to join a union (p. 809)

urban renewal government programs that attempt to eliminate poverty and revitalize urban areas (p. 829)

utopia community based on a vision of a perfect society sought by reformers (p. 277)

vaquero men who herded cattle on haciendas (p. 55)

vaudeville stage entertainment made up of various acts, such as dancing, singing, comedy, and magic shows (p. 480)

vertical integration the combining of companies that supply equipment and services needed for a particular industry (p. 449)

veto power of the chief executive to reject laws passed by the legislature (p. 169)

victory garden gardens planted by American citizens during war to raise vegetables for home use, leaving more for the troops (pp. 586, 754)

Vietcong the guerrilla soldiers of the Communist faction in Vietnam, also known as the National Liberation Front (p. 897)

Vietnamization the process of making South Vietnam assume more of the war effort by slowly withdrawing American troops from Vietnam (p. 911)

War Hawks members of Congress during Madison's presidency who pressed for war with Britain (p. 229)

war on poverty antipoverty program under President Lyndon Johnson (p. 856)

welfare capitalism system in which companies enable employees to buy stock, participate in profit sharing, and receive benefits such as medical care common in the 1920s (p. 645)

white-collar jobs in fields not requiring work clothes or protective clothing, such as sales (p. 815)

wigwam conical or dome-shaped dwelling built by Native Americans using bent poles covered with hides or bark (p. 23)

writ of assistance a search warrant enabling customs officers to enter any location to look for evidence of smuggling (p. 122)

yellow journalism type of sensational, biased, and often false reporting for the sake of attracting readers (p. 528)

yeoman farmer owner of a small farm with four or fewer enslaved persons, and usually none (p. 253)

yuppie a young college-educated adult who is employed in a well-paying profession and who lives and works in or near a large city (p. 995)

Spanish Glossary

A

abolition/abolición el final inmediato de la esclavitud (p. 285)

affirmative action/acción afirmativa un esfuerzo activo para mejorar las oportunidades educacionales y de empleo para las minorías (p. 933)

agrarianism/agrarismo filosofía de que la agricultura y la propiedad de tierras son los elementos principales de la economía (p. 214)

agricultural revolution/revolución agrícola período cuando los primeros americanos aprendieron plantar y cultivar la cosecha (p. 13)

alien/extranjero una persona que vive en un país del cual no es ciudadano (p. 219)

allotment/parcela un terreno asignado a un individuo o familia para su cultivación (p. 430)

amendment/enmienda un cambio a la Constitución (p.169)

Americanization/americanización causar que una persona adquiera características y rasgos americanos (p. 485)

amnesty/amnistía el acto de otorgar perdón a un número grande de personas (p. 387)

amphtrac/*amphtrac* un tractor anfibio utilizado para mover tropas desde barcos a la orilla del mar (p. 760)

anarchist/anarquista una persona que cree que no debe haber ningún gobierno (p. 611)

annexation/anexión incorporar un territorio dentro del dominio de un país (p. 304)

annuity/anualidad dinero pagado por contrato en intervalos regulares (p. 426)

Antifederalist/antifederalista oponente a la Constitución (p. 173)

appeasement/apaciguamiento demandas aceptadas a fin de evitar conflictos (p. 714)

appropriate/asignar apartar fondos para gastos (p. 183)

arbitration/arbitraje arreglar una disputa acordando aceptar la decisión de una persona imparcial (pp. 458, 557)

armistice/armisticio acuerdo temporal de paz para terminar con una lucha (p. 596)

artisan/artesano trabajador diestro que practica las artesanías y habilidades manuales (p. 95)

assembly line/línea de montaje sistema de producción con máquinas y trabajadores arreglados para que cada persona haga su trabajo designado una y otra vez mientras el artículo pasa frente a ellos (p. 641)

assimilate/asimilar incorporar a un grupo dentro de la cultura de una población más grande (p. 430)

astrolabe/astrolabio instrumento usado para determinar la dirección, latitud y la hora de una localidad (p. 36)

attrition/atrición acto de desalentar por constantes ataques o acoso (p. 355)

B

baby boom/auge de nacimientos aumento marcado en la taza de natalidad, tal como ocurrió en Estados Unidos después de la Segunda Guerra Mundial (p. 816)

bailiff/alguacil oficial en rango menor de las Cortes (p. 662)

benevolent society/sociedad de beneficencia una asociación enfocada en llevar la palabra de Dios y combatir problemas sociales (p. 279)

bilingualism/bilingualismo la práctica de enseñar a estudiantes inmigrantes en su propio lenguaje (p. 935)

bill/proyecto de ley una ley propuesta (p. 183)

bill of exchange/letra de cambio crédito en papel dado por mercaderes ingleses a colonos a cambio de azúcar (p. 95)

binding arbitration/arbitraje obligatorio proceso por el cual un partido neutral escucha argumentos de dos partidos opositores y toma una decisión que ambos deben aceptar (p. 692)

black codes/códigos negros leyes aprobadas en el Sur al terminar la Guerra Civil para controlar a los libertos y permitir a los dueños de plantaciones la explotación de los trabajadores afroamericanos (p. 393)

black power/poder negro mobilización del poder económico y político de afroamericanos especialmente para imponer respeto por sus derechos y para mejorar su condiciones (p. 884)

blitzkrieg/guerra relámpago nombre dado a los ataques repentinos ofensivos violentos que los alemanes usaron durante la Segunda Guerra Mundial (p. 715)

blockade runner/forzador de bloqueo un barco que navega a través de un bloqueo, usualmente para pasar contrabando a través de un área protegida (p. 359)

blue-collar/collar azul trabajos de mano de obra, particularmente aquellos que requieren ropa protectora (p. 815)

blues/*blues* estilo de música que evolucionó de la música espiritual de los afroamericanos, distinguida por su sonido melancólico (p. 626)

Bohemian/bohemio una persona (como artista o escritor) que lleva un estilo de vida poco convencional (p. 621)

bonanza farm/granja en bonanza extensa granja de trigo que produce muchas ganancias (p. 422)

bond/bono una obligación emitida por el gobierno que promete pagar un préstamo con interés (p. 212)

bounty/recompensa dinero dado para animar el alistamiento en el ejército (p. 358)

brinkmanship/política arriesgada la buena voluntad para ir al borde de guerra para forzar a un oponente a que se retracte (p. 799)

broker state/estado intermediario el papel del gobierno para resolver conflictos entre grupos con intereses competitivos (p. 700)

budget deficit/déficit del presupuesto la cantidad por la cual los gastos exceden los ingresos (p. 987)

bull market/bolsa al alza largo período durante el cual los precios de acciones en la bolsa se incrementan (p. 657)

burgesses/burgueses representantes elegidos para la asamblea general de la colonia de Virginia (p. 64)

busing/traslado obligatorio la política de transportar estudiantes a escuelas fuera de sus vecindarios para alcanzar un balance racial (p. 934)

cabinet/gabinete grupo de consejeros al presidente (p. 184, 211)

capital gains tax/impuestos a las ganancias del capital impuesto federal pagado por inversionistas y negocios cuando ellos venden acciones y bienes raíces (p. 1006)

capitalist/capitalista persona que invierte riqueza, particularmente dinero, en un negocio (p. 97)

caravel/carabela buque capaz de explorar largas distancias (p. 37)

carpetbagger/*carpetbagger* nombre dado a muchos norteños que se mudaron al Sur después de la Guerra Civil y apoyaron a los republicanos (p. 399)

cash crop/cultivo comercial cosecha cultivada para ganancia (p. 85)

caucus system/sistema de junta electoral sistema en el cual los miembros de un partido político se reúnen para escoger el candidato a la presidencia de su partido o para decidir políticas (p. 268)

cede/ceder darse por vencido por un tratado (p. 311)

censure/censura expresar la desaprobación formal sobre una acción (p. 795)

chad/agujereado pedazo pequeño de cartón producido taladrando una tarjeta de computadora (p. 1028)

charter/carta de privilegio una constitución (p. 771)

checks and balances/control y balances sistema en el cual cada ramo de gobierno tiene la habilidad para limitar el poder a los otros ramos para que ninguno vuelva a ser demasiado poderoso (p. 168)

circumnavigate/circunnavegar navegar alrededor de (p. 43)

civilization/civilización cultura sumamente desarrollada distinguida por un conocimiento de comercio, gobierno, las artes, las ciencias, y frecuentemente lenguaje escrito (p. 14)

closed shop/taller cerrado acuerdo en el que una compañía contrata solamente a miembros del sindicato (pp. 458, 809)

cloture/clausura una moción que termina con el debate y requiere un voto inmediato, posible en el Senado de EEUU por un voto de 60 senadores (p. 878)

Cold War/Guerra Fría conflicto ideológico caracterizado por frecuentes confrontaciones entre Estados Unidos y la Unión Soviética entre los años 1946 y 1990 (p. 778)

Columbian Exchange/Intercambio Colombiano una serie de interacciones complejas sociales y del medio ambiente entre Europa y las Américas que empezó con el primer viaje de Colón (p. 43)

commission plan/gobierno por comisión plan en el cual el gobierno municipal está dividido dentro de diferentes departamentos con diferentes funciones, cada uno bajo la dirección de un comisionado (p. 548)

committee of correspondence/comité de correspondencia comité organizado en cada colonia para comunicar entre las colonias y unificarlas (p. 127)

commune/comuna un arreglo de vivienda en el cual los miembros de un grupo trabajan juntos y comparten todo (p. 923)

concentration camp/campo de concentración un campamento donde personas están detenidas o encerradas (p. 723)

concurrent powers/poderes concurrentes poderes compartidos por los estados y el gobierno federal (p. 181)

Confederacy/Confederación nación formada por los estados sureños que se separaron de la Unión en 1860-1861 (p. 343)

conference committee/comité de conferencia una comisión paritaria especial organizada para ayudar a la Cámara y al Senado a forjar un compromiso de ley aceptable para ambas cámaras (p. 183)

conquistador/conquistador los hombres que condujeron las expediciones para conquistar las Américas (p. 52)

conscription/reclutamiento requerir que personas ingresen en el servicio militar (pp. 353, 585)

consensus/consenso acuerdo general (p. 856)

conservative/conservador una persona que cree que el poder del gobierno, particularmente en la economía, debe estar limitado para llevar al máximo la libertad individual (p. 981)

constituent/elector residente de un distrito electoral (p. 183)

containment/contención la política o proceso de prevenir la expansión de un poder hostil (p. 784)

contra/contra contrarevolucionario, la fuerza guerilla anti-Sandinista en Nicaragua (p. 990)

contraband/contrabando artículos de los que la importación, exportación o posesión es ilegal (pp. 581)

convoy/convoy un grupo que viaja junto con algo, tal como un barco, para protegerlo (p. 594)

convoy system/sistema de convoy un sistema en el cual barcos mercantes viajan con buques navales para protección (p. 746)

cooperative/cooperativa tienda donde los granjeros compraban productos el uno del otro; empresa poseída y operada por los que usan sus servicios (p. 502)

cooperative individualism/individualismo cooperativo política del Presidente Hoover para alentar a los manufactureros y distribuidores a formar sus propias organizaciones y pasar información voluntariamente al gobierno federal en un esfuerzo para estimular la economía (p. 648)

corporation/sociedad anónima organización autorizada por ley a montar una actividad, tratada como si fuera una sola persona (p. 448, 686)

"corrupt bargain"/trato corrupto un acuerdo ilegítimo entre políticos (p. 259)

cost of living/costo de vida el costo de comprar artículos y servicios esenciales para la supervivencia (p. 599)

cost-plus/costo más beneficio contrato del gobierno para pagar el costo de fabricación para producir un artículo más un porcentaje garantizado (p. 737)

cotton gin/despepitadora de algodón máquina que sacaba las semillas de las fibras de algodón (p. 252)

counterculture/contracultura una cultura con valores y creencias diferentes de los de la cultura principal (p. 922)

coureur de bois/coureur de bois franceses que comerciaban con pieles y vivían entre los Nativos Americanos (p. 56)

covert/secreto no hecho o mostrado abiertamente (p. 801)

creationism/creacionismo la creencia que Dios creó al mundo y todo lo que hay en él, usualmente como se describe en Génesis (p. 614)

credibility gap/barrera de credibilidad falta de confianza (p. 905)

crop lien/derecho de cultivo obligación impuesta a un agricultor para cubrir la deuda por medio de cosecha (p. 407)

customs duty/derecho de aduana impuesto sobre importaciones y exportaciones (p.119)

de facto segregation/segregación de facto segregación por costumbre y tradición (p. 867)

debt peonage/esclavitud deudora condición de aparceros que no podían pagar sus deudas y por lo tanto no podían abandonar la propiedad que trabajaban (p. 407)

deficit spending/gastos déficits práctica del gobierno de gastar dinero prestado en vez de aumentar impuestos, usualmente una tentativa para levantar la economía (p. 690)

deflation/deflación un decremento de la cantidad de dinero o crédito disponible el cual resulta en precios reducidos y por lo tanto aumenta el poder adquisitivo de la moneda (pp. 455, 501)

deport/deportar expulsar del país a individuos (p. 602)

détente/détente una política que intenta relajar o borrar la tensión entre naciones (p. 956)

developing nation/nación en desarrollo nación en donde la economía es principalmente agrícola (p. 801)

direct primary/elección primaria voto tomado por todos los miembros de un partido político para elegir a su candidato para un puesto público (p. 549)

disco/música disco música popular para danza caracterizada por ritmo hipnótico, cantos repetitivos y sonidos producidos electrónicamente (p. 973)

disfranchise/privación civil privar el derecho al voto (p. 740)

DNA/ADN material genético de las células que determina toda forma de vida (p. 1015)

dollar diplomacy/diplomacia del dólar política de juntar los intereses comerciales de un país con sus intereses diplomáticos en el extranjero (p. 541)

domino theory/teoría dominó la creencia que si una nación en Asia se derrumbara ante los comunistas, sus países vecinos hubieran caído en seguida (p. 894)

dove/paloma persona a favor de que Estados Unidos se retirara de la guerra en Vietnam (p. 907)

dry farming/cultivo seco manera de cultivar tierra seca plantando las semillas en la profundidad de la tierra donde hay algo de humedad (p. 422)

due process/proceso justo requerimiento judicial de que las leyes no deben tratar individuos injusta, arbitraria, o irracionalmente y que las cortes deben de seguir procesos y reglamentos justos al jurar casos (pp. 186, 844)

Dust Bowl/Cuenca Polvada nombre dado al área sureña de las Grandes Planicies severamente dañada por sequías y tormentas de polvo durante los años 1930 (p. 663)

duty/impuesto un impuesto sobre importaciones (p.159)

dynamic conservatism/conservatismo dinámico política de alcanzar un balance entre el conservatismo económico y algún activismo (p. 811)

economies of scale/economía a gran escala reducción del costo de un producto a causa de la producción aumentada en una fábrica de producción (p. 448)

emancipation/emancipación el proceso de liberar a personas esclavizadas (p. 150, 286)

embargo/embargo prohibición gubernamental contra el comercio con otros países (pp. 225, 964)

empresario/**empresario** persona que arreglaba el asentamiento de tierras en Texas durante los años 1800 (p. 301)

encomienda/**encomienda** sistema de recompensar a los conquistadores con extensiones de tierra y el derecho de recaudar impuestos y exigir mano de obra a los indígenas americanos (p. 54)

Enlightenment/Siglo Ilustrado movimiento durante los años 1700 que promovió el conocimiento, la razón, y las ciencias (p. 108)

entrepreneur/empresario persona que organiza, dirige y asume el riesgo de un negocio o empresa (pp. 97, 438)

enumerated powers/poderes enumerados poderes nombrados en la Constitución que pertenecen solamente al gobierno federal (pp. 181, 213)

espionage/espionaje espiar, especialmente para obtener secretos gubernamentales (p. 588)

ethnic cleansing/purificación étnica expulsión, encarcelamiento o asesinato de minorías étnicas por un grupo mayoritario dominante (p. 1020)

eugenics/eugenesia seudociencia que trata con el perfeccionamiento de las cualidades hereditarias de una raza o especie (p. 611)

euro/eurodólar moneda básica compartida por los países de la Unión Europea desde 1999 (p. 1023)

evolution/evolución teoría científica que los humanos y otras formas de vida se han evolucionado tras el tiempo (p. 614)

executive branch/ramo ejecutivo ramo de gobierno que implementa y refuerza las leyes (p. 168)

executive privilege/privilegio ejecutivo el principio de que las comunicaciones del ramo ejecutivo deben de permanecer confidenciales para proteger la seguridad nacional (p. 961)

extermination camp/campo de exterminación campo donde los prisioneros eran enviados para ser ejecutados (p. 723)

F

---

fallout/caída radioactiva partículas radioactivas dispersadas por una explosión nuclear (p. 796)

fallout shelter/refugio atómico un refugio construido para proteger a las personas de la caída radioactiva (p. 796)

fascism/fascismo un sistema político encabezado por un dictador que pide por nacionalismo y racismo extremo y poca tolerancia de la oposición (p. 709)

favorite son/hijo favorito hombres que disfrutaban del apoyo de los líderes de su estado y región natales (p. 259)

featherbedding/paro técnico práctica de limitar la producción con el fin de crear más trabajos (p. 809)

federalism/federalismo sistema político en el cual el poder está dividido entre los estados y el gobierno federal (pp. 168, 181)

Federalist/federalista persona que apoya la Constitución (p. 173)

feminism/feminismo la creencia que los hombres y las mujeres deben ser iguales política, económica y socialmente (p. 927)

feudalism/feudalismo un sistema político en el cual los líderes poderosos dieron tierra a los nobles a cambio de compromisos de lealtad y servicio (p. 33)

filibuster/filibustero un atentado para acabar con un proyecto de ley hablando continuamente a turnos un grupo de senadores para que no pueda haber un voto (p. 878)

fireside chats/pláticas hogareñas emisiones de radio transmitidas por FDR al pueblo americano para explicar sus iniciativas (p. 684)

fixed costs/costos fijos costos que una compañía debe pagar si está operando o no (p. 448)

flapper/*flapper* mujer jóven de los años 1920 que demostró libertad de las costumbres tradicionales especialmente en vestido (p. 613)

flexible response/respuesta flexible formación de tropas y armas convencionales para permitir que un país entre en una guerra limitada sin usar armas nucleares (p. 847)

forage/forrajear buscar alimento (p. 370)

foreclose/ejecutar una hipoteca tomar posesión de una propiedad por falta de pagos hipotecarios (p. 671)

fossil fuel/combustible fósil un combustible formado en la tierra de los restos descompuestos de plantas o animales (p. 942)

franchise/concesión derecho o licencia para vender los bienes o servicios de una compañía en un área tal como una cadena de tiendas (p. 815)

freedman/liberto persona liberada de la esclavitud (p. 389)

Freedom Riders/Jinetes de la Libertad nombre dado a un grupo de personas que viajaron al Sur en 1961 para protestar la negativa del Sur para integrar las terminales de autobuses (p. 755)

fundamentalist/fundamentalista un cristiano protestante evangélico que cree en ser salvado de pecados volviendo a nacer otra vez y haciendo un compromiso personal para seguir a Cristo Jesus (p. 984)

furnishing merchant/mercader usurero comerciante que proporciona abastos a los aparceros a crédito con un interés muy alto (p. 407)

general strike/huelga general una huelga por todos los trabajadores de un lugar geográfico (p. 600)

generation gap/barrera generacional una separación cultural entre padres e hijos (p. 824)

gentry/pequeña nobleza ricos terratenientes del Sur, también llamados plantadores de la élite (p. 86)

glacier/glaciar trozo enorme de hielo (p. 13)

glasnost/glasnost política soviética que permitía discusión abierta de temas políticos y sociales y diseminación más libre de noticias e información (p. 1002)

global warming/calentamiento global aumento en la temperatura promedio mundial tras un período (p. 1025)

gold standard/patrón oro norma monetaria en la cual una onza de oro igualaba a un número fijo de dólares (p. 681)

goldbug/goldbug persona que cree que la moneda americana debe de estar basada en un patrón oro (p. 506)

gradualism/gradualismo teoría de que la esclavitud debería terminarse gradualmente (p. 285)

graduated income tax/impuesto graduado de utilidades impuesto basado en los ingresos netos de un individuo o empresa en el cual la taza del impuesto se diferencia de acuerdo a diferentes niveles de salario (p. 504)

graft/soborno adquisición de dinero de manera deshonesta tal como el sobornar a un político (pp. 400, 473)

grandfather clause/cláusula de abuelo cláusula que permitió votar a los que no aprobaron el examen de leer si sus padres o sus abuelos habían votado antes de que empezara la Reconstrucción; excepción a una ley basada en circunstancias preexistentes (p. 510)

grassroots movement/movimiento local grupo de personas que se organiza a nivel local y popular lejos de centros políticos o culturales (p. 1006)

Great Awakening/Gran Despertar movimiento durante los años 1700 que enfatizó la dependencia en Dios (p. 108)

greenback/billete dorso verde billete de papel moneda de EEUU expedido por primera vez por el Norte durante la Guerra Civil (pp. 352, 501)

gross national product/producto nacional bruto valor total de bienes y servicios producidos por un país durante un año (p. 436)

guerrilla/guerrilla banda armada que usa ataques sorpresas o sabotaje en vez de la guerra organizada (pp. 577, 894)

guerrilla warfare/guerra de guerrillas técnica de tirar y darse a la huida usada en combates de guerra; peleas por pequeñas bandas de guerreros usando tácticas tales como emboscadas repentinas (p. 139)

guru/gurú persona con conocimiento y experiencia, dicho especialmente de un maestro religioso y guía espiritual en el indoísmo (p. 971)

habeas corpus/hábeas corpus orden legal para una encuesta para determinar si una persona ha sido encarcelada legalmente (p. 353)

hacienda/hacienda un rancho extenso (p. 55)

hardtack/hardtack galleta dura hecha de harina de trigo (p. 366)

hawk/halcón persona que creía que Estados Unidos debía continuar sus esfuerzos militares en Vietnam (p. 907)

headright/derecho de terreno sistema en el cual los colonizadores recibían tierra a cambio de establecerse en Virginia (p. 64)

hedgerow/seto fila de arbustos o árboles cercando un campo a menudo sobre un muro de tierra (p. 765)

hemispheric defense zone/zona de defensa hemisférica política nacional durante la Segunda Guerra Mundial que declaró que el Hemisferio Oeste fue neutral y que Estados Unidos patrullaría esta región en contra de submarinos alemanes (p. 727)

heretic/hereje disidente de creencias establecidas por la iglesia (p. 69)

hidalgo/hidalgo noble de bajo rango que vino a América como conquistador (p. 54)

hobo/vagabundo persona errante sin hogar y usualmente sin dinero (p. 662)

holding company/compañía de valores compañía de la cual el negocio principal es poseer el control de acciones en otras compañías (p. 450)

Holocaust/Holocausto nombre dado a la exterminación masiva de judíos y otros grupos hecha por los nazis durante la Segunda Guerra Mundial (p. 719)

homestead/posesionar método de adquirir una extensión de tierra pública de EEUU viviendo en ella y cultivándola (p. 421)

Hooverville/Hooverville apodo dado a los barrios en Estados Unidos durante la Depresión (p. 662)

horizontal integration/integración horizontal asociación de firmas competitivas en una sociedad anónima (p. 449)

Ice Age/Época Glacial período de temperaturas extremadamente frías cuando parte de la superficie del planeta estaba cubierta de capas masivas de hielo (p. 13)

immunity/inmunidad libertad de prosecusión (p. 638)

impeach/acusar acusar formalmente a un oficial público de mala conducta en la oficina (pp. 169, 183, 394, 961)

imperialism/imperialismo acciones usadas por una nación para ejercer el control político o económico sobre naciones más pequeñas o débiles (p. 521)

implied powers/poderes implícitos poderes no nombrados específicamente en la Constitución pero reclamados por el gobierno federal (p. 213)

impound/confiscar tomar posesión de (p. 955)

impressment/requisición un tipo de secuestro legalizado en el cual personas son forzadas a servir en el servicio militar (p. 225)

income tax/impuesto de utilidades impuesto basado en el ingreso neto de una persona o empresa (p. 568)

indentured servant/sirviente contratado individuo contratado para trabajar para un colono durante cierto número de años a cambio de transportación a las colonias, alimento, ropa y refugio (p. 86)

industrial union/sindicato industrial organización de trabajadores comunes y obreros calificados en una industria (p. 455)

inflation/inflación pérdida del valor del dinero (pp. 120, 501, 844)

initiative/iniciativa derecho de los ciudadanos de poner una propuesta o tema ante los votantes o la legislatura para su aprobación (p. 549)

installment/pago a plazos compra de un artículo a crédito con un plan de pago mensual para pagar el valor del artículo (p. 662)

insubordination/insubordinación desobediencia (p. 565)

insurrection/insurrección un acto de rebelión en contra del gobierno establecido (p. 337)

interchangeable parts/partes intercambiables piezas uniformes que pueden ser hechas en grandes cantidades para reemplazar otras piezas idénticas (p. 248)

internationalism/internacionalismo política nacional de intercambio comercial activo con países extranjeros para promover la paz y la prosperidad (p. 712)

Internet/*Internet* red de comunicaciones electrónicas que conecta redes de computación y facilidades de computación de organizaciones alrededor del mundo (p. 1014)

interposition/interposición teoría que un estado debiera poder intervenir entre el gobierno federal y la gente para detener una acción ilegal (p. 220)

iron curtain/cortina de hierro barrera política y militar que aisló a los países de Europa Oriental controlados por los soviéticos después de la Segunda Guerra Mundial (p. 782)

isolationism/aislacionismo política nacional de evitar el involucramiento en asuntos mundiales (pp. 649, 711)

jazz/*jazz* estilo de música americana que se desarrolló de *ragtime* y *blues* y que usa melodías y ritmos sincopados (p. 627)

Jim Crow Laws/Leyes de Jim Crow leyes creadas para reforzar la segregación (p. 510)

jingoism/patriotismo extremo nacionalismo marcado por la agresiva política extranjera (p. 529)

joint committee/comité paritaria comité organizado con miembros de la Cámara y el Senado para trabajar en temas específicos (p. 183)

joint-stock company/compañía por acciones forma de organización de negocios en la cual muchos inversionistas compran acciones para juntar grandes cantidades de dinero para grandes proyectos (p. 61)

judicial branch/ramo judicial ramo del gobierno que interpreta las leyes dando juicios de los casos involucrando esas leyes (p. 168)

judicial review/revisión judicial derecho de la Suprema Corte para determinar si las leyes del Congreso son constitucionales y para derribar aquellas que no lo son (pp. 185, 223)

juvenile delinquency/delincuencia juvenil comportamiento antisocial o criminal de los jóvenes (p. 831)

kachina/kachina espíritu bueno que la gente Pueblo creyó traía mensajes de los dioses a su pueblo cada año (p. 21)

kamikaze/kamikase durante la Segunda Guerra Mundial un piloto suicida japonés de quien la misión fue chocar en su objetivo (p. 761)

kinship group/grupo de parentesco grupo grande de familias (p. 23)

kiva/kiva cuarto circular ceremonial construido por los Anasazi (p. 16)

labor union/sindicato organización de trabajadores formada con el propósito de promover los intereses de sus miembros (p. 249)

laissez-faire/*laissez-faire* política que el gobierno debe interferir tan poco como sea posible en la economía del país (p. 438)

land-grant/concesión de tierras una concesión de terrenos por el gobierno federal especialmente para carreteras, vías de ferrocarril y colegios agrícolas (p. 445)

legislative branch/ramo legislativo ramo del gobierno que hace las leyes de una nación (p. 168)

letters of marque/patente de corso cédula autorizada por el Congreso para propietarios de naves privadas autorizándoles a atacar barcos mercantes británicos (p. 143)

liberal/liberal persona que generalmente cree que el gobierno debe desempeñar un papel active en la economía y programas sociales pero que el gobierno no debe dictar el comportamiento social (p. 981)

Liberty ship/barco de Libertad barco de carga básico utilizado por Estados Unidos durante la Segunda Guerra Mundial (p. 738)

limited war/guerra limitada guerra peleada con compromisos limitados de recursos para alcanzar un objetivo limitado, tal como la contención del comunismo (p. 789)

line of demarcation/línea de demarcación línea de longitud de norte a sur a través del Océano Atlántico que dividía las tierras en las Américas reclamadas por España y Portugal (p. 42)

linkage/enlace política de mejorar relaciones con la Unión Soviética y China con la esperanza de persuadirlas a que redujeran su ayuda a Vietnam del Norte (p. 910)

lockout/cierre patronal práctica de una empresa para rechazar las demandas sindicales negándose a permitir a los empleados a entrar al área de trabajo (p. 456)

long drive/manejo largo conducción de ganado por largas distancias a estaciones de ferrocarril para la transportación rápida y grandes ganancias (p. 417)

longhouse/casa comunal edificio grande rectangular con techo en forma de barril cubierto de corteza de árbol utilizado por unos indígenas americanos (p. 23)

Loyalist/lealista colono americano que apoyó a la Gran Bretaña y se opuso a la guerra para la independencia (p. 129)

lynching/linchamiento ejecución hecha sin aprobación legal (p. 511)

— M —

maize/maíz una de las primeras cosechas cultivadas por los antiguos americanos, conocido hoy en día como elote (p. 14)

mandate/mandato autorización dado a un representante (p. 379)

Manifest Destiny/Destino Manifiesto idea popular en Estados Unidos durante los años 1800 de que el país debía extender sus fronteras hasta el Océano Pacífico (p. 295)

manorialism/señorialismo sistema económico en el cual los campesinos proporcionan sus servicios a un lord feudal a cambio de protección (p. 33)

manumission/manumisión liberación voluntaria de personas esclavizadas (p. 151)

margin/margen comprar acciones pagando solamente una fracción del precio y pidiendo prestado el resto (p. 657)

margin call/llamada de reserva demanda de un accionista a que los inversionistas paguen los préstamos hechos para la compra de acciones al margen (p. 657)

martial law/derecho marcial derecho administrado por fuerzas militares que es invocado por un gobierno en una emergencia (p. 345)

Marxism/marxismo teoría de socialismo en la cual una lucha de clases sociales existiría hasta que los trabajadores salieran finalmente victoriosos, creando una sociedad sin distinción de clases (p. 456)

mass media/medios informativos medios de comunicación (como televisión y radio) con la intención de llegar a la audiencia extensa (p. 623)

mass production/fabricación en serie producción de grandes cantidades de productos usando máquinas y a menudo una línea de montaje (p. 641)

massive retaliation/represalia masiva una política que amenaza una respuesta masiva, incluyendo el uso de armas nucleares, contra un estado comunista que trata de captar un país pacífico por la fuerza (p. 798)

matrilineal/por línea materna relacionado o basado en la línea materna (p. 30)

maverick/*maverick* un res descarriado sin ningún símbolo de identificación (p. 418)

mercantilism/mercantilismo teoría que el poder de una estado depende de su riqueza (p. 98)

microprocessor/microprocesador procesador de computadora que contiene memoria y funciones de computación en un solo chip (p. 1013)

military-industrial complex/compejo militar industrial relación informal que algunas personas creen que existe entre lo militar y la industria de defensa para promover mayores gastos militares y para influenciar la política gubernamental (p. 802)

minutemen/*minutemen* compañías de soldados civiles que se jactaban de que podrían estar listos para tomar armas en sólo un minuto (p. 129)

missile gap/diferencia de proyectiles creencia que la Unión Soviética tenía más armas nucleares que Estados Unidos (p. 841)

monopoly/monopolio control total de una industria por una persona o una compañía (p. 449)

moratorium/moratoria suspensión de actividad (p. 650)

most-favored nation/nación más favorecida política entre países asegurando prácticas de tratado de comercio justo (p. 216)

muckraker/*muckraker* periodista que revela abusos y corrupción en una sociedad (p. 547)

mudslinging/*mudslinging* intentar arruinar la reputación de un adversario con insultos (p. 260)

multinational corporation/corporación multinacional grandes corporaciones de inversión extranjera (p. 815)

napalm/*napalm* gasolina gelatinosa utilizada para bombas incendiarias (pp. 768, 900)

nationalism/nacionalismo lealtad y devoción a una nación (p. 232, 578)

nativism/nativismo sentimientos de hostilidad hacia imigrantes (pp. 274, 468)

natural rights/derechos naturales derechos fundamentales de las personas que nacen con ellos, incluyendo el derecho a vivir, de libertad y propiedad (p. 102)

naturalism/naturalismo filosofía y perspectiva en arte y literatura en la cual la naturaleza es tratada realísticamente, puede ser entendida a través de observación científica y que la sociedad funcionará mejor con algunas regulaciones gubernamentales (p. 483)

nomad/nómada persona que se mueve de un lugar a otro, generalmente en busca de alimentos o pastos (pp. 13, 425)

nonimportation agreement/acuerdo de no importación compromiso por mercaderes de no comprar artículos importados de una fuente indicada (p. 121)

normalcy/normalidad estado de ser normal (p. 637)

Northwest Passage/Pasaje del Noroeste ruta acuática mítica del norte a través de América del Norte al Océano Pacífico (p. 55)

nuclear proliferation/proliferación nuclear distribución de armas nucleares a nuevas naciones (p. 1025)

nullification/anulación teoría que los estados tienen el derecho de declarar inválida una ley federal (p. 220, 268)

obsidian/obsidiana vidrio obscuro formado por el enfriamiento de la lava líquida (p. 14)

Open Door policy/política de Puertas Abiertas política que permitió a cada nación extranjera en China intercambiar libremente en las esferas de influencia de otras naciones (p. 538)

open range/terreno abierto gran extensión de pastos propiedad del gobierno federal (p. 416)

open shop/taller abierto lugar de trabajo donde los trabajadores no son requeridos de ser miembros del sindicato (p. 645)

operating cost/costos de operación costos que ocurren operando una compañía (p. 448)

overlander/viajero persona que viaja al oeste por tierra (p. 296)

override/anular habilidad del Congreso de rechazar un veto presidencial por el voto de una mayoría de dos tercios (p. 182)

pacifism/pacifismo oposición a la guerra o violencia como un medio para arreglar disputas (p. 75)

party boss/jefe de partido persona que lleva el control de la maquinaria política (p. 473)

Patriot/Patriota colono americano que apoyó la guerra para independencia (p. 129)

patronage/patronazgo otro nombre para el sistema de despojos política en el cual puestos y favores gubernamentales son dados a aliados políticos y amigos (p. 492)

penitentiary/penitenciaría prisión cuyo propósito es de reformar prisioneros (p. 280)

perestroika/*perestroika* política de reestructuración económica y gubernamental instituida por Mikhail Gorbachev en la Unión Soviética en los años 1980 (p. 1002)

periphery/periferia frontera externa de algo (p. 745)

perjury/perjurio mentir cuando uno ha jurado decir la verdad (p. 1020)

philanthropy/filantropía proporcionar dinero para apoyar metas humanitarias o sociales (p. 478)

pietism/piedad movimiento en los años 1700 que enfatizó la piedad individual y la unión emocional con Dios (p. 108)

Pilgrim/peregrino Separatista que viajó a las colonias americanas durante los años 1600 para libertad religiosa (p. 67)

pillage/saquear botín y robo (p. 379)

placer mining/explotación de placeres método para extraer mineral a mano utilizando simples herramientas manuales como picos, palas y bateas (p. 415)

plantation/plantación hacienda comercial y agrícola muy grande (p. 85)

planter/plantador dueño de plantación que tenía 20 ó más esclavos (p. 253)

pocket veto/veto indirecto vetar indirectamente un proyecto de ley permitiendo que una sesión del Congreso expire sin firmar el proyecto (p. 388)

police power/fuerza policiaca poder gubernamental para controlar a personas y propiedades para la seguridad, salud, bienestar, y moral pública (p. 615)

political machine/maquinaria política organización aliada con un partido político que a menudo controlaba el gobierno local (p. 473)

poll tax/impuesto de capitación impuesto de cantidad fija por cada persona, el cual tenía que ser pagado antes de que una persona pudiera votar (pp. 510, 879)

pool/consorcio grupo compartiendo una actividad; por ejemplo, dueños de ferrocarril que tomaban acuerdos secretos y fijaban tipos entre ellos mismos (p. 448)

popular sovereignty/soberanía popular teoría política de que el gobierno está sujeto a la voluntad del pueblo; antes de la Guerra Civil, la idea de que la gente que vivía en un territorio tenía el derecho de decidir votando si ahí sería permitida la esclavitud (pp. 180, 321)

populism/populismo movimiento político fundado en los años 1890 representando principalmente a los granjeros que favoreció libre acuñación de plata y el control gubernamental de ferrocarriles y otras industrias grandes (p. 500)

poverty line/línea de pobreza nivel de ingreso individual o familiar bajo del cual uno es clasificado por el gobierno federal como pobre (p. 828)

presidio/presidio fuerte construido por los españoles en las Américas (p. 54)

privateer/buque corsario buque de propiedad privada autorizado por el gobierno para atacar a buques de otros países (p. 61)

progressivism/progresivismo movimiento político que cruzó las líneas partidarias que creyó que la industria y la urbanización habían creados muchos problemas sociales y que el gobierno debía tomar un papel más activo para resolver estos problemas (p. 547)

prohibition/prohibición leyes que prohibían la manufactura, transportación y venta de bebidas alcohólicas (p. 553)

propaganda/propaganda diseminación de ideas sobre una institución o individuo con el propósito de influenciar la opinión (p. 581)

proprietary colony/colonia propietaria colonia propiedad de un individuo (p. 64)

protective tariff/arancel protectora impuesto en importaciones diseñado para proteger a los manufactureros americanos (p. 241)

protectorate/protectorado país que es técnicamente independiente pero que en realidad queda bajo el control de otro país (p. 521)

public works/obras públicas proyectos como carreteras, parques y bibliotecas construidos con fondos públicos para uso público (p. 669)

pueblo/pueblo término usado por los primeros exploradores españoles para denotar grandes estructuras habitacionales construidas por los Anasazi (p. 16)

Puritan/puritano persona que quería purificar la Iglesia Anglicana en los años 1500 y 1600 (p. 60)

quartz mining/minería de cuarzo método para extraer minerales excavando debajo de la superficie (p. 415)

racism/racismo prejuicio o discriminación en contra de alguien por su raza (p. 882)

radiocarbon dating/datar con carbó radioactivo método para determinar la edad de objetos biológicos midiendo la radioactividad en una clase especial de carbón (p. 13)

ragtime/*ragtime* tipo de música con un ritmo fuerte y una melodía animada con notas acentuadas (p. 480)

rationalism/racionalismo filosofía que enfatiza el papel de la lógica y la razón para obtener el conocimiento (p. 108)

rationing/racionamiento proporcionar escasos artículos de manera limitada (p. 753)

realism/realismo perspectiva de literatura, arte, y teatro que intenta representar las cosas tal como son y que la sociedad funcionará mejor si la dejan en paz (p. 478)

reapportionment/nueva repartición método usado por los estados para formar distritos políticos basados en los cambios de población (p. 843)

rebate/descuento devolución parcial para reducir el costo de un producto o bien (p. 495)

recall/elección de revocación derecho que permite a los votantes quitar del cargo a los oficiales elegidos que son inadecuados (p. 549)

recession/recesión retraso económico (p. 160)

Reconstruction/Reconstrucción reorganización y reconstrucción de los estados de la ex-Confederación después de la Guerra Civil (p. 387)

referendum/referéndum práctica de permitir a los votantes aceptar o rechazar medidas propuestas por la legislatura (pp. 335, 549)

relief/asistencia pública ayuda para los necesitados; beneficencia (p. 670)

Renaissance/Renacimiento período en Europa desde 1350 hasta 1600 durante el cual ocurrió el renacimiento de interés en la cultura de la antigua Grecia y Roma (p. 36)

reparations/indemnización pago hecho por el país perdedor de una guerra al país ganador por los daños causados por la guerra (pp. 596, 649)

republic/república forma de gobierno en el cual el poder reside en un cuerpo de ciudadanos con derecho al voto (p. 147)

reserved powers/poderes reservados los poderes nombrados en la Constitución que son retenidos por los estados (p. 181)

Restoration/Restauración término usado para describir cuando el Parlamento Inglés decidió reponer a la monarquía en el año 1660 (p. 73)

revenue tariff/arancel de ingresos impuesto en las importaciones con el propósito de recaudar dinero (p. 241)

revival/asamblea evangelista reunión pública grande para predicar y rezar (p. 108)

right-to-work law/derecho a trabajar ley que hace ilegal la demanda que los trabajadores se unan a un sindicato (p. 809)

romanticism/romanticismo movimiento literario, artístico, y filosófico del siglo XVIII que enfatizó la imaginación y las emociones, promoviendo el sentido en lugar de la razón, la espiritualidad interior en lugar de reglas externas, el individuo en lugar de la sociedad, y la naturaleza en lugar de medios ambientes credos por los humanos (p. 276)

safety net/red de seguridad algo que proporciona seguridad en contra de desgracias, específicamente, programas de beneficencia gubernamentales para proteger en contra del desastre económico (p.700)

savannah/sabana pasto ondulante (p. 27)

scalawag/scalawag nombre dado a los sureños que apoyaron la Reconstrucción republicana del Sur (p. 399)

secede/separarse abandonar o retirar (p. 268)

secession/secesión retiro de la Unión (p. 323)

sedition/sedición incitación a la rebelión (p. 219)

segregation/segregación separación o aislamiento de una raza, clase o grupo (p. 510)

select committee/comité selecto comité organizado en la Cámara o el Senado para hacer una tarea específica (p. 183)

selectmen/concejales hombres escogidos para manejar los asuntos de un pueblo (p. 94)

self-determination/autodeterminación creencia que las personas en un territorio deberían tener la habilidad para escoger su propio gobierno (p. 578)

separate-but-equal/separados pero iguales doctrina establecida por la Suprema Corte en el caso *Plessy contra Ferguson* en 1896 que las leyes que segregaron a los afroamericanos fueron permitidas si facilidades iguales fueron proporcionadas (p. 867)

separation of powers/separación de poderes principio de gobierno en el cual el poder está dividido entre diferentes ramos (p. 168)

Separatist/separatista puritano que dejó la Iglesia Anglicana (p. 66)

serf/siervo persona atada a un señorío (p. 33)

settlement house/casa de beneficencia institución establecida en una vecindad pobre que proveía numerosos servicios comunitarios tal como cuidado médico, cuidado de niños, bibliotecas, e instrucción en inglés (p. 485)

shantytown/villa miseria barrio pobre de un pueblo que consiste de viviendas mal construidas, normalmente hechas de madera (p. 662)

sharecropper/aparcero agricultor que labra la tierra para un dueño que proporciona equipo y semillas y recibe una porción de la cosecha (pp. 407, 509)

siege/sitio bloqueo militar de una ciudad o un recinto fortificado para forzarlo a rendirse (p. 370)

silverite/defensor de plata persona que cree que la acuñación de monedas de plata en cantidades sin límite eliminará la crisis económica (p. 506)

sin tax/impuesto pecadero impuesto federal sobre el alcohol y tabaco (p. 404)

sit-down strike/huelga de brazos caídos método de boicotear el trabajo por medio de sentarse en el lugar de trabajo y de rehusar a abandonar el establecimiento (p. 693)

sit-in/plantón forma de protesta ocupando las sillas o sentándose en el piso de un establecimiento (p. 868)

skyscraper/rascacielos edificio de gran altura (p. 470)

slash-and-burn agriculture/agrícola de tala y quema técnica agrícola en la cual la tierra es preparada y fertilizada derrumbando los bosques y quemándolos (p. 23)

slave code/código de esclavos leyes aprobadas que regularon formalmente la esclavitud y definieron la relación entre los africanos esclavizados y la gente libre (p. 90, 254)

smog/smog niebla hecha más pesada y oscura por el humo y vapores químicos (p. 940)

soap opera/novela drama en serie de radio o televisión utilizando situaciones melodramáticas (p. 664)

Social Security Act/Acta de Seguro Social ley que requiere que los trabajadores y empleados paguen un impuesto; el dinero proporciona un ingreso mensual para la gente jubilada (p. 694)

socialism/socialismo creencia que los negocios deben ser propiedad del gobierno y dirigidos por él (p. 553)

sodbuster/rompeterrón nombre dado a los granjeros de las Grandes Planicies (p. 422)

software/software programa de computadora (p. 1013)

space race/carrera espacial se refiere a la competencia durante la Guerra Fría sobre el dominio de la exploración espacial (p. 847)

space shuttle/puente espacial nave espacial diseñada para transportar personas y carga entre la tierra y el espacio la cual puede ser usada una y otra vez (p. 998)

space station/estación espacial satélite grande diseñado para ser ocupado por largos períodos y para servir como base para operaciones en el espacio (p. 999)

speakeasy/*speakeasy* lugar donde son vendidas clandestinamente bebidas alcohólicas (p. 615)

speculation/especulación acciones compradas con alto riesgo con la anticipación que los precios subirán (p. 657)

speculator/especulador persona que arriesga dinero con la esperanza de obtener una ganancia financiera (p. 212)

sphere of influence/esfera de influencia sección de un país donde una nación extranjera tiene derechos y poderes especiales (p. 538)

spoils system/sistema de despojos práctica de dar puestos gubernamentales a los partidarios; reemplazando a los empleados del gobierno con los partidarios del candidato victorioso (p. 267)

Square Deal/Trato Justo promesa de Theodore Roosevelt para un trato justo e igual para todos (p. 556)

squatter/colono usurpador persona que se establece en tierras públicas bajo reglamento gubernamental con la esperanza de adquirir el título de propiedad (p. 295)

stagflation/*stagflación* inflación persistente combinado con la demanda estancada y una taza de desempleo alta (p. 964)

standing committee/comité permanente comité permanente en la Cámara o el Senado organizado para enfocarse en un área específica (p. 183)

state-sponsored terrorism/terrorismo patrocinado por el estado actos violentos en contra de civiles que son secretamente apoyados por un gobierno con el motivo de atacar a otras naciones sin entrar en la guerra (p. 1033)

steerage/tercera clase cuarteles apretados de las cubiertas bajas de un barco para los pasajeros que pagan los pasajes más bajos (p. 465)

stock market/bolsa de valores sistema para comprar y vender acciones de corporaciones (p. 657)

strategic defense/defensa estratégica plan para desarrollar proyectiles y otras armas que pueden derribar proyectiles nucleares antes de que estos golpeen en Estados Unidos (p. 1029)

strategic materials/materiales estratégicos materiales necesarios para una guerra (p. 729)

strike/huelga paro de trabajo por los trabajadores para forzar al empresario a satisfacer sus demandas (p. 249)

subsistence farming/agricultura de subsistencia labranza que sólo produce la cosecha que se necesita para alimentar a la familia de uno (p. 87)

subversion/subversión intento sistemático para derrocar un gobierno utilizando personas que trabajan secretamente desde adentro (p. 791)

suffrage/sufragio derecho al voto (p. 549)

summit/cumbre junta de jefes de gobiernos (p. 957)

Sunbelt/Región Solada nueva región industrial en el sur de California y el Bajo Sur que se desarrolló durante la Segunda Guerra Mundial (p. 751)

supply-side economics/economía de oferta teoría económica de que los impuestos bajos levantarían la economía invirtiendo su dinero los negocios y los individuos, así creando un alto ingreso del impuesto (pp. 648, 987)

syndicate/sindicato grupo de negocios (p. 564)

teach-in/plantón educacional junta o clase extendida para discutir un asunto político o social (p. 905)

***Tejano*/tejano** habitante de Texas de habla española (p. 300)

telecommute/viajar electrónicamente trabajar en casa por medio de conexión electrónica con una oficina central (p. 1013)

televangelist/televangelista evangelista que transmite regularmente programas evangélicos por televisión (p. 984)

temperance/templanza moderación o abstinencia del uso del alcohol (pp. 279, 553)

tenant farmer/granjero arrendatario granjero que labra la tierra de un terrateniente y paga la renta ya sea con dinero efectivo o cosecha (p. 407)

tenement/casa de vecindad apartamentos para varias familias, normalmente obscuros, apretados que apenas cumplen con los estándares mínimos de viviendas (p. 471)

termination policy/política de terminación política gubernamental para traer a los Nativos Americanos dentro de la sociedad principal retirando el reconocimiento de los grupos Nativos Americanos como entidades legales (p. 830)

terrorism/terrorismo el uso de violencia por grupos no del gobierno en contra de civiles para alcanzar una meta política impartiendo miedo y amenazando gobiernos para que cambien su política (p. 1032)

time zone/huso horario región geográfica en la cual la misma norma horaria es mantenida (p. 444)

Title IX/Título IX sección de las Enmiendas Educacionales de 1972 prohibiendo que las escuelas que recibían fondos federales discriminaran contra niñas y mujeres jóvenes en casi todo aspecto de su operación (p. 929)

town meeting/junta municipal asamblea de hombres libres de un pueblo de Nueva Inglaterra para elegir líderes la cual desarrolló en gobierno local (p. 94)

trade deficit/déficit de intercambio diferencia entre el valor de las importaciones de un país y las exportaciones (p. 1023)

trade union/gremio organización de trabajadores con el mismo oficio o destreza (p. 455)

Spanish Glossary

transcendental meditation/meditación transcendental técnica de meditación en la cual una persona repite una palabra una y otra vez como manera de alcanzar la máxima inteligencia, armonía y salud (p. 971)

transcendentalism/transcendentalismo filosofía que acentúa la relación entre los seres humanos y la naturaleza, cosas espirituales sobre las materiales y la importancia de la conciencia del individuo (p. 276)

transcontinental railroad/ferrocarril transcontinental sistema de ferrocarril que se extiende a través del continente (p. 328)

triangular trade/comercio triangular una ruta comercial de tres ramas para intercambiar productos entre las colonias americanas y otros dos asociados comerciales (p. 95)

trust/cártel combinación de empresas o sociedades anónimas formada por acuerdo legal, especialmente para reducir la competición (p. 450)

U-boat/nave-U apodo inglés para submarino alemán, de *Unterseeboot,* término que significa barco submarino (p. 581)

Underground Railroad/Ferrocarril Clandestino sistema que ayudó a los afroamericanos esclavizados a seguir una red de rutas de escape fuera del Sur hacia la libertad en el Norte (p. 327)

unfair trade practices/prácticas comerciales injustas prácticas comerciales que ganan el beneficio perjudicando a la competencia (p. 569)

union shop/taller sindicalizado taller que requiere que los trabajadores se unan al sindicato (p. 809)

urban renewal/renovación urbana programas gubernamentales que intentan eliminar la pobreza y revitalizar las áreas urbanas (p. 829)

utopia/utopía comunidad basada en una visión de la sociedad perfecta buscada por los reformistas (p. 277)

vaquero/vaquero hombres que conducían el ganado en las haciendas (p. 55)

vaudeville/vodevil entretenimiento compuesto de varios actos, tal como baile, canción, comedia, y espectáculos de magia (p. 480)

vertical integration/integración vertical asociación de compañías que abastecen equipo y servicios necesarios a una industria particular (p. 449)

veto/veto poder del jefe del ejecutivo de rechazar leyes aprobadas por la legislatura (p. 169)

victory garden/huerto de victoria huertos plantados por ciudadanos americanos durante la guerra para cultivar vegetales para usar en casa así dejando más para las tropas (pp. 586, 754)

Vietcong/*Vietcong* soldados guerrilleros de la facción comunista en Vietnam, también conocidos como Frente Nacional de Liberación (p. 897)

Vietnamization/vietnamización el proceso de hacer que el Vietnam del Sur asumiera más de los esfuerzos de la guerra sacando poco a poco a las tropas americanas de Vietnam (p. 911)

War Hawks/halcones de guerra miembros del Congreso durante la presidencia de Madison que insistían en la guerra contra la Gran Bretaña (p. 229)

war on poverty/guerra contra la pobreza programa antipobreza bajo el Presidente Lyndon Johnson (p. 856)

welfare capitalism/capitalismo de beneficencia sistema en el cual las compañías permiten a los trabajadores comprar acciones, compartir las ganancias, y recibir beneficios tal como atención médica, común en los años 1920 (p. 645)

white-collar/collar blanco trabajos que no requieren ropa de protección o de trabajo, asi como los vendedores (p. 815)

wigwam/*wigwam* vivienda en forma de cono o domo construida por Nativos Americanos utilizando palos curvados cubiertos con piel o corteza de árbol (p. 23)

writ of assistance/escrito de asistencia documento legal que permitió a los oficiales aduanales entrar cualquier lugar en busca de evidencia de contrabando (p. 122)

yellow journalism/periodismo amarillista tipo de reportaje sensacional, tendencioso, y a menudo falso con el propósito de atraer a los lectores (p. 528)

yeoman farmer/terrateniente menor dueño de una granja pequeña con cuatro o menos esclavos, normalmente ninguno (p. 253)

yuppie/*yuppie* adulto joven educado en la universidad empleado en una profesión de buen salario y que vive y trabaja en o cerca de una ciudad grande (p. 995)

Spanish Glossary

Index

Italicized page numbers refer to illustrations. The following abbreviations are used in the index:
m = map; c = chart; p = photograph or picture; g = graph; crt = cartoon; ptg = painting; q = quote

Index

Index

Index

Index

Index

Index

Index

Index

Index

Index

Index

Index

Index

Index

Independence National Historic Park Collection, ...um, New York; 167 Yale University Art Gallery. ...hite, BA1859; 168 Library of Philadelphia, Rare ...Colonial Williamsburg Collection; 173 American ...74 (l)The Thomas Gilcrease Museum, Tulsa OK, ...nce National Historic Park Collection; 208 (l)Christie's ...nsonian Institution, (r)Missouri Historical Society; ...ettmann; 209 Field Museum of Natural History; ...Institution; 211 North Wind Picture Archives; ...r Museum; 215 National Portrait Gallery, Smithsonian ...Resource, NY; 216 The Library of Congress; ...nce National Historical Park, (r)Doug Martin; 218 The ...ess; 219 Boston Public Library; 221 White House Historical ...2 Courtesy Monticello, photo by Colonial Williamsburg ...22–223 Maryland Historical Society; 223 (t)Picture Research ...(b)The Historical Society of Washington, DC; 224 Colorado ...ociety; 227 The Thomas Gilcrease Museum, Tulsa, OK; ...nd Historical Society; 229 Smithsonian Institution; 230 Field ...f Natural History; 232 Anne S.K. Brown, Brown Military ...Brown University Library; 234 (tl tr br)National Portrait Gallery, ...ian Institution/Art Resource, NY, (bl)Yale University Art ...Trumbull Collection; 236 The New York Historical Society; ...Canajoharie Library & Art Gallery; 237 Gilbert Stuart, 1907. ...n College Museum of Art, Brunswick ME; 238 (l)National Portrait ...y/Smithsonian Institution/Art Resource, NY, (r)private collection; ...39 Winterthur Museum; 239 (l)The New York Historical Society, ...ek Naylor Collection; 240 National Portrait Gallery/Smithsonian ...itution/Art Resource, NY; 241 (l)New York Historical Society, ...(r)Greenville County Museum of Art; 242 Washington and Lee University, ...Lexington VA; 243 The Library of Congress; 245 The New York Historical ...Society; 246 The Library of Congress; 247 B&O Railroad Museum; ...248 Courtesy Jack Naylor; 249 (t)The Metropolitan Museum of Art. Gift of ...I.N. Phelps Stokes, Edward S. Hawes, Alice Mary Hawes, Marion Augusta ...Hawes, 1937, (b)Bob Rowan/Progressive Image/CORBIS; 250 The Bicycle ...Museum of America; 251 Trustees of the Boston Public Library; 254 (l)The ...Library of Congress, (r)Fitchburg Art Museum; 255 CORBIS/Bettmann; ...256 Picture Research Consultants; 257 West Point Museum Collections, ...1822. United States Military Academy; 259 The Metropolitan Museum of ...Art. Gift of I.N. Phelps Stokes, Edward S. Hawes, Alice Mary Hawes, ...Marion Augusta Hawes, 1937. (37.14.34); 292 Texas Department of ...Highways and Public Transportation; 292–293 The Corcoran Gallery of Art, ...Washington DC. Gift of Mr. and Mrs. Lansdell K. Christie; 293 (l)Lake ...County Museum/CORBIS, (c)Texas State Library/Archives Division, ...(r)California State Capitol; 294 The Henry E. Huntington Library and Art ...Center; 297 (t)National Archives, (b)courtesy Museum of Art, Brigham ...Young University; 298 (l)Edwards S. Curtis/CORBIS, (r)O. Pierre Havens/ ...CORBIS; 299 (l)The Library of Congress/CORBIS, (r)CORBIS/Bettmann; ...300 Texas State Archives; 301 Center for American History/Barker ...Collection/University of Texas, Austin; 302 (l)Texas State Library & Archive ...Commission, photo by Eric Beggs, (r)Texas State Library & Archives ...Commision #1983/74-1; 303 Texas Department of Transportation; ...04 (l)Texas State Library & Archive Commission, photo by Eric Beggs, ...)San Jacinto Museum History Association; 306 Chicago Historical Society, ...20; 307 Henry Groskinsky; 308 The Library of Congress; 310 Courtesy ...merican Antiquarian Society; 311 The Library of Congress; 313 George ...H. Huey; 316 First Image; 316–317 National Park Service; 317 McLellan ...coln Collection. Gift of John D. Rockefeller Jr., Class of 1897; ...Courtesy Wells Fargo Bank; 318–319 Courtesy Robert M. Hicklin Jr., Inc.; ...(l c) Chicago Historical Society, (r)Fort Sumter National Monument; ...(l)Illinois State Historical Library, Old State Capitol, (r)Chicago ...orical Society; 321 American Antiquarian Society; 322 California State ...ry, Sacramento; 323 New York Public Library Print Division; ...hlesinger Library; 328 The Library of Congress; 329 Raymond Bial; ...e Kansas State Historical Society, Topeka; 331 (l)McKissick Museum, ...BIS; 332 The Library of Congress; 334 Illinois State Historical Library, ...e Capitol; 335 (l)The Supreme Court of the United States Office of ...tor, #1991.402.2, (r)The Library of Congress; 336–337 Henry Horner ...Collection; 338 Boston Athenaeum; 339 (l)CORBIS/Bettmann, ...rary Company of Philadelphia; 340 Private collection/Art ...NY; 342 (l)Museum of American Political Life/photo by Steve ...(r)Museum of American Political Life; 343 The Library of ...44 The "Richmond Grays" Valentine Museum/Richmond

History Center, VA; 348 (l)Museum of the Confederacy, (r)The Library of Congress; 348–349 Don Troiani, courtesy Historical Art Prints Inc., Southbury CT; 349 Illinois State Historical Library; 350 Cunningham Memorial Library, Indiana State University; 351 Kean E. Wilcox Collection; 352 (t)American Numismatic Association, (b)CORBIS; 353 The Library of Congress; 355 (t)Collection of David & Kevin Kyl, (b)Washington & Lee University, VA; 357 CORBIS; 359 (t)The Library of Congress, (b)Chicago Historical Society; 360 The Cincinnati Historical Society; 361 file photo; 364 CORBIS; 366 Chicago Historical Society; 367 (l)Burns Archive, (r)US Army Military History Institute; 368 National Archives/Picture Research Consultants; 369 Amanita Pictures; 370 The Library of Congress; 371 Al Freni; 372 (l)The Library of Congress, (r)CORBIS; 374 Courtesy Atlanta History Center, Dubose Collection; 375 Steen Cannons, Ashland, KY; (b)Kunstler Enterprises, Ltd. *It's My Fault*, National Geographic Society; 376 National Portrait Gallery; 377 The Library of Congress; 378–379 National Archives; 381 Bob Daemmrich; 384 (l)American Museum of Political Life, (r)Collection of Janice L. and David J. Frent; 384–385 Los Angeles County Museum; 385 The Library of Congress; 386 Gladstone; 387 (t)Thaddeus Stevens by Edward Dalton, The Library of the Union League of Philadelphia, photo by Rick Echelmeyer, (b)The Library of Congress; 388 Photographic History Collection, National Museum of American History, Smithsonian Institution; 390 The Library of Congress; 391 The Library of Congress; 392 (t)Carl Iwasaki/TimePix, (b)CORBIS/ Bettmann; 393 (t)Flip Schulke/Black Star, (b)Reuters NewMedia Inc./CORBIS; 398 Picture Research Consultants; 399 (l)Herbert F. Johnson Museum of Art, Cornell University, (r)The Library of Congress; 400 Cook Collection/Valentine Museum; 402 CORBIS; 403 Mississippi Department of Archives & History, Archives & Library Division, Special Collections Section, Graphics Records; 404 The Library of Congress; 406 Southern Light/Hinklin; 407 CORBIS; 410 Picture Research Consultants; 410–411 Curt Teich Postcard Archives; 411 Mark Steinmetz; 412 (tl)Oakland Museum History Department, (tr)Fenimore House Museum, Cooperstown NY; 412–413 Wyoming Division of Cultural Resources; 413 (tl)CORBIS, (tr)Trustees of the Boston Public Library; 414 US Department of the Interior/Geological Survey; 416 (t)Nevada Historical Society, (b)Roy Bishop/Stock Boston; 417 (l)Thomas Gilcrease Museum, Tulsa OK, (r)Montana Historical Society, Helena; 418 (t)Amon Carter Museum, Fort Worth TX, (b)Robert Holmes/CORBIS; 419 Panhandle-Plains Historical Museum; 420 Runk-Schoenberger from Grant Heilman; 421 State Historical Society of Wisconsin; 422 (tl)Frank Siteman/Stock Boston, (bl)Doug Martin, (r)Bob Daemmrich/Stock Boston; 425 Smithsonian Institution; 426 National Anthropological Archives, Smithsonian Institution; 427 The Library of Congress; 429 Picture Research Consultants; 431 (l)National Portrait Gallery, Smithsonian Institution/Art Resource, NY, (r)Chick Harrity; 434 (l)The New York Historical Society, (r)Chicago Historical Society; 434–435 Private collection; 435 Picture Research Consultants; 436 The Library of Congress; 437 CORBIS/Bettman; 438 (l)CORBIS/Bettmann, (tr)Smithsonian Institution, (br)Culver Pictures; 439 (l)US Department of the Interior/National Park Service/Edison National Historic Site, (c)Smithsonian Institution, (r)CORBIS/Bettmann; 441 Courtesy George Eastman House; 442 Union Pacific Historical Collection; 443 Union Pacific Railroad Museum; 447 The New York Historical Society; 450 Brown Brothers; 451 New York Stock Exchange; 452 (l)CORBIS, (tr)courtesy Rockefeller Archive Center, (br)CORBIS/Bettmann; 453 (tl)E.O. Hoppe/CORBIS, (bl)PhotoDisc, (tr)file photo; 454 Culver Pictures; 455 The Library of Congress; 456 CORBIS/ Bettmann; 458 George Meany Memorial Archives; 459 Chicago Historical Society; 462 The Library of Congress; 462–463 Brown Brothers; 463 (l)Doug Martin, (r)CORBIS; 464 American Jewish Archives; 466 Picture Research Consultants; 467 National Archives; 469 Frank Lloyd Wright Archives; 470 (l)The Museum of the City of New York. Gift of Mr. Shirley C. Burden, (r)The Library of Congress; 471 Berry-Hill Galleries; 475 Mark Seider/ National Geographic Society; 477 (t)Brown Brothers, (b)Frank & Marie Wood/The Picture Bank; 478 Museum of Art, Rhode Island School of Design; Jesse Metcalf and Walter H. Kimball Funds; 479 Baseball Hall of Fame Library, Cooperstown NY; 480 Frank Driggs Collection; 481 Brown Brothers; 483 United Charities Collection/Chicago Historical Society; 485 (l)Brown Brothers, (r)The Library of Congress; 486 Lake County Museum/CORBIS; 487 Bob Daemmrich; 488 (l)Michael J. Howell/Stock Boston, (r)Collection of Janice L. and David J. Frent; 490 (tl)East Carolina University, (tc)Collection of Janice L. and David J. Frent, (tr)Picture Research Consultants; 490–491 E.L. Henry; 491 (l)Amistad Foundation/Wadsworth Athenaeum, (r)Collection of Janice L. and David J. Frent; 492 Collection of

Acknowledgments

631 "The Negro Speaks of Rivers" and "I, Too," from *The Collected Poems of Langston Hughes* by Langston Hughes. Copyright © 1994 by the Estate of Langston Hughes. Used by permission of Alfred A. Knopf, a division of Random House, Inc.

773 From *Farewell to Manzanar* by Jeanne Wakatsuki Houston and James D. Houston. Copyright © 1973 by James D. Houston. Reprinted by permission of Houghton Mifflin Company.

1007 From *Hunger of Memory* by Richard Rodriguez (Boston: David R. Godine, Publisher, 1981). Copyright © 1981 by Richard Rodriguez. Reprinted by permission of Georges Borchardt, Inc., for the author.

1054 From *The Grapes of Wrath* by John Steinbeck. Copyright © 1939, renewed 1967 by John Steinbeck. Used by permission of Viking Penguin, a division of Penguin Putnam, Inc.

1055 "Alone and Far Removed" by Audie Murphy. Reprinted by permission of the Estate of Audie Murphy.

1056 "Letter from Birmingham Jail" reprinted by arrangement with the Estate of Martin Luther King, Jr., c/o Writers House, Inc. as agent for the proprietor. Copyright Martin Luther King 1963, copyright renewed 1991 by Coretta Scott King.

1057 From *Barefoot Heart: Stories of a Migrant Child* by Elva Trevino Hart. Reprinted by permission of Bilingual Press.

1078 From "I Have a Dream," reprinted by arrangement with the Estate of Martin Luther King, Jr., c/o Writers House, Inc. as agent for the proprietor. Copyright Martin Luther King 1968, copyright renewed 1996 by Coretta Scott King.

Glencoe would like to acknowledge the artists and agencies that participated in illustrating this program: Morgan Cain & Associates; Ortelius Design, Inc.; and QA Digital.

Photo Credits

Cover: (left to right) (steamboat)Sean Sexton/CORBIS, (covered wagon)David Muench/CORBIS, (Ellis Island)CORBIS, (assembling Model T automobiles) Bettmann/CORBIS, (Asian American holding flag)Catherine Karnow/CORBIS, (express train)Reuters NewMedia Inc./CORBIS, (firemen raising flag)Thomas E. Franklin/Bergen Record/CORBIS Saba, (naturalization ceremony)CORBIS/Bettmann, (child worker)Lewis Hine/CORBIS, (Air Force jet)CORBIS, (Thomas Edison & son)CORBIS/Bettmann, (Martin Luther King Jr.)Robert Mills/CORBIS, (Roberto Clemente, Mulberry Street)CORBIS/Bettmann, (Condoleeza Rice)AFP/CORBIS, (others)PhotoDisc CORBIS; **iv** (tr)Lee Boltin Picture Library; (bl)CORBIS/Bettmann, (br)J. McGrail/H. Armstrong Roberts; **v** (t)Panhandle-Plains Historical Museum, (b)The Library of Congress; **vi** (tl)Michael J. Howell/Stock Boston, (tr)National Air and Space Museum, Smithsonian Institution, (cl)courtesy Baylor University/Wings Across America, (bl)Air Force Museum Foundation, Inc.; **vii** (tr)Picture Research Consultants, (bl bc)Collection of Janice L. and David J. Frent, (br)Collection of Chester Stott/Picture Research Consultants; **viii** CORBIS; **xxii–xxiii** PhotoDisc; **xxiv** CORBIS/Bettmann; **xxv** Courtesy Ford Motor Company; **RA20** PhotoDisc; **1** NASA; **4** (t)PhotoDisc, (b)Mark Newman/Folio, Inc.; **5** (tl)Ron Jautz/Folio, Inc., (tr)PhotoDisc, (inset)David R. Frazier Photolibrary/Folio, Inc., (bl)Grant Heilman, (br)Picture Research Consultants, (inset)US Geological Survey; **8** CORBIS; **8–9** Courtesy Schwarz Gallery, Philadelphia; **9** Archivo de Indias, Seville, Spain/Mithra-Index/Bridgeman Art Library; **10** (l)Boltin Picture Library, (r)Richard A. Cooke III; **10–11** The City of Plainfield, NJ; **11** (tl)Field Museum of Natural History, Chicago, (tr)The Detroit Institute of Art, Dirk Bakker, (bl)The British Museum, (br)National Maritime Museum; **12** Photo Archives, Denver Museum of Natural History; **14** (l)Lee Boltin Picture Library, (r)Runk/Schoenberger from Grant Heilman; **15** Lee Boltin Picture Library; **16** (l)MarkFiennes/Chequers/Buckinghamshire, UK/Bridgeman Art Library, (r)Richard A. Cooke III; **17** (t)Richard A. Cooke III, (b)Ohio Historical Society; **18** Jacques Cinq-Mars/CMC; **20** Richard A. Cooke III; **21** Werner Forman Archive/Art Resource, NY; **22** Richard A. Cooke III; **23** The Library of Congress; **24** Picture Research

Library of Congress; 166 (...
(b)Fraunces Tavern Mus...
Gift of Roger Sherman...
Books Room; 172 The...
Antiquarian Society;...
(r)courtesy Independe...
Images, NY, (c)Smi...
208–209 CORBIS...
210 Smithsonian...
212 213 Winterth...
Institution/Art...
217 (l)Independe...
Library of Con...
Association;...
Foundation...
Consult...
Resource...
UK/Brid...
Bridgeman...
S.A./CORBIS...

37 CORBIS; 3...
(b)Canadian Mus...
London, (r)The Britis...
(r)The Thomas Gilcrea...
43 Picture Research C...
Numismatic Society; **48–4**...
49 Pilgrim Society; **50** The L...
52 (l)Picture Research Consulta...
erican Museum of Natural H...
55 Biblioteca Colombina, Sevilla, Spa...
(r)Historical Society of Pennsylvania;...
Virginia, CA9-92; **60–61** National Maritim...
Portrait Gallery, Washington DC; **63** (t)Asse...
Virginia Antiquities, (b)Virginia State Libra...
66 Pilgrim Hall Museum, Plymouth MA; **67** Priv...
Galleries; **69** American Antiquarian Society; **72** T...
Society; **73** Art Resource, NY; **74** (l)file photo, (r)cou...
82 (l)Association for the Preservation of Virginia Antiqu...
Library of Virginia, (r)Philadelphia Museum of Art/ph...
Wood; **82–83** The Warner Collection of Gulf States Paper...
Tuscaloosa, AL; **83** (l)William Gladstone, (r)Josh Nefslay; 8...
Nowitz/CORBIS; **86** Picture Research Consultants; **87** The N...
Library; **88** (l)Inko Production; **88–89** Maggie Steber/CORBIS...
89 National Maritime Museum, London; **90** Exeter City Museum &...
Gallery; **91** Fine Arts Photographic Library, London/Art Resources, N...
94 (t)The Folger Shakespeare Library, (b)Peabody Essex Museum/photo by...
Mark Sexton; **97** Miriam & Ira D. Wallach Division of Art, Prints and...
Photographs, The New York Public Library, Astor Lenox and Tilden...
Foundation; **98** Picture Research Consultants; **99** Miriam & Ira D. Wallach...
Division of Art, Prints and Photographs, The New York Public Library...
Astor Lenox and Tilden Foundation; **101** Courtesy The Massachusett...
Historical Society; **102** CORBIS/Bettmann; **103** Museum of Fine Art...
Boston; **104** Harvard University Art Museum; **105** Philadelphia Museum...
Art/photo by Graydon Wood; **106** Josh Nefslay; **109** National Por...
Gallery, London; **112** Charles H. Phillips/Smithsonian Instit...
112–113 Lora Robins Collection of Virginia Art, Virginia Historical...
113 Museum of Fine Arts, Boston; **114** Colonial Willi...
114–115 CORBIS; **115** (l)Gwynn M. Kibbe/Stock Boston, (c)The...
Congress, (r)National Archives; **116** The British Library; **117**...
118 The Library of Congress; **120** American Antiqua...
121 (t)Picture Research Consultants, (b)Karie Hamilton/C...
122 National Portrait Gallery/Smithsonian Institution/A...
123 John Carter Brown Library; **124** The Libra...
124–125 PhotoDisc; **125** (l)Kevin Fleming, (r)The Li...
126 DAR Museum on loan from Boston Tea Party Ch...
Picture Archives; **128** CORBIS; **129** J. McGrail/...
131 Chicago Historical Society; **132** The Librar...
University Art Gallery; **137** CORBIS; **138** Henry...
courtesy Beverly Historical Society; **141** The Vall...
142 (l)Yale University Art Gallery/Trumbull C...
Gallery, Washington DC/Art Resource, NY...
State Library; **146** The British Library; **147** N...
Merseyside, Liverpool; **149** Courtesy The M...
151 New York State Historical Association, C...
of The New York Historical Society; **156** All...
The White House Historical Association; **156**...
(r)National Postal Museum; **156–157** The L...
Antiquarian Society; **157** (t)Picture Research...
Historical Society; **158** Independence Natio...
Hamerman/Folio, Inc; **161** Joseph Sohm,...
164 Independence National Historical Par...

Library of Congress; 166 (...
(b)Fraunces Tavern Mus...
318...
319...
Hist...
Libra...
326 S...
330 Th...
(r)COR...
Old Sta...
the Cur...
Lincoln...
(r)The L...
Resources...
schever...
ss;...